BELLAMY & CHILD

MATERIALS ON
EUROPEAN COMMUNITY
LAW OF COMPETITION

2008 Edition

BELLAMY & CHILD

MATERIALS ON EUROPEAN COMMUNITY LAW OF COMPETITION

2008 Edition

Edited by

ANDREW MACNAB

Barrister, Monckton Chambers

Consultant Editors

PETER ROTH QC

Barrister, Visiting Professor of Law, King's College, London

VIVIEN ROSE

Barrister, Chairman of the Competition Appeal Tribunal

OXFORD
UNIVERSITY PRESS

OXFORD

UNIVERSITY PRESS

Great Clarendon Street, Oxford OX2 6DP

Oxford University Press is a department of the University of Oxford.
It furthers the University's objective of excellence in research, scholarship,
and education by publishing worldwide in

Oxford New York

Auckland Cape Town Dar es Salaam Hong Kong Karachi
Kuala Lumpur Madrid Melbourne Mexico City Nairobi
New Delhi Shanghai Taipei Toronto

With offices in

Argentina Austria Brazil Chile Czech Republic France Greece
Guatemala Hungary Italy Japan Poland Portugal Singapore
South Korea Switzerland Thailand Turkey Ukraine Vietnam

Oxford is a registered trade mark of Oxford University Press
in the UK and in certain other countries

Published in the United States
by Oxford University Press Inc., New York

British Library Cataloguing in Publication Data
Data available

Library of Congress Cataloging in Publication Data
Data available

Typeset by Cepha Imaging Private Ltd., Bangalore, India
Printed in Great Britain
on acid-free paper by
Legoprint S.p.A

ISBN 978–0–19–928652–2

1 3 5 7 9 10 8 6 4 2

INTRODUCTION TO MATERIALS ON EUROPEAN COMMUNITY LAW OF COMPETITION 2008 EDITION

Welcome to *Bellamy & Child Materials on European Community Law of Competition*. This book started life as the volume of Appendices to *Bellamy & Child, European Community Law of Competition*. Its role has now been expanded to serve three aims:

- First, it continues its role as the volume of Appendices to *Bellamy & Child, European Community Law of Competition* (6th edition). A copy of the Materials volume will be bundled with the main work.
- Second, it acts as a companion to *Faull and Nikpay, The EC Law of Competition* (2nd edition).
- Third, it is intended to be a self-standing volume of EC competition law materials.

Readers' attention is drawn to the following features, which have been incorporated into the book to optimise utility and ease of use:

- The book is divided into seven main Parts (treaty provisions, modernisation and procedural matters, substantive antitrust matters, mergers and concentrations, sectoral regimes, public undertakings and state aids) and are, indicated by headings and thumb-tabs.
- Within each Part, materials are, in the main, sub-divided into legislation and notices and are, in the main, arranged chronologically within each sub-division.
- The arrangement of the seven main Parts broadly follows the structure of *Bellamy & Child* and the Parts and Chapter headings cross-refer to *Bellamy & Child* (6th edition).
- In addition, documents include pinpoint cross-references to paragraphs in *Bellamy & Child* (6th edition) and *Faull & Nikpay* (2nd edition).
- Helpful tables of contents and page-headings throughout aim to optimise accessibility of content and to ensure easy navigation.
- Documents are reproduced with details of their publication in the Official Journal and their Celex numbers.
- Original Official Journal footnotes are reproduced, together with editorial annotations regarding amendments, etc.
- Where applicable, details of instruments' EEA application are included.

Selection of materials for inclusion in this book has been dictated largely by the content of *Bellamy & Child* (6th edition). Having regard to the book's third aim, however, selection has not been limited only to materials referred to in *Bellamy & Child* (particularly in relation to state aids) and we have sought to ensure comprehensive coverage of the major areas. Lack of space and a desire to save trees mean that, in some cases, we have not included full versions of certain documents (*viz.* the EEA Agreement, the country rail maps annexed to Directive 91/440/EC and Annex I to Commission Regulation 794/2004/EC), we have had to be selective as to the materials to be included in respect of sectoral regimes and we have omitted some of the more specialised sector-specific state aids instruments.

Documents (and drafts) reproduced in this book are up to date as at 1st October 2007 (although in some cases it has been possible to include later updates). The content will be kept updated by:

- A companion website, tracking new material and amendments on an ongoing basis. This can be found by following this link: www.oup.co.uk/law/practitioner/cws, and clicking on the listing for this book.
- Annual new editions of this book, fully updated to take account of changes and developments in the preceding 12 months.

The recommended retail price of this book has been set at less than £50 in the hope that this will make it affordable for firms to purchase multiple copies, and to replace it on an annual basis, thus keeping their EC competition law teams optimally equipped.

For the convenience of the reader, references to articles of the EC Treaty in the materials reproduced have been amended to state the articles as renumbered in accordance with Article 12 of the Treaty of Amsterdam and the Tables of Equivalences annexed thereto (reproduced at A1).

CONTENTS

A. TREATY PROVISIONS

B. MODERNISATION AND PROCEDURAL MATTERS

Regulations, etc

Notices, etc

C. SUBSTANTIVE ANTITRUST MATTERS

Regulations

Notices, etc

D. MERGERS AND CONCENTRATIONS

Regulations, etc

Notices, etc

US, EEA

E. SECTORAL REGIMES

Electronic Communications

Legislation

Information and Notices

Insurance

Postal Services

Agriculture

F. PUBLIC UNDERTAKINGS

G. STATE AIDS

Block Exemptions

Horizontal Rules

Specific Aid Instruments

Reference/Discount Rates and Recovery Interest Rates

1. Methodology

2. Rates

Part A

TREATY PROVISIONS

A1

TABLES OF EQUIVALENCES REFERRED TO IN ARTICLE 12 OF THE TREATY OF AMSTERDAM

Article 12 of the Treaty of Amsterdam provides as follows:

1. The articles, titles and sections of the Treaty on European Union and of the Treaty establishing the European Community, as amended by the provisions of this Treaty, shall be renumbered in accordance with the tables of equivalences set out in the Annex to this Treaty, which shall form an integral part thereof.
2. The cross-references to articles, titles and sections in the Treaty on European Union and in the Treaty establishing the European Community, as well as between them, shall be adapted in consequence. The same shall apply as regards references to articles, titles and sections of those treaties contained in the other Community treaties.
3. The references to the articles, titles and sections of the Treaties referred to in paragraph 2 contained in other instruments or acts shall be understood as references to the articles, titles and sections of the Treaties as renumbered pursuant to paragraph 1 and, respectively, to the paragraphs of the said articles, as renumbered by certain provisions of Article 6.

The tables of equivalences set out in the Annex to the Treaty of Amsterdam are reproduced below.

Notes

* New Article introduced by the Treaty of Amsterdam.
** New Title introduced by the Treaty of Amsterdam.
*** Chapter or Title restructured by the Treaty of Amsterdam.

A. Treaty on European Union

Old number	New number
TITLE I	TITLE I
Article A	Article 1
Article B	Article 2
Article C	Article 3
Article D	Article 4
Article E	Article 5
Article F	Article 6
Article F.1*	Article 7
TITLE II	TITLE II
Article G	Article 8
TITLE III	TITLE III
Article H	Article 9
TITLE IV	TITLE IV
Article I	Article 10
TITLE V***	TITLE V
Article J.1	Article 11
Article J.2	Article 12
Article J.3	Article 13
Article J.4	Article 14
Article J.5	Article 15

Old number	New number
Article J.6	Article 16
Article J.7	Article 17
Article J.8	Article 18
Article J.9	Article 19
Article J.10	Article 20
Article J.11	Article 21
Article J.12	Article 22
Article J.13	Article 23
Article J.14	Article 24
Article J.15	Article 25
Article J.16	Article 26
Article J.17	Article 27
Article J.18	Article 28
TITLE VI***	TITLE VI
Article K.1	Article 29
Article K.2	Article 30
Article K.3	Article 31
Article K.4	Article 32
Article K.5	Article 33
Article K.6	Article 34
Article K.7	Article 35
Article K.8	Article 36
Article K.9	Article 37
Article K.10	Article 38
Article K.11	Article 39
Article K.12	Article 40
Article K.13	Article 41
Article K.14	Article 42
TITLE VIa**	TITLE VII
Article K.15*	Article 43
Article K.16*	Article 44
Article K.17*	Article 45
TITLE VII	TITLE VIII
Article L	Article 46
Article M	Article 47
Article N	Article 48
Article O	Article 49
Article P	Article 50
Article Q	Article 51
Article R	Article 52
Article S	Article 53

B. Treaty establishing the European Community

Old number	New number
PART ONE	PART ONE
Article 1	Article 1
Article 2	Article 2
Article 3	Article 3
Article 3 a	Article 4
Article 3 b	Article 5
Article 3 c*	Article 6

Old number	New number
Article 4	Article 7
Article 4 a	Article 8
Article 4 b	Article 9
Article 5	Article 10
Article 5 a*	Article 11
Article 6	Article 12
Article 6 a*	Article 13
Article 7 (repealed)	—
Article 7 a	Article 14
Article 7 b (repealed)	—
Article 7 c	Article 15
Article 7 d*	Article 16
PART TWO	PART TWO
Article 8	Article 17
Article 8 a	Article 18
Article 8 b	Article 19
Article 8 c	Article 20
Article 8 d	Article 21
Article 8 e	Article 22
PART THREE TITLE I	PART THREE TITLE I
Article 9	Article 23
Article 10	Article 24
Article 11 (repealed)	—
CHAPTER 1	CHAPTER 1
Section 1 (deleted)	—
Article 12	Article 25
Article 13 (repealed)	—
Article 14 (repealed)	—
Article 15 (repealed)	—
Article 16 (repealed)	—
Article 17 (repealed)	—
Section 2 (deleted)	—
Article 18 (repealed)	—
Article 19 (repealed)	—
Article 20 (repealed)	—
Article 21 (repealed)	—
Article 22 (repealed)	—
Article 23 (repealed)	—
Article 24 (repealed)	—
Article 25 (repealed)	—
Article 26 (repealed)	—
Article 27 (repealed)	—
Article 28	Article 26
Article 29	Article 27
CHAPTER 2	CHAPTER 2
Article 30	Article 28
Article 31 (repealed)	—
Article 32 (repealed)	—
Article 33 (repealed)	—
Article 34	Article 29

5

Old number	New number
Article 35 (repealed)	—
Article 36	Article 30
Article 37	Article 31
TITLE II	TITLE II
Article 38	Article 32
Article 39	Article 33
Article 40	Article 34
Article 41	Article 35
Article 42	Article 36
Article 43	Article 37
Article 44 (repealed)	—
Article 45 (repealed)	—
Article 46	Article 38
Article 47 (repealed)	—
TITLE III CHAPTER 1	TITLE III CHAPTER 1
Article 48	Article 39
Article 49	Article 40
Article 50	Article 41
Article 51	Article 42
CHAPTER 2	CHAPTER 2
Article 52	Article 43
Article 53 (repealed)	—
Article 54	Article 44
Article 55	Article 45
Article 56	Article 46
Article 57	Article 47
Article 58	Article 48
CHAPTER 3	CHAPTER 3
Article 59	Article 49
Article 60	Article 50
Article 61	Article 51
Article 62 (repealed)	—
Article 63	Article 52
Article 64	Article 53
Article 65	Article 54
Article 66	Article 55
CHAPTER 4	CHAPTER 4
Article 67 (repealed)	—
Article 68 (repealed)	—
Article 69 (repealed)	—
Article 70 (repealed)	—
Article 71 (repealed)	—
Article 72 (repealed)	—
Article 73 (repealed)	—
Article 73 a (repealed)	—
Article 73 b	Article 56
Article 73 c	Article 57
Article 73 d	Article 58
Article 73 e (repealed)	—
Article 73 f	Article 59

Old number	New number
Article 73 g	Article 60
Article 73 h (repealed)	—
TITLE III a**	TITLE IV
Article 73 i*	Article 61
Article 73 j*	Article 62
Article 73 k*	Article 63
Article 73 l*	Article 64
Article 73 m*	Article 65
Article 73 n*	Article 66
Article 73 o*	Article 67
Article 73 p*	Article 68
Article 73 q*	Article 69
TITLE IV	TITLE V
Article 74	Article 70
Article 75	Article 71
Article 76	Article 72
Article 77	Article 73
Article 78	Article 74
Article 79	Article 75
Article 80	Article 76
Article 81	Article 77
Article 82	Article 78
Article 83	Article 79
Article 84	Article 80
TITLE V	TITLE VI
CHAPTER 1 Section 1	CHAPTER 1 Section 1
Article 85	Article 81
Article 86	Article 82
Article 87	Article 83
Article 88	Article 84
Article 89	Article 85
Article 90	Article 86
Section 2 (deleted)	—
Article 91 (repealed)	—
Section 3	Section 2
Article 92	Article 87
Article 93	Article 88
Article 94	Article 89
CHAPTER 2	CHAPTER 2
Article 95	Article 90
Article 96	Article 91
Article 97 (repealed)	—
Article 98	Article 92
Article 99	Article 93
CHAPTER 3	CHAPTER 3
Article 100	Article 94
Article 100 a	Article 95
Article 100 b (repealed)	—
Article 100 c (repealed)	—

Old number	New number
Article 100 d (repealed)	—
Article 101	Article 96
Article 102	Article 97

TITLE VI	TITLE VII
CHAPTER 1	CHAPTER 1
Article 102 a	Article 98
Article 103	Article 99
Article 103 a	Article 100
Article 104	Article 101
Article 104 a	Article 102
Article 104 b	Article 103
Article 104 c	Article 104

CHAPTER 2	CHAPTER 2
Article 105	Article 105
Article 105 a	Article 106
Article 106	Article 107
Article 107	Article 108
Article 108	Article 109
Article 108 a	Article 110
Article 109	Article 111

CHAPTER 3	CHAPTER 3
Article 109 a	Article 112
Article 109 b	Article 113
Article 109 c	Article 114
Article 109 d	Article 115

CHAPTER 4	CHAPTER 4
Article 109 e	Article 116
Article 109 f	Article 117
Article 109 g	Article 118
Article 109 h	Article 119
Article 109 i	Article 120
Article 109 j	Article 121
Article 109 k	Article 122
Article 109 l	Article 123
Article 109 m	Article 124

TITLE VI a**	TITLE VIII
Article 109 n*	Article 125
Article 109 o*	Article 126
Article 109 p*	Article 127
Article 109 q*	Article 128
Article 109 r*	Article 129
Article 109 s*	Article 130

TITLE VII	TITLE IX
Article 110	Article 131
Article 111 (repealed)	—
Article 112	Article 132
Article 113	Article 133
Article 114 (repealed)	—
Article 115	Article 134

Old number	New number
TITLE VII a**	TITLE X
Article 116*	Article 135
TITLE VIII CHAPTER 1***	TITLE XI CHAPTER 1
Article 117	Article 136
Article 118	Article 137
Article 118 a	Article 138
Article 118 b	Article 139
Article 118 c	Article 140
Article 119	Article 141
Article 119 a	Article 142
Article 120	Article 143
Article 121	Article 144
Article 122	Article 145
CHAPTER 2	CHAPTER 2
Article 123	Article 146
Article 124	Article 147
Article 125	Article 148
CHAPTER 3	CHAPTER 3
Article 126	Article 149
Article 127	Article 150
TITLE IX	TITLE XII
Article 128	Article 151
TITLE X	TITLE XIII
Article 129	Article 152
TITLE XI	TITLE XIV
Article 129 a	Article 153
TITLE XII	TITLE XV
Article 129 b	Article 154
Article 129 c	Article 155
Article 129 d	Article 156
TITLE XIII	TITLE XVI
Article 130	Article 157
TITLE XIV	TITLE XVII
Article 130 a	Article 158
Article 130 b	Article 159
Article 130 c	Article 160
Article 130 d	Article 161
Article 130 e	Article 162
TITLE XV	TITLE XVIII
Article 130 f	Article 163
Article 130 g	Article 164
Article 130 h	Article 165
Article 130 i	Article 166
Article 130 j	Article 167
Article 130 k	Article 168
Article 130 l	Article 169
Article 130 m	Article 170

Old number	New number
Article 130 n	Article 171
Article 130 o	Article 172
Article 130 p	Article 173
Article 130 q (repealed)	—

TITLE XVI	TITLE XIX
Article 130 r	Article 174
Article 130 s	Article 175
Article 130 t	Article 176

TITLE XVII	TITLE XX
Article 130 u	Article 177
Article 130 v	Article 178
Article 130 w	Article 179
Article 130 x	Article 180
Article 130 y	Article 181

PART FOUR	PART FOUR
Article 131	Article 182
Article 132	Article 183
Article 133	Article 184
Article 134	Article 185
Article 135	Article 186
Article 136	Article 187
Article 136 a	Article 188

PART FIVE TITLE I CHAPTER 1 Section 1	PART FIVE TITLE I CHAPTER 1 Section 1
Article 137	Article 189
Article 138	Article 190
Article 138 a	Article 191
Article 138 b	Article 192
Article 138 c	Article 193
Article 138 d	Article 194
Article 138 e	Article 195
Article 139	Article 196
Article 140	Article 197
Article 141	Article 198
Article 142	Article 199
Article 143	Article 200
Article 144	Article 201
Section 2	Section 2
Article 145	Article 202
Article 146	Article 203
Article 147	Article 204
Article 148	Article 205
Article 149 (repealed)	—
Article 150	Article 206
Article 151	Article 207
Article 152	Article 208
Article 153	Article 209
Article 154	Article 210

Old number	New number
Section 3	Section 3
Article 155	Article 211
Article 156	Article 212
Article 157	Article 213
Article 158	Article 214
Article 159	Article 215
Article 160	Article 216
Article 161	Article 217
Article 162	Article 218
Article 163	Article 219
Section 4	Section 4
Article 164	Article 220
Article 165	Article 221
Article 166	Article 222
Article 167	Article 223
Article 168	Article 224
Article 168 a	Article 225
Article 169	Article 226
Article 170	Article 227
Article 171	Article 228
Article 172	Article 229
Article 173	Article 230
Article 174	Article 231
Article 175	Article 232
Article 176	Article 233
Article 177	Article 234
Article 178	Article 235
Article 179	Article 236
Article 180	Article 237
Article 181	Article 238
Article 182	Article 239
Article 183	Article 240
Article 184	Article 241
Article 185	Article 242
Article 186	Article 243
Article 187	Article 244
Article 188	Article 245
Section 5	Section 5
Article 188 a	Article 246
Article 188 b	Article 247
Article 188 c	Article 248
CHAPTER 2	CHAPTER 2
Article 189	Article 249
Article 189 a	Article 250
Article 189 b	Article 251
Article 189 c	Article 252
Article 190	Article 253
Article 191	Article 254
Article 191 a*	Article 255
Article 192	Article 256
CHAPTER 3	CHAPTER 3
Article 193	Article 257

Old number	New number
Article 194	Article 258
Article 195	Article 259
Article 196	Article 260
Article 197	Article 261
Article 198	Article 262
CHAPTER 4	CHAPTER 4
Article 198 a	Article 263
Article 198 b	Article 264
Article 198 c	Article 265
CHAPTER 5	CHAPTER 5
Article 198 d	Article 266
Article 198 e	Article 267
TITLE II	TITLE II
Article 199	Article 268
Article 200 (repealed)	—
Article 201	Article 269
Article 201 a	Article 270
Article 202	Article 271
Article 203	Article 272
Article 204	Article 273
Article 205	Article 274
Article 205 a	Article 275
Article 206	Article 276
Article 206 a (repealed)	—
Article 207	Article 277
Article 208	Article 278
Article 209	Article 279
Article 209 a	Article 280
PART SIX	PART SIX
Article 210	Article 281
Article 211	Article 282
Article 212*	Article 283
Article 213	Article 284
Article 213 a*	Article 285
Article 213 b*	Article 286
Article 214	Article 287
Article 215	Article 288
Article 216	Article 289
Article 217	Article 290
Article 218*	Article 291
Article 219	Article 292
Article 220	Article 293
Article 221	Article 294
Article 222	Article 295
Article 223	Article 296
Article 224	Article 297
Article 225	Article 298
Article 226 (repealed)	—
Article 227	Article 299
Article 228	Article 300
Article 228 a	Article 301
Article 229	Article 302

Old number	New number
Article 230	Article 303
Article 231	Article 304
Article 232	Article 305
Article 233	Article 306
Article 234	Article 307
Article 235	Article 308
Article 236*	Article 309
Article 237 (repealed)	—
Article 238	Article 310
Article 239	Article 311
Article 240	Article 312
Article 241 (repealed)	—
Article 242 (repealed)	—
Article 243 (repealed)	—
Article 244 (repealed)	—
Article 245 (repealed)	—
Article 246 (repealed)	—
FINAL PROVISIONS	FINAL PROVISIONS
Article 247	Article 313
Article 248	Article 314

A2

EC TREATY: RULES ON COMPETITION

(Amsterdam consolidated version: Articles 81–89)

Commentary

Arts 81–86: B&C: 1.018, 12.200 **F&N:** 3.03
Arts 81–89: B&C: 1.015, 1.018, 1.027, 2.015, 11.009, 11.029, 12.194, 15.068 **F&N:** 6.08, 6.09, 6.50
Arts 87–89: B&C: Arts 87–89 1.018, 1.025, 15.001, 15.006, 15.128 **F&N:** 4.413

Section 1
Rules Applying to Undertakings

Article 81

1. The following shall be prohibited as incompatible with the common market: all agreements between undertakings, decisions by associations of undertakings and concerted practices which may affect trade between Member States and which have as their object or effect the prevention, restriction or distortion of competition within the common market, and in particular those which:

(a) directly or indirectly fix purchase or selling prices or any other trading conditions;

(b) limit or control production, markets, technical development, or investment;

(c) share markets or sources of supply;

(d) apply dissimilar conditions to equivalent transactions with other trading parties, thereby placing them at a competitive disadvantage;

(e) make the conclusion of contracts subject to acceptance by the other parties of supplementary obligations which, by their nature or according to commercial usage, have no connection with the subject of such contracts.

2. Any agreements or decisions prohibited pursuant to this Article shall be automatically void.

3. The provisions of paragraph 1 may, however, be declared inapplicable in the case of:

— any agreement or category of agreements between undertakings;
— any decision or category of decisions by associations of undertakings;
— any concerted practice or category of concerted practices,

which contributes to improving the production or distribution of goods or to promoting technical or economic progress, while allowing consumers a fair share of the resulting benefit, and which does not:

(a) impose on the undertakings concerned restrictions which are not indispensable to the attainment of these objectives;
(b) afford such undertakings the possibility of eliminating competition in respect of a substantial part of the products in question.

Commentary

Art 81: B&C: 1.002, 1.004, 1.019–1.021, 1.023–1.024, 1.029–1.030, 1.032, 1.057–1.059, 1.061–1.063, 1.090, 1.096–1.098, 1.108, 1.112, 1.115–1.116, 1.119, 1.124, 1.127–1.128, 1.130, 1.132–1.133, 2.003–2.004, 2.012, 2.018, 2.020, 2.029, 2.035–2.036, 2.046, 2.055, 2.078, 2.088–2.089, 2.101, 2.118, 2.121, 2.129, 3.004, 3.007–3.008, 3.019, 3.057, 3.094–3.095, 4.002, 4.005–4.006, 4.011, 4.013, 4.017, 4.092, 5.002, 5.004, 5.011, 5.016, 5.018, 5.023, 5.032, 5.038, 5.040, 5.045, 5.055, 5.078, 5.080, 5.089–5.090, 5.094, 5.104, 5.110–5.112, 5.133–5.134, 5.149, 5.156–5.157, **5.159–5.162**, 6.002, 6.053, 6.055–6.056, 6.059, 6.067, 6.092, 6.108, 6.137, 7.001, 7.003, 7.008, 7.011, 7.013–7.018, 7.021, 7.024–7.025, 7.027, 7.032, 7.034, 7.055, 7.070, 7.087, 7.090–7.091, 7.100, 7.111, 7.113, 7.118, 7.128, 7.131, 7.138, 8.006, 8.009, 8.016, 8.024, 8.052–8.053, 8.097, 8.127, 8.130, 8.142, 8.150, 8.185, 8.188, 8.233–8.234, 8.238, 8.257–8.258, **8.260–8.263**, 8.273–8.274, 9.004–9.005, 9.007, 9.014, 9.017, 9.064, 9.066, 9.069, 9.071, 9.075, 9.083–9.084, 9.087–9.088, 9.091, 9.097, 9.101, 9.124, 9.126, 9.131, 9.168, 9.172, 10.003, 10.005–10.008, 10.037, 10.048, 10.050, 10.054, 10.063, 10.086, 10.098, 10.100, 10.102, 10.118, 10.129, 10.138, 10.150, 11.001, 11.004, 11.006–11.008, 11.013, 11.015, 11.021–11.022, 11.029–11.031, 11.033–11.035, 11.047, 11.053–11.054, 12.003–12.004, 12.006–12.007, 12.019, 12.021, 12.023, 12.036, 12.042, 12.049, 12.057, 12.071–12.072, 12.078, 12.122, 12.124, 12.126–12.127, 12.129–12.130, 12.136, 12.140, 12.144–12.145, 12.169, 12.180, 12.188, 12.195, 12.205–12.206, 12.209, 13.001–13.002, 13.004, 13.011, 13.015, 13.017, 13.022, 13.034, 13.040, 13.052, 13.061–13.062, 13.069, 13.071, 13.080, 13.082, 13.087, 13.093, 13.097, 13.107, 13.109, 13.112–13.113, 13.128, 13.134, 13.136, 13.139, 13.160, 13.169–13.170, 13.179, 13.183, 13.196, 13.201, 13.207, 13.211, 13.221, 13.228, 13.236, 14.002–14.004, 14.006–14.011, 14.013, 14.015–14.017, 14.019, 14.021, 14.024, 14.026–14.027, 14.034, 14.036, 14.038, 14.041–14.044, 14.047, 14.049, 14.051, **14.053–14.059**, 14.061–14.062, **14.069–14.074**, 14.076–14.078, **14.080–14.084**, 14.086–14.088, 14.090, 14.092, 14.094–14.096, 14.098, 14.108, 14.110–14.112, 14.115–14.117, 14.119, 14.132, **14.136–14.139**, 14.142, 14.144, 14.146–14.147, 14.149, 14.151, 14.159, 14.162–14.164, 14.167–14.168, 14.170, 15.026–15.028, 15.111, 15.133 **F&N:** 1.17, 1.21, 1.114, 1.115, 2.03, 2.05, 2.07, 2.08, 2.11, 2.19–2.25, 2.27, 2.30, 2.31, 2.32, 2.33, 2.39–2.43, 2.46, 2.47, 2.48, 2.53–2.57, 2.59, 2.62–2.65, 2.67, 2.73, 2.74, 2.75, 2.78, 2.79, 2.81, 2.83, 2.85, 2.87, 2.88, 2.90, 2.91, 2.92, 2.94, 2.100, 2.106, 2.108, 2.110, 2.111, 2.133, 2.135, 2.139, 2.141–2.147, 2.149, 2.150, 2.151, 2.153, 2.154, 2.158, 2.164, 2.176, 2.177, 2.181, 2.198, 2.201, 2.203, 2.205, 2.208, 2.218, 2.219, 2.228, 2.235, 2.240, 2.242, 2.243, 2.244, 2.246, 2.248, 2.250, 2.253, 2.254, 2.260, 2.261, 2.270, 2.274, **3.01–3.460**, 4.01–4.03, 4.05, 4.07, 4.10, 4.15, 4.115, 4.125, 4.357, 4.410–4.418, 4.420, 4.421, 4.423, 4.432, 4.450, 4.459, 5.24, 5.25, 5.54, 5.57, 5.241, 5.297, 5.347, 5.350, 6.02, 6.04–6.07, 6.09–6.13, 6.34, 6.53, 6.89, 6.91, 6.92, 6.93, 6.157, 6.218, 6.222, 7.08, 7.23–7.26, 7.34, 7.38, 7.39, 7.48, 7.51, 7.53, 7.78, 7.87, 7.113, 7.114, 7.148, 7.149, 7.168, 7.213, 7.225, 7.229, 7.257, 7.260, 7.263, 7.281, 7.310, 7.334, 7.341, 8.03, 8.04, 8.49–8.52, 8.54, 8.56, 8.57, 8.70, 8.101, 8.129, 8.130, 8.143, 8.144, 8.160, 8.161, 8.205, 8.215, 8.216, 8.218, 8.220, 8.236, 8.237, 8.238, 8.239, 8.240, 8.244, 8.245, 8.246, 8.250, 8.258, 8.260, 8.263, 8.270, 8.303, 8.320, 8.323, 8.329, 8.352, 8.353, 8.399, 8.420, 8.424, 8.434, 8.436, 8.449, 8.450, 8.452, 8.453, 8.457, 8.458, 8.466, 8.487, 8.488, 8.491, 8.493, 8.494, 8.497, 8.502, 8.504, 8.507, 8.511, 8.535, 8.553, 8.556, 8.586, 8.590– 8.592, 8.596, 8.681, 8.715, 8.717, 8.822, 8.846, 8.857, 8.859, 8.875, 9.01–9.04, 9.09, 9.24, 9.29, 9.39, 9.40, 9.50, 9.52, 9.55, 9.58, 9.62, 9.64, 9.65, 9.69, 9.86, 9.90, 9.96, 9.101, 9.117, 9.119, 9.120, 9.149, 9.156, 9.165, 9.172, 9.176, 9.187, 9.199, 9.213, 9.245, 9.291, 10.11, 10.59, 10.62, 10.63, 10.69, 10.88, 10.89, 10.114, 10.125, 10.126, 10.127, 10.140, 10.144, 10.148, 10.153, 10.165, 10.171, 10.196, 10.202, 10.203, 10.205, 10.207, 10.208, 11.03, 11.08, 11.22, 11.40, 11.51, 11.52, 11.71, 11.72, 11.97, 11.100, 11.131, 11.138, 11.154, 11.161, 12.31, 12.53, 12.67, 12.91, 12.105, 12.122, 12.123, **12.174–12.368**, 13.01, 13.32, 13.46, 13.55, 13.61, 13.77, 13.96, 13.114, 13.128, 13.214, 13.361, 13.365, 14.10, 14.28, 14.43, 14.55, 14.67, 14.87, 14.88, 14.114, 14.122, 14.126, 14.131, 14.176, 14.200, 14.212, 14.232, 15.09, 15.13, 15.18, 15.46, 15.48, 15.55, 15.63, 15.63

13.240, 13.242, 13.250, 14.004–14.005, 14.010, 14.042–14.043, 14.060, 14.081, 14.087–14.088, 14.092, 14.098, 14.153, 14.163 **F&N:** 2.2, 2.3, 2.5, 2.7, 2.19, 2.20, 2.21, 2.24, 2.25, 2.43, 2.45, 2.52, 2.71, 2.74, 2.87, 2.139, 2.208, 2.240, 2.244, 3.12, 3.13, 3.15, 3.133, 3.136, 3.137, 3.163, 3.189, 3.205, 3.210, 3.213, 3.223, 3.224, 3.229, 3.266, 3.281, 3.282, 3.323, 3.393, 3.394, **3.395–3.460**, 4.157, 4.158, 4.415, 4.418, 4.419, 4.421, 4.450, 4.459, 4.460, 4.461, 5.332, 5.334, 5.336, 5.343, 5.344, 6.212, 7.24, 7.52, 7.56–7.58 7.62, 7.132, 7.165, 7.183, 7.192, 7.211, 7.238, 7.244, 7.245, 7.273, 7.281, 7.283, 7.287, 7.303, 7.391, 7.394, 7.398, 7.411, 7.413, 8.03, 8.04, 8.488, 9.10, 9.12, 9.14, 9.18, 9.24, 9.26, 9.42, 9.45, 9.55, 9.56, 9.69, 9.78–9.81, 9.104, 9.108, 9.125, 9.127, 9.155, 9.156, 9.158, 9.159, 9.160, 9.164, 9.165, 9.207, 9.262, 9.264, 9.273, 9.290, 9.291, 9.292, 9.293, 9.317, 9.337, 9.356, 10.62, 10.63, 10.64, 10.65, 10.91, 10.96, 10.116, 10.117, 10.122, 10.125, 10.128, 10.137, 10.138, 10.140, 10.164, 10.165, 10.186, 11.42, 11.43, 11.45, 11.47, 11.49, 11.112, 11.122, 11.128, 12.22, 12.105, 12.174, 12.176, 12.178, 12.191, 12.198, 12.217, 12.218, 12.219, 12.223, 12.229, 12.231, 12.232, 12.236, 12.237, 12.239, 12.240, 12.257, 12.278, 12.280, 12.281, 12.291, 12.323, 12.326, 12.346, 12.360, 12.362, 12.422, 13.87, 13.92, 13.96, 13.106, 13.109, 13.110, 13.258, 13.361, 13.363, 14.15, 14.30, 14.34, 14.43, 14.48, 14.78, 14.102, 14.104, 14.111, 14.124, 14.145, 14.148, 14.177, 14.219, 15.02, 15.05, 15.08, 15.16, 15.17, 15.19, 15.21, 15.22, 15.23, 15.25, 15.58, 15.93, 15.143, 15.149, 15.152, 15.162, 16.58
Art 81(3)(b): B&C: 7.013, 7.062–7.063 **F&N:** 3.455

Article 82

Any abuse by one or more undertakings of a dominant position within the common market or in a substantial part of it shall be prohibited as incompatible with the common market in so far as it may affect trade between Member States.

Such abuse may, in particular, consist in:

(a) directly or indirectly imposing unfair purchase or selling prices or other unfair trading conditions;
(b) limiting production, markets or technical development to the prejudice of consumers;
(c) applying dissimilar conditions to equivalent transactions with other trading parties, thereby placing them at a competitive disadvantage;
(d) making the conclusion of contracts subject to acceptance by the other parties of supplementary obligations which, by their nature or according to commercial usage, have no connection with the subject of such contracts.

Commentary
Art 82: B&C: 1.002, 1.020–1.021, 1.023–1.024, 1.029–1.030, 1.057–1.059, 1.061–1.063, 1.075, 1.090, 1.096–1.098, 1.105, 1.107, 1.110, 1.115–1.117, 1.119–1.121, 1.126, 1.128, 1.130–1.133, 2.003, 2.008–2.011, 2.024, 2.029–2.030, 2.035, 2.041, 2.052, 2.055, 2.101, 2.114, 2.119, 3.012, 3.018, 3.050, 3.086, 3.095, 4.002, 4.011, 4.013, 4.015, 4.017–4.018, 4.026, 4.030–4.031, 4.034, 4.052, 4.082, 4.092, 5.075, 5.100, 5.107, 5.112, 5.116, 5.134, 5.156–5.157, 5.163, 6.001, 6.007, 6.101, 6.105, 6.144, 6.159, 6.163, 7.025, 7.034, 7.063, 7.113, 7.131, 7.138, 8.006, 8.009, 8.016, 8.097, 8.127, 8.142, 8.150, 8.188, 8.195, 8.218, 8.255, 8.257, **8.259–8.263**, 8.273–8.276, 9.004, 9.006–9.007, 9.014, 9.066, **9.071–9.075**, 9.083, 9.115, 9.118, 9.124, 9.172, 9.179–9.180, 9.182, **10.001–10.015**, 10.019–10.020, 10.026, 10.028, 10.030, 10.033, 10.036, 10.041, 10.043, 10.045, 10.047–10.051, 10.054, 10.058–10.059, 10.061, 10.063–10.065, 10.069, 10.073, 10.075, 10.080, 10.084, 10.086, 10.090–10.093, 10.097–10.100, 10.102, 10.106, 10.110–10.111, 10.113, 10.117–10.120, 10.122–10.123, 10.125–10.127, 10.129, 10.132, 10.138, 10.141, 10.144–10.146, 10.149–10.150, 10.152–10.153, 11.001, 11.004, 11.007–11.009, 11.013, 11.015–11.022, 11.029–11.030, 11.033–11.034, 11.047, 11.053–11.054, 12.003–12.004, 12.006–12.007, 12.014, 12.019, 12.021, 12.026, 12.034–12.036, 12.046, 12.049–12.050, 12.057, 12.067–12.068, 12.078, 12.082, 12.099–12.100, 12.122–12.127, 12.136, 12.144, 12.147–12.148, 12.150, 12.152–12.154, 12.156, 12.158–12.159, 12.164, 12.168–12.169, 12.180, 12.188, 12.191–12.193, 12.195, 12.200, 12.205–12.206, 13.001–13.002, 13.004–13.005, 13.015, 13.017, 13.022, 13.034, 13.040, 13.052, 13.061–13.062, 13.069, 13.080, 13.082, 13.087, 13.093, 13.097, 13.107, 13.109, 13.112–13.113, 13.116, 13.126, 13.128, 13.131, 13.134–13.136, 13.140, 13.160, 13.167, 13.169, 13.179, 13.196, 13.201–13.202, 13.207, 13.211, 13.227, 13.236, 14.002–14.011, 14.013, 14.015–14.017, 14.019, 14.021, 14.024, 14.026–14.027, 14.034, 14.036, 14.038, 14.041–14.044, 14.047, 14.049, 14.051, 14.053–14.056, 14.057–14.059, 14.061–14.062, 14.069–14.074, 14.076–14.078, 14.081–14.084, 14.086–14.087, 14.090, 14.092, 14.095–14.096, 14.098, 14.108, 14.110–14.111, 14.116, 14.119, 14.123, 14.130, 14.132–14.133, 14.136–14.138, 14.140–14.142, 14.144, 14.146–14.147, 14.149, 14.151–14.152, 14.159, 14.161–14.164, 14.170 **F&N:** 1.17, 1.21, 1.114, 1.185, 2.3, 2.5, 2.11, 2.19–2.23, 2.25, 2.27, 2.30–2.36, 2.39–2.43, 2.47, 2.48, 2.53–2.57, 2.59, 2.61–2.67, 2.73, 2.74, 2.75, 2.78, 2.79, 2.81, 2.83, 2.85, 2.90, 2.91, 2.92, 2.94, 2.100, 2.105, 2.106, 2.108, 2.110, 2.111, 2.133, 2.135, 2.139, 2.141, 2.142, 2.143, 2.144, 2.145, 2.146, 2.147, 2.149, 2.150, 2.151, 2.153, 2.154, 2.158, 2.164, 2.176, 2.177, 2.181, 2.198, 2.201, 2.203, 2.205, 2.208, 2.218, 2.219, 2.228, 2.235, 2.240, 2.242, 2.243, 2.244, 2.246, 2.248, 2.250, 2.253, 2.254, 2.260, 2.261, 2.270, 2.274, 4.01–4.464, 5.168, 5.181, 5.186, 5.244, 5.284, 5.296, 5.298, 5.301–5.306, 5.347, 5.350, 6.02, 6.04–6.07, 6.10–6.13, 6.33, 6.53, 6.54–6.83, 6.86–6.88, 6.129, 6.157, 6.158, 6.178, 6.183, 6.186, 6.187, 6.198, 6.218, 6.222,

6.245, 7.23, 8.101, 8.160, 8.237, 8.238, 8.240, 8.244, 8.245, 8.250, 8.258, 8.260, 8.263, 8.270, 8.320, 8.323,
8.329, 8.352, 8.353, 8.399, 8.420, 8.424, 8.434, 8.436, 8.449, 8.452, 8.457, 8.458, 8.466, 8.488, 8.491, 8.500,
8.502, 8.511, 8.535, 8.586, 8.590, 8.596, 8.715, 8.749, 8.822, 8.857, 8.859, 9.02, 9.38, 9.39, 9.50, 9.58, 9.65,
9.117, 9.119, 9.120, 9.121, 9.185, 9.291, 9.292, 9.305, 9.356, 10.6, 10.11, 10.15, 10.209–10.255, 11.03, 11.22,
11.40, 11.71, 11.73, 11.97, 11.120, 11.138, 11.154, 11.156, 11.157, 11.161, 12.31, 12.53, 12.67, 12.91, 12.105,
12.122, 12.123, 12.176, 12.178, 12.213, 12.239, 12.259, 12.263, 12.273, 12.275, 12.333, 12.370, 12.371,
12.373, 12.379, 12.385, 12.395, 12.401, 12.411, 12.413, 12.416, 12.417, 13.01, 13.32, 13.33, 13.46, 13.55,
13.56, 13.99, 13.117, 13.131, 13.175, 13.184, 13.200, 13.208, 13.213, 13.214, 13.215, 13.234, 13.236, 13.245,
13.251, 13.253, 13.261, 13.291, 13.308, 13.311, 13.361, 13.365, 14.08, 14.10, 14.13, 14.28, 14.49, 14.55,
14.62, 14.65, 14.66, 14.67, 14.69, 14.88, 14.121, 14.122, 14.126, 14.131, 14.192, 14.200, 14.212, 14.225,
14.226, 14.228, 14.230, 14.232, 14.236, 14.244, 14.250–14.252, 14.256, 15.154
Art 82(a)–(d): B&C: 10.058, 10.068
Art 82(a): B&C: 10.088, 10.104, 10.146, 10.150 F&N: 4.362
Art 82(b): B&C: 10.133, 10.144, 10.151, 10.155–10.156 F&N: 4.390, 4.392, 6.66, 10.238, 15.154
Art 82(c): B&C: 10.080–10.081, 10.083–10.084, 10.088, 10.097, 10.144 F&N: 4.321, 4.322, 4.397, 4.401,
12.389, 13.136, 14.246, 14.247
Art 82(d): B&C: 10.119, 10.144, 12.193 F&N: 4.238, 4.317, 13.135

Article 83

1. The appropriate regulations or directives to give effect to the principles set out in Articles 81 and 82 shall be laid down by the Council, acting by a qualified majority on a proposal from the Commission and after consulting the European Parliament.

2. The regulations or directives referred to in paragraph 1 shall be designed in particular:

(a) to ensure compliance with the prohibitions laid down in Article 81(1) and in Article 82 by making provision for fines and periodic penalty payments;

(b) to lay down detailed rules for the application of Article 81(3), taking into account the need to ensure effective supervision on the one hand, and to simplify administration to the greatest possible extent on the other;

(c) to define, if need be, in the various branches of the economy, the scope of the provisions of Articles 81 and 82;

(d) to define the respective functions of the Commission and of the Court of Justice in applying the provisions laid down in this paragraph;

(e) to determine the relationship between national laws and the provisions contained in this Section or adopted pursuant to this Article.

Commentary
Art 83: B&C: 1.021–1.022, 1.042, 8.257, 8.260, 11.025, 14.022, 14.042 F&N: 2.73, 2.176, 4.351, 4.413, 8.250,
8.590, 11.03, 14.99
Art 83(2): F&N: 8.590
Art 83(2)(b): F&N: 2.19
Art 83(2)(e): B&C: 14.054 F&N: 4.421

Article 84

Until the entry into force of the provisions adopted in pursuance of Article 83, the authorities in Member States shall rule on the admissibility of agreements, decisions and concerted practices and on abuse of a dominant position in the common market in accordance with the law of their country and with the provisions of Article 81, in particular paragraph 3, and of Article 82.

Commentary
Art 84: B&C: 1.023, 3.095, 7.017, 8.261, 12.036 F&N: 4.351, 4.413

Article 85

1. Without prejudice to Article 84, the Commission shall ensure the application of the principles laid down in Articles 81 and 82. On application by a Member State or on its own initiative, and in cooperation with the competent authorities in the Member States, who shall give it their assistance, the Commission shall investigate cases of suspected infringement of these principles. If it finds that there has been an infringement, it shall propose appropriate measures to bring it to an end.

2. If the infringement is not brought to an end, the Commission shall record such infringement of the principles in a reasoned decision. The Commission may publish its decision and authorise Member States to take the measures, the conditions and details of which it shall determine, needed to remedy the situation.

Commentary

Art 85: **B&C:** 1.023, 3.094–3.095, 7.017, 7.138, 8.261, 12.036, 13.089 **F&N:** 4.413, 5.24, 14.84, 14.93, 14.94, 14.130, 14.252, 14.254
Art 85(1): **F&N:** 2.91
Art 85(2): **B&C:** 12.036

Article 86

1. In the case of public undertakings and undertakings to which Member States grant special or exclusive rights, Member States shall neither enact nor maintain in force any measure contrary to the rules contained in this Treaty, in particular to those rules provided for in Article 12 and Articles 81 to 89.

2. Undertakings entrusted with the operation of services of general economic interest or having the character of a revenue-producing monopoly shall be subject to the rules contained in this Treaty, in particular to the rules on competition, in so far as the application of such rules does not obstruct the performance, in law or in fact, of the particular tasks assigned to them. The development of trade must not be affected to such an extent as would be contrary to the interests of the Community.

3. The Commission shall ensure the application of the provisions of this Article and shall, where necessary, address appropriate directives or decisions to Member States.

Commentary

Art 86: **B&C:** 1.024, 1.090, 1.096, 2.008, 2.029, 10.009, 10.086, 10.097, 11.002–11.003, 11.009, 11.011, 11.014, 11.018–11.020, 11.023, 11.028, 12.003, 12.089, 12.116, 12.168, 12.180, 12.188, 13.071, 13.089, 15.068 **F&N:** 4.33, 4.102, 4.128, 4.135, 4.196, 4.395, 4.411, 6.01–6.257, 6.07, 6.35, 6.41, 6.72, 6.78, 6.131, 6.135, 6.178, 6.191, 6.213, 6.214, 6.221, 6.222, 6.224, 6.225, 6.227, 6.229, 6.233, 6.239, 6.240, 6.255, 11.138, 11.154, 11.157, 12.28, 12.59, 12.91, 12.105–12.107, 12.278, 12.426, 13.14, 13.23, 13.29, 13.32, 13.33, 13.159, 14.08, 14.10, 14.88, 14.93, 14.232
Art 86(1): **B&C:** 2.015, 10.009, 11.001, 11.007–11.009, 11.011–11.018, 11.020–11.023, 11.026, 11.046, 12.057, 14.123 **F&N:** 6.08–6.130, 6.134, 6.137, 6.158, 6.169, 6.186, 6.187, 6.211, 6.217, 6.218, 6.219, 6.222, 6.223, 6.226, 6.228, 6.229, 6.242, 6.243, 6.245, 6.250, 11.155, 11.157, 11.160, 14.88, 14.244, 14.253
Art 86(2): **B&C:** 1.024, 2.015, 6.162, 10.009, 11.001, 11.021, 11.026, 11.045–11.050, 11.052–11.056, 12.057, 12.071, 12.123, 12.182, 15.012, 15.041, 15.043, 15.068–15.069, 15.077, 15.134 **F&N:** 4.102, 6.22, 6.25, 6.78, 6.83, 6.87, 6.131–6.216, 6.243, 6.246, 6.250, 11.157, 11.158, 11.161, 12.40, 12.107, 12.108, 12.294, 12.362, 13.106, 16.223, 16.227, 16.229, 16.230, 16.232, 16.255
Art 86(3): **B&C:** 1.043, 11.014, 11.022–11.025, 11.027, 11.056, 12.082, 12.168, 13.220, 13.245, 15.090, 15.134 **F&N:** 6.98, 6.100, 6.122, 6.159, 6.203, 6.213, 6.215, 6.217–6.257, 16.262

SECTION 2
AIDS GRANTED BY STATES

Article 87

1. Save as otherwise provided in this Treaty, any aid granted by a Member State or through State resources in any form whatsoever which distorts or threatens to distort competition by favouring certain undertakings or the production of certain goods shall, in so far as it affects trade between Member States, be incompatible with the common market.

2. The following shall be compatible with the common market:

(a) aid having a social character, granted to individual consumers, provided that such aid is granted without discrimination related to the origin of the products concerned;
(b) aid to make good the damage caused by natural disasters or exceptional occurrences;
(c) aid granted to the economy of certain areas of the Federal Republic of Germany affected by the division of Germany, in so far as such aid is required in order to compensate for the economic disadvantages caused by that division.

3. The following may be considered to be compatible with the common market:

(a) aid to promote the economic development of areas where the standard of living is abnormally low or where there is serious underemployment;

(b) aid to promote the execution of an important project of common European interest or to remedy a serious disturbance in the economy of a Member State;

(c) aid to facilitate the development of certain economic activities or of certain economic areas, where such aid does not adversely affect trading conditions to an extent contrary to the common interest;

(d) aid to promote culture and heritage conservation where such aid does not affect trading conditions and competition in the Community to an extent that is contrary to the common interest;

(e) such other categories of aid as may be specified by decision of the Council acting by a qualified majority on a proposal from the Commission.

Commentary

Art 87: **B&C:** 1.022, 1.115, 11.003, 11.009, 11.025, 11.047–11.048, 15.004, 15.006–15.007, 15.013, 15.015, 15.018, 15.022–15.023, 15.025–15.027, 15.044, 15.066, 15.068, 15.074, 15.080, 15.090, 15.108, 15.122, 15.129–15.135 **F&N:** 6.07, 6.159, 6.190, 6.213, 6.218, 14.232, 16.78, 16.197, 16.204, 16.274

Art 87(1): **B&C:** 1.025, 4.014, 15.001, 15.006–15.008, 15.010, 15.012, 15.017–15.018, 15.023–15.024, 15.026, 15.028, 15.030, 15.034, 15.039, 15.068, 15.071, 15.080, 15.108–15.109, 15.120, 15.122 **F&N:** 6.159, 16.02, 16.03, 16.04, 16.06, 16.28, 16.44, 16.58, 16.59, 16.82, 16.98, 16.227, 16.229, 16.233, 16.236, 16.241, 16.277, 16.285

Art 87(2): **B&C:** 15.001, 15.006, 15.039, 15.108 **F&N:** 16.79, 16.90, 16.277

Art 87(2)(a): **B&C:** 15.039

Art 87(2)(b): **B&C:** 15.039 **F&N:** 8.788, 16.82, 16.84, 16.86, 16.87

Art 87(2)(c): **B&C:** 15.004, 15.040 **F&N:** 16.89

Art 87(3): **B&C:** 15.001, 15.008, 15.042–15.044, 15.047, 15.064, 15.067, 15.122 **F&N:** 16.90, 16.277, 16.424

Art 87(3)(a)–(d) **B&C:** 15.041, 15.065

Art 87(3)(a): **B&C:** 15.040, 15.042–15.043, 15.045–15.046, 15.049, 15.054–15.055 **F&N:** 16.64, 16.70, 16.77, 16.91, 16.101, 16.103, 16.105, 16.106, 16.108

Art 87(3)(b): **B&C:** 15.053–15.054 **F&N:** 6.92, 16.94, 16.97

Art 87(3)(c): **B&C:** 15.040, 15.042–15.043, 15.046, 15.050, 15.054–15.057, 15.064 **F&N:** 16.64, 16.90, 16.99, 16.100, 16.101, 16.103, 16.105, 16.119, 16.136

Art 87(3)(d): **B&C:** 4.014, 15.004, 15.064 **F&N:** 16.98, 16.146

Art 87(3)(e): **B&C:** 15.041, 15.065–15.066

Article 88

1. The Commission shall, in cooperation with Member States, keep under constant review all systems of aid existing in those States. It shall propose to the latter any appropriate measures required by the progressive development or by the functioning of the common market.

2. If, after giving notice to the parties concerned to submit their comments, the Commission finds that aid granted by a State or through State resources is not compatible with the common market having regard to Article 87, or that such aid is being misused, it shall decide that the State concerned shall abolish or alter such aid within a period of time to be determined by the Commission.

If the State concerned does not comply with this decision within the prescribed time, the Commission or any other interested State may, in derogation from the provisions of Articles 226 and 227, refer the matter to the Court of Justice direct.

On application by a Member State, the Council may, acting unanimously, decide that aid which that State is granting or intends to grant shall be considered to be compatible with the common market, in derogation from the provisions of Article 87 or from the regulations provided for in Article 89, if such a decision is justified by exceptional circumstances. If, as regards the aid in question, the Commission has already initiated the procedure provided for in the first subparagraph of this paragraph, the fact that the State concerned has made its application to the Council shall have the effect of suspending that procedure until the Council has made its attitude known.

If, however, the Council has not made its attitude known within three months of the said application being made, the Commission shall give its decision on the case.

3. The Commission shall be informed, in sufficient time to enable it to submit its comments, of any plans to grant or alter aid. If it considers that any such plan is not compatible with the common market

Part A Treaty Provisions

having regard to Article 87, it shall without delay initiate the procedure provided for in paragraph 2. The Member State concerned shall not put its proposed measures into effect until this procedure has resulted in a final decision.

Commentary
Art 88: B&C: 1.022, 1.025, 1.090, 15.004, 15.006, 15.013, 15.015, 15.027, 15.044, 15.069, 15.090, 15.108, 15.129–15.131, 15.133–15.135 **F&N**: 6.07, 6.159, 6.215, 6.218, 6.246, 16.258, 16.370
Art 88(1): B&C: 15.070, 15.074, 15.111–15.112 **F&N**: 16.322, 16.347
Art 88(2): B&C: 15.041, 15.066, 15.073, 15.078, 15.080–15.086, 15.088, 15.092–15.093, 15.098, 15.102, 15.105, 15.110, 15.112–15.114, 15.116–15.117, 15.119, 15.122, 15.125, 15.135 **F&N**: 16.111, 16.193, 16.204, 16.207, 16.281, 16.292, 16.295, 16.375, 16.409
Art 88(3): B&C: 15.028, 15.067, 15.074–15.075, 15.077–15.078, 15.082, 15.090–15.092, 15.096–15.097, 15.107–15.109, 15.111–15.112, 15.121, 15.125, 15.128, 15.130, 15.134–15.135 **F&N**: 16.02, 16.58, 16.60, 16.66, 16.74, 16.79, 16.173, 16.226, 16.227, 16.228, 16.232, 16.274, 16.278, 16.279, 16.309, 16.368, 16.381, 16.408, 16.422, 16.424, 16.427

Article 89

The Council, acting by a qualified majority on a proposal from the Commission and after consulting the European Parliament, may make any appropriate regulations for the application of Articles 87 and 88 and may in particular determine the conditions in which Article 88(3) shall apply and the categories of aid exempted from this procedure.

Commentary
Art 89: B&C: 1.022, 1.025, 11.025, 15.006, 15.066, 15.090 **F&N**: 8.534, 16.58, 16.204

A3

EC TREATY: GENERAL PRINCIPLES

(Amsterdam consolidated version: Articles 1–3, 5–11a, 14–16)

Commentary
EC Treaty: B&C: 1.002–1.004, 1.006–1.008, 1.013, 1.028, 1.035, 1.038, 1.040, 1.043, 1.045–1.046, 1.048, 1.051, 1.070–1.071, 1.079, 1.090–1.092, 1.120, 1.130, 12.056, 14.001 **F&N**: 2.164, 2.197, 2.244, 2.245, 3.04, 4.364, 8.459, 8.476, 10.17, 12.06, 12.09, 12.12, 12.15, 14.05, 16.01, 16.56, 16.265, 16.386
Arts 1–16: B&C: 1.014
Arts 7–9: B&C: 1.014

Article 1

By this Treaty, the HIGH CONTRACTING PARTIES establish among themselves a EUROPEAN COMMUNITY.

Article 2

The Community shall have as its task, by establishing a common market and an economic and monetary union and by implementing common policies or activities referred to in Articles 3 and 4, to promote throughout the Community a harmonious, balanced and sustainable development of economic activities, a high level of employment and of social protection, equality between men and women, sustainable and non-inflationary growth, a high degree of competitiveness and convergence of economic performance, a high level of protection and improvement of the quality of the environment, the raising of the standard of living and quality of life, and economic and social cohesion and solidarity among Member States.

Commentary

Art 2: **B&C:** 1.007, 1.013–1.015, 2.034, 3.044, 8.183 **F&N:** 4.411, 5.653, 6.04, 9.38, 16.113

Article 3

1. For the purposes set out in Article 2, the activities of the Community shall include, as provided in this Treaty and in accordance with the timetable set out therein:

(a) the prohibition, as between Member States, of customs duties and quantitative restrictions on the import and export of goods, and of all other measures having equivalent effect;

(b) a common commercial policy;

(c) an internal market characterised by the abolition, as between Member States, of obstacles to the free movement of goods, persons, services and capital;

(d) measures concerning the entry and movement of persons as provided for in Title IV;

(e) a common policy in the sphere of agriculture and fisheries;

(f) a common policy in the sphere of transport;

(g) a system ensuring that competition in the internal market is not distorted;

(h) the approximation of the laws of Member States to the extent required for the functioning of the common market;

(i) the promotion of coordination between employment policies of the Member States with a view to enhancing their effectiveness by developing a coordinated strategy for employment;

(j) a policy in the social sphere comprising a European Social Fund;

(k) the strengthening of economic and social cohesion;

(l) a policy in the sphere of the environment;

(m) the strengthening of the competitiveness of Community industry;

(n) the promotion of research and technological development;

(o) encouragement for the establishment and development of trans-European networks;

(p) a contribution to the attainment of a high level of health protection;

(q) a contribution to education and training of quality and to the flowering of the cultures of the Member States;

(r) a policy in the sphere of development cooperation;

(s) the association of the overseas countries and territories in order to increase trade and promote jointly economic and social development;

(t) a contribution to the strengthening of consumer protection;

(u) measures in the spheres of energy, civil protection and tourism.

2. In all the activities referred to in this Article, the Community shall aim to eliminate inequalities, and to promote equality, between men and women.

Commentary

Art 3: **B&C:** 1.013–1.015, 1.026–1.027, 2.089, 12.052, 12.194 **F&N:** 3.02, 3.13, 6.04, 12.91

Art 3(1): **B&C:** 1.026

Art 3(1)(c): **F&N:** 9.38

Art 3(1)(e): **B&C:** 12.194

Art 3(1)(f): **B&C:** 12.005

Art 3(1)(g): **B&C:** 1.018, 1.027, 2.094, 5.038, 10.002, 10.006, 10.059, 11.007–11.008, 11.030, 11.033, 11.035, 12.124, 12.194, 14.055, 14.064, 14.167 **F&N:** 2.57, 2.142, 3.341, 4.01, 4.350, 4.411, 6.04, 6.05, 6.06, 6.92, 9.38, 14.88

Art 3(1)(l): **B&C:** 12.084

Art 3(1)(u): **B&C:** 12.052

Article 5

The Community shall act within the limits of the powers conferred upon it by this Treaty and of the objectives assigned to it therein.

In areas which do not fall within its exclusive competence, the Community shall take action, in accordance with the principle of subsidiarity, only if and in so far as the objectives of the proposed action cannot be sufficiently achieved by the Member States and can therefore, by reason of the scale or effects of the proposed action, be better achieved by the Community.

Any action by the Community shall not go beyond what is necessary to achieve the objectives of this Treaty.

Commentary
Art 5: B&C: 1.014–1.015, 1.028 F&N: 4.102
Art 5(2): F&N: 16.255
Art 5(3): B&C: 1.015

Article 6

Environmental protection requirements must be integrated into the definition and implementation of the Community policies and activities referred to in Article 3, in particular with a view to promoting sustainable development.

Commentary
Art 6: B&C: 1.014, 1.037 F&N: 3.13, 16.113
Art 6(3): F&N: 14.14

Article 7

1. The tasks entrusted to the Community shall be carried out by the following institutions:

— a EUROPEAN PARLIAMENT,
— a COUNCIL,
— a COMMISSION,
— a COURT OF JUSTICE,
— a COURT OF AUDITORS.

Each institution shall act within the limits of the powers conferred upon it by this Treaty.

2. The Council and the Commission shall be assisted by an Economic and Social Committee and a Committee of the Regions acting in an advisory capacity.

Commentary
Art 7: B&C: 1.009, 1.014, 1.038, 13.032

Article 8

A European system of central banks (hereinafter referred to as "ESCB") and a European Central Bank (hereinafter referred to as "ECB") shall be established in accordance with the procedures laid down in this Treaty; they shall act within the limits of the powers conferred upon them by this Treaty and by the Statute of the ESCB and of the ECB (hereinafter referred to as "Statute of the ESCB") annexed thereto.

Commentary
Art 8: B&C: 1.003, 1.014, 1.038
Art 8(1): F&N: 4.417
Art 8(2): F&N: 4.343, 4.344, 4.350, 4.416, 4.417

Article 9

A European Investment Bank is hereby established, which shall act within the limits of the powers conferred upon it by this Treaty and the Statute annexed thereto.

Commentary
Art 9: B&C: 1.014, 1.038

Article 10

Member States shall take all appropriate measures, whether general or particular, to ensure fulfilment of the obligations arising out of this Treaty or resulting from action taken by the institutions of the Community. They shall facilitate the achievement of the Community's tasks.

They shall abstain from any measure which could jeopardise the attainment of the objectives of this Treaty.

Commentary
Art 10: B&C: 1.015, 1.030, 2.012, 2.029, 2.118, 5.038, 11.001, 11.007–11.009, 11.029–11.035, 12.124, 13.052, 13.116–13.117, 14.001, 14.054–14.055, 14.064, 14.068, 14.089, 14.095, 14.110, 15.103 **F&N:** 2.155, 2.164, 2.195, 2.270, 6.04–6.06, 6.92, 8.244, 8.407, 12.91, 13.32, 13.33, 14.87, 16.334
Art 10(2): F&N: 14.88

Article 11[1]

1. Member States which intend to establish enhanced cooperation between themselves in one of the areas referred to in this Treaty shall address a request to the Commission, which may submit a proposal to the Council to that effect. In the event of the Commission not submitting a proposal, it shall inform the Member States concerned of the reasons for not doing so.

2. Authorisation to establish enhanced cooperation as referred to in paragraph 1 shall be granted, in compliance with Articles 43 to 45 of the Treaty on European Union, by the Council, acting by a qualified majority on a proposal from the Commission and after consulting the European Parliament. When enhanced cooperation relates to an area covered by the procedure referred to in Article 251 of this Treaty, the assent of the European Parliament shall be required.

A member of the Council may request that the matter be referred to the European Council. After that matter has been raised before the European Council, the Council may act in accordance with the first subparagraph of this paragraph.

3. The acts and decisions necessary for the implementation of enhanced cooperation activities shall be subject to all the relevant provisions of this Treaty, save as otherwise provided in this Article and in Articles 43 to 45 of the Treaty on European Union.

Notes
[1] Article 11 amended by the Treaty of Nice.

Article 11a[1]

Any Member State which wishes to participate in enhanced cooperation established in accordance with Article 11 shall notify its intention to the Council and to the Commission, which shall give an opinion to the Council within three months of the date of receipt of that notification. Within four months of the date of receipt of that notification, the Commission shall take a decision on it, and on such specific arrangements as it may deem necessary.

Notes
[1] Article 11a inserted by the Treaty of Nice (former Article 11(3)).

Article 14

1. The Community shall adopt measures with the aim of progressively establishing the internal market over a period expiring on 31 December 1992, in accordance with the provisions of this Article and of Articles 15, 26, 47(2), 49, 80, 93 and 95 and without prejudice to the other provisions of this Treaty.

2. The internal market shall comprise an area without internal frontiers in which the free movement of goods, persons, services and capital is ensured in accordance with the provisions of this Treaty.

3. The Council, acting by a qualified majority on a proposal from the Commission, shall determine the guidelines and conditions necessary to ensure balanced progress in all the sectors concerned.

Article 15

When drawing up its proposals with a view to achieving the objectives set out in Article 14, the Commission shall take into account the extent of the effort that certain economies showing differences in development will have to sustain during the period of establishment of the internal market and it may propose appropriate provisions.

If these provisions take the form of derogations, they must be of a temporary nature and must cause the least possible disturbance to the functioning of the common market.

Article 16

Without prejudice to Articles 73, 86 and 87, and given the place occupied by services of general economic interest in the shared values of the Union as well as their role in promoting social and territorial cohesion, the Community and the Member States, each within their respective powers and within the scope of application of this Treaty, shall take care that such services operate on the basis of principles and conditions which enable them to fulfil their missions.

Commentary

Art 16: **B&C:** 10.009, 11.003 **F&N:** 6.213, 6.214, 16.217

A4

EC TREATY: FREE MOVEMENT OF GOODS

(Amsterdam consolidated version: Articles 23–25; 28–31)

Commentary

Arts 23–31: **B&C:** 1.014
Arts 23–27: **B&C:** 1.032
Arts 28–30: **B&C:** 1.032, 1.036, 9.007, 9.053, 9.068, 9.075, 9.098–9.099
Arts 28–32: **F&N:** 10.17

Article 23

1. The Community shall be based upon a customs union which shall cover all trade in goods and which shall involve the prohibition between Member States of customs duties on imports and exports and of all charges having equivalent effect, and the adoption of a common customs tariff in their relations with third countries.

2. The provisions of Article 25 and of Chapter 2 of this title shall apply to products originating in Member States and to products coming from third countries which are in free circulation in Member States.

Commentary

Art 23: **B&C:** 1.014, 1.026, 1.032

Article 24

Products coming from a third country shall be considered to be in free circulation in a Member State if the import formalities have been complied with and any customs duties or charges having equivalent effect which are payable have been levied in that Member State, and if they have not benefited from a total or partial drawback of such duties or charges.

CHAPTER 1
THE Customs Union

Article 25

Customs duties on imports and exports and charges having equivalent effect shall be prohibited between Member States. This prohibition shall also apply to customs duties of a fiscal nature.

Commentary
Art 25: B&C: 1.014, 1.026, 1.032

CHAPTER 2
PROHIBITION OF QUANTITATIVE RESTRICTIONS BETWEEN MEMBER STATES

Article 28

Quantitative restrictions on imports and all measures having equivalent effect shall be prohibited between Member States.

Commentary
Art 28: B&C: 1.014, 1.026, 1.032–1.035, 1.036, 9.004, 9.007, 9.008–9.011, 9.016, 9.019, 9.026–9.027, 9.043, 9.048, 9.053, 9.057, 9.059, 9.062–9.063, 9.068, 9.075, 9.098–9.099, 9.100, 9.179, 11.009, 11.014–11.015, 11.033, 11.038, 14.137, 15.128–15.130 **F&N:** 6.49, 6.51, 6.97, 6.100–6.105, 6.120, 6.121, 6.130, 6.158, 6.245, 7.386, 10.10, 10.17, 10.49, 10.173

Article 29

Quantitative restrictions on exports, and all measures having equivalent effect, shall be prohibited between Member States.

Commentary
Art 29: B&C: 1.014, 1.026, 1.032, 1.034–1.035, 1.036, 1.084, 9.007, 9.008, 9.011,9.053, 9.068, 9.075, 9.088–9.099

Article 30

The provisions of Articles 28 and 29 shall not preclude prohibitions or restrictions on imports, exports or goods in transit justified on grounds of public morality, public policy or public security; the protection of health and life of humans, animals or plants; the protection of national treasures possessing artistic, historic or archaeological value; or the protection of industrial and commercial property. Such prohibitions or restrictions shall not, however, constitute a means of arbitrary discrimination or a disguised restriction on trade between Member States.

Commentary
Art 30: B&C: 1.014, 1.026, 1.032–1.033, 1.035, 1.036, 9.001, 9.004, 9.007–9.011, 9.013, 9.016, 9.018–9.019, 9.026–9.027, 9.032, 9.035, 9.037–9.038, 9.041, 9.043, 9.049, 9.053, 9.056, 9.059, 9.062–9.063, 9.068, 9.075, 9.098–9.099, 9.100, 9.179, 14.137 **F&N:** 6.164, 6.165, 6.166, 6.167, 6.168, 10.17, 10.19, 10.38, 10.49

Article 31

1. Member States shall adjust any State monopolies of a commercial character so as to ensure that no discrimination regarding the conditions under which goods are procured and marketed exists between nationals of Member States.

The provisions of this Article shall apply to any body through which a Member State, in law or in fact, either directly or indirectly supervises, determines or appreciably influences imports or exports between Member States. These provisions shall likewise apply to monopolies delegated by the State to others.

2. Member States shall refrain from introducing any new measure which is contrary to the principles laid down in paragraph 1 or which restricts the scope of the articles dealing with the prohibition of customs duties and quantitative restrictions between Member States.

3. If a State monopoly of a commercial character has rules which are designed to make it easier to dispose of agricultural products or obtain for them the best return, steps should be taken in applying the rules contained in this article to ensure equivalent safeguards for the employment and standard of living of the producers concerned.

Commentary
Art 31: B&C: 1.014, 1.036, 2.015, 11.001, 11.037–11.042, 11.044, 11.047, 11.051–11.052, 12.057, 12.071, 15.128, 15.131 F&N: 6.100, 6.101, 6.105–6.110, 6.111, 6.116–6.121, 6.130, 6.134, 6.135, 6.158, 6.169, 6.245, 12.40
Art 31(1): B&C: 11.036, 11.039, 11.041–11.045, 15.128 F&N: 6.106, 6.107, 6.110, 6.114, 6.115
Art 31(2): B&C: 11.043–11.045, 15.128 F&N: 6.106, 6.112
Art 31(3): B&C: 11.044 F&N: 6.106

A5

EC TREATY: AGRICULTURE

(Amsterdam consolidated version: Articles 32–37)

Commentary
Arts 32–38: B&C: 1.014, 1.026, 1.037, 12.196

Article 32

1. The common market shall extend to agriculture and trade in agricultural products. "Agricultural products" means the products of the soil, of stockfarming and of fisheries and products of first-stage processing directly related to these products.

2. Save as otherwise provided in Articles 33 to 38, the rules laid down for the establishment of the common market shall apply to agricultural products.

3. The products subject to the provisions of Articles 33 to 38 are listed in Annex I to this Treaty.

4. The operation and development of the common market for agricultural products must be accompanied by the establishment of a common agricultural policy.

Commentary
Art 32(1) B&C: 12.196
Art 32(3) B&C: 12.196

Article 33

1. The objectives of the common agricultural policy shall be:

(a) to increase agricultural productivity by promoting technical progress and by ensuring the rational development of agricultural production and the optimum utilisation of the factors of production, in particular labour;

(b) thus to ensure a fair standard of living for the agricultural community, in particular by increasing the individual earnings of persons engaged in agriculture;

(c) to stabilise markets;

(d) to assure the availability of supplies;

(e) to ensure that supplies reach consumers at reasonable prices.

2. In working out the common agricultural policy and the special methods for its application, account shall be taken of:

(a) the particular nature of agricultural activity, which results from the social structure of agriculture and from structural and natural disparities between the various agricultural regions;

(b) the need to effect the appropriate adjustments by degrees;

(c) the fact that in the Member States agriculture constitutes a sector closely linked with the economy as a whole.

Commentary
Art 33: B&C: 12.001, 12.194, 12.200, 12.203, 12.205, 12.209 F&N: 3.03

Article 34

1. In order to attain the objectives set out in Article 33, a common organisation of agricultural markets shall be established.

This organisation shall take one of the following forms, depending on the product concerned:

(a) common rules on competition;

(b) compulsory coordination of the various national market organisations;

(c) a European market organisation.

2. The common organisation established in accordance with paragraph 1 may include all measures required to attain the objectives set out in Article 33, in particular regulation of prices, aids for the production and marketing of the various products, storage and carryover arrangements and common machinery for stabilising imports or exports.

The common organisation shall be limited to pursuit of the objectives set out in Article 33 and shall exclude any discrimination between producers or consumers within the Community.

Any common price policy shall be based on common criteria and uniform methods of calculation.

3. In order to enable the common organisation referred to in paragraph 1 to attain its objectives, one or more agricultural guidance and guarantee funds may be set up.

Commentary
Art 34: F&N: 6.104

Article 35

To enable the objectives set out in Article 33 to be attained, provision may be made within the framework of the common agricultural policy for measures such as:

(a) an effective coordination of efforts in the spheres of vocational training, of research and of the dissemination of agricultural knowledge; this may include joint financing of projects or institutions;

(b) joint measures to promote consumption of certain products.

Article 36

The provisions of the chapter relating to rules on competition shall apply to production of and trade in agricultural products only to the extent determined by the Council within the framework of Article 37(2) and (3) and in accordance with the procedure laid down therein, account being taken of the objectives set out in Article 33.

The Council may, in particular, authorise the granting of aid:

(a) for the protection of enterprises handicapped by structural or natural conditions;

(b) within the framework of economic development programmes.

Commentary
Art 36: B&C: 12.195 F&N: 3.03, 6.214

Article 37

1. In order to evolve the broad lines of a common agricultural policy, the Commission shall, immediately this Treaty enters into force, convene a conference of the Member States with a view to making a comparison of their agricultural policies, in particular by producing a statement of their resources and needs.

2. Having taken into account the work of the Conference provided for in paragraph 1, after consulting the Economic and Social Committee and within two years of the entry into force of this Treaty, the Commission shall submit proposals for working out and implementing the common agricultural policy, including the replacement of the national organisations by one of the forms of common organisation provided for in Article 34(1), and for implementing the measures specified in this title.

These proposals shall take account of the interdependence of the agricultural matters mentioned in this title.

The Council shall, on a proposal from the Commission and after consulting the European Parliament, acting by a qualified majority, make regulations, issue directives, or take decisions, without prejudice to any recommendations it may also make.

3. The Council may, acting by a qualified majority and in accordance with paragraph 2, replace the national market organisations by the common organisation provided for in Article 34(1) if:

(a) the common organisation offers Member States which are opposed to this measure and which have an organisation of their own for the production in question equivalent safeguards for the employment and standard of living of the producers concerned, account being taken of the adjustments that will be possible and the specialisation that will be needed with the passage of time;

(b) such an organisation ensures conditions for trade within the Community similar to those existing in a national market.

4. If a common organisation for certain raw materials is established before a common organisation exists for the corresponding processed products, such raw materials as are used for processed products intended for export to third countries may be imported from outside the Community.

Commentary
Art 37: F&N: 3.03
Art 37(2): B&C: 12.1947, 12.197
Art 37(3): B&C: 12.194, 12.197

A6

EC TREATY: THE COMMUNITY COURTS

(Amsterdam consolidated version: Articles 220–222; 225–234; 242–243)

Article 220[1]

The Court of Justice and the Court of First Instance, each within its jurisdiction, shall ensure that in the interpretation and application of this Treaty the law is observed.

In addition, judicial panels may be attached to the Court of First Instance under the conditions laid down in Article 225a in order to exercise, in certain specific areas, the judicial competence laid down in this Treaty.

Notes
[1] Article amended by the Treaty of Nice.

Commentary
Art 220: **B&C:** 1.045–1.046, 13.212

Article 221[1]

The Court of Justice shall consist of one judge per Member State.

The Court of Justice shall sit in chambers or in a Grand Chamber, in accordance with the rules laid down for that purpose in the Statute of the Court of Justice.

When provided for in the Statute, the Court of Justice may also sit as a full Court.

Notes
[1] Article amended by the Treaty of Nice.

Commentary
Art 221: **B&C:** 1.047

Article 222[1]

The Court of Justice shall be assisted by eight Advocates-General. Should the Court of Justice so request, the Council, acting unanimously, may increase the number of Advocates-General.

It shall be the duty of the Advocate-General, acting with complete impartiality and independence, to make, in open court, reasoned submissions on cases which, in accordance with the Statute of the Court of Justice, require his involvement.

Notes
[1] Article amended by the Treaty of Nice.

Commentary
Art 222: **B&C:** 1.047

Article 225[1]

1. The Court of First Instance shall have jurisdiction to hear and determine at first instance actions or proceedings referred to in Articles 230, 232, 235, 236 and 238, with the exception of those assigned to a judicial panel and those reserved in the Statute for the Court of Justice. The Statute may provide for the Court of First Instance to have jurisdiction for other classes of action or proceeding.

Decisions given by the Court of First Instance under this paragraph may be subject to a right of appeal to the Court of Justice on points of law only, under the conditions and within the limits laid down by the Statute.

2. The Court of First Instance shall have jurisdiction to hear and determine actions or proceedings brought against decisions of the judicial panels set up under Article 225a.

Decisions given by the Court of First Instance under this paragraph may exceptionally be subject to review by the Court of Justice, under the conditions and within the limits laid down by the Statute, where there is a serious risk of the unity or consistency of Community law being affected.

3. The Court of First Instance shall have jurisdiction to hear and determine questions referred for a preliminary ruling under Article 234, in specific areas laid down by the Statute.

Where the Court of First Instance considers that the case requires a decision of principle likely to affect the unity or consistency of Community law, it may refer the case to the Court of Justice for a ruling.

Decisions given by the Court of First Instance on questions referred for a preliminary ruling may exceptionally be subject to review by the Court of Justice, under the conditions and within the limits laid down by the Statute, where there is a serious risk of the unity or consistency of Community law being affected.

Notes
[1] Article amended by the Treaty of Nice.

Commentary
Art 225: B&C: 1.046, 13.032, 13.212, 13.252–13.253 **F&N:** 8.476, 8.479
Art 225(1): B&C: 1.047, 13.212
Art 225(3): B&C: 1.046, 13.212

Article 225a[1]

The Council, acting unanimously on a proposal from the Commission and after consulting the European Parliament and the Court of Justice or at the request of the Court of Justice and after consulting the European Parliament and the Commission, may create judicial panels to hear and determine at first instance certain classes of action or proceeding brought in specific areas.

The decision establishing a judicial panel shall lay down the rules on the organisation of the panel and the extent of the jurisdiction conferred upon it.

Decisions given by judicial panels may be subject to a right of appeal on points of law only or, when provided for in the decision establishing the panel, a right of appeal also on matters of fact, before the Court of First Instance.

The members of the judicial panels shall be chosen from persons whose independence is beyond doubt and who possess the ability required for appointment to judicial office. They shall be appointed by the Council, acting unanimously.

The judicial panels shall establish their Rules of Procedure in agreement with the Court of Justice. Those Rules shall require the approval of the Council, acting by a qualified majority.

Unless the decision establishing the judicial panel provides otherwise, the provisions of this Treaty relating to the Court of Justice and the provisions of the Statute of the Court of Justice shall apply to the judicial panels.

Notes
[1] Article inserted by the Treaty of Nice.

Commentary
Art 225a: B&C: 1.045

Article 226

If the Commission considers that a Member State has failed to fulfil an obligation under this Treaty, it shall deliver a reasoned opinion on the matter after giving the State concerned the opportunity to submit its observations.

If the State concerned does not comply with the opinion within the period laid down by the Commission, the latter may bring the matter before the Court of Justice.

Commentary
Art 226: B&C: 1.049, 11.007, 11.022, 11.025, 11.045–11.046, 11.058, 12.056, 12.071, 12.089, 13.244, 15.088, 15.102, 15.113, 15.125 **F&N:** 3.07, 6.218, 6.219, 6.223, 6.238, 12.40, 13.21, 14.88

Article 227

A Member State which considers that another Member State has failed to fulfil an obligation under this Treaty may bring the matter before the Court of Justice.

Before a Member State brings an action against another Member State for an alleged infringement of an obligation under this Treaty, it shall bring the matter before the Commission.

The Commission shall deliver a reasoned opinion after each of the States concerned has been given the opportunity to submit its own case and its observations on the other party's case both orally and in writing.

If the Commission has not delivered an opinion within three months of the date on which the matter was brought before it, the absence of such opinion shall not prevent the matter from being brought before the Court of Justice.

Commentary
Art 227: B&C: 11.058, 15.088 **F&N:** 3.07, 16.279

Article 228

1. If the Court of Justice finds that a Member State has failed to fulfil an obligation under this Treaty, the State shall be required to take the necessary measures to comply with the judgment of the Court of Justice.

2. If the Commission considers that the Member State concerned has not taken such measures it shall, after giving that State the opportunity to submit its observations, issue a reasoned opinion specifying the points on which the Member State concerned has not complied with the judgment of the Court of Justice.

If the Member State concerned fails to take the necessary measures to comply with the Court's judgment within the time limit laid down by the Commission, the latter may bring the case before the Court of Justice. In so doing it shall specify the amount of the lump sum or penalty payment to be paid by the Member State concerned which it considers appropriate in the circumstances.

If the Court of Justice finds that the Member State concerned has not complied with its judgment it may impose a lump sum or penalty payment on it.

This procedure shall be without prejudice to Article 227.

Commentary
Art 228: B&C: 15.102
Art 228(2): F&N: 16.375

Article 229

Regulations adopted jointly by the European Parliament and the Council, and by the Council, pursuant to the provisions of this Treaty, may give the Court of Justice unlimited jurisdiction with regard to the penalties provided for in such regulations.

Commentary
Art 229: B&C: 1.046, 13.081, 13.145, 13.213–13.214, 13.232, 13.234, 13.242, 13.254 **F&N:** 8.478, 8.608, 8.845, 8.847, 8.849

Article 229a[1]

Without prejudice to the other provisions of this Treaty, the Council, acting unanimously on a proposal from the Commission and after consulting the European Parliament, may adopt provisions to confer jurisdiction, to the extent that it shall determine, on the Court of Justice in disputes relating to the application of acts adopted on the basis of this Treaty which create Community industrial property rights. The Council shall recommend those provisions to the Member States for adoption in accordance with their respective constitutional requirements.

Notes
[1] Article inserted by the Treaty of Nice.

Article 230[1]

The Court of Justice shall review the legality of acts adopted jointly by the European Parliament and the Council, of acts of the Council, of the Commission and of the ECB, other than recommendations and opinions, and of acts of the European Parliament intended to produce legal effects vis-à-vis third parties.

It shall for this purpose have jurisdiction in actions brought by a Member State, the European Parliament, the Council or the Commission on grounds of lack of competence, infringement of an essential procedural requirement, infringement of this Treaty or of any rule of law relating to its application, or misuse of powers.

The Court of Justice shall have jurisdiction under the same conditions in actions brought by the Court of Auditors and by the ECB for the purpose of protecting their prerogatives.

Any natural or legal person may, under the same conditions, institute proceedings against a decision addressed to that person or against a decision which, although in the form of a regulation or a decision addressed to another person, is of direct and individual concern to the former.

The proceedings provided for in this article shall be instituted within two months of the publication of the measure, or of its notification to the plaintiff, or, in the absence thereof, of the day on which it came to the knowledge of the latter, as the case may be.

Notes

[1] Article amended by the Treaty of Nice.

Commentary

Art 230: **B&C:** 1.046, 1.048, 3.010, 8.235, 8.238–8.239, 8.244, 13.049, 13.065, 13.069–13.071, 13.081–13.083, 13.213–13.214, 13.217–13.218, 13.220–13.222, 13.232, 13.234, 13.241, 13.244–13.246, 14.077, 14.089, 15.084, 15.088, 15.110, 15.112, 15.114–15.115, 15.117–15.118, 15.121 **F&N:** 2.138, 2.144, 2.223, 5.650, 5.654, 5.658, 5.659–5.661, 5.665, 6.222, 6.227, 6.229, 6.237, 8.315, 8.353, 8.357, 8.403, 8.452, 8.466, 8.476–8.478, 8.847, 16.304, 16.399
Art 230(4): **F&N:** 16.389, 16.409
Art 230(5): **F&N:** 16.304, 16.400

Article 231

If the action is well founded, the Court of Justice shall declare the act concerned to be void.

In the case of a regulation, however, the Court of Justice shall, if it considers this necessary, state which of the effects of the regulation which it has declared void shall be considered as definitive.

Commentary

Art 231: **F&N:** 8.477

Article 232

Should the European Parliament, the Council or the Commission, in infringement of this Treaty, fail to act, the Member States and the other institutions of the Community may bring an action before the Court of Justice to have the infringement established.

The action shall be admissible only if the institution concerned has first been called upon to act. If, within two months of being so called upon, the institution concerned has not defined its position, the action may be brought within a further period of two months.

Any natural or legal person may, under the conditions laid down in the preceding paragraphs, complain to the Court of Justice that an institution of the Community has failed to address to that person any act other than a recommendation or an opinion.

The Court of Justice shall have jurisdiction, under the same conditions, in actions or proceedings brought by the ECB in the areas falling within the latter's field of competence and in actions or proceedings brought against the latter.

Commentary

Art 232: **B&C:** 1.047, 8.235, 8.238, 13.069–13.070, 13.213, 13.243–13.246, 15.112, 15.121 **F&N:** 5.659, 6.227, 16.403

Article 233

The institution or institutions whose act has been declared void or whose failure to act has been declared contrary to this Treaty shall be required to take the necessary measures to comply with the judgment of the Court of Justice.

This obligation shall not affect any obligation which may result from the application of the second paragraph of Article 288.

This article shall also apply to the ECB.

Commentary
Art 233: B&C: 13.239–13.240 **F&N:** 5.686

Article 234

The Court of Justice shall have jurisdiction to give preliminary rulings concerning:

(a) the interpretation of this Treaty;
(b) the validity and interpretation of acts of the institutions of the Community and of the ECB;
(c) the interpretation of the statutes of bodies established by an act of the Council, where those statutes so provide.

Where such a question is raised before any court or tribunal of a Member State, that court or tribunal may, if it considers that a decision on the question is necessary to enable it to give judgment, request the Court of Justice to give a ruling thereon.

Where any such question is raised in a case pending before a court or tribunal of a Member State against whose decisions there is no judicial remedy under national law, that court or tribunal shall bring the matter before the Court of Justice.

Commentary
Art 234: B&C: 1.047–1.049, 1.120, 3.010, 5.021, 5.034, 5.102, 10.128, 10.137, 13.123, 13.213, 14.006, 14.077, 14.079, 14.089–14.094, 14.137, 14.142, 14.161, 14.166–14.167, 15.105, 15.110, 15.115 **F&N:** 2.16, 2.144, 2.145, 2.227, 2.232, 2.245, 2.246, 2.262, 2.273, 3.128, 3.191, 9.01, 9.39, 9.48, 9.75, 9.83, 9.94, 9.101, 9.116, 9.146, 10.242, 11.162, 16.07, 16.10, 16.405
Art 234(2): B&C: 14.093, 14.166
Art 234(3): B&C: 14.093

Article 242

Actions brought before the Court of Justice shall not have suspensory effect. The Court of Justice may, however, if it considers that circumstances so require, order that application of the contested act be suspended.

Commentary
Art 242: B&C: 13.213, 13.246–13.247, 13.255 **F&N:** 5.672, 8.397, 8.403, 8.835, 16.344, 16.405

Article 243

The Court of Justice may in any cases before it prescribe any necessary interim measures.

Commentary
Art 243: B&C: 13.213, 13.246–13.247, 13.250, 13.255 **F&N:** 5.672, 16.405

A7

EC TREATY: ART 296 AND LIST

(Amsterdam consolidated version)

Article 296

1. The provisions of this Treaty shall not preclude the application of the following rules:

(a) No Member State shall be obliged to supply information the disclosure of which it considers contrary to the essential interests of its security;

(b) Any Member State may take such measures as it considers necessary for the protection of the essential interests of its security which are connected with the production of or trade in arms, munitions and war material; such measures shall not adversely affect the conditions of competition in the common market regarding products which are not intended for specifically military purposes.

2. The Council may, acting unanimously on a proposal from the Commission, make changes to the list, which it drew up on 15 April 1958, of the products to which the provisions of paragraph 1(b) apply.

List of Products Referred to in Article 296 of the Treaty

The provisions of Article [296] paragraph 1(b) of the [EC Treaty] are applicable to the arms, munition and war material specified below, including nuclear arms:

1. Portable and automatic firearms, such as rifles, carbines, revolvers, pistols, sub-machine guns and machine guns, except for hunting weapons, pistols and other low calibre weapons of the calibre less than 7mm.
2. Artillery, and smoke, gas and flame throwing weapons such as:
   (a) cannon, howitzers, mortars, artillery, anti-tank guns, rocket launchers, flame-throwers, recoilless guns;
   (b) military smoke and gas guns.
3. Ammunition for the weapons at 1 and 2 above.
4. Bombs, torpedoes, rockets and guided missiles:
   (a) bombs, torpedoes, grenades, including smoke grenades, smoke bombs, rockets, mines, guided missiles, underwater grenades, incendiary bombs;
   (b) military apparatus and components specially designed for the handling, assembly, dismantling, firing or detection of the articles at (a) above.
5. Military fire control equipment:
   (a) firing computers and guidance systems in infra-red and other night guidance devices;
   (b) telemeters, position indicators, altimeters;
   (c) electronic tracking components, gyroscopic, optical and acoustic;
   (d) bomb sights and gun sights, periscopes for the equipment specified in this list.
6. Tanks and specialist fighting vehicles:
   (a) tanks;
   (b) military type vehicles, armed or armoured including amphibious vehicles;
   (c) armoured cars;
   (d) half-tracked military vehicles;
   (e) military vehicles with tank bodies;
   (f) trailers specially designed for the transportation of ammunition specified at paragraphs 3 and 4.
7. Toxic and radioactive agents:
   (a) toxic, biological or chemical agents and radioactive agents adapted for destructive use in war against persons, animals or crops;

    (b) military apparatus for the propagation, detection and identification of substances at paragraph (a) above;

    (c) counter–measures material related to paragraph (a) above.

8. Powders, explosives and liquid or solid propellants:

    (a) powders and liquid or solid propellants specially designed and constructed for use with the material at paragraphs 3, 4 and 7 above;

    (b) military explosives;

    (c) incendiary and freezing agents for military use.

9. Warships and their specialist equipment:

    (a) warships of all kinds;

    (b) equipment specially designed for laying, detecting and sweeping mines;

    (c) underwater cables.

10. Aircraft and equipment for military use.

11. Military electronic equipment.

12. Camera equipment specially designed for military use.

13. Other equipment and material:

    (a) parachutes and parachute fabric;

    (b) water purification plant specially designed for military use;

    (c) military command relay electrical equipment.

14. Specialised parts and items of material included in this list in so far as they are of a military nature.

15. Machines, equipment and items exclusively designed for the study, manufacture, testing and control of arms, munitions and apparatus of an exclusively military nature included in this list.

Commentary
Art 296: B&C: 1.037, 8.102, 8.105, 8.177, 11.045, 11.058 F&N: 3.06, 3.11

A8

AGREEMENT ON THE EUROPEAN ECONOMIC AREA

(As amended:[1] Articles 1, 2, 53–65 and 108–110)

THE EUROPEAN COMMUNITY,[2]

THE KINGDOM OF BELGIUM,

THE CZECH REPUBLIC,

THE KINGDOM OF DENMARK,

THE FEDERAL REPUBLIC OF GERMANY,

THE REPUBLIC OF ESTONIA,

THE HELLENIC REPUBLIC,

THE KINGDOM OF SPAIN,

THE FRENCH REPUBLIC,

IRELAND,

THE ITALIAN REPUBLIC,

THE REPUBLIC OF CYPRUS,

THE REPUBLIC OF LATVIA,

THE REPUBLIC OF LITHUANIA,

THE GRAND DUCHY OF LUXEMBOURG,

THE REPUBLIC OF HUNGARY,

THE REPUBLIC OF MALTA,

THE KINGDOM OF THE NETHERLANDS,

THE REPUBLIC OF AUSTRIA,

THE REPUBLIC OF POLAND,

THE PORTUGUESE REPUBLIC,

THE REPUBLIC OF SLOVENIA,

THE SLOVAK REPUBLIC,

THE REPUBLIC OF FINLAND,

THE KINGDOM OF SWEDEN,

THE UNITED KINGDOM OF GREAT BRITAIN AND NORTHERN IRELAND, AND

[ ]³

THE REPUBLIC OF ICELAND,

THE PRINCIPALITY OF LIECHTENSTEIN,

THE KINGDOM OF NORWAY,³

[ ]⁴

hereinafter referred to as the CONTRACTING PARTIES;

Notes

[1] As amended by the Adjusting Protocol and subsequently by the EEA Enlargement Agreement (OJ L 130, 29.4.2004, p. 3 and EEA Supplement No 23, 29.4.2004, p. 1), with effect from 1 May 2004.

[2] As amended by the EEA Enlargement Agreement (OJ L 130, 29.4.2004, p. 3 and EEA Supplement No 23, 29.4.2004, p. 1), with effect from 1 May 2004.

[3] Austria, Finland and Sweden acceded to the European Union on 1 January 1995.

[4] Reference to "the Swiss Confederation" deleted by the Adjusting Protocol.
   For information regarding the EEA generally, see the Website of the EFTA Secretariat at http://secretariat.efta.int/.

Commentary

EEA Agreement: B&C: 1.002, 1.015, 1.085–1.086, 1.089–1.090, 2.128, 8.007, 8.280, 12.008
Arts 17–20: B&C: 12.199

CONVINCED of the contribution that a European Economic Area will bring to the construction of a Europe based on peace, democracy and human rights;

REAFFIRMING the high priority attached to the privileged relationship between the European Community, its Member States and the EFTA States, which is based on proximity, long-standing common values and European identity;

DETERMINED to contribute, on the basis of market economy, to world-wide trade liberalization and cooperation, in particular in accordance with the provisions of the General Agreement on Tariffs and Trade and the Convention on the Organisation for Economic Cooperation and Development;

CONSIDERING the objective of establishing a dynamic and homogeneous European Economic Area, based on common rules and equal conditions of competition and providing for the adequate means of enforcement including at the judicial level, and achieved on the basis of equality and reciprocity and of an overall balance of benefits, rights and obligations for the Contracting Parties;

DETERMINED to provide for the fullest possible realization of the free movement of goods, persons, services and capital within the whole European Economic Area, as well as for strengthened and broadened cooperation in flanking and horizontal policies;

AIMING to promote a harmonious development of the European Economic Area and convinced of the need to contribute through the application of this Agreement to the reduction of economic and social regional disparities;

DESIROUS of contributing to the strengthening of the cooperation between the members of the European Parliament and of the Parliaments of the EFTA States, as well as between the social partners in the European Community and in the EFTA States;

CONVINCED of the important role that individuals will play in the European Economic Area through the exercise of the rights conferred on them by this Agreement and through the judicial defence of these rights;

DETERMINED to preserve, protect and improve the quality of the environment and to ensure a prudent and rational utilization of natural resources on the basis, in particular, of the principle of sustainable development, as well as the principle that precautionary and preventive action should be taken;

DETERMINED to take, in the further development of rules, a high level of protection concerning health, safety and the environment as a basis;

NOTING the importance of the development of the social dimension, including equal treatment of men and women, in the European Economic Area and wishing to ensure economic and social progress and to promote conditions for full employment, an improved standard of living and improved working conditions within the European Economic Area;

DETERMINED to promote the interests of consumers and to strengthen their position in the market place, aiming at a high level of consumer protection;

ATTACHED to the common objectives of strengthening the scientific and technological basis of European industry and of encouraging it to become more competitive at the international level;

CONSIDERING that the conclusion of this Agreement shall not prejudge in any way the possibility of any EFTA State to accede to the European Communities;

WHEREAS, in full deference to the independence of the courts, the objective of the Contracting Parties is to arrive at, and maintain, a uniform interpretation and application of this Agreement and those provisions of Community legislation which are substantially reproduced in this Agreement and to arrive at an equal treatment of individuals and economic operators as regards the four freedoms and the conditions of competition;

WHEREAS this Agreement does not restrict the decision-making autonomy or the treaty-making power of the Contracting Parties, subject to the provisions of this Agreement and the limitations set by public international law;

HAVE DECIDED to conclude the following Agreement:

PART I
OBJECTIVES AND PRINCIPLES

Article 1

1. The aim of this Agreement of association is to promote a continuous and balanced strengthening of trade and economic relations between the Contracting Parties with equal conditions of competition, and the respect of the same rules, with a view to creating a homogeneous European Economic Area, hereinafter referred to as the EEA.

2. In order to attain the objectives set out in paragraph 1, the association shall entail, in accordance with the provisions of this Agreement:
   (a) the free movement of goods;
   (b) the free movement of persons;
   (c) the free movement of services;
   (d) the free movement of capital;
   (e) the setting up of a system ensuring that competition is not distorted and that the rules thereon are equally respected; as well as
   (f) closer cooperation in other fields, such as research and development, the environment, education and social policy.

Article 2

For the purposes of this Agreement:
(a) the term "Agreement" means the main Agreement, its Protocols and Annexes as well as the acts referred to therein;
[(b) the term "EFTA States" means the Republic of Iceland, the Principality of Liechtenstein and the Kingdom of Norway;][1]
(c) the term "Contracting Parties" means, concerning the Community and the EC Member States, the Community and the EC Member States, or the Community, or the EC Member States. The meaning to be attributed to this expression in each case is to be deduced from the relevant provisions of this Agreement and from the respective competences of the Community and the EC Member States as they follow from the Treaty establishing the European Economic Community [...];[2]
[(d) the term "Act of Accession of 16 April 2003" shall mean the Act concerning the conditions of Accession of the Czech Republic, the Republic of Estonia, the Republic of Cyprus, the Republic of Latvia, the Republic of Lithuania, the Republic of Hungary, the Republic of Malta, the Republic of Poland, the Republic of Slovenia and the Slovak Republic and the adjustments to the Treaties on which the European Union is founded, adopted in Athens on 16 April 2003.][3]

Notes
[1] As replaced by the Adjusting Protocol and subsequently by the EEA Enlargement Agreement (OJ L 130, 29.4.2004, p. 3 and EEA Supplement No 23, 29.4.2004, p. 1), with effect from 1 May 2004.
[2] Words "and the Treaty establishing the European Coal and Steel Community" deleted by the EEA Enlargement Agreement (OJ L 130, 29.4.2004, p. 3 and EEA Supplement No 23, 29.4.2004, p. 1), with effect from 1 May 2004.
[3] Point added by the EEA Enlargement Agreement (OJ L 130, 29.4.2004, p. 3 and EEA Supplement No 23, 29.4.2004, p. 1), with effect from 1 May 2004.

[Articles 3 to 52]

Notes
Articles 3 to 52 are not reproduced in this volume. They are available at:
<http://secretariat.efta.int/Web/EuropeanEconomicArea/EEAAgreement/EEAAgreement>.

PART IV
COMPETITION AND OTHER COMMON RULES

CHAPTER 1
Rules Applicable to Undertakings

Article 53

1. The following shall be prohibited as incompatible with the functioning of this Agreement: all agreements between undertakings, decisions by associations of undertakings and concerted practices which may affect trade between Contracting Parties and which have as their object or effect the prevention, restriction or distortion of competition within the territory covered by this Agreement, and in particular those which:
   (a) directly or indirectly fix purchase or selling prices or any other trading conditions;
   (b) limit or control production, markets, technical development, or investment;
   (c) share markets or sources of supply;
   (d) apply dissimilar conditions to equivalent transactions with other trading parties, thereby placing them at a competitive disadvantage;
   (e) make the conclusion of contracts subject to acceptance by the other parties of supplementary obligations which, by their nature or according to commercial usage, have no connection with the subject of such contracts.
2. Any agreements or decisions prohibited pursuant to this Article shall be automatically void.
3. The provisions of paragraph 1 may, however, be declared inapplicable in the case of:
   — any agreement or category of agreements between undertakings;

— any decision or category of decisions by associations of undertakings;

— any concerted practice or category of concerted practices;

which contributes to improving the production or distribution of goods or to promoting technical or economic progress, while allowing consumers a fair share of the resulting benefit, and which does not:

(a) impose on the undertakings concerned restrictions which are not indispensable to the attainment of these objectives;

(b) afford such undertakings the possibility of eliminating competition in respect of a substantial part of the products in question.

Commentary

Art 53(1): **B&C:** 1.088, 1.090, 2.014, 2.034, 2.036, 5.128, 8.006, 13.003 **F&N:** 3.281

Art 53(2): **B&C:** 2.023, 2.036, 3.092, 5.094, 6.064

Art 53(3): **B&C:** 3.001, 3.090–3.091

Article 54

Any abuse by one or more undertakings of a dominant position within the territory covered by this Agreement or in a substantial part of it shall be prohibited as incompatible with the functioning of this Agreement in so far as it may affect trade between Contracting Parties.

Such abuse may, in particular, consist in:

(a) directly or indirectly imposing unfair purchase or selling prices or other unfair trading conditions;

(b) limiting production, markets or technical development to the prejudice of consumers;

(c) applying dissimilar conditions to equivalent transactions with other trading parties, thereby placing them at a competitive disadvantage;

(d) making the conclusion of contracts subject to acceptance by the other parties of supplementary obligations which, by their nature or according to commercial usage, have no connection with the subject of such contracts.

Commentary

Art 54: **B&C:** 1.088, 1.090–1.091, 8.006, 13.003

Article 55

1. Without prejudice to the provisions giving effect to Articles 53 and 54 as contained in Protocol 21 and Annex XIV of this Agreement, the EC Commission and the EFTA Surveillance Authority provided for in Article 108(1) shall ensure the application of the principles laid down in Articles 53 and 54.

   The competent surveillance authority, as provided for in Article 56, shall investigate cases of suspected infringement of these principles, on its own initiative, or on application by a State within the respective territory or by the other surveillance authority. The competent surveillance authority shall carry out these investigations in cooperation with the competent national authorities in the respective territory and in cooperation with the other surveillance authority, which shall give it its assistance in accordance with its internal rules. If it finds that there has been an infringement, it shall propose appropriate measures to bring it to an end.

2. If the infringement is not brought to an end, the competent surveillance authority shall record such infringement of the principles in a reasoned decision.

   The competent surveillance authority may publish its decision and authorize States within the respective territory to take the measures, the conditions and details of which it shall determine, needed to remedy the situation. It may also request the other surveillance authority to authorize States within the respective territory to take such measures.

Notes

Protocol 21 and Annex XIV are not reproduced in this volume.

Protocol 21 is available at:

<http://secretariat.efta.int/Web/EuropeanEconomicArea/EEAAgreement/EEAAgreement/protocols/>.

Annex XIV is available at:

<http://secretariat.efta.int/Web/EuropeanEconomicArea/EEAAgreement/annexes>.

Commentary

Art 55(1): B&C: 1.088

Article 56

1. Individual cases falling under Article 53 shall be decided upon by the surveillance authorities in accordance with the following provisions:
   (a) individual cases where only trade between EFTA States is affected shall be decided upon by the EFTA Surveillance Authority;
   (b) without prejudice to subparagraph (c), the EFTA Surveillance Authority decides, as provided for in the provisions set out in Article 58, Protocol 21 and the rules adopted for its implementation, Protocol 23 and Annex XIV, on cases where the turnover of the undertakings concerned in the territory of the EFTA States equals 33 per cent or more of their turnover in the territory covered by this Agreement;
   (c) the EC Commission decides on the other cases as well as on cases under (b) where trade between EC Member States is affected, taking into account the provisions set out in Article 58, Protocol 21, Protocol 23 and Annex XIV.
2. Individual cases falling under Article 54 shall be decided upon by the surveillance authority in the territory of which a dominant position is found to exist. The rules set out in paragraph 1(b) and (c) shall apply only if dominance exists within the territories of both surveillance authorities.
3. Individual cases falling under subparagraph (c) of paragraph 1, whose effects on trade between EC Member States or on competition within the Community are not appreciable, shall be decided upon by the EFTA Surveillance Authority.
4. The terms "undertaking" and "turnover" are, for the purposes of this Article, defined in Protocol 22.

Notes

Protocols 21, 22, and 23 and Annex XIV are not reproduced in this volume.

Protocols 21, 22, and 23 are available at:

<http://secretariat.efta.int/Web/EuropeanEconomicArea/EEAAgreement/EEAAgreement/protocols/>.

Annex XIV is available at:

<http://secretariat.efta.int/Web/EuropeanEconomicArea/EEAAgreement/annexes>.

Commentary

Art 56: B&C: 1.091

Article 57

1. Concentrations the control of which is provided for in paragraph 2 and which create or strengthen a dominant position as a result of which effective competition would be significantly impeded within the territory covered by this Agreement or a substantial part of it, shall be declared incompatible with this Agreement.
2. The control of concentrations falling under paragraph 1 shall be carried out by:
   (a) the EC Commission in cases falling under Regulation (EEC) No 4064/89 in accordance with that Regulation and in accordance with Protocols 21 and 24 and Annex XIV to this Agreement. The EC Commission shall, subject to the review of the EC Court of Justice, have sole competence to take decisions on these cases;
   (b) the EFTA Surveillance Authority in cases not falling under subparagraph (a) where the relevant thresholds set out in Annex XIV are fulfilled in the territory of the EFTA States in accordance with Protocols 21 and 24 and Annex XIV. This is without prejudice to the competence of EC Member States.

Notes

Protocols 21 and 24 and Annex XIV are not reproduced in this volume.

Protocols 21 and 24 are available at:
<http://secretariat.efta.int/Web/EuropeanEconomicArea/EEAAgreement/EEAAgreement/protocols/>.
Annex XIV is available at:
<http://secretariat.efta.int/Web/EuropeanEconomicArea/EEAAgreement/annexes>.

Commentary
Art 57: **B&C:** 1.090, 8.012, 8.061, 8.119, 8.184, 8.282 **F&N:** 5.409
Art 57(2)(a): **B&C:** 8.280–8.281
Art 57(2)(b): **B&C:** 8.280

Article 58

With a view to developing and maintaining a uniform surveillance throughout the European
Economic Area in the field of competition and to promoting a homogeneous implementation,
application and interpretation of the provisions of this Agreement to this end, the competent authorities shall cooperate in accordance with the provisions set out in Protocols 23 and 24.

Notes
Protocols 23 and 24 are not reproduced in this volume.
Protocols 23 and 24 are available at:
<http://secretariat.efta.int/Web/EuropeanEconomicArea/EEAAgreement/EEAAgreement/protocols/>.

Commentary
Art 58: **B&C:** 1.093 **F&N:** 5.409

Article 59

1. In the case of public undertakings and undertakings to which EC Member States or EFTA States
   grant special or exclusive rights, the Contracting Parties shall ensure that there is neither enacted
   nor maintained in force any measure contrary to the rules contained in this Agreement, in particular to those rules provided for in Articles 4 and 53 to 63.
2. Undertakings entrusted with the operation of services of general economic interest or having
   the character of a revenue-producing monopoly shall be subject to the rules contained in this
   Agreement, in particular to the rules on competition, in so far as the application of such rules does
   not obstruct the performance, in law or in fact, of the particular tasks assigned to them. The development of trade must not be affected to such an extent as would be contrary to the interests of the
   Contracting Parties.
3. The EC Commission as well as the EFTA Surveillance Authority shall ensure within their respective competence the application of the provisions of this Article and shall, where necessary, address
   appropriate measures to the States falling within their respective territory.

Commentary
Art 59: **B&C:** 1.090, 11.013

Article 60

Annex XIV contains specific provisions giving effect to the principles set out in Articles 53, 54, 57
and 59.

Notes
Annex XIV is not reproduced in this volume.
Annex XIV is available at:
<http://secretariat.efta.int/Web/EuropeanEconomicArea/EEAAgreement/annexes>.

Commentary
Art 60: **B&C:** 1.090

CHAPTER 2
STATE AID

Article 61

1. Save as otherwise provided in this Agreement, any aid granted by EC Member States, EFTA States or through State resources in any form whatsoever which distorts or threatens to distort competition by favouring certain undertakings or the production of certain goods shall, in so far as it affects trade between Contracting Parties, be incompatible with the functioning of this Agreement.
2. The following shall be compatible with the functioning of this Agreement:
    (a) aid having a social character, granted to individual consumers, provided that such aid is granted without discrimination related to the origin of the products concerned;
    (b) aid to make good the damage caused by natural disasters or exceptional occurrences;
    (c) aid granted to the economy of certain areas of the Federal Republic of Germany affected by the division of Germany, in so far as such aid is required in order to compensate for the economic disadvantages caused by that division.
3. The following may be considered to be compatible with the functioning of this Agreement:
    (a) aid to promote the economic development of areas where the standard of living is abnormally low or where there is serious underemployment;
    (b) aid to promote the execution of an important project of common European interest or to remedy a serious disturbance in the economy of an EC Member State or an EFTA State;
    (c) aid to facilitate the development of certain economic activities or of certain economic areas, where such aid does not adversely affect trading conditions to an extent contrary to the common interest;
    (d) such other categories of aid as may be specified by the EEA Joint Committee in accordance with Part VII.

Commentary
Art 61: B&C: 1.090, 15.004
Art 61(1)(a): B&C: 15.004
Art 61(1)(b): B&C: 15.004
Art 61(2): B&C: 15.004, 15.040
Art 61(3): B&C: 15.004

Article 62

1. All existing systems of State aid in the territory of the Contracting Parties, as well as any plans to grant or alter State aid, shall be subject to constant review as to their compatibility with Article 61 This review shall be carried out:
    (a) as regards the EC Member States, by the EC Commission according to the rules laid down in Article 93 of the Treaty establishing the European Economic Community;[1]
    (b) as regards the EFTA States, by the EFTA Surveillance Authority according to the rules set out in an agreement between the EFTA States establishing the EFTA Surveillance Authority which is entrusted with the powers and functions laid down in Protocol 26.
2. With a view to ensuring a uniform surveillance in the field of State aid throughout the territory covered by this Agreement, the EC Commission and the EFTA Surveillance Authority shall cooperate in accordance with the provisions set out in Protocol 27.

Notes
[1] Now Art 88 of the EC Treaty.
Protocols 26 and 27 are not reproduced in this volume.
Protocols 26 and 27 are available at:
<http://secretariat.efta.int/Web/EuropeanEconomicArea/EEAAgreement/EEAAgreement/protocols/>.

Commentary
Art 62: B&C: 1.090, 15.004
Art 62(2): B&C: 15.004

Article 63

Annex XV contains specific provisions on State aid.

Notes

Annex XV is not reproduced in this volume.
Annex XV is available at:
<http://secretariat.efta.int/Web/EuropeanEconomicArea/EEAAgreement/annexes>.

Commentary
Art 63: B&C: 15.004

Article 64

1. If one of the surveillance authorities considers that the implementation by the other surveillance authority of Articles 61 and 62 of this Agreement and Article 5 of Protocol 14 is not in conformity with the maintenance of equal conditions of competition within the territory covered by this Agreement, exchange of views shall be held within two weeks according to the procedure of Protocol 27, paragraph (f).
   If a commonly agreed solution has not been found by the end of this two-week period, the competent authority of the affected Contracting Party may immediately adopt appropriate interim measures in order to remedy the resulting distortion of competition.
   Consultations shall then be held in the EEA Joint Committee with a view to finding a commonly acceptable solution.
   If within three months the EEA Joint Committee has not been able to find such a solution, and if the practice in question causes, or threatens to cause, distortion of competition affecting trade between the Contracting Parties, the interim measures may be replaced by definitive measures, strictly necessary to offset the effect of such distortion. Priority shall be given to such measures that will least disturb the functioning of the EEA.
2. The provisions of this Article will also apply to State monopolies, which are established after the date of signature of the Agreement.

Notes

Protocols 14 and 27 are not reproduced in this volume.
Protocols 14 and 27 are available at:
<http://secretariat.efta.int/Web/EuropeanEconomicArea/EEAAgreement/EEAAgreement/protocols/>.

CHAPTER 3
Other Common Rules

Article 65

1. Annex XVI contains specific provisions and arrangements concerning procurement which, unless otherwise specified, shall apply to all products and to services as specified.
2. Protocol 28 and Annex XVII contain specific provisions and arrangements concerning intellectual, industrial and commercial property, which, unless otherwise specified, shall apply to all products and services.

Notes

Protocol 28 and Annexes XVI and XVII are not reproduced in this volume.
Protocol 28 is available at:
<http://secretariat.efta.int/Web/EuropeanEconomicArea/EEAAgreement/EEAAgreement/protocols/>.
Annexes XVI and XVII are available at:
<http://secretariat.efta.int/Web/EuropeanEconomicArea/EEAAgreement/annexes>.

Commentary
Art 65(2): B&C: 9.011

Notes
Articles 66 to 107 are not reproduced in this volume. They are available at:
<http://secretariat.efta.int/Web/EuropeanEconomicArea/EEAAgreement/EEAAgreement>.

PART VII
INSTITUTIONAL PROVISIONS

CHAPTER 3
Homogeneity, Surveillance Procedure and Settlement of Disputes

Section 2
Surveillance procedure

Article 108

1. The EFTA States shall establish an independent surveillance authority (EFTA Surveillance Authority) as well as procedures similar to those existing in the Community including procedures for ensuring the fulfilment of obligations under this Agreement and for control of the legality of acts of the EFTA Surveillance Authority regarding competition.
2. The EFTA States shall establish a court of justice (EFTA Court).
   The EFTA Court shall, in accordance with a separate agreement between the EFTA States, with regard to the application of this Agreement be competent, in particular, for:
   (a) actions concerning the surveillance procedure regarding the EFTA States;
   (b) appeals concerning decisions in the field of competition taken by the EFTA Surveillance Authority;
   (c) the settlement of disputes between two or more EFTA States.

Commentary
Art 108: B&C: 1.087

Article 109

1. The fulfilment of the obligations under this Agreement shall be monitored by, on the one hand, the EFTA Surveillance Authority and, on the other, the EC Commission acting in conformity with the Treaty establishing the European Economic Community […].[1]
2. In order to ensure a uniform surveillance throughout the EEA, the EFTA Surveillance Authority and the EC Commission shall cooperate, exchange information and consult each other on surveillance policy issues and individual cases.
3. The EC Commission and the EFTA Surveillance Authority shall receive any complaints concerning the application of this Agreement. They shall inform each other of complaints received.
4. Each of these bodies shall examine all complaints falling within its competence and shall pass to the other body any complaints which fall within the competence of that body.
5. In case of disagreement between these two bodies with regard to the action to be taken in relation to a complaint or with regard to the result of the examination, either of the bodies may refer the matter to the EEA Joint Committee which shall deal with it in accordance with Article 111.

Notes
[1] Words "and the Treaty establishing the European Coal and Steel Community" deleted by the EEA Enlargement Agreement (OJ L 130, 29.4.2004, p. 3 and EEA Supplement No 23, 29.4.2004, p. 1), with effect from 1 May 2004.

Commentary
Art 109: B&C: 1.093

Article 110

Decisions under this Agreement by the EFTA Surveillance Authority and the EC Commission which impose a pecuniary obligation on persons other than States, shall be enforceable. The same shall apply to such judgments under this Agreement by the Court of Justice of the European Communities, the Court of First Instance of the European Communities and the EFTA Court.

Enforcement shall be governed by the rules of civil procedure in force in the State in the territory of which it is carried out.

The order for its enforcement shall be appended to the decision, without other formality than verification of the authenticity of the decision, by the authority which each Contracting Party shall designate for this purpose and shall make known to the other Contracting Parties, the EFTA Surveillance Authority, the EC Commission, the Court of Justice of the European Communities, the Court of First Instance of the European Communities and the EFTA Court.

When these formalities have been completed on application by the party concerned, the latter may proceed to enforcement, in accordance with the law of the State in the territory of which enforcement is to be carried out, by bringing the matter directly before the competent authority.

Enforcement may be suspended only by a decision of the Court of Justice of the European Communities, as far as decisions by the EC Commission, the Court of First Instance of the European Communities or the Court of Justice of the European Communities are concerned, or by a decision of the EFTA Court as far as decisions by the EFTA Surveillance Authority or the EFTA Court are concerned. However, the courts of the States concerned shall have jurisdiction over complaints that enforcement is being carried out in an irregular manner.

[*Articles 111 to 129*]

Notes

Articles 111 to 129 are not reproduced in this volume. They are available at:
<http://secretariat.efta.int/Web/EuropeanEconomicArea/EEAAgreement/EEAAgreement>.

PART B

MODERNISATION AND PROCEDURAL MATTERS

B1

REGULATION No 17

First Regulation implementing Articles [81] and [82] of the Treaty

Official Journal P 13, 21.2.1962, p. 204

Celex No: 31962R0017

Notes

Regulation No 17 was repealed and superseded with effect from 1 May 2004 (with the exception of Article 8(3), which continues to apply to decisions adopted pursuant to Article 81(3) of the Treaty prior to 1 May 2004 until the date of expiration of those decisions) by Council Regulation 1/2003/EC (OJ L 1, 4.1.2003, p. 1), Article 43. The repealed provisions of Regulation No 17 are nonetheless reproduced here, in italics, in the form in which they stood immediately before repeal.

Commentary

Reg 17/62: **B&C:** 1.003, 1.019, 1.022, 1.057, 3.003, 3.005, 3.008–3.010, 3.012, 3.015–3.017, 3.072, 5.028, 5.099, 7.021, 7.023, 7.072, 7.096, 8.130, 8.276, 12.006–12.007, 12.010, 12.023, 13.004, 13.006, 13.015, 13.026, 13.033, 13.049, 13.052, 13.113, 13.118, 13.128, 13.136, 13.181, 13.195, 13.240, 14.010, 14.025, 14.034, 14.042, 14.086, 14.088 **F&N:** 2.01, 2.02, 2.07, 2.09, 2.20, 2.54, 2.110, 2.127, 2.141, 2.148, 2.149, 2.157, 2.158, 2.251, 3.188, 3.420, 4.351, 4.439, 6.230, 8.09, 8.106, 8.245, 8.264, 8.310, 8.359, 8.367, 8.369, 8.370, 8.416, 8.512, 8.602, 8.603, 9.12, 9.13, 9.18, 9.96, 12.55, 12.351, 13.290, 13.361, 14.08, 14.123, 14.124, 14.182, 14.183, 14.185, 14.188

THE COUNCIL OF THE EUROPEAN ECONOMIC COMMUNITY,

Having regard to the Treaty establishing the European Economic Community, and in particular Article [83] thereof;

Having regard to the proposal from the Commission;

Having regard to the Opinion of the Economic and Social Committee;

Having regard to the Opinion of the European Parliament;

[1] Whereas, in order to establish a system ensuring that competition shall not be distorted in the common market, it is necessary to provide for balanced application of Articles [81] and [82] in a uniform manner in the Member States;

[2] Whereas in establishing the rules for applying Article [81](3) account must be taken of the need to ensure effective supervision and to simplify administration to the greatest possible extent;

[3] Whereas it is accordingly necessary to make it obligatory, as a general principle, for undertakings which seek application of Article [81](3) to notify to the Commission their agreements, decisions and concerted practices;

[4] Whereas, on the one hand, such agreements, decisions and concerted practices are probably very numerous and cannot therefore all be examined at the same time and, on the other hand, some of them have special features which may make them less prejudicial to the development of the common market;

[5] Whereas there is consequently a need to make more flexible arrangements for the time being in respect of certain categories of agreement, decision and concerted practice without prejudging their validity under Article [81];

[6] Whereas it may be in the interest of undertakings to know whether any agreements, decisions or practices to which they are party, or propose to become party, may lead to action on the part of the Commission pursuant to Article [81](1) or Article [82];

[7] Whereas, in order to secure uniform application of Articles [81] and [82] in the common market, rules must be made under which the Commission, acting in close and constant liaison with the competent authorities of the Member States, may take the requisite measures for applying those Articles;

[8] Whereas for this purpose the Commission must have the co-operation of the competent authorities of the Member States and be empowered, throughout the common market, to require such information to be supplied and to undertake such investigations as are necessary to bring to light any agreement, decision or concerted practice prohibited by Article [81](1) or any abuse of a dominant position prohibited by Article [82];

[9] Whereas, in order to carry out its duty of ensuring that the provisions of the Treaty are applied, the Commission must be empowered to address to undertakings or associations of undertakings recommendations and decisions for the purpose of bringing to an end infringements of Articles [81] and [82];

[10] Whereas compliance with Articles [81] and [82] and the fulfilment of obligations imposed on undertakings and associations of undertakings under this Regulation must be enforceable by means of fines and periodic penalty payments;

[11] Whereas undertakings concerned must be accorded the right to be heard by the Commission, third parties whose interests may be affected by a decision must be given the opportunity of submitting their comments beforehand, and it must be ensured that wide publicity is given to decisions taken;

[12] Whereas all decisions taken by the Commission under this Regulation are subject to review by the Court of Justice under the conditions specified in the Treaty; whereas it is moreover desirable to confer upon the Court of Justice, pursuant to Article [229], unlimited jurisdiction in respect of decisions under which the Commission imposes fines or periodic penalty payments;

[13] Whereas this Regulation may enter into force without prejudice to any other provisions that may hereafter be adopted pursuant to Article [83];

HAS ADOPTED THIS REGULATION:

Article 1
Basic provision

Without prejudice to Articles 6, 7 and 23 of this Regulation, agreements, decisions and concerted practices of the kind described in Article [81](1) of the Treaty and the abuse of a dominant position in the market, within the meaning of Article [82] of the Treaty, shall be prohibited, no prior decision to that effect being required.

Commentary
Art 1: **B&C:** 1.057

Article 2
Negative clearance

Upon application by the undertakings or associations of undertakings concerned, the Commission may certify that, on the basis of the facts in its possession, there are no grounds under Article [81](1) or Article [82] of the Treaty for action on its part in respect of an agreement, decision or practice.

Commentary
Art 2: **B&C:** 13.005, 14.086 **F&N:** 15.142

Article 3
Termination of infringements

1. Where the Commission, upon application or upon its own initiative, finds that there is infringement of Article [81] or Article [82] of the Treaty, it may by decision require the undertakings or associations of undertakings concerned to bring such infringement to an end.

2. Those entitled to make application are:

(a) Member States;

(b) natural or legal persons who claim a legitimate interest.

3. Without prejudice to the other provisions of this Regulation, the Commission may, before taking a decision under paragraph 1, address to the undertakings or associations of undertakings concerned recommendations for termination of the infringement.

Commentary
Art 3: **B&C:** 13.065 **F&N:** 13.46, 15.05
Art 3(1): **B&C:** 13.118
Art 3(2): **B&C:** 13.218
Art 3(3): **B&C:** 13.133

Article 4
Notification of new agreements, decisions and practices

1. Agreements, decisions and concerted practices of the kind described in Article [81](1) of the Treaty which come into existence after the entry into force of this Regulation and in respect of which the parties seek application of Article [81](3) must be notified to the Commission. Until they have been notified, no decision in application of Article [81](3) may be taken.

2. Paragraph 1 shall not apply to agreements, decisions and concerted practices where:

(1) the only parties thereto are undertakings from one Member State and the agreements, decisions or practices do not relate either to imports or to exports between Member States;

(2) (a) the agreements or concerted practices are entered into by two or more undertakings, each operating, for the purposes of the agreement, at a different level of the production or distribution chain, and relate to the conditions under which the parties may purchase, sell or resell certain goods or services;

(b) not more than two undertakings are party thereto, and the agreements only impose restrictions on the exercise of the rights of the assignee or user of industrial property rights, in particular patents, utility models, designs or trade marks, or of the person entitled under a contract to the assignment, or grant, of the right to use a method of manufacture or knowledge relating to the use and to the application of industrial processes;

(3) they have as their sole object:

(a) the development or uniform application of standards or types; or

(b) joint research and development;

(c) specialisation in the manufacture of products, including agreements necessary for achieving this:

— where the products which are the subject of specialisation do not, in a substantial part of the common market, represent more than 15% of the volume of business done in identical products or those considered by consumers to be similar by reason of their characteristics, price and use, and

— where the total annual turnover of the participating undertakings does not exceed 200 million unit of account. These agreements, decisions and practices may be notified to the Commission.

Commentary
Art 4: **B&C:** 1.057 **F&N:** 15.142
Art 4(2): **B&C:** 13.007, 14.088 **F&N:** 2.02, 2.20, 2.21, 2.28

Article 5
Notification of existing agreements, decisions and practices

1. Agreements, decisions and concerted practices of the kind described in Article [81] (1) of the Treaty which are in existence at the date of entry into force of this Regulation and in respect of which the parties seek application of Article [81](3) shall be notified to the Commission before 1 November 1962. However, notwithstanding the foregoing provisions, any agreements, decisions and concerted practices to which not more than two undertakings are party shall be notified before 1 February 1963.

2. Paragraph 1 shall not apply to agreements, decisions or concerted practices falling within Article 4(2); these may be notified to the Commission.

51

Article 6
Decisions pursuant to Article [81](3)

1. Whenever the Commission takes a decision pursuant to Article [81](3) of the Treaty, it shall specify therein the date from which the decision shall take effect. Such a date shall not be earlier than the date of notification.

2. The second sentence of paragraph 1 shall not apply to agreements, decisions or concerted practices falling within Article 4(2) and Article 5(2), nor to those falling within Article 5(1) which have been notified within the time limit specified in Article 5(1).

Commentary
Art 6: **B&C:** 13.006

Article 7
Special provisions for existing agreements, decisions and practices

1. Where agreements, decisions and concerted practices in existence at the date of entry into force of this Regulation and notified within the time limits specified in Article 5(1) do not satisfy the requirements of Article [81](3) of the Treaty and the undertakings or associations of undertakings concerned cease to give effect to them or modify them in such a manner that they no longer fall within the prohibition contained in Article [81](1) or that they satisfy the requirements of Article [81](3), the prohibition contained in Article [81](1) shall apply only for a period fixed by the Commission. A decision by the Commission pursuant to the foregoing sentence shall not apply as against undertakings and associations of undertakings which did not expressly consent to the notification.

2. Paragraph 1 shall apply to agreements, decisions and concerted practices falling within Article 4(2) which are in existence at the date of entry into force of this Regulation if they are notified before 1 January 1967.

Article 8
Duration and revocation of decisions under Article [81](3)

1. A decision in application of Article [81](3) of the Treaty shall be issued for a specified period and conditions and obligations may be attached thereto.

2. A decision may on application be renewed if the requirements of Article [81](3) of the Treaty continue to be satisfied.

(3) The Commission may revoke or amend its decision or prohibit specified acts by the parties:

    (a) where there has been a change in any of the facts which were basic to the making of the decision;

    (b) where the parties commit a breach of any obligation attached to the decision;

    (c) where the decision is based on incorrect information or was induced by deceit;

    (d) where the parties abuse the exemption from the provisions of Article [81](1) of the Treaty granted to them by the decision. In cases to which subparagraphs (b), (c) or (d) apply, the decision may be revoked with retroactive effect.

Notes
Article 8(3) continues to apply to decisions adopted pursuant to Article 81(3) of the Treaty prior to 1 May 2004 until the date of expiration of those decisions: Council Regulation 1/2003/EC (OJ L 1, 4.1.2003, p. 1), Article 43.

Commentary
Art 8: **F&N:** 2.127, 2.137
Art 8(1): **B&C:** 13.006, 13.013
Art 8(3): **B&C:** 3.008, 13.201, 14.085

Article 9
Powers

1. Subject to review of its decision by the Court of Justice, the Commission shall have sole power to declare Article [81](1) inapplicable pursuant to Article [81](3) of the Treaty.

2. The Commission shall have power to apply Article [81](1) and Article [82] of the Treaty; this power may be exercised notwithstanding that the time limits specified in Article 5(1) and in Article 7(2) relating to notification have not expired.

3. As long as the Commission has not initiated any procedure under Articles 2, 3 or 6, the authorities of the Member States shall remain competent to apply Article [81](1) and Article [82] in accordance with Article 88 of the Treaty; they shall remain competent in this respect notwithstanding that the time limits specified in Article 5(1) and in Article 7(2) relating to notification have not expired.

Commentary
Art 9(1): B&C: 3.003
Art 9(3): B&C: 14.010 F&N: 2.220, 2.226, 2.246

Article 10
Liaison with the authorities of the Member States

1. The Commission shall forthwith transmit to the competent authorities of the Member States a copy of the applications and notifications together with copies of the most important documents lodged with the Commission for the purpose of establishing the existence of infringements of Articles [81] or [82] of the Treaty or of obtaining negative clearance or a decision in application of Article [81](3).

2. The Commission shall carry out the procedure set out in paragraph 1 in close and constant liaison with the competent authorities of the Member States; such authorities shall have the right to express their views upon that procedure.

3. An Advisory Committee on Restrictive Practices and Monopolies shall be consulted prior to the taking of any decision following upon a procedure under paragraph 1, and of any decision concerning the renewal, amendment or revocation of a decision pursuant to Article [81](3) of the Treaty.

4. The Advisory Committee shall be composed of officials competent in the matter of restrictive practices and monopolies. Each Member State shall appoint an official to represent it who, if prevented from attending, may be replaced by another official.

5. The consultation shall take place at a joint meeting convened by the Commission; such a meeting shall be held not earlier than fourteen days after dispatch of the notice convening it. The notice shall, in respect of each case to be examined, be accompanied by a summary of the case together with an indication of the most important documents, and a preliminary draft decision.

6. The Advisory Committee may deliver an opinion notwithstanding that some of its members or their alternates are not present. A report of the outcome of the consultative proceedings shall be annexed to the draft decision. It shall not be made public.

Commentary
Art 10: B&C: 13.223 F&N: 2.157
Art 10(1): F&N: 2.157, 2.158
Art 10(3): F&N: 2.150

Article 11
Requests for information

1. In carrying out the duties assigned to it by Article [85] and by provisions adopted under Article [83] of the Treaty, the Commission may obtain all necessary information from the Governments and competent authorities of the Member States and from undertakings and associations of undertakings.

2. When sending a request for information to an undertaking or association of undertakings, the Commission shall at the same time forward a copy of the request to the competent authority of the Member State in whose territory the seat of the undertaking or association of undertakings is situated.

3. In its request the Commission shall state the legal basis and the purpose of the request and also the penalties provided for in Article 15(1)(b) for supplying incorrect information.

4. The owners of the undertakings or their representatives and, in the case of legal persons, companies or firms, or of associations having no legal personality, the persons authorised to represent them by law or by their constitution shall supply the information requested.

Part B Modernisation and Procedural Matters

5. *Where an undertaking or association of undertakings does not supply the information requested within the time limit fixed by the Commission, or supplies incomplete information, the Commission shall by decision require the information to be supplied. The decision shall specify what information is required, fix an appropriate time limit within which it is to be supplied and indicate the penalties provided for in Article 15(1)(b) and Article 16(1)(c) and the right to have the decision reviewed by the Court of Justice.*

6. *The Commission shall at the same time forward a copy of its decision to the competent authority of the Member State in whose territory the seat of the undertaking or association of undertakings is situated.*

Commentary
Art 11: B&C: 13.032 F&N: 2.158, 8.99, 8.224, 8.294, 8.295, 8.296, 8.308, 8.310, 8.312, 8.370
Art 11(1): F&N: 2.150, 2.157
Art 11(2): F&N: 2.157
Art 11(4): B&C: 13.032
Art 11(5): B&C: 13.032
Art 11(6): F&N: 2.157

Article 12
Inquiry into sectors of the economy

1. *If in any sector of the economy the trend of trade between Member States, price movements, inflexibility of prices or other circumstances suggest that in the economic sector concerned competition is being restricted or distorted within the common market, the Commission may decide to conduct a general inquiry into that economic sector and in the course thereof may request undertakings in the sector concerned to supply the information necessary for giving effect to the principles formulated in Articles [81] and [82] of the Treaty and for carrying out the duties entrusted to the Commission.*

2. *The Commission may in particular request every undertaking or association of undertakings in the economic sector concerned to communicate to it all agreements, decisions and concerted practices which are exempt from notification by virtue of Article 4(2) and Article 5(2).*

3. *When making inquiries pursuant to paragraph 2, the Commission shall also request undertakings or groups of undertakings whose size suggests that they occupy a dominant position within the common market or a substantial part thereof to supply to the Commission such particulars of the structure of the undertakings and of their behaviour as are requisite to an appraisal of their position in the light of Article [82] of the Treaty.*

4. *Article 10(3) to (6) and Articles 11, 13 and 14 shall apply correspondingly.*

Article 13
Investigations by the authorities of the Member States

1. *At the request of the Commission, the competent authorities of the Member States shall undertake the investigations which the Commission considers to be necessary under Article 14(1), or which it has ordered by decision pursuant to Article 14(3). The officials of the competent authorities of the Member States responsible for conducting these investigations shall exercise their powers upon production of an authorisation in writing issued by the competent authority of the Member State in whose territory the investigation is to be made. Such authorisation shall specify the subject matter and purpose of the investigation.*

2. *If so requested by the Commission or by the competent authority of the Member State in whose territory the investigation is to be made, the officials of the Commission may assist the officials of such authorities in carrying out their duties.*

Commentary
Art 13: F&N: 2.154

Article 14
Investigating powers of the Commission

1. *In carrying out the duties assigned to it by Article [85] and by provisions adopted under Article [83] of the Treaty, the Commission may undertake all necessary investigations into undertakings and associations of undertakings. To this end the officials authorised by the Commission are empowered:*

(a) to examine the books and other business records;

(b) to take copies of or extracts from the books and business records;

(c) to ask for oral explanations on the spot;

(d) to enter any premises; land and means of transport of undertakings.

2. The officials of the Commission authorised for the purpose of these investigations shall exercise their powers upon production of an authorisation in writing specifying the subject matter and purpose of the investigation and the penalties provided for in Article 15(1)(c) in cases where production of the required books or other business records is incomplete. In good time before the investigation, the Commission shall inform the competent authority of the Member State in whose territory the same is to be made of the investigation and of the identity of the authorised officials.

3. Undertakings and associations of undertakings shall submit to investigations ordered by decision of the Commission. The decision shall specify the subject matter and purpose of the investigation, appoint the date on which it is to begin and indicate the penalties provided for in Article 15(1)(c) and Article 16(1)(d) and the right to have the decision reviewed by the Court of Justice.

4. The Commission shall take decisions referred to in paragraph 3 after consultation with the competent authority of the Member State in whose territory the investigation is to be made.

5. Officials of the competent authority of the Member State in whose territory the investigation is to be made may, at the request of such authority or of the Commission, assist the officials of the Commission in carrying out their duties.

6. Where an undertaking opposes an investigation ordered pursuant to this Article, the Member State concerned shall afford the necessary assistance to the officials authorised by the Commission to enable them to make their investigation. Member States shall, after consultation with the Commission, take the necessary measures to this end before 1 October 1962.

Commentary

Art 14: **B&C:** 2.036, 13.032, 13.047–13.048 **F&N:** 8.263, 8.296, 8.346, 8.393

Art 14(1): **F&N:** 8.345

Art 14(1)(c): **F&N:** 8.367

Art 14(2): **F&N:** 2.157, 8.337, 8.399

Art 14(3): **B&C:** 13.043 **F&N:** 8.139, 8.271, 8.346, 8.392

Art 14(4): **F&N:** 2.157

Art 14(5): **F&N:** 2.150

Art 14(6): **F&N:** 8.392

Article 15

Fines

1. The Commission may by decision impose on undertakings or associations of undertakings fines of 100 to 5,000 euros where, intentionally or negligently:

(a) they supply incorrect or misleading information in an application pursuant to Article 2 or in a notification pursuant to Articles 4 or 5; or

(b) they supply incorrect information in response to a request made pursuant to Article 11(3) or (5) or to Article 12, or do not supply information within the time limit fixed by a decision taken under Article 11(5); or

(c) they produce the required books or other business records in incomplete form during investigations under Article 13 or 14, or refuse to submit to an investigation ordered by decision issued in implementation of Article 14(3).

2. The Commission may by decision impose on undertakings or associations of undertakings fines of 1,000 to 1,000,000 euros, or a sum in excess thereof but not exceeding 10% of the turnover in the preceding business year of each of the undertakings participating in the infringement where, either intentionally or negligently:

(a) they infringe Article [81](1) or Article [82] of the Treaty; or

(b) they commit a breach of any obligation imposed pursuant to Article 8(1). In fixing the amount of the fine, regard shall be had both to the gravity and to the duration of the infringement.

3. *Article 10(3) to (6) shall apply.*

4. *Decisions taken pursuant to paragraphs 1 and 2 shall not be of a criminal law nature.*

5. *The fines provided for in paragraph 2(a) shall not be imposed in respect of acts taking place:*

(a) *after notification to the Commission and before its decision in application of Article [81](3) of the Treaty, provided they fall within the limits of the activity described in the notification;*

(b) *before notification and in the course of agreements, decisions or concerted practices in existence at the date of entry into force of this Regulation, provided that notification was effected within the time limits specified in Article 5(1) and Article 7(2).*

6. *Paragraph 5 shall not have effect where the Commission has informed the undertakings concerned that after preliminary examination it is of opinion that Article [81](1) of the Treaty applies and that application of Article [81](3) is not justified.*

Commentary

Art 15(1)(b): **B&C**: 13.035 **F&N**: 8.316
Art 15(1)(c): **F&N**: 8.384, 8.721
Art 15(2): **B&C**: 13.030, 13.144 **F&N**: 8.10, 8.420, 8.471, 8.501, 8.587, 8.590, 8.591, 8.594, 8.595, 8.611, 8.615, 8.622, 8.707, 8.777, 8.780
Art 15(2)(b): **B&C**: 3.008
Art 15(4): **F&N**: 8.596
Art 15(5): **B&C**: 13.006
Art 15(6): **B&C**: 13.010, 13.078, 13.156

Article 16
Periodic penalty payments

1. *The Commission may by decision impose on undertakings or associations of undertakings periodic penalty payments of 50 to 1,000 euros per day, calculated from the date appointed by the decision, in order to compel them:*

(a) *to put an end to an infringement of Article [81] or 86 of the Treaty, in accordance with a decision taken pursuant to Article 3 of this Regulation;*

(b) *to refrain from any act prohibited under Article 8(3);*

(c) *to supply complete and correct information which it has requested by decision taken pursuant to Article 11(5);*

(d) *to submit to an investigation which it has ordered by decision taken pursuant to Article 14(3).*

2. *Where the undertakings or associations of undertakings have satisfied the obligation which it was the purpose of the periodic penalty payment to enforce, the Commission may fix the total amount of the periodic penalty payment at a lower figure than that which would arise under the original decision.*

3. *Article 10(3) to (6) shall apply.*

Commentary

Art 16(1)(b): **B&C**: 13.201
Art 16(1)(c): **F&N**: 8.315
Art 16(1)(d): **B&C**: 13.043

Article 17
Review by the Court of Justice

The Court of Justice shall have unlimited jurisdiction within the meaning of Article [229] of the Treaty to review decisions whereby the Commission has fixed a fine or periodic penalty payment; it may cancel, reduce or increase the fine or periodic penalty payment imposed.

Commentary

Art 17: **B&C**: 13.214 **F&N**: 8.845, 8.849

Article 18
Unit of account

For the purposes of applying Articles 15 to 17 the unit of account shall be that adopted in drawing up the budget of the Community in accordance with Articles [277] and [279] of the Treaty.

Article 19
Hearing of the parties and of third persons

1. Before taking decisions as provided for in Articles 2, 3, 6, 7, 8, 15 and 16, the Commission shall give the undertakings or associations of undertakings concerned the opportunity of being heard on the matters to which the Commission has taken objection.

2. If the Commission or the competent authorities of the Member States consider it necessary, they may also hear other natural or legal persons. Applications to be heard on the part of such persons shall, where they show a sufficient interest, be granted.

3. Where the Commission intends to give negative clearance pursuant to Article 2 or take a decision in application of Article [81](3) of the Treaty, it shall publish a summary of the relevant application or notification and invite all interested third parties to submit their observations within a time limit which it shall fix being not less than one month. Publication shall have regard to the legitimate interest of undertakings in the protection of their business secrets.

Commentary
Art 19: **B&C:** 13.100
Art 19(3): **B&C:** 5.090, 5.092, 5.140, 5.144, 5.151, 6.064, 6.079, 6.084, 6.107, 6.165, 6.169, 6.194, 7.072, 7.113, 13.008–13.009, 13.011, 15.133 **F&N:** 2.127, 10.214, 11.72, 12.55, 12.94, 12.95, 12.135, 12.276, 12.279, 12.304, 12.325, 12.349, 13.80, 13.86, 13.91, 13.104, 13.112, 13.196, 13.290, 13.303, 13.312

Article 20
Professional secrecy

1. Information acquired as a result of the application of Articles 11, 12, 13 and 14 shall be used only for the purpose of the relevant request or investigation.

2. Without prejudice to the provisions of Articles 19 and 21, the Commission and the competent authorities of the Member States, their officials and other servants shall not disclose information acquired by them as a result of the application of this Regulation and of the kind covered by the obligation of professional secrecy.

3. The provisions of paragraphs 1 and 2 shall not prevent publication of general information or surveys which do not contain information relating to particular undertakings or associations of undertakings.

Commentary
Art 20: **F&N:** 2.158
Art 20(2): **F&N:** 2.188

Article 21
Publication of decisions

1. The Commission shall publish the decisions which it takes pursuant to Articles 2, 3, 6, 7 and 8.

2. The publication shall state the names of the parties and the main content of the decision; it shall have regard to the legitimate interest of undertakings in the protection of their business secrets.

Commentary
Art 21: **F&N:** 8.475

Article 22
Special provisions

1. The Commission shall submit to the Council proposals for making certain categories of agreement, decision and concerted practice falling within Article 4(2) or Article 5(2) compulsorily notifiable under Article 4 or 5.

2. *Within one year from the date of entry into force of this Regulation, the Council shall examine, on a proposal from the Commission, what special provisions might be made for exempting from the provisions of this Regulation agreements, decisions and concerted practices falling within Article 4(2) or Article 5(2).*

Article 23
Transitional provisions applicable to decisions of authorities of the Member States

1. *Agreements, decisions and concerted practices of the kind described in Article [81](1) of the Treaty to which, before the entry into force of this Regulation, the competent authority of a Member State has declared Article [81](1) to be inapplicable pursuant to Article [81](3) shall not be subject to compulsory notification under Article 5. The decision of the competent authority of the Member State shall be deemed to be a decision within the meaning of Article 6; it shall cease to be valid upon expiration of the period fixed by such authority but in any event not more than three years after the entry into force of this Regulation. Article 8(3) shall apply.*

2. *Applications for renewal of decisions of the kind described in paragraph 1 shall be decided upon by the Commission in accordance with Article 8(2).*

Article 24
Implementing provisions

The Commission shall have power to adopt implementing provisions concerning the form, content and other details of applications pursuant to Articles 2 and 3 and of notifications pursuant to Articles 4 and 5, and concerning hearings pursuant to Article 19(1) and (2).

Article 25

1. *As regards agreements, decisions and concerted practices to which Article [81] of the Treaty applies by virtue of accession, the date of accession shall be substituted for the date of entry into force of this Regulation in every place where reference is made in this Regulation to this latter date.*

2. *Agreements, decisions and concerted practices existing at the date of accession to which Article [81] of the Treaty applies by virtue of accession shall be notified pursuant to Article 5(1) or Article 7(1) and (2) within six months from the date of accession.*

3. *Fines under Article 15(2)(a) shall not be imposed in respect of any act prior to notification of the agreements, decisions and practices to which paragraph 2 applies and which have been notified within the period therein specified.*

4. *New Member States shall take the measures referred to in Article 14(6) within six months from the date of accession after consulting the Commission.*

5. *The provisions of paragraphs 1 to 4 above still apply in the same way in the case of the accession of the Hellenic Republic, the Kingdom of Spain and of the Portuguese Republic.*

6. *The provisions of paragraphs 1 to 4 still apply in the same way in the case of the accession of Austria, Finland and Sweden. However, they do not apply to agreements, decisions and concerted practises which at the date of accession already fall under Article 53 of the EEA Agreement.*

Commentary
Art 25: B&C: 1.079

This Regulation shall be binding in its entirety and directly applicable in all Member States.

B2

COMMISSION DECISION

of 23 May 2001

on the terms of reference of hearing officers in certain competition proceedings
(notified under document number C(2001) 1461)

(Text with EEA relevance)

(2001/462/EC, ECSC)

Official Journal L 162, 19.6.2001, p. 21

Celex No: 32001D0462

Part B Modernisation and
Procedural Matters

THE COMMISSION OF THE EUROPEAN COMMUNITIES,

Having regard to the Treaty establishing the European Community,

Having regard to the Treaty establishing the European Coal and Steel Community,

Having regard to the Agreement on the European Economic Area,

Having regard to the Rules of Procedure of the Commission,[1] and in particular Article 20 thereof,

Notes
[1] OJ L 308, 8.12.2000, p. 26.

Commentary
Decision: B&C: 1.056, 13.101, 13.102

Whereas:

(1) The right of the parties concerned and of third parties to be heard before a final decision affecting their interests is taken is a fundamental principle of Community law. That right is also set out in Council Regulation (EEC) No 4064/89 of 21 December 1989 on the control of concentrations between undertakings,[1] as last amended by Regulation (EC) No 1310/97,[2] Commission Regulation (EC) No 2842/98 of 22 December 1998 on the hearing of parties in certain proceedings under Articles 85 and 86 of the EC Treaty[3] and Commission Regulation (EC) No 447/98 of 1 March 1998 on the notifications, time limits and hearings provided for in Council Regulation (EEC) No 4064/89 on the control of concentrations between undertakings.[4]

Notes
[1] OJ L 395, 30.12.1989, p. 1 (corrected version in OJ L 257, 21.9.1990, p. 13).
[2] OJ L 180, 9.7.1997, p. 1.
[3] OJ L 354, 30.12.1998, p. 18.
[4] OJ L 61, 2.3.1998, p. 1.

(2) The Commission must ensure that that right is guaranteed in its competition proceedings, having regard in particular to the Charter of Fundamental Rights of the European Union.[1]

Notes
[1] OJ C 364, 18.12.2000, p. 1.

(3) The conduct of administrative proceedings should therefore be entrusted to an independent person experienced in competition matters who has the integrity necessary to contribute to the objectivity, transparency and efficiency of those proceedings.

(4) The Commission created the post of hearing officer for these purposes in 1982 and last laid down the terms of reference for that post in Commission Decision 94/810/ECSC, EC of 12 December 1994 on the terms of reference of hearing officers in competition procedures before the Commission.[1]

Notes
[1] OJ L 330, 21.12.1994, p. 67.

(5) It is necessary to further strengthen the role of the hearing officer and to adapt and consolidate those terms of reference in the light of developments in competition law.
(6) In order to ensure the independence of the hearing officer, he should be attached, for administrative purposes, to the member of the Commission with special responsibility for competition. Transparency as regards the appointment, termination of appointment and transfer of hearing officers should be increased.
(7) The hearing officer should be appointed in accordance with the rules laid down in the Staff Regulations of Officials and the Conditions of Employment of Other Servants of the European Communities. In accordance with those rules, consideration may be given to candidates who are not officials of the Commission.
(8) The terms of reference of the hearing officer in competition proceedings should be framed in such a way as to safeguard the right to be heard throughout the whole procedure.
(9) When disclosing information on natural persons, particular attention should be paid to Regulation (EC) No 45/2001 of the European Parliament and of the Council of 18 December 2000 on the protection of individuals with regard to the processing of personal data by the Community institutions and bodies and on the free movement of such data.[1]

Notes
[1] OJ L 8, 12.1.2001, p. 1.

(10) This Decision should be without prejudice to the general rules granting or excluding access to Commission documents.
(11) Decision 94/810/ECSC, EC should be repealed,

HAS DECIDED AS FOLLOWS:

Article 1

The Commission shall appoint one or more hearing officers (hereinafter "the hearing officer"), who shall ensure that the effective exercise of the right to be heard is respected in competition proceedings before the Commission under Articles 81 and 82 of the EC Treaty, Articles 65 and 66 of the ECSC Treaty, and Regulation (EEC) No 4064/89.

Article 2

1. The appointment of the hearing officer shall be published in the *Official Journal of the European Communities*. Any interruption, termination of appointment or transfer by whatever procedure, shall be the subject of a reasoned decision of the Commission. That decision shall be published in the *Official Journal of the European Communities*.

2. The hearing officer shall be attached, for administrative purposes, to the member of the Commission with special responsibility for competition (hereinafter "the competent member of the Commission").

3. Where the hearing officer is unable to act, the competent member of the Commission, where appropriate after consultation of the hearing officer, shall designate another official, who is not involved in the case in question, to carry out the hearing officer's duties.

Commentary
Art 2(1): B&C: 13.102

Article 3

1. In performing his duties, the hearing officer shall take account of the need for effective application of the competition rules in accordance with the Community legislation in force and the principles laid down by the Court of Justice and the Court of First Instance of the European Communities.

2. The hearing officer shall be kept informed by the director responsible for investigating the case (hereinafter "the director responsible") about the development of the procedure up to the stage of the draft [decision] to be submitted to the competent member of the Commission.

3. The hearing officer may present observations on any matter arising out of any Commission competition proceeding to the competent member of the Commission.

Commentary
Art 3(3): **B&C**: 13.102

Article 4

1. The hearing officer shall organise and conduct the hearings provided for in the provisions implementing Articles 81 and 82 of the EC Treaty, Articles 65 and 66 of the ECSC Treaty and Regulation (EEC) No 4064/89, in accordance with Articles 5 to 13 of this Decision.

2. The provisions referred to in paragraph 1 are:

(a) the first paragraph of Article 36 of the ECSC Treaty;
(b) Regulation (EC) No 2842/98;
(c) Regulation (EC) No 447/98.

Article 5

The hearing officer shall ensure that the hearing is properly conducted and contributes to the objectivity of the hearing itself and of any decision taken subsequently. The hearing officer shall seek to ensure in particular that, in the preparation of draft Commission decisions, due account is taken of all the relevant facts, whether favourable or unfavourable to the parties concerned, including the factual elements related to the gravity of any infringement.

Commentary
Art 5: **B&C**: 13.101, 13.102

Article 6

1. Applications to be heard from third parties, be they persons, undertakings or associations of persons or undertakings, shall be submitted in writing, together with a written statement explaining the applicant's interest in the outcome of the procedure.

2. Decisions as to whether third parties are to be heard shall be taken after consulting the director responsible.

3. Where it is found that an application has not shown a sufficient interest to be heard, he shall be informed in writing of the reasons for such finding. A time limit shall be fixed within which he may submit any further written comments.

Article 7

1. Applications to be heard orally shall be made in the applicant's written comments on letters which the Commission has addressed to him.

2. The letters referred to in paragraph 1 are those:

(a) communicating a statement of objections;
(b) inviting the written comments of a third party having shown sufficient interest to be heard;
(c) informing a complainant that in the Commission's view there are insufficient grounds for finding an infringement and inviting him to submit any further written comments.

3. Decisions as to whether applicants are to be heard orally shall be taken after consulting the director responsible.

Article 8

1. Where a person, an [undertaking] or an association of persons or undertakings has received one or more of the letters listed in Article 7(2) and has reason to believe that the Commission has in its possession documents which have not been disclosed to it and that those documents are necessary for

the proper exercise of the right to be heard, access to those documents may be sought by means of a reasoned request.

2. The reasoned decision on any such request shall be communicated to the person, undertaking or association that made the request and to any other person, undertaking or association concerned by the procedure.

Article 9

Where it is intended to disclose information which may constitute a business secret of an undertaking, it shall be informed in writing of this intention and the reasons for it. A time limit shall be fixed within which the undertaking concerned may submit any written comments.

Where the undertaking concerned objects to the disclosure of the information but it is found that the information is not protected and may therefore be disclosed, that finding shall be stated in a reasoned decision which shall be notified to the undertaking concerned. The decision shall specify the date after which the information will be disclosed. This date shall not be less than one week from the date of notification.

The first and second paragraphs shall apply mutatis mutandis to the disclosure of information by publication in the *Official Journal of the European Communities*.

Commentary
Art 9: B&C: 13.219

Article 10

Where a person, undertaking or association of persons or undertakings considers that the time limit imposed for its reply to a letter referred to in Article 7(2) is too short, it may, within the original time limit, seek an extension of that time limit by means of a reasoned request. The applicant shall be informed in writing whether the request has been granted.

Article 11

Where appropriate, in view of the need to ensure that the hearing is properly prepared and particularly that questions of fact are clarified as far as possible, the hearing officer may, after consulting the director responsible, supply in advance to the parties invited to the hearing a list of the questions on which he wishes them to make known their views.

For this purpose, after consulting the director responsible, the hearing officer may hold a meeting with the parties invited to the hearing and, where appropriate, the Commission staff, in order to prepare for the hearing itself.

The hearing officer may also ask for prior written notification of the essential contents of the intended statement of persons whom the parties invited to the hearing have proposed for hearing.

Article 12

1. After consulting the director responsible, the hearing officer shall determine the date, the duration and the place of the hearing. Where a postponement is requested, the hearing officer shall decide whether or not to allow it.

2. The hearing officer shall be fully responsible for the conduct of the hearing.

3. The hearing officer shall decide whether fresh documents should be admitted during the hearing, what persons should be heard on behalf of a party and whether the persons concerned should be heard separately or in the presence of other persons attending the hearing.

4. Where appropriate, in view of the need to ensure the right to be heard, the hearing officer may, after consulting the Director responsible, afford persons, undertakings, and associations of persons or undertakings the opportunity of submitting further written comments after the oral hearing. The hearing officer shall fix a date by which such submissions may be made. The Commission shall not be obliged to take into account written comments received after that date.

Commentary
Art 12(1): **B&C**: 13.101
Art 12(3): **B&C**: 13.103
Art 12(4): **B&C**: 13.103

Article 13

1. The hearing officer shall report to the competent member of the Commission on the hearing and the conclusions he draws from it, with regard to the respect of the right to be heard. The observations in this report shall concern procedural issues, including disclosure of documents and access to the file, time limits for replying to the statement of objections and the proper conduct of the oral hearing.

A copy of the report shall be given to the Director-General for Competition and to the director responsible.

2. In addition to the report referred to in paragraph 1, the hearing officer may make observations on the further progress of the proceedings. Such observations may relate among other things to the need for further information, the withdrawal of certain objections, or the formulation of further objections.

Commentary
Art 13: **B&C**: 13.102

Article 14

Where appropriate, the hearing officer may report on the objectivity of any enquiry conducted in order to assess the competition impact of commitments proposed in relation to any proceeding initiated by the Commission in application of the provisions referred to in Article 1. This shall cover in particular the selection of respondents and the methodology used.

Article 15

The hearing officer shall, on the basis of the draft decision to be submitted to the Advisory Committee in the case in question, prepare a final report in writing on the respect of the right to be heard, as referred to in Article 13(1). This report will also consider whether the draft decision deals only with objections in respect of which the parties have been afforded the opportunity of making known their views, and, where appropriate, the objectivity of any enquiry within the meaning of Article 14.

The final report shall be submitted to the competent member of the Commission, the Director-General for Competition and the director responsible. It shall be communicated to the competent authorities of the Member States and, in accordance with the provisions on cooperation laid down in Protocol 23 and Protocol 24 of the EEA Agreement, to the EFTA Surveillance Authority.

Commentary
Art 15: **B&C**: 13.102

Article 16

1. The hearing officer's final report shall be attached to the draft decision submitted to the Commission, in order to ensure that, when it reaches a decision on an individual case, the Commission is fully apprised of all relevant information as regards the course of the procedure and respect of the right to be heard.

2. The final report may be modified by the hearing officer in the light of any amendments to the draft decision up to the time the decision is adopted by the Commission.

3. The Commission shall communicate the hearing officer's final report, together with the decision, to the addressees of the decision. It shall publish the hearing officer's final report in the *Official Journal of the European Communities*, together with the decision, having regard to the legitimate interest of undertakings in the protection of their business secrets.

Commentary
Art 16: **B&C**: 13.102

Part B Modernisation and Procedural Matters

Article 17

Decision 94/810/ECSC, EC is repealed.

Procedural steps already taken under that Decision shall continue to have effect.

Done at Brussels, 23 May 2001.

Notes

Communication from the Commission (2004/C 197/03) (OJ C 197, 4.8.2004, p. 10):
On 16 and 30 October 2001 respectively, the Commission appointed Ms Karen WILLIAMS and Mr Serge DURANDE to the post of hearing officer, in accordance to Article 1 of the Commission Decision of 23 May 2001 on the terms of reference of hearing officers in certain competition cases (OJ L 162, 19.6.2001, p. 21).

B3

COUNCIL REGULATION (EC) NO 1/2003

of 16 December 2002

on the implementation of the rules on competition laid down
in Articles 81 and 82 of the Treaty

(Text with EEA relevance)

Official Journal L 1, 4.1.2003, p. 1

Celex No: 32003R0001

Notes

EEA application: see the Surveillance and Court Agreement, Protocol 4, Part I, Chapter II, as amended by the Agreement of 24 September 2004 (entry into force 20 May 2005). See also EEA Agreement, Protocol 21, Article 3(1), Point 1 (as replaced by EEA Joint Committee Decision No 130/2004 of 24 September 2004 (OJ L 64, 10.3.2005, p. 57 and EEA Supplement No 12, 10.2.3005, p. 42) with effect from 19 May 2005.

Commentary

Reg 1/2003/EC: B&C: 1.019, 1.022–1.023, 1.030, **1.058–1.060**, 1.063, 1.115, 2.088, 3.003–3.004, 3.007–3.008, 3.016, 3.082, 3.086–3.087, 3.090, 3.094, 4.017, 5.006, 6.137, 7.001, 7.012, 7.017–7.018, 7.024, 7.057, 7.066, 7.074, 7.133, 7.138, 8.234, 8.260, 8.263, 9.167, 10.008, 11.022, 12.003, 12.007, 12.009–12.010, 12.021, 12.039, 12.047, 12.122, 12.208, 13.002, 13.004, 13.016–13.018, 13.023–13.024, 13.044, 13.061, 13.074, 13.113, 13.118, 13.133, 13.196, 13.218, 13.251, 14.003, 14.005, 14.008, 14.010, 14.012, 14.033, 14.035–14.036, 14.043, 14.055, 14.088 F&N: 2.01, 2.03, 2.05, 2.08, 2.10, 2.21, 2.24, 2.28, 2.29, 2.39, 2.40, 2.47, 2.54, 2.55, 2.64, 2.68, 2.69, 2.73, 2.75, 2.76, 2.77, 2.84, 2.87, 2.92, 2.96, 2.98, 2.109, 2.119, 2.130, 2.143, 2.147, 2.148, 2.149, 2.154, 2.159, 2.160, 2.172, 2.181, 2.195, 2.200, 2.201, 2.204, 2.209, 2.231, 2.241, 2.242, 2.244, 2.253, 2.261, 2.268, 2.270, 2.278, 3.338, 3.395, 3.406, 3.416, 3.420, 4.413, 4.425, 5.24, 5.335, 5.345, 5.347, 5.350, 7.23, 7.24, 7.34, 7.86, 8.04, 8.10, 8.102, 8.166, 8.221, 8.235, 8.237, 8.244, 8.250, 8.260, 8.262–8.265, 8.281, 8.324, 8.336, 8.345, 8.357, 8.358, 8.363, 8.365, 8.367, 8.369, 8.371, 8.378, 8.410, 8.434, 8.459, 8.488, 8.514, 8.515, 8.858, 8.738, 9.12, 9.18, 10.122, 11.08, 12.325, 13.106, 14.09, 14.10, 14.14, 14.15, 14.26, 14.84, 14.93, 14.94, 14.100, 14.128, 14.131, 14.176, 14.182, 15.17
Arts 4–6: B&C: 3.003
Arts 6–9: F&N: 15.25
Arts 7–10: B&C: 13.109, 13.232 F&N: 2.23, 2.83, 2.90, 2.258, 14.132
Arts 11–16: F&N: 2.149, 8.434
Arts 17–22: B&C: 13.051, 14.024 F&N: 2.195, 14.132
Arts 18–21: F&N: 2.90, 8.259

THE COUNCIL OF THE EUROPEAN UNION,

Having regard to the Treaty establishing the European Community, and in particular Article 83 thereof,

Having regard to the proposal from the Commission,[1]

Having regard to the opinion of the European Parliament,[2]

Having regard to the opinion of the European Economic and Social Committee,[3]

Notes
[1] OJ C 365 E, 19.12.2000, p. 284.
[2] OJ C 72 E, 21.3.2002, p. 305.
[3] OJ C 155, 29.5.2001, p. 73.

Commentary
Preamble: B&C: 1.029, 14.062 F&N: 2.270, 8.323, 8.488

Part B Modernisation and Procedural Matters

Whereas:

(1) In order to establish a system which ensures that competition in the common market is not distorted, Articles 81 and 82 of the Treaty must be applied effectively and uniformly in the Community. Council Regulation No 17 of 6 February 1962, First Regulation implementing Articles 81 and 82[1] of the Treaty,[2] has allowed a Community competition policy to develop that has helped to disseminate a competition culture within the Community. In the light of experience, however, that Regulation should now be replaced by legislation designed to meet the challenges of an integrated market and a future enlargement of the Community.

Notes
[1] The title of Regulation No 17 has been adjusted to take account of the renumbering of the Articles of the EC Treaty, in accordance with Article 12 of the Treaty of Amsterdam; the original reference was to Articles 85 and 86 of the Treaty.
[2] OJ 13, 21.2.1962, p. 204/62. Regulation as last amended by Regulation (EC) No 1216/1999 (OJ L 148, 15.6.1999, p. 5).

(2) In particular, there is a need to rethink the arrangements for applying the exception from the prohibition on agreements, which restrict competition, laid down in Article 81(3) of the Treaty. Under Article 83(2)(b) of the Treaty, account must be taken in this regard of the need to ensure effective supervision, on the one hand, and to simplify administration to the greatest possible extent, on the other.

(3) The centralised scheme set up by Regulation No 17 no longer secures a balance between those two objectives. It hampers application of the Community competition rules by the courts and competition authorities of the Member States, and the system of notification it involves prevents the Commission from concentrating its resources on curbing the most serious infringements. It also imposes considerable costs on undertakings.

Commentary
Recital 3: F&N: 2.86, 2.148

(4) The present system should therefore be replaced by a directly applicable exception system in which the competition authorities and courts of the Member States have the power to apply not only Article 81(1) and Article 82 of the Treaty, which have direct applicability by virtue of the case-law of the Court of Justice of the European Communities, but also Article 81(3) of the Treaty.

Commentary
Recital 4: **B&C:** 14.005 **F&N:** 2.86

(5) In order to ensure an effective enforcement of the Community competition rules and at the same time the respect of fundamental rights of defence, this Regulation should regulate the burden of proof under Articles 81 and 82 of the Treaty. It should be for the party or the authority alleging an infringement of Article 81(1) and Article 82 of the Treaty to prove the existence thereof to the required legal standard. It should be for the undertaking or association of undertakings invoking the benefit of a defence against a finding of an infringement to demonstrate to the required legal standard that the conditions for applying such defence are satisfied. This Regulation affects neither national rules on the standard of proof nor obligations of competition authorities and courts of the Member States to ascertain the relevant facts of a case, provided that such rules and obligations are compatible with general principles of Community law.

Commentary
Recital 5: **B&C:** 14.006, 14.095, 14.154 **F&N:** 2.24, 2.25, 2.26, 2.27, 8.491

(6) In order to ensure that the Community competition rules are applied effectively, the competition authorities of the Member States should be associated more closely with their application. To this end, they should be empowered to apply Community law.

Commentary
Recital 6: **F&N:** 2.148

(7) National courts have an essential part to play in applying the Community competition rules. When deciding disputes between private individuals, they protect the subjective rights under Community law, for example by awarding damages to the victims of infringements. The role of the national courts here complements that of the competition authorities of the Member States. They should therefore be allowed to apply Articles 81 and 82 of the Treaty in full.

Commentary
Recital 7: **B&C:** 14.042, 14.057

(8) In order to ensure the effective enforcement of the Community competition rules and the proper functioning of the cooperation mechanisms contained in this Regulation, it is necessary to oblige the competition authorities and courts of the Member States to also apply Articles 81 and 82 of the Treaty where they apply national competition law to agreements and practices which may affect trade between Member States. In order to create a level playing field for agreements, decisions by associations of undertakings and concerted practices within the internal market, it is also necessary to determine pursuant to Article 83(2)(e) of the Treaty the relationship between national laws and Community competition law. To that effect it is necessary to provide that the application of national competition laws to agreements, decisions or concerted practices within the meaning of Article 81(1) of the Treaty may not lead to the prohibition of such agreements, decisions and concerted practices if they are not also prohibited under Community competition law. The notions of agreements, decisions and concerted practices are autonomous concepts of Community competition law covering the coordination of behaviour of undertakings on the market as interpreted by the Community Courts. Member States should not under this Regulation be precluded from adopting and applying on their territory stricter national competition laws which prohibit or impose sanctions on unilateral conduct engaged in by undertakings. These stricter national laws may include provisions which prohibit or impose sanctions on abusive behaviour toward economically dependent undertakings. Furthermore, this Regulation does not apply to national laws

which impose criminal sanctions on natural persons except to the extent that such sanctions are the means whereby competition rules applying to undertakings are enforced.

Commentary
Recital 8: B&C: 14.016, 14.022, 14.056, 14.060–14.062, 14.075 **F&N:** 2.38, 2.43, 2.55, 2.69, 2.70, 2.71, 2.72, 2.73

(9) Articles 81 and 82 of the Treaty have as their objective the protection of competition on the market. This Regulation, which is adopted for the implementation of these Treaty provisions, does not preclude Member States from implementing on their territory national legislation, which protects other legitimate interests provided that such legislation is compatible with general principles and other provisions of Community law. In so far as such national legislation pursues predominantly an objective different from that of protecting competition on the market, the competition authorities and courts of the Member States may apply such legislation on their territory. Accordingly, Member States may under this Regulation implement on their territory national legislation that prohibits or imposes sanctions on acts of unfair trading practice, be they unilateral or contractual. Such legislation pursues a specific objective, irrespective of the actual or presumed effects of such acts on competition on the market. This is particularly the case of legislation which prohibits undertakings from imposing on their trading partners, obtaining or attempting to obtain from them terms and conditions that are unjustified, disproportionate or without consideration.

Commentary
Recital 9: B&C: 14.062 **F&N:** 2.43, 2.57, 2.59, 2.69

(10) Regulations such as 19/65/EEC,[1] (EEC) No 2821/71,[2] (EEC) No 3976/87,[3] (EEC) No 1534/91,[4] or (EEC) No 479/92[5] empower the Commission to apply Article 81(3) of the Treaty by Regulation to certain categories of agreements, decisions by associations of undertakings and concerted practices. In the areas defined by such Regulations, the Commission has adopted and may continue to adopt so called "block" exemption Regulations by which it declares Article 81(1) of the Treaty inapplicable to categories of agreements, decisions and concerted practices. Where agreements, decisions and concerted practices to which such Regulations apply nonetheless have effects that are incompatible with Article 81(3) of the Treaty, the Commission and the competition authorities of the Member States should have the power to withdraw in a particular case the benefit of the block exemption Regulation.

Notes
[1] Council Regulation No 19/65/EEC of 2 March 1965 on the application of Article 81(3) (the titles of the Regulations have been adjusted to take account of the renumbering of the Articles of the EC Treaty, in accordance with Article 12 of the Treaty of Amsterdam; the original reference was to Article 85(3) of the Treaty) of the Treaty to certain categories of agreements and concerted practices (OJ 36, 6.3.1965, p. 533). Regulation as last amended by Regulation (EC) No 1215/1999 (OJ L 148, 15.6.1999, p. 1).
[2] Council Regulation (EEC) No 2821/71 of 20 December 1971 on the application of Article 81(3) (the titles of the Regulations have been adjusted to take account of the renumbering of the Articles of the EC Treaty, in accordance with Article 12 of the Treaty of Amsterdam; the original reference was to Article 85(3) of the Treaty) of the Treaty to categories of agreements, decisions and concerted practices (OJ L 285, 29.12.1971, p. 46). Regulation as last amended by the Act of Accession of 1994.
[3] Council Regulation (EEC) No 3976/87 of 14 December 1987 on the application of Article 81(3) (the titles of the Regulations have been adjusted to take account of the renumbering of the Articles of the EC Treaty, in accordance with Article 12 of the Treaty of Amsterdam; the original reference was to Article 85(3) of the Treaty) of the Treaty to certain categories of agreements and concerted practices in the air transport sector (OJ L 374, 31.12.1987, p. 9). Regulation as last amended by the Act of Accession of 1994.
[4] Council Regulation (EEC) No 1534/91 of 31 May 1991 on the application of Article 81(3) (the titles of the Regulations have been adjusted to take account of the renumbering of the Articles of the EC Treaty, in accordance with Article 12 of the Treaty of Amsterdam; the original reference was to Article 85(3) of the Treaty) of the Treaty to certain categories of agreements, decisions and concerted practices in the insurance sector (OJ L 143, 7.6.1991, p. 1).
[5] Council Regulation (EEC) No 479/92 of 25 February 1992 on the application of Article 81(3) (the titles of the Regulations have been adjusted to take account of the renumbering of the Articles of the EC Treaty, in accordance with Article 12 of the Treaty of Amsterdam; the original reference was to Article 85(3) of the Treaty) of the Treaty to certain categories of agreements, decisions and concerted practices between liner shipping companies (Consortia) (OJ L 55, 29.2.1992, p. 3). Regulation amended by the Act of Accession of 1994.

(11) For it to ensure that the provisions of the Treaty are applied, the Commission should be able to address decisions to undertakings or associations of undertakings for the purpose of bringing to an end infringements of Articles 81 and 82 of the Treaty. Provided there is a legitimate interest in doing so, the Commission should also be able to adopt decisions which find that an infringement has been committed in the past even if it does not impose a fine. This Regulation should also make explicit provision for the Commission's power to adopt decisions ordering interim measures, which has been acknowledged by the Court of Justice.

Commentary
Recital 11: B&C: 13.104

(12) This Regulation should make explicit provision for the Commission's power to impose any remedy, whether behavioural or structural, which is necessary to bring the infringement effectively to an end, having regard to the principle of proportionality. Structural remedies should only be imposed either where there is no equally effective behavioural remedy or where any equally effective behavioural remedy would be more burdensome for the undertaking concerned than the structural remedy. Changes to the structure of an undertaking as it existed before the infringement was committed would only be proportionate where there is a substantial risk of a lasting or repeated infringement that derives from the very structure of the undertaking.

Commentary
Recital 12: F&N: 2.104, 2.105, 4.434

(13) Where, in the course of proceedings which might lead to an agreement or practice being prohibited, undertakings offer the Commission commitments such as to meet its concerns, the Commission should be able to adopt decisions which make those commitments binding on the undertakings concerned. Commitment decisions should find that there are no longer grounds for action by the Commission without concluding whether or not there has been or still is an infringement. Commitment decisions are without prejudice to the powers of competition authorities and courts of the Member States to make such a finding and decide upon the case. Commitment decisions are not appropriate in cases where the Commission intends to impose a fine.

Commentary
Recital 13: B&C: 13.114, 13.116, 14.083 **F&N:** 2.116, 2.121, 2.147, 8.482

(14) In exceptional cases where the public interest of the Community so requires, it may also be expedient for the Commission to adopt a decision of a declaratory nature finding that the prohibition in Article 81 or Article 82 of the Treaty does not apply, with a view to clarifying the law and ensuring its consistent application throughout the Community, in particular with regard to new types of agreements or practices that have not been settled in the existing case-law and administrative practice.

Commentary
Recital 14: B&C: 3.007, 7.025, 13.022 **F&N:** 2.140, 2.141, 2.143, 2.145

(15) The Commission and the competition authorities of the Member States should form together a network of public authorities applying the Community competition rules in close cooperation. For that purpose it is necessary to set up arrangements for information and consultation. Further modalities for the cooperation within the network will be laid down and revised by the Commission, in close cooperation with the Member States.

Commentary
Recital 15: B&C: 13.018, 14.013 **F&N:** 2.148, 2.204

(16) Notwithstanding any national provision to the contrary, the exchange of information and the use of such information in evidence should be allowed between the members of the network even where the information is confidential. This information may be used for the application of Articles 81 and 82 of the Treaty as well as for the parallel application of national competition law,

provided that the latter application relates to the same case and does not lead to a different outcome. When the information exchanged is used by the receiving authority to impose sanctions on undertakings, there should be no other limit to the use of the information than the obligation to use it for the purpose for which it was collected given the fact that the sanctions imposed on undertakings are of the same type in all systems. The rights of defence enjoyed by undertakings in the various systems can be considered as sufficiently equivalent. However, as regards natural persons, they may be subject to substantially different types of sanctions across the various systems. Where that is the case, it is necessary to ensure that information can only be used if it has been collected in a way which respects the same level of protection of the rights of defence of natural persons as provided for under the national rules of the receiving authority.

Commentary
Recital 16: **B&C:** 14.022, 14.027 **F&N:** 2.174

(17) If the competition rules are to be applied consistently and, at the same time, the network is to be managed in the best possible way, it is essential to retain the rule that the competition authorities of the Member States are automatically relieved of their competence if the Commission initiates its own proceedings. Where a competition authority of a Member State is already acting on a case and the Commission intends to initiate proceedings, it should endeavour to do so as soon as possible. Before initiating proceedings, the Commission should consult the national authority concerned.

Commentary
Recital 17: **F&N:** 2.220, 2.238

(18) To ensure that cases are dealt with by the most appropriate authorities within the network, a general provision should be laid down allowing a competition authority to suspend or close a case on the ground that another authority is dealing with it or has already dealt with it, the objective being that each case should be handled by a single authority. This provision should not prevent the Commission from rejecting a complaint for lack of Community interest, as the case-law of the Court of Justice has acknowledged it may do, even if no other competition authority has indicated its intention of dealing with the case.

Commentary
Recital 18: **F&N:** 2.11, 2.151, 2.153

(19) The Advisory Committee on Restrictive Practices and Dominant Positions set up by Regulation No 17 has functioned in a very satisfactory manner. It will fit well into the new system of decentralised application. It is necessary, therefore, to build upon the rules laid down by Regulation No 17, while improving the effectiveness of the organisational arrangements. To this end, it would be expedient to allow opinions to be delivered by written procedure. The Advisory Committee should also be able to act as a forum for discussing cases that are being handled by the competition authorities of the Member States, so as to help safeguard the consistent application of the Community competition rules.

(20) The Advisory Committee should be composed of representatives of the competition authorities of the Member States. For meetings in which general issues are being discussed, Member States should be able to appoint an additional representative. This is without prejudice to members of the Committee being assisted by other experts from the Member States.

(21) Consistency in the application of the competition rules also requires that arrangements be established for cooperation between the courts of the Member States and the Commission. This is relevant for all courts of the Member States that apply Articles 81 and 82 of the Treaty, whether applying these rules in lawsuits between private parties, acting as public enforcers or as review courts. In particular, national courts should be able to ask the Commission for information or for its opinion on points concerning the application of Community competition law. The Commission and the competition authorities of the Member States should also be able to submit written or oral observations to courts called upon to apply Article 81 or Article 82 of the Treaty. These observations should be submitted within the framework of national procedural rules and

Part B Modernisation and Procedural Matters

practices including those safeguarding the rights of the parties. Steps should therefore be taken to ensure that the Commission and the competition authorities of the Member States are kept sufficiently well informed of proceedings before national courts.

(22) In order to ensure compliance with the principles of legal certainty and the uniform application of the Community competition rules in a system of parallel powers, conflicting decisions must be avoided. It is therefore necessary to clarify, in accordance with the case-law of the Court of Justice, the effects of Commission decisions and proceedings on courts and competition authorities of the Member States. Commitment decisions adopted by the Commission do not affect the power of the courts and the competition authorities of the Member States to apply Articles 81 and 82 of the Treaty.

Commentary
Recital 22: B&C: 14.076, 14.083

(23) The Commission should be empowered throughout the Community to require such information to be supplied as is necessary to detect any agreement, decision or concerted practice prohibited by Article 81 of the Treaty or any abuse of a dominant position prohibited by Article 82 of the Treaty. When complying with a decision of the Commission, undertakings cannot be forced to admit that they have committed an infringement, but they are in any event obliged to answer factual questions and to provide documents, even if this information may be used to establish against them or against another undertaking the existence of an infringement.

Commentary
Recital 23: F&N: 8.270

(24) The Commission should also be empowered to undertake such inspections as are necessary to detect any agreement, decision or concerted practice prohibited by Article 81 of the Treaty or any abuse of a dominant position prohibited by Article 82 of the Treaty. The competition authorities of the Member States should cooperate actively in the exercise of these powers.

Commentary
Recital 24: F&N: 8.329, 8.407

(25) The detection of infringements of the competition rules is growing ever more difficult, and, in order to protect competition effectively, the Commission's powers of investigation need to be supplemented. The Commission should in particular be empowered to interview any persons who may be in possession of useful information and to record the statements made. In the course of an inspection, officials authorised by the Commission should be empowered to affix seals for the period of time necessary for the inspection. Seals should normally not be affixed for more than 72 hours. Officials authorised by the Commission should also be empowered to ask for any information relevant to the subject matter and purpose of the inspection.

Commentary
Recital 25: F&N: 8.323

(26) Experience has shown that there are cases where business records are kept in the homes of directors or other people working for an undertaking. In order to safeguard the effectiveness of inspections, therefore, officials and other persons authorised by the Commission should be empowered to enter any premises where business records may be kept, including private homes. However, the exercise of this latter power should be subject to the authorisation of the judicial authority.

Commentary
Recital 26: B&C: 13.041 F&N: 8.416

(27) Without prejudice to the case-law of the Court of Justice, it is useful to set out the scope of the control that the national judicial authority may carry out when it authorises, as foreseen by national law including as a precautionary measure, assistance from law enforcement authorities in order to overcome possible opposition on the part of the undertaking or the execution of the decision to carry out inspections in non-business premises. It results from the case-law that the national judicial authority may in particular ask the Commission for further information which it needs to carry out its control and in the absence of which it could refuse the authorisation. The case-law also confirms the competence of the national courts to control the application of national rules governing the implementation of coercive measures.

(28) In order to help the competition authorities of the Member States to apply Articles 81 and 82 of the Treaty effectively, it is expedient to enable them to assist one another by carrying out inspections and other fact-finding measures.

Commentary
Recital 28: F&N: 2.154

(29) Compliance with Articles 81 and 82 of the Treaty and the fulfilment of the obligations imposed on undertakings and associations of undertakings under this Regulation should be enforceable by means of fines and periodic penalty payments. To that end, appropriate levels of fine should also be laid down for infringements of the procedural rules.

(30) In order to ensure effective recovery of fines imposed on associations of undertakings for infringements that they have committed, it is necessary to lay down the conditions on which the Commission may require payment of the fine from the members of the association where the association is not solvent. In doing so, the Commission should have regard to the relative size of the undertakings belonging to the association and in particular to the situation of small and medium-sized enterprises. Payment of the fine by one or several members of an association is without prejudice to rules of national law that provide for recovery of the amount paid from other members of the association.

(31) The rules on periods of limitation for the imposition of fines and periodic penalty payments were laid down in Council Regulation (EEC) No 2988/74,[1] which also concerns penalties in the field of transport. In a system of parallel powers, the acts, which may interrupt a limitation period, should include procedural steps taken independently by the competition authority of a Member State. To clarify the legal framework, Regulation (EEC) No 2988/74 should therefore be amended to prevent it applying to matters covered by this Regulation, and this Regulation should include provisions on periods of limitation.

Notes
[1] Council Regulation (EEC) No 2988/74 of 26 November 1974 concerning limitation periods in proceedings and the enforcement of sanctions under the rules of the European Economic Community relating to transport and competition (OJ L 319, 29.11.1974, p. 1).

Commentary
Recital 31: B&C: 14.017

(32) The undertakings concerned should be accorded the right to be heard by the Commission, third parties whose interests may be affected by a decision should be given the opportunity of submitting their observations beforehand, and the decisions taken should be widely publicised. While ensuring the rights of defence of the undertakings concerned, in particular, the right of access to the file, it is essential that business secrets be protected. The confidentiality of information exchanged in the network should likewise be safeguarded.

(33) Since all decisions taken by the Commission under this Regulation are subject to review by the Court of Justice in accordance with the Treaty, the Court of Justice should, in accordance with Article 229 thereof be given unlimited jurisdiction in respect of decisions by which the Commission imposes fines or periodic penalty payments.

(34) The principles laid down in Articles 81 and 82 of the Treaty, as they have been applied by Regulation No 17, have given a central role to the Community bodies. This central role should be retained, whilst associating the Member States more closely with the application of the

Part B Modernisation and Procedural Matters

71

Community competition rules. In accordance with the principles of subsidiarity and proportionality as set out in Article 5 of the Treaty, this Regulation does not go beyond what is necessary in order to achieve its objective, which is to allow the Community competition rules to be applied effectively.

(35) In order to attain a proper enforcement of Community competition law, Member States should designate and empower authorities to apply Articles 81 and 82 of the Treaty as public enforcers. They should be able to designate administrative as well as judicial authorities to carry out the various functions conferred upon competition authorities in this Regulation. This Regulation recognises the wide variation which exists in the public enforcement systems of Member States. The effects of Article 11(6) of this Regulation should apply to all competition authorities. As an exception to this general rule, where a prosecuting authority brings a case before a separate judicial authority, Article 11(6) should apply to the prosecuting authority subject to the conditions in Article 35(4) of this Regulation. Where these conditions are not fulfilled, the general rule should apply. In any case, Article 11(6) should not apply to courts insofar as they are acting as review courts.

Commentary
Recital 35: B&C: 14.016 F&N: 8.365

---

(36) As the case-law has made it clear that the competition rules apply to transport, that sector should be made subject to the procedural provisions of this Regulation. Council Regulation No 141 of 26 November 1962 exempting transport from the application of Regulation No 17[1] should therefore be repealed and Regulations (EEC) No 1017/68,[2] (EEC) No 4056/86[3] and (EEC) No 3975/87[4] should be amended in order to delete the specific procedural provisions they contain.

Notes
[1] OJ 124, 28.11.1962, p. 2751/62; Regulation as last amended by Regulation No 1002/67/EEC (OJ 306, 16.12.1967, p. 1).
[2] Council Regulation (EEC) No 1017/68 of 19 July 1968 applying rules of competition to transport by rail, road and inland waterway (OJ L 175, 23.7.1968, p. 1). Regulation as last amended by the Act of Accession of 1994.
[3] Council Regulation (EEC) No 4056/86 of 22 December 1986 laying down detailed rules for the application of Articles 81 and 82 (the title of the Regulation has been adjusted to take account of the renumbering of the Articles of the EC Treaty, in accordance with Article 12 of the Treaty of Amsterdam; the original reference was to Articles 85 and 86 of the Treaty) of the Treaty to maritime transport (OJ L 378, 31.12.1986, p. 4). Regulation as last amended by the Act of Accession of 1994.
[4] Council Regulation (EEC) No 3975/87 of 14 December 1987 laying down the procedure for the application of the rules on competition to undertakings in the air transport sector (OJ L 374, 31.12.1987, p. 1). Regulation as last amended by Regulation (EEC) No 2410/92 (OJ L 240, 24.8.1992, p. 18).
Commentary
Recital 36: F&N: 8.263

---

(37) This Regulation respects the fundamental rights and observes the principles recognised in particular by the Charter of Fundamental Rights of the European Union. Accordingly, this Regulation should be interpreted and applied with respect to those rights and principles.

Commentary
Recital 37: B&C: 1.010, 13.026, 14.026 F&N: 8.266

---

(38) Legal certainty for undertakings operating under the Community competition rules contributes to the promotion of innovation and investment. Where cases give rise to genuine uncertainty because they present novel or unresolved questions for the application of these rules, individual undertakings may wish to seek informal guidance from the Commission. This Regulation is without prejudice to the ability of the Commission to issue such informal guidance,

---

Commentary
Recital 38: B&C: 7.025, 13.023, 14.084

HAS ADOPTED THIS REGULATION:

CHAPTER I

PRINCIPLES

Article 1

Application of Articles 81 and 82 of the Treaty

1. Agreements, decisions and concerted practices caught by Article 81(1) of the Treaty which do not satisfy the conditions of Article 81(3) of the Treaty shall be prohibited, no prior decision to that effect being required.

2. Agreements, decisions and concerted practices caught by Article 81(1) of the Treaty which satisfy the conditions of Article 81(3) of the Treaty shall not be prohibited, no prior decision to that effect being required.

3. The abuse of a dominant position referred to in Article 82 of the Treaty shall be prohibited, no prior decision to that effect being required.

Commentary
Art 1: F&N: 2.22, 2.74
Art 1(1): B&C: 3.007 F&N: 2.21, 2.87
Art 1(2): B&C: 1.059, 3.003, 3.005, 14.005 F&N: 2.03, 2.21, 3.395
Art 1(3): B&C: 7.024 F&N: 2.21

Article 2

Burden of proof

In any national or Community proceedings for the application of Articles 81 and 82 of the Treaty, the burden of proving an infringement of Article 81(1) or of Article 82 of the Treaty shall rest on the party or the authority alleging the infringement. The undertaking or association of undertakings claiming the benefit of Article 81(3) of the Treaty shall bear the burden of proving that the conditions of that paragraph are fulfilled.

Commentary
Art 2: B&C: 2.088, 3.015, 3.068, 3.072, 13.076, 13.226, 14.153 F&N: 2.25, 2.26, 2.241, 3.399, 4.424, 8.488, 8.491, 10.133, 12.230, 12.231, 12.402

Article 3

Relationship between Articles 81 and 82 of the Treaty and national competition laws

1. Where the competition authorities of the Member States or national courts apply national competition law to agreements, decisions by associations of undertakings or concerted practices within the meaning of Article 81(1) of the Treaty which may affect trade between Member States within the meaning of that provision, they shall also apply Article 81 of the Treaty to such agreements, decisions or concerted practices. Where the competition authorities of the Member States or national courts apply national competition law to any abuse prohibited by Article 82 of the Treaty, they shall also apply Article 82 of the Treaty.

2. The application of national competition law may not lead to the prohibition of agreements, decisions by associations of undertakings or concerted practices which may affect trade between Member States but which do not restrict competition within the meaning of Article 81(1) of the Treaty, or which fulfil the conditions of Article 81(3) of the Treaty or which are covered by a Regulation for the application of Article 81(3) of the Treaty. Member States shall not under this Regulation be precluded from adopting and applying on their territory stricter national laws which prohibit or sanction unilateral conduct engaged in by undertakings.

3. Without prejudice to general principles and other provisions of Community law, paragraphs 1 and 2 do not apply when the competition authorities and the courts of the Member States apply national merger control laws nor do they preclude the application of provisions of national law that predominantly pursue an objective different from that pursued by Articles 81 and 82 of the Treaty.

Commentary

Art 3: **B&C:** 1.059, 1.115, 7.018, 13.196, 14.015, 14.054, 14.062–14.063 **F&N:** 2.05, 2.29, 2.30, 2.31–2.42, 2.47, 2.53, 2.55, 2.56, 2.58, 2.61, 2.63, 2.64–2.70, 2.74, 2.177, 2.220, 2.271, 3.339, 3.343, 4.410, 4.421, 8.236, 8.245, 8.325, 9.50

Art 3(1): **B&C:** 14.008, 14.036, 14.056 **F&N:** 2.05, 2.30, 2.31–2.42, 2.49–2.51, 2.55, 2.67, 2.71, 2.87, 2.88, 2.242, 2.243, 3.338, 4.422, 8.434

Art 3(2): **B&C:** 1.059, 14.008, 14.026, 14.060–14.061 **F&N:** 2.30, 2.35, 2.37, 2.42, 2.43–2.51, 2.53, 2.54, 2.55, 2.56, 2.67, 2.87, 2.178, 2.271, 3.338, 3.357, 4.423

Art 3(3): **B&C:** 14.062 **F&N:** 2.53, 2.54, 2.55, 2.57, 2.59, 2.66, 2.67, 2.68, 2.70, 2.73

CHAPTER II
POWERS

Article 4
Powers of the Commission

For the purpose of applying Articles 81 and 82 of the Treaty, the Commission shall have the powers provided for by this Regulation.

Commentary

Art 4: **F&N:** 2.90, 2.150

Article 5
Powers of the competition authorities of the Member States

The competition authorities of the Member States shall have the power to apply Articles 81 and 82 of the Treaty in individual cases. For this purpose, acting on their own initiative or on a complaint, they may take the following decisions:

— requiring that an infringement be brought to an end,
— ordering interim measures,
— accepting commitments,
— imposing fines, periodic penalty payments or any other penalty provided for in their national law.

Where on the basis of the information in their possession the conditions for prohibition are not met they may likewise decide that there are no grounds for action on their part.

Commentary

Art 5: **B&C:** 7.024, 11.035, 13.062, 14.005, 14.036, 14.056–14.057 **F&N:** 2.5, 2.22, 2.74, 2.75, 2.78, 2.79, 2.80, 2.82, 2.83, 2.84, 2.85, 2.86, 2.150, 2.181, 2.209, 2.224, 2.225, 2.231, 2.272, 3.416, 13.55

Article 6
Powers of the national courts

National courts shall have the power to apply Articles 81 and 82 of the Treaty.

Commentary

Art 6: **B&C:** 3.003, 7.024, 14.005, 14.042 **F&N:** 2.05, 2.242, 8.859, 13.55

CHAPTER III
COMMISSION DECISIONS

Article 7
Finding and termination of infringement

1. Where the Commission, acting on a complaint or on its own initiative, finds that there is an infringement of Article 81 or of Article 82 of the Treaty, it may by decision require the undertakings and associations of undertakings concerned to bring such infringement to an end. For this purpose, it may impose on them any behavioural or structural remedies which are proportionate to the infringement

committed and necessary to bring the infringement effectively to an end. Structural remedies can only be imposed either where there is no equally effective behavioural remedy or where any equally effective behavioural remedy would be more burdensome for the undertaking concerned than the structural remedy. If the Commission has a legitimate interest in doing so, it may also find that an infringement has been committed in the past.

2. Those entitled to lodge a complaint for the purposes of paragraph 1 are natural or legal persons who can show a legitimate interest and Member States.

Commentary
Art 7: **B&C:** 12.054, 13.065, 13.071, 13.080, 13.092, 13.104, 13.116, 13.118, 13.120, 13.128, 13.130, 13.134, 13.201, 13.208, 13.219 **F&N:** 2.93, 2.107, 2.111, 2.112, 2.116, 2.121, 2.122, 2.127, 2.133, 2.208, 3.419, 4.426, 4.431, 8.471, 8.483, 8.484, 8.488, 8.511, 8.715, 12.71
Art 7(1): **B&C:** 2.032, 13.100, 13.124–13.125, 13.130–13.131 **F&N:** 2.94, 2.97, 2.101, 2.102, 2.103, 12.75
Art 7(2): **B&C:** 13.062–13.063, 13.065–13.066, 13.068, 13.094, 13.221 **F&N:** 2.107

Article 8
Interim measures

1. In cases of urgency due to the risk of serious and irreparable damage to competition, the Commission, acting on its own initiative may by decision, on the basis of a prima facie finding of infringement, order interim measures.

2. A decision under paragraph 1 shall apply for a specified period of time and may be renewed in so far this is necessary and appropriate.

Commentary
Art 8: **B&C:** 13.080, 13.092, 13.104, 13.118–13.120, 13.219 **F&N:** 2.110, 2.111, 8.303
Art 8(1): **F&N:** 2.110
Art 8(2): **F&N:** 2.110

Article 9
Commitments

1. Where the Commission intends to adopt a decision requiring that an infringement be brought to an end and the undertakings concerned offer commitments to meet the concerns expressed to them by the Commission in its preliminary assessment, the Commission may by decision make those commitments binding on the undertakings. Such a decision may be adopted for a specified period and shall conclude that there are no longer grounds for action by the Commission.

2. The Commission may, upon request or on its own initiative, reopen the proceedings:

(a) where there has been a material change in any of the facts on which the decision was based;
(b) where the undertakings concerned act contrary to their commitments; or
(c) where the decision was based on incomplete, incorrect or misleading information provided by the parties.

Commentary
Art 9: **B&C:** 1.059, 3.007, 5.118, 12.141, 13.114–13.116, 13.201, 13.219, 13.221, 13.227, 14.036, 14.083, 14.086 **F&N:** 2.112–2.138, 2.139, 2.146, 2.147, 2.208, 3.419, 4.436, 4.437, 4.439, 8.303, 8.482, 10.206, 12.118, 13.95, 13.120, 13.121, 14.43
Art 9(1): **B&C:** 6.152, 13.082 **F&N:** 2.113, 2.116, 2.126, 2.129, 2.135
Art 9(2): **B&C:** 13.116–13.117 **F&N:** 2.131, 2.136
Art 9(2)(a): **F&N:** 2.132
Art 9(2)(b): **F&N:** 2.133

Article 10
Finding of inapplicability

Where the Community public interest relating to the application of Articles 81 and 82 of the Treaty so requires, the Commission, acting on its own initiative, may by decision find that Article 81 of the Treaty is not applicable to an agreement, a decision by an association of undertakings or a concerted practice, either because the conditions of Article 81(1) of the Treaty are not fulfilled, or because the conditions of Article 81(3) of the Treaty are satisfied.

The Commission may likewise make such a finding with reference to Article 82 of the Treaty.

Commentary
Art 10: **B&C:** 1.062, 3.007, 7.025, 13.022, 13.082, 13.087, 13.219, 14.081, 14.086 **F&N:** 2.54, 2.79, 2.80, 2.81, 2.139–2.147, 2.165, 2.209, 2.264, 2.265

CHAPTER IV
COOPERATION

Article 11
Cooperation between the Commission and the competition authorities of the Member States

1. The Commission and the competition authorities of the Member States shall apply the Community competition rules in close cooperation.

2. The Commission shall transmit to the competition authorities of the Member States copies of the most important documents it has collected with a view to applying Articles 7, 8, 9, 10 and Article 29(1). At the request of the competition authority of a Member State, the Commission shall provide it with a copy of other existing documents necessary for the assessment of the case.

3. The competition authorities of the Member States shall, when acting under Article 81 or Article 82 of the Treaty, inform the Commission in writing before or without delay after commencing the first formal investigative measure. This information may also be made available to the competition authorities of the other Member States.

4. No later than 30 days before the adoption of a decision requiring that an infringement be brought to an end, accepting commitments or withdrawing the benefit of a block exemption Regulation, the competition authorities of the Member States shall inform the Commission. To that effect, they shall provide the Commission with a summary of the case, the envisaged decision or, in the absence thereof, any other document indicating the proposed course of action. This information may also be made available to the competition authorities of the other Member States. At the request of the Commission, the acting competition authority shall make available to the Commission other documents it holds which are necessary for the assessment of the case. The information supplied to the Commission may be made available to the competition authorities of the other Member States. National competition authorities may also exchange between themselves information necessary for the assessment of a case that they are dealing with under Article 81 or Article 82 of the Treaty.

5. The competition authorities of the Member States may consult the Commission on any case involving the application of Community law.

6. The initiation by the Commission of proceedings for the adoption of a decision under Chapter III shall relieve the competition authorities of the Member States of their competence to apply Articles 81 and 82 of the Treaty. If a competition authority of a Member State is already acting on a case, the Commission shall only initiate proceedings after consulting with that national competition authority.

Commentary
Art 11: **B&C:** 1.059, 1.115, 13.051, 13.094, 14.028–14.029, 14.031, 14.072 **F&N:** 2.41, 2.165, 2.196, 8.238, 8.239, 8.305
Art 11(1): **B&C:** 13.017, 14.020 **F&N:** 2.155, 2.204
Art 11(2): **B&C:** 13.195, 14.018 **F&N:** 2.41, 2.151, 8.239, 16.329
Art 11(3): **B&C:** 13.018, 14.018, 14.031, 14.072 **F&N:** 2.41, 2.151, 2.229, 2.237, 8.239, 8.313
Art 11(4): **B&C:** 14.019, 14.072 **F&N:** 2.41, 2.50, 2.195, 2.205–2.218, 2.220
Art 11(5): **B&C:** 14.019
Art 11(6): **B&C:** 7.017, 13.017, 13.020, 13.082, 13.196, 14.011, 14.015–14.016, 14.018, 14.072–14.073, 14.090
   F&N: 2.41, 2.42, 2.50, 2.151, 2.205, 2.212, 2.213, 2.218, 2.219–2.239, 2.246, 2.254, 8.236, 8.245

Article 12
Exchange of information

1. For the purpose of applying Articles 81 and 82 of the Treaty the Commission and the competition authorities of the Member States shall have the power to provide one another with and use in evidence any matter of fact or of law, including confidential information.

2. Information exchanged shall only be used in evidence for the purpose of applying Article 81 or Article 82 of the Treaty and in respect of the subject-matter for which it was collected by the transmitting authority. However, where national competition law is applied in the same case and in parallel to Community competition law and does not lead to a different outcome, information exchanged under this Article may also be used for the application of national competition law.

3. Information exchanged pursuant to paragraph 1 can only be used in evidence to impose sanctions on natural persons where:

— the law of the transmitting authority foresees sanctions of a similar kind in relation to an infringement of Article 81 or Article 82 of the Treaty or, in the absence thereof,
— the information has been collected in a way which respects the same level of protection of the rights of defence of natural persons as provided for under the national rules of the receiving authority. However, in this case, the information exchanged cannot be used by the receiving authority to impose custodial sanctions.

Commentary
Art 12: B&C: 1.059, 1.064, 1.115, 13.040, 13.051, 13.053, 13.094, 13.109, 13.195, 14.022, 14.025, 14.027–14.028, 14.030–14.031 F&N: 2.69, 2.154, 2.155, 2.156, 2.159, 2.161–2.168, 2.169, 2.170, 2.173, 2.174, 2.175, 2.196, 2.197, 2.272, 8.99, 8.101, 8.238, 8.240, 8.242, 8.269, 8.327, 8.431, 8.435, 8.436, 8.488, 12.67
Art 12(1): B&C: 14.022–14.023, 14.026 F&N: 2.176, 2.178, 2.181, 2.272, 12.67
Art 12(2): B&C: 13.053, 14.024, 14.026 F&N: 2.42, 2.176, 2.177, 2.178, 2.179, 2.268, 2.269, 2.270, 2.271, 8.520
Art 12(3): B&C: 13.053, 14.024, 14.027 F&N: 2.173, 2.181, 2.183, 2.184, 2.268, 2.272, 8.242, 8.372, 8.436

Article 13
Suspension or termination of proceedings

1. Where competition authorities of two or more Member States have received a complaint or are acting on their own initiative under Article 81 or Article 82 of the Treaty against the same agreement, decision of an association or practice, the fact that one authority is dealing with the case shall be sufficient grounds for the others to suspend the proceedings before them or to reject the complaint. The Commission may likewise reject a complaint on the ground that a competition authority of a Member State is dealing with the case.

2. Where a competition authority of a Member State or the Commission has received a complaint against an agreement, decision of an association or practice which has already been dealt with by another competition authority, it may reject it.

Commentary
Art 13: B&C: 13.068, 14.017–14.018 F&N: 2.122, 2.151, 2.152, 2.153, 2.155
Art 13(1): B&C: 14.017 F&N: 2.152
Art 13(2): B&C: 14.017

Article 14
Advisory Committee

1. The Commission shall consult an Advisory Committee on Restrictive Practices and Dominant Positions prior to the taking of any decision under Articles 7, 8, 9, 10, 23, Article 24(2) and Article 29(1).

2. For the discussion of individual cases, the Advisory Committee shall be composed of representatives of the competition authorities of the Member States. For meetings in which issues other than individual cases are being discussed, an additional Member State representative competent in competition matters may be appointed. Representatives may, if unable to attend, be replaced by other representatives.

3. The consultation may take place at a meeting convened and chaired by the Commission, held not earlier than 14 days after dispatch of the notice convening it, together with a summary of the case, an indication of the most important documents and a preliminary draft decision. In respect of decisions pursuant to Article 8, the meeting may be held seven days after the dispatch of the operative part of a draft decision. Where the Commission dispatches a notice convening the meeting which gives a shorter period of notice than those specified above, the meeting may take place on the proposed date in the absence of an objection by any Member State. The Advisory Committee shall deliver a written opinion on the Commission's preliminary draft decision. It may deliver an opinion even if some members are absent and are not represented. At the request of one or several members, the positions stated in the opinion shall be reasoned.

4. Consultation may also take place by written procedure. However, if any Member State so requests, the Commission shall convene a meeting. In case of written procedure, the Commission shall determine a time-limit of not less than 14 days within which the Member States are to put forward their observations for circulation to all other Member States. In case of decisions to be taken pursuant to Article 8, the time-limit of 14 days is replaced by seven days. Where the Commission determines a time-limit for the written procedure which is shorter than those specified above, the proposed time-limit shall be applicable in the absence of an objection by any Member State.

5. The Commission shall take the utmost account of the opinion delivered by the Advisory Committee. It shall inform the Committee of the manner in which its opinion has been taken into account.

6. Where the Advisory Committee delivers a written opinion, this opinion shall be appended to the draft decision. If the Advisory Committee recommends publication of the opinion, the Commission shall carry out such publication taking into account the legitimate interest of undertakings in the protection of their business secrets.

7. At the request of a competition authority of a Member State, the Commission shall include on the agenda of the Advisory Committee cases that are being dealt with by a competition authority of a Member State under Article 81 or Article 82 of the Treaty. The Commission may also do so on its own initiative. In either case, the Commission shall inform the competition authority concerned.

A request may in particular be made by a competition authority of a Member State in respect of a case where the Commission intends to initiate proceedings with the effect of Article 11(6).

The Advisory Committee shall not issue opinions on cases dealt with by competition authorities of the Member States. The Advisory Committee may also discuss general issues of Community competition law.

Commentary
Art 14: **B&C:** 13.039, 13.080, 13.223, 14.020 **F&N:** 2.196, 8.472, 14.132
Art 14(1): **B&C:** 13.035, 13.050, 13.107, 13.115, 13.120
Art 14(2): **B&C:** 13.107
Art 14(3): **B&C:** 13.107
Art 14(4): **B&C:** 13.107
Art 14(5): **B&C:** 13.107
Art 14(6): **F&N:** 2.195
Art 14(7): **B&C:** 13.107

Article 15
Cooperation with national courts

1. In proceedings for the application of Article 81 or Article 82 of the Treaty, courts of the Member States may ask the Commission to transmit to them information in its possession or its opinion on questions concerning the application of the Community competition rules.

2. Member States shall forward to the Commission a copy of any written judgment of national courts deciding on the application of Article 81 or Article 82 of the Treaty. Such copy shall be forwarded without delay after the full written judgment is notified to the parties.

3. Competition authorities of the Member States, acting on their own initiative, may submit written observations to the national courts of their Member State on issues relating to the application of

Article 81 or Article 82 of the Treaty. With the permission of the court in question, they may also submit oral observations to the national courts of their Member State. Where the coherent application of Article 81 or Article 82 of the Treaty so requires, the Commission, acting on its own initiative, may submit written observations to courts of the Member States. With the permission of the court in question, it may also make oral observations.

For the purpose of the preparation of their observations only, the competition authorities of the Member States and the Commission may request the relevant court of the Member State to transmit or ensure the transmission to them of any documents necessary for the assessment of the case.

4. This Article is without prejudice to wider powers to make observations before courts conferred on competition authorities of the Member States under the law of their Member State.

Commentary

Art 15: B&C: 13.051–13.052, 14.028, 14.032, 14.074 **F&N:** 2.148, 2.196, 2.241, 2.247, 2.258, 2.262, 2.263, 2.274, 12.230
Art 15(1): B&C: 14.067, 14.069 **F&N:** 2.145, 2.250, 2.264, 2.268, 2.270, 2.272, 8.237, 8.244
Art 15(2): B&C: 14.066, 14.071 **F&N:** 2.253, 2.275
Art 15(3): B&C: 14.070, 14.074 **F&N:** 2.227, 2.274

Article 16
Uniform application of Community competition law

1. When national courts rule on agreements, decisions or practices under Article 81 or Article 82 of the Treaty which are already the subject of a Commission decision, they cannot take decisions running counter to the decision adopted by the Commission. They must also avoid giving decisions which would conflict with a decision contemplated by the Commission in proceedings it has initiated. To that effect, the national court may assess whether it is necessary to stay its proceedings. This obligation is without prejudice to the rights and obligations under Article 234 of the Treaty.

2. When competition authorities of the Member States rule on agreements, decisions or practices under Article 81 or Article 82 of the Treaty which are already the subject of a Commission decision, they cannot take decisions which would run counter to the decision adopted by the Commission.

Commentary

Art 16: B&C: 1.059, 3.007, 14.008, 14.054, 14.076, 14.080–14.081, 14.085–14.086 **F&N:** 2.54, 2.92, 2.116, 2.120, 2.144, 2.145, 2.223, 2.227, 8.473
Art 16(1): B&C: 3.007–3.008, 5.038, 14.074, 14.077, 14.089, 14.146 **F&N:** 2.148, 2.254, 2.257
Art 16(2): B&C: 3.007–3.008, 7.017, 14.078 **F&N:** 2.148

Chapter V
Powers of Investigation

Article 17
Investigations into sectors of the economy and into types of agreements

1. Where the trend of trade between Member States, the rigidity of prices or other circumstances suggest that competition may be restricted or distorted within the common market, the Commission may conduct its inquiry into a particular sector of the economy or into a particular type of agreements across various sectors. In the course of that inquiry, the Commission may request the undertakings or associations of undertakings concerned to supply the information necessary for giving effect to Articles 81 and 82 of the Treaty and may carry out any inspections necessary for that purpose.

The Commission may in particular request the undertakings or associations of undertakings concerned to communicate to it all agreements, decisions and concerted practices.

The Commission may publish a report on the results of its inquiry into particular sectors of the economy or particular types of agreements across various sectors and invite comments from interested parties.

2. Articles 14, 18, 19, 20, 22, 23 and 24 shall apply *mutatis mutandis*.

Commentary
Art 17: B&C: 5.047, 5.143, 12.054, 13.039 F&N: 2.45, 8.98, 11.164, 12.23
Art 17(1): B&C: 13.039 F&N: 8.98
Art 17(2): B&C: 13.039

Article 18
Requests for information

1. In order to carry out the duties assigned to it by this Regulation, the Commission may, by simple request or by decision, require undertakings and associations of undertakings to provide all necessary information.

2. When sending a simple request for information to an undertaking or association of undertakings, the Commission shall state the legal basis and the purpose of the request, specify what information is required and fix the time-limit within which the information is to be provided, and the penalties provided for in Article 23 for supplying incorrect or misleading information.

3. Where the Commission requires undertakings and associations of undertakings to supply information by decision, it shall state the legal basis and the purpose of the request, specify what information is required and fix the time-limit within which it is to be provided. It shall also indicate the penalties provided for in Article 23 and indicate or impose the penalties provided for in Article 24. It shall further indicate the right to have the decision reviewed by the Court of Justice.

4. The owners of the undertakings or their representatives and, in the case of legal persons, companies or firms, or associations having no legal personality, the persons authorised to represent them by law or by their constitution shall supply the information requested on behalf of the undertaking or the association of undertakings concerned. Lawyers duly authorised to act may supply the information on behalf of their clients. The latter shall remain fully responsible if the information supplied is incomplete, incorrect or misleading.

5. The Commission shall without delay forward a copy of the simple request or of the decision to the competition authority of the Member State in whose territory the seat of the undertaking or association of undertakings is situated and the competition authority of the Member State whose territory is affected.

6. At the request of the Commission the governments and competition authorities of the Member States shall provide the Commission with all necessary information to carry out the duties assigned to it by this Regulation.

Commentary
Art 18: B&C: 1.094, 13.025, 13.032, 13.039, 13.051, 14.022 F&N: 8.224, 8.259, 8.279, 8.290, 8.293, 8.296,
    8.305, 8.307, 8.309, 8.310, 8.311, 8.312, 8.313, 8.318, 8.319, 8.321, 8.324, 8.328, 8.428
Art 18(1): B&C: 13.032–13.033 F&N: 8.294, 8.295
Art 18(2): B&C: 13.032, 13.035 F&N: 8.274, 8.312, 8.313, 8.315, 8.316, 8.320, 8.328
Art 18(3): B&C: 13.032, 13.035 F&N: 8.274, 8.312, 8.313, 8.315, 8.320, 8.322
Art 18(4): B&C: 13.032 F&N: 8.292, 8.322
Art 18(5): B&C: 13.032
Art 18(6): B&C: 13.036, 13.094 F&N: 2.156, 2.164

Article 19
Power to take statements

1. In order to carry out the duties assigned to it by this Regulation, the Commission may interview any natural or legal person who consents to be interviewed for the purpose of collecting information relating to the subject-matter of an investigation.

2. Where an interview pursuant to paragraph 1 is conducted in the premises of an undertaking, the Commission shall inform the competition authority of the Member State in whose territory the interview takes place. If so requested by the competition authority of that Member State, its officials may assist the officials and other accompanying persons authorised by the Commission to conduct the interview.

Commentary
Art 19: B&C: 1.059, 13.025, 13.039, 14.022 F&N: 8.103, 8.259, 8.292, 8.323–8.328, 8.367, 8.537, 8.539, 8.546
Art 19(2): B&C: 13.037 F&N: 8.328

Article 20
The Commission's powers of inspection

1. In order to carry out the duties assigned to it by this Regulation, the Commission may conduct all necessary inspections of undertakings and associations of undertakings.

2. The officials and other accompanying persons authorised by the Commission to conduct an inspection are empowered:

(a) to enter any premises, land and means of transport of undertakings and associations of undertakings;

(b) to examine the books and other records related to the business, irrespective of the medium on which they are stored;

(c) to take or obtain in any form copies of or extracts from such books or records;

(d) to seal any business premises and books or records for the period and to the extent necessary for the inspection;

(e) to ask any representative or member of staff of the undertaking or association of undertakings for explanations on facts or documents relating to the subject-matter and purpose of the inspection and to record the answers.

3. The officials and other accompanying persons authorised by the Commission to conduct an inspection shall exercise their powers upon production of a written authorisation specifying the subject matter and purpose of the inspection and the penalties provided for in Article 23 in case the production of the required books or other records related to the business is incomplete or where the answers to questions asked under paragraph 2 of the present Article are incorrect or misleading. In good time before the inspection, the Commission shall give notice of the inspection to the competition authority of the Member State in whose territory it is to be conducted.

4. Undertakings and associations of undertakings are required to submit to inspections ordered by decision of the Commission. The decision shall specify the subject matter and purpose of the inspection, appoint the date on which it is to begin and indicate the penalties provided for in Articles 23 and 24 and the right to have the decision reviewed by the Court of Justice. The Commission shall take such decisions after consulting the competition authority of the Member State in whose territory the inspection is to be conducted.

5. Officials of as well as those authorised or appointed by the competition authority of the Member State in whose territory the inspection is to be conducted shall, at the request of that authority or of the Commission, actively assist the officials and other accompanying persons authorised by the Commission. To this end, they shall enjoy the powers specified in paragraph 2.

6. Where the officials and other accompanying persons authorised by the Commission find that an undertaking opposes an inspection ordered pursuant to this Article, the Member State concerned shall afford them the necessary assistance, requesting where appropriate the assistance of the police or of an equivalent enforcement authority, so as to enable them to conduct their inspection.

7. If the assistance provided for in paragraph 6 requires authorisation from a judicial authority according to national rules, such authorisation shall be applied for. Such authorisation may also be applied for as a precautionary measure.

8. Where authorisation as referred to in paragraph 7 is applied for, the national judicial authority shall control that the Commission decision is authentic and that the coercive measures envisaged are neither arbitrary nor excessive having regard to the subject matter of the inspection. In its control of the proportionality of the coercive measures, the national judicial authority may ask the Commission, directly or through the Member State competition authority, for detailed explanations in particular on the grounds the Commission has for suspecting infringement of Articles 81 and 82 of the Treaty, as well as on the seriousness of the suspected infringement and on the nature of the involvement of the undertaking concerned. However, the national judicial authority may not call into question the necessity

for the inspection nor demand that it be provided with the information in the Commission's file. The lawfulness of the Commission decision shall be subject to review only by the Court of Justice.

Commentary
Art 20: B&C: 1.094, 8.174, 13.025, 13.031–13.032, 13.039, 13.041, 13.045, 13.047, 13.050, 13.109, 14.022, 14.025, 14.036 F&N: 2.165, 8.174, 8.259, 8.263, 8.279, 8.290, 8.293, 8.308, 8.319, 8.329, 8.340, 8.390, 8.407, 8.415, 8.418, 8.419, 8.423, 8.428
Art 20(1): F&N: 8.294
Art 20(2): B&C: 13.045 F&N: 8.298, 8.345, 8.347, 8.356, 8.414, 8.415
Art 20(2)(a): F&N: 8.401
Art 20(2)(d): B&C: 14.036 F&N: 8.365
Art 20(2)(e): F&N: 8.274, 8.325, 8.367, 8.368, 8.546
Art 20(3): B&C: 13.041–13.042 F&N: 8.308, 8.331, 8.334, 8.335, 8.337, 8.344, 8.401, 8.402
Art 20(4): B&C: 13.041–13.043, 13.050 F&N: 8.139, 8.173, 8.174, 8.274, 8.331, 8.334, 8.336, 8.337, 8.344, 8.392, 8.395, 8.397–8.399, 8.401, 8.413, 8.424
Art 20(5): B&C: 13.045 F&N: 8.358, 8.380, 8.402, 8.407, 8.415, 8.429, 8.430
Art 20(6): B&C: 13.045 F&N: 8.339, 8.348, 8.384, 8.392, 8.408, 8.410, 8.429, 8.430
Art 20(7): B&C: 13.045, 14.065 F&N: 8.339, 8.409
Art 20(8): B&C: 13.047, 14.065 F&N: 8.338, 8.339, 8.403, 8.409, 8.425

Article 21
Inspection of other premises

1. If a reasonable suspicion exists that books or other records related to the business and to the subject-matter of the inspection, which may be relevant to prove a serious violation of Article 81 or Article 82 of the Treaty, are being kept in any other premises, land and means of transport, including the homes of directors, managers and other members of staff of the undertakings and associations of undertakings concerned, the Commission can by decision order an inspection to be conducted in such other premises, land and means of transport.

2. The decision shall specify the subject matter and purpose of the inspection, appoint the date on which it is to begin and indicate the right to have the decision reviewed by the Court of Justice. It shall in particular state the reasons that have led the Commission to conclude that a suspicion in the sense of paragraph 1 exists. The Commission shall take such decisions after consulting the competition authority of the Member State in whose territory the inspection is to be conducted.

3. A decision adopted pursuant to paragraph 1 cannot be executed without prior authorisation from the national judicial authority of the Member State concerned. The national judicial authority shall control that the Commission decision is authentic and that the coercive measures envisaged are neither arbitrary nor excessive having regard in particular to the seriousness of the suspected infringement, to the importance of the evidence sought, to the involvement of the undertaking concerned and to the reasonable likelihood that business books and records relating to the subject matter of the inspection are kept in the premises for which the authorisation is requested. The national judicial authority may ask the Commission, directly or through the Member State competition authority, for detailed explanations on those elements which are necessary to allow its control of the proportionality of the coercive measures envisaged.

However, the national judicial authority may not call into question the necessity for the inspection nor demand that it be provided with information in the Commission's file. The lawfulness of the Commission decision shall be subject to review only by the Court of Justice.

4. The officials and other accompanying persons authorised by the Commission to conduct an inspection ordered in accordance with paragraph 1 of this Article shall have the powers set out in Article 20(2)(a), (b) and (c). Article 20(5) and (6) shall apply *mutatis mutandis*.

Commentary
Art 21: B&C: 1.059, 13.025, 13.041, 13.048, 14.022, 14.025, 14.036 F&N: 2.165, 8.259, 8.292, 8.293, 8.331, 8.416, 8.417, 8.418, 8.420– 8.424, 8.426, 8.428, 8.430, 8.431, 8.432
Art 21(1): B&C: 13.044–13.045 F&N: 8.424
Art 21(3): B&C: 13.044 F&N: 8.422, 8.425, 8.428, 8.429
Art 21(4): B&C: 13.045, 13.048 F&N: 8.430

Article 22
Investigations by competition authorities of Member States

1. The competition authority of a Member State may in its own territory carry out any inspection or other fact-finding measure under its national law on behalf and for the account of the competition authority of another Member State in order to establish whether there has been an infringement of Article 81 or Article 82 of the Treaty. Any exchange and use of the information collected shall be carried out in accordance with Article 12.

2. At the request of the Commission, the competition authorities of the Member States shall undertake the inspections which the Commission considers to be necessary under Article 20(1) or which it has ordered by decision pursuant to Article 20(4). The officials of the competition authorities of the Member States who are responsible for conducting these inspections as well as those authorised or appointed by them shall exercise their powers in accordance with their national law.

If so requested by the Commission or by the competition authority of the Member State in whose territory the inspection is to be conducted, officials and other accompanying persons authorised by the Commission may assist the officials of the authority concerned.

Commentary
Art 22: B&C: 13.039, 14.021–14.022 F&N: 2.148, 2.165, 2.175, 2.195, 8.333, 8.411, 8.412, 8.414, 8.429, 8.438, 13.371
Art 22(1): B&C: 14.021, 14.030, 14.036 F&N: 2.154, 2.155, 2.156, 8.411, 8.413
Art 22(2): B&C: 13.045, 14.036 F&N: 2.154, 2.156, 8.332, 8.411–8.415

CHAPTER VI
PENALTIES

Article 23
Fines

1. The Commission may by decision impose on undertakings and associations of undertakings fines not exceeding 1% of the total turnover in the preceding business year where, intentionally or negligently:

(a) they supply incorrect or misleading information in response to a request made pursuant to Article 17 or Article 18(2);

(b) in response to a request made by decision adopted pursuant to Article 17 or Article 18(3), they supply incorrect, incomplete or misleading information or do not supply information within the required time-limit;

(c) they produce the required books or other records related to the business in incomplete form during inspections under Article 20 or refuse to submit to inspections ordered by a decision adopted pursuant to Article 20(4);

(d) in response to a question asked in accordance with Article 20(2)(e),
— they give an incorrect or misleading answer,
— they fail to rectify within a time-limit set by the Commission an incorrect, incomplete or misleading answer given by a member of staff, or
— they fail or refuse to provide a complete answer on facts relating to the subject-matter and purpose of an inspection ordered by a decision adopted pursuant to Article 20(4);

(e) seals affixed in accordance with Article 20(2)(d) by officials or other accompanying persons authorised by the Commission have been broken.

2. The Commission may by decision impose fines on undertakings and associations of undertakings where, either intentionally or negligently:

(a) they infringe Article 81 or Article 82 of the Treaty; or

(b) they contravene a decision ordering interim measures under Article 8; or

(c) they fail to comply with a commitment made binding by a decision pursuant to Article 9.

For each undertaking and association of undertakings participating in the infringement, the fine shall not exceed 10% of its total turnover in the preceding business year.

Where the infringement of an association relates to the activities of its members, the fine shall not exceed 10% of the sum of the total turnover of each member active on the market affected by the infringement of the association.

3. In fixing the amount of the fine, regard shall be had both to the gravity and to the duration of the infringement.

4. When a fine is imposed on an association of undertakings taking account of the turnover of its members and the association is not solvent, the association is obliged to call for contributions from its members to cover the amount of the fine.

Where such contributions have not been made to the association within a time-limit fixed by the Commission, the Commission may require payment of the fine directly by any of the undertakings whose representatives were members of the decision-making bodies concerned of the association.

After the Commission has required payment under the second subparagraph, where necessary to ensure full payment of the fine, the Commission may require payment of the balance by any of the members of the association which were active on the market on which the infringement occurred.

However, the Commission shall not require payment under the second or the third subparagraph from undertakings which show that they have not implemented the infringing decision of the association and either were not aware of its existence or have actively distanced themselves from it before the Commission started investigating the case.

The financial liability of each undertaking in respect of the payment of the fine shall not exceed 10% of its total turnover in the preceding business year.

5. Decisions taken pursuant to paragraphs 1 and 2 shall not be of a criminal law nature.

Commentary

Art 23: B&C: 13.039, 13.080, 13.092, 13.104, 13.152, 13.201, 13.219, 13.232 F&N: 2.83, 2.98, 2.118, 2.133, 2.181, 4.440, 8.305, 8.313, 8.315, 8.316, 8.317, 8.319, 8.339, 8.348, 8.354, 8.355, 8.379, 8.396, 8.401, 8.430, 8.464, 8.483, 8.553, 8.595, 14.132
Art 23(1): F&N: 8.375, 8.396, 8.596
Art 23(1)(a): B&C: 13.035 F&N: 8.315, 8.316
Art 23(1)(b): B&C: 13.035 F&N: 8.315, 8.316
Art 23(1)(c): B&C: 13.043, 13.050 F&N: 8.384, 8.410
Art 23(1)(d): B&C: 13.050 F&N: 8.368, 8.376, 8.378
Art 23(1)(e): B&C: 13.050 F&N: 8.363, 8.366
Art 23(2): B&C: 2.052, 13.181 F&N: 4.439, 8.315, 8.498, 8.558, 8.590, 8.591, 8.592, 8.594, 8.595, 8.596, 8.615, 8.622, 8.698, 8.777, 8.778, 8.779, 8.783, 8.811, 8.827, 8.833
Art 23(2)(a): B&C: 4.010, 13.135, 13.137 F&N: 8.486, 8.501, 8.587, 8.611, 8.808
Art 23(2)(b): B&C: 13.122
Art 23(2)(c): B&C: 13.117
Art 23(3): B&C: 13.135, 13.144, 13.156 F&N: 8.593
Art 23(4): B&C: 13.030, 13.201, 13.204 F&N: 8.595
Art 23(5): B&C: 13.136 F&N: 8.596

Article 24
Periodic penalty payments

1. The Commission may, by decision, impose on undertakings or associations of undertakings periodic penalty payments not exceeding 5% of the average daily turnover in the preceding business year per day and calculated from the date appointed by the decision, in order to compel them:

(a) to put an end to an infringement of Article 81 or Article 82 of the Treaty, in accordance with a decision taken pursuant to Article 7;
(b) to comply with a decision ordering interim measures taken pursuant to Article 8;
(c) to comply with a commitment made binding by a decision pursuant to Article 9;
(d) to supply complete and correct information which it has requested by decision taken pursuant to Article 17 or Article 18(3);
(e) to submit to an inspection which it has ordered by decision taken pursuant to Article 20(4).

2. Where the undertakings or associations of undertakings have satisfied the obligation which the periodic penalty payment was intended to enforce, the Commission may fix the definitive amount of the periodic penalty payment at a figure lower than that which would arise under the original decision. Article 23(4) shall apply correspondingly.

Commentary

Art 24: B&C: 13.039, 13.201, 13.219, 13.232 F&N: 2.83, 2.98, 2.133, 2.181, 8.305, 8.317, 8.319, 8.339, 8.348, 8.354, 8.355, 8.379, 8.396, 8.401, 8.430

Art 24(1): B&C: 13.050, 13.201

Art 24(1)(a): B&C: 13.134, 13.202

Art 24(1)(b): B&C: 13.123, 13.201

Art 24(1)(c): B&C: 13.117, 13.201

Art 24(1)(d): B&C: 13.035 F&N: 8.315

Art 24(1)(e): B&C: 13.043 F&N: 8.336, 8.384, 8.398

Art 24(2): B&C: 13.035, 13.080, 13.092, 13.104, 13.134, 13.201–13.202 F&N: 8.315

Part B Modernisation and Procedural Matters

Chapter VII
Limitation Periods

Article 25
Limitation periods for the imposition of penalties

1. The powers conferred on the Commission by Articles 23 and 24 shall be subject to the following limitation periods:

(a) three years in the case of infringements of provisions concerning requests for information or the conduct of inspections;

(b) five years in the case of all other infringements.

2. Time shall begin to run on the day on which the infringement is committed. However, in the case of continuing or repeated infringements, time shall begin to run on the day on which the infringement ceases.

3. Any action taken by the Commission or by the competition authority of a Member State for the purpose of the investigation or proceedings in respect of an infringement shall interrupt the limitation period for the imposition of fines or periodic penalty payments. The limitation period shall be interrupted with effect from the date on which the action is notified to at least one undertaking or association of undertakings which has participated in the infringement. Actions which interrupt the running of the period shall include in particular the following:

(a) written requests for information by the Commission or by the competition authority of a Member State;

(b) written authorisations to conduct inspections issued to its officials by the Commission or by the competition authority of a Member State;

(c) the initiation of proceedings by the Commission or by the competition authority of a Member State;

(d) notification of the statement of objections of the Commission or of the competition authority of a Member State.

4. The interruption of the limitation period shall apply for all the undertakings or associations of undertakings which have participated in the infringement.

5. Each interruption shall start time running afresh. However, the limitation period shall expire at the latest on the day on which a period equal to twice the limitation period has elapsed without the Commission having imposed a fine or a periodic penalty payment. That period shall be extended by the time during which limitation is suspended pursuant to paragraph 6.

6. The limitation period for the imposition of fines or periodic penalty payments shall be suspended for as long as the decision of the Commission is the subject of proceedings pending before the Court of Justice.

Commentary

Art 25: B&C: 5.011, 13.160, 13.180 F&N: 8.307, 8.597

Art 25(1)–(5): F&N: 8.307
Art 25(1): B&C: 2.033, 13.035, 13.050
Art 25(1)(a): B&C: 13.208 F&N: 8.307
Art 25(1)(b): B&C: 13.208
Art 25(2): B&C: 2.052, 13.208
Art 25(3): B&C: 13.082, 13.208, 14.017 F&N: 8.307
Art 25(4): B&C: 13.208
Art 25(5): B&C: 13.208 F&N: 8.307
Art 25(6): B&C: 13.208 F&N: 8.307

Article 26
Limitation period for the enforcement of penalties

1. The power of the Commission to enforce decisions taken pursuant to Articles 23 and 24 shall be subject to a limitation period of five years.

2. Time shall begin to run on the day on which the decision becomes final.

3. The limitation period for the enforcement of penalties shall be interrupted:

(a) by notification of a decision varying the original amount of the fine or periodic penalty payment or refusing an application for variation;

(b) by any action of the Commission or of a Member State, acting at the request of the Commission, designed to enforce payment of the fine or periodic penalty payment.

4. Each interruption shall start time running afresh.

5. The limitation period for the enforcement of penalties shall be suspended for so long as:

(a) time to pay is allowed;

(b) enforcement of payment is suspended pursuant to a decision of the Court of Justice.

Commentary
Art 26: B&C: 13.210 F&N: 8.307, 8.473
Art 26(1): B&C: 13.035, 13.050
Art 26(3): B&C: 13.035, 13.050
Art 26(4): B&C: 13.035, 13.050

CHAPTER VIII
HEARINGS AND PROFESSIONAL SECRECY

Article 27
Hearing of the parties, complainants and others

1. Before taking decisions as provided for in Articles 7, 8, 23 and Article 24(2), the Commission shall give the undertakings or associations of undertakings which are the subject of the proceedings conducted by the Commission the opportunity of being heard on the matters to which the Commission has taken objection. The Commission shall base its decisions only on objections on which the parties concerned have been able to comment. Complainants shall be associated closely with the proceedings.

2. The rights of defence of the parties concerned shall be fully respected in the proceedings. They shall be entitled to have access to the Commission's file, subject to the legitimate interest of undertakings in the protection of their business secrets. The right of access to the file shall not extend to confidential information and internal documents of the Commission or the competition authorities of the Member States. In particular, the right of access shall not extend to correspondence between the Commission and the competition authorities of the Member States, or between the latter, including documents drawn up pursuant to Articles 11 and 14. Nothing in this paragraph shall prevent the Commission from disclosing and using information necessary to prove an infringement.

3. If the Commission considers it necessary, it may also hear other natural or legal persons. Applications to be heard on the part of such persons shall, where they show a sufficient interest, be granted.

The competition authorities of the Member States may also ask the Commission to hear other natural or legal persons.

4. Where the Commission intends to adopt a decision pursuant to Article 9 or Article 10, it shall publish a concise summary of the case and the main content of the commitments or of the proposed course of action. Interested third parties may submit their observations within a time limit which is fixed by the Commission in its publication and which may not be less than one month. Publication shall have regard to the legitimate interest of undertakings in the protection of their business secrets.

Commentary
Art 27: B&C: 13.051, 13.096, 13.100, 13.120 F&N: 2.196, 8.293, 8.315, 8.319, 8.484, 8.515, 8.546
Art 27(1): B&C: 13.035, 13.050, 13.080, 13.104 F&N: 2.202, 8.450, 8.455, 8.457, 8.469
Art 27(2): B&C: 13.075, 13.089, 13.093–13.094, 13.097 F&N: 2.195, 2.198, 2.200
Art 27(3): B&C: 13.104
Art 27(4): B&C: 6.052, 13.022, 13.087, 13.115 F&N: 2.83, 2.114, 2.127, 2.128, 2.131, 2.138, 2.139, 2.195, 2.258, 10.206

Article 28
Professional secrecy

1. Without prejudice to Articles 12 and 15, information collected pursuant to Articles 17 to 22 shall be used only for the purpose for which it was acquired.

2. Without prejudice to the exchange and to the use of information foreseen in Articles 11, 12, 14, 15 and 27, the Commission and the competition authorities of the Member States, their officials, servants and other persons working under the supervision of these authorities as well as officials and civil servants of other authorities of the Member States shall not disclose information acquired or exchanged by them pursuant to this Regulation and of the kind covered by the obligation of professional secrecy. This obligation also applies to all representatives and experts of Member States attending meetings of the Advisory Committee pursuant to Article 14.

Commentary
Art 28: B&C: 1.093, 13.052–13.053 F&N: 2.172, 2.186, 8.101, 8.240, 8.298, 8.448, 8.459, 8.475
Art 28(1): B&C: 13.051, 14.024 F&N: 8.372
Art 28(2): B&C: 13.051, 14.023 F&N: 2.172, 2.185, 2.186, 2.188, 2.195, 2.196, 2.197, 2.200

CHAPTER IX
EXEMPTION REGULATIONS

Article 29
Withdrawal in individual cases

1. Where the Commission, empowered by a Council Regulation, such as Regulations 19/65/EEC, (EEC) No 2821/71, (EEC) No 3976/87, (EEC) No 1534/91 or (EEC) No 479/92, to apply Article 81(3) of the Treaty by regulation, has declared Article 81(1) of the Treaty inapplicable to certain categories of agreements, decisions by associations of undertakings or concerted practices, it may, acting on its own initiative or on a complaint, withdraw the benefit of such an exemption Regulation when it finds that in any particular case an agreement, decision or concerted practice to which the exemption Regulation applies has certain effects which are incompatible with Article 81(3) of the Treaty.

2. Where, in any particular case, agreements, decisions by associations of undertakings or concerted practices to which a Commission Regulation referred to in paragraph 1 applies have effects which are incompatible with Article 81(3) of the Treaty in the territory of a Member State, or in a part thereof, which has all the characteristics of a distinct geographic market, the competition authority of that Member State may withdraw the benefit of the Regulation in question in respect of that territory.

Commentary
Art 29: B&C: 13.072 F&N: 4.419
Art 29(1): B&C: 3.086 F&N: 3.419
Art 29(2): B&C: 3.087 F&N: 3.419

CHAPTER X
GENERAL PROVISIONS

Article 30
Publication of decisions

1. The Commission shall publish the decisions, which it takes pursuant to Articles 7 to 10, 23 and 24.

2. The publication shall state the names of the parties and the main content of the decision, including any penalties imposed. It shall have regard to the legitimate interest of undertakings in the protection of their business secrets.

Commentary
Art 30:   **B&C:** 1.063, 13.032, 13.043, 13.112, 13.232   **F&N:** 8.474, 8.475
Art 30(1):   **B&C:** 13.115, 13.125
Art 30(2):   **F&N:** 2.195, 8.459, 8.475

Article 31
Review by the Court of Justice

The Court of Justice shall have unlimited jurisdiction to review decisions whereby the Commission has fixed a fine or periodic penalty payment. It may cancel, reduce or increase the fine or periodic penalty payment imposed.

Commentary
Art 31:   **B&C:** 13.032, 13.214   **F&N:** 8.478, 8.484, 8.608, 8.845

[Article 32]

Notes
Article 32(c) was repealed by Council Regulation 411/2004/EC of 26 February 2004 (OJ L 68, 6.3.2004, p. 1), Article 3, with effect from 1 May 2004.
Article 32 was deleted by Council Regulation 1419/2006/EC of 28 September 2006 (OJ L 269, 28.9.2006, p. 1), Article 2, with effect from 18 October 2006.

Commentary
Art 32:   **B&C:** 3.094, 12.007   **F&N:** 8.263, 14.126, 14.132

Article 33
Implementing provisions

1. The Commission shall be authorised to take such measures as may be appropriate in order to apply this Regulation. The measures may concern, inter alia:

(a) the form, content and other details of complaints lodged pursuant to Article 7 and the procedure for rejecting complaints;
(b) the practical arrangements for the exchange of information and consultations provided for in Article 11;
(c) the practical arrangements for the hearings provided for in Article 27.

2. Before the adoption of any measures pursuant to paragraph 1, the Commission shall publish a draft thereof and invite all interested parties to submit their comments within the time-limit it lays down, which may not be less than one month. Before publishing a draft measure and before adopting it, the Commission shall consult the Advisory Committee on Restrictive Practices and Dominant Positions.

Commentary
Art 33:   **B&C:** 1.060

CHAPTER XI
TRANSITIONAL, AMENDING AND FINAL PROVISIONS

Article 34
Transitional provisions

1. Applications made to the Commission under Article 2 of Regulation No 17, notifications made under Articles 4 and 5 of that Regulation and the corresponding applications and notifications made under Regulations (EEC) No 1017/68, (EEC) No 4056/86 and (EEC) No 3975/87 shall lapse as from the date of application of this Regulation.

2. Procedural steps taken under Regulation No 17 and Regulations (EEC) No 1017/68, (EEC) No 4056/86 and (EEC) No 3975/87 shall continue to have effect for the purposes of applying this Regulation.

Commentary
Art 34: B&C: 14.085
Art 34(1): B&C: 3.009, 14.085

Article 35
Designation of competition authorities of Member States

1. The Member States shall designate the competition authority or authorities responsible for the application of Articles 81 and 82 of the Treaty in such a way that the provisions of this regulation are effectively complied with. The measures necessary to empower those authorities to apply those Articles shall be taken before 1 May 2004. The authorities designated may include courts.

2. When enforcement of Community competition law is entrusted to national administrative and judicial authorities, the Member States may allocate different powers and functions to those different national authorities, whether administrative or judicial.

3. The effects of Article 11(6) apply to the authorities designated by the Member States including courts that exercise functions regarding the preparation and the adoption of the types of decisions foreseen in Article 5. The effects of Article 11(6) do not extend to courts insofar as they act as review courts in respect of the types of decisions foreseen in Article 5.

4. Notwithstanding paragraph 3, in the Member States where, for the adoption of certain types of decisions foreseen in Article 5, an authority brings an action before a judicial authority that is separate and different from the prosecuting authority and provided that the terms of this paragraph are complied with, the effects of Article 11(6) shall be limited to the authority prosecuting the case which shall withdraw its claim before the judicial authority when the Commission opens proceedings and this withdrawal shall bring the national proceedings effectively to an end.

Commentary
Art 35: B&C: 1.061, 14.032, 14.038, 14.074
Art 35(1): B&C: 14.011, 14.013 F&N: 2.22, 2.75, 2.76, 2.81, 2.210, 2.272
Art 35(2): F&N: 2.76, 2.210
Art 35(3): B&C: 14.016, 14.074 F&N: 2.224, 2.225, 2.226, 2.254
Art 35(4): B&C: 14.016, 14.074 F&N: 2.224, 2.225, 2.226, 2.254

[*Articles 36 to 42*]

Notes
Articles 36 to 42 amend Regulations 1017/68/EEC, 2988/74/EEC, 4056/86/EEC, 3975/87/EEC, 19/65/EEC, 2821/71/EEC, 1534/91/EEC, 3976/87/EEC and 479/92. Those Regulations are reproduced as amended elsewhere in this volume.

Article 43
Repeal of Regulations No 17 and No 141

1. Regulation No 17 is repealed with the exception of Article 8(3) which continues to apply to decisions adopted pursuant to Article 81(3) of the Treaty prior to the date of application of this Regulation until the date of expiration of those decisions.

2. Regulation No 141 is repealed.

3. References to the repealed Regulations shall be construed as references to this Regulation.

Commentary
Art 43: B&C: 13.201
Art 43(1): B&C: 3.008, 14.085

Article 44
Report on the application of the present Regulation

Five years from the date of application of this Regulation, the Commission shall report to the European Parliament and the Council on the functioning of this Regulation, in particular on the application of Article 11(6) and Article 17.

On the basis of this report, the Commission shall assess whether it is appropriate to propose to the Council a revision of this Regulation.

Article 45
Entry into force

This Regulation shall enter into force on the 20th day following that of its publication in the *Official Journal of the European Communities.*

It shall apply from 1 May 2004.

Commentary
Art 45: B&C: 14.088

This Regulation shall be binding in its entirety and directly applicable in all Member States.
Done at Brussels, 16 December 2002.

B4

COMMISSION REGULATION (EC)
No 773/2004

of 7 April 2004

relating to the conduct of proceedings by the Commission pursuant to Articles 81 and 82 of the
EC Treaty

(Text with EEA relevance)

Official Journal L 123, 27.4.2004, p. 18

Celex No: 32004R0773

Notes

EEA application: see the Surveillance and Court Agreement, Protocol 4, Part I, Chapter III, as replaced by the Agreement amending Protocol 4 of 3 December 2004 with effect from 1 July 2005.

Commentary

Reg 773/2004/EC: F&N: 2.108, 2.136, 2.258, 8.102, 8.215, 8.260, 8.281, 8.336, 8.363, 8.365, 8.366, 8.398, 8.422, 8.423, 8.459

THE COMMISSION OF THE EUROPEAN COMMUNITIES,

Having regard to the Treaty establishing the European Community,

Having regard to the Agreement on the European Economic Area,

Having regard to Council Regulation (EC) No 1/2003 of 16 December 2002 on the implementation of the rules on competition laid down in Articles 81 and 82 of the Treaty,[1] and in particular Article 33 thereof,

---

Notes

[1] OJ L 1, 4.1.2003, p. 1. Regulation as amended by Regulation (EC) No 411/2004 (OJ L 68, 6.3.2004, p. 1).

After consulting the Advisory Committee on Restrictive Practices and Dominant Positions,

Whereas:

(1) Regulation (EC) No 1/2003 empowers the Commission to regulate certain aspects of proceedings for the application of Articles 81 and 82 of the Treaty. It is necessary to lay down rules concerning the initiation of proceedings by the Commission as well as the handling of complaints and the hearing of the parties concerned.

(2) According to Regulation (EC) No 1/2003, national courts are under an obligation to avoid taking decisions which could run counter to decisions envisaged by the Commission in the same case. According to Article 11(6) of that Regulation, national competition authorities are relieved from their competence once the Commission has initiated proceedings for the adoption of a decision under Chapter III of Regulation (EC) No 1/2003. In this context, it is important that courts and competition authorities of the Member States are aware of the initiation of proceedings by the Commission. The Commission should therefore be able to make public its decisions to initiate proceedings.

(3) Before taking oral statements from natural or legal persons who consent to be interviewed, the Commission should inform those persons of the legal basis of the interview and its voluntary nature. The persons interviewed should also be informed of the purpose of the interview and of any record which may be made. In order to enhance the accuracy of the statements, the persons

interviewed should also be given an opportunity to correct the statements recorded. Where information gathered from oral statements is exchanged pursuant to Article 12 of Regulation (EC) No 1/2003, that information should only be used in evidence to impose sanctions on natural persons where the conditions set out in that Article are fulfilled.

(4) Pursuant to Article 23(1)(d) of Regulation (EC) No 1/2003 fines may be imposed on undertakings and associations of undertakings where they fail to rectify within the time limit fixed by the Commission an incorrect, incomplete or misleading answer given by a member of their staff to questions in the course of inspections. It is therefore necessary to provide the undertaking concerned with a record of any explanations given and to establish a procedure enabling it to add any rectification, amendment or supplement to the explanations given by the member of staff who is not or was not authorised to provide explanations on behalf of the undertaking. The explanations given by a member of staff should remain in the Commission file as recorded during the inspection.

(5) Complaints are an essential source of information for detecting infringements of competition rules. It is important to define clear and efficient procedures for handling complaints lodged with the Commission.

(6) In order to be admissible for the purposes of Article 7 of Regulation (EC) No 1/2003, a complaint must contain certain specified information.

(7) In order to assist complainants in submitting the necessary facts to the Commission, a form should be drawn up. The submission of the information listed in that form should be a condition for a complaint to be treated as a complaint as referred to in Article 7 of Regulation (EC) No 1/2003.

(8) Natural or legal persons having chosen to lodge a complaint should be given the possibility to be associated closely with the proceedings initiated by the Commission with a view to finding an infringement. However, they should not have access to business secrets or other confidential information belonging to other parties involved in the proceedings.

(9) Complainants should be granted the opportunity of expressing their views if the Commission considers that there are insufficient grounds for acting on the complaint. Where the Commission rejects a complaint on the grounds that a competition authority of a Member State is dealing with it or has already done so, it should inform the complainant of the identity of that authority.

(10) In order to respect the rights of defence of undertakings, the Commission should give the parties concerned the right to be heard before it takes a decision.

(11) Provision should also be made for the hearing of persons who have not submitted a complaint as referred to in Article 7 of Regulation (EC) No 1/2003 and who are not parties to whom a statement of objections has been addressed but who can nevertheless show a sufficient interest. Consumer associations that apply to be heard should generally be regarded as having a sufficient interest, where the proceedings concern products or services used by the end-consumer or products or services that constitute a direct input into such products or services. Where it considers this to be useful for the proceedings, the Commission should also be able to invite other persons to express their views in writing and to attend the oral hearing of the parties to whom a statement of objections has been addressed. Where appropriate, it should also be able to invite such persons to express their views at that oral hearing.

(12) To improve the effectiveness of oral hearings, the Hearing Officer should have the power to allow the parties concerned, complainants, other persons invited to the hearing, the Commission services and the authorities of the Member States to ask questions during the hearing.

(13) When granting access to the file, the Commission should ensure the protection of business secrets and other confidential information. The category of "other confidential information" includes information other than business secrets, which may be considered as confidential, insofar as its disclosure would significantly harm an undertaking or person. The Commission should be able to request undertakings or associations of undertakings that submit or have submitted documents or statements to identify confidential information.

Commentary
Recital 13: F&N: 2.194

(14) Where business secrets or other confidential information are necessary to prove an infringement, the Commission should assess for each individual document whether the need to disclose is greater than the harm which might result from disclosure.

Commentary
Recital 14: F&N: 2.199

(15) In the interest of legal certainty, a minimum time-limit for the various submissions provided for in this Regulation should be laid down.

(16) This Regulation replaces Commission Regulation (EC) No 2842/98 of 22 December 1998 on the hearing of parties in certain proceedings under Articles 85 and 86 of the EC Treaty,[1] which should therefore be repealed.

Notes
[1] OJ L 354, 30.12.1998, p. 18.

(17) This Regulation aligns the procedural rules in the transport sector with the general rules of procedure in all sectors. Commission Regulation (EC) No 2843/98 of 22 December 1998 on the form, content and other details of applications and notifications provided for in Council Regulations (EEC) No 1017/68, (EEC) No 4056/86 and (EEC) No 3975/87 applying the rules on competition to the transport sector[1] should therefore be repealed.

Notes
[1] OJ L 354, 30.12.1998, p. 22.

(18) Regulation (EC) No 1/2003 abolishes the notification and authorisation system. Commission Regulation (EC) No 3385/94 of 21 December 1994 on the form, content and other details of applications and notifications provided for in Council Regulation No 17[1] should therefore be repealed,

Notes
[1] OJ L 377, 31.12.1994, p. 28.

HAS ADOPTED THIS REGULATION:

CHAPTER I
SCOPE

Article 1
Subject-matter and scope

This regulation applies to proceedings conducted by the Commission for the application of Articles 81 and 82 of the Treaty.

CHAPTER II
INITIATION OF PROCEEDINGS

Article 2
Initiation of proceedings

1. The Commission may decide to initiate proceedings with a view to adopting a decision pursuant to Chapter III of Regulation (EC) No 1/2003 at any point in time, but no later than the date on which it issues a preliminary assessment as referred to in Article 9(1) of that Regulation or a statement of objections or the date on which a notice pursuant to Article 27(4) of that Regulation is published, whichever is the earlier.

2. The Commission may make public the initiation of proceedings, in any appropriate way. Before doing so, it shall inform the parties concerned.

3. The Commission may exercise its powers of investigation pursuant to Chapter V of Regulation (EC) No 1/2003 before initiating proceedings.

4. The Commission may reject a complaint pursuant to Article 7 of Regulation (EC) No 1/2003 without initiating proceedings.

Commentary
Art 2(1): B&C: 13.082 F&N: 2.124, 8.452
Art 2(2): B&C: 13.082, 14.074
Art 2(3): B&C: 13.082

CHAPTER III
INVESTIGATIONS BY THE COMMISSION

Article 3
Power to take statements

1. Where the Commission interviews a person with his consent in accordance with Article 19 of Regulation (EC) No 1/2003, it shall, at the beginning of the interview, state the legal basis and the purpose of the interview, and recall its voluntary nature. It shall also inform the person interviewed of its intention to make a record of the interview.

2. The interview may be conducted by any means including by telephone or electronic means.

3. The Commission may record the statements made by the persons interviewed in any form. A copy of any recording shall be made available to the person interviewed for approval. Where necessary, the Commission shall set a time-limit within which the person interviewed may communicate to it any correction to be made to the statement.

Commentary
Art 3: F&N: 8.488, 8.511
Art 3(1): B&C: 13.037 F&N: 8.328
Art 3(2): B&C: 13.037 F&N: 8.328
Art 3(3): B&C: 13.037 F&N: 8.328

Article 4
Oral questions during inspections

1. When, pursuant to Article 20(2)(e) of Regulation (EC) No 1/2003, officials or other accompanying persons authorised by the Commission ask representatives or members of staff of an undertaking or of an association of undertakings for explanations, the explanations given may be recorded in any form.

2. A copy of any recording made pursuant to paragraph 1 shall be made available to the undertaking or association of undertakings concerned after the inspection.

3. In cases where a member of staff of an undertaking or of an association of undertakings who is not or was not authorised by the undertaking or by the association of undertakings to provide explanations on behalf of the undertaking or association of undertakings has been asked for explanations, the Commission shall set a time-limit within which the undertaking or the association of undertakings may communicate to the Commission any rectification, amendment or supplement to the explanations given by such member of staff. The rectification, amendment or supplement shall be added to the explanations as recorded pursuant to paragraph 1.

Commentary
Art 4: F&N: 8.299, 8.368, 8.369, 8.372, 8.488, 8.511
Art 4(1): B&C: 13.049 F&N: 8.373
Art 4(2): B&C: 13.049 F&N: 8.373
Art 4(3): B&C: 13.049 F&N: 8.378

CHAPTER IV

HANDLING OF COMPLAINTS

Article 5

Admissibility of complaints

1. Natural and legal persons shall show a legitimate interest in order to be entitled to lodge a complaint for the purposes of Article 7 of Regulation (EC) No 1/2003.

Such complaints shall contain the information required by Form C, as set out in the Annex. The Commission may dispense with this obligation as regards part of the information, including documents, required by Form C.

2. Three paper copies as well as, if possible, an electronic copy of the complaint shall be submitted to the Commission. The complainant shall also submit a non-confidential version of the complaint, if confidentiality is claimed for any part of the complaint.

3. Complaints shall be submitted in one of the official languages of the Community.

Commentary
Art 5: B&C: 13.221 F&N: 8.102
Art 5(1): B&C: 13.066
Art 5(2): B&C: 13.066
Art 5(3): B&C: 13.066

Article 6

Participation of complainants in proceedings

1. Where the Commission issues a statement of objections relating to a matter in respect of which it has received a complaint, it shall provide the complainant with a copy of the non-confidential version of the statement of objections and set a time-limit within which the complainant may make known its views in writing.

2. The Commission may, where appropriate, afford complainants the opportunity of expressing their views at the oral hearing of the parties to which a statement of objections has been issued, if complainants so request in their written comments.

Commentary
Art 6: F&N: 8.486
Art 6(1): B&C: 13.073
Art 6(2): B&C: 13.073

Article 7

Rejection of complaints

1. Where the Commission considers that on the basis of the information in its possession there are insufficient grounds for acting on a complaint, it shall inform the complainant of its reasons and set a time-limit within which the complainant may make known its views in writing. The Commission shall not be obliged to take into account any further written submission received after the expiry of that time-limit.

2. If the complainant makes known its views within the time-limit set by the Commission and the written submissions made by the complainant do not lead to a different assessment of the complaint, the Commission shall reject the complaint by decision.

3. If the complainant fails to make known its views within the time-limit set by the Commission, the complaint shall be deemed to have been withdrawn.

Commentary
Art 7: B&C: 13.068, 13.073, 13.219, 13.244 F&N: 12.399
Art 7(1): B&C: 13.069
Art 7(3): B&C: 13.069

Article 8
Access to information

1. Where the Commission has informed the complainant of its intention to reject a complaint pursuant to Article 7(1) the complainant may request access to the documents on which the Commission bases its provisional assessment. For this purpose, the complainant may however not have access to business secrets and other confidential information belonging to other parties involved in the proceedings.

2. The documents to which the complainant has had access in the context of proceedings conducted by the Commission under Articles 81 and 82 of the Treaty may only be used by the complainant for the purposes of judicial or administrative proceedings for the application of those Treaty provisions.

Commentary
Art 8: B&C: 13.069 F&N: 2.202
Art 8(2): F&N: 8.458

Article 9
Rejections of complaints pursuant to Article 13 of Regulation (EC) No 1/2003

Where the Commission rejects a complaint pursuant to Article 13 of Regulation (EC) No 1/2003, it shall inform the complainant without delay of the national competition authority which is dealing or has already dealt with the case.

Commentary
Art 9: B&C: 13.068

Chapter V
Exercise of the Right to be Heard

Article 10
Statement of objections and reply

1. The Commission shall inform the parties concerned in writing of the objections raised against them. The statement of objections shall be notified to each of them.

2. The Commission shall, when notifying the statement of objections to the parties concerned, set a time-limit within which these parties may inform it in writing of their views. The Commission shall not be obliged to take into account written submissions received after the expiry of that time-limit.

3. The parties may, in their written submissions, set out all facts known to them which are relevant to their defence against the objections raised by the Commission. They shall attach any relevant documents as proof of the facts set out. They shall provide a paper original as well as an electronic copy or, where they do not provide an electronic copy, [30] paper copies of their submission and of the documents attached to it. They may propose that the Commission hear persons who may corroborate the facts set out in their submission.

Notes
Amendment in square brackets in Article 10(3) made by Commission Regulation (EC) No 1792/2006 of 23 October 2006 (OJ L 362, 20.12.2006, p. 1), with effect from 1 January 2007.

Commentary
Art 10(1): B&C: 13.080, 13.082, 13.083
Art 10(2): B&C: 13.086 F&N: 8.456
Art 10(3): B&C: 13.080, 13.086 F&N: 8.456

Article 11
Right to be heard

1. The Commission shall give the parties to whom it has addressed a statement of objections the opportunity to be heard before consulting the Advisory Committee referred to in Article 14(1) of Regulation (EC) No 1/2003.

2. The Commission shall, in its decisions, deal only with objections in respect of which the parties referred to in paragraph 1 have been able to comment.

Commentary
Art 11(1): **B&C:** 13.080 **F&N:** 8.464
Art 11(2): **B&C:** 13.080, 13.084 **F&N:** 8.450, 8.455, 8.457, 8.469, 8.470, 8.515

Article 12
Right to an oral hearing

The Commission shall give the parties to whom it has addressed a statement of objections the opportunity to develop their arguments at an oral hearing, if they so request in their written submissions.

Commentary
Art 12: **B&C:** 13.080, 13.101 **F&N:** 8.456, 8.464, 8.520

Article 13
Hearing of other persons

1. If natural or legal persons other than those referred to in Articles 5 and 11 apply to be heard and show a sufficient interest, the Commission shall inform them in writing of the nature and subject matter of the procedure and shall set a time-limit within which they may make known their views in writing.

2. The Commission may, where appropriate, invite persons referred to in paragraph 1 to develop their arguments at the oral hearing of the parties to whom a statement of objections has been addressed, if the persons referred to in paragraph 1 so request in their written comments.

3. The Commission may invite any other person to express its views in writing and to attend the oral hearing of the parties to whom a statement of objections has been addressed. The Commission may also invite such persons to express their views at that oral hearing.

Commentary
Art 13: **B&C:** 13.073 **F&N:** 8.452, 8.465
Art 13(1): **B&C:** 13.104
Art 13(2): **B&C:** 13.104 **F&N:** 8.464
Art 13(3): **B&C:** 13.104

Article 14
Conduct of oral hearings

1. Hearings shall be conducted by a Hearing Officer in full independence.

2. The Commission shall invite the persons to be heard to attend the oral hearing on such date as it shall determine.

3. The Commission shall invite the competition authorities of the Member States to take part in the oral hearing. It may likewise invite officials and civil servants of other authorities of the Member States.

4. Persons invited to attend shall either appear in person or be represented by legal representatives or by representatives authorised by their constitution as appropriate. Undertakings and associations of undertakings may also be represented by a duly authorised agent appointed from among their permanent staff.

5. Persons heard by the Commission may be assisted by their lawyers or other qualified persons admitted by the Hearing Officer.

6. Oral hearings shall not be public. Each person may be heard separately or in the presence of other persons invited to attend, having regard to the legitimate interest of the undertakings in the protection of their business secrets and other confidential information.

Part B Modernisation and Procedural Matters

7. The Hearing Officer may allow the parties to whom a statement of objections has been addressed, the complainants, other persons invited to the hearing, the Commission services and the authorities of the Member States to ask questions during the hearing.

8. The statements made by each person heard shall be recorded. Upon request, the recording of the hearing shall be made available to the persons who attended the hearing. Regard shall be had to the legitimate interest of the parties in the protection of their business secrets and other confidential information.

Commentary
Art 14: F&N: 8.456, 8.465
Art 14(1): B&C: 13.101 F&N: 8.464
Art 14(3): B&C: 13.101
Art 14(4): B&C: 13.101
Art 14(5): B&C: 13.101
Art 14(6): B&C: 13.103 F&N: 8.464
Art 14(7): B&C: 13.103 F&N: 8.465
Art 14(8): B&C: 13.103 F&N: 8.465

CHAPTER VI
ACCESS TO THE FILE AND TREATMENT OF CONFIDENTIAL INFORMATION

Article 15
Access to the file and use of documents

1. If so requested, the Commission shall grant access to the file to the parties to whom it has addressed a statement of objections. Access shall be granted after the notification of the statement of objections.

2. The right of access to the file shall not extend to business secrets, other confidential information and internal documents of the Commission or of the competition authorities of the Member States. The right of access to the file shall also not extend to correspondence between the Commission and the competition authorities of the Member States or between the latter where such correspondence is contained in the file of the Commission.

3. Nothing in this Regulation prevents the Commission from disclosing and using information necessary to prove an infringement of Articles 81 or 82 of the Treaty.

4. Documents obtained through access to the file pursuant to this Article shall only be used for the purposes of judicial or administrative proceedings for the application of Articles 81 and 82 of the Treaty.

Commentary
Art 15: B&C: 13.073 F&N: 8.458, 8.459
Art 15(1): B&C: 13.089, 13.092 F&N: 2.200
Art 15(2): B&C: 13.093-13.094, 13.097 F&N: 2.200, 8.459
Art 15(3): F&N: 2.198, 8.459
Art 15(4): F&N: 8.160, 8.218, 8.458

Article 16
Identification and protection of confidential information

1. Information, including documents, shall not be communicated or made accessible by the Commission in so far as it contains business secrets or other confidential information of any person.

2. Any person which makes known its views pursuant to Article 6(1), Article 7(1), Article 10(2) and Article 13(1) and (3) or subsequently submits further information to the Commission in the course of the same procedure, shall clearly identify any material which it considers to be confidential, giving reasons, and provide a separate non-confidential version by the date set by the Commission for making its views known.

3. Without prejudice to paragraph 2 of this Article, the Commission may require undertakings and associations of undertakings which produce documents or statements pursuant to Regulation (EC)

No 1/2003 to identify the documents or parts of documents which they consider to contain business secrets or other confidential information belonging to them and to identify the undertakings with regard to which such documents are to be considered confidential. The Commission may likewise require undertakings or associations of undertakings to identify any part of a statement of objections, a case summary drawn up pursuant to Article 27(4) of Regulation (EC) No 1/2003 or a decision adopted by the Commission which in their view contains business secrets.

The Commission may set a time-limit within which the undertakings and associations of undertakings are to:

(a) substantiate their claim for confidentiality with regard to each individual document or part of document, statement or part of statement;
(b) provide the Commission with a non-confidential version of the documents or statements, in which the confidential passages are deleted;
(c) provide a concise description of each piece of deleted information.

4. If undertakings or associations of undertakings fail to comply with paragraphs 2 and 3, the Commission may assume that the documents or statements concerned do not contain confidential information.

Commentary
Art 16: B&C: 13.096 F&N: 8.458, 8.459, 8.462, 8.475
Art 16(1): B&C: 13.093, 13.095 F&N: 2.200, 8.459
Art 16(2): B&C: 13.098
Art 16(3): B&C: 13.098
Art 16(4): B&C: 13.098

Chapter VII
General and Final Provisions

Article 17
Time-limits

1. In setting the time-limits provided for in Article 3(3), Article 4(3), Article 6(1), Article 7(1), Article 10(2) and Article 16(3), the Commission shall have regard both to the time required for preparation of the submission and to the urgency of the case.

2. The time-limits referred to in Article 6(1), Article 7(1) and Article 10(2) shall be at least four weeks. However, for proceedings initiated with a view to adopting interim measures pursuant to Article 8 of Regulation (EC) No 1/2003, the time-limit may be shortened to one week.

3. The time-limits referred to in Article 3(3), Article 4(3) and Article 16(3) shall be at least two weeks.

4. Where appropriate and upon reasoned request made before the expiry of the original time-limit, time-limits may be extended.

Commentary
Art 17(1): F&N: 8.456
Art 17(2): B&C: 13.121 F&N: 8.456

Article 18
Repeals

Regulations (EC) No 2842/98, (EC) No 2843/98 and (EC) No 3385/94 are repealed.

References to the repealed regulations shall be construed as references to this Regulation.

Article 19
Transitional provisions

Procedural steps taken under Regulations (EC) No 2842/98 and (EC) No 2843/98 shall continue to have effect for the purpose of applying this Regulation.

Commentary
Art 19: B&C: 13.080

Article 20
Entry into force

This Regulation shall enter into force on 1 May 2004.

This Regulation shall be binding in its entirety and directly applicable in all Member States.

Done at Brussels, 7 April 2004.

ANNEX
FORM C
COMPLAINT PURSUANT TO ARTICLE 7 OF REGULATION (EC) No 1/2003

I. INFORMATION REGARDING THE COMPLAINANT AND THE UNDERTAKING(S) OR ASSOCIATION OF UNDERTAKINGS GIVING RISE TO THE COMPLAINT

1. Give full details on the identity of the legal or natural person submitting the complaint. Where the complainant is an undertaking, identify the corporate group to which it belongs and provide a concise overview of the nature and scope of its business activities. Provide a contact person (with telephone number, postal and e-mail-address) from which supplementary explanations can be obtained.

2. Identify the undertaking(s) or association of undertakings whose conduct the complaint relates to, including, where applicable, all available information on the corporate group to which the undertaking(s) complained of belong and the nature and scope of the business activities pursued by them. Indicate the position of the complainant vis-à-vis the undertaking(s) or association of undertakings complained of (e.g. customer, competitor).

II. DETAILS OF THE ALLEGED INFRINGEMENT AND EVIDENCE

3. Set out in detail the facts from which, in your opinion, it appears that there exists an infringement of Article 81 or 82 of the Treaty and/or Article 53 or 54 of the EEA agreement. Indicate in particular the nature of the products (goods or services) affected by the alleged infringements and explain, where necessary, the commercial relationships concerning these products. Provide all available details on the agreements or practices of the undertakings or associations of undertakings to which this complaint relates. Indicate, to the extent possible, the relative market positions of the undertakings concerned by the complaint.

4. Submit all documentation in your possession relating to or directly connected with the facts set out in the complaint (for example, texts of agreements, minutes of negotiations or meetings, terms of transactions, business documents, circulars, correspondence, notes of telephone conversations . . .). State the names and address of the persons able to testify to the facts set out in the complaint, and in particular of persons affected by the alleged infringement. Submit statistics or other data in your possession which relate to the facts set out, in particular where they show developments in the marketplace (for example information relating to prices and price trends, barriers to entry to the market for new suppliers etc.).

5. Set out your view about the geographical scope of the alleged infringement and explain, where that is not obvious, to what extent trade between Member States or between the Community and one or more EFTA States that are contracting parties of the EEA Agreement may be affected by the conduct complained of.

III. FINDING SOUGHT FROM THE COMMISSION AND LEGITIMATE INTEREST

6. Explain what finding or action you are seeking as a result of proceedings brought by the Commission.

7. Set out the grounds on which you claim a legitimate interest as complainant pursuant to Article 7 of Regulation (EC) No 1/2003. State in particular how the conduct complained of affects you and explain how, in your view, intervention by the Commission would be liable to remedy the alleged grievance.

IV. Proceedings before National Competition Authorities or National Courts

8. Provide full information about whether you have approached, concerning the same or closely related subject-matters, any other competition authority and/or whether a lawsuit has been brought before a national court. If so, provide full details about the administrative or judicial authority contacted and your submissions to such authority.

Declaration that the information given in this form and in the Annexes thereto is given entirely in good faith.

Date and signature

B5

GUIDELINES ON THE METHOD OF SETTING FINES IMPOSED PURSUANT TO ARTICLE 15(2) OF REGULATION No 17 AND ARTICLE 65(5) OF THE ECSC TREATY

(98/C 9/03)

(Text with EEA relevance)

Official Journal C 9, 14.1.1998, p3

Celex No: 31998Y0114(01)

Notes

EEA application: the EFTA Surveillance Authority has adopted a parallel notice on the method of setting fines imposed pursuant to the EEA competition rules under Article 5(2)(b) of the Surveillance and Court Agreement: OJ C 10, 16.1.2003, p. 16 and EEA Supplement No 3, 16.1.2003, p. 6.

Commentary

Guidelines: **B&C:** 4.010, 13.146–13.147, 13.149, 13.152, 13.161, 13.166, 13.169, 13.178 **F&N:** 2.83, 4.150, 4.441, 4.443, 4.444, 8.10, 8.112, 8.234, 8.501, 8.552, 8.587, 8.599, 8.611, 8.613, 8.614–8.621, 8.623, 8.624, 8.626–8.630, 8.634, 8.636, 8.638, 8.640, 8.641, 8.643, 8.645, 8.646, 8.648, 8.650, 8.652, 8.653, 8.654, 8.660, 8.661, 8.664, 8.665, 8.667, 8.668, 8.698, 8.699, 8.700, 8.702, 8.703, 8.705, 8.707, 8.710, 8.712, 8.713, 8.718, 8.722, 8.723, 8.737, 8.739, 8.742, 8.744, 8.745, 8.748, 8.751, 8.761, 8.766, 8.774, 8.792, 8.800, 8.801, 8.802, 8.805, 8.806, 8.809, 8.817, 8.820, 8.823, 8.825, 8.829, 8.831, 8.832, 8.833

The principles outlined here should ensure the transparency and impartiality of the Commission's decisions, in the eyes of the undertakings and of the Court of Justice alike, while upholding the discretion which the Commission is granted under the relevant legislation to set fines within the limit of 10% of overall turnover. This discretion must, however, follow a coherent and non-discriminatory policy which is consistent with the objectives pursued in penalizing infringements of the competition rules.

The new method of determining the amount of a fine will adhere to the following rules, which start from a basic amount that will be increased to take account of aggravating circumstances or reduced to take account of attenuating circumstances.

1. Basic amount

The basic amount will be determined according to the gravity and duration of the infringement, which are the only criteria referred to in Article 15(2) of Regulation No 17.

A. *Gravity*

In assessing the gravity of the infringement, account must be taken of its nature, its actual impact on the market, where this can be measured, and the size of the relevant geographic market.

Infringements will thus be put into one of three categories: minor infringements, serious infringements and very serious infringements.

— *minor infringements:*
These might be trade restrictions, usually of a vertical nature, but with a limited market impact and affecting only a substantial but relatively limited part of the Community market.
Likely fines: ECU 1 000 to ECU 1 million.

— *serious infringements:*
These will more often than not be horizontal or vertical restrictions of the same type as above, but more rigorously applied, with a wider market impact, and with effects in extensive areas of the common market. There might also be abuse of a dominant position (refusals to supply, discrimination, exclusion, loyalty discounts made by dominant firms in order to shut competitors out of the market, etc.).
Likely fines: ECU 1 million to ECU 20 million.

— *very serious infringements:*
These will generally be horizontal restrictions such as price cartels and market-sharing quotas, or other practices which jeopardize the proper functioning of the single market, such as the partitioning of national markets and clear-cut abuse of a dominant position by undertakings holding a virtual monopoly (see Decisions 91/297/EEC, 91/298/EEC, 91/299/EEC, 91/300/EEC and 91/301/EEC[1] — Soda Ash, 94/815/EC[2] — Cement, 94/601/EC[3] — Cartonboard, 92/163/EC[4] — Tetra Pak, and 94/215/ECSC[5] — Steel beams).
Likely fines: above ECU 20 million

Within each of these categories, and in particular as far as serious and very serious infringements are concerned, the proposed scale of fines will make it possible to apply differential treatment to undertakings according to the nature of the infringement committed.

It will also be necessary to take account of the effective economic capacity of offenders to cause significant damage to other operators, in particular consumers, and to set the fine at a level which ensures that it has a sufficiently deterrent effect.

Generally speaking, account may also be taken of the fact that large undertakings usually have legal and economic knowledge and infrastructures which enable them more easily to recognize that their conduct constitutes an infringement and be aware of the consequences stemming from it under competition law.

Where an infringement involves several undertakings (e.g. cartels), it might be necessary in some cases to apply weightings to the amounts determined within each of the three categories in order to take account of the specific weight and, therefore, the real impact of the offending conduct of each undertaking on competition, particularly where there is considerable disparity between the sizes of the undertakings committing infringements of the same type.

Thus, the principle of equal punishment for the same conduct may, if the circumstances so warrant, lead to different fines being imposed on the undertakings concerned without this differentiation being governed by arithmetic calculation.

Commentary
point 1A: **B&C:** 4.010, 13.152, 13.177 **F&N:** 8.626, 8.654, 8.655, 8.656, 8.663, 8.672, 8.708, 8.724, 8.727

B. *Duration*

A distinction should be made between the following:

— infringements of short duration (in general, less than one year): no increase in amount,
— infringements of medium duration (in general, one to five years): increase of up to 50% in the amount determined for gravity,
— infringements of long duration (in general, more than five years): increase of up to 10% per year in the amount determined for gravity.

This approach will therefore point to a possible increase in the amount of the fine.

Generally speaking, the increase in the fine for long-term infringements represents a considerable strengthening of the previous practice with a view to imposing effective sanctions on restrictions which have had a harmful impact on consumers over a long period. Moreover, this new approach is consistent with the expected effect of the notice of 18 July 1996 on the non-imposition or reduction of fines in cartel cases.[6] The risk of having to pay a much larger fine, proportionate to the duration of the infringement, will necessarily increase the incentive to denounce it or to cooperate with the Commission.

The basic amount will result from the addition of the two amounts established in accordance with the above:

$$x \text{ gravity} + y \text{ duration} = \text{basic amount}$$

Notes
[1] OJ L 152, 15.6.1991, p. 54.
[2] OJ L 343, 30.12.1994, p. 1.
[3] OJ L 243, 19.9.1994, p. 1.
[4] OJ L 72, 18.3.1992, p. 1.
[5] OJ L 116, 6.5.1994, p. 1.
[6] OJ C 207, 18.7.1996, p. 4. [See now Commission notice on immunity from fines and reduction of fines in cartel cases (2002/C 45/03), OJ C 045, 19.2.2002, p 3.]

Commentary
point 1B: **B&C:** 13.155 **F&N:** 8.551

2. Aggravating circumstances

The basic amount will be increased where there are aggravating circumstances such as:

— repeated infringement of the same type by the same undertaking(s),
— refusal to cooperate with or attempts to obstruct the Commission in carrying out its investigations,
— role of leader in, or instigator of the infringement,
— retaliatory measures against other undertakings with a view to enforcing practices which constitute an infringement,
— need to increase the penalty in order to exceed the amount of gains improperly made as a result of the infringement when it is objectively possible to estimate that amount,
— other.

Commentary
point 2: **F&N:** 8.471, 8.708

3. Attenuating circumstances

The basic amount will be reduced where there are attenuating circumstances such as:

— an exclusively passive or "follow-my-leader" role in the infringement,
— non-implementation in practice of the offending agreements or practices,
— termination of the infringement as soon as the Commission intervenes (in particular when it carries out checks),
— existence of reasonable doubt on the part of the undertaking as to whether the restrictive conduct does indeed constitute an infringement,
— infringements committed as a result of negligence or unintentionally,
— effective cooperation by the undertaking in the proceedings, outside the scope of the Notice of 18 July 1996 on the non-imposition or reduction of fines in cartel cases,
— other.

Commentary
point 3: F&N: 8.708, 8.709

4. Application of the Notice of 18 July 1996 on the non-imposition or reduction of fines [7]

Notes
[7] See footnote 6.

Commentary
point 4: F&N: 8.784

5. General comments

(a) It goes without saying that the final amount calculated according to this method (basic amount increased or reduced on a percentage basis) may not in any case exceed 10% of the worldwide turnover of the undertakings, as laid down by Article 15(2) of Regulation No 17. In the case of agreements which are illegal under the ECSC Treaty, the limit laid down by Article 65(5) is twice the turnover on the products in question, increased in certain cases to a maximum of 10% of the undertaking's turnover on ECSC products.
    The accounting year on the basis of which the worldwide turnover is determined must, as far as possible, be the one preceding the year in which the decision is taken or, if figures are not available for that accounting year, the one immediately preceding it.
(b) Depending on the circumstances, account should be taken, once the above calculations have been made, of certain objective factors such as a specific economic context, any economic or financial benefit derived by the offenders (see Twenty-first report on competition policy, point 139), the specific characteristics of the undertakings in question and their real ability to pay in a specific social context, and the fines should be adjusted accordingly.
(c) In cases involving associations of undertakings, decisions should as far as possible be addressed to and fines imposed on the individual undertakings belonging to the association. If this is not possible (e.g. where there are several thousands of affiliated undertakings), and except for cases falling within the ECSC Treaty, an overall fine should be imposed on the association, calculated according to the principles outlined above but equivalent to the total of individual fines which might have been imposed on each of the members of the association.
(d) The Commission will also reserve the right, in certain cases, to impose a "symbolic" fine of ECU 1 000, which would not involve any calculation based on the duration of the infringement or any aggravating or attenuating circumstances. The justification for imposing such a fine should be given in the text of the decision.

Commentary
point 5(b): F&N: 8.785, 8.786, 8.787, 8.788, 8.793

B6

COMMISSION NOTICE ON IMMUNITY FROM FINES AND REDUCTION OF FINES IN CARTEL CASES

(2002/C 45/03)

(Text with EEA relevance)

Official Journal C 45, 19.2.2002, p. 3

Celex No: 52002XC0219(02)

Notes

EEA application: the EFTA Surveillance Authority has adopted a parallel notice on immunity from fines and reduction of fines in cartel cases under Article 5(2)(b) of the Surveillance and Court Agreement: OJ C 10, 16.1.2003, p. 13 and EEA Supplement OJ No 3, 16.1.2003, p. 1.

Commentary

Notice: **B&C:** 13.182, 13.192 **F&N:** 8.107, 8.111, 8.112, 8.118, 8.126, 8.134, 8.136, 8.137, 8.149, 8.154, 8.156, 8.157, 8.159, 8.160, 8.164, 8.166, 8.170, 8.174, 8.177, 8.186, 8.187, 8.190, 8.191, 8.192, 8.196, 8.198, 8.208, 8.211, 8.216, 8.222, 8.248, 8.255, 8.328, 8.488, 8.511, 8.578, 8.757, 8.782, 8.783, 8.784, 8.811
section A: **F&N:** 8.137, 8.178
section B: **F&N:** 8.138, 8.149, 8.154, 8.178, 8.180, 8.189, 8.198, 8.207, 8.327, 8.546, 8.758

INTRODUCTION

1. This notice concerns secret cartels between two or more competitors aimed at fixing prices, production or sales quotas, sharing markets including bid-rigging or restricting imports or exports. Such practices are among the most serious restrictions of competition encountered by the Commission and ultimately result in increased prices and reduced choice for the consumer. They also harm European industry.

Commentary
point 1: **F&N:** 8.166

---

2. By artificially limiting the competition that would normally prevail between them, undertakings avoid exactly those pressures that lead them to innovate, both in terms of product development and the introduction of more efficient production methods. Such practices also lead to more expensive raw materials and components for the Community companies that purchase from such producers. In the long term, they lead to a loss of competitiveness and reduced employment opportunities.

3. The Commission is aware that certain undertakings involved in this type of illegal agreements are willing to put an end to their participation and inform it of the existence of such agreements, but are dissuaded from doing so by the high fines to which they are potentially exposed. In order to clarify its position in this type of situation, the Commission adopted a notice on the non-imposition or reduction of fines in cartel cases,[1] hereafter "the 1996 notice."

Notes
[1] OJ C 207, 18.7.1996, p. 4.

---

4. The Commission considered that it is in the Community interest to grant favourable treatment to undertakings which cooperate with it. The interests of consumers and citizens in ensuring that secret cartels are detected and punished outweigh the interest in fining those undertakings that enable the Commission to detect and prohibit such practices.

5. In the 1996 notice, the Commission announced that it would examine whether it was necessary to modify the notice once it had acquired sufficient experience in applying it. After five years of implementation, the Commission has the experience necessary to modify its policy in this matter. Whilst the validity of the principles governing the notice has been confirmed, experience has shown that its effectiveness would be improved by an increase in the transparency and certainty of the conditions on which any reduction of fines will be granted. A closer alignment between the level of reduction of fines and the value of a company's contribution to establishing the infringement could also increase this effectiveness. This notice addresses these issues.

6. The Commission considers that the collaboration of an undertaking in the detection of the existence of a cartel has an intrinsic value. A decisive contribution to the opening of an investigation or to the finding of an infringement may justify the granting of immunity from any fine to the undertaking in question, on condition that certain additional requirements are fulfilled.

7. Moreover, cooperation by one or more undertakings may justify a reduction of a fine by the Commission. Any reduction of a fine must reflect an undertaking's actual contribution, in terms of quality and timing, to the Commission's establishment of the infringement. Reductions are to be limited to those undertakings that provide the Commission with evidence that adds significant value to that already in the Commission's possession.

A. Immunity from Fines

8. The Commission will grant an undertaking immunity from any fine which would otherwise have been imposed if:

   (a) the undertaking is the first to submit evidence which in the Commission's view may enable it to adopt a decision to carry out an investigation in the sense of Article 14(3) of Regulation No 17[2] in connection with an alleged cartel affecting the Community; or

   (b) the undertaking is the first to submit evidence which in the Commission's view may enable it to find an infringement of Article 81 EC[3] in connection with an alleged cartel affecting the Community.

Notes

[2] OJ 13, 21.2.1962, p. 204/62. (Or the equivalent procedural regulations: Article 21(3) of Regulation (EEC) No 1017/68 of the Council; Article 18(3) of Council Regulation (EEC) No 4056/86 and Article 11(3) of Council Regulation (EEC) No 3975/87.)

[3] Reference in this text to Article 81 EC also covers Article 53 EEA when applied by the Commission according to the rules laid down in Article 56 of the EEA Agreement.

Commentary

point 8: F&N: 8.138
point 8(a): F&N: 8.138, 8.139, 8.144, 8.154, 8.167, 8.172, 8.173, 8.174, 8.189
point 8(b): F&N: 8.138, 8.143, 8.144, 8.154, 8.167, 8.170, 8.172, 8.189

---

9. Immunity pursuant to point 8(a) will only be granted on the condition that the Commission did not have, at the time of the submission, sufficient evidence to adopt a decision to carry out an investigation in the sense of Article 14(3) of Regulation No 17 in connection with the alleged cartel.

10. Immunity pursuant to point 8(b) will only be granted on the cumulative conditions that the Commission did not have, at the time of the submission, sufficient evidence to find an infringement of Article 81 EC in connection with the alleged cartel and that no undertaking had been granted conditional immunity from fines under point 8(a) in connection with the alleged cartel.

11. In addition to the conditions set out in points 8(a) and 9 or in points 8(b) and 10, as appropriate, the following cumulative conditions must be met in any case to qualify for any immunity from a fine:

   (a) the undertaking cooperates fully, on a continuous basis and expeditiously throughout the Commission's administrative procedure and provides the Commission with all evidence that comes into its possession or is available to it relating to the suspected infringement. In particular, it remains at the Commission's disposal to answer swiftly any request that may contribute to the establishment of the facts concerned;

(b) the undertaking ends its involvement in the suspected infringement no later than the time at which it submits evidence under points 8(a) or 8(b), as appropriate;

(c) the undertaking did not take steps to coerce other undertakings to participate in the infringement.

Commentary
point 11: F&N: 8.170
point 11(a): F&N: 8.145, 8.148, 8.536
point 11(b): F&N: 8.150
point 11(c): F&N: 8.153

Procedure

12. An undertaking wishing to apply for immunity from fines should contact the Commission's Directorate-General for Competition. Should it become apparent that the requirements set out in points 8 to 10, as appropriate, are not met, the undertaking will immediately be informed that immunity from fines is not available for the suspected infringement.

Commentary
point 12: F&N: 8.154

13. If immunity from fines is available for a suspected infringement, the undertaking may, in order to meet conditions 8(a) or 8(b), as appropriate:

(a) immediately provide the Commission with all the evidence relating to the suspected infringement available to it at the time of the submission; or

(b) initially present this evidence in hypothetical terms, in which case the undertaking must present a descriptive list of the evidence it proposes to disclose at a later agreed date. This list should accurately reflect the nature and content of the evidence, whilst safeguarding the hypothetical nature of its disclosure. Expurgated copies of documents, from which sensitive parts have been removed, may be used to illustrate the nature and content of the evidence.

Commentary
point 13(b): F&N: 8.159

14. The Directorate-General for Competition will provide a written acknowledgement of the undertaking's application for immunity from fines, confirming the date on which the undertaking either submitted evidence under 13(a) or presented to the Commission the descriptive list referred to in 13(b).

15. Once the Commission has received the evidence submitted by the undertaking under point 13(a) and has verified that it meets the conditions set out in points 8(a) or 8(b), as appropriate, it will grant the undertaking conditional immunity from fines in writing.

16. Alternatively, the Commission will verify that the nature and content of the evidence described in the list referred to in point 13(b) will meet the conditions set out in points 8(a) or 8(b), as appropriate, and inform the undertaking accordingly. Following the disclosure of the evidence no later than on the date agreed and having verified that it corresponds to the description made in the list, the Commission will grant the undertaking conditional immunity from fines in writing.

Commentary
point 16: F&N: 8.159

17. An undertaking which fails to meet the conditions set out in points 8(a) or 8(b), as appropriate, may withdraw the evidence disclosed for the purposes of its immunity application or request the Commission to consider it under section B of this notice. This does not prevent the Commission from using its normal powers of investigation in order to obtain the information.

Commentary
point 17: F&N: 8.154

18. The Commission will not consider other applications for immunity from fines before it has taken a position on an existing application in relation to the same suspected infringement.

Commentary
point 18: F&N: 8.162

19. If at the end of the administrative procedure, the undertaking has met the conditions set out in point 11, the Commission will grant it immunity from fines in the relevant decision.

B. Reduction of a Fine

20. Undertakings that do not meet the conditions under section A above may be eligible to benefit from a reduction of any fine that would otherwise have been imposed.
21. In order to qualify, an undertaking must provide the Commission with evidence of the suspected infringement which represents significant added value with respect to the evidence already in the Commission's possession and must terminate its involvement in the suspected infringement no later than the time at which it submits the evidence.

Commentary
point 21: F&N: 8.198

22. The concept of "added value" refers to the extent to which the evidence provided strengthens, by its very nature and/or its level of detail, the Commission's ability to prove the facts in question. In this assessment, the Commission will generally consider written evidence originating from the period of time to which the facts pertain to have a greater value than evidence subsequently established. Similarly, evidence directly relevant to the facts in question will generally be considered to have a greater value than that with only indirect relevance.

Commentary
point 22: F&N: 8.180, 8.184, 8.191, 8.199, 8.204, 8.205, 8.260, 8.488, 8.511

23. The Commission will determine in any final decision adopted at the end of the administrative procedure:
    (a) whether the evidence provided by an undertaking represented significant added value with respect to the evidence in the Commission's possession at that same time;
    (b) the level of reduction an undertaking will benefit from, relative to the fine which would otherwise have been imposed, as follows. For the:
       — first undertaking to meet point 21: a reduction of 30–50%,
       — second undertaking to meet point 21: a reduction of 20–30%,
       — subsequent undertakings that meet point 21: a reduction of up to 20%.

    In order to determine the level of reduction within each of these bands, the Commission will take into account the time at which the evidence fulfilling the condition in point 21 was submitted and the extent to which it represents added value. It may also take into account the extent and continuity of any cooperation provided by the undertaking following the date of its submission.

    In addition, if an undertaking provides evidence relating to facts previously unknown to the Commission which have a direct bearing on the gravity or duration of the suspected cartel, the Commission will not take these elements into account when setting any fine to be imposed on the undertaking which provided this evidence.

Commentary
point 23: F&N: 8.179, 8.182, 8.196, 8.327, 8.488, 8.511, 8.757
point 23(b): F&N: 8.182, 8.184, 8.185, 8.186, 8.191, 8.208

Procedure

24. An undertaking wishing to benefit from a reduction of a fine should provide the Commission with evidence of the cartel in question.

25. The undertaking will receive an acknowledgement of receipt from the Directorate-General for Competition recording the date on which the relevant evidence was submitted. The Commission will not consider any submissions of evidence by an applicant for a reduction of a fine before it has taken a position on any existing application for a conditional immunity from fines in relation to the same suspected infringement.

Commentary
point 25: **F&N:** 8.188

26. If the Commission comes to the preliminary conclusion that the evidence submitted by the undertaking constitutes added value within the meaning of point 22, it will inform the undertaking in writing, no later than the date on which a statement of objections is notified, of its intention to apply a reduction of a fine within a specified band as provided in point 23(b).

Commentary
point 26: **F&N:** 8.184, 8.185, 8.186, 8.190

27. The Commission will evaluate the final position of each undertaking which filed an application for a reduction of a fine at the end of the administrative procedure in any decision adopted.

GENERAL CONSIDERATIONS

28. From 14 February 2002, this notice replaces the 1996 notice for all cases in which no undertaking has contacted the Commission in order to take advantage of the favourable treatment set out in that notice. The Commission will examine whether it is necessary to modify this notice once it has acquired sufficient experience in applying it.

Commentary
point 28: **F&N:** 8.112

29. The Commission is aware that this notice will create legitimate expectations on which undertakings may rely when disclosing the existence of a cartel to the Commission.

30. Failure to meet any of the requirements set out in sections A or B, as the case may be, at any stage of the administrative procedure may result in the loss of any favourable treatment set out therein.

31. In line with the Commission's practice, the fact that an undertaking cooperated with the Commission during its administrative procedure will be indicated in any decision, so as to explain the reason for the immunity or reduction of the fine. The fact that immunity or reduction in respect of fines is granted cannot protect an undertaking from the civil law consequences of its participation in an infringement of Article 81 EC.

32. The Commission considers that normally disclosure, at any time, of documents received in the context of this notice would undermine the protection of the purpose of inspections and investigations within the meaning of Article 4(2) of Regulation (EC) No 1049/2001 of the European Parliament and of the Council.

Commentary
point 32: **F&N:** 8.220

33. Any written statement made vis-à-vis the Commission in relation to this notice, forms part of the Commission's file. It may not be disclosed or used for any other purpose than the enforcement of Article 81 EC.

Commentary
point 33: **F&N:** 8.160, 8.215, 8.216, 8.458

B7

JOINT STATEMENT OF THE COUNCIL AND THE COMMISSION ON THE FUNCTIONING OF THE NETWORK OF COMPETITION AUTHORITIES

Notes
Date of document: 10 December 2002
This document is available from the website of the Council of the European Union at the following address:
<http://register.consilium.europa.eu/pdf/en/02/st15/15435-a1en2.pdf>

Commentary
Statement: B&C: 1.061, 13.018

"STATEMENTS TO BE ENTERED IN THE COUNCIL MINUTES:

JOINT STATEMENT OF THE COUNCIL AND THE COMMISSION ON THE FUNCTIONING OF THE NETWORK OF COMPETITION AUTHORITIES"

"1. The today adopted Regulation on the implementation of the rules on competition laid down in Articles 81 and 82 of the Treaty establishes a directly applicable exception system in which the competition authorities and courts of the Member States, along with the Commission, have the power to apply not only Articles 81(1) and 82 of the Treaty, which have direct applicability by virtue of the case-law of the Court of Justice of the European Communities, but also Article 81(3) of the Treaty.

2. In order to ensure that the Community competition rules are applied effectively and consistently, the Commission and the national competition authorities designated by the Member States (hereafter NCAs) form together a network of competition authorities (hereafter the Network) for the application in close cooperation of Articles 81 and 82 of the Treaty.

3. This Joint Statement is political in nature and does therefore not create any legal rights or obligations. It is limited to setting out common political understanding shared by all Member States and the Commission on the principles of the functioning of the Network.

Commentary
para 3: B&C: 13.021

4. Details will be set out in a Commission notice which will be drafted and updated as necessary in close cooperation with Member States.

General principles

5. The cooperation within the Network is dedicated to the effective enforcement of EC competition rules throughout the Community.

6. Decentralization of the implementation of Community competition rules strengthens the position of the NCAs. These will be fully competent to apply Article 81 and 82 of the Treaty, actively contributing to the development of competition policy, law and practice.

7. All competition authorities within the Network are independent from one another. Cooperation between NCAs and with the Commission takes place on the basis of equality, respect and solidarity.

8. Member States accept that their enforcement systems differ but nonetheless mutually recognize the standards of each other's system as a basis for cooperation.

9. The Commission, as the guardian of the Treaty, has the ultimate but not the sole responsibility for developing policy and safeguarding efficiency and consistency. Therefore, the instruments of the

Commission on the one hand and of the NCAs on the other hand are not identical. The additional powers the Commission has been granted to fulfil its responsibilities will be exercised with the utmost regard for the cooperative nature of the Network.

10. Cooperation within the Network and the management of information will be as efficient as possible. All members of the Network will minimize the administrative burden of participating in the Network on the understanding that any information exchanged under Article 11 of the Regulation will be made available and easily accessible to all Network members.

Division of work

11. Without prejudice to Article 11(6) of the Regulation, all Network members have full parallel competence to apply Articles 81 and 82 of the Treaty.
12. Case allocation will be completed as quickly as possible. An indicative time limit (up to 3 months) will be used within the Network. Normally, this allocation will remain definitive to the end of the proceedings provided that the facts known about the case remain substantially the same. If so, this implies that the competition authority which has notified the case to the Network, will normally remain the responsible competition authority if it is well placed to deal with the case and no other competition authority raises objections during the indicative time period.

Commentary
para 12: B&C: 13.018

13. All members of the Network will endeavour to make allocation a predictable process with business and other interested parties receiving guidance as to where to direct complaints.
14. Members of the Network will ensure that those cases which merit a detailed investigation by a competition authority are adequately allocated and assessed. This principle does not prejudice the discretion of all Network members to decide whether or not to investigate a case.

Authority (-ies) well placed to act

15. Members of the Network will ensure an effective enforcement of Articles 81 and 82 of the Treaty. Cases will be dealt with by an authority, or by authorities, able to restore or maintain competition in the market. To that effect, the members of the Network will take into account all relevant factors in particular in which markets the main anti-competitive effects are felt and which authority is most able to deal with a case successfully depending on the ability of the authority to gather evidence, to bring the infringement to an end and to apply sanctions effectively.
16. Cases will be dealt with by a single competition authority as often as possible. A single NCA will be usually well placed to act if only one Member State is substantially affected by an agreement or practice, particularly when the main anti-competitive effects appear in the same Member State and all participating companies to an agreement or an abusive behaviour have their seat in that Member State.
17. Where an agreement or practice substantially affects competition in more than one Member State, the Network members will seek to agree between them who is best placed to deal with the case successfully.
18. In cases where single action is not possible (when competition in several Member States is affected and no NCA can deal with the case alone successfully), the Network members should coordinate their action and seek to designate one competition authority as the lead institution.
19. The Commission will be particularly well placed to deal with a case if more than three Member States are substantially affected by an agreement or practice, if it is closely linked to other Community provisions which may be exclusively or more effectively applied by the Commission, if Community interest requires the adoption of a Commission decision to develop Community competition policy particularly when a new competition issue arises or to ensure effective enforcement.

Consistent application of Community competition rules

20. After the initial allocation period, when the same case (same market, same parties, same conduct/agreement) is being dealt with by more than one NCA well placed to do so, one national

competition authority will take a formal decision, whilst others stay their proceedings or, if this is not possible, the NCAs will deal with the case in close cooperation.

21. After the initial allocation period, when a case is being dealt with by one or several competition authority (-ies) which is (are) well placed to do so, the Commission will normally not open proceedings with the effects of relieving them of their competence pursuant to Article 11(6) of the Regulation unless one of the following situations arises:

(a) Network members envisage conflicting decisions in the same case;

(b) Network members envisage a decision which is obviously in conflict with consolidated case law; the standards defined in the judgements of the Community courts and in previous decisions and regulations of the Commission should serve as a yardstick; concerning facts, only a significant divergence will trigger an intervention of the Commission;

(c) Network member(s) is (are) unduly drawing out proceedings;

(d) There is a need to adopt a Commission decision to develop Community competition policy in particular when a similar competition issue arises in several Member States;

(e) The national competition authority does not object.

Should the Commission decide to open proceedings with the effects of Article 11(6) of the Regulation, it will do so as soon as possible.

22. If an NCA is already acting on a case, the Commission will explain the reasons for the application of Article 11(6) of the Regulation in writing to the NCA concerned and to the other members of the Network.

23. The Commission will normally not—and to the extent that Community interest is not at stake—adopt a decision which is in conflict with a decision of an NCA after proper information pursuant to both Article 11(3) and (4) of the Regulation has been provided and the Commission has made no use of Article 11(6) of the Regulation.

24. Network members will inform the other members of the Network about rejections of complaints and the termination of investigations on all cases which have been notified within the Network pursuant to Article 11(2) and 11(3) of the Regulation."

STATEMENT BY THE COMMISSION

"The today adopted Regulation establishes a directly applicable exception system. It is without prejudice to the ability of the Commission to issue informal guidance to individual undertakings seeking it, where individual cases give rise to genuine uncertainty because they present novel or unresolved questions for the application of Articles 81 or 82.

The Commission is prepared to issue a Notice which sets out the circumstances under which guidance in the form of written opinions could be provided. The Commission shall have no obligation to provide guidance in any individual case."

STATEMENT BY THE GERMAN DELEGATION ON ARTICLE 2 OF THE REGULATION

"With a view to supplementing in particular recital 5 of this Regulation, the Government of the Federal Republic of Germany confirms its view that Article 83 of the Treaty is not a sufficient legal basis for introducing or amending criminal law or criminal procedural law provisions. This applies in particular to fundamental procedural safeguards in criminal proceedings such as the presumption of innocence on the part of the defendant. The Government of the Federal Republic of Germany would point out that these procedural safeguards also apply to criminal-law-related proceedings such as monetary fine proceedings and enjoy constitutional status. It accordingly assumes that the present Regulation, and in particular Article 2 thereof, cannot amend or adversely affect such criminal law or criminal procedural law provisions applicable to criminal proceedings or criminal-law-related proceedings and legal principles of the Member States."

B8

COMMISSION NOTICE ON COOPERATION WITHIN THE NETWORK OF COMPETITION AUTHORITIES

(2004/C 101/03)

(Text with EEA relevance)

Official Journal C 101, 27.4.2004, p. 43

Celex No: 52004XC0427(02)

Notes

EEA application: the EFTA Surveillance Authority has adopted a parallel notice on cooperation within the EFTA Network of Competition Authorities under Article 5(2)(b) of the Surveillance and Court Agreement: OJ C 227, 12.9.2006, p. 7 and EEA Supplement No 47, 21.9.2006, p. 1.

Commentary

Notice: **B&C:** 1.060-1.061, 7.017, 13.195, 14.012, 14.017, 14.060, 15.111 **F&N:** 2.11, 2.148, 2.168, 2.228, 2.229, 2.230, 8.99, 8.236, 8.239, 8.240, 8.243, 8.244, 8.246, 8.520, 12.66

1. INTRODUCTION

1. Council Regulation (EC) No 1/2003 of 16 December 2002 on the implementation of the rules on competition laid down in Articles 81 and 82 of the Treaty[1] (hereafter the "Council Regulation") creates a system of parallel competences in which the Commission and the Member States' competition authorities (hereafter the "NCAs")[2] can apply Article 81 and Article 82 of the EC Treaty (hereafter the "Treaty"). Together the NCAs and the Commission form a network of public authorities: they act in the public interest and cooperate closely in order to protect competition. The network is a forum for discussion and cooperation in the application and enforcement of EC competition policy. It provides a framework for the cooperation of European competition authorities in cases where Articles 81 and 82 of the Treaty are applied and is the basis for the creation and maintenance of a common competition culture in Europe. The network is called "European Competition Network" (ECN).

Notes

[1] OJ L 1, 4.1.2003, p. 1.
[2] In this notice, the European Commission and the NCAs are collectively referred to as "the competition authorities".

2. The structure of the NCAs varies between Member States. In some Member States, one body investigates cases and takes all types of decisions. In other Member States, the functions are divided between two bodies, one which is in charge of the investigation of the case and another, often a college, which is responsible for deciding the case. Finally, in certain Member States, prohibition decisions and/or decisions imposing a fine can only be taken by a court: another competition authority acts as a prosecutor bringing the case before that court. Subject to the general principle of effectiveness, Article 35 of the Council Regulation allows Member States to choose the body or bodies which will be designated as national competition authorities and to allocate functions between them. Under general principles of Community law, Member States are under an obligation to set up a sanctioning system providing for sanctions which are effective, proportionate and dissuasive for

113

infringements of EC law.[3] The enforcement systems of the Member States differ but they have recognised the standards of each other"s systems as a basis for cooperation.[4]

Notes
[3] Cf. ECJ Case 68/88 *Commission v Greece* [1989] ECR 2965 (Recitals 23 to 25).
[4] See paragraph 8 of the Joint Statement of the Council and the Commission on the functioning of the network available from the Council register at http://register.consilium.eu.int (document No 15435/02 ADD 1).

Commentary
para 2: B&C: 14.013

3. The network formed by the competition authorities should ensure both an efficient division of work and an effective and consistent application of EC competition rules. The Council Regulation together with the joint statement of the Council and the Commission on the functioning of the European Competition Network sets out the main principles of the functioning of the network. This notice presents the details of the system.

4. Consultations and exchanges within the network are matters between public enforcers and do not alter any rights or obligations arising from Community or national law for companies. Each competition authority remains fully responsible for ensuring due process in the cases it deals with.

2. DIVISION OF WORK

2.1 Principles of allocation

5. The Council Regulation is based on a system of parallel competences in which all competition authorities have the power to apply Articles 81 or 82 of the Treaty and are responsible for an efficient division of work with respect to those cases where an investigation is deemed to be necessary. At the same time each network member retains full discretion in deciding whether or not to investigate a case. Under this system of parallel competences, cases will be dealt with by:

— a single NCA, possibly with the assistance of NCAs of other Member States; or
— several NCAs acting in parallel; or
— the Commission.

Commentary
para 5: F&N: 2.150, 2.151

6. In most instances the authority that receives a complaint or starts an *ex-officio* procedure[5] will remain in charge of the case. Re-allocation of a case would only be envisaged at the outset of a procedure (see paragraph 18 below) where either that authority considered that it was not well placed to act or where other authorities also considered themselves well placed to act (see paragraphs 8 to 15 below).

Notes
[5] In this Notice the term "procedure" is used for investigations and/or formal proceedings for the adoption of a decision pursuant to the Council Regulation conducted by an NCA or the Commission, as the case may be.

7. Where re-allocation is found to be necessary for an effective protection of competition and of the Community interest, network members will endeavour to re-allocate cases to a single well placed competition authority as often as possible.[6] In any event, re-allocation should be a quick and efficient process and not hold up ongoing investigations.

Notes
[6] See Recital 18 of the Council Regulation.

8. An authority can be considered to be well placed to deal with a case if the following three cumulative conditions are met:

1. the agreement or practice has substantial direct actual or foreseeable effects on competition within its territory, is implemented within or originates from its territory;

2. the authority is able to effectively bring to an end the entire infringement, i.e. it can adopt a cease-and-desist order the effect of which will be sufficient to bring an end to the infringement and it can, where appropriate, sanction the infringement adequately;

3. it can gather, possibly with the assistance of other authorities, the evidence required to prove the infringement.

Commentary
para 8: **F&N:** 2.151

9. The above criteria indicate that a material link between the infringement and the territory of a Member State must exist in order for that Member State's competition authority to be considered well placed. It can be expected that in most cases the authorities of those Member States where competition is substantially affected by an infringement will be well placed provided they are capable of effectively bringing the infringement to an end through either single or parallel action unless the Commission is better placed to act (see below paragraphs 14 and 15).

10. It follows that a single NCA is usually well placed to deal with agreements or practices that substantially affect competition mainly within its territory.

> Example 1: *Undertakings situated in Member State A are involved in a price fixing cartel on products that are mainly sold in Member State A.*
>
> *The NCA in A is well placed to deal with the case.*

11. Furthermore single action of an NCA might also be appropriate where, although more than one NCA can be regarded as well placed, the action of a single NCA is sufficient to bring the entire infringement to an end.

> Example 2: *Two undertakings have set up a joint venture in Member State A. The joint venture provides services in Member States A and B and gives rise to a competition problem. A cease-and-desist order is considered to be sufficient to deal with the case effectively because it can bring an end to the entire infringement. Evidence is located mainly at the offices of the joint venture in Member State A.*
>
> *The NCAs in A and B are both well placed to deal with the case but single action by the NCA in A would be sufficient and more efficient than single action by NCA in B or parallel action by both NCAs.*

12. Parallel action by two or three NCAs may be appropriate where an agreement or practice has substantial effects on competition mainly in their respective territories and the action of only one NCA would not be sufficient to bring the entire infringement to an end and/or to sanction it adequately.

> Example 3: *Two undertakings agree on a market sharing agreement, restricting the activity of the company located in Member State A to Member State A and the activity of the company located in Member State B to Member State B.*
>
> *The NCAs in A and B are well placed to deal with the case in parallel, each one for its respective territory.*

Commentary
para 12: **F&N:** 2.151

13. The authorities dealing with a case in parallel action will endeavour to coordinate their action to the extent possible. To that effect, they may find it useful to designate one of them as a lead authority and to delegate tasks to the lead authority such as for example the coordination of investigative measures, while each authority remains responsible for conducting its own proceedings.

14. The Commission is particularly well placed if one or several agreement(s) or practice(s), including networks of similar agreements or practices, have effects on competition in more than three Member States (cross-border markets covering more than three Member States or several national markets).

Commentary
para 14: **B&C:** 13.196 **F&N:** 2.151, 8.99, 8.245, 8.246

> Example 4: *Two undertakings agree to share markets or fix prices for the whole territory of the Community. The Commission is well placed to deal with the case.*

> Example 5: *An undertaking, dominant in four different national markets, abuses its position by imposing fidelity rebates on its distributors in all these markets. The Commission is well placed to deal with the case. It could also deal with one national market so as to create a "leading"case and other national markets could be dealt with by NCAs, particularly if each national market requires a separate assessment.*

15. Moreover, the Commission is particularly well placed to deal with a case if it is closely linked to other Community provisions which may be exclusively or more effectively applied by the Commission, if the Community interest requires the adoption of a Commission decision to develop Community competition policy when a new competition issue arises or to ensure effective enforcement.

Commentary
para 15: **F&N:** 2.151

2.2. Mechanisms of cooperation for the purpose of case allocation and assistance

2.2.1. Information at the beginning of the procedure (Article 11 of the Council Regulation)

16. In order to detect multiple procedures and to ensure that cases are dealt with by a well placed competition authority, the members of the network have to be informed at an early stage of the cases pending before the various competition authorities.[7] If a case is to be re-allocated, it is indeed in the best interest both of the network and of the undertakings concerned that the re-allocation takes place quickly.

Notes
[7] For cases initiated following a leniency application see paragraphs 37 *et subseq.*

---

17. The Council Regulation creates a mechanism for the competition authorities to inform each other in order to ensure an efficient and quick re-allocation of cases. Article 11(3) of the Council Regulation lays down an obligation for NCAs to inform the Commission when acting under Article 81 or 82 of the Treaty before or without delay after commencing the first formal investigative measure. It also states that the information may be made available to other NCAs.[8] The rationale of Article 11(3) of the Council Regulation is to allow the network to detect multiple procedures and address possible case re-allocation issues as soon as an authority starts investigating a case. Information should therefore be provided to NCAs and the Commission before or just after any step similar to the measures of investigation that can be undertaken by the Commission under Articles 18 to 21 of the Council Regulation. The Commission has accepted an equivalent obligation to inform NCAs under Article 11(2) of the Council Regulation. Network members will inform each other of pending cases by means of a standard form containing limited details of the case, such as the authority dealing with the case, the product, territories and parties concerned, the alleged infringement, the suspected duration of the infringement and the origin of the case. They will also provide each other with updates when a relevant change occurs.

Commentary
para 17: B&C: 14.018 F&N: 2.151

18. Where case re-allocation issues arise, they should be resolved swiftly, normally within a period of two months, starting from the date of the first information sent to the network pursuant to Article 11 of the Council Regulation. During this period, competition authorities will endeavour to reach an agreement on a possible re-allocation and, where relevant, on the modalities for parallel action.
19. In general, the competition authority or authorities that is/are dealing with a case at the end of the re-allocation period should continue to deal with the case until the completion of the proceedings. Re-allocation of a case after the initial allocation period of two months should only occur where the facts known about the case change materially during the course of the proceedings.

2.2.2. Suspension or termination of proceedings (Article 13 of the Council Regulation)

20. If the same agreement or practice is brought before several competition authorities, be it because they have received a complaint or have opened a procedure on their own initiative, Article 13 of the Council Regulation provides a legal basis for suspending proceedings or rejecting a complaint on the grounds that another authority is dealing with the case or has dealt with the case. In Article 13 of the Council Regulation, "dealing with the case" does not merely mean that a complaint has been lodged with another authority. It means that the other authority is investigating or has investigated the case on its own behalf.

Commentary
para 20: B&C: 14.017 F&N: 2.153

21. Article 13 of the Council Regulation applies when another authority has dealt or is dealing with the competition issue raised by the complainant, even if the authority in question has acted or acts on the basis of a complaint lodged by a different complainant or as a result of an *ex-officio* procedure. This implies that Article 13 of the Council Regulation can be invoked when the agreement or practice involves the same infringement(s) on the same relevant geographic and product markets.

Commentary
para 21: F&N: 2.153

22. An NCA may suspend or close its proceedings but it has no obligation to do so. Article 13 of the Council Regulation leaves scope for appreciation of the peculiarities of each individual case. This flexibility is important: if a complaint was rejected by an authority following an investigation of the substance of the case, another authority may not want to re-examine the case. On the other hand, if a complaint was rejected for other reasons (e.g. the authority was unable to collect the evidence necessary to prove the infringement), another authority may wish to carry out its own investigation and deal with the case. This flexibility is also reflected, for pending cases, in the choice open to each NCA as to whether it closes or suspends its proceedings. An authority may be unwilling to close a case before the outcome of another authority's proceedings is clear. The ability to suspend its proceedings allows the authority to retain its ability to decide at a later point whether or not to terminate its proceedings. Such flexibility also facilitates consistent application of the rules.

Commentary
para 22: F&N: 2.152

23. Where an authority closes or suspends proceedings because another authority is dealing with the case, it may transfer — in accordance with Article 12 of the Council Regulation — the information provided by the complainant to the authority which is to deal with the case.

24. Article 13 of the Council Regulation can also be applied to part of a complaint or to part of the proceedings in a case. It may be that only part of a complaint or of an *ex-officio* procedure overlaps with a case already dealt or being dealt with by another competition authority. In that case, the competition authority to which the complaint is brought is entitled to reject part of the complaint on the basis of Article 13 of the Council Regulation and to deal with the rest of the complaint in an appropriate manner. The same principle applies to the termination of proceedings.

Commentary
para 24: B&C: 14.017 F&N: 2.152

25. Article 13 of the Council Regulation is not the only legal basis for suspending or closing *ex-officio* proceedings or rejecting complaints. NCAs may also be able to do so according to their national procedural law. The Commission may also reject a complaint for lack of Community interest or other reasons pertaining to the nature of the complaint.[9]

Notes
[9] See Commission Notice on complaints.

Commentary
para 25: F&N: 2.152

2.2.3. Exchange and use of confidential information (Article 12 of the Council Regulation)

26. A key element of the functioning of the network is the power of all the competition authorities to exchange and use information (including documents, statements and digital information) which has been collected by them for the purpose of applying Article 81 or Article 82 of the Treaty. This power is a precondition for efficient and effective allocation and handling of cases.

Commentary
para 26: F&N: 2.165, 8.269, 8.437

27. Article 12 of the Council Regulation states that for the purpose of applying Articles 81 and 82 of the Treaty, the Commission and the competition authorities of the Member States shall have the power to provide one another with and use in evidence any matter of fact or of law, including confidential information. This means that exchanges of information may not only take place between an NCA and the Commission but also between and amongst NCAs. Article 12 of the Council Regulation takes precedence over any contrary law of a Member State. The question whether information was gathered in a legal manner by the transmitting authority is governed on the basis of the law applicable to this authority. When transmitting information the transmitting authority may inform the receiving authority whether the gathering of the information was contested or could still be contested.

Commentary
para 27: B&C: 14.022, 14.032 F&N: 2.175, 8.269, 8.437

28. The exchange and use of information contains in particular the following safeguards for undertakings and individuals.
    (a) First, Article 28 of the Council Regulation states that "the Commission and the competition authorities of the Member States, their officials, servants and other persons working under the supervision of these authorities (...) shall not disclose information acquired or exchanged by them pursuant to the" Council Regulation which is "of the kind covered by the obligation of professional secrecy". However, the legitimate interest of undertakings in the protection of their business secrets may not prejudice the disclosure of information necessary to prove an infringement of Articles 81 and 82 of the Treaty. The term "professional secrecy" used in Article 28 of the Council Regulation is a Community law concept and includes in particular business secrets and other confidential information. This will create a common minimum level of protection throughout the Community.

(b) The second safeguard given to undertakings relates to the use of information which has been exchanged within the network. Under Article 12(2) of the Council Regulation, information so exchanged can only be used in evidence for the application of Articles 81 and 82 of the Treaty and for the subject matter for which it was collected.[10] According to Article 12(2) of the Council Regulation, the information exchanged may also be used for the purpose of applying national competition law in parallel in the same case. This is, however, only possible if the application of national law does not lead to an outcome as regards the finding of an infringement different from that under Articles 81 and 82 of the Treaty.

(c) The third safeguard given by the Council Regulation relates to sanctions on individuals on the basis of information exchanged pursuant to Article 12(1). The Council Regulation only provides for sanctions on undertakings for violations of Articles 81 and 82 of the Treaty. Some national laws also provide for sanctions on individuals in connection with violations of Articles 81 and 82 of the Treaty. Individuals normally enjoy more extensive rights of defence (e.g. a right to remain silent compared to undertakings which may only refuse to answer questions which would lead them to admit that they have committed an infringement.[11]) Article 12(3) of the Council Regulation ensures that information collected from undertakings cannot be used in a way which would circumvent the higher protection of individuals. This provision precludes sanctions being imposed on individuals on the basis of information exchanged pursuant to the Council Regulation if the laws of the transmitting and the receiving authorities do not provide for sanctions of a similar kind in respect of individuals, unless the rights of the individual concerned as regards the collection of evidence have been respected by the transmitting authority to the same standard as they are guaranteed by the receiving authority. The qualification of the sanctions by national law ("administrative" or "criminal") is not relevant for the purpose of applying Article 12(3) of the Council Regulation. The Council Regulation intends to create a distinction between sanctions which result in custody and other types of sanctions such as fines on individuals and other personal sanctions. If both the legal system of the transmitting and that of the receiving authority provide for sanctions of a similar kind (e.g. in both Member States, fines can be imposed on a member of the staff of an undertaking who has been involved in the violation of Article 81 or 82 of the Treaty), information exchanged pursuant to Article 12 of the Council Regulation can be used by the receiving authority. In that case, procedural safeguards in both systems are considered to be equivalent. If on the other hand, both legal systems do not provide for sanctions of a similar kind, the information can only be used if the same level of protection of the rights of the individual has been respected in the case at hand (see Article 12(3) of the Council Regulation). In that latter case however, custodial sanctions can only be imposed where both the transmitting and the receiving authority have the power to impose such a sanction.

Notes

[10] See ECJ Case 85/87 *Dow Benelux* [1989] ECR 3137 (Recitals 17–20).

[11] See ECJ Case 374/87 *Orkem* [1989] ECR 3283 and CFI Case T-112/98 *Mannesmannröhren-Werke AG* [2001] ECR II-729.

Commentary

para 28: F&N: 8.269, 8.437
para 28(a): B&C: 14.023
para 28(b): F&N: 2.179
para 28(c): F&N: 2.183, 2.272

2.2.4. Investigations (Article 22 of the Council Regulation)

29. The Council Regulation provides that an NCA may ask another NCA for assistance in order to collect information on its behalf. An NCA can ask another NCA to carry out fact-finding measures on its behalf. Article 12 of the Council Regulation empowers the assisting NCA to transmit the information it has collected to the requesting NCA. Any exchange between or amongst NCAs and use in evidence by the requesting NCA of such information shall be carried out in accordance with Article 12 of the Council Regulation. Where an NCA acts on behalf of another NCA, it acts pursuant to its own rules of procedure, and under its own powers of investigation.

30. Under Article 22(2) of the Council Regulation, the Commission can ask an NCA to carry out an inspection on its behalf. The Commission can either adopt a decision pursuant to Article 20(4) of the Council Regulation or simply issue a request to the NCA. The NCA officials will exercise their powers in accordance with their national law. The agents of the Commission may assist the NCA during the inspection.

2.3. Position of undertakings

2.3.1. General

31. All network members will endeavour to make the allocation of cases a quick and efficient process. Given the fact that the Council Regulation has created a system of parallel competences, the allocation of cases between members of the network constitutes a mere division of labour where some authorities abstain from acting. The allocation of cases therefore does not create individual rights for the companies involved in or affected by an infringement to have the case dealt with by a particular authority.

Commentary
para 31: B&C: 14.014

32. If a case is re-allocated to a given competition authority, it is because the application of the allocation criteria set out above led to the conclusion that this authority is well placed to deal with the case by single or parallel action. The competition authority to which the case is re-allocated would have been in a position, in any event, to commence an *ex-officio* procedure against the infringement.
33. Furthermore, all competition authorities apply Community competition law and the Council Regulation sets out mechanisms to ensure that the rules are applied in a consistent way.
34. If a case is re-allocated within the network, the undertakings concerned and the complainant(s) are informed as soon as possible by the competition authorities involved.

2.3.2. Position of complainants

35. If a complaint is lodged with the Commission pursuant to Article 7 of the Council Regulation and if the Commission does not investigate the complaint or prohibit the agreement or practice complained of, the complainant has a right to obtain a decision rejecting his complaint. This is without prejudice to Article 7(3) of the Commission implementing regulation.[12] The rights of complainants who lodge a complaint with an NCA are governed by the applicable national law.

Notes
[12] Commission Regulation (EC) No 773/2004, OJ L 123, 27.4.2004.

36. In addition, Article 13 of the Council Regulation gives all NCAs the possibility of suspending or rejecting a complaint on the ground that another competition authority is dealing or has dealt with the same case. That provision also allows the Commission to reject a complaint on the ground that a competition authority of a Member State is dealing or has dealt with the case. Article 12 of the Council Regulation allows the transfer of information between competition authorities within the network subject to the safeguards provided in that Article (see paragraph 28 above).

2.3.3. Position of applicants claiming the benefit of a leniency programme

37. The Commission considers[13] that it is in the Community interest to grant favourable treatment to undertakings which co-operate with it in the investigation of cartel infringements. A number of Member States have also adopted leniency programmes[14] relating to cartel investigations. The aim of these leniency programmes is to facilitate the detection by competition authorities of cartel activity and also thereby to act as a deterrent to participation in unlawful cartels.

Notes

[13] OJ C 45, 19.2.2002, p. 3, at paragraph 3.

[14] In this Notice, the term "leniency programme" is used to describe all programmes (including the Commission's programme) which offer either full immunity or a significant reduction in the penalties which would otherwise have been imposed on a participant in a cartel, in exchange for the freely volunteered disclosure of information on the cartel which satisfies specific criteria prior to or during the investigative stage of the case. The term does not cover reductions in the penalty granted for other reasons. The Commission will publish on its website a list of those authorities that operate a leniency programme.

38. In the absence of a European Union-wide system of fully harmonised leniency programmes, an application for leniency to a given authority is not to be considered as an application for leniency to any other authority. It is therefore in the interest of the applicant to apply for leniency to all competition authorities which have competence to apply Article 81 of the Treaty in the territory which is affected by the infringement and which may be considered well placed to act against the infringement in question.[15] In view of the importance of timing in most existing leniency programmes, applicants will also need to consider whether it would be appropriate to file leniency applications with the relevant authorities simultaneously. It is for the applicant to take the steps which it considers appropriate to protect its position with respect to possible proceedings by these authorities.

Notes

[15] See paragraphs 8 to 15 above.

Commentary

para 38: **B&C:** 13.196

39. As for all cases where Articles 81 and 82 of the Treaty are applied, where an NCA deals with a case which has been initiated as a result of a leniency application, it must inform the Commission and may make the information available to other members of the network pursuant to Article 11(3) of the Council Regulation (cf. paragraphs 16 *et subseq.*). The Commission has accepted an equivalent obligation to inform NCAs under Article 11(2) of the Council Regulation. In such cases, however, information submitted to the network pursuant to Article 11 will not be used by other members of the network as the basis for starting an investigation on their own behalf whether under the competition rules of the Treaty or, in the case of NCAs, under their national competition law or other laws.[16] This is without prejudice to any power of the authority to open an investigation on the basis of information received from other sources or, subject to paragraphs 40 and 41 below, to request, be provided with and use information pursuant to Article 12 from any member of the network, including the network member to whom the leniency application was submitted.

Notes

[16] Similarly, information transmitted with a view to obtaining assistance from the receiving authority under Articles 20 or 21 of the Council Regulation or of carrying out an investigation or other fact-finding measure under Article 22 of the Council Regulation may only be used for the purpose of the application of the said Articles.

Commentary

para 39: **B&C:** 14.029 **F&N:** 2.165, 8.239

40. Save as provided under paragraph 41, information voluntarily submitted by a leniency applicant will only be transmitted to another member of the network pursuant to Article 12 of the Council Regulation with the consent of the applicant. Similarly other information that has been obtained during or following an inspection or by means of or following any other fact-finding measures which, in each case, could not have been carried out except as a result of the leniency application will only be transmitted to another authority pursuant to Article 12 of the Council Regulation if the applicant has consented to the transmission to that authority of information it has voluntarily submitted in its application for leniency. The network members will encourage leniency applicants to give such consent, in particular as regards disclosure to authorities in respect of which it would be open to the applicant to obtain lenient treatment. Once the leniency applicant has given consent to the transmission of information to another authority, that consent may not be

withdrawn. This paragraph is without prejudice, however, to the responsibility of each applicant to file leniency applications to whichever authorities it may consider appropriate.

Commentary
para 40: B&C: 14.030-14.031 F&N: 2.165, 2.266, 8.240, 8.250

41. Notwithstanding the above, the consent of the applicant for the transmission of information to another authority pursuant to Article 12 of the Council Regulation is not required in any of the following circumstances:

    1. No consent is required where the receiving authority has also received a leniency application relating to the same infringement from the same applicant as the transmitting authority, provided that at the time the information is transmitted it is not open to the applicant to withdraw the information which it has submitted to that receiving authority.

    2. No consent is required where the receiving authority has provided a written commitment that neither the information transmitted to it nor any other information it may obtain following the date and time of transmission as noted by the transmitting authority, will be used by it or by any other authority to which the information is subsequently transmitted to impose sanctions:

       (a) on the leniency applicant;
       (b) on any other legal or natural person covered by the favourable treatment offered by the transmitting authority as a result of the application made by the applicant under its leniency programme;
       (c) on any employee or former employee of any of the persons covered by (a) or (b).
       A copy of the receiving authority's written commitment will be provided to the applicant.

    3. In the case of information collected by a network member under Article 22(1) of the Council Regulation on behalf of and for the account of the network member to whom the leniency application was made, no consent is required for the transmission of such information to, and its use by, the network member to whom the application was made.

Commentary
para 41: B&C: 14.030-14.031 F&N: 2.165, 2.191, 2.266, 8.240, 8.520
para 41(2): B&C: 14.030 F&N: 2.168

42. Information relating to cases initiated as a result of a leniency application and which has been submitted to the Commission under Article 11(3) of the Council Regulation[17] will only be made available to those NCAs that have committed themselves to respecting the principles set out above (see paragraph 72). The same principle applies where a case has been initiated by the Commission as a result of a leniency application made to the Commission. This does not affect the power of any authority to be provided with information under Article 12 of the Council Regulation, provided however that the provisions of paragraphs 40 and 41 are respected.

Notes
[17] See paragraph 17.

Commentary
para 42: B&C: 14.031

3. Consistent Application of EC Competition Rules[18]

Notes
[18] Article 15 of the Council Regulation empowers NCAs and the Commission to submit written and, with the permission of the Court, oral submissions in court proceedings for the application of Articles 81 and 82 of the Treaty. This is a very important tool for ensuring consistent application of Community rules. In exercising this power NCAs and the Commission will cooperate closely.

3.1. Mechanism of Cooperation (Article 11(4) and 11(5) of the Council Regulation)

43. The Council Regulation pursues the objective that Articles 81 and 82 of the Treaty are applied in a consistent manner throughout the Community. In this respect NCAs will respect the convergence rule contained in Article 3(2) of the Council Regulation. In line with Article 16(2) they cannot — when ruling on agreements, decisions and practices under Article 81 or Article 82 of the Treaty which are already the subject of a Commission decision — take decisions, which would run counter to the decisions adopted by the Commission. Within the network of competition authorities the Commission, as the guardian of the Treaty, has the ultimate but not the sole responsibility for developing policy and safeguarding consistency when it comes to the application of EC competition law.

Commentary
para 43: B&C: 14.060

44. According to Article 11(4) of the Council Regulation, no later than 30 days before the adoption of a decision applying Articles 81 or 82 of the Treaty and requiring that an infringement be brought to an end, accepting commitments or withdrawing the benefit of a block-exemption regulation, NCAs shall inform the Commission. They have to send to the Commission, at the latest 30 days before the adoption of the decision, a summary of the case, the envisaged decision or, in the absence thereof, any other document indicating the proposed course of action.

45. As under Article 11(3) of the Council Regulation, the obligation is to inform the Commission, but the information may be shared by the NCA informing the Commission with the other members of the network

Commentary
para 45: B&C: 14.019

46. Where an NCA has informed the Commission pursuant to Article 11(4) of the Council Regulation and the 30 days deadline has expired, the decision can be adopted as long as the Commission has not initiated proceedings. The Commission may make written observations on the case before the adoption of the decision by the NCA. The NCA and the Commission will make the appropriate efforts to ensure the consistent application of Community law (cf. paragraph 3 above).

47. If special circumstances require that a national decision is taken in less than 30 days following the transmission of information pursuant to Article 11(4) of the Council Regulation, the NCA concerned may ask the Commission for a swifter reaction. The Commission will endeavour to react as quickly as possible.

48. Other types of decisions, i.e. decisions rejecting complaints, decisions closing an *ex-officio* procedure or decisions ordering interim measures, can also be important from a competition policy point of view, and the network members may have an interest in informing each other about them and possibly discussing them. NCAs can therefore on the basis of Article 11(5) of the Council Regulation inform the Commission and thereby inform the network of any other case in which EC competition law is applied.

Commentary
para 48: B&C: 14.019

49. All members of the network should inform each other about the closure of their procedures which have been notified to the network pursuant to Article 11(2) and (3) of the Council Regulation.[19]

Notes
[19] See paragraph 24 of the Joint Statement on the functioning of the network mentioned above in footnote 4.

Commentary
para 49: B&C: 14.019

3.2. The initiation of proceedings by the Commission under Article 11(6) of the Council Regulation

50. According to the case law of the Court of Justice, the Commission, entrusted by Article 85(1) of the Treaty with the task of ensuring the application of the principles laid down in Articles 81 and 82 of the Treaty, is responsible for defining and implementing the orientation of Community competition policy.[20] It can adopt individual decisions under Articles 81 and 82 of the Treaty at any time.

Notes

[20] See ECJ Case C-344/98 *Masterfoods Ltd* [2000] ECR I-11369.

51. Article 11(6) of the Council Regulation states that the initiation by the Commission of proceedings for the adoption of a decision under the Council Regulation shall relieve all NCAs of their competence to apply Articles 81 and 82 of the Treaty. This means that once the Commission has opened proceedings, NCAs cannot act under the same legal basis against the same agreement(s) or practice(s) by the same undertaking(s) on the same relevant geographic and product market.

52. The initiation of proceedings by the Commission is a formal act[21] by which the Commission indicates its intention to adopt a decision under Chapter III of the Council Regulation. It can occur at any stage of the investigation of the case by the Commission. The mere fact that the Commission has received a complaint is not in itself sufficient to relieve NCAs of their competence.

Notes

[21] The ECJ has defined that concept in Case 48/72 *SA Brasserie de Haecht* [1973] ECR 77: "the initiation of a procedure within the meaning of Article 9 of Regulation No 17 implies an authoritative act of the Commission, evidencing its intention of taking a decision."

Commentary

para 52: **B&C:** 14.015, 14.073 **F&N:** 2.221

53. Two situations can arise. First, where the Commission is the first competition authority to initiate proceedings in a case for the adoption of a decision under the Council Regulation, national competition authorities may no longer deal with the case. Article 11(6) of the Council Regulation provides that once the Commission has initiated proceedings, the NCAs can no longer start their own procedure with a view to applying Articles 81 and 82 of the Treaty to the same agreement(s) or practice(s) by the same undertaking(s) on the same relevant geographic and product market.

54. The second situation is where one or more NCAs have informed the network pursuant to Article 11(3) of the Council Regulation that they are acting on a given case. During the initial allocation period (indicative time period of two months, see paragraph 18 above), the Commission can initiate proceedings with the effects of Article 11(6) of the Council Regulation after having consulted the authorities concerned. After the allocation phase, the Commission will in principle only apply Article 11(6) of the Council Regulation if one of the following situations arises:
    (a) Network members envisage conflicting decisions in the same case.
    (b) Network members envisage a decision which is obviously in conflict with consolidated case law; the standards defined in the judgements of the Community courts and in previous decisions and regulations of the Commission should serve as a yardstick; concerning the assessment of the facts (e.g. market definition), only a significant divergence will trigger an intervention of the Commission;
    (c) Network member(s) is (are) unduly drawing out proceedings in the case;
    (d) There is a need to adopt a Commission decision to develop Community competition policy in particular when a similar competition issue arises in several Member States or to ensure effective enforcement;
    (e) The NCA(s) concerned do not object.

Commentary

para 54: **F&N:** 2.230
para 54(b): **B&C:** 14.080

55. If an NCA is already acting on a case, the Commission will explain the reasons for the application of Article 11(6) of the Council Regulation in writing to the NCA concerned and to the other members of the Network.[22]

Notes

[22] See paragraph 22 of the Joint Statement mentioned above in footnote 4.

56. The Commission will announce to the network its intention of applying Article 11(6) of the Council Regulation in due time, so that Network members will have the possibility of asking for a meeting of the Advisory Committee on the matter before the Commission initiates proceedings.

57. The Commission will normally not — and to the extent that Community interest is not at stake — adopt a decision which is in conflict with a decision of an NCA after proper information pursuant to both Article 11(3) and (4) of the Council Regulation has taken place and the Commission has not made use of Article 11(6) of the Council Regulation.

Commentary

para 57: B&C: 14.072

4. The Role and the Functioning of the Advisory Committee in the New System

58. The Advisory Committee is the forum where experts from the various competition authorities discuss individual cases and general issues of Community competition law.[23]

Notes

[23] In accordance with Article 14(2) of the Council Regulation, where horizontal issues such as block-exemption regulations and guidelines are being discussed, Member States can appoint an additional representative competent in competition matters and who does not necessarily belong to the competition authority.

4.1. Scope of the Consultation

4.1.1. Decisions of the Commission

59. The Advisory Committee is consulted prior to the Commission taking any decision pursuant to Articles 7, 8, 9, 10, 23, 24(2) or 29(1) of the Council Regulation. The Commission must take the utmost account of the opinion of the Advisory Committee and inform the Committee of the manner in which its opinion has been taken into account.

60. For decisions adopting interim measures, the Advisory Committee is consulted following a swifter and lighter procedure, on the basis of a short explanatory note and the operative part of the decision.

4.1.2. Decisions of NCAs

61. It is in the interest of the network that important cases dealt with by NCAs under Articles 81 and 82 of the Treaty can be discussed in the Advisory Committee. The Council Regulation enables the Commission to put a given case being dealt with by an NCA on the agenda of the Advisory Committee. Discussion can be requested by the Commission or by any Member State. In either case, the Commission will put the case on the agenda after having informed the NCA(s) concerned. This discussion in the Advisory Committee will not lead to a formal opinion.

62. In important cases, the Advisory Committee could also serve as a forum for the discussion of case allocation. In particular, where the Commission intends to apply Article 11(6) of the Council Regulation after the initial allocation period, the case can be discussed in the Advisory Committee before the Commission initiates proceedings. The Advisory Committee may issue an informal statement on the matter.

4.1.3. *Implementing measures, block-exemption regulations, guidelines and other notices (Article 33 of the Council Regulation)*

63. The Advisory Committee will be consulted on draft Commission regulations as provided for in the relevant Council Regulations.

64. Beside regulations, the Commission may also adopt notices and guidelines. These more flexible tools are very useful for explaining and announcing the Commission's policy, and for explaining its interpretation of the competition rules. The Advisory Committee will also be consulted on these notices and guidelines.

4.2. Procedure

4.2.1. *Normal procedure*

65. For consultation on Commission draft decisions, the meeting of the Advisory Committee takes place at the earliest 14 days after the invitation to the meeting is sent by the Commission. The Commission attaches to the invitation a summary of the case, a list of the most important documents, i.e. the documents needed to assess the case, and a draft decision. The Advisory Committee gives an opinion on the Commission draft decision. At the request of one or several members, the opinion shall be reasoned.

66. The Council Regulation allows for the possibility of the Member States agreeing upon a shorter period of time between the sending of the invitation and the meeting.

4.2.2. *Written procedure*

67. The Council Regulation provides for the possibility of a written consultation procedure. If no Member State objects, the Commission can consult the Member States by sending the documents to them and setting a deadline within which they can comment on the draft. This deadline would not normally be shorter than 14 days, except for decisions on interim measures pursuant to Article 8 of the Council Regulation. Where a Member State requests that a meeting takes place, the Commission will arrange for such a meeting.

4.3. Publication of the Opinion of the Advisory Committee

68. The Advisory Committee can recommend the publication of its opinion. In that event, the Commission will carry out such publication simultaneously with the decision, taking into account the legitimate interest of undertakings in the protection of their business secrets.

5. FINAL REMARKS

69. This Notice is without prejudice to any interpretation of the applicable Treaty and regulatory provisions by the Court of First Instance and the Court of Justice.

70. This Notice will be the subject of periodic review carried out jointly by the NCAs and the Commission. On the basis of the experience acquired, it will be reviewed no later than at the end of the third year after its adoption.

71. This notice replaces the Commission notice on cooperation between national competition authorities and the Commission in handling cases falling within the scope of Articles 81 and 82 of the Treaty published in 1997.[24]

Notes
[24] OJ C 313, 15.10.1997, p. 3.

---

6. STATEMENT BY OTHER NETWORK MEMBERS

72. The principles set out in this notice will also be abided by those Member States' competition authorities which have signed a statement in the form of the Annex to this Notice. In this statement they acknowledge the principles of this notice, including the principles relating to the protection of applicants claiming the benefit of a leniency programme[25] and declare that they will

abide by them. A list of these authorities is published on the website of the European Commission. It will be updated if appropriate.

Notes

[25] See paragraphs 37 *et subseq.*

Commentary

para 72: B&C: 14.031

ANNEX
STATEMENT REGARDING THE COMMISSION NOTICE ON COOPERATION WITHIN THE NETWORK OF COMPETITION AUTHORITIES

In order to cooperate closely with a view to protecting competition within the European Union in the interest of consumers, the undersigned competition authority:

Acknowledges the principle set out in the Commission Notice on Cooperation within the Network of Competition Authorities; and

Declares that it will abide by those principles, which include principles relating to the protection of applicants claiming the benefit of a leniency programme, in any case in which it is acting or may act and to which those principles apply.

(place)   (date)

B9

COMMISSION NOTICE ON THE COOPERATION BETWEEN THE COMMISSION AND THE COURTS OF THE EU MEMBER STATES IN THE APPLICATION OF ARTICLES 81 AND 82 EC

(2004/C 101/04)
(Text with EEA relevance)

Official Journal C 101, 27.4.2004, p. 54

Celex No: 52004XC0427(03)

Note

EEA application: the EFTA Surveillance Authority has adopted a parallel notice on the co-operation between the EFTA Surveillance Authority and the courts of the EFTA States in the application of Articles 53 and 54 of the EEA Agreement under Article 5(2)(b) of the Surveillance and Court Agreement: OJ C 305, 14.12.2006, p. 19 and EE Supplement No 62, 14.12.2006, p. 21.

Commentary

Notice: B&C: 1.060, 3.010, 13.052, 14.006 **F&N:** 2.148
points 11–14: B&C: 8.262
points 21–26: B&C: 14.074 **F&N:** 2.196
points 21–30: B&C: 3.010, 14.069
points 31–35: B&C: 14.070

I. THE SCOPE OF THE NOTICE

1. The present notice addresses the co-operation between the Commission and the courts of the EU Member States, when the latter apply Articles 81 and 82 EC. For the purpose of this notice, the "courts of the EU Member States" (hereinafter "national courts") are those courts and tribunals within an EU Member State that can apply Articles 81 and 82 EC and that are authorised to ask a preliminary question to the Court of Justice of the European Communities pursuant to Article 234 EC.[1]

Notes

[1] For the criteria to determine which entities can be regarded as courts or tribunals within the meaning of Article 234 EC, see e.g. Case C-516/99 *Schmid* [2002] ECR I-4573, 34: "The Court takes account of a number of factors, such as whether the body is established by law, whether it is permanent, whether its jurisdiction is compulsory, whether its procedure is inter partes, whether it applies rules of law and whether it is independent".

Commentary
point 1: F&N: 2.246

2. The national courts may be called upon to apply Articles 81 or 82 EC in lawsuits between private parties, such as actions relating to contracts or actions for damages. They may also act as public enforcer or as review court. A national court may indeed be designated as a competition authority of a Member State (hereinafter "the national competition authority") pursuant to Article 35(1) of Regulation (EC) No 1/2003 (hereinafter "the regulation").[2] In that case, the co-operation between the national courts and the Commission is not only covered by the present notice, but also by the notice on the co-operation within the network of competition authorities.[3]

Notes

[2] Council Regulation (EC) No 1/2003 of 16 December 2002 on the implementation of the rules on competition laid down in Articles 81 and 82 of the Treaty (OJ L 1, 4.1.2003, p. 1).

[3] Notice on co-operation within the network of competition authorities (OJ C 101, 27.4.2004, p. 43). For the purpose of this notice, a "national competition authority" is the authority designated by a Member State in accordance with Article 35(1) of the regulation.

II. THE APPLICATION OF EC COMPETITION RULES BY NATIONAL COURTS

A. THE COMPETENCE OF NATIONAL COURTS TO APPLY EC COMPETITION RULES

3. To the extent that national courts have jurisdiction to deal with a case[4], they have the power to apply Articles 81 and 82 EC.[5] Moreover, it should be remembered that Articles 81 and 82 EC are a matter of public policy and are essential to the accomplishment of the tasks entrusted to the Community, and, in particular, for the functioning of the internal market.[6] According to the Court of Justice, where, by virtue of domestic law, national courts must raise of their own motion points of law based on binding domestic rules which have not been raised by the parties, such an obligation also exists where binding Community rules, such as the EC competition rules, are concerned. The position is the same if domestic law confers on national courts a discretion to apply of their own motion binding rules of law: national courts must apply the EC competition rules, even when the party with an interest in application of those provisions has not relied on them, where domestic law allows such application by the national court. However, Community law does not require national courts to raise of their own motion an issue concerning the breach of provisions of Community law where examination of that issue would oblige them to abandon the passive role assigned to them by going beyond the ambit of the dispute defined by the parties themselves and relying on facts and circumstances other than those on which the party with an interest in application of those provisions bases his claim.[7]

Notes

[4] The jurisdiction of a national court depends on national, European and international rules of jurisdiction. In this context, it may be recalled that Council Regulation (EC) No 44/2001 of 22 December 2000 on jurisdiction and the

recognition and enforcement of judgements in civil and commercial matters (OJ L 12, 16.1.2001, p. 1) is applicable to all competition cases of a civil or commercial nature.
5   See Article 6 of the regulation.
6   See Articles 2 and 3 EC, Case C-126/97 *Eco Swiss* [1999] ECR I-3055, 36; Case T-34/92 *Fiatagri UK and New Holland Ford* [1994] ECR II-905, 39 and Case T-128/98 *Aéroports de Paris* [2000] ECR II-3929, 241.
7   Joined Cases C-430/93 and C-431/93 *van Schijndel* [1995] ECR I-4705, 13 to 15 and 22.

Commentary
point 3: B&C: 14.058 **F&N:** 2.243

4. Depending on the functions attributed to them under national law, national courts may be called upon to apply Articles 81 and 82 EC in administrative, civil or criminal proceedings.[8] In particular, where a natural or legal person asks the national court to safeguard his individual rights, national courts play a specific role in the enforcement of Articles 81 and 82 EC, which is different from the enforcement in the public interest by the Commission or by national competition authorities.[9] Indeed, national courts can give effect to Articles 81 and 82 EC by finding contracts to be void or by awards of damages.

Notes

8   According to the last sentence of Recital 8 of Regulation (EC) No 1/2003, the regulation does not apply to national laws which impose criminal sanctions on natural persons except to the extent that such sanctions are the means whereby competition rules applying to undertakings are enforced.
9   Case T-24/90 *Automec* [1992] ECR II-2223, 85.

Commentary
point 4: B&C: 14.006

5. National courts can apply Articles 81 and 82 EC, without it being necessary to apply national competition law in parallel. However, where a national court applies national competition law to agreements, decisions by associations of undertakings or concerted practices which may affect trade between Member States within the meaning of Article 81(1) EC[10] or to any abuse prohibited by Article 82 EC, they also have to apply EC competition rules to those agreements, decisions or practices.[11]

Notes

10   For further clarification of the effect on trade concept, see the notice on this issue (OJ L 101, 27.4.2004, p. 81).
11   Article 3(1) of the regulation.

6. The regulation does not only empower the national courts to apply EC competition law. The parallel application of national competition law to agreements, decisions of associations of undertakings and concerted practices which affect trade between Member States may not lead to a different outcome from that of EC competition law. Article 3(2) of the regulation provides that agreements, decisions or concerted practices which do not infringe Article 81(1) EC or which fulfil the conditions of Article 81(3) EC cannot be prohibited either under national competition law.[12] On the other hand, the Court of Justice has ruled that agreements, decisions or concerted practices that violate Article 81(1) and do not fulfil the conditions of Article 81(3) EC cannot be upheld under national law.[13] As to the parallel application of national competition law and Article 82 EC in the case of unilateral conduct, Article 3 of the regulation does not provide for a similar convergence obligation. However, in case of conflicting provisions, the general principle of primacy of Community law requires national courts to disapply any provision of national law which contravenes a Community rule, regardless of whether that national law provision was adopted before or after the Community rule.[14]

Notes

12   See also the notice on the application of Article 81(3) EC (OJ L 101, 27.4.2004, p. 2).
13   Case 14/68 *Walt Wilhelm* [1969] ECR 1 and Joined Cases 253/78 and 1 to 3/79 *Giry and Guerlain* [1980] ECR 2327, 15 to 17.
14   Case 106/77 *Simmenthal* [1978] ECR 629, 21 and Case C-198/01 *Consorzio Industrie Fiammiferi (CIF)* [2003] ECR I-49.

Part B Modernisation and Procedural Matters

7. Apart from the application of Articles 81 and 82 EC, national courts are also competent to apply acts adopted by EU institutions in accordance with the EC Treaty or in accordance with the measures adopted to give the Treaty effect, to the extent that these acts have direct effect. National courts may thus have to enforce Commission decisions[15] or regulations applying Article 81(3) EC to certain categories of agreements, decisions or concerted practices. When applying these EC competition rules, national courts act within the framework of Community law and are consequently bound to observe the general principles of Community law.[16]

Notes

[15] E.g. a national court may be asked to enforce a Commission decision taken pursuant to Articles 7 to 10, 23, and 24 of the regulation.

[16] See e.g. Case 5/88 *Wachauf* [1989] ECR 2609, 19.

8. The application of Articles 81 and 82 EC by national courts often depends on complex economic and legal assessments.[17] When applying EC competition rules, national courts are bound by the case law of the Community courts as well as by Commission regulations applying Article 81(3) EC to certain categories of agreements, decisions or concerted practices.[18] Furthermore, the application of Articles 81 and 82 EC by the Commission in a specific case binds the national courts when they apply EC competition rules in the same case in parallel with or subsequent to the Commission.[19] Finally, and without prejudice to the ultimate interpretation of the EC Treaty by the Court of Justice, national courts may find guidance in Commission regulations and decisions which present elements of analogy with the case they are dealing with, as well as in Commission notices and guidelines relating to the application of Articles 81 and 82 EC[20] and in the annual report on competition policy.[21]

Notes

[17] Joined Cases C-215/96 and C-216/96 *Bagnasco* [1999] ECR I-135, 50.

[18] Case 63/75 *Fonderies Roubaix* [1976] ECR 111, 9 to 11 and Case C-234/89 *Delimitis* [1991] ECR I-935, 46.

[19] On the parallel or consecutive application of EC competition rules by national courts and the Commission, see also points 11 to 14.

[20] Case 66/86 *Ahmed Saeed Flugreisen* [1989] ECR 803, 27 and Case C-234/89 *Delimitis* [1991] ECR I-935, 50. A list of Commission guidelines, notices and regulations in the field of competition policy, in particular the regulations applying Article 81(3) EC to certain categories of agreements, decisions or concerted practices, [is] annexed to this notice. For the decisions of the Commission applying Articles 81 and 82 EC (since 1964), see http://www.europa.eu.int/comm/competition/antitrust/cases/.

[21] Joined Cases C-319/93, C-40/94 and C-224/94 *Dijkstra* [1995] ECR I-4471, 32.

Commentary
point 8: **B&C**: 8.262, 14.080

B. Procedural Aspects of the Application of EC Competition Rules by National Courts

9. The procedural conditions for the enforcement of EC competition rules by national courts and the sanctions they can impose in case of an infringement of those rules, are largely covered by national law. However, to some extent, Community law also determines the conditions in which EC competition rules are enforced. Those Community law provisions may provide for the faculty of national courts to avail themselves of certain instruments, e.g. to ask for the Commission's opinion on questions concerning the application of EC competition rules[22] or they may create rules that have an obligatory impact on proceedings before them, e.g. allowing the Commission and national competition authorities to submit written observations.[23] These Community law provisions prevail over national rules. Therefore, national courts have to set aside national rules which, if applied, would conflict with these Community law provisions. Where such Community law provisions are directly applicable, they are a direct source of rights and duties for all those affected, and must be fully and uniformly applied in all the Member States from the date of their entry into force.[24]

Part B Modernisation and Procedural Matters

Notes

22 On the possibility for national courts to ask the Commission for an opinion, see further in points 27 to 30.

23 On the submission of observations, see further in points 31 to 35.

24 Case 106/77 *Simmenthal* [1978] ECR 629, 14 and 15.

10. In the absence of Community law provisions on procedures and sanctions related to the enforcement of EC competition rules by national courts, the latter apply national procedural law and — to the extent that they are competent to do so — impose sanctions provided for under national law. However, the application of these national provisions must be compatible with the general principles of Community law. In this regard, it is useful to recall the case law of the Court of Justice, according to which:

(a) where there is an infringement of Community law, national law must provide for sanctions which are effective, proportionate and dissuasive;[25]

(b) where the infringement of Community law causes harm to an individual, the latter should under certain conditions be able to ask the national court for damages; [26]

(c) the rules on procedures and sanctions which national courts apply to enforce Community law

— must not make such enforcement excessively difficult or practically impossible (the principle of effectiveness)[27] and they

— must not be less favourable than the rules applicable to the enforcement of equivalent national law (the principle of equivalence).[28]

On the basis of the principle of primacy of Community law, a national court may not apply national rules that are incompatible with these principles.

Notes

25 Case 68/88 *Commission v Greece* [1989] ECR 2965, 23 to 25.

26 On damages in case of an infringement by an undertaking, see Case C-453/99 *Courage v Crehan* [2001] ECR 6297, 26 and 27. On damages in case of an infringement by a Member State or by an authority which is an emanation of the State and on the conditions of such State liability, see e.g. Joined Cases C-6/90 and C-9/90 *Francovich* [1991] ECR I-5357, 33 to 36; Case C-271/91 *Marshall v Southampton and South West Hampshire Area Health Authority* [1993] ECR I-4367, 30 and 34 to 35; Joined Cases C-46/93 and C-48/93 *Brasserie du Pêcheur and Factortame* [1996] ECR I-1029; Case C-392/93 *British Telecommunications* [1996] ECR I-1631, 39 to 46 and Joined Cases C-178/94, C-179/94 and C-188/94 to 190/94 *Dillenkofer* [1996] ECR I-4845, 22 to 26 and 72.

27 See e.g. Case 33/76 *Rewe* [1976] ECR 1989, 5; Case 45/76 *Comet* [1976] ECR 2043, 12 and Case 79/83 *Harz* [1984] ECR 1921, 18 and 23.

28 See eg Case 33/76 *Rewe* [1976] ECR 1989, 5; Case 158/80 *Rewe* [1981] ECR 1805, 44; Case 199/82 *San Giorgio* [1983] ECR 3595, 12 and Case C-231/96 *Edis* [1998] ECR I-4951, 36 and 37.

Commentary
point 10: B&C: 14.055

C. Parallel or Consecutive Application of EC Competition Rules by the Commission and by National Courts

11. A national court may be applying EC competition law to an agreement, decision, concerted practice or unilateral behaviour affecting trade between Member States at the same time as the Commission or subsequent to the Commission.[29] The following points outline some of the obligations national courts have to respect in those circumstances.

Notes

29 Article 11(6), juncto Article 35(3) and (4) of the regulation prevents a parallel application of Articles 81 or 82 EC by the Commission and a national court only when the latter has been designated as a national competition authority.

Commentary
point 11: B&C: 14.074

12. Where a national court comes to a decision before the Commission does, it must avoid adopting a decision that would conflict with a decision contemplated by the Commission.[30] To that effect, the

national court may ask the Commission whether it has initiated proceedings regarding the same agreements, decisions or practices[31] and if so, about the progress of proceedings and the likelihood of a decision in that case.[32] The national court may, for reasons of legal certainty, also consider staying its proceedings until the Commission has reached a decision.[33] The Commission, for its part, will endeavour to give priority to cases for which it has decided to initiate proceedings within the meaning of Article 2(1) of Commission Regulation (EC) No 773/2004 and that are the subject of national proceedings stayed in this way, in particular when the outcome of a civil dispute depends on them. However, where the national court cannot reasonably doubt the Commission's contemplated decision or where the Commission has already decided on a similar case, the national court may decide on the case pending before it in accordance with that contemplated or earlier decision without it being necessary to ask the Commission for the information mentioned above or to await the Commission's decision.

Notes

[30] Article 16(1) of the regulation.

[31] The Commission makes the initiation of its proceedings with a view to adopting a decision pursuant to Articles 7 to 10 of the regulation public (see Article 2(2) of Commission Regulation (EC) No 773/2004 of 7 April relating to proceedings pursuant to Articles 81 and 82 of the EC Treaty (OJ C 101, 27.4.2004). According to the Court of Justice, the initiation of proceedings implies an authoritative act of the Commission, evidencing its intention of taking a decision (Case 48/72 *Brasserie de Haecht* [1973] ECR 77, 16).

[32] Case C-234/89 *Delimitis* [1991] ECR I-935, 53, and Joined Cases C-319/93, C-40/94 and C-224/94 *Dijkstra* [1995] ECR I-4471, 34. See further on this issue point 21 of this notice.

[33] See Article 16(1) of the regulation and Case C-234/89 I [1991] ECR I-935, 47 and Case C-344/98 *Masterfoods* [2000] ECR I-11369, 51.

Commentary
point 12: B&C: 14.074 F&N: 2.258

13. Where the Commission reaches a decision in a particular case before the national court, the latter cannot take a decision running counter to that of the Commission. The binding effect of the Commission's decision is of course without prejudice to the interpretation of Community law by the Court of Justice. Therefore, if the national court doubts the legality of the Commission's decision, it cannot avoid the binding effects of that decision without a ruling to the contrary by the Court of Justice.[34] Consequently, if a national court intends to take a decision that runs counter to that of the Commission, it must refer a question to the Court of Justice for a preliminary ruling (Article 234 EC). The latter will then decide on the compatibility of the Commission's decision with Community law. However, if the Commission's decision is challenged before the Community courts pursuant to Article 230 EC and the outcome of the dispute before the national court depends on the validity of the Commission's decision, the national court should stay its proceedings pending final judgment in the action for annulment by the Community courts unless it considers that, in the circumstances of the case, a reference to the Court of Justice for a preliminary ruling on the validity of the Commission decision is warranted.[35]

Notes

[34] Case 314/85 *Foto-Frost* [1987] ECR 4199, 12 to 20.

[35] See Article 16(1) of the regulation and Case C-344/98 *Masterfoods* [2000] ECR I-11369, 52 to 59.

Commentary
point 13: B&C: 14.077

14. When a national court stays proceedings, e.g. awaiting the Commission's decision (situation described in point 12 of this notice) or pending final judgement by the Community courts in an action for annulment or in a preliminary ruling procedure (situation described in point 13), it is incumbent on it to examine whether it is necessary to order interim measures in order to safeguard the interests of the parties.[36]

Notes

[36] Case C-344/98 *Masterfoods* [2000] ECR, I-11369, 58.

III. THE CO-OPERATION BETWEEN THE COMMISSION AND NATIONAL COURTS

15. Other than the co-operation mechanism between the national courts and the Court of Justice under Article 234 EC, the EC Treaty does not explicitly provide for co-operation between the national courts and the Commission. However, in its interpretation of Article 10 EC, which obliges the Member States to facilitate the achievement of the Community's tasks, the Community courts found that this Treaty provision imposes on the European institutions and the Member States mutual duties of loyal co-operation with a view to attaining the objectives of the EC Treaty. Article 10 EC thus implies that the Commission must assist national courts when they apply Community law.[37] Equally, national courts may be obliged to assist the Commission in the fulfilment of its tasks.[38]

Notes
[37] Case C-2/88 *Imm Zwartveld* [1990] ECR I-3365, 16 to 22 and Case C-234/89 *Delimitis* [1991] I-935, 53.
[38] C-94/00 *Roquette Frères* [2002] ECR 9011, 31.

Commentary
point 15: B&C: 14.064 F&N: 2.277

16. It is also appropriate to recall the co-operation between national courts and national authorities, in particular national competition authorities, for the application of Articles 81 and 82 EC. While the co-operation between these national authorities is primarily governed by national rules, Article 15(3) of the regulation provides for the possibility for national competition authorities to submit observations before the national courts of their Member State. Points 31 and 33 to 35 of this notice are *mutatis mutandis* applicable to those submissions.

A. THE COMMISSION AS *AMICUS CURIAE*

17. In order to assist national courts in the application of EC competition rules, the Commission is committed to help national courts where the latter find such help necessary to be able to decide on a case. Article 15 of the regulation refers to the most frequent types of such assistance: the transmission of information (points 21 to 26) and the Commission's opinions (points 27 to 30), both at the request of a national court and the possibility for the Commission to submit observations (points 31 to 35). Since the regulation provides for these types of assistance, it cannot be limited by any Member States' rule. However, in the absence of Community procedural rules to this effect and to the extent that they are necessary to facilitate these forms of assistance, Member States must adopt the appropriate procedural rules to allow both the national courts and the Commission to make full use of the possibilities the regulation offers.[39]

Notes
[39] On the compatibility of such national procedural rules with the general principles of Community law, see points 9 and 10 of this notice.

Commentary
point 17: B&C: 14.065

18. The national court may send its request for assistance in writing to

European Commission
Directorate General for Competition
B-1049 Brussels
Belgium

or send it electronically to comp-amicus@cec.eu.int

19. It should be recalled that whatever form the co-operation with national courts takes, the Commission will respect the independence of national courts. As a consequence, the assistance offered by the Commission does not bind the national court. The Commission has also to make sure that it respects its duty of professional secrecy and that it safeguards its own functioning and independence.[40] In fulfilling its duty under Article 10 EC, of assisting national courts in the application of EC competition rules, the Commission is committed to remaining neutral and

133

objective in its assistance. Indeed, the Commission's assistance to national courts is part of its duty to defend the public interest. It has therefore no intention to serve the private interests of the parties involved in the case pending before the national court. As a consequence, the Commission will not hear any of the parties about its assistance to the national court. In case the Commission has been contacted by any of the parties in the case pending before the court on issues which are raised before the national court, it will inform the national court thereof, independent of whether these contacts took place before or after the national court's request for co-operation.

Notes
[40] On these duties, see e.g. points 23 to 26 of this notice.

Commentary
point 19: **B&C:** 14.065 **F&N:** 2.277

20. The Commission will publish a summary concerning its co-operation with national courts pursuant to this notice in its annual Report on Competition Policy. It may also make its opinions and observations available on its website.

Commentary
point 20: **F&N:** 2.273

1. The Commission's duty to transmit information to national courts

21. The duty for the Commission to assist national courts in the application of EC competition law is mainly reflected in the obligation for the Commission to transmit information it holds to national courts. A national court may, e.g., ask the Commission for documents in its possession or for information of a procedural nature to enable it to discover whether a certain case is pending before the Commission, whether the Commission has initiated a procedure or whether it has already taken a position. A national court may also ask the Commission when a decision is likely to be taken, so as to be able to determine the conditions for any decision to stay proceedings or whether interim measures need to be adopted.[41]

Notes
[41] Case C-234/89 *Delimitis* [1991] ECR I-935, 53, and Joined Cases C-319/93, C-40/94 and C-224/94 *Dijkstra* [1995] ECR I-4471, 34.

22. In order to ensure the efficiency of the co-operation with national courts, the Commission will endeavour to provide the national court with the requested information within one month from the date it receives the request. Where the Commission has to ask the national court for further clarification of its request or where the Commission has to consult those who are directly affected by the transmission of the information, that period starts to run from the moment that it receives the required information.

Commentary
point 22: **B&C:** 14.067

23. In transmitting information to national courts, the Commission has to uphold the guarantees given to natural and legal persons by Article 287 EC.[42] Article 287 EC prevents members, officials and other servants of the Commission from disclosing information covered by the obligation of professional secrecy. The information covered by professional secrecy may be both confidential information and business secrets. Business secrets are information of which not only disclosure to the public but also mere transmission to a person other than the one that provided the information might seriously harm the latter's interests.[43]

Notes
[42] Case C-234/89 *Delimitis* [1991] I-935, 53.
[43] Case T-353/94 *Postbank* [1996] ECR II-921, 86 and 87 and Case 145/83 *Adams* [1985] ECR 3539, 34.

24. The combined reading of Articles 10 and 287 EC does not lead to an absolute prohibition for the Commission to transmit information which is covered by the obligation of professional secrecy to national courts. The case law of the Community courts confirms that the duty of loyal co-operation requires the Commission to provide the national court with whatever information the latter asks for, even information covered by professional secrecy. However, in offering its co-operation to the national courts, the Commission may not in any circumstances undermine the guarantees laid down in Article 287 EC.

25. Consequently, before transmitting information covered by professional secrecy to a national court, the Commission will remind the court of its obligation under Community law to uphold the rights which Article 287 EC confers on natural and legal persons and it will ask the court whether it can and will guarantee protection of confidential information and business secrets. If the national court cannot offer such guarantee, the Commission shall not transmit the information covered by professional secrecy to the national court.[44] Only when the national court has offered a guarantee that it will protect the confidential information and business secrets, will the Commission transmit the information requested, indicating those parts which are covered by professional secrecy and which parts are not and can therefore be disclosed.

Notes
[44] Case C-2/88 *Zwartveld* [1990] ECR I-4405, 10 and 11 and Case T-353/94 *Postbank* [1996] ECR II-921, 93.

Commentary
point 25: B&C: 13.052

26. There are further exceptions to the disclosure of information by the Commission to national courts. Particularly, the Commission may refuse to transmit information to national courts for overriding reasons relating to the need to safeguard the interests of the Community or to avoid any interference with its functioning and independence, in particular by jeopardising the accomplishment of the tasks entrusted to it.[45] Therefore, the Commission will not transmit to national courts information voluntarily submitted by a leniency applicant without the consent of that applicant.

Notes
[45] Case C-2/88 *Zwartveld* [1990] ECR I-4405, 10 and 11; Case C-275/00 *First and Franex* [2002] ECR I-10943, 49 and Case T-353/94 *Postbank* [1996] ECR II-921, 93.

Commentary
point 26: F&N: 2.266

2. Request for an opinion on questions concerning the application of EC competition rules

27. When called upon to apply EC competition rules to a case pending before it, a national court may first seek guidance in the case law of the Community courts or in Commission regulations, decisions, notices and guidelines applying Articles 81 and 82 EC.[46] Where these tools do not offer sufficient guidance, the national court may ask the Commission for its opinion on questions concerning the application of EC competition rules. The national court may ask the Commission for its opinion on economic, factual and legal matters.[47] The latter is of course without prejudice to the possibility or the obligation for the national court to ask the Court of Justice for a preliminary ruling regarding the interpretation or the validity of Community law in accordance with Article 234 EC.

Notes
[46] See point 8 of this notice.
[47] Case C-234/89 *Delimitis* [1991] ECR I-935, 53, and Joined Cases C-319/93, C-40/94 and C-224/94 *Dijkstra* [1995] ECR I-4471, 34.

28. In order to enable the Commission to provide the national court with a useful opinion, it may request the national court for further information.[48] In order to ensure the efficiency of the co-operation with national courts, the Commission will endeavour to provide the national court with the requested opinion within four months from the date it receives the request. Where the Commission has requested the national court for further information in order to enable it to formulate its opinion, that period starts to run from the moment that it receives the additional information.

Notes
48 Compare with Case 96/81 *Commission v The Netherlands* [1982] ECR 1791, 7 and Case 272/86 *Commission v Greece* [1988] ECR 4875, 30.

29. When giving its opinion, the Commission will limit itself to providing the national court with the factual information or the economic or legal clarification asked for, without considering the merits of the case pending before the national court. Moreover, unlike the authoritative interpretation of Community law by the Community courts, the opinion of the Commission does not legally bind the national court.

30. In line with what has been said in point 19 of this notice, the Commission will not hear the parties before formulating its opinion to the national court. The latter will have to deal with the Commission's opinion in accordance with the relevant national procedural rules, which have to respect the general principles of Community law.

3. The Commission's submission of observations to the national court

31. According to Article 15(3) of the regulation, the national competition authorities and the Commission may submit observations on issues relating to the application of Articles 81 or 82 EC to a national court which is called upon to apply those provisions. The regulation distinguishes between written observations, which the national competition authorities and the Commission may submit on their own initiative, and oral observations, which can only be submitted with the permission of the national court.[49]

Notes
49 According to Article 15(4) of the regulation, this is without prejudice to wider powers to make observations before courts conferred on national competition authorities under national law.

32. The regulation specifies that the Commission will only submit observations when the coherent application of Articles 81 or 82 EC so requires. That being the objective of its submission, the Commission will limit its observations to an economic and legal analysis of the facts underlying the case pending before the national court.

Commentary
point 32: B&C: 14.065

33. In order to enable the Commission to submit useful observations, national courts may be asked to transmit or ensure the transmission to the Commission of a copy of all documents that are necessary for the assessment of the case. In line with Article 15(3), second subparagraph, of the regulation, the Commission will only use those documents for the preparation of its observations.[50]

Notes
50 See also Article 28(2) of the regulation, which prevents the Commission from disclosing the information it has acquired and which is covered by the obligation of professional secrecy.

34. Since the regulation does not provide for a procedural framework within which the observations are to be submitted, Member States' procedural rules and practices determine the relevant procedural framework. Where a Member State has not yet established the relevant procedural framework, the national court has to determine which procedural rules are appropriate for the submission of observations in the case pending before it.

35. The procedural framework should respect the principles set out in point 10 of this notice. That implies amongst others that the procedural framework for the submission of observations on issues relating to the application of Articles 81 or 82 EC
    (a) has to be compatible with the general principles of Community law, in particular the fundamental rights of the parties involved in the case;

(b) cannot make the submission of such observations excessively difficult or practically imposs-ible (the principle of effectiveness);[51] and

(c) cannot make the submission of such observations more difficult than the submission of observations in court proceedings where equivalent national law is applied (the principle of equivalence).

Notes
[51] Joined Cases 46/87 and 227/88 *Hoechst* [1989] ECR, 2859, 33. See also Article 15(3) of the regulation.

Commentary
point 35: F&N: 2.278

B. The National Courts Facilitating the Role of the Commission in the Enforcement of EC Competition Rules

36. Since the duty of loyal co-operation also implies that Member States' authorities assist the European institutions with a view to attaining the objectives of the EC Treaty,[52] the regula-tion provides for three examples of such assistance: (1) the transmission of documents necessary for the assessment of a case in which the Commission would like to submit observations (see point 33), (2) the transmission of judgements applying Articles 81 or 82 EC, and (3) the role of national courts in the context of a Commission inspection.

Notes
[52] Case C-69/90 *Commission v Italy* [1991] ECR 6011, 15.

1. The transmission of judgements of national courts applying Articles 81 or 82 EC

37. According to Article 15(2) of the regulation, Member States shall send to the Commission a copy of any written judgement of national courts applying Articles 81 or 82 EC without delay after the full written judgement is notified to the parties. The transmission of national judge-ments on the application of Articles 81 or 82 EC and the resulting information on proceedings before national courts primarily enable the Commission to become aware in a timely fashion of cases for which it might be appropriate to submit observations where one of the parties lodges an appeal against the judgement.

2. The role of national courts in the context of a Commission inspection

38. Finally, national courts may play a role in the context of a Commission inspection of undertak-ings and associations of undertakings. The role of the national courts depends on whether the inspections are conducted in business premises or in non-business premises.

39. With regard to the inspection of business premises, national legislation may require authorisation from a national court to allow a national enforcement authority to assist the Commission in case of opposition of the undertaking concerned. Such authorisation may also be sought as a precau-tionary measure. When dealing with the request, the national court has the power to control that the Commission's inspection decision is authentic and that the coercive measures envisaged are neither arbitrary nor excessive having regard to the subject matter of the inspection. In its control of the proportionality of the coercive measures, the national court may ask the Commission, directly or through the national competition authority, for detailed explanations in particular on the grounds the Commission has for suspecting infringement of Articles 81 and 82 EC, as well as on the seriousness of the suspected infringement and on the nature of the involvement of the undertaking concerned.[53]

Notes
[53] Article 20(6) to (8) of the regulation and Case C-94/00 *Roquette Frères* [2002] ECR 9011.

40. With regard to the inspection of non-business premises, the regulation requires the authorisation from a national court before a Commission decision ordering such an inspection can be executed.

In that case, the national court may control that the Commission's inspection decision is authentic and that the coercive measures envisaged are neither arbitrary nor excessive having regard in particular to the seriousness of the suspected infringement, to the importance of the evidence sought, to the involvement of the undertaking concerned and to the reasonable likelihood that business books and records relating to the subject matter of the inspection are kept in the premises for which the authorisation is requested. The national court may ask the Commission, directly or through the national competition authority, for detailed explanations on those elements that are necessary to allow its control of the proportionality of the coercive measures envisaged.[54]

Notes

[54] Article 21(3) of the regulation.

---

41. In both cases referred to in points 39 and 40, the national court may not call into question the lawfulness of the Commission's decision or the necessity for the inspection nor can it demand that it be provided with information in the Commission's file.[55] Furthermore, the duty of loyal co-operation requires the national court to take its decision within an appropriate timeframe that allows the Commission to effectively conduct its inspection.[56]

Notes

[55] Case C-94/00 *Roquette Frères* [2002] ECR 9011, 39 and 62 to 66.
[56] See also *ibidem*, 91 and 92.

IV. Final Provisions

42. This notice is issued in order to assist national courts in the application of Articles 81 and 82 EC. It does not bind the national courts, nor does it affect the rights and obligations of the EU Member States and natural or legal persons under Community law.
43. This notice replaces the 1993 notice on co-operation between national courts and the Commission in applying Articles 85 and 86 of the EEC Treaty.[57]

Notes

[57] OJ C 39, 13.2.93, p. 6.

Annex
Commission Block Exemption Regulations, Notices and Guidelines

This list is also available and updated on the website of the Directorate General for Competition of the European Commission:

http://europa.eu.int/comm/competition/antitrust/legislation/

A. Non-sector Specific Rules

1. Notices of a general nature

— Notice on the definition of the relevant market for the purposes of Community competition law (OJ C 372, 9.12.1997, p. 5)
— Notice on agreements of minor importance which do not appreciably restrict competition under Article 81(1) of the Treaty establishing the European Community (*de minimis*) (OJ C 368, 22.12.2001, p. 13)
— Notice on the effect on trade concept contained in Articles 81 and 82 of the Treaty (OJ C 101, 27.4.2004, p. 81)
— Guidelines on the application of Article 81(3) of the Treaty (OJ C 101, 27.4.2004, p. 2)

2. Vertical agreements

— Regulation (EC) No 2790/1999 of 22 December 1999 on the application of Article 81(3) of the Treaty to categories of vertical agreements and concerted practices (OJ L 336, 29.12.1999, p. 21)

— Guidelines on Vertical Restraints (OJ C 291, 13.10.2000, p. 1)

3. Horizontal co-operation agreements

— Regulation (EC) No 2658/2000 of 29 November 2000 on the application of Article 81(3) of the Treaty to categories of specialisation agreements (OJ L 304, 5.12.2000, p. 3)

— Regulation (EC) No 2659/2000 of 29 November 2000 on the application of Article 81(3) of the Treaty to categories of research and development agreements (OJ L 304, 5.12.2000, p. 7)

— Guidelines on the applicability of Article 81 to horizontal co-operation agreements (OJ C 3, 6.1.2001, p. 2)

4. Licensing agreements for the transfer of technology

— Regulation (EC) No 773/2004 of 27 April 2004 on the application of Article 81(3) of the Treaty to categories of technology transfer agreements (OJ L 123, 27.4.2004)

— Guidelines on the application of Article 81 of the EC Treaty to technology transfer agreements (OJ C 101, 27.4.2004, p. 2)

B. Sector Specific Rules

1. Insurance

— Regulation (EC) No 358/2003 of 27 February 2003 on the application of Article 81(3) of the Treaty to certain categories of agreements, decisions and concerted practices in the insurance sector (OJ L 53, 28.2.2003, p. 8)

2. Motor vehicles

— Regulation (EC) No 1400/2002 of 31 July 2002 on the application of Article 81(3) of the Treaty to categories of vertical agreements and concerted practices in the motor vehicle sector (OJ L 203, 1.8.2002, p. 30)

3. Telecommunications and postal services

— Guidelines on the application of EEC competition rules in the telecommunications sector (OJ C 233, 6.9.1991, p. 2)

— Notice on the application of the competition rules to the postal sector and on the assessment of certain State measures relating to postal services (OJ C 39, 6.2.1998, p. 2)

— Notice on the application of the competition rules to access agreements in the telecommunications sector — Framework, relevant markets and principles (OJ C 265, 22.8.1998, p. 2)

— Guidelines on market analysis and the assessment of significant market power under the Community regulatory framework for electronic communications networks and services (OJ C 165, 11.7.2002, p. 6)

4. Transport

— Regulation (EEC) No 1617/93 on the application of Article 81(3) of the Treaty to certain categories of agreements and concerted practices concerning joint planning and co-ordination of schedules, joint operations, consultations on passenger and cargo tariffs on scheduled air services and slot allocation at airports (OJ L 155, 26.6.1993, p. 18)

— Communication on clarification of the Commission recommendations on the application of the competition rules to new transport infrastructure projects (OJ C 298, 30.9.1997, p. 5)

— Regulation (EC) No 823/2000 of 19 April 2000 on the application of Article 81(3) of the Treaty to certain categories of agreements, decisions and concerted practices between liner shipping companies (consortia) (OJ L 100, 20.4.2000, p. 24)

B10

COMMISSION NOTICE ON THE HANDLING OF COMPLAINTS BY THE COMMISSION UNDER ARTICLES 81 AND 82 OF THE EC TREATY

(2004/C 101/05)
(Text with EEA relevance)

Official Journal C 101, 27.4.2004, p. 65

Celex No: 52004XC0427(04)

Notes

EEA application: the EFTA Surveillance Authority has adopted a parallel notice under Article 5(2)(b) of the Surveillance and Court Agreement: see College Decision No 175/05/COL of 15 July 2005, not yet published.

Commentary
Notice: B&C: 1.060, 13.024, 13.061 F&N: 2.108, 8.102
Part III: B&C: 13.061

I. Introduction and Subject-matter of the Notice

1. Regulation 1/2003[1] establishes a system of parallel competence for the application of Articles 81 and 82 of the EC Treaty by the Commission and the Member States' competition authorities and courts. The Regulation recognises in particular the complementary functions of the Commission and Member States' competition authorities acting as public enforcers and the Member States' courts that rule on private lawsuits in order to safeguard the rights of individuals deriving from Articles 81 and 82.[2]

Notes
[1] Council Regulation (EC) No 1/2003 of 16 December 2002 on the implementation of the rules on competition laid down in Articles 81 and 82 of the Treaty (OJ L 1, 4.1.2003, pages 1–25).
[2] Cf. in particular Recitals 3–7 and 35 of Regulation 1/2003.

---

2. Under Regulation 1/2003, the public enforcers may focus their action on the investigation of serious infringements of Articles 81 and 82 which are often difficult to detect. For their enforcement activity, they benefit from information supplied by undertakings and by consumers in the market.

Commentary
point 2: B&C: 13.061

---

3. The Commission therefore wishes to encourage citizens and undertakings to address themselves to the public enforcers to inform them about suspected infringements of the competition rules. At the level of the Commission, there are two ways to do this, one is by lodging a complaint pursuant to Article 7(2) of Regulation 1/2003. Under Articles 5 to 9 of Regulation 773/2004,[3] such complaints must fulfil certain requirements.

Notes
[3] Commission Regulation (EC) No 773/2004 of 7 April 2004 relating to the conduct of proceedings by the Commission pursuant to Articles 81 and 82 of the EC Treaty (OJ 123, 27.4.2004).

Commentary
para 3: B&C: 13.061 F&N: 8.102

---

4. The other way is the provision of market information that does not have to comply with the requirements for complaints pursuant to Article 7(2) of Regulation 1/2003. For this purpose, the Commission has created a special website to collect information from citizens and undertakings and their associations who wish to inform the Commission about suspected infringements of Articles 81 and 82. Such information can be the starting point for an investigation by the Commission.[4] Information about suspected infringements can be supplied to the following address:

http://europa.eu.int/dgcomp/info-on-anti-competitivepractices

or to:

Commission européenne/Europese Commissie
Competition DG
B-1049 Bruxelles/Brussel

Notes

[4] The Commission handles correspondence from informants in accordance with its principles of good administrative practice.

Commentary
point 4: **B&C:** 13.062 **F&N:** 8.102

5. Without prejudice to the interpretation of Regulation 1/2003 and of Commission Regulation 773/2004 by the Community Courts, the present Notice intends to provide guidance to citizens and undertakings that are seeking relief from suspected infringements of the competition rules. The Notice contains two main parts:

— Part II gives indications about the choice between complaining to the Commission or bringing a lawsuit before a national court. Moreover, it recalls the principles related to the work-sharing between the Commission and the national competition authorities in the enforcement system established by Regulation 1/2003 that are explained in the Notice on cooperation within the network of competition authorities.[5]

— Part III explains the procedure for the treatment of complaints pursuant to Article 7(2) of Regulation 1/2003 by the Commission.

Notes

[5] Notice on cooperation within the Network of competition authorities (OJ C 101, 27.4.2004, p. 43).

6. This Notice does not address the following situations:

— complaints lodged by Member States pursuant to Article 7(2) of Regulation 1/2003,
— complaints that ask the Commission to take action against a Member State pursuant to Article 86(3) in conjunction with Articles 81 or 82 of the Treaty,
— complaints relating to Article 87 of the Treaty on state aids,
— complaints relating to infringements by Member States that the Commission may pursue in the framework of Article 226 of the Treaty.[6]

Notes

[6] For the handling of such complaints, cf. Commission communication of 10 October 2002, COM(2002) 141.

II. DIFFERENT POSSIBILITIES FOR LODGING COMPLAINTS ABOUT SUSPECTED INFRINGEMENTS OF ARTICLES 81 OR 82

A. COMPLAINTS IN THE NEW ENFORCEMENT SYSTEM ESTABLISHED BY REGULATION 1/2003

7. Depending on the nature of the complaint, a complainant may bring his complaint either to a national court or to a competition authority that acts as public enforcer. The present chapter of this Notice intends to help potential complainants to make an informed choice about whether to

address themselves to the Commission, to one of the Member States' competition authorities or to a national court.

8. While national courts are called upon to safeguard the rights of individuals and are thus bound to rule on cases brought before them, public enforcers cannot investigate all complaints, but must set priorities in their treatment of cases. The Court of Justice has held that the Commission, entrusted by Article 85(1) of the EC Treaty with the task of ensuring application of the principles laid down in Articles 81 and 82 of the Treaty, is responsible for defining and implementing the orientation of Community competition policy and that, in order to perform that task effectively, it is entitled to give differing degrees of priority to the complaints brought before it.[7]

Notes

[7] Case C-344/98 *Masterfoods v HB Ice Cream* [2000] ECR I-11369, para 46; Case C-119/97 P *Union française de l'express (Ufex) and Others v Commission of the European Communities* [1999] ECR I-1341, para 88; Case T-24/90 *Automec v Commission of the European Communities* [1992] ECR II-2223, paras 73–77.

---

9. Regulation 1/2003 empowers Member States' courts and Member States' competition authorities to apply Articles 81 and 82 in their entirety alongside the Commission. Regulation 1/2003 pursues as one principal objective that Member States' courts and competition authorities should participate effectively in the enforcement of Articles 81 and 82.[8]

Notes

[8] Cf. in particular Articles 5, 6, 11, 12, 15, 22, 29, 35 and Recitals 2 to 4 and 6 to 8 of Regulation 1/2003.

---

10. Moreover, Article 3 of Regulation 1/2003 provides that Member States' courts and competition authorities have to apply Articles 81 and 82 to all cases of agreements or conduct that are capable of affecting trade between Member States to which they apply their national competition laws. In addition, Articles 11 and 15 of the Regulation create a range of mechanisms by which Member States' courts and competition authorities cooperate with the Commission in the enforcement of Articles 81 and 82.

11. In this new legislative framework, the Commission intends to refocus its enforcement resources along the following lines:
   — enforce the EC competition rules in cases for which it is well placed to act,[9] concentrating its resources on the most serious infringements;[10]
   — handle cases in relation to which the Commission should act with a view to define Community competition policy and/or to ensure coherent application of Articles 81 or 82.

Notes

[9] Cf. Notice on cooperation within the network of competition authorities [OJ C 101, 27.4.2004, p 43], points 5 [ff].
[10] Cf. Recital 3 of Regulation 1/2003.

Commentary
point 11: B&C: 13.024

B. The Complementary Roles of Private and Public Enforcement

12. It has been consistently held by the Community Courts that national courts are called upon to safeguard the rights of individuals created by the direct effect of Articles 81(1) and 82.[11]

Notes

[11] Settled case law, cf. Case 127/73 *Belgische Radio en Televisie (BRT) v SABAM and Fonior* [1974] ECR 51, para 16; Case C-282/95 P *Guérin automobiles v Commission of the European Communities* [1997] ECR I-1503, para 39; Case C-453/99 *Courage v Bernhard Crehan* [2001] ECR I-6297, para 23.

---

13. National courts can decide upon the nullity or validity of contracts and only national courts can grant damages to an individual in case of an infringement of Articles 81 and 82. Under the case law of the Court of Justice, any individual can claim damages for loss caused to him by a contract or by conduct which restricts or distorts competition, in order to ensure the full effectiveness of

the Community competition rules. Such actions for damages before the national courts can make a significant contribution to the maintenance of effective competition in the Community as they discourage undertakings from concluding or applying restrictive agreements or practices.[12]

Notes

[12] Case C-453/99 *Courage v Bernhard Crehan* [2001] ECR I-6297, paras 26 and 27; the power of national courts to grant damages is also underlined in Recital 7 of Regulation 1/2003.

14. Regulation 1/2003 takes express account of the fact that national courts have an essential part to play in applying the EC competition rules.[13] By extending the power to apply Article 81(3) to national courts it removes the possibility for undertakings to delay national court proceedings by a notification to the Commission and thus eliminates an obstacle for private litigation that existed under Regulation No 17.[14]

Notes

[13] Cf Articles 1, 6 and 15 as well as Recital 7 of Regulation 1/2003.

[14] Regulation No 17: First Regulation implementing Articles 85 and 86 of the Treaty; OJ P 13 of 21 February 1962, p. 204–211; English special edition: Series I Chapter 1959–1962, p. 87. Regulation No 17 is repealed by Article 43 of Regulation 1/2003 with effect from 1 May 2004.

15. Without prejudice to the right or obligation of national courts to address a preliminary question to the Court of Justice in accordance with Article 234 EC, Article 15(1) of Regulation 1/2003 provides expressly that national courts may ask for opinions or information from the Commission. This provision aims at facilitating the application of Articles 81 and 82 by national courts.[15]

Notes

[15] For more detailed explanations of this mechanism, cf. Notice on co-operation between the Commission and the courts of the EU Member States in the application of Articles 81 and 82 EC [OJ C 101, 27.4.2004, p 54].

16. Action before national courts has the following advantages for complainants:
   — National courts may award damages for loss suffered as a result of an infringement of Article 81 or 82.
   — National courts may rule on claims for payment or contractual obligations based on an agreement that they examine under Article 81.
   — It is for the national courts to apply the civil sanction of nullity of Article 81(2) in contractual relationships between individuals.[16] They can in particular assess, in the light of the applicable national law, the scope and consequences of the nullity of certain contractual provisions under Article 81(2), with particular regard to all the other matters covered by the agreement.[17]
   — National courts are usually better placed than the Commission to adopt interim measures.[18]
   — Before national courts, it is possible to combine a claim under Community competition law with other claims under national law.
   — Courts normally have the power to award legal costs to the successful applicant. This is never possible in an administrative procedure before the Commission.

Notes

[16] Case T-24/90 *Automec v Commission of the European Communities* [1992] ECR II-2223, para 93.

[17] Case C-230/96 *Cabour and Nord Distribution Automobile v Arnor "SOCO"* [1998] ECR I-2055, para 51; Joined Cases T-185/96, T-189/96 and T-190/96 *Dalmasso and Others v Commission of the European Communities* [1999] ECR II-93, para 50.

[18] Cf. Article 8 of Regulation 1/2003 and [point] 80 below. Depending on the case, Member States' competition authorities may equally be well placed to adopt interim measures.

17. The fact that a complainant can secure the protection of his rights by an action before a national court, is an important element that the Commission may take into account in its examination of the Community interest for investigating a complaint.[19]

Notes

[19] Cf. points 41 [ff] below.

18. The Commission holds the view that the new enforcement system established by Regulation 1/2003 strengthens the possibilities for complainants to seek and obtain effective relief before national courts.

C. Work-sharing between the Public Enforcers in the European Community

19. Regulation 1/2003 creates a system of parallel competence for the application of Articles 81 and 82 by empowering Member States' competition authorities to apply Articles 81 and 82 in their entirety (Article 5). Decentralised enforcement by Member States' competition authorities is further encouraged by the possibility to exchange information (Article 12) and to provide each other assistance with investigations (Article 22).

20. The Regulation does not regulate the work-sharing between the Commission and the Member States' competition authorities but leaves the division of case work to the cooperation of the Commission and the Member States' competition authorities inside the European Competition Network (ECN). The Regulation pursues the objective of ensuring effective enforcement of Articles 81 and 82 through a flexible division of case work between the public enforcers in the Community.

21. Orientations for the work sharing between the Commission and the Member States' competition authorities are laid down in a separate Notice.[20] The guidance contained in that Notice, which concerns the relations between the public enforcers, will be of interest to complainants as it permits them to address a complaint to the authority most likely to be well placed to deal with their case.

Notes

[20] Notice on cooperation within the Network of competition authorities (p. 43).

---

22. The Notice on cooperation within the Network of Competition Authorities states in particular:[21]

"An authority can be considered to be well placed to deal with a case if the following three cumulative conditions are met:
— the agreement or practice has substantial direct actual or foreseeable effects on competition within its territory, is implemented within or originates from its territory;
— the authority is able effectively to bring to an end the entire infringement, i.e. it can adopt a cease-and desist order, the effect of which will be sufficient to bring an end to the infringement and it can, where appropriate, sanction the infringement adequately;
— it can gather, possibly with the assistance of other authorities, the evidence required to prove the infringement.
The above criteria indicate that a material link between the infringement and the territory of a Member State must exist in order for that Member State's competition authority to be considered well placed. It can be expected that in most cases the authorities of those Member States where competition is substantially affected by an infringement will be well placed provided they are capable of effectively bringing the infringement to an end through either single or parallel action unless the Commission is better placed to act (see below [. . .]).
It follows that a single NCA is usually well placed to deal with agreements or practices that substantially affect competition mainly within its territory [. . .].
Furthermore single action of an NCA might also be appropriate where, although more than one NCA can be regarded as well placed, the action of a single NCA is sufficient to bring the entire infringement to an end [. . .].
Parallel action by two or three NCAs may be appropriate where an agreement or practice has substantial effects on competition mainly in their respective territories and the action of only one NCA would not be sufficient to bring the entire infringement to an end and/or to sanction it adequately [. . .].
The authorities dealing with a case in parallel action will endeavour to coordinate their action to the extent possible. To that effect, they may find it useful to designate one of them as a lead

authority and to delegate tasks to the lead authority such as for example the coordination of investigative measures, while each authority remains responsible for conducting its own proceedings. The Commission is particularly well placed if one or several agreement(s) or practice(s), including networks of similar agreements or practices, have effects on competition in more than three Member States (crossborder markets covering more than three Member States or several national markets) [. . .].

Moreover, the Commission is particularly well placed to deal with a case if it is closely linked to other Community provisions which may be exclusively or more effectively applied by the Commission, if the Community interest requires the adoption of a Commission decision to develop Community competition policy when a new competition issue arises or to ensure effective enforcement".

Notes

[21] Notice on cooperation within the Network of competition authorities [OJ C 101, 27.4.2004, p 43], points 8–15.

23. Within the European Competition Network, information on cases that are being investigated following a complaint will be made available to the other members of the network before or without delay after commencing the first formal investigative measure.[22] Where the same complaint has been lodged with several authorities or where a case has not been lodged with an authority that is well placed, the members of the network will endeavour to determine within an indicative time-limit of two months which authority or authorities should be in charge of the case.

Notes

[22] Article 11(2) and (3) of Regulation 1/2003; Notice on cooperation within the Network of Competition Authorities [OJ C 101, 27.4.2004, p 43], points 16 and 17.

24. Complainants themselves have an important role to play in further reducing the potential need for reallocation of a case originating from their complaint by referring to the orientations on work sharing in the network set out in the present chapter when deciding on where to lodge their complaint. If nonetheless a case is reallocated within the network, the undertakings concerned and the complainant(s) are informed as soon as possible by the competition authorities involved.[23]

Notes

[23] Notice on cooperation within the Network of Competition Authorities [OJ C 101, 27.4.2004, p 43], point 34.

25. The Commission may reject a complaint in accordance with Article 13 of Regulation 1/2003, on the grounds that a Member State competition authority is dealing or has dealt with the case. When doing so, the Commission must, in accordance with Article 9 of Regulation 773/2004, inform the complainant without delay of the national competition authority which is dealing or has already dealt with the case.

III. The Commission's Handling of Complaints Pursuant to Article 7(2) of Regulation 1/2003

A. General

26. According to Article 7(2) of Regulation 1/2003 natural or legal persons that can show a legitimate interest[24] are entitled to lodge a complaint to ask the Commission to find an infringement of Articles 81 and 82 EC and to require that the infringement be brought to an end in accordance with Article 7(1) of Regulation 1/2003. The present part of this Notice explains the requirements applicable to complaints based on Article 7(2) of Regulation 1/2003, their assessment and the procedure followed by the Commission.

Notes

[24] For more extensive explanations on this notion in particular, cf. points 33 [ff] below.

27. The Commission, unlike civil courts, whose task is to safeguard the individual rights of private persons, is an administrative authority that must act in the public interest. It is an inherent feature of the Commission's task as public enforcer that it has a margin of discretion to set priorities in its enforcement activity.[25]

Notes

[25] Case C-119/97 P *Union française de l'express (Ufex) and Others v Commission of the European Communities* [1999] ECR I-1341, para 88; Case T-24/90 *Automec v Commission of the European Communities* [1992] ECR II-2223, paras 73–77 and 85.

28. The Commission is entitled to give different degrees of priority to complaints made to it and may refer to the Community interest presented by a case as a criterion of priority.[26] The Commission may reject a complaint when it considers that the case does not display a sufficient Community interest to justify further investigation. Where the Commission rejects a complaint, the complainant is entitled to a decision of the Commission[27] without prejudice to Article 7(3) of Regulation 773/2004.

Notes

[26] Settled case law since Case T-24/90 *Automec v Commission of the European Communities* [1992] ECR II-2223, para 85.

[27] Case C-282/95 P *Guérin automobiles v Commission of the European Communities* [1997] ECR I-1503, para 36.

B. Making a Complaint pursuant to Article 7(2) of Regulation 1/2003

(a) Complaint form

29. A complaint pursuant to Article 7(2) of Regulation 1/2003 can only be made about an alleged infringement of Articles 81 or 82 with a view to the Commission taking action under Article 7(1) of Regulation 1/2003. A complaint under Article 7(2) of Regulation 1/2003 has to comply with Form C mentioned in Article 5(1) of Regulation 773/2004 and annexed to that Regulation.

30. Form C is available at http://europa.eu.int/dgcomp/ complaints-form and is also annexed to this Notice. The complaint must be submitted in three paper copies as well as, if possible, an electronic copy. In addition, the complainant must provide a non-confidential version of the complaint (Article 5(2) of Regulation 773/2004). Electronic transmission to the Commission is possible via the website indicated, the paper copies should be sent to the following address:

Commission européenne/Europese Commissie
Competition DG
B-1049 Bruxelles/Brussel

Commentary
point 30: B&C: 13.066

31. Form C requires complainants to submit comprehensive information in relation to their complaint. They should also provide copies of relevant supporting documentation reasonably available to them and, to the extent possible, provide indications as to where relevant information and documents that are unavailable to them could be obtained by the Commission. In particular cases, the Commission may dispense with the obligation to provide information in relation to part of the information required by Form C (Article 5(1) of Regulation 773/2004). The Commission holds the view that this possibility can in particular play a role to facilitate complaints by consumer associations where they, in the context of an otherwise substantiated complaint, do not have access to specific pieces of information from the sphere of the undertakings complained of.

Commentary
point 31: B&C: 13.066

32. Correspondence to the Commission that does not comply with the requirements of Article 5 of Regulation 773/2004 and therefore does not constitute a complaint within the meaning of

Article 7(2) of Regulation 1/2003 will be considered by the Commission as general information that, where it is useful, may lead to an own-initiative investigation (cf. point 4 above).

Commentary
point 32: B&C: 13.066

(b) Legitimate interest

33. The status of formal complainant under Article 7(2) of Regulation 1/2003 is reserved to legal and natural persons who can show a legitimate interest.[28] Member States are deemed to have a legitimate interest for all complaints they choose to lodge.

Notes
[28] Cf. Article 5(1) of Regulation 773/2004.

Commentary
point 33: B&C: 13.063

34. In the past practice of the Commission, the condition of legitimate interest was not often a matter of doubt as most complainants were in a position of being directly and adversely affected by the alleged infringement. However, there are situations where the condition of a "legitimate interest" in Article 7(2) requires further analysis to conclude that it is fulfilled. Useful guidance can best be provided by a non-exhaustive set of examples.

35. The Court of First Instance has held that an association of undertakings may claim a legitimate interest in lodging a complaint regarding conduct concerning its members, even if it is not directly concerned, as an undertaking operating in the relevant market, by the conduct complained of, provided that, first, it is entitled to represent the interests of its members and secondly, the conduct complained of is liable to adversely affect the interests of its members.[29] Conversely, the Commission has been found to be entitled not to pursue the complaint of an association of undertakings whose members were not involved in the type of business transactions complained of.[30]

Notes
[29] Case T-114/92 *Bureau Européen des Médias et de l'Industrie Musicale (BEMIM) v Commission of the European Communities* [1995] ECR II-147, para 28. Associations of undertakings were also the complainants in the cases underlying the judgments in Case 298/83 *Comité des industries cinématographiques des Communautés Européennes (CICCE) v Commission of the European Communities* [1985] ECR 1105 and Case T-319/99 *Federacion Nacional de Empresas (FENIN) v Commission of the European Communities* [2003] ECR II-357 [and see, on appeal, Case C-205/03 P *FENIN v Commission of the European Communities* [2006] ECR, judgment of 11 July 2006].
[30] Joined Cases T-133/95 and T-204/95 *International Express Carriers Conference (IECC) v Commission of the European Communities* [1998] ECR II-3645, paras 79–83.

36. From this case law, it can be inferred that undertakings (themselves or through associations that are entitled to represent their interests) can claim a legitimate interest where they are operating in the relevant market or where the conduct complained of is liable to directly and adversely affect their interests. This confirms the established practice of the Commission which has accepted that a legitimate interest can, for instance, be claimed by the parties to the agreement or practice which is the subject of the complaint, by competitors whose interests have allegedly been damaged by the behaviour complained of or by undertakings excluded from a distribution system.

37. Consumer associations can equally lodge complaints with the Commission.[31] The Commission moreover holds the view that individual consumers whose economic interests are directly and adversely affected insofar as they are the buyers of goods or services that are the object of an infringement can be in a position to show a legitimate interest.[32]

Notes
[31] Case T-37/92 *Bureau Européen des Unions des Consommateurs (BEUC) v Commission of the European Communities* [1994] ECR II-285, para 36.
[32] This question is currently raised in a pending procedure before the Court of First Instance (Joined Cases T-213 and 214/01). The Commission has also accepted as complainant an individual consumer in its Decision of 9 December 1998 in Case IV/D-2/34.466, Greek Ferries, OJ L 109/24 of 27 April 1999, para 1.

Commentary
point 37: B&C: 13.064

38. However, the Commission does not consider as a legitimate interest within the meaning of
Article 7(2) the interest of persons or organisations that wish to come forward on general interest
considerations without showing that they or their members are liable to be directly and adversely
affected by the infringement (*pro bono publico*).

Commentary
point 38: B&C: 13.064

39. Local or regional public authorities may be able to show a legitimate interest in their capacity as buyers or users of goods or services affected by the conduct complained of. Conversely,
they cannot be considered as showing a legitimate interest within the meaning of Article 7(2)
of Regulation 1/2003 to the extent that they bring to the attention of the Commission alleged
infringements *pro bono publico.*
40. Complainants have to demonstrate their legitimate interest. Where a natural or legal person
lodging a complaint is unable to demonstrate a legitimate interest, the Commission is entitled,
without prejudice to its right to initiate proceedings of its own initiative, not to pursue the
complaint. The Commission may ascertain whether this condition is met at any stage of the
investigation.[33]

Notes

[33] Joined Cases T-133/95 and T-204/95 *International Express Carriers Conference (IECC) v Commission of the European
Communities* [1998] ECR II-3645, para 79.

Commentary
point 40: B&C: 13.063

C. Assessment of Complaints

(a) Community interest

41. Under the settled case law of the Community Courts, the Commission is not required to conduct
an investigation in each case[34] or, *a fortiori*, to take a decision within the meaning of Article 249
EC on the existence or non-existence of an infringement of Articles 81 or 82,[35] but is entitled to
give differing degrees of priority to the complaints brought before it and refer to the Community
interest in order to determine the degree of priority to be applied to the various complaints it
receives.[36] The position is different only if the complaint falls within the exclusive competence
of the Commission.[37]

Notes

[34] Case T-24/90 *Automec v Commission of the European Communities* [1992] ECR II-2223, para 76; Case C-91/95
P *Roger Tremblay and Others v Commission of the European Communities* [1996] ECR I-5547, para 30.
[35] Case 125/78 *GEMA v Commission of the European Communities* [1979] ECR 3173, para 17; Case C-119/97/P *Union
française de l'express (Ufex) and Others v Commission of the European Communities* [1999] ECR I-1341, para 87.
[36] Settled case law since Case T-24/90 *Automec v Commission of the European Communities* [1992] ECR II-2223, paras
77 and 85; Recital 18 of Regulation 1/2003 expressly confirms this possibility.
[37] Settled case law since Case T-24/90 *Automec v Commission of the European Communities* [1992] ECR II-2223, para
75. Under Regulation 1/2003, this principle may only be relevant in the context of Article 29 of that Regulation.

42. The Commission must however examine carefully the factual and legal elements brought to
its attention by the complainant in order to assess the Community interest in further investigation of a case.[38]

Notes

[38] Case 210/81 *Oswald Schmidt, trading as Demo-Studio Schmidt v Commission of the European Communities* [1983]
ECR 3045, para 19; Case C-119/97 P *Union française de l'express (Ufex) and Others v Commission of the European
Communities* [1999] ECR I-1341, para 86.

43. The assessment of the Community interest raised by a complaint depends on the circumstances of each individual case. Accordingly, the number of criteria of assessment to which the Commission may refer is not limited, nor is the Commission required to have recourse exclusively to certain criteria. As the factual and legal circumstances may differ considerably from case to case, it is permissible to apply new criteria which had not before been considered.[39] Where appropriate, the Commission may give priority to a single criterion for assessing the Community interest.[40]

Notes

[39] Case C-119/97 P *Union française de l'express (Ufex) and Others v Commission of the European Communities* [1999] ECR I-1341, paras 79–80.

[40] Case C-450/98 P *International Express Carriers Conference (IECC) v Commission of the European Communities* [2001] ECR I-3947, paras 57–59.

Commentary
point 43: B&C: 13.072

44. Among the criteria which have been held relevant in the case law for the assessment of the Community interest in the (further) investigation of a case are the following:
   — The Commission can reject a complaint on the ground that the complainant can bring an action to assert its rights before national courts.[41]
   — The Commission may not regard certain situations as excluded in principle from its purview under the task entrusted to it by the Treaty but is required to assess in each case how serious the alleged infringements are and how persistent their consequences are. This means in particular that it must take into account the duration and the extent of the infringements complained of and their effect on the competition situation in the Community.[42]
   — The Commission may have to balance the significance of the alleged infringement as regards the functioning of the common market, the probability of establishing the existence of the infringement and the scope of the investigation required in order to fulfil its task of ensuring that Articles 81 and 82 of the Treaty are complied with.[43]
   — While the Commission's discretion does not depend on how advanced the investigation of a case is, the stage of the investigation forms part of the circumstances of the case which the Commission may have to take into consideration.[44]
   — The Commission may decide that it is not appropriate to investigate a complaint where the practices in question have ceased. However, for this purpose, the Commission will have to ascertain whether anticompetitive effects persist and if the seriousness of the infringements or the persistence of their effects does not give the complaint a Community interest.[45]
   — The Commission may also decide that it is not appropriate to investigate a complaint where the undertakings concerned agree to change their conduct in such a way that it can consider that there is no longer a sufficient Community interest to intervene.[46]

Notes

[41] Case T-24/90 *Automec v Commission of the European Communities* [1992] ECR II-2223, paras 88 [ff]; Case T-5/93 *Roger Tremblay and Others v Commission of the European Communities* [1995] ECR II-185, paras 65 [ff]; Case T-575/93 *Casper Koelman v Commission of the European Communities* [1996] ECR II-1, paras 75–80; see also Part II above, where more detailed explanations concerning this situation are given.

[42] Case C-119/97 P *Union française de l'express (Ufex) and Others v Commission of the European Communities* [1999] ECR I-1341, paras 92 and 93.

[43] Settled case law since Case T-24/90 *Automec v Commission of the European Communities* [1992] ECR II-2223, para 86.

[44] Case C-449/98 P *International Express Carriers Conference (IECC) v Commission of the European Communities* [2001] ECR I-3875, para 37.

[45] Case T-77/95 *Syndicat français de l'Express International and Others v Commission of the European Communities* [1997] ECR II-1, para 57; Case C-119/97 P *Union française de l'express (Ufex) and Others v Commission of the European Communities* [1999] ECR I-1341, para 95. Cf. also Case T-37/92 *Bureau Européen des Unions des Consommateurs (BEUC) v Commission of the European Communities* [1994] ECR II-285, para 113, where an unwritten commitment between a Member State and a third county outside the common commercial policy was held not to suffice to establish that the conduct complained of had ceased.

[46] Case T-110/95 *International Express Carriers (IECC) v Commission of the European Communities and Others* [1998] ECR II-3605, para 57, upheld by Case 449/98 P *International Express Carriers (IECC) v Commission of the European Communities and Others* [2001] ECR I-3875, paras 44–47.

Commentary
point 45: B&C: 13.072

45. Where it forms the view that a case does not display sufficient Community interest to justify (further) investigation, the Commission may reject the complaint on that ground. Such a decision can be taken either before commencing an investigation or after taking investigative measures.[47] However, the Commission is not obliged to set aside a complaint for lack of Community interest.[48]

Notes
[47] Case C-449/98 P *International Express Carriers (IECC) v Commission of the European Communities e.a.* [2001] ECR I-3875, para 37.
[48] Cf. Case T-77/92 *Parker Pen v Commission of the European Communities* [1994] ECR II-549, paras 64/65.

(b) Assessment under Articles 81 and 82

46. The examination of a complaint under Articles 81 and 82 involves two aspects, one relating to the facts to be established to prove an infringement of Articles 81 or 82 and the other relating to the legal assessment of the conduct complained of.

47. Where the complaint, while complying with the requirements of Article 5 of Regulation 773/2004 and Form C, does not sufficiently substantiate the allegations put forward, it may be rejected on that ground.[49] In order to reject a complaint on the ground that the conduct complained of does not infringe the EC competition rules or does not fall within their scope of application, the Commission is not obliged to take into account circumstances that have not been brought to its attention by the complainant and that it could only have uncovered by the investigation of the case.[50]

Notes
[49] Case 298/83 *Comité des industries cinématographiques des Communautés Européennes (CICCE) v Commission of the European Communities* [1985] ECR 1105, paras 21–24; Case T-198/98 *Micro Leader Business v Commission of the European Communities* [1999] ECR II-3989, paras 32–39.
[50] Case T-319/99 *Federación Nacional de Empresas (FENIN) v Commission of the European Communities* [2003] ECR II-357, para 43 [and see, on appeal, Case C-205/03 P *FENIN v Commission of the European Communities* [2006] ECR I-6295, judgment of 11 July 2006].

48. The criteria for the legal assessment of agreements or practices under Articles 81 and 82 cannot be dealt with exhaustively in the present Notice. However, potential complainants should refer to the extensive guidance available from the Commission,[51] in addition to other sources and in particular the case law of the Community Courts and the case practice of the Commission. Four specific issues are mentioned in the following points with indications on where to find further guidance.

Notes
[51] Extensive guidance can be found on the Commission's website at http://europa.eu.int/comm/competition/index_en.html.

49. Agreements and practices fall within the scope of application of Articles 81 and 82 where they are capable of affecting trade between Member States. Where an agreement or practice does not fulfil this condition, national competition law may apply, but not EC competition law. Extensive guidance on this subject can be found in the Notice on the effect on trade concept.[52]

Notes
[52] Notice on the effect on trade concept contained in Articles 81 and 82 of the Treaty [OJ C 101, 27.4.2004, p. 81].

50. Agreements falling within the scope of Article 81 may be agreements of minor importance which are deemed not to restrict competition appreciably. Guidance on this issue can be found in the Commission's *de minimis* Notice.[53]

Notes

[53] Commission Notice on agreements of minor importance which do not appreciably restrict competition under Article 81(1) of the Treaty establishing the European Community (*de minimis*), OJ C 368 of 22 December [2001], p. 13.

51. Agreements that fulfil the conditions of a block exemption regulation are deemed to satisfy the conditions of Article 81(3).[54] For the Commission to withdraw the benefit of the block exemption pursuant to Article 29 of Regulation 1/2003, it must find that upon individual assessment an agreement to which the exemption regulation applies has certain effects which are incompatible with Article 81(3).

Notes

[54] The texts of all block exemption regulations are available on the Commission's website at http://europa.eu.int/comm/competition/index_en.html.

52. Agreements that restrict competition within the meaning of Article 81(1) EC may fulfil the conditions of Article 81(3) EC. Pursuant to Article 1(2) of Regulation 1/2003 and without a prior administrative decision being required, such agreements are not prohibited. Guidance on the conditions to be fulfilled by an agreement pursuant to Article 81(3) can be found in the Notice on Article 81(3).[55]

Notes

[55] Commission Notice — Guidelines on the application of Article 81(3) of the Treaty [OJ C 101, 27.4.2004, p. 97].

D. THE COMMISSION'S PROCEDURES WHEN DEALING WITH COMPLAINTS

(a) Overview

53. As recalled above, the Commission is not obliged to carry out an investigation on the basis of every complaint submitted with a view to establishing whether an infringement has been committed. However, the Commission is under a duty to consider carefully the factual and legal issues brought to its attention by the complainant, in order to assess whether those issues indicate conduct which is liable to infringe Articles 81 and 82.[56]

Notes

[56] Case 210/81 *Oswald Schmidt, trading as Demo-Studio Schmidt v Commission of the European Communities* [1983] ECR 3045, para 19; Case T-24/90 *Automec v Commission of the European Communities* [1992] ECR II-2223, para 79.

54. In the Commission's procedure for dealing with complaints, different stages can be distinguished.[57]

Notes

[57] Cf. Case T-64/89 *Automec v Commission of the European Communities* [1990] ECR II-367, paras 45–47; Case T-37/92 *Bureau Européen des Unions des Consommateurs (BEUC) v Commission of the European Communities* [1994] ECR II-285, para 29.

55. During the first stage, following the submission of the complaint, the Commission examines the complaint and may collect further information in order to decide what action it will take on the complaint. That stage may include an informal exchange of views between the Commission and the complainant with a view to clarifying the factual and legal issues with which the complaint is concerned. In this stage, the Commission may give an initial reaction to the complainant allowing the complainant an opportunity to expand on his allegations in the light of that initial reaction.

Commentary
point 55: B&C: 13.068

56. In the second stage, the Commission may investigate the case further with a view to initiating proceedings pursuant to Article 7(1) of Regulation 1/2003 against the undertakings complained of.

Where the Commission considers that there are insufficient grounds for acting on the complaint, it will inform the complainant of its reasons and offer the complainant the opportunity to submit any further comments within a time-limit which it fixes (Article 7(1) of Regulation 773/2004).

Commentary
point 56: B&C: 13.069

57. If the complainant fails to make known its views within the time-limit set by the Commission, the complaint is deemed to have been withdrawn (Article 7(3) of Regulation 773/2004). In all other cases, in the third stage of the procedure, the Commission takes cognisance of the observations submitted by the complainant and either initiates a procedure against the subject of the complaint or adopts a decision rejecting the complaint.[58]

Notes
[58] Case C-282/95 P, *Guérin automobiles v Commission of the European Communities* [1997] ECR I-1503, para 36.
Commentary
point 57: B&C: 13.069

58. Where the Commission rejects a complaint pursuant to Article 13 of Regulation 1/2003 on the grounds that another authority is dealing or has dealt with the case, the Commission proceeds in accordance with Article 9 of Regulation 773/2004.
59. Throughout the procedure, complainants benefit from a range of rights as provided in particular in Articles 6 to 8 of Regulation 773/2004. However, proceedings of the Commission in competition cases do not constitute adversarial proceedings between the complainant on the one hand and the companies which are the subject of the investigation on the other hand. Accordingly, the procedural rights of complainants are less far-reaching than the right to a fair hearing of the companies which are the subject of an infringement procedure.[59]

Notes
[59] Joined Cases 142 and 156/84 *British American Tobacco Company and R. J. Reynolds Industries v Commission of the European Communities* [1987] ECR 249, paras 19 and 20.

(b) Indicative time limit for informing the complainant of the Commission's proposed action

60. The Commission is under an obligation to decide on complaints within a reasonable time.[60] What is a reasonable duration depends on the circumstances of each case and in particular, its context, the various procedural steps followed by the Commission, the conduct of the parties in the course of the procedure, the complexity of the case and its importance for the various parties involved.[61]

Notes
[60] Case C-282/95 P *Guérin automobiles v Commission of the European Communities* [1997] ECR I-1503, para 37.
[61] Joined Cases T-213/95 and T-18/96 *Stichting Certificatie Kraanverhuurbedrijf (SCK) and Federatie van Nederlandse Kraanbedrijven (FNK) v Commission of the European Communities* [1997] ECR 1739, para 57.

61. The Commission will in principle endeavour to inform complainants of the action that it proposes to take on a complaint within an indicative time frame of four months from the reception of the complaint. Thus, subject to the circumstances of the individual case and in particular the possible need to request complementary information from the complainant or third parties, the Commission will in principle inform the complainant within four months whether or not it intends to investigate its case further. This time-limit does not constitute a binding statutory term.

Commentary
point 61: B&C: 13.068

62. Accordingly, within this four month period, the Commission may communicate its proposed course of action to the complainant as an initial reaction within the first phase of the procedure (see point 55 above). The Commission may also, where the examination of the complaint has progressed to the second stage (see point 56 above), directly proceed to informing the complainant about its provisional assessment by a letter pursuant to Article 7(1) of Regulation 773/2004.

63. To ensure the most expeditious treatment of their complaint, it is desirable that complainants cooperate diligently in the procedures,[62] for example by informing the Commission of new developments.

Notes

[62] The notion of "diligence" on the part of the complainant is used by the Court of First Instance in Case T-77/94 *Vereniging van Groothandelaren in Bloemkwekerijprodukten and Others v Commission of the European Communities* [1997] ECR II-759, para 75.

(c) Procedural rights of the complainant

64. Where the Commission addresses a statement of objections to the companies complained of pursuant to Article 10(1) of Regulation 773/2004, the complainant is entitled to receive a copy of this document from which business secrets and other confidential information of the companies concerned have been removed (non-confidential version of the statement of objections; cf. Article 6(1) of Regulation 773/2004). The complainant is invited to comment in writing on the statement of objections. A time-limit will be set for such written comments.

Commentary
point 64: B&C: 13.073

65. Furthermore, the Commission may, where appropriate, afford complainants the opportunity of expressing their views at the oral hearing of the parties to which a statement of objections has been addressed, if the complainants so request in their written comments.[63]

Notes
[63] Article 6(2) of Commission Regulation 773/2004.

Commentary
point 65: B&C: 13.073 F&N: 8.452

66. Complainants may submit, of their own initiative or following a request by the Commission, documents that contain business secrets or other confidential information. Confidential information will be protected by the Commission.[64] Under Article 16 of Regulation 773/2004, complainants are obliged to identify confidential information, give reasons why the information is considered confidential and submit a separate non-confidential version when they make their views known pursuant to Article 6(1) and 7(1) of Regulation 773/2004, as well as when they subsequently submit further information in the course of the same procedure. Moreover, the Commission may, in all other cases, request complainants which produce documents or statements to identify the documents or parts of the documents or statements which they consider to be confidential. It may in particular set a deadline for the complainant to specify why it considers a piece of information to be confidential and to provide a non-confidential version, including a concise description or non-confidential version of each piece of information deleted.

Notes
[64] Article 287 EC, Article 28 of Regulation 1/2003 and Articles 15 and 16 of Regulation 773/2004.

67. The qualification of information as confidential does not prevent the Commission from disclosing and using information where that is necessary to prove an infringement of Articles 81 or 82.[65] Where business secrets and confidential information are necessary to prove an infringement, the Commission must assess for each individual document whether the need to disclose is greater than the harm which might result from disclosure.

Notes
65 Article 27(2) of Regulation 1/2003.

68. Where the Commission takes the view that a complaint should not be further examined, because there is no sufficient Community interest in pursuing the case further or on other grounds, it will inform the complainant in the form of a letter which indicates its legal basis (Article 7(1) of Regulation 773/2004), sets out the reasons that have led the Commission to provisionally conclude in the sense indicated and provides the complainant with the opportunity to submit supplementary information or observations within a time-limit set by the Commission. The Commission will also indicate the consequences of not replying pursuant to Article 7(3) of Regulation 773/2004, as explained below.

69. Pursuant to Article 8(1) of Regulation 773/2004, the complainant has the right to access the information on which the Commission bases its preliminary view. Such access is normally provided by annexing to the letter a copy of the relevant documents.

Commentary
point 69: B&C: 13.069

70. The time-limit for observations by the complainant on the letter pursuant to Article 7(1) of Regulation 773/2004 will be set in accordance with the circumstances of the case. It will not be shorter than four weeks (Article 17(2) of Regulation 773/2004). If the complainant does not respond within the time-limit set, the complaint is deemed to have been withdrawn pursuant to Article 7(3) of Regulation 773/2004. Complainants are also entitled to withdraw their complaint at any time if they so wish.

Commentary
point 70: B&C: 13.069

71. The complainant may request an extension of the time-limit for the provision of comments. Depending on the circumstances of the case, the Commission may grant such an extension.

Commentary
point 71: B&C: 13.069

72. In that case, where the complainant submits supplementary observations, the Commission takes cognisance of those observations. Where they are of such a nature as to make the Commission change its previous course of action, it may initiate a procedure against the companies complained of. In this procedure, the complainant has the procedural rights explained above.

73. Where the observations of the complainant do not alter the Commission's proposed course of action, it rejects the complaint by decision.[66]

Notes
66 Article 7(2) of Regulation 773/2004; Case C-282/95 P *Guérin automobiles v Commission of the European Communities* [1997] ECR I-1503, para 36.

(d) The Commission decision rejecting a complaint

74. Where the Commission rejects a complaint by decision pursuant to Article 7(2) of Regulation 773/2004, it must state the reasons in accordance with Article 253 EC, i.e. in a way that is appropriate to the act at issue and takes into account the circumstances of each case.

75. The statement of reasons must disclose in a clear and unequivocal fashion the reasoning followed by the Commission in such a way as to enable the complainant to ascertain the reasons for the decision and to enable the competent Community Court to exercise its power of review. However, the Commission is not obliged to adopt a position on all the arguments relied on by the complainant in support of its complaint. It only needs to set out the facts and legal considerations which are of decisive importance in the context of the decision.[67]

Notes
67 Settled case law, cf. i.a. Case T-114/92 *Bureau Européen des Médias et de l'Industrie Musicale (BEMIM) v Commission of the European Communities* [1995] ECR II-147, para 41.

76. Where the Commission rejects a complaint in a case that also gives rise to a decision pursuant to Article 10 of Regulation 1/2003 (Finding of inapplicability of Articles 81 or 82) or Article 9 of Regulation 1/2003 (Commitments), the decision rejecting a complaint may refer to that other decision adopted on the basis of the provisions mentioned.

77. A decision to reject a complaint is subject to appeal before the Community Courts.[68]

Notes
68 Settled case law since Case 210/81 *Oswald Schmidt, trading as Demo-Studio Schmidt v Commission of the European Communities* [1983] ECR 3045.

78. A decision rejecting a complaint prevents complainants from requiring the reopening of the investigation unless they put forward significant new evidence. Accordingly, further correspondence on the same alleged infringement by former complainants cannot be regarded as a new complaint unless significant new evidence is brought to the attention of the Commission. However, the Commission may re-open a file under appropriate circumstances.

Commentary
point 78: B&C: 13.070

79. A decision to reject a complaint does not definitively rule on the question of whether or not there is an infringement of Articles 81 or 82, even where the Commission has assessed the facts on the basis of Articles 81 and 82. The assessments made by the Commission in a decision rejecting a complaint therefore do not prevent a Member State court or competition authority from applying Articles 81 and 82 to agreements and practices brought before it. The assessments made by the Commission in a decision rejecting a complaint constitute facts which Member States' courts or competition authorities may take into account in examining whether the agreements or conduct in question are in conformity with Articles 81 and 82.[69]

Notes
69 Case T-575/93 *Casper Koelman v Commission of the European Communities* [1996] ECR II-1, paras 41–43.

(e) Specific situations

80. According to Article 8 of Regulation 1/2003 the Commission may on its own initiative order interim measures where there is the risk of serious and irreparable damage to competition. Article 8 of Regulation 1/2003 makes it clear that interim measures cannot be applied for by complainants under Article 7(2) of Regulation 1/2003. Requests for interim measures by undertakings can be brought before Member States' courts which are well placed to decide on such measures.[70]

Notes
70 Depending on the case, Member States' competition authorities may equally be well placed to adopt interim measures.

Commentary
point 80: B&C: 13.072, 13.118

81. Some persons may wish to inform the Commission about suspected infringements of Articles 81 or 82 without having their identity revealed to the undertakings concerned by the allegations. These persons are welcome to contact the Commission. The Commission is bound to respect an informant's request for anonymity,[71] unless the request to remain anonymous is manifestly unjustified.

Notes
71 Case 145/83 *Stanley George Adams v Commission of the European Communities* [1985] ECR 3539.

ANNEX
FORM C
COMPLAINT PURSUANT TO ARTICLE 7 OF REGULATION (EC) NO 1/2003

I. INFORMATION REGARDING THE COMPLAINANT AND THE UNDERTAKING(S) OR ASSOCIATION OF UNDERTAKINGS GIVING RISE TO THE COMPLAINT

1. Give full details on the identity of the legal or natural person submitting the complaint. Where the complainant is an undertaking, identify the corporate group to which it belongs and provide a concise overview of the nature and scope of its business activities. Provide a contact person (with telephone number, postal and e-mail-address) from which supplementary explanations can be obtained.

2. Identify the undertaking(s) or association of undertakings whose conduct the complaint relates to, including, where applicable, all available information on the corporate group to which the undertaking(s) complained of belong and the nature and scope of the business activities pursued by them. Indicate the position of the complainant vis-à-vis the undertaking(s) or association of undertakings complained of (e.g. customer, competitor).

II. DETAILS OF THE ALLEGED INFRINGEMENT AND EVIDENCE

3. Set out in detail the facts from which, in your opinion, it appears that there exists an infringement of Article 81 or 82 of the Treaty and/or Article 53 or 54 of the EEA agreement. Indicate in particular the nature of the products (goods or services) affected by the alleged infringements and explain, where necessary, the commercial relationships concerning these products. Provide all available details on the agreements or practices of the undertakings or associations of undertakings to which this complaint relates. Indicate, to the extent possible, the relative market positions of the undertakings concerned by the complaint.

4. Submit all documentation in your possession relating to or directly connected with the facts set out in the complaint (for example, texts of agreements, minutes of negotiations or meetings, terms of transactions, business documents, circulars, correspondence, notes of telephone conversations . . .). State the names and address of the persons able to testify to the facts set out in the complaint, and in particular of persons affected by the alleged infringement. Submit statistics or other data in your possession which relate to the facts set out, in particular where they show developments in the marketplace (for example information relating to prices and price trends, barriers to entry to the market for new suppliers etc.).

5. Set out your view about the geographical scope of the alleged infringement and explain, where that is not obvious, to what extent trade between Member States or between the Community and one or more EFTA States that are contracting parties of the EEA Agreement may be affected by the conduct complained of.

III. FINDING SOUGHT FROM THE COMMISSION AND LEGITIMATE INTEREST

6. Explain what finding or action you are seeking as a result of proceedings brought by the Commission.

7. Set out the grounds on which you claim a legitimate interest as complainant pursuant to Article 7 of Regulation (EC) No 1/2003. State in particular how the conduct complained of affects you and explain how, in your view, intervention by the Commission would be liable to remedy the alleged grievance.

IV. PROCEEDINGS BEFORE NATIONAL COMPETITION AUTHORITIES OR NATIONAL COURTS

8. Provide full information about whether you have approached, concerning the same or closely related subject-matters, any other competition authority and/or whether a lawsuit has been brought before a national court. If so, provide full details about the administrative or judicial authority contacted and your submissions to such authority.

Declaration that the information given in this form and in the Annexes thereto is given entirely in good faith.

Date and signature.

B11

COMMISSION NOTICE ON INFORMAL GUIDANCE RELATING TO NOVEL QUESTIONS CONCERNING ARTICLES 81 AND 82 OF THE EC TREATY THAT ARISE IN INDIVIDUAL CASES (GUIDANCE LETTERS)

(2004/C 101/06)
(Text with EEA relevance)

Official Journal C 101, 27.04.2004, p. 78

Celex No: 52004XC0427(05)

Notes
EEA application: the EFTA Surveillance Authority has adopted a parallel notice on informal guidance relating to novel questions concerning Articles 53 and 54 of the EEA Agreement that arise in individual cases (guidance letters) under Article 5(2)(b) of the Surveillance and Court Agreement: OJ C 305, 14.12.2006, p. 34 and EEA Supplement No 62, 14.12.2006, p. 17.

Commentary
Notice: F&N: 2.13, 2.15
sections III–VI: B&C: 13.023

I. Regulation 1/2003

1. Regulation 1/2003[1] sets up a new enforcement system for Articles 81 and 82 of the Treaty. While designed to restore the focus on the primary task of effective enforcement of the competition rules, the Regulation also creates legal certainty inasmuch as it provides that agreements[2] which fall under Article 81(1) but fulfil the conditions in Article 81(3) are valid and fully enforceable *ab initio* without a prior decision by a competition authority (Article 1 of Regulation 1/2003).

Notes
[1] Council Regulation (EC) No 1/2003 of 16 December 2002 on the implementation of the rules on competition laid down in Articles 81 and 82 of the Treaty (OJ L 1, 4.1.2003, pages 1–25).
[2] In this notice, the term "agreement" is used for agreements, decisions by associations of undertakings and concerted practices. The term "practices" refers to the conduct of dominant undertakings. The term "undertakings" equally covers "associations of undertakings".

2. The framework of Regulation 1/2003, while introducing parallel competence of the Commission, Member States' competition authorities and Member States' courts to apply Article 81 and 82 in their entirety, limits risks of inconsistent application by a range of measures, thereby ensuring the

Part B Modernisation and Procedural Matters

primary aspect of legal certainty for companies as reflected in the case law of the Court of Justice, i.e. that the competition rules are applied in a consistent way throughout the Community.

3. Undertakings are generally well placed to assess the legality of their actions in such a way as to enable them to take an informed decision on whether to go ahead with an agreement or practice and in what form. They are close to the facts and have at their disposal the framework of block exemption regulations, case law and case practice as well as extensive guidance in Commission guidelines and notices.[3]

Notes

[3] All texts mentioned are available at [http://ec.europa.eu./comm/competition/index_en.html].

4. Alongside the reform of the rules implementing Articles 81 and 82 brought about by Regulation 1/2003, the Commission has conducted a review of block exemption regulations, Commission notices and guidelines, with a view to further assist self-assessment by economic operators. The Commission has also produced guidelines on the application of Article 81(3).[4] This allows undertakings in the vast majority of cases to reliably assess their agreements with regard to Article 81. Furthermore, it is the practice of the Commission to impose more than symbolic fines[5] only in cases where it is established, either in horizontal instruments or in the case law and practice that a certain behaviour constitutes an infringement.

Notes

[4] Commission Notice — Guidelines on the application of Article 81(3) of the Treaty [OJ C 101, 27.4.2004, p. 97].

[5] Symbolic fines are normally set at 1000 EUR; cf. Commission Guidelines on the method of setting fines imposed pursuant to Article 15(2) of Regulation No 17 and Article 65(5) of the ECSC Treaty (OJ C 9, 14.1.1998).

5. Where cases, despite the above elements, give rise to genuine uncertainty because they present novel or unresolved questions for the application of Articles 81 and 82, individual undertakings may wish to seek informal guidance from the Commission.[6] Where it considers it appropriate and subject to its enforcement priorities, the Commission may provide such guidance on novel questions concerning the interpretation of Articles 81 and/or 82 in a written statement (guidance letter). The present Notice sets out details of this instrument.

Notes

[6] Cf. Recital 38 of Regulation 1/2003.

II. Framework for Assessing Whether to Issue a Guidance Letter

6. Regulation 1/2003 confers powers on the Commission to effectively prosecute infringements of Articles 81 and 82 and to impose sanctions.[7] One major objective of the Regulation is to ensure efficient enforcement of the EC competition rules by removing the former notification system and thus allowing the Commission to focus its enforcement policy on the most serious infringements.[8]

Notes

[7] Cf. in particular Articles 7 to 9, 12, 17–24, 29 of Regulation 1/2003.

[8] Cf. in particular Recital 3 of Regulation 1/2003.

7. While Regulation 1/2003 is without prejudice to the ability of the Commission to issue informal guidance to individual undertakings,[9] as set out in this Notice, this ability should not interfere with the primary objective of the Regulation, which is to ensure effective enforcement. The Commission may therefore only provide informal guidance to individual undertakings in so far as this is compatible with its enforcement priorities.

Notes
9 Cf. Recital 38 of Regulation 1/2003.

8. Subject to point 7, the Commission, seized of a request for a guidance letter, will consider whether it is appropriate to process it. Issuing a guidance letter may only be considered if the following cumulative conditions are fulfilled:

   (a) The substantive assessment of an agreement or practice with regard to Articles 81 and/or 82 of the Treaty, poses a question of application of the law for which there is no clarification in the existing EC legal framework including the case law of the Community Courts, nor publicly available general guidance or precedent in decision-making practice or previous guidance letters.

   (b) A prima facie evaluation of the specificities and background of the case suggests that the clarification of the novel question through a guidance letter is useful, taking into account the following elements:
   — the economic importance from the point of view of the consumer of the goods or services concerned by the agreement or practice, and/or
   — the extent to which the agreement or practice corresponds or is liable to correspond to more widely spread economic usage in the marketplace, and/or
   — the extent of the investments linked to the transaction in relation to the size of the companies concerned and the extent to which the transaction relates to a structural operation such as the creation of a non-full function joint venture.

   (c) It is possible to issue a guidance letter on the basis of the information provided, i.e. no further fact-finding is required.

Commentary
point 8: **B&C**: 13.023

9. Furthermore, the Commission will not consider a request for a guidance letter in either of the following circumstances:
   — the questions raised in the request are identical or similar to issues raised in a case pending before the European Court of First Instance or the European Court of Justice;
   — the agreement or practice to which the request refers is subject to proceedings pending with the Commission, a Member State court or Member State competition authority.

Commentary
point 9: **B&C**: 13.023

10. The Commission will not consider hypothetical questions and will not issue guidance letters on agreements or practices that are no longer being implemented by the parties. Undertakings may however present a request for a guidance letter to the Commission in relation to questions raised by an agreement or practice that they envisage, i.e. before the implementation of that agreement or practice. In this case the transaction must have reached a sufficiently advanced stage for a request to be considered.

Commentary
point 10: **B&C**: 13.023

11. A request for a guidance letter is without prejudice to the power of the Commission to open proceedings in accordance with Regulation 1/2003 with regard to the facts presented in the request.

III. INDICATIONS ON HOW TO REQUEST GUIDANCE

12. A request can be presented by an undertaking or undertakings which have entered into or intend to enter into an agreement or practice that could fall within the scope of Articles 81 and/or 82 of the Treaty with regard to questions of interpretation raised by such agreement or practice.

13. A request for a guidance letter should be addressed to the following address:
    Commission européenne/Europese Commissie

Competition DG
B–1049 Bruxelles/Brussel.

14. There is no form. A memorandum should be presented which clearly states:
    — the identity of all undertakings concerned as well as a single address for contacts with the Commission;
    — the specific questions on which guidance is sought;
    — full and exhaustive information on all points relevant for an informed evaluation of the questions raised, including pertinent documentation;
    — a detailed reasoning, having regard to point 8 a), why the request presents (a) novel question(s);
    — all other information that permits an evaluation of the request in the light of the aspects explained in points 8–10 of this Notice, including in particular a declaration that the agreement or practice to which the request refers is not subject to proceedings pending before a Member State court or competition authority;
    — where the request contains elements that are considered business secrets, a clear identification of these elements;
    — any other information or documentation relevant to the individual case.

IV. PROCESSING OF THE REQUEST

15. The Commission will in principle evaluate the request on the basis of the information provided. Notwithstanding point 8 c), the Commission may use additional information at its disposal from public sources, former proceedings or any other source and may ask the applicant(s) to provide supplementary information. The normal rules on professional secrecy apply to the information supplied by the applicant(s).

16. The Commission may share the information submitted to it with the Member States' competition authorities and receive input from them. It may discuss the substance of the request with the Member States' competition authorities before issuing a guidance letter.

17. Where no guidance letter is issued, the Commission shall inform the applicant(s) accordingly.

18. An undertaking can withdraw its request at any point in time. In any case, information supplied in the context of a request for guidance remains with the Commission and can be used in subsequent procedures under Regulation 1/2003 (cf. point 11 above).

V. GUIDANCE LETTERS

19. A guidance letter sets out:
    — a summary description of the facts on which it is based;
    — the principal legal reasoning underlying the understanding of the Commission on novel questions relating to Articles 81 and/or 82 raised by the request.

20. A guidance letter may be limited to part of the questions raised in the request. It may also include additional aspects to those set out in the request.

21. Guidance letters will be posted on the Commission's [web-site], having regard to the legitimate interest of undertakings in the protection of their business secrets. Before issuing a guidance letter, the Commission will agree with the applicants on a public version.

VI. THE EFFECTS OF GUIDANCE LETTERS

22. Guidance letters are in the first place intended to help undertakings carry out themselves an informed assessment of their agreements and practices.

23. A guidance letter cannot prejudge the assessment of the same question by the Community Courts.

24. Where an agreement or practice has formed the factual basis for a guidance letter, the Commission is not precluded from subsequently examining that same agreement or practice in a procedure under Regulation 1/2003, in particular following a complaint. In that case, the Commission will take the previous guidance letter into account, subject in particular to changes in the underlying facts, to any new aspects raised by a complaint, to developments in the case law of the European Courts or wider changes of the Commission's policy.

25. Guidance letters are not Commission decisions and do not bind Member States' competition authorities or courts that have the power to apply Articles 81 and 82. However, it is open to Member States' competition authorities and courts to take account of guidance letters issued by the Commission as they see fit in the context of a case.

Commentary
point 25: B&C: 14.084

B12

COMMISSION NOTICE ON THE RULES FOR ACCESS TO THE COMMISSION FILE IN CASES PURSUANT TO ARTICLES 81 AND 82 OF THE EC TREATY, ARTICLES 53, 54 AND 57 OF THE EEA AGREEMENT AND COUNCIL REGULATION (EC) No 139/2004

(2005/C 325/07)

Text with EEA relevance)

Official Journal C 325, 22.12.2005, p. 7

Celex No: 52005XC1222(03)

Notes
EEA application: the EFTA Surveillance Authority has adopted a parallel notice on the rules for access to the EFTA Surveillance Authority file in cases pursuant to Articles 53, 54 and 57 of the EEA Agreement under Article 5(2)(b) of the Surveillance and Court Agreement: see College Decision 229/06/COL of 19 July 2006, not yet published.

Commentary
Notice: B&C: 8.009, 8.146, 13.089 F&N: 5.569, 5.580, 5.583, 5.588, 8.260, 8.352, 8.353, 8.458, 8.461, 8.488, 8.518
paras 21–25: B&C: 8.177 F&N: 5.584
paras 29–32: B&C: 13.100
paras 35–43: F&N: 5.584
section IV(B): F&N: 8.459

I. Introduction and Subject-matter of the Notice

1. Access to the Commission file is one of the procedural guarantees intended to apply the principle of equality of arms and to protect the rights of the defence. Access to the file is provided for in Article 27(1) and (2) of Council Regulation (EC) No 1/2003,[1] Article 15(1) of Commission Regulation (EC) No 773/2004 ("the Implementing Regulation"),[2] Article 18(1) and (3) of the Council Regulation (EC) No 139/2004 ("Merger Regulation")[3] and Article 17(1) of Commission Regulation (EC) No 802/2004 ("the Merger Implementing Regulation").[4] In accordance with

these provisions, before taking decisions on the basis of Articles 7, 8, 23 and 24(2) of Regulation (EC) No 1/2003 and Articles 6(3), 7(3), 8(2) to (6), 14 and 15 of the Merger Regulation, the Commission shall give the persons, undertakings or associations of undertakings, as the case may be, an opportunity of making known their views on the objections against them and they shall be entitled to have access to the Commission's file in order to fully respect their rights of defence in the proceedings. The present notice provides the framework for the exercise of the right set out in these provisions. It does not cover the possibility of the provision of documents in the context of other proceedings. This notice is without prejudice to the interpretation of such provisions by the Community Courts. The principles set out in this Notice apply also when the Commission enforces Articles 53, 54 and 57 of the EEA Agreement.[5]

Notes

[1] Council Regulation (EC) No 1/2003 of 16 December 2002 on the implementation of the rules on competition laid down in Articles 81 and 82 of the Treaty, OJ L 1, 4.1.2003, p. 1–25.

[2] Commission Regulation (EC) No 773/2004 of 7 April 2004 relating to the conduct of proceedings by the Commission pursuant to Articles 81 and 82 of the EC Treaty, OJ L 123, 27.4.2004, p. 18–24.

[3] Council Regulation (EC) No 139/2004 of 20 January 2004 on the control of concentrations between undertakings, OJ L 24, 29.1.2004, p. 1–22.

[4] Commission Regulation (EC) No 802/2004 of 21 April 2004 implementing Council Regulation (EC) No 139/2004 on the control of concentrations between undertakings, OJ L 133, 30.4.2004, p. 1–39. Corrected in the OJ L 172, 6.5.2004, p. 9.

[5] References in this Notice to Articles 81 and 82 therefore apply also to Articles 53 and 54 of the EEA Agreement.

Commentary
para 1: F&N: 8.457

2. This specific right outlined above is distinct from the general right to access to documents under Regulation (EC) No 1049/2001,[1] which is subject to different criteria and exceptions and pursues a different purpose.

Notes

[1] Regulation (EC) No 1049/2001 of the European Parliament and of the Council of 30 May 2001 regarding public access to European Parliament, Council and Commission documents, OJ L 145, 31.5.2001, p. 43. See for instance Case T-2/03, *Verein für Konsumenteninformation v Commission*, judgment of 13 April 2005 [[2005] ECR II-1121].

3. The term access to the file is used in this notice exclusively to mean the access granted to the persons, undertakings or association of undertakings to whom the Commission has addressed a statement of objections. This notice clarifies who has access to the file for this purpose.

4. The same term, or the term access to documents, is also used in the above-mentioned regulations in respect of complainants or other involved parties. These situations are, however, distinct from that of the addressees of a statement of objections and therefore do not fall under the definition of access to the file for the purposes of this notice. These related situations are dealt with in a separate section of the notice.

5. This notice also explains to which information access is granted, when access takes place and what are the procedures for implementing access to the file.

6. As from its publication, this notice replaces the 1997 Commission notice on access to the file.[1] The new rules take account of the legislation applicable as of 1 May 2004, namely the above referred Regulation (EC) No 1/2003, Merger Regulation, Implementing Regulation and Merger Implementing Regulation, as well as the Commission Decision of 23 May 2001 on the terms of reference of Hearing Officers in certain competition proceedings.[2] It also takes into account the recent case law of the Court of Justice and the Court of First Instance of the European Communities[3] and the practice developed by the Commission since the adoption of the 1997 notice.

Notes

[1] Commission notice on the internal rules of procedure for processing requests for access to the file in cases under Articles 85 and 86 [now 81 and 82] of the EC Treaty, Articles 65 and 66 of the ECSC Treaty and Council Regulation (EEC) No 4064/89, OJ C 23, 23.1.1997, p. 3.

[2] OJ L 162, 19.6.2001, p. 21.
[3] In particular Joint Cases T-25/95 et al., *Cimenteries CBR SA et al. v Commission* [2000] ECR II-0491.

II. SCOPE OF ACCESS TO THE FILE

A. Who is entitled to access to the file?

7. Access to the file pursuant to the provisions mentioned in paragraph 1 is intended to enable the effective exercise of the rights of defence against the objections brought forward by the Commission. For this purpose, both in cases under Articles 81 and 82 EC and in cases under the Merger Regulation, access is granted, upon request, to the persons, undertakings or associations of undertakings,[1] as the case may be, to which the Commission addresses its objections[2] (hereinafter, "the parties").

Notes
[1] In the remainder of this Notice, the term "undertaking" includes both undertakings and associations of undertakings. The term "person" encompasses natural and legal persons. Many entities are legal persons and undertakings at the same time; in this case, they are covered by both terms. The same applies where a natural person is an undertaking within the meaning of Articles 81 and 82. In Merger proceedings, account must also be taken of persons referred to in Article 3(1)(b) of the Merger Regulation, even when they are natural persons. Where entities without legal personality which are also not undertakings become involved in Commission competition proceedings, the Commission applies, where appropriate, the principles set out in this Notice mutatis mutandis.
[2] Cf. Article 15(1) of the Implementing Regulation, Article 18(3) of the Merger Regulation and Article 17(1) of the Merger Implementing Regulation.

Commentary
para 7: F&N: 2.200, 5.390, 5.420, 5.570, 8.457

B. To which documents is access granted?

1. The content of the Commission file

8. The "Commission file" in a competition investigation (hereinafter also referred to as "the file") consists of all documents,[1] which have been obtained, produced and/or assembled by the Commission Directorate General for Competition, during the investigation.

Notes
[1] In this notice the term "document" is used for all forms of information support, irrespective of the storage medium. This covers also any electronic data storage device as may be or become available.

Commentary
para 8: B&C: 8.146, 13.093 F&N: 5.577, 8.458

9. In the course of investigation under Articles 20, 21 and 22(2) of Regulation (EC) No 1/2003 and Articles 12 and 13 of the Merger Regulation, the Commission may collect a number of documents, some of which may, following a more detailed examination, prove to be unrelated to the subject matter of the case in question. Such documents may be returned to the undertaking from which those have been obtained. Upon return, these documents will no longer constitute part of the file.

Commentary
para 9: B&C: 13.049

2. Accessible documents

10. The parties must be able to acquaint themselves with the information in the Commission's file, so that, on the basis of this information, they can effectively express their views on the preliminary conclusions reached by the Commission in its objections. For this purpose they will be granted access to all documents making up the Commission file, as defined in paragraph 8, with the

exception of internal documents, business secrets of other undertakings, or other confidential information.[1]

11. Results of a study commissioned in connection with proceedings are accessible together with the terms of reference and the methodology of the study. Precautions may however be necessary in order to protect intellectual property rights.

3. Non-accessible documents

3.1. Internal documents

3.1.1 General principles

12. Internal documents can be neither incriminating nor exculpatory.[1] They do not constitute part of the evidence on which the Commission can rely in its assessment of a case. Thus, the parties will not be granted access to internal documents in the Commission file.[2] Given their lack of evidential value, this restriction on access to internal documents does not prejudice the proper exercise of the parties" right of defence.[3]

13. There is no obligation on the Commission departments to draft any minutes of meetings[1] with any person or undertaking. If the Commission chooses to make notes of such meetings, such documents constitute the Commission's own interpretation of what was said at the meetings, for which reason they are classified as internal documents. Where, however, the person or undertaking in question has agreed the minutes, such minutes will be made accessible after deletion of any business secrets or other confidential information. Such agreed minutes constitute part of the evidence on which the Commission can rely in its assessment of a case.[2]

14. In the case of a study commissioned in connection with proceedings, correspondence between the Commission and its contractor containing evaluation of the contractor's work or relating to financial aspects of the study, are considered internal documents and will thus not be accessible.

Commentary
para 14: **B&C:** 13.094 **F&N:** 5.581

3.1.2 Correspondence with other public authorities

15. A particular case of internal documents is the Commission's correspondence with other public authorities and the internal documents received from such authorities (whether from EC
Member States ("the Member States') or non-member countries). Examples of such non-accessible documents include:
    — correspondence between the Commission and the competition authorities of the Member
      States, or between the latter;[1]
    — correspondence between the Commission and other public authorities of the Member
      States;[2]
    — correspondence between the Commission, the EFTA Surveillance Authority and public
      authorities of EFTA States;[3]
    — correspondence between the Commission and public authorities of non-member countries,
      including their competition authorities, in particular where the Community and a third
      country have concluded an agreement governing the confidentiality of the information
      exchanged.[4]

Notes

[1] Cf. Article 27(2) of Regulation (EC) No 1/2003, Article 15(2) of the Implementing Regulation, Article 17(3) of the
Merger Implementing Regulation.

[2] Cf. Order of the Court of First Instance in Cases T-134/94 et al. *NMH Stahlwerke and Others v Commission* [1997]
ECR II-2293, paragraph 36, and Case T-65/89 *BPB Industries and British Gypsum* [1993] ECR II-389, paragraph 33.

[3] In this notice the term "EFTA States' includes the EFTA States that are parties to the EEA Agreement.

[4] For example, Article VIII.2 of the Agreement between the European Communities and the Government of the United
States of America regarding the application of their competition laws (OJ No L 95, 27.4.1995, p. 47) stipulates that
information provided to it in confidence under the Agreement must be protected "to the fullest extent possible". That
Article creates an international-law obligation binding the Commission.

Commentary
para 15: **B&C:** 13.094

16. In certain exceptional circumstances, access is granted to documents originating from Member
States, the EFTA Surveillance Authority or EFTA States, after deletion of any business secrets or
other confidential information. The Commission will consult the entity submitting the document prior to granting access to identify business secrets or other confidential information.
    This is the case where the documents originating from Member States contain allegations
brought against the parties, which the Commission must examine, or form part of the evidence
in the investigative process, in a way similar to documents obtained from private parties. These
considerations apply, in particular, as regards:
    — documents and information exchanged pursuant to Article 12 of Regulation (EC) No 1/2003,
      and information provided to the Commission pursuant to Article 18(6) of Regulation (EC)
      No 1/2003;
    — complaints lodged by a Member State under Article 7(2) of Regulation (EC) No 1/2003.
    Access will also be granted to documents originating from Member States or the EFTA
Surveillance Authority in so far as they are relevant to the parties' defence with regard to the
exercise of competence by the Commission.[1]

Notes

[1] In the merger control area, this may apply in particular to submissions by a Member State under Article 9(2) of the
Merger Regulation with regard to a case referral.

Commentary
para 16: **B&C:** 13.094 **F&N:** 5.581

3.2. Confidential information

17. The Commission file may also include documents containing two categories of information, namely business secrets and other confidential information, to which access may be partially or totally restricted.[1] Access will be granted, where possible, to non-confidential versions of the original information. Where confidentiality can only be assured by summarising the relevant information, access will be granted to a summary. All other documents are accessible in their original form.

Notes

[1] Cf. Article 16(1) of the Implementing Regulation and Article 17(3) of the Merger Implementing Regulation; Case T-7/89, *Hercules Chemicals NV v Commission* [1991] ECR II-1711, paragraph 54; Case T-23/99, *LR AF 1998 A/S v Commission* [2002] ECR II-1705, paragraph 170.

Commentary

para 17: **B&C:** 8.177, 13.095

3.2.1 Business secrets

18. In so far as disclosure of information about an undertaking's business activity could result in a serious harm to the same undertaking, such information constitutes business secrets.[1] Examples of information that may qualify as business secrets include: technical and/or financial information relating to an undertaking's know-how, methods of assessing costs, production secrets and processes, supply sources, quantities produced and sold, market shares, customer and distributor lists, marketing plans, cost and price structure and sales strategy.

Notes

[1] Judgement of 18.9.1996 in Case T-353/94 *Postbank NV v Commission* [1996] ECR II-921, paragraph 87.

Commentary

para 18: **B&C:** 8.177, 13.051, 13.095 **F&N:** 2.191, 5.581, 8.460

3.2.2 Other confidential information

19. The category "other confidential information" includes information other than business secrets, which may be considered as confidential, insofar as its disclosure would significantly harm a person or undertaking. Depending on the specific circumstances of each case, this may apply to information provided by third parties about undertakings which are able to place very considerable economic or commercial pressure on their competitors or on their trading partners, customers or suppliers. The Court of First Instance and the Court of Justice have acknowledged that it is legitimate to refuse to reveal to such undertakings certain letters received from their customers, since their disclosure might easily expose the authors to the risk of retaliatory measures.[1] Therefore the notion of other confidential information may include information that would enable the parties to identify complainants or other third parties where those have a justified wish to remain anonymous.

Notes

[1] The Community Courts have pronounced upon this question both in cases of alleged abuse of a dominant position (Article 82 of the EC Treaty) (Case T-65/89, *BPB Industries and British Gypsum* [1993] ECR II-389; and Case C-310/93P, *BPB Industries and British Gypsum* [1995] ECR I-865), and in merger cases (Case T-221/95 *Endemol v Commission* [1999] ECR II-1299, paragraph 69; and Case T-5/02 *Laval v Commission* [2002] ECR II-4381, paragraph 98 et seq.).

Commentary

para 19: **B&C:** 8.177, 13.096 **F&N:** 2.194, 5.582, 8.461

20. The category of other confidential information also includes military secrets.

Commentary

para 20: **B&C:** 8.178 **F&N:** 2.194, 5.582

3.2.3 Criteria for the acceptance of requests for confidential treatment

21. Information will be classified as confidential where the person or undertaking in question has made a claim to this effect and such claim has been accepted by the Commission.[1]

Notes
[1] See paragraph 40 below.
Commentary
para 21: B&C: 13.098

22. Claims for confidentiality must relate to information which is within the scope of the above descriptions of business secrets or other confidential information. The reasons for which information is claimed to be a business secret or other confidential information must be substantiated.[1] Confidentiality claims can normally only pertain to information obtained by the Commission from the same person or undertaking and not to information from any other source.

Notes
[1] See paragraph 35 below.
Commentary
para 22: B&C: 13.098

23. Information relating to an undertaking but which is already known outside the undertaking (in case of a group, outside the group), or outside the association to which it has been communicated by that undertaking, will not normally be considered confidential.[1] Information that has lost its commercial importance, for instance due to the passage of time, can no longer be regarded as confidential. As a general rule, the Commission presumes that information pertaining to the parties' turnover, sales, market-share data and similar information which is more than 5 years old is no longer confidential.[2]

Notes
[1] However, business secrets or other confidential information which are given to a trade or professional association by its members do not lose their confidential nature with regard to third parties and may therefore not be passed on to complainants. Cf. Joined Cases 209 to 215 and 218/78, *Fedetab* [1980] ECR 3125, paragraph 46.
[2] See paragraphs 35–38 below on asking undertakings to identify confidential information.
Commentary
para 23: B&C: 8.177, 13.098 F&N: 8.460

24. In proceedings under Articles 81 and 82 of the Treaty, the qualification of a piece of information as confidential is not a bar to its disclosure if such information is necessary to prove an alleged infringement ("inculpatory document") or could be necessary to exonerate a party ("exculpatory document"). In this case, the need to safeguard the rights of the defence of the parties through the provision of the widest possible access to the Commission file may outweigh the concern to protect confidential information of other parties.[1] It is for the Commission to assess whether those circumstances apply to any specific situation. This calls for an assessment of all relevant elements, including:
   — the relevance of the information in determining whether or not an infringement has been committed, and its probative value;
   — whether the information is indispensable;
   — the degree of sensitivity involved (to what extent would disclosure of the information harm the interests of the person or undertaking in question);
   — the preliminary view of the seriousness of the alleged infringement.
Similar considerations apply to proceedings under the Merger Regulation when the disclosure of information is considered necessary by the Commission for the purpose of the procedure.[2]

Notes
[1] Cf. Article 27(2) of Regulation (EC) No 1/2003 and Article 15(3) of the Implementing Regulation.
[2] Article 18(1) of the Merger Implementing Regulation.

Commentary
para 24: B&C: 13.097 F&N: 8.459

25. Where the Commission intends to disclose information, the person or undertaking in question shall be granted the possibility to provide a non-confidential version of the documents where that information is contained, with the same evidential value as the original documents.[1]

Notes
[1] Cf. paragraph 42 below.

Commentary
para 25: B&C: 13.097 F&N: 8.459

C. When is access to the file granted?

26. Prior to the notification of the Commission's statement of objections pursuant to the provisions mentioned in paragraph 1, the parties have no right of access to the file.

Commentary
para 26: B&C: 8.146, 13.092

1. In antitrust proceedings under Articles 81 and 82 of the Treaty

27. Access to the file will be granted upon request and, normally, on a single occasion, following the notification of the Commission's objections to the parties, in order to ensure the principle of equality of arms and to protect their rights of defence. As a general rule, therefore, no access will be granted to other parties" replies to the Commission's objections.

A party will, however, be granted access to documents received after notification of the objections at later stages of the administrative procedure, where such documents may constitute new evidence — whether of an incriminating or of an exculpatory nature —, pertaining to the allegations concerning that party in the Commission's statement of objections. This is particularly the case where the Commission intends to rely on new evidence.

Commentary
para 27: B&C: 8.146, 13.092, 13.098 F&N: 8.458

2. In proceedings under the Merger Regulation

28. In accordance with Article 18(1) and (3) of the Merger Regulation and Article 17(1) of the Merger Implementing Regulation, the notifying parties will be given access to the Commission's file upon request at every stage of the procedure following the notification of the Commission's objections up to the consultation of the Advisory Committee. In contrast, this notice does not address the possibility of the provision of documents before the Commission states its objections to undertakings under the Merger Regulation.[1]

Notes
[1] This question is dealt with in the Directorate General Competition document "DG COMP Best Practices on the conduct of EC merger control proceedings" available on the web-site of the Directorate General for Competition: http://europa.eu.int/comm/competition/index_en.html.

Commentary
para 28: B&C: 8.146 F&N: 5.572, 5.576

III. Particular Questions Regarding Complainants and Other Involved Parties

29. The present section relates to situations where the Commission may or has to provide access to certain documents contained in its file to the complainants in antitrust proceedings and other involved parties in merger proceedings. Irrespective of the wording used in the antitrust and merger implementing regulations,[1] these two situations are distinct — in terms of scope, timing, and rights — from access to the file, as defined in the preceding section of this notice.

Notes

[1] Cf. Article 8(1) of the Implementing Regulation, which speaks about "access to documents" to complainants and Article 17(2) of the Merger Implementing Regulation, which speaks about "access to file" to other involved parties "in so far as this is necessary for the purposes of preparing their comments".

A. Provision of documents to complainants in antitrust proceedings

30. The Court of First Instance has ruled[1] that complainants do not have the same rights and guarantees as the parties under investigation. Therefore complainants cannot claim a right of access to the file as established for parties.

Notes

[1] See Case T-17/93 *Matra-Hachette SA v Commission* [1994] ECR II-595, paragraph 34. The Court ruled that the rights of third parties, as laid down by Article 19 of the Council Regulation No 17 of 6.2.1962 (now replaced by Article 27 of Regulation (EC) No 1/2003), were limited to the right to participate in the administrative procedure.

31. However, a complainant who, pursuant to Article 7(1) of the Implementing Regulation, has been informed of the Commission's intention to reject its complaint,[1] may request access to the documents on which the Commission has based its provisional assessment.[2] The complainant will be provided access to such documents on a single occasion, following the issuance of the letter informing the complainant of the Commission's intention to reject its complaint.

Notes

[1] By means of a letter issued in accordance with Article 7(1) of the Implementing Regulation.
[2] Cf. Article 8(1) of the Implementing Regulation.

32. Complainants do not have a right of access to business secrets or other confidential information which the Commission has obtained in the course of its investigation.[1]

Notes

[1] Cf. Article 8(1) of the Implementing Regulation.

B. Provision of documents to other involved parties in merger proceedings

33. In accordance with Article 17(2) of the Merger Implementing Regulation, access to the file in merger proceedings shall also be given, upon request, to other involved parties who have been informed of the objections in so far as this is necessary for the purposes of preparing their comments.

Commentary
para 33: **B&C:** 8.146 **F&N:** 5.570

34. Such other involved parties are parties to the proposed concentration other than the notifying parties, such as the seller and the undertaking which is the target of the concentration.[1]

Notes

[1] Cf. Article 11(b) of the Merger Implementing Regulation.

IV. Procedure for Implementing Access to the File

A. Preparatory procedure

35. Any person which submits information or comments in one of the situations listed hereunder, or subsequently submits further information to the Commission in the course of the same procedures, has an obligation to clearly identify any material which it considers to be confidential, giving reasons, and provide a separate non-confidential version by the date set by the Commission for making its views known:[1]

   (a) In antitrust proceedings
      — an addressee of a Commission's statement of objections making known its views on the objections;[2]
      — a complainant making known its views on a Commission statement of objections;[3]
      — any other natural or legal person, which applies to be heard and shows a sufficient interest, or which is invited by the Commission to express its views, making known its views in writing or at an oral hearing;[4]
      — a complainant making known his views on a Commission letter informing him on the Commission's intention to reject the complaint.[5]

   (b) In merger proceedings
      — notifying parties or other involved parties making known their views on Commission objections adopted with a view to take a decision with regard to a request for a derogation from suspension of a concentration and which adversely affects one or more of those parties, or on a provisional decision adopted in the matter;[6]
      — notifying parties to whom the Commission has addressed a statement of objections, other involved parties who have been informed of those objections or parties to whom the Commission has addressed objections with a view to inflict a fine or a periodic penalty payment, submitting their comments on the objections;[7]
      — third persons who apply to be heard, or any other natural or legal person invited by the Commission to express their views, making known their views in writing or at an oral hearing;[8]
      — any person which supplies information pursuant to Article 11 of the Merger Regulation.

Notes
[1] Cf. Article 16(2) of the Implementing Regulation and Article 18(2) of the Merger Implementing Regulation.
[2] pursuant to Article 10(2) of the Implementing Regulation.
[3] pursuant to Article 6(1) of the Implementing Regulation.
[4] pursuant to Article 13(1) and (3) of the Implementing Regulation.
[5] pursuant to Article 7(1) of the Implementing Regulation.
[6] Article 12 of the Merger Implementing Regulation.
[7] Article 13 of the Merger Implementing Regulation.
[8] pursuant to Article 16 of the Merger Implementing Regulation.

36. Moreover, the Commission may require undertakings,[1] in all cases where they produce or have produced documents, to identify the documents or parts of documents, which they consider to contain business secrets or other confidential information belonging to them, and to identify the undertakings with regard to which such documents are to be considered confidential.[2]

Notes
[1] In merger proceedings the principles set out in the present and subsequent paragraphs also apply to the persons referred to in Article 3(1)(b) of Merger Regulation.
[2] Cf. Article 16(3) of the Implementing Regulation and Article 18(3) of the Merger Implementing Regulation. This also applies to documents gathered by the Commission in an inspection pursuant to Article 13 of the Merger Regulation and Articles 20 and 21 of Regulation (EC) No 1/2003.

37. For the purposes of quickly dealing with confidentiality claims referred to in paragraph 36 above, the Commission may set a time-limit within which the undertakings shall: (i) substantiate their claim for confidentiality with regard to each individual document or part of document; (ii) provide the Commission with a non-confidential version of the documents, in which the confidential passages are deleted.[1] In antitrust proceedings the undertakings in question shall also provide within the said time-limit a concise description of each piece of deleted information.[2]

Notes
[1] Cf. Article 16(3) of the Implementing Regulation and Article 18(3) of the Merger Implementing Regulation.
[2] Cf. Article 16(3) of the Implementing Regulation.

38. The non-confidential versions and the descriptions of the deleted information must be established in a manner that enables any party with access to the file to determine whether the information deleted is likely to be relevant for its defence and therefore whether there are sufficient grounds to request the Commission to grant access to the information claimed to be confidential.

Commentary
para 38: B&C: 13.099

B. Treatment of confidential information

39. In antitrust proceedings, if undertakings fail to comply with the provisions set out in paragraphs 35 to 37 above, the Commission may assume that the documents or statements concerned do not contain confidential information.[1] The Commission may consequently assume that the undertaking has no objections to the disclosure of the documents or statements concerned in their entirety.

Notes
[1] Cf. Article 16 of the Implementing Regulation.

Commentary
para 39: B&C: 13.098 F&N: 8.462

40. In both antitrust proceedings and in proceedings under the Merger Regulation, should the person or undertaking in question meet the conditions set out in paragraphs 35 to 37 above, to the extent they are applicable, the Commission will either:
   — provisionally accept the claims which seem justified; or
   — inform the person or undertaking in question that it does not agree with the confidentiality claim in whole or in part, where it is apparent that the claim is unjustified.

Commentary
para 40: B&C: 13.098

41. The Commission may reverse its provisional acceptance of the confidentiality claim in whole or in part at a later stage.

Commentary
para 41: B&C: 13.098

42. Where the Directorate General for Competition does not agree with the confidentiality claim from the outset or where it takes the view that the provisional acceptance of the confidentiality claim should be reversed, and thus intends to disclose information, it will grant the person or undertaking in question an opportunity to express its views. In such cases, the Directorate General for Competition will inform the person or undertaking in writing of its intention to disclose information, give its reasons and set a time-limit within which such person or undertaking may inform it in writing of its views. If, following submission of those views, a disagreement on the confidentiality claim persists, the matter will be dealt with by the Hearing Officer according to the applicable Commission terms of reference of Hearing Officers.[1]

Notes

[1] Cf. Article 9 of the Commission Decision of 23.5.2001 on the terms of reference of hearing officers in certain competition proceedings, OJ L 162, 19.6.2001, p. 21.

Commentary

para 42: B&C: 8.150, 8.177 **F&N:** 5.591, 8.462

43. Where there is a risk that an undertaking which is able to place very considerable economic or commercial pressure on its competitors or on its trading partners, customers or suppliers will adopt retaliatory measures against those, as a consequence of their collaboration in the investigation carried out by the Commission[1], the Commission will protect the anonymity of the authors by providing access to a non-confidential version or summary of the responses in question[2]. Requests for anonymity in such circumstances, as well as requests for anonymity according to point 81 of the Commission Notice on the handling of complaints[3] will be dealt with according to paragraphs 40 to 42 above.

Notes

[1] Cf. paragraph 19 above.
[2] Cf. Case T-5/02, *Tetra Laval vs Commission* [2002] ECR II-4381, paragraph 98, 104 and 105.
[3] Commission Notice on the handling of complaints by the Commission under Articles 81 and 82 of the EC Treaty, OJ C 101, 27.4.2004, p. 65.

Commentary

para 43: B&C: 8.177, 13.098

C. Provision of access to file

44. The Commission may determine that access to the file shall be granted in one of the following ways, taking due account of the technical capabilities of the parties:
    — by means of a CD-ROM(s) or any other electronic data storage device as may become available in future;
    — through copies of the accessible file in paper form sent to them by mail;
    — by inviting them to examine the accessible file on the Commission's premises.
    The Commission may choose any combination of these methods.

Commentary

para 44: B&C: 8.146, 13.099 **F&N:** 5.586, 8.458

45. In order to facilitate access to the file, the parties will receive an enumerative list of documents setting out the content of the Commission file, as defined in paragraph 8 above.

Commentary

para 45: B&C: 13.099

46. Access is granted to evidence as contained in the Commission file, in its original form: the Commission is under no obligation to provide a translation of documents in the file.[1]

Notes

[1] Cf Case T-25/95 et al. *Cimenteries*, paragraph 635.

Commentary

para 46: B&C: 13.099

47. If a party considers that, after having obtained access to the file, it requires knowledge of specific non-accessible information for its defence, it may submit a reasoned request to that end to the Commission. If the services of the Directorate General for Competition are not in a position to accept the request and if the party disagrees with that view, the matter will be resolved by the Hearing Officer, in accordance with the applicable terms of reference of Hearing Officers.[1]

Notes
[1] Cf. Article 8 of the Commission Decision of 23.5.2001 on the terms of reference of hearing officers in certain competition proceedings, OJ L 162, 19.6.2001, p. 21.

Commentary
para 47: **B&C:** 8.150, 13.099 **F&N:** 8.458, 8.462

48. Access to the file in accordance with this notice is granted on the condition that the information thereby obtained may only be used for the purposes of judicial or administrative proceedings for the application of the Community competition rules at issue in the related administrative proceedings.[1] Should the information be used for a different purpose, at any point in time, with the involvement of an outside counsel, the Commission may report the incident to the bar of that counsel, with a view to disciplinary action.

Notes
[1] Cf. Articles 15(4) and 8(2) of the Implementing Regulation, respectively, and Article 17(4) of the Merger Implementing Regulation.

Commentary
para 48: **F&N:** 8.160, 8.215

49. With the exception of paragraphs 45 and 47, this section C applies equally to the grant of access to documents to complainants (in antitrust proceedings) and to other involved parties (in merger proceedings).

Part B Modernisation and Procedural Matters

B13

GUIDELINES ON THE METHOD OF SETTING FINES IMPOSED PURSUANT TO ARTICLE 23(2)(A) OF REGULATION No 1/2003

(2006/C 210/02)

(Text with EEA relevance)

Official Journal C 210, 1.9.2006, p. 2

Celex No: 52006XC0901(01)

Notes

EEA application: the EFTA Surveillance Authority has adopted a parallel notice on the method of setting fines imposed pursuant to Article 23(2)(a) of Chapter II of Protocol 4 to the Surveillance and Court Agreement under Article 5(2)(b) of the Surveillance and Court Agreement: see College Decision 343/06/COL of 15 November 2006 OJ C 314, 21.12.2006, p. 84 and EEA Supplement No 63, 14.12.2006, p. 44.

Commentary

Guidelines: B&C: 1.066, 4.010, 5.007, 13.135, 13.146, 13.148, 13.151–13.154, 13.157, 13.159, 13.160, 13.163, 13.164, 13.166, 13.167, 13.171, 13.177, 13.179 **F&N:** 8.501, 8.587, 8.599, 8.611, 8.629, 8.808–8.834

points 15–17: F&N: 8.814

section C: F&N: 8.823

INTRODUCTION

1. Pursuant to Article 23(2)(a) of Regulation No 1/2003,[1] the Commission may, by decision, impose fines on undertakings or associations of undertakings where, either intentionally or negligently, they infringe Article 81 or 82 of the Treaty.

Notes

[1] Council Regulation (EC) No 1 of 16 December 2002 on the implementation of the rules on competition laid down in Articles 81 and 82 of the Treaty (OJ L 1, 4.1.2003, p. 1).

2. In exercising its power to impose such fines, the Commission enjoys a wide margin of discretion[1] within the limits set by Regulation No 1/2003. First, the Commission must have regard both to the gravity and to the duration of the infringement. Second, the fine imposed may not exceed the limits specified in Article 23(2), second and third subparagraphs, of Regulation No 1/2003.

Notes

[1] See, for example, Case C-189/02 P, C-202/02 P, C-205/02 P to C-208/02 P and C-213/02 P, *Dansk Rørindustri A/S and others v Commission* [2005] ECR I-5425, paragraph 172.

3. In order to ensure the transparency and impartiality of its decisions, the Commission published on 14 January 1998 guidelines on the method of setting fines.[1] After more than eight years of implementation, the Commission has acquired sufficient experience to develop further and refine its policy on fines.

Notes

[1] Guidelines on the method of setting fines imposed pursuant to Article 15(2) of Regulation No 17 and Article 65(5) of the ECSC Treaty (OJ C 9, 14.1.1998, p.3).

4. The Commission's power to impose fines on undertakings or associations of undertakings which, intentionally or negligently, infringe Article 81 or 82 of the Treaty is one of the means conferred on it in order for it to carry out the task of supervision entrusted to it by the Treaty. That task not only includes the duty to investigate and sanction individual infringements, but it also encompasses the duty to pursue a general policy designed to apply, in competition matters, the principles laid down by the Treaty and to steer the conduct of undertakings in the light of those principles.[1] For this purpose, the Commission must ensure that its action has the necessary deterrent effect.[2] Accordingly, when the Commission discovers that Article 81 or 82 of the Treaty has been infringed, it may be necessary to impose a fine on those who have acted in breach of the law. Fines should have a sufficiently deterrent effect, not only in order to sanction the undertakings concerned (specific deterrence) but also in order to deter other undertakings from engaging in, or continuing, behaviour that is contrary to Articles 81 and 82 of the EC Treaty (general deterrence).

Notes
[1] See, for example, *Dansk Rørindustri A/S and others v Commission*, cited above, paragraph 170.
[2] See Joined Cases 100/80 to 103/80 *Musique Diffusion française and others v Commission* [1983] ECR 1825, paragraph 106.

5. In order to achieve these objectives, it is appropriate for the Commission to refer to the value of the sales of goods or services to which the infringement relates as a basis for setting the fine. The duration of the infringement should also play a significant role in the setting of the appropriate amount of the fine. It necessarily has an impact on the potential consequences of the infringement on the market. It is therefore considered important that the fine should also reflect the number of years during which an undertaking participated in the infringement.
6. The combination of the value of sales to which the infringement relates and of the duration of the infringement is regarded as providing an appropriate proxy to reflect the economic importance of the infringement as well as the relative weight of each undertaking in the infringement. Reference to these factors provides a good indication of the order of magnitude of the fine and should not be regarded as the basis for an automatic and arithmetical calculation method.
7. It is also considered appropriate to include in the fine a specific amount irrespective of the duration of the infringement, in order to deter companies from even entering into illegal practices.
8. The sections below set out the principles which will guide the Commission when it sets fines imposed pursuant to Article 23(2)(a) of Regulation No 1/2003.

METHOD FOR THE SETTING OF FINES

9. Without prejudice to point 37 below, the Commission will use the following two-step methodology when setting the fine to be imposed on undertakings or associations of undertakings.
10. First, the Commission will determine a basic amount for each undertaking or association of undertakings (see Section 1 below).

Commentary
point 10: **B&C:** 13.148

11. Second, it may adjust that basic amount upwards or downwards (see Section 2 below).

1. Basic amount of the fine

12. The basic amount will be set by reference to the value of sales and applying the following methodology.

A. Calculation of the value of sales

13. In determining the basic amount of the fine to be imposed, the Commission will take the value of the undertaking's sales of goods or services to which the infringement directly or indirectly[1] relates in the relevant geographic area within the EEA. It will normally take the sales made by the undertaking during the last full business year of its participation in the infringement (hereafter "value of sales").

Notes
1 Such will be the case for instance for horizontal price fixing arrangements on a given product, where the price of that product then serves as a basis for the price of lower or higher quality products.

Commentary
point 13: B&C: 13.149 F&N: 8.813

14. Where the infringement by an association of undertakings relates to the activities of its members, the value of sales will generally correspond to the sum of the value of sales by its members.

Commentary
point 14: F&N: 8.814

15. In determining the value of sales by an undertaking, the Commission will take that undertaking's best available figures.
16. Where the figures made available by an undertaking are incomplete or not reliable, the Commission may determine the value of its sales on the basis of the partial figures it has obtained and/or any other information which it regards as relevant and appropriate.
17. The value of sales will be determined before VAT and other taxes directly related to the sales.
18. Where the geographic scope of an infringement extends beyond the EEA (e.g. worldwide cartels), the relevant sales of the undertakings within the EEA may not properly reflect the weight of each undertaking in the infringement. This may be the case in particular with worldwide market-sharing arrangements. In such circumstances, in order to reflect both the aggregate size of the relevant sales within the EEA and the relative weight of each undertaking in the infringement, the Commission may assess the total value of the sales of goods or services to which the infringement relates in the relevant geographic area (wider than the EEA), may determine the share of the sales of each undertaking party to the infringement on that market and may apply this share to the aggregate sales within the EEA of the undertakings concerned. The result will be taken as the value of sales for the purpose of setting the basic amount of the fine.

Commentary
point 18: F&N: 8.815

B. Determination of the basic amount of the fine

19. The basic amount of the fine will be related to a proportion of the value of sales, depending on the degree of gravity of the infringement, multiplied by the number of years of infringement.

Commentary
point 19: B&C: 13.150 F&N: 8.812

20. The assessment of gravity will be made on a case-by-case basis for all types of infringement, taking account of all the relevant circumstances of the case.

Commentary
point 20: F&N: 8.812

21. As a general rule, the proportion of the value of sales taken into account will be set at a level of up to 30% of the value of sales.

Commentary
point 21: B&C: 5.007, 13.150 F&N: 8.816, 8.830

22. In order to decide whether the proportion of the value of sales to be considered in a given case should be at the lower end or at the higher end of that scale, the Commission will have regard to a number of factors, such as the nature of the infringement, the combined market share of all the undertakings concerned, the geographic scope of the infringement and whether or not the infringement has been implemented.

Commentary
point 22: B&C: 4.010, 5.007, 13.150 **F&N:** 8.816

23. Horizontal price-fixing, market-sharing and output-limitation agreements,[1] which are usually secret, are, by their very nature, among the most harmful restrictions of competition. As a matter of policy, they will be heavily fined. Therefore, the proportion of the value of sales taken into account for such infringements will generally be set at the higher end of the scale.

Notes
[1] This includes agreements, concerted practices and decisions by associations of undertakings within the meaning of Article 81 of the Treaty.

Commentary
point 23: B&C: 5.007, 13.153 **F&N:** 8.818

24. In order to take fully into account the duration of the participation of each undertaking in the infringement, the amount determined on the basis of the value of sales (see points 20 to 23 above) will be multiplied by the number of years of participation in the infringement. Periods of less than six months will be counted as half a year; periods longer than six months but shorter than one year will be counted as a full year.

Commentary
point 24: B&C: 13.155 **F&N:** 8.819

25. In addition, irrespective of the duration of the undertaking's participation in the infringement, the Commission will include in the basic amount a sum of between 15% and 25% of the value of sales as defined in Section A above in order to deter undertakings from even entering into horizontal price-fixing, market-sharing and output-limitation agreements. The Commission may also apply such an additional amount in the case of other infringements. For the purpose of deciding the proportion of the value of sales to be considered in a given case, the Commission will have regard to a number of factors, in particular those referred in point 22.

Commentary
point 25: B&C: 5.007, 13.157 **F&N:** 8.821

26. Where the value of sales by undertakings participating in the infringement is similar but not identical, the Commission may set for each of them an identical basic amount. Moreover, in determining the basic amount of the fine, the Commission will use rounded figures.

Commentary
para 26: B&C: 13.151

2. Adjustments to the basic amount

27. In setting the fine, the Commission may take into account circumstances that result in an increase or decrease in the basic amount as determined in Section 1 above. It will do so on the basis of an overall assessment which takes account of all the relevant circumstances.

A. Aggravating circumstances

28. The basic amount may be increased where the Commission finds that there are aggravating circumstances, such as:
   — where an undertaking continues or repeats the same or a similar infringement after the Commission or a national competition authority has made a finding that the undertaking infringed Article 81 or 82: the basic amount will be increased by up to 100% for each such infringement established;
   — refusal to cooperate with or obstruction of the Commission in carrying out its investigations;

— role of leader in, or instigator of, the infringement; the Commission will also pay particular attention to any steps taken to coerce other undertakings to participate in the infringement and/or any retaliatory measures taken against other undertakings with a view to enforcing the practices constituting the infringement.

Commentary
point 28: B&C: 13.159 F&N: 4.71, 8.822

B. Mitigating circumstances

29. The basic amount may be reduced where the Commission finds that mitigating circumstances exist, such as:
— where the undertaking concerned provides evidence that it terminated the infringement as soon as the Commission intervened: this will not apply to secret agreements or practices (in particular, cartels);
— where the undertaking provides evidence that the infringement has been committed as a result of negligence;
— where the undertaking provides evidence that its involvement in the infringement is substantially limited and thus demonstrates that, during the period in which it was party to the offending agreement, it actually avoided applying it by adopting competitive conduct in the market: the mere fact that an undertaking participated in an infringement for a shorter duration than others will not be regarded as a mitigating circumstance since this will already be reflected in the basic amount;
— where the undertaking concerned has effectively cooperated with the Commission outside the scope of the Leniency Notice and beyond its legal obligation to do so;
— where the anti-competitive conduct of the undertaking has been authorized or encouraged by public authorities or by legislation.[1]

Notes
[1] This is without prejudice to any action that may be taken against the Member State concerned.

Commentary
point 29: B&C: 13.163 F&N: 8.824, 8.825

C. Specific increase for deterrence

30. The Commission will pay particular attention to the need to ensure that fines have a sufficiently deterrent effect; to that end, it may increase the fine to be imposed on undertakings which have a particularly large turnover beyond the sales of goods or services to which the infringement relates.

Commentary
para 30: B&C: 13.177

31. The Commission will also take into account the need to increase the fine in order to exceed the amount of gains improperly made as a result of the infringement where it is possible to estimate that amount.

Commentary
point 31: B&C: 13.178 F&N: 8.826

D. Legal maximum

32. The final amount of the fine shall not, in any event, exceed 10% of the total turnover in the preceding business year of the undertaking or association of undertakings participating in the infringement, as laid down in Article 23(2) of Regulation No 1/2003.

Commentary
point 32: F&N: 8.827

33. Where an infringement by an association of undertakings relates to the activities of its members, the fine shall not exceed 10% of the sum of the total turnover of each member active on the market affected by that infringement.

Commentary
point 33: F&N: 8.827

E. Leniency Notice

34. The Commission will apply the leniency rules in line with the conditions set out in the applicable notice.

Commentary
point 34: F&N: 8.828

F. Ability to pay

35. In exceptional cases, the Commission may, upon request, take account of the undertaking's inability to pay in a specific social and economic context. It will not base any reduction granted for this reason in the fine on the mere finding of an adverse or loss-making financial situation. A reduction could be granted solely on the basis of objective evidence that imposition of the fine as provided for in these Guidelines would irretrievably jeopardise the economic viability of the undertaking concerned and cause its assets to lose all their value.

Commentary
point 35: B&C: 13.179 F&N: 8.829

FINAL CONSIDERATIONS

36. The Commission may, in certain cases, impose a symbolic fine. The justification for imposing such a fine should be given in its decision.

Commentary
point 36: B&C: 13.169 F&N: 8.830

37. Although these Guidelines present the general methodology for the setting of fines, the particularities of a given case or the need to achieve deterrence in a particular case may justify departing from such methodology or from the limits specified in point 21.

Commentary
point 37: F&N: 8.830

38. These Guidelines will be applied in all cases where a statement of objections is notified after their date of publication in the Official Journal, regardless of whether the fine is imposed pursuant to Article 23(2) of Regulation No 1/2003 or Article 15(2) of Regulation 17/62.[1]

Notes

[1] Article 15(2) of Regulation 17/62 of 6 February 1962: First Regulation implementing Articles [81 and 82] of the Treaty (OJ 13, 21.2.1962, p. 204).

B14

COMMISSION NOTICE ON IMMUNITY FROM FINES AND REDUCTION OF FINES IN CARTEL CASES

(Text with EEA relevance)
(2006/C 298/11)

Official Journal C 298, 8.12.2006, p 17

Celex No: 52006XC1208(04)

Commentary
Notice: **B&C:** 13.182, 13.198, 14.028 **F&N:** 8.10, 8.94, 8.104, 8.107, 8.112, 8.126, 8.134–8.137, 8.139, 8.143, 8.145, 8.150, 8.154, 8.158, 8.161, 8.162, 8.164, 8.166, 8.173, 8.174, 8.177, 8.179, 8.181, 8.183, 8.184, 8.186, 8.190, 8.191, 8.192, 8.197, 8.198, 8.201–8.204, 8.208, 8.210, 8.222, 8.234, 8.248, 8.327, 8.328, 8.458, 8.488, 8.536, 8.546, 8.581
section II: F&N: 8.137, 8.178
section III: F&N: 8.137, 8.154, 8.178, 8.180, 8.186, 8.207
section IV: F&N: 8.161

I. INTRODUCTION

(1) This notice sets out the framework for rewarding cooperation in the Commission investigation by undertakings which are or have been party to secret cartels affecting the Community. Cartels are agreements and/or concerted practices between two or more competitors aimed at coordinating their competitive behaviour on the market and/or influencing the relevant parameters of competition through practices such as the fixing of purchase or selling prices or other trading conditions, the allocation of production or sales quotas, the sharing of markets including bid-rigging, restrictions of imports or exports and/or anticompetitive actions against other competitors. Such practices are among the most serious violations of Article 81 EC.[1]

Notes

[1] Reference in this text to Article 81 EC also covers Article 53 EEA when applied by the Commission according to the rules laid down in Article 56 of the EEA Agreement.

Commentary
point 1: **F&N:** 8.166

---

(2) By artificially limiting the competition that would normally prevail between them, undertakings avoid exactly those pressures that lead them to innovate, both in terms of product development and the introduction of more efficient production methods. Such practices also lead to more expensive raw materials and components for the Community companies that purchase from such producers. They ultimately result in artificial prices and reduced choice for the consumer. In the long term, they lead to a loss of competitiveness and reduced employment opportunities.

(3) By their very nature, secret cartels are often difficult to detect and investigate without the cooperation of undertakings or individuals implicated in them. Therefore, the Commission considers that it is in the Community interest to reward undertakings involved in this type of illegal practices which are willing to put an end to their participation and co-operate in the Commission's investigation. The interests of consumers and citizens in ensuring that secret cartels are detected and punished outweigh the interest in fining those undertakings that enable the Commission to detect and prohibit such practices.

(4) The Commission considers that the collaboration of an undertaking in the detection of the existence of a cartel has an intrinsic value. A decisive contribution to the opening of an investigation or to the finding of an infringement may justify the granting of immunity from any fine to the undertaking in question, on condition that certain additional requirements are fulfilled.

(5) Moreover, co-operation by one or more undertakings may justify a reduction of a fine by the Commission. Any reduction of a fine must reflect an undertaking's actual contribution, in terms of quality and timing, to the Commission's establishment of the infringement. Reductions are to be limited to those undertakings that provide the Commission with evidence that adds significant value to that already in the Commission's possession.

(6) In addition to submitting pre-existing documents, undertakings may provide the Commission with voluntary presentations of their knowledge of a cartel and their role therein prepared specially to be submitted under this leniency program. These initiatives have proved to be useful for the effective investigation and termination of cartel infringements and they should not be discouraged by discovery orders issued in civil litigation. Potential leniency applicants might be dissuaded from cooperating with the Commission under this Notice if this could impair their position in civil proceedings, as compared to companies who do not cooperate. Such undesirable effect would significantly harm the public interest in ensuring effective public enforcement of Article 81 EC in cartel cases and thus their subsequent or parallel effective private enforcement.

Commentary
point 6: F&N: 8.161, 8.215

(7) The supervisory task conferred on the Commission by the Treaty in competition matters does not only include the duty to investigate and punish individual infringements, but also encompasses the duty to pursue a general policy. The protection of corporate statements in the public interest is not a bar to their disclosure to other addressees of the statement of objections in order to safeguard their rights of defence in the procedure before the Commission, to the extent that it is technically possible to combine both interests by rendering corporate statements accessible only at the Commission premises and normally on a single occasion following the formal notification of the objections. Moreover, the Commission will process personal data in the context of this notice in conformity with its obligations under Regulation (EC) No 45/2001.[1]

Notes
[1] OJ L 8, 12.1.2001, p. 1.

Commentary
point 7: F&N: 8.215

II. Immunity from Fines

A. Requirements to qualify for immunity from fines

(8) The Commission will grant immunity from any fine which would otherwise have been imposed to an undertaking disclosing its participation in an alleged cartel affecting the Community if that undertaking is the first to submit information and evidence which in the Commission's view will enable it to:

(a) carry out a targeted inspection in connection with the alleged cartel;[1] or

(b) find an infringement of Article 81 EC in connection with the alleged cartel.

Notes
[1] The assessment of the threshold will have to be carried out *ex ante*, *i.e.* without taking into account whether a given inspection has or has not been successful or whether or not an inspection has or has not been carried out. The assessment will be made exclusively on the basis of the type and the quality of the information submitted by the applicant.

Commentary
point 8: F&N: 8.138
point 8(a): F&N: 8.138, 8.139, 8.144, 8.146, 8.159, 8.164, 8.167, 8.172
point 8(b): F&N: 8.139, 8.143, 8.144, 8.159, 8.164, 8.167, 8.172

(9) For the Commission to be able to carry out a targeted inspection within the meaning of point (8)(a), the undertaking must provide the Commission with the information and evidence listed below, to the extent that this, in the Commission's view, would not jeopardize the inspections:

    (a) A corporate statement[1] which includes, in so far as it is known to the applicant at the time of the submission:

        — A detailed description of the alleged cartel arrangement, including for instance its aims, activities and functioning; the product or service concerned, the geographic scope, the duration of and the estimated market volumes affected by the alleged cartel; the specific dates, locations, content of and participants in alleged cartel contacts, and all relevant explanations in connection with the pieces of evidence provided in support of the application;

        — The name and address of the legal entity submitting the immunity application as well as the names and addresses of all the other undertakings that participate(d) in the alleged cartel;

        — The names, positions, office locations and, where necessary, home addresses of all individuals who, to the applicant's knowledge, are or have been involved in the alleged cartel, including those individuals which have been involved on the applicant's behalf;

        — Information on which other competition authorities, inside or outside the EU, have been approached or are intended to be approached in relation to the alleged cartel; and

    (b) Other evidence relating to the alleged cartel in possession of the applicant or available to it at the time of the submission, including in particular any evidence contemporaneous to the infringement.

Notes

[1] Corporate statements may take the form of written documents signed by or on behalf of the undertaking or be made orally.

Commentary
point 9: F&N: 8.141, 8.146
point 9(a): F&N: 8.142, 8.143

(10) Immunity pursuant to point (8)(a) will not be granted if, at the time of the submission, the Commission had already sufficient evidence to adopt a decision to carry out an inspection in connection with the alleged cartel or had already carried out such an inspection.

Commentary
point 10: F&N: 8.146

(11) Immunity pursuant to point (8)(b) will only be granted on the cumulative conditions that the Commission did not have, at the time of the submission, sufficient evidence to find an infringement of Article 81 EC in connection with the alleged cartel and that no undertaking had been granted conditional immunity from fines under point (8)(a) in connection with the alleged cartel. In order to qualify, an undertaking must be the first to provide contemporaneous, incriminating evidence of the alleged cartel as well as a corporate statement containing the kind of information specified in point (9)(a), which would enable the Commission to find an infringement of Article 81 EC.

Commentary
point 11: F&N: 8.143, 8.144, 8.146

(12) In addition to the conditions set out in points (8)(a), (9) and (10) or in points (8)(b) and 11, all the following conditions must be met in any case to qualify for any immunity from a fine:

    (a) The undertaking cooperates genuinely,[1] fully, on a continuous basis and expeditiously from the time it submits its application throughout the Commission's administrative procedure. This includes:

        — providing the Commission promptly with all relevant information and evidence relating to the alleged cartel that comes into its possession or is available to it;

— remaining at the Commission's disposal to answer promptly to any request that may contribute to the establishment of the facts;

— making current (and, if possible, former) employees and directors available for interviews with the Commission;

— not destroying, falsifying or concealing relevant information or evidence relating to the alleged cartel; and

— not disclosing the fact or any of the content of its application before the Commission has issued a statement of objections in the case, unless otherwise agreed;

(b) The undertaking ended its involvement in the alleged cartel immediately following its application, except for what would, in the Commission's view, be reasonably necessary to preserve the integrity of the inspections;

(c) When contemplating making its application to the Commission, the undertaking must not have destroyed, falsified or concealed evidence of the alleged cartel nor disclosed the fact or any of the content of its contemplated application, except to other competition authorities.

Notes

[1] This requires in particular that the applicant provides accurate, not misleading, and complete information. [Cf] judgement of the European Court of Justice of 29 June 2006 in case C-301/04 P, *Commission v SGL Carbon AG a.o.,* at paragraphs 68–70, and judgement of the European Court of Justice of 28 June 2005 in cases C-189/02 P, C-202/02 P, C-205/02 P, C-208/02 P and C- 213/02 P, *Dansk Rørindustri A/S a.o. v Commission* [[2005] ECR I-5425], at paragraphs 395–399.

Commentary
point 12: F&N: 8.145, 8.146, 8.170, 8.184, 8.219, 8.327, 8.328
point 12(a): F&N: 8.186, 8.196, 8.536
point 12(b): F&N: 8.150, 8.186, 8.196
point 12(c): F&N: 8.151, 8.152, 8.153, 8.186, 8.196

(13) An undertaking which took steps to coerce other undertakings to join the cartel or to remain in it is not eligible for immunity from fines. It may still qualify for a reduction of fines if it fulfils the relevant requirements and meets all the conditions therefor.

Commentary
point 13: F&N: 8.146

B. Procedure

(14) An undertaking wishing to apply for immunity from fines should contact the Commission's Directorate General for Competition. The undertaking may either initially apply for a marker or immediately proceed to make a formal application to the Commission for immunity from fines in order to meet the conditions in points (8)(a) or (8)(b), as appropriate. The Commission may disregard any application for immunity from fines on the ground that it has been submitted after the statement of objections has been issued.

Commentary
point 14: F&N: 8.154, 8.157

(15) The Commission services may grant a marker protecting an immunity applicant's place in the queue for a period to be specified on a case-by-case basis in order to allow for the gathering of the necessary information and evidence. To be eligible to secure a marker, the applicant must provide the Commission with information concerning its name and address, the parties to the alleged cartel, the affected product(s) and territory(-ies), the estimated duration of the alleged cartel and the nature of the alleged cartel conduct. The applicant should also inform the Commission on other past or possible future leniency applications to other authorities in relation to the alleged cartel and justify its request for a marker. Where a marker is granted, the Commission services determine the period within which the applicant has to perfect the marker by submitting the information and evidence required to meet the relevant threshold for immunity. Undertakings which have been granted a marker cannot perfect it by making a formal application in hypothetical terms. If the applicant perfects the marker within the period set by the Commission

services, the information and evidence provided will be deemed to have been submitted on the date when the marker was granted.

Commentary
point 15: F&N: 8.158

(16) An undertaking making a formal immunity application to the Commission must:
  (a) provide the Commission with all information and evidence relating to the alleged cartel available to it, as specified in points (8) and (9), including corporate statements; or
  (b) initially present this information and evidence in hypothetical terms, in which case the undertaking must present a detailed descriptive list of the evidence it proposes to disclose at a later agreed date. This list should accurately reflect the nature and content of the evidence, whilst safeguarding the hypothetical nature of its disclosure. Copies of documents, from which sensitive parts have been removed, may be used to illustrate the nature and content of the evidence. The name of the applying undertaking and of other undertakings involved in the alleged cartel need not be disclosed until the evidence described in its application is submitted. However, the product or service concerned by the alleged cartel, the geographic scope of the alleged cartel and the estimated duration must be clearly identified.

Commentary
point 16: F&N: 8.196
point 16(b): F&N: 8.159

(17) If requested, the Directorate General for Competition will provide an acknowledgement of receipt of the undertaking's application for immunity from fines, confirming the date and, where appropriate, time of the application.

Commentary
point 17: F&N: 8.164

(18) Once the Commission has received the information and evidence submitted by the undertaking under point (16)(a) and has verified that it meets the conditions set out in points (8)(a) or (8)(b), as appropriate, it will grant the undertaking conditional immunity from fines in writing.
(19) If the undertaking has presented information and evidence in hypothetical terms, the Commission will verify that the nature and content of the evidence described in the detailed list referred to in point (16)(b) will meet the conditions set out in points (8)(a) or (8)(b), as appropriate, and inform the undertaking accordingly. Following the disclosure of the evidence no later than on the date agreed and having verified that it corresponds to the description made in the list, the Commission will grant the undertaking conditional immunity from fines in writing.

Commentary
point 19: F&N: 8.159

(20) If it becomes apparent that immunity is not available or that the undertaking failed to meet the conditions set out in points (8)(a) or (8)(b), as appropriate, the Commission will inform the undertaking in writing. In such case, the undertaking may withdraw the evidence disclosed for the purposes of its immunity application or request the Commission to consider it under section III of this notice. This does not prevent the Commission from using its normal powers of investigation in order to obtain the information.

Commentary
point 20: F&N: 8.154

(21) The Commission will not consider other applications for immunity from fines before it has taken a position on an existing application in relation to the same alleged infringement, irrespective of whether the immunity application is presented formally or by requesting a marker.

Commentary
point 21: F&N: 8.163

(22) If at the end of the administrative procedure, the undertaking has met the conditions set out in point (12), the Commission will grant it immunity from fines in the relevant decision. If at the end of the administrative procedure, the undertaking has not met the conditions set out in point (12), the undertaking will not benefit from any favourable treatment under this Notice. If the Commission, after having granted conditional immunity ultimately finds that the immunity applicant has acted as a coercer, it will withhold immunity.

III. Reduction of a Fine

A. Requirements to qualify for reduction of a fine

(23) Undertakings disclosing their participation in an alleged cartel affecting the Community that do not meet the conditions under section II above may be eligible to benefit from a reduction of any fine that would otherwise have been imposed.

(24) In order to qualify, an undertaking must provide the Commission with evidence of the alleged infringement which represents significant added value with respect to the evidence already in the Commission's possession and must meet the cumulative conditions set out in points (12)(a) to (12)(c) above.

Commentary
point 24: F&N: 8.184, 8.191, 8.196, 8.198, 8.327, 8.328, 8.536, 8.538

(25) The concept of "added value" refers to the extent to which the evidence provided strengthens, by its very nature and/or its level of detail, the Commission's ability to prove the alleged cartel. In this assessment, the Commission will generally consider written evidence originating from the period of time to which the facts pertain to have a greater value than evidence subsequently established. Incriminating evidence directly relevant to the facts in question will generally be considered to have a greater value than that with only indirect relevance. Similarly, the degree of corroboration from other sources required for the evidence submitted to be relied upon against other undertakings involved in the case will have an impact on the value of that evidence, so that compelling evidence will be attributed a greater value than evidence such as statements which require corroboration if contested.

Commentary
point 25: F&N: 8.180, 8.181, 8.183, 8.184, 8.191, 8.199, 8.201, 8.204, 8.205, 8.488

(26) The Commission will determine in any final decision adopted at the end of the administrative procedure the level of reduction an undertaking will benefit from, relative to the fine which would otherwise be imposed. For the:
— first undertaking to provide significant added value: a reduction of 30–50 %,
— second undertaking to provide significant added value: a reduction of 20–30 %,
— subsequent undertakings that provide significant added value: a reduction of up to 20%.
In order to determine the level of reduction within each of these bands, the Commission will take into account the time at which the evidence fulfilling the condition in point (24) was submitted and the extent to which it represents added value.
If the applicant for a reduction of a fine is the first to submit compelling evidence in the sense of point (25) which the Commission uses to establish additional facts increasing the gravity or the duration of the infringement, the Commission will not take such additional facts into account when setting any fine to be imposed on the undertaking which provided this evidence.

Commentary
point 26: F&N: 8.179, 8.181, 8.184, 8.191, 8.208

B. Procedure

(27) An undertaking wishing to benefit from a reduction of a fine must make a formal application to the Commission and it must present it with sufficient evidence of the alleged cartel to qualify for a reduction of a fine in accordance with point (24) of this Notice. Any voluntary submission of evidence to the Commission which the undertaking that submits it wishes to be considered for the beneficial treatment of section III of this Notice must be clearly identified at the time of its submission as being part of a formal application for a reduction of a fine.

Commentary
point 27: F&N: 8.184, 8.187, 8.219

(28) If requested, the Directorate General for Competition will provide an acknowledgement of receipt of the undertaking's application for a reduction of a fine and of any subsequent submissions of evidence, confirming the date and, where appropriate, time of each submission. The Commission will not take any position on an application for a reduction of a fine before it has taken a position on any existing applications for conditional immunity from fines in relation to the same alleged cartel.

Commentary
point 28: F&N: 8.188

(29) If the Commission comes to the preliminary conclusion that the evidence submitted by the undertaking constitutes significant added value within the meaning of points (24) and (25), and that the undertaking has met the conditions of points (12) and (27), it will inform the undertaking in writing, no later than the date on which a statement of objections is notified, of its intention to apply a reduction of a fine within a specified band as provided in point (26). The Commission will also, within the same time frame, inform the undertaking in writing if it comes to the preliminary conclusion that the undertaking does not qualify for a reduction of a fine. The Commission may disregard any application for a reduction of fines on the grounds that it has been submitted after the statement of objections has been issued.

Commentary
point 29: F&N: 8.190

(30) The Commission will evaluate the final position of each undertaking which filed an application for a reduction of a fine at the end of the administrative procedure in any decision adopted. The Commission will determine in any such final decision:
   (a) whether the evidence provided by an undertaking represented significant added value with respect to the evidence in the Commission's possession at that same time;
   (b) whether the conditions set out in points (12)(a) to (12)(c) above have been met;
   (c) the exact level of reduction an undertaking will benefit from within the bands specified in point (26). If the Commission finds that the undertaking has not met the conditions set out in point (12), the undertaking will not benefit from any favourable treatment under this Notice.

Commentary
point 30(b): F&N: 8.208

IV. Corporate Statements Made to Qualify under this Notice

(31) A corporate statement is a voluntary presentation by or on behalf of an undertaking to the Commission of the undertaking's knowledge of a cartel and its role therein prepared specially to be submitted under this Notice. Any statement made vis-à-vis the Commission in relation to this notice, forms part of the Commission's file and can thus be used in evidence.
(32) Upon the applicant's request, the Commission may accept that corporate statements be provided orally unless the applicant has already disclosed the content of the corporate statement to third parties. Oral corporate statements will be recorded and transcribed at the

Commission's premises. In accordance with Article 19 of Council Regulation (EC) No 1/2003[1] and Articles 3 and 17 of Commission Regulation (EC) No 773/2004,[2] undertakings making oral corporate statements will be granted the opportunity to check the technical accuracy of the recording, which will be available at the Commission's premises and to correct the substance of their oral statements within a given time limit. Undertakings may waive these rights within the said time limit, in which case the recording will from that moment on be deemed to have been approved. Following the explicit or implicit approval of the oral statement or the submission of any corrections to it, the undertaking shall listen to the recordings at the Commission's premises and check the accuracy of the transcript within a given time limit. Non-compliance with the last requirement may lead to the loss of any beneficial treatment under this Notice.

Notes
[1] OJ L 1 of 4.1.2003, p. 1.
[2] OJ L 123 of 27.4.2004, p. 18.

Commentary
point 32: F&N: 8.162

(33) Access to corporate statements is only granted to the addressees of a statement of objections, provided that they commit, — together with the legal counsels getting access on their behalf —, not to make any copy by mechanical or electronic means of any information in the corporate statement to which access is being granted and to ensure that the information to be obtained from the corporate statement will solely be used for the purposes mentioned below. Other parties such as complainants will not be granted access to corporate statements. The Commission considers that this specific protection of a corporate statement is not justified as from the moment when the applicant discloses to third parties the content thereof.

Commentary
point 33: F&N: 8.217, 8.458

(34) In accordance with the Commission Notice on rules for access to the Commission file,[1] access to the file is only granted to the addressees of a statement of objections on the condition that the information thereby obtained may only be used for the purposes of judicial or administrative proceedings for the application of the Community competition rules at issue in the related administrative proceedings. The use of such information for a different purpose during the proceeding may be regarded as lack of cooperation within the meaning of points (12) and (27) of this Notice. Moreover, if any such use is made after the Commission has already adopted a prohibition decision in the proceeding, the Commission may, in any legal proceedings before the Community Courts, ask the Court to increase the fine in respect of the responsible undertaking. Should the information be used for a different purpose, at any point in time, with the involvement of an outside counsel, the Commission may report the incident to the bar of that counsel, with a view to disciplinary action.

Notes
[1] OJ C 325, 22.12.2005, p. 7.

Commentary
point 34: F&N: 8.215, 8.216, 8.458

(35) Corporate statements made under the present Notice will only be transmitted to the competition authorities of the Member States pursuant to Article 12 of Regulation No 1/2003, provided that the conditions set out in the Network Notice[1] are met and provided that the level of protection against disclosure awarded by the receiving competition authority is equivalent to the one conferred by the Commission.

Notes
[1] Commission Notice on cooperation within the Network of Competition Authorities, OJ C 101, 27.4.2004, p. 43.

V. General Considerations

(36) The Commission will not take a position on whether or not to grant conditional immunity, or otherwise on whether or not to reward any application, if it becomes apparent that the application concerns infringements covered by the five years limitation period for the imposition of penalties stipulated in Article 25(1)(b) of Regulation 1/2003, as such applications would be devoid of purpose.

Commentary
point 36: F&N: 8.171

(37) From the date of its publication in the Official Journal, this notice replaces the 2002 Commission notice on immunity from fines and reduction of fines in cartel cases for all cases in which no undertaking has contacted the Commission in order to take advantage of the favourable treatment set out in that notice. However, points (31) to (35) of the current notice will be applied from the moment of its publication to all pending and new applications for immunity from fines or reduction of fines.

Commentary
point 37: F&N: 8.111, 8.162

(38) The Commission is aware that this notice will create legitimate expectations on which undertakings may rely when disclosing the existence of a cartel to the Commission.

(39) In line with the Commission's practice, the fact that an undertaking cooperated with the Commission during its administrative procedure will be indicated in any decision, so as to explain the reason for the immunity or reduction of the fine. The fact that immunity or reduction in respect of fines is granted cannot protect an undertaking from the civil law consequences of its participation in an infringement of Article 81 EC.

Commentary
point 39: F&N: 8.215

(40) The Commission considers that normally public disclosure, at any time, of documents or written or recorded statements received in the context of this notice would undermine certain public or private interests, for example the protection of the purpose of inspections and investigations, within the meaning of Article 4 of Regulation (EC) No 1049/2001,[1] even after the decision has been taken.

Notes
[1] OJ L 145, 31.5.2001, p. 43.

Commentary
point 40: F&N: 8.220

B15

LENIENCY APPLICATION

Note

This document is published on the Europa website at the following address:
<http://ec.europa.eu/comm/competition/cartels/leniency/leniency.html>

Leniency

The penalties for companies that breach the competition rules can be very severe. For cartel infringements, the largest fine imposed on a single company is EUR 462 million; the largest fine imposed on all members of a single cartel is EUR 790 million. In June 2006 the Commission revised its guidelines for setting fines in competition cases. These revised guidelines will often lead to fines for cartels being significantly higher than previously. However, companies that have participated in illegal cartels have a limited opportunity to avoid or reduce a fine. The Commission operates a leniency policy whereby companies that provide information about a cartel in which they participated might receive full or partial immunity from fines.

About the leniency policy

Along with the other detection and investigation tools at the Commission's disposal, the leniency policy proves very successful in fighting cartels. In essence, the leniency policy offers companies involved in a cartel — which self-report and hand over evidence — either total immunity from fines or a reduction of fines which the Commission would have otherwise imposed on them. It also benefits the Commission, allowing it not only to pierce the cloak of secrecy in which cartels operate but also to obtain insider evidence of the cartel infringement. The leniency policy also has a very deterrent effect on cartel formation and it destabilizes the operation of existing cartels as it seeds distrust and suspicion among cartel members.

In order to obtain total **immunity** under the leniency policy, a company which participated in a cartel must be the first one to inform the Commission of an undetected cartel by providing sufficient information to allow the Commission to launch an inspection at the premises of the companies allegedly involved in the cartel. If the Commission is already in possession of enough information to launch an inspection or has already undertaken one, the company must provide evidence that enables the Commission to prove the cartel infringement. In all cases, the company must also fully cooperate with the Commission throughout its procedure, provide it with all evidence in its possession and put an end to the infringement immediately. The cooperation with the Commission implies that the existence and the content of the application cannot be disclosed to any other company. The company may not benefit from immunity if it took steps to coerce other undertakings to participate in the cartel.

Companies which do not qualify for immunity may benefit from a **reduction of fines** if they provide evidence that represents "significant added value" to that already in the Commission's possession and have terminated their participation in the cartel. Evidence is considered to be of a "significant added value" for the Commission when it reinforces its ability to prove the infringement. The first company to meet these conditions is granted 30 to 50% reduction, the second 20 to 30% and subsequent companies up to 20%.

The Commission considers that any statement submitted to it within the context of its leniency policy forms part of the Commission's file and may therefore not be disclosed or used for any other purpose than the Commission's own cartel proceedings.

Leniency applications

In order to benefit from the Notice, companies can approach the Commission directly or through a legal adviser. To apply for leniency please contact the Commission only through the following dedicated fax number:

Leniency fax: + 32 2 299 45 85

The use of this fax ensures that the precise time and date of the contact is duly recorded and that the information is treated with the utmost confidentiality within the Commission. Before sending the actual submission by fax, however, it is advisable to seek assistance from one of the Commission officials involved in leniency by calling the following dedicated telephone numbers:

Telephone numbers: + 32 2 298 41 90 or + 32 2 298 41 91

Because of the confidentiality, companies are requested not to send any application to the Commission by any other channel than the leniency fax!

B16

ECN MODEL LENIENCY PROGRAMME

Notes

This document is published on the Europa website at the following address:
<http://ec.europa.eu/comm/competition/ecn/model_leniency_en.pdf>

I. INTRODUCTION

1. In a system of parallel competences between the Commission and National Competition Authorities, an application for leniency[1] to one authority is not to be considered as an application for leniency to another authority. It is therefore in the interest of the applicant to apply for leniency to all Competition Authorities which have competence to apply Article 81 of the EC Treaty (hereafter CAs) in the territory which is affected by the infringement and which may be considered well placed to act against the infringement in question.[2]

Notes

[1] The term "leniency" refers to immunity as well as a reduction of any fine which would otherwise have been imposed on a participant in a cartel, in exchange for the voluntary disclosure of information regarding the cartel which satisfies specific criteria prior to or during the investigative stage of the case (see paragraph 37 of the Commission Notice on cooperation within the Network of Competition Authorities (hereafter the Network Notice)).
[2] See paragraph 38 of the Network Notice.

---

2. The purpose of the ECN Model Leniency Programme (hereafter the ECN Model Programme) is to ensure that potential leniency applicants are not discouraged from applying as a result of the discrepancies between the existing leniency programmes within the ECN. The ECN Model Programme therefore sets out the treatment which an applicant can anticipate in any ECN jurisdiction once alignment of all programmes has taken place. In addition, the ECN Model Programme aims to alleviate the burden associated with multiple filings in cases for which the Commission is particularly well placed by introducing a model for a uniform summary application system.
3. The ECN Model Programme sets out a framework for rewarding the cooperation of undertakings which are party to agreements and practices falling within its scope. The ECN members commit to using their best efforts, within the limits of their competence, to align their respective programmes

with the ECN Model Programme. The ECN Model Programme does not prevent a CA from adopting a more favourable approach towards applicants within its programme..

II. SCOPE OF THE PROGRAMME

4. The ECN Model Programme concerns secret cartels, in particular agreements and/or concerted practices between two or more competitors aimed at restricting competition through the fixing of purchase or selling prices, the allocation of production or sales quotas or the sharing of markets including bid-rigging.

III. IMMUNITY FROM FINES

Type 1A

5. The CA will grant an undertaking immunity from any fine which would otherwise have been imposed provided:

   a) The undertaking is the first to submit evidence which in the CA's view, at the time it evaluates the application, will enable the CA to carry out targeted inspections in connection with an alleged cartel;

   b) The CA did not, at the time of the application, already have sufficient evidence to adopt an inspection decision/seek a court warrant for an inspection or had not already carried out an inspection in connection with the alleged cartel arrangement; and

   c) The conditions attached to leniency are met.

6. With a view to enabling the CA to carry out targeted inspections, the undertaking should be in a position to provide the CA with the following:

   — The name and address of the legal entity submitting the immunity application;
   — The other parties to the alleged cartel;
   — A detailed description of the alleged cartel, including:
      — The affected products;
      — The affected territory (-ies);
      — The duration; and
      — The nature of the alleged cartel conduct;
   — Evidence of the alleged cartel in its possession or under its control (in particular any contemporaneous evidence);
   — Information on any past or possible future leniency applications to any other CAs and competition authorities outside the EU in relation to the alleged cartel.

Type 1B

7. In cases where no undertaking had been granted conditional immunity from fines before the CA carried out an inspection or before it had sufficient evidence to adopt an inspection decision/seek a court warrant for an inspection, the CA will grant an undertaking immunity from any fine which would otherwise have been imposed if:

   a) The undertaking is the first to submit evidence which in the CA's view, enables the finding of an infringement of Article 81[3] in respect of an alleged cartel;

   b) At the time of the submission, the CA did not have sufficient evidence to find an infringement of Article 81 in connection with the alleged cartel; and

   c) The conditions attached to leniency are met.

Notes
[3] For national programmes, the equivalent national legal basis should be added.

Excluded immunity applicants

8. An undertaking which took steps to coerce another undertaking to participate in the cartel will not be eligible for immunity from fines under the programme.[4]

Notes
[4] Germany and Greece note that the sole ringleader is not eligible for immunity from fines under their respective programmes.

IV. Reduction of Fines: Type 2

9. Undertakings that do not qualify for immunity may benefit from a reduction of any fine that would otherwise have been imposed.

10. In order to qualify for a reduction of fines, an undertaking must provide the CA with evidence of the alleged cartel which, in the CA's view, represents significant added value relative to the evidence already in the CA's possession at the time of the application. The concept of "significant added value' refers to the extent to which the evidence provided strengthens, by its very nature and/or its level of detail, the CA's ability to prove the alleged cartel.

11. In order to determine the appropriate level of reduction of the fine, the CA will take into account the time at which the evidence was submitted (including whether the applicant was the first, second or third, etc. undertaking to apply) and the CA's assessment of the overall value added to its case by that evidence. Reductions granted to an applicant following a Type 2 application shall not exceed 50% of the fine which would otherwise have been imposed.

12. If a Type 2 applicant submits compelling evidence which the CA uses to establish additional facts which have a direct bearing on the amount of the fine, this will be taken into account when setting any fine to be imposed on the undertaking which provided this evidence.

V. Conditions Attached to Leniency

13. In order to qualify for leniency under this programme, the applicant must satisfy the following cumulative conditions:

    (1) It ends its involvement in the alleged cartel immediately following its application[5] save to the extent that its continued involvement would, in the CA's view, be reasonably necessary to preserve the integrity of the CA's inspections;

    (2) It cooperates genuinely, fully and on a continuous basis from the time of its application with the CA until the conclusion of the case; this includes:

        (a) providing the CA promptly with all relevant information and evidence that comes into the applicant's possession or under its control;

        (b) remaining at the disposal of the CA to reply promptly to any requests that, in the CA's view, may contribute to the establishment of relevant facts;

        (c) making current and, to the extent possible, former employees and directors available for interviews with the CA;

        (d) not destroying, falsifying or concealing relevant information or evidence; and

        (e) not disclosing the fact or any of the content of the leniency application before the CA has notified its objections[6] to the parties (unless otherwise agreed with the CA).

    (3) When contemplating making an application to the CA but prior to doing so, it must not have:

        (a) destroyed evidence which falls within the scope of the application; or

        (b) disclosed, directly or indirectly, the fact or any of the content of the application it is contemplating except to other CAs or any competition authority outside the EU.

Notes
[5] "Application" in this paragraph 13 refers to an application for a marker, a summary application or a full leniency application (as the case may be).
[6] Due to the variety of procedures and investigative measures applied in the various jurisdictions, the ECN Model Programme has been drafted in a manner that takes into account both administrative and judicial proceedings. The terms "objections" and "statement of objections" should be read as covering all equivalent steps under the relevant procedures where the investigative stage has been completed and the parties are formally notified of the CA's objections.

VI. Procedure

Approaching the CA

14. An undertaking wishing to benefit from leniency must apply to the CA and provide it with the information specified above. Before making a formal application, the applicant may on an anonymous basis approach the CA in order to seek informal guidance on the application of the leniency programme.

15. Once a formal application has been made, the CA will, upon request, provide an acknowledgement of receipt confirming the date and time of the application. The CA will assess applications in relation to the same alleged cartel in the order of receipt.

Procedure for immunity applications

Marker for immunity applicants

16. An undertaking wishing to make an application for immunity may initially apply for a "marker". A marker protects an applicant's place in the queue for a given period of time and allows it to gather the necessary information and evidence in order to meet the relevant evidential threshold for immunity.

17. The CA has discretion as to whether or not it grants a marker. Where a marker is granted, the CA determines the period within which the applicant has to "perfect" the marker by submitting the information required to meet the relevant evidential threshold for immunity. If the applicant perfects the marker within the set period, the information and evidence provided will be deemed to have been submitted on the date when the marker was granted.

18. To be eligible to secure a marker, the applicant must provide the CA with its name and address as well as information concerning:
    — The basis for the concern which led to the leniency approach;
    — The parties to the alleged cartel;
    — The affected product(s);
    — The affected territory (-ies);
    — The duration of the alleged cartel;
    — The nature of the alleged cartel conduct; and
    — Information on any past or possible future leniency applications to any other CAs and competition authorities outside the EU in relation to the alleged cartel.

Granting immunity

19. Once the CA has verified that the evidence submitted is sufficient to meet the relevant evidential threshold for immunity, it will grant the undertakings conditional immunity from fines in writing.

20. If the relevant evidential threshold is not met, the CA will inform the undertaking in writing that its application for immunity is rejected. The undertaking may in that case request the CA to consider its application for a reduction of the fine.

21. The CA will take its final position on the grant of immunity at the end of the procedure. If the CA, having granted conditional immunity, ultimately finds that the immunity applicant acted as a coercer or that the applicant has not fulfilled all of the conditions attached to leniency, the CA will inform the applicant of this promptly. If immunity is withheld because the CA finds at the end of the procedure that the conditions attached to leniency have not been fulfilled, the undertaking will not benefit from any other favourable treatment under this programme in respect of the same proceedings.

Summary applications in Type 1A cases

22. In cases where the Commission is "particularly well placed" to deal with a case in accordance with paragraph 14 of the Network Notice, the applicant that has or is in the process of filing an application for immunity with the Commission may file summary applications with any NCAs

which the applicant considers might be "well placed" to act under the Network Notice. Summary applications should include a short description of the following:

— The name and address of the applicant;
— The other parties to the alleged cartel;
— The affected product(s);
— The affected territory(-ies);
— The duration;
— The nature of the alleged cartel conduct;
— The Member State(s) where the evidence is likely to be located; and
— Information on its other past or possible future leniency applications in relation to the alleged cartel.

23. Having received a summary application, the NCA will acknowledge receipt and confirm to the applicant that it is the first to apply to that CA for immunity.

24. Should an NCA having received a summary application decide to request specific further information, the applicant should provide such information promptly. Should an NCA decide to act upon the case, it will determine a period of time within which the applicant must make a full submission of all relevant evidence and information required to meet the threshold. If the applicant submits such information within the set period, the information provided will be deemed to have been submitted on the date when the summary application was made.

25. Summary applications are deemed to be applications within the meaning of paragraph 41(1) of the Network Notice.

Procedure for reductions of fines applications

26. If the CA comes to the preliminary conclusion that the evidence submitted by an undertaking constitutes "significant added value" within the meaning of the programme, it will inform the undertaking in writing of its intention to apply a reduction of fines. This confirmation will be given as early as possible and no later than the date the statement of objections is notified to the parties. The final amount of reduction will be determined at the latest by the end of the procedure.

27. If the CA finds that one or more of the conditions attached to leniency have not been fulfilled, the undertaking will not benefit from any favourable treatment under this programme in respect of the same proceedings.

Oral procedure

28. Upon the applicant's request, the CA may allow oral applications. In such cases the statements[7] may be provided orally and recorded in any form deemed appropriate by the CA. The applicant will still need to provide the CA with copies of all pre-existing documentary evidence of the cartel.

Notes

[7] The term "statement" refers both to corporate statements given by legal representatives on behalf of their clients and witness statements made by employees and directors of the undertakings.

---

29. No access to any records of the applicant's oral statements will be granted before the CA has issued its statement of objections to the parties.

30. Oral statements made under the present programme will only be exchanged between CAs pursuant to Article 12 of Regulation No 1/2003 if the conditions set out in the Network Notice are met and provided that the protection against disclosure granted by the receiving CA is equivalent to the one conferred by the transmitting CA.

VII. REVIEW OF THE ECN MODEL PROGRAMME

31. The ECN Model Programme may be reviewed on the basis of the experience gathered by the ECN members. In any event, no later than at the end of the second year after the publication of the ECN Model Programme, the state of convergence of the leniency programmes of ECN members will be assessed.

ECN Model Leniency Programme

Explanatory Notes

I. Introduction

Importance of leniency programmes in the fight against cartels

1. Cartel activities are very serious violations of competition law. They injure consumers by raising prices and restricting supply. In the long term, they lead to a loss of competitiveness and reduced employment opportunities. Undertakings involved in these types of illegal activities that are willing to put an end to their participation and inform the European Commission and the National Competition Authorities (i.e. CAs) of the existence of such activities should not be dissuaded from doing so by the high fines to which they are potentially exposed. The CAs consider that it is in the public interest to grant favourable treatment to undertakings which co-operate with them.

2. The purpose of leniency programmes is to assist CAs in their efforts to detect and terminate cartels and to punish cartel participants. The CAs consider that the voluntary assistance with the above objectives has an intrinsic value for the economic well-being of individual Member States as well as the Common Market which may justify immunity in certain cases (Type 1A and 1B) and a reduction of a any fine in others (Type 2).

Safeguards for leniency information within the ECN

3. In order to prevent the mechanisms for cooperation between CAs established by Regulation No 1/2003[8] discouraging applicants from voluntarily reporting cartel activities, the Network Notice sets out special safeguards for leniency related information.[9] These safeguards enable the CAs to exchange and use in evidence leniency related information without jeopardising the effectiveness of their respective programmes.

Notes

[8] OJ L 1, 4.1.2003, page 1.

[9] See paragraphs 39–42 of the Network Notice. Leniency related information covers not only information contained in the leniency application itself, but all information that has been collected following any fact-finding measures that could not have been carried out but for the leniency application.

4. According to paragraph 39 of the Network Notice, leniency related information submitted pursuant to Article 11 of Regulation 1/2003 cannot be used by other CAs to start an investigation.

5. According to paragraph 41, information submitted by a leniency applicant or collected on that basis, may only be exchanged between two CAs in the following circumstances:

— The applicant consents to the exchange; or
— The applicant has applied for leniency with both CAs in the same case; or
— The receiving CA provides a written commitment not to use the information transmitted or any information it may obtain after the date of the transmission to impose sanctions on the applicant, its subsidiaries or its employees. A copy of the written commitment is sent to the applicant.

Purpose of the ECN Model Programme

6. Making multiple parallel applications across the ECN is a complex exercise given the existing discrepancies between the different leniency regimes. Certain discrepancies may have adverse effects on the effectiveness of individual programmes. In addition, for cases involving a significant number of jurisdictions and for which the Commission is particularly well placed to act within the meaning of the Network Notice, the multiple filing of complete applications to all other possibly well placed CAs can be a cumbersome process which could discourage certain applicants from applying for leniency under any programme.

7. The purpose of the ECN Model Programme is to address the issue of multiple parallel applications and to provide a greater degree of predictability for potential applicants. The ECN Model Programme is based on the common experience of the CAs having operated a leniency programme for a number of years and has two principal objectives. Firstly, the ECN Model Programme is meant to trigger soft harmonisation of the existing leniency programmes and to facilitate the

adoption of such programmes by the few CAs who do not currently operate one. Secondly, it sets out the features of a uniform type of short form applications (so-called summary applications) designed to alleviate the burden on both undertakings and CAs associated with multiple filing in large, cross-border cartel cases.

8. While it is highly desirable to ensure that all CAs operate a leniency programme, the variety of legislative frameworks, procedures and sanctions across the EU makes it difficult to adopt one uniform system. The ECN Model Programme therefore sets out the principal elements which, after the soft harmonisation process has occurred, should be common to all leniency programmes across the ECN. This would be without prejudice to the possibility for a CA to add further detailed provisions which suit its own enforcement system or to provide for a more favourable treatment of its applicants if it considers it to be necessary in order to ensure effective enforcement.

9. The Commission and the NCAs are committed to seeking the alignment of the programmes in their jurisdictions within the framework specified by the ECN Model Programme. It is recognised that some ECN members do not have the power to implement changes in their national leniency programmes as this power is held by other bodies. However, the existence of the ECN Model Programme should assist all relevant bodies (ECN members as well as other decision-making bodies) in implementing an efficient policy and making sure that cooperation within the ECN works as efficiently and effectively as possible.

II. The ECN Model Programme

10. The ECN Model Programme sets out a framework for rewarding the cooperation of undertakings which are party to agreements and practices falling within its scope.
   The ECN Model Programme does not give rise to any legal or other legitimate expectations on the part of any undertaking.

A. Scope of the programme

11. The ECN Model Programme concerns secret cartels.

12. Cartels constitute very serious violations of competition rules which are often extremely difficult to detect and investigate without the cooperation of at least one of the participants. The interests of consumers and citizens in ensuring that such cartels are detected, terminated and punished outweighs the interest in fining those undertakings that enable a CA to detect, terminate and punish such illegal practices.

13. For the purpose of the ECN Model Programme cartels are agreements and/or concerted practices between competitors aimed at restricting competition by coordinating their competitive behaviour or influencing the relevant parameters of competition within the EEA. Cartel participants would typically collude to fix their purchase or selling prices, and/or to allocate production or sales quotas and/or to share markets. These cartel practices include arrangements which either directly or indirectly affect prices, volumes, market shares and other relevant parameters of competition. By way of example, collusive practices such as restrictions on imports or exports, bid-rigging or joint boycotts fall within the scope of the ECN Model Programme.

14. Other types of restriction such as vertical agreements and horizontal restrictions other than cartels are normally less difficult to detect and/or investigate and therefore do not justify being dealt with under a leniency programme. In addition, including agreements other than cartels within the scope of a leniency programme may risk re-introducing a kind of de facto notification system which would be undesirable.

15. The ECN Model Programme only concerns corporate leniency. It does not cover sanctions on natural persons which are not undertakings. In order to ensure that corporate leniency programmes work efficiently, it is however important to protect to the greatest extent possible employees and directors of the undertakings applying for immunity. It may also be appropriate to offer protection from individual sanctions to employees and directors of applicants for a reduction of any fine.

B. Immunity from fines: Type 1A and 1B

Evidential thresholds for immunity

16. The ECN Model Programme contains two different evidential thresholds for granting immunity:
    — one for the first undertaking that provides the CA with sufficient evidence to enable it to carry out targeted inspections in connection with an alleged cartel (Type 1A); and
    — one for the first undertaking that submits evidence which in the CA's view may enable the finding of an infringement of Article 81 EC in connection with an alleged cartel (Type 1B).

17. Immunity is no longer available under Type 1B if it has already been granted under Type 1A.

18. Immunity is available under a lower threshold in Type 1A compared to Type 1B in order to create an incentive for cartel participants to leave the cartel and to report infringements which are not yet known to the CAs.

19. The threshold in a Type 1A situation is that the applicant must provide the CA with sufficient information to allow it to carry out targeted inspections. The assessment of the threshold will have to be carried out *ex ante*, i.e. without taking into account whether a given inspection has or has not been successful or whether or not an inspection has or has not been carried out. The assessment will be made exclusively on the basis of the type and the quality of the information submitted by the applicant. The list contained in the ECN Model Programme and described in more detail below should serve as guidance for the applicant to anticipate what is usually required by a CA.

20. In order to meet the evidential threshold in Type 1A cases, undertakings should generally be in a position to provide the CA with the following information and evidence:
    — The name and address of the legal entity submitting the immunity application, as well as the names of individuals who are or have been involved in the alleged cartel on its behalf;
    — The identity of all the other undertakings which participate(d) in the alleged cartel as well as of the individuals who, to the applicant's knowledge, are or have been involved in the alleged cartel;
    — A detailed description of the alleged cartel conduct, including for instance its aims, activities and functioning; the product(s) or service(s) concerned, the geographic coverage, the duration and the estimated market volumes affected by the alleged cartel; the dates, locations, content and participants of alleged cartel contacts; all relevant explanations in connection with evidence provided in support of the application;
    — Evidence relating to the alleged cartel in the possession of the applicant or available to it at the time of the submission, in particular contemporaneous evidence; and
    — Information on which other CAs, inside or outside the EU, have been approached or are intended to be approached by the applicant in relation to the alleged cartel.

21. If a CA has carried out an inspection or already has in its possession sufficient evidence to carry out an inspection, immunity under Type 1A will no longer be available.

Excluded applicants

22. An undertaking which has taken steps to coerce one or more undertakings to join or remain in the cartel should, as a matter of principle, be excluded from the benefit of immunity. Considerations of natural justice prevent an undertaking that has played such a role from escaping sanction altogether. The scope of the exclusion is narrow, however, so as to avoid creating uncertainty for potential applicants.

C. Reduction of fines: Type 2

23. It is in the interest of CAs to obtain the cooperation in the proceedings of those undertakings which do not qualify for immunity, either because they failed to meet the relevant evidential threshold or because of the role they played in the cartel. Such cooperation ensures that cartel activities are more efficiently investigated and penalised.

24. The value of the cooperation depends on the timing (including whether the applicant was the first, second or third, etc. to apply) and the quality and nature of the evidence submitted. There are various ways of combining these parameters to reward the contribution of the applicant. However, all systems should ensure that there is a significant difference between immunity from fines and reductions of fines in order to make applications for immunity significantly more

attractive. Significant added value for type 2 applications should therefore not be rewarded with a reduction of any fine of more than 50%.

25. Applicants are required to adduce evidence which constitutes in the CA's view significant added value with respect to the evidence already in its possession at the time the application was submitted. The CA will generally consider written evidence originating from the period to which the facts pertain to have a greater value than evidence subsequently created, and incriminating evidence directly relevant to the facts in question will generally be considered to have a greater value than that with only indirect relevance. Similarly, the degree of corroboration from other sources required to rely on the evidence submitted will have an impact on the value of that evidence.

26. The ECN Model Programme contains a provision to counter any potentially adverse consequences for Type 2 applicants when they submit compelling evidence relating to additional facts which have a direct bearing on the amount of the fines.

D. Conditions attached to leniency

27. Qualifying for conditional immunity or bringing significant added value to an investigation will entitle an applicant to immunity or a reduction of fines provided that three cumulative conditions are met.

28. The final assessment of full compliance with the conditions attached to leniency is made at the end of the procedure.

29. The first condition relates to the termination of the alleged cartel conduct. Undertakings should terminate all cartel activities as soon as possible. However, experience shows that immediate termination, e.g. sudden unexplained absences from regular cartel meetings, after the application and before the CA has undertaken inspections can seriously undermine the effectiveness of subsequent inspections by alerting other cartel participants and allowing them to conceal or destroy evidence.

It is therefore in the public interest to delay the complete termination of all cartel activities until the point in time necessary to safeguard the integrity of the inspection. This strikes the appropriate balance between bringing an end to the illegal activities of the applicant as soon as possible and protecting the effectiveness of the CA's investigation. This is also necessary to allow coordination between the various CAs in the event of parallel proceedings and to avoid applicants from being exposed to conflicting demands. The need to continue with certain cartel conduct should be discussed between the applicant and the CA at a very early stage.

30. The second condition is the obligation to cooperate with the CA throughout the procedure. This obligation starts from the date of application to the CA. Cooperation is an essential feature of the programme which rewards assistance to the CA in the investigation. The cooperation has to be sincere and there is no reason to distinguish between applicants for immunity and those for a reduction of fines. It has various facets. It involves providing without delay any pre-existing evidence and information which is available to the applicant or comes into its possession or under its control during the investigation. It also requires answering without delay any question from the CA and making current and, where possible former, individual employees and directors available for interviews with the CA. It encompasses not destroying, falsifying or concealing evidence which falls within the scope of the application after having applied for leniency. It also requires the applicant not to reveal (directly or indirectly) without the CA's prior consent the fact or any of the content of its leniency application before the CA has notified its objections to the parties.

31. The third condition requires that the applicant should not, when contemplating making a leniency application to the CA but before doing so, have:
    a) destroyed evidence which falls within the scope of the application; or
    b) disclosed, directly or indirectly, the fact or any of the content of its contemplated application except to other CAs.

32. Failure to comply fully with any of these conditions will disqualify the applicant from the leniency programme in the relevant proceedings.

E. Procedure

Approaching the CA

33. All CAs accept anonymous approaches by potential applicants wishing to obtain guidance on their respective programmes. Some CAs have more formalised systems for such approaches, such as hypothetical applications.

Marker for immunity applicants

34. A marker protects an applicant's place in the queue for a given period of time. It allows the applicant to complete its internal investigation to gather the required information and evidence in order to meet the threshold.

35. In the ECN Model Programme, markers are available at the discretion of the CA. Some CAs may choose only to grant markers when it is clear that immunity is available or in certain type of situations, whereas certain others may grant markers in every case. Taking account of the specificities of each individual case the CA may decide the duration of the marker. In the event of parallel action by a number of CAs, the CAs will endeavour to use their discretion in a manner that allows their respective investigations to be coordinated smoothly.

36. The ECN Model Programme specifies the information required to secure a marker within the meaning of this programme. It is broadly equivalent to what is required to file a summary application. Some CAs however may decide to protect the applicant's place in the queue on the basis of more limited information, depending on the case at hand. In any event, an applicant would as a minimum have to provide its name and address and to satisfy a CA that it has a concrete basis for a reasonable concern that it has participated in cartel conduct.

Procedure for immunity and reduction of fines applications

37. CAs should deal with an application in a manner which ensures a high degree of legal certainty for the applicant. This implies that the applicant is informed as early as possible of the status of its application and that it will receive an acknowledgement of receipt of its submission(s).

38. If a CA has granted conditional immunity, no fines will be imposed on the applicant in relation to the cartel which is the subject of the application, provided that the conditions attached to leniency are fulfilled during the procedure and that it is not found that the applicant has acted as a coercer. Similarly, any position taken on an application for reduction of fines is subject to the conditions set out in the programme.

Summary applications in Type 1A cases

39. Experience has shown that applicants often choose to apply to several CAs simultaneously in cases for which the Commission is particularly well placed to act under paragraph 14 of the Network Notice. Such precautionary multiple applications are time-consuming both for the CAs and the applicants. They are however useful to allow network members to have an informed view on whether or not they want to act on a case and to protect the applicant in the event of a case being reallocated, given that an application to one CA does not count as an application to all CAs.

40. In order to alleviate the burden associated with multiple parallel applications on both undertakings and national CAs, the ECN Model Programme introduces a model for a uniform system of summary applications. By filing a summary application, the applicant protects its position as the first in the queue with the CA concerned for the alleged cartel.

41. A summary application is an application for immunity and CAs having received such an application are entitled to exchange information without the consent of the applicant, in accordance with paragraph 41(1) of the Network Notice.

42. The national CAs will not process summary applications, i.e. they will not grant or deny conditional immunity. They will only confirm to the applicant that (a) it is the first to file an application with that CA and (b) it would have a given period of time in which to complete the application, should the CA at any point later decide to take action in respect of the case.

43. As long as the CA has not decided to take action in the case, the applicant's duty to provide further information and generally assist with the investigation only exists towards the Commission.[10] However, the applicant must comply with any specific additional information requests of an NCA which has received a summary application in particular for the NCA to reach an informed view on the issue of case allocation. Failure to comply with such requests by an NCA fully and expeditiously would result in loss of the summary application protection.

Notes

[10] The duties specified under paragraphs 13(2)(d) and (e) of the ECN Model Programme will also be owed to the CA which has accepted the summary application.

---

44. The timing of the termination by the applicant of its participation in the cartel in summary application cases is for the Commission to determine.
45. The ECN Model Programme lists the information which must be contained in a summary application. Firstly, the information and the level of detail must be sufficient to enable the CA to decide whether it wants to act in the case. Secondly, it must allow the CA to determine whether the applicant is in a Type 1A situation. NCAs agree to show flexibility (to the extent legally permissible) as to the language(s) in which summary applications can be made.
46. The ECN Model Programme only provides for the filing of summary applications in Type 1A cases. Summary applications in Type 1B and Type 2 cases are neither necessary nor always practicable. They are unnecessary because, at the time of the approaches and unlike in Type 1A cases, the applicant normally knows which of the well placed CAs is (or are) dealing with the case. They are not always practicable because, unlike Type 1A cases, such applications are generally assessed against what is already in the CA's file at the time of the application. In a re-allocation scenario the CA would not normally have its own file by reference to which the application could be assessed, with the result that it might have been necessary to interlink the CAs' respective files in order to avoid over- or under protection of such applicants[11].

Notes

[11] The information from the leniency applicant could be compared to: (i) only the information provided by the immunity applicant; (ii) the information gathered at the point of re-allocation by the previous acting CA(s); or (iii) the information gathered by the previous acting CA(s) before the date of the summary application.

Oral procedure

47. The ECN members are strong proponents of effective civil proceedings for damages against cartel participants. However, they consider it inappropriate that undertakings which cooperate with them in revealing cartels should be placed in a worse position in respect of civil damage claims than cartel members that refuse to cooperate. The discovery in civil damage proceedings of statements which have been made specifically to a CA in the context of its leniency programme risks creating this very result and, by dissuading cooperation in the CAs' leniency programmes, could undermine the effectiveness of the CAs' fight against cartels. Such a result could also have a negative impact on the fight against cartels in other jurisdictions. The risk that an applicant becomes subject to a discovery order depends to some extent on the affected territories and the nature of the cartel in which it has participated. Experience has so far shown that it is more likely that discovery orders will be made in cases which the Commission is particularly well placed to deal with than in cartels that are limited to a certain region or a certain Member State.
48. In order to limit any such negative consequences for the CAs' leniency programmes, the ECN Model Programme allows for oral applications (summary, marker or full applications) in all cases where this would appear to be justified and proportionate. Oral applications are always justified and proportionate in cases where the Commission is particularly well placed to act under paragraph 14 of the Network Notice. Some CAs will accept oral applications without requiring the applicant to demonstrate that its request is justified and proportionate.

49. The ECN Model Programme also stipulates that no access will be granted to any records of any oral statements before the statement of objections has been issued. In addition, given the differences in the rules concerning access to the file and/or public access to documents in the various jurisdictions, the ECN Model Programme stipulates that the exchange of records of oral statements between CAs is limited to cases where the protections afforded to such records by the receiving CA are equivalent to those afforded by the transmitting CA

PART C

SUBSTANTIVE ANTITRUST MATTERS

C1

REGULATION No 19/65/EEC
OF THE COUNCIL

of 2 March 1965

on application of Article [[81]](3) of the Treaty to certain categories of agreements and concerted practices

Official Journal P 36, 6.3.1965, p. 533

Celex No: 31965R0019

Commentary

Regulation 19/65/EEC: B&C: 1.022, 1.065, 3.075, 3.089, 6.006 F&N: 9.18, 9.19, 9.20, 9.22, 9.191, 10.66

THE COUNCIL OF THE EUROPEAN ECONOMIC COMMUNITY,

Having regard to the Treaty establishing the European Economic Community, and in particular Article [83] thereof;

Having regard to the proposal from the Commission;

Having regard to the Opinion of the European Parliament;[1]

Having regard to the Opinion of the Economic and Social Committee;[2]

Notes

[1] OJ No [81], 27.5.1964, p. 1275/64.
[2] OJ No 197, 30.11.1964, p. 3320/64.

[1] Whereas Article [81](1) of the Treaty may in accordance with Article [81](3) be declared inapplicable to certain categories of agreements, decisions and concerted practices which fulfil the conditions contained in Article [81](3);

[2] Whereas the provisions for implementation of Article [81](3) must be adopted by way of regulation pursuant to Article [83];

[3] Whereas in view of the large number of notifications submitted in pursuance of Regulation No 17[1] it is desirable that in order to facilitate the task of the Commission it should be enabled to declare by way of regulation that the provisions of Article [81](1) do not apply to certain categories of agreements and concerted practices;

Notes

[1] OJ No 13, 21.2.1962, p. 204/62 (Regulation No 17 as amended by Regulation No 59 — OJ No 58, 10.7.1962,
  p. 1655/62 — and Regulation No 118/63/ EEC — OJ No 162, 7.11.1963, p. 2696/63.

---

[4] Whereas it should be laid down under what conditions the Commission, in close and constant liaison with the competent authorities of the Member States, may exercise such powers after sufficient experience has been gained in the light of individual decisions and it becomes possible to define categories of agreements and concerted practices in respect of which the conditions of Article [81](3) may be considered as being fulfilled;

[5] Whereas the Commission has indicated by the action it has taken, in particular by Regulation No 153,[1] that there can be no easing of the procedures prescribed by Regulation No 17 in respect of certain types of agreements and concerted practices that are particularly liable to distort competition in the common market;

Notes
[1] OJ No 139, 24.12.1962, p. 2918/62.

[6] Whereas under Article 6 of Regulation No 17 the Commission may provide that a decision taken pursuant to Article [81](3) of the Treaty shall apply with retroactive effect; whereas it is desirable that the Commission be also empowered to adopt, by regulation, provisions to the like effect;

[7] Whereas under Article 7 of Regulation No 17 agreements, decisions and concerted practices may, by decision of the Commission, be exempted from prohibition in particular if they are modified in such manner that they [satisfy] the requirements of Article [81](3); whereas it is desirable that the Commission be enabled to grant like exemption by regulation to such agreements and concerted practices if they are modified in such manner as to fall within a category defined in an exempting regulation;

[8] Whereas, since there can be no exemption if the conditions set out in Article [81](3) are not satisfied, the Commission must have power to lay down by decision the conditions that must be satisfied by an agreement or concerted practice which owing to special circumstances has certain effects incompatible with Article [81](3);

HAS ADOPTED THIS REGULATION:

Article 1

[1. Without prejudice to the application of Regulation No 17 and in accordance with Article [81](3) of the Treaty the Commission may by regulation declare that Article [81](1) shall not apply to:

(a) categories of agreements which are entered into by two or more undertakings, each operating, for the purposes of the agreement, at a different level of the production or distribution chain, and which relate to the conditions under which the parties may purchase, sell or resell certain goods or services,

(b) categories of agreements to which only two undertakings are party and which include restrictions imposed in relation to the acquisition or use of industrial property rights, in particular of patents, utility models, designs or trade marks, or to the rights arising out of contracts for assignment of, or the right to use, a method of manufacture or knowledge relating to the use or to the application of industrial processes.]

2. The regulation shall define the categories of agreements to which it applies and shall specify in particular:

(a) the restrictions or clauses which must not be contained in the agreements;

(b) [. . .] the other conditions which must be satisfied.

3. Paragraphs 1 and 2 shall apply by analogy to categories of concerted practices [. . .]

Notes
The amendments in square brackets were made by Council Regulation (EC) No 1215/1999 of 10 June 1999 (OJ L 148, 15.6.1999, p. 1) with effect from 18 June 1999.

Commentary
Art 1: B&C: 3.089 F&N: 9.20
Art 1(2): F&N: 9.23, 9.25
Art 1(3): F&N: 9.25
Art 1(4): F&N: 9.26

[*Article 1a*

A regulation pursuant to Article 1 may stipulate the conditions which may lead to the exclusion from its application of certain parallel networks of similar agreements or concerted practices operating on particular market; when these circumstances are fulfilled the Commission may establish this by means of regulation and fix a period at the expiry of which the Regulation pursuant to Article 1 would no longer be applicable in respect of the relevant agreements or concerted practices on that market; such period must not be shorter than six months.]

Notes
Article 1a was added by Council Regulation (EC) No 1215/1999 of 10 June 1999 (OJ L 148, 15.6.1999, p. 1) with effect from 18 June 1999.

Article 2

1. A regulation pursuant to Article 1 shall be made for a specified period.

2. It may be repealed or amended where circumstances have changed with respect to any factor which was basic to its being made; in such case, a period shall be fixed for modification of the agreements and concerted practices to which the earlier regulation applies.

Article 3

A regulation pursuant to Article 1 may stipulate that it shall apply with retroactive effect to agreements and concerted practices to which, at the date of entry into force of that regulation, a decision issued with retroactive effect in pursuance of Article 6 of Regulation No 17 would have applied.

Article 4

1. A regulation pursuant to Article 1 may stipulate that the prohibition contained in Article [81](1) of the Treaty shall not apply, for such period as shall be fixed by that regulation, to agreements and concerted practices already in existence on 13 March 1962 which do not satisfy the conditions of Article [81](3)[; or]

[A regulation pursuant to Article 1 may stipulate that the prohibition contained in Article [81](1) of the Treaty shall not apply, for such period as shall be fixed by that regulation, to agreements and concerted practices already in existence at the date of accession to which Article [81] applies by virtue of accession and which do not satisfy the conditions of Article [81](3), where:][1]

— within three months from the entry into force of the Regulation, they are so modified as to satisfy the said conditions in accordance with the provisions of the regulation; and

— the modifications are brought to the notice of the Commission within the time limit fixed by the regulation.

[The provisions of the preceding subparagraph shall apply in the same way in the case of the accession of the Hellenic Republic, the Kingdom of Spain and of the Portuguese Republic.][2]

[The provisions of the preceding subparagraphs shall apply in the same way in the case of the accession of Austria, Finland and Sweden.][3]

2. Paragraph 1 shall apply to agreements and concerted practices which had to be notified before 1 February 1963, in accordance with Article 5 of Regulation No 17, only where they have been so notified before that date.

[Paragraph 1 shall not apply to agreements and concerted practices to which Article [81](1) of the Treaty applies by virtue of accession and which must be notified before 1 July 1973, in accordance with Articles 5 and 25 of Regulation No 17, unless they have been so notified before that date.][1]

[Paragraph 1 shall not apply to agreements and concerted practices to which Article [81](1) of the Treaty applies by virtue of the accession of the Hellenic Republic and which must be notified before 1 July 1981, in accordance with Articles 5 and 25 of Regulation No 17, unless they have been so notified before that date.][4]

[Paragraph 2 shall not apply to agreements and concerted practices to which Article [81](1) of the Treaty applies by virtue of the accession of the Kingdom of Spain and of the Portuguese Republic and which must be notified before 1 July 1986, in accordance with Articles 5 and 25 of Regulation No 17, unless they have been so notified before that date.][5]

[Paragraph 1 shall not apply to agreements and concerted practices to which Article [81](1) of the Treaty applies by virtue of the accession of Austria, Finland and Sweden and which must be notified within six months of accession, in accordance with Articles 5 and 25 of Regulation No 17, unless they have been so notified within that period. The present paragraph shall not apply to agreements and concerted practices which at the date of accession already fall under Article 53 (1) of the EEA Agreement.][3]

Part C Substantive Antitrust Matters

3. The benefit of the provisions laid down pursuant to paragraph 1 may not be claimed in actions pending at the date of entry into force of a regulation adopted pursuant to Article 1; neither may it be relied on as grounds for claims for damages against third parties.

Notes

(1) The words in square brackets were added by the Act of Accession of Denmark, Ireland and the United Kingdom of Great Britain and Northern Ireland (OJ L 73, 27.3.1972, p. 14).

(2) The words in square brackets were added by the Act of Accession of Greece (OJ L 291, 19.11.1979, p. 17); subsequently amended by the Act of Accession of Spain and Portugal (OJ L 302, 15.11.1985, p. 23).

(3) The words in square brackets were added by the Act of Accession of Austria, Sweden and Finland (OJ C 241, 29.8.1994, p. 21), as amended by Council Decision 95/1/EC (OJ L 1, 1.1.1995, p. 1).

(4) The words in square brackets were added by the Act of Accession of Greece (OJ L 291, 19.11.1979, p. 17).

(5) The words in square brackets were added by the Act of Accession of Spain and Portugal (OJ L 302, 15/11/1985, p. 23).

Article 5

Before adopting a regulation, the Commission shall publish a draft thereof and invite all persons concerned to submit their comments within such time limit, being not less than one month, as the Commission shall fix.

Article 6

1. The Commission shall consult the [Advisory] Committee on Restrictive Practices and Monopolies:

(a) [with regard to a regulation pursuant to Article 1 before publishing a draft regulation and before adopting a regulation;

(b) with regard to a regulation pursuant to Article 1a before publishing a draft regulation if requested by a Member State, and before adopting a regulation.]

2. Article 10(5) and (6) of Regulation No 17, relating to consultation with the Advisory Committee, shall apply by analogy, it being understood that joint meetings with the Commission shall take place not earlier than one month after dispatch of the notice convening them.

Notes

The amendments in square brackets were made by Council Regulation (EC) No 1215/1999 of 10 June 1999 (OJ L 148, 15.6.1999, p. 1) with effect from 18 June 1999.

Article 7

[. . .]

Notes

Article 7 was repealed by Council Regulation (EC) No 1/2003 of 16 December 2002 (OJ L 1, 4.1.2003, p.1), Article 40, with effect from 1 May 2004.

Article 8

The Commission shall, before 1 January 1970, submit to the Council a proposal for a Regulation for such amendment of this Regulation as may prove necessary in the light of experience.

This Regulation shall be binding in its entirety and directly applicable in all Member States.

Done at Brussels, 2 March 1965

C2

REGULATION (EEC) No 2821/71
OF THE COUNCIL

of 20 December 1971

on application of Article [81](3) of the Treaty to categories of
agreements, decisions and concerted practices

Official Journal L 281, 29.12.1971, p 46

Celex No: 31971R2821

Commentary
Regulation 2821/71/EEC: F&N: 3.416

THE COUNCIL OF THE EUROPEAN COMMUNITIES,

Having regard to the Treaty establishing the European Economic Community, and in particular Article [83] thereof;

Having regard to the proposal from the Commission;

Having regard to the Opinion of the European Parliament;

Having regard to the Opinion of the Economic and Social Committee;

[1] Whereas Article [81](1) of the Treaty may in accordance with Article [81](3) be declared inapplicable to categories of agreements, decisions and concerted practices which fulfil the conditions contained in Article [81](3);

[2] Whereas the provisions for implementation of Article [81](3) must be adopted by way of regulation pursuant to Article [83];

[3] Whereas the creation of a common market requires that undertakings be adapted to the conditions of the enlarged market and whereas co-operation between undertakings can be a suitable means of achieving this;

[4] Whereas agreements, decisions and concerted practices for co-operation between undertakings which enable the undertakings to work more rationally and adapt their productivity and competitiveness to the enlarged market may, in so far as they fall within the prohibition contained in Article [81](1), be exempted therefrom under certain conditions; whereas this measure is necessary in particular as regards agreements, decisions and concerted practices relating to the application of standards and types, research and development of products or processes up to the stage of industrial application, exploitation of the results thereof and specialisation;

[5] Whereas it is desirable that the Commission be enabled to declare by way of regulation that the provisions of Article [81](1) do not apply to those categories of agreements, decisions and concerted practices, in order to make it easier for undertakings to co-operate in ways which are economically desirable and without adverse effect from the point of view of competition policy;

[6] Whereas it should be laid down under what conditions the Commission, in close and constant liaison with the competent authorities of the Member States, may exercise such powers;

[7] Whereas under Article 6 of Regulation No 17[1] the Commission may provide that a decision taken in accordance with Article [81](3) of the Treaty shall apply with retroactive effect; whereas it is desirable that the Commission be empowered to issue regulations whose provisions are to the like effect;

Notes
[1] OJ No 13, 21.2.1962, p. 204/62.

[8] Whereas under Article 7 of Regulation No 17 agreements, decisions and concerted practices may by decision of the Commission be exempted from prohibition, in particular if they are modified in such manner that Article [81](3) applies to them; whereas it is desirable that the Commission be enabled to grant by regulation like exemption to such agreements, decisions and concerted practices if they are modified in such manner as to fall within a category defined in an exempting regulation;

[9] Whereas the possibility cannot be excluded that, in a specific case, the conditions set out in Article [81](3) may not be fulfilled; whereas the Commission must have power to regulate such a case in pursuance of Regulation No 17 by way of decision having effect for the future;

HAS ADOPTED THIS REGULATION:

Article 1

1. Without prejudice to the application of Regulation No 17 the Commission may, by regulation and in accordance with Article [81](3) of the Treaty, declare that Article [81](1) shall not apply to categories of agreements between undertakings, decisions of associations of undertakings and concerted practices which have as their object:

(a) the application of standards or types;
(b) the research and development of products or processes up to the stage of industrial application, and exploitation of the results, including provisions regarding industrial property rights and confidential technical knowledge;
(c) specialisation, including agreements necessary for achieving it.

2. Such regulation shall define the categories of agreements, decisions and concerted practices to which it applies and shall specify in particular:

(a) the restrictions or clauses which may, or may not, appear in the agreements, decisions and concerted practices;
(b) the clauses which must be contained in the agreements, decisions and concerted practices or the other conditions which must be satisfied.

Article 2

1. Any regulation pursuant to Article 1 shall be made for a specified period.

2. It may be repealed or amended where circumstances have changed with respect to any of the facts which were basic to its being made; in such case, a period shall be fixed for modification of the agreements, decisions and concerted practices to which the earlier regulation applies.

Article 3

A regulation pursuant to Article 1 may provide that it shall apply with retroactive effect to agreements, decisions and concerted practices to which, at the date of entry into force of that regulation, a decision issued with retroactive effect in pursuance of Article 6 of Regulation No 17 would have applied.

Article 4

1. A regulation pursuant to Article 1 may provide that the prohibition contained in Article [81](1) of the Treaty shall not apply, for such period as shall be fixed by that regulation, to agreements, decisions and concerted practices already in existence on 13 March 1962 which do not satisfy the conditions of Article [81](3), where:

— within six months from the entry into force of the regulation, they are so modified as to satisfy the said conditions in accordance with the provisions of the regulation; and
— the modifications are brought to the notice of the Commission within the time limit fixed by the regulation.

[A Regulation adopted pursuant to Article 1 may lay down that the prohibition referred to in Article [81](1) of the Treaty shall not apply, for the period fixed in the same Regulation, to agreements and concerted practices which existed at the date of accession and which, by virtue of accession, come within the scope of Article [81] and do not fulfil the conditions set out in Article [81](3).][1]

[The provisions of the preceding subparagraph shall apply in the same way in the case of the accession of the Hellenic Republic, the Kingdom of Spain and of the Portuguese Republic.][2]

[The provisions of the preceding subparagraphs shall apply in the same way in the case of the accession of Austria, Finland and Sweden.][3]

2. Paragraph 1 shall apply to agreements, decisions and concerted practices which had to be notified before 1 February 1963, in accordance with Article 5 of Regulation No 17, only where they have been so notified before that date.

[Paragraph 1 shall be applicable to those agreements and concerted practices which, by virtue of the accession, come within the scope of Article [81](1) of the Treaty and for which notification before 1 July 1973 is mandatory, in accordance with Articles 5 and 25 of Regulation No 17, only if notification was given before that date.][1]

[Paragraph 1 shall not apply to agreements and concerted practices to which Article [81](1) of the Treaty applies by virtue of the accession of the Hellenic Republic and which must be notified before 1 July 1981, in accordance with Articles 5 and 25 of Regulation No 17, unless they have been so notified before that date.][4]

[Paragraph 1 shall not apply to agreements and concerted practices to which Article [81](1) of the Treaty applies by virtue of the accession of the Kingdom of Spain and of the Portuguese Republic and which must be notified before 1 July 1986, in accordance with Articles 5 and 25 of Regulation No 17, unless they have been so notified before that date.][5]

[Paragraph 1 shall not apply to agreements and concerted practices to which Article [81](1) of the Treaty applies by virtue of the accession of Austria, Finland and Sweden and which must be notified within six months of accession, in accordance with Articles 5 and 25 of Regulation No 17, unless they have been so notified within that period. The present paragraph shall not apply to agreements and concerted practices which at the date of accession already fall under Article 53(1) of the EEA Agreement.][3]

3. The benefit of the provisions laid down pursuant to paragraph 1 may not be claimed in actions pending at the date of entry into force of a regulation adopted pursuant to Article 1; neither may it be relied on as grounds for claims for damages against third parties.

Notes

[1] The words in square brackets were added by the Regulation (EEC) No 2743/72 of the Council of 19 December 1972 (OJ L 291, 28.12.1972, p. 144).

[2] The words in square brackets were added by the Act of Accession of Greece (OJ L 291, 19.11.1979, p. 17); subsequently amended by the Act of Accession of Spain and Portugal (OJ L 302, 15.11.1985, p. 23).

[3] The words in square brackets were added by the Act of Accession of Austria, Sweden and Finland (OJ C 241, 29.8.1994, p. 21) as amended by Council Decision 95/1/EC (OJ L 1, 1.1.1995, p. 1).

[4] The words in square brackets were added by the Act of Accession of Greece (OJ L 291, 19.11.1979, p. 17).

[5] The words in square brackets were added by the Act of Accession of Spain and Portugal (OJ L 302, 15.11.1985, p. 23).

Article 5

Before making a regulation, the Commission shall publish a draft thereof to enable all persons and organisations concerned to submit their comments within such time limit, being not less than one month, as the Commission shall fix.

Article 6

1. The Commission shall consult the Advisory Committee on Restrictive Practices and Monopolies:

(a) before publishing a draft regulation;
(b) before making a regulation.

2. Paragraphs 5 and 6 of Article 10 of Regulation No 17, relating to consultation with the Advisory Committee, shall apply by analogy, it being understood that joint meetings with the Commission shall take place not earlier than one month after dispatch of the notice convening them.

Article 7

[. . .]

Notes

Article 7 was repealed by Council Regulation (EC) No 1/2003 (OJ L 4.1.2003, p. 1), Article 40, with effect from 1 May 2004.

This Regulation shall be binding in its entirety and directly applicable in all Member States.

Done at Brussels, 20 December 1971.

C3

COMMISSION REGULATION (EC) No 2790/1999

of 22 December 1999

on the application of Article 81(3) of the Treaty to categories
of vertical agreements and concerted practices

(Text with EEA relevance)

Official Journal L 336, 29.12.1999, p. 21

Celex No: 31999R2790

Notes

EEA application: this instrument was adopted with appropriate adaptations by EEA Joint Committee Decision No 18/2000, OJ L 103, 12.4.2001, p. 36 and EEA Supplement No 20, 12.4.2001, p. 179, with effect from 29 January 2000: see EEA Agreement, Annex XIV, Chapter B, Point 2 (as subsequently amended by Decision No 29/2004, OJ L 127, 29.4.2004, p. 137 and EEA Supplement No 22, 29.4.2004, the EEA Enlargement Agreement, OJ L 130, 29.4.2004, p. 3 and EEA Supplement No 23, 29.4.2004, and Decision No 130/2004, OJ L 64, 10.3.2005, p. 57 and EEA Supplement No 12, 10.3.2005).

Commentary

Regulation 2790/1999/EC: B&C: 2.070, 2.083, 2.087, 2.097, 2.110, 2.130, 3.062, 3.068–3.069, 3.078–3.079, 3.086, 3.089, 3.092–3.093, 5.124, 6.006, 6.008–6.011, 6.017, 6.038, 6.043, 6.045–6.048, 6.050, 6.066, 6.079–6.080, 6.082–6.083, 6.086, 6.099, 6.110, 6.142, 6.150, 6.152, 6.160, 6.164, 6.166, 6.168, 6.172, 6.182, 6.184, 6.187–6.188, 6.190, 6.192, 6.194, 9.005, 13.007, 14.105 **F&N:** 3.142, 3.143, 3.314–3.316, 3.323, 3.324, 7.183, 9.27, 9.127, 9.163, 9.189, 9.190, 9.195, 9.196, 9.198, 9.201, 9.202, 9.203, 9.204, 9.206, 9.218, 9.223, 9.234, 9.237, 9.267, 9.273, 9.275, 9.276, 9.280, 9.302, 9.309, 9.334, 10.61, 10.76, 10.77, 10.92, 10.106, 10.125, 12.174, 12.178, 15.11, 15.12, 15.13, 15.14, 15.32, 15.33, 15.34, 15.35, 15.91, 15.126, 15.148, 15.156 **Recitals 8–9: B&C:** 6.017

THE COMMISSION OF THE EUROPEAN COMMUNITIES,

Having regard to the Treaty establishing the European Community,

Having regard to Council Regulation No 19/65/EEC of 2 March 1965 on the application of Article [81](3) of the Treaty to certain categories of agreements and concerted practices,[1] as last amended by Regulation (EC) No 1215/1999,[2] and in particular Article 1 thereof,

Having published a draft of this Regulation,[3]

Having consulted the Advisory Committee on Restrictive Practices and Dominant Positions,

Notes
[1] OJ 36, 6.3.1965, p. 533/65
[2] OJ L 148, 15.6.1999, p. 1
[3] OJ C 270, 24.9.1999, p. 7

Whereas:

(1) Regulation No 19/65/EEC empowers the Commission to apply Article 81(3) of the Treaty (formerly Article 85(3)) by regulation to certain categories of vertical agreements and corresponding concerted practices falling within Article 81(1).

(2) Experience acquired to date makes it possible to define a category of vertical agreements which can be regarded as normally satisfying the conditions laid down in Article 81(3).

(3) This category includes vertical agreements for the purchase or sale of goods or services where these agreements are concluded between non-competing undertakings, between certain competitors or by certain associations of retailers of goods; it also includes vertical agreements containing ancillary provisions on the assignment or use of intellectual property rights; for the purposes of this Regulation, the term "vertical agreements" includes the corresponding concerted practices.

(4) For the application of Article 81(3) by regulation, it is not necessary to define those vertical agreements which are capable of falling within Article 81(1); in the individual assessment of agreements under Article 81(1), account has to be taken of several factors, and in particular the market structure on the supply and purchase side.

Commentary
Recital 4: B&C: 6.017

(5) The benefit of the block exemption should be limited to vertical agreements for which it can be assumed with sufficient certainty that they satisfy the conditions of Article 81(3).

(6) Vertical agreements of the category defined in this Regulation can improve economic efficiency within a chain of production or distribution by facilitating better coordination between the participating undertakings; in particular, they can lead to a reduction in the transaction and distribution costs of the parties and to an optimisation of their sales and investment levels.

(7) The likelihood that such efficiency-enhancing effects will outweigh any anti-competitive effects due to restrictions contained in vertical agreements depends on the degree of market power of the undertakings concerned and, therefore, on the extent to which those undertakings face competition from other suppliers of goods or services regarded by the buyer as interchangeable or substitutable for one another, by reason of the products' characteristics, their prices and their intended use.

(8) It can be presumed that, where the share of the relevant market accounted for by the supplier does not exceed 30%, vertical agreements which do not contain certain types of severely anti-competitive restraints generally lead to an improvement in production or distribution and allow consumers a fair share of the resulting benefits; in the case of vertical agreements containing exclusive supply obligations, it is the market share of the buyer which is relevant in determining the overall effects of such vertical agreements on the market.

Commentary
Recital 8: F&N: 3.314

(9) Above the market share threshold of 30%, there can be no presumption that vertical agreements falling within the scope of Article 81(1) will usually give rise to objective advantages of such a character and size as to compensate for the disadvantages which they create for competition.

Commentary
Recital 9: F&N: 3.316, 3.324

(10) This Regulation should not exempt vertical agreements containing restrictions which are not indispensable to the attainment of the positive effects mentioned above; in particular, vertical agreements containing certain types of severely anti-competitive restraints such as minimum

and fixed resale-prices, as well as certain types of territorial protection, should be excluded from the benefit of the block exemption established by this Regulation irrespective of the market share of the undertakings concerned.

Commentary
Recital 10: B&C: 6.185

(11) In order to ensure access to or to prevent collusion on the relevant market, certain conditions are to be attached to the block exemption; to this end, the exemption of non-compete obligations should be limited to obligations which do not exceed a definite duration; for the same reasons, any direct or indirect obligation causing the members of a selective distribution system not to sell the brands of particular competing suppliers should be excluded from the benefit of this Regulation.

Commentary
Recital 11: B&C: 6.024

(12) The market-share limitation, the non-exemption of certain vertical agreements and the conditions provided for in this Regulation normally ensure that the agreements to which the block exemption applies do not enable the participating undertakings to eliminate competition in respect of a substantial part of the products in question.

(13) In particular cases in which the agreements falling under this Regulation nevertheless have effects incompatible with Article 81(3), the Commission may withdraw the benefit of the block exemption; this may occur in particular where the buyer has significant market power in the relevant market in which it resells the goods or provides the services or where parallel networks of vertical agreements have similar effects which significantly restrict access to a relevant market or competition therein; such cumulative effects may for example arise in the case of selective distribution or non-compete obligations.

Commentary
Recital 13: B&C: 6.025, 6.155

(14) Regulation No 19/65/EEC empowers the competent authorities of Member States to withdraw the benefit of the block exemption in respect of vertical agreements having effects incompatible with the conditions laid down in Article 81(3), where such effects are felt in their respective territory, or in a part thereof, and where such territory has the characteristics of a distinct geographic market; Member States should ensure that the exercise of this power of withdrawal does not prejudice the uniform application throughout the common market of the Community competition rules or the full effect of the measures adopted in implementation of those rules.

(15) In order to strengthen supervision of parallel networks of vertical agreements which have similar restrictive effects and which cover more than 50% of a given market, the Commission may declare this Regulation inapplicable to vertical agreements containing specific restraints relating to the market concerned, thereby restoring the full application of Article 81 to such agreements.

(16) This Regulation is without prejudice to the application of Article 82.

(17) In accordance with the principle of the primacy of Community law, no measure taken pursuant to national laws on competition should prejudice the uniform application throughout the common market of the Community competition rules or the full effect of any measures adopted in implementation of those rules, including this Regulation,

HAS ADOPTED THIS REGULATION:

Article 1

For the purposes of this Regulation:

(a) "competing undertakings" means actual or potential suppliers in the same product market; the, product market includes goods or services which are regarded by the buyer as interchangeable with or substitutable for the contract goods or services, by reason of the products' characteristics, their prices and their intended use;

(b) "non-compete obligation" means any direct or indirect obligation causing the buyer not to manu-facture, purchase, sell or resell goods or services which compete with the contract goods or ser-vices, or any direct or indirect obligation on the buyer to purchase from the supplier or from another undertaking designated by the supplier more than 80% of the buyer's total purchases of the contract goods or services and their substitutes on the relevant market, calculated on the basis of the value of its purchases in the preceding calendar year;

(c) "exclusive supply obligation" means any direct or indirect obligation causing the supplier to sell the goods or services specified in the agreement only to one buyer inside the Community for the purposes of a specific use or for resale;

(d) "Selective distribution system" means a distribution system where the supplier undertakes to sell the contract goods or services, either directly or indirectly, only to distributors selected on the basis of specified criteria and where these distributors undertake not to sell such goods or services to unauthorised distributors;

(e) "intellectual property rights" includes industrial property rights, copyright and neighbouring rights;

(f) "know-how" means a package of non-patented practical information, resulting from experience and testing by the supplier, which is secret, substantial and identified: in this context, "secret" means that the know-how, as a body or in the precise configuration and assembly of its compo-nents, is not generally known or easily accessible; "substantial" means that the know-how includes information which is indispensable to the buyer for the use, sale or resale of the contract goods or services; "identified" means that the know-how must be described in a sufficiently comprehensive manner so as to make it possible to verify that it fulfils the criteria of secrecy and substantiality;

(g) "buyer" includes an undertaking which, under an agreement falling within Article 81(1) of the Treaty, sells goods or services on behalf of another undertaking.

Commentary

Art 1: B&C: 3.078
Art 1(a): **B&C:** 6.012, 6.085, 6.193 **F&N:** 9.194, 12.177
Art 1(b): **B&C:** 6.024, 6.074, 6.107, 6.157 **F&N:** 4.233, 9.234, 9.299, 12.186, 12.210, 12.215, 12.226, 12.227, 12.231
Art 1(c): **B&C:** 6.018, 6.039 **F&N:** 3.314, 9.190, 9.221, 9.226, 9.267, 9.268, 12.244
Art 1(d): **B&C:** 6.023, 6.086, 6.099, 6.108, 6.185
Art 1(e): **B&C:** 6.193, 9.001
Art 1(f): **B&C:** 6.024, 6.186, 6.193 **F&N:** 9.238
Art 1(g): **B&C:** 6.038

Article 2

1. Pursuant to Article 81(3) of the Treaty and subject to the provisions of this Regulation, it is hereby declared that Article 81(1) shall not apply to agreements or concerted practices entered into between two or more undertakings each of which operates, for the purposes of the agreement, at a different level of the production or distribution chain, and relating to the conditions under which the parties may purchase, sell or resell certain goods or services ("vertical agreements").

This exemption shall apply to the extent that such agreements contain restrictions of competition falling within the scope of Article 81(1) ("vertical restraints").

2. The exemption provided for in paragraph 1 shall apply to vertical agreements entered into between an association of undertakings and its members, or between such an association and its suppliers, only if all its members are retailers of goods and if no individual member of the association, together with its connected undertakings, has a total annual turnover exceeding EUR 50 million; vertical agree-ments entered into by such associations shall be covered by this Regulation without prejudice to the application of Article 81 to horizontal agreements concluded between the members of the association or decisions adopted by the association.

3. The exemption provided for in paragraph 1 shall apply to vertical agreements containing provisions which relate to the assignment to the buyer or use by the buyer of intellectual property rights, provided that those provisions do not constitute the primary object of such agreements and are directly related to the use, sale or resale of goods or services by the buyer or its customers. The exemption applies on

condition that, in relation to the contract goods or services, those provisions do not contain restrictions of competition having the same object or effect as vertical restraints which are not exempted under this Regulation.

4. The exemption provided for in paragraph 1 shall not apply to vertical agreements entered into between competing undertakings; however, it shall apply where competing undertakings enter into a non-reciprocal vertical agreement and:

(a) the buyer has a total annual turnover not exceeding EUR 100 million, or
(b)   the supplier is a manufacturer and a distributor of goods, while the buyer is a distributor not manufacturing goods competing with the contract goods, or
(c) the supplier is a provider of services at several levels of trade, while the buyer does not provide competing services at the level of trade where it purchases the contract services.

5. This Regulation shall not apply to vertical agreements the subject matter of which falls within the scope of any other block exemption regulation.

Commentary
Art 2: B&C: 6.011 F&N: 9.209, 9.266
Art 2(1): B&C: 4.009, 6.193 F&N: 9.163, 9.191
Art 2(2): B&C: 6.013 F&N: 9.193, 9.198, 12.286
Art 2(3): B&C: 6.016, 6.183, 6.193, 9.171 F&N: 9.193, 9.200
Art 2(4): B&C: 5.076, 5.110, 6.012, 6.085, 6.193 F&N: 9.193, 12.177, 12.286
Art 2(4)(a): F&N: 12.177
Art 2(4)(b): F&N: 12.177
Art 2(4)(c): F&N: 12.177
Art 2(5): B&C: 6.015, 6.115 F&N: 9.193, 9.205, 15.17

Article 3

1. Subject to paragraph 2 of this Article, the exemption provided for in Article 2 shall apply on condition that the market share held by the supplier does not exceed 30% of the relevant market on which it sells the contract goods or services.

2. In the case of vertical agreements containing exclusive supply obligations, the exemption provided for in Article 2 shall apply on condition that the market share held by the buyer does not exceed 30% of the relevant market on which it purchases the contract goods or services.

Commentary
Art 3: B&C: 3.078, 6.017, 14.100 F&N: 9.266, 12.176
Art 3(1): B&C: 4.009, 6.018–6.019, 6.088, 6.184 F&N: 9.266
Art 3(2): B&C: 4.009, 6.018 F&N: 9.266, 9.344, 12.244

Article 4

The exemption provided for in Article 2 shall not apply to vertical agreements which, directly or indirectly, in isolation or in combination with other factors under the control of the parties, have as their object:

(a) the restriction of the buyer's ability to determine its sale price, without prejudice to the possibility of the supplier's imposing a maximum sale price or recommending a sale price, provided that they do not amount to a fixed or minimum sale price as a result of pressure from, or incentives offered by, any of the parties;
(b) the restriction of the territory into which, or of the customers to whom, the buyer may sell the contract goods or services, except:
— the restriction of active sales into the exclusive territory or to an exclusive customer group reserved to the supplier or allocated by the supplier to another buyer, where such a restriction does not limit sales by the customers of the buyer,
— the restriction of sales to end users by a buyer operating at the wholesale level of trade,
— the restriction of sales to unauthorised distributors by the members of a selective distribution system, and

— the restriction of the buyer's ability to sell components, supplied for the purposes of incorporation, to customers who would use them to manufacture the same type of goods as those produced by the supplier;

(c) the restriction of active or passive sales to end users by members of a selective distribution system operating at the retail level of trade, without prejudice to the possibility of prohibiting a member of the system from operating out of an unauthorised place of establishment;

(d) the restriction of cross-supplies between distributors within a selective distribution system, including between distributors operating at different level of trade;

(e) the restriction agreed between a supplier of components and a buyer who incorporates those components, which limits the supplier to selling the components as spare parts to end-users or to repairers or other service providers not entrusted by the buyer with the repair or servicing of its goods.

Commentary

Art 4: B&C: 3.078, 6.022–6.023, 6.128, 6.185, 14.105 F&N: 3.314, 9.42, 9.67, 9.127, 9.164, 9.201, 9.206, 9.207, 9.208, 9.232, 12.184

Art 4(a): B&C: 6.023, 6.038, 6.050, 6.102, 6.161, 6.185, 6.187 F&N: 3.155, 9.209, 9.210, 9.212, 9.241, 9.255, 12.184

Art 4(b): B&C: 6.023, 6.058, 6.065–6.066, 6.095, 6.101, 6.161, 6.185 F&N: 3.155, 9.209, 9.213, 9.214, 9.217, 9.220, 9.221, 9.222, 9.226, 9.227, 9.229, 9.230, 9.241, 9.248, 9.251, 9.258, 10.63, 12.189, 12.192, 12.197, 12.199

Art 4(c): B&C: 6.023, 6.043, 6.054, 6.095, 6.101, 6.185 F&N: 9.209, 9.227, 9.229, 9.230, 9.255

Art 4(d): B&C: 6.023, 6.101, 6.185 F&N: 9.209, 9.227, 9.228

Art 4(e): B&C: 6.023 F&N: 9.209, 9.216, 9.231

Article 5

The exemption provided for in Article 2 shall not apply to any of the following obligations contained in vertical agreements:

(a) any direct or indirect non-compete obligation, the duration of which is indefinite or exceeds five years. A non-compete obligation which is tacitly renewable beyond a period of five years is to be deemed to have been concluded for an indefinite duration. However, the time limitation of five years shall not apply where the contract goods or services are sold by the buyer from premises and land owned by the supplier or leased by the supplier from third parties not connected with the buyer, provided that the duration of the non-compete obligation does not exceed the period of occupancy of the premises and land by the buyer;

(b) any direct or indirect obligation causing the buyer, after termination of the agreement, not to manufacture, purchase, sell or resell goods or services, unless such obligation:

— relates to goods or services which compete with the contract goods or services, and

— is limited to the premises and land from which the buyer has operated during the contract period, and

— is indispensable to protect know-how transferred by the supplier to the buyer, and provided that the duration of such non-compete obligation is limited to a period of one year after termination of the agreement; this obligation is without prejudice to the possibility of imposing a restriction which is unlimited in time on the use and disclosure of know-how which has not entered the public domain;

(c) any direct or indirect obligation causing the members of a selective distribution system not to sell the brands of particular competing suppliers.

Commentary

Art 5: B&C: 6.022, 6.024, 14.105 F&N: 3.155, 3.314, 9.201, 9.206, 9.232, 9.233, 9.299, 9.302

Art 5(a): B&C: 6.024, 6.037, 6.062, 6.081, 6.107, 6.150, 6.152, 6.186 F&N: 9.233, 9.234, 12.186, 12.215, 12.220, 12.231, 15.142

Art 5(b): B&C: 6.024, 6.186 F&N: 9.233, 9.238

Art 5(c): B&C: 6.024, 6.107 F&N: 9.233, 9.240

Article 6

The Commission may withdraw the benefit of this Regulation, pursuant to Article 7(1) of Regulation No 19/65/EEC, where it finds in any particular case that vertical agreements to which this Regulation applies nevertheless have effects which are incompatible with the conditions laid down in Article 81(3) of the Treaty, and in particular where access to the relevant market or competition therein is significantly restricted by the cumulative effect of parallel networks of similar vertical restraints implemented by competing suppliers or buyers.

Commentary
Art 6: B&C: 3.086, 6.025, 6.027, 6.155 F&N: 9.155, 9.156, 9.262, 9.264

Article 7

Where in any particular case vertical agreements to which the exemption provided for in Article 2 applies have effects incompatible with the conditions laid down in Article 81(3) of the Treaty in the territory of a Member State, or in a part thereof, which has all the characteristics of a distinct geographic market, the competent authority of that Member State may withdraw the benefit of application of this Regulation in respect of that territory, under the same conditions as provided in Article 6.

Commentary
Art 7: B&C: 3.087, 6.026 F&N: 9.262

Article 8

1. Pursuant to Article 1a of Regulation No 19/65/EEC, the Commission may by regulation declare that, where parallel networks of similar vertical restraints cover more than 50% of a relevant market, this Regulation shall not apply to vertical agreements containing specific restraints relating to that market.

2. A regulation pursuant to paragraph 1 shall not become applicable earlier than six months following its adoption.

Commentary
Art 8: B&C: 3.089, 6.027, 6.100, 6.155 F&N: 9.156, 9.264, 9.265
Art 8(1): B&C: 6.027
Art 8(2): B&C: 6.027 F&N: 15.165

Article 9

1. The market share of 30% provided for in Article 3(1) shall be calculated on the basis of the market sales value of the contract goods or services and other goods or services sold by the supplier, which are regarded as interchangeable or substitutable by the buyer, by reason of the products' characteristics, their prices and their intended use; if market sales value data are not available, estimates based on other reliable market information, including market sales volumes, may be used to establish the market share of the undertaking concerned. For the purposes of Article 3(2), it is either the market purchase value or estimates thereof which shall be used to calculate the market share.

2. For the purposes of applying the market share, threshold provided for in Article 3 the following rules shall apply:

(a) the market share shall be calculated on the basis of data relating to the preceding calendar year;

(b) the market share shall include any goods or services supplied to integrated distributors for the purposes of sale;

(c) if the market share is initially not more than 30% but subsequently rises above that level without exceeding 35%, the exemption provided for in Article 2 shall continue to apply for a period of two consecutive calendar years following the year in which the 30% market share threshold was first exceeded;

(d) if the market share is initially not more than 30% but subsequently rises above 35%, the exemption provided for in Article 2 shall continue to apply for one calendar year following the year in which the level of 35% was first exceeded;

(e) the benefit of points (c) and (d) may not be combined so as to exceed a period of two calendar years.

Commentary
Art 9: **B&C:** 6.019, 14.100 **F&N:** 9.269
Art 9(1): **B&C:** 6.019 **F&N:** 9.269
Art 9(2): **B&C:** 6.020
Art 9(2)(a): **F&N:** 9.269
Art 9(2)(b): **B&C:** 6.019, 6.153 **F&N:** 9.269

Article 10

1. For the purpose of calculating total annual turnover within the meaning of Article 2(2) and (4), the turnover achieved during the previous financial year by the relevant party to the vertical agreement and the turnover achieved by its connected undertakings in respect of all goods and services, excluding all taxes and other duties, shall be added together. For this purpose, no account shall be taken of dealings between the party to the vertical agreement and its connected undertakings or between its connected undertakings.

2. The exemption provided for in Article 2 shall remain applicable where, for any period of two consecutive financial years, the total annual turnover threshold is exceeded by no more than 10%.

Commentary
Art 10(1): **B&C:** 6.014
Art 10(2): **B&C:** 6.014

Article 11

1. For the purposes of this Regulation, the terms "undertaking", "supplier" and "buyer" shall include their respective connected undertakings.

2. "Connected undertakings" are:

(a) undertakings in which a party to the agreement, directly or indirectly:
   — has the power to exercise more than half the voting rights, or
   — has the power to appoint more than half the members of the supervisory board, board of management or bodies legally representing the undertaking, or
   — has the right to manage the undertaking's affairs;

(b) undertakings which directly or indirectly have, over a party to the agreement, the rights or powers listed in (a);

(c) undertakings in which an undertaking referred to in (b) has, directly or indirectly, the rights or powers listed in (a);

(d) undertakings in which a party to the agreement together with one or more of the undertakings referred to in (a), (b) or (c), or in which two or more of the latter undertakings, jointly have the rights or powers listed in (a);

(e) undertakings in which the rights or the powers listed in (a) are jointly held by:
   — parties to the agreement or their respective connected undertakings referred to in (a) to (d), or
   — one or more of the parties to the agreement or one or more of their connected undertakings referred to in (a) to (d) and one or more third parties.

3. For the purposes of Article 3, the market share held by the undertakings referred to in paragraph 2(e) of this Article shall be apportioned equally to each undertaking having the rights or the powers listed in paragraph 2(a).

Commentary
Art 11(1): **B&C:** 6.018
Art 11(2): **B&C:** 6.014
Art 11(3): **B&C:** 6.019

Article 12

1. The exemptions provided for in Commission Regulations (EEC) No 1983/83,[1] (EEC) No 1984/83[2] and (EEC) No 4087/88[3] shall continue to apply until 31 May 2000.

2. The prohibition laid down in Article 81(1) of the EC Treaty shall not apply during the period from 1 June 2000 to 31 December 2001 in respect of agreements already in force on 31 May 2000 which do not satisfy the conditions for exemption provided for in this Regulation but which satisfy the conditions for exemption provided for in Regulations (EEC) No 1983/83, (EEC) No 1984/83 or (EEC) No 4087/88.

Notes
[1] OJ L 173, 30.6.1983, p. 1
[2] OJ L 173, 30.6.1983, p. 5
[3] OJ L 359, 28.12.1988, p. 46

Commentary
Art 12: F&N: 9.261

[Article 12a

The prohibition in Article 81(1) of the Treaty shall not apply to agreements which were in existence at the date of accession of the Czech Republic, Estonia, Cyprus, Latvia, Lithuania, Hungary, Malta, Poland, Slovenia and Slovakia and which, by reason of accession, fall within the scope of Article 81(1) if, within six months from the date of accession, they are so amended that they comply with the conditions laid down in this Regulation.]

Notes
Article 12a was inserted with effect from 1 May 2004 by the Act concerning the conditions of accession of the Czech Republic, the Republic of Estonia, the Republic of Cyprus, the Republic of Latvia, the Republic of Lithuania, the Republic of Hungary, the Republic of Malta, the Republic of Poland, the Republic of Slovenia and the Slovak Republic and the adjustments to the Treaties on which the European Union is founded — Annex II: List referred to in Article 20 of the Act of Accession — 5. Competition policy (OJ L 236, 23.9.2003, p. 344)

Article 13

This Regulation shall enter into force on 1 January 2000.

It shall apply from 1 June 2000, except for Article 12(1) which shall apply from 1 January 2000.

This Regulation shall expire on 31 May 2010.

Commentary
Art 13: B&C: 3.078, 6.010 F&N: 9.261

This Regulation shall be binding in its entirety and directly applicable in all Member States.

Done at Brussels, 22 December 1999.

C4

COMMISSION REGULATION (EC) No 2658/2000

of 29 November 2000
on the application of Article 81(3) of the Treaty to
categories of specialisation agreements

(Text with EEA relevance)

Official Journal L 304, 5.12.2000, p. 3

Celex No: 32000R2658

Notes

EEA application: this instrument was adopted with appropriate adaptations by EEA Joint Committee Decision No 113/2000, OJ L 52, 22.2.2001, p. 38 and EEA Supplement No 9, 22.2.01: see EEA Agreement, Annex XIV, Chapter D, Point 6 (as subsequently amended by the EEA Enlargement Agreement, OJ L 130, 29.4.2004, p. 3 and EEA Supplement No 23, 29.4.2004, and Decision No 130/2004, OJ L 64, 10.3.2005, p. 57 and EEA Supplement No 12, 10.3.2005).

Commentary

Regulation 2658/2000/EC: B&C: 3.004, 3.076, 3.093, 5.004, 5.056–5.057, 5.074, 6.015, 7.015, 7.018, 7.030, 7.087, 7.089–7.090, **7.097–7.101**, 9.169–9.170 **F&N:** 3.323, 3.324, 3.325, 7.213, 7.218–7.222, 9.164, 10.61, 10.78, 10.92, 12.316

THE COMMISSION OF THE EUROPEAN COMMUNITIES,

Having regard to the Treaty establishing the European Community,

Having regard to Council Regulation (EEC) No 2821/71 of 20 December 1971 on the application of Article [81](3) of the Treaty to categories of agreements, decisions and concerted practices,[1] as last amended by the Act of Accession of Austria, Finland and Sweden, and in particular Article 1(1)(c) thereof,

Having published a draft of this Regulation,[2]

Having consulted the Advisory Committee on Restrictive Practices and Dominant Positions,

---

Notes

[1] OJ L 285, 29.12.1971, p. 46.
[2] OJ C 118, 27.4.2000, p. 3.

Whereas:

(1) Regulation (EEC) No 2821/71 empowers the Commission to apply Article 81(3) (formerly Article 85(3)) of the Treaty by regulation to certain categories of agreements, decisions and concerted practices falling within the scope of Article 81(1) which have as their object specialisation, including agreements necessary for achieving it.

(2) Pursuant to Regulation (EEC) No 2821/71, in particular, the Commission has adopted Regulation (EEC) No 417/85 of 19 December 1984 on the application of Article [81](3) of the Treaty to categories of specialisation agreements,[1] as last amended by Regulation (EC) No 2236/97.[2] Regulation (EEC) No 417/85 expires on 31 December 2000.

Notes

[1] OJ L 53, 22.2.1985, p. 1
[2] OJ L 306, 11.11.1997, p. 12.

---

(3) A new regulation should meet the two requirements of ensuring effective protection of competition and providing adequate legal security for undertakings. The pursuit of these objectives should take account of the need to simplify administrative supervision and the legislative framework to as great an extent as possible. Below a certain level of market power it can, for the application of Article 81(3), in general be presumed that the positive effects of specialisation agreements will outweigh any negative effects on competition.

(4) Regulation (EEC) No 2821/71 requires the exempting regulation of the Commission to define the categories of agreements, decisions and concerted practices to which it applies, to specify the restrictions or clauses which may, or may not, appear in the agreements, decisions and concerted practices, and to specify the clauses which must be contained in the agreements, decisions and concerted practices or the other conditions which must be satisfied.

(5) It is appropriate to move away from the approach of listing exempted clauses and to place greater emphasis on defining the categories of agreements which are exempted up to a certain level of market power and on specifying the restrictions or clauses which are not to be contained in such agreements. This is consistent with an economics-based approach which assesses the impact of agreements on the relevant market.

(6) For the application of Article 81(3) by regulation, it is not necessary to define those agreements which are capable of falling within Article 81(1). In the individual assessment of agreements under Article 81(1), account has to be taken of several factors, and in particular the market structure on the relevant market.

(7) The benefit of the block exemption should be limited to those agreements for which it can be assumed with sufficient certainty that they satisfy the conditions of Article 81(3).

(8) Agreements on specialisation in production generally contribute to improving the production or distribution of goods, because the undertakings concerned can concentrate on the manufacture of certain products and thus operate more efficiently and supply the products more cheaply. Agreements on specialisation in the provision of services can also be said to generally give rise to similar improvements. It is likely that, given effective competition, consumers will receive a fair share of the resulting benefit.

(9) Such advantages can arise equally from agreements whereby one participant gives up the manufacture of certain products or provision of certain services in favour of another participant ("unilateral specialisation"), from agreements whereby each participant gives up the manufacture of certain products or provision of certain services in favour of another participant ("reciprocal specialisation") and from agreements whereby the participants undertake to jointly manufacture certain products or provide certain services ("joint production").

(10) As unilateral specialisation agreements between non-competitors may benefit from the block exemption provided by Commission Regulation (EC) No 2790/1999 of 22 December 1999 on the application of Article 81(3) of the Treaty to categories of vertical agreements and concerted practices,[1] the application of the present Regulation to unilateral specialisation agreements should be limited to agreements between competitors.

Notes
[1] OJ L 336, 29.12.1999, p. 21.

(11) All other agreements entered into between undertakings relating to the conditions under which they specialise in the production of goods and/or services should fall within the scope of this Regulation. The block exemption should also apply to provisions contained in specialisation agreements which do not constitute the primary object of such agreements, but are directly related to and necessary for their implementation, and to certain related purchasing and marketing arrangements.

Commentary
Recital 11: F&N: 12.317

(12) To ensure that the benefits of specialisation will materialise without one party leaving the market downstream of production, unilateral and reciprocal specialisation agreements should only be

covered by this Regulation where they provide for supply and purchase obligations. These obligations may, but do not have to, be of an exclusive nature.

(13) It can be presumed that, where the participating undertakings' share of the relevant market does not exceed 20%, specialisation agreements as defined in this Regulation will, as a general rule, give rise to economic benefits in the form of economies of scale or scope or better production technologies, while allowing consumers a fair share of the resulting benefits.

(14) This Regulation should not exempt agreements containing restrictions which are not indispensable to attain the positive effects mentioned above. In principle certain severe anti-competitive restraints relating to the fixing of prices charged to third parties, limitation of output or sales, and allocation of markets or customers should be excluded from the benefit of the block exemption established by this Regulation irrespective of the market share of the undertakings concerned.

(15) The market share limitation, the non-exemption of certain agreements and the conditions provided for in this Regulation normally ensure that the agreements to which the block exemption applies do not enable the participating undertakings to eliminate competition in respect of a substantial part of the products or services in question.

(16) In particular cases in which the agreements falling under this Regulation nevertheless have effects incompatible with Article 81(3) of the Treaty, the Commission may withdraw the benefit of the block exemption.

(17) In order to facilitate the conclusion of specialisation agreements, which can have a bearing on the structure of the participating undertakings, the period of validity of this Regulation should be fixed at 10 years.

(18) This Regulation is without prejudice to the application of Article 82 of the Treaty.

(19) In accordance with the principle of the primacy of Community law, no measure taken pursuant to national laws on competition should prejudice the uniform application throughout the common market of the Community competition rules or the full effect of any measures adopted in implementation of those rules, including this Regulation,

HAS ADOPTED THIS REGULATION:

Article 1
Exemption

1. Pursuant to Article 81(3) of the Treaty and subject to the provisions of this Regulation, it is hereby declared that Article 81(1) shall not apply to the following agreements entered into between two or more undertakings (hereinafter referred to as "the parties") which relate to the conditions under which those undertakings specialise in the production of products (hereinafter referred to as "specialisation agreements"):

(a) unilateral specialisation agreements, by virtue of which one party agrees to cease production of certain products or to refrain from producing those products and to purchase them from a competing undertaking, while the competing undertaking agrees to produce and supply those products; or

(b) reciprocal specialisation agreements, by virtue of which two or more parties on a reciprocal basis agree to cease or refrain from producing certain but different products and to purchase these products from the other parties, who agree to supply them; or

(c) joint production agreements, by virtue of which two or more parties agree to produce certain products jointly.

This exemption shall apply to the extent that such specialisation agreements contain restrictions of competition falling within the scope of Article 81(1) of the Treaty.

2. The exemption provided for in paragraph 1 shall also apply to provisions contained in specialisation agreements, which do not constitute the primary object of such agreements, but are directly related to and necessary for their implementation, such as those concerning the assignment or use of intellectual property rights.

The first subparagraph does, however, not apply to provisions which have the same object as the restrictions of competition enumerated in Article 5(1).

Commentary
Art 1: B&C: 3.076 F&N: 7.219, 12.316
Art 1(1)(c): B&C: 9.170
Art 1(2): B&C: 7.099

Article 2
Definitions

For the purposes of this Regulation:

1. "Agreement" means an agreement, a decision of an association of undertakings or a concerted practice.
2. "Participating undertakings" means undertakings party to the agreement and their respective connected undertakings.
3. "Connected undertakings" means:
    (a) undertakings in which a party to the agreement, directly or indirectly:
        (i) has the power to exercise more than half the voting rights, or
        (ii) has the power to appoint more than half the members of the supervisory board, board of management or bodies legally representing the undertaking, or
        (iii) has the right to manage the undertaking's affairs;
    (b) undertakings which directly or indirectly have, over a party to the agreement, the rights or powers listed in (a);
    (c) undertakings in which an undertaking referred to in (b) has, directly or indirectly, the rights or powers listed in (a);
    (d) undertakings in which a party to the agreement together with one or more of the undertakings referred to in (a), (b) or (c), or in which two or more of the latter undertakings, jointly have the rights or powers listed in (a);
    (e) undertakings in which the rights or the powers listed in (a) are jointly held by:
        (i) parties to the agreement or their respective connected undertakings referred to in (a) to (d), or
        (ii) one or more of the parties to the agreement or one or more of their connected undertakings referred to in (a) to (d) and one or more third parties.
4. "Product" means a good and/or a service, including both intermediary goods and/or services and final goods and/or services, with the exception of distribution and rental services.
5. "Production" means the manufacture of goods or the provision of services and includes production by way of subcontracting.
6. "Relevant market" means the relevant product and geographic market(s) to which the products, which are the subject matter of a specialisation agreement, belong.
7. "Competing undertaking" means an undertaking that is active on the relevant market (an actual competitor) or an undertaking that would, on realistic grounds, undertake the necessary additional investments or other necessary switching costs so that it could enter the relevant market in response to a small and permanent increase in relative prices (a potential competitor).
8. "Exclusive supply obligation" means an obligation not to supply a competing undertaking other than a party to the agreement with the product to which the specialisation agreement relates.
9. "Exclusive purchase obligation" means an obligation to purchase the product to which the specialisation agreement relates only from the party which agrees to supply it.

Commentary
Art 2(2): B&C: 7.102

Article 3
Purchasing and marketing arrangements

The exemption provided for in Article 1 shall also apply where:

(a) the parties accept an exclusive purchase and/or exclusive supply obligation in the context of a unilateral or reciprocal specialisation agreement or a joint production agreement, or

(b) the parties do not sell the products which are the object of the specialisation agreement independently but provide for joint distribution or agree to appoint a third party distributor on an exclusive or non-exclusive basis in the context of a joint production agreement provided that the third party is not a competing undertaking.

Commentary
Art 3: B&C: 7.100 F&N: 7.221, 12.316
Art 3(b): F&N: 12.317

Article 4
Market share threshold

The exemption provided for in Article 1 shall apply on condition that the combined market share of the participating undertakings does not exceed 20% of the relevant market.

Commentary
Art 4: B&C: 3.076, 4.009, 7.102 F&N: 7.222

Article 5
Agreements not covered by the exemption

1. The exemption provided for in Article 1 shall not apply to agreements which, directly or indirectly, in isolation or in combination with other factors under the control of the parties, have as their object:

(a) the fixing of prices when selling the products to third parties;
(b) the limitation of output or sales; or
(c) the allocation of markets or customers.

2. Paragraph 1 shall not apply to:

(a) provisions on the agreed amount of products in the context of unilateral or reciprocal specialisation agreements or the setting of the capacity and production volume of a production joint venture in the context of a joint production agreement;

(b) the setting of sales targets and the fixing of prices that a production joint venture charges to its immediate customers in the context of point (b) of Article 3.

Commentary
Art 5: B&C: 7.102 F&N: 12.323
Art 5(1): B&C: 7.101
Art 5(2): F&N: 3.162
Art 5(2)(a): B&C: 7.101
Art 5(2)(b): B&C: 7.101

Article 6
Application of the market share threshold

1. For the purposes of applying the market share threshold provided for in Article 4 the following rules shall apply:

(a) he market share shall be calculated on the basis of the market sales value; if market sales value data are not available, estimates based on other reliable market information, including market sales volumes, may be used to establish the market share of the undertaking concerned;

(b) the market share shall be calculated on the basis of data relating to the preceding calendar year;

(c) the market share held by the undertakings referred to in point 3(e) of Article 2 shall be apportioned equally to each undertaking having the rights or the powers listed in point 3(a) of Article 2.

2. If the market share referred to in Article 4 is initially not more than 20% but subsequently rises above this level without exceeding 25%, the exemption provided for in Article 1 shall continue to apply for a period of two consecutive calendar years following the year in which the 20% threshold was first exceeded.

3. If the market share referred to in Article 4 is initially not more than 20% but subsequently rises above 25%, the exemption provided for in Article 1 shall continue to apply for one calendar year following the year in which the level of 25% was first exceeded.

4. The benefit of paragraphs 2 and 3 may not be combined so as to exceed a period of two calendar years.

Commentary
Art 6: B&C: 7.102

Article 7
Withdrawal

The Commission may withdraw the benefit of this Regulation, pursuant to Article 7 of Regulation (EEC) No 2821/71, where, either on its own initiative or at the request of a Member State or of a natural or legal person claiming a legitimate interest, it finds in a particular case that an agreement to which the exemption provided for in Article 1 applies nevertheless has effects which are incompatible with the conditions laid down in Article 81(3) of the Treaty, and in particular where:

(a) the agreement is not yielding significant results in terms of rationalisation or consumers are not receiving a fair share of the resulting benefit, or

(b) the products which are the subject of the specialisation are not subject in the common market or a substantial part thereof to effective competition from identical products or products considered by users to be equivalent in view of their characteristics, price and intended use.

Commentary
Art 7: B&C: 3.086, 7.103

Article 8
Transitional period

The prohibition laid down in Article 81(1) of the Treaty shall not apply during the period from 1 January 2001 to 30 June 2002 in respect of agreements already in force on 31 December 2000 which do not satisfy the conditions for exemption provided for in this Regulation but which satisfy the conditions for exemption provided for in Regulation (EEC) No 417/85.

[Article 8a

The prohibition in Article 81(1) of the Treaty shall not apply to agreements which were in existence at the date of accession of the Czech Republic, Estonia, Cyprus, Latvia, Lithuania, Hungary, Malta, Poland, Slovenia and Slovakia and which, by reason of accession, fall within the scope of Article 81(1) if, within six months from the date of accession, they are so amended that they comply with the conditions laid down in this Regulation.]

Notes

Article 8a was inserted with effect from 1 May 2004 by Act concerning the conditions of accession of the Czech Republic, the Republic of Estonia, the Republic of Cyprus, the Republic of Latvia, the Republic of Lithuania, the Republic of Hungary, the Republic of Malta, the Republic of Poland, the Republic of Slovenia and the Slovak Republic and the adjustments to the Treaties on which the European Union is founded — Annex II: List referred to in Article 20 of the Act of Accession — 5. Competition policy (OJ L 236, 23.9.2003, p. 344).

Article 9
Period of validity

This Regulation shall enter into force on 1 January 2001.

It shall expire on 31 December 2010.

Commentary
Art 9: B&C: 3.076

This Regulation shall be binding in its entirety and directly applicable in all Member States.
Done at Brussels, 29 November 2000.

C5

COMMISSION REGULATION (EC)
No 2659/2000

of 29 November 2000
on the application of Article 81(3) of the Treaty to categories
of research and development agreements

(Text with EEA relevance)

Official Journal, L 304, 5.12.2000, p. 7

Celex No: 32000R2658

Notes

EEA application: this instrument was adopted with appropriate adaptations by EEA Joint Committee Decision No 113/2000, OJ L 52, 22.2.2001, p. 38 and EEA Supplement No 9, 22.2.2001: see EEA Agreement, Annex XIV, Chapter D, Point 7 (as subsequently amended by the EEA Enlargement Agreement, OJ L 130, 29.4.2004, p. 3 and EEA Supplement No 23, 29.4.2004, and Decision No 130/2004, OJ L 64, 10.3.2005, p. 57 and EEA Supplement No 12, 10.3.2005).

Commentary

Regulation 2659/2000/EC: B&C: 2.087, 3.004, 3.077, 3.093, 5.004, 5.074, 6.015, 6.186, 7.015, 7.018, 7.030, 7.067, 7.069, 7.078–7.079, 7.083, 7.086, 7.090, 9.169–9.170, 12.142–12.143 **F&N:** 3.323, 3.324, 3.325, 7.115, 7.116, 7.172, 9.164, 10.61, 10.79, 10.92, 11.117

THE COMMISSION OF THE EUROPEAN COMMUNITIES,

Having regard to the Treaty establishing the European Community,

Having regard to Council Regulation (EEC) No 2821/71 of 20 December 1971 on application of Article [81](3) of the Treaty to categories of agreements, decisions and concerted practices,[1] as last amended by the Act of Accession of Austria, Finland and Sweden, and in particular Article 1(1)(b) thereof,

Having published a draft of this Regulation,[2]

Having consulted the Advisory Committee on Restrictive Practices and Dominant Positions,

Notes
[1] OJ L 285, 29.12.1971, p. 46.
[2] OJ C 118, 27.4.2000, p. 3.

Whereas:

(1) Regulation (EEC) No 2821/71 empowers the Commission to apply Article 81(3) (formerly Article 85(3)) of the Treaty by regulation to certain categories of agreements, decisions and concerted practices falling within the scope of Article 81(1) which have as their object the research

and development of products or processes up to the stage of industrial application, and exploitation of the results, including provisions regarding intellectual property rights.

(2) Article 163(2) of the Treaty calls upon the Community to encourage undertakings, including small and medium-sized undertakings, in their research and technological development activities of high quality, and to support their efforts to cooperate with one another. Pursuant to Council Decision 1999/65/EC of 22 December 1998 concerning the rules for the participation of undertakings, research centres and universities and for the dissemination of research results for the implementation of the fifth framework programme of the European Community (1998–2002)[1] and Commission Regulation (EC) No 996/1999[2] on the implementation of Decision 1999/65/EC, indirect research and technological development (RTD) actions supported under the fifth framework programme of the Community are required to be carried out cooperatively.

Notes
[1] OJ L 26, 1.2.1999, p. 46.
[2] OJ L 122, 12.5.1999, p. 9.

(3) Agreements on the joint execution of research work or the joint development of the results of the research, up to but not including the stage of industrial application, generally do not fall within the scope of Article 81(1) of the Treaty. In certain circumstances, however, such as where the parties agree not to carry out other research and development in the same field, thereby forgoing the opportunity of gaining competitive advantages over the other parties, such agreements may fall within Article 81(1) and should therefore be included within the scope of this Regulation.

Commentary
Recital 3: B&C: 7.079 F&N: 7.163

(4) Pursuant to Regulation (EEC) No 2821/71, the Commission has, in particular, adopted Regulation (EEC) No 418/85 of 19 December 1984 on the application of Article [81](3) of the Treaty to categories of research and development agreements,[1] as last amended by Regulation (EC) No 2236/97.[2] Regulation (EEC) No 418/85 expires on 31 December 2000.

Notes
[1] OJ L 53, 22.2.1985, p. 5.
[2] OJ L 306, 11.11.1997, p. 12.

(5) A new regulation should meet the two requirements of ensuring effective protection of competition and providing adequate legal security for undertakings. The pursuit of these objectives should take account of the need to simplify administrative supervision and the legislative framework to as great an extent possible. Below a certain level of market power it can, for the application of Article 81(3), in general be presumed that the positive effects of research and development agreements will outweigh any negative effects on competition.

(6) Regulation (EEC) No 2821/71 requires the exempting regulation of the Commission to define the categories of agreements, decisions and concerted practices to which it applies, to specify the restrictions or clauses which may, or may not, appear in the agreements, decisions and concerted practices, and to specify the clauses which must be contained in the agreements, decisions and concerted practices or the other conditions which must be satisfied.

(7) It is appropriate to move away from the approach of listing exempted clauses and to place greater emphasis on defining the categories of agreements which are exempted up to a certain level of market power and on specifying the restrictions or clauses which are not to be contained in such agreements. This is consistent with an economics based approach which assesses the impact of agreements on the relevant market.

Commentary
Recital 7: B&C: 7.083 F&N: 7.172

(8) For the application of Article 81(3) by regulation, it is not necessary to define those agreements which are capable of falling within Article 81(1). In the individual assessment of agreements under

Article 81(1), account has to be taken of several factors, and in particular the market structure on the relevant market.

(9) The benefit of the block exemption should be limited to those agreements for which it can be assumed with sufficient certainty that they satisfy the conditions of Article 81(3).

Commentary
Recital 9: B&C: 7.083

(10) Cooperation in research and development and in the exploitation of the results generally promotes technical and economic progress by increasing the dissemination of know-how between the parties and avoiding duplication of research and development work, by stimulating new advances through the exchange of complementary know-how, and by rationalising the manufacture of the products or application of the processes arising out of the research and development.

(11) The joint exploitation of results can be considered as the natural consequence of joint research and development. It can take different forms such as manufacture, the exploitation of intellectual property rights that substantially contribute to technical or economic progress, or the marketing of new products.

(12) Consumers can generally be expected to benefit from the increased volume and effectiveness of research and development through the introduction of new or improved products or services or the reduction of prices brought about by new or improved processes.

(13) In order to attain the benefits and objectives of joint research and development the benefit of this Regulation should also apply to provisions contained in research and development agreements which do not constitute the primary object of such agreements, but are directly related to and necessary for their implementation.

(14) In order to justify the exemption, the joint exploitation should relate to products or processes for which the use of the results of the research and development is decisive, and each of the parties is given the opportunity of exploiting any results that interest it. However, where academic bodies, research institutes or undertakings which supply research and development as a commercial service without normally being active in the exploitation of results participate in research and development, they may agree to use the results of research and development solely for the purpose of further research. Similarly, non-competitors may agree to limit their right to exploitation to one or more technical fields of application to facilitate cooperation between parties with complementary skills.

Commentary
Recital 14: B&C: 7.082

(15) The exemption granted under this Regulation should be limited to research and development agreements which do not afford the undertakings the possibility of eliminating competition in respect of a substantial part of the products or services in question. It is necessary to exclude from the block exemption agreements between competitors whose combined share of the market for products or services capable of being improved or replaced by the results of the research and development exceeds a certain level at the time the agreement is entered into.

Commentary
Recital 15: F&N: 7.118

(16) In order to guarantee the maintenance of effective competition during joint exploitation of the results, provision should be made for the block exemption to cease to apply if the parties' combined share of the market for the products arising out of the joint research and development becomes too great. The exemption should continue to apply, irrespective of the parties' market shares, for a certain period after the commencement of joint exploitation, so as to await stabilisation of their market shares, particularly after the introduction of an entirely new product, and to guarantee a minimum period of return on the investments involved.

(17) This Regulation should not exempt agreements containing restrictions which are not indispensable to attain the positive effects mentioned above. In principle certain severe anti-competitive restraints such as limitations on the freedom of parties to carry out research and development in

a field unconnected to the agreement, the fixing of prices charged to third parties, limitations on output or sales, allocation of markets or customers, and limitations on effecting passive sales for the contract products in territories reserved for other parties should be excluded from the benefit of the block exemption established by this Regulation irrespective of the market share of the undertakings concerned.

(18) The market share limitation, the non-exemption of certain agreements, and the conditions provided for in this Regulation normally ensure that the agreements to which the block exemption applies do not enable the participating undertakings to eliminate competition in respect of a substantial part of the products or services in question.

(19) In particular cases in which the agreements falling under this Regulation nevertheless have effects incompatible with Article 81(3) of the Treaty, the Commission may withdraw the benefit of the block exemption.

(20) Agreements between undertakings which are not competing manufacturers of products capable of being improved or replaced by the results of the research and development will only eliminate effective competition in research and development in exceptional circumstances. It is therefore appropriate to enable such agreements to benefit from the block exemption irrespective of market share and to address such exceptional cases by way of withdrawal of its benefit.

(21) As research and development agreements are often of a long-term nature, especially where the cooperation extends to the exploitation of the results, the period of validity of this Regulation should be fixed at 10 years.

(22) This Regulation is without prejudice to the application of Article 82 of the Treaty.

(23) In accordance with the principle of the primacy of Community law, no measure taken pursuant to national laws on competition should prejudice the uniform application throughout the common market of the Community competition rules or the full effect of any measures adopted in implementation of those rules, including this Regulation,

HAS ADOPTED THIS REGULATION:

Article 1
Exemption

1. Pursuant to Article 81(3) of the Treaty and subject to the provisions of this Regulation, it is hereby declared that Article 81(1) shall not apply to agreements entered into between two or more undertakings (hereinafter referred to as "the parties") which relate to the conditions under which those undertakings pursue:

(a) joint research and development of products or processes and joint exploitation of the results of that research and development;

(b) joint exploitation of the results of research and development of products or processes jointly carried out pursuant to a prior agreement between the same parties; or

(c) joint research and development of products or processes excluding joint exploitation of the results.

This exemption shall apply to the extent that such agreements (hereinafter referred to as "research and development agreements") contain restrictions of competition falling within the scope of Article 81(1).

2. The exemption provided for in paragraph 1 shall also apply to provisions contained in research and development agreements which do not constitute the primary object of such agreements, but are directly related to and necessary for their implementation, such as an obligation not to carry out, independently or together with third parties, research and development in the field to which the agreement relates or in a closely connected field during the execution of the agreement.

The first subparagraph does, however, not apply to provisions which have the same object as the restrictions of competition enumerated in Article 5(1).

Commentary

Art 1(1): **B&C:** 7.079 **F&N:** 7.116, 7.196, 7.202
Art 1(1)(b): **F&N:** 7.191
Art 1(2): **B&C:** 7.085 **F&N:** 7.116

Article 2

Definitions

For the purposes of this Regulation:

1. "agreement" means an agreement, a decision of an association of undertakings or a concerted practice;
2. "participating undertakings" means undertakings party to the research and development agreement and their respective connected undertakings;
3. "connected undertakings" means:
   (a) undertakings in which a party to the research and development agreement, directly or indirectly:
      (i) has the power to exercise more than half the voting rights,
      (ii) has the power to appoint more than half the members of the supervisory board, board of management or bodies legally representing the undertaking, or
      (iii) has the right to manage the undertaking's affairs;
   (b) undertakings which directly or indirectly have, over a party to the research and development agreement, the rights or powers listed in (a);
   (c) undertakings in which an undertaking referred to in (b) has, directly or indirectly, the rights or powers listed in (a);
   (d) undertakings in which a party to the research and development agreement together with one or more of the undertakings referred to in (a), (b) or (c), or in which two or more of the latter undertakings, jointly have the rights or powers listed in (a);
   (e) undertakings in which the rights or the powers listed in (a) are jointly held by:
      (i) parties to the research and development agreement or their respective connected undertakings referred to in (a) to (d), or
      (ii) one or more of the parties to the research and development agreement or one or more of their connected undertakings referred to in (a) to (d) and one or more third parties;
4. "research and development" means the acquisition of know-how relating to products or processes and the carrying out of theoretical analysis, systematic study or experimentation, including experimental production, technical testing of products or processes, the establishment of the necessary facilities and the obtaining of intellectual property rights for the results;
5. "product" means a good and/or a service, including both intermediary goods and/or services and final goods and/or services;
6. "contract process" means a technology or process arising out of the joint research and development;
7. "contract product" means a product arising out of the joint research and development or manufactured or provided applying the contract processes;
8. "exploitation of the results" means the production or distribution of the contract products or the application of the contract processes or the assignment or licensing of intellectual property rights or the communication of know-how required for such manufacture or application;
9. "intellectual property rights" includes industrial property rights, copyright and neighbouring rights;
10. "know-how" means a package of non-patented practical information, resulting from experience and testing, which is secret, substantial and identified: in this context, "secret" means that the know-how is not generally known or easily accessible; "substantial" means that the know-how includes information which is indispensable for the manufacture of the contract products or the application of the contract processes; "identified" means that the know-how is described in a sufficiently comprehensive manner so as to make it possible to verify that it fulfils the criteria of secrecy and substantiality;
11. research and development, or exploitation of the results, are carried out "jointly" where the work involved is:
    (a) carried out by a joint team, organisation or undertaking,
    (b) jointly entrusted to a third party, or
    (c) allocated between the parties by way of specialisation in research, development, production or distribution;

12. "competing undertaking" means an undertaking that is supplying a product capable of being improved or replaced by the contract product (an actual competitor) or an undertaking that would, on realistic grounds, undertake the necessary additional investments or other necessary switching costs so that it could supply such a product in response to a small and permanent increase in relative prices (a potential competitor);
13. "relevant market for the contract products" means the relevant product and geographic market(s) to which the contract products belong.

Commentary
Art 2(1): B&C: 7.079
Art 2(2): B&C: 7.084
Art 2(3): B&C: 7.084
Art 2(6): B&C: 7.080
Art 2(7): B&C: 7.080
Art 2(8): B&C: 7.080–7.081 F&N: 7.191
Art 2(10): B&C: 7.080
Art 2(11): F&N: 7.180
Art 2(12): B&C: 7.084

Article 3
Conditions for exemption

1. The exemption provided for in Article 1 shall apply subject to the conditions set out in paragraphs 2 to 5.

2. All the parties must have access to the results of the joint research and development for the purposes of further research or exploitation. However, research institutes, academic bodies, or undertakings which supply research and development as a commercial service without normally being active in the exploitation of results may agree to confine their use of the results for the purposes of further research.

3. Without prejudice to paragraph 2, where the research and development agreement provides only for joint research and development, each party must be free independently to exploit the results of the joint research and development and any pre-existing know-how necessary for the purposes of such exploitation. Such right to exploitation may be limited to one or more technical fields of application, where the parties are not competing undertakings at the time the research and development agreement is entered into.

4. Any joint exploitation must relate to results which are protected by intellectual property rights or constitute know-how, which substantially contribute to technical or economic progress and the results must be decisive for the manufacture of the contract products or the application of the contract processes.

5. Undertakings charged with manufacture by way of specialisation in production must be required to fulfil orders for supplies from all the parties, except where the research and development agreement also provides for joint distribution.

Commentary
Art 3: F&N: 7.173
Art 3(2): B&C: 7.072, 7.082 F&N: 7.179
Art 3(3): B&C: 7.073, 7.082 F&N: 7.179, 7.207
Art 3(4): B&C: 7.073, 7.082, 12.143 F&N: 7.175
Art 3(5): B&C: 7.082 F&N: 7.176

Article 4
Market share threshold and duration of exemption

1. Where the participating undertakings are not competing undertakings, the exemption provided for in Article 1 shall apply for the duration of the research and development. Where the results are

jointly exploited, the exemption shall continue to apply for seven years from the time the contract products are first put on the market within the common market.

2. Where two or more of the participating undertakings are competing undertakings, the exemption provided for in Article 1 shall apply for the period referred to in paragraph 1 only if, at the time the research and development agreement is entered into, the combined market share of the participating undertakings does not exceed 25% of the relevant market for the products capable of being improved or replaced by the contract products.

3. After the end of the period referred to in paragraph 1, the exemption shall continue to apply as long as the combined market share of the participating undertakings does not exceed 25% of the relevant market for the contract products.

Commentary
Art 4: B&C: 3.077 F&N: 7.119, 7.211
Art 4(1): B&C: 7.084 F&N: 7.120
Art 4(2): B&C: 4.009, 7.084 F&N: 7.123, 7.191
Art 4(3): B&C: 4.009, 7.084 F&N: 7.122

Article 5
Agreements not covered by the exemption

1. The exemption provided for in Article 1 shall not apply to research and development agreements which, directly or indirectly, in isolation or in combination with other factors under the control of the parties, have as their object:
(a) the restriction of the freedom of the participating undertakings to carry out research and development independently or in cooperation with third parties in a field unconnected with that to which the research and development relates or, after its completion, in the field to which it relates or in a connected field;
(b) the prohibition to challenge after completion of the research and development the validity of intellectual property rights which the parties hold in the common market and which are relevant to the research and development or, after the expiry of the research and development agreement, the validity of intellectual property rights which the parties hold in the common market and which protect the results of the research and development, without prejudice to the [possibility] to provide for termination of the research and development agreement in the event of one of the parties challenging the validity of such intellectual property rights;
(c) the limitation of output or sales;
(d) the fixing of prices when selling the contract product to third parties;
(e) the restriction of the customers that the participating undertakings may serve, after the end of seven years from the time the contract products are first put on the market within the common market;
(f) the prohibition to make passive sales of the contract products in territories reserved for other parties;
(g) the prohibition to put the contract products on the market or to pursue an active sales policy for them in territories within the common market that are reserved for other parties after the end of seven years from the time the contract products are first put on the market within the common market;
(h) the requirement not to grant licences to third parties to manufacture the contract products or to apply the contract processes where the exploitation by at least one of the parties of the results of the joint research and development is not provided for or does not take place;
(i) the requirement to refuse to meet demand from users or resellers in their respective territories who would market the contract products in other territories within the common market; or
(j) the requirement to make it difficult for users or resellers to obtain the contract products from other resellers within the common market, and in particular to exercise intellectual property rights or take measures so as to prevent users or resellers from obtaining, or from putting on the market within the common market, products which have been lawfully put on the market within the Community by another party or with its consent.

2. Paragraph 1 shall not apply to:

(a) the setting of production targets where the exploitation of the results includes the joint production of the contract products;

(b) the setting of sales targets and the fixing of prices charged to immediate customers where the
exploitation of the results includes the joint distribution of the contract products.

Commentary
Art 5: F&N: 7.125, 7.184
Art 5(1): B&C: 7.085 F&N: 3.163, 7.113
Art 5(1)(a): F&N: 7.204, 7.207
Art 5(1)(f): F&N: 7.200
Art 5(1)(g): F&N: 7.199
Art 5(2): B&C: 7.085 F&N: 3.162, 7.125

Article 6
Application of the market share threshold

1. For the purposes of applying the market share threshold provided for in Article 4 the following
rules shall apply:

(a) the market share shall be calculated on the basis of the market sales value; if market sales value data
are not available, estimates based on other reliable market information, including market sales
volumes, may be used to establish the market share of the undertaking concerned;

(b) the market share shall be calculated on the basis of data relating to the preceding calendar year;

(c) the market share held by the undertakings referred to in point 3(e) of Article 2 shall be apportioned
equally to each undertaking having the rights or the powers listed in point 3(a) of Article 2.

2. If the market share referred to in Article 4(3) is initially not more than 25% but subsequently rises
above this level without exceeding 30%, the exemption provided for in Article 1 shall continue to
apply for a period of two consecutive calendar years following the year in which the 25% threshold
was first exceeded.

3. If the market share referred to in Article 4(3) is initially not more than 25% but subsequently rises
above 30%, the exemption provided for in Article 1 shall continue to apply for one calendar year following the year in which the level of 30% was first exceeded.

4. The benefit of paragraphs 2 and 3 may not be combined so as to exceed a period of two
calendar years.

Commentary
Art 6: B&C: 7.084

Article 7
Withdrawal

The Commission may withdraw the benefit of this Regulation, pursuant to Article 7 of Regulation
(EEC) No 2821/71, where, either on its own initiative or at the request of a Member State or of a
natural or legal person claiming a legitimate interest, it finds in a particular case that a research and
development agreement to which the exemption provided for in Article 1 applies nevertheless has
effects which are incompatible with the conditions laid down in Article 81(3) of the Treaty, and in
particular where:

(a) the existence of the research and development agreement substantially restricts the scope for third
parties to carry out research and development in the relevant field because of the limited research
capacity available elsewhere;

(b) because of the particular structure of supply, the existence of the research and development agreement substantially restricts the access of third parties to the market for the contract products;

(c) without any objectively valid reason, the parties do not exploit the results of the joint research and
development;

(d) the contract products are not subject in the whole or a substantial part of the common market to effective competition from identical products or products considered by users as equivalent in view of their characteristics, price and intended use;

(e) the existence of the research and development agreement would eliminate effective competition in research and development on a particular market.

Commentary
Art 7: B&C: 3.086, 7.086

Article 8
Transitional period

The prohibition laid down in Article 81(1) of the Treaty shall not apply during the period from 1 January 2001 to 30 June 2002 in respect of agreements already in force on 31 December 2000 which do not satisfy the conditions for exemption provided for in this Regulation but which satisfy the conditions for exemption provided for in Regulation (EEC) No 418/85.

Commentary
Art 8: B&C: 7.078

[Article 8a

The prohibition in Article 81(1) of the Treaty shall not apply to agreements which were in existence at the date of accession of the Czech Republic, Estonia, Cyprus, Latvia, Lithuania, Hungary, Malta, Poland, Slovenia and Slovakia and which, by reason of accession, fall within the scope of Article 81(1) if, within six months from the date of accession, they are so amended that they comply with the conditions laid down in this Regulation.]

Notes
Article 8a was inserted with effect from 1 May 2004 by the Act concerning the conditions of accession of the Czech Republic, the Republic of Estonia, the Republic of Cyprus, the Republic of Latvia, the Republic of Lithuania, the Republic of Hungary, the Republic of Malta, the Republic of Poland, the Republic of Slovenia and the Slovak Republic and the adjustments to the Treaties on which the European Union is founded — Annex II: List referred to in Article 20 of the Act of Accession — 5. Competition policy (OJ L 236, 23.9.2003, p. 344).

Article 9
Period of validity

This Regulation shall enter into force on 1 January 2001.

It shall expire on 31 December 2010.

Commentary
Art 9: B&C: 3.077

This Regulation shall be binding in its entirety and directly applicable in all Member States.

Done at Brussels, 29 November 2000.

C6

COMMISSION REGULATION (EC)
No 1400/2002

of 31 July 2002

on the application of Article 81(3) of the Treaty to categories of vertical
agreements and concerted practices in the motor vehicle sector

Official Journal L 203, 1.8.2002, p. 30

Celex No: 32002R1400

Notes

EEA application: this instrument was adopted with appropriate adaptations by EEA Joint Committee Decision No 136/2002 of 27 September 2002, OJ 2002 L336, 12.12.2002, p. 38 and EEA Supplement No 61/31: see EEA Agreement, Annex XIV, Chapter B, Point 4b (as subsequently amended by Decision No 29/2004, OJ L 127, 29.4.2004, p. 137 and EEA Supplement No 22, 29.4.2004, the EEA Enlargement Agreement, OJ L 130, 29.4.2004, p. 3 and EEA Supplement No 23, 29.4.2004, and Decision No 130/2004, OJ L 64, 10.3.2005, p. 57 and EEA Supplement No 12, 10.3.2005).

Commentary

Regulation 1400/2002/EC: **B&C:** 3.069, 3.093, 6.006, 6.009, 6.015, 6.088, 6.109-6.110, 6.117, 6.127-6.128, 6.133 **F&N:** 9.205, 15.02, 15.03, 15.15, 15.17, 15.19, 15.57, 15.62, 15.83, 15.84, 15.85, 15.92, 15.99, 15.121, 15.125, 15.126, 15.148, 15.159, 15.161, 15.163, 15.165
Recitals 12–26: **B&C:** 6.124

THE COMMISSION OF THE EUROPEAN COMMUNITIES,

Having regard to the Treaty establishing the European Community,

Having regard to Council Regulation No 19/65/EEC of 2 March 1965 on the application of Article [81](3) of the Treaty to certain categories of agreements and concerted practices,[1] as last amended by Regulation (EC) No 1215/1999,[2] and in particular Article 1 thereof,

Having published a draft of this Regulation,[3]

Having consulted the Advisory Committee on Restrictive Practices and Dominant Positions,

---

Notes
[1] OJ 36, 6.3.1965, p. 533/65.
[2] OJ L 148, 15.6.1999, p. 1.
[3] OJ C 67, 16.3.2002, p. 2.

Whereas:

(1) Experience acquired in the motor vehicle sector regarding the distribution of new motor vehicles, spare parts and after sales services makes it possible to define categories of vertical agreements which can be regarded as normally satisfying the conditions laid down in Article 81(3).

(2) This experience leads to the conclusion that rules stricter than those provided for by Commission Regulation (EC) No 2790/1999 of 22 December 1999 on the application of Article 81(3) of the Treaty to categories of vertical agreements and concerted practices[1] are necessary in this sector.

Notes
[1] OJ L 336, 29.12.1999, p. 21.

Commentary
Recital 2: **B&C:** 3.069 **F&N:** 15.18

---

(3) These stricter rules for exemption by category (the exemption) should apply to vertical agreements for the purchase or sale of new motor vehicles, vertical agreements for the purchase or sale of spare parts for motor vehicles and vertical agreements for the purchase or sale of repair and maintenance services for such vehicles where these agreements are concluded between non-competing undertakings, between certain competitors, or by certain associations of retailers or repairers. This includes vertical agreements concluded between a distributor acting at the retail level or an authorised repairer and a (sub)distributor or repairer. This Regulation should also apply to these vertical agreements when they contain ancillary provisions on the assignment or use of intellectual property rights. The term "vertical agreements" should be defined accordingly to include both such agreements and the corresponding concerted practices.

(4) The benefit of the exemption should be limited to vertical agreements for which it can be assumed with sufficient certainty that they satisfy the conditions of Article 81(3).

(5) Vertical agreements falling within the categories defined in this Regulation can improve economic efficiency within a chain of production or distribution by facilitating better coordination between the participating undertakings. In particular, they can lead to a reduction in the transaction and distribution costs of the parties and to an optimisation of their sales and investment levels.

(6) The likelihood that such efficiency-enhancing effects will outweigh any anti-competitive effects due to restrictions contained in vertical agreements depends on the degree of market power held by the undertakings concerned and therefore on the extent to which those undertakings face competition from other suppliers of goods or services regarded by the buyer as interchangeable or substitutable for one another, by reason of the products' characteristics, prices or intended use.

(7) Thresholds based on market share should be fixed in order to reflect suppliers' market power. Furthermore, this sector-specific Regulation should contain stricter rules than those provided for by Regulation (EC) No 2790/1999, in particular for selective distribution. The thresholds below which it can be presumed that the advantages secured by vertical agreements outweigh their restrictive effects should vary with the characteristics of different types of vertical agreement. It can therefore be presumed that in general, vertical agreements have such advantages where the supplier concerned has a market share of up to 30% on the markets for the distribution of new motor vehicles or spare parts, or of up to 40% where quantitative selective distribution is used for the sale of new motor vehicles. As regards after sales services it can be presumed that, in general, vertical agreements by which the supplier sets criteria on how its authorised repairers have to provide repair or maintenance services for the motor vehicles of the relevant make and provides them with equipment and training for the provision of such services have such advantages where the network of authorised repairers of the supplier concerned has a market share of up to 30%. However, in the case of vertical agreements containing exclusive supply obligations, it is the market share of the buyer which is relevant for determining the overall effects of such vertical agreements on the market.

(8) Above those market share thresholds, there can be no presumption that vertical agreements falling within the scope of Article 81(1) will usually give rise to objective advantages of such a character and magnitude as to compensate for the disadvantages which they create for competition. However, such advantages can be anticipated in the case of qualitative selective distribution, irrespective of the supplier's market share.

(9) In order to prevent a supplier from terminating an agreement because a distributor or a repairer engages in pro-competitive behaviour, such as active or passive sales to foreign consumers, multi-branding or subcontracting of repair and maintenance services, every notice of termination must clearly set out in writing the reasons, which must be objective and transparent. Furthermore, in order to strengthen the independence of distributors and repairers from their suppliers, minimum periods of notice should be provided for the non-renewal of agreements concluded for a limited duration and for the termination of agreements of unlimited duration.

Commentary
Recital 9: B&C: 6.137

(10) In order to foster market integration and to allow distributors or authorised repairers to seize additional business opportunities, distributors or authorised repairers have to be allowed to purchase other undertakings of the same type that sell or repair the same brand of motor vehicles within the distribution system. To this end, any vertical agreement between a supplier and a distributor or authorised repairer has to provide for the latter to have the right to transfer all of its rights and obligations to any other undertaking of its choice of the same type that sell or repairs the same brand of motor vehicles within the distribution system.

(11) In order to favour the quick resolution of disputes which arise between the parties to a distribution agreement and which might otherwise hamper effective competition, agreements should only benefit from exemption if they provide for each party to have a right of recourse to an independent expert or arbitrator, in particular where notice is given to terminate an agreement.

(12) Irrespective of the market share of the undertakings concerned, this Regulation does not cover vertical agreements containing certain types of severely anti-competitive restraints (hardcore restrictions) which in general appreciably restrict competition even at low market shares and which are not indispensable to the attainment of the positive effects mentioned above. This concerns in particular vertical agreements containing restraints such as minimum or fixed resale prices and, with certain exceptions, restrictions of the territory into which, or of the customers to whom, a distributor or repairer may sell the contract goods or services. Such agreements should not benefit from the exemption.

(13) It is necessary to ensure that effective competition within the common market and between distributors located in different Member States is not restricted if a supplier uses selective distribution in some markets and other forms of distribution in others. In particular selective distribution agreements which restrict passive sales to any end user or unauthorised distributor located in markets where exclusive territories have been allocated should be excluded from the benefit of the exemption, as should those selective distribution agreements which restrict passive sales to customer groups which have been allocated exclusively to other distributors. The benefit of the exemption should also be withheld from exclusive distribution agreements if active or passive sales to any end user or unauthorised distributor located in markets where selective distribution is used are restricted.

Commentary
Recital 13: B&C: 6.121

(14) The right of any distributor to sell new motor vehicles passively or, where relevant, actively to end users should include the right to sell such vehicles to end users who have given authorisation to an intermediary or purchasing agent to purchase, take delivery of, transport or store a new motor vehicle on their behalf.

Commentary
Recital 14: B&C: 6.113

(15) The right of any distributor to sell new motor vehicles or spare parts or of any authorised repairer to sell repair and maintenance services to any end user passively or, where relevant, actively should include the right to use the Internet or Internet referral sites.

Commentary
Recital 15: B&C: 6.128 F&N: 15.41

(16) Limits placed by suppliers on their distributors' sales to any end user in other Member States, for instance where distributor remuneration or the purchase price is made dependent on the destination of the vehicles or on the place of residence of the end users, amount to an indirect restriction on sales. Other examples of indirect restrictions on sales include supply quotas based on a sales territory other than the common market, whether or not these are combined with sales targets. Bonus systems based on the destination of the vehicles or any form of discriminatory product supply to distributors, whether in the case of product shortage or otherwise, also amount to an indirect restriction on sales.

Commentary
Recital 16: B&C: 6.126

(17) Vertical agreements that do not oblige the authorised repairers within a supplier's distribution system to honour warranties, perform free servicing and carry out recall work in respect of any motor vehicle of the relevant make sold in the common market amount to an indirect restriction of sales and should not benefit from the exemption. This obligation is without prejudice to the right of a motor vehicle supplier to oblige a distributor to make sure as regards the new motor vehicles that he has sold that the warranties are honoured and that free servicing and recall work is carried out, either by the distributor itself or, in case of subcontracting, by the authorised repairer(s) to whom these services have been subcontracted. Therefore consumers should in these cases be able to turn to the distributor if the above obligations have not been properly fulfilled by the authorised repairer to whom the distributor has subcontracted these services. Furthermore, in order to allow sales by motor vehicle distributors to end users throughout the common market, the exemption should apply only to distribution agreements which require the repairers within the supplier's network to carry out repair and maintenance services for the contract goods and corresponding goods irrespective of where these goods are sold in the common market.

Commentary
Recital 17: F&N: 15.88, 15.100, 15.121

(18) In markets where selective distribution is used, the exemption should apply in respect of a prohibition on a distributor from operating out of an additional place of establishment where he is a distributor of vehicles other than passenger cars or light commercial vehicles. However, this prohibition should not be exempted if it limits the expansion of the distributor's business at the authorised place of establishment by, for instance, restricting the development or acquisition of the infrastructure necessary to allow increases in sales volumes, including increases brought about by Internet sales.

Commentary
Recital 18: F&N: 15.56

(19) It would be inappropriate to exempt any vertical agreement that restricts the sale of original spare parts or spare parts of matching quality by members of the distribution system to independent repairers which use them for the provision of repair or maintenance services. Without access to such spare parts, these independent repairers would not be able to compete effectively with authorised repairers, since they could not provide consumers with good quality services which contribute to the safe and reliable functioning of motor vehicles.

(20) In order to give end users the right to purchase new motor vehicles with specifications identical to those sold in any other Member State, from any distributor selling corresponding models and established in the common market, the exemption should apply only to vertical agreements which enable a distributor to order, stock and sell any such vehicle which corresponds to a model within its contract range. Discriminatory or objectively unjustified supply conditions, in particular those regarding delivery times or prices, applied by the supplier to corresponding vehicles, are to be considered a restriction on the ability of the distributor to sell such vehicles.

(21) Motor vehicles are expensive and technically complex mobile goods which require repair and maintenance at regular and irregular intervals. However, it is not indispensable for distributors of new motor vehicles also to carry out repair and maintenance. The legitimate interests of suppliers and end users can be fully satisfied if the distributor subcontracts these services, including the honouring of warranties, free servicing and recall work, to a repairer or to a number of repairers within the supplier's distribution system. It is nevertheless appropriate to facilitate access to repair and maintenance services. Therefore, a supplier may require distributors who have subcontracted repair and maintenance services to one or more authorised repairers to give end users the name and address of the repair shop or shops in question. If any of these authorised repairers is not established in the vicinity of the sales outlet, the supplier may also require the distributor

to tell end users how far the repair shop or shops in question are from the sales outlet. However, a supplier can only impose such obligations if he also imposes similar obligations on distributors whose own repair shop is not on the same premises as their sales outlet.

(22) Furthermore, it is not necessary, in order to adequately provide for repair and maintenance services, for authorised repairers to also sell new motor vehicles. The exemption should therefore not cover vertical agreements containing any direct or indirect obligation or incentive which leads to the linking of sales and servicing activities or which makes the performance of one of these activities dependent on the performance of the other; this is in particular the case where the remuneration of distributors or authorised repairers relating to the purchase or sale of goods or services necessary for one activity is made dependent on the purchase or sale of goods or services relating to the other activity, or where all such goods or services are indistinctly aggregated into a single remuneration or discount system.

(23) In order to ensure effective competition on the repair and maintenance markets and to allow repairers to offer end users competing spare parts such as original spare parts and spare parts of matching quality, the exemption should not cover vertical agreements which restrict the ability of authorised repairers within the distribution system of a vehicle manufacturer, independent distributors of spare parts, independent repairers or end users to source spare parts from the manufacturer of such spare parts or from another third party of their choice. This does not affect spare part manufacturers' liability under civil law.

(24) Furthermore, in order to allow authorised and independent repairers and end users to identify the manufacturer of motor vehicle components or of spare parts and to choose between competing spare parts, the exemption should not cover agreements by which a manufacturer of motor vehicles limits the ability of a manufacturer of components or original spare parts to place its trade mark or logo on these parts effectively and in a visible manner. Moreover, in order to facilitate this choice and the sale of spare parts, which have been manufactured according to the specifications and production and quality standards provided by the vehicle manufacturer for the production of components or spare parts, it is presumed that spare parts constitute original spare parts, if the spare part producer issues a certificate that the parts are of the same quality as the components used for the assembly of a motor vehicle and have been manufactured according to these specifications and standards. Other spare parts for which the spare part producer can issue a certificate at any moment attesting that they match the quality of the components used for the assembly of a certain motor vehicle, may be sold as spare parts of matching quality.

(25) The exemption should not cover vertical agreements which restrict authorised repairers from using spare parts of matching quality for the repair or maintenance of a motor vehicle. However, in view of the vehicle manufacturers' direct contractual involvement in repairs under warranty, free servicing, and recall operations, agreements containing obligations on authorised repairers to use original spare parts supplied by the vehicle manufacturer for these repairs should be covered by the exemption.

(26) In order to protect effective competition on the market for repair and maintenance services and to prevent foreclosure of independent repairers, motor vehicle manufacturers must allow all interested independent operators to have full access to all technical information, diagnostic and other equipment, tools, including all relevant software, and training required for the repair and maintenance of motor vehicles. Independent operators who must be allowed such access include in particular independent repairers, manufacturers of repair equipment or tools, publishers of technical information, automobile clubs, roadside assistance operators, operators offering inspection and testing services and operators offering training for repairers. In particular, the conditions of access must not discriminate between authorised and independent operators, access must be given upon request and without undue delay, and the price charged for the information should not discourage access to it by failing to take into account the extent to which the independent operator uses it. A supplier of motor vehicles should be required to give independent operators access to technical information on new motor vehicles at the same time as such access is given to its authorised repairers and must not oblige independent operators to purchase more than the information necessary to carry out the work in question. Suppliers should be obliged to give access to the technical information necessary for re-programming electronic devices in a motor vehicle. It is, however, legitimate and proper for them to withhold access to

technical information which might allow a third party to bypass or disarm on-board anti-theft devices, to recalibrate electronic devices or to tamper with devices which for instance limit the speed of a motor vehicle, unless protection against theft, re-calibration or tampering can be attained by other less restrictive means. Intellectual property rights and rights regarding know-how including those which relate to the aforementioned devices must be exercised in a manner which avoids any type of abuse.

Commentary
Recital 26: F&N: 15.153

(27) In order to ensure access to and to prevent collusion on the relevant markets and to give distributors opportunities to sell vehicles of brands from two or more manufacturers that are not connected undertakings, certain specific conditions are attached to the exemption. To this end, the exemption should not be accorded to non-compete obligations. In particular, without prejudice to the ability of the supplier to require the distributor to display the vehicles in brand-specific areas of the showroom in order to avoid brand confusion, any prohibition on sales of competing makes should not be exempted. The same applies to an obligation to display the full range of motor vehicles if it makes the sale or display of vehicles manufactured by undertakings which are not connected impossible or unreasonably difficult. Furthermore, an obligation to have brand-specific sales personnel is considered to be an indirect non-compete obligation and therefore should not be covered by the exemption, unless the distributor decides to have brand-specific sales personnel and the supplier pays all the additional costs involved.

Commentary
Recital 27: B&C: 6.132

(28) In order to ensure that repairers are able to carry out repairs or maintenance on all motor vehicles, the exemption should not apply to any obligation limiting the ability of repairers of motor vehicles to provide repair or maintenance services for brands of competing suppliers.

(29) In addition, specific conditions are required to exclude certain restrictions, sometimes imposed in the context of a selective distribution system, from the scope of the exemption. This applies in particular to obligations which have the effect of preventing the members of a selective distribution system from selling the brands of particular competing suppliers, which could easily lead to foreclosure of certain brands. Additional conditions are necessary in order to foster intra-brand competition and market integration within the common market, to create opportunities for distributors and authorised repairers who wish to seize business opportunities outside their place of establishment, and to create conditions which allow the development of multi-brand distributors. In particular a restriction on operating out of an unauthorised place of establishment for the distribution of passenger cars and light commercial vehicles or the provision of repair and maintenance services should not be exempted. The supplier may require additional sales or delivery outlets for passenger cars and light commercial vehicles or repair shops to comply with the relevant qualitative criteria applicable for similar outlets located in the same geographic area.

Commentary
Recital 29: F&N: 15.57

(30) The exemption should not apply to restrictions limiting the ability of a distributor to sell leasing services for motor vehicles.

(31) The market share limitations, the fact that certain vertical agreements are not covered, and the conditions provided for in this Regulation, should normally ensure that the agreements to which the exemption applies do not enable the participating undertakings to eliminate competition in respect of a substantial part of the goods or services in question.

(32) In particular cases in which agreements which would otherwise benefit from the exemption nevertheless have effects incompatible with Article 81(3), the Commission is empowered to withdraw the benefit of the exemption; this may occur in particular where the buyer has significant market power on the relevant market on which it resells the goods or provides the services or where parallel networks of vertical agreements have similar effects which significantly restrict

access to a relevant market or competition thereon; such cumulative effects may for example arise in the case of selective distribution. The Commission may also withdraw the benefit of the exemption if competition is significantly restricted on a market due to the presence of a supplier with market power or if prices and conditions of supply to motor vehicle distributors differ substantially between geographic markets. It may also withdraw the benefit of the exemption if discriminatory prices or sales conditions, or unjustifiably high supplements, such as those charged for right hand drive vehicles, are applied for the supply of goods corresponding to the contract range.

(33) Regulation No 19/65/EEC empowers the national authorities of Member States to withdraw the benefit of the exemption in respect of vertical agreements having effects incompatible with the conditions laid down in Article 81(3), where such effects are felt in their territory, or in a part thereof, and where such territory has the characteristics of a distinct geographic market; the exercise of this national power of withdrawal should not prejudice the uniform application throughout the common market of the Community competition rules or the full effect of the measures adopted in implementation of those rules.

(34) In order to allow for better supervision of parallel networks of vertical agreements which have similar restrictive effects and which cover more than 50% of a given market, the Commission should be permitted to declare the exemption inapplicable to vertical agreements containing specific restraints relating to the market concerned, thereby restoring the full application of Article 81(1) to such agreements.

(35) The exemption should be granted without prejudice to the application of the provisions of Article 82 of the Treaty on the abuse by an undertaking of a dominant position.

(36) Commission Regulation (EC) No 1475/95 of 28 June 1995 on the application of Article [81](3) of the Treaty to certain categories of motor vehicle distribution and servicing agreements[1] is applicable until 30 September 2002. In order to allow all operators time to adapt vertical agreements which are compatible with that regulation and which are still in force when the exemption provided for therein expires, it is appropriate for such agreements to benefit from a transition period until 1 October 2003, during which time they should be exempted from the prohibition laid down in Article 81(1) under this Regulation.

Notes
[1] OJ L 145, 29.6.1995, p. 25.

---

(37) In order to allow all operators within a quantitative selective distribution system for new passenger cars and light commercial vehicles to adapt their business strategies to the non-application of the exemption to location clauses, it is appropriate to stipulate that the condition set out in Article 5(2)(b) shall enter into force on 1 October 2005.

(38) The Commission should monitor the operation of this Regulation on a regular basis, with particular regard to its effects on competition in motor vehicle retailing and in after sales servicing in the common market or relevant parts of it. This should include monitoring the effects of this Regulation on the structure and level of concentration of motor vehicle distribution and any resulting effects on competition. The Commission should also carry out an evaluation of the operation of this Regulation and draw up a report not later than 31 May 2008.

HAS ADOPTED THIS REGULATION:

Article 1
Definitions

1. For the purposes of this Regulation:

(a) "competing undertakings" means actual or potential suppliers on the same product market; the product market includes goods or services which are regarded by the buyer as interchangeable with or substitutable for the contract goods or services, by reason of the products' characteristics, their prices and their intended use;

(b) "non-compete obligation" means any direct or indirect obligation causing the buyer not to manufacture, purchase, sell or resell goods or services which compete with the contract goods or services, or any direct or indirect obligation on the buyer to purchase from the supplier or from another undertaking designated by the supplier more than 30% of the buyer's total purchases of the contract goods, corresponding goods or services and their substitutes on the relevant market, calculated on the basis of the value of its purchases in the preceding calendar year. An obligation that the distributor sell motor vehicles from other suppliers in separate areas of the showroom in order to avoid confusion between the makes does not constitute a non-compete obligation for the purposes of this Regulation. An obligation that the distributor have brand-specific sales personnel for different brands of motor vehicles constitutes a non-compete obligation for the purposes of this Regulation, unless the distributor decides to have brand-specific sales personnel and the supplier pays all the additional costs involved;

(c) "vertical agreements" means agreements or concerted practices entered into by two or more undertakings, each of which operates, for the purposes of the agreement, at a different level of the production or distribution chain;

(d) "vertical restraints" means restrictions of competition falling within the scope of Article 81(1), when such restrictions are contained in a vertical agreement;

(e) "exclusive supply obligation" means any direct or indirect obligation causing the supplier to sell the contract goods or services only to one buyer inside the common market for the purposes of a specific use or for resale;

(f) "selective distribution system" means a distribution system where the supplier undertakes to sell the contract goods or services, either directly or indirectly, only to distributors or repairers selected on the basis of specified criteria and where these distributors or repairers undertake not to sell such goods or services to unauthorised distributors or independent repairers, without prejudice to the ability to sell spare parts to independent repairers or the obligation to provide independent operators with all technical information, diagnostic equipment, tools and training required for the repair and maintenance of motor vehicles or for the implementation of environmental protection measures;

(g) "quantitative selective distribution system" means a selective distribution system where the supplier uses criteria for the selection of distributors or repairers which directly limit their number;

(h) "qualitative selective distribution system" means a selective distribution system where the supplier uses criteria for the selection of distributors or repairers which are only qualitative in nature, are required by the nature of the contract goods or services, are laid down uniformly for all distributors or repairers applying to join the distribution system, are not applied in a discriminatory manner, and do not directly limit the number of distributors or repairers;

(i) "intellectual property rights" includes industrial property rights, copyright and neighbouring rights;

(j) "know-how" means a package of non-patented practical information, derived from experience and testing by the supplier, which is secret, substantial and identified; in this context, "secret" means that the know-how, as a body or in the precise configuration and assembly of its components, is not generally known or easily accessible; "substantial" means that the know-how includes information which is indispensable to the buyer for the use, sale or resale of the contract goods or services; "identified" means that the know-how must be described in a sufficiently comprehensive manner so as to make it possible to verify that it fulfils the criteria of secrecy and substantiality;

(k) "buyer", whether distributor or repairer, includes an undertaking which sells goods or services on behalf of another undertaking;

(l) "authorised repairer" means a provider of repair and maintenance services for motor vehicles operating within the distribution system set up by a supplier of motor vehicles;

(m) "independent repairer" means a provider of repair and maintenance services for motor vehicles not operating within the distribution system set up by the supplier of the motor vehicles for which it provides repair or maintenance. An authorised repairer within the distribution system of a given supplier shall be deemed to be an independent repairer for the purposes of this Regulation to the extent that he provides repair or maintenance services for motor vehicles in respect of which he is not a member of the respective supplier's distribution system;

(n) "motor vehicle" means a self propelled vehicle intended for use on public roads and having three or more road wheels;

(o) "passenger car" means a motor vehicle intended for the carriage of passengers and comprising no more than eight seats in addition to the driver's seat;

(p) "light commercial vehicle" means a motor vehicle intended for the transport of goods or passengers with a maximum mass not exceeding 3.5 tonnes; if a certain light commercial vehicle is also sold in a version with a maximum mass above 3.5 tonnes, all versions of that vehicle are considered to be light commercial vehicles;

(q) the "contract range" means all the different models of motor vehicles available for purchase by the distributor from the supplier;

(r) a "motor vehicle which corresponds to a model within the contract range" means a vehicle which is the subject of a distribution agreement with another undertaking within the distribution system set up by the manufacturer or with his consent and which is:

— manufactured or assembled in volume by the manufacturer, and

— identical as to body style, drive-line, chassis, and type of motor to a vehicle within the contract range;

(s) "spare parts" means goods which are to be installed in or upon a motor vehicle so as to replace components of that vehicle, including goods such as lubricants which are necessary for the use of a motor vehicle, with the exception of fuel;

(t) "original spare parts" means spare parts which are of the same quality as the components used for the assembly of a motor vehicle and which are manufactured according to the specifications and production standards provided by the vehicle manufacturer for the production of components or spare parts for the motor vehicle in question. This includes spare parts which are manufactured on the same production line as these components. It is presumed, unless the contrary is proven, that parts constitute original spare parts if the part manufacturer certifies that the parts match the quality of the components used for the assembly of the vehicle in question and have been manufactured according to the specifications and production standards of the vehicle manufacturer;

(u) "spare parts of matching quality" means exclusively spare parts made by any undertaking which can certify at any moment that the parts in question match the quality of the components which are or were used for the assembly of the motor vehicles in question;

(v) "undertakings within the distribution system" means the manufacturer and undertakings which are entrusted by the manufacturer or with the manufacturer's consent with the distribution or repair or maintenance of contract goods or corresponding goods;

(w) "end user" includes leasing companies unless the leasing contracts used provide for a transfer of ownership or an option to purchase the vehicle prior to the expiry of the contract.

2. The terms "undertaking", "supplier", "buyer", "distributor" and "repairer" shall include their respective connected undertakings.

"Connected undertakings" are:

(a) undertakings in which a party to the agreement, directly or indirectly:

(i) has the power to exercise more than half the voting rights, or

(ii) has the power to appoint more than half the members of the supervisory board, board of management or bodies legally representing the undertaking, or

(iii) has the right to manage the undertaking's affairs;

(b) undertakings which directly or indirectly have, over a party to the agreement, the rights or powers listed in (a);

(c) undertakings in which an undertaking referred to in (b) has, directly or indirectly, the rights or powers listed in (a);

(d) undertakings in which a party to the agreement together with one or more of the undertakings referred to in (a), (b) or (c), or in which two or more of the latter undertakings, jointly have the rights or powers listed in (a);

(e) undertakings in which the rights or the powers listed in (a) are jointly held by:

(i) parties to the agreement or their respective connected undertakings referred to in (a) to (d), or

(ii) one or more of the parties to the agreement or one or more of their connected undertakings referred to in (a) to (d) and one or more third parties.

Commentary
Art 1: F&N: 15.20
Art 1(1)(b): B&C: 6.132 F&N: 15.53, 15.73, 15.77, 15.79, 15.133, 15.140, 15.141, 15.142
Art 1(1)(c): B&C: 6.118
Art 1(1)(e): B&C: 6.122
Art 1(1)(f): B&C: 6.134 F&N: 15.38, 15.76, 15.102, 15.119
Art 1(1)(g): B&C: 6.121, 6.134 F&N: 15.39
Art 1(1)(h): B&C: 6.097, 6.121, 6.134 F&N: 15.40, 15.102, 15.109, 15.117, 15.129, 15.131
Art 1(1)(i): F&N: 15.154
Art 1(1)(j): F&N: 15.127
Art 1(1)(k): F&N: 15.127, 15.154
Art 1(1)(l): F&N: 15.127
Art 1(1)(m): B&C: 6.114
Art 1(1)(n): B&C: 6.116 F&N: 15.36
Art 1(1)(p): B&C: 6.134
Art 1(1)(q): F&N: 15.59
Art 1(1)(r): F&N: 15.36, 15.59, 15.133
Art 1(1)(s): F&N: 15.126
Art 1(1)(t): F&N: 15.127, 15.133
Art 1(1)(u): F&N: 15.127, 15.133
Art 1(1)(w): F&N: 15.60

Article 2
Scope

1. Pursuant to Article 81(3) of the Treaty and subject to the provisions of this Regulation, it is hereby declared that the provisions of Article 81(1) shall not apply to vertical agreements where they relate to the conditions under which the parties may purchase, sell or resell new motor vehicles, spare parts for motor vehicles or repair and maintenance services for motor vehicles.

The first subparagraph shall apply to the extent that such vertical agreements contain vertical restraints.

The exemption declared by this paragraph shall be known for the purposes of this Regulation as "the exemption".

2. The exemption shall also apply to the following categories of vertical agreements:

(a) Vertical agreements entered into between an association of undertakings and its members, or between such an association and its suppliers, only if all its members are distributors of motor vehicles or spare parts for motor vehicles or repairers and if no individual member of the association, together with its connected undertakings, has a total annual turnover exceeding EUR 50 million; vertical agreements entered into by such associations shall be covered by this Regulation without prejudice to the application of Article 81 to horizontal agreements concluded between the members of the association or decisions adopted by the association;

(b) vertical agreements containing provisions which relate to the assignment to the buyer or use by the buyer of intellectual property rights, provided that those provisions do not constitute the primary object of such agreements and are directly related to the use, sale or resale of goods or services by the buyer or its customers. The exemption shall apply on condition that those provisions do not contain restrictions of competition relating to the contract goods or services which have the same object or effect as vertical restraints which are not exempted under this Regulation.

3. The exemption shall not apply to vertical agreements entered into between competing undertakings.

However, it shall apply where competing undertakings enter into a non-reciprocal vertical agreement and:

(a) the buyer has a total annual turnover not exceeding EUR 100 million, or
(b) the supplier is a manufacturer and a distributor of goods, while the buyer is a distributor not manufacturing goods competing with the contract goods, or
(c) the supplier is a provider of services at several levels of trade, while the buyer does not provide competing services at the level of trade where it purchases the contract services.

Commentary
Art 2: B&C: 6.115 F&N: 15.21, 15.29
Art 2(1): B&C: 3.079, 4.009, 6.116 F&N: 15.137
Art 2(2)(a): B&C: 6.119
Art 2(2)(b): F&N: 15.32
Art 2(3): B&C: 6.119 F&N: 15.33

Article 3
General conditions

1. Subject to paragraphs 2, 3, 4, 5, 6 and 7, the exemption shall apply on condition that the supplier's market share on the relevant market on which it sells the new motor vehicles, spare parts for motor vehicles or repair and maintenance services does not exceed 30%.

However, the market share threshold for the application of the exemption shall be 40% for agreements establishing quantitative selective distribution systems for the sale of new motor vehicles.

Those thresholds shall not apply to agreements establishing qualitative selective distribution systems.

2. In the case of vertical agreements containing exclusive supply obligations, the exemption shall apply on condition that the market share held by the buyer does not exceed 30% of the relevant market on which it purchases the contract goods or services.

3. The exemption shall apply on condition that the vertical agreement concluded with a distributor or repairer provides that the supplier agrees to the transfer of the rights and obligations resulting from the vertical agreement to another distributor or repairer within the distribution system and chosen by the former distributor or repairer.

4. The exemption shall apply on condition that the vertical agreement concluded with a distributor or repairer provides that a supplier who wishes to give notice of termination of an agreement must give such notice in writing and must include detailed, objective and transparent reasons for the termination, in order to prevent a supplier from ending a vertical agreement with a distributor or repairer because of practices which may not be restricted under this Regulation.

5. The exemption shall apply on condition that the vertical agreement concluded by the supplier of new motor vehicles with a distributor or authorised repairer provides

(a) that the agreement is concluded for a period of at least five years; in this case each party has to undertake to give the other party at least six months' prior notice of its intention not to renew the agreement;

(b) or that the agreement is concluded for an indefinite period; in this case the period of notice for regular termination of the agreement has to be at least two years for both parties; this period is reduced to at least one year where:

    (i) the supplier is obliged by law or by special agreement to pay appropriate compensation on termination of the agreement, or

    (ii) the supplier terminates the agreement where it is necessary to re-organise the whole or a substantial part of the network.

6. The exemption shall apply on condition that the vertical agreement provides for each of the parties the right to refer disputes concerning the fulfilment of their contractual obligations to an independent expert or arbitrator. Such disputes may relate, inter alia, to any of the following:

(a) supply obligations;

(b) the setting or attainment of sales targets;

(c) the implementation of stock requirements;

(d) the implementation of an obligation to provide or use demonstration vehicles;

(e) the conditions for the sale of different brands;

(f) the issue whether the prohibition to operate out of an unauthorised place of establishment limits the ability of the distributor of motor vehicles other than passenger cars or light commercial vehicles to expand its business, or

(g) the issue whether the termination of an agreement is justified by the reasons given in the notice.

The right referred to in the first sentence is without prejudice to each party's right to make an application to a national court.

7. For the purposes of this Article, the market share held by the undertakings referred to in Article 1(2)(e) shall be apportioned equally to each undertaking having the rights or the powers listed in Article 1(2)(a).

Commentary
Art 3: B&C: 6.111, 6.122–6.123 F&N: 15.15, 15.22, 15.29, 15.120
Art 3(1): B&C: 3.079, 4.009, 6.122 F&N: 15.70, 15.94, 15.160
Art 3(2): B&C: 3.079, 6.122 F&N: 15.70
Art 3(3): B&C: 6.123 F&N: 15.80
Art 3(4): B&C: 6.123, 6.137 F&N: 15.82
Art 3(5): B&C: 6.137 F&N: 15.83
Art 3(5)(a): B&C: 6.123
Art 3(5)(b): B&C: 6.123
Art 3(6): B&C: 6.123 F&N: 15.07, 15.76, 15.85
Art 3(6)(f): F&N: 15.56
Art 3(6)(g): B&C: 6.123
Art 3(7): B&C: 6.122 F&N: 15.70

Article 4
Hardcore restrictions

(Hardcore restrictions concerning the sale of new motor vehicles, repair and maintenance services or spare parts)

1. The exemption shall not apply to vertical agreements which, directly or indirectly, in isolation or in combination with other factors under the control of the parties, have as their object:

(a) the restriction of the distributor's or repairer's ability to determine its sale price, without prejudice to the supplier's ability to impose a maximum sale price or to recommend a sale price, provided that this does not amount to a fixed or minimum sale price as a result of pressure from, or incentives offered by, any of the parties;

(b) the restriction of the territory into which, or of the customers to whom, the distributor or repairer may sell the contract goods or services; however, the exemption shall apply to:

   (i) the restriction of active sales into the exclusive territory or to an exclusive customer group reserved to the supplier or allocated by the supplier to another distributor or repairer, where such a restriction does not limit sales by the customers of the distributor or repairer;

   (ii) the restriction of sales to end users by a distributor operating at the wholesale level of trade;

   (iii) the restriction of sales of new motor vehicles and spare parts to unauthorised distributors by the members of a selective distribution system in markets where selective distribution is applied, subject to the provisions of point (i);

   (iv) the restriction of the buyer's ability to sell components, supplied for the purposes of incorporation, to customers who would use them to manufacture the same type of goods as those produced by the supplier;

(c) the restriction of cross-supplies between distributors or repairers within a selective distribution system, including between distributors or repairers operating at different levels of trade;

(d) the restriction of active or passive sales of new passenger cars or light commercial vehicles, spare parts for any motor vehicle or repair and maintenance services for any motor vehicle to end users by members of a selective distribution system operating at the retail level of trade in markets where selective distribution is used. The exemption shall apply to agreements containing a prohibition on a member of a selective distribution system from operating out of an unauthorised place of establishment. However, the application of the exemption to such a prohibition is subject to Article 5(2)(b);

(e) the restriction of active or passive sales of new motor vehicles other than passenger cars or light commercial vehicles to end users by members of a selective distribution system operating at the retail level of trade in markets where selective distribution is used, without prejudice to the ability of the supplier to prohibit a member of that system from operating out of an unauthorised place of establishment;

247

(Hardcore restrictions only concerning the sale of new motor vehicles)

(f) the restriction of the distributor's ability to sell any new motor vehicle which corresponds to a model within its contract range;

(g) the restriction of the distributor's ability to subcontract the provision of repair and maintenance services to authorised repairers, without prejudice to the ability of the supplier to require the distributor to give end users the name and address of the authorised repairer or repairers in question before the conclusion of a sales contract and, if any of these authorised repairers is not in the vicinity of the sales outlet, to also tell end users how far the repair shop or repair shops in question are from the sales outlet; however, such obligations may only be imposed provided that similar obligations are imposed on distributors whose repair shop is not on the same premises as their sales outlet;

(Hardcore restrictions only concerning the sale of repair and maintenance services and of spare parts)

(h) the restriction of the authorised repairer's ability to limit its activities to the provision of repair and maintenance services and the distribution of spare parts;

(i) the restriction of the sales of spare parts for motor vehicles by members of a selective distribution system to independent repairers which use these parts for the repair and maintenance of a motor vehicle;

(j) the restriction agreed between a supplier of original spare parts or spare parts of matching quality, repair tools or diagnostic or other equipment and a manufacturer of motor vehicles, which limits the supplier's ability to sell these goods or services to authorised or independent distributors or to authorised or independent repairers or end users;

(k) the restriction of a distributor's or authorised repairer's ability to obtain original spare parts or spare parts of matching quality from a third undertaking of its choice and to use them for the repair or maintenance of motor vehicles, without prejudice to the ability of a supplier of new motor vehicles to require the use of original spare parts supplied by it for repairs carried out under warranty, free servicing and vehicle recall work;

(l) the restriction agreed between a manufacturer of motor vehicles which uses components for the initial assembly of motor vehicles and the supplier of such components which limits the latter's ability to place its trade mark or logo effectively and in an easily visible manner on the components supplied or on spare parts.

2. The exemption shall not apply where the supplier of motor vehicles refuses to give independent operators access to any technical information, diagnostic and other equipment, tools, including any relevant software, or training required for the repair and maintenance of these motor vehicles or for the implementation of environmental protection measures.

Such access must include in particular the unrestricted use of the electronic control and diagnostic systems of a motor vehicle, the programming of these systems in accordance with the supplier's standard procedures, the repair and training instructions and the information required for the use of diagnostic and servicing tools and equipment.

Access must be given to independent operators in a non-discriminatory, prompt and proportionate way, and the information must be provided in a usable form. If the relevant item is covered by an intellectual property right or constitutes know-how, access shall not be withheld in any abusive manner.

For the purposes of this paragraph "independent operator" shall mean undertakings which are directly or indirectly involved in the repair and maintenance of motor vehicles, in particular independent repairers, manufacturers of repair equipment or tools, independent distributors of spare parts, publishers of technical information, automobile clubs, roadside assistance operators, operators offering inspection and testing services and operators offering training for repairers.

Commentary
Art 4: F&N: 15.15, 15.23, 15.29
Art 4(1): B&C: 6.111, 6.124, 6.138 F&N: 3.163, 15.27, 15.31
Art 4(1)(a): B&C: 6.124–6.125
Art 4(1)(b): B&C: 6.124, 6.126 F&N: 15.121
Art 4(1)(b)(i): B&C: 6.121 F&N: 15.42
Art 4(1)(b)(ii): F&N: 15.42

Article 5
Specific conditions

1. As regards the sale of new motor vehicles, repair and maintenance services or spare parts, the exemption shall not apply to any of the following obligations contained in vertical agreements:

(a) any direct or indirect non-compete obligation;

(b) any direct or indirect obligation limiting the ability of an authorised repairer to provide repair and maintenance services for vehicles from competing suppliers;

(c) any direct or indirect obligation causing the members of a distribution system not to sell motor vehicles or spare parts of particular competing suppliers or not to provide repair and maintenance services for motor vehicles of particular competing suppliers;

(d) any direct or indirect obligation causing the distributor or authorised repairer, after termination of the agreement, not to manufacture, purchase, sell or resell motor vehicles or not to provide repair or maintenance services.

2. As regards the sale of new motor vehicles, the exemption shall not apply to any of the following obligations contained in vertical agreements:

(a) any direct or indirect obligation causing the retailer not to sell leasing services relating to contract goods or corresponding goods;

(b) any direct or indirect obligation on any distributor of passenger cars or light commercial vehicles within a selective distribution system, which limits its ability to establish additional sales or delivery outlets at other locations within the common market where selective distribution is applied.

3. As regards repair and maintenance services or the sale of spare parts, the exemption shall not apply to any direct or indirect obligation as to the place of establishment of an authorised repairer where selective distribution is applied.

Commentary

Article 6
Withdrawal of the benefit of the Regulation

1. The Commission may withdraw the benefit of this Regulation, pursuant to Article 7(1) of Regulation No 19/65/EEC, where it finds in any particular case that vertical agreements to which this Regulation applies nevertheless have effects which are incompatible with the conditions laid down in Article 81(3) of the Treaty, and in particular:

(a) where access to the relevant market or competition therein is significantly restricted by the cumulative effect of parallel networks of similar vertical restraints implemented by competing suppliers or buyers, or

Part C Substantive Antitrust Matters

(b) where competition is restricted on a market where one supplier is not exposed to effective competition from other suppliers, or

(c) where prices or conditions of supply for contract goods or for corresponding goods differ substantially between geographic markets, or

(d) where discriminatory prices or sales conditions are applied within a geographic market.

2. Where in any particular case vertical agreements to which the exemption applies have effects incompatible with the conditions laid down in Article 81(3) of the Treaty in the territory of a Member State, or in a part thereof, which has all the characteristics of a distinct geographic market, the relevant authority of that Member State may withdraw the benefit of application of this Regulation in respect of that territory, under the same conditions as those provided in paragraph 1.

Commentary
Art 6: B&C: 6.135 F&N: 15.25, 15.162, 15.163
Art 6(1): B&C: 3.086
Art 6(2): B&C: 3.087, 6.135 F&N: 15.162

Article 7
Non-application of the Regulation

1. Pursuant to Article 1a of Regulation No 19/65/EEC, the Commission may by regulation declare that, where parallel networks of similar vertical restraints cover more than 50% of a relevant market, this Regulation shall not apply to vertical agreements containing specific restraints relating to that market.

2. A regulation pursuant to paragraph 1 shall not become applicable earlier than one year following its adoption.

Commentary
Art 7: B&C: 3.089, 6.136 F&N: 15.25, 15.165
Art 7(1): F&N: 15.164
Art 7(2): B&C: 6.136

Article 8
Market share calculation

1. The market shares provided for in this Regulation shall be calculated:

(a) for the distribution of new motor vehicles on the basis of the volume of the contract goods and corresponding goods sold by the supplier, together with any other goods sold by the supplier which are regarded as interchangeable or substitutable by the buyer, by reason of the products' characteristics, prices and intended use;

(b) for the distribution of spare parts on the basis of the value of the contract goods and other goods sold by the supplier, together with any other goods sold by the supplier which are regarded as interchangeable or substitutable by the buyer, by reason of the products' characteristics, prices and intended use;

(c) for the provision of repair and maintenance services on the basis of the value of the contract services sold by the members of the supplier's distribution network together with any other services sold by these members which are regarded as interchangeable or substitutable by the buyer, by reason of their characteristics, prices and intended use.

If the volume data required for those calculations are not available, value data may be used or vice versa. If such information is not available, estimates based on other reliable market information may be used. For the purposes of Article 3(2), the market purchase volume or the market purchase value respectively, or estimates thereof shall be used to calculate the market share.

2. For the purposes of applying the market share thresholds of 30% and 40% provided for in this Regulation the following rules shall apply:

(a) the market share shall be calculated on the basis of data relating to the preceding calendar year;

(b) the market share shall include any goods or services supplied to integrated distributors for the purposes of sale;

250

(c) if the market share is initially not more than 30% or 40% respectively but subsequently rises above that level without exceeding 35% or 45% respectively, the exemption shall continue to apply for a period of two consecutive calendar years following the year in which the market share threshold of 30% or 40% respectively was first exceeded;

(d) if the market share is initially not more than 30% or 40% respectively but subsequently rises above 35% or 45% respectively, the exemption shall continue to apply for one calendar year following the year in which the level of 30% or 40% respectively was first exceeded;

(e) the benefit of points (c) and (d) may not be combined so as to exceed a period of two calendar years.

Commentary
Art 8: **B&C**: 6.122 **F&N**: 15.25
Art 8(1)(a): **F&N**: 15.66

Article 9
Turnover calculation

1. For the purposes of calculating total annual turnover figures referred to in Article 2(2)(a) and 2(3)(a) respectively, the turnover achieved during the previous financial year by the relevant party to the vertical agreement and the turnover achieved by its connected undertakings in respect of all goods and services, excluding all taxes and other duties, shall be added together. For this purpose, no account shall be taken of dealings between the party to the vertical agreement and its connected undertakings or between its connected undertakings.

2. The exemption shall remain applicable where, for any period of two consecutive financial years, the total annual turnover threshold is exceeded by no more than 10%.

Commentary
Art 9: **B&C**: 6.119 **F&N**: 15.25

Article 10
Transitional period

[1.] The prohibition laid down in Article 81(1) shall not apply during the period from 1 October 2002 to 30 September 2003 in respect of agreements already in force on 30 September 2002 which do not satisfy the conditions for exemption provided for in this Regulation but which satisfy the conditions for exemption provided for in Regulation (EC) No 1475/95.

[2. The prohibition laid down in Article 81(1) shall not apply to agreements existing at the date of accession for the Czech Republic, Estonia, Cyprus, Latvia, Lithuania, Hungary, Malta, Poland, Slovenia and Slovakia and which, by reason of accession, fall within the scope of Article 81(1) if, within six months from the date of accession, they are amended and thereby comply with the conditions laid down in this Regulation.]

Notes
The amendments in square brackets were made with effect from 1 May 2004 by the Act concerning the conditions of accession of the Czech Republic, the Republic of Estonia, the Republic of Cyprus, the Republic of Latvia, the Republic of Lithuania, the Republic of Hungary, the Republic of Malta, the Republic of Poland, the Republic of Slovenia and the Slovak Republic and the adjustments to the Treaties on which the European Union is founded. Annex II: List referred to in Article 20 of the Act of Accession—5. Competition policy (OJ L 236, 23.9 2003, p. 344).

Commentary
Art 10: **B&C**: 6.110, 6.138 **F&N**: 5.26, 15.158

Article 11
Monitoring and evaluation report

1. The Commission shall monitor the operation of this Regulation on a regular basis, with particular regard to its effects on:

(a) competition in motor vehicle retailing and in after sales servicing in the common market or relevant parts of it;

251

(b) the structure and level of concentration of motor vehicle distribution and any resulting effects on competition.

2. The Commission shall draw up a report on this Regulation not later than 31 May 2008 having regard in particular to the conditions set out in Article 81(3).

Commentary
Art 11: **F&N:** 15.27, 15.166

Article 12
Entry into force and expiry

1. This Regulation shall enter into force on 1 October 2002.

2. Article 5(2)(b) shall apply from 1 October 2005.

3. This Regulation shall expire on 31 May 2010.

Commentary
Art 12: **B&C:** 3.079, 6.110 **F&N:** 15.28
Art 12(1): **B&C:** 6.138
Art 12(2): **B&C:** 6.113, 6.134 **F&N:** 15.57
Art 12(3): **B&C:** 6.138

This Regulation shall be binding in its entirety and directly applicable in all Member States.

Done at Brussels, 31 July 2002.

C7

COMMISSION REGULATION (EC) No 772/2004

of [7] April 2004

on the application of Article 81(3) of the Treaty to categories of technology transfer agreements

(Text with EEA relevance)

Official Journal L 123, 27.4.2004, p. 11

Celex No: 32004R0772

Notes
The date of this Regulation is shown as corrected by the Corrigendum at OJ L 127, 29.4.2004, p. 158.
EEA application: this instrument was adopted with appropriate adaptations by EEA Joint Committee Decision No 42/2005 of 11 March 2005, OJ L 198, 28.7.2005, p. 42 and EEA Supplement No 38, 28.7.2005, p. 24: see EEA Agreement, Annex XIV, Chapter C, Point 5.

Commentary
Regulation 772/2004/EC: B&C: 2.017, 2.031, 2.087, 2.111, 3.080, 3.093, 5.081, 6.015, 6.186, 9.005–9.006, 9.075, 9.078, 9.082–9.083, 9.086, 9.094, 9.097, 9.100, 9.106, 9.111, 9.115–9.116, 9.129–9.131, 9.169–9.171, 9.173 **F&N:** 3.376, 3.377, 9.108, 9.164, 9.205, 9.267, 10.60, 10.63, 10.68, 10.69, 10.70, 10.71, 10.94, 10.111, 10.222

THE COMMISSION OF THE EUROPEAN COMMUNITIES,

Having regard to the Treaty establishing the European Community,

Having regard to Council Regulation No 19/65/EEC of 2 March 1965 on application of Article 81(3) of the Treaty to certain categories of agreements and concerted practices,[1] and in particular Article 1 thereof,

Having published a draft of this Regulation,[2]

After consulting the Advisory Committee on Restrictive Practices and Dominant Positions,

Notes
[1] OJ 36, 6.3.1965, p. 533/65. Regulation as last amended by Regulation (EC) No 1/2003 (OJ L 1, 4.1.2003, p. 1).
[2] OJ C 235, 1.10.2003, p. 10.

Whereas:

(1) Regulation No 19/65/EEC empowers the Commission to apply Article 81(3) of the Treaty by Regulation to certain categories of technology transfer agreements and corresponding concerted practices to which only two undertakings are party which fall within Article 81(1).

(2) Pursuant to Regulation No 19/65/EEC, the Commission has, in particular, adopted Regulation (EC) No 240/96 of 31 January 1996 on the application of Article 81(3) of the Treaty to certain categories of technology transfer agreements.[1]

Notes
[1] OJ L 31, 9.2.1996, p. 2. Regulation as amended by the 2003 Act of Accession.

(3) On 20 December 2001 the Commission published an evaluation report on the transfer of technology block exemption Regulation (EC) No 240/96.[1] This generated a public debate on the application of Regulation (EC) No 240/96 and on the application in general of Article 81(1) and (3) of the Treaty to technology transfer agreements. The response to the evaluation report from Member States and third parties has been generally in favour of reform of Community competition policy on technology transfer agreements. It is therefore appropriate to repeal Regulation (EC) No 240/96.

Notes
[1] COM(2001) 786 final.

(4) This Regulation should meet the two requirements of ensuring effective competition and providing adequate legal security for undertakings. The pursuit of these objectives should take account of the need to simplify the regulatory framework and its application. It is appropriate to move away from the approach of listing exempted clauses and to place greater emphasis on defining the categories of agreements which are exempted up to a certain level of market power and on specifying the restrictions or clauses which are not to be contained in such agreements. This is consistent with an economics-based approach which assesses the impact of agreements on the relevant market. It is also consistent with such an approach to make a distinction between agreements between competitors and agreements between non-competitors.

Commentary
Recital 4: B&C: 9.129

(5) Technology transfer agreements concern the licensing of technology. Such agreements will usually improve economic efficiency and be pro-competitive as they can reduce duplication of research and development, strengthen the incentive for the initial research and development, spur incremental innovation, facilitate diffusion and generate product market competition.

(6) The likelihood that such efficiency-enhancing and pro-competitive effects will outweigh any anti-competitive effects due to restrictions contained in technology transfer agreements depends on the degree of market power of the undertakings concerned and, therefore, on the extent to which

those undertakings face competition from undertakings owning substitute technologies or undertakings producing substitute products.

(7) This Regulation should only deal with agreements where the licensor permits the licensee to exploit the licensed technology, possibly after further research and development by the licensee, for the production of goods or services. It should not deal with licensing agreements for the purpose of subcontracting research and development. It should also not deal with licensing agreements to set up technology pools, that is to say, agreements for the pooling of technologies with the purpose of licensing the created package of intellectual property rights to third parties.

Commentary
Recital 7: B&C: 9.139

---

(8) For the application of Article 81(3) by regulation, it is not necessary to define those technology transfer agreements that are capable of falling within Article 81(1). In the individual assessment of agreements pursuant to Article 81(1), account has to be taken of several factors, and in particular the structure and the dynamics of the relevant technology and product markets.

(9) The benefit of the block exemption established by this Regulation should be limited to those agreements which can be assumed with sufficient certainty to satisfy the conditions of Article 81(3). In order to attain the benefits and objectives of technology transfer, the benefit of this Regulation should also apply to provisions contained in technology transfer agreements that do not constitute the primary object of such agreements, but are directly related to the application of the licensed technology.

(10) For technology transfer agreements between competitors it can be presumed that, where the combined share of the relevant markets accounted for by the parties does not exceed 20% and the agreements do not contain certain severely anti-competitive restraints, they generally lead to an improvement in production or distribution and allow consumers a fair share of the resulting benefits.

(11) For technology transfer agreements between non-competitors it can be presumed that, where the individual share of the relevant markets accounted for by each of the parties does not exceed 30% and the agreements do not contain certain severely anti-competitive restraints, they generally lead to an improvement in production or distribution and allow consumers a fair share of the resulting benefits.

(12) There can be no presumption that above these market-share thresholds technology transfer agreements do fall within the scope of Article 81(1). For instance, an exclusive licensing agreement between non-competing undertakings does often not fall within the scope of Article 81(1). There can also be no presumption that, above these market-share thresholds, technology transfer agreements falling within the scope of Article 81(1) will not satisfy the conditions for exemption. However, it can also not be presumed that they will usually give rise to objective advantages of such a character and size as to compensate for the disadvantages which they create for competition.

Commentary
Recital 12: B&C: 9.131, 9.141

---

(13) This Regulation should not exempt technology transfer agreements containing restrictions which are not indispensable to the improvement of production or distribution. In particular, technology transfer agreements containing certain severely anti-competitive restraints such as the fixing of prices charged to third parties should be excluded from the benefit of the block exemption established by this Regulation irrespective of the market shares of the undertakings concerned. In the case of such hardcore restrictions the whole agreement should be excluded from the benefit of the block exemption.

(14) In order to protect incentives to innovate and the appropriate application of intellectual property rights, certain restrictions should be excluded from the block exemption. In particular exclusive grant back obligations for severable improvements should be excluded. Where such a restriction is included in a licence agreement only the restriction in question should be excluded from the benefit of the block exemption.

(15) The market-share thresholds, the non-exemption of technology transfer agreements containing severely anti-competitive restraints and the excluded restrictions provided for in this Regulation will normally ensure that the agreements to which the block exemption applies do not enable the participating undertakings to eliminate competition in respect of a substantial part of the products in question.

(16) In particular cases in which the agreements falling under this Regulation nevertheless have effects incompatible with Article 81(3), the Commission should be able to withdraw the benefit of the block exemption. This may occur in particular where the incentives to innovate are reduced or where access to markets is hindered.

(17) Council Regulation (EC) No 1/2003 of 16 December 2002 on the implementation of the rules on competition laid down in Articles 81 and 82 of the Treaty[1] empowers the competent authorities of Member States to withdraw the benefit of the block exemption in respect of technology transfer agreements having effects incompatible with Article 81(3), where such effects are felt in their respective territory, or in a part thereof, and where such territory has the characteristics of a distinct geographic market. Member States must ensure that the exercise of this power of withdrawal does not prejudice the uniform application throughout the common market of the Community competition rules or the full effect of the measures adopted in implementation of those rules.

Notes

[1] OJ L 1, 4.1.2003, p. 1. Regulation as amended by Regulation (EC) No 411/2004 (OJ L 68, 6.3.2004, p. 1).

---

(18) In order to strengthen supervision of parallel networks of technology transfer agreements which have similar restrictive effects and which cover more than 50% of a given market, the Commission should be able to declare this Regulation inapplicable to technology transfer agreements containing specific restraints relating to the market concerned, thereby restoring the full application of Article 81 to such agreements.

(19) This Regulation should cover only technology transfer agreements between a licensor and a licensee. It should cover such agreements even if conditions are stipulated for more than one level of trade, by, for instance, requiring the licensee to set up a particular distribution system and specifying the obligations the licensee must or may impose on resellers of the products produced under the licence. However, such conditions and obligations should comply with the competition rules applicable to supply and distribution agreements. Supply and distribution agreements concluded between a licensee and its buyers should not be exempted by this Regulation.

Commentary
Recital 19: F&N: 3.376. 10.76

---

(20) This Regulation is without prejudice to the application of Article 82 of the Treaty,

HAS ADOPTED THIS REGULATION:

Article 1
Definitions

1. For the purposes of this Regulation, the following definitions shall apply:

(a) "agreement" means an agreement, a decision of an association of undertakings or a concerted practice;

(b) "technology transfer agreement" means a patent licensing agreement, a know-how licensing agreement, a software copyright licensing agreement or a mixed patent, know-how or software copyright licensing agreement, including any such agreement containing provisions which relate to the sale and purchase of products or which relate to the licensing of other intellectual property rights or the assignment of intellectual property rights, provided that those provisions do not constitute the primary object of the agreement and are directly related to the production of the contract products; assignments of patents, know-how, software copyright or a combination thereof where part of the risk associated with the exploitation of the technology remains with the assignor, in particular where the sum payable in consideration of the assignment is dependent on the turnover obtained by the assignee in respect of products produced with the assigned technology, the

255

quantity of such products produced or the number of operations carried out employing the technology, shall also be deemed to be technology transfer agreements;

(c) "reciprocal agreement" means a technology transfer agreement where two undertakings grant each other, in the same or separate contracts, a patent licence, a know-how licence, a software copyright licence or a mixed patent, know-how or software copyright licence and where these licences concern competing technologies or can be used for the production of competing products;

(d) "non-reciprocal agreement" means a technology transfer agreement where one undertaking grants another undertaking a patent licence, a know-how licence, a software copyright licence or a mixed patent, know-how or software copyright licence, or where two undertakings grant each other such a licence but where these licences do not concern competing technologies and cannot be used for the production of competing products;

(e) "product" means a good or a service, including both intermediary goods and services and final goods and services;

(f) "contract products" means products produced with the licensed technology;

(g) "intellectual property rights" includes industrial property rights, know-how, copyright and neighbouring rights;

(h) "patents" means patents, patent applications, utility models, applications for registration of utility models, designs, topographies of semiconductor products, supplementary protection certificates for medicinal products or other products for which such supplementary protection certificates may be obtained and plant breeder's certificates;

(i) "know-how" means a package of non-patented practical information, resulting from experience and testing, which is:

  (i) secret, that is to say, not generally known or easily accessible,

  (ii) substantial, that is to say, significant and useful for the production of the contract products, and

  (iii) identified, that is to say, described in a sufficiently comprehensive manner so as to make it possible to verify that it fulfils the criteria of secrecy and substantiality;

(j) "competing undertakings" means undertakings which compete on the relevant technology market and/or the relevant product market, that is to say:

  (i) competing undertakings on the relevant technology market, being undertakings which license out competing technologies without infringing each others' intellectual property rights (actual competitors on the technology market); the relevant technology market includes technologies which are regarded by the licensees as interchangeable with or substitutable for the licensed technology, by reason of the technologies' characteristics, their royalties and their intended use,

  (ii) competing undertakings on the relevant product market, being undertakings which, in the absence of the technology transfer agreement, are both active on the relevant product and geographic market(s) on which the contract products are sold without infringing each others' intellectual property rights (actual competitors on the product market) or would, on realistic grounds, undertake the necessary additional investments or other necessary switching costs so that they could timely enter, without infringing each others' intellectual property rights, the(se) relevant product and geographic market(s) in response to a small and permanent increase in relative prices (potential competitors on the product market); the relevant product market comprises products which are regarded by the buyers as interchangeable with or substitutable for the contract products, by reason of the products' characteristics, their prices and their intended use;

(k) "selective distribution system" means a distribution system where the licensor undertakes to license the production of the contract products only to licensees selected on the basis of specified criteria and where these licensees undertake not to sell the contract products to unauthorised distributors;

(l) "exclusive territory" means a territory in which only one undertaking is allowed to produce the contract products with the licensed technology, without prejudice to the possibility of allowing within that territory another licensee to produce the contract products only for a particular customer where this second licence was granted in order to create an alternative source of supply for that customer;

(m) "exclusive customer group" means a group of customers to which only one undertaking is allowed actively to sell the contract products produced with the licensed technology;

(n) "severable improvement" means an improvement that can be exploited without infringing the licensed technology.

2. The terms "undertaking", "licensor" and "licensee" shall include their respective connected undertakings.

"Connected undertakings" means:

(a) undertakings in which a party to the agreement, directly or indirectly:

(i) has the power to exercise more than half the voting rights, or

(ii) has the power to appoint more than half the members of the supervisory board, board of management or bodies legally representing the undertaking, or

(iii) has the right to manage the undertaking's affairs;

(b) undertakings which directly or indirectly have, over a party to the agreement, the rights or powers listed in (a);

(c) undertakings in which an undertaking referred to in (b) has, directly or indirectly, the rights or powers listed in (a);

(d) undertakings in which a party to the agreement together with one or more of the undertakings referred to in (a), (b) or (c), or in which two or more of the latter undertakings, jointly have the rights or powers listed in (a);

(e) undertakings in which the rights or the powers listed in (a) are jointly held by:

(i) parties to the agreement or their respective connected undertakings referred to in (a) to (d), or

(ii) one or more of the parties to the agreement or one or more of their connected undertakings referred to in (a) to (d) and one or more third parties.

Commentary

Art 1(1): B&C: 9.133
Art 1(1)(a): B&C: 9.134
Art 1(1)(b): B&C: 3.080, 9.134–9.137 F&N: 10.74
Art 1(1)(c): B&C: 9.091
Art 1(1)(d): B&C: 9.091
Art 1(1)(e): B&C: 9.091, 9.135
Art 1(1)(f): B&C: 9.135
Art 1(1)(h): B&C: 9.134
Art 1(1)(i): B&C: 6.186, 9.086, 9.088, 9.134
Art 1(1)(j): B&C: 4.068, 9.088, 9.144 F&N: 10.83, 10.87
Art 1(1)(j)(ii): F&N: 10.86
Art 1(1)(n): B&C: 9.164
Art 1(2): B&C: 9.138

Article 2
Exemption

Pursuant to Article 81(3) of the Treaty and subject to the provisions of this Regulation, it is hereby declared that Article 81(1) of the Treaty shall not apply to technology transfer agreements entered into between two undertakings permitting the production of contract products.

This exemption shall apply to the extent that such agreements contain restrictions of competition falling within the scope of Article 81(1). The exemption shall apply for as long as the intellectual property right in the licensed technology has not expired, lapsed or been declared invalid or, in the case of know-how, for as long as the know-how remains secret, except in the event where the know-how becomes publicly known as a result of action by the licensee, in which case the exemption shall apply for the duration of the agreement.

Commentary
Art 2: B&C: 3.080, 9.119, 9.133, 9.138, 9.140–9.141, 9.144 F&N: 10.66, 10.67, 10.93

Article 3
Market-share thresholds

1. Where the undertakings party to the agreement are competing undertakings, the exemption provided for in Article 2 shall apply on condition that the combined market share of the parties does not exceed 20% on the affected relevant technology and product market.

2. Where the undertakings party to the agreement are not competing undertakings, the exemption provided for in Article 2 shall apply on condition that the market share of each of the parties does not exceed 30% on the affected relevant technology and product market.

3. For the purposes of paragraphs 1 and 2, the market share of a party on the relevant technology market(s) is defined in terms of the presence of the licensed technology on the relevant product market(s). A licensor's market share on the relevant technology market shall be the combined market share on the relevant product market of the contract products produced by the licensor and its licensees.

Commentary
Art 3: B&C: 3.080 F&N: 10.117
Art 3(1): B&C: 4.009, 9.144
Art 3(2): B&C: 4.009, 9.144
Art 3(3): B&C: 4.068 F&N: 10.118

Article 4
Hardcore restrictions

1. Where the undertakings party to the agreement are competing undertakings, the exemption provided for in Article 2 shall not apply to agreements which, directly or indirectly, in isolation or in combination with other factors under the control of the parties, have as their object:

(a) the restriction of a party's ability to determine its prices when selling products to third parties;

(b) the limitation of output, except limitations on the output of contract products imposed on the licensee in a non-reciprocal agreement or imposed on only one of the licensees in a reciprocal agreement;

(c) the allocation of markets or customers except:

    (i) the obligation on the licensee(s) to produce with the licensed technology only within one or more technical fields of use or one or more product markets,

    (ii) the obligation on the licensor and/or the licensee, in a non-reciprocal agreement, not to produce with the licensed technology within one or more technical fields of use or one or more product markets or one or more exclusive territories reserved for the other party,

    (iii) the obligation on the licensor not to license the technology to another licensee in a particular territory,

    (iv) the restriction, in a non-reciprocal agreement, of active and/or passive sales by the licensee and/or the licensor into the exclusive territory or to the exclusive customer group reserved for the other party,

    (v) the restriction, in a non-reciprocal agreement, of active sales by the licensee into the exclusive territory or to the exclusive customer group allocated by the licensor to another licensee provided the latter was not a competing undertaking of the licensor at the time of the conclusion of its own licence,

    (vi) the obligation on the licensee to produce the contract products only for its own use provided that the licensee is not restricted in selling the contract products actively and passively as spare parts for its own products,

    (vii) the obligation on the licensee, in a non-reciprocal agreement, to produce the contract products only for a particular customer, where the licence was granted in order to create an alternative source of supply for that customer;

(d) the restriction of the licensee's ability to exploit its own technology or the restriction of the ability of any of the parties to the agreement to carry out research and development, unless such latter restriction is indispensable to prevent the disclosure of the licensed know-how to third parties.

2. Where the undertakings party to the agreement are not competing undertakings, the exemption provided for in Article 2 shall not apply to agreements which, directly or indirectly, in isolation or in combination with other factors under the control of the parties, have as their object:

(a) the restriction of a party's ability to determine its prices when selling products to third parties, without prejudice to the possibility of imposing a maximum sale price or recommending a sale price, provided that it does not amount to a fixed or minimum sale price as a result of pressure from, or incentives offered by, any of the parties;

(b) the restriction of the territory into which, or of the customers to whom, the licensee may passively sell the contract products, except:

   (i) the restriction of passive sales into an exclusive territory or to an exclusive customer group reserved for the licensor,

   (ii) the restriction of passive sales into an exclusive territory or to an exclusive customer group allocated by the licensor to another licensee during the first two years that this other licensee is selling the contract products in that territory or to that customer group,

   (iii) the obligation to produce the contract products only for its own use provided that the licensee is not restricted in selling the contract products actively and passively as spare parts for its own products,

   (iv) the obligation to produce the contract products only for a particular customer, where the licence was granted in order to create an alternative source of supply for that customer,

   (v) the restriction of sales to end-users by a licensee operating at the wholesale level of trade,

   (vi) the restriction of sales to unauthorised distributors by the members of a selective distribution system;

(c) the restriction of active or passive sales to end-users by a licensee which is a member of a selective distribution system and which operates at the retail level, without prejudice to the possibility of prohibiting a member of the system from operating out of an unauthorised place of establishment.

3. Where the undertakings party to the agreement are not competing undertakings at the time of the conclusion of the agreement but become competing undertakings afterwards, paragraph 2 and not paragraph 1 shall apply for the full life of the agreement unless the agreement is subsequently amended in any material respect.

Commentary

Art 4: B&C: 3.080, 9.077, 9.145, 14.105 F&N: 3.163, 10.90, 10.91, 10.167
Art 4(1): B&C: 9.106, 9.145 F&N: 10.91, 10.92, 10.93, 10.98, 10.99
Art 4(1)(a): B&C: 9.108, 9.147 F&N: 10.93, 10.95, 10.96
Art 4(1)(b): B&C: 9.149 F&N: 10.93, 10.97, 10.139
Art 4(1)(c): B&C: 9.095, 9.150 F&N: 10.93, 10.104
Art 4(1)(c)(i): B&C: 9.151 F&N: 10.93, 10.102
Art 4(1)(c)(ii): B&C: 9.105, 9.151 F&N: 10.93, 10.101
Art 4(1)(c)(iii): B&C: 9.152 F&N: 10.93, 10.102, 10.103
Art 4(1)(c)(iv): B&C: 9.097, 9.152–9.153 F&N: 10.93, 10.101
Art 4(1)(c)(v): B&C: 9.152–9.153 F&N: 10.93, 10.104
Art 4(1)(c)(vi): B&C: 9.153 F&N: 10.93, 10.105
Art 4(1)(c)(vii): B&C: 9.153 F&N: 10.93, 10.105
Art 4(1)(d): B&C: 9.154, 9.166 F&N: 10.93, 10.96, 10.102, 10.103, 10.110, 10.116
Art 4(2): B&C: 9.145, 9.155 F&N: 10.91, 10.92, 10.93, 10.98, 10.99
Art 4(2)(a): B&C: 9.104, 9.108, 9.156 F&N: 10.93, 10.95
Art 4(2)(b): F&N: 9.108, 10.93, 10.106, 10.107, 10.109
Art 4(2)(b)(i): B&C: 9.158 F&N: 10.93
Art 4(2)(b)(ii): B&C: 9.099, 9.158 F&N: 10.93, 10.109
Art 4(2)(b)(iii): B&C: 9.160 F&N: 10.93, 10.109
Art 4(2)(b)(iv): B&C: 9.160 F&N: 10.93, 10.109
Art 4(2)(b)(v): B&C: 9.161–9.162 F&N: 10.93, 10.109

Article 5
Excluded restrictions

1. The exemption provided for in Article 2 shall not apply to any of the following obligations contained in technology transfer agreements:

(a) any direct or indirect obligation on the licensee to grant an exclusive licence to the licensor or to a third party designated by the licensor in respect of its own severable improvements to or its own new applications of the licensed technology;

(b) any direct or indirect obligation on the licensee to assign, in whole or in part, to the licensor or to a third party designated by the licensor, rights to its own severable improvements to or its own new applications of the licensed technology;

(c) any direct or indirect obligation on the licensee not to challenge the validity of intellectual property rights which the licensor holds in the common market, without prejudice to the possibility of providing for termination of the technology transfer agreement in the event that the licensee challenges the validity of one or more of the licensed intellectual property rights.

2. Where the undertakings party to the agreement are not competing undertakings, the exemption provided for in Article 2 shall not apply to any direct or indirect obligation limiting the licensee's ability to exploit its own technology or limiting the ability of any of the parties to the agreement to carry out research and development, unless such latter restriction is indispensable to prevent the disclosure of the licensed know-how to third parties.

Article 6
Withdrawal in individual cases

1. The Commission may withdraw the benefit of this Regulation, pursuant to Article 29(1) of Regulation (EC) No 1/2003, where it finds in any particular case that a technology transfer agreement to which the exemption provided for in Article 2 applies nevertheless has effects which are incompatible with Article 81(3) of the Treaty, and in particular where:

(a) access of third parties' technologies to the market is restricted, for instance by the cumulative effect of parallel networks of similar restrictive agreements prohibiting licensees from using third parties' technologies;

(b) access of potential licensees to the market is restricted, for instance by the cumulative effect of parallel networks of similar restrictive agreements prohibiting licensors from licensing to other licensees;

(c) without any objectively valid reason, the parties do not exploit the licensed technology.

2. Where, in any particular case, a technology transfer agreement to which the exemption provided for in Article 2 applies has effects which are incompatible with Article 81(3) of the Treaty in the territory of a Member State, or in a part thereof, which has all the characteristics of a distinct geographic market, the competition authority of that Member State may withdraw the benefit of this Regulation, pursuant to Article 29(2) of Regulation (EC) No 1/2003, in respect of that territory, under the same circumstances as those set out in paragraph 1 of this Article.

Commentary
Art 6: B&C: 9.167 F&N: 10.122
Art 6(1): B&C: 3.086 F&N: 10.123
Art 6(1)(a): B&C: 9.167 F&N: 10.123
Art 6(1)(b): B&C: 9.167 F&N: 10.123, 10.124
Art 6(1)(c): B&C: 9.167 F&N: 10.123
Art 6(2): B&C: 3.087, 9.167

Article 7
Non-application of this Regulation

1. Pursuant to Article 1a of Regulation No 19/65/EEC, the Commission may by regulation declare that, where parallel networks of similar technology transfer agreements cover more than 50% of a relevant market, this Regulation is not to apply to technology transfer agreements containing specific restraints relating to that market.

2. A regulation pursuant to paragraph 1 shall not become applicable earlier than six months following its adoption.

Commentary
Art 7: B&C: 3.089 F&N: 10.125
Art 7(1): B&C: 9.168
Art 7(2): B&C: 9.168

Article 8
Application of the market-share thresholds

1. For the purposes of applying the market-share thresholds provided for in Article 3 the rules set out in this paragraph shall apply.

The market share shall be calculated on the basis of market sales value data. If market sales value data are not available, estimates based on other reliable market information, including market sales volumes, may be used to establish the market share of the undertaking concerned.

The market share shall be calculated on the basis of data relating to the preceding calendar year.

The market share held by the undertakings referred to in point (e) of the second subparagraph of Article 1(2) shall be apportioned equally to each undertaking having the rights or the powers listed in point (a) of the second subparagraph of Article 1(2).

2. If the market share referred to in Article 3(1) or (2) is initially not more than 20% respectively 30% but subsequently rises above those levels, the exemption provided for in Article 2 shall continue to apply for a period of two consecutive calendar years following the year in which the 20% threshold or 30% threshold was first exceeded.

Commentary
Art 8: B&C: 9.144
Art 8(1): B&C: 9.144

Article 9
Repeal

Regulation (EC) No 240/96 is repealed.

References to the repealed Regulation shall be construed as references to this Regulation.

Article 10
Transitional period

The prohibition laid down in Article 81(1) of the Treaty shall not apply during the period from 1 May 2004 to 31 March 2006 in respect of agreements already in force on 30 April 2004 which do not satisfy the conditions for exemption provided for in this Regulation but which, on 30 April 2004, satisfied the conditions for exemption provided for in Regulation (EC) No 240/96.

Commentary
Art 10: **B&C:** 9.086, 9.130 **F&N:** 10.24

Article 11
Period of validity

This Regulation shall enter into force on 1 May 2004.

It shall expire on 30 April 2014.

Commentary
Art 11: **B&C:** 3.080

This Regulation shall be binding in its entirety and directly applicable in all Member States.

Done at Brussels, [7] April 2004.

Notes
The date of this Regulation is shown as corrected by the Corrigendum at OJ L 127, 29.4.2004, p. 158.

C8

COMMISSION NOTICE

of 18 December 1978
**concerning its assessment of certain subcontracting agreements
in relation to Article [81](1) of the EEC Treaty**

Official Journal C 1, 3.1.1979, p. 2

Celex No: 31979Y0103(01)

Notes
EEA application: the EFTA Surveillance Authority has adopted a parallel notice concerning its assessment of certain subcontracting agreements in relation to Article 53(1) of the EEA Agreement under Article 5(2)(b) of the Surveillance and Court Agreement: OJ L 153, 18.6.1994, p. 30 and EEA Supplement No 15, 18.6.1994, p. 29.
Commentary
Notice: **B&C:** 2.113, 6.190, 6.194, 9.139 **F&N:** 3.30

1. In this notice the Commission of the European Communities gives its view as to subcontracting agreements in relation to Article [81](1) of the Treaty establishing the European Economic Community. This class of agreement is at the present time a form of work distribution which concerns firms of all sizes, but which offers opportunities for development in particular to small and medium sized firms.

The Commission considers that agreements under which one firm, called "the contractor", whether or not in consequence of a prior order from a third party, entrusts to another, called "the subcontractor", the manufacture of goods, the supply of services or the performance of work under the contractor's instructions, to be provided to the contractor or performed on his behalf, are not of themselves caught by the prohibition in Article [81](1).

To carry out certain subcontracting agreements in accordance with the contractor's instructions, the subcontractor may have to make use of particular technology or equipment which the contractor will have to provide. In order to protect the economic value of such technology or equipment, the contractor may wish to restrict their use by the subcontractor to whatever is necessary for the purpose of the agreement. The question arises whether such restrictions are caught by Article [81](1). They are assessed in this notice with due regard to the purpose of such agreements, which distinguishes them from ordinary patent and know-how licensing agreements.

2. In the Commission's view, Article [81](1) does not apply to clauses whereby:
   — technology or equipment provided by the contractor may not be used except for the purposes of the subcontracting agreement,
   — technology or equipment provided by the contractor may not be made available to third parties,
   — the goods, services or work resulting from the use of such technology or equipment may be supplied only to the contractor or performed on his behalf,

   provided that and in so far as this technology or equipment is necessary to enable the subcontractor under reasonable conditions to manufacture the goods, to supply the services or to carry out the work in accordance with the contractor's instructions. To that extent the subcontractor is providing goods, services or work in respect of which he is not an independent supplier in the market.

   The above proviso is satisfied where performance of the subcontracting agreement makes necessary the use by the subcontractor of:
   — industrial property rights of the contractor or at his disposal, in the form of patents, utility models, designs protected by copyright, registered designs or other rights, or
   — secret knowledge or manufacturing processes (know-how) of the contractor or at his disposal, or of
   — studies, plans or documents accompanying the information given which have been prepared by or for the contractor, or
   — dies, patterns or tools, and accessory equipment that are distinctively the contractor's,

   which, even though not covered by industrial property rights nor containing any element of secrecy, permit the manufacture of goods which differ in form, function or composition from other goods manufactured or supplied on the market.

   However, the restrictions mentioned above are not justifiable where the subcontractor has at his disposal or could under reasonable conditions obtain access to the technology and equipment needed to produce the goods, provide the services or carry out the work. Generally, this is the case when the contractor provides no more than general information which merely describes the work to be done. In such circumstances the restrictions could deprive the subcontractor of the possibility of developing his own business in the fields covered by the agreement.

Commentary
para 2: **B&C:** 6.190

3. The following restrictions in connection with the provision of technology by the contractor may in the Commission's view also be imposed by subcontracting agreements without giving grounds for objection under Article [81](1):
   — an undertaking by either of the parties not to reveal manufacturing processes or other know-how of a secret character, or confidential information given by the other party during the negotiation and performance of the agreement, as long as the know-how or information in question has not become public knowledge,
   — an undertaking by the subcontractor not to make use, even after expiry of the agreement, of manufacturing processes or other know-how of a secret character received by him during the currency of the agreement, as long as they have not become public knowledge,
   — an undertaking by the subcontractor to pass on to the contractor on a non-exclusive basis any technical improvements which he has made during the currency of the agreement, or, where a patentable invention has been discovered by the subcontractor, to grant non-exclusive licences in respect of inventions relating to improvements and new applications of the original invention to the contractor for the term of the patent held by the latter.

This undertaking by the subcontractor may be exclusive in favour of the contractor in so far as improvements and inventions made by the subcontractor during the currency of the agreement are incapable of being used independently of the contractor's secret know-how or patent, since this does not constitute an appreciable restriction of competition.

However, any undertaking by the subcontractor regarding the right to dispose of the results of his own research and development work may restrain competition, where such results are capable of being used independently. In such circumstances, the subcontracting relationship is not sufficient to displace the ordinary competition rules on the disposal of industrial property rights or secret know-how.

Commentary
para 3: **B&C:** 6.191 **F&N:** 10.69

4. Where the subcontractor is authorized by a subcontracting agreement to use a specified trade mark, trade name or get up, the contractor may at the same time forbid such use by the subcontractor in the case of goods, services or work which are not to be supplied to the contractor.
5. Although this notice should in general obviate the need for firms to obtain a ruling on the legal position by an individual Commission Decision, it does not affect the right of the firms concerned to apply for negative [clearance] as defined by Article 2 of Regulation No 17 or to notify the agreement to the Commission under Article 4(1) of that Regulation.[1]

Notes
[1] First Regulation implementing Articles [81] and [82] of the EEC Treaty (OJ No 13, 21.2.1962, p. 204/62).

The 1968 notice on cooperation between enterprises,[2] which lists a number of agreements that by their nature are not to be regarded as anti-competitive, is thus supplemented in the subcontracting field. The Commission also reminds firms that, in order to promote cooperation between small and medium sized businesses, it has published a notice concerning agreements of minor importance which do not fall under Article [81](1) of the Treaty establishing the European Economic Community.[3]

Notes
[2] Notice concerning agreements, decisions and concerted practices relating to cooperation between enterprises (OJ No C 75, 29.7.1968, p. 3). [See now Commission Notice 2001/C 3/02, Guidelines on the applicability of Article 81 of the EC Treaty to horizontal cooperation agreements (OJ C 3, 06.01.2001, p. 2).]
[3] OJ C 313, 29.12.1977, p. 3. [See now Commission Notice on agreements of minor importance which do not appreciably restrict competition under Article 81(1) of the Treaty establishing the European Community (*de minimis*) (OJ C 368, 22.12.2001 p. 13).]

This notice is without prejudice to the view that may be taken of subcontracting agreements by the Court of Justice of the European Communities.

C9

COMMISSION NOTICE

concerning the assessment of cooperative joint ventures pursuant to
Article [81] of the [EC] Treaty

(93/C 43/02)

Official Journal C43, 16.2.93, p. 2

Notes

This notice is no longer in force, but remains of assistance.

Commentary

Notice: B&C: 2.113, 7.011, 7.026–7.027, 7.055 F&N: 7.86, 7.223–7.226, 7.260, 7.310
paras 27–31: F&N: 7.83
paras 59–62: B&C: 7.003
paras 70–76: B&C: 7.055

I. INTRODUCTION

1. Joint Ventures (JVs), as referred to in this Notice, embody a special, institutionally fixed form of cooperation between undertakings. They are versatile instruments at the disposal of the parents, with the help of which different goals can be pursued and attained.
2. JVs can form the basis and the framework for cooperation in all fields of business activity. Their potential area of application includes, inter alia, the procuring and processing of data, the organization of working systems and procedures, taxation and business consultancy, the planning and financing of investment, the implementation of research and development plans, the acquisition and granting of licences for the use of intellectual property rights, the supply of raw materials or semi-finished products, the manufacture of goods, the provision of services, advertising, distribution and customer service.

Commentary
para 2: B&C: 7.003

---

3. JVs can fulfil one or more of the aforementioned tasks. Their activity can be limited in time or be of an unlimited duration. The broader the concrete and temporal framework of the cooperation, the stronger it will influence the business policy of the parents in relation to each other and to third parties. If the JV concerns market-orientated matters such as purchasing, manufacturing, sales or the provision of services, it will normally lead to coordination, if not even to a uniformity of the competitive behaviour of the parents at that particular economic level. This is all the more true where a JV fulfils all the functions of a normal undertaking and consequently behaves on the market as an independent supplier or purchaser. The creation of a JV which combines wholly or in part the existing activities of the parents in a particular economic area or takes over new activities for the parents, brings, over and above that, a change in the structure of the participating enterprises.
4. The assessment of cooperative joint ventures pursuant to Article [81](1) and (3) does not depend on the legal form which the parents choose for their cooperation. The applicability of the prohibition of restrictive practices depends, on the contrary, on whether the creation or the activities of the JV may affect trade between Member States and have as their object or effect the prevention, restriction or distortion of competition within the common market. The question whether an exemption can be granted to a JV will depend on the one hand on its overall economic benefits and on the other hand on the nature and scope of the restrictions of competition it entails.
5. In view of the variety of situations which come into consideration it is impossible to make general comments on the compliance of JVs with competition law. For a large proportion of JVs, whether or not they fall within the scope of application of Article [81] depends on their particular activity.[1]

For other JVs, prohibition will occur only if particular legal and factual circumstances coincide, the existence of which must be determined on a case-by-case basis.[2] Exemptions from the prohibition are based on the analysis of the overall economic balance, the results of which can turn out differently.[3] Cooperative joint ventures can however be divided into different categories, which are each open to the same competition law analysis.

Notes

[1] See below III. 1, point 15.

[2] See below III.2 and 3, points 17 et seq. 32 et seq.

[3] See below IV.1 and 2, points 43 et seq. and 52 et seq.

6. In the Commission Notice of 1968 concerning agreements, decisions and concerted practices in the field of cooperation between enterprises,[4] the Commission listed a series of types of cooperation which by their nature are not prohibited because they do not have as their object or effect the restriction of competition within the meaning of Article [81](1). The 1986 Notice on agreements of minor importance[5] sets out quantitative criteria for those arrangements which are not prohibited because they have no appreciable impact on competition or inter-State trade. Both Notices apply to JVs. Commission Regulations (EEC) No 417/85, (EEC) No 418/ 85, (EEC) No 2349/84 and (EEC) No 556/89 on the application of Article [81](3) of the Treaty to specialization agreements,[6] research and development agreements,[7] patent licensing agreements[8] and know-how licensing agreements,[9] as amended by Regulation (EEC) [151/93],[10] include JVs amongst the beneficiaries of these group exemptions,[11] Further general indications on the assessment of cooperative JVs for competition purposes can be found in the numerous decisions and notices of the Commission in individual cases.[12]

Notes

[4] OJ C75, 29.7.68, p. 3; corrected by OJ C84, 28.8.68, p.14.

[5] OJ C 231, 12.9.86, p. 2.

[6] OJ L 53, 22.2.85, p. 1.

[7] OJ L 53, 22.2.85, p. 5.

[8] OJ L 219, 16.8.84, p. 15; corrected by OJ L 280, 22.10.85, p. 32.

[9] OJ L 61, 4.3.89, p. 1.

[10] [OJ L 21, 29.1.1993, p. 8].

[11] See below IV.1, points 43 et seq.

[12] For references and summaries see the Commission Competition Policy Reports.

7. The Commission will hereinafter summarize its administrative practice to date. In this way undertakings will be informed about both the legal and economic criteria which will guide the Commission in the future application of Article [81](1) and (3) to cooperative joint ventures. This Notice applies to all JVs which do not fall within the scope of application of Article 3 of Council Regulation (EEC) No 4064/89 of 21.12.1989 on the control of concentrations between undertakings.[13] It forms the counterpart of the Notice regarding concentrative and cooperative operations[14] and the Notice on restrictions ancillary to concentrations[15] which clarify the above-mentioned Regulation. Links between undertakings other than JVs will not be dealt with in this Notice, even though they often have similar effects on competition in the common market and on trade between Member States. Having regard to the experience of the Commission, however, no generally applicable conclusions can yet be drawn.

Notes

[13] OJ L 395, 30.12.1989, p. 1; corrected by OJ No L 257, 21.1990, p. 13.

[14] OJ C 203, 14.8. 1990, p. 10.

[15] OJ C 203, 14.8.1990, p. 5.

8. This notice is without prejudice to the power of national courts in the Member States to apply Article [81](1) and group exemptions under Article [81](3) on the basis of their own jurisdiction. Nevertheless it constitutes a factor which the national courts can take into account when deciding

a dispute before them. It is also without prejudice to any interpretation which may be given by the Court of Justice of the European Communities.

II. The Concept of Cooperative Joint Ventures

9. The concept of cooperative joint ventures can be derived from Regulation (EEC) No 4064/89. According to Article 3(1), a JV is an undertaking under the joint control of several other undertakings, the parents. Control, according to Article 3(3), consists of the possibility of exercising a decisive influence on the activities of the undertaking. Whether joint control, the prerequisite of every JV, exists, is determined by the legal and factual circumstances of the individual case. For details refer to the Notice regarding concentrative and cooperative operations.[16]

Notes
[16] See points 6 to 14.

10. According to Article 3(2) of Regulation (EEC) No 4064/89, any JV which does not fulfil the criteria of a concentration, is cooperative in nature. Under the second subparagraph, this applies to:
   — all JVs, the activities of which are not to be performed on a lasting basis, especially those limited in advance by the parents to a short time period,
   — JVs which do not perform all the functions of an autonomous economic entity, especially those charged by their parents simply with the operation of particular functions of an undertaking (partial-function JVs),
   — JVs which perform all the functions of an autonomous economic entity (full-function JVs) where they give rise to coordination of competitive behaviour by the parents in relation to each other or to the JV.
   The delimitation of cooperative and concentrative operations can be difficult in individual cases. The abovementioned Commission Notice[17] contains detailed instructions for the solution of this problem. Additional indications can also be gained from the practice of the Commission under Regulation (EEC) No 4064/89.[18]

Notes
[17] See points 15 and 16.
[18] See on the one hand Decisions (pursuant to Article 6(1)(a) of Regulation (EEC) No 4064/89); *Renault/Volvo*; *Baxter/Nestlé/Salvia*; *Apollinaris/Schweppes*; *Elf Enterprise*; *Sunrise*; *BSN/Nestlé/Cokoladovny*; *Flachglas/Vegla*; *Eureko, Herba/IRR*; *Koipe-Tabacalera/Elosua*; on the other hand Decisions (pursuant to Article 6(1)(b) of Regulation (EEC) No 4064/89): *Sanofi/Sterling Drugs*; *Elf/BC/Cepsa*; *Dräger/IBM/HMP*; *Thomson/Pilkington*; *UAP/Transatlantic/Sun Life*; *TNT/GD Net*; *Lucas/Eaton*; *Courtaulds/SNIA*; *Volvo/Atlas*; *Ericsson/Kolbe*; *Spar/Dansk Supermarket*; *Generali/ BCHA*; *Mondi/Frantschach*; *Eucom/Digital*; *Ericsson/Ascom*; *Thomas Cook/LTU/West LB*; *Elf-Atochem/Rohm & Haas*; *Rhône-Poulenc/SNIA*; *Northern Telecom/Matra Telecommunications*; *Avesta/British Steel*; *NCC/AGA/Axel Johnson*; (References and summaries in the Commission Competition Policy Reports).

11. Cooperative JVs are outside the scope of the provisions on merger control. The determination of the cooperative character of a JV has however no substantive legal effects. It simply means that the JV is subject to the procedures set out in Regulation No 17[19] or Regulations (EEC) No 1017/68,[20] (EEC) No 4056/86[21] or (EEC) No 3975/87[22] in the determination of its compliance with Article [81](1) and (3).

Notes:
[19] OJ 13, 21.2.1962, p. 204/62. [See now Council Regulation (EC) 1/2003, L1, 4.1.2003, p. 1.]
[20] OJ L 175, 23.7 1968, p. 10.
[21] OJ L 378, 31.12.1986, p. 4.
[22] OJ L 374, 31.12. 1987, p. 1.

III. Assessment Pursuant to Article 81

1. General comments

12. JVs can be caught by the prohibition of cartels only where they fulfil all the requisite elements pursuant to Article [81](1).

13. The creation of a JV is usually based on an agreement between undertakings and sometimes on a decision of an association of undertakings. The exercise of control as well as the management of the business is likewise usually governed by contract. Where there is no agreement, which is the case for instance in the acquisition of a joint controlling interest in an existing company by the purchase of shares on the stock exchange, the continued existence of the JV depends on the parent companies their policy towards the JV and their manner of controlling it.

14. Whether the aforementioned agreements, decisions or concerted practices are likely to affect trade between Member States, can be decided only on a case-by-case basis. Where the JVs actual or foreseeable effects on competition are limited to the territory of one Member State or to territories outside the Community, Article [81](1) will not apply.

15. Article [81](1) does not therefore apply to certain categories of JV because they do not have as their object or effect the prevention, restriction or distortion of competition. This is particularly true for:
    — JVs formed by parents which all belong to the same group and which are not in a position freely to determine their market behaviour: in such a case its creation is merely a matter of internal organization and allocation of tasks within the group,
    — JVs of minor economic importance within the meaning of the 1986 Notice;[23] there is no appreciable restriction of competition where the combined turnover of the participating undertakings does not exceed ECU 200 million and their market share is not more than 5%,
    — JVs with activities neutral to competition within the meaning of the 1968 Notice on cooperation between enterprises:[24] the types of cooperation referred to therein do not restrict competition because:
    — they have as their sole object the procurement of non-confidential information and therefore serve in the preparation of autonomous decisions of the participating enterprises,[25]
    — they have as their sole object management cooperation;[26]
    — they have as their sole object cooperation in fields removed from the market,[27]
    — they are concerned solely with technical and organizational arrangements;[28]
    — they concern solely arrangements between non-competitors,[29]
    — even though they concern arrangements between competitors, they neither limit the parties competitive behaviour nor affect the market position of third parties.[30]

The aforementioned characteristics for distinguishing between conduct restrictive of competition and conduct which is neutral from a competition point of view are not fixed, but form part of the general development of Community law. They must therefore be construed and applied in the light of the case-law of the Court of Justice as well as of the Commissions decisions. In addition, general Commission notices are modified from time to time in order to adapt them to the evolution of the law.

Notes
[23] OJ C 231, 12.9.1986, p. 2.
[24] OJ C 75, 29.7.1968, p. 3; corrected by OJ C 93, 18.9.1968, p. 14.
[25] See II, point 1.
[26] See II, point 2.
[27] See II, point 3.
[28] See II, point 4.
[29] See II, points 5 and 6.
[30] See II, points 7 and 8.

Commentary
para 15: B&C: 7.011

16. JVs which do not fall into any of the abovementioned categories must be individually examined to see whether they have the object or effect of restricting competition. The basic principles of the Notice on cooperation can be useful in such examination. The Commission will explain below on what criteria it assesses the restrictive character of a JV.

2. Criteria for the establishment of restrictions of competition

17. The appraisal of a cooperative JV in the light of the competition rules will focus on the relationship between the enterprises concerned and on the effects of their cooperation on third parties. In this respect the first task is to check whether the creation or operation of the JV is likely to prevent, restrict or distort competition between the parents. Secondly, it is necessary to examine whether the operation in question is likely to affect appreciably the competitive position of third parties, especially with regard to supply and sales possibilities. The relationship of the parents to the JV requires a separate legal assessment only if the JV is a full-function undertaking. However, even here the assessment must always take into account the relationship of the parents to each other and to third parties. Prevention, restriction or distortion of competition will be brought about by a JV only if its creation or activity affects the conditions of competition on the relevant market. The evaluation of a JV pursuant to Article [81](1) therefore always implies defining the relevant geographic and product market. The criteria to apply in that process are to be drawn from the de minimis Notice and the Commissions previous decisions. Special attention must be paid to networks of JVs which are set up by the same parents, by one parent with different partners or by different parents in parallel. They form an important element of the market structure and may therefore be of decisive influence in determining whether the creation of a JV leads to restrictions of competition.

Commentary
para 17: B&C: 7.034

(a) *Competition between parent companies*

18. Competition between parent companies can be prevented, restricted or distorted through cooperation in a JV only to the extent that companies are already actual or potential competitors. The assumption of potential competitive circumstances presupposes that each parent alone is in a position to fulfil the tasks assigned to the JV and that it does not forfeit its capabilities to do so by the creation of the JV. An economically realistic approach is necessary in the assessment of any particular case.

Commentary
para 18: B&C: 7.026

19. The Commission has developed a set of questions, which aim to clarify the theoretical and practical existing possibilities for the parents to perform the tasks individually instead of together.[31] Although these questions are designed to apply in particular to the case of manufacturing of goods, they are also relevant to the provision of services. They are as follows:
   — *Contribution to the JV*
      Does each parent company have sufficient financial resources to carry out the planned investment? Does each parent company have sufficient managerial qualifications to run the JV? Does each parent company have access to the necessary input products?
   — *Production of the JV*
      Does each parent know the production technique?
      Does each parent make the upstream or downstream products himself and does it have access to the necessary production facilities?
   — *Sales by the JV*
      Is actual or potential demand such as to enable each parent company to manufacture the product on its own? Does each parent company have access to the distribution channels needed to sell the product manufactured by the JV?
   — *Risk factors*
      Can each parent company on its own bear the technical and financial risks associated with the production operations of the JV?

— *Access to the relevant market*

What is the relevant geographic and product market? What are the barriers to entry into that market? Is each parent company capable of entering that market on its own? Can each parent overcome existing barriers within a reasonable time and without undue effort or cost?

Notes

[31] See Thirteenth Competition Policy Report (1983), point 55.

Commentary

para 19: B&C: 7.045

20. The parents of a JV are potential competitors, in so far as in the light of the above factors, which may be given different weight from case to case, they could reasonably be expected to act autonomously. In that connection, analysis must focus on the various stages of the activity of an undertaking. The economic pressure towards cooperation at the R&D stage does not normally eliminate the possibility of competition between the participating undertakings at the production and distribution stages. The pooling of the production capacity of several undertakings, when it is economically unavoidable and thus unobjectionable as regards competition law, does not necessarily imply that these undertakings should also cooperate in the distribution of the products concerned.

(b) *Competition between the parent companies and the JV*

21. The relationship between the parents and the JV takes a specific significance when the JV is a full-function JV and is in competition with, or is a supplier or a customer of, at least one of the parents. The applicability of the prohibition on cartels depends on the circumstances of the individual case. As anti-competitive behaviour between the parents will as a rule also influence business relationships between the parents and the JV and conversely, anti-competitive behaviour by the JV and one of the parents will always affect relationships between the parents, a global analysis of all the different relationships is necessary. The Commissions decisions offer plenty of examples of this.

22. The restriction of competition, within the meaning of Article [81](1), between parents and JVs typically manifests itself in the division of geographical markets, product markets (especially through specialization) or customers. In such cases the participating undertakings reduce their activity to the role of potential competitors. If they remain active competitors, they will usually be tempted to reduce the intensity of competition by coordinating their business policy, especially as to prices and volume of production or sales or by voluntarily restraining their efforts.

(c) *Effects of the JV on the position of third parties*

23. The restrictive effect on third parties depends on the JVs activities in relation to those of its parents and on the combined market power of the undertakings concerned.

24. Where the parent companies leave it to the JV to handle their purchases or sales, the choice available to suppliers or customers may be appreciably restricted. The same is true when the parents arrange for the JV to manufacture primary or intermediate products or to process products which they themselves have produced. The creation of a JV may even exclude from the market the parents traditional suppliers and customers. That risk increases in step with the degree of oligopolisation of the market and the existence of exclusive or preferential links between the JV and its parents.

25. The existence of a JV in which economically significant undertakings pool their respective market power may even be a barrier to market entry by potential competitors and/or impede the growth of the parent competitors.

(d) *Assessment of the appreciable effect of restrictions of competition*

26. The scale of a JVs effects on competition depends on a number of factors, the most important of which are:

— the market shares of the parent companies and the JV, the structure of the relevant market and the degree of concentration in the sector concerned,

— the economic and financial strength of the parent companies, and any commercial or technical edge which they may have in comparison to their competitors,

— the market proximity of the activities carried out by the JV,

— whether the fields of activity of the parent companies and the JV are identical or interdependent,

— the scale and significance of the JVs activities in relation to those of its parents,

— the extent to which the arrangements between the firms concerned are restrictive,

— the extent to which market access by third parties is restricted.

(e) *JV networks*

27. JV networks can particularly restrict competition because they increase the influence of the individual JV on the business policy of the parents and on the market position of third parties. The assessment under competition law must take into account the different ways of arranging JV networks just as much as the cumulative effects of parallel existing networks.

28. Often competing parent companies set up several JVs which are active in the same product market but in different geographical markets. On the top of the restrictions of competition which can already be attributed to each JV, there will then be those which arise in the relationships between the individual JVs. The ties between the parents are strengthened by the creation of every further JV so that any competition which still exists between them will be further reduced.

29. The same is true in the case where competing parents set up several JVs for complementary products which they themselves intend to process or for non-complementary products which they themselves distribute. The extent and intensity of the restrictive effects on competition are also increased in such cases. Competition is most severely restricted where undertakings competing within the same oligopolistic economic sector set up a multitude of JVs for related products or for a great variety of intermediate products. These considerations are also valid for the service sector.

30. Even where a JV is created by non-competing undertakings and does not, on its own, cause any restriction of competition, it can be anti-competitive if it belongs to a network of JVs set up by one of the parents for the same product market with different partners, because competition between the JVs may then be prevented, restricted or distorted.[32] If the different partners are actual or potential competitors, there will additionally be restrictive effects in the relationships between them.

Notes

[32] See Decision *Optical Fibres*, OJ L 236, 22.8.1986, p. 30.

31. Parallel networks of JVs, involving different parent companies, simply reveal the degree of personal and financial connection between the undertakings of an economic sector or between several economic sectors. They form, in so far as they are comparable to the degree of concentration on the relevant market, an important aspect of the economic environment which has to be taken into account in the assessment from a competition point of view of both the individual networks and the participating JVs.

3. Assessment of the most important types of JV

(a) *Joint ventures between non-competitors*

32. This group rarely causes problems for competition, whether the JV fulfils merely partial or the full functions of an undertaking. In the first case one must simply examine whether market access of third parties is significantly affected by the cooperation between the parents.[33] In the second case the emphasis of the examination is on the same question and the problem of competition restrictions between one of the parents and the JV[34] is usually only of secondary significance.

Notes

[33] See above III.2(c), points 23, 24 and 25.
[34] See above III.2(b), points 21 and 22.

33. JVs between non-competitors created for research and development, for production or for distribution of goods including customer service do not in principle fall within Article [81](1). The non-application of the prohibition is justified by the combination of complementary knowledge, products and services in the JV. That is, however, subject to the reservation that there remains room for a sufficient number of R&D centres, production units and sales channels in the

respective area of economic activity of the JV.[35] The same reasoning also applies to the assessment of purchasing JVs for customers from different business sectors. Such JVs are unobjectionable from a competition point of view as long as they leave suppliers with sufficient possibilities of customer choice.

Notes

[35] See Section II of the Notice on cooperation, points 3 and 6, and Regulation (EEC) No 418/85 on the application of Article [81](3) of the Treaty to categories of research and development agreements, OJ L 53, 22.2.1985, p. 5.

34. JVs which manufacture exclusively for their parents primary or intermediate products or undertake processing for one or more of their parents do not, as a rule, restrict competition. A significant restriction of the supply and sales possibilities of third parties, a prerequisite for the application of the prohibition, can occur only if the parents have a strong market position in the supply or demand of the relevant products.

35. In the assessment of a full-function JV it is essential whether the activities the JV pursues are closely linked to those of the parents. In addition, the relationship of the activities of the parents to each other is of importance. If the JV trades in a product market which is upstream or downstream of the market of a parent, restrictions of competition can occur in relation to third parties, if the participants are undertakings with market power.[36] If the market of the JV is upstream of the market of one of the parents and at the same time downstream of the market of another parent, the JV functions as a connection between the two parents and also possibly as a vertical multi-level integration instrument. In such a situation the exclusive effects with regard to third parties are reinforced. Whether it fulfils the requisite minimum degree for the application of Article [81](1) can be decided only on an individual basis. If the JV and one of the parents trade in the same product market, then coordination of their market behaviour is probable if not inevitable.[37]

Notes

[36] No negative effect was found by the Commission in Decision 86/405/EEC (*Optical Fibres*), OJ L 236, 22.8.1986, p. 30, and in Decision 90/410/EEC (*Elopak/Metal Box-Odin*), OJ L 209, 8.8.1990, p. 15.
[37] See above III.2(b), point 22, and Decision 87/100/EEC (*Mitchell Cotts/Sofiltra*), OJ L 41, 11.2.1987, p. 31.

(b) *Joint ventures by competitors*

36. In this situation the effects of the JV on competition between the parents and on the market position of third parties must be analysed. The relationship between the activities of the JV and those of the parents is of decisive importance. In the absence of any interplay, Article [81](1) will usually not be applicable. The competition law assessment of the different types of JV leads to the following results.

37. A research and development JV may, in exceptional cases, restrict competition if it excludes individual activity in this area by the parents or if competition by the parents on the market for the resulting products will be restricted. This will normally be the case where the JV also assumes the exploitation of the newly developed or improved products or processes.[38] Whether the restriction of competition between the parents and the ensuing possible secondary effects on third parties are appreciable can be decided only on a case-by-case basis.

Notes

[38] See Notice in cooperation, II, point 3 and Regulation (EEC) No 418/85 (cited in footnote 7).

38. Sales JVs, selling the products of competing manufacturers, restrict competition between the parents on the supply side and limit the choice of purchasers. They belong to the category of traditional horizontal cartels which are subject to the prohibition of Article [81](1),[39] when they have an appreciable effect on the market.

Notes

[39] See the following decisions: NCH, OJ L 22, 26.1.1972, p. 16; *Cementregeling voor Nederland*, OJ L 303, 31.12.1972, p. 7; *Cimbel*, OJ L 303, 31.12.1972, p. 24; *CSV*, OJ L 242, 4.9. 1978, p. 15; *UIP*, OJ L 226, 3.8.1989, p. 25 and *Astra*, [OJ L 20, 28.1.1993, p. 23].

Commentary
para 38: F&N: 7.260

39. Purchasing JVs set up by competitors can give the participants an advantageous position on the demand side and reduce the choice of suppliers. Depending on the importance of the jointly-sold products to the production and sales activities of the parents, the cooperation can also lead to a considerable weakening of price competition between the participating undertakings. This applies even more so when the purchase price makes up a significant part of the total cost of the products distributed by the parents. The application of Article [81](1) depends on the circumstances of the individual case.[40]

Notes
[40] See the following decisions: *Socemas*, OJ L 201, 12.8.1968, p. 4; *Intergroup*, OJ L 212, 9.8.1975, p. 23; *National Sulphuric Acid Association*, I, OJ L 260, 3.10.1980, p. 24 and (II) OJ L 190, 5.7.1989, p. 25; *Filmeinkauf Deutscher Fernsehanstalten*, OJ L 284, 3.10.1989, p. 36; and *IJsselcentrale*, OJ L 28, 2.2.1991, p. 32.

40. JVs which manufacture primary or intermediate products for competing parent companies, which are further processed by them into the final product, must be assessed on the same principles. On the other hand, if the JV undertakes the processing of basic materials supplied by the parents, or the processing of half-finished into fully-finished products, with the aim of resupplying the parents, then competition between the participating undertakings, taking into consideration the market proximity of their cooperation and the inherent tendency to align prices, will usually exist only in a weaker form.[41] This is particularly so when the entire production activities of the parents are concentrated in the JV and the parents withdraw to the role of pure distributors. This leads to the standardization of manufacturing costs and the quality of the products so that essentially the only competition between the parents is on trade margins. This is a considerable restriction of competition which cannot be remedied by the parents marketing the products under different brand names.[42]

Notes
[41] See Notice in *Exxon/Shell*, [OJ C 92, 2.4.1993, p. 2].
[42] See Decision 91/38/EEC (*KSB/Goulds/Lowara/ITT*), OJ 19, 25.1.1991, p. 25; the anticompetitive character of joint economic production is acknowledged in principle in Regulation (EEC) No 417/85 on the application of Article [81](3) of the EEC Treaty to categories of specialization agreements, OJ L 53, 22.2.1985, p. 1.

41. Different situations must be distinguished when assessing full-function JVs between competing undertakings.[43]
   — Where the JV operates on the same market as its parents, the normal consequence is that competition between all participating undertakings will be restricted.
   — Where the JV operates on a market upstream or downstream of that of the parents with which it has supply or delivery links, the effects on competition will be the same as in the case of a production JV.
   — Where the JV operates on a market adjacent to that of its parents, competition can only be restricted when there is a high degree of interdependence between the two markets. This is especially the case when the JV manufactures products which are complementary to those of its parents.
   Combinations of various types of JV are often found in economic life so that an overall assessment of the resultant restrictions of competition between participating undertakings and the consequences of the cooperation on third parties must be carried out. In addition the economic circumstances must be taken into account, especially the association of a JV to a network with other JVs and the existence of several parallel JV networks within the same economic sector.[44]

Notes
[43] See in particular the following decisions: *Bayer/Gist-Brocades*, OJ L 30, 5.2.1976, p. 13; *United Reprocessors and KEWA*, OJ L 51, 26.2.1976, pp. 7, 15; *Vacuum Interrupters I*, OJ L 48, 19.2.1977, p. 32, and *II*, OJ L 383, 31.12.1980, p. 1; *De Laval/Stork I*, OJ L 215, 23.8.1977, p. 11, and *II*, OJ L 59, 4.3.1988, p. 32; *GEC/Weir*, OJ L 327, 20.12.1977, p. 26; *WANO/Schwarzpulver*, OJ L 322, 16.11.1978, p. 26; *Langenscheidt/Hachette*, OJ L 39, 11.2.1982, p. 25; *Amersham/Buchler*, OJ L 314, 10.11.1982, p. 34; *Rockwell/Iveco*, OJ L 224, 17.8.1983, p. 19; *Carbon Gas Technologie*, OJ L 376, 31.12.1983, p. 17; *Enichem/ICI*, OJ L 50, 24.2.1988, p. 18; *Bayer/BP Chemicals*,

OJ L 150, 16.6.1988, p. 35; *Iveco/Ford*, OJ L 230, 19.8.1988, p. 39; *Alcatel Espace/ANT*, OJ L 32, 3.2.1990, p. 19; *Konsortium ECR 900*, OJ L 228, 22.8.1990, p. 31; *Screensport/EBU — Eurosport*, OJ L 63, 9.3.1991, p. 32; *Eirpage*, OJ L 306, 7.11.1991, p. 22; *Procter and Gamble/Finaf*, OJ C 3, 7.1.1992, p. 2 and *Infonet*, OJ C 7, 11.1.1992, p. 3.
[44] See above III.2 (e), points 27 to 31.

Commentary
para 41: F&N: 7.75

42. Even JVs between competitors, which are usually caught by the prohibition in Article [81](1), must be examined to see whether in the actual circumstances of the individual case they have as their object or effect the restriction, prevention or distortion of competition. This will not be the case where cooperation in the form of a JV can objectively be seen as the only possibility for the parents to enter a new market or to remain in their existing market, provided that their presence will strengthen competition or prevent it from being weakened. Under these conditions the JV will neither reduce existing competition nor prevent potential competition from being realized. The prohibition in Article [81](1) will therefore not apply.[45]

Notes
[45] See the following decisions: *Alliance des constructeurs français de machines-outils*, OJ L 201, 12.8.1968, p. 1; *SAFCO*, OJ L 13, 17.1.1972, p. 44; *Metaleurop*, OJ L 179, 12.7.1990, p. 41; *Elopak/Metal Box-Odin*, OJ L 209, 8.8.1990, p. 15; *Konsortium ECR 900*, OJ L 228, 22.8.1990, p. 31.

IV. ASSESSMENT PURSUANT TO ARTICLE [81](3)

1. Group exemptions

43. JVs falling within the scope of Article [81](1) are exempted from the prohibition if they fulfil the conditions of a group exemption. Two Commission regulations legalize cooperation between undertakings in the form of JVs. Two other Commission regulations authorize certain restrictive agreements on the transfer of technology to a JV by its parents. The field of application of these group exemption regulations will be considerably expanded, notably for JVs, by Regulation (EEC) No [151/93].[46]

Notes
[46] [OJ L 21, 29.1.1993, p.8.]

(a) *Specialization Regulation*

44. Regulation (EEC) No 417/85 on the application of Article [81](3) to categories of specialization agreements[47] includes, *inter alia*, agreements whereby several undertakings leave the manufacture of certain products to a JV set up by them. This transfer can be for existing or future production. The creation and use of production JVs are exempted only if the aggregate market share of the participating undertakings does not exceed 20% and the cumulated turnover does not exceed ECU 1 000 million. Agreements between more sizable undertakings, the turnover of which exceeds ECU 1 000 million, also benefit from the group exemption if they are properly notified and the Commission does not object to the agreement within six months. This procedure is not applicable when the market share threshold is exceeded.

Notes
[47] OJ L 53, 22.2.1985, p. 1. [See now Commission Regulation (EC) No 2658/2000, OJ L 304, 5.12.2000, p. 3.]

45. The abovementioned rules apply exclusively to cooperation at the production level. The JV must supply all its production — which can include primary, intermediate or finished products — to its parents. The latter are not permitted to be active as manufacturers in the JVs area of production, but they may manufacture other products belonging to that product market. Products made by the JV are then sold by the parents, each of which can deal as exclusive distributor for a given territory.

46. Agreements in which the parents entrust JVs with the distribution of the contract products are also covered by the group exemption, though only under more rigorous conditions.

The aggregate market share of the participating undertakings must not exceed 10%. In this case also, there is a turnover threshold of ECU 1 000 million, the effect of which undertakings can avoid by resorting to the opposition procedure. Regulation (EEC) No 417/85 leaves the undertakings concerned free to organize their cooperation at the production and distribution stages. It allows for separate production followed by joint distribution of the contract products through a sales JV, as well as for the merging of production and distribution in a full-function JV, or the separation of both functions through the creation of a production JV and a sales JV. The production and/or distribution of the contract products can be entrusted to several JVs instead of one, which may, as the case may be, fulfil their function on the basis of exclusive contracts in various territories.

(b) *Research and development Regulation*

47. Regulation (EEC) No 418/85 on the application of Article [81](3) to categories of research and development agreements[48] provides for the exemption of JVs whose activities can range from R&D to the joint exploitation of results. The term exploitation covers the manufacture of new or improved products as well as the use of new or improved production processes, the marketing of products derived from R&D activities and the granting of manufacturing, use or distribution licences to third parties. The exemption is subject to the requirement that the joint R&D contributes substantially to technical or economic progress and is essential to the manufacture of new or improved products.

Notes
[48] OJ L 53, 22.2.1985, p. 5. [See now Commission Regulation (EC) No 2659/2000, OJ L 304, 15.12.2000, p. 7]

---

48. Regulation (EEC) No 418/85 also links exemption from the prohibition to quantitative conditions in the form of a two-fold market share limit. Cooperation in the form of a JV dealing with R&D, production and licensing policy will be permitted for parents who have an aggregate market share of up to 20%. In the area of R&D as well as manufacture, the Regulation allows all forms of coordination of behaviour because it does not require specialization. The parents can themselves remain or become active within the field of activity of the JV. They are also allowed to determine in what way they wish to use the possibilities of production by themselves or the licensing of third parties. By the allocation of contract territories the parents can protect themselves for the duration of the contract from the manufacture and use of the contract products by other partners in the reserved territories; furthermore, they can prevent other partners from pursuing an active marketing policy in those territories for five years after the introduction of the new or improved product into the common market. If, on the contrary, the partners entrust one or more JVs with the distribution of the contract products, a market share threshold of 10% is applicable to the whole of their cooperation. As Regulation (EEC) No 418/85 does not provide for a turnover threshold, all undertakings regardless of their size can benefit from the group exemption.

(c) *Patent-licensing and know-how licensing Regulations*

49. Regulation (EEC) No 2349/84 on the application of Article [81](3) of the Treaty to categories of patent licensing agreements[49] applies also to such agreements between any one of the parents and the JV affecting the activities of the JV. If the parents are competitors on the market of the contract products, the group exemption applies only up to a certain market share limit. This is 20% if the JV simply carries on manufacturing or 10% if it carries on the manufacture and marketing of the licensed products.

Notes
[49] OJ L 219, 16.8.1984, p. 15. [See now Commission Regulation 772/2004, OJ L 123, 27.4.2004, p. 11.]

---

50. Regulation (EEC) No 2349/84 also permits the granting of exclusive territorial manufacture and distribution licences to the JV, the protection of the licence territories of the JV and of the parents against active and passive competition by other participants for the duration of the contract and the protection of the licence territory of the JV against other licensees. The parents can protect the JV from an active distribution policy by other licensees for the full duration of the contract. During an initial five-year period from the introduction of a product into the common market,

it is possible to forbid direct imports of contract products by other licensees into the JVs licensed territory.

51. Regulation (EEC) No 556/89 on the application of Article [81](3) of the Treaty to certain categories of know-how licensing agreements[50] contains similar provisions, except that the territorial protection between the JV and the parents is limited to 10 years, beginning from the signature of the first know-how agreement concluded for a territory inside the Community. This point in time also marks the beginning of the period for which the JV can be protected against active competition (10 years) and passive competition (five years) by other licensees.

Notes
[50] OJ L 61, 4.3.1989, p. 1.

---

2. Individual Exemptions

(a) *General comments*

52. JVs which fall within Article [81](1) without fulfilling the conditions for the application of a group exemption regulation are not inevitably unlawful. They can be exempted by an individual decision of the Commission in so far as they fulfil the four conditions of Article [81](3). According to Articles 4, 5 and 15 of Regulation No 17 an individual exemption can be issued only if the participating undertakings have notified the agreement, decision or concerted practice on which cooperation is based, to the Commission. Certain arrangements which are less harmful to the development of the common market are dispensed from the requirement to notify by Article 4(2) of Regulation No 17. They can therefore be exempted without prior notification. The same applies to transport cartels within the meaning of Regulations (EEC) No 1017/68, (EEC) No 4056/86 and (EEC) No 3975/87.

53. The Commission must, pursuant to Article [81](3), examine:
    — whether the JV contributes to improving the production or distribution of goods or to promoting technical or economic progress,
    — whether consumers are allowed a fair share of the resulting benefit,
    — whether the parents or the JV are subject to restrictions which are not indispensable for the attainment of these objectives, and
    — whether the cooperation in the JV affords the undertakings concerned the possibility of eliminating competition in respect of a substantial part of the products or services in question.

    An exemption from the prohibition in Article [81](1) can be issued only if the answer to the first two questions is in the affirmative and the answer to the second two questions is negative.

(b) *Principles of assessment*

54. In order to fulfil the first two conditions of Article [81](3) the JV must bring appreciable objective advantages for third parties, especially consumers, which at least equal the consequent detriment to competition.

55. Advantages in the abovementioned sense, which can be pursued and attained with the aid of a JV, include, in the Commissions opinion, in particular, the development of new or improved products and processes which are marketed by the originator or by third parties under licence. In addition, measures opening up new markets, leading to the sales expansion of the undertaking in new territories or the enlargement of its supply range by new products, will in principle be assessed favourably. In all these cases the undertakings in question contribute to dynamic competition, consolidating the internal market and strengthening the competitiveness of the relevant economic sector. Production and sales increases can also be a pro-competitive stimulant. On the other hand, the rationalization of production activities and distribution networks are rather a means of adapting supply to a shrinking or stagnant demand. It leads, however, to cost savings which, under effective competition, are usually passed on to customers as lower prices. Plans for the reduction of production capacity however lead mostly to price rises. Agreements of this latter type will be judged favourably only if they serve to overcome a structural crisis, to accelerate the removal of unprofitable production capacity from the market and thereby to re-establish competition in the medium term.

56. The Commission will give a negative assessment to agreements which have as their main purpose the coordination of actual or potential competition between the participating undertakings. This is especially so for joint price-fixing, the reduction of production and sales by establishing quotas, the division of markets and contractual prohibitions or restrictions on investment. JVs which are created or operated essentially to achieve such aims are nothing but classic cartels the anti-competitive effects of which are well known.

57. The pros and cons of a JV will be weighed against each other on an overall economic balance, by means of which the type and the extent of the respective advantages and risks can be assessed. If the parents are economically and financially powerful and have, over and above that a high market-share, their exemption applications will need a rigorous examination. The same applies to JVs which reinforce an existing narrow oligopoly or belong to a network of JVs.

Commentary
para 57: B&C: 7.057

58. The acceptance pursuant to Article [81](3) (a) of restrictions on the parents or the JV depends above all on the type and aims of the cooperation. In this context, the decisive factor is usually whether the contractual restriction on the parties economic freedom is directly connected with the creation of the JV and can be considered indispensable for its existence.[51] It is only for the restriction of global competition that Article [81](3)(b) sets an absolute limit. Competition must be fully functioning at all times. Agreements which endanger its effectiveness cannot benefit from individual exemption. This category includes JVs which, through the combination of activities of the parents, achieve, consolidate or strengthen a dominant position.

Notes
[51] See below V.2, point 70 et seq.

(c) *Assessment of the most important types of JV*

59. Pure research and development JVs which do not fulfil the conditions for group exemption under Regulation (EEC) No 418/85 can still in general be viewed positively. This type of cooperation normally offers important economic benefits without adversely affecting competition. That is also the case where the parents entrust the JV with the further task of granting licences to third parties. If the JV also takes on the manufacture of the jointly researched and developed product, the assessment for the purpose of exemption must include the principles which apply to production JVs.[52] JVs which are responsible for R&D, licensing, production and distribution are full-function JVs and must be analysed accordingly.[53]

Notes
[52] See below points 62 and 63.
[53] See below point 64.

60. Sales JVs belong to the category of classic horizontal cartels. They have as a rule the object and effect of coordinating the sales policy of competing manufacturers. In this way they not only close off price competition between the parents but also restrict the volume of goods to be delivered by the participants within the framework of the system for allocating orders. The Commission will therefore in principle assess sales JVs negatively.[54] The Commission takes a positive view however of those cases where joint distribution of the contract products is part of a global cooperation project which merits favourable treatment pursuant to Article [81](3) and for the success of which it is indispensable. The most important examples are sales JVs between manufacturers who have concluded a reciprocal specialization agreement, but wish to continue to offer the whole range of products concerned, or sales JVs set up for the joint exploitation of the results of joint R and D, even at the distribution stage. In other cases, an exemption can be envisaged only in certain specific circumstances.[55]

Notes
[54] See the NCH, *Cementregeling voor Nederland*, *Cimbel* and *CSV* decisions (all cited in footnote 39) and *Astra*, [OJ L 20, 28.1.1993, p. 23.]

[55] See Decision 89/467/EEC (*UIP*) (cited in footnote 40).

Commentary
para 60: F&N: 7.260, 7.287

61. Purchasing JVs contribute to the rationalization of ordering and to the better use of transport and store facilities but are at the same time an instrument for the setting of uniform purchase prices and conditions and often of purchase quotas. By combining their demand power in a JV, the parents can obtain a position of excessive influence vis-à-vis the other side of the market and distort competition between suppliers. Consequently, the disadvantages often outweigh the possible benefits which can accompany purchasing JVs, particularly those between competing producers. The Commission is correspondingly prepared to grant exemptions only in exceptional cases and then only if the parents retain the possibility of purchasing individually.[56] No decision has, however, concerned the most important of the purchasing JVs so far.

Notes
[56] See the *National Sulphuric Acid Association, Filmeinkauf deutscher Fernsehanstalten, IJsselcentrale* decisions (all cited in footnote 40).

Commentary
para 61: F&N: 7.310

62. Production JVs can serve different economic purposes. They will often be set up to create new capacity for the manufacture of particular products which are also manufactured by the parents.[57] In other cases the JV will be entrusted with the manufacture of a new product in the place of parents.[58] Finally, the JV can be entrusted with the combination of the production capacities of the parents and their expansion or reduction as necessary.

Notes
[57] See *Exxon/Shell* (footnote 41).
[58] See the *KSB/Goulds/Lowara/ITT* decision (cited in footnote 42).

63. In view of the various tasks of production JVs their assessment for exemption purposes will be carried out according to different yardsticks. JVs, for the expansion of production capacity or product range, can contribute not only to the prevention of parallel investment — which results in costs savings — but also to the stimulation of competition. The combination or reduction of existing production capacity is primarily a rationalization measure and is usually of a defensive nature. It is not always obvious that measures of this kind benefit third parties, especially consumers and they must therefore be justified individually. Generally applicable quantitative thresholds, for instance in the form of market share limits, cannot be fixed for production JVs. The more the competition between the parents is restricted, the more emphasis must be put on the maintenance of competition with third parties. The market share limit of 20% in the group exemption regulations can serve as a starting point for the assessment of production JVs in individual cases.

64. Full-function JVs, in so far as they are not price-fixing, quota-fixing or market-sharing cartels or vehicles for a coordination of the investment policies conducted by the parents which goes beyond the individual case, often form elements of dynamic competition and then deserve a favourable assessment.[59] As cooperation also includes distribution, the Commission has to take special care in assessing individual cases that no position of market power will be created or strengthened by entrusting the JV with all the functions of an undertaking, combined with the placing at its disposal of all the existing resources of the parents. To assess whether a full-function JV raises problems of compatibility with the competition rules or not, an important point of reference is the aggregate market share limit of 10% contained in the group exemption regulations. Below this threshold it can be assumed that the effect of exclusion from the market of third parties and the danger of creating, or reinforcing barriers to market entry will be kept within justifiable limits. A prerequisite is however that the market structure will continue to guarantee effective competition. If the said threshold is exceeded, an exemption will be considered only after a careful examination of each individual case.

Notes
[59] See the following decisions: *Amersham//Buchler*, OJ L 314, 10.11.1982, p. 34; *Rockwell/Iveco*, OJ L 224, 17.8.1983, p. 19; *Carbon Gas Technologie*, OJ L 376, 31.12.1983, p. 17; *Enichem/ICI*, OJ L 50, 24.2.1988, p. 18; *Bayer/BP Chemicals*, OJ L 150, 16.6.1988, p. 35; *Iveco/Ford*, OJ L 230, 19.8.1988, p. 39; *Alcatel Espace/ANT*, OJ L 32, 3.2.1990, p. 19; *Eirpage*, OJ L 306, 7.11.1991, p. 22; *Bayer/Gist-Brocades*, OJ L 30, 5.2.1976, p. 13; *United Reprocessors and KEWA*, OJ L 51, 26.2.1976, p. 7; *Vacuum Interrupters I*, OJ L 48, 19.2.1977, p. 32 and II, OJ L 383, 31.12.1980, p. 1; *De Laval/Stork I*, OJ L 215, 23.8.1977, p. 11 and *II*, OJ L 59, 4.3.1988, p. 32; *GEC/Weir*, OJ L 327, 20.12.1977, p. 26; *Langenscheidt/Hachette*, OJ L 39, 11.2.1982, p. 25; *Procter and Gamble/Finaf*, OJ C 3, 7.1.1992, p. 2; and *INFONET*, OJ C 7, 11.1.1992, p. 3.

V. Ancillary Restrictions

1. Principles of assessment

65. A distinction must be made between restrictions of competition which arise from the creation and operation of a JV, and additional agreements which would, on their own, also constitute restrictions of competition by limiting the freedom of action in the market of the participating undertakings. Such additional agreements are either directly related to and necessary for the establishment and operation of the JV in so far as they cannot be dissociated from it without jeopardizing its existence, or are simply concluded at the same time as the JVs creation without having those features.

66. Additional agreements which are directly related to the JV and necessary for its existence must be assessed together with the JV. They are treated under the rules of competition as ancillary restrictions if they remain subordinate in importance to the main object of the JV. In particular, in determining the necessity of the restriction, it is proper not only to take account of its nature, but equally to ensure that its duration, subject matter and geographical field of application do not exceed what the creation and operation of the JV normally requires.

67. If a JV does not fall within the scope of Article [81](1), then neither do any additional agreements which, while restricting competition on their own, are ancillary to the JV in the manner described above. Conversely, if a JV falls within the scope of Article [81](1), then so will any ancillary restrictions. The exemption from prohibition is based for both on the same principles. Ancillary restrictions require no special justification under Article [81](3). They will generally be exempted for the same period as the JV.

68. Additional agreements which are not ancillary to the JV normally fall within the scope of Article [81](1), even though the JV itself may not. For them to be granted an exemption under Article [81](3), a specific assessment of their benefits and disadvantages must be made. This assessment must be carried out separately from that of the JV.

69. In view of the diversity of JVs and of the additional restrictions that may be linked to them, only a few examples can be given of the application of existing principles. They are drawn from previous Commission practice.

2. Assessment of certain additional restrictions

70. Assessment of whether additional restrictions constitute an ancillary agreement must distinguish between those which affect the JV and those which affect the parents.

(a) *Restrictions on the JV*

71. Of the restrictions which affect the JV, those which give concrete expression to its object, such as contract clauses which specify the product range or the location of production, may be regarded as ancillary. Additional restrictions which go beyond the definition of the ventures object and which relate to quantities, prices or customers may not. The same can be said for export bans.

72. When the setting-up of the JV involves the creation of new production capacity or the transfer of technology from the parent, the obligation imposed on the JV not to manufacture or market products competing with the licensed products may usually be regarded as ancillary. The JV must seek to ensure the success of the new production unit, without depriving the parent companies of the necessary control over exploitation and dissemination of their technology.[60]

73. In certain circumstances, other restrictions on the JV can be classified as ancillary such as con-
    tract clauses which limit the cooperation to a certain area or to a specific technical application of
    the transferred technology. Such restrictions must be seen as the inevitable consequences of the
    parents wish to limit the cooperation to a specific field of activity without jeopardizing the object
    and existence of the JV.[61]

Notes
[61] *Elopak/Metal Box-Odin* (footnote 36).

74. Lastly, where the parent companies assign to the JV certain stages of production or the manufac-
    ture of certain products, obligations on the JV to purchase from or supply its parents may also be
    regarded as ancillary, at least during the JVs starting-up period.

(b) *Restrictions on the parent companies*

75. Restrictions which prohibit the parent companies from competing with the JV or from actively
    competing with it in its area of activity, may be regarded as ancillary at least during the JVs start-
    ing-up period. Additional restrictions relating to quantities, prices or customers, and export bans
    obviously go beyond what is required for the setting-up and operation of the JV.

76. The Commission has in one case regarded as ancillary, a territorial restriction imposed on a
    parent company where the JV was granted an exclusive manufacturing licence in respect of fields
    of technical application and product markets in which both the JV and the parent were to be
    active.[62] This decision was limited, however, to the starting-up period of the JV and appeared
    necessary for the parents to become established in a new geographical market with the help of the
    JV. In another case, the grant to the JV of an exclusive exploitation licence without time-limit was
    regarded as indispensable for its creation and operation. In this case the parent company granting
    the licence was not active in the same field of application or on the same product market as that for
    which the licence was granted.[63] This will generally be the case with JVs undertaking new activi-
    ties in respect of which the parent companies are neither actual nor potential competitors.

Notes
[62] *Mitchell Cotts/Sofiltra* (footnote 37).
[63] *Elopak/Metal Box-Odin* (footnote 36).

C10

COMMISSION NOTICE

on the definition of relevant market for the purposes of Community competition law

(97/C 372/03)

(Text with EEA relevance)

Official Journal C 372, 9.12.1997, p. 5

Celex No: 31997Y1209(01)

Notes
EEA application: the EFTA Surveillance Authority has adopted a parallel notice on the definition of the relevant market
for the purpose of competition law in the EEA under Article 5(2)(b) of the Surveillance and Court Agreement: OJ L
200, 16.7.1998, p. 48 and EEA Supplement No 28, 16.7.1998, p. 3.

Commentary
Notice: B&C: 1.066, 2.101, 2.128, 4.002, 4.004, 4.016–4.017, 4.056, 6.019, 8.009, 8.083, 10.033, 12.148 **F&N:**
1.132, 1.138, 1.156, 2.250, 4.43, 4.108, 5.208, 7.230, 7.333, 9.66, 9.270, 11.102, 14.16, 14.192, 15.66, 15.95

paras 28–30: B&C: 4.071
paras 28–31: B&C: 10.033

I. INTRODUCTION

1. The purpose of this notice is to provide guidance as to how the Commission applies the concept of relevant product and geographic market in its ongoing enforcement of Community competition law, in particular the application of Council Regulation No 17 and (EEC) No 4064/89, their equivalents in other sectoral applications such as transport, coal and steel, and agriculture, and the relevant provisions of the EEA Agreement.[1] Throughout this notice, references to Articles [81] and [82] of the Treaty and to merger control are to be understood as referring to the equivalent provisions in the EEA Agreement and the ECSC Treaty.

Notes

[1] The focus of assessment in State aid cases is the aid recipient and the industry/sector concerned rather than identification of competitive constraints faced by the aid recipient. When consideration of market power and therefore of the relevant market are raised in any particular case, elements of the approach outlined here might serve as a basis for the assessment of State aid cases.

2. Market definition is a tool to identify and define the boundaries of competition between firms. It serves to establish the framework within which competition policy is applied by the Commission. The main purpose of market definition is to identify in a systematic way the competitive constraints that the undertakings involved[2] face. The objective of defining a market in both its product and geographic dimension is to identify those actual competitors of the undertakings involved that are capable of constraining those undertakings' behaviour and of preventing them from behaving independently of effective competitive pressure. It is from this perspective that the market definition makes it possible inter alia to calculate market shares that would convey meaningful information regarding market power for the purposes of assessing dominance or for the purposes of applying Article [81].

Notes

[2] For the purposes of this notice, the undertakings involved will be, in the case of a concentration, the parties to the concentration; in investigations within the meaning of Article [82] of the Treaty, the undertaking being investigated or the complainants; for investigations within the meaning of Article [81], the parties to the Agreement.

3. It follows from point 2 that the concept of "relevant market" is different from other definitions of market often used in other contexts. For instance, companies often use the term "market" to refer to the area where it sells its products or to refer broadly to the industry or sector where it belongs.

Commentary
para 3: B&C: 4.003

4. The definition of the relevant market in both its product and its geographic dimensions often has a decisive influence on the assessment of a competition case. By rendering public the procedures which the Commission follows when considering market definition and by indicating the criteria and evidence on which it relies to reach a decision, the Commission expects to increase the transparency of its policy and decision-making in the area of competition policy.
5. Increased transparency will also result in companies and their advisers being able to better anticipate the possibility that the Commission may raise competition concerns in an individual case. Companies could, therefore, take such a possibility into account in their own internal decision-making when contemplating, for instance, acquisitions, the creation of joint ventures, or the establishment of certain agreements. It is also intended that companies should be in a better position to understand what sort of information the Commission considers relevant for the purposes of market definition.
6. The Commission's interpretation of "relevant market" is without prejudice to the interpretation which may be given by the Court of Justice or the Court of First Instance of the European Communities.

II. Definition of Relevant Market

Definition of relevant product market and relevant geographic market

7. The Regulations based on Article [81] and [82] of the Treaty, in particular in section 6 of Form A/B with respect to Regulation No 17, as well as in section 6 of Form CO with respect to Regulation (EEC) No 4064/89 on the control of concentrations having a Community dimension have laid down the following definitions, "Relevant product markets" are defined as follows:

> "A relevant product market comprises all those products and/or services which are regarded as interchangeable or substitutable by the consumer, by reason of the products' characteristics, their prices and their intended use".

Commentary
para 7: **B&C:** 2.101, 8.187, 8.190

8. "Relevant geographic markets" are defined as follows:
> "The relevant geographic market comprises the area in which the undertakings concerned are involved in the supply and demand of products or services, in which the conditions of competition are sufficiently homogeneous and which can be distinguished from neighbouring areas because the conditions of competition are appreciably different in those area".

Commentary
para 8: **B&C:** 2.101

9. The relevant market within which to assess a given competition issue is therefore established by the combination of the product and geographic markets. The Commission interprets the definitions in paragraphs 7 an 8 (which reflect the case-law of the Court of Justice and the Court of First Instance as well as its own decision-making practice) according to the orientations defined in this notice.

Commentary
para 9: **B&C:** 4.016

Concept of relevant market and objectives of Community competition policy

10. The concept of relevant market is closely related to the objectives pursued under Community competition policy. For example, under the Community's merger control, the objective in controlling structural changes in the supply of a product/service is to prevent the creation or reinforcement of a dominant position as a result of which effective competition would be significantly impeded in a substantial part of the common market. Under the Community's competition rules, a dominant position is such that a firm or group of firms would be in a position to behave to an appreciable extent independently of its competitors, customers and ultimately of its consumers.[3] Such a position would usually arise when a firm or group of firms accounted for a large share of the supply in any given market, provided that other factors analysed in the assessment (such as entry barriers, customers' capacity to react, etc.) point in the same direction.

Notes
[3] Definition given by the Court of Justice in its judgment of 13 February 1979 in Case 85/76, *Hoffmann-La Roche* [1979] ECR 461, and confirmed in subsequent judgments.

11. The same approach is followed by the Commission in its application of Article [82] of the Treaty to firms that enjoy a single or collective dominant position. Within the meaning of Regulation No 17, the Commission has the power to investigate and bring to an end abuses of such a dominant position, which must also be defined by reference to the relevant market. Markets may also need to be defined in the application of Article [81] of the Treaty, in particular, in determining whether an appreciable restriction of competition exists or in establishing if the condition pursuant to Article [81](3)(b) for an exemption from the application of Article [81](1) is met.

12. The criteria for defining the relevant market are applied generally for the analysis of certain types of behaviour in the market and for the analysis of structural changes in the supply of

products. This methodology, though, might lead to different results depending on the nature of the competition issue being examined. For instance, the scope of the geographic market might be different when analysing a concentration, where the analysis is essentially prospective, from an analysis of past behaviour. The different time horizon considered in each case might lead to the result that different geographic markets are defined for the same products depending on whether the Commission is examining a change in the structure of supply, such as a concentration or a cooperative joint venture, or examining issues relating to certain past behaviour.

Commentary
para 12: B&C: 4.021

Basic principles for market definition

Competitive constraints

13. Firms are subject to three main sources or competitive constraints: demand substitutability, supply substitutability and potential competition. From an economic point of view, for the definition of the relevant market, demand substitution constitutes the most immediate and effective disciplinary force on the suppliers of a given product, in particular in relation to their pricing decisions. A firm or a group of firms cannot have a significant impact on the prevailing conditions of sale, such as prices, if its customers are in a position to switch easily to available substitute products or to suppliers located elsewhere. Basically, the exercise of market definition consists in identifying the effective alternative sources of supply for the customers of the undertakings involved, in terms both of products/services and of geographic location of suppliers.

Commentary
para 13: B&C: 4.019

14. The competitive constraints arising from supply side substitutability other then those described in paragraphs 20 to 23 and from potential competition are in general less immediate and in any case require an analysis of additional factors. As a result such constraints are taken into account at the assessment stage of competition analysis.

Demand substitution

15. The assessment of demand substitution entails a determination of the range of products which are viewed as substitutes by the consumer. One way of making this determination can be viewed as a speculative experiment, postulating a hypothetical small, lasting change in relative prices and evaluating the likely reactions of customers to that increase. The exercise of market definition focuses on prices for operational and practical purposes, and more precisely on demand substitution arising from small, permanent changes in relative prices. This concept can provide clear indications as to the evidence that is relevant in defining markets.

Commentary
para 15: B&C: 4.016

16. Conceptually, this approach means that, starting from the type of products that the undertakings involved sell and the area in which they sell them, additional products and areas will be included in, or excluded from, the market definition depending on whether competition from these other products and areas affect or restrain sufficiently the pricing of the parties' products in the short term.

Commentary
para 16: B&C: 4.025

17. The question to be answered is whether the parties' customers would switch to readily available substitutes or to suppliers located elsewhere in response to a hypothetical small (in the range 5% to 10%) but permanent relative price increase in the products and areas being considered. If substitution were enough to make the price increase unprofitable because of the resulting loss

of sales, additional substitutes and areas are included in the relevant market. This would be done until the set of products and geographical areas is such that small, permanent increases in relative prices would be profitable. The equivalent analysis is applicable in cases concerning the [concentration] of buying power, where the starting point would then be the supplier and the price test serves to identify the alternative distribution channels or outlets for the supplier's products. In the application of these principles, careful account should be taken of certain particular situations as described within paragraphs 56 and 58.

18. A practical example of this test can be provided by its application to a merger of, for instance, soft-drink bottlers. An issue to examine in such a case would be to decide whether different flavours of soft drinks belong to the same market. In practice, the question to address would be whether consumers of flavour A would switch to other flavours when confronted with a permanent price increase of 5% to 10% for flavour A. If a sufficient number of consumers would switch to, say, flavour B, to such an extent that the price increase for flavour A would not be profitable owing to the resulting loss of sales, then the market would comprise at least flavours A and B. The process would have to be extended in addition to other available flavours until a set of products is identified for which a price rise would not induce a sufficient substitution in demand.

19. Generally, and in particular for the analysis of merger cases, the price to take into account will be the prevailing market price. This may not be the case where the prevailing price has been determined in the absence of sufficient competition. In particular for the investigation of abuses of dominant positions, the fact that the prevailing price might already have been substantially increased will be taken into account.

Commentary
para 19: F&N: 4.43

Supply substitution

20. Supply-side substitutability may also be taken into account when defining markets in those [situations] in which its effects are equivalent to those of demand substitution in terms of effectiveness and immediacy. This means that suppliers are able to switch production to the relevant products and market them in the short term[4] without incurring significant additional costs or risks in response to small and permanent changes in relative prices. When these conditions are met, the additional production that is put on the market will have a disciplinary effect on the competitive behaviour of the companies involved. Such an impact in terms of effectiveness and immediacy is equivalent to the demand substitution effect.

Notes
[4] That is such a period that does not entail a significant adjustment of existing tangible and intangible assets (see paragraph 23).

Commentary
para 20: F&N: 1.156

21. These situations typically arise when companies market a wide range of qualities or grades of one product; even if, for a given final customer or group of consumers, the different qualities are not substitutable, the different qualities will be grouped into one product market, provided that most of the suppliers are able to offer and sell the various qualities immediately and without the significant increases in costs described above. In such cases, the relevant product market will encompass all products that are substitutable in demand and supply, and the current sales of those products will be aggregated so as to give the total value or volume of the market. The same reasoning may lead to group different geographic areas.

Commentary
para 21: F&N: 1.159

22. A practical example of the approach to supply-side substitutability when defining product markets is to be found in the case of paper. [Paper] is usually supplied in a range of different qualities, from standard writing paper to high quality papers to be used, for instance, to publish art books.

From a demand point of view, different qualities of paper cannot be used for any given use, i.e. an art book or a high quality publication cannot be based on lower quality papers. However, paper plants are prepared to manufacture the different qualities, and production can be adjusted with negligible costs and in a short time-frame. In the absence of particular difficulties in distribution, paper manufacturers are able therefore, to compete for orders of the various qualities, in particular if orders are placed with sufficient lead time to allow for modification of production plans. Under such circumstances, the Commission would not define a separate market for each quality of paper and its respective use. The various qualities of paper are included in the relevant market, and their sales added up to estimate total market [value] and volume.

Commentary
para 22: B&C: 4.052 F&N: 1.157

23. When supply-side substitutability would entail the need to adjust significantly existing tangible and intangible assets, additional investments, strategic decisions or time delays, it will not be considered at the stage of market definition. Examples where supply-side substitution did not induce the Commission to enlarge the market are offered in the area of consumer products, in particular for branded beverages. Although bottling plants may in principle bottle different beverages, there are costs and lead times involved (in terms of advertising, product testing and distribution) before the products can actually be sold. In these cases, the effects of supply-side substitutability and other forms of potential competition would then be examined at a later stage.

Commentary
para 23: B&C: 4.053

Potential competition

24. The third source of competitive constraint, potential competition, is not taken into account when defining markets, since the conditions under which potential competition will actually represent an effective competitive constraint depend on the analysis of specific factors and circumstances related to the conditions of entry. If required, this analysis is only carried out at a subsequent stage, in general once the position of the companies involved in the relevant market has already been ascertained, and when such position gives rise to concerns from a competition point of view.

Commentary
para 24: B&C: 4.003, 4.020, 10.033

III. Evidence Relied on to Define Relevant Markets

The process of defining the relevant market in practice

Product dimension

25. There is a range of evidence permitting an assessment of the extent to which substitution would take place. In individual cases, certain types of evidence will be determinant, depending very much on the characteristics and specificity of the industry and products or services that are being examined. The same type of evidence may be of no importance in other cases. In most cases, a decision will have to be based on the consideration of a number of criteria and different items of evidence. The Commission follows an open approach to empirical evidence, aimed at making an effective use of all available information which may be relevant in individual cases. The Commission does not follow a rigid hierarchy of different sources of information or types of evidence.

Commentary
para 25: B&C: 4.033

26. The process of defining relevant markets may be summarized as follows: on the basis of the preliminary information available or information submitted by the undertakings involved, the

Commission will usually be in a position to broadly establish the possible relevant markets within which, for instance, a concentration or a restriction of competition has to be assessed. In general, and for all practical purposes when handling individual cases, the question will usually be to decide on a few alternative possible relevant markets. For instance, with respect to the product market, the issue will often be to establish whether product A and product B belong or do not belong to the same product market. it is often the case that the inclusion of product B would be enough to remove any competition concerns.

Commentary
para 26: B&C: 4.021, 4.027

27. In such situations it is not necessary to consider whether the market includes additional products, or to reach a definitive conclusion on the precise product market. If under the conceivable alternative market definitions the operation in question does not raise competition concerns, the question of market definition will be left open, reducing thereby the burden on companies to supply information.

Commentary
para 27: B&C: 8.187

Geographic dimension

28. The Commission's approach to geographic market definition might be summarized as follows: it will take a preliminary view of the scope of the geographic market on the basis of broad indications as to the distribution of market shares between the parties and their competitors, as well as a preliminary analysis of pricing and price differences at national and Community or EEA level. This initial view is used basically as a working hypothesis to focus the Commission's enquiries for the purposes of arriving at a precise geographic market definition.

Commentary
para 28: B&C: 4.078

29. The reasons behind any particular configuration of prices and market shares need to be explored. Companies might enjoy high market shares in their domestic markets just because of the weight of the past, and conversely, a homogeneous presence of companies throughout the EEA might be consistent with national or regional geographic markets. The initial working hypothesis will therefore be checked against an analysis of demand characteristics (importance of national or local preferences, current patterns of purchases of customers, product differentiation/brands, other) in order to establish whether companies in different areas do indeed constitute a real alternative source of supply for consumers. The theoretical experiment is again based on substitution arising from changes in relative prices, and the question to answer is again whether the customers of the parties would switch their orders to companies located elsewhere in the short term and at a negligible cost.

Commentary
para 29: F&N: 1.164

30. If necessary, a further check on supply factors will be carried out to ensure that those companies located in differing areas do not face impediments in developing their sales on competitive terms throughout the whole geographic market. This analysis will include an examination of requirements for a local presence in order to sell in that area the conditions of access to distribution channels, costs associated with setting up a distribution network, and the presence or absence of regulatory barriers arising from public procurement, price regulations, quotas and tariffs limiting trade or production, technical standards, monopolies, freedom of establishment, requirements for administrative authorizations, packaging regulations, etc. In short, the Commission will identify possible obstacles and barriers isolating companies located in a given area from the

competitive pressure of companies located outside that area, so as to determine the precise degree of market interpenetration at national, European or global level.

31. The actual pattern and evolution of trade flows offers useful supplementary indications as to the economic importance of each demand or supply factor mentioned above, and the extent to which they may or may not constitute actual barriers creating different geographic markets. The analysis of trade flows will generally address the question of transport costs and the extent to which these may hinder trade between different areas, having regard to plant location, costs of production and relative price levels.

Market integration in the Community

32. Finally, the Commission also takes into account the continuing process of market integration, in particular in the Community, when defining geographic markets, especially in the area of concentrations and structural joint ventures. The measures adopted and implemented in the internal market programme to remove barriers to trade and further integrate the Community markets cannot be ignored when assessing the effects on competition of a concentration or a structural joint venture. A situation where national markets have been [artificially] isolated from each other because of the existence of legislative barriers that have now been removed will generally lead to a cautious assessment of past evidence regarding prices, market shares or trade patterns. A process of market integration that would, in the short term, lead to wider geographic markets may therefore be taken into consideration when defining the geographic market for the purposes of assessing concentrations and joint ventures.

Commentary
para 32: B&C: 4.072

The process of gathering evidence

33. When a precise market definition is deemed necessary, the Commission will often contact the main customers and the main companies in the industry to enquire into their views about the [boundaries] of product and geographic markets and to obtain the necessary factual evidence to reach a conclusion. The Commission might also contact the relevant professional associations, and companies active in upstream markets, so as to be able to define, in so far as necessary, separate product and geographic markets, for different levels of production or distribution of the products/services in question. It might also request additional information to the undertakings involved.

34. Where appropriate, the Commission will address written requests for information to the market players mentioned above. These requests will usually include questions relating to the perceptions of companies about reactions to hypothetical price increases and their views of the boundaries of the relevant market. They will also ask for provision of the factual information the Commission deems necessary to reach a conclusion on the extent of the relevant market. The Commission might also discuss with marketing directors or other officers of those companies to gain a better understanding on how negotiations between suppliers and customers take place and better understand issues relating to the definition of the relevant market. Where appropriate, they might also carry out visits or inspections to the premises of the parties, their customers and/or their competitors, in order to better understand how products are manufactured and sold.

35. The type of evidence relevant to reach a conclusion as to the product market can be categorized as follows:

Evidence to define markets — product dimension

36. An analysis of the product characteristics and its intended use allows the Commission, as a first step, to limit the field of investigation of possible substitutes. However, product characteristics and intended use are insufficient to show whether two products are demand substitutes. Functional interchangeability or similarity in characteristics may not, in themselves, provide sufficient criteria, because the responsiveness of customers to relative price changes may be [determined] by other considerations as well. For example, there may be different competitive [constraints] in the original equipment market for car components and in spare parts, thereby leading to a separate

delineation of two relevant markets. Conversely, differences in product characteristics are not in themselves sufficient to exclude demand substitutability, since this will depend to a large extent on how customers value different characteristics.

Commentary
para 36: B&C: 4.034

37. The type of evidence the Commission considers relevant to assess whether two products are demand substitutes can be categorized as follows:

38. *Evidence of substitution in the recent past.* In certain cases, it is possible to analyse evidence relating to recent past events or shocks in the market that offer actual examples of [substitution] between two products. When available, this sort of information will normally be fundamental for market definition. If there have been changes in relative prices in the past (all else being equal), the reactions in terms of quantities demanded will be determinant in establishing substitutability. Launches of new products in the past can also offer useful information, when it is possible to precisely analyse which products have lost sales to the new product.

Commentary
para 38: B&C: 4.040

39. There are a number of *quantitative tests* that have specifically been designed for the purpose of delineating markets. These tests consist of various econometric and statistical approaches estimates of elasticities and cross-price elasticities[5] for the demand of a product, tests based on similarity of price movements over time, the analysis of causality between price series and similarity of price levels and/or their convergence. The Commission takes into account the available quantitative evidence capable of withstanding rigorous scrutiny for the purposes of establishing patterns of substitution in the past.

Notes

[5] Own-price elasticity of demand for product X is a measure of the responsiveness of demand for X to percentage change in its own price. Cross-price elasticity between products X and Y is the responsiveness of demand for product X to percentage change in the price of product Y.

Commentary
para 39: B&C: 4.043

40. *Views of customers and competitors.* The Commission often contacts the main customers and competitors of the companies involved in its enquiries, to gather their views on the boundaries of the product market as well as most of the factual information it requires to reach a conclusion on the scope of the market. Reasoned answers of customers and competitors as to what would happen if relative prices for the candidate products were to increase in the candidate geographic area by a small amount (for instance of 5% to 10%) are taken into account when they are sufficiently backed by factual evidence.

Commentary
para 40: B&C: 4.049

41. *Consumer preferences.* In the case of consumer goods, it may be difficult for the Commission to gather the direct views of end consumers about substitute products. Marketing studies that companies have commissioned in the past and that are used by companies in their own decision-making as to pricing of their products and/or marketing actions may provide useful information for the Commission's delineation of the relevant market. Consumer surveys on usage patterns and attitudes, data from consumer's purchasing patterns, the views expressed by retailers and more generally, market research studies submitted by the parties and their competitors are taken into account to establish whether an economically significant proportion of consumers consider two products as substitutable, also taking into account the importance of brands for the products in question. The methodology followed in consumer surveys carried out ad hoc by the undertakings involved or their competitors for the purposes of a merger procedure or a procedure pursuant to

Regulation No 17 will usually be scrutinized with utmost care. Unlike pre-existing studies, they have not been prepared in the normal course of business for the adoption of business decisions.

Commentary
para 41: B&C: 4.050

42. *Barriers and costs associated with switching demand to potential substitutes.* There are a number of barriers and costs that might prevent the Commission from considering two prima facie demand substitutes as belonging to one single product market. It is not possible to provide an exhaustive list of all the possible barriers to substitution and of switching costs. These barriers or obstacles might have a wide range of origins, and in its decisions, the Commission has been confronted with regulatory barriers or other forms of State intervention, constraints arising in downstream markets, need to incur specific capital investment or loss in current output in order to switch to alternative inputs, the location of customers, specific investment in production process, learning and human capital investment, retooling costs or other investments, uncertainty about quality and reputation of unknown suppliers, and others.

Commentary
para 42: B&C: 4.038

43. *Different categories of customers and price discrimination.* The extent of the product market might be narrowed in the presence of distinct groups of customers. A distinct group of customers for the relevant product may constitute a narrower, distinct market when such ha group could be subject to price discrimination. This will usually be the case when two conditions are met: (a) it is possible to identify clearly which group an individual customer belongs to at the moment of selling the relevant products to him, and (b) trade among customers or arbitrage by third parties should not be feasible.

Commentary
para 43: B&C: 4.046

Evidence for defining markets — geographic dimension

44. The type of evidence the Commission considers relevant to reach a conclusion as to the geographic market can be categorized as follows:
45. *Past evidence of diversion of orders to other areas.* In certain cases, evidence on changes in prices between different areas and consequent reactions by customers might be available. Generally, the same quantitative tests used for product market definition might as well be used in geographic market definition, bearing in mind that international comparisons of prices might be more complex due to a number of factors such as exchange rate movements, taxation and product differentiation.

Commentary
para 45: B&C: 4.086

46. *Basic demand characteristics.* The nature of demand for the relevant product may in itself determine the scope of the geographical market. Factors such as national preferences or preferences for national brands, language, culture and life style, and the need for a local presence have a strong potential to limit the geographic scope of competition.

Commentary
para 46: B&C: 4.076

47. *Views of customers and competitors.* Where appropriate, the Commission will contact the main customers and competitors of the parties in its enquiries, to gather their views on the boundaries of the geographic market as well as most of the factual information it requires to reach a conclusion on the scope of the market when they are sufficiently backed by factual evidence.

Commentary
para 47: **B&C:** 4.082

48. *Current geographic pattern of purchases.* An examination of the customers' current geographic pattern of purchases provides useful evidence as to the possible scope of the geographic market. When customers purchase from companies located anywhere in the Community or the EEA on similar terms, or they procure their supplies through effective tendering procedures in which companies from anywhere in the Community or the EEA submit bids, usually the geographic market will be considered to be Community-wide.

Commentary
para 48: **B&C:** 4.077

49. *Trade flows/pattern of shipments.* When the number of customers is so large that it is not possible to obtain through them a clear picture of geographic purchasing patterns, information on trade flows might be used alternatively, provided that the trade statistics are available with a sufficient degree of detail for the relevant products. Trade flows, and above all, the rationale behind trade flows provide useful insights and information for the purpose of establishing the scope of the geographic market but are not in themselves conclusive.

Commentary
para 49: **B&C:** 4.077

50. *Barriers and switching costs associated to divert orders to companies located in other areas.* The absence of trans-border purchases or trade flows, for instance, does not necessarily mean that the market is at most national in scope. Still, barriers isolating the national market have to identified before it is concluded that the relevant geographic market in such a case is national. Perhaps the clearest obstacle for a customer to divert its orders to other areas is the impact of transport costs and transport restrictions arising from legislation or from the nature of the relevant products. The impact of transport costs will usually limit the scope of the geographic market for bulky, low-value products, bearing in mind that a transport disadvantage might also be compensated by a comparative advantage in other costs (labour costs or raw materials). Access to distribution in a given area, regulatory barriers still existing in certain sectors, quotas and custom tariffs might also constitute barriers isolating a geographic area from the competitive pressure of companies located outside that area. Significant switching costs in procuring supplies from companies located in other countries constitute additional sources of such barriers.

Commentary
para 50: **B&C:** 4.076–4.077

51. On the basis of the evidence gathered, the Commission will then define a geographic market that could range from a local dimension to a global one, and there are examples of both local and global markets in past decisions of the Commission.
52. The paragraphs above describe the different factors which might be relevant to define markets. This does not imply that in each individual case it will be necessary to obtain evidence and assess each of these factors. Often in practice the evidence provided by a [subset] of these factors will be sufficient to reach a conclusion, as shown in the past decisional practice of the Commission.

IV. Calculation of Market Share

53. The definition of the relevant market in both its product and [geographic] dimensions allows the identification the suppliers and the customers/consumers active on that market. On that basis, a total market size and market shares for each supplier can be calculated on the basis of their sales of the relevant products in the relevant area. In practice, the total market size and market shares are often available from market sources, i.e. companies' estimates, studies commissioned from industry consultants and/or trade associations. When this is not the case, or when available estimates are not reliable, the Commission will usually ask each supplier in the relevant market to provide its own sales in order to calculate total market size and market shares.

54. If sales are usually the reference to calculate market shares, there are nevertheless other indications that, depending on the specific products or industry in question, can offer useful information such as, in particular, capacity, the number of players in bidding markets, units of fleet as in aerospace, or the reserves held in the case of sectors such as mining.

55. As a rule of thumb, both volume sales and value sales provide useful information. In cases of differentiated products, sales in value and their associated market share will usually be considered to better reflect the relative position and strength of each supplier.

V. ADDITIONAL CONSIDERATIONS

56. There are certain areas where the application of the principles above has to be undertaken with care. This is the case when considering primary and secondary markets, in particular, when the behaviour of undertakings at a point in time has to be analysed pursuant to Article [82]. The method of defining markets in these cases is the same, i.e. assessing the responses of customers based on their purchasing decisions to relative price changes, but taking into account as well, constraints on substitution imposed by conditions in the connected markets. A narrow definition of market for secondary products, for instance, spare parts, may result when compatibility with the primary product is important. Problems of finding compatible secondary products together with the existence of high prices and a long lifetime of the primary products may render relative price increases of secondary products profitable. A different market definition may result if significant substitution between secondary products is possible or if the characteristics of the primary products make quick and direct consumer responses to relative price increases of the secondary products feasible.

Commentary
para 56: F&N: 4.108, 9.275

57. In certain cases, the existence of chains of substitution might lead to the definition of a relevant market where products or areas at the extreme of the market are not directly substitutable. An example might be provided by the geographic dimension of a product with significant transport costs. In such cases, deliveries from a given plant are limited to a certain area around each plant by the impact of transport costs. In principle, such an area could constitute the relevant geographic market. However, if the distribution of plants is such that there are considerable overlaps between the areas around different plants, it is possible that the pricing of those products will be constrained by a chain substitution effect, and lead to the definition of a broader geographic market. The same reasoning may apply if product B is a demand substitute for products A and C. Even if products A and C are not direct demand substitutes, they might be found to be in the same relevant product market since their respective pricing might be constrained by substitution to B.

Commentary
para 57: B&C: 4.066

58. From a practical perspective, the concept of chains of substitution has to be corroborated by actual evidence, for instance related to price interdependence at the extremes of the chains of substitution, in order to lead to an extension of the relevant market in an individual case. Price levels at the extremes of the chains would have to be of the same magnitude as well.

Commentary
para 58: B&C: 4.066, 4.088

Part C Substantive
Antitrust Matters

C11

COMMISSION NOTICE

Guidelines on Vertical Restraints

(2000/C 291/01)

(Text with EEA relevance)

Official Journal C 291, 13.10.2000, p. 1

Celex No : 32000Y1013(01)

Notes

EEA application: the EFTA Surveillance Authority has adopted a parallel notice under Article 5(2)(b) of the Surveillance and Court Agreement: OJ C 122, 23.5.2002, p. 1 and EEA Supplement No 26, 23.5.2002, p. 7.

Commentary

Guidelines: **B&C:** 1.066, 2.097, 2.110, 2.115, 2.128, 2.130–2.131, 3.004, 4.007, 6.003, 6.006, 6.008, 6.010, 6.088, 6.120, 6.173, 9.005 **F&N:** 3.30, 3.136, 3.138, 3.142, 3.143, 3.309, 3.317–3.322, 3.446, 3.456, 3.1050, 4.230, 9.27, 9.57, 9.82, 9.163, 9.164, 9.165, 9.166, 9.182–9.186, 9.213, 9.218, 9.223, 9.224, 9.225, 9.235, 9.236, 9.237, 9.261, 9.265, 9.270, 9.277, 9.280, 9.287, 9.288, 9.292, 9.293, 9.294, 9.297, 9.299, 9.303, 9.304, 9.305, 9.306, 9.309, 9.312, 9.313, 9.314, 9.315, 9.318, 9.319, 9.320, 9.321, 9.326, 9.329, 9.332, 9.337, 9.339, 9.341, 9.343, 9.344, 9.345, 9.348, 9.349, 9.350, 9.351, 9.356, 9.357, 10.76, 11.130, 12.174, 12.176, 12.177, 12.208, 15.47

paras 8–11: **F&N:** 9.167
paras 12–20: **B&C:** 6.029, 12.179 **F&N:** 9.1082, 15.47
paras 39–41: **F&N:** 9.202
paras 42–44: **B&C:** 6.016
paras 71–74: **F&N:** 9.263
paras 71–79: **B&C:** 3.086 **F&N:** 15.162
paras 80–81: **F&N:** 9.264
paras 80–87: **B&C:** 3.089 **F&N:** 15.164
paras 80–89: **B&C:** 6.136
paras 104–114: **B&C:** 6.008
paras 106–108: **F&N:** 9.283
paras 109–110: **F&N:** 9.284
paras 111–112: **F&N:** 9.285
paras 113–114: **F&N:** 9.286
paras 115–118: **F&N:** 9.293
paras 115–166: **B&C:** 3.031
paras 121–125: **B&C:** 4.007
paras 121–133: **B&C:** 6.044, 6.156 **F&N:** 9.288
paras 137–228: **B&C:** 6.008
paras 138–158: **F&N:** 15.143
paras 140–146: **F&N:** 3.319
paras 171–179: **B&C:** 6.135
paras 186–198: **B&C:** 6.104
paras 225–228: **B&C:** 9.108
section IV: **F&N:** 9.298

CONTENTS

Part C Substantive Antitrust Matters

I. INTRODUCTION

1. Purpose of the Guidelines

(1) These Guidelines set out the principles for the assessment of vertical agreements under Article 81 of the EC Treaty. What are considered vertical agreements is defined in Article 2(1) of Commission Regulation (EC) No 2790/1999 of 22 December 1999 on the application of Article 81(3) of the Treaty to categories of vertical agreements and concerted practices[1] (Block Exemption Regulation) (see paragraphs 23 to 45). These Guidelines are without prejudice to the possible parallel application of Article 82 of the Treaty to vertical agreements. The Guidelines are structured in the following way:

— Section II (paragraphs 8 to 20) describes vertical agreements which generally fall outside Article 81(1);

— Section III (paragraphs 21 to 70) comments on the application of the Block Exemption Regulation;

— Section IV (paragraphs 71 to 87) describes the principles concerning the withdrawal of the block exemption and the disapplication of the Block Exemption Regulation;
— Section V (paragraphs 88 to 99) addresses market definition and market share calculation issues;
— Section VI (paragraphs 100 to 229) describes the general framework of analysis and the enforcement policy of the Commission in individual cases concerning vertical agreements.

Notes
[1] OJ L 336, 29.12.1999, p. 21.

(2) Throughout these Guidelines the analysis applies to both goods and services, although certain vertical restraints are mainly used in the distribution of goods. Similarly, vertical agreements can be concluded for intermediate and final goods and services. Unless otherwise stated, the analysis and arguments in the text apply to all types of goods and services and to all levels of trade. The term "products" includes both goods and services. The terms "supplier" and "buyer" are used for all levels of trade.

(3) By issuing these Guidelines the Commission aims to help companies to make their own assessment of vertical agreements under the EC competition rules. The standards set forth in these Guidelines must be applied in circumstances specific to each case. This rules out a mechanical application. Each case must be evaluated in the light of its own facts. The Commission will apply the Guidelines reasonably and flexibly.

(4) These Guidelines are without prejudice to the interpretation that may be given by the Court of First Instance and the Court of Justice of the European Communities in relation to the application of Article 81 to vertical agreements.

Commentary
para 1: B&C: 6.163
para 1(3): B&C: 6.008

2. Applicability of Article 81 to vertical agreements

(5) Article 81 of the EC Treaty applies to vertical agreements that may affect trade between Member States and that prevent, restrict or distort competition (hereinafter referred to as "vertical restraints").[1] For vertical restraints, Article 81 provides an appropriate legal framework for assessment, recognising the distinction between anti-competitive and pro-competitive effects: Article 81(1) prohibits those agreements which appreciably restrict or distort competition, while Article 81(3) allows for exemption of those agreements which confer sufficient benefits to outweigh the anti-competitive effects.

Notes

[1] See inter alia judgment of the Court of Justice of the European Communities in Joined Cases 56/64 and 58/64 *Grundig-Consten v Commission* [1966] ECR 299; Case 56/65 *Technique Minière v Machinenbau Ulm* [1966] ECR 235; and of the Court of First Instance of the European Communities in Case T-77/92 *Parker Pen v Commission* [1994] ECR II 549.

Commentary
para 5: F&N: 9.163

(6) For most vertical restraints, competition concerns can only arise if there is insufficient inter-brand competition, i.e. if there is some degree of market power at the level of the supplier or the buyer or at both levels. If there is insufficient inter-brand competition, the protection of inter- and intra-brand competition becomes important.

Commentary
para 6: B&C: 6.007, 6.040 F&N: 9.187

(7) The protection of competition is the primary objective of EC competition policy, as this enhances consumer welfare and creates an efficient allocation of resources. In applying the EC competition rules, the Commission will adopt an economic approach which is based on the effects on the market; vertical agreements have to be analysed in their legal and economic context. However, in the case of restrictions by object as listed in Article 4 of the Block Exemption Regulation, the Commission is not required to assess the actual effects on the market. Market integration is an additional goal of EC competition policy. Market integration enhances competition in the Community. Companies should not be allowed to recreate private barriers between Member States where State barriers have been successfully abolished.

II. Vertical Agreements which Generally Fall Outside Article 81(1)

1. Agreements of minor importance and SMEs

(8) Agreements which are not capable of appreciably affecting trade between Member States or capable of appreciably restricting competition by object or effect are not caught by Article 81(1). The Block Exemption Regulation applies only to agreements falling within the scope of application of Article 81(1). These Guidelines are without prejudice to the application of the present or any future "*de minimis*" notice.[1]

Notes

[1] See Notice on agreements of minor importance of 9 December 1997, OJ C 372, 9.12.1997, p. 13. [See now Commission Notice on agreements of minor importance which do not appreciably restrict competition under Article 81(1) of the Treaty establishing the European Community (*de minimis*), OJ C 368, 22.12.2001 p. 13.]

Commentary
para 8: B&C: 6.003

(9) Subject to the conditions set out in points 11, 18 and 20 of the "*de minimis*" notice concerning hardcore restrictions and cumulative effect issues, vertical agreements entered into by undertakings whose market share on the relevant market does not exceed 10% are generally considered to fall outside the scope of Article 81(1). There is no presumption that vertical agreements concluded by undertakings having more than 10% market share automatically infringe Article 81(1). Agreements between undertakings whose market share exceeds the 10% threshold may still not have an appreciable effect on trade between Member States or may not constitute an appreciable restriction of competition.[1] Such agreements need to be assessed in their legal and economic context. The criteria for the assessment of individual agreements are set out in paragraphs 100 to 229.

Notes

[1] See judgment of the Court of First Instance in Case T-7/93 *Langnese-Iglo v Commission* [1995] ECR II-1533, paragraph 98.

Commentary
para 9: B&C: 2.130

(10) As regards hardcore restrictions defined in the "*de minimis*" notice, Article 81(1) may apply below the 10% threshold, provided that there is an appreciable effect on trade between Member States and on competition. The applicable case-law of the Court of Justice and the Court of First Instance is relevant in this respect.[1] Reference is also made to the particular situation of launching a new product or entering a new market which is dealt with in these Guidelines (paragraph 119, point 10).

Notes

[1] See judgment of the Court of Justice in Case 5/69 *Völk v Vervaecke* [1969] ECR 295; Case 1/71 *Cadillon v Höss* [1971] ECR 351 and Case C-306/96 *Javico v Yves Saint Laurent* [1998] ECR I-1983, paragraphs 16 and 17.

Commentary
para 10: B&C: 2.129, 6.050

Part C Substantive
Antitrust Matters

(11) In addition, the Commission considers that, subject to cumulative effect and hardcore restrictions, agreements between small and medium-sized undertakings as defined in the Annex to Commission Recommendation 96/280/EC[1] are rarely capable of appreciably affecting trade between Member States or of appreciably restricting competition within the meaning of Article 81(1), and therefore generally fall outside the scope of Article 81(1). In cases where such agreements nonetheless meet the conditions for the application of Article 81(1), the Commission will normally refrain from opening proceedings for lack of sufficient Community interest unless those undertakings collectively or individually hold a dominant position in a substantial part of the common market.

Notes

[1] OJ L 107, 30.4.1996, p. 4. [See now Commission Recommendation of 6 May 2003 concerning the definition of micro, small and medium-sized enterprises, OJ L 124, 20.5.2003, p. 36.]

Commentary
para 11: B&C: 2.130

2. Agency agreements

(12) Paragraphs 12 to 20 replace the Notice on exclusive dealing contracts with commercial agents of 1962.[1] They must be read in conjunction with Council Directive 86/653/EEC.[2]

Agency agreements cover the situation in which a legal or physical person (the agent) is vested with the power to negotiate and/or conclude contracts on behalf of another person (the principal), either in the agent's own name or in the name of the principal, for the:

— purchase of goods or services by the principal, or

— sale of goods or services supplied by the principal.

Notes

[1] OJ 139, 24.12.1962, p. 2921/62.
[2] OJ L 382, 31.12.1986, p. 17.

Commentary
para 12: B&C: 6.029 **F&N:** 15.21

(13) In the case of genuine agency agreements, the obligations imposed on the agent as to the contracts negotiated and/or concluded on behalf of the principal do not fall within the scope of application of Article 81(1). The determining factor in assessing whether Article 81(1) is applicable is the financial or commercial risk borne by the agent in relation to the activities for which he has been appointed as an agent by the principal. In this respect it is not material for the assessment whether the agent acts for one or several principals. Non-genuine agency agreements may be caught by Article 81(1), in which case the Block Exemption Regulation and the other sections of these Guidelines will apply.

Commentary
para 13: B&C: 6.033 **F&N:** 9.183, 15.44, 15.45

(14) There are two types of financial or commercial risk that are material to the assessment of the genuine nature of an agency agreement under Article 81(1). First there are the risks which are directly related to the contracts concluded and/or negotiated by the agent on behalf of the principal, such as financing of stocks. Secondly, there are the risks related to market-specific investments. These are investments specifically required for the type of activity for which the agent has been appointed by the principal, i.e. which are required to enable the agent to conclude and/or negotiate this type of contract. Such investments are usually sunk, if upon leaving that particular field of activity the investment cannot be used for other activities or sold other than at a significant loss.

Commentary
para 14: B&C: 6.032 F&N: 9.184

(15) The agency agreement is considered a genuine agency agreement and consequently falls outside Article 81(1) if the agent does not bear any, or bears only insignificant, risks in relation to the contracts concluded and/or negotiated on behalf of the principal and in relation to market-specific investments for that field of activity. In such a situation, the selling or purchasing function forms part of the principal's activities, despite the fact that the agent is a separate undertaking. The principal thus bears the related financial and commercial risks and the agent does not exercise an independent economic activity in relation to the activities for which he has been appointed as an agent by the principal. In the opposite situation the agency agreement is considered a non-genuine agency agreement and may fall under Article 81(1). In that case the agent does bear such risks and will be treated as an independent dealer who must remain free in determining his marketing strategy in order to be able to recover his contract- or market-specific investments. Risks that are related to the activity of providing agency services in general, such as the risk of the agent's income being dependent upon his success as an agent or general investments in for instance premises or personnel, are not material to this assessment.

Commentary
para 15: F&N: 9.185

(16) The question of risk must be assessed on a case-by-case basis, and with regard to the economic reality of the situation rather than the legal form. Nonetheless, the Commission considers that Article 81(1) will generally not be applicable to the obligations imposed on the agent as to the contracts negotiated and/or concluded on behalf of the principal where property in the contract goods bought or sold does not vest in the agent, or the agent does not himself supply the contract services and where the agent:
— does not contribute to the costs relating to the supply/purchase of the contract goods or services, including the costs of transporting the goods. This does not preclude the agent from carrying out the transport service, provided that the costs are covered by the principal;
— is not, directly or indirectly, obliged to invest in sales promotion, such as contributions to the advertising budgets of the principal;
— does not maintain at his own cost or risk stocks of the contract goods, including the costs of financing the stocks and the costs of loss of stocks and can return unsold goods to the principal without charge, unless the agent is liable for fault (for example, by failing to comply with reasonable security measures to avoid loss of stocks);
— does not create and/or operate an after-sales service, repair service or a warranty service unless it is fully reimbursed by the principal;
— does not make market-specific investments in equipment, premises or training of personnel, such as for example the petrol storage tank in the case of petrol retailing or specific software to sell insurance policies in case of insurance agents;
— does not undertake responsibility towards third parties for damage caused by the product sold (product liability), unless, as agent, he is liable for fault in this respect;
— does not take responsibility for customers' non-performance of the contract, with the exception of the loss of the agent's commission, unless the agent is liable for fault (for example, by failing to comply with reasonable security or anti-theft measures or failing to comply with reasonable measures to report theft to the principal or police or to communicate to the principal all necessary information available to him on the customer's financial reliability).

Commentary
para 16: F&N: 9.186

(17) This list is not exhaustive. However, where the agent incurs one or more of the above risks or costs, then Article 81(1) may apply as with any other vertical agreement.
(18) If an agency agreement does not fall within the scope of application of Article 81(1), then all obligations imposed on the agent in relation to the contracts concluded and/or negotiated on

Part C Substantive Antitrust Matters

behalf of the principal fall outside Article 81(1). The following obligations on the agent's part will generally be considered to form an inherent part of an agency agreement, as each of them relates to the ability of the principal to fix the scope of activity of the agent in relation to the contract goods or services, which is essential if the principal is to take the risks and therefore to be in a position to determine the commercial strategy:
— limitations on the territory in which the agent may sell these goods or services;
— limitations on the customers to whom the agent may sell these goods or services;
— the prices and conditions at which the agent must sell or purchase these goods or services.

Commentary
para 18: B&C: 6.036

(19) In addition to governing the conditions of sale or purchase of the contract goods or services by the agent on behalf of the principal, agency agreements often contain provisions which concern the relationship between the agent and the principal. In particular, they may contain a provision preventing the principal from appointing other agents in respect of a given type of transaction, customer or territory (exclusive agency provisions) and/or a provision preventing the agent from acting as an agent or distributor of undertakings which compete with the principal (non-compete provisions). Exclusive agency provisions concern only intra-brand competition and will in general not lead to anti-competitive effects. Non-compete provisions, including post-term non-compete provisions, concern inter-brand competition and may infringe Article 81(1) if they lead to foreclosure on the relevant market where the contract goods or services are sold or purchased (see Section VI.2.1).

Commentary
para 19: B&C: 6.036 **F&N:** 11.130

(20) An agency agreement may also fall within the scope of Article 81(1), even if the principal bears all the relevant financial and commercial risks, where it facilitates collusion. This could for instance be the case when a number of principals use the same agents while collectively excluding others from using these agents, or when they use the agents to collude on marketing strategy or to exchange sensitive market information between the principals.

Commentary
para 20: B&C: 6.034

III. Application of the Block Exemption Regulation

1. Safe harbour created by the Block Exemption Regulation

(21) The Block Exemption Regulation creates a presumption of legality for vertical agreements depending on the market share of the supplier or the buyer. Pursuant to Article 3 of the Block Exemption Regulation, it is in general the market share of the supplier on the market where it sells the contract goods or services which determines the applicability of the block exemption. This market share may not exceed the threshold of 30% in order for the block exemption to apply. Only where the agreement contains an exclusive supply obligation, as defined in Article 1(c) of the Block Exemption Regulation, is it the buyer's market share on the market where it purchases the contract goods or services which may not exceed the threshold of 30% in order for the block exemption to apply. For market share issues see Section V (paragraphs 88 to 99).

(22) From an economic point of view, a vertical agreement may have effects not only on the market between supplier and buyer but also on markets downstream of the buyer. The simplified approach of the Block Exemption Regulation, which only takes into account the market share of the supplier or the buyer (as the case may be) on the market between these two parties, is justified by the fact that below the threshold of 30% the effects on downstream markets will in general be limited. In addition, only having to consider the market between supplier and buyer makes the application of the Block Exemption Regulation easier and enhances the level of

legal certainty, while the instrument of withdrawal (see paragraphs 71 to 87) remains available to remedy possible problems on other related markets.

Commentary
para 22: F&N: 9.190, 9.267

2. Scope of the Block Exemption Regulation

(i) Definition of vertical agreements

(23) Vertical agreements are defined in Article 2(1) of the Block Exemption Regulation as "agreements or concerted practices entered into between two or more undertakings each of which operates, for the purposes of the agreement, at a different level of the production or distribution chain, and relating to the conditions under which the parties may purchase, sell or resell certain goods or services".

(24) There are three main elements in this definition:
   — the agreement or concerted practice is between two or more undertakings. Vertical agreements with final consumers not operating as an undertaking are not covered; More generally, agreements with final consumers do not fall under Article 81(1), as that article applies only to agreements between undertakings, decisions by associations of undertakings and concerted practices. This is without prejudice to the possible application of Article 82 of the Treaty;
   — the agreement or concerted practice is between undertakings each operating, for the purposes of the agreement, at a different level of the production or distribution chain. This means for instance that one undertaking produces a raw material which the other undertaking uses as an input, or that the first is a manufacturer, the second a wholesaler and the third a retailer. This does not preclude an undertaking from being active at more than one level of the production or distribution chain;
   — the agreements or concerted practices relate to the conditions under which the parties to the agreement, the supplier and the buyer, "may purchase, sell or resell certain goods or services". This reflects the purpose of the Block Exemption Regulation to cover purchase and distribution agreements. These are agreements which concern the conditions for the purchase, sale or resale of the goods or services supplied by the supplier and/or which concern the conditions for the sale by the buyer of the goods or services which incorporate these goods or services. For the application of the Block Exemption Regulation both the goods or services supplied by the supplier and the resulting goods or services are considered to be contract goods or services. Vertical agreements relating to all final and intermediate goods and services are covered. The only exception is the automobile sector, as long as this sector remains covered by a specific block exemption such as that granted by Commission Regulation (EC) No 1475/95.[1] The goods or services provided by the supplier may be resold by the buyer or may be used as an input by the buyer to produce his own goods or services.

Notes

[1] OJ L 145, 29.6.1995, p. 25. [See now Commission Regulation (EC) No 1400/2002 of 31 July 2002 on the application of Article 81(3) of the Treaty to categories of vertical agreements and concerted practices in the motor vehicle sector OJ L 203 1.8.2002, p. 30.]

(25) The Block Exemption Regulation also applies to goods sold and purchased for renting to third parties. However, rent and lease agreements as such are not covered, as no good or service is being sold by the supplier to the buyer. More generally, the Block Exemption Regulation does not cover restrictions or obligations that do not relate to the conditions of purchase, sale and resale, such as an obligation preventing parties from carrying out independent research and development which the parties may have included in an otherwise vertical agreement. In addition, Articles 2(2) to (5) directly or indirectly exclude certain vertical agreements from the application of the Block Exemption Regulation.

Commentary
para 25: F&N: 9.192

(ii) Vertical agreements between competitors

(26) Article 2(4) of the Block Exemption Regulation explicitly excludes from its application "vertical agreements entered into between competing undertakings". Vertical agreements between competitors will be dealt with, as regards possible collusion effects, in the forthcoming Guidelines on the applicability of Article 81 to horizontal cooperation.[1] However, the vertical aspects of such agreements need to be assessed under these Guidelines. Article 1(a) of the Block Exemption Regulation defines competing undertakings as "actual or potential suppliers in the same product market", irrespective of whether or not they are competitors on the same geographic market. Competing undertakings are undertakings that are actual or potential suppliers of the contract goods or services or goods or services that are substitutes for the contract goods or services. A potential supplier is an undertaking that does not actually produce a competing product but could and would be likely to do so in the absence of the agreement in response to a small and permanent increase in relative prices. This means that the undertaking would be able and likely to undertake the necessary additional investments and supply the market within 1 year. This assessment has to be based on realistic grounds; the mere theoretical possibility of entering a market is not sufficient.[2]

Notes

[1] Draft text published in OJ C 118, 27.4.2000, p. 14. [See now Commission Notice — Guidelines on the applicability of Article 81 of the EC Treaty to horizontal cooperation agreements (2001/C 3/02) OJ C 3, 6.1.2001, p. 2.]

[2] See Commission Notice on the definition of the relevant market for the purposes of Community competition law, OJ C 372, 9.12.1997, p. 5, at paras 20–24, the Commission's Thirteenth Report on Competition Policy, point 55, and Commission Decision 90/410/EEC in Case No IV/32.009 — *Elopak/Metal Box-Odin*, OJ L 209, 8.8.1990, p. 15.

Commentary
para 26: F&N: 9.193, 9.194, 12.177

---

(27) There are three exceptions to the general exclusion of vertical agreements between competitors, all three being set out in Article 2(4) and relating to non-reciprocal agreements. Non-reciprocal means, for instance, that while one manufacturer becomes the distributor of the products of another manufacturer, the latter does not become the distributor of the products of the first manufacturer. Non-reciprocal agreements between competitors are covered by the Block Exemption Regulation where (1) the buyer has a turnover not exceeding EUR 100 million, or (2) the supplier is a manufacturer and distributor of goods, while the buyer is only a distributor and not also a manufacturer of competing goods, or (3) the supplier is a provider of services operating at several levels of trade, while the buyer does not provide competing services at the level of trade where it purchases the contract services. The second exception covers situations of dual distribution, i.e. the manufacturer of particular goods also acts as a distributor of the goods in competition with independent distributors of his goods. A distributor who provides specifications to a manufacturer to produce particular goods under the distributor's brand name is not to be considered a manufacturer of such own-brand goods. The third exception covers similar situations of dual distribution, but in this case for services, when the supplier is also a provider of services at the level of the buyer.

Commentary
para 27: B&C: 6.193 F&N: 9.195, 9.196, 12.177

(iii) Associations of retailers

(28) Article 2(2) of the Block Exemption Regulation includes in its application vertical agreements entered into by an association of undertakings which fulfils certain conditions and thereby excludes from the Block Exemption Regulation vertical agreements entered into by all other associations. Vertical agreements entered into between an association and its members, or between an association and its suppliers, are covered by the Block Exemption Regulation only

if all the members are retailers of goods (not services) and if each individual member of the association has a turnover not exceeding EUR 50 million. Retailers are distributors reselling goods to final consumers. Where only a limited number of the members of the association have a turnover not significantly exceeding the EUR 50 million threshold, this will normally not change the assessment under Article 81.

(29) An association of undertakings may involve both horizontal and vertical agreements. The horizontal agreements have to be assessed according to the principles set out in the forthcoming Guidelines on the applicability of Article 81 to horizontal cooperation. If this assessment leads to the conclusion that a cooperation between undertakings in the area of purchasing or selling is acceptable, a further assessment will be necessary to examine the vertical agreements concluded by the association with its suppliers or its individual members. The latter assessment will follow the rules of the Block Exemption Regulation and these Guidelines. For instance, horizontal agreements concluded between the members of the association or decisions adopted by the association, such as the decision to require the members to purchase from the association or the decision to allocate exclusive territories to the members have to be assessed first as a horizontal agreement. Only if this assessment is positive does it become relevant to assess the vertical agreements between the association and individual members or between the association and suppliers.

(iv) Vertical agreements containing provisions on intellectual property rights (IPRs)

(30) Article 2(3) of the Block Exemption Regulation includes in its application vertical agreements containing certain provisions relating to the assignment of IPRs to or use of IPRs by the buyer and thereby excludes from the Block Exemption Regulation all other vertical agreements containing IPR provisions. The Block Exemption Regulation applies to vertical agreements containing IPR provisions when five conditions are fulfilled:
  — The IPR provisions must be part of a vertical agreement, i.e. an agreement with conditions under which the parties may purchase, sell or resell certain goods or services;
  — The IPRs must be assigned to, or for use by, the buyer;
  — The IPR provisions must not constitute the primary object of the agreement;
  — The IPR provisions must be directly related to the use, sale or resale of goods or services by the buyer or his customers. In the case of franchising where marketing forms the object of the exploitation of the IPRs, the goods or services are distributed by the master franchisee or the franchisees;
  — The IPR provisions, in relation to the contract goods or services, must not contain restrictions of competition having the same object or effect as vertical restraints which are not exempted under the Block Exemption Regulation.

(31) These conditions ensure that the Block Exemption Regulation applies to vertical agreements where the use, sale or resale of goods or services can be performed more effectively because IPRs are assigned to or transferred for use by the buyer. In other words, restrictions concerning the assignment or use of IPRs can be covered when the main object of the agreement is the purchase or distribution of goods or services.

Part C Substantive
Antitrust Matters

(32) The first condition makes clear that the context in which the IPRs are provided is an agreement to purchase or distribute goods or an agreement to purchase or provide services and not an agreement concerning the assignment or licensing of IPRs for the manufacture of goods, nor a pure licensing agreement. The Block Exemption Regulation does not cover for instance:
   — agreements where a party provides another party with a recipe and licenses the other party to produce a drink with this recipe;
   — agreements under which one party provides another party with a mould or master copy and licenses the other party to produce and distribute copies;
   — the pure licence of a trade mark or sign for the purposes of merchandising;
   — sponsorship contracts concerning the right to advertise oneself as being an official sponsor of an event;
   — copyright licensing such as broadcasting contracts concerning the right to record and/or the right to broadcast an event.

(33) The second condition makes clear that the Block Exemption Regulation does not apply when the IPRs are provided by the buyer to the supplier, no matter whether the IPRs concern the manner of manufacture or of distribution. An agreement relating to the transfer of IPRs to the supplier and containing possible restrictions on the sales made by the supplier is not covered by the Block Exemption Regulation. This means in particular that subcontracting involving the transfer of know-how to a subcontractor[1] does not fall within the scope of application of the Block Exemption Regulation. However, vertical agreements under which the buyer provides only specifications to the supplier which describe the goods or services to be supplied are covered by the Block Exemption Regulation.

Notes

[1]   See Notice on subcontracting, OJ C 1, 3.1.1979, p. 2.

Commentary
para 33: B&C: 6.193

(34) The third condition makes clear that in order to be covered by the Block Exemption Regulation the primary object of the agreement must not be the assignment or licensing of IPRs. The primary object must be the purchase or distribution of goods or services and the IPR provisions must serve the implementation of the vertical agreement.

(35) The fourth condition requires that the IPR provisions facilitate the use, sale or resale of goods or services by the buyer or his customers. The goods or services for use or resale are usually supplied by the licensor but may also be purchased by the licensee from a third supplier. The IPR provisions will normally concern the marketing of goods or services. This is for instance the case in a franchise agreement where the franchisor sells to the franchisee goods for resale and in addition licenses the franchisee to use his trade mark and know-how to market the goods. Also covered is the case where the supplier of a concentrated extract licenses the buyer to dilute and bottle the extract before selling it as a drink.

(36) The fifth condition signifies in particular that the IPR provisions should not have the same object or effect as any of the hardcore restrictions listed in Article 4 of the Block Exemption Regulation or any of the restrictions excluded from the coverage of the Block Exemption Regulation by Article 5 (see paragraphs 46 to 61).

(37) Intellectual property rights which may be considered to serve the implementation of vertical agreements within the meaning of Article 2(3) of the Block Exemption Regulation generally concern three main areas: trade marks, copyright and know-how.

Trade mark

(38) A trade mark licence to a distributor may be related to the distribution of the licensor's products in a particular territory. If it is an exclusive licence, the agreement amounts to exclusive distribution.

Copyright

(39) Resellers of goods covered by copyright (books, software, etc.) may be obliged by the copyright holder only to resell under the condition that the buyer, whether another reseller or the end user, shall not infringe the copyright. Such obligations on the reseller, to the extent that they fall under Article 81(1) at all, are covered by the Block Exemption Regulation.

(40) Agreements under which hard copies of software are supplied for resale and where the reseller does not acquire a licence to any rights over the software but only has the right to resell the hard copies, are to be regarded as agreements for the supply of goods for resale for the purpose of the Block Exemption Regulation. Under this form of distribution the licence of the software only takes place between the copyright owner and the user of the software. This may take the form of a "shrink wrap" licence, i.e. a set of conditions included in the package of the hard copy which the end user is deemed to accept by opening the package.

(41) Buyers of hardware incorporating software protected by copyright may be obliged by the copyright holder not to infringe the copyright, for example not to make copies and resell the software or not to make copies and use the software in combination with other hardware. Such use-restrictions, to the extent that they fall within Article 81(1) at all, are covered by the Block Exemption Regulation.

Know-how

(42) Franchise agreements, with the exception of industrial franchise agreements, are the most obvious example where know-how for marketing purposes is communicated to the buyer. Franchise agreements contain licences of intellectual property rights relating to trade marks or signs and know-how for the use and distribution of goods or the provision of services. In addition to the licence of IPR, the franchisor usually provides the franchisee during the life of the agreement with commercial or technical assistance, such as procurement services, training, advice on real estate, financial planning etc. The licence and the assistance are integral components of the business method being franchised.

Commentary
para 42: B&C: 6.171 **F&N:** 9.203

---

(43) Licensing contained in franchise agreements is covered by the Block Exemption Regulation if all five conditions listed in point 30 are fulfilled. This is usually the case, as under most franchise agreements, including master franchise agreements, the franchisor provides goods and/or services, in particular commercial or technical assistance services, to the franchisee. The IPRs help the franchisee to resell the products supplied by the franchisor or by a supplier designated by the franchisor or to use those products and sell the resulting goods or services. Where the franchise agreement only or primarily concerns licensing of IPRs, such an agreement is not covered by the Block Exemption Regulation, but it will be treated in a way similar to those franchise agreements which are covered by the Block Exemption Regulation.

Commentary
para 43: B&C: 6.183, 6.188 **F&N:** 9.204

---

(44) The following IPR-related obligations are generally considered to be necessary to protect the franchisor's intellectual property rights and are, if these obligations fall under Article 81(1), also covered by the Block Exemption Regulation:

(a) an obligation on the franchisee not to engage, directly or indirectly, in any similar business;

(b) an obligation on the franchisee not to acquire financial interests in the capital of a competing undertaking such as would give the franchisee the power to influence the economic conduct of such undertaking;

(c) an obligation on the franchisee not to disclose to third parties the know-how provided by the franchisor as long as this know-how is not in the public domain;

(d) an obligation on the franchisee to communicate to the franchisor any experience gained in exploiting the franchise and to grant it, and other franchisees, a non-exclusive licence for the know-how resulting from that experience;

(e) an obligation on the franchisee to inform the franchisor of infringements of licensed intellectual property rights, to take legal action against infringers or to assist the franchisor in any legal actions against infringers;

(f) an obligation on the franchisee not to use know-how licensed by the franchisor for purposes other than the exploitation of the franchise;

(g) an obligation on the franchisee not to assign the rights and obligations under the franchise agreement without the franchisor's consent.

Commentary
para 44: B&C: 6.187 F&N: 12.236

(v) Relationship to other block exemption regulations

(45) Article 2(5) states that the Block Exemption Regulation does "not apply to vertical agreements the subject matter of which falls within the scope of any other block exemption regulation." This means that the Block Exemption Regulation does not apply to vertical agreements covered by Commission Regulation (EC) No 240/96[1] on technology transfer, Commission Regulation (EC) No 1475/1995[2] for car distribution or Regulations (EEC) No 417/85[3] and (EEC) No 418/85[4] exempting vertical agreements concluded in connection with horizontal agreements, as last amended by Regulation (EC) No 2236/97[5] or any future regulations of that kind.

Notes

[1] OJ L 31, 9.2.1996, p. 2. [See now Commission Regulation (EC) No 772/2004 of 27 April 2004 on the application of Article 81(3) of the Treaty to categories of technology transfer agreements OJ L 123, 27.4.2004, p. 11.]

[2] OJ L 145, 29.6.1995, p. 25. [See now Commission Regulation (EC) No 1400/2002 of 31 July 2002 on the application of Article 81(3) of the Treaty to categories of vertical agreements and concerted practices in the motor vehicle sector OJ L 203, 1.8.2002, p. 30.]

[3] OJ L 53, 22.2.1985, p. 1. [See now Commission Regulation (EC) No 2658/2000 of 29 November 2000 on the application of Article 81(3) of the Treaty to categories of specialisation agreements OJ L 304, 5.12.2000, p. 3.]

[4] OJ L 53, 22.2.1985, p. 5. [See now Commission Regulation (EC) No 2659/2000 of 29 November 2000 on the application of Article 81(3) of the treaty to categories of research and development agreements, OJ L 304, 5.12.2000, p. 7.]

[5] OJ L 306, 11.11.1997, p. 12.

3. Hardcore restrictions under the Block Exemption Regulation

(46) The Block Exemption Regulation contains in Article 4 a list of hardcore restrictions which lead to the exclusion of the whole vertical agreement from the scope of application of the Block Exemption Regulation. This list of hardcore restrictions applies to vertical agreements concerning trade within the Community. In so far as vertical agreements concern exports outside the Community or imports/re-imports from outside the Community see the judgment in Javico v Yves Saint Laurent. Individual exemption of vertical agreements containing such hardcore restrictions is also unlikely.

Commentary
para 46: B&C: 6.170 F&N: 9.207, 12.191, 12.198, 15.23, 15.152

(47) The hardcore restriction set out in Article 4(a) of the Block Exemption Regulation concerns resale price maintenance (RPM), that is agreements or concerted practices having as their direct or indirect object the establishment of a fixed or minimum resale price or a fixed or minimum price level to be observed by the buyer. In the case of contractual provisions or concerted practices that directly establish the resale price, the restriction is clear cut. However, RPM can also be achieved through indirect means. Examples of the latter are an agreement fixing the distribution margin, fixing the maximum level of discount the distributor can grant from a prescribed price level, making the grant of rebates or reimbursement of promotional costs by the supplier subject to the observance of a given price level, linking the prescribed resale price to the resale prices of competitors, threats, intimidation, warnings, penalties, delay or suspension of deliveries or contract terminations in relation to observance of a given price level. Direct or indirect means of achieving price fixing can be made more effective when combined with measures to

identify price-cutting distributors, such as the implementation of a price monitoring system, or the obligation on retailers to report other members of the distribution network who deviate from the standard price level. Similarly, direct or indirect price fixing can be made more effective when combined with measures which may reduce the buyer's incentive to lower the resale price, such as the supplier printing a recommended resale price on the product or the supplier obliging the buyer to apply a most-favoured-customer clause. The same indirect means and the same "supportive" measures can be used to make maximum or recommended prices work as RPM. However, the provision of a list of recommended prices or maximum prices by the supplier to the buyer is not considered in itself as leading to RPM.

Commentary
para 47: **B&C:** 6.023, 6.051 **F&N:** 9.210, 9.211

(48) In the case of agency agreements, the principal normally establishes the sales price, as the agent does not become the owner of the goods. However, where an agency agreement falls within Article 81(1) (see paragraphs 12 to 20), an obligation preventing or restricting the agent from sharing his commission, fixed or variable, with the customer would be a hardcore restriction under Article 4(a) of the Block Exemption Regulation. The agent should thus be left free to lower the effective price paid by the customer without reducing the income for the principal.[1]

Notes
[1] See, for instance, Commission Decision 91/562/EEC in Case No IV/32.737 — *Eirpage*, OJ L 306, 7.11.1991, p. 22, in particular point (6).

Commentary
para 48: **B&C:** 6.038 **F&N:** 9.212

(49) The hardcore restriction set out in Article 4(b) of the Block Exemption Regulation concerns agreements or concerted practices that have as their direct or indirect object the restriction of sales by the buyer, in as far as those restrictions relate to the territory into which or the customers to whom the buyer may sell the contract goods or services. That hardcore restriction relates to market partitioning by territory or by customer. That may be the result of direct obligations, such as the obligation not to sell to certain customers or to customers in certain territories or the obligation to refer orders from these customers to other distributors. It may also result from indirect measures aimed at inducing the distributor not to sell to such customers, such as refusal or reduction of bonuses or discounts, refusal to supply, reduction of supplied volumes or limitation of supplied volumes to the demand within the allocated territory or customer group, threat of contract termination or profit pass-over obligations. It may further result from the supplier not providing a Community-wide guarantee service, whereby all distributors are obliged to provide the guarantee service and are reimbursed for this service by the supplier, even in relation to products sold by other distributors into their territory. These practices are even more likely to be viewed as a restriction of the buyer's sales when used in conjunction with the implementation by the supplier of a monitoring system aimed at verifying the effective destination of the supplied goods, e.g. the use of differentiated labels or serial numbers. However, a prohibition imposed on all distributors to sell to certain end users is not classified as a hardcore restriction if there is an objective justification related to the product, such as a general ban on selling dangerous substances to certain customers for reasons of safety or health. It implies that also the supplier himself does not sell to these customers. Nor are obligations on the reseller relating to the display of the supplier's brand name classified as hardcore.

Commentary
para 49: **B&C:** 6.023, 6.068 **F&N:** 9.214, 9.215

(50) There are four exceptions to the hardcore restriction in Article 4(b) of the Block Exemption Regulation. The first exception allows a supplier to restrict active sales by his direct buyers to a territory or a customer group which has been allocated exclusively to another buyer or which the supplier has reserved to itself. A territory or customer group is exclusively allocated when the supplier agrees to sell his product only to one distributor for distribution in a particular territory

or to a particular customer group and the exclusive distributor is protected against active selling into his territory or to his customer group by the supplier and all the other buyers of the supplier inside the Community. The supplier is allowed to combine the allocation of an exclusive territory and an exclusive customer group by for instance appointing an exclusive distributor for a particular customer group in a certain territory. This protection of exclusively allocated territories or customer groups must, however, permit passive sales to such territories or customer groups. For the application of Article 4(b) of the Block Exemption Regulation, the Commission interprets "active" and "passive" sales as follows:

— "Active" sales mean actively approaching individual customers inside another distributor's exclusive territory or exclusive customer group by for instance direct mail or visits; or actively approaching a specific customer group or customers in a specific territory allocated exclusively to another distributor through advertisement in media or other promotions specifically targeted at that customer group or targeted at customers in that territory; or establishing a warehouse or distribution outlet in another distributor's exclusive territory.

— "Passive" sales mean responding to unsolicited requests from individual customers including delivery of goods or services to such customers. General advertising or promotion in media or on the Internet that reaches customers in other distributors' exclusive territories or customer groups but which is a reasonable way to reach customers outside those territories or customer groups, for instance to reach customers in non-exclusive territories or in one's own territory, are passive sales.

Commentary
para 50: **B&C:** 6.023, 6.054, 9.152, 9.158 **F&N:** 9.11, 9.218, 10.108, 12.192, 12.199, 15.41

---

(51) Every distributor must be free to use the Internet to advertise or to sell products. A restriction on the use of the Internet by distributors could only be compatible with the Block Exemption Regulation to the extent that promotion on the Internet or sales over the Internet would lead to active selling into other distributors' exclusive territories or customer groups. In general, the use of the Internet is not considered a form of active sales into such territories or customer groups, since it is a reasonable way to reach every customer. The fact that it may have effects outside one's own territory or customer group results from the technology, i.e. the easy access from everywhere. If a customer visits the web site of a distributor and contacts the distributor and if such contact leads to a sale, including delivery, then that is considered passive selling. The language used on the website or in the communication plays normally no role in that respect. Insofar as a web site is not specifically targeted at customers primarily inside the territory or customer group exclusively allocated to another distributor, for instance with the use of banners or links in pages of providers specifically available to these exclusively allocated customers, the website is not considered a form of active selling. However, unsolicited e-mails sent to individual customers or specific customer groups are considered active selling. The same considerations apply to selling by catalogue. Notwithstanding what has been said before, the supplier may require quality standards for the use of the Internet site to resell his goods, just as the supplier may require quality standards for a shop or for advertising and promotion in general. The latter may be relevant in particular for selective distribution. An outright ban on Internet or catalogue selling is only possible if there is an objective justification. In any case, the supplier cannot reserve to itself sales and/or advertising over the Internet.

Commentary
para 51: **B&C:** 6.023, 6.054, 6.095 **F&N:** 9.223, 9.224

---

(52) There are three other exceptions to the second hardcore restriction set out in Article 4(b) of the Block Exemption Regulation. All three exceptions allow for the restriction of both active and passive sales. Thus, it is permissible to restrict a wholesaler from selling to end users, to restrict an appointed distributor in a selective distribution system from selling, at any level of trade, to unauthorised distributors in markets where such a system is operated, and to restrict a buyer of components supplied for incorporation from reselling them to competitors of the supplier.

The term "component" includes any intermediate goods and the term "incorporation" refers to the use of any input to produce goods.

Commentary
para 52: B&C: 6.023 F&N: 9.230

(53) The hardcore restriction set out in Article 4(c) of the Block Exemption Regulation concerns the restriction of active or passive sales to end users, whether professional end users or final consumers, by members of a selective distribution network. This means that dealers in a selective distribution system, as defined in Article 1(d) of the Block Exemption Regulation, cannot be restricted in the users or purchasing agents acting on behalf of these users to whom they may sell. For instance, also in a selective distribution system the dealer should be free to advertise and sell with the help of the Internet. Selective distribution may be combined with exclusive distribution provided that active and passive selling is not restricted anywhere. The supplier may therefore commit itself to supplying only one dealer or a limited number of dealers in a given territory.

Commentary
para 53: B&C: 6.023, 6.187 F&N: 9.227

(54) In addition, in the case of selective distribution, restrictions can be imposed on the dealer's ability to determine the location of his business premises. Selected dealers may be prevented from running their business from different premises or from opening a new outlet in a different location. If the dealer's outlet is mobile ("shop on wheels"), an area may be defined outside which the mobile outlet cannot be operated.

Commentary
para 54: B&C: 6.023 F&N: 9.227, 15.56

(55) The hardcore restriction set out in Article 4(d) of the Block Exemption Regulation concerns the restriction of cross-supplies between appointed distributors within a selective distribution system. This means that an agreement or concerted practice may not have as its direct or indirect object to prevent or restrict the active or passive selling of the contract products between the selected distributors. Selected distributors must remain free to purchase the contract products from other appointed distributors within the network, operating either at the same or at a different level of trade. This means that selective distribution cannot be combined with vertical restraints aimed at forcing distributors to purchase the contract products exclusively from a given source, for instance exclusive purchasing. It also means that within a selective distribution network no restrictions can be imposed on appointed wholesalers as regards their sales of the product to appointed retailers.

Commentary
para 55: 9.228, 15.53

(56) The hardcore restriction set out in Article 4(e) of the Block Exemption Regulation concerns agreements that prevent or restrict end-users, independent repairers and service providers from obtaining spare parts directly from the manufacturer of these spare parts. An agreement between a manufacturer of spare parts and a buyer who incorporates these parts into his own products (original equipment manufacturer (OEM)), may not, either directly or indirectly, prevent or restrict sales by the manufacturer of these spare parts to end users, independent repairers or service providers. Indirect restrictions may arise in particular when the supplier of the spare parts is restricted in supplying technical information and special equipment which are necessary for the use of spare parts by users, independent repairers or service providers. However, the agreement may place restrictions on the supply of the spare parts to the repairers or service providers entrusted by the original equipment manufacturer with the repair or servicing of his own goods. In other words, the original equipment manufacturer may require his own repair and service network to buy the spare parts from it.

Commentary
para 56: F&N: 9.231

4. Conditions under the Block Exemption Regulation

(57) Article 5 of the Block Exemption Regulation excludes certain obligations from the coverage of the Block Exemption Regulation even though the market share threshold is not exceeded. However, the Block Exemption Regulation continues to apply to the remaining part of the vertical agreement if that part is severable from the non-exempted obligations.

Commentary
para 57: F&N: 9.232, 15.24

(58) The first exclusion is provided in Article 5(a) of the Block Exemption Regulation and concerns non-compete obligations. Non-compete obligations are obligations that require the buyer to purchase from the supplier or from another undertaking designated by the supplier more than 80% of the buyer's total purchases during the previous year of the contract goods and services and their substitutes (see the definition in Article 1(b) of the Block Exemption Regulation), thereby preventing the buyer from purchasing competing goods or services or limiting such purchases to less than 20% of total purchases. Where for the year preceding the conclusion of the contract no relevant purchasing data for the buyer are available, the buyer's best estimate of his annual total requirements may be used. Such non-compete obligations are not covered by the Block Exemption Regulation when their duration is indefinite or exceeds five years. Non-compete obligations that are tacitly renewable beyond a period of five years are also not covered by the Block Exemption Regulation. However, non-compete obligations are covered when their duration is limited to five years or less, or when renewal beyond five years requires explicit consent of both parties and no obstacles exist that hinder the buyer from effectively terminating the non-compete obligation at the end of the five year period. If for instance the agreement provides for a five-year non-compete obligation and the supplier provides a loan to the buyer, the repayment of that loan should not hinder the buyer from effectively terminating the non-compete obligation at the end of the five-year period; the repayment needs to be structured in equal or decreasing instalments and should not increase over time. This is without prejudice to the possibility, in the case for instance of a new distribution outlet, to delay repayment for the first one or two years until sales have reached a certain level. The buyer must have the possibility to repay the remaining debt where there is still an outstanding debt at the end of the non-compete obligation. Similarly, when the supplier provides the buyer with equipment which is not relationship-specific, the buyer should have the possibility to take over the equipment at its market asset value at the end of the non-compete obligation.

Commentary
para 58: B&C: 6.024, 6.166 F&N: 4.233, 9.234, 9.236

(59) The five-year duration limit does not apply when the goods or services are resold by the buyer "from premises and land owned by the supplier or leased by the supplier from third parties not connected with the buyer." In such cases the non-compete obligation may be of the same duration as the period of occupancy of the point of sale by the buyer (Article 5(a) of the Block Exemption Regulation). The reason for this exception is that it is normally unreasonable to expect a supplier to allow competing products to be sold from premises and land owned by the supplier without his permission. Artificial ownership constructions intended to avoid the five-year limit cannot benefit from this exception.

Commentary
para 59: B&C: 6.152 F&N: 9.235

(60) The second exclusion from the block exemption is provided for in Article 5(b) of the Block Exemption Regulation and concerns post term non-compete obligations. Such obligations are normally not covered by the Block Exemption Regulation, unless the obligation is indispensable

to protect know-how transferred by the supplier to the buyer, is limited to the point of sale from which the buyer has operated during the contract period, and is limited to a maximum period of one year. According to the definition in Article 1(f) of the Block Exemption Regulation the know-how needs to be "substantial", meaning "that the know-how includes information which is indispensable to the buyer for the use, sale or resale of the contract goods or services".

(61) The third exclusion from the block exemption is provided for in Article 5(c) of the Block Exemption Regulation and concerns the sale of competing goods in a selective distribution system. The Block Exemption Regulation covers the combination of selective distribution with a non-compete obligation, obliging the dealers not to resell competing brands in general. However, if the supplier prevents his appointed dealers, either directly or indirectly, from buying products for resale from specific competing suppliers, such an obligation cannot enjoy the benefit of the Block Exemption Regulation. The objective of the exclusion of this obligation is to avoid a situation whereby a number of suppliers using the same selective distribution outlets prevent one specific competitor or certain specific competitors from using these outlets to distribute their products (foreclosure of a competing supplier which would be a form of collective boycott).[1]

Notes
[1] An example of indirect measures having such exclusionary effects can be found in Commission Decision 92/428/EEC in Case No IV/33.542 — *Parfum Givenchy* (OJ L 236, 19.8.1992, p. 11).

Commentary
para 61: B&C: 6.024, 6.107

5. No presumption of illegality outside the block exemption regulation

(62) Vertical agreements falling outside the Block Exemption Regulation will not be presumed to be illegal but may need individual examination. Companies are encouraged to do their own assessment without notification. In the case of an individual examination by the Commission, the latter will bear the burden of proof that the agreement in question infringes Article 81(1). When appreciable anti-competitive effects are demonstrated, undertakings may substantiate efficiency claims and explain why a certain distribution system is likely to bring about benefits which are relevant to the conditions for exemption under Article 81(3).

Commentary
para 62: B&C: 3.068–3.069 F&N: 3.316, 9.165, 15.93

6. No need for precautionary notification

(63) Pursuant to Article 4(2) of Council Regulation No 17 of 6 February 1962, First Regulation implementing Articles [81] and [82] of the Treaty,[1] as last amended by Regulation (EC) No 1216/1999,[2] vertical agreements can benefit from an exemption under Article 81(3) from their date of entry into force, even if notification occurs after that date. This means in practice that no precautionary notification needs to be made. If a dispute arises, an undertaking can still notify, in which case the Commission can exempt the vertical agreement with retroactive effect from the date of entry into force of the agreement if all four conditions of Article 81(3) are fulfilled. A notifying party does not have to explain why the agreement was not notified earlier and will not be denied retroactive exemption simply because it did not notify earlier. Any notification will be reviewed on its merits. This amendment to Article 4(2) of Regulation No 17 should eliminate artificial litigation before national courts and thus strengthen the civil enforceability of contracts. It also takes account of the situation where undertakings have not notified because they assumed the agreement was covered by the Block Exemption Regulation.

Notes
[1] OJ 13, 21.2.1962, p. 204/62. [See now Council Regulation (EC) 1/2003, OJ L 1, 4.1.2003, p. 1.]
[2] OJ L 148, 15.6.1999, p. 5.

Commentary
para 63: B&C: 6.017

Part C Substantive
Antitrust Matters

(64) Since the date of notification no longer limits the possibility of exemption by the Commission, national courts have to assess the likelihood that Article 81(3) will apply in respect of vertical agreements falling within Article 81(1). If such likelihood exists, they should suspend proceedings pending adoption of a position by the Commission. However, national courts may adopt interim measures pending the assessment by the Commission of the applicability of Article 81(3), in the same way as they do when they refer a preliminary question to the Court of Justice under Article 234 of the EC Treaty. No suspension is necessary in respect of injunction proceedings, where national courts themselves are empowered to assess the likelihood of application of Article 81(3).[1]

Notes

[1] Case C-234/89 *Delimitis v Henninger Bräu* [1991] ECR I-935, at paragraph 52.

(65) Unless there is litigation in national courts or complaints, notifications of vertical agreements will not be given priority in the Commission's enforcement policy. Notifications as such do not provide provisional validity for the execution of agreements. Where undertakings have not notified an agreement because they assumed in good faith that the market share threshold under the Block Exemption Regulation was not exceeded, the Commission will not impose fines.

7. Severability

(66) The Block Exemption Regulation exempts vertical agreements on condition that no hardcore restriction, as set out in Article 4, is contained in or practised with the vertical agreement. If there are one or more hardcore restrictions, the benefit of the Block Exemption Regulation is lost for the entire vertical agreement. There is no severability for hardcore restrictions.

Commentary
para 66: F&N: 9.207

(67) The rule of severability does apply, however, to the conditions set out in Article 5 of the Block Exemption Regulation. Therefore, the benefit of the block exemption is only lost in relation to that part of the vertical agreement which does not comply with the conditions set out in Article 5.

Commentary
para 67: F&N: 9.207, 9.232

8. Portfolio of products distributed through the same distribution system

(68) Where a supplier uses the same distribution agreement to distribute several goods/services some of these may, in view of the market share threshold, be covered by the Block Exemption Regulation while others may not. In that case, the Block Exemption Regulation applies to those goods and services for which the conditions of application are fulfilled.

(69) In respect of the goods or services which are not covered by the Block Exemption Regulation, the ordinary rules of competition apply, which means:

— there is no block exemption but also no presumption of illegality;
— if there is an infringement of Article 81(1) which is not exemptable, consideration may be given to whether there are appropriate remedies to solve the competition problem within the existing distribution system;
— if there are no such appropriate remedies, the supplier concerned will have to make other distribution arrangements.

This situation can also arise where Article 82 applies in respect of some products but not in respect of others.

Commentary
para 69: B&C: 6.021 F&N: 9.273

9. Transitional period

(70) The Block Exemption Regulation applies from 1 June 2000. Article 12 of the Block Exemption Regulation provides for a transitional period for vertical agreements already in force before 1 June 2000 which do not satisfy the conditions for exemption provided in the Block Exemption Regulation, but which do satisfy the conditions for exemption under the Block Exemption Regulations which expired on 31 May 2000 (Commissions Regulations (EEC) No 1983/83, (EEC) No 1984/83 and (EEC) No 4087/88). The Commission Notice concerning Regulations (EEC) Nos 1983/83 and 1984/83 also ceases to apply on 31 May 2000. The latter agreements may continue to benefit from these outgoing Regulations until 31 December 2001. Agreements of suppliers with a market share not exceeding 30% who signed with their buyers non-compete agreements with a duration exceeding five years are covered by the Block Exemption Regulation if on 1 January 2002 the non-compete agreements have no more than five years to run.

Commentary
para 70: F&N: 9.261

IV. WITHDRAWAL OF THE BLOCK EXEMPTION AND DISAPPLICATION OF THE BLOCK EXEMPTION REGULATION

1. Withdrawal procedure

(71) The presumption of legality conferred by the Block Exemption Regulation may be withdrawn if a vertical agreement, considered either in isolation or in conjunction with similar agreements enforced by competing suppliers or buyers, comes within the scope of Article 81(1) and does not fulfil all the conditions of Article 81(3). This may occur when a supplier, or a buyer in the case of exclusive supply agreements, holding a market share not exceeding 30%, enters into a vertical agreement which does not give rise to objective advantages such as to compensate for the damage which it causes to competition. This may particularly be the case with respect to the distribution of goods to final consumers, who are often in a much weaker position than professional buyers of intermediate goods. In the case of sales to final consumers, the disadvantages caused by a vertical agreement may have a stronger impact than in a case concerning the sale and purchase of intermediate goods. When the conditions of Article 81(3) are not fulfilled, the Commission may withdraw the benefit of the Block Exemption Regulation under Article 6 and establish an infringement of Article 81(1).

Commentary
para 71: B&C: 6.025

(72) Where the withdrawal procedure is applied, the Commission bears the burden of proof that the agreement falls within the scope of Article 81(1) and that the agreement does not fulfil all four conditions of Article 81(3).

(73) The conditions for an exemption under Article 81(3) may in particular not be fulfilled when access to the relevant market or competition therein is significantly restricted by the cumulative effect of parallel networks of similar vertical agreements practised by competing suppliers or buyers. Parallel networks of vertical agreements are to be regarded as similar if they contain restraints producing similar effects on the market. Similar effects will normally occur when vertical restraints practised by competing suppliers or buyers come within one of the four groups listed in paragraphs 104 to 114. Such a situation may arise for example when, on a given market, certain suppliers practise purely qualitative selective distribution while other suppliers practise quantitative selective distribution. In such circumstances, the assessment must take account of the anti-competitive effects attributable to each individual network of agreements. Where appropriate, withdrawal may concern only the quantitative limitations imposed on the number of authorised distributors. Other cases in which a withdrawal decision may be taken include situations where the buyer, for example in the context of exclusive supply or exclusive distribution, has significant market power in the relevant downstream market where he resells the goods or provides the services.

(74) Responsibility for an anti-competitive cumulative effect can only be attributed to those under-takings which make an appreciable contribution to it. Agreements entered into by undertakings whose contribution to the cumulative effect is insignificant do not fall under the prohibition provided for in Article 81(1)[1] and are therefore not subject to the withdrawal mechanism. The assessment of such a contribution will be made in accordance with the criteria set out in para-graphs 137 to 229.

Notes

[1] Judgment in the *Delimitis* Case [Case C-234/89 *Delimitis v Henninger Bräu* [1991] ECR I-935].

(75) A withdrawal decision can only have *ex nunc* effect, which means that the exempted status of the agreements concerned will not be affected until the date at which the withdrawal becomes effective.

(76) Under Article 7 of the Block Exemption Regulation, the competent authority of a Member State may withdraw the benefit of the Block Exemption Regulation in respect of vertical agreements whose anti-competitive effects are felt in the territory of the Member State concerned or a part thereof, which has all the characteristics of a distinct geographic market. Where a Member State has not enacted legislation enabling the national competition authority to apply Community competition law or at least to withdraw the benefit of the Block Exemption Regulation, the Member State may ask the Commission to initiate proceedings to this effect.

(77) The Commission has the exclusive power to withdraw the benefit of the Block Exemption Regulation in respect of vertical agreements restricting competition on a relevant geographic market which is wider than the territory of a single Member State. When the territory of a single Member State, or a part thereof, constitutes the relevant geographic market, the Commission and the Member State concerned have concurrent competence for withdrawal. Often, such cases lend themselves to decentralised enforcement by national competition authorities. However, the Commission reserves the right to take on certain cases displaying a particular Community interest, such as cases raising a new point of law.

Commentary
para 77: B&C: 3.087, 6.026

(78) National decisions of withdrawal must be taken in accordance with the procedures laid down under national law and will only have effect within the territory of the Member State concerned. Such national decisions must not prejudice the uniform application of the Community com-petition rules and the full effect of the measures adopted in implementation of those rules.[1] Compliance with this principle implies that national competition authorities must carry out their assessment under Article 81 in the light of the relevant criteria developed by the Court of Justice and the Court of First Instance and in the light of notices and previous decisions adopted by the Commission.

Notes

[1] Judgment of the Court of Justice in Case 14/68 *Walt Wilhelm and Others v Bundeskartellamt* [1969] ECR 1, paragraph 4, and judgment in *Delimitis*.

Commentary
para 78: B&C: 6.026

(79) The Commission considers that the consultation mechanisms provided for in the Notice on cooperation between national competition authorities and the Commission[1] should be used to avert the risk of conflicting decisions and duplication of procedures.

Notes

[1] OJ C 313, 15.10.1997, p. 3, points 49 to 53. [See now Commission Notice on the co-operation between the Commission and the courts of the EU Member States in the application of Articles 81 and 82 EC, OJ C 101, 27.4.2004, p. 54.]

2. Disapplication of the Block Exemption Regulation

(80) Article 8 of the Block Exemption Regulation enables the Commission to exclude from the scope of the Block Exemption Regulation, by means of regulation, parallel networks of similar vertical restraints where these cover more than 50% of a relevant market. Such a measure is not addressed to individual undertakings but concerns all undertakings whose agreements are defined in the regulation disapplying the Block Exemption Regulation.

(81) Whereas the withdrawal of the benefit of the Block Exemption Regulation under Article 6 implies the adoption of a decision establishing an infringement of Article 81 by an individual company, the effect of a regulation under Article 8 is merely to remove, in respect of the restraints and the markets concerned, the benefit of the application of the Block Exemption Regulation and to restore the full application of Article 81(1) and (3). Following the adoption of a regulation declaring the Block Exemption inapplicable in respect of certain vertical restraints on a particular market, the criteria developed by the relevant case-law of the Court of Justice and the Court of First Instance and by notices and previous decisions adopted by the Commission will guide the application of Article 81 to individual agreements. Where appropriate, the Commission will take a decision in an individual case, which can provide guidance to all the undertakings operating on the market concerned.

Commentary
para 81: **B&C:** 3.089, 6.025, 6.027

(82) For the purpose of calculating the 50% market coverage ratio, account must be taken of each individual network of vertical agreements containing restraints, or combinations of restraints, producing similar effects on the market. Similar effects normally result when the restraints come within one of the four groups listed in paragraphs 104 to 114.

Commentary
para 82: **B&C:** 6.027

(83) Article 8 does not entail an obligation on the part of the Commission to act where the 50% market-coverage ratio is exceeded. In general, disapplication is appropriate when it is likely that access to the relevant market or competition therein is appreciably restricted. This may occur in particular when parallel networks of selective distribution covering more than 50% of a market make use of selection criteria which are not required by the nature of the relevant goods or discriminate against certain forms of distribution capable of selling such goods.

Commentary
para 83: **F&N:** 15.165

(84) In assessing the need to apply Article 8, the Commission will consider whether individual withdrawal would be a more appropriate remedy. This may depend, in particular, on the number of competing undertakings contributing to a cumulative effect on a market or the number of affected geographic markets within the Community.

Commentary
para 84: **B&C:** 6.027

(85) Any regulation adopted under Article 8 must clearly set out its scope. This means, first, that the Commission must define the relevant product and geographic market(s) and, secondly, that it must identify the type of vertical restraint in respect of which the Block Exemption Regulation will no longer apply. As regards the latter aspect, the Commission may modulate the scope of its regulation according to the competition concern which it intends to address. For instance, while all parallel networks of single-branding type arrangements shall be taken into account in view of establishing the 50% market coverage ratio, the Commission may nevertheless restrict the scope of the disapplication regulation only to non-compete obligations exceeding a certain duration. Thus, agreements of a shorter duration or of a less restrictive nature might be left unaffected,

in consideration of the lesser degree of foreclosure attributable to such restraints. Similarly, when on a particular market selective distribution is practised in combination with additional restraints such as non-compete or quantity-forcing on the buyer, the disapplication regulation may concern only such additional restraints. Where appropriate, the Commission may also provide guidance by specifying the market share level which, in the specific market context, may be regarded as insufficient to bring about a significant contribution by an individual undertaking to the cumulative effect.

(86) The transitional period of not less than six months that the Commission will have to set under Article 8(2) should allow the undertakings concerned to adapt their agreements to take account of the regulation disapplying the Block Exemption Regulation.

Commentary
para 86: B&C: 6.027

(87) A regulation disapplying the Block Exemption Regulation will not affect the exempted status of the agreements concerned for the period preceding its entry into force.

Commentary
para 87: B&C: 6.027

V. Market Definition and Market Share Calculation Issues

1. Commission notice on definition of the relevant market

(88) The Commission Notice on definition of the relevant market for the purposes of Community competition law[1] provides guidance on the rules, criteria and evidence which the Commission uses when considering market definition issues. That Notice will not be further explained in these Guidelines and should serve as the basis for market definition issues. These Guidelines will only deal with specific issues that arise in the context of vertical restraints and that are not dealt with in the general notice on market definition.

Notes
[1] OJ C 372, 9.12.1997, p. 5.

2. The relevant market for calculating the 30% market share threshold under the Block Exemption Regulation

(89) Under Article 3 of the Block Exemption Regulation, it is in general the market share of the supplier that is decisive for the application of the block exemption. In the case of vertical agreements concluded between an association of retailers and individual members, the association is the supplier and needs to take into account its market share as a supplier. Only in the case of exclusive supply as defined in Article 1(c) of the Block Exemption Regulation is it the market share of the buyer, and only that market share, which is decisive for the application of the Block Exemption Regulation.

(90) In order to calculate the market share, it is necessary to determine the relevant market. For this, the relevant product market and the relevant geographic market must be defined. The relevant product market comprises any goods or services which are regarded by the buyer as interchangeable, by reason of their characteristics, prices and intended use. The relevant geographic market comprises the area in which the undertakings concerned are involved in the supply and demand of relevant goods or services, in which the conditions of competition are sufficiently homogeneous, and which can be distinguished from neighbouring geographic areas because, in particular, conditions of competition are appreciably different in those areas.

Commentary
para 90: F&N: 9.270

(91) For the application of the Block Exemption Regulation, the market share of the supplier is his share on the relevant product and geographic market on which he sells to his buyers.[1]

In the example given in paragraph 92, this is market A. The product market depends in the first place on substitutability from the buyers' perspective. When the supplied product is used as an input to produce other products and is generally not recognisable in the final product, the product market is normally defined by the direct buyers' preferences. The customers of the buyers will normally not have a strong preference concerning the inputs used by the buyers. Usually the vertical restraints agreed between the supplier and buyer of the input only relate to the sale and purchase of the intermediate product and not to the sale of the resulting product. In the case of distribution of final goods, what are substitutes for the direct buyers will normally be influenced or determined by the preferences of the final consumers. A distributor, as reseller, cannot ignore the preferences of final consumers when he purchases final goods. In addition, at the distribution level the vertical restraints usually concern not only the sale of products between supplier and buyer, but also their resale. As different distribution formats usually compete, markets are in general not defined by the form of distribution that is applied. Where suppliers generally sell a portfolio of products, the entire portfolio may determine the product market when the portfolios and not the individual products are regarded as substitutes by the buyers. As the buyers on market A are professional buyers, the geographic market is usually wider than the market where the product is resold to final consumers. Often, this will lead to the definition of national markets or wider geographic markets.

Notes

[1] For example, the Dutch market for new replacement truck and bus tyres in the *Michelin* case (Case 322/81 *Nederlandsche Banden-Industrie Michelin v Commission* [1983] ECR 3461), the various meat markets in the Danish slaughter-house case: Commission Decision 2000/42/EC in Case No IV/M.1313 — *Danish Crown/Vestjyske Slagterier*, OJ L 20, 25.1.2000, p. 1.

Commentary
para 91: F&N: 9.271, 9.272, 9.273

(92) In the case of exclusive supply, the buyer's market share is his share of all purchases on the relevant purchase market.[1] In the example below, this is also market A.

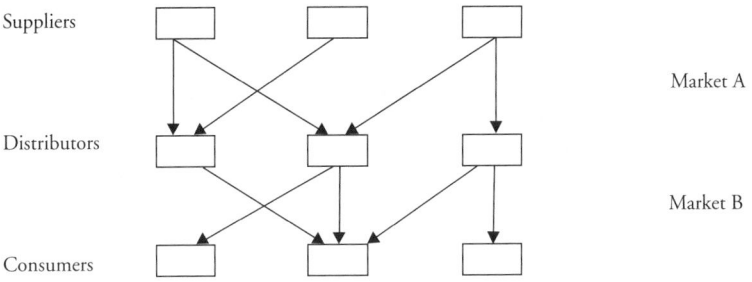

Notes

[1] For an example of purchase markets, see Commission Decision 1999/674/EC in Case No IV/M.1221 — *Rewe/Meinl*, OJ L 274, 23.10.1999, p. 1.

(93) Where a vertical agreement involves three parties, each operating at a different level of trade, their market shares will have to be below the market share threshold of 30% at both levels in order to benefit from the block exemption. If for instance, in an agreement between a manufacturer, a wholesaler (or association of retailers) and a retailer, a non-compete obligation is agreed, then the market share of both the manufacturer and the wholesaler (or association of retailers) must not exceed 30% in order to benefit from the block exemption.

Commentary
para 93: B&C: 6.019 **F&N:** 9.274

(94) Where a supplier produces both original equipment and the repair or replacement parts for this equipment, the supplier will often be the only or the major supplier on the after-market for the repair and replacement parts. This may also arise where the supplier (OEM supplier) subcontracts the manufacturing of the repair or replacement parts. The relevant market for application of the Block Exemption Regulation may be the original equipment market including the spare parts or a separate original equipment market and after-market depending on the circumstances of the case, such as the effects of the restrictions involved, the lifetime of the equipment and importance of the repair or replacement costs.[1]

Notes

[1] See for example *Pelikan/Kyocera* in XXV Report on Competition Policy, point 87, and Commission Decision 91/595/EEC in Case No IV/M.12 — *Varta/Bosch*, OJ L 320, 22.11.1991, p. 26, Commission Decision in Case No IV/M.1094 — *Caterpillar/Perkins Engines*, OJ C 94, 28.3.1998, p. 23, and Commission Decision in Case No IV/M.768 — *Lucas/Varity*, OJ C 266, 13.9.1996, p. 6. See also *Eastman Kodak Co v Image Technical Services, Inc et al*, Supreme Court of the United States, No 90 1029. See also point 56 of the Commission Notice on the definition of relevant market for the purposes of Community competition law.

Commentary
para 94: B&C: 6.019 **F&N:** 9.275

(95) Where the vertical agreement, in addition to the supply of the contract goods, also contains IPR provisions — such as a provision concerning the use of the supplier's trademark — which help the buyer to market the contract goods, the supplier's market share on the market where he sells the contract goods is decisive for the application of the Block Exemption Regulation. Where a franchisor does not supply goods to be resold but provides a bundle of services combined with IPR provisions which together form the business method being franchised, the franchisor needs to take account of his market share as a provider of a business method. For that purpose, the franchisor needs to calculate his market share on the market where the business method is exploited, which is the market where the franchisees exploit the business method to provide goods or services to end users. The franchisor must base his market share on the value of the goods or services supplied by his franchisees on this market. On such a market the competitors may be providers of other franchised business methods but also suppliers of substitutable goods or services not applying franchising. For instance, without prejudice to the definition of such market, if there was a market for fast-food services, a franchisor operating on such a market would need to calculate his market share on the basis of the relevant sales figures of his franchisees on this market. If the franchisor, in addition to the business method, also supplies certain inputs, such as meat and spices, then the franchisor also needs to calculate his market share on the market where these goods are sold.

Commentary
para 95: B&C: 6.019, 6.184 **F&N:** 9.276, 9.277

3. The relevant market for individual assessment

(96) For individual assessment of vertical agreements not covered by the Block Exemption Regulation, additional markets may need to be investigated besides the relevant market defined for the application of the Block Exemption Regulation. A vertical agreement may not only have effects on the market between supplier and buyer but may also have effects on downstream markets. For an individual assessment of a vertical agreement the relevant markets at each level of trade affected by restraints contained in the agreement will be examined:

    (i) For "intermediate goods or services" that are incorporated by the buyer into his own goods or services, vertical restraints generally have effects only on the market between supplier and buyer. A non-compete obligation imposed on the buyer for instance may foreclose other suppliers but will not lead to reduced in-store competition downstream. However, in cases of exclusive supply the position of the buyer on his downstream market is also relevant because the buyer's foreclosing behaviour may only have appreciable negative effects if he has market power on the downstream market.

(ii) For "final products" an analysis limited to the market between supplier and buyer is less likely to be sufficient since vertical restraints may have negative effects of reduced inter-brand and/or intra-brand competition on the resale market, that is on the market downstream of the buyer. For instance, exclusive distribution may not only lead to foreclosure effects on the market between the supplier and the buyer, but may above all lead to less intra-brand competition in the resale territories of the distributors. The resale market is in particular important if the buyer is a retailer selling to final consumers. A non-compete obligation agreed between a manufacturer and a wholesaler may foreclose this wholesaler to other manufacturers but a loss of in-store competition is not very likely at the wholesale level. The same agreement concluded with a retailer may however cause this added loss of in-store inter-brand competition on the resale market.

(iii) In cases of individual assessment of an "after-market", the relevant market may be the original equipment market or the after-market depending on the circumstances of the case. In any event, the situation on a separate after-market will be evaluated taking account of the situation on the original equipment market. A less significant position on the original equipment market will normally reduce possible anti-competitive effects on the after-market.

Commentary
para 96: B&C: 6.045 F&N: 9.275, 9.278

4. Calculation of the market share under the Block Exemption Regulation

(97) The calculation of the market share needs to be based in principle on value figures. Where value figures are not available substantiated estimates can be made. Such estimates may be based on other reliable market information such as volume figures (see Article 9(1) of the Block Exemption Regulation).

(98) In-house production, that is production of an intermediate product for own use, may be very important in a competition analysis as one of the competitive constraints or to accentuate the market position of a company. However, for the purpose of market definition and the calculation of market share for intermediate goods and services, in-house production will not be taken into account.

Commentary
para 98: B&C: 6.019 F&N: 9.279

(99) However, in the case of dual distribution of final goods, i.e. where a producer of final goods also acts as a distributor on the market, the market definition and market share calculation need to include the goods sold by the producer and competing producers through their integrated distributors and agents (see Article 9(2)(b) of the Block Exemption Regulation). "Integrated distributors" are connected undertakings within the meaning of Article 11 of the Block Exemption Regulation.

VI. Enforcement Policy in Individual Cases

(100) Vertical restraints are generally less harmful than horizontal restraints. The main reason for treating a vertical restraint more leniently than a horizontal restraint lies in the fact that the latter may concern an agreement between competitors producing identical or substitutable goods or services. In such horizontal relationships the exercise of market power by one company (higher price of its product) may benefit its competitors. This may provide an incentive to competitors to induce each other to behave anti-competitively. In vertical relationships the product of the one is the input for the other. This means that the exercise of market power by either the upstream or downstream company would normally hurt the demand for the product

Part C Substantive
Antitrust Matters

of the other. The companies involved in the agreement therefore usually have an incentive to prevent the exercise of market power by the other.

Commentary
para 100: F&N: 9.188, 10.80

(101) However, this self-restraining character should not be over-estimated. When a company has no market power it can only try to increase its profits by optimising its manufacturing and distribution processes, with or without the help of vertical restraints. However, when it does have market power it can also try to increase its profits at the expense of its direct competitors by raising their costs and at the expense of its buyers and ultimately consumers by trying to appropriate some of their surplus. This can happen when the upstream and downstream company share the extra profits or when one of the two uses vertical restraints to appropriate all the extra profits.

Commentary
para 101: F&N: 10.80

(102) In the assessment of individual cases, the Commission will adopt an economic approach in the application of Article 81 to vertical restraints. This will limit the scope of application of Article 81 to undertakings holding a certain degree of market power where inter-brand competition may be insufficient. In those cases, the protection of inter-brand and intra-brand competition is important to ensure efficiencies and benefits for consumers.

Commentary
para 102: B&C: 6.044 F&N: 9.187

1. The framework of analysis

1.1. *Negative effects of vertical restraints*

(103) The negative effects on the market that may result from vertical restraints which EC competition law aims at preventing are the following:
  (i) foreclosure of other suppliers or other buyers by raising barriers to entry;
  (ii) reduction of inter-brand competition between the companies operating on a market, including facilitation of collusion amongst suppliers or buyers; by collusion is meant both explicit collusion and tacit collusion (conscious parallel behaviour);
  (iii) reduction of intra-brand competition between distributors of the same brand;
  (iv) the creation of obstacles to market integration, including, above all, limitations on the freedom of consumers to purchase goods or services in any Member State they may choose.

Commentary
para 103: F&N: 9.281

(104) Such negative effects may result from various vertical restraints. Agreements which are different in form may have the same substantive impact on competition. To analyse these possible negative effects, it is appropriate to divide vertical restraints into four groups: a single branding group, a limited distribution group, a resale price maintenance group and a market partitioning group. The vertical restraints within each group have largely similar negative effects on competition.

(105) The classification into four groups is based upon what can be described as the basic components of vertical restraints. In paragraphs 103 to 136, the four different groups are analysed. In 137 to 229, vertical agreements are analysed as they are used in practice because many vertical agreements make use of more than one of these components.

Single branding group

(106) Under the heading of "single branding" come those agreements which have as their main element that the buyer is induced to concentrate his orders for a particular type of product with

one supplier. This component can be found amongst others in non-compete and quantity-forcing on the buyer, where an obligation or incentive scheme agreed between the supplier and the buyer makes the latter purchase his requirements for a particular product and its substitutes only, or mainly, from one supplier. The same component can be found in tying, where the obligation or incentive scheme relates to a product that the buyer is required to purchase as a condition of purchasing another distinct product. The first product is referred to as the "tied" product and the second is referred to as the "tying" product.

(107) There are four main negative effects on competition: (1) other suppliers in that market cannot sell to the particular buyers and this may lead to foreclosure of the market or, in the case of tying, to foreclosure of the market for the tied product; (2) it makes market shares more rigid and this may help collusion when applied by several suppliers; (3) as far as the distribution of final goods is concerned, the particular retailers will only sell one brand and there will therefore be no inter-brand competition in their shops (no in-store competition); and (4) in the case of tying, the buyer may pay a higher price for the tied product than he would otherwise do. All these effects may lead to a reduction in inter-brand competition.

Commentary
para 107: F&N: 9.301

(108) The reduction in inter-brand competition may be mitigated by strong initial competition between suppliers to obtain the single branding contracts, but the longer the duration of the non-compete obligation, the more likely it will be that this effect will not be strong enough to compensate for the reduction in inter-brand competition.

Limited distribution group

(109) Under the heading of "limited distribution" come those agreements which have as their main element that the manufacturer sells to only one or a limited number of buyers. This may be to restrict the number of buyers for a particular territory or group of customers, or to select a particular kind of buyers. This component can be found amongst others in:
— exclusive distribution and exclusive customer allocation, where the supplier limits his sales to only one buyer for a certain territory or class of customers;
— exclusive supply and quantity-forcing on the supplier, where an obligation or incentive scheme agreed between the supplier and the buyer makes the former sell only or mainly to one buyer;
— selective distribution, where the conditions imposed on or agreed with the selected dealers usually limit their number;
— after-market sales restrictions which limit the component supplier's sales possibilities.

Commentary
para 109: B&C: 6.039

(110) There are three main negative effects on competition: (1) certain buyers within that market can no longer buy from that particular supplier, and this may lead in particular in the case of exclusive supply, to foreclosure of the purchase market, (2) when most or all of the competing suppliers limit the number of retailers, this may facilitate collusion, either at the distributor's level or at the supplier's level, and (3) since fewer distributors will offer the product it will also lead to a reduction of intra-brand competition. In the case of wide exclusive territories or exclusive customer allocation the result may be total elimination of intra-brand competition. This reduction of intra-brand competition can in turn lead to a weakening of inter-brand competition.

Commentary
para 110: B&C: 6.040

Part C Substantive Antitrust Matters

Resale price maintenance group

(111) Under the heading of "resale price maintenance" (RPM) come those agreements whose main element is that the buyer is obliged or induced to resell not below a certain price, at a certain price or not above a certain price. This group comprises minimum, fixed, maximum and recommended resale prices. Maximum and recommended resale prices, which are not hardcore restrictions, may still lead to a restriction of competition by effect.

(112) There are two main negative effects of RPM on competition: (1) a reduction in intra-brand price competition, and (2) increased transparency on prices. In the case of fixed or minimum RPM, distributors can no longer compete on price for that brand, leading to a total elimination of intra-brand price competition. A maximum or recommended price may work as a focal point for resellers, leading to a more or less uniform application of that price level. Increased transparency on price and responsibility for price changes makes horizontal collusion between manufacturers or distributors easier, at least in concentrated markets. The reduction in intra-brand competition may, as it leads to less downward pressure on the price for the particular goods, have as an indirect effect a reduction of inter-brand competition.

Market partitioning group

(113) Under the heading of "market partitioning" come agreements whose main element is that the buyer is restricted in where he either sources or resells a particular product. This component can be found in exclusive purchasing, where an obligation or incentive scheme agreed between the supplier and the buyer makes the latter purchase his requirements for a particular product, for instance beer of brand X, exclusively from the designated supplier, but leaving the buyer free to buy and sell competing products, for instance competing brands of beer. It also includes territorial resale restrictions, the allocation of an area of primary responsibility, restrictions on the location of a distributor and customer resale restrictions.

Commentary
para 113: B&C: 6.144

(114) The main negative effect on competition is a reduction of intra-brand competition that may help the supplier to partition the market and thus hinder market integration. This may facilitate price discrimination. When most or all of the competing suppliers limit the sourcing or resale possibilities of their buyers this may facilitate collusion, either at the distributors' level or at the suppliers' level.

Commentary
para 114: B&C: 6.140

1.2. *Positive effects of vertical restraints*

(115) It is important to recognise that vertical restraints often have positive effects by, in particular, promoting non-price competition and improved quality of services. When a company has no market power, it can only try to increase its profits by optimising its manufacturing or distribution processes. In a number of situations vertical restraints may be helpful in this respect since the usual arm's length dealings between supplier and buyer, determining only price and quantity of a certain transaction, can lead to a sub-optimal level of investments and sales.

(116) While trying to give a fair overview of the various justifications for vertical restraints, these Guidelines do not claim to be complete or exhaustive. The following reasons may justify the application of certain vertical restraints:

(1) To "solve a "free-rider' problem". One distributor may free-ride on the promotion efforts of another distributor. This type of problem is most common at the wholesale and retail level. Exclusive distribution or similar restrictions may be helpful in avoiding such free-riding. Free-riding can also occur between suppliers, for instance where one invests in promotion at the buyer's premises, in general at the retail level, that may also attract customers for its competitors. Non-compete type restraints can help to overcome this situation of free-riding.

For there to be a problem, there needs to be a real free-rider issue. Free-riding between buyers can only occur on pre-sales services and not on after-sales services. The product will usually need to be relatively new or technically complex as the customer may otherwise very well know what he or she wants, based on past purchases. And the product must be of a reasonably high value as it is otherwise not attractive for a customer to go to one shop for information and to another to buy. Lastly, it must not be practical for the supplier to impose on all buyers, by contract, effective service requirements concerning pre-sales services.

Free-riding between suppliers is also restricted to specific situations, namely in cases where the promotion takes place at the buyer's premises and is generic, not brand specific.

(2) To "open up or enter new markets". Where a manufacturer wants to enter a new geographic market, for instance by exporting to another country for the first time, this may involve special "first time investments" by the distributor to establish the brand in the market. In order to persuade a local distributor to make these investments it may be necessary to provide territorial protection to the distributor so that he can recoup these investments by temporarily charging a higher price. Distributors based in other markets should then be restrained for a limited period from selling in the new market. This is a special case of the free-rider problem described under point (1).

(3) The "certification free-rider issue". In some sectors, certain retailers have a reputation for stocking only "quality" products. In such a case, selling through these retailers may be vital for the introduction of a new product. If the manufacturer cannot initially limit his sales to the premium stores, he runs the risk of being de-listed and the product introduction may fail. This means that there may be a reason for allowing for a limited duration a restriction such as exclusive distribution or selective distribution. It must be enough to guarantee introduction of the new product but not so long as to hinder large-scale dissemination. Such benefits are more likely with "experience" goods or complex goods that represent a relatively large purchase for the final consumer.

(4) The so-called "hold-up problem". Sometimes there are client-specific investments to be made by either the supplier or the buyer, such as in special equipment or training. For instance, a component manufacturer that has to build new machines and tools in order to satisfy a particular requirement of one of his customers. The investor may not commit the necessary investments before particular supply arrangements are fixed.

However, as in the other free-riding examples, there are a number of conditions that have to be met before the risk of under-investment is real or significant. Firstly, the investment must be relationship-specific. An investment made by the supplier is considered to be relationship-specific when, after termination of the contract, it cannot be used by the supplier to supply other customers and can only be sold at a significant loss. An investment made by the buyer is considered to be relationship-specific when, after termination of the contract, it cannot be used by the buyer to purchase and/or use products supplied by other suppliers and can only be sold at a significant loss. An investment is thus relationship-specific because for instance it can only be used to produce a brand-specific component or to store a particular brand and thus cannot be used profitably to produce or resell alternatives. Secondly, it must be a long-term investment that is not recouped in the short run. And thirdly, the investment must be asymmetric; i.e. one party to the contract invests more than the other party. When these conditions are met, there is usually a good reason to have a vertical restraint for the duration it takes to depreciate the investment. The appropriate vertical restraint will be of the non-compete type or quantity-forcing type when the investment is made by the supplier and of the exclusive distribution, exclusive customer allocation or exclusive supply type when the investment is made by the buyer.

(5) The "specific hold-up problem that may arise in the case of transfer of substantial know-how". The know-how, once provided, cannot be taken back and the provider of the know-how may not want it to be used for or by his competitors. In as far as the know-how was not readily available to the buyer, is substantial and indispensable for the operation of the agreement, such a transfer may justify a non-compete type of restriction. This would normally fall outside Article 81(1).

321

(6) "Economies of scale in distribution". In order to have scale economies exploited and thereby see a lower retail price for his product, the manufacturer may want to concentrate the resale of his products on a limited number of distributors. For this he could use exclusive distribution, quantity forcing in the form of a minimum purchasing requirement, selective distribution containing such a requirement or exclusive purchasing.

(7) "Capital market imperfections". The usual providers of capital (banks, equity markets) may provide capital sub-optimally when they have imperfect information on the quality of the borrower or there is an inadequate basis to secure the loan. The buyer or supplier may have better information and be able, through an exclusive relationship, to obtain extra security for his investment. Where the supplier provides the loan to the buyer this may lead to non-compete or quantity forcing on the buyer. Where the buyer provides the loan to the supplier this may be the reason for having exclusive supply or quantity forcing on the supplier.

(8) "Uniformity and quality standardisation". A vertical restraint may help to increase sales by creating a brand image and thereby increasing the attractiveness of a product to the final consumer by imposing a certain measure of uniformity and quality standardisation on the distributors. This can for instance be found in selective distribution and franchising.

Commentary
para 116: B&C: 6.140 F&N: 9.294, 9.317
para 116(1): B&C: 6.040
para 116(4): B&C: 6.140, 6.166
para 116(5): B&C: 6.166
para 116(6): B&C: 6.040, 6.080
para 116(7): B&C: 6.140, 6.166

---

(117) The eight situations mentioned in paragraph 116 make clear that under certain conditions vertical agreements are likely to help realise efficiencies and the development of new markets and that this may offset possible negative effects. The case is in general strongest for vertical restraints of a limited duration which help the introduction of new complex products or protect relationship-specific investments. A vertical restraint is sometimes necessary for as long as the supplier sells his product to the buyer (see in particular the situations described in paragraph 116, points (1), (5), (6) and (8).

(118) There is a large measure of substitutability between the different vertical restraints. This means that the same inefficiency problem can be solved by different vertical restraints. For instance, economies of scale in distribution may possibly be achieved by using exclusive distribution, selective distribution, quantity forcing or exclusive purchasing. This is important as the negative effects on competition may differ between the various vertical restraints. This plays a role when indispensability is discussed under Article 81(3).

Commentary
para 118: B&C: 6.080

1.3. *General rules for the evaluation of vertical restraints*

(119) In evaluating vertical restraints from a competition policy perspective, some general rules can be formulated:

(1) For most vertical restraints competition concerns can only arise if there is insufficient inter-brand competition, i.e. if there exists a certain degree of market power at the level of the supplier or the buyer or both. Conceptually, market power is the power to raise price above the competitive level and, at least in the short term, to obtain supra-normal profits. Companies may have market power below the level of market dominance, which is the threshold for the application of Article 82. Where there are many firms competing in an unconcentrated market, it can be assumed that non-hardcore vertical restraints will not have appreciable negative effects. A market is deemed unconcentrated when the HHI index, i.e. the sum of the squares of the individual market shares of all companies in the relevant market, is below 1000.

(2) Vertical restraints which reduce inter-brand competition are generally more harmful than vertical restraints that reduce intra-brand competition. For instance, non-compete obligations are likely to have more net negative effects than exclusive distribution. The former, by possibly foreclosing the market to other brands, may prevent those brands from reaching the market. The latter, while limiting intra-brand competition, does not prevent goods from reaching the final consumer.

(3) Vertical restraints from the limited distribution group, in the absence of sufficient inter-brand competition, may significantly restrict the choices available to consumers. They are particularly harmful when more efficient distributors or distributors with a different distribution format are foreclosed. This can reduce innovation in distribution and denies consumers the particular service or price-service combination of these distributors.

(4) Exclusive dealing arrangements are generally worse for competition than non-exclusive arrangements. Exclusive dealing makes, by the express language of the contract or its practical effects, one party fulfil all or practically all its requirements from another party. For instance, under a non-compete obligation the buyer purchases only one brand. Quantity forcing, on the other hand, leaves the buyer some scope to purchase competing goods. The degree of foreclosure may therefore be less with quantity forcing.

(5) Vertical restraints agreed for non-branded goods and services are in general less harmful than restraints affecting the distribution of branded goods and services. Branding tends to increase product differentiation and reduce substitutability of the product, leading to a reduced elasticity of demand and an increased possibility to raise price. The distinction between branded and non-branded goods or services will often coincide with the distinction between intermediate goods and services and final goods and services.

Intermediate goods and services are sold to undertakings for use as an input to produce other goods or services and are generally not recognisable in the final goods or services. The buyers of intermediate products are usually well-informed customers, able to assess quality and therefore less reliant on brand and image. Final goods are, directly or indirectly, sold to final consumers who often rely more on brand and image. As distributors (retailers, wholesalers) have to respond to the demand of final consumers, competition may suffer more when distributors are foreclosed from selling one or a number of brands than when buyers of intermediate products are prevented from buying competing products from certain sources of supply.

The undertakings buying intermediate goods or services normally have specialist departments or advisers who monitor developments in the supply market. Because they effect sizeable transactions, search costs are in general not prohibitive. A loss of intra-brand competition is therefore less important at the intermediate level.

(6) In general, a combination of vertical restraints aggravates their negative effects. However, certain combinations of vertical restraints are better for competition than their use in isolation from each other. For instance, in an exclusive distribution system, the distributor may be tempted to increase the price of the products as intra-brand competition has been reduced. The use of quantity forcing or the setting of a maximum resale price may limit such price increases.

(7) Possible negative effects of vertical restraints are reinforced when several suppliers and their buyers organise their trade in a similar way. These so-called cumulative effects may be a problem in a number of sectors.

(8) The more the vertical restraint is linked to the transfer of know-how, the more reason there may be to expect efficiencies to arise and the more a vertical restraint may be necessary to protect the know-how transferred or the investment costs incurred.

(9) The more the vertical restraint is linked to investments which are relationship-specific, the more justification there is for certain vertical restraints. The justified duration will depend on the time necessary to depreciate the investment.

(10) In the case of a new product, or where an existing product is sold for the first time on a different geographic market, it may be difficult for the company to define the market or its market share may be very high. However, this should not be considered a major problem, as vertical restraints linked to opening up new product or geographic markets in general

do not restrict competition. This rule holds, irrespective of the market share of the company, for two years after the first putting on the market of the product. It applies to all non-hardcore vertical restraints and, in the case of a new geographic market, to restrictions on active and passive sales imposed on the direct buyers of the supplier located in other markets to intermediaries in the new market. In the case of genuine testing of a new product in a limited territory or with a limited customer group, the distributors appointed to sell the new product on the test market can be restricted in their active selling outside the test market for a maximum period of 1 year without being caught by Article 81(1).

Commentary
para 119: B&C: 2.131 F&N: 3.140, 9.81, 9.82, 9.297, 12.236
para 119(1): B&C: 2.124, 6.007, 6.040, 6.045
para 119(2): B&C: 6.144
para 119(3): B&C: 6.046
para 119(6): B&C: 6.052
para 119(10): B&C: 6.045

1.4. *Methodology of analysis*

(120) The assessment of a vertical restraint involves in general the following four steps:
- (1) First, the undertakings involved need to define the relevant market in order to establish the market share of the supplier or the buyer, depending on the vertical restraint involved (see paragraphs 88 to 99, in particular 89 to 95).
- (2) If the relevant market share does not exceed the 30% threshold, the vertical agreement is covered by the Block Exemption Regulation, subject to the hardcore restrictions and conditions set out in that regulation.
- (3) If the relevant market share is above the 30% threshold, it is necessary to assess whether the vertical agreement falls within Article 81(1).
- (4) If the vertical agreement falls within Article 81(1), it is necessary to examine whether it fulfils the conditions for exemption under Article 81(3).

Commentary
para 120(2): B&C: 6.008

1.4.1. *Relevant factors for the assessment under Article 81(1)*

(121) In assessing cases above the market share threshold of 30%, the Commission will make a full competition analysis. The following factors are the most important to establish whether a vertical agreement brings about an appreciable restriction of competition under Article 81(1):
- (a) market position of the supplier;
- (b) market position of competitors;
- (c) market position of the buyer;
- (d) entry barriers;
- (e) maturity of the market;
- (f) level of trade;
- (g) nature of the product;
- (h) other factors.

(122) The importance of individual factors may vary from case to case and depends on all other factors. For instance, a high market share of the supplier is usually a good indicator of market power, but in the case of low entry barriers it may not indicate market power. It is therefore not possible to provide strict rules on the importance of the individual factors. However the following can be said:

Market position of the supplier

(123) The market position of the supplier is established first and foremost by his market share on the relevant product and geographic market. The higher his market share, the greater his market power is likely to be. The market position of the supplier is further strengthened if he has

certain cost advantages over his competitors. These competitive advantages may result from a first mover advantage (having the best site, etc.), holding essential patents, having superior technology, being the brand leader or having a superior portfolio.

Market position of competitors

(124) The same indicators, that is market share and possible competitive advantages, are used to describe the market position of competitors. The stronger the established competitors are and the greater their number, the less risk there is that the supplier or buyer in question will be able to foreclose the market individually and the less there is a risk of a reduction of inter-brand competition. However, if the number of competitors becomes rather small and their market position (size, costs, R & D potential, etc.) is rather similar, this market structure may increase the risk of collusion. Fluctuating or rapidly changing market shares are in general an indication of intense competition.

Market position of the buyer

(125) Buying power derives from the market position of the buyer. The first indicator of buying power is the market share of the buyer on the purchase market. This share reflects the importance of his demand for his possible suppliers. Other indicators focus on the market position of the buyer on his resale market including characteristics such as a wide geographic spread of his outlets, own brands of the buyer/distributor and his image amongst final consumers. The effect of buying power on the likelihood of anti-competitive effects is not the same for the different vertical restraints. Buying power may in particular increase the negative effects in case of restraints from the limited distribution and market partitioning groups such as exclusive supply, exclusive distribution and quantitative selective distribution.

Entry barriers

(126) Entry barriers are measured by the extent to which incumbent companies can increase their price above the competitive level, usually above minimum average total cost, and make supra-normal profits without attracting entry. Without any entry barriers, easy and quick entry would eliminate such profits. In as far as effective entry, which would prevent or erode the supra-normal profits, is likely to occur within one or two years, entry barriers can be said to be low.

(127) Entry barriers may result from a wide variety of factors such as economies of scale and scope, government regulations, especially where they establish exclusive rights, state aid, import tariffs, intellectual property rights, ownership of resources where the supply is limited due to for instance natural limitations,[1] essential facilities, a first mover advantage and brand loyalty of consumers created by strong advertising. Vertical restraints and vertical integration may also work as an entry barrier by making access more difficult and foreclosing (potential) competitors. Entry barriers may be present at only the supplier or buyer level or at both levels.

Notes
[1] See Commission Decision 97/26/EC (Case No IV/M.619 — *Gencor/Lonrho*), (OJ L 11, 14.1.1997, p. 30).

(128) The question whether certain of these factors should be described as entry barriers depends on whether they are related to sunk costs. Sunk costs are those costs that have to be incurred to enter or be active on a market but that are lost when the market is exited. Advertising costs to build consumer loyalty are normally sunk costs, unless an exiting firm could either sell its brand name or use it somewhere else without a loss. The more costs are sunk, the more potential entrants have to weigh the risks of entering the market and the more credibly incumbents can threaten that they will match new competition, as sunk costs make it costly for incumbents to leave the market. If, for instance, distributors are tied to a manufacturer via a non-compete obligation, the foreclosing effect will be more significant if setting up its own distributors will impose sunk costs on the potential entrant.

(129) In general, entry requires sunk costs, sometimes minor and sometimes major. Therefore, actual competition is in general more effective and will weigh more in the assessment of a case than potential competition.

Maturity of the market

(130) A mature market is a market that has existed for some time, where the technology used is well known and widespread and not changing very much, where there are no major brand innovations and in which demand is relatively stable or declining. In such a market negative effects are more likely than in more dynamic markets.

Level of trade

(131) The level of trade is linked to the distinction between intermediate and final goods and services. As indicated earlier, negative effects are in general less likely at the level of intermediate goods and services.

Nature of the product

(132) The nature of the product plays a role in particular for final products in assessing both the likely negative and the likely positive effects. When assessing the likely negative effects, it is important whether the products on the market are more homogeneous or heterogeneous, whether the product is expensive, taking up a large part of the consumer's budget, or is inexpensive and whether the product is a one-off purchase or repeatedly purchased. In general, when the product is more heterogeneous, less expensive and resembles more a one-off purchase, vertical restraints are more likely to have negative effects.

Other factors

(133) In the assessment of particular restraints other factors may have to be taken into account. Among these factors can be the cumulative effect, i.e. the coverage of the market by similar agreements, the duration of the agreements, whether the agreement is "imposed" (mainly one party is subject to the restrictions or obligations) or "agreed" (both parties accept restrictions or obligations), the regulatory environment and behaviour that may indicate or facilitate collusion like price leadership, pre-announced price changes and discussions on the "right" price, price rigidity in response to excess capacity, price discrimination and past collusive behaviour.

Commentary
para 133: B&C: 6.047

1.4.2. *Relevant factors for the assessment under Article 81(3)*

(134) There are four cumulative conditions for the application of Article 81(3):
— the vertical agreement must contribute to improving production or distribution or to promoting technical or economic progress;
— the vertical agreement must allow consumers a fair share of these benefits;
— the vertical agreement must not impose on the undertakings concerned vertical restraints which are not indispensable to the attainment of these benefits;
— the vertical agreement must not afford such undertakings the possibility of eliminating competition in respect of a substantial part of the products in question.

Commentary
para 134: F&N: 9.290

---

(135) The last criterion of elimination of competition for a substantial part of the products in question is related to the question of dominance. Where an undertaking is dominant or becoming dominant as a consequence of the vertical agreement, a vertical restraint that has appreciable anti-competitive effects can in principle not be exempted. The vertical agreement may however fall outside Article 81(1) if there is an objective justification, for instance if it is necessary for the protection of relationship-specific investments or for the transfer of substantial know-how without which the supply or purchase of certain goods or services would not take place.

Commentary
para 135: B&C: 3.062, 6.080

(136) Where the supplier and the buyer are not dominant, the other three criteria become important. The first, concerning the improvement of production or distribution and the promotion of technical or economic progress, refers to the type of efficiencies described in paragraphs 115 to 118. These efficiencies have to be substantiated and must produce a net positive effect. Speculative claims on avoidance of free-riding or general statements on cost savings will not be accepted. Cost savings that arise from the mere exercise of market power or from anti-competitive conduct cannot be accepted. Secondly, economic benefits have to favour not only the parties to the agreement, but also the consumer. Generally the transmission of the benefits to consumers will depend on the intensity of competition on the relevant market. Competitive pressures will normally ensure that cost-savings are passed on by way of lower prices or that companies have an incentive to bring new products to the market as quickly as possible. Therefore, if sufficient competition which effectively constrains the parties to the agreement is maintained on the market, the competitive process will normally ensure that consumers receive a fair share of the economic benefits. The third criterion will play a role in ensuring that the least anti-competitive restraint is chosen to obtain certain positive effects.

Commentary
para 136: B&C: 6.080 F&N: 3.446

2. Analysis of specific vertical restraints

(137) Vertical agreements may contain a combination of two or more of the components of vertical restraints described in paragraphs 103 to 114. The most common vertical restraints and combinations of vertical restraints are analysed below following the methodology of analysis developed in paragraphs 120 to 136.

2.1. *Single branding*

(138) A non-compete arrangement is based on an obligation or incentive scheme which makes the buyer purchase practically all his requirements on a particular market from only one supplier. It does not mean that the buyer can only buy directly from the supplier, but that the buyer will not buy and resell or incorporate competing goods or services. The possible competition risks are foreclosure of the market to competing suppliers and potential suppliers, facilitation of collusion between suppliers in case of cumulative use and, where the buyer is a retailer selling to final consumers, a loss of in-store inter-brand competition. All three restrictive effects have a direct impact on inter-brand competition.

Commentary
para 138: B&C: 6.139 F&N: 9.301

(139) Single branding is exempted by the Block Exemption Regulation when the supplier's market share does not exceed 30% and subject to a limitation in time of five years for the non-compete obligation. Above the market share threshold or beyond the time limit of five years, the following guidance is provided for the assessment of individual cases.

(140) The "market position of the supplier" is of main importance to assess possible anti-competitive effects of non-compete obligations. In general, this type of obligation is imposed by the supplier and the supplier has similar agreements with other buyers.

Commentary
para 140: F&N: 9.304

(141) It is not only the market position of the supplier that is of importance but also the extent to and the duration for which he applies a non-compete obligation. The higher his tied market share, i.e. the part of his market share sold under a single branding obligation, the more significant foreclosure is likely to be. Similarly, the longer the duration of the non-compete obligations,

the more significant foreclosure is likely to be. Non-compete obligations shorter than one year entered into by non-dominant companies are in general not considered to give rise to appreciable anti-competitive effects or net negative effects. Non-compete obligations between one and five years entered into by non-dominant companies usually require a proper balancing of pro- and anti-competitive effects, while non-compete obligations exceeding five years are for most types of investments not considered necessary to achieve the claimed efficiencies or the efficiencies are not sufficient to outweigh their foreclosure effect. Dominant companies may not impose non-compete obligations on their buyers unless they can objectively justify such commercial practice within the context of Article 82.

Commentary
para 141: B&C: 6.150 F&N: 3.141, 9.305, 9.307, 12.215

(142) In assessing the supplier's market power, the "market position of his competitors" is important. As long as the competitors are sufficiently numerous and strong, no appreciable anti-competitive effects can be expected. It is only likely that competing suppliers will be foreclosed if they are significantly smaller than the supplier applying the non-compete obligation. Foreclosure of competitors is not very likely where they have similar market positions and can offer similarly attractive products. In such a case foreclosure may however occur for potential entrants when a number of major suppliers enter into non-compete contracts with a significant number of buyers on the relevant market (cumulative effect situation). This is also a situation where non-compete agreements may facilitate collusion between competing suppliers. If individually these suppliers are covered by the Block Exemption Regulation, a withdrawal of the block exemption may be necessary to deal with such a negative cumulative effect. A tied market share of less than 5% is not considered in general to contribute significantly to a cumulative foreclosure effect.

Commentary
para 142: B&C: 6.155

(143) In cases where the market share of the largest supplier is below 30% and the market share of the five largest suppliers (concentration rate (CR) 5) is below 50%, there is unlikely to be a single or a cumulative anti-competitive effect situation. If a potential entrant cannot penetrate the market profitably, this is likely to be due to factors other than non-compete obligations, such as consumer preferences. A competition problem is unlikely to arise when, for instance, 50 companies, of which none has an important market share, compete fiercely on a particular market.

Commentary
para 143: B&C: 2.124, 6.007, 6.155 F&N: 9.308

(144) "Entry barriers" are important to establish whether there is real foreclosure. Wherever it is relatively easy for competing suppliers to create new buyers or find alternative buyers for the product, foreclosure is unlikely to be a real problem. However, there are often entry barriers, both at the manufacturing and at the distribution level.

(145) "Countervailing power" is relevant, as powerful buyers will not easily allow themselves to be cut off from the supply of competing goods or services. Foreclosure which is not based on efficiency and which has harmful effects on ultimate consumers is therefore mainly a risk in the case of dispersed buyers. However, where non-compete agreements are concluded with major buyers this may have a strong foreclosure effect.

(146) Lastly, "the level of trade" is relevant for foreclosure. Foreclosure is less likely in case of an intermediate product. When the supplier of an intermediate product is not dominant, the competing suppliers still have a substantial part of demand that is "free". Below the level of dominance a serious foreclosure effect may however arise for actual or potential competitors where there is a cumulative effect. A serious cumulative effect is unlikely to arise as long as less than 50% of the market is tied. When the supplier is dominant, any obligation to buy the products only

or mainly from the dominant supplier may easily lead to significant foreclosure effects on the market. The stronger his dominance, the higher the risk of foreclosure of other competitors.

Commentary
para 146: B&C: 6.156 F&N: 10.154

(147) Where the agreement concerns supply of a final product at the wholesale level, the question whether a competition problem is likely to arise below the level of dominance depends in large part on the type of wholesaling and the entry barriers at the wholesale level. There is no real risk of foreclosure if competing manufacturers can easily establish their own wholesaling operation. Whether entry barriers are low depends in part on the type of wholesaling, i.e. whether or not wholesalers can operate efficiently with only the product concerned by the agreement (for example ice cream) or whether it is more efficient to trade in a whole range of products (for example frozen foodstuffs). In the latter case, it is not efficient for a manufacturer selling only one product to set up his own wholesaling operation. In that case anti-competitive effects may arise below the level of dominance. In addition, cumulative effect problems may arise if several suppliers tie most of the available wholesalers.

Commentary
para 147: B&C: 6.156

(148) For final products, foreclosure is in general more likely to occur at the retail level, given the significant entry barriers for most manufacturers to start retail outlets just for their own products. In addition, it is at the retail level that non-compete agreements may lead to reduced in-store inter-brand competition. It is for these reasons that for final products at the retail level, significant anti-competitive effects may start to arise, taking into account all other relevant factors, if a non-dominant supplier ties 30% or more of the relevant market. For a dominant company, even a modest tied market share may already lead to significant anti-competitive effects. The stronger its dominance, the higher the risk of foreclosure of other competitors.

Commentary
para 148: B&C: 6.156 F&N: 9.315

(149) At the retail level a cumulative foreclosure effect may also arise. When all companies have market shares below 30% a cumulative foreclosure effect is unlikely if the total tied market share is less than 40% and withdrawal of the block exemption is therefore unlikely. This figure may be higher when other factors like the number of competitors, entry barriers etc. are taken into account. When not all companies have market shares below the threshold of the Block Exemption Regulation but none is dominant, a cumulative foreclosure effect is unlikely if the total tied market share is below 30 %.

Commentary
para 149: B&C: 6.156 F&N: 9.316

(150) Where the buyer operates from premises and land owned by the supplier or leased by the supplier from a third party not connected with the buyer, the possibility of imposing effective remedies for a possible foreclosure effect will be limited. In that case intervention by the Commission below the level of dominance is unlikely.

Commentary
para 150: B&C: 6.152

(151) In certain sectors the selling of more than one brand from a single site may be difficult, in which case a foreclosure problem can better be remedied by limiting the effective duration of contracts.

(152) A so-called "English clause", requiring the buyer to report any better offer and allowing him only to accept such an offer when the supplier does not match it, can be expected to have the same effect as a non-compete obligation, especially when the buyer has to reveal who makes the

better offer. In addition, by increasing the transparency of the market it may facilitate collusion between the suppliers. An English clause may also work as quantity-forcing. Quantity-forcing on the buyer is a weaker form of non-compete, where incentives or obligations agreed between the supplier and the buyer make the latter concentrate his purchases to a large extent with one supplier. Quantity-forcing may for example take the form of minimum purchase requirements or non-linear pricing, such as quantity rebate schemes, loyalty rebate schemes or a two-part tariff (fixed fee plus a price per unit). Quantity-forcing on the buyer will have similar but weaker foreclosure effects than a non-compete obligation. The assessment of all these different forms will depend on their effect on the market. In addition, Article 82 specifically prevents dominant companies from applying English clauses or fidelity rebate schemes.

Commentary
para 152: B&C: 6.139, 6.159 F&N: 4.236, 9.298

(153) Where appreciable anti-competitive effects are established, the question of a possible exemption under Article 81(3) arises as long as the supplier is not dominant. For non-compete obligations, the efficiencies described in paragraph 116, points 1 (free riding between suppliers), 4, 5 (hold-up problems) and 7 (capital market imperfections) may be particularly relevant.

Commentary
para 153: F&N: 9.317

(154) In the case of an efficiency as described in paragraph 116, points 1, 4 and 7, quantity forcing on the buyer could possibly be a less restrictive alternative. A non-compete obligation may be the only viable way to achieve an efficiency as described in paragraph 116, point 5 (hold-up problem related to the transfer of know-how).

(155) In the case of a relationship-specific investment made by the supplier (see efficiency 4 in paragraph 116), a non-compete or quantity forcing agreement for the period of depreciation of the investment will in general fulfil the conditions of Article 81(3). In the case of high relationship-specific investments, a non-compete obligation exceeding five years may be justified. A relationship-specific investment could, for instance, be the installation or adaptation of equipment by the supplier when this equipment can be used afterwards only to produce components for a particular buyer. General or market-specific investments in (extra) capacity are normally not relationship-specific investments. However, where a supplier creates new capacity specifically linked to the operations of a particular buyer, for instance a company producing metal cans which creates new capacity to produce cans on the premises of or next to the canning facility of a food producer, this new capacity may only be economically viable when producing for this particular customer, in which case the investment would be considered to be relationship-specific.

(156) Where the supplier provides the buyer with a loan or provides the buyer with equipment which is not relationship-specific, this in itself is normally not sufficient to justify the exemption of a foreclosure effect on the market. The instances of capital market imperfection, whereby it is more efficient for the supplier of a product than for a bank to provide a loan, will be limited (see efficiency 7 in paragraph 116). Even if the supplier of the product were to be the more efficient provider of capital, a loan could only justify a non-compete obligation if the buyer is not prevented from terminating the non-compete obligation and repaying the outstanding part of the loan at any point in time and without payment of any penalty. This means that the repayment of the loan should be structured in equal or decreasing instalments and should not increase over time and that the buyer should have the possibility to take over the equipment provided by the supplier at its market asset value. This is without prejudice to the possibility, in case for example of a new point of distribution, to delay repayment for the first one or two years until sales have reached a certain level.

Commentary
para 156: B&C: 6.166 F&N: 15.143

(157) The transfer of substantial know-how (efficiency 5 in paragraph 116) usually justifies a non-compete obligation for the whole duration of the supply agreement, as for example in the context of franchising.

(158) Below the level of dominance the combination of non-compete with exclusive distribution may also justify the non-compete obligation lasting the full length of the agreement. In the latter case, the non-compete obligation is likely to improve the distribution efforts of the exclusive distributor in his territory (see paragraphs 161 to 177).

Commentary
para 158: B&C: 6.168

(159) Example of non-compete

The market leader in a national market for an impulse consumer product, with a market share of 40%, sells most of its products (90%) through tied retailers (tied market share 36%). The agreements oblige the retailers to purchase only from the market leader for at least four years. The market leader is especially strongly represented in the more densely populated areas like the capital. Its competitors, 10 in number, of which some are only locally available, all have much smaller market shares, the biggest having 12%. These 10 competitors together supply another 10% of the market via tied outlets. There is strong brand and product differentiation in the market. The market leader has the strongest brands. It is the only one with regular national advertising campaigns. It provides its tied retailers with special stocking cabinets for its product.

The result on the market is that in total 46% (36% + 10%) of the market is foreclosed to potential entrants and to incumbents not having tied outlets. Potential entrants find entry even more difficult in the densely populated areas where foreclosure is even higher, although it is there that they would prefer to enter the market. In addition, owing to the strong brand and product differentiation and the high search costs relative to the price of the product, the absence of in-store inter-brand competition leads to an extra welfare loss for consumers.

The possible efficiencies of the outlet exclusivity, which the market leader claims result from reduced transport costs and a possible hold-up problem concerning the stocking cabinets, are limited and do not outweigh the negative effects on competition. The efficiencies are limited, as the transport costs are linked to quantity and not exclusivity and the stocking cabinets do not contain special know-how and are not brand specific. Accordingly, it is unlikely that the conditions for exemption are fulfilled.

(160) Example of quantity forcing

A producer X with a 40% market share sells 80% of its products through contracts which specify that the reseller is required to purchase at least 75% of its requirements for that type of product from X. In return X is offering financing and equipment at favourable rates. The contracts have a duration of five years in which repayment of the loan is foreseen in equal instalments. However, after the first two years buyers have the possibility to terminate the contract with a six-month notice period if they repay the outstanding loan and take over the equipment at its market asset value. At the end of the five-year period the equipment becomes the property of the buyer. Most of the competing producers are small, twelve in total with the biggest having a market share of 20%, and engage in similar contracts with different durations. The producers with market shares below 10% often have contracts with longer durations and with less generous termination clauses. The contracts of producer X leave 25% of requirements free to be supplied by competitors. In the last three years, two new producers have entered the market and gained a combined market share of around 8%, partly by taking over the loans of a number of resellers in return for contracts with these resellers.

Producer X's tied market share is 24% ($0{,}75 \times 0{,}80 \times 40\%$). The other producers' tied market share is around 25%. Therefore, in total around 49% of the market is foreclosed to potential entrants and to incumbents not having tied outlets for at least the first two years of the supply contracts. The market shows that the resellers often have difficulty in obtaining loans from banks and are too small in general to obtain capital through other means like the issuing of shares. In addition, producer X is able to demonstrate that concentrating his sales on a limited number of resellers allows him to plan his sales better and to save transport costs. In the light of the 25% non-tied part in the contracts of producer X, the real possibility for early termination of the contract, the recent entry of new producers and the fact that around half the resellers are not tied, the quantity forcing of 75 % applied by producer X is likely to fulfil the conditions for exemption.

2.2. *Exclusive distribution*

(161) In an exclusive distribution agreement the supplier agrees to sell his products only to one distributor for resale in a particular territory. At the same time the distributor is usually limited in his active selling into other exclusively allocated territories. The possible competition risks are mainly reduced intra-brand competition and market partitioning, which may in particular facilitate price discrimination. When most or all of the suppliers apply exclusive distribution this may facilitate collusion, both at the suppliers' and distributors' level.

Commentary
para 161: B&C: 6.039–6.040 F&N: 3.321, 9.318

(162) Exclusive distribution is exempted by the Block Exemption Regulation when the supplier's market share does not exceed 30%, even if combined with other non-hardcore vertical restraints, such as a non-compete obligation limited to five years, quantity forcing or exclusive purchasing. A combination of exclusive distribution and selective distribution is only exempted by the Block Exemption Regulation if active selling in other territories is not restricted. Above the 30% market share threshold, the following guidance is provided for the assessment of exclusive distribution in individual cases.

(163) The market position of the supplier and his competitors is of major importance, as the loss of intra-brand competition can only be problematic if inter-brand competition is limited. The stronger the "position of the supplier", the more serious is the loss of intra-brand competition. Above the 30% market share threshold there may be a risk of a significant reduction of intra-brand competition. In order to be exemptable, the loss of intra-brand competition needs to be balanced with real efficiencies.

Commentary
para 163: B&C: 6.081

(164) The "position of the competitors" can have a dual significance. Strong competitors will generally mean that the reduction in intra-brand competition is outweighed by sufficient interbrand competition. However, if the number of competitors becomes rather small and their market position is rather similar in terms of market share, capacity and distribution network, there is a risk of collusion. The loss of intra-brand competition can increase this risk, especially when several suppliers operate similar distribution systems. Multiple exclusive dealerships, i.e. when different suppliers appoint the same exclusive distributor in a given territory, may further increase the risk of collusion. If a dealer is granted the exclusive right to distribute two or more important competing products in the same territory, inter-brand competition is likely to be substantially restricted for those brands. The higher the cumulative market share of the brands distributed by the multiple dealer, the higher the risk of collusion and the more inter-brand competition will be reduced. Such cumulative effect situations may be a reason to withdraw the benefit of the Block Exemption Regulation when the market shares of the suppliers are below the threshold of the Block Exemption Regulation.

Commentary
para 164: B&C: 6.048 F&N: 9.322

(165) "Entry barriers" that may hinder suppliers from creating new distributors or finding alternative distributors are less important in assessing the possible anti-competitive effects of exclusive distribution. Foreclosure of other suppliers does not arise as long as exclusive distribution is not combined with single branding.

Commentary
para 165: B&C: 6.046

(166) Foreclosure of other distributors is not a problem if the supplier which operates the exclusive distribution system appoints a high number of exclusive distributors in the same market and these exclusive distributors are not restricted in selling to other non-appointed distributors. Foreclosure of other distributors may however become a problem where there is "buying power" and market power downstream, in particular in the case of very large territories where the exclusive distributor becomes the exclusive buyer for a whole market. An example would be a supermarket chain which becomes the only distributor of a leading brand on a national food retail market. The foreclosure of other distributors may be aggravated in the case of multiple exclusive dealership. Such a case, covered by the Block Exemption Regulation when the market share of each supplier is below 30 %, may give reason for withdrawal of the block exemption.

Commentary
para 166: B&C: 6.046

(167) "Buying power" may also increase the risk of collusion on the buyers' side when the exclusive distribution arrangements are imposed by important buyers, possibly located in different territories, on one or several suppliers.

Commentary
para 167: F&N: 9.323

(168) "Maturity of the market" is important, as loss of intra-brand competition and price discrimination may be a serious problem in a mature market but may be less relevant in a market with growing demand, changing technologies and changing market positions.

(169) "The level of trade" is important as the possible negative effects may differ between the wholesale and retail level. Exclusive distribution is mainly applied in the distribution of final goods and services. A loss of intra-brand competition is especially likely at the retail level if coupled with large territories, since final consumers may be confronted with little possibility of choosing between a high price/high service and a low price/low service distributor for an important brand.

(170) A manufacturer which chooses a wholesaler to be his exclusive distributor will normally do so for a larger territory, such as a whole Member State. As long as the wholesaler can sell the products without limitation to downstream retailers there are not likely to be appreciable anti-competitive effects if the manufacturer is not dominant. A possible loss of intra-brand competition at the wholesale level may be easily outweighed by efficiencies obtained in logistics, promotion etc, especially when the manufacturer is based in a different country. Foreclosure of other wholesalers within that territory is not likely as a supplier with a market share above 30% usually has enough bargaining power not to choose a less efficient wholesaler. The possible risks for inter-brand competition of multiple exclusive dealerships are however higher at the wholesale than at the retail level.

Commentary
para 170: B&C: 6.066 F&N: 9.324

(171) The combination of exclusive distribution with single branding may add the problem of foreclosure of the market to other suppliers, especially in case of a dense network of exclusive distributors with small territories or in case of a cumulative effect. This may necessitate application of the principles set out above on single branding. However, when the combination does not lead to significant foreclosure, the combination of exclusive distribution and single branding may be pro-competitive by increasing the incentive for the exclusive distributor to focus his efforts on the particular brand. Therefore, in the absence of such a foreclosure effect, the combination of exclusive distribution with non-compete is exemptable for the whole duration of the agreement, particularly at the wholesale level.

Commentary
para 171: **B&C:** 6.046–6.047, 6.168 **F&N:** 9.327

(172) The combination of exclusive distribution with exclusive purchasing increases the possible competition risks of reduced intra-brand competition and market partitioning which may in particular facilitate price discrimination. Exclusive distribution already limits arbitrage by customers, as it limits the number of distributors and usually also restricts the distributors in their freedom of active selling. Exclusive purchasing, requiring the exclusive distributors to buy their supplies for the particular brand directly from the manufacturer, eliminates in addition possible arbitrage by the exclusive distributors, who are prevented from buying from other distributors in the system. This enhances the possibilities for the supplier to limit intra-brand competition while applying dissimilar conditions of sale. The combination of exclusive distribution and exclusive purchasing is therefore unlikely to be exempted for suppliers with a market share above 30 % unless there are very clear and substantial efficiencies leading to lower prices to all final consumers. Lack of such efficiencies may also lead to withdrawal of the block exemption where the market share of the supplier is below 30 %.

Commentary
para 172: **B&C:** 6.063, 6.081, 6.168 **F&N:** 9.327

(173) The "nature of the product" is not very relevant to assessing the possible anti-competitive effects of exclusive distribution. It is, however, relevant when the issue of possible efficiencies is discussed, that is after an appreciable anti-competitive effect is established.

(174) Exclusive distribution may lead to efficiencies, especially where investments by the distributors are required to protect or build up the brand image. In general, the case for efficiencies is strongest for new products, for complex products, for products whose qualities are difficult to judge before consumption (so-called experience products) or of which the qualities are difficult to judge even after consumption (so-called credence products). In addition, exclusive distribution may lead to savings in logistic costs due to economies of scale in transport and distribution.

Commentary
para 174: **B&C:** 6.081 **F&N:** 9.328

(175) Example of exclusive distribution at the wholesale level

In the market for a consumer durable, A is the market leader. A sells its product through exclusive wholesalers. Territories for the wholesalers correspond to the entire Member State for small Member States, and to a region for larger Member States. These exclusive distributors take care of sales to all the retailers in their territories. They do not sell to final consumers. The wholesalers are in charge of promotion in their markets. This includes sponsoring of local events, but also explaining and promoting the new products to the retailers in their territories. Technology and product innovation are evolving fairly quickly on this market, and pre-sale service to retailers and to final consumers plays an important role. The wholesalers are not required to purchase all their requirements of the brand of supplier A from the producer himself, and arbitrage by wholesalers or retailers is practicable because the transport costs are relatively low compared to the value of the product. The wholesalers are not under a non-compete obligation. Retailers also sell a number of brands of competing suppliers, and there are no exclusive or selective distribution agreements at the retail level. On the European market of sales to wholesalers A has around 50% market share. Its market share on the various national retail markets varies between 40% and 60%. A has between 6 and 10 competitors on every national market: B, C and D are its biggest competitors and are also present on each national market, with market shares varying between 20% and 5%. The remaining producers are national producers, with smaller market shares. B, C and D have similar distribution networks, whereas the local producers tend to sell their products directly to retailers.

On the wholesale market described above, the risk of reduced intra-brand competition and price discrimination is low. Arbitrage is not hindered, and the absence of intra-brand competition is not very relevant at the wholesale level. At the retail level neither intra- nor inter-brand competition are hindered. Moreover, inter-brand competition is largely unaffected by the exclusive arrangements at the wholesale level. This makes it likely, if anti-competitive effects exist, that the conditions for exemption are fulfilled.

(176) Example of multiple exclusive dealerships in an oligopolistic market

In a national market for a final product, there are four market leaders, who each have a market share of around 20%. These four market leaders sell their product through exclusive distributors at the retail level. Retailers are given an exclusive territory which corresponds to the town in which they are located or a district of the town for large towns. In most territories, the four market leaders happen to appoint the same exclusive retailer ("multiple dealership"), often centrally located and rather specialised in the product. The remaining 20% of the national market is composed of small local producers, the largest of these producers having a market share of 5% on the national market. These local producers sell their products in general through other retailers, in particular because the exclusive distributors of the four largest suppliers show in general little interest in selling less well-known and cheaper brands. There is strong brand and product differentiation on the market. The four market leaders have large national advertising campaigns and strong brand images, whereas the fringe producers do not advertise their products at the national level. The market is rather mature, with stable demand and no major product and technological innovation. The product is relatively simple.

In such an oligopolistic market, there is a risk of collusion between the four market leaders. This risk is increased through multiple dealerships. Intra-brand competition is limited by the territorial exclusivity. Competition between the four leading brands is reduced at the retail level, since one retailer fixes the price of all four brands in each territory. The multiple dealership implies that, if one producer cuts the price for its brand, the retailer will not be eager to transmit this price cut to the final consumer as it would reduce its sales and profits made with the other brands. Hence, producers have a reduced interest in entering into price competition with one another. Inter-brand price competition exists mainly with the low brand image goods of the fringe producers. The possible efficiency arguments for (joint) exclusive distributors are limited, as the product is relatively simple, the resale does not require any specific investments or training and advertising is mainly carried out at the level of the producers.

Even though each of the market leaders has a market share below the threshold, exemption under Article 81(3) may not be justified and withdrawal of the block exemption may be necessary.

(177) Example of exclusive distribution combined with exclusive purchasing

Manufacturer A is the European market leader for a bulky consumer durable, with a market share of between 40% and 60% in most national retail markets. In every Member State, it has about seven competitors with much smaller market shares, the largest of these competitors having a market share of 10%. These competitors are present on only one or two national markets. A sells its product through its national subsidiaries to exclusive distributors at the retail level, which are not allowed to sell actively into each other's territories. In addition, the retailers are obliged to purchase manufacturer A's products exclusively from the national subsidiary of manufacturer A in their own country. The retailers selling the brand of manufacturer A are the main resellers of that type of product in their territory. They handle competing brands, but with varying degrees of success and enthusiasm. A applies price differences of 10% to 15% between markets and smaller differences within markets. This is translated into smaller price differences at the retail level. The market is relatively stable on the demand and the supply side, and there are no significant technological changes.

In these markets, the loss of intra-brand competition results not only from the territorial exclusivity at the retail level but is aggravated by the exclusive purchasing obligation imposed on the retailers. The exclusive purchase obligation helps to keep markets and territories separate by making arbitrage between the exclusive retailers impossible. The exclusive retailers also cannot sell actively into each other's territory and in practice tend to avoid delivering outside their own territory. This renders price discrimination possible. Arbitrage by consumers or independent traders is limited due to the bulkiness of the product.

The possible efficiency arguments of this system, linked to economies of scale in transport and promotion efforts at the retailers' level, are unlikely to outweigh the negative effect of price discrimination and reduced intra-brand competition. Consequently, it is unlikely that the conditions for exemption are fulfilled.

Commentary
para 177: B&C: 6.081

2.3. *Exclusive customer allocation*

(178) In an exclusive customer allocation agreement, the supplier agrees to sell his products only to one distributor for resale to a particular class of customers. At the same time, the distributor is usually limited in his active selling to other exclusively allocated classes of customers. The possible competition risks are mainly reduced intra-brand competition and market partitioning, which may in particular facilitate price discrimination. When most or all of the suppliers apply exclusive customer allocation, this may facilitate collusion, both at the suppliers' and the distributors' level.

Commentary
para 178: B&C: 6.039

(179) Exclusive customer allocation is exempted by the Block Exemption Regulation when the supplier's market share does not exceed the 30% market share threshold, even if combined with other non-hardcore vertical restraints such as non-compete, quantity-forcing or exclusive purchasing. A combination of exclusive customer allocation and selective distribution is normally hardcore, as active selling to end-users by the appointed distributors is usually not left free. Above the 30% market share threshold, the guidance provided in paragraphs 161 to 177 applies mutatis mutandis to the assessment of exclusive customer allocation, subject to the following specific remarks.

Commentary
para 179: B&C: 6.065, 6.082, 6.106

(180) The allocation of customers normally makes arbitrage by the customers more difficult. In addition, as each appointed distributor has his own class of customers, non-appointed distributors not falling within such a class may find it difficult to obtain the product. This will reduce possible arbitrage by non-appointed distributors. Therefore, above the 30% market share threshold of the Block Exemption Regulation exclusive customer allocation is unlikely to be exemptable unless there are clear and substantial efficiency effects.

Commentary
para 180: B&C: 6.041, 6.065, 6.082 F&N: 9.329

(181) Exclusive customer allocation is mainly applied to intermediate products and at the wholesale level when it concerns final products, where customer groups with different specific requirements concerning the product can be distinguished.

(182) Exclusive customer allocation may lead to efficiencies, especially when the distributors are required to make investments in for instance specific equipment, skills or know-how to adapt to the requirements of their class of customers. The depreciation period of these investments indicates the justified duration of an exclusive customer allocation system. In general the case is strongest for new or complex products and for products requiring adaptation to the needs of the individual customer. Identifiable differentiated needs are more likely for intermediate products, that is products sold to different types of professional buyers. Allocation of final consumers is unlikely to lead to any efficiencies and is therefore unlikely to be exempted.

Commentary
para 182: B&C: 6.041, 6.082 F&N: 9.330

(183) Example of exclusive customer allocation

A company has developed a sophisticated sprinkler installation. The company has currently a market share of 40 % on the market for sprinkler installations. When it started selling the sophisticated sprinkler it had a market share of 20% with an older product. The installation of the new type of sprinkler depends on the type of building that it is installed in and on the use of the building (office, chemical plant, hospital etc.). The company has appointed a number of distributors to sell and install the sprinkler installation. Each distributor needed to train its employees for the general and specific requirements of installing the sprinkler installation for a particular class of customers. To ensure that distributors would specialise the company assigned to each distributor an exclusive class of customers and prohibited active sales to each others' exclusive customer classes. After five years, all the exclusive distributors will be allowed to sell actively to all classes of customers, thereby ending the system of exclusive customer allocation. The supplier may then also start selling to new distributors. The market is quite dynamic, with two recent entries and a number of technological developments. Competitors, with market shares between 25% and 5%, are also upgrading their products.

As the exclusivity is of limited duration and helps to ensure that the distributors may recoup their investments and concentrate their sales efforts first on a certain class of customers in order to learn the trade, and as the possible anti-competitive effects seem limited in a dynamic market, the conditions for exemption are likely to be fulfilled.

Commentary
para 183: B&C: 6.082

2.4. *Selective distribution*

(184) Selective distribution agreements, like exclusive distribution agreements, restrict on the one hand the number of authorised distributors and on the other the possibilities of resale. The difference with exclusive distribution is that the restriction of the number of dealers does not depend on the number of territories but on selection criteria linked in the first place to the nature of the product. Another difference with exclusive distribution is that the restriction on resale is not a restriction on active selling to a territory but a restriction on any sales to non-authorised distributors, leaving only appointed dealers and final customers as possible buyers. Selective distribution is almost always used to distribute branded final products.

Commentary
para 184: F&N: 12.185

(185) The possible competition risks are a reduction in intra-brand competition and, especially in case of cumulative effect, foreclosure of certain type(s) of distributors and facilitation of collusion between suppliers or buyers. To assess the possible anti-competitive effects of selective distribution under Article 81(1), a distinction needs to be made between purely qualitative selective distribution and quantitative selective distribution. Purely qualitative selective distribution selects dealers only on the basis of objective criteria required by the nature of the product such as training of sales personnel, the service provided at the point of sale, a certain range of the products being sold etc.[1] The application of such criteria does not put a direct limit on the number of dealers. Purely qualitative selective distribution is in general considered to fall outside Article 81(1) for lack of anti-competitive effects, provided that three conditions are satisfied. First, the nature of the product in question must necessitate a selective distribution system, in the sense that such a system must constitute a legitimate requirement, having regard to the nature of the product concerned, to preserve its quality and ensure its proper use. Secondly, resellers must be chosen on the basis of objective criteria of a qualitative nature which are laid down uniformly for all potential resellers and are not applied in a discriminatory manner. Thirdly, the criteria laid down must not go beyond what is necessary.[2]

Quantitative selective distribution adds further criteria for selection that more directly limit the potential number of dealers by, for instance, requiring minimum or maximum sales, by fixing the number of dealers, etc.

Notes

[1] See for example judgment of the Court of First Instance in Case T-88/92 *Groupement d'achat Édouard Leclerc v Commission* [1996] ECR II-1961.

[2] See judgments of the Court of Justice in Case 31/80 *L'Oréal v PVBA* [1980] ECR 3775, paragraphs 15 and 16; Case 26/76 *Metro I* [1977] ECR 1875, paragraphs 20 and 21; Case 107/82 *AEG* [1983] ECR 3151, paragraph 35; and of the Court of First Instance in Case T-19/91 *Vichy v Commission* [1992] ECR II-415, paragraph 65.

Commentary
para 185: B&C: 6.091

(186) Qualitative and quantitative selective distribution is exempted by the Block Exemption Regulation up to 30% market share, even if combined with other non-hardcore vertical restraints, such as non-compete or exclusive distribution, provided active selling by the authorised distributors to each other and to end users is not restricted. The Block Exemption Regulation exempts selective distribution regardless of the nature of the product concerned. However, where the nature of the product does not require selective distribution, such a distribution system does not generally bring about sufficient efficiency enhancing effects to counterbalance a significant reduction in intra-brand competition. If appreciable anti-competitive effects occur, the benefit of the Block Exemption Regulation is likely to be withdrawn. In addition, the following guidance is provided for the assessment of selective distribution in individual cases which are not covered by the Block Exemption Regulation or in the case of cumulative effects resulting from parallel networks of selective distribution.

Commentary
para 186: B&C: 6.099 F&N: 9.334

(187) The market position of the supplier and his competitors is of central importance in assessing possible anti-competitive effects, as the loss of intra-brand competition can only be problematic if inter-brand competition is limited. The stronger the position of the supplier, the more problematic is the loss of intra-brand competition. Another important factor is the number of selective distribution networks present in the same market. Where selective distribution is applied by only one supplier in the market which is not a dominant undertaking, quantitative selective distribution does not normally create net negative effects provided that the contract goods, having regard to their nature, require the use of a selective distribution system and on condition that the selection criteria applied are necessary to ensure efficient distribution of the goods in question. The reality, however, seems to be that selective distribution is often applied by a number of the suppliers in a given market.

Commentary
para 187: B&C: 6.099, 6.105 F&N: 9.335

(188) The position of competitors can have a dual significance and plays in particular a role in case of a cumulative effect. Strong competitors will mean in general that the reduction in intra-brand competition is easily outweighed by sufficient inter-brand competition. However, when a majority of the main suppliers apply selective distribution there will be a significant loss of intra-brand competition and possible foreclosure of certain types of distributors as well as an increased risk of collusion between those major suppliers. The risk of foreclosure of more efficient distributors has always been greater with selective distribution than with exclusive distribution, given the restriction on sales to non-authorised dealers in selective distribution. This is designed to give selective distribution systems a closed character, making it impossible for non-authorised dealers to obtain supplies. This makes selective distribution particularly well suited to avoid pressure by price discounters on the margins of the manufacturer, as well as on the margins of the authorised dealers.

Commentary
para 188: B&C: 6.087, 6.105

(189) Where the Block Exemption Regulation applies to individual networks of selective distribution, withdrawal of the block exemption or disapplication of the Block Exemption Regulation may be considered in case of cumulative effects. However, a cumulative effect problem is unlikely to arise when the share of the market covered by selective distribution is below 50%. Also, no problem is likely to arise where the market coverage ratio exceeds 50 %, but the aggregate market share of the five largest suppliers (CR5) is below 50%. Where both the CR5 and the share of the market covered by selective distribution exceed 50%, the assessment may vary depending on whether or not all five largest suppliers apply selective distribution. The stronger the position of the competitors not applying selective distribution, the less likely the foreclosure of other distributors. If all five largest suppliers apply selective distribution, competition concerns may in particular arise with respect to those agreements that apply quantitative selection criteria by directly limiting the number of authorised dealers. The conditions of Article 81(3) are in general unlikely to be fulfilled if the selective distribution systems at issue prevent access to the market by new distributors capable of adequately selling the products in question, especially price discounters, thereby limiting distribution to the advantage of certain existing channels and to the detriment of final consumers. More indirect forms of quantitative selective distribution, resulting for instance from the combination of purely qualitative selection criteria with the requirement imposed on the dealers to achieve a minimum amount of annual purchases, are less likely to produce net negative effects, if such an amount does not represent a significant proportion of the dealer's total turnover achieved with the type of products in question and it does not go beyond what is necessary for the supplier to recoup his relationship-specific investment and/or realise economies of scale in distribution. As regards individual contributions, a supplier with a market share of less than 5% is in general not considered to contribute significantly to a cumulative effect.

Commentary
para 189: B&C: 2.124, 6.007, 6.099–6.100, 6.105 F&N: 9.337

(190) "Entry barriers" are mainly of interest in the case of foreclosure of the market to non-authorised dealers. In general entry barriers will be considerable as selective distribution is usually applied by manufacturers of branded products. It will in general take time and considerable investment for excluded retailers to launch their own brands or obtain competitive supplies elsewhere.

Commentary
para 190: F&N: 9.338

(191) "Buying power" may increase the risk of collusion between dealers and thus appreciably change the analysis of possible anti-competitive effects of selective distribution. Foreclosure of the market to more efficient retailers may especially result where a strong dealer organisation imposes selection criteria on the supplier aimed at limiting distribution to the advantage of its members.

Commentary
para 191: F&N: 9.339

(192) Article 5(c) of the Block Exemption Regulation provides that the supplier may not impose an obligation causing the authorised dealers, either directly or indirectly, not to sell the brands of particular competing suppliers. This condition aims specifically at avoiding horizontal collusion to exclude particular brands through the creation of a selective club of brands by the leading suppliers. This kind of obligation is unlikely to be exemptable when the CR5 is equal to or above 50%, unless none of the suppliers imposing such an obligation belongs to the five largest suppliers in the market.

Part C Substantive
Antitrust Matters

Commentary
para 192: **B&C:** 6.024

(193) Foreclosure of other suppliers is normally not a problem as long as other suppliers can use the same distributors, i.e. as long as the selective distribution system is not combined with single branding. In the case of a dense network of authorised distributors or in the case of a cumulative effect, the combination of selective distribution and a non-compete obligation may pose a risk of foreclosure to other suppliers. In that case the principles set out above on single branding apply. Where selective distribution is not combined with a non-compete obligation, foreclosure of the market to competing suppliers may still be a problem when the leading suppliers apply not only purely qualitative selection criteria, but impose on their dealers certain additional obligations such as the obligation to reserve a minimum shelf-space for their products or to ensure that the sales of their products by the dealer achieve a minimum percentage of the dealer's total turnover. Such a problem is unlikely to arise if the share of the market covered by selective distribution is below 50% or, where this coverage ratio is exceeded, if the market share of the five largest suppliers is below 50%.

Commentary
para 193: **B&C:** 6.87, 6.107

(194) Maturity of the market is important, as loss of intra-brand competition and possible foreclosure of suppliers or dealers may be a serious problem in a mature market but is less relevant in a market with growing demand, changing technologies and changing market positions.

(195) Selective distribution may be efficient when it leads to savings in logistical costs due to economies of scale in transport and this may happen irrespective of the nature of the product (efficiency 6 in paragraph 116). However, this is usually only a marginal efficiency in selective distribution systems. To help solve a free-rider problem between the distributors (efficiency 1 in paragraph 116) or to help create a brand image (efficiency 8 in paragraph 116), the nature of the product is very relevant. In general the case is strongest for new products, for complex products, for products of which the qualities are difficult to judge before consumption (so-called experience products) or of which the qualities are difficult to judge even after consumption (so-called credence products). The combination of selective and exclusive distribution is likely to infringe Article 81 if it is applied by a supplier whose market share exceeds 30% or in case of cumulative effects, even though active sales between the territories remain free. Such a combination may exceptionally fulfil the conditions of Article 81(3) if it is indispensable to protect substantial and relationship-specific investments made by the authorised dealers (efficiency 4 in paragraph 116).

Commentary
para 195: **B&C:** 6.107 **F&N:** 9.341

(196) To ensure that the least anti-competitive restraint is chosen, it is relevant to see whether the same efficiencies can be obtained at a comparable cost by for instance service requirements alone.

(197) Example of quantitative selective distribution:

In a market for consumer durables, the market leader (brand A), with a market share of 35%, sells its product to final consumers through a selective distribution network. There are several criteria for admission to the network: the shop must employ trained staff and provide pre-sales services, there must be a specialised area in the shop devoted to the sales of the product and similar hi-tech products, and the shop is required to sell a wide range of models of the supplier and to display them in an attractive manner. Moreover, the number of admissible retailers in the network is directly limited through the establishment of a maximum number of retailers per number of inhabitants in each province or urban area. Manufacturer A has 6 competitors in this market. Its largest competitors, B, C and D, have market shares of respectively 25, 15 and 10%, whilst the other producers have smaller market shares. A is the only manufacturer to use selective distribution. The selective distributors of brand A always handle a few competing brands. However, competing brands are also widely sold in shops which are not member of A's selective distribution network. Channels of distribution are various: for instance, brands B and C are sold in most of A's selected shops, but also in other shops providing a high quality service and in hypermarkets. Brand D is mainly sold in high service shops. Technology is evolving quite rapidly in this market, and the main suppliers maintain a strong quality image for their products through advertising.

In this market, the coverage ratio of selective distribution is 35%. Inter-brand competition is not directly affected by the selective distribution system of A. Intra-brand competition for brand A may be reduced, but consumers have access to low service/low price retailers for brands B and C, which have a comparable quality image to brand A. Moreover, access to high service retailers for other brands is not foreclosed, since there is no limitation on the capacity of selected distributors to sell competing brands, and the quantitative limitation on the number of retailers for brand A leaves other high service retailers free to distribute competing brands. In this case, in view of the service requirements and the efficiencies these are likely to provide and the limited effect on intra-brand competition the conditions for exempting A's selective distribution network are likely to be fulfilled.

Commentary
para 197: B&C: 6.105

(198) Example of selective distribution with cumulative effects:

On a market for a particular sports article, there are seven manufacturers, whose respective market shares are: 25%, 20%, 15%, 15%, 10%, 8% and 7%. The five largest manufacturers distribute their products through quantitative selective distribution, whilst the two smallest use different types of distribution systems, which results in a coverage ratio of selective distribution of 85%. The criteria for access to the selective distribution networks are remarkably uniform amongst manufacturers: shops are required to have trained personnel and to provide pre-sale services, there must be a specialised area in the shop devoted to the sales of the article and a minimum size for this area is specified. The shop is required to sell a wide range of the brand in question and to display the article in an attractive manner, the shop must be located in a commercial street, and this type of article must represent at least 30% of the total turnover of the shop. In general, the same dealer is appointed selective distributor for all five brands. The two brands which do not use selective distribution usually sell through less specialised retailers with lower service levels. The market is stable, both on the supply and on the demand side, and there is strong brand image and product differentiation. The five market leaders have strong brand images, acquired through advertising and sponsoring, whereas the two smaller manufacturers have a strategy of cheaper products, with no strong brand image.

In this market, access by general price discounters to the five leading brands is denied. Indeed, the requirement that this type of article represents at least 30% of the activity of the dealers and the criteria on presentation and pre-sales services rule out most price discounters from the network of authorised dealers. As a consequence, consumers have no choice but to buy the five leading brands in high service/high price shops. This leads to reduced inter-brand competition between the five leading brands. The fact that the two smallest brands can be bought in low service/low price shops does [not] compensate for this, because the brand image of the five market leaders is much better. Inter-brand competition is also limited through multiple dealership. Even though there exists some degree of intra-brand competition and the number of retailers is not directly limited, the criteria for admission are strict enough to lead to a small number of retailers for the five leading brands in each territory.

The efficiencies associated with these quantitative selective distribution systems are low: the product is not very complex and does not justify a particularly high service. Unless the manufacturers can prove that there are clear efficiencies linked to their network of selective distribution, it is probable that the block exemption will have to be withdrawn because of its cumulative effects resulting in less choice and higher prices for consumers.

Commentary
para 198: B&C: 6.100

2.5. *Franchising*

(199) Franchise agreements contain licences of intellectual property rights relating in particular to trade marks or signs and know-how for the use and distribution of goods or services. In addition to the licence of IPRs, the franchisor usually provides the franchisee during the life of the agreement with commercial or technical assistance. The licence and the assistance are integral components of the business method being franchised. The franchisor is in general paid a franchise fee by the franchisee for the use of the particular business method. Franchising may enable the franchisor to establish, with limited investments, a uniform network for the distribution of his products. In addition to the provision of the business method, franchise agreements usually contain a combination of different vertical restraints concerning the products being distributed, in particular selective distribution and/or non-compete and/or exclusive distribution or weaker forms thereof.

(200) The coverage by the Block Exemption Regulation of the licensing of IPRs contained in franchise agreements is dealt with in paragraphs 23 to 45. As for the vertical restraints on the purchase, sale and resale of goods and services within a franchising arrangement, such as selective distribution, non-compete or exclusive distribution, the Block Exemption Regulation applies up to the 30% market share threshold for the franchisor or the supplier designated by the franchisor.[1] The guidance provided earlier in respect of these types of restraints applies also to franchising, subject to the following specific remarks:

1) In line with general rule 8 (see paragraph 119), the more important the transfer of know-how, the more easily the vertical restraints fulfil the conditions for exemption.

2) A non-compete obligation on the goods or services purchased by the franchisee falls outside Article 81(1) when the obligation is necessary to maintain the common identity and reputation of the franchised network. In such cases, the duration of the non-compete obligation is also irrelevant under Article 81(1), as long as it does not exceed the duration of the franchise agreement itself.

Notes

[1] See also [Case 107/82] *AEG* [1983] ECR 3151, paragraph 35; and [the judgment] of the Court of First Instance in Case T-19/91 *Vichy v Commission* [1992] ECR II-415, paragraph 65. See also paragraphs 89 to 95, in particular paragraph 95.

Commentary
para 200: F&N: 9.342
para 200(1): B&C: 6.188
para 200(2): B&C: 6.175–6.176, 6.186

(201) Example of franchising:

A manufacturer has developed a new format for selling sweets in so-called fun shops where the sweets can be coloured specially on demand from the consumer. The manufacturer of the sweets has also developed the machines to colour the sweets. The manufacturer also produces the colouring liquids. The quality and freshness of the liquid is of vital importance to producing good sweets. The manufacturer made a success of its sweets through a number of own retail outlets all operating under the same trade name and with the uniform fun image (style of layout of the shops, common advertising etc.). In order to expand sales the manufacturer started a franchising system. The franchisees are obliged to buy the sweets, liquid and colouring machine from the manufacturer, to have the same image and operate under the trade name, pay a franchise fee, contribute to common advertising and ensure the confidentiality of the operating manual prepared by the franchisor. In addition, the franchisees are only allowed to sell from the agreed premises, are only allowed to sell to end users or other franchisees and are not allowed to sell other sweets. The franchisor is obliged not to appoint another franchisee nor operate a retail outlet himself in a given contract territory. The franchisor is also under the obligation to update and further develop its products, the business outlook and the operating manual and make these improvements available to all retail franchisees. The franchise agreements are concluded for a duration of 10 years.

Sweet retailers buy their sweets on a national market from either national producers that cater for national tastes or from wholesalers which import sweets from foreign producers in addition to selling products from national producers. On this market the franchisor's products compete with other brands of sweets. The franchisor has a market share of 30 % on the market for sweets sold to retailers. Competition comes from a number of national and international brands, sometimes produced by large diversified food companies. There are many potential points of sale of sweets in the form of tobacconists, general food retailers, cafeterias and specialised sweet shops. On the market for machines for colouring food the franchisor's market share is below 10%.

Most of the obligations contained in the franchise agreements can be assessed as being necessary to protect the intellectual property rights or maintain the common identity and reputation of the franchised network and fall outside Article 81(1). The restrictions on selling (contract territory and selective distribution) provide an incentive to the franchisees to invest in the colouring machine and the franchise concept and, if not necessary for, at least help to maintain the common identity, thereby offsetting the loss of intra-brand competition. The non-compete clause excluding other brands of sweets from the shops for the full duration of the agreements does allow the franchisor to keep the outlets uniform and prevent competitors from benefiting from its trade name. It does not lead to any serious foreclosure in view of the great number of potential outlets available to other sweet producers. The franchise agreements of this franchisor are likely to fulfil the conditions for exemption under Article 81(3) in as far as the obligations contained therein fall under Article 81(1).

Commentary
para 201: **B&C:** 6.185, 6.188

2.6. *Exclusive supply*

(202) Exclusive supply as defined in Article 1(c) of the Block Exemption Regulation is the extreme form of limited distribution in as far as the limit on the number of buyers is concerned: in the agreement it is specified that there is only one buyer inside the Community to which the supplier may sell a particular final product. For intermediate goods or services, exclusive supply means that there is only one buyer inside the Community or that there is only one buyer inside the Community for the purposes of a specific use. For intermediate goods or services, exclusive supply is often referred to as industrial supply.

Commentary
para 202: **B&C:** 6.039 **F&N:** 9.343, 9.354

---

(203) Exclusive supply as defined in Article 1(c) of the Block Exemption Regulation is exempted by Article 2(1) read in conjunction with Article 3(2) of the Block Exemption Regulation up to 30% market share of the buyer, even if combined with other non-hardcore vertical restraints such as non-compete. Above the market share threshold the following guidance is provided for the assessment of exclusive supply in individual cases.

(204) The main competition risk of exclusive supply is foreclosure of other buyers. The market share of the buyer on the upstream purchase market is obviously important for assessing the ability of the buyer to "impose" exclusive supply which forecloses other buyers from access to supplies. The importance of the buyer on the downstream market is however the factor which determines whether a competition problem may arise. If the buyer has no market power downstream, then no appreciable negative effects for consumers can be expected. Negative effects can however be expected when the market share of the buyer on the downstream supply market as well as the upstream purchase market exceeds 30%. Where the market share of the buyer on the upstream market does not exceed 30%, significant foreclosure effects may still result, especially when the market share of the buyer on his downstream market exceeds 30%. In such cases withdrawal of the block exemption may be required. Where a company is dominant on

the downstream market, any obligation to supply the products only or mainly to the dominant buyer may easily have significant anti-competitive effects.

Commentary
para 204: B&C: 6.025, 6.040

(205) It is not only the market position of the buyer on the upstream and downstream market that is important but also the extent to and the duration for which he applies an exclusive supply obligation. The higher the tied supply share, and the longer the duration of the exclusive supply, the more significant the foreclosure is likely to be. Exclusive supply agreements shorter than five years entered into by non-dominant companies usually require a balancing of pro- and anti-competitive effects, while agreements lasting longer than five years are for most types of investments not considered necessary to achieve the claimed efficiencies or the efficiencies are not sufficient to outweigh the foreclosure effect of such long-term exclusive supply agreements.

Commentary
para 205: B&C: 6.083 F&N: 9.344

(206) The market position of the competing buyers on the upstream market is important as it is only likely that competing buyers will be foreclosed for anti-competitive reasons, i.e. to increase their costs, if they are significantly smaller than the foreclosing buyer. Foreclosure of competing buyers is not very likely where these competitors have similar buying power and can offer the suppliers similar sales possibilities. In such a case, foreclosure could only occur for potential entrants, who may not be able to secure supplies when a number of major buyers all enter into exclusive supply contracts with the majority of suppliers on the market. Such a cumulative effect may lead to withdrawal of the benefit of the Block Exemption Regulation.

Commentary
para 206: F&N: 9.346

(207) Entry barriers at the supplier level are relevant to establishing whether there is real foreclosure. In as far as it is efficient for competing buyers to provide the goods or services themselves via upstream vertical integration, foreclosure is unlikely to be a real problem. However, often there are significant entry barriers.

(208) Countervailing power of suppliers is relevant, as important suppliers will not easily allow themselves to be cut off from alternative buyers. Foreclosure is therefore mainly a risk in the case of weak suppliers and strong buyers. In the case of strong suppliers the exclusive supply may be found in combination with non-compete. The combination with non-compete brings in the rules developed for single branding. Where there are relationship-specific investments involved on both sides (hold-up problem) the combination of exclusive supply and non-compete i.e. reciprocal exclusivity in industrial supply agreements is usually justified below the level of dominance.

Commentary
para 208: F&N: 9.347

(209) Lastly, the level of trade and the nature of the product are relevant for foreclosure. Foreclosure is less likely in the case of an intermediate product or where the product is homogeneous. Firstly, a foreclosed manufacturer that uses a certain input usually has more flexibility to respond to the demand of his customers than the wholesaler/retailer has in responding to the demand of the final consumer for whom brands may play an important role. Secondly, the loss of a possible source of supply matters less for the foreclosed buyers in the case of homogeneous products than in the case of a heterogeneous product with different grades and qualities.

(210) For homogeneous intermediate products, anti-competitive effects are likely to be exemptable below the level of dominance. For final branded products or differentiated intermediate products where there are entry barriers, exclusive supply may have appreciable anti-competitive

effects where the competing buyers are relatively small compared to the foreclosing buyer, even if the latter is not dominant on the downstream market.

Commentary
para 210: B&C: 6.083

(211) Where appreciable anti-competitive effects are established, an exemption under Article 81(3) is possible as long as the company is not dominant. Efficiencies can be expected in the case of a hold-up problem (paragraph 116, points 4 and 5), and this is more likely for intermediate products than for final products. Other efficiencies are less likely. Possible economies of scale in distribution (paragraph 116, point 6) do not seem likely to justify exclusive supply.

Commentary
para 211: B&C: 6.083

(212) In the case of a hold-up problem and even more so in the case of scale economies in distribution, quantity forcing on the supplier, such as minimum supply requirements, could well be a less restrictive alternative.

(213) Example of exclusive supply:

On a market for a certain type of components (intermediate product market) supplier A agrees with buyer B to develop, with his own know-how and considerable investment in new machines and with the help of specifications supplied by buyer B, a different version of the component. B will have to make considerable investments to incorporate the new component. It is agreed that A will supply the new product only to buyer B for a period of five years from the date of first entry on the market. B is obliged to buy the new product only from A for the same period of five years. Both A and B can continue to sell and buy respectively other versions of the component elsewhere. The market share of buyer B on the upstream component market and on the downstream final goods market is 40%. The market share of the component supplier is 35%. There are two other component suppliers with around 20–25% market share and a number of small suppliers.

Given the considerable investments, the agreement is likely to fulfil the conditions for exemption in view of the efficiencies and the limited foreclosure effect. Other buyers are foreclosed from a particular version of a product of a supplier with 35% market share and there are other component suppliers that could develop similar new products. The foreclosure of part of buyer B's demand to other suppliers is limited to maximum 40% of the market.

Commentary
para 213: B&C: 6.083, 6.193

(214) Exclusive supply is based on a direct or indirect obligation causing the supplier only to sell to one buyer. Quantity forcing on the supplier is based on incentives agreed between the supplier and the buyer that make the former concentrate his sales mainly with one buyer. Quantity forcing on the supplier may have similar but more mitigated effects than exclusive supply. The assessment of quantity forcing will depend on the degree of foreclosure of other buyers on the upstream market.

Commentary
para 214: B&C: 6.039

2.7. *Tying*

(215) Tying exists when the supplier makes the sale of one product conditional upon the purchase of another distinct product from the supplier or someone designated by the latter. The first product is referred to as the tying product and the second is referred to as the tied product. If the tying is not objectively justified by the nature of the products or commercial usage, such practice may constitute an abuse within the meaning of Article 82.[1] Article 81 may apply to horizontal agreements or concerted practices between competing suppliers which make the

sale of one product conditional upon the purchase of another distinct product. Tying may also constitute a vertical restraint falling under Article 81 where it results in a single branding type of obligation (see paragraphs 138 to 160) for the tied product. Only the latter situation is dealt with in these Guidelines.

Notes

[1] Judgment of the Court of Justice in Case C-333/94 P *Tetrapak v Commission* [1996] ECR I-5951, paragraph 37.

(216) What is to be considered as a distinct product is determined first of all by the demand of the buyers. Two products are distinct if, in the absence of tying, from the buyers' perspective, the products are purchased by them on two different markets. For instance, since customers want to buy shoes with laces, it has become commercial usage for shoe manufacturers to supply shoes with laces. Therefore, the sale of shoes with laces is not a tying practice. Often combinations have become accepted practice because the nature of the product makes it technically difficult to supply one product without the supply of another product.

(217) The main negative effect of tying on competition is possible foreclosure on the market of the tied product. Tying means that there is at least a form of quantity-forcing on the buyer in respect of the tied product. Where in addition a non-compete obligation is agreed in respect of the tied product, this increases the possible foreclosure effect on the market of the tied product. Tying may also lead to supra-competitive prices, especially in three situations. Firstly, when the tying and tied product are partly substitutable for the buyer. Secondly, when the tying allows price discrimination according to the use the customer makes of the tying product, for example the tying of ink cartridges to the sale of photocopying machines (metering). Thirdly, when in the case of long-term contracts or in the case of after-markets with original equipment with a long replacement time, it becomes difficult for the customers to calculate the consequences of the tying. Lastly, tying may also lead to higher entry barriers both on the market of the tying and on the market of the tied product.

(218) Tying is exempted by Article 2(1) read in conjunction with Article 3 of the Block Exemption Regulation when the market share of the supplier on both the market of the tied product and the market of the tying product does not exceed 30%. It may be combined with other non-hardcore vertical restraints such as non-compete or quantity forcing in respect of the tying product, or exclusive purchasing. Above the market share threshold the following guidance is provided for the assessment of tying in individual cases.

(219) The market position of the supplier on the market of the tying product is obviously of main importance to assess possible anti-competitive effects. In general this type of agreement is imposed by the supplier. The importance of the supplier on the market of the tying product is the main reason why a buyer may find it difficult to refuse a tying obligation.

(220) To assess the supplier's market power, the market position of his competitors on the market of the tying product is important. As long as his competitors are sufficiently numerous and strong, no anti-competitive effects can be expected, as buyers have sufficient alternatives to purchase the tying product without the tied product, unless other suppliers are applying similar tying. In addition, entry barriers on the market of the tying product are relevant to establish the market position of the supplier. When tying is combined with a non-compete obligation in respect of the tying product, this considerably strengthens the position of the supplier.

(221) Buying power is relevant, as important buyers will not easily be forced to accept tying without obtaining at least part of the possible efficiencies. Tying not based on efficiency is therefore mainly a risk where buyers do not have significant buying power.

(222) Where appreciable anti-competitive effects are established, the question of a possible exemption under Article 81(3) arises as long as the company is not dominant. Tying obligations may help to produce efficiencies arising from joint production or joint distribution. Where the tied product is not produced by the supplier, an efficiency may also arise from the supplier buying large quantities of the tied product. For tying to be exemptable, it must, however, be shown that at least part of these cost reductions are passed on to the consumer. Tying is therefore normally not exemptable when the retailer is able to obtain, on a regular basis, supplies of the same or equivalent products on the same or better conditions than those offered by the supplier which applies the tying practice. Another efficiency may exist where tying helps to ensure a

certain uniformity and quality standardisation (see efficiency 8 in paragraph 116). However, it needs to be demonstrated that the positive effects cannot be realised equally efficiently by requiring the buyer to use or resell products satisfying minimum quality standards, without requiring the buyer to purchase these from the supplier or someone designated by the latter. The requirements concerning minimum quality standards would not normally fall within Article 81(1). Where the supplier of the tying product imposes on the buyer the suppliers from which the buyer must purchase the tied product, for instance because the formulation of minimum quality standards is not possible, this may also fall outside Article 81(1), especially where the supplier of the tying product does not derive a direct (financial) benefit from designating the suppliers of the tied product.

Commentary
para 222: F&N: 9.356

(223) The effect of supra-competitive prices is considered anti-competitive in itself. The effect of foreclosure depends on the tied percentage of total sales on the market of the tied product. On the question of what can be considered appreciable foreclosure under Article 81(1), the analysis for single branding can be applied. Above the 30% market share threshold exemption of tying is unlikely, unless there are clear efficiencies that are transmitted, at least in part, to consumers. Exemption is even less likely when tying is combined with non-compete, either in respect of the tied or in respect of the tying product.

(224) Withdrawal of the block exemption is likely where no efficiencies result from tying or where such efficiencies are not passed on to the consumer (see paragraph 222). Withdrawal is also likely in the case of a cumulative effect where a majority of the suppliers apply similar tying arrangements without the possible efficiencies being transmitted at least in part to consumers.

2.8. *Recommended and maximum resale prices*

(225) The practice of recommending a resale price to a reseller or requiring the reseller to respect a maximum resale price is — subject to the comments in paragraphs 46 to 56 concerning RPM — covered by the Block Exemption Regulation when the market share of the supplier does not exceed the 30% threshold. For cases above the market share threshold and for cases of withdrawal of the block exemption the following guidance is provided.

Commentary
para 225: F&N: 12.184

(226) The possible competition risk of maximum and recommended prices is firstly that the maximum or recommended price will work as a focal point for the resellers and might be followed by most or all of them. A second competition risk is that maximum or recommended prices may facilitate collusion between suppliers.

(227) The most important factor for assessing possible anti-competitive effects of maximum or recommended resale prices is the market position of the supplier. The stronger the market position of the supplier, the higher the risk that a maximum resale price or a recommended resale price leads to a more or less uniform application of that price level by the resellers, because they may use it as a focal point. They may find it difficult to deviate from what they perceive to be the preferred resale price proposed by such an important supplier on the market. Under such circumstances the practice of imposing a maximum resale price or recommending a resale price may infringe Article 81(1) if it leads to a uniform price level.

Commentary
para 227: B&C: 6.052

(228) The second most important factor for assessing possible anti-competitive effects of the practice of maximum and recommended prices is the market position of competitors. Especially in a narrow oligopoly, the practice of using or publishing maximum or recommended prices may facilitate collusion between the suppliers by exchanging information on the preferred price level and by reducing the likelihood of lower resale prices. The practice of imposing a

maximum resale price or recommending resale prices leading to such effects may also infringe Article 81(1).

Commentary
para 228: B&C: 6.052

2.9. *Other vertical restraints*

(229) The vertical restraints and combinations described above are only a selection. There are other restraints and combinations for which no direct guidance is provided here. They will however be treated according to the same principles, with the help of the same general rules and with the same emphasis on the effect on the market.

C12

COMMISSION NOTICE

Guidelines on the applicability of Article 81 of the EC Treaty
to horizontal cooperation agreements

(2001/C 3/02)

(Text with EEA relevance)

Official Journal C 3, 6.1.2001, p. 2

Celex No: 32001Y0106

Notes

EEA application: the EFTA Surveillance Authority has adopted a parallel notice on the applicability of Article 53 of the EEA Agreement to horizontal co-operation agreements under Article 5(2)(b) of the Surveillance and Court Agreement: OJ C 266, 31.10.2002, p. 1 and EEA Supplement No 55, 31.10.2002, p. 1.

Commentary

Guidelines: B&C: 1.037, 1.066, 1.100, 2.097, 2.113, 2.128, 2.132, 3.004, 4.007, 5.004, 5.147, 7.003, 7.018, 7.027–7.028, 7.030, 7.041, 7.055, 7.057, 7.087, 7.089, 7.091, 7.094, 7.131, 8.008, 8.190, 9.005, 12.086, 12.145 F&N: 3.136, 3.291, 3.336, 3.446, 3.456, 7.08, 7.11, 7.112, 7.115, 7.141, 7.146, 7.148, 7.187, 7.213, 7.228, 7.257, 7.297, 7.309, 7.322, 7.364, 7.388, 7.403, 7.404, 7.406–7.413, 8.51, 9.155, 12.284, 12.343
paras 21–23: F&N: 3.180
paras 44–46: F&N: 7.142
paras 47–49: F&N: 7.143
paras 55–58: F&N: 7.115
paras 68–71: B&C: 7.057
paras 71–74: F&N: 9.155
paras 79–81: B&C: 6.189
paras 80–81: F&N: 9.156
paras 115–118: F&N: 12.339
paras 119–122: F&N: 12.339
paras 128–131: B&C: 5.128
paras 144–146: B&C: 5.147
paras 148–150: B&C: 5.147
paras 193–194: B&C: 5.145
paras 192–197: F&N: 7.413
paras 192–198: B&C: 3.022, 3.044
paras 193–194: B&C: 5.145
Chap 3: F&N: 7.214
Chap 5: F&N: 7.262

1. INTRODUCTION

1.1. Purpose

1. These guidelines set out the principles for the assessment of horizontal cooperation agreements under Article 81 of the Treaty. A cooperation is of a "horizontal nature" if an agreement or concerted practice is entered into between companies operating at the same level(s) in the market. In most instances, horizontal cooperation amounts to cooperation between competitors. It covers for example areas such as research and development (R & D), production, purchasing or commercialisation.

2. Horizontal cooperation may lead to competition problems. This is for example the case if the parties to a cooperation agree to fix prices or output, to share markets, or if the cooperation enables the parties to maintain, gain or increase market power and thereby causes negative market effects with respect to prices, output, innovation or the variety and quality of products.

Commentary

para 2: F&N: 9.56, 9.60, 12.287

---

3. On the other hand, horizontal cooperation can lead to substantial economic benefits. Companies need to respond to increasing competitive pressure and a changing market place driven by globalisation, the speed of technological progress and the generally more dynamic nature of markets. Cooperation can be a means to share risk, save costs, pool know-how and launch innovation faster. In particular for small and medium-sized enterprises cooperation is an important means to adapt to the changing market place.

Commentary

para 3: F&N: 9.62

---

4. The Commission, while recognising the economic benefits that can be generated by cooperation, has to ensure that effective competition is maintained. Article 81 provides the legal framework for a balanced assessment taking into account both anti-competitive effects as well as economic benefits.

5. In the past, two Commission notices and two block exemption regulations provided guidance for the assessment of horizontal cooperation under Article 81. Commission Regulation (EEC) No 417/85,[1] as last amended by Regulation (EC) No 2236/97[2] and Commission Regulation (EEC) No 418/85,[3] as last amended by Regulation (EC) No 2236/97, provided for the exemption of certain forms of specialisation agreement and research and development agreement (R & D) respectively. Those two Regulations have now been replaced by Commission Regulation (EC) No 2658/2000 of 29 November 2000 on the application of Article 81(3) of the Treaty to categories of specialisation agreements[4] ("the Specialisation block exemption Regulation") and Commission Regulation (EC) No 2659/2000 of 29 November 2000 on the application of Article 81(3) of the Treaty to categories of research and development agreements[5] ("the R & D block exemption Regulation"). The two notices provided guidance in respect of certain types of cooperation agreement falling outside Article 81[6] and the [assessment] of cooperative joint ventures.[7]

Notes

[1] OJ L 53, 22.2.1985, p. 1.
[2] OJ L 306, 11.11.1997, p. 12.
[3] OJ L 53, 22.2.1985, p. 5.
[4] OJ L 304, 5.12.2000, p. 3.
[5] OJ L 304, 5.12.2000, p. 7.
[6] OJ C 75, 29.7.1968, p. 3.
[7] OJ C 43, 16.2.1993, p. 2.

---

6. Changing markets have generated an increasing variety and use of horizontal cooperation. More complete and updated guidance is needed to improve clarity and transparency regarding the applicability of Article 81 in this area. Within the assessment greater emphasis has to be put on

economic criteria to better reflect recent developments in enforcement practice and the case law of the Court of Justice and Court of First Instance of the European Communities.

7. The purpose of these guidelines is to provide an analytical framework for the most common types of horizontal cooperation. This framework is primarily based on criteria that help to analyse the economic context of a cooperation agreement. Economic criteria such as the market power of the parties and other factors relating to the market structure, form a key element of the assessment of the market impact likely to be caused by a cooperation and therefore for the assessment under Article 81. Given the enormous variety in types and combinations of horizontal cooperation and market circumstances in which they operate, it is impossible to provide specific answers for every possible scenario. The present analytical framework based on economic criteria will nevertheless assist businesses in assessing the compatibility of an individual cooperation agreement with Article 81.

Commentary
para 7: B&C: 7.003

8. The guidelines not only replace the Notices referred to in paragraph 5, but also cover a wider range of the most common types of horizontal agreements. They complement the R & D block exemption Regulation and the Specialisation block exemption Regulation.

Commentary
para 8: B&C: 5.091 F&N: 9.61, 9.145

1.2. Scope of the Guidelines

9. These guidelines cover agreements or concerted practices (hereinafter referred to as "agreements") entered into between two or more companies operating at the same level(s) in the market, e.g. at the same level of production or distribution. Within this context the focus is an cooperation between competitors. The term "competitors" as used in these guidelines includes both actual[8] and potential.[9]

Notes

[8] A firm is treated as an actual competitor if it is either active on the same relevant market or if, in the absence of the agreement, it is able to switch production to the relevant products and market them in the short term without incurring significant additional costs or risks in response to a small and permanent increase in relative prices (immediate supply-side substitutability). The same reasoning may lead to the grouping of different geographic areas. However, when supply-side substitutability would entail the need to adjust significantly existing tangible and intangible assets, to make additional investments, to take strategic decisions or to incur time delays, a company will not be treated as a competitor but as a potential competitor (see below). See Commission Notice on the definition of the relevant market for the purposes of Community competition law (OJ C372, 9.12.1997, p. 5, paragraphs 20–23).

[9] A firm is treated as a potential competitor if there is evidence that, absent the agreement, this firm could and would be likely to undertake the necessary additional investments or other necessary switching costs so that it could enter the relevant market in response to a small and permanent increase in relative prices. This assessment has to be based on realistic grounds, the mere theoretical possibility to enter a market is not sufficient (see Commission Notice on the definition of the relevant market for the purposes of Community competition law (paragraph 24); see also the Commission's Thirteenth Report on Competition Policy, point 55 and Commission Decision 90/410/EEC in case *Elopak/Metal Box-Odin* (OJ L 209, 8.8.1990, p. 15)). Market entry needs to take place sufficiently fast so that the threat of potential entry is a constraint on the market participants' behaviour. Normally, this means that entry has to occur within a short period. The Guidelines on Vertical Restraints (OJ C 291, 13.10.2000, p. 1, paragraph 26), consider a period of maximum 1 year for the purposes of application of the Block Exemption Regulation on Vertical Restraints (see footnote 11). However, in individual cases longer time periods can be taken into account. The time period needed by companies already active on the market to adjust their capacities can be used as a yardstick to determine this period.

Commentary
para 9: F&N: 3.225

10. The present guidelines do not, however, address all possible horizontal agreements. They are only concerned with those types of cooperation which potentially generate efficiency gains, namely agreements on R & D, production, purchasing, commercialisation, standardisation,

and environmental agreements. Other types of horizontal agreements between competitors, for example on the exchange of information or on minority shareholdings, are to be addressed separately.

Commentary
para 10: B&C: 2.132, 5.091, 8.186

11. Agreements that are entered into between companies operating at a different level of the production or distribution chain, that is to say vertical agreements, are in principle excluded from these guidelines and dealt with in Commission Regulation (EC) No 2790/1999[10] (the "Block Exemption Regulation on Vertical Restraints") and the Guidelines on vertical restraints.[11] However, to the extent that vertical agreements, e.g. distribution agreements, are concluded between competitors, the effects of the agreement on the market and the possible competition problems can be similar to horizontal agreements. Therefore, these agreements have to be assessed according to the principles described in the present guidelines. This does not exclude the additional application of the Guidelines on Vertical Restraints to these agreements to assess the vertical restraints included in such agreements.[12]

Notes
[10] OJ L 336, 29.12.1999, p. 21.
[11] OJ C 291, 13.10.2000, p. 1.
[12] The delineation between horizontal and vertical agreements will be further developed in the chapters on joint purchasing (Chapter 4) and joint commercialisation (Chapter 5). See also the Guidelines on Vertical Restraints, paragraph 26 and 29.

12. Agreements may combine different stages of cooperation, for example R & D and the production of its results. Unless they fall under Council Regulation (EEC) No 4064/89 of 21 December 1989 on the control of concentrations between undertakings,[13] as last amended by Regulation (EC) No 1310/97[14] ("the Merger Regulation"), these agreements are covered by the guidelines. The centre of gravity of the cooperation determines which section of the present guidelines applies to the agreement in question. In the determination of the centre of gravity, account is taken in particular of two factors: firstly, the starting point of the cooperation, and, secondly, the degree of integration of the different functions which are being combined. A cooperation involving both joint R & D and joint production of the results would thus normally be covered in the section on "Agreements on Research and Development", as the joint production will only take place if the joint R & D is successful. This implies that the results of the joint R & D are decisive for production. The R & D agreement can thus be regarded as the starting point of the cooperation. This assessment would change if the agreement foresaw a full integration in the area of production and only a partial integration of some R & D activities. In this case, the possible anti-competitive effects and economic benefits of the cooperation would largely relate to the joint production, and the agreement would therefore be examined according to the principles set out in the section on "Production Agreements". More complex arrangements such as strategic alliances that combine a number of different areas and instruments of cooperation in varying ways are not covered by the guidelines. The assessment of each individual area of cooperation within an alliance may be carried out with the help of the corresponding chapter in the guidelines. However, complex arrangements must also be analysed in their totality. Due to the variety of areas an alliance may combine, it is impossible to give general guidance for such an overall assessment. Alliances or other forms of cooperation that primarily declare intentions are impossible to assess under the competition rules as long as they lack a precise scope.

Notes
[13] OJ L 395, 30.12.1989, p. 1. Corrected version OJ L 257, 21.9.1990, p. 13.
[14] OJ L 180, 9.7.1997, p. 1.

Commentary
para 12: B&C: 7.009, 7.029 F&N: 7.13

13. The criteria set out in these guidelines apply to cooperation concerning both goods and services, collectively referred to as "products". However, the guidelines do not apply to the extent that sector-specific rules apply, as is the case for agriculture, transport or insurance.[15] Operations that come under the Merger Regulation are also not the subject of the present guidelines.

Notes

[15] Council Regulation 26/62 (OJ 30, 20.4.1962, p. 993) (agriculture). [See now Council Regulation (EC) No 1184/2006 of 24 July 2006, OJ L 214, 4.8.2006, p. 7.]

14. Article 81 only applies to those horizontal cooperation agreements which may affect trade between Member States. These guidelines are not concerned with the analysis of the capability of a given agreement to affect trade. The following principles on the applicability of Article 81 are therefore based on the assumption that trade between Member States is affected. In practice, however, this issue needs to be examined on a case-by-case basis.

15. Article 81 does not apply to agreements which are of minor importance because they are not capable of appreciably restricting competition by object or effect. These guidelines are without prejudice to the application of the present or any future "de minimis" notice.[16]

Notes

[16] See Notice on agreements of minor importance (OJ C 372, 9.12.1997, p. 13). [See now Commission Notice on agreements of minor importance which do not appreciably restrict competition under Article 81(1) of the Treaty establishing the European Community (*de minimis*) OJ C 368, 22.12.2001, p. 13.]

16. The assessment under Article 81 as described in these guidelines is without prejudice to the possible parallel application of Article 82 of the Treaty to horizontal cooperation agreements. Furthermore, these guidelines are without prejudice to the interpretation that may be given by the Court of First Instance and the Court of Justice of the European Communities in relation to the application of Article 81 to horizontal cooperation agreements.

1.3. Basic Principles for the Assessment under Article 81

1.3.1. Article 81(1)

17. Article 81(1) applies to horizontal cooperation agreements which have as their object or effect the prevention, restriction or distortion of competition (hereinafter referred to as "restrictions of competition").

18. In some cases the nature of a cooperation indicates from the outset the applicability of Article 81(1). This is the case for agreements that have as their object a restriction of competition by means of price fixing, output limitation or sharing of markets or customers. These agreements are presumed to have negative market effects. It is therefore not necessary to examine their actual effects on competition and the market in order to establish that they fall within Article 81(1).

19. Many horizontal cooperation agreements, however, do not have as their object a restriction of competition. Therefore, an analysis of the effects of the agreement is necessary. For this analysis it is not sufficient that the agreement limits competition between the parties. It must also be likely to affect competition in the market to such an extent that negative market effects as to prices, output, innovation or the variety or quality of goods and services can be expected.

Commentary
para 19: B&C: 7.041 F&N:.292

20. Whether the agreement is able to cause such negative market effects depends on the economic context taking into account both the nature of the agreement and the parties' combined market power which determines — together with other structural factors — the capability of the cooperation to affect overall competition to such a significant extent.

Commentary
para 20: F&N: 3.291

Nature of the agreement

21. The nature of an agreement relates to factors such as the area and objective of the cooperation, the competitive relationship between the parties and the extent to which they combine their activities. These factors indicate the likelihood of the parties coordinating their behaviour in the market.

22. Certain types of agreement, for instance most R & D agreements or cooperation to set standards or improve environmental conditions, are less likely to include restrictions with respect to prices and output. If these types of agreements have negative effects at all these are likely to be on innovation or the variety of products. They may also give rise to foreclosure problems.

23. Other types of cooperation such as agreements on production or purchasing typically cause a certain degree of commonality in (total) costs. If this degree is significant, the parties may more easily coordinate market prices and output. A significant degree of commonality in costs can only be achieved under certain conditions: First, the area of cooperation, e.g. production and purchasing, has to account for a high proportion of the total costs in a given market. Secondly, the parties need to combine their activities in the area of cooperation to a significant extent. This is, for instance, the case, where they jointly manufacture or purchase an important intermediate product or a high proportion of their total output of a final product.

Agreements that do not fall under Article 81(1)

24. Some categories of agreements do not fall under Article 81(1) because of their very nature. This is normally true for cooperation that does not imply a coordination of the parties' competitive behaviour in the market such as
    — cooperation between non-competitors,
    — cooperation between competing companies that cannot independently carry out the project or activity covered by the cooperation,
    — cooperation concerning an activity which does not influence the relevant parameters of competition.
    These categories of cooperation could only come under Article 81(1) if they involve firms with significant market power[17] and are likely to cause foreclosure problems vis-à-vis third parties.

Notes

[17] Companies may have significant market power below the level of market dominance, which is the threshold for the application of Article 82.

Commentary
para 24: **B&C:** 7.036 **F&N:** 12.344

Agreements that almost always fall under Article 81(1)

25. Another category of agreements can be assessed from the outset as normally falling under Article 81(1). This concerns cooperation agreements that have the object to restrict competition by means of price fixing, output limitation or sharing of markets or customers. These restrictions are considered to be the most harmful, because they directly interfere with the outcome of the competitive process. Price fixing and output limitation directly lead to customers paying higher prices or not receiving the desired quantities. The sharing of markets or customers reduces the choice available to customers and therefore also leads to higher prices or reduced output. It can therefore be presumed that these restrictions have negative market effects. They are therefore almost always prohibited.[18]

Notes

[18] This does, however, exceptionally not apply to a production joint venture. It is inherent to the functioning of such a joint venture that decisions on output are taken jointly by the parties. If the joint venture also markets the jointly manufactured goods, then decisions on prices need to be taken jointly by the parties to such an agreement. In this case, the inclusion of provisions on prices or output does not automatically cause the agreement to fall under Article 81(1). The provisions on prices or output will have to be assessed together with the other effects of the joint venture on the market to determine the applicability of Article 81(1) (see paragraph 90).

Agreements that may fall under Article 81(1)

26. Agreements that do not belong to the above-mentioned categories need further analysis in order to decide whether they fall under Article 81(1). The analysis has to include market-related criteria such as the market position of the parties and other structural factors.

Commentary
para 26: F&N: 7.10

Market power and market structure

27. The starting point for the analysis is the position of the parties in the markets affected by the cooperation. This determines whether or not they are likely to maintain, gain or increase market power through the cooperation, i.e. have the ability to cause negative market effects as to prices, output, innovation or the variety or quality of goods and services. To carry out this analysis the relevant market(s) have to be defined by using the methodology of the Commission's market definition notice.[19] Where specific types of markets are concerned such as purchasing or technology markets, these guidelines will provide additional guidance.

Notes
[19] See Commission Notice on the definition of the relevant market for the purposes of Community competition law (OJ C 372, 9.12.1997, p. 5).

Commentary
para 27: B&C: 4.007

28. If the parties together have a low combined market share,[20] a restrictive effect of the cooperation is unlikely and no further analysis normally is required. If one of just two parties has only an insignificant market share and if it does not possess important resources, even a high combined market share normally cannot be seen as indicating a restrictive effect on competition in the market,[21] Given the variety of cooperation types and the different effects they may cause in different market situations, it is impossible to give a general market share threshold above which sufficient market power for causing restrictive effects can be assumed.

Notes
[20] Market shares should normally be calculated on the basis of the market sales value (see Article 6 of the R & D Block Exemption Regulation and Article 6 of the Specialisation Block Exemption Regulation). In determining the market share of a party in a given market, account must be taken of the undertakings which are connected to the parties (see point 2 of Article 2 of the R & D Block Exemption Regulation and point 2 of Article 2 of the Specialisation Block Exemption Regulation).
[21] If there are more than two parties, then the collective share of all cooperating competitors has to be significantly greater than the share of the largest single participating competitor.

Commentary
para 28: B&C: 2.132

29. In addition to the market position of the parties and the addition of market shares, the market concentration, i.e. the position and number of competitors, may have to be taken into account as an additional factor to assess the impact of the cooperation on market competition. As an indicator the Herfindahl-Hirshman Index ("HHI"), which sums up the squares of the individual market shares of all competitors,[22] can be used: With an HHI below 1000 the market concentration can be characterised as low, between 1000 and 1800 as moderate and above 1800 as high. Another possible indicator would be the leading firm concentration ratio, which sums up the individual market shares of the leading competitors.[23]

Notes
[22] A market consisting of four firms with shares of 30%, 25%, 25% and 20%, has a HHI of 2550 (900+625+625+400) pre-cooperation. If the first two market leaders would cooperate, the HHI would change to 4050 (3025+625+400) post-cooperation. The HHI post-cooperation is relevant for the assessment of the possible market effects of a cooperation.

[23] E.g. the three-firm concentration ratio CR3 is the sum of the market shares of the leading three competitors in a market.

Commentary
para 29: B&C: 2.124, 6.007, 7.042

30. Depending on the market position of the parties and the concentration in the market, other factors such as the stability of market shares over time, entry barriers and the likelihood of market entry, the countervailing power of buyers/suppliers or the nature of the products (e.g. homogeneity, maturity) have to be considered as well. Where an impact on competition in innovation is likely and can not be assessed adequately on the basis of existing markets, specific factors to analyse these impacts may have to be taken into account (see Chapter 2, R & D agreements).

Commentary
para 30: B&C: 7.042

1.3.2. Article 81(3)

31. Agreements that come under Article 81(1) may be exempted provided the conditions of Article 81(3) are fulfilled. This is the case if the agreement
   — contributes to improving the production or distribution of products or to promoting technical or economic progress
   — allows consumers a fair share of the resulting benefit

   and does not

   — impose restrictions which are not indispensable to the attainment of the above listed objectives
   — afford the possibility of eliminating competition in respect of a substantial part of the products in question.

Economic benefits

32. The first condition requires that the agreement contributes to improving the production or distribution of products or to promoting technical or economic progress. As these benefits relate to static or dynamic efficiencies, they can be referred to as "economic benefits". Economic benefits may outweigh restrictive effects on: competition. For instance, a cooperation may enable firms to offer goods or services at lower prices, better quality or to launch innovation more quickly. Most efficiencies stem from the combination and integration of different skills or resources. The parties must demonstrate that the efficiencies are likely to be caused by the cooperation and cannot be achieved by less restrictive means (see also below). Efficiency claims must be substantiated. Speculations or general statements on cost savings are not sufficient.

33. The Commission does not take into account cost savings that arise from output reduction, market sharing, or from the mere exercise of market power.

Commentary
para 33: B&C: 3.032, 7.058

Fair share for the consumers

34. Economic benefits have to favour not only the parties to the agreement, but also the consumers. Generally, the transmission of the benefits to the consumers will depend on the intensity of competition within the relevant market. Competitive pressures will normally ensure that cost-savings are passed on by way of lower prices or that companies have an incentive to bring new products to the market as quickly as possible. Therefore, if sufficient competition which effectively constrains the parties to the agreement is maintained on the market, the competitive process will normally ensure that the consumers receive a fair share of the economic benefits.

Commentary
para 34: F&N: .446

Part C Substantive Antitrust Matters

Indispensability

35. The restriction of competition must be necessary to achieve the economic benefits. If there are less restrictive means to achieve similar benefits, the claimed efficiencies cannot be used to justify the restrictions of competition. Whether or not individual restrictions are necessary depends on market circumstances and on the duration of the agreement. For instance, exclusivity agreements may prevent a participating party from free riding and may therefore be acceptable. Under certain circumstances they may, however, not be necessary and worsen a restrictive effect.

Commentary
para 35: B&C: 7.060

No elimination of competition

36. The last criterion of elimination of competition for a substantial part of the products in question is related to the question of dominance. Where an undertaking is dominant or becoming dominant as a consequence of a horizontal agreement, an agreement which produces anti-competitive effects in the meaning of Article 81 can in principle not be exempted.

Commentary
para 36: B&C: 3.062, 7.063 F&N: 9.291

Block Exemption Regulations for R & D and Specialisation

37. Under certain conditions the criteria of Article 81(3) can be assumed to be fulfilled for specified categories of agreements. This is in particular the case for R & D and production agreements where the combination of complementary skills or assets can be the source of substantial efficiencies. These guidelines should be seen as a complement to the R & D and Specialisation block exemption Regulations. Those block exemption Regulations exempt most common forms of agreements in the fields of production/specialisation up to a market share threshold of 20% and in the field of R & D up to a market share threshold of 25% provided that the agreements fulfil the conditions for application of the block exemption and do not contain "hard core" restrictions ("black clauses") that render the block exemption inapplicable. The block exemption Regulations do not provide severability for hardcore restrictions. If there are one or more hardcore restrictions, the benefit of the block exemption Regulation is lost for the entire agreement.

1.4. Structure of the following chapters on types of cooperation

38. The guidelines are divided into chapters relating to certain types of agreements. Each chapter is structured according to the analytical framework described above under point 1.3. Where necessary, specific guidance on the definition of relevant markets is given (e.g. in the field of R & D or with respect to purchasing markets).

2. AGREEMENTS ON RESEARCH AND DEVELOPMENT

2.1. Definition

39. R & D agreements may vary in form and scope. They range from outsourcing certain R & D activities to the joint improvement of existing technologies or to a cooperation concerning the research, development and marketing of completely new products. They may take the form of a cooperation agreement or of a jointly controlled company. This chapter applies to all forms of R & D agreements including related agreements concerning the production or commercialisation of the R & D results provided that the cooperation's centre of gravity lies in R & D, with the exception of mergers and joint ventures falling under the Merger Regulation.

40. Cooperation in R & D may reduce duplicative, unnecessary costs, lead to significant cross fertilisation of ideas and experience and thus result in products and technologies being developed more rapidly than would otherwise be the case. As a general rule, R & D cooperation tends to increase overall R & D activities.

Commentary
para 40: F&N: 7.108

41. Small and medium-sized enterprises (SMEs) form a dynamic and heterogeneous community which is confronted by many challenges, including the growing demands of larger companies for which they often work as sub-contractors. In R & D intensive sectors, fast growing SMEs, more often called "start-up companies", also aim at becoming a leader in fast-developing market segments. To meet those challenges and to remain competitive, SMEs need constantly to innovate. Through R & D cooperation there is a likelihood that overall R & D by SMEs will increase and that they will be able to compete more vigorously with stronger market players.

42. Under certain circumstances, however, R & D agreements may cause competition problems such as restrictive effects on prices, output, innovation, or variety or quality of products.

2.2. Relevant Markets

43. The key to defining the relevant market when assessing the effects of an R & D agreement is to identify those products, technologies or R & D efforts, that will act as a competitive constraint on the parties. At one end of the spectrum of possible situations, the innovation may result in a product (or technology) which competes in an existing product (or technology) market. This is the case with R & D directed towards slight improvements or variations, such as new models of certain products. Here, possible effects concern the market for existing products. At the other end, innovation may result in an entirely new product which creates its own new market (e.g. of the spectrum of a new vaccine for a previously incurable disease). In such a case, existing markets are only relevant if they are somehow related to the innovation in question. Consequently, and if possible, the effects of the cooperation on innovation have to be assessed. However, most of the cases probably concern situations in between these two extremes, i.e. situations in which innovation efforts may create products (or technology) which, over time, replace existing ones (e.g. CDs which have replaced records). A careful analysis of those situations may have to cover both existing markets and the impact of the agreement on innovation.

Existing markets

(a) Product markets

44. When the cooperation concerns R & D for the improvement of existing products, these existing products including its close substitutes form the relevant market concerned by the cooperation.[24]

Notes
[24] For market definition see the Commission Notice on the definition of the relevant market

45. If the R & D efforts aim at a significant change of an existing product or even at a new product replacing existing ones, substitution with the existing products may be imperfect or long-term. Consequently, the old and the potentially emerging new products are not likely to belong to the same relevant market. The market for existing products may nevertheless be concerned, if the pooling of R & D efforts is likely to result in the coordination of the parties' behaviour as suppliers of existing products. An exploitation of power in the existing market, however, is only possible if the parties together have a strong position with respect to both the existing product market and R & D efforts.

46. If the R & D concerns an important component of a final product, not only the market for this component may be relevant for the assessment, but the existing market for the final product as well. For instance, if car manufacturers cooperate in R & D related to a new type of engine, the car market may be affected by this R & D cooperation. The market for final products, however, is only relevant for the assessment, if the component at which the R & D is aimed, is technically or economically a key element of these final products and if the parties to the R & D agreement are important competitors with respect to the final products.

(b) Technology markets

47. R & D cooperation may not only concern products but also technology. When rights to intellectual property are marketed separately from the products concerned to which they relate, the relevant technology market has to be defined as well. Technology markets consist of the intellectual property that is licensed and its close substitutes, i.e. other technologies which customers could use as a substitute.

Commentary
para 47: B&C: 4.068

48. The methodology for defining technology markets follows the same principles as product market definition.[25] Starting from the technology which is marketed by the parties, one needs to identify those other technologies to which customers could switch in response to a small but permanent increase in relative prices. Once these technologies are identified, one can calculate market shares by dividing the licensing income generated by the parties with the total licensing income of all sellers of substitutable technologies.

Notes
[25] See Commission Notice on the definition of the relevant market; see also, for example, Commission Decision 94/811/EC of 8 June 1994 in Case No IV/M269 —*Shell/Montecatini* (OJ L 332, 22.12.1994, p. 48).

Commentary
para 48: B&C: 4.068

49. The parties' position in the market for existing technology is a relevant assessment criterion where the R & D cooperation concerns the significant improvement of existing technology or a new technology that is likely to replace the existing technology. The parties' market share can however only be taken as a starting point for this analysis. In technology markets, particular emphasis must be put on potential competition. If companies, who do not currently license their technology, are potential entrants on the technology market they could constrain the ability of the parties to raise the price for their technology (see Example 3 below).

Competition in innovation (R & D efforts)

50. R & D cooperation may not — or not only — affect competition in existing markets, but competition in innovation. This is the case where cooperation concerns the development of new products/technology which either may — if emerging — one day replace existing ones or which are being developed for a new intended use and will therefore not replace existing products but create a completely new demand. The effects on competition in innovation are important in these situations, but can in some cases not be sufficiently assessed by analysing actual or potential competition in existing product/technology markets. In this respect, two scenarios can be distinguished, depending on the nature of the innovative process in a given industry.

51. In the first scenario, which is for instance present in the pharmaceutical industry, the process of innovation is structured in such a way that it is possible at an early stage to identify R & D poles. R & D poles are R & D efforts directed towards a certain new product or technology, and the substitutes for that R & D, i.e. R & D aimed at developing substitutable products or technology for those developed by the cooperation and having comparable access to resources as well as a similar timing. In this case, it can be analysed if after the agreement there will be a sufficient number of R & D poles left. The starting point of the analysis is the R & D of the parties. Then credible competing R & D poles have to be identified. In order to assess the credibility of competing poles, the following aspects have to be taken into account: the nature, scope and size of possible other R & D efforts, their access to financial and human resources, know-how/patents, or other specialised assets as well as their timing and their capability to exploit possible results. An R & D pole is not a credible competitor if it can not be regarded as a close substitute for the parties' R & D effort from the viewpoint of, for instance, access to resources or timing.

52. In the second scenario, the innovative efforts in an industry are not clearly structured so as to allow the identification of R & D poles. In this situation, the Commission would, absent exceptional circumstances, not try to assess the impact of a given R & D cooperation on innovation,

but would limit its assessment to product and/or technology markets which are related to the R & D cooperation in question.

Calculation of market shares

53. The calculation of market shares, both for the purposes of the R & D block exemption Regulation and of these guidelines, has to reflect the distinction between existing markets and competition in innovation. At the beginning of a cooperation the reference point is the market for products capable of being improved or replaced by the products under development. If the R & D agreement only aims at improving or refining existing products, this market includes the products directly concerned by the R & D. Market shares can thus be calculated on the basis of the sales value of the existing products. If the R & D aims at replacing an existing product, the new product will, if [successful], become a substitute to the existing products. To assess the competitive position of the parties, it is again possible to calculate market shares on the basis of the sales value of the existing products. Consequently, the R & D block exemption Regulation bases its exemption of these situations on the market share in "the relevant market for the products capable of being improved or replaced by the contract products". For an automatic exemption, this market share may not exceed 25%.[26]

Notes

[26] Article 4(2) of the R & D Block Exemption Regulation.

54. If the R & D aims at developing a product which will create a complete new demand, market shares based on sales cannot be calculated. Only an analysis of the effects of the agreement on competition in innovation is possible. Consequently, the R & D block exemption Regulation exempts these agreements irrespective of market share for a period of seven years after the product is first put on the market.[27] However, the benefit of the block exemption may be withdrawn if the agreement would eliminate effective competition in innovation.[28] After the seven year period, market shares based on sales value can be calculated, and the market share threshold of 25% applies.[29]

Notes

[27] Article 4(1) of the R & D Block Exemption Regulation.
[28] Article 7(e) of the R & D Block Exemption Regulation.
[29] Article 4(3) of the R & D Block Exemption Regulation.

Commentary
para 54: B&C: 7.084

2.3. Assessment under Article 81(1)

2.3.1. Nature of the agreement

2.3.1.1. Agreements that do not fall under Article 81(1)

55. Most R & D agreements do not fall under Article 81(1). First, this can be said for agreements relating to cooperation in R & D at a rather theoretical stage, far removed from the exploitation of possible results.

Commentary
para 55: B&C: 7.070 F&N: 7.162

56. Moreover, R & D cooperation between non-competitors does generally not restrict competition.[30] The competitive relationship between the parties has to be analysed in the context of affected existing markets and/or innovation. If the parties are not able to carry out the necessary R & D independently, there is no competition to be restricted. This can apply, for example, to firms bringing together complementary skills, technologies and other resources. The issue of potential competition has to be assessed on a realistic basis. For instance, parties cannot be defined as potential competitors simply because the cooperation enables them to carry out the R & D activities. The decisive question is whether each party independently has the necessary means as to assets, know-how and other resources.

Commentary
para 56: F&N: 7.126, 7.168

57. R & D cooperation by means of outsourcing of previously captive R & D is often carried out by specialised companies, research institutes or academic bodies which are not active in the exploitation of the results. Typically such agreements are combined with a transfer of know-how and/or an exclusive supply clause concerning possible results. Due to the complementary nature of the cooperating parties in these scenarios, Article 81(1) does not apply.

58. R & D cooperation which does not include the joint exploitation of possible results by means of licensing, production and/or marketing rarely falls under Article 81(1). Those "pure" R & D agreements can only cause a competition problem, if effective competition with respect to innovation is significantly reduced.

Commentary
para 58: F&N: 7.115

2.3.1.2. Agreements that almost always fall under Article 81(1)

59. If the true object of an agreement is not R & D but the creation of a disguised cartel, i.e. otherwise prohibited price fixing, output limitation or market allocation, it falls under Article 81(1). However, an R & D agreement which includes the joint exploitation of possible future results is not necessarily restrictive of competition.

Commentary
para 59: F&N: 7.116

2.3.1.3. Agreements that may fall under Article 81(1)

60. R & D agreements that cannot be assessed from the outset as clearly non-restrictive may fall under Article 81(1)[31] and have to be analysed in their economic context. This applies to R & D cooperation which is set up at a stage rather close to the market launch and which is agreed between companies that are competitors on either existing product/technology markets or on innovation markets.

2.3.2. Market power and market structures

61. R & D cooperation can cause negative market effects in three respects: First, it may restrict innovation, secondly it may cause the coordination of the parties' behaviour in existing markets and thirdly, foreclosure problems may occur at the level of the exploitation of possible results. These types of negative market effects, however, are only likely to emerge when the parties to the cooperation have significant power on the existing markets and/or competition with respect to innovation is significantly reduced. Without market power there is no incentive to coordinate behaviour on existing markets or to reduce or slow down innovation. A foreclosure problem may only arise in the context of cooperation involving at least one player with significant market power for a key technology and the exclusive exploitation of results.

62. There is no absolute market share threshold which indicates that an R & D agreement creates some degree of market power and thus falls under Article 81(1). However, R & D agreements are exempted provided that they are concluded between parties with a combined market share not exceeding 25% and that the other conditions for the application of the R & D Block Exemption Regulation are fulfilled. Therefore, for most R & D agreements, restrictive effects only have to be analysed if the parties' combined market share exceeds 25%.

63. Agreements falling outside the R & D Block Exemption Regulation due to a stronger market position of the parties do not necessarily restrict competition. However, the stronger the combined position of the parties on existing markets and/or the more competition in innovation is restricted, the more likely is the application of Article 81(1) and the assessment requires a more detailed analysis.

64. If the R & D is directed at the improvement or refinement of existing products/technology possible effects concern the relevant market(s) for these existing products/technology. Effects on prices, output and/or innovation in existing markets are, however, only likely if the parties together have a strong position, entry is difficult and few other innovation activities are identifiable. Furthermore, if the R & D only concerns a relatively minor input of a final product, effects as to competition in these final products are, if invariably, very limited. In general, a distinction has to be made between pure R & D agreements and more comprehensive cooperation involving different stages of the exploitation of results (i.e. licensing, production, marketing). As said above, pure R & D agreements rarely come under Article 81(1). This is in particular true for R & D directed towards a limited improvement of existing products/technology. If, in such a scenario, the R & D cooperation includes joint exploitation only by means of licensing, restrictive effects such as foreclosure problems are unlikely. If, however, joint production and/or marketing of the slightly improved products/technology are included, the cooperation has to be examined more closely. First, negative effects as to prices and output in existing markets are more likely if strong competitors are involved in such a situation. Secondly, the cooperation may come closer to a production agreement because the R & D activities may de facto not form the centre of gravity of such a collaboration.

65. If the R & D is directed at an entirely new product (or technology) which creates its own new market, price and output effects on existing markets are rather unlikely. The analysis has to focus on possible restrictions of innovation concerning, for instance, the quality and variety of possible future products/technology or the speed of innovation. Those restrictive effects can arise where two or more of the few firms engaged in the development of such a new product, start to cooperate at a stage where they are each independently rather near to the launch of the product. In such a case, innovation may be restricted even by a pure R & D agreement. In general, however, R & D cooperation concerning entirely new products is pro-competitive. This principle does not change significantly if the joint exploitation of the results, even joint marketing, is involved. Indeed, the issue of joint exploitation in these situations is only relevant where foreclosure from key technologies plays a role. Those problems would, however, not arise where the parties grant licences to third parties.

66. Most R & D agreements will lie somewhere in between the two situations described above. They may therefore have effects on innovation as well as repercussions on existing markets. Consequently, both the existing market and the effect on innovation may be of relevance for the assessment with respect to the parties' combined positions, concentration ratios, number of players/innovators and entry conditions. In some cases there can be restrictive price/output effects on existing markets and a negative impact on innovation by means of slowing down the speed of development. For instance, if significant competitors on an existing technology market cooperate to develop a new technology which may one day replace existing products, this cooperation is likely to have restrictive effects if the parties have significant market power on the existing market (which would give an incentive to exploit it), and if they also have a strong position with respect to R & D. A similar effect can occur, if the major player in an existing market cooperates with a much smaller or even potential competitor who is just about to emerge with a new product/technology which may endanger the incumbent's position.

67. Agreements may also fall outside the block exemption irrespective of the market power of the parties. This applies for instance to agreements which restrict access of a party to the results of the work because they do not, as a general rule, promote technical and economic progress by increasing the dissemination of technical knowledge between the parties.[32] The Block exemption provides for a specific exception to this general rule in the case of academic bodies, research institutes or specialised companies which provide R & D as a service and which are not active in the industrial exploitation of the results of research and development.[33] Nevertheless, it should be noted that agreements containing exclusive access rights may, where they fall under

Article 81(1), meet the criteria for exemption under Article 81(3), particularly where exclusive access rights are economically indispensable in view of the market, risks and scale of the investment required to exploit the results of the research and development.

Notes
[32] See [Article] 3(2) of the R & D Block Exemption Regulation.
[33] See [Article] 3(2) of the R & D Block Exemption Regulation.

Commentary
para 67: **B&C:** 7.073

2.4. Assessment under Article 81(3)

2.4.1. Economic benefits

68. Most R & D agreements — with or without joint exploitation of possible results — bring about economic benefits by means of cost savings and cross fertilisation of ideas and experience, thus resulting in improved or new products and technologies being developed more rapidly than would otherwise be the case. Under these conditions it appears reasonable to provide for the exemption of such agreements which result in a restriction of competition up to a market share threshold below which it can, for the application of Article 81(3), in general, be presumed that the positive effects of research and development agreements will outweigh any negative effects on competition. Therefore, the R & D Block Exemption Regulation exempts those R & D agreements which [fulfil] certain conditions (see Article 3) and which do not include hard core restrictions (see Article 5), provided that the combined market share of the parties in the affected existing market(s) does not exceed 25%.

Commentary
para 68: **F&N:** 7.184

69. If considerable market power is created or increased by the cooperation, the parties have to demonstrate significant benefits in carrying out R & D, a quicker launch of new products/technology or other efficiencies.

2.4.2. Indispensability

70. An R & D agreement can not be exempted if it imposes restrictions that are not indispensable to the attainment of the above-mentioned benefits. The individual clauses listed in Article 5 of the R & D Block Exemption Regulation will in most cases render an exemption impossible following an individual assessment too, and can therefore be regarded as a good indication of restrictions that are not indispensable to the cooperation.

2.4.3. No elimination of competition

71. No exemption will be possible, if the parties are afforded the possibility of eliminating competition in respect of a substantial part of the products (or technologies) in question. Where as a consequence of a R & D agreement an undertaking is dominant or becoming dominant either on an existing markets or with respect to innovation, such an agreement which produces anticompetitive effects in the meaning of Article 81 can in principle not be exempted. For innovation this is the case, for example, if the agreement combines the only two existing poles of research.

Commentary
para 71: **F&N:** 9.291

Time of the assessment and duration of the exemption

72. R & D agreements extending to the joint production and marketing of new products/technology require particular attention as to the time of the assessment.
73. At the beginning of an R & D cooperation, its success and factors such as the parties' future market position as well as the development of future product or technology markets are often not known. Consequently, the assessment at the point in time when the cooperation is formed is

limited to the (then) existing product or technology markets and/or innovation markets as described in this chapter. If, on the basis of this analysis, competition is not likely to be eliminated, the R & D agreement can benefit from an exemption. This will normally cover the duration of the R & D phase plus, in as far as the joint production and marketing of the possible results is concerned, an additional phase for a possible launch and market introduction. The reason for this additional exemption phase is that the first companies to reach the market with a new product/technology will often enjoy very high initial market shares and successful R & D is also often rewarded by intellectual property protection. A strong market position due to this "first mover advantage" cannot normally be interpreted as elimination of competition. Therefore, the block exemption covers R & D agreements for an additional period of seven years (i.e. beyond the R & D phase) irrespective of whether or not the parties obtain with their new products/technology a high share within this period. This also applies to the individual assessment of cases falling outside the block exemption provided that the criteria of Article 81(3) as to the other aspects of the agreement are fulfilled. This does not exclude the possibility that a period of more than 7 years also meets the criteria of Article 81(3) if it can be shown to be the minimum period of time necessary to guarantee an adequate return on the investment involved.

Commentary
para 73: B&C: 7.074

74. If a new assessment of an R & D cooperation is made after that period — for instance, following a complaint — the analysis has to be based on the (then) existing market situation. The block exemption still continues to apply if the parties' share on the (then) relevant market does not exceed 25%. Similarly, Article 81(3) continues to apply to R & D agreements falling outside the block exemption provided that the criteria for an exemption are fulfilled.

Commentary
para 74: B&C: 7.066, 7.074

2.5. Examples

75. Example 1

Situation: There are two major companies on the European market for the manufacture of existing electronic components: A (30%) and B (30%). They have each made significant investment in the R & D necessary to develop miniaturised electronic components and have developed early prototypes. They now agree to pool these R & D efforts by setting up a JV to complete the R & D and produce the components, which will be sold back to the parents, who will commercialise them separately. The remainder of the market consists of small firms without sufficient resources to undertake the necessary investments.

Analysis: Miniaturised electronic components, while likely to compete with the existing components in some areas, are essentially a new technology and an analysis must be made of the poles of research destined towards this future market. If the JV goes ahead then only one route to the necessary manufacturing technology will exist, whereas it would appear likely that A and B could reach the market individually with separate products. While the agreement could have advantages in bringing a new technology forward quicker, it also reduces variety and creates a commonality of costs between the parties. Furthermore, the possibility for the parties to exploit their strong position on the existing market must be taken into account. Since they would face no competition at the R & D level, their incentives to pursue the new technology at a high pace could be severely reduced. Although some of these concerns could be remedied by requiring the parties to license key know-how for manufacturing miniature components to third parties on reasonable terms, it may not be possible to remedy all concerns and fulfil the conditions for an exemption.

76. Example 2

Situation: A small research company A which does not have its own marketing organisation has discovered and patented a pharmaceutical substance based on new technology that will revolutionise the treatment of a certain disease. Company A enters into an R & D agreement with a large pharmaceutical producer B of products that have so far been used for treating the disease. Company B lacks any similar R & D programme. For the existing products company B has a market share of around 75% in all Member States, but patents are expiring over the next five-year period. There exist two other poles of research at approximately the same stage of development using the same basic new technology. Company B will provide considerable funding and know-how for product development, as well as future access to the market. Company B is granted a license for the exclusive production and distribution of the resulting product for the duration of the patent. It is expected that the parties could jointly bring the product to market in five to seven years.

Analysis: The product is likely to belong to a new relevant market. The parties bring complementary resources and skills to the cooperation, and the probability of the product coming to market increases substantially. Although Company B is likely to have considerable market power on the existing market, this power will be decreasing shortly and the existence of other poles of research are likely to eliminate any incentive to reduce R & D efforts. The exploitation rights during the remaining patent period are likely to be necessary for Company B to make the considerable investments needed and Company A has no own marketing resources. The agreement is therefore unlikely to restrict competition.

77. Example 3

Situation: Two engineering companies that produce vehicle components, agree to set up a JV to combine their R & D efforts to improve the production and performance of an existing component. They also pool their existing technology licensing businesses in this area, but will continue to manufacture separately. The two companies have market shares in Europe of 15% and 20% on the OEM product market. There are two other major competitors together with several in-house research programmes by large vehicle manufacturers. On the world-wide market for the licensing of technology for these products they have shares of 20% and 25%, measured in terms of revenue generated, and there are two other major technologies. The product life cycle for the component is typically two to three years. In each of the last five years one of the major firms has introduced a new version or upgrade.

Analysis: Since neither company's R & D effort is aimed at a completely new product, the markets to consider are for the existing components and for the licensing of relevant technology. Although their existing R & D programmes broadly overlap, the reduced duplication through the cooperation could allow them to spend more on R & D than individually. Several other technologies exist and the parties' combined market share on the OEM market does not bring them into a dominant position. Although their market share on the technology market, at 45%, is very high, there are competing technologies. In addition, the vehicle manufacturers, who do not currently licence their technology, are also potential entrants on this market thus constraining the ability of the parties to raise price. As described, the JV is likely to benefit from an exemption.

3. PRODUCTION AGREEMENTS (INCLUDING SPECIALISATION AGREEMENTS)

3.1. Definition

78. Production agreements may vary in form and scope. They may take the form of joint production through a joint venture,[34] i.e. a jointly controlled company that runs one or several production facilities, or can be carried out by means of specialisation or subcontracting agreements whereby one party agrees to carry out the production of a certain product.

Notes

34 As indicated above, joint ventures which fall under the Merger Regulation are not the subject of these guidelines. Full-function joint ventures below Community dimension are normally dealt with by the competition authorities of the Member States. The application of Regulation No 17 could be relevant only where such a full-function joint venture would lead to a restriction of competition resulting from the coordination of the parent companies outside the joint venture ("spill-over effect"). In this respect, the Commission has declared that it will leave the assessment of such operations to the Member States as far as possible (see Statement for the Council Minutes on Regulation (EC) No 1310/97, pt. 4).

79. Generally, one can distinguish three categories of production agreements: Joint production agreements, whereby the parties agree to produce certain products jointly, (unilateral or reciprocal) specialisation agreements, whereby the parties agree unilaterally or reciprocally to cease production of a product and to purchase it from the other party, and subcontracting agreements whereby one party (the "contractor") entrusts to another party (the "subcontractor") the production of a product.

80. Subcontracting agreements are vertical agreements. They are therefore, to the extent that they contain restrictions of competition, covered by the Block Exemption Regulation and the Guidelines on Vertical Restraints. There are however two exceptions to this rule: Subcontracting agreements between competitors,[35] and subcontracting agreements between non-competitors involving the transfer of know-how to the subcontractor.[36]

Notes

35 Article 2(4) of the Block Exemption Regulation on Vertical Restraints.
36 Article 2(3) of the Block Exemption Regulation on Vertical Restraints. See also Guidelines on Vertical Restraints, paragraph 33, which notes that subcontracting arrangements between non-competitors under which the buyer provides only specifications to the supplier which describe the goods or services to be supplied are covered by the Block Exemption Regulation on Vertical Restraints.

Commentary
para 80: B&C: 6.190

81. Subcontracting agreements between competitors are covered by these guidelines.[37] Guidance for the assessment of subcontracting agreements between non-competitors involving the transfer of know-how to the subcontractor is given in a separate Notice.[38]

Notes

37 If a subcontracting agreement between competitors stipulates that the contractor will cease production of the product to which the agreement relates, the agreement constitutes a unilateral specialisation agreement which is covered, subject to certain conditions, by the Specialisation Block Exemption Regulation.
38 Notice concerning the assessment of certain subcontracting agreements in relation to Article [81](1) of the EEC Treaty, OJ C 1, 3.1.1979, p. 2.

Commentary
para 81: B&C: 2.113, 6.190

3.2. Relevant Markets

82. In order to assess the competitive relationship between the cooperating parties, the relevant product and geographic market(s) directly concerned by the cooperation (i.e. the market(s) to which products subject to the agreement belong) must first be defined. Secondly, a production agreement in one market may also affect the competitive behaviour of the parties in a market which is downstream or upstream or a neighbouring market closely related to the market directly concerned by the cooperation[39] (so-called "spill-over markets"). However, spill-over effects only occur if the cooperation in one market necessarily results in the coordination of competitive behaviour in another market, i.e. if the markets are linked by interdependencies, and if the parties are in a strong position on the spill-over market.

Notes

39 As also referred to in Article 2(4) of the Merger Regulation.

Commentary
para 82: B&C: 7.044

3.3. Assessment under Article 81(1)

3.3.1. Nature of the agreement

83. The main source of competition problems that may arise from production agreements is the coordination of the parties' competitive behaviour as suppliers. This type of competition problem arises where the cooperating parties are actual or potential competitors on at least one of these relevant market(s), i.e. on the markets directly concerned by the cooperation and/or on possible spill-over markets.

84. The fact that the parties are competitors does not automatically cause the coordination of their behaviour. In addition, the parties normally need to cooperate with regard to a significant part of their activities in order to achieve a substantial degree of commonality of costs. The higher the degree of commonality of costs, the greater the potential for a limitation of price competition, especially in the case of homogenous products.

85. In addition to coordination concerns, production agreements may also create foreclosure problems and other negative effects towards third parties. They are not caused by a competitive relationship between the parties, but by a strong market position of at least one of the parties (e.g. on an upstream market for a key component, which enables the parties to raise the costs of their rivals in a downstream market) in the context of a more vertical or complementary relationship between the cooperating parties. Therefore, the [possibility] of foreclosure mainly needs to be examined in the case of joint production of an important component and of subcontracting agreements (see below).

3.3.1.1. Agreements that do not fall under Article 81(1)

86. Unless foreclosure problems arise, production agreements between non-competitors are not normally caught by Article 81(1). This is also true for agreements whereby inputs or components which have so far been manufactured for own consumption (captive production) are purchased from a third party by way of subcontracting or unilateral specialisation, unless there are indications that the company which so far has only produced for own consumption could have entered the merchant market for sales to third parties without incurring significant additional costs or risks in response to small, permanent changes in relative market prices.

87. Even production agreements between competitors do not necessarily come under Article 81(1). First, cooperation between firms which compete on markets closely related to the market directly concerned by the cooperation, cannot be defined as restricting competition, if the cooperation is the only commercially justifiable possible way to enter a new market, to launch a new product or service or to carry out a specific project.

Commentary
para 87: B&C: 7.090 F&N: 12.344

88. Secondly, an effect on the parties' competitive behaviour as market suppliers is highly unlikely if the parties have a small proportion of their total costs in common. For instance, a low degree of commonality in total costs can be assumed where two or more companies agree on specialisation/joint production of an intermediate product which only accounts for a small proportion of the production costs of the final product and, consequently, the total costs. The same applies to a subcontracting agreement between competitors where the input which one competitor purchases from another only accounts for a small proportion of the production costs of the final product. A low degree of commonality of total costs can also be assumed where the parties jointly manufacture a final product, but only a small proportion as compared to their total output of the final product. Even if a significant proportion is jointly manufactured, the degree of commonality of total costs may nevertheless be low or moderate, if the cooperation concerns heterogeneous products which require costly marketing.

Commentary
para 88: B&C: 7.036, 7.044, 7.094

89. Thirdly, subcontracting agreements between competitors do not fall under Article 81(1) if they are limited to individual sales and purchases on the merchant market without any further obligations and without forming part of a wider commercial relationship between the parties.[40]

Notes

[40] As any subcontracting agreement such an agreement can however fall under Article 81(1) if it contains vertical restraints, such as restrictions on passive sales, resale price maintenance, etc.

3.3.1.2. Agreements that almost always fall under Article 81(1)

90. Agreements which fix the prices for market supplies of the parties, limit output or share markets or customer groups have the object of restricting competition and almost always fall under Article 81(1). This does, however, not apply to cases
    — where the parties agree on the output directly concerned by the production agreement (e.g. the capacity and production volume of a joint venture or the agreed amount of outsourced products), or
    — where a production joint venture that also carries out the distribution of the manufactured products sets the sales prices for these products, provided that the price fixing by the joint venture is the effect of integrating the various functions.[41]
    In both scenarios the agreement on output or prices will not be assessed separately, but in light of the overall effects of the joint venture on the market in order to determine the applicability of Article 81(1).

Notes

[41] A production joint venture which also carries out joint distribution is, however, in most of the cases a full-function joint venture.

3.3.1.3. Agreements that may fall under Article 81(1)

91. Production agreements that cannot be characterised as clearly restrictive or non-restrictive on the basis of the above factors may fall under Article 81(1)[42] and have to be analysed in their economic context. This applies to cooperation agreements between competitors which create a significant degree of commonality of costs, but do not involve hard core restrictions as described above.

Notes

[42] Pursuant to Article 4(2)(3) of Council Regulation No 17, agreements which have as their sole object specialisation in the manufacture of products need, under certain conditions, not to be notified to the Commission. They may, however, be notified.

3.3.2. *Market power and market structures*

92. The starting point for the analysis is the position of the parties in the market(s) concerned. This is due to the fact that without market power the parties to a production agreement do not have an incentive to coordinate their competitive behaviour as suppliers. Secondly, there is no effect on competition in the market without market power of the parties, even if the parties would coordinate their behaviour.

93. There is no absolute market share threshold which indicates that a production agreement creates some degree of market power and thus falls under Article 81(1). However, agreements concerning unilateral or reciprocal specialisation as well as joint production are block exempted provided that they are concluded between parties with a combined market share not exceeding 20% in the relevant market(s) and that the other conditions for the application of the Specialisation block exemption Regulation are fulfilled. Therefore, for agreements covered by the block exemption, restrictive effects only have to be analysed if the parties combined market share exceeds 20%.

94. Agreements which are not covered by the block exemption Regulation require a more detailed analysis. The starting point is the market position of the parties. This will normally be followed by the concentration ratio and the number of players as well as by other factors as described in Chapter 1.

95. Usually the analysis will only involve the relevant market(s) with which the cooperation is directly concerned. Under certain circumstances, e.g. if the parties have a very strong combined position

on up- or downstream markets or on markets otherwise closely related to the markets with which the cooperation is directly concerned, these spill-over markets may however have to be analysed as well. This applies in particular to cooperation in upstream markets by firms which also enjoy a strong combined market position further downstream. Similarly, problems of foreclosure may need to be examined if the parties individually have a strong position as either suppliers or buyers of an input.

Market position of the parties, concentration ratio, number of players and other structural factors

96. If the parties' combined market share is larger than 20%, the likely impact of the production agreement on the market must be assessed. In this respect market concentration as well as market shares will be a significant factor. The higher the combined market share of the parties, the higher the concentration in the market concerned. However, a moderately higher market share than allowed for in the block exemption does not necessarily imply a high concentration ratio. Far instance, a combined market share of the parties of slightly more than 20% may occur in a market with a moderate concentration (HHI below 1800). In such a scenario a restrictive effect is unlikely. In a more concentrated market, however, a market share of more than 20% may, alongside other elements, lead to a restriction of competition (see also example 1 below). The picture may nevertheless change, if the market is very dynamic with new participants entering the market and market positions changing frequently.

Commentary
para 96: F&N: 7.228

97. For joint production, network effects, i.e. links between a significant number of competitors, can also play an important role. In a concentrated market the creation of an additional link may tip the balance and make collusion in this market likely, even if the parties have a significant, but still moderate, combined market share (see example 2 below).

Commentary
para 97: F&N: 12.306

98. Under specific circumstances a cooperation between potential competitors may also raise competition concerns. This is, however, limited to cases where a strong player in one market cooperates with a realistic potential entrant, for instance, with a strong supplier of the same product or service in a neighbouring geographic market. The reduction of potential competition creates particular problems if actual competition is already weak and threat of entry is a major source of competition.

Commentary
para 98: F&N: 12.307

Cooperation in upstream markets

99. Joint production of an important component or other input to the parties' final product can cause negative market effects under certain circumstances:
   — Foreclosure problems (see example 3 below) provided that the parties have a strong position on the relevant input market (non-captive use) and that switching between captive and non-captive use would not occur in the presence of a small but permanent relative price increase for the product in question.
   — Spill-over effects (see example 4 below) provided that the input is an important component of costs and that the parties have a strong position in the downstream market for the final product.

Subcontracting agreements between competitors

100. Similar problems can arise if a competitor subcontracts an important component or other input to its final product from a competitor. This can also lead to:
    — Foreclosure problems provided that the parties have a strong position as either suppliers or buyers on the relevant input market (non-captive use). Subcontracting could then either lead to other competitors not being able to obtain this input at a competitive price or to other suppliers not being able to supply the input competitively if they will be losing a large part of their demand.
    — Spill-over effects provided that the input is an important component of costs and that the parties have a strong position in the downstream market for the final product.

Commentary
para 100: **B&C:** 6.193

Specialisation agreements

101. Reciprocal specialisation agreements with market shares beyond the threshold of the block exemption will almost always fall under Article 81(1) and have to be examined carefully because of the risk of market partitioning (see example 5 below).

Commentary
para 101: **B&C:** 5.058

3.4. Assessment under Article 81(3)

3.4.1. Economic benefits

102. Most common types of production agreements can be assumed to cause some economic benefits in the form of economies of scale or scope or better production technologies unless they are an instrument for price fixing, output restriction or market and customer allocation. Under these conditions it appears reasonable to provide for the exemption of such agreements which result in a restriction of competition up to a market share threshold below which it can, for the application of Article 81(3), in general, be presumed that the positive effects of production agreements will outweigh any negative effects on competition. Therefore, agreements concerning unilateral or reciprocal specialisation as well as joint production are block exempted (Specialisation block exemption Regulation) provided that they do not contain hard core restrictions (see Article 5) and that they are concluded between parties with a combined market share not exceeding 20% in the relevant market(s).

103. For those agreements not covered by the block exemption the parties have to demonstrate improvements of production or other efficiencies. Efficiencies that only benefit the parties or cost savings that are caused by output reduction or market allocation cannot be taken into account.

3.4.2. Indispensability

104. Restrictions that go beyond what is necessary to achieve the economic benefits described above will not be accepted. For instance, parties should not be restricted in their competitive behaviour on output outside the cooperation.

3.4.3. No elimination of competition

105. No exemption will be possible, if the parties are afforded the possibility of eliminating competition in respect of a substantial part of the products in question. Where as a consequence of a production agreement an undertaking is dominant or becoming dominant, such an agreement which produces anti-competitive effects in the meaning of Article 81 can in principle not be exempted. This has to be analysed on the relevant market to which the products subject to the cooperation belong and on possible spill-over markets.

Commentary
para 105: **F&N:** 9.291

3.5. Examples

Joint production

106. The following two examples concern hypothetical cases causing competition problems on the relevant market to which the jointly manufactured products belong.

---

107. **Example 1**

Situation: Two suppliers, A and B, of the basic chemical product X decide to build a new production plant controlled by a joint venture. This plant will produce roughly 50% of their total output. X is a homogeneous product and is not substitutable with other products, i.e. forms a relevant market on its own. The market is rather stagnant. The parties will not significantly increase total output, but close down two old factories and shift capacity to the new plant. A and B each have a market share of 20%. There are three other significant suppliers each with 10–15% market share and several smaller players.

Analysis: It is likely that this joint venture would have an effect on the competitive behaviour of the parties because coordination would give them considerable market power, if not even a dominant position. Severe restrictive effects in the market are probable. High efficiency gains which may outweigh these effects are unlikely in such a scenario where a significant increase in output cannot be expected.

---

108. **Example 2**

Situation: Two suppliers, A and B, form a production joint venture on the same relevant market as in example 1. The joint venture also produces 50% of the parties' total output. A and B each have 15% market share. There are 3 other players: C with a market share of 30%, D with 25% and E with 15%. B already has a joint production plant with E.

Analysis: Here the market is characterised by very few players and rather symmetric structures. The joint venture creates an additional link between the players. Coordination between A and B would de facto further increase concentration and also link E to A and B. This cooperation is likely to cause a severe restrictive effect, and — as in example 1 — high efficiency gains cannot be expected.

---

109. Example 3 also concerns the relevant market to which the jointly manufactured products belong, but demonstrates the importance of criteria other than market share (here: switching between captive and non-captive production).

---

110. **Example 3**

Situation: A and B set up a production joint venture for an intermediate product X through restructuring current plants. The joint venture sells X exclusively to A and B. It produces 40% of A's total output of X and 50% of B's total output. A and B are captive users of X and are also suppliers of the non-captive market. A's share of total industry output of X is 10%, B's share amounts to 20% and the share of the joint venture to 14%. On the non-captive market, however, A and B have respectively 25% and 35% market share.

Analysis: Despite the parties' strong position on the non-captive market the cooperation may not eliminate effective competition in the market for X, if switching costs between captive and non-captive use are small. However, only very rapid switching would counteract the high market share of 60%. Otherwise this production venture raises serious competition concerns which cannot be outweighed even by significant economic benefits.

---

111. Example 4 concerns cooperation regarding an important intermediate product with spill-over effects on a downstream market.

112. Example 4

Situation: A and B set up a production joint venture for an intermediate product X. They will close their own factories, which have been manufacturing X, and will cover their needs of X exclusively from the joint venture. The intermediate product accounts for 50% of the total costs of the final product Y. A and B each have a share of 20% in the market for Y. There are two other significant suppliers of Y each with 15% market share and several smaller competitors.

Analysis: Here the commonality of costs is high; furthermore, the parties would gain market power through coordination of their behaviour on the market Y. The case raises competition problems and the assessment is almost identical to example 1 although here the cooperation is taking place in an upstream market.

Reciprocal specialisation

113. Example 5

Situation: A and B each manufacture and supply the homogeneous products X and Y, which belong to different markets. A's market share of X is 28% and of Y it is 10%. B's share of X is 10% and of Y it is 30%. Because of scale economies they conclude a reciprocal specialisation agreement according to which A will in future only produce X and B will produce only Y. Both agree on cross-supplies so that they will both remain in the markets as suppliers. Due to the homogeneous nature of the products, distribution costs are minor. There are two other manufacturing suppliers of X and Y with market shares of roughly 15% each, the remaining suppliers have 5–10% shares.

Analysis: The degree of commonality of costs is extremely high, only the relatively minor distribution costs remain separate. Consequently, there is very little room for competition left. The parties would gain market power through coordination of their behaviour on the markets for X and Y. Furthermore, it is likely that the market supplies of Y from A and X from B will diminish over time. The case raises competition problems which the economies of scale are unlikely to outweigh.

The scenario may change if X and Y were heterogeneous products with a very high proportion of marketing and distribution costs (e.g. 65–70% of total costs). Furthermore, if the offer of a complete range of the differentiated products was a condition for competing successfully, the withdrawal of one or more parties as suppliers of X and/or Y would be unlikely. In such a scenario the criteria for exemption may be fulfilled (provided that the economies are significant), despite the high market shares.

Subcontracting between competitors

114. Example 6

Situation: A and B are competitors in the market for the final product X. A has a market share of 15%, B of 20%. Both also produce the intermediate product Y, which is an input into the production of X, but is also used to produce other products. It accounts for 10% of the cost of X. A only produces Y for internal consumption, while B is also selling Y to third party customers. Its market share for Y is 10%. A and B agree on a subcontracting agreement, whereby A will purchase 60% of its requirements of Y from B. It will continue to produce 40% of its requirements internally to not lose the know-how related to the production of Y.

Analysis: As A has only produced Y for internal consumption, it first needs to be analysed if A is a realistic potential entrant into the merchant market for sales of Y to third parties. If this is not the case, then the agreement does not restrict competition with respect to Y. Spill-over effects into the market for X are also unlikely in view of the low degree of commonality of costs created by the agreement.

371

> If A were to be regarded a realistic potential entrant into the merchant market for sales of Y to third parties, the market position of B in the market for Y would need to be taken into account. As B's market share is rather low, the result of the analysis would not change.

Commentary
para 114: B&C: 6.193

4. Purchasing Agreements

4.1. Definition

115. This chapter focuses on agreements concerning the joint buying of products. Joint buying can be carried out by a jointly controlled company, by a company in which many firms hold a small stake, by a contractual arrangement or even looser form of cooperation.
116. Purchasing agreements are often concluded by small and medium-sized enterprises to achieve volumes and discounts similar to their bigger competitors. These agreements between small and medium-sized enterprises are therefore normally pro-competitive. Even if a moderate degree of market power is created, this may be outweighed by economies of scale provided the parties actually bundle volume.

Commentary
para 116: B&C: 5.128

117. Joint purchasing may involve both horizontal and vertical agreements. In these cases a two-step analysis is necessary. First, the horizontal agreements have to be assessed according to the principles described in the present guidelines. If this assessment leads to the conclusion that a cooperation between competitors in the area of purchasing is acceptable, a further assessment will be necessary to examine the vertical agreements concluded with suppliers or individual sellers. The latter assessment will follow the rules of the Block Exemption Regulation and the Guidelines on Vertical Restraints.[43]

Notes
[43] See Guidelines on Vertical Restraints, paragraph 29.

118. An example would be an association formed by a group of retailers for the joint purchasing of products. Horizontal agreements concluded between the members of the association or decisions adopted by the association have to be assessed first as a horizontal agreement according to the present guidelines. Only if this assessment is positive does it become relevant to assess the resulting vertical agreements between the association and an individual members or between the association and suppliers. These agreements are covered — up to a certain limit — by the block exemption for vertical restraints.[44] Those agreements falling outside the vertical block exemption will not be presumed to be illegal but may need individual examination.

Notes
[44] Article 2(2) of Block Exemption Regulation on Vertical Restraints.

4.2. Relevant Markets

119. There are two markets which may be affected by joint buying: First, the market(s) with which the cooperation is directly concerned, i.e. the relevant purchasing market(s). Secondly, the selling market(s), i.e. the market(s) downstream where the participants of the joint purchasing arrangement are active as sellers.

Commentary
para 119: F&N: 7.332

120. The definition of relevant purchasing markets follows the principles described in the Commission Notice on the definition of the relevant market and is based on the concept of substitutability

to identify competitive constraints. The only difference to the definition of "selling markets" is that substitutability has to be defined from the viewpoint of supply and not from the viewpoint of demand. In other words: the suppliers' alternatives are decisive in identifying the competitive constraints on purchasers. These could be analysed for instance by examining the suppliers' reaction to a small but lasting price decrease. If the market is defined, the market share can be calculated as the percentage for which the purchases by the parties concerned account out of the total sales of the purchased product or service in the relevant market.

---

121. Example 1

A group of car manufacturers agree to buy product X jointly. Their combined purchases of X account for 15 units. All the sales of X to car manufacturers account for 50 units. However, X is also sold to manufacturers of products other than cars. All sales of X account for 100 units. Thus, the (purchasing) market share of the group is 15%.

---

122. If the parties are in addition competitors on one or more selling markets, these markets are also relevant for the assessment. Restrictions of competition on these markets are more likely if the parties will achieve market power by coordinating their behaviour and if the parties have a significant proportion of their total costs in common. This is, for instance, the case if retailers which are active in the same relevant retail market(s) jointly purchase a significant amount of the products they offer for resale. It may also be the case if competing manufacturers and sellers of a final product jointly purchase a high proportion of their input together. The selling markets have to be defined by applying the methodology described in the Commission Notice on the definition of the relevant market.

4.3. Assessment under Article 81(1)

4.3.1. Nature of the agreement

4.3.1.1. Agreements that do not fall under Article 81(1)

123. By their very nature joint buying agreements will be concluded between companies that are at least competitors on the purchasing markets. If, however, competing purchasers cooperate who are not active on the same relevant market further downstream (e.g. retailers which are active in different geographic markets and cannot be regarded as realistic potential competitors), Article 81(1) will rarely apply unless the parties have a very strong position in the buying markets, which could be used to harm the competitive position of other players in their respective selling markets.

4.3.1.2. Agreements that almost always fall under Article 81(1)

124. Purchasing agreements only come under Article 81(1) by their nature if the cooperation does not truly concern joint buying, but serves as a tool to engage in a disguised cartel, i.e. otherwise prohibited price fixing, output limitation or market allocation.

Commentary
para 124: B&C: 5.128

4.3.1.3. Agreements that may fall under Article 81(1)

125. Most purchasing agreements have to be analysed in their legal and economic context. The analysis has to cover both the purchasing and the selling markets.

4.3.2. Market power and market structures

126. The starting point for the analysis is the examination of the parties' buying power. Buying power can be assumed if a purchasing agreement accounts for a sufficiently large proportion of the total volume of a purchasing market so that prices can be driven down below the competitive level or access to the market can be foreclosed to competing buyers. A high degree of buying power over the suppliers of a market may bring about inefficiencies such as quality reductions, lessening of innovation efforts, or ultimately sub-optimal supply. However, the primary concerns in the context of buying power are that lower prices may not be passed on to customers further downstream and that it may cause cost increases for the purchasers' competitors on the selling markets because

Part C Substantive Antitrust Matters

either suppliers will try to recover price reductions for one group of customers by increasing prices for other customers or competitors have less access to efficient suppliers. Consequently, purchasing markets and selling markets are characterised by interdependencies as set out below.

Commentary
para 126: F&N: 7.335

Interdependencies between purchasing and selling market(s)

127. The cooperation of competing purchasers can appreciably restrict competition by means of creating buying power. Whilst the creation of buying power can lead to lower prices for consumers, buying power is not always pro-competitive and may even, under certain circumstances, cause severe negative effects on competition.

Commentary
para 127: F&N: 7.305

128. First, lower purchasing costs resulting from the exercise of buying power cannot be seen as pro-competitive, if the purchasers together have power on the selling markets. In this case, the cost savings are probably not passed on to consumers. The more combined power the parties have on their selling markets, the higher is the incentive for the parties to coordinate their behaviour as sellers. This may be facilitated if the parties achieve a high degree of commonality of costs through joint purchasing. For instance, if a group of large retailers buys a high proportion of their products together, they will have a high proportion of their total cost in common. The negative effects of joint buying can therefore be rather similar to joint production.

129. Secondly, power on the selling markets may be created or increased through buying power which is used to foreclose competitors or to raise rivals' costs. Significant buying power by one group of customers may lead to foreclosure of competing buyers by limiting their access to efficient suppliers. It can also cause cost increases for its competitors because suppliers will try to recover price reductions for one group of customers by increasing prices for other customers (e.g. rebate discrimination by suppliers of retailers). This is only possible if the suppliers of the purchasing markets also have a certain degree of market power. In both cases, competition in the selling markets can be further restricted by buying power.

130. There is no absolute threshold which indicates that a buying cooperation creates some degree of market power and thus falls under Article 81(1). However, in most cases, it is unlikely that market power exists if the parties to the agreement have a combined market share of below 15% on the purchasing market(s) as well as a combined market share of below 15% on the selling market(s). In any event, at that level of market share it is likely that the conditions of Article 81(3) explained below are fulfilled by the agreement in question.

Commentary
para 130: F&N: 12.340

131. A market share above this threshold does not automatically indicate that a negative market effect is caused by the cooperation but requires a more detailed assessment of the impact of a joint buying agreement on the market, involving factors such as the market concentration and possible countervailing power of strong suppliers. Joint buying that involves parties with a combined market share significantly above 15% in a concentrated market is likely to come under Article 81(1), and efficiencies that may outweigh the restrictive effect have to be shown by the parties.

Commentary
para 131: F&N:.325

4.4. Assessment under Article 81(3)

4.4.1. Economic benefits

132. Purchasing agreements can bring about economic benefits such as economies of scale in ordering or transportation which may outweigh restrictive effects. If the parties together have significant buying or selling power, the issue of efficiencies has to be examined carefully. Cost savings

that are caused by the mere exercise of power and which do not benefit consumers cannot be taken into account.

4.4.2. Indispensability

133. Purchasing agreements cannot be exempted if they impose restrictions that are not indispensable to the attainment of the above mentioned benefits. An obligation to buy exclusively through the cooperation can in certain cases be indispensable to achieve the necessary volume for the realisation of economies of scale. However, such an obligation has to be assessed in the context of the individual case.

4.4.3. No elimination of competition

134. No exemption will be possible, if the parties are afforded the possibility of eliminating competition in respect of a substantial part of the products in question. This assessment has to cover buying and selling markets. The combined market shares of the parties can be regarded as a starting point. It then needs to be evaluated whether these market shares are indicative of a dominant position, and whether there are any mitigating factors, such as countervailing power of suppliers on the purchasing markets or potential for market entry in the selling markets. Where as a consequence of a purchasing agreement an undertaking is dominant or becoming dominant on either the buying or selling market, such an agreement which produces anti-competitive effects in the meaning of Article 81 can in principle not be exempted.

Commentary
para 134: F&N: 9.291

4.5. Examples

---

135. **Example 2**

Situation: Two manufacturers, A and B, decide to jointly buy component X. They are competitors on their selling market. Together their purchases represent 35% of the total sales of X in the EEA, which is assumed to be the relevant geographic market. There are 6 other manufacturers (competitors of A and B on their selling market) accounting for the remaining 65% of the purchasing market; one having 25%, the others accounting for significantly less. The supply side is rather concentrated with 6 suppliers of component X, two with 30% market share each, and the rest with between 10 and 15% (HHI of 2300–2500). On their selling market, A and B achieve a combined market share of 35%.

Analysis: Due to the parties' market power in their selling market, the benefits of possible cost savings may not be passed on to final consumers. Furthermore, the joint buying is likely to increase the costs of the parties' smaller competitors because the two powerful suppliers probably recover price reductions for the group by increasing smaller customers' prices. Increasing concentration in the downstream market may be the result. In addition, the cooperation may lead to further concentration among suppliers because smaller ones, which may already work near or below minimum optimal scale, may be driven out of business if they cannot reduce prices further. Such a case probably causes a significant restriction of competition which may not be outweighed by possible efficiency gains from bundling volume.

---

136. **Example 3**

Situation: 150 small retailers conclude an agreement to form a joint buying organisation. They are obliged to buy a minimum volume through the organisation which accounts for roughly 50% of each retailer's total costs. The retailers can buy more than the minimum volume through the organisation, and they may also buy outside the cooperation. They have a combined market share of 20% on each of the purchasing and the selling market(s). A and B are their two large competitors, A has a 25% share on each of the markets concerned, B 35%. The remaining smaller competitors have also formed a buying group. The 150 retailers achieve economies by combinig a significant amount of volume and buying tasks.

Analysis: The retailers may achieve a high degree of commonality of costs if they ultimately buy more than the agreed minimum volume together. However, together they only have a moderate market position on the buying and the selling market. Furthermore, the cooperation brings about some economies of scale. This cooperation is likely to be exempted.

Commentary
para 136: B&C: 5.128

---

137. Example 4

Situation: Two supermarket chains conclude an agreement to jointly buy products which account for roughly 50% of their total costs. On the relevant buying markets for the different categories of products the parties have shares between 25% and 40%, on the relevant selling market (assuming there is only one geographic market concerned) they achieve 40%. There are five other significant retailers each with 10–15% market share. Market entry is not likely.

Analysis: It is likely that this joint buying arrangement would have an effect on the competitive behaviour of the parties because coordination would give them significant market power. This is particularly the case if entry is weak. The incentive to coordinate behaviour is higher if the costs are similar. Similar margins of the parties would add an incentive to have the same prices. Even if efficiencies are caused by the cooperation, it is not likely to be exempted due to the high degree of market power.

---

138. Example 5

Situation: small cooperatives conclude an agreement to form a joint buying organisation. They are obliged to buy a minimum volume through the organisation. The parties can buy more than the minimum volume through the organisation, but they may also buy outside the cooperation. Each of the parties has a total market share of 5% on each of the purchasing and selling markets, giving a combined market share of 25%. There are two other significant retailers each with 20–25% market share and a number of smaller retailers with market shares below 5%.

Analysis: The setting up of the joint buying organisation is likely to give the parties a market position on both the purchasing and selling markets of a degree which enables them to compete with the two largest retailers. Moreover, the presence of these two other players with similar levels of market position is likely to result in the efficiencies of the agreement being passed on to consumers. In such a scenario the agreement is likely to be exempted.

Commentary
para 138: B&C: 5.128

---

5. COMMERCIALISATION AGREEMENTS

5.1. Definition

139. The agreements covered in this section involve cooperation between competitors in the selling, distribution or promotion of their products. These agreements can have a widely varying scope, depending on the marketing functions which are being covered by the cooperation. At one end of the spectrum, there is joint selling that leads to a joint determination of all commercial aspects related to the sale of the product including price. At the other end, there are more limited agreements that only address one specific marketing function, such as distribution, service, or advertising.

140. The most important of these more limited agreements would seem to be distribution agreements. These agreements are generally covered by the Block Exemption Regulation and Guidelines on Vertical Restraints unless the parties are actual or potential competitors. In this case, the Block Exemption Regulation only covers non-reciprocal vertical agreements between competitors,

if (a) the buyer, together with its connected undertakings, has an annual turnover not exceeding EUR 100 million, or (b) the supplier is a manufacturer and a distributor of products and the buyer is a distributor who is not also a manufacturer of products competing with the contract products, or (c) the supplier is a provider of services at several levels of trade, while the buyer does not provide competing services at the level of trade where it purchases the contract services.[45] If competitors agree to distribute their products on a reciprocal basis there is a possibility in certain cases that the agreements have as their object or effect the partitioning of markets between the parties or that they lead to collusion. The same is true for non-reciprocal agreements between competitors exceeding a certain size. These agreements have thus first to be assessed according to the principles set out below. If this assessment leads to the conclusion that a cooperation between competitors in the area of distribution would in principle be acceptable, a further assessment will be necessary to examine the vertical restraints included in such agreements. This assessment should be based on the principles set out in the Guidelines on Vertical Restraints.

Notes

[45] Article 2(4) of Block Exemption Regulation on Vertical Restraints.

141. A further distinction should be drawn between agreements where the parties agree only on joint commercialisation and agreements where the commercialisation is related to another cooperation. This can be for instance the case as regards joint production or joint purchasing. These agreements will be dealt with as in the assessment of those types of cooperation.

5.2. Relevant Markets

142. To assess the competitive relationship between the cooperating parties, first the relevant product and geographic market(s) directly concerned by the cooperation (i.e. the market(s) to which products subject to the agreement belong) have to be defined. Secondly, a commercialisation agreement in one market may also affect the competitive behaviour of the parties in a neighbouring market closely related to the market directly concerned by the cooperation.

5.3. Assessment under Article 81(1)

5.3.1. Nature of the agreement

5.3.1.1. Agreements that do not fall under Article 81(1)

143. The commercialisation agreements covered by this section only fall under the competition rules if the parties to the agreements are competitors. If the parties clearly do not compete with regard to the products or services covered by the agreement, the agreement cannot create competition problems of a horizontal nature. However, the agreement can fall under Article 81(1) if it contains vertical restraints, such as restrictions on passive sales, resale price maintenance, etc. This also applies if a cooperation in commercialisation is objectively necessary to allow one party to enter a market it could not have entered individually, for example because of the costs involved. A specific application of this principle would be consortia arrangements that allow the companies involved to mount a credible tender for projects that they would not be able to fulfil, or would not have bid for, individually. As they are therefore not potential competitors for the tender, there is no restriction of competition.

Commentary

para 143: **B&C:** 5.110 **F&N:** 7.255, 7.257, 12.344

5.3.1.2. Agreements that almost always fall under Article 81(1)

144. The principal competition concern about a commercialisation agreement between competitors is price fixing. Agreements limited to joint selling have as a rule the object and effect of coordinating the pricing policy of competing manufacturers. In this case they not only eliminate price competition between the parties but also restrict the volume of products to be delivered by the participants within the framework of the system for allocating orders. They therefore restrict competition between the parties on the supply side and limit the choice of purchasers and fall under Article 81(1).

Commentary
para 144: F&N: 12.323

145. This appreciation does not change if the agreement is non-exclusive. Article 81(1) continues to apply even where the parties are free to sell outside the agreement, as long as it can be presumed that the agreement will lead to an overall coordination of the prices charged by the parties.

Commentary
para 145: F&N: 7.279

5.3.1.3. Agreements that may fall under Article 81(1)

146. For commercialisation arrangements that fall short of joint selling there will be two major concerns. The first is that the joint commercialisation provides a clear opportunity for exchanges of sensitive commercial information particularly on marketing strategy and pricing. The second is that, depending on the cost structure of the commercialisation, a significant input to the parties' final costs may be common. As a result the actual scope for price competition at the final sales level may be limited. Joint commercialisation agreements therefore can fall under Article 81(1) if they either allow the exchange of sensitive commercial information, or if they influence a significant part of the parties' final cost.

147. A specific concern related to distribution arrangements between competitors which are active in different geographic markets is that they can lead to or be an instrument of market partitioning. In the case of reciprocal agreements to distribute each other's products, the parties to the agreement allocate markets or customers and eliminate competition between themselves. The key question in assessing an agreement of this type is if the agreement in question is objectively necessary for the parties to enter each other's market. If it is, the agreement does not create competition problems of a horizontal nature. However, the distribution agreement can fall under Article 81(1) if it contains vertical restraints, such as restrictions on passive sales, resale price maintenance, etc. If the agreement is not objectively necessary for the parties to enter each other's market, it falls under 81(1). If the agreement is not reciprocal, the risk of market partitioning is less pronounced. It needs however to be assessed if the non-reciprocal agreement constitutes the basis for a mutual understanding to not enter each other's market or is a means to control access to or competition on the "importing" market.

Commentary
para 146: B&C: 5.110

5.3.2. *Market power and market structure*

148. As indicated above, agreements that involve price fixing will always fall under Article 81(1) irrespective of the market power of the parties. They may, however, be exemptable under Article 81(3) under the conditions described below.

149. Commercialisation agreements between competitors which do not involve price fixing are only subject to Article 81(1) if the parties to the agreement have some degree of market power. In most cases, it is unlikely that market power exists if the parties to the agreement have a combined market share of below 15%. In any event, at that level of market share it is likely that the conditions of Article 81(3) explained below are fulfilled by the agreement in question.

150. If the parties' combined market share is greater than 15%, the likely impact of the joint commercialisation agreement on the market must be assessed. In this respect market concentration, as well as market shares will be a significant factor. The more concentrated the market the more useful information about prices or marketing strategy to reduce uncertainty and the greater the incentive for the parties to exchange such information.[46]

Notes

[46] The exchange of sensitive and detailed information which takes place in an oligopolistic market might as such be caught by Article 81(1). The judgments of 28 May 1998 in the "Tractor" cases (C-8/958 P: *New Holland Ford* and C-7/95 P: *John Deere*) and of 11 March 1999 in the "Steel Beams" cases (T-134/94, T-136/94, T-137/94, T-138/94,

T-141/94, T-145/94, T-147/94, T-148/94, T-151/94, T-156/94 and T-157/94) provide useful clarification in this respect.

Commentary
para 150: B&C: 5.110

5.4. Assessment under Article 81(3)

5.4.1. Economic benefits

151. The efficiencies to be taken into account when assessing whether a joint commercialisation agreement can be exempted will depend upon the nature of the activity. Price fixing can generally not be justified, unless it is indispensable for the integration of other marketing functions, and this integration will generate substantial efficiencies. The size of the efficiencies generated depends inter alia on the importance of the joint marketing activities for the overall cost structure of the product in question. Joint distribution is thus more likely to generate significant efficiencies for producers of widely distributed consumer products than for producers of industrial products which are only bought by a limited number of users.

152. In addition, the claimed efficiencies should not be savings which result only from the elimination of costs that are inherently part of competition, but must result from the integration of economic activities. A reduction of transport cost which is only a result of customer allocation without any integration of the logistical system can therefore not be regarded as an efficiency that would make an agreement exemptable.

153. Claimed efficiency benefits must be demonstrated. An important element in this respect would be the contribution by both parties of significant capital, technology, or other assets. Cost savings through reduced duplication of resources and facilities can also be accepted. If, on the other hand, the joint commercialisation represents no more than a sales agency with no investment, it is likely to be a disguised cartel and as such cannot fulfil the conditions of Article 81(3).

Commentary
para 153: F&N: 12.317

5.4.2. Indispensability

154. A commercialisation agreement cannot be exempted if it imposes restrictions that are not indispensable to the attainment of the abovementioned benefits. As discussed above, the question of indispensability is especially important for those agreements involving price fixing or the allocation of markets.

5.4.3. No elimination of competition

155. No exemption will be possible, if the parties are afforded the possibility of eliminating competition in respect of a substantial part of the products in question. In making this assessment, the combined market shares of the parties can be regarded as a starting point. One then needs to evaluate whether these market shares are indicative of a dominant position, and whether there are any mitigating factors, such as the potential for market entry. Where as a consequence of a commercialisation agreement an undertaking is dominant or becoming dominant, such an agreement which produces anti-competitive effects in the meaning of Article 81 can in principle not be exempted.

Commentary
para 155: F&N: 9.291

5.5. Examples

156. Example 1

Situation: 5 small food producers, each with 2% market share of the overall food market, agree to: combine their distribution facilities; market under a common brand name; and sell their products at a common price. This involves significant investment in warehousing, transport, advertising, marketing and a sales force. It significantly reduces their cost base, representing typically 50% of the price at which they sell, and allows them to offer a quicker, more efficient distribution system. The customers of the food producers are large retail chains.

Three large multinational food groups dominate the market, each with 20% market share. The rest of the market is made up of small independent producers. The product ranges of the parties to this agreement overlap in some significant areas, but in no product market does their combined market share exceed 15%.

Analysis: The agreement involves price fixing and thus falls under Article 81(1), even though the parties to the agreement cannot be considered as having market power. However, the integration of the marketing and distribution appears to provide significant efficiencies which are of benefit to customers both in terms of improved service, and lower costs. The question is therefore whether the agreement is exemptable under Article 81(3). To answer this question it must be established whether the price fixing is indispensable for the integration of the other marketing functions and the attainment of the economic benefits. In this case, the price fixing can be regarded as indispensable, as the clients — large retail chains — do not want to deal with a multitude of prices. It is also indispensable, as the aim — a common brand — can only be credibly achieved if all aspects of marketing, including price, are standardised. As the parties do not have market power and the agreement creates significant efficiencies it is compatible with Article 81.

---

157. Example 2

Situation: 2 producers of ball bearings, each having a market share of 5%, create a sales joint venture which will market the products, determine the prices and allocate orders to the parent companies. They retain the right to sell outside this structure. Deliveries to customers continue to be made directly from the parents' factories. They claim that this will create efficiencies as the joint sales force can demonstrate the parties' products at the same time to the same client thus eliminating a wasteful duplication of sales efforts. In addition, the joint venture would, wherever possible, allocate orders to the closest factory possible, thus reducing transport costs.

Analysis: The agreement involves price fixing and thus falls under Article 81(1), even though the parties to the agreement cannot be considered as having market power. It is not exemptable under Article 81(3), as the claimed efficiencies are only cost reductions derived from the elimination of competition between the parties.

---

158. Example 3

Situation: 2 producers of soft drinks are active in 2 different, neighbouring Member States. Both have a market share of 20% in their home market. They agree to reciprocally distribute each other's product in their respective geographic market.
Both markets are dominated by a large multi-national soft drink producer, having a market share of 50% in each market.

Analysis: The agreement falls under Article 81(1) if the parties can be presumed to be potential competitors. Answering this question would thus require an analysis of the barriers to entry into the respective geographic markets. If the parties could have entered each other's market independently, then their agreement eliminates competition between them. However, even though the market shares of the parties indicate that they could have some market power, an analysis of the market structure indicates that this is not the case. In addition, the reciprocal distribution agreement benefits customers as it increases the available choice in each geographic market. The agreement would thus be exemptable even if it were considered to be restrictive of competition.

Commentary
para 158: B&C: 5.110

6. Agreement on Standards

6.1. Definition

159. Standardisation agreements have as their primary objective the definition of technical or quality requirements with which current or future products, production processes or methods may comply.[47] Standardisation agreements can cover various issues, such as standardisation of different grades or sizes of a particular product or technical specifications in markets where compatibility and interoperability with other products or systems is essential. The terms of access to a particular quality mark or for approval by a regulatory body can also be regarded as a standard.

Notes

[47] Standardisation can take different forms, ranging from the adoption of national consensus based standards by the recognised European or national standards bodies, through consortia and fora, to agreements between single companies. Although Community law defines standards in a narrow way, these guidelines qualify as standards all agreements as defined in this paragraph.

Commentary
para 159: F&N: 7.385

160. Standards related to the provision of professional services, such as rules of admission to a liberal profession, are not covered by these guidelines.

Commentary
para 160: F&N: 7.389

6.2. Relevant Markets

161. Standardisation agreements produce their effects on three possible markets, which will be defined according to the Commission notice on market definition. First, the product market(s) to which the standard(s) relates. Standards on entirely new products may raise issues similar to those raised for R & D agreements, as far as market definition is concerned (see Point 2.2). Second, the service market for standard setting, if different standard setting bodies or agreements exist. Third, where relevant, the distinct market for testing and certification.

Commentary
para 161: F&N: 7.388

6.3. Assessment under Article 81(1)

162. Agreements to set standards[48] may be either concluded between private undertakings or set under the aegis of public bodies or bodies entrusted with the operation of services of general economic interest, such as the standards bodies recognised under Directive 98/34/EC.[49] The involvement of such bodies is subject to the obligations of Member States regarding the preservation of non-distorted competition in the Community.

Notes

[48] Pursuant to Article 4(2)(3) of Regulation No 17, agreements which have as their sole object the development or the uniform application of standards and types need not, but may, be notified to the Commission. [As regards Regulation No 17, see now Council Regulation (EC) 1/2003, OJ L 1, 4.1.2003, p. 1.]

[49] Directive 98/34/EC of the European Parliament and of the Council on 22 June 1998 laying down a procedure for the provision of information in the field of technical standards and regulations (OJ L 204, 21.7.1998, p. 37).

Commentary
para 162: F&N: 7.389

6.3.1. *Nature of the agreement*

6.3.1.1. Agreements that do not fall under Article 81(1)

163. Where participation in standard setting is unrestricted and transparent, standardisation agreements as defined above, which set no obligation to comply with the standard or which are parts of a wider agreement to ensure compatibility of products, do not restrict competition. This normally

Part C Substantive Antitrust Matters

381

applies to standards adopted by the recognised standards bodies which are based on non-discriminatory, open and transparent procedures.

164. No appreciable restriction exists for those standards that have a negligible coverage of the relevant market, as long as it remains so. No appreciable restriction is found either in agreements which pool together SMEs to standardise access forms or conditions to collective tenders or those that standardise aspects such as minor product characteristics, forms and reports, which have an insignificant effect on the main factors affecting competition in the relevant markets.

6.3.1.2. Agreements that almost always fall under Article 81(1)

165. Agreements that use a standard as a means amongst other parts of a broader restrictive agreement aimed at excluding actual or potential competitors will almost always be caught by Article 81(1). For instance, an agreement whereby a national association of manufacturers set a standard and put pressure on third parties not to market products that did not comply with the standard would be in this category.

6.3.1.3. Agreements that may fall under Article 81(1)

166. Standardisation agreements may be caught by Article 81(1) insofar as they grant the parties joint control over production and/or innovation, thereby restricting their ability to compete on product characteristics, while affecting third parties like suppliers or purchasers of the standardised products. The assessment of each agreement must take into account the nature of the standard and its likely effect on the markets concerned, on the one hand, and the scope of possible restrictions that go beyond the primary objective of standardisation, as defined above, on the other.

167. The existence of a restriction of competition in standardisation agreements depends upon the extent to which the parties remain free to develop alternative standards or products that do not comply with the agreed standard. Standardisation agreements may restrict competition where they prevent the parties from either developing alternative standards or commercialising products that do not comply with the standard. Agreements that entrust certain bodies with the exclusive right to test compliance with the standard go beyond the primary objective of defining the standard and may also restrict competition. Agreements that impose restrictions on marking of conformity with standards, unless imposed by regulatory provisions, may also restrict competition.

6.3.2. Market power and market structures

168. High market shares held by the parties in the market(s) affected will not necessarily be a concern for standardisation agreements. Their effectiveness is often proportional to the share of the industry involved in setting and/or applying the standard. On the other hand, standards that are not accessible to third parties may discriminate or foreclose third parties or segment markets according to their geographic scope of application. Thus, the assessment whether the agreement restricts competition will focus, necessarily on an individual basis, on the extent to which such barriers to entry are likely to be overcome.

6.4. Assessment under Article 81(3)

6.4.1. Economic benefits

169. The Commission generally takes a positive approach towards agreements that promote economic interpenetration in the common market or encourage the development of new markets and improved supply conditions. To materialise those economic benefits, the necessary information to apply the standard must be available to those wishing to enter the market and an appreciable proportion of the industry must be involved in the setting of the standard in a transparent manner. It will be for the parties to demonstrate that any restrictions on the setting, use or access to the standard provide economic benefits.

Commentary
para 169: B&C: 5.144

170. In order to reap technical or economic benefits, standards should not limit innovation. This will depend primarily on the lifetime of the associated products, in connection with the market development stage (fast growing, growing, stagnant. . .). The effects on innovation must be analysed on a case-by-case basis. The parties may also have to provide evidence that collective standardisation is efficiency-enhancing for the consumer when a new standard may trigger unduly rapid obsolescence of existing products, without objective additional benefits.

Commentary
para 170: F&N: 7.395

6.4.2. Indispensability

171. By their nature, standards will not include all possible specifications or technologies. In some cases, it would be necessary for the benefit of the consumers or the economy at large to have only one technological solution. However, this standard must be set on a non-discriminatory basis. Ideally, standards should be technology neutral. In any event, it must be justifiable why one standard is chosen over another.

172. All competitors in the market(s) affected by the standard should have the possibility of being involved in discussions. Therefore, participation in standard setting should be open to all, unless the parties demonstrate important inefficiencies in such participation or unless recognised procedures are foreseen for the collective representation of interests, as in formal standards bodies.

Commentary
para 172: F&N: 7.396

173. As a general rule there should be a clear distinction between the setting of a standard and, where necessary, the related R & D, and the commercial exploitation of that standard. Agreements on standards should cover no more than what is necessary to ensure their aims, whether this is technical compatibility or a certain level of quality. For instance, it should be very clearly demonstrated why it is indispensable to the emergence of the economic benefits that an agreement to disseminate a standard in an industry where only one competitor offers an alternative should oblige the parties to the agreement to boycott the alternative.

6.4.3. No elimination of competition

174. There will clearly be a point at which the specification of a private standard by a group of firms that are jointly dominant is likely to lead to the creation of a de facto industry standard. The main concern will then be to ensure that these standards are as open as possible and applied in a clear non-discriminatory manner. To avoid elimination of competition in the relevant market(s), access to the standard must be possible for third parties on fair, reasonable and non-discriminatory terms.

175. To the extent that private organisations or groups of companies set a standard or their proprietary technology becomes a de facto standard, then competition will be eliminated if third parties are foreclosed from access to this standard.

6.5. Examples

> 176. Example 1
>
> **Situation**: EN 60603–7:1993 defines the requirements to connect television receivers to video-generating accessories such as video recorders and video games. Although the standard is not legally binding, in practice manufacturers both of television receivers and of video games use the standard, as the market requires so.
>
> **Analysis**: Article 81(1) is not infringed. The standard has been adopted by recognised standards bodies, at national, European and international level, through open and transparent procedures, and is based on national consensus reflecting the position of manufacturers and consumers. All manufacturers are allowed to use the standard.

Commentary
para 176: B&C: 5.140

> 177. Example 2
>
> **Situation**: A number of videocassette manufacturers agree to develop a quality mark or standard to denote the fact that the videocassette meets certain minimum technical specifications. The manufacturers are free to produce videocassettes which do not conform to the standard and the standard is freely available to other developers.
>
> **Analysis**: Provided that the agreement does not otherwise restrict competition, Article 81(1) is not infringed, as participation in standard setting is unrestricted and transparent, and the standardisation agreement does not set an obligation to comply with the standard. If the parties. agreed only to produce videocassettes which conform to the new standard, the agreement would limit technical development and prevent the parties from selling different products, which would infringe Article 81(1).

> 178. Example 3
>
> **Situation**: A group of competitors active in various markets which are interdependent with products that must be compatible, and with over 80% of the relevant markets, agree to jointly develop a new standard that will be introduced in competition with other standards already present in the market, widely applied by their competitors. The various products complying with the new standard will not be compatible with existing standards. Because of the significant investment needed to shift and to maintain production under the new standard, the parties agree to commit a certain volume of sales to products complying with the new standard so as to create a "critical mass" in the market. They also agree to limit their individual production volume of products not complying with the standard to the level attained last year.
>
> **Analysis**: This agreement, owing to the parties' market power and the restrictions on production, falls under Article 81(1) while not being likely to fulfil the conditions of paragraph 3, unless access to technical information were provided on a non-discriminatory basis and reasonable terms to other suppliers wishing to compete.

7. ENVIRONMENTAL AGREEMENTS

7.1. Definition

179. Environmental agreements[50] are those by which the parties undertake to achieve pollution abatement, as defined in environmental law, or environmental objectives, in particular, those set out in Article 174 of the Treaty. Therefore, the target or the measures agreed need to be directly linked to the reduction of a pollutant or a type of waste identified as such in relevant regulations.[51] This excludes agreements that trigger pollution abatement as a by-product of other measures.

Notes

[50] The term "agreement" is used in the sense defined by the Court of Justice and the Court of First Instance in the case law on Article 81. It does not necessarily correspond to the definition of an "agreement" in Commission documents dealing with environmental issues such as the Communication on environmental agreements COM(96) 561 final of 27.11.1996.

[51] For instance, a national agreement phasing out a pollutant or waste identified as such in relevant Community directives may not be assimilated to a collective boycott on a product which circulates freely in the Community.

Commentary
para 179: F&N: 7.404

180. Environmental agreements may set out standards on the environmental performance of products (inputs or outputs) or production processes.[52] Other possible categories may include agreements at the same level of trade, whereby the parties provide for the common attainment of an environmental target such as recycling of certain materials, emission reductions, or the improvement of energy-efficiency.

Notes

[52] To the extent that some environmental agreements could be assimilated to standardisation, the same assessment principles for standardisation apply to them.

181. Comprehensive, industry-wide schemes are set up in many Member States for complying with environmental obligations on take-back or recycling. Such schemes usually comprise a complex set of arrangements, some of which are horizontal, while others are vertical in character. To the extent that these arrangements contain vertical restraints they are not subject to these guidelines.

7.2. Relevant Markets

182. The effects are to be assessed on the markets to which the agreement relates, which will be defined according to the Notice on the definition of the relevant market for the purposes of Community competition law. When the pollutant is not itself a product, the relevant market encompasses that of the product into which the pollutant is incorporated. As for collection/recycling agreements, in addition to their effects on the market(s) on which the parties are active as producers or distributors, the effects on the market of collection services potentially covering the good in question must be assessed as well.

Commentary
para 182: F&N: 7.405

7.3. Assessment under Article 81(1)

183. Some environmental agreements may be encouraged or made necessary by State authorities in the exercise of their public prerogatives. The present guidelines do not deal with the question of whether such State intervention is in conformity with the Member State's obligations under the Treaty. They only address the assessment that must be made as to the compatibility of the agreement with Article 81.

7.3.1. Nature of the agreement

7.3.1.1. Agreements that do not fall under Article 81(1)

184. Some environmental agreements are not likely to fall within the scope of the prohibition of Article 81(1), irrespective of the aggregated market share of the parties.

185. This may arise if no precise individual obligation is placed upon the parties or if they are loosely committed to contributing to the attainment of a sector-wide environmental target. In this latter case, the assessment will focus on the discretion left to the parties as to the means that are technically and economically available in order to attain the environmental objective agreed upon. The more varied such means, the less appreciable the potential restrictive effects.

Commentary
para 185: F&N: 7.408

186. Similarly, agreements setting the environmental performance of products or processes that do not appreciably affect product and production diversity in the relevant market or whose importance is marginal for influencing purchase decisions do not fall under Article 81(1). Where some categories of a product are banned or phased out from the market, restrictions cannot be deemed appreciable in so far as their share is minor in the relevant geographic market or, in the case of Community-wide markets, in all Member States.

Commentary
para 186: F&N: 7.409

187. Finally, agreements which give rise to genuine market creation, for instance recycling agreements, will not generally restrict competition, provided that and for as long as, the parties would not be capable of conducting the activities in isolation, whilst other alternatives and/or competitors do not exist.

Commentary
para 187: F&N: 7.410

7.3.1.2. Agreements that almost always come under Article 81(1)

188. Environmental agreements come under Article 81(1) by their nature if the cooperation does not truly concern environmental objectives, but serves as a tool to engage in a disguised cartel, i.e. otherwise prohibited price fixing, output limitation or market allocation, or if the cooperation is used as a means amongst other parts of a broader restrictive agreement which aims at excluding actual or potential competitors.

7.3.1.3. Agreements that may fall under Article 81(1)

189. Environmental agreements covering a major share of an industry at national or EC level are likely to be caught by Article 81(1) where they appreciably restrict the parties' ability to devise the characteristics of their products or the way in which they produce them, thereby granting them influence over each other's production or sales. In addition to restrictions between the parties, an environmental agreement may also reduce or substantially affect the output of third parties, either as suppliers or as purchasers.

Commentary
para 189: F&N: 7.411

190. For instance, environmental agreements, which may phase out or significantly affect an important proportion of the parties' sales as regards their products or production processes, may fall under Article 81(1) when the parties hold a significant proportion of the market. The same applies to agreements whereby the parties allocate individual pollution quotas.

Commentary
para 190: F&N: 7.411

191. Similarly, agreements whereby parties holding significant market shares in a substantial part of the common market appoint an undertaking as exclusive provider of collection and/or recycling services for their products, may also appreciably restrict competition, provided other actual or realistic potential providers exist.

Commentary
para 191: F&N: 7.411

7.4. Assessment under Article 81(3)

7.4.1. Economic benefits

192. The Commission takes a positive stance on the use of environmental agreements as a policy instrument to achieve the goals enshrined in Article 2 and Article 174 of the Treaty as well as

in Community environmental action plans,[53] provided such agreements are compatible with competition rules.[54]

Notes

[53] Vth Environmental Action Programme (OJ C 138, 17.5.1993), p. 1; European Parliament and Council Decision No 2179/98/EC of 24 September 1998 (OJ L 275, 10.10.1998, p. 1).

[54] Communication on environmental agreements COM(96) 561 final of 27.11.1996, paragraphs 27–29 and Article 3(1)f of EP and Council Decision *ut supra*. The communication includes a "Checklist for Environmental Agreements" identifying the elements that should generally be included in such an agreement.

Commentary
para 192: B&C: 3.044

193. Environmental agreements caught by Article 81(1) may attain economic benefits which, either at individual or aggregate consumer level, outweigh their negative effects on competition. To fulfil this condition, there must be net benefits in terms of reduced environmental pressure resulting from the agreement, as compared to a baseline where no action is taken. In other words, the expected economic benefits must outweigh the costs.[55]

Notes

[55] This is consistent with the requirement to take account of the potential benefits and costs of action or lack of action set forth in Article 174(3) of the Treaty and Article 7(d) of European Parliament and Council Decision *ut supra*.

194. Such costs include the effects of lessened competition along with compliance costs for economic operators and/or effects on third parties. The benefits might be assessed in two stages. Where consumers individually have a positive rate of return from the agreement under reasonable payback periods, there is no need for the aggregate environmental benefits to be objectively established. Otherwise, a cost–benefit analysis may be necessary to assess whether net benefits for consumers in general are likely under reasonable assumptions.

7.4.2. Indispensability

195. The more objectively the economic efficiency of an environmental agreement is demonstrated, the more clearly each provision might be deemed indispensable to the attainment of the environmental goal within its economic context.

196. An objective evaluation of provisions which might "prima facie" be deemed not to be indispensable must be supported with a cost-effectiveness analysis showing that alternative means of attaining the expected environmental benefits, would be more economically or financially costly, under reasonable assumptions. For instance, it should be very clearly demonstrated that a uniform fee, charged irrespective of individual costs for waste collection, is indispensable for the functioning of an industry-wide collection system.

7.4.3. No elimination of competition

197. Whatever the environmental and economic gains and the necessity of the intended provisions, the agreement must not eliminate competition in terms of product or process differentiation, technological innovation or market entry in the short or, where relevant, medium run. For instance, in the case of exclusive collection rights granted to a collection/recycling operator who has potential competitors, the duration of such rights should take into account the possible emergence of an alternative to the operator.

7.5. Examples

198. Example

Situation: Almost all Community producers and importers of a given domestic appliance (e.g. washing machines) agree, with the encouragement of a public body, to no longer manufacture and import into the Community products which do not comply with certain environmental criteria (e.g. energy efficiency). Together, the parties hold 90% of the Community market. The products which will be thus phased out of the market account for a significant proportion of total sales. They will be replaced with more environmentally friendly, but also more expensive products. Furthermore, the agreement indirectly reduces the output of third parties (e.g. electric utilities, suppliers of components incorporated in the products phased out).

Analysis: The agreement grants the parties control of individual production and imports and concerns an appreciable proportion of their sales and total output, whilst also reducing third parties' output. Consumer choice, which is partly focused on the environmental characteristics of the product, is reduced and prices will probably rise. Therefore, the agreement is caught by Article 81(1). The involvement of the public authority is irrelevant for this assessment.

However, newer products are more technically advanced and by reducing the environmental problem indirectly aimed at (emissions from electricity generation), they will not inevitably create or increase another environmental problem (e.g. water consumption, detergent use). The net contribution to the improvement of the environmental situation overall outweighs increased costs. Furthermore, individual purchasers of more expensive products will also rapidly recoup the cost increase as the more environmentally friendly products have lower running costs. Other alternatives to the agreement are shown to be less certain and less cost-effective in delivering the same net benefits. Varied technical means are economically available to the parties in order to manufacture products which do comply with the environmental characteristics agreed upon and competition will still take place for other product characteristics. Therefore, the conditions for an exemption under Article 81(3) are fulfilled.

C13

COMMISSION NOTICE

on agreements of minor importance which do not
appreciably restrict competition under Article 81(1) of the Treaty establishing
the European Community (*de minimis*)[1]

(Text with EEA relevance)

(2001/C 368/07)

Official Journal C 368, 22.12.2001, p. 13

Celex No: 52001XC1222(03)

Notes
[1] This notice replaces the notice on agreements of minor importance published in OJ C 372, 9.12.1997.
EEA application: the EFTA Surveillance Authority has adopted a parallel notice under Article 5(2)(b) of the Surveillance and Court Agreement: OJ C 67, 20.3.2003, p. 20 and EEA Supplement No 15, 20.3.2003, p. 11.

Commentary
Notice: B&C: 1.066, 1.124, 2.128–2.130, 4.007, 5.007, 6.003, 6.049–6.050, 6.147, 9.005 **F&N:** 3.162, 3.163, 3.238, 3.240, 3.308, 3.309, 3.310–3.313, 3.368, 7.264, 9.42, 9.50, 9.60, 9.61, 9.62, 9.64, 9.67, 9.72, 9.127, 9.145, 9.166, 9.167, 9.267, 9.309, 9.479, 12.123, 14.230

I

1. Article 81(1) prohibits agreements between undertakings which may affect trade between Member States and which have as their object or effect the prevention, restriction or distortion of competition within the common market. The Court of Justice of the European Communities has clarified

that this provision is not applicable where the impact of the agreement on intra-Community trade or on competition is not appreciable.

Commentary
point 1: F&N: 9.62, 9.66

2. In this notice the Commission quantifies, with the help of market share thresholds, what is not an appreciable restriction of competition under Article 81 of the EC Treaty. This negative definition of appreciability does not imply that agreements between undertakings which exceed the thresholds set out in this notice appreciably restrict competition. Such agreements may still have only a negligible effect on competition and may therefore not be prohibited by Article 81(1).[1]

Notes
[1] See, for instance, the judgment of the Court of Justice in Joined Cases C-215/96 and C-216/96 *Bagnasco (Carlos) v Banca Popolare di Novara and Casa di Risparmio di Genova e Imperia* [1999] ECR I-135, points 34–35. This notice is also without prejudice to the principles for assessment under Article 81(1) as expressed in the Commission notice "Guidelines on the applicability of Article 81 of the EC Treaty to horizontal cooperation agreements", OJ C 3, 6.1.2001, in particular points 17–31 inclusive, and in the Commission notice "Guidelines on vertical restraints", OJ C 291, 13.10.2000, in particular points 5–20 inclusive.

Commentary
point 2: F&N: 3.240, 3.313

3. Agreements may in addition not fall under Article 81(1) because they are not capable of appreciably affecting trade between Member States. This notice does not deal with this issue. It does not quantify what does not constitute an appreciable effect on trade. It is however acknowledged that agreements between small and medium-sized undertakings, as defined in the Annex to Commission Recommendation 96/280/EC,[1] are rarely capable of appreciably affecting trade between Member States. Small and medium-sized undertakings are currently defined in that recommendation as undertakings which have fewer than 250 employees and have either an annual turnover not exceeding EUR 40 million or an annual balance-sheet total not exceeding EUR 27 million.

Notes
[1] OJ L 107, 30.4.1996, p. 4. This recommendation will be revised. It is envisaged to increase the annual turnover threshold from EUR 40 million to EUR 50 million and the annual balance-sheet total from EUR 27 million to EUR 43 million. [See now Commission Recommendation of 6 May 2003 concerning the definition of micro, small and medium-sized enterprises (notified under document number C(2003) 1422) OJ L 124, 20.5.2003, p. 36.]

Commentary
point 3: B&C: 1.124, 2.130 F&N: 9.63

4. In cases covered by this notice the Commission will not institute proceedings either upon application or on its own initiative. Where undertakings assume in good faith that an agreement is covered by this notice, the Commission will not impose fines. Although not binding on them, this notice also intends to give guidance to the courts and authorities of the Member States in their application of Article 81.

Commentary
point 4: F&N: 3.238, 3.310, 9.59

5. This notice also applies to decisions by associations of undertakings and to concerted practices.

Commentary
point 5: B&C: 1.066

6. This notice is without prejudice to any interpretation of Article 81 which may be given by the Court of Justice or the Court of First Instance of the European Communities.

Part C Substantive Antitrust Matters

II

7. The Commission holds the view that agreements between undertakings which affect trade between Member States do not appreciably restrict competition within the meaning of Article 81(1):

    (a) if the aggregate market share held by the parties to the agreement does not exceed 10% on any of the relevant markets affected by the agreement, where the agreement is made between undertakings which are actual or potential competitors on any of these markets (agreements between competitors);[1] or

    (b) if the market share held by each of the parties to the agreement does not exceed 15% on any of the relevant markets affected by the agreement, where the agreement is made between undertakings which are not actual or potential competitors on any of these markets (agreements between non-competitors).

    In cases where it is difficult to classify the agreement as either an agreement between competitors or an agreement between non-competitors the 10% threshold is applicable.

Notes

[1] On what are actual or potential competitors, see the Commission notice "Guidelines on the applicability of Article 81 of the EC Treaty to horizontal cooperation agreements", OJ C 3, 6.1.2001, paragraph 9. A firm is treated as an actual competitor if it is either active on the same relevant market or if, in the absence of the agreement, it is able to switch production to the relevant products and market them in the short term without incurring significant additional costs or risks in response to a small and permanent increase in relative prices (immediate supply-side substitutability). A firm is treated as a potential competitor if there is evidence that, absent the agreement, this firm could and would be likely to undertake the necessary additional investments or other necessary switching costs so that it could enter the relevant market in response to a small and permanent increase in relative prices.

Commentary
point 7: **B&C:** 6.003
point 7(a): **F&N:** 3.162
point 7(b): **F&N:** 3.162

8. Where in a relevant market competition is restricted by the cumulative effect of agreements for the sale of goods or services entered into by different suppliers or distributors (cumulative foreclosure effect of parallel networks of agreements having similar effects on the market), the market share thresholds under point 7 are reduced to 5%, both for agreements between competitors and for agreements between non-competitors. Individual suppliers or distributors with a market share not exceeding 5% are in general not considered to contribute significantly to a cumulative foreclosure effect.[1] A cumulative foreclosure effect is unlikely to exist if less than 30% of the relevant market is covered by parallel (networks of) agreements having similar effects.

Notes

[1] See also the Commission notice "Guidelines on vertical restraints", OJ C 291, 13.10.2000, in particular paragraphs 73, 142, 143 and 189. While in the guidelines on vertical restraints in relation to certain restrictions reference is made not only to the total but also to the tied market share of a particular supplier or buyer, in this notice all market share thresholds refer to total market shares.

Commentary
point 8: **B&C:** 6.005 **F&N:** 9.156, 9.263

9. The Commission also holds the view that agreements are not restrictive of competition if the market shares do not exceed the thresholds of respectively 10%, 15% and 5% set out in point 7 and 8 during two successive calendar years by more than 2 percentage points.

Commentary
point 9: **B&C:** 2.129 **F&N:** 3.238

10. In order to calculate the market share, it is necessary to determine the relevant market. This consists of the relevant product market and the relevant geographic market. When defining the relevant market, reference should be had to the notice on the definition of the relevant market for the purposes of Community competition law.[1] The market shares are to be calculated on the

basis of sales value data or, where appropriate, purchase value data. If value data are not available, estimates based on other reliable market information, including volume data, may be used.

Notes

[1] OJ C 372, 9.12.1997, p. 5.

11. Points 7, 8 and 9 do not apply to agreements containing any of the following hardcore restrictions:
   (1) as regards agreements between competitors as defined in point 7, restrictions which, directly or indirectly, in isolation or in combination with other factors under the control of the parties, have as their object:[1]
      (a) the fixing of prices when selling the products to third parties;
      (b) the limitation of output or sales;
      (c) the allocation of markets or customers;
   (2) as regards agreements between non-competitors as defined in point 7, restrictions which, directly or indirectly, in isolation or in combination with other factors under the control of the parties, have as their object:
      (a) the restriction of the buyer's ability to determine its sale price, without prejudice to the possibility of the supplier imposing a maximum sale price or recommending a sale price, provided that they do not amount to a fixed or minimum sale price as a result of pressure from, or incentives offered by, any of the parties;
      (b) the restriction of the territory into which, or of the customers to whom, the buyer may sell the contract goods or services, except the following restrictions which are not hardcore:
         — the restriction of active sales into the exclusive territory or to an exclusive customer group reserved to the supplier or allocated by the supplier to another buyer, where such a restriction does not limit sales by the customers of the buyer,
         — the restriction of sales to end users by a buyer operating at the wholesale level of trade,
         — the restriction of sales to unauthorised distributors by the members of a selective distribution system, and
         — the restriction of the buyer's ability to sell components, supplied for the purposes of incorporation, to customers who would use them to manufacture the same type of goods as those produced by the supplier;
      (c) the restriction of active or passive sales to end users by members of a selective distribution system operating at the retail level of trade, without prejudice to the possibility of prohibiting a member of the system from operating out of an unauthorised place of establishment;
      (d) the restriction of cross-supplies between distributors within a selective distribution system, including between distributors operating at different levels of trade;
      (e) the restriction agreed between a supplier of components and a buyer who incorporates those components, which limits the supplier's ability to sell the components as spare parts to end users or to repairers or other service providers not entrusted by the buyer with the repair or servicing of its goods;
   (3) as regards agreements between competitors as defined in point 7, where the competitors operate, for the purposes of the agreement, at a different level of the production or distribution chain, any of the hardcore restrictions listed in paragraph (1) and (2) above.

Notes

[1] Without prejudice to situations of joint production with or without joint distribution as defined in Article 5, paragraph 2, of Commission Regulation (EC) No 2658/2000 and Article 5, paragraph 2, of Commission Regulation (EC) No 2659/2000, OJ L 304, 5.12.2000, pp. 3 and 7 respectively.

Commentary

point 11: B&C: 4.007, 5.007 **F&N:** 3.155, 3.162, 238, 3.310
point 11(2): F&N: 9.67

12. (1) For the purposes of this notice, the terms "undertaking," "party to the agreement," "distributor," "supplier" and "buyer" shall include their respective connected undertakings.
    (2) "Connected undertakings" are:
       (a) undertakings in which a party to the agreement, directly or indirectly:
          — has the power to exercise more than half the voting rights, or
          — has the power to appoint more than half the members of the supervisory board, board of management or bodies legally representing the undertaking, or
          — has the right to manage the undertaking's affairs;
       (b) undertakings which directly or indirectly have, over a party to the agreement, the rights or powers listed in (a);
       (c) undertakings in which an undertaking referred to in (b) has, directly or indirectly, the rights or powers listed in (a);
       (d) undertakings in which a party to the agreement together with one or more of the undertakings referred to in (a), (b) or (c), or in which two or more of the latter undertakings, jointly have the rights or powers listed in (a);
       (e) undertakings in which the rights or the powers listed in (a) are jointly held by:
          — parties to the agreement or their respective connected undertakings referred to in (a) to (d), or
          — one or more of the parties to the agreement or one or more of their connected undertakings referred to in (a) to (d) and one or more third parties.
    (3) For the purposes of paragraph 2(e), the market share held by these jointly held undertakings shall be apportioned equally to each undertaking having the rights or the powers listed in paragraph 2(a).

Commentary
point 12: B&C: 2.129
point 12(2): F&N: 3.36814

C14

DISTRIBUTION AND SERVICING OF MOTOR VEHICLES IN THE EUROPEAN UNION COMMISSION REGULATION (EC) NO 1400/2002

of 31 July 2002[1] on the application of Article 81(3) of the Treaty to categories of vertical agreements and concerted practices in the motor vehicle sector

EXPLANATORY BROCHURE
EUROPEAN COMMISSION — DIRECTORATE GENERAL FOR COMPETITION

Notes
[1] OJ L 203, 1.8.2002, p. 30. "This document is available on the Europa website at the following address: http://ec.europa.eu/comm/competition/sectors/motors_vehicles/legislation/explanatory_brochure_en.pdf".

FOREWORD

Motor vehicle distribution and repair are areas that are of crucial interest for the European consumer. This sector has been associated with specific competition problems— particularly as regards consumers' Single Market rights to buy a car wherever it suits them in the European Union. The new Regulation 1400/2002, which is explained in this brochure, has been designed to sort out these problems, while recognising the special features of the motor vehicle sector. The new Regulation also deals with issues related to repair and maintenance and the supply of spare parts, since over the lifetime of a vehicle, the costs associated with these services are around as high as the initial purchase price of the vehicle itself.

The new Regulation is designed to increase competition and bring tangible benefits to European consumers. It opens the way to greater use of new distribution techniques, such as Internet sales and multi-brand dealerships. It will lead to more competition between dealers, make cross-border purchases of new vehicles significantly easier, and lead to greater price competition. Car owners will have more opportunity to choose where they have repair and maintenance carried out and what spare parts are used.

This explanatory brochure, drawn up by DG Competition, is intended as a legally non-binding guide to the Regulation. It aims at providing different categories of interested parties, in particular consumers, dealers and repairers, with guidance and information. Such information is all the more important in view of the fundamental changes which the Regulation introduces. The brochure contains separate sections for these parties, and provides answers to questions which are likely to be raised. This should make it easier for the reader to find information in accordance with his or her needs.

DG Competition will be vigilant in monitoring the implementation of this important Regulation and will not hesitate to take action, where necessary, to ensure that the competition rules are respected and that the Regulation operates to the benefit of European consumers.

Philip Lowe

Director-General for Competition

TABLE OF CONTENTS

Part C Substantive Antitrust Matters

1. Introduction

In the Member States of the European Union, motor vehicle and spare part manufacturers distribute their products through networks of distributors. As far as motor vehicles are concerned, these distributors are commonly known as dealers, and will be referred to as such in this brochure. Motor vehicle manufacturers and other undertakings also operate networks of authorised repairers. Such a distribution or repair network consists of a bundle of similar agreements between the manufacturer and the individual distributors or repairers. For the purposes of competition law, these agreements are referred to as vertical agreements, as the manufacturer and distributor or repairer each operate at different levels of the production or distribution chain.

Article 81 of the EC Treaty applies to agreements that may affect trade between Member States and which prevent, restrict or distort competition. The first condition for Article 81 to apply is that the agreements in question are capable of having an appreciable effect on trade between Member States. This will usually be the case if a network extends across the whole territory of a Member State. Where the first condition is met, Article 81(1) prohibits agreements which appreciably restrict or distort competition.[2] This may be the case if the vertical agreements not only determine the price and quantity for a specific sale and purchase transaction but contain restraints on the supplier or the buyer (hereinafter referred to as "vertical restraints"). Article 81(3) renders this prohibition inapplicable for those agreements which create sufficient benefits, such as improvements in efficiency, to outweigh the anti-competitive effects. Such agreements are said to be exempted under Article 81(3). Agreements can only be exempted if consumers receive a fair share of the benefits resulting from the improvements.[3]

Whether a vertical agreement actually restricts competition and whether in that case the benefits outweigh the anti-competitive effects will often depend on the market structure. In principle, this requires an individual assessment. However, the Commission can also grant an exemption by regulation for whole categories of agreements. Such regulations are commonly referred to as "block exemption regulations". For instance, the Commission has adopted a block exemption regulation for supply and distribution agreements known as Commission Regulation 2790/1999.[4] This block exemption Regulation applies in principle to vertical agreements in all sectors of industry and trade. However, where the Commission has adopted a sector specific block exemption regulation, Regulation 2790/1999 is not applicable.[5]

The motor vehicle sector has had a sector-specific block exemption regulation for some time. Commission Regulation 1475/95,[6] the former sector-specific regulation for the motor vehicle sector, expired on 30 September 2002 and was replaced by Commission Regulation 1400/2002 of 31 July 2002 on the application of Article 81(3) of the Treaty to categories of vertical agreements and concerted practices in the motor vehicle sector[7] (hereafter: "the Regulation" or "the new Regulation").

The new Regulation is applicable in the European Union. It is also applicable in the EEA.[8]

The new Regulation, which entered into force on 1 October 2002, introduces a number of substantial changes as regards the exemption of distribution agreements for new motor vehicles and spare parts. It also introduces major changes as regards the exemption of agreements for the provision of repair and maintenance services by authorised and independent repairers and other independent operators, such as on-road assistance operators, distributors of spare parts and providers of training for repairers.

The Commission has, however, a general policy to give stakeholders sufficient time to adapt to a new legal framework, and the new Regulation will therefore only become fully applicable after the end of the transition periods.[9]

This brochure is intended to serve as a guide to the Regulation for consumers[10] and other operators. It is also meant to help companies to make their own assessment as to the conformity of their vertical agreements with EC competition rules. It contains technical analysis and explanation, and gives answers to questions with which manufacturers, dealers, spare part producers and distributors, authorised and independent repairers and other independent operators involved in the sale and/or repair and maintenance of motor vehicles are likely to be confronted in practice. The brochure does not, however, give a detailed commentary on each provision of the Regulation, and is not legally binding.

Notes

[2] Article 81(1) provides that:

> *"The following shall be prohibited as incompatible with the common market: all agreements between undertakings, decisions by associations of undertakings and concerted practices which may affect trade between Member States and which have as their object or effect the prevention, restriction or distortion of competition within the common market, and in particular those which:*
> *(a) directly or indirectly fix purchase or selling prices or any other trading conditions;*
> *(b) limit or control production, markets, technical development, or investment;*
> *(c) share markets or sources of supply;*
> *(d) apply dissimilar conditions to equivalent transactions with other trading parties, thereby placing them at a competitive disadvantage;*
> *(e) make the conclusion of contracts subject to acceptance by the other parties of supplementary obligations which, by their nature or according to commercial usage, have no connection with the subject of such contracts."*

[3] Article 81(3) provides that:

> *"The provisions of paragraph 1 may, however, be declared inapplicable in the case of:*
> *— any agreement or category of agreements between undertakings;*
> *— any decision or category of decisions by associations of undertakings;*
> *— any concerted practice or category of concerted practices, which contributes to improving the production or distribution of goods or to promoting technical or economic progress, **while allowing consumers a fair share of the resulting benefit, (. . .)"***

[4] Commission Regulation (EC) No 2790/1999 of 22 December 1999 on the application of Article 81(3) of the Treaty to categories of vertical agreements and concerted practices (OJ L 336, 29.12.1999, p. 21).

[5] See Article 2(5) of Regulation 2790/1999.

[6] Commission Regulation (EC) No 1475/95 of 28 June 1995 on the application of Article 81(3) of the Treaty to certain categories of motor vehicle distribution and servicing agreements (OJ L 145, 29.6.1995, p. 25).

[7] OJ L 203, 1.8.2002, p. 30.

⁸ See Decision of the EEA Joint Committee 136/2002 of 27 September 2002 amending Annex XIV (Competition) to the EEA Agreement [OJ L 336, 12.12.2002, p. 38]; see also EEA Joint Committee Decision 46/96 of 19 July 1996 amending Annex XIV (Competition) to the EEA Agreement (OJ L 291, 14.11.1996, p. 39), according to which Regulation 1475/95 was also applicable in the EEA Member States.

⁹ See below section 4.8 and Articles 10 and 12 of the Regulation. Agreements which are compatible with the requirements of Regulation 1475/95 are exempted until 30.9.2003. Moreover, dealers of new motor vehicles in a selective distribution system may be prohibited until 30.9.2005 from opening additional outlets elsewhere in the European Union.

¹⁰ One of the main objectives of this brochure is to let consumers and their intermediaries know how the Regulation guarantees the freedom to buy a car anywhere in the European Union in accordance with the principles of the Single Market.

2. Structure of the Brochure

The brochure has the following structure:

Chapter 3 explains the <u>philosophy and aims</u> behind the Regulation, both as regards the distribution of motor vehicles and repair and maintenance services.

Chapter 4 contains an <u>explanation of the structure</u> of the Regulation and of certain legal aspects of each of its provisions. This may be of particular interest to lawyers and others who wish to better understand the scope and content of the various clauses of this Regulation.

Chapter 5 is particularly aimed at <u>consumers</u>, including their <u>intermediaries</u>, and at <u>dealers</u> in new vehicles, and <u>repairers</u>. It gives <u>answers to questions which are likely to arise</u> for each of these categories of stakeholder, in separate sections for each category. The replies to these questions may also be relevant for vehicle and spare part manufacturers and their wholesalers. Rights conferred on, for example, consumers or independent repairers, may also correspond to obligations incumbent on other operators, such as vehicle manufacturers.

Chapter 6 deals with technical issues relating to <u>market definition</u>.

Chapter 7 deals with <u>spare parts distribution</u> from a technical perspective.

Finally, a list of reference documents relevant to the new regime and the full text of the new Regulation are annexed to this brochure and are also available on DG Competition's web site.¹¹

Notes

¹¹ http://europa.eu.int/comm/competition/car_sector/

3. Philosophy of Regulation (EC) No 1400/2002

3.1. General Approach

Regulation 1400/2002 is a <u>block exemption regulation that is specific to the motor vehicle sector</u>. It covers agreements concerning the distribution of new motor vehicles and spare parts, and distribution agreements governing the provision of repair and maintenance services by authorised repairers. It also deals with the issue of access to technical information for independent operators which are directly or indirectly involved in the repair or maintenance of motor vehicles, such as independent repairers, and with access to spare parts.

Regulation 1400/2002 is <u>stricter</u> than its predecessor, Regulation 1475/95, and than Regulation 2790/1999, with a view to remedying the competition problems identified in this sector.¹²

Regulation 1400/2002 is however based on the Commission's general policy for the assessment of vertical restraints as laid down in Regulation 2790/1999 and in the accompanying Guidelines on Vertical Restraints.¹³ It is thus based on a more economic approach and on the principle that it is for the economic operators (manufacturers, dealers) to organise distribution according to their own needs. Consequently, the new Regulation is <u>less prescriptive</u> than Commission Regulation 1475/95, with a view to avoid the "straitjacket" effect¹⁴ observed in the case of Regulation 1475/95 and to allow the development of innovative distribution formats. The new Regulation takes account of the general policy that block exemption regulations should cover restrictive agreements only up to certain market share thresholds, in this case the threshold is generally 30%, although it is 40% for quantitative selection distribution of new motor vehicles. In addition, the new Regulation only covers agreements when certain general conditions,[15] for instance in relation to dispute resolution by an arbitrator, are fulfilled. An important part of the Regulation focuses on practices and behaviour which seriously restrict competition within the Common Market and which are detrimental to consumers. To this end, and in line with the Commission's general approach for block exemption regulations[16] it sets out a list of very serious restrictions (often referred to as "black clauses" or "hardcore restrictions") clarifying what is not normally permitted.[17] This list has been drawn up in order to remedy the drawbacks of Regulation 1475/95 and in order to take account of issues specific to the motor vehicle sector, in particular as regards repair and maintenance. Where these restrictions are present, not only will the agreement no longer benefit from the block exemption, but individual exemption is also unlikely. In addition to the hardcore list the new regulation imposes specific conditions on certain vertical restraints, in particular non-compete obligations and location clauses.[18] When these specific conditions are not fulfilled, these vertical restraints are excluded from the block exemption. However, the Regulation continues to apply to the rest of a vertical agreement if the remainder of the agreement can operate independently from the non-exempted vertical restraint. The non exempted vertical restraint will need an individual assessment under Article 81.

Notes

[12] See the Commission's report of 15 November 2000 on the evaluation of Regulation (EC) No 1475/95 on the application of Article 85(3) of the Treaty to certain categories of motor vehicle distribution and servicing agreements. Document COM(2000)743 final, published on the Internet under: http://europa.eu.int/comm/competition/car_sector/

[13] Commission Notice Guidelines on Vertical Restraints (OJ C 291, 13.10.2000, p. 1).

[14] This is an effect whereby, by exempting only one model for distribution, the Regulation encourages all suppliers to use near identical distribution systems, leading to rigidity.

[15] See Article 3 for general conditions.

[16] Commission Regulation 2790/1999; Commission Regulation (EC) No 2658/2000 of 29 November 2000 on the application of Article 81(3) of the Treaty to categories of specialisation agreements (OJ L 304, 5.12.2000 p. 3); Commission Regulation (EC) No 2659/2000 of 29 November 2000 on the application of Article 81(3) of the Treaty to categories of research and development agreements (OJ L 304, 5.12.2000 p. 7).

[17] See Article 4 for hardcore restrictions.

[18] See Article 5 for specific conditions.

3.2. Result of the New General Approach as Regards the Distribution and Servicing of Motor Vehicles

Figures available show[19] that the purchase price and the cost of repairing and maintaining a car each account for about 40% of the total cost of ownership.[20] Competition on the distribution and repair and maintenance markets is therefore of equal importance to consumers, and the Regulation therefore addresses competition issues relating to both.

The evaluation report adopted by the Commission on 15 November 2000 concluded that Regulation 1475/95 did not achieve certain of its principal aims.[21] Applying the general vertical block exemption regulation (Regulation 2790/1999) would also not solve all the problems identified in the evaluation report. Although it is based on the same non-prescriptive approach as Regulation 2790/1999, Regulation 1400/2002 therefore introduces a stricter approach.

As regards the **distribution of new motor vehicles**, the Regulation is built around the following principles:

— banning the combination of selective and exclusive distribution permitted by Regulation 1475/95. To benefit from the new Regulation, manufacturers have to choose between creating selective and exclusive distribution systems when appointing their distributors;

— reinforcing competition between dealers in different Member States (intra-brand competition) and improving market integration in particular by not exempting distribution agreements which restrict passive sales, by not exempting distribution agreements in selective distribution systems which restrict active sales, and by not exempting clauses (commonly referred to as "location clauses") prohibiting dealers in selective distribution systems from establishing additional outlets elsewhere in the Common Market;[22]

- <u>removing</u> the obligation for the same firm to carry out both sales and servicing[23] by not exempting agreements that do not allow dealers to subcontract servicing and repair to authorised repairers who belong to the authorised repair network of the brand in question and who therefore fulfil the manufacturer's quality standards;[24]
- <u>facilitating</u> multi-branding by not exempting restrictions on the sale of motor vehicles of different brands by one dealer.[25] Suppliers may however impose an obligation for motor vehicles of different brands to be exhibited in different areas of the same showroom;
- <u>maintaining</u> the "availability clause" by not exempting agreements that limit a dealer's ability to sell cars with different specifications to the equivalent models within the dealer's contract range. This should make it possible for a consumer to obtain vehicles from a dealer in another Member State with the specifications current in the consumer's home Member State, for example allowing UK and Irish consumers to buy new right-hand-drive cars in mainland Europe;[26]
- <u>supporting</u> the use of intermediaries or purchasing agents by consumers.[27] These operators are an important tool to help consumers to buy a vehicle in another part of the Common Market;
- <u>strengthening</u> dealers' independence from manufacturers, both by stimulating multi-brand sales and by strengthening minimum standards of contractual protection (including retaining the existing minimum notice periods provided for in Regulation 1475/95) and by allowing them to realise the value that they have built up by giving them the freedom to sell their businesses to other dealers authorised to sell the same brand.[28]

In sum, Regulation 1400/2002 sets up a regime which should stimulate the development of innovative distribution methods and thereby enhance competition.

As regards **repair and maintenance of motor vehicles**, Regulation 1400/2002 is based on the same stricter approach while retaining certain elements of the previous Regulation 1475/95, since Regulation 2790/1999 does not contain provisions that are sufficiently adapted to repair and maintenance of motor vehicles. Given the size of consumer expenditure on repair and maintenance, it is important to ensure that they can choose between different alternatives and that all operators (dealers, authorised repairers, independent repairers including body shops, fast fit chains and service centres) can offer good quality services and thereby contribute to vehicle safety and reliability.

Consequently, as regards repair and maintenance, Regulation 1400/2002 pursues the following aims:
- to allow manufacturers to set selection criteria for authorised repairers, so long as these do not prevent the exercise of any of the rights enshrined in the Regulation;
- to ensure that if a supplier of new motor vehicles sets qualitative criteria for the authorised repairers belonging to its network, all operators who fulfil those criteria can join the network. This approach will enhance competition between authorised repairers by making sure that operators with the necessary technical expertise can establish themselves wherever there is a business opportunity;
- to improve authorised repairers' access to spare parts which compete with parts sold by the vehicle manufacturer;
- to preserve and reinforce the competitive position of independent repairers; these currently carry out on average about 50% of all repairs on motor cars.[29] The Regulation improves their position by reinforcing their ability to gain access to spare parts and technical information in line with technical advances, especially in the field of electronic devices and diagnostic equipment. The access right is also extended to training and to all types of tools since access to all four of these elements is necessary if an operator is to be able to provide after sales services. A desirable and important side effect of this wider access is to encourage improvement in independent repairers' technical skills, to the benefit of road safety and consumers in general.

Taking all of these elements into account, Regulation 1400/2002 reinforces competition on the markets for the distribution of new motor vehicles and for the provision of after sales services.

Notes

[19] Andersen, Study on the impact of possible future legislative scenarios for motor vehicle distribution on all parties concerned, p. 43, chapter II.2.1.B; published on the Internet: http://europa.eu.int/comm/competition/car_sector/.

[20] The remaining 20% being for financing, insurance and other costs.

[21] See Commission Report on the evaluation of Regulation 1475/95.

---

[22] After 30 September 2005. See Article 5(2)(b) and Article 12(2). With a location clause, a manufacturer obliges a dealer only to operate from a certain place of establishment, which may be an address, a town or a territory.

[23] This is commonly referred to as the sales-service link.

[24] Article 4(1)(g).

[25] Article 5(1)(a) and (c).

[26] Article 4(1)(f).

[27] Recital 14.

[28] Article 3(3) and 3(5).

[29] Andersen study, p. 254, appendix 8; Accenture, Study on the Impact of Legislative Scenarios on Motor Vehicle Distribution, September 2001, commissioned by ACEA, p. 11.

---

4. Contents of the Regulation

This chapter surveys the contents of various Articles of the Regulation and aims at illustrating certain provisions which may require interpretation. It contains an enumeration and explanation of the Articles, illustrated as much as possible with references to the recitals of the Regulation, examples and answers to questions that legal practitioners and suppliers of motor vehicles or spare parts which organise a distribution network may ask The section also contains references to other Commission Notices which provide conceptual guidance on enforcement issues.

4.1. Definitions Used in the Regulation (Article 1)

Article 1 contains a list of definitions which clarify the meaning which needs to be given to certain words or expressions used in the text of other Articles of the Regulation. When relevant, the precise definition is provided below with the text of the Article(s) in which such words or expressions are used.

4.2. Scope of application of the Regulation (Article 2)

Article 2
Scope

1. Pursuant to Article 81(3) of the Treaty and subject to the provisions of this Regulation, it is hereby declared that the provisions of Article 81(1) shall not apply to vertical agreements where they relate to the conditions under which the parties may purchase, sell or resell new motor vehicles, spare parts for motor vehicles or repair and maintenance services for motor vehicles.

   The first subparagraph shall apply to the extent that such vertical agreements contain vertical restraints.

   The exemption declared by this paragraph shall be known for the purposes of this Regulation as "the exemption".

   (. . .)

4.2.1. Products and services covered by the scope of the Regulation

---

Article 1
Definitions

1. For the purposes of this Regulation:

   (. . .)

   (n) "Motor vehicle" means a self propelled vehicle intended for use on public roads and having three or more road wheels.

   (. . .)

   (s) "Spare parts" means goods which are to be installed in or upon a motor vehicle so as to replace components of that vehicle, including goods such as lubricants which are necessary for the use of a motor vehicle, with the exception of fuel.

   (. . .)

Question 1: Where does the borderline lie between the new Regulation 1400/2002 and Regulation 2790/1999 on vertical agreements?

Article 2(5) of Regulation 2790/1999 on vertical agreements declares that it does not apply to vertical agreements whose subject matter falls within the scope of any other block exemption regulation. It follows that Regulation 2790/1999 does not apply to vertical agreements that concern new motor vehicles, repair and maintenance services for motor vehicles and spare parts for motor vehicles, as defined in the Regulation. An agreement whose subject matter falls within the scope of application of the Regulation[30] but which fails to meet other requirements set out therein,[31] does not fall within the scope of application of Regulation 2790/1999.

Notes
[30] See Article 2, Scope.
[31] For instance Articles 3, 4 or 5.

Question 2: Does the Regulation apply to all agreements regarding vehicles and spare parts?

No. The Regulation does not apply, *inter alia*, to vehicles which are not motor vehicles,[32] to motor vehicles which are not new,[33] to loans by banks which finance the purchase of a vehicle by an end-user or to goods which are not spare parts as defined in the Regulation.[34]

Notes
[32] The definition of motor vehicles is the same as under Regulation 1475/95. Some vehicles do not fall within this definition because they are not self-propelled, like horse-drawn wagons, because they have less than three wheels, like motor-bikes, or because they are not intended for use on public roads, though they may occasionally circulate on public roads, like tractors or earthmoving machines.
[33] For instance the second-hand car market.
[34] For instance because they are not necessary for the use of a motor vehicle, though they may be fitted in it, like accessories such as a tape, CD or other accessories according to trade usage (for an explanation see below Chapter 7).

Many replacement products are specific to motor vehicles as defined in the Regulation and therefore fall clearly within the definition of spare parts in Article 1(1)(s). However, certain goods, such as lubricants, paint and generic products such as screws, nuts and bolts, may have dual — or multiple — uses. While they can be installed in or upon a motor vehicle so as to replace components of that vehicle, they may also have end uses in relation to types of vehicles not covered by the Regulation (e.g. motor bikes, tractors) or in even more diverse contexts. Therefore, such goods should only be regarded as spare parts within the meaning of Article 1(1)(s), with the result that vertical agreements for their distribution fall within the scope of the Regulation, where it is reasonably certain that they are destined for installation in or upon a motor vehicle. In practice, this will occur where the buyer's activity is in the motor vehicle repair sector or in the supply of that sector.

This would exclude from the scope of the Regulation, at one level of trade, vertical agreements whereby wholesalers purchase such products for onward distribution to a wide variety of customers and, at quite another level of trade, agreements regarding products destined for direct sale to end users, as the circumstances of final use will in both cases be far from clear. For instance, a vertical agreement between a manufacturer of screws and a do-it-yourself store does not fall within the scope of the Regulation, even though the manufacturer also supplies the same screws to a manufacturer of motor vehicles or to the motor vehicle repair sector. Nor does an agreement with a distributor of, for instance, paints or lubricants, unless his type of activity leads to reasonable certainty that such goods will be used only for installation in or upon a motor vehicle which falls under the Regulation. Such reasonable certainty does not exist for the sale of paints or lubricants for retail to filling stations, supermarkets or do-it-yourself stores. To the extent that vertical agreements relate to vehicles, goods or services not covered by the Regulation, they fall, in principle, within the scope of Regulation 2790/1999.

4.2.2. Categories of agreements falling within the scope of the Regulation

---

Article 1
Definitions

1. For the purposes of this Regulation:

   (...)

   (c) "Vertical agreements" means agreements or concerted practices entered into by two or more undertakings, each of which operates, for the purposes of the agreement, at a different level of the production or distribution chain.

   (...).

Article 2
Scope

(...)

2. The exemption shall also apply to the following categories of vertical agreements:

   (a) Vertical agreements entered into between an association of undertakings and its members, or between such an association and its suppliers, only if all its members are distributors of motor vehicles or spare parts for motor vehicles or repairers and if no individual member of the association, together with its connected undertakings, has a total annual turnover exceeding EUR 50 million; vertical agreements entered into by such associations shall be covered by this Regulation without prejudice to the application of Article 81 to horizontal agreements concluded between the members of the association or decisions adopted by the association;

   (b) vertical agreements containing provisions which relate to the assignment to the buyer or use by the buyer of intellectual property rights, provided that those provisions do not constitute the primary object of such agreements and are directly related to the use, sale or resale of goods or services by the buyer or its customers. The exemption shall apply on condition that those provisions do not contain restrictions of competition relating to the contract goods or services which have the same object or effect as vertical restraints which are not exempted under this Regulation.

3. The exemption shall not apply to vertical agreements entered into between competing undertakings.

   However, it shall apply where competing undertakings enter into a non-reciprocal vertical agreement and:

   (a) the buyer has a total annual turnover not exceeding EUR 100 million, or

   (b) the supplier is a manufacturer and a distributor of goods, while the buyer is a distributor not manufacturing goods competing with the contract goods, or

   (c) the supplier is a provider of services at several levels of trade, while the buyer does not provide competing services at the level of trade where it purchases the contract services.

Question 3: Which types of vertical agreements are covered by the Regulation?

The Regulation applies to vertical agreements in the motor vehicle sector at all levels of trade from the stage first supply of a new motor vehicle by its manufacturer to the final resale to end consumers and from the first supply of spare parts by their manufacturer to the provision of repair and maintenance services to end consumers. The Regulation covers, inter alia, vertical agreements between:

— a manufacturer of motor vehicles or its subsidiary and independent importers or wholesalers, that are not subsidiaries of the manufacturer and that may be entrusted with the supply and management of the manufacturer's distribution and repair network in one or several Member States, even where the manufacturer has incorporated import and wholesale subsidiaries in those or other Member States;[35]

— a manufacturer of motor vehicles or its subsidiary and individual members of its authorised network of distributors and repairers, including the licensing of intellectual property rights held by the manufacturer;[36]

— a manufacturer of motor vehicles, a main distributor and a sub-distributor or an agent in two or three-tier distribution networks.[37] Such agreements are covered irrespective of whether the sub-distributors are selected by and contractually linked with the vehicle manufacturer or whether main distributors select and enter into contracts with sub-distributors on the basis of criteria set by the manufacturer;[38]

— a manufacturer of motor vehicles or spare parts and an association of authorised or independent dealers or repairers who jointly buy motor vehicles or spare parts, if none of the individual members of the association has a total annual turnover exceeding EUR 50 million;[39]

— a supplier of spare parts and individual members of a network of independent or authorised repairers who use these spare parts to provide repair and maintenance services.

The scope of application of the Regulation is thus broader than Regulation 1475/95 as it includes agreements, for instance, with importers or wholesalers of motor vehicles which do not provide after-sales services, with repairers who do not sell cars and with suppliers who provide spare parts to repairers.

Notes

[35] Article 2(3)(a) and (b).

[36] Article 2(2)(b), e.g. the use of the trade-mark affixed in the showroom in which vehicles are sold or the disclosure of know-how for the provision of repair services of a particular brand.

[37] Recital 3.

[38] The Regulation does not prevent the use of single tier distribution systems. The choice as to whether and how systems are organised lies with the manufacturer or supplier whose motor vehicles and spare parts are supplied through the network. Distribution agreements concluded by a dealer with other undertakings were also subject to the supplier's consent, pursuant to Article 3(6) of Regulation 1475/95.

[39] Article 2(2)(a).

Question 4: Do vertical agreements fall within the scope of the Regulation when the supplier also sells motor vehicles directly to end consumers in competition with its distribution network?

In general the Regulation does not apply to vertical agreements entered into between competing undertakings. However, certain vertical agreements between competitors fall within the scope of the Regulation. In particular, Article 2(3) extends the scope of the Regulation to situations of dual distribution so as to cover the various vertical agreements that a motor vehicle manufacturer that sells directly to end users may conclude with individual members of its network(s) of authorised distributors. The Regulation does not set out any specific requirements as to the coexistence of manufacturer-owned outlets and those owned and run by authorised distributor's.

Question 5: Do agency agreements fall within the scope of the Regulation?

Agency agreements are common in the motor vehicle sector. The Commission draws a dividing line between "genuine" and "non-genuine" agency agreements for the purposes of EC competition law following the criteria set out in its Guidelines on Vertical Restraints, irrespective of how such agreements are categorised under national civil law.[40] Genuine agency agreements, that is, those where the agent bears insignificant or no financial and commercial risk in respect of the contract concluded or negotiated on behalf of its principal and in respect of market-specific investments for that field of activity, are not prohibited under Article 81(1) and do not fall within the scope of the Regulation. Non-genuine agency agreements, on the other hand, do fall within the scope of the Regulation.[41]

Notes

[40] Guidelines on Vertical Restraints, Section II.2 Agency agreements, paragraphs 12 to 20.

[41] Such non-genuine agency agreements may fall under Article 81(1) and also fell under Regulation 1475/95, see also Commission Decision of 10.10.2001 — *DaimlerChrysler* — (case COMP/36.264 — *Mercedes-Benz*), OJ L 257, 25.9.2002, p. 1.

Question 6: What are the requirements that the agreements must, in general, fulfil to comply with the Regulation and what are the consequences of this compliance?

In order for the Regulation to apply to agreements which fall within its scope of application, the general conditions set out in Article 3 must be met and clauses or stipulations between the parties must neither directly nor indirectly amount to hardcore restrictions, as enumerated in Article 4.

Specific obligations which do not meet the conditions enumerated in Article 5 are not exempted, but it may be possible under national contract law to sever such obligations from the remainder of the agreement leaving the remainder to be covered by the block exemption. The use of pressure, financial incentives or disincentives, leases of commercial premises, or other measures[42] which limit or attempt at limiting the independent behaviour of a distributor or repairer to carry out the types of pro-competitive behaviour which Articles 4 and 5 favour or which undermine the rights enshrined in Article 3 are not exempted under the Regulation. All other restraints or stipulations contained in agreements which meet these requirements may benefit from the block exemption, as Article 2 renders the prohibition laid down in Article 81(1) inapplicable in respect of such agreements.

The Regulation relieves the parties from the task of showing that in their specific economic and legal context, their agreements meet the conditions of Article 81(3). The Regulation, which is binding and directly applicable in all Member States, ensures throughout the European Union that such agreements cannot be held null and void pursuant to Article 81(2). In accordance with the principle of primacy of Community law, no measure taken in pursuance of national laws on competition by national authorities or courts should prejudice the uniform application of the Regulation throughout the Common Market.

Notes

[42] For example, if the manufacturer is a minority shareholder of one of its dealers and agrees with the other shareholders that the dealer will no longer engage in multi-branding or not open further sales or delivery outlets after 30 September 2005 this would be regarded as a disguised vertical agreement which would fall within the definition of Article (1)(1)(c) and which would not be exempted under Article 5(1)(a) or 5(2)(b).

4.3. General Conditions of Application (Article 3)

Article 3 of the Regulation sets out five general conditions which agreements must fulfil for the block exemption to apply. The first of these limits the application of the exemption to situations where certain market share thresholds are not exceeded and below which it can be safely assumed that the conditions of Article 81(3) will in general be fulfilled. The other conditions require the inclusion of several provisions in the agreement which promote contractual stability, hence enabling distributors or repairers to compete vigorously and pass on to consumers the benefits of improved distribution.

4.3.1. Market share thresholds

Article 3
General conditions

1. Subject to paragraphs 2, 3, 4, 5, 6 and 7, the exemption shall apply on condition that the supplier's market share on the relevant market on which it sells the new motor vehicles, spare parts for motor vehicles or repair and maintenance services does not exceed 30%.

   However, the market share threshold for the application of the exemption shall be 40% for agreements establishing quantitative selective distribution systems for the sale of new motor vehicles.

   Those thresholds shall not apply to agreements establishing qualitative selective distribution systems.

2. In the case of vertical agreements containing exclusive supply obligations, the exemption shall apply on condition that the market share held by the buyer does not exceed 30% of the relevant market on which it purchases the contract goods or services.

   (. . .)

Article 1

Definitions

1. For the purposes of this Regulation:

   (. . .)

   (e) "Exclusive supply obligation" means any direct or indirect obligation causing the supplier to sell the contract goods or services only to one buyer inside the common market for the purposes of a specific use or for resale.

   (f) "Selective distribution system" means a distribution system where the supplier undertakes to sell the contract goods or services, either directly or indirectly, only to distributors or repairers selected on the basis of specified criteria and where these distributors or repairers undertake not to sell such goods or services to unauthorised distributors or independent repairers, without prejudice to the ability to sell spare parts to independent repairers or the obligation to provide independent operators with all technical information, diagnostic equipment, tools and training required for the repair and maintenance of motor vehicles or for the implementation of environmental protection measures.

   (g) "Quantitative selective distribution system" means a selective distribution system where the supplier uses criteria for the selection of distributors or repairers which directly limit their number.

   (h) "Qualitative selective distribution system" means a selective distribution system where the supplier uses criteria for the selection of distributors or repairers which are only qualitative in nature, are required by the nature of the contract goods or services, are laid down uniformly for all distributors or repairers applying to join the distribution system, are not applied in a discriminatory manner, and do not directly limit the number of distributors or repairers.

   (. . .)

As with Regulation 2790/1999, the application of the Regulation requires, in principle, a definition of the relevant product market(s) and of the relevant geographic market(s) affected by the vertical agreements ("relevant market"). Except where qualitative selective distribution is used,[43] vertical agreements can only benefit from the block exemption when certain market share thresholds are not exceeded; generally the relevant threshold is 30%, although it is 40% for quantitative selective distribution agreements for the sale of new motor vehicles. The application of the Regulation to distribution agreements other than those providing for qualitative selective distribution thus implies firstly the definition of the relevant market(s) affected by the agreements and secondly, the calculation of market shares.

To calculate its market share, a company has to take into account its connected undertakings.[44] If a company or its connected undertakings supply vehicles of different brands which belong to the same product market, it has to take them all into account when calculating its market share. If its market share exceeds the threshold, the Regulation will not cover any of the distribution agreements even if, taken individually, none of these brands exceeds those thresholds. Similarly, if the same agreement is used in different geographic areas to distribute motor vehicles or spare parts or to provide repair and maintenance services pertaining to different relevant markets and the thresholds are exceeded for some of them, the Regulation covers the agreements only on the relevant markets for which the thresholds are not exceeded.

The Guidelines on Vertical Restraints indicate the policy which the Commission follows in such cases.[45] Further issues of market definition and calculation of market shares are dealt with in chapter 6.

Notes

[43] See definition of Article 1(1)(h).

[44] See definition of connected undertakings at Article 1(2) and section 6.2. below.

[45] Guidelines on Vertical Restraints, paragraphs 62, 68–69. More generally, for the analysis of individual cases, see paragraphs 100 to 229 and in particular paragraphs 184–198 on selective distribution.

Question 7: Can agreements in the motor vehicle sector be covered by the De Minimis Notice?[46]

Yes, whereas the Regulation provides an exemption from the prohibition in Article 81(1) because the positive effects of the agreement outweigh the negative effects, the de *minimis* Notice quantifies with the help of lower market share thresholds, what is not, in the Commission's view, an appreciable restriction of competition in the first place and for that reason not prohibited by Article 81(1). A vertical agreement between non-competitors whose market share on the relevant market does not exceed 15% is generally considered not to have appreciable anti-competitive effects, unless the agreement contains a hardcore restriction.[47] The same is true for vertical agreements between competitors, like in situations of dual distribution[48] when their market share does not exceed 10%.

Where the market is foreclosed by the application of parallel networks of similar vertical agreements by several companies, the *de minimis* threshold is set at 5%. For instance, a cumulative effect may arise where more than 30% of competing motor vehicles are marketed through selective distribution systems, which by their criteria prevent access to the market to categories of distributors capable of adequately selling the vehicles in question.[49] Cumulative effects also arise if non-compete obligations on distributors or repairers foreclose access to the market to certain suppliers. These *de-minimis* thresholds are important in relation to the conditions as contained in articles 3 and 5 of the Regulation. These conditions do not apply to agreements below the *de minimis* thresholds.

In practice, on the basis of the information available, *de minimis* market share thresholds are very likely to be exceeded in the case of agreements entered into by a motor vehicle manufacturer and its authorised repair network as regards the provision of brand-specific spare parts, repair and maintenance services.[50]

Notes

[46] Commission Notice on agreements of minor importance which do not appreciably restrict competition under Article 81(1) of the Treaty establishing the European Community, OJ C 368, 22.12.2001, p. 13.

[47] Severely anti-competitive restraints, that is, those listed in Article 4 of the Regulation (hardcore restrictions) generally constitute appreciable restrictions of competition even at low market shares; see Recital 12.

[48] Article 1(1)(a) of the Regulation defines competitors as "actual or potential suppliers on the same product market" irrespective of where they supply the products. It follows from the definition that suppliers which also sell vehicles or provide services to end-users are considered as competitors of their distribution or repair network who sell the same vehicles or provide the same services.

[49] Article 1(1)(f), (g) and (h). See also the Commission's report on the evaluation of Regulation 1475/95, paragraphs 20 and 82, and Guidelines on Vertical Restraints, paragraphs 82 and 104 to 114.

[50] See below Chapter 6 on market definition.

4.3.2. General conditions on specific provisions which must be included in the agreements

Article 3
General conditions

(. . .)

3. The exemption shall apply on condition that the vertical agreement concluded with a distributor or repairer provides that the supplier agrees to the transfer of the rights and obligations resulting from the vertical agreement to another distributor or repairer within the distribution system and chosen by the former distributor or repairer.

4. The exemption shall apply on condition that the vertical agreement concluded with a distributor or repairer provides that a supplier who wishes to give notice of termination of an agreement must give such notice in writing and must include detailed, objective and transparent reasons for the termination, in order to prevent a supplier from ending a vertical agreement with a distributor or repairer because of practices which may not be restricted under this Regulation.

5. The exemption shall apply on condition that the vertical agreement concluded by the supplier of new motor vehicles with a distributor or authorised repairer provides

(a) that the agreement is concluded for a period of at least five years; in this case each party has to undertake to give the other party at least six months' prior notice of its intention not to renew the agreement;

> (b) or that the agreement is concluded for an indefinite period; in this case the period of notice for regular termination of the agreement has to be at least two years for both parties; this period is reduced to at least one year where:
>
> > (i) the supplier is obliged by law or by special agreement to pay appropriate compensation on termination of the agreement, or
> > (ii) the supplier terminates the agreement where it is necessary to re-organise the whole or a substantial part of the network.
>
> 6. The exemption shall apply on condition that the vertical agreement provides for each of the parties the right to refer disputes concerning the fulfilment of their contractual obligations to an independent expert or arbitrator. Such disputes may relate *inter alia* to any of the following:
>   (a) supply obligations;
>   (b) the setting or attainment of sales targets;
>   (c) the implementation of stock requirements;
>   (d) the implementation of an obligation to provide or use demonstration vehicles;
>   (e) the conditions for the sale of different brands;
>   (f) the issue whether the prohibition to operate out of an unauthorised place of establishment limits the ability of the distributor of motor vehicles other than passenger cars or light commercial vehicles to expand its business; or
>   (g) the issue whether the termination of an agreement is justified by the reasons given in the notice.
>
> > The right referred to in the first sentence is without prejudice to each party's right to make an application to a national court.
>
> (. . .)

The four other general conditions of Article 3 of the Regulation aim at safeguarding a relatively stable contractual framework in which sellers of new vehicles or providers of repair services can engage in vigorous competition. The Regulation requires that there be a right to transfer a dealership or authorised repair business together with all related rights and obligations to another member of the brand network,[51] an obligation to give reasons for contract termination,[52] a right of referral of contract disputes to an arbitrator[53] and a minimum duration for i) fixed-term contracts ii) periods of notice for non-renewal or termination of the contract.[54] The obligation to give reasons for contract termination and the ability to transfer rights and obligations were not provided for by Regulation 1475/95.

Notes
[51] Article 3(3).
[52] Article 3(4).
[53] Article 3(6).
[54] Article 3(5).

Question 8: Can an individual exemption be granted in respect of an agreement which does not meet the general conditions of the Regulation as to contractual protection?

If a vertical agreement in this sector is caught by Article 81(1),[55] and the Regulation does not apply, the parties can only avoid the agreement being null and void pursuant to Article 81(2) by meeting the requirements for an individual exemption pursuant to Article 81(3). When the Regulation does not apply, it is the entire combination of restrictive provisions in the agreement which needs to be taken into account in respect of the application of Article 81.

The introduction of the general conditions on contractual protection is part of the specific, stricter rules devised by the Commission for this sector compared to other economic sectors. This is based on the Commission's experience that a stable contractual framework allows for the benefits of distribution and for cost savings to be passed on to consumers.[56] Therefore, a party which applies for an individual exemption should show why, in its specific case, the absence of relevant provisions on contractual protection in its vertical agreements helps to attain or does not obstruct the attainment of the positive effects referred to in Article 81(3).

Notes
[55] See above, question 7.
[56] Recitals 1 and 4.

Question 9: Do all vertical agreements falling within the scope of the Regulation need to comply with all the conditions which relate to contractual matters to be able to benefit from the block exemption?

The right to refer disputes concerning the fulfilment of their contractual obligations to an independent expert or arbitrator as set out in Article 3(6) applies to all vertical agreements falling within the scope of the Regulation. The conditions on contractual protection set out in Article 3(3) and (4) apply to restrictive agreements to which distributors or repairers are a party. The relevant general condition regarding the minimum duration of contracts and periods of notice set out in Article 3(5) only applies to agreements between suppliers of new motor vehicles and their distributors or authorised repairers.

Question 10: Can a supplier restrict the transfer of rights and obligations to another member of the supplier's network, if the other member does not carry out the same kind of activity as the member selling its business?

Yes. The Regulation fosters competition and market integration by facilitating acquisitions of businesses by prospective acquirers who are members of the distribution or the repair network.[57] Such prospective acquirers fulfil the criteria set out by the supplier elsewhere and thus benefit from a presumption that they also fulfil those criteria in respect of the business operations of the selling member of the network. For instance, differences as to selection or sales criteria between network members who carry out the same kind of activity, even in other Member States, cannot be used to prevent transfers of rights and obligations. However, there may be no such presumption if the activities of the acquirer and the seller, such as selling new motor vehicles and repairing them, differ completely. The Regulation therefore does   not stop suppliers from preventing transfers in such cases.

Notes
[57] Article 3(3). See Recital 10 regarding transfers to "undertakings of the same type . . . within the distribution system".

4.4. Hardcore Restrictions (Article 4)

Article 4
Hardcore restrictions

(Hardcore restrictions concerning the sale of new motor vehicles, repair and maintenance services or spare parts)

1. The exemption shall not apply to vertical agreements which, directly or indirectly, in isolation or in combination with other factors under the control of the parties, have as their object:

    (a) the restriction of the distributor's or repairer's ability to determine its sale price, without prejudice to the supplier's ability to impose a maximum sale price or to recommend a sale price, provided that this does not amount to a fixed or minimum sale price as a result of pressure from, or incentives offered by, any of the parties;

    (b) the restriction of the territory into which, or of the customers to whom, the distributor or repairer may sell the contract goods or services; however, the exemption shall apply to:

        (i) the restriction of active sales into the exclusive territory or to an exclusive customer group reserved to the supplier or allocated by the supplier to another distributor or repairer, where such a restriction does not limit sales by the customers of the distributor or repairer,

        (ii) the restriction of sales to end users by a distributor operating at the wholesale level of trade,

        (iii) the restriction of sales of new motor vehicles and spare parts to unauthorised distributors by the members of a selective distribution system in markets where selective distribution is applied, subject to the provisions of point (i),

        (iv) the restriction of the buyer's ability to sell components, supplied for the purposes of incorporation, to customers who would use them to manufacture the same type of goods as those produced by the supplier;

(c) the restriction of cross-supplies between distributors or repairers within a selective distribution system, including between distributors or repairers operating at different levels of trade;

(d) the restriction of active or passive sales of new passenger cars or light commercial vehicles, spare parts for any motor vehicle or repair and maintenance services for any motor vehicle to end users by members of a selective distribution system operating at the retail level of trade in markets where selective distribution is used. The exemption shall apply to agreements containing a prohibition on a member of a selective distribution system from operating out of an unauthorised place of establishment. However, the application of the exemption to such a prohibition is subject to Article 5(2)(b);

(e) the restriction of active or passive sales of new motor vehicles other than passenger cars or light commercial vehicles to end users by members of a selective distribution system operating at the retail level of trade in markets where selective distribution is used, without prejudice to the ability of the supplier to prohibit a member of that system from operating out of an unauthorised place of establishment;

(Hardcore restrictions only concerning the sale of new motor vehicles)

(f) the restriction of the distributor's ability to sell any new motor vehicle which corresponds to a model within its contract range;

(g) the restriction of the distributor's ability to subcontract the provision of repair and maintenance services to authorised repairers, without prejudice to the ability of the supplier to require the distributor to give end users the name and address of the authorised repairer or repairers in question before the conclusion of a sales contract and, if any of these authorised repairers is not in the vicinity of the sales outlet, to also tell end users how far the repair shop or repair shops in question are from the sales outlet; however, such obligations may only be imposed provided that similar obligations are imposed on distributors whose repair shop is not on the same premises as their sales outlet;

(Hardcore restrictions only concerning the sale of repair and maintenance services and of spare parts)

(h) the restriction of the authorised repairer's ability to limit its activities to the provision of repair and maintenance services and the distribution of spare parts;

(i) the restriction of the sales of spare parts for motor vehicles by members of a selective distribution system to independent repairers which use these parts for the repair and maintenance of a motor vehicle;

(j) the restriction agreed between a supplier of original spare parts or spare parts of matching quality, repair tools or diagnostic or other equipment and a manufacturer of motor vehicles, which limits the supplier's ability to sell these goods or services to authorised or independent distributors or to authorised or independent repairers or end users;

(k) the restriction of a distributor's or authorised repairer's ability to obtain original spare parts or spare parts of matching quality from a third undertaking of its choice and to use them for the repair or maintenance of motor vehicles, without prejudice to the ability of a supplier of new motor vehicles to require the use of original spare parts supplied by it for repairs carried out under warranty, free servicing and vehicle recall work;

(l) the restriction agreed between a manufacturer of motor vehicles which uses components for the initial assembly of motor vehicles and the supplier of such components which limits the latter's ability to place its trade mark or logo effectively and in an easily visible manner on the components supplied or on spare parts.

2. The exemption shall not apply where the supplier of motor vehicles refuses to give independent operators access to any technical information, diagnostic and other equipment, tools, including any relevant software, or training required for the repair and maintenance of these motor vehicles or for the implementation of environmental protection measures.

Such access must include in particular the unrestricted use of the electronic control and diagnostic systems of a motor vehicle, the programming of these systems in accordance with the supplier's standard procedures, the repair and training instructions and the information required for the use of diagnostic and servicing tools and equipment.

Access must be given to independent operators in a non-discriminatory, prompt and proportionate way, and the information must be provided in a usable form. If the relevant item is covered by an intellectual property right or constitutes know-how, access shall not be withheld in any abusive manner.

For the purposes of this paragraph "independent operator" shall mean undertakings which are directly or indirectly involved in the repair and maintenance of motor vehicles, in particular independent repairers, manufacturers of repair equipment or tools, independent distributors of spare parts, publishers of technical information, automobile clubs, roadside assistance operators, operators offering inspection and testing services and operators offering training for repairers.

Article 4 of the Regulation contains a list of 13 severely anti-competitive restraints (hardcore restrictions). The presence of one or more of these restraints in an agreement would automatically lead to the benefit of the block exemption being lost in respect of the entire agreement, and not only the vertical restraint concerned. In its enforcement of EC competition rules, the Commission considers that the individual exemption of vertical agreements containing hardcore restrictions is unlikely.[58]

Notes
[58] Guidelines on Vertical Restraints, paragraph 46.

Question 11: Can the same hardcore restriction be arrived at in different ways?

To avoid circumvention, the Regulation defines hardcore restraints as provisions which, directly or indirectly, in isolation or in combination with other factors under the control of the parties, have the object of restricting a certain ability,[59] or a certain type of sale.[60] This broad definition indicates that each of the hardcore restrictions can be brought about through one or more indirect means, and that in practice this may result in an anticompetitive outcome similar to that resulting from the express inclusion of the restriction in question in the written contract. Hardcore restrictions may of course take the form of outright prohibitions, but may also consist of limitations, financial disincentives, pressures or obstacles to certain activities or transactions. Recitals 12 to 26 set out some of many possible examples of agreements or practices which may indirectly constitute hardcore restrictions for the purposes of the Regulation.[61]

For instance, several provisions or practices listed in Recitals 16 and 17 may constitute hardcore restrictions by indirectly restricting active or passive sales of a distributor.

(. . .)

WHEREAS:

(. . .)

(16) Limits placed by suppliers on their distributors' sales to any end user in other Member States, for instance where distributor remuneration or the purchase price is made dependent on the destination of the vehicles or on the place of residence of the end users, amount to an indirect restriction on sales. Other examples of indirect restrictions on sales include supply quotas based on a sales territory other than the common market, whether or not these are combined with sales targets. Bonus systems based on the destination of the vehicles or any form of discriminatory product supply to distributors, whether in the case of product shortage or otherwise, also amount to an indirect restriction on sales.

(. . .)

(17) Vertical agreements that do not oblige the authorised repairers within a supplier's distribution system to honour warranties, perform free servicing and carry out recall work in respect of any motor vehicle of the relevant make sold in the common market amount to an indirect restriction of sales and should not benefit from the exemption. [.] Furthermore, in order to allow sales by motor vehicle distributors to end users throughout the common market, the exemption should apply only to distribution agreements which require the repairers within the supplier's network to carry out repair and maintenance services for the contract goods and corresponding goods irrespective of where these goods are sold in the common market.

(. . .)

Notes
59 Article 4(1)(a), (f), (g), (h), (j), (k) and (l).
60 Article 4(1)(b), (c), (d), (e), and (i).
61 See also examples given in question 6.

Question 12: What are active and passive sales?

"Active sales" means actively approaching individual customers by for instance direct mail or visits, through advertisement in media, or by other promotions not normally available or in circulation at the authorised place of establishment of a dealer or repairer;62 or by establishing a warehouse or sales or delivery outlet at another place of establishment to facilitate dealings with customers or their intermediaries.

"Passive sales" means responding to unsolicited requests from customers or their duly authorised intermediaries including delivery of motor vehicles or spare parts to such customers or intermediaries. General advertising or promotions in media which are normally available or in circulation at the authorised place of establishment of the dealer or repairer or on the Internet are passive sales methods.

Notes
62 In a distribution system based on territorial exclusivity the place of establishment is deemed to be his exclusive territory.

4.5. Specific Conditions (Article 5)

> *Article 5*
> **Specific conditions**
> 1. As regards the sale of new motor vehicles, repair and maintenance services or spare parts, the exemption shall not apply to any of the following obligations contained in vertical agreements:
>   (a) any direct or indirect non-compete obligation;
>   (b) any direct or indirect obligation limiting the ability of an authorised repairer to provide repair and maintenance services for vehicles from competing suppliers;
>   (c) any direct or indirect obligation causing the members of a distribution system not to sell motor vehicles or spare parts of particular competing suppliers or not to provide repair and maintenance services for motor vehicles of particular competing suppliers;
>   (d) any direct or indirect obligation causing the distributor or authorised repairer, after termination of the agreement, not to manufacture, purchase, sell or resell motor vehicles or not to provide repair or maintenance services.
> 2. As regards the sale of new motor vehicles, the exemption shall not apply to any of the following obligations contained in vertical agreements:
>   (a) any direct or indirect obligation causing the retailer not to sell leasing services relating to contract goods or corresponding goods;
>   (b) any direct or indirect obligation on any distributor of passenger cars or light commercial vehicles within a selective distribution system, which limits its ability to establish additional sales or delivery outlets at other locations within the common market where selective distribution is applied.
> 3. As regards repair and maintenance services or the sale of spare parts, the exemption shall not apply to any direct or indirect obligation as to the place of establishment of an authorised repairer where selective distribution is applied.

Article 5 contains a list of seven specific obligations which may not benefit from exemption under the Regulation. Where such obligations can be severed from the rest of the agreement, the remaining part of the agreement continues to benefit from the block exemption. The specific conditions exclude both direct and indirect means to attain the anti-competitive outcome of such obligations.

4.5.1. Multi-branding

The Regulation seeks to ensure access to markets and to give distributors and repairers in particular opportunities to sell and repair vehicles from different suppliers, i.e. "multi-branding". Article 5 excludes obligations contrary to this aim from the block exemption. As regards the sale of vehicles, repair and maintenance services or spare parts, the Regulation does not cover any direct or indirect non-compete obligations. In many instances, the activity of providing repair and maintenance services for motor vehicles of one brand does not actually compete with the provision of such services for a different brand. In order to allow authorised repairers to repair vehicles of different brands, the specific condition excluding non-compete obligations is therefore complemented with another condition excluding from the block exemption any obligation limiting the ability of authorised repairers to provide such services for vehicles from competing suppliers.[63]

Notes
[63] Article 5(1)(a) and (b).

Article 1
Definitions

1. For the purposes of this Regulation:

   (. . .)
   (b) "Non-compete obligation" means any direct or indirect obligation causing the buyer not to manufacture, purchase, sell or resell goods or services which compete with the contract goods or services, or any direct or indirect obligation on the buyer to purchase from the supplier or from another undertaking designated by the supplier more than 30% of the buyer's total purchases of the contract goods, corresponding goods or services and their substitutes on the relevant market, calculated on the basis of the value of its purchases in the preceding calendar year. An obligation that the distributor sell motor vehicles from other suppliers in separate areas of the showroom in order to avoid confusion between the makes does not constitute a non-compete obligation for the purposes of this Regulation. An obligation that the distributor have brand-specific sales personnel for different brands of motor vehicles constitutes a non-compete obligation for the purposes of this Regulation, unless the distributor decides to have brand-specific sales personnel and the supplier pays all the additional costs involved. (. . .)

Non-compete obligations are notably those which make benefits or incentives expressly dependent on the member of the network only selling the supplier's goods or not selling goods which compete with the contract goods.

The Regulation excludes direct or indirect obligations which make distributors or repairers buy more than 30% of their purchases of vehicles or spare parts pertaining to the same relevant market from a single supplier. It does, however, not mean that the distributor or repairer can be required to buy the specified quantity (up to 30% of purchases) directly from the supplier. It can also buy the same goods from other sources designated by the supplier, such as any other undertaking within the distribution system. General obligations or requirements which objectively speaking do not hamper members of a suppliers' network from purchasing 70% of their requirements of substitutable goods or services from other suppliers producing competing goods are covered by the block exemption.[64] Insofar as access to the market is not foreclosed to competing suppliers, such obligations may not raise competition problems. For instance, fidelity rebates based on a specific proportion (greater than 30%) of a buyer's purchases would be an indirect non-compete obligation, whereas a scale of reducing prices based on absolute volumes purchased and linked to economies of scale would not. Disputes as to whether direct or indirect non-compete obligations hamper the sale of different brands in specific cases may be referred to an independent third party or arbitrator.[65]

Notes
[64] Article 4(1)(b) and (c).
[65] Article 3(6)(e).

Part C Substantive Antitrust Matters

Question 13: Does the maximum 30% limit on annual purchases prevent buyers from purchasing the goods only from one supplier?

No. The non-compete obligation relates to the freedom of the dealer or repairer to purchase and resell competing products. The Regulation only provides that the block exemption does not apply to direct or indirect obligations that induce or oblige the distributor to purchase more than 30% of his requirements of a particular type of product from one supplier. The 30% limit on direct or indirect non-compete obligations should thus enable those network members who wish to do so, to buy and sell goods from at least three different competing suppliers. This does not prevent the exemption from applying if the distributor or repairer freely chooses to sell goods from a single supplier.

Question 14: May a supplier impose specific conditions for the sale of its motor vehicles by a multi-brand distributor?

The block exemption no longer covers obligations as to sales of competing motor vehicles which were allowed under Regulation 1475/95, such as having separate sales premises and management for each brand, or selling each brand through a distinct legal entity.[66] The Regulation nonetheless covers requirements to sell vehicles of different brands in separate areas of a single showroom. It also covers situations where the dealer decides to have brand-specific sales personnel and the supplier pays all the additional costs involved.[67] The Regulation does not, however, cover the provision of any advantage in excess of the actual costs incurred in having such personnel. The Regulation also covers an obligation to display the full range of motor vehicles in the showroom provided that such an obligation does not prevent the display or sale of motor vehicles from other suppliers or render the display or sale of such vehicles unreasonably difficult.[68]

Notes

[66] Article 3(3) of Regulation 1475/95.
[67] Article 1(1)(b).
[68] Recital 27.

Question 15: Does the Regulation cover non-compete obligations agreed to by the buyer in return for the supplier making trade loans to the buyer or investing directly in the buyer's business premises or equipment?

Unlike Regulation 2790/1999,[69] the Regulation neither covers non-compete obligations of certain duration nor makes any exception regarding goods being sold or services being provided in premises and land owned or leased by the supplier. Partial investments in such premises or equipment or financing used by the supplier to hinder the sale of competing brands or products are not covered either. However, trade loans for the purchase of lubricants, for instance, which can be repaid at any moment and which do not directly or indirectly hinder the buyer from selling competing goods are not non-compete obligations.

Notes

[69] Articles 5(a) and 1(1)(b).

4.5.2. Location of authorised distributors or repairers in selective distribution systems

The Regulation does not cover any restriction on the freedom of an authorised repairer to locate its workshops in the area of the Common Market where selective distribution, whether quantitative or qualitative is applied.[70] Moreover, as of 1 October 2005, the Regulation will no longer cover any restriction on any authorised distributor of passenger cars or light commercial vehicles freely establishing additional sales or delivery outlets in the area of the Common Market where selective distribution, whether quantitative or qualitative, is applied. The use of location clauses in agreements for the distribution of such vehicles will thus be incompatible with the Regulation.

Notes

[70] Article 5(3). See also definitions of selective distribution in Article 1(1)(f), (g) and (h).

Article 1
Definitions

1. For the purposes of this Regulation:

 (...)

 (o) "Passenger car" means a motor vehicle intended for the carriage of passengers and comprising no more than eight seats in addition to the driver's seat.

 (p) "Light commercial vehicle" means a motor vehicle intended for the transport of goods or passengers with a maximum mass not exceeding 3.5 tonnes; if a certain light commercial vehicle is also sold in a version with a maximum mass above 3.5 tonnes, all versions of that vehicle are considered to be light commercial vehicles.

 (...)

Question 16: For the distribution of which type of vehicles are location clauses still allowed under the Regulation?

The freedom to establish additional outlets concerns the sale through a selective distribution network of passenger cars and light commercial vehicles with a maximum mass below 3.5 tonnes. If distributors of commercial vehicles in selective distribution systems sell models of light commercial vehicles which exist in versions both below and above a maximum mass of 3.5 tonnes, location clauses for these models, are also not covered by the Regulation. Location clauses restricting the establishment of additional outlets for other motor vehicles such as trucks and buses are however allowed.[71]

Notes

[71] Articles 4(1)(d) and 5(2)(b) for passenger cars and light commercial vehicles and Article 4(1)(e) for other motor vehicles.

Question 17: Can obligations contrary to the specific conditions of the Regulation meet the conditions for an individual exemption?

The specific conditions set out in the Regulation are more numerous and stricter than the corresponding provisions in Regulation 2790/1999 or those in the previous block exemption regulations in the motor vehicle sector, Regulations 1475/95 and 123/85.[72] In order to ensure that the requirements of Article 81(3) are met, the specific conditions set out in Article 5 exclude several obligations which are or were exempted under these other regulations. By placing vertical agreements in the motor vehicle sector under a more demanding legal framework, the Regulation indicates that obligations contrary to Article 5 may raise serious competition concerns that can only be assessed in an individual examination. Companies are encouraged to do their own assessment and may find guidance for this in the Commission Guidelines on Vertical Restraints, which indicate the policy which the Commission follows in the assessment of individual cases.[73]

Notes

[72] See Recitals 1 to 4.

[73] Guidelines on Vertical Restraints, section VI. Enforcement Policy in Individual Cases.

4.6. Withdrawal of the Benefit of the Block Exemption (Article 6)

Article 6
Withdrawal of the benefit of the Regulation

1. The Commission may withdraw the benefit of this Regulation, pursuant to Article 7(1) of Regulation No 19/65/EEC, where it finds in any particular case that vertical agreements to which this Regulation applies nevertheless have effects which are incompatible with the conditions laid down in Article 81(3) of the Treaty, and in particular:

 (a) where access to the relevant market or competition therein is significantly restricted by the cumulative effect of parallel networks of similar vertical restraints implemented by competing suppliers or buyers, or

---

413

> (b) where competition is restricted on a market where one supplier is not exposed to effective competition from other suppliers, or
> (c) where prices or conditions of supply for contract goods or for corresponding goods differ substantially between geographic markets, or
> (d) where discriminatory prices or sales conditions are applied within a geographic market.
> 2. Where in any particular case vertical agreements to which the exemption applies have effects incompatible with the conditions laid down in Article 81(3) of the Treaty in the territory of a Member State, or in a part thereof, which has all the characteristics of a distinct geographic market, the relevant authority of that Member State may withdraw the benefit of application of this Regulation in respect of that territory, under the same conditions as those provided in paragraph 1.

The Commission, and in certain cases the competition authority of a Member State, may withdraw the benefit of the exemption in respect of individual agreements if it finds that due to specific circumstances the conditions for exemption set out in Article 81(3) are not met.

Question 18: In which circumstances may the Commission withdraw the Regulation?

Article 6 contains a non-exhaustive list of circumstances in which the Commission may decide to use its prerogative to withdraw the benefit of the block exemption from specific vertical agreements. These give an indication to suppliers and distributors about what circumstances or behaviour might lead the Commission to withdraw the block exemption. However, the precise levels at which, for instance, restricted access to or effective competition on a relevant market may lead to one or more of the four cumulative conditions of Article 81(3) not being met can only be established on a case by case basis. The Commission's Guidelines on Vertical Restraints provide indications of procedure and substance about withdrawal by the Commission and the Member States.[74]

Notes

[74] Guidelines on Vertical Restraints, section IV, paragraphs 71 to 79.

4.7. Disapplication in a Relevant Market (Article 7)

> *Article 7*
> **Non-application of the Regulation**
> 1. Pursuant to Article 1a of Regulation No 19/65/EEC, the Commission may by regulation declare that, where parallel networks of similar vertical restraints cover more than 50% of a relevant market, this Regulation shall not apply to vertical agreements containing specific restraints relating to that market.
> 2. A regulation pursuant to paragraph 1 shall not become applicable earlier than one year following its adoption.

Question 19: In which circumstances may the Regulation be disapplied on a relevant market?

Where there is a cumulative effect, the Regulation enables, but does not oblige, the Commission to disapply the block exemption in respect of specific vertical restraints. The fact that parallel networks of similar vertical restraints cover more than 50% of a relevant market need not in itself trigger disapplication of the Regulation. Nor will the Regulation necessarily be disapplied in respect of entire vertical agreements. The Regulation may also be disapplied in respect of specific restrictions or stipulations.

For instance, if more than 50% of suppliers on a relevant market were to set the exact total number of distributors by operating quantitative selective distribution systems clearly aimed at preventing categories of distributors capable of adequately selling the vehicles in question from having access to the market, this might result in less intra- and inter-brand competition, and lead to higher prices for consumers. Disapplication of the Regulation with regard to restrictions limiting the number of distributors may be in the interest of consumers. If the block exemption were only disapplied in respect of this quantitative criterion, this would mean that the exemption still applied to selective distribution and to quantitative selection criteria, such as minimum sales obligations, which limit the number of distributors by less direct means. As under the Regulation 2790/1999, the disapplication requires the adoption of a specific regulation disapplying the block exemption from the vertical restraints in question. The Commission's Guidelines on Vertical Restraints provide indications of procedure and substance about the disapplication.[75] However, any such specific regulation disapplying the Regulation may not become applicable earlier than one year following its adoption.[76]

Notes

[75] Guidelines on Vertical Restraints, section IV, paragraphs 80 to 89.
[76] Instead of the six months provided for in Regulation 2790/1999.

4.8. Entry into Force and Transitional Period (Articles 12 and 10)

> *Article 12*
> **Entry into force and expiry**
>
> 1. This Regulation shall enter into force on 1 October 2002.
> 2. Article 5(2)(b) shall apply from 1 October 2005.
> 3. This Regulation shall expire on 31 May 2010.
>
> *Article 10*
> **Transitional period**
>
> The prohibition laid down in Article 81(1) shall not apply during the period from 1 October 2002 to 30 September 2003 in respect of agreements already in force on 30 September 2002 which do not satisfy the conditions for exemption provided for in this Regulation but which satisfy the conditions for exemption provided for in Regulation (EC) No 1475/95.

The Regulation applies between 1 October 2002 and 31 May 2010. New agreements entering into force from 1 October 2002 will have to be compatible with the new Regulation for the benefit of the block exemption to apply. However, in order to allow all operators time to adapt existing vertical agreements which are compatible with Regulation 1475/95 and which are still in force after the exemption provided for in Regulation 1475/95 expires on 30 September 2002, such agreements benefit from a transitional period until 30 September 2003, during which time the new Regulation exempts them from the prohibition laid down in Article 81(1).[77] If such agreements subsist on 1 October 2003 and conflict with the application of the Regulation, Article 10 no longer exempts them from the prohibition laid down in Article 81(1). In practice, these agreements and all their relevant provisions must conform to the requirements of the Regulation as of 1 October 2003 if they are to benefit from the block exemption.

Notes

[77] See section 5.3.8.

Question 20: How can termination of contracts which comply with Regulation 1475/95 be effected during the transitional period?

Regulation 1475/95 only applied provided, among other things, that the period of notice given to dealers was at least two years or, in case of compensation or reorganisation of the whole or a substantial part of the network, at least one year. In the event of disagreement, disputes were to be referred to an expert third party or arbitrator or to a competent court to rule in conformity with national law.[78] The expiry of Regulation 1475/95 on 30 September 2002 and its replacement by a new Regulation does not in itself imply that there should be a reorganisation of the network. After the entry into force of the Regulation, a vehicle manufacturer may nonetheless decide to substantially reorganise its network.[79] To comply with Regulation 1475/95 and thus, to benefit from the transitional period, notices of regular contract termination should thus be given two years in advance unless a reorganisation is decided upon or if there is an obligation to pay compensation.

Notes
[78] Article 5(2)(2) and (3) of Regulation 1475/95.
[79] See section 5.3.8.

Question 21: During the transitional period, is there any conflict between rights conferred by agreements complying with the Regulation and rights conferred by agreements complying with Regulation 1475/95, having particular regard to the innovations introduced by the Regulation?

No. The automatic protection which the transitional period allows should ensure that, before 1 October 2003 the Regulation does not call into question rights or obligations which existed on 30 September 2002. Until 30 September 2003, the prohibition laid down in Article 81(1) does not apply to "old agreements" which meet two cumulative conditions, namely that their relevant express provisions i) are in force on 30 September 2002 and ii) satisfy the conditions for exemption provided for in Regulation 1475/95.

Question 22: May the rights of a dealer over a certain territory call into question the appointment of a candidate authorised repairer for one brand during the transition period?

Only in certain circumstances. For instance, a repairer may wish, as of 19 December 2002, to be appointed as authorised repairer of a particular brand in a particular territory in respect of which the supplier applies qualitative selective distribution, and may wish the supplier to supply him with spare parts for that brand. If an agreement which was in force on 30 September 2002 and remains in force on 19 December 2002 expressly stipulates that only one dealer within the distribution system will be supplied with spare parts of that particular brand for the territory in question,[80] the repairer cannot possibly argue that such a stipulation infringes Article 81 until 1 October 2003.

Notes
[80] See Article 5(3) of the new Regulation and Article 1 of Regulation 1475/95.

Question 23: Can dealers be prevented from taking on additional brands during the transition period?

Only in certain circumstances. For instance, on 1 January 2003, a distributor of brand A may wish to sell new motor vehicles of another brand B at his current and sole sales premises, in which he sells new motor vehicles of brand A. If his agreement with manufacturer A which was in force on 30 September 2002 and remains in force on 1 January 2003 expressly prevents him from selling a different brand within the same premises,[81] the distributor cannot possibly argue that such a stipulation infringes Article 81 until 1 October 2003. However, manufacturer A cannot object to the use of the same sales premises unless the old agreement contains express provisions to that effect.

Notes
[81] See Article 5(1)(a) and Article 1(1)(b) of the new Regulation and Article 3(3) of Regulation 1475/95.

Question 24: Does the fact that additional products, such as lubricants, and additional agreements, such as those entered into by part wholesalers, have been brought within the scope of the Regulation cause conflicts during the transition period with the regime formerly applied to such products and agreements under Regulation 2790/1999?

No. Agreements in respect of products or services which were not formerly within the scope of Regulation 1475/95 and which meet the conditions for exemption set out in block exemption Regulation 2790/1999 will not in normal circumstances constitute a priority for Commission enforcement of the new Regulation during the transitional period set out in Article 10. It is likely that such agreements could, during that period, benefit from individual exemption. After the end of the transitional period on 30 September 2003, their situation will be identical to those of products and agreements which fell under Regulation 1475/95 (see above).

4.9. Monitoring and Evaluation Report (Article 11)

Article 11
Monitoring and evaluation report

1. The Commission shall monitor the operation of this Regulation on a regular basis, with particular regard to its effects on:

   (a) competition in motor vehicle retailing and in after sales servicing in the common market or relevant parts of it,

   (b) the structure and level of concentration of motor vehicle distribution and any resulting effects on competition.

2. The Commission shall draw up a report on this Regulation not later than 31 May 2008 having regard in particular to the conditions set out in Article 81(3).

The Commission will monitor the operation of the Regulation on a regular basis, with particular regard to its effects on competition in motor vehicle retailing and in after sales servicing in the Common Market or relevant parts of it.[82] This will include regular monitoring of price differentials within the Single Market and, if need be, specific inquiries in the circumstances mentioned at Articles 6 and 7 of the Regulation. This will also include monitoring the effects of this Regulation on the structure and level of concentration of motor vehicle distribution and any resulting effects on competition. In the context of the future decentralised application of Article 81, it can be expected that this monitoring will be carried out in close co-operation with national competition authorities.

As with Regulation 1475/95, the Commission will carry out an evaluation of the operation of the Regulation before it expires, and will draw up a report not later than 31 May 2008.

Notes
[82] See Recital 38.

5. Rights, Obligations and Opportunities Conferred by the Regulation

This chapter looks at the Regulation in a "question and answer" format from the perspective of various types of interested party, including consumers. Where possible, the issues discussed are cross-referenced to the other parts of this brochure, where a more technical explanation is given.

5.1. Consumers: Increasing Consumer Choice in Accordance with single Market Principles

The need to increase the benefits that distribution systems bring to the consumer is at the heart of Commission policy for the motor vehicle sector. By injecting greater competition into vehicle sales, servicing and repair, and the sale of spare parts, Regulation 1400/2002 promotes consumer choice.

Although the Regulation is not aimed at bringing about price harmonisation, it contains a number of measures to make it easier for consumers to exercise their Single Market right to take advantage of price differentials between the various Member States and buy their vehicle where it suits them. In particular, most restrictions on consumers' use of intermediaries will no longer be covered by the block exemption. Furthermore, by promoting active sales and the opening of additional outlets, and by clarifying the position on Internet use, the new rules make it easier for dealers to sell to consumers wherever they wish within the Single Market. The availability clause, which under the previous Regulation 1475/95 allowed consumers to buy a car with their home country specification in another Member State, including right-hand drive cars in mainland Europe, has also been carried forward into the new rules. The availability clause provided for in Article 4(1)(f) of Regulation 1400/2002 covers all motor vehicles, including light commercial vehicles which are sold anywhere in the Common Market.

By only exempting agreements that oblige authorised repairers to repair vehicles sold by any dealer in the distribution system, the Regulation ensures that a consumer can take his vehicle to any authorised repairer anywhere in the European Union to be repaired and serviced. The Regulation also contains measures which aim to ensure that consumers continue to be able to get their cars repaired and serviced by independent repairers, and that safety and environmental protection will be maintained.

Many of these measures are dealt with in other sections of this brochure, since they have a more direct impact on other classes of operator. Listed below are a series of questions and issues of more direct interest to the consumer.

5.1.1. Sales

Question 25: Is a consumer free to buy a vehicle wherever he/she considers it to be most advantageous in the Single Market?

The consumer's freedom to buy anywhere in the Single Market is one of the fundamental achievements of the European Union, and the Regulation reinforces the right to buy a motor vehicle in another Member State. A manufacturer, importer, or area distributor may never restrict a dealer from selling to any consumer who contacts him directly, through an intermediary, or via the Internet. If a supplier were to instruct a dealer not to sell to consumers from other Member States, sought to deter him from doing so or imposed any restrictions on sales to such consumers, this would be a serious restriction of competition, which would mean that the supplier's distribution agreements would not be covered by the block exemption. In recent years, the Commission has detected several infringements of EC competition rules which involved restrictions on sales to foreign consumers and has fined the undertakings involved.[83]

Notes
[83] Commission decisions imposing fines on Volkswagen (1998 and 2001), Opel (2000) and DaimlerChrysler (2001). See annex I for exact references of these decisions.

Question 26: Can a dealer in another Member State refuse to sell a consumer a car?

Business sense would normally lead a dealer to sell as many cars as possible, as the more he sells the greater his profits. However, a dealer (referred to in the Regulation as a distributor), like a retailer of other goods, may refuse to sell to any consumer, so long as he decides on his own initiative and not on instructions from the supplier. If however the supplier[84] were to instruct its dealers not to sell to consumers from other Member States or sought to deter them from doing so,[85] this would be a serious restriction of competition, and most probably a breach of Article 81 of the EC Treaty.

Notes
[84] *I.e.* the manufacturer, importer, or area distributor.
[85] For instance, by restricting their supplies of vehicles.

Question 27: Should a consumer who orders a vehicle from a dealer in another Member State have to wait a longer time for his order to be fulfilled?

Normally, delays should be no longer than for a similarly specified vehicle in the local version. If it were to be shown that a supplier had caused deliveries of vehicles to its dealers for sale to foreign customers to suffer unduly long delays, with the object of discouraging those customers from buying in another Member State, this would be a serious restriction of competition. If, for example, a Danish consumer orders a left-hand-drive car of a given model with tinted windows, 16 valve engine and a sunroof from an Irish dealership, delays in fulfilling such an order[86] should be comparable to those experienced by an Irish consumer ordering a right-hand-drive car of that model with tinted windows, 16 valve engine and a sunroof from the same dealership. Any additional delivery time must be justifiable.

Notes
[86] See Article 4(1)(f).

Question 28: Can a supplier make a consumer from another Member State wait before supplying a certificate of conformity?

No. Suppliers must systematically make available the full certificate of conformity documentation to the dealer at the time the vehicle is delivered to the consumer or to his intermediary. If this is not done, the consumer will not be able to register the vehicle for use within another Member State. This may amount to an indirect restriction on sales, and a serious restriction of competition.[87]

Notes
[87] Article 4(1)(b), (d) and (e).

Question 29: Can a dealer in a selective distribution system make his customers sign an undertaking/other document to the effect that the vehicle will not be resold for commercial gain while new?

It is legitimate for a supplier operating a selective distribution system to prevent sales to resellers who are not members of that system. However, the consumer is free to sell the motor vehicle at any time provided he is not a disguised independent reseller. If a dealer, acting on instructions from his supplier, were to take measures to prevent a purchaser from reselling a vehicle for reasons other than commercial gain,[88] or to prevent a purchaser from re-selling a vehicle once it was no longer new, this would be an indirect restriction on sales.

Notes
[88] For example, because the consumer's personal circumstances have changed since he placed the order and he now needs a larger car.

Question 30: What if a dealer tells a consumer who tries to buy his car in another Member State, or tells an intermediary acting for a consumer, that he cannot order the model in question with the specifications current in the consumer's home country, or that he cannot obtain a price quotation for such a vehicle?

Suppliers must provide dealers with motor vehicles built to specifications current in other Member States.[89] If a supplier were not to do so, this would amount to a serious restriction of competition and a breach of the consumer's Single Market rights. However, a supplier can refuse to supply such a vehicle if the dealer does not normally sell the local variant of the model in question: in other words, if the vehicle does not correspond to a vehicle within the dealer's contract range.[90]

For example, a Dutch dealer of brand A should be able to order a right-hand-drive car of model X for a UK consumer unless

1) the Dutch dealer does not normally sell cars of model X, or

2) cars of model X are not normally made in a right-hand-drive version.

If the dealer sells the model in question, he must be able to obtain a price quotation for versions of that model with specifications current in other Member States. If he cannot obtain such a price quotation promptly, this could amount to a serious restriction on competition by the supplier.

Notes
[89] See Article 4(1)(f).
[90] For example, because the model in question has not yet been launched in the Member State where the dealer is established.

Question 31: Can the dealer charge a right-hand-drive supplement or another similar kind of surcharge?

Surcharges, such as right-hand-drive supplements, which take account of differences in vehicle specification between Member States, and reflect differences in the cost of production or distribution, are not in themselves restrictive of competition. However, the level of surcharge must be objectively justifiable, particularly with regard to the real additional cost of producing or delivering the vehicle. There is no rule of thumb for calculating what an objectively justified level of surcharge in any given case might be, since amongst other things, the additional cost of producing or delivering the vehicle in question will vary depending on the model.

Question 32: What if the dealer says that he has been told not to grant discounts on a certain model?

Dealers must be free to sell vehicles below the supplier's recommended price.[91] Manufacturers cannot fix actual selling prices or minimum prices. If a supplier were to restrict a dealer's ability to grant discounts, this would be a serious restriction of competition,[92] which would mean that the supplier's distribution agreements would not be covered by the block exemption.

Notes

[91] Or indeed above it, provided that the supplier has not set a maximum price. See Article 4(1)(a).

[92] See Commission Decision of 29.6.2001 in case COMP/36.693 — *Volkswagen*, OJ L 262, 2.10.2001, p. 14, see also *Press Release — IP/01/760 — 30.05.2001*. The decision imposed a fine for this infringement.

Question 33: Can a supplier set up a special scheme in a Member State, under which consumers get a rebate if they register the car in that country, but consumers who register their vehicles in other Member States don't qualify for the rebate?

No. This scheme amounts to a restriction on sales to consumers from another Member State and is a serious restriction of competition and would mean that the supplier's distribution agreements would not be covered by the block exemption.[93]

Notes

[93] See Article 4(1)(b) and (c).

5.1.2. After-sales servicing

Question 34: Does a consumer have to take his vehicle back to the dealer he bought it from to have warranty work/servicing done?

No. For the Regulation to apply the consumer should be able to take the vehicle to any authorised repairer within the supplier's network anywhere in the EU. The Regulation[94] only exempts agreements with authorised repairers when the supplier imposes an obligation on all its authorised repairers to repair all vehicles of the brand in question, to honour warranties, perform free servicing and carry out recall work irrespective of where the car was bought. If the authorised repairer is not able to service a car which is not sold in his Member State, he will be in a position to liaise with the supplier or another authorised repairer in another Member State. The consumer does not have to re-register the warranty in his home Member State in order to have warranty repairs done. The warranty period starts with the delivery of a car by the authorised dealer. If a manufacturer, importer, dealer, repairer or another company within the network were to impede consumers from availing themselves of the manufacturer's EU-wide warranty, this would mean that one of the basic conditions for the exemption to apply to the agreements in question would not be met.

Notes

[94] Article 4(1)(b), first sentence, and (d) and Recital 17.

Question 35: What if a consumer's car has a problem, covered by warranty, that his local authorised repairer cannot fix?

In these circumstances, the consumer may have to take the vehicle back to the dealership where it was purchased, just as he would for any other product.[95] Alternatively, if he bought the car through an intermediary (see section 5.2) he may give the intermediary a mandate to take the vehicle back to the dealer he bought it from.

Notes

[95] This problem is governed by national contract law, and not by EC competition rules.

Question 36: What if the authorised dealer from whom a consumer buys his car does not service vehicles, the vehicle develops a fault during the warranty period, and the repairer to whom the dealer has sub-contracted servicing can't repair it?

The consumer can take the vehicle back to the place he bought it from, just as he would with any other consumer goods. The dealer who sold the vehicle will then either have to arrange for repairs to be carried out, or give the consumer a replacement vehicle, although the consumer's rights to this will depend on national contract law and the terms of the contract of sale.[96]

Notes

[96] See Recital 17.

Question 37: If a consumer has his vehicle repaired or maintained by an independent repairer during the warranty period, can the manufacturer refuse to honour the warranty?

If the consumer has his vehicle repaired or maintained by an independent repairer during the manufacturer's warranty period the warranty may be lost if the work carried out is faulty. However, a general obligation to have the car maintained or repaired only within the authorised network during such a period would deprive consumers of their right to choose to have their vehicle maintained or repaired by an independent repairer and it would, especially in the case of "extended warranties", prevent such repairers from competing effectively with the authorised network.

Question 38: What can a consumer do if he thinks he has been the victim of restrictive behaviour?

He can complain to the European Commission or to a national competition authority.[97] He may also be able to bring a claim for damages in a national court. The ability to bring such an action may, however, depend on national procedural rules, and the consumer should therefore take legal advice before bringing a claim.

Since not all problems that consumers encounter buying a vehicle in other Member States stem from a breach of competition rules, the Commission has published a list of contact points ("hot-lines") for most manufacturers on its web site in order to encourage the resolution of disputes of various types and deal with other types of problems relating to the purchase of vehicles.[98]

Notes

[97] A list of these is available at http://europa.eu.int/comm/competition/national_authorities/

[98] At http://europa.eu.int/comm/competition/car_sector/

5.2. Intermediaries

An intermediary or purchase agent is a person or an undertaking which purchases a new motor vehicle on behalf of the consumer without being a member of the distribution network. Intermediaries are to be distinguished from independent resellers, who purchase a vehicle for resale and do not operate for the account of a named consumer. They are also to be distinguished from sales agents, who find customers for one or more dealers. Suppliers can only oblige their dealers to make sure that an intermediary has a prior valid Authorisation[99] from the consumer to purchase and/or collect a specified vehicle. The only limitation on an intermediary's activities permitted in an agreement covered by Regulation 1400/2002 is therefore the need to show a valid mandate from an individual consumer. The mandate must give the consumer's name and address and must be signed and dated. It is up to the consumer to determine how specific the mandate is as regards the vehicle.[100] No further requirements may be imposed if an intermediary is involved in the purchase of a new motor vehicle. The Commission has abolished its two notices[101] which dealt with the activity of intermediaries.

Notes

[99] This may be a written or electronically signed authorisation. See Recital 14.

[100] For instance, the mandate could relate to a class of vehicle, a given model or be more detailed.

[101] Commission Notice concerning Regulation (EEC) No 123/85 of 12 December 1984 on the application of Article [81](3) of the Treaty to certain categories of motor vehicle distribution and servicing agreements, OJ C 17, 18.1.1985, p. 4, and the Information from the Commission — Clarification of the activities of motor vehicle intermediaries, OJ C 329, 18.12.1991, p. 20. Based on these notices, intermediaries could be requested, for example, not have their office within the same premises as a supermarket. Another element hampering their activities was that a car dealer could be requested not to sell more than 10% of the new vehicles through a given intermediary.

Question 39: Can the dealer ask an intermediary to provide photocopies of his customers' identity cards or other documentation,[102] in addition to the signed mandate?

Yes, in certain circumstances. It should be borne in mind that within a selective distribution system a dealer may not sell new[103] motor vehicles to independent resellers. Therefore a dealer may, if he feels it necessary, ask an intermediary for evidence of the buyer's identity so as to prevent sales to independent resellers.

Part C Substantive
Antitrust Matters

Although a dealer may, of his own volition, decide to ask his customers for further documentation, if a supplier instructs a dealer to systematically ask for such documentation, this would not be covered by the Regulation.

Notes

[102] Such as a passport or other documentation proving the consumer's identity (utility bill etc.).

[103] Whether a vehicle is still new has to be decided on the basis of trade usage. For a buyer a vehicle is no longer new once it has been registered and driven on the road by another consumer. In contrast, a vehicle which has been registered by a dealer for one day without having been used is still new.

5.3. Authorised Distributors of New Motor Vehicles
(Also Referred to in this Brochure as Dealers)

Dealers play a key role as regards the development of the Single Market for new motor vehicles. A strong and independent dealer sector is more likely to engage in pro-competitive behaviour and to be more innovative, to the benefit of consumers. Regulation 1400/2002 therefore gives dealers more freedom to run their businesses as they see fit. The new Regulation has in particular considerably reduced the opportunities for manufacturers and their importers to impose measures on their dealers which are not indispensable for the distribution of new motor vehicles or for the provision of repair and maintenance services.

Unlike the previous motor vehicle block exemption, Regulation 1475/95, Regulation 1400/2002 only provides coverage if:

— the vehicle manufacturer or its importer does not oblige dealers to carry out repair and maintenance or to distribute spare parts themselves. Dealers should be free to subcontract repair and maintenance to authorised repairers belonging to the network of the same brand;
— dealers can take on additional brands;
— manufacturers or importers do not limit supplies of new vehicles to their dealers if such behaviour restricts their dealers' ability to sell vehicles to particular consumers within the European Union;
— dealers <u>in a selective distribution system</u> may sell actively and passively to any end consumer and after 1st October 2005 may open additional sales or delivery outlets for the distribution of new passenger cars and light commercial vehicles wherever selective distribution is used;
— Dealers within an exclusive distribution system are entirely free to sell actively within their territory and in territories which are not subject to exclusive distribution and passively into other distributors' exclusive territories.

5.3.1. Sales of new vehicles by dealers

Regulation 1400/2002 aims to give dealers more opportunities to supply new motor vehicles to all consumers, whether these are local, national or from another Member State. Direct restrictions on sales, active or passive as the case may be, are not covered by the Regulation.[104]

Under the new Regulation, any distribution system, be it selective or exclusive, has to be organised in such a way that all categories of consumer can purchase new vehicles from any dealer even if they purchase a large number of vehicles.[105]

Notes

[104] See Recital 16.

[105] For example a rent-a-car company or another fleet operator such as a leasing company normally buys large quantities of cars from a single supplier.

Question 40: Does the Regulation cover restrictions on active and passive sales by dealers?

Dealers within a selective distribution system must be able to sell actively to any end user resident in an area within the European Union where selective distribution is used. Suppliers are however allowed to impose an obligation on the dealer not to sell new vehicles to independent resellers in areas where selective distribution is used. If the supplier uses exclusive distribution in certain areas of the European Union, the dealers within the selective distribution system must be allowed to sell passively to end users or unauthorised distributors within those areas.[106]

If a supplier sets up an exclusive distribution system, its dealers must be free to sell actively within their exclusive territory or to their exclusive customer group. As regards all other buyers within an exclusive distribution system, be they end users or resellers of new motor vehicles, they may be able to supply them passively. If the supplier uses selective distribution in certain other areas of the European Union, the dealers within the exclusive distribution system must be allowed to sell actively to end users and unauthorised distributors within those areas.[107]

Notes
[106] See Recital 13. For a definition of active and passive sales, see above question 12.
[107] Article 4(1) 1st part of the sentence and Guidelines on Vertical Restraints, paragraph 52.

Question 41: How does the new Regulation ensure that a dealer can sell new vehicles to any consumer, including local consumers, consumers from other areas of the same Member State and those from another Member State?

The supply of new motor vehicles has to be organised in such a way that a dealer can supply all consumers who wish to buy from him. The manufacturer should honour orders for new motor vehicles for supply to consumers from other areas of the Common Market in the same way as for sales to local consumers, in particular as regards pricing and delivery times. Under the new Regulation manufacturers will therefore have to put in place ordering and delivery systems which comply with this requirement. To this end they may for example put in place an ordering system based on the "first come first served" principle. A distribution system which is based on supply quotas relating to a sales territory smaller than the Common Market amounts to an indirect restriction on sales and is not exempted by the Regulation.[108]

The Regulation does not oblige manufacturers to put in place a distribution system which ensures that delivery times are the same throughout the Common Market. They must however ensure that dealers are in a position to supply new vehicles under the same conditions to their local, national customers and to customers from other Member States.

It may happen that a supplier is forced to limit product supply to its dealers in certain circumstances, for example where there is a strike or where overall demand is higher than product output. In such circumstances the supplier may not allocate vehicles to its dealers in such a way as to discriminate between dealers who sell many vehicles to consumers from other Member States and those who do not. For example, imagine a situation where dealer A sells fifty vehicles a month, mainly to consumers in the town where he is established. Whereas dealer B also sells fifty vehicles a month, he sells twenty-five of them to consumers in his home town, and twenty-five to consumers from another Member State. If one month there are production difficulties, and the supplier is forced to reduce the number of vehicles it delivers by forty percent, it must supply thirty vehicles to dealer A and the same number to dealer B.

In order to avoid any discrimination between local sales and sales to buyers located in other areas of the Common Market, bonus systems or other kinds of financial or non-financial incentives may not be based on the buyers' place of residence or establishment, or on the place where the vehicle is to be registered, but must take account of all sales.

Notes
[108] See Recital 16.

Question 42: Should the way in which new vehicles are supplied to a dealer differ according to whether the supplier operates a selective distribution system or another kind of distribution system, such as one based on territorial exclusivity?

The above principles apply whatever distribution system is put in place by the supplier, since it is paramount for the operation of the Single Market that a dealer can sell new vehicles to all consumers without regard to the residence or place of establishment of the buyer of a new motor vehicle. This applies irrespective of whether the dealer is entitled to engage in active sales, or only in passive sales to certain customer groups or territories.

Question 43: Can a supplier agree with its dealer on sales targets which the dealer has to endeavour to achieve within a certain territory?

The new Regulation allows a supplier to agree with its dealer on sales targets based on a given geographic area which may be smaller than the Common Market. However, such agreed sales targets may not be used to limit deliveries of new motor vehicles to dealers.[109] Nor may product allocation, dealer remuneration or bonus schemes be based on whether or not a vehicle is sold within the agreed geographic area since such measures would indirectly restrict the dealer's right to sell passively to all consumers within the Common Market.

Notes
[109] See Recital 16

Question 44: Is a dealer free to advertise on the Internet and to sell new vehicles over the Internet?

A dealership web site is a passive selling[110] tool and the dealer may use it for advertising and for carrying out transactions, and this use may not be restricted under the Regulation. Nor may the dealer be restricted under the Regulation in his use of the Internet or of email instead of more traditional methods, such as normal mail or fax, to conclude sales Contracts.[111]

A dealer must also be free to make agreements with Internet referral sites, which put consumers in contact with the dealer who is able to supply a vehicle. A vehicle manufacturer may require the dealer using the Internet to comply with the qualitative requirements regarding the promotion of the relevant brand of motor vehicles over the Internet. A supplier may also require an Internet referral site to which a dealer out-sources its advertising to comply with its quality requirements. Such sites, which may promote the sales of new motor vehicles of one or more brands, may also refer consumers who wish to purchase a new vehicle to one of the dealers which is connected to the referral site.

Notes
[110] See Recital 15 and Article 4(1)(e), also Guidelines on Vertical Restraints, paragraph 51.
[111] Recital 15.

Question 45: Is a dealer free to use e-mail or personalised letters to contact potential customers?

Using e-mail or personalised letters to actively market vehicles and services to end users throughout the Common Market is an active selling method. Under the Regulation[112] suppliers may not restrict dealers in selective distribution systems from making use of such methods. Dealers in exclusive distribution systems must be free to actively contact customers exclusively allocated to them, and may not be restricted from responding to unsolicited requests from customers even if these are allocated exclusively to other dealers. For example, in an exclusive distribution system in which a territory is allocated to each dealer, the supplier can prohibit the marketing of new vehicles via e-mail or personalised letters to customers located in another dealer's exclusive sales territory. Such dealers can engage in such active sales methods in other areas, where selective distribution applies.

Notes
[112] See Article 4(1)(d) and 4(1)(e).

5.3.1.1. The sale of new motor vehicles to consumers using the services of an intermediary

Questions relating to the supply of new motor vehicles to end users who have given an authorisation to an intermediary are dealt with in section 5.2.

5.3.1.2. Sales of new vehicles to leasing companies

The Regulation does not cover obligations restricting a dealer's ability to sell leasing Services.[113] This includes leasing by the dealer himself, through a leasing company connected with the dealer, or as an agent of a leasing company of his choice.

Notes
[113] See Recital 30 and Article 5(2)(a).

Question 46: Is a dealer entitled to sell new motor vehicles to leasing companies?

Yes, supplying new vehicles to leasing companies is a legitimate part of a dealer's activities, as leasing companies are normally considered to be end users.[114] However, a supplier using selective distribution may prevent dealers from supplying contract goods to leasing companies when there is a verifiable risk that the leasing company will resell these motor vehicles while they are new. Article 1(1)(w) makes it clear that leasing contracts which involve a transfer of ownership or a purchase option prior to the expiry of the contract and which would allow the lessee to purchase the vehicle from the leasing company at any moment, including while the vehicle is still new, would in reality turn the leasing company into an independent reseller.

Notes
[114] See Article 1(1)(w).

Question 47: Can a supplier operating a selective distribution system oblige a leasing company to whom a dealer sells a new vehicle to sign an undertaking to the effect that it will not re-sell the vehicle while it is new for commercial gain?

It is legitimate for a supplier operating a selective distribution system to take appropriate measures to ensure that its dealers do not sell new motor vehicles to resellers who are not members of that system. It may therefore ask the dealers to take appropriate measures to prevent purchasers from re-selling vehicles while they are new. In order to prevent a leasing company from reselling a motor vehicle while it is new the dealer may request the leasing company to sign a declaration that it will not resell the cars when new.

Question 48: Can a supplier require a dealer to obtain and provide it with copies of each leasing agreement before the dealer sells a vehicle to a leasing company?

No. This would amount to an indirect restriction on sales and a serious restriction of Competition.[115] Moreover, it would allow the dealer and the supplier to get information on the terms and conditions of the leasing contract and the identity of the lessee. However, a supplier can require a dealer to check, before selling the first time to a particular leasing company, the general conditions applied by the leasing company so as to avoid sales to an unauthorised reseller.

Notes
[115] Article 4(1)(b).

Question 49: Can a leasing company buy new cars from a dealer for whom it has not yet found lessees?

Yes, and the supplier cannot refuse to honour the relevant orders even if the leasing company uses the new vehicles to build a stock.[116] Any requirement on a leasing company to name a customer before purchase would constitute an indirect restriction on sales and would be a serious restriction of competition.[117]

Notes
[116] See Commission Decision 10.10.2001 — *DaimlerChrysler* — (case COMP/36.264 — *Mercedes-Benz*), paragraphs 176 and 201 et seq.
[117] See Article 4(1)(b).

5.3.2. The distribution of different brands of motor vehicles by the dealer (multi-branding)

Regulation 1400/2002 simplifies the conditions which a supplier may impose on dealers who want to take on one or more additional brands (sometimes referred to as "multi-branding"). A supplier that wants its agreements to be exempted under the Regulation must allow any dealer to sell vehicles from competing suppliers. The only restriction that it may impose is an obligation on the dealer to exhibit the models of other suppliers in separate areas of the same showroom. In addition, if the dealer decides to employ brand specific sales personnel and the supplier agrees to it and pays all the additional costs involved, this will be covered by the Regulation.

The supplier may impose on such dealers all the quality criteria it imposes on mono-brand dealers, including that relating to showroom decoration and training of sales personnel. However, if the dealer's showroom is not large enough to allow the display of all the vehicles or to use all the decoration which a mono-brand dealer has normally to exhibit or use, then the supplier must moderate this obligation in an appropriate way as regards the space needed to exhibit such vehicles, in order to allow the dealer to also display vehicles of the other manufacturer in its existing showroom.[118] Whether these conditions are fulfilled in a specific case is a question of fact. Agreements must provide for the parties to have the right to refer any disputes on this subject to an independent expert or arbitrator or to a national court.[119]

Notes
[118] See Recital 27.
[119] Article 3(6).

Question 50: May a dealer receive higher margins or a bonus if he only sells the vehicles from one supplier?

No. Such measures would amount to an indirect restriction of a dealer's right to sell competing brands and would not be covered by the Regulation.[120] Equivalent margins or bonuses therefore have to be made available to all dealers, irrespective of whether they sell motor vehicles from only one supplier or from several.

Notes
[120] See Article 5(1)(a) and Article 1(1)(b).

Question 51: What degree of separation may a supplier require as regards the display of different brands in the same showroom?

The Regulation allows suppliers to oblige dealers to exhibit vehicles of their brands in brand-specific areas of the same showroom. Any obligation for further separation, such as the installation of a wall or a curtain or an obligation to leave a distance between displays of vehicles from different brands that was so large that it made display of other brands impossible (for example, because the showroom was too small) or unreasonably difficult (for example, because the supplier required its vehicles to be exhibited alongside the windows of the showroom) would not be covered by the Regulation.

Question 52: Can a supplier oblige a dealer to have brand-specific features in his showroom?

A supplier may oblige all his dealers to have decoration that promotes the brand image, provided that this does not restrict the sale of other brands. For example, a supplier could oblige all his dealers to install a luxury carpet in that part of the showroom used to display his brands or to erect brand-related signage that could be seen from the street. He could also oblige the dealer to only display his vehicles in a high quality building. A supplier could not, however, require the dealer who wanted to take on an additional brand to have a separate customer entrance for each brand. Nor could he, for example, require a dealer who also sold the brands of competing suppliers to modify the whole of the inside or outside of the showroom in a way that was brand-related.

5.3.3. The right to open additional sales outlets (the prohibition of a "location clause")

After 1 October 2005, Regulation 1400/2002[121] does not cover obligations preventing <u>dealers of passenger cars and light commercial vehicles within selective distribution systems</u> from opening additional sales or delivery outlets in other areas of the Common Market where selective distribution is applied. This allows dealers to exploit new business opportunities by establishing a physical presence close to potential customers further away from their initial outlet, including customers in other Member States. This freedom will strengthen intra-brand competition throughout Europe to the benefit of consumers, and will moreover allow dealers to expand their businesses and to become more independent from their suppliers. It will also allow such dealers to become pan-European distributors of new motor vehicles.

Restrictions on opening additional outlets are, however, covered under Regulation 1400/2002, as regards dealers in motor vehicles other than passenger cars and light commercial vehicles, i.e. medium and heavy trucks, buses and coaches.[122] It is assumed that most of the buyers of these vehicles use such vehicles in a commercial context, and that they are therefore in a better position to buy from a dealer located in another area of the Common Market and to have access to more favourable sales conditions than private consumers.

The Regulation allows suppliers to prohibit dealers within exclusive distribution systems from opening additional outlets in markets covered by such systems. However, since such dealers can sell new vehicles to all customers, including unauthorised resellers, throughout the Common Market, it is assumed that these resellers will organise arbitrage between the different markets and seize additional business opportunities which arise in other areas of the Common Market.

Notes
[121] See Article 5(2)(b) and Article 12(2).
[122] See also reply to question 16.

Question 53: What sort of outlets may a dealer acting within a selective distribution system covered by the Regulation open after 1 October 2005?

After 1 October 2005, a dealer acting within a selective distribution system covered by the Regulation may open additional sales outlets or delivery outlets in other areas of the Common Market where the supplier uses selective distribution.

A <u>sales outlet</u> includes the showroom and the necessary infrastructure to sell new motor vehicles. This will for example include a showroom to exhibit the new motor vehicles, the necessary offices, sales personnel and demonstration vehicles. It is up to the dealer who operates the sales outlet whether he delivers new cars at the sales outlet or delivers them elsewhere.

A <u>delivery outlet</u> is a place where vehicles sold elsewhere are handed over (delivered) to the end consumer. It may include the necessary office space, a storage facility or an area for the preparation of the cars for their delivery and the necessary staff for carrying out the deliveries. A dealer must be allowed to combine a delivery outlet with a sales outlet providing he meets the relevant quality criteria for both. Under the Regulation dealers within a selective distribution system should be allowed to actively sell new motor vehicles.[123] A dealer may therefore not be prevented from erecting advertising hoardings at a delivery point or making available brochures about vehicles or services offered by the dealership.

Notes
[123] Article 4(1)(b) and (d).

Question 54: If a dealer in a selective distribution system decides to open an additional outlet elsewhere, what standards will the new outlet have to meet?

It will have to meet the same standards as similar sales outlets in the area where it is to be located. For example, if a dealer in a rural area decides to open additional sales premises on a main street in a large city, the supplier can oblige him to meet the same quality standards as regards signage and display of vehicles as existing sales premises in that area or in similar urban areas.

If a dealer in one area finds it expedient to open a delivery point in another area, that delivery point will have to meet the quality standards as other delivery points in that area or in similar areas.[124] However, a supplier may not, for example, require a delivery point to have the same staffing levels as a showroom, since this would represent an indirect restriction on active sales and would be an indirect means of reintroducing a location clause.

Notes
[124] See Recital 29 at the end.

Question 55: Can a dealer in a selective distribution system close the initial outlet, in respect of which he is authorised by the supplier, and set up another outlet elsewhere?

Not without the approval of the supplier, which will continue to be able to agree with the dealer where his initial outlet is located. Suppliers of new motor vehicles can thus ensure that their networks cover all geographic areas within the Common Market.

Question 56: If a dealer in a selective distribution system wants to open an additional sales or delivery outlet, does he have to obtain the supplier's consent, and will he have to enter into a further distribution agreement with the supplier in respect of that outlet?

In order to be covered by the Regulation a dealer operating within a selective distribution system should be allowed to open additional outlets without having to ask the supplier's permission. It will therefore not be necessary to enter into any additional agreement. The supplier may however require the additional outlet to comply with the quality standards applicable to the outlets of the same type in the same geographic area.

Question 57: From where can the dealer source the vehicles he sells in the additional sales outlet?

The dealer may source the vehicles for his additional outlet from the same supplier(s) that supply vehicles to his initial (main) outlet. In addition, he will be free to source vehicles from any other dealer or wholesaler of the brand in question, anywhere in the Common Market.

This supplier will have to make the necessary arrangements to ensure that a dealer can buy sufficient quantities of new motor vehicles to satisfy both the demand at his initial (main) outlet and any additional outlet(s). Any supply restriction would amount to an indirect restriction of the dealer's right to open additional outlets in other areas of the Common Market. This would also be the case if wholesale prices or other financial incentives were made to depend on whether the vehicle was sold through the dealer's initial (main) outlet or through its additional outlet.

5.3.4. *The supply of new vehicles to the dealer*

Question 58: Can a dealer in a selective distribution system be prevented from obtaining vehicles from another authorised dealer of the same brand established in the same or another Member State?

No. Under the Regulation, authorised dealers in a selective distribution system may not be prevented from purchasing from other authorised dealers established anywhere in the Single Market.[125]

Notes
[125] Article 4(1)(c).

Question 59: Can a supplier arrange for motor vehicles which are due to be sold to a foreign end user or sold through an additional outlet to be subject to longer delivery times?

Such a system would restrict (active or passive) sales to end users, and would be a serious restriction of competition.

5.3.5. *Disputes regarding contractual matters*

In order to favour the quick resolution of any disputes which arise between the parties to distribution agreements, which might otherwise hamper effective competition, such agreements will only be covered by the exemption if they provide for each party to have a right of recourse to an independent expert or arbitrator. This right does not affect each party's right to make an application to a national court.[126]

Notes
[126] See Recital 11 and Article 3(6).

Question 60: In what circumstances does the Regulation provide for disputes between a supplier and a dealer to be referred to an expert third party or an arbitrator?

The Regulation stipulates that any vertical agreement has to provide for each of the parties to have the right to refer disputes concerning the fulfilment of their contractual obligations to an independent expert, such as a mediator, or to an arbitrator. Such disputes may relate *inter alia* to supply obligations, the setting and attainment of stock requirements or agreed sales targets, the implementation of an obligation to provide or use demonstration vehicles, the conditions for the sale of different brands (multi-branding), the issue as to whether a prohibition to operate out of an unauthorised place of establishment limits the ability of the distributor of motor vehicles other than passenger cars or light commercial vehicles to expand its business[127] or where notice is given to terminate an agreement, in particular the issue whether the termination of an agreement is justified by the reasons given in the notice.[128]

Notes
[127] See Recital 18.
[128] See Recital 11 and Article 3(6).

Question 61: Who can act as an expert third party or an arbitrator and how should an expert third party or arbitrator be nominated?

Any person accepted by both parties as being qualified to act in such a capacity may be appointed as expert third party or arbitrator. The parties are free to decide, should the situation arise, whom they wish to nominate and whether they prefer to appoint one, two, three or more people to act as expert(s) or arbitrator(s). However, no party may decide unilaterally who the expert or arbitrator will be. In the event of disagreement the parties must adopt the nomination procedures which are normally used in such cases, such as nomination by the president of a court, or by the president of a chamber for commerce and industry. It seems advisable that the vertical agreement should specify what kind of nomination procedure they wish to use should the situation arise.

5.3.6. The right for the dealer to choose whether or not to carry out repair and maintenance services

Unlike Regulation 1475/95[129] the new Regulation does not allow manufacturers to oblige their dealers to offer repair and maintenance services. It therefore allows dealers to specialise in vehicle distribution, which might be a particularly attractive option for those dealers who wish to sell new vehicles from different manufacturers.

If a dealer decides not to carry out repair and maintenance himself, the supplier may require him to subcontract these services to an authorised repairer belonging to the same brand network.[130] To make things more transparent for consumers the manufacturer may also require the dealer to give the name and address of the authorised repairer in question before the conclusion of the sales contract. Moreover, where the repair shop is not in the vicinity of the showroom, the supplier may also require the dealer to tell its customers how far the repair shop is from the showroom; however, he may only do so if he imposes a similar obligation on dealers whose own repair shop is not in the vicinity of the sales outlet.

Under a sub-contract, an authorised repairer undertakes to co-operate as a sort of privileged service partner of the dealer, and to offer all types of after sales services to the dealer's customers. This includes normal repair and maintenance but also the honouring of warranties, repairs following a vehicle recall or free servicing offered by the vehicle manufacturer through the authorised repairer.[131]

Notes
[129] See in particular Article 4(1)(1) and (6) and Article 5(1)(1)(a) and (b).
[130] Article 4(1)(g).
[131] See Recital 17.

Question 62: Can an authorised dealer of a given brand be prevented under the Regulation from also being an independent repairer of that brand?

No. However, as an independent repairer, he may not have the same benefits as an authorised repairer. Most notably, he may have no right to remuneration from the supplier for repairs carried out under warranty. In addition, he may have to sub-contract the provision of repair and maintenance under warranty for the new vehicles he sells to an authorised repairer within the manufacturer's network.

5.3.7. Transferring/selling a dealership or authorised repair business

In order to foster market integration and to allow distributors and authorised repairers to seize additional business opportunities and to expand their businesses and become more independent, Regulation 1400/2002 provides that they have to be allowed to purchase other undertakings of the same type that sell or repair the same brand of motor vehicles. To this end, any vertical agreement between a supplier and a distributor or authorised repairer has to provide for the latter to have the right to transfer all of its rights and obligations to any other undertaking of its choice of the same type that sells or repairs, respectively, the same brand of motor vehicles within the distribution system.[132]

Notes
[132] Recital 10 and Article 3(3).

Question 63: Can a supplier prevent a dealer from selling his dealership to another dealer within the same manufacturer's network?

In order to benefit from Regulation 1400/2002 distribution agreements for new motor vehicles have to contain a clause by which the supplier agrees to the transfer of ownership of the dealership with all of the attendant rights and obligations to another dealer within the manufacturer's network.[133]

For example, imagine that the car manufacturer A has dealership agreements compatible with the Regulation with Dupont in Paris, and with Smith in London. Dupont and Smith are owned and run by Franco S.A. and Anglo Plc respectively. If Anglo wishes to sell Smith[134] to Franco, neither manufacturer A nor its importer may oppose the sale.[135] In this example, both Franco and Anglo are considered to be "distributors" within the meaning of the Regulation, since they are connected undertakings of Dupont and Smith.

Notes
[133] Including dealers authorised by the manufacturer in other Member States of the EU.
[134] It is irrelevant whether Smith is a limited company, of which a controlling part of the share capital is transferred, or whether it operates under a simpler legal form, and is sold as a business, together with all assets, rights and obligations.
[135] For example by invoking a contractual clause such as a "change of ownership" clause, which would otherwise permit the supplier to veto any such transfer of ownership.

Question 64: Can a supplier prevent a dealer from selling his dealership to another dealer who is under notice of termination?

If the distribution agreement is to be covered by the Regulation, the supplier may not prevent the transfer of the dealership, provided that the dealer under notice meets all of the supplier's quality criteria.

Question 65: Can a supplier whose distribution agreement is covered by the Regulation prevent a dealer who is under notice of termination from transferring his dealership to another dealer?

No. The Regulation does not cover such a restriction. However, this transfer will not alter the fact that the dealership agreement which is transferred will end once the notice period expires. The dealer will therefore only get an additional dealership for a limited period of time until the end of the notice period.

Question 66: Under the Regulation, can a dealer be prevented from transferring his dealership to an authorised repairer?

Yes. The right to sell only exists in respect of transfers to a network member of the same type, i.e. dealer to dealer, authorised repairer to authorised repairer.[136]

Notes
[136] Article 3(3) and Recital 10.

5.3.8. The end of the dealer agreement

Question 67: Does the Regulation provide for a dealership agreement to have a minimum term?

Under the Regulation an agreement may be entered into for an indefinite period[137] or for a fixed term.[138] If an agreement is for a fixed term, that term may not be shorter than five years. For the purposes of this regulation, a five-year agreement which provides for either party to have the right to bring the agreement to an end part-way through the term[139] is taken to be an agreement for a fixed term of less than five years.

Notes
[137] In other words, the agreement does not provide for a set termination date.
[138] Article 3(5).
[139] In the absence of failure to perform a basic obligation.

Question 68: Does the Regulation provide for minimum periods of notice?

A party who does not wish to renew a fixed-term agreement must inform the other party of its intention not to renew six months prior to the end of the agreement.[140]

A party who wishes to bring an indefinite-term agreement to an end must normally give at least two years' notice of its intention to end the agreement. However, if a supplier is obliged by law or special agreement to pay appropriate compensation on termination of the agreement or if he wishes to terminate an agreement where it is necessary to reorganise the whole or a substantial part of its network, he must give at least one year's notice.[141]

A need for re-organisation may arise due to the behaviour of competitors or due to other economic developments, irrespective of whether these are motivated by internal decisions of a manufacturer or external influences, for example, the closure of a company employing a large workforce in a specific area. In view of the wide variety of situations which may arise, it would be unrealistic to list all the possible reasons for re-organisation.

The question as to whether or not it is necessary to re-organise the network is an objective one, and the fact that the supplier deems such a re-organisation to be necessary does not settle the matter in case of dispute. In such a case it shall be for the national judge or arbitrator to determine the matter with reference to the circumstances.

Whether or not a "substantial part" of the network is affected must be decided in the light of the specific organisation of a manufacturer's network in each case. "Substantial" implies both an economic and a geographical aspect, which may be limited to the network, or a part of it, in a given Member State.

Notes
140 Article 3(5)(a). The consequences of omitting to notify in this way have to be assessed under national law.
141 Article 3(5)(b).

Question 69: Are there exceptional circumstances in which a party to a vertical agreement which is compatible with the Regulation can terminate it without notice?

It is a matter for national law whether the parties to an agreement have the right to terminate it at any time without notice, where the other party fails to perform one of its basic obligations. The parties must establish whether the reason for early termination is sufficient, by common accord or, in case of disagreement, by recourse to an expert third party or an arbitrator and/or by application to the appropriate court, as provided by national law.[142]

Notes
142 Article 3(6).

Question 70: Does the Regulation oblige a supplier to give justified reasons for terminating an agreement with a dealer or authorised repairer?

In order to be covered by the Regulation a supplier who wishes to terminate a dealer agreement must give detailed, objective, and transparent reasons in writing.[143] This condition was introduced in order to prevent a supplier from terminating an agreement because a distributor or a repairer engages in pro-competitive behaviour, such as active or passive sales to foreign consumers, sales of brands from other suppliers or subcontracting repair and maintenance.

In the event of dispute, it will be for the arbitrator or national court to decide whether the reasons given justify the termination of the dealer agreement and, amongst other things, to choose an appropriate remedy if the reasons given do not justify the termination. In coming to a decision as to whether the reasons for termination are well-founded, the arbitrator or judge may have regard to a number of elements including the dealer agreement itself, the requirements of national contract law, as well as the text of the Regulation.

The Regulation sets out a number of types of dealer behaviour that a supplier may not prohibit. If, rather than prohibiting these types of behaviour, a supplier were to seek to prevent such behaviour or bring it to an end by terminating a dealer agreement, this would amount to a serious indirect restriction of competition and would mean that the distribution agreement would no longer be covered by the exemption. The issue as to whether the supplier has chosen to terminate the agreement for the reasons given in the notice, or rather in order to bring pro-competitive behaviour to an end, is a question of fact that may be determined by the independent third party or arbitrator or national judge.

Question 71: Does a supplier have to give reasons for issuing a notice that a fixed-term contract will not be renewed?

No. The Regulation does not require the supplier to give reasons for not wishing to renew a fixed-term contract.[144]

Notes
[144] However, there may be civil law provisions in some Member States that require such reasons to be given.

5.4. Authorised Repairers

An authorised repairer is defined in Article 1(1)(l) of the Regulation. It is an undertaking that belongs to the network of "official" providers of repair and maintenance services put in place by a supplier (vehicle manufacturer or its importer). The term "authorised repairer" is a new one, since under Regulation 1475/95, both car retailing and repair and maintenance were commonly carried out within the suppliers' networks by the same kind of business, commonly referred to as "dealers". In contrast, Regulation 1400/2002 is based on a different concept: the distribution of new motor vehicle and the provision of repair and maintenance services are no longer rigidly linked and may be carried out by separate undertakings.

Regulation 1400/2002 therefore does not allow suppliers to impose an obligation on dealers to carry out repair and maintenance services.[145] Nor does it allow a supplier to oblige its authorised repairers to distribute new motor vehicles.[146]

The Regulation covers a supplier's use of quantitative selective distribution or of exclusive distribution for its network of authorised repairers up to a market share of 30%.[147] For authorised repair networks which exceed this threshold, the Regulation only covers qualitative selection of authorised repairers.[148]

Notes
[145] See Article 4(1)(g). See also Recital 22, which explains an important aspect of the very serious restrictions set out in Article 4(1)(g) and (h) and which explicitly refers to any direct or indirect obligation or incentive which leads to the linking of sales and servicing activities or which makes the performance of one of these activities dependent on the performance of the other.
[146] Article 4(1)(h).
[147] Article 3(1) 1st subparagraph.
[148] Article 3(1) 3rd subparagraph.

5.4.1. How to become an authorised repairer

Question 72: Has the supplier of new motor vehicles to allow a repairer to become a member of its network of authorised repairers?

In principle the supplier is free to choose the members of its network. However, if the supplier wants its agreements to be covered by the Regulation the reply to this question depends on the market share held by the supplier's network of authorised repairers in respect of repairs carried out on all motor vehicles of the brand in question. If this market share is not above 30%, the supplier can base its network of authorised repairers either on quantitative selective distribution or on exclusive distribution and may choose not to appoint particular repairers even though they meet the quality criteria for appointment. If the market share of the authorised repair network of the brand in question is above 30%, the Regulation only covers qualitative selective distribution. If the supplier wishes his distribution agreement to be covered by the Regulation it may thus only impose qualitative criteria for its authorised repairers, and must allow all repairers which fulfil these criteria to operate as authorised repairers, including authorised dealers whose contracts have been terminated but who would like to continue as authorised repairers.

Question 73: Does the supplier have to let all interested repairers know what the criteria are if it applies qualitative selective distribution?

432

Yes. If the supplier were not to disclose the quality criteria, repairers would have no way of knowing how to fulfil them and would not be able to demonstrate that they met them. It seems advisable for suppliers to make these conditions available to any repairer upon request or even to make them public, for example on the Internet.

Question 74: How must a supplier whose authorised repair network is based on purely qualitative criteria apply those criteria?

A supplier which sets qualitative criteria for its network of authorised repairers has to apply the same criteria in the same manner to all repairers. This means in particular:

— As soon as a repairer meets these criteria, he has to be admitted as an authorised repairer. It is however legitimate for a supplier to check whether the repairer meets these criteria before concluding an agreement with him;

— The criteria must be the same for authorised repairers who are dealers selling new motor vehicles of the relevant brand and those who do not. In particular, the supplier must allow all authorised repairers to honour warranties, perform free servicing and carry out recall work in respect of all motor vehicles of the brand in question sold in the Common Market.[149]

Notes
[149] See Recital 17.

5.4.2. No location clause for authorised repairers

Question 75: Does the Regulation cover a restriction on the ability of an authorised repairer within a selective distribution system to decide freely where to locate his repair shop or his additional outlet(s)?

No. Such a restriction is not covered by the Regulation. The authorised repairer must be free to decide on the location of his repair shop and the location of any additional outlet where he provides repair and maintenance services.[150]

Notes
[150] Article 5(3).

5.4.3. Spare parts and the authorised repairer

Please refer also to chapter 7 of this brochure.

Question 76: May a vehicle supplier seek to prevent an authorised repairer from sourcing original spare parts directly from the part manufacturer?

No. This would be a serious restriction of competition.[151]

Notes
[151] See Article 4(1)(k)

Question 77: May a supplier oblige an authorised repairer to inform its customers whether he uses original spare parts or spare parts of matching quality?

Outside the context of warranty work where the supplier may insist on the use of spare parts supplied by himself, it is considered a hardcore restriction if the supplier uses an obligation on the repairer to inform its customers on the use of original spare parts or of spare parts of matching quality as a means to directly or indirectly restrict the right of the authorised repairer to purchase and use such spare parts. In particular, it may not use such an obligation to create the impression in the mind of consumers that these parts are of lesser quality than original spare parts supplied by the vehicle manufacturer.

Question 78: May an authorised repairer be obliged to carry out repairs under warranty, free servicing and vehicle recall work using original spare parts supplied by the vehicle supplier?

Yes. Article 4(1)(k) provides that a vehicle supplier may stipulate that parts supplied by it be used for the above types of repair[152] work. However, as regards the normal repair and maintenance of a motor vehicle, which is not provided for free to the customer, (for example the 30,000 km service of a car) the vehicle supplier may not require the use of original spare parts supplied by it since this would amount to a restriction of the authorised repairers' freedom to use for such maintenance services original or matching quality spare parts from other suppliers.[153]

Question 79: May a supplier oblige an authorised repairer to exclusively use spare parts of this supplier's brand?

Such arrangements, known as non-compete obligations,[154] entered into between the authorised repairer and the vehicle supplier or between the authorised repairer and the supplier of spare parts, would not be covered by the block exemption. However, an obligation to use spare parts of a particular brand for up to 30%[155] of the authorised repairer's purchases of competing spare parts is not considered to be a non-compete obligation and would be covered by the Regulation[156] as long as the authorised repairer is free to buy these goods from the supplier or from other sources designated by the supplier, e.g. as cross-supplies from other authorised distributors or repairers.[157]

Notes
[154] See Articles 1(1)(b) and 5(1)(a).
[155] Calculated on the basis of the value of its purchases of competing goods in the preceding calendar year.
[156] See Article 1(1)(b).
[157] Article 4(1)(b) and (c).

Question 80: Does the Regulation cover an agreement where a vehicle supplier obliges an authorised repairer to keep spare parts for vehicles of different brands in different areas of the repair shop?

No. This would be an indirect restriction on an authorised repairer's right to repair vehicles of other brands. Such a restriction is not covered by the Regulation.[158] A supplier could, however, oblige an authorised repairer to keep an orderly system for storing spare parts.

Notes
[158] See Article 5(1)(b).

Question 81: May a vehicle supplier seek to prevent an authorised repairer from selling original spare parts to independent repairers?

No. This would be a serious restriction of competition.[159]

Notes
[159] See Article 4(1)(i).

5.4.4. Non compete obligations for authorised repairers

Question 82: Does the Regulation cover a vehicle supplier preventing authorised repairers from repairing different brands in the same workshop?

No. Such a restriction, whether direct or indirect, is not covered by the Regulation.[160]

Notes
[160] Article 5(1)(b).

5.4.5. Transfer of the authorised repair business

Question 83: Has an authorised repairer the right to sell his repair shop to a dealership/distributorship?

In order to be covered by the Regulation an agreement between a supplier and a distributor or authorised repairer has to provide for the distributor or repairer to have the right to transfer all of its rights and obligations to any other undertaking *of the same type* chosen by the former distributor or repairer that sells or repairs the same brand of motor vehicles within the distribution system.[161]

An authorised repairer therefore has to be free to sell his repair business to another repairer authorised to repair the same brand.[162] However, a supplier does not have to allow an authorised repairer to sell its repair shop to a dealer, since a dealer is not an undertaking *of the same type*. However, if the dealer to whom the repairer wishes to sell his authorised repair business is also an authorised repairer for the brand in question, the supplier may not oppose the sale.

Notes
[161] Article 3(3) and Recital 10.
[162] Article 3(3).

5.5. Independent Operators on the After-market

One of the main aims of Regulation 1400/2002 is to create the conditions for effective competition on the motor vehicle repair and maintenance markets, and to enable all operators on those markets, including independent repairers, to offer high quality services.

Effective competition is in the interest of consumers and allows them to choose between alternative providers of repair and maintenance services, including those authorised by the vehicle manufacturer and those in the independent sector.

5.5.1. Access to technical information

If competition is to be effective, all independent operators involved in repair and maintenance must have access to the same technical information, training, tools and equipment, as authorised repairers. The approach of Regulation 1400/2002[163] is wider than that of Regulation 1475/95[164] both as regards the operators which are entitled to have access, and the items to which access has to be given.

Access has to be given in a non-discriminatory,[165] prompt and proportionate way, which takes account of the needs of the independent operator in question; it has also to be provided in a usable format.

It would be abusive to deny access to information covered by an intellectual property right or constituting know how in circumstances where such denial would amount to an abuse of a dominant position under Article 82.

Notes
[163] See Article 4(2).
[164] See Article 6(1)(12) of Regulation 1475/95.
[165] There must be no discrimination between independent and authorised repairers.

Question 84: Who qualifies as an independent operator under the Regulation?

Article 4(2) of the Regulation gives a non-exhaustive list of those who are to be considered as "independent operators". Broadly speaking, for the purposes of the Regulation, an independent operator is an undertaking[166] that is directly or indirectly involved in the repair and maintenance of motor vehicles.[167] Independent operators directly involved in repair or maintenance include independent repairers (for example body repairers, independent garages, fast fit chains), roadside assistance operators and automobile clubs. Those who are considered to be indirectly involved in repair and maintenance include publishers of technical information, distributors of spare parts, manufacturers of repair equipment or tools and operators offering testing services or providing training for repairers since these facilitate the work of repairers.

Notes
[166] The term "undertaking" can include an individual, a partnership, an association or a company.
[167] This is, for example, not the case for experts involved in the analysis of road accidents or manufacturers who wish to produce spare parts.

Question 85: Who has to give access to technical information?

It is the responsibility of the supplier of new motor vehicles[168] to make the necessary arrangements to allow independent operators to have the required access. It is however compatible with this obligation if the supplier delegates the responsibility of providing this access to an undertaking which has been entrusted by the vehicle manufacturer with the distribution of technical information, such as a national importer of the brand in question.

Notes
168 See Article 4(2) 1st subparagraph.

Question 86: To what kinds of technical information should an independent operator have access?

Independent operators must have access to the same technical information as authorised repairers. This covers all information needed to carry out repair and maintenance,[169] including that necessary to access and service electronic on-board systems, including diagnostic systems. It covers information in natural language form,[170] as well as electronic data. If a manufacturer provides technical assistance to its authorised repairers via a telephone or Internet help line, independent operators must also be given such assistance.

Notes
169 The access only concerns information needed to carry out repair and maintenance activities. Access therefore does not have to be given to training relating for example to managing a repair business or running an accounting system.
170 Whether printed, voice recorded, or held in electronic form.

Question 87: To what kinds of tools and equipment should an independent operator have access?

Independent operators must have access to the same tools as authorised repairers. This includes hand and machine tools, software and hardware tools,[171] diagnostic and other equipment required for repair and maintenance services. Where a supplier leases tools to authorised repairers, the same facility also has to be made available to independent operators.

Notes
171 Including hardware and software needed to interface with and re-program on-board systems.

Question 88: Does an independent operator have the right to receive training?

Independent operators have to have access to the same technical training required for repair and maintenance services as authorised repairers. This includes both on-line training and training where the mechanic or technician has to be present in person.

Question 89: Can the supplier charge for technical information, tools or training?

Yes. But the price should be no higher than that charged to authorised repairers. If the item in question is supplied free of charge to authorised repairers, it should also be supplied without charge to independent operators.

Question 90: Can a supplier charge an independent operator for a large package of information when all he needs is the information necessary to do a particular job?

No.[172] The price charged for information should take account of the use to which the independent operator intends to put it[173] and should not be so high as to discourage access. Even though information may usually be made available in a large package to authorised repairers, independent operators must be allowed to buy smaller packages or individual items. If, for example, a repairer wishes to service a particular model, he should not have to pay for servicing-related information for the whole range. Similarly, if a "fastfit" operator wishes to know the correct tyre pressures for the entire range of vehicles, he should not be obliged to purchase information not related to tyres.

Notes
172 Article 4(2) and Recital 26.
173 Recital 26.

Question 91: How quickly is an independent operator entitled to receive the information?

The information must be provided to independent operators as quickly as it is made available to authorised repairers.[174] It is therefore not permissible for suppliers to only provide information to independent operators after they have provided it to their authorised repairers. Suppliers have to make the necessary arrangements as regards infrastructure and staff to be able to achieve this. Where information has already been provided to all authorised repairers, it must be made available on request to independent operators quickly enough to enable them to carry out a repair for a customer without undue delay. Where technical information is commonly supplied to authorised repairers via individual data links of a type not commonly used by independent operators, it must be available on request to independent operators via other rapid electronic means such as email or Internet download.

Information on new models should be made available to independent operators at the same time as it is made available to authorised repairers.

Notes
[174] Recital 26.

Question 92: Can publishers of technical information redistribute technical information which they have received from a motor vehicle supplier?

Publishers of technical information normally collect the information from different suppliers and publish it in a standardised format which can easily be used by independent repairers, thereby simplifying access. This is in particular important for small independent operators which repair motor vehicles from different manufacturers and for which direct access to different vehicle manufacturers' systems might be too difficult or complex.

Question 93: Under the Regulation can an independent distributor of spare parts ask a manufacturer to give him the right to resell information?

Like publishers of technical information, independent resellers of spare parts are entitled to access to technical information for their own use; in other words, to enable them to market spare parts efficiently and accurately. Without such access they would not be in a position to keep their customers, the repairers, informed as to which spare parts are needed to a particular job.

If such information were not available at the point of sale, independent repairers would have to obtain it later from the motor vehicle supplier. This would be much more time-consuming and complicated and would put independent repairers at a competitive disadvantage compared to authorised repairers, who get both parts and technical information from the same source. If a supplier were to refuse to grant independent spare part distributors the right to resell technical information, this would prevent effective competition between independent and authorised repairers and would amount to a serious indirect restriction of competition.[175]

Notes
[175] Article 4(2) of the Regulation.

Question 94: Are there any exceptional circumstances in which a supplier can refuse to grant access to technical information?

As an exception to the general rule, the Regulation specifies[176] that it is legitimate and proper for a supplier to withhold access to technical information which might allow a third party to bypass or disarm on-board anti-theft devices, to recalibrate electronic devices[177] or to tamper with devices which, for instance, limit the speed of a vehicle.

However, it is clear that many independent operators will regularly come across situations where access to this kind of information is necessary for them to carry out their tasks. Roadside assistance operators,[178] for instance, must be allowed to do their job without undue difficulty. Information made available to the Commission shows that a large percentage of call-outs relate to consumers who are unable to start their vehicle despite having the ignition key on their person. Another frequent problem concerns consumers who have locked themselves out of their vehicle, leaving the key inside. Clearly in these circumstances it is necessary for roadside operators to be able to have the information necessary to do whatever is necessary to put the consumer back behind the wheel of his vehicle, even if the vehicle is equipped with an electronic anti-theft device. Similarly, independent repairers may also come across situations where they cannot service a vehicle without access to information of this type. One example might be where the removal of the battery or of an electronic component during routine maintenance engaged a device intended to immobilise the vehicle in case of theft.

The exception is therefore to be interpreted narrowly, and suppliers may only withhold information concerning devices of this type if no other less restrictive means exist to attain protection against theft, re-calibration or tampering. One less restrictive method might be to protect a speed limitation device through separate access codes or encryption which prevent any modification of the relevant standard hardware or software, but which allow an independent repairer to install software updates in the course of repair and maintenance work.

As far as anti-theft protection is concerned, it is clear that information could be made available to roadside operators and independent repairers which could only be used by someone who also had the consumer's ignition key. An alternative secure way of transmitting the information needed for maintaining or repairing a motor vehicle could also be the use of a data link compatible with the requirements of ISO DIS 15764 concerning Data Link Security or so called "pass-through-programming techniques" by which a vehicle is directly connected to the vehicle manufacturer, who carries out the reprogramming on the motor vehicle.

Notes

[176] See Recital 26.
[177] Commonly referred to as "chip-tuning".
[178] Such as automobile clubs.

5.5.2. *The relationship between independent and authorised repairers*

An independent repairer, as defined in Article 1(1)(m) of the Regulation, is an independent operator that repairs and maintains vehicles of a given brand without having been appointed by the manufacturer of the brand in question. Independent repairers provide healthy competition to the authorised repair network. A repairer may act as an independent repairer in respect of some brands and as an authorised repairer in respect of others. An independent repairer may also be an authorised distributor (i.e. a "dealer") in respect of one or more brands of new motor vehicle.

6. Market Definition and Calculation of Market Shares

6.1. Principles of Market Definition

The correct delineation of a relevant market raises questions of fact and may evolve over time, amongst other things as a result of the new opportunities which the Regulation opens up. Vertical agreements in the motor vehicle sector relate to numerous and very different products. As a consequence, despite the fact that the Regulation is sector-specific, it does not fix the product and geographic boundaries of the markets to which it applies. With regard to market definition, the Commission follows the approach defined in its Notice on this subject.[179] It also takes into account previous decisions which have precisely defined relevant markets,[180] subject to an assessment of the changes which may have occurred since the decision and taking into account the level of trade at which the decision has defined the market.[181] The Commission Guidelines on Vertical Restraints also clarify specific issues which may arise in respect of vertical agreements.[182]

Notes

[179] Commission Notice on the definition of the relevant market for the purposes of Community competition law, OJ C 372, 9.12.1997, p. 5.
[180] For instance, in Commission Decision of 14.3.2000 in case No COMP/M.1672 — *Volvo/Scania* (OJ L 143, 29.5.2001, p. 74), trucks were subdivided into the light-duty segment (below 5 tonnes), medium duty segment (between 5 and 16 tonnes) and heavy duty segment (above 16 tonnes) and markets were defined as national. The list of decisions adopted by the Commission in application of EC competition rules can be consulted at: http://europa. eu.int/comm/competition/index_en.html
[181] It follows that a definition of a relevant product and geographic market in a decision assessing say, a merger between manufacturers of automotive components, may not always be appropriate to establish the relevant product market affected by a distribution and servicing agreement which concerns the same component used as spare part along with all the other spare parts which are necessary to provide repair services.
[182] Guidelines on Vertical Restraints, section V, paragraphs 88 to 99.

Several principles set out in these notices, which may serve as a guide for the way that markets are to be defined under the Regulation, are illustrated below. This illustration is provided for convenience of the reader and neither supersedes these notices nor prejudges how the Commission would define markets in a specific case.

(1) The Regulation prescribes that product substitutability for the purposes of market definition is to be assessed from the perspective of the buyer.[183] So does the market definition Notice, which places emphasis on demand substitution in response to small but lasting price increases, among other factors. The assessment of demand substitution entails a determination of the range of products or geographic areas which are viewed as substitutes by the buyer and an assessment as to the extent to which demand would react to small and lasting price increases of, say, 5–10%.[184]

Notes

[183] Article 8(1)(a), (b) and (c).

[184] Small but significant and not transitory increase in selling prices, "SSNIP test". The Commission Notice privileges demand substitutability over supply substitutability for the purposes of market definition.

(2) In line with the distinction which the Regulation operates, as a general rule, one should separately examine the activity of selling new motor vehicles and that of selling spare parts and providing repair and maintenance services.[185] For spare parts, the existence of actual substitutes on the market needs to be carefully assessed. In some cases there may be substitutes,[186] in some cases not.[187]

Notes

[185] Single markets which would include motor vehicles and spare parts together may be defined, taking into account, inter alia, the life-time of the motor-vehicle as well as the preferences and buying behaviour of the users, see Notice on market definition, paragraph 56. In practice, the issue to decide is whether a significant proportion of buyers make their choice taking into account the lifetime costs of the vehicle or not. Buying behaviour may significantly differ, for instance, between buyers of trucks who purchase and operate a fleet which take into account maintenance costs at the moment of purchasing the vehicle (e.g. bundled purchase and use contracts of trucks billed on price per km) and buyers of individual vehicles.

[186] For instance products used in unsophisticated repair or maintenance operations. In the case of batteries, for instance, several alternatives present on the market may be safely fitted in a particular car model.

[187] For many brand-specific spare parts, as there may be no readily alternative sources of supply in the market, end-consumers would not get their cars repaired with a different spare part. In the absence of substitutes, spare parts for a particular brand may thus be defined as a relevant product market affected by the agreement between a supplier and its authorised repair network.

(3) The level of trade at which a vertical agreement is entered into must be taken into account in order to assess substitutability and, hence, to define the market(s) affected.[188] It cannot be excluded, for instance, that the same spare part pertains to different relevant markets depending on the stage of the production or distribution chain at which the agreement is entered into, e.g. first supply ex works, wholesaling trade or retail.[189]

Notes

[188] Guidelines on Vertical Restraints, paragraphs 91 to 94.

[189] Supply or wholesaling agreements as to components or spare parts may be entered into between parties which have all or several Member States as geographic scope of activity, hence leading to defining the geographic markets accordingly (see, for instance, Commission Decision of 25.1.2002 in case No COMP/M.2696 — *TMD/MENETA/ MAST*, in which the Commission was of the opinion that the relevant geographic market for the production of anti-vibration shims for automotive disc brakes was at least EU-wide). Vertical agreements further downstream at the stage of distribution may affect more narrowly defined markets. The agreements immediately prior to the retailing stage may typically involve buyers for which a national or a regional delineation of the relevant market is appropriate.

(4) For distribution of final goods, such as motor vehicles, or provision of repair and maintenance services to end-consumers, what is substitutable from the point of view of buyers which are active as retailers, such as authorised distributors or repairers who are members of the distribution system, will normally be determined by the preferences of end-users. If different motor vehicles are not substitutable for end-users, they will be deemed not to be substitutable for distributors who retail them.[190] However, for an intermediate product which is not recognisable in the final good,

the preferences of end-users will not greatly determine those of the buyer, for example the vehicle manufacturer.[191]

Notes

[190] For instance, two different motor vehicles, say a light commercial vehicle and a luxury limousine will not be held to be substitutable for the buyer if they are not substitutable for the final consumer, irrespective of whether the same distributor actually buys both for resale.

[191] For instance, a component to be assembled in the vehicle, may lead to defining the product market according to the preferences of the vehicle manufacturer. A vertical agreement concluded between the latter and a component supplier would affect a hypothetical market of, say, "diesel fuel injection systems for light vehicles, including passenger cars and light commercial vehicles" (see, for instance, Commission Decision of 11.7.1996 in case No IV/M.768 — *Lucas/Varity*).

(5) The existence of chains of substitution between products which are not directly substitutable needs to be assessed. If no well established precedent for definition of the relevant market is available, possible chains of substitution are particularly relevant and need to be investigated for different ranges of motor vehicles.[192]

Notes

[192] Notice on market definition, paragraph 57. For instance, given three categories (e.g. segments) of vehicles A, B and C, of which A is held to be substitutable with B but not with C, but B is held to be substitutable with C, the relevant product market may include vehicles from categories A, B and C altogether. Notwithstanding the absence of direct substitutability between the extremes A and C, their substitutability with their "neighbour" category B may constrain sufficiently the competitive behaviour of suppliers of A and C.

(6) As regards after-sales services and spare parts, the vertical agreement between a supplier of motor vehicles and its brand network of authorised repairers often covers a bundle of contract goods, as well as service, support and licensing of intellectual property rights. This bundling, combined with sizeable brand-specific investments enables the authorised network to provide repair services for the vehicles of the brand in question. In such cases, the supplier calculates its market shares on the value of both the goods, in particular spare parts, which it supplies to its network, that is, on the market between suppliers and repairers and of the services which the network provides, that is, on the market downstream between repairers and end-users.[193]

Notes

[193] Recital 7. Guidelines on Vertical Restraints, paragraph 95.

6.2. Examples of Market Definition and Calculation of Market Shares

Article 8
Market share calculation

1. The market shares provided for in this Regulation shall be calculated

(a) for the distribution of new motor vehicles on the basis of the volume of the contract goods and corresponding goods sold by the supplier, together with any other goods sold by the supplier which are regarded as interchangeable or substitutable by the buyer, by reason of the products' characteristics, prices and intended use;

(b) for the distribution of spare parts on the basis of the value of the contract goods and other goods sold by the supplier, together with any other goods sold by the supplier which are regarded as interchangeable or substitutable by the buyer, by reason of the products' characteristics, prices and intended use;

(c) for the provision of repair and maintenance services on the basis of the value of the contract services sold by the members of the supplier's distribution network together with any other services sold by these members which are regarded as interchangeable or substitutable by the buyer, by reason of their characteristics, prices and intended use.

If the volume data required for those calculations are not available, value data may be used or vice versa. If such information is not available, estimates based on other reliable market information may be used. For the purposes of Article 3(2), the market purchase volume or the market purchase value respectively, or estimates thereof shall be used to calculate the market share.

Article 1
Definitions

(. . .)

2. The terms "undertaking", "supplier", "buyer", "distributor" and "repairer" shall include their respective connected undertakings. "Connected undertakings" are:
   (a) undertakings in which a party to the agreement, directly or indirectly:
       (i) has the power to exercise more than half the voting rights, or
       (ii) has the power to appoint more than half the members of the supervisory board, board of management or bodies legally representing the undertaking, or
       (iii) has the right to manage the undertaking's affairs;
   (b) undertakings which directly or indirectly have, over a party to the agreement, the rights or powers listed in (a);
   (c) undertakings in which an undertaking referred to in (b) has, directly or indirectly, the rights or powers listed in (a);
   (d) undertakings in which a party to the agreement together with one or more of the undertakings referred to in (a), (b) or (c), or in which two or more of the latter undertakings, jointly have the rights or powers listed in (a);
   (e) undertakings in which the rights or the powers listed in (a) are jointly held by:
       (i) parties to the agreement or their respective connected undertakings referred to in (a) to (d), or
       (ii) one or more of the parties to the agreement or one or more of their connected undertakings referred to in (a) to (d) and one or more third parties.

For the purposes of application of the Regulation, the relevant market shares are those held by the supplier, except for agreements containing exclusive supply obligations,[194] for which the market shares of the buyer are pertinent. The terms "supplier" and "buyer" within the meaning of the Regulation are not limited to the legal entity which is a party to the agreement. They also include the other connected companies which together form an undertaking within the meaning of Article 81(1). As a consequence, the calculation of market shares for the agreement entered into by one brand which is a separate legal entity should, for the purposes of the Regulation, add altogether the sales in the relevant market of the other brands which are part of the same undertaking including its connected undertakings.

Notes
[194] See definition of Article 1(1)(e).

The calculation of market shares can be illustrated with four typical, yet hypothetical examples. This illustration is provided for convenience of the reader and does not prejudge how the Commission would define markets in a specific case.

Example a): Calculation of market shares for a specific car model when there is a chain of substitution between candidate product markets

A supplier is concerned by the success in its home Member State of its new model of car targeted at urban consumers (segment C following, for instance, the classification used by the Commission in its twice-yearly reports on car prices or similar classifications used in industry surveys). Previous Commission decisions have not precisely defined passenger car market(s).[195] The supplier wishes to analyse whether the high market share held by this model compared to competing models which pertain to the same segment has any consequence on the coverage by the Regulation of its distribution agreements. Let us assume that as distributors purchase on a national basis, wide differences in price and market penetration exist among Member States and parallel trading is minor, the retail markets are normally deemed to be national.

The basic model of the car is sold for 15 000 Euro, but additional options may increase the price by 33%, up to 20 000 Euro, at a price level similar to the selling prices of basic models in the higher-end segment D. A market survey shows that a similar price overlap exists with the lower segment B. In such situations, a chain of substitution between the three candidate product markets may justify establishing a single relevant product market which encompass all three segments if sufficient substitution between the segments can be established.[196] The supplier thus calculates its market share on the basis of the number of all its car models pertaining to segments B, C, and D, supplied to its distribution network and sold in the relevant geographic market, that is, the Member State, divided by the total number of models pertaining to segments B, C, and D sold on this market.

Notes

[195] Passenger cars can be subdivided according to objective factors such as horsepower, body and price into different segments. No previous Commission decision has defined precisely the relevant market for sales of passenger cars under Article 81 or under Council Regulation (EEC) No 4064/89 of 21 December 1989 on the control of concentrations between undertakings (OJ L 395, 30.12.1989; corrected version OJ L 257, 21.9.1990, p. 13). Concerning mergers among car manufacturers even with the narrowest market definitions taking into account industry classification of different cars within different segments, the precise definition did not alter the assessment of the case. For the application of Article 81, the infringements at hand concerned restrictions of competition by object, appreciable under alternative market definitions, and the precise definition were left open. For mergers, see, for instance, cases M.416 *BMW/Rover*, M.741 *Ford/Mazda*, M.1204 *DaimlerBenz/Chrysler*, M. 1283, *Volkswagen/Rolls Royce*, M.1326 *Toyota/Daihatsu*, M.1416 *Hyundai/Kia*, M.1452 *Ford/Volvo*, M.1847 *GM/Saab*, M.1998 *Ford/Land-Rover*, M.2832 *General Motors/Daewoo*. None of these concentrations raised concerns under the narrowest possible market definition. For the application of Article 81, see, for instance, *Volkswagen I* (1998) and II (2001), *Opel* (2000), *DaimlerChrysler* (2001).

[196] An example of segmentation examined by the Commission is the following: A: mini-cars (e.g. Smart), B: small cars (Fiat Punto), C: medium cars (VW Golf), D: large cars (Volvo S-70), E: executive cars (Audi A6), F: luxury cars (Mercedes Class S), S: sport cars (Ferrari), M: Multi-purpose cars (or MPV-VAN, Renault Espace), J: sport utility cars (including four-wheel drive, Suzuki Vitara). See cases M.416 *BMW/Rover* and M.1452 *Ford/Volvo*. With a chain of substitution, several of these segments may be aggregated into separate product markets, so that there would be less relevant markets than segments. It is however questionable whether such a chain of substitution could be extended to cover all segments.

Example b): Distribution agreements concerning retail sales of passenger cars between a vehicle manufacturer and its network of authorised distributors

A supplier of passenger cars commercialises its product range through a network of authorised distributors in the 15 Member States of the European Union, following a system of quantitative selective distribution. Such a system is covered by the Regulation if the supplier holds less than a 40% share of the relevant markets affected by the distribution agreements. Following the Commission's Guidelines on Vertical Restraints and previous decisions, retailing of cars is normally viewed as a market distinct from that of manufacturing and wholesaling.[197] As currently seems to be the case distributors actually purchase on a national basis, wide differences in price and market penetration exist among Member States and parallel trading is minor, the retail markets are deemed to be national. The product range includes several car models, which are mainly purchased by consumers, whose individual preferences for a particular type of car determine those of the authorised distributor.[198] The car models sold by the network are classified into segments B, C and D.

The supplier then calculates its market share(s) in the preceding calendar year for each of these three "candidate" product markets, based for instance, on public data on car registrations in each Member State. The calculation also includes retail sales made by the supplier through directly-operated sales points.[199]

If the total sales of all the brands pertaining to the same supplier are lower than 40% in each of the candidate product markets B, C and D and for each Member State, the agreements fulfil the general condition set out in Article 3(1) of the Regulation.[200] If, in one or several Member States, the threshold is exceeded on one candidate market, the issue whether a chain of substitution would lead to defining a broader product market encompassing these three candidate product markets needs to be explored.

Notes

197 Guidelines on Vertical Restraints, paragraphs 91–92. See, for instance, as regards car distribution, cases M.182 *Inchape/IEP*, M.1592 *Toyota Motor/Toyota Denmark*, M.1036 *Chrysler/Distributors (BeNeLux, Germany)*, M.1761 *Toyota Motor/Toyota France*.

198 See above Section 6.1, point (4).

199 Article 8(2)(b).

200 In this example, high market shares held by a different brand under the control of the same undertaking for sport cars would be irrelevant if such cars were not included in the same relevant market affected by the distribution agreements. The same would be true if the high market shares are held in other Member States which are not part of the relevant market affected by the agreement or for products which do not compete with passenger cars, whether covered by the Regulation, e.g. coaches, or not, e.g. motor-bikes.

Example c): Servicing agreements between a vehicle manufacturer and its network of authorised repairers

A manufacturer of passenger cars organises a network of authorised repairers for its brand, which are entrusted to honour its warranty. The manufacturer also supplies the network with spare parts and gives them access to supply-chain logistics, software and items which are protected by intellectual property rights. Members of the system are allowed to mention their standing as authorised repairers for that brand and to use the brand's trademark in their repair shop and adverts. Authorised repairers have to make sizeable brand-specific investments, which put them in a position to provide the entire range of repair and maintenance services for all the vehicles of the brand. As the supply to the network is organised on a national basis and network members can and do purchase at similar trading conditions on such a basis, the national market is held to be the geographic market affected by the agreement.

The provision of spare parts, repair and maintenance services is held to be distinct from the market of sale of new vehicles in question.201 Assume that market surveys indicate in this example that, although other repairers do effectively service cars of the brand in question which have a certain age or carry out unsophisticated maintenance or repair operations, e.g. exhaust, batteries, tyres, only the authorised network is able to and does actually provide servicing of most cars of the brand operated in each geographic market. If car owners do not view brand-specific repair services as substitutable with non-brand specific repair services, and if many brand-specific spare parts are not substitutable with non-brand specific parts for providing those services, the total value of the market for the authorised network is the value of the services provided for the vehicles of the brand in question in the national market the preceding calendar year, or estimates thereof.202

In this situation, the supplier should calculate its market share(s) on the national market(s) both on the basis of the value of the repair and maintenance services which the network provides and on the value of the spare parts, some of which are unique to the brand, which it sells to its network.203 Spare parts supplied at no profit for the purposes of honouring legal obligations of warranty are not included in the calculation. In this example it is likely that the supplier and its network's market share(s) will be above the 30% threshold set out in Article 3(1) of the Regulation, for those spare parts fitted in its product range which are not substitutable with spare parts from other brands and for those repair services provided by the authorised network which are not provided by independent repairers. This will depend on market penetration by independent suppliers of brand-specific original spare parts and parts of matching quality.

Notes

201 See above Section 6.1, point (4), e.g. the cars in question are mainly purchased by end-consumers, have on average a useful life of 12 years, and change ownership several times. Servicing costs do not greatly influence the choice between buying competing vehicles. See also Case M.416 *BMW/Rover*.

202 See Section 6.1, point (2) above and Article 8(1) last sub-paragraph. Estimates of the value of the services provided may be calculated based on the park of vehicles operated in a particular area.

203 See Article 8(1), in particular, (b) and (c) and section 6.1, point (2).

Example d): Calculation of market shares for a franchise network of independent repairers

A supplier which does not manufacture motor vehicles organises a network of repairers as an exclusive distribution system, that is, a system in which exclusive geographic areas are allotted to each repairer. It also applies qualitative standards on the provision of repair services and allows the network to use intellectual property rights and provides it with technical and commercial assistance for the operation and maintenance of a distinctive brand-image. It also supplies directly spare parts or sets out standards for parts to be used by the network in the provision of repair and maintenance services. The network provides only unsophisticated repair and maintenance services for all brands of motor vehicles. As the supply to the network is organised on a national basis and network members can and do actually purchase at similar trading conditions on such basis, the national market is held to be the geographic market affected by the agreement.

The Regulation covers the agreements implementing the network if the supplier's market share does not exceed 30% on any of the product or service markets affected. The network provides no brand-specific service and consumers have, in respect of the range of services offered by the network, the choice between alternative providers of the relevant service, e.g. car manufacturers' repair networks, other fast-fit networks, individual independent repairers. The general condition laid down in Article 3(1) of the Regulation is thus met if competitors provide 70% or more on the relevant repair and maintenance markets for all passenger cars in that Member State and if, for each category of spare parts, the value of the spare parts which the supplier sells to the network amounts to 30% or less of the purchase value of the spare parts used in such repairs on the market as a whole.

7. DISTRIBUTION OF AND ACCESS TO SPARE PARTS

Regulation 1400/2002 aims at ensuring competition in the spare part market. To this end it lists a number of hardcore restrictions and does not allow suppliers, in particular vehicle manufacturers and their importers, to restrict the right of their distributors and authorised repairers to obtain original spare parts and spare parts of matching quality from any third undertaking of their choice and to use them for the repair and maintenance of motor vehicles.[204] Nor may vehicle manufacturers restrict the right of spare part manufacturers to sell original spare parts or spare parts of matching quality to authorised or independent repairers.[205] Moreover, Regulation 1400/2002 does not allow suppliers to restrict the right of their distributors and authorised repairers to sell spare parts to independent repairers, who use them for the repair and maintenance of motor vehicles.[206]

Notes

[204] Article 4(1)(k).

[205] Article 4(1)(j).

[206] Article 4(1)(i) clarifies this for selective distribution systems of spare parts; within an exclusive distribution system this follows from Article 4(1)(b)(i) which prevents a supplier using exclusive distribution to restrict passive sales to any type of customer.

In order to improve the conditions for effective competition, Regulation 1400/2002 introduces the new term "original spare part".[207] These are spare parts of the same quality as the components used for the assembly of a new motor vehicle. Original spare parts can be manufactured by the vehicle manufacturer, but most are manufactured by part manufacturers based on supply agreements with the vehicle manufacturer. They are manufactured according to the specifications and production standards provided by the vehicle manufacturer and in many cases they are produced on the same production line as the components used for the assembly of the motor vehicle.

Notes

[207] See the definition in Article 1(1)(t).

The word "provided" means that these specifications and production standards are employed by the spare part manufacturer in question with the vehicle manufacturer's consent with a view to the incorporation of parts corresponding to those specifications and standards in its vehicles. It is however not necessary for the vehicle manufacturer to have developed these specifications and standards; these may also result from a joint development programme or may even have been developed exclusively by the component or spare part manufacturer. In the latter case the specifications and production standards are deemed to be provided to the spare part manufacturer with the vehicle manufacturer's consent and the spare part manufacturer can use them for the production of original spare parts. It is also not necessary under Regulation 1400/2002 for the vehicle manufacturer to explicitly give permission for the part manufacturer, which produces components, to use these specifications and standards for the production and distribution of original spare parts: the fact that these standards are available to the spare part manufacturer allows it to also use them for the production of original spare parts which are not supplied to the vehicle manufacturer, but are rather sold directly to spare part distributors or repairers.[208]

Notes

[208] Indeed any restriction on this ability would constitute a hardcore restraint under Article 4(1)(k).

Since in nearly all cases the same part manufacturer makes both components and spare parts for a vehicle using the same specifications and production standards, the spare parts in question are clearly "original". However, in some specific cases manufacturers have supply agreements with part manufacturers that only manufacture and supply spare parts for a vehicle and do not manufacture its components. If these parts are made according to specifications and production standards provided by the vehicle manufacturer which are the same as those used for the production of the components, they also are "original spare parts".

"Original spare parts" are to be distinguished from "matching quality spare parts."[209] Matching quality parts match the quality of the components used for the assembly of the relevant vehicle but are not produced according to the specifications and production standards provided by the vehicle manufacturer. This means that these parts are of the same or even higher quality, but may for example be made of another material or be painted in another colour.

Notes

[209] See the definition in Article 1(1)(u).

Question 95: Is an accessory a spare part?

It follows from the definition in Article 1(1)(s) that goods which are not necessary for the use of the motor vehicle in question, such as a radio set or a CD player, a GSM hands-free installation, a navigation system or a luggage rack, which are normally referred to as accessories, are not considered to be spare parts. However, if such goods are installed on the production line of the new vehicle and integrated with other parts or systems of the vehicle then these goods become components of that vehicle and the parts needed to repair or replace these goods are spare parts (e.g. Hi-fi controls integrated in a car steering wheel). Air conditioning or temperature control equipment which is installed on a truck or bus or an alarm system or hi-fi system installed on a car after the vehicle has left the vehicle manufacturer's production line has therefore to be considered as an accessory.

Regulation 1400/2002 is not applicable to the distribution, repair and maintenance of accessories. Their distribution may come under Regulation 2790/1999.

Question 96: Are lubricants or other liquids spare parts and if so what are the consequences?

Please refer to question 2.

Question 97: What are "original spare parts"?

There are three categories of "original spare parts".

The first category of original spare parts consists of parts which are manufactured by the vehicle manufacturer. The following rules apply to these original spare parts:

— the vehicle manufacturer may require its authorised repairers to use this category of original spare parts for repairs carried out under warranty, free servicing and vehicle recall work;[210]
— the vehicle manufacturer may not limit the right of its distributors to sell this category of parts, actively or passively as the case may be, on to independent repairers which use them for the repair and maintenance of motor vehicles;[211] in this respect it is irrelevant whether these repairers use them in their workshop or for the provision of roadside assistance services.

Notes

[210] See Article 4(1)(k).
[211] See Article 4(1)(i) or 4(1)(b)(i).

The <u>second category</u> of "original spare parts" refers to parts which are supplied by the spare part manufacturer to the vehicle manufacturer, who sells them on to its distributors. The following rules apply to these original spare parts:

— the spare part producer may not be restricted from placing its trade mark or logo effectively and in an easily visible manner on these parts.[212] This right also includes the right to place the trademark or logo on the packaging and on any accompanying document;
— the vehicle manufacturer may also place its trademark or logo on these parts;
— the spare part producer may not be restricted from supplying these spare parts to any authorised or independent spare part distributor or any authorised or independent repairer,[213] and the authorised repairer may not be restricted from using these parts;[214]
— the vehicle manufacturer may require its authorised repairers to use this category of original spare parts for repairs carried out under warranty, free servicing and vehicle recall work;[215]
— the vehicle manufacturer may not limit the right of its distributors to sell this category of parts, actively or passively as the case may be, on to independent repairers which use them for the repair and maintenance of motor vehicles;[216] in this respect it is irrelevant whether these repairers use them in their workshop or for the provision of roadside assistance services.

Notes
[212] See Article 4(1)(l).
[213] See Article 4(1)(j).
[214] See Article 4(1)(k).
[215] See Article 4(1)(k).
[216] See Article 4(1)(i) or 4(1)(b)(i).

The <u>third category</u> of "original spare parts" consists of those which are not supplied to the relevant vehicle manufacturer, but which are nevertheless manufactured according to the specifications and production standards provided by it. The spare part manufacturer either supplies these parts to independent spare part distributors or directly to repairers. The following rules apply to this category of original spare parts:

— the spare part producer may not be restricted from placing its trade mark or logo effectively and in an easily visible manner on these parts. This also includes the right to place the trademark or logo on the packaging;[217]
— the spare part producer may not be restricted from supplying these spare parts to any authorised or independent spare part distributor or any authorised or independent repairer,[218] and the authorised repairer may not be restricted from using these parts.[219]

Notes
[217] See Article 4(1)(l).
[218] See Article 4 (1)(j).
[219] See Article 4(1)(k).

Question 98: May the supplier require its authorised repairers to only use original spare parts supplied by it for the normal maintenance or the repair of motor vehicles?

No. An obligation on an authorised repairer to only use original spare parts supplied to it by the vehicle manufacturer for the normal maintenance[220] or repair[221] of a motor vehicle would amount to a restriction of the repairer's liberty to use original spare parts or spare parts of matching quality sourced from other suppliers of his choice.[222]

Notes
[220] For instance routine servicing.
[221] For instance after an accident.
[222] See Article 4(1)(k).

Question 99: May the use of original spare parts from other sources than the supplier or of spare parts of matching quality have an impact on the vehicle manufacturer's warranty?

If a vehicle manufacturer's warranty were to require authorised or independent repairers to use original spare parts supplied by it for normal repair and maintenance during the warranty period (but not covered by the warranty), this would be a hard core restriction, as set out in Article 4(1)(k), and the manufacturer's distribution system would no longer be covered by Regulation 1400/2002.

Question 100: Are authorised repairers or spare part distributors allowed to sell spare parts, which have been supplied to them by the vehicle manufacturer, to independent repairers?

Yes. A restriction on sales of spare parts by members of a selective distribution system to independent repairers, which use them for the provision of repair and maintenance services, is a serious restriction of competition.[223] A restriction of passive sales of spare parts for motor vehicles by members of an exclusive distribution system is also a serious restriction.[224] In both cases, the manufacturer's distribution system would no longer be covered by Regulation 1400/2002.

Notes
[223] See Article 4(1)(i); Article 3(10)(b) and Article 6(1)(3) Regulation 1475/95.
[224] See Article 4(1)(b).

Question 101: How is the quality of original spare parts demonstrated?

A part producer which produces spare parts based on specifications and production standards provided to it by the vehicle manufacturer has to issue a certificate confirming that the spare parts have been produced accordingly and that the parts are of the same quality as the components used for the assembly of the vehicle in question.[225] Such an affirmation by the part producer can be printed on the packaging or on a paper which accompanies the part or be published on the Internet. It is for the part manufacturer to decide whether it wants to issue such a certificate itself or whether it wishes to go further and to refer to a certification carried out by an independent body such as a certification organisation. Certification by an independent body is however not a requirement for parts to qualify as original spare parts.

If such a declaration has been issued, it is to be presumed that these spare parts are original spare parts, and an authorised repairer may use them for the repair and maintenance. However, if the vehicle manufacturer or any third party, for example a consumer association or automobile club, could prove that a certain spare part or a certain number of spare parts belonging to the same production lot is of lesser quality or has not been manufactured according to the specifications or production standards of the vehicle manufacturer, these spare parts cannot be sold as original spare parts.

Notes
[225] See Article 1(1)(t), 3rd sentence.

Question 102: How is the quality of matching quality spare parts demonstrated?

If a spare part is to qualify as being of matching quality, the spare part manufacturer must be able to certify at any moment that it matches the quality of the corresponding component of the motor vehicle in question.[226] It is for the spare part manufacturer to issue such a declaration and to make it known to the user in the same way as for original spare parts (see above). Such a certification has to be made available at any moment, that is to say not only when the part is sold, but also at a later stage, for example if the part is alleged to be faulty.

Notes
[226] See Article 1(1)(u).

Question 103: May the vehicle manufacturer or its importer prevent its authorised repairers from sourcing and using spare parts from the independent aftermarket which are of the same quality as its "Economy Line" spare parts?

Vehicle manufacturers themselves nowadays also sell "Economy Line" spare parts through their own distribution networks. These spare parts are made according to newly defined standards (which differ from the standards for components) for vehicles which are no longer in serial production. Such a restriction would not be covered by the Regulation because this would amount to a non-compete obligation.[227]

Notes
[227] See Article 5(1)(a).

Question 104: If a vehicle manufacturer enters into an agreement with a spare part manufacturer which provides that any intellectual property rights (IPR) or know how that the spare part manufacturer has developed is to be transferred to the vehicle manufacturer, can the vehicle manufacturer use these rights to restrict the right of the spare part manufacturer to distribute the spare parts manufactured using those rights?

No. Even though the Regulation does not rule out such a transfer of rights, IPRs or know how may not be used by the supplier (vehicle manufacturer or its importer) to restrict the spare part manufacturer's right to sell the spare parts in question to authorised and independent repairers.[228] If the supplier were to use IPRs or know how in this way, Regulation 1400/2002 would not apply to the its distribution system.

Notes
[228] Article 4(1)(j) and (k).

8. Annex I — Reference to the Most Important Documents Concerning the Competition Rules for Motor Vehicle Distribution in the European Union

Some of these documents are also available on the Commission web site

http://europa.eu.int/comm/competition/car_sector

Motor vehicle block exemption regulation

- Commission Regulation (EC) No 1400/2002 of 31 July 2002 on the application of Article 81(3) of the Treaty to categories of vertical agreements and concerted practices in the motor vehicle sector. *Published in the Official Journal L 203, 1.8.2002, p. 30.*
- Decision of the EEA Joint Committee No 136/2002 of 27 September 2002 amending Annex XIV (Competition) to the EEA Agreement incorporating Commission Regulation (EC) No 1400/2002 of 31 July 2002 into the EEA Agreement [*Published in the Official Journal L 336, 12.12.2002, p. 38*].

Previous regulations and notices

- Commission Regulation (EC) No 1475/95 of 28 June 1995 on the application of Article 85(3) of the Treaty to certain categories of motor vehicle distribution and servicing agreements. *Published in the Official Journal L 145, 29.6.1995, p. 25.*
- Explanatory brochure on the Commission Regulation (EC) No 1475/95 of 28 June 1995 on the application of Article 85(3) of the Treaty to certain categories of motor vehicle distribution and servicing agreements. *Published by Directorate General IV – Competition, IV/9509/95.*
- Commission Regulation (EEC) No 123/85 of 12 December 1984 on the application of Article 85(3) of the Treaty to certain categories of motor vehicle distribution and servicing agreements. *Published in the Official Journal L 15, 18.1.1985, p. 16.*
- Commission notice concerning Regulation (EEC) No 123/85 of 12 December 1984 on the application of Article 85(3) of the Treaty to certain categories of motor vehicle distribution and servicing agreements. *Published in the Official Journal C 17, 18.1.1985, p.4.*
- Information from the Commission — Clarification of the activities of motor vehicle intermediaries. *Published in the Official Journal C 329, 18.12.1991, p. 20.*

General regulation and notices on vertical restraints

- Commission Regulation (EC) No 2790/1999 of 22 December 1999 on the application of Article 81(3) of the Treaty to categories of vertical agreements and concerted practices. *Published in the Official Journal L 336, 29.12.1999, p. 21.*

- Commission Notice — Guidelines on Vertical Restraints. *Published in the Official Journal C 291, 13.10.2000, p. 1.*
- Commission Notice on agreements of minor importance which do not appreciably restrict competition under Article 81(1) of the Treaty establishing the European Community (de minimis). *Published in the Official Journal C 368, 22.12.2001, p. 13.*

Studies

- Quantitative Study on the demand for new cars to define the relevant market in the passenger car sector by Frank Verboven, K.U. Leuven and C.E.P.R., *September 2002*
- Customer preferences for existing and potential sales and servicing alternatives in automotive distribution by Dr. Lademann & Partner, *December 2001*
- Study on the impact of possible future legislative scenarios for motor vehicle distribution on all parties concerned by Andersen, *December 2001*
- Car price differentials in the European Union: An economic analysis by Hans Degryse and Frank Verboven, K.U. Leuven and C.E.P.R, *November 2000*
- The Natural Link between Sales and Service by Autopolis, *November 2000*

Recent decisions (Article 81)

- Commission Decision of 10.10.2001 against DaimlerChrysler AG. *Press release IP/01/1394 of 10.10.2001. Published in the Official Journal L 257, 25.9.2002, p. 1.*
- Commission Decision of 29.6.2001 against Volkswagen AG. *Press release IP/01/760 of 30.5.2001. Published in the Official Journal L 262, 2.10.2001, p. 14.*
- Commission Decision of 20.9.2000 against Opel Nederland BV / General Motors Nederland BV. *Press release IP/00/1028 of 20.9.2000. Published in the Official Journal L 59, 28.2.2001, p. 1.*
- Commission Decision of 28.1.1998 against Volkswagen AG. *Press release IP/98/94 of 28.1.1998. Published in the Official Journal L 124, 25.4.1998, p. 60.*
- The Commission Decision of 28.1.1998 against Volkswagen AG was largely confirmed by the European Court of First Instance in its judgment of 6.7.2000 in case T-62/98, Volkswagen v Commission. *Commission Press release IP/00/725 of 6.7.2000. Court of First Instance Press release 50/00 of 6.7.2000. Published in the European Court reports 2000, p. II-02707.*

Other documents

- Commission Report on the evaluation of Regulation (EC) No 1475/95 on the application of Article 85(3) [now 81(3)] of the Treaty to certain categories of motor vehicle distribution and servicing agreements, *15.11.2000 — COM(2000)743 final.*
- Public hearing of 13–14 February 2001 on motor vehicle distribution — Speaking notes and presentation slides.
- Car price report, published twice a year by the Directorate General for Competition of the European Commission.

9. ANNEX II — TEXT OF REGULATION 1400/2002

Official Journal L 203, 1.8.2002, p. 30

Also available in all the official Community languages on the Internet:
http://europa.eu.int/comm/competition/car_sector/

Notes

The text of Regulation 1400/2002/EC is reproduced at page [236 et seq] above.

10. INDEX

A

Agent

451

Part C Substantive Antitrust Matters

C15

COMMISSION RECOMMENDATION

of 6 May 2003

concerning the definition of micro, small and medium-sized enterprises
(notified under document number C(2003) 1422)

(Text with EEA relevance)

(2003/361/EC)

Official Journal L 124, 20.5.2003, p. 36

Celex No: 32003H0361

Notes

EEA application: this Recommendation was incorporated (as Annex I to Commission Regulation (EC) No 70/2001, as amended) into the EEA Agreement by EEA Joint Committee Decision of 25 September 2004 No 131/2004 (OJ L 264, 10.3.2005, p. 67 and EEA supplement No 12, 10.3.2005, p. 49). See also the EFTA Surveillance Authority's Procedural and Substantive Rules in the Field of State Aid (Guidelines on the application and interpretation of Articles 61 and 62 of the EEA Agreement and Article 1 of Protocol 3 to the Surveillance and Court Agreement), Part III, Chapter 10 (as introduced by EFTA Surveillance Authority Decision of 19 April 2006, not yet published).

Commentary

Recommendation: B&C: 1.124 F&N: 9.63

THE COMMISSION OF THE EUROPEAN COMMUNITIES,

Having regard to the Treaty establishing the European Community, and in particular Article 211, second indent, thereof,

Whereas:

(1) In a report submitted to the Council in 1992 at the request of the "Industry" Council held on 28 May 1990, the Commission had proposed limiting the proliferation of definitions of small and medium-sized enterprises in use at Community level. Commission Recommendation 96/280/EC of 3 April 1996 concerning the definition of small and medium-sized enterprises[1] was based on the idea that the existence of different definitions at Community level and at national level could create inconsistencies. Following the logic of a single market without internal frontiers, the treatment of enterprises should be based on a set of common rules. The pursuit of such an approach is all the more necessary in view of the extensive interaction between national and Community measures assisting micro, small and medium-sized enterprises (SME), for example in connection with Structural Funds or research. It means that situations in which the Community focuses its action on a given category of SMEs and the Member States on another must be avoided. In addition, it was considered that the application of the same definition by the Commission, the Member States, the European Investment Bank (EIB) and the European Investment Fund (EIF) would improve the consistency and effectiveness of policies targeting SMEs and would, therefore, limit the risk of distortion of competition.

Notes

[1] OJ L 107, 30.4.1996, p. 4.

---

(2) Recommendation 96/280/EC has been applied widely by the Member States, and the definition contained in the Annex thereto has been taken over in Commission Regulation (EC) No 70/2001 of 12 January 2001 on the application of Articles 87 and 88 of the EC Treaty to State aid to small and medium-sized enterprises.[1] Apart from the need to adapt Recommendation 96/280/EC to

economic developments, pursuant to Article 2 of the Annex thereto, consideration must be given to a number of difficulties of interpretation which have emerged in its application, as well as the observations received from enterprises. In view of the number of amendments now requiring to be made to Recommendation 96/280/EC, and for the sake of clarity, it is appropriate to replace the Recommendation.

Notes
[1] OJ L 10, 13.1.2001, p. 33.

(3) It should also be made clear that, in accordance with Articles 48, 81 and 82 of the Treaty, as interpreted by the Court of Justice of the European Communities, an enterprise should be considered to be any entity, regardless of its legal form, engaged in economic activities, including in particular entities engaged in a craft activity and other activities on an individual or family basis, partnerships or associations regularly engaged in economic activities.

(4) The criterion of staff numbers (the "staff headcount criterion") remains undoubtedly one of the most important, and must be observed as the main criterion; introducing a financial criterion is nonetheless a necessary adjunct in order to grasp the real scale and performance of an enterprise and its position compared to its competitors. However, it would not be desirable to use turnover as the sole financial criterion, in particular because enterprises in the trade and distribution sector have by their nature higher turnover figures than those in the manufacturing sector. Thus the turnover criterion should be combined with that of the balance sheet total, a criterion which reflects the overall wealth of a business, with the possibility of either of these two criteria being exceeded.

(5) The turnover ceiling refers to enterprises engaged in very different types of economic activity. In order not to restrict unduly the usefulness of applying the definition, it should be updated to take account of changes in both prices and productivity.

(6) As regards the ceiling for the balance sheet total, in the absence of any new element, it is justified to maintain the approach whereby the turnover ceilings are subjected to a coefficient based on the statistical ratio between the two variables. The statistical trend requires a greater increase to be made to the turnover ceiling. Since the trend differs according to the size-category of the enterprise, it is also appropriate to adjust the coefficient in order to reflect the economic trend as closely as possible and not to penalise microenterprises and small enterprises as opposed to medium-sized enterprises. This coefficient is very close to 1 in the case of microenterprises and small enterprises. To simplify matters, therefore, a single value must be chosen for those categories for the turnover ceiling and balance sheet total ceiling.

(7) As in Recommendation 96/280/EC, the financial ceilings and the staff ceilings represent maximum limits and the Member States, the EIB and the EIF may fix ceilings lower than the Community ceilings if they wish to direct their measures towards a specific category of SME. In the interests of administrative simplification, the Member States, the EIB and the EIF may use only one criterion — the staff headcount — for the implementation of some of their policies. However, this does not apply to the various rules in competition law where the financial criteria must also be used and adhered to.

(8) Following the endorsement of the European Charter for Small Enterprises by the European Council of Santa Maria da Feira in June 2000, microenterprises — a category of small enterprises particularly important for the development of entrepreneurship and job creation — should also be better defined.

(9) To gain a better understanding of the real economic position of SMEs and to remove from that category groups of enterprises whose economic power may exceed that of genuine SMEs, a distinction should be made between various types of enterprises, depending on whether they are autonomous, whether they have holdings which do not entail a controlling position (partner enterprises), or whether they are linked to other enterprises. The current limit shown in Recommendation 96/280/EC, of a 25% holding below which an enterprise is considered autonomous, is maintained.

(10) In order to encourage the creation of enterprises, equity financing of SMEs and rural and local development, enterprises can be considered autonomous despite a holding of 25% or more by

certain categories of investors who have a positive role in business financing and creation. However, conditions for these investors have not previously been specified. The case of "business angels" (individuals or groups of individuals pursuing a regular business of investing venture capital) deserves special mention because — compared to other venture capital investors — their ability to give relevant advice to new entrepreneurs is extremely valuable. Their investment in equity capital also complements the activity of venture capital companies, as they provide smaller amounts at an earlier stage of the enterprise's life.

(11) To simplify matters, in particular for Member States and enterprises, use should be made when defining linked enterprises of the conditions laid down in Article 1 of Council Directive 83/349/EEC of 13 June 1983 based on Article 54(3)(g) of the Treaty on consolidated accounts,[1] as last amended by Directive 2001/65/EC of the European Parliament and of the Council,[2] in so far as these conditions are suitable for the purposes of this Recommendation. To strengthen the incentives for investing in the equity funding of an SME, the presumption of absence of dominant influence on the enterprise in question was introduced, in pursuance of the criteria of Article 5(3), of Council Directive 78/660/EEC of 25 July 1978 based on Article 54(3)(g) of the Treaty on the annual accounts of certain types of companies,[3] as last amended by Directive 2001/65/EC.

Notes
[1] OJ L 193, 18.7.1983, p. 1.
[2] OJ L 283, 27.10.2001, p. 28.
[3] OJ L 222, 14.8.1978, p. 11.

(12) Account should also be taken, in suitable cases, of relations between enterprises which pass through natural persons, with a view to ensuring that only those enterprises which really need the advantages accruing to SMEs from the different rules or measures in their favour actually benefit from them. In order to limit the examination of these situations to the strict minimum, the account taken of such relationships has been restricted to the relevant market or to adjacent markets — reference being had, where necessary, to the Commission's definition of "relevant markets" in the Commission notice on the definition of relevant market for the purposes of Community competition law.[1]

Notes
[1] OJ C 372, 9.12.1997, p. 5.

(13) In order to avoid arbitrary distinctions between different public bodies of a Member State, and given the need for legal certainty, it is considered necessary to confirm that an enterprise with 25% or more of its capital or voting rights controlled by a public body is not an SME.

(14) In order to ease the administrative burden for enterprises, and to simplify and speed up the administrative handling of cases for which SME status is required, it is appropriate to allow enterprises to use solemn declarations to certify certain of their characteristics.

(15) It is necessary to establish in detail the composition of the staff headcount for SME definition purposes. In order to promote the development of vocational training and sandwich courses, it is desirable, when calculating staff numbers, to disregard apprentices and students with a vocational training contract. Similarly, maternity or parental leave periods should not be counted.

(16) The various types of enterprise defined according to their relationship with other enterprises correspond to objectively differing degrees of integration. It is therefore appropriate to apply distinct procedures to each of those types of enterprise when calculating the quantities representing their activities and economic power,

HEREBY RECOMMENDS:

Article 1

1. This Recommendation concerns the definition of micro, small and medium-sized enterprises used in Community policies applied within the Community and the European Economic Area.

2. Member States, the European Investment Bank (EIB) and the European Investment Fund (EIF), are invited:

(a) to comply with Title I of the Annex for their programmes directed towards medium-sized enterprises, small enterprises or microenterprises;

(b) to take the necessary steps with a view to using the size classes set out in Article 7 of the Annex, especially where the monitoring of their use of Community financial instruments is concerned.

Article 2

The ceilings shown in Article 2 of the Annex are to be regarded as maximum values. Member States, the EIB and the EIF may fix lower ceilings. In implementing certain of their policies, they may also choose to apply only the criterion of number of employees, except in fields governed by the various rules on State aid.

Article 3

This Recommendation will replace Recommendation 96/280/EC as from 1 January 2005.

Article 4

This Recommendation is addressed to the Member States, the EIB and the EIF.

They are requested to inform the Commission by 31 December 2004 of any measures they have taken further to it and, no later than 30 September 2005, to inform it of the first results of its implementation.

Done at Brussels, 6 May 2003.

ANNEX

TITLE I
DEFINITION OF MICRO, SMALL AND MEDIUM-SIZED ENTERPRISES ADOPTED BY THE COMMISSION

Article 1
Enterprise

An enterprise is considered to be any entity engaged in an economic activity, irrespective of its legal form. This includes, in particular, self-employed persons and family businesses engaged in craft or other activities, and partnerships or associations regularly engaged in an economic activity.

Commentary
Art 1: B&C: 1.124

Article 2
Staff headcount and financial ceilings determining enterprise categories

1. The category of micro, small and medium-sized enterprises (SMEs) is made up of enterprises which employ fewer than 250 persons and which have an annual turnover not exceeding EUR 50 million, and/or an annual balance sheet total not exceeding EUR 43 million.

2. Within the SME category, a small enterprise is defined as an enterprise which employs fewer than 50 persons and whose annual turnover and/or annual balance sheet total does not exceed EUR 10 million.

3. Within the SME category, a microenterprise is defined as an enterprise which employs fewer than 10 persons and whose annual turnover and/or annual balance sheet total does not exceed EUR 2 million.

Article 3

Types of enterprise taken into consideration in calculating staff numbers and financial amounts

1. An "autonomous enterprise" is any enterprise which is not classified as a partner enterprise within the meaning of paragraph 2 or as a linked enterprise within the meaning of paragraph 3.

2. "Partner enterprises" are all enterprises which are not classified as linked enterprises within the meaning of paragraph 3 and between which there is the following relationship: an enterprise (upstream enterprise) holds, either solely or jointly with one or more linked enterprises within the meaning of paragraph 3, 25% or more of the capital or voting rights of another enterprise (downstream enterprise).

However, an enterprise may be ranked as autonomous, and thus as not having any partner enterprises, even if this 25% threshold is reached or exceeded by the following investors, provided that those investors are not linked, within the meaning of paragraph 3, either individually or jointly to the enterprise in question:

(a) public investment corporations, venture capital companies, individuals or groups of individuals with a regular venture capital investment activity who invest equity capital in unquoted businesses ("business angels"), provided the total investment of those business angels in the same enterprise is less than EUR 1250000;

(b) universities or non-profit research centres;

(c) institutional investors, including regional development funds;

(d) autonomous local authorities with an annual budget of less than EUR 10 million and fewer than 5000 inhabitants.

3. "Linked enterprises" are enterprises which have any of the following relationships with each other:

(a) an enterprise has a majority of the shareholders' or members' voting rights in another enterprise;

(b) an enterprise has the right to appoint or remove a majority of the members of the administrative, management or supervisory body of another enterprise;

(c) an enterprise has the right to exercise a dominant influence over another enterprise pursuant to a contract entered into with that enterprise or to a provision in its memorandum or articles of association;

(d) an enterprise, which is a shareholder in or member of another enterprise, controls alone, pursuant to an agreement with other shareholders in or members of that enterprise, a majority of shareholders' or members' voting rights in that enterprise.

There is a presumption that no dominant influence exists if the investors listed in the second subparagraph of paragraph 2 are not involving themselves directly or indirectly in the management of the enterprise in question, without prejudice to their rights as stakeholders.

Enterprises having any of the relationships described in the first subparagraph through one or more other enterprises, or any one of the investors mentioned in paragraph 2, are also considered to be linked.

Enterprises which have one or other of such relationships through a natural person or group of natural persons acting jointly are also considered linked enterprises if they engage in their activity or in part of their activity in the same relevant market or in adjacent markets.

An "adjacent market" is considered to be the market for a product or service situated directly upstream or downstream of the relevant market.

4. Except in the cases set out in paragraph 2, second subparagraph, an enterprise cannot be considered an SME if 25% or more of the capital or voting rights are directly or indirectly controlled, jointly or individually, by one or more public bodies.

5. Enterprises may make a declaration of status as an autonomous enterprise, partner enterprise or linked enterprise, including the data regarding the ceilings set out in Article 2. The declaration may be made even if the capital is spread in such a way that it is not possible to determine exactly by whom it is held, in which case the enterprise may declare in good faith that it can legitimately presume that it is not owned as to 25% or more by one enterprise or jointly by enterprises linked to one another. Such declarations are made without prejudice to the checks and investigations provided for by national or Community rules.

Article 4

Data used for the staff headcount and the financial amounts and reference period

1. The data to apply to the headcount of staff and the financial amounts are those relating to the latest approved accounting period and calculated on an annual basis. They are taken into account from the date of closure of the accounts. The amount selected for the turnover is calculated excluding value added tax (VAT) and other indirect taxes.

2. Where, at the date of closure of the accounts, an enterprise finds that, on an annual basis, it has exceeded or fallen below the headcount or financial ceilings stated in Article 2, this will not result in the loss or acquisition of the status of medium-sized, small or microenterprise unless those ceilings are exceeded over two consecutive accounting periods.

3. In the case of newly established enterprises whose accounts have not yet been approved, the data to apply is to be derived from a bona fide estimate made in the course of the financial year.

Article 5

Staff headcount

The headcount corresponds to the number of annual work units (AWU), i.e. the number of persons who worked full-time within the enterprise in question or on its behalf during the entire reference year under consideration. The work of persons who have not worked the full year, the work of those who have worked part-time, regardless of duration, and the work of seasonal workers are counted as fractions of AWU. The staff consists of:

(a) employees;
(b) persons working for the enterprise being subordinated to it and deemed to be employees under national law;
(c) owner-managers;
(d) partners engaging in a regular activity in the enterprise and benefiting from financial advantages from the enterprise.

Apprentices or students engaged in vocational training with an apprenticeship or vocational training contract are not included as staff. The duration of maternity or parental leaves is not counted.

Article 6

Establishing the data of an enterprise

1. In the case of an autonomous enterprise, the data, including the number of staff, are determined exclusively on the basis of the accounts of that enterprise.

2. The data, including the headcount, of an enterprise having partner enterprises or linked enterprises are determined on the basis of the accounts and other data of the enterprise or, where they exist, the consolidated accounts of the enterprise, or the consolidated accounts in which the enterprise is included through consolidation.

To the data referred to in the first subparagraph are added the data of any partner enterprise of the enterprise in question situated immediately upstream or downstream from it. Aggregation is proportional to the percentage interest in the capital or voting rights (whichever is greater). In the case of cross-holdings, the greater percentage applies.

To the data referred to in the first and second subparagraph is added 100% of the data of any enterprise, which is linked directly or indirectly to the enterprise in question, where the data were not already included through consolidation in the accounts.

3. For the application of paragraph 2, the data of the partner enterprises of the enterprise in question are derived from their accounts and their other data, consolidated if they exist. To these is added 100% of the data of enterprises which are linked to these partner enterprises, unless their accounts data are already included through consolidation.

For the application of the same paragraph 2, the data of the enterprises which are linked to the enterprise in question are to be derived from their accounts and their other data, consolidated if they exist. To these is added, pro rata, the data of any possible partner enterprise of that linked enterprise, situated immediately upstream or downstream from it, unless it has already been included in the consolidated accounts with a percentage at least proportional to the percentage identified under the second subparagraph of paragraph 2.

4. Where in the consolidated accounts no staff data appear for a given enterprise, staff figures are calculated by aggregating proportionally the data from its partner enterprises and by adding the data from the enterprises to which the enterprise in question is linked.

TITLE II
SUNDRY PROVISIONS

Article 7
Statistics

The Commission will take the necessary measures to present the statistics that it produces in accordance with the following size-classes of enterprises:

(a) 0 to 1 person;
(b) 2 to 9 persons;
(c) 10 to 49 persons;
(d) 50 to 249 persons.

Article 8
References

1. Any Community legislation or any Community programme to be amended or adopted and in which the term "SME", "microenterprise", "small enterprise" or "medium-sized enterprise", or any other similar term occurs, should refer to the definition contained in this Recommendation.

2. As a transitional measure, current Community programmes using the SME definition in Recommendation 96/280/EC will continue to be implemented for the benefit of the enterprises which were considered SMEs when those programmes were adopted. Legally binding commitments entered into by the Commission on the basis of such programmes will remain unaffected.

Without prejudice to the first subparagraph, any amendment of the SME definition within the programmes can be made only by adopting the definition contained in this Recommendation in accordance with paragraph 1.

Article 9
Revision

On the basis of a review of the application of the definition contained in this Recommendation, to be drawn up by 31 March 2006, and taking account of any amendments to Article 1 of Directive 83/349/EEC on the definition of linked enterprises within the meaning of that Directive, the Commission will, if necessary, adapt the definition contained in this Recommendation, and in particular the ceilings for turnover and the balance-sheet total in order to take account of experience and economic developments in the Community.

Notes

For a model declaration on the information relating to the qualification of an enterprise as an SME, see Commission communication — Model declaration on the information relating to the qualification of an enterprise as an SME, OJ C 118, 20.5.2003, p. 5.

C16

COMMISSION NOTICE

Guidelines on the application of Article 81 of the EC Treaty to technology transfer agreements (2004/C 101/02)

(Text with EEA relevance)

Official Journal C 101, 27.4.2004, p. 2

Celex No: 52004XC0427(01)

Notes

EEA application: the EFTA Surveillance Authority has adopted a parallel notice on the application of Article 53 of the EEA Agreement to technology transfer agreements under Article 5(2)(b) of the Surveillance and Court Agreement: see College Decision 228/05/COL of 21 September 2005, OJ L 259, 4.10.2007, p. 1 and EEA Supplement No 46, 4.10.2007, p. 1.

Commentary

Notice: B&C: 3.013, 9.083, 9.131 10.59, 10.60, 10.62, 10.63, 10.67, 10.68, 10.70, 10.72, 10.73, 10.75, 10.77, 10.78, 10.80, 10.81, 10.82, 10.83, 10.86, 10.87, 10.96, 10.103, 10.116, 10.121, 10.126, 10.128, 10.129, 10.137, 10.140, 10.141, 10.142, 10.143, 10.145, 10.146, 10.148, 10.152, 10.154, 10.158, 10.162, 10.163, 10.165, 10.166, 10.167, 10.168, 10.169
paras 19–25: B&C: 9.142
paras 41–46: B&C: 9.139
paras 79–81: F&N: 10.96
paras 114–116: B&C: 9.166 **F&N:** 10.116
paras 162–167: B&C: 9.095
paras 162–174: B&C: 9.107
paras 176–178: B&C: 9.101
paras 179–183: B&C: 9.151
paras 186–190: B&C: 9.153, 9.160
paras 196–203: B&C: 9.106

I. INTRODUCTION

1. These guidelines set out the principles for the assessment of technology transfer agreements under Article 81 of the Treaty. Technology transfer agreements concern the licensing of technology where the licensor permits the licensee to exploit the licensed technology for the production of goods or services, as defined in Article 1(1)(b) of Commission Regulation (EC) No 773/2004 on the application of Article 81(3) of the Treaty to categories of technology transfer agreements (the TTBER).[1]

Notes

[1] OJ L 123, 27.4.2004. The TTBER replaces Commission Regulation (EC) No 240/96 of 31 January 1996 on the application of Article 85(3) of the Treaty to certain categories of technology transfer agreements (OJ L 31, 9.2. 1996, p. 2).

2. The purpose of the guidelines is to provide guidance on the application of the TTBER as well as on the application of Article 81 to technology transfer agreements that fall outside the scope of the TTBER. The TTBER and the guidelines are without prejudice to the possible parallel application of Article 82 of the Treaty to licensing agreements.[2]

Notes

[2] See Joined Cases C-395/96 P and C-396/96 P, *Compagnie Maritime Belge*, [2000] ECR I-1365, paragraph 130, and paragraph 106 of the Commission Guidelines on the application of Article 81(3) of the Treaty, [OJ C 101, 27.4.2004, p. 97].

Commentary
para 2: F&N: 9.56

3. The standards set forth in these guidelines must be applied in light of the circumstances specific to each case. This excludes a mechanical application. Each case must be assessed on its own facts and the guidelines must be applied reasonably and flexibly. Examples given serve as illustrations only and are not intended to be exhaustive. The Commission will keep under review the functioning of the TTBER and the guidelines in the new enforcement system created by Regulation 1/2003[3] to consider whether changes need to be made.

Notes

[3] Council Regulation (EC) No 1/2003 on the implementation of the rules on competition laid down in Articles 81 and 82 of the Treaty (OJ L 1, 4.1.2003, p. 1).

4. The present guidelines are without prejudice to the interpretation of Article 81 and the TTBER that may be given by the Court of Justice and the Court of First Instance.

II. GENERAL PRINCIPLES

1. Article 81 and intellectual property rights

5. The aim of Article 81 as a whole is to protect competition on the market with a view to promoting consumer welfare and an efficient allocation of resources. Article 81(1) prohibits all agreements and concerted practices between undertakings and decisions by associations of undertakings[4] which may affect trade between Member States[5] and which have as their object or effect the prevention, restriction or distortion of competition.[6] As an exception to this rule Article 81(3) provides that the prohibition contained in Article 81(1) may be declared inapplicable in the case of agreements between undertakings which contribute to improving the production or distribution of products or to promoting technical or economic progress, while allowing consumers a fair share of the resulting benefits and which do not impose restrictions which are not indispensable to the attainment of these objectives and do not afford such undertakings the possibility of eliminating competition in respect of a substantial part of the products concerned.

Notes

[4] In the following the term "agreement" includes concerted practices and decisions of associations of undertakings.

[5] See Commission Notice on the concept of effect on trade between Member States contained in Articles 81 and 82 of the Treaty [OJ C 101, 27.04.2004, p. 81].

[6] In the following the term "restriction" includes the prevention and distortion of competition.

Commentary

para 5: F&N: 2.11

6. Intellectual property laws confer exclusive rights on holders of patents, copyright, design rights, trademarks and other legally protected rights. The owner of intellectual property is entitled under intellectual property laws to prevent unauthorised use of his intellectual property and to exploit it, *inter alia*, by licensing it to third parties. Once a product incorporating an intellectual property right has been put on the market inside the EEA by the holder or with his consent, the intellectual property right is exhausted in the sense that the holder can no longer use it to control the sale of the product[7] (principle of Community exhaustion). The right holder has no right under intellectual property laws to prevent sales by licensees or buyers of such products incorporating the licensed technology.[8] The principle of Community exhaustion is in line with the essential function of intellectual property rights, which is to grant the holder the right to exclude others from exploiting his intellectual property without his consent.

Notes

[7] This principle of Community exhaustion is for example enshrined in Article 7(1) of Directive 104/89/EEC to approximate the laws of the Member States relating to trade marks (OJ L 40, 11.2.1989, p. 1), which provides that the trade mark shall not entitle the proprietor to prohibit its use in relation to goods which have been put on the market in the Community under that trade mark by the proprietor or with his consent.

[8] On the other hand, the sale of copies of a protected work does not lead to the exhaustion of performance rights, including rental rights, in the work, see in this respect Case 158/86, *Warner Brothers and Metronome Video*, [1988] ECR 2605, and Case C-61/97, *Foreningen af danske videogramdistributører*, [1998] ECR I-5171.

7. The fact that intellectual property laws grant exclusive rights of exploitation does not imply that intellectual property rights are immune from competition law intervention. Articles 81 and 82 are in particular applicable to agreements whereby the holder licenses another undertaking to exploit his intellectual property rights.[9] Nor does it imply that there is an inherent conflict between intellectual property rights and the Community competition rules. Indeed, both bodies of law share the same basic objective of promoting consumer welfare and an efficient allocation of resources. Innovation constitutes an essential and dynamic component of an open and competitive market economy. Intellectual property rights promote dynamic competition by encouraging undertakings to invest in developing new or improved products and processes. So does competition by putting pressure on undertakings to innovate. Therefore, both intellectual property rights and competition are necessary to promote innovation and ensure a competitive exploitation thereof.

Notes
[9] See e.g. Joined Cases 56/64 and 58/64, *Consten and Grundig*, [1966] ECR 429.

Commentary
para 7: F&N: 10.59

8. In the assessment of licence agreements under Article 81 it must be kept in mind that the creation of intellectual property rights often entails substantial investment and that it is often a risky endeavour. In order not to reduce dynamic competition and to maintain the incentive to innovate, the innovator must not be unduly restricted in the exploitation of intellectual property rights that turn out to be valuable. For these reasons the innovator should normally be free to seek compensation for successful projects that is sufficient to maintain investment incentives, taking failed projects into account. Technology licensing may also require the licensee to make significant sunk investments in the licensed technology and production assets necessary to exploit it. Article 81 cannot be applied without considering such *ex ante* investments made by the parties and the risks relating thereto. The risk facing the parties and the sunk investment that must be committed may thus lead to the agreement falling outside Article 81(1) or fulfilling the conditions of Article 81(3), as the case may be, for the period of time required to recoup the investment.

Commentary
para 8: B&C: 9.083 F&N: 10.63

9. In assessing licensing agreements under Article 81, the existing analytical framework is sufficiently flexible to take due account of the dynamic aspects of technology licensing. There is no presumption that intellectual property rights and licence agreements as such give rise to competition concerns. Most licence agreements do not restrict competition and create pro-competitive efficiencies. Indeed, licensing as such is pro-competitive as it leads to dissemination of technology and promotes innovation. In addition, even licence agreements that do restrict competition may often give rise to pro-competitive efficiencies, which must be considered under Article 81(3) and balanced against the negative effects on competition.[10] The great majority of licence agreements are therefore compatible with Article 81.

Notes
[10] The methodology for the application of Article 81(3) is set out in the Commission Guidelines on the application of Article 81(3) of the Treaty [OJ C 101, 27.4.2004, p. 97].

Commentary
para 9: B&C: 9.083 F&N: 10.63, 10.127

2. The general framework for applying Article 81

10. Article 81(1) prohibits agreements which have as their object or effect the restriction of competition. Article 81(1) applies both to restrictions of competition between the parties to an agreement and to restrictions of competition between any of the parties and third parties.

11. The assessment of whether a licence agreement restricts competition must be made within the actual context in which competition would occur in the absence of the agreement with its alleged restrictions.[11] In making this assessment it is necessary to take account of the likely impact of the

agreement on inter-technology competition (i.e. competition between undertakings using competing technologies) and on intra-technology competition (i.e. competition between undertakings using the same technology).[12] Article 81(1) prohibits restrictions of both inter-technology competition and intra-technology competition. It is therefore necessary to assess to what extent the agreement affects or is likely to affect these two aspects of competition on the market.

Notes

[11] See Case 56/65, *Société Technique Minière*, [1966] ECR 337, and Case C-7/95 P, *John Deere*, [1998] ECR I-3111, paragraph 76.

[12] See in this respect e.g. judgment in *Consten and Grundig* cited in note 9.

Commentary
para 11: **B&C:** 9.087 **F&N:** 10.128

12. The following two questions provide a useful framework for making this assessment. The first question relates to the impact of the agreement on inter-technology competition while the second question relates to the impact of the agreement on intra-technology competition. As restraints may be capable of affecting both inter-technology competition and intra-technology competition at the same time, it may be necessary to analyse a restraint in the light of both questions before it can be concluded whether or not competition within the meaning of Article 81(1) is restricted:

    (a) Does the licence agreement restrict actual or potential competition that would have existed without the contemplated agreement? If so, the agreement may be caught by Article 81(1). In making this assessment it is necessary to take into account competition between the parties and competition from third parties. For instance, where two undertakings established in different Member States cross licence competing technologies and undertake not to sell products in each other's home markets, (potential) competition that existed prior to the agreement is restricted. Similarly, where a licensor imposes obligations on his licensees not to use competing technologies and these obligations foreclose third party technologies, actual or potential competition that would have existed in the absence of the agreement is restricted.

    (b) Does the agreement restrict actual or potential competition that would have existed in the absence of the contractual restraint(s)? If so, the agreement may be caught by Article 81(1). For instance, where a licensor restricts its licensees from competing with each other, (potential) competition that could have existed between the licensees absent the restraints is restricted. Such restrictions include vertical price fixing and territorial or customer sales restrictions between licensees. However, certain restraints may in certain cases not be caught by Article 81(1) when the restraint is objectively necessary for the existence of an agreement of that type or that nature.[13] Such exclusion of the application of Article 81(1) can only be made on the basis of objective factors external to the parties themselves and not the subjective views and characteristics of the parties. The question is not whether the parties in their particular situation would not have accepted to conclude a less restrictive agreement, but whether, given the nature of the agreement and the characteristics of the market, a less restrictive agreement would not have been concluded by undertakings in a similar setting. For instance, territorial restraints in an agreement between non-competitors may fall outside Article 81(1) for a certain duration if the restraints are objectively necessary for a licensee to penetrate a new market. Similarly, a prohibition imposed on all licensees not to sell to certain categories of end users may not be restrictive of competition if such a restraint is objectively necessary for reasons of safety or health related to the dangerous nature of the product in question. Claims that in the absence of a restraint the supplier would have resorted to vertical integration are not sufficient. Decisions on whether or not to vertically integrate depend on a broad range of complex economic factors, a number of which are internal to the undertaking concerned.

Notes

[13] See in this respect the judgment in *Société Technique Minière* cited in note 11 and Case 258/78, *Nungesser*, [1982] ECR 2015.

Commentary
para 12: B&C: 9.087 F&N: 10.65, 10.128
para 12(b): F&N: 10.65, 10.138

13. In the application of the analytical framework set out in the previous paragraph it must be taken into account that Article 81(1) distinguishes between those agreements that have a restriction of competition as their object and those agreements that have a restriction of competition as their effect. An agreement or contractual restraint is only prohibited by Article 81(1) if its object or effect is to restrict inter-technology competition and/or intra-technology competition.

14. Restrictions of competition by object are those that by their very nature restrict competition. These are restrictions which in light of the objectives pursued by the Community competition rules have such a high potential for negative effects on competition that it is not necessary for the purposes of applying Article 81(1) to demonstrate any actual effects on the market.[14] Moreover, the conditions of Article 81(3) are unlikely to be fulfilled in the case of restrictions by object. The assessment of whether or not an agreement has as its object a restriction of competition is based on a number of factors. These factors include, in particular, the content of the agreement and the objective aims pursued by it. It may also be necessary to consider the context in which it is (to be) applied or the actual conduct and behaviour of the parties on the market.[15] In other words, an examination of the facts underlying the agreement and the specific circumstances in which it operates may be required before it can be concluded whether a particular restriction constitutes a hardcore restriction of competition. The way in which an agreement is actually implemented may reveal a restriction by object even where the formal agreement does not contain an express provision to that effect. Evidence of subjective intent on the part of the parties to restrict competition is a relevant factor but not a necessary condition. For licence agreements, the Commission considers that the restrictions covered by the list of hardcore restrictions of competition contained in Article 4 of the TTBER are restrictive by their very object.

Notes

[14] See in this respect e.g. Case C-49/92 P, *Anic Partecipazioni*, [1999] ECR I-4125, paragraph 99.

[15] See Joined Cases 29/83 and 30/83, *CRAM and Rheinzink*, [1984] ECR 1679, paragraph 26, and Joined Cases 96/82 and others, *ANSEAU-NAVEWA*, [1983] ECR 3369, paragraphs 23–25.

Commentary
para 14: F&N: 10.91

15. If an agreement is not restrictive of competition by object it is necessary to examine whether it has restrictive effects on competition. Account must be taken of both actual and potential effects.[16] In other words the agreement must have likely anti-competitive effects. For licence agreements to be restrictive of competition by effect they must affect actual or potential competition to such an extent that on the relevant market negative effects on prices, output, innovation or the variety or quality of goods and services can be expected with a reasonable degree of probability. The likely negative effects on competition must be appreciable.[17] Appreciable anti-competitive effects are likely to occur when at least one of the parties has or obtains some degree of market power and the agreement contributes to the creation, maintenance or strengthening of that market power or allows the parties to exploit such market power. Market power is the ability to maintain prices above competitive levels or to maintain output in terms of product quantities, product quality and variety or innovation below competitive levels for a not insignificant period of time. The degree of market power normally required for a finding of an infringement under Article 81(1) is less than the degree of market power required for a finding of dominance under Article 82.

Notes

[16] See the judgment in *John Deere*, [1998] cited in note 11.

[17] Guidance on the issue of appreciability can be found in Commission notice on agreements of minor importance which do not appreciably restrict competition under Article 81(1) of the Treaty (OJ C 368, 22.12.2001, p. 13). The notice defines appreciability in a negative way. Agreements, which fall outside the scope of the de minimis notice, do not necessarily have appreciable restrictive effects. An individual assessment is required.

16. For the purposes of analysing restrictions of competition by effect it is normally necessary to define the relevant market and to examine and assess, inter alia, the nature of the products and technologies concerned, the market position of the parties, the market position of competitors, the market position of buyers, the existence of potential competitors and the level of entry barriers. In some cases, however, it may be possible to show anti-competitive effects directly by analysing the conduct of the parties to the agreement on the market. It may for example be possible to ascertain that an agreement has led to price increases.

17. Licence agreements, however, also have substantial pro-competitive potential. Indeed, the vast majority of licence agreements are pro-competitive. Licence agreements may promote innovation by allowing innovators to earn returns to cover at least part of their research and development costs. Licence agreements also lead to a dissemination of technologies, which may create value by reducing the production costs of the licensee or by enabling him to produce new or improved products. Efficiencies at the level of the licensee often stem from a combination of the licensor's technology with the assets and technologies of the licensee. Such integration of complementary assets and technologies may lead to a cost/output configuration that would not otherwise be possible. For instance, the combination of an improved technology of the licensor with more efficient production or distribution assets of the licensee may reduce production costs or lead to the production of a higher quality product. Licensing may also serve the pro-competitive purpose of removing obstacles to the development and exploitation of the licensee's own technology. In particular in sectors where large numbers of patents are prevalent licensing often occurs in order to create design freedom by removing the risk of infringement claims by the licensor. When the licensor agrees not to invoke his intellectual property rights to prevent the sale of the licensee's products, the agreement removes an obstacle to the sale of the licensee's product and thus generally promotes competition.

Commentary
para 17: F&N: 10.63

18. In cases where a licence agreement is caught by Article 81(1) the pro-competitive effects of the agreement must be balanced against its restrictive effects in the context of Article 81(3). When all four conditions of Article 81(3) are satisfied, the restrictive licence agreement in question is valid and enforceable, no prior decision to that effect being required.[18] Hardcore restrictions of competition only fulfil the conditions of Article 81(3) in exceptional circumstances. Such agreements generally fail (at least) one of the first two conditions of Article 81(3). They generally do not create objective economic benefits or benefits for consumers. Moreover, these types of agreements generally also fail the indispensability test under the third condition. For example, if the parties fix the price at which the products produced under the licence must be sold, this will generally lead to a lower output and a misallocation of resources and higher prices for consumers. The price restriction is also not indispensable to achieve the possible efficiencies resulting from the availability to both competitors of the two technologies.

Notes
[18] See Article 1(2) of Council Regulation No 1/2003 cited in note 3.

Commentary
para 18: F&N: 10.65, 10.91

3. Market definition

19. The Commission's approach to defining the relevant market is laid down in its market definition guidelines.[19] The present guidelines only address aspects of market definition that are of particular importance in the field of technology licensing.

Notes
[19] Commission notice on the definition of the relevant market for the purposes of Community competition law (OJ C 372, 9.12.1997, p. 5).

20. Technology is an input, which is integrated either into a product or a production process. Technology licensing can therefore affect competition both in input markets and in output markets.

For instance, an agreement between two parties which sell competing products and which cross license technologies relating to the production of these products may restrict competition on the product market concerned. It may also restrict competition on the market for technology and possibly also on other input markets. For the purposes of assessing the competitive effects of licence agreements it may therefore be necessary to define relevant goods and service markets (product markets) as well as technology markets.[20] The term "product market" used in Article 3 of the TTBER refers to relevant goods and service markets in both their geographic and product dimension. As is clear from Article 1(1)(j) of the TTBER, the term is used merely to distinguish relevant goods and service markets from relevant technology markets.

Notes

[20] As to these distinctions see also Commission Guidelines on the applicability of Article 81 of the EC Treaty to horizontal cooperation agreements (OJ C 3, 6.1.2001, p. 2, paragraphs 44 to 52).

Commentary
para 20: F&N: 3.374, 9.79

21. The TTBER and these guidelines are concerned with effects both on product markets for final products and on product markets for intermediate products. The relevant product market includes products which are regarded by the buyers as interchangeable with or substitutable for the contract products incorporating the licensed technology, by reason of the products' characteristics, their prices and their intended use.

22. Technology markets consist of the licensed technology and its substitutes, i.e. other technologies which are regarded by the licensees as interchangeable with or substitutable for the licensed technology, by reason of the technologies' characteristics, their royalties and their intended use. The methodology for defining technology markets follows the same principles as the definition of product markets. Starting from the technology which is marketed by the licensor, one needs to identify those other technologies to which licensees could switch in response to a small but permanent increase in relative prices, i.e. the royalties. An alternative approach is to look at the market for products incorporating the licensed technology (cf. paragraph [23] below).

Commentary
para 22: B&C: 9.088 F&N: 3.374

23. Once relevant markets have been defined, market shares can be assigned to the various sources of competition in the market and used as an indication of the relative strength of market players. In the case of technology markets one way to proceed is to calculate market shares on the basis of each technology's share of total licensing income from royalties, representing a technology's share of the market where competing technologies are licensed. However, this may often be a mere theoretical and not a practical way to proceed because of lack of clear information on royalties etc. An alternative approach, which is the one used in Article 3(3) of the TTBER, is to calculate market shares on the technology market on the basis of sales of products incorporating the licensed technology on downstream product markets (see paragraph 70 below). Under this approach all sales on the relevant product market are taken into account, irrespective of whether the product incorporates a technology that is being licensed. In the case of technology markets the approach of Article 3(3) to take into account technologies that are (only) being used in-house, is justified. Indeed, this approach is in general a good indicator of the strength of the technology. First, it captures any potential competition from undertakings that are producing with their own technology and that are likely to start licensing in the event of a small but permanent increase in the price for licenses. Secondly, even where it is unlikely that other technology owners would start licensing, the licensor does not necessarily have market power on the technology market even if he has a high share of licensing income. If the downstream product market is competitive, competition at this level may effectively constrain the licensor. An increase in royalties upstream affects the costs of the licensee, making him less competitive, causing him to lose sales. A technology's market share on the product market also captures this element and is thus normally a good indicator of licensor market power. In individual cases outside the safe harbour of the TTBER it may be necessary, where practically possible, to apply both of the described approaches in order to assess more accurately the market strength of the licensor.

Commentary
para 23: B&C: 4.068

24. Moreover, outside the safe harbour of the TTBER it must also be taken into account that market share may not always be a good indication of the relative strength of available technologies. The Commission will therefore, inter alia, also have regard to the number of independently controlled technologies available in addition to the technologies controlled by the parties to the agreement that may be substitutable for the licensed technology at a comparable cost to the user (see paragraph 131 below).

25. Some licence agreements may affect innovation markets. In analysing such effects, however, the Commission will normally confine itself to examining the impact of the agreement on competition within existing product and technology markets.[21] Competition on such markets may be affected by agreements that delay the introduction of improved products or new products that over time will replace existing products. In such cases innovation is a source of potential competition which must be taken into account when assessing the impact of the agreement on product markets and technology markets. In a limited number of cases, however, it may be useful and necessary to also define innovation markets. This is particularly the case where the agreement affects innovation aiming at creating new products and where it is possible at an early stage to identify research and development poles.[22] In such cases it can be analysed whether after the agreement there will be a sufficient number of competing research and development poles left for effective competition in innovation to be maintained.

Notes

[21] See to that effect paragraphs 50 to 52 of the Guidelines on horizontal cooperation agreements, cited in the previous note.

[22] Idem, paragraph 51.

Commentary
para 25: B&C: 4.069 F&N: 10.83

4. The distinction between competitors and non-competitors

26. In general, agreements between competitors pose a greater risk to competition than agreements between non-competitors. However, competition between undertakings that use the same technology (intra-technology competition between licensees) constitutes an important complement to competition between undertakings that use competing technologies (inter-technology competition). For instance, intra-technology competition may lead to lower prices for the products incorporating the technology in question, which may not only produce direct and immediate benefits for consumers of these products, but also spur further competition between undertakings that use competing technologies. In the context of licensing it must also be taken into account that licensees are selling their own product. They are not re-selling a product supplied by another undertaking. There may thus be greater scope for product differentiation and quality-based competition between licensees than in the case of vertical agreements for the resale of products.

Commentary
para 26: F&N: 10.80, 10.81

27. In order to determine the competitive relationship between the parties it is necessary to examine whether the parties would have been actual or potential competitors in the absence of the agreement. If without the agreement the parties would not have been actual or potential competitors in any relevant market affected by the agreement they are deemed to be non-competitors.

Commentary
para 27: F&N: 10.82

28. Where the licensor and the licensee are both active on the same product market or the same technology market without one or both parties infringing the intellectual property rights of the other party, they are actual competitors on the market concerned. The parties are deemed to be

actual competitors on the technology market if the licensee is already licensing out his technology and the licensor enters the technology market by granting a license for a competing technology to the licensee.

Commentary
para 28: F&N: 10.85, 10.86

29. The parties are considered to be potential competitors on the product market if in the absence of the agreement and without infringing the intellectual property rights of the other party it is likely that they would have undertaken the necessary additional investment to enter the relevant market in response to a small but permanent increase in product prices. In order to constitute a realistic competitive constraint entry has to be likely to occur within a short period. Normally a period of one to two years is appropriate. However, in individual cases longer periods can be taken into account. The period of time needed for undertakings already on the market to adjust their capacities can be used as a yardstick to determine this period. For instance, the parties are likely to be considered potential competitors on the product market where the licensee produces on the basis of its own technology in one geographic market and starts producing in another geographic market on the basis of a licensed competing technology. In such circumstances, it is likely that the licensee would have been able to enter the second geographic market on the basis of its own technology, unless such entry is precluded by objective factors, including the existence of blocking patents (see paragraph 32 below).

Commentary
para 29: B&C: 9.088 F&N: 10.86

30. The parties are considered to be potential competitors on the technology market where they own substitutable technologies if in the specific case the licensee is not licensing his own technology, provided that he would be likely to do so in the event of a small but permanent increase in technology prices. However, for the application of the TTBER potential competition on the technology market is not taken into account (see paragraph 66 below).

Commentary
para 30: B&C: 9.088 F&N: 10.84

31. In some cases the parties may become competitors subsequent to the conclusion of the agreement because the licensee develops and starts exploiting a competing technology. In such cases it must be taken into account that the parties were non-competitors at the time of conclusion of the agreement and that the agreement was concluded in that context. The Commission will therefore mainly focus on the impact of the agreement on the licensee's ability to exploit his own (competing) technology. In particular, the list of hardcore restrictions applying to agreements between competitors will not be applied to such agreements unless the agreement is subsequently amended in any material respect after the parties have become competitors (cf. Article 4(3) of the TTBER). The undertakings party to an agreement may also become competitors subsequent to the conclusion of the agreement where the licensee was already active on the product market prior to the licence and where the licensor subsequently enters the product market either on the basis of the licensed technology or a new technology. Also in this case the hardcore list relevant for agreements between non-competitors will continue to apply to the agreement unless the agreement is subsequently amended in any material respect (cf. article 4(3) of the TTBER).

Commentary
para 31: B&C: 9.089 F&N: 10.89

32. If the parties own technologies that are in a one-way or two-way blocking position, the parties are considered to be non-competitors on the technology market. A one-way blocking position exists when a technology cannot be exploited without infringing upon another technology. This is for

instance the case where one patent covers an improvement of a technology covered by another patent. In that case the exploitation of the improvement patent pre-supposes that the holder obtains a licence to the basic patent. A two-way blocking position exists where neither technology can be exploited without infringing upon the other technology and where the holders thus need to obtain a licence or a waiver from each other. In assessing whether a blocking position exists the Commission will rely on objective factors as opposed to the subjective views of the parties. Particularly convincing evidence of the existence of a blocking position is required where the parties may have a common interest in claiming the existence of a blocking position in order to be qualified as non-competitors, for instance where the claimed two-way blocking position concerns technologies that are technological substitutes. Relevant evidence includes court decisions including injunctions and opinions of independent experts. In the latter case the Commission will, in particular, closely examine how the expert has been selected. However, also other convincing evidence, including expert evidence from the parties that they have or had good and valid reasons to believe that a blocking position exists or existed, can be relevant to substantiate the existence of a blocking position.

Commentary
para 32: B&C: 9.090 F&N: 10.87

33. In some cases it may also be possible to conclude that while the licensor and the licensee produce competing products, they are non-competitors on the relevant product market and the relevant technology market because the licensed technology represents such a drastic innovation that the technology of the licensee has become obsolete or uncompetitive. In such cases the licensor's technology either creates a new market or excludes the licensee's technology from the market. Often, however, it is not possible to come to this conclusion at the time the agreement is concluded. It is usually only when the technology or the products incorporating it have been available to consumers for some time that it becomes apparent that the older technology has become obsolete or uncompetitive. For instance, when CD technology was developed and players and discs were put on the market, it was not obvious that this new technology would replace LP technology. This only became apparent some years later. The parties will therefore be considered to be competitors if at the time of the conclusion of the agreement it is not obvious that the licensee's technology is obsolete or uncompetitive. However, given that both Articles 81(1) and Article 81(3) must be applied in light of the actual context in which the agreement occurs, the assessment is sensitive to material changes in the facts. The classification of the relationship between the parties will therefore change into a relationship of non-competitors, if at a later point in time the licensee's technology becomes obsolete or uncompetitive on the market.

Commentary
para 33: B&C: 9.089 F&N: 10.87

III. APPLICATION OF THE BLOCK EXEMPTION REGULATION

1. The effects of the Block Exemption Regulation

34. Technology transfer agreements that fulfil the conditions set out in the TTBER are block exempted from the prohibition rule contained in Article 81(1). Block exempted agreements are legally valid and enforceable. Such agreements can only be prohibited for the future and only upon withdrawal of the block exemption by the Commission or a Member State competition authority. Block exempted agreements cannot be prohibited under Article 81 by national courts in the context of private litigation.

35. Block exemption of categories of technology transfer agreements is based on the presumption that such agreements — to the extent that they are caught by Article 81(1) — fulfil the four conditions laid down in Article 81(3). It is thus presumed that the agreements give rise to economic efficiencies, that the restrictions contained in the agreements are indispensable to the attainment of these efficiencies, that consumers within the affected markets receive a fair share of the

efficiency gains and that the agreements do not afford the undertakings concerned the possibility of eliminating competition in respect of a substantial part of the products in question. The market share thresholds (Article 3), the hardcore list (Article 4) and the excluded restrictions (Article 5) set out in the TTBER aim at ensuring that only restrictive agreements that can reasonably be presumed to fulfil the four conditions of Article 81(3) are block exempted.

36. As set out in section IV below, many licence agreements fall outside Article 81(1), either because they do not restrict competition at all or because the restriction of competition is not appreciable.[23] To the extent that such agreements would anyhow fall within the scope of the TTBER, there is no need to determine whether they are caught by Article 81(1).[24]

Notes

[23] See in this respect the Notice on agreements of minor importance cited in note 17.

[24] According to Article 3(2) of Regulation 1/2003, agreements which may affect trade between Member States but which are not prohibited by Article 81 cannot be prohibited by national competition law.

Commentary
para 36: B&C: 9.083

37. Outside the scope of the block exemption it is relevant to examine whether in the individual case the agreement is caught by Article 81(1) and if so whether the conditions of Article 81(3) are satisfied. There is no presumption that technology transfer agreements falling outside the block exemption are caught by Article 81(1) or fail to satisfy the conditions of Article 81(3). In particular, the mere fact that the market shares of the parties exceed the market share thresholds set out in Article 3 of the TTBER is not a sufficient basis for finding that the agreement is caught by Article 81(1). Individual assessment of the likely effects of the agreement is required. It is only when agreements contain hardcore restrictions of competition that it can normally be presumed that they are prohibited by Article 81.

Commentary
para 37: B&C: 3.013, 3.069 F&N: 3.418, 10.62

2. Scope and duration of the Block Exemption Regulation

2.1. Agreements between two parties

38. According to Article 2(1) of the TTBER, the Regulation covers technology transfer agreements "between two undertakings." Technology transfer agreements between more than two undertakings are not covered by the TTBER.[25] The decisive factor in terms of distinguishing between agreements between two undertakings and multiparty agreements is whether the agreement in question is concluded between more than two undertakings.

Notes

[25] Under Council Regulation 19/65, OJ Special Edition Series I 1965–1966, p. 35, the Commission is not empowered to block exempt technology transfer agreements concluded between more than two undertakings.

39. Agreements concluded by two undertakings fall within the scope of the TTBER even if the agreement stipulates conditions for more than one level of trade. For instance, the TTBER applies to a licence agreement concerning not only the production stage but also the distribution stage, stipulating the obligations that the licensee must or may impose on resellers of the products produced under the licence.[26]

Notes

[26] See recital 19 of the TTBER and further section 2.5 below.

40. Licence agreements concluded between more than two undertakings often give rise to the same issues as licence agreements of the same nature concluded between two undertakings. In its individual assessment of licence agreements which are of the same nature as those covered by the block exemption but which are concluded between more than two undertakings, the Commission will apply by analogy the principles set out in the TTBER.

Commentary
para 40: B&C: 9.138 F&N: 10.66

2.2. Agreements for the production of contract products

41. It follows from Article 2 that for licence agreements to be covered by the TTBER they must concern "the production of contract products", i.e. products incorporating or produced with the licensed technology. In other words, to be covered by the TTBER the licence must permit the licensee to exploit the licensed technology for production of goods or services (see recital 7 of the TTBER). The TTBER does not cover technology pools. The notion of technology pools covers agreements whereby two or more parties agree to pool their respective technologies and license them as a package. The notion of technology pools also covers arrangements whereby two or more undertakings agree to license a third party and authorise him to license on the package of technologies. Technology pools are dealt with in section IV.4 below.

Commentary
para 41: F&N: 10.159

42. The TTBER applies to licence agreements for the production of contract products whereby the licensee is also permitted to sublicense the licensed technology to third parties provided, however, that the production of contract products constitutes the primary object of the agreement. Conversely, the TTBER does not apply to agreements that have sublicensing as their primary object. However, the Commission will apply by analogy the principles set out in the TTBER and these guidelines to such "master licensing" agreements between licensor and licensee. Agreements between the licensee and sub-licensees are covered by the TTBER.

Commentary
para 42: B&C: 9.139 F&N: 10.67

43. The term "contract products" encompasses goods and services produced with the licensed technology. This is the case both where the licensed technology is used in the production process and where it is incorporated into the product itself. In these guidelines the term "products incorporating the licensed technology" covers both situations. The TTBER applies in all cases where technology is licensed for the purposes of producing goods and services. It is sufficient in this respect that the licensor undertakes not to exercise his intellectual property rights against the licensee. Indeed, the essence of a pure patent licence is the right to operate inside the scope of the exclusive right of the patent. It follows that the TTBER also covers so-called non-assertion agreements and settlement agreements whereby the licensor permits the licensee to produce within the scope of the patent.

Commentary
para 43: F&N: 10.70

44. The TTBER covers "subcontracting" whereby the licensor licenses technology to the licensee who undertakes to produce certain products on the basis thereof exclusively for the licensor. Subcontracting may also involve the supply of equipment by the licensor to be used in the production of the goods and services covered by the agreement. For the latter type of subcontracting to be covered by the TTBER, the licensed technology and not the supplied equipment must constitute the primary object of the agreement. Subcontracting is also covered by the Commission's Notice concerning the assessment of certain subcontracting agreements in relation to Article 81(1) of the Treaty.[27] According to this notice, which remains applicable, subcontracting agreements whereby the subcontractor undertakes to produce certain products exclusively for the contractor generally fall outside Article 81(1). However, other restrictions imposed on the subcontractor such as the obligation not to conduct or exploit his own research and development may be caught by Article 81.[28]

Notes
[27] OJ C 1, 3.1.1979, p. 2.
[28] See paragraph 3 of the subcontracting notice.

Commentary
para 44: **B&C:** 9.139

45. The TTBER also applies to agreements whereby the licensee must carry out development work before obtaining a product or a process that is ready for commercial exploitation, provided that a contract product has been identified. Even if such further work and investment is required, the object of the agreement is the production of an identified contract product. On the other hand, the TTBER and the guidelines do not cover agreements whereby a technology is licensed for the purpose of enabling the licensee to carry out further research and development in various fields. For instance, the TTBER and the guidelines do not cover the licensing of a technological research tool used in the process of further research activity. The framework of the TTBER and the guidelines is based on the premise that there is a direct link between the licensed technology and an identified contract product. In cases where no such link exists the main object of the agreement is research and development as opposed to bringing a particular product to the market; in that case the analytical framework of the TTBER and the guidelines may not be appropriate. For the same reasons the TTBER and the guidelines do not cover research and development sub-contracting whereby the licensee undertakes to carry out research and development in the field of the licensed technology and to hand back the improved technology package to the licensor. The main object of such agreements is the provision of research and development services aimed at improving the technology as opposed to the production of goods and services on the basis of the licensed technology.

Commentary
para 45: **F&N:** 10.68

2.3. The concept of technology transfer agreements

46. The TTBER and these guidelines cover agreements for the transfer of technology. According to Article 1(1)(b) and (h) of the TTBER the concept of "technology" covers patents and patent applications, utility models and applications for utility models, design rights, plant breeders rights, topographies of semiconductor products, supplementary protection certificates for medicinal products or other products for which such supplementary protection certificates may be obtained, software copyright, and know-how. The licensed technology should allow the licensee with or without other inputs to produce the contract products.

Commentary
para 46: **B&C:** 9.134 **F&N:** 9.80

47. Know-how is defined in Article 1(1)(i) as a package of non-patented practical information, resulting from experience and testing, which is secret, substantial and identified. "Secret" means that the know-how is not generally known or easily accessible. "Substantial" means that the know-how includes information which is significant and useful for the production of the products covered by the licence agreement or the application of the process covered by the licence agreement. In other words, the information must significantly contribute to or facilitate the production of the contract products. In cases where the licensed know-how relates to a product as opposed to a process, this condition implies that the know-how is useful for the production the contract product. This condition is not satisfied where the contract product can be produced on the basis of freely available technology. However, the condition does not require that the contract product is of higher value than products produced with freely available technology. In the case of process technologies, this condition implies that the know-how is useful in the sense that it can reasonably be expected at the date of conclusion of the agreement to be capable of significantly improving the competitive position of the licensee, for instance by reducing his production costs. "Identified" means that it is possible to verify that the licensed know-how fulfils the criteria of

secrecy and substantiality. This condition is satisfied where the licensed know-how is described in manuals or other written form. However, in some cases this may not be reasonably possible. The licensed know-how may consist of practical knowledge possessed by the licensor's employees. For instance, the licensor's employees may possess secret and substantial knowledge about a certain production process which is passed on to the licensee in the form of training of the licensee's employees. In such cases it is sufficient to describe in the agreement the general nature of the know-how and to list the employees that will be or have been involved in passing it on to the licensee.

Commentary
para 47: B&C: 9.134

48. The concept of "transfer" implies that technology must flow from one undertaking to another. Such transfers normally take the form of licensing whereby the licensor grants the licensee the right to use his technology against payment of royalties. It can also take the form of sub-licensing, whereby a licensee, having been authorised to do so by the licensor, grants licenses to third parties (sub-licensees) for the exploitation of the technology.

Commentary
para 48: B&C: 9.134

49. The TTBER only applies to agreements that have as their primary object the transfer of technology as defined in that Regulation as opposed to the purchase of goods and services or the licensing of other types of intellectual property. Agreements containing provisions relating to the purchase and sale of products are only covered by the TTBER to the extent that those provisions do not constitute the primary object of the agreement and are directly related to the application of the licensed technology. This is likely to be the case where the tied products take the form of equipment or process input which is specifically tailored to efficiently exploit the licensed technology. If, on the other hand, the product is simply another input into the final product, it must be carefully examined whether the licensed technology constitutes the primary object of the agreement. For instance, in cases where the licensee is already manufacturing a final product on the basis of another technology, the licence must lead to a significant improvement of the licensee's production process, exceeding the value of the product purchased from the licensor. The requirement that the tied products must be related to the licensing of technology implies that the TTBER does not cover the purchase of products that have no relation with the products incorporating the licensed technology. This is for example the case where the tied product is not intended to be used with the licensed product, but relates to an activity on a separate product market.

Commentary
para 49: B&C: 9.135, 9.138, 9.139 F&N: 10.75

50. The TTBER only covers the licensing of other types of intellectual property such as trademarks and copyright, other than software copyright, to the extent that they are directly related to the exploitation of the licensed technology and do not constitute the primary object of the agreement. This condition ensures that agreements covering other types of intellectual property rights are only block exempted to the extent that these other intellectual property rights serve to enable the licensee to better exploit the licensed technology. The licensor may for instance authorise the licensee to use his trademark on the products incorporating the licensed technology. The trademark licence may allow the licensee to better exploit the licensed technology by allowing consumers to make an immediate link between the product and the characteristics imputed to it by the licensed technology. An obligation on the licensee to use the licensor's trademark may also promote the dissemination of technology by allowing the licensor to identify himself as the source of the underlying technology. However, where the value of the licensed technology to the licensee is limited because he already employs an identical or very similar technology and the main object of the agreement is the trademark, the TTBER does not apply.[29]

Notes
[29] See in this respect Commission Decision in *Moosehead/Whitbread* (OJ L 100, 20.4.1990, p. 32).

Commentary
para 50: B&C: 9.136

51. The licensing of copyright for the purpose of reproduction and distribution of the protected work, i.e. the production of copies for resale, is considered to be similar to technology licensing. Since such licence agreements relate to the production and sale of products on the basis of an intellectual property right, they are considered to be of a similar nature as technology transfer agreements and normally raise comparable issues. Although the TTBER does not cover copyright other than software copyright, the Commission will as a general rule apply the principles set out in the TTBER and these guidelines when assessing such licensing of copyright under Article 81.

Commentary
para 51: B&C: 9.136

52. On the other hand, the licensing of rights in performances and other rights related to copyright is considered to raise particular issues and it may not be warranted to assess such licensing on the basis of the principles developed in these guidelines. In the case of the various rights related to performances value is created not by the reproduction and sale of copies of a product but by each individual performance of the protected work. Such exploitation can take various forms including the performance, showing or the renting of protected material such as films, music or sporting events. In the application of Article 81 the specificities of the work and the way in which it is exploited must be taken into account.[30] For instance, resale restrictions may give rise to less competition concerns whereas particular concerns may arise where licensors impose on their licensees to extend to each of the licensors more favourable conditions obtained by one of them. The Commission will therefore not apply the TTBER and the present guidelines by way of analogy to the licensing of these other rights.

Notes
[30] See in this respect Case 262/81, *Coditel (II)*, [1982] ECR 3381.

Commentary
para 52: B&C: 9.136 **F&N:** 10.72

53. The Commission will also not extend the principles developed in the TTBER and these guidelines to trademark licensing. Trademark licensing often occurs in the context of distribution and resale of goods and services and is generally more akin to distribution agreements than technology licensing. Where a trademark licence is directly related to the use, sale or resale of goods and services and does not constitute the primary object of the agreement, the licence agreement is covered by Commission Regulation (EC) No 2790/1999 on the application of Article 81(3) of the Treaty to categories of vertical agreements and concerted practices.[31]

Notes
[31] OJ L 336, 29.12.1999, p. 21.

Commentary
para 53: B&C: 9.136, 9.173

2.4. Duration

54. Subject to the duration of the TTBER, the block exemption applies for as long as the licensed property right has not lapsed, expired or been declared invalid. In the case of know-how the block exemption applies as long as the licensed know-how remains secret, except where the know-how becomes publicly known as a result of action by the licensee, in which case the exemption shall apply for the duration of the agreement (cf. Article 2 of the TTBER).

Commentary
para 54: B&C: 9.119

55. The block exemption applies to each licensed property right covered by the agreement and ceases to apply on the date of expiry, invalidity or the coming into the public domain of the last intellectual property right which constitutes "technology" within the meaning of the TTBER (cf. paragraph above).

Commentary
para 55: B&C: 9.140

2.5. Relationship with other block exemption regulations

56. The TTBER covers agreements between two undertakings concerning the licensing of technology for the purpose of the production of contract products. However, technology can also be an element of other types of agreements. In addition, the products incorporating the licensed technology are subsequently sold on the market. It is therefore necessary to address the interface between the TTBER and Commission Regulation (EC) No 2658/2000 on the application of Article 81(3) of the Treaty to categories of specialisation agreements,[32] Commission Regulation 2659/2000 on the application of Article 81(3) to categories of research and development agreements[33] and Commission Regulation (EC) No 2790/1999 on the application of Article 81(3) of the Treaty to categories of vertical agreements and concerted practices.[34]

Notes
[32] OJ L 304, 5.12.2000, p. 3.
[33] OJ L 304, 5.12.2000, p. 7.
[34] [OJ L 336, 29.12.1999, p. 21.]

Commentary
para 56: B&C: 9.169

2.5.1. The Block Exemption Regulations on specialisation and R&D agreements

57. According to Article 1(1)(c) of Regulation 2658/2000 on specialisation agreements, that Regulation covers, inter alia, joint production agreements by virtue of which two or more undertakings agree to produce certain products jointly. The Regulation extends to provisions concerning the assignment or use of intellectual property rights, provided that they do not constitute the primary object of the agreement, but are directly related to and necessary for its implementation.

58. Where undertakings establish a production joint venture and license the joint venture to exploit technology, which is used in the production of the products produced by the joint venture, such licensing is subject to Regulation 2658/2000 and not the TTBER. Accordingly, licensing in the context of a production joint venture normally falls to be considered under Regulation 2658/2000. However, where the joint venture engages in licensing of the technology to third parties, the activity is not linked to production by the joint venture and therefore not covered by that Regulation. Such licensing arrangements, which bring together the technologies of the parties, constitute technology pools, which are dealt with in section IV.4 below.

Commentary
para 58: B&C: 9.170

59. Regulation 2659/2000 on research and development agreements covers agreements whereby two or more undertakings agree to jointly carry out research and development and to jointly exploit the results thereof. According to Article 2(11), research and development and the exploitation of the results are carried out jointly where the work involved is carried out by a joint team, organisation or undertakings, jointly entrusted to a third party or allocated between the parties by way of specialisation in research, development, production and distribution, including licensing.

60. It follows that Regulation 2659/2000 covers licensing between the parties and by the parties to a joint entity in the context of a research and development agreement. In the context of such agreements the parties can also determine the conditions for licensing the fruits of the research

Part C Substantive Antitrust Matters

and development agreement to third parties. However, since third party licensees are not party to the research and development agreement, the individual licence agreement concluded with third parties is not covered by Regulation 2659/2000. Such licence agreements are block exempted by the TTBER where they fulfil the conditions of that Regulation.

Commentary
para 60: B&C: 9.170

2.5.2. The Block Exemption Regulation on vertical agreements

61. Commission Regulation (EC) No 2790/1999 on vertical agreements covers agreements entered into between two or more undertakings each operating, for the purposes of the agreement, at different levels of the production or distribution chain, and relating to the conditions under which the parties may purchase, sell or resell certain goods or services. It thus covers supply and distribution agreements.[35]

Notes
[35] See the guide "Competition policy in Europe — The competition rules for supply and distribution agreements", 2002.

62. Given that the TTBER only covers agreements between two parties and that a licensee, selling products incorporating the licensed technology, is a supplier for the purposes of Regulation 2790/1999, these two block exemption regulations are closely related. The agreement between licensor and licensee is subject to the TTBER whereas agreements concluded between a licensee and buyers are subject to Regulation 2790/1999 and the Guidelines on Vertical Restraints.[36]

Notes
[36] OJ C 291, 13.10.2000, p. 1, and note 31.

63. The TTBER also block exempts agreements between the licensor and the licensee where the agreement imposes obligations on the licensee as to the way in which he must sell the products incorporating the licensed technology. In particular, the licensee can be obliged to establish a certain type of distribution system such as exclusive distribution or selective distribution. However, the distribution agreements concluded for the purposes of implementing such obligations must, in order to be block exempted, comply with Regulation 2790/1999. For instance, the licensor can oblige the licensee to establish a system based on exclusive distribution in accordance with specified rules. However, it follows from Article 4(b) of Regulation 2790/1999 that distributors must be free to make passive sales into the territories of other exclusive distributors.

64. Furthermore, distributors must in principle be free to sell both actively and passively into territories covered by the distribution systems of other licensees producing their own products on the basis of the licensed technology. This is because for the purposes of Regulation 2790/1999 each licensee is a separate supplier. However, the reasons underlying the block exemption contained in that Regulation may also apply where the products incorporating the licensed technology are sold by the licensees under a common brand belonging to the licensor. When the products incorporating the licensed technology are sold under a common brand identity there may be the same efficiency reasons for applying the same types of restraints between licensees' distribution systems as within a single vertical distribution system. In such cases the Commission would be unlikely to challenge restraints where by analogy the requirements of Regulation 2790/1999 are fulfilled. For a common brand identity to exist the products must be sold and marketed under a common brand, which is predominant in terms of conveying quality and other relevant information to the consumer. It does not suffice that in addition to the licensees' brands the product carries the licensor's brand, which identifies him as the source of the licensed technology.

Commentary
para 64: B&C: 9.171 F&N: 10.77

3. *The safe harbour established by the Block Exemption Regulation*

65. According to Article 3 of the TTBER the block exemption of restrictive agreements is subject to market share thresholds, confining the scope of the block exemption to agreements that although they may be restrictive of competition can generally be presumed to fulfil the conditions of Article 81(3). Outside the safe harbour created by the market share thresholds individual assessment is required. The fact that market shares exceed the thresholds does not give rise to any presumption either that the agreement is caught by Article 81(1) or that the agreement does not fulfil the conditions of Article 81(3). In the absence of hardcore restrictions, market analysis is required.

Commentary
para 65: **B&C:** 9.131, 9.141 **F&N:** 10.62

66. The market share threshold to be applied for the purpose of the safe harbour of the TTBER depends on whether the agreement is concluded between competitors or non-competitors. For the purposes of the TTBER undertakings are competitors on the relevant technology market when they license competing technologies. Potential competition on the technology market is not taken into account for the application of the market share threshold or the hardcore list. Outside the safe harbour of the TTBER potential competition on the technology market is taken into account but does not lead to the application of the hardcore list relating to agreements between competitors (see also paragraph 31 above).

Commentary
para 66: **B&C:** 9.088 **F&N:** 10.84

67. Undertakings are competitors on the relevant product market where both undertakings are active on the same product and geographic market(s) on which the products incorporating the licensed technology are sold (actual competitors). They are also considered competitors where they would be likely, on realistic grounds, to undertake the necessary additional investments or other necessary switching costs to enter the relevant product and geographic market(s) within a reasonably short period of time[37] in response to a small and permanent increase in relative prices (potential competitors).

Notes
[37] See paragraph 29 above.

68. It follows from paragraphs 66 and 67 that two undertakings are not competitors for the purposes of the TTBER where the licensor is neither an actual nor a potential supplier of products on the relevant market and the licensee, already present on the product market, is not licensing out a competing technology even if he owns a competing technology and produces on the basis of that technology. However, the parties become competitors if at a later point in time the licensee starts licensing out his technology or the licensor becomes an actual or potential supplier of products on the relevant market. In that case the hardcore list relevant for agreements between non-competitors will continue to apply to the agreement unless the agreement is subsequently amended in any material respect, see Article 4(3) of the TTBER and paragraph 31 above.

69. In the case of agreements between competitors the market share threshold is 20% and in the case of agreements between non-competitors it is 30% (cf. Article 3(1) and (2) of the TTBER). Where the undertakings party to the licensing agreement are not competitors the agreement is covered if the market share of neither party exceeds 30% on the affected relevant technology and product markets. Where the undertakings party to the licensing agreement are competitors the agreement is covered if the combined market shares of the parties do not exceed 20% on the relevant technology and product markets. The market share thresholds apply both to technology markets and markets for products incorporating the licensed technology. If the applicable market share threshold is exceeded on an affected relevant market, the block exemption does not apply to the agreement for that relevant market. For instance, if the licence agreement concerns two separate product markets or two separate geographic markets, the block exemption may apply to one of the markets and not to the other.

Part C Substantive Antitrust Matters

70. In the case of technology markets, it follows from Article 3(3) of the TTBER that the licensor's market share is to be calculated on the basis of the sales of the licensor and all his licensees of products incorporating the licensed technology and this for each relevant market separately.[38] Where the parties are competitors on the technology market, sales of products incorporating the licensee's own technology must be combined with the sales of the products incorporating the licensed technology. In the case of new technologies that have not yet generated any sales, a zero market share is assigned. When sales commence the technology will start accumulating market share.

Notes
[38] The reasons for this calculation rule are explained in paragraph 23 above.

71. In the case of product markets, the licensee's market share is to be calculated on the basis of the licensee's sales of products incorporating the licensor's technology and competing products, i.e. the total sales of the licensee on the product market in question. Where the licensor is also a supplier of products on the relevant market, the licensor's sales on the product market in question must also be taken into account. In the calculation of market shares for product markets, however, sales made by other licensees are not taken into account when calculating the licensee's and/or licensor's market share.

72. Market shares should be calculated on the basis of sales value data where such data are available. Such data normally provide a more accurate indication of the strength of a technology than volume data. However, where value based data are not available, estimates based on other reliable market information may be used, including market sales volume data.

73. The principles set out above can be illustrated by the following examples:

Licensing between non-competitors

Example 1

Company A is specialised in developing bio-technological products and techniques and has developed a new product Xeran. It is not active as a producer of Xeran, for which it has neither the production nor the distribution facilities. Company B is one of the producers of competing products, produced with freely available non-proprietary technologies. In year 1, B was selling EUR 25 million worth of products produced with the freely available technologies. In year 2, A gives a licence to B to produce Xeran. In that year B sells EUR 15 million produced with the help of the freely available technologies and EUR 15 million of Xeran. In year 3 and the following years B produces and sells only Xeran worth EUR 40 million annually. In addition in year 2, A is also licensing to C. C was not active on that product market before. C produces and sells only Xeran, EUR 10 million in year 2 and EUR 15 million in year 3 and thereafter. It is established that the total market of Xeran and its substitutes where B and C are active is worth EUR 200 million in each year.

In year 2, the year the licence agreement is concluded, A's market share on the technology market is 0% as its market share has to be calculated on the basis of the total sales of Xeran in the preceding year. In year 3 A's market share on the technology market is 12,5%, reflecting the value of Xeran produced by B and C in the preceding year 2. In year 4 and thereafter A's market share on the technology market is 27,5%, reflecting the value of Xeran produced by B and C in the preceding year.

In year 2 B's market share on the product market is 12,5%, reflecting B's EUR 25 million sales in year 1. In year 3 B's market share is 15% because its sales have increased to EUR 30 million in year 2. In year 4 and thereafter B's market share is 20% as its sales are EUR 40 million annually. C's market share on the product market is 0% in year 1 and 2,5% in year 3 and 7,5% thereafter.

As the licence agreements are between non-competitors and the individual market shares of A, B and C are below 30% each year, the agreements fall within the safe harbour of the TTBER.

Example 2

The situation is the same as in example 1, however now B and C are operating in different geographic markets. It is established that the total market of Xeran and its substitutes is worth EUR 100 million annually in each geographic market.

In this case, A's market share on the technology market has to be calculated for each of the two geographic markets. In the market where B is active A's market share depends on the sale of Xeran by B. As in this example the total market is assumed to be EUR 100 million, i.e. half the size of the market in example 1, the market share of A is 0% in year 2, 15% in year 3 and 40% thereafter. B's market share is 25% in year 2, 30% in year 3 and 40% thereafter. In year 2 and 3 both A's and B's market share does not exceed the 30% threshold. The threshold is however exceeded from year 4 and this means that, in line with Article 8(2) of the TTBER, after year 6 the licence agreement between A and B can no longer benefit from the safe harbour but has to be assessed on an individual basis.

In the market where C is active A's market share depends on the sale of Xeran by C. A's market share on the technology market, based on C's sales in the previous year, is therefore 0% in year 2, 10% in year 3 and 15% thereafter. The market share of C on the product market is the same: 0% in year 2, 10% in year 3 and 15% thereafter. The licence agreement between A and C therefore falls within the safe harbour for the whole period.

Licensing between competitors

Example 3

Companies A and B are active on the same relevant product and geographic market for a certain chemical product. They also each own a patent on different technologies used to produce this product. In year 1 A and B sign a cross licence agreement licensing each other to use their respective technologies. In year 1 A and B produce only with their own technology and A sells EUR 15 million of the product and B sells EUR 20 million of the product. From year 2 they both use their own and the other's technology. From that year onward A sells EUR 10 million of the product produced with its own technology and EUR 10 million of the product produced with B's technology. B sells from year 2 EUR 15 million of the product produced with its own technology and EUR 10 million of the product produced with A's technology. It is established that the total market of the product and its substitutes is worth EUR 100 million in each year.

To assess the licence agreement under the TTBER, the market shares of A and B have to be calculated both on the technology market and the product market. The market share of A on the technology market depends on the amount of the product sold in the preceding year that was produced, by both A and B, with A's technology. In year 2 the market share of A on the technology market is therefore 15%, reflecting its own production and sales of EUR 15 million in year 1. From year 3 A's market share on the technology market is 20%, reflecting the EUR 20 million sale of the product produced with A's technology and produced and sold by A and B (EUR 10 million each). Similarly, in year 2 B's market share on the technology market is 20% and thereafter 25%.

The market shares of A and B on the product market depend on their respective sales of the product in the previous year, irrespective of the technology used. The market share of A on the product market is 15% in year 2 and 20% thereafter. The market share of B on the product market is 20% in year 2 and 25% thereafter.

As the agreement is between competitors, their combined market share, both on the technology and on the product market, has to be below the 20% market share threshold in order to benefit from the safe harbour. It is clear that this is not the case here. The combined market share on the technology market and on the product market is 35% in year 2 and 45% thereafter. This agreement between competitors will therefore have to be assessed on an individual basis.

Commentary
para 73: B&C: 9.143, 9.144 F&N: 10.120

4. Hardcore restrictions of competition under the Block Exemption Regulation

4.1. General principles

74. Article 4 of the TTBER contains a list of hardcore restrictions of competition. The classification of a restraint as a hardcore restriction of competition is based on the nature of the restriction and experience showing that such restrictions are almost always anti-competitive. In line with the case law of the Community Courts[39] such a restriction may result from the clear objective of the agreement or from the circumstances of the individual case (cf. paragraph 14 above).

Notes
[39] See e.g. the case law cited in note 15.

75. When a technology transfer agreement contains a hardcore restriction of competition, it follows from Article 4(1) and 4(2) of the TTBER that the agreement as a whole falls outside the scope of the block exemption. For the purposes of the TTBER hardcore restrictions cannot be severed from the rest of the agreement. Moreover, the Commission considers that in the context of individual assessment hardcore restrictions of competition will only in exceptional circumstances fulfil the four conditions of Article 81(3) (cf. paragraph 18 above).

Commentary
para 75: F&N: 10.91

76. Article 4 of the TTBER distinguishes between agreements between competitors and agreements between non-competitors.

4.2. Agreements between competitors

77. Article 4(1) lists the hardcore restrictions for licensing between competitors. According to Article 4(1), the TTBER does not cover agreements which, directly or indirectly, in isolation or in combination with other factors under the control of the parties, have as their object:

(a) The restriction of a party's ability to determine its prices when selling products to third parties;

(b) The limitation of output, except limitations on the output of contract products imposed on the licensee in a non-reciprocal agreement or imposed on only one of the licensees in a reciprocal agreement;

(c) The allocation of markets or customers except

  (i) the obligation on the licensee(s) to produce with the licensed technology only within one or more technical fields of use or one or more product markets;

  (ii) the obligation on the licensor and/or the licensee, in a non-reciprocal agreement, not to produce with the licensed technology within one or more technical fields of use or one or more product markets or one or more exclusive territories reserved for the other party;

  (iii) the obligation on the licensor not to license the technology to another licensee in a particular territory;

  (iv) the restriction, in a non-reciprocal agreement, of active and/or passive sales by the licensee and/or the licensor into the exclusive territory or to the exclusive customer group reserved for the other party;

  (v) the restriction, in a non-reciprocal agreement, of active sales by the licensee into the exclusive territory or to the exclusive customer group allocated by the licensor to another licensee provided that the latter was not a competing undertaking of the licensor at the time of the conclusion of its own licence;

  (vi) the obligation on the licensee to produce the contract products only for its own use provided that the licensee is not restricted in selling the contract products actively and passively as spare parts for its own products;

      (vii) the obligation on the licensee in a non-reciprocal agreement to produce the contract products only for a particular customer, where the licence was granted in order to create an alternative source of supply for that customer;

    (d) The restriction of the licensee's ability to exploit its own technology or the restriction of the ability of any of the parties to the agreement to carry out research and development, unless such latter restriction is indispensable to prevent the disclosure of the licensed know-how to third parties.

78. For a number of hardcore restrictions the TTBER makes a distinction between reciprocal and non-reciprocal agreements. The hardcore list is stricter for reciprocal agreements than for non-reciprocal agreements between competitors. Reciprocal agreements are cross-licensing agreements where the licensed technologies are competing technologies or can be used for the production of competing products. A non-reciprocal agreement is an agreement where only one of the parties is licensing its technology to the other party or where in case of cross-licensing the licensed technologies are not competing technologies and cannot be used for the production of competing products. An agreement is not reciprocal merely because the agreement contains a grant back obligation or because the licensee licenses back own improvements of the licensed technology. In case at a later point in time a non-reciprocal agreement becomes a reciprocal agreement due to the conclusion of a second licence between the same parties, they may have to revise the first licence in order to avoid that the agreement contains a hardcore restriction. In the assessment of the individual case the Commission will take into account the time lapsed between the conclusion of the first and the second licence.

Commentary
para 78: B&C: 9.091 **F&N:** 10.94

---

79. The hardcore restriction of competition contained in Article 4(1)(a) concerns agreements between competitors that have as their object the fixing of prices for products sold to third parties, including the products incorporating the licensed technology. Price fixing between competitors constitutes a restriction of competition by its very object. Price fixing can for instance take the form of a direct agreement on the exact price to be charged or on a price list with certain allowed maximum rebates. It is immaterial whether the agreement concerns fixed, minimum, maximum or recommended prices. Price fixing can also be implemented indirectly by applying disincentives to deviate from an agreed price level, for example, by providing that the royalty rate will increase if product prices are reduced below a certain level. However, an obligation on the licensee to pay a certain minimum royalty does not in itself amount to price fixing.

Commentary
para 79: B&C: 9.092, 9.108, 9.147

---

80. When royalties are calculated on the basis of individual product sales, the amount of the royalty has a direct impact on the marginal cost of the product and thus a direct impact on product prices.[40] Competitors can therefore use cross licensing with reciprocal running royalties as a means of co-ordinating prices on downstream product markets.[41] However, the Commission will only treat cross licences with reciprocal running royalties as price fixing where the agreement is devoid of any pro-competitive purpose and therefore does not constitute a bona fide licensing arrangement. In such cases where the agreement does not create any value and therefore has no valid business justification, the arrangement is a sham and amounts to a cartel.

Notes
[40] See in this respect paragraph 98 of the Guidelines on the application of Article 81(3) of the Treaty cited in note 2.
[41] This is also the case where one party grants a licence to the other party and accepts to buy a physical input from the licensee. The purchase price can serve the same function as the royalty.

Commentary
para 80: B&C: 9.148

---

81. The hardcore restriction contained in Article 4(1)(a) also covers agreements whereby royalties are calculated on the basis of all product sales irrespective of whether the licensed technology

is being used. Such agreements are also caught by Article 4(1)(d) according to which the licensee must not be restricted in his ability to use his own technology (see paragraph 95 below). In general such agreements restrict competition since the agreement raises the cost of using the licensee's own competing technology and restricts competition that existed in the absence of the agreement.[42] This is so both in the case of reciprocal and non-reciprocal arrangements. Exceptionally, however, an agreement whereby royalties are calculated on the basis of all product sales may fulfil the conditions of Article 81(3) in an individual case where on the basis of objective factors it can be concluded that the restriction is indispensable for pro-competitive licensing to occur. This may be the case where in the absence of the restraint it would be impossible or unduly difficult to calculate and monitor the royalty payable by the licensee, for instance because the licensor's technology leaves no visible trace on the final product and practicable alternative monitoring methods are unavailable.

Notes

[42] See in this respect Case 193/83, *Windsurfing International*, [1986] ECR 611, paragraph 67.

Commentary
para 81: B&C: 9.147

82. The hardcore restriction of competition set out in Article 4(1)(b) concerns reciprocal output restrictions on the parties. An output restriction is a limitation on how much a party may produce and sell. Article 4(1)(b) does not cover output limitations on the licensee in a non-reciprocal agreement or output limitations on one of the licensees in a reciprocal agreement provided that the output limitation only concerns products produced with the licensed technology. Article 4(1)(b) thus identifies as hardcore restrictions reciprocal output restrictions on the parties and output restrictions on the licensor in respect of his own technology. When competitors agree to impose reciprocal output limitations, the object and likely effect of the agreement is to reduce output in the market. The same is true of agreements that reduce the incentive of the parties to expand output, for example by obliging each other to make payments if a certain level of output is exceeded.

Commentary
para 82: B&C: 9.149 F&N: 10.97

83. The more favourable treatment of non-reciprocal quantity limitations is based on the consideration that a one-way restriction does not necessarily lead to a lower output on the market while also the risk that the agreement is not a bona fide licensing arrangement is less when the restriction is non-reciprocal. When a licensee is willing to accept a one-way restriction, it is likely that the agreement leads to a real integration of complementary technologies or an efficiency enhancing integration of the licensor's superior technology with the licensee's productive assets. In a reciprocal agreement an output restriction on one of the licensees is likely to reflect the higher value of the technology licensed by one of the parties and may serve to promote pro-competitive licensing.

Commentary
para 83: B&C: 9.149 F&N: 10.97

84. The hardcore restriction of competition set out in Article 4(1)(c) concerns the allocation of markets and customers. Agreements whereby competitors share markets and customers have as their object the restriction of competition. It is a hardcore restriction where competitors in a reciprocal agreement agree not to produce in certain territories or not to sell actively and/or passively into certain territories or to certain customers reserved for the other party.

85. Article 4(1)(c) applies irrespective of whether the licensee remains free to use his own technology. Once the licensee has tooled up to use the licensor's technology to produce a given product, it may be costly to maintain a separate production line using another technology in order to serve customers covered by the restrictions. Moreover, given the anti-competitive potential of the restraint the licensee may have little incentive to produce under his own technology. Such restrictions are also highly unlikely to be indispensable for pro-competitive licensing to occur.

Commentary
para 85: F&N: 10.100

86. Under Article 4(1)(c)(ii) it is not a hardcore restriction for the licensor in a non-reciprocal agreement to grant the licensee an exclusive licence to produce on the basis of the licensed technology in a particular territory and thus agree not to produce himself the contract products in or provide the contract products from that territory. Such exclusive licences are block exempted irrespective of the scope of the territory. If the licence is world-wide, the exclusivity implies that the licensor abstains from entering or remaining on the market. The block exemption also applies where the licence is limited to one or more technical fields of use or one or more product markets. The purpose of agreements covered by Article 4(1)(c)(ii) may be to give the licensee an incentive to invest in and develop the licensed technology. The object of the agreement is therefore not necessarily to share markets.

Commentary
para 86: B&C: 9.151, 9.152

87. According to Article 4(1)(c)(iv) and for the same reason, the block exemption also applies to non-reciprocal agreements whereby the parties agree not to sell actively or passively[43] into an exclusive territory or to an exclusive customer group reserved for the other party.

Notes
[43] For a general definition of active and passive sales, reference is made to paragraph 50 of the Guidelines on vertical restraints cited in note 36.

88. According to Article 4(1)(c)(iii) it is also not a hardcore restriction if the licensor appoints the licensee as his sole licensee in a particular territory, implying that third parties will not be licensed to produce on the basis of the licensor's technology in the territory in question. In the case of such sole licences the block exemption applies irrespective of whether the agreement is reciprocal or not given that the agreement does not affect the ability of the parties to fully exploit their own technology in the respective territories.

Commentary
para 88: B&C: 9.152 F&N: 10.103

89. Article 4(1)(c)(v) excludes from the hardcore list and thus block exempts up to the market share threshold restrictions in a non-reciprocal agreement on active sales by a licensee into the territory or to the customer group allocated by the licensor to another licensee. It is a condition, however, that the protected licensee was not a competitor of the licensor when the agreement was concluded. It is not warranted to hardcore such restrictions. By allowing the licensor to grant a licensee, who was not already on the market, protection against active sales by licensees which are competitors of the licensor and which for that reason are already established on the market, such restrictions are likely to induce the licensee to exploit the licensed technology more efficiently. On the other hand, if the licensees agree between themselves not to sell actively or passively into certain territories or to certain customer groups, the agreement amounts to a cartel amongst the licensees. Given that such agreements do not involve any transfer of technology they fall outside the scope of the TTBER.

Commentary
para 89: B&C: 9.152, 9.153

90. According to Article 4(1)(c)(i) restrictions in agreements between competitors that limit the licence to one or more product markets or technical fields of use[44] are not hardcore restrictions. Such restrictions are block exempted up to the market share threshold of 20% irrespective of whether the agreement is reciprocal or not. It is a condition for the application of the block exemption, however, that the field of use restrictions do not go beyond the scope of the licensed technologies. It is also a condition that licensees are not limited in the use of their own technology (see Article 4(1)(d)). Where licensees are limited in the use of their own technology the agreement amounts to market sharing.

Notes
[44] Field of use restrictions are further dealt with in section IV.2.4 below.

Commentary
para 90: B&C: 9.151 **F&N:** 10.102

91. The block exemption applies irrespective of whether the field of use restriction is symmetrical or asymmetrical. An asymmetrical field of use restriction in a reciprocal licence agreement implies that both parties are allowed to use the respective technologies that they license in only within different fields of use. As long as the parties are unrestricted in the use of their own technologies, it is not assumed that the agreement leads the parties to abandon or refrain from entering the field(s) covered by the licence to the other party. Even if the licensees tool up to use the licensed technology within the licensed field of use, there may be no impact on assets used to produce outside the scope of the licence. It is important in this regard that the restriction relates to distinct product markets or fields of use and not to customers, allocated by territory or by group, who purchase products falling within the same product market or technical field of use. The risk of market sharing is considered substantially greater in the latter case (see paragraph 85 above). In addition, field of use restrictions may be necessary to promote pro-competitive licensing (see paragraph 182 below).

Commentary
para 91: F&N: 10.102

92. Article 4(1)(c)(vi) contains a further exception, namely captive use restrictions, i.e. a requirement whereby the licensee may produce the products incorporating the licensed technology only for his own use. Where the contract product is a component the licensee can thus be obliged to produce that component only for incorporation into his own products and can be obliged not to sell the components to other producers. The licensee must be able, however, to sell the components as spare parts for his own products and must thus be able to supply third parties that perform after sale services on these products. Captive use restrictions as defined may be necessary to encourage the dissemination of technology, particularly between competitors, and are covered by the block exemption. Such restrictions are also dealt with in section IV.2.5 below.

Commentary
para 92: B&C: 9.153

93. Finally, Article 4(1)(c)(vii) excludes from the hardcore list an obligation on the licensee in a non-reciprocal agreement to produce the contract products only for a particular customer with a view to creating an alternative source of supply for that customer. It is thus a condition for the application of Article 4(1)(c)(vii) that the licence is limited to creating an alternative source of supply for that particular customer. It is not a condition, however, that only one such licence is granted. Article 4(1)(c)(vii) also covers situations where more than one undertaking is licensed to supply the same specified customer. The potential of such agreements to share markets is limited where the licence is granted only for the purpose of supplying a particular customer. In particular, in such circumstances it cannot be assumed that the agreement will cause the licensee to cease exploiting his own technology.

94. The hardcore restriction of competition set out in Article 4(1)(d) covers firstly restrictions on any of the parties' ability to carry out research and development. Both parties must be free to carry out independent research and development. This rule applies irrespective of whether the restriction applies to a field covered by the licence or to other fields. However, the mere fact that the parties agree to provide each other with future improvements of their respective technologies does not amount to a restriction on independent research and development. The effect on competition of such agreements must be assessed in light of the circumstances of the individual case. Article 4(1)(d) also does not extend to restrictions on a party to carry out research and development with third parties, where such restriction is necessary to protect the licensor's know-how against disclosure. In order to be covered by the exception, the restrictions imposed to protect the licensor's know-how against disclosure must be necessary and proportionate to ensure such protection.

For instance, where the agreement designates particular employees of the licensee to be trained in and responsible for the use of the licensed know-how, it may be sufficient to oblige the licensee not to allow those employees to be involved in research and development with third parties. Other safeguards may be equally appropriate.

Commentary
para 94: B&C: 9.154, 9.174

95. According to Article 4(1)(d) the licensee must also be unrestricted in the use of his own competing technology provided that in so doing he does not make use of the technology licensed from the licensor. In relation to his own technology the licensee must not be subject to limitations in terms of where he produces or sells, how much he produces or sells and at what price he sells. He must also not be obliged to pay royalties on products produced on the basis of his own technology (cf. paragraph 81 above). Moreover, the licensee must not be restricted in licensing his own technology to third parties. When restrictions are imposed on the licensee's use of his own technology or to carry out research and development, the competitiveness of the licensee's technology is reduced. The effect of this is to reduce competition on existing product and technology markets and to reduce the licensee's incentive to invest in the development and improvement of his technology.

Commentary
para 95: B&C: 9.154 F&N: 10.103

4.3. Agreements between non-competitors

96. Article 4(2) lists the hardcore restrictions for licensing between non-competitors. According to this provision, the TTBER does not cover agreements which, directly or indirectly, in isolation or in combination with other factors under the control of the parties, have as their object:
    (a) the restriction of a party's ability to determine its prices when selling products to third parties, without prejudice to the possibility to impose a maximum sale price or recommend a sale price, provided that it does not amount to a fixed or minimum sale price as a result of pressure from, or incentives offered by, any of the parties;
    (b) the restriction of the territory into which, or of the customers to whom, the licensee may passively sell the contract products, except:
        (i) the restriction of passive sales into an exclusive territory or to an exclusive customer group reserved for the licensor;
        (ii) the restriction of passive sales into an exclusive territory or to an exclusive customer group allocated by the licensor to another licensee during the first two years that this other licensee is selling the contract products in that territory or to that customer group;
        (iii) the obligation to produce the contract products only for its own use provided that the licensee is not restricted in selling the contract products actively and passively as spare parts for its own products;
        (iv) the obligation to produce the contract products only for a particular customer, where the licence was granted in order to create an alternative source of supply for that customer;
        (v) the restriction of sales to end users by a licensee operating at the wholesale level of trade;
        (vi) the restriction of sales to unauthorised distributors by the members of a selective distribution system;
    (c) the restriction of active or passive sales to end users by a licensee which is a member of a selective distribution system and which operates at the retail level, without prejudice to the possibility of prohibiting a member of the system from operating out of an unauthorised place of establishment.
97. The hardcore restriction of competition set out in Article 4(2)(a) concerns the fixing of prices charged when selling products to third parties. More specifically, this provision covers restrictions which have as their direct or indirect object the establishment of a fixed or a minimum selling price or a fixed or minimum price level to be observed by the licensor or the licensee when selling

products to third parties. In the case of agreements that directly establish the selling price, the restriction is clear-cut. However, the fixing of selling prices can also be achieved through indirect means. Examples of the latter are agreements fixing the margin, fixing the maximum level of discounts, linking the sales price to the sales prices of competitors, threats, intimidation, warnings, penalties, or contract terminations in relation to observance of a given price level. Direct or indirect means of achieving price fixing can be made more effective when combined with measures to identify price-cutting, such as the implementation of a price monitoring system, or the obligation on licensees to report price deviations. Similarly, direct or indirect price fixing can be made more effective when combined with measures that reduce the licensee's incentive to lower his selling price, such as the licensor obliging the licensee to apply a most-favoured-customer clause, i.e. an obligation to grant to a customer any more favourable terms granted to any other customer. The same means can be used to make maximum or recommended prices work as fixed or minimum selling prices. However, the provision of a list of recommended prices to or the imposition of a maximum price on the licensee by the licensor is not considered in itself as leading to fixed or minimum selling prices.

Commentary
para 97: **B&C:** 9.108, 9.114, 9.156 **F&N:** 10.96

---

98. Article 4(2)(b) identifies as hardcore restrictions of competition agreements or concerted practices that have as their direct or indirect object the restriction of passive sales by licensees of products incorporating the licensed technology.[45] Passive sales restrictions on the licensee may be the result of direct obligations, such as the obligation not to sell to certain customers or to customers in certain territories or the obligation to refer orders from these customers to other licensees. It may also result from indirect measures aimed at inducing the licensee to refrain from making such sales, such as financial incentives and the implementation of a monitoring system aimed at verifying the effective destination of the licensed products. Quantity limitations may be an indirect means to restrict passive sales. The Commission will not assume that quantity limitations as such serve this purpose. However, it will be otherwise where quantity limitations are used to implement an underlying market partitioning agreement. Indications thereof include the adjustment of quantities over time to cover only local demand, the combination of quantity limitations and an obligation to sell minimum quantities in the territory, minimum royalty obligations linked to sales in the territory, differentiated royalty rates depending on the destination of the products and the monitoring of the destination of products sold by individual licensees. The general hardcore restriction covering passive sales by licensees is subject to a number of exceptions, which are dealt with below.

Notes
[45] This hardcore restriction applies to licence agreements concerning trade within the Community. As regards agreements concerning exports outside the Community or imports/re-imports from outside the Community see Case C-306/96, *Javico*, [1998] ECR I-1983.

Commentary
para 98: **B&C:** 9.159 **F&N:** 10.107, 10.141

---

99. Article 4(2)(b) does not cover sales restrictions on the licensor. All sales restrictions on the licensor are block exempted up to the market share threshold of 30%. The same applies to all restrictions on active sales by the licensee, with the exception of what is said on active selling in paragraphs 105 and 106 below. The block exemption of restrictions on active selling is based on the assumption that such restrictions promote investments, non-price competition and improvements in the quality of services provided by the licensees by solving free rider problems and hold-up problems. In the case of restrictions of active sales between licensees' territories or customer groups, it is not a condition that the protected licensee has been granted an exclusive territory or an exclusive customer group. The block exemption also applies to active sales restrictions where more than one licensee has been appointed for a particular territory or customer group. Efficiency enhancing investment is likely to be promoted where a licensee can be ensured that he will only face

active sales competition from a limited number of licensees inside the territory and not also from licensees outside the territory.

Commentary
para 99: B&C: 9.157, 9.158 F&N: 10.108

100. Restrictions on active and passive sales by licensees into an exclusive territory or to an exclusive customer group reserved for the licensor do not constitute hardcore restrictions of competition (cf. Article 4(2)(b)(i)). Indeed, they are block exempted. It is presumed that up to the market share threshold such restraints, where restrictive of competition, promote pro-competitive dissemination of technology and integration of such technology into the production assets of the licensee. For a territory or customer group to be reserved for the licensor, it is not required that the licensor is actually producing with the licensed technology in the territory or for the customer group in question. A territory or customer group can also be reserved by the licensor for later exploitation.

Commentary
para 100: B&C: 9.159 F&N: 10.109

101. Restrictions on passive sales by licensees into an exclusive territory or customer group allocated to another licensee are block exempted for two years calculated from the date on which the protected licensee first markets the products incorporating the licensed technology inside his exclusive territory or to his exclusive customer group (cf. Article 4(2)(b)(ii)). Licensees often have to commit substantial investments in production assets and promotional activities in order to start up and develop a new territory. The risks facing the new licensee are therefore likely to be substantial, in particular since promotional expenses and investment in assets required to produce on the basis of a particular technology are often sunk, i.e. they cannot be recovered if the licensee exits the market. In such circumstances, it is often the case that licensees would not enter into the licence agreement without protection for a certain period of time against (active and) passive sales into their territory by other licensees. Restrictions on passive sales into the exclusive territory of a licensee by other licensees therefore often fall outside Article 81(1) for a period of up to two years from the date on which the product incorporating the licensed technology was first put on the market in the exclusive territory by the licensee in question. However, to the extent that in individual cases such restrictions are caught by Article 81(1) they are block exempted. After the expiry of this two-year period restrictions on passive sales between licensees constitute hardcore restrictions. Such restrictions are generally caught by Article 81(1) and are unlikely to fulfil the conditions of Article 81(3). In particular, passive sales restrictions are unlikely to be indispensable for the attainment of efficiencies.[46]

Notes
[46] See in this respect paragraph 77 of the judgment in *Nungesser* cited in note 13.

Commentary
para 101: B&C: 9.159 F&N: 3.302, 3.413, 10.65, 10.109

102. Article 4(2)(b)(iii) brings under the block exemption a restriction whereby the licensee is obliged to produce products incorporating the licensed technology only for his own (captive) use. Where the contract product is a component the licensee can thus be obliged to use that product only for incorporation into his own products and can be obliged not to sell the product to other producers. The licensee must however be able to actively and passively sell the products as spare parts for his own products and must thus be able to supply third parties that perform after sale services on these products. Captive use restrictions are also dealt with in section IV.2.5 below.

Commentary
para 102: B&C: 9.160

103. As in the case of agreements between competitors (cf. paragraph 93 above) the block exemption also applies to agreements whereby the licensee is obliged to produce the contract products only

for a particular customer in order to provide that customer with an alternative source of supply (cf. Article 4(2)(b)(iv)). In the case of agreements between non-competitors, such restrictions are unlikely to be caught by Article 81(1).

Commentary
para 103: B&C: 9.160

104. Article 4(2)(b)(v) brings under the block exemption an obligation on the licensee not to sell to end users and thus only to sell to retailers. Such an obligation allows the licensor to assign the wholesale distribution function to the licensee and normally falls outside Article 81(1).[47]

Notes
[47] See in this respect Case 26/76, *Metro (I)*, [1977] ECR 1875.

Commentary
para 104: B&C: 9.161

105. Finally Article 4(2)(b)(vi) brings under the block exemption a restriction on the licensee not to sell to unauthorised distributors. This exception allows the licensor to impose on the licensees an obligation to form part of a selective distribution system. In that case, however, the licensees must according to Article 4(2)(c) be permitted to sell both actively and passively to end users, without prejudice to the possibility to restrict the licensee to a wholesale function as foreseen in Article 4(2)(b)(v) (cf. the previous paragraph).

106. It is recalled (cf. paragraph 39 above) that the block exemption covers licence agreements whereby the licensor imposes obligations which the licensee must or may impose on his buyers, including distributors. However, these obligations must comply with the competition rules applicable to supply and distribution agreements. Since the TTBER is limited to agreements between two parties the agreements concluded between the licensee and his buyers implementing such obligations are not covered by the TTBER. Such agreements are only block exempted when they comply with Regulation 2790/1999 (cf. section 2.5.2 above).

Commentary
para 106: B&C: 9.162

5. Excluded restrictions

107. Article 5 of the TTBER lists four types of restrictions that are not block exempted and which thus require individual assessment of their anti-competitive and pro-competitive effects. It follows from Article 5 that the inclusion in a licence agreement of any of the restrictions contained in these provisions does not prevent the application of the block exemption to the rest of the agreement. It is only the individual restriction in question that is not block exempted, implying that individual assessment is required. Accordingly, the rule of severability applies to the restrictions set out in Article 5.

108. Article 5(1) provides that the block exemption shall not apply to the following three obligations:
   (a) Any direct or indirect obligation on the licensee to grant an exclusive licence to the licensor or to a third party designated by the licensor in respect of its own severable improvements to or its new applications of the licensed technology.
   (b) Any direct or indirect obligation on the licensee to assign to the licensor or to a third party designated by the licensor rights to severable improvements to or new applications of the licensed technology.
   (c) Any direct or indirect obligation on the licensee not to challenge the validity of intellectual property rights held by the licensor in the common market. However, the TTBER does cover the possibility for the licensor to terminate the licence agreement in the event that the licensee challenges the validity of the licensed technology.
   The purpose of Article 5(1)(a), (b) and (c) is to avoid block exemption of agreements that may reduce the incentive of licensees to innovate.

109. Article 5(1)(a) and 5(1)(b) concerns exclusive grant backs or assignments to the licensor of severable improvements of the licensed technology. An improvement is severable if it can be exploited without infringing upon the licensed technology. An obligation to grant the licensor an exclusive licence to severable improvements of the licensed technology or to assign such improvements to the licensor is likely to reduce the licensee's incentive to innovate since it hinders the licensee in exploiting his improvements, including by way of licensing to third parties. This is the case both where the severable improvement concerns the same application as the licensed technology and where the licensee develops new applications of the licensed technology. According to Article 5(1)(a) and (b) such obligations are not block exempted. However, the block exemption does cover non-exclusive grant back obligations in respect of severable improvements. This is so even where the grant back obligation is non-reciprocal, i.e. only imposed on the licensee, and where under the agreement the licensor is entitled to feed-on the severable improvements to other licensees. A non-reciprocal grant back obligation may promote innovation and the dissemination of new technology by permitting the licensor to freely determine whether and to what extent to pass on his own improvements to his licensees. A feed-on clause may also promote the dissemination of technology because each licensee knows at the time of contracting that he will be on an equal footing with other licensees in terms of the technology on the basis of which he is producing. Exclusive grant backs and obligations to assign non-severable improvements are not restrictive of competition within the meaning of Article 81(1) since non-severable improvements cannot be exploited by the licensee without the licensor's permission.

Commentary
para 109: B&C: 9.164 **F&N:** 10.114

110. The application of Article 5(1)(a) and (b) does not depend on whether or not the licensor pays consideration in return for acquiring the improvement or for obtaining an exclusive licence. However, the existence and level of such consideration may be a relevant factor in the context of an individual assessment under Article 81. When grant backs are made against consideration it is less likely that the obligation creates a disincentive for the licensee to innovate. In the assessment of exclusive grant backs outside the scope of the block exemption the market position of the licensor on the technology market is also a relevant factor. The stronger the position of the licensor, the more likely it is that exclusive grant back obligations will have restrictive effects on competition in innovation. The stronger the position of the licensor's technology the more likely it is that the licensee will be an important source of innovation and future competition. The negative impact of grant back obligations can also be increased in case of parallel networks of licence agreements containing such obligations. When available technologies are controlled by a limited number of licensors that impose exclusive grant back obligations on licensees, the risk of anti-competitive effects is greater than where there are a number of technologies only some of which are licensed on exclusive grant back terms.

Commentary
para 110: B&C: 9.164 **F&N:** 10.114

111. The risk of negative effects on innovation is higher in the case of cross licensing between competitors where a grant back obligation on both parties is combined with an obligation on both parties to share with the other party improvements of his own technology. The sharing of all improvements between competitors may prevent each competitor from gaining a competitive lead over the other (see also paragraph 208 below). However, the parties are unlikely to be prevented from gaining a competitive lead over each other where the purpose of the licence is to permit them to develop their respective technologies and where the licence does not lead them to use the same technological base in the design of their products. This is the case where the purpose of the licence is to create design freedom rather than to improve the technological base of the licensee.

112. The excluded restriction set out in Article 5(1)(c) concerns non-challenge clauses, i.e. obligations not to challenge the validity of the licensor's intellectual property. The reason for

excluding non-challenge clauses from the scope of the block exemption is the fact that licensees are normally in the best position to determine whether or not an intellectual property right is invalid. In the interest of undistorted competition and in conformity with the principles underlying the protection of intellectual property, invalid intellectual property rights should be eliminated. Invalid intellectual property stifles innovation rather than promoting it. Article 81(1) is likely to apply to non-challenge clauses where the licensed technology is valuable and therefore creates a competitive disadvantage for undertakings that are prevented from using it or are only able to use it against payment of royalties.[48] In such cases the conditions of Article 81(3) are unlikely to be fulfilled.[49] However, the Commission takes a favourable view of non-challenge clauses relating to know-how where once disclosed it is likely to be impossible or very difficult to recover the licensed know-how. In such cases, an obligation on the licensee not to challenge the licensed know-how promotes dissemination of new technology, in particular by allowing weaker licensors to license stronger licensees without fear of a challenge once the know-how has been absorbed by the licensee.

Notes

[48] If the licensed technology is outdated no restriction of competition arises, see in this respect Case 65/86, *Bayer v Süllhofer*, [1988] ECR 5249.

[49] As to non-challenge clauses in the context of settlement agreements see point 209 below.

Commentary
para 112: B&C: 9.165 F&N: 10.115

113. The TTBER covers the possibility for the licensor to terminate the licence agreement in the event of a challenge of the licensed technology. Accordingly, the licensor is not forced to continue dealing with a licensee that challenges the very subject matter of the licence agreement, implying that upon termination any further use by the licensee of the challenged technology is at the challenger's own risk. Article 5(1)(c) ensures, however, that the TTBER does not cover contractual obligations obliging the licensee not to challenge the licensed technology, which would permit the licensor to sue the licensee for breach of contract and thereby create a further disincentive for the licensee to challenge the validity of the licensor's technology. The provision thereby ensures that the licensee is in the same position as third parties.

Commentary
para 113: F&N: 10.115

114. Article 5(2) excludes from the scope of the block exemption, in the case of agreements between non-competitors, any direct or indirect obligation limiting the licensee's ability to exploit his own technology or limiting the ability of the parties to the agreement to carry out research and development, unless such latter restriction is indispensable to prevent the disclosure of licensed know-how to third parties. The content of this condition is the same as that of Article 4(1)(d) of the hardcore list concerning agreements between competitors, which is dealt with in paragraphs 94 and 95 above. However, in the case of agreements between non-competitors it cannot be considered that such restrictions generally have negative effects on competition or that the conditions of Article 81(3) are generally not satisfied.[50] Individual assessment is required.

Notes
[50] See paragraph 14 above.

115. In the case of agreements between non-competitors, the licensee normally does not own a competing technology. However, there may be cases where for the purposes of the block exemption the parties are considered non-competitors in spite of the fact that the licensee does own a competing technology. This is the case where the licensee owns a technology but does not license it and the licensor is not an actual or potential supplier on the product market. For the purposes of the block exemption the parties are in such circumstances neither competitors on the technology market nor competitors on the product market.[51] In such cases it is important to ensure that the licensee is not restricted in his ability to exploit his own technology and further

develop it. This technology constitutes a competitive constraint in the market, which should be preserved. In such a situation restrictions on the licensee's use of his own technology or on research and development are normally considered to be restrictive of competition and not to satisfy the conditions of Article 81(3). For instance, an obligation on the licensee to pay royalties not only on the basis of products it produces with the licensed technology but also on the basis of products it produces with its own technology will generally limit the ability of the licensee to exploit its own technology and thus be excluded from the scope of the block exemption.

Notes
[51] See paragraphs 66 and 67 above.

116. In cases where the licensee does not own a competing technology or is not already developing such a technology, a restriction on the ability of the parties to carry out independent research and development may be restrictive of competition where only a few technologies are available. In that case the parties may be an important (potential) source of innovation in the market. This is particularly so where the parties possess the necessary assets and skills to carry out further research and development. In that case the conditions of Article 81(3) are unlikely to be fulfilled. In other cases where several technologies are available and where the parties do not possess special assets or skills, the restriction on research and development is likely to either fall outside Article 81(1) for lack of an appreciable restrictive effect or satisfy the conditions of Article 81(3). The restraint may promote the dissemination of new technology by assuring the licensor that the licence does not create a new competitor and by inducing the licensee to focus on the exploitation and development of the licensed technology. Moreover, Article 81(1) only applies where the agreement reduces the licensee's incentive to improve and exploit his own technology. This is for instance not likely to be the case where the licensor is entitled to terminate the licence agreement once the licensee commences to produce on the basis of his own competing technology. Such a right does not reduce the licensee's incentive to innovate, since the agreement can only be terminated when a commercially viable technology has been developed and products produced on the basis thereof are ready to be put on the market.

6. *Withdrawal and disapplication of the Block Exemption Regulation*

6.1. Withdrawal procedure

117. According to Article 6 of the TTBER, the Commission and the competition authorities of the Member States may withdraw the benefit of the block exemption in respect of individual agreements that do not fulfil the conditions of Article 81(3). The power of the competition authorities of the Member States to withdraw the benefit of the block exemption is limited to cases where the relevant geographic market is no wider than the territory of the Member State in question.

118. The four conditions of Article 81(3) are cumulative and must all be fulfilled for the exception rule to be applicable.[52] The block exemption can therefore be withdrawn where a particular agreement fails one or more of the four conditions.

Notes
[52] See in this respect paragraph 42 of the Guidelines on the application of Article 81(3) of the Treaty, cited in note 2.

119. Where the withdrawal procedure is applied, the withdrawing authority bears the burden of proving that the agreement falls within the scope of Article 81(1) and that the agreement does not satisfy all four conditions of Article 81(3). Given that withdrawal implies that the agreement in question restricts competition within the meaning of Article 81(1) and does not fulfil the conditions of Article 81(3), withdrawal is necessarily accompanied by a negative decision based on Articles 5, 7 or 9 of Regulation 1/2003.

Commentary
para 119: B&C: 9.167

Part C Substantive Antitrust Matters

120. According to Article 6, withdrawal may in particular be warranted in the following circumstances:
    1. access of third parties' technologies to the market is restricted, for instance by the cumulative effect of parallel networks of similar restrictive agreements prohibiting licensees from using third party technology;
    2. access of potential licensees to the market is restricted, for instance by the cumulative effect of parallel networks of similar restrictive agreements preventing licensors from licensing to other licensees;
    3. without any objectively valid reason the parties refrain from exploiting the licensed technology.

121. Articles 4 and 5 of the TTBER, containing the list of hardcore restrictions of competition and excluded restrictions, aim at ensuring that block exempted agreements do not reduce the incentive to innovate, do not delay the dissemination of technology, and do not unduly restrict competition between the licensor and licensee or between licensees. However, the list of hard-core restrictions and the list of excluded restrictions do not take into account all the possible impacts of licence agreements. In particular, the block exemption does not take account of any cumulative effect of similar restrictions contained in networks of licence agreements. Licence agreements may lead to foreclosure of third parties both at the level of the licensor and at the level of the licensee. Foreclosure of other licensors may stem from the cumulative effect of networks of licence agreements prohibiting the licensees from exploiting competing technologies, leading to the exclusion of other (potential) licensors. Foreclosure of licensors is likely to arise in cases where most of the undertakings on the market that could (efficiently) take a competing licence are prevented from doing so as a consequence of restrictive agreements and where potential licensees face relatively high barriers to entry. Foreclosure of other licensees may stem from the cumulative effect of licence agreements prohibiting licensors from licensing other licensees and thereby preventing potential licensees from gaining access to the necessary technology. The issue of foreclosure is examined in more detail in section IV.2.7 below. In addition, the Commission is likely to withdraw the benefit of the block exemption where a significant number of licensors of competing technologies in individual agreements impose on their licensees to extend to them more favourable conditions agreed with other licensors.

122. The Commission is also likely to withdraw the benefit of the block exemption where the parties refrain from exploiting the licensed technology, unless they have an objective justification for doing so. Indeed, when the parties do not exploit the licensed technology, no efficiency enhancing activity takes place, in which case the very rationale of the block exemption disappears. However, exploitation does not need to take the form of an integration of assets. Exploitation also occurs where the licence creates design freedom for the licensee by allowing him to exploit his own technology without facing the risk of infringement claims by the licensor. In the case of licensing between competitors, the fact that the parties do not exploit the licensed technology may be an indication that the arrangement is a disguised cartel. For these reasons the Commission will examine very closely cases of non-exploitation.

Commentary
para 122: B&C: 9.167

6.2. Disapplication of the Block Exemption Regulation

123. Article 7 of the TTBER enables the Commission to exclude from the scope of the TTBER, by means of regulation, parallel networks of similar agreements where these cover more than 50% of a relevant market. Such a measure is not addressed to individual undertakings but concerns all undertakings whose agreements are defined in the regulation disapplying the TTBER.

124. Whereas withdrawal of the benefit of the TTBER by the Commission under Article 6 implies the adoption of a decision under Articles 7 or 9 of Regulation 1/2003, the effect of a Commission disapplication regulation under Article 7 of the TTBER is merely to remove, in respect of the restraints and the markets concerned, the benefit of the TTBER and to restore the full application of Article 81(1) and (3). Following the adoption of a regulation declaring the TTBER inapplicable for a particular market in respect of agreements containing certain restraints, the

criteria developed by the relevant case law of the Community Courts and by notices and previous decisions adopted by the Commission will give guidance on the application of Article 81 to
individual agreements. Where appropriate, the Commission will take a decision in an individual
case, which can provide guidance to all the undertakings operating on the market concerned.

125. For the purpose of calculating the 50% market coverage ratio, account must be taken of each
individual network of licence agreements containing restraints, or combinations of restraints,
producing similar effects on the market.

126. Article 7 does not entail an obligation on the part of the Commission to act where the 50%
market-coverage ratio is exceeded. In general, disapplication is appropriate when it is likely that
access to the relevant market or competition therein is appreciably restricted. In assessing the
need to apply Article 7, the Commission will consider whether individual withdrawal would
be a more appropriate remedy. This may depend, in particular, on the number of competing
undertakings contributing to a cumulative effect on a market or the number of affected geographic markets within the Community.

Commentary
para 126: B&C: 9.168

127. Any regulation adopted under Article 7 must clearly set out its scope. This means, first, that the
Commission must define the relevant product and geographic market(s) and, secondly, that
it must identify the type of licensing restraint in respect of which the TTBER will no longer
apply. As regards the latter aspect, the Commission may modulate the scope of its regulation
according to the competition concern which it intends to address. For instance, while all parallel
networks of non-compete arrangements will be taken into account for the purpose of establishing the 50% market coverage ratio, the Commission may nevertheless restrict the scope of
the disapplication regulation only to non-compete obligations exceeding a certain duration.
Thus, agreements of a shorter duration or of a less restrictive nature might be left unaffected,
due to the lesser degree of foreclosure attributable to such restraints. Where appropriate, the
Commission may also provide guidance by specifying the market share level which, in the specific market context, may be regarded as insufficient to bring about a significant contribution
by an individual undertaking to the cumulative effect. In general, when the market share of the
products incorporating a technology licensed by an individual licensor does not exceed 5 %, the
agreement or network of agreements covering that technology is not considered to contribute
significantly to a cumulative foreclosure effect.[53]

Notes
[53] See in this respect paragraph 8 of the Commission Notice on agreements of minor importance, cited in note 17.

Commentary
para 127: B&C: 9.168

128. The transitional period of not less than six months that the Commission will have to set under
Article 7(2) should allow the undertakings concerned to adapt their agreements to take account
of the regulation disapplying the TTBER.

129. A regulation disapplying the TTBER will not affect the block exempted status of the agreements
concerned for the period preceding its entry into force.

IV. Application of Article 81(1) and 81(3) Outside the Scope of the Block Exemption Regulation

1. The general framework for analysis

130. Agreements that fall outside the block exemption, for example because the market share thresholds are exceeded or the agreement involves more than two parties, are subject to individual
assessment. Agreements that either do not restrict competition within the meaning of Article
81(1) or which fulfil the conditions of Article 81(3) are valid and enforceable. It is recalled
that there is no presumption of illegality of agreements that fall outside the scope of the block

exemption provided that they do not contain hardcore restrictions of competition. In particular, there is no presumption that Article 81(1) applies merely because the market share thresholds are exceeded. Individual assessment based on the principles described in these guidelines is required.

Commentary
para 130: F&N: 10.62

131. In order to promote predictability beyond the application of the TTBER and to confine detailed analysis to cases that are likely to present real competition concerns, the Commission takes the view that outside the area of hardcore restrictions Article 81 is unlikely to be infringed where there are four or more independently controlled technologies in addition to the technologies controlled by the parties to the agreement that may be substitutable for the licensed technology at a comparable cost to the user. In assessing whether the technologies are sufficiently substitutable the relative commercial strength of the technologies in question must be taken into account. The competitive constraint imposed by a technology is limited if it does not constitute a commercially viable alternative to the licensed technology. For instance, if due to network effects in the market consumers have a strong preference for products incorporating the licensed technology, other technologies already on the market or likely to come to market within a reasonable period of time may not constitute a real alternative and may therefore impose only a limited competitive constraint. The fact that an agreement falls outside the safe harbour described in this paragraph does not imply that the agreement is caught by Article 81(1) and, if so, that the conditions of Article 81(3) are not satisfied. As for the market share safe harbour of the TTBER, this additional safe harbour merely creates a negative presumption that the agreement is not prohibited by Article 81. Outside the safe harbour individual assessment of the agreement based on the principles developed in these guidelines is required.

Commentary
para 131: B&C: 9.083–9.084 F&N: 10.121

1.1. The relevant factors

132. In the application of Article 81 to individual cases it is necessary to take due account of the way in which competition operates on the market in question. The following factors are particularly relevant in this respect:
(a) the nature of the agreement;
(b) the market position of the parties;
(c) the market position of competitors;
(d) the market position of buyers of the licensed products;
(e) entry barriers;
(f) maturity of the market; and
(g) other factors.
The importance of individual factors may vary from case to case and depends on all other factors. For instance, a high market share of the parties is usually a good indicator of market power, but in the case of low entry barriers it may not be indicative of market power. It is therefore not possible to provide firm rules on the importance of the individual factors.

Commentary
para 132: B&C: 9.083

133. Technology transfer agreements can take many shapes and forms. It is therefore important to analyse the nature of the agreement in terms of the competitive relationship between the parties and the restraints that it contains. In the latter regard it is necessary to go beyond the express terms of the agreement. The existence of implicit restraints may be derived from the way in which the agreement has been implemented by the parties and the incentives that they face.

134. The market position of the parties provides an indication of the degree of market power, if any, possessed by the licensor, the licensee or both. The higher their market share the greater their market power is likely to be. This is particularly so where the market share reflects cost advantages or other competitive advantages vis-à-vis competitors. These competitive advantages may for instance result from being a first mover in the market, from holding essential patents or from having superior technology.

135. In analysing the competitive relationship between the parties it is sometimes necessary to go beyond the analysis set out in the above sections II.3 on market definition and II.4 on the distinction between competitors and non-competitors. Even where the licensor is not an actual or potential supplier on the product market and the licensee is not an actual or potential competitor on the technology market, it is relevant to the analysis whether the licensee owns a competing technology, which is not being licensed. If the licensee has a strong position on the product market, an agreement granting him an exclusive licence to a competing technology can restrict competition significantly compared to the situation where the licensor does not grant an exclusive licence or licences other undertakings.

136. Market shares and possible competitive advantages and disadvantages are also used to assess the market position of competitors. The stronger the actual competitors and the greater their number the less risk there is that the parties will be able to individually exercise market power. However, if the number of competitors is rather small and their market position (size, costs, R & D potential, etc.) is rather similar, this market structure may increase the risk of collusion.

137. The market position of buyers provides an indication of whether or not one or more buyers possess buyer power. The first indicator of buying power is the market share of the buyer on the purchase market. This share reflects the importance of his demand for possible suppliers. Other indicators focus on the position of the buyer on his resale market, including characteristics such as a wide geographic spread of his outlets, and his brand image amongst final consumers. In some circumstances buyer power may prevent the licensor and/or the licensee from exercising market power on the market and thereby solve a competition problem that would otherwise have existed. This is particularly so when strong buyers have the capacity and the incentive to bring new sources of supply on to the market in the case of a small but permanent increase in relative prices. Where the strong buyers merely extract favourable terms from the supplier or simply pass on any price increase to their customers, the position of the buyers is not such as to prevent the exercise of market power by the licensee on the product market and therefore not such as to solve the competition problem on that market.[54]

Notes
[54] See in this respect Case T-228/97, *Irish Sugar*, [1999] ECR II-2969, paragraph 101.

138. Entry barriers are measured by the extent to which incumbent companies can increase their price above the competitive level without attracting new entry. In the absence of entry barriers, easy and quick entry would render price increases unprofitable. When effective entry, preventing or eroding the exercise of market power, is likely to occur within one or two years, entry barriers can, as a general rule, be said to be low. Entry barriers may result from a wide variety of factors such as economies of scale and scope, government regulations, especially where they establish exclusive rights, state aid, import tariffs, intellectual property rights, ownership of resources where the supply is limited due to for instance natural limitations, essential facilities, a first mover advantage or brand loyalty of consumers created by strong advertising over a period of time. Restrictive agreements entered into by undertakings may also work as an entry barrier by making access more difficult and foreclosing (potential) competitors. Entry barriers may be present at all stages of the research and development, production and distribution process. The question whether certain of these factors should be described as entry barriers depends particularly on whether they entail sunk costs. Sunk costs are those costs which have to be incurred to enter or be active on a market but which are lost when the market is exited. The more costs are sunk, the more potential entrants have to weigh the risks of entering the market and the more credibly incumbents can threaten that they will match new competition, as sunk costs make it costly for incumbents to leave the market. In general, entry requires sunk costs, sometimes

minor and sometimes major. Therefore, actual competition is in general more effective and will weigh more heavily in the assessment of a case than potential competition.

139. A mature market is a market that has existed for some time, where the technology used is well known and widespread and not changing very much and in which demand is relatively stable or declining. In such a market restrictions of competition are more likely to have negative effects than in more dynamic markets.

140. In the assessment of particular restraints other factors may have to be taken into account. Such factors include cumulative effects, i.e. the coverage of the market by similar agreements, the duration of the agreements, the regulatory environment and behaviour that may indicate or facilitate collusion like price leadership, pre-announced price changes and discussions on the "right" price, price rigidity in response to excess capacity, price discrimination and past collusive behaviour.

Commentary
para 140: B&C: 9.083

1.2. Negative effects of restrictive licence agreements

141. The negative effects on competition on the market that may result from restrictive technology transfer agreements include the following:
    1. reduction of inter-technology competition between the companies operating on a technology market or on a market for products incorporating the technologies in question, including facilitation of collusion, both explicit and tacit;
    2. foreclosure of competitors by raising their costs, restricting their access to essential inputs or otherwise raising barriers to entry; and
    3. reduction of intra-technology competition between undertakings that produce products on the basis of the same technology.

142. Technology transfer agreements may reduce inter-technology competition, i.e. competition between undertakings that license or produce on the basis of substitutable technologies. This is particularly so where reciprocal obligations are imposed. For instance, where competitors transfer competing technologies to each other and impose a reciprocal obligation to provide each other with future improvements of their respective technologies and where this agreement prevents either competitor from gaining a technological lead over the other, competition in innovation between the parties is restricted (see also paragraph 208 below).

Commentary
para 142: B&C: 9.087

---

143. Licensing between competitors may also facilitate collusion. The risk of collusion is particularly high in concentrated markets. Collusion requires that the undertakings concerned have similar views on what is in their common interest and on how the co-ordination mechanisms function. For collusion to work the undertakings must also be able to monitor each other's market behaviour and there must be adequate deterrents to ensure that there is an incentive not to depart from the common policy on the market, while entry barriers must be high enough to limit entry or expansion by outsiders. Agreements can facilitate collusion by increasing transparency in the market, by controlling certain behaviour and by raising barriers to entry. Collusion can also exceptionally be facilitated by licensing agreements that lead to a high degree of commonality of costs, because undertakings that have similar costs are more likely to have similar views on the terms of coordination.[55]

Notes
[55] See in this respect paragraph 23 of the Guidelines on horizontal cooperation agreements, cited in note 20.

---

144. Licence agreements may also affect inter-technology competition by creating barriers to entry for and expansion by competitors. Such foreclosure effects may stem from restraints that prevent licensees from licensing from third parties or create disincentives for them to do so. For instance, third parties may be foreclosed where incumbent licensors impose non-compete obligations on

licensees to such an extent that an insufficient number of licensees are available to third parties and where entry at the level of licensees is difficult. Suppliers of substitutable technologies may also be foreclosed where a licensor with a sufficient degree of market power ties together various parts of a technology and licenses them together as a package while only part of the package is essential to produce a certain product.

145. Licence agreements may also reduce intra-technology competition, i.e. competition between undertakings that produce on the basis of the same technology. An agreement imposing territorial restraints on licensees, preventing them from selling into each other's territory reduces competition between them. Licence agreements may also reduce intra-technology competition by facilitating collusion between licensees. Moreover, licence agreements that reduce intra-technology competition may facilitate collusion between owners of competing technologies or reduce inter-technology competition by raising barriers to entry.

Commentary
para 145: B&C: 9.087

1.3. Positive effects of restrictive licence agreements and the framework for analysing such effects

146. Even restrictive licence agreements mostly also produce pro-competitive effects in the form of efficiencies, which may outweigh their anti-competitive effects. This assessment takes place within the framework of Article 81(3), which contains an exception from the prohibition rule of Article 81(1). For this exception to be applicable the licence agreement must produce objective economic benefits, the restrictions on competition must be indispensable to attain the efficiencies, consumers must receive a fair share of the efficiency gains, and the agreement must not afford the parties the possibility of eliminating competition in respect of a substantial part of the products concerned.

147. The assessment of restrictive agreements under Article 81(3) is made within the actual context in which they occur[56] and on the basis of the facts existing at any given point in time. The assessment is sensitive to material changes in the facts. The exception rule of Article 81(3) applies as long as the four conditions are fulfilled and ceases to apply when that is no longer the case.[57] However, when applying Article 81(3) in accordance with these principles it is necessary to take into account the initial sunk investments made by any of the parties and the time needed and the restraints required to commit and recoup an efficiency enhancing investment. Article 81 cannot be applied without considering the *ex ante* investment and the risks relating thereto. The risk facing the parties and the sunk investment that must be committed to implement the agreement can thus lead to the agreement falling outside Article 81(1) or fulfilling the conditions of Article 81(3), as the case may be, for the period of time required to recoup the investment.

Notes
[56] See Joined Cases 25/84 and 26/84, *Ford*, [1985] ECR 2725.
[57] See in this respect for example Commission Decision in TPS (OJ L 90, 2.4.1999, p. 6). Similarly, the prohibition of Article 81(1) also only applies as long as the agreement has a restrictive object or restrictive effects.

148. The first condition of Article 81(3) requires an assessment of what are the objective benefits in terms of efficiencies produced by the agreement. In this respect, licence agreements have the potential of bringing together complementary technologies and other assets allowing new or improved products to be put on the market or existing products to be produced at lower cost. Outside the context of hardcore cartels, licensing often occurs because it is more efficient for the licensor to licence the technology than to exploit it himself. This may particularly be the case where the licensee already has access to the necessary production assets. The agreement allows the licensee to gain access to a technology that can be combined with these assets, allowing him to exploit new or improved technologies. Another example of potentially efficiency enhancing licensing is where the licensee already has a technology and where the combination of this technology and the licensor's technology gives rise to synergies. When the two technologies are combined the licensee may be able to attain a cost/output configuration that would not otherwise be possible. Licence agreements may also give rise to efficiencies at the distribution stage in the same way as vertical distribution agreements. Such efficiencies can take the form of cost savings

Part C Substantive Antitrust Matters

or the provision of valuable services to consumers. The positive effects of vertical agreements are described in the Guidelines on Vertical Restraints.[58] A further example of possible efficiency gains is agreements whereby technology owners assemble a technology package for licensing to third parties. Such pooling arrangements may in particular reduce transaction costs, as licensees do not have to conclude separate licence agreements with each licensor. Pro-competitive licensing may also occur to ensure design freedom. In sectors where large numbers of intellectual property rights exist and where individual products may infringe upon a number of existing and future property rights, licence agreements whereby the parties agree not to assert their property rights against each other are often pro-competitive because they allow the parties to develop their respective technologies without the risk of subsequent infringement claims.

Notes
[58] Cited in note 36. See in particular paragraphs 115 et seq.

149. In the application of the indispensability test contained in Article 81(3) the Commission will in particular examine whether individual restrictions make it possible to perform the activity in question more efficiently than would have been the case in the absence of the restriction concerned. In making this assessment the market conditions and the realities facing the parties must be taken into account. Undertakings invoking the benefit of Article 81(3) are not required to consider hypothetical and theoretical alternatives. They must, however, explain and demonstrate why seemingly realistic and significantly less restrictive alternatives would be significantly less efficient. If the application of what appears to be a commercially realistic and less restrictive alternative would lead to a significant loss of efficiencies, the restriction in question is treated as indispensable. In some cases, it may also be necessary to examine whether the agreement as such is indispensable to achieve the efficiencies. This may for example be so in the case of technology pools that include complementary but non-essential technologies,[59] in which case it must be examined to what extent such inclusion gives rise to particular efficiencies or whether, without a significant loss of efficiencies, the pool could be limited to technologies for which there are no substitutes. In the case of simple licensing between two parties it is generally not necessary to go beyond an examination of the indispensability of individual restraints. Normally there is no less restrictive alternative to the licence agreement as such.

Notes
[59] As to these concepts see section IV.4.1 below.

150. The condition that consumers must receive a fair share of the benefits implies that consumers of the products produced under the licence must at least be compensated for the negative effects of the agreement.[60] This means that the efficiency gains must fully off-set the likely negative impact on prices, output and other relevant factors caused by the agreement. They may do so by changing the cost structure of the undertakings concerned, giving them an incentive to reduce price, or by allowing consumers to gain access to new or improved products, compensating for any likely price increase.[61]

Notes
[60] See paragraph 85 of the Guidelines on the application of Article 81(3) of the Treaty, cited in note 2.
[61] Idem, paragraphs 98 and 102.

151. The last condition of Article 81(3), according to which the agreement must not afford the parties the possibility of eliminating competition in respect of a substantial part of the products concerned, presupposes an analysis of remaining competitive pressures on the market and the impact of the agreement on such sources of competition. In the application of the last condition of Article 81(3) the relationship between Article 81(3) and Article 82 must be taken into account. According to settled case law, the application of Article 81(3) cannot prevent the application of Article 82 of the Treaty.[62] Moreover, since Articles 81 and 82 both pursue the aim of maintaining effective competition on the market, consistency requires that Article 81(3) be interpreted as precluding any application of the exception rule to restrictive agreements that constitute an abuse of a dominant position.[63]

[62] See paragraph 130 of the judgment cited in note 2. Similarly, the application of Article 81(3) does not prevent the application of the Treaty rules on the free movement of goods, services, persons and capital. These provisions are in certain circumstances applicable to agreements, decisions and concerted practices within the meaning of Article 81(1), see to that effect Case C-309/99, *Wouters*, [2002] ECR I-1577, paragraph 120.

[63] See in this respect Case T-51/89, *Tetra Pak (I)*, [1990] ECR II-309. See also paragraph 106 of the Guidelines on the application of Article 81(3) of the Treaty cited in note 2 above.

152. The fact that the agreement substantially reduces one dimension of competition does not necessarily mean that competition is eliminated within the meaning of Article 81(3). A technology pool, for instance, can result in an industry standard, leading to a situation in which there is little competition in terms of the technological format. Once the main players in the market adopt a certain format, network effects may make it very difficult for alternative formats to survive. This does not imply, however, that the creation of a de facto industry standard always eliminates competition within the meaning of the last condition of Article 81(3). Within the standard, suppliers may compete on price, quality and product features. However, in order for the agreement to comply with Article 81(3), it must be ensured that the agreement does not unduly restrict competition and does not unduly restrict future innovation.

2. The application of Article 81 to various types of licensing restraints

153. This section deals with various types of restraints that are commonly included in licence agreements. Given their prevalence it is useful to provide guidance as to how they are assessed outside the safe harbour of the TTBER. Restraints that have already been dealt with in the preceding parts of these guidelines, in particular sections III.4 and III.5, are only dealt with briefly in the present section.

154. This section covers both agreements between non-competitors and agreements between competitors. In respect of the latter a distinction is made — where appropriate — between reciprocal and non-reciprocal agreements. No such distinction is required in the case of agreements between non-competitors. When undertakings are neither actual nor potential competitors on a relevant technology market or on a market for products incorporating the licensed technology, a reciprocal licence is for all practical purposes no different from two separate licences. Arrangements whereby the parties assemble a technology package, which is then licensed to third parties, are technology pools, which are dealt with in section 4 below.

155. This section does not deal with obligations in licence agreements that are generally not restrictive of competition within the meaning of Article 81(1). These obligations include but are not limited to:
    (a) confidentiality obligations;
    (b) obligations on licensees not to sub-license;
    (c) obligations not to use the licensed technology after the expiry of the agreement, provided that the licensed technology remains valid and in force;
    (d) obligations to assist the licensor in enforcing the licensed intellectual property rights;
    (e) obligations to pay minimum royalties or to produce a minimum quantity of products incorporating the licensed technology; and
    (f) obligations to use the licensor's trade mark or indicate the name of the licensor on the product.

Commentary

para 155: B&C: 9.112, 9.117, 9.118
para 155(d): B&C: 9.113
para 155(e): B&C: 9.104
para 155(f): B&C: 9.109

2.1. Royalty obligations

156. The parties to a licence agreement are normally free to determine the royalty payable by the licensee and its mode of payment without being caught by Article 81(1). This principle applies both to agreements between competitors and agreements between non-competitors. Royalty

obligations may for instance take the form of lump sum payments, a percentage of the selling price or a fixed amount for each product incorporating the licensed technology. In cases where the licensed technology relates to an input which is incorporated into a final product it is as a general rule not restrictive of competition that royalties are calculated on the basis of the price of the final product, provided that it incorporates the licensed technology. In the case of software licensing royalties based on the number of users and royalties calculated on a per machine basis are generally compatible with Article 81(1).

Commentary
para 156: B&C: 9.093 F&N: 10.131

157. In the case of licence agreements between competitors it is recalled, see paragraphs and above, that in a limited number of circumstances royalty obligations may amount to price fixing, which is a hardcore restriction (cf. Article 4(1)(a)). It is a hardcore restriction under Article 4(1)(a) if competitors provide for reciprocal running royalties in circumstances where the licence is a sham, in that its purpose is not to allow an integration of complementary technologies or to achieve another pro-competitive aim. It is also a hardcore restriction under Article 4(1)(a) and 4(1)(d) if royalties extend to products produced solely with the licensee's own technology.

Commentary
para 157: B&C: 9.092

158. Other types of royalty arrangements between competitors are block exempted up to the market share threshold of 20% even if they restrict competition. Outside the safe harbour of the block exemption Article 81(1) may be applicable where competitors cross license and impose running royalties that are clearly disproportionate compared to the market value of the licence and where such royalties have a significant impact on market prices. In assessing whether the royalties are disproportionate it is relevant to have regard to the royalties paid by other licensees on the product market for the same or substitute technologies. In such cases it is unlikely that the conditions of Article 81(3) are satisfied. Article 81(1) may also apply where reciprocal running royalties per unit increase as output increases. If the parties have a significant degree of market power, such royalties may have the effect of limiting output.

Commentary
para 158: B&C: 9.092 F&N: 10.133

159. Notwithstanding the fact that the block exemption only applies as long as the technology is valid and in force, the parties can normally agree to extend royalty obligations beyond the period of validity of the licensed intellectual property rights without falling foul of Article 81(1). Once these rights expire, third parties can legally exploit the technology in question and compete with the parties to the agreement. Such actual and potential competition will normally suffice to ensure that the obligation in question does not have appreciable anti-competitive effects.

Commentary
para 159: B&C: 9.119

160. In the case of agreements between non-competitors the block exemption covers agreements whereby royalties are calculated on the basis of both products produced with the licensed technology and products produced with technologies licensed from third parties. Such arrangements may facilitate the metering of royalties. However, they may also lead to foreclosure by increasing the cost of using third party inputs and may thus have similar effects as a non-compete obligation. If royalties are paid not just on products produced with the licensed technology but also on products produced with third party technology, then the royalties will increase the cost of the latter products and reduce demand for third party technology. Outside the scope of the block exemption it must therefore be examined whether the restriction has foreclosure effects. For that purpose it is appropriate to use the analytical framework set out in section 2.7 below. In the case of appreciable foreclosure effects such agreements are caught by Article 81(1)

and unlikely to fulfil the conditions of Article 81(3), unless there is no other practical way of calculating and monitoring royalty payments.

Commentary
para 160: B&C: 9.092

2.2. Exclusive licensing and sales restrictions

161. For the present purposes it is useful to distinguish between restrictions as to production within a given territory (exclusive or sole licences) and restrictions on the sale of products incorporating the licensed technology into a given territory and to a given customer group (sales restrictions).

2.2.1. Exclusive and sole licences

162. A licence is deemed to be exclusive if the licensee is the only one who is permitted to produce on the basis of the licensed technology within a given territory. The licensor thus undertakes not to produce itself or license others to produce within a given territory. This territory may cover the whole world. Where the licensor undertakes only not to licence third parties to produce within a given territory, the licence is a sole licence. Often exclusive or sole licensing is accompanied by sales restrictions that limit the parties in where they may sell products incorporating the licensed technology.

163. Reciprocal exclusive licensing between competitors falls under Article 4(1)(c), which identifies market sharing between competitors as a hardcore restriction. Reciprocal sole licensing between competitors is block exempted up to the market share threshold of 20%. Under such an agreement the parties mutually commit not to license their competing technologies to third parties. In cases where the parties have a significant degree of market power such agreements may facilitate collusion by ensuring that the parties are the only sources of output in the market based on the licensed technologies.

Commentary
para 163: B&C: 9.095

164. Non-reciprocal exclusive licensing between competitors is block exempted up to the market share threshold of 20%. Above the market share threshold it is necessary to analyse what are the likely anti-competitive effects of such exclusive licensing. Where the exclusive licence is world-wide it implies that the licensor leaves the market. In cases where exclusivity is limited to a particular territory such as a Member State the agreement implies that the licensor abstains from producing goods and services inside the territory in question. In the context of Article 81(1) it must in particular be assessed what is the competitive significance of the licensor. If the licensor has a limited market position on the product market or lacks the capacity to effectively exploit the technology in the licensee's territory, the agreement is unlikely to be caught by Article 81(1). A special case is where the licensor and the licensee only compete on the technology market and the licensor, for instance being a research institute or a small research based undertaking, lacks the production and distribution assets to effectively bring to market products incorporating the licensed technology. In such cases Article 81(1) is unlikely to be infringed.

Commentary
para 164: B&C: 9.095 F&N: 10.124, 10.135

165. Exclusive licensing between non-competitors — to the extent that it is caught by Article 81(1)[64] — is likely to fulfil the conditions of Article 81(3). The right to grant an exclusive licence is generally necessary in order to induce the licensee to invest in the licensed technology and to bring the products to market in a timely manner. This is in particular the case where the licensee must make large investments in further developing the licensed technology. To intervene against the exclusivity once the licensee has made a commercial success of the licensed technology would deprive the licensee of the fruits of his success and would be detrimental to competition,

the dissemination of technology and innovation. The Commission will therefore only exceptionally intervene against exclusive licensing in agreements between non-competitors, irrespective of the territorial scope of the licence.

Notes
[64] See the judgment in *Nungesser* cited in note 13.

Commentary
para 165: B&C: 9.095 F&N: 10.124, 10.135

166. The main situation in which intervention may be warranted is where a dominant licensee obtains an exclusive licence to one or more competing technologies. Such agreements are likely to be caught by Article 81(1) and unlikely to fulfil the conditions of Article 81(3). It is a condition however that entry into the technology market is difficult and the licensed technology constitutes a real source of competition on the market. In such circumstances an exclusive licence may foreclose third party licensees and allow the licensee to preserve his market power.

Commentary
para 166: B&C: 9.095 F&N: 10.136

167. Arrangements whereby two or more parties cross licence each other and undertake not to licence third parties give rise to particular concerns when the package of technologies resulting from the cross licences creates a de facto industry standard to which third parties must have access in order to compete effectively on the market. In such cases the agreement creates a closed standard reserved for the parties. The Commission will assess such arrangements according to the same principles as those applied to technology pools (see section 4 below). It will normally be required that the technologies which support such a standard be licensed to third parties on fair, reasonable and non-discriminatory terms.[65] Where the parties to the arrangement compete with third parties on an existing product market and the arrangement relates to that product market a closed standard is likely to have substantial exclusionary effects. This negative impact on competition can only be avoided by licensing also to third parties.

Notes
[65] See in this respect the Commission's Notice in the *Canon/Kodak Case* (OJ C 330, 1.11.1997, p. 10) and the *IGR Stereo Television* Case mentioned in the XI Report on Competition Policy, paragraph 94.

2.2.2. Sales restrictions

168. Also as regards sales restrictions there is an important distinction to be made between licensing between competitors and between non-competitors.
169. Restrictions on active and passive sales by one or both parties in a reciprocal agreement between competitors are hardcore restrictions of competition under Article 4(1)(c). Sales restrictions on either party in a reciprocal agreement between competitors are caught by Article 81(1) and are unlikely to fulfil the conditions of Article 81(3). Such restrictions are generally considered market sharing, since they prevent the affected party from selling actively and passively into territories and to customer groups which he actually served or could realistically have served in the absence of the agreement.

Commentary
para 169: B&C: 9.097

170. In the case of non-reciprocal agreements between competitors the block exemption applies to restrictions on active and passive sales by the licensee or the licensor into the exclusive territory or to the exclusive customer group reserved for the other party (cf. Article 4(1)(c)(iv). Above the market share threshold of 20% sales restrictions between licensor and licensee are caught by Article 81(1) when one or both of the parties have a significant degree of market power. Such restrictions, however, may be indispensable for the dissemination of valuable technologies and therefore fulfil the conditions of Article 81(3). This may be the case where the licensor has a

relatively weak market position in the territory where he exploits himself the technology. In such circumstances restrictions on active sales in particular may be indispensable to induce the licensor to grant the licence. In the absence thereof the licensor would risk facing active competition in his main area of activity. Similarly, restrictions on active sales by the licensor may be indispensable, in particular, where the licensee has a relatively weak market position in the territory allocated to him and has to make significant investments in order to efficiently exploit the licensed technology.

Commentary
para 170: **B&C:** 9.097 **F&N:** 10.137

171. The block exemption also covers restrictions on active sales into the territory or to the customer group allocated to another licensee, who was not a competitor of the licensor at the time when he concluded the licence agreement with the licensor. It is a condition, however, that the agreement between the parties in question is non-reciprocal. Above the market share threshold such active sales restrictions are likely to be caught by Article 81(1) when the parties have a significant degree of market power. However, the restraint is likely to be indispensable within the meaning of Article 81(3) for the period of time required for the protected licensee to penetrate a new market and establish a market presence in the allocated territory or vis-à-vis the allocated customer group. This protection against active sales allows the licensee to overcome the asymmetry, which he faces due to the fact that some of the licensees are competing undertakings of the licensor and thus already established on the market. Restrictions on passive sales by licensees into a territory or to a customer group allocated to another licensee are hardcore restrictions under Article 4(1)(c) of the TTBER.

Commentary
para 171: **B&C:** 9.099

172. In the case of agreements between non-competitors sales restrictions between the licensor and a licensee are block exempted up to the market share threshold of 30 %. Above the market share threshold restrictions on active and passive sales by licensees to territories or customer groups reserved for the licensor may fall outside Article 81(1) where on the basis of objective factors it can be concluded that in the absence of the sales restrictions licensing would not occur. A technology owner cannot normally be expected to create direct competition with himself on the basis of his own technology. In other cases sales restrictions on the licensee may be caught by Article 81(1) both where the licensor individually has a significant degree of market power and in the case of a cumulative effect of similar agreements concluded by licensors which together hold a strong position on the market.

Commentary
para 172: **B&C:** 9.097 **F&N:** 10.138

173. Sales restrictions on the licensor, when caught by Article 81(1), are likely to fulfil the conditions of Article 81(3) unless there are no real alternatives to the licensor's technology on the market or such alternatives are licensed by the licensee from third parties. Such restrictions and in particular restrictions on active sales are likely to be indispensable within the meaning of Article 81(3) in order to induce the licensee to invest in the production, marketing and sale of the products incorporating the licensed technology. It is likely that the licensee's incentive to invest would be significantly reduced if he would face direct competition from the licensor whose production costs are not burdened by royalty payments, possibly leading to sub-optimal levels of investment.

Commentary
para 173: **B&C:** 9.096

174. As regards restrictions on sales between licensees in agreements between non-competitors, the TTBER block exempts restrictions on active selling between territories or customer groups.

Part C Substantive Antitrust Matters

Above the market share threshold restrictions on active sales between licensees' territories and customer groups limit intra-technology competition and are likely to be caught by Article 81(1) when the individual licensee has a significant degree of market power. Such restrictions, however, may fulfil the conditions of Article 81(3) where they are necessary to prevent free riding and to induce the licensee to make the investment necessary for efficient exploitation of the licensed technology inside his territory and to promote sales of the licensed product. Restrictions on passive sales are covered by the hardcore list of Article 4(2)(b), cf. paragraph 101 above, when they exceed two years from the date on which the licensee benefiting from the restrictions first put the product incorporating the licensed technology on the market inside his exclusive territory. Passive sales restrictions exceeding this two-year period are unlikely to fulfil the conditions of Article 81(3).

Commentary
para 174: B&C: 9.099 F&N: 10.138

2.3. Output restrictions

175. Reciprocal output restrictions in licence agreements between competitors constitute a hardcore restriction covered by Article 4(1)(b) of the TTBER (cf. point 82 above). Article 4(1)(b) does not cover output restrictions imposed on the licensee in a non-reciprocal agreement or on one of the licensees in an reciprocal agreement. Such restrictions are block exempted up to the market share threshold of 20%. Above the market share threshold, output restrictions on the licensee may restrict competition where the parties have a significant degree of market power. However, Article 81(3) is likely to apply in cases where the licensor's technology is substantially better than the licensee's technology and the output limitation substantially exceeds the output of the licensee prior to the conclusion of the agreement. In that case the effect of the output limitation is limited even in markets where demand is growing. In the application of Article 81(3) it must also be taken into account that such restrictions may be necessary in order to induce the licensor to disseminate his technology as widely as possible. For instance, a licensor may be reluctant to license his competitors if he cannot limit the licence to a particular production site with a specific capacity (a site licence). Where the licence agreement leads to a real integration of complementary assets, output restrictions on the licensee may therefore fulfil the conditions of Article 81(3). However, this is unlikely to be the case where the parties have substantial market power.

Commentary
para 175: B&C: 9.101 F&N: 10.64, 10.139

176. Output restrictions in licence agreements between non-competitors are block exempted up to the market share threshold of 30%. The main anti-competitive risk flowing from output restrictions on licensees in agreements between non-competitors is reduced intra-technology competition between licensees. The significance of such anti-competitive effects depends on the market position of the licensor and the licensees and the extent to which the output limitation prevents the licensee from satisfying demand for the products incorporating the licensed technology.

177. When output restrictions are combined with exclusive territories or exclusive customer groups, the restrictive effects are increased. The combination of the two types of restraints makes it more likely that the agreement serves to partition markets.

Commentary
para 177: B&C: 9.101

178. Output limitations imposed on the licensee in agreements between non-competitors may also have pro-competitive effects by promoting the dissemination of technology. As a supplier of technology, the licensor should normally be free to determine the output produced with the licensed technology by the licensee. If the licensor were not free to determine the output of the

licensee, a number of licence agreements might not come into existence in the first place, which would have a negative impact on the dissemination of new technology. This is particularly likely to be the case where the licensor is also a producer, since in that case the output of the licensees may find their way back into the licensor's main area of operation and thus have a direct impact on these activities. On the other hand, it is less likely that output restrictions are necessary in order to ensure dissemination of the licensor's technology when combined with sales restrictions on the licensee prohibiting him from selling into a territory or customer group reserved for the licensor.

Commentary
para 178: F&N: 10.141

2.4. Field of use restrictions

179. Under a field of use restriction the licence is either limited to one or more technical fields of application or one or more product markets. There are many cases in which the same technology can be used to make different products or can be incorporated into products belonging to different product markets. A new moulding technology may for instance be used to make plastic bottles and plastic glasses, each product belonging to separate product markets. However, a single product market may encompass several technical fields of use. For instance a new engine technology may be employed in four cylinder engines and six cylinder engines. Similarly, a technology to make chipsets may be used to produce chipsets with up to four CPUs and more than four CPUs. A licence limiting the use of the licensed technology to produce say four cylinder engines and chipsets with up to four CPUs constitutes a technical field of use restriction.

Commentary
para 179: F&N: 10.142

180. Given that field of use restrictions are block exempted and that certain customer restrictions are hardcore restrictions under Articles 4(1)(c) and 4(2)(b) of the TTBER, it is important to distinguish the two categories of restraints. A customer restriction presupposes that specific customer groups are identified and that the parties are restricted in selling to such identified groups. The fact that a technical field of use restriction may correspond to certain groups of customers within a product market does not imply that the restraint is to be classified as a customer restriction. For instance, the fact that certain customers buy predominantly or exclusively chipsets with more than four CPUs does not imply that a licence which is limited to chipsets with up to four CPUs constitutes a customer restriction. However, the field of use must be defined objectively by reference to identified and meaningful technical characteristics of the licensed product.

Commentary
para 180: B&C: 9.105, 9.151

181. A field of use restriction limits the exploitation of the licensed technology by the licensee to one or more particular fields of use without limiting the licensor's ability to exploit the licensed technology. In addition, as with territories, these fields of use can be allocated to the licensee under an exclusive or sole licence. Field of use restrictions combined with an exclusive or sole licence also restrict the licensor's ability to exploit his own technology, by preventing him from exploiting it himself, including by way of licensing to others. In the case of a sole license only licensing to third parties is restricted. Field of use restrictions combined with exclusive and sole licences are treated in the same way as the exclusive and sole licenses dealt with in section 2.2.1 above. In particular, for licensing between competitors, this means that reciprocal exclusive licensing is hardcore under Article 4(1)(c).

Commentary
para 181: B&C: 9.105

182. Field of use restrictions may have pro-competitive effects by encouraging the licensor to license his technology for applications that fall outside his main area of focus. If the licensor could not prevent licensees from operating in fields where he exploits the technology himself or in fields where the value of the technology is not yet well established, it would be likely to create a disincentive for the licensor to license or would lead him to charge a higher royalty. It must also be taken into account that in certain sectors licensing often occurs to ensure design freedom by preventing infringement claims. Within the scope of the licence the licensee is able to develop his own technology without fearing infringement claims by the licensor.

Commentary
para 182: F&N: 10.64, 10.143

183. Field of use restrictions on licensees in agreements between actual or potential competitors are block exempted up to the market share threshold of 20%. The main competitive concern in the case of such restrictions is the risk that the licensee ceases to be a competitive force outside the licensed field of use. This risk is greater in the case of cross licensing between competitors where the agreement provides for asymmetrical field of use restrictions. A field of use restriction is asymmetrical where one party is permitted to use the licensed technology within one product market or technical field of use and the other party is permitted to use the other licensed technology within another product market or technical field of use. Competition concerns may in particular arise where the licensee's production facility, which is tooled up to use the licensed technology, is also used to produce with his own technology products outside the licensed field of use. If the agreement is likely to lead the licensee to reduce output outside the licensed field of use, the agreement is likely to be caught by Article 81(1). Symmetrical field of use restrictions, i.e. agreements whereby the parties are licensed to use each other's technologies within the same field(s) of use, are unlikely to be caught by Article 81(1). Such agreements are unlikely to restrict competition that existed in the absence of the agreement. Article 81(1) is also unlikely to apply in the case of agreements that merely enable the licensee to develop and exploit his own technology within the scope of the licence without fearing infringement claims by the licensor. In such circumstances field of use restrictions do not in themselves restrict competition that existed in the absence of the agreement. In the absence of the agreement the licensee also risked infringement claims outside the scope of the licensed field of use. However, if the licensee without business justification terminates or scales back his activities in the area outside the licensed field of use this may be an indication of an underlying market sharing arrangement amounting to a hardcore restriction under Article 4(1)(c) of the TTBER.

Commentary
para 183: B&C: 9.105 F&N: 10.143, 10.145

184. Field of use restrictions on licensee and licensor in agreements between non-competitors are block exempted up to the market share threshold of 30%. Field of use restrictions in agreements between non-competitors whereby the licensor reserves one or more product markets or technical fields of use for himself are generally either non-restrictive of competition or efficiency enhancing. They promote dissemination of new technology by giving the licensor an incentive to license for exploitation in fields in which he does not want to exploit the technology himself. If the licensor could not prevent licensees from operating in fields where the licensor exploits the technology himself, it would be likely to create a disincentive for the licensor to licence.

Commentary
para 184: B&C: 9.105 F&N: 10.146

185. In agreements between non-competitors the licensor is normally also entitled to grant sole or exclusive licences to different licensees limited to one or more fields of use. Such restrictions limit intra-technology competition between licensees in the same way as exclusive licensing and are analysed in the same way (cf. section 2.2.1 above).

Commentary
para 185: B&C: 9.105

2.5. Captive use restrictions

186. A captive use restriction can be defined as an obligation on the licensee to limit his production of the licensed product to the quantities required for the production of his own products and for the maintenance and repair of his own products. In other words, this type of use restriction takes the form of an obligation on the licensee to use the products incorporating the licensed technology only as an input for incorporation into his own production; it does not cover the sale of the licensed product for incorporation into the products of other producers. Captive use restrictions are block exempted up to the respective market share thresholds of 20% and 30%. Outside the scope of the block exemption it is necessary to examine what are the pro-competitive and anti-competitive effects of the restraint. In this respect it is necessary to distinguish agreements between competitors from agreements between non-competitors.

Commentary
para 186: B&C: 9.102   F&N: 10.147

187. In the case of licence agreements between competitors a restriction that imposes on the licensee to produce under the licence only for incorporation into his own products prevents him from being a supplier of components to third party producers. If prior to the conclusion of the agreement, the licensee was not an actual or likely potential supplier of components to other producers, the captive use restriction does not change anything compared to the pre-existing situation. In those circumstances the restriction is assessed in the same way as in the case of agreements between non-competitors. If, on the other hand, the licensee is an actual or likely component supplier, it is necessary to examine what is the impact of the agreement on this activity. If by tooling up to use the licensor's technology the licensee ceases to use his own technology on a stand alone basis and thus to be a component supplier, the agreement restricts competition that existed prior to the agreement. It may result in serious negative market effects when the licensor has a significant degree of market power on the component market.

Commentary
para 187: B&C: 9.102   F&N: 10.147

188. In the case of licence agreements between non-competitors there are two main competitive risks stemming from captive use restrictions: (a) a restriction of intra-technology competition on the market for the supply of inputs and (b) an exclusion of arbitrage between licensees enhancing the possibility for the licensor to impose discriminatory royalties on licensees.

189. Captive use restrictions, however, may also promote pro-competitive licensing. If the licensor is a supplier of components, the restraint may be necessary in order for the dissemination of technology between non-competitors to occur. In the absence of the restraint the licensor may not grant the licence or may do so only against higher royalties, because otherwise he would create direct competition to himself on the component market. In such cases a captive use restriction is normally either not restrictive of competition or covered by Article 81(3). It is a condition, however, that the licensee is not restricted in selling the licensed product as replacement parts for his own products. The licensee must be able to serve the after market for his own products, including independent service organisations that service and repair the products produced by him.

Commentary
para 189: F&N: 10.148

190. Where the licensor is not a component supplier on the relevant market, the above reason for imposing captive use restrictions does not apply. In such cases a captive use restriction may in principle promote the dissemination of technology by ensuring that licensees do not sell

to producers that compete with the licensor on other markets. However, a restriction on the licensee not to sell into certain customer groups reserved for the licensor normally constitutes a less restrictive alternative. Consequently, in such cases a captive use restriction is normally not necessary for the dissemination of technology to take place.

Commentary
para 190: B&C: 9.102

2.6. Tying and bundling

191. In the context of technology licensing tying occurs when the licensor makes the licensing of one technology (the tying product) conditional upon the licensee taking a licence for another technology or purchasing a product from the licensor or someone designated by him (the tied product). Bundling occurs where two technologies or a technology and a product are only sold together as a bundle. In both cases, however, it is a condition that the products and technologies involved are distinct in the sense that there is distinct demand for each of the products and technologies forming part of the tie or the bundle. This is normally not the case where the technologies or products are by necessity linked in such a way that the licensed technology cannot be exploited without the tied product or both parts of the bundle cannot be exploited without the other. In the following the term "tying" refers to both tying and bundling.

192. Article 3 of the TTBER, which limits the application of the block exemption by market share thresholds, ensures that tying and bundling are not block exempted above the market share thresholds of 20% in the case of agreements between competitors and 30% in the case of agreements between non-competitors. The market share thresholds apply to any relevant technology or product market affected by the licence agreement, including the market for the tied product. Above the market share thresholds it is necessary to balance the anti-competitive and pro-competitive effects of tying.

193. The main restrictive effect of tying is foreclosure of competing suppliers of the tied product. Tying may also allow the licensor to maintain market power in the market for the tying product by raising barriers to entry since it may force new entrants to enter several markets at the same time. Moreover, tying may allow the licensor to increase royalties, in particular when the tying product and the tied product are partly substitutable and the two products are not used in fixed proportion. Tying prevents the licensee from switching to substitute inputs in the face of increased royalties for the tying product. These competition concerns are independent of whether the parties to the agreement are competitors or not. For tying to produce likely anti-competitive effects the licensor must have a significant degree of market power in the tying product so as to restrict competition in the tied product. In the absence of market power in the tying product the licensor cannot use his technology for the anti-competitive purpose of foreclosing suppliers of the tied product. Furthermore, as in the case of non-compete obligations, the tie must cover a certain proportion of the market for the tied product for appreciable foreclosure effects to occur. In cases where the licensor has market power on the market for the tied product rather than on the market for the tying product, the restraint is analysed as non-compete or quantity forcing, reflecting the fact that any competition problem has its origin on the market for the "tied" product and not on the market for the "tying" product.[66]

Notes
[66] For the applicable analytical framework see section 2.7 below and paragraphs 138 et seq. of the Guidelines on Vertical Restraints cited in note 36.

Commentary
para 193: F&N: 10.151

194. Tying can also give rise to efficiency gains. This is for instance the case where the tied product is necessary for a technically satisfactory exploitation of the licensed technology or for ensuring that production under the licence conforms to quality standards respected by the licensor and other licensees. In such cases tying is normally either not restrictive of competition or covered by Article 81(3). Where the licensees use the licensor's trademark or brand name or where it

is otherwise obvious to consumers that there is a link between the product incorporating the licensed technology and the licensor, the licensor has a legitimate interest in ensuring that the quality of the products are such that it does not undermine the value of his technology or his reputation as an economic operator. Moreover, where it is known to consumers that the licensees (and the licensor) produce on the basis of the same technology it is unlikely that licensees would be willing to take a licence unless the technology is exploited by all in a technically satisfactory way.

Commentary
para 194: B&C: 9.103, 9.111 F&N: 10.152

195. Tying is also likely to be pro-competitive where the tied product allows the licensee to exploit the licensed technology significantly more efficiently. For instance, where the licensor licenses a particular process technology the parties can also agree that the licensee buys a catalyst from the licensor which is developed for use with the licensed technology and which allows the technology to be exploited more efficiently than in the case of other catalysts. Where in such cases the restriction is caught by Article 81(1), the conditions of Article 81(3) are likely to be fulfilled even above the market share thresholds.

Commentary
para 195: F&N: 10.152

2.7. Non-compete obligations

196. Non-compete obligations in the context of technology licensing take the form of an obligation on the licensee not to use third party technologies which compete with the licensed technology. To the extent that a non-compete obligation covers a product or additional technology supplied by the licensor the obligation is dealt with in the preceding section on tying.

197. The TTBER exempts non-compete obligations both in the case of agreements between competitors and in the case of agreements between non-competitors up to the market share thresholds of 20% and 30% respectively.

198. The main competitive risk presented by non-compete obligations is foreclosure of third party technologies. Non-compete obligations may also facilitate collusion between licensors in the case of cumulative use. Foreclosure of competing technologies reduces competitive pressure on royalties charged by the licensor and reduces competition between the incumbent technologies by limiting the possibilities for licensees to substitute between competing technologies. As in both cases the main problem is foreclosure, the analysis can in general be the same in the case of agreements between competitors and agreements between non-competitors. However, in the case of cross licensing between competitors where both agree not to use third party technologies the agreement may facilitate collusion between them on the product market, thereby justifying the lower market share threshold of 20%.

199. Foreclosure may arise where a substantial part of potential licensees are already tied to one or, in the case of cumulative effects, more sources of technology and are prevented from exploiting competing technologies. Foreclosure effects may result from agreements concluded by a single licensor with a significant degree of market power or by a cumulative effect of agreements concluded by several licensors, even where each individual agreement or network of agreements is covered by the TTBER. In the latter case, however, a serious cumulative effect is unlikely to arise as long as less than 50% of the market is tied. Above this threshold significant foreclosure is likely to occur when there are relatively high barriers to entry for new licensees. If barriers to entry are low, new licensees are able to enter the market and exploit commercially attractive technologies held by third parties and thus represent a real alternative to incumbent licensees. In order to determine the real possibility for entry and expansion by third parties it is also necessary to take account of the extent to which distributors are tied to licensees by non-compete obligations. Third party technologies only have a real possibility of entry if they have access to the necessary production and distribution assets. In other words, the ease of entry depends not only on the availability of licensees but also the extent to which they have access to distribution.

In assessing foreclosure effects at the distribution level the Commission will apply the analytical framework set out in section IV.2.1 of the Guidelines on Vertical Restraints.[67]

Notes
[67] See note 36.

Commentary
para 199: F&N: 10.154

200. When the licensor has a significant degree of market power, obligations on licensees to obtain the technology only from the licensor can lead to significant foreclosure effects. The stronger the market position of the licensor the higher the risk of foreclosing competing technologies. For appreciable foreclosure effects to occur the non-compete obligations do not necessarily have to cover a substantial part of the market. Even in the absence thereof, appreciable foreclosure effects may occur where non-compete obligations are targeted at undertakings that are the most likely to license competing technologies. The risk of foreclosure is particularly high where there is only a limited number of potential licensees and the licence agreement concerns a technology which is used by the licensees to make an input for their own use. In such cases the entry barriers for a new licensor are likely to be high. Foreclosure may be less likely in cases where the technology is used to make a product that is sold to third parties; although in this case the restriction also ties production capacity for the input in question, it does not tie demand for the product incorporating the input produced with the licensed technology. To enter the market in the latter case licensors only need access to one or more licensee(s) that have suitable production capacity and unless only few undertakings possess or are able to obtain the assets required to take a licence, it is unlikely that by imposing non-compete obligations on its licensees the licensor is able to deny competitors access to efficient licensees.

Commentary
para 200: F&N: 10.154

201. Non-compete obligations may also produce pro-competitive effects. First, such obligations may promote dissemination of technology by reducing the risk of misappropriation of the licensed technology, in particular know-how. If a licensee is entitled to license competing technologies from third parties, there is a risk that particularly licensed know-how would be used in the exploitation of competing technologies and thus benefit competitors. When a licensee also exploits competing technologies, it normally also makes monitoring of royalty payments more difficult, which may act as a disincentive to licensing.

Commentary
para 201: F&N: 10.155

202. Second, non-compete obligations possibly in combination with an exclusive territory may be necessary to ensure that the licensee has an incentive to invest in and exploit the licensed technology effectively. In cases where the agreement is caught by Article 81(1) because of an appreciable foreclosure effect, it may be necessary in order to benefit from Article 81(3) to choose a less restrictive alternative, for instance to impose minimum output or royalty obligations, which normally have less potential to foreclose competing technologies.

Commentary
para 202: F&N: 10.155

203. Third, in cases where the licensor undertakes to make significant client specific investments for instance in training and tailoring of the licensed technology to the licensee's needs, non-compete obligations or alternatively minimum output or minimum royalty obligations may be necessary to induce the licensor to make the investment and to avoid hold-up problems. However, normally the licensor will be able to charge directly for such investments by way of a lump sum payment, implying that less restrictive alternatives are available.

3. Settlement and non-assertion agreements

204. Licensing may serve as a means of settling disputes or avoiding that one party exercises his intellectual property rights to prevent the other party from exploiting his own technology. Licensing including cross licensing in the context of settlement agreements and non-assertion agreements is not as such restrictive of competition since it allows the parties to exploit their technologies post agreement. However, the individual terms and conditions of such agreements may be caught by Article 81(1). Licensing in the context of settlement agreements is treated like other licence agreements. In the case of technologies that from a technical point of view are substitutes, it is therefore necessary to assess to what extent it is likely that the technologies in question are in a one-way or two-way blocking position (cf. paragraph 32 above). If so, the parties are not deemed to be competitors.

Commentary
para 204: B&C: 9.120 F&N: 10.156

205. The block exemption applies provided that the agreement does not contain any hardcore restrictions of competition as set out in Article 4 of the TTBER. The hardcore list of Article 4(1) may in particular apply where it was clear to the parties that no blocking position exists and that consequently they are competitors. In such cases the settlement is merely a means to restrict competition that existed in the absence of the agreement.

206. In cases where it is likely that in the absence of the licence the licensee could be excluded from the market, the agreement is generally pro-competitive. Restrictions that limit intra-technology competition between the licensor and the licensee are often compatible with Article 81, see section 2 above.

207. Agreements whereby the parties cross license each other and impose restrictions on the use of their technologies, including restrictions on the licensing to third parties, may be caught by Article 81(1). Where the parties have a significant degree of market power and the agreement imposes restrictions that clearly go beyond what is required in order to unblock, the agreement is likely to be caught by Article 81(1) even if it is likely that a mutual blocking position exists. Article 81(1) is particularly likely to apply where the parties share markets or fix reciprocal running royalties that have a significant impact on market prices.

Commentary
para 207: F&N: 10.156

208. Where under the agreement the parties are entitled to use each other's technology and the agreement extends to future developments, it is necessary to assess what is the impact of the agreement on the parties' incentive to innovate. In cases where the parties have a significant degree of market power the agreement is likely to be caught by Article 81(1) where the agreement prevents the parties from gaining a competitive lead over each other. Agreements that eliminate or substantially reduce the possibilities of one party to gain a competitive lead over the other reduce the incentive to innovate and thus adversely affect an essential part of the competitive process. Such agreements are also unlikely to satisfy the conditions of Article 81(3). It is particularly unlikely that the restriction can be considered indispensable within the meaning of the third condition of Article 81(3). The achievement of the objective of the agreement, namely to ensure that the parties can continue to exploit their own technology without being blocked by the other party, does not require that the parties agree to share future innovations. However, the parties are unlikely to be prevented from gaining a competitive lead over each other where the purpose of the licence is to allow the parties to develop their respective technologies and where the licence does not lead them to use the same technological solutions. Such agreements merely create design freedom by preventing future infringement claims by the other party.

Commentary
para 208: F&N: 10.158

209. In the context of a settlement and non-assertion agreement, non-challenge clauses are generally considered to fall outside Article 81(1). It is inherent in such agreements that the parties agree not to challenge *ex post* the intellectual property rights covered by the agreement. Indeed, the very purpose of the agreement is to settle existing disputes and/or to avoid future disputes.

Commentary
para 209: F&N: 10.157

4. Technology pools

210. Technology pools are defined as arrangements whereby two or more parties assemble a package of technology which is licensed not only to contributors to the pool but also to third parties. In terms of their structure technology pools can take the form of simple arrangements between a limited number of parties or elaborate organisational arrangements whereby the organisation of the licensing of the pooled technologies is entrusted to a separate entity. In both cases the pool may allow licensees to operate on the market on the basis of a single licence.

Commentary
para 210: F&N: 10.159

211. There is no inherent link between technology pools and standards, but in some cases the technologies in the pool support (wholly or partly) a de facto or de jure industry standard. When technology pools do support an industry standard they do not necessarily support a single standard. Different technology pools may support competing standards.[68]

Notes

[68] See in this respect the Commission's press release IP/02/1651 concerning the licensing of patents for third generation (3G) mobile services. This case involved five technology pools creating five different technologies, each of which could be used to produce 3G equipment.

212. Agreements establishing technology pools and setting out the terms and conditions for their operation are not — irrespective of the number of parties — covered by the block exemption (cf. section III.2.2 above). Such agreements are addressed only by these guidelines. Pooling arrangements give rise to a number of particular issues regarding the selection of the included technologies and the operation of the pool, which do not arise in the context of other types of licensing. The individual licences granted by the pool to third party licensees, however, are treated like other licence agreements, which are block exempted when the conditions set out in the TTBER are fulfilled, including the requirements of Article 4 of the TTBER containing the list of hardcore restrictions.

Commentary
para 212: F&N: 10.159

213. Technology pools may be restrictive of competition. The creation of a technology pool necessarily implies joint selling of the pooled technologies, which in the case of pools composed solely or predominantly of substitute technologies amounts to a price fixing cartel. Moreover, in addition to reducing competition between the parties, technology pools may also, in particular when they support an industry standard or establish a de facto industry standard, result in a reduction of innovation by foreclosing alternative technologies. The existence of the standard and the related technology pool may make it more difficult for new and improved technologies to enter the market.

214. Technology pools can also produce pro-competitive effects, in particular by reducing transaction costs and by setting a limit on cumulative royalties to avoid double marginalisation. The creation of a pool allows for one-stop licensing of the technologies covered by the pool. This is particularly important in sectors where intellectual property rights are prevalent and where in order to operate on the market licences need to be obtained from a significant number of licensors. In cases where licensees receive on-going services concerning the application of the licensed technology, joint licensing and servicing can lead to further cost reductions.

4.1. The nature of the pooled technologies

215. The competitive risks and the efficiency enhancing potential of technology pools depend to a large extent on the relationship between the pooled technologies and their relationship with technologies outside the pool. Two basic distinctions must be made, namely (a) between technological complements and technological substitutes and (b) between essential and non-essential technologies.

216. Two technologies[69] are complements as opposed to substitutes when they are both required to produce the product or carry out the process to which the technologies relate. Conversely, two technologies are substitutes when either technology allows the holder to produce the product or carry out the process to which the technologies relate. A technology is essential as opposed to non-essential if there are no substitutes for that technology inside or outside the pool and the technology in question constitutes a necessary part of the package of technologies for the purposes of producing the product(s) or carrying out the process(es) to which the pool relates. A technology for which there are no substitutes, remains essential as long as the technology is covered by at least one valid intellectual property right. Technologies that are essential are by necessity also complements.

Notes

[69] The term "technology" is not limited to patents. It covers also patent applications and intellectual property rights other than patents.

Commentary
para 216: F&N: 10.161

---

217. When technologies in a pool are substitutes, royalties are likely to be higher than they would otherwise be, because licensees do not benefit from rivalry between the technologies in question. When the technologies in the pool are complements the arrangement reduces transaction costs and may lead to lower overall royalties because the parties are in a position to fix a common royalty for the package as opposed to each fixing a royalty which does not take account of the royalty fixed by others.

218. The distinction between complementary and substitute technologies is not clear-cut in all cases, since technologies may be substitutes in part and complements in part. When due to efficiencies stemming from the integration of two technologies licensees are likely to demand both technologies the technologies are treated as complements even if they are partly substitutable. In such cases it is likely that in the absence of the pool licensees would want to licence both technologies due to the additional economic benefit of employing both technologies as opposed to employing only one of them.

219. The inclusion in the pool of substitute technologies restricts inter-technology competition and amounts to collective bundling. Moreover, where the pool is substantially composed of substitute technologies, the arrangement amounts to price fixing between competitors. As a general rule the Commission considers that the inclusion of substitute technologies in the pool constitutes a violation of Article 81(1). The Commission also considers that it is unlikely that the conditions of Article 81(3) will be fulfilled in the case of pools comprising to a significant extent substitute technologies. Given that the technologies in question are alternatives, no transaction cost savings accrue from including both technologies in the pool. In the absence of the pool licensees would not have demanded both technologies. It is not sufficient that the parties remain free to license independently. In order not to undermine the pool, which allows them to jointly exercise market power, the parties are likely to have little incentive to do so.

Commentary
para 219: B&C: 9.126 F&N: 10.164

---

220. When a pool is composed only of technologies that are essential and therefore by necessity also complements, the creation of the pool as such generally falls outside Article 81(1) irrespective of the market position of the parties. However, the conditions on which licences are granted may be caught by Article 81(1).

Commentary
para 220: B&C: 9.126 F&N: 10.164

221. Where non-essential but complementary patents are included in the pool there is a risk of fore-closure of third party technologies. Once a technology is included in the pool and is licensed as part of the package, licensees are likely to have little incentive to license a competing technology when the royalty paid for the package already covers a substitute technology. Moreover, the inclusion of technologies which are not necessary for the purposes of producing the product(s) or carrying out the process(es) to which the technology pool relates also forces licensees to pay for technology that they may not need. The inclusion of complementary patents thus amounts to collective bundling. When a pool encompasses non-essential technologies, the agreement is likely to be caught by Article 81(1) where the pool has a significant position on any relevant market.

Commentary
para 221: B&C: 9.126 F&N: 10.165

222. Given that substitute and complementary technologies may be developed after the creation of the pool, the assessment of essentiality is an on-going process. A technology may therefore become non-essential after the creation of the pool due to the emergence of new third party technologies. One way to ensure that such third party technologies are not foreclosed is to exclude from the pool technologies that have become non-essential. However, there may be other ways to ensure that third party technologies are not foreclosed. In the assessment of tech-nology pools comprising non-essential technologies, i.e. technologies for which substitutes exist outside the pool or which are not necessary in order to produce one or more products to which the pool relates, the Commission will in its overall assessment, inter alia, take account of the following factors:
    (a) whether there are any pro-competitive reasons for including the non-essential technologies in the pool;
    (b) whether the licensors remain free to license their respective technologies independently. Where the pool is composed of a limited number of technologies and there are substitute technologies outside the pool, licensees may want to put together their own technological package composed partly of technology forming part of the pool and partly of technology owned by third parties;
    (c) whether, in cases where the pooled technologies have different applications some of which do not require use of all of the pooled technologies, the pool offers the technologies only as a single package or whether it offers separate packages for distinct applications. In the latter case it is avoided that technologies which are not essential to a particular product or process are tied to essential technologies;
    (d) whether the pooled technologies are available only as a single package or whether licensees have the possibility of obtaining a licence for only part of the package with a corresponding reduction of royalties. The possibility to obtain a licence for only part of the package may reduce the risk of foreclosure of third party technologies outside the pool, in particular where the licensee obtains a corresponding reduction in royalties. This requires that a share of the overall royalty has been assigned to each technology in the pool. Where the licence agreements concluded between the pool and individual licensees are of relatively long dura-tion and the pooled technology supports a de facto industry standard, it must also be taken into account that the pool may foreclose access to the market of new substitute technologies. In assessing the risk of foreclosure in such cases it is relevant to take into account whether or not licensees can terminate at reasonable notice part of the licence and obtain a correspond-ing reduction of royalties.

Commentary
para 222: B&C: 9.126 F&N: 10.166

4.2. Assessment of individual restraints

223. The purpose of this section is to address a certain number of restraints that in one form or another are commonly found in technology pools and which need to be assessed in the overall context of the pool. It is recalled, cf. paragraph 212 above, that the TTBER applies to licence agreements concluded between the pool and third party licensees. This section is therefore limited to addressing the creation of the pool and licensing issues that are particular to licensing in the context of technology pools.

224. In making its assessment the Commission will be guided by the following main principles:
    1. The stronger the market position of the pool the greater the risk of anti-competitive effects.
    2. Pools that hold a strong position on the market should be open and non-discriminatory.
    3. Pools should not unduly foreclose third party technologies or limit the creation of alternative pools.

225. Undertakings setting up a technology pool that is compatible with Article 81, and any industry standard that it may support, are normally free to negotiate and fix royalties for the technology package and each technology's share of the royalties either before or after the standard is set. Such agreement is inherent in the establishment of the standard or pool and cannot in itself be considered restrictive of competition and may in certain circumstances lead to more efficient outcomes. In certain circumstances it may be more efficient if the royalties are agreed before the standard is chosen and not after the standard is decided upon, to avoid that the choice of the standard confers a significant degree of market power on one or more essential technologies. On the other hand, licensees must remain free to determine the price of products produced under the licence. Where the selection of technologies to be included in the pool is carried out by an independent expert this may further competition between available technological solutions.

Commentary
para 225: F&N: 10.164, 10.168

---

226. Where the pool has a dominant position on the market, royalties and other licensing terms should be fair and non-discriminatory and licences should be non-exclusive. These requirements are necessary to ensure that the pool is open and does not lead to foreclosure and other anti-competitive effects on down stream markets. These requirements, however, do not preclude different royalties for different uses. It is in general not considered restrictive of competition to apply different royalty rates to different product markets, whereas there should be no discrimination within product markets. In particular, the treatment of licensees should not depend on whether they are licensors or not. The Commission will therefore take into account whether licensors are also subject to royalty obligations.

Commentary
para 226: F&N: 10.167

---

227. Licensors and licensees must be free to develop competing products and standards and must also be free to grant and obtain licences outside the pool. These requirements are necessary in order to limit the risk of foreclosure of third party technologies and ensure that the pool does not limit innovation and preclude the creation of competing technological solutions. Where a pool supports a (de facto) industry standard and where the parties are subject to non-compete obligations, the pool creates a particular risk of preventing the development of new and improved technologies and standards.

Commentary
para 227: F&N: 10.167

---

228. Grant back obligations should be non-exclusive and be limited to developments that are essential or important to the use of the pooled technology. This allows the pool to feed on and benefit from improvements to the pooled technology. It is legitimate for the parties to ensure that the exploitation of the pooled technology cannot be held up by licensees that hold or obtain essential patents.

229. One of the problems identified with regard to patent pools is the risk that they shield invalid patents. Pooling raises the costs/risks for a successful challenge, because the challenge fails if only one patent in the pool is valid. The shielding of invalid patents in the pool may oblige licensees to pay higher royalties and may also prevent innovation in the field covered by an invalid patent. In order to limit this risk any right to terminate a licence in the case of a challenge must be limited to the technologies owned by the licensor who is the addressee of the challenge and must not extend to the technologies owned by the other licensors in the pool.

4.3. The institutional framework governing the pool

230. The way in which a technology pool is created, organised and operated can reduce the risk of it having the object or effect of restricting competition and provide assurances to the effect that the arrangement is pro-competitive.

231. When participation in a standard and pool creation process is open to all interested parties representing different interests it is more likely that technologies for inclusion into the pool are selected on the basis of price/quality considerations than when the pool is set up by a limited group of technology owners. Similarly, when the relevant bodies of the pool are composed of persons representing different interests, it is more likely that licensing terms and conditions, including royalties, will be open and non-discriminatory and reflect the value of the licensed technology than when the pool is controlled by licensor representatives.

232. Another relevant factor is the extent to which independent experts are involved in the creation and operation of the pool. For instance, the assessment of whether or not a technology is essential to a standard supported by a pool is often a complex matter that requires special expertise. The involvement in the selection process of independent experts can go a long way in ensuring that a commitment to include only essential technologies is implemented in practice.

233. The Commission will take into account how experts are selected and what are the exact functions that they are to perform. Experts should be independent from the undertakings that have formed the pool. If experts are connected to the licensors or otherwise depend on them, the involvement of the expert will be given less weight. Experts must also have the necessary technical expertise to perform the various functions with which they have been entrusted. The functions of independent experts may include, in particular, an assessment of whether or not technologies put forward for inclusion into the pool are valid and whether or not they are essential.

234. It is also relevant to consider the arrangements for exchanging sensitive information among the parties. In oligopolistic markets exchanges of sensitive information such as pricing and output data may facilitate collusion.[70] In such cases the Commission will take into account to what extent safeguards have been put in place, which ensure that sensitive information is not exchanged. An independent expert or licensing body may play an important role in this respect by ensuring that output and sales data, which may be necessary for the purposes of calculating and verifying royalties is not disclosed to undertakings that compete on affected markets.

Notes

[70] See in this respect the judgment in *John Deere* cited in note 11.

235. Finally, it is relevant to take account of the dispute resolution mechanism foreseen in the instruments setting up the pool. The more dispute resolution is entrusted to bodies or persons that are independent of the pool and the members thereof, the more likely it is that the dispute resolution will operate in a neutral way.

C17

COMMISSION NOTICE

Guidelines on the effect on trade concept contained in Articles 81 and 82
of the Treaty (2004/C 101/07)

(Text with EEA relevance)

Official Journal C 101, 27.4.2004, p. 81

Celex No: 52004XC0427(06)

Notes

EEA application: the EFTA Surveillance Authority has adopted a parallel notice on the effect on trade concept contained in Articles 53 and 54 of the EEA Agreement under Article 5(2)(b) of the Surveillance and Court Agreement: OJ C 291, 30.11.2006, p. 46 and EEA Supplement No 59, 30.11.2006, p. 18.

Commentary

Notice: **B&C:** 1.060, 1.115–1.116, 1.121–1.124 **F&N:** 2.250, 3.339, 3.368, 3.372, 3.376, 3.378, 3.379, 3.392, 5.171, 9.50, 9.58, 9.65, 9.167, 13.52
paras 77–99: **B&C:** 1.131
paras 79–80: **B&C:** 1.131
paras 89–92: **B&C:** 1.133
paras 93–96: **B&C:** 1.132
paras 97–98: **B&C:** 1.133
paras 97–99: **B&C:** 1.133

1. Introduction

1. Articles 81 and 82 of the Treaty are applicable to horizontal and vertical agreements and practices on the part of undertakings which "may affect trade between Member States".
2. In their interpretation of Articles 81 and 82, the Community Courts have already substantially clarified the content and scope of the concept of effect on trade between Member States.
3. The present guidelines set out the principles developed by the Community Courts in relation to the interpretation of the effect on trade concept of Articles 81 and 82. They further spell out a rule indicating when agreements are in general unlikely to be capable of appreciably affecting trade between Member States (the non-appreciable affectation of trade rule or NAAT-rule). The guidelines are not intended to be exhaustive. The aim is to set out the methodology for the application of the effect on trade concept and to provide guidance on its application in frequently occurring situations. Although not binding on them, these guidelines also intend to give guidance to the courts and authorities of the Member States in their application of the effect on trade concept contained in Articles 81 and 82.

Commentary
para 3: **F&N:** 3.379

4. The present guidelines do not address the issue of what constitutes an appreciable restriction of competition under Article 81(1). This issue, which is distinct from the ability of agreements to appreciably affect trade between Member States, is dealt with in the Commission Notice on agreements of minor importance which do not appreciably restrict competition under Article 81(1) of the Treaty[1] (the *de minimis* rule). The guidelines are also not intended to provide guidance on the effect on trade concept contained in Article 87(1) of the Treaty on State aid.

Notes
[1] OJ C 368, 22.12.2001, p. 13.

Part C Substantive Antitrust Matters

5. These guidelines, including the NAAT-rule, are without prejudice to the interpretation of Articles 81 and 82 which may be given by the Court of Justice and the Court of First Instance.

2. The Effect on Trade Criterion

2.1. General principles

6. Article 81(1) provides that "the following shall be prohibited as incompatible with the common market: all agreements between undertakings, decisions of associations of undertakings and concerted practices which may affect trade between Member States and which have as their object or effect the prevention, restriction or distortion of competition within the common market". For the sake of simplicity the terms "agreements, decisions of associations of undertakings and concerted practices" are collectively referred to as "agreements".

7. Article 82 on its part stipulates that "any abuse by one or more undertakings of a dominant position within the common market or in a substantial part thereof shall be prohibited as incompatible with the common market insofar as it may affect trade between Member States." In what follows the term "practices" refers to the conduct of dominant undertakings.

8. The effect on trade criterion also determines the scope of application of Article 3 of Regulation 1/2003 on the implementation of the rules on competition laid down in Articles 81 and 82 of the Treaty.[2]

Notes

[2] OJ L 1, 4.1.2003, p. 1.

9. According to Article 3(1) of that Regulation the competition authorities and courts of the Member States must apply Article 81 to agreements, decisions by associations of undertakings or concerted practices within the meaning of Article 81(1) of the Treaty which may affect trade between Member States within the meaning of that provision, when they apply national competition law to such agreements, decisions or concerted practices. Similarly, when the competition authorities and courts of the Member States apply national competition law to any abuse prohibited by Article 82 of the Treaty, they must also apply Article 82 of the Treaty. Article 3(1) thus obliges the competition authorities and courts of the Member States to also apply Articles 81 and 82 when they apply national competition law to agreements and abusive practices which may affect trade between Member States. On the other hand, Article 3(1) does not oblige national competition authorities and courts to apply national competition law when they apply Articles 81 and 82 to agreements, decisions and concerted practices and to abuses which may affect trade between Member States. They may in such cases apply the Community competition rules on a stand alone basis.

10. It follows from Article 3(2) that the application of national competition law may not lead to the prohibition of agreements, decisions by associations of undertakings or concerted practices which may affect trade between Member States but which do not restrict competition within the meaning of Article 81(1) of the Treaty, or which fulfil the conditions of Article 81(3) of the Treaty or which are covered by a Regulation for the application of Article 81(3) of the Treaty. Member States, however, are not under Regulation 1/2003 precluded from adopting and applying on their territory stricter national laws which prohibit or sanction unilateral conduct engaged in by undertakings.

11. Finally it should be mentioned that Article 3(3) stipulates that without prejudice to general principles and other provisions of Community law, Article 3(1) and (2) do not apply when the competition authorities and the courts of the Member States apply national merger control laws, nor do they preclude the application of provisions of national law that predominantly pursue an objective different from that pursued by Articles 81 and 82 of the Treaty.

12. The effect on trade criterion is an autonomous Community law criterion, which must be assessed separately in each case. It is a jurisdictional criterion, which defines the scope of application of Community competition law.[3] Community competition law is not applicable to agreements and practices that are not capable of appreciably affecting trade between Member States.

Notes
[3] See e.g. Joined Cases 56/64 and 58/64, *Consten and Grundig*, [1966] ECR p. 429, and Joined Cases 6/73 and 7/73, *Commercial Solvents*, [1974] ECR p. 223.

Commentary
para 12: B&C: 1.115

13. The effect on trade criterion confines the scope of application of Articles 81 and 82 to agreements and practices that are capable of having a minimum level of cross-border effects within the Community. In the words of the Court of Justice, the ability of the agreement or practice to affect trade between Member States must be "appreciable".[4]

Notes
[4] See in this respect Case 22/71, *Béguelin*, [1971] ECR p. 949, paragraph 16.

14. In the case of Article 81 of the Treaty, it is the agreement that must be capable of affecting trade between Member States. It is not required that each individual part of the agreement, including any restriction of competition which may flow from the agreement, is capable of doing so.[5] If the agreement as a whole is capable of affecting trade between Member States, there is Community law jurisdiction in respect of the entire agreement, including any parts of the agreement that individually do not affect trade between Member States. In cases where the contractual relations between the same parties cover several activities, these activities must, in order to form part of the same agreement, be directly linked and form an integral part of the same overall business arrangement.[6] If not, each activity constitutes a separate agreement.

Notes
[5] See Case 193/83, *Windsurfing*, [1986] ECR p. 611, paragraph 96, and Case T-77/94, *Vereniging van Groothandelaren in Bloemkwekerijprodukten*, [1997] ECR II-759, paragraph 126.
[6] See paragraphs 142 to 144 of the judgment in *Vereniging van Groothandelaren in Bloemkwekerijprodukteten* cited in the previous footnote.

Commentary
para 14: B&C: 1.127 F&N: 3.344

15. It is also immaterial whether or not the participation of a particular undertaking in the agreement has an appreciable effect on trade between Member States.[7] An undertaking cannot escape Community law jurisdiction merely because of the fact that its own contribution to an agreement, which itself is capable of affecting trade between Member States, is insignificant.

Notes
[7] See e.g. Case T-2/89, *Petrofina*, [1991] ECR II-1087, paragraph 226.

16. It is not necessary, for the purposes of establishing Community law jurisdiction, to establish a link between the alleged restriction of competition and the capacity of the agreement to affect trade between Member States. Non-restrictive agreements may also affect trade between Member States. For example, selective distribution agreements based on purely qualitative selection criteria justified by the nature of the products, which are not restrictive of competition within the meaning of Article 81(1), may nevertheless affect trade between Member States. However, the alleged restrictions arising from an agreement may provide a clear indication as to the capacity of the agreement to affect trade between Member States. For instance, a distribution agreement prohibiting exports is by its very nature capable of affecting trade between Member States, although not necessarily to an appreciable extent.[8]

Notes
[8] The concept of appreciability is dealt with in section 2.4 below.

17. In the case of Article 82 it is the abuse that must affect trade between Member States. This does not imply, however, that each element of the behaviour must be assessed in isolation. Conduct that forms part of an overall strategy pursued by the dominant undertaking must be assessed in

terms of its overall impact. Where a dominant undertaking adopts various practices in pursuit of the same aim, for instance practices that aim at eliminating or foreclosing competitors, in order for Article 82 to be applicable to all the practices forming part of this overall strategy, it is sufficient that at least one of these practices is capable of affecting trade between Member States.[9]

Notes

[9] See in this respect Case 85/76, *Hoffmann-La Roche*, [1979] ECR p. 461, paragraph 126.

Commentary
para 17: B&C: 1.128 F&N: 3.346

18. It follows from the wording of Articles 81 and 82 and the case law of the Community Courts that in the application of the effect on trade criterion three elements in particular must be addressed:
    (a) The concept of "trade between Member States",
    (b) The notion of "may affect", and
    (c) The concept of "appreciability".

2.2. The concept of "trade between Member States"

19. The concept of "trade" is not limited to traditional exchanges of goods and services across borders.[10] It is a wider concept, covering all cross-border economic activity including establishment.[11] This interpretation is consistent with the fundamental objective of the Treaty to promote free movement of goods, services, persons and capital.

Notes

[10] Throughout these guidelines the term "products" covers both goods and services.
[11] See Case 172/80, *Züchner*, [1981] ECR p. 2021, paragraph 18. See also Case C-309/99, *Wouters*, [2002] ECR I-1577, paragraph 95, Case C-475/99, *Ambulanz Glöckner*, [2001] ECR I-8089, paragraph 49, Joined Cases C-215/96 and 216/96, *Bagnasco*, [1999] ECR I-135, paragraph 51, Case C-55/96, *Job Centre*, [1997] ECR I-7119, paragraph 37, and Case C-41/90, *Höfner and Elser*, [1991] ECR I-1979, paragraph 33.

20. According to settled case law the concept of "trade" also encompasses cases where agreements or practices affect the competitive structure of the market. Agreements and practices that affect the competitive structure inside the Community by eliminating or threatening to eliminate a competitor operating within the Community may be subject to the Community competition rules.[12] When an undertaking is or risks being eliminated the competitive structure within the Community is affected and so are the economic activities in which the undertaking is engaged.

Notes

[12] See e.g. Joined Cases T-24/93 and others, *Compagnie maritime belge*, [1996] ECR II-1201, paragraph 203, and paragraph 23 of the judgment in *Commercial Solvents* cited in footnote [3].

Commentary
para 20: B&C: 1.121

21. The requirement that there must be an effect on trade "between Member States" implies that there must be an impact on cross-border economic activity involving at least two Member States. It is not required that the agreement or practice affect trade between the whole of one Member State and the whole of another Member State. Articles 81 and 82 may be applicable also in cases involving part of a Member State, provided that the effect on trade is appreciable.[13]

Notes

[13] See e.g. Joined Cases T-213/95 and T-18/96, *SCK and FNK*, [1997] ECR II-1739, and sections 3.2.4 and 3.2.6 below.

22. The application of the effect on trade criterion is independent of the definition of relevant geographic markets. Trade between Member States may be affected also in cases where the relevant market is national or sub-national.[14]

2.3. The notion "may affect"

23. The function of the notion "may affect" is to define the nature of the required impact on trade between Member States. According to the standard test developed by the Court of Justice, the notion "may affect" implies that it must be possible to foresee with a sufficient degree of probability on the basis of a set of objective factors of law or fact that the agreement or practice may have an influence, direct or indirect, actual or potential, on the pattern of trade between Member States.[15,16] As mentioned in paragraph 20 above the Court of Justice has in addition developed a test based on whether or not the agreement or practice affects the competitive structure. In cases where the agreement or practice is liable to affect the competitive structure inside the Community, Community law jurisdiction is established.

Notes
[15] See e.g. the judgment in *Züchner* cited in footnote 11 and Case 319/82 *Kerpen & Kerpen* [1983] ECR 4173, Joined Cases 240/82 and others *Stichting Sigarettenindustrie* [1985] ECR 3831, paragraph 48, and Joined Cases T-25/95 and others *Cimenteries CBR* [2000] ECR II-491, paragraph 3930.
[16] In some judgments mainly relating to vertical agreements the Court of Justice has added wording to the effect that the agreement was capable of hindering the attainment of the objectives of a single market between Member States, see e.g. Case T-62/98 *Volkswagen* [2000] ECR II-2707, paragraph 179, and paragraph 47 of the *Bagnasco* judgment cited in footnote 11, and Case 56/65 *Société Technique Minière* [1966] ECR 337. The impact of an agreement on the single market objective is thus a factor which can be taken into account.

24. The "pattern of trade"-test developed by the Court of Justice contains the following main elements, which are dealt with in the following sections:
    (a) "A sufficient degree of probability on the basis of a set of objective factors of law or fact",
    (b) An influence on the "pattern of trade between Member States",
    (c) "A direct or indirect, actual or potential influence" on the pattern of trade.

2.3.1. A sufficient degree of probability on the basis of a set of objective factors of law or fact

25. The assessment of effect on trade is based on objective factors. Subjective intent on the part of the undertakings concerned is not required. If, however, there is evidence that undertakings have intended to affect trade between Member States, for example because they have sought to hinder exports to or imports from other Member States, this is a relevant factor to be taken into account.
26. The words "may affect" and the reference by the Court of Justice to "a sufficient degree of probability" imply that, in order for Community law jurisdiction to be established, it is not required that the agreement or practice will actually have or has had an effect on trade between Member States. It is sufficient that the agreement or practice is "capable" of having such an effect.[17]

Notes
[17] See e.g. Case T-228/97 *Irish Sugar* [1999] ECR II-2969, paragraph 170, and Case 19/77 *Miller* [1978] ECR 131, paragraph 15.

27. There is no obligation or need to calculate the actual volume of trade between Member States affected by the agreement or practice. For example, in the case of agreements prohibiting exports to other Member States there is no need to estimate what would have been the level of parallel trade between the Member States concerned, in the absence of the agreement. This interpretation is consistent with the jurisdictional nature of the effect on trade criterion. Community law jurisdiction extends to categories of agreements and practices that are capable of having cross-border effects, irrespective of whether a particular agreement or practice actually has such effects.
28. The assessment under the effect on trade criterion depends on a number of factors that individually may not be decisive.[18] The relevant factors include the nature of the agreement and practice,

the nature of the products covered by the agreement or practice and the position and importance of the undertakings concerned.[19]

Notes
[18] See e.g. Case C-250/92, *Gøttrup-Klim* [1994] ECR II-5641, paragraph 54.
[19] See e.g. Case C-306/96, *Javico*, [1998] ECR I-1983, paragraph 17, and paragraph 18 of the judgment in *Béguelin* cited in footnote 4.

Commentary
para 28: F&N: 3.350

29. The nature of the agreement and practice provides an indication from a qualitative point of view of the ability of the agreement or practice to affect trade between Member States. Some agreements and practices are by their very nature capable of affecting trade between Member States, whereas others require more detailed analysis in this respect. Cross-border cartels are an example of the former, whereas joint ventures confined to the territory of a single Member State are an example of the latter. This aspect is further examined in section 3 below, which deals with various categories of agreements and practices.

30. The nature of the products covered by the agreements or practices also provides an indication of whether trade between Member States is capable of being affected. When by their nature products are easily traded across borders or are important for undertakings that want to enter or expand their activities in other Member States, Community jurisdiction is more readily established than in cases where due to their nature there is limited demand for products offered by suppliers from other Member States or where the products are of limited interest from the point of view of cross-border establishment or the expansion of the economic activity carried out from such place of establishment.[20] Establishment includes the setting-up by undertakings in one Member State of agencies, branches or subsidiaries in another Member State.

Notes
[20] Compare in this respect the judgments in *Bagnasco* and *Wouters* cited in footnote 11.

Commentary
para 30: B&C: 1.118

31. The market position of the undertakings concerned and their sales volumes are indicative from a quantitative point of view of the ability of the agreement or practice concerned to affect trade between Member States. This aspect, which forms an integral part of the assessment of appreciability, is addressed in section 2.4 below.

32. In addition to the factors already mentioned, it is necessary to take account of the legal and factual environment in which the agreement or practice operates. The relevant economic and legal context provides insight into the potential for an effect on trade between Member States. If there are absolute barriers to cross-border trade between Member States, which are external to the agreement or practice, trade is only capable of being affected if those barriers are likely to disappear in the foreseeable future. In cases where the barriers are not absolute but merely render cross-border activities more difficult, it is of the utmost importance to ensure that agreements and practices do not further hinder such activities. Agreements and practices that do so are capable of affecting trade between Member States.

Commentary
para 32: B&C: 1.129 F&N: 3.355

2.3.2. An influence on the "pattern of trade between Member States"

33. For Articles 81 and 82 to be applicable there must be an influence on the "pattern of trade between Member States".

34. The term "pattern of trade" is neutral. It is not a condition that trade be restricted or reduced.[21] Patterns of trade can also be affected when an agreement or practice causes an increase in trade. Indeed, Community law jurisdiction is established if trade between Member States is likely to

develop differently with the agreement or practice compared to the way in which it would probably have developed in the absence of the agreement or practice.[22]

Notes

[21] See e.g. Case T-141/89, *Tréfileurope*, [1995] ECR II-791, Case T-29/92, *Vereniging van Samenwerkende Prijsregelende Organisaties in de Bouwnijverheid (SPO)*, [1995] ECR II-289, as far as exports were concerned, and Commission Decision in *Volkswagen (II)* (OJ L 264, 2.10.2001, p. 14).

[22] See in this respect Case 71/74, *Frubo*, [1975] ECR 563, paragraph 38, Joined Cases 209/78 and others, *Van Landewyck*, [1980] ECR 3125, paragraph 172, Case T-61/89, *Dansk Pelsdyravler Forening*, [1992] ECR II-1931, paragraph 143, and Case T-65/89, *BPB Industries and British Gypsum*, [1993] ECR II-389, paragraph 135.

35. This interpretation reflects the fact that the effect on trade criterion is a jurisdictional one, which serves to distinguish those agreements and practices which are capable of having cross-border effects, so as to warrant an examination under the Community competition rules, from those agreements and practices which do not.

2.3.3. A "direct or indirect, actual or potential influence" on the pattern of trade

36. The influence of agreements and practices on patterns of trade between Member States can be "direct or indirect, actual or potential".

37. Direct effects on trade between Member States normally occur in relation to the products covered by an agreement or practice. When, for example, producers of a particular product in different Member States agree to share markets, direct effects are produced on trade between Member States on the market for the products in question. Another example of direct effects being produced is when a supplier limits distributor rebates to products sold within the Member State in which the distributors are established. Such practices increase the relative price of products destined for exports, rendering export sales less attractive and less competitive.

38. Indirect effects often occur in relation to products that are related to those covered by an agreement or practice. Indirect effects may, for example, occur where an agreement or practice has an impact on cross-border economic activities of undertakings that use or otherwise rely on the products covered by the agreement or practice.[23] Such effects can, for instance, arise where the agreement or practice relates to an intermediate product, which is not traded, but which is used in the supply of a final product, which is traded. The Court of Justice has held that trade between Member States was capable of being affected in the case of an agreement involving the fixing of prices of spirits used in the production of cognac.[24] Whereas the raw material was not exported, the final product — cognac — was exported. In such cases Community competition law is thus applicable, if trade in the final product is capable of being appreciably affected.

Notes

[23] See in this respect Case T-86/95, *Compagnie Générale Maritime and others*, [2002] ECR II-1011, paragraph 148, and paragraph 202 of the judgment in *Compagnie maritime belge* cited in footnote 12.

[24] See Case 123/83, *BNIC v Clair*, [1985] ECR 391, paragraph 29.

39. Indirect effects on trade between Member States may also occur in relation to the products covered by the agreement or practice. For instance, agreements whereby a manufacturer limits warranties to products sold by distributors within their Member State of establishment create disincentives for consumers from other Member States to buy the products because they would not be able to invoke the warranty.[25] Export by official distributors and parallel traders is made more difficult because in the eyes of consumers the products are less attractive without the manufacturer's warranty.[26]

Notes

[25] See Commission Decision in *Zanussi*, OJ L 322, 16.11.1978, p. 36, paragraph 11.

[26] See in this respect Case 31/85, *ETA Fabrique d'Ébauches*, [1985] ECR 3933, paragraphs 12 and 13.

Commentary

para 39: F&N: 3.359

40. Actual effects on trade between Member States are those that are produced by the agreement or practice once it is implemented. An agreement between a supplier and a distributor within the

same Member State, for instance one that prohibits exports to other Member States, is likely to produce actual effects on trade between Member States. Without the agreement the distributor would have been free to engage in export sales. It should be recalled, however, that it is not required that actual effects are demonstrated. It is sufficient that the agreement or practice be capable of having such effects.

41. Potential effects are those that may occur in the future with a sufficient degree of probability. In other words, foreseeable market developments must be taken into account.[27] Even if trade is not capable of being affected at the time the agreement is concluded or the practice is implemented, Articles 81 and 82 remain applicable if the factors which led to that conclusion are likely to change in the foreseeable future. In this respect it is relevant to consider the impact of liberalisation measures adopted by the Community or by the Member State in question and other foreseeable measures aiming at eliminating legal barriers to trade.

Notes

[27] See Joined Cases C-241/91 P and C-242/91 P, *RTE (Magill)*, [1995] ECR I-743, paragraph 70, and Case 107/82, *AEG*, [1983] ECR 3151, paragraph 60.

Commentary
para 41: **B&C:** 1.129

42. Moreover, even if at a given point in time market conditions are unfavourable to cross-border trade, for example because prices are similar in the Member States in question, trade may still be capable of being affected if the situation may change as a result of changing market conditions.[28] What matters is the ability of the agreement or practice to affect trade between Member States and not whether at any given point in time it actually does so.

Notes

[28] See paragraph 60 of the *AEG* judgment cited in the previous footnote.

Commentary
para 42: **F&N:** 3.406

43. The inclusion of indirect or potential effects in the analysis of effects on trade between Member States does not mean that the analysis can be based on remote or hypothetical effects. The likelihood of a particular agreement to produce indirect or potential effects must be explained by the authority or party claiming that trade between Member States is capable of being appreciably affected. Hypothetical or speculative effects are not sufficient for establishing Community law jurisdiction. For instance, an agreement that raises the price of a product which is not tradable reduces the disposable income of consumers. As consumers have less money to spend they may purchase fewer products imported from other Member States. However, the link between such income effects and trade between Member States is generally in itself too remote to establish Community law jurisdiction.

Commentary
para 43: **B&C:** 1.123 **F&N:** 3.364

2.4. The concept of appreciability

2.4.1. General principle

44. The effect on trade criterion incorporates a quantitative element, limiting Community law jurisdiction to agreements and practices that are capable of having effects of a certain magnitude. Agreements and practices fall outside the scope of application of Articles 81 and 82 when they affect the market only insignificantly having regard to the weak position of the undertakings concerned on the market for the products in question.[29] Appreciability can be appraised in particular by reference to the position and the importance of the relevant undertakings on the market for the products concerned.[30]

45. The assessment of appreciability depends on the circumstances of each individual case, in particular the nature of the agreement and practice, the nature of the products covered and the market position of the undertakings concerned. When by its very nature the agreement or practice is capable of affecting trade between Member States, the appreciability threshold is lower than in the case of agreements and practices that are not by their very nature capable of affecting trade between Member States. The stronger the market position of the undertakings concerned, the more likely it is that an agreement or practice capable of affecting trade between Member States can be held to do so appreciably.[31]

46. In a number of cases concerning imports and exports the Court of Justice has considered that the appreciability requirement was fulfilled when the sales of the undertakings concerned accounted for about 5% of the market.[32] Market share alone, however, has not always been considered the decisive factor. In particular, it is necessary also to take account of the turnover of the undertakings in the products concerned.[33]

47. Appreciability can thus be measured both in absolute terms (turnover) and in relative terms, comparing the position of the undertaking(s) concerned to that of other players on the market (market share). This focus on the position and importance of the undertakings concerned is consistent with the concept "may affect", which implies that the assessment is based on the ability of the agreement or practice to affect trade between Member States rather than on the impact on actual flows of goods and services across borders. The market position of the undertakings concerned and their turnover in the products concerned are indicative of the ability of an agreement or practice to affect trade between Member States. These two elements are reflected in the presumptions set out in paragraphs and 53 below.

48. The application of the appreciability test does not necessarily require that relevant markets be defined and market shares calculated.[34] The sales of an undertaking in absolute terms may be sufficient to support a finding that the impact on trade is appreciable. This is particularly so in the case of agreements and practices that by their very nature are liable to affect trade between Member States, for example because they concern imports or exports or because they cover several Member States. The fact that in such circumstances turnover in the products covered by the agreement may be sufficient for a finding of an appreciable effect on trade between Member States is reflected in the positive presumption set out in paragraph below.

49. Agreements and practices must always be considered in the economic and legal context in which they occur. In the case of vertical agreements it may be necessary to have regard to any cumulative effects of parallel networks of similar agreements.[35] Even if a single agreement or network of agreements is not capable of appreciably affecting trade between Member States, the effect of parallel networks of agreements, taken as a whole, may be capable of doing so. For that to be the case, however, it is necessary that the individual agreement or network of agreements makes a significant contribution to the overall effect on trade.[36]

Notes
[35] See e.g. Case T-7/93, *Langnese-Iglo*, [1995] ECR II-1533, paragraph 120.
[36] See paragraphs 140 and 141 of the judgment in *Vereniging van Groothandelaren in Bloemkwekerijprodukten* cited in footnote 5.

2.4.2. Quantification of appreciability

50. It is not possible to establish general quantitative rules covering all categories of agreements indicating when trade between Member States is capable of being appreciably affected. It is possible, however, to indicate when trade is normally not capable of being appreciably affected. Firstly, in its notice on agreements of minor importance which do not appreciably restrict competition in the meaning of Article 81(1) of the Treaty (the de minimis rule)[37] the Commission has stated that agreements between small and medium-sized undertakings (SMEs) as defined in the Annex to Commission Recommendation 96/280/EC[38] are normally not capable of affecting trade between Member States. The reason for this presumption is the fact that the activities of SMEs are normally local or at most regional in nature. However, SMEs may be subject to Community law jurisdiction in particular where they engage in cross-border economic activity. Secondly, the Commission considers it appropriate to set out general principles indicating when trade is normally not capable of being appreciably affected, i.e. a standard defining the absence of an appreciable effect on trade between Member States (the NAAT-rule). When applying Article 81, the Commission will consider this standard as a negative rebuttable presumption applying to all agreements within the meaning of Article 81(1) irrespective of the nature of the restrictions contained in the agreement, including restrictions that have been identified as hardcore restrictions in Commission block exemption regulations and guidelines. In cases where this presumption applies the Commission will normally not institute proceedings either upon application or on its own initiative. Where the undertakings assume in good faith that an agreement is covered by this negative presumption, the Commission will not impose fines.

Notes
[37] See Commission Notice on agreements of minor importance which do not appreciably restrict competition under Article 81(1) of the Treaty (OJ C 368, 22.12.2001, p. 13, paragraph 3).
[38] OJ L 107, 30.4.1996, p. 4. With effect from 1.1.2005 this recommendation will be replaced by Commission Recommendation 2003/361/EC concerning the definition of micro, small and medium-sized enterprises (OJ L 124, 20.5.2003, p. 36).

Commentary
para 50: B&C: 1.124 **F&N:** 3.372

51. Without prejudice to paragraph below, this negative definition of appreciability does not imply that agreements, which do not fall within the criteria set out below, are automatically capable of appreciably affecting trade between Member States. A case by case analysis is necessary.

Commentary
para 51: B&C: 1.126 **F&N:** 9.58, 9.65

52. The Commission holds the view that in principle agreements are not capable of appreciably affecting trade between Member States when the following cumulative conditions are met:
    (a) The aggregate market share of the parties on any relevant market within the Community affected by the agreement does not exceed 5%, and

(b) In the case of horizontal agreements, the aggregate annual Community turnover of the under-takings concerned[39] in the products covered by the agreement does not exceed 40 million euro. In the case of agreements concerning the joint buying of products the relevant turnover shall be the parties' combined purchases of the products covered by the agreement.

In the case of vertical agreements, the aggregate annual Community turnover of the supplier in the products covered by the agreement does not exceed 40 million euro. In the case of licence agreements the relevant turnover shall be the aggregate turnover of the licensees in the products incorporating the licensed technology and the licensor's own turnover in such prod-ucts. In cases involving agreements concluded between a buyer and several suppliers the rele-vant turnover shall be the buyer's combined purchases of the products covered by the agreements.

The Commission will apply the same presumption where during two successive calendar years the above turnover threshold is not exceeded by more than 10% and the above market threshold is not exceeded by more than 2 percentage points. In cases where the agreement concerns an emerging not yet existing market and where as a consequence the parties neither generate relevant turnover nor accumulate any relevant market share, the Commission will not apply this presumption. In such cases appreciability may have to be assessed on the basis of the position of the parties on related product markets or their strength in technologies relating to the agreement.

Notes

[39] The term "undertakings concerned" shall include connected undertakings as defined in paragraph 12.2 of the Commission's Notice on agreements of minor importance which do not appreciably restrict competition under Article 81(1) of the Treaty establishing the European Community (OJ C 368, 22.12.2001, p. 13).

Commentary
para 52: B&C: 1.125 F&N: 3.368, 3.369, 9.65
para 52(a): F&N: 3.373
para 52(b): F&N: 3.374, 3.375

53. The Commission will also hold the view that where an agreement by its very nature is capable of affecting trade between Member States, for example, because it concerns imports and exports or covers several Member States, there is a rebuttable positive presumption that such effects on trade are appreciable when the turnover of the parties in the products covered by the agreement calcu-lated as indicated in paragraphs 52 and 54 exceeds 40 million euro. In the case of agreements that by their very nature are capable of affecting trade between Member States it can also often be pre-sumed that such effects are appreciable when the market share of the parties exceeds the 5% threshold set out in the previous paragraph. However, this presumption does not apply where the agreement covers only part of a Member State (see paragraph 90 below).

Commentary
para 53: B&C: 1.126 F&N: 3.377

54. With regard to the threshold of 40 million euro (cf. paragraph 52 above), the turnover is calcu-lated on the basis of total Community sales excluding tax during the previous financial year by the undertakings concerned, of the products covered by the agreement (the contract products). Sales between entities that form part of the same undertaking are excluded.[40]

Notes
[40] See the previous footnote.

55. In order to apply the market share threshold, it is necessary to determine the relevant market.[41] This consists of the relevant product market and the relevant geographic market. The market shares are to be calculated on the basis of sales value data or, where appropriate, purchase value data. If value data are not available, estimates based on other reliable market information, includ-ing volume data, may be used.

Notes
⁴¹ When defining the relevant market, reference should be made to the notice on the definition of the relevant market for the purposes of Community competition law (OJ C 372, 9.12.1997, p. 5).

Commentary
para 55: B&C: 1.125

56. In the case of networks of agreements entered into by the same supplier with different distributors, sales made through the entire network are taken into account.

Commentary
para 56: B&C: 1.125 **F&N:** 3.370, 3.376

57. Contracts that form part of the same overall business arrangement constitute a single agreement for the purposes of the NAAT-rule.⁴² Undertakings cannot bring themselves inside these thresholds by dividing up an agreement that forms a whole from an economic perspective.

Notes
⁴² See also paragraph 14 above.

Commentary
para 57: F&N: 3.370

3. The Application of the Above Principles to Common Types of Agreements and Abuses

58. The Commission will apply the negative presumption set out in the preceding section to all agreements, including agreements that by their very nature are capable of affecting trade between Member States as well as agreements that involve trade with undertakings located in third countries (cf. section 3.3 below).
59. Outside the scope of negative presumption, the Commission will take account of qualitative elements relating to the nature of the agreement or practice and the nature of the products that they concern (see paragraphs and above). The relevance of the nature of the agreement is also reflected in the positive presumption set out in paragraph 53 above relating to appreciability in the case of agreements that by their very nature are capable of affecting trade between Member States. With a view to providing additional guidance on the application of the effect on trade concept it is therefore useful to consider various common types of agreements and practices.
60. In the following sections a primary distinction is drawn between agreements and practices that cover several Member States and agreements and practices that are confined to a single Member State or to part of a single Member State. These two main categories are broken down into further subcategories based on the nature of the agreement or practice involved. Agreements and practices involving third countries are also dealt with.

3.1. Agreements and abuse covering or implemented in several Member States

61. Agreements and practices covering or implemented in several Member States are in almost all cases by their very nature capable of affecting trade between Member States. When the relevant turnover exceeds the threshold set out in paragraph above it will therefore in most cases not be necessary to conduct a detailed analysis of whether trade between Member States is capable of being affected. However, in order to provide guidance also in these cases and to illustrate the principles developed in section 2 above, it is useful to explain what are the factors that are normally used to support a finding of Community law jurisdiction.

Commentary
para 61: B&C: 1.120

3.1.1. Agreements concerning imports and exports

62. Agreements between undertakings in two or more Member States that concern imports and exports are by their very nature capable of affecting trade between Member States. Such agreements, irrespective of whether they are restrictive of competition or not, have a direct impact on patterns of trade between Member States. In Kerpen & Kerpen, for example, which concerned an agreement between a French producer and a German distributor covering more than 10% of exports of cement from France to Germany, amounting in total to 350000 tonnes per year, the Court of Justice held that it was impossible to take the view that such an agreement was not capable of (appreciably) affecting trade between Member States.[43]

Notes

[43] See paragraph 8 of the judgment in *Kerpen & Kerpen* cited in footnote 15. It should be noted that the Court does not refer to market share but to the share of French exports and to the product volumes involved.

63. This category includes agreements that impose restrictions on imports and exports, including restrictions on active and passive sales and resale by buyers to customers in other Member States.[44] In these cases there is an inherent link between the alleged restriction of competition and the effect on trade, since the very purpose of the restriction is to prevent flows of goods and services between Member States, which would otherwise be possible. It is immaterial whether the parties to the agreement are located in the same Member State or in different Member States.

Notes

[44] See e.g. the judgment in *Volkswagen* cited in footnote 16 and Case T-175/95, *BASF Coatings*, [1999] ECR II-1581. For a horizontal agreement to prevent parallel trade see Joined Cases 96/82 and others, *IAZ International*, [1983] ECR 3369, paragraph 27.

3.1.2. Cartels covering several Member States

64. Cartel agreements such as those involving price fixing and market sharing covering several Member States are by their very nature capable of affecting trade between Member States. Cross-border cartels harmonise the conditions of competition and affect the interpenetration of trade by cementing traditional patterns of trade.[45] When undertakings agree to allocate geographic territories, sales from other areas into the allocated territories are capable of being eliminated or reduced. When undertakings agree to fix prices, they eliminate competition and any resulting price differentials that would entice both competitors and customers to engage in cross-border trade. When undertakings agree on sales quotas traditional patterns of trade are preserved. The undertakings concerned abstain from expanding output and thereby from serving potential customers in other Member States.

Notes

[45] See e.g. Case T-142/89, *Usines Gustave Boël*, [1995] ECR II-867, paragraph 102.

65. The effect on trade produced by cross-border cartels is generally also by its very nature appreciable due to the market position of the parties to the cartel. Cartels are normally only formed when the participating undertakings together hold a large share of the market, as this allows them to raise price or reduce output.

3.1.3. Horizontal cooperation agreements covering several Member States

66. This section covers various types of horizontal cooperation agreements. Horizontal cooperation agreements may for instance take the form of agreements whereby two or more undertakings cooperate in the performance of a particular economic activity such as production and distribution.[46] Often such agreements are referred to as joint ventures. However, joint ventures that perform on a lasting basis all the functions of an autonomous economic entity are covered by the Merger Regulation.[47] At the level of the Community such full function joint ventures are not dealt with under Articles 81 and 82 except in cases where Article 2(4) of the Merger Regulation is applicable.[48] This section therefore does not deal with full-function joint ventures. In the case

of non-full function joint ventures the joint entity does not operate as an autonomous supplier (or buyer) on any market. It merely serves the parents, who themselves operate on the market.[49]

Notes

[46] Horizontal cooperation agreements are dealt with in the Commission Guidelines on the applicability of Article 81 of the EC Treaty to horizontal cooperation agreements (OJ C 3, 6.1.2001, p. 2). Those guidelines deal with the substantive competition assessment of various types of agreements but do not deal with the effect on trade issue.

[47] See Council Regulation (EC) No 139/2004 on the control of concentrations between undertakings (OJ L 24, 29.1.2004, p. 1).

[48] The Commission Notice on the concept of full-function joint ventures under the Merger Regulation (OJ C 66, 2.3.1998, p. 1) gives guidance on the scope of this concept.

[49] See e.g. the Commission Decision in *Ford/Volkswagen* (OJ L 20, 28.1.1993, p. 14).

67. Joint ventures which engage in activities in two or more Member States or which produce an output that is sold by the parents in two or more Member States affect the commercial activities of the parties in those areas of the Community. Such agreements are therefore normally by their very nature capable of affecting trade between Member States compared to the situation without the agreement.[50] Patterns of trade are affected when undertakings switch their activities to the joint venture or use it for the purpose of establishing a new source of supply in the Community.

Notes

[50] See in this respect paragraph 146 of the *Compagnie Générale Maritime* judgment cited in footnote 23 above.

68. Trade may also be capable of being affected where a joint venture produces an input for the parent companies, which is subsequently further processed or incorporated into a product by the parent undertakings. This is likely to be the case where the input in question was previously sourced from suppliers in other Member States, where the parents previously produced the input in other Member States or where the final product is traded in more than one Member State.

69. In the assessment of appreciability it is important to take account of the parents' sales of products related to the agreement and not only those of the joint entity created by the agreement, given that the joint venture does not operate as an autonomous entity on any market.

3.1.4. Vertical agreements implemented in several Member States

70. Vertical agreements and networks of similar vertical agreements implemented in several Member States are normally capable of affecting trade between Member States if they cause trade to be channelled in a particular way. Networks of selective distribution agreements implemented in two or more Member States for example, channel trade in a particular way because they limit trade to members of the network, thereby affecting patterns of trade compared to the situation without the agreement.[51]

Notes

[51] See in this respect Joined Cases 43/82 and 63/82, *VBVB and VBBB*, [1984] ECR 19, paragraph 9.

71. Trade between Member States is also capable of being affected by vertical agreements that have foreclosure effects. This may for instance be the case of agreements whereby distributors in several Member States agree to buy only from a particular supplier or to sell only its products. Such agreements may limit trade between the Member States in which the agreements are implemented, or trade from Member States not covered by the agreements. Foreclosure may result from individual agreements or from networks of agreements. When an agreement or networks of agreements that cover several Member States have foreclosure effects, the ability of the agreement or agreements to affect trade between Member States is normally by its very nature appreciable.

72. Agreements between suppliers and distributors which provide for resale price maintenance (RPM) and which cover two or more Member States are normally also by their very nature capable of affecting trade between Member States.[52] Such agreements alter the price levels that would have been likely to exist in the absence of the agreements and thereby affect patterns of trade.

Notes

52 See in this respect Case T-66/89, *Publishers Association*, [1992] ECR II-1995.

3.1.5. *Abuses of dominant positions covering several Member States*

73. In the case of abuse of a dominant position it is useful to distinguish between abuses that raise barriers to entry or eliminate competitors (exclusionary abuses) and abuses whereby the dominant undertaking exploits its economic power for instance by charging excessive or discriminatory prices (exploitative abuses). Both kinds of abuse may be carried out either through agreements, which are equally subject to Article 81(1), or through unilateral conduct, which as far as Community competition law is concerned is subject only to Article 82.

74. In the case of exploitative abuses such as discriminatory rebates, the impact is on downstream trading partners, which either benefit or suffer, altering their competitive position and affecting patterns of trade between Member States.

Commentary
para 74: B&C: 1.128

75. When a dominant undertaking engages in exclusionary conduct in more than one Member State, such abuse is normally by its very nature capable of affecting trade between Member States. Such conduct has a negative impact on competition in an area extending beyond a single Member State, being likely to divert trade from the course it would have followed in the absence of the abuse. For example, patterns of trade are capable of being affected where the dominant undertaking grants loyalty rebates. Customers covered by the exclusionary rebate system are likely to purchase less from competitors of the dominant firm than they would otherwise have done. Exclusionary conduct that aims directly at eliminating a competitor such as predatory pricing is also capable of affecting trade between Member States because of its impact on the competitive market structure inside the Community.[53] When a dominant firm engages in behaviour with a view to eliminating a competitor operating in more than one Member State, trade is capable of being affected in several ways. First, there is a risk that the affected competitor will cease to be a source of supply inside the Community. Even if the targeted undertaking is not eliminated, its future competitive conduct is likely to be affected, which may also have an impact on trade between Member States. Secondly, the abuse may have an impact on other competitors. Through its abusive behaviour the dominant undertaking can signal to its competitors that it will discipline attempts to engage in real competition. Thirdly, the very fact of eliminating a competitor may be sufficient for trade between Member States to be capable of being affected. This may be the case even where the undertaking that risks being eliminated mainly engages in exports to third countries.[54] Once the effective competitive market structure inside the Community risks being further impaired, there is Community law jurisdiction.

Notes

53 See in this respect the judgment in *Commercial Solvents* cited in footnote 3, in the judgment in *Hoffmann-La Roche*, cited in footnote, paragraph 125, and in *RTE and ITP* cited in footnote, as well as Case 6/72, *Continental Can*, [1973] ECR 215, paragraph 16, and Case 27/76, *United Brands*, [1978] ECR 207, paragraphs 197 to 203.
54 See paragraphs 32 and 33 of the judgment in *Commercial Solvents* cited in footnote 3.

Commentary
para 75: B&C: 1.128

76. Where a dominant undertaking engages in exploitative or exclusionary abuse in more than one Member State, the capacity of the abuse to affect trade between Member States will normally also by its very nature be appreciable. Given the market position of the dominant undertaking concerned, and the fact that the abuse is implemented in several Member States, the scale of the abuse and its likely impact on patterns of trade is normally such that trade between Member States is capable of being appreciably affected. In the case of an exploitative abuse such as price discrimination, the abuse alters the competitive position of trading partners in several Member States. In the case of exclusionary abuses, including abuses that aim at eliminating a competitor, the economic activity engaged in by competitors in several Member States is affected. The very

existence of a dominant position in several Member States implies that competition in a substantial part of the common market is already weakened.[55] When a dominant undertaking further weakens competition through recourse to abusive conduct, for example by eliminating a competitor, the ability of the abuse to affect trade between Member States is normally appreciable.

Notes

[55] According to settled case law dominance is a position of economic strength enjoyed by an undertaking which enables it to prevent effective competition being maintained on the relevant market by affording it the power to act to an appreciable extent independently of its competitors, its customers and ultimately of the consumers, see e.g. paragraph 38 of the judgment in *Hoffmann-La Roche* cited in footnote 9.

3.2. Agreements and abuses covering a single, or only part of a, Member State

77. When agreements or abusive practices cover the territory of a single Member State, it may be necessary to proceed with a more detailed inquiry into the ability of the agreements or abusive practices to affect trade between Member States. It should be recalled that for there to be an effect on trade between Member States it is not required that trade is reduced. It is sufficient that an appreciable change is capable of being caused in the pattern of trade between Member States. Nevertheless, in many cases involving a single Member State the nature of the alleged infringement, and in particular, its propensity to foreclose the national market, provides a good indication of the capacity of the agreement or practice to affect trade between Member States. The examples mentioned hereafter are not exhaustive. They merely provide examples of cases where agreements confined to the territory of a single Member State can be considered capable of affecting trade between Member States.

3.2.1. Cartels covering a single Member State

78. Horizontal cartels covering the whole of a Member State are normally capable of affecting trade between Member States. The Community Courts have held in a number of cases that agreements extending over the whole territory of a Member State by their very nature have the effect of reinforcing the partitioning of markets on a national basis by hindering the economic penetration which the Treaty is designed to bring about.[56]

Notes

[56] See for a recent example paragraph 95 of the *Wouters* judgment cited in footnote 11.

79. The capacity of such agreements to partition the internal market follows from the fact that undertakings participating in cartels in only one Member State, normally need to take action to exclude competitors from other Member States.[57] If they do not, and the product covered by the agreement is tradable,[58] the cartel risks being undermined by competition from undertakings from other Member States. Such agreements are normally also by their very nature capable of having an appreciable effect on trade between Member States, given the market coverage required for such cartels to be effective.

Notes

[57] See e.g. Case 246/86, *Belasco*, [1989] ECR 2117, paragraph 32–38.

[58] See paragraph 34 of the *Belasco* judgment cited in the previous footnote and more recently Joined Cases T-202/98 a.o., *British Sugar*, [2001] ECR II-2035, paragraph 79. On the other hand this is not so when the market is not susceptible to imports, see paragraph 51 of the *Bagnasco* judgment cited in footnote 11.

80. Given the fact that the effect on trade concept encompasses potential effects, it is not decisive whether such action against competitors from other Member States is in fact adopted at any given point in time. If the cartel price is similar to the price prevailing in other Member States, there may be no immediate need for the members of the cartel to take action against competitors from other Member States. What matters is whether or not they are likely to do so, if market conditions change. The likelihood of that depends on the existence or otherwise of natural barriers to trade in the market, including in particular whether or not the product in question is tradable. In a case involving certain retail banking services[59] the Court of Justice has, for example, held that trade was not capable of being appreciably affected because the potential for trade in the specific

products concerned was very limited and because they were not an important factor in the choice made by undertakings from other Member States regarding whether or not to establish themselves in the Member State in question.[60]

Notes
[59] Guarantees for current account credit facilities.
[60] See paragraph 51 of the *Bagnasco* judgment cited in footnote 11.

81. The extent to which the members of a cartel monitor prices and competitors from other Member States can provide an indication of the extent to which the products covered by the cartel are tradable. Monitoring suggests that competition and competitors from other Member States are perceived as a potential threat to the cartel. Moreover, if there is evidence that the members of the cartel have deliberately fixed the price level in the light of the price level prevailing in other Member States (limit pricing), it is an indication that the products in question are tradable and that trade between Member States is capable of being affected.

82. Trade is normally also capable of being affected when the members of a national cartel temper the competitive constraint imposed by competitors from other Member States by inducing them to join the restrictive agreement, or if their exclusion from the agreement places the competitors at a competitive disadvantage.[61] In such cases the agreement either prevents these competitors from exploiting any competitive advantage that they have, or raises their costs, thereby having a negative impact on their competitiveness and their sales. In both cases the agreement hampers the operations of competitors from other Member States on the national market in question. The same is true when a cartel agreement confined to a single Member State is concluded between undertakings that resell products imported from other Member States.[62]

Notes
[61] See in this respect Case 45/85, *Verband der Sachversicherer*, [1987] ECR 405, paragraph 50, and Case C-7/95 P, *John Deere*, [1998] ECR I-3111. See also paragraph 172 of the judgment in *Van Landewyck* cited in footnote 22, where the Court stressed that the agreement in question reduced appreciably the incentive to sell imported products.
[62] See e.g. the judgment in *Stichting Sigarettenindustrie*, cited in footnote 15, paragraphs 49 and 50.

3.2.2. Horizontal cooperation agreements covering a single Member State

83. Horizontal cooperation agreements and in particular non-full function joint ventures (cf. paragraph 66 above), which are confined to a single Member State and which do not directly relate to imports and exports, do not belong to the category of agreements that by their very nature are capable of affecting trade between Member States. A careful examination of the capacity of the individual agreement to affect trade between Member States may therefore be required.

84. Horizontal cooperation agreements may, in particular, be capable of affecting trade between Member States where they have foreclosure effects. This may be the case with agreements that establish sector-wide standardisation and certification regimes, which either exclude undertakings from other Member States or which are more easily fulfilled by undertakings from the Member State in question due to the fact that they are based on national rules and traditions. In such circumstances the agreements make it more difficult for undertakings from other Member States to penetrate the national market.

Commentary
para 84: F&N: 3.381

85. Trade may also be affected where a joint venture results in undertakings from other Member States being cut off from an important channel of distribution or source of demand. If, for example, two or more distributors established within the same Member State, and which account for a substantial share of imports of the products in question, establish a purchasing joint venture combining their purchases of that product, the resulting reduction in the number of distribution channels limits the possibility for suppliers from other Member States of gaining access to the national market in question. Trade is therefore capable of being affected.[63] Trade may also be affected where undertakings which previously imported a particular product form a joint venture

which is entrusted with the production of that same product. In this case the agreement causes a change in the patterns of trade between Member States compared to the situation before the agreement.

Notes
[63] See in this respect Case T-22/97, *Kesko*, [1999] ECR II-3775, paragraph 109.

3.2.3. Vertical agreements covering a single Member State

86. Vertical agreements covering the whole of a Member State may, in particular, be capable of affecting patterns of trade between Member States when they make it more difficult for undertakings from other Member States to penetrate the national market in question, either by means of exports or by means of establishment (foreclosure effect). When vertical agreements give rise to such foreclosure effects, they contribute to the partitioning of markets on a national basis, thereby hindering the economic interpenetration which the Treaty is designed to bring about.[64]

Notes
[64] See e.g. Case T-65/98, *Van den Bergh Foods*, [2003] ECR II-[4653], and the judgment in *Langnese-Iglo*, cited in footnote 35 paragraph 120.

Commentary
para 86: F&N: 3.381

87. Foreclosure may, for example, occur when suppliers impose exclusive purchasing obligations on buyers.[65] In *Delimitis*,[66] which concerned agreements between a brewer and owners of premises where beer was consumed whereby the latter undertook to buy beer exclusively from the brewer, the Court of Justice defined foreclosure as the absence, due to the agreements, of real and concrete possibilities of gaining access to the market. Agreements normally only create significant barriers to entry when they cover a significant proportion of the market. Market share and market coverage can be used as an indicator in this respect. In making the assessment account must be taken not only of the particular agreement or network of agreements in question, but also of other parallel networks of agreements having similar effects.[67]

Notes
[65] See e.g. judgment of 7.12.2000, Case C-214/99, *Neste*, ECR I-11121.
[66] See judgment of 28.2.1991, Case C-234/89, *Delimitis*, ECR I-935.
[67] See paragraph 120 of the *Langnese-Iglo* judgment cited in footnote 35.

88. Vertical agreements which cover the whole of a Member State and which relate to tradable products may also be capable of affecting trade between Member States, even if they do not create direct obstacles to trade. Agreements whereby undertakings engage in resale price maintenance (RPM) may have direct effects on trade between Member States by increasing imports from other Member States and by decreasing exports from the Member State in question.[68] Agreements involving RPM may also affect patterns of trade in much the same way as horizontal cartels. To the extent that the price resulting from RPM is higher than that prevailing in other Member States this price level is only sustainable if imports from other Member States can be controlled.

Notes
[68] See e.g. Commission Decision in *Volkswagen (II)*, cited in footnote 21, paragraphs 81 et seq.

3.2.4. Agreements covering only part of a Member State

89. In qualitative terms the assessment of agreements covering only part of a Member State is approached in the same way as in the case of agreements covering the whole of a Member State. This means that the analysis in section 2 applies. In the assessment of appreciability, however, the two categories must be distinguished, as it must be taken into account that only part of a Member State is covered by the agreement. It must also be taken into account what proportion of the national territory is susceptible to trade. If, for example, transport costs or the operating radius of

equipment render it economically unviable for undertakings from other Member States to serve the entire territory of another Member State, trade is capable of being affected if the agreement forecloses access to the part of the territory of a Member State that is susceptible to trade, provided that this part is not insignificant.[69]

Notes
[69] See in this respect paragraphs 177 to 181 of the judgment in *SCK and FNK* cited in footnote 13.

Commentary
para 89: F&N: 3.383

90. Where an agreement forecloses access to a regional market, then for trade to be appreciably affected, the volume of sales affected must be significant in proportion to the overall volume of sales of the products concerned inside the Member State in question. This assessment cannot be based merely on geographic coverage. The market share of the parties to the agreement must also be given fairly limited weight. Even if the parties have a high market share in a properly defined regional market, the size of that market in terms of volume may still be insignificant when compared to total sales of the products concerned within the Member State in question. In general, the best indicator of the capacity of the agreement to (appreciably) affect trade between Member States is therefore considered to be the share of the national market in terms of volume that is being foreclosed. Agreements covering areas with a high concentration of demand will thus weigh more heavily than those covering areas where demand is less concentrated. For Community jurisdiction to be established the share of the national market that is being foreclosed must be significant.

Commentary
para 90: B&C: 1.133 F&N: 3.385

91. Agreements that are local in nature are in themselves not capable of appreciably affecting trade between Member States. This is the case even if the local market is located in a border region. Conversely, if the foreclosed share of the national market is significant, trade is capable of being affected even where the market in question is not located in a border region.

Commentary
para 91: F&N: 3.385

92. In cases in this category some guidance may be derived from the case law concerning the concept in Article 82 of a substantial part of the common market.[70] Agreements that, for example, have the effect of hindering competitors from other Member States from gaining access to part of a Member State, which constitutes a substantial part of the common market, should be considered to have an appreciable effect on trade between Member States.

Notes
[70] See as to this notion the judgment in *Ambulanz Glöckner*, cited in footnote 11, paragraph 38, and Case C-179/90, *Merci convenzionali porto di Genova*, [1991] ECR I-5889, and Case C-242/95, *GT-Link*, [1997] ECR I-4449.

Commentary
para 92: B&C: 1.133 F&N: 3.386

3.2.5. *Abuses of dominant positions covering a single Member State*

93. Where an undertaking, which holds a dominant position covering the whole of a Member State, engages in exclusionary abuses, trade between Member States is normally capable of being affected. Such abusive conduct will generally make it more difficult for competitors from other Member States to penetrate the market, in which case patterns of trade are capable of being affected.[71] In Michelin,[72] for example, the Court of Justice held that a system of loyalty rebates foreclosed competitors from other Member States and therefore affected trade within the meaning of Article 82. In Rennet[73] the Court similarly held that an abuse in the form of an exclusive purchasing obligation on customers foreclosed products from other Member States.

537

Notes

[71] See e.g. paragraph 135 of the judgment in *BPB Industries and British Gypsum* cited in footnote [22].
[72] See Case 322/81, *Nederlandse Banden Industrie Michelin*, [1983] ECR 3461
[73] See Case 61/80, *Coöperative Stremsel- en Kleurselfabriek*, [1981] ECR 851, paragraph 15.

94. Exclusionary abuses that affect the competitive market structure inside a Member State, for instance by eliminating or threatening to eliminate a competitor, may also be capable of affecting trade between Member States. Where the undertaking that risks being eliminated only operates in a single Member State, the abuse will normally not affect trade between Member States. However, trade between Member States is capable of being affected where the targeted undertaking exports to or imports from other Member States[74] and where it also operates in other Member States.[75] An effect on trade may arise from the dissuasive impact of the abuse on other competitors. If through repeated conduct the dominant undertaking has acquired a reputation for adopting exclusionary practices towards competitors that attempt to engage in direct competition, competitors from other Member States are likely to compete less aggressively, in which case trade may be affected, even if the victim in the case at hand is not from another Member State.

Notes

[74] See in this respect judgment in *Irish Sugar*, cited in footnote 17 paragraph 169.
[75] See paragraph 70 of the judgment in *RTE (Magill)* cited in footnote 27.

Commentary
para 94: B&C: 1.132

95. In the case of exploitative abuses such as price discrimination and excessive pricing, the situation may be more complex. Price discrimination between domestic customers will normally not affect trade between Member States. However, it may do so if the buyers are engaged in export activities and are disadvantaged by the discriminatory pricing or if this practice is used to prevent imports.[76] Practices consisting of offering lower prices to customers that are the most likely to import products from other Member States may make it more difficult for competitors from other Member States to enter the market. In such cases trade between Member States is capable of being affected.

Notes

[76] See the judgment in *Irish Sugar* cited in footnote 17.

Commentary
para 95: B&C: 1.132

96. As long as an undertaking has a dominant position which covers the whole of a Member State it is normally immaterial whether the specific abuse engaged in by the dominant undertaking only covers part of its territory or affects certain buyers within the national territory. A dominant firm can significantly impede trade by engaging in abusive conduct in the areas or vis-à-vis the customers that are the most likely to be targeted by competitors from other Member States. For example, it may be the case that a particular channel of distribution constitutes a particularly important means of gaining access to broad categories of consumers. Hindering access to such channels can have a substantial impact on trade between Member States. In the assessment of appreciability it must also be taken into account that the very presence of the dominant undertaking covering the whole of a Member State is likely to make market penetration more difficult. Any abuse which makes it more difficult to enter the national market should therefore be considered to appreciably affect trade. The combination of the market position of the dominant undertaking and the anti-competitive nature of its conduct implies that such abuses have normally by their very nature an appreciable effect on trade. However, if the abuse is purely local in nature or involves only an insignificant share of the sales of the dominant undertaking within the Member State in question, trade may not be capable of being appreciably affected.

Commentary
para 96: B&C: 1.132 F&N: 3.385

3.2.6. *Abuse of a dominant position covering only part of a Member State*

97. Where a dominant position covers only part of a Member State some guidance may, as in the case of agreements, be derived from the condition in Article 82 that the dominant position must cover a substantial part of the common market. If the dominant position covers part of a Member State that constitutes a substantial part of the common market and the abuse makes it more difficult for competitors from other Member States to gain access to the market where the undertaking is dominant, trade between Member States must normally be considered capable of being appreciably affected.

Commentary
para 97: F&N: 3.386

98. In the application of this criterion regard must be had in particular to the size of the market in question in terms of volume. Regions and even a port or an airport situated in a Member State may, depending on their importance, constitute a substantial part of the common market.[77] In the latter cases it must be taken into account whether the infrastructure in question is used to provide cross-border services and, if so, to what extent. When infrastructures such as airports and ports are important in providing cross-border services, trade between Member States is capable of being affected.

Notes
[77] See e.g. the case law cited in footnote 70.

99. As in the case of dominant positions covering the whole of a Member State (cf. paragraph 95 above), trade may not be capable of being appreciably affected if the abuse is purely local in nature or involves only an insignificant share of the sales of the dominant undertaking.

Commentary
para 99: B&C: 1.133

3.3. Agreements and abuses involving imports and exports with undertakings located in third countries, and agreements and practices involving undertakings located in third countries

3.3.1. *General remarks*

100. Articles 81 and 82 apply to agreements and practices that are capable of affecting trade between Member States even if one or more of the parties are located outside the Community.[78] Articles 81 and 82 apply irrespective of where the undertakings are located or where the agreement has been concluded, provided that the agreement or practice is either implemented inside the Community,[79] or produce effects inside the Community.[80] Articles 81 and 82 may also apply to agreements and practices that cover third countries, provided that they are capable of affecting trade between Member States. The general principle set out in section 2 above according to which the agreement or practice must be capable of having an appreciable influence, direct or indirect, actual or potential, on the pattern of trade between Member States, also applies in the case of agreements and abuses which involve undertakings located in third countries or which relate to imports or exports with third countries.

Notes
[78] See in this respect Case 28/77, *Tepea*, [1978] ECR 1391, paragraph 48, and paragraph 16 of the judgment in *Continental Can* cited in footnote 53.
[79] See Joined Cases C-89/85 and others, *Ahlström Osakeyhtiö (Woodpulp)*, [1988] ECR 651, paragraph 16.
[80] See in this respect Case T-102/96, *Gencor*, [1999] ECR II-753, which applies the effects test in the field of mergers.

Commentary
para 100: B&C: 1.134 F&N: 3.387

101. For the purposes of establishing Community law jurisdiction it is sufficient that an agreement or practice involving third countries or undertakings located in third countries is capable of affecting cross-border economic activity inside the Community. Import into one Member State may be sufficient to trigger effects of this nature. Imports can affect the conditions of competition in the importing Member State, which in turn can have an impact on exports and imports of competing products to and from other Member States. In other words, imports from third countries resulting from the agreement or practice may cause a diversion of trade between Member States, thus affecting patterns of trade.

102. In the application of the effect on trade criterion to the above mentioned agreements and practices it is relevant to examine, inter alia, what is the object of the agreement or practice as indicated by its content or the underlying intent of the undertakings involved.[81]

Notes

[81] See to that effect paragraph 19 of the judgment in *Javico* cited in footnote 19.

103. Where the object of the agreement is to restrict competition inside the Community the requisite effect on trade between Member States is more readily established than where the object is predominantly to regulate competition outside the Community. Indeed in the former case the agreement or practice has a direct impact on competition inside the Community and trade between Member States. Such agreements and practices, which may concern both imports and exports, are normally by their very nature capable of affecting trade between Member States.

3.3.2. Arrangements that have as their object the restriction of competition inside the Community

104. In the case of imports, this category includes agreements that bring about an isolation of the internal market.[82] This is, for instance, the case of agreements whereby competitors in the Community and in third countries share markets, e.g. by agreeing not to sell in each other's home markets or by concluding reciprocal (exclusive) distribution agreements.[83]

Notes

[82] See in this respect Case 51/75, *EMI v CBS*, [1976] ECR 811, paragraphs 28 and 29.
[83] See Commission Decision in *Siemens/Fanuc* (OJ L 376, 31.12.1985, p. 29).

105. In the case of exports, this category includes cases where undertakings that compete in two or more Member States agree to export certain (surplus) quantities to third countries with a view to co-ordinating their market conduct inside the Community. Such export agreements serve to reduce price competition by limiting output inside the Community, thereby affecting trade between Member States. Without the export agreement these quantities might have been sold inside the Community.[84]

Notes

[84] See in this respect Joined Cases 29/83 and 30/83, *CRAM and Rheinzinc*, [1984] ECR 1679, and Joined Cases 40/73 and others, *Suiker Unie*, [1975] ECR 1663, paragraphs 564 and 580.

3.3.3. Other arrangements

106. In the case of agreements and practices whose object is not to restrict competition inside the Community, it is normally necessary to proceed with a more detailed analysis of whether or not cross-border economic activity inside the Community, and thus patterns of trade between Member States, are capable of being affected.

Commentary
para 106: B&C: 1.134, 2.128

107. In this regard it is relevant to examine the effects of the agreement or practice on customers and other operators inside the Community that rely on the products of the undertakings that are parties to the agreement or practice.[85] In Compagnie maritime belge,[86] which concerned agreements between shipping companies operating between Community ports and West African ports, the agreements were held to be capable of indirectly affecting trade between Member

States because they altered the catchment areas of the Community ports covered by the agreements and because they affected the activities of other undertakings inside those areas. More specifically, the agreements affected the activities of undertakings that relied on the parties for transportation services, either as a means of transporting goods purchased in third countries or sold there, or as an important input into the services that the ports themselves offered.

Notes
[85] See paragraph 22 of the judgment in *Javico* cited in footnote 19.
[86] See paragraph 203 of the judgment in *Compagnie maritime belge* cited in footnote 12.

108. Trade may also be capable of being affected when the agreement prevents re-imports into the Community. This may, for example, be the case with vertical agreements between Community suppliers and third country distributors, imposing restrictions on resale outside an allocated territory, including the Community. If in the absence of the agreement resale to the Community would be possible and likely, such imports may be capable of affecting patterns of trade inside the Community.[87]

Notes
[87] See in this respect the judgment in *Javico* cited in footnote 19.

109. However, for such effects to be likely, there must be an appreciable difference between the prices of the products charged in the Community and those charged outside the Community, and this price difference must not be eroded by customs duties and transport costs. In addition, the product volumes exported compared to the total market for those products in the territory of the common market must not be insignificant.[88] If these product volumes are insignificant compared to those sold inside the Community, the impact of any re-importation on trade between Member States is considered not to be appreciable. In making this assessment, regard must be had not only to the individual agreement concluded between the parties, but also to any cumulative effect of similar agreements concluded by the same and competing suppliers. It may be, for example, that the product volumes covered by a single agreement are quite small, but that the product volumes covered by several such agreements are significant. In that case the agreements taken as a whole may be capable of appreciably affecting trade between Member States. It should be recalled, however (cf. paragraph 49 above), that the individual agreement or network of agreements must make a significant contribution to the overall effect on trade.

Notes
[88] See in this respect paragraphs 24 to 26 of the *Javico* judgment cited in footnote 19.

Commentary
para 109: F&N: 3.392

C18

COMMUNICATION FROM THE COMMISSION

Notice

Guidelines on the application of Article 81(3) of the Treaty

(2004/C 101/08)

(Text with EEA relevance)

Official Journal C 101, 27.4.2004, p. 97

Celex No: 52004XC0427(07)

Notes

EEA application: the EFTA Surveillance Authority has adopted a parallel notice on the application of Article 53(3) of the EEA Agreement under Article 5(2)(b) of the Surveillance and Court Agreement: see College Decision 123/05/COL of 18 May 2005, OJ C 208, 6.9.2007, p.1.

---

1. INTRODUCTION

1. Article 81(3) of the Treaty sets out an exception rule, which provides a defence to undertakings against a finding of an infringement of Article 81[1] of the Treaty. Agreements, decisions of associations of undertakings and concerted practices(1) caught by Article 81(1) which satisfy the conditions of Article 81(3) are valid and enforceable, no prior decision to that effect being required.

Notes

[1] In the following the term "agreement" includes concerted practices and decisions of associations of undertakings.

---

2. Article 81(3) can be applied in individual cases or to categories of agreements and concerted practices by way of block exemption regulation. Regulation 1/2003 on the implementation of the competition rules laid down in Articles 81 and 82[2] does not affect the validity and legal nature of block exemption regulations. All existing block exemption regulations remain in force and agreements covered by block exemption regulations are legally valid and enforceable even if they are restrictive of competition within the meaning of Article 81(1).[3] Such agreements can only be prohibited for the future and only upon formal withdrawal of the block exemption by the Commission or a national competition authority.[4] Block exempted agreements cannot be held invalid by national courts in the context of private litigation.

Notes

[2] OJ L 1, 4.1.2003, p. 1.

[3] All existing block exemption regulations and Commission notices are available on the DG Competition web-site: http://www.europa.eu.int/comm/ dgs/competition

[4] See paragraph 36 below.

---

3. The existing guidelines on vertical restraints, horizontal cooperation agreements and technology transfer agreements[5] deal with the application of Article 81 to various types of agreements and concerted practices. The purpose of those guidelines is to set out the Commission's view of the substantive assessment criteria applied to the various types of agreements and practices.

Notes

[5] See Commission Notice on Guidelines on vertical restraints (OJ C 291, 13.10.2000, p. 1), Commission Notice on Guidelines on the application of Article 81 of the Treaty to horizontal cooperation agreements (OJ C 3, 6.1.2001, p. 2), and Commission Notice on Guidelines on the application of Article 81 of the Treaty to technology transfer agreements, [OJ C 101, 27.04.2004, p. 2].

4. The present guidelines set out the Commission's interpretation of the conditions for exception contained in Article 81(3). It thereby provides guidance on how it will apply Article 81 in individual cases. Although not binding on them, these guidelines also intend to give guidance to the courts and authorities of the Member States in their application of Article 81(1) and (3) of the Treaty.

5. The guidelines establish an analytical framework for the application of Article 81(3). The purpose is to develop a methodology for the application of this Treaty provision. This methodology is based on the economic approach already introduced and developed in the guidelines on vertical restraints, horizontal co-operation agreements and technology transfer agreements. The Commission will follow the present guidelines, which provide more detailed guidance on the application of the four conditions of Article 81(3) than the guidelines on vertical restraints, horizontal co-operation agreements and technology transfer agreements, also with regard to agreements covered by those guidelines.

Commentary
para 5: F&N: 12.229

6. The standards set forth in the present guidelines must be applied in light of the circumstances specific to each case. This excludes a mechanical application. Each case must be assessed on its own facts and the guidelines must be applied reasonably and flexibly.

7. With regard to a number of issues, the present guidelines outline the current state of the case law of the Court of Justice. However, the Commission also intends to explain its policy with regard to issues that have not been dealt with in the case law, or that are subject to interpretation. The Commission's position, however, is without prejudice to the case law of the Court of Justice and the Court of First Instance concerning the interpretation of Article 81(1) and (3), and to the interpretation that the Community Courts may give to those provisions in the future.

2. The General Framework of Article 81 EC

2.1. The Treaty provisions

8. Article 81(1) prohibits all agreements between undertakings, decisions by associations of undertakings and concerted practices which may affect trade between Member States[6] and which have as their object or effect the prevention, restriction or distortion of competition.[7]

Notes

[6] The concept of effect on trade between Member States is dealt with in separate guidelines.
[7] In the following the term "restriction" includes the prevention and distortion of competition.

9. As an exception to this rule Article 81(3) provides that the prohibition contained in Article 81(1) may be declared inapplicable in case of agreements which contribute to improving the production or distribution of goods or to promoting technical or economic progress, while allowing consumers a fair share of the resulting benefits, and which do not impose restrictions which are not indispensable to the attainment of these objectives, and do not afford such undertakings the possibility of eliminating competition in respect of a substantial part of the products concerned.

10. According to Article 1(1) of Regulation 1/2003 agreements which are caught by Article 81(1) and which do not satisfy the conditions of Article 81(3) are prohibited, no prior decision to that effect being required.[8] According to Article 1(2) of the same Regulation agreements which are

caught by Article 81(1) but which satisfy the conditions of Article 81(3) are not prohibited, no prior decision to that effect being required. Such agreements are valid and enforceable from the moment that the conditions of Article 81(3) are satisfied and for as long as that remains the case.

Notes
[8] According to Article 81(2) such agreements are automatically void.

11. The assessment under Article 81 thus consists of two parts. The first step is to assess whether an agreement between undertakings, which is capable of affecting trade between Member States, has an anti-competitive object or actual or potential[9] anti-competitive effects. The second step, which only becomes relevant when an agreement is found to be restrictive of competition, is to determine the pro-competitive benefits produced by that agreement and to assess whether these pro-competitive effects outweigh the anti-competitive effects. The balancing of anticompetitive and pro-competitive effects is conducted exclusively within the framework laid down by Article 81(3).[10]

Notes
[9] Article 81(1) prohibits both actual and potential anti-competitive effects, see e.g. Case C-7/95 P *John Deere* [1998] ECR I-3111, paragraph 77.
[10] See Case T-65/98 *Van den Bergh Foods* [2003] ECR II-[4653], paragraph 107 and Case T-112/99 *Métropole télévision (M6) and others* [2001] ECR II-2459, paragraph 74, where the Court of First Instance held that it is only in the precise framework of Article 81(3) that the pro- and anti-competitive aspects of a restriction may be weighed.

12. The assessment of any countervailing benefits under Article 81(3) necessarily requires prior determination of the restrictive nature and impact of the agreement. To place Article 81(3) in its proper context it is appropriate to briefly outline the objective and principal content of the prohibition rule of Article 81(1). The Commission guidelines on vertical restraints, horizontal co-operation agreements and technology transfer agreements[11] contain substantial guidance on the application of Article 81(1) to various types of agreements. The present guidelines are therefore limited to recalling the basic analytical framework for applying Article 81(1).

Notes
[11] See note above.

2.2. The prohibition rule of Article 81(1)

2.2.1. General remarks

13. The objective of Article 81 is to protect competition on the market as a means of enhancing consumer welfare and of ensuring an efficient allocation of resources. Competition and market integration serve these ends since the creation and preservation of an open single market promotes an efficient allocation of resources throughout the Community for the benefit of consumers.

Commentary
para 13: F&N: 2.11, 2.27, 2.61, 3.136, 3.140

14. The prohibition rule of Article 81(1) applies to restrictive agreements and concerted practices between undertakings and decisions by associations of undertakings in so far as they are capable of affecting trade between Member States. A general principle underlying Article 81(1) which is expressed in the case law of the Community Courts is that each economic operator must determine independently the policy, which he intends to adopt on the market.[12] In view of this the Community Courts have defined "agreements", "decisions" and "concerted practices" as Community law concepts which allow a distinction to be made between the unilateral conduct of an undertaking and co-ordination of behaviour or collusion between undertakings.[13] Unilateral conduct is subject only to Article 82 of the Treaty as far as Community competition law is concerned. Moreover, the convergence rule set out in Article 3(2) of Regulation 1/2003 does not apply to unilateral conduct. This provision applies only to agreements, decisions and concerted practices, which are capable of affecting trade between Member States. Article 3(2) provides that

when such agreements, decisions and concerted practices are not prohibited by Article 81, they cannot be prohibited by national competition law. Article 3 is without prejudice to the fundamental principle of primacy of Community law, which entails in particular that agreements and abusive practices that are prohibited by Articles 81 and 82 cannot be upheld by national law.[14]

Notes

[12] See e.g. Case C-49/92 P *Anic Partecipazioni* [1999] ECR I-4125, paragraph 116; and Joined Cases 40/73 to 48/73 and others, *Suiker Unie* [1975] ECR page 1663, paragraph 173.

[13] See in this respect paragraph 108 of the judgment in *Anic Partecipazioni* cited in the previous note and Case C-277/87 *Sandoz Prodotti* [1990] ECR I-45.

[14] See in this respect e.g. Case 14/68 *Walt Wilhelm* [1969] ECR 1, and more recently Case T-203/01 *Michelin (II)* [2003] ECR II -[4071], paragraph 112.

15. The type of co-ordination of behaviour or collusion between undertakings falling within the scope of Article 81(1) is that where at least one undertaking vis-à-vis another undertaking undertakes to adopt a certain conduct on the market or that as a result of contacts between them uncertainty as to their conduct on the market is eliminated or at least substantially reduced.[15] It follows that co-ordination can take the form of obligations that regulate the market conduct of at least one of the parties as well as of arrangements that influence the market conduct of at least one of the parties by causing a change in its incentives. It is not required that co-ordination is in the interest of all the undertakings concerned.[16] Co-ordination must also not necessarily be express. It can also be tacit. For an agreement to be capable of being regarded as having been concluded by tacit acceptance there must be an invitation from an undertaking to another undertaking, whether express or implied, to fulfil a goal jointly.[17] In certain circumstances an agreement may be inferred from and imputed to an ongoing commercial relationship between the parties.[18] However, the mere fact that a measure adopted by an undertaking falls within the context of on-going business relations is not sufficient.[19]

Notes

[15] See Joined Cases T-25/95 and others, *Cimenteries CBR* [2000] ECR II-491, paragraphs 1849 and 1852; and Joined Cases T-202/98 and others, *British Sugar* [2001] ECR II-2035, paragraphs 58 to 60.

[16] See to that effect Case C-453/99 *Courage v Crehan* [2001] ECR I-6297, and paragraph 3444 of the judgment in *Cimenteries CBR* cited in the previous note.

[17] See in this respect Joined Cases C-2/01 P and C-3/01 P *Bundesverband der Arzneimittel-Importeure* [2004] ECR I-[23], paragraph 102.

[18] See e.g. Joined Cases 25/84 and 26/84 *Ford* [1985] ECR 2725.

[19] See in this respect paragraph 141 of the judgment in *Bundesverband der Arzneimittel-Importeure* cited in note [17].

16. Agreements between undertakings are caught by the prohibition rule of Article 81(1) when they are likely to have an appreciable adverse impact on the parameters of competition on the market, such as price, output, product quality, product variety and innovation. Agreements can have this effect by appreciably reducing rivalry between the parties to the agreement or between them and third parties.

2.2.2. The basic principles for assessing agreements under Article 81(1)

17. The assessment of whether an agreement is restrictive of competition must be made within the actual context in which competition would occur in the absence of the agreement with its alleged restrictions.[20] In making this assessment it is necessary to take account of the likely impact of the agreement on inter-brand competition (i.e. competition between suppliers of competing brands) and on intra-brand competition (i.e. competition between distributors of the same brand). Article 81(1) prohibits restrictions of both inter-brand competition and intra-brand competition.[21]

Notes

[20] See Case 56/65 *Société Technique Minière* [1966] ECR 337, and paragraph 76 of the judgment in *John Deere*, cited in note 9.

[21] See in this respect e.g. Joined Cases 56/64 and 58/66 *Consten and Grundig* [1966] ECR 429.

Commentary

para 17: F&N: 3.142

18. For the purpose of assessing whether an agreement or its individual parts may restrict inter-brand competition and/or intra-brand competition it needs to be considered how and to what extent the agreement affects or is likely to affect competition on the market. The following two questions provide a useful framework for making this assessment. The first question relates to the impact of the agreement on inter-brand competition while the second question relates to the impact of the agreement on intra-brand competition. As restraints may be capable of affecting both inter-brand competition and intra-brand competition at the same time, it may be necessary to analyse a restraint in light of both questions before it can be concluded whether or not competition is restricted within the meaning of Article 81(1):

    (1) Does the agreement restrict actual or potential competition that would have existed without the agreement? If so, the agreement may be caught by Article 81(1). In making this assessment it is necessary to take into account competition between the parties and competition from third parties. For instance, where two undertakings established in different Member States undertake not to sell products in each other's home markets, (potential) competition that existed prior to the agreement is restricted. Similarly, where a supplier imposes obligations on his distributors not to sell competing products and these obligations foreclose third party access to the market, actual or potential competition that would have existed in the absence of the agreement is restricted. In assessing whether the parties to an agreement are actual or potential competitors the economic and legal context must be taken into account. For instance, if due to the financial risks involved and the technical capabilities of the parties it is unlikely on the basis of objective factors that each party would be able to carry out on its own the activities covered by the agreement the parties are deemed to be non-competitors in respect of that activity.[22] It is for the parties to bring forward evidence to that effect.

    (2) Does the agreement restrict actual or potential competition that would have existed in the absence of the contractual restraint(s)? If so, the agreement may be caught by Article 81(1). For instance, where a supplier restricts its distributors from competing with each other, (potential) competition that could have existed between the distributors absent the restraints is restricted. Such restrictions include resale price maintenance and territorial or customer sales restrictions between distributors. However, certain restraints may in certain cases not be caught by Article 81(1) when the restraint is objectively necessary for the existence of an agreement of that type or that nature.[23] Such exclusion of the application of Article 81(1) can only be made on the basis of objective factors external to the parties themselves and not the subjective views and characteristics of the parties. The question is not whether the parties in their particular situation would not have accepted to conclude a less restrictive agreement, but whether given the nature of the agreement and the characteristics of the market a less restrictive agreement would not have been concluded by undertakings in a similar setting. For instance, territorial restraints in an agreement between a supplier and a distributor may for a certain period of time fall outside Article 81(1), if the restraints are objectively necessary in order for the distributor to penetrate a new market.[24] Similarly, a prohibition imposed on all distributors not to sell to certain categories of end users may not be restrictive of competition if such restraint is objectively necessary for reasons of safety or health related to the dangerous nature of the product in question. Claims that in the absence of a restraint the supplier would have resorted to vertical integration are not sufficient. Decisions on whether or not to vertically integrate depend on a broad range of complex economic factors, a number of which are internal to the undertaking concerned.

Notes

[22] See in this respect e.g. Commission Decision in *Elopak/Metal Box–Odin* (OJ 1990 L 209, p. 15) and in *TPS* (OJ 1999 L 90, p. 6).

[23] See in this respect the judgment in *Société Technique Minière* cited in note 20 and Case 258/78 *Nungesser* [1982] ECR 2015.

[24] See rule 10 in paragraph 119 of the Guidelines on vertical restraints cited in note above, according to which *inter alia* passive sales restrictions — a hardcore restraint — are held to fall outside Article 81(1) for a period of 2 years when the restraint is linked to opening up new product or geographic markets.

Commentary

para 18: F&N: 3.295, 9.57

para 18(1): F&N: 3.295, 3.298, 3.437
para 18(2): F&N: 3.217, 3.298, 3.300, 3.301, 3.302, 3.303

19. In the application of the analytical framework set out in the previous paragraph it must be taken into account that Article 81(1) distinguishes between those agreements that have a restriction of competition as their object and those agreements that have a restriction of competition as their effect. An agreement or contractual restraint is only prohibited by Article 81(1) if its object or effect is to restrict inter-brand competition and/or intra-brand competition.

20. The distinction between restrictions by object and restrictions by effect is important. Once it has been established that an agreement has as its object the restriction of competition, there is no need to take account of its concrete effects.[25] In other words, for the purpose of applying Article 81(1) no actual anti-competitive effects need to be demonstrated where the agreement has a restriction of competition as its object. Article 81(3), on the other hand, does not distinguish between agreements that restrict competition by object and agreements that restrict competition by effect. Article 81(3) applies to all agreements that fulfil the four conditions contained therein.[26]

Notes

[25] See e.g. paragraph 99 of the judgment in *Anic Partecipazioni* cited in note 12.
[26] See paragraph 46 below.

21. Restrictions of competition *by object* are those that by their very nature have the potential of restricting competition. These are restrictions which in light of the objectives pursued by the Community competition rules have such a high potential of negative effects on competition that it is unnecessary for the purposes of applying Article 81(1) to demonstrate any actual effects on the market. This presumption is based on the serious nature of the restriction and on experience showing that restrictions of competition by object are likely to produce negative effects on the market and to jeopardise the objectives pursued by the Community competition rules. Restrictions by object such as price fixing and market sharing reduce output and raise prices, leading to a misallocation of resources, because goods and services demanded by customers are not produced. They also lead to a reduction in consumer welfare, because consumers have to pay higher prices for the goods and services in question.

Commentary
para 21: F&N: 3.153, 3.159

22. The assessment of whether or not an agreement has as its object the restriction of competition is based on a number of factors. These factors include, in particular, the content of the agreement and the objective aims pursued by it. It may also be necessary to consider the context in which it is (to be) applied and the actual conduct and behaviour of the parties on the market.[27] In other words, an examination of the facts underlying the agreement and the specific circumstances in which it operates may be required before it can be concluded whether a particular restriction constitutes a restriction of competition by object. The way in which an agreement is actually implemented may reveal a restriction by object even where the formal agreement does not contain an express provision to that effect. Evidence of subjective intent on the part of the parties to restrict competition is a relevant factor but not a necessary condition.

Notes

[27] See Joined Cases 29/83 and 30/83 *CRAM and Rheinzink* [1984] ECR 1679, paragraph 26, and Joined Cases 96/82 and others, *ANSEAU-NAVEWA* [1983] ECR 3369, paragraphs 23–25.

Commentary
para 22: F&N: 3.146, 3.153, 3.154, 9.45

23. Non-exhaustive guidance on what constitutes restrictions by object can be found in Commission block exemption regulations, guidelines and notices. Restrictions that are black-listed in block exemptions or identified as hardcore restrictions in guidelines and notices are generally considered by the Commission to constitute restrictions by object. In the case of horizontal agreements restrictions of competition by object include price fixing, output limitation and sharing

of markets and customers.[28] As regards vertical agreements the category of restrictions by object includes, in particular, fixed and minimum resale price maintenance and restrictions providing absolute territorial protection, including restrictions on passive sales.[29]

Notes

[28] See the Guidelines on horizontal cooperation agreements, cited in note, paragraph 25, and Article 5 of Commission Regulation 2658/2000 on the application of Article 81(3) of the Treaty to categories of specialisation agreements (OJ L 304, 5.12.2000, p. 3).

[29] See Article 4 Commission Regulation 2790/1999 on the application of Article 81(3) of the Treaty to categories of vertical agreements and concerted practices (OJ L 336, 29.12.1999, p. 21) and the Guidelines on Vertical Restraints, cited in note, paragraph 46 et seq. See also Case 279/87 *Tipp-Ex* [1990] ECR I-261, and Case T-62/98 *Volkswagen v Commission* [2000] ECR II-2707, paragraph 178.

Commentary

para 23: F&N: 9.127

24. If an agreement is not restrictive of competition by object it must be examined whether it has restrictive effects on competition. Account must be taken of both actual and potential effects.[30] In other words the agreement must have likely anti-competitive effects. In the case of restrictions of competition by effect there is no presumption of anti-competitive effects. For an agreement to be restrictive by effect it must affect actual or potential competition to such an extent that on the relevant market negative effects on prices, output, innovation or the variety or quality of goods and services can be expected with a reasonable degree of probability.[31] Such negative effects must be appreciable. The prohibition rule of Article 81(1) does not apply when the identified anti-competitive effects are insignificant.[32] This test reflects the economic approach which the Commission is applying. The prohibition of Article 81(1) only applies where on the basis of proper market analysis it can be concluded that the agreement has likely anti-competitive effects on the market.[33] It is insufficient for such a finding that the market shares of the parties exceed the thresholds set out in the Commission's de minimis notice.[34] Agreements falling within safe harbours of block exemption regulations may be caught by Article 81(1) but this is not necessarily so. Moreover, the fact that due to the market shares of the parties, an agreement falls outside the safe harbour of a block exemption is in itself an insufficient basis for finding that the agreement is caught by Article 81(1) or that it does not fulfil the conditions of Article 81(3). Individual assessment of the likely effects produced by the agreement is required.

Notes

[30] See paragraph 77 of the judgment in *John Deere* cited in note 9.

[31] It is not sufficient in itself that the agreement restricts the freedom of action of one or more of the parties, see paragraphs 76 and 77 of the judgment in *Métropole television (M6)* cited in note 10. This is in line with the fact that the object of Article 81 is to protect competition on the market for the benefit of consumers.

[32] See e.g. Case 5/69 *Völk* [1969] ECR 295, paragraph 7. Guidance on the issue of appreciability can be found in the Commission Notice on agreements of minor importance which do not appreciably restrict competition under Article 81(1) of the Treaty (OJ C 368, 22.12.2001, p. 13) The notice defines appreciability in a negative way. Agreements, which fall outside the scope of the de minimis notice, do not necessarily have appreciable restrictive effects. An individual assessment is required.

[33] See in this respect Joined Cases T-374/94 and others, *European Night Services* [1998] ECR II-3141.

[34] See note 32.

Commentary

para 24: F&N: 2.45, 3.136, 3.294, 3.402, 9.56, 13.92

25. Negative effects on competition within the relevant market are likely to occur when the parties individually or jointly have or obtain some degree of market power and the agreement contributes to the creation, maintenance or strengthening of that market power or allows the parties to exploit such market power. Market power is the ability to maintain prices above competitive levels for a significant period of time or to maintain output in terms of product quantities, product quality and variety or innovation below competitive levels for a significant period of time. In markets with high fixed costs undertakings must price significantly above their marginal costs of production in order to ensure a competitive return on their investment. The fact that undertakings price above their marginal costs is therefore not in itself a sign that competition in

the market is not functioning well and that undertakings have market power that allows them to price above the competitive level. It is when competitive constraints are insufficient to maintain prices and output at competitive levels that undertakings have market power within the meaning of Article 81(1).

Commentary
para 25: F&N: 3.307

26. The creation, maintenance or strengthening of market power can result from a restriction of competition between the parties to the agreement. It can also result from a restriction of competition between any one of the parties and third parties, e.g. because the agreement leads to foreclosure of competitors or because it raises competitors' costs, limiting their capacity to compete effectively with the contracting parties. Market power is a question of degree. The degree of market power normally required for the finding of an infringement under Article 81(1) in the case of agreements that are restrictive of competition by effect is less than the degree of market power required for a finding of dominance under Article 82.

27. For the purposes of analysing the restrictive effects of an agreement it is normally necessary to define the relevant market.[35] It is normally also necessary to examine and assess, *inter alia*, the nature of the products, the market position of the parties, the market position of competitors, the market position of buyers, the existence of potential competitors and the level of entry barriers. In some cases, however, it may be possible to show anti-competitive effects directly by analysing the conduct of the parties to the agreement on the market. It may for example be possible to ascertain that an agreement has led to price increases. The guidelines on horizontal cooperation agreements and on vertical restraints set out a detailed framework for analysing the competitive impact of various types of horizontal and vertical agreements under Article 81(1).[36]

Notes

[35] See in this respect Commission notice on the definition of the relevant market for the purposes of Community competition law (OJ C 372, 9.12.1997, p. 1).

[36] For the reference in the OJ see note 5.

Commentary
para 27: F&N: 3.307

2.2.3. Ancillary restraints

28. Paragraph 18 above sets out a framework for analysing the impact of an agreement and its individual restrictions on inter-brand competition and intra-brand competition. If on the basis of those principles it is concluded that the main transaction covered by the agreement is not restrictive of competition, it becomes relevant to examine whether individual restraints contained in the agreement are also compatible with Article 81(1) because they are ancillary to the main non-restrictive transaction.

29. In Community competition law the concept of ancillary restraints covers any alleged restriction of competition which is directly related and necessary to the implementation of a main non-restrictive transaction and proportionate to it.[37] If an agreement in its main parts, for instance a distribution agreement or a joint venture, does not have as its object or effect the restriction of competition, then restrictions, which are directly related to and necessary for the implementation of that transaction, also fall outside Article 81(1).[38] These related restrictions are called ancillary restraints. A restriction is directly related to the main transaction if it is subordinate to the implementation of that transaction and is inseparably linked to it. The test of necessity implies that the restriction must be objectively necessary for the implementation of the main transaction and be proportionate to it. It follows that the ancillary restraints test is similar to the test set out in paragraph 18(2) above. However, the ancillary restraints test applies in all cases where the main transaction is not restrictive of competition.[39] It is not limited to determining the impact of the agreement on intra-brand competition.

Notes

[37] See paragraph 104 of the judgment in *Métropole télévision (M6) and others*, cited in note 10.

Part C Substantive
Antitrust Matters

[38] See e.g. Case C-399/93 *Luttikhuis* [1995] ECR I-4515, paragraphs 12 to 14.
[39] See in this respect paragraphs 118 et seq. of the *Métropole television* judgment cited in note 10.

Commentary
para 29: F&N: 3.217, 3.300, 3.302

30. The application of the ancillary restraint concept must be distinguished from the application of the defence under Article 81(3) which relates to certain economic benefits produced by restrictive agreements and which are balanced against the restrictive effects of the agreements. The application of the ancillary restraint concept does not involve any weighing of pro-competitive and anti-competitive effects. Such balancing is reserved for Article 81(3).[40]

Notes
[40] See paragraph 107 of the judgment in *Métropole télévision* judgement cited in note 10.

Commentary
para 30: F&N: 3.302

31. The assessment of ancillary restraints is limited to determining whether, in the specific context of the main non-restrictive transaction or activity, a particular restriction is necessary for the implementation of that transaction or activity and proportionate to it. If on the basis of objective factors it can be concluded that without the restriction the main non-restrictive transaction would be difficult or impossible to implement, the restriction may be regarded as objectively necessary for its implementation and proportionate to it.[41] If, for example, the main object of a franchise agreement does not restrict competition, then restrictions, which are necessary for the proper functioning of the agreement, such as obligations aimed at protecting the uniformity and reputation of the franchise system, also fall outside Article 81(1).[42] Similarly, if a joint venture is not in itself restrictive of competition, then restrictions that are necessary for the functioning of the agreement are deemed to be ancillary to the main transaction and are therefore not caught by Article 81(1). For instance in TPS[43] the Commission concluded that an obligation on the parties not to be involved in companies engaged in distribution and marketing of television programmes by satellite was ancillary to the creation of the joint venture during the initial phase. The restriction was therefore deemed to fall outside Article 81(1) for a period of three years. In arriving at this conclusion the Commission took account of the heavy investments and commercial risks involved in entering the market for pay-television.

Notes
[41] See e.g. Commission Decision in *Elopak/Metal Box–Odin* cited in note 22.
[42] See Case 161/84 *Pronuptia* [1986] ECR 353.
[43] See note 22. The decision was upheld by the Court of First Instance in the judgment in *Métropole télévision (M6)* cited in note 10.

Commentary
para 31: F&N: 3.302, 3.316

2.3. The exception rule of Article 81(3)

32. The assessment of restrictions by object and effect under Article 81(1) is only one side of the analysis. The other side, which is reflected in Article 81(3), is the assessment of the positive economic effects of restrictive agreements.

Commentary
para 32: F&N: 9.56

33. The aim of the Community competition rules is to protect competition on the market as a means of enhancing consumer welfare and of ensuring an efficient allocation of resources. Agreements that restrict competition may at the same time have pro-competitive effects by way of efficiency gains.[44] Efficiencies may create additional value by lowering the cost of producing an output, improving the quality of the product or creating a new product. When the pro-competitive

effects of an agreement outweigh its anti-competitive effects the agreement is on balance pro-competitive and compatible with the objectives of the Community competition rules. The net effect of such agreements is to promote the very essence of the competitive process, namely to win customers by offering better products or better prices than those offered by rivals. This analytical framework is reflected in Article 81(1) and Article 81(3). The latter provision expressly acknowledges that restrictive agreements may generate objective economic benefits so as to outweigh the negative effects of the restriction of competition.[45]

Notes

[44] Cost savings and other gains to the parties that arise from the mere exercise of market power do not give rise to objective benefits and cannot be taken into account, cf. paragraph 49 below.

[45] See the judgment in *Consten and Grundig*, cited in note 21.

34. The application of the exception rule of Article 81(3) is subject to four cumulative conditions, two positive and two negative:
    (a) The agreement must contribute to improving the production or distribution of goods or contribute to promoting technical or economic progress,
    (b) Consumers must receive a fair share of the resulting benefits,
    (c) The restrictions must be indispensable to the attainment of these objectives, and finally
    (d) The agreement must not afford the parties the possibility of eliminating competition in respect of a substantial part of the products in question. When these four conditions are fulfilled the agreement enhances competition within the relevant market, because it leads the undertakings concerned to offer cheaper or better products to consumers, compensating the latter for the adverse effects of the restrictions of competition.

35. Article 81(3) can be applied either to individual agreements or to categories of agreements by way of a block exemption regulation. When an agreement is covered by a block exemption the parties to the restrictive agreement are relieved of their burden under Article 2 of Regulation 1/2003 of showing that their individual agreement satisfies each of the conditions of Article 81(3). They only have to prove that the restrictive agreement benefits from a block exemption. The application of Article 81(3) to categories of agreements by way of block exemption regulation is based on the presumption that restrictive agreements that fall within their scope[46] fulfil each of the four conditions laid down in Article 81(3).

Notes

[46] The fact that an agreement is block exempted does not in itself indicate that the individual agreement is caught by Article 81(1).

Commentary
para 35: F&N: 3.454

36. If in an individual case the agreement is caught by Article 81(1) and the conditions of Article 81(3) are not fulfilled the block exemption may be withdrawn. According to Article 29(1) of Regulation 1/2003 the Commission is empowered to withdraw the benefit of a block exemption when it finds that in a particular case an agreement covered by a block exemption regulation has certain effects which are incompatible with Article 81(3) of the Treaty. Pursuant to Article 29(2) of Regulation 1/2003 a competition authority of a Member State may also withdraw the benefit of a Commission block exemption regulation in respect of its territory (or part of its territory), if this territory has all the characteristics of a distinct geographic market. In the case of withdrawal it is for the competition authorities concerned to demonstrate that the agreement infringes Article 81(1) and that it does not fulfil the conditions of Article 81(3).

37. The courts of the Member States have no power to withdraw the benefit of block exemption regulations. Moreover, in their application of block exemption regulations Member State courts may not modify their scope by extending their sphere of application to agreements not covered by the block exemption regulation in question.[47] Outside the scope of block exemption regulations Member State courts have the power to apply Article 81 in full (cf. Article 6 of Regulation 1/2003).

Notes
[47] See e.g. Case C-234/89 *Delimitis* [1991] ECR I-935, paragraph 46.

3. The Application of the Four Conditions of Article 81(3)

38. The remainder of these guidelines will consider each of the four conditions of Article 81(3).[48] Given that these four conditions are cumulative[49] it is unnecessary to examine any remaining conditions once it is found that one of the conditions of Article 81(3) is not fulfilled. In individual cases it may therefore be appropriate to consider the four conditions in a different order.

Notes
[48] Article 36(4) of Regulation 1/2003 has, *inter alia*, repealed Article 5 of Regulation 1017/68 applying rules of competition to transport by rail, road and inland waterway. However, the Commission's case practice adopted under Regulation 1017/68 remains relevant for the purposes of applying Article 81(3) in the inland transport sector.
[49] See paragraph 42 below.

39. For the purposes of these guidelines it is considered appropriate to invert the order of the second and the third condition and thus deal with the issue of indispensability before the issue of pass-on to consumers. The analysis of pass-on requires a balancing of the negative and positive effects of an agreement on consumers. This analysis should not include the effects of any restrictions, which already fail the indispensability test and which for that reason are prohibited by Article 81.

3.1. General principles

40. Article 81(3) of the Treaty only becomes relevant when an agreement between undertakings restricts competition within the meaning of Article 81(1). In the case of non-restrictive agreements there is no need to examine any benefits generated by the agreement.

41. Where in an individual case a restriction of competition within the meaning of Article 81(1) has been proven, Article 81(3) can be invoked as a defence. According to Article 2 of Regulation 1/2003 the burden of proof under Article 81(3) rests on the undertaking(s) invoking the benefit of the exception rule. Where the conditions of Article 81(3) are not satisfied the agreement is null and void, cf. Article 81(2). However, such automatic nullity only applies to those parts of the agreement that are incompatible with Article 81, provided that such parts are severable from the agreement as a whole.[50] If only part of the agreement is null and void, it is for the applicable national law to determine the consequences thereof for the remaining part of the agreement.[51]

Notes
[50] See the judgment in *Société Technique Minière* cited in note 20.
[51] See in this respect Case 319/82 *Kerpen & Kerpen* [1983] ECR 4173, paragraphs 11 and 12.

42. According to settled case law the four conditions of Article 81(3) are cumulative,[52] i.e. they must all be fulfilled for the exception rule to be applicable. If they are not, the application of the exception rule of Article 81(3) must be refused.[53] The four conditions of Article 81(3) are also exhaustive. When they are met the exception is applicable and may not be made dependant on any other condition. Goals pursued by other Treaty provisions can be taken into account to the extent that they can be subsumed under the four conditions of Article 81(3).[54]

Notes
[52] See e.g. Case T-185/00 and others, *Métropole télévision SA (M6)* [2002] ECR II-3805, paragraph 86, Case T-17/93 *Matra* [1994] ECR II-595, paragraph 85; and Joined Cases 43/82 and 63/82 *VBVB and VBBB* [1984] ECR 19, paragraph 61.
[53] See Case T-213/00 *CMA CGM and others* [2003] ECR II –[913], paragraph 226.
[54] See to that effect implicitly paragraph 139 of the *Matra* judgment cited in note 52 and Case 26/76 *Metro (I)* [1977] ECR 1875, paragraph 43.

Commentary
para 42: **B&C:** 3.021, 3.043 **F&N:** 3.404, 3.426, 12.105

43. The assessment under Article 81(3) of benefits flowing from restrictive agreements is in principle made within the confines of each relevant market to which the agreement relates. The Community competition rules have as their objective the protection of competition on the market and cannot be detached from this objective. Moreover, the condition that consumers[55] must receive a fair share of the benefits implies in general that efficiencies generated by the restrictive agreement within a relevant market must be sufficient to outweigh the anti-competitive effects produced by the agreement within that same relevant market.[56] Negative effects on consumers in one geographic market or product market cannot normally be balanced against and compensated by positive effects for consumers in another unrelated geographic market or product market. However, where two markets are related, efficiencies achieved on separate markets can be taken into account provided that the group of consumers affected by the restriction and benefiting from the efficiency gains are substantially the same.[57] Indeed, in some cases only consumers in a downstream market are affected by the agreement in which case the impact of the agreement on such consumers must be assessed. This is for instance so in the case of purchasing agreements.[58]

Notes

[55] As to the concept of consumers see paragraph 84 below where it is stated that consumers are the customers of the parties and subsequent buyers. The parties themselves are not "consumers" for the purposes of Article 81(3).

[56] The test is market specific, see to that effect Case T-131/99 *Shaw* [2002] ECR II-2023, paragraph 163, where the Court of First Instance held that the assessment under Article 81(3) had to be made within the same analytical framework as that used for assessing the restrictive effects, and Case C-360/92 P *Publishers Association* [1995] ECR I-23, paragraph 29, where in a case where the relevant market was wider than national the Court of Justice held that in the application of Article 81(3) it was not correct only to consider the effects on the national territory.

[57] In Case T-86/95 *Compagnie Générale Maritime and others* [2002] ECR II-1011, paragraphs 343 to 345, the Court of First Instance held that Article 81(3) does not require that the benefits are linked to a specific market and that in appropriate cases regard must be had to benefits "for every other market on which the agreement in question might have beneficial effects, and even, in a more general sense, for any service the quality or efficiency of which might be improved by the existence of that agreement". Importantly, however, in this case the affected group of consumers was the same. The case concerned intermodal transport services encompassing a bundle of, *inter alia*, inland and maritime transportation provided to shipping companies across the Community. The restrictions related to inland transport services, which were held to constitute a separate market, whereas the benefits were claimed to occur in relation to maritime transport services. Both services were demanded by shippers requiring intermodal transport services between northern Europe and South-East and East Asia. The judgment in *CMA CGM*, cited in note 53 above, also concerned a situation where the agreement, while covering several distinct services, affected the same group of consumers, namely shippers of containerised cargo between northern Europe and the Far East. Under the agreement the parties fixed charges and surcharges relating to inland transport services, port services and maritime transport services. The Court of First Instance held (cf. paragraphs 226 to 228) that in the circumstances of the case there was no need to define relevant markets for the purpose of applying Article 81(3). The agreement was restrictive of competition by its very object and there were no benefits for consumers.

[58] See paragraphs 126 and 132 of the Guidelines on horizontal co-operation agreements cited in note 5 above.

Commentary
para 43: **B&C:** 3.022, 3.039 **F&N:** 3.409, 14.30

44. The assessment of restrictive agreements under Article 81(3) is made within the actual context in which they occur[59] and on the basis of the facts existing at any given point in time. The assessment is sensitive to material changes in the facts. The exception rule of Article 81(3) applies as long as the four conditions are fulfilled and ceases to apply when that is no longer the case.[60] When applying Article 81(3) in accordance with these principles it is necessary to take into account the initial sunk investments made by any of the parties and the time needed and the restraints required to commit and recoup an efficiency enhancing investment. Article 81 cannot be applied without taking due account of such *ex ante* investment. The risk facing the parties and the sunk investment that must be committed to implement the agreement can thus lead to the agreement falling outside Article 81(1) or fulfilling the conditions of Article 81(3), as the case may be, for the period of time required to recoup the investment.

Notes

[59] See the *Ford* judgment cited in note 18.

[60] See in this respect for example Commission Decision in *TPS* (OJ L 90, 2.4.1999, p. 6). Similarly, the prohibition of Article 81(1) also only applies as long as the agreement has a restrictive object or restrictive effects.

Commentary
para 44: B&C: 3.017 F&N: 2.45, 3.413, 12.281

45. In some cases the restrictive agreement is an irreversible event. Once the restrictive agreement has been implemented the *ex ante* situation cannot be re-established. In such cases the assessment must be made exclusively on the basis of the facts pertaining at the time of implementation. For instance, in the case of a research and development agreement whereby each party agrees to abandon its respective research project and pool its capabilities with those of another party, it may from an objective point of view be technically and economically impossible to revive a project once it has been abandoned. The assessment of the anti-competitive and pro-competitive effects of the agreement to abandon the individual research projects must therefore be made as of the time of the completion of its implementation. If at that point in time the agreement is compatible with Article 81, for instance because a sufficient number of third parties have competing research and development projects, the parties' agreement to abandon their individual projects remains compatible with Article 81, even if at a later point in time the third party projects fail. However, the prohibition of Article 81 may apply to other parts of the agreement in respect of which the issue of irreversibility does not arise. If for example in addition to joint research and development, the agreement provides for joint exploitation, Article 81 may apply to this part of the agreement if due to subsequent market developments the agreement becomes restrictive of competition and does not (any longer) satisfy the conditions of Article 81(3) taking due account of *ex ante* sunk investments, cf. the previous paragraph.

Commentary
para 45: B&C: 3.017 F&N: 3.414

46. Article 81(3) does not exclude *a priori* certain types of agreements from its scope. As a matter of principle all restrictive agreements that fulfil the four conditions of Article 81(3) are covered by the exception rule.[61] However, severe restrictions of competition are unlikely to fulfil the conditions of Article 81(3). Such restrictions are usually black-listed in block exemption regulations or identified as hardcore restrictions in Commission guidelines and notices. Agreements of this nature generally fail (at least) the two first conditions of Article 81(3). They neither create objective economic benefits[62] nor do they benefit consumers.[63] For example, a horizontal agreement to fix prices limits output leading to misallocation of resources. It also transfers value from consumers to producers, since it leads to higher prices without producing any countervailing value to consumers within the relevant market. Moreover, these types of agreements generally also fail the indispensability test under the third condition.[64]

Notes
[61] See paragraph 85 of the *Matra* judgment cited in note 52.
[62] As to this requirement see paragraph 49 below.
[63] See e.g. Case T-29/92 *Vereniging van Samenwerkende Prijsregelende Organisaties in de Bouwnijverheid (SPO)* [1995] ECR II-289.
[64] See e.g. Case 258/78 *Nungesser* [1982] ECR 2015, paragraph 77, concerning absolute territorial protection.

Commentary
para 46: B&C: 3.013 F&N: 3.140, 3.405, 3.418, 14.102

47. Any claim that restrictive agreements are justified because they aim at ensuring fair conditions of competition on the market is by nature unfounded and must be discarded.[65] The purpose of Article 81 is to protect effective competition by ensuring that markets remain open and competitive. The protection of fair conditions of competition is a task for the legislator in compliance with Community law obligations[66] and not for undertakings to regulate themselves.

Notes
[65] See in this respect e.g. the judgment in *SPO* cited in note 63.
[66] National measures must, inter alia, comply with the Treaty rules on free movement of goods, services, persons and capital.

3.2. First condition of Article 81(3): Efficiency gains

3.2.1. General remarks

48. According to the first condition of Article 81(3) the restrictive agreement must contribute to improving the production or distribution of goods or to promoting technical or economic progress. The provision refers expressly only to goods, but applies by analogy to services.

Commentary
para 48: B&C: 3.021, 3.026 **F&N:** 3.421

49. It follows from the case law of the Court of Justice that only objective benefits can be taken into account.[67] This means that efficiencies are not assessed from the subjective point of view of the parties.[68] Cost savings that arise from the mere exercise of market power by the parties cannot be taken into account. For instance, when companies agree to fix prices or share markets they reduce output and thereby production costs. Reduced competition may also lead to lower sales and marketing expenditures. Such cost reductions are a direct consequence of a reduction in output and value. The cost reductions in question do not produce any pro-competitive effects on the market. In particular, they do not lead to the creation of value through an integration of assets and activities. They merely allow the undertakings concerned to increase their profits and are therefore irrelevant from the point of view of Article 81(3).

Notes
[67] See e.g. the judgment in *Consten and Grundig* cited in note 21.
[68] See in this respect Commission Decision in *Van den Bergh Foods* (OJ 1998 L 246, p. 1).

Commentary
para 49: B&C: 3.020 **F&N:** 3.424

50. The purpose of the first condition of Article 81(3) is to define the types of efficiency gains that can be taken into account and be subject to the further tests of the second and third conditions of Article 81(3). The aim of the analysis is to ascertain what are the objective benefits created by the agreement and what is the economic importance of such efficiencies. Given that for Article 81(3) to apply the pro-competitive effects flowing from the agreement must outweigh its anti-competitive effects, it is necessary to verify what is the link between the agreement and the claimed efficiencies and what is the value of these efficiencies.

51. All efficiency claims must therefore be substantiated so that the following can be verified:
    (a) The *nature* of the claimed efficiencies;
    (b) The *link* between the agreement and the efficiencies;
    (c) The *likelihood* and *magnitude* of each claimed efficiency; and
    (d) *How* and *when* each claimed efficiency would be achieved.

52. Letter (a) allows the decision-maker to verify whether the claimed efficiencies are objective in nature, cf. paragraph 49 above.

53. Letter (b) allows the decision-maker to verify whether there is a sufficient causal link between the restrictive agreement and the claimed efficiencies. This condition normally requires that the efficiencies result from the economic activity that forms the object of the agreement. Such activities may, for example, take the form of distribution, licensing of technology, joint production or joint research and development. To the extent, however, that an agreement has wider efficiency enhancing effects within the relevant market, for example because it leads to a reduction in industry wide costs, these additional benefits are also taken into account.

Commentary
para 53: F&N: 3.423, 3.432

54. The causal link between the agreement and the claimed efficiencies must normally also be direct.[69] Claims based on indirect effects are as a general rule too uncertain and too remote to be taken into account. A direct causal link exists for instance where a technology transfer agreement allows the licensees to produce new or improved products or a distribution agreement allows products to be distributed at lower cost or valuable services to be produced. An example of indirect effect would

be a case where it is claimed that a restrictive agreement allows the undertakings concerned to increase their profits, enabling them to invest more in research and development to the ultimate benefit of consumers. While there may be a link between profitability and research and development, this link is generally not sufficiently direct to be taken into account in the context of Article 81(3).

Notes

[69] See in this respect Commission Decision in *Glaxo Wellcome* (OJ 2001 L 302, p. 1).

Commentary
para 54: B&C: 3.024 F&N: 3.433

55. Letters (c) and (d) allow the decision-maker to verify the value of the claimed efficiencies, which in the context of the third condition of Article 81(3) must be balanced against the anti-competitive effects of the agreement, see paragraph 101 below. Given that Article 81(1) only applies in cases where the agreement has likely negative effects on competition and consumers (in the case of hardcore restrictions such effects are presumed) efficiency claims must be substantiated so that they can be verified. Unsubstantiated claims are rejected.

Commentary
para 55: F&N: 3.434

56. In the case of claimed cost efficiencies the undertakings invoking the benefit of Article 81(3) must as accurately as reasonably possible calculate or estimate the value of the efficiencies and describe in detail how the amount has been computed. They must also describe the method(s) by which the efficiencies have been or will be achieved. The data submitted must be verifiable so that there can be a sufficient degree of certainty that the efficiencies have materialised or are likely to materialise.

Commentary
para 56: F&N: 3.434

57. In the case of claimed efficiencies in the form of new or improved products and other non-cost based efficiencies, the undertakings claiming the benefit of Article 81(3) must describe and explain in detail what is the nature of the efficiencies and how and why they constitute an objective economic benefit.

Commentary
para 57: F&N: 3.434

58. In cases where the agreement has yet to be fully implemented the parties must substantiate any projections as to the date from which the efficiencies will become operational so as to have a significant positive impact in the market.

Commentary
para 58: F&N: 3.434

3.2.2. The different categories of efficiencies

59. The types of efficiencies listed in Article 81(3) are broad categories which are intended to cover all objective economic efficiencies. There is considerable overlap between the various categories mentioned in Article 81(3) and the same agreement may give rise to several kinds of efficiencies. It is therefore not appropriate to draw clear and firm distinctions between the various categories. For the purpose of these guidelines, a distinction is made between cost efficiencies and efficiencies of a qualitative nature whereby value is created in the form of new or improved products, greater product variety etc.

60. In general, efficiencies stem from an integration of economic activities whereby undertakings combine their assets to achieve what they could not achieve as efficiently on their own or whereby

they entrust another undertaking with tasks that can be performed more efficiently by that other undertaking.

Commentary
para 60: F&N: 3.423, 12.105

61. The research and development, production and distribution process may be viewed as a value chain that can be divided into a number of stages. At each stage of this chain an undertaking must make a choice between performing the activity itself, performing it together with (an)other undertaking(s) or outsourcing the activity entirely to (an)other undertaking(s).

Commentary
para 61: F&N: 3.423

62. In each case where the choice made involves cooperation on the market with another undertaking, an agreement within the meaning of Article 81(1) normally needs to be concluded. These agreements can be vertical, as is the case where the parties operate at different levels of the value chain or horizontal, as is the case where the firms operate at the same level of the value chain. Both categories of agreements may create efficiencies by allowing the undertakings in question to perform a particular task at lower cost or with higher added value for consumers. Such agreements may also contain or lead to restrictions of competition in which case the prohibition rule of Article 81(1) and the exception rule of Article 81(3) may become relevant.

63. The types of efficiencies mentioned in the following are only examples and are not intended to be exhaustive.

3.2.2.1. Cost efficiencies

64. Cost efficiencies flowing from agreements between undertakings can originate from a number of different sources. One very important source of cost savings is the development of new production technologies and methods. In general, it is when technological leaps are made that the greatest potential for cost savings is achieved. For instance, the introduction of the assembly line led to a very substantial reduction in the cost of producing motor vehicles.

Commentary
para 64: F&N: 3.428

65. Another very important source of efficiency is synergies resulting from an integration of existing assets. When the parties to an agreement combine their respective assets they may be able to attain a cost/output configuration that would not otherwise be possible. The combination of two existing technologies that have complementary strengths may reduce production costs or lead to the production of a higher quality product. For instance, it may be that the production assets of firm A generate a high output per hour but require a relatively high input of raw materials per unit of output, whereas the production assets of firm B generate lower output per hour but require a relatively lower input of raw materials per unit of output. Synergies are created if by establishing a production joint venture combining the production assets of A and B the parties can attain a high(er) level of output per hour with a low(er) input of raw materials per unit of output. Similarly, if one undertaking has optimised one part of the value chain and another undertaking has optimised another part of the value chain, the combination of their operations may lead to lower costs. Firm A may for instance have a highly automated production facility resulting in low production costs per unit whereas B has developed an efficient order processing system. The system allows production to be tailored to customer demand, ensuring timely delivery and reducing warehousing and obsolescence costs. By combining their assets A and B may be able to obtain cost reductions.

Commentary
para 65: F&N: 3.428

Part C Substantive Antitrust Matters

66. Cost efficiencies may also result from economies of scale, i.e. declining cost per unit of output as output increases. To give an example: investment in equipment and other assets often has to be made in indivisible blocks. If an undertaking cannot fully utilise a block, its average costs will be higher than if it could do so. For instance, the cost of operating a truck is virtually the same regardless of whether it is almost empty, half-full or full. Agreements whereby undertakings combine their logistics operations may allow them to increase the load factors and reduce the number of vehicles employed. Larger scale may also allow for better division of labour leading to lower unit costs. Firms may achieve economies of scale in respect of all parts of the value chain, including research and development, production, distribution and marketing. Learning economies constitute a related type of efficiency. As experience is gained in using a particular production process or in performing particular tasks, productivity may increase because the process is made to run more efficiently or because the task is performed more quickly.

67. Economies of scope are another source of cost efficiency, which occur when firms achieve cost savings by producing different products on the basis of the same input. Such efficiencies may arise from the fact that it is possible to use the same components and the same facilities and personnel to produce a variety of products. Similarly, economies of scope may arise in distribution when several types of goods are distributed in the same vehicles. For instance, a producer of frozen pizzas and a producer of frozen vegetables may obtain economies of scope by jointly distributing their products. Both groups of products must be distributed in refrigerated vehicles and it is likely that there are significant overlaps in terms of customers. By combining their operations the two producers may obtain lower distribution costs per distributed unit.

68. Efficiencies in the form of cost reductions can also follow from agreements that allow for better planning of production, reducing the need to hold expensive inventory and allowing for better capacity utilisation. Efficiencies of this nature may for example stem from the use of "just in time" purchasing, i.e. an obligation on a supplier of components to continuously supply the buyer according to its needs thereby avoiding the need for the buyer to maintain a significant stock of components which risks becoming obsolete. Cost savings may also result from agreements that allow the parties to rationalise production across their facilities.

3.2.2.2. Qualitative efficiencies

69. Agreements between undertakings may generate various efficiencies of a qualitative nature which are relevant to the application of Article 81(3). In a number of cases the main efficiency enhancing potential of the agreement is not cost reduction; it is quality improvements and other efficiencies of a qualitative nature. Depending on the individual case such efficiencies may therefore be of equal or greater importance than cost efficiencies.

Commentary
para 69: F&N: 3.429

---

70. Technical and technological advances form an essential and dynamic part of the economy, generating significant benefits in the form of new or improved goods and services. By cooperating undertakings may be able to create efficiencies that would not have been possible without the restrictive agreement or would have been possible only with substantial delay or at higher cost. Such efficiencies constitute an important source of economic benefits covered by the first condition of Article 81(3). Agreements capable of producing efficiencies of this nature include, in particular, research and development agreements. An example would be A and B creating a joint venture for the development and, if successful, joint production of a cell-based tyre. The puncture of one cell does not affect other cells, which means that there is no risk of collapse of the tyre in the event of a puncture. The tyre is thus safer than traditional tyres. It also means that there is no immediate need to change the tyre and thus to carry a spare. Both types of efficiencies constitute objective benefits within the meaning of the first condition of Article 81(3).

71. In the same way that the combination of complementary assets can give rise to cost savings, combinations of assets may also create synergies that create efficiencies of a qualitative nature. The combination of production assets may for instance lead to the production of higher quality products or products with novel features. This may for instance be the case for licence agreements,

and agreements providing for joint production of new or improved goods or services. Licence agreements may, in particular, ensure more rapid dissemination of new technology in the Community and enable the licensee(s) to make available new products or to employ new production techniques that lead to quality improvements. Joint production agreements may, in particular, allow new or improved products or services to be introduced on the market more quickly or at lower cost.[70] In the telecommunications sector, for example, cooperation agreements have been held to create efficiencies by making available more quickly new global services.[71] In the banking sector cooperation agreements that made available improved facilities for making crossborder payments have also been held to create efficiencies falling within the scope of the first condition of Article 81(3).[72]

Notes

[70] See e.g. Commission Decision in *GEAE/P&W* (OJ 2000 L 58, p. 16); in *British Interactive Broadcasting/Open* (OJ 1999 L 312, p. 1) and in *Asahi/Saint Gobain* (OJ 1994 L 354, page 87).
[71] See e.g. Commission Decision in *Atlas* (OJ 1996 L 239, p. 23), and in *Phoenix/Global One* (OJ 1996 L 239, p. 57).
[72] See e.g. Commission Decision in *Uniform Eurocheques* (OJ 1985 L 35, p. 43).

72. Distribution agreements may also give rise to qualitative efficiencies. Specialised distributors, for example, may be able to provide services that are better tailored to customer needs or to provide quicker delivery or better quality assurance throughout the distribution chain.[73]

Notes

[73] See e.g. Commission Decision in *Cégétel + 4* (OJ 1999 L 88, p. 26).

3.3. Third condition of Article 81(3): Indispensability of the restrictions

73. According to the third condition of Article 81(3) the restrictive agreement must not impose restrictions, which are not indispensable to the attainment of the efficiencies created by the agreement in question. This condition implies a two-fold test. First, the restrictive agreement as such must be reasonably necessary in order to achieve the efficiencies. Secondly, the individual restrictions of competition that flow from the agreement must also be reasonably necessary for the attainment of the efficiencies.

Commentary
para 73: F&N: 3.438

74. In the context of the third condition of Article 81(3) the decisive factor is whether or not the restrictive agreement and individual restrictions make it possible to perform the activity in question more efficiently than would likely have been the case in the absence of the agreement or the restriction concerned. The question is not wheth er in the absence of the restriction the agreement would not have been concluded, but whether more efficiencies are produced with the agreement or restriction than in the absence of the agreement or restriction.[74]

Notes

[74] As to the former question, which may be relevant in the context of Article 81(1), see paragraph 18 above.

Commentary
para 74: F&N: 3.437

75. The first test contained in the third condition of Article 81(3) requires that the efficiencies be specific to the agreement in question in the sense that there are no other economically practicable and less restrictive means of achieving the efficiencies. In making this latter assessment the market conditions and business realities facing the parties to the agreement must be taken into account. Undertakings invoking the benefit of Article 81(3) are not required to consider hypothetical or theoretical alternatives. The Commission will not second guess the business judgment of the parties. It will only intervene where it is reasonably clear that there are realistic and attainable alternatives. The parties must only explain and demonstrate why such seemingly realistic and significantly less restrictive alternatives to the agreement would be significantly less efficient.

Commentary
para 75: **B&C**: 3.059 **F&N**: 3.440

76. It is particularly relevant to examine whether, having due regard to the circumstances of the individual case, the parties could have achieved the efficiencies by means of another less restrictive type of agreement and, if so, when they would likely be able to obtain the efficiencies. It may also be necessary to examine whether the parties could have achieved the efficiencies on their own. For instance, where the claimed efficiencies take the form of cost reductions resulting from economies of scale or scope the undertakings concerned must explain and substantiate why the same efficiencies would not be likely to be attained through internal growth and price competition. In making this assessment it is relevant to consider, *inter alia*, what is the minimum efficient scale on the market concerned. The minimum efficient scale is the level of output required to minimise average cost and exhaust economies of scale.[75] The larger the minimum efficient scale compared to the current size of either of the parties to the agreement, the more likely it is that the efficiencies will be deemed to be specific to the agreement. In the case of agreements that produce substantial synergies through the combination of complementary assets and capabilities the very nature of the efficiencies give rise to a presumption that the agreement is necessary to attain them.

Notes

[75] Scale economies are normally exhausted at a certain point. Thereafter average costs will stabilise and eventually rise due to, for example, capacity constraints and bottlenecks.

Commentary
para 76: **B&C**: 3.059, 7.061

77. These principles can be illustrated by the following hypothetical example: A and B combine within a joint venture their respective production technologies to achieve higher output and lower raw material consumption. The joint venture is granted an exclusive licence to their respective production technologies. The parties transfer their existing production facilities to the joint venture. They also transfer key staff in order to ensure that existing learning economies can be exploited and further developed. It is estimated that these economies will reduce production costs by a further 5%. The output of the joint venture is sold independently by A and B. In this case the indispensability condition necessitates an assessment of whether or not the benefits could be substantially achieved by means of a licence agreement, which would be likely to be less restrictive because A and B would continue to produce independently. In the circumstances described this is unlikely to be the case since under a licence agreement the parties would not be able to benefit in the same seamless and continued way from their respective experience in operating the two technologies, resulting in significant learning economies.

Commentary
para 77: **B&C**: 7.061

78. Once it is found that the agreement in question is necessary in order to produce the efficiencies, the indispensability of each restriction of competition flowing from the agreement must be assessed. In this context it must be assessed whether individual restrictions are reasonably necessary in order to produce the efficiencies. The parties to the agreement must substantiate their claim with regard to both the nature of the restriction and its intensity.

79. A restriction is indispensable if its absence would eliminate or significantly reduce the efficiencies that follow from the agreement or make it significantly less likely that they will materialise. The assessment of alternative solutions must take into account the actual and potential improvement in the field of competition by the elimination of a particular restriction or the application of a less restrictive alternative. The more restrictive the restraint the stricter the test under the third condition.[76] Restrictions that are black listed in block exemption regulations or identified as hardcore restrictions in Commission guidelines and notices are unlikely to be considered indispensable.

Notes

[76] See in this respect paragraphs 392 to 395 of the judgment in *Compagnie Générale Maritime* cited in note 57.

Commentary
para 79: **B&C:** 3.060, 3.061 **F&N:** 3.441

80. The assessment of indispensability is made within the actual context in which the agreement operates and must in particular take account of the structure of the market, the economic risks related to the agreement, and the incentives facing the parties. The more uncertain the success of the product covered by the agreement, the more a restriction may be required to ensure that the efficiencies will materialise. Restrictions may also be indispensable in order to align the incentives of the parties and ensure that they concentrate their efforts on the implementation of the agreement. A restriction may for instance be necessary in order to avoid hold-up problems once a substantial sunk investment has been made by one of the parties. Once for instance a supplier has made a substantial relationship-specific investment with a view to supplying a customer with an input, the supplier is locked into the customer. In order to avoid that *ex post* the customer exploits this dependence to obtain more favourable terms, it may be necessary to impose an obligation not to purchase the component from third parties or to purchase minimum quantities of the component from the supplier.[77]

Notes
[77] See for more detail paragraph 116 of the Guidelines on Vertical Restraints cited in note 5.

Commentary
para 80: **F&N:** 3.439

81. In some cases a restriction may be indispensable only for a certain period of time, in which case the exception of Article 81(3) only applies during that period. In making this assessment it is necessary to take due account of the period of time required for the parties to achieve the efficiencies justifying the application of the exception rule.[78] In cases where the benefits cannot be achieved without considerable investment, account must, in particular, be taken of the period of time required to ensure an adequate return on such investment, see also paragraph 44 above.

Notes
[78] See Joined Cases T-374/94 and others, *European Night Services* [1998] ECR II-3141, paragraph 230.

Commentary
para 81: **B&C:** 3.060 **F&N:** 12.346

82. These principles can be illustrated by the following hypothetical examples: P produces and distributes frozen pizzas, holding 15% of the market in Member State X. Deliveries are made directly to retailers. Since most retailers have limited storage capacity, relatively frequent deliveries are required, leading to low capacity utilisation and use of relatively small vehicles. T is a wholesaler of frozen pizzas and other frozen products, delivering to most of the same customers as P. The pizza products distributed by T hold 30% of the market. T has a fleet of larger vehicles and has excess capacity. P concludes an exclusive distribution agreement with T for Member State X and undertakes to ensure that distributors in other Member States will not sell into T's territory either actively or passively. T undertakes to advertise the products, survey consumer tastes and satisfaction rates and ensure delivery to retailers of all products within 24 hours. The agreement leads to a reduction in total distribution costs of 30% as capacity is better utilised and duplication of routes is eliminated. The agreement also leads to the provision of additional services to consumers. Restrictions on passive sales are hardcore restrictions under the block exemption regulation on vertical restraints[79] and can only be considered indispensable in exceptional circumstances. The established market position of T and the nature of the obligations imposed on it indicate this is not an exceptional case. The ban on active selling, on the other hand, is likely to be indispensable. T is likely to have less incentive to sell and advertise the P brand, if distributors in other Member States could sell actively in Member State X and thus get a free ride on the efforts of T. This is particularly so, as T also distributes competing brands and thus has the possibility of pushing more of the brands that are the least exposed to free riding. S is a producer of carbonated soft drinks, holding 40% of the market. The nearest competitor holds 20%. S concludes supply agreements with customers accounting for 25% of demand, whereby they undertake to purchase

exclusively from S for 5 years. S concludes agreements with other customers accounting for 15% of demand whereby they are granted quarterly target rebates, if their purchases exceed certain individually fixed targets. S claims that the agreements allow it to predict demand more accurately and thus to better plan production, reducing raw material storage and warehousing costs and avoiding supply shortages. Given the market position of S and the combined coverage of the restrictions, the restrictions are very unlikely to be considered indispensable. The exclusive purchasing obligation exceeds what is required to plan production and the same is true of the target rebate scheme. Predictability of demand can be achieved by less restrictive means. S could, for example, provide incentives for customers to order large quantities at a time by offering quantity rebates or by offering a rebate to customers that place firm orders in advance for delivery on specified dates.

Notes

[79] See Commission Regulation No 2790/1999 on the application of Article 81(3) of the Treaty on categories of vertical agreements and concerted practices (OJ 1999 L 336, page 21).

Commentary
para 82: B&C: 6.165

3.4. Second condition of Article 81(3): Fair share for consumers

3.4.1. General remarks

83. According to the second condition of Article 81(3) consumers must receive a fair share of the efficiencies generated by the restrictive agreement.

84. The concept of "consumers" encompasses all direct or indirect users of the products covered by the agreement, including producers that use the products as an input, wholesalers, retailers and final consumers, i.e. natural persons who are acting for purposes which can be regarded as outside their trade or profession. In other words, consumers within the meaning of Article 81(3) are the customers of the parties to the agreement and subsequent purchasers. These customers can be undertakings as in the case of buyers of industrial machinery or an input for further processing or final consumers as for instance in the case of buyers of impulse ice-cream or bicycles.

Commentary
para 84: B&C: 3.053 F&N: 3.442

---

85. The concept of *"fair share"* implies that the pass-on of benefits must at least compensate consumers for any actual or likely negative impact caused to them by the restriction of competition found under Article 81(1). In line with the overall objective of Article 81 to prevent anti-competitive agreements, the net effect of the agreement must at least be neutral from the point of view of those consumers directly or likely affected by the agreement.[80] If such consumers are worse off following the agreement, the second condition of Article 81(3) is not fulfilled. The positive effects of an agreement must be balanced against and compensate for its negative effects on consumers.[81] When that is the case consumers are not harmed by the agreement. Moreover, society as a whole benefits where the efficiencies lead either to fewer resources being used to produce the output consumed or to the production of more valuable products and thus to a more efficient allocation of resources.

Notes

[80] See in this respect the judgment in *Consten and Grundig* cited in note 21, where the Court of Justice held that the improvements within the meaning of the first condition of Article 81(3) must show appreciable objective advantages of such a character as to compensate for the disadvantages which they cause in the field of competition.

[81] It is recalled that positive and negative effects on consumers are in principle balanced within each relevant market (cf. paragraph 43 above).

Commentary
para 85: B&C: 3.054 F&N: 3.444

86. It is not required that consumers receive a share of each and every efficiency gain identified under the first condition. It suffices that sufficient benefits are passed on to compensate for the negative effects of the restrictive agreement. In that case consumers obtain a fair share of the overall benefits.[82] If a restrictive agreement is likely to lead to higher prices, consumers must be fully compensated through increased quality or other benefits. If not, the second condition of Article 81(3) is not fulfilled.

Notes

[82] See in this respect paragraph 48 of the *Metro (I)* judgment cited in note 54.

Commentary

para 86: B&C: 3.054

87. The decisive factor is the overall impact on consumers of the products within the relevant market and not the impact on individual members of this group of consumers[83]. In some cases a certain period of time may be required before the efficiencies materialise. Until such time the agreement may have only negative effects. The fact that pass-on to the consumer occurs with a certain time lag does not in itself exclude the application of Article 81(3). However, the greater the time lag, the greater must be the efficiencies to compensate also for the loss to consumers during the period preceding the pass-on.

Notes

[83] See paragraph 163 of the judgment in *Shaw* cited in note 56.

88. In making this assessment it must be taken into account that the value of a gain for consumers in the future is not the same as a present gain for consumers. The value of saving 100 euro today is greater than the value of saving the same amount a year later. A gain for consumers in the future therefore does not fully compensate for a present loss to consumers of equal nominal size. In order to allow for an appropriate comparison of a present loss to consumers with a future gain to consumers, the value of future gains must be discounted. The discount rate applied must reflect the rate of inflation, if any, and lost interest as an indication of the lower value of future gains.

Commentary

para 88: B&C: 3.054

89. In other cases the agreement may enable the parties to obtain the efficiencies earlier than would otherwise be possible. In such circumstances it is necessary to take account of the likely negative impact on consumers within the relevant market once this lead-time has lapsed. If through the restrictive agreement the parties obtain a strong position on the market, they may be able to charge a significantly higher price than would otherwise have been the case. For the second condition of Article 81(3) to be satisfied the benefit to consumers of having earlier access to the products must be equally significant. This may for instance be the case where an agreement allows two tyre manufacturers to bring to market three years earlier a new substantially safer tyre but at the same time, by increasing their market power, allows them to raise prices by 5%. In such a case it is likely that having early access to a substantially improved product outweighs the price increase.

90. The second condition of Article 81(3) incorporates a sliding scale. The greater the restriction of competition found under Article 81(1) the greater must be the efficiencies and the pass-on to consumers. This sliding scale approach implies that if the restrictive effects of an agreement are relatively limited and the efficiencies are substantial it is likely that a fair share of the cost savings will be passed on to consumers. In such cases it is therefore normally not necessary to engage in a detailed analysis of the second condition of Article 81(3), provided that the three other conditions for the application of this provision are fulfilled.

Commentary

para 90: F&N: 3.435, 3.452

91. If, on the other hand, the restrictive effects of the agreement are substantial and the cost savings are relatively insignificant, it is very unlikely that the second condition of Article 81(3) will be fulfilled. The impact of the restriction of competition depends on the intensity of the restriction and the degree of competition that remains following the agreement.

Commentary
para 91: F&N: 3.452

92. If the agreement has both substantial anti-competitive effects and substantial pro-competitive effects a careful analysis is required. In the application of the balancing test in such cases it must be taken into account that competition is an important long-term driver of efficiency and innovation. Undertakings that are not subject to effective competitive constraints — such as for instance dominant firms — have less incentive to maintain or build on the efficiencies. The more substantial the impact of the agreement on competition, the more likely it is that consumers will suffer in the long run.

Commentary
para 92: F&N: 3.456

93. The following two sections describe in more detail the analytical framework for assessing consumer pass-on of efficiency gains. The first section deals with cost efficiencies, whereas the section that follows covers other types of efficiencies such as new or improved products (qualitative efficiencies). The framework, which is developed in these two sections, is particularly important in cases where it is not immediately obvious that the competitive harms exceed the benefits to consumers or *vice versa*.[84]

Notes
[84] In the following sections, for convenience the competitive harm is referred to in terms of higher prices; competitive harm could also mean lower quality, less variety or lower innovation than would otherwise have occurred.

94. In the application of the principles set out below the Commission will have regard to the fact that in many cases it is difficult to accurately calculate the consumer pass-on rate and other types of consumer pass-on. Undertakings are only required to substantiate their claims by providing estimates and other data to the extent reasonably possible, taking account of the circumstances of the individual case.

3.4.2. Pass-on and balancing of cost efficiencies

95. When markets, as is normally the case, are not perfectly competitive, undertakings are able to influence the market price to a greater or lesser extent by altering their output.[85] They may also be able to price discriminate amongst customers.

Notes
[85] In perfectly competitive markets individual undertakings are price-takers. They sell their products at the market price, which is determined by overall supply and demand. The output of the individual undertaking is so small that any individual undertaking's change in output does not affect the market price.

96. Cost efficiencies may in some circumstances lead to increased output and lower prices for the affected consumers. If due to cost efficiencies the undertakings in question can increase profits by expanding output, consumer pass-on may occur. In assessing the extent to which cost efficiencies are likely to be passed on to consumers and the outcome of the balancing test contained in Article 81(3) the following factors are in particular taken into account:
(a) The characteristics and structure of the market,
(b) The nature and magnitude of the efficiency gains,
(c) The elasticity of demand, and
(d) The magnitude of the restriction of competition.
All factors must normally be considered. Since Article 81(3) only applies in cases where competition on the market is being appreciably restricted, see paragraph 24 above, there can be no presumption that residual competition will ensure that consumers receive a fair share of the benefits.

However, the degree of competition remaining on the market and the nature of this competition influences the likelihood of pass-on.

Commentary
para 96: F&N: 3.447

97. The greater the degree of residual competition the more likely it is that individual undertakings will try to increase their sales by passing on cost efficiencies. If undertakings compete mainly on price and are not subject to significant capacity constraints, pass-on may occur relatively quickly. If competition is mainly on capacity and capacity adaptations occur with a certain time lag, pass-on will be slower. Pass-on is also likely to be slower when the market structure is conducive to tacit collusion.[86] If competitors are likely to retaliate against an increase in output by one or more parties to the agreement, the incentive to increase output may be tempered, unless the competitive advantage conferred by the efficiencies is such that the undertakings concerned have an incentive to break away from the common policy adopted on the market by the members of the oligopoly. In other words, the efficiencies generated by the agreement may turn the undertakings concerned into so-called "mavericks".[87]

Notes
[86] Undertakings collude tacitly when in an oligopolistic market they are able to coordinate their action on the market without resorting to an explicit cartel agreement.
[87] This term refers to undertakings that constrain the pricing behaviour of other undertakings in the market who might otherwise have tacitly colluded.

98. The nature of the efficiency gains also plays an important role. According to economic theory undertakings maximise their profits by selling units of output until marginal revenue equals marginal cost. Marginal revenue is the change in total revenue resulting from selling an additional unit of output and marginal cost is the change in total cost resulting from producing that additional unit of output. It follows from this principle that as a general rule output and pricing decisions of a profit maximising undertaking are not determined by its fixed costs (i.e. costs that do not vary with the rate of production) but by its variable costs (i.e. costs that vary with the rate of production). After fixed costs are incurred and capacity is set, pricing and output decisions are determined by variable cost and demand conditions. Take for instance a situation in which two companies each produce two products on two production lines operating only at half their capacities. A specialisation agreement may allow the two undertakings to specialise in producing one of the two products and scrap their second production line for the other product. At the same time the specialisation may allow the companies to reduce variable input and stocking costs. Only the latter savings will have a direct effect on the pricing and output decisions of the undertakings, as they will influence the marginal costs of production. The scrapping by each undertaking of one of their production lines will not reduce their variable costs and will not have an impact on their production costs. It follows that undertakings may have a direct incentive to pass on to consumers in the form of higher output and lower prices efficiencies that reduce marginal costs, whereas they have no such direct incentive with regard to efficiencies that reduce fixed costs. Consumers are therefore more likely to receive a fair share of the cost efficiencies in the case of reductions in variable costs than they are in the case of reductions in fixed costs.

Commentary
para 98: F&N: 3.430, 3.450

99. The fact that undertakings may have an incentive to pass on certain types of cost efficiencies does not imply that the pass-on rate will necessarily be 100%. The actual pass-on rate depends on the extent to which consumers respond to changes in price, i.e. the elasticity of demand. The greater the increase in demand caused by a decrease in price, the greater the pass-on rate. This follows from the fact that the greater the additional sales caused by a price reduction due to an increase in output the more likely it is that these sales will offset the loss of revenue caused by the lower price resulting from the increase in output. In the absence of price discrimination the lowering of prices affects all units sold by the undertaking, in which case marginal revenue is less than the price

obtained for the marginal product. If the undertakings concerned are able to charge different prices to different customers, i.e. price discriminate, pass-on will normally only benefit price-sensitive consumers.[88]

Notes

[88] The restrictive agreement may even allow the undertakings in question to charge a higher price to customers with a low elasticity of demand.

Commentary
para 99: F&N: 3.451

100. It must also be taken into account that efficiency gains often do not affect the whole cost structure of the undertakings concerned. In such event the impact on the price to consumers is reduced. If for example an agreement allows the parties to reduce production costs by 6%, but production costs only make up one third of the costs on the basis of which prices are determined, the impact on the product price is 2%, assuming that the full amount is passed-on.

101. Finally, and very importantly, it is necessary to balance the two opposing forces resulting from the restriction of competition and the cost efficiencies. On the one hand, any increase in market power caused by the restrictive agreement gives the undertakings concerned the ability and incentive to raise price. On the other hand, the types of cost efficiencies that are taken into account may give the undertakings concerned an incentive to reduce price, see paragraph 98 above. The effects of these two opposing forces must be balanced against each other. It is recalled in this regard that the consumer pass-on condition incorporates a sliding scale. When the agreement causes a substantial reduction in the competitive constraint facing the parties, extraordinarily large cost efficiencies are normally required for sufficient pass-on to occur.

3.4.3. *Pass-on and balancing of other types of efficiencies*

102. Consumer pass-on can also take the form of qualitative efficiencies such as new and improved products, creating sufficient value for consumers to compensate for the anticompetitive effects of the agreement, including a price increase.

Commentary
para 102: F&N: 3.430

103. Any such assessment necessarily requires value judgment. It is difficult to assign precise values to dynamic efficiencies of this nature. However, the fundamental objective of the assessment remains the same, namely to ascertain the overall impact of the agreement on the consumers within the relevant market. Undertakings claiming the benefit of Article 81(3) must substantiate that consumers obtain countervailing benefits (see in this respect paragraphs 57 and 86 above).

Commentary
para 103: B&C: 3.056

104. The availability of new and improved products constitutes an important source of consumer welfare. As long as the increase in value stemming from such improvements exceeds any harm from a maintenance or an increase in price caused by the restrictive agreement, consumers are better off than without the agreement and the consumer pass-on requirement of Article 81(3) is normally fulfilled. In cases where the likely effect of the agreement is to increase prices for consumers within the relevant market it must be carefully assessed whether the claimed efficiencies create real value for consumers in that market so as to compensate for the adverse effects of the restriction of competition.

Commentary
para 104: B&C: 3.056

3.5. Fourth condition of Article 81(3): No elimination of competition

105. According to the fourth condition of Article 81(3) the agreement must not afford the undertakings concerned the possibility of eliminating competition in respect of a substantial part of the products concerned. Ultimately the protection of rivalry and the competitive process is given priority over potentially pro-competitive efficiency gains which could result from restrictive agreements. The last condition of Article 81(3) recognises the fact that rivalry between undertakings is an essential driver of economic efficiency, including dynamic efficiencies in the shape of innovation. In other words, the ultimate aim of Article 81 is to protect the competitive process. When competition is eliminated the competitive process is brought to an end and short-term efficiency gains are outweighed by longer-term losses stemming *inter alia* from expenditures incurred by the incumbent to maintain its position (rent seeking), misallocation of resources, reduced innovation and higher prices.

Commentary
para 105: F&N: 3.453

106. The concept in Article 81(3) of elimination of competition in respect of a substantial part of the products concerned is an autonomous Community law concept specific to Article 81(3).[89] However, in the application of this concept it is necessary to take account of the relationship between Article 81 and Article 82. According to settled case law the application of Article 81(3) cannot prevent the application of Article 82 of the Treaty.[90] Moreover, since Articles 81 and 82 both pursue the aim of maintaining effective competition on the market, consistency requires that Article 81(3) be interpreted as precluding any application of this provision to restrictive agreements that constitute an abuse of a dominant position.[91,92] However, not all restrictive agreements concluded by a dominant undertaking constitute an abuse of a dominant position. This is for instance the case where a dominant undertaking is party to a non-full function joint venture,[93] which is found to be restrictive of competition but at the same time involves a substantial integration of assets.

Notes

[89] See Joined Cases T-191/98, T-212/98 and T-214/98 *Atlantic Container Line (TACA)* [2003] ECR II-[3275], paragraph 939, and Case T-395/94 *Atlantic Container Line* [2002] ECR II-875, paragraph 330.

[90] See Joined Cases C-395/96 P and C-396/96 P *Compagnie maritime belge* [2000] ECR I-1365, paragraph 130. Similarly, the application of Article 81(3) does not prevent the application of the Treaty rules on the free movement of goods, services, persons and capital. These provisions are in certain circumstances applicable to agreements, decisions and concerted practices within the meaning of Article 81(1), see to that effect Case C-309/99 *Wouters* [2002] ECR I-1577, paragraph 120.

[91] See in this respect Case T-51/89 *Tetra Pak (I)* [1990] ECR II-309, and Joined Cases T-191/98, T-212/98 and T-214/98 *Atlantic Container Line (TACA)* [2003] ECR II-[3275], paragraph 1456.

[92] This is how paragraph 135 of the Guidelines on vertical restraints and paragraphs 36, 71, 105, 134 and 155 of the Guidelines on horizontal cooperation agreements, cited in note 5, should be understood when they state that in principle restrictive agreements concluded by dominant undertakings cannot be exempted.

[93] Full function joint ventures, i.e. joint ventures that perform on a lasting basis all the functions of an autonomous economic entity, are covered by Council Regulation (EEC) No 4064/89 on the control of concentrations between undertakings (OJ 1990 L 257, p. 13).

Commentary
para 106: B&C: 3.018 F&N: 3.456

107. Whether competition is being eliminated within the meaning of the last condition of Article 81(3) depends on the degree of competition existing prior to the agreement and on the impact of the restrictive agreement on competition, i.e. the reduction in competition that the agreement brings about. The more competition is already weakened in the market concerned, the slighter the further reduction required for competition to be eliminated within the meaning of Article 81(3). Moreover, the greater the reduction of competition caused by the agreement, the greater the likelihood that competition in respect of a substantial part of the products concerned risks being eliminated.

Commentary
para 107: F&N: 3.458

108. The application of the last condition of Article 81(3) requires a realistic analysis of the various sources of competition in the market, the level of competitive constraint that they impose on the parties to the agreement and the impact of the agreement on this competitive constraint. Both actual and potential competition must be considered.

109. While market shares are relevant, the magnitude of remaining sources of actual competition cannot be assessed exclusively on the basis of market share. More extensive qualitative and quantitative analysis is normally called for. The capacity of actual competitors to compete and their incentive to do so must be examined. If, for example, competitors face capacity constraints or have relatively higher costs of production their competitive response will necessarily be limited.

Commentary
para 109: B&C: 3.065

110. In the assessment of the impact of the agreement on competition it is also relevant to examine its influence on the various parameters of competition. The last condition for exception under Article 81(3) is not fulfilled, if the agreement eliminates competition in one of its most important expressions. This is particularly the case when an agreement eliminates price competition[94] or competition in respect of innovation and development of new products.

Notes
[94] See paragraph 21 of the judgment in *Metro (I)* cited in note 54.

111. The actual market conduct of the parties can provide insight into the impact of the agreement. If following the conclusion of the agreement the parties have implemented and maintained substantial price increases or engaged in other conduct indicative of the existence of a considerable degree of market power, it is an indication that the parties are not subject to any real competitive pressure and that competition has been eliminated with regard to a substantial part of the products concerned.

112. Past competitive interaction may also provide an indication of the impact of the agreement on future competitive interaction. An undertaking may be able to eliminate competition within the meaning of Article 81(3) by concluding an agreement with a competitor that in the past has been a "maverick".[95] Such agreement may change the competitive incentives and capabilities of the competitor and thereby remove an important source of competition in the market.

Notes
[95] See paragraph 97 above.

113. In cases involving differentiated products, i.e. products that differ in the eyes of consumers, the impact of the agreement may depend on the competitive relationship between the products sold by the parties to the agreement. When undertakings offer differentiated products the competitive constraint that individual products impose on each other differs according to the degree of substitutability between them. It must therefore be considered what is the degree of substitutability between the products offered by the parties, i.e. what is the competitive constraint that they impose on each other. The more the products of the parties to the agreement are close substitutes the greater the likely restrictive effect of the agreement. In other words, the more substitutable the products the greater the likely change brought about by the agreement in terms of restriction of competition on the market and the more likely it is that competition in respect of a substantial part of the products concerned risks being eliminated.

Commentary
para 113: F&N: 3.460

114. While sources of actual competition are usually the most important, as they are most easily verified, sources of potential competition must also be taken into account. The assessment of potential competition requires an analysis of barriers to entry facing undertakings that are not already competing within the relevant market. Any assertions by the parties that there are low barriers to market entry must be supported by information identifying the sources of potential competition and the parties must also substantiate why these sources constitute a real competitive pressure on the parties.

115. In the assessment of entry barriers and the real possibility for new entry on a significant scale, it is relevant to examine, *inter alia,* the following:

   (i) The regulatory framework with a view to determining its impact on new entry.

  (ii) The cost of entry including sunk costs. Sunk costs are those that cannot be recovered if the entrant subsequently exits the market. The higher the sunk costs the higher the commercial risk for potential entrants.

 (iii) The minimum efficient scale within the industry, i.e. the rate of output where average costs are minimised. If the minimum efficient scale is large compared to the size of the market, efficient entry is likely to be more costly and risky.

 (iv) The competitive strengths of potential entrants. Effective entry is particularly likely where potential entrants have access to at least as cost efficient technologies as the incumbents or other competitive advantages that allow them to compete effectively. When potential entrants are on the same or an inferior technological trajectory compared to the incumbents and possess no other significant competitive advantage entry is more risky and less effective.

  (v) The position of buyers and their ability to bring onto the market new sources of competition. It is irrelevant that certain strong buyers may be able to extract more favourable conditions from the parties to the agreement than their weaker competitors.[96] The presence of strong buyers can only serve to counter a prima facie finding of elimination of competition if it is likely that the buyers in question will pave the way for effective new entry.

 (vi) The likely response of incumbents to attempted new entry. Incumbents may for example through past conduct have acquired a reputation of aggressive behaviour, having an impact on future entry.

 (vii) The economic outlook for the industry may be an indicator of its longer-term attractiveness. Industries that are stagnating or in decline are less attractive candidates for entry than industries characterised by growth.

(viii) Past entry on a significant scale or the absence thereof.

Notes
[96] See in this respect Case T-228/97 *Irish Sugar* [1999] ECR II-2969, paragraph 101.

Commentary
para 115(v): F&N: 3.459

116. The above principles can be illustrated by the following hypothetical examples, which are not intended to establish thresholds: Firm A is brewer, holding 70% of the relevant market, comprising the sale of beer through cafés and other on-trade premises. Over the past 5 years A has increased its market share from 60%. There are four other competitors in the market, B, C, D and E with market shares of 10%, 10%, 5% and 5%. No new entry has occurred in the recent past and price changes implemented by A have generally been followed by competitors. A concludes agreements with 20% of the on-trade premises representing 40% of sales volumes whereby the contracting parties undertake to purchase beer only from A for a period of 5 years. The agreements raise the costs and reduce the revenues of rivals, which are foreclosed from the most attractive outlets. Given the market position of A, which has been strengthened in recent years, the absence of new entry and the already weak position of competitors it is likely that competition in the market is eliminated within the meaning of Article 81(3). Shipping firms A, B, C, and D, holding collectively more than 70% of the relevant market, conclude an agreement whereby they agree to coordinate their schedules and their tariffs. Following the

implementation of the agreement prices rise between 30% and 100%. There are four other suppliers, the largest holding about 14% of the relevant market. There has been no new entry in recent years and the parties to the agreement did not lose significant market share following the price increases. The existing competitors brought no significant new capacity to the market and no new entry occurred. In light of the market position of the parties and the absence of competitive response to their joint conduct it can reasonably be concluded that the parties to the agreement are not subject to real competitive pressures and that the agreement affords them the possibility of eliminating competition within the meaning of Article 81(3). A is a producer of electric appliances for professional users with a market share of 65% of a relevant national market. B is a competing manufacturer with 5% market share which has developed a new type of motor that is more powerful while consuming less electricity. A and B conclude an agreement whereby they establish a production joint venture for the production of the new motor. B undertakes to grant an exclusive licence to the joint venture. The joint venture combines the new technology of B with the efficient manufacturing and quality control process of A. There is one other main competitor with 15% of the market. Another competitor with 5% market share has recently been acquired by C, a major international producer of competing electric appliances, which itself owns efficient technologies. C has thus far not been active on the market mainly due to the fact that local presence and servicing is desired by customers. Through the acquisition C gains access to the service organisation required to penetrate the market. The entry of C is likely to ensure that competition is not being eliminated.

Commentary
para 116: B&C: 7.096 F&N: 12.235

PART D

MERGERS AND CONCENTRATIONS

D1

COUNCIL REGULATION (EC) NO 139/2004

of 20 January 2004
on the control of concentrations between undertakings
(the EC Merger Regulation)

(Text with EEA relevance)

Official Journal L 24, 29.1.2004, p. 1

Celex No: 32004R0139

Notes

EEA application: Articles 1 to 5 of the Merger Regulation were adopted with appropriate adaptations by EEA Joint Committee Decision No 78/2004 of 8 June 2004, OJ L 219, 19.6.2004, p. 13 and EEA Supplement No 32, 19.6.2004, p. 1, and EEA Joint Committee Decision No 79/2004 of 8 June 2004, OJ L 219, 19.6.2004, p. 24 and EEA Supplement No 32, 19.6.2004, p. 10: see EEA Agreement, Annex XIV, Chapter A, Point 1 and Protocol 21, Article 3(1), Point 1. The procedural provisions of Articles 4(4), 4(5) and 6 to 25 were adopted with appropriate adaptations, by agreement of 4 June 2004: see the Surveillance and Court Agreement, Protocol 4, Part III, Chapter XIII.

Commentary

Regulation 139/2004/EC: B&C: 1.022, 1.106, 1.110, 1.113, 1.115, 2.003, 2.035, 7.001, 7.047, 8.001, 8.004, 8.008–8.010, 8.012, 8.015, 8.044, 8.060, 8.162, 14.043 **F&N:** 1.17, 1.185, 3.11, 3.389, 4.39, 4.40, 4.41, 4.117, 4.119, 4.123, 4.124, 5.07, 5.7, 5.16, 5.17, 5.21, 5.24, 5.25, 5.28, 5.31, 5.33, 5.34, 5.37, 5.48, 5.53, 5.54, 5.55, 5.56, 5.57, 5.58, 5.68, 5.73, 5.77, 5.80, 5.113, 5.181, 5.182, 5.197, 5.200, 5.205, 5.241, 5.257, 5.270, 5.278, 5.295, 5.296, 5.297, 5.301, 5.302, 5.319, 5.320, 5.335, 5.343, 5.344, 5.345, 5.346, 5.362, 5.364, 5.365, 5.380, 5.385, 5.386, 5.395, 5.399, 5.408, 5.409, 5.412, 5.414, 5.416, 5.421, 5.422, 5.424, 5.463, 5.481, 5.487, 5.497, 5.502, 5.552, 5.556, 5.557, 5.570, 5.645, 5.646, 5.649, 5.652, 5.655, 5.675, 6.27, 7.23, 7.32, 7.36, 7.87, 7.213, 7.253, 8.160, 8.215, 8.260, 8.262, 8.352, 8.353, 8.457, 8.561, 11.68, 13.39, 13.191, 13.290, 13.361, 14.25, 14.26, 14.85, 14.230
Arts 11–13: F&N: 5.386

THE COUNCIL OF THE EUROPEAN UNION,

Having regard to the Treaty establishing the European Community, and in particular Articles 83 and 308 thereof,

Having regard to the proposal from the Commission,[1]

Having regard to the opinion of the European Parliament,[2]

Having regard to the opinion of the European Economic and Social Committee,[3]

Notes

[1] OJ C 20, 28.1.2003, p. 4.
[2] Opinion delivered on 9.10.2003 (not yet published in the Official Journal).
[3] Opinion delivered on 24.10.2003 [OJ C 10, 14.1.2004].

Whereas:

(1) Council Regulation (EEC) No 4064/89 of 21 December 1989 on the control of concentrations between undertakings[1] has been substantially amended. Since further amendments are to be made, it should be recast in the interest of clarity.

Notes

[1] OJ L 395, 30.12.1989, p. 1. Corrected version in OJ L 257, 21.9.1990, p. 13. Regulation as last amended by Regulation (EC) No 1310/97 (OJ L 180, 9.7.1997, p. 1). Corrigendum in OJ L 40, 13.2.1998, p. 17.

---

(2) For the achievement of the aims of the Treaty, Article 3(1)(g) gives the Community the objective of instituting a system ensuring that competition in the internal market is not distorted. Article 4(1) of the Treaty provides that the activities of the Member States and the Community are to be conducted in accordance with the principle of an open market economy with free competition. These principles are essential for the further development of the internal market.

(3) The completion of the internal market and of economic and monetary union, the enlargement of the European Union and the lowering of international barriers to trade and investment will continue to result in major corporate reorganisations, particularly in the form of concentrations.

Commentary
Recital 3: B&C: 8.255

(4) Such reorganisations are to be welcomed to the extent that they are in line with the requirements of dynamic competition and capable of increasing the competitiveness of European industry, improving the conditions of growth and raising the standard of living in the Community.

Commentary
Recital 4: B&C: 8.255

(5) However, it should be ensured that the process of reorganisation does not result in lasting damage to competition; Community law must therefore include provisions governing those concentrations which may significantly impede effective competition in the common market or in a substantial part of it.

(6) A specific legal instrument is therefore necessary to permit effective control of all concentrations in terms of their effect on the structure of competition in the Community and to be the only instrument applicable to such concentrations. Regulation (EEC) No 4064/89 has allowed a Community policy to develop in this field. In the light of experience, however, that Regulation should now be recast into legislation designed to meet the challenges of a more integrated market and the future enlargement of the European Union. In accordance with the principles of subsidiarity and of proportionality as set out in Article 5 of the Treaty, this Regulation does not go beyond what is necessary in order to achieve the objective of ensuring that competition in the common market is not distorted, in accordance with the principle of an open market economy with free competition.

Commentary
Recital 6: B&C: 8.260

(7) Articles 81 and 82, while applicable, according to the case-law of the Court of Justice, to certain concentrations, are not sufficient to control all operations which may prove to be incompatible with the system of undistorted competition envisaged in the Treaty. This Regulation should therefore be based not only on Article 83 but, principally, on Article 308 of the Treaty, under which the Community may give itself the additional powers of action necessary for the attainment of its objectives, and also powers of action with regard to concentrations on the markets for agricultural products listed in Annex I to the Treaty.

Commentary
Recital 7: B&C: 8.257, 8.260

(8) The provisions to be adopted in this Regulation should apply to significant structural changes, the impact of which on the market goes beyond the national borders of any one Member State. Such concentrations should, as a general rule, be reviewed exclusively at Community level, in application of a "one-stop shop" system and in compliance with the principle of subsidiarity. Concentrations not covered by this Regulation come, in principle, within the jurisdiction of the Member States.

Commentary
Recital 8: B&C: 8.012

(9) The scope of application of this Regulation should be defined according to the geographical area of activity of the undertakings concerned and be limited by quantitative thresholds in order to cover those concentrations which have a Community dimension. The Commission should report to the Council on the implementation of the applicable thresholds and criteria so that the Council, acting in accordance with Article 202 of the Treaty, is in a position to review them regularly, as well as the rules regarding pre-notification referral, in the light of the experience gained; this requires statistical data to be provided by the Member States to the Commission to enable it to prepare such reports and possible proposals for amendments. The Commission's reports and proposals should be based on relevant information regularly provided by the Member States.

(10) A concentration with a Community dimension should be deemed to exist where the aggregate turnover of the undertakings concerned exceeds given thresholds; that is the case irrespective of whether or not the undertakings effecting the concentration have their seat or their principal fields of activity in the Community, provided they have substantial operations there.

(11) The rules governing the referral of concentrations from the Commission to Member States and from Member States to the Commission should operate as an effective corrective mechanism in the light of the principle of subsidiarity; these rules protect the competition interests of the Member States in an adequate manner and take due account of legal certainty and the "one-stop shop" principle.

Commentary
Recital 11: **B&C:** 8.012 **F&N:** 5.119

---

(12) Concentrations may qualify for examination under a number of national merger control systems if they fall below the turnover thresholds referred to in this Regulation. Multiple notification of the same transaction increases legal uncertainty, effort and cost for undertakings and may lead to conflicting assessments. The system whereby concentrations may be referred to the Commission by the Member States concerned should therefore be further developed.

Commentary
Recital 12: **F&N:** 5.144

---

(13) The Commission should act in close and constant liaison with the competent authorities of the Member States from which it obtains comments and information.

(14) The Commission and the competent authorities of the Member States should together form a network of public authorities, applying their respective competences in close cooperation, using efficient arrangements for information-sharing and consultation, with a view to ensuring that a case is dealt with by the most appropriate authority, in the light of the principle of subsidiarity and with a view to ensuring that multiple notifications of a given concentration are avoided to the greatest extent possible. Referrals of concentrations from the Commission to Member States and from Member States to the Commission should be made in an efficient manner avoiding, to the greatest extent possible, situations where a concentration is subject to a referral both before and after its notification.

(15) The Commission should be able to refer to a Member State notified concentrations with a Community dimension which threaten significantly to affect competition in a market within that Member State presenting all the characteristics of a distinct market. Where the concentration affects competition on such a market, which does not constitute a substantial part of the common market, the Commission should be obliged, upon request, to refer the whole or part of the case to the Member State concerned. A Member State should be able to refer to the Commission a concentration which does not have a Community dimension but which affects trade between Member States and threatens to significantly affect competition within its territory. Other Member States which are also competent to review the concentration should be able to join the request. In such a situation, in order to ensure the efficiency and predictability of the system, national time limits should be suspended until a decision has been reached as to the referral of the case. The Commission should have the power to examine and deal with a concentration on behalf of a requesting Member State or requesting Member States.

(16) The undertakings concerned should be granted the possibility of requesting referrals to or from the Commission before a concentration is notified so as to further improve the efficiency of the system for the control of concentrations within the Community. In such situations, the Commission and national competition authorities should decide within short, clearly defined time limits whether a referral to or from the Commission ought to be made, thereby ensuring the efficiency of the system. Upon request by the undertakings concerned, the Commission should be able to refer to a Member State a concentration with a Community dimension which may significantly affect competition in a market within that Member State presenting all the characteristics of a distinct market; the undertakings concerned should not, however, be required to demonstrate that the effects of the concentration would be detrimental to competition. A concentration should not be referred from the Commission to a Member State which has expressed its disagreement to such a referral. Before notification to national authorities, the undertakings concerned should also be able to request that a concentration without a Community dimension which is capable of being reviewed under the national competition laws of at least three Member States be referred to the Commission. Such requests for pre-notification referrals to the Commission would be particularly pertinent in situations where the concentration would affect competition beyond the territory of one Member State. Where a concentration capable of being reviewed under the competition laws of three or more Member States is referred to the Commission prior to any national notification, and no Member State competent to review the case expresses its disagreement, the Commission should acquire exclusive competence to review the concentration and such a concentration should be deemed to have a Community dimension. Such pre-notification referrals from Member States to the Commission should not, however, be made where at least one Member State competent to review the case has expressed its disagreement with such a referral.

Commentary
Recital 16: F&N: 5.139, 5.144

(17) The Commission should be given exclusive competence to apply this Regulation, subject to review by the Court of Justice.

(18) The Member States should not be permitted to apply their national legislation on competition to concentrations with a Community dimension, unless this Regulation makes provision therefor. The relevant powers of national authorities should be limited to cases where, failing intervention by the Commission, effective competition is likely to be significantly impeded within the territory of a Member State and where the competition interests of that Member State cannot be sufficiently protected otherwise by this Regulation. The Member States concerned must act promptly in such cases; this Regulation cannot, because of the diversity of national law, fix a single time limit for the adoption of final decisions under national law.

Commentary
Recital 18: F&N: 2.11

(19) Furthermore, the exclusive application of this Regulation to concentrations with a Community dimension is without prejudice to Article 296 of the Treaty, and does not prevent the Member States from taking appropriate measures to protect legitimate interests other than those pursued by this Regulation, provided that such measures are compatible with the general principles and other provisions of Community law.

(20) It is expedient to define the concept of concentration in such a manner as to cover operations bringing about a lasting change in the control of the undertakings concerned and therefore in the structure of the market. It is therefore appropriate to include, within the scope of this Regulation, all joint ventures performing on a lasting basis all the functions of an autonomous economic entity. It is moreover appropriate to treat as a single concentration transactions that are closely connected in that they are linked by condition or take the form of a series of transactions in securities taking place within a reasonably short period of time.

(21) This Regulation should also apply where the undertakings concerned accept restrictions directly related to, and necessary for, the implementation of the concentration. Commission decisions declaring concentrations compatible with the common market in application of this Regulation should automatically cover such restrictions, without the Commission having to assess such restrictions in individual cases. At the request of the undertakings concerned, however, the Commission should, in cases presenting novel or unresolved questions giving rise to genuine uncertainty, expressly assess whether or not any restriction is directly related to, and necessary for, the implementation of the concentration. A case presents a novel or unresolved question giving rise to genuine uncertainty if the question is not covered by the relevant Commission notice in force or a published Commission decision.

(22) The arrangements to be introduced for the control of concentrations should, without prejudice to Article 86(2) of the Treaty, respect the principle of non-discrimination between the public and the private sectors. In the public sector, calculation of the turnover of an undertaking concerned in a concentration needs, therefore, to take account of undertakings making up an economic unit with an independent power of decision, irrespective of the way in which their capital is held or of the rules of administrative supervision applicable to them.

(23) It is necessary to establish whether or not concentrations with a Community dimension are compatible with the common market in terms of the need to maintain and develop effective competition in the common market. In so doing, the Commission must place its appraisal within the general framework of the achievement of the fundamental objectives referred to in Article 2 of the Treaty establishing the European Community and Article 2 of the Treaty on European Union.

(24) In order to ensure a system of undistorted competition in the common market, in furtherance of a policy conducted in accordance with the principle of an open market economy with free competition, this Regulation must permit effective control of all concentrations from the point of view of their effect on competition in the Community. Accordingly, Regulation (EEC) No 4064/89 established the principle that a concentration with a Community dimension which creates or strengthens a dominant position as a result of which effective competition in the common market or in a substantial part of it would be significantly impeded should be declared incompatible with the common market.

(25) In view of the consequences that concentrations in oligopolistic market structures may have, it is all the more necessary to maintain effective competition in such markets. Many oligopolistic markets exhibit a healthy degree of competition. However, under certain circumstances, concentrations involving the elimination of important competitive constraints that the merging parties had exerted upon each other, as well as a reduction of competitive pressure on the remaining competitors, may, even in the absence of a likelihood of coordination between the members of the oligopoly, result in a significant impediment to effective competition. The Community courts have, however, not to date expressly interpreted Regulation (EEC) No 4064/89 as requiring concentrations giving rise to such non-coordinated effects to be declared incompatible with the common market. Therefore, in the interests of legal certainty, it should be made clear that this Regulation permits effective control of all such concentrations by providing that any concentration which would significantly impede effective competition, in the common market or

in a substantial part of it, should be declared incompatible with the common market. The notion of "significant impediment to effective competition" in Article 2(2) and (3) should be interpreted as extending, beyond the concept of dominance, only to the anti-competitive effects of a concentration resulting from the non-coordinated behaviour of undertakings which would not have a dominant position on the market concerned.

Commentary
Recital 25: **B&C:** 8.194, 8.196 **F&N:** 5.199

(26) A significant impediment to effective competition generally results from the creation or strengthening of a dominant position. With a view to preserving the guidance that may be drawn from past judgments of the European courts and Commission decisions pursuant to Regulation (EEC) No 4064/89, while at the same time maintaining consistency with the standards of competitive harm which have been applied by the Commission and the Community courts regarding the compatibility of a concentration with the common market, this Regulation should accordingly establish the principle that a concentration with a Community dimension which would significantly impede effective competition, in the common market or in a substantial part thereof, in particular as a result of the creation or strengthening of a dominant position, is to be declared incompatible with the common market.

Commentary
Recital 26: **B&C:** 4.012, 8.196 **F&N:** 5.199

(27) In addition, the criteria of Article 81(1) and (3) of the Treaty should be applied to joint ventures performing, on a lasting basis, all the functions of autonomous economic entities, to the extent that their creation has as its consequence an appreciable restriction of competition between undertakings that remain independent.

Commentary
Recital 27: **F&N:** 5.3334

(28) In order to clarify and explain the Commission's appraisal of concentrations under this Regulation, it is appropriate for the Commission to publish guidance which should provide a sound economic framework for the assessment of concentrations with a view to determining whether or not they may be declared compatible with the common market.

(29) In order to determine the impact of a concentration on competition in the common market, it is appropriate to take account of any substantiated and likely efficiencies put forward by the undertakings concerned. It is possible that the efficiencies brought about by the concentration counteract the effects on competition, and in particular the potential harm to consumers, that it might otherwise have and that, as a consequence, the concentration would not significantly impede effective competition, in the common market or in a substantial part of it, in particular as a result of the creation or strengthening of a dominant position. The Commission should publish guidance on the conditions under which it may take efficiencies into account in the assessment of a concentration.

Commentary
Recital 29: **B&C:** 8.228 **F&N:** 4.351, 5.319

(30) Where the undertakings concerned modify a notified concentration, in particular by offering commitments with a view to rendering the concentration compatible with the common market, the Commission should be able to declare the concentration, as modified, compatible with the common market. Such commitments should be proportionate to the competition problem and entirely eliminate it. It is also appropriate to accept commitments before the initiation of proceedings where the competition problem is readily identifiable and can easily be remedied. It should be expressly provided that the Commission may attach to its decision conditions and obligations in order to ensure that the undertakings concerned comply with their commitments in a timely and effective manner so as to render the concentration compatible with the

common market. Transparency and effective consultation of Member States as well as of interested third parties should be ensured throughout the procedure.

Commentary
Recital 30: B&C: 8.163, 8.165

(31) The Commission should have at its disposal appropriate instruments to ensure the enforcement of commitments and to deal with situations where they are not fulfilled. In cases of failure to fulfil a condition attached to the decision declaring a concentration compatible with the common market, the situation rendering the concentration compatible with the common market does not materialise and the concentration, as implemented, is therefore not authorised by the Commission. As a consequence, if the concentration is implemented, it should be treated in the same way as a non-notified concentration implemented without authorisation. Furthermore, where the Commission has already found that, in the absence of the condition, the concentration would be incompatible with the common market, it should have the power to directly order the dissolution of the concentration, so as to restore the situation prevailing prior to the implementation of the concentration. Where an obligation attached to a decision declaring the concentration compatible with the common market is not fulfilled, the Commission should be able to revoke its decision. Moreover, the Commission should be able to impose appropriate financial sanctions where conditions or obligations are not fulfilled.

Commentary
Recital 31: B&C: 8.171 F&N: 5.640

(32) Concentrations which, by reason of the limited market share of the undertakings concerned, are not liable to impede effective competition may be presumed to be compatible with the common market. Without prejudice to Articles 81 and 82 of the Treaty, an indication to this effect exists, in particular, where the market share of the undertakings concerned does not exceed 25% either in the common market or in a substantial part of it.

Commentary
Recital 32: F&N: 5.213

(33) The Commission should have the task of taking all the decisions necessary to establish whether or not concentrations with a Community dimension are compatible with the common market, as well as decisions designed to restore the situation prevailing prior to the implementation of a concentration which has been declared incompatible with the common market.

(34) To ensure effective control, undertakings should be obliged to give prior notification of concentrations with a Community dimension following the conclusion of the agreement, the announcement of the public bid or the acquisition of a controlling interest. Notification should also be possible where the undertakings concerned satisfy the Commission of their intention to enter into an agreement for a proposed concentration and demonstrate to the Commission that their plan for that proposed concentration is sufficiently concrete, for example on the basis of an agreement in principle, a memorandum of understanding, or a letter of intent signed by all undertakings concerned, or, in the case of a public bid, where they have publicly announced an intention to make such a bid, provided that the intended agreement or bid would result in a concentration with a Community dimension. The implementation of concentrations should be suspended until a final decision of the Commission has been taken. However, it should be possible to derogate from this suspension at the request of the undertakings concerned, where appropriate. In deciding whether or not to grant a derogation, the Commission should take account of all pertinent factors, such as the nature and gravity of damage to the undertakings concerned or to third parties, and the threat to competition posed by the concentration. In the interest of legal certainty, the validity of transactions must nevertheless be protected as much as necessary.

Commentary
Recital 34: B&C: 8.111 F&N: 5.160, 5.440

Part D Mergers and Concentrations

(35) A period within which the Commission must initiate proceedings in respect of a notified concentration and a period within which it must take a final decision on the compatibility or incompatibility with the common market of that concentration should be laid down. These periods should be extended whenever the undertakings concerned offer commitments with a view to rendering the concentration compatible with the common market, in order to allow for sufficient time for the analysis and market testing of such commitment offers and for the consultation of Member States as well as interested third parties. A limited extension of the period within which the Commission must take a final decision should also be possible in order to allow sufficient time for the investigation of the case and the verification of the facts and arguments submitted to the Commission.

(36) The Community respects the fundamental rights and observes the principles recognised in particular by the Charter of Fundamental Rights of the European Union.[1] Accordingly, this Regulation should be interpreted and applied with respect to those rights and principles.

Notes

[1] OJ C 364, 18.12.2000, p. 1.

Commentary

Recital 36: **B&C:** 8.144

(37) The undertakings concerned must be afforded the right to be heard by the Commission when proceedings have been initiated; the members of the management and supervisory bodies and the recognised representatives of the employees of the undertakings concerned, and interested third parties, must also be given the opportunity to be heard.

Commentary

Recital 37: **B&C:** 8.131

(38) In order properly to appraise concentrations, the Commission should have the right to request all necessary information and to conduct all necessary inspections throughout the Community. To that end, and with a view to protecting competition effectively, the Commission's powers of investigation need to be expanded. The Commission should, in particular, have the right to interview any persons who may be in possession of useful information and to record the statements made.

(39) In the course of an inspection, officials authorised by the Commission should have the right to ask for any information relevant to the subject matter and purpose of the inspection; they should also have the right to affix seals during inspections, particularly in circumstances where there are reasonable grounds to suspect that a concentration has been implemented without being notified; that incorrect, incomplete or misleading information has been supplied to the Commission; or that the undertakings or persons concerned have failed to comply with a condition or obligation imposed by decision of the Commission. In any event, seals should only be used in exceptional circumstances, for the period of time strictly necessary for the inspection, normally not for more than 48 hours.

(40) Without prejudice to the case-law of the Court of Justice, it is also useful to set out the scope of the control that the national judicial authority may exercise when it authorises, as provided by national law and as a precautionary measure, assistance from law enforcement authorities in order to overcome possible opposition on the part of the undertaking against an inspection, including the affixing of seals, ordered by Commission decision. It results from the case-law that the national judicial authority may in particular ask of the Commission further information which it needs to carry out its control and in the absence of which it could refuse the authorisation. The case-law also confirms the competence of the national courts to control the application of national rules governing the implementation of coercive measures. The competent authorities of the Member States should cooperate actively in the exercise of the Commission's investigative powers.

(41) When complying with decisions of the Commission, the undertakings and persons concerned cannot be forced to admit that they have committed infringements, but they are in any event obliged to answer factual questions and to provide documents, even if this information may be used to establish against themselves or against others the existence of such infringements.

(42) For the sake of transparency, all decisions of the Commission which are not of a merely procedural nature should be widely publicised. While ensuring preservation of the rights of defence
of the undertakings concerned, in particular the right of access to the file, it is essential that business secrets be protected. The confidentiality of information exchanged in the network and with
the competent authorities of third countries should likewise be safeguarded.

Commentary
Recital 42: F&N: 5.515

(43) Compliance with this Regulation should be enforceable, as appropriate, by means of fines and
periodic penalty payments. The Court of Justice should be given unlimited jurisdiction in that
regard pursuant to Article 229 of the Treaty.

Commentary
Recital 43: B&C: 8.235

(44) The conditions in which concentrations, involving undertakings having their seat or their principal fields of activity in the Community, are carried out in third countries should be observed,
and provision should be made for the possibility of the Council giving the Commission an
appropriate mandate for negotiation with a view to obtaining non-discriminatory treatment for
such undertakings.

Commentary
Recital 44: B&C: 8.286

(45) This Regulation in no way detracts from the collective rights of employees, as recognised in the
undertakings concerned, notably with regard to any obligation to inform or consult their recognised representatives under Community and national law.

(46) The Commission should be able to lay down detailed rules concerning the implementation of
this Regulation in accordance with the procedures for the exercise of implementing powers conferred on the Commission. For the adoption of such implementing provisions, the Commission
should be assisted by an Advisory Committee composed of the representatives of the Member
States as specified in Article 23,

HAS ADOPTED THIS REGULATION:

Article 1
Scope

1. Without prejudice to Article 4(5) and Article 22, this Regulation shall apply to all concentrations
with a Community dimension as defined in this Article.

2. A concentration has a Community dimension where:

(a) the combined aggregate worldwide turnover of all the undertakings concerned is more than EUR
5000 million; and

(b) the aggregate Community-wide turnover of each of at least two of the undertakings concerned is
more than EUR 250 million,

unless each of the undertakings concerned achieves more than two-thirds of its aggregate Community-
wide turnover within one and the same Member State.

3. A concentration that does not meet the thresholds laid down in paragraph 2 has a Community
dimension where:

(a) the combined aggregate worldwide turnover of all the undertakings concerned is more than EUR
2500 million;

(b) in each of at least three Member States, the combined aggregate turnover of all the undertakings
concerned is more than EUR 100 million;

(c) in each of at least three Member States included for the purpose of point (b), the aggregate turnover of each of at least two of the undertakings concerned is more than EUR 25 million; and

(d) the aggregate Community-wide turnover of each of at least two of the undertakings concerned is more than EUR 100 million,

unless each of the undertakings concerned achieves more than two-thirds of its aggregate Community-wide turnover within one and the same Member State.

4. On the basis of statistical data that may be regularly provided by the Member States, the Commission shall report to the Council on the operation of the thresholds and criteria set out in paragraphs 2 and 3 by 1 July 2009 and may present proposals pursuant to paragraph 5.

5. Following the report referred to in paragraph 4 and on a proposal from the Commission, the Council, acting by a qualified majority, may revise the thresholds and criteria mentioned in paragraph 3.

Commentary
Art 1: B&C: 8.008 F&N: 5.81, 5.82, 5.97, 5.98, 5.119
Art 1(1)–(3): B&C: 8.060
Art 1(2): F&N: 5.94, 5.95, 5.96, 5.98, 5.100, 5.111, 5.166
Art 1(3): F&N: 5.94, 5.95, 5.97, 5.98, 5.99, 5.111
Art 1(4)–(5): B&C: 8.060

Article 2
Appraisal of concentrations

1. Concentrations within the scope of this Regulation shall be appraised in accordance with the objectives of this Regulation and the following provisions with a view to establishing whether or not they are compatible with the common market.

In making this appraisal, the Commission shall take into account:

(a) the need to maintain and develop effective competition within the common market in view of, among other things, the structure of all the markets concerned and the actual or potential competition from undertakings located either within or outwith the Community;

(b) the market position of the undertakings concerned and their economic and financial power, the alternatives available to suppliers and users, their access to supplies or markets, any legal or other barriers to entry, supply and demand trends for the relevant goods and services, the interests of the intermediate and ultimate consumers, and the development of technical and economic progress provided that it is to consumers' advantage and does not form an obstacle to competition.

2. A concentration which would not significantly impede effective competition in the common market or in a substantial part of it, in particular as a result of the creation or strengthening of a dominant position, shall be declared compatible with the common market.

3. A concentration which would significantly impede effective competition, in the common market or in a substantial part of it, in particular as a result of the creation or strengthening of a dominant position, shall be declared incompatible with the common market.

4. To the extent that the creation of a joint venture constituting a concentration pursuant to Article 3 has as its object or effect the coordination of the competitive behaviour of undertakings that remain independent, such coordination shall be appraised in accordance with the criteria of Article 81(1) and (3) of the Treaty, with a view to establishing whether or not the operation is compatible with the common market.

5. In making this appraisal, the Commission shall take into account in particular:

— whether two or more parent companies retain, to a significant extent, activities in the same market as the joint venture or in a market which is downstream or upstream from that of the joint venture or in a neighbouring market closely related to this market,

— whether the coordination which is the direct consequence of the creation of the joint venture affords the undertakings concerned the possibility of eliminating competition in respect of a substantial part of the products or services in question.

Commentary
Art 2: B&C: 2.089, 2.095, 8.251, 12.127 F&N: 4.39, 4.85, **5.182–5.207**, 5.331, 5.338, 5.652, 5.674, 12.433
Art 2(1): B&C: 8.183, 8.204

Art 2(1)(a): F&N: 5.182
Art 2(1)(b): F&N: 5.324, 53.182
Art 2(1)–(3): F&N: 5.334
Art 2(2): B&C: 4.012, 8.184, 8.255 F&N: 5.183, 5.199
Art 2(3): B&C: 8.184, 8.255, 10.010 F&N: 4.119, 5.183, 5.199, 7.23
Art 2(4): B&C: 7.007, 7.017, 7.034, 8.052, 8.185, 8.233 F&N: 5.332, 5.334, 5.335, 5.337, 5.338, 5.344, 5.448,
   7.24, 7.88, 7.89, 7.90, 7.93, 7.97, 7.106
Art 2(5): B&C: 8.052, 8.185, 8.233 F&N: 5.333, 5.334, 5.336, 5.337, 7.24

Article 3
Definition of concentration

1. A concentration shall be deemed to arise where a change of control on a lasting basis results from:

(a) the merger of two or more previously independent undertakings or parts of undertakings, or
(b) the acquisition, by one or more persons already controlling at least one undertaking, or by one or more undertakings, whether by purchase of securities or assets, by contract or by any other means, of direct or indirect control of the whole or parts of one or more other undertakings.

2. Control shall be constituted by rights, contracts or any other means which, either separately or in combination and having regard to the considerations of fact or law involved, confer the possibility of exercising decisive influence on an undertaking, in particular by:

(a) ownership or the right to use all or part of the assets of an undertaking;
(b) rights or contracts which confer decisive influence on the composition, voting or decisions of the organs of an undertaking.

3. Control is acquired by persons or undertakings which:

(a) are holders of the rights or entitled to rights under the contracts concerned; or
(b) while not being holders of such rights or entitled to rights under such contracts, have the power to exercise the rights deriving therefrom.

4. The creation of a joint venture performing on a lasting basis all the functions of an autonomous economic entity shall constitute a concentration within the meaning of paragraph 1(b).

5. A concentration shall not be deemed to arise where:

(a) credit institutions or other financial institutions or insurance companies, the normal activities of which include transactions and dealing in securities for their own account or for the account of others, hold on a temporary basis securities which they have acquired in an undertaking with a view to reselling them, provided that they do not exercise voting rights in respect of those securities with a view to determining the competitive behaviour of that undertaking or provided that they exercise such voting rights only with a view to preparing the disposal of all or part of that undertaking or of its assets or the disposal of those securities and that any such disposal takes place within one year of the date of acquisition; that period may be extended by the Commission on request where such institutions or companies can show that the disposal was not reasonably possible within the period set;
(b) control is acquired by an office-holder according to the law of a Member State relating to liquidation, winding up, insolvency, cessation of payments, compositions or analogous proceedings;
(c) the operations referred to in paragraph 1(b) are carried out by the financial holding companies referred to in Article 5(3) of Fourth Council Directive 78/660/EEC of 25 July 1978 based on Article 54(3)(g) of the Treaty on the annual accounts of certain types of companies[1] provided however that the voting rights in respect of the holding are exercised, in particular in relation to the appointment of members of the management and supervisory bodies of the undertakings in which they have holdings, only to maintain the full value of those investments and not to determine directly or indirectly the competitive conduct of those undertakings.

Notes
[1] OJ L 222, 14. 8. 1978, p. 11. Directive as last amended by Directive 2003/51/EC of the European Parliament and of the Council (OJ L 178, 17.7.2003, p. 16).

Commentary
Art 3: B&C: 8.019, 8.074, 8.087, 8.260, 10.011 F&N: 5.24, 5.27–5.30, 5.80, 5.133, 5.143, 5.159, 7.24, 7.92

Article 4
Prior notification of concentrations and pre-notification referral at the request of the notifying parties

1. Concentrations with a Community dimension defined in this Regulation shall be notified to the Commission prior to their implementation and following the conclusion of the agreement, the announcement of the public bid, or the acquisition of a controlling interest.

Notification may also be made where the undertakings concerned demonstrate to the Commission a good faith intention to conclude an agreement or, in the case of a public bid, where they have publicly announced an intention to make such a bid, provided that the intended agreement or bid would result in a concentration with a Community dimension.

For the purposes of this Regulation, the term "notified concentration" shall also cover intended concentrations notified pursuant to the second subparagraph. For the purposes of paragraphs 4 and 5 of this Article, the term "concentration" includes intended concentrations within the meaning of the second subparagraph.

2. A concentration which consists of a merger within the meaning of Article 3(1)(a) or in the acquisition of joint control within the meaning of Article 3(1)(b) shall be notified jointly by the parties to the merger or by those acquiring joint control as the case may be. In all other cases, the notification shall be effected by the person or undertaking acquiring control of the whole or parts of one or more undertakings.

3. Where the Commission finds that a notified concentration falls within the scope of this Regulation, it shall publish the fact of the notification, at the same time indicating the names of the undertakings concerned, their country of origin, the nature of the concentration and the economic sectors involved. The Commission shall take account of the legitimate interest of undertakings in the protection of their business secrets.

4. Prior to the notification of a concentration within the meaning of paragraph 1, the persons or undertakings referred to in paragraph 2 may inform the Commission, by means of a reasoned submission, that the concentration may significantly affect competition in a market within a Member State which presents all the characteristics of a distinct market and should therefore be examined, in whole or in part, by that Member State.

The Commission shall transmit this submission to all Member States without delay. The Member State referred to in the reasoned submission shall, within 15 working days of receiving the submission, express its agreement or disagreement as regards the request to refer the case. Where that Member State takes no such decision within this period, it shall be deemed to have agreed.

Unless that Member State disagrees, the Commission, where it considers that such a distinct market exists, and that competition in that market may be significantly affected by the concentration, may decide to refer the whole or part of the case to the competent authorities of that Member State with a view to the application of that State's national competition law.

The decision whether or not to refer the case in accordance with the third subparagraph shall be taken within 25 working days starting from the receipt of the reasoned submission by the Commission. The Commission shall inform the other Member States and the persons or undertakings concerned of its decision. If the Commission does not take a decision within this period, it shall be deemed to have adopted a decision to refer the case in accordance with the submission made by the persons or undertakings concerned.

If the Commission decides, or is deemed to have decided, pursuant to the third and fourth sub-paragraphs, to refer the whole of the case, no notification shall be made pursuant to paragraph 1 and national competition law shall apply. Article 9(6) to (9) shall apply mutatis mutandis.

5. With regard to a concentration as defined in Article 3 which does not have a Community dimension within the meaning of Article 1 and which is capable of being reviewed under the national competition laws of at least three Member States, the persons or undertakings referred to in paragraph 2 may, before any notification to the competent authorities, inform the Commission by means of a reasoned submission that the concentration should be examined by the Commission.

The Commission shall transmit this submission to all Member States without delay.

Any Member State competent to examine the concentration under its national competition law may, within 15 working days of receiving the reasoned submission, express its disagreement as regards the request to refer the case.

Where at least one such Member State has expressed its disagreement in accordance with the third subparagraph within the period of 15 working days, the case shall not be referred. The Commission shall, without delay, inform all Member States and the persons or undertakings concerned of any such expression of disagreement.

Where no Member State has expressed its disagreement in accordance with the third subparagraph within the period of 15 working days, the concentration shall be deemed to have a Community dimension and shall be notified to the Commission in accordance with paragraphs 1 and 2. In such situations, no Member State shall apply its national competition law to the concentration.

6. The Commission shall report to the Council on the operation of paragraphs 4 and 5 by 1 July 2009. Following this report and on a proposal from the Commission, the Council, acting by a qualified majority, may revise paragraphs 4 and 5.

Commentary

Art 4: **B&C:** 8.180 **F&N:** 5.386, 5.476, 5.557
Art 4(1): **B&C:** 8.110–8.111, 8.238 **F&N:** 5.78, 5.122, 5.148, 5.156, 5.160, 5.437, 5.439, 5.440, 5.470
Art 4(2): **B&C:** 8.015, 8.112 **F&N:** 5.78, 5.438
Art 4(3): **B&C:** 8.133, 8.176 **F&N:** 5.480, 5.487
Art 4(4): **B&C:** 8.081–8.084, 8.086, 8.089, 8.091, 8.094, 8.100, 8.110–8.111, 8.184, 8.261, 8.277 **F&N:** 5.110, 5.114, 5.115, 5.118, 5.120, 5.122, 5.123, 5.125, 5.126, 5.127, 5.133, 5.140, 5.145, 5.147, 5.148, 5.156, 5.159, 5.160, 5.164, 5.166, 5.179, 5.423
Art 4(5): **B&C:** 7.017, 8.085–8.089, 8.097, 8.100, 8.110, 8.261, 8.278 **F&N:** 5.110, 5.114, 5.115, 5.120, 5.123, 5.132–5.144, 5.145, 5.149, 5.154, 5.159, 5.160, 5.180, 5.423, 5.437
Art 4(6): **B&C:** 8.090

Article 5
Calculation of turnover

1. Aggregate turnover within the meaning of this Regulation shall comprise the amounts derived by the undertakings concerned in the preceding financial year from the sale of products and the provision of services falling within the undertakings' ordinary activities after deduction of sales rebates and of value added tax and other taxes directly related to turnover. The aggregate turnover of an undertaking concerned shall not include the sale of products or the provision of services between any of the undertakings referred to in paragraph 4.

Turnover, in the Community or in a Member State, shall comprise products sold and services provided to undertakings or consumers, in the Community or in that Member State as the case may be.

2. By way of derogation from paragraph 1, where the concentration consists of the acquisition of parts, whether or not constituted as legal entities, of one or more undertakings, only the turnover relating to the parts which are the subject of the concentration shall be taken into account with regard to the seller or sellers.

However, two or more transactions within the meaning of the first subparagraph which take place within a two-year period between the same persons or undertakings shall be treated as one and the same concentration arising on the date of the last transaction.

3. In place of turnover the following shall be used:

(a) for credit institutions and other financial institutions, the sum of the following income items as defined in Council Directive 86/635/EEC,[1] after deduction of value added tax and other taxes directly related to those items, where appropriate:
   (i)   interest income and similar income;
   (ii) income from securities:
       — income from shares and other variable yield securities,
       — income from participating interests,
       — income from shares in affiliated undertakings;
   (iii) commissions receivable;
   (iv) net profit on financial operations;
   (v)   other operating income.

   The turnover of a credit or financial institution in the Community or in a Member State shall comprise the income items, as defined above, which are received by the branch or division of that institution established in the Community or in the Member State in question, as the case may be;

(b) for insurance undertakings, the value of gross premiums written which shall comprise all amounts received and receivable in respect of insurance contracts issued by or on behalf of the insurance undertakings, including also outgoing reinsurance premiums, and after deduction of taxes and parafiscal contributions or levies charged by reference to the amounts of individual premiums or the total volume of premiums; as regards Article 1(2)(b) and (3)(b), (c) and (d) and the final part of Article 1(2) and (3), gross premiums received from Community residents and from residents of one Member State respectively shall be taken into account.

4. Without prejudice to paragraph 2, the aggregate turnover of an undertaking concerned within the meaning of this Regulation shall be calculated by adding together the respective turnovers of the following:

(a) the undertaking concerned;
(b) those undertakings in which the undertaking concerned, directly or indirectly:
   (i)   owns more than half the capital or business assets, or
   (ii) has the power to exercise more than half the voting rights, or
   (iii) has the power to appoint more than half the members of the supervisory board, the administrative board or bodies legally representing the undertakings, or
   (iv) has the right to manage the undertakings' affairs;
(c) those undertakings which have in the undertaking concerned the rights or powers listed in (b);
(d) those undertakings in which an undertaking as referred to in (c) has the rights or powers listed in (b);
(e) those undertakings in which two or more undertakings as referred to in (a) to (d) jointly have the rights or powers listed in (b).

5. Where undertakings concerned by the concentration jointly have the rights or powers listed in paragraph 4(b), in calculating the aggregate turnover of the undertakings concerned for the purposes of this Regulation:

(a) no account shall be taken of the turnover resulting from the sale of products or the provision of services between the joint undertaking and each of the undertakings concerned or any other undertaking connected with any one of them, as set out in paragraph 4(b) to (e);
(b) account shall be taken of the turnover resulting from the sale of products and the provision of services between the joint undertaking and any third undertakings. This turnover shall be apportioned equally amongst the undertakings concerned.

Notes
[1] OJ L 372, 31. 12. 1986, p. 1. Directive as last amended by Directive 2003/51/EC of the European Parliament and of the Council.

Commentary
Art 5: **B&C:** 8.008, 8.180–8.181 **F&N:** 5.94
Art 5(1): **B&C:** 8.062, 8.066 **F&N:** 5.85
Art 5(2): **B&C:** 8.044, 8.064–8.065 **F&N:** 5.68, 5.85
Art 5(3): **B&C:** 8.067
Art 5(3)(a): **B&C:** 8.067 **F&N:** 5.109
Art 5(4): **B&C:** 8.062, 8.069, 8.076–8.078 **F&N:** 5.82, 5.88
Art 5(4)(b)(i)–(iii): **B&C:** 8.076
Art 5(4)(b)(iv): **B&C:** 8.076

Article 6
Examination of the notification and initiation of proceedings

1. The Commission shall examine the notification as soon as it is received.

(a) Where it concludes that the concentration notified does not fall within the scope of this Regulation, it shall record that finding by means of a decision.

(b) Where it finds that the concentration notified, although falling within the scope of this Regulation, does not raise serious doubts as to its compatibility with the common market, it shall decide not to oppose it and shall declare that it is compatible with the common market.
A decision declaring a concentration compatible shall be deemed to cover restrictions directly related and necessary to the implementation of the concentration.

(c) Without prejudice to paragraph 2, where the Commission finds that the concentration notified falls within the scope of this Regulation and raises serious doubts as to its compatibility with the common market, it shall decide to initiate proceedings. Without prejudice to Article 9, such proceedings shall be closed by means of a decision as provided for in Article 8(1) to (4), unless the undertakings concerned have demonstrated to the satisfaction of the Commission that they have abandoned the concentration.

2. Where the Commission finds that, following modification by the undertakings concerned, a notified concentration no longer raises serious doubts within the meaning of paragraph 1(c), it shall declare the concentration compatible with the common market pursuant to paragraph 1(b).

The Commission may attach to its decision under paragraph 1(b) conditions and obligations intended to ensure that the undertakings concerned comply with the commitments they have entered into vis-à-vis the Commission with a view to rendering the concentration compatible with the common market.

3. The Commission may revoke the decision it took pursuant to paragraph 1(a) or (b) where:

(a) the decision is based on incorrect information for which one of the undertakings is responsible or where it has been obtained by deceit,
or

(b) the undertakings concerned commit a breach of an obligation attached to the decision.

4. In the cases referred to in paragraph 3, the Commission may take a decision under paragraph 1, without being bound by the time limits referred to in Article 10(1).

5. The Commission shall notify its decision to the undertakings concerned and the competent authorities of the Member States without delay.

Commentary
Art 6: **F&N:** 5.154, 5.180, 5.470, 5.479, 5.482, 5.483, 5.509, 5.511, 5.512, 5.513, 5.515, 5.516, 5.517, 5.632, 5.683
Art 6(1): **B&C:** 8.256
Art 6(1)(a): **B&C:** 8.038, 8.136, 8.138, 8.238, 8.243 **F&N:** 5.90, 5.154, 5.155, 5.510, 5.655
Art 6(1)(b): **B&C:** 8.136, 8.138, 8.181–8.182, 8.263 **F&N:** 5.90, 5.345, 5.510, 5.634, 5.638, 5.655
Art 6(1)(c): **B&C:** 8.093, 8.131, 8.136, 8.142, 8.145, 8.157, 8.163, 8.165, 8.238, 8.282 **F&N:** 5.149, 5.448,
    5.466, 5.467, 5.468, 5.510, 5.518, 5.524, 5.526, 5.528, 5.533, 5.536, 5.624, 5.656, 7.106
Art 6(2): **B&C:** 8.133, 8.136, 8.163 **F&N:** 5.365, 5.510, 5.615, 5.655, 12.455
Art 6(3): **F&N:** 5.516, 5.615
Art 6(3)(a): **B&C:** 8.140 **F&N:** 5.154, 5.462
Art 6(3)(b): **B&C:** 8.140, 8.171
Art 6(4): **B&C:** 8.171 **F&N:** 5.527
Art 6(5): **B&C:** 8.138 **F&N:** 5.513

Part D Mergers and
Concentrations

Article 7
Suspension of concentrations

1. A concentration with a Community dimension as defined in Article 1, or which is to be examined by the Commission pursuant to Article 4(5), shall not be implemented either before its notification or until it has been declared compatible with the common market pursuant to a decision under Articles 6(1)(b), 8(1) or 8(2), or on the basis of a presumption according to Article 10(6).

2. Paragraph 1 shall not prevent the implementation of a public bid or of a series of transactions in securities including those convertible into other securities admitted to trading on a market such as a stock exchange, by which control within the meaning of Article 3 is acquired from various sellers, provided that:

(a) the concentration is notified to the Commission pursuant to Article 4 without delay; and
(b) the acquirer does not exercise the voting rights attached to the securities in question or does so only to maintain the full value of its investments based on a derogation granted by the Commission under paragraph 3.

3. The Commission may, on request, grant a derogation from the obligations imposed in paragraphs 1 or 2. The request to grant a derogation must be reasoned. In deciding on the request, the Commission shall take into account inter alia the effects of the suspension on one or more undertakings concerned by the concentration or on a third party and the threat to competition posed by the concentration. Such a derogation may be made subject to conditions and obligations in order to ensure conditions of effective competition. A derogation may be applied for and granted at any time, be it before notification or after the transaction.

4. The validity of any transaction carried out in contravention of paragraph 1 shall be dependent on a decision pursuant to Article 6(1)(b) or Article 8(1), (2) or (3) or on a presumption pursuant to Article 10(6).

This Article shall, however, have no effect on the validity of transactions in securities including those convertible into other securities admitted to trading on a market such as a stock exchange, unless the buyer and seller knew or ought to have known that the transaction was carried out in contravention of paragraph 1.

Commentary
Art 7: **B&C:** 8.048 **F&N:** 5.78, 5.386, **5.470–5.478**, 5.634
Art 7(1): **B&C:** 8.046, 8.126–8.127 **F&N:** 5.77, 5.470, 5.471, 5.475, 5.477
Art 7(2): **B&C:** 8.128 **F&N:** 5.78, 5.471, 5.476
Art 7(3): **B&C:** 8.129, 8.181–8.182 **F&N:** 5.137, 5.471, 5.476, 5.477, 5.478, 5.634, 5.638, 5.655
Art 7(4): **B&C:** 8.130, 8.144

Article 8
Powers of decision of the Commission

1. Where the Commission finds that a notified concentration fulfils the criterion laid down in Article 2(2) and, in the cases referred to in Article 2(4), the criteria laid down in Article 81(3) of the Treaty, it shall issue a decision declaring the concentration compatible with the common market.

A decision declaring a concentration compatible shall be deemed to cover restrictions directly related and necessary to the implementation of the concentration.

2. Where the Commission finds that, following modification by the undertakings concerned, a notified concentration fulfils the criterion laid down in Article 2(2) and, in the cases referred to in Article 2(4), the criteria laid down in Article 81(3) of the Treaty, it shall issue a decision declaring the concentration compatible with the common market.

The Commission may attach to its decision conditions and obligations intended to ensure that the undertakings concerned comply with the commitments they have entered into vis-à-vis the Commission with a view to rendering the concentration compatible with the common market.

A decision declaring a concentration compatible shall be deemed to cover restrictions directly related and necessary to the implementation of the concentration.

3. Where the Commission finds that a concentration fulfils the criterion defined in Article 2(3) or, in the cases referred to in Article 2(4), does not fulfil the criteria laid down in Article 81(3) of the Treaty, it shall issue a decision declaring that the concentration is incompatible with the common market.

4. Where the Commission finds that a concentration:

(a) has already been implemented and that concentration has been declared incompatible with the common market, or

(b) has been implemented in contravention of a condition attached to a decision taken under paragraph 2, which has found that, in the absence of the condition, the concentration would fulfil the criterion laid down in Article 2(3) or, in the cases referred to in Article 2(4), would not fulfil the criteria laid down in Article 81(3) of the Treaty,

the Commission may:

— require the undertakings concerned to dissolve the concentration, in particular through the dissolution of the merger or the disposal of all the shares or assets acquired, so as to restore the situation prevailing prior to the implementation of the concentration; in circumstances where restoration of the situation prevailing before the implementation of the concentration is not possible through dissolution of the concentration, the Commission may take any other measure appropriate to achieve such restoration as far as possible,

— order any other appropriate measure to ensure that the undertakings concerned dissolve the concentration or take other restorative measures as required in its decision.

In cases falling within point (a) of the first subparagraph, the measures referred to in that subparagraph may be imposed either in a decision pursuant to paragraph 3 or by separate decision.

5. The Commission may take interim measures appropriate to restore or maintain conditions of effective competition where a concentration:

(a) has been implemented in contravention of Article 7, and a decision as to the compatibility of the concentration with the common market has not yet been taken;

(b) has been implemented in contravention of a condition attached to a decision under Article 6(1)(b) or paragraph 2 of this Article;

(c) has already been implemented and is declared incompatible with the common market.

6. The Commission may revoke the decision it has taken pursuant to paragraphs 1 or 2 where:

(a) the declaration of compatibility is based on incorrect information for which one of the undertakings is responsible or where it has been obtained by deceit; or

(b) the undertakings concerned commit a breach of an obligation attached to the decision.

7. The Commission may take a decision pursuant to paragraphs 1 to 3 without being bound by the time limits referred to in Article 10(3), in cases where:

(a) it finds that a concentration has been implemented
   (i) in contravention of a condition attached to a decision under Article 6(1)(b), or
   (ii) in contravention of a condition attached to a decision taken under paragraph 2 and in accordance with Article 10(2), which has found that, in the absence of the condition, the concentration would raise serious doubts as to its compatibility with the common market; or

(b) a decision has been revoked pursuant to paragraph 6.

8. The Commission shall notify its decision to the undertakings concerned and the competent authorities of the Member States without delay.

Commentary
Art 8: B&C: 8.144 F&N: 5.154, 5.180, 5.399, 5.471, 5.518, 5.520, 5.526, 5.527, 5.528, 5.549, 5.552, 5.616, 5.624, 5.629, 5.631, 5.632, 5.683
Art 8(1): B&C: 8.156, 8.263 F&N: 5.345, 5.528, 5.625
Art 8(2): B&C: 8.156, 8.161, 8.164, 8.181–8.182, 8.263 F&N: 5.22, 5.129, 5.345, 5.528, 5.615, 5.625, 5.634, 5.638, 5.641, 5.655, 12.455
Art 8(2)–(5): B&C: 8.158
Art 8(3): B&C: 8.156, 8.181 F&N: 5.625, 5.634, 5.641, 5.643, 5.655
Art 8(4): B&C: 8.099, 8.156, 8.160, 8.178, 8.181–8.182, 8.236 F&N: 5.77, 5.475, 5.615, 5.625, 5.638, 5.640, 5.641, 5.642, 5.655

Part D Mergers and Concentrations

Article 9
Referral to the competent authorities of the Member States

1. The Commission may, by means of a decision notified without delay to the undertakings concerned and the competent authorities of the other Member States, refer a notified concentration to the competent authorities of the Member State concerned in the following circumstances.

2. Within 15 working days of the date of receipt of the copy of the notification, a Member State, on its own initiative or upon the invitation of the Commission, may inform the Commission, which shall inform the undertakings concerned, that:

(a) a concentration threatens to affect significantly competition in a market within that Member State, which presents all the characteristics of a distinct market, or

(b) a concentration affects competition in a market within that Member State, which presents all the characteristics of a distinct market and which does not constitute a substantial part of the common market.

3. If the Commission considers that, having regard to the market for the products or services in question and the geographical reference market within the meaning of paragraph 7, there is such a distinct market and that such a threat exists, either:

(a) it shall itself deal with the case in accordance with this Regulation; or

(b) it shall refer the whole or part of the case to the competent authorities of the Member State concerned with a view to the application of that State's national competition law.

If, however, the Commission considers that such a distinct market or threat does not exist, it shall adopt a decision to that effect which it shall address to the Member State concerned, and shall itself deal with the case in accordance with this Regulation.

In cases where a Member State informs the Commission pursuant to paragraph 2(b) that a concentration affects competition in a distinct market within its territory that does not form a substantial part of the common market, the Commission shall refer the whole or part of the case relating to the distinct market concerned, if it considers that such a distinct market is affected.

4. A decision to refer or not to refer pursuant to paragraph 3 shall be taken:

(a) as a general rule within the period provided for in Article 10(1), second subparagraph, where the Commission, pursuant to Article 6(1)(b), has not initiated proceedings; or

(b) within 65 working days at most of the notification of the concentration concerned where the Commission has initiated proceedings under Article 6(1)(c), without taking the preparatory steps in order to adopt the necessary measures under Article 8(2), (3) or (4) to maintain or restore effective competition on the market concerned.

5. If within the 65 working days referred to in paragraph 4(b) the Commission, despite a reminder from the Member State concerned, has not taken a decision on referral in accordance with paragraph 3 nor has taken the preparatory steps referred to in paragraph 4(b), it shall be deemed to have taken a decision to refer the case to the Member State concerned in accordance with paragraph 3(b).

6. The competent authority of the Member State concerned shall decide upon the case without undue delay.

Within 45 working days after the Commission's referral, the competent authority of the Member State concerned shall inform the undertakings concerned of the result of the preliminary competition assessment and what further action, if any, it proposes to take. The Member State concerned may exceptionally suspend this time limit where necessary information has not been provided to it by the undertakings concerned as provided for by its national competition law.

Where a notification is requested under national law, the period of 45 working days shall begin on the working day following that of the receipt of a complete notification by the competent authority of that Member State.

7. The geographical reference market shall consist of the area in which the undertakings concerned are involved in the supply and demand of products or services, in which the conditions of competition are sufficiently homogeneous and which can be distinguished from neighbouring areas because, in particular, conditions of competition are appreciably different in those areas. This assessment should take account in particular of the nature and characteristics of the products or services concerned, of the existence of entry barriers or of consumer preferences, of appreciable differences of the undertakings' market shares between the area concerned and neighbouring areas or of substantial price differences.

8. In applying the provisions of this Article, the Member State concerned may take only the measures strictly necessary to safeguard or restore effective competition on the market concerned.

9. In accordance with the relevant provisions of the Treaty, any Member State may appeal to the Court of Justice, and in particular request the application of Article 243 of the Treaty, for the purpose of applying its national competition law.

Commentary

Art 9: **B&C:** 4.012, 4.071, 4.076, 6.026, 8.081, 8.083–8.084, 8.091–8.093, 8.096, 8.100–8.101, 8.104, 8.106, 8.136, 8.154, 8.184, 8.190, 8.261, 8.277, 8.281 **F&N:** 5.110, 5.112, 5.113, 5.115, 5.118, 5.129, 5.159, 5.161, 5.169, 5.178, 5.449, 5.484, 5.655, 5.656
Art 9(1): **B&C:** 8.091
Art 9(2): **B&C:** 6.026, 8.093, 8.133 **F&N:** 5.177, 5.484
Art 9(2)(a): **B&C:** 8.083, 8.091–8.092 **F&N:** 5.162, 5.163, 5.178
Art 9(2)(b): **B&C:** 8.091–8.092 **F&N:** 5.162, 5.167, 5.168, 5.178
Art 9(3): **B&C:** 8.092, 8.136 **F&N:** 5.179
Art 9(3)(b): **B&C:** 8.092, 8.190
Art 9(4)(a): **B&C:** 8.093
Art 9(4)(b): **B&C:** 8.093 **F&N:** 5.178
Art 9(5): **B&C:** 8.093 **F&N:** 5.178
Art 9(6): **B&C:** 8.084, 8.093 **F&N:** 5.178, 5.179
Art 9(6)–(9): **F&N:** 5.148
Art 9(7): **B&C:** 4.071, 6.026, 8.083, 8.094, 8.190
Art 9(8): **B&C:** 8.092–8.093 **F&N:** 5.178
Art 9(9): **B&C:** 8.093

Article 10
Time limits for initiating proceedings and for decisions

1. Without prejudice to Article 6(4), the decisions referred to in Article 6(1) shall be taken within 25 working days at most. That period shall begin on the working day following that of the receipt of a notification or, if the information to be supplied with the notification is incomplete, on the working day following that of the receipt of the complete information.

That period shall be increased to 35 working days where the Commission receives a request from a Member State in accordance with Article 9(2)or where, the undertakings concerned offer commitments pursuant to Article 6(2) with a view to rendering the concentration compatible with the common market.

2. Decisions pursuant to Article 8(1) or (2) concerning notified concentrations shall be taken as soon as it appears that the serious doubts referred to in Article 6(1)(c) have been removed, particularly as a result of modifications made by the undertakings concerned, and at the latest by the time limit laid down in paragraph 3.

3. Without prejudice to Article 8(7), decisions pursuant to Article 8(1) to (3) concerning notified concentrations shall be taken within not more than 90 working days of the date on which the proceedings are initiated. That period shall be increased to 105 working days where the undertakings

concerned offer commitments pursuant to Article 8(2), second subparagraph, with a view to rendering the concentration compatible with the common market, unless these commitments have been offered less than 55 working days after the initiation of proceedings.

The periods set by the first subparagraph shall likewise be extended if the notifying parties make a request to that effect not later than 15 working days after the initiation of proceedings pursuant to Article 6(1)(c). The notifying parties may make only one such request. Likewise, at any time following the initiation of proceedings, the periods set by the first subparagraph may be extended by the Commission with the agreement of the notifying parties. The total duration of any extension or extensions effected pursuant to this subparagraph shall not exceed 20 working days.

4. The periods set by paragraphs 1 and 3 shall exceptionally be suspended where, owing to circumstances for which one of the undertakings involved in the concentration is responsible, the Commission has had to request information by decision pursuant to Article 11 or to order an inspection by decision pursuant to Article 13.

The first subparagraph shall also apply to the period referred to in Article 9(4)(b).

5. Where the Court of Justice gives a judgment which annuls the whole or part of a Commission decision which is subject to a time limit set by this Article, the concentration shall be re-examined by the Commission with a view to adopting a decision pursuant to Article 6(1).

The concentration shall be re-examined in the light of current market conditions.

The notifying parties shall submit a new notification or supplement the original notification, without delay, where the original notification becomes incomplete by reason of intervening changes in market conditions or in the information provided. Where there are no such changes, the parties shall certify this fact without delay.

The periods laid down in paragraph 1 shall start on the working day following that of the receipt of complete information in a new notification, a supplemented notification, or a certification within the meaning of the third subparagraph.

The second and third subparagraphs shall also apply in the cases referred to in Article 6(4) and Article 8(7).

6. Where the Commission has not taken a decision in accordance with Article 6(1)(b), (c), 8(1), (2) or (3) within the time limits set in paragraphs 1 and 3 respectively, the concentration shall be deemed to have been declared compatible with the common market, without prejudice to Article 9.

Commentary
Art 10: F&N: 5.386, 5.456, 5.527
Art 10(1): B&C: 8.093, 8.133, 8.163 F&N: 5.464, 5.482, 5.484, 5.685
Art 10(2): B&C: 8.142, 8.164
Art 10(3): B&C: 8.142, 8.161, 8.164 F&N: 5.412, 5.527, 5.528, 5.529, 5.530, 5.533, 5.610
Art 10(4): B&C: 8.134, 8.143
Art 10(5): B&C: 8.140, 8.161, 8.180, 8.256 F&N: 5.493, 5.532, 5.649, 5.682, 5.683, 5.684, 5.685, 5.686
Art 10(6): B&C: 8.126, 8.137, 8.156, 8.235, 8.255 F&N: 5.483, 5.527

Article 11
Requests for information

1. In order to carry out the duties assigned to it by this Regulation, the Commission may, by simple request or by decision, require the persons referred to in Article 3(1)(b), as well as undertakings and associations of undertakings, to provide all necessary information.

2. When sending a simple request for information to a person, an undertaking or an association of undertakings, the Commission shall state the legal basis and the purpose of the request, specify what information is required and fix the time limit within which the information is to be provided, as well as the penalties provided for in Article 14 for supplying incorrect or misleading information.

3. Where the Commission requires a person, an undertaking or an association of undertakings to supply information by decision, it shall state the legal basis and the purpose of the request, specify what information is required and fix the time limit within which it is to be provided. It shall also

indicate the penalties provided for in Article 14 and indicate or impose the penalties provided for in Article 15. It shall further indicate the right to have the decision reviewed by the Court of Justice.

4. The owners of the undertakings or their representatives and, in the case of legal persons, companies or firms, or associations having no legal personality, the persons authorised to represent them by law or by their constitution, shall supply the information requested on behalf of the undertaking concerned. Persons duly authorised to act may supply the information on behalf of their clients. The latter shall remain fully responsible if the information supplied is incomplete, incorrect or misleading.

5. The Commission shall without delay forward a copy of any decision taken pursuant to paragraph 3 to the competent authorities of the Member State in whose territory the residence of the person or the seat of the undertaking or association of undertakings is situated, and to the competent authority of the Member State whose territory is affected. At the specific request of the competent authority of a Member State, the Commission shall also forward to that authority copies of simple requests for information relating to a notified concentration.

6. At the request of the Commission, the governments and competent authorities of the Member States shall provide the Commission with all necessary information to carry out the duties assigned to it by this Regulation.

7. In order to carry out the duties assigned to it by this Regulation, the Commission may interview any natural or legal person who consents to be interviewed for the purpose of collecting information relating to the subject matter of an investigation. At the beginning of the interview, which may be conducted by telephone or other electronic means, the Commission shall state the legal basis and the purpose of the interview.

Where an interview is not conducted on the premises of the Commission or by telephone or other electronic means, the Commission shall inform in advance the competent authority of the Member State in whose territory the interview takes place. If the competent authority of that Member State so requests, officials of that authority may assist the officials and other persons authorised by the Commission to conduct the interview.

Commentary

Art 11: **B&C:** 8.132, 8.134, 8.142, 8.172, 8.175, 8.180 **F&N:** 5.488, 5.489, 5.491, 5.492, 5.493, 5.504, 5.534, 5.613, 5.639, 8.262
Art 11(1): **B&C:** 8.172 **F&N:** 5.488, 5.489
Art 11(2): **B&C:** 8.172 **F&N:** 5.505, 5.636
Art 11(3): **B&C:** 8.172, 8.175 **F&N:** 5.489, 5.490, 5.505, 5.506, 5.532, 5.636, 5.638
Art 11(5): **B&C:** 8.172 **F&N:** 5.492
Art 11(6): **B&C:** 8.172 **F&N:** 5.488, 8.452
Art 11(7): **B&C:** 8.173 **F&N:** 5.495, 5.496, 5.500, 5.504, 8.262

Article 12
Inspections by the authorities of the Member States

1. At the request of the Commission, the competent authorities of the Member States shall undertake the inspections which the Commission considers to be necessary under Article 13(1), or which it has ordered by decision pursuant to Article 13(4). The officials of the competent authorities of the Member States who are responsible for conducting these inspections as well as those authorised or appointed by them shall exercise their powers in accordance with their national law.

2. If so requested by the Commission or by the competent authority of the Member State within whose territory the inspection is to be conducted, officials and other accompanying persons authorised by the Commission may assist the officials of the authority concerned.

Commentary

Art 12: **B&C:** 8.174 **F&N:** 5.503
Art 12(1): **F&N:** 5.503
Art 12(2): **F&N:** 5.503

Article 13
The Commission's powers of inspection

1. In order to carry out the duties assigned to it by this Regulation, the Commission may conduct all necessary inspections of undertakings and associations of undertakings.

2. The officials and other accompanying persons authorised by the Commission to conduct an inspection shall have the power:

(a) to enter any premises, land and means of transport of undertakings and associations of undertakings;

(b) to examine the books and other records related to the business, irrespective of the medium on which they are stored;

(c) to take or obtain in any form copies of or extracts from such books or records;

(d) to seal any business premises and books or records for the period and to the extent necessary for the inspection;

(e) to ask any representative or member of staff of the undertaking or association of undertakings for explanations on facts or documents relating to the subject matter and purpose of the inspection and to record the answers.

3. Officials and other accompanying persons authorised by the Commission to conduct an inspection shall exercise their powers upon production of a written authorisation specifying the subject matter and purpose of the inspection and the penalties provided for in Article 14, in the production of the required books or other records related to the business which is incomplete or where answers to questions asked under paragraph 2 of this Article are incorrect or misleading. In good time before the inspection, the Commission shall give notice of the inspection to the competent authority of the Member State in whose territory the inspection is to be conducted.

4. Undertakings and associations of undertakings are required to submit to inspections ordered by decision of the Commission. The decision shall specify the subject matter and purpose of the inspection, appoint the date on which it is to begin and indicate the penalties provided for in Articles 14 and 15 and the right to have the decision reviewed by the Court of Justice. The Commission shall take such decisions after consulting the competent authority of the Member State in whose territory the inspection is to be conducted.

5. Officials of, and those authorised or appointed by, the competent authority of the Member State in whose territory the inspection is to be conducted shall, at the request of that authority or of the Commission, actively assist the officials and other accompanying persons authorised by the Commission. To this end, they shall enjoy the powers specified in paragraph 2.

6. Where the officials and other accompanying persons authorised by the Commission find that an undertaking opposes an inspection, including the sealing of business premises, books or records, ordered pursuant to this Article, the Member State concerned shall afford them the necessary assistance, requesting where appropriate the assistance of the police or of an equivalent enforcement authority, so as to enable them to conduct their inspection.

7. If the assistance provided for in paragraph 6 requires authorisation from a judicial authority according to national rules, such authorisation shall be applied for. Such authorisation may also be applied for as a precautionary measure.

8. Where authorisation as referred to in paragraph 7 is applied for, the national judicial authority shall ensure that the Commission decision is authentic and that the coercive measures envisaged are neither arbitrary nor excessive having regard to the subject matter of the inspection. In its control of proportionality of the coercive measures, the national judicial authority may ask the Commission, directly or through the competent authority of that Member State, for detailed explanations relating to the subject matter of the inspection. However, the national judicial authority may not call into question the necessity for the inspection nor demand that it be provided with the information in the Commission's file. The lawfulness of the Commission's decision shall be subject to review only by the Court of Justice.

Commentary
Art 13: B&C: 8.001, 8.134, 8.143, 8.174 **F&N:** 5.493, 5.499, 5.504, 5.532, 5.549, 5.636, 8.262
Art 13(2): B&C: 8.147 **F&N:** 5.501, 5.558, 5.559

Article 14
Fines

1. The Commission may by decision impose on the persons referred to in Article 3(1)(b), undertakings or associations of undertakings, fines not exceeding 1% of the aggregate turnover of the undertaking or association of undertakings concerned within the meaning of Article 5 where, intentionally or negligently:

(a) they supply incorrect or misleading information in a submission, certification, notification or supplement thereto, pursuant to Article 4, Article 10(5) or Article 22(3);

(b) they supply incorrect or misleading information in response to a request made pursuant to Article 11(2);

(c) in response to a request made by decision adopted pursuant to Article 11(3), they supply incorrect, incomplete or misleading information or do not supply information within the required time limit;

(d) they produce the required books or other records related to the business in incomplete form during inspections under Article 13, or refuse to submit to an inspection ordered by decision taken pursuant to Article 13(4);

(e) in response to a question asked in accordance with Article 13(2)(e),
   — they give an incorrect or misleading answer,
   — they fail to rectify within a time limit set by the Commission an incorrect, incomplete or misleading answer given by a member of staff, or
   — they fail or refuse to provide a complete answer on facts relating to the subject matter and purpose of an inspection ordered by a decision adopted pursuant to Article 13(4);

(f) seals affixed by officials or other accompanying persons authorised by the Commission in accordance with Article 13(2)(d) have been broken.

2. The Commission may by decision impose fines not exceeding 10% of the aggregate turnover of the undertaking concerned within the meaning of Article 5 on the persons referred to in Article 3(1)(b) or the undertakings concerned where, either intentionally or negligently, they:

(a) fail to notify a concentration in accordance with Articles 4 or 22(3) prior to its implementation, unless they are expressly authorised to do so by Article 7(2) or by a decision taken pursuant to Article 7(3);

(b) implement a concentration in breach of Article 7;

(c) implement a concentration declared incompatible with the common market by decision pursuant to Article 8(3) or do not comply with any measure ordered by decision pursuant to Article 8(4) or (5);

(d) fail to comply with a condition or an obligation imposed by decision pursuant to Articles 6(1)(b), Article 7(3) or Article 8(2), second subparagraph.

3. In fixing the amount of the fine, regard shall be had to the nature, gravity and duration of the infringement.

4. Decisions taken pursuant to paragraphs 1, 2 and 3 shall not be of a criminal law nature.

Art 14(1)(f): F&N: 5.505
Art 14(2): B&C: 8.181 F&N: 5.634, 5.635
Art 14(2)(a): F&N: 5.475
Art 14(2)(b): B&C: 8.127, 8.130 F&N: 5.475
Art 14(2)(c): B&C: 8.156, 8.160
Art 14(2)(d): B&C: 8.171
Art 14(3): B&C: 8.179 F&N: 5.633
Art 14(4): B&C: 8.179 F&N: 5.633

Article 15
Periodic penalty payments

1. The Commission may by decision impose on the persons referred to in Article 3(1)(b), undertakings or associations of undertakings, periodic penalty payments not exceeding 5% of the average daily aggregate turnover of the undertaking or association of undertakings concerned within the meaning of Article 5 for each working day of delay, calculated from the date set in the decision, in order to compel them:

(a) to supply complete and correct information which it has requested by decision taken pursuant to Article 11(3);

(b) to submit to an inspection which it has ordered by decision taken pursuant to Article 13(4);

(c) to comply with an obligation imposed by decision pursuant to Article 6(1)(b), Article 7(3) or Article 8(2), second subparagraph; or

(d) to comply with any measures ordered by decision pursuant to Article 8(4) or (5).

2. Where the persons referred to in Article 3(1)(b), undertakings or associations of undertakings have satisfied the obligation which the periodic penalty payment was intended to enforce, the Commission may fix the definitive amount of the periodic penalty payments at a figure lower than that which would arise under the original decision.

Commentary
Art 15: B&C: 8.172, 8.179, 8.182 F&N: 5.386, 5.490, 5.504, 5.505, 5.506, 5.616, 5.633, 5.638, 5.655
Art 15(1)(a): F&N: 5.506
Art 15(1)(b): F&N: 5.506
Art 15(1)(c): B&C: 8.171
Art 15(2): B&C: 8.182

Article 16
Review by the Court of Justice

The Court of Justice shall have unlimited jurisdiction within the meaning of Article 229 of the Treaty to review decisions whereby the Commission has fixed a fine or periodic penalty payments; it may cancel, reduce or increase the fine or periodic penalty payment imposed.

Commentary
Art 16: B&C: 8.235, 13.214 F&N: 5.386, 5.649

Article 17
Professional secrecy

1. Information acquired as a result of the application of this Regulation shall be used only for the purposes of the relevant request, investigation or hearing.

2. Without prejudice to Article 4(3), Articles 18 and 20, the Commission and the competent authorities of the Member States, their officials and other servants and other persons working under the supervision of these authorities as well as officials and civil servants of other authorities of the Member States shall not disclose information they have acquired through the application of this Regulation of the kind covered by the obligation of professional secrecy.

3. Paragraphs 1 and 2 shall not prevent publication of general information or of surveys which do not contain information relating to particular undertakings or associations of undertakings.

Commentary
Art 17: F&N: 5.146, 5.386, 5.419
Art 17(1): B&C: 8.176
Art 17(2): B&C: 8.176 F&N: 5.416, 5.487

Article 18
Hearing of the parties and of third persons

1. Before taking any decision provided for in Article 6(3), Article 7(3), Article 8(2) to (6), and Articles 14 and 15, the Commission shall give the persons, undertakings and associations of undertakings concerned the opportunity, at every stage of the procedure up to the consultation of the Advisory Committee, of making known their views on the objections against them.

2. By way of derogation from paragraph 1, a decision pursuant to Articles 7(3) and 8(5) may be taken provisionally, without the persons, undertakings or associations of undertakings concerned being given the opportunity to make known their views beforehand, provided that the Commission gives them that opportunity as soon as possible after having taken its decision.

3. The Commission shall base its decision only on objections on which the parties have been able to submit their observations. The rights of the defence shall be fully respected in the proceedings. Access to the file shall be open at least to the parties directly involved, subject to the legitimate interest of undertakings in the protection of their business secrets.

4. In so far as the Commission or the competent authorities of the Member States deem it necessary, they may also hear other natural or legal persons. Natural or legal persons showing a sufficient interest and especially members of the administrative or management bodies of the undertakings concerned or the recognised representatives of their employees shall be entitled, upon application, to be heard.

Commentary
Art 18: B&C: 8.148, 8.176, 8.242 F&N: 5.386, 5.487, 5.548
Art 18(1): B&C: 8.140, 8.144, 8.148, 8.161, 13.089 F&N: 5.478, 5.549, 5.553, 5.572, 5.575, 5.597
Art 18(2): B&C: 8.144, 8.171 F&N: 5.478
Art 18(3): B&C: 8.144, 8.146, 13.089 F&N: 5.551, 5.556, 5.569, 5.570, 5.572, 5.575, 5.645
Art 18(4): B&C: 2.021, 8.131, 8.148, 8.242 F&N: 5.553, 5.556

Article 19
Liaison with the authorities of the Member States

1. The Commission shall transmit to the competent authorities of the Member States copies of notifications within three working days and, as soon as possible, copies of the most important documents lodged with or issued by the Commission pursuant to this Regulation. Such documents shall include commitments offered by the undertakings concerned vis-à-vis the Commission with a view to rendering the concentration compatible with the common market pursuant to Article 6(2) or Article 8(2), second subparagraph.

2. The Commission shall carry out the procedures set out in this Regulation in close and constant liaison with the competent authorities of the Member States, which may express their views upon those procedures. For the purposes of Article 9 it shall obtain information from the competent authority of the Member State as referred to in paragraph 2 of that Article and give it the opportunity to make known its views at every stage of the procedure up to the adoption of a decision pursuant to paragraph 3 of that Article; to that end it shall give it access to the file.

3. An Advisory Committee on concentrations shall be consulted before any decision is taken pursuant to Article 8(1) to (6), Articles 14 or 15 with the exception of provisional decisions taken in accordance with Article 18(2).

4. The Advisory Committee shall consist of representatives of the competent authorities of the Member States. Each Member State shall appoint one or two representatives; if unable to attend, they may be replaced by other representatives. At least one of the representatives of a Member State shall be competent in matters of restrictive practices and dominant positions.

5. Consultation shall take place at a joint meeting convened at the invitation of and chaired by the Commission. A summary of the case, together with an indication of the most important documents and a preliminary draft of the decision to be taken for each case considered, shall be sent with the invitation. The meeting shall take place not less than 10 working days after the invitation has been sent. The Commission may in exceptional cases shorten that period as appropriate in order to avoid serious harm to one or more of the undertakings concerned by a concentration.

6. The Advisory Committee shall deliver an opinion on the Commission's draft decision, if necessary by taking a vote. The Advisory Committee may deliver an opinion even if some members are absent and unrepresented. The opinion shall be delivered in writing and appended to the draft decision. The Commission shall take the utmost account of the opinion delivered by the Committee. It shall inform the Committee of the manner in which its opinion has been taken into account.

7. The Commission shall communicate the opinion of the Advisory Committee, together with the decision, to the addressees of the decision. It shall make the opinion public together with the decision, having regard to the legitimate interest of undertakings in the protection of their business secrets.

Commentary
Art 19: F&N: 5.386, 5.407
Art 19(1): B&C: 8.154, 8.165
Art 19(2): B&C: 8.093, 8.146, 8.154 F&N: 5.616
Art 19(3): B&C: 8.155, 8.161, 8.165, 8.171 F&N: 5.616
Art 19(4): B&C: 8.155 F&N: 5.615
Art 19(5): B&C: 8.155 F&N: 5.523, 5.617, 5.618
Art 19(6): B&C: 8.155 F&N: 5.621, 5.622
Art 19(7): F&N: 5.623, 5.628

Article 20
Publication of decisions

1. The Commission shall publish the decisions which it takes pursuant to Article 8(1) to (6), Articles 14 and 15 with the exception of provisional decisions taken in accordance with Article 18(2) together with the opinion of the Advisory Committee in the *Official Journal of the European Union*.

2. The publication shall state the names of the parties and the main content of the decision; it shall have regard to the legitimate interest of undertakings in the protection of their business secrets.

Commentary
Art 20: B&C: 8.176 F&N: 5.386, 5.487
Art 20(1): B&C: 8.158, 8.163 F&N: 5.630
Art 20(2): B&C: 8.176 F&N: 5.630

Article 21
Application of the Regulation and jurisdiction

1. This Regulation alone shall apply to concentrations as defined in Article 3, and Council Regulations (EC) No 1/2003,[1] (EEC) No 1017/68,[2] (EEC) No 4056/86[3] and (EEC) No 3975/87[4] shall not apply, except in relation to joint ventures that do not have a Community dimension and which have as their object or effect the coordination of the competitive behaviour of undertakings that remain independent.

2. Subject to review by the Court of Justice, the Commission shall have sole jurisdiction to take the decisions provided for in this Regulation.

3. No Member State shall apply its national legislation on competition to any concentration that has a Community dimension.

The first subparagraph shall be without prejudice to any Member State's power to carry out any enquiries necessary for the application of Articles 4(4), 9(2) or after referral, pursuant to Article 9(3), first subparagraph, indent (b), or Article 9(5), to take the measures strictly necessary for the application of Article 9(8).

4. Notwithstanding paragraphs 2 and 3, Member States may take appropriate measures to protect legitimate interests other than those taken into consideration by this Regulation and compatible with the general principles and other provisions of Community law.

Public security, plurality of the media and prudential rules shall be regarded as legitimate interests within the meaning of the first subparagraph.

Any other public interest must be communicated to the Commission by the Member State concerned and shall be recognised by the Commission after an assessment of its compatibility with the general principles and other provisions of Community law before the measures referred to above may be taken. The Commission shall inform the Member State concerned of its decision within 25 working days of that communication.

Notes
[1] OJ L 1, 4.1.2003, p. 1.
[2] OJ L 175, 23. 7. 1968, p. 1. Regulation as last amended by Regulation (EC) No 1/2003 (OJ L 1, 4.1.2003, p. 1).
[3] OJ L 378, 31. 12. 1986, p. 4. Regulation as last amended by Regulation (EC) No 1/2003.
[4] OJ L 374. 31. 12. 1987, p. 1. Regulation as last amended by Regulation (EC) No 1/2003.

Commentary
Art 21: B&C: 8.101, 8.104
Art 21(1): B&C: 7.017, 8.234, 8.260, 14.005, 14.043 F&N: 5.24, 5.54, 5.345
Art 21(2): B&C: 8.012, 8.260 F&N: 5.649
Art 21(3): B&C: 7.011, 8.012, 8.101, 8.104, 8.281 F&N: 5.54, 5.159
Art 21(4): B&C: 8.013, 8.101–8.102, 8.104–8.105, 8.281

Article 22
Referral to the Commission

1. One or more Member States may request the Commission to examine any concentration as defined in Article 3 that does not have a Community dimension within the meaning of Article 1 but affects trade between Member States and threatens to significantly affect competition within the territory of the Member State or States making the request.

Such a request shall be made at most within 15 working days of the date on which the concentration was notified, or if no notification is required, otherwise made known to the Member State concerned.

2. The Commission shall inform the competent authorities of the Member States and the undertakings concerned of any request received pursuant to paragraph 1 without delay.

Any other Member State shall have the right to join the initial request within a period of 15 working days of being informed by the Commission of the initial request.

All national time limits relating to the concentration shall be suspended until, in accordance with the procedure set out in this Article, it has been decided where the concentration shall be examined. As soon as a Member State has informed the Commission and the undertakings concerned that it does not wish to join the request, the suspension of its national time limits shall end.

3. The Commission may, at the latest 10 working days after the expiry of the period set in paragraph 2, decide to examine, the concentration where it considers that it affects trade between Member States and threatens to significantly affect competition within the territory of the Member State or States making the request. If the Commission does not take a decision within this period, it shall be deemed to have adopted a decision to examine the concentration in accordance with the request.

The Commission shall inform all Member States and the undertakings concerned of its decision. It may request the submission of a notification pursuant to Article 4.

The Member State or States having made the request shall no longer apply their national legislation on competition to the concentration.

4. Article 2, Article 4(2) to (3), Articles 5, 6, and 8 to 21 shall apply where the Commission examines a concentration pursuant to paragraph 3. Article 7 shall apply to the extent that the concentration has not been implemented on the date on which the Commission informs the undertakings concerned that a request has been made.

Where a notification pursuant to Article 4 is not required, the period set in Article 10(1) within which proceedings may be initiated shall begin on the working day following that on which the Commission informs the undertakings concerned that it has decided to examine the concentration pursuant to paragraph 3.

5. The Commission may inform one or several Member States that it considers a concentration fulfils the criteria in paragraph 1. In such cases, the Commission may invite that Member State or those Member States to make a request pursuant to paragraph 1.

Commentary
Art 22: B&C: 1.115, 1.121, 7.017, 8.001, 8.087, 8.097–8.098, 8.100, 8.261 **F&N:** 5.110, 5.112, 5.113, 5.114, 5.115, 5.159, 5.161, 5.170–5.177, 5.180
Art 22(1): B&C: 7.017, 8.097–8.098 **F&N:** 5.177
Art 22(2): B&C: 8.098
Art 22(3): B&C: 8.082, 8.098–8.100, 8.180 **F&N:** 5.159, 5.655
Art 22(4): B&C: 8.098–8.099 **F&N:** 5.180
Art 22(5): B&C: 8.098

Article 23
Implementing provisions

1. The Commission shall have the power to lay down in accordance with the procedure referred to in paragraph 2:

(a) implementing provisions concerning the form, content and other details of notifications and submissions pursuant to Article 4;
(b) implementing provisions concerning time limits pursuant to Article 4(4), (5) Articles 7, 9, 10 and 22;
(c) the procedure and time limits for the submission and implementation of commitments pursuant to Article 6(2) and Article 8(2);
(d) implementing provisions concerning hearings pursuant to Article 18.

2. The Commission shall be assisted by an Advisory Committee, composed of representatives of the Member States.

(a) Before publishing draft implementing provisions and before adopting such provisions, the Commission shall consult the Advisory Committee.
(b) Consultation shall take place at a meeting convened at the invitation of and chaired by the Commission. A draft of the implementing provisions to be taken shall be sent with the invitation. The meeting shall take place not less than 10 working days after the invitation has been sent.
(c) The Advisory Committee shall deliver an opinion on the draft implementing provisions, if necessary by taking a vote. The Commission shall take the utmost account of the opinion delivered by the Committee.

Commentary
Art 23: F&N: 5.387

Article 24
Relations with third countries

1. The Member States shall inform the Commission of any general difficulties encountered by their undertakings with concentrations as defined in Article 3 in a third country.

2. Initially not more than one year after the entry into force of this Regulation and, thereafter periodically, the Commission shall draw up a report examining the treatment accorded to undertakings having their seat or their principal fields of activity in the Community, in the terms referred to in paragraphs 3 and 4, as regards concentrations in third countries. The Commission shall submit those reports to the Council, together with any recommendations.

3. Whenever it appears to the Commission, either on the basis of the reports referred to in paragraph 2 or on the basis of other information, that a third country does not grant undertakings having their seat or their principal fields of activity in the Community, treatment comparable to that granted by the Community to undertakings from that country, the Commission may submit proposals to the Council for an appropriate mandate for negotiation with a view to obtaining comparable treatment for undertakings having their seat or their principal fields of activity in the Community.

4. Measures taken under this Article shall comply with the obligations of the Community or of the Member States, without prejudice to Article 307 of the Treaty, under international agreements, whether bilateral or multilateral.

Article 25
Repeal

1. Without prejudice to Article 26(2), Regulations (EEC) No 4064/89 and (EC) No 1310/97 shall be repealed with effect from 1 May 2004.

2. References to the repealed Regulations shall be construed as references to this Regulation and shall be read in accordance with the correlation table in the Annex.

Article 26
Entry into force and transitional provisions

1. This Regulation shall enter into force on the 20th day following that of its publication in the *Official Journal of the European Union.*

It shall apply from 1 May 2004.

2. Regulation (EEC) No 4064/89 shall continue to apply to any concentration which was the subject of an agreement or announcement or where control was acquired within the meaning of Article 4(1) of that Regulation before the date of application of this Regulation, subject, in particular, to the provisions governing applicability set out in Article 25(2) and (3) of Regulation (EEC) No 4064/89 and Article 2 of Regulation (EEC) No 1310/97.

3. As regards concentrations to which this Regulation applies by virtue of accession, the date of accession shall be substituted for the date of application of this Regulation.

This Regulation shall be binding in its entirety and directly applicable in all Member States.

Commentary
Art 24: **B&C:** 8.286

Done at Brussels, 20 January 2004.

Aɴɴᴇx
Correlation Table

Regulation (EEC) No 4064/89	This Regulation
Article 1(1), (2) and (3)	Article 1(1), (2) and (3)
Article 1(4)	Article 1(4)
Article 1(5)	Article 1(5)
Article 2(1)	Article 2(1)
—	Article 2(2)
Article 2(2)	Article 2(3)
Article 2(3)	Article 2(4)
Article 2(4)	Article 2(5)
Article 3(1)	Article 3(1)
Article 3(2)	Article 3(4)
Article 3(3)	Article 3(2)
Article 3(4)	Article 3(3)
—	Article 3(4)
Article 3(5)	Article 3(5)

Regulation (EEC) No 4064/89	This Regulation
Article 4(1) first sentence	Article 4(1) first subparagraph
Article 4(1) second sentence	—
—	Article 4(1) second and third subparagraphs
Article 4(2) and (3)	Article 4(2) and (3)
—	Article 4(4) to (6)
Article 5(1) to (3)	Article 5(1) to (3)
Article 5(4), introductory words	Article 5(4), introductory words
Article 5(4) point (a)	Article 5(4) point (a)
Article 5(4) point (b), introductory words	Article 5(4) point (b), introductory words
Article 5(4) point (b), first indent	Article 5(4) point (b)(i)
Article 5(4) point (b), second indent	Article 5(4) point (b)(ii)
Article 5(4) point (b), third indent	Article 5(4) point (b)(iii)
Article 5(4) point (b), fourth indent	Article 5(4) point (b)(iv)
Article 5(4) points (c), (d) and (e)	Article 5(4) points (c), (d) and (e)
Article 5(5)	Article 5(5)
Article 6(1), introductory words	Article 6(1), introductory words
Article 6(1) points (a) and (b)	Article 6(1) points (a) and (b)
Article 6(1) point (c)	Article 6(1) point (c), first sentence
Article 6(2) to (5)	Article 6(2) to (5)
Article 7(1)	Article 7(1)
Article 7(3)	Article 7(2)
Article 7(4)	Article 7(3)
Article 7(5)	Article 7(4)
Article 8(1)	Article 6(1) point (c), second sentence
Article 8(2)	Article 8(1) and (2)
Article 8(3)	Article 8(3)
Article 8(4)	Article 8(4)
—	Article 8(5)
Article 8(5)	Article 8(6)
Article 8(6)	Article 8(7)
—	Article 8(8)
Article 9(1) to (9)	Article 9(1) to (9)
Article 9(10)	—
Article 10(1) and (2)	Article 10(1) and (2)
Article 10(3)	Article 10(3) first subparagraph, first sentence
—	Article 10(3) first subparagraph, second sentence
—	Article 10(3) second subparagraph
Article 10(4)	Article 10(4) first subparagraph
—	Article 10(4), second subparagraph
Article 10(5)	Article 10(5), first and fourth subparagraphs
—	Article 10(5), second, third and fifth subparagraphs
Article 10(6)	Article 10(6)
Article 11(1)	Article 11(1)
Article 11(2)	—
Article 11(3)	Article 11(2)
Article 11(4)	Article 11(4) first sentence
—	Article 11(4) second and third sentences
—	Article 11(5) second sentence
Article 11(3)	Article 11(6)
Article 11(5)	—
Article 11(6) and (7)	Article 12
Article 12	Article 13(1) first subparagraph
Article 13(1)	Article 13(1) second subparagraph, introductory words

Regulation (EEC) No 4064/89	This Regulation
Article 13(2) introductory words	Article 13(1) second subparagraph, point (a)
Article 13(2) point (b)	Article 13(1) second subparagraph, point (b)
Article 13(2) point (c)	Article 13(1) second subparagraph, point (c)
Article 13(2) point (e)	Article 13(1) second subparagraph, point (d)
Article 13(2) point (a)	—
Article 13(2) point (d)	Article 13(2)
Article 13(3)	Article 13(3)
Article 13(4) first and second sentences	Article 13(4)
Article 13(4) third sentence	Article 13(5)
Article 13(5), first sentence	—
Article 13(5), second sentence	Article 13(6) first sentence
Article 13(6)	Article 13(6) second sentence
—	—
Article 13(7) and (8)	Article 14(1) introductory words
Article 14(1) introductory words	Article 14(1) point (a)
Article 14(2) point (a)	Article 14(1) point (b)
Article 14(1) point (a)	Article 14(1) point (c)
Article 14(1) points (b) and (c)	Article 14(1) point (d)
Article 14(1) point (d)	—
Article 14(1) points (e) and (f)	Article 14(2) introductory words
Article 14(2) introductory words	Article 14(2) point (a)
Article 14(2) point (d)	Article 14(2) points (b) and (c)
Article 14(2) points (b) and (c)	Article 14(3)
Article 14(3)	Article 14(4)
Article 14(4)	Article 15(1) introductory words
Article 15(1) introductory words	Article 15(1) points (a) and (b)
Article 15(1) points (a) and (b)	Article 15(2) introductory words
Article 15(1) introductory words	Article 15(2) point (a)
Article 15(1) point (c)	Article 15(2) point (b)
Article 15(1) point (d)	Article 15(3)
Article 15(2)	Articles 16 to 20
Articles 16 to 20	Article 21(1)
Article 21(2)	Article 21(2)
Article 21(3)	Article 21(3)
Article 21(4)	Article 22(1)
Article 21(1)	Article 22(3)
—	—
Article 22(1) to (3)	Article 22(4)
Article 22(4)	Article 22(5)
—	—
Article 22(5)	Article 23
Article 23(1)	—
Article 23(2)	Article 24
Article 24	—
Article 25	Article 25(1)
Article 26(1), first subparagraph	—
Article 26(1), second subparagraph	Article 25(2)
Article 26(2)	Article 25(3)
Article 26(3)	—
Annex	

D2

COMMISSION REGULATION (EC) NO 802/2004

of [21] April 2004

implementing Council Regulation (EC) No 139/2004 on the control of concentrations
between undertakings

(Text with EEA relevance)

Official Journal L 133, 30.4.2004, p. 1

Celex No: 32004R0802

Notes

The date of this Regulation is shown as corrected by the Corrigendum at OJ L 172, 6.5.2004, p. 9.
EEA application: not yet incorporated.

Commentary

Regulation 802/2004/EC: B&C: 8.008, 8.082 F&N: 5.17, 5.386, 5.412, 5.450, 5.570, 5.611
Arts 7–10: B&C: 8.142

THE COMMISSION OF THE EUROPEAN COMMUNITIES,

Having regard to the Treaty establishing the European Community,

Having regard to the Agreement on the European Economic Area,

Having regard to Council Regulation (EC) No 139/2004 of 20 January 2004 on the control of concentrations between undertakings (EC Merger Regulation),[1] and in particular Article 23(1) thereof,

Having regard to Council Regulation (EEC) No 4064/89 of 21 December 1989 on the control of concentrations between undertakings,[2] as last amended by Regulation (EC) No 1310/97,[3] and in particular Article 23 thereof,

Having consulted the Advisory Committee,

Notes

[1] OJ L 24, 29.1.2004, p. 1.
[2] OJ L 395, 30.12.1989, p. 1.
[3] OJ L 180, 9.7.1997, p. 1.

Whereas:

(1) Council Regulation (EEC) No 4064/89 of 21 December 1989 on the control of concentrations between undertakings has been recast, with substantial amendments to various provisions of that Regulation.

(2) Commission Regulation (EC) No 447/98[1] of 1 March 1998 on the notifications, time-limits and hearings provided for in Council Regulation (EEC) No 4064/89 must be modified in order to take account of those amendments. For the sake of clarity it should therefore be repealed and replaced by a new regulation.

Notes

[1] OJ L 61, 2.3.1998, p. 1. Regulation as amended by the 2003 Act of Accession.

---

(3) The Commission has adopted measures concerning the terms of reference of hearing officers in certain competition proceedings.

(4) Regulation (EC) No 139/2004 is based on the principle of compulsory notification of concentrations before they are put into effect. On the one hand, a notification has important legal consequences which are favourable to the parties to the proposed concentration, while, on the other hand, failure to comply with the obligation to notify renders the parties liable to fines and may also entail civil law disadvantages for them. It is therefore necessary in the interests of legal certainty to define precisely the subject matter and content of the information to be provided in the notification.

(5) It is for the notifying parties to make a full and honest disclosure to the Commission of the facts and circumstances which are relevant for taking a decision on the notified concentration.

(6) Regulation (EC) No 139/2004 also allows the undertakings concerned to request, in a reasoned submission, prior to notification, that a concentration fulfilling the requirements of that Regulation be referred to the Commission by one or more Member States, or referred by the Commission to one or more Member States, as the case may be. It is important to provide the Commission and the competent authorities of the Member States concerned with sufficient information, in order to enable them to assess, within a short period of time, whether or not a referral ought to be made. To that end, the reasoned submission requesting the referral should contain certain specific information.

(7) In order to simplify and expedite examination of notifications and of reasoned submissions, it is desirable to prescribe that forms be used.

(8) Since notification sets in motion legal time-limits pursuant to Regulation (EC) No 139/2004, the conditions governing such time-limits and the time when they become effective should also be determined.

(9) Rules must be laid down in the interests of legal certainty for calculating the time-limits provided for in Regulation (EC) No 139/2004. In particular, the beginning and end of time periods and the circumstances suspending the running of such periods must be determined, with due regard to the requirements resulting from the exceptionally tight legal timeframe available for the proceedings.

(10) The provisions relating to the Commission's procedure must be framed in such a way as to safeguard fully the right to be heard and the rights of defence. For these purposes, the Commission should distinguish between the parties who notify the concentration, other parties involved in the proposed concentration, third parties and parties regarding whom the Commission intends to take a decision imposing a fine or periodic penalty payments.

(11) The Commission should give the notifying parties and other parties involved in the proposed concentration, if they so request, an opportunity before notification to discuss the intended concentration informally and in strict confidence. In addition, the Commission should, after notification, maintain close contact with those parties, to the extent necessary to discuss with them any practical or legal problems which it discovers on a first examination of the case, with a view, if possible, to resolving such problems by mutual agreement.

Commentary
Recital 11: **B&C:** 8.109, 8.135

(12) In accordance with the principle of respect for the rights of defence, the notifying parties must be given the opportunity to submit their comments on all the objections which the Commission proposes to take into account in its decisions. The other parties involved in the proposed concentration should also be informed of the Commission's objections and should be granted the opportunity to express their views.

(13) Third parties demonstrating a sufficient interest must also be given the opportunity of expressing their views, if they make a written application to that effect.

(14) The various persons entitled to submit comments should do so in writing, both in their own interests and in the interests of sound administration, without prejudice to their right to request a formal oral hearing, where appropriate, to supplement the written procedure. In urgent cases, however, the Commission must be enabled to proceed immediately to formal oral hearings of the notifying parties, of other parties involved or of third parties.

(15) It is necessary to define the rights of persons who are to be heard, to what extent they should be granted access to the Commission's file and on what conditions they may be represented or assisted.

(16) When granting access to the file, the Commission should ensure the protection of business secrets and other confidential information. The Commission should be able to ask undertakings that have submitted documents or statements to identify confidential information.

Commentary
Recital 16: B&C: 8.146

---

(17) In order to enable the Commission to carry out a proper assessment of commitments offered by the notifying parties with a view to rendering the concentration compatible with the common market, and to ensure due consultation with other parties involved, with third parties and with the authorities of the Member States as provided for in Regulation (EC) No 139/2004, in particular Article 18(1), 18(4), Article 19(1), 19(2), 19(3) and 19(5) thereof, the procedure and time-limits for submitting the commitments referred to in Article 6(2) and Article 8(2) of that Regulation should be laid down.

(18) It is also necessary to define the rules applicable to certain time limits set by the Commission.

(19) The Advisory Committee on Concentrations must deliver its opinion on the basis of a preliminary draft decision. It must therefore be consulted on a case after the inquiry in to that case has been completed. Such consultation does not, however, prevent the Commission from reopening an inquiry if need be.

HAS ADOPTED THIS REGULATION:

CHAPTER I
SCOPE

Article 1
Scope

This Regulation shall apply to the control of concentrations conducted pursuant to Regulation (EC) No 139/2004.

CHAPTER II
NOTIFICATIONS AND OTHER SUBMISSIONS

Article 2
Persons entitled to submit notifications

1. Notifications shall be submitted by the persons or undertakings referred to in Article 4(2) of Regulation (EC) No 139/2004.

2. Where notifications are signed by representatives of persons or of undertakings, such representatives shall produce written proof that they are authorised to act.

3. Joint notifications shall be submitted by a joint representative who is authorised to transmit and to receive documents on behalf of all notifying parties.

Commentary
Art 2(1): B&C: 8.112 F&N: 5.438
Art 2(2): B&C: 8.118 F&N: 5.454

Article 3
Submission of notifications

1. Notifications shall be submitted in the manner prescribed by Form CO as set out in Annex I. Under the conditions set out in Annex II, notifications may be submitted in Short Form as defined therein. Joint notifications shall be submitted on a single form.

2. One original and [37] copies of the Form CO and the supporting documents shall be submitted to the Commission. The notification shall be delivered to the address referred to in Article 23(1) and in the format specified by the Commission.

3. The supporting documents shall be either originals or copies of the originals; in the latter case the notifying parties shall confirm that they are true and complete.

4. Notifications shall be in one of the official languages of the Community. For the notifying parties, this language shall also be the language of the proceeding, as well as that of any subsequent proceedings relating to the same concentration. Supporting documents shall be submitted in their original language. Where the original language is not one of the official languages of the Community, a translation into the language of the proceeding shall be attached.

5. Where notifications are made pursuant to Article 57 of the Agreement on the European Economic Area, they may also be submitted in one of the official languages of the EFTA States or the working language of the EFTA Surveillance Authority. If the language chosen for the notifications is not an official language of the Community, the notifying parties shall simultaneously supplement all documentation with a translation into an official language of the Community. The language which is chosen for the translation shall determine the language used by the Commission as the language of the proceeding for the notifying parties.

Notes

The amendment shown in square brackets in Article 3(2) was made by Commission Regulation (EC) No 1792/2006 of 23 October 2006 (OJ L 362, 20.12.2006, p. 1), with effect from 1 January 2007.

Commentary

Art 3(1): **B&C:** 8.117, 8.121, 8.124 **F&N:** 5.436, 5,444
Art 3(2): **B&C:** 8.118 **F&N:** 5.453, 5,455
Art 3(3): **B&C:** 8.118
Art 3(4): **B&C:** 8.119 **F&N:** 5.451
Art 3(5): **B&C:** 8.119

Article 4
Information and documents to be provided

1. Notifications shall contain the information, including documents, requested in the applicable forms set out in the Annexes. The information shall be correct and complete.

2. The Commission may dispense with the obligation to provide any particular information in the notification, including documents, or with any other requirement specified in Annexes I and II where the Commission considers that compliance with those obligations or requirements is not necessary for the examination of the case.

3. The Commission shall without delay acknowledge in writing to the notifying parties or their representatives receipt of the notification and of any reply to a letter sent by the Commission pursuant to Article 5(2) and 5(3).

Commentary

Art 4(1): **B&C:** 8.121
Art 4(2): **B&C:** 8.114 **F&N:** 5.434

Article 5
Effective date of notification

1. Subject to paragraphs 2, 3 and 4, notifications shall become effective on the date on which they are received by the Commission.

2. Where the information, including documents, contained in the notification is incomplete in any material respect, the Commission shall inform the notifying parties or their representatives in writing without delay. In such cases, the notification shall become effective on the date on which the complete information is received by the Commission.

3. Material changes in the facts contained in the notification coming to light subsequent to the notification which the notifying parties know or ought to know, or any new information coming to light subsequent to the notification which the parties know or ought to know and which would have had to be notified if known at the time of notification, shall be communicated to the Commission without delay. In such cases, when these material changes or new information could have a significant effect on the appraisal of the concentration, the notification may be considered by the Commission as becoming effective on the date on which the relevant information is received by the Commission; the Commission shall inform the notifying parties or their representatives of this in writing and without delay.

4. Incorrect or misleading information shall be considered to be incomplete information.

5. When the Commission publishes the fact of the notification pursuant to Article 4(3) of Regulation (EC) No 139/2004, it shall specify the date upon which the notification has been received. Where, further to the application of paragraphs 2, 3 and 4 of this Article, the effective date of notification is later than the date specified in that publication, the Commission shall issue a further publication in which it shall state the later date.

Commentary
Art 5(1): B&C: 8.113 F&N: 5.456
Art 5(2): B&C: 8.113 F&N: 5.458
Art 5(3): B&C: 8.113, 8.121 F&N: 5.458
Art 5(4): F&N: 5.457
Art 5(5): B&C: 8.133 F&N: 5.458

Article 6
Specific provisions relating to reasoned submissions, supplements and certifications

1. Reasoned submissions within the meaning of Article 4(4) and 4(5) of Regulation (EC) No 139/2004 shall contain the information, including documents, requested in accordance with Annex III to this Regulation.

2. Article 2, Article 3(1), third sentence, 3(2) to (5), Article 4, Article 5(1), 5(2) first sentence, 5(3), 5(4), Article 21 and Article 23 of this Regulation shall apply *mutatis mutandis* to reasoned submissions within the meaning of Article 4(4) and 4(5) of Regulation (EC) No 139/2004.

Article 2, Article 3(1), third sentence, 3(2) to (5), Article 4, Article 5(1) to (4), Article 21 and Article 23 of this Regulation shall apply *mutatis mutandis* to supplements to notifications and certifications within the meaning of Article 10(5) of Regulation (EC) No 139/2004.

Commentary
Art 6: B&C: 8.089
Art 6(2): B&C: 8.118 F&N: 5.685

CHAPTER III
TIME-LIMITS

Article 7
Beginning of time periods

Time periods shall begin on the working day, as defined in Article 24 of this Regulation, following the event to which the relevant provision of Regulation (EC) No 139/2004 refers.

Commentary
Art 7: B&C: 8.133 F&N: 5.481, 5.526

Article 8
Expiry of time periods

A time period calculated in working days shall expire at the end of its last working day.

A time period set by the Commission in terms of a calendar date shall expire at the end of that day.

Commentary
Art 8: B&C: 8.133 F&N: 5.481, 5.526

Article 9
Suspension of time limit

1. The time limits referred to in Articles 9(4), Article 10(1) and 10(3) of Regulation (EC) No 139/2004 shall be suspended where the Commission has to take a decision pursuant to Article 11(3) or Article 13(4) of that Regulation, on any of the following grounds:

(a) information which the Commission has requested pursuant to Article 11(2) of Regulation (EC) No 139/2004 from one of the notifying parties or another involved party, as defined in Article 11 of this Regulation, is not provided or not provided in full within the time limit fixed by the Commission;

(b) information which the Commission has requested pursuant to Article 11(2) of Regulation (EC) No 139/2004 from a third party, as defined in Article 11 of this Regulation, is not provided or not provided in full within the time limit fixed by the Commission owing to circumstances for which one of the notifying parties or another involved party, as defined in Article 11 of this Regulation, is responsible;

(c) one of the notifying parties or another involved party, as defined in Article 11 of this Regulation, has refused to submit to an inspection deemed necessary by the Commission on the basis of Article 13(1) of Regulation (EC) No 139/2004 or to cooperate in the carrying out of such an inspection in accordance with Article 13(2) of that Regulation;

(d) the notifying parties have failed to inform the Commission of material changes in the facts contained in the notification, or of any new information of the kind referred to in Article 5(3) of this Regulation.

2. The time limits referred to in Articles 9(4), Article 10(1) and 10(3) of Regulation (EC) No 139/2004 shall be suspended where the Commission has to take a decision pursuant to Article 11(3) of that Regulation, without proceeding first by way of simple request for information, owing to circumstances for which one of the undertakings involved in the concentration is responsible.

3. The time limits referred to in Articles 9(4), Article 10(1) and (3) of Regulation (EC) No 139/2004 shall be suspended:

(a) in the cases referred to in points (a) and (b) of paragraph 1, for the period between the expiry of the time limit set in the simple request for information, and the receipt of the complete and correct information required by decision;

(b) in the cases referred to in point (c) of paragraph 1, for the period between the unsuccessful attempt to carry out the inspection and the completion of the inspection ordered by decision;

(c) in the cases referred to in point (d) of paragraph 1, for the period between the occurrence of the change in the facts referred to therein and the receipt of the complete and correct information.

(d) in the cases referred to in paragraph 2 for the period between the expiry of the time limit set in the decision and the receipt of the complete and correct information required by decision.

4. The suspension of the time limit shall begin on the working day following the date on which the event causing the suspension occurred. It shall expire with the end of the day on which the reason for suspension is removed. Where such a day is not a working day, the suspension of the time-limit shall expire with the end of the following working day.

Commentary
Art 9: F&N: 5.493, 5.532
Art 9(1): B&C: 8.175
Art 9(1)(a): B&C: 8.134, 8.143
Art 9(1)(b): B&C: 8.134, 8.143
Art 9(1)(c): B&C: 8.134, 8.143
Art 9(1)(d): B&C: 8.134, 8.143
Art 9(2): B&C: 8.143, 8.175
Art 9(3): B&C: 8.143
Art 9(4): B&C: 8.143

Article 10
Compliance with the time-limits

1. The time limits referred to in Article 4(4), fourth subparagraph, Article 9(4), Article 10(1) and (3), and Article 22(3) of Regulation (EC) No 139/2004 shall be met where the Commission has taken the relevant decision before the end of the period.

2. The time limits referred to in Article 4(4), second subparagraph, Article 4(5), third subparagraph, Article 9(2), Article 22(1), second subparagraph, and 22(2), second subparagraph, of Regulation (EC) No 139/2004 shall be met by a Member State concerned where that Member State, before the end of the period, informs the Commission in writing or makes or joins the request in writing, as the case may be.

3. The time limit referred to in Article 9(6) of Regulation (EC) No 139/2004 shall be met where the competent authority of a Member State concerned informs the undertakings concerned in the manner set out in that provision before the end of the period.

CHAPTER IV
EXERCISE OF THE RIGHT TO BE HEARD; HEARINGS

Article 11
Parties to be heard

For the purposes of the rights to be heard pursuant to Article 18 of Regulation (EC) No 139/2004, the following parties are distinguished:

(a) notifying parties, that is, persons or undertakings submitting a notification pursuant to Article 4(2) of Regulation (EC) No 139/2004;

(b) other involved parties, that is, parties to the proposed concentration other than the notifying parties, such as the seller and the undertaking which is the target of the concentration;

(c) third persons, that is natural or legal persons, including customers, suppliers and competitors, provided they demonstrate a sufficient interest within the meaning of Article 18(4), second sentence, of Regulation (EC) No 139/2004, which is the case in particular
   — for members of the administrative or management bodies of the undertakings concerned or the recognised representatives of their employees;
   — for consumer associations, where the proposed concentration concerns products or services used by final consumers[;]

(d) parties regarding whom the Commission intends to take a decision pursuant to Article 14 or Article 15 of Regulation (EC) No 139/2004.

Commentary
Art 11: **B&C:** 8.112, 8.146 **F&N:** 5.33

Article 12
Decisions on the suspension of concentrations

1. Where the Commission intends to take a decision pursuant to Article 7(3) of Regulation (EC) No 139/2004 which adversely affects one or more of the parties, it shall, pursuant to Article 18(1) of that Regulation, inform the notifying parties and other involved parties in writing of its objections and shall set a time limit within which they may make known their views in writing.

2. Where the Commission, pursuant to Article 18(2) of Regulation (EC) No 139/2004, has taken a decision referred to in paragraph 1 of this Article provisionally without having given the notifying parties and other involved parties the opportunity to make known their views, it shall without delay send them the text of the provisional decision and shall set a time limit within which they may make known their views in writing.

Once the notifying parties and other involved parties have made known their views, the Commission shall take a final decision annulling, amending or confirming the provisional decision. Where they have not made known their views in writing within the time limit set, the Commission's provisional decision shall become final with the expiry of that period.

Commentary
Art 12(1): **B&C:** 8.129 **F&N:** 5.478
Art 12(2): **B&C:** 8.129 **F&N:** 5.478, 5.566

Article 13
Decisions on the substance of the case

1. Where the Commission intends to take a decision pursuant to Article 6(3) or Article 8(2) to (6) of Regulation (EC) No 139/2004, it shall, before consulting the Advisory Committee on Concentrations, hear the parties pursuant to Article 18(1) and (3) of that Regulation.

Article 12(2) of this Regulation shall apply *mutatis mutandis* where, in application of Article 18(2) of Regulation (EC) No 139/2004, the Commission has taken a decision pursuant to Article 8(5) of that Regulation provisionally.

2. The Commission shall address its objections in writing to the notifying parties.

The Commission shall, when giving notice of objections, set a time limit within which the notifying parties may inform the Commission of their comments in writing.

The Commission shall inform other involved parties in writing of these objections.

The Commission shall also set a time limit within which those other involved parties may inform the Commission of their comments in writing.

The Commission shall not be obliged to take into account comments received after the expiry of a time limit which it has set.

3. The parties to whom the Commission's objections have been addressed or who have been informed of those objections shall, within the time limit set, submit in writing their comments on the objections. In their written comments, they may set out all facts and matters known to them which are relevant to their defence, and shall attach any relevant documents as proof of the facts set out. They may also propose that the Commission hear persons who may corroborate those facts. They shall submit one original and 10 copies of their comments to the Commission to the address of the Commission's Directorate General for Competition. An electronic copy shall also be submitted at the same address and in the format specified by the Commission. The Commission shall forward copies of such written comments without delay to the competent authorities of the Member States.

4. Where the Commission intends to take a decision pursuant to Article 14 or Article 15 of Regulation (EC) No 139/2004, it shall, before consulting the Advisory Committee on Concentrations, hear pursuant to Article 18(1) and (3) of that Regulation the parties regarding whom the Commission intends to take such a decision.

The procedure provided for in paragraph 2, first and second subparagraphs, and paragraph 3 shall apply, *mutatis mutandis*.

Commentary
Art 13(2): **B&C:** 8.145, 8.147 **F&N:** 5.565, 5.566
Art 13(3): **F&N:** 5.566, 5.567
Art 13(5): **F&N:** 5.566

Article 14
Oral hearings

1. Where the Commission intends to take a decision pursuant to Article 6(3) or Article 8(2) to (6) of Regulation (EC) No 139/2004, it shall afford the notifying parties who have so requested in their written comments the opportunity to develop their arguments in a formal oral hearing. It may also, at other stages in the proceedings, afford the notifying parties the opportunity of expressing their views orally.

2. Where the Commission intends to take a decision pursuant to Article 6(3) or Article 8(2) to (6) of Regulation (EC) No 139/2004, it shall also afford other involved parties who have so requested in their written comments the opportunity to develop their arguments in a formal oral hearing. It may also, at other stages in the proceedings, afford other involved parties the opportunity of expressing their views orally.

3. Where the Commission intends to take a decision pursuant to Article 14 or Article 15 of Regulation (EC) No 139/2004, it shall afford parties on whom it proposes to impose a fine or periodic penalty payment the opportunity to develop their arguments in a formal oral hearing, if so requested in their written comments. It may also, at other stages in the proceedings, afford such parties the opportunity of expressing their views orally.

Commentary
Art 14(1): **B&C:** 8.115, 8.140, 8.148, 8.161 **F&N:** 5.560, 5.597
Art 14(2): **B&C:** 8.112, 8.148 **F&N:** 5.560

Article 15
Conduct of formal oral hearings

1. Formal oral hearings shall be conducted by the Hearing Officer in full independence.

2. The Commission shall invite the persons to be heard to attend the formal oral hearing on such date as it shall determine.

3. The Commission shall invite the competent authorities of the Member States to take part in any formal oral hearing.

4. Persons invited to attend shall either appear in person or be represented by legal representatives or by representatives authorised by their constitution as appropriate. Undertakings and associations of undertakings may also be represented by a duly authorised agent appointed from among their permanent staff.

5. Persons heard by the Commission may be assisted by their lawyers or other qualified and duly authorised persons admitted by the Hearing Officer.

6. Formal oral hearings shall not be public. Each person may be heard separately or in the presence of other persons invited to attend, having regard to the legitimate interest of the undertakings in the protection of their business secrets and other confidential information.

7. The Hearing Officer may allow all parties within the meaning of Article 11, the Commission services and the competent authorities of the Member States to ask questions during the formal oral hearing.

The Hearing Officer may hold a preparatory meeting with the parties and the Commission services, so as to facilitate the efficient organisation of the formal oral hearing.

8. The statements made by each person heard shall be recorded. Upon request, the recording of the formal oral hearing shall be made available to the persons who attended that hearing. Regard shall be had to the legitimate interest of the undertakings in the protection of their business secrets and other confidential information.

Commentary
Art 15(2): **F&N:** 5.597, 5.598
Art 15(3): **B&C:** 8.148, 8.154
Art 15(5): **F&N:** 5.598
Art 15(6): **F&N:** 5.596
Art 15(7): **F&N:** 5.599, 5.600
Art 15(8): **F&N:** 5.602

Article 16
Hearing of third persons

1. If third persons apply in writing to be heard pursuant to Article 18(4), second sentence, of Regulation (EC) No 139/2004, the Commission shall inform them in writing of the nature and subject matter of the procedure and shall set a time limit within which they may make known their views.

2. The third persons referred to in paragraph 1 shall make known their views in writing within the time limit set. The Commission may, where appropriate, afford such third parties who have so requested in their written comments the opportunity to participate in a formal hearing. It may also in other cases afford such third parties the opportunity of expressing their views orally.

3. The Commission may likewise invite any other natural or legal person to express its views, in writing as well as orally, including at a formal oral hearing.

Commentary
Art 16(1): **B&C:** 8.131 **F&N:** 5.553, 5.558, 5.565
Art 16(2): **B&C:** 8.131, 8.148 **F&N:** 5.560, 5.597
Art 16(3): **B&C:** 8.131, 8.148 **F&N:** 5.563, 5.595

CHAPTER V

ACCESS TO THE FILE AND TREATMENT OF CONFIDENTIAL INFORMATION

Article 17
Access to the file and use of documents

1. If so requested, the Commission shall grant access to the file to the parties to whom it has addressed a statement of objections, for the purpose of enabling them to exercise their rights of defence. Access shall be granted after the notification of the statement of objections.

2. The Commission shall, upon request, also give the other involved parties who have been informed of the objections access to the file in so far as this is necessary for the purposes of preparing their comments.

3. The right of access to the file shall not extend to confidential information, or to internal documents of the Commission or of the competent authorities of the Member States. The right of access to the file shall equally not extend to correspondence between the Commission and the competent authorities of the Member States or between the latter.

4. Documents obtained through access to the file pursuant to this Article may only be used for the purposes of the relevant proceeding pursuant to Regulation (EC) No 139/2004.

Commentary
Art 17(1): **B&C:** 8.146 **F&N:** 5.561, 5.569, 5.572, 5.575
Art 17(2): **B&C:** 8.120, 8.146 **F&N:** 5.561, 5.570, 5.574
Art 17(3): **B&C:** 8.146 **F&N:** 5.579
Art 17(4): **B&C:** 8.146

Article 18
Confidential information

1. Information, including documents, shall not be communicated or made accessible by the Commission in so far as it contains business secrets or other confidential information the disclosure of which is not considered necessary by the Commission for the purpose of the procedure.

2. Any person which makes known its views or comments pursuant to Articles 12, Article 13 and Article 16 of this Regulation, or supplies information pursuant to Article 11 of Regulation (EC) No 139/2004, or subsequently submits further information to the Commission in the course of the same procedure, shall clearly identify any material which it considers to be confidential, giving reasons, and provide a separate non-confidential version by the date set by the Commission.

3. Without prejudice to paragraph 2, the Commission may require persons referred to in Article 3 of Regulation (EC) No 139/2004, undertakings and associations of undertakings in all cases where they produce or have produced documents or statements pursuant to Regulation (EC) No 139/2004 to identify the documents or parts of documents which they consider to contain business secrets or other confidential information belonging to them and to identify the undertakings with regard to which such documents are to be considered confidential.

The Commission may also require persons referred to in Article 3 of Regulation (EC) No 139/2004, undertakings or associations of undertakings to identify any part of a statement of objections, case summary or a decision adopted by the Commission which in their view contains business secrets.

Where business secrets or other confidential information are identified, the persons, undertakings and associations of undertakings shall give reasons and provide a separate non-confidential version by the date set by the Commission.

Commentary
Art 18: F&N: 5.419
Art 18(1): B&C: 8.177, 8.179
Art 18(2): B&C: 8.120, 8.177 F&N: 5.584
Art 18(3): B&C: 8.138, 8.177 F&N: 5.419, 5.584
Art 18(4): B&C: 8.131

Chapter VI
Commitments Offered by the Undertakings Concerned

Article 19
Time limits for submission of commitments

1. Commitments offered by the undertakings concerned pursuant to Article 6(2) of Regulation (EC) No 139/2004 shall be submitted to the Commission within not more than 20 working days from the date of receipt of the notification.

2. Commitments offered by the undertakings concerned pursuant to Article 8(2) of Regulation (EC) No 139/2004 shall be submitted to the Commission within not more than 65 working days from the date on which proceedings were initiated.

Where pursuant to Article 10(3), second subparagraph, of Regulation (EC) No 139/2004 the period for the adoption of a decision pursuant to Article 8(1), (2) and (3) is extended, the period of 65 working days for the submission of commitments shall automatically be extended by the same number of working days.

In exceptional circumstances, the Commission may accept commitments offered after the expiry of the time limit for their submission within the meaning of this paragraph provided that the procedure provided for in Article 19(5) of Regulation (EC) No 139/2004 is complied with.

3. Articles 7, 8 and 9 shall apply *mutatis mutandis*.

Commentary
Art 19(1): B&C: 8.163 F&N: 5.484, 5.508
Art 19(2): B&C: 8.164 F&N: 5.609, 5.611
Art 19(3): B&C: 8.179 F&N: 5.611

Article 20
Procedure for the submission of commitments

1. One original and 10 copies of commitments offered by the undertakings concerned pursuant to Article 6(2) or Article 8(2) of Regulation (EC) No 139/2004 shall be submitted to the Commission at the address of the Commission's Directorate General for Competition. An electronic copy shall also be submitted at the same address and in the format specified by the Commission. The Commission shall forward copies of such commitments without delay to the competent authorities of the Member States.

2. When offering commitments pursuant to Articles 6(2) or Article 8(2) of Regulation (EC) No 139/2004, the undertakings concerned shall at the same time clearly identify any information which they consider to be confidential, giving reasons, and shall provide a separate non-confidential version.

Commentary
Art 20(1): B&C: 8.164 F&N: 5.612
Art 20(2): F&N: 5.612

CHAPTER VII
MISCELLANEOUS PROVISIONS

Article 21
Transmission of documents

1. Transmission of documents and invitations from the Commission to the addressees may be effected in any of the following ways:

(a) delivery by hand against receipt;
(b) registered letter with acknowledgement of receipt;
(c) fax with a request for acknowledgement of receipt;
(d) telex;
(e) electronic mail with a request for acknowledgement of receipt.

2. Unless otherwise provided in this Regulation, paragraph 1 also applies to the transmission of documents from the notifying parties, from other involved parties or from third parties to the Commission.

3. Where a document is sent by telex, by fax or by electronic mail, it shall be presumed that it has been received by the addressee on the day on which it was sent.

Commentary
Art 21: B&C: 8.138, 8.158

Article 22
Setting of time limits

In setting the time limits provided for pursuant to Article 12(1) and (2), Article 13(2) and Article 16(1), the Commission shall have regard to the time required for the preparation of statements and to the urgency of the case. It shall also take account of working days as well as public holidays in the country of receipt of the Commission's communication.

Time limits shall be set in terms of a precise calendar date.

Commentary
Art 22: B&C: 8.133, 8.147

Article 23
Receipt of documents by the Commission

1. In accordance with the provisions of Article 5(1) of this Regulation, notifications shall be delivered to the Commission at the address of the Commission's Directorate General for Competition as published by the Commission in the *Official Journal of the European Union*.

2. Additional information requested to complete notifications must reach the Commission at the address referred to in paragraph 1.

3. Written comments on Commission communications pursuant to Article 12(1) and (2), Article 13(2) and Article 16(1) of this Regulation must have reached the Commission at the address referred to in paragraph 1 before the expiry of the time limit set in each case.

Commentary
Art 23: B&C: 8.118
Art 23(1): F&N: 5.455

Article 24
Definition of working days

The expression working days in Regulation (EC) No 139/2004 and in this Regulation means all days other than Saturdays, Sundays, and Commission holidays as published in the *Official Journal of the European Union* before the beginning of each year.

Part D Mergers and Concentrations

Commentary
Art 24: B&C: 8.133 F&N: 5.481

Article 25
Repeal and transitional provision

1. Without prejudice to paragraphs 2 and 3, Regulation (EC) No 447/98 is repealed with effect from 1 May 2004.

References to the repealed Regulation shall be construed as references to this Regulation.

2. Regulation (EC) No 447/98 shall continue to apply to any concentration falling within the scope of Regulation (EEC) No 4064/89.

3. For the purposes of paragraph 2, Sections 1 to 12 of the Annex to Regulation (EC) No 447/98 shall be replaced by Sections 1 to 11 of Annex I to this Regulation. In such cases references in those sections to the "EC Merger Regulation" and to the "Implementing Regulation" shall be read as referring to the corresponding provisions of Regulation (EEC) No 4064/89 and Regulation (EC) No 447/98, respectively.

Article 26
Entry into force

This Regulation shall enter into force on 1 May 2004.

This Regulation shall be binding in its entirety and directly applicable in all Member States.

Done at Brussels, [21] April 2004.

Notes

The date of this Regulation is shown as corrected by the Corrigendum at OJ L 172, 6.5.2004, p. 9.

Annex I
Form CO Relating to the Notification of a Concentration Pursuant to Regulation (EC) No 139/2004

Commentary
Annex I: B&C: 8.114, 8.117

1. Introduction

1.1. The purpose of this Form

This Form specifies the information that must be provided by notifying parties when submitting a notification to the European Commission of a proposed merger, acquisition or other concentration. The merger control system of the European Union is laid down in Council Regulation (EC) No 139/2004 (hereinafter referred to as "the EC Merger Regulation"), and in Commission Regulation (EC) No [802]/2004 (hereinafter referred to as "the Implementing Regulation"), to which this Form CO is annexed.[1] The text of these regulations, as well as other relevant documents, can be found on the Competition page of the Commission's Europa web site.

In order to limit the time and expense involved in complying with various merger control procedures in several individual countries, the European Union has put in place a system of merger control by which concentrations having a Community dimension (normally, where the parties to the concentration fulfil certain turnover thresholds)[2] are assessed by the European Commission in a single procedure (the "one stop shop" principle). Mergers which do not meet the turnover thresholds may fall within the competence of the Member States' authorities in charge of merger control.

The EC Merger Regulation requires the Commission to reach a decision within a legal deadline. In an initial phase the Commission normally has 25 working days to decide whether to clear the concentration or to "initiate proceedings", i.e., to undertake an in-depth investigation.[3] If the Commission decides to initiate proceedings, it normally has to take a final decision on the operation within no more than 90 working days of the date when proceedings are initiated.[4]

In view of these deadlines, and for the "one stop shop" principle to work, it is essential that the Commission is provided, in a timely fashion, with the information required to carry out the necessary investigation and to assess the impact of the concentration on the markets concerned. This requires that a certain amount of information be provided at the time of notification.

It is recognised that the information requested in this Form is substantial. However, experience has shown that, depending on the specific characteristics of the case, not all information is always necessary for an adequate examination of the proposed concentration. Accordingly, if you consider that any particular information requested by this Form may not be necessary for the Commission's examination of the case, you are encouraged to ask the Commission to dispense with the obligation to provide certain information ("waiver"). See Section 1.3(g) for more details.

Pre-notification contacts are extremely valuable to both the notifying parties and the Commission in determining the precise amount of information required in a notification and, in the majority of cases, will result in a significant reduction of the information required. Notifying parties may refer to the Commission's Best Practices on the Conduct of EC Merger Control Proceedings, which provides guidance on pre-notification contacts and the preparation of notifications.

In addition, it should be noted that certain concentrations, which are unlikely to pose any competition concerns, can be notified using a Short Form, which is attached to the Implementing Regulation, as Annex II.

Notes

[1] Council Regulation (EC) No 139/2004 of 20 January 2004, OJ L 24, 29.01.2004, p. 1. Your attention is drawn to the corresponding provisions of the Agreement on the European Economic Area (hereinafter referred to as "the EEA Agreement"). See in particular Article 57 of the EEA Agreement, point 1 of Annex XIV to the EEA Agreement and Protocol 4 to the Agreement between the EFTA States on the establishment of a Surveillance Authority and a Court of Justice, as well as Protocols 21 and 24 to the EEA Agreement and Article 1 and the Agreed Minutes of the Protocol adjusting the EEA Agreement. Any reference to EFTA States shall be understood to mean those EFTA States which are Contracting Parties to the EEA Agreement. As of 1 May 2004, these States are Iceland, Liechtenstein and Norway.

[2] The term "concentration" is defined in Article 3 of the EC Merger Regulation and the term "Community dimension" in Article 1 thereof. Furthermore, Article 4(5) provides that in certain circumstances where the Community turnover thresholds are not met, notifying parties may request that the Commission treat their proposed concentration as having a Community dimension.

[3] See Article 10(1) of the EC Merger Regulation.

[4] See Article 10(3) of the EC Merger Regulation.

1.2. Who must notify

In the case of a merger within the meaning of Article 3(1)(a) of the EC Merger Regulation or the acquisition of joint control of an undertaking within the meaning of Article 3(1)(b) of the EC Merger Regulation, the notification shall be completed jointly by the parties to the merger or by those acquiring joint control, as the case may be.[1]

In case of the acquisition of a controlling interest in one undertaking by another, the acquirer must complete the notification.

In the case of a public bid to acquire an undertaking, the bidder must complete the notification.

Each party completing the notification is responsible for the accuracy of the information which it provides.

Notes

[1] See Article 4(2) of the EC Merger Regulation.

1.3. The requirement for a correct and complete notification

All information required by this Form must be correct and complete. The information required must be supplied in the appropriate Section of this Form.

In particular you should note that:

(a) In accordance with Article 10(1) of the EC Merger Regulation and Article 5(2) and (4) of the Implementing Regulation, the time-limits of the EC Merger Regulation linked to the notification will not begin to run until all the information that has to be supplied with the notification has been received by the Commission. This requirement is to ensure that the Commission is able to assess the notified concentration within the strict time-limits provided by the EC Merger Regulation.

(b) The notifying parties should verify, in the course of preparing their notification, that contact names and numbers, and in particular fax numbers and e-mail addresses, provided to the Commission are accurate, relevant and up-to-date.

(c) Incorrect or misleading information in the notification will be considered to be incomplete information (Article 5(4) of the Implementing Regulation).

(d) If a notification is incomplete, the Commission will inform the notifying parties or their representatives in writing and without delay. The notification will only become effective on the date on which the complete and accurate information is received by the Commission (Article 10(1) of the EC Merger Regulation, Articles 5(2) and (4) of the Implementing Regulation).

(e) Under Article 14(1)(a) of the EC Merger Regulation, notifying parties who, either intentionally or negligently, supply incorrect or misleading information, may be liable to fines of up to 1% of the aggregate turnover of the undertaking concerned. In addition, pursuant to Article 6(3)(a) and Article 8(6)(a) of the EC Merger Regulation the Commission may revoke its decision on the compatibility of a notified concentration where it is based on incorrect information for which one of the undertakings is responsible.

(f) You may request in writing that the Commission accept that the notification is complete notwithstanding the failure to provide information required by this Form, if such information is not reasonably available to you in part or in whole (for example, because of the unavailability of information on a target company during a contested bid).

The Commission will consider such a request, provided that you give reasons for the unavailability of that information, and provide your best estimates for missing data together with the sources for the estimates. Where possible, indications as to where any of the requested information that is unavailable to you could be obtained by the Commission should also be provided.

(g) You may request in writing that the Commission accept that the notification is complete notwithstanding the failure to provide information required by this Form, if you consider that any particular information required, in the full or short form version, may not be necessary for the Commission's examination of the case.

The Commission will consider such a request, provided that you give adequate reasons why that information is not relevant and necessary to its inquiry into the notified operation. You should explain this during your pre-notification contacts with the Commission and, submit a written request for a waiver, asking the Commission to dispense with the obligation to provide that information, pursuant to Article 4(2) of the Implementing Regulation.

1.4. How to notify

The notification must be completed in one of the official languages of the European Community. This language will thereafter be the language of the proceedings for all notifying parties. Where notifications are made in accordance with Article 12 of Protocol 24 to the EEA Agreement in an official language of an EFTA State which is not an official language of the Community, the notification must simultaneously be supplemented with a translation into an official language of the Community.

The information requested by this Form is to be set out using the sections and paragraph numbers of the Form, signing a declaration as provided in Section 11, and annexing supporting documentation. In completing Sections 7 to 9 of this Form, the notifying parties are invited to consider whether, for purposes of clarity, these sections are best presented in numerical order, or whether they can be grouped together for each individual affected market (or group of affected markets).

For the sake of clarity, certain information may be put in annexes. However, it is essential that all key substantive pieces of information, and in particular market share information for the parties and their largest competitors, are presented in the body of Form CO. Annexes to this Form shall only be used to supplement the information supplied in the Form itself.

Contact details must be provided in a format provided by the Commission's Directorate-General for Competition (DG Competition). For a proper investigatory process, it is essential that the contact details are accurate. Multiple instances of incorrect contact details may be a ground for declaring a notification incomplete.

Supporting documents are to be submitted in their original language; where this is not an official language of the Community, they must be translated into the language of the proceeding (Article 3(4) of the Implementing Regulation).

Supporting documents may be originals or copies of the originals. In the latter case, the notifying party must confirm that they are true and complete.

One original and [37] copies of the Form CO and the supporting documents shall be submitted to the Commission's Directorate-General for Competition.

The notification shall be delivered to the address referred to in Article 23 (1) of the Implementing Regulation and in the format specified by the Commission from time to time. This address is published in the *Official Journal of the European Union*. The notification must be delivered to the Commission on working days as defined by Article 24 of the Implementing Regulation. In order to enable it to be registered on the same day, it must be delivered before 17.00 hrs on Mondays to Thursdays and before 16.00 hrs on Fridays and workdays preceding public holidays and other holidays as determined by the Commission and published in the *Official Journal of the European Union*. The security instructions given on DG Competition's website must be adhered to.

Notes

The amendment shown in square brackets was made by Commission Regulation (EC) No 1792/2006 of 23 October 2006 (OJ L 362, 20.12.2006, p. 1), with effect from 1 January 2007.

1.5. Confidentiality

Article 287 of the Treaty and Article 17(2) of the EC Merger Regulation as well as the corresponding provisions of the EEA Agreement[1] require the Commission, the Member States, the EFTA Surveillance Authority and the EFTA States, their officials and other servants not to disclose information they have acquired through the application of the Regulation of the kind covered by the obligation of professional secrecy. The same principle must also apply to protect confidentiality between notifying parties.

If you believe that your interests would be harmed if any of the information you are asked to supply were to be published or otherwise divulged to other parties, submit this information separately with each page clearly marked "Business Secrets". You should also give reasons why this information should not be divulged or published.

In the case of mergers or joint acquisitions, or in other cases where the notification is completed by more than one of the parties, business secrets may be submitted under separate cover, and referred to in the notification as an annex. All such annexes must be included in the submission in order for a notification to be considered complete.

Notes

[1] See, in particular, Article 122 of the EEA Agreement, Article 9 of Protocol 24 to the EEA Agreement and Article 17(2) of Chapter XIII of Protocol 4 to the Agreement between the EFTA States on the establishment of a Surveillance Authority and a Court of Justice (ESA Agreement).

1.6. Definitions and instructions for purposes of this Form

Notifying party or parties: in cases where a notification is submitted by only one of the undertakings who is a party to an operation, "notifying parties" is used to refer only to the undertaking actually submitting the notification.

Party(ies) to the concentration or parties: these terms relate to both the acquiring and acquired parties, or to the merging parties, including all undertakings in which a controlling interest is being acquired or which is the subject of a public bid.

Except where otherwise specified, the terms notifying party(ies) and party(ies) to the concentration include all the undertakings which belong to the same groups as those parties.

Affected markets: Section 6 of this Form requires the notifying parties to define the relevant product markets, and further to identify which of those relevant markets are likely to be affected by the notified operation. This definition of affected market is used as the basis for requiring information for a number of other questions contained in this Form. The definitions thus submitted by the notifying parties are referred to in this Form as the affected market(s). This term can refer to a relevant market made up either of products or of services.

Year: all references to the word year in this Form should be read as meaning calendar year, unless otherwise stated. All information requested in this Form must, unless otherwise specified, relate to the year preceding that of the notification.

The financial data requested in Sections 3.3 to 3.5 must be provided in euros at the average exchange rates prevailing for the years or other periods in question.

All references contained in this Form are to the relevant articles and paragraphs of the EC Merger Regulation, unless otherwise stated.

1.7. Provision of Information to Employees and their Representatives

The Commission would like to draw attention to the obligations to which the parties to a concentration may be subject under Community and/or national rules on information and consultation regarding transactions of a concentrative nature vis-à-vis employees and/or their representatives.

SECTION 1
Description of the concentration

1.1. Provide an executive summary of the concentration, specifying the parties to the concentration, the nature of the concentration (for example, merger, acquisition, or joint venture), the areas of activity of the notifying parties, the markets on which the concentration will have an impact (including the main affected markets),[1] and the strategic and economic rationale for the concentration.

Notes
[1] See Section 6.III for the definition of affected markets.

1.2. Provide a summary (up to 500 words) of the information provided under Section 1.1. It is intended that this summary will be published on the Commission's website at the date of notification. The summary must be drafted so that it contains no confidential information or business secrets.

SECTION 2
Information about the parties

2.1. Information on notifying party (or parties)

Give details of:
2.1.1. name and address of undertaking;
2.1.2. nature of the undertaking's business;
2.1.3. name, address, telephone number, fax number and e-mail address of, and position held by, the appropriate contact person; and
2.1.4. an address for service of the notifying party (or each of the notifying parties) to which documents and, in particular, Commission decisions may be delivered. The name, telephone number and e-mail address of a person at this address who is authorised to accept service must be provided.

2.2. Information on other parties[1] to the concentration

For each party to the concentration (except the notifying party or parties) give details of:
2.2.1. name and address of undertaking;
2.2.2. nature of undertaking's business;

2.2.3. name, address, telephone number, fax number and e-mail address of, and position held by, the appropriate contact person; and

2.2.4. an address for service of the party (or each of the parties) to which documents and, in particular, Commission Decisions may be delivered. The name, e-mail address and telephone number of a person at this address who is authorised to accept service must be provided.

Notes

[1] This includes the target company in the case of a contested bid, in which case the details should be completed as far as is possible.

2.3. Appointment of representatives

Where notifications are signed by representatives of undertakings, such representatives must produce written proof that they are authorised to act. The written proof must contain the name and position of the persons granting such authority.

Provide the following contact details of any representatives who have been authorised to act for any of the parties to the concentration, indicating whom they represent:

2.3.1. name of representative;

2.3.2. address of representative;

2.3.3. name, address, telephone number, fax number and e-mail address of person to be contacted; and

2.3.4. an address of the representative (in Brussels if available) to which correspondence may be sent and documents delivered.

SECTION 3
Details of the concentration

3.1. Describe the nature of the concentration being notified. In doing so, state:

(a) whether the proposed concentration is a full legal merger, an acquisition of sole or joint control, a full-function joint venture within the meaning of Article 3(4) of the EC Merger Regulation or a contract or other means of conferring direct or indirect control within the meaning of Article 3(2) of the EC Merger Regulation;

(b) whether the whole or parts of parties are subject to the concentration;

(c) a brief explanation of the economic and financial structure of the concentration;

(d) whether any public offer for the securities of one party by another party has the support of the former's supervisory boards of management or other bodies legally representing that party;

(e) the proposed or expected date of any major events designed to bring about the completion of the concentration;

(f) the proposed structure of ownership and control after the completion of the concentration;

(g) any financial or other support received from whatever source (including public authorities) by any of the parties and the nature and amount of this support; and

(h) the economic sectors involved in the concentration.

3.2. State the value of the transaction (the purchase price or the value of all the assets involved, as the case may be).

3.3. For each of the undertakings concerned by the concentration[1] provide the following data[2] for the last financial year:

3.3.1. world-wide turnover;

3.3.2. Community-wide turnover;

3.3.3. EFTA-wide turnover;

3.3.4. turnover in each Member State;

3.3.5. turnover in each EFTA State;

3.3.6. the Member State, if any, in which more than two-thirds of Community-wide turnover is achieved; and

3.3.7. the EFTA State, if any, in which more than two-thirds of EFTA-wide turnover is achieved.

Notes
[1] See Commission Notice on the concept of undertakings concerned.
[2] See, generally, the Commission Notice on calculation of turnover. Turnover of the acquiring party or parties to the concentration should include the aggregated turnover of all undertakings within the meaning of Article 5(4) of the EC Merger Regulation. Turnover of the acquired party or parties should include the turnover relating to the parts subject to the transaction within the meaning of Article 5(2) of the EC Merger Regulation. Special provisions are contained in Articles 5(3), (4) and 5(5) of the EC Merger Regulation for credit, insurance, other financial institutions and joint undertakings.

3.4. For the purposes of Article 1(3) of the EC Merger Regulation, if the operation does not meet the thresholds set out in Article 1(2), provide the following data for the last financial year:

    3.4.1. the Member States, if any, in which the combined aggregate turnover of all the undertakings concerned is more than EUR 100 million; and

    3.4.2. the Member States, if any, in which the aggregate turnover of each of at least two of the undertakings concerned is more than EUR 25 million.

3.5. For the purposes of determining whether the concentration qualifies as an EFTA cooperation case,[1] provide the following information with respect to the last financial year:

    3.5.1. does the combined turnover of the undertakings concerned in the territory of the EFTA States equal 25% or more of their total turnover in the EEA territory?

    3.5.2. does each of at least two undertakings concerned have a turnover exceeding EUR 250 million in the territory of the EFTA States?

Notes
[1] See Article 57 of the EEA Agreement and, in particular, Article 2(1) of Protocol 24 to the EEA Agreement. A case qualifies as a cooperation case if the combined turnover of the undertakings concerned in the territory of the EFTA States equals 25% or more of their total turnover within the territory covered by the EEA Agreement; or each of at least two undertakings concerned has a turnover exceeding EUR 250 million in the territory of the EFTA States; or the concentration is liable to create or strengthen a dominant position as a result of which effective competition would be significantly impeded in the territories of the EFTA States or a substantial part thereof.

3.6. Describe the economic rationale of the concentration.

Section 4
Ownership and control[1]

Notes
[1] See Articles 3(3), 3(4) and 3(5) and Article 5(4) of the EC Merger Regulation.

4.1. For each of the parties to the concentration provide a list of all undertakings belonging to the same group.
This list must include:

    4.1.1. all undertakings or persons controlling these parties, directly or indirectly;

    4.1.2. all undertakings active on any affected market[1] that are controlled, directly or indirectly:
        (a) by these parties;
        (b) by any other undertaking identified in 4.1.1.

For each entry listed above, the nature and means of control should be specified.
The information sought in this section may be illustrated by the use of organization charts or diagrams to show the structure of ownership and control of the undertakings.

Notes
[1] See Section 6 for the definition of affected markets.

4.2. With respect to the parties to the concentration and each undertaking or person identified in response to Section 4.1, provide:

    4.2.1. a list of all other undertakings which are active in affected markets (affected markets are defined in Section 6) in which the undertakings, or persons, of the group hold individually or collectively 10% or more of the voting rights, issued share capital or other securities; in each case, identify the holder and state the percentage held;

4.2.2. a list for each undertaking of the members of their boards of management who are also members of the boards of management or of the supervisory boards of any other undertaking which is active in affected markets; and (where applicable) for each undertaking a list of the members of their supervisory boards who are also members of the boards of management of any other undertaking which is active in affected markets;

in each case, identify the name of the other undertaking and the positions held;

4.2.3. details of acquisitions made during the last three years by the groups identified above (Section 4.1) of undertakings active in affected markets as defined in Section 6.

Information provided here may be illustrated by the use of organization charts or diagrams to give a better understanding.

SECTION 5
Supporting documentation

Notifying parties must provide the following:

5.1. copies of the final or most recent versions of all documents bringing about the concentration, whether by agreement between the parties to the concentration, acquisition of a controlling interest or a public bid;

5.2. in a public bid, a copy of the offer document; if it is unavailable at the time of notification, it should be submitted as soon as possible and not later than when it is posted to shareholders;

5.3. copies of the most recent annual reports and accounts of all the parties to the concentration; and

5.4. copies of all analyses, reports, studies, surveys, and any comparable documents prepared by or for any member(s) of the board of directors, or the supervisory board, or the other person(s) exercising similar functions (or to whom such functions have been delegated or entrusted), or the shareholders' meeting, for the purpose of assessing or analysing the concentration with respect to market shares, competitive conditions, competitors (actual and potential), the rationale of the concentration, potential for sales growth or expansion into other product or geographic markets, and/or general market conditions.[1]

For each of these documents, indicate (if not contained in the document itself) the date of preparation, the name and title of each individual who prepared each such document.

Notes

[1] As set out in introductory Parts 1.1 and 1.3(g), in the context of pre-notification, you may want to discuss with the Commission to what extent dispensation (waivers) to provide the requested documents would be appropriate. Where waivers are sought, the Commission may specify the documents to be provided in a particular case in a request for information under Article 11 of the EC Merger Regulation.

SECTION 6
Market definitions

The relevant product and geographic markets determine the scope within which the market power of the new entity resulting from the concentration must be assessed.[1]

Notes

[1] See Commission Notice on the definition of the relevant market for the purposes of Community competition law.

The notifying party or parties must provide the data requested having regard to the following definitions:

I. Relevant product markets:

A relevant product market comprises all those products and/or services which are regarded as interchangeable or substitutable by the consumer, by reason of the products' characteristics, their prices and their intended use. A relevant product market may in some cases be composed of a number of individual products and/or services which present largely identical physical or technical character-istics and are interchangeable.

Factors relevant to the assessment of the relevant product market include the analysis of why the products or services in these markets are included and why others are excluded by using the above definition, and having regard to, for example, substitutability, conditions of competition, prices, cross-price elasticity of demand or other factors relevant for the definition of the product markets (for example, supply-side substitutability in appropriate cases).

II. **Relevant geographic markets:**

The relevant geographic market comprises the area in which the undertakings concerned are involved in the supply and demand of relevant products or services, in which the conditions of competition are sufficiently homogeneous and which can be distinguished from neighbouring geographic areas because, in particular, conditions of competition are appreciably different in those areas.

Factors relevant to the assessment of the relevant geographic market include inter alia the nature and characteristics of the products or services concerned, the existence of entry barriers, consumer prefer-ences, appreciable differences in the undertakings' market shares between neighbouring geographic areas or substantial price differences.

III. **Affected markets:**

For purposes of information required in this Form, affected markets consist of relevant product markets where, in the EEA territory, in the Community, in the territory of the EFTA States, in any Member State or in any EFTA State:

(a) two or more of the parties to the concentration are engaged in business activities in the same product market and where the concentration will lead to a combined market share of 15% or more. These are horizontal relationships;

(b) one or more of the parties to the concentration are engaged in business activities in a product market, which is upstream or downstream of a product market in which any other party to the concentration is engaged, and any of their individual or combined market shares at either level is 25% or more, regardless of whether there is or is not any existing supplier/customer relationship between the parties to the concentration.[1] These are vertical relationships.

Notes

[1] For example, if a party to the concentration holds a market share larger than 25% in a market that is upstream to a market in which the other party is active, then both the upstream and the downstream markets are affected markets. Similarly, if a vertically integrated company merges with another party which is active at the downstream level, and the merger leads to a combined market share downstream of 25% or more, then both the upstream and the down-stream markets are affected markets.

On the basis of the above definitions and market share thresholds, provide the following information:[1]

— Identify each affected market within the meaning of Section III, at:
— the EEA, Community or EFTA level;
— the individual Member States or EFTA States level.

Notes

[1] As set out in introductory Parts 1.1 and 1.3(g), in the context of pre-notification, you may want to discuss with the Commission to what extent dispensation (waivers) to provide the requested information would be appropriate for certain affected markets, or for certain other markets (as described under IV).

6.2. In addition, state and explain the parties' view regarding the scope of the relevant geographic market within the meaning of Section II that applies in relation to each affected market identi-fied above.

Notes

There is no paragraph 6.1 in the original instrument.

IV. Other markets in which the notified operation may have a significant impact

6.3. On the basis of the above definitions, describe the product and geographic scope of markets other than affected markets identified in Section 6.1 in which the notified operation may have a significant impact, for example, where:

(a) any of the parties to the concentration has a market share larger than 25% and any other party to the concentration is a potential competitor into that market. A party may be considered a potential competitor, in particular, where it has plans to enter a market, or has developed or pursued such plans in the past two years;

(b) any of the parties to the concentration has a market share larger than 25% and any other party to the concentration holds important intellectual property rights for that market;

(c) any of the parties to the concentration is present in a product market, which is a neighbouring market closely related to a product market in which any other party to the concentration is engaged, and the individual or combined market shares of the parties in any one of these markets is 25% or more. Product markets are closely related neighbouring markets when the products are complementary to each other[1] or when they belong to a range of products that is generally purchased by the same set of customers for the same end use;[2]

where such markets include the whole or a part of the EEA.

In order to enable the Commission to consider, from the outset, the competitive impact of the proposed concentration in the markets identified under this Section 6.3, notifying parties are invited to submit the information under Sections 7 and 8 of this Form in relation to those markets.

Notes

[1] Products (or services) are called complementary when, for example, the use (or consumption) of one product essentially implies the use (or consumption) of the other product, such as for staple machines and staples, and printers and printer cartridges.

[2] Examples of products belonging to such a range would be whisky and gin sold to bars and restaurants, and different materials for packaging a certain category of goods sold to producers of such goods.

SECTION 7
Information on affected markets

For each affected relevant product market, for each of the last three financial years:[1]

Notes

[1] Without prejudice to Article 4(2) of the Implementing Regulation.

(a) for the EEA territory;

(b) for the Community as a whole;

(c) for the territory of the EFTA States as a whole;

(d) individually for each Member State and EFTA State where the parties to the concentration do business; and

(e) where in the opinion of the notifying parties, the relevant geographic market is different;

provide the following:

7.1. an estimate of the total size of the market in terms of sales value (in euros) and volume (units).[1] Indicate the basis and sources for the calculations and provide documents where available to confirm these calculations;

Notes

[1] The value and volume of a market should reflect output less exports plus imports for the geographic areas under consideration. If readily available, please provide disaggregated information on imports and exports by country of origin and destination, respectively.

7.2. the sales in value and volume, as well as an estimate of the market shares, of each of the parties to the concentration;

7.3. an estimate of the market share in value (and where appropriate, volume) of all competitors (including importers) having at least 5% of the geographic market under consideration. On this basis, provide an estimate of the HHI index[1] pre- and post-merger, and the difference between the two (the delta).[2] Indicate the proportion of market shares used as a basis to calculate the HHI. Identify the sources used to calculate these market shares and provide documents where available to confirm the calculation;

Notes

[1] HHI stands for Herfindahl-Hirschman Index, a measure of market concentration. The HHI is calculated by summing the squares of the individual market shares of all the firms in the market. For example, a market containing five firms with market shares of 40%, 20%, 15%, 15%, and 10%, respectively, has an HHI of 2550 ($40^2 + 20^2 + 15^2 + 15^2 + 10^2 = 2{,}550$). The HHI ranges from close to zero (in an atomistic market) to 10000 (in the case of a pure monopoly). The post-merger HHI is calculated on the working assumption that the individual market shares of the companies do not change. Although it is best to include all firms in the calculation, lack of information about very small firms may not be important because such firms do not affect the HHI significantly.

[2] The increase in concentration as measured by the HHI can be calculated independently of the overall market concentration by doubling the product of the market shares of the merging firms. For example, a merger of two firms with market shares of 30% and 15% respectively would increase the HHI by 900 ($30 \times 15 \times 2 = 900$). The explanation for this technique is as follows: Before the merger, the market shares of the merging firms contribute to the HHI by their squares individually: $(a)^2 + (b)^2$. After the merger, the contribution is the square of their sum: $(a + b)^2$, which equals $(a)^2 + (b)^2 + 2ab$. The increase in the HHI is therefore represented by $2ab$.

7.4. the name, address, telephone number, fax number and e-mail address of the head of the legal department (or other person exercising similar functions; and in cases where there is no such person, then the chief executive) for the competitors identified under 7.3;

7.5. an estimate of the total value and volume and source of imports from outside the EEA territory and identify:
   (a) the proportion of such imports that are derived from the groups to which the parties to the concentration belong;
   (b) an estimate of the extent to which any quotas, tariffs or non-tariff barriers to trade, affect these imports; and
   (c) an estimate of the extent to which transportation and other costs affect these imports;

7.6. the extent to which trade among States within the EEA territory is affected by:
   (a) transportation and other costs; and
   (b) other non-tariff barriers to trade;

7.7. the manner in which the parties to the concentration produce, price and sell the products and/or services; for example, whether they manufacture and price locally, or sell through local distribution facilities;

7.8. a comparison of price levels in each Member State and EFTA State by each party to the concentration and a similar comparison of price levels between the Community, the EFTA States and other areas where these products are produced (e.g. Russia, the United States of America, Japan, China, or other relevant areas); and

7.9. the nature and extent of vertical integration of each of the parties to the concentration compared with their largest competitors.

SECTION 8
General conditions in affected markets

8.1. Identify the five largest independent[1] suppliers to the parties to the concentration and their individual shares of purchases from each of these suppliers (of raw materials or goods used for purposes of producing the relevant products). Provide the name, address, telephone number, fax number and e-mail address of the head of the legal department (or other person exercising similar functions; and in cases where there is no such person, then the chief executive) for each of these suppliers.

Notes

[1] That is, suppliers which are not subsidiaries, agents or undertakings forming part of the group of the party in question. In addition to those five independent suppliers the notifying parties can, if they consider it necessary for a proper assessment of the case, identify the intra-group suppliers. The same will apply in 8.6 in relation to customers.

Structure of supply in affected markets

8.2. Explain the distribution channels and service networks that exist in the affected markets. In so doing, take account of the following where appropriate:

(a) the distribution systems prevailing in the market and their importance. To what extent is distribution performed by third parties and/or undertakings belonging to the same group as the parties identified in Section 4?

(b) the service networks (for example, maintenance and repair) prevailing and their importance in these markets. To what extent are such services performed by third parties and/or undertakings belonging to the same group as the parties identified in Section 4?

8.3. Provide an estimate of the total Community-wide and EFTA-wide capacity for the last three years. Over this period what proportion of this capacity is accounted for by each of the parties to the concentration, and what have been their respective rates of capacity utilization. If applicable, identify the location and capacity of the manufacturing facilities of each of the parties to the concentration in affected markets.

8.4. Specify whether any of the parties to the concentration, or any of the competitors, have "pipeline products", products likely to be brought to market in the near term, or plans to expand (or contract) production or sales capacity. If so, provide an estimate of the projected sales and market shares of the parties to the concentration over the next three to five years.

8.5. If you consider any other supply-side considerations to be relevant, they should be specified.

Structure of demand in affected markets

8.6. Identify the five[1] largest independent customers of the parties in each affected market and their individual share of total sales for such products accounted for by each of those customers. Provide the name, address, telephone number, fax number and e-mail address of the head of the legal department (or other person exercising similar functions; and in cases where there is no such person, then the chief executive) for each of these customers.

Notes

[1] Experience has shown that the examination of complex cases often requires more customer contact details. In the course of pre-notification contacts, the Commission's services may ask for more customer contact details for certain affected markets.

8.7. Explain the structure of demand in terms of:

(a) the phases of the markets in terms of, for example, take-off, expansion, maturity and decline, and a forecast of the growth rate of demand;

(b) the importance of customer preferences, for example in terms of brand loyalty, the provision of pre- and after-sales services, the provision of a full range of products, or network effects;

(c) the role of product differentiation in terms of attributes or quality, and the extent to which the products of the parties to the concentration are close substitutes;

(d) the role of switching costs (in terms of time and expense) for customers when changing from one supplier to another;

(e) the degree of concentration or dispersion of customers;

(f) segmentation of customers into different groups with a description of the "typical customer" of each group;

(g) the importance of exclusive distribution contracts and other types of long-term contracts; and

(h) the extent to which public authorities, government agencies, State enterprises or similar bodies are important participants as a source of demand.

Market entry

8.8. Over the last five years, has there been any significant entry into any affected markets? If so, identify such entrants and provide the name, address, telephone number, fax number and e-mail address of the head of the legal department (or other person exercising similar functions; and in cases where there is no such person, then the chief executive) and an estimate of the current market share of each such entrant. If any of the parties to the concentration entered an affected market in the past five years, provide an analysis of the barriers to entry encountered.

8.9. In the opinion of the notifying parties, are there undertakings (including those at present operating only outside the Community or the EEA) that are likely to enter the market? If so, identify such entrants and provide the name, address, telephone number, fax number and e-mail address of the head of the legal department (or other person exercising similar functions; and in cases where there is no such person, then the chief executive). Explain why such entry is likely and provide an estimate of the time within which such entry is likely to occur.

8.10. Describe the various factors influencing entry into affected markets, examining entry from both a geographical and product viewpoint. In so doing, take account of the following where appropriate:

(a) the total costs of entry (R& D, production, establishing distribution systems, promotion, advertising, servicing, and so forth) on a scale equivalent to a significant viable competitor, indicating the market share of such a competitor;

(b) any legal or regulatory barriers to entry, such as government authorization or standard setting in any form, as well as barriers resulting from product certification procedures, or the need to have a proven track record;

(c) any restrictions created by the existence of patents, know-how and other intellectual property rights in these markets and any restrictions created by licensing such rights;

(d) the extent to which each of the parties to the concentration are holders, licensees or licensors of patents, know-how and other rights in the relevant markets;

(e) the importance of economies of scale for the production or distribution of products in the affected markets; and

(f) access to sources of supply, such as availability of raw materials and necessary infrastructure.

Research and development

8.11. Give an account of the importance of research and development in the ability of a firm operating the relevant market(s) to compete in the long term. Explain the nature of the research and development in affected markets carried out by the parties to the concentration.

In so doing, take account of the following, where appropriate:

(a) trends and intensities of research and development[1] in these markets and for the parties to the concentration;

(b) the course of technological development for these markets over an appropriate time period (including developments in products and/or services, production processes, distribution systems, and so on);

(c) the major innovations that have been made in these markets and the undertakings responsible for these innovations; and

(d) the cycle of innovation in these markets and where the parties are in this cycle of innovation.

Notes
[1] Research and development intensity is defined as research development expenditure as a proportion of turnover.

Cooperative agreements

8.12. To what extent do cooperative agreements (horizontal, vertical, or other) exist in the affected markets?

8.13. Give details of the most important cooperative agreements engaged in by the parties to the concentration in the affected markets, such as research and development, licensing, joint production, specialization, distribution, long term supply and exchange of information agreements and, where deemed useful, provide a copy of these agreements.

Trade associations

8.14. With respect to the trade associations in the affected markets:

(a) identify those of which the parties to the concentration are members; and

(b) identify the most important trade associations to which the customers and suppliers of the parties to the concentration belong.

Provide the name, address, telephone number, fax number and e-mail address of the appropriate contact person for all trade associations listed above.

SECTION 9
Overall market context and efficiencies

9.1. Describe the world wide context of the proposed concentration, indicating the position of each of the parties to the concentration outside of the EEA territory in terms of size and competitive strength.

9.2. Describe how the proposed concentration is likely to affect the interests of intermediate and ultimate consumers and the development of technical and economic progress.

9.3. Should you wish the Commission specifically to consider from the outset[1] whether efficiency gains generated by the concentration are likely to enhance the ability and incentive of the new entity to act pro-competitively for the benefit of consumers, please provide a description of, and supporting documents relating to, each efficiency (including cost savings, new product introductions, and service or product improvements) that the parties anticipate will result from the proposed concentration relating to any relevant product.[2]

For each claimed efficiency, provide:

(i) a detailed explanation of how the proposed concentration would allow the new entity to achieve the efficiency. Specify the steps that the parties anticipate taking to achieve the efficiency, the risks involved in achieving the efficiency, and the time and costs required to achieve it;

(ii) where reasonably possible, a quantification of the efficiency and a detailed explanation of how the quantification was calculated. Where relevant, also provide an estimate of the significance of efficiencies related to new product introductions or quality improvements. For efficiencies that involve cost savings, state separately the one-time fixed cost savings, recurring fixed cost savings, and variable cost savings (in euros per unit and euros per year);

(iii) the extent to which customers are likely to benefit from the efficiency and a detailed explanation of how this conclusion is arrived at; and

(iv) the reason why the party or parties could not achieve the efficiency to a similar extent by means other than through the concentration proposed, and in a manner that is not likely to raise competition concerns.

Notes

[1] It should be noted that submitting information in response to Section 9.3 is voluntary. Parties are not required to offer any justification for not completing this section. Failure to provide information on efficiencies will not be taken to imply that the proposed concentration does not create efficiencies or that the rationale for the concentration is to increase market power. Not providing the requested information on efficiencies at the notification stage does not preclude providing the information at a later stage. However, the earlier the information is provided, the better the Commission can verify the efficiency claim.

[2] For further guidance on the assessment of efficiencies, see the Commission Notice on the assessment of horizontal mergers.

SECTION 10
Cooperative effects of a joint venture

10. For the purpose of Article 2(4) of the EC Merger Regulation, answer the following questions:

(a) Do two or more parents retain to a significant extent activities in the same market as the joint venture or in a market which is upstream or downstream from that of the joint venture or in a neighbouring market closely related to this market?[1]

If the answer is affirmative, please indicate for each of the markets referred to here:
— the turnover of each parent company in the preceding financial year;
— the economic significance of the activities of the joint venture in relation to this turnover;
— the market share of each parent.

If the answer is negative, please justify your answer.

(b) If the answer to (a) is affirmative and in your view the creation of the joint venture does not lead to coordination between independent undertakings that restricts competition within the meaning of Article 81(1) of the EC Treaty, give your reasons.

(c) Without prejudice to the answers to (a) and (b) and in order to ensure that a complete assessment of the case can be made by the Commission, please explain how the criteria of Article 81(3) apply. Under Article 81(3), the provisions of Article 81(1) may be declared inapplicable if the operation:

  (i) contributes to improving the production or distribution of goods, or to promoting technical or economic progress;

  (ii) allows consumers a fair share of the resulting benefit;

  (iii) does not impose on the undertakings concerned restrictions which are not indispensable to the attainment of these objectives; and

  (iv) does not afford such undertakings the possibility of eliminating competition in respect of a substantial part of the products in question.

Notes

[1] For market definitions refer to Section 6.

Section 11
Declaration

Article 2(2) of the Implementing Regulation states that where notifications are signed by representatives of undertakings, such representatives must produce written proof that they are authorized to act. Such written authorization must accompany the notification.

The notification must conclude with the following declaration which is to be signed by or on behalf of all the notifying parties:

The notifying party or parties declare that, to the best of their knowledge and belief, the information given in this notification is true, correct, and complete, that true and complete copies of documents required by Form CO have been supplied, that all estimates are identified as such and are their best estimates of the underlying facts, and that all the opinions expressed are sincere.

They are aware of the provisions of Article 14(1)(a) of the EC Merger Regulation.

Place and date:

Signatures:

Name/s and positions:

On behalf of:

Annex II
Short Form for the Notification of a Concentration Pursuant to Regulation (EC) No 139/2004

Commentary
Annex II: B&C: 8.114, 8.124

---

1. Introduction

1.1. The purpose of the Short Form

The Short Form specifies the information that must be provided by the notifying parties when submitting a notification to the European Commission of certain proposed mergers, acquisitions or other concentrations that are unlikely to raise competition concerns.

In completing this Form, your attention is drawn to Council Regulation (EC) No 139/2004 (hereinafter referred to as "the EC Merger Regulation"), and Commission Regulation (EC) No [802]/2004 (hereinafter referred to as "the Implementing Regulation"), to which this Form is annexed[1]. The text of these regulations, as well as other relevant documents, can be found on the Competition page of the Commission's Europa web site.

As a general rule, the Short Form may be used for the purpose of notifying concentrations, where one of the following conditions is met:

1. in the case of a joint venture, the joint venture has no, or negligible, actual or foreseen activities within the territory of the European Economic Area (EEA). Such cases occur where:
   (a) the turnover of the joint venture and/or the turnover of the contributed activities is less than EUR 100 million in the EEA territory; and
   (b) the total value of the assets transferred to the joint venture is less than EUR 100 million in the EEA territory;
2. none of the parties to the concentration are engaged in business activities in the same relevant product and geographic market (no horizontal overlap), or in a market which is upstream or downstream of a market in which another party to the concentration is engaged (no vertical relationship);
3. two or more of the parties to the concentration are engaged in business activities in the same relevant product and geographic market (horizontal relationships), provided that their combined market share is less than 15%; and/or one or more of the parties to the concentration are engaged in business activities in a product market which is upstream or downstream of a product market in which any other party to the concentration is engaged (vertical relationships), and provided that none of their individual or combined market shares at either level is 25% or more; or
4. a party is to acquire sole control of an undertaking over which it already has joint control.

The Commission may require a full form notification where it appears either that the conditions for using the Short Form are not met, or, exceptionally, where they are met, the Commission determines, nonetheless, that a notification under Form CO is necessary for an adequate investigation of possible competition concerns.

Examples of cases where a notification under Form CO may be necessary are concentrations where it is difficult to define the relevant markets (for example, in emerging markets or where there is no established case practice); where a party is a new or potential entrant, or an important patent holder; where it is not possible to adequately determine the parties' market shares; in markets with high entry barriers, with a high degree of concentration or known competition problems; where at least two parties to the concentration are present in closely related neighbouring markets;[2] and in concentrations where an issue of coordination arises, as referred to in Article 2(4) of the EC Merger Regulation. Similarly, a Form CO notification may be required in the case of a party acquiring sole control of a joint venture in which it currently holds joint control, where the acquiring party and the joint venture, together, have a strong market position, or the joint venture and the acquiring party have strong positions in vertically related markets.

Notes

[1] Council Regulation (EC) No 139/2004 of 20 January 2004, OJ L 24, 29.01.2004, p. 1. Your attention is drawn to the corresponding provisions of the Agreement on the European Economic Area (hereinafter referred to as "the EEA Agreement". See in particular Article 57 of the EEA Agreement, point 1 of Annex XIV to the EEA Agreement and Protocol 4 to the Agreement between the EFTA States on the establishment of a Surveillance Authority and a Court of Justice, as well as Protocols 21 and 24 to the EEA Agreement and Article 1, and the Agreed Minutes of the Protocol adjusting the EEA Agreement. Any reference to EFTA States shall be understood to mean those EFTA States which are Contracting Parties to the EEA Agreement. As of 1 May 2004, these States are Iceland, Liechtenstein and Norway.

[2] Product markets are closely related neighbouring markets when the products are complementary to each other or when they belong to a range of products that is generally purchased by the same set of customers for the same end use.

1.2. Reversion to the full Form CO notification

In assessing whether a concentration may be notified under the Short Form, the Commission will ensure that all relevant circumstances are established with sufficient clarity. In this respect, the responsibility to provide correct and complete information rests with the notifying parties.

Part D Mergers and Concentrations

If, after the concentration has been notified, the Commission considers that the case is not appropriate for notification under the Short Form, the Commission may require full, or where appropriate partial, notification under Form CO. This may be the case where:

— it appears that the conditions for using the Short Form are not met;

— although the conditions for using the Short Form are met, a full or partial notification under Form CO appears to be necessary for an adequate investigation of possible competition concerns or to establish that the transaction is a concentration within the meaning of Article 3 of the EC Merger Regulation;

— the Short Form contains incorrect or misleading information;

— a Member State expresses substantiated competition concerns about the notified concentration within 15 working days of receipt of the copy of the notification; or

— a third party expresses substantiated competition concerns within the time-limit laid down by the Commission for such comments.

In such cases, the notification may be treated as being incomplete in a material respect pursuant to Article 5(2) of the Implementing Regulation. The Commission will inform the notifying parties or their representatives of this in writing and without delay. The notification will only become effective on the date on which all information required is received.

1.3. Importance of pre-notification contacts

Experience has shown that pre-notification contacts are extremely valuable to both the notifying parties and the Commission in determining the precise amount of information required in a notification. Also, in cases where the parties wish to submit a Short Form notification, they are advised to engage in pre-notification contacts with the Commission in order to discuss whether the case is one for which it is appropriate to use a Short Form. Notifying parties may refer to the Commission's Best Practices on the Conduct of EC Merger Control Proceedings, which provides guidance on pre-notification contacts and the preparation of notifications.

1.4. Who must notify

In the case of a merger within the meaning of Article 3(1)(a) of the EC Merger Regulation or the acquisition of joint control of an undertaking within the meaning of Article 3(1)(b) of the EC Merger Regulation, the notification shall be completed jointly by the parties to the merger or by those acquiring joint control, as the case may be.[1]

In the case of the acquisition of a controlling interest in one undertaking by another, the acquirer must complete the notification.

In the case of a public bid to acquire an undertaking, the bidder must complete the notification.

Each party completing the notification is responsible for the accuracy of the information which it provides.

Notes
[1] See Article 4(2) of the EC Merger Regulation.

1.5. The requirement for a correct and complete notification

All information required by this Form must be correct and complete. The information required must be supplied in the appropriate Section of this Form.

In particular you should note that:

(a) In accordance with Article 10(1) of the EC Merger Regulation and Article 5(2) and (4) of the Implementing Regulation, the time-limits of the EC Merger Regulation linked to the notification will not begin to run until all the information that must be supplied with the notification has been received by the Commission. This requirement is to ensure that the Commission is able to assess the notified concentration within the strict time-limits provided by the EC Merger Regulation.

(b) The notifying parties should verify, in the course of preparing their notification, that contact names and numbers, and in particular fax numbers and e-mail addresses, provided to the Commission are accurate, relevant and up-to-date.

(c) Incorrect or misleading information in the notification will be considered to be incomplete information (Article 5(4) of the Implementing Regulation).

(d) If a notification is incomplete, the Commission will inform the notifying parties or their representatives in writing and without delay. The notification will only become effective on the date on which the complete and accurate information is received by the Commission (Article 10(1) of the EC Merger Regulation, Article 5(2) and (4) of the Implementing Regulation).

(e) Under Article 14(1)(a) of the EC Merger Regulation, notifying parties who, either intentionally or negligently, supply incorrect or misleading information, may be liable to fines of up to 1% of the aggregate turnover of the undertaking concerned. In addition, pursuant to Article 6(3)(a) and Article 8(6)(a) of the EC Merger Regulation the Commission may revoke its decision on the compatibility of a notified concentration where it is based on incorrect information for which one of the undertakings is responsible.

(f) You may request in writing that the Commission accept that the notification is complete notwithstanding the failure to provide information required by this Form, if such information is not reasonably available to you in part or in whole (for example, because of the unavailability of information on a target company during a contested bid).

The Commission will consider such a request, provided that you give reasons for the unavailability of that information, and provide your best estimates for missing data together with the sources for the estimates. Where possible, indications as to where any of the requested information that is unavailable to you could be obtained by the Commission should also be provided.

(g) You may request in writing that the Commission accept that the notification is complete notwithstanding the failure to provide information required by this Form, if you consider that any particular information required may not be necessary for the Commission's examination of the case.

The Commission will consider such a request, provided that you give adequate reasons why that information is not relevant and necessary to its inquiry into the notified operation. You should explain this during your pre-notification contacts with the Commission and submit a written request for a waiver, asking the Commission to dispense with the obligation to provide that information, pursuant to Article 4(2) of the Implementing Regulation.

1.6. How to notify

The notification must be completed in one of the official languages of the European Community. This language will thereafter be the language of the proceedings for all notifying parties. Where notifications are made in accordance with Article 12 of Protocol 24 to the EEA Agreement in an official language of an EFTA State which is not an official language of the Community, the notification must simultaneously be supplemented with a translation into an official language of the Community.

The information requested by this Form is to be set out using the sections and paragraph numbers of the Form, signing a declaration as provided in Section 9, and annexing supporting documentation. In completing Section 7 of this Form, the notifying parties are invited to consider whether, for purposes of clarity, this section is best presented in numerical order, or whether information can be grouped together for each individual reportable market (or group of reportable markets).

For the sake of clarity, certain information may be put in annexes. However, it is essential that all key substantive pieces of information, in particular, market share information for the parties and their largest competitors, are presented in the body of this Form. Annexes to this Form shall only be used to supplement the information supplied in the Form itself.

Contact details must be provided in a format provided by the Commission's Directorate-General for Competition (DG Competition). For a proper investigatory process, it is essential that the contact details are accurate. Multiple instances of incorrect contact details may be a ground for declaring a notification incomplete.

Part D Mergers and Concentrations

Supporting documents are to be submitted in their original language; where this is not an official language of the Community, they must be translated into the language of the proceeding (Article 3(4) of the Implementing Regulation).

Supporting documents may be originals or copies of the originals. In the latter case, the notifying party must confirm that they are true and complete.

One original and [37] copies of the Short Form and the supporting documents shall be submitted to the Commission's Directorate-General for Competition.

The notification shall be delivered to the address referred to in Article 23(1) of the Implementing Regulation and in the format specified by the Commission from time to time. This address is published in the *Official Journal of the European Union*. The notification must be delivered to the Commission on working days as defined by Article 24 of the Implementing Regulation. In order to enable it to be registered on the same day, it must be delivered before 17.00 hrs on Mondays to Thursdays and before 16.00 hrs on Fridays and workdays preceding public holidays and other holidays as determined by the Commission and published in the *Official Journal of the European Union*. The security instructions given on DG Competition's website must be adhered to.

Notes

The amendment shown in square brackets was made by Commission Regulation (EC) No 1792/2006 of 23 October 2006 (OJ L 362, 20.12.2006, p. 1), with effect from 1 January 2007.

1.7. Confidentiality

Article 287 of the Treaty and Article 17(2) of the EC Merger Regulation as well as the corresponding provisions of the EEA Agreement[1] require the Commission, the Member States, the EFTA Surveillance Authority and the EFTA States, their officials and other servants not to disclose information they have acquired through the application of the Regulation of the kind covered by the obligation of professional secrecy. The same principle must also apply to protect confidentiality between notifying parties.

If you believe that your interests would be harmed if any of the information you are asked to supply were to be published or otherwise divulged to other parties, submit this information separately with each page clearly marked "Business Secrets". You should also give reasons why this information should not be divulged or published.

In the case of mergers or joint acquisitions, or in other cases where the notification is completed by more than one of the parties, business secrets may be submitted under separate cover, and referred to in the notification as an annex. All such annexes must be included in the submission in order for a notification to be considered complete.

Notes

[1] See, in particular, Article 122 of the EEA Agreement, Article 9 of Protocol 24 to the EEA Agreement and Article 17(2) of Chapter XIII of Protocol 4 to the Agreement between the EFTA States on the establishment of a Surveillance Authority and a Court of Justice (ESA Agreement).

1.8. Definitions and instructions for purposes of this Form

Notifying party or parties: in cases where a notification is submitted by only one of the undertakings who is a party to an operation, "notifying parties" is used to refer only to the undertaking actually submitting the notification.

Party(ies) to the concentration or parties: these terms relate to both the acquiring and acquired parties, or to the merging parties, including all undertakings in which a controlling interest is being acquired or which is the subject of a public bid.

Except where otherwise specified, the terms notifying party(ies) and party(ies) to the concentration include all the undertakings which belong to the same groups as those parties.

Year: all references to the word year in this Form should be read as meaning calendar year, unless otherwise stated. All information requested in this Form must, unless otherwise specified, relate to the year preceding that of the notification.

The financial data requested in Sections 3.3 to 3.5 must be provided in euros at the average exchange rates prevailing for the years or other periods in question.

All references contained in this Form are to the relevant articles and paragraphs of the EC Merger Regulation, unless otherwise stated.

1.9. Provision of information to employees and their representatives

The Commission would like to draw attention to the obligations to which the parties to a concentration may be subject under Community and/or national rules on information and consultation regarding transactions of a concentrative nature vis-à-vis employees and/or their representatives.

SECTION 1
Description of the concentration

1.1. Provide an executive summary of the concentration, specifying the parties to the concentration, the nature of the concentration (for example, merger, acquisition, joint venture), the areas of activity of the notifying parties, the markets on which the concentration will have an impact (including the main reportable markets),[1] and the strategic and economic rationale for the concentration.

Notes

[1] See Section 6.III for the definition of reportable markets.

1.2. Provide a summary (up to 500 words) of the information provided under Section 1.1. It is intended that this summary will be published on the Commission's website at the date of notification. The summary must be drafted so that it contains no confidential information or business secrets.

SECTION 2
Information about the parties

2.1. Information on notifying party (or parties)

Give details of:
2.1.1. name and address of undertaking;
2.1.2. nature of the undertaking's business;
2.1.3. name, address, telephone number, fax number and e-mail address of, and position held by, the appropriate contact person; and
2.1.4. an address for service of the notifying party (or each of the notifying parties) to which documents and, in particular, Commission Decisions may be delivered. The name, e-mail address and telephone number of a person at this address who is authorised to accept service must be provided.

2.2. Information on other parties[1] to the concentration

For each party to the concentration (except the notifying party or parties) give details of:
2.2.1. name and address of undertaking;
2.2.2. nature of undertaking's business;
2.2.3. name, address, telephone number, fax number and e-mail address of, and position held by, the appropriate contact person; and
2.2.4. an address for service of the party (or each of the parties) to which documents and, in particular, Commission Decisions may be delivered. The name, e-mail address and telephone number of a person at this address who is authorised to accept service must be provided.

Part D Mergers and Concentrations

Notes

[1] This includes the target company in the case of a contested bid, in which case the details should be completed as far as is possible.

2.3. Appointment of representatives

Where notifications are signed by representatives of undertakings, such representatives must produce written proof that they are authorised to act. The written proof must contain the name and position of the persons granting such authority.

Provide the following contact details of information of any representatives who have been authorised to act for any of the parties to the concentration, indicating whom they represent:

2.3.1. name of representative;

2.3.2. address of representative;

2.3.3. name, address, telephone number, fax number and e-mail address of person to be contacted; and

2.3.4. an address of the representative for service (in Brussels if available) to which correspondence may be sent and documents delivered.

Section 3
Details of the concentration

3.1. Describe the nature of the concentration being notified. In doing so state:

(a) whether the proposed concentration is a full legal merger, an acquisition of sole or joint control, a full-function joint venture within the meaning of Article 3(4) of the EC Merger Regulation or a contract or other means of conferring direct or indirect control within the meaning of Article 3(2) of the EC Merger Regulation;

(b) whether the whole or parts of parties are subject to the concentration;

(c) a brief explanation of the economic and financial structure of the concentration;

(d) whether any public offer for the securities of one party by another party has the support of the former's supervisory boards of management or other bodies legally representing that party;

(e) the proposed or expected date of any major events designed to bring about the completion of the concentration;

(f) the proposed structure of ownership and control after the completion of the concentration;

(g) any financial or other support received from whatever source (including public authorities) by any of the parties and the nature and amount of this support; and

(h) the economic sectors involved in the concentration.

3.2. State the value of the transaction (the purchase price or the value of all the assets involved, as the case may be);

3.3. For each of the undertakings concerned by the concentration[1] provide the following data[2] for the last financial year:

3.3.1. world-wide turnover;

3.3.2. Community-wide turnover;

3.3.3. EFTA-wide turnover;

3.3.4. turnover in each Member State;

3.3.5. turnover in each EFTA State;

3.3.6. the Member State, if any, in which more than two-thirds of Community-wide turnover is achieved; and

3.3.7. the EFTA State, if any, in which more than two-thirds of EFTA-wide turnover is achieved.

Notes

[1] See Commission Notice on the concept of undertakings concerned.

[2] See, generally, the Commission Notice on calculation of turnover. Turnover of the acquiring party or parties to the concentration should include the aggregated turnover of all undertakings within the meaning of Article 5(4) of the

---

EC Merger Regulation. Turnover of the acquired party or parties should include the turnover relating to the parts subject to the transaction within the meaning of Article 5(2) of the EC Merger Regulation. Special provisions are contained in Articles 5(3), (4) and 5(5) of the EC Merger Regulation for credit, insurance, other financial institutions and joint undertakings.

3.4. For the purposes of Article 1(3) of the EC Merger Regulation, if the operation does not meet the thresholds set out in Article 1(2), provide the following data for the last financial year:

    3.4.1. the Member States, if any, in which the combined aggregate turnover of all the undertakings concerned is more than EUR 100 million; and

    3.4.2. the Member States, if any, in which the aggregate turnover of each of at least two of the undertakings concerned is more than EUR 25 million.

3.5. For the purposes of determining whether the concentration qualifies as an EFTA cooperation case,[1] provide the following information with respect to the last financial year:

    3.5.1. does the combined turnover of the undertakings concerned in the territory of the EFTA States equal 25% or more of their total turnover in the EEA territory?

    3.5.2. does each of at least two undertakings concerned have a turnover exceeding EUR 250 million in the territory of the EFTA States?

Notes

[1] See Article 57 of the EEA Agreement and, in particular, Article 2(1) of Protocol 24 to the EEA Agreement. A case qualifies to be treated as a cooperation case if the combined turnover of the undertakings concerned in the territory of the EFTA States equals 25% or more of their total turnover within the territory covered by the EEA Agreement; or each of at least two undertakings concerned has a turnover exceeding EUR 250 million in the territory of the EFTA States; or the concentration is liable to create or strengthen a dominant position as a result of which effective competition would be significantly impeded in the territories of the EFTA States or a substantial part thereof.

3.6. In case the transaction concerns the acquisition of joint control of a joint venture, provide the following information:

    3.6.1. the turnover of the joint venture and/or the turnover of the contributed activities to the joint venture; and/or

    3.6.2. the total value of assets transferred to the joint venture.

3.7. Describe the economic rationale of the concentration.

SECTION 4
Ownership and control[1]

Notes

[1] See Articles 3(3), 3(4) and 3(5) and Article 5(4) of the EC Merger Regulation.

For each of the parties to the concentration provide a list of all undertakings belonging to the same group.

This list must include:

4.1. all undertakings or persons controlling these parties, directly or indirectly;

4.2. all undertakings active in any reportable market[1] that are controlled, directly or indirectly:

    (a) by these parties;

    (b) by any other undertaking identified in 4.1.

For each entry listed above, the nature and means of control should be specified.

The information sought in this section may be illustrated by the use of organisation charts or diagrams to show the structure of ownership and control of the undertakings.

Notes

[1] See Section 6.III for the definition of reportable markets.

SECTION 5

Supporting documentation

Notifying parties must provide the following:

5.1. copies of the final or most recent versions of all documents bringing about the concentration, whether by agreement between the parties to the concentration, acquisition of a controlling interest or a public bid; and

5.2. copies of the most recent annual reports and accounts of all the parties to the concentration.

SECTION 6

Market definitions

The relevant product and geographic markets determine the scope within which the market power of the new entity resulting from the concentration must be assessed.[1]

Notes

[1] See Commission Notice on the definition of the relevant market for the purposes of Community competition law.

The notifying party or parties must provide the data requested having regard to the following definitions:

I. **Relevant product markets**

A relevant product market comprises all those products and/or services which are regarded as interchangeable or substitutable by the consumer, by reason of the products' characteristics, their prices and their intended use. A relevant product market may in some cases be composed of a number of individual products and/or services which present largely identical physical or technical characteristics and are interchangeable.

Factors relevant to the assessment of the relevant product market include the analysis of why the products or services in these markets are included and why others are excluded by using the above definition, and having regard to, for example, substitutability, conditions of competition, prices, cross-price elasticity of demand or other factors relevant for the definition of the product markets (for example, supply-side substitutability in appropriate cases).

II. **Relevant geographic markets**

The relevant geographic market comprises the area in which the undertakings concerned are involved in the supply and demand of relevant products or services, in which the conditions of competition are sufficiently homogeneous and which can be distinguished from neighbouring geographic areas because, in particular, conditions of competition are appreciably different in those areas.

Factors relevant to the assessment of the relevant geographic market include inter alia the nature and characteristics of the products or services concerned, the existence of entry barriers, consumer preferences, appreciable differences in the undertakings' market shares between neighbouring geographic areas, or substantial price differences.

III. **Reportable markets**

For purposes of information required in this Form, reportable markets consist of all relevant product and geographic markets, as well as plausible alternative relevant product and geographic market definitions, on the basis of which:

(a) two or more of the parties to the concentration are engaged in business activities in the same relevant market (horizontal relationships);

(b) one or more of the parties to the concentration are engaged in business activities in a product market, which is upstream or downstream of a market in which any other party to the concentration is engaged, regardless of whether there is or is not any existing supplier/customer relationship between the parties to the concentration (vertical relationships).

6.1. On the basis of the above market definitions, identify all reportable markets.

Information on markets

For each reportable market described in Section 6, for the year preceding the operation, provide the following:[1]

Notes

[1] In the context of pre-notification, you may want to discuss with the Commission to what extent dispensation (waivers) to provide the requested information would be appropriate for certain reportable markets.

7.1. an estimate of the total size of the market in terms of sales value (in euros) and volume (units).[1] Indicate the basis and sources for the calculations and provide documents where available to confirm these calculations;

Notes

[1] The value and volume of a market should reflect output less exports plus imports for the geographic areas under consideration.

7.2. the sales in value and volume, as well as an estimate of the market shares, of each of the parties to the concentration. Indicate if there have been significant changes to the sales and market shares for the last three financial years; and

7.3. for horizontal and vertical relationships, an estimate of the market share in value (and where appropriate, volume) of the three largest competitors (indicating the basis for the estimates). Provide the name, address, telephone number, fax number and e-mail address of the head of the legal department (or other person exercising similar functions; and in cases where there is no such person, then the chief executive) for these competitors.

SECTION 8
Cooperative effects of a joint venture

8. For the purpose of Article 2(4) of the EC Merger Regulation, please answer the following questions:
   (a) Do two or more parents retain to a significant extent activities in the same market as the joint venture or in a market which is upstream or downstream from that of the joint venture or in a neighbouring market closely related to this market?[1]

Notes

[1] For market definitions refer to Section 6.

If the answer is affirmative, please indicate for each of the markets referred to here:
   — the turnover of each parent company in the preceding financial year;
   — the economic significance of the activities of the joint venture in relation to this turnover;
   — the market share of each parent.
If the answer is negative, please justify your answer.
   (b) If the answer to (a) is affirmative and in your view the creation of the joint venture does not lead to coordination between independent undertakings that restricts competition within the meaning of Article 81(1) of the EC Treaty, give your reasons.
   (c) Without prejudice to the answers to (a) and (b) and in order to ensure that a complete assessment of the case can be made by the Commission, please explain how the criteria of Article 81(3) apply. Under Article 81(3), the provisions of Article 81(1) may be declared inapplicable if the operation:
      (i) contributes to improving the production or distribution of goods, or to promoting technical or economic progress;
      (ii) allows consumers a fair share of the resulting benefit;
      (iii) does not impose on the undertakings concerned restrictions which are not indispensable to the attainment of these objectives; and

(iv) does not afford such undertakings the possibility of eliminating competition in respect of a substantial part of the products in question.

SECTION 9

Declaration

Article 2(2) of the Implementing Regulation states that where notifications are signed by representatives of undertakings, such representatives must produce written proof that they are authorized to act. Such written authorization must accompany the notification.

The notification must conclude with the following declaration which is to be signed by or on behalf of all the notifying parties:

The notifying party or parties declare that, to the best of their knowledge and belief, the information given in this notification is true, correct, and complete, that true and complete copies of documents required by this Form have been supplied, that all estimates are identified as such and are their best estimates of the underlying facts, and that all the opinions expressed are sincere.

They are aware of the provisions of Article 14(1)(a) of the EC Merger Regulation.

Place and date:

Signatures:

Name/s and positions:

On behalf of:

ANNEX III

FORM RS

(RS = REASONED SUBMISSION PURSUANT TO ARTICLE 4(4) AND (5)
OF COUNCIL REGULATION (EC) NO 139/2004)

FORM RS RELATING TO REASONED SUBMISSIONS

Pursuant to Articles 4(4) and 4(5) of Regulation (EC) No 139/2004

INTRODUCTION

A. The purpose of this Form

This Form specifies the information that requesting parties should provide when making a reasoned submission for a pre-notification referral under Article 4(4) or (5) of Council Regulation (EC) No 139/2004 (hereinafter referred to as "the EC Merger Regulation").

Your attention is drawn to the EC Merger Regulation and to Commission Regulation (EC) No [802/2004] (hereinafter referred to as "the EC Merger Implementing Regulation"). The text of these regulations, as well as other relevant documents, can be found on the Competition page of the Commission's Europa web site.

Experience has shown that prior contacts are extremely valuable to both the parties and the relevant authorities in determining the precise amount and type of information required. Accordingly, parties are encouraged to consult the Commission and the relevant Member State/s regarding the adequacy of the scope and type of information on which they intend to base their reasoned submission.

B. The requirement for a reasoned submission to be correct and complete

All information required by this Form must be correct and complete. The information required must be supplied in the appropriate section of this Form.

Incorrect or misleading information in the reasoned submission will be considered to be incomplete information (Article 5(4) of the EC Merger Implementing Regulation).

If parties submit incorrect information, the Commission will have the power to revoke any Article 6 or 8 decision it adopts following an Article 4(5) referral, pursuant to Article 6(3)(a) or 8(6)(a) of the EC Merger Regulation. Following revocation, national competition laws would once again be applicable to the transaction. In the case of referrals under Article 4(4) made on the basis of incorrect information, the Commission may require a notification pursuant to Article 4(1). In addition, the Commission will have the power to impose fines for submission of incorrect or misleading information pursuant to Article 14(1)(a) of the EC Merger Regulation. (See point d below). Finally, parties should also be aware that, if a referral is made on the basis of incorrect, misleading or incomplete information included in Form RS, the Commission and/or the Member States may consider making a post-notification referral rectifying any referral made at pre-notification.

In particular you should note that:

(a) In accordance with Articles 4(4) and (5) of the EC Merger Regulation, the Commission is obliged to transmit reasoned submissions to Member States without delay. The time-limits for considering a reasoned submission will begin upon receipt of the submission by the relevant Member State or States. The decision whether or not to accede to a reasoned submission will normally be taken on the basis of the information contained therein, without further investigation efforts being undertaken by the authorities involved.

(b) The submitting parties should therefore verify, in the course of preparing their reasoned submission, that all information and arguments relied upon are sufficiently supported by independent sources.

(c) Under Article 14(1)(a) of the EC Merger Regulation, parties making a reasoned submission who, either intentionally or negligently, provide incorrect or misleading information, may be liable to fines of up to 1 % of the aggregate turnover of the undertaking concerned.

(d) You may request in writing that the Commission accept that the reasoned submission is complete notwithstanding the failure to provide information required by this Form, if such information is not reasonably available to you in part or in whole (for example, because of the unavailability of information on a target company during a contested bid).

The Commission will consider such a request, provided that you give reasons for the non-availability of that information, and provide your best estimates for missing data together with the sources for the estimates. Where possible, indications as to where any of the requested information that is unavailable to you could be obtained by the Commission or the relevant Member State/s should also be provided.

(e) You may request that the Commission accept that the reasoned submission is complete notwithstanding the failure to provide information required by this Form, if you consider that any particular information requested by this Form may not be necessary for the Commission's or the relevant Member State/s' examination of the case.

The Commission will consider such a request, provided that you give adequate reasons why that information is not relevant and necessary to dealing with your request for a pre-notification referral. You should explain this during your prior contacts with the Commission and with the relevant Member State/s, and submit a written request for a waiver asking the Commission to dispense with the obligation to provide that information, pursuant to Article 4(2) of the EC Merger Implementing Regulation. The Commission may consult with the relevant Member State authority or authorities before deciding whether to accede to such a request.

C. Persons entitled to submit a reasoned submission

In the case of a merger within the meaning of Article 3(1)(a) of the EC Merger Regulation or the acquisition of joint control of an undertaking within the meaning of Article 3(1)(b) of the Merger Regulation, the reasoned submission must be completed jointly by the parties to the merger or by those acquiring joint control as the case may be.

In case of the acquisition of a controlling interest in one undertaking by another, the acquirer must complete the reasoned submission.

In the case of a public bid to acquire an undertaking, the bidder must complete the reasoned submission.

Each party completing a reasoned submission is responsible for the accuracy of the information which it provides.

D. How to make a reasoned submission

The reasoned submission must be completed in one of the official languages of the European Union. This language will thereafter be the language of the proceedings for all submitting parties.

In order to facilitate treatment of Form RS by Member State authorities, parties are strongly encouraged to provide the Commission with a translation of their reasoned submission in a language or languages which will be understood by all addressees of the information. As regards requests for referral to a Member State or States, the requesting parties are strongly encouraged to include a copy of the request in the language/s of the Member State/s to which referral is being requested.

The information requested by this Form is to be set out using the sections and paragraph numbers of the Form, signing the declaration at the end, and annexing supporting documentation. For the sake of clarity, certain information may be put in annexes. However, it is essential that all key substantive pieces of information are presented in the body of Form RS. Annexes to this Form shall only be used to supplement the information supplied in the Form itself.

Supporting documents are to be submitted in their original language; where this is not an official language of the Community, they must be translated into the language of the proceeding.

Supporting documents may be originals or copies of the originals. In the latter case, the submitting party must confirm that they are true and complete.

One original and [37] copies of the Form RS and of the supporting documents must be submitted to the Commission. The reasoned submission shall be delivered to the address referred to in Article 23 (1) of the EC Merger Implementing Regulation and in the format specified by the Commission services.

The submission must be delivered to the address of the Commission's Directorate-General for Competition (DG Competition). This address is published in the *Official Journal of the European Union*. The submission must be delivered to the Commission on working days as defined by Article 24 of the EC Merger Implementing Regulation. In order to enable it to be registered on the same day, it must be delivered before 17.00 hrs on Mondays to Thursdays and before 16.00 hrs on Fridays and workdays preceding public holidays and other holidays as determined by the Commission and published in the *Official Journal of the European Union*. The security instructions given on DG Competition's website must be adhered to.

Notes

The amendment shown in square brackets was made by Commission Regulation (EC) No 1792/2006 of 23 October 2006 (OJ L 362, 20.12.2006, p. 1), with effect from 1 January 2007.

E. Confidentiality

Article 287 of the Treaty and Article 17(2) of the EC Merger Regulation require the Commission and the competent authorities of the Member States, their officials and other servants and other persons working under the supervision of these authorities as well as officials and civil servants of other authorities of the Member States, not to disclose information of the kind covered by the obligation of professional secrecy and which they have acquired through the application of the Regulation. The same principle must also apply to protect confidentiality between submitting parties.

If you believe that your interests would be harmed if any of the information supplied were to be published or otherwise divulged to other parties, submit this information separately with each page clearly marked "Business Secrets". You should also give reasons why this information should not be divulged or published.

In the case of mergers or joint acquisitions, or in other cases where the reasoned submission is completed by more than one of the parties, business secrets may be submitted in separate annexes, and referred to in the submission as an annex. All such annexes must be included in the reasoned submission.

F. Definitions and instructions for the purposes of this Form

Submitting party or parties: in cases where a reasoned submission is made by only one of the undertakings who is a party to an operation, "submitting parties" is used to refer only to the undertaking actually making the submission.

Party(ies) to the concentration or parties: these terms relate to both the acquiring and acquired parties, or to the merging parties, including all undertakings in which a controlling interest is being acquired or which is the subject of a public bid.

Except where otherwise specified, the terms "submitting party(ies)" and "party(ies) to the concentration" include all the undertakings which belong to the same groups as those "parties".

Affected markets: Section 4 of this Form requires the submitting parties to define the relevant product markets, and further to identify which of those relevant markets are likely to be affected by the operation. This definition of affected market is used as the basis for requiring information for a number of other questions contained in this Form. The definitions thus submitted by the submitting parties are referred to in this Form as the affected market(s). This term can refer to a relevant market made up either of products or of services.

Year: all references to the word "year" in this Form should be read as meaning calendar year, unless otherwise stated. All information requested in this Form relates, unless otherwise specified, to the year preceding that of the reasoned submission.

The financial data requested in this Form must be provided in Euros at the average exchange rates prevailing for the years or other periods in question.

All references contained in this Form are to the relevant Articles and paragraphs of the EC Merger Regulation, unless otherwise stated.

Section 1
Background information

1.0. Indicate whether the reasoned submission is made under Article 4(4) or (5).
   — Article 4(4) referral
   — Article 4(5) referral

1.1. Information on the submitting party (or parties)

   Give details of:
   1.1.1. the name and address of undertaking;
   1.1.2. the nature of the undertaking's business;
   1.1.3. the name, address, telephone number, fax number and electronic address of, and position held by, the appropriate contact person; and
   1.1.4. an address for service of the submitting party (or each of the submitting parties) to which documents and, in particular, Commission decisions may be delivered. The name, telephone number and e-mail address of a person at this address who is authorised to accept service must be provided.

1.2. Information on the other parties[1] to the concentration

   For each party to the concentration (except the submitting party or parties) give details of:
   1.2.1. the name and address of undertaking;
   1.2.2. the nature of undertaking's business;
   1.2.3. the name, address, telephone number, fax number and electronic address of, and position held by the appropriate contact person;
   1.2.4. an address for service of the party (or each of the parties) to which documents and, in particular, Commission Decisions may be delivered. The name, e-mail address and telephone number of a person at this address who is authorised to accept service must be provided.

Notes

[1] This includes the target company in the case of a contested bid, in which case the details should be completed as far as is possible.

1.3. Appointment of representatives

Where reasoned submissions are signed by representatives of undertakings, such representatives must produce written proof that they are authorized to act. The written proof must contain the name and position of the persons granting such authority.

Provide the following contact details of any representatives who have been authorized to act for any of the parties to the concentration, indicating whom they represent:

1.3.1. the name of the representative;

1.3.2. the address of the representative;

1.3.3. the name, address, telephone number, fax number and e-mail address of the person to be contacted; and

1.3.4. an address of the representative (in Brussels if available) to which correspondence may be sent and documents delivered.

SECTION 2
General background and details of the concentration

2.1. Describe the general background to the concentration. In particular, give an overview of the main reasons for the transaction, including its economic and strategic rationale.

Provide an executive summary of the concentration, specifying the parties to the concentration, the nature of the concentration (for example, merger, acquisition, or joint venture.), the areas of activity of the submitting parties, the markets on which the concentration will have an impact (including the main affected markets[1]), and the strategic and economic rationale for the concentration.

Notes
[1] See Section 4 for the definition of affected markets.

2.2. Describe the legal nature of the transaction which is the subject of the reasoned submission. In doing so, indicate:

(a) whether the whole or parts of the parties are subject to the concentration;

(b) the proposed or expected date of any major events designed to bring about the completion of the concentration;

(c) the proposed structure of ownership and control after the completion of the concentration; and

(d) whether the proposed transaction is a concentration within the meaning of Article 3 of the EC Merger Regulation.

2.3. List the economic sectors involved in the concentration.

2.3.1. State the value of the transaction (the purchase price or the value of all the assets involved, as the case may be).

2.4. Provide sufficient financial or other data to show that the concentration meets OR does not meet the jurisdictional thresholds under Article 1 of the EC Merger Regulation.

2.4.1. Provide a breakdown of the Community-wide turnover achieved by the undertakings concerned, indicating, where applicable, the Member State, if any, in which more than two-thirds of this turnover is achieved.

SECTION 3
Ownership and control[1]

Notes
[1] See Article 3(3), 3(4) and 3(5) and Article 5(4).

For each of the parties to the concentration provide a list of all undertakings belonging to the same group.

This list must include:

3.1. all undertakings or persons controlling these parties, directly or indirectly;

3.2. all undertakings active on any affected market[1] that are controlled, directly or indirectly:

    (a) by these parties;

    (b) by any other undertaking identified in 3.1.

For each entry listed above, the nature and means of control should be specified.

The information sought in this section may be illustrated by the use of organization charts or diagrams to show the structure of ownership and control of the undertakings.

Notes

[1] See Section 4 for the definition of affected markets.

SECTION 4
Market definitions

The relevant product and geographic markets determine the scope within which the market power of the new entity resulting from the concentration must be assessed.[1]

Notes

[1] See Commission Notice on the definition of the relevant market for the purposes of Community competition law.

The submitting party or parties must provide the data requested having regard to the following definitions:

I. Relevant product markets

A relevant product market comprises all those products and/or services which are regarded as interchangeable or substitutable by the consumer, by reason of the products' characteristics, their prices and their intended use. A relevant product market may in some cases be composed of a number of individual products and/or services which present largely identical physical or technical characteristics and are interchangeable.

Factors relevant to the assessment of the relevant product market include the analysis of why the products or services in these markets are included and why others are excluded by using the above definition, and having regard to, for example, substitutability, conditions of competition, prices, cross-price elasticity of demand or other factors relevant for the definition of the product markets (for example, supply-side substitutability in appropriate cases).

II. Relevant geographic markets

The relevant geographic market comprises the area in which the undertakings concerned are involved in the supply and demand of relevant products or services, in which the conditions of competition are sufficiently homogeneous and which can be distinguished from neighbouring geographic areas because, in particular, conditions of competition are appreciably different in those areas.

Factors relevant to the assessment of the relevant geographic market include inter alia the nature and characteristics of the products or services concerned, the existence of entry barriers, consumer preferences, appreciable differences in the undertakings' market shares between neighbouring geographic areas, or substantial price differences.

III. Affected markets

For the purposes of the information required in this Form, affected markets consist of relevant product markets where, in the Community, or in any Member State:

(a) two or more of the parties to the concentration are engaged in business activities in the same product market and where the concentration will lead to a combined market share of 15% or more. These are horizontal relationships;

(b) one or more of the parties to the concentration are engaged in business activities in a product market, which is upstream or downstream of a product market in which any other party to the concentration is engaged, and any of their individual or combined market shares at either level is 25% or more, regardless of whether there is or is not any existing supplier/customer relationship between the parties to the concentration.[1] These are vertical relationships.

Part D Mergers and Concentrations

Notes

[1] For example, if a party to the concentration holds a market share larger than 25% in a market that is upstream to a market in which the other party is active, then both the upstream and the downstream markets are affected markets. Similarly, if a vertically integrated company merges with another party which is active at the downstream level, and the merger leads to a combined market share downstream of 25% or more, then both the upstream and the downstream markets are affected markets.

On the basis of the above definitions and market share thresholds, provide the following information:

4.1. Identify each affected market within the meaning of Section III:

    (a) at the Community level;

    (b) in the case of a request for referral pursuant to Article 4(4), at the level of each individual Member State;

    (c) in the case of a request for referral pursuant to Article 4(5), at the level of each Member State identified at Section 6.3.1 of this Form as capable of reviewing the concentration.

4.2. In addition, explain the submitting parties' view as to the scope of the relevant geographic market within the meaning of Section II in relation to each affected market identified at 4.1 above.

SECTION 5
Information on affected markets

For each affected relevant product market, for the last financial year,

(a) for the Community as a whole;

(b) in the case of a request for referral pursuant to Article 4(4), individually for each Member State where the parties to the concentration do business; and

(c) in the case of a request for referral pursuant to Article 4(5), individually for each Member State identified at Section 6.3.1 of this Form as capable of reviewing the concentration where the parties to the concentration do business; and

(d) where in the opinion of the submitting parties, the relevant geographic market is different;

provide the following information:

5.1. an estimate of the total size of the market in terms of sales value (in Euros) and volume (units).[1] Indicate the basis and sources for the calculations and provide documents where available to confirm these calculations;

Notes

[1] The value and volume of a market should reflect output less exports plus imports for the geographic areas under consideration.

5.2. the sales in value and volume, as well as an estimate of the market shares, of each of the parties to the concentration;

5.3. an estimate of the market share in value (and where appropriate volume) of all competitors (including importers) having at least 5% of the geographic market under consideration;
On this basis, provide an estimate of the HHI index[1] pre- and post-merger, and the difference between the two (the delta).[2] Indicate the proportion of market shares used as a basis to calculate the HHI; Identify the sources used to calculate these market shares and provide documents where available to confirm the calculation;

Notes

[1] HHI stands for Herfindahl-Hirschman Index, a measure of market concentration. The HHI is calculated by summing the squares of the individual market shares of all the firms in the market. For example, a market containing five firms with market shares of 40%, 20%, 15%, 15%, and 10%, respectively, has an HHI of 2550 ($40^2 + 20^2 + 15^2 + 15^2 + 10^2 = 2,550$). The HHI ranges from close to zero (in an atomistic market) to 10,000 (in the case of a pure monopoly). The post-merger HHI is calculated on the working assumption that the individual market shares of the companies do not change. Although it is best to include all firms in the calculation, lack of information about very small firms may not be important because such firms do not affect the HHI significantly.

[2] The increase in concentration as measured by the HHI can be calculated independently of the overall market concentration by doubling the product of the market shares of the merging firms. For example, a merger of two firms with

market shares of 30% and 15% respectively would increase the HHI by 900 ($30 \times 15 \times 2 = 900$). The explanation for this technique is as follows: Before the merger, the market shares of the merging firms contribute to the HHI by their squares individually: $(a)^2 + (b)^2$. After the merger, the contribution is the square of their sum: $(a + b)^2$, which equals $(a)^2 + (b)^2 + 2ab$. The increase in the HHI is therefore represented by $2ab$.

5.4. the five largest independent customers of the parties in each affected market and their individual share of total sales for such products accounted for by each of those customers;

5.5. the nature and extent of vertical integration of each of the parties to the concentration compared with their largest competitors;

5.6. identify the five largest independent[1] suppliers to the parties;

Notes

[1] That is suppliers which are not subsidiaries, agents or undertakings forming part of the group of the party in question. In addition to those five independent suppliers the notifying parties can, if they consider it necessary for a proper assessment of the case, identify the intra-group suppliers. The same applies in relation to customers.

5.7. Over the last five years, has there been any significant entry into any affected markets? In the opinion of the submitting parties are there undertakings (including those at present operating only in extra-Community markets) that are likely to enter the market? Please specify.

5.8. To what extent do cooperative agreements (horizontal or vertical) exist in the affected markets?

5.9. If the concentration is a joint venture, do two or more parents retain to a significant extent activities in the same market as the joint venture or in a market which is downstream or upstream from that of the joint venture or in a neighbouring market closely related to this market?[1]

Notes

[1] For market definitions refer to Section 4.

5.10. Describe the likely impact of the proposed concentration on competition in the affected markets and how the proposed concentration is likely to affect the interests of intermediate and ultimate consumers and the development of technical and economic progress.

Section 6

Details of the referral request and reasons why the case should be referred

6.1. Indicate whether the reasoned submission is made pursuant to Article 4(4) or 4(5) of the EC Merger Regulation, and fill in only the relevant sub-section:
— Article 4.4. referral
— Article 4.5 referral

Sub-section 6.2

ARTICLE 4(4) REFERRAL

6.2.1. Identify the Member State or Member States which, pursuant to Article 4(4), you submit should examine the concentration, indicating whether or not you have made informal contact with this Member State/s.

6.2.2. Specify whether you are requesting referral of the whole or part of the case.
If you are requesting referral of part of the case, specify clearly the part or parts of the case for which you request the referral.
If you are requesting referral of the whole of the case, you must confirm that there are no affected markets outside the territory of the Member State/s to which you request the referral to be made.

6.2.3. Explain in what way each of the affected markets in the Member State or States to which referral is requested presents all the characteristics of a distinct market within the meaning of Article 4(4).

6.2.4. Explain in what way competition may be significantly affected in each of the above-mentioned distinct markets within the meaning of Article 4(4).

6.2.5. In the event of a Member State/s becoming competent to review the whole or part of the case following a referral pursuant to Article 4(4), do you consent to the information contained in this Form being relied upon by the Member State/s in question for the purpose of its/their national proceedings relating to that case or part thereof? YES or NO

Sub-section 6.3

ARTICLE 4(5) REFERRAL

6.3.1. For each Member State, specify whether the concentration is or is not capable of being reviewed under its national competition law. You must tick one box for each and every Member State. Is the concentration capable of being reviewed under the national competition law of each of the following Member States? You must reply for each Member State. Only indicate YES or NO for each Member State. Failure to indicate YES or NO for any Member State shall be deemed to constitute an indication of YES for that Member State.

Austria	YES	NO
Belgium	YES	NO
Cyprus	YES	NO
Czech Republic	YES	NO
Denmark	YES	NO
Estonia	YES	NO
Finland	YES	NO
France	YES	NO
Germany	YES	NO
Greece	YES	NO
Hungary	YES	NO
Ireland	YES	NO
Italy	YES	NO
Latvia	YES	NO
Lithuania	YES	NO
Luxembourg	YES	NO
Malta	YES	NO
Netherlands	YES	NO
Poland	YES	NO
Portugal	YES	NO
Slovakia	YES	NO
Slovenia	YES	NO
Spain	YES	NO
Sweden	YES	NO
United Kingdom	YES	NO

6.3.2. For each Member State, provide sufficient financial or other data to show that the concentration meets or does not meet the relevant jurisdictional criteria under the applicable national competition law.

6.3.4. Explain why the case should be examined by the Commission. Explain in particular whether the concentration might affect competition beyond the territory of one Member State.

Notes

There is no paragraph 6.3.3 in the original instrument.

SECTION 7

Declaration

It follows from Articles 2(2) and 6(2) of the EC Merger Implementing Regulation that where reasoned submissions are signed by representatives of undertakings, such representatives must produce written proof that they are authorized to act. Such written authorization must accompany the submission.

The reasoned submission must conclude with the following declaration which is to be signed by or on behalf of all the submitting parties:

The submitting party or parties declare that, following careful verification, the information given in this reasoned submission is to the best of their knowledge and belief true, correct, and complete, that true and complete copies of documents required by Form RS, have been supplied, and that all estimates are identified as such and are their best estimates of the underlying facts and that all the opinions expressed are sincere.

They are aware of the provisions of Article 14(1)(a) of the EC Merger Regulation.

Place and date:

Signatures:

Name/s and positions:

On behalf of:

Commentary
Annex IV: B&C: 8.165

D3

PROPOSAL FOR A
COMMISSION REGULATION (EC) NO 802/2004

of [. . .]
**amending Regulation (EC) No 802/2004 implementing Council Regulation (EC)
No 139/2004 on the control of concentrations between undertakings**
(Text with EEA relevance)

Notes
This document was published for consultation on 24 April 2007, together with a draft Commission Notice on remedies acceptable under Council Regulation (EEC) No 139/2004 and under Commission Regulation (EC) No 802/2004. The document is available on the Europa website at the following address:
http://ec.europa.eu/comm/competition/mergers/legislation/draft_amendments_regulation.pdf

THE COMMISSION OF THE EUROPEAN COMMUNITIES,

Having regard to the Treaty establishing the European Community,

Having regard to the Agreement on the European Economic Area,

Having regard to Council Regulation (EC) No 139/2004 of 20 January 2004 on the control of concentrations between undertakings (the EC Merger Regulation),[1] and in particular Article 23(1) thereof,

After consulting the Advisory Committee on Concentrations,

Notes
[1] OJ L 24, 29.1.2004, p. 1.

Whereas:

(1) Commission Regulation (EC) No 802/2004 of 7 April 2004 implementing Council Regulation (EC) No 139/2004 on the control of concentrations between undertakings[2] sets out procedural rules for the notification and examination of concentrations. In order to take account of the accession of Bulgaria and Romania to the Community it is necessary to update the notification form

used for concentrations which requires certain information based on a list of all Member States of the Community.

(2) In order to ensure that the Commission is in a position to carry out a proper assessment of commitments offered by the notifying parties pursuant to Article 6(2) or Article 8(2) of Regulation (EC) No 139/2004 with a view to rendering a concentration compatible with the common market, the notifying parties should be required to submit detailed information concerning the commitments offered and, in particular, to submit specific information if the commitments offered consist in the divestiture of a business.

(3) Regulation (EC) No 802/2004 should therefore be amended accordingly,

---

Notes
2 OJ L 133, 30.4.2004, p. 1. Regulation as amended by Regulation (EC) No 1792/2006 (OJ L 362, 20.12.2006, p. 1).

HAS ADOPTED THIS REGULATION:

Article 1

Regulation (EC) No 802/2004 is amended as follows:

(1) In Article 20, the following paragraph 3 is added:

3. When offering commitments pursuant to Article 6(2) or Article 8(2) of Regulation (EC) No 139/2004, the undertakings concerned shall simultaneously submit the information and documents prescribed by Form RM as set out in Annex IV. The information submitted shall be correct and complete.

(2) The Annexes are amended in accordance with the Annex to this Regulation.

Article 2
Entry into force

This Regulation shall enter into force on []

This Regulation shall be binding in its entirety and directly applicable in all Member States.

Done at Brussels, [. . .]

ANNEX

The Annexes to Regulation (EC) No 802/2004 are amended as follows:

(1) In Annex III, subsection 6.3.1 is replaced by the following:

"6.3.1. For each Member State, specify whether the concentration is or is not capable of being reviewed under its national competition law. You must tick one box for each and every Member State.

Is the concentration capable of being reviewed under the national competition law of each of the following Member States? You must reply for **each** Member State. Only indicate YES **or** NO for each Member State. Failure to indicate YES or NO for any Member State shall be deemed to constitute an indication of YES for that Member State.

Belgium:	YES	NO
Bulgaria:	YES	NO
Czech Republic:	YES	NO
Denmark:	YES	NO
Germany:	YES	NO
Estonia:	YES	NO
Ireland:	YES	NO
Greece:	YES	NO
Spain:	YES	NO
France:	YES	NO

Italy:	YES	NO
Cyprus:	YES	NO
Latvia:	YES	NO
Lithuania:	YES	NO
Luxembourg:	YES	NO
Hungary:	YES	NO
Malta:	YES	NO
Netherlands:	YES	NO
Austria:	YES	NO
Poland:	YES	NO
Portugal:	YES	NO
Romania:	YES	NO
Slovenia:	YES	NO
Slovakia:	YES	NO
Finland:	YES	NO
Sweden:	YES	NO
United Kingdom:	YES	NO"

(2) The following Annex IV is added:

"ANNEX IV:
FORM RM RELATING TO THE INFORMATION CONCERNING COMMITMENTS SUBMITTED PURSUANT TO ARTICLE 6(2) AND ARTICLE 8(2) OF REGULATION (EC) No 139/2004

INTRODUCTION

This form specifies the information and documents to be submitted by the undertakings concerned simultaneously when offering commitments pursuant to Article 6(2) or Article 8(2) of Regulation (EC) No 139/2004. The information requested is necessary to allow the Commission to examine whether the commitments are capable of rendering the concentration compatible with the common market in that they will prevent a significant impediment to effective competition. The Commission may dispense with the obligation to provide any particular information in respect of the commitments offered, including documents, or with any other requirement laid down in this form where it considers that compliance with those obligations or requirements is not necessary for the examination of the commitments offered. If you consider that any particular information requested by this Form may not be necessary for the Commission's assessment, you may approach the Commission asking to dispense with certain requirements, giving adequate reasons why that information is not relevant.

SECTION 1
Description of the commitment

1.1 Provide detailed information on
   (i) the object of the commitments offered, and
   (ii) the conditions for their implementation.
1.2 In case the commitments offered consist in the divestiture of a business, Section 5 provides for the specific information required.

SECTION 2
Suitability to remove competition concerns

2. Provide information showing the suitability of the commitments offered to remove the significant impediment of effective competition identified.

Part D Mergers and Concentrations

651

Section 3
Deviation from Model Texts

3. Identify any deviations of the commitments offered from the pertinent Model Commitments texts published by the Commission's services, as revised from time-to-time, and explain the reasons for the deviations.

Section 4
Summary of the commitments

4. Provide a non-confidential summary of the nature and scope of the commitments offered and why, in your view, they are suitable to remove any significant impediment to effective competition. The Commission may use this summary for the market test of the commitments offered with third parties.

Section 5
Information on a business to be divested

5. In case the commitments offered consist in the divestiture of a business, provide the following information and documents.

General information on the business to be divested

The following information should be provided as to the current operation of the business to be divested and changes already planned for the future:

5.1 Describe the business to be divested generally, including the entities belonging to it, their seat and place of management, other locations for production or provisions of services, the general organisational structure, etc.

5.2 State whether there are and describe any legal obstacles for the transfer of the business to be divested or the assets, including third party rights and administrative approvals required.

5.3 List and describe the products manufactured or services provided, in particular their technical and other characteristics, the brands involved, the turnover generated with each of these products or services, and any innovations or new products or services planned.

5.4 Describe the level on which the essential functions of the business to be divested are operated if they are not operated on the level of the business to be divested itself, including such functions as R&D, production, marketing & sales, logistics, relations with customers, relations with suppliers, IT systems, etc. The description should contain the role performed by those other levels, the relations with the business to be divested and the resources (personnel, assets, financial resources, etc.) involved in the function.

5.5 Describe in detail the links between the business to be divested and other undertakings controlled by the notifying parties (irrespective of the direction of the link), such as
   • Supply, production, distribution, service or other contracts;
   • Shared tangible or intangible assets;
   • Shared or seconded personnel;
   • Shared IT systems or other systems; and
   • Shared customers.

5.6 Describe in general terms all relevant tangible and intangible assets used and/or owned by the business to be divested, including, in any case, IP rights and brands.

5.7 Submit an organisational chart identifying the number of personnel currently working in each of the functions of the business to be divested and a list of those employees who are indispensable for the operation of the business to be divested, describing their functions.

5.8 Describe the customers of the business to be divested, including a list of customers, a description of the corresponding records available, and a quantification of the importance of each of the customers.

5.9 Provide financial data for the business to be divested, including the turnover and the EBITDA achieved in the last two years, and the forecast for the next two years.

5.10 Identify and describe any changes, having occurred in the last two years, in the organisation of the business to be divested or in the links with other undertakings controlled by the notifying parties.

5.11 Identify and describe any changes, planned for the next two years, in the organisation of the business to be divested or in the links with other undertakings controlled by the notifying parties.

General information on the business to be divested as described in the commitments

5.12 Describe any areas where the business to be divested as set out in the commitments offered differs from the nature and scope of the business as currently operated.

Acquisition by a suitable purchaser

5.13 Explain the reasons why, in your view, the business will be acquired by a suitable purchaser in the time-frame proposed in the commitments offered.

D4

COMMISSION NOTICE

on remedies acceptable under Council Regulation (EEC) No 4064/89 and under Commission Regulation (EC) No 447/98
(2001/C 68/03)
(Text with EEA relevance)

Official Journal C 68, 2.3.2001, p. 3

Celex No: 52001XC0302(01)

Commentary
Notice: **B&C:** 8.008, 8.133, 8.162 **F&N:** 5.366, 5.392, 5.608, 14.55

I. INTRODUCTION

1. Council Regulation (EEC) No 4064/89 of 21 December 1989 on the control of concentrations between undertakings,[1] as last amended by Regulation (EC) No 1310/97[2] (hereinafter referred to as "the Merger Regulation") expressly provides that the Commission may decide to declare a concentration compatible with the common market following modification by the parties. Recital 8 of Council Regulation (EC) No 1310/97 states that "the Commission may declare a concentration compatible with the common market in the second phase[4] of the procedure, following commitments by the parties that are proportional to and would entirely eliminate the competition problem . . . ". Recital 8 also provides for "commitments in the first phase[5] of the procedure where the competition problem is readily identifiable and can easily be remedied . . . Transparency and effective consultation of Member States and interested third parties should be ensured in both phases of the procedure".

Notes
[1] OJ L 395, 30.12.1989, p. 1; corrected version OJ L 257, 21.9.1990, p. 13.
[2] OJ L 180, 9.7.1997, p. 1.
[3] The references to "parties" and "merging parties" also cover situations with one notifying party.
[4] Referred to hereinafter as "phase II".
[5] Referred to hereinafter as "phase I".

Part D Mergers and Concentrations

2. The purpose of this notice is to provide guidance on modifications to concentrations, including, in particular, commitments to modify a concentration. Such modifications are more commonly described as "remedies" since their object is to reduce the merging parties' market power and to restore conditions for effective competition which would be distorted as a result of the merger creating or strengthening a dominant position. The guidance set out in this notice reflects the Commission's evolving experience with the assessment, acceptance and implementation of remedies under the Merger Regulation since its entry into force on 21 September 1990. The principles contained here will be applied and further developed and refined by the Commission in individual cases. The guidance provided on commitments is without prejudice to the interpretation which may be given by the Court of Justice or by the Court of First Instance of the European Communities.

3. This notice sets out the general principles applicable to remedies acceptable to the Commission, the main types of commitments that have been accepted by the Commission in cases under the Merger Regulation, the specific requirements which proposals of commitments need to fulfil in both phases of the procedure, and the main requirements for the implementation of commitments.

II. General Principles

4. Under the Merger Regulation, the Commission assesses the compatibility of a notified concentration with the common market on the basis of its effect on the structure of competition in the Community.[6] The test for compatibility under Article 2(2) and (3) of the Merger Regulation is whether or not a concentration would create or strengthen a dominant position as a result of which effective competition would be significantly impeded in the common market or a substantial part of it.[7] A concentration that creates or strengthens a dominant position as described above is incompatible with the common market and the Commission is required to prohibit it.

Notes

[6] Recital 7 of the Merger Regulation.

[7] In the case of the creation of a joint venture, the Commission will also examine the concentration under Article 2(4) of the Merger Regulation. In this respect, the Commission examines whether or not the creation of the joint venture has as its object or effect the coordination of the competitive behaviour of undertakings that remain independent. Such coordination will be appraised in accordance with the criteria of Article 81(1) and (3) of the Treaty, with a view to establishing whether or not the operation is compatible with the common market. The principles set out in this notice would normally also apply to cases dealt with under Article 2(4).

5. Where a concentration raises competition concerns in that it could lead to the creation or strengthening of a dominant position, the parties may seek to modify the concentration in order to resolve the competition concerns raised by the Commission and thereby gain clearance of their merger. Such modifications may be offered and implemented in advance of a clearance decision. However, it is more common that the parties submit commitments with a view to rendering the concentration compatible with the common market within a specific period following clearance.

6. It is the responsibility of the Commission to show that a concentration creates or strengthens market structures which are liable to impede significantly effective competition in the common market. It is the responsibility of the parties to show that the proposed remedies, once implemented, eliminate the creation or strengthening of such a dominant position identified by the Commission. To this end, the parties are required to show clearly, to the Commission's satisfaction in accordance with its obligations under the Merger Regulation, that the remedy restores conditions of effective competition in the common market on a permanent basis.

Commentary
para 6: **B&C:** 8.165

7. In assessing whether or not a remedy will restore effective competition the Commission will consider all relevant factors relating to the remedy itself, including *inter alia* the type, scale and scope of the remedy proposed, together with the likelihood of its successful, full and timely implementation by the parties. Moreover, these factors have to be judged by reference to the structure and particular characteristics of the market in which the competition concerns arise, including of

course the position of the parties and other players on the market. It follows that it is incumbent on the parties from the outset to remove any uncertainties as to any of these factors which might cause the Commission to reject the remedy proposed.

Commentary
para 7: **B&C:** 8.165

8. More generally, the Commission will take into account the fact that any remedy, so long as it remains a commitment which is not yet fulfilled, carries with it certain uncertainties as to its eventual outcome. This general factor must also be taken into consideration by the parties when presenting a remedy to the Commission.

9. In the Gencor case,[8] the Court of First Instance established the principle that the basic aim of commitments is to ensure competitive market structures. Accordingly, commitments that would amount merely to a promise to behave in a certain way, for example a commitment not to abuse a dominant position created or strengthened by the proposed concentration, are as such not considered suitable to render the concentration compatible with the common market. According to the Court,[9] commitments which are structural in nature, such as the commitment to sell a subsidiary, are, as a rule, preferable from the point of view of the Regulation's objective, inasmuch as such a commitment prevents the creation or strengthening of a dominant position previously identified by the Commission and does not, moreover, require medium or long-term monitoring measures. Nevertheless, the possibility cannot automatically be ruled out that other types of commitments may themselves also be capable of preventing the emergence or strengthening of a dominant position. However, whether such commitments can be accepted has to be determined on a case-by-case basis.

Notes
[8] Judgment of the Court of First Instance of 25 March 1999 in Case T-102/96 *Gencor v Commission* [1999] ECR II-753, at paragraph 316.
[9] *Op. cit.*, at paragraph 319.

Commentary
para 9: **B&C:** 8.166

10. Once the concentration has been implemented, despite the possibility of some interim safeguards, the desired conditions of competition on the market cannot actually be restored until the commitments have been fulfilled. Therefore, commitments must be capable of being implemented effectively and within a short period. Commitments should not require additional monitoring once they have been implemented.[10]

Notes
[10] Only in exceptional circumstances will the Commission consider commitments which require further monitoring: Commission Decision 97/816/EC (IV/M.877 — *Boeing/McDonnell Douglas*; OJ L 336, 8.12.1997, p. 16).

Commentary
para 10: **B&C:** 8.165

11. The Commission may accept commitments in either phase of the procedure. However, given the fact that an in-depth market investigation is only carried out in phase II, commitments submitted to the Commission in phase I must be sufficient to clearly rule out "serious doubts" within the meaning of Article 6(1)(c) of the Merger Regulation.[11] Pursuant to Article 10(2) of the Merger Regulation, the Commission has to take a clearance decision as soon as the serious doubts established in the decision pursuant to Article 6(1)(c) of the Merger Regulation are removed as a result of commitments submitted by the parties. This rule applies in particular to commitments proposed at an early stage of phase II-proceedings.[12] After an in-depth investigation and where the Commission in a Statement of Objections has reached the preliminary view that the merger leads to the creation or strengthening of a dominant position within the meaning of Article 2(3) of the Merger Regulation, the commitments have to eliminate the creation or strengthening of such a dominant position.

Notes

[11] Commitments in phase I can only be accepted in certain types of situation. The competition problem needs to be so straightforward and the remedies so clear-cut that it is not necessary to enter into an in-depth investigation.

[12] Commission Decision of 30 March 1999 (IV/JV.15 — *BT/AT & T*); Commission Decision 2000/45/EC (IV/M.1532 — *BP Amoco/Arco*; OJ L 18, 19.1.2001, p. 1).

Commentary
para 11: B&C: 8.163

12. Whilst commitments have to be offered by the parties, the Commission may ensure the enforce-ability of commitments by making its authorisation subject to compliance with them.[13] A dis-tinction must be made between conditions and obligations. The requirement for achievement of each measure that gives rise to the structural change of the market is a condition — for example, that a business is to be divested. The implementing steps which are necessary to achieve this result are generally obligations on the parties, e.g. such as the appointment of a trustee with an irrevocable mandate to sell the business. Where the undertakings concerned commit a breach of an obligation, the Commission may revoke clearance decisions issued either under Article 6(2) or Article 8(2) of the Merger Regulation, acting pursuant to Article 6(3) or Article 8(5)(b), respectively. The parties may also be subject to fines and periodic penalty payments as provided in Article 14(2)(a) and 15(2)(a) respectively of the Merger Regulation. Where, however, the situation rendering the concentration compatible with the common market does not materi-alise,[14] that is, where the condition is not fulfilled, the compatibility decision no longer stands. In such circumstances, the Commission may, pursuant to Article 8(4) of the Merger Regulation, order any appropriate action necessary to restore conditions of effective competition.[15] In addition, the parties may also be subject to fines as provided in Article 14(2)(c).

Notes

[13] If the Commission's final assessment of a case shows that there are no competition concerns or that the resolution of the concerns does not depend on a particular element of the submitted commitments, the parties, being informed, may withdraw them. If the parties do not withdraw them, the Commission may either take note of their proposals in the decision or ignore them. Where the Commission takes note of them, it will explain in its decision that they do not constitute a condition for clearance.

[14] The same principle applies where the situation that originally rendered the concentration compatible is subsequently reversed; see the last sentence of paragraph 49.

[15] These measures may also lead to periodic penalty payments as provided in Article 15(2)(b).

Commentary
para 12: B&C: 8.162, 8.171

III. Types of Remedy Acceptable to the Commission[16]

Notes

[16] The following overview is non-exhaustive.

1. Divestiture

13. Where a proposed merger threatens to create or strengthen a dominant position which would impede effective competition, the most effective way to restore effective competition, apart from prohibition, is to create the conditions for the emergence of a new competitive entity or for the strengthening of existing competitors via divestiture.

Viable business

14. The divested activities must consist of a **viable business** that, if operated by a suitable purchaser, can compete effectively with the merged entity on a lasting basis. Normally a viable business is an **existing** one that can operate on a **stand-alone-basis**, which means independently of the merging parties as regards the supply of input materials or other forms of cooperation other than during a transitory period.

Commentary
para 14: **B&C:** 8.167

15. In proposing a viable business for divestiture, the parties must take into account the uncertainties and risks related to the transfer of a business to a new owner. These risks may limit the competitive impact of the divested business, and, therefore, may lead to a market situation where the competition concerns of the Commission will not necessarily be eliminated.

Object of the divestiture

16. Where the competition problem results from horizontal overlap, the most appropriate business has to be divested.[17] This might be the business of the acquiring company in cases of a hostile bid where the notifying party's knowledge of the business to be acquired is more limited. A commitment to divest activities of the target company might, in such circumstances, increase the risk that this business might not result in a viable competitor which could effectively compete in the market on a lasting basis.

Notes

[17] Where the competition problem arises in vertical integration cases, divestiture may also resolve the competition concern.

17. In determining which overlapping business should be divested, the ability of the business to be operated on a stand-alone-basis is an important consideration.[18] In order to assure a viable business, it might be necessary to include in a divestiture those activities which are related to markets where the Commission did not raise competition concerns because this would be the only possible way to create an effective competitor in the affected markets.[19]

Notes

[18] Commission Decision of 29 September 1999 (IV/M.1383 — *Exxon/Mobil*, at paragraph 860); Commission Decision of 9 February 2000 (COMP/M.1641 *Linde/AGA*, at paragraph 94).

[19] Commission Decision 1999/229/EC (IV/M.913 — *Siemens/Elektrowatt*; OJ L 88, 31.3.1999, p. 1, at paragraph 134); Commission Decision 2000/718/EC (COMP/M.1578 — *Sanitec/Sphinx*; OJ L 294, 22.11.2000, p. 1, at paragraph 255); Commission Decision of 8 March 2000 (COMP/M.1802 — *Unilever/Amora Maille*); Commission Decision of 28 September 2000 (COMP/M.1990 — *Unilever/Bestfoods*; OJ C 311, 31.10.2000, p. 6).

18. Although it has been accepted in certain specific circumstances,[20] a divestiture consisting of a combination of certain assets from both the purchaser and the target may create additional risks as to the viability and efficiency of the resulting business. It will, therefore, be assessed with great care. In exceptional cases, a divestiture package including only brands and supporting production assets may be sufficient to create the conditions for effective competition.[21] In such circumstances, the Commission would have to be convinced that the buyer could integrate these assets effectively and immediately.

Notes

[20] Commission Decision 96/222/EC (IV/M.603 — *Crown Cork & Seal/CarnaudMetalbox*; OJ L 75, 23.3.1996, p. 38).

[21] Commission Decision 96/435/EC (IV/M.623 — *Kimberly-Clark/Scott Paper*; OJ L 183, 23.7.1996, p. 1).

Suitable purchaser

19. The condition for a clearance decision by the Commission is that the viable business will have been transferred to a suitable purchaser[22] within a specific deadline. The two elements of the viable business and the suitable purchaser are thus inter-linked. The potential of a business to attract a suitable purchaser is, therefore, an important element of the Commission's assessment of the appropriateness of the proposed commitment.[23]

Notes

[22] See paragraph 49 for the purchaser standards.

[23] IV/M.913 — *Siemens/Elektrowatt*: cited above.

Commentary
para 19: B&C: 8.162

20. There are cases where the viability of the divestiture package depends, in view of the assets being part of the business, to a large extent on the identity of the purchaser. In such circumstances, the Commission will not clear the merger unless the parties undertake not to complete the notified operation before having entered into a binding agreement with a purchaser for the divested business (known as the "upfront buyer"), approved by the Commission.[24]

Notes
[24] Commission Decision of 13 December 2000 (COMP/M.2060 — *Bosch/Rexroth*).

Commentary
para 20: B&C: 8.162, 8.168

21. Once a divestiture of a business is made a condition of the clearance decision, it is a matter for the parties to find a suitable purchaser for this business. The parties may therefore add, on their own initiative, other assets to make the package more attractive to buyers.[25]

Notes
[25] IV/M.1532 — *BP Amoco/Arco* (cited above) where the commitment was to divest the interests in certain gas pipelines and processing facilities in the North Sea, also the interests in the related gas fields were divested.

Alternative divestiture commitments

22. In certain cases, the implementation of the parties' preferred divestiture option (of a viable business solving the competition concerns) might be uncertain or difficult in view of, for instance, third parties' pre-emption rights or uncertainty as to the transferability of key contracts, intellectual property rights or employees, as the case may be. Nevertheless, the parties may consider that they would be able to divest this business within the appropriate short time period.

Commentary
para 22: B&C: 8.168

23. In such circumstances, the Commission cannot take the risk that, in the end, effective competition will not be restored. Accordingly, it is up to the parties to set out in the commitment an alternative proposal, which has to be at least equal if not better suited to restore effective competition, as well as a clear timetable as to how and when the other alternative will be implemented.[26]

Notes
[26] Commission Decision of 8 April 1999 (COMP/M.1453 — *AXA/GRE*; OJ C 30, 2.2.2000, p. 6).

Commentary
para 23: B&C: 8.168

Removal of structural links

24. Divestiture commitments may not be limited to overcoming competition problems created by horizontal overlaps. The divestiture of an existing shareholding in a joint venture may be necessary in order to sever a structural link with a major competitor.[27]

Notes
[27] Commission Decision 98/455/EC (IV/M.942 — *VEBA/Degussa*; OJ L 201, 17.7.1998, p. 102).

25. In other cases, a possible remedy could be the divestiture of minority shareholdings or the elimination of interlocking directorates in order to increase the incentives for competing on the market.[28]

Notes

[28] Commission Decision of 9 February 2000 (COMP/M.1628 — *TotalFina/Elf*); Commission Decision of 13 June 2000 (COMP/M.1673 — *VEBA/ VIAG*); Commission Decision of 1 September 2000 (COMP/M.1980 — *Volvo/ Renault*; OJ C 301, 21.10.2000, p. 23).

2. Other remedies

26. Whilst being the preferred remedy, divestiture is not the only remedy acceptable to the Commission. First, there may be situations where a divestiture of a business is impossible.[29] Secondly, competition problems can also result from specific features, such as the existence of exclusive agreements, the combination of networks ("network effects") or the combination of key patents. In such circumstances, the Commission has to determine whether or not other types of remedy may have a sufficient effect on the market to restore effective competition.

Notes

[29] IV/M.877 — *Boeing/McDonnell Douglas* (cited above). The Commission's investigations revealed that no existing aircraft manufacturer was interested in acquiring Douglas Aircraft Company (DAC, the commercial aircraft division of McDonell Douglas) from Boeing, nor was it possible to find a potential entrant to the commercial jet aircraft market who might achieve entry through the acquisition of DAC.

27. The change in the market structure resulting from a proposed concentration can cause existing contractual arrangements to be inimical to effective competition. This is in particular true for exclusive long-term supply and distribution agreements if such agreements limit the market potential available for competitors. Where the merged entity will have a considerable market share, the foreclosure effects resulting from **existing exclusive agreements** may contribute to the creation of a dominant position.[30] In such circumstances, the termination of existing exclusive agreements[31] may be considered appropriate to eliminate the competitive concerns if there is clearly no evidence that de facto exclusivity is being maintained.

Notes

[30] Commission Decision 98/475/EC (IV/M.986 — *AGFA Gevaert/DuPont*; OJ L 211, 29.7.1998, p. 22).
[31] Commission Decision of 28 October 1999 (IV/M.1571 — *New Holland/Case*: OJ C 130, 11.5.2000, p. 11); Commission Decision of 19 April 1999 (IV/M.1467 — *Rohm and Haas/Morton*; OJ C 157, 4.6.1999, p. 7).

28. The change in the market structure resulting from a proposed concentration can lead to major barriers or impediments to entry into the relevant market. Such barriers may arise from control over infrastructure, in particular networks, or key technology including patents, know-how or other intellectual property rights. In such circumstances, remedies may aim at facilitating market entry by ensuring that competitors will have **access to the necessary infrastructure**[32] or **key technology**.

Notes

[32] Commission Decision of 5 October 1992 (IV/M.157 — *Air France/Sabena*; OJ C 272, 21.10.1992, p. 1); Commission Decision of 27 November 1992 (IV/M.259 — *British Airways/TAT*; OJ C 326, 11.12.1992, p. 1); Commission Decision of 20 July 1995 (IV/M.616 — *Swissair/Sabena*; OJ C 200, 4.8.1995, p. 10); Commission Decision of 13 October 1999 (IV/M.1439 — *Telia/Telenor*); Commission Decision of 12 April 2000 (COMP/M. 1795 — *Vodafone/Mannesmann*).

29. Where the competition problem is created by control over key technology, a divestiture of such technology[33] is the preferable remedy as it eliminates a lasting relationship between the merged entity and its competitors. However, the Commission may accept licensing arrangements (preferably exclusive licences without any field-of-use restrictions on the licensee) as an alternative to divestiture where, for instance, a divestiture would have impeded efficient, on-going research. The Commission has pursued this approach in mergers involving, for example, the pharmaceutical industry.[34]

Notes

[33] Commission Decision of 9 August 1999 (IV/M.1378 — *Hoechst/Rhône-Poulenc*; OJ C 254, 7.9.1999, p. 5); Commission Decision of 1 December 1999 (COMP/M.1601 — *Allied Signal/Honeywell*); Commission Decision of 3 May 2000 (COMP/M.1671 — *Dow/UCC*).
[34] Commission Decision of 28 February 1995 (IV/M.555 — *Glaxo/Wellcome*; OJ C 65, 16.3.1995, p. 3).

Part D Mergers and Concentrations

30. Owing to the specifics of the competition problems raised by a given concentration in several markets, the parties may have to offer **remedy packages** which comprise a combination of divestiture remedies and other remedies that facilitate market entry by granting network access or access to specific content.[35] Such packages may be appropriate to remedy specific foreclosure problems arising, for instance, in concentrations in the telecommunication and media sectors. In addition, there may be transactions affecting mainly one product market where, however, only a package including a variety of other commitments will be able to remedy the competitive concerns raised by the specific concentration on an overall basis.[36]

Notes

[35] COMP/M.1439 — *Telia/Telenor*; COMP/M.1795 — *Vodafone Airtouch/Mannesmann* (cited above); Commission Decision of 13 October 2000 (COMP/M.2050 — *Vivendi/Canal+/Seagram*; OJ C 311, 31.10.2000, p. 3).

[36] Commission Decision 97/816/EC (IV/M.877 — *Boeing/McDonnell Douglas*; OJ L 336, 8.12.1997, p. 16); COMP/M.1673 — *VEBA/VIAG*.

IV. Situations where Remedies are Difficult, if not Impossible

31. The Commission is willing to explore solutions to the competition problems raised by a concentration, provided that these solutions are convincing and effective. There are, however, concentrations where remedies adequate to eliminate competition concerns within the common market cannot be found.[37] In such circumstances, the only possibility is prohibition.

Notes

[37] Commission Decision 94/922/EC (*MSG Media Service*, OJ L 364, 31.12.1994, p. 1); Commission Decision 96/177/EC (*Nordic Satellite Distribution*, OJ L 53, 2.3.1996, p. 20); Commission Decision 96/342/EC (*RTL/Veronica/Endemol*, OJ L 134, 5.6.1996, p. 32); Commission Decision 1999/153/EC (*Bertelsmann/Kirch/Premiere*, OJ L 53, 27.2.1999, p. 1); Commission Decision 1999/154/EC (*Deutsche Telekom BetaResearch*, OJ L 53, 27.2.1999, p. 31); Commission Decision 97/610/EC (*St Gobain/Wacker Chemie/NOM*, OJ L 247, 10.9.1997, p. 1); Commission Decision 91/619/EEC (*Aerospatiale/Alenia/De Havilland*, OJ L 334, 5.12.1991, p. 42); Commission Decision 97/26/EC *Gencor/Lonrho*, OJ L 11, 14.1.1997, p. 30); Commission Decision 2000/276/EC (M.1524. *Airtours/First Choice*; OJ L 93, 13.4.2000, p. 1).

32. Where the parties submit proposed remedies that are so extensive and complex that it is not possible for the Commission to determine with the required degree of certainty that effective competition will be restored in the market, an authorisation decision cannot be granted.[38]

Notes

[38] Commission Decision of 15 March 2000 (COMP/M.1672 — *Volvo/Scania*); Commission Decision of 28 June 2000 (COMP/M.1741 — *WorldCom/ Sprint*).

V. Specific Requirements for Submission of Commitments

1. Phase I

33. Pursuant to Article 6(2) of the Merger Regulation the Commission may declare a concentration compatible with the common market, where it is confident that following modification a notified concentration no longer raises serious doubts within the meaning of paragraph 1(c). Parties can submit proposals for commitments to the Commission on an informal basis, even before notification. Where the parties submit proposals for commitments together with the notification or within three weeks from the date of receipt of the notification,[39] the deadline for the Commission's decision pursuant to Article 6(1) of the Merger Regulation is extended from one month to six weeks.

Notes

[39] Article 18(1) of Commission Regulation (EC) No 447/98 (Implementing Regulation), OJ L 61, 2.3.1998, p. 1.

Commentary
para 33: B&C: 8.133

34. In order to form the basis of a decision pursuant to Article 6(2), proposals for commitments must meet the following requirements:

    (a) they shall be submitted in due time, at the latest on the last day of the three-week period;

    (b) they shall specify the commitments entered into by the parties in a sufficient degree of detail to enable a full assessment to be carried out;

    (c) they shall explain how the commitments offered solve the competition concerns identified by the Commission.

    At the same time as submitting the commitments, the parties need to supply a non-confidential version of the commitments, for purposes of market testing.[40]

Notes

[40] By way of a market test, customers, competitors, suppliers and other companies which might be affected or have specific expertise are requested to indicate to the Commission their reasoned opinion as to the effectiveness of the commitment.

Commentary

para 34: **B&C:** 8.163

35. Proposals submitted by the parties in accordance with these requirements will be assessed by the Commission. The Commission will consult the authorities of the Member States on the proposed commitments and, when considered appropriate, also third parties in the form of a market test. In addition, in cases involving a geographic market that is wider than the European Economic Area ("EEA") or where, for reasons related to the viability of the business, the scope of the business to be divested is wider than the EEA territory, the proposed remedies may also be discussed with non-EEA competition authorities in the framework of the Community's bilateral cooperation agreements with these countries.

Commentary

para 35: **B&C:** 8.163

36. Where the assessment confirms that the proposed commitments remove the grounds for serious doubts, the Commission clears the merger in phase I.

37. Where the assessment shows that the commitments offered are not sufficient to remove the competitive concerns raised by the merger, the parties will be informed accordingly. Given that phase I remedies are designed to provide a straightforward answer to a readily identifiable competition concern,[41] only limited modifications can be accepted to the proposed commitments. Such modifications, presented as an immediate response to the result of the consultations, include clarifications, refinements and/or other improvements which ensure that the commitments are workable and effective.

Notes

[41] See Recital 8 of Council Regulation (EC) No 1310/97 referred to in paragraph 1.

Commentary

para 37: **B&C:** 8.163

38. If the parties have not removed the serious doubts, the Commission will issue an Article 6(1)(c) decision and open proceedings.

2. Phase II

39. Pursuant to Article 8(2) of the Merger Regulation, the Commission must declare a concentration compatible with the common market, where following modification a notified concentration no longer creates or strengthens a dominant position within the meaning of Article 2(3) of the Merger Regulation. Commitments proposed to the Commission pursuant to Article 8(2) must be submitted to the Commission within not more than three months from the day on which proceedings were initiated. An extension of this period shall only be taken into consideration on request by the parties setting forth the exceptional circumstances which, according to them, justify it. The request for extension must be received within the three-month-period. An extension is only

possible in case of exceptional circumstances and where in the particular case there is sufficient time to make a proper assessment of the proposal by the Commission and to allow adequate consultation with Member States and third parties.[42]

Notes
[42] M.1439 — *Telia/Telenor*, and in Commission Decision 98/335/EC (M.754 — *Anglo American/Lonrho*; OJ L 149, 20.5.1998, p. 21).
Commentary
para 39: B&C: 8.164

40. The Commission is available to discuss suitable commitments prior to the end of the three-month period. The parties are encouraged to submit draft proposals dealing with both substantive and procedural aspects which are necessary to ensure that the commitments are fully workable.

Commentary
para 40: B&C: 8.164

41. Proposals for commitments submitted in order to form the basis for a decision pursuant to Article 8(2) must meet the following requirements:
    (a) they shall be submitted in due time, at the latest on the last day of the three-month period;
    (b) they shall address all competition problems raised in the Statement of Objections and not subsequently abandoned. In this respect, they must specify the substantive and implementing terms entered into by the parties in sufficient detail to enable a full assessment to be carried out;
    (c) they shall explain how the commitments offered solve the competition concerns. At the same time as submitting the commitments, the parties shall supply a non-confidential version of the commitments, for purposes of market testing.

Commentary
para 41: B&C: 8.164

42. Proposals submitted by the parties in accordance with these requirements will be assessed by the Commission. If the assessment confirms that the proposed commitments remove the competition concerns, following consultation with the authorities of the Member States, discussions with non-Member States authorities[43] and, when considered appropriate, with third parties in the form of a market test, a clearance decision will be submitted for Commission approval.

Notes
[43] See paragraph 35.
Commentary
para 42: B&C: 8.164

43. Conversely, where the assessment leads to the conclusion that the proposed commitments appear not to be sufficient to resolve the competition concerns raised by the concentration, the parties will be informed accordingly. Where the parties subsequently modify the proposed commitments, the Commission may only accept these modified commitments[44] where it can clearly determine — on the basis of its assessment of information already received in the course of the investigation, including the results of prior market testing, and without the need for any other market test — that such commitments, once implemented, resolve the competition problems identified and allow sufficient time for proper consultation of Member States.

Notes
[44] COMP/M.1628 — *TotalFina/Elf*, LPG, cited above, at paragraph 345.
Commentary
para 43: F&N: 5.611

VI. REQUIREMENTS FOR IMPLEMENTATION OF COMMITMENTS

44. Commitments are offered as a means of securing a clearance, with the implementation normally taking place after the decision. These commitments require safeguards to ensure their successful and timely implementation. These implementing provisions will form part of the commitments entered into by the parties *vis-à-vis* the Commission. They have to be considered on a case-by-case basis. This is in particular true for the fixed time periods laid down for the implementation, which should in general be as short as is feasible. Consequently, it is not possible to standardise these requirements totally.

45. The following guidance is intended to assist the parties in framing commitment proposals. The principles are based on the framework of a divestiture commitment, which, as was seen above, is the most typical commitment. However, many of the principles discussed below are equally applicable to other types of commitments.

1. Essential features of divestment commitments

46. In a typical divestment commitment, the business to be divested normally consists of a combination of tangible and intangible assets, which could take the form of a pre-existing company or group of companies, or of a business activity which was not previously incorporated in its own right. Thus the parties,[45] when submitting a divestiture commitment, have to give a precise and exhaustive definition of the intended subject of divestment (hereafter referred to as "the description of the business" or "the description"). The description has to contain all the elements of the business that are necessary for the business to act as a viable competitor in the market: tangible (such as R & D, production, distribution, sales and marketing activities) and intangible (such as intellectual property rights, goodwill) assets, personnel, supply and sales agreements (with appropriate guarantees about the transferability of these), customer lists, third party service agreements, technical assistance (scope, duration, cost, quality) and so forth. In order to avoid any misunderstanding about the business to be divested, assets that are used within the business but that should not, according to the parties, be divested, have to be identified separately.

Notes
[45] Commitments must be signed by a person duly authorised to do so.

Commentary
para 46: B&C: 8.167

47. The description has to provide for a mechanism whereby the acquirer of the business can retain and select the appropriate personnel. Such a mechanism is required both for the personnel that are currently working in the business unit as it is operated and for the personnel that provide essential functions for the business such as, for instance, group R & D and information technology staff even where such personnel are currently employed by another business unit of the parties. This mechanism is without prejudice to the application of the Council Directives on collective redundancies;[46] on safeguarding employees rights in the event of transfers of undertakings;[47] and on informing and consulting employees[48] as well as national provisions implementing those Directives.

Notes
[46] Council Directive 98/59/EC of 20 July 1998 on the approximation of the laws of the Member States relating to collective redundancies (OJ L 225, 12.8.1998, p. 16).
[47] Council Directive 77/187/EEC of 14 February 1977 on the approximation of the laws of the Member States relating to the safeguarding of employees' rights in the event of transfers of undertakings, businesses or parts of a business (OJ L 61, 5.3.1977, p. 26) as amended by Council Directive 98/50/EC (OJ L 201, 17.7.1998, p. 88).
[48] Council Directive 94/45/EC of 22 September 1994 on the establishment of a European Works Council or a procedure in Community-scale undertakings and Community-scale groups of undertakings for the purposes of informing and consulting employees (OJ L 254, 30.9.1994, p. 64), as amended by Directive 97/74/EC (OJ L 10, 16.1.1998, p. 22).

48. The divestment has to be completed within a fixed time period agreed between the parties and the Commission, which takes account of all relevant circumstances. The package will specify

Part D Mergers and Concentrations

what kind of agreement — binding letter of intent, final agreement, transfer of legal title — is required by what date. The deadline for the divestment should start on the day of the adoption of the Commission decision.

Commentary
para 48: B&C: 8.167

49. In order to ensure the effectiveness of the commitment, the sale to a proposed purchaser is subject to prior approval by the Commission. The purchaser is normally required to be a viable existing or potential competitor, independent of and unconnected to the parties, possessing the financial resources,[49] proven expertise and having the incentive to maintain and develop the divested business as an active competitive force in competition with the parties. In addition, the acquisition of the business by a particular proposed purchaser must neither be likely to create new competition problems nor give rise to a risk that the implementation of the commitment will be delayed. These conditions are hereinafter referred to as "the purchaser standards". In order to maintain the structural effect of a remedy, the merged entity cannot, even in the absence of an explicit clause in the commitments, subsequently acquire influence over the whole or parts of the divested business unless the Commission has previously found that the structure of the market has changed to such an extent that the absence of influence over the divested business is no longer necessary to render the concentration compatible with the common market.

Notes
[49] The Commission does not accept seller-financed divestitures because of the impact this has on the divested company's independence.

Commentary
para 49: B&C: 8.167 **F&N:** 5.375

2. Interim preservation of the business to be divested — the hold-separate trustee

50. It is the parties' responsibility to reduce to the minimum any possible risk of loss of competitive potential of the business to be divested resulting from the uncertainties inherent to the transfer of a business. Pending divestment, the Commission will require the parties to offer commitments to maintain the independence, economic viability, marketability and competitiveness of the business.

Commentary
para 50: B&C: 8.170

51. These commitments will be designed to keep the business separate from the business retained by the parties, and to ensure that it is managed as a distinct and saleable business. The parties will be required to ensure that all relevant tangible and intangible assets of the divestiture package are maintained, pursuant to good business practice and in the ordinary course of business. This relates in particular to the maintenance of fixed assets, know-how or commercial information of a confidential or proprietary nature, the customer base and the technical and commercial competence of the employees. Furthermore, the parties must maintain the same conditions of competition as regards the divestiture package as those applied before the merger, so as to continue the business as it is currently conducted. This includes providing relevant administrative and management functions, sufficient capital, and a line of credit, and it may include other conditions specific to maintaining competition in an industry.

Commentary
para 51: B&C: 8.170

52. As the Commission cannot, on a daily basis, be directly involved in overseeing compliance with these interim preservation measures, it therefore approves the appointment of a trustee to oversee the parties' compliance with such preservation measures (a so-called "hold-separate trustee"). The hold-separate trustee will act in the best interests of the business to be divested. The commitment

will set out the specific details of the trustee's mandate. The trustee's mandate, to be approved by the Commission, together with the trustee appointment, will include for example, responsibilities for supervision, which include the right to propose, and, if deemed necessary, impose, all measures which the trustee considers necessary to ensure compliance with any of the commitments, and periodic compliance reports.

Commentary
para 52: B&C: 8.170

3. Implementation of the commitments — the divestiture trustee

53. The commitment will also set out the specific details and procedures relating to the Commission's oversight of the implementation of the divestiture: for example, criteria for approval of the purchaser, periodic reporting requirements, and approval of the prospectus or advertising material. Here, too, it is noted that the Commission cannot, on a daily basis, be directly involved in managing the divestment. Consequently, in most cases, the Commission considers it appropriate to approve the appointment a trustee with responsibilities for overseeing the implementation of the commitments (the "divestiture trustee").

54. The divestiture trustee's role will vary on a case-by-case basis, but will generally include supervision which includes the right to propose, and if deemed necessary, impose, all measures which the trustee requires to ensure compliance with any of the commitments, and reporting at regular intervals. Where appropriate, the trustee's role will span two phases: in the first phase, he or she will be responsible for overseeing the parties' efforts to find a potential purchaser. If the parties do not succeed in finding an acceptable purchaser within the time frame set out in their commitments, then in the second phase, the trustee will be given an irrevocable mandate to dispose of the business within a specific deadline at any price, subject to the prior approval of the Commission.

4. Approval of the trustee and the trustee mandate

55. Depending on the types of commitments involved and the facts of the case, the divestiture trustee may or may not be the same person or institution as the hold-separate trustee. The trustee will normally be an investment bank, management consulting or accounting company or similar institution. The parties shall suggest the trustee (or a number of trustees) to the Commission. The trustee shall be independent of the parties, possess the necessary qualifications to carry out the job and shall not be, or become, exposed to a conflict of interests. It is the parties' responsibility to supply the Commission with adequate information for it to verify that the trustee fulfils these requirements. The Commission will review and approve the terms of the trustee's appointment, which should be irrevocable unless "good cause" is shown to the Commission for the appointment of a new trustee.

Commentary
para 55: B&C: 8.170

56. The parties are responsible for remuneration of each trustee for all services rendered in the execution of their responsibilities, and the remuneration structure must be such as to not impede the trustee's independence and effectiveness in fulfilling his mandate. The trustee will assume specified duties designed to ensure compliance in good faith with the commitments on behalf of the Commission, and these duties will be defined in the trustee's mandate. The mandate must include all provisions necessary to enable the trustee to fulfil its duties under the commitments accepted by the Commission. It is subject to Commission's approval.

Commentary
para 56: B&C: 8.168

57. When the specific commitments with which the trustee has been entrusted have been implemented — that is to say, when legal title for the divestiture package to be divested has passed or at the end of some specific obligations which continue post-divestiture — the mandate will

provide for the trustee to request the Commission for a discharge from further responsibilities. Even after the discharge has been given, the Commission has the discretion to require the reappointment of the trustee, if subsequently it appears to the Commission that the relevant commitments might not have been fully and properly implemented.

Commentary
para 57: B&C: 8.168

5. Approval of the purchaser and the purchase agreement

58. The parties or the trustee can only proceed with the sale if the Commission approves a proposed purchaser and the purchase agreement on the basis of the arrangements set out in the commitment. The parties or the trustee will be required to demonstrate satisfactorily to the Commission that the proposed buyer meets the requirements of the commitments, which means the purchaser's standards, and that the business is sold in a manner consistent with the commitment. The Commission will formally communicate its view to the parties. Before doing so, the Commission officials may have discussed with the proposed purchaser its incentives for competing with the merged entity on the basis of its business plans. Where different purchasers are being proposed for different parts of the package, the Commission will assess whether each individual proposed purchaser is acceptable and that the total package solves the competition problem.

Commentary
para 58: B&C: 8.167

59. Where the Commission determines that the acquisition of the divestiture package by the proposed purchaser, in the light of the information available to the Commission, threatens to create *prima facie* competition problems[50] or other difficulties, which may delay the timely implementation of the commitment or indicate the lack of appropriate incentives for the purchaser to compete with the merged entity, the proposed purchaser will not be considered acceptable. In this case, the Commission will formally communicate its view that the buyer does not satisfy the purchaser's standards.[51]

Notes
[50] This is most likely to arise where the market structure is already highly concentrated and where the remedy would transfer the market share to another market player.
[51] COMP/M.1628 — *TotalFina/Elf* — motorway service stations.

60. Where the purchase results in a concentration that has a Community dimension, this new operation will have to be notified under the Merger Regulation and cleared under normal procedures.[52] Where this is not the case, the Commission's approval of a purchaser is without prejudice to the jurisdiction of merger control of national authorities.

Notes
[52] Commission Decision of 29 September 1999 (Case M.1383 — *Exxon/Mobil*) and the Commission Decisions of 2 February 2000 in the follow-up Cases M.1820 — *BP/JV Dissolution* (not published) and M.1822 — *Mobil/JV Dissolution* (OJ C 112, 19.4.2000, p. 6).

D5

BEST PRACTICE GUIDELINES: THE COMMISSION'S MODEL TEXTS FOR DIVESTITURE COMMITMENTS AND THE TRUSTEE MANDATE UNDER THE EC MERGER REGULATION

Note

This document is published on the Europa website at:
http://ec.europa.eu/comm/competition/mergers/legislation/explanatory_note.pdf

---

1. The European Commission's model texts for divestiture commitments and trustee mandates are designed to serve as best practice guidelines for notifying parties submitting commitments under the EC Merger Regulation.[1] These texts are (1) the model to be used for divestiture commitments (the "*Standard Model for Divestiture Commitments*" or the "*Standard Commitments*"); and (2) the model for the mandate of the two types of trustees referred to in the Standard Commitments, that is, the mandate appointing monitoring and divestiture trustees (the "*Standard Trustee Mandate*").

Notes

[1] Council Regulation (EEC) No 4064/89 of 21 December 1989 on the control of concentrations between undertakings, as amended, OJ L 395, 30.12.1989, p. 1; corrigendum OJ L 257, 21.9.1990, p. 13.

---

2. The model texts (the "*Standard Models*") are based upon the experience the Commission has gained to date in fashioning remedies from previous merger cases and are drafted in line with the remedies policy set out in the Commission's Notice on Remedies[2] (the "*Remedies Notice*"). The Standard Models are neither intended to provide an exhaustive coverage of all issues that may become relevant in all cases, nor are they legally binding upon parties in a merger procedure. Rather, they contain the elements for all standard provisions that should be included in commitments and trustee mandates relating to divestitures. In providing a framework for commitments and trustee mandates to be submitted in concrete cases, the Standard Models leave the flexibility to adapt the texts to the specific requirements of the case in question.

Notes

[2] See Commission Notice on remedies acceptable under Council Regulation (EEC) No 4064/89 and Regulation (EC) No 447/98 at *Official Journal* C 68, 02.03.2001, pages 3–11; published on http://europa.eu.int/eur-lex/pri/en/oj/dat/2001/c_068/c_06820010302en00030011.pdf.

---

3. The Standard Models are designed to apply to all remedy proceedings in both Phase I and Phase II, therefore to all Commission decisions according to Articles 6(2) and 8(2) of the Merger Regulation. The Standard Models deal specifically with divestiture commitments inasmuch as the Commission's Remedies Notice stipulates that divestiture commitments are normally the preferred form of merger remedies; they are also the most common. However, it should be underlined that the Commission will consider the acceptability of other types of commitments in appropriate circumstances, as set out in the Remedies Notice. Individual provisions contained in the Standard Models can be used in cases involving such other types of commitments.

4. Finally, it is expected that the text of these models will evolve, based on ongoing practice, and will be regularly up-dated by the Commission, taking into consideration both the developments of the Commission's remedies policy and the experience gained from working with the merging parties and trustees in future matters.

The Purpose of the Standard Models

5. The Commission recognises that timing is crucial when merging parties reach the remedies stage in merger review procedures, where they offer commitments in order to resolve the Commission's competition concerns in a given case. Through the use of standardised models, the merging parties and the Commission will be relieved of the heavy demands — both in terms of time and resources — that would otherwise be required to negotiate the standard terms and provisions for commitments and trustee mandates under tight time constraints. The use of standardised models will expedite the proceedings and allow the merging parties to concentrate more on the actual substance and implementation of the commitments.

6. The use of the standard models will ensure consistency across cases and will thereby contribute to increasing the level of transparency and legal certainty for the merging parties offering commitments to the Commission.

Overview of the Contents of the Standard Models

7. The <u>Standard Model for Divestiture Commitments</u> sets out all requirements for achieving full and effective compliance with divestiture commitments offered by the merging parties (the "*Parties*") to obtain a clearance decision. More specifically, this Model is designed (i) to describe clearly the business to be divested ("*Divestment Business*"), the divestiture procedure and the obligations of the parties in relation to the Divestment Business for the interim period until divestiture has been completed, (ii) to set out the various responsibilities that the merging parties will thereby have, respectively, to the Commission, the Trustee, and the Divestment Business; and (iii) to enshrine the importance which the Commission places upon requiring an acceptable purchaser for the Divestment Business in order to ensure the viability and competitiveness of the new entity in the market where the divestiture takes place.

8. The <u>Standard Model for Trustee Mandates</u> sets out the role and functions of the Trustee, as provided in the Standard Commitments, in a contractual relationship between the Parties responsible for the divestiture and the Trustee. As the Commitments set out the basis for the responsibilities of the Trustee, the Standard Trustee Mandate has been prepared in conformity with the requirements laid down for the Trustee in the Standard Model for Divestiture Commitments.

9. Although the Standard Trustee Mandate is a bilateral contract between the Parties responsible for the divestiture and the Trustee, this document forms the basis for a tri-partite relationship among the Commission, the Trustee, and the Parties. The relationship between the Parties and the Trustee is not a traditional trusteeship. The Trustee rather benefits from a status which makes it independent from the Parties and which is characterised by the role of the Trustee to monitor (Monitoring Trustee) or even to effectuate (Divestiture Trustee) the Parties' compliance with the commitments. Accordingly, the Parties are not entitled to give instructions to the Trustee, whereas the Commission is allowed to do so. This specific relationship is also confirmed by the fact that the Trustee Mandate requires the Commission's approval.

10. The Standard Trustee Mandate is designed (i) to facilitate the smooth and timely appointment of the Trustee and the approval of the Trustee Mandate; (ii) to clarify the relationship among the Commission, the Trustee, and the Parties; and (iii) to set out the tasks of the Trustee in the process in order to enable the Trustee to expedite compliance with the commitments. Whereas the Standard Trustee Mandate defines the role of a Monitoring and a Divestiture Trustee in one text, they can be assigned to different Trustees in practice.

11. In providing guidance for the interpretation of the Standard Texts, a certain hierarchy is established. The Standard Trustee Mandate should be interpreted in the light of the Standard Commitments, as they lay the foundation for the application of the Trustee Mandate. To the extent that they are attached as conditions and obligations, the commitments are to be interpreted in the light of the respective Commission decision. Moreover, both Standard Texts should be interpreted in the general framework of Community law, in particular in the light of the EC Merger Regulation, and by reference to the Commission's Remedies Notice setting out the Commission's remedies policy.

Description of the Provisions of the Standard Models

12. The most important provisions contained in both Standard Models are briefly set out below.

Standard Model for Divestiture Commitments

13. The Standard Model for Commitments consists of the following main elements:

14. Section A contains a definitions section.

15. Section B contains the commitment to divest and the definition of the Divestment Business. After spelling out the general obligation to divest the Divestment Business as a going concern, paragraph 1 describes the divestiture procedure, which may take two phases. The Commitments provide that in the first phase (that is, the *Divestiture Period*), the Parties have the sole responsibility for finding a suitable purchaser for the Divestment Business. If the Parties do not succeed in divesting the business on their own in the Divestiture Period, then a Divestiture Trustee will be appointed with an exclusive mandate to dispose of the Divestment Business at no minimum price, in the Extended Divestiture Period. The individual deadlines are determined in the definitions section. The experience of the Commission has shown that short divestiture periods contribute largely to the success of the divestiture as, otherwise, the Divestment Business will be exposed to an extended period of uncertainty. The Commission will normally consider a period of around 6 months for the Divestiture Period and an additional period of 3 to 6 months for the Extended Divestiture Period as appropriate. These periods may be modified according to the particular requirements of the case in question.

16. The divestiture commitment will take a special form in those cases where the Parties propose an up-front buyer. The Parties commit not to implement the proposed concentration unless and until they have entered into a binding agreement with a purchaser for the Divestment Business, approved by the Commission. The qualification of the buyer are the same as in other divestiture commitments. The up-front buyer concept has been applied in several cases[3] and will be used in the specific circumstances as described in the Notice.[4] The structure of the divestiture commitment also needs to be adapted in cases of alternative divestitures, in particular "Crown Jewels" structures, i.e. structures in which the Parties commit to divest a very attractive business if they have not divested the originally proposed business until the end of a period fixed in the commitments. The circumstances in which the Commission will accept alternative divestiture commitments are also set out in the Remedies Notice.[5]

Notes

[3] Cases COMP/M.2060 — *Bosch/Rexroth*; COMP/M.1915 — *The Post Office/TPG/SPPL*; COMP/M.2544 — *Masterfood/Royal Canin*.

[4] Paragraph 18 of the Remedies Notice.

[5] Paragraphs 22, 23 of the Remedies Notice.

---

17. The divestiture commitment includes the commitment not to re-acquire direct or indirect influence over the Divestment Business (paragraph 3). This re-acquisition prohibition is limited to ten years after the date of the decision and serves to maintain the structural effects of the Commitments. The Commission may grant a waiver if the structure of the market has changed to such an extent that the absence of influence over the Divestment Business is no longer necessary to render the concentration compatible with the common market.

18. Section B, together with the Schedule to the Commitments, defines what is included in the Divestment Business. The clear identification of the Divestment Business is of great importance as thereby the scope of the divestiture and of the hold-separate obligations are defined. As set out in the Notice, the Divestment Business is considered to be an existing entity that can operate on a stand-alone-basis.[6] The Divestment Business is the minimum which is to be divested by the Parties in order to comply with the Commitments. In order to make the package more attractive to buyers, the Parties may add, on their own initiative, other assets.[7] The Divestment Business must include all the assets and personnel necessary to ensure the viability of the divested activities. Whereas this principle is set out as an undertaking of the Parties in paragraph 3 of the Standard Commitments, the Parties have to give a detailed factual description of the Divestment Business in the Schedule to the Standard Commitments.

Notes

[6] Cf. paragraph 14 of the Remedies Notice. The importance of the divestiture of an on-going business for the success of the remedy has also been underlined by the FTC in a published study entitled A Study of the Commission's Divestiture Process, prepared by the Staff of the Bureau of Competition of the Federal Trade Commission, p. 10 ff.

[7] Cf. paragraph 21 of the Remedies Notice.

19. The Divestment Business must comprise the <u>Personnel and the Key Personnel</u> retained by the Divestment Business as well as the personnel providing essential functions for the Divestment Business, such as the central R&D staff. The personnel (according to groups and functions performed) is to be listed in the Schedule to the Commitments, the Key Personnel is to be listed separately. The principle, indicated in paragraph 4(d), is that the personnel should be transferred with the Divestment Business. If the Divestment Business takes the form of a company or if the transfer of undertakings legislation applies, the personnel will normally be transferred by operation of law. In other cases, the acquirer of the business can retain and select the personnel and can make offers of employment. The transfer — whichever form it takes — is without prejudice to the application of Council Directives, where applicable, on collective redundancies;[8] on safeguarding employees rights in the event of transfers of undertakings;[9] and on informing and consulting employees,[10] as well as relevant national law on these matters.

Notes

[8] Council Directive 98/59/EC of 20 July 1998 on the approximation of the laws of the Member States relating to collective redundancies (OJ L 225, 12.8.1998, p.16).

[9] Council Directive 77/187/EEC on the approximation of the laws of the Member States relating to the safeguarding of employees rights in the event of transfers of undertakings, businesses or parts of a business (OJ L 61, 5.3.1977, p. 26) as amended by Council Directive 98/50/EC (OJ L 201, 17.7.1998, p. 88).

[10] Council Directive 94/45/EC of 22 September 1994 on the establishment of a European Works Council or a procedure in Community-scale undertakings and Community-scale groups of undertakings for the purposes of informing and consulting employees (OJ L 254, 30.9.1994, p. 64) as amended by Directive 97/74/EC (OJ L 10, 16.1.1998, p. 22).

20. Furthermore, the Standard Commitments foresee that the Divestment Business shall be <u>entitled to benefit from products or services</u> provided by the Parties for a transitional period, determined on a case-by-case basis, if this is necessary to maintain the full economic viability and competitiveness of the Divestment Business (paragraph 4(e) of the Standard Commitments referring to the products or services listed in the Schedule).

21. <u>Section C</u> contains a number of <u>related commitments</u>, which are designed to maintain, pending divestiture, the viability, marketability and competitiveness of the Divestment Business. These provisions deal with the <u>preservation of the divested entity's viability and independence, as well as the hold-separate and ring-fencing obligations</u>. The Hold Separate Manager, to be appointed by the Parties and normally the manager of the Divestment Business, is responsible for the management of the Divestment Business as a distinct entity separate from the businesses retained by the Parties, and is supervised by the Monitoring Trustee.

22. In certain cases it may also be necessary for the <u>hold-separate obligation to apply to the corporate structure</u> itself. That is, in cases where the Divestment Business takes the form of a company and a strict separation of the corporate structure is necessary, the Monitoring Trustee must be given the authority to (i) exercise the Parties' rights as shareholders in the Divestment Business and (ii) to replace members of the supervisory board or non-executive directors on the board of directors who have been appointed on behalf of the Parties (cf. paragraph 8 of the Standard Commitments and paragraph 6(d) of the Standard Trustee Mandate).

23. Of particular importance is the <u>ring-fencing of competitively sensitive information</u> of the Divestment Business. The parties are obliged to implement all necessary measures to ensure that they do not obtain such information of the Divestment Business and, in particular, to sever its participation in a central information technology network. The Monitoring Trustee may allow the disclosure of information to the divesting party if this is reasonably necessary for the divestiture of the Divestment Business or required by law (e.g. information necessary for group accounts).

24. The related commitments further contain a <u>non-solicitation</u> clause for Key Personnel of the Divestment Business. According to the experience of the Commission, the non-solicitation

period, dependent on the circumstances of the case, should normally be two years. In addition, the Commission may request the inclusion of a <u>non-compete</u> clause in the commitments protecting the customers of the Divestment Business for a start-up period. This may be required to enable the Divestment Business to be active as a viable competitor in the market. The period for such customer protection clause will depend on the market in question.

25. During the Divestiture Phase, the divestiture lies in the hands of the divesting party. The Commission does not have a preference as to the method the parties use to select an acceptable purchaser as long as they meet the objective of the divestiture, to maintain or restore competition. However, as part of the <u>due diligence procedure</u>, it is foreseen that the divesting party shall provide to potential purchasers sufficient information as regards the Divestment Business and allow them access to its personnel (paragraph 11 of the Standard Commitments) in order to enable them to determine whether it will be possible to maintain and to develop the Divestment Business as active and viable competitive force in the market after the divestiture.

26. The divesting party shall further submit regular <u>reports</u> on potential purchasers and developments in the divestiture process to the Commission and the Monitoring Trustee (paragraph 12 of the Standard Commitments). This reporting mechanism gives the Monitoring Trustee the basis on which to assess the progress of the divestiture process as well as potential purchasers (for the Trustee's report, see paragraph 23(vi) of the Standard Commitments) and keeps the Commission informed.

27. <u>Section D</u> sets out the requirements to be met by the <u>Purchaser</u>. The aim of this section is to ensure that the Divestment Business will be sold to a suitable purchaser who is independent of and unconnected to the Parties, and who possesses the financial resources, proven expertise and incentive to maintain and develop the Divestment Business as a viable and active competitive force in the marketplace. These Purchaser Requirements can generally be met by either industrial or financial investors. The latter must demonstrate the necessary management capabilities and "proven expertise" which can in particular be met by financing a management buy-out.

28. Section D also deals with the <u>approval process</u>. After finalising the agreement(s), the divesting party shall submit a fully documented and reasoned proposal to the Commission. The Commission will verify that the purchaser will fulfil the requirements and that the Divestment Business is being sold in a manner consistent with the Commitments. One element for its assessment will be the report of the Monitoring Trustee according to paragraph 23(vii). The Commission may approve the sale of the Divestment Business without parts of the assets or personnel of the Divestment Business if this does not affect the viability and competitiveness of the Divestment Business, in particular if the Purchaser provides for such assets or personnel itself.

29. <u>Section E</u> deals with both the <u>Monitoring and Divestiture Trustees</u>. It identifies the terms for their appointment, as well as the content of the Trustee Mandates, and conditions for replacement of the Trustee during the divestiture periods if that becomes necessary. A Monitoring Trustee must be proposed by the Parties within one week after the adoption of the decision, whereas a Divestiture Trustee must be proposed no later than one month before the end of the Divestiture Period, (paragraph 16 of the Standard Commitments). The Commission wishes to emphasise the importance it attaches to compliance with these deadlines in practise, as otherwise the Parties are in breach of the commitments and the divestiture procedure is endangered.

30. <u>Section E</u> also sets out the <u>duties and obligations of both types of Trustees</u>. The Monitoring Trustee's responsibilities (mainly set out in paragraph 23 Standard Commitments) relate to both the management of the Divestment Business during the hold-separate period and the monitoring of the divestiture process itself. The supervision of the management shall in particular ensure the viability, marketability and competitiveness of the Divestment Business and the compliance with the hold-separate and ring-fencing obligations. The Standard Commitments further assign certain monitoring tasks concerning the divestiture process to the Monitoring Trustee in the Divestiture Period. Once the Parties have proposed a purchaser for the Divestment Business, the Monitoring Trustee assesses the independence and suitability of the proposed purchaser and the viability of the Divestment Business after the sale to the purchaser, in order to assist the Commission in assessing the suitability of the proposed purchaser.

31. In the <u>Extended Divestiture Period</u>, the <u>Divestiture Trustee</u> will have an exclusive mandate to sell the Divestment Business at no minimum price and is empowered to include in the sale and

purchase agreement such terms and conditions as it considers appropriate for an expedient sale. However, it is foreseen that the Trustee has to protect the legitimate financial interests of the divesting parties, subject to its unconditional obligation to divest at no minimum price. The Divestiture Trustee must report regularly on the progress of the divestiture process.

32. Also in Section E (paragraphs 26–30), the <u>duties and obligations of the Parties vis-à-vis the Trustee are</u> defined. Beside the provision of information, the Parties are in particular obliged to provide the Monitoring Trustee with all managerial and administrative support necessary for the Divestment Business and to grant to the Divestiture Trustee comprehensive powers of attorney covering all steps of the sale of the Divestment Business. An indemnification clause is included in order to reinforce the independent status of the Trustee from the Parties. Such a clause is already common practice in the trustee mandates submitted to the Commission for approval. The Trustee may further, at the expense of the Parties, retain advisors with specialised skills, in particular for corporate finance or legal advice.

33. Section E further foresees that trustees may only be removed in exceptional circumstances and with the approval of the Commission before the complete implementation of the Commitments.

34. <u>Section F</u> contains a <u>review clause</u>, which allows the Commission to extend the periods specified in the Commitments and to waive or modify the undertakings in the Commitments. The Parties must show good cause in order to be able to benefit from the exercise of the review clause. Requests for the extension of time periods shall, normally, be submitted no later than one month before the expiry of the time period in question.

Standard Model for Trustee Mandates

35. The <u>Standard Model for Trustee Mandates</u> sets out the duties and responsibilities of both Monitoring and Divestiture Trustee in a single text. However, the language makes clear that the Commission does not have a preference for the appointment of a single person to serve in the dual role of both Monitoring and Divestiture Trustee. Rather, the decision as to whether one or more trustees are appointed should be determined on a case-by-case basis by the Parties. If more than one trustee shall serve in these roles, only the provisions relevant for the Monitoring or Divestiture Trustee, respectively, have to be included in the individual mandate.

36. The Standard Trustee Mandate consists of the <u>following main elements</u>:

37. <u>Section A</u> contains <u>some definitions</u> and references the definitions included in the Standard Commitments.

38. <u>Sections B to G</u> contain provisions regarding the appointment of the Trustee (Section B), its general duties (Section C), the specific duties and obligations of the Monitoring and Divestiture Trustees (Sections D and E), reporting obligations identifying certain important subjects that should be discussed in each report (Section G), and duties and obligations of the Parties vis-à-vis the Trustee (Section F). These arrangements are based on the provisions established in the Standard Commitments in relation to the Trustee and described above.

39. <u>Sections H to J</u> cover additional trustee-related provisions, including provisions regarding the remuneration of the Trustee(s), procedures concerning the termination of the Mandate, and certain additional provisions, such as determination of applicable national law.

40. In particular, the independence of the trustee and the absence of <u>conflicts of interests of the trustee</u> are of great importance for the Commission in deciding on the approval of the Trustee and the respective mandate. The provisions in the Standard Trustee Mandate (paragraphs 20 to 23) ensuring the independence of the trustee from the parties and the absence of conflicts of interest foresee the following procedure: (1) The Trustee must disclose all current relationships with the Parties (paragraph 20) at the time at which the Trustee Mandate is entered into. (2) During the term of the mandate, the Trustee undertakes not to create a conflict of interest by having or accepting employment or appointment as a Member of the Board of the Parties or by having or accepting any assignments or other business relationships with, or financial interests in, the Parties. (3) As legal consequences it is foreseen that, if the Trustee becomes aware of a conflict of interest during the Mandate, the Trustee must notify the Commission and resolve the problem immediately and, if the conflict of interest cannot subsequently be resolved, the Commission

may require the termination of the trustee mandate. These rules concerning conflicts of interests apply to the Trustee itself, members of the Trustee Team and the Trustee Partner Firms as members of the same organisation. (4) For a period of one year following termination of the Mandate, the members of the Trustee Team shall not provide services to the Parties without the Commission's prior approval and must establish measures to ensure the integrity of the members of the Trustee Team.

41. In addition to the rules laid down in the Standard Trustee Mandate, it is up to the Parties and the Trustee to include provisions dealing with other potential conflicts of interests, such as conflicts of interests of the Trustee with potential purchasers.

MODEL TEXTS FOR DIVESTITURE COMMITMENTS

Note

The following texts are published on the Europa website at:
http://ec.europa.eu/comm/competition/mergers/legislation/commitments.pdf
All square brackets in the following document are original and not editorial.

By hand and by fax: 00 32 2 296 4301
European Commission — Merger Task Force
DG Competition
Rue Joseph II 70 Jozef-II straat
B-1000 BRUSSELS

Case M. [*No . . .*] — [*Title . . .*]

Commitments To The European Commission

Pursuant to [Article 6(2), *if Phase I Commitments*] [Article 8(2), *if Phase II Commitments*] [Articles 8(2) and 10(2), *if in Phase II Commitments prior to the sending out of the Statement of Objections*] of Council Regulation (EEC) No. 4064/89 as amended (the "*Merger Regulation*"), [*Indicate the name of the Undertakings offering the Commitments*] (the "*Parties*") hereby provide the following Commitments (the "*Commitments*") in order to enable the European Commission (the "*Commission*") to declare [*Description of the operation: e.g. the acquisition of . . .; the creation of a full-function joint venture between . . .*] compatible with the common market and the EEA Agreement by its decision pursuant to [Article 6(1)(b) of the Merger Regulation, *if Phase I Commitments*] [Article 8(2), *if Phase II Commitments*] of the Merger Regulation (the "*Decision*").

The Commitments shall take effect upon the date of adoption of the Decision.

This text shall be interpreted in the light of the Decision to the extent that the Commitments are attached as conditions and obligations, in the general framework of Community law, in particular in the light of the Merger Regulation, and by reference to the Commission Notice on remedies acceptable under Council Regulation (EEC) No 4064/89 and under Commission Regulation (EC) No 447/98.

Section A. Definitions

For the purpose of the Commitments, the following terms shall have the following meaning:

Affiliated Undertakings: undertakings controlled by the Parties and/or by the ultimate parents of the Parties, including the JV [*Only in the case when the proposed operation is a creation of a JV*], whereby the notion of control shall be interpreted pursuant to Article 3 Merger Regulation and in the light of the Commission Notice on the concept of concentration under Council Regulation (EEC) No 4064/89.

Closing: the transfer of the legal title of the Divestment Business to the Purchaser.

Divestment Business: the business or businesses as defined in Section B and the Schedule that the Parties commit to divest.

Divestiture Trustee: one or more natural or legal person(s), independent from the Parties, who is approved by the Commission and appointed by [*X*] and who has received from [*X*] the exclusive Trustee Mandate to sell the Divestment Business to a Purchaser at no minimum price.

Effective Date: the date of adoption of the Decision.

First Divestiture Period: the period of [•] months from the Effective Date.

Hold Separate Manager: the person appointed by [*X*] for the Divestment Business to manage the day-to-day business under the supervision of the Monitoring Trustee.

Key Personnel: all personnel necessary to maintain the viability and competitiveness of the Divestment Business, as listed in the Schedule.

Monitoring Trustee: one or more natural or legal person(s), independent from the Parties, who is approved by the Commission and appointed by [*X*], and who has the duty to monitor [*X*'s] compliance with the conditions and obligations attached to the Decision.

Personnel: all personnel currently employed by the Divestment Business, including Key Personnel, staff seconded to the Divestment Business, shared personnel and the additional personnel listed in the Schedule.

Purchaser: the entity approved by the Commission as acquirer of the Divestment Business in accordance with the criteria set out in Section D.

Trustee(s): the Monitoring Trustee and the Divestiture Trustee.

Trustee Divestiture Period: the period of [•] months from the end of the First Divestiture Period.

[*X*]: [*Indicate the short name of the Undertaking Concerned that will divest its business/es*], incorporated under the laws of [•], with its registered office at [•] and registered with the Commercial/Company Register at [•] under number [•].

Section B. The Divestment Business

<u>Commitment to divest</u>

1. In order to restore effective competition, [*X*] commits to divest, or procure the divestiture of the Divestment Business by the end of the Trustee Divestiture Period as a going concern to a purchaser and on terms of sale approved by the Commission in accordance with the procedure described in paragraph 15. To carry out the divestiture, [*X*] commits to find a purchaser and to enter into a final binding sale and purchase agreement for the sale of the Divestment Business within the First Divestiture Period. If [*X*] has not entered into such an agreement at the end of the First Divestiture Period, [*X*] shall grant the Divestiture Trustee an exclusive mandate to sell the Divestment Business in accordance with the procedure described in paragraph 24 in the Trustee Divestiture Period. [*The following sentence should be inserted in case of an "up-front buyer"*: The proposed concentration shall not be implemented unless and until [*X*] or the Divestiture Trustee has entered into a final binding sale and purchase agreement for the sale of the Divestment Business and the Commission has approved the purchaser and the terms of sale in accordance with paragraph 15].

2. [*X*] shall be deemed to have complied with this commitment if, by the end of the Trustee Divestiture Period, [*X*] has entered into a final binding sale and purchase agreement, if the Commission approves the Purchaser and the terms in accordance with the procedure described in paragraph 15 and if the closing of the sale of the Divestment Business takes place within a period not exceeding 3 months after the approval of the purchaser and the terms of sale by the Commission.

3. In order to maintain the structural effect of the Commitments, the Parties shall, for a period of 10 years after the Effective Date, not acquire direct or indirect influence over the whole or part of the Divestment Business, unless the Commission has previously found that the structure of the market has changed to such an extent that the absence of influence over the Divestment Business is no longer necessary to render the proposed concentration compatible with the common market.

<u>Structure and definition of the Divestment Business</u>

4. The Divestment Business consists of [*Provide a summary description of the Divestment Business*]. The present legal and functional structure of the Divestment Business as operated to date is described in the Schedule. The Divestment Business, described in more detail in the Schedule, includes

   (a) all tangible and intangible assets (including intellectual property rights), which contribute to the current operation or are necessary to ensure the viability and competitiveness of the Divestment Business;

   (b) all licences, permits and authorisations issued by any governmental organisation for the benefit of the Divestment Business;

   (c) all contracts, leases, commitments and customer orders of the Divestment Business; all customer, credit and other records of the Divestment Business (items referred to under (a)-(c) hereinafter collectively referred to as "*Assets*");

   (d) the Personnel; and

   (e) [*To be included in cases in which the Divestment Business needs an on-going relationship with the Parties in order to be fully competitive and viable:* the benefit, for a transitional period of up to [*insert*] years after Closing and on terms and conditions equivalent to those at present afforded to the Divestment Business, of all current arrangements under which [X] or Affiliated Undertakings supply products or services to the Divestment Business, as detailed in the Schedule, unless otherwise agreed with the Purchaser.]

Section C. Related commitments

<u>Preservation of Viability, Marketability and Competitiveness</u>

5. From the Effective Date until Closing, [X] shall preserve the economic viability, marketability and competitiveness of the Divestment Business, in accordance with good business practice, and shall minimise as far as possible any risk of loss of competitive potential of the Divestment Business. In particular [X] undertakes:

   (a) not to carry out any act upon its own authority that might have a significant adverse impact on the value, management or competitiveness of the Divestment Business or that might alter the nature and scope of activity, or the industrial or commercial strategy or the investment policy of the Divestment Business;

   (b) to make available sufficient resources for the development of the Divestment Business, on the basis and continuation of the existing business plans;

   (c) to take all reasonable steps, including appropriate incentive schemes (based on industry practice), to encourage all Key Personnel to remain with the Divestment Business.

<u>Hold-separate obligations of Parties</u>

6. [X] commits, from the Effective Date until Closing, to keep the Divestment Business separate from the businesses it is retaining and to ensure that Key Personnel of the Divestment Business – including the Hold Separate Manager – have no involvement in any business retained and vice versa. [X] shall also ensure that the Personnel does not report to any individual outside the Divestment Business.

7. Until Closing, [X] shall assist the Monitoring Trustee in ensuring that the Divestment Business is managed as a distinct and saleable entity separate from the businesses retained by the Parties. [X] shall appoint a Hold Separate Manager who shall be responsible for the management of the Divestment Business, under the supervision of the Monitoring Trustee. The Hold Separate Manager shall manage the Divestment Business independently and in the best interest of the business with a view to ensuring its continued economic viability, marketability and competitiveness and its independence from the businesses retained by the Parties.

8. [*The following is to be inserted in cases in which a company or a share in a company is to be divested and a strict separation of the corporate structure is necessary:* To ensure that the Divestment Business is held and managed as a separate entity the Monitoring Trustee shall exercise [X's] rights as shareholder in the Divestment Business (except for its rights for dividends that are due before Closing), with the aim of acting in the best interest of the business, determined on a stand-alone basis, as an

independent financial investor, and with a view to fulfilling [*X*'s] obligations under the Commitments. Furthermore, the Monitoring Trustee shall have the power to replace members of the supervisory board or non-executive directors of the board of directors, who have been appointed on behalf of [*X*]. Upon request of the Monitoring Trustee, [*X*] shall resign as member of the boards or shall cause such members of the boards to resign.]

Ring-fencing

9. [*X*] shall implement all necessary measures to ensure that it does not after the Effective Date obtain any business secrets, know-how, commercial information, or any other information of a confidential or proprietary nature relating to the Divestment Business. In particular, the participation of the Divestment Business in a central information technology network shall be severed to the extent possible, without compromising the viability of the Divestment Business. [*X*] may obtain information relating to the Divestment Business which is reasonably necessary for the divestiture of the Divestment Business or whose disclosure to [*X*] is required by law.

Non-solicitation clause

10. The Parties undertake, subject to customary limitations, not to solicit, and to procure that Affiliated Undertakings do not solicit, the Key Personnel transferred with the Divestment Business for a period of [●] after Closing.

Due Diligence

11. In order to enable potential purchasers to carry out a reasonable due diligence of the Divestment Business, [*X*] shall, subject to customary confidentiality assurances and dependent on the stage of the divestiture process:
    (a) provide to potential purchasers sufficient information as regards the Divestment Business;
    (b) provide to potential purchasers sufficient information relating to the Personnel and allow them reasonable access to the Personnel.

Reporting

12. [*X*] shall submit written reports in [*Indicate the language of the procedure or another language agreed with the Commission*] on potential purchasers of the Divestment Business and developments in the negotiations with such potential purchasers to the Commission and the Monitoring Trustee no later than 10 days after the end of every month following the Effective Date (or otherwise at the Commission's request).

13. The Parties shall inform the Commission and the Monitoring Trustee on the preparation of the data room documentation and the due diligence procedure and shall submit a copy of an information memorandum to the Commission and the Monitoring Trustee before sending the memorandum out to potential purchasers.

Section D. The Purchaser

14. In order to ensure the immediate restoration of effective competition, the Purchaser, in order to be approved by the Commission, must:
    (a) be independent of and unconnected to the Parties;
    (b) have the financial resources, proven expertise and incentive to maintain and develop the Divestment Business as a viable and active competitive force in competition with the Parties and other competitors;
    (c) neither be likely to create, in the light of the information available to the Commission, *prima facie* competition concerns nor give rise to a risk that the implementation of the Commitments will be delayed, and must, in particular, reasonably be expected to obtain all necessary approvals from the relevant regulatory authorities for the acquisition of the Divestment Business (the before-mentioned criteria for the purchaser hereafter the "*Purchaser Requirements*").

15. The final binding sale and purchase agreement shall be conditional on the Commission's approval. When [*X*] has reached an agreement with a purchaser, it shall submit a fully documented and reasoned proposal, including a copy of the final agreement(s), to the Commission and the Monitoring Trustee. [*X*] must be able to demonstrate to the Commission that the purchaser meets the Purchaser Requirements and that the Divestment Business is being sold in a

manner consistent with the Commitments. For the approval, the Commission shall verify that the purchaser fulfils the Purchaser Requirements and that the Divestment Business is being sold in a manner consistent with the Commitments. The Commission may approve the sale of the Divestment Business without one or more Assets or parts of the Personnel, if this does not affect the viability and competitiveness of the Divestment Business after the sale, taking account of the proposed purchaser.

Section E. Trustee

I. Appointment Procedure

16. [*X*] shall appoint a Monitoring Trustee to carry out the functions specified in the Commitments for a Monitoring Trustee. If [*X*] has not entered into a binding sales and purchase agreement one month before the end of the First Divestiture Period or if the Commission has rejected a purchaser proposed by [*X*] at that time or thereafter, [*X*] shall appoint a Divestiture Trustee to carry out the functions specified in the Commitments for a Divestiture Trustee. The appointment of the Divestiture Trustee shall take effect upon the commencement of the Extended Divestment Period.

17. The Trustee shall be independent of the Parties, possess the necessary qualifications to carry out its mandate, for example as an investment bank or consultant or auditor, and shall neither have nor become exposed to a conflict of interest. The Trustee shall be remunerated by the Parties in a way that does not impede the independent and effective fulfilment of its mandate. In particular, where the remuneration package of a Divestiture Trustee includes a success premium linked to the final sale value of the Divestment Business, the fee shall also be linked to a divestiture within the Trustee Divestiture Period.

Proposal by the Parties

18. No later than one week after the Effective Date, [*X*] shall submit a list of one or more persons whom [*X*] proposes to appoint as the Monitoring Trustee to the Commission for approval. No later than one month before the end of the First Divestiture Period, [*X*] shall submit a list of one or more persons whom [*X*] proposes to appoint as Divestiture Trustee to the Commission for approval. The proposal shall contain sufficient information for the Commission to verify that the proposed Trustee fulfils the requirements set out in paragraph 17 and shall include:
    (a) the full terms of the proposed mandate, which shall include all provisions necessary to enable the Trustee to fulfil its duties under these Commitments;
    (b) the outline of a work plan which describes how the Trustee intends to carry out its assigned tasks;
    (c) an indication whether the proposed Trustee is to act as both Monitoring Trustee and Divestiture Trustee or whether different trustees are proposed for the two functions.

Approval or rejection by the Commission

19. The Commission shall have the discretion to approve or reject the proposed Trustee(s) and to approve the proposed mandate subject to any modifications it deems necessary for the Trustee to fulfil its obligations. If only one name is approved, [*X*] shall appoint or cause to be appointed, the individual or institution concerned as Trustee, in accordance with the mandate approved by the Commission. If more than one name is approved, [*X*] shall be free to choose the Trustee to be appointed from among the names approved. The Trustee shall be appointed within one week of the Commission's approval, in accordance with the mandate approved by the Commission.

New proposal by the Parties

20. If all the proposed Trustees are rejected, [*X*] shall submit the names of at least two more individuals or institutions within one week of being informed of the rejection, in accordance with the requirements and the procedure set out in paragraphs 16 and 19.

Trustee nominated by the Commission

21. If all further proposed Trustees are rejected by the Commission, the Commission shall nominate a Trustee, whom [*X*] shall appoint, or cause to be appointed, in accordance with a trustee mandate approved by the Commission.

II. <u>Functions of the Trustee</u>

22. The Trustee shall assume its specified duties in order to ensure compliance with the Commitments. The Commission may, on its own initiative or at the request of the Trustee or [X], give any orders or instructions to the Trustee in order to ensure compliance with the conditions and obligations attached to the Decision.

Duties and obligations of the Monitoring Trustee

23. The Monitoring Trustee shall:
    (i) propose in its first report to the Commission a detailed work plan describing how it intends to monitor compliance with the obligations and conditions attached to the Decision.
    (ii) oversee the on-going management of the Divestment Business with a view to ensuring its continued economic viability, marketability and competitiveness and monitor compliance by [X] with the conditions and obligations attached to the Decision. To that end the Monitoring Trustee shall:
        (a) monitor the preservation of the economic viability, marketability and competitiveness of the Divestment Business, and the keeping separate of the Divestment Business from the business retained by the Parties, in accordance with paragraphs 5 and 6 of the Commitments;
        (b) supervise the management of the Divestment Business as a distinct and saleable entity, in accordance with paragraph 7 of the Commitments;
        (c) (i) in consultation with [X], determine all necessary measures to ensure that [X] does not after the effective date obtain any business secrets, knowhow, commercial information, or any other information of a confidential or proprietary nature relating to the Divestment Business, in particular strive for the severing of the Divestment Business' participation in a central information technology network to the extent possible, without compromising the viability of the Divestment Business, and (ii) decide whether such information may be disclosed to [X] as the disclosure is reasonably necessary to allow [X] to carry out the divestiture or as the disclosure is required by law;
        (d) monitor the splitting of assets and the allocation of Personnel between the Divestment Business and [X] or Affiliated Undertakings;
    (iii) assume the other functions assigned to the Monitoring Trustee under the conditions and obligations attached to the Decision;
    (iv) propose to [X] such measures as the Monitoring Trustee considers necessary to ensure [X]'s compliance with the conditions and obligations attached to the Decision, in particular the maintenance of the full economic viability, marketability or competitiveness of the Divestment Business, the holding separate of the Divestment Business and the non-disclosure of competitively sensitive information;
    (v) review and assess potential purchasers as well as the progress of the divestiture process and verify that, dependent on the stage of the divestiture process, (a) potential purchasers receive sufficient information relating to the Divestment Business and the Personnel in particular by reviewing, if available, the data room documentation, the information memorandum and the due diligence process, and (b) potential purchasers are granted reasonable access to the Personnel;
    (vi) provide to the Commission, sending [X] a non-confidential copy at the same time, a written report within 15 days after the end of every month. The report shall cover the operation and management of the Divestment Business so that the Commission can assess whether the business is held in a manner consistent with the Commitments and the progress of the divestiture process as well as potential purchasers. In addition to these reports, the Monitoring Trustee shall promptly report in writing to the Commission, sending [X] a non-confidential copy at the same time, if it concludes on reasonable grounds that [X] is failing to comply with these Commitments;
    (vii) within one week after receipt of the documented proposal referred to in paragraph 15, submit to the Commission a reasoned opinion as to the suitability and independence of the proposed purchaser and the viability of the Divestment Business after the Sale and as to whether the Divestment Business is sold in a manner consistent with the conditions and

obligations attached to the Decision, in particular, if relevant, whether the Sale of the Divestment Business without one or more Assets or not all of the Personnel affects the viability of the Divestment Business after the sale, taking account of the proposed purchaser.

Duties and obligations of the Divestiture Trustee

24. Within the Trustee Divestiture Period, the Divestiture Trustee shall sell at no minimum price the Divestment Business to a purchaser, provided that the Commission has approved both the purchaser and the final binding sale and purchase agreement in accordance with the procedure laid down in paragraph 15. The Divestiture Trustee shall include in the sale and purchase agreement such terms and conditions as it considers appropriate for an expedient sale in the Trustee Divestiture Period. In particular, the Divestiture Trustee may include in the sale and purchase agreement such customary representations and warranties and indemnities as are reasonably required to effect the sale. The Divestiture Trustee shall protect the legitimate financial interests of [X], subject to the Parties' unconditional obligation to divest at no minimum price in the Trustee Divestiture Period.

25. In the Trustee Divestiture Period (or otherwise at the Commission's request), the Divestiture Trustee shall provide the Commission with a comprehensive monthly report written in [*Please indicate the language of the procedure or a different language agreed with the Commission*] on the progress of the divestiture process. Such reports shall be submitted within 15 days after the end of every month with a simultaneous copy to the Monitoring Trustee and a non-confidential copy to the Parties.

III. Duties and obligations of the Parties

26. [X] shall provide and shall cause its advisors to provide the Trustee with all such cooperation, assistance and information as the Trustee may reasonably require to perform its tasks. The Trustee shall have full and complete access to any of [X's] or the Divestment Business' books, records, documents, management or other personnel, facilities, sites and technical information necessary for fulfilling its duties under the Commitments and [X] and the Divestment Business shall provide the Trustee upon request with copies of any document. [X] and the Divestment Business shall make available to the Trustee one or more offices on their premises and shall be available for meetings in order to provide the Trustee with all information necessary for the performance of its tasks.

27. [X] shall provide the Monitoring Trustee with all managerial and administrative support that it may reasonably request on behalf of the management of the Divestment Business. This shall include all administrative support functions relating to the Divestment Business which are currently carried out at headquarters level. [X] shall provide and shall cause its advisors to provide the Monitoring Trustee, on request, with the information submitted to potential purchasers, in particular give the Monitoring Trustee access to the data room documentation and all other information granted to potential purchasers in the due diligence procedure. [X] shall inform the Monitoring Trustee on possible purchasers, submit a list of potential purchasers, and keep the Monitoring Trustee informed of all developments in the divestiture process.

28. [X] shall grant or procure Affiliated Undertakings to grant comprehensive powers of attorney, duly executed, to the Divestiture Trustee to effect the sale, the Closing and all actions and declarations which the Divestiture Trustee considers necessary or appropriate to achieve the sale and the Closing, including the appointment of advisors to assist with the sale process. Upon request of the Divestiture Trustee, [X] shall cause the documents required for effecting the sale and the Closing to be duly executed.

29. [X] shall indemnify the Trustee and its employees and agents (each an "*Indemnified Party*") and hold each Indemnified Party harmless against, and hereby agrees that an Indemnified Party shall have no liability to [X] for any liabilities arising out of the performance of the Trustee's duties under the Commitments, except to the extent that such liabilities result from the wilful default, recklessness, gross negligence or bad faith of the Trustee, its employees, agents or advisors.

30. At the expense of [X], the Trustee may appoint advisors (in particular for corporate finance or legal advice), subject to [X's] approval (this approval not to be unreasonably withheld or delayed) if the Trustee considers the appointment of such advisors necessary or appropriate for the performance of its duties and obligations under the Mandate, provided that any fees and

other expenses incurred by the Trustee are reasonable. Should [X] refuse to approve the advisors proposed by the Trustee the Commission may approve the appointment of such advisors instead, after having heard [X]. Only the Trustee shall be entitled to issue instructions to the advisors. Paragraph 29 shall apply mutatis mutandis. In the Trustee Divestiture Period, the Divestiture Trustee may use advisors who served [X] during the Divestiture Period if the Divestiture Trustee considers this in the best interest of an expedient sale.

IV. Replacement, discharge and reappointment of the Trustee

31. If the Trustee ceases to perform its functions under the Commitments or for any other good cause, including the exposure of the Trustee to a conflict of interest:
   (a) the Commission may, after hearing the Trustee, require [X] to replace the Trustee; or
   (b) [X], with the prior approval of the Commission, may replace the Trustee.

32. If the Trustee is removed according to paragraph 31, the Trustee may be required to continue in its function until a new Trustee is in place to whom the Trustee has effected a full hand over of all relevant information. The new Trustee shall be appointed in accordance with the procedure referred to in paragraphs 16–21.

33. Beside the removal according to paragraph 31, the Trustee shall cease to act as Trustee only after the Commission has discharged it from its duties after all the Commitments with which the Trustee has been entrusted have been implemented. However, the Commission may at any time require the reappointment of the Monitoring Trustee if it subsequently appears that the relevant remedies might not have been fully and properly implemented.

Section F. The Review Clause

34. The Commission may, where appropriate, in response to a request from [X] showing good cause and accompanied by a report from the Monitoring Trustee:
   (i) Grant an extension of the time periods foreseen in the Commitments, or
   (ii) Waive, modify or substitute, in exceptional circumstances, one or more of the undertakings in these Commitments.

   Where [X] seeks an extension of a time period, it shall submit a request to the Commission no later than one month before the expiry of that period, showing good cause. Only in exceptional circumstances shall [X] be entitled to request an extension within the last month of any period.

....

duly authorised for and on behalf of

[*Indicate the name of each of the Parties*]

SCHEDULE

1. The Divestment Business as operated to date has the following legal and functional structure: [*Describe the legal and functional structure of the Divestment Business, including the organisational chart*].

2. Following paragraph [4] of these Commitments, the Divestment Business includes, but is not limited to:
   (a) the following main tangible assets: [*Indicate the essential tangible assets, e.g. xyz factory/warehouse/pipelines located at abc and the real estate/property on which the factory/warehouse is located; the R&D facilities*];
   (b) the following main intangible assets: [*Indicate the main intangible assets. This should in particular include (i) the brand names and (ii) all other Intellectual Property Rights used in conducting the Divestment Business.*];
   (c) the following main licences, permits and authorisations: [*Indicate the main licences, permits and authorisations*];
   (d) the following main contracts, agreements, leases, commitments and understandings [*Indicate the main contracts, etc.*];
   (e) the following customer, credit and other records: [*Indicate the main customer, credit and other records, according to further sector specific indications, where appropriate*];

(f) the following Personnel: [*Indicate the personnel to be transferred in general, including personnel providing essential functions for the Divestment Business, such as central R&D staff*];

(g) the following Key Personnel: [*Indicate the names and functions of the Key Personnel, including the Hold Separate Manager, where appropriate*]; and

(h) the arrangements for the supply with the following products or services by [X] or Affiliated Undertakings for a transitional period of up to [•] after Closing: [*Indicate the products or services to be provided for a transitional period in order to maintain the economic viability and competitiveness of the Divestment Business*].

3. The Divestment Business shall not include:

(i) . . .;

(ii) [*It is the responsibility of the Parties to indicate clearly what the Divestment Business will not encompass*].

MODELS TEXTS FOR TRUSTEE MANDATES

Note

The following texts are published on the Europa website at:
http://ec.europa.eu/comm/competition/mergers/legislation/trustee_mandate.pdf
All square brackets in the following document are original and not editorial.

TRUSTEE MANDATE

BETWEEN:

1. [X] [*Indicate a short name(s) of the Undertaking(s) Concerned that will divest its/their businesses*] (hereafter [X]), a company organised under the laws of [*Indicate law of origin*], which has its registered seat at [*Indicate complete address*], represented by [*Indicate name and title of individual representing X for the Mandate*],

AND

2. [*Insert name, address, and, as the case may be, company details of the Trustee*], (the "*Trustee*").

[X] and the Trustee are hereafter referred to as the "*Mandate Parties*".

WHEREAS

In [*Indicate full case name and number*] and pursuant to [*Article 6(2)/Article 8(2)*] of Council Regulation (EEC) No. 4064/89 as amended (the "*Merger Regulation*"), [X] offered commitments (the "*Commitments*"), attached hereto as Annex 1, in order to enable the European Commission (the "*Commission*") to declare [*Description of the operation: e.g. the acquisition of . . .; the creation of a full-function joint venture between . . .*] compatible with the common market and the functioning of the EEA Agreement. The Commission approved the operation by its decision pursuant to [*Article 6(1)(b)/Article 8(2)*] of the Merger Regulation (the "*Decision*"), subject to full compliance with the conditions and obligations attached to the Decision (the " *Conditions and Obligations*").

According to the Conditions and Obligations, [X] undertakes to divest the [*Indicate the business to be divested*] and, in the meantime, to preserve the economic viability, marketability and competitiveness of this business. Therefore, [X] undertakes to appoint a Monitoring Trustee for the monitoring of the hold separate obligations and of the divestiture procedure, and to appoint a Divestiture Trustee for the divestiture of the said business if [X] has not succeeded in divesting it during the First Divestiture Period. In accordance with the Conditions and Obligations, [X] hereby engages the Trustee and this agreement forms the mandate referred to in the Commitments (hereafter the "*Mandate*").

The appointment of the Trustee and the terms of this Mandate were approved by the Commission on [*Indicate date of approval letter*].

In case of doubt or conflict, this Mandate shall be interpreted in the light of (1) the Conditions and Obligations and the Decision, (2) the general framework of Community law, in particular in the light of the Merger Regulation, and (3) the Commission Notice on remedies acceptable under Council Regulation (EEC) No 4064/89 and under Commission Regulation (EC) No 447/98.

IT HAS BEEN AGREED AS FOLLOWS:

Section A. Definitions

Terms used in this Mandate shall have the meaning set out in Section 1 of the Commitments. For the purpose of this Mandate, the following terms shall have the following meaning:

Sale: the entering into a binding sale and purchase agreement for the selling of the Divestment Business to the Purchaser.

Trustee Partner Firms: the other firms belonging to the same organisation of individual partnerships and companies as the Trustee.

Trustee Team: The key persons responsible for carrying out the tasks assigned by the Mandate and identified in paragraph [3] below of the Mandate.

Work-Plan: the outline of the work-plan submitted to the Commission by the Trustee before the approval of the Trustee and attached hereto as Annex [●], a more detailed version of which will be prepared by the Trustee and submitted to the Commission in its first report.

Section B. Appointment of Trustee

1. [X] hereby appoints the Trustee to act as its exclusive trustee for fulfilling the tasks of a [Monitoring Trustee and/or Divestiture Trustee] according to the Conditions and Obligations and the Trustee hereby accepts the said appointment in accordance with the terms of this Mandate.
2. The appointment and this Mandate shall become effective on the date hereof except for the provisions specifically addressing the duties and obligations of the Divestiture Trustee which shall become effective with the beginning of the Trustee Divestiture Period.
3. The Trustee Team consists of the following key persons: [*Indicate name and title of each of the key persons (partners/leading persons)*]. The Trustee shall not replace the persons of the Trustee Team without prior approval of the Commission and [X].

Section C. General Duties and Obligations of the Trustee

4. The Trustee shall act on behalf of the Commission to ensure [X's] compliance with the Conditions and Obligations and assume the duties specified in the Conditions and Obligations for a [*Monitoring and/or Divestiture Trustee*]. The Trustee shall carry out the duties under this Mandate in accordance with the Work-Plan as well as revisions of the Work-Plan, approved by the Commission. The Commission may, on its own initiative or at the request of the Trustee or [X], give any orders or instructions to the Trustee in order to ensure compliance with the Conditions and Obligations. [X] is not entitled to give instructions to the Trustee.
5. The Trustee shall propose to [X] such measures as the Trustee considers necessary to ensure [X's] compliance with the Commitments and/or the Mandate, and the Trustee shall propose necessary measures to the Commission in the event that [X] does not comply with the Trustee's proposals within the timeframe set by the Trustee.

Section D. Duties and Obligations of the Monitoring Trustee

Monitoring and Management of the Divestment Business

6. The Monitoring Trustee shall, in conformity with the Conditions and Obligations, oversee the on-going management of the Divestment Business with a view to ensuring its continued economic viability, marketability and competitiveness and monitor the compliance of [X] with the Conditions and Obligations. To that end, the Monitoring Trustee shall until Closing in particular:
   (a) monitor (i) the preservation of the economic viability, marketability and competitiveness of the Divestment Business in accordance with good business practice, (ii) the minimisation, as far as possible, of any risk of loss of competitive potential of the Divestment Business; (iii) the not carrying out by [X] or Affiliated Undertakings of any act on its own authority that might have a significant adverse impact on the value, management or competitiveness of the Divestment Business or that might to alter the nature and scope of activity, or the industrial or commercial strategy or the investment policy of the Divestment Business; and (iv) the making available by [X] of sufficient resources for the Divestment Business to develop, based on the existing business plans and their continuation, and (v) the taking of all reasonable steps by [X],

including appropriate incentive schemes (based on business practice), to encourage all Key Personnel to remain with the Divestment Business;

(b) monitor (i) the holding separate of the Divestment Business from the businesses retained by [X] and Affiliated Undertakings, (ii) the absence of involvement of Key Employees of the Divestment Business — including the Hold Separate Manager — in any business retained and vice versa, and (iii) the absence of reporting of the Personnel of the Divestment Business to any individual outside the Divestment Business, except where permitted in the Commitments;

(c) seek to ensure that the Divestment Business is managed as a distinct and saleable entity separate from [X's] or Affiliated Undertakings' businesses and that the Hold Separate Manager manages the Divestment Business independently and in the best interest of the business and ensuring its continued economic viability, marketability and competitiveness as well as its independence from the businesses retained by the Parties;

[(d) *the following paragraph to be inserted in cases in which the Commitments foresee the voting of shares by the Monitoring Trustee and/or the replacement of member of the supervisory board/board of directors*: exercise [X's] rights as shareholder in the Divestment Business (except for its rights for dividends that are due before Closing), with the aim of acting in the best interest of the business, determined on a stand-alone basis, as an independent financial investor, and with a view to fulfilling [X's] obligation under the Conditions and Obligations. Consequently, [X] grants a comprehensive and duly executed proxy to the Monitoring Trustee in Annex [●] for the exercise of the voting rights attached to [X's] shares in the Divestment Business. The Monitoring Trustee shall have the power to replace members of the supervisory board or non-executive directors of the board of directors of the Divestment Business, who have been appointed on behalf of [X]. Upon request of the Monitoring Trustee, [X] shall resign as a member of the boards or shall cause such members of the boards to resign. The representatives of the Monitoring Trustee to be appointed to the board shall be one or more persons of the Trustee Team. In the event that appointments outside these named individuals are envisaged the prior approval of the Commission is required;]

(e) monitor the splitting of assets and the allocation of Personnel between the Divestment Business and [X] or Affiliated Undertakings;

(f) (i) in consultation with [X], determine all necessary measures to ensure that [X] does not after the Effective Date obtain any business secrets, know-how, commercial information, or any other information of a confidential or proprietary nature relating to the Divestment Business, in particular strive for the severing of the Divestment Business' participation in a central information technology network to the extent possible, without compromising the viability of the Divestment Business, and (ii) decide whether such information may be disclosed to [X] as the disclosure is reasonably necessary to allow [X] to carry out the divestiture or as the disclosure is required by law.

Monitoring of Divestiture

7. Until the end of the First Divestiture Period, the Monitoring Trustee shall assist the Commission in reviewing the divestiture process and assessing proposed purchasers. Therefore the Monitoring Trustee shall during the First Divestiture Period:

(a) review and assess the progress of the divestiture process and potential purchasers;

(b) verify that, dependent on the stage of the divestiture process, (i) potential purchasers receive sufficient information relating to the Divestment Business and the Personnel, in particular by reviewing, if available, the data room documentation, the information memorandum and the due diligence process, and (ii) potential purchasers are granted reasonable access to the Personnel;

8. Once [X] has submitted to the Commission a proposal for a purchaser, the Trustee shall, within one week after receipt of the documented proposal by the Parties, submit to the Commission a reasoned opinion as to the suitability and independence of the proposed purchaser and the viability of the Divestment Business after the Sale and as to whether the Divestment Business is sold in a manner consistent with the Conditions and Obligations, in particular, if relevant, whether the Sale of the Divestment Business without one or more Assets or not all of the Personnel affects the viability of the Divestment Business after the Sale, taking account of the proposed purchaser.

Section E. Duties and Obligations of the Divestiture Trustee

9. With the commencement of the Trustee Divestiture Period, [X] hereby gives the Trustee an exclusive mandate to sell the Divestment Business to a purchaser according to the provisions of this section of the Mandate and the Commitments.

10. The purchaser shall fulfil the Purchaser Requirements and both the purchaser and the final sale and purchase agreement shall be approved by the Commission in accordance with the procedure laid down in paragraph [15] of the Commitments.

11. The Divestiture Trustee shall sell the Divestment Business at no minimum price and at such terms and conditions as it considers appropriate for an expedient sale in the Trustee Divestiture Period. In particular, the Divestiture Trustee may include in the sale and purchase agreement such customary representations and warranties and indemnities as are reasonably required to effect the Sale. At the same time, the Divestiture Trustee shall protect the legitimate financial interests of [X], subject to the Parties' unconditional obligation to divest at no minimum price in the Trustee Divestiture Period.

12. [X] grants a comprehensive and duly executed power of attorney to the Divestiture Trustee in Annex [•] to effect the Sale of the Divestment Business, the Closing and all actions and declarations which the Trustee considers necessary or appropriate for achieving the Sale of the Divestment Business or the Closing, including the power to appoint advisors to assist with the sale process. The power of attorney shall include the authority to grant sub-powers of attorney to members of the Trustee Team. If necessary to accomplish the Sale, [X] shall grant the Divestiture Trustee further powers of attorney, duly executed, or cause the documents required for the effecting of the Sale and the Closing to be duly executed. Any power of attorney granted by [X], including any sub-powers of attorney granted pursuant to them, shall expire on the earlier of the termination of this Mandate or the discharge of the Trustee.

13. The Trustee shall comply with the Commission's instructions as regards any aspects of the conduct or conclusion of the sale, in particular in ending negotiations with any prospective purchaser, if the Commission notifies the Trustee and [X] of the Commission's determination that the negotiations are being conducted with an unacceptable purchaser.

Section F. Reporting Obligations

14. Within 15 days of the end of each month or as otherwise agreed with the Commission, the Monitoring Trustee shall submit a written report to the Commission, sending [X] a non-confidential copy at the same time. The report shall cover the Monitoring Trustee's fulfilment of its obligations under the Mandate and the compliance of the Parties with the Conditions and Obligations. The reports shall cover in particular the following topics:
    - Operational and financial performance of the Divestment Business in the relevant period;
    - Any issues or problems which have arisen in the execution of the obligations as Monitoring Trustee, in particular any issues of non-compliance by [X] or the Divestment Business with the Conditions and Obligations;
    - Monitoring of the preservation of the economic viability, marketability and competitiveness of the Divestment Business and of [X's] compliance with the hold-separate and ring-fencing obligations as well as monitoring of the splitting of assets and of the allocation of Personnel between the Divestment Business and the businesses retained by [X] or Affiliated Undertakings;
    - Review and assessment of the progress of the divestiture process, including reporting on potential purchasers and all other information received from [X] regarding the divestiture;
    - Any particular issues as set out in the Work-Plan;
    - Estimated future timetable, including the date of next anticipated reporting;
    - A proposal for a detailed Work-Plan in the first report as well as revisions in subsequent reports.

15. In the Trustee Divestiture Period, within 15 days after the end of every month, the Divestiture Trustee shall provide to the Commission, with a simultaneous copy to the Monitoring Trustee and a non-confidential copy to [X], a comprehensive report written in [*Indicate the language*] on

the discharge of its obligations under the Mandate and the progress of the divestiture process, covering in particular the following information:

- List of potential purchasers and a preliminary assessment of each of them;
- State of negotiations with potential purchasers;
- Any issues or problems regarding the sale of the Divestment Business, including any issues and problems regarding the negotiation of the necessary agreement(s);
- Need for advisers for the sale of the Divestment Business and a list of advisers selected by the Trustee for this purpose;
- Any particular issues as set out in the Work-Plan;
- A proposal for a detailed Work-Plan in the first report as well as revisions in subsequent reports.

16. At any time, the Trustee will provide to the Commission, at its request (or on the Trustee's own initiative), a written or oral report on matters falling within the Trustee's Mandate. [X] shall receive simultaneously a non-confidential copy of such additional written reports and shall be informed promptly of the non-confidential content of any oral reports.

Section G. Duties and Obligations of [X]

17. [X] shall provide and shall cause its advisors to provide the Trustee with all such cooperation, assistance and information as the Trustee may reasonably require to perform its tasks. The Trustee shall have full and complete access to any of [X's] or the Divestment Business' books, records, documents, management or other personnel, facilities, sites and technical information necessary for fulfilling its duties under the Mandate and [X] and the Divestment Business shall provide the Trustee upon request with copies of any document. [X] and the Divestment Business shall make available to the Trustee one or more offices on their premises and shall be available for meetings in order to provide the Trustee with all information necessary for the performance of its tasks.

18. [X] shall provide the Monitoring Trustee with all managerial and administrative support that it may reasonably request on behalf of the management of the Divestment Business. This shall include all administrative support functions relating to the Divestment Business which are currently carried out at headquarters level. [X] shall provide and shall cause its advisors to provide the Monitoring Trustee, on request, with access to the information submitted to potential purchasers, in particular to the data room documentation and all other information granted to potential purchasers in the due diligence procedure. [X] shall inform the Monitoring Trustee on possible purchasers, submit a list of potential purchasers, and keep the Monitoring Trustee informed of all developments in the divestiture process. Once a purchaser has been chosen, [X] shall submit the fully documented and reasoned proposal, including a copy of the final agreement(s), to the Monitoring Trustee and allow the Monitoring Trustee to have confidential contacts with the proposed purchaser in order for the Monitoring Trustee to determine whether or not, in its opinion, it meets the Purchaser Criteria.

19. At the expense of [X], the Trustee may appoint advisors (in particular for corporate finance or legal advice), subject to [X's] approval (this approval not to be unreasonably withheld or delayed) if the Trustee considers the appointment of such advisors necessary or appropriate for the performance of its duties and obligations under the Mandate, provided that any fees and other expenses incurred by the Trustee are reasonable. Should [X] refuse to approve the advisors proposed by the Trustee, the Commission may, after having heard [X], approve the appointment of such advisors instead. Only the Trustee shall be entitled to issue instructions to the advisors. Paragraph 25 of this Mandate shall apply to the advisors mutatis mutandis. In the Trustee Divestiture Period, the Divestiture Trustee may use advisors who served [X] during the First Divestiture Period if the Divestiture Trustee considers this in the best interest of an expedient sale.

Section H. Trustee Related Provisions

Conflict of Interests

20. The Trustee's, the Trustee Team's and the Trustee Partner Firms' current relationships with [X] and Affiliated Undertakings are disclosed in Annex [•] to this Mandate. On this basis, the Trustee confirms that, as of the date of this Mandate, the Trustee and each member of the Trustee Team is independent of [X] and Affiliated Undertakings and has no conflict of interest that impairs the

Trustee's objectivity and independence in discharging its duties under the Mandate ("*Conflict of Interest*").

21. The Trustee undertakes not to create a Conflict of Interest during the term of the Mandate. The Trustee, members of the Trustee Team and the Trustee Partner Firms may therefore not during the term of this Mandate:

    (a) Have or accept any employment by or be or accept any appointment as Member of the Board or member of other management bodies of the Parties or Affiliated Undertakings other than appointments pertaining to the establishment and performance of the Mandate;

    (b) Have or accept any assignments or other business relationships with or financial interests in the Parties or Affiliated Undertakings that might lead to a Conflict of Interest. This affects neither assignments or other business relationships between the Trustee or Trustee Partner Firms and the Parties or Affiliated Undertakings nor investments by the Trustee or Trustee Partner Firms in the stock or securities of the Parties or Affiliated Undertakings if such assignments, business relationships or investments are in the normal course of business and are material neither to the Trustee or the Trustee Partner Firms nor to the undertaking concerned.

    Should the Trustee, the Trustee Partner Firms or members of the Trustee Team wish to undertake an assignment, business relationship or investment, such a person must seek the prior approval of the Commission. Should the Trustee become aware of a Conflict of Interest, the Trustee shall promptly inform [X] and the Commission, of such Conflict of Interest. In the event that [X] becomes aware that the Trustee or the Trustee Partner Firms have or may have a Conflict of Interest, [X] shall promptly notify the Trustee and the Commission, of such Conflict of Interest. Where a Conflict of Interest occurs during the term of the Mandate the Trustee undertakes to resolve it immediately. In case the Conflict of Interest cannot be resolved or is not resolved by the Trustee in a timely manner, the Mandate may be terminated in accordance with paragraph 30 below.

22. [*It is up to the Mandate Parties to insert suitable provisions regarding conflict of interests of the Trustee and the Trustee Partner Firms with (potential) purchasers.*]

23. The Trustee undertakes that, during the term of the Mandate and for a period of one year following termination of the Mandate, members of the Trustee Team shall not provide services to the Parties or Affiliated Undertakings without first obtaining the Commission's prior approval. Moreover, the Trustee undertakes to establish measures to ensure the independence and integrity of the Trustee Team and the Trustee's employees and agents directly assigned to the Trustee Team ("*Assigned Persons*") during the term of the Mandate and for a period of one year following termination of the Mandate, from any undue influence that might interfere with or in any way compromise the Trustee Team in the performance of its duties under the Mandate. In particular:

    (a) Access to confidential information shall be limited to the Trustee Team and Assigned Persons; and

    (b) The Trustee Team and Assigned Persons shall be prohibited from communicating any information relating to this Mandate to any other of the Trustee's personnel, except for information of a general nature (e.g. Trustee's appointment, fees, etc.), and except for information whose disclosure is required by law.

Remuneration

24. [*It is up to the Mandate Parties to agree on a suitable fee structure. As set out in the Standard Commitments Text, the Trustee shall be remunerated in such a way that it does not impede its independence and effectiveness in fulfilling the Mandate. Regarding the Divestiture Trustee, the Commission is in favour of fee structures that, at least to a significant part, are contingent on the Divestiture Trustee's accomplishing a timely divestiture. In particular, if the remuneration package includes a success premium linked to the final sale value of the Divestment Business, the fee should also be linked to a divestiture within the Trustee Divestiture Period as specified in the Commitments. It should be noted that the fee structure — as well as the entire Mandate — is subject to the Commission's approval.*]

Indemnity

25. [*X*] shall indemnify the Trustee and its employees and agents (each an "***Indemnified Party***") and hold each Indemnified Party harmless against, and hereby agrees that an Indemnified Party shall have no liability to [*X*] for any liabilities arising out of the performance of the Mandate, except to the extent that such liabilities result from the wilful default, recklessness, gross negligence or bad faith of the Trustee, its employees, agents or advisors.

Confidentiality

26. [*It is up to the Mandate Parties to agree a suitable confidentiality provision prohibiting the use, or disclosure to anyone other than the Commission of any sensitive or proprietary information gained as a result of performing the Trustee role. As a matter of course, the Mandate cannot limit the disclosure of information by the Trustee vis-à-vis the Commission. However, the Trustee must not disclose certain information gained as a result of the Trustee role to the Parties. This in particular applies to information gained on the Divestment Business to which the ring-fencing provisions apply and to information received from (potential) purchasers of the Divestment Business.*]

Section I. Termination of the Mandate

27. The Mandate may only be terminated under the conditions set out in paragraphs 28–31.

Regular Termination of the Mandate

28. The Mandate shall automatically terminate if the Commission approves the discharge in writing of the Trustee from its obligations under this Mandate. The approval of the discharge of the Trustee may be requested after the Trustee has completed the performance of its obligations under the Mandate.

29. The Mandate Parties acknowledge that the Commission may at any time request the reappointment of the Trustee by [*X*] if it subsequently appears that the Conditions and Obligations might not have been fully and properly implemented. The Trustee hereby accepts such a reappointment in accordance with the terms and conditions of this Mandate.

Termination of the Mandate before the Discharge

30. [*X*] may only terminate the Mandate before the discharge of the Trustee in accordance with paragraph 31 of the Commitments. The Trustee may only terminate the Mandate for good cause by giving written notice to [*X*], with a copy to the Commission. The Trustee shall continue carrying out its functions under the Mandate until it has effected a full handover of all relevant information to a new trustee appointed by [*X*] pursuant to the procedure laid down in the Commitments.

Surviving Provisions

31. Paragraphs [*23*]–[*26*] shall survive the termination of the Mandate.

Section J. Additional Provisions

Amendments to the Mandate

32. The Mandate may only be amended in writing and with the Commission's prior approval. The Mandate Parties agree to amend this Mandate if required by the Commission, after consultation with the Mandate Parties, in order to secure compliance with the Commitments, in particular if the amendment is necessary in order to adapt the Mandate to amendments of the Commitments under the Review Clause.

Governing Law and Dispute Resolution

33. This Mandate shall be governed by, and construed in accordance with, the laws of [*Indicate the state by whose laws the Mandate shall be governed*].

34. In the event that a dispute arises concerning the Mandate Parties' obligations under the Mandate, such dispute shall be submitted to the non-exclusive jurisdiction of the [*Indicate the state whose courts shall have jurisdiction for disputes regarding the Mandate*] courts.

Severability

35. [*It is up to the Mandate Parties to agree on a suitable provision on severability, taking into account the rules under the governing law*].

Part D Mergers and Concentrations

<u>Notices</u>

36. All notices sent under this Mandate shall be made in writing and be deemed to have been duly given if served by personal delivery upon the party for whom it is intended or the Commission or delivered by registered or certified mail; return receipt requested, or if sent by fax, upon receipt of oral confirmation that such transmission has been received, to the person at the address set forth below:

If to [X], addressed as follows:

[●]

If to the Trustee, addressed as follows:

[●]

If to the Commission, addressed as follows:

To the attention of the Director
Director of Directorate B
European Commission
Directorate General for Competition
70 rue Joseph II / Jozef II-straat 70
B-1000 Brussels
Ref: Case No COMP/M . . . . . .
Fax: + 32 2 296 43 01

Or to any such other address or person as the relevant party may from time to time advise by notice in writing given pursuant to this section. The date of receipt of any such notice, request, consent, agreement or approval shall be deemed to be the date of delivery thereof.

[Indicate place and date]

_____

By:

Title:

_____

By:

Title:

Annex [●]

Power of Attorney, duly executed, for the exercise of [X's] rights as shareholder (pursuant to paragraph 6(d) of the Mandate)

Annex [●] Power of Attorney, duly executed, for the Divestiture Trustee (pursuant to paragraph 12 of the Mandate)

Annex [●] Disclosure of current relationships between the Trustee, the Trustee Team and the Trustees Partner Firm and [X] and Affiliated Undertakings.

D6

GUIDELINES

on the assessment of horizontal mergers under the Council Regulation on the control of
concentrations between undertakings

(2004/C 31/03)

Official Journal C 31, 5.2.2004, p. 5

Celex No: 52004XC0205(02)

I. INTRODUCTION

1. Article 2 of Council Regulation (EC) No 139/2004 of 20 January 2004 on the control of concentrations between undertakings[1] (hereinafter: the "Merger Regulation") provides that the
Commission has to appraise concentrations within the scope of the Merger Regulation with a view
to establishing whether or not they are compatible with the common market. For that purpose, the
Commission must assess, pursuant to Article 2(2) and (3), whether or not a concentration would
significantly impede effective competition, in particular as a result of the creation or strengthening
of a dominant position, in the common market or a substantial part of it.

Notes
[1] Council Regulation (EC) No 139/2004 of 20 January 2004 (OJ L 24, 29.1.2004, p. 1).

---

2. Accordingly, the Commission must take into account any significant impediment to effective competition likely to be caused by a concentration. The creation or the strengthening of a dominant
position is a primary form of such competitive harm. The concept of dominance was defined in
the context of Council Regulation (EEC) No 4064/89 of 21 December 1989 on the control of
concentrations between undertakings (hereinafter "Regulation No 4064/89") as:

"a situation where one or more undertakings wield economic power which would enable them to
prevent effective competition from being maintained in the relevant market by giving them the
opportunity to act to a considerable extent independently of their competitors, their customers
and, ultimately, of consumers".[2]

689

Notes

[2] Case T-102/96 *Gencor v Commission* [1999] ECR II-753, paragraph 200. See Joined Cases C-68/94 and C-30/95 *France and others v Commission* (hereinafter "*Kali and Salz*"), [1998] ECR I-1375, paragraph 221. In exceptional circumstances, a merger may give rise to the creation or the strengthening of a dominant position on the part of an undertaking which is not a party to the notified transaction (see Case IV/M.1383 —*Exxon/Mobil*, points 225–229; Case COMP/M.2434 — *Grupo Villar MIR/EnBW/Hidroelectrica del Cantabrico*, points 67–71).

Commentary
para 2: B&C: 8.196

---

3. For the purpose of interpreting the concept of dominance in the context of Regulation No 4064/89, the Court of Justice referred to the fact that it "is intended to apply to all concentrations with a Community dimension insofar as they are likely, because of their effect on the structure of competition within the Community, to prove incompatible with the system of undistorted competition envisaged by the Treaty".[3]

Notes

[3] See also Joined Cases C-68/94 and C-30/95, *Kali and Salz*, paragraph 170.

4. The creation or strengthening of a dominant position held by a single firm as a result of a merger has been the most common basis for finding that a concentration would result in a significant impediment to effective competition. Furthermore, the concept of dominance has also been applied in an oligopolistic setting to cases of collective dominance. As a consequence, it is expected that most cases of incompatibility of a concentration with the common market will continue to be based upon a finding of dominance. That concept therefore provides an important indication as to the standard of competitive harm that is applicable when determining whether a concentration is likely to impede effective competition to a significant degree, and hence, as to the likelihood of intervention.[4] To that effect, the present notice is intended to preserve the guidance that can be drawn from past decisional practice and to take full account of past case-law of the Community Courts.

Notes

[4] See Recitals 25 and 26 of the Merger Regulation.

Commentary
para 4: B&C: 8.197 F&N: 5.200

---

5. The purpose of this notice is to provide guidance as to how the Commission assesses concentrations[5] when the undertakings concerned are actual or potential competitors on the same relevant market.[6] In this notice such mergers will be denoted "horizontal mergers". While the notice presents the analytical approach used by the Commission in its appraisal of horizontal mergers it cannot provide details of all possible applications of this approach. The Commission applies the approach described in the notice to the particular facts and circumstances of each case.

Notes

[5] The term "concentration" used in the Merger Regulation covers various types of transactions such as mergers, acquisitions, takeovers, and certain types of joint ventures. In the remainder of this notice, unless otherwise specified, the term "merger" will be used as a synonym for concentration and therefore cover all the above types of transactions.

[6] The notice does not cover the assessment of the effects of competition that a merger has in other markets, including vertical and conglomerate effects. Nor does it cover the assessment of the effects of a joint venture as referred to in Article 2(4) of the Merger Regulation.

6. The guidance set out in this notice draws and elaborates on the Commission's evolving experience with the appraisal of horizontal mergers under Regulation No 4064/89 since its entry into force on 21 September 1990 as well as on the case-law of the Court of Justice and the Court of First Instance of the European Communities. The principles contained here will be applied and further developed and refined by the Commission in individual cases. The Commission may revise this notice from time to time in the light of future developments.

7. The Commission's interpretation of the Merger Regulation as regards the appraisal of horizontal mergers is without prejudice to the interpretation which may be given by the Court of Justice or the Court of First Instance of the European Communities.

II. OVERVIEW

8. Effective competition brings benefits to consumers, such as low prices, high quality products, a wide selection of goods and services, and innovation. Through its control of mergers, the Commission prevents mergers that would be likely to deprive customers of these benefits by significantly increasing the market power of firms. By "increased market power" is meant the ability of one or more firms to profitably increase prices, reduce output, choice or quality of goods and services, diminish innovation, or otherwise influence parameters of competition. In this notice, the expression "increased prices" is often used as shorthand for these various ways in which a merger may result in competitive harm.[7] Both suppliers and buyers can have market power. However, for clarity, market power will usually refer here to a supplier's market power. Where a buyer's market power is the issue, the term "buyer power" is employed.

Notes

[7] The expression should be understood to also cover situations where, for instance, prices are decreased less, or are less likely to decrease, than they otherwise would have without the merger and where prices are increased more, or are more likely to increase, than they otherwise would have without the merger.

Commentary
para 8: B&C: 8.200

9. In assessing the competitive effects of a merger, the Commission compares the competitive conditions that would result from the notified merger with the conditions that would have prevailed without the merger.[8] In most cases the competitive conditions existing at the time of the merger constitute the relevant comparison for evaluating the effects of a merger. However, in some circumstances, the Commission may take into account future changes to the market that can reasonably be predicted.[9] It may, in particular, take account of the likely entry or exit of firms if the merger did not take place when considering what constitutes the relevant comparison.[10]

Notes

[8] By analogy, in the case of a merger that has been implemented without having been notified, the Commission would assess the merger in the light of the competitive conditions that would have prevailed without the implemented merger.

[9] See, e.g. Commission Decision 98/526/EC in Case IV/M.950 — *Hoffmann La Roche/Boehringer Mannheim*, OJ L 234, 21.8.1998, p. 14, point 13; Case IV/M.1846 — *Glaxo Wellcome/SmithKline Beecham*, points 70–72; Case COMP/M.2547 — *Bayer/Aventis Crop Science*, points 324 et seq.

[10] See, e.g. Case T-102/96 *Gencor v Commission* [1999] ECR II-753, paragraphs 247–263.

10. The Commission's assessment of mergers normally entails:
    (a) definition of the relevant product and geographic markets;
    (b) competitive assessment of the merger.
    The main purpose of market definition is to identify in a systematic way the immediate competitive constraints facing the merged entity. Guidance on this issue can be found in the Commission's Notice on the definition of the relevant market for the purposes of Community competition law.[11] Various considerations leading to the delineation of the relevant markets may also be of importance for the competitive assessment of the merger.

Notes

[11] OJ C 372, 9.12.1997, p. 5.

11. This notice is structured around the following elements:
    (a) The approach of the Commission to market shares and concentration thresholds (Section III).
    (b) The likelihood that a merger would have anti-competitive effects in the relevant markets, in the absence of countervailing factors (Section IV).

(c) The likelihood that buyer power would act as a countervailing factor to an increase in market power resulting from the merger (Section V).

(d) The likelihood that entry would maintain effective competition in the relevant markets (Section VI).

(e) The likelihood that efficiencies would act as a factor counteracting the harmful effects on competition which might otherwise result from the merger (Section VII).

(f) The conditions for a failing firm defence (Section VIII).

12. In order to assess the foreseeable impact[12] of a merger on the relevant markets, the Commission analyses its possible anti-competitive effects and the relevant countervailing factors such as buyer power, the extent of entry barriers and possible efficiencies put forward by the parties. In exceptional circumstances, the Commission considers whether the conditions for a failing firm defence are met.

Notes

[12] See Case T-102/96 *Gencor v Commission* [1999] ECR II-753, paragraph 262, and Case T-342/99 *Airtours v Commission* [2002] ECR II-2585, paragraph 280.

Commentary
para 12: B&C: 8.200

---

13. In the light of these elements, the Commission determines, pursuant to Article 2 of the Merger Regulation, whether the merger would significantly impede effective competition, in particular through the creation or the strengthening of a dominant position, and should therefore be declared incompatible with the common market. It should be stressed that these factors are not a "checklist" to be mechanically applied in each and every case. Rather, the competitive analysis in a particular case will be based on an overall assessment of the foreseeable impact of the merger in the light of the relevant factors and conditions. Not all the elements will always be relevant to each and every horizontal merger, and it may not be necessary to analyse all the elements of a case in the same detail.

III. Market Share and Concentration Levels

14. Market shares and concentration levels provide useful first indications of the market structure and of the competitive importance of both the merging parties and their competitors.

Commentary
para 14: B&C: 8.203

---

15. Normally, the Commission uses current market shares in its competitive analysis.[13] However, current market shares may be adjusted to reflect reasonably certain future changes, for instance in the light of exit, entry or expansion.[14] Post-merger market shares are calculated on the assumption that the post-merger combined market share of the merging parties is the sum of their pre-merger market shares.[15] Historic data may be used if market shares have been volatile, for instance when the market is characterised by large, lumpy orders. Changes in historic market shares may provide useful information about the competitive process and the likely future importance of the various competitors, for instance, by indicating whether firms have been gaining or losing market shares. In any event, the Commission interprets market shares in the light of likely market conditions, for instance, if the market is highly dynamic in character and if the market structure is unstable due to innovation or growth.[16]

Notes

[13] As to the calculation of market shares, see also Commission Notice on the definition of the relevant market for the purposes of Community competition law, OJ C 372, 9.12.1997, p. 3, paragraphs 54–55.

[14] See, e.g. Case COMP/M.1806 — *Astra Zeneca/Novartis*, points 150 and 415.

[15] When relevant, market shares may be adjusted, in particular, to account for controlling interests in other firms (see, e.g. Case IV/M.1383 — *Exxon/Mobil*, points 446–458; Case COMP/M.1879 — *Boeing/Hughes*, points 60–79; Case COMP/JV 55 — *Hutchison/RCPM/ECT*, points 66–75), or for other arrangements with third parties (see, for

instance, as regards sub-contractors, Commission Decision 2001/769/EC in Case COMP/M.1940 — *Framatome/Siemens/Cogema*, OJ L 289, 6.11.2001, p. 8, point 142).

[16] See, e.g. Case COMP/M.2256 — *Philips/Agilent Health Care Technologies*, points 31–32, and Case COMP/M.2609 — *HP/Compaq*, point 39.

Commentary
para 15: B&C: 8.204

16. The overall concentration level in a market may also provide useful information about the competitive situation. In order to measure concentration levels, the Commission often applies the Herfindahl-Hirschman Index (HHI).[17] The HHI is calculated by summing the squares of the individual market shares of all the firms in the market.[18] The HHI gives proportionately greater weight to the market shares of the larger firms. Although it is best to include all firms in the calculation, lack of information about very small firms may not be important because such firms do not affect the HHI significantly. While the absolute level of the HHI can give an initial indication of the competitive pressure in the market post-merger, the change in the HHI (known as the "delta") is a useful proxy for the change in concentration directly brought about by the merger.[19]

Notes

[17] See, e.g. Case IV/M.1365 — *FCC/Vivendi*, point 40; Case COMP/JV 55 — *Hutchison/RCPM/ECT*, point 50. If appropriate, the Commission may also use other concentration measures such as, for instance, concentration ratios, which measure the aggregate market share of a small number (usually three or four) of the leading firms in a market.

[18] For example, a market containing five firms with market shares of 40%, 20%, 15%, 15%, and 10%, respectively, has an HHI of 2550 ($40^2 + 20^2 + 15^2 + 15^2 + 10^2 = 2,550$). The HHI ranges from close to zero (in an atomistic market) to 10000 (in the case of a pure monopoly).

[19] The increase in concentration as measured by the HHI can be calculated independently of the overall market concentration by doubling the product of the market shares of the merging firms. For example, a merger of two firms with market shares of 30% and 15% respectively would increase the HHI by 900 ($30 \times 15 \times 2 = 900$). The explanation for this technique is as follows: Before the merger, the market shares of the merging firms contribute to the HHI by their squares individually: $(a)^2 + (b)^2$. After the merger, the contribution is the square of their sum: $(a + b)^2$, which equals $(a)^2 + (b)^2 + 2ab$. The increase in the HHI is therefore represented by $2ab$.

Market share levels

17. According to well-established case law, very large market shares — 50 % or more — may in themselves be evidence of the existence of a dominant market position.[20] However, smaller competitors may act as a sufficient constraining influence if, for example, they have the ability and incentive to increase their supplies. A merger involving a firm whose market share will remain below 50% after the merger may also raise competition concerns in view of other factors such as the strength and number of competitors, the presence of capacity constraints or the extent to which the products of the merging parties are close substitutes. The Commission has thus in several cases considered mergers resulting in firms holding market shares between 40% and 50%,[21] and in some cases below 40%,[22] to lead to the creation or the strengthening of a dominant position.

Notes

[20] Case T-221/95 *Endemol v Commission*, [1999] ECR II-1299, paragraph 134, and Case T-102/96, *Gencor v Commission*, [1999] ECR II-753, paragraph 205. It is a distinct question whether a dominant position is created or strengthened as a result of the merger.

[21] See, e.g. Case COMP/M.2337 — *Nestlé/Ralston Purina*, points 48–50.

[22] See, e.g. Commission Decision 1999/674/EC in Case IV/M.1221 — *Rewe/Meinl*, OJ L 274, 23.10.1999, p. 1, points 98–114; Case COMP/M.2337 — *Nestlé/Ralston Purina*, points 44–47.

Commentary
para 17: B&C: 8.205 F&N: 3.334, 5.213

18. Concentrations which, by reason of the limited market share of the undertakings concerned, are not liable to impede effective competition may be presumed to be compatible with the common market. Without prejudice to Articles 81 and 82 of the Treaty, an indication to this effect exists, in particular, where the market share of the undertakings concerned does not exceed 25%[23] either in the common market or in a substantial part of it.[24]

Part D Mergers and Concentrations

Notes

[23] The calculation of market shares depends critically on market definition. It must be emphasised that the Commission does not necessarily accept the parties' proposed market definition.

[24] Recital 32 of the Merger Regulation. However, such an indication does not apply to cases where the proposed merger creates or strengthens a collective dominant position involving the "undertakings concerned" and other third parties (see Joined Cases C-68/94 and C-30/95, *Kali and Salz*, [1998] ECR I-1375, paragraphs 171 et seq.; and Case T-102/96, *Gencor v Commission*, [1999] ECR II-753, paragraphs 134 et seq.).

Commentary
para 18: B&C: 8.204 F&N: 5.213

HHI levels

19. The Commission is unlikely to identify horizontal competition concerns in a market with a post-merger HHI below 1000. Such markets normally do not require extensive analysis.

Commentary
para 19: B&C: 8.204 F&N: 3.326

---

20. The Commission is also unlikely to identify horizontal competition concerns in a merger with a post-merger HHI between 1000 and 2000 and a delta below 250, or a merger with a post-merger HHI above 2000 and a delta below 150, except where special circumstances such as, for instance, one or more of the following factors are present:
    (a) a merger involves a potential entrant or a recent entrant with a small market share;
    (b) one or more merging parties are important innovators in ways not reflected in market shares;
    (c) there are significant cross-shareholdings among the market participants;[25]
    (d) one of the merging firms is a maverick firm with a high likelihood of disrupting coordinated conduct;
    (e) indications of past or ongoing coordination, or facilitating practices, are present;
    (f) one of the merging parties has a pre-merger market share of 50% of more.[26]

Notes

[25] In markets with cross-shareholdings or joint ventures the Commission may use a modified HHI, which takes into account such share-holdings (see, e.g. Case IV/M.1383 — *Exxon/Mobil*, point 256).

[26] See paragraph 17.

Commentary
para 20: B&C: 8.204 F&N: 3.326

---

21. Each of these HHI levels, in combination with the relevant deltas, may be used as an initial indicator of the absence of competition concerns. However, they do not give rise to a presumption of either the existence or the absence of such concerns.

IV. POSSIBLE ANTI-COMPETITIVE EFFECTS OF HORIZONTAL MERGERS

22. There are two main ways in which horizontal mergers may significantly impede effective competition, in particular by creating or strengthening a dominant position:
    (a) by eliminating important competitive constraints on one or more firms, which consequently would have increased market power, without resorting to coordinated behaviour (non-coordinated effects);
    (b) by changing the nature of competition in such a way that firms that previously were not coordinating their behaviour, are now significantly more likely to coordinate and raise prices or otherwise harm effective competition. A merger may also make coordination easier, more stable or more effective for firms which were coordinating prior to the merger (coordinated effects).

Commentary
para 22: B&C: 8.202 F&N: 5.220

---

23. The Commission assesses whether the changes brought about by the merger would result in any of these effects. Both instances mentioned above may be relevant when assessing a particular transaction.

Non-coordinated effects [27]

24. A merger may significantly impede effective competition in a market by removing important competitive constraints on one or more sellers, who consequently have increased market power. The most direct effect of the merger will be the loss of competition between the merging firms. For example, if prior to the merger one of the merging firms had raised its price, it would have lost some sales to the other merging firm. The merger removes this particular constraint. Non-merging firms in the same market can also benefit from the reduction of competitive pressure that results from the merger, since the merging firms' price increase may switch some demand to the rival firms, which, in turn, may find it profitable to increase their prices.[28] The reduction in these competitive constraints could lead to significant price increases in the relevant market.

Notes

[27] Also often called "unilateral" effects.

[28] Such expected reactions by competitors may be a relevant factor influencing the merged entity's incentives to increase prices.

25. Generally, a merger giving rise to such non-coordinated effects would significantly impede effective competition by creating or strengthening the dominant position of a single firm, one which, typically, would have an appreciably larger market share than the next competitor post-merger. Furthermore, mergers in oligopolistic markets[29] involving the elimination of important competitive constraints that the merging parties previously exerted upon each other together with a reduction of competitive pressure on the remaining competitors may, even where there is little likelihood of coordination between the members of the oligopoly, also result in a significant impediment to competition. The Merger Regulation clarifies that all mergers giving rise to such non-coordinated effects shall also be declared incompatible with the common market.[30]

Notes

[29] An oligopolistic market refers to a market structure with a limited number of sizeable firms. Because the behaviour of one firm has an appreciable impact on the overall market conditions, and thus indirectly on the situation of each of the other firms, oligopolistic firms are interdependent.

[30] Recital 25 of the Merger Regulation.

Commentary
para 25: **B&C:** 8.206: **F&N:** 1.228

26. A number of factors, which taken separately are not necessarily decisive, may influence whether significant non-coordinated effects are likely to result from a merger. Not all of these factors need to be present for such effects to be likely. Nor should this be considered an exhaustive list.

Merging firms have large market shares

27. The larger the market share, the more likely a firm is to possess market power. And the larger the addition of market share, the more likely it is that a merger will lead to a significant increase in market power. The larger the increase in the sales base on which to enjoy higher margins after a price increase, the more likely it is that the merging firms will find such a price increase profitable despite the accompanying reduction in output. Although market shares and additions of market shares only provide first indications of market power and increases in market power, they are normally important factors in the assessment.[31]

Notes

[31] See, in particular, paragraphs 17 and 18.

Commentary
para 27: **F&N:** 3.327

Merging firms are close competitors

28. Products may be differentiated[32] within a relevant market such that some products are closer substitutes than others.[33] The higher the degree of substitutability between the merging firms' products, the more likely it is that the merging firms will raise prices significantly.[34] For example, a merger between two producers offering products which a substantial number of customers regard as their first and second choices could generate a significant price increase. Thus, the fact that rivalry between the parties has been an important source of competition on the market may be a central factor in the analysis.[35] High pre-merger margins[36] may also make significant price increases more likely. The merging firms' incentive to raise prices is more likely to be constrained when rival firms produce close substitutes to the products of the merging firms than when they offer less close substitutes.[37] It is therefore less likely that a merger will significantly impede effective competition, in particular through the creation or strengthening of a dominant position, when there is a high degree of substitutability between the products of the merging firms and those supplied by rival producers.

Notes

[32] Products may be differentiated in various ways. There may, for example, be differentiation in terms of geographic location, based on branch or stores location; location matters for retail distribution, banks, travel agencies, or petrol stations. Likewise, differentiation may be based on brand image, technical specifications, quality or level of service. The level of advertising in a market may be an indicator of the firms' effort to differentiate their products. For other products, buyers may have to incur switching costs to use a competitor's product.

[33] For the definition of the relevant market, see the Commission's Notice on the definition of the relevant market for the purposes of Community competition law, cited above.

[34] See for example Case COMP/M.2817 — *Barilla/BPS/Kamps*, point 34; Commission Decision 2001/403/EC in Case COMP/M.1672 — *Volvo/Scania*, OJ L 143, 29.5.2001, p. 74, points 107–148.

[35] See, e.g. Commission Decision 94/893/EC in Case IV/M.430 — *Procter & Gamble/VP Schickedanz (II)*, OJ L 354, 21.6.1994, p. 32, Case T-290/94, *Kaysersberg v Commission*, [1997] II-2137, paragraph 153; Commission Decision 97/610/EC in Case IV/M.774 — *Saint-Gobain/Wacker-Chemie/NOM*, OJ L 247, 10.9.1997, p. 1, point 179; Commission Decision 2002/156/EC in Case COMP/M.2097 — *SCA/Metsä Tissue*, OJ L 57, 27.2.2002, p. 1, points 94–108; Case T-310/01, *Schneider v Commission*, [2002] II-4071, paragraph 418.

[36] Typically, the relevant margin (m) is the difference between price (p) and the incremental cost (c) of supplying one more unit of output expressed as a percentage of price (m = (p – c)p)).

[37] See, e.g. Case IV/M.1980 —*Volvo/Renault VI*, point 34; Case COMP/M.2256 — *Philips Agilent/Health Care Solutions*, points 33–35; Case COMP/M.2537 — *Philips/Marconi Medical Systems*, points 31–34.

Commentary

para 28: B&C: 8.207 F&N: 3.328

29. When data are available, the degree of substitutability may be evaluated through customer preference surveys, analysis of purchasing patterns, estimation of the cross-price elasticities of the products involved,[38] or diversion ratios.[39] In bidding markets it may be possible to measure whether historically the submitted bids by one of the merging parties have been constrained by the presence of the other merging party.[40]

Notes

[38] The cross-price elasticity of demand measures the extent to which the quantity of a product demanded changes in response to a change in the price of some other product, all other things remaining equal. The own-price elasticity measures the extent to which demand for a product changes in response to the change in the price of the product itself.

[39] The diversion ratio from product A to product B measures the proportion of the sales of product A lost due to a price increase of A that are captured by product B.

[40] Commission Decision 97/816/EC in Case IV/M.877 — *Boeing/McDonnell Douglas*, OJ L 336, 8.12.1997, p. 16, points 58 et seq.; Case COMP/M.3083 — *GE/Instrumentarium*, points 125 et seq.

30. In some markets it may be relatively easy and not too costly for the active firms to reposition their products or extend their product portfolio. In particular, the Commission examines whether the possibility of repositioning or product line extension by competitors or the merging parties may influence the incentive of the merged entity to raise prices. However, product repositioning or product line extension often entails risks and large sunk costs[41] and may be less profitable than the current line.

Customers have limited possibilities of switching supplier

31. Customers of the merging parties may have difficulties switching to other suppliers because there are few alternative suppliers[42] or because they face substantial switching costs.[43] Such customers are particularly vulnerable to price increases. The merger may affect these customers' ability to protect themselves against price increases. In particular, this may be the case for customers that have used dual sourcing from the two merging firms as a means of obtaining competitive prices. Evidence of past customer switching patterns and reactions to price changes may provide important information in this respect.

Notes

[42] See e.g. Commission Decision 2002/156/EC in Case IV/M.877 — *Boeing/McDonnell Douglas*, OJ L 336, 8.12.1997, p. 16, point 70.
[43] See, e.g. Case IV/M. 986 — *Agfa Gevaert/DuPont*, OJ L 211, 29.7.1998, p. 22, points 63–71.

Commentary

para 31: B&C: 8.207

Competitors are unlikely to increase supply if prices increase

32. When market conditions are such that the competitors of the merging parties are unlikely to increase their supply substantially if prices increase, the merging firms may have an incentive to reduce output below the combined pre-merger levels, thereby raising market prices.[44] The merger increases the incentive to reduce output by giving the merged firm a larger base of sales on which to enjoy the higher margins resulting from an increase in prices induced by the output reduction.

Notes

[44] See, e.g. Case COMP/M.2187 — *CVC/Lenzing*, points 162–170.

33. Conversely, when market conditions are such that rival firms have enough capacity and find it profitable to expand output sufficiently, the Commission is unlikely to find that the merger will create or strengthen a dominant position or otherwise significantly impede effective competition.
34. Such output expansion is, in particular, unlikely when competitors face binding capacity constraints and the expansion of capacity is costly[45] or if existing excess capacity is significantly more costly to operate than capacity currently in use.

Notes

[45] When analysing the possible expansion of capacity by rivals, the Commission considers factors similar to those described in Section VI on entry. See, e.g. Case COMP/M.2187 — *CVC/Lenzing*, points 162–173.

35. Although capacity constraints are more likely to be important when goods are relatively homogeneous, they may also be important where firms offer differentiated products.

Merged entity able to hinder expansion by competitors

36. Some proposed mergers would, if allowed to proceed, significantly impede effective competition by leaving the merged firm in a position where it would have the ability and incentive to make the expansion of smaller firms and potential competitors more difficult or otherwise restrict the ability of rival firms to compete. In such a case, competitors may not, either individually or in the aggregate, be in a position to constrain the merged entity to such a degree that it would not increase prices or take other actions detrimental to competition. For instance, the merged entity may have such a degree of control, or influence over, the supply of inputs[46] or distribution possibilities[47] that expansion or entry by rival firms may be more costly. Similarly, the merged entity's control over patents[48] or other types of intellectual property (e.g. brands[49]) may make

expansion or entry by rivals more difficult. In markets where interoperability between different infrastructures or platforms is important,[50] a merger may give the merged entity the ability and incentive to raise the costs or decrease the quality of service of its rivals.[51] In making this assessment the Commission may take into account, inter alia, the financial strength of the merged entity relative to its rivals.[52]

Notes

[46] See, e.g. Case T-221/95 *Endemol v Commission* [1999] ECR II-1299, paragraph 167.

[47] See, e.g. Case T-22/97 *Kesko v Commission* [1999], ECR II-3775, paragraphs 141 et seq.

[48] See, e.g. Commission Decision 2001/684/EC in Case M.1671 — *Dow Chemical/Union Carbides* OJ L 245, 14.9.2001, p. 1, points 107–114.

[49] See, e.g. Commission Decision 96/435/EC in Case IV/M.623 — *Kimberly-Clark/Scott*, OJ L 183, 23.7.1996, p. 1; Case T-114/02, *Babyliss SA v Commission* ("*Seb/Moulinex*"), [2003] ECR II-[1279], paragraphs 343 et seq.

[50] This is, for example, the case in network industries such as energy, telecommunications and other communication industries.

[51] Commission Decision 99/287/EC in Case IV/M.1069 — *Worldcom/MCI*, OJ L 116, 4.5.1999, p. 1, points 117 et seq.; Case IV/M.1741 — *MCI Worldcom/Sprint*, points 145 et seq.; Case IV/M.1795 — *Vodafone Airtouch/Mannesmann*, points 44 et seq.

[52] Case T-156/98 *RJB Mining v Commission* [2001] ECR II-337.

Commentary
para 36: B&C: 8.207

Merger eliminates an important competitive force

37. Some firms have more of an influence on the competitive process than their market shares or similar measures would suggest. A merger involving such a firm may change the competitive dynamics in a significant, anti-competitive way, in particular when the market is already concentrated.[53] For instance, a firm may be a recent entrant that is expected to exert significant competitive pressure in the future on the other firms in the market.

Notes

[53] Commission Decision 2002/156/EC in Case IV/M.877 — *Boeing/McDonnell Douglas*, OJ L 336, 8.12.1997, p. 16, point 58; Case COMP/M.2568 — *Haniel/Ytong*, point 126.

Commentary
para 37: B&C: 8.207

38. In markets where innovation is an important competitive force, a merger may increase the firms' ability and incentive to bring new innovations to the market and, thereby, the competitive pressure on rivals to innovate in that market. Alternatively, effective competition may be significantly impeded by a merger between two important innovators, for instance between two companies with "pipeline" products related to a specific product market. Similarly, a firm with a relatively small market share may nevertheless be an important competitive force if it has promising pipeline products.[54]

Notes

[54] For an example of pipeline products of one merging party likely to compete with the other party's pipeline or existing products, see, e.g. Case IV/M.1846 — *Glaxo Wellcome/SmithKline Beecham*, point 188.

Commentary
para 38: B&C: 4.069, 8.207

Coordinated effects

39. In some markets the structure may be such that firms would consider it possible, economically rational, and hence preferable, to adopt on a sustainable basis a course of action on the market aimed at selling at increased prices. A merger in a concentrated market may significantly impede effective competition, through the creation or the strengthening of a collective dominant position, because it increases the likelihood that firms are able to coordinate their behaviour in this way and raise prices, even without entering into an agreement or resorting to a concerted practice

within the meaning of Article 81 of the Treaty.[55] A merger may also make coordination easier, more stable or more effective for firms, that were already coordinating before the merger, either by making the coordination more robust or by permitting firms to coordinate on even higher prices.

Notes

[55] Case T-102/96 *Gencor v Commission* [1999] ECR II-753, paragraph 277; Case T-342/99 *Airtours v Commission* [2002] ECR II-2585, paragraph 61.

Commentary
para 39: **B&C:** 8.209

40. Coordination may take various forms. In some markets, the most likely coordination may involve keeping prices above the competitive level. In other markets, coordination may aim at limiting production or the amount of new capacity brought to the market. Firms may also coordinate by dividing the market, for instance by geographic area[56] or other customer characteristics, or by allocating contracts in bidding markets.

Notes

[56] This may be the case if the oligopolists have tended to concentrate their sales in different areas for historic reasons.

Commentary
para 40: **B&C:** 8.210

41. Coordination is more likely to emerge in markets where it is relatively simple to reach a common understanding on the terms of coordination. In addition, three conditions are necessary for coordination to be sustainable. First, the coordinating firms must be able to monitor to a sufficient degree whether the terms of coordination are being adhered to. Second, discipline requires that there is some form of credible deterrent mechanism that can be activated if deviation is detected. Third, the reactions of outsiders, such as current and future competitors not participating in the coordination, as well as customers, should not be able to jeopardise the results expected from the coordination.[57]

Notes

[57] Case T-342/99, *Airtours v Commission*, [2002] ECR II-2585, paragraph 62.

Commentary
para 41: **F&N:** 5.245

42. The Commission examines whether it would be possible to reach terms of coordination and whether the coordination is likely to be sustainable. In this respect, the Commission considers the changes that the merger brings about. The reduction in the number of firms in a market may, in itself, be a factor that facilitates coordination. However, a merger may also increase the likelihood or significance of coordinated effects in other ways. For instance, a merger may involve a "maverick" firm that has a history of preventing or disrupting coordination, for example by failing to follow price increases by its competitors, or has characteristics that gives it an incentive to favour different strategic choices than its coordinating competitors would prefer. If the merged firm were to adopt strategies similar to those of other competitors, the remaining firms would find it easier to coordinate, and the merger would increase the likelihood, stability or effectiveness of coordination.

43. In assessing the likelihood of coordinated effects, the Commission takes into account all available relevant information on the characteristics of the markets concerned, including both structural features and the past behaviour of firms.[58] Evidence of past coordination is important if the relevant market characteristics have not changed appreciably or are not likely to do so in the near future.[59] Likewise, evidence of coordination in similar markets may be useful information.

Notes

[58] See Commission Decision 92/553/EC in Case IV/M.190 — *Nestlé/Perrier*, OJ L 356, 5.12.1992, p. 1, points 117–118.
[59] See, e.g. Case IV/M.580 — *ABB/Daimler-Benz*, point 95.

Commentary
para 43: B&C: 8.210

Reaching terms of coordination

44. Coordination is more likely to emerge if competitors can easily arrive at a common perception as to how the coordination should work. Coordinating firms should have similar views regarding which actions would be considered to be in accordance with the aligned behaviour and which actions would not.

Commentary
para 44: B&C: 8.210

45. Generally, the less complex and the more stable the economic environment, the easier it is for the firms to reach a common understanding on the terms of coordination. For instance, it is easier to coordinate among a few players than among many. It is also easier to coordinate on a price for a single, homogeneous product, than on hundreds of prices in a market with many differentiated products. Similarly, it is easier to coordinate on a price when demand and supply conditions are relatively stable than when they are continuously changing.[60] In this context volatile demand, substantial internal growth by some firms in the market or frequent entry by new firms may indicate that the current situation is not sufficiently stable to make coordination likely.[61] In markets where innovation is important, coordination may be more difficult since innovations, particularly significant ones, may allow one firm to gain a major advantage over its rivals.

Notes

[60] See, e.g. Commission Decision 2002/156/EC in Case COMP/M.2097 — *SCA/Metsä Tissue*, OJ L 57, 27.2.2002, p. 1, point 148.

[61] See, e.g. Case IV/M.1298 — *Kodak/Imation*, point 60.

46. Coordination by way of market division will be easier if customers have simple characteristics that allow the coordinating firms to readily allocate them. Such characteristics may be based on geography; on customer type or simply on the existence of customers who typically buy from one specific firm. Coordination by way of market division may be relatively straightforward if it is easy to identify each customer's supplier and the coordination device is the allocation of existing customers to their incumbent supplier.

47. Coordinating firms may, however, find other ways to overcome problems stemming from complex economic environments short of market division. They may, for instance, establish simple pricing rules that reduce the complexity of coordinating on a large number of prices. One example of such a rule is establishing a small number of pricing points, thus reducing the coordination problem. Another example is having a fixed relationship between certain base prices and a number of other prices, such that prices basically move in parallel. Publicly available key information, exchange of information through trade associations, or information received through cross-shareholdings or participation in joint ventures may also help firms reach terms of coordination. The more complex the market situation is, the more transparency or communication is likely to be needed to reach a common understanding on the terms of coordination.

Commentary
para 47: B&C: 8.212

48. Firms may find it easier to reach a common understanding on the terms of coordination if they are relatively symmetric,[62] especially in terms of cost structures, market shares, capacity levels and levels of vertical integration.[63] Structural links such as cross-shareholding or participation in joint ventures may also help in aligning incentives among the coordinating firms.[64]

Notes

[62] Case T-102/96 *Gencor v Commission* [1999] ECR II-753, paragraph 222; Commission Decision 92/553/EC in Case IV/M.190 — *Nestlé/Perrier*, OJ L 356, 5.12.1992, p. 1, points 63–123.

63 In assessing whether or not a merger may increase the symmetry of the various firms present on the market, efficiency gains may provide important indications (see also paragraph 82 of the notice).
64 See, e.g. Commission Decision 2001/519/EC in Case COMP/M.1673 — *VEBA/VIAG*, OJ L 188, 10.7.2001, p. 1, point 226; Case COMP/M.2567 — *Nordbanken/Postgirot*, point 54.

Monitoring deviations

49. Coordinating firms are often tempted to increase their share of the market by deviating from the terms of coordination, for instance by lowering prices, offering secret discounts, increasing product quality or capacity or trying to win new customers. Only the credible threat of timely and sufficient retaliation keeps firms from deviating. Markets therefore need to be sufficiently transparent to allow the coordinating firms to monitor to a sufficient degree whether other firms are deviating, and thus know when to retaliate.[65]

Notes

65 See, e.g. Case COMP/M.2389 — *Shell/DEA*, points 112 et seq.; and Case COMP/M.2533 — *BP/E.ON*, points 102 et seq.

50. Transparency in the market is often higher, the lower the number of active participants in the market. Further, the degree of transparency often depends on how market transactions take place in a particular market. For example, transparency is likely to be high in a market where transactions take place on a public exchange or in an open outcry auction.[66] Conversely, transparency may be low in a market where transactions are confidentially negotiated between buyers and sellers on a bilateral basis.[67] When evaluating the level of transparency in the market, the key element is to identify what firms can infer about the actions of other firms from the available information.[68] Coordinating firms should be able to interpret with some certainty whether unexpected behaviour is the result of deviation from the terms of coordination. For instance, in unstable environments it may be difficult for a firm to know whether its lost sales are due to an overall low level of demand or due to a competitor offering particularly low prices. Similarly, when overall demand or cost conditions fluctuate, it may be difficult to interpret whether a competitor is lowering its price because it expects the coordinated prices to fall or because it is deviating.

Notes

66 See also Commission Decision 2000/42/EC in Case IV/M.1313 — *Danish Crown/Vestjyske Slagterier*, OJ L 20, 25.1.2000, p. 1, points 176–179.
67 See, e.g. Case COMP/M.2640 — *Nestlé/Schöller*, point 37; Commission Decision 1999/641/EC in Case COMP/M.1225 — *Enso/Stora*, OJ L 254, 29.9.1999, p. 9, points 67–68.
68 See, e.g. Case IV/M.1939 — *Rexam (PLM)/American National Can*, point 24.

51. In some markets where the general conditions may seem to make monitoring of deviations difficult, firms may nevertheless engage in practices which have the effect of easing the monitoring task, even when these practices are not necessarily entered into for such purposes. These practices, such as meeting-competition or most-favoured-customer clauses, voluntary publication of information, announcements, or exchange of information through trade associations, may increase transparency or help competitors interpret the choices made. Cross-directorships, participation in joint ventures and similar arrangements may also make monitoring easier.

Deterrent mechanisms

52. Coordination is not sustainable unless the consequences of deviation are sufficiently severe to convince coordinating firms that it is in their best interest to adhere to the terms of coordination. It is thus the threat of future retaliation that keeps the coordination sustainable.[69] However the threat is only credible if, where deviation by one of the firms is detected, there is sufficient certainty that some deterrent mechanism will be activated.[70]

Notes

69 See Case COMP/M.2389 — *Shell/DEA*, point 121, and Case COMP/M.2533 — *BP/E.ON*, point 111.
70 Although deterrent mechanisms are sometimes called "punishment" mechanisms, this should not be understood in the strict sense that such a mechanism necessarily punishes individually a firm that has deviated. The expectation that

coordination may break down for a certain period of time, if a deviation is identified as such, may in itself constitute a sufficient deterrent mechanism.

53. Retaliation that manifests itself after some significant time lag, or is not certain to be activated, is less likely to be sufficient to offset the benefits from deviating. For example, if a market is characterised by infrequent, large-volume orders, it may be difficult to establish a sufficiently severe deterrent mechanism, since the gain from deviating at the right time may be large, certain and immediate, whereas the losses from being punished may be small and uncertain and only materialise after some time. The speed with which deterrent mechanisms can be implemented is related to the issue of transparency. If firms are only able to observe their competitors' actions after a substantial delay, then retaliation will be similarly delayed and this may influence whether it is sufficient to deter deviation.

54. The credibility of the deterrence mechanism depends on whether the other coordinating firms have an incentive to retaliate. Some deterrent mechanisms, such as punishing the deviator by temporarily engaging in a price war or increasing output significantly, may entail a short-term economic loss for the firms carrying out the retaliation. This does not necessarily remove the incentive to retaliate since the short-term loss may be smaller than the long-term benefit of retaliating resulting from the return to the regime of coordination.

55. Retaliation need not necessarily take place in the same market as the deviation.[71] If the coordinating firms have commercial interaction in other markets, these may offer various methods of retaliation.[72] The retaliation could take many forms, including cancellation of joint ventures or other forms of cooperation or selling of shares in jointly owned companies.

Notes
[71] See, e.g. Commission Decision 2000/42/EC in Case IV/M.1313 — *Danish Crown/Vestjyske Slagterier*, OJ L 20, 25.1.2000, p. 1, point 177.
[72] See Case T-102/96 *Gencor v Commission* [1999] ECR II-753, paragraph 281.

Commentary
para 55: B&C: 8.213

Reactions of outsiders

56. For coordination to be successful, the actions of non-coordinating firms and potential competitors, as well as customers, should not be able to jeopardise the outcome expected from coordination. For example, if coordination aims at reducing overall capacity in the market, this will only hurt consumers if non-coordinating firms are unable or have no incentive to respond to this decrease by increasing their own capacity sufficiently to prevent a net decrease in capacity, or at least to render the coordinated capacity decrease unprofitable.[73]

Notes
[73] These elements are analysed in a similar way to non-coordinated effects.

57. The effects of entry and countervailing buyer power of customers are analysed in later sections. However, special consideration is given to the possible impact of these elements on the stability of coordination. For instance, by concentrating a large amount of its requirements with one supplier or by offering long-term contracts, a large buyer may make coordination unstable by successfully tempting one of the coordinating firms to deviate in order to gain substantial new business.

Merger with a potential competitor

58. Concentrations where an undertaking already active on a relevant market merges with a potential competitor in this market can have similar anti-competitive effects to mergers between two undertakings already active on the same relevant market and, thus, significantly impede effective competition, in particular through the creation or the strengthening of a dominant position.

59. A merger with a potential competitor can generate horizontal anti-competitive effects, whether coordinated or non-coordinated, if the potential competitor significantly constrains the behaviour of the firms active in the market. This is the case if the potential competitor possesses assets that could easily be used to enter the market without incurring significant sunk costs. Anti-competitive effects may also occur where the merging partner is very likely to incur the necessary

sunk costs to enter the market in a relatively short period of time after which this company would constrain the behaviour of the firms currently active in the market.[74]

Notes
[74] See, e.g. Case IV/M.1630 — *Air Liquide/BOC*, points 201 et seq. For an example of a case where entry by the other merging firm was not sufficiently likely in the short to medium term (Case T-158/00, *ARD v Commission*, [2003] ECR II-000, paragraphs 115–127).

60. For a merger with a potential competitor to have significant anti-competitive effects, two basic conditions must be fulfilled. First, the potential competitor must already exert a significant constraining influence or there must be a significant likelihood that it would grow into an effective competitive force. Evidence that a potential competitor has plans to enter a market in a significant way could help the Commission to reach such a conclusion.[75] Second, there must not be a sufficient number of other potential competitors, which could maintain sufficient competitive pressure after the merger.[76]

Notes
[75] Commission Decision 2001/98/EC in Case IV/M.1439 — *Telia/Telenor*, OJ L 40, 9.2.2001, p. 1, points 330–331, and Case IV/M.1681 — *Akzo Nobel/Hoechst Roussel Vet*, point 64.
[76] Case IV/M.1630 — *Air Liquide/BOC*, point 219; Commission Decision 2002/164/EC in Case COMP/M. 1853 — *EDF/EnBW*, OJ L 59, 28.2.2002, p. 1, points 54–64.

Commentary
para 60: F&N: 5.268

Mergers creating or strengthening buyer power in upstream markets

61. The Commission may also analyse to what extent a merged entity will increase its buyer power in upstream markets. On the one hand, a merger that creates or strengthens the market power of a buyer may significantly impede effective competition, in particular by creating or strengthening a dominant position. The merged firm may be in a position to obtain lower prices by reducing its purchase of inputs. This may, in turn, lead it also to lower its level of output in the final product market, and thus harm consumer welfare.[77] Such effects may in particular arise when upstream sellers are relatively fragmented. Competition in the downstream markets could also be adversely affected if, in particular, the merged entity were likely to use its buyer power vis-à-vis its suppliers to foreclose its rivals.[78]

Notes
[77] See Commission Decision 1999/674/EC in Case M.1221 — *Rewe/Meinl*, OJ L 274, 23.10.1999, p. 1, points 71–74.
[78] Case T-22/97, *Kesko v Commission*, [1999] ECR II-3775, paragraph 157; Commission Decision 2002/156/EC in Case M.877 — *Boeing/McDonnell Douglas*, OJ L 336, 8.12.1997, p. 16, points 105–108.

Commentary
para 61: F&N: 5.272

62. On the other hand, increased buyer power may be beneficial for competition. If increased buyer power lowers input costs without restricting downstream competition or total output, then a proportion of these cost reductions are likely to be passed onto consumers in the form of lower prices.

63. In order to assess whether a merger would significantly impede effective competition by creating or strengthening buyer power, an analysis of the competitive conditions in upstream markets and an evaluation of the possible positive and negative effects described above are therefore required.

V. COUNTERVAILING BUYER POWER

64. The competitive pressure on a supplier is not only exercised by competitors but can also come from its customers. Even firms with very high market shares may not be in a position, post-merger, to significantly impede effective competition, in particular by acting to an appreciable extent

independently of their customers, if the latter possess countervailing buyer power.[79] Countervailing buyer power in this context should be understood as the bargaining strength that the buyer has vis-à-vis the seller in commercial negotiations due to its size, its commercial significance to the seller and its ability to switch to alternative suppliers.

Notes

[79] See, e.g. Case IV/M.1882 — *Pirelli/BICC*, points 73–80.

65. The Commission considers, when relevant, to what extent customers will be in a position to counter the increase in market power that a merger would otherwise be likely to create. One source of countervailing buyer power would be if a customer could credibly threaten to resort, within a reasonable timeframe, to alternative sources of supply should the supplier decide to increase prices[80] or to otherwise deteriorate quality or the conditions of delivery. This would be the case if the buyer could immediately switch to other suppliers,[81] credibly threaten to vertically integrate into the upstream market or to sponsor upstream expansion or entry[82] for instance by persuading a potential entrant to enter by committing to placing large orders with this company. It is more likely that large and sophisticated customers will possess this kind of countervailing buyer power than smaller firms in a fragmented industry.[83] A buyer may also exercise countervailing buying power by refusing to buy other products produced by the supplier or, particularly in the case of durable goods, delaying purchases.

Notes

[80] See, e.g. Case IV/M.1245 — *Valeo/ITT Industries*, point 26.

[81] Even a small number of customers may not have sufficient buyer power if they are to a large extent "locked in" because of high switching costs (see Case COMP/M.2187 — *CVC/Lenzing*, point 223).

[82] Commission Decision 1999/641/EC in Case COMP/M.1225 — *Enso/Stora*, OJ L 254, 29.9.1999, p. 9, points 89–91.

[83] It may also be appropriate to compare the concentration existing on the customer side with the concentration on the supply side (Case COMP/JV 55 — *Hutchison/RCPM/ECT*, point 119, and Commission Decision 1999/641/EC in Case COMP/M.1225 — *Enso/Stora*, OJ L 254, 29.9.1999, p. 9, point 97).

66. In some cases, it may be important to pay particular attention to the incentives of buyers to utilise their buyer power.[84] For example, a downstream firm may not wish to make an investment in sponsoring new entry if the benefits of such entry in terms of lower input costs could also be reaped by its competitors.

Notes

[84] Case COMP/JV 55 — *Hutchison/RCPM/ECT*, points 129–130.

67. Countervailing buyer power cannot be found to sufficiently off-set potential adverse effects of a merger if it only ensures that a particular segment of customers,[85] with particular bargaining strength, is shielded from significantly higher prices or deteriorated conditions after the merger.[86] Furthermore, it is not sufficient that buyer power exists prior to the merger, it must also exist and remain effective following the merger. This is because a merger of two suppliers may reduce buyer power if it thereby removes a credible alternative.

Notes

[85] Commission Decision 2002/156/EC in Case COMP/M.2097 — *SCA/Metsä Tissue*, OJ L 57, 27.2.2002, point 88. Price discrimination between different categories of customers may be relevant in some cases in the context of market definition (see the Commission's notice on the definition of the relevant market, cited above, at paragraph 43).

[86] Accordingly, the Commission may assess whether the various purchasers will hold countervailing buyer power, see, e.g. Commission Decision 1999/641/EC in Case COMP/M.1225 — *Enso/Stora*, OJ L 254, 29.9.1999, p. 9, points 84–97.

VI. ENTRY

68. When entering a market is sufficiently easy, a merger is unlikely to pose any significant anti-competitive risk. Therefore, entry analysis constitutes an important element of the overall

competitive assessment. For entry to be considered a sufficient competitive constraint on the merging parties, it must be shown to be likely, timely and sufficient to deter or defeat any potential anti-competitive effects of the merger.

Likelihood of entry

69. The Commission examines whether entry is likely or whether potential entry is likely to constrain the behaviour of incumbents post-merger. For entry to be likely, it must be sufficiently profitable taking into account the price effects of injecting additional output into the market and the potential responses of the incumbents. Entry is thus less likely if it would only be economically viable on a large scale, thereby resulting in significantly depressed price levels. And entry is likely to be more difficult if the incumbents are able to protect their market shares by offering long-term contracts or giving targeted pre-emptive price reductions to those customers that the entrant is trying to acquire. Furthermore, high risk and costs of failed entry may make entry less likely. The costs of failed entry will be higher, the higher is the level of sunk cost associated with entry.[87]

Notes

[87] Commission Decision 97/610/EC in Case IV/M.774 — *Saint-Gobain/Wacker-Chemie/NOM*, OJ L 247, 10.9.1997, p. 1, point 184.

70. Potential entrants may encounter barriers to entry which determine entry risks and costs and thus have an impact on the profitability of entry. Barriers to entry are specific features of the market, which give incumbent firms advantages over potential competitors. When entry barriers are low, the merging parties are more likely to be constrained by entry. Conversely, when entry barriers are high, price increases by the merging firms would not be significantly constrained by entry. Historical examples of entry and exit in the industry may provide useful information about the size of entry barriers.

71. Barriers to entry can take various forms:
    (a) Legal advantages encompass situations where regulatory barriers limit the number of market participants by, for example, restricting the number of licences.[88] They also cover tariff and non-tariff trade barriers.[89]
    (b) The incumbents may also enjoy technical advantages, such as preferential access to essential facilities, natural resources,[90] innovation and R & D,[91] or intellectual property rights,[92] which make it difficult for any firm to compete successfully. For instance, in certain industries, it might be difficult to obtain essential input materials, or patents might protect products or processes. Other factors such as economies of scale and scope, distribution and sales networks,[93] access to important technologies, may also constitute barriers to entry.
    (c) Furthermore, barriers to entry may also exist because of the established position of the incumbent firms on the market. In particular, it may be difficult to enter a particular industry because experience or reputation is necessary to compete effectively, both of which may be difficult to obtain as an entrant. Factors such as consumer loyalty to a particular brand,[94] the closeness of relationships between suppliers and customers, the importance of promotion or advertising, or other advantages relating to reputation[95] will be taken into account in this context. Barriers to entry also encompass situations where the incumbents have already committed to building large excess capacity,[96] or where the costs faced by customers in switching to a new supplier may inhibit entry.

Notes

[88] Case IV/M.1430 — *Vodafone/Airtouch*, point 27; Case IV/M.2016 — *France Télécom/Orange*, point 33.
[89] Commission Decision 2002/174/EC in Case COMP/M.1693 — *Alcoa/Reynolds*, OJ L 58, 28.2.2002, point 87.
[90] Commission Decision 95/335/EC in Case IV/M.754 — *Anglo American Corp./Lonrho*, OJ L 149, 20.5.1998, p. 21, points 118–119.
[91] Commission Decision 97/610/EC in Case IV/M.774 — *Saint-Gobain/Wacker-Chemie/NOM*, OJ L 247, 10.9.1997, p. 1, points 184–187.
[92] Commission Decision 94/811/EC in Case IV/M.269 — *Shell/Montecatini*, OJ L 332, 22.12.1994, p. 48, point 32.
[93] Commission Decision 98/327/EC in Case IV/M.833 — *The Coca-Cola Company/Carlsberg A/S*, OJ L 145, 15.5.1998, p. 41, point 74.

[94] Commission Decision 98/327/EC in Case IV/M.833 — *The Coca-Cola Company/Carlsberg A/S*, OJ L 145, 15.5.1998, p. 41, points 72–73.
[95] Commission Decision 2002/156/EC in Case COMP/M.2097 — *SCA/Metsä Tissue*, OJ L 57, 27.2.2002, p. 1, points 83–84.
[96] Commission Decision 2001/432/EC in Case IV/M.1813 — *Industri Kapital Nordkem/Dyno*, OJ L 154, 9.6.2001, p. 41, point 100.

72. The expected evolution of the market should be taken into account when assessing whether or not entry would be profitable. Entry is more likely to be profitable in a market that is expected to experience high growth in the future[97] than in a market that is mature or expected to decline.[98] Scale economies or network effects may make entry unprofitable unless the entrant can obtain a sufficiently large market share.[99]

Notes

[97] See, e.g. Commission Decision 98/475/EC in Case IV/M.986 — *Agfa-Gevaert/Dupont*, OJ L 211, 29.7.1998, p. 22, points 84–85.
[98] Case T-102/96 *Gencor v Commission* [1999] ECR II-753, paragraph 237.
[99] See, e.g. Commission Decision 2000/718/EC in Case IV/M.1578 — *Sanitec/Sphinx*, OJ L 294, 22.11.2000, p. 1, point 114.

73. Entry is particularly likely if suppliers in other markets already possess production facilities that could be used to enter the market in question, thus reducing the sunk costs of entry. The smaller the difference in profitability between entry and non-entry prior to the merger, the more likely such a reallocation of production facilities.

Timeliness

74. The Commission examines whether entry would be sufficiently swift and sustained to deter or defeat the exercise of market power. What constitutes an appropriate time period depends on the characteristics and dynamics of the market, as well as on the specific capabilities of potential entrants.[100] However, entry is normally only considered timely if it occurs within two years.

Notes

[100] See, e.g. Commission Decision 2002/174/EC in Case COMP/M.1693 — *Alcoa/Reynolds*, L 58, 28.2.2002, points 31–32, 38.

Commentary
para 74: F&N: 4.67

Sufficiency

75. Entry must be of sufficient scope and magnitude to deter or defeat the anti-competitive effects of the merger.[101] Small-scale entry, for instance into some market "niche", may not be considered sufficient.

Notes

[101] Commission Decision 91/535/EEC in Case IV/M.68 — *Tetra Pak/Alfa Laval*, OJ L 290, 22.10.1991, p. 35, point 3.4.

Commentary
para 75: F&N: 4.67

VII. Efficiencies

76. Corporate reorganisations in the form of mergers may be in line with the requirements of dynamic competition and are capable of increasing the competitiveness of industry, thereby improving the conditions of growth and raising the standard of living in the Community.[102] It is possible that efficiencies brought about by a merger counteract the effects on competition and in particular the potential harm to consumers that it might otherwise have.[103] In order to assess whether a merger would significantly impede effective competition, in particular through the creation or the strengthening of a dominant position, within the meaning of Article 2(2) and (3) of the

Merger Regulation, the Commission performs an overall competitive appraisal of the merger. In making this appraisal, the Commission takes into account the factors mentioned in Article 2(1), including the development of technical and economic progress provided that it is to the consumers' advantage and does not form an obstacle to competition.[104]

Notes
[102] See Recital 4 of the Merger Regulation.
[103] See Recital 29 of the Merger Regulation.
[104] Cf. Article 2(1)(b) of the Merger Regulation.

77. The Commission considers any substantiated efficiency claim in the overall assessment of the merger. It may decide that, as a consequence of the efficiencies that the merger brings about, there are no grounds for declaring the merger incompatible with the common market pursuant to Article 2(3) of the Merger Regulation. This will be the case when the Commission is in a position to conclude on the basis of sufficient evidence that the efficiencies generated by the merger are likely to enhance the ability and incentive of the merged entity to act pro-competitively for the benefit of consumers, thereby counteracting the adverse effects on competition which the merger might otherwise have.

78. For the Commission to take account of efficiency claims in its assessment of the merger and be in a position to reach the conclusion that as a consequence of efficiencies, there are no grounds for declaring the merger to be incompatible with the common market, the efficiencies have to benefit consumers, be merger-specific and be verifiable. These conditions are cumulative.

Benefit to consumers

79. The relevant benchmark in assessing efficiency claims is that consumers[105] will not be worse off as a result of the merger. For that purpose, efficiencies should be substantial and timely, and should, in principle, benefit consumers in those relevant markets where it is otherwise likely that competition concerns would occur.

Notes
[105] Pursuant to Article 2(1)(b), the concept of "consumers" encompasses intermediate and ultimate consumers, i.e. users of the products covered by the merger. In other words, consumers within the meaning of this provision include the customers, potential and/or actual, of the parties to the merger.

Commentary
para 79: F&N: 3.409

80. Mergers may bring about various types of efficiency gains that can lead to lower prices or other benefits to consumers. For example, cost savings in production or distribution may give the merged entity the ability and incentive to charge lower prices following the merger. In line with the need to ascertain whether efficiencies will lead to a net benefit to consumers, cost efficiencies that lead to reductions in variable or marginal costs[106] are more likely to be relevant to the assessment of efficiencies than reductions in fixed costs; the former are, in principle, more likely to result in lower prices for consumers.[107] Cost reductions, which merely result from anti-competitive reductions in output, cannot be considered as efficiencies benefiting consumers.

Notes
[106] Variable costs should be viewed as those costs that vary with the level of production or sales over the relevant time period. Marginal costs are those costs associated with expanding production or sales at the margin.
[107] Generally, fixed cost savings are not given such weight as the relationship between fixed costs and consumer prices is normally less direct, at least in the short run.

81. Consumers may also benefit from new or improved products or services, for instance resulting from efficiency gains in the sphere of R & D and innovation. A joint venture company set up in order to develop a new product may bring about the type of efficiencies that the Commission can take into account.

82. In the context of coordinated effects, efficiencies may increase the merged entity's incentive to increase production and reduce prices, and thereby reduce its incentive to coordinate its market

behaviour with other firms in the market. Efficiencies may therefore lead to a lower risk of coordinated effects in the relevant market.

83. In general, the later the efficiencies are expected to materialise in the future, the less weight the Commission can assign to them. This implies that, in order to be considered as a counteracting factor, the efficiencies must be timely.

84. The incentive on the part of the merged entity to pass efficiency gains on to consumers is often related to the existence of competitive pressure from the remaining firms in the market and from potential entry. The greater the possible negative effects on competition, the more the Commission has to be sure that the claimed efficiencies are substantial, likely to be realised, and to be passed on, to a sufficient degree, to the consumer. It is highly unlikely that a merger leading to a market position approaching that of a monopoly, or leading to a similar level of market power, can be declared compatible with the common market on the ground that efficiency gains would be sufficient to counteract its potential anti-competitive effects.

Merger specificity

85. Efficiencies are relevant to the competitive assessment when they are a direct consequence of the notified merger and cannot be achieved to a similar extent by less anticompetitive alternatives. In these circumstances, the efficiencies are deemed to be caused by the merger and thus, merger-specific.[108] It is for the merging parties to provide in due time all the relevant information necessary to demonstrate that there are no less anti-competitive, realistic and attainable alternatives of a non-concentrative nature (e.g. a licensing agreement, or a cooperative joint venture) or of a concentrative nature (e.g. a concentrative joint venture, or a differently structured merger) than the notified merger which preserve the claimed efficiencies. The Commission only considers alternatives that are reasonably practical in the business situation faced by the merging parties having regard to established business practices in the industry concerned.

Notes

[108] In line with the general principle set out in paragraph 9 of this notice.

Verifiability

86. Efficiencies have to be verifiable such that the Commission can be reasonably certain that the efficiencies are likely to materialise, and be substantial enough to counteract a merger's potential harm to consumers. The more precise and convincing the efficiency claims are, the better the Commission can evaluate the claims. Where reasonably possible, efficiencies and the resulting benefit to consumers should therefore be quantified. When the necessary data are not available to allow for a precise quantitative analysis, it must be possible to foresee a clearly identifiable positive impact on consumers, not a marginal one. In general, the longer the start of the efficiencies is projected into the future, the less probability the Commission may be able to assign to the efficiencies actually being brought about.

87. Most of the information, allowing the Commission to assess whether the merger will bring about the sort of efficiencies that would enable it to clear a merger, is solely in the possession of the merging parties. It is, therefore, incumbent upon the notifying parties to provide in due time all the relevant information necessary to demonstrate that the claimed efficiencies are merger-specific and likely to be realised. Similarly, it is for the notifying parties to show to what extent the efficiencies are likely to counteract any adverse effects on competition that might otherwise result from the merger, and therefore benefit consumers.

88. Evidence relevant to the assessment of efficiency claims includes, in particular, internal documents that were used by the management to decide on the merger, statements from the management to the owners and financial markets about the expected efficiencies, historical examples of efficiencies and consumer benefit, and pre-merger external experts' studies on the type and size of efficiency gains, and on the extent to which consumers are likely to benefit.

VIII. Failing Firm

89. The Commission may decide that an otherwise problematic merger is nevertheless compatible with the common market if one of the merging parties is a failing firm. The basic requirement is that the deterioration of the competitive structure that follows the merger cannot be said to be caused by the merger.[109] This will arise where the competitive structure of the market would deteriorate to at least the same extent in the absence of the merger.[110]

Notes

[109] Joined Cases C-68/94 and C-30/95 *Kali and Salz*, paragraph 110.

[110] Joined Cases C-68/94 and C-30/95 *Kali and Salz*, paragraph 114. See also Commission Decision 2002/365/EC in Case COMP/M.2314 — *BASF/Pantochim/Eurodiol*, OJ L 132, 17.5.2002, p. 45, points 157–160. This requirement is linked to the general principle set out in paragraph 9 of this notice.

90. The Commission considers the following three criteria to be especially relevant for the application of a "failing firm defence". First, the allegedly failing firm would in the near future be forced out of the market because of financial difficulties if not taken over by another undertaking. Second, there is no less anti-competitive alternative purchase than the notified merger. Third, in the absence of a merger, the assets of the failing firm would inevitably exit the market.[111]

Notes

[111] The inevitability of the assets of the failing firm leaving the market in question may, in particular in a case of merger to monopoly, underlie a finding that the market share of the failing firm would in any event accrue to the other merging party. See Joined Cases C-68/94 and C-30/95 *Kali and Salz*, paragraphs 115–116.

91. It is for the notifying parties to provide in due time all the relevant information necessary to demonstrate that the deterioration of the competitive structure that follows the merger is not caused by the merger.

D7

DG COMPETITION: BEST PRACTICES ON THE CONDUCT OF EC MERGER CONTROL PROCEEDINGS

Note

This document is published on the Europa website at:
http://ec.europa.eu/comm/competition/mergers/legislation/regulation/best_practices.pdf

Commentary

Best Practices: F&N: 5.389, 5.395, 5.410, 5.413, 5.420, 5.423, 5.425, 5.429, 5.433, 5.538

paras 10–23: F&N: 5.429

paras 16–18: F&N: 5.430

paras 26–28: F&N: 5.489

1. Scope and Purpose of the Best Practices

1. The principal aim of these Best Practices is to provide guidance for interested parties on the day-to-day conduct of EC merger control proceedings. They are intended to foster and build upon a spirit of co-operation and better understanding between DG Competition and the legal and business community. In this regard, the Best Practices seek to increase understanding of the investigation process and thereby to further enhance the efficiency of investigations and to ensure a high degree

Part D Mergers and Concentrations

of transparency and predictability of the review process. In particular, they aim at making the short time available in EC merger procedures as productive and efficient as possible for all parties concerned.

Commentary
para 1: F&N: 5.395

2. The Best Practices are built on the experience to date of DG Competition in the application of Council Regulation (EEC) No 4064/89[1] (the Merger Regulation) and replace the current Best Practices of 1999. They reflect the views and practice of DG Competition at the time of publication.[2]
The specificity of an individual case may require an adaptation of, or deviation from these Best Practices depending on the case at hand.

Notes
[1] Council Regulation No 4064/89, OJ L 395, 30.12.1989 p. 1; corrigendum OJ L 257 of 21.9.1990, p. 13; Regulation as last amended by Regulation (EC) No 1310/97 (OJ L 180, 9.7.1997, p. 1, corrigendum OJ L 40, 13.2.1998, p. 17).
[2] It is to be noted that a recast Merger Regulation replacing Regulation 4064/89 will apply from 1 May 2004. The Best Practices are equally applicable under Regulation 4064/89 and will continue to be applicable, possibly with further amendments, under the recast Merger Regulation. Appropriate references to the recast Merger Regulation are made throughout the Best Practices by means of footnotes. Those references will only become applicable from 1st of May 2004.

2. RELATIONSHIP TO COMMUNITY LAW

3. These Best Practices should not be taken as a full or comprehensive account of the relevant legislative, interpretative and administrative measures which govern Community merger control. They should be read in conjunction with such measures.
4. The Best Practices do not create or alter any rights or obligations as set out in the Treaty establishing the European Community, the Merger Regulation, its Implementing Regulation[3] as amended from time to time and as interpreted by the case-law of the Community Courts. Nor do they alter the Commission's interpretative notices. The Best Practices do not apply to proceedings under Council Regulation No 17,[4] to be replaced by Council Regulation No 1/2003[5] as of 1 May 2004, implementing Articles 81 and 82 of the Treaty.

Notes
[3] Commission Regulation (EC) No 447/98 of 1 March 1998 on the notifications, time limits and hearings provided for in the Merger Regulation, OJ L 61, 2.3.1998, p. 1.
[4] OJ P 013, 21/02/1962, p. 204–211.
[5] Council Regulation (EC) No 1/2003 of 16 December 2002 on the implementation of the rules on competition laid down in Articles 81 and 82 of the Treaty, OJ L 1, 04.01.2003, p. 1–25.

3. PRE-NOTIFICATION

Purpose of pre-notification contacts

5. In DG Competition's experience the pre-notification phase of the procedure is an important part of the whole review process. As a general rule, DG Competition finds it useful to have pre-notification contacts with notifying parties even in seemingly non-problematic cases. DG Competition will therefore always give notifying parties and other involved parties the opportunity, if they so request, to discuss an intended concentration informally and in confidence prior to notification (cf. also Recital 10 Implementing Regulation).

Commentary
para 5: F&N: 5.413

6. Pre-notification contacts provide DG Competition and the notifying parties with the possibility, prior to notification, to discuss jurisdictional and other legal issues. They also serve to discuss issues such as the scope of the information to be submitted and to prepare for the upcoming investigation by identifying key issues and possible competition concerns (theories of harm) at an early stage.

7. Further, it is in the interests of DG Competition and the business and legal community to ensure that notification forms are complete from the outset so that declarations of incompleteness are avoided as far as possible. It is DG Competition's experience that in cases in which notifications have been declared incomplete, usually there were no or very limited pre-notification contacts. Accordingly, for this reason it is recommended that notifying parties contact DG Competition prior to notification.

Commentary
para 7: F&N: 5.433, 5.542

8. Pre-notification discussions are held in strict confidence. The discussions are a voluntary part of the process and remain without prejudice to the handling and investigation of the case following formal notification. However, the mutual benefits for DG Competition and the parties of a fruitful pre-notification phase can only materialise if discussions are held in an open and co-operative atmosphere, where all potential issues are addressed in a constructive way.

Commentary
para 8: F&N: 5.417

9. In DG Competition's experience it is generally preferable that both legal advisers and business representatives, who have a good understanding of the relevant markets, are available for pre-notification discussions with the case-team. This normally results in more informed discussions on the business rationale for the transaction and the functioning of the markets in question.

Timing and extent of pre-notification contacts

10. Pre-notification contacts should preferably be initiated at least two weeks before the expected date of notification. The extent and format of the pre-notification contacts required is, however, linked to the complexity of the individual case in question. In more complex cases a more extended pre-notification period may be appropriate and in the interest of the notifying parties. In all cases it is advisable to make contact with DG Competition as soon as possible as this will facilitate planning of the case.

Commentary
para 10: F&N: 5.423

11. Pre-notification contacts should be launched with a submission that allows the selection of an appropriate DG Competition case-team.[6] This memorandum should provide a brief background to the transaction, a brief description of the relevant sector(s) and market(s) involved and the likely impact of the transaction on competition in general terms. It should also indicate the case language. In straightforward cases, the parties may chose to submit a draft Form CO as a basis for further discussions with DG Competition.

Notes
[6] Case teams for new cases are normally set up in weekly DG Competition's Merger Management Meetings.

12. After initial contacts have been made between the case-team and the notifying parties, it will be decided, whether it will suffice for DG Competition to make comments orally or in writing on the submissions made. This would typically be considered in straightforward cases. In more complex cases and cases that raise jurisdictional or other procedural issues, one or more pre-notification meetings are normally considered appropriate.
13. The first pre-notification meeting is normally held on the basis of a more substantial submission or a first draft Form CO. This allows for a more fruitful discussion about the proposed transaction in question or potential issue in point. Subsequent meetings may cover additional information submitted or outstanding issues.
14. Any submission sent to DG Competition should be provided sufficiently ahead of meetings or other contacts in order to allow for well prepared and fruitful discussions. In this regard, preparatory briefing memoranda/ draft Form COs sent in preparation of meetings should be filed in good time before the meeting (at least three working days) unless agreed otherwise with

the case team. In case of voluminous submissions and in less straightforward cases, this time may need to be extended to allow DG Competition to properly prepare for the meeting.

15. Irrespective of whether pre-notification meetings have taken place or not, it is advisable that the notifying parties systematically provide a substantially complete draft Form CO before filing a formal notification. DG Competition would thereafter normally require five working days to review the draft before being asked to comment, at a meeting or on the telephone, on the adequacy of the draft. In case of voluminous submissions, this time will normally be extended.

Commentary
para 15: F&N: 5.433

Information to be provided / preparation of the Form CO

16. The format and the timing of all pre-notification submissions should be decided together with the case-team. Notifying parties are advised to fully and frankly disclose information relating to all potentially affected markets and possible competition concerns, even if they may ultimately consider that they are not affected and notwithstanding that they may take a particular view in relation to, for example, the issue of market definition. This will allow for an early market testing of alternative market definitions and/or the notifying parties' position on the market/s in question. In DG Competition's experience this approach minimises surprise submissions from third parties, and may avoid requests for additional information from the notifying parties at a late stage in the procedure and possible declarations of incompleteness under Article 4(2) of the Implementing Regulation or a decision under Article 11(5) of the Merger Regulation.

17. In addition, DG Competition recommends that notifying parties should, as early as possible in pre-notification, submit internal documents such as board presentations, surveys, analyses, reports and studies discussing the proposed concentration, the economic rationale for the concentration and competitive significance or the market context in which it takes place. Such documents provide DG Competition with an early and informed view of the transaction and its potential competitive impact and can thus allow for a productive discussion and finalisation of the Form CO.

18. Where appropriate, it is also recommended that notifying parties put forward, already at the pre-notification stage, any elements demonstrating that the merger leads to efficiency gains that they would like the Commission to take into account for the purposes of its competitive assessment of the proposed transaction. Such claims are likely to require extensive analysis. It is thus in the interests of the notifying parties to present these claims as early as possible to allow sufficient time for DG Competition to appropriately consider these elements in its assessment of a proposed transaction.

19. Pre-notification discussions provide the opportunity for the Commission and the notifying parties to discuss the amount of information to be provided in a notification. The notifying parties may in pre-notification request the Commission to waive the obligation to provide certain information that is not necessary for the examination of the case. All requests to omit any part of the information specified should be discussed in detail and any waiver has to be agreed with DG Competition prior to notification.[7]

Notes
[7] See Article 3(2) Implementing Regulation. See also Commission Notice on a simplified procedure for treatment of certain concentrations under Council Regulation (EEC) No 4064/89, OJ C 217, 29.07.2000, p. 32.

Completeness of the notification

20. Given that a notification is not considered effective until the information to be submitted in Form CO is complete in all material respects, the notifying parties and their advisers should ensure that the information contained in Form CO has been carefully prepared and verified: incorrect and misleading information is considered incomplete information.[8] In this regard, the notifying parties should take special care that the appropriate contact details are provided for customers, suppliers and competitors. If such information is not correct or provided in full it will significantly delay the investigation and therefore may lead to a declaration of incompleteness.

Notes
[8] In addition, the Commission may impose fines on the notifying parties where they supply incorrect or misleading information in a notification under Article 14 (1)(b) Merger Regulation.

Commentary
para 20: F&N: 5.457

21. Further, to facilitate the effective and expeditious handling of their notification, notifying parties should also endeavour to provide the contact details required in Form CO electronically, at the latest on the day of notification, using the appropriate electronic form which can be provided by the case team.

22. Provided that the notifying parties follow the above described guidance, DG Competition will in principle, be prepared to confirm informally the adequacy of a draft notification at the pre-notification stage or, if appropriate, to identify in what material respects the draft Form CO is incomplete. However it has to be recognised that it will not be possible for DG Competition to exclude the fact that it may have to declare a notification incomplete in appropriate cases after notification.

23. In the event that DG Competition discovers omissions in the Form CO after formal notification, the notifying parties may be given an opportunity to urgently put right such omissions before a declaration of incompleteness is adopted. Due to the time constraints in merger procedures, the time allowed for such rectification is normally limited to 1 or 2 days. This opportunity will not be granted, however, in cases where DG Competition finds that the omissions immediately hinder the proper investigation of the proposed transaction.

Commentary
para 24: F&N: 5.421

Procedural questions and inter-agency co-operation

24. In addition to substantive issues, the notifying parties may in the pre-notification phase seek DG Competition's opinion on procedural matters such as jurisdictional questions.

25. Informal guidance may be provided if they are directly related to an actual, planned transaction and if sufficiently detailed background information is submitted by the notifying parties to properly assess the issue in question.[9] Further matters for pre-notification discussions include the possibility of referrals to or from national EU jurisdictions,[10] parallel proceedings in other non-EU jurisdictions and the issue of waivers on information sharing with other jurisdictions. As regards transactions likely to be reviewed in more than one jurisdiction, DG Competition invites the notifying parties to discuss the timing of the case with a view to enhance efficiency of the respective investigations, to reduce burdens on the merging parties and third parties, and to increase overall transparency of the merger review process. In this regard, notifying parties should also have regard to the EU-US Best Practices on cooperation in merger investigations.[11]

Notes
[9] Such informal guidance cannot be regarded as creating legitimate expectations regarding the proper interpretation of applicable jurisdictional or other rules.
[10] Such jurisdictional discussions will become particularly pertinent under the recast Merger Regulation, which becomes applicable from 1 May 2004. Pursuant to Articles 4(4) and 4(5) of the recast Merger Regulation, notifying parties may, before notification, request on the basis of a reasoned submission, referral of a case to or from the Commission. DG Competition will be ready to discuss with notifying parties informally the possibility of such pre-notification referrals and to guide them through the pre-notification referral process.
[11] http://europa.eu.int/comm/competition/mergers/others/eu_us.pdf

Commentary
para 25: F&N: 5.422, 5.425

4. FACT FINDING/REQUESTS FOR INFORMATION

26. In carrying out its duties the Commission may obtain all necessary information from relevant persons, undertakings, associations of undertakings and competent authorities of Member States

(see Article 11(1) Merger Regulation). That investigation normally starts after the notification of a proposed concentration. However, DG Competition may exceptionally decide that, in the interest of its investigation, market contacts could be initiated informally prior to notification. Such pre-notification contacts/enquiries would only take place if the existence of the transaction is in the public domain and once the notifying parties have had the opportunity to express their views on such measures.

27. The Commission's investigation is mainly conducted in the form of written Requests for Information (requests pursuant to Article 11 of the Merger Regulation) to customers, suppliers, competitors and other relevant parties. Such requests may also be addressed to the notifying parties. In addition to such Article 11 requests, the views of the notifying parties, other involved parties and third parties are also sought orally.

28. In the interest of an efficient investigation, DG Competition may consult the notifying parties, other involved parties or third parties on methodological issues regarding data and information gathering in the relevant economic sector. It may also seek external economic and/or industrial expertise and launch its own economic studies.

5. COMMUNICATION AND MEETINGS WITH THE NOTIFYING PARTIES, OTHER INVOLVED PARTIES AND 3RD PARTIES

29. One of the aims of these Best Practices is to enhance transparency in the day to day handling of merger cases and in particular, to ensure good communication between DG Competition, the merging parties and third parties. In this regard, DG Competition endeavours to give all parties involved in the proceeding ample opportunity for open and frank discussions and to make their points of view known throughout the procedure.

5.1. State of Play meetings with notifying parties

Aim and format of the State of Play meetings

30. The objective of the State of Play meetings is to contribute to the quality and efficiency of the decision-making process and to ensure transparency and communication between DG Competition and the notifying parties. As such these meetings should provide a forum for the mutual exchange of information between DG Competition and the notifying parties at key points in the procedure. They are entirely voluntary in nature.

31. State of Play meetings may be conducted in the form of meetings at the Commission's premises, or alternatively, if appropriate, by telephone or videoconference. In order for the meetings to operate properly they should be carefully prepared on the basis of an agenda agreed in advance. Further, senior DG Competition management will normally chair the meetings.

32. The State of Play meetings will not exclude discussions and exchanges of information between the notifying parties and DG Competition at other occasions throughout the procedure as appropriate. In this regard, notifying parties are advised to inform DG Competition, as soon as possible, about any important procedural or substantive developments that may be of relevance for the assessment of the proposed transaction. Such developments may include any remedy proposals the notifying parties are offering or are considering to offer in other jurisdictions, so as to facilitate co-ordination of the timing and substance of such remedy proposals. This also concerns matters already discussed at a State of Play meeting, in respect of which the parties consider it necessary to provide additional comments.

Timing of the State of Play meetings

33. Notifying parties will normally be offered the opportunity of attending a State of Play meeting at the following five different points in the Phase I and Phase II procedure:
   a) where it appears that "serious doubts" within the meaning of Article 6(1)(c) of the Merger Regulation are likely to be present a meeting will be offered <u>before the expiry of 3 weeks</u>[12] <u>into Phase I</u>. In addition to informing the notifying parties of the preliminary result of the initial investigation, this meeting provides an opportunity for the notifying parties to prepare the formulation of a possible remedy proposal in Phase I before expiry of the deadline provided in Article 18 of the Implementing Regulation.

b) <u>normally within 2 weeks following the adoption of the Article 6(1)(c) decision</u>. In order to prepare for this meeting, the notifying parties should provide DG Competition with their comments on the Article 6(1)(c) decision and on any documents in the Commission's file, which they may have had the opportunity to review (see below section 7.2) by way of a written memorandum in advance of the meeting. The notifying parties should contact the case team to discuss an appropriate schedule for the filing of this memorandum.

The main purpose of the post Article 6(1)(c) meeting is to facilitate the notifying parties' understanding of the Commission's concerns at an early stage of the Phase II proceedings. The meeting also serves to assist DG Competition in deciding the appropriate framework for its further investigation by discussing with the notifying parties matters such as the market definition and competition concerns outlined in the Article 6(1)(c) decision. The meeting is also intended to serve as a forum for mutually informing each other of any planned economic or other studies. The approximate timetable of the Phase II procedure may also be discussed.[13]

c) <u>before the issuing of a Statement of Objections (SO)</u>. This pre-SO meeting gives the notifying parties an opportunity to understand DG Competition's preliminary view on the outcome of the Phase II investigation and to be informed of the type of objections DG Competition may set out in the SO. The meeting may also be used by DG Competition to clarify certain issues and facts before it finalises its proposal on the issuing of a SO.

d) <u>following the reply to the SO and the Oral Hearing</u>. This post-SO State of Play meeting provides the notifying parties with an opportunity to understand DG Competition's position after it has considered their reply and heard them at an Oral Hearing. If DG Competition indicates that it is minded to maintain some or all of its objections, the meeting may also serve as an opportunity to discuss the scope and timing of possible remedy proposals.[14]

e) <u>before the Advisory Committee meets</u>. The primary purpose of this meeting is to enable the notifying parties to discuss with DG Competition its views on any proposed remedies and where relevant, the results of the market testing of such remedies. It also provides the notifying parties where necessary, with the opportunity to formulate improvements to their remedies proposal.[15]

Notes

[12] Fifteen working days under the recast Merger Regulation.

[13] Once the recast Merger Regulation becomes applicable, this post Article 6(1)(c) State of Play meeting will also serve to discuss the possibility of any extensions to the Phase II deadline pursuant to Article 10(3) of the recast Merger Regulation.

[14] It is to be noted that, under the recast Merger Regulation (Article 10(3)), the submission of remedies could lead to an automatic extension of the Phase II deadline.

[15] Modifications to remedies are only possible under those conditions set out in Article 18 of the Implementing Regulation and point 43 of the Commission's Notice on Remedies.

Commentary

para 33: F&N: 5.507, 5.524
para 33(a): F&N: 5.485
para 33(b): F&N: 5.533
para 33(c): F&N: 5.543
para 33(d): F&N: 5.606
para 33(e): F&N: 5.606

5.2. Involvement of third parties

34. According to Community merger control law, third parties considered as having a "sufficient interest" in the Commission's procedure include customers, suppliers, competitors, members of the administration or management organs of the undertakings concerned or recognised workers' representatives of those undertakings.[16] Their important role in the Commission's procedure is stressed in particular in Article 18(4) of the Merger Regulation and Articles 16(1) and (2) of the Implementing Regulation. In addition, the Commission also welcomes the views of any other interested third parties including consumer organisations.[17]

Part D Mergers and Concentrations

Notes
[16] See Article 11 of the Implementing Regulation.
[17] Article 16(3) Implementing Regulation. To this effect, DG Competition has appointed a Consumer Liaison Officer responsible for contacts with consumer organisations.

35. The primary way for third parties to contribute to the Commission's investigation is by means of replies to requests for information (Article 11 Merger Regulation).[18] However, DG Competition also welcomes any individual submission apart from direct replies to questionnaires, where third parties provide information and comments they consider relevant for the assessment of a given transaction. DG Competition may also invite third parties for meetings to discuss and clarify specific issues raised.

Notes
[18] Article 11(7) of the recast Merger Regulation expressly provides for the Commission's competence to interview any natural or legal person who consents to be interviewed for the purpose of collecting information relating to the subject-matter of an investigation.

36. In addition, DG Competition may in the interest of the investigation in appropriate cases provide third parties that have shown a sufficient interest in the procedure with an edited version of the SO from which business secrets have been removed, in order to allow them to make their views known on the Commission's preliminary assessment. In such cases, the SO is provided under strict confidentiality obligations and restrictions of use, which the third parties have to accept prior to receipt.

Commentary
para 36: F&N: 5.555

37. If third parties wish to express competition concerns as regards the transaction in question or to put forward views on key market data or characteristics that deviate from the notifying parties' position, it is essential that they are communicated as early as possible to DG Competition, so that they can be considered, verified and taken into account properly. Any point raised should be substantiated and supported by examples, documents and other factual evidence. Furthermore, in accordance with Article 17(2) of the Implementing Regulation, third parties should always provide the DG Competition with a non-confidential version of their submissions at the time of filing or shortly thereafter to facilitate access to the file and other measures intended to ensure transparency for the benefit of the decision making process (see further below section 7).

Commentary
para 37: F&N: 5.420

5.3. "Triangular" and other meetings

38. In addition to bilateral meetings between DG Competition and the notifying parties, other involved parties or third parties, DG Competition may decide to invite third parties and the notifying parties to a "triangular" meeting where DG Competition believes it is desirable, in the interests of the fact-finding investigation, to hear the views of the notifying parties and such third parties in a single forum. Such triangular meetings, which will be on a voluntary basis and which are not intended to replace the formal oral hearing, would take place in situations where two or more opposing views have been put forward as to key market data and characteristics and the effects of the concentration on competition in the markets concerned.

Commentary
para 38: F&N: 5.539

39. Triangular meetings should ideally be held as early in the investigation as possible in order to enable DG Competition to reach a more informed conclusion as to the relevant market characteristics and to clarify issues of substance before deciding on the issuing of an SO. Triangular meetings are normally chaired by senior DG Competition management. They are prepared in

advance on the basis of an agenda established by DG Competition after consultation of all parties that agreed to attend the meeting. The preparation will normally include a mutual exchange of non-confidential submissions between the notifying parties and the third party in question sufficiently in advance of the meeting. The meeting will not require the disclosure of confidential information or business secrets, unless otherwise agreed by the parties.

Commentary
para 39: F&N: 5.540

6. Remedies Discussions

40. As stated above, the State of Play meetings in both Phase I and Phase II, in addition to providing a forum for discussing issues related to the investigation, also serve to discuss possible remedy proposals. Detailed guidance on the requirements for such proposals is set out in the Commission Notice on remedies acceptable under Council Regulation (EEC) No 4064/89 and under Commission Regulation (EC) No 447/98[19] (the Remedies Notice). In particular, the Remedies Notice sets out the general principles applicable to remedies, the main types of commitments that have previously been accepted by the Commission, the specific requirements which proposals of remedies need to fulfil in both phases of the procedure, and guidance on the implementation of remedies. As regards the design of divestiture commitment proposals, the notifying parties are advised to take due account of the Commission's "Best Practice Guidelines on Divestiture Commitments".[20]

Notes
[19] OJ C 68, 02.03.2001, p. 3–11.
[20] Available under: http://europa.eu.int/comm/competition/mergers/legislation/divestiture_commitments/

41. Although it is for the notifying parties to formulate suitable remedies proposals, DG Competition will provide guidance to the parties as to the general appropriateness of their draft proposal in advance of submission. In order to allow for such discussions, a notifying party should contact DG Competition in good time before the relevant deadline in Phase I or Phase II, in order to be able to address comments DG Competition may have on the draft proposal.[21]

Notes
[21] It is to be noted that under the recast Merger Regulation (Articles 10(1) and (3)), the submission of remedies could lead to an automatic extension of the Phase I and II deadlines.

Commentary
para 41: F&N: 5.609

7. Provision of Documents in the Commission's file/Confidentiality

7.1. Access to the file

42. According to Community law, the notifying parties have upon request a right to access the Commission's file after the Commission has issued an SO (see Article 18(3) of the Merger Regulation and Article 13(3) of the Implementing Regulation).

43. Further, the notifying parties will be given the opportunity to have access to documents received after the issuing of the SO up until the consultation of the Advisory Committee.

Commentary
para 43: F&N: 5.575, 5.613

44. Access to the file will be provided subject to the legitimate interest of the protection of third parties' business secrets and other confidential information.

Part D Mergers and Concentrations

7.2. Review of key documents

45. DG Competition believes in the merits of an open exchange of views with ample opportunities for the notifying parties and third parties to make their points of view known throughout the procedure. This enables DG Competition to assess the main issues arising during the investigation with as much information at its disposal as possible. In this spirit, DG Competition's objective will be to provide the notifying parties with the opportunity of reviewing and commenting on "key documents" obtained by the Commission. Such documents would comprise substantiated submissions of third parties running counter to the notifying parties' own contentions received during Phase I and thereafter,[22] including key submissions to which specific reference is made in the Article 6(1)(c) decision and market studies.

Notes

[22] This would in particular include substantiated "complaints" contending that the notified transaction may give rise to competition concerns. The word "complaint" is to be understood in the non-technical sense of the term as no formal complaints procedure exists in merger cases.

Commentary
para 45: F&N: 5.576

46. DG Competition will use its best endeavours to provide notifying parties in a timely fashion, with the opportunity to review such documents following the initiation of proceedings and thereafter on an *ad hoc* basis. DG Competition will respect justified requests by third parties for non-disclosure of their submissions prior to the issuing of the SO relating to genuine concerns regarding confidentiality, including fears of retaliation and the protection of business secrets.

Commentary
para 46: F&N: 5.542, 5.576

7.3. Confidentiality Rules

47. In accordance with Article 287 of the EC Treaty and Article 17(1) of the Implementing Regulation, the Commission will, throughout its investigation, protect confidential information and business secrets contained in submissions provided by all parties involved in EC merger proceedings. Given the short legal deadlines of EC merger procedures, parties are encouraged to clarify as soon as possible any queries related to confidentiality claims with members of the case team. Guidance on what is considered to be business secrets or other confidential information is provided in the Commission's Notice on Access to file.[23]

Notes

[23] OJ C 23, 23/01/97, p. 3. [See now Commission Notice of 13 December 2005 on the rules for access to the Commission file in cases pursuant to Articles 81 and 82 of the EC Treaty, Articles 53, 54 and 57 of the EEA Agreement and Council Regulation (EC) No 139/2004, (2005/C 325/07), OJ C 225, 22.12.2005, p. 7.]

Commentary
para 47: F&N: 5.420

8. Right to be Heard and Other Procedural Rights

48. The right of the parties concerned to be heard before a final decision affecting their interests is taken is a fundamental principle of Community law. That right is also set out in the Merger Regulation (Article 18) and the Implementing Regulation (Articles 14–16). These Best Practices do not alter any such rights under Community law.

49. Any issues related to the right to be heard and other procedural issues, including access to the file, time limits for replying to the SO and the objectivity of any enquiry conducted in order to assess the competition impact of commitments proposed in EC merger proceedings can be raised with the Hearing Officer, in accordance with Commission Decision of 23 May 2001 on the terms of reference of hearing officers in certain competition proceedings.[24]

Notes
[24] Official Journal L 162, 19/06/2001 p. 21–24. The text can also be found at: http://europa.eu.int/comm/competition/
hearings/officers/

9. FUTURE REVIEW

50. These Best Practices may be revised to reflect changes to legislative, interpretative and administrative measures or due to case law of the European Courts, which govern EC merger control or any experience gained in applying such framework. DG Competition further intends to engage, on a regular basis, in a dialogue with the business and legal community on the experience gained through the application of the Merger Regulation in general, and these Best Practices in particular.

D8

COMMUNICATION FROM THE COMMISSION

Communication pursuant to Article 23(1) of Commission Regulation (EC) No 802/2004[1] implementing Council Regulation (EC) No 139/2004[2] on the control of concentrations between undertakings

(2004/C 139/02)

(Text with EEA relevance)

Official Journal C 139, 19.5.2004, p. 2

Celex No: 52004XC0519(01)

Commentary
Communication: F&N: 5.455

Address of the Commission's Directorate General for Competition

European Commission
Directorate General for Competition
Merger Registry
Rue Joseph II / Jozef II Straat, 70
B-1000 Bruxelles / Brussel

Notes
[1] OJ L 133, 30.04.2004, pages 1–39.
[2] Council Regulation (EC) No 139/2004 of 20 January 2004 on the control of concentrations between undertakings, OJ L 24, 29.01.2004, pages 1–22.

D9

COMMISSION NOTICE

on Case Referral in respect of concentrations

(2005/C 56/02)

(Text with EEA relevance)

Official Journal C 56, 5.3.2005, p. 2

Celex No: 52005XC0305(01)

Commentary
Notice: **B&C:** 8.008, 8.014 **F&N:** 5.115
paras 8–14: **B&C:** 8.014

---

1. The purpose of this Notice is to describe in a general way the rationale underlying the case referral system in Article 4(4) and (5), Article 9 and Article 22 of Council Regulation (EC) No 139/2004 of 20 January 2004 on the control of concentrations between undertakings (the EC Merger Regulation)[1] (hereinafter "the Merger Regulation"), including the recent changes made to the system, to catalogue the legal criteria that must be fulfilled in order for referrals to be possible, and to set out the factors which may be taken into consideration when referrals are decided upon. The Notice also provides practical guidance regarding the mechanics of the referral system, in particular regarding the pre-notification referral mechanism provided for in Article 4(4) and (5) of the Merger Regulation. The guidance provided in this notice applies, *mutatis mutandis*, to the referral rules contained in the EEA Agreement.[2]

Notes

[1] OJ L 24, 29.1.2004, p. 1. This Regulation has recast Council Regulation (EEC) No 4064/89 of 21 December 1989 on the control of concentrations between undertakings (OJ L 395, 30.12.1989, p. 1. Corrected version in OJ L 257, 21.9.1990, p. 13).

[2] See EEA Joint Committee Decision No 78/2004 of 8 June 2004 (OJ L 219, 8.6.2004, p. 13).

I. INTRODUCTION

2. Community jurisdiction in the field of merger control is defined by the application of the turnover-related criteria contained in Articles 1(2) and 1(3) of the Merger Regulation. When dealing with concentrations, the Commission and Member States do not have concurrent jurisdiction. Rather, the Merger Regulation establishes a clear division of competence. Concentrations with a "Community dimension", i.e. those above the turnover thresholds in Article 1 of the Merger Regulation, fall within the exclusive jurisdiction of the Commission; Member States are precluded from applying national competition law to such concentrations by virtue of Article 21 of the Merger Regulation. Concentrations falling below the thresholds remain within the competence of the Member States; the Commission has no jurisdiction to deal with them under the Merger Regulation.

3. Determining jurisdiction exclusively by reference to fixed turnover-related criteria provides legal certainty for merging companies. While the financial criteria generally serve as effective proxies for the category of transactions for which the Commission is the more appropriate authority, Regulation (EEC) No 4064/89 complemented this "bright-line" jurisdictional scheme with a possibility for cases to be re-attributed by the Commission to Member States and vice versa, upon request and provided certain criteria were fulfilled.

4. When Regulation (EEC) No 4064/89 was first introduced, it was envisaged by the Council and Commission that case referrals would only be resorted to in "exceptional circumstances" and where "the interests in respect of competition of the Member State concerned could not be adequately

720

protected in any other way".[3] There have, however, been a number of developments since the adoption of Regulation (EEC) No 4064/89. First, merger control laws have been introduced in almost all Member States. Second, the Commission has exercised its discretion to refer a number of cases to Member States pursuant to Article 9 in circumstances where it was felt that the Member State in question was in a better position to carry out the investigation than the Commission.[4] Likewise, in a number of cases,[5] several Member States decided to make a joint referral of a case pursuant to Article 22 in circumstances where it was felt that the Commission was the authority in a better position to carry out the investigation.[6] Third, there has been an increase in the number of transactions not meeting the thresholds in Article 1 of the Merger Regulation which must be filed in multiple Member State jurisdictions, a trend which is likely to continue in line with the Community's growing membership. Many of these transactions affect competition beyond the territories of individual Member States.[7]

Notes

[3] See the Notes on Council Regulation (EEC) No 4064/89 ["Merger Control in the European union", European Commission, Brussels–Luxembourg, 1998, at p. 54]. See also Case T-119/02 *Philips v Commission* [2003] ECR II-1433 (Case M.2621 *SEB/Moulinex*) at paragraph 354.

[4] It is a fact that some concentrations of Community dimension affect competition in national or sub-national markets within one or more Member States.

[5] M.2698 *Promatech/Sulzer*; M.2738 *GE/Unison*; M.3136 *GE/AGFA*.

[6] In the same vein, Member States" competition authorities, in the context of the European Competition Authorities' association, have issued a recommendation designed to provide guidance as to the principles upon which national competition authorities should deal with cases eligible for joint referrals under Article 22 of the Merger Regulation — *Principles on the application, by National Competition Authorities within the ECA network, of Article 22 of the EC Merger Regulation.*

[7] While the introduction of Article 1(3) in 1997 has brought some such cases under the jurisdiction of the Merger Regulation, many are unaffected. See paragraph 21 et seq of the Commission's Green Paper of 11 December 2001 (COM(2001) 745 final).

5. The revisions made to the referral system in the Merger Regulation are designed to facilitate the reattribution of cases between the Commission and Member States, consistent with the principle of subsidiarity, so that the more appropriate authority or authorities for carrying out a particular merger investigation should in principle deal with the case. At the same time, the revisions are intended to preserve the basic features of the Community merger control system introduced in 1989, in particular the provision of a "one-stop-shop" for the competition scrutiny of mergers with a cross-border impact and an alternative to multiple merger control notifications within the Community.[8] Such multiple filings often entail considerable cost for competition authorities and businesses alike.

Notes

[8] See Recitals 11, 12 and 14 to the Merger Regulation.

6. The case re-attribution system now provides that a referral may also be triggered before a formal filing has been made in any Member State jurisdiction, thereby affording merging companies the possibility of ascertaining, at as early as possible a stage, where jurisdiction for scrutiny of their transaction will ultimately lie. Such pre-notification referrals have the advantage of alleviating the additional cost, notably in terms of time delay, associated with post-filing referral.

7. The revisions made to the referral system in Regulation (EC) No. 139/2004 were motivated by a desire that it should operate as a jurisdictional mechanism which is flexible[9] but which at the same time ensures effective protection of competition and limits the scope for "forum shopping" to the greatest extent possible. However, having regard in particular to the importance of legal certainty, it should be stressed that referrals remain a derogation from the general rules which determine jurisdiction based upon objectively determinable turnover thresholds. Moreover, the Commission and Member States retain a considerable margin of discretion in deciding whether to refer cases falling within their "original jurisdiction", or whether to accept to deal with cases not falling within their "original jurisdiction", pursuant to Article 4(4) and (5), Article 9(2)(a) and Article 22.[10] To that extent, the current Notice is intended to provide no more than general guidance regarding the appropriateness of particular cases or categories of cases for referral.

Part D Mergers and Concentrations

⁹ See Recital 11 to the Merger Regulation.

¹⁰ See, however, *infra*, footnote 14. It should moreover be noted that, pursuant to Article 4(5), the Commission has no discretion as to whether or not to accept a case not falling within its original jurisdiction.

II. REFERRAL OF CASES

Guiding principles

8. The system of merger control established by the Merger Regulation, including the mechanism for re-attributing cases between the Commission and Member States contained therein, is consistent with the principle of subsidiarity enshrined in the EC Treaty.[11] Decisions taken with regard to the referral of cases should accordingly take due account of all aspects of the application of the principle of subsidiarity in this context, in particular which is the authority more appropriate for carrying out the investigation, the benefits inherent in a "one-stop-shop" system, and the importance of legal certainty with regard to jurisdiction.[12] These factors are inter-linked and the respective weight placed upon each of them will depend upon the specificities of a particular case. Above all, in considering whether or not to exercise their discretion to make or accede to a referral, the Commission and Member States should bear in mind the need to ensure effective protection of competition in all markets affected by the transaction.[13]

Notes

[11] See Article 5 of the EC Treaty.

[12] See Recitals 11 and 14 to the Merger Regulation.

[13] See Article 9(8) of the Merger Regulation; see also *Philips v Commission* (paragraph 343) where the Court of First Instance of the European Communities states that ". . . although the first subparagraph of Article 9(3) of Regulation (EEC) No 4064/89 confers on the Commission broad discretion as to whether or not to refer a concentration, it cannot decide to make such a referral if, when the Member State's request for referral is examined, it is clear, on the basis of a body of precise and coherent evidence, that such a referral cannot safeguard effective competition on the relevant market"; see also T-346/02 and T-347/02 *Cableuropa SA v Commission* of 30 September 2003, [[2003] ECR II-4251] (paragraph 215). Circumstances relevant for the purpose of the Commission assessment include, *inter alia*, the fact that a Member State: (i) has specific laws for the control of concentrations on competition grounds and specialised bodies to ensure that these laws are implemented under the supervision of the national courts; (ii) has accurately identified the competition concerns raised by the concentration on the relevant markets in that Member State (see paragraphs 346–347 of *Philips v Commission*, cited above).

More appropriate authority

9. In principle, jurisdiction should only be re-attributed to another competition authority in circumstances where the latter is the more appropriate for dealing with a merger, having regard to the specific characteristics of the case as well as the tools and expertise available to the authority. Particular regard should be had to the likely locus of any impact on competition resulting from the merger. Regard may also be had to the implications, in terms of administrative effort, of any contemplated referral.[14]

Notes

[14] This may involve consideration of the relative cost, time delay, legal uncertainty and the risk of conflicting assessment which may be associated with the investigation, or a part of the investigation, being carried out by multiple authorities.

10. The case for re-attributing jurisdiction is likely to be more compelling where it appears that a particular transaction may have a significant impact on competition and thus may deserve careful scrutiny.

One-stop-shop

11. Decisions on the referral of cases should also have regard to the benefits inherent in a "one-stop-shop", which is at the core of the Merger Regulation.[15] The provision of a one-stop-shop is beneficial to competition authorities and businesses alike. The handling of a merger by a single competition authority normally increases administrative efficiency, avoiding duplication

and fragmentation of enforcement effort as well as potentially incoherent treatment (regarding investigation, assessment and possible remedies) by multiple authorities. It normally also brings advantages to businesses, in particular to merging firms, by reducing the costs and burdens arising from multiple filing obligations and by eliminating the risk of conflicting decisions resulting from the concurrent assessment of the same transaction by a number of competition authorities under diverse legal regimes.

Notes
[15] See Recital 11 of the Merger Regulation.

12. Fragmentation of cases through referral should therefore be avoided where possible,[16] unless it appears that multiple authorities would be in a better position to ensure that competition in all markets affected by the transaction is effectively protected. Accordingly, while partial referrals are possible under Article 4(4) and Article 9, it would normally be appropriate for the whole of a case (or at least all connected parts thereof) to be dealt with by a single authority.[17]

Notes
[16] The Court of First Instance in *Philips v Commission* took the view, *obiter dictum*, that "fragmentation" of cases, while possible as a result of the application of Article 9, is "undesirable in view of the 'one-stop-shop' principle on which Regulation (EEC) No 4064/89 is based". Moreover, the Court, while recognising that the risk of "inconsistent, or even irreconcilable" decisions by the Commission and Member States "is inherent in the referral system established by Article 9", made it clear that this is not, in its view, desirable. (See paragraphs 350 and 380.)
[17] This is consistent with the Commission's decision in cases M.2389 *Shell/DEA* and M.2533 *BP/E.ON* to refer to Germany all of the markets for downstream oil products. The Commission retained the parts of the cases involving upstream markets. Likewise, in M.2706 *P&O Princess/Carnival*, the Commission exercised its discretion not to refer a part of the case to the United Kingdom, because it wished to avoid a fragmentation of the case. (See Commission press release of 11.4.2002, IP/02/552.)

Legal certainty

13. Due account should also be taken of the importance of legal certainty regarding jurisdiction over a particular concentration, from the perspective of all concerned.[18] Accordingly, referral should normally only be made when there is a compelling reason for departing from "original jurisdiction" over the case in question, particularly at the post-notification stage. Similarly, if a referral has been made prior to notification, a post-notification referral in the same case should be avoided to the greatest extent possible.[19]

Notes
[18] See Recital 11 of the Merger Regulation.
[19] See Recital 14 to the Merger Regulation. This is of course subject to the parties having made a full and honest disclosure of all relevant facts in their request for a pre-filing referral.

14. The importance of legal certainty should also be borne in mind with regard to the legal criteria for referral, and particularly — given the tight deadlines — at the pre-notification stage. Accordingly, pre-filing referrals should in principle be confined to those cases where it is relatively straightforward to establish, from the outset, the scope of the geographic market and/or the existence of a possible competitive impact, so as to be able to promptly decide upon such requests

Case referrals: legal requirements and other factors to be considered

Pre-notification referrals

15. The system of pre-notification referrals is triggered by a reasoned submission lodged by the parties to the concentration. When contemplating such a request, the parties to the concentration are required, first, to verify whether the relevant legal requirements set out in the Merger Regulation are fulfilled, and second, whether a pre-notification referral would be consistent with the guiding principles outlined above.

Referral of cases by the Commission to Member States under Article 4(4)

Legal requirements

16. In order for a referral to be made by the Commission to one or more Member States pursuant to Articles 4(4), two legal requirements must be fulfilled:
    (i) there must be indications *that the concentration may significantly affect competition* in a market or markets;
    (ii) the market(s) in question must be within a Member State and *present all the characteristics of a distinct market.*

17. As regards the *first criterion*, the requesting parties are in essence required to demonstrate that the transaction is liable to have a potential impact on competition on a distinct market in a Member State, which may prove to be significant, thus deserving close scrutiny. Such indications may be no more than preliminary in nature, and would be without prejudice to the outcome of the investigation. While the parties are not required to demonstrate that the effect on competition is likely to be an adverse one,[20] they should point to indicators which are generally suggestive of the existence of some competitive effects stemming from the transaction.[21]

Notes

[20] See Recital 16, which states that "the undertakings concerned should not . . . be required to demonstrate that the effects of the concentration would be detrimental to competition".

[21] The existence of "affected markets" within the meaning of Form RS would generally be considered sufficient to meet the requirements of Article 4(4). However, the parties can point to any factors which may be relevant for the competitive analysis of the case (market overlap, vertical integration, etc).

---

18. As regards the *second criterion*, the requesting parties are required to show that a geographic market in which competition is affected by the transaction in the manner just described (paragraph 17) is national, or narrower than national in scope.[22]

Notes

[22] To this end, the requesting parties should consider those factors which are typically suggestive of national or narrower than national markets, such as, primarily, the product characteristics (e.g. low value of the product as opposed to significant costs of transport), specific characteristics of demand (e.g. end consumers sourcing in proximity to their centre of activity) and supply, significant variation of prices and market shares across countries national consumer habits, different regulatory frameworks, taxation or other legislation. Further guidance can be found in the Commission Notice on the definition of the relevant market for the purposes of Community competition law (OJ C 372, 9.12.1997, p. 5).

Other factors to be considered

19. Other than verification of the legal requirements, in order to anticipate to the greatest extent possible the likely outcome of a referral request, merging parties contemplating a request should also consider whether referral of the case is likely to be considered appropriate. This will involve an examination of the application of the guiding principles referred to above (paragraphs 8 to 14), and in particular whether the competition authority or authorities to which they are contemplating requesting the referral of the case is the most appropriate authority for dealing with the case. To this end, consideration should be given in turn both to the likely locus of the competitive effects of the transaction and to how appropriate the national competition authority (NCA) would be for scrutinising the operation.

20. Concentrations with a Community dimension which are likely to affect competition in markets that have a national or narrower than national scope, and the effects of which are likely to be confined to, or have their main economic impact in, a single Member State,[23] are the most appropriate candidate cases for referral to that Member State. This applies in particular to cases where the impact would occur on a distinct market which does not constitute a substantial part of the common market. To the extent that referral is made to one Member State only, the benefit of a "one-stop-shop" is also preserved.

Notes

[23] See, for example, the Commission's referral of certain distinct oil storage markets for assessment by the French authorities in Cases M.1021 *Compagnie Nationale de Navigation-SOGELF*, M.1464 *Total/Petrofina*, and Case

M.1628 *Totalfina/Elf Aquitaine*, Case M.1030 *Lafarge/Redland*, Case M.1220 *Alliance Unichem/Unifarma*, Case M.2760 *Nehlsen/Rethmann/SWB/Bremerhavener Energiewirtschaft*, and Case M.2154 *C3D/Rhone/Go-ahead*; Case M.2845 *Sogecable/Canal Satelite Digital/Vias Digital*.

21. The extent to which a concentration with a Community dimension which, despite having a potentially significant impact on competition in a nation-wide market, nonetheless potentially engenders substantial cross-border effects (e.g. because the effects of the concentration in one geographic market may have significant repercussions in geographic markets in other Member States, or because it may involve potential foreclosure effects and consequent fragmentation of the common market),[24] may be an appropriate candidate for referral will depend on the specific circumstances of the case. As both the Commission and Member States may be equally well equipped or be in an equally good position to deal with such cases, a considerable margin of discretion should be retained in deciding whether or not to refer such cases.

Notes

[24] See Case M.580 *ABB/Daimler Benz*, where the Commission did not accede to Germany's request for referral of a case under Article 9 in circumstances where, while the competition concerns were confined to German markets, the operation (which would create the largest supplier of railway equipment in the world) would have significant repercussions throughout Europe. See also Case M.2434 *Hidroelectrica del Cantabrico/EnBW/Grupo Vilar Mir*, where, despite a request by Spain to have the case referred under Article 9, the Commission pursued the investigation and adopted a decision pursuant to Article 8(2).

22. The extent to which concentrations with a Community dimension, and potentially affecting competition in a series of national or narrower than national markets in more than one Member State, may be appropriate candidates for referral to Member States will depend on factors specific to each individual case, such as the number of national markets likely to be significantly affected, the prospect of addressing any possible concerns by way of proportionate, non-conflicting remedies, and the investigative efforts that the case may require. To the extent that a case may engender competition concerns in a number of Member States, and require coordinated investigations and remedial action, this may militate in favour of the Commission retaining jurisdiction over the entirety of the case in question.[25] On the other hand, to the extent that the case gives rise to competition concerns which, despite involving national markets in more than one Member State, do not appear to require coordinated investigation and/or remedial action, a referral may be appropriate. In a limited number of cases,[26] the Commission has even found it appropriate to refer a concentration to more than one Member State, in view of the significant differences in competitive conditions that characterised the affected markets in the Member States concerned. While fragmentation of the treatment of a case deprives the merging parties of the benefit of a one-stop-shop in such cases, this consideration is less pertinent at the pre-notification stage, given that the referral is triggered by a voluntary request from the merging parties.

Notes

[25] For some examples, see M.1383 *Exxon/Mobil*, where the Commission, despite the United Kingdom request to have the part of the concentration relating to the market for motor fuel retailing in North west of Scotland referred to it, pursued the investigation as the case required a single and coherent remedy package designed to address all the problematic issues in the sector concerned; see also M.2706 *P&O Princess/Carnival*, where, despite the fact that the UK authorities were assessing a rival bid by Royal Caribbean, the Commission did not accede to a request for a partial referral, so as to avoid a fragmentation of the case and secure a single investigation of the various national markets affected by the operation.

[26] See M. 2898, *Le Roy Merlin/Brico*, M.1030, *Redland/Lafarge*, M. 1684, *Carrefour/Promodes*.

23. Consideration should also, to the extent possible, be given to whether the NCA(s) to which referral of the case is contemplated may possess specific expertise concerning local markets,[27] or be examining, or about to examine, another transaction in the sector concerned.[28]

Notes

[27] In Case M.330 *MacCormick/CPC/Rabobank/Ostmann*, the Commission referred a case to Germany, because it was better placed to investigate local conditions in 85,000 sales points in Germany; a referral to the Netherlands was made in Case M.1060 *Vendex/KBB*, because it was better placed to assess local consumer tastes and habits; See also Case M.1555 *Heineken/Cruzcampo*, Case M.2621 *SEB/Moulinex* (where consumer preferences and commercial and

marketing practices were specific to the French market); Case M.2639 *Compass/Restorama/Rail Gourmet/Gourmet*, and Case M.2662 *Danish-Crown/Steff-Houlberg*.

[28] In Case M.716 *Gehe/Lloyds Chemists*, for example, the Commission referred a case because Lloyds was also subject to another bid not falling under ECMR thresholds but being scrutinised by the UK authorities: the referral allowed both bids to be scrutinised by the same authority; in M.1001/M.1019 *Preussag/Hapag-Lloyd/TUI*, a referral was made to Germany of two transactions, which together with a third one notified in Germany, would present competition concerns: the referral ensured that all three operations were dealt with in like manner; in case M.2044 *Interbrew/Bass*, the Commission referred the case to the UK authorities, because they were at the same time assessing Interbrew's acquisition of another brewer, Whitbread, and because of their experience in recent investigations in the same markets; similarly, see also Cases M.2760 *Nehlsen/Rethmann/SWB/Bremerhavener Energiewirtschaft*, M.2234 *Metsalilitto Osuuskunta/Vapo Oy/JV*, M.2495 *Haniel/Fels*, M.2881 *Koninklijke BAM NBM/HBG*, and M.2857/M.3075–3080 *ECS/IEH* and six other acquisitions by Electrabel of local distributors. In M.2706 *P&O Princess/Carnival*, however, despite the fact that the UK authorities were already assessing a rival bid by Royal Caribbean, the Commission did not accede to a request for a partial referral. The Commission had identified preliminary competition concerns in other national markets affected by the merger and thus wished to avoid a fragmentation of the case (see Commission press release of 11.4.2002, IP/02/552).

Referral of cases from Member States to the Commission under Article 4(5)

Legal requirements

24. Under Article 4(5), only two legal requirements must be met in order for the parties to the transaction to request the referral of the case to the Commission: the transaction must be a concentration within the meaning of Article 3 of the Merger Regulation, and the concentration must be *capable of being reviewed under the national competition laws for the control of mergers of at least three Member States* (see also paragraphs 65 et seq and 70 et seq).

Other factors to be considered

25. Other than verification of the legal requirements, in order to anticipate to the greatest extent possible the likely outcome of a referral request, merging parties contemplating a request should also consider whether referral of the case is likely to be considered appropriate. This will involve an examination of the application of the guiding principles referred to above, and in particular whether the Commission is the more appropriate authority for dealing with the case.

26. In this regard, Recital 16 to the Merger Regulation states that "requests for pre-notification referrals to the Commission would be particularly pertinent in situations where the concentration would affect competition beyond the territory of one Member State." Particular consideration should therefore be given to the likely locus of any competitive effects resulting from the transaction, and to how appropriate it would be for the Commission to scrutinise the operation.

27. It should in particular be assessed whether the case is genuinely cross-border in nature, having regard to elements such as its likely effects on competition and the investigative and enforcement powers likely to be required to address any such effects. In this regard, particular consideration should be given to whether the case is liable to have a potential impact on competition in one or more markets affected by the concentration. In any case, indications of possible competitive impact may be no more than preliminary in nature,[29] and would be without prejudice to the outcome of the investigation. Nor would it be necessary for the parties to demonstrate that the effect on competition is likely to be an adverse one.

Notes

[29] The existence of "affected markets" within the meaning of Form RS would generally be considered sufficient. However, the parties can point to any factors which may be relevant for the competitive analysis of the case (market overlap, vertical integration, etc).

28. Cases where the market(s) in which there may be a potential impact on competition is/are wider than national in geographic scope,[30] or where some of the potentially affected markets are wider than national and the main economic impact of the concentration is connected to such markets, are the most appropriate candidate cases for referral to the Commission. In such cases, as the competitive dynamics extend over territories reaching beyond national boundaries, and may consequently require investigative efforts in several countries as well as appropriate enforcement powers, the Commission is likely to be in the best position to carry out the investigation.

Notes

[30] See the joint referral by seven Member States to the Commission of a transaction affecting worldwide markets in M.2738 *GE/Unison*, and the joint referral by seven Member States to the Commission of a transaction affecting a Western European market in M.2698 *Promatech/Sulzer*; See also *Principles on the application, by National Competition Authorities within the ECA network, of Article 22 of the EC Merger Regulation*, a paper published by the European Competition Authorities (ECA), at paragraph 11.

29. The Commission may be more appropriately placed to treat cases (including investigation, assessment and possible remedial action) that give rise to potential competition concerns in a series of national or narrower than national markets located in a number of different Member States.[31] The Commission is likely to be in the best position to carry out the investigation in such cases, given the desirability of ensuring consistent and efficient scrutiny across the different countries, of employing appropriate investigative powers, and of addressing any competition concerns by way of coherent remedies.

Notes

[31] This may, for example, be the case in relation to operations where the affected markets, while national (or even narrower than national in scope for the purposes of a competition assessment), are nonetheless characterised by common Europe-wide or world-wide brands, by common Europe-wide or world-wide intellectual property rights, or by centralised manufacture or distribution — at least to the extent that such centralised manufacture or distribution would be likely to impact upon any remedial measures.

30. Similarly to what has been said above in relation to Article 4(4), the appropriateness of referring concentrations which, despite having a potentially significant impact on competition in a nation-wide market, nonetheless potentially engender substantial cross-border effects, will depend on the specific circumstances of the case. As both the Commission and Member States may be in an equally good position to deal with such cases, a considerable margin of discretion should be retained in deciding whether or not to refer such cases.

31. Consideration should also, to the extent possible, be given to whether the Commission is particularly well equipped to properly scrutinise the case, in particular having regard to factors such as specific expertise, or past experience in the sector concerned. The greater a merger's potential to affect competition beyond the territory of one Member State, the more likely it is that the Commission will be better equipped to conduct the investigation, particularly in terms of fact finding and enforcement powers.

32. Finally, the parties to the concentration might submit that, despite the apparent absence of an effect on competition, there is a compelling case for having the operation treated by the Commission, having regard in particular to factors such as the cost and time delay involved in submitting multiple Member State filings.[32]

Notes

[32] See Recitals 12 and 16 of the Merger Regulation.

Post-notification referrals

Referrals from the Commission to Member States pursuant to Article 9

33. Under Article 9 there are two options for a Member State wishing to request referral of a case following its notification to the Commission: Articles 9(2)(a) and 9(2)(b) respectively.

Article 9(2)(a)

Legal requirements

34. In order for a referral to be made to a Member State or States pursuant to Article 9(2)(a), the following legal requirements must be fulfilled:
   (i)   the concentration must *threaten to affect significantly competition in a market*; and
   (ii) the market in question must be *within the requesting Member State, and present all the characteristics of a distinct market*.

35. As regards the *first criterion*, in essence a requesting Member State is required to demonstrate that, based on a preliminary analysis, there is a real risk that the transaction may have a significant

adverse impact on competition, and thus that it deserves close scrutiny. Such preliminary indications may be in the nature of *prima facie* evidence of such a possible significant adverse impact, but would be without prejudice to the outcome of a full investigation.

36. As regards the *second criterion*, the Member State is required to show that a geographic market(s) in which competition is affected by the transaction in the manner just described (paragraph 35) is/are national, or narrower than national in scope.[33]

Notes

[33] See Commission notice on the definition of relevant market for the purposes of Community competition law (OJ C372, 9.12.1997, p. 5).

Other factors to be considered

37. Other than verification of the legal requirements, other factors should also be considered in assessing whether referral of a case is likely to be considered appropriate. This will involve an examination of the application of the guiding principles referred to above, and in particular whether the competition authority or authorities requesting the referral of the case is/are in the best position to deal with the case. To this end, consideration should be given in turn both to the likely locus of the competitive effects of the transaction and to how well equipped the NCA would be to scrutinise the operation (see above at paragraphs 19–23).

Article 9(2)(b)

Legal requirements

38. In order for a referral to be made to a Member State or States pursuant to Article 9(2)(b), the following legal requirements must be fulfilled:
    (i)   the concentration *must affect competition in a market*; and
    (ii) the market in question must be *within the requesting Member State, present all the characteristics of a distinct market, and must not constitute a substantial part of the common market*.

39. As regards the *first criterion*, a requesting Member State is required to show, based on a preliminary analysis, that the concentration is liable to have an impact on competition in a market. Such preliminary indications may be in the nature of *prima facie* evidence of a possible adverse impact, but would be without prejudice to the outcome of a full investigation.

40. As to the *second criterion*, a requesting Member State is required to show not only that the market in which competition is affected by the operation in the manner just described (paragraph 38) constitutes a distinct market within a Member State, but also that the market in question does not constitute a substantial part of the common market. In this respect, based on the past practice and case-law,[34] it appears that such situations are generally limited to markets with a narrow geographic scope, within a Member State.

Notes

[34] See Commission referrals granted under Article 9(2)(b) in: M.2446, *Govia/Connex South Central*, where the operation affected competition on specific railway routes in the London/Gatwick-Brighton area in the United Kingdom; in M.2730, *Connex/DNVBVG*, where the transaction affected competition in local public transport services in the Riesa area (Saxony, Germany); and in M. 3130, *Arla Foods/Express Diaries*, where the transaction affected competition in the market for the supply of bottled milk to doorstep deliverers in the London, Yorkshire and Lancashire regions of the United Kingdom. For the purpose of defining the notion of a non-substantial part of the common market, some guidance can also be found in the case-law relating to the application of Article 82 of EC Treaty. In that context, the Court of Justice has articulated quite a broad notion of what may constitute a substantial part of the common market, resorting *inter alia* to empirical evidence. In the case-law there can be found, for instance, indications essentially based on practical criteria such as "the pattern and volume of the production and consumption of the said product as well as the habits and economic opportunities of vendors and purchasers", see Case 40/73, *Suiker Unie v Commission*, [1975] ECR 1663. See also Case C-179/90, *Porto di Genova* [1991] ECR 5889, where the Port of Genova was considered as constituting a substantial part of the common market. In its case-law the Court has also stated that a series of separate markets may be regarded as together constituting a substantial part of the common market. See, for example, Case C-323/93, *Centre d'insémination de la Crespelle* [1994] ECR I-5077, paragraph. 17,

where the Court stated "In this case, by making the operation of the insemination centres subject to authorization and providing that each centre should have the exclusive right to serve a defined area, the national legislation granted those centres exclusive rights. By thus establishing, in favour of those undertakings, a contiguous series of monopolies territorially limited but together covering the entire territory of a Member State, those national provisions create a dominant position, within the meaning of Article 86 of the Treaty, in a substantial part of the common market".

41. If these conditions are met, the Commission has an obligation to refer the case.

Referrals from Member States to the Commission pursuant to Article 22

Legal requirements

42. In order for a referral to be made by one or more Member States to the Commission pursuant to Article 22, two legal requirements must be fulfilled:
    (i) the concentration must *affect trade between Member States*; and
    (ii) it must *threaten to significantly affect competition within the territory of the Member State or States making the request.*

43. As to the *first criterion*, a concentration fulfils this requirement to the extent that it is liable to have some discernible influence on the pattern of trade between Member States.[35]

Notes

[35] See also, by analogy, the Commission Notice — Guidelines on the effect on trade concept contained in Articles 81 and 82 of the Treaty (OJ C 101, 27.4.2004, p. 81).

---

44. As to the *second criterion*, as under Article 9(2)(a), a referring Member State or States is/are required in essence to demonstrate that, based on a preliminary analysis, there is a real risk that the transaction may have a significant adverse impact on competition, and thus that it deserves close scrutiny. Such preliminary indications may be in the nature of *prima facie* evidence of such a possible significant adverse impact, but would be without prejudice to the outcome of a full investigation.

Other factors to be considered

45. As post-notification referrals to the Commission may entail additional cost and time delay for the merging parties, they should normally be limited to those cases which appear to present a real risk of negative effects on competition and trade between Member States, and where it appears that these would be best addressed at the Community level.[36] The categories of cases normally most appropriate for referral to the Commission pursuant to Article 22 are accordingly the following:
    — cases which give rise to serious competition concerns in one or more markets which are wider than national in geographic scope, or where some of the potentially affected markets are wider than national, and where the main economic impact of the concentration is connected to such markets,
    — cases which give rise to serious competition concerns in a series of national or narrower than national markets located in a number of Member States, in circumstances where coherent treatment of the case (regarding possible remedies, but also, in appropriate cases, the investigative efforts as such) is considered desirable, and where the main economic impact of the concentration is connected to such markets.

Notes

[36] See the joint referral by seven Member States to the Commission of a transaction affecting worldwide markets in M.2738 *GE/Unison*, and the joint referral by seven Member States to the Commission of a transaction affecting a Western European market in M.2698 *Promatech/Sulzer*; See also *Principles on the application, by National Competition Authorities within the ECA network, of Article 22 of the EC Merger Regulation*, a paper published by the European Competition Authorities (ECA), at paragraph 11.

III. Mechanics of the Referral System

A. Overview of the Referral System

46. The Merger Regulation sets out the relevant legal rules for the functioning of the referral system. The rules contained in Article 4(4) and (5), Article 9 and Article 22 set out in detail the various steps required for a case to be referred from the Commission to Member States and vice versa.

47. Each of the four relevant referral provisions establishes a self-contained mechanism for the referral of a given category of concentration. The provisions can be categorised in the following way:
    (a) Pre-notification referrals:
        (i) From the Commission to Member States (Article 4(4))
        (ii) From Member States to the Commission (Article 4(5))
    (b) Post-notification referrals:
        (i) From the Commission to Member States (Article 9)
        (ii) From Member States to the Commission (Article 22).

48. The flowcharts in Annex I to this Notice describe in graphical form the various procedural steps to be followed in the referral mechanisms set out in Articles 4(4) and (5), Article 9 and Article 22.

Pre-notification referrals

49. Pre-notification referrals can only be requested by the undertakings concerned.[37] It is for the undertakings concerned to verify whether the concentration meets the criteria specified in Article 4(4) (that the concentration has a Community dimension but may significantly affect competition in a distinct market within a Member State) or Article 4(5) (that the concentration does not have a Community dimension but is capable of being reviewed under the national competition laws of at least three Member States). The undertakings concerned may then decide to request a referral to or from the Commission by submitting a reasoned request on Form RS. The request is transmitted without delay by the Commission to all Member States. The remainder of the process differs under Article 4(4) and Article 4(5).
    — Under Article 4(4), the Member State or States concerned[38] have 15 working days from the date they receive the submission to express agreement or disagreement with the request. Silence on the part of a Member State is deemed to constitute agreement.[39] If the Member State or States concerned agree to the referral, the Commission has an additional period of approximately 10 working days (25 working days from the date the Commission received Form RS) in which it may decide to refer the case. Silence on the part of the Commission is deemed to constitute assent. If the Commission assents, the case (or one or more parts thereof) is referred to the Member States or States as requested by the undertakings concerned. If the referral is made, the Member State or States concerned apply their national law to the referred part of the case.[40] Articles 9(6) to 9(9) apply.
    — Under Article 4(5), the Member States concerned[41] have 15 working days from the date they receive the submission to express agreement or disagreement with the request. At the end of that period, the Commission checks whether any Member State competent to examine the concentration under its national competition law has expressed disagreement. If there is no expression of disagreement by any such competent Member State, the case is deemed to acquire a Community dimension and is thus referred to the Commission which has exclusive jurisdiction over it. It is then for the parties to notify the case to the Commission, using Form CO. On the other hand, if one or more competent Member States have expressed their disagreement, the Commission informs all Member States and the undertakings concerned without delay of any such expression of disagreement and the referral process ends. It is then for the parties to comply with any applicable national notification rules.

Notes

[37] The term "undertakings concerned" includes "persons" within the meaning of Article 3(1)(b).

[38] The Member State or States concerned are the ones identified in Form RS to which the case will be referred if the request is granted.

[39] This mechanism is an essential feature of all referral procedures set out in the Merger Regulation. The mechanism may be termed "positive silence" or non-opposition: that is to say that failure to take a decision on the part of the Commission or a Member State will be deemed to constitute the taking of a positive decision. This mechanism was already a feature of Regulation (EEC) No 4064/89, in Article 9(5). It is now included in Article 4(4) (second and fourth sub-paragraphs), Article 4(5) (fourth sub-paragraph), Article 9(5) and Article 22(3) (first sub-paragraph, last sentence) of the Merger Regulation. The positive silence mechanism is, however, not applicable with regard to decisions by Member States to join a request under Article 22(2).

[40] Article 4(4) allows merging parties to request partial or full referrals. The Commission and Member States must either accede to or refuse the request, and may not vary its scope by, for example, referring only a part of case when a referral of the whole of the case had been requested. In the case of a partial referral, the Member State concerned will apply its national competition law to the referred part of the case. For the remainder of the case, the Merger Regulation will continue to apply in the normal way, that is the undertakings concerned will be obliged to make a notification of the non-referred part of the concentration on Form CO pursuant to Article 4(1) of the Merger Regulation. By contrast, if the whole of the case is referred to a Member State, Article 4(4) final subparagraph specifies that there will be no obligation to notify the case also to the Commission. The case will thus not be examined by the Commission. The Member State concerned will apply its national law to the whole of the case; no other Member State can apply national competition law to the concentration in question.

[41] That is, those that would be competent to review the case under their national competition law in the absence of a referral. For the concept of "competent to review the case", see section B5 below.

Post-notification referrals

50. Pursuant to Article 9(2) and Article 22(1), post-notification referrals are triggered by Member States either on their own initiative or following an invitation by the Commission pursuant to Article 9(2) and Article 22(5) respectively. The procedures differ according to whether the referral is from or to the Commission.

— Under Article 9, a Member State may request that the Commission refer to it a concentration with Community dimension, or a part thereof, which has been notified to the Commission and which threatens to significantly affect competition within a distinct market within that Member State (Article 9(2)(a)), or which affects such a distinct market not constituting a substantial part of the common market (Article 9(2)(b)). The request must be made within 15 working days from the date the Member State received a copy of Form CO. The Commission must first verify whether those legal criteria are met. It may then decide to refer the case, or a part thereof, exercising its administrative discretion. In the case of a referral request made pursuant to Article 9(2)(b), the Commission must (i.e. has no discretion) make the referral if the legal criteria are met. The decision must be taken within 35 working days from notification or, where the Commission has initiated proceedings, within 65 working days.[42] If the referral is made, the Member State concerned applies its own national competition law, subject only to Article 9(6) and (8).

— Under Article 22, a Member State may request that the Commission examine a concentration which has no Community dimension but which affects trade between Member States and threatens to significantly affect competition within its territory. The request must be made within 15 working days from the date of national notification or, where no notification is required, the date when the concentration was "made known"[43] to the Member State concerned. The Commission transmits the request to all Member States. Any other Member States can decide to join the request[44] within a period of 15 working days from the date they receive a copy of the initial request. All national time limits relating to the concentration are suspended a decision has been taken as to where it will be examined; a Member State can re-start the national time limits before the expiry of the 15 working day period by informing the Commission and the merging parties that it does not wish to join the request. At the latest 10 working days following the expiry of the 15 working day period, the Commission must decide whether to accept the case from the requesting Member State(s). If the Commission accepts jurisdiction, national proceedings in the referring Member State(s) are terminated and the Commission examines the case pursuant to Article 22(4) of the Merger Regulation on behalf of the requesting State(s).[45] Non-requesting States can continue to apply national law.

Notes
⁴² As regards cases where the Commission takes preparatory steps within 65 working days, see Article 9(4)(b) and (5).
⁴³ The notion of "made known", derived from the wording of Article 22, should in this context be interpreted as imply- ing sufficient information to make a preliminary assessment as to the existence of the criteria for the making of a referral request pursuant to Article 22.
⁴⁴ It should be noted that Article 22 enables a Member State to join the initial request even if the concentration has not yet been notified to it. However, Member States may be unable to do so if they have not yet received the necessary information from the merging parties at the time of being informed by the Commission that a referral request has been lodged by another Member State. Notwithstanding the Member State's ability to contact the merging parties in order to verify whether they are competent to review any particular transaction, the notifying parties are therefore strongly encouraged to file, where feasible, their notification to all competent Member States simultaneously.
⁴⁵ Where the Commission examines a concentration on behalf of one or more Member States pursuant to Article 22, it can adopt all the substantive decisions provided for in Articles 6 and 8 of the Merger Regulation. This is established in Article 22(4) of that Regulation. It is to be noted that the Commission examines the concentration upon the request of and on behalf of the requesting Member States. This provision should therefore be interpreted as requiring the Commission to examine the impact of the concentration within the territory of those Member States. The Commission will not examine the effects of the concentration in the territory of Member States which have not joined the request unless this examination is necessary for the assessment of the effects of the concentration within the territory of the requesting Member States (for example, where the geographic market extends beyond the terri- tory/or territories of the requesting Member State(s).

51. The following section of the Notice focuses on a number of detailed elements of the system with the aim in particular of providing further guidance to undertakings contemplating making requests at the pre-notification stage, or who may be party to transactions subject to the possibility of post-notification referral.

B. Details of the Referral Mechanism

52. This section of this Notice provides guidance regarding certain aspects of the functioning of the referral system set out in Article 4(4) and(5), Article 9 and Article 22 of the Merger Regulation.

1. The network of competition authorities

53. Article 19(2) of the Merger Regulation provides that the Commission is to carry out the proce- dures set out in that Regulation in close and constant liaison with the competent authorities of the Member States (the NCAs). Cooperation and dialogue between the Commission and the NCAs, and between the NCAs themselves, is particularly important in the case of concentrations which are subject to the referral system set out in the Merger Regulation.

54. According to Recital 14 to the Merger Regulation, "the Commission and the NCAs should form together a network of public authorities, applying their respective competences in close coop- eration using efficient arrangements for information sharing and consultation with a view to ensuring that a case is dealt with by the most appropriate authority, in the light of the principle of subsidiarity, and with a view to ensuring that multiple notifications of a given concentration are avoided to the greatest extent possible".

55. The network should ensure the efficient re-attribution of concentrations according to the principles described in section II above. This involves facilitating the smooth operation of the pre-notification referral mechanism, as well as providing, to the extent foreseeable, a system whereby potential post-notification referral requests are identified as soon as possible.⁴⁶

56. Pursuant to Article 4(4) and (5), the Commission must transmit reasoned requests made by the undertakings concerned "without delay".⁴⁷ The Commission will endeavour to transmit such documents on the working day following that on which they are received or issued. Information within the network will be exchanged by various means, depending on the circumstances: e-mail, surface mail, courier, fax, telephone. It should be noted that for sensitive information or

confidential information exchanges will be carried out by secure e-mail or by any other protected means of communication between these contact points.

Notes

[47] It should be noted that, as provided for in Article 19(1) of the Merger Regulation, the Commission is also under an obligation to transmit to the NCAs copies of notifications and of the most important documents lodged with or issued by the Commission.

57. All members of the network, including the Commission and all NCAs, their officials and other servants, and other persons working under the supervision of those authorities as well as officials and civil servants of other authorities of the Member States, will be bound by the professional secrecy obligations set out in Article 17 of the Merger Regulation. They must not disclose non-public information they have acquired through the application of the Merger Regulation, unless the natural or legal person who provided that information has consented to its disclosure.

58. Consultations and exchanges within the network is a matter between public enforcement agencies and do not alter any rights or obligations arising from Community or national law for companies. Each competition authority remains fully responsible for ensuring that due process is observed in the cases it deals with.

2. Triggering the pre-notification referral system; information to be provided by the requesting parties

59. For the referral system to work swiftly and smoothly, it is crucial that the requesting parties, provide complete and accurate information, whenever required, in a timely fashion and in the most efficient way possible. Legal requirements concerning the information to be provided and the consequences of providing incorrect, incomplete or misleading information are set out in the Merger Regulation, Regulation (EC) No 802/2004 (hereinafter "the Merger Implementing Regulation") and Form RS.[48]

Notes

[48] Form RS is annexed to Commission Regulation (EC) No 802/2004 of 7 April 2004 implementing Council Regulation (EC) No 139/2004 on the control of concentrations between undertakings (OJ L 133, 30.4.2004, p. 1).

60. Form RS states that all information submitted in a reasoned submission must be correct and complete. If parties submit incorrect or incomplete information, the Commission has the power to either adopt a decision pursuant to Article 6(1)(a) of the Merger Regulation (where failure to fulfil the conditions of Article 4(5) comes to its attention during the course of the investigation), or to revoke any decision it adopts pursuant to Article 6 or Article 8, following an Article 4(5) referral, pursuant to Article 6(3)(a) or 8(6)(a) of the Merger Regulation. Following the adoption of a decision pursuant to Article 6(1)(a) or following revocation, national competition laws would once again be applicable to the transaction. In the case of referrals under Article 4(4) made on the basis of incorrect or incomplete information, the Commission may require a notification pursuant to Article 4(1). In addition, the Commission has the power to impose fines under Article 14(1)(a) of the Merger Regulation. Finally, parties should also be aware that, if a referral is made on the basis of incorrect or incomplete information included in Form RS, the Commission and/or the Member States may consider making a post-notification referral reversing a pre-notification referral based on such incorrect or incomplete information.[49]

Notes

[49] This would be the appropriate "remedy" where the requesting parties have submitted incorrect or incomplete information not affecting fulfilment of the conditions of Article 4(5), which comes to the Commission's attention during the course of the investigation.

61. When providing information on Form RS or generally in making a request for a pre-notification referral, it is not envisaged or necessary for the undertakings concerned to show that their concentration will lead to detrimental effects on competition.[50] They should, however, provide as much information as possible showing clearly in what way the concentration meets the relevant

legal criteria set out in Article 4(4) and (5) and why the concentration would be most appropriately dealt with by the competition authority or authorities specified in the request. The Merger Regulation does not require publication of the fact that a Form RS has been lodged, and it is not intended to do so. A non-public transaction can consequently be the subject of a pre-notification referral request.

Notes

[50] See Recital 16 to the Merger Regulation.

62. Even though, according to the Merger Implementing Regulation, the Commission will accept Form RS in any official Community language, undertakings concerned providing information which is to be distributed to the network are strongly encouraged to use a language which will be understood by all addressees of the information. This will facilitate Member State treatment of such requests. Moreover, as regards requests for referral to a Member State or States, the requesting parties are strongly encouraged to include a copy of the request in the language(s) of the Member State(s) to which the referral is being requested.

63. Beyond the legal requirements specified in Form RS, the undertakings concerned should be prepared to provide additional information, if required, and to discuss the matter with the Commission and the NCAs in a frank and open manner in order to enable the Commission and the NCAs to assess whether the concentration in question should be the subject of referral.

64. Informal contacts between merging parties contemplating lodging a pre-filing referral request, on the one hand, and the Commission and/or Member State authorities, on the other, are actively encouraged, even following the submission of Form RS. The Commission is committed to providing informal, early guidance to firms wishing to use the pre-notification referrals system set out in Article 4(4) and (5) of the Merger Regulation.[51]

Notes

[51] A request for derogation from the suspensive effect pursuant to Article 7(3) of the Merger Regulation would normally be inconsistent with an intention to make a pre-notification referral request pursuant to Article 4(4).

3. Concentrations eligible for referral

65. Only concentrations within the meaning of Article 3 of the Merger Regulation are eligible for referral pursuant to Article 4(5) and Article 22. Only concentrations falling within the ambit of the relevant national competition laws for the control of mergers are eligible for referral pursuant to Article 4(4) and Article 9.[52]

Notes

[52] By contrast, the reference to "national legislation on competition" in Article 21(3) and Article 22(3) should be understood as referring to all aspects of national competition law.

66. Pre-filing referral requests pursuant to Article 4(4) and (5) of the Merger Regulation must concern concentrations the plans for which are sufficiently concrete. In that regard, there must at least exist a good faith intention to merge on the part of the undertakings concerned, or, in the case of a public bid, at least a public announcement of an intention to make such a bid.[53]

Notes

[53] See Recital 34 to, and Article 4(1) of, the Merger Regulation.

4. The concept of "prior to notification" under Article 4(4) and (5)

67. Article 4(4) and (5) only apply at the pre-notification stage.

68. Article 4(4) specifies that the undertakings concerned may make a referral request by means of reasoned submission (Form RS), "prior to the notification of a concentration within the meaning of paragraph 1". This means that the request can only be made where no Form CO has been submitted pursuant to Article 4(1).

69. Likewise, Article 4(5) specifies that the request may be made "before any notification to the competent [national] authorities". This means that the concentration in question must not have been formally notified in any Member State jurisdiction for that provision to apply. Even one notification anywhere in the Community will preclude the undertakings concerned from triggering the mechanism of Article 4(5). In the Commission's view, no penalty should be imposed for non-notification of a transaction at the national level while a request pursuant to Article 4(5) is pending.

5. The concept of a "concentration capable of being reviewed under national competition law" and the concept of "competent Member State" in Article 4(5)

70. Article 4(5) enables the undertakings concerned to request a pre-notification referral of a concentration which does not have a Community dimension and which is "capable of being reviewed under the national competition laws of at least three Member States".

71. "Capable of being reviewed" or reviewable should be interpreted as meaning a concentration which falls within the jurisdiction of a Member State under its national competition law for the control of mergers. There is no need for a mandatory notification requirement, i.e. it is not necessary for the concentration to be required to be notified under national law.[54]

Notes

[54] Even in circumstances where a notification is voluntary *de jure*, the parties may in practice wish or be expected to file a notification.

---

72. Pursuant to the third and fourth subparagraphs of Article 4(5), where at least one Member State "competent to examine the concentration under its national competition law" has expressed its disagreement with the referral, the case must not be referred. A "competent" Member State is one where the concentration is reviewable and which therefore has the power to examine the concentration under its national competition law.

73. All Member States, and not only those "competent" to review the case, receive a copy of the Form RS. However, only Member States "competent" to review the case are counted for the purposes of the third and fourth subparagraphs of Article 4(5). Pursuant to the third subparagraph of Article 4(5), "competent" Member States have 15 working days from the date they receive the Form RS to express their agreement or disagreement with the referral. If they all agree, the case will be deemed to acquire a Community dimension pursuant to the fifth subparagraph of Article 4(5). According to the fourth subparagraph of Article 4(5), by contrast, if even only one "competent" Member State disagrees, no referral will take place from any Member State.

74. Given the above mechanism, it is crucial to the smooth operation of Article 4(5) that *all* Member States where the case is reviewable under national competition law, and which are hence "competent" to examine the case under national competition law, are identified correctly. Form RS therefore requires the undertakings concerned to provide sufficient information to enable each and every Member State to identify whether or not it is competent to review the concentration pursuant to its own national competition law.

75. In situations where Form RS has been filled in correctly, no complications should arise. The undertakings concerned will have identified correctly all Member States which are competent to review the case. In situations, however, where the undertakings concerned have not filled in Form RS correctly, or where there is a genuine disagreement as to which Member States are "competent" to review the case, complications may arise.

— Within the period of 15 working days provided for in the third subparagraph of Article 4(5), a Member State which is not identified in Form RS as being competent may inform the Commission that it is competent and may, like any other competent Member State, express its agreement or disagreement with the referral.

— Likewise, within the period of 15 working days provided for in the third subparagraph of Article 4(5), a Member State which has been identified as competent in Form RS may inform the Commission that it is not "competent". That Member State would then be disregarded for the purposes of Article 4(5).

76. Once the period of 15 working days has expired without any disagreement having been expressed, the referral, will be considered valid. This ensures the validity of Commission decisions taken under Articles 6 or 8 of the Merger Regulation following an Article 4(5) referral.

77. This is not to say, however, that undertakings concerned can abuse the system by negligently or intentionally providing incorrect information, including as regards the reviewability of the concentration in the Member States, on Form RS. As noted at paragraph 60 above, the Commission may take measures to rectify the situation and to deter such violations. The undertakings concerned should also be aware that, in such circumstances, where a referral has been made on the basis of incorrect or incomplete information, a Member State which believes it was competent to deal with the case but did not have the opportunity to veto the referral due to incorrect information being supplied, may request a post-notification referral.

6. Notification and Publication of Decisions

78. According to the fourth subparagraph of Article 4(4), the fourth subparagraph of Article 4(5), Article 9(1) and the second subparagraph of Article 22(3), the Commission is obliged to inform the undertakings or persons concerned and all Member States of any decision taken pursuant to those provisions as to the referral of a concentration.

79. The information will be provided by means of a letter addressed to the undertakings concerned (or for decisions adopted pursuant to Article 9(1) or Article 22(3), a letter addressed to the Member State concerned). All Member States will receive a copy thereof.

80. There is no requirement that such decisions be published in the *Official Journal of the European Union*.[55] The Commission will, however, give adequate publicity to such decisions on DG Competition's website, subject to confidentiality requirements.

Notes

[55] Pursuant to Article 20 of the Merger Regulation this is only required for decisions taken under Article 8(1)–(6) and Articles 14 and 15.

---

7. Article 9(6)

81. Article 9(6) provides that, when the Commission refers a notified concentration to a Member State in accordance with Article 4(4) or Article 9(3), the NCA concerned must deal with the case "without undue delay". Accordingly, the competent authority concerned should deal as expeditiously as possible with the case under national law.

82. In addition, Article 9(6) provides that the competent national authority must, within 45 working days after the Commission's referral or following receipt of a notification at the national level if requested inform the undertakings concerned of the result of the "preliminary competition assessment" and what "further action", if any, it proposes to take. Accordingly, within 45 working days after the referral or notification, as appropriate, the merging parties should be provided with sufficient information to enable them to understand the nature of any preliminary competition concerns the authority may have and be informed of the likely extent and duration of the investigation. The Member State concerned may only exceptionally suspend this time limit, where necessary information has not been provided to it by the undertakings concerned as required under its national competition law.

IV. FINAL REMARKS

83. This Notice will be the subject of periodic review, in particular following any revision of the referral provisions in the Merger Regulation. In that regard, it should be noted that, according to Article 4(6) of the Merger Regulation, the Commission must report to the Council on the operation of the pre-notification referral provisions in Article 4(4) and (5), by 1 July 2009.

84. This Notice is without prejudice to any interpretation of the applicable Treaty and regulatory provisions by the Court of First Instance and the Court of Justice of the European Communities.

ANNEXES

REFERRAL CHARTS

Article 4(4)
Concentration with Community Dimension

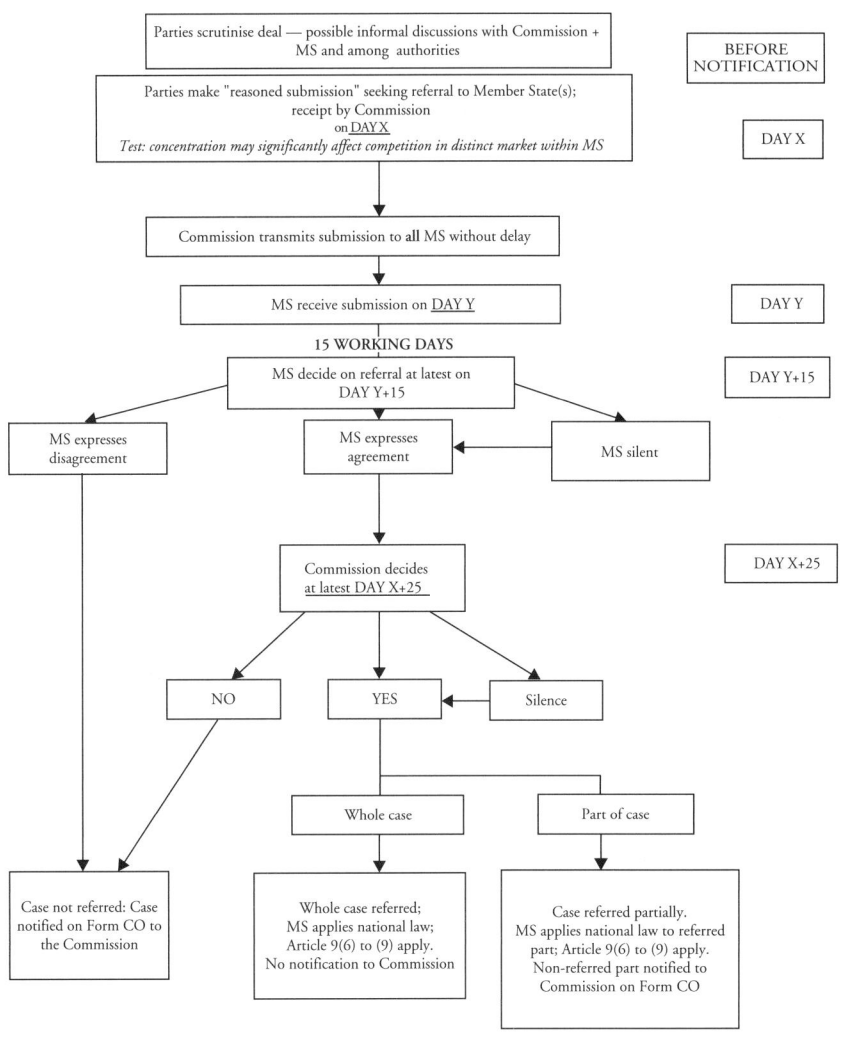

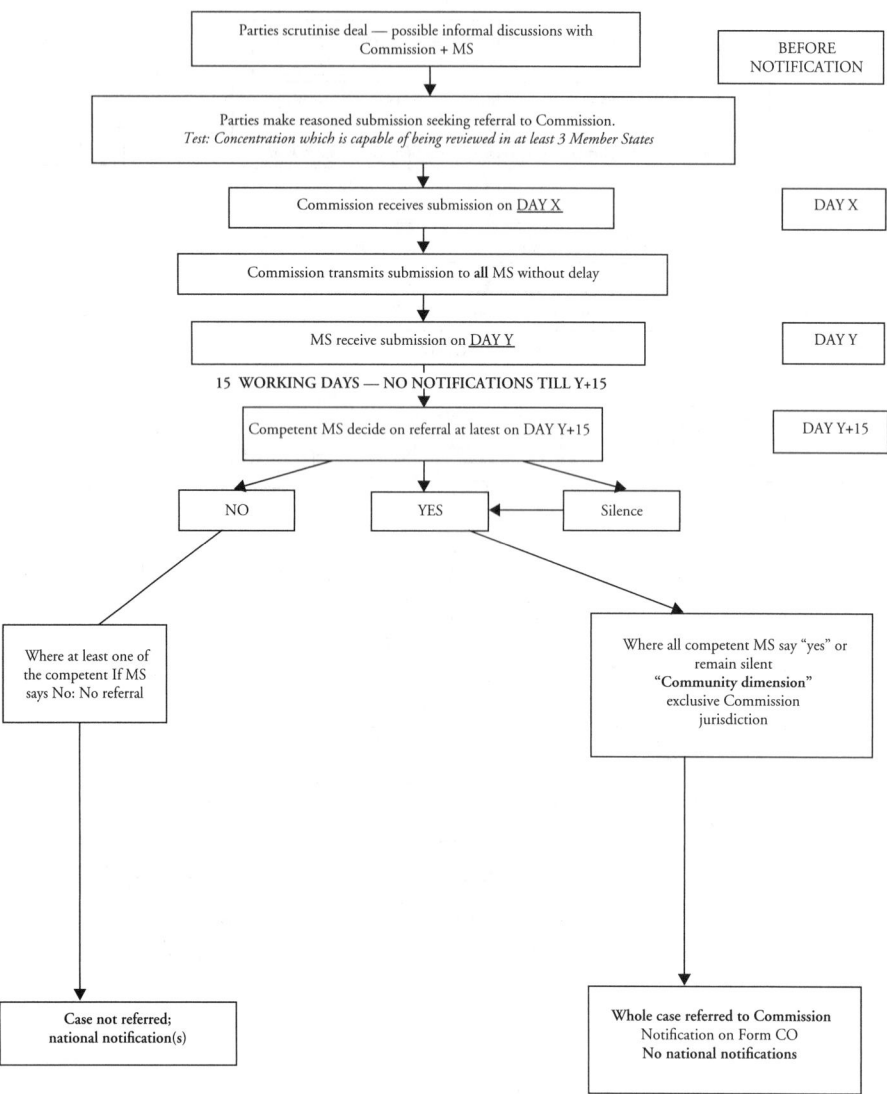

Article 4(5)
Concentration without Community Dimension
reviewable in at least three MS under national law

Parties scrutinise deal — possible informal discussions with Commission + MS	BEFORE NOTIFICATION
Parties make reasoned submission seeking referral to Commission. *Test: Concentration which is capable of being reviewed in at least 3 Member States*	
Commission receives submission on <u>DAY X</u>	DAY X
Commission transmits submission to **all** MS without delay	
MS receive submission on <u>DAY Y</u>	DAY Y
15 WORKING DAYS — NO NOTIFICATIONS TILL Y+15	
Competent MS decide on referral at latest on DAY Y+15	DAY Y+15

NO YES Silence

Where at least one of the competent If MS says No: No referral

Where all competent MS say "yes" or remain silent **"Community dimension"** exclusive Commission jurisdiction

Case not referred;
national notification(s)

Whole case referred to Commission
Notification on Form CO
No national notifications

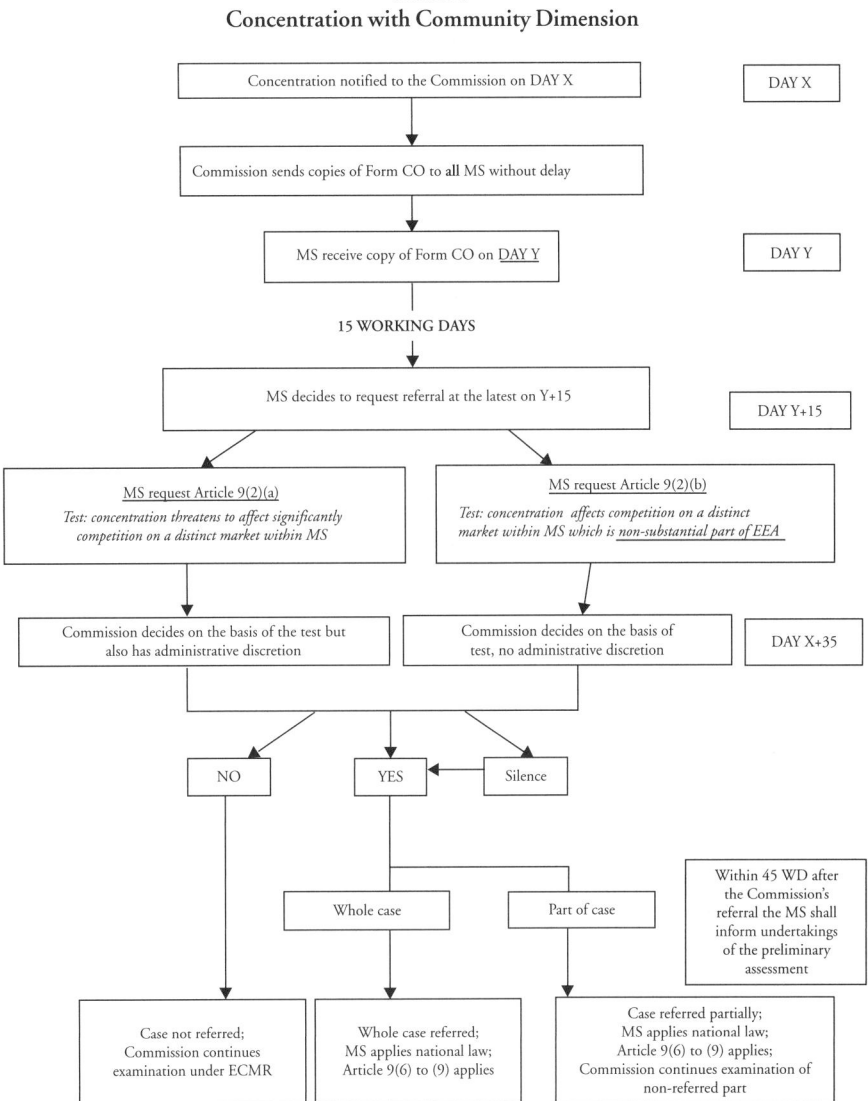

**Article 9
Concentration with Community Dimension**

Concentration notified to the Commission on DAY X	DAY X

Commission sends copies of Form CO to **all** MS without delay

MS receive copy of Form CO on <u>DAY Y</u>	DAY Y

15 WORKING DAYS

MS decides to request referral at the latest on Y+15	DAY Y+15

MS request Article 9(2)(a)
Test: concentration threatens to affect significantly competition on a distinct market within MS

MS request Article 9(2)(b)
Test: concentration affects competition on a distinct market within MS which is <u>non-substantial part of EEA</u>

Commission decides on the basis of the test but also has administrative discretion	
Commission decides on the basis of test, no administrative discretion	DAY X+35

NO — YES — Silence

Whole case — Part of case

Within 45 WD after the Commission's referral the MS shall inform undertakings of the preliminary assessment

Case not referred; Commission continues examination under ECMR

Whole case referred; MS applies national law; Article 9(6) to (9) applies

Case referred partially; MS applies national law; Article 9(6) to (9) applies; Commission continues examination of non-referred part

Part D Mergers and Concentrations

739

Article 22
Concentration without Community Dimension

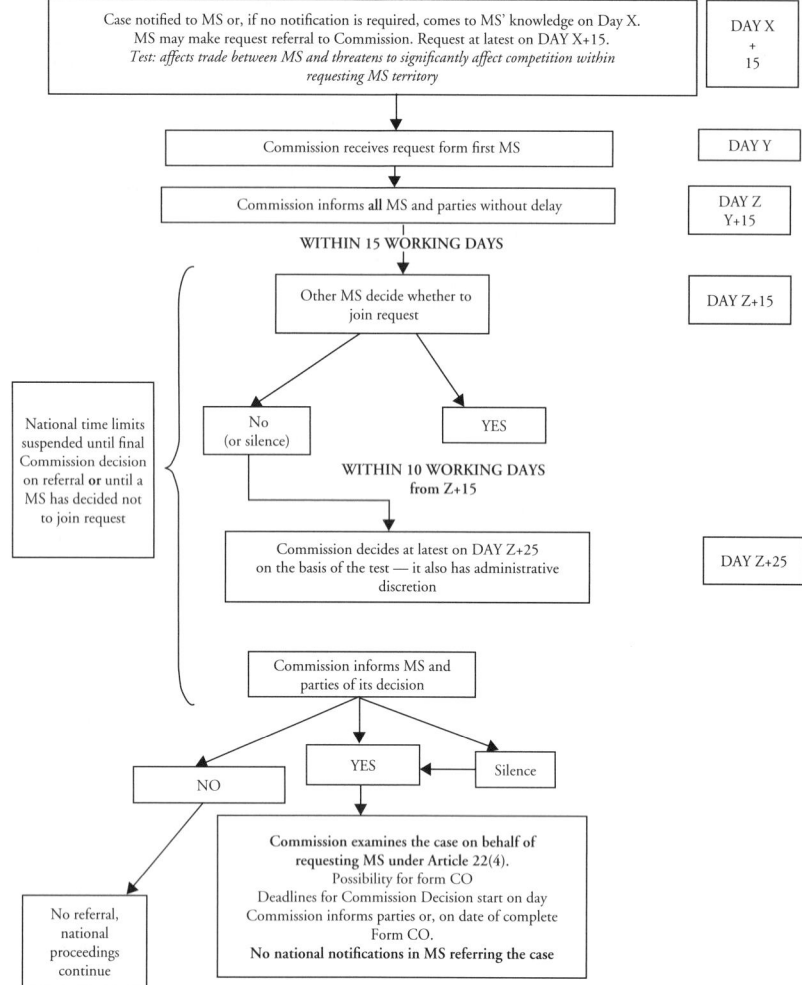

Case notified to MS or, if no notification is required, comes to MS' knowledge on Day X. MS may make request referral to Commission. Request at latest on DAY X+15. *Test: affects trade between MS and threatens to significantly affect competition within requesting MS territory*	DAY X + 15
Commission receives request form first MS	DAY Y
Commission informs **all** MS and parties without delay	DAY Z Y+15

WITHIN 15 WORKING DAYS

Other MS decide whether to join request — DAY Z+15

National time limits suspended until final Commission decision on referral **or** until a MS has decided not to join request

No (or silence)   YES

WITHIN 10 WORKING DAYS from Z+15

Commission decides at latest on DAY Z+25 on the basis of the test — it also has administrative discretion — DAY Z+25

Commission informs MS and parties of its decision

NO   YES   Silence

No referral, national proceedings continue

Commission examines the case on behalf of requesting MS under Article 22(4). Possibility for form CO Deadlines for Commission Decision start on day Commission informs parties or, on date of complete Form CO. **No national notifications in MS referring the case**

740

D10

COMMISSION NOTICE

on restrictions directly related and necessary to concentrations

(2005/C 56/03)

(Text with EEA relevance)

Official Journal C 56, 5.3.2005, p. 24

Celex No: 52005XC0305(02)

Commentary
Notice: B&C: 2.113, 7.012, 8.008, 8.083, 8.263–8.264 F&N: 5.17, 5.349, 7.86
paras 36–44: B&C: 7.053
paras 37–39: B&C: 7.055
paras 42–45: B&C: 8.097

I. Introduction

1. Council Regulation (EC) No 139/2004 of 20 January 2004 on the control of concentrations between undertakings (the EC Merger Regulation)[1] provides in Article 6(1)(b), second subparagraph, in Article 8(1), second subparagraph and in Article 8(2), third subparagraph that a decision declaring a concentration compatible with the common market *"shall be deemed to cover restrictions directly related and necessary to the implementation of the concentration"*.

Notes
[1] OJ L 24, 29.1.2004, p. 1.

---

2. The amendment of the rules governing the assessment of restrictions directly related and necessary to the implementation of the concentration (hereinafter also referred to as "ancillary restraints") introduces a principle of self-assessment of such restrictions. This reflects the intention of the legislature not to oblige the Commission to assess and individually address ancillary restraints. The treatment of ancillary restraints under the EC Merger Regulation is further explained in recital 21 in the preamble to the EC Merger Regulation, which states that *"Commission decisions declaring concentrations compatible with the common market in application of this Regulation should automatically cover such restrictions, without the Commission having to assess such restrictions in individual cases"*. While the Recital envisages that the Commission will exercise a residual function with regard to specific novel or unresolved issues giving rise to genuine uncertainty, it is in all other scenarios the task of the undertakings concerned to assess for themselves whether and to what extent their agreements can be regarded as ancillary to a transaction. Disputes as to whether restrictions are directly related and necessary to the implementation of the concentration, and thus automatically covered by the Commission's clearance decision, may be resolved before national courts.

Commentary
para 2: B&C: 8.263

---

3. The Commission's residual function is addressed in recital 21 of the Merger Regulation, where it is stated that the Commission should, at the request of the undertakings concerned, expressly assess the ancillary character of restrictions if a case presents *"novel and unresolved questions giving rise to genuine uncertainty"*. The Recital subsequently defines a "novel or unresolved question giving rise to genuine uncertainty" as a question that is *"not covered by the relevant Commission notice in force or a published Commission decision."*

4. In order to provide legal certainty to the undertakings concerned, this Notice provides guidance on the interpretation of the notion of ancillary restraints. The guidance given in the following sections reflects the essence of the Commission's practice, and sets out principles for assessing whether and to what extent the most common types of agreements are deemed to be ancillary restraints.

5. However, cases involving exceptional circumstances that are not covered by this Notice may justify departing from these principles. Parties may find further guidance in published Commission decisions[1] as to whether their agreements can be regarded as ancillary restraints or not. To the extent that cases involving exceptional circumstances have been previously addressed by the Commission in its published decisions,[2] they do not constitute "novel or unresolved questions" within the meaning of recital 21 of the Merger Regulation.

Notes

[1] For the purpose of this Notice, a decision is considered to be published when it is published in the *Official Journal of the European Union* or when it is made available to the public on the Commission's web site.

[2] See for example Commission Decision of 1 September 2000 (COMP/M.1980 — *Volvo/Renault V.I.*, paragraph 56) — *high degree of customer loyalty*; Commission Decision of 23 October 1998 (IV/M.1298 — *Kodak/Imation*, paragraph 73) — *long product life cycle*; Commission Decision of 13 March 1995 (IV/M.550 — *Union Carbide/Enichem*, paragraph 99) — *limited number of alternative producers*; Commission Decision of 30 April 1992 (IV/M.197 — *Solvay-Laporte/Interox*, paragraph 50) — *longer protection of know-how required*.

Commentary
para 5: B&C: 8.263

6. Accordingly, a case presents a "novel and unresolved question giving rise to genuine uncertainty" if those restrictions are not covered by this Notice and have not been previously addressed by the Commission in its published decisions. As envisaged in recital 21 of the Merger Regulation, the Commission will, at the request of the parties, expressly assess such restrictions in these cases. Subject to confidentiality requirements, the Commission will provide adequate publicity as regards such assessments that further develop the principles set out in this Notice.

7. To the extent that restrictions are directly related and necessary to the implementation of the concentration, Article 21(1) of the Merger Regulation provides that this Regulation alone applies, to the exclusion of Council Regulations (EC) No 1/2003,[1] (EEC) No 1017/68[2] and (EEC) No 4056/86.[3] By contrast, for restrictions that cannot be regarded as directly related and necessary to the implementation of the concentration, Articles 81 and 82 of the EC Treaty remain potentially applicable. However, the mere fact that an agreement or arrangement is not deemed to be ancillary to a concentration is not, as such, prejudicial to the legal status thereof. Such agreements or arrangements are to be assessed in accordance with Article 81 and 82 of the EC Treaty and the related regulatory texts and notices.[4] They may also be subject to any applicable national competition rules. Hence, agreements which contain a restriction on competition, but are not considered directly related and necessary to the implementation of the concentration pursuant to this notice, may nevertheless be covered by those provisions.

Notes

[1] Council Regulation (EC) No 1/2003 of 16 December 2002 on the implementation of the rules on competition laid down in Articles 81 and 82 of the Treaty, OJ L 1, 4.1.2003, p. 1; Regulation as last amended by Regulation (EC) No 411/2004 (OJ L 68, 6.3.2004, p. 1).

[2] Council Regulation (EEC) No 1017/68 of 19 July 1968 applying rules of competition to transport by rail, road and inland waterway, OJ L 175, 23.7.1968, p. 1; Regulation as last amended by Regulation (EC) No 1/2003.

[3] Council Regulation (EEC) No 4056/86 of 22 December 1986 laying down detailed rules for the application of Articles 81 and 82 of the Treaty to maritime transport, OJ L 378, 31.12.1986, p. 4; Regulation as last amended by Regulation (EC) No 1/2003.

[4] See, for example, for licence agreements Regulation (EC) No 772/2004 of 27 April 2004 on the application of Article 81(3) of the Treaty to categories of technology transfer agreements, OJ L 123, 27.4.2004, p. 11; see for supply and purchase agreements e.g. Commission Regulation (EC) No 2790/1999 of 22 December 1999 on the application of Article 81(3) of the Treaty to categories of vertical agreements and concerted practices, OJ L 336, 29.12.1999, p. 21.

8. The Commission's interpretation of Article 6(1)(b), second subparagraph, and Article 8(1), second subparagraph, and (2), third subparagraph, of the Merger Regulation is without prejudice

to the interpretation which may be given by the Court of Justice or the Court of First Instance of the European Communities.

9. This Notice replaces the Commission's previous Notice regarding restrictions directly related and necessary to concentrations.[1]

Notes

[1] OJ C 188, 4.7.2001, p. 5.

II. General Principles

10. A concentration consists of contractual arrangements and agreements establishing control within the meaning of Article 3(2) of the Merger Regulation. All agreements which carry out the main object of the concentration,[1] such as those relating to the sale of shares or assets of an undertaking, are integral parts of the concentration. In addition to these arrangements and agreements, the parties to the concentration may enter into other agreements which do not form an integral part of the concentration but can restrict the parties' freedom of action in the market. If such agreements contain ancillary restraints, these are automatically covered by the decision declaring the concentration compatible with the Common Market.

Notes

[1] See e.g. Commission Decision of 10 August 1992 (IV/M.206 — *Rhône-Poulenc/SNIA*, paragraph 8.3); Commission Decision of 19 December 1991 (IV/M.113 — *Courtaulds/SNIA*, paragraph 35); Commission Decision of 2 December 1991 (IV/M.102 — *TNT/Canada Post/DBP Postdienst/La Poste/PTT Poste & Sweden Post*, paragraph 46).

Commentary
para 10: B&C: 8.264

11. The criteria of direct relation and necessity are objective in nature. Restrictions are not directly related and necessary to the implementation of a concentration simply because the parties regard them as such.

12. For restrictions to be considered "directly related to the implementation of the concentration", they must be closely linked to the concentration itself. It is not sufficient that an agreement has been entered into in the same context or at the same time as the concentration.[1] Restrictions which are directly related to the concentration are economically related to the main transaction and intended to allow a smooth transition to the changed company structure after the concentration.

Notes

[1] Likewise, a restriction could, if all other requirements are fulfilled, be "directly related" even if it has not been entered into at the same time as the agreement carrying out the main object of the concentration.

13. Agreements must be "necessary to the implementation of the concentration",[1] which means that, in the absence of those agreements, the concentration could not be implemented or could only be implemented under considerably more uncertain conditions, at substantially higher cost, over an appreciably longer period or with considerably greater difficulty.[2] Agreements necessary to the implementation of a concentration are typically aimed at protecting the value transferred,[3] maintaining the continuity of supply after the break-up of a former economic entity,[4] or enabling the start-up of a new entity.[5] In determining whether a restriction is necessary, it is appropriate not only to take account of its nature, but also to ensure that its duration, subject matter and geographical field of application does not exceed what the implementation of the concentration reasonably requires. If equally effective alternatives are available for attaining the legitimate aim pursued, the undertakings must choose the one which is objectively the least restrictive of competition.

Notes

[1] See European Court of Justice, Case 42/84 (*Remia*), [1985] ECR 2545, paragraph 20; Court of First Instance, Case T-112/99 (*Métropole Télévision — M6*), [2001] ECR II-2459, paragraph 106.
[2] Commission Decision of 18 December 2000 (COMP/M.1863 — *Vodafone/BT/Airtel JV*, paragraph 20).

[3] Commission Decision of 30 July 1998 (IV/M.1245 — *VALEO/ITT Industries*, paragraph 59); Commission Decision of 3 March 1999 (IV/M.1442 — *MMP/AFP*, paragraph 17); Commission Decision of 9 March 2001 (COMP/M.2330 — *Cargill/Banks*, paragraph 30); Commission Decision of 20 March 2001 (COMP/M.2227 — *Goldman Sachs/Messer Griesheim*, paragraph 11).

[4] Commission Decision of 25 February 2000 (COMP/M.1841 — *Celestica/IBM*, paragraph 21).

[5] Commission Decision of 30 March 1999 (IV/JV.15 — *BT/AT&T*, paragraphs 207–214); Commission Decision of 22 December 2000 (COMP/M.2243 — *Stora Enso/Assidoman/JV*, paragraphs 49, 56 and 57).

Commentary
para 13: **B&C:** 8.264

14. For concentrations which are carried out in stages, the contractual arrangements relating to the stages before the establishment of control within the meaning of Article 3(1) and (2) of the Merger Regulation cannot normally be considered directly related and necessary to the implementation of the concentration. However, an agreement to abstain from material changes in the target's business until completion is considered directly related and necessary to the implementation of the joint bid.[1] The same applies, in the context of a joint bid, to an agreement by the joint purchasers of an undertaking to abstain from making separate competing offers for the same undertaking, or otherwise acquiring control.

Notes

[1] Commission Decision of 27 July 1998 (IV/M.1226 — *GEC/GPTH*, paragraph 22); Commission Decision of 2 October 1997 (IV/M.984 — *Dupont/ICI*, paragraph 55); Commission Decision of 19 December 1997 (IV/M.1057 — *Terra Industries/ ICI*, paragraph 16); Commission Decision of 18 December 1996 (IV/M.861 — *Textron/Kautex*, paragraphs 19 and 22); Commission Decision of 7 August 1996 (IV/M.727 — *BP/Mobil*, paragraph 50).

Commentary
para 14: **B&C:** 8.127, 8.264

15. Agreements which serve to facilitate the joint acquisition of control are to be considered directly related and necessary to the implementation of the concentration. This will apply to arrangements between the parties for the joint acquisition of control aimed at implementing the division of assets in order to divide the production facilities or distribution networks among themselves, together with the existing trademarks of the undertaking acquired jointly.

Commentary
para 15: **B&C:** 8.264

16. To the extent that such a division involves the break-up of a pre-existing economic entity, arrangements that make the break-up possible under reasonable conditions are to be considered directly related and necessary to the implementation of the concentration, under the principles set out below.

Commentary
para 16: **B&C:** 8.264

III. Principles Applicable to Commonly Encountered Restrictions in Cases of Acquisition of an Undertaking

17. Restrictions agreed between the parties in the context of a transfer of an undertaking may be to the benefit of the purchaser or of the vendor. In general terms, the need for the purchaser to benefit from certain protection is more compelling than the corresponding need for the vendor. It is the purchaser who needs to be assured that she/he will be able to acquire the full value of the acquired business. Thus, as a general rule, restrictions which benefit the vendor are either not directly related and necessary to the implementation of the concentration at all,[1] or their scope and/or duration need to be more limited than that of clauses which benefit the purchaser.[2]

Notes

[1] Commission Decision of 27 July 1998 (IV/M.1226 — *GEC/GPTH*, paragraph 24).

[2] See, for example, for a clause aiming at the protection of a part of the business remaining with the vendor: Commission Decision of 30 August 1993 (IV/M.319 — *BHF/CCF/Charterhouse*, paragraph 16).

Commentary
para 17: B&C: 8.083

A. Non-competition clauses

18. Non-competition obligations which are imposed on the vendor in the context of the transfer of an undertaking or of part of it can be directly related and necessary to the implementation of the concentration. In order to obtain the full value of the assets transferred, the purchaser must be able to benefit from some protection against competition from the vendor in order to gain the loyalty of customers and to assimilate and exploit the know-how. Such non-competition clauses guarantee the transfer to the purchaser of the full value of the assets transferred, which in general include both physical assets and intangible assets, such as the goodwill accumulated or the know-how[1] developed by the vendor. These are not only directly related to the concentration but are also necessary to its implementation because, without them, there would be reasonable grounds to expect that the sale of the undertaking or of part of it could not be accomplished.

Notes
[1] As defined in Article 1(1)(i) of Regulation (EC) No 772/2004.

Commentary
para 18: B&C: 8.083, 8.094

19. However, such non-competition clauses are only justified by the legitimate objective of implementing the concentration when their duration, their geographical field of application, their subject matter and the persons subject to them do not exceed what is reasonably necessary to achieve that end.[1]

Notes
[1] See European Court of Justice, Case 42/84 (*Remia*), [1985] ECR 2545, paragraph 20; Court of First Instance, Case T-112/99 (*Métropole Télévision — M6*), [2001] ECR II-2459, paragraph 106.

20. Non-competition clauses are justified for periods of up to three years,[1] when the transfer of the undertaking includes the transfer of customer loyalty in the form of both goodwill and know-how.[2] When only goodwill is included, they are justified for periods of up to two years.[3]

Notes
[1] See for exceptional cases in which longer periods may be justified e.g. Commission Decision of 1 September 2000 (COMP/M.1980 — *Volvo/Renault V.I.*, paragraph 56); Commission Decision of 27 July 1995 (IV/M.612 — *RWE-DEA/ Enichem Augusta*, paragraph 37); Commission decision of 23 October 1998 (IV/M.1298 — *Kodak/Imation*, paragraph 74).
[2] Commission Decision of 2 April 1998 (IV/M.1127 — *Nestlé/Dalgety*, paragraph 33); Commission Decision of 1 September 2000 (COMP/M.2077 — *Clayton Dubilier & Rice/Iteltel*, paragraph 15); Commission Decision of 2 March 2001 (COMP/M.2305 — *Vodafone Group PLC/EIRCELL*, paragraphs 21 and 22).
[3] Commission Decision of 12 April 1999 (IV/M.1482 — *KingFisher/Grosslabor*, paragraph 26); Commission Decision of 14 December 1997 (IV/M.884 — *KNP BT/Bunzl/Wilhelm Seiler*, paragraph 17).

Commentary
para 20: B&C: 8.266

21. By contrast, non-competition clauses cannot be considered necessary when the transfer is in fact limited to physical assets (such as land, buildings or machinery) or to exclusive industrial and commercial property rights (the holders of which could immediately take action against infringements by the transferor of such rights).

Commentary
para 21: B&C: 8.266

Part D Mergers and Concentrations

22. The geographical scope of a non-competition clause must be limited to the area in which the vendor has offered the relevant products or services before the transfer, since the purchaser does not need to be protected against competition from the vendor in territories not previously penetrated by the vendor.[1] That geographical scope can be extended to territories which the vendor was planning to enter at the time of the transaction, provided that he had already invested in preparing this move.

Notes

[1] Commission Decision of 14 December 1997 (IV/M.884 — *KNP BT/Bunzl/Wilhelm Seiler*, paragraph 17); Commission Decision of 12 April 1999 (IV/M.1482 — *KingFisher/Grosslabor*, paragraph 27); Commission Decision of 6 April 2001 (COMP/M.2355 — *Dow/Enichem Polyurethane*, paragraph 28); Commission Decision of 4 August 2000 (COMP/M.1979 — *CDC/Banco Urquijo/JV*, paragraph 18).

Commentary
para 22: B&C: 8.083

23. Similarly, non-competition clauses must remain limited to products (including improved versions or updates of products as well as successor models) and services forming the economic activity of the undertaking transferred. This can include products and services at an advanced stage of development at the time of the transaction, or products which are fully developed but not yet marketed. Protection against competition from the vendor in product or service markets in which the transferred undertaking was not active before the transfer is not considered necessary.[1]

Notes

[1] Commission Decision of 14 December 1997 (IV/M.884 — *KNP BT/Bunzl/Wilhelm Seiler*, paragraph 17); Commission Decision of 2 March 2001 (COMP/M.2305 — *Vodafone Group PLC/EIRCELL*, paragraph 22); Commission Decision of 6 April 2001 (COMP/M.2355 — *Dow/Enichem Polyurethane*, paragraph 28); Commission Decision of 4 August 2000 (COMP/M.1979 — *CDC/Banco Urquijo/JV*, paragraph 18).

Commentary
para 23: B&C: 8.083

24. The vendor may bind herself/himself, her/his subsidiaries and commercial agents. However, an obligation to impose similar restrictions on others would not be regarded as directly related and necessary to the implementation of the concentration. This applies, in particular, to clauses which would restrict the freedom of resellers or users to import or export.

25. Clauses which limit the vendor's right to purchase or hold shares in a company competing with the business transferred shall be considered directly related and necessary to the implementation of the concentration under the same conditions as outlined above for non-competition clauses, unless they prevent the vendor from purchasing or holding shares purely for financial investment purposes, without granting him/her, directly or indirectly, management functions or any material influence in the competing company.[1]

Notes

[1] Commission Decision of 4 February 1993 (IV/M.301 — *Tesco/Catteau*, paragraph 14); Commission Decision of 14 December 1997 (IV/M.884 — *KNP BT/Bunzl/Wilhelm Seiler*, paragraph 19); Commission Decision of 12 April 1999 (IV/M.1482 — *Kingfisher/Grosslabor*, paragraph 27); Commission Decision of 6 April 2000 (COMP/M.1832 — *Ahold/ ICA Förbundet/Canica*, paragraph 26).

26. Non-solicitation and confidentiality clauses have a comparable effect and are therefore evaluated in a similar way to non-competition clauses.[1]

Notes

[1] Accordingly, confidentiality clauses on customer details, prices and quantities cannot be extended. By contrast, confidentiality clauses concerning technical know-how may exceptionally be justified for longer periods, see Commission Decision of 29 April 1998 (IV/M.1167 — *ICI/Williams*, paragraph 22); Commission Decision of 30 April 1992 (IV/ M.197 — *Solvay-Laporte/Interox*, paragraph 50).

Commentary
para 26: B&C: 8.087

B. Licence agreements

27. The transfer of an undertaking or of part of it can include the transfer to the purchaser, with a view to the full exploitation of the assets transferred, of intellectual property rights or know-how. However, the vendor may remain the owner of the rights in order to exploit them for activities other than those transferred. In these cases, the usual means for ensuring that the purchaser will have the full use of the assets transferred is to conclude licensing agreements in his/her favour. Likewise, where the vendor has transferred intellectual property rights with the business, she/he may still want to continue using some or all of these rights for activities other than those transferred; in such a case the purchaser will grant a licence to the vendor.

Commentary
para 27: B&C: 8.087, 8.267

28. Licences of patents,[1] of similar rights, or of know-how,[2] can be considered necessary to the implementation of the concentration. They may equally be considered an integral part of the concentration and, in any event, need not be limited in time. These licences can be simple or exclusive and may be limited to certain fields of use, to the extent that they correspond to the activities of the undertaking transferred.

Notes
[1] Including patent applications, utility models, applications for registration of utility models, designs, topographies of semiconductor products, supplementary protection certificates for medicinal products or other products for which such supplementary protection certificates may be obtained and plant breeder's certificates (as referred to in Article 1(1)(h) of Regulation (EC) No 772/2004).
[2] As defined in Article 1(1)(i) of Regulation (EC) No 772/2004.

29. However, territorial limitations on manufacture reflecting the territory of the transferred activity are not necessary to the implementation of the operation. As regards licences granted by the seller of a business to the buyer, the seller can be made subject to territorial restrictions in the licence agreement under the same conditions as laid down for non-competition clauses in the context of the sale of a business.
30. Restrictions in licence agreements going beyond the above provisions, such as those which protect the licensor rather than the licensee, are not necessary to the implementation of the concentration.[1]

Notes
[1] To the extent that they fall within Article 81(1) of the EC Treaty, such agreements may nevertheless fall under Regulation (EC) No 772/2004, or other Community legislation.

Commentary
para 30: B&C: 8.267

31. Similarly, in the case of licences of trademarks, business names, design rights, copyrights or similar rights, there may be situations in which the vendor wishes to remain the owner of such rights in relation to activities retained, but the purchaser needs those rights in order to market the goods or services produced by the undertaking or part of the undertaking transferred. Here, the same considerations as above apply.[1]

Notes
[1] Commission Decision of 1 September 2000 (COMP/M.1980 — *Volvo/Renault V.I.*, paragraph 54).

C. Purchase and supply obligations

32. In many cases, the transfer of an undertaking or of part of it can entail the disruption of traditional lines of purchase and supply which have existed as a result of the previous integration of activities within the economic unity of the vendor. In order to enable the break-up of the economic unity of the vendor and the partial transfer of the assets to the purchaser under reasonable conditions, it is often necessary to maintain, for a transitional period, the existing or similar links between

the vendor and the purchaser. This objective is normally attained by purchase and supply obligations for the vendor and/or the purchaser of the undertaking or of part of it. Taking into account
the particular situation resulting from the break-up of the economic unity of the vendor, such
obligations can be recognised as directly related and necessary to the implementation of the
concentration. They may be in favour of the vendor as well as the purchaser, depending on the
particular circumstances of the case.

Commentary
para 32: **B&C**: 8.268

33. The aim of such obligations may be to ensure the continuity of supply to either of the parties
of products necessary for carrying out the activities retained by the vendor or taken over by the
purchaser. However, the duration of purchase and supply obligations must be limited to a period
necessary for the replacement of the relationship of dependency by autonomy in the market.
Thus, purchase or supply obligations aimed at guaranteeing the quantities previously supplied
can be justified for a transitional period of up to five years.[1]

Notes
[1] Commission Decision of 5 February 1996 (IV/M.651 — *AT&T/Philips*, VII.); Commission Decision of 30 March
1999 (IV/JV.15 — *BT/AT&T*, paragraph 209); see for exceptional cases Commission Decision of 13 March 1995
(IV/M.550 — *Union Carbide/Enichem*, paragraph 99); Commission Decision of 27 July 1995 (IV/M.612 — *RWE-
DEA/Enichem Augusta*, paragraph 45).

34. Both supply and purchase obligations providing for fixed quantities, possibly with a variation
clause, are recognised as directly related and necessary to the implementation of the concentration.
However, obligations providing for unlimited quantities,[1] exclusivity or conferring preferred-
supplier or preferred-purchaser status,[2] are not necessary to the implementation of the concentration.

Notes
[1] In line with the principle of proportionality, obligations providing for fixed quantities with a variation clause are, in
these cases, less restrictive on competition, see e.g. Commission Decision of 18 September 1998 (IV/M.1292 —
Continental/ ITT, paragraph 19).
[2] Commission Decision of 30 July 1998 (IV/M.1245 — *VALEO/ITT Industries*, paragraph 64); see for exceptional
cases (e.g. absence of a market) Commission Decision of 13 March 1995 (IV/M.550 — *Union Carbide/Enichem*,
paragraphs 92 to 96); Commission Decision of 27 July 1995 (IV/M.612 — *RWE-DEA/Enichem Augusta*, paragraphs
38 et seq.).

35. Service and distribution agreements are equivalent in their effect to supply arrangements;
consequently the same considerations as above shall apply.

Commentary
para 35: **B&C**: 8.091

IV. Principles Applicable to Commonly Encountered Restrictions in Cases of Joint Ventures within the Meaning of Article 3(4) of the Merger Regulation

A. Non-competition obligations

36. A non-competition obligation between the parent undertakings and a joint venture may be
considered directly related and necessary to the implementation of the concentration where such
obligations correspond to the products, services and territories covered by the joint venture agreement or its bylaws. Such non-competition clauses reflect, *inter alia*, the need to ensure good faith
during negotiations; they may also reflect the need to fully utilise the joint venture's assets or to
enable the joint venture to assimilate know-how and goodwill provided by its parents; or the need
to protect the parents' interests in the joint venture against competitive acts facilitated, *inter alia*,
by the parents' privileged access to the know-how and goodwill transferred to or developed by

the joint venture. Such non-competition obligations between the parent undertakings and a joint venture can be regarded as directly related and necessary to the implementation of the concentration for the lifetime of the joint venture.[1]

Notes

[1] Commission Decision of 15 January 1998 (IV/M.1042 — *Eastman Kodak/Sun Chemical*, paragraph 40); Commission Decision of 7 August 1996 (IV/M.727 — *BP/Mobil*, paragraph 51); Commission Decision of 3 July 1996 (IV/M.751 — *Bayer/Hüls*, paragraph 31); Commission Decision of 6 April 2000 (COMP/M.1832 — *Ahold/ICA Förbundet/Canica*, paragraph 26).

Commentary
para 36: **B&C:** 7.055, 8.083, 8.091, 8.094, 8.270

37. The geographical scope of a non-competition clause must be limited to the area in which the parents offered the relevant products or services before establishing the joint venture.[1] That geographical scope can be extended to territories which the parent companies were planning to enter at the time of the transaction, provided that they had already invested in preparing this move.

Notes

[1] Commission Decision of 29 August 2000 (COMP/M.1913 — *Lufthansa/Menzies/LGS/JV*; paragraph 18); Commission Decision of 22 December 2000 (COMP/M.2243 — *Stora Enso/Assidoman/JV*, paragraph 49, last sentence).

38. Similarly, non-competition clauses must be limited to products and services constituting the economic activity of the joint venture. This may include products and services at an advanced stage of development at the time of the transaction, as well as products and services which are fully developed but not yet marketed.

39. If the joint venture is set up to enter a new market, reference will be made to the products, services and territories in which it is to operate under the joint venture agreement or by-laws. However, the presumption is that one parent's interest in the joint venture does not need to be protected against competition from the other parent in markets other than those in which the joint venture will be active from the outset.

Commentary
para 39: **B&C:** 7.055, 8.091

40. Additionally, non-competition obligations between non-controlling parents and a joint venture are not directly related and necessary to the implementation of the concentration.

Commentary
para 40: **B&C:** 8.091

41. The same principles as for non-competition clauses apply to non-solicitation and confidentiality clauses.

Commentary
para 41: **B&C:** 7.055

B. Licence agreements

42. A licence granted by the parent undertakings to the joint venture may be considered directly related and necessary to the implementation of the concentration. This applies regardless of whether or not the licence is an exclusive one and whether or not it is limited in time. The licence may be restricted to a particular field of use which corresponds to the activities of the joint venture.

Commentary
para 42: **B&C:** 7.055, 8.271

43. Licences granted by the joint venture to one of its parents, or cross-licence agreements, can be regarded as directly related and necessary to the implementation of the concentration under the same conditions as in the case of the acquisition of an undertaking. Licence agreements between the parents are not considered directly related and necessary to the implementation of a joint venture.

Commentary
para 43: B&C: 8.271

C. Purchase and supply obligations

44. If the parent undertakings remain present in a market upstream or downstream of that of the joint venture, any purchase and supply agreements, including service and distribution agreements are subject to the principles applicable in the case of the transfer of an undertaking.

Commentary
para 44: B&C: 7.055, 8.272

D11

COMMISSION NOTICE

on a simplified procedure for treatment of certain concentrations under
Council Regulation (EC) No 139/2004

(2005/C 56/04)

(Text with EEA relevance)

Official Journal C 56, 5.3.2005, p 32

Celex No: 52005XC0305(03)

Commentary
Notice: B&C: 8.110 F&N: 5.447
points 6–11: B&C: 8.125
points 12–13: B&C: 8.125
points 17–18: B&C: 8.122

I. Introduction

1. This Notice sets out a simplified procedure under which the Commission intends to treat certain concentrations pursuant to Council Regulation (EC) No 139/2004 of 20 January 2004, on the control of concentrations between undertakings (the EC Merger Regulation)[1] on the basis that they do not raise competition concerns. This Notice replaces the Notice on a simplified procedure for treatment of certain concentrations under Council Regulation (EEC) No 4064/89.[2] The Commission's experience gained in applying Council Regulation (EEC) No 4064/89 of 21 December 1989 on the control of concentrations between undertakings[3] has shown that certain categories of notified concentrations are normally cleared without having raised any substantive doubts, provided that there were no special circumstances.

Notes
[1] OJ L 24, 29.1.2004, p. 1.
[2] OJ C 217, 29.7.2000, p. 32.
[3] OJ L 395, 30.12.1989, p. 1; corrected version OJ L 257, 21.9.1990, p. 13.

2. The purpose of this Notice is to set out the conditions under which the Commission usually adopts a short-form decision declaring a concentration compatible with the common market pursuant to the simplified procedure and to provide guidance in respect of the procedure itself. When all necessary conditions set forth at point 5 of this Notice are met and provided there are no special circumstances, the Commission adopts a short-form clearance decision within 25 working days from the date of notification, pursuant to Article 6(1)(b) of the EC Merger Regulation.[4]

Notes
[4] The notification requirements are set out in Annexes I and II to Commission Regulation (EC) No 802/2004 implementing Council Regulation (EC) No 139/2004 on the control of concentrations between undertakings.

3. However, if the safeguards or exclusions set forth at points 6 to 11 of this Notice are applicable, the Commission may launch an investigation and/or adopt a full decision under the EC Merger Regulation.
4. By following the procedure outlined in the following sections, the Commission aims to make Community merger control more focused and effective.

II. CATEGORIES OF CONCENTRATIONS SUITABLE FOR TREATMENT UNDER THE SIMPLIFIED PROCEDURE

Eligible concentrations

5. The Commission will apply the simplified procedure to the following categories of concentrations:
   (a) two or more undertakings acquire joint control of a joint venture, provided that the joint venture has no, or negligible, actual or foreseen activities within the territory of the European Economic Area (EEA). Such cases occur where:
      (i) the turnover[5] of the joint venture and/or the turnover of the contributed activities[6] is less than EUR 100 million in the EEA territory; and
      (ii) the total value of assets[7] transferred to the joint venture is less than EUR 100 million in the EEA territory;[8]
   (b) two or more undertakings merge, or one or more undertakings acquire sole or joint control of another undertaking, provided that none of the parties to the concentration are engaged in business activities in the same product and geographical market, or in a product market which is upstream or downstream of a product market in which any other party to the concentration is engaged;[9]
   (c) two or more undertakings merge, or one or more undertakings acquire sole or joint control of another undertaking and:
      (i) two or more of the parties to the concentration are engaged in business activities in the same product and geographical market (horizontal relationships) provided that their combined market share is less than 15%; or
      (ii) one or more of the parties to the concentration are engaged in business activities in a product market which is upstream or downstream of a product market in which any other party to the concentration is engaged (vertical relationships),[10] provided that none of their individual or combined market shares is at either level 25% or more;[11]
   (d) a party is to acquire sole control of an undertaking over which it already has joint control.

Notes
[5] The turnover of the joint venture should be determined according to the most recent audited accounts of the parent companies, or the joint venture itself, depending upon the availability of separate accounts for the resources combined in the joint venture.

[6] The expression "and/or" refers to the variety of situations covered; for example:
— in the case of a joint acquisition of a target company, the turnover to be taken into account is the turnover of this target (the joint venture),
— in the case of the creation of a joint venture to which the parent companies contribute their activities, the turnover to be taken into account is that of the contributed activities,
— in the case of entry of a new controlling party into an existing joint venture, the turnover of the joint venture and the turnover of the activities contributed by the new parent company (if any) must be taken into account.

[7] The total value of assets of the joint venture should be determined according to the last prepared and approved balance sheet of each parent company. The term "assets" includes: (1) all tangible and intangible assets that will be transferred to the joint venture (examples of tangible assets include production plants, wholesale or retail outlets, and inventory of goods; examples of intangible assets include intellectual property, goodwill, etc.), and (2) any amount of credit or any obligations of the joint venture which any parent company of the joint venture has agreed to extend or guarantee.

[8] Where the assets transferred generate turnover, then neither the value of the assets nor that of the turnover may exceed EUR 100 million.

[9] See Commission Notice on the definition of relevant market for the purposes of Community competition law (OJ C 372, 9.12.1997, p. 5).

[10] See footnote 6.

[11] This means that only concentrations, which do not lead to affected markets, as defined in Section 6 III of Form CO, fall into this category. The thresholds for horizontal and vertical relationships apply to market shares both at national and at EEA levels and to any plausible alternative product market definition that may have to be considered in a given case. It is important that the underlying market definitions set out in the notification are precise enough to justify the assessment that these thresholds are not met, and that all plausible alternative market definitions are mentioned (including geographic markets narrower than national).

Safeguards and exclusions

6. In assessing whether a concentration falls into one of the categories referred to in point 5, the Commission will ensure that all relevant circumstances are established with sufficient clarity. Given that market definitions are likely to be a key element in this assessment, the parties should provide information on all plausible alternative market definitions during the pre-notification phase (see point 15). Notifying parties are responsible for describing all alternative relevant product and geographic markets on which the notified concentration could have an impact and for providing data and information relating to the definition of such markets.[12] The Commission retains the discretion to take the ultimate decision on market definition, basing its decision on an analysis of the facts of the case. Where it is difficult to define the relevant markets or to determine the parties' market shares, the Commission will not apply the simplified procedure. In addition, to the extent that concentrations involve novel legal issues of a general interest, the Commission would normally abstain from adopting short-form decisions, and would normally revert to a normal first phase merger procedure.

Notes
[12] As with all other notifications, the Commission may revoke the short-form decision if it is based on incorrect information for which one of the undertakings concerned is responsible (Article 6(3)(a), of the EC Merger Regulation).

7. While it can normally be assumed that concentrations falling into the categories referred to in point 5 will not raise serious doubts as to their compatibility with the common market, there may nonetheless be certain situations, which exceptionally require a closer investigation and/or a full decision. In such cases, the Commission may revert to a normal first phase merger procedure.

8. The following are indicative examples of types of cases which may be excluded from the simplified procedure. Certain types of concentrations may increase the parties' market power, for instance by combining technological, financial or other resources, even if the parties to the concentration do not operate in the same market. Concentrations where at least two parties to the concentration are present in closely related neighbouring markets[13] may also be unsuitable for the simplified procedure, in particular, where one or more of the parties to the concentration holds individually a market share of 25% or more in any product market in which there is no horizontal or vertical relationship between the parties but which is a neighbouring market to a market where another party is active. In other cases, it may not be possible to determine the parties' precise market shares. This is often the case when the parties operate in new or little developed markets. Concentrations in markets with high entry barriers, with a high degree of concentration[14] or other known competition problems may also be unsuitable.

Notes

[13] Product markets are closely related neighbouring markets when the products are complementary to each other or when they belong to a range of products that is generally purchased by the same set of customers for the same end use.

[14] See Guidelines on the assessment of horizontal mergers under the Council Regulation on the control of concentrations between undertakings OJ C 31, 5.2.2004, p. 5, points 14–21.

9. The Commission's experience to date has shown that a change from joint to sole control may exceptionally require closer investigation and/or a full decision. A particular competition concern could arise in circumstances where the former joint venture is integrated into the group or network of its remaining single controlling shareholder, whereby the disciplining constraints exercised by the potentially diverging incentives of the different controlling shareholders are removed and its strategic market position could be strengthened. For example, in a scenario in which undertaking A and undertaking B jointly control a joint venture C, a concentration pursuant to which A acquires sole control of C may give rise to competition concerns in circumstances in which C is a direct competitor of A and where C and A will hold a substantial combined market position and where this removes a degree of independence previously held by C.[15] In cases where such scenarios require a closer analysis, the Commission may revert to a normal first phase merger procedure.[16]

Notes

[15] Case No. IV/M.1328 *KLM/Martinair*, XXIXth Report on Competition Policy 1999 — SEC(2000) 720 final, points 165–166.

[16] Case No COMP/M.2908 *Deutsche Post/DHL (II)*, Decision of 18.9.2002.

10. The Commission may also revert to a normal first phase merger procedure where neither the Commission nor the competent authorities of Member States have reviewed the prior acquisition of joint control of the joint venture in question.
11. Furthermore, the Commission may revert to a normal first phase merger procedure where an issue of coordination as referred to in Article 2(4) of the EC Merger Regulation arises.
12. If a Member State expresses substantiated concerns about the notified concentration within 15 working days of receipt of the copy of the notification, or if a third party expresses substantiated concerns within the time-limit laid down for such comments, the Commission will adopt a full decision. The time-limits set out in Article 10(1) of the EC Merger Regulation apply.

Referral requests

13. The simplified procedure will not be applied if a Member State requests the referral of a notified concentration pursuant to Article 9 of the EC Merger Regulation or if the Commission accepts a request from one or more Member States for referral of a notified concentration pursuant to Article 22 of the EC Merger Regulation.

Pre-notification referrals at the request of the notifying parties

14. Subject to the safeguards and exclusions set out in this Notice, the Commission may apply the simplified procedure to concentrations where:
    (i) following a reasoned submission pursuant to Article 4(4) of the EC Merger Regulation, the Commission decides not to refer the case to a Member State; or
    (ii) following a reasoned submission pursuant to Article 4(5) of the EC Merger Regulation the case is referred to the Commission.

III. Procedural Provisions

Pre-notification contacts

15. The Commission has found pre-notification contacts between notifying parties and the Commission beneficial even in seemingly unproblematic cases.[17] The Commission's experience of the simplified procedure has shown that candidate cases for the simplified procedure may raise complex issues for instance, of market definition (see point 6) which should preferably be resolved prior to notification. Such contacts allow the Commission and the notifying parties to determine the precise amount of information to be provided in a notification. Pre-notification

contacts should be initiated at least two weeks prior to the expected date of notification. Notifying parties are therefore advised to engage in pre-notification contacts, particularly where they request the Commission to waive full-form notification in accordance with Article 3(1) of Commission Regulation (EC) No 802/2004 of 7 April 2004 implementing Council Regulation (EC) No 139/2004 on the control of concentrations between undertakings[18] on the grounds that the operation to be notified will not raise competition concerns.

Notes

[17] See DG Competition Best Practices on the conduct of EC merger control proceedings available at: http://europa.eu.int/comm/competition/mergers/legislation/regulation/ best_practices.pdf

[18] OJ L 133, 30.4.2004, p. 1.

Commentary
point 15: B&C: 8.110

Publication of the fact of notification

16. The information to be published in the *Official Journal of the European Union* upon receipt of a notification[19] will include the names of the parties to the concentration, their country of origin, the nature of the concentration and the economic sectors involved, as well as an indication that, on the basis of the information provided by the notifying party, the concentration may qualify for a simplified procedure. Interested parties will then have the opportunity to submit observations, in particular on circumstances which might require an investigation.

Notes

[19] Article 4(3) of the EC Merger Regulation.

Short-form decision

17. If the Commission is satisfied that the concentration fulfils the criteria for the simplified procedure (see point 5), it will normally issue a short-form decision. This includes appropriate cases not giving rise to any competition concerns where it receives a full form notification. The concentration will thus be declared compatible with the common market, within 25 working days from the date of notification, pursuant to Article 10(1) and (6) of the EC Merger Regulation. The Commission will endeavour to issue a short-form decision as soon as practicable following expiry of the 15 working day period during which Member States may request referral of a notified concentration pursuant to Article 9 of the EC Merger Regulation. However, in the period leading up to the 25 working day deadline, the option of reverting to a normal first phase merger procedure and thus launching investigations and/or adopting a full decision remains open to the Commission, should it judge such action appropriate in the case in question.

Publication of the short-form decision

18. The Commission will publish a notice of the fact of the decision in the *Official Journal of the European Union* as it does for full clearance decisions. The public version of the decision will be made available on DG Competition's Internet website for a limited period. The short-form decision will contain the information about the notified concentration published in the Official Journal at the time of notification (names of the parties, their country of origin, nature of the concentration and economic sectors concerned) and a statement that the concentration is declared compatible with the common market because it falls within one or more of the categories described in this Notice, with the applicable category(ies) being explicitly identified.

IV. ANCILLARY RESTRICTIONS

19. The simplified procedure is not suited to cases in which the undertakings concerned request an express assessment of restrictions which are directly related to, and necessary for, the implementation of the concentration.

D12

COMMUNICATION FROM THE COMMISSION

Communication pursuant to Article 3(2) of Commission Regulation (EC) No 802/2004[1] implementing Council Regulation (EC) No 139/2004[2] on the control of concentrations between undertakings.

(2006/C 251/02)

(Text with EEA relevance)

Official Journal C 251, 17.10.2006, p. 2

Celex No: 52006XC1017(01)

Notes

[1] OJ L 133, 30.4.2004, pages 1–39.
[2] OJ L 24, 29.1.2004, pages 1–22.

Introduction

The Commission hereby lays down, pursuant to Article 3(2) of Commission Regulation (EC) No 802/2004,[3] the format in which notifications and reasoned submissions should be delivered. Article 3(2) of Regulation 802/2004 requires notifications and reasoned submissions to be delivered in one original and 35 copies.

Notes

[3] Article 3(2) should be read together with Article 6(2) of Commission Regulation (EC) No 802/2004.

Notifications: Form CO and Short Form CO (Annexes I and II to Commission Regulation (EC) No 802/2004)

1) One signed original on paper.
2) Five paper copies of the entire Form CO or Short Form CO and its annexes ("notification").
3) Thirty copies of the notification in CD- or DVD-ROM format (the "medium"). The following specifications shall be adhered to:
   a) The files comprising the notification in this medium shall be in Portable Document Format (*.pdf) and should preferably not exceed 5 MB (mega-bytes) each in size. The copy of the notification may be contained on several CD- or DVD-ROMs. Documents which were originally produced in *.doc, *.xls and *.ppt format shall also be saved in this format in the same medium.
   b) Files should be named in a way which allows easy identification of the section in the Form CO or Short Form CO they refer to.
   c) A list of all files in the medium shall be delivered as a separate file in the medium.
   d) Each file shall bear the number and name of the proceeding for which the notification is submitted.

Reasoned submissions:[4]— Form RS (Annex III to Commission Regulation (EC) No 802/2004)

1) One signed original on paper.
2) Five paper copies of the entire Form RS and its annexes ("Reasoned submission")
3) One CD- or DVD-ROM (the "medium") which contains the complete reasoned submission. The following specifications shall be adhered to:
   a) The files comprising the reasoned submission in this medium shall be in Portable Document Format (*.pdf) and may not exceed 1 MB (mega-byte) each in size. Documents which were originally produced in *.doc, *.xls and *.ppt format shall also be saved in this format in the same medium.

b) Files should be named in a way which allows easy identification of the section in the Form RS they refer to.

c) A list of files in the medium shall be delivered as a separate file in the medium itself.

d) Each file shall bear the number and name of the proceeding for which the Reasoned submission is made.

4) If the files on the CD- or DVD-ROM cannot be kept under 1MB (mega-byte) each in size and/or if the total size of the files on the CD- or DVD-ROM exceeds 5MB, the instructions for submitting Form CO should be followed instead, i.e. 30 copies in CD- or DVD-ROM format should be submitted.

Notes

[4] Reasoned submissions within the meaning of Article 4(4) and 4(5) of Council Regulation (EC) No 139/2004.

Date of Applicability of this Communication

The instructions contained in this communication shall be applicable 20 days following the date of publication of this communication in the *Official Journal of the European Union*.

Notes

Date of applicability: 6 November 2006.

D13

COMMISSION CONSOLIDATED JURISDICTIONAL NOTICE

UNDER COUNCIL REGULATION (EC) No 139/2004
on the control of concentrations between undertakings

Official Journal [not yet published]

Celex No: [not yet published]

Notes

The Commission adopted this Notice on 10 July 2007. It has not yet been published in the Official Journal. It is published on the European website at the following address: http://ec.europa.eu/comm/competition/mergers/legislation/jn_en.pdf

A. Introduction

1. The purpose of this Notice is to provide guidance as to jurisdictional issues under Council Regulation (EC) No 139/2004, OJ L 24, 29.1.2003, p. 1 (the "Merger Regulation").[1] This formal guidance should enable firms to establish more quickly, in advance of any contact with the Commission, whether and to what extent their operations may be covered by Community control of concentrations.

Notes

[1] Where it is necessary in this Notice to distinguish between Regulation 139/2004 and Council Regulation (EEC) No 4064/89 (OJ L 395, 30.12.19989, corrected version in OJ L 257, 21.9.1990, p. 13, Regulation last amended by Regulation (EC) No 1310/97, OJ L 180, 9.7.1997, p. 1, corrigendum in OJ L 40, 13.2.1998, p. 17), the former will be referred to as the "recast Merger Regulation" whereas the latter will be referred to as the "former Merger Regulation". Articles without reference refer to the recast Merger Regulation.

2. This Notice replaces the Notice on the concept of concentration,[2] the Notice on the concept of full-function joint ventures,[3] the Notice on the concept of undertakings concerned[4] and the Notice on calculation of turnover.[5]

Notes

[2] OJ C 66, 02.03.1998, p. 5.
[3] OJ C 66, 02.03.1998, p. 1.
[4] OJ C 66, 02.03.1998, p. 14.
[5] OJ C 66, 02.03.1998, p. 25

3. This Notice deals with the concepts of a concentration and of a full-function joint venture, undertakings concerned and the calculation of turnover as set out in Articles 1, 3 and 5 of the Merger Regulation. Issues concerning referrals are dealt with in the Notice on referrals.[6] The Commission's interpretation of Articles 1, 3 and 5 in the present Notice is without prejudice to the interpretation which may be given by the Court of Justice or by the Court of First Instance of the European Communities.

Notes

[6] OJ C 56, 05.03.2005, p. 2.

4. The guidance set out in this Notice reflects the Commission's experience in applying the recast Merger Regulation and the former Merger Regulation since the latter entered into force on 21 September 1990. The general principles governing the issues dealt with in this Notice have not been changed by the entry into force of Regulation (EC) No 139/2004, but where changes have occurred, the Notice deals with them explicitly. The principles contained in the Notice will be applied and further developed by the Commission in individual cases.
5. According to Article 1, the Merger Regulation only applies to operations that satisfy two conditions. First, there must be a concentration of two or more undertakings within the meaning of Article 3 of the Merger Regulation. Secondly, the turnover of the undertakings concerned, calculated in accordance with Article 5, must satisfy the thresholds set out in Article 1 of the Regulation. The notion of a concentration (including the particular requirements for joint ventures), as the first condition, is dealt with under Part B; the identification of undertakings concerned and the calculation of their turnover as relevant for the second condition are dealt with under Part C.
6. The Commission addresses the question of its jurisdiction over a concentration in decisions according to Article 6 of the Merger Regulation.[7]

Notes

[7] See also opinion of AG Kokott in Case C-202/06, *Cementbouw v Commission* of 26 April 2007, paragraph 56 (not yet reported).

B. The Concept of Concentration

7. According to Article 3(1) of the Merger Regulation, a concentration only covers operations where a change of control in the undertakings concerned occurs on a lasting basis. Recital 20 in the

preamble to the Merger Regulation further explains that the concept of concentration is intended to relate to operations which bring about a lasting change in the structure of the market. Because the test in Article 3 is centred on the concept of control, the existence of a concentration is to a great extent determined by qualitative rather than quantitative criteria.

8. Article 3(1) of the Merger Regulation defines two categories of concentrations: – those arising from a merger between previously independent undertakings (point (a)); –those arising from an acquisition of control (point (b)). These are treated respectively in Sections I and II below.

I. MERGERS BETWEEN PREVIOUSLY INDEPENDENT UNDERTAKINGS

9. A merger within the meaning of Article 3(1)(a) of the Merger Regulation occurs when two or more independent undertakings amalgamate into a new undertaking and cease to exist as separate legal entities. A merger may also occur when an undertaking is absorbed by another, the latter retaining its legal identity while the former ceases to exist as a legal entity.[8]

Notes

[8] See, for example, Case COMP/M.1673 – *Veba/VIAG* of 13 June 2000; Case COMP/M.1806 – *AstraZeneca/Novartis* of 26 July 2000; Case COMP/M.2208 – *Chevron/Texaco* of 26 January 2001; and Case IV/M.1383 – *Exxon/Mobil* of 29 September 1999. A merger in the meaning of Article 3(1)(a) is not deemed to occur if a target company is merged with a subsidiary of the acquiring company to the effect that the parent company acquires control of the target undertaking under Article 3(1)(b), see Case COMP/M.2510 – *Cendant/Galileo* of 24 September 2001.

---

10. A merger within the meaning of Article 3(1)(a) may also occur where, in the absence of a legal merger, the combining of the activities of previously independent undertakings results in the creation of a single economic unit.[9] This may arise in particular where two or more undertakings, while retaining their individual legal personalities, establish contractually a common economic management[10] or the structure of a dual listed company.[11] If this leads to a *de facto* amalgamation of the undertakings concerned into a single economic unit, the operation is considered to be a merger. A prerequisite for the determination of such a *de facto* merger is the existence of a permanent, single economic management. Other relevant factors may include internal profit and loss compensation or a revenue distribution as between the various entities within the group, and their joint liability or external risk sharing. The *de facto* amalgamation may be solely based on contractual arrangements,[12] but it can also be reinforced by cross-shareholdings between the undertakings forming the economic unit.

Notes

[9] In determining the previous independence of undertakings, the issue of control may be relevant as the merger might otherwise only be an internal restructuring within the group. In this specific context, the assessment of control also follows the general concept set out below and includes *de jure* as well as *de facto* control.

[10] This could apply for example in the case of a "Gleichordnungskonzern" in German law, certain "Groupements d'Intérêt Economique" in French law, and the amalgamation of partnerships, as in Case IV/M.1016 – *Price Waterhouse/Coopers&Lybrand* of 20 May 1998.

[11] Case IV/M.660 – *RTZ/CRA* of 7 December 1995; Case COMP/M.3071 – *Carnival Corporation/P&O Princess II* of 24 July 2002.

[12] See Case IV/M.1016 – *Price Waterhouse/Coopers&Lybrand* of 20 May 1998; Case COMP/M.2824 – *Ernst & Young/ Andersen Germany* of 27 August 2002.

II. ACQUISITION OF CONTROL

1. Concept of control

1.1 Person or undertaking acquiring control

11. Article 3(1)(b) provides that a concentration occurs in the case of an acquisition of control. Such control may be acquired by one undertaking acting alone or by several undertakings acting jointly.

Person controlling another undertaking

12. Control may also be acquired by a person in circumstances where that person already controls (whether solely or jointly) at least one other undertaking or, alternatively, by a combination

of persons (which control another undertaking) and undertakings. The term "person" in this context extends to public bodies[13] and private entities, as well as natural persons. Acquisitions of control by natural persons are only considered to bring about a lasting change in the structure of the undertakings concerned if those natural persons carry out further economic activities on their own account or if they control at least one other undertaking.[14]

Notes

[13] Including the State itself, e.g. Case IV/M.157 – *Air France/Sabena*, of 5 October 1992 in relation to the Belgian State, or other public bodies such as the Treuhandanstalt in Case IV/M.308 – *Kali und Salz/MDK/Treuhand*, of 14 December 1993. See, however, recital 22 of the Merger Regulation.

[14] Case IV/M.82 – *Asko/Jakobs/Adia* of 16 May 1991 including a private individual as undertaking concerned.; Case COMP/M3762 – *Apax/Travelex* of 16 June 2005 in which a private individual acquiring joint control was not considered an undertaking concerned.

Acquirer of control

13. Control is normally acquired by persons or undertakings which are the holders of the rights or are entitled to rights conferring control under the contracts concerned (Article 3(3)(a)). However, there are also situations where the formal holder of a controlling interest differs from the person or undertaking having in fact the real power to exercise the rights resulting from this interest. This may be the case, for example, where an undertaking uses another person or undertaking for the acquisition of a controlling interest and has the power to exercise the rights conferring control through this person or undertaking, i.e. the latter is formally the holder of the rights, but acts only as a vehicle. In such a situation, control is acquired by the undertaking which in reality is behind the operation and in fact enjoys the power to control the target undertaking (Article 3(3)(b)). The Court of First Instance concluded from this provision that control held by commercial companies can be attributed to their exclusive shareholder, their majority shareholders or to those jointly controlling the companies since these companies comply in any event with the decisions of those shareholders.[15] A controlling shareholding which is held by different entities in a group is normally attributed to the undertaking exercising control over the different formal holders of the rights. In other cases, the evidence needed to establish this type of indirect control may include, either separately or in combination and to be assessed on a case-by-case basis, factors such as shareholdings, contractual relations, source of financing or family links.[16]

Notes

[15] Judgment in Case T-282/02 *Cementbouw v Commission*, paragraph 72, [2006] ECR II-319.

[16] See Case M.754 – *Anglo American Corporation/Lonrho* of 23 April 1997.

Acquisition of control by investment funds

14. Specific issues may arise in the case of acquisitions of control by investment funds. The Commission will analyse structures involving investment funds on a case-by-case basis, but some general features of such structures can be set out on the basis of the Commission's past experience.

15. Investment funds are often set up in the legal form of limited partnerships, in which the investors participate as limited partners and normally do not exercise control, either individually or collectively. The investment funds usually acquire the shares and voting rights which confer control over the portfolio companies. Depending on the circumstances, control is normally exercised by the investment company which has set up the fund as the fund itself is typically a mere investment vehicle; in more exceptional circumstances, control may be exercised by the fund itself. The investment company usually exercises control by means of the organisational structure, *e.g.* by controlling the general partner of fund partnerships, or by contractual arrangements, such as advisory agreements, or by a combination of both. This may be the case even if the investment company itself does not own the company acting as a general partner, but their shares are held by natural persons (who may be linked to the investment company) or by a trust. Contractual arrangements with the investment company, in particular advisory agreements, will become even more important if the general partner does not have any own resources and personnel for the management of the portfolio companies, but only constitutes a company structure whose acts are performed by persons linked to the investment company. In these circumstances, the investment

company normally acquires indirect control within the meaning of Article 3(1)(b) and 3(3)(b) of the Merger Regulation, and has the power to exercise the rights which are directly held by the investment fund.[17]

Notes

[17] This structure also has an effect on how the turnover is calculated in situations involving investment funds, see paras 189ff.

1.2 Means of control

16. Control is defined by Article 3(2) of the Merger Regulation as the possibility of exercising decisive influence on an undertaking. It is therefore not necessary to show that the decisive influence is or will be actually exercised. However, the possibility of exercising that influence must be effective.[18] Article 3(2) further provides that the possibility of exercising decisive influence on an undertaking can exist on the basis of rights, contracts or any other means, either separately or in combination, and having regard to the considerations of fact and law involved. A concentration therefore may occur on a legal or a *de facto* basis, may take the form of sole or joint control, and extend to the whole or parts of one or more undertakings (cf Article 3(1)(b)).

Notes

18 Judgment in Case T-282/02 *Cementbouw v Commission*, paragraph 58, [2006] ECR II-319

Control by the acquisition of shares or assets

17. Whether an operation gives rise to an acquisition of control therefore depends on a number of legal and/or factual elements. The most common means for the acquisition of control is the acquisition of shares, possibly combined with a shareholders' agreement in cases of joint control, or the acquisition of assets.

Control on a contractual basis

18. Control can also be acquired on a contractual basis. In order to confer control, the contract must lead to a similar control of the management and the resources of the other undertaking as in the case of acquisition of shares or assets. In addition to transferring control over the management and the resources, such contracts must be characterised by a very long duration (ordinarily without a possibility of early termination for the party granting the contractual rights). Only such contracts can result in a structural change in the market.[19] Examples of such contracts are organisational contracts under national company law [20] or other types of contracts, *e.g.* in the form of agreements for the lease of the business, giving the acquirer control over the management and the resources despite the fact that property rights or shares are not transferred. In this respect, Article 3(2)(a) specifies that control may also be constituted by a right to use the assets of an undertaking.[21] Such contracts may also lead to a situation of joint control if both the owner of the assets as well as the undertaking controlling the management enjoy veto rights over strategic business decisions.[22]

Notes

[19] In Case COMP/M.3858 – *Lehman Brothers/SCG/Starwood/Le Meridien* of 20 July 2005 the management agreements had a duration of 10–15 years; in Case COMP/M.2632 – *Deutsche Bahn/ECT International/United Depots/JV* of 11 February 2002 the contract had a duration of 8 years.
[20] Examples of such specific contracts under national company law are the "Beherrschungsvertrag" in German law or the "*Contrato de subordinação*" in Portuguese law; such contracts do not exist in all Member States.
[21] See Case COMP/M.2060 – *Bosch/Rexroth* of 12 January 2001 concerning a control contract (Beherrschungsvertrag) in combination with a business lease; Case COMP/M.3136 – *GE/Agfa NDT* of 5 December 2003 concerning a specific contract to transfer control over entrepreneurial resources, management and risks; Case COMP/M.2632 – *Deutsche Bahn/ECT International/United Depots/JV* of 11 February 2002 concerning a business lease.
[22] Case COMP/M.3858 – *Lehman Brothers/SCG/Starwood/Le Meridien* of 20 July 2005; see also case IV/M. 126 – *Accor/Wagon-Lits* of 28 April 1992 in the context of Article 5(4)(b) of the Merger Regulation.

Control by other means

19. In line with these considerations, franchising agreements as such do not normally confer control over the franchisee's business on the franchisor. The franchisee usually exploits the entrepreneurial resources on its own account even if essential parts of the assets may belong to the

franchisor.[23] Furthermore, purely financial agreements, such as sale-and-lease-back transactions with arrangements for a buyback of the assets at the end of the term, do not normally constitute a concentration as they do not change control over the management and the resources.

Notes

[23] Case M.940 – *UBS/Mister Minit*, in the context of Article 5(4)(b) of the Merger Regulation. For the treatment of franchising relationships in the competitive assessment, see Case COMP/M.4220 – *Food Service Project/ Tele Pizza* of 6 June 2006. The situation in Case IV/M.126 – *Accor/Wagon-Lits* of 28 April 1992 has to be distinguished from franchising agreements. In this case, again in the context of Article 5(4)(b), the hotel company had a right to manage also hotels in which it only owned a minority stake as it had entered into long-term hotel management agreements giving it decisive influence over the day-to-day operations of these hotels, including decisions on budgetary matters.

20. Furthermore, control can also be established by any other means. Purely economic relationships may play a decisive role for the acquisition of control. In exceptional circumstances, a situation of economic dependence may lead to control on a *de facto* basis where, for example, very important long-term supply agreements or credits provided by suppliers or customers, coupled with structural links, confer decisive influence.[24] In such a situation, the Commission will carefully analyse whether such economic links, combined with other links, are sufficient to lead to a change of control on a lasting basis.[25]

Notes

[24] See Case IV/M.794 – *Coca-Cola/Amalgamated Beverages GB* of 22 January 1997; Case IV/ESCS.1031 – *US/Sollac/ Bamesa* of 28 July 1993; Case IV/M.625 – *Nordic Capital/Transpool* of 23 August 1995; for the criteria see also Case IV/M.697 – *Lockheed Martin Corporation/Loral Corporation*, of 27 March 1996.

[25] See Case IV/M.258 – *CCIE/GTE*, of 25 September 1992 where the Commission did not find control due to the temporary nature of the commercial agreements involved.

21. There may be an acquisition of control even if it is not the declared intention of the parties or if the acquirer is only passive and the acquisition of control is triggered by action of third parties. Examples are situations where the change of control results from the inheritance of a shareholder or where the exit of a shareholder triggers a change of control, in particular a change from joint to sole control.[26] Article 3(1)(b) covers such scenarios in specifying that control may also be acquired "by any other means".

Notes

[26] See Case COMP/M.3330 – *RTL/M6* of 12 March 2004; Case COMP/M.452 – *Avesta (II)* of 9 June 1994.

Control and national company law

22. National legislation within a Member State may provide specific rules on the structure of bodies representing the organization of decision-making within an undertaking. While such legislation may confer some power of control upon persons other than the shareholders, in particular on representatives of employees, the concept of control under the Merger Regulation is not related to such a means of influence as the Merger Regulation focuses on decisive influence enjoyed on the basis of rights, assets or contracts or equivalent de facto means. Restrictions in the articles of association or in general law concerning the persons eligible to sit on the board, such as a provisions requiring the appointment of independent members or excluding persons holding office or employment in the parent companies, do not exclude the existence of control as long as the shareholders decide the composition of the decision-making bodies.[27] Similarly, despite provisions of national law foreseeing that decisions of a company must be taken by its company organs in its interests, those persons holding the voting rights have the power to adopt those decisions and therefore have the possibility to exercise decisive influence on the company.[28]

Notes

[27] Judgment in Case T-282/02 *Cementbouw v Commission*, paragraphs 70, 73, 74 [2006] ECR II-319.

[28] Judgment in Case T-282/02 *Cementbouw v Commission*, paragraphs 79 [2006] ECR II-319.

Control in other areas of legislation

23. The concept of control under the Merger Regulation may be different from that applied in specific areas of Community and national legislation concerning, for example, prudential rules,

taxation, air transport or the media. The interpretation of "control" in other areas is therefore not necessarily decisive for the concept of control under the Merger Regulation.

1.3 Object of control

24. The Merger Regulation provides in Article 3(1)(b), (2) that the object of control can be one or more, or also parts of, undertakings which constitute legal entities, or the assets of such entities, or only some of these assets. The acquisition of control over assets can only be considered a concentration if those assets constitute the whole or a part of an undertaking, i.e. a business with a market presence, to which a market turnover can be clearly attributed.[29] The transfer of the client base of a business can fulfil these criteria if this is sufficient to transfer a business with a market turnover.[30] A transaction confined to intangible assets such as brands, patents or copyrights may also be considered to be a concentration if those assets constitute a business with a market turnover. In any case, the transfer of licences for brands, patents or copyrights, without additional assets, can only fulfil these criteria if the licences are exclusive at least in a certain territory and the transfer of such licences will transfer the turnover-generating activity.[31] For non-exclusive licences it can be excluded that they may constitute on their own a business to which a market turnover is attached.

Notes

[29] See, e.g., Case COMP/M.3867 – *Vattenfall/Elsam and E2 Assets* of 22 December 2005.

[30] Case COMP/M.2857 – *ECS/IEH* of 23 December 2002.

[31] In addition, the granting of licences and the transfer of patent licences will only constitute a concentration if this is done on a lasting basis. In this respect, similar considerations as set out above in paragraph 18 for the acquisition of control by (long-term) agreements apply.

---

25. Specific issues arise in cases where an undertaking outsources in-house activities, such as the provision of services or the manufacturing of products, to a service provider. Typical cases are the outsourcing of IT services to specialised IT companies. Outsourcing contracts can take several forms; their common characteristic is that the outsourcing service supplier shall provide those services to the customer which the latter has performed in-house before. Cases of simple outsourcing do not involve any transfer of assets or employees to the outsourcing service suppliers, but it is usually the case that any assets or employees are retained by the customer. Such an outsourcing contract is akin to a normal service contract and even if the outsourcing service supplier acquires a right to direct those assets and employees of the customer, no concentration arises if the assets and employees will be used exclusively to service the customer.

26. The situation may be different if the outsourcing service supplier, in addition to taking over a certain activity which was previously provided internally, is transferred the associated assets and/or personnel. A concentration only arises in these circumstances if the assets constitute the whole or part of an undertaking, i.e. a business with access to the market. This requires that the assets previously dedicated to in-house activities of the seller will enable the outsourcing service supplier to provide services not only to the outsourcing customer but also to third parties, either immediately or within a short period after the transfer. This will be the case if the transfer relates to an internal business unit or a subsidiary already engaged in the provision of services to third parties. If third parties are not yet supplied, the assets transferred in the case of manufacturing should contain production facilities, the product know-how (it is sufficient if the assets transferred allow the build-up of such capabilities in the near future) and, if there is no existing market access, the means for the purchaser to develop a market access within a short period of time (e.g. including existing contracts or brands).[32] As regards the provision of services, the assets transferred should include the required know-how (e.g. the relevant personnel and intellectual property) and those facilities which allow market access (such as, eg, marketing facilities).[33] The assets transferred therefore have to include at least those core elements that would allow an acquirer to build up a market presence in a time-frame similar to the start-up period for joint ventures as set out below under paragraphs 97, 100. As in the case of joint ventures, the Commission will take account of substantiated business plans and general market features for assessing this.

Notes

[32] See Case COMP/M.1841 – *Celestica/IBM* of 25 February 2000; Case COMP/M.1849 – *Solectron/Ericsson* of 29 February 2000; Case COMP/M.2479 – *Flextronics/Alcatel* – of 29 June 2001; Case COMP/M.2629 – *Flextronics/Xerox* of 12 November 2001.

[33] See, in the context of joint ventures, Case IV/M.560 – *EDS/Lufthansa* of 11 May 1995; Case COMP/M.2478 – *IBM Italia/Business Solutions/JV* of 29 June 2001.

27. If the assets transferred do not allow the purchaser to at least develop a market presence, it is likely that they will be used only for providing services to the outsourcing customer. In such circumstances, the transaction will not result in a lasting change in the market structure and the outsourcing contract is again similar to a service contract. The transaction will not constitute a concentration. The specific requirements under which a joint venture for the provision of outsourcing services is qualified as a concentration are assessed in the present Notice in the section on full-function joint ventures.

1.4 Change of control on a lasting basis

28. Article 3(1) of the Merger Regulation defines the concept of a concentration in such a manner as to cover operations only if they bring about a lasting change in the control of the undertakings concerned and, as recital 20 adds, in the structure of the market. The Merger Regulation therefore does not deal with transactions resulting only in a temporary change of control. However, a change of control on a lasting basis is not excluded by the fact that the underlying agreements are entered into for a definite period of time, provided those agreements are renewable. A concentration may arise even in cases in which agreements envisage a definite end-date, if the period envisaged is sufficiently long to lead to a lasting change in the control of the undertakings concerned.[34]

Notes

[34] See, in cases of joint ventures, Case COMP/M.2903 – *DaimlerChrysler/Deutsche Telekom/JV* of 30 April 2003 where a period of 12 years was considered sufficient; Case COMP/M.2632 – *Deutsche Bahn/ECT International/ United Depots/JV* of 11 February 2002 with a contract duration of 8 years. In Case COMP/M.3858 *Lehman Brothers/ Starwood/Le Meridien* of 20 July 2005, the Commission considered a minimum period of 10–15 years sufficient, but not a period of three years. The acquisition of control by the acquisition of shares or assets is not normally confined to a definite period of time and is therefore assumed to lead to a change of control on a lasting basis. Only in the scenarios set out in paragraphs 29 ff., will an acquisition of control by shares or assets be exceptionally considered to be transitory in nature and thus not to lead to a lasting change in the control of the undertakings concerned.

29. The question whether an operation results in a lasting change in the market structure is also relevant for the assessment of several operations occurring in succession, where the first transaction is only transitory in nature. Several scenarios can be distinguished in this respect.

30. In one scenario, several undertakings come together solely for the purpose of acquiring another company on the basis of an agreement to divide up the acquired assets according to a pre-existing plan immediately upon completion of the transaction. In such circumstances, in a first step, the acquisition of the entire target company is carried out by one or several undertakings. In a second step, the acquired assets are divided among several undertakings. The question is then whether the first transaction is to be considered as a separate concentration, involving an acquisition of sole control (in the case of a single purchaser) or of joint control (in the case of a joint purchase) of the entire target undertaking, or whether only the acquisitions in the second step constitute concentrations, whereby each of the acquiring undertakings acquires its relevant part of the target undertaking.

31. The Commission considers that the first transaction does not constitute a concentration, and examines the acquisitions of control by the ultimate acquirers, provided a number of conditions are met: First, the subsequent break-up must be agreed between the different purchasers in a legally binding way. Second, there must not be any uncertainty that the second step, the division of the acquired assets, will take place within a short time period after the first acquisition. The Commission considers that normally the maximum time-frame for the division of the assets should be one year.[35]

Notes

[35] See, e.g., Cases COMP/M. Case No COMP/M.3779 – *Pernod Ricard/Allied Domecq* of 24 June 2005 and COMP/ M.3813 – *Fortune Brands/Allied Domecq* of 10 June 2005, where the split-up of the assets was foreseen to become effective within 6 months after the acquisition

32. If both conditions are met, the first acquisition does not result in a structural change on a lasting basis. There is no effective concentration of economic power between the acquirer(s) and the target company as a whole since the acquired assets are not held in an undivided way on a lasting basis, but only for the time necessary to carry out the immediate split-up of the acquired assets. In those circumstances, only the acquisitions of the different parts of the undertaking in the second step will constitute concentrations, whereby each of these acquisitions by different purchasers will constitute a separate concentration. This is irrespective of whether the first acquisition is carried out by only one undertaking[36] or jointly by the undertakings which are also involved in the second step.[37] In any case, it must be noted that the scope of a clearance decision will only allow for a takeover of the entire target if the break-up can proceed within a short time-frame afterwards and the different parts of the target undertaking are directly sold on to the respective ultimate buyer.

33. However, if these conditions are not fulfilled, in particular if it is not certain that the second step will proceed within a short time-frame after the first acquisition, the Commission will consider the first transaction as a separate concentration, involving the entire target undertaking. This, *e.g.*, is the case if the first transaction may also proceed independently of the second transaction[38] or if a longer transitory period is needed to divide up the target undertaking.[39]

Notes

[36] For a first acquisition by only one undertaking see Case COMP/M.3779 – *Pernod Ricard/Allied Domecq* of 24 June 2005 and Case COMP/M.3813 – *Fortune Brands/Allied Domecq/Pernod Ricard* of 10 June 2005; Case COMP/M.2060 – *Bosch/Rexroth* of 12 January 2001.

[37] For a joint acquisition see Case COMP/M.1630 – *Air Liquide/BOC* of 18 January 2000; Case COMP/M.1922 – *Siemens/Bosch/Atecs* of 11 August 2000; Case COMP/M.2059 – *Siemens/Dematic/VDO Sachs* of 29 August 2000.

[38] See Case COMP/M.2498 – *UPM-Kymmene/Haindl* of 21 November 2001 and Case COMP/M.2499 – *Norske Skog/Parenco/Walsum* of 21 November 2001.

[39] Case COMP/M.3372 – *Carlsberg/Holsten* of 16 March 2004.

34. A second scenario is an operation leading to joint control for a starting-up period but, according to legally binding agreements, this joint control will be converted to sole control by one of the shareholders. As the joint control situation may not constitute a lasting change of control, the whole operation may be considered to be an acquisition of sole control. In the past, the Commission accepted that such a start-up period could last up to three years.[40] Such a period seems to be too long to exclude that the joint control scenario has an impact on the structure of the market. The period therefore should, in general, not exceed one year and the joint control period should be only transitory in nature.[41] Only such a relatively short period will make it unlikely that the joint control period will have a distinct impact on the market structure and can therefore be considered as not leading to a change in control on a lasting basis.

Notes

[40] Case IV/M.425 – *British Telecom/Santander* of 28 March 1994.

[41] See Case M.2389 – *Shell/DEA* of 20 December 2001 where the ultimate acquirer of sole control had a strong influence in the operational management during the joint control period; Case M.2854 – *RAG/Degussa* of 18 November 2002 where the transitional period was designed to facilitate internal post-merger restructuring.

35. In a third scenario, an undertaking is "parked" with an interim buyer, often a bank, on the basis of an agreement on the future onward sale of the business to an ultimate acquirer. The interim buyer generally acquires shares "on behalf" of the ultimate acquirer, which often bears the major part of the economic risks and may also be granted specific rights. In such circumstances, the first transaction is only undertaken to facilitate the second transaction and the first buyer is directly linked to the ultimate acquirer. Contrary to the situation described in the first scenario in paragraphs 30–33, no other ultimate acquirer is involved, the target business remains unchanged, and the sequence of transactions is initiated alone by the sole ultimate acquirer. From the date of the adoption of this Notice, the Commission will examine the acquisition of control by the ultimate acquirer, as provided for in the agreements entered into by the parties. The Commission will consider the transaction by which the interim buyer acquires control in such circumstances as the first step of a single concentration comprising the lasting acquisition of control by the ultimate buyer.

1.5 Interrelated transactions

1.5.1 Relation between Article 3 and Article 5(2) second subparagraph

36. Several transactions can be treated as a single concentration under the Merger Regulation either according to the general rule of Article 3 – as the transactions are interdependent – or according to the specific provision of Article 5(2) second subparagraph.

37. Article 5(2) second subparagraph governs a different question from that referred to by Article 3 of the Merger Regulation. Article 3 defines the existence of a "concentration" in general and material terms, but does not directly determine the question of the Commission's competence in respect of concentrations. Article 5 intends to specify the scope of the Merger Regulation, in particular by defining the turnover to be taken into account for the purpose of determining whether a concentration has Community dimension, and Article 5(2) second subparagraph allows the Commission in this respect to consider two or more concentrative transactions to constitute a single concentration for the purposes of calculating the turnover of the undertakings concerned. The assessment whether, in application of Article 3, a number of transactions give rise to a single concentration or whether those transactions must be regarded as giving rise to a number of concentrations, is thereby logically precedent to the question addressed in Article 5(2) second subparagraph.[42]

Notes

[42] Judgment in Case T-282/02 *Cementbouw v Commission*, paragraphs 113–119 [2006] ECR II-319.

1.5.2 Interdependent transactions under Article 3

38. The general and teleological definition of a concentration set out in Article 3(1) – the result being control of one or more undertakings – implies that it makes no difference whether control was acquired by one or several legal transactions, provided that the end result constitutes a single concentration. Two or more transactions constitute a single concentration for the purposes of Article 3 if they are unitary in nature. It should therefore be determined whether the result leads to conferring one or more undertakings direct or indirect economic control over the activities of one or more other undertakings. For the assessment, the economic reality underlying the transactions is to be identified and thus the economic aim pursued by the parties. In other words, in order to determine the unitary nature of the transactions in question, it is necessary, in each individual case, to ascertain whether those transactions are interdependent, in such a way that one transaction would not have been carried out without the other.[43]

Notes

[43] Judgment in Case T-282/02 *Cementbouw v Commission*, paragraphs 104–109 [2006] ECR II-319:

---

39. Recital 20 to the Merger Regulation explains in this respect that it is appropriate to treat as a single concentration transactions that are closely connected in that they are linked by condition. The requirement that the transactions are interdependent as set out by the Court of First Instance in the *Cementbouw* judgment[44] thereby corresponds to the explanation set out in recital 20 that the transactions are linked by condition.

Notes

[44] Judgment in Case T-282/02 *Cementbouw v Commission*, paragraphs 106–109 [2006] ECR II-319.

---

40. This general approach reflects, on the one hand, that under the Merger Regulation transactions which stand or fall together according to the economic objectives pursued by the parties should also be analysed in one procedure. In these circumstances, the change of the market structure is brought about by these transactions together. On the other hand, if different transactions are not interdependent and if the parties would proceed with one of the transactions if the other ones would not succeed, it seems appropriate to assess these transactions individually under the Merger Regulation.

41. However, several transactions, even if linked by condition upon each other, can only be treated as a single concentration, if control is acquired ultimately by the same undertaking(s). Only in these

circumstances two or more transactions can be considered to be unitary in nature and therefore to constitute a single concentration for the purposes of Article 3.[45] This excludes de-mergers of joint ventures by which different parts of an undertaking are split between its former parent companies. The Commission will consider those transactions as separate concentrations.[46] The same applies to transactions where two (or more) companies exchange assets in transactions involving de-mergers of joint ventures or assets swaps. Although the parties will normally consider those transactions as interdependent, the purpose of the Merger Regulation requires a separate assessment of the results of each of the transactions: Several undertakings acquire control of different assets; a separate combination of resources takes place for each of the acquiring undertakings; and the impact on the market of each of those acquisitions of control needs to be analysed separately under the Merger Regulation.

Notes

[45] This also covers situations where an undertaking sells a business to a purchaser and then acquirers the seller including the business sold, see Case COMP/M.4521 – *LGI/Telenet* of 26 February 2007.

[46] See parallel cases COMP/M.3293 – *Shell/BEB* and COMP/M.3294 – *ExxonMobil/BEB* of 20 November 2003; case IV/M.197 – *Solvay/Laporte* of 30 April 1992.

42. The acquisition of different degrees of control (for example joint control of one business and sole control of another business) raises specific questions. An operation involving the acquisition of joint control of one part of an undertaking and sole control of another part is in principle regarded as two separate concentrations under the Merger Regulation.[47] Those transactions constitute only one concentration if they are interdependent and if the undertaking acquiring sole control is also acquiring joint control. In any case, such a scenario is considered to constitute one concentration where a corporate entity is acquired to which both the solely controlled and the jointly controlled undertaking belong. On the basis of the interpretation in recital 20, the situation where the same undertaking acquires sole and joint control of other undertakings based on interdependent agreements is not to be treated differently. These transactions, if they are interdependent, therefore constitute a single concentration.

Notes

[47] See Case IV/M.409 *ABB/Renault Automation* of 9 March 1994.

Requirement of conditionality of transactions

43. The required conditionality implies that none of the transactions would take place without the others and they therefore constitute a single operation.[48] Such conditionality is normally demonstrated if the transactions are linked *de jure*, i.e. the agreements themselves are linked by mutual conditionality. If *de facto* conditionality can be satisfactorily demonstrated, it may also suffice for treating the transactions as a single concentration. This requires an economic assessment of whether each of the transactions necessarily depends on the conclusion of the others.[49] Further indications of the interdependence of several transactions may be the statements of the parties themselves or the simultaneous conclusion of the relevant agreements. A conclusion of *de facto* interconditionality of several transactions will be difficult to reach in the absence of their simultaneity. A pronounced lack of simultaneity of legally interconditional transactions may likewise put into doubt their true interdependence.

Notes

[48] Judgment in Case T-282/02 *Cementbouw v Commission*, paragraphs 127 et seq. [2006] ECR II-319.

[49] Judgment in Case T-282/02 *Cementbouw v Commission*, paragraphs 131 et seq. [2006] ECR II-319. See Case COMP/M.4521 – *LGI/Telenet* of 26 February 2007, where the interdependence was based on the fact that two transactions were decided and carried out simultaneously and that, according to the economic aims of the parties, each of the transactions would not have been carried out without the other.

44. The principle that several transactions can be treated as a single concentration under the mentioned conditions only applies if the result is that control of one or more undertakings is acquired by the same person(s) or undertaking(s). First, this may be the case if a single business or undertaking is acquired via several legal transactions. Second, also the acquisition of control of several

undertakings – which could constitute concentrations in themselves - can be linked in such a way that it constitutes a single concentration. However, it is not possible under the Merger Regulation to link different legal transactions which only partly concern the acquisition of control of undertakings, but partly also the acquisition of other assets, such as non-controlling minority stakes in other companies. It would not be in line with the general framework and the purpose of the Merger Regulation if different transactions, linked by conditionality, were assessed as a whole under the Merger Regulations if only some of these transactions lead to a change in control of a given target.

Acquisition of a single business

45. A single concentration may therefore exist if the same purchaser(s) acquire control of a single business, i.e. a single economic entity, via several legal transactions if those are inter-conditional. This is the case irrespective of whether the business is acquired in a corporate structure, consisting of one or several companies, or whether various assets are acquired which form a single business, i.e. a single economic entity managed for a common commercial purpose to which all the assets contribute. Such a business may comprise majority and minority stakes in companies as well as tangible and intangible assets. If several legal transactions which are interdependent are required to transfer such a business, these transactions constitute one concentration.[50]

Notes
[50] See Case IV/M.470 – *Gencor/Shell* of 29 August 1994; COMP/M.3410 – *Total/Gaz de France* of 8 October 2004; Case IV/M.957 – *L'Oreal/Procasa/Cosmetique Iberica/Albesa* of 19 September 1997; Case IV/M.861 – *Textron/Kautex* of 18 December 1996 where all the assets were also used in the same product market. The same considerations apply if a joint venture is created by several companies, forming a single business, see Case M.4048, *Sonae Industria/Tarkett* of 12 June 2006, where the interdependence of transactions establishing, respectively, a production and a distribution joint venture was necessary in order to demonstrate that there was a single concentration that would create a full-function joint venture.

Parallel and serial acquisitions of control

46. For the treatment of several acquisitions of control as a single concentration, several scenarios have arisen in the Commission's past decisional practice. One such scenario is a parallel acquisition of control, i.e. undertaking A acquires control of undertaking B and C in parallel from separate sellers on condition that A is not obliged to buy either and neither seller is obliged to sell, unless both transactions proceed.[51] Another scenario is a serial acquisition of control, i.e. undertaking A acquires control of undertaking B conditional on B's prior or simultaneous acquisition of undertaking C, as illustrated by the Kingfisher case.[52]

Notes
[51] Case COMP/M.2926 – *EQT/H&R/Dragoco* – of 16 September 2002; the same considerations apply to the question when several mergers constitute one concentration in the meaning of Article 3(1)(a), Case COMP/M.2824 – *Ernst & Young/Andersen Germany* of 27 August 2002.
[52] Case IV/M.1188 – *Kingfisher/Wegert/ProMarkt* of 18 June 1998; case COMP/M.2650 – *Haniel/Cementbouw/JV* (CVK) of 26 June 2002.

Serial acquisition of sole/joint control

47. In the same way as the Kingfisher scenario, the Commission approaches cases where, in a serial transaction, an undertaking agrees to acquire first sole control of a target undertaking, with a view to directly selling on parts of the acquired stake in the target to another undertaking, finally resulting in joint control of both acquirers over the target company. If both acquisitions are inter-conditional, the two transactions constitute a single concentration and only the acquisition of joint control, as the final result of the transactions, will be considered by the Commission.[53]

Notes
[53] Case COMP/M.2420 – *Mitsui/CVRD/Caemi* of 30 October 2001.

1.5.3 Series of transactions in securities

48. Recital 20 of the Merger Regulation further explains that a single concentration will also arise in cases where control over one undertaking is acquired by a series of transactions in securities from

one or several sellers taking place within a reasonably short period of time. The concentration in these scenarios is not limited to the acquisition of the "one and decisive" share, but will cover all the acquisitions of securities which take place in the reasonably short period of time.

1.5.4 Article 5(2) subparagraph 2

49. Article 5(2) subparagraph 2 provides a specific rule which allows the Commission. to consider successive transactions occurring in a fixed period of time a single concentration for the purposes of calculating the turnover of the undertakings concerned. The purpose of this provision is to ensure that the same persons do not break a transaction down into series of sales of assets over a period of time, with the aim of avoiding the competence conferred on the Commission by the Merger Regulation.[54]

Notes

[54] Judgment in Case T-282/02 *Cementbouw v Commission*, paragraph 118 [2006] ECR II-319.

50. If two or more transactions (each of them bringing about an acquisition of control) take place within a two-year period between the same persons or undertakings, they shall be qualified as a single concentration,[55] irrespective of whether or not those transactions relate to parts of the same business or concern the same sector. This does not apply where the same persons or undertakings are joined by other persons or undertakings for only some of the transactions involved. It is sufficient if the transactions, although not carried out between the same companies, are carried out between companies belonging to the same respective groups. The provision also applies to two or more transactions between the same persons or undertakings if they are carried out simultaneously. Whenever they lead to acquisitions of control by the same undertaking, such simultaneous transactions between the same parties form a single concentration even if they are not conditional upon each other.[56] However, Article 5(2) subparagraph 2 would not appear to apply to different transactions at least one of which involves an undertaking concerned which is distinct from the common seller(s) and buyer(s). In situations involving two transactions where one transaction results in sole control and the other in joint control, Article 5(2) subparagraph 2 therefore does not apply unless the other jointly controlling parent(s) in the latter transaction are the seller(s) of the solely controlling stake in the former transaction.

Notes

[55] See Case COMP/M.3173 – *E.ON/Fortum Burghausen/Smaland/Endenderry* of 13 June 2003. This also applies to situations where sole control is acquired whereby only parts of the undertaking were previously jointly controlled by the acquiring undertaking, case COMP/M.2679 – *EdF/TXU/ Europe/24 Seven* of 20 December 2001.
[56] Case IV/M.1283 – *Volkswagen/RollsRoyce/Cosworth* of 24 August 1998.

1.6 Internal Restructuring

51. A concentration within the meaning of the Merger Regulation is limited to changes in control. An internal restructuring within a group of companies does not constitute a concentration. This applies, e.g., to increases in shareholdings not accompanied by changes of control or to restructuring operations such as a merger of a dual listed company into a single legal entity or a merger of subsidiaries. A concentration could only arise if the operation leads to a change in the quality of control of one undertaking and therefore is no longer purely internal.

1.7 Concentrations involving State-owned undertakings

52. An exceptional situation exists where both the acquiring and acquired undertakings are companies owned by the same State (or by the same public body or municipality). In this case, whether the operation is to be regarded as an internal restructuring depends in turn on the question whether both undertakings were formerly part of the same economic unit. Where the undertakings were formerly part of different economic units having an independent power of decision, the operation will be deemed to constitute a concentration and not an internal restructuring.[57] However, where the different economic units will continue to have an independent power of decision also after the operation, the operation is only to be regarded as an internal restructuring, even if the shares of the undertakings, constituting different economic units, should be held by a single entity, such as a pure holding company.[58]

Notes

[57] Case IV/M.097 – *Péchiney/Usinor*, of 24 June 1991; Case IV/M.216 – *CEA Industrie/France Telecom/SGS-Thomson*, of 22 February 1993; Case IV/M.931 – *Neste/IVO* of 2 June 1998. See also Recital 22 of the Merger Regulation.

[58] Specific issues concerning the calculation of turnover for state-owned companies are dealt with in paragraphs 192–194

53. However, the prerogatives exercised by a State acting as a public authority rather than as a shareholder, in so far as they are limited to the protection of the public interest, do not constitute control within the meaning of the Merger Regulation to the extent that they have neither the aim nor the effect of enabling the State to exercise a decisive influence over the activity of the undertaking.[59]

Notes

[59] Case IV/M.493 – *Tractebel/Distrigaz II*, of 1 September 1994.

2. Sole control

54. Sole control is acquired if one undertaking alone can exercise decisive influence on an undertaking. Two general situations in which an undertaking has sole control can be distinguished. First, the solely controlling undertaking enjoys the power to determine the strategic commercial decisions of the other undertaking. This power is typically achieved by the acquisition of a majority of voting rights in a company. Second, a situation also conferring sole control exists where only one shareholder is able to veto strategic decisions in an undertaking, but this shareholder does not have the power, on his own, to impose such decisions (the so-called negative sole control). In these circumstances, a single shareholder possesses the same level of influence as that usually enjoyed by an individual shareholder which jointly-controls a company, i.e. the power to block the adoption of strategic decisions. In contrast to the situation in a jointly controlled company, there are no other shareholders enjoying the same level of influence and the shareholder enjoying negative sole control does not necessarily have to cooperate with specific other shareholders in determining the strategic behaviour of the controlled undertaking. Since this shareholder can produce a deadlock situation, the shareholder acquires decisive influence within the meaning of Article 3(2) and therefore control within the meaning of the Merger Regulation.[60]

Notes

[60] Since this shareholder is the only undertaking acquiring a controlling influence, only this shareholder is obliged to submit a notification under the Merger Regulation.

55. Sole control can be acquired on a *de jure* and/or *de facto* basis.

De jure sole control

56. Sole control is normally acquired on a legal basis where an undertaking acquires a majority of the voting rights of a company. In the absence of other elements, an acquisition which does not include a majority of the voting rights does not normally confer control even if it involves the acquisition of a majority of the share capital. Where the company statutes require a supermajority for strategic decisions, the acquisition of a simple majority of the voting rights may not confer the power to determine strategic decisions, but may be sufficient to confer a blocking right on the acquirer and therefore negative control.

57. Even in the case of a minority shareholding, sole control may occur on a legal basis in situations where specific rights are attached to this shareholding. These may be preferential shares to which special rights are attached enabling the minority shareholder to determine the strategic commercial behaviour of the target company, such as the power to appoint more than half of the members of the supervisory board or the administrative board. Sole control can also be exercised by a minority shareholder who has the right to manage the activities of the company and to determine its business policy on the basis of the organisational structure (e.g. as a general partner in a limited partnership which often does not even have a shareholding).

58. A typical situation of negative sole control occurs where one shareholder holds 50% in an undertaking whilst the remaining 50% is held by several other shareholders (assuming this does not lead

to positive sole control on a *de facto* basis), or where there is a supermajority required for strategic decisions which in fact confers a veto right upon only one shareholder, irrespective of whether it is a majority or a minority shareholder.[61]

Notes

[61] See consecutive Cases COMP/M.3537 – *BBVA/BNL* of 20 August 2004 and M.3768 – *BBVA/BNL* of 27 April 2005; Case M.3198 – *VW-Audi/VW-Audi Vertriebszentren* of 29 July 2003; Case COMP/M.2777 – *Cinven Limited/ Angel Street Holdings* of 8 May 2002; Case IV/M.258 – *CCIE/GTE*, of 25 September 1992. In Case COMP/M. 3876 – *Diester Industrie/Bunge/JV* of 30 September 2005, there was the specific situation that a joint venture held a stake in a company by which it had negative sole control over this company.

De facto sole control

59. A minority shareholder may also be deemed to have sole control on a *de facto* basis. This is in particular the case where the shareholder is highly likely to achieve a majority at the shareholders" meetings, given the level of its shareholding and the evidence resulting from the presence of shareholders in the shareholders' meetings in previous years.[62] Based on the past voting pattern, the Commission will carry out a prospective analysis and take into account foreseeable changes of the shareholders' presence which might arise in future following the operation.[63] The Commission will further analyse the position of other shareholders and assess their role. Criteria for such an assessment are in particular whether the remaining shares are widely dispersed, whether other important shareholders have structural, economic or family links with the large minority shareholder or whether other shareholders have a strategic or a purely financial interest in the target company; these criteria will be assessed on a case-by-case basis.[64] Where, on the basis of its shareholding, the historic voting pattern at the shareholders' meeting and the position of other shareholders, a minority shareholder is likely to have a stable majority of the votes at the shareholders' meeting, then that large minority shareholder is taken to have sole control.[65]

Notes

[62] Case IV/M.343 – *Société Générale de Belgique/Générale de Banque*, of 3 August 1993; Case COMP/M.3330 – *RTL/ M6* of 12 March 2004; Case IV/M.159 – *Mediobanca/Generali* of 19 December 1991.

[63] See Case COMP/M.4336 – *MAN/Scania* of 20 December 2007 as regards the question whether Volkswagen hat acquired control of MAN.

[64] Case IV/M.754 – *Anglo American/Lonrho* of 23 April 1997; Case IV/M.025 – *Arjomari/Wiggins Teape*, of 10 February 1990.

[65] See also Case COMP/M.2574 – *Pirelli/Edizione/Olivetti/Telecom Italia* of 20 September 2001; Case IV/M.1519 – *Renault/Nissan* of 12 May 1999.

60. An option to purchase or convert shares cannot in itself confer sole control unless the option will be exercised in the near future according to legally binding agreements.[66] However, in exceptional circumstances an option, together with other elements, may lead to the conclusion that there is *de facto* sole control.[67]

Notes

[66] Judgment in Case T 2/93, *Air France v Commission* [1994] ECR II-323. Even though an option does normally not in itself lead to a concentration, it can be taken into account for the substantive assessment in a related concentration, see Case COMP/M.3696 – *E.ON/MOL* of 21 December 2005, at paragraphs 12–14, 480, 762 et subseq.

[67] Case IV/M.397 – *Ford/Hertz* of 7 March 1994.

Sole control acquired by other means than voting rights

61. Apart from the acquisition of sole control on the basis of voting rights, the considerations outlined in section 1.2 concerning the acquisition of sole control by purchase of assets, by contract, or by any other means also apply.

3. Joint Control

62. Joint control exists where two or more undertakings or persons have the possibility of exercising decisive influence over another undertaking. Decisive influence in this sense normally means the power to block actions which determine the strategic commercial behaviour of an undertaking.

Unlike sole control, which confers upon a specific shareholder the power to determine the strategic decisions in an undertaking, joint control is characterized by the possibility of a deadlock situation resulting from the power of two or more parent companies to reject proposed strategic decisions. It follows, therefore, that these shareholders must reach a common understanding in determining the commercial policy of the joint venture and that they are required to cooperate.[68]

Notes

[68] See also Judgment in Case T-282/02 *Cementbouw v Commission*, paragraphs 42, 52, 67 [2006] ECR II-319.

---

63. As in the case of sole control, the acquisition of joint control can also be established on a *de jure* or *de facto* basis. There is joint control if the shareholders (the parent companies) must reach agreement on major decisions concerning the controlled undertaking (the joint venture).

3.1 Equality in voting rights or appointment to decision-making bodies

64. The clearest form of joint control exists where there are only two parent companies which share equally the voting rights in the joint venture. In this case, it is not necessary for a formal agreement to exist between them. However, where there is a formal agreement, it must be consistent with the principle of equality between the parent companies, by laying down, for example, that each is entitled to the same number of representatives in the management bodies and that none of the members has a casting vote.[69] Equality may also be achieved where both parent companies have the right to appoint an equal number of members to the decision-making bodies of the joint venture.

Notes

[69] Case COMP/M.3097 – *Maersk Data/Eurogate IT; Global Transport Solutions JV* of 12 March 2003; Case IV/M.272 – *Matra/CAP Gemini Sogeti*, of 17 March 1993.

3.2 Veto rights

65. Joint control may exist even where there is no equality between the two parent companies in votes or in representation in decision-making bodies or where there are more than two parent companies. This is the case where minority shareholders have additional rights which allow them to veto decisions which are essential for the strategic commercial behaviour of the joint venture.[70] These veto rights may be set out in the statute of the joint venture or conferred by agreement between its parent companies. The veto rights themselves may operate by means of a specific quorum required for decisions taken at the shareholders' meeting or by the board of directors to the extent that the parent companies are represented on this board. It is also possible that strategic decisions are subject to approval by a body, e.g. supervisory board, where the minority shareholders are represented and form part of the quorum needed for such decisions.

Notes

[70] Case T 2/93, *Air France v Commission* [1994] ECR II-323; Case IV/M.010 – *Conagra/Idea*, of 3 May 1991.

---

66. These veto rights must be related to strategic decisions on the business policy of the joint venture. They must go beyond the veto rights normally accorded to minority shareholders in order to protect their financial interests as investors in the joint venture. This normal protection of the rights of minority shareholders is related to decisions on the essence of the joint venture, such as changes in the statute, an increase or decrease in the capital or liquidation. A veto right, for example, which prevents the sale or winding-up of the joint venture does not confer joint control on the minority shareholder concerned.[71]

Notes

[71] Case IV/M.062 – *Eridania/ISI*, of 30 July 1991.

---

67. In contrast, veto rights which confer joint control typically include decisions on issues such as the budget, the business plan, major investments or the appointment of senior management. The acquisition of joint control, however, does not require that the acquirer has the power to exercise decisive

influence on the day-to-day running of an undertaking. The crucial element is that the veto rights are sufficient to enable the parent companies to exercise such influence in relation to the strategic business behaviour of the joint venture. Moreover, it is not necessary to establish that an acquirer of joint control of the joint venture will actually make use of its decisive influence. The possibility of exercising such influence and, hence, the mere existence of the veto rights, is sufficient.

68. In order to acquire joint control, it is not necessary for a minority shareholder to have all the veto rights mentioned above. It may be sufficient that only some, or even one such right, exists. Whether or not this is the case depends upon the precise content of the veto right itself and also the importance of this right in the context of the specific business of the joint venture.

Appointment of senior management and determination of budget

69. Very important are the veto rights concerning decisions on the appointment and dismissal of the senior management and the approval of the budget. The power to codetermine the structure of the senior management, such as the members of the board, usually confers upon the holder the power to exercise decisive influence on the commercial policy of an undertaking. The same is true with respect to decisions on the budget since the budget determines the precise framework of the activities of the joint venture and, in particular, the investments it may make.

Business plan

70. The business plan normally provides details of the aims of a company together with the measures to be taken in order to achieve those aims. A veto right over this type of business plan may be sufficient to confer joint control even in the absence of any other veto right. In contrast, where the business plan contains merely general declarations concerning the business aims of the joint venture, the existence of a veto right will be only one element in the general assessment of joint control but will not, on its own, be sufficient to confer joint control.

Investments

71. In the case of a veto right on investments, the importance of this right depends, first, on the level of investments which are subject to the approval of the parent companies and, secondly, on the extent to which investments constitute an essential feature of the market in which the joint venture is active. In relation to the first criterion, where the level of investments necessitating approval of the parent companies is extremely high, this veto right may be closer to the normal protection of the interests of a minority shareholder than to a right conferring a power of co-determination over the commercial policy of the joint venture. With regard to the second, the investment policy of an undertaking is normally an important element in assessing whether or not there is joint control. However, there may be some markets where investment does not play a significant role in the market behaviour of an undertaking.

Market-specific rights

72. Apart from the typical veto rights mentioned above, there exist a number of other possible veto rights related to specific decisions which are important in the context of the particular market of the joint venture. One example is the decision on the technology to be used by the joint venture where technology is a key feature of the joint venture's activities. Another example relates to markets characterized by product differentiation and a significant degree of innovation. In such markets, a veto right over decisions relating to new product lines to be developed by the joint venture may also be an important element in establishing the existence of joint control.

Overall context

73. In assessing the relative importance of veto rights, where there are a number of them, these rights should not be evaluated in isolation. On the contrary, the determination of whether or not joint control exists is based upon an assessment of these rights as a whole. However, a veto right which does not relate either to strategic commercial policy, to the appointment of senior management or to the budget or business plan cannot be regarded as giving joint control to its owner.[72]

Notes

[72] Case IV/M.295 – *SITA-RPC/SCORI*, of 19 March 1993.

3.3 Joint exercise of voting rights

74. Even in the absence of specific veto rights, two or more undertakings acquiring minority share-holdings in another undertaking may obtain joint control. This may be the case where the minor-ity shareholdings together provide the means for controlling the target undertaking. This means that the minority shareholders, together, will have a majority of the voting rights; and they will act together in exercising these voting rights. This can result from a legally binding agreement to this effect, or it may be established on a *de facto* basis.

75. The legal means to ensure the joint exercise of voting rights can be in the form of a (jointly con-trolled) holding company to which the minority shareholders transfer their rights, or an agree-ment by which they undertake to act in the same way (pooling agreement).

76. Very exceptionally, collective action can occur on a de facto basis where strong common interests exist between the minority shareholders to the effect that they would not act against each other in exercis-ing their rights in relation to the joint venture. The greater the number of parent companies involved in such a joint venture, however, the more remote is the likelihood of this situation occurring.

77. Indicative for such a commonality of interests is a high degree of mutual dependency as between the parent companies to reach the strategic objectives of the joint venture. This is in particular the case when each parent company provides a contribution to the joint venture which is vital for its operation (e.g. specific technologies, local know-how or supply agreements).[73] In these circum-stances, the parent companies may be able to block the strategic decisions of the joint venture and, thus, they can operate the joint venture successfully only with each other's agreement on the strategic decisions even if there is no express provision for any veto rights. The parent companies will therefore be required to cooperate.[74] Further factors are decision making procedures which are tailored in such a way as to allow the parent companies to exercise joint control even in the absence of explicit agreements granting veto rights or other links between the minority sharehold-ers related to the joint venture.[75]

Notes

[73] Case COMP/JV.55 *Hutchinson/RCPM/ECT* of 3 July 2001; see also Case IV/M.553 – *RTL/Veronica/Endemol* of 20 September 1995.

[74] Judgment in Case T-282/02 *Cementbouw v Commission*, paragraphs 42, 52, 67 [2006] ECR II-319.

[75] Case COMP/JV.55 *Hutchinson/RCPM/ECT* of 3 July 2001. See also Case IV/M.553 – *RTL/Veronica/Endemol* of 20 September 1995.

78. Such a scenario may not only occur in a situation where two or more minority shareholders jointly control an undertaking on a *de facto* basis, but also where there is high degree of dependency of a majority shareholder on a minority shareholder. This may be the case where the joint venture economically and financially depends on the minority shareholder or where only the minority shareholder has the required know-how for, and will play a major role in, the operation of the joint undertaking whereas the majority shareholder is a mere financial investor.[76] In such circum-stances, the majority shareholder will not be able to enforce its position, but the joint venture partner may be able to block strategic decisions so that both parent undertakings will be required to cooperate permanently. This leads to a situation of *de facto* joint control which prevails over a pure *de jure* assessment according to which the majority shareholder could have been considered to have sole control.

Notes

[76] Case IV/M.967 – *KLM/Air UK* of 22 September 1997; Case COMP/M.4085 – *Arcelor/Oyak/Erdemir* of 13 February 2006.

79. These criteria apply to the formation of a new joint venture as well as to acquisitions of minority shareholdings, together conferring joint control. In case of acquisitions of shareholdings, there is a higher probability of a commonality of interests if the shareholdings are acquired by means of concerted action. However, an acquisition by way of a concerted action is not alone sufficient for the purposes of establishing *de facto* joint control. In general, a common interest as financial investors (or creditors) of a company in a return on investment does not constitute a commonality of interests leading to the exercise of *de facto* joint control.

80. In the absence of strong common interests such as those outlined above, the possibility of changing coalitions between minority shareholders will normally exclude the assumption of joint control. Where there is no stable majority in the decision-making procedure and the majority can on each occasion be any of the various combinations possible amongst the minority shareholders, it cannot be assumed that the minority shareholders (or a certain group thereof) will jointly control the undertaking.[77] In this context, it is not sufficient that there are agreements between two or more parties having an equal shareholding in the capital of an undertaking which establish identical rights and powers between the parties, where these fall short of strategic veto rights. For example, in the case of an undertaking where three shareholders each own one-third of the share capital and each elect one-third of the members of the Board of Directors, the shareholders do not have joint control since decisions are required to be taken on the basis of a simple majority.

Notes

[77] Case IV/JV.12 – *Ericsson/Nokia/Psion/Motorola* of 22 December 1998.

3.4 Other considerations related to joint control

Unequal role of the parent companies

81. Joint control is not incompatible with the fact that one of the parent companies enjoys specific knowledge of and experience in the business of the joint venture. In such a case, the other parent company can play a modest or even non-existent role in the daily management of the joint venture where its presence is motivated by considerations of a financial, long-term-strategy, brand image or general policy nature. Nevertheless, it must always retain the real possibility of contesting the decisions taken by the other parent company on the basis of equality in voting rights or rights of appointment to decision making bodies or of veto rights related to strategic issues. Without this, there would be sole control.

Casting Vote

82. For joint control to exist, there should not be a casting vote for one parent company only as this would lead to sole control of the company enjoying the casting vote. However, there can be joint control when this casting vote is in practice of limited relevance and effectiveness. This may be the case when the casting vote can be exercised only after a series of stages of arbitration and attempts at reconciliation or in a very limited field or if the exercise of the casting vote triggers a put option implying a serious financial burden or if the mutual interdependence of the parent companies would make the exercise of the casting vote unlikely.[78]

Notes

[78] Case COMP/M.2574 – *Pirelli/Edizione/Olivetti/Telecom Italia* of 20 September 2001; Case IV/M.553 – *RTL/ Veronica/Endemol* of 20 September 1995; Case IV/M.425 – *British Telecom/Banco Santander*, of 28 March 1994.

III. CHANGES IN THE QUALITY OF CONTROL

83. The Merger Regulation covers operations resulting in the acquisition of sole or joint control, including operations leading to changes in the quality of control. First, such a change in the quality of control, resulting in a concentration, occurs if there is a change between sole and joint control. Second, a change in the quality of control occurs between joint control scenarios before and after the transaction if there is an increase in the number or a change in the identity of controlling shareholders. However, there is no change in the quality of control if a change from negative to positive sole control occurs. Such a change affects neither the incentives of the negatively controlling shareholder nor the nature of the control structure, as the controlling shareholder did not necessarily have to cooperate with specific shareholders at the time when it enjoyed negative control. In any case, mere changes in the level of shareholdings of the same controlling shareholders, without changes of the powers they hold in a company and of the composition of the control structure of the company, do not constitute a change in the quality of control and therefore are not a notifiable concentration.

84. These changes in the quality of control will be discussed in two categories: first, an entrance of one or more new controlling shareholders irrespective of whether or not they replace existing controlling shareholders and, second, a reduction of the number of controlling shareholders.

1. Entry of controlling shareholders

85. An entry of new controlling shareholders leading to a joint control scenario can either result from a change from sole to joint control, or from the entry of an additional shareholder or a replacement of an existing shareholder in an already jointly controlled undertaking.

86. A move from sole control to joint control is considered a notifiable operation as this changes the quality of control of the joint venture. First, there is a new acquisition of control for the shareholder entering the controlled undertaking. Second, only the new acquisition of control makes the controlled undertaking to a joint venture which changes decisively also the situation for the remaining controlling undertaking under the Merger Regulation: In the future, it has to take into account the interests of one or more other controlling shareholder(s) and it is required to cooperate permanently with the new shareholder(s). Before, it could either determine the strategic behaviour of the controlled undertaking alone (in the case of sole control) or was not forced to take into account the interests of specific other shareholders and was not forced to cooperate with those shareholders permanently.

87. The entry of a new shareholder in a jointly controlled undertaking – either in addition to the already controlling shareholders or in replacement of one of them – also constitutes a notifiable concentration, although the undertaking is jointly controlled before and after the operation.[79] First, also in this scenario there is a shareholder newly acquiring control of the joint venture. Second, the quality of control of the joint venture is determined by the identity of all controlling shareholders. It lies in the nature of joint control that, since each shareholder alone has a blocking right concerning strategic decisions, the jointly controlling shareholders have to take into account each others interests and are required to cooperate for the determination of the strategic behaviour of the joint venture.[80] The nature of joint control therefore does not exhaust itself in a pure mathematical addition of the blocking rights exercised by several shareholders, but is determined by the composition of the jointly controlling shareholders. One of the most obvious scenarios leading to a decisive change in the nature of the control structure of a jointly controlled undertaking is a situation where in a joint venture, jointly controlled by a competitor of the joint venture and a financial investor, the financial investor is replaced by another competitor. In these circumstances, the control structure and the incentives of the joint venture may entirely change, not only because of the entry of the new controlling shareholder, but also due to the change in the behaviour of the remaining shareholder. The replacement of a controlling shareholder or the entry of a new shareholder in a jointly controlled undertaking therefore constitutes a change in the quality of control.[81]

Notes

[79] See, e.g., Case COMP/M.3440 – *ENI/EDP/GdP* of 9 December 2004.

[80] Judgment in Case T-282/02 *Cementbouw v Commission*, paragraph 67 [2006] ECR II-319.

[81] Generally, it should be noted that the Commission will not assess as a separate concentration the indirect replacement of a controlling shareholder in a joint control scenario which takes place via an acquisition of control of one of its parent undertakings. The Commission will assess any changes occurring in the competitive situation of the joint venture in the framework of the overall acquisition of control of its parent undertaking. In those circumstances, the other controlling shareholders in the joint venture will therefore not be undertakings concerned by the concentration which relates to its parent undertaking.

---

88. However, the entry of new shareholders only results in a notifiable concentration if one or several shareholders acquire sole or joint control by virtue of the operation. The entry of new shareholders may lead to a situation where joint control can neither be established on a *de jure* basis nor on a *de facto* basis as the entry of the new shareholder leads to the consequence that changing coalitions between minority shareholders are possible.[82]

Notes

[82] Case IV/JV.12 – *Ericsson/Nokia/Psion/Motorola* of 22 December 1998.

2. Reduction in the number of shareholders

89. A reduction in the number of controlling shareholders constitutes a change in the quality of control and is thus to be considered as a concentration if the exit of one or more controlling shareholders results in a change from joint to sole control. Decisive influence exercised alone is substantially different from decisive influence exercised jointly, since in the latter case the jointly controlling shareholders have to take into account the potentially different interests of the other party or parties involved.[83]

Notes

[83] See Case IV/M023 – *ICI/Tioxide*, of 28 November 1990; see also paragraph 5(d) of the Commission Notice on a simplified procedure for treatment of certain concentrations under Council Regulation (EC) No 139/2004.

90. Where the operation involves a reduction in the number of jointly controlling shareholders, without leading to a change from joint to sole control, the transaction will normally not lead to a notifiable concentration.

IV. Joint Ventures – the Concept of Full-Functionality

91. Article 3(1)(b) provides that a concentration shall be deemed to arise where control is acquired by *one or more* undertakings of the whole or parts of another undertaking. The new acquisition of another undertaking by several jointly controlling undertakings therefore constitutes a concentration under the Merger Regulation. As in the case of the acquisition of sole control of an undertaking, such an acquisition of joint control will lead to a structural change in the market even if, according to the plans of the acquiring undertakings, the acquired undertaking would no longer be considered full-function after the transaction (e.g. because it will sell exclusively to the parent undertakings in future). Thus, a transaction involving several undertakings acquiring joint control of another undertaking or parts of another undertaking, fulfilling the criteria set out in paragraph 24, from third parties will constitute a concentration according to Article 3(1) without it being necessary to consider the full-functionality criterion.[84]

Notes

[84] These considerations do not apply to Article 2(4) in the same way. Whereas the interpretation of Article 3, paragraphs (1) and (4) relates to the applicability of the Merger Regulation to joint ventures, Article 2(4) relates to the substantive analysis of joint ventures. The "creation of a joint venture constituting a concentration pursuant to Article 3", as provided for in Article 2(4), comprises the acquisition of joint control according to Article 3, paragraphs (1) and (4).

92. Article 3(4) provides in addition that the creation of a joint venture performing on a lasting basis all the functions of an autonomous economic entity (so called full-function joint ventures) shall constitute a concentration within the meaning of the Merger Regulation. The full-functionality criterion therefore delineates the application of the Merger Regulation for the creation of joint ventures by the parties, irrespective of whether such a joint venture is created as a "greenfield operation" or whether the parties contribute assets to the joint venture which they previously owned individually. In these circumstances, the joint venture must fulfil the full-functionality criterion in order to constitute a concentration.

93. The fact that a joint venture may be a full-function undertaking and therefore economically autonomous from an operational viewpoint does not mean that it enjoys autonomy as regards the adoption of its strategic decisions. Otherwise, a jointly controlled undertaking could never be considered a full-function joint venture and therefore the condition laid down in Article 3(4) would never be complied with.[85] It is therefore sufficient for the criterion of full-functionality if the joint venture is autonomous in operational respect.

Notes

[85] Judgment in Case T-282/02 *Cementbouw v Commission*, paragraph 62 [2006] ECR II-319.

1. Sufficient resources to operate independently on a market

94. Full function character essentially means that a joint venture must operate on a market, performing the functions normally carried out by undertakings operating on the same market. In order
to do so the joint venture must have a management dedicated to its day-to-day operations and
access to sufficient resources including finance, staff, and assets (tangible and intangible) in order
to conduct on a lasting basis its business activities within the area provided for in the joint-venture
agreement.[86] The personnel do not necessarily need to be employed by the joint venture itself.
If it is standard practice in the industry where the joint venture is operating, it may be sufficient
if third parties envisage the staffing under an operational agreement or if staff is assigned by an
interim employment agency. The secondment of personnel by the parent companies may also be
sufficient if this is done either only for a start-up period or if the joint venture deals with the parent companies in the same way as with third parties. The latter case requires that the joint venture
deals with the parents at arm's length on the basis of normal commercial conditions and that the
joint venture is also free to recruit its own employees or to obtain staff via third parties.

Notes

[86] Case IV/M.527 – *Thomson CSF/Deutsche Aerospace*, of 2 December 1994 -intellectual rights, Case IV/M.560 *EDS/
Lufthansa* of 11 May 1995 – outsourcing, Case IV/M.585 – *Voest Alpine Industrieanlagenbau GmbH/Davy
International Ltd*, of 7 September 1995 – joint venture's right to demand additional expertise and staff from its parent
companies, Case IV/M.686 – *Nokia/Autoliv*, of 5 February 1996, joint venture able to terminate "service agreements" with parent company and to move from site retained by parent company, Case IV/M.791 – *British Gas
Trading Ltd/Group 4 Utility Services Ltd*, of 7 October 1996, joint venture's intended assets will be transferred to leasing company and leased by joint venture.

2. Activities beyond one specific function for the parents

95. A joint venture is not full-function if it only takes over one specific function within the parent
companies' business activities without its own access to or presence on the market. This is the case,
for example, for joint ventures limited to R&D or production. Such joint ventures are auxiliary to
their parent companies' business activities. This is also the case where a joint venture is essentially
limited to the distribution or sales of its parent companies' products and, therefore, acts principally as a sales agency. However, the fact that a joint venture makes use of the distribution network
or outlet of one or more of its parent companies normally will not disqualify it as "full-function"
as long as the parent companies are acting only as agents of the joint venture.[87]

Notes

[87] Case IV/M.102 – *TNT/Canada Post etc.* of 2 December 1991.

96. A frequent example where this question arises are joint ventures involved in the holding of
real estate property, which are typically set up for tax and other financial reasons. As long as
the purpose of the joint venture is limited to the acquisition and/or holding of certain real estate
for the parents and based on financial resources provided by the parents, it will not usually be
considered to be full-function, as it lacks an autonomous, long term business activity on the
market and will typically also lack the necessary resources to operate independently. This has
to be distinguished from joint ventures that are actively managing a real estate portfolio and who
act on their own behalf on the market, which typically indicates full-functionality.[88]

Notes

[88] See Case IV/M.929 – *DIA/Veba Immobilien/Deutschbau* of 23 June 1997; Case COMP/M.3325 – *Morgan Stanley/
Glick/Canary Wharf* of 23 January 2004.

3. Sale/purchase relations with the parents

97. The strong presence of the parent companies in upstream or downstream markets is a factor to
be taken into consideration in assessing the full-function character of a joint venture where this
presence results in substantial sales or purchases between the parent companies and the joint
venture. The fact that, for an initial start-up period only, the joint venture relies almost entirely

on sales to or purchases from its parent companies does not normally affect its full-function character. Such a start-up period may be necessary in order to establish the joint venture on a market. But the period will normally not exceed a period of three years, depending on the specific conditions of the market in question.[89]

Notes
[89] Case IV/M.560 – *EDS/Lufthansa* of 11 May 1995; Case IV/M.686 *Nokia/Autoliv* of 5 February 1996; to be contrasted with Case IV/M.904 – *RSB/Tenex/Fuel Logistics* of 2 April 1997 and Case IV/M.979 – *Preussag/Voest-Alpine* of 1 October 1997. A special case exists where sales by the joint venture to its parent are caused by a legal monopoly downstream of the joint venture, see Case IV/M.468 – *Siemens/Italtel* of 17 February 1995, or where the sales to a parent company consist of by-products, which are of minor importance to the joint venture, see Case IV/M.550 – *Union Carbide/Enichem* of 13 March 1995.

Sales to the parents

98. Where sales from the joint venture to the parent companies are intended to be made on a lasting basis, the essential question is whether, regardless of these sales, the joint venture is geared to play an active role on the market and can be considered economically autonomous from an operational viewpoint. In this respect the relative proportion of sales made to its parents compared with the total production of the joint venture is an important factor. Due to the particularities of each individual case, it is impossible to define a specific turnover ratio which distinguishes full-function from other joint ventures. If the joint venture achieves more than 50% of its turnover with third parties, this will typically be an indication of full-functionality. Below this indicative threshold, a case-by-case analysis is required, whereby, for the finding of operational autonomy, the relationship between the joint venture and its parents must be truly commercial in character. For this purpose, it is to be demonstrated that the joint venture will supply its goods or services to the purchaser who values them most and will pay most and that the joint venture will also deal with its parents' companies at arm's length on the basis of normal commercial conditions.[90] Under these circumstances, i.e. if the joint venture will treat its parent companies in the same commercial way as third parties, it may be sufficient that at least 20% of the joint venture's predicted sales will go to third parties. However, the greater the proportion of sales likely to be made to the parents, the greater will be the need for clear evidence of the commercial character of the relationship.

Notes
[90] Case IV/M.556 – *Zeneca/Vanderhave* of 9 April 1996; Case IV/M.751 – *Bayer/Hüls* of 3 July 1996.

99. For the determination of the proportion between sales to the parents and to third parties, the Commission will take past accounts and substantiated business plans into account. However, especially where substantial third–party sales cannot be readily foreseen, the Commission will base its finding also on the general market structure. This may be a relevant factor as well for the assessment whether the joint venture will deal with its parents on an arm's length basis.

100. These issues frequently arise with regard to outsourcing agreements, where an undertaking creates a joint venture with a service provider[91] which will carry out functions that were previously dealt with by the undertaking in-house. The JV typically cannot be considered to be full-function in these scenarios: it provides its services exclusively to the client undertaking, and it is dependent for its services on input from the service provider. The fact that the joint venture's business plan often at least does not exclude that the joint venture can provide its services to third parties does not alter this assessment, as in the typical outsourcing setup any third party revenues are likely to remain ancillary to the joint venture's main activities for the client undertaking. However, this general rule does not exclude that there are outsourcing situations where the joint venture partners, for example for reasons of economies of scale, set up a joint venture with the perspective of significant market access. This could qualify the joint venture as full function if significant third-party sales are foreseen and if the relationship between the joint venture and its parent will be truly commercial in character and if the joint venture deals with its parents on the basis of normal commercial conditions.

Notes

The question under which circumstances an outsourcing arrangement qualifies as a concentration is dealt with in paragraphs 25ff. of this Notice.

Purchases from the parents

101. In relation to purchases made by the joint venture from its parent companies, the full-function character of the joint venture is questionable in particular where little value is added to the products or services concerned at the level of the joint venture itself. In such a situation, the joint venture may be closer to a joint sales agency.

Trade markets

102. However, in contrast to this situation where a joint venture is active in a trade market and performs the normal functions of a trading company in such a market, it normally will not be an auxiliary sales agency but a full-function joint venture. A trade market is characterised by the existence of companies which specialise in the selling and distribution of products without being vertically integrated in addition to those which are integrated, and where different sources of supply are available for the products in question. In addition, many trade markets may require operators to invest in specific facilities such as outlets, stockholding, warehouses, depots, transport fleets and sales and service personnel. In order to constitute a full-function joint venture in a trade market, an undertaking must have the necessary facilities and be likely to obtain a substantial proportion of its supplies not only from its parent companies but also from other competing sources.[92]

Notes

92 Case IV/M.788 – *AgrEVO/Marubeni* of 3 September 1996.

4. Operation on a lasting basis

103. Furthermore, the joint venture must be intended to operate on a lasting basis. The fact that the parent companies commit to the joint venture the resources described above normally demonstrates that this is the case. In addition, agreements setting up a joint venture often provide for certain contingencies, for example, the failure of the joint venture or fundamental disagreement as between the parent companies.[93] This may be achieved by the incorporation of provisions for the eventual dissolution of the joint venture itself or the possibility for one or more parent companies to withdraw from the joint venture. This kind of provision does not prevent the joint venture from being considered as operating on a lasting basis. The same is normally true where the agreement specifies a period for the duration of the joint venture where this period is sufficiently long in order to bring about a lasting change in the structure of the undertakings concerned,[94] or where the agreement provides for the possible continuation of the joint venture beyond this period.

Notes

93 Case IV/M.891 – *Deutsche Bank/Commerzbank/JM Voith* of 23 April 1997.

94 See Case COMP/M.2903 – *DaimlerChrysler/Deutsche Telekom/JV* of 30 April 2003 where a period of 12 years was considered sufficient; Case COMP/M.2632 – *Deutsche Bahn/ECT International/United Depots/JV* of 11 February 2002 with a contract duration of 8 years. In Case COMP/M.3858 *Lehman Brothers/Starwood/Le Meridien* of 20 July 2005, the Commission considered a minimum period of 10–15 years sufficient, but not a period of three years.

104. By contrast, the joint venture will not be considered to operate on a lasting basis where it is established for a short finite duration. This would be the case, for example, where a joint venture is established in order to construct a specific project such as a power plant, but it will not be involved in the operation of the plant once its construction has been completed.

105. A joint venture also lacks the sufficient operations on a lasting basis at a stage where there are decisions of third parties outstanding that are of an essential core importance for starting the joint venture's business activity. Only decisions that go beyond mere formalities and the award of which is typically uncertain qualify for these scenarios. Examples are the award of a contract (e.g., in public tenders), licences (e.g., in the telecoms sector) or access rights to property (e.g., exploration rights for oil and gas). Pending the decision on such factors, it is unclear whether

the joint venture will become operational at all. Thus, at that stage the joint venture cannot be considered to perform economic functions on a lasting basis and consequently does not qualify as full function. However, once a decision has been taken in favour of the joint venture in question, this criterion is fulfilled and a concentration arises.[95]

Notes

[95] Subject to the other criteria mentioned in this chapter of the Notice.

5. Changes in the activities of the joint venture

106. The parents may decide to enlarge the scope of the activities of the joint venture in the course of its lifetime. This will be considered as a new concentration that may trigger a notification requirement if this enlargement entails the acquisition of the whole or part of another undertaking from the parents that would, considered in isolation, qualify as a concentration as explained in paragraph 24 of this Notice.[96]

Notes

[96] See Case COMP/M.3039 – *Soprol/Céréol/Lesieur* of 30 January 2003.

107. A concentration may also arise if the parent companies transfer significant additional assets, contracts, know-how or other rights to the joint venture and these assets and rights constitute the basis or nucleus of an extension of the activities of the joint venture into other product or geographic markets which were not the object of the original joint venture, and if the joint venture performs such activities on a full-function basis. As the transfer of the assets or rights shows that the parents are the real players behind the extension of the joint venture's scope, the enlargement of the activities of the joint venture can be considered in the same way as the creation of a new joint venture within the meaning of Article 3(4).[97]

Notes

[97] The triggering event for the notification in such a case will be the agreement or other legal act underlying the transfer of the assets, contracts, know-how or other rights.

108. If the scope of a joint venture is enlarged without additional assets, contracts, know-how or rights being transferred, no concentration will be deemed to arise.
109. A concentration arises if a change in the activity of an existing non-full-function joint venture occurs so that a full-function joint venture within the meaning of Article 3(4) is created. The following examples may be given: a change of the organisational structure of a joint venture so that it fulfils the full functionality criterion;[98] a joint venture that used to supply only the parent companies, which subsequently starts a significant activity on the market; or scenarios, as described in paragraph 105 above, where a joint venture can only start its activity on the market once it has essential input (such as a licence for a joint venture in the telecoms sector). Such a change in the activity of the joint venture will frequently require a decision by its shareholders or its management. Once the decision is taken that leads to the joint venture meeting the full functionality criterion, a concentration arises.

Notes

[98] Case COMP/M.2276 – *The Coca-Cola Company/Nestlé/JV* of 27 September 2001.

V. Exceptions

110. Article 3(5) sets out three exceptional situations where the acquisition of a controlling interest does not constitute a concentration under the Merger Regulation.
111. First, the acquisition of securities by companies whose normal activities include transactions and dealing in securities for their own account or for the account of others is not deemed to constitute a concentration if such an acquisition is made in the framework of these businesses and if the securities are held on only a temporary basis (Article 3(5)(a)). In order to fall within this exception, the following requirements must be fulfilled:

— the acquiring undertaking must be a credit or other financial institution or insurance company the normal activities of which are described above;
— the securities must be acquired with a view to their resale;
— the acquiring undertaking must not exercise the voting rights with a view to determining the strategic commercial behaviour of the target company or must exercise these rights only with a view to preparing the total or partial disposal of the undertaking, its assets or the securities;
— the acquiring undertaking must dispose of its controlling interest within one year of the date of the acquisition, that is, it must reduce its shareholding within this one-year period at least to a level which no longer confers control. This period, however, may be extended by the Commission where the acquiring undertaking can show that the disposal was not reasonably possible within the one-year period.

112. Second, there is no change of control, and hence no concentration within the meaning of the Merger Regulation, where control is acquired by an office-holder according to the law of a Member State relating to liquidation, winding-up, insolvency, cessation of payments, compositions or analogous proceedings (Article 3(5)(b));

113. Third, a concentration does not arise where a financial holding company within the meaning of Article 5(3) of the Council Directive 78/660/EEC[99] acquires control. The notion of "financial holding company" is thus limited to companies whose sole purpose it is to acquire holdings in other undertakings without involving themselves directly or indirectly in the management of those undertakings, the foregoing without prejudice to their rights as shareholders. Such investment companies must be further structured in a way that compliance with these limitations can be supervised by an administrative or judicial authority. The Merger Regulation provides for an additional condition for this exception to apply: such companies may exercise the voting rights in the other undertakings only to maintain the full value of those investments and not to determine directly or indirectly the strategic commercial conduct of the controlled undertaking.

Notes

[99] Fourth Council Directive 78/660/EEC of 25 July 1978 based on Article 54(3)(g) of the Treaty on the annual accounts of certain types of companies, OJ L 222, 14.8.1978, p. 11, as last amended by Directive 2003/51/EC of 18 June 2003, OJ L 178, 17.7.2003, p.16. Article 5(3) of this Directive defines financial holding companies as "those companies the sole objective of which is to acquire holdings in other undertakings, and to manage such holdings and turn them to profit, without involving themselves directly or indirectly in the management of those undertakings, the foregoing without prejudice to their rights as shareholders. The limitations imposed on the activities of these companies must be such that compliance with them can be supervised by an administrative or judicial authority".

114. The exceptions under Article 3(5) of the Merger Regulation only apply to a very limited field. First, these exceptions only apply if the operation would otherwise be a concentration in its own right, but not if the transaction is part of a broader, single concentration, in circumstances in which the ultimate acquirer of control would not fall within the terms of Article 3(5) (see e.g. paragraph 35 above). Second, the exceptions under Article 3(5)(a) and (c) only apply to acquisitions of control by way of purchase of securities, not to acquisitions of assets.

115. The exceptions do not apply to typical investment fund structures. According to their objectives, these funds usually do not limit themselves in the exercise of the voting rights, but adopt decisions to appoint the members of the management and the supervisory bodies of the undertakings or to even restructure those undertakings. This would not be compatible with the requirement under both Article 3(5)(a) and (c) that the acquiring companies do not exercise the voting rights with a view to determine the competitive conduct of the other undertaking.[100]

Notes

[100] Case IV/M.669 – *Charterhouse/Porterbrook*, of 11 December 1995.

116. The question may arise whether an operation to rescue an undertaking before or from insolvency proceedings constitutes a concentration under the Merger Regulation. Such a rescue operation typically involves the conversion of existing debt into a new company, through which a syndicate of banks may acquire joint control of the company concerned. Where such an operation meets the criteria for joint control, as outlined above, it will normally be considered to be a

concentration.[101] Although the primary intention of the banks is to restructure the financing of the undertaking concerned for its subsequent resale, the exception set out in Article 3(5)(a) is normally not applicable to such an operation. In a similar way as set out for investment funds, the restructuring programme normally requires the controlling banks to determine the strategic commercial behaviour of the rescued undertaking. Furthermore, it is not normally a realistic proposition to transform a rescued company into a commercially viable entity and to resell it within the permitted one-year period. Moreover, the length of time needed to achieve this aim may be so uncertain that it would be difficult to grant an extension of the disposal period.

Notes
[101] Case IV/M.116 – *Kelt/American Express*, of 28 August 1991.

VI. Abandonment of Concentrations

117. A concentration ceases to exist and the Merger Regulation ceases to be applicable if the undertakings concerned abandon the concentration.

118. In this respect, the revised Merger Regulation 139/2004 introduced a new provision related to the closure of procedures concerning the control of concentrations without a final decision after the Commission has initiated proceedings under Article 6(1)(c) 1st sentence. That sentence reads as follows: "Without prejudice to Article 9, such proceedings shall be closed by means of a decision as provided for in Article 8(1) to (4), unless the undertakings concerned have demonstrated to the satisfaction of the Commission that they have abandoned the concentration". Prior to the initiation of proceedings, such requirements do not apply.

119. As a general principle, the requirements for the proof of the abandonment must correspond in terms of legal form, intensity etc. to the initial act that was considered sufficient to make the concentration notifiable. In case the parties proceed from that initial act to a strengthening of their contractual links during the procedure, for example by concluding a binding agreement after the transaction was notified on the basis of a good faith intention, the requirements for the proof of the abandonment must correspond also to the nature of the latest act.

120. In line with this principle, in case of implementation of the concentration prior to a Commission decision, the re-establishment of the *status quo ante* has to be shown. The mere withdrawal of the notification is not considered as sufficient proof that the concentration has been abandoned in the sense of Article 6(1)(c). Likewise, minor modifications of a concentration which do not affect the change in control or the quality of that change, cannot be considered as an abandonment of the original concentration.[102]
    - Binding agreement: proof of the legally binding cancellation of the agreement in the form envisaged by the initial agreement (i.e. usually a document signed by all the parties) will be required. Expressions of intention to cancel the agreement or not to implement the notified concentration, as well as unilateral declarations by (one of) the parties will not be considered sufficient.[103]
    - Good faith intention to conclude an agreement: In case of a letter of intent or memorandum of understanding reflecting such good faith intention, documents proving that this basis for the good faith intention has been cancelled will be required. As for possible other forms that indicated the good faith intention, the abandonment must reverse this good faith intention and correspond in terms of form and intensity to the initial expression of intent.
    - Public announcement of a public bid or of the intention to make a public bid: a public announcement terminating the bidding procedure or renouncing to the intention to make a public bid will be required. The format and public reach of this announcement must be comparable to the initial announcement.
    - Implemented concentrations: In case the concentration has been implemented prior to a Commission decision, the parties will be required to show that the situation prevailing before the implementation of the concentration has been re-established.

Notes
[102] This paragraph does not prejudge the assessment whether the modification requires submitting additional information to the Commission under Art. 5(3) Reg. 802/2004.

121. It is for the parties to submit the necessary documentation to meet these requirements in due time.

VII. Changes of Transactions after a Commission Authorisation Decision

122. In some cases, parties may wish not to implement the concentration in the form foreseen after authorisation of the concentration by the Commission. The question arises whether the Commission's authorisation decision still covers the changed structure of the transaction.

123. Broadly speaking, if, before implementation of the authorised concentration, the transactional structure is changed from an acquisition of control, falling under Article 3(1)(b), to a merger according to Article 3(1)(a), or *vice versa*, then the change in the transactional structure is considered a different concentration under the Merger Regulation and a new notification is required.[104] However, less significant modifications of the transaction, for example minor changes in the shareholding percentages which do not affect the change in control or the quality of that change, changes in the offer price in the case of public bids or changes in the corporate structure by which the transaction is implemented without effects on the relevant control situation under the Merger Regulation, are considered as being covered by the Commission's authorisation decision.

Notes

C. Community Dimension

I. Thresholds

124. A two fold test defines the operations to which the Merger Regulation applies. The first test is that the operation must be a concentration within the meaning of Article 3. The second comprises the turnover thresholds contained in Article 1, designed to identify those operations which have an impact upon the Community and can be deemed to be of "Community dimension". Turnover is used as a proxy for the economic resources being combined in a concentration, and is allocated geographically in order to reflect the geographic distribution of those resources.

125. Two sets of thresholds are set out in Article 1 to establish whether the operation has a Community dimension. Article 1(2) establishes three different criteria: The worldwide turnover threshold is intended to measure the overall dimension of the undertakings concerned; the Community turnover threshold seek to determine whether the concentration involves a minimum level of activities in the Community; and the two-thirds rule aims to exclude purely domestic transactions from Community jurisdiction.

126. This second set of thresholds, contained in Article 1(3), is designed to tackle those concentrations which fall short of achieving Community dimension under Article 1(2), but would have a substantial impact in at least three Member States leading to multiple notifications under national competition rules of those Member States. For this purpose, Article 1(3) provides for lower turnover thresholds, both worldwide and Community-wide, and for a minimum level of activities of the undertakings concerned, jointly and individually, in at least three Member States. Similarly to Article 1(2), Article 1(3) also contains a two-thirds rule excluding predominantly domestic concentrations.[105]

Notes
105 A concentration is further deemed to have a Community dimension if it is referred to the Commission under Article 4(5) of the Merger Regulation. These cases are dealt with in the Commission Notice on Case Referral in respect of concentrations, OJ C 56, 05.03.2005, p. 2.

127. The thresholds as such are designed to govern jurisdiction and not to assess the market position of the parties to the concentration nor the impact of the operation. In so doing they include turnover derived from, and thus the resources devoted to, all areas of activity of the parties, and not just those directly involved in the concentration. The thresholds are purely quantitative, since they are only based on turnover calculation instead of market share or other criteria. They pursue the objective to provide a simple and objective mechanism that can be easily handled by the companies involved in a merger in order to determine if their transaction has a Community dimension and is therefore notifiable.

128. Whereas Article 1 sets out the numerical thresholds to establish jurisdiction, the purpose of Article 5 is to explain how turnover should be calculated to ensure that the resulting figures are a true representation of economic reality.

II. Notion of Undertaking Concerned

1. General

129. From the point of view of determining jurisdiction, the undertakings concerned are those participating in a concentration, i.e. a merger or an acquisition of control as foreseen in Article 3(1). The individual and aggregate turnover of those undertakings will be decisive in determining whether the thresholds are met.

130. Once the undertakings concerned have been identified in a given transaction, their turnover for the purposes of determining jurisdiction is to be calculated according to the rules set out in Article 5. Article 5(4) sets out detailed criteria to identify undertakings whose turnover may be attributed to the undertaking concerned because of certain direct or indirect links with the latter. The legislator's intention was to lay down concrete rules which, seen together, can be taken to establish the notion of a "group" for the purposes of the turnover thresholds in the Merger Regulation. The term "group" will be used in the following sections exclusively to refer to the collection of undertakings whose relations with an undertaking concerned come within the terms of one or more of the sub-paragraphs of Article 5(4) of the Merger Regulation.

131. It is important, when referring to the various undertakings which may be involved in a procedure, not to confuse the concept of "undertakings concerned" under Articles 1 and 5 with the terminology used elsewhere in the Merger Regulation and in Commission Regulation (EC) No 802/2004 of 7 April 2004 implementing Council Regulation (EC) No 139/2004 on the control of concentrations between undertakings (hereinafter referred to as the "Implementing Regulation")[106] referring to the various undertakings which may be involved in a procedure. This terminology refers to the notifying parties, other involved parties, third parties and parties who may be subject to fines or periodic penalty payments, and they are defined in Chapter IV of the Implementing Regulation, along with their respective rights and duties.

Notes
106 OJ L 133, 30 April 2004, p. 1.

2. Mergers

132. In a merger the undertakings concerned are each of the merging entities.

3. Acquisition of control

133. In the remaining cases, it is the concept of "acquiring control" that will determine which are the undertakings concerned. On the acquiring side, there can be one or more undertakings acquiring sole or joint control. On the acquired side, there can be one or more undertakings as a whole or parts thereof. As a general rule, each of these undertakings will be an undertaking concerned within the meaning of the Merger Regulation.

Acquisition of sole control

134. Acquisition of sole control of the whole undertaking is the most straightforward case of acquisition of control. The undertakings concerned will be the acquiring undertaking and the target undertaking.

135. Where the target undertaking is acquired by a group through one of its subsidiaries, the undertakings concerned are the target undertaking and the acquiring subsidiary if this is not a mere acquisition vehicle. However, even though the subsidiary is normally the undertaking concerned for the purpose of calculating turnover, the turnover of all undertakings with which the undertaking concerned has the links as specified in Article 5(4) shall be included in the threshold calculations. In this respect, the group is considered to be a single economic unit and the different companies belonging to the same group cannot be considered as different undertakings concerned for jurisdictional purposes under the Merger Regulation. The actual notification can be made by the subsidiary concerned or by its parent company.

Acquisition of parts of an undertaking and staggered operations – Article 5(2)

136. The first subparagraph of Article 5(2) of the Merger Regulation provides that when the operation concerns the acquisition of parts of one or more undertakings, only those parts which are the subject of the transaction shall be taken into account with regard to the seller. The possible impact of the transaction on the market will depend only on the combination of the economic and financial resources that are the subject of the transaction with those of the acquirer and not on the remaining business of the seller. In this case, the undertakings concerned will be the acquirer(s) and the acquired part(s) of the target undertaking, but the remaining businesses of the seller will be ignored.

137. The second subparagraph of Article 5(2) includes a special provision on staggered operations or follow-up deals. The previous concentrations (within two years) involving the same parties become (re)notifiable with the most recent transaction, provided this constitutes a concentration, if the thresholds are met whether for one or more of the transactions taken in isolation or cumulatively. In this case, the undertakings concerned are the acquirer(s) and the different acquired part(s) of the target company taken as a whole.

Change from joint to sole control

138. If the acquisition of control occurs by way of a change from joint control to sole control, one shareholder normally acquires the stake previously held by the other shareholder(s). In this situation, the undertakings concerned are the acquiring shareholder and the joint venture. As is the case for any other seller, the "exiting" shareholder is not an undertaking concerned.[107]

Notes
[107] Case IV/M.023 – *ICI/Tioxide*, of 28 November 1990.

Acquisition of joint control

139. In the case of acquisition of joint control of a newly-created undertaking, the undertakings concerned are each of the companies acquiring control of the newly setup joint venture (which, as it does not yet exist, cannot be considered to be an undertaking concerned and moreover, as yet, has no turnover of its own). The same rule applies where one undertaking contributes a pre-existing subsidiary or a business (over which it previously exercised sole control) to a newly created joint venture. In these circumstances, each of the jointly-controlling undertakings is considered an undertaking concerned whereas any company or business contributed to the joint venture is not an undertaking concerned, and its turnover is part of the turnover of the initial parent company.

140. The situation is different if undertakings newly acquire joint control of a pre-existing undertaking or business. The undertakings concerned are each of the undertakings acquiring joint control on the one hand, and the pre-existing acquired undertaking or business on the other.

141. The acquisition of a company with a view to immediately split up the assets is, as explained above in paragraph 32, mostly not considered as an acquisition of joint control of the entire target company, but as the acquisition of sole control by each of the ultimate acquirers of the

respective parts of the target company. In line with the considerations for the acquisition of sole control, undertakings concerned are the acquiring undertakings and the acquired parts in each of the transactions.

Changes of controlling shareholders in cases of joint control of an existing joint venture

142. A notifiable concentration may arise, as explained above, where a change in the quality of control occurs in a joint control structure due to the entrance of new controlling shareholders, irrespective of whether or not they replace existing controlling shareholders.

143. In the case where one or more shareholders acquire control, either by entry or by substitution of one or more shareholders, in a situation of joint control both before and after the operation, the undertakings concerned are the shareholders (both existing and new) who exercise joint control and the joint venture itself.[108] On the one hand, similar to the acquisition of joint control of an existing company, the joint venture itself can be considered as an undertaking concerned as it is an already pre-existing undertaking. On the other hand, as set out above, the entry of a new shareholder is not only in itself a new acquisition of control, but also leads to a change in the quality of control for the remaining controlling shareholders as the quality of control of the joint venture is determined by the identity and composition of the controlling shareholders and therefore also by the relationship between them. Furthermore, the Merger Regulation considers a joint venture as a combination of the economic resources of the parent companies, together with the joint venture if it already generates turnover on the market. For these reasons, the newly entering controlling shareholders are undertakings concerned alongside with the remaining controlling shareholders. Due to the change of the quality in control, all of them are considered to undertake an acquisition of control.

Notes
[108] See Case IV/M.376 – *Synthomer/Yule Catto*, of 22 October 1993.

144. As Article 4(2) first sentence of the Merger Regulation foresees that all acquisitions of joint control shall be notified jointly by the undertakings acquiring joint control, existing and new shareholders in principle have to notify concentrations arising from such changes in joint control scenarios jointly.

Acquisition of control by a joint venture

145. In transactions where a joint venture acquires control of another company, the question arises whether or not the joint venture should be regarded as the undertaking concerned (the turnover of which would include the turnover of its parent companies), or whether each of its parent companies should individually be regarded as undertakings concerned. This question may be decisive for jurisdictional purposes.[109] Whereas, in principle, the undertaking concerned is the joint venture as the direct participant in the acquisition of control, there may be circumstances where companies set up "shell" companies and the parent companies will individually be considered as undertakings concerned. In this type of situation, the Commission will look at the economic reality of the operation to determine which are the undertakings concerned.

Notes
[109] Assume the following scenario: The target company has an aggregate Community turnover of less than EUR 250 million, and the acquiring parties are two (or more) undertakings, each with a Community turnover exceeding EUR 250 million. If the target is acquired by a "shell" company set up between the acquiring undertakings, there would only be one undertaking (the "shell" company) with a Community turnover exceeding EUR 250 million, and thus one of the cumulative threshold conditions for Community jurisdiction, namely, the existence of at least two undertakings with a Community turnover exceeding EUR 250 million, would not be fulfilled. Conversely, if instead of acting through a "shell" company, the acquiring undertakings acquire the target undertaking themselves, then the turnover threshold would be met and the Merger Regulation would apply to this transaction. The same considerations apply to the national turnover thresholds referred to in Article 1(3).

146. Where the acquisition is carried out by a full-function joint venture, with the features set out above, and already operates on the same market, the Commission will normally consider the joint venture itself and the target undertaking to be the undertakings concerned (and not the joint venture's parent companies).

147. Conversely, where the joint venture can be regarded as a mere vehicle for an acquisition by the parent companies, the Commission will consider each of the parent companies themselves to be the undertakings concerned, rather than the joint venture, together with the target company. This is the case in particular where the joint venture is set up especially for the purpose of acquiring the target company or has not yet started to operate, where an existing joint venture has no full-function character as referred to above or where the joint venture is an association of undertakings. The same applies where there are elements which demonstrate that the parent companies are in fact the real players behind the operation. These elements may include a significant involvement by the parent companies themselves in the initiation, organisation and financing of the operation. In those cases, the parent companies are regarded as undertakings concerned.

Break-up of joint ventures and exchange of assets

148. When two (or more) undertakings break up a joint venture and split the assets (constituting businesses) between them, this will normally be considered as more than one acquisition of control, as explained above in paragraph 41. For example, undertakings A and B form a joint venture and subsequently split it up, in particular with a new asset configuration. The break-up of the joint venture involves a change from joint control over the joint venture's entire assets to sole control over the divided assets by each of the acquiring undertakings.[110]

Notes
[110] See parallel cases COMP/M.3293 – *Shell/BEB* and COMP/M.3294 – *ExxonMobil/BEB* of 20 November 2003; Case IV/M.197 – *Solvay/Laporte* of 30 April 1992.

---

149. For each break-up operation, and in line with the consideration to the acquisition of sole control, the undertakings concerned will be, on the one hand, the acquiring party and, on the other, the assets that this undertaking will acquire.

150. Similar to the break-up scenario is the situation where two (or more) companies exchange assets constituting a business on each side. In this case, each acquisition of control is considered an independent acquisition of sole control. The undertakings concerned will be, for each transaction, the acquiring companies and the acquired undertaking or assets.

Acquisitions of control by natural persons

151. Control may also be acquired by natural persons, within the meaning of Article 3 of the Merger Regulation, if those persons themselves carry out further economic activities (and are therefore classified as economic undertakings in their own right) or if they control one or more other economic undertakings. In such a situation, the undertakings concerned are the target undertaking and the individual acquirer (with the turnover of the undertaking(s) controlled by that natural person being included in the calculation of the natural person's turnover to the extent that the terms of Article 5(4) are satisfied).[111]

Notes
[111] See Case IV/M.082 – *Asko/Jacobs/Adia*, of 16 May 1991 where a private individual with other economic activities acquired joint control of an undertaking and was considered an undertaking concerned.

---

152. An acquisition of control of an undertaking by its managers is also an acquisition by natural persons, and paragraph 151 above is also relevant. However, the managers may pool their interests through a "vehicle company", so that it acts with a single voice and also to facilitate decision-making. Such a vehicle company may be, but is not necessarily, an undertaking concerned. The general guidance given above in paragraphs 145–147 on acquisitions of control by a joint venture also applies here.

Acquisition of control by a State-owned undertaking

153. As described above, a merger or an acquisition of control arising between two undertakings owned by the same State (or the same public body) may constitute a concentration if the undertakings were formerly part of different economic units having an independent power of decision. If this is the case, both of them will qualify as undertakings concerned although both are owned by the same State.[112]

Notes

112 See recital 22 of the Merger Regulation, directly related to the calculation of turnover of a state-owned undertaking concerned in the context of Article 5(4).

III. Relevant Date for Establishing Jurisdiction

154. The legal situation for establishing the Commission's jurisdiction has been changed under the recast Merger Regulation. Under the former Merger Regulation, the relevant date was the triggering event for a notification according to Article 4(1) of this Regulation – the conclusion of a final agreement or the announcement of a public bid or the acquisition of a controlling interest – or, at the latest, the time when the parties were obliged to notify (i.e. one week after a triggering event for a notification).[113]

Notes

113 See Case COMP/M.1741 – *MCI Worldcom/Sprint* of 28 June 2000.

155. Under the recast Merger Regulation, there is no longer an obligation for the parties to notify within a certain time-frame (provided the parties do not implement the planned concentration before notification). Moreover, according to Article 4(1) second subparagraph, the undertakings concerned can already notify the transaction on the basis of a good faith intention to conclude an agreement or, in the case of a public bid, where they have publicly announced an intention to make such a bid. At the time of the notification at the latest, the Commission – as well as national competition authorities – must be able to determine their jurisdiction. Article 4(1) subparagraph 1 of the Merger Regulation provides, generally, that concentrations shall be notified following the conclusion of the agreement, the announcement of the public bid, or the acquisition of a controlling interest. The dates of these events are therefore still decisive under the recast Merger Regulation in order to determine the relevant date for establishing jurisdiction, if a notification does not occur before such events on the basis of a good faith intention or an announced intention.[114]

Notes

114 The alternative possibility that turnover should be defined on the latest date when the relevant parties are obliged to notify (seven days after the "triggering event" under the former Merger Regulation) cannot be retained under the recast merger Regulation, because there is no deadline for notification.

156. The relevant date for establishing Community jurisdiction over a concentration is therefore the date of the conclusion of the binding legal agreement, the announcement of a public bid or the acquisition of a controlling interest or the date of the first notification, whichever date is earlier.[115] Regarding the date of notification, a notification to either the Commission or to a Member State authority is relevant. The relevant date needs in particular to be considered for the question whether acquisitions or divestitures which occur after the period covered by the relevant account, but before the relevant date, require adaptations to those accounts according to the principles set out in paragraphs 172, 173.

Notes

115 See also opinion of AG Kokott in Case C-202/06 *Cementbouw v Commission* of 26 April 2007, paragraph 46 (not yet reported). Only the recast merger Regulation has provided for the possibility to take into account the first notification if this is earlier than the date of the conclusion of the binding legal agreement, the announcement of a public bid or the acquisition of a controlling interest, see footnote 35 of the opinion.

IV. Turnover

1. The concept of turnover

157. The concept of turnover as used in Article 5 of the Merger Regulation comprises "the amounts derived [...] from the sale of products and the provision of services". Those amounts generally appear in company accounts under the heading "sales". In the case of products, turnover can be

Part D Mergers and Concentrations

determined without difficulty, namely by identifying each commercial act involving a transfer of ownership.

158. In the case of services, the method of calculating turnover in general does not differ from that used in the case of products: the Commission takes into consideration the total amount of sales. However, the calculation of the amounts derived from the provision of services may be more complex as this depends on the exact service provided and the underlying legal and economic arrangements in the sector in question. Where one undertaking provides the entire service directly to the customer, the turnover of the undertaking concerned consists of the total amount of sales for the provision of services in the last financial year.

159. In other areas, this general principle may have to be adapted to the specific conditions of the service provided. In certain sectors of activity (such as package holidays and advertising), the service may be sold through intermediaries.[116] Even if the intermediary invoices the entire amount to the final customer, the turnover of the undertaking acting as an intermediary consists solely of the amount of its commission. For package holidays, the entire amount paid by the final customer is then allocated to the tour operator which uses the travel agency as distribution network. In the case of advertising, only the amounts received (without the commission) are considered to constitute the turnover of the TV channel or the magazine since media agencies, as intermediaries, do not constitute the distribution channel for the sellers of advertising space, but are chosen by the customers, i.e. those undertakings wishing to place advertising.

Notes

[116] An undertaking will normally not act as an intermediary if it sells products via a commercial act which involves a transfer of ownership, Judgment in Case T-417/05, *Endesa v Commission*, paragraph 213, [2006] ECR II-2533.

160. The examples mentioned show that, due to the diversity of services, many different situations may arise and the underlying legal and economic relations have to be carefully analysed. Similarly, specific situations for the calculation of turnover may arise in the areas of credit, financial services and insurance. These issues will be dealt with in Section VI.

2. Ordinary activities

161. Article 5(1) provides that the amounts to be included in the calculation of turnover should correspond to the "ordinary activities" of the undertakings concerned. This is the turnover achieved from the sale of products or the provision of services in the normal course of its business. It generally excludes those items which are listed under the headers "financial income" or "extraordinary income" in the company's accounts. Such extraordinary income may be derived from the sale of businesses or of fixed assets. However, company accounts do not necessarily delineate the revenues derived from ordinary activities in the way required for the purposes of turnover calculation under the Merger Regulation. In some cases, the qualification of the items in the accounts may have to be adapted to the requirements of the Merger Regulation.[117]

Notes

[117] In Case IV/M.126 – *Accor/Wagons-Lits*, of 28 April 1992, the Commission decided to consider certain income from car-hire activities as revenues from ordinary activities although they were included as "other operating proceeds" in Wagons-Lits' profit and loss account.

162. The revenues do not necessarily have to be derived from the customer of the products or services. With regard to aid granted to undertakings by public bodies, any aid has to be included in the calculation of turnover if the undertaking is itself the recipient of the aid and if the aid is directly linked to the sale of products and the provision of services by the undertaking. The aid is therefore an income of the undertaking from the sale of products or provision of services in addition to the price paid by the consumer.[118]

Notes

[118] See Case IV/M.156 – *Cereol/Continentale Italiana* of 27 November 1991. In this case, the Commission excluded Community aid from the calculation of turnover because the aid was not intended to support the sale of products manufactured by one of the undertakings involved in the merger, but the producers of the raw materials (grain) used by the undertaking, which specialized in the crushing of grain.

163. Specific issues have arisen for the calculation of turnover of a business unit which only had internal revenues in the past. This may in particular apply for transactions involving the outsourcing of services by transfer of a business unit. If such a transaction constitutes a concentration on the basis of the considerations outlined in paragraphs 25 ff. of this Notice, the Commission's practice is that the turnover should normally be calculated on the basis of the previously internal turnover or of publicly quoted prices where such prices exist (e.g. in the oil industry). Where the previously internal turnover does not appear to correspond to a market valuation of the activities in question (and, thus, to the expected future turnover on the market), the forecast revenues to be received on the basis of an agreement with the former parent may be a suitable proxy.

3. "Net" turnover

164. The turnover to be taken into account is "net" turnover, after deduction of a number of components specified in the Regulation. The aim is to adjust turnover in such a way as to enable it to reflect the real economic strength of the undertaking.

3.1 Deduction of rebates and taxes

165. Article 5(1) provides for the "deduction of sales rebates and of value added tax and other taxes directly related to turnover". "Sales rebates" mean all rebates or discounts which are granted by the undertakings to their customers and which have a direct influence on the amounts of sales.

166. As regards the deduction of taxes, the Merger Regulation refers to VAT and "other taxes directly related to turnover". The concept of "taxes directly related to turnover" refers to indirect taxation linked to turnover, such as, for example, taxes on alcoholic beverages or cigarettes.

3.2 The treatment of "internal" turnover

167. The first subparagraph of Article 5(1) states that "the aggregate turnover of an undertaking concerned shall not include the sale of products or the provision of services between any of the undertakings referred to in paragraph 4", i.e. the group to which the undertaking concerned belongs. The aim is to exclude the proceeds of business dealings within a group so as to take account of the real economic weight of each entity in the form of market turnover. Thus, the "amounts" taken into account by the Merger Regulation reflect only the transactions which take place between the group of undertakings on the one hand and third parties on the other.

168. Article 5(5)(a) of the Merger Regulation applies the principle that double counting is to be avoided specifically to the situation where two or more undertakings concerned in a concentration jointly have the rights or powers listed in Article 5(4)(b) in another company. According to this provision, the turnover resulting from the sale of products or the provision of services between the joint venture and each of the undertakings concerned (or any other undertaking connected with any one of them in the sense of Article 5(4)) should be excluded. As regards joint ventures between undertakings concerned and third parties, insofar as their turnover is taken into account according to Article 5(4)(b) as set out in paragraph 181 below, the turnover generated by sales between the joint venture and the undertaking concerned (as well as undertakings linked to the undertaking concerned in accordance with the criteria set out in Article 5(4)) is not taken into account according to Article 5(1).

4. Turnover calculation and financial accounts

4.1 The general rule

169. The Commission seeks to base itself upon the most accurate and reliable figures available. Generally, the Commission will refer to accounts which relate to the closest financial year to the date of the transaction and which are audited under the standard applicable to the undertaking in question and compulsory for the relevant financial year.[119] An adjustment of the audited figures should only take place if this is required by the provisions of the Merger Regulation, including the cases explained in more detail in paragraph 172.

Notes

[119] See Case COMP/M.3986 – *Gas Natural/Endesa* of 15 November 2005; confirmed by Judgment in Case T-417/05, *Endesa v Commission*, paragraphs 128, 131, [2006] ECR II-2533.

170. The Commission is reluctant to rely on management or any other form of provisional accounts in any but exceptional circumstances.[120] Where a concentration takes place within the first months of the year and audited accounts are not yet available for the most recent financial year, the figures to be taken into account are those relating to the previous year. Where there is a major divergence between the two sets of accounts, due to significant and permanent changes in the undertaking concerned, and, in particular, when the final draft figures for the most recent year have been approved by the board of management, the Commission may decide to take those figures into account.

Notes

[120] See Case COMP/M.3986 – *Gas Natural/Endesa* of 15 November 2005; confirmed by Judgment in Case T-417/05, *Endesa v Commission*, paragraphs 176,179, [2006] ECR II-2533.

171. Despite the general rule, in cases where major differences between the Community's accounting standards and those of a non-member country are observed, the Commission may consider it necessary to restate these accounts in accordance with Community standards in respect of turnover.

4.2 Adjustments after the date of the last audited accounts

172. Notwithstanding the foregoing paragraphs, an adjustment must always be made to account for permanent changes in the economic reality of the undertakings concerned, such as acquisitions or divestments which are not or not fully reflected in the audited accounts. Such changes have to be taken into account in order to identify the true resources being concentrated and to better reflect the economic situation of the undertakings concerned. Those adjustments are only selective in nature and do not endanger the principle that there should be a simple and objective mechanism to determine the Commission's jurisdiction as they do not require a complete revision of the audited accounts.[121] First, this applies to acquisitions, divestments or closure of part of its business subsequent to the date of the audited accounts. This is relevant if a company closes a transaction concerning the divestment and closure of part of its business at any time before the relevant date for establishing jurisdiction (see paragraph 154) or where such a divestment or closure of a business is a pre-condition for the operation.[122] In this case, the turnover to be attributed to that part of the business must be subtracted from the turnover of the notifying party as shown in its last audited accounts. If an agreement for the sale of part of its business is signed, but the closing of the sale (in other words, its legal implementation and the transfer of the legal title to the shares or assets acquired) has not yet occurred, such a change is not taken into account,[123] unless the sale is a pre-condition for the notified operation. Conversely, the turnover of those businesses whose acquisition has been closed subsequent to the preparation of the most recent audited accounts, but before the relevant date for establishing jurisdiction, must be added to a company's turnover for notification purposes.

Notes

[121] Judgment in Case T-417/05, *Endesa v Commission*, paragraph 209, [2006] ECR II-2533.
[122] See Judgment in Case T-3/93, *Air France v Commission*, [1994] ECR II-121 paragraphs 100 et seq. in relation to Case IV/M.278 – *British Airways/Dan Air*; Case IV/M.588 – *Ingersoll-Rand/Clark Equipment*.
[123] Case IV/M.632 – *Rhône Poulenc Rorer/Fisons* of 21 September 1995; Case COMP/M.1741 – *MCI Worldcom/Sprint* of 28 June 2000.

173. Second, an adjustment may also be necessary for acquisitions, divestments or closure of part of the business which have taken place during the financial year for which the audited accounts are drawn up. If acquisitions, divestments or closure of part of the business within this period are made, the changes in the economic resources may only partly be reflected in the audited accounts of the undertaking concerned. As the turnover of the businesses acquired may be included in the accounts only from the time of their acquisition, this may not reflect the full annual turnover of the acquired business. Conversely, the turnover of the businesses divested or

closed may still be included in the audited accounts up to the point in time of their actual divest-ment or closure. In these cases, adjustments have to be made to remove the turnover generated by the divested or closed businesses from the audited accounts until the time of deconsolidation and to add the turnover which the acquired businesses have generated in the year until the time they have been consolidated in the accounts. As a result, the turnover of the businesses divested or closed must be excluded in full and the full annual turnover of the businesses acquired must be included.

174. Other factors that may affect turnover on a temporary basis such as a decrease in orders for the product or a slow-down in the production process within the period prior to the transaction will be ignored for the purposes of calculating turnover. No adjustment to the definitive accounts will be made to incorporate them.

5. Attribution of turnover under Article 5(4)

5.1 Identification of undertakings whose turnover is taken into account

175. When an undertaking concerned by a concentration belongs to a group, not only the turnover of the undertaking concerned is considered, but the Merger Regulation requires to also take into account the turnover of those undertakings with which the undertaking concerned has links consisting in the rights or powers listed in Article 5(4) in order to determine whether the thresholds contained in Article 1 of the Merger Regulation are met. The aim is again to capture the total volume of the economic resources that are being combined through the operation irrespective of whether the economic activities are carried out directly by the undertaking con-cerned or whether they are undertaken indirectly via undertakings with which the undertaking concerned possesses the links described in Article 5(4).

176. The Merger Regulation does not delineate the concept of a group in a single abstract definition, but sets out in Article 5(4)(b) certain rights or powers. If an undertaking concerned directly or indirectly has such links with other companies, those are to be regarded as part of its group for purposes of turnover calculation under the Merger Regulation.

177. Article 5(4) of the Merger Regulation provides the following:
"Without prejudice to paragraph 2 [acquisitions of parts], the aggregate turnover of an under-taking concerned within the meaning of Article 1(2) and (3) shall be calculated by adding together the respective turnovers of the following:
(a) the undertaking concerned;
(b) those undertakings in which the undertaking concerned directly or indirectly:
   (i) owns more than half the capital or business assets, or
   (ii) has the power to exercise more than half the voting rights, or
   (iii) has the power to appoint more than half the members of the supervisory board, the administrative board or bodies legally representing the undertakings, or
   (iv) has the right to manage the undertaking's affairs;
(c) those undertakings which have in an undertaking concerned the rights or powers listed in (b);
(d) those undertakings in which an undertaking as referred to in (c) has the rights or powers listed in (b);
(e) those undertakings in which two or more undertakings as referred to in (a) to (d) jointly have the rights or powers listed in (b)."
An undertaking which has in another undertaking the rights and powers mentioned in Article 5(4)(b) will be referred to as the "parent" of the latter in the present section of this Notice dealing with the calculation of turnover, whereas the latter is referred to as "subsidiary" of the former. In short, Article 5(4) therefore provides that the turnover of the undertaking concerned by the concentration (point (a)) should include its subsidiaries (point (b)), its parent companies (point (c)), the other subsidiaries of its parent undertakings (point (d)) and any other subsidiary jointly held by two or more of the undertakings identified under (a)-(d) (point (e)).

178. A graphic example is as follows:
The undertaking concerned and its group:

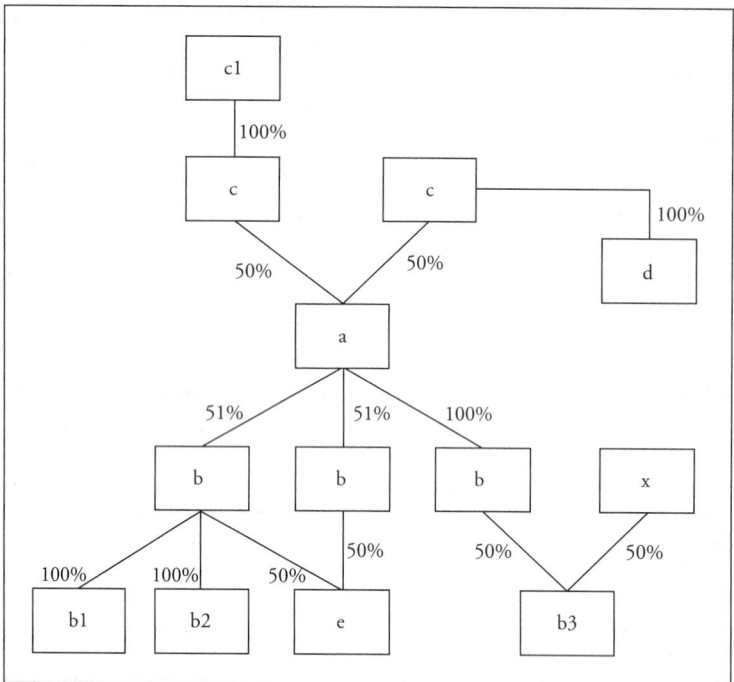

a: The undertaking concerned[124]
b: Its subsidiaries, jointly held companies together with third parties (b3) and their own subsidiaries (b1 and b2)
c: Its parent companies and their own parent companies (c1)
d: Other subsidiaries of the parent companies of the undertaking concerned
e: Companies jointly held by two (or more) companies of the group
x: Third party

Note: the letters a–e correspond to the relevant points of Article 5(4). Percentages set out in the graph
relate to the percentage of voting rights held by the respective parent company.

Notes
[124] For the graph it is assumed that the joint venture itself is the undertaking concerned according to the criteria set out
in paragraph 146 (acquisition by a full-function JV operating on the same market).

179. The rights or powers listed in Article 5(4)(b)(i)-(iii) can be identified in a rather straightforward
way as they refer to quantitative thresholds. These thresholds are fulfilled if the undertaking
concerned owns more than half of the capital or business assets of other undertakings, has
more than half of the voting rights or has legally the power to appoint more than half of the
board members in other undertakings. However, the thresholds are also met if the undertaking concerned *de facto* has the power to exercise more than half of the voting rights in the
shareholders' assembly or the power to appoint more than half of the board members in other
undertakings.[125]

Notes
[125] Case IV/M.187 – *Ifint/Exor* of 2 March 1992; Case IV/M.062 – *Eridania/ISI* of 30 July 1991.

180. The provision contained in Article 5(4)(b)(iv) refers to the right to manage the undertaking's
affairs. Such a right to manage exists under company law in particular on the basis of organisational contracts such as a "*Beherrschungsvertrag*" under German law, on the basis of business lease agreements or on the basis of the organisation structure for the general partner in

a limited partnership.[126] However, the "right to manage" may also result from the holding of voting rights (alone or in combination with contractual arrangements, such as a shareholders' agreement) which enable, on a stable, *de jure* basis, to determine the strategic behaviour of an undertaking.

Notes

[126] Case IV/M.126 – *Accor/WagonLits* of 28 April 1992.

181. The right to manage also covers situations in which the undertaking concerned jointly has the right to manage an undertaking's affairs together with third parties.[127] The underlying consideration is that the undertakings exercising joint control have jointly the right to manage the controlled undertakings' affairs even if each of them individually may have those rights only in a negative sense, i.e. in the form of veto rights. In the example, the undertaking (b3) which is jointly controlled by the undertaking concerned (a) and a third party (x) is taken into account as both (a) and (x) have veto rights in (b3) on the basis of their equal shareholding in (b3).[128] Under Article 5(4)(b)(iv) the Commission only takes into account those joint ventures in which the undertaking concerned and third parties have *de jure* rights that give rise to a clear-cut right to manage. The inclusion of joint ventures is therefore limited to situations where the undertaking concerned and third parties have a joint *right* to manage on the basis of an agreement, *e.g.* a shareholders' agreement, or where the undertaking concerned and a third party have an equality of voting rights to the effect that they have the right to appoint an equal number of members to the decision-making bodies of the joint venture.

Notes

[127] Case COMP/M.1741 – *MCI Worldcom/Sprint*; Case IV/ M.187 – *Ifint/Exor*; Case IV/ M.1046 – *Ameritech/Tele Danmark*.
[128] However, only half of the turnover generated by b3 is taken into account, see paragraph 187.

182. In the same way, where two or more companies jointly control the undertaking concerned in the sense that the agreement of each and all of them is needed in order to manage the undertaking affairs, the turnover of all of them is included. In the example, the two parent companies (c) of the undertaking concerned (a) would be taken into account as well as their own parent companies (c1 in the example). This interpretation results from the referral from Article 5(4)(c), dealing with this case, to Article 5(4)(b), which is applicable to jointly controlled companies as set out in the preceding paragraph.
183. When any of the companies identified on the basis of Article 5(4) also has links as defined in Article 5(4) with other undertakings, these should also be brought into the calculation. In the example, one of the subsidiaries of the undertaking concerned a (called b) has in turn its own subsidiaries b1 and b2 and one of the parent companies (called c) has its own subsidiary (d).
184. Article 5(4) sets out specific criteria for identifying undertakings whose turnover can be attributed to the undertaking concerned. These criteria, including the "right to manage the undertaking's affairs", are not coextensive with the notion of "control" under Article 3(2). There are significant differences between Articles 3 and 5, as those provisions fulfil different roles. The differences are most apparent in the field of *de facto* control. Whereas under Article 3(2) even a situation of economic dependence may lead to control on a *de facto* basis (see in detail above), a solely controlled subsidiary is only taken into account on a *de facto* basis under Article 5(4)(b) if it is clearly demonstrated that the undertaking concerned has the power to exercise more than half of the voting rights or to appoint more than half of the board members. Concerning joint control scenarios, Article 5(4)(b)(iv) covers those scenarios where the controlling undertakings jointly have a right to manage on the basis of individual veto rights. However, Article 5(4) would not cover situations where joint control occurs on a *de facto* basis due to strong common interests between different minority shareholders of the joint venture company on the basis of shareholders' attendance. The difference is reflected in the fact that Article 5(4)(b)(iv) refers to the *right* to manage, and not a *power* (as in subparagraph (b)(ii) and (iii)) and is explained by the need for precision and certainty in the criteria used for calculating turnover so that jurisdiction can be readily verified. Under Article 3(3), however, the question whether a concentration arises can be much more comprehensively investigated. In addition, situations of negative sole control are only exceptionally covered

(if the conditions of Article 5(4)(b)(i)-(iii) are met in the specific case); the "right to manage" under Article 5(4)(b)(iv) does not cover negative control scenarios. Finally, Article 5(4)(b)(i), for example, covers situations where "control" under Article 3(2) may not exist.

5.2 Allocation of turnover of the undertakings identified

185. In general, as long as the test under Article 5(4)(b) is fulfilled, the whole turnover of the subsidiary in question will be taken into account regardless of the actual shareholding which the undertaking concerned holds in the subsidiary. In the chart, the whole turnover of the subsidiaries called b of the undertaking concerned a will be taken into account.

186. However, the Merger Regulation includes specific rules for joint ventures. Article 5(5)(b) provides that for joint ventures between two or more undertakings concerned, the turnover of the joint venture (as far as the turnover is generated from activities with third parties as set out above in paragraph 168) should be apportioned equally amongst the undertakings concerned, irrespective of their share of the capital or the voting rights.

187. The principle contained in Article 5(5)(b) is followed by analogy for the allocation of turnover for joint ventures between undertakings concerned and third parties if their turnover is taken into account according to Article 5(4)(b) as set out above in paragraph 181. The Commission's practice has been to allocate to the undertaking concerned the turnover of the joint venture on a per capita basis according to the number of undertakings exercising joint control. In the example, half of the turnover of b3 is taken into account.

188. The rules of Article 5(4) also have to be adapted in situations involving a change from joint to sole control in order to avoid double counting of the turnover of the joint venture. Even if the acquiring undertaking has rights or powers in the joint venture which satisfy the requirements of Article 5(4), the turnover of the acquiring shareholder has to be calculated without the turnover of the joint venture, and the turnover of the joint venture has to be taken without the turnover of the acquiring shareholder.

5.3 Allocation of turnover in case of investment funds

189. The investment company, as set out above in paragraph 15, normally acquires indirect control over portfolio companies held by an investment fund. In the same way, the investment company may be considered to indirectly have the powers and rights which are set out in Article 5(4)(b), in particular to indirectly have the power to exercise the voting rights held by the investment fund in the portfolio companies.

190. The same considerations, as set out above in the framework of Article 3 (paragraph 15), may also apply if an investment company sets up several investment funds with possibly different investors. Typically, on the basis of the organisational structure, in particular links between the investment company and the general partner(s) of the different funds organised as limited partnerships, or contractual arrangements, especially advisory agreements between the general partner or the investment fund and the investment company, the investment company will indirectly have the power to exercise the voting rights held by the investment fund in the portfolio companies or indirectly have one of the other powers or rights set out in Article 5(4)(b). In these circumstances, the investment company may exercise a common control structure over the different funds which it has set up and the common operation of the different funds by the investment company is often indicated by a common brand for the funds.

191. Consequently, such an organisation of the different funds by the investment company may lead to the result that the turnover of all portfolio companies held by different funds is taken into account for the purpose of assessing whether the turnover thresholds in Article 1 are met if the investment company acquires indirect control of a portfolio company via one of the funds.

5.4 Allocation of turnover for State-owned undertakings

192. As regards the calculation of turnover of State-owned undertakings, Article 5(4) should be read in conjunction with recital 22 of the Merger Regulation. This recital declares that, in order to avoid discrimination between the public and private sectors, "in the public sector, calculation of the turnover of an undertaking concerned in a concentration needs, therefore, to take account of undertakings making up an economic unit with an independent power of decision, irrespective of the way in which their capital is held or of the rules of administrative supervision applicable to them".[129]

Notes
[129] See also Case IV/M.216 – *CEA Industrie/France Telecom/Finmeccanica/SGS-Thomson*, of 22 February 1993.

193. This recital clarifies that Member States (or other public bodies) are not considered as "undertakings" under Article 5(4) simply because they have interests in other undertakings which satisfy the conditions of Article 5(4). Therefore, for the purposes of calculating turnover of State-owned undertakings, account is only taken of those undertakings which belong to the same economic unit, having the same independent power of decision.

194. Thus, where a State-owned company is not subject to any coordination with other State-controlled holdings, it should be treated as independent for the purposes of Article 5, and the turnover of other companies owned by that State should not be taken into account. Where, however, several State-owned companies are under the same independent centre of commercial decision-making, then the turnover of those businesses should be considered part of the group of the undertaking concerned for the purposes of Article 5.

V. Geographic Allocation of Turnover

195. The thresholds concerning Community-wide and Member State turnover in Article 1(2) and (3) aim to identify cases which have sufficient turnover within the Community in order to be of Community interest and which are primarily cross-border in nature. They require turnover to be allocated geographically to the Community and to individual Member States. Since audited accounts often do not provide a geographical breakdown as required by the Merger Regulation, the Commission will rely on the best figures available provided by the undertakings. The second subparagraph of Article 5(1) provides that the location of turnover is determined by the location of the customer at the time of the transaction: "Turnover, in the Community or in a Member State, shall comprise products sold and services provided to undertakings or consumers, in the Community or in that Member State as the case may be."

General rule

196. The Merger Regulation does not discriminate between "products sold" and "services provided" for the geographic allocation of turnover. In both cases, the general rule is that turnover should be attributed to the place where the customer is located. The underlying principle is that turnover should be allocated to the location where competition with alternative suppliers takes place. This location is normally also the place where the characteristic action under the contract in question is to be performed, i.e. where the service is actually provided and the product is actually delivered. In the case of Internet transactions, it may be difficult for the undertakings to determine the location of the customer at the time when the contract is concluded via the Internet. If the product or the service itself is not supplied via the Internet, focusing on the place where the characteristic action under the contract is performed may avoid those difficulties. In the following, the sale of goods and the provision of services are dealt with separately as they exhibit certain different features in terms of allocation of turnover.

Sale of goods

197. For the sale of goods, particular situations may arise in situations in which the place where the customer was located at the time of concluding the purchase agreement is different from the billing address and/or the place of delivery. In these situations, the place where the purchase agreement was entered into and the place of delivery are more important than the billing address. As the delivery is in general the characteristic action for the sale of goods, the place of delivery may even be prevailing over the place where the customer was located at the time when the purchase agreement was concluded. This will depend on whether the place of delivery is to be considered the place where competition takes place for the sale of goods or whether competition rather takes place at the residence of the customer. In the case of a sale of mobile goods, such as a motor car, to a final consumer, the place where the car is delivered to the customer is decisive even if the agreement was concluded via the phone or the Internet before.

198. A specific situation arises in cases where a multinational corporation has a Community buying strategy and sources all its requirements for a good from one location. As a central purchasing

organisation can take different forms, it is necessary to consider its concrete form since this may determine how to allocate the turnover. Where goods are purchased by and delivered to the central purchasing organisation and are subsequently re-distributed internally to different plants in a variety of Member States, turnover is allocated only to the Member State where the central purchasing organisation is located. In this case, competition takes place at the location of the central purchasing organisation and this is also the place where the characteristic action under the sales contract is performed. The situation is different in case of direct links between the seller and the different subsidiaries. This comprises the case where the central purchasing organisation concludes a mere framework agreement, but the individual orders are placed by and the products are directly delivered to the subsidiaries in different Member States as well as the case where the individual orders are placed via the central purchasing organisation, but the products are directly delivered to the subsidiaries. In both cases, turnover is to be allocated to the different Member States in which the subsidiaries are located, irrespective of whether the central purchasing organisation or the subsidiaries receive the bills and effect the payment. The reason is that in both cases competition with alternative suppliers takes place for the delivery of products to the different subsidiaries even though the contract is concluded centrally. In the first case, in addition, the subsidiaries actually decide upon the quantities to be delivered and on an element essential for competition on their own.

Provision of services

199. For services, the Merger Regulation foresees that the place of their provision to the customer is relevant. Services containing cross-border elements can be considered to fall into three general categories. The first category comprises cases where the service provider travels, the second category cases where the customer travels. The third category comprises those cases where a service is provided without either the service provider or the customer having to travel. In the first two categories, the turnover generated is to be allocated to the place of destination of the traveller, i.e. the place where the service is actually provided to the customer. In the third category, the turnover is generally to be allocated to the location of the customer. For the central sourcing of services the above outlined principles for the central purchasing of goods apply in an analogous way.

200. An example of the first category would be a situation where a non-European company provides special airplane maintenance services to a carrier in a Member State. In this case, the service provider travels to the Community where the service is actually provided and where also competition for this service takes place. If a European tourist hires a car or books a hotel directly in the United States, this falls into the second category as the service is provided outside the Community and also competition takes place between hotels and rental car companies at the location chosen. However, the case is different for package holidays. For this kind of holiday, the service starts with the sale of the package through a travel agent at the customer's location and competition for the sale of holidays through travel agents takes place locally, as with retail shopping, even though parts of the service may be provided in a number of distant locations. The case therefore falls into the third category and the turnover generated is to be allocated to the customer's location. The third category also comprises cases like the supply of software or the distribution of films which are made outside the Community, but are supplied to a customer in a Member State so that the service is actually provided to the customer within the Community.

201. Cases concerning the transport of goods are different as the customer, to whom those services are provided, does not travel, but the transport service is provided to the customer at its location. Those cases fall into the third category and the location of the customer is the relevant criterion for the allocation of the turnover.

202. In telecom cases, the qualification of call termination services may raise problems. Although call termination would appear to fall into the third category, there are reasons to treat it differently. Call termination services are provided, *e.g.*, in situations where a call, originating from a European operator, is being terminated in the United States. Although neither the European nor the US operator travels, the signal travels and the service is provided by the US network to the European operator in the United States. This is also the place where competition takes place (if any). The turnover is therefore to be considered as non-Community turnover.[130]

Notes
[130] This does not affect the turnover which the European telephony operator generates vis-à-vis its own customer with this call.

Specific sectors

203. Certain sectors do, however, pose very particular problems with regard to the geographical allocation of turnover. These will be dealt with in Section VI below.

VI. CONVERSION OF TURNOVER INTO EURO

204. When converting turnover figures into Euro great care should be taken with the exchange rate used. The annual turnover of a company should be converted at the average rate for the twelve months concerned. This average can be obtained via DG Competition's website.[131] The audited annual turnover figures should be converted as such and not be broken down into quarterly or monthly figures which would then be converted individually.

Notes
[131] See http://europa.eu.int/comm/competition/mergers/others/exchange_rates. html#footnote_1. The website makes reference to the European Central Bank's Monthly Bulletin.

205. When a company has sales in a range of currencies, the procedure is no different. The total turnover given in the consolidated audited accounts and in that company's reporting currency is converted into Euros at the yearly average rate. Local currency sales should not be converted directly into Euros since these figures are not from the consolidated audited accounts of the company.

VII. PROVISIONS FOR CREDIT AND OTHER FINANCIAL INSTITUTIONS AND INSURANCE UNDERTAKINGS

1. Scope of application

206. Due to the specific nature of the sector, Article 5(3) contains specific rules for the calculation of turnover of credit and other financial institutions as well as insurance undertakings.

207. In order to define the terms "credit institutions and other financial institutions" under the Merger Regulation, the Commission in its practice has consistently adopted the definitions provided in the applicable European regulation in the banking sector. The Directive on the taking up and pursuit of the business of credit institutions foresees that:[132]

— "Credit institution shall mean an undertaking whose business is to receive deposits or other repayable funds from the public and to grant credits for its own account."

— "Financial institution shall mean an undertaking other than a credit institution, the principal activity of which is to acquire holdings or to carry on one or more of the activities listed in points 2 to 12 of Annex I."

Notes
[132] The definitions are to be found in Article 1(1) and (5) of Directive 2000/12/EC of the European Parliament and of the Council of 20 March 2000 relating to the taking up and pursuit of the business of credit institutions (OJ L 126, 26.5.2000, p. 1).

208. Financial institutions within the meaning of Article 5(3) of the Merger Regulation are, accordingly, on the one hand holding companies and, on the other hand, undertakings which perform on a regular basis as a principal activity one or more activities expressly mentioned in points 2 to 12 of the Annex of the banking Directive. These activities include:

• lending (comprising activities such as consumer credit, mortgage credit, factoring);
• financial leasing;
• money transmission services;
• issuing and administering means of payment (e.g. credit cards, travellers' cheques and bankers' drafts);
• guarantees and commitments;

- trading for own account or for account of customers in money market instruments (cheques, bills, certificates of deposit, etc.), foreign exchange, financial futures and options, exchange and interest-rate instruments, transferable securities;
- participation in securities issues and the provision of services related to such issues;
- money broking;
- portfolio management and advice; and
- safekeeping and administration of securities.

2. Calculation of turnover

209. Article 5(3) of the Merger Regulation sets out the methods of calculation of turnover for credit and other financial institutions and for insurance undertakings. In the following Section, some supplementary questions related to turnover calculation for the abovementioned types of undertakings are addressed.

2.1 Calculation of turnover of credit and financial institutions (other than financial holding companies)

2.1.1 General

210. There are normally no particular difficulties in applying the banking income criterion for the definition of the worldwide turnover to credit institutions and other kinds of financial institutions. For the geographic allocation of turnover to the Community and to individual Member States, the specific provision of Article 5(3)(a) second subparagraph applies. It specifies that the turnover is to be allocated to the branch or division established in the Community or in the Member State which receives this income.

2.1.2 Turnover of leasing companies

211. There is a fundamental distinction to be made between financial leases and operating leases. Basically, financial leases are made for longer periods than operating leases and ownership is generally transferred to the lessee at the end of the lease term by means of a purchase option included in the lease contract. Under an operating lease, on the contrary, ownership is not transferred to the lessee at the end of the lease term and the costs of maintenance, repair and insurance of the leased equipment are included in the lease payments. A financial lease therefore functions as a loan by the lessor to enable the lessee to purchase a given asset.

212. As already mentioned above, a company performing as its principal activity financial leasing is a financial institution within the meaning of Article 5(3)(a) and its turnover is to be calculated according to the specific rules set out in this provision. All payments on financial leasing contracts, except for the redemption part, are to be taken into account; a sale of future leasing payments at the beginning of the contract for refinancing purposes is not relevant.

213. Operational leasing activities are, however, not considered to be carried out by financial institutions, and therefore the general turnover calculation rules of Article 5(1) apply.[133]

Notes
[133] See Case IV/M.234 – *GECC/Avis Lease*, 15 July 1992.

2.2 Insurance undertakings

214. In order to measure the turnover of insurance undertakings, Article 5(3)(b) of the Merger Regulation provides that gross premiums written are taken into account. The gross premiums written are the sum of received premiums, including any received reinsurance premiums if the undertaking concerned has activities in the field of reinsurance. Outgoing or outward reinsurance premiums, i.e. all amounts paid and payable by the undertaking concerned to get reinsurance cover, are only costs related to the provision of insurance coverage and are not to be deducted from the gross premiums written.

215. The premiums to be taken into account are not only related to new insurance contracts made during the accounting year being considered but also to all premiums related to contracts made in previous years which remain in force during the period taken into consideration.

216. In order to constitute appropriate reserves allowing for the payment of claims, insurance undertakings, usually hold a portfolio of investments in shares, interest-bearing securities, land and property and other assets providing annual revenues. The annual revenues coming from those sources are not considered as turnover for insurance undertakings under Article 5(3)(b). However, a distinction has to be made between pure financial investments, which do not confer the rights and powers specified in Article 5(4) to the insurance undertaking in the undertakings in which the investment has been made, and those investments leading to the acquisition of an interest which meets the criteria specified in Article 5(4)(b). In the latter case, Article 5(4) of the Merger Regulation applies, and the turnover of this undertaking has to be added to the turnover of the insurance undertaking, as calculated according to Article 5(3)(b), for the determination of the thresholds laid down in the Merger Regulation.[134]

Notes
[134] See Case IV/M.018 – *AG/AMEV*, of 21 November 1990.

2.3 Financial holding companies

217. As an "other financial institution" within the meaning of Article 5(3)(a) of the Merger Regulation, the turnover of a financial holding company has to be calculated according to the specific rules set out in this provision. However, in the same way as mentioned above for insurance undertakings, Article 5(4) applies to those participations which meet the criteria specified in Article 5(4)(b). Thus, the turnover of a financial holding is to be basically calculated according to Article 5(3), but it may be necessary to add turnover of undertakings falling within the categories set out in Article 5(4) ("Art. 5(4) companies").[135]

Notes
[135] The principles for financial holding companies may to a certain extent be applied to fund management companies.

218. In practice, the turnover of the financial holding company (non-consolidated) must first be taken into account. Then the turnover of the Art 5(4) companies must be added, whilst taking care to deduct dividends and other income distributed by those companies to the financial holdings. The following provides an example for this kind of calculation:

	EURO Million
1. Turnover related to financial activities (from non-consolidated P&L)	3 000
2. Turnover related to insurance Art. 5(4) companies (gross premiums written)	300
3. Turnover of industrial Art. 5(4) companies	2 000
4. Deduct dividends and other income derived from Art. 5(4) companies 2 and 3	<200>
Total turnover financial holding and its group	5 100

219. In such calculations different accounting rules may need to be taken into consideration. Whilst this consideration applies to any type of undertaking concerned by the Merger Regulation, it is particularly important in the case of financial holding companies[136] where the number and the diversity of enterprises controlled and the degree of control the holding holds on its subsidiaries, affiliated companies and other companies in which it has shareholding requires careful examination.

Notes
[136] See, for example, Case IV/M.166 – *Torras/Sarrió*, of 24 February 1992.

220. Turnover calculation for financial holding companies as described above may in practice prove onerous. Therefore a strict and detailed application of this method will be necessary only in cases where it seems that the turnover of a financial holding company is likely to be close to the Merger Regulation thresholds; in other cases it may well be obvious that the turnover is far from the thresholds of the Merger Regulation, and therefore the published accounts are adequate for the establishment of jurisdiction.

D14

DRAFT COMMISSION NOTICE

Guidelines on the assessment of non-horizontal mergers under the Council Regulation on the control of concentrations between undertakings
Draft – for the purpose of public consultation

Notes

This draft notice was published by the Commission for the purpose of public consultation on 13 February 2007. It is published on the Europa website at:
http://ec.europa.eu/comm/competition/mergers/legislation/merger_guidelines.html
On 28 November 2007 the Commission adopted the final version of these draft guidelines. [It has not been possible to include the final version in this volume, but] it is published on the Europa website at the following address:
http://ec.europa.eu/comm/competition/mergers/legislation/nonhorizontalguidelines.pdf.

I. Introduction

1. Article 2 of Council Regulation (EC) No 139/2004 of 20 January 2004 on the control of concentrations between undertakings[1] (hereinafter: the "Merger Regulation") provides that the Commission has to appraise concentrations within the scope of the Merger Regulation with a view to establishing whether or not they are compatible with the common market. For that purpose, the Commission must assess, pursuant to Article 2(2) and (3), whether or not a concentration would significantly impede effective competition, in particular as a result of the creation or strengthening of a dominant position, in the common market or a substantial part of it.

Notes

[1] Council Regulation (EC) No 139/2004 of 20 January 2004, Official Journal L 24, 29.01.2004, p. 1.

---

2. This document develops guidance as to how the Commission assesses concentrations[2] where the undertakings concerned are active on distinct relevant markets.[3] In this document, these concentrations will be called "non-horizontal mergers".

Notes

[2] The term *concentration* used in the Merger Regulation covers various types of transactions such as mergers, acquisitions, takeovers, and certain types of joint ventures. In the remainder of this Document, unless otherwise specified, the term "merger" will be used as a synonym for concentration and therefore cover all the above types of transactions.

[3] Guidance on the assessment of mergers involving undertakings which are actual or potential competitors on the same relevant market ("horizontal mergers") is given in the Commission Notice: Guidelines on the assessment of horizontal mergers under the Council Regulation on the control of concentrations between undertakings. OJ C 31, 05.02.2004, pages 5–18 ("Notice on Horizontal Mergers").

---

3. Two broad types of non-horizontal mergers can be distinguished: vertical mergers and conglomerate mergers.

4. Vertical mergers involve companies operating at different levels of the supply chain. For example, when a manufacturer of a certain product (the "upstream firm") merges with one of its distributors (the "downstream firm"), this is called a vertical merger.[4]

Notes

[4] In the present Document, the terms "downstream" and "upstream" are used to describe the (potential) commercial relationship that the merging entities have with each other. Generally the commercial relationship is one where the "downstream" firm purchases the output from the "upstream" firm and uses it as an input in its own production, which it then sells on to its customers. The market where the former transactions take place is referred to as the intermediate market (upstream market). The latter market is referred to as the downstream market.

---

5. Conglomerate mergers are mergers between firms that are in a relationship, which is neither purely horizontal (as competitors in the same relevant market) nor vertical (as suppliers or customers).[5]

In practice, the focus of the present guidelines is on mergers between companies that are active in closely related markets (e.g. mergers involving suppliers of complementary products or products that belong to the same product range).

Notes
[5] The distinction between conglomerate mergers and horizontal mergers may be subtle, e.g. when a conglomerate merger involves products that are weak substitutes for each other. The same holds true for the distinction between conglomerate mergers and vertical mergers. For instance, products may be supplied by some companies with the inputs already integrated (vertical relationship), whereas other producers leave it to the customers to select and assemble the inputs themselves (conglomerate relationship).

---

6. The general guidance already given in the Notice on horizontal mergers is also relevant in the context of non-horizontal mergers. The purpose of the present document is to concentrate on the competition aspects that are relevant to the specific context of non-horizontal mergers. In addition, it will set out the Commission's approach to market shares and concentration thresholds in this context.
7. In practice, mergers may entail both horizontal and non-horizontal effects. This may for instance be the case where the merging firms are not only in a vertical or conglomerate relationship, but are also actual or potential competitors of each other in one or more of the relevant markets concerned.[6] In such a case, the Commission will appraise horizontal, vertical and/or conglomerate effects in accordance with the guidance set out in the relevant notices.[7]

Notes
[6] For instance, in certain markets upstream or downstream firms are often well-placed potential entrants. See, e.g., in the electricity and gas sector, Case COMP/M.3440 –EDP/ENI/GDP (2004). The same may hold for producers of complementary products. See, e.g. in the liquid packaging sector, Case COMP/M.2416 – TetraLaval/Sidel (2001).
[7] Guidance on the assessment of mergers with a potential competitor is given in the Notice on horizontal mergers, in particular at paragraphs 58 to 60 thereof.

---

8. The guidance set out in this document draws and elaborates on the Commission's evolving experience with the appraisal of non-horizontal mergers under Regulation No 4064/89 since its entry into force on 21 September 1990, the Merger Regulation presently in force as well as on the case-law of the Court of Justice and the Court of First Instance of the European Communities. The principles contained here will be applied and further developed and refined by the Commission in individual cases. The Commission may revise the notice on non-horizontal mergers from time to time in the light of future developments and of evolving insight.
9. The Commission's interpretation of the Merger Regulation as regards the appraisal of non-horizontal mergers is without prejudice to the interpretation which may be given by the Court of Justice or the Court of First Instance of the European Communities.

II. Overview

10. Effective competition brings benefits to consumers, such as low prices, high quality products, a wide selection of goods and services, and innovation. Through its control of mergers, the Commission prevents mergers that would be likely to deprive customers of these benefits by significantly increasing the market power of firms. An "increase in market power" in this context refers to the ability of one or more firms to profitably increase prices, reduce output, choice or quality of goods and services, diminish innovation, or otherwise influence parameters of competition.[8]

Notes
[8] In this Document, the expression "increased prices" is often used as shorthand for these various ways in which a merger may result in competitive harm. The expression should be understood to also cover situations where, for instance, prices are decreased less, or are less likely to decrease, than they otherwise would have without the merger and where prices are increased more, or are more likely to increase, than they otherwise would have without the merger.

---

11. Non-horizontal mergers are generally less likely to create competition concerns than horizontal mergers.
12. First, unlike horizontal mergers, vertical or conglomerate mergers do not entail the loss of direct competition between the merging firms in the same relevant market.[9] As a result, the main source of anti-competitive effect in horizontal mergers is absent from vertical and conglomerate mergers.

Notes
9 Such a loss of direct competition can, nevertheless, arise where one of the merging firms is a potential competitor in the relevant market where the other merging firm operates. See paragraph 7 above.

13. Second, vertical and conglomerate mergers provide substantial scope for efficiencies. A characteristic of vertical mergers and certain conglomerate mergers is that the activities and/or the products of the companies involved are *complementary* to each other.[10] The integration of complementary activities or products within a single firm may produce significant efficiencies and be pro-competitive. For instance, in vertical mergers, efforts to increase sales at one level (e.g. by lowering price, or by stepping up innovation) will benefit sales at the other level. Depending on the market conditions, integration may increase the incentive to carry out such efforts. In particular, after the vertical integration, lowering the mark-up downstream may lead to increased sales not only downstream but also upstream and vice versa. This is often referred to as the "internalisation of double mark-ups".

Notes
10 In this document, products or services are called "complementary" (or "economic complements") when they are worth more to a customer when used or consumed together than when used or consumed separately. Also a merger between upstream and downstream activities can be seen as a combination of complements which go into the final product. For instance, both production and distribution fulfil an indispensable role in getting a product to the market.

14. Integration may also decrease transaction costs and allow for a better co-ordination in terms of product design, the organisation of the production process, and the way in which the products are sold. Similarly, mergers which involve products belonging to a range of products that are generally sold to the same set of customers (be they complementary products or not) may give rise to customer benefits such as one-stop-shopping.

15. However, there are circumstances in which non-horizontal mergers may significantly impede effective competition, in particular as a result of the creation or strengthening of a dominant position. This is essentially because a non-horizontal merger may change the ability and incentive to compete on the part of the merging companies and their competitors in ways that cause harm to consumers.

16. In the context of competition law, the concept of "consumers" encompasses intermediate and ultimate consumers.[11] When intermediate customers are actual or potential competitors of the parties to the merger, the Commission focuses on the effects of the merger on the customers to which the merged entity and those competitors are selling. Consequently, the fact that a merger affects competitors is not in and of itself a problem. It is the impact on effective competition that matters, not the mere impact on competitors at some level of the supply chain.[12]

Notes
11 See Article 2(1)(b) of the Merger Regulation.
12 One example of this approach can be found in the case COMP/M.3653 Siemens/VA Tech (2005), in which the Commission assessed the effect of the transaction on the two complementary markets for electrical rail vehicles and electrical traction systems for rail vehicles, which combine into a full rail vehicle. While the merger allegedly reduced the independent supply of electrical traction systems, there would still be several integrated suppliers which could deliver the rail vehicle. The Commission thus concluded that even if the merger had negative consequences for independent suppliers of electrical rail vehicles "sufficient competition would remain in the relevant downstream market for rail vehicles"

17. There are two main ways in which non-horizontal mergers may significantly impede effective competition: non-coordinated effects and coordinated effects.[13]

Notes
13 See Section II of the Notice on Horizontal Mergers.

18. Non-coordinated effects may principally arise when non-horizontal mergers give rise to *foreclosure*. In this document, the term "foreclosure" will be used to describe any instance where actual or potential rivals' access to supplies or markets is hampered or eliminated as a result of the merger, thereby reducing these companies' ability and/or incentive to compete. As a result

of such foreclosure, the merging companies – and, possibly, some of its competitors as well – may be able to profitably increase the price[14] charged to consumers. These instances will be referred to as "anticompetitive foreclosure".

Notes

[14] For the meaning of the expression "increased prices" see footnote 8.

19. Coordinated effects arise where the merger changes the nature of competition in such a way that firms that previously were not coordinating their behaviour, are now significantly more likely to coordinate and raise prices or otherwise harm effective competition. A merger may also make coordination easier, more stable or more effective for firms, which were coordinating prior to the merger.

20. In assessing the competitive effects of a merger, the Commission compares the competitive conditions that would result from the notified merger with the conditions that would have prevailed without the merger.[15] In most cases the competitive conditions existing at the time of the merger constitute the relevant comparison for evaluating the effects of a merger. However, in some circumstances, the Commission may take into account future changes to the market that can reasonably be predicted. It may, in particular, take account of the likely entry or exit of firms if the merger did not take place when considering what constitutes the relevant comparison. The Commission may take into account future market developments that result from expected regulatory changes.[16]

Notes

[15] By analogy, in the case of a merger that has been implemented without having been notified, the Commission would assess the merger in the light of the competitive conditions that would have prevailed without the implemented merger.

[16] This may be particularly relevant in cases where effective competition is expected to arise in the future as a result of market opening. See e.g. Case COMP/M.3696 – *E.ON/MOL* (2005), at points 457 to 463.

21. In its assessment, the Commission will consider both the possible anti-competitive effects arising from the merger and the pro-competitive effects stemming from efficiencies identified and substantiated by the parties. The Commission examines the various chains of cause and effect with a view to ascertaining which of them is the most likely. The more immediate and direct the overall anti-competitive effect of a merger, the more likely the Commission is to raise competition concerns.

22. This document describes the main scenarios of competitive harm and sources of efficiencies in the context of vertical mergers and, subsequently, in the context of conglomerate mergers.

III. Market Share and Concentration Levels

23. Non-horizontal mergers pose no threat to effective competition unless the merged entity has market power in at least one of the markets concerned.

24. Market shares and concentration levels provide useful first indications of the market power and the competitive importance of both the merging parties and their competitors.[17]

Notes

[17] See also Section III of the Notice on Horizontal Mergers. The calculation of market shares depends critically on market definition (see Commission notice on the definition of the relevant market for the purposes of Community competition law, OJ C 372/5, 9 December 1997). Special care must be taken in contexts where vertically integrated companies supply products internally.

25. The Commission is unlikely to find concern in non-horizontal mergers, be it of a coordinated or of a non-coordinated nature, where the market share post-merger of the new entity in each of the markets concerned is below [30%][18] and where the post-merger HHI is below [2000]. In practice, it will not extensively investigate such mergers, except where special circumstances such as, for instance, one or more of the following factors are present:

(a) a merger involves a company that is likely to expand significantly in the near future, e.g. because of a recent innovation;

(b) there are significant cross-shareholdings or cross-directorships among the market participants;

(c) one of the merging firms is a firm with a high likelihood of disrupting coordinated conduct;

(d) indications of past or ongoing coordination, or facilitating practices, are present.

Notes

[18] In analogy to the indications given in Commission Regulation (EC) No 2790/1999 of 22 December 1999 on the application of Article 81(3) of the Treaty to categories of vertical agreements and concerted practices, Official Journal L 336, 29.12.1999, pages 21–25.

26. The Commission will use the above market share thresholds and HHI levels as an initial indicator of the absence of competition concerns. However, they do not give rise to a legal presumption. The Commission is of the opinion that presenting market share and concentration levels above which there are competition concerns is less appropriate in this context. Indeed, market power in at least one of the markets concerned is a necessary condition for competitive harm, not a sufficient condition.[19]

Notes

[19] See Sections III and IV.

IV. VERTICAL MERGERS

27. This section sets out the Commission's framework of analysis in the context of vertical mergers. In its assessment, the Commission will consider both the possible anti-competitive effects arising from vertical mergers and the pro-competitive effects stemming from efficiencies identified and substantiated by the parties.

A. Non-coordinated effects: foreclosure

28. A vertical merger may significantly impede effective competition through non-coordinated effects mainly when it gives rise to foreclosure. Foreclosure may discourage entry or expansion of rivals or encourage their exit. Foreclosure thus can be found even if the foreclosed rivals are not forced to exit the market: it is sufficient that the rivals are disadvantaged and consequently led to compete less effectively. As a result of such foreclosure, the merging companies – and, possibly, some of its competitors as well – may be able to profitably increase the price charged to consumers.[20]

Notes

[20] For the meaning of the expression "increased prices" see footnote 8. For the meaning of "consumers", see paragraph 16.

29. Two forms of foreclosure can be distinguished. The first is where the merger is likely to raise the costs of downstream rivals by restricting their access to an important input (input foreclosure). The second is where the merger is likely to foreclose upstream rivals by restricting their access to a sufficient customer base (customer foreclosure).[21]

Notes

[21] See Merger Regulation, Article 2(1)(b), referring to "*access to supplies*" and "*access to [. . .] markets*", respectively.

1. Input foreclosure

30. A merger may significantly impede effective competition through input foreclosure where, post-merger, the new entity would be likely to restrict access to the products or services that it would have otherwise supplied absent the merger, thereby raising its downstream rivals' costs by making it harder for them to obtain supplies of the input under similar prices and conditions as absent the merger. This may lead the merged entity to profitably increase the price charged to consumers. Any efficiencies resulting from the merger, however, may lead the merged entity to reduce price, so that the overall likely impact on consumers is neutral or positive. A graphical presentation of this mechanism is provided in Figure 1.

Figure 1 - Input foreclosure

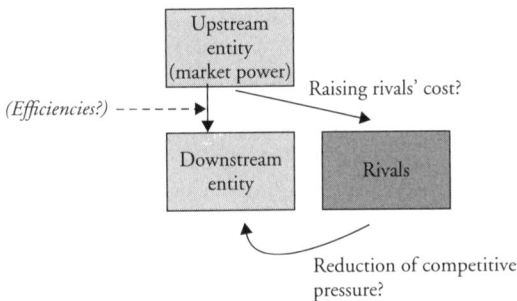

31. In assessing the likelihood of an anticompetitive input foreclosure scenario, the Commission examines, first, whether the merged entity would have, post-merger, the ability to substantially foreclose access to inputs, second, whether it would have the incentive to do so, and third, whether a foreclosure strategy would have a significant detrimental effect on competition downstream. In practice, these factors are often examined together since they are closely intertwined.

A. Ability to foreclose access to inputs[22]

32. Input foreclosure may occur in various forms. The merged entity may decide not to deal with its actual or potential competitors in the vertically related market. Alternatively, the merged firm may decide to restrict supplies and/or to raise the price it charges in supplying competitors and/or to otherwise make the conditions of supply less favourable than they would have been absent the merger.[23] Further, the merged entity may opt for a specific choice of technology within the new firm which is not compatible with the technologies chosen by rival firms.[24] Foreclosure may also take more subtle forms, such as the degradation of the quality of input supplied. In its assessment, the Commission may consider a series of alternative or complementary possible strategies.

Notes

[22] The term "inputs" is used here as a generic term and may also cover services, access to infrastructure and access to intellectual property rights.

[23] See e.g. Case COMP/M.1693 – *Alcoa/Reynolds* (2000).

[24] See, e.g., Case COMP/M.2861 – *Siemens/Dragerwerk/JV* (2003).

---

33. Input foreclosure may raise competition problems only if it concerns an important input for the downstream product. This is the case, in particular, when the input concerned represents a significant cost factor relative to the price of the downstream product. Irrespective of its cost, an input may also be sufficiently important for other reasons. For instance, the input may be a critical component without which the downstream product could not be manufactured or effectively sold on the market,[25] or it may represent a significant source of product differentiation for the downstream product.[26] It may also be that the cost of switching to alternative inputs is relatively high.

Notes

[25] For instance, an engine starter can be considered a critical component to an engine (Case T-210/01 *General Electric v Commission* [2005] ECR II-[5575]).

[26] For instance, personal computers are often sold with specific reference to the type of microprocessor they contain.

---

34. For input foreclosure to be a concern, the vertically integrated firm resulting from the merger must have market power in the upstream market. It is only in these circumstances that the merged firm can be expected to have a significant influence on the conditions of competition

in the upstream market and thus, possibly, on prices and supply conditions in the downstream market.

35. The merged entity would only have the ability to foreclose downstream competitors if, by reducing access to its own upstream products or services, it could negatively affect the overall availability of inputs for the downstream market in terms of price or quality. This may be the case where the remaining upstream suppliers are less efficient, offer less preferred alternatives, or lack the ability to expand output in response to the supply restriction, for example because they face binding capacity constraints or, more generally, face decreasing returns to scale.[27] Also, the presence of exclusive contracts between the merged entity and independent input providers may limit the ability of downstream rivals to have adequate access to inputs.

Notes

[27] For instance, in Case COMP/M.2322 – *CRH/Addtek* (2001; case withdrawn), the merger involved an upstream dominant supplier of cement and a downstream producer of pre-cast concrete products, both active in Finland. Imports of cement from the Baltic countries were capacity constrained, whereas imports from Russia at that time were deemed not be of sufficient quality to be a real alternative to the merged entity's supply of cement.

---

36. When determining the extent to which input foreclosure may occur, it must be taken into account that the decision of the merged entity to rely on its upstream division's supply of inputs may also free up capacity on the part of the remaining input suppliers from which the downstream division used to purchase before. In fact, the merger may merely realign purchase patterns among competing firms.

37. When competition in the input market is oligopolistic, a decision of the merged entity to restrict access to its inputs reduces the competitive pressure exercised on remaining input suppliers, which may allow them to raise the input price they charge to non-integrated downstream competitors. In essence, input foreclosure by the merged entity may expose its downstream rivals to independent suppliers with increased market power.[28] This increase in third-party market power will be greater the lower the degree of product differentiation between the merged entity and other upstream suppliers and the higher the degree of upstream concentration. However, the attempt to raise the input price may fail when independent input suppliers, faced with a reduction in the demand for their products (from the downstream division of the merged entity or from independent downstream firms), respond by pricing more aggressively.[29]

Notes

[28] The analysis of the likely effect of the removal of a competitive constraint is similar to the analysis of non-coordinated effects with horizontal mergers (See Section IV of the Notice on Horizontal Mergers)

[29] Also the nature of the supply contracts between upstream suppliers and the downstream independent firms may be important in this respect. For instance, when these contracts use a price system combining a fixed fee and a per-unit supply price, the effect on downstream competitors' marginal costs may be affected less than when these contracts involve only per-unit supply prices.

---

38. In its assessment, the Commission may consider, on the basis of the information available, whether there are effective and timely counter-strategies that the rival firms would be likely to deploy. Such counterstrategies include the possibility of changing their production process so as to be less reliant on the input concerned or sponsoring the entry of new suppliers upstream.

B. Incentive to foreclose access to inputs

39. The incentive to foreclose depends on the degree to which foreclosure would be profitable. The vertically integrated firm will take into account how its supplies of inputs to competitors downstream will affect not only the profits of its upstream division, but also of its downstream division. Essentially, the merged entity faces a trade-off between the profit lost in the upstream market due to a reduction of input sales to (actual or potential) rivals and the profit gain from expanding sales downstream or, as the case may be, being able to raise price in that market.

40. The trade-off is likely to depend on the level of profits the merged entity obtains upstream and downstream. Other things constant, the lower the margins upstream, the lower the loss from restricting input sales. Similarly, the higher the downstream margins, the higher the profit gain from increasing market share downstream at the expense of foreclosed rivals.[30]

41. The incentive for the integrated firm to raise rivals' costs further depends on the extent to which downstream demand is likely to be diverted away from foreclosed rivals and the share of that diverted demand that the downstream division of the integrated firm can capture.[31] This share will normally be higher the less capacity constrained the merged entity will be relative to non-foreclosed downstream rivals and the more the products of the merged entity and foreclosed competitors are close substitutes.[32]

42. The incentive to foreclose actual or potential rivals may also depend on the extent to which the downstream division of the integrated firm can be expected to benefit from higher price levels downstream as a result of a strategy to raise rivals' costs. The greater the market shares of the merged entity downstream, the greater the base of sales on which to enjoy increased margins.[33]

43. In its assessment of the likely incentives of the merged firm, the Commission may take into account various considerations such as the ownership structure of the merged entity,[34] the type of strategies adopted on the market in the past[35] or the content of internal strategic documents such as business plans.

44. In addition, when the adoption of a specific course of conduct by the merged entity is an essential step in foreclosure, the Commission examines both the incentives to adopt such conduct and the factors liable to reduce, or even eliminate, those incentives, including the possibility that the conduct is unlawful. Conduct may be unlawful *inter alia* because of competition rules or sector-specific rules at the EU or national levels. This appraisal, however, does not require an exhaustive and detailed examination of the rules of the various legal orders which might be applicable and of the enforcement policy practised within them.[36] Moreover, the illegality of a conduct may be likely to provide significant disincentives for the merged entity to engage in such conduct only in certain circumstances. In particular, the Commission will consider, on the basis of a summary analysis: (i) the likelihood that this conduct would be clearly, or highly probably, unlawful under Community law,[37] (ii) the likelihood that this illegal conduct could be detected,[38] and (iii) the penalties which could be imposed.

Notes

[36] Case C-12/03 P *Commission v Tetra Laval BV* [[2005] ECR I-987], paragraphs 74–76. Case T-210/01 *General Electric v Commission* [2005], ECR II-[5575], at paragraph 73.

[37] Case T-210/01 *General Electric v Commission* [2005] ECR II-[5575], specifically at points 74–75 and 311–312.

[38] For instance, in Case M.3696 *E.ON/MOL* (2005), points 433 and 443–446, the Commission attached importance to the fact that the national Hungarian regulator for the gas sector indicated that in a number of settings, although it has the right to control and to force market players to act without discrimination, it would not be able to obtain adequate information on the commercial behaviour of the operators. See also Case COMP/M.3440 – *EDP/ENI/GDP* (2004), point 424.

C. Overall likely impact on effective competition

45. A merger will raise competition concerns because of input foreclosure only if it would significantly impede effective competition in the downstream market.

46. First, such anticompetitive foreclosure may occur when a vertical merger allows the merging parties to increase the costs of downstream rivals in the market thereby leading to an upward pressure on their sales prices.[39] Significant harm to effective competition normally requires that the foreclosed firms play a sufficiently important role in the competitive process on the downstream market. The higher the proportion of rivals which would be foreclosed on the downstream market, the more likely the merger can be expected to result in a significant price increase in the downstream market and, therefore, to significantly impede effective competition therein. Despite a relatively small market share compared to other players, a specific firm may play a significant competitive role compared to other players,[40] for instance because it is a close competitor of the vertically integrated firm.[41]

Notes

[39] Where downstream prices are not likely to increase in the short run, foreclosed rivals may still lose significant sales to the merged entity. As a result of lower revenue streams, foreclosed rivals may be restricted in their ability to invest so as to further compete downstream, to the detriment of consumers in the future (See, for related concerns, the section on customer foreclosure)

[40] See e.g. Case COMP/M.3440 – *EDP/ENI/GDP* (2004).

[41] A vertical merger may also allow an upstream supplier to exercise its market power more effectively. For example, a downstream buyer may be willing to pay a high price from an upstream monopolist if the latter does not subsequently sell additional quantities to a competitor. But once the terms of supply are fixed with one downstream firm, the upstream supplier may have an incentive to increase its supplies to other downstream firms, thereby making the first purchase unprofitable. Since downstream firms will anticipate this kind of opportunistic behaviour, the upstream supplier will be unable to fully exploit its market power. Vertical integration may restore the upstream supplier's ability to commit not to expand input sales as this would harm its own downstream division.

47. Second, effective competition may be significantly impeded by raising barriers to entry to potential competitors. A vertical merger may foreclose potential competition on the downstream market when the merged entity would be likely not to supply potential downstream entrants, or only on less favourable terms than absent the merger. The mere likelihood that the merged entity would carry out a foreclosure strategy post-merger may also create a strong deterrent effect on potential entrants.[42] Effective competition on the downstream market may be significantly impeded by raising barriers to entry, in particular if input foreclosure would entail for such potential competitors the need to enter at both the downstream and the upstream level in order to compete effectively on either market. The concern of raising entry barriers is particularly relevant in those industries that are opening up to competition or are expected to do so in the foreseeable future.[43]

Notes

[42] See Case COMP/M.3696 – *E.ON/MOL* (2005), at point 662 et seq.

[43] See paragraph 20. It is important that regulatory measures aimed at opening a market are not rendered ineffective through the merger of vertically related incumbent with market power thereby potentially closing off the market, or eliminating each other as potential entrants.

48. If there remain sufficient credible downstream competitors whose costs are not likely to be raised, for example because they are themselves vertically integrated[44] or they are capable of switching to

adequate alternative inputs, competition from those firms may constitute a sufficient constraint on the merged entity and therefore prevent output prices from rising above pre-merger levels.

Notes
[44] See e.g. Case COMP/M.3653 – *Siemens / VA Tech* (2005), at point 164.

49. The effect on competition on the downstream market must also be assessed in light of counter-vailing factors such as the presence of buyer power [45] or the likelihood that entry upstream would maintain effective competition. [46]

Notes
[45] See Section V on countervailing buyer power in the Notice on Horizontal Mergers.
[46] See Section VI on entry in the Notice on Horizontal Mergers.

50. Further, the effect on competition needs to be assessed in light of efficiencies identified and sub-stantiated by the merging parties. [47] The Commission may decide that, as a consequence of the efficiencies that the merger brings about, there are no grounds for declaring the merger incompat-ible with the common market pursuant to Article 2(3) of the Merger Regulation. This will be the case when the Commission is in a position to conclude on the basis of sufficient evidence that the efficiencies generated by the merger are likely to enhance the ability and incentive of the merged entity to act pro-competitively for the benefit of consumers, thereby counteracting the adverse effects on competition which the merger might otherwise have.

Notes
[47] See Section VII on efficiencies in the Notice on Horizontal Mergers.

51. When assessing efficiencies in the context of non-horizontal mergers, the Commission applies the principles already set out in Section VII of the Notice on Horizontal Mergers In particular, for the Commission to take account of efficiency claims in its assessment of the merger, the efficiencies have to benefit consumers, be merger-specific and be verifiable. These conditions are cumulative. [48]

Notes
[48] See, more specifically, paragraphs 79 to 88 of the Notice on Horizontal Mergers.

52. Vertical mergers may entail some specific sources of efficiencies, the list of which is not exhaustive.
53. A vertical merger may allow the merged entity to internalise any pre-existing double mark-ups resulting from both parties setting their prices independently pre-merger. [49] Depending on the market conditions, reducing the combined mark-up (relative to a situation where pricing deci-sions at both levels are not aligned) may allow the vertically integrated firm to profitably expand output on the downstream market. [50]

Notes
[49] See also paragraph 13 above.
[50] It is important to recognise, however, that the problem of double mark-ups is not always present or significant pre-merger, for instance because the merging parties had already concluded a supply agreement with a price mechanism providing for volume discounts eliminating the mark-up. Besides, a merger may not fully eliminate the double mark-up when the supply of the input is capacity constrained and there is an important alternative use for the input. In such circumstances, the internal use of the input entails an opportunity cost for the vertically integrated company: using more of the input internally to increase output downstream means selling less in the alternative market. As a result, the incentive to use the input internally and increase output downstream is less than when there is no oppor-tunity cost.

54. A vertical merger may further allow the parties to better coordinate the production and distribu-tion process, and therefore to save on inventories costs.
55. More generally, a vertical merger may align the incentives of the parties with regard to invest-ments in new products, new production processes and in the marketing of products. For instance, whereas before the merger, the upstream entity might have been reluctant to invest in the sales

force of the downstream entity when such investment would also have benefited the sale of other upstream firms' products, the merged entity does not face such incentive problems.

56. The above mentioned efficiencies may not always be merger specific in that vertical cooperation or vertical agreements may, short of a merger, achieve similar benefits with less anti-competitive effects.

2. Foreclosing access to customers

57. Customer foreclosure may occur when a supplier integrates with an important customer in the downstream market.[51] Because of this downstream presence, the merged entity may foreclose access to a sufficient customer base to its actual or potential rivals in the upstream market (the input market) and reduce their ability or incentive to compete. In turn, this may raise downstream rivals' costs by making it harder for them to obtain supplies of the input under similar prices and conditions as absent the merger. This may allow the merged entity profitably to establish higher prices on the downstream market. Any efficiencies resulting from the merger, however, may lead the merged entity to reduce price, so that there is overall not a negative impact on consumers. A graphical presentation of this mechanism is provided in Figure 2.

Figure 2 – Customer foreclosure

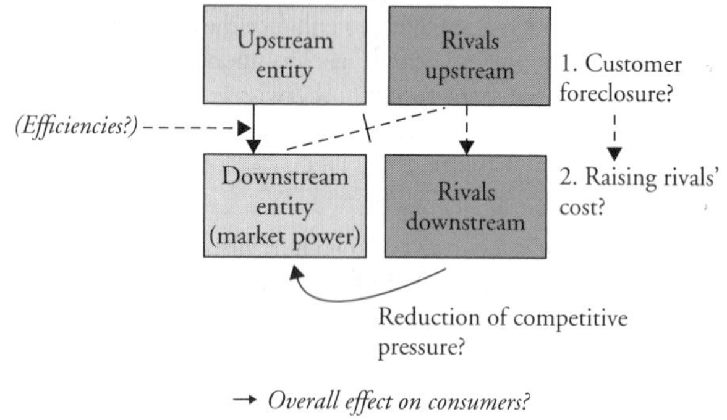

Notes
[51] See footnote 4 for the definition of "downstream" and "upstream".

---

58. In assessing the likelihood of an anticompetitive customer foreclosure scenario, the Commission examines, first, whether the merged entity would have the ability to foreclose access to downstream markets by reducing its purchases from its upstream rivals, second, whether it would have the incentive to reduce its purchases upstream, and third, whether a foreclosure strategy would have a significant detrimental effect on consumers in the downstream market.

A. Ability to foreclose access to downstream markets

59. A vertical merger may affect upstream competitors by increasing their cost to access downstream customers or by restricting access to a significant customer base. Customer foreclosure may take various forms. For instance, the merged entity may decide to source all of its internal needs from its upstream division and, as a result, may stop purchasing from its upstream competitors. It may also reduce its purchases from upstream rivals, or purchase from those rivals on less favourable terms than it would have done absent the merger.[52]

Notes
[52] For instance, in cases involving distribution, the merged entity may be less likely to grant access to its outlets under the same conditions as absent the merger.

---

60. When considering whether the merged entity would have the ability to foreclose access to downstream markets, the Commission examines whether there are sufficient economic alternatives in the downstream market for the upstream rivals (actual or potential) to sell their output.[53] For customer foreclosure to be a concern, it must be the case that the vertical merger involves an

undertaking which is an important customer in the downstream market.[54] If, on the contrary, there is a sufficiently large customer base, at present or in the future, that is likely to turn to independent suppliers, the Commission is unlikely to raise competition concerns on that ground.[55]

Notes

[53] The loss of the integrated firm as a customer is normally less significant if that firm's pre-merger purchases from non-integrated firms are a small share of the available sales base for those firms. In that case, sufficient alternative customers are more likely to be available. The presence of exclusive contracts between the merged entity and other downstream firms may limit the ability of upstream rivals to reach a sufficient sales volume.

[54] See e.g. Case COMP/M.2822 – *ENBW/ENI/GVS* (2002) at points 54–57.

[55] See e.g. Case COMP/M.81 – *VIAG / Continental Can* (1991), point 51

61. Customer foreclosure can lead to higher input prices only if there are significant economies of scale or scope in the input market.[56] It is only in such circumstances that the ability to compete of upstream rivals, be they actual or potential, can be impaired.

Notes

[56] A production process exhibits economies of scale or scope when the increased scale or scope of production leads to a reduction in unit cost. This includes, for example, also network effects.

62. In the presence of economies of scale or scope, customer foreclosure may render entry upstream by potential entrants unattractive by significantly reducing the revenue prospects of potential entrants. When customer foreclosure effectively results in entry deterrence, input prices may remain at a higher level than otherwise would have been the case, thereby raising the cost of input supply to downstream competitors of the merged firm.

63. Customer foreclosure can also lead to higher input prices when existing upstream rivals operate at or close to their minimum efficient scale. To the extent that customer foreclosure and the corresponding loss of output for the upstream rivals increases their variable costs of production, this may result in an upward pressure on the prices they charge to their customers operating in the downstream market.

64. Further, when customer foreclosure primarily impacts upon the revenue streams of upstream rivals, it may significantly reduce their ability and incentive to invest in cost reduction, R&D and product quality.[57] This may reduce their ability to compete in the long run and possibly even cause their exit from the market.

Notes

[57] An input supplier foreclosed from an important customer may prefer to stay out of the market if it fails to reach some minimum viable scale following the investment. Such minimum viable scale may be achieved, however, if a potential entrant has access to a broader customer base including customers in other relevant markets. See Case No COMP/M. 1879 – *Boeing/Hughes* (2000); Case No COMP/M.2978 – *Lagardère/Natexis/VUP* (2003).

65. In its assessment, the Commission may take into account the existence of different markets corresponding to different uses for the input. If a substantial part of the downstream market is foreclosed, an upstream supplier may fail to reach efficient scale and may also operate at higher costs in the other market(s). Conversely, an upstream supplier may continue to operate efficiently scale if it finds other uses or secondary markets for its input without incurring significantly higher costs.

66. In its assessment, the Commission may consider, on the basis of the information available, whether there are effective and timely counter-strategies, sustainable over time, that the rival firms would be likely to deploy. Such counterstrategies include the likelihood that upstream rivals decide to price more aggressively to maintain sales levels in the downstream market, so as to mitigate the effect of foreclosure.[58]

Notes

[58] For instance, in Case COMP/M.1879 – *Boeing/Hughes* (2000), point 100, it was considered, among several other factors, that in view of the high fixed costs involved, if competing satellite launch vehicle providers were to become less cost-competitive relative to the merged entity, they would try to cut prices in order to salvage volume and recoup

at least part of their fixed costs rather than accept losing a contract and incur a higher loss. The most likely impact would therefore be greater price competition rather than market monopolisation.

B. *Incentive to foreclose access to downstream markets*

67. The incentive to foreclose depends on the degree to which it is profitable. The merged entity faces a trade-off between the possible costs associated with not procuring products from upstream rivals and the possible gains from doing so, for instance, because it allows the merged entity to raise price in the upstream or downstream markets.

68. The costs associated with reducing purchases from rival upstream suppliers are higher, when the upstream division of the integrated firm is less efficient than the foreclosed suppliers. Such costs are also higher if the upstream division of the merged firm is capacity constrained or rivals' products are more attractive due to product differentiation.

69. The incentive to engage in customer foreclosure further depends on the extent to which the upstream division of the merged entity can benefit from possibly higher price levels in the upstream market arising as a result of upstream rivals being foreclosed. The incentive to engage in customer foreclosure also becomes higher, the more the downstream division of the integrated firm can be expected to enjoy the benefits of higher price levels downstream resulting from the foreclosure strategy. In this context, the greater the market shares of the merged entity's down-stream operations, the greater the base of sales on which to enjoy increased margins.[59]

Notes

[59] If the vertically integrated firm partially supplies inputs to downstream competitors it may benefit from the ability to expand sales, or as the case may be, to increase input prices.

70. When the adoption of a specific conduct by the merged entity is an essential step in foreclosure, the Commission examines both the incentives to adopt such conduct and the factors liable to reduce, or even eliminate, those incentives, including the possibility that the conduct is unlawful.[60]

Notes

[60] The analysis of these incentives will be conducted as set out in para 44 above.

C. *Overall likely impact on effective competition*

71. Foreclosing rivals in the upstream market may have an adverse impact in the downstream market and harm consumers. By denying competitive access to a significant customer base for the fore-closed rivals' (upstream) products, the merger may reduce their ability to compete in the foresee-able future. As a result, rivals downstream are likely to be put at a competitive disadvantage, for example in the form of raised input costs. In turn, this may allow the merged entity profitably to reduce the overall output on the downstream market, thus leading to price increases.

72. The negative impact on consumers may take some time to materialise when the primary impact of customer foreclosure is on the revenue streams of upstream rivals, reducing their incentives to make investments in cost reduction, product quality or in other competitive dimensions so as to remain competitive.

73. It is only when a sufficiently large fraction of upstream output is affected by the revenue decreases resulting from the vertical merger that the merger may significantly impede effective competition on the upstream market. If there remain a number of upstream competitors that are not affected, competition from those firms may be sufficient to prevent prices from rising in the upstream mar-ket and, consequently, in the downstream market. Sufficient competition from these non-fore-closed upstream firms requires that they do not face barriers to expansion e.g. through capacity constraints or product differentiation.[61] When the reduction of competition upstream affects a significant fraction of output downstream, the merger is likely, as with input foreclosure, to result in a significant increase of the price level in the downstream market and, therefore, to significantly impede effective competition.[62]

74. Effective competition on the upstream market may also be significantly impeded by raising barriers to entry to potential competitors. This may be so in particular if customer foreclosure would entail for such potential competitors the need to enter at both the downstream and the upstream level in order to compete effectively on either market. In such a context, customer foreclosure and input foreclosure may thus be part of the same strategy. The concern of raising entry barriers is particularly relevant in those industries that are opening up to competition or are expected to do so in the foreseeable future.[63]

75. The effect on competition must be assessed in light of countervailing factors such as the presence of countervailing buyer power[64] or the likelihood that entry would maintain effective competition in the upstream or downstream markets.[65]

76. Further, the effect on competition needs to be assessed in light of efficiencies identified and substantiated by the merging parties.[66]

B. Other non-coordinated effects

77. The merged entity may, by vertically integrating, gain access to commercially sensitive information regarding the upstream or downstream activities of rivals.[67] For instance, by becoming the supplier of a downstream competitor, a company may obtain critical information, which allows it to price less aggressively in the downstream market to the detriment of consumers.[68] It may also put competitors at a competitive disadvantage, thereby dissuading them to enter or expand in the market.

C. Coordinated effects

78. As set out in Section IV of the Notice on Horizontal Mergers, a merger may change the nature of competition in such a way that firms that previously were not coordinating their behaviour, are now significantly more likely to coordinate and raise prices or otherwise harm effective competition. A merger may also make coordination easier, more stable or more effective for firms which were coordinating prior to the merger.[69]

79. Market coordination may arise where competitors are able, without entering into an agreement or resorting to a concerted practice within the meaning of Article 81 of the Treaty, to identify and pursue common objectives, avoiding the normal mutual competitive pressure by a coherent system of implicit threats. In a normal competitive setting, each firm constantly has an incentive to compete. This incentive is ultimately what keeps prices low, and what prevents firms from jointly maximising their profits. Coordination involves a departure form normal competitive conditions in that firms, are able to sustain prices in excess of what independent short term profit maximisation would yield. Firms will refrain from undercutting the high prices charged by their competitors in a coordinated way because they anticipate that such behaviour would jeopardise coordination in the future. For coordinated effects to arise, the profit that firms could make by competing aggressively in the short term ("deviating") has to be less than the expected reduction in revenues that this behaviour would entail in the longer term, as it would be expected to trigger an aggressive response by competitors ("a punishment").

80. Coordination is more likely to emerge in markets where it is relatively simple to reach a common understanding on the terms of coordination. In addition, three conditions are necessary for coordination to be sustainable. First, the coordinating firms must be able to monitor to a sufficient degree whether the terms of coordination are being adhered to. Second, discipline requires that there is some form of credible deterrent mechanism that can be activated if deviation is detected. Third, the reactions of outsiders, such as current and future competitors not participating in the coordination, as well as customers, should not be able to jeopardise the results expected from the coordination.[70]

Notes

[70] See Case T-342/99, *Airtours v Commission* [2002] ECR II-2585, paragraph 62.

Reaching terms of coordination

81. A vertical merger may make it easier for the firms in the upstream or downstream market to reach a common understanding on the terms of coordination.

82. For instance, when a vertical merger leads to foreclosure,[71] it results in a reduction in the number of effective competitors in the market. Generally speaking, a reduction in the number of players makes it easier to coordinate among the remaining market players.

Notes

[71] Foreclosure would have to be shown by the Commission along the lines of Part A of this section.

83. Vertical mergers may also increase the degree of symmetry between firms active in the market.[72] This may increase the likelihood of coordination by making it easier to reach a common understanding on the terms of coordination. Likewise, vertical integration may increase the level of market transparency, making it easier to coordinate among the remaining market players.

Notes

[72] See Case COMP/M.2389 – *Shell/DEA*; Case COMP/M.2533 – *BP/EON*.

84. Further, a merger may involve the elimination of a maverick in a market. A maverick is a supplier that for its own reasons is unwilling to accept the co-ordinated outcome and thus maintains aggressive competition. The vertical integration of the maverick may alter its incentives to such an extent that co-ordination will no longer be prevented.[73]

Notes

[73] The incentive of a vertically integrated firm to participate in coordination at the upstream level may be increased when such a course of action is in line with a strategy of raising downstream rivals' cost, which, in turn, may confer market power to the merged entity's downstream division. Alternatively, coordination downstream may avoid that downstream competitors turn to other, possibly less attractive sources of supply.

Monitoring deviations

85. Vertical integration may facilitate coordination by increasing the level of market transparency between firms through access to sensitive information on rivals or by making it easier to monitor pricing. Such concerns may arise, for example, if the level of price transparency is higher downstream than upstream. This could be the case when prices to final consumers are public, while transactions at the intermediate market are confidential. Vertical integration may give upstream producers control over final prices and thus base co-ordination on those prices.

86. When it leads to foreclosure, a vertical merger may also induce a reduction in the number of effective competitors in a market. A reduction in the number of players may make it easier to monitor each other's actions in the market.

Deterrent mechanisms

87. Vertical mergers may further improve the scope for ensuring that coordinating firms find it in their best interest to adhere to the terms of coordination. For instance, a vertical integrated company may be in a position to more effectively punish rival companies when they chose to deviate from the terms of coordination, because it is either a crucial customer or supplier to them.[74]

Notes

[74] For instance, in Case COMP/M.2322 – *CRH/Addtek* (2001; case withdrawn), the merger involved an upstream dominant supplier of cement and a downstream producer or pre-cast concrete products, both active in Finland. The Commission held that the new entity would be able to discipline the downstream rivals by using the fact that they would be highly dependent on cement supplies of the merged entity. As a result, the downstream entity would be able to increase the price of its pre-cast concrete products while making sure that the competitors would follow these price increases and avoiding that they turn to cement imports from the Baltic states and Russia.

Reactions of outsiders

88. Vertical mergers may reduce the scope for outsiders to destabilise the coordination by increasing barriers to enter the market or otherwise limiting the ability to compete on the part of outsiders to the coordination.

89. A vertical merger may also involve the elimination of a disruptive buyer in a market. If upstream firms view sales to a particular buyer as sufficiently important, they may be tempted to deviate from the terms of co-ordination in an effort to secure their business. Similarly, a large buyer may be able to tempt the co-ordinating firms to deviate from these terms by concentrating a large amount of its requirements on one supplier or by offering long term contracts. The acquisition of such a buyer may increase the risk of co-ordination in a market.

V. Conglomerate Mergers

90. Conglomerate mergers are mergers between firms that are in a relationship which is neither purely horizontal (as competitors in the same relevant market) nor vertical (as supplier and customer). In practice, the focus is on mergers between companies that are active in closely related markets[75] (e.g. mergers involving suppliers of complementary products or of products which belong to a range of products that is generally purchased by the same set of customers for the same end use).

Notes

[75] See also Form CO, Section IV, 6.3 (c).

91. Whereas it is acknowledged that conglomerate mergers in the majority of circumstances will not lead to any competition problems, in certain specific cases there may be harm to competition.

A. Non-coordinated effects: foreclosure

92. The main concern in the context of conglomerate mergers is that of foreclosure. The combination of products in related markets may confer on the merged entity the ability and incentive to leverage[76] a strong market position from one market to another by means of tying or bundling or other exclusionary practices.[77] Tying and bundling as such are common practices that often have no anticompetitive consequences. Companies engage in tying and bundling in order to provide

their customers with better products or offerings in cost-effective ways. Nevertheless, in certain circumstances, these practices may lead to a reduction in actual or potential rivals' ability or incentive to compete. This may reduce the competitive pressure on the merged entity allowing it to increase prices.

Notes

[76] There is no received definition of "leveraging" but, in a neutral sense, it is being able to increase sales of a product in one market (the "tied market" or "bundled market"), by virtue of the strong market position of the product to which it is tied or bundled (the "tying market" or "leveraging market").

[77] These concepts are defined further below.

93. In assessing the likelihood of such a scenario, the Commission examines, first, whether the merged firm would have the ability to foreclose its rivals, second, whether it would have the economic incentive to do so and, third, whether a foreclosure strategy would have a significant detrimental effect on competition, thus causing harm to consumers.[78] In practice, these factors are often examined together as they are closely intertwined.

Notes

[78] See Case T-210/01 *General Electric v Commission* [2005], ECR II-[5575], para. 327, 362–363, 405; Case COMP/M.3304 – GE/Amersham (2004), point 37.

A. Ability to foreclose

94. The most immediate way in which the merged entity may be able to use its market power in one market to foreclose competitors in another is by conditioning sales in a way that links the products in the separate markets together. This is done most directly either by bundling or tying.

95. "Bundling" relates to the way products are offered and priced by the merged entity. One can distinguish in this respect between pure bundling and mixed bundling. In the case of pure bundling the products are only sold jointly. With mixed bundling the products are still available separately, but the sum of the stand-alone prices is higher than the bundled price.[79] Rebates, when made dependent on the purchase of other goods, are a form of mixed bundling.[80]

Notes

[79] The distinction between mixed bundling and pure bundling is not necessarily clear-cut. Mixed bundling may come close to pure bundling when the prices charged for the individual offerings are high.

[80] Accordingly, mixed bundling is sometimes also referred to as multi-product rebates.

96. "Tying" occurs when customers that purchase one good (the tying good) are required also to purchase another good from the producer (the tied good). Tying can take place on a technical or contractual basis. For instance, technical tying occurs when the tying product is designed in such a way that it only works with the tied product (and not with the alternatives offered by competitors). Contractual tying entails that the customer when purchasing the tying good undertakes only to purchase the tied product (and not the alternatives offered by competitors).

97. The specific characteristics of the products may be relevant for determining whether any of these means of linking sales between separate markets are available to the merged entity. For instance, pure bundling is very unlikely to be possible if products are not bought simultaneously or by the same customers.[81] Similarly, technical tying is only an option in certain industries.

Notes

[81] See, e.g., Case COMP.M.3304 – *GE/Amersham* (2004), point 35.

98. Foreclosure is unlikely to give rise to concern if the new entity, prior to it engaging in exclusionary practices, has no market power in any of the markets concerned. The effects of bundling or tying can only be expected to be substantial when at least one of the merging parties' products is viewed by many customers as particularly important and there are few relevant alternatives for that product, e.g. because of product differentiation[82] or capacity constraints on the part of rivals.

99. Further, for foreclosure to be a potential concern it must be the case that there is a large common pool of customers for the individual products concerned. The more customers tend to buy both products (instead of only one of the products), the more demand for the individual products may be affected through bundling or tying. Such a correspondence in purchasing behaviour is more likely to be significant when the products in question are complementary.

100. Generally speaking, the foreclosure effects of bundling and tying are likely to be more pronounced in industries where there are economies of scale and the demand pattern at any given point in time has dynamic implications on the conditions of supply in the market in the future. Notably, where a supplier of complementary goods has market power in one of the products (product A), the decision to bundle or tie may result in reduced sales by the non-integrated suppliers of the complementary good (product B). If further there are network externalities at play[83] this will significantly reduce these rivals' scope for expanding sales of product B in the future. Alternatively, where entry into the market for the complementary product is contemplated by potential entrants, the decision to bundle by the merged entity may have the effect of deterring such entry. The limited availability of complementary products with which to combine may, in turn, discourage potential entrants to enter market A.

101. It can also be noted that the scope for foreclosure tends to be smaller where the merging parties cannot commit to making their tying or bundling strategy a lasting one, for example through technical tying or bundling which is costly to reverse.

102. In its assessment, the Commission considers, on the basis of the information available, whether there are effective and timely counter-strategies that the rival firms may deploy. One such example is when a strategy of bundling would be defeated by single-product companies combining their offers so as to make them more attractive to customers.[84] Bundling is further less likely to lead to foreclosure if a company in the market would purchase the bundled products and profitably resell them unbundled. In addition, rivals may decide to price more aggressively to maintain market share, mitigating the effect of foreclosure.[85]

103. Customers may have a strong incentive to buy the range of products concerned from a single source (one-stop-shopping) rather than from many suppliers, e.g. because it saves on transaction costs ("portfolio effect"). However, the fact that the merged entity will have a broad range of products does not, as such, raise competition concerns.

B. Incentive to foreclose

104. The incentive to foreclose rivals through bundling or tying depends on the degree to which this strategy is profitable. The merged entity faces a trade-off between the possible costs associated with bundling or tying its products and the possible gains from expanding market shares in the market(s) concerned or, as the case may be, being able to raise price in those market(s) due to its market power.

105. Pure bundling and tying may entail losses for the merged company itself. For instance, if a significant number of customers is not interested in buying the bundle, but instead prefers to

buy only one product (e.g. the product used to leverage), sales of that product (as contained in the bundle) may significantly fall. Furthermore, losses on the leveraging product may arise where customers who, before the merger, used to "mix and match" the leveraging product of a merging party with the product of another company, decide to purchase the bundle offered by rivals or no longer to purchase at all.[86]

Notes
[86] See, e.g., Case COMP/M.3304 – *GE/Amersham* (2004), point 59.

106. In this context it may thus be relevant to assess the relative value of the different products. By way of example, it is unlikely that the merged entity would be willing to forego sales on one highly profitable market in order to gain market shares on another market where turnover is relatively small and profits are modest.

107. However, the decision to bundle and tie may also increase profits by gaining market power in the tied goods market, protecting market power in the tying goods market, or a combination of the two (See Section C. below).

108. When the adoption of a specific conduct by the merged entity is an essential step in foreclosure, the Commission examines both the incentives to adopt such conduct and the factors liable to reduce, or even eliminate, those incentives, including the possibility that the conduct is unlawful.[87]

Notes
[87] The analysis of these incentives will be conducted as set out in para 44 above.

C. Overall likely impact on prices and choice

109. Bundling or tying may result in a significant reduction of sales prospects faced by single-component rivals in the market. The reduction in sales by competitors is not in and of itself a problem. Yet, in particular industries, if this reduction is significant enough, it may lead to a reduction in rivals' ability or incentive to compete. This may allow the merged entity to subsequently acquire market power (in the market for the tied or bundled good) and/or to maintain market power (in the market for the tying or leveraging good).

110. In particular, foreclosure practices may deter entry by potential competitors.. They may do so for a specific market by reducing sales prospects for potential rivals in that market to a level below minimum viable scale. In the case of complementary products, deterring entry in one market through bundling or tying may also allow the merged entity to deter entry in another market if the bundling or tying forces potential competitors to enter both product markets at the same time rather than entering only one of them or entering them sequentially. The latter may have a significant impact in particular in those industries where the demand pattern at any given point in time has dynamic implications on the conditions of supply in the market in the future.

111. It is only when a sufficiently large fraction of market output is affected by foreclosure resulting from the merger that the merger may significantly impede effective competition. If there remain effective single-product players in either market, competition is unlikely to deteriorate following a conglomerate merger. The same holds when few single-product rivals remain, but these have the ability and incentive to expand output.

112. The effect on competition needs to be assessed in light of countervailing factors such as the presence of countervailing buyer power[88] or the likelihood that entry would maintain effective competition in the upstream or downstream markets.[89]

Notes
[88] See Section V on countervailing buyer power in the Notice on Horizontal Mergers.
[89] See, e.g., Case COMP/M.3732 – *Procter&Gamble/Gillette* (2005), point 131. See also Section VI on entry in the Notice on Horizontal Mergers.

113. Further, the effect on competition needs to be assessed in light of the efficiencies identified and substantiated by the merging parties.[90]

Notes
[90] See Section VII on efficiencies in the Notice on Horizontal Mergers.

114. Many of the efficiencies identified in the context of vertical mergers may, mutatis mutandis, also apply to conglomerate mergers involving complementary products.
115. Notably, when producers of complementary goods are pricing independently, they will not take into account the positive effect of a drop in the price of their product on the sales of the other product. Depending on the market conditions, a merged firm may internalise this effect and may have a certain incentive to lower margins if this leads to higher overall profits (this incentive is often referred to as the "Cournot effect"). In most cases, the merged firm will make the most out of this effect by means of mixed bundling, i.e. by making the price drop conditional upon whether or not the customer buys both products from the merged entity.[91]

Notes
[91] It is important to recognise however that the problem of double mark-ups is not always present or significant pre-merger. In the context of mixed bundling, it must further be noted that while the merged entity may have an incentive to reduce the price for the bundle, the effect on the prices of the individual products is less clear cut. The incentive for the merged entity to raise its single product prices may come from the fact that it counts on selling more bundled products instead. The merged entity's bundle price and prices of the individually sold products (if any) will further depend on the price reactions of rivals in the market.

116. Specific to conglomerate mergers is that they may produce cost savings in the form of economies of scope (either on the production or the consumption side), yielding an inherent advantage to supplying the goods together rather than apart.[92] For instance, it may be more efficient that certain components are marketed together as a bundle rather than separately. Value enhancements for the customer can result from better compatibility and quality assurance of complementary components. Such economies of scope however are necessary but not sufficient to provide an efficiency justification for bundling or tying. Indeed, benefits from economies of scope frequently can be realised without any need for technical or contractual bundling.

Notes
[92] See, e.g., Case COMP/M.3732 – *Procter&Gamble/Gillette* (2005), point 131.

B. Co-ordinated effects

117. Conglomerate mergers may in certain circumstances facilitate anticompetitive coordination in markets, even in the absence of an agreement or a concerted practice within the meaning of Article 81 of the Treaty. The framework set out in Section IV of the Notice on Horizontal Mergers also applies in this context. In particular, coordination is more likely to emerge in markets where it is fairly easy to identify the terms of co-ordination and where such co-ordination is sustainable.
118. One way in which a conglomerate merger may influence the likelihood of a coordinated outcome in a given market is by reducing the number of effective competitors to such an extent that tacit coordination becomes a real possibility. Also when rivals are not excluded from the market, they may find themselves in a more vulnerable situation. As a result, foreclosed rivals may choose not to contest the situation of co-ordination, but may prefer instead to live under the shelter of the increased price level.
119. Further, a conglomerate merger may increase the extent and importance of multi-market competition. Competitive interaction on several markets may increase the scope and effectiveness of disciplining mechanisms in ensuring that the terms of coordination are being adhered to.

D15

DRAFT COMMISSION NOTICE ON REMEDIES ACCEPTABLE UNDER COUNCIL REGULATION (EEC) NO 139/2004 AND UNDER COMMISSION REGULATION (EC) NO 802/2004

(2007)

(Text with EEA relevance)

Notes

This document was published for consultation on 24 April 2007, together with proposed amendments to the Merger Implementing Regulation (Commission Regulation (EC) No 802/2004 of 7 April 2004). The document is published on the Europa website at the following address:

http://ec.europa.eu/comm/competition/mergers/legislation/draft_remedies_notice.pdf

Commentary

Notice: B&C: 8.162
paras 11–12: B&C: 8.165
paras 15–17: B&C: 8.166
paras 19–20: B&C: 8.162, 8.171
paras 38–42: B&C: 8.166
paras 47–52: B&C: 8.167
paras 53–55: B&C: 8.168
paras 56–57: B&C: 8.168
paras 61–69: B&C: 8.166
paras 70–75: B&C: 8.171
paras 76–84: B&C: 8.163
paras 90–92: B&C: 8.164
paras 95–98: B&C: 8.169
paras 105–109: B&C: 8.170
paras 115–117: B&C: 8.170
paras 120–124: B&C: 8.170
paras 126–127: B&C: 8.166

I. INTRODUCTION

1. Council Regulation (EEC) No 139/2004 of 20 January 2004 on the control of concentrations between undertakings[1] (hereinafter referred to as "the Merger Regulation") in Articles 6 (2) and 8 (2) expressly provides that the Commission may decide to declare a concentration compatible with the common market following modification by the parties,[2] both before and after the initiation of proceedings. To that end, the Commission may attach to its decision conditions and obligations intended to ensure that the undertakings concerned comply with the commitments they have entered into vis-à-vis the Commission with a view to rendering the concentration compatible with the common market.[3]

Notes

[1] L 24, 29.01.2004, p. 1–22.

[2] The references to "parties" and "merging parties" also cover situations with one notifying party.

[3] Articles 6 (2) and 8 (2), second subparagraphs respectively. See also Recital 30 of the Merger Regulation which states that "where the undertakings concerned modify a notified concentration, in particular by offering commitments with a view to rendering the concentration compatible with the common market, the Commission should be able to declare

the concentration, as modified, compatible with the common market. Such commitments should be proportionate to the competition problem and entirely eliminate it". Recital 30 further explains that "it is also appropriate to accept commitments before the initiation of proceedings where the competition problem is readily identifiable and can easily be remedied".

2. The purpose of this Notice is to provide guidance on modifications to concentrations, including, in particular, commitments to modify a concentration. Such modifications are more commonly described as "remedies" since their object is to eliminate the competition concerns[4] identified by the Commission. The guidance set out in this notice reflects the Commission's evolving experience with the assessment, acceptance and implementation of remedies under the Merger Regulation since its entry into force on 21 September 1990.[5] The revision of the Commission's 2001 Notice on remedies[6] is entailed by the entry into force of the recast Merger Regulation (EC) No 139/2004[7] and of Commission Regulation (EC) No 802/2004[8] (the "Implementing Regulation") on 1 May 2004, case-law of the Court of Justice and the Court of First Instance, the conclusions drawn from the systematic *ex post* review of the Commission of past remedies case,[9] and decisional practice of the Commission in cases involving remedies in recent years. The principles contained herein will be applied and further developed and refined by the Commission in individual cases. The guidance provided in this Notice is without prejudice to the interpretation which may be given by the Court of Justice or by the Court of First Instance of the European Communities.

Notes

[4] Save where the contrary is indicated, in the following, the term "competition concerns" corresponds, according to the stage of the procedure, to serious doubts or preliminary findings that the concentration is likely to significantly impede effective competition in the common market or in a substantial part of it, in particular as a result of the creation or strengthening of a dominant position.

[5] *Ex post* review under the Merger Remedies Study and experience acquired since the publication of the last Notice on remedies.

[6] Commission Notice on remedies acceptable under Council Regulation (EEC) No 4064/89 and under Commission Regulation (EC) No 47/98, OJ C 68, 02.03.2001, p. 3.

[7] Replacing Council Regulation (EEC) No 4064/89 (OJ L 395, 30.12.19989, corrected version in OJ L257, 21.9.1990, p.13, Regulation last amended by Regulation (EC) No 1310/97, OJ L 180, 9.7.1997, p.1, corrigendum in OJ L 40, 13.2.1998, p.17).

[8] Commission Regulation (EC) No 802/2004 implementing Council Regulation (EC) No 139/2004 on the control of concentrations between undertakings, OJ L 133, 30.0.2004, p. 1. This regulation replaces Commission Regulation (EC) No 447/98 implementing Council Regulation (EEC) No 4064/89 on the control of concentrations between undertakings, OJ L 61, 2.3.1998, p. 1.

[9] DG COMP, Merger Remedies Study, October 2005.

3. This Notice sets out the general principles applicable to remedies acceptable to the Commission, the main types of commitments that may be accepted by the Commission in cases under the Merger Regulation, the specific requirements which proposals of commitments need to fulfil in both phases of the procedure, and the main requirements for the implementation of commitments.

II. General Principles

4. Under the Merger Regulation, the Commission assesses the compatibility of a notified concentration with the common market on the basis of its effect on the structure of competition in the Community.[10] The test for compatibility under Article 2(2) and (3) of the Merger Regulation is whether or not a concentration would significantly impede effective competition in the common market or a substantial part of it, in particular as a result of the creation or strengthening of a dominant position. A concentration that significantly impedes effective competition as described above is incompatible with the common market and the Commission is required to prohibit it. For the creation of a joint venture, the Commission will also examine the concentration under Article 2(4) of the Merger Regulation. The principles set out in this Notice will generally also apply to remedies submitted to eliminate competition concerns identified under Article 2(4).

Notes

[10] Recital 6 of the Merger Regulation.

5. Where a concentration raises competition concerns in that it could significantly impede effective competition, in particular the creation or strengthening of a dominant position, the parties may seek to modify the concentration in order to resolve the competition concerns and thereby gain clearance of their merger. Such modifications may be fully implemented in advance of a clearance decision. However, it is more common that the parties submit commitments with a view to rendering the concentration compatible with the common market and that those commitments are implemented following clearance.

Allocation of responsibilities

6. Under the structure of the Merger Regulation, it is the responsibility of the Commission to show that a concentration would significantly impede competition. The Commission communicates its competition concerns to the parties to allow them to formulate appropriate and corresponding remedies proposals.[11] It is then for the parties of a concentration to put forward commitments; the Commission is not in a position to impose unilaterally any conditions to an authorisation decision, but only on the basis of the parties' commitments.[12] Even if the parties choose to address the competition concerns by proposing commitments which go further than what is necessary to maintain the competitive situation existing before the concentration, the Commission does not have any discretion to refuse them and to impose unilaterally other conditions to the authorisation decision.[13] If, however, the parties do not validly propose remedies adequate to eliminate the competition concerns, the only possibility will be to adopt a prohibition.[14]

Notes

[11] The Merger Regulation provides for formal steps where the parties are informed of the competition concerns identified by the Commission (6 (1) c decision, Statement of Objections). In addition, the DG COMPETITION Best Practices on the conduct of EC merger control proceedings foresee that "state of play" meetings will normally be offered at key stages of the procedure where the Commission services will explain their concerns to the parties in order to allow them to respond with remedies proposals.

[12] Judgment of the CFI in Case T-210/01 *General Electric v Commission* [2005] ECR II-[5575], paragraph 52; see judgment of the CFI in Case T-87/05 *EDP v Commission* [2005] ECR II-[3745], paragraph 105.

[13] As to the treatment of commitment proposals unnecessary to eliminate the competition concern see below paragraph 83.

[14] See Case COMP/M.2220 – *GE/Honeywell* of 3 July 2001, confirmed by judgment of the CFI in Case T-210/01 *General Electric v Commission* [2005] ECR II-[5575], paragraph 555 et seq., 612 et seq.; Case COMP/M.3440 – *EDP/ENI/GDP* of 9 December 2004, confirmed by judgment of the CFI in Case T-87/05 *EDP v Commission* [2005] ECR II-[3745], paragraphs 63 et seq., 75 et seq.; Case IV/M.469 – *MSG Media Service* of 9 November 1994; Case IV/M. 490 – *Nordic Satellite Distribution* of 19 July 1995; Case IV/M.553 – *RTL/Veronica/Endemol* of 20 September 1995; Case IV/M.993 – *Bertelsmann/Kirch/Premiere* of 27 May 1998; Case IV/M.1027 – *Deutsche Telekom BetaResearch* of 27 May 1998; Case IV/M.774 – *St Gobain/Wacker Chemie* of 4 December 1996; Case IV/M.53 – *Aerospatiale/Alenia/De Havilland* of 2 October 1991; Case IV/M.619 – *Gencor/Lonrho* of 24 April 1996, confirmed by judgment of the CFI in Case T-102/96 *Gencor v Commission* [1999] ECR II-753.

7. The Commission has to assess whether the proposed remedies, once implemented, eliminate the competition concerns identified. It is only the parties that have all the relevant information necessary for such an assessment, in particular as to the feasibility of the commitments proposed and the viability and competitiveness of the assets proposed to divest. It is therefore the responsibility of the parties to provide all such information available that is necessary for the Commission's assessment of the remedies proposal. To this end, the Implementing Regulation obliges the notifying parties, together with the commitments, to provide detailed information on the content of the commitments offered, the conditions for their implementation and showing their suitability to remove any significant impediment of effective competition, as set out in the annex to the Implementing Regulation ("Form RM"). Specifically for commitments consisting in the divestiture of a business, parties have to describe in detail in particular how the business to be divested is currently operated. This information will enable the Commission to assess the viability, competitiveness and marketability of the business by comparing its current operation to its proposed scope under the commitments. The Commission can adapt the precise requirements to the information necessary in the individual case at hand on the basis of waivers.

8. Whereas the parties have to propose commitments sufficient to remove the competition concerns and submit the necessary information to assess them, it is for the Commission to establish whether or not a concentration, as modified by commitments validly submitted, must be declared incompatible with the common market because it leads, despite the commitments, to a significant impediment of effective competition. The burden of proof for a prohibition or authorisation of a concentration modified by commitments is therefore subject to the same criteria as an unmodified concentration.[15]

Notes
[15] See judgment of the CFI in Case T-87/05 *EDP v Commission* [2005] ECR II- [3745], paragraphs 62 ff.

Basic conditions to accept remedies

9. Under the Merger Regulation, the Commission has power to accept only such commitments that are deemed capable of rendering the concentration compatible with the common market so that they will prevent a significant impediment of effective competition. The commitments have to eliminate the competition concerns entirely[16] and have to be comprehensive and effective from all points of view.[17] Furthermore, commitments must be capable of being implemented effectively within a short period of time as the conditions of competition on the market will not be maintained until the commitments have been fulfilled.

Notes
[16] See recital 30 of the Merger Regulation and judgment of the CFI in Case T-282/02 Cementbouw v Commission [2006] ECR II-[319], paragraph 307.
[17] CFI, Case 210/01 *General Electrics v Commission* [2005] ECR II-[5575], paragraph 52; Case T-87/05 *EDP v Commission* [2005] ECR II-[3749], paragraph 105.

10. Structural commitments, in particular divestitures, proposed by the parties will meet that condition only in so far as the Commission is able to conclude with the requisite degree of certainty that it will be possible to implement them and that it will be likely that the new commercial structures resulting from them will be sufficiently workable and lasting to ensure that the significant impediment to effective competition will not materialise.[18]

Notes
[18] CFI, Case T-210/01 *General Electric v Commission* [2005] ECR II-[5575], paragraphs 555, 612.

11. The requisite degree of certainty concerning the implementation of the proposed commitments may in particular be affected by risks in relation to the transfer of a business to be divested, such as conditions attached by the parties to the divestiture, third party rights in relation to the business or the risks of finding a suitable purchaser, as well as risks in relation to the degradation of the assets until the divestiture has taken place. It is incumbent on the parties to remove such uncertainties as to the implementation of the remedy when submitting it to the Commission.[19]

Notes
[19] Depending on the nature of the risks, specific safeguards may aim at compensating for them. For example, the risk arising from third party rights in relation to the assets to be divested may be compensated by the proposal of an alternative divestiture. Such safeguards will be discussed in more detail below.

12. In assessing the second condition, whether the proposed commitment are sufficiently workable and lasting to ensure that the commitments will likely eliminate the competition concerns identified, the Commission will consider all relevant factors relating to the proposed remedy itself, including, *inter alia,* the type, scale and scope of the remedy proposed, judged by reference to the structure and particular characteristics of the market in which the competition concerns arise, including the position of the parties and other players on the market.

13. In order for the commitments to comply with these principles, there has to be an effective implementation and ability to monitor the commitments.[20] Whereas divestitures, once implemented, do not require any further monitoring measures, other types of commitments require effective

monitoring mechanisms in order to ensure that their effect is not reduced or even eliminated by the parties. Otherwise, such commitments would have to be considered as mere declarations of intentions by the parties and would not amount to binding obligations, as, due to the lack of effective monitoring mechanisms, any breach of them could not result in the revocation of the decision according to the provisions of the Merger Regulation.[21]

Notes

[20] CFI, Case T-177/04 *easyJet v Commission* [2006] ECR II-[1931], paragraph 188.

[21] CFI, Case T-177/04 *easyJet v Commission* [2006] ECR II-[1931], paragraph 186 et seq.; CFI, judgment in Case T-87/05 *EDP v Commission* [2005] ECR II-[3745], paragraph 72.

Commentary

para 13: B&C: 8.165

14. Where, however, the parties submit remedies proposals that are so extensive and complex that it is not possible for the Commission to determine, at the time of the Commission decision, with the requisite degree of certainty that they will be fully implemented and that they are likely to maintain effective competition in the market, an authorisation decision cannot be granted.[22] The Commission may reject those remedies in particular on the grounds that the implementation of the remedies cannot be monitored and that the lack of effective monitoring reduces, or even eliminates, the effect of the commitments proposed.

Notes

[22] See, as an example for such a complex and inappropriate remedy, Case COMP/M.3440 – *ENI/EDP/GDP* of 9 December 2004; confirmed by CFI, judgment in Case T-87/05 *EDP v Commission* of 21 September 2005, [2005] ECR-II-[3745], paragraph 102; Case COMP/ M.1672 - *Volvo/Scania* of 15 March 2000.

Appropriateness of different types of remedies

15. According to the case law of the Court, the basic aim of commitments is to ensure competitive market structures.[23] Accordingly, commitments which are structural in nature, such as the commitment to sell a business unit, are, as a rule, preferable from the point of view of the Regulation's objective, inasmuch as such commitments prevent, durably, the competition problem which the Commission considers would be caused by the merger as notified, and do not, moreover, require medium or long-term monitoring measures. Nevertheless, the possibility cannot automatically be ruled out that other types of commitments may also be capable of preventing the significant impediment of effective competition.[24]

Notes

[23] See recital 8 of the Merger Regulation; judgment of CFI in Case T-102/96 *Gencor v Commission* [1999] ECR II-753, at paragraph 316; ECJ in Case C-12/03 P *Commission v Tetra Laval* [2005] ECR I-987, paragraph 86; judgment of CFI in Case T-158/00 *ARD v Commission* [2003] ECR II-3825, at paragraphs 192 et seq.

[24] ECJ, judgment in Case C-12/03 P *Commission v Tetra Laval* [2005] ECR I-987, paragraph 86; CFI, judgment of 25 March 1999 in Case T-102/96 *Gencor v Commission* [1999] ECR II-753, paragraphs 319 et seq.; CFI; judgment of 30 September 2003 in Case T-158/00 *ARD v Commission* [2003] ECR II-3825, paragraph 193; CFI in Case T-177/04 *easyJet v Commission* [2006] ECR II-[1931], paragraph 182; CFI, judgment in Case T- 87/05 *EDP v Commission* [2005] ECR II-[3745], paragraph 101.

16. Whether a remedy and, more specifically, which type of remedy is suitable to eliminate the competition problems identified, has to be examined on a case-by-case basis.

17. Nevertheless, a general distinction can be made between divestitures, other structural remedies, such as granting access to key infrastructure or inputs on non-discriminatory terms, and commitments relating to the future behaviour of the merged entity. Divestiture commitments are the best way to eliminate competition problems resulting from horizontal overlaps, and may also be the best means of resolving problems resulting from vertical or conglomerate concerns.[25] Other structural commitments may be suitable to resolve all types of concerns if those remedies

are equivalent to divestitures in their effects, as explained in more detail below in paragraphs 61 et seq. Commitments relating to the future behaviour of the merged entity may be acceptable only exceptionally in very specific circumstances.[26] In particular, for competition problems resulting from horizontal overlaps, such commitments in the form of undertakings not to raise prices, to reduce product ranges or to remove brands, etc., will generally not eliminate the competition concerns. In any case, those types of remedies can only exceptionally be accepted if their workability is fully ensured by effective implementation and monitoring in line with the considerations set out in paragraphs 13–14, 66, 69, and if they do not risk leading to distorting effects on competition.[27]

Notes

[25] See divestiture of storage facilities in Case COMP/M.3868 – *DONG/Elsam/Energi* E2 of 14 March 2006, paragraphs 170 et seq.; Case COMP/M.3696 – *E.ON/MOL* of 21 December 2005, paragraphs 735 et seq., for an example of "ownership unbundling" to eliminate structural links between the parties in the gas storage sector; further Case COMP./M.4314 – *Johnson & Johnson/Pfizer* of 11 December 2006, Case COMP/M.4494 *Evraz/Highveld* of 20 February 2007.

[26] See, in relation to conglomerate effects of a concentration, ECJ, judgment of 15 February 2005 in Case C 12/03 P *Commission v Tetra Laval* [2005] ECR I-987, paragraphs 85, 89.

[27] For example, commitments regarding a certain pricing behaviour such as price caps which contain the risk to lead to an anticompetitive alignment of prices among competitors.

Procedure

18. The Commission may accept commitments in either phase of the procedure.[28] However, given the fact that an in-depth market investigation is only carried out in phase II, commitments submitted to the Commission in phase I must be sufficient to clearly rule out "serious doubts" within the meaning of Article 6(1)(c) of the Merger Regulation.[29] Pursuant to Article 10(2) of the Merger Regulation, the Commission has to take a clearance decision as soon as the serious doubts established in the decision pursuant to Article 6(1)(c) of the Merger Regulation are removed as a result of commitments submitted by the parties. This rule applies in particular to commitments proposed at an early stage of phase II-proceedings.[30] After an in-depth investigation and where the Commission in a Statement of Objections has reached the preliminary view that the merger leads to a significant impediment to effective competition the commitments have to eliminate such significant impediments to effective competition.

Notes

[28] As foreseen in recital 30 of the Merger Regulation, the Commission will ensure transparency and effective consultation of Member States in both phases of the procedure.

[29] Commitments in phase I can only be accepted in certain types of situations; see below in paragraph 80.

[30] See, *inter alia*, Case COMP/M.2972 – *DSM/Roche Vitamins* of 23 July 2003; Case COMP/M.2861 *Siemens/Drägerwerk/JV* of 30 April 2003; Case IV/JV.15 – *BT/AT & T* of 30 March 1999; Case IV/M.1532 – *BP Amoco/Arco* of 29 September 1999.

Commentary
para 18: B&C: 8.163

19. Whilst commitments have to be offered by the parties, the Commission will ensure the enforceability of commitments by making the authorisation of the merger subject to compliance with the commitments. A distinction must be made between conditions and obligations. The requirement for achievement of each measure that gives rise to the structural change of the market is a condition - for example, that a business is to be divested. The implementing steps which are necessary to achieve this result are generally obligations on the parties, e.g. such as the appointment of a trustee with an irrevocable mandate to sell the business.

20. Where the undertakings concerned commit a breach of an obligation, the Commission may revoke clearance decisions issued either under Article 6(2) or Article 8(2) of the Merger Regulation, acting pursuant to Article 6(3) or Article 8(6), respectively. In case of a breach of an obligation, the parties may also be subject to fines and periodic penalty payments as provided in Article 14(2)(d) and 15(1)(c) respectively of the Merger Regulation. Where, however, a condition is breached, *e.g.* a business is not divested in the time-frame foreseen in the commitments or

afterwards re-acquired, the compatibility decision is no longer applicable. In such circumstances, the Commission may, first, take interim measures appropriate to maintain conditions of effective competition pursuant to Article 8(5)(b) of the Merger Regulation. Second, it may, if the conditions of Article 8(4)(b) are met, order any appropriate measure to ensure that the undertakings concerned dissolve the concentration or take other restorative measures or, according to Article 8(7), take a decision pursuant to Article 8 (1)–(3). In addition, the parties may also be subject to fines as provided in Article 14(2)(d).

Model Texts for divestiture commitments

21. The Commission services have issued Best Practice Guidelines for divestiture commitments, consisting of a Model Text for Divestiture Commitments and a Model Text for Trustee Mandates.[31] These model texts are neither intended to provide an exhaustive coverage of all issues that may become relevant in all cases, nor are they legally binding upon parties in a merger procedure. They complement the present Notice as they set out the standard requirements for divestiture commitments in a format which can be used by the parties. At the same time, the model texts leave the flexibility to adapt them to the requirements of the specific case. Those model texts for divestiture commitments may be continuously up-dated and, if there should be a need, further best practice guidelines in the field of remedies may be issued.

Notes
[31] See Web-site of DG COMP, released in May 2003.

III. Different Types of Remedies

1. Divestiture of a Business to a Suitable Purchaser

22. Where a proposed concentration threatens to significantly impede effective competition the most effective way to maintain effective competition, apart from prohibition, is to create the conditions for the emergence of a new competitive entity or for the strengthening of existing competitors via divestiture by the merging parties.

1.1 Divestiture of a viable and competitive business

23. The divested activities must consist of a viable business that, if operated by a suitable purchaser, can compete effectively with the merged entity on a lasting basis and that is divested as a going concern.[32] For the business to be viable, it may also be necessary to include activities which are related to markets where the Commission did not identify competition concerns if this is required to create an effective competitor in the affected markets.[33]

Notes
[32] This includes, under certain conditions, businesses that have to be carved out from a party's business or individual assets; see below paragraphs 35 ff.
[33] Case IV/M.913 – *Siemens/Elektrowatt* of 18 November 1997; Case IV/M.1578 – *Sanitec/Sphinx* of 1 December 1999, at paragraph 255; Case COMP/M.1802 – *Unilever/Amora-Maille* of 8 March 2000; Case COMP/M.1990 – *Unilever/Bestfoods* of 28 September 2000.

24. In proposing a viable business for divestiture, it is necessary to take into account the uncertainties and risks related to the transfer of a business to a new owner. These risks may limit the competitive impact of the divested business, and, therefore, may lead to a market situation where the competition concerns at stake will not necessarily be eliminated.

Scope of the business to be divested

25. The business has to include all the assets which contribute to its current operation or which are necessary to ensure its viability and competitiveness and all personnel which is currently employed or which is necessary to ensure the business' viability and competitiveness.[34]

26. Also personnel and assets which are currently shared between the business to be divested and other businesses of the parties, but which contribute to the operation of the business or are necessary to ensure its viability and competitiveness, have to be included. Otherwise, the viability and competitiveness of the business to be divested would be endangered. Therefore, the divested business has to contain the personnel providing essential functions for the business such as, for instance, group R & D and information technology staff even where such personnel is currently employed by another business unit of the parties - at least in a sufficient proportion to meet the ongoing needs of the divested business. In the same way shared assets have to be included even if those assets are owned by or allocated to another business unit.

27. In order for the Commission to be able to identify the scope of the business to be divested, the parties have to include a precise definition of the scope of the divested business in the commitments (the "description of the business"). The description of the business has to be adapted to the individual case at hand and should contain all the elements that are part of the business to be divested: tangible (*e.g.*, R & D, production, marketing, distribution, sales and marketing activities) and intangible assets (such as intellectual property rights, know-how and goodwill); licences, permits and authorisations by governmental organisations granted to the business; contracts, leases and commitments (*e.g.*, arrangements with suppliers and customers) for the benefit of the business to be divested; and customer, credit and other records. In the description of the business, the parties have to include the personnel to be transferred in general terms, including staff seconded and temporary employees, and to insert a list of the key personnel, *i.e.* the personnel essential for the viability and competitiveness of the business. The transfer of those employees is without prejudice to the application of the Council Directives on collective redundancies;[35] on safeguarding employees' rights in the event of transfers of undertakings;[36] and on informing and consulting employees[37] as well as national provisions implementing those Directives and other national laws. The remedy has to include a non-solicitation commitment by the parties with regard to the key personnel.

28. In the description of the business, the parties also have to set out the arrangements for the supply of products and services by them to the divested business or by the divested business to them. Such on-going relationships of the divested business may be necessary to maintain the full economic viability and competitiveness of the divested business for a transitional basis. The Commission will only accept such arrangements if they do not affect the independence of the divested business from the parties.

29. In order to avoid any misunderstanding about the business to be divested, assets or personnel that are used within or employed by the business but that should not, according to the parties, be transferred with the divestiture, have to be expressly excluded by the parties in the commitments text. The Commission will only be able to accept such exclusion of assets or personnel if the parties can clearly show that this does not affect the viability and competitiveness of the business.

Part D Mergers and Concentrations

30. The business to be divested has to be viable as such. Therefore, the resources of a possible or even presumed future purchaser are not taken into account by the Commission at the stage of assessing the remedy. The situation is different if already during the procedure a sale and purchase agreement with a specific purchaser is concluded whose resources can be taken into account at the time of the assessment of the commitment. This situation will be dealt with in more detail below in paragraphs 56 ff.

31. Once a purchaser is identified after adoption of an authorisation decision, some of the assets or personnel included in the divested business may not be needed by the proposed purchaser. In the purchaser approval process, the Commission may, upon request by the parties, approve the divestiture of the business to the proposed purchaser without one or more assets or parts of the personnel if this does not affect the viability and competitiveness of the business to be divested after the sale, taking account of the own resources of the proposed purchaser.

1.2 Stand-alone business and conditions for acceptability of alternatives

32. Normally, a viable business is a business that can operate on a stand-alone-basis, which means independently of the merging parties as regards the supply of input materials or other forms of cooperation other than during a transitory period.

33. The Commission has a clear preference for an existing stand-alone business. This may take the form of a pre-existing company or group of companies, or of a business division which was not previously legally incorporated as such.

34. Where the competition problem results from a horizontal overlap, the parties may be able to choose between two businesses. In cases of a hostile bid, it may be more appropriate for the parties to propose to divest activities of the acquiring company. A commitment to divest activities of the target company may, in such circumstances of limited information available to the notifying parties about the business to be divested, increase the risk that this business might not, after a divestiture, result in a viable competitor which could effectively compete in the market on a lasting basis.

Carve-outs

35. Even though normally the divestiture of an existing viable stand-alone business is required, the Commission, taking into account the principle of proportionality, may also consider the divestiture of businesses which have existing strong links or are partially integrated with businesses retained by the parties and therefore need to be "carved out" in those respects. In order to reduce the risks for the viability and competitiveness to a minimum in such circumstances, an option for the parties is to submit commitments proposing to carve out those parts of an existing business which do not necessarily have to be divested. In effect, an existing, stand-alone business is being divested in those circumstances although, by way of a "reverse carve-out", the parties may carve-out the limited parts which they may keep.

36. In any case, the Commission will only be able to accept commitments which require the carve-out of a business if it can be certain that, at least at the time when the business is transferred to the purchaser, a viable business on a stand-alone basis will be divested and the risks for the viability and competitiveness caused by the carve-out will thereby be reduced to a minimum. The parties therefore have to ensure, as set out in detail below in paragraph 111, that the carve-out is started in the interim period, *i.e.* the period between the adoption of the Commission decision up to the completion of the divestiture (meaning the legal and factual transfer of the business to the purchaser). Consequently, at the end of this period, a viable business on a stand-alone basis will be divested. If this should not be possible or if the carve-out should be particularly difficult, parties may provide the requisite degree of certainty for the Commission by proposing an up-front buyer solution, as further detailed below in paragraph 55.

Divestiture of assets, in particular of brands and licences

37. A divestiture consisting of a combination of certain assets which did not form a uniform and viable business in the past creates risks as to the viability and competitiveness of the resulting business. This is in particular the case if assets from more than one party are involved. Such an approach may be accepted by the Commission only if the viability of the business is ensured

notwithstanding the fact that the assets did not form a uniform business in the past. This may be the case if already the individual assets can be considered a viable and competitive business.[38] Similarly, only in exceptional cases a divestiture package including only brands and supporting production and/or distribution assets may be sufficient to create the conditions for effective competition.[39] In such circumstances, the package consisting of brands and assets must be sufficient to allow the Commission to conclude that the resulting business will be immediately viable in the hands of a suitable purchaser.

Notes

[38] Case COMP/M.1806 – *AstraZeneca/Novartis* of 26 July 2000; COMP/M.1628 – *TotalFina/Elf* of 9 February 2000; Case IV/ M.603 – *Crown Cork & Seal/ CarnaudMetalbox* of 14 November 1995.
[39] Case COMP/M.2544 – *Masterfoods/Royal Canin* of 15 February 2002; Case COMP/M.2337 – *Nestle/Ralston Purina* of 27 July 2001; Case IV/ M.623 – *Kimberly-Clark/ Scott* Paper of 16 January 1996; Case COMP/M.3779 – *Pernod Ricard/Allied Domecq* of 24 June 2005.

38. The granting of licences to IP rights instead of a divestiture may be acceptable to the Commission only if a divestiture of a business is not possible and the granting of a licence is as effective as a divestiture. Where the competition problem is caused by the market position held for such a technology or such IP rights, a divestiture of the technology or the IP rights is the preferable remedy as it eliminates a lasting relationship between the merged entity and its competitors.[40] However, the Commission may accept licensing arrangements as an alternative to divestiture where, for instance, a divestiture would impede efficient, on-going research or where a divestiture would be impossible due to the nature of the business.[41] Such licences will normally be exclusive licences and have to be without any field-of-use and any geographical restrictions on the licensee. Where there might be any uncertainty as regards the scope of the licence or its terms and conditions, the parties will have to divest the underlying IP right, but may obtain a licence back. If there is uncertainty that the license will actually be granted to a suitable licensee, the parties may consider to propose an up-front licensee or a fix-it-first solution according to the considerations set out below in paragraphs 56, in order to enable the Commission to conclude with the requisite degree of certainty that the remedy will be implemented.[42]

Notes

[40] See Case COMP/M.2972 – *DSM/Roche Vitamins* of 23 July 2003; Case IV/ M.1378 – *Hoechst/Rhône- Poulenc* of 9 August 1999; Case COMP/ M.1601 – *Allied Signal/ Honeywell* of 1 December 1999; Case COMP/ M.1671 – *Dow/ UCC* of 3 May 2000.
[41] Case COMP/M.2949 – *Finmeccanica/Alenia Telespazio* of 30 October 2002; Case M. 3593 – *Apollo/Bakelite* of 11 April 2005, commitment on carbon bond refractory licence; for cases from the pharmaceutical industry see Case COMP/M.2972 – *DSM/Roche Vitamins* of 23 July 2003; Case IV/M.555 – *Glaxo/Wellcome* of 28 February 1995.
[42] Case COMP/M.2972 – *DSM/Roche Vitamins* of 23 July 2003.

Re-branding

39. In exceptional cases, the Commission has accepted commitments to grant an exclusive, time-limited license for a brand with the purpose to allow the licensee to re-brand the product in the period foreseen. After the first licence phase of these so-called re-branding commitments, the parties commit in a second phase to abstain from any use of the brand (blackout phase). The goal of such commitments is to allow the licensee to transfer the customers from the licensed brand to its own brand in order to create a viable competitor, without the licensed brand being permanently divested.

40. A re-branding remedy carries substantially higher risks for restoring effective competition than a divestiture, including the divestiture of a brand as there is considerable uncertainty whether the licensee will succeed in establishing itself as an active competitor in the market on the basis of the re-branded product. A re-branding remedy may be acceptable in circumstances where the brand at stake is widely used and a high proportion of its turnover is generated in markets outside those in which competition problems have been identified.[43] In those circumstances, a re-branding remedy has to be defined in such a way as to ensure that the granting of the license will effectively

maintain competition in the market on a lasting basis and that the licensee will be an effective competitor after re-branding the products.

Notes

[43] However, even in these conditions a divestiture of the brand may be more appropriate, especially if the resulting split in the ownership of the brand corresponds to common practice in the industry, see for the pharmaceutical industry Case COMP/M.3544 – *Bayer Healthcare/Roche* (OTC) of 19 November 2004, paragraph 59 concerning the divestiture of the Desenex brand.

41. As the success of re-branding commitments is substantially linked to the viability of the licensed brand a number of preconditions have to be met for the design of such commitments. Firstly, the brand to be transferred must be well-known and one of considerable strength to guarantee both immediate viability of the licensed brand and its economic survival in the re-branding period. Secondly, part of the assets related to the production or the distribution of the products marketed under the licensed brand or the transfer of know-how may be necessary to ensure the viability of the remedy.[44] Thirdly, the licence has to be exclusive and normally comprehensive, *i.e.* not limited to a certain range of products within a specific market, and has to include the intellectual property rights to ensure that customers will acknowledge the familiarity of the re-branded product. The parties will not be allowed to use similar words or signs as this could undermine the effect of the re-branding exercise.[45] Fourthly, both the licence and the black-out period have to be sufficiently long, account taken of the particularities of the case, so that the re-branding remedy is in its effects similar to a divestiture.[46]

Notes

[44] COMP/M.3149 *Procter&Gamble/Wella* paragraph 60; IV/M.623 – *Kimberly-Clark/Scott Paper* of 16 January 1996, paragraph 236 (i). This is particularly important during the licence phase in which the licensee has to prepare for the launch of a new competitive brand. Such a launch of a new brand appears to not be feasible if the purchaser had to spend considerable resources on the production process, marketing and distribution of the licensed brand; COMP/M.2337 – *Nestlé/Ralston Purina* of 27 July 2001, paragraphs 67 et seq.; COMP/M.2621 – *SEB/Moulinex* of 8 January 2002, paragraph 140.
[45] COMP/M.3149 – *Procter&Gamble/Wella* of 30 July 2003, paragraph 61; COMP/M.2337 – *Nestlé/Ralstone Purina* of 27 July 2001, paragraph 68; COMP/M.2621 – *SEB/Moulinex* of 8 January 2002, paragraph 141; IV/M.623 – *Kimberly-Clark/Scott Paper* of 16 January 1996, paragraph 236 (ii).
[46] For example taking into account the life cycle of products, c.f. COMP/M.2621 – *SEB/Moulinex* of 8 January 2002, paragraph 141, where effectively the duration of the commitments covered a period equal to about three product life cycles; confirmed by judgment of CFI in Case T-119/02 *Royal Philips Electronics v Commission* [2003] ECR II-1433, paragraphs 112 et seq.

42. The identity of the potential licensee will be a key factor for the success of the commitment. If there is uncertainty that a number of suitable licensees are available, being able and having strong incentives to carry out the re-branding exercise, the parties may consider to propose a fix-it-first solution, in line with the considerations set out below in paragraph 56.

1.3 Non-reacquisition clause

43. In order to maintain the structural effect of a remedy, the commitments have to foresee that the merged entity cannot subsequently acquire influence[47] over the whole or parts of the divested business, unless the Commission subsequently finds that the structure of the market has changed to such an extent that the absence of influence over the divested business is no longer necessary to render the concentration compatible with the common market. The commitments will normally have to foresee that no reacquisition of influence is possible for a period of 10 years. Even in the absence of an explicit clause, a re-acquisition of the business would violate an implicit obligation on the parties under the commitments as this would affect the effectiveness of the remedies.

Notes

[47] Such influence does not have to amount to control in the sense of Art. 3 of the Merger Regulation.

1.4 Alternative divestiture commitments: Crown Jewels

44. In certain cases, the implementation of the parties' preferred divestiture option (of a viable business solving the competition concerns) might be uncertain in view of third parties' pre-emption rights or uncertainty as to the transferability of key contracts, intellectual property rights, or the uncertainty to find a suitable purchaser. Nevertheless, the parties may consider that they would be able to divest this business to a suitable purchaser within a very short time period.

45. In such circumstances, the Commission cannot take the risk that, in the end, effective competition will not be maintained. Accordingly, the Commission will only accept such divestiture commitments under the following conditions: (a) absent the uncertainty, the first divestiture proposed in the commitments would consist of a viable business, and (b) the parties will have to propose a second alternative divestiture which the parties will be obliged to implement if they are not able to implement the first commitment.[48] Such an alternative commitment normally has to be a "crown jewel",[49] *i.e.* it should be as least as good as the first proposed divestiture in terms of creating a viable competitor once implemented, it should not involve any uncertainties as to its implementation and it should be capable of being implemented quickly in order to avoid that the overall implementation period exceeds what would normally be regarded as acceptable in the conditions of the market in question. In order to limit the risks in the interim period, it is indispensable that interim preservation and holding separate measures apply to all assets included in both divestiture alternatives. Furthermore, the commitment has to establish clear criteria and a strict timetable as to how and when the alternative divestiture obligation will become effective and the Commission will require shorter periods for its implementation.

Notes

[48] See judgment of the CFI in Case T-210/01 *General Electric v Commission* [2005] ECR II-[5575], paragraph 617; COMP/M.1453 – *AXA/GRE* of 8 April 1999.

[49] The alternative may consist of an entirely different business or, in case of uncertainty as to finding a suitable buyer, of additional businesses and assets that are added to the initial package.

46. If there is uncertainty as to the implementation of the divestiture due to third party rights or as to finding a suitable purchaser crown jewel commitments and up-front buyers as discussed below in paragraphs 54 address the same concerns, and the parties may therefore choose between both structures.

1.5 Transfer to a suitable purchaser

47. The intended effect of the divestiture will only be achieved if and once the business is transferred to a suitable purchaser in whose hands it will become an active competitive force in the market. The potential of a business to attract a suitable purchaser is an important element already of the Commission's assessment of the appropriateness of the proposed commitment.[50] In order to ensure that the business is divested to a suitable purchaser, the commitments have to include criteria to define its suitability which will allow the Commission to conclude that the divestiture of the business to such a purchaser will likely remove the competition concerns identified.

Notes

[50] Case IV/ M.913 – *Siemens/ Elektrowatt* of 18 November 1997.

(a) Suitability of a purchaser

48. The standard purchaser requirements are the following:
   - the purchaser is required to be independent of and unconnected to the parties,
   - the purchaser must possess the financial resources, proven relevant expertise and have the incentive and ability to maintain and develop the divested business as a viable and active competitive force in competition with the parties and other competitors; and
   - the acquisition of the business by a proposed purchaser must neither be likely to create new competition problems nor give rise to a risk that the implementation of the commitments will be delayed. Therefore, the proposed purchaser must reasonably be expected to obtain all

necessary approvals from the relevant regulatory authorities for the acquisition of the business to be divested.

49. The standard purchaser requirements may have to be supplemented on a case-by-case basis. An example is the requirement, where appropriate, that the purchaser should be an industrial, rather than a financial purchaser.[51] The commitments will have to contain such a clause where a financial buyer will not be able or will not have the incentives to develop the business as a viable and competitive force in the market even considering that it could obtain the necessary management expertise (*e.g.*, by recruiting managers experienced in the sector at stake) and therefore the acquisition by a financial buyer will not remove the competition concerns.

Notes

[51] See commitments in Case COMP/M.2621 – *SEB/Moulinex* of 8 January 2002, which foresee that the licensee needs to have its own trademark used in the sector concerned. Certain markets may require a sufficient degree of recognition by customers for a purchaser to be able to translate the business to be divested into a competitive force on the market.

(b) Identification of a suitable purchaser

50. In general, there are three ways to ensure that the business is transferred to a suitable purchaser. First, the business is transferred within a fixed time-limit after adoption of the decision to a purchaser which is approved by the Commission on the basis of the purchaser requirements. Second, in addition to the conditions set out for the first category, the commitments foresee that the parties may not complete the notified operation before having entered into a binding agreement with a purchaser for the business, approved by the Commission (so-called "up-front-buyer"). Third, the parties identify a purchaser for the business and enter into a binding agreement already during the Commission's procedure[52] (so-called "fix-it-first" remedy). The main difference between the two latter options is that in the case of an up-front buyer, the identity of the purchaser is not know to the Commission prior to the authorisation decision.

Notes

[52] The transfer of the business may be implemented after the Commission decision.

51. The choice of the category depends on the risks involved in the case and therefore on the measures which enable the Commission to conclude with the requisite degree of certainty that the commitment will be implemented. This will depend on the nature and the scope of the business to be divested, the risks of degradation of the business in the interim period up to divestiture and any uncertainties inherent in the transfer and implementation, in particular the risks of finding a suitable purchaser.

(1) Sale of the divested business within a fixed time-limit after the decision

52. In the first category, the parties may proceed with the sale of the divested business on the basis of the purchaser requirements within a fixed time-limit after the adoption of the decision. This procedure is appropriate in cases where a number of purchasers can be envisaged for a viable business and where no specific issues interfere with the divestiture. Where the purchaser needs to have special qualifications, this procedure may be appropriate if there are sufficient interested potential purchasers available which fulfil the specific purchaser requirements to be included in the commitments in such cases. In these circumstances the Commission may be able to conclude that the divestiture will be implemented and there are no reasons for the implementation of the notified concentration to be suspended after the Commission decision.

(2) Up-front buyer

53. There are cases where only the proposal of an up-front buyer will allow the Commission to conclude with the requisite degree of certainty that the business will be effectively divested to a suitable purchaser. The parties therefore have to undertake in the commitments that they are not going to complete the notified operation before having entered into a binding agreement with a purchaser for the divested business, approved by the Commission.[53]

Notes
[53] Case COMP/M.3796 – *Omya/Huber PCC* of 19 July 2006; Case COMP/M.2972 – *DSM/Roche Vitamins* of 23 July 2003; Case COMP/M.2060 – *Bosch/Rexroth* of 13 December 2000; Case COMP/M.2337 *Nestlé/Ralston Purina* of 27 July 2001; COMP/M.2544 *Masterfoods/Royal Canin* of 15 February 2002; COMP/M.2947 *Verbund/ Energie Allianz* of 11 June 2003.

54. First, this concerns cases where there are considerable obstacles for a divestiture, such as third party rights, or uncertainties as to finding a suitable purchaser[54]. In such cases, an up-front buyer will allow the Commission to conclude with the requisite degree of certainty that the commitments will be implemented, as such a commitment creates greater incentives for the parties to close the divestiture in order to be able to complete their own concentration. In these circumstances, parties may choose between proposing an up-front buyer and an alternative divestiture commitment, as set out above in paragraph 46.

Notes
[54] See Case COMP/ M.2060 – *Bosch/Rexroth* of 13 December 2000, paragraph 92.

55. Second, an up-front buyer may be necessary in cases which cause considerable risks of preserving the competitiveness and saleability of the divestment business in the interim period until divestiture. This category comprises cases where the risks of a degradation of the divestment business appear to be high, in particular due to a risk of losing employees being key for the business, or where the interim risks are increased as the parties are not able to undertake the carve-out process in the interim period, but the carve-out process can only take place once a sales and purchase agreement with a purchaser is entered into. The up-front buyer provision may accelerate the transfer of the business to be divested -given the increased incentives for the parties to close the divestiture in order to be able to complete their own concentration- to such an extent that the commitments may allow the Commission to conclude with the requisite degree of certainty that those risks are limited and the divestiture will be effectively implemented.[55]

Notes
[55] See Case COMP/ M.2060 – *Bosch/Rexroth* of 13 December 2000, paragraph 95.

(3) Fix-it-first remedies

56. The third category contains cases where the parties already during the Commission procedure identify and enter into a legally binding agreement with a buyer outlining the essentials of the purchase.[56] The Commission will be able to decide in the final decision whether the transfer of the divested business to the identified purchaser will remove the competition concerns. If the Commission authorises the notified concentration, no additional Commission decision for the purchaser approval will be needed and the closing of the sale of the divested business may take place shortly afterwards.

Notes
[56] Such agreements are normally conditional to the final Commission decision accepting the remedy in question.

57. The Commission welcomes such a fix-it-first remedy in particular in cases where the identity of the purchaser is crucial for the effectiveness of the proposed remedy. This concerns cases where, given the circumstances, only very few potential purchasers can be considered suitable, in particular as the divested business is not a viable business in itself, but its viability will only be ensured by specific assets of the purchaser, or where the purchaser needs to have specific characteristics in order for the remedy to solve the competition concerns.[57] If the parties choose to enter into a binding agreement with a suitable purchaser during the procedure by way of a fix-it-first solution, the Commission can in those circumstances conclude with the requisite degree of certainty that the commitments will be implemented with a sale to a suitable purchaser. In these situations, an "upfront buyer" solution containing specific requirements as to a suitable buyer will generally be considered equivalent and acceptable.

Notes

[57] See Case COMP/M.3916 – *T-Mobile Austria/tele.ring* of April 2006, the divestiture of certain mobile telephony sites and frequencies, not constituting a viable business, could only take place to a competitor which was likely to play a similar role in the market as tele.ring; COMP/M.4000 – *Inco/Falconbridge* of 4 July 2006, the divestiture of a nickel processing business could only take place to a competitor vertically integrated into the supply of nickel; Case COMP/M. 4187 – *Metso/Aker Kvaerner* of 12 December 2006, only one purchaser was suitable for acquiring the businesses to be divested as it was the only one with the necessary know-how and the necessary presence in neighbouring markets; Case COMP/M. 3436 – *Continental/Phoenix* of 26 October 2004, only the partner in the distribution joint venture was able to render the divested business viable; Case COMP/M.3136 – *GE/Agfa* of 5 December 2003.

2. Removal of Links with Competitors

58. Divestiture commitments may also be used for removing links between the parties and competitors in cases where these links contribute to the competition concerns raised by the merger. The divestiture of a minority shareholding in a joint venture may be necessary in order to sever a structural link with a major competitor,[58] or, similarly, the divestiture of a minority shareholding in a competitor.[59]

Notes

[58] Case IV/ M.942 - VEBA/ Degussa of 3 December 1997. Divestitures of stakes in joint ventures may, of course, also be suitable remedies for other situations apart from removing links with competitors.
[59] Case COMP/M. 3653 – Siemens/VA Tech of 13 July 2005, paragraphs 491, 493 ff.

59. Whereas the divestiture of such stakes is the preferable solution, the Commission may exceptionally accept the waiving of rights linked to minority stakes in a competitor where it can be excluded, given the specific circumstances of the case, that the minority shareholding in a competitor would raise competition concerns in financial respect.[60] In such circumstances, the parties have to waive all the rights linked to such a shareholding which were relevant for behaviour in terms of competition, such as representations on the board, veto rights and also information rights.[61] The Commission may only be able to accept such a severing of the link with a competitor if those rights are waived comprehensively and in a permanent way.[62]

Notes

[60] See Case COMP/M. 3653 – *Siemens/VA Tech* of 13 July 2005, paragraphs 327 ff., where effects from the minority stake in financial respect could be excluded as a put option for the sale of this stake had already been exercised.
[61] Case COMP/M.4153 – *Toshiba/Westinghouse* of 19 September 2006.
[62] See Case COMP/M.3440 – *ENI/EDP/GDP* of 9 December 2004, paragraphs 648 f., 672.

60. Where competition concerns result from agreements with companies supplying the same products or providing the same services, a suitable remedy may be the termination of the respective agreement, such as distribution agreements with competitors[63] or agreements resulting in the coordination of certain commercial behaviour.[64] However, the termination of a distribution agreement alone will only remove the competition concerns if it is ensured that the product of a competitor will also be distributed in the future and exercise effective competitive pressure on the parties.

Notes

[63] See for the termination of distribution agreements Case COMP/M.3779 – *Pernod Ricard/Allied Domecq* of 24 June 2005; Case COMP/M. 3658 – *Orkla/Chips* of 3 March 2005.
[64] See particularly the sea transport sector, Case COMP/M. 3829 – *Maersk/PONL* of 29 July 2005 and Case COMP/M.3863 – *TUI/CP* Ships of 12 October 2005. In those cases, the parties committed to withdraw from certain liner conferences and consortia.

3. Other Remedies

61. Whilst being the preferred remedy, divestitures or the removal of links with competitors are not the only remedy possible to eliminate certain competition concerns. The Commission may accept other types of commitments in circumstances where the other remedy proposed is equivalent in its effects to a divestiture.[65]

Notes

[65] Case COMP/M.3680 – *Alcatel/Finmeccanica/Alcatel Alenia Space & Telespazio* of 28 April 2005, where a divestiture was impossible.

Access remedies

62. In a number of cases, the Commission has accepted remedies foreseeing the granting of access to key infrastructure, networks, key technology, including patents, know-how or other intellectual property rights, and essential inputs. Normally, the parties grant such access to third parties on a non-discriminatory and transparent basis.

63. Commitments granting access to infrastructure and networks may be submitted in order to facilitate market entry by competitors. They may be acceptable to the Commission in circumstances where it is sufficiently clear that there will be actual entry of new competitors that would eliminate any significant impediment to effective competition.[66] Examples are commitments granting access to pay-TV platforms,[67] to airports slots in air transport cases[68] and to energy via gas release programs or electricity auctions.[69] Often, a sufficient reduction of entry barriers is not achieved by individual measures, but by a package comprising a combination of divestiture remedies and access commitments or a commitments package aimed at overall facilitating entry of competitors by a whole range of different measures. If those commitments actually make the entry of sufficient new competitors timely and likely, they can be considered to have a similar effect on competition in the market as a divestiture. If it cannot be concluded that the lowering of the entry barriers by the proposed commitments will likely lead to the entry of new competitors in the market, the Commission will reject such a remedies package.

Notes

[66] See judgment of the CFI in Case T-177/04 *easyJet v Commission* [2006] ECR II-[1931], at paragraphs 197 et seq.

[67] See Case COMP/M.2876 – *Newscorp/Telepiù* of 2 April 2003, paragraphs 225 et seq., where the commitments package included access of competitors to all essential elements of a pay-TV network, such as (1) access to the necessary content, (2) access to the technical platform as well as (3) access to the necessary technical services. Similarly, in Case COMP/JV.37 – *BskyB/Kirch Pay TV* of 21 March 2000, confirmed by judgment of CFI in Case T-158/00 *ARD v Commission* [2003] ECR II-3825, the Commission accepted a commitments package which allowed other operators comprehensive access to the pay-TV market.

[68] In those cases, comprehensive commitments packages were accepted, consisting, *inter alia*, of transfer of slots, access to interlining and intermodal services as well as access to frequent flyer programs; see; Case COMP/M.3770 – *Lufthansa/Swiss* of 4 July 2005; Case COMP/M.3940 – *Lufthansa/Eurowings* of 22 December 2005, and Case COMP/M. 3280 – *Air France/KLM* of 11 February 2004, confirmed by judgment of the CFI in Case T-177/04 *easyJet v Commission* [2006] ECR II-[1931].

[69] See Case COMP/M.3696 – *E.ON/MOL* of 21 December 2005; Case COMP/M.3868 – *DONG/Elsam/Energi E2* of 14 March 2006; Case COMP/M.1853 – *EDF/ENBW* of 7 February 2001.

64. Commitments granting non-discriminatory access to infrastructure or networks of the merging parties may also be submitted in order to ensure that competition is not significantly impeded as a result of foreclosure. In past Commission decisions, commitments have foreseen the granting of access to pipelines[70] and to telecom or similar networks.[71] The Commission will only accept such commitments if it can be concluded that competitors will likely use these commitments so that foreclosure concerns will be eliminated. In specific cases, it may be appropriate to link such a commitment with an up-front or fix-it-first provision in order to allow the Commission to conclude with the requisite degree of certainty that the commitment will be implemented.[72]

Notes

[70] Case COMP/M.2533 – *BP/E.ON* of 20 December 2001, access to pipelines in addition to divestiture of shares in a pipeline company; Case COMP/M.2389 – *Shell/DEA* of 20 December 2001, access to an ethylene import terminal.

[71] For access to telecom networks, see Case COMP/M.2803 – *Telia/Sonera* of 10 July 2002; Case IV/ M.1439 – *Telia/Telenor* of 13 October 1999; Case COMP/ M.1795 – *Vodafone/ Mannesmann* of 12 April 2000. See also Case COMP/M.2903 – *DaimlerChrysler/Deutsche Telekom/JV* of 30 April 2003, where the Commission accepted a commitments package to grant third parties access to a telematics network and to reduce the entry barriers by allowing them to use parts of a telematics device, designed for toll collection, provided by the parties.

Part D Mergers and Concentrations

[72] See the "qualitative moratorium" in Case COMP/M.2903 – *DaimlerChrysler/Deutsche Telekom/JV* of 30 April 2003, paragraph 76.

65. Similarly, the control of key technology or IP rights may lead to concerns of foreclosure of competitors which depend on the technology or IP rights as essential input for the activities in a downstream market. This, for example, concerns cases where competition problems arise as the parties may withhold information necessary for the interoperability of different equipment. In such circumstances, commitments to grant competitors access to the necessary information may eliminate the competition concerns.[73] Similarly, in sectors where players commonly have to cooperate by licensing patents to each other, concerns that the merged entity would no longer have the incentive to provide licences to the same extent and under the same conditions as before may be eliminated by commitments to grant licenses on the same basis also in the future.[74] In those cases, commitments should foresee non-exclusive licences or the disclosure of information on a non-exclusive basis to all third parties which depend on the IP rights or information for their activities. As regards the terms and conditions, it may be appropriate to rely on commonly accepted licensing terms in the industry at stake, *e.g.*, if appropriate, on "reasonable and non-discriminatory licensing" ("RAND") as used in some standardisation processes. As set out in the preceding paragraph, the Commission will only accept such commitments if it can be concluded that competitors will likely use them.

Notes
[73] Case COMP/M.3083 – *GE/Instrumentarium* of 2 September 2003; Case COMP/M.2861 – *Siemens/Draegerwerk* of 30 April 2003.
[74] See Case COMP/M. 3998 – *Axalto/Gemplus* of 19 May 2006.

66. Access commitments are often complex in nature and necessarily include general terms for determining the terms and conditions under which access is granted. In order to render them effective, those commitments have to contain the procedural requirements necessary for monitoring them, such as the requirement of separate accounts for the infrastructure in order to allow a review of the costs involved,[75] and suitable monitoring devices. Normally, such monitoring has to be done by the market participants themselves, *e.g.* by those undertakings wishing to benefit from the commitments. Measures allowing third parties themselves to enforce the commitments are in particular access to a fast dispute resolution mechanism via arbitration proceedings (together with trustees).[76] If the Commission can conclude that the mechanisms foreseen in the commitments will allow the market participants themselves to effectively enforce them in a timely manner, no permanent monitoring of the commitments by the Commission is required. In those cases, an intervention by the Commission would only be necessary in cases where the parties do not comply with the solutions found by those dispute resolution mechanisms.[77] However, the Commission will only be able to accept such commitments where the complexity does not lead to a risk of their effectiveness from the outset and where the monitoring devices proposed ensure that those commitments will be effectively implemented and the enforcement mechanism will lead to timely results.[78]

Notes
[75] See, *e.g.*, Case COMP/M.2803 – *Telia/Sonera* of 10 July 2002; Case COMP/M.2903 – *DaimlerChrysler/Deutsche Telekom/JV* of 30 April 2003.
[76] As to the effects of arbitration clauses, see judgment of CFI in Case T-158/00 *ARD v Commission* [2003] ECR II-3825, paragraphs 212, 295, 352; CFI judgment in Case T-177/04 *easyJet v Commission*, [2006] ECR II-[1931], paragraph 186.
[77] CFI; judgment in Case T-158/00 *ARD v Commission* [2003] ECR II-3825, paragraphs 212, 295, 352.
[78] See judgments of the CFI in Case T-87/05 *EDP v Commission*, [2005] ECR II-[3745], at paragraphs 102 et seq.; and Case T-177/04 *easyJet v Commission* [2006] ECR II-[1931], at paragraph 188.

Change of long-term exclusive contracts

67. The change in the market structure resulting from a proposed concentration can cause existing contractual arrangements to be inimical to effective competition. This is in particular true

for exclusive long-term supply agreements if such agreements foreclose either, up-stream, the input for competitors or, down-stream, their access to customers. Where the merged entity will have the ability and the incentives to foreclose competitors in this way, the foreclosure effects resulting from existing exclusive agreements may contribute to significantly impeding effective competition.[79]

Notes

[79] See Commission Notice on non-horizontal mergers [...]; Case IV/ M. 986 – *AGFA Gevaert/DuPont* of 11 February 1998.

68. In such circumstances, the termination or change of existing exclusive agreements may be considered appropriate to eliminate the competition concerns.[80] However, the available evidence must allow the Commission to clearly determine that no *de facto* exclusivity will be maintained. Furthermore, such change of long-term agreements will normally only be sufficient as part of a remedies package to remove the competition concerns identified.

Notes

[80] Case COMP/M.2876 – *Newscorp/Telepiù* of 2 April 2003, paragraphs 225 et seq., granting unilateral termination rights to suppliers of TV content, limiting the scope of the exclusivity clauses and limiting the duration of future exclusive agreements relating to supply of content; Case COMP/M. 2822 – *ENI/EnBW/GVS* of 17 December 2002, granting of early termination rights to all local gas distributors concerning long-term gas supply agreements; Case IV/ M.1571 – *New Holland* of 28 October 1999; Case IV/ M.1467 – *Rohm and Haas/ Morton* of 19 April 1999.

Other non-divestiture remedies

69. As indicated above in paragraph 17, non-structural types of remedies, such as promises by the parties to abstain from certain commercial behaviour (e.g. bundling products), will generally not eliminate the competition concerns resulting from horizontal overlaps. In any case, it may be difficult to achieve the required degree of effectiveness of such a remedy due to the absence of effective monitoring of its implementation, as already set out above in paragraph 13 f.[81] Indeed, it may be impossible for the Commission to verify whether or not the commitment is complied with and even other market participants, such as competitors, may not be able to establish at all or with the requisite degree of certainty whether the parties meet the conditions of the commitment in practice. In addition, competitors may also not have an incentive to alert the Commission as they do not directly benefit from the commitments. Therefore, the Commission may examine other types of non-divestiture remedies, such as behavioural promises, only exceptionally in specific circumstances, such as in respect of competition concerns arising in conglomerate structures.[82]

Notes

[81] See, as an example for such remedies, Case COMP/M.3440 – *ENI/EDP/GDP* of 9 December 2004, paragraphs 663, 719.

[82] See, in relation to conglomerate effects of a concentration, ECJ, judgment of 15 February 2005 in Case C 12/03 P *Commission v Tetra Laval* [2005] ECR I-987, paragraphs 85, 89.

4. REVIEW CLAUSE

70. Irrespective of the type of remedy, commitments will usually include a review clause.[83] This may allow the Commission, upon request by the parties showing good cause, to grant an extension of deadlines or to waive, modify or substitute, in exceptional circumstances, the commitments.

Notes

[83] However, the review clause is of particular relevance for access remedies, which systematically should include such a clause; see below paragraph 73.

71. Modifying commitments by extending the deadlines is in particular relevant for divestiture commitments. Parties have to submit a request for an extension within the deadline. Where parties apply for an extension for the first divestiture period, the Commission will only accept that they have shown good cause if the parties were not able to meet the deadline for reasons outside their

responsibility and if it can be expected that the parties will succeed in divesting the business within a short timeframe. Otherwise, the divestiture trustee may be better placed to undertake the divestiture and to fulfil the commitments for the parties.

72. The Commission may grant waivers or accept modifications or substitutions of the commitments only in exceptional circumstances. This will very rarely be relevant for divestiture commitments. As divestiture commitments have to be implemented within a short time-frame after the decision, no changes of market circumstances will have occurred in such a short time-frame and the Commission will normally not accept any modifications under the general review clause. For specific situations the commitments normally foresee more targeted review clauses.[84]

Notes

[84] As mentioned in paragraph 30, the Commission may approve a purchaser without some of the assets or personnel foreseen if this does not affect the competitiveness and viability of the divested business. Similarly, the non-requisition clause, as explained in paragraph 43, prohibits the re-acquisition of control over the assets divested only if the Commission has not previously found that that the market structure has changed to such an extent that the divestiture is no longer necessary.

73. A waiver, modification or substitution of commitments may be more relevant for non-divestiture commitments, such as access commitments, which may be on-going for a number of years and for which not all contingencies can be predicted at the time of the adoption of the Commission decision. Exceptional circumstances justifying a waiver, modification or substitution may, first, be accepted for such commitments if parties show that market circumstances have changed significantly and on a permanent basis. For showing this, a sufficient long time-span, normally at least several years, between the Commission decision and a request by the parties is required. Second, exceptional circumstances may also be present if the parties can show that the experience gained in the application of the remedy demonstrates that the objective pursued with the remedy will be better achieved if modalities of the commitment are changed. For any waiver, modification or substitution of commitments, the Commission will also take into account the view of third parties and the impact a modification may have on the position of third parties and thereby on the overall effectiveness of the remedy. In this regard, the Commission will also consider whether modifications affect the right already acquired by third parties after implementation of the remedy.[85]

Notes

[85] See examples in judgment of CFI in Case T-119/02 *Royal Philips Electronics v Commission* [2003] ECR II-1433, paragraph 184.

74. If at the time of the adoption of the decision the Commission for particular reasons cannot anticipate all contingencies in relation to the implementation of such commitments, it may also be appropriate to include a clause in the commitments allowing the Commission to trigger a limited modification of the commitments, agreed in advance by the parties, on its own. Such modifications may be necessary if the original commitments do not achieve the envisaged results defined in the commitments, in particular as specific modalities prevent an effective implementation of the commitments, and the original commitments therefore do not effectively remove the competition concerns. Procedurally, the parties may be obliged in such cases to propose a change of the commitments in order to achieve the result defined in the commitments, or the Commission may change the conditions and obligations on its own to this purpose, after hearing the parties. Such clauses were used, for example, in relation to the modalities of gas release programs.[86]

Notes

[86] See Case COMP/M.3868 – *DONG/Elsam/Energi E2* of 14 March 2006, paragraph 24 of the annex.

75. The Commission may adopt a formal decision for any waiver, modification or substitution of commitments or simply take note of satisfactory amendments of the remedy by the parties, where such amendments improve the effectiveness of the remedy and result in legally binding obligations of the parties, *e.g.* by contractual arrangements. A change of the commitments will

normally only be effective *ex nunc*. Consequently, a modification of the commitments will not heal retroactively any breach of the commitments which has been committed before the time of the modification. The Commission may therefore, where appropriate, further pursue a breach under Articles 14, 15 of the Merger Regulation.

IV. Aspects of Procedure for Submission of Commitments

1. Phase I

76. Pursuant to Article 6(2) of the Merger Regulation the Commission may declare a concentration compatible with the common market also before the initiation of proceedings, where it is confident that following modification a notified concentration no longer raises serious doubts within the meaning of paragraph 1(c).

77. Parties can submit proposals for commitments to the Commission on an informal basis, even before notification. Parties have to submit commitments within not more than 20 working days from the date of the receipt of the notification.[87] The Commission informs the parties about its serious doubts in due time before that deadline.[88] Where the parties submit commitments, the deadline for the Commission's decision pursuant to Article 6(1) of the Merger Regulation is extended from 25 to 35 working days.[89]

Notes

[87] Article 18(1) of the Implementing Regulation.

[88] The notifying parties will normally be offered the opportunity of attending a state of play meeting in such circumstances, see point 33 of the DG COMPETITION Best Practices on the conduct of EC merger control proceedings.

[89] Article 10 (1) subparagraph 2 of the Merger Regulation.

---

78. In order to form the basis of a decision pursuant to Article 6(2), proposals for commitments must meet the following requirements:
    (a) they shall fully specify the substantive and implementing commitments entered into by the parties;
    (b) they shall be signed by a person duly authorised to do so;
    (c) they shall be accompanied by the information on the commitments offered as provided for in the Implementing Regulation (as explained above in paragraph 7); and
    (d) they shall be accompanied by a non-confidential version of the commitments[90] for the purposes of market testing them with third parties. The non-confidential version of the commitments must allow third parties to fully assess the workability and the effectiveness of the proposed remedies to remove the competition concerns.

Notes

[90] Article 20 (2) of the Implementing Regulation.

---

79. Proposals submitted by the parties in accordance with these requirements will be assessed by the Commission. The Commission will consult the authorities of the Member States on the proposed commitments and, when considered appropriate, also third parties in the form of a market test. In addition, in cases involving a geographic market that is wider than the European Economic Area ("EEA") or where, for reasons related to the viability of the business, the scope of the business to be divested is wider than the EEA territory, the non-confidential version of the proposed remedies may also be discussed with non-EEA competition authorities in the framework of the Community's bilateral cooperation agreements with these countries.

Commentary
para 79: **B&C:** 8.164

---

80. Commitments in phase I can only be accepted where the competition problem is readily identifiable and can easily be remedied.[91] The competition problem therefore needs to be so straightforward and the remedies so clear-cut that it is not necessary to enter into an in-depth investigation

and that the commitments are sufficient to clearly rule out "serious doubts" within the meaning of Article 6(1)(c) of the Merger Regulation.[92] Where the assessment confirms that the proposed commitments remove the grounds for serious doubts on this basis, the Commission clears the merger in phase I.

Notes

[91] See recital 30 of the Merger Regulation.

[92] See judgment of CFI in Case T-119/02 *Royal Philips Electronics v Commission* [2003] ECR II-1433, paragraphs 79 et seq.

81. Due to the time-constraints in phase I, it is particularly important for the parties to submit in a timely manner to the Commission the information required in the Implementing Regulation to properly assess the content and workability of the commitments and their suitability to maintain conditions of effective competition in the common market on a permanent basis. If the parties do not comply with the obligation in the Implementing Regulation, the Commission will not be able to conclude that the proposed commitments will remove the grounds for serious doubts.

82. Where the assessment shows that the commitments offered are not sufficient to remove the competition concerns raised by the concentration, the parties will be informed accordingly. Given that phase I remedies are designed to provide a clear-cut answer to a readily identifiable competition concern, only limited modifications can be accepted to the proposed commitments. Such modifications, presented as an immediate response to the result of the consultations, may include clarifications, refinements and/or other improvements designed to ensure that the commitments are workable and effective. However, such modifications may only be accepted in circumstances where it is ensured that the Commission can carry out a proper assessment of those commitments.[93]

Notes

[93] See recital 17 of the Implementing Regulation and judgment of the CFI, Case T-119/02 *Royal Philips Electronics v Commission* [2003] ECR II-1433, paragraphs 237 et seq.

83. If the Commission's final assessment of a case shows that there are no competition concerns in one or more markets, the parties will be informed accordingly and may withdraw the unnecessary commitments for such markets. If the parties do not withdraw them, the Commission may either take note of their proposals in the decision or ignore them. In any event, such commitment proposals do not constitute a condition for clearance. This also applies to commitments in phase-II.

84. If the Commission concludes that the commitments offered by the parties do not remove the serious doubts, it will issue an Article 6(1)(c) decision and open proceedings.

2. Phase II

85. Pursuant to Article 8(2) of the Merger Regulation, the Commission must declare a concentration compatible with the common market, where following modification a notified concentration does no longer significantly impede effective competition within the meaning of Article 2(3) of the Merger Regulation.

86. Commitments proposed to the Commission pursuant to Article 8(2) must be submitted to the Commission within not more than 65 working days from the day on which proceedings were initiated. Where the deadlines for the final decision have been extended according to Article 10(3) of the Merger Regulation, also the deadline for remedies is automatically extended by the same number of days.[94] Only in exceptional circumstances, the Commission may accept that commitments are submitted for the first time after the expiry of this period. The request by the parties for an extension of the deadline must be received within the period and has to set forth the exceptional circumstances which, according to the parties, justify it. In addition to the existence of exceptional circumstances, an extension is only possible where there is sufficient time to make a proper assessment of the proposal by the Commission and to allow adequate consultation with Member States and third parties.[95]

Notes

[94] Article 19 (2) subparagraph 2 of the Implementing Regulation.

[95] Article 19 (2) subparagraph 3 of the Implementing Regulation. See Case COMP/M.1439 – *Telia/Telenor* of 13 October 1999; Case IV/M.754 – *Anglo American Corporation/Lonrho* of 23 April 1997.

87. The question whether or not submitting remedies will extend the deadline for the Commission to take a final decision depends on the time in the procedure when the commitments are submitted. Where the parties submit commitments within less than 55 working days after the initiation of proceedings, the Commission has to take a final decision within not more than 90 working days of the date of initiation of proceedings.[96] Where the parties submit commitments on working day 55 or afterwards (even after working day 65, if those commitments should be acceptable due to exceptional circumstances as described above in paragraph 86), the period for the Commission to take a final decision is increased to 105 working days according to Article 10(3) subparagraph 2. Where the parties submit commitments within less than 55 working days, but submit a modified version on day 55 or thereafter, the period to take a final decision will also be extended to 105 working days.

Notes

[96] Where the deadlines for the final decision have been extended according to Article 10(3) subparagraph 2 of the Merger Regulation before working day 55, this period is also extended.

88. The Commission is available to discuss suitable commitments well in advance of the end of the 65 working day period. The parties are encouraged to submit draft proposals dealing with both substantive and implementation aspects which are necessary to ensure that the commitments are fully workable. If the parties are of the opinion that more time is needed for the investigation of the competition concerns and for the corresponding design of appropriate commitments, they may also suggest to the Commission to extend the final deadline under Article 10(3) subparagraph 1. Such a request will have to be made before the end of the 65 working day period. Indeed, the Commission will normally not extend the period for adopting a final decision according to Article 10(3) subparagraph 1 where the request for extension is presented after the deadline for submitting remedies foreseen in the Implementing Regulation, *i.e.* after working day 65.[97]

Notes

[97] The Court of First Instance confirmed that the Merger Regulation and the Implementing Regulation do not impose any obligations on the Commission to accept commitments which are submitted after the legal deadline, as set out below in paragraph 92, see Case T-87/05 *EDP v Commission* judgment [2005] ECR II-[3745], at paragraph 161. Therefore, the Commission is not bound to consider any remedies which are submitted by the parties after the deadline for remedies, even if the parties were to agree to extend the final deadline. Moreover, this would not correspond to the purpose, as explained in recital 35 of the Merger Regulation, of the extensions foreseen in Article 10(3). The extension foreseen in Article 10(3) subparagraph 1 is to allow for sufficient time for the investigation of the competitive concerns, whereas it is the purpose of the extension laid down in Article 10(3) subparagraph 2 to allow for sufficient time for the analysis and market testing of commitments.

Commentary
para 88: B&C: 8.164

89. In order to meet the requirements for a decision pursuant to Article 8 (2), commitments must meet the following requirements:
   (a) they shall address all competition problems raised by the concentration and shall fully specify the substantive and implementing commitments entered into by the parties;
   (b) they shall be signed by a person duly authorised to do so;
   (c) they shall by accompanied by the information on the commitments offered as provided for in the Implementing Regulation (as explained above in paragraph 7); and (d) they shall be accompanied by a non-confidential version of the commitments[98] for the purposes of market testing them with third parties, fulfilling the requirements set out above in paragraph 78.

Notes
[98] Article 20 (2) of the Implementing Regulation.

90. Proposals submitted by the parties in accordance with these requirements will be assessed by the Commission. If the assessment confirms that the proposed commitments remove the serious doubts (if no Statement of Objection has been issued yet by the Commission) or the competition concerns raised in the Statement of Objections, following the consultations as set out in paragraph 79 above, the Commission will adopt a conditional clearance decision.

91. Conversely, where the assessment leads to the conclusion that the proposed commitments appear not to be sufficient to resolve the competition concerns raised by the concentration, the parties will be informed accordingly.[99]

Notes
[99] See paragraphs 30ff of the DG Competition Best Practices on the conduct of EC merger proceedings which provide for several state of play meetings between the Commission and the parties throughout the procedure.

92. The Merger Regulation does not impose any obligation on the Commission to accept commitments after the legal deadline for remedies, unless the Commission voluntarily undertakes to assess commitments in specific circumstances.[100] In view of this, where parties subsequently modify the proposed commitments after the deadline of 65 working days, the Commission will only accept these modified commitments where it can clearly determine - on the basis of its assessment of information already received in the course of the investigation, including the results of prior market testing, and without the need for any other market test - that such commitments, once implemented, fully and unambiguously resolve the competition problems identified and where there is sufficient time to allow for an adequate assessment by the Commission and for proper consultation with Member States.[101,102] The Commission will normally reject modified commitments which do not fulfil those conditions.[103]

Notes
[100] See judgment of CFI in Case T-87/05 *EDP v Commission* [2005] ECR II-[3745], at paragraphs 161 et seq. See also judgement of CFI in case T-290/94 *Kaysersberg SA v Commission* [1997] ECR II-2137.
[101] Case COMP/M.3440 – *ENI/EDP/GDP* of 9 December 2004, paragraphs 855 et seq.; confirmed by Judgment of CFI in Case T-87/05 *EDP v Commission* [2005] ECR II-[3745], at paragraphs 162 et seq.; COMP/M.1628 – *TotalFina/Elf* of 9 March 2000, at paragraph 345.
[102] This consultation normally requires that the Commission has to be able to send a draft of the final decision, including an assessment of the modified commitments, to the Member States not less than 10 working days before the Advisory Committee with Member States. This period may only be shortened in exceptional circumstances (Article 19(5) of the Merger Regulation).
[103] See Case COMP/M.3440 – *ENI/EDP/GDP* of 9 December 2004, paragraph 913.

V. REQUIREMENTS FOR IMPLEMENTATION OF COMMITMENTS

93. Commitments are offered as a means of securing a clearance, with the implementation normally taking place after the decision. Commitments therefore require safeguards to ensure their effective and timely implementation. These implementing provisions will normally form part of the commitments entered into by the parties vis-à-vis the Commission.

94. In the following, detailed guidance is given on the implementation of divestiture commitments, as the most typical commitment. Afterwards, some aspects of the implementation of other types of commitments are discussed.

1. DIVESTITURE PROCESS

95. The divestiture has to be completed within a fixed time period agreed between the parties and the Commission. In the Commission's practice, the total time period is divided into a period for entering into a final agreement and a further period for the closing, the transfer of legal title, of the transaction. The period for entering into a binding agreement is further normally divided into a first period in which the parties can look for a suitable purchaser (the "first divestiture period")

and, if the parties do not succeed to divest the business, a second period in which a divestiture trustee obtains the mandate to divest the business at no minimum price (the "trustee divestiture period").

96. The Commission's experience has shown that short divestiture periods contribute largely to the success of the divestiture as, otherwise, the business to be divested will be exposed to an extended period of uncertainty. The time periods should therefore be as short as feasible. The Commission will normally consider a period of around six months for the first divestiture period and an additional period of three months for the trustee divestiture period as appropriate. A period of further three months is normally foreseen for closing the transaction. These periods may be modified on a case-by-case basis. In particular, they may have to be shortened if there is a high risk of degradation of the business' viability in the interim period.

97. The deadline for the divestiture shall normally start on the day of the adoption of the Commission decision. In exceptional cases, the Commission may accept that the periods only start running on the day of closing of the notified concentration.[104] An example could be a transaction via public bid where the parties commit to divest a business belonging to the target. Where in such circumstances the parties cannot prepare for the divestiture of the target's business before closing of the notified concentration, the Commission might accept that the periods for such a divestiture only start with that date. Similarly, such a solution may be considered if the date of closing of the concentration is not under the control of the parties as it, *e.g.*, requires state approval. In return, it may be appropriate to shorten the deadlines in order to reduce the time of uncertainty for the business to be divested.

Notes

[104] However, also in those circumstances, other provisions in the commitments, in particular the provisions establishing the safeguards in the interim period, should start running on the date of the adoption of the decision.

---

98. Whereas for up-front buyer solutions the above-described procedure applies, the procedure will be different for fix-it-first solutions. In general, a binding agreement with a purchaser will already be entered into during the procedure so that after the decision only a further period for the closing of the transaction has to be foreseen. If before the decision only a framework agreement has been concluded with the purchaser, the periods to be foreseen for entering into a full agreement and the closing afterwards will have to be decided on a case-by-case basis.[105]

Notes

[105] See Case COMP/M.3916 – *T-Mobile Austria/tele.ring* of 20 April 2006.

---

2. APPROVAL OF THE PURCHASER AND OF THE SALE AND PURCHASE AGREEMENT

99. In order to ensure the effectiveness of the commitment, the sale to a proposed purchaser is subject to prior approval by the Commission. When the parties (or the divestiture trustee) have reached a final agreement with a purchaser, they have to submit a reasoned and documented proposal to the Commission. The parties or the divestiture trustee, as the case may be, will be required to demonstrate to the satisfaction of the Commission that the proposed purchaser meets the purchaser requirements, and that the business is divested in a manner consistent with the Commission's decision and the commitments. Where the commitments allow that different purchasers are being proposed for different parts of the package, the Commission will assess whether each individual proposed purchaser is acceptable and that the total package solves the competition problem.

100. In assessing any proposed purchaser, the Commission will interpret the purchaser requirements in the light of the purpose of the commitments, to immediately maintain effective competition in the market where competition concerns had been found, and of the market circumstances as set out in the decision.[106] Generally, the basis for the Commission's assessment of the purchaser requirements will be the submission of the parties, the assessment of the monitoring trustee and, in particular, discussions with the proposed purchaser and its business plan. The Commission will further analyse whether the underlying assumptions of the purchaser appear plausible according to the market circumstances.

Notes

[106] See judgment of the CFI in Case T-342–00 *Petrolessence v Commission* [2003] ECR II-1161.

101. The requirement that the purchaser has to have the necessary financial resources extends in particular to the way the acquisition is financed by the proposed purchaser. The Commission will normally not accept any financing of the divestiture by the seller, and, in particular, any seller financing if this were to give the seller a share in the profits of the divested business in the future.

102. In assessing whether the proposed purchaser threatens to create competition problems, the Commission will undertake a prima facie assessment in the light of the information available to the Commission in the purchaser approval process. Where the purchase results in a concentration that has a Community dimension, this new operation will have to be notified under the Merger Regulation and cleared under normal procedures.[107] Where this is not the case, the Commission's approval of a proposed purchaser is without prejudice to the merger control jurisdiction of national authorities. In addition, the proposed purchaser must be expected to obtain all other necessary approvals from the relevant regulatory authorities. Where it can be foreseen, in the light of the information available to the Commission, that difficulties in obtaining merger control clearance or other approvals may unduly delay the timely implementation of the commitment, it will be considered that the proposed purchaser does not meet the purchaser requirements. Otherwise, the competition concerns identified by the Commission would not be removed in the appropriate time-frame.

Notes

[107] Case IV/M.1383 – *Exxon/Mobil* of 29 September 1999 and the follow-up Cases COMP/M.1820 – *BP/JV Dissolution* of 2 February 2000 and COMP/M.1822 – *Mobil/JV Dissolution* of 2 February 2000.

103. The requirement for an approval by the Commission does usually not only extend to the identity of the purchaser, but also to the sale and purchase agreement and any other agreement entered into between the parties and the proposed purchaser, including transitory agreements. The Commission will verify whether the divestiture according to the agreements is in line with the commitments.[108]

Notes

[108] As discussed above, the parties may apply to the Commission to approve the divestiture of the business to the proposed purchaser without one or more assets or parts of the personnel if this does not affect the viability and competitiveness of the Divestment Business after the sale, taking account of the resources of the proposed purchaser.

104. The Commission will communicate its view as to the suitability of the proposed purchaser to the parties. If the Commission concludes that the proposed purchaser does not meet the purchaser requirements, it will adopt a decision that the proposed purchaser is not a suitable purchaser under the commitments.[109] If the Commission concludes that the sale and purchase agreement (or any ancillary agreements) does not foresee a divestiture in line with the commitments, the Commission will communicate this to the parties without necessarily rejecting the purchaser as such. If the Commission concludes that the purchaser is suitable under the commitments and that the contracts agree a divestiture in line with the commitments, the Commission will approve the divestiture to the proposed purchaser.[110]

Notes

[109] COMP/M.1628 – *TotalFina/Elf* of 9 February 2000, motorway service stations; confirmed by judgment of the CFI in Case T-342/00 *Petrolessence v Commission* [2003] ECR II-1161.

[110] The parties have to ensure, for example through appropriate provisions in the purchase agreement, that the purchaser will maintain the divested business as a competitive force in the market and will not sell on the business within a short time-span.

3. Obligations of the Parties in the Interim Period

105. Parties have to fulfil certain obligations in the interim period (as defined above in paragraph 36). The following should normally be included in the commitments in this respect: (i) safeguards for the interim preservation of the viability to the business, (ii) the necessary steps for a carve-out process, if relevant, and (iii) the necessary steps to prepare the divestiture of the business.

Interim preservation of the divested business

106. It is the parties' responsibility to reduce to the minimum any possible risk of loss of competitive potential of the business to be divested resulting from the uncertainties inherent in the transfer of a business. Up to the transfer of the business to the purchaser, the Commission will require the parties to offer commitments to maintain the independence, economic viability, marketability and competitiveness of the business. Only such commitments will allow the Commission to conclude with the requisite degree of certainty that the divestiture of the business will be implemented in the way as proposed by the parties in the commitments.

107. Generally, these commitments should be designed to keep the business separate from the business retained by the parties, and to ensure that it is managed as a distinct and saleable business in its best interest, with a view to ensuring its continued economic viability, marketability and competitiveness and its independence from the businesses retained by the parties.

108. The parties will be required to ensure that all assets of the business are maintained, pursuant to good business practice and in the ordinary course of business, and that no acts which might have a significant adverse impact on the business are carried out. This relates in particular to the maintenance of fixed assets, know-how or commercial information of a confidential or proprietary nature, the customer base and the technical and commercial competence of the employees. Furthermore, the parties must maintain the business in the same conditions as before the concentration, in particular provide sufficient resources, such as capital or a line of credit, on the basis and continuation of existing business plans, the same administrative and management functions, or other factors relevant for maintaining competition in the specific sector. The commitments also have to foresee that the parties should take all reasonable steps, including appropriate incentive schemes, to encourage all key personnel to remain with the business, and that the parties may not solicit or move any personnel to their remaining businesses.

109. The parties should further hold the business separate from its retained business and ensure that the key personnel of the business to be divested do not have any involvement into the retained businesses and *vice versa*. If the business to be divested is in corporate form and a strict separation of the corporate structure appears necessary, the parties' rights as shareholders, in particular the voting rights, should be exercised by the monitoring trustee which should also have the power to replace the board members appointed on behalf of the parties. In relation to information, the parties must ring-fence the business to be divested and take all necessary measures to ensure that the parties do not obtain any business secrets or other confidential information. Any documents or information confidential to the business obtained by the parties before adoption of the decision have to be returned to the business or destroyed.

110. The parties are further generally required to appoint a hold separate manager with the necessary expertise, who will be responsible for the management of the business and the implementation of the hold-separate and ring-fencing obligations. The hold separate-manager should act under the supervision of the monitoring trustee who may issue instructions to the hold-separate manager. The commitments have to provide that the appointment should take place immediately after the adoption of the decision and even before the parties may close the notified concentration. Whereas the parties can appoint the hold-separate manager on their own, the commitments have to foresee that the monitoring trustee is able to remove the hold-separate manager if s/he does not act in line with the commitments or endangers their timely and proper implementation. A new appointment of a hold-separate manager afterwards will be subject to the approval of the monitoring trustee.

Commentary
para 110: B&C: 8.170

111. As outlined above in paragraph 35, the Commission may accept in appropriate circumstances that the divestiture of a business which needs to be carved out from the remaining businesses of the parties can be considered a suitable remedy. Nevertheless, also in such circumstances only the transfer of a viable business to a purchaser which can maintain and develop this business as an active competitive force in the market will remove the Commission's competition concerns. Therefore, the parties have to commit to a result-oriented obligation to carry out, in the interim period, a carve-out of the assets that contribute to the divested business. The result has to be that a viable and competitive business, which is stand-alone and separate from the other businesses of the parties, can be transferred to a suitable purchaser at the end of the interim period. The parties will have to bear the costs and risks of such a carve-out in the interim period.

112. The carve-out will need to be carried out by the parties under the supervision of the trustee and in cooperation with the hold-separate manager. First, those assets and parts of the personnel which are shared between the business to be divested and remaining businesses of the parties have to be allocated to the business to the extent that this is not excluded in the commitments.[111] The allocation of the assets and the personnel will be monitored and has to be approved by the monitoring trustee. Second, the carve-out process may also require a replication for the business of assets held or functions performed by other parts of the parties' businesses if this is necessary to ensure the viability and competitiveness of the business to be divested. An example is the termination of the business' participation in a central information technology network and an installation of a separate IT system for the business. In general, the major steps of such a carve-out process and the functions to be replicated should be decided on a case-by-case basis and described in the commitments.

Notes
[111] See paragraph 26 above for the question how shared assets have to be dealt with in commitments.

113. At the same time, it has to be ensured that the viability of the business to be divested is not affected by such measures. In the interim period, the parties therefore have to maintain the use of shared assets by and to continue to provide services to the business to the same extent as in the past as long as the business is not yet viable on a stand-alone basis.

Specific obligations of the parties concerning the divestiture process

114. For the divestiture process, the commitments should foresee that potential purchasers can carry out a due diligence exercise and obtain, dependent on the stage of the procedure, sufficient information concerning the divested business and have direct access to its personnel. The parties further have to submit periodic reports on potential purchasers and developments in the negotiations. The divestiture will only be implemented once the transaction is closed, that is the legal title has passed to the approved purchaser, and the assets have been actually transferred. At the end of the process, the parties will have to send a final report, confirming the closing and the transfer of the assets.

4. The Monitoring and the Divestiture Trustee

Role of the Monitoring Trustee

115. As the Commission cannot, on a daily basis, be directly involved in overseeing the implementation of the commitments, the parties have to propose the appointment of a trustee to oversee the parties' compliance with the commitments, in particular with their obligations in the interim period and the divestiture process (the so-called "monitoring trustee"). The monitoring trustee is to be considered the "eyes and ears" of the Commission and shall be the guardian that the business is managed and kept properly on a stand-alone basis in the interim period. The Commission may therefore give any orders and instructions to the monitoring trustee in order to ensure compliance with the commitments, and the trustee may propose to the parties any measures it considers necessary for carrying out its tasks. The parties, however, may not issue any instructions to the trustee without approval by the Commission.

116. The Commitments will generally set out the tasks of the monitoring trustee. Its duties and obligations will be specified in detail in the trustee mandate, to be concluded between the parties and the trustee, and its tasks shall be further detailed in a work-plan. The tasks of the monitoring trustee will normally start immediately after the adoption of the Commission decision and last until the legal and actual transfer of the business to the approved purchaser. Five main, non-exhaustive tasks of the monitoring trustee can be distinguished:

    • First, the monitoring trustee will be called upon to oversee the safeguards for the business to be divested in the interim period.
    • Second, in carve-out cases, the monitoring trustee has to monitor the splitting of assets and the allocation of the personnel between the divested business and retained businesses by the parties as well as the replication of assets and functions in the business previously provided by the parties.
    • Third, the monitoring trustee shall be responsible for overseeing the parties' efforts to find a potential purchaser and to transfer the business. In general, it shall review the progress of the divestiture process and the potential purchasers included in the process. It shall verify that potential purchasers receive sufficient information relating to the business - in particular by reviewing the information memorandum (if available), the data room or the due diligence process. Once a purchaser is proposed, the monitoring trustee shall submit to the Commission a reasoned opinion as to whether the proposed purchaser fulfils the purchaser requirements in the commitments and whether the business is sold in a manner consistent with the commitments. At the end of the process, the monitoring trustee has to oversee the legal and actual transfer of the business to the purchaser and make a final report, confirming the transfer.
    • Fourth, the monitoring trustee shall act as a contact point for any requests by third parties, in particular potential purchasers, in relation to the commitments. The parties shall inform interested third parties of the identity and the tasks of the monitoring trustee, including any potential purchasers. In case of disagreement between the parties and third parties in relation to matters dealt with by the commitments, the monitoring trustee shall discuss those matters with both sides and try to find a suitable solution. In order to be able to carry out its role, the monitoring trustee will keep confidential any business secrets of the parties and third parties.
    • Fifth, the monitoring trustee shall report on these issues to the Commission in periodic compliance reports and shall also submit additional reports upon request by the Commission.

117. The commitments will also comprehensively set out the parties' obligations to support and cooperate with the monitoring trustee. In order to fulfil its tasks, the trustee shall have access to all books and records of the parties and of the divested business, may request managerial and administrative support by the parties, shall be informed of potential purchasers and all developments in the divestiture process, and shall be provided with the information submitted to potential purchasers. In addition, the parties shall indemnify the trustee and allow the trustee to appoint advisors, if appropriate for the fulfilment of its tasks under the commitments.

Role of the Divestiture Trustee

118. If the parties do not succeed in finding a suitable purchaser within the first divestiture period, then in the trustee divestiture period, the divestiture trustee will be given an irrevocable and exclusive mandate to dispose of the business within a specific deadline at no minimum price to a suitable purchaser. The commitments shall allow the divestiture trustee to include in the sale and purchase agreement such terms and conditions as it considers appropriate for an expedient sale, in particular customary representations, warranties and indemnities. The sale of the business by the divestiture trustee is in the same way subject to the prior approval of the Commission as the sale by the parties.

119. The commitments will set out that the parties are obliged to support and inform the divestiture trustee and fully cooperate with the trustee in the same way as this is foreseen for the monitoring trustee. For the divestiture, the parties have to grant to the divestiture trustee comprehensive powers of attorney, covering all stages of the divestiture.

Approval of the trustee and the trustee mandate

120. Depending on the commitment, the monitoring trustee may or may not be the same person or institution as the divestiture trustee. The parties shall propose one or several potential trustees to the Commission, including the full terms of the mandate and an outline of a work-plan. It is of the essence that the monitoring trustee is in place immediately after the Commission decision. Therefore, the parties should propose a suitable trustee immediately after the Commission decision and the commitments normally have to foresee that the notified concentration can only be implemented once the monitoring trustee is appointed, after being approved by the Commission.[112] The situation is different for the divestiture trustee who should be appointed well ahead of the end of the first divestiture period[113] so that its mandate can take effect with the beginning of the trustee divestiture period.

Notes

[112] See Case COMP/M.4180 – *GdF/Suez* of 14 November 2006; Case COMP/M.4187 – *Metso/Aker Kvaerner* of 12 December 2006; Case COMP/M.3916 – *T-Mobile/Tele.ring* of 20 April 2006.

[113] The Commission will normally require an appointment at least one month ahead of the end of the first divestiture period.

---

121. Both types of trustees will be appointed by the parties on the basis of a trustee mandate, entered into by the parties and the trustee. The appointment and the mandate will be subject to the approval by the Commission which will have discretion in the selection of the trustee and will assess whether the proposed candidate is suitable for the tasks in the specific case. The trustee shall be independent of the parties, possess the necessary qualifications to carry out its mandate and shall not be, or become, exposed to a conflict of interests.

122. The Commission will assess the necessary qualifications in the light of the requirements of the specific case, including the geographic area and the sector concerned. According to the Commission's experience, auditing firms and other consulting firms may be particularly well placed to fulfil the tasks of a monitoring trustee. Individuals who have worked in the specific industry may also be suitable candidates for performing such a role if they have the necessary resources available to deal with the tasks at stake. Investment banks seem to be particularly suitable for the role of a divestiture trustee. The independence of the trustee is crucial in order to enable the trustee to properly fulfil its role of monitoring the parties' compliance for the Commission and to ensure its credibility vis-à-vis third parties. In particular, the Commission will not accept persons or institutions as trustees which are at the same time the parties' auditors or their investment advisors in the divestiture. However, no conflicts of interests will arise by relations of the trustee with the parties if those relations will not impair the Trustee's objectivity and independence in discharging its tasks. It is the parties' responsibility to supply the Commission with adequate information for it to verify that the trustee fulfils the requirements. The appointment of the trustee after approval by the parties is irrevocable unless the trustee is replaced with the approval of or upon request by the Commission.

123. The trustee mandate shall define the tasks as specified in the commitments further and shall include all provisions necessary to enable the trustee to fulfil its tasks under the commitments accepted by the Commission. The parties are responsible for remuneration of the trustee under the mandate, and the remuneration structure must be such as to not impede the trustee's independence and effectiveness in fulfilling the mandate. The Commission will approve a trustee only together with a suitable mandate. In appropriate cases, it may publish the identity of the trustee and a summary of its tasks.

124. When the specific commitments with which the trustee has been entrusted have been implemented - that is to say, when legal title for the business to be divested has passed, the assets have been actually transferred to the purchaser and specific arrangements which may continue post-divestiture have been fulfilled - the mandate will provide for the trustee to request the Commission for a discharge from further responsibilities. Even after the discharge has been given, it may be necessary for the Commission to require the reappointment of the trustee on the basis of the commitments, if it appears subsequently to the Commission that the relevant commitments might not have been fully and properly implemented.

5. Obligations of the Parties Following Implementation of the Divestiture

125. The Commitments also have to foresee that for a period of 10 years after the adoption of the decision accepting the commitments the Commission may request information from the parties. This will allow the Commission to monitor the implementation of the remedy.

6. Implementation of Other Commitments

126. Many of the principles discussed above for the implementation of divestiture commitments can equally be applied to other types of commitments if those commitments need to be implemented subsequent to the Commission decision. For example, if it is foreseen that the beneficiary of a licence needs to be approved by the Commission, the considerations regarding the purchaser approval can be applied. Given the wide range of non-divestiture commitments, no general and comprehensive requirements for the implementation of non-divestiture commitments can be set out.

127. However, given the long duration of non-divestiture commitments and their frequent complexity, they often require a very high monitoring effort and specific monitoring tools in order to allow the Commission to conclude that they will effectively be implemented. Therefore, the Commission will often require the involvement of a trustee to oversee the implementation of such commitments and the establishment of a fast-track arbitration procedure in order to provide for a dispute resolution mechanism and to render the commitments enforceable by the market participants themselves. In past cases, the Commission has often required both the appointment of a trustee and an arbitration clause.[114] In those circumstances, the trustee will oversee the implementation of the commitments, but will also be able to assist in arbitral proceedings to the effect that they may be finalised in a short period of time.

Notes

[114] Such an approach of combined monitoring by arbitration and a monitoring trustee was, *e.g.*, used in Case COMP/M.2803 – *Telia/Sonera* of 10 July 2002; Case COMP/M.3083 – *GE/Instrumentarium* of 2 September 2003; and Case COMP/M.3225 – *Alcan/Pechiney II* of 29 September 2003.

D16

SCHEDULE OF PUBLIC HOLIDAYS FOR 2008

(2006/C 169/03)

Official Journal C 169, 21.7.2006, p. 3

Celex No: 52006XC0721(02)

1st January	Tuesday, New Year's Day
2nd January	Wednesday, day following New Year's Day
20th March	Maundy Thursday
21st March	Good Friday
24th March	Easter Monday
1st May	Thursday, Ascension Day
2nd May	Friday, day following Ascension Day

9th May	Friday, Anniversary of the Declaration made by President Robert Schuman in 1950
12th May	Whit Monday
21st July	Monday, Belgian National Holiday
15th August	Friday, Assumption Day
24th December to	Wednesday
	} 6 days — Christmas and end of year
31st December	Wednesday

TOTAL: 17 days

The above-mentioned dates also apply to Luxembourg, except that Monday 21 July is replaced by Monday 23 June, Luxembourg National Holiday.

Work will resume as normal on Monday 5 January 2009.

Without prejudice to the schedule of public holidays for 2009, Thursday 1 January 2009 and Friday 2 January 2009 will be holidays.

The Commission reserves the right to modify the decisions, should the needs of service so require.

D17

SCHEDULE OF PUBLIC HOLIDAYS FOR 2009

(2007/C 171/08)

Official Journal C 171, 24.7.2007, p. 10

Celex No: 5200 7XC0724(02)

1st January	Thursday, New Year's Day
2nd January	Friday, day following New Year's Day
9th April	Maundy Thursday
10th April	Good Friday
13th April	Easter Monday
1st May	Friday, Labour Day
21st May	Thursday, Ascension Day
22nd May	Friday, day following Ascension Day
1st June	Whit Monday
21st July	Tuesday, Belgian National Holiday
2nd November	Monday, All Souls' Day
24th December to	Thursday
	} 6 days — Christmas and end of year
31st December	Thursday

TOTAL: 17 days

The above-mentioned dates also apply to Luxembourg, except that Tuesday 21 July is replaced by Tuesday 23 June, Luxembourg National Holiday.

Work will resume as normal on Monday 4 January 2010. Without prejudice to the schedule of public holidays for 2010, Friday 1 January 2010 will be holidays.

The Commission reserves the right to modify the decisions, should the needs of service so require.

D18

US–EU MERGER WORKING GROUP: BEST PRACTICES ON COOPERATION IN MERGER INVESTIGATIONS

Note

This document is published on the Europa website at:
http://ec.europa.eu/comm/competition/mergers/others/eu_us.pdf

---

This document sets forth best practices which the United States federal antitrust agencies and the Commission of the European Union will seek to apply, to the extent consistent with their respective laws and enforcement responsibilities, when they simultaneously review the same merger transaction.[1] A number of these best practices already are routinely employed informally between the US and EU. With that in mind, this statement of best practices seeks to set out the conditions under which trans-Atlantic inter-agency cooperation in merger investigations should be conducted, while at the same time confirming and building upon current good practice.

Notes

[1] This document is intended to set forth an advisory framework for interagency cooperation. The agencies reserve their full discretion in the implementation of these best practices and nothing in this document is intended to create any enforceable rights.

Objectives

1. In today's global economy, many sizeable transactions involving international businesses are likely to be subject to review by the EU and by the US. Where the US and EU are reviewing the same transaction, both jurisdictions have an interest in reaching, insofar as possible, consistent, or at least non-conflicting, outcomes.[2] Divergent approaches to assessment of the likely impact on competition of the same transaction undermine public confidence in the merger review process, risk imposing inconsistent requirements on the firms involved, and may frustrate the agencies' respective remedial objectives.

Notes

[2] Cooperation between the US and EU agencies is based primarily upon the 1991 US–EC Agreement on the Application of their Competition Laws, a principal purpose of which is to avoid conflict in the enforcement of their antitrust laws.

---

2. These best practices are designed to further enhance cooperation in merger review between the United States Department of Justice ("DOJ") or the U.S. Federal Trade Commission ("FTC") (hereafter referred to as the "US"),[3] on the one hand, and the European Commission (hereafter referred to as the "EU"), on the other. They are intended to promote fully-informed decision-making on the part of both sides' authorities, to minimize the risk of divergent outcomes on

both sides of the Atlantic, to facilitate coherence and compatibility in remedies, to enhance the efficiency of their respective investigations, to reduce burdens on merging parties and third parties, and to increase the overall transparency of the merger review processes.

Notes

[3] This document assumes that, consistent with past practice, only one US agency — either the DOJ or FTC — reviews each pertinent transaction and, accordingly, coordinates with the EU regarding that transaction.

---

3. Given legal constraints existing in both jurisdictions, effective inter-agency coordination between the US and the EU depends to a considerable extent on the cooperation and good will of the merging parties, and to a lesser extent on third parties. In particular, cooperation is more complete and effective when the merging parties allow the agencies to share information the disclosure of which is subject to confidentiality restrictions. In addition, coordination between the agencies is most effective when the investigation timetables of the US and the EU run more or less in parallel so that the investigative staffs of each agency can engage with one another and with the parties on substantive issues at similar points in their investigations. The agencies intend, therefore, to work cooperatively with one another and with the parties, as appropriate, to promote such timetable coordination. At the same time, the EU and US agencies recognize that many considerations go into confidentiality waiver and transaction timing and/or notification decisions and that these decisions are within the discretion of the merging parties. Accordingly, it should be emphasized that any party's choice not to abide by some or all of the agencies' recommendations will not in any way prejudice the conduct or outcome of the agencies' investigations.

Coordination on Timing

4. Cooperation is most effective when the investigation timetables of the reviewing agencies run more or less in parallel, recognizing there are differences between US and EU merger review processes. To that end, the agencies should endeavour to keep one another apprised of important developments related to the timing of their respective investigations throughout the course of their reviews of merger transactions subject to review by the US and the EU.

5. In appropriate cases, the reviewing agencies should offer the merging parties an opportunity to confer with the relevant EU and US staffs jointly to discuss timing issues. Such a conference will be most beneficial if held as soon as feasible after the transaction has been announced. At this conference, the agencies and parties should be prepared to discuss ways to synchronize the timing of the US and EU investigations, to the extent possible under EU and US law respectively. Topics addressed may include the appropriate times to file in the US and EU, suggested timeframes for the submission of documents or other information, and, where appropriate, the prospect of a timing agreement (in the US) and/or a waiver from the obligation to notify within seven days of the conclusion of a binding agreement (in the EU). The success of this effort depends on the active participation and cooperation of the parties, and would, in most cases, require the parties to discuss timing with the agencies before filing in either jurisdiction.

Collection and Evaluation of Evidence

6. In significant matters under review by both jurisdictions, the agencies should seek to coordinate with one another throughout the course of their investigations and keep one another apprised of their progress. This may include sharing publicly available information and, consistent with their confidentiality obligations, discussing their respective analyses at various stages of an investigation, including tentative market definitions, assessment of competitive effects, efficiencies, theories of competitive harm, economic theories, and the empirical evidence needed to test those theories. Views on necessary remedial measures, and similar past investigations and cases, also may be discussed. The agencies also may discuss and coordinate information or discovery requests to the merging parties and third parties, including exchanging draft questionnaires to the extent permitted by the respective jurisdictions' laws and regulations.

7. Waivers of confidentiality executed by merging parties enable more complete communication between the reviewing agencies and with the merging parties regarding evidence that is relevant to the investigation. This results in more informed decision-making and more effective coordination between the reviewing agencies, thereby helping to avoid divergent analyses and outcomes, as

well as expediting merger review. Accordingly, as soon as feasible after the announcement of a transaction that requires review by the US and EU, the staffs of the reviewing agencies should, in appropriate cases, enter into discussion with the parties with a view to requesting the possible execution by the merging parties of confidentiality waivers, providing sample waiver letters if necessary. The reviewing agencies should, where appropriate and feasible, also encourage the merging parties to allow joint EU/US agency interviews with party executives and joint conferences with the parties.

8. Similarly, waivers of confidentiality executed by third parties enable more complete communication between the reviewing agencies and with third parties and can reduce the investigative burden imposed on third parties. Where appropriate, the reviewing agencies may, therefore, request that third parties waive confidentiality, or simply request that third parties provide the same information divulged to one reviewing agency to the other. The agencies may also encourage joint interviews and conferences with third parties, where appropriate and feasible.

Communication Between the Reviewing Agencies

9. The reviewing agencies will, via liaison officers or otherwise, contact one other upon learning of a transaction that appears to require review by both the US and EU.

10. At the start of any investigation in which it appears that substantial cooperation between the US and EU may be beneficial, each agency should designate a contact person who will be responsible for: setting up a schedule for conferences between the relevant investigative staffs of each agency; discussing with the merging parties the possibility of coordinating investigation timetables (see Section II above); and coordinating information gathering or discovery efforts, including seeking waivers from the merging parties and from third-parties.

11. At the start of any investigation in which it appears that substantial cooperation between the US and EU may be beneficial, the relevant DOJ Section Chiefs/FTC Assistant Directors and the EU Merger Task Force Unit Head (or their designees) should seek to agree on a tentative timetable for regular consultations between them on the progress of their investigations. The timetable for consultations will take into account the nature and timing of the transaction. Consultations normally should occur: (a) before the US closes its investigation without taking action; (b) before the US issues a second request; (c) no later than three weeks following the initiation of a Phase I investigation in the EU; (d) before the EU opens a Phase II investigation or clears the merger without going to Phase II; (e) before the EU closes a Phase II investigation without issuing a Statement of Objections or approximately two weeks before the EU anticipates issuing its Statement of Objections; (f) before the relevant US DOJ/FTC section/division investigating the merger makes its case recommendation to the relevant DOJ DAAG or the FTC Bureau Director; and (g) at the commencement of remedies negotiations with the merging parties. Discussions may also take place at any other point the DOJ Chiefs/FTC Assistant Directors and the EU Unit Head find useful.

12. In some cases, consultations may be appropriate between senior competition officials for the EU (the Competition Commissioner, Director General for Competition, or Deputy Director General for Mergers, as appropriate) and their counterparts at the Antitrust Division of the Department of Justice (the Assistant Attorney General for Antitrust or the relevant DOJ Deputy Assistant Attorney General ("DAAG"), as appropriate) or the Federal Trade Commission (the Chairman, Director of the Bureau of Competition, or Deputy Director of the Bureau of Competition, as appropriate). In such cases, consultations are likely to be particularly useful: (a) shortly before or after the US issues a second request and the EU initiates a Phase II investigation; (b) approximately one week before the EU anticipates issuing its Statement of Objections; (c) approximately one week after the relevant DOJ/FTC section/division investigating the merger makes its case recommendation to the relevant DOJ DAAG or FTC Bureau Director; and (d) prior to a decision by the Antitrust Division or FTC to challenge a merger or by the Competition Commissioner to recommend that the European Commission prohibit a merger. Consultations may also take place between their economic counterparts. These officials may find it useful to confer at other points in the investigation as well.

13. Pursuant to the terms of the Administrative Arrangements on Attendance of 1999, the US and EU, as appropriate, may attend certain key events in the other's investigative process.

Part D Mergers and Concentrations

These include (a) the EU's Oral Hearing and (b) the merging parties' presentations to the Assistant Attorney General or Deputy Assistant Attorney General or to the Director or Deputy Director of the Bureau of Competition at which the parties present their arguments prior to the agency's decision whether to take enforcement action.

Remedies/Settlements

14. The reviewing agencies recognize that the remedies offered by the merging parties may not always be identical, in particular because the effects of a transaction may be different in the US than in the EU. Nevertheless, a remedy accepted in one jurisdiction may have an impact on the other. To the extent consistent with their respective law enforcement responsibilities, the reviewing agencies should strive to ensure that the remedies they accept do not impose inconsistent obligations upon the merging parties. The agencies should, therefore, advise that the parties consider coordinating the timing and substance of remedy proposals being made to the EU and US agencies, so as to minimize the risk of inconsistent results or subsequent difficulties in implementation.

15. Consistent with their confidentiality and/or non-disclosure obligations, the reviewing agencies should seek to keep one another informed of remedy offers being considered and of other relevant developments with respect to remedies to the extent they may impact the other jurisdiction's review. Where appropriate, and consistent with confidentiality and/or non-disclosure obligations, the agencies should share draft remedy proposals or settlement papers, on which they may provide comments to one another, and participate in joint conferences with the parties, buyers, and trustees.

D19

CASE REFERRAL UNDER
THE EEA AGREEMENT

Note

This document is published on the Europa website at:
http://ec.europa.eu/comm/competition/mergers/legislation/regulation/regulation139/eea_referral.pdf

1. Introduction

When the Commission has jurisdiction to deal with a case under the Merger Regulation,[1] it is the sole competent authority in the EEA,[2] which means that it exercises its powers not only with respect to the EC Member States, but also with respect to the territories of the EFTA States.[3] The rules on referral of cases under the EEA Agreement are included in Protocol 24 to the EEA Agreement. These are based on the Merger Regulation's system for referral of cases, but have been subject to certain adaptations. Following the adoption of Council Regulation 139/2004, many of the new rules on referral (pre-notification and post-notification) of cases included in the Regulation have likewise been incorporated into the EEA Agreement.[4]

The referral rules in Protocol 24 of the EEA Agreement apply with regard to cases referred to or from the EFTA States. The referral rules in the Merger Regulation are applicable in parallel with regard to cases referred to or from the EC Member States. Thus, in a case which involves referrals involving both EFTA States and EC Member States, the two sets of rules are applicable. When a referral involves EFTA States only, the EEA Agreement alone applies. Similarly, when a referral involves exclusively EC Member States, only the rules of the Merger Regulation apply.

According to the referral rules in the EEA Agreement, there is a more limited scope for the EFTA States than for the EC Member States to request the referral of a case to the Commission. The rules on referral of cases from the Commission to the EFTA States are, however, essentially identical to those in the Merger Regulation.

Notes

[1] Council Regulation (EC) No 139/2004 of 20 January 2004 on the control of concentrations between undertakings, OJ L 24/1, 29.1.2004.

[2] This follows from Article 57(2) and Annex XIV to the EEA Agreement. The EEA Agreement and its Annexes and Protocols can be found of the web-site of the EFTA.

[3] For the purpose of this note, the term EFTA States, which is the term used in the EEA Agreement, refers to Iceland, Liechtenstein and Norway, and not to Switzerland which has not ratified the EEA Agreement.

[4] See the Commission's web-site:
http://europa.eu.int/comm/competition/mergers/legislation/regulation/regulation139/

---

2. Pre-notification referrals under the EEA Agreement

The EEA Agreement provides for **pre-notification referrals from the EFTA States to the Commission**, by allowing the parties to a concentration to request the Commission to examine a concentration which is "capable of being reviewed under the national competition laws of at least three EC Member States and at least one EFTA State".[5] Such a request is optional for the parties. It constitutes an "add-on" to a request for referral from three or more EC Member States under Article 4(5) of Regulation 139/2004. This means that if a case is capable of being reviewed under the competition laws of, e.g., France, Poland, and Norway, this is not sufficient for the case to be referred to the Commission; it is necessary that the case is reviewable also under the national law of a third EC Member State.

If one or more EFTA States vetoes the referral, the competent EFTA State(s) shall retain its/their competence to examine the case under its national competition law and the case shall not be referred from any EFTA State. However, a veto by an EFTA State has no impact on the fate of the request for referral from the EC Member States concerned and the Commission.

The parties can also request the **pre-notification referral of a case from the Commission to a competent EFTA State**. In this situation, the rules of the EEA Agreement are essentially identical to those of the Merger Regulation.[6] They provide that an undertaking concerned may inform the Commission by means of a reasoned submission that the "concentration may significantly affect competition in a market within an EFTA State, which presents all the characteristics of a distinct market and should therefore be examined, in whole or in part, by that EFTA State.. In such circumstances, the rules applicable to the assessment of that request by the Commission and by the EFTA State(s) concerned are in substance the same as those set out in the Merger Regulation.

Notes

[5] See Article 6(5) of Protocol 24 to the EEA Agreement, and Article 4(5) of the Merger Regulation. EEA referrals — 14/10/2004

[6] See Article 6(4) of Protocol 24 to the EEA Agreement, and Article 4(4) of the Merger Regulation.

---

3. Post-notification referrals under the EEA Agreement

The EEA Agreement enables **post-notification referral from the Commission to an EFTA State** of a case or of a part or parts of a case.[7]

The Commission may refer a notified concentration to an EFTA State in two situations. First, a case may be referred where the concentration "threatens to affect significantly competition in a market within that EFTA State, which presents all the characteristics of a distinct market". Second, the Commission may refer a case to an EFTA State where the concentration "affects competition in a market within that EFTA State, which presents all the characteristics of a distinct market and which does not constitute a substantial part of the territory covered by the Agreement".[8]

As regards **post-notification referral of cases to the Commission**, an EFTA State may only join a referral request made by an EC Member State; it may not initiate such a request itself. This is consistent with the "two-pillar" system of the EEA-Agreement, and means that the powers of the EFTA States are in this regard somewhat more limited than those of the EC Member States.

Part D Mergers and Concentrations

Accordingly, where a concentration may affect trade between one or more EC Member States and one or more EFTA States, and it threatens to significantly affect competition in one or more EFTA States, that State or these States may join a request for referral put forward by one or more EC Member States.[9]

As under the Merger Regulation, the EEA Agreement provides that when the EFTA States receive the request by an EC Member State to refer a case to the Commission, all national time limits relating to the concentration shall be suspended in all the EFTA States competent to review the case until it has been decided whether the Commission will examine the case or not. Once an EFTA State has informed the Commission that it does not wish to join the request, that EFTA State retains its competence to examine the case and its national time limits start running anew. If the Commission decides to examine the referred concentration, the EFTA State or the EFTA States that joined the request are no longer competent to examine the case under their national competition law. An EFTA State that does not join the request can apply its national competition law to the concentration.

Notes

[7] See Article 6(1) of Protocol 24 to the EEA Agreement.
[8] These provisions closely correspond to the provisions in Article 9(2)(a) and 9(2)(b) of the Merger Regulation, but are not identical to them. In particular, it should be noted that the Commission has no discretion regarding a case meeting the requirements set out in Article 9(2)(b) of the Merger Regulation, but does enjoy discretion regarding referral of the corresponding category of cases under Article 6(1) of Protocol 24 to the EEA Agreement.
[9] See Article 6(3) of Protocol 24 to the EEA Agreement. EEA referrals — 14/10/2004

4. Calculation of time limits

In general, the procedure governing referral requests including the EFTA States is the same as for requests applicable to requests involving only EC Member States. However, although the time limits are the same for the EFTA States as for the EC Member States, the manner in which they are calculated differs somewhat. The time limits start to run, for pre- and post notification referrals involving the EFTA States, upon receipt of the request for referral and other relevant documents by the EFTA Surveillance Authority, and not upon the receipt by the EFTA States of the documents in question.[10]

Notes

[10] See Article 13 of Protocol 24 to the EEA Agreement.

5. Submission of pre-notification referral requests

As regards the submission of requests for pre-notification referrals, an unofficial version of the Form RS, which is intended to give guidance on the information undertakings may wish to provide should they seek a referral involving any of the EFTA States, has been published on the web site of DG Competition.[11] Merging parties are therefore encouraged to use this form.

According to Section D of that unofficial version of the Form RS, where a reasoned submission is made according to the EEA Agreement[12] in an official language of an EFTA State which is not an official language of the Community, the submission must simultaneously be supplemented by a translation into an official language of the Community.

Notes

[11] http://europa.eu.int/comm/competition/mergers/legislation/regulation/regulation139/form_rs_eea_en.pdf
[12] See Article 12 of Protocol 24 to the EEA Agreement.

PART E

SECTORAL REGIMES

E1

REGULATION (EEC) No 1017/68 OF THE COUNCIL

of 19 July 1968
applying rules of competition to transport by rail, road and inland waterway

Official Journal L 175, 23.7.1968, p. 1

Celex No: 31968R1017

Notes

EEA application: this Regulation is incorporated, with appropriate adaptations, in the EEA Agreement, Annex XIV, Chapter G, Point 10 (as subsequently amended by EEA Joint Committee Decision No 130/2004 (OJ No L 64, 10.3.2005, p. 57 and EEA Supplement No 12, 10.3.2005, p. 42) and Decision No 43/2005 (OJ No L 198, 28.7.2005, p. 45 and EEA Supplement No 38, 28.7.2005, p. 26)).

On 27 November 2006, the Commission presented a proposal for a codified Regulation applying rules of competition to transport by rail, road and inland waterway in substitution for Regulation 1017/68/EEC: see http://eur-lex.europa.eu/LexUriServ/site/en/com/2006/com2006_0722en01.pdf

Commentary

Regulation 1017/68: B&C: 2.085, 3.082, 3.093, 5.033, 5.080, 7.015, 12.006–12.007, 12.023, 13.015, 13.169, 13.223, 14.085 **F&N**: 14.08, 14.10, 14.123, 14.149, 14.175, 14.176, 14.181, 14.182, 14.183, 14.188

THE COUNCIL OF THE EUROPEAN COMMUNITIES,

Having regard to the Treaty establishing the European Economic Community, and in particular Articles [71] and [83] thereof;

Having regard to the proposal from the Commission;

Having regard to the Opinion of the European Parliament;[1]

Having regard to the Opinion of the Economic and Social Committee;[2]

Notes

[1] OJ No 205, 11.12.1964, p. 3505/64.
[2] OJ No 103, 12.6.1965, p. 1792/65.

---

[1] Whereas Council Regulation No 141[1] exempting transport from the application of Regulation No 17 provides that the said Regulation No 17[2] shall not apply to agreements, decisions and concerted practices in the transport sector the effect of which is to fix transport rates and conditions, to limit or control the supply of transport or to share transport markets, nor to dominant positions, within the meaning of Article [82] of the Treaty, on the transport market;

Notes

[1] OJ No 124, 28.11.1962, p. 2751/62.
[2] OJ No 13, 21.2.1962, p. 204/62.

---

[2] Whereas, for transport by rail, road and inland waterway, Regulation No 1002/67/CEE[1] provides that such exemption shall not extend beyond 30 June 1968;

Notes

[1] OJ No 306, 16.12.1967, p. 1.

---

[3] Whereas the establishing of rules of competition for transport by rail, road and inland waterway is part of the common transport policy and of general economic policy;

[4] Whereas, when rules of competition for these sectors are being settled, account must be taken of the distinctive features of transport;

[5] Whereas, since the rules of competition for transport derogate from the general rules of competition, it must be made possible for undertakings to ascertain what rules apply in any particular case;

[6] Whereas, with the introduction of a system of rules on competition for transport, it is desirable that such rules should apply equally to the joint financing or acquisition of transport equipment for the joint operation of services by certain groupings of undertakings, and also to certain operations in connection with transport by rail, road or inland waterway of providers of services ancillary to transport;

[7] Whereas, in order to ensure that trade between Member States is not affected or competition within the common market distorted, it is necessary to prohibit in principle for the three modes of transport specified above all agreements between undertakings, decisions of associations of undertakings and concerted practices between undertakings and all instances of abuse of a dominant position within the common market which could have such effects;

[8] Whereas certain types of agreement, decision and concerted practice in the transport sector the object and effect of which is merely to apply technical improvements or to achieve technical co-operation may be exempted from the prohibition on restrictive agreements since they contribute to improving productivity; whereas, in the light of experience following application of this Regulation, the Council may, on a proposal from the Commission, amend the list of such types of agreement;

Commentary
Recital 8: B&C: 12.011

[9] Whereas, in order that an improvement may be fostered in the sometimes too dispersed structure of the industry in the road and inland waterway sectors, there should also be exempted from the prohibition on restrictive agreements those agreements, decisions and concerted practices providing for the creation and operation of groupings of undertakings in these two transport sectors whose object is the carrying on of transport operations, including the joint financing or acquisition of transport equipment for the joint operation of services; whereas such overall exemption can be granted only on condition that the total carrying capacity of a grouping does not exceed a fixed maximum, and that the individual capacity of undertakings belonging to the grouping does not exceed certain limits so fixed as to ensure that no one undertaking can hold a dominant position within the grouping; whereas the Commission must, however, have power to intervene if, in specific cases, such agreements should have effects incompatible with the conditions under which a restrictive agreement may be recognised as lawful, and should constitute an abuse of the exemption; whereas, nevertheless, the fact that a grouping has a total carrying capacity greater than the fixed maximum, or cannot claim the overall exemption because of the individual capacity of the undertakings belonging to the grouping, does not in itself prevent such a grouping from constituting a lawful agreement, decision or concerted practice if it satisfies the conditions therefor laid down in this Regulation;

[10] Whereas, where an agreement, decision or concerted practice contributes towards improving the quality of transport services, or towards promoting greater continuity and stability in the satisfaction of transport needs on markets where supply and demand may be subject to considerable temporal fluctuation, or towards increasing the productivity of undertakings, or towards furthering technical or economic progress, it must be made possible for the prohibition to be declared not to apply, always provided, however, that the agreement, decision or concerted practice takes fair account of the interests of transport users, and neither imposes on the undertakings concerned any restriction not indispensable to the attainment of the above objectives nor makes it possible for such undertakings to eliminate competition in respect of a substantial part of the transport market concerned, having regard to competition from alternative modes of transport;

[11] Whereas it is desirable until such time as the Council, acting in pursuance of the common transport policy, introduces appropriate measures to ensure a stable transport market, and subject to the

condition that the Council shall have found that a state of crisis exists, to authorise, for the market in question, such agreements as are needed in order to reduce disturbance resulting from the structure of the transport market;

[12] Whereas, in respect of transport by rail, road and inland waterway, it is desirable that Member States should neither enact nor maintain in force measures contrary to this Regulation concerning public undertakings or undertakings to which they grant special or exclusive rights; whereas it is also desirable that undertakings entrusted with the operation of services of general economic importance should be subject to the provisions of this Regulation in so far as the application thereof does not obstruct, in law or in fact, the accomplishment of the particular tasks assigned to them, always provided that the development of trade is not thereby affected to such an extent as would be contrary to the interests of the Community; whereas the Commission must have power to see that these principles are applied and to address the appropriate directives or decisions for this purpose to Member States;

[13] Whereas the detailed rules for application of the basic principles of this Regulation must be so drawn that they not only ensure effective supervision while simplifying administration as far as possible but also meet the needs of undertakings for certainty in the law;

[14] Whereas it is for the undertakings themselves, in the first instance, to judge whether the predominant effects of their agreements, decisions or concerted practices are the restriction of competition or the economic benefits acceptable as justification for such restriction and to decide accordingly, on their own responsibility, as to the illegality or legality of such agreements, decisions or concerted practices;

[15] Whereas, therefore, undertakings should be allowed to conclude or operate agreements without declaring them; whereas this exposes such agreements to the risk of being declared void with retroactive effect should they be examined following a complaint or on the Commission's own initiative, but does not prevent their being retroactively declared lawful in the event of such subsequent examination;

[16] Whereas, however, undertakings may, in certain cases, desire the assistance of the competent authorities to ensure that their agreements, decisions of concerted practices are in conformity with the rules applicable; whereas for this purpose there should be made available to undertakings a procedure whereby they may submit applications to the Commission and a summary of each such application is published in the *Official Journal of the European Communities*, enabling any interested third parties to submit their comments on the agreement in question; whereas, in the absence of any complaint from Member States or interested third parties and unless the Commission notifies applicants within a fixed time limit, that there are serious doubts as to the legality of the agreement in question, that agreement should be deemed exempt from the prohibition for the time already elapsed and for a further period of three years;

[17] Whereas, in view of the exceptional nature of agreements needed in order to reduce disturbances resulting from the structure of the transport market, once the Council has found that a state of crisis exists undertakings wishing to obtain authorisation for such an agreement should be required to notify it to the Commission; whereas authorisation by the Commission should have effect only from the date when it is decided to grant it; whereas the period of validity of such authorisation should not exceed three years from the finding of a state of crisis by the Council; whereas renewal of the decision should depend upon renewal of the finding of a state of crisis by the Council; whereas, in any event, the authorisation should cease to be valid not later than six months from the bringing into operation by the Council of appropriate measures to ensure the stability of the transport market to which the agreement relates;

[18] Whereas, in order to secure uniform application within the common market of the rules of competition for transport, rules must be made under which the Commission, acting in close and constant liaison with the competent authorities of the Member States, may take the measures required for the application of such rules of competition;

[19] Whereas for this purpose the Commission must have the co-operation of the competent authorities of the Member States and be empowered throughout the common market to request such information and to carry out such investigations as are necessary to bring to light any agreement, decision

or concerted practice prohibited under this Regulation, or any abuse of a dominant position prohibited under this Regulation.

[20] Whereas, if, on the application of the Regulation to a specific case, a Member State is of the opinion that a question of principle concerning the common transport policy is involved, it should be possible for such questions of principle to be examined by the Council; whereas it should be possible for any general questions raised by the implementation of the competition policy in the transport sector to be referred to the Council; whereas a procedure must be provided for which ensures that any decision to apply the Regulation in a specific case will be taken by the Commission only after the questions of principle have been examined by the Council, and in the light of the policy guidelines that emerge from that examination;

[21] Whereas, in order to carry out its duty of ensuring that the provisions of this Regulation are applied, the Commission must be empowered to address to undertakings or associations of undertakings recommendations and decisions for the [purpose] of bringing to an end infringements of the provisions of this Regulation prohibiting certain agreements, decisions or practices;

[22] Whereas compliance with the prohibitions laid down in this Regulation and the fulfilment of obligations imposed on undertakings and associations of undertakings under this Regulation must be enforceable by means of fines and periodic penalty payments;

[23] Whereas undertakings concerned must be accorded the right to be heard by the Commission, third parties whose interests may be affected by a decision must be given the opportunity of submitting their comments beforehand, and it must be ensured that wide publicity is given to decisions taken;

[24] Whereas it is desirable to confer upon the Court of Justice, pursuant to Article [229], unlimited jurisdiction in respect of decisions under which the Commission imposes fines or periodic penalty payments;

[25] Whereas it is expedient to postpone for six months, as regards agreements, decisions and concerted practices in existence at the date of publication of this Regulation in the Official Journal of the European Communities, the entry into force of the prohibition laid down in the Regulation, in order to make it easier for undertakings to adjust their operations so as to conform to its provisions;

[26] Whereas, following discussions with the third countries signatories to the Revised Convention for the Navigation of the Rhine, and within an appropriate period of time from the conclusion of those discussions, this Regulation as a whole should be amended as necessary in the light of the obligations arising out of the Revised Convention for the Navigation of the Rhine;

[27] Whereas the Regulation should be amended as necessary in the light of the experience gained over a three-year period; whereas it will in particular be desirable to consider whether, in the light of the development of the common transport policy over that period, the scope of the Regulation should be extended to agreements, decisions and concerted practices, and to instances of abuse of a dominant position, not affecting trade between Member States;

HAS ADOPTED THIS REGULATION:

Article 1
Basic provision

The provisions of this Regulation shall, in the field of transport by rail, road and inland waterway, apply both to all agreements, decisions and concerted practices which have as their object or effect the fixing of transport rates and conditions, the limitation or control of the supply of transport, the sharing of transport markets, the application of technical improvements or technical co-operation, or the joint financing or acquisition of transport equipment or supplies where such operations are directly related to the provision of transport services and are necessary for the joint operation of services by a grouping within the meaning of Article 4 of road or inland waterway transport undertakings, and to the abuse of a dominant position on the transport market. These provisions shall apply also to operations of providers of services ancillary to transport which have any of the objects or effects listed above.

Commentary
Art 1: B&C: 12.009–12.010 F&N: 14.185–14.186

[Article 2]

Notes

Article 2 was repealed by Council Regulation 1/2003/EC (OJ L1, 4.1.2003, p. 1), Article 36, with effect from 1 May 2004.

Commentary

Art 2: F&N: 14.200–14.204, 14.218

Article 3
Exception for technical agreements

1. [The prohibition in Article 81(1) of the Treaty] shall not apply to agreements, decisions or concerted practices the object and effect of which is to apply technical improvements or to achieve technical co-operation by means of:

(a) the standardisation of equipment, transport supplies, vehicles or fixed installations;

(b) the exchange or pooling, for the purpose of operating transport services, of staff, equipment, vehicles or fixed installations;

(c) the organisation and execution of successive, complementary, substitute or combined transport operations, and the fixing and application of inclusive rates and conditions for such operations, including special competitive rates;

(d) the use, for journeys by a single mode of transport, of the routes which are most rational from the operational point of view;

(e) the co-ordination of transport timetables for connecting routes;

(f) the grouping of single consignments;

(g) the establishment of uniform rules as to the structure of tariffs and their conditions of application, provided such rules do not lay down transport rates and conditions.

2. The Commission shall, where appropriate, submit proposals to the Council with a view to extending or reducing the list in paragraph 1.

Note

The words shown in square brackets were inserted by Council Regulation (EC) No 1/2003 (OJ L1, 4.1.2003, p. 1), Article 36, with effect from 1 May 2004.

Commentary

Art 3: B&C: 3.074, 12.009, 12.011, 12.020 F&N: 14.212–14.213

Article 4
Exemption for groups of small and medium-sized undertakings

1. [Agreements, decisions and concerted practices pursuant to Article [81](1) of the Treaty] shall be exempt from the prohibition in that Article where their purpose is:

— the constitution and operation of groupings of road or inland waterway transport undertakings with a view to carrying on transport activities;

— the joint financing or acquisition of transport equipment or supplies, where these operations are directly related to the provision of transport services and are necessary for the joint operations of the aforesaid groupings;

always provided that the total carrying capacity of any grouping does not exceed:

— 10,000 metric tons in the case of road transport,

— 500,000 metric tons in the case of transport by inland waterway.

The individual capacity of each undertaking belonging to a grouping shall not exceed 1,000 metric tons in the case of road transport or 50,000 metric tons in the case of transport by inland waterway.

[2. If the implementation of any agreement, decision or concerted practice covered by paragraph 1 has, in a given case, effects which are incompatible with the requirements of Article 81(3) of the Treaty, undertakings or associations of undertakings may be required to make such effects cease.]

Notes

The amendments shown in square brackets were made by Council Regulation (EC) No 1/2003 (OJ L1, 4.1.2003, p. 1), Article 36, with effect from 1 May 2004.

Commentary

Art 4: B&C: 3.074, 3.082, 12.009–12.010, 12.012 F&N: 14.217
Art 4(2): B&C: 3.086

[*Article 5–Article 12*]

Notes

Articles 5 to 12 were repealed by Council Regulation EC No 1/2003 (OJ L1, 4.1.2003, p. 1), Article 36, with effect from 1 May 2004.

Commentary

Art 5: B&C: 3.002, 12.013 F&N: 14.218–14.219, 14.224
Art 12(2): F&N: 14.222

Article 13
Duration and revocation of decisions applying Article 5

[...]

3. The Commission may revoke or amend its decision or prohibit specified acts by the parties:

(a) where there has been a change in any of the facts which were basic to the making of the decision;

(b) where the parties commit a breach of any obligation attached to the decision;

(c) where the decision is based on incorrect information or was induced by deceit;

(d) where the parties abuse the exemption from the provisions of Article 2 granted to them by the decision.

In cases falling within (b), (c) or (d), the decision may be revoked with retroactive effect.

Notes

Article 13(1) and 13(2) were repealed by Council Regulation (EC) No 1/2003 (OJ L1, 4.1.2003, p. 1), Article 36, with effect from 1 May 2004. Article 13(3) continues to apply to decisions adopted pursuant to Article 5 prior to 1 May 2004 until the date of expiration of those decisions: Council Regulation (EC) 1/2003, Article 36.

Commentary

Art 13(3): B&C: 3.008

[*Article 14–Article 29*]

Notes

Articles 14 to 29 were repealed by Council Regulation (EC) No 1/2003 (OJ L1, 4.1.2003, p. 1), Article 36, with effect from 1 May 2004.

Article 30
Entry into force, existing agreements

1. This Regulation shall enter into force on 1 July 1968.

[...]

Notes

Paragraphs 2, 3 and 4 were deleted by Council Regulation (EC) No 1/2003 (OJ L1, 4.1.2003, p. 1), Article 36, with effect from 1 May 2004.

Commentary

Art 30: B&C: 3.082

Article 31
Review of the Regulation

1. Within six months of the conclusion of discussions with the third countries signatories to the Revised Convention for the Navigation of the Rhine[,] the Council, on a proposal from the Commission, shall make any amendments to this Regulation which may prove necessary in the light of the obligations arising out of the Revised Convention for the Navigation of the Rhine.

2. The Commission shall submit to the Council, before 1 January 1971, a general report on the operation of this Regulation and, before 1 July 1971, a proposal for a Regulation to make the necessary amendments to this Regulation.

This Regulation shall be binding in its entirety and directly applicable in all Member States.

Done at Brussels, 19 July 1968.

E2

COUNCIL DIRECTIVE 91/440/EEC

of 29 July 1991
on the development of the Community's railways

Official Journal L 237, 24.8.1991, p. 25

Celex No: 31991L0440

Notes

This document is reproduced as amended by Directive 2001/12/EC of 26 February 2001 (OJ L 75, 15.3.2001, p. 1), Directive 2004/51/EC of 29 April 2004 (OJ L 220, 21.6.2004, p. 58) and the Act of Accession of the Czech Republic, Estonia, Cyprus, Latvia, Lithuania, Hungary, Malta, Poland, Slovenia and the Slovak Republic (OJ L 236, 23.9.2003, p. 33) and Council Directive 2006/103/EC of 20 November 2006, adapting certain Directives in the field of transport policy, by reason of the accession of Bulgaria and Romania (OJ L 363, 20.12.2006, p.344) and as corrected by the Corrigendum to 91/440/EEC (OJ L 305, 6.11.1991, p. 22), the Corrigendum to 2001/12/EC (OJ L 334, 18.12.2001, p. 34) and the Corrigendum to Directive 2004/51/EC (OJ L 220, 21.6.2004, p. 58). Amendments made by Directive 2001/12/EC (as corrected) and Directive 2004/51/EC (as corrected) are marked; amendments made by the Act of Accession and Directive 2006/103 (EC), and other corrections, are not.

EEA application: this Directive was adopted with appropriate adaptations by EEA Joint Committee Decision No 7/94: see EEA Agreement, Annex XIII, Chapter III, Point 37 (as subsequently amended by Decision No 118/2001 (OJ L 322, 6.12.2001, p. 32 and EEA Supplement No 60, 6.12.2001, p. 29), Decision No 151/2004 (OJ No L 102, 21.4.2005, p. 27 and EEA Supplement No 20, 21.4.2005, p. 17) and the EEA Enlargement Agreement (OJ L 130, 29.4.2004, p. 3 and EEA Supplement No 23, 29.4.2004, p. 1)).

Commentary

Directive 91/440: B&C: 12.015–12.016, 12.018 F&N: 14.164–14.165, 14.171, 14.201, 14.211, 14.220, 14.238

THE COUNCIL OF THE EUROPEAN COMMUNITIES,

Having regard to the Treaty establishing the European Economic Community, and in particular Article [71] thereof,

Having regard to the proposal from the Commission,[1]

Having regard to the opinion of the European Parliament,[2]

Having regard to the opinion of the Economic and Social Committee,[3]

Notes
[1] OJ No C 34, 14.2.1990, p. 8 and OJ No C 87, 4.4.1991, p. 7.
[2] OJ No C 19, 28.1.1991, p. 254.
[3] OJ No C 225, 10.9.1990, p. 27.

[1] Whereas greater integration of the Community transport sector is an essential element of the internal market, and Whereas the railways are a vital part of the Community transport sector;

[2] Whereas the efficiency of the railway system should be improved, in order to integrate it into a competitive market, whilst taking account of the special features of the railways;

[3] Whereas, in order to render railway transport efficient and competitive as compared with other modes of transport, Member States must guarantee that railway undertakings are afforded a status of independent operators behaving in a commercial manner and adapting to market needs;

[4] Whereas the future development and efficient operation of the railway system may be made easier if a distinction is made between the provision of transport services and the operation of infrastructure;

[5] Whereas given this situation, it is necessary for these two activities to be separately managed and have separate accounts;

[6] Whereas, in order to boost competition in railway service management in terms of improved comfort and the services provided to users, it is appropriate for Member States to retain general responsibility for the development of the appropriate railway infrastructure;

[7] Whereas, in the absence of common rules on allocation of infrastructure costs, Member States shall, after consulting the infrastructure management, lay down rules providing for the payment by railway undertakings and their groupings for the use of railway infrastructure;

[8] Whereas such payments must comply with the principle of non-discrimination between railway undertakings;

[9] Whereas Member States should ensure in particular that existing publicly owned or controlled railway transport undertakings are given a sound financial structure, whilst taking care that any financial rearrangement as may be necessary shall be made in accordance with the relevant rules lid down in the Treaty;

[10] Whereas, in order to facilitate transport between Member States, railway undertakings should be free to form groupings with railway undertakings established in other Member States;

[11] Whereas, such international groupings should be granted rights of access and transit in the Member States of establishment of their constituent undertakings, as well as transit rights in other Member States as required for the international service concerned;

[12] Whereas, with a view to encouraging combined transport, it is appropriate that access to the railway infrastructure of the other Member States should be granted to railway undertakings engaged in the international combined transport of goods;

[13] Whereas it is necessary to establish an advisory committee to monitor and assist the Commission with the implementation of this Directive;

[14] Whereas, as a result, Council Directive 75/327/EEC of 20 May 1975 on the improvement of the situation of railway undertakings and the harmonization of rules governing financial relations between such undertakings and States[1] should be repealed,

Notes
[1] OJ No L 152, 12.6.1975, p. 3.

HAS ADOPTED THIS DIRECTIVE:

Section I
[Scope and definitions]

[Article 1]

Notes

The title of Section I was amended and Article 1 was repealed with effect from 15 March 2001 by Directive 2001/12/EC by (OJ L 75, 15.3.2001, p. 1).

Article 2

1. This Directive shall apply to the management of railway infrastructure and to rail transport activities of the railway undertakings established or to be established in a Member State.

2. Railway undertakings whose activity is limited to the provision of solely urban, suburban or regional services shall be excluded from the scope of this Directive.

[3. Undertakings the train operations of which are limited to providing solely shuttle services for road vehicles through the Channel Tunnel are excluded from the scope of this Directive except Articles 6(1), 10 and 10a.]

Notes

The amendment shown in square brackets was made by Directive 2001/12/EC (OJ L 75, 15.3.2001, p. 1) with effect from 15 March 2001.

Article 3

For the purpose of this Directive:

[— "railway undertaking" shall mean any public or private undertaking licensed according to applicable Community legislation, the principal business of which is to provide services for the transport of goods and/or passengers by rail with a requirement that the undertaking must ensure traction; this also includes undertakings which provide traction only;
— "infrastructure manager" shall mean any body or undertaking responsible in particular for establishing and maintaining railway infrastructure. This may also include the management of infrastructure control and safety systems. The functions of the infrastructure manager on a network or part of a network may be allocated to different bodies or undertakings]
— "railway infrastructure" shall mean all the items listed in Annex I.A to Commission Regulation (EEC) No 2598/70 of 18 December 1970 specifying the items to be included under the various headings in the forms of accounts shown in Annex I to Regulation (EEC) No 1108/ 70,[1] with the exception of the final indent which, for the purposes of this Directive only, shall read as follows: "Buildings used by the infrastructure department",
— "international grouping" shall mean any association of at least two railway undertakings established in different Member States for the purpose of providing international transport services between Member States;
[— "international freight service" shall mean transport services where the train crosses at least one border of a Member State; the train may be joined and/or split and the different sections may have different origins and destinations, provided that all wagons cross at least one border]
— "urban and suburban services" shall mean transport services operated to meet the transport needs of an urban centre or conurbation, as well as the transport needs between such centre or conurbation and surrounding areas;
— "regional services" shall mean transport services operated to meet the transport needs of a region.

Notes

[1] OJ No L 278, 23.12.1970, p. 1, Regulation amended by Regulation (EEC) No 2116/78 (OJ No L 246, 8.9.1978, p. 7).

The amendments shown in square brackets were made by Directive 2001/12/EC (OJ L 75, 15.2.2001, p. 1) with effect from 15 March 2001.

Commentary
Art 3: **B&C:** 12.015

871

Section II
[Management independence

Article 4

1. Member States shall take the measures necessary to ensure that as regards management, administration and internal control over administrative, economic and accounting matters railway undertakings have independent status in accordance with which they will hold, in particular, assets, budgets and accounts which are separate from those of the State.

2. While respecting the framework and specific charging and allocation rules established by the Member States, the infrastructure manager shall have responsibilities for its own management, administration and internal control.]

Notes

The title of Section II and Article 4 were replaced by Directive 2001/12/EC (OJ L 75, 15.3.2001, p. 1) with effect from 15 March 2001.

Article 5

1. Member States shall take the measure necessary to enable railway undertakings to adjust their activities to the market and to manage those activities under the responsibility of their management bodies, in the interests of providing efficient and appropriate services at the lowest possible cost for the quality of service required. Railway undertakings shall be managed according to the principles which apply to commercial companies; this shall also apply to their public services obligations imposed by the State and to public services contracts which they conclude with the competent authorities of the Member State.

2. Railway undertakings shall determine their business plans, including their investment and financing programmes. Such plans shall be designed to achieve the undertakings' financial equilibrium and the other technical, commercial and financial management objectives; they must also provide for the means enabling these objectives to be obtained.

3. In the context of the general policy guidelines determined by the State and taking into account national plans and contracts (which may be multiannual) including investment and financing plans, railway undertakings shall, in particular, be free to:

— establish with one or more other railway undertakings an international grouping;
— establish their internal organization, without prejudice to the provisions of Section III;
— control the supply and marketing of services and fix the pricing thereof, without prejudice to Council Regulation (EEC) No 1191/69 of 26 June 1969 on action by Member States concerning the obligation inherent in the concept of a public service in transport by rail, road and inland waterway,[1]
— take decisions on staff, assets and own procurement,
— expand their market share, develop new technologies and new services and adopt any innovative management techniques;
— establish new activities in fields associated with railway business.

Notes

[1] OJ No L 156, 28.6.1969, p. 1; Regulation last amended by Regulation (EEC) No 1893/91 (OJ No L 169, 29.6.1991, p. 1).

Section III
Separation between infrastructure management and transport operations

[Article 6

1. Member States shall take the measures necessary to ensure that separate profit and loss accounts and balance sheets are kept and published, on the one hand, for business relating to the provision of

transport services by railway undertakings and, on the other, for business relating to the management of railway infrastructure. Public funds paid to one of these two areas of activity may not be transferred to the other.

The accounts for the two areas of activity shall be kept in a way that reflects this prohibition.

2. Member States may also provide that this separation shall require the organisation of distinct divisions within a single undertaking or that the infrastructure shall be managed by a separate entity.

3. Member States shall take the measures necessary to ensure that the functions determining equitable and non-discriminatory access to infrastructure, listed in Annex II, are entrusted to bodies or firms that do not themselves provide any rail transport services. Regardless of the organisational structures, this objective must be shown to have been achieved. Member States may, however, assign to railway undertakings or any other body the collecting of the charges and the responsibility for managing the railway infrastructure, such as investment, maintenance and funding.

4. The application of paragraph 3 shall be subject to a report by the Commission in accordance with Article 10b, to be submitted by 15 March 2006.]

Notes

Article 6 was replaced as shown in square brackets by Directive 2001/12/EC (OJ L 75, 15.3.2001, p. 1) with effect from 15 March 2001.

Commentary
Art 6(3): F&N: 14.228

[*Article 7*

1. Member States shall take the necessary measures for the development of their national railway infrastructure taking into account, where necessary, the general needs of the Community.

2. …

3. Member States may also accord the infrastructure manager, having due regard to Articles 73, 87 and 88 of the Treaty, financing consistent with the tasks, size and financial requirements, in particular in order to cover new investments.

4. Within the framework of general policy determined by the State, the infrastructure manager shall draw up a business plan including investment and financial programmes. The plan shall be designed to ensure optimal and efficient use and development of the infrastructure while ensuring financial balance and providing means for these objectives to be achieved.]

Notes

Article 7 was replaced as shown in square brackets by Directive 2001/12/EC (OJ L 75, 15.3.2001, p. 1) with effect from 15 March 2001.
Paragraph 2 was subsequently deleted by Directive 2004/51/EC (OJ L 220, 21.6.2004, p. 58) with effect from 30 April 2004.

Commentary
Art 7: F&N: 14.168

Article 8

The manager of the infrastructure shall charge a fee for the use of the railway infrastructure for which he is responsible, payable by railway undertakings and international groupings using that infrastructure. After consulting the manager, Member States shall lay down the rules for determining this fee.

The user fee, which shall be calculated in such a way as to avoid any discrimination between railway undertakings, may in particular take into account the mileage, the composition of the train and any specific requirements in terms of such factors as speed, axle load and the degree or period of utilization of the infrastructure.

Section IV
Improvement of the financial situation

Article 9

1. In conjunction with the existing publicly owned or controlled railway undertakings, Member States shall set up appropriate mechanisms to help reduce the indebtedness of such undertakings to a level which does not impede sound financial management and to improve their financial situation.

2. To that end, Member States may take the necessary measures requiring a separate debt amortization unit to be set up within the accounting departments of such undertakings. The balance sheet of the unit may be charged, until they are extinguished, with all the loans raised by the undertaking both to finance investment and to cover excess operating expenditure resulting from the business of rail transport or from railway infrastructure management. Debts arising from subsidiaries" operations may not be taken into account.

[3. Aid accorded by Member States to cancel the debts referred to in this Article shall be granted in accordance with Articles 73, 87 and 88 of the Treaty.

4. In the case of railway undertakings profit and loss accounts and either balance sheets or annual statement of assets and liabilities shall be kept and published for business relating to the provision of rail freight-transport services. Funds paid for activities relating to the provision of passenger-transport services as public-service remits must be shown separately in the relevant accounts and may not be transferred to activities relating to the provision of other transport services or any other business.]

Notes

The amendments shown in square brackets were made by Directive 2001/12/EC (OJ L 75, 15.3.2001, p. 1) with effect from 15 March 2001.

Section V
Access to railway infrastructure

[Article 10

1. International groupings shall be granted access and transit rights in the Member States of establishment of their constituent railway undertakings, as well as transit rights in other Member States, for international services between the Member States where the undertakings constituting the said groupings are established.

2. Railway undertakings within the scope of Article 2 shall be granted, on equitable conditions, access to the infrastructure in other Member States for the purpose of operating international combined transport goods services.][1]

[3. Railway undertakings within the scope of Article 2 shall be granted, on equitable conditions, access to the Trans-European Rail Freight Network defined in Article 10a and in Annex I and, at the latest by 1 January 2006, to the entire rail network, for the purpose of operating international freight services.

In addition, at the latest by 1 January 2007, railway undertakings within the scope of Article 2 shall be granted, on equitable conditions, access to the infrastructure in all Member States for the purpose of operating all types of rail freight services.][2]

[4. At the request of a Member State or on its own initiative the Commission shall, in a specific case, examine the application and enforcement of this Article, and within two months of receipt of such a request and after consulting the Committee referred to in Article 11a (2), decide whether the related measure may continue to be applied. The Commission shall communicate its decision to the European Parliament, the Council and to the Member States.

Without prejudice to Article 226 of the Treaty, any Member State may refer the Commission"s decision to the Council within a time limit of one month. The Council, acting by a qualified majority, may in exceptional circumstances take a different decision within a period of one month.][1]

[5. Any railway undertaking engaged in rail transport services shall conclude the necessary agreements on the basis of public or private law with the infrastructure managers of the railway infrastructure used. The conditions governing such agreements shall be non-discriminatory and transparent, in conformity with the provisions of Directive 2001/ 14/EC of the European Parliament and of the Council of 26 February 2001 on the allocation of railway infrastructure capacity and the levying of charges for the use of railway infrastructure and safety certification.[1]

6. Track access to, and supply of services in, the terminals and ports linked to rail activities referred to in paragraphs 1, 2 and 3, serving or potentially serving more than one final customer, shall be provided to all railway undertakings in a non-discriminatory and transparent manner and requests by railway undertakings may be subject to restrictions only if viable alternatives by rail under market conditions exist.][2]

[7. Without prejudice to Community and national regulations concerning competition policy and the institutions with responsibility in that area, the regulatory body established pursuant to Article 30 of Directive 2000/14/EC, or any other body enjoying the same degree of independence shall monitor the competition in the rail services markets, including the rail freight transport market.

That body shall be set up in accordance with the rules in Article 30(1) of the said Directive. Any applicant or interested party may lodge a complaint with this body if it feels that it has been treated unjustly, has been the subject of discrimination or has been injured in any other way. On the basis of the complaint and, where appropriate, on its own initiative, the regulatory body shall decide at the earliest opportunity on appropriate measures to correct undesirable developments in these markets. In order to ensure the necessary possibility of judicial control and the requisite cooperation between national regulatory bodies, Article 30(6) and Article 31 of the said Directive shall apply in this context.]

[8. By 1 January 2006, the Commission shall submit to the European Parliament, the European Economic and Social Committee, the Committee of the Regions and the Council a report on the implementation of this Directive.]

This report shall address:

— implementation of this Directive in the Member States and the effective working of the various bodies involved,
— market development, in particular international traffic trends, activities and market share of all market actors, including new entrants,
— impact on the overall transport sector, in particular as regards modal shift,
— impact on the level of safety in each Member State,
— working conditions in the sector, for each Member State.

If necessary, it shall be accompanied by suitable proposals or recommendations on continuing Community action to develop the railway market and the legal framework governing it.][2]

Notes

[OJ L 75, 15.3.2001, p. 29. Directive as amended by Commission Decision 2002/844/EC (OJ L 289, 26.10.2002, p. 30)].
[1] The amendments shown in square brackets were made by Directive 2001/12/EC (OJ L 75, 15.3.2001, p. 1) with effect from 15 March 2001.
[2] The amendments shown in square brackets were made by Directive 2004/51/EC, as corrected, (OJ L 230, 21.6.2004, p. 58) with effect from 30 April 2004.

Commentary
Art 10: **F&N:** 14.168, 14.233

[*Article 10a*

1. The Trans-European Rail Freight Network consists of the following elements:

a) Railway lines as indicated in the maps in Annex I.

b) Diversionary routes, where appropriate, particularly around congested infrastructure within the meaning of Directive 2000/14/ EC. When these routes are offered, overall journey times shall be safeguarded as far as this is feasible.
c) Track access to terminals serving or potentially serving more than one final customer and to other sites and facilities, including feeder lines to and from these.
d) Track access to and from ports as listed in Annex I, including feeder lines.

2. The feeder lines mentioned in paragraph 1(c) and (d) cover at either end of the journey 50 km or 20% of the length of the journey on the railway lines referred to in paragraph 1(a), whichever is greater. Belgium and Luxembourg, as Member States with a relatively small or concentrated network, may limit the length of the feeder lines in the first year after 15 March 2003 to at least 20 km and until the end of the second year to at least 40 km.]

Notes

Article 10a was added by Directive 2001/12/EC (OJ L 75, 15.3.2001, p. 1) with effect from 15 March 2001.

[Section Va
Monitoring tasks of the Commission

Article 10b

1. Not later than 15 September 2001 the Commission shall make the necessary arrangements to monitor technical and economic conditions and market developments of European rail transport. The Commission shall ensure that adequate resources are made available to enable the effective monitoring of this sector.

2. In this context, the Commission shall closely involve representatives of the Member States and of the sectors concerned in its work, including users, so that they are able better to monitor the development of the railway sector and the evolution of the market, assess the effect of the measures adopted and analyse the impact of the measures planned by the Commission.

3. The Commission shall monitor the use of the networks and the evolution of the framework conditions in the rail sector, in particular infrastructure charging, capacity allocation, safety regulation and licensing and the degree of harmonisation that evolves. It shall ensure an active cooperation between the appropriate regulatory bodies in the Member States.

4. The Commission shall report to the European Parliament and the Council on:

  a) the evolution of the internal market in rail services
  b) the framework conditions][1]
  [c) the state of the European railway network][2]
  [d) the utilisation of access rights
  e) barriers to more effective rail services
  f) infrastructure limitations, and
  g) the need for legislation.][1]

Notes

[1] Section Va and Article 10b were added by Directive 2001/12/EC (OJ L 75, 15.3.2001, p. 1) with effect from 15 March 2001.

[2] The amendment in Article 10b(4)(c) shown in square brackets was made by Directive 2004/51/EC, as corrected (OJ L 220, 21.6.2004, p. 58). with effect from 30 April 2004.

Section VI
Final provisions

[*Article 11*

1. Member States may bring any question concerning the implementation of this Directive to the attention of the Commission. Appropriate decisions shall be adopted by use of the advisory procedure referred to in Article 11a(2).

2. The amendments necessary to adapt the Annexes shall be adopted by use of the regulatory procedure referred to in Article 11a(3).]

Notes

Article 11 was replaced as shown in square brackets by Directive 2001/12/EC (OJ L75, 15.3.2001, p. 1) with effect from 15 March 2001.

[*Article 11a*

1. The Commission shall be assisted by a Committee.

2. Where reference is made to this paragraph, Articles 3 and 7 of Decision 1999/468/EC shall apply, having regard to the provisions of Article 8 thereof.

3. Where reference is made to this paragraph, Articles 5 and 7 of Decision 1999/468/EC shall apply, having regard to the provisions of Article 8 thereof.

The period laid down in Article 5(6) of Decision 1999/468/EC shall be set at three months.

4. The Committee shall adopt its rules of procedure.]

Notes

Article 11a was inserted as shown in square brackets by Directive 2001/12/EC (OJ L75, 15.3.2001, p. 1) with effect from 15 March 2001.

Article 12

The provisions of this Directive shall be without prejudice to Council Directive 90/531/EEC of 17 September 1990 on the procurement procedure of entities operating in the water, energy, transport and telecommunications sectors.[1]

Notes

[1] OJ No L 297, 29.10.1990, p. 1.

Article 13

Decision 75/327/EEC is hereby repealed as from 1 January 1993.

Reference to the repealed Decision shall be understood to refer to this Directive.

[*Article 14*]

Notes

Article 14 was deleted by Directive 2004/51/EC, as corrected (OJ L220, 21.6.2004, p. 58) with effect from 30 April 2004.

[*Article 14a*

1. For a period of five years from 15 March 2003, the following Member States:

— Ireland, as a Member State located on an island with a rail link to only one other Member State
— the United Kingdom, in respect of Northern Ireland, on the same basis, and
— Greece, as a Member State that does not have any direct rail link to any other Member State,

do not need to apply the requirement to entrust to an independent body the functions determining equitable and non-discriminatory access to infrastructure, as provided for in Article 6(3), first subparagraph and the tasks set out in Article 7(2), first subparagraph, in so far as those Articles oblige Member States to establish independent bodies performing the tasks referred to in the said Articles.

2. However, where:

a) more than one railway undertaking licensed in accordance with Article 4 of Directive 95/18/EC, or, in the case of Ireland and of Northern Ireland, a railway company so licensed elsewhere, submits an official application to operate competing railway services in, to or from Ireland, Northern Ireland or Greece, the continued applicability of this derogation will be decided upon in accordance with the advisory procedure referred to out in Article 11a(2); or

b) a railway undertaking operating railway services in Ireland, Northern Ireland or Greece submits an official application to operate railway services on, to or from the territory of another Member State (in the case of Ireland, or the United Kingdom, in respect of Northern Ireland, or both, another Member State outside their territories), the derogation referred to in paragraph 1 shall not apply.

Within one year from the receipt of either the decision referred to in point (a) adopted in accordance with the advisory procedure referred to in Article 11a(2), or notification of the official application referred to in point (b), the Member State or States concerned (Ireland, the United Kingdom with respect to Northern Ireland, or Greece) shall put in place legislation to implement the Articles referred to in paragraph 1.

3. A derogation referred to in paragraph 1, may be renewed for periods not longer than five years. Not later than 12 months before the expiry date of the derogation a Member State availing itself of such derogation may address a request to the Commission for a renewed derogation. Any such request must be substantiated. The Commission shall examine such a request and adopt a decision in accordance with the advisory procedure referred to in Article 11a(2). The said advisory procedure shall apply to any decision related to the request. When adopting its decision the Commission shall take into account any development in the geopolitical situation and the development of the rail market in, from and to the Member State having requested the renewed derogation.

4. Luxembourg as a Member State with a relatively small rail network does not need to apply until 31 August 2004 the requirement to award to an independent body the functions determining equitable and non-discriminatory access to infrastructure, as provided for in Article 6(3), first subparagraph, in so far as it obliges Member States to establish independent bodies performing the tasks referred to in that Article.]

Notes

Article 14a was inserted as shown in square brackets by Directive 2001/12/EC (OJ L75, 15.3.2001, p. 1) with effect from 15 March 2001.

Article 15

Member States shall, after consultation with the Commission, adopt the laws, regulations and administrative provisions necessary to comply with this Directive not later than 1 January 1993. They shall forthwith inform the Commission thereof. When Member States adopt these provisions, they shall contain a reference to this Directive or be accompanied by such reference on the occasion of their official publication. The methods of making such a reference shall be laid down by the Member States.

Article 16

This Directive is addressed to the Member States.

ANNEX I

Notes

Annex I was added by Directive 2001/12/EC (OJ L75, 15.3.2001, p. 1) with effect from 15 March 2001. It has been subsequently amended by the instruments listed in the first editorial note on page 869 above.

Ports

Belgie/Belgique
Antwerpen/Anvers
Gent/Gand
Zeebrugge/Zeebruges

БЪЛГАРИЯ

Варна

Бургас

Русе

Лом

Видин

Česká Republika

Danmark

Ålborg

Århus

Esbjerg

Fredericia

København

Nyborg

Odense

Deutschland

Brake

Bremen/Bremerhaven

Brunsbüttel

Cuxhaven

Emden

Hamburg

Kiel

Lübeck

Nordenham

Puttgarden

Rostock

Sassnitz

Wilhelmshaven

Wismar

Eesti

Muuga sadam

Paljassaare sadam

Vanasadam

Paldiski põhjasadam

Paldiski lõunasadam

Kopli põhjasadam

Kopli lõunasadam

Bekkeri sadam

Kunda sadam

Ελλασ

Αλεξανδρούπολις

Ελευσίνα

Πάτρα

Πειραιάς

Θεσσαλονίκη

Βόλος

España

Algeciras

Almería

Barcelona

Bilbao

Cartagena-Escombreras

Gijón

Huelva

Tarragona

Valencia

Vigo

France

Bayonne

Bordeaux

Boulogne

Calais

Cherbourg

Dunkerque

Fos-Marseille

La Rochelle

Le Havre

Nantes

Port-la-Nouvelle

Rouen

Sète

St-Nazaire

Ireland

Cork

Dublin

Italia

Ancona

Bari

Brindisi

C. Vecchia

Genova

Gioia Tauro

La Spezia

Livorno

Napoli

Piombino

Ravenna

Salerno

Savona

Taranto

Trieste

Venezia

Κυπροσ

Latvija

Rīga

Ventspils

Liepāja

Lietuva

Klaipėda

Luxembourg

Magyarország

Malta

Nederland

Amsterdam Zeehaven

Delfzijl/Eemshaven

Vlissingen

Rotterdam Zeehaven

Terneuzen

Österreich

Polska

Szczecin

Świnoujście

Gdańsk

Gdynia

Portugal

Leixões

Lisboa

Setúbal
Sines

ROMÂNIA
Constanţa
Mangalia
Midia
Tulcea
Galaţi
Brăila
Medgidia
Olteniţa
Giurgiu
Zimnicea
Calafat
Turnu Severin
OrŞova

Slovenija
Koper

Slovensko

Suomi/Finland
Hamina
Hanko
Helsinki
Kemi
Kokkola
Kotka
Oulu
Pori
Rauma
Tornio
Turku

Sverige
Göteborg-Varberg
Helsingborg
Luleå
Malmö
Norrköping
Oxelösund
Stockholm
Trelleborg-Ystad

Umeå

United Kingdom

All rail-connected ports

Note

Individual country rail maps are not reproduced in this volume.

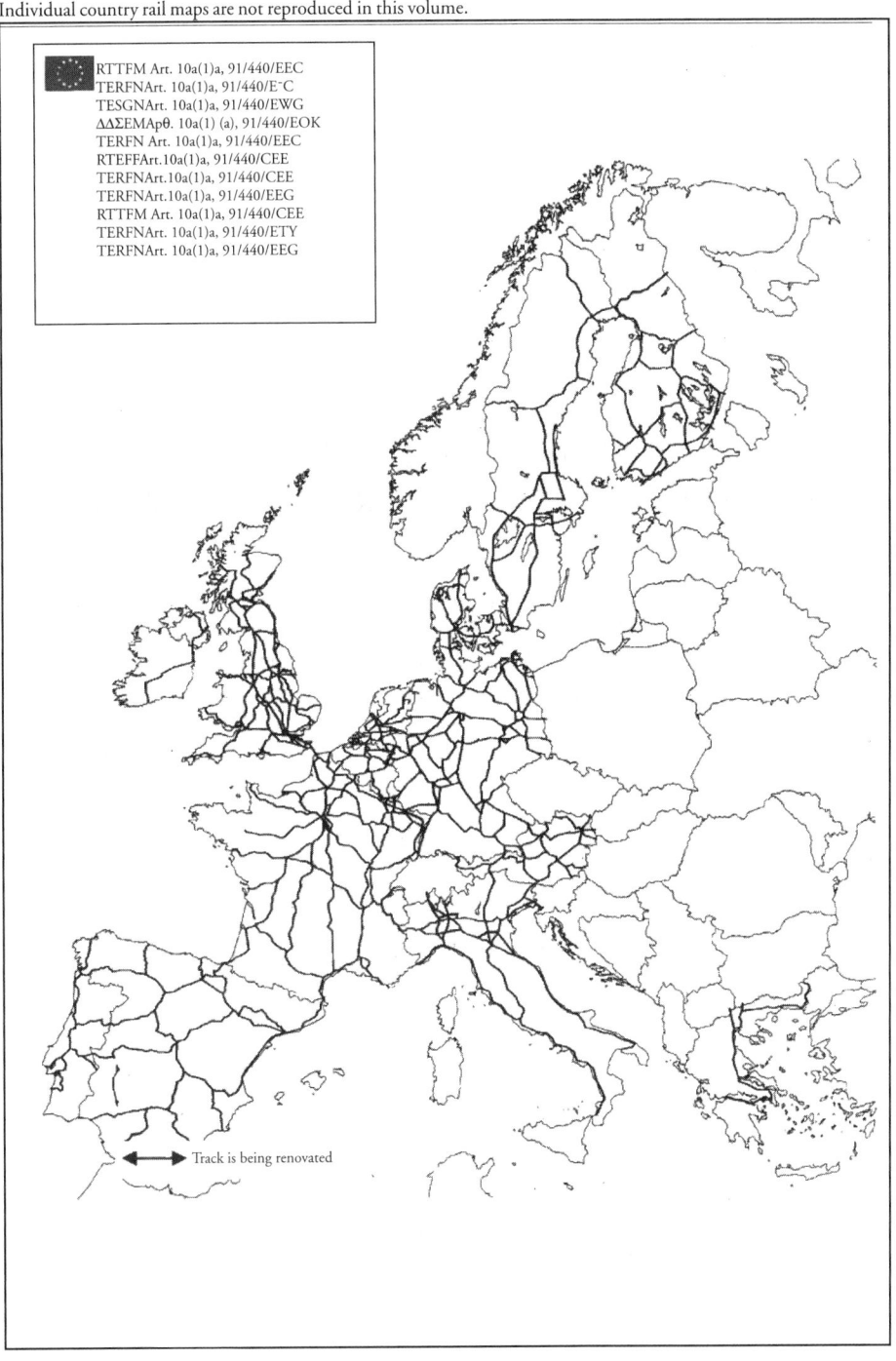

RTTFM Art. 10a(1)a, 91/440/EEC
TERFNArt. 10a(1)a, 91/440/E⁻C
TESGNArt. 10a(1)a, 91/440/EWG
ΔΔΣΕΜΑρθ. 10a(1) (a), 91/440/EOK
TERFN Art. 10a(1)a, 91/440/EEC
RTEFFArt.10a(1)a, 91/440/CEE
TERFNArt.10a(1)a, 91/440/CEE
TERFNArt.10a(1)a, 91/440/EEG
RTTFM Art. 10a(1)a, 91/440/CEE
TERFNArt. 10a(1)a, 91/440/ETY
TERFNArt. 10a(1)a, 91/440/EEG

◀▶ Track is being renovated

ANNEX II

List of essential functions referred to in Article 6(3):

— preparation and decision making related to the licensing of railway undertakings including granting of individual licenses,

— decision making related to the path allocation including both the definition and the assessment of availability and the allocation of individual train paths,

— decision making related to infrastructure charging,

— monitoring observance of public service obligations required in the provision of certain services.

Notes

Annex II was added by Directive 2001/12/EC (OJ L75, 15.3.2001, p. 1) with effect from 15 March 2001.

Commentary
Annex II: F&N: 14.228

E3

[DIRECTIVE 2001/14/EC OF THE EUROPEAN PARLIAMENT AND OF THE COUNCIL

of 26 February 2001
on the allocation of railway infrastructure capacity and the levying of
charges for the use of railway infrastructure]

Official Journal L 75, 15.3.2001, p. 29

Celex No: 32001L0014

Notes

The title was replaced as shown in square brackets by Directive 2004/49/EC (OJ L 164, 30.4.2004, as corrected by Corrigendum at OJ L 220, 21.6.2004, p. 16) with effect from 30 April 2004.

EEA application: this Directive was adopted, with appropriate adaptations, by EEA Joint Committee Decision No 118/2001 (OJ L 322, 6.12.2001, p. 32 and EEA Supplement No 60, 6.12.2001, p. 29): see the EEA Agreement, Annex XIII, Chapter III, Point 41(b) (as subsequently amended by Decision No 35/2003 (OJ No L 137, 5.6.2003, p. 40 and EEA Supplement No 29, p. 26), and Decision No 151/2004 (OJ No L 102, 21.4.2005, p. 27 and EEA Supplement No 20, 21.4.2005, p. 17)).

Commentary
Directive 2001/14/EC: B&C: 12.016 F&N: 4.227

THE EUROPEAN PARLIAMENT AND THE COUNCIL OF THE EUROPEAN UNION,

Having regard to the Treaty establishing the European Community, and in particular Article 71 thereof,

Having regard to the proposal from the Commission,[1]

Having regard to the opinion of the Economic and Social Committee,[2]

Having regard to the opinion of the Committee of the Regions,[3]

Acting in accordance with the procedure laid down in Article 251 of the Treaty[4] in the light of the joint text approved on 22 November 2000 by the Conciliation Committee,

Notes

[1] OJ C 321, 20.10.1998, p. 10, and OJ C 116 E, 26.4.2000, p. 40.

[2] OJ C 209, 22.7.1999, p. 22.

[3] OJ C 57, 29.2.2000, p. 40.

[4] Opinion of the European Parliament of 10 March 1999 (OJ C 175, 21.6.1999, p. 120), confirmed on 27 October 1999 (OJ C 154, 5.6.2000, p. 22), Council Common Position of 28 March 2000 (OJ C 178, 27.6.2000, p. 28) and Decision of the European Parliament of 5 July 2000 [OJ C 121, 24.4.2001, p. 34–113], Decision of the European Parliament of 1 February 2001 and Council Decision of 20 December 2000.

Whereas:

(1) Greater integration of the Community railway sector is an essential element of the completion of the internal market and moving towards achieving sustainable mobility.

(2) Council Directive 91/440/EEC of 29 July 1991 on the development of the Community's railways[1] provides for certain access rights in international rail transport for railway undertakings, and international groupings of railway undertakings; these rights mean that railway infrastructure can be used by multiple users.

Notes

[1] OJ L 237, 24.8.1991, p. 25. Directive as amended by Directive 2001/12/EC of the European Parliament and of the Council [OJ L 75, 15.3.2001, p. 1].

(3) Council Directive 95/19/EC of 19 June 1995 on the allocation of railway infrastructure capacity and the charging of infrastructure fees[1] set out a broad framework for the allocation of railway infrastructure capacity.

Notes

[1] OJ L 143, 27.6.1995, p. 75.

(4) Those Directives have not prevented a considerable variation in the structure and level of railway infrastructure charges and the form and duration of capacity allocation processes.

(5) To ensure transparency and non-discriminatory access to rail infrastructure for all railway undertakings all the necessary information required to use access rights are to be published in a network statement.

(6) Appropriate capacity-allocation schemes for rail infrastructure coupled with competitive operators will result in a better balance of transport between modes.

(7) Encouraging optimal use of the railway infrastructure will lead to a reduction in the cost of transport to society.

(8) An efficient freight sector, especially across borders, requires action for the opening up of the market.

(9) It should be possible for Member States to allow purchasers of railway services to enter directly the capacity-allocation process.

(10) The revitalisation of European railways by means of extended access for international freight on the Trans-European Rail Freight Network requires fair intermodal competition between rail and road, particularly by taking appropriate account of the different external effects; appropriate charging schemes for rail infrastructure coupled with appropriate charging schemes for other transport infrastructures and competitive operators will result in an optimal balance of different transport modes.

(11) The charging and capacity allocation schemes should permit equal and non-discriminatory access for all undertakings and attempt as far as possible to meet the needs of all users and traffic types in a fair and non-discriminatory manner.

(12) Within the framework set out by Member States charging and capacity-allocation schemes should encourage railway infrastructure managers to optimise use of their infrastructure.

(13) Railway undertakings should receive clear and consistent signals from capacity allocation schemes which lead them to make rational decisions.

(14) In order to take into account the needs of users, or potential users, of railway infrastructure capacity to plan their business, and to the needs of customers and funders, it is important that the infrastructure manager ensures that infrastructure capacity is allocated in a way which reflects the need to maintain and improve service reliability levels.

(15) It is desirable for railway undertakings and the infrastructure manager to be provided with incentives to minimise disruption and improve performance of the network.

(16) Charging and capacity allocation schemes should allow for fair competition in the provision of railway services.

(17) It is important to have regard to the business requirements of both applicants and the infrastructure manager.

(18) It is important to maximise the flexibility available to the infrastructure managers with regard to the allocation of infrastructure capacity, but this must be consistent with satisfaction of the applicant's reasonable requirements.

(19) The capacity allocation process must prevent the imposition of undue constraints on the wishes of other undertakings holding, or intending to hold, rights to use the infrastructure to develop their business.

(20) It is desirable to grant some degree of flexibility to infrastructure managers to enable a more efficient use to be made of the infrastructure network.

(21) Capacity allocation and charging schemes may need to take account of the fact that different components of the rail infrastructure network may have been designed with different principal users in mind.

(22) The requirements for passenger services may often conflict with the requirements for freight; the requirements for passenger services may result in a network which is more costly to build and maintain than one designed solely for freight; the increasing speed differential between freight and passenger rolling stock can lead to an exacerbation of the conflict between these two types of traffic.

(23) Different users and types of users will frequently have a different impact on infrastructure capacity and the needs of different services need to be properly balanced.

(24) Services operated under contract to a public authority may require special rules to safeguard their attractiveness to users.

(25) The charging and capacity allocation schemes must take account of the effects of increasing saturation of infrastructure capacity and ultimately the scarcity of capacity.

(26) The different time-frames for planning traffic types mean that it is desirable to ensure that requests for infrastructure capacity which are made after the completion of the timetabling process can be satisfied.

(27) The use of information technology can enhance the speed and responsiveness of the timetabling process and improve the ability of applicants to bid for infrastructure capacity, as well as improving the ability to establish train paths which cross more than one infrastructure manager's network.

(28) To ensure the optimum outcome for railway undertakings, it is desirable to require an examination of the use of infrastructure capacity when the coordination of requests for capacity is required to meet the needs of users.

(29) In view of the monopolistic position of the infrastructure managers it is desirable to require an examination of the available infrastructure capacity, and methods of enhancing it when the capacity allocation process is unable to meet the requirements of users.

(30) A lack of information about other railway undertakings" requests as well as about the constraints within the system may make it difficult for railway undertakings to seek to optimise their infrastructure capacity requests.

(31) It is important to ensure the better coordination of allocation schemes so as to ensure the improved attractiveness of rail for traffic which uses the network of more than one infrastructure manager, in particular for international traffic.

(32) It is important to minimise the distortions of competition which may arise, either between railway infrastructures or between transport modes, from significant differences in charging principles.

(33) It is desirable to define those components of the infrastructure service which are essential to enable an operator to provide a service and which should be provided in return for minimum access charges.

(34) Investment in railway infrastructure is desirable and infrastructure charging schemes should provide incentives for infrastructure managers to make appropriate investments where they are economically attractive.

(35) Any charging scheme will send economic signals to users. It is important that those signals to railway undertakings should be consistent and lead them to make rational decisions.

(36) To enable the establishment of appropriate and fair levels of infrastructure charges, infrastructure managers need to record and establish the valuation of their assets and develop a clear understanding of cost factors in the operation of the infrastructure.

(37) It is desirable to ensure that account is taken of external costs when making transport decisions.

(38) It is important to ensure that charges for international traffic are such as to permit rail to meet the needs of the market; consequently infrastructure charging should be set at the cost that is directly incurred as a result of operating the train service.

(39) The overall level of cost recovery through infrastructure charges affects the necessary level of government contribution; Member States may require different levels of overall cost recovery through charges including mark-ups or a rate of return which the market can bear while balancing cost recovery with intermodal competitiveness of rail freight. However, it is desirable for any infrastructure charging scheme to enable traffic to use the rail network which can at least pay for the additional cost which it imposes.

(40) A railway infrastructure is a natural monopoly. It is therefore necessary to provide infrastructure managers with incentives to reduce costs and manage their infrastructure efficiently.

(41) Account should be taken of the fact that for a great many years the level of investment in infrastructure and technology has not made it possible to create the conditions for any real development of railway transport. It is therefore advisable, against this background, for appropriate upgrading to be carried out, in particular in the context of setting up the Trans-European Rail Freight Network, by using *inter alia* the Community instruments available, without prejudice to priorities already established.

(42) Discounts which are allowed to railway undertakings must relate to actual administrative cost savings experienced; discounts may also be used to promote the efficient use of infrastructure.

(43) It is desirable for railway undertakings and the infrastructure manager to be provided with incentives to minimise disruption of the network.

(44) The allocation of capacity is associated with a cost to the infrastructure manager, payment for which should be required.

(45) Measures are needed to ensure that all railway undertakings licensed under Community law are required to hold an appropriate safety certificate before operating on the territory of a Member State; the granting of safety certificates must comply with Community law.

(46) The efficient management and fair and non-discriminatory use of rail infrastructure require the establishment of a regulatory body that oversees the application of these Community rules and acts as an appeal body, notwithstanding the possibility of judicial review.

(47) Specific measures are required to take account of the specific geopolitical and geographical situation of certain Member States as well as a specific organisation of the railway sector in various Member States while ensuring the integrity of the internal market.

(48) The measures necessary for the implementation of this Directive should be adopted in accordance with Council Decision 1999/468/EC of 28 June 1999 laying down the procedures for the exercise of implementing powers conferred on the Commission.[1]

Notes
[1] OJ L 184, 17.7.1999, p. 23.

(49) In accordance with the principles of subsidiarity and proportionality as set out in Article 5 of the
Treaty, the objectives of this Directive, namely to coordinate arrangements in the Member States
governing the allocation of railway infrastructure capacity and the charges made for the use
thereof as well as safety certification, cannot be sufficiently achieved by the Member States in
view of the need to ensure fair and non-discriminatory terms for access to the infrastructure as
well as to take account of the manifestly international dimensions involved in the operation of
significant elements of the railway networks, and can therefore, by reason of the need for coordinated trans-national action, be better achieved by the Community. This Directive does not go
beyond what is necessary to achieve those objectives.

(50) Council Regulation (EEC) No 2830/77 of 12 December 1977 on the measures necessary to
achieve comparability between the accounting systems and annual accounts of railway undertakings,[1] Council Regulation (EEC) No 2183/78 of 19 September 1978 laying down uniform
costing principles for railway undertakings,[2] Council Decision 82/529/EEC of 19 July 1982 on
the fixing of rates for the international carriage of goods by rail,[3] Council Decision 83/418/EEC
of 25 July 1983 on the commercial independence of the railways in the management of their
international passenger and luggage traffic,[4] and Directive 95/19/EC are superseded by this
Directive and should therefore be repealed,

Notes
[1] OJ L 334, 24.12.1977, p. 13. Regulation as last amended by the 1994 Act of Accession.
[2] OJ L 258, 21.9.1978, p. 1. Regulation as last amended by the 1994 Act of Accession.
[3] OJ L 234, 9.8.1982, p. 5. Regulation as last amended by the 1994 Act of Accession.
[4] OJ L 237, 26.8.1983, p. 32. Regulation as last amended by the 1994 Act of Accession.

HAVE ADOPTED THIS DIRECTIVE:

CHAPTER I
INTRODUCTORY PROVISIONS

Article 1
Scope

1. This Directive concerns the principles and procedures to be applied with regard to the setting and
charging of railway infrastructure charges and the allocation of railway infrastructure capacity.

Member States shall ensure that charging and capacity allocation schemes for railway infrastructure
follow the principles set down in this Directive and thus allow the infrastructure manager to market
and make optimum effective use of the available infrastructure capacity.

2. This Directive applies to the use of railway infrastructure for domestic and international rail
services.

3. Member States may exclude from the scope of this Directive:

a) stand-alone local and regional networks for passenger services on railway infrastructure;
b) networks intended only for the operation of urban or suburban passenger services;
c) regional networks which are used for regional freight services solely by a railway undertaking that
is not covered by the scope of Directive 91/440/EEC until capacity on that network is requested
by another applicant;
d) privately owned railway infrastructure that exists solely for use by the infrastructure owner for its
own freight operations.

4. Transport operations in the form of shuttle services for road vehicles through the Channel Tunnel
are excluded from the scope of this Directive.

Article 2
Definitions

For the purpose of this Directive:

a) "allocation" means the allocation of railway infrastructure capacity by an infrastructure manager;

b) "applicant" means a licensed railway undertaking and/or an international grouping of railway undertakings, and, in Member States which provide for such a possibility, other persons and/or legal entities with public service or commercial interest in procuring infrastructure capacity, such as public authorities under Regulation (EEC) No 1191/69[1] and shippers, freight forwarders and combined transport operators, for the operation of railway service on their respective territories;

c) "congested infrastructure" means a section of infrastructure for which demand for infrastructure capacity cannot be fully satisfied during certain periods even after coordination of the different requests for capacity;

d) "capacity enhancement plan" means a measure or series of measures with a calendar for their implementation which are proposed to alleviate the capacity constraints leading to the declaration of a section of infrastructure as "congested infrastructure";

e) "coordination" means the process through which the allocation body and applicants will attempt to resolve situations in which there are conflicting applications for infrastructure capacity;

f) "framework agreement" means a legally binding general agreement on the basis of public or private law, setting out the rights and obligations of an applicant and the infrastructure manager or the allocation body in relation to the infrastructure capacity to be allocated and the charges to be levied over a period longer than one working timetable period;

g) "infrastructure capacity" means the potential to schedule train paths requested for an element of infrastructure for a certain period;

h) "infrastructure manager" means any body or undertaking that is responsible in particular for establishing and maintaining railway infrastructure. This may also include the management of infrastructure control and safety systems. The functions of the infrastructure manager on a network or part of a network may be allocated to different bodies or undertakings;

i) "network" means the entire railway infrastructure owned and/or managed by an infrastructure manager;

j) "network statement" means the statement which sets out in detail the general rules, deadlines, procedures and criteria concerning the charging and capacity allocation schemes. It shall also contain such other information as is required to enable application for infrastructure capacity;

k) "railway undertaking" means any public or private undertaking, licensed according to applicable Community legislation, the principal business of which is to provide services for the transport of goods and/or passengers by rail with a requirement that the undertaking must ensure traction; this also includes undertakings which provide traction only;

l) "train path" means the infrastructure capacity needed to run a train between two places over a given time-period;

m) "working timetable" means the data defining all planned train and rolling-stock movements which will take place on the relevant infrastructure during the period for which it is in force.

Notes

[1] Regulation (EEC) No 1191/69 of the Council of 26 June 1969 on action by Member States concerning the obligations inherent in the concept of a public service in transport by rail, road and inland waterway (OJ L 156, 28.6.1969, p. 1). Regulation as last amended by Regulation (EC) No 1893/91 (OJ L 169, 29.6.1991, p. 1).

Article 3
Network statement

1. The infrastructure manager shall, after consultation with the interested parties, develop and publish a network statement obtainable against payment of a duty which may not exceed the cost of publishing that statement.

2. The network statement shall set out the nature of the infrastructure which is available to railway undertakings. It shall contain information setting out the conditions for access to the relevant railway infrastructure. The content of the network statement is laid down in Annex I.

3. The network statement shall be kept up to date and modified as necessary.

4. The network statement shall be published no less than four months in advance of the deadline for requests for infrastructure capacity.

CHAPTER II
INFRASTRUCTURE CHARGES

Article 4
Establishing, determining and collecting charges

1. Member States shall establish a charging framework while respecting the management independence laid down in Article 4 of Directive 91/440/EEC.

Subject to the said condition of management independence, Member States shall also establish specific charging rules or delegate such powers to the infrastructure manager. The determination of the charge for the use of infrastructure and the collection of this charge shall be performed by the infrastructure manager.

2. Where the infrastructure manager, in its legal form, organisation or decision-making functions, is not independent of any railway undertaking, the functions, described in this chapter, other than collecting the charges shall be performed by a charging body that is independent in its legal form, organisation and decision-making from any railway undertaking.

3. Infrastructure managers shall cooperate to achieve the efficient operation of train services which cross more than one infrastructure network. They shall in particular aim to guarantee the optimum competitiveness of international rail freight and ensure the efficient utilisation of the Trans-European Rail Freight Network. They may establish such joint organisations as are appropriate to enable this to take place. Any cooperation or joint organisation shall be bound by the rules set out in this Directive.

4. Except where specific arrangements are made under Article 8(2), infrastructure managers shall ensure that the charging scheme in use is based on the same principles over the whole of their network.

5. Infrastructure managers shall ensure that the application of the charging scheme results in equivalent and non-discriminatory charges for different railway undertakings that perform services of equivalent nature in a similar part of the market and that the charges actually applied comply with the rules laid down in the network statement.

6. An infrastructure manager or charging body shall respect the commercial confidentiality of information provided to it by applicants.

Commentary
Art 4(2): F&N: 14.229

Article 5
Services

1. Railway undertakings shall, on a non-discriminatory basis, be entitled to the minimum access package and track access to service facilities that are described in Annex II. The supply of services referred to in Annex II, point 2 shall be provided in a non-discriminatory manner and requests by railway undertakings may only be rejected if viable alternatives under market conditions exist. If the services are not offered by one infrastructure manager, the provider of the "main infrastructure" shall use all reasonable endeavours to facilitate the provision of these services.

2. Where the infrastructure manager offers any of the range of services described in Annex II, point 3 as additional services he shall supply them upon request to a railway undertaking.

3. Railway undertakings may request a further range of ancillary services, listed in Annex II, point 4 from the infrastructure manager or from other suppliers. The infrastructure manager is not obliged to supply these services.

Commentary
Art 5: F&N: 14.234

Article 6
Infrastructure cost and accounts

1. Member States shall lay down conditions, including where appropriate advance payments, to ensure that, under normal business conditions and over a reasonable time period, the accounts of an infrastructure manager shall at least balance income from infrastructure charges, surpluses from other commercial activities and State funding on the one hand, and infrastructure expenditure on the other.

Without prejudice to the possible long-term aim of user cover of infrastructure costs for all modes of transport on the basis of fair, non-discriminatory competition between the various modes, where rail transport is able to compete with other modes of transport, within the charging framework of Articles 7 and 8, a Member State may require the infrastructure manager to balance his accounts without State funding.

2. Infrastructure managers shall, with due regard to safety and to maintaining and improving the quality of the infrastructure service, be provided with incentives to reduce the costs of provision of infrastructure and the level of access charges.

3. Member States shall ensure that the provision set out in paragraph 2 is implemented, either through a contractual agreement between the competent authority and infrastructure manager covering a period of not less than three years which provides for State funding or through the establishment of appropriate regulatory measures with adequate powers.

4. Where a contractual agreement exists, the terms of the contract and the structure of the payments agreed to provide funding to the infrastructure manager shall be agreed in advance to cover the whole of the contract period.

5. A method for apportioning costs shall be established. Member States may require prior approval. This method should be updated from time to time to the best international practice.

Article 7
Principles of charging

1. Charges for the use of railway infrastructure shall be paid to the infrastructure manager and used to fund his business.

2. Member States may require the infrastructure manager to provide all necessary information on the charges imposed. The infrastructure manager must, in this regard, be able to justify that infrastructure charges actually invoiced to each operator, pursuant to Articles 4 to 12, comply with the methodology, rules, and where applicable, scales laid down in the network statement.

3. Without prejudice to paragraphs 4 or 5 or to Article 8, the charges for the minimum access package and track access to service facilities shall be set at the cost that is directly incurred as a result of operating the train service.

4. The infrastructure charge may include a charge which reflects the scarcity of capacity of the identifiable segment of the infrastructure during periods of congestion.

5. The infrastructure charge may be modified to take account of the cost of the environmental effects caused by the operation of the train. Such a modification shall be differentiated according to the magnitude of the effect caused.

Charging of environmental costs which results in an increase in the overall revenue accruing to the infrastructure manager shall however be allowed only if such charging is applied at a comparable level to competing modes of transport.

In the absence of any comparable level of charging of environmental costs in other competing modes of transport, such modification shall not result in any overall change in revenue to the infrastructure manager. If a comparable level of charging of environmental costs has been introduced for rail and competing modes of transport and that generates additional revenue, it shall be for Member States to decide how the revenue shall be used.

6. To avoid undesirable disproportionate fluctuations, the charges referred to in paragraphs 3, 4 and 5 may be averaged over a reasonable spread of train services and times. Nevertheless, the relative magnitudes of the infrastructure charges shall be related to the costs attributable to the services.

7. The supply of services referred to in Annex II, point 2, shall not be covered by this Article. Without prejudice to the foregoing, account shall be taken, in setting the prices for the services set out in Annex II, point 2, of the competitive situation of rail transport.

8. Where services listed in Annex II, points 3 and 4 as additional and ancillary services are offered only by one supplier the charge imposed for such a service shall relate to the cost of providing it, calculated on the basis of the actual level of use.

9. Charges may be levied for capacity used for the purpose of infrastructure maintenance. Such charges shall not exceed the net revenue loss to the infrastructure manager caused by the maintenance.

Commentary
Art 7: F&N: 14.232

Article 8
Exceptions to charging principles

1. In order to obtain full recovery of the costs incurred by the infrastructure manager a Member State may, if the market can bear this, levy mark-ups on the basis of efficient, transparent and non-discriminatory principles, while guaranteeing optimum competitiveness in particular of international rail freight. The charging system shall respect the productivity increases achieved by railway undertakings.

The level of charges must not, however, exclude the use of infrastructure by market segments which can pay at least the cost that is directly incurred as a result of operating the railway service, plus a rate of return which the market can bear.

2. For specific investment projects, in the future, or that have been completed not more than 15 years before the entry into force of this Directive, the infrastructure manager may set or continue to set higher charges on the basis of the long-term costs of such projects if they increase efficiency and/or cost-effectiveness and could not otherwise be or have been undertaken. Such a charging arrangement may also incorporate agreements on the sharing of the risk associated with new investments.

3. To prevent discrimination, it shall be ensured that any given infrastructure manager's average and marginal charges for equivalent uses of his infrastructure are comparable and that comparable services in the same market segment are subject to the same charges. The infrastructure manager shall show in the network statement that the charging system meets these requirements in so far as this can be done without disclosing confidential business information.

4. If an infrastructure manager intends to modify the essential elements of the charging system referred to in paragraph 1, it shall make them public at least three months in advance.

Commentary
Art 8: F&N: 14.232

Article 9
Discounts

1. Without prejudice to Articles 81, 82, 86 and 87 of the Treaty and notwithstanding Article 7(3) of this Directive, any discount on the charges levied on a railway undertaking by the infrastructure manager, for any service, shall comply with the criteria set out in this Article.

2. With the exception of paragraph 3, discounts shall be limited to the actual saving of the administrative cost to the infrastructure manager. In determining the level of discount, no account may be taken of cost savings already internalised in the charge levied.

3. Infrastructure managers may introduce schemes available to all users of the infrastructure, for specified traffic flows, granting time limited discounts to encourage the development of new rail services, or discounts encouraging the use of considerably underutilised lines.

4. Discounts may relate only to charges levied for a specified infrastructure section.

5. Similar discount schemes shall apply for similar services.

Commentary
Art 9: F&N: 14.232

Article 10
Compensation schemes for unpaid environmental, accident and infrastructure costs

1. Member States may put in place a time-limited compensation scheme for the use of railway infrastructure for the demonstrably unpaid environmental, accident and infrastructure costs of competing transport modes in so far as these costs exceed the equivalent costs of rail.

2. Where an operator receiving compensation enjoys an exclusive right, the compensation must be accompanied by comparable benefits to users.

3. The methodology used and calculations performed must be publicly available. It shall in particular be possible to demonstrate the specific uncharged costs of the competing transport infrastructure that are avoided and to ensure that the scheme is granted on non-discriminatory terms to undertakings.

4. Member States shall ensure that such a scheme is compatible with Articles 73, 87 and 88 of the Treaty.

Article 11
Performance scheme

1. Infrastructure charging schemes shall through a performance scheme encourage railway undertakings and the infrastructure manager to minimise disruption and improve the performance of the railway network. This may include penalties for actions which disrupt the operation of the network, compensation for undertakings which suffer from disruption and bonuses that reward better than planned performance.

2. The basic principles of the performance scheme shall apply throughout the network.

Article 12
Reservation charges

Infrastructure managers may levy an appropriate charge for capacity that is requested but not used. This charge shall provide incentives for efficient use of capacity.

The infrastructure manager shall always be able to inform any interested party of the infrastructure capacity which has been allocated to user railway undertakings.

CHAPTER III
ALLOCATION OF INFRASTRUCTURE CAPACITY

Article 13
Capacity rights

1. Infrastructure capacity shall be allocated by an infrastructure manager, and once allocated to an applicant may not be transferred by the recipient to another undertaking or service.

Any trading in infrastructure capacity shall be prohibited and shall lead to exclusion from the further allocation of capacity.

The use of capacity by a railway undertaking when carrying out the business of an applicant who is not a railway undertaking shall not be considered a transfer.

2. The right to use specific infrastructure capacity in the form of a train path may be granted to applicants for a maximum duration of one working timetable period.

An infrastructure manager and an applicant may enter into a framework agreement as laid down in Article 17 for the use of capacity on the relevant railway infrastructure for a longer term than one working timetable period.

3. The definition of respective rights and obligations between infrastructure managers and applicants in respect of any allocation of capacity shall be laid down in contracts or legislation.

Article 14
Capacity allocation

1. Member States may establish a framework for the allocation of infrastructure capacity while respecting the management independence laid down in Article 4 of Directive 91/440/EEC. Specific capacity allocation rules shall be established. The infrastructure manager shall perform the capacity allocation processes. In particular, the infrastructure manager shall ensure that infrastructure capacity is allocated on a fair and non-discriminatory basis and in accordance with Community law.

2. Where the infrastructure manager, in its legal form, organisation or decision-making functions is not independent of any railway undertaking, the functions referred to in paragraph 1 and described in this chapter shall be performed by an allocation body that is independent in its legal form, organisation and decision-making from any railway undertaking.

3. Infrastructure managers and allocation bodies shall respect the commercial confidentiality of information provided to them.

Commentary
Art 14(2): F&N: 14.229

Article 15
Cooperation in the allocation of infrastructure capacity on more than one network

1. Infrastructure managers shall cooperate to enable the efficient creation and allocation of infrastructure capacity which crosses more than one network. They shall organise international train paths, in particular within the framework of the Trans-European Rail Freight Network. They shall establish such procedures as are appropriate to enable this to take place. These procedures shall be bound by the rules set out in this Directive.

The procedure established in order to coordinate the allocation of infrastructure capacity at an international level shall associate representatives of infrastructure managers for all railway infrastructures whose allocation decisions have an impact on more than one other infrastructure manager. Appropriate representatives of infrastructure managers from outside the Community may be associated with these procedures. The Commission shall be informed and invited to attend as an observer.

2. At any meeting or other activity undertaken to permit the allocation of infrastructure capacity for trans-network train services, decisions shall only be taken by representatives of infrastructure managers.

3. The participants in the cooperation referred to paragraph 1 shall ensure that its membership, methods of operation and all relevant criteria which are used for assessing and allocating infrastructure capacity be made publicly available.

4. Working in cooperation as referred to in paragraph 1, infrastructure managers shall assess the need for, and may where necessary propose and organise international train paths to facilitate the operation of freight trains which are subject to an ad hoc request as referred to in Article 23.

Such prearranged international train paths shall be made available to applicants via any of the participating infrastructure managers.

Article 16
Applicants

1. Applications for infrastructure capacity may be made by railway undertakings and their international groupings and, in the territories of those Member States which so allow, by other applicants complying with the definition in Article 2(b). Member States may also allow other applicants to apply for infrastructure capacity on their territories.

2. The infrastructure manager may set requirements with regard to applicants to ensure that its legitimate expectations about future revenues and utilisation of the infrastructure are safeguarded. Such requirements shall be appropriate, transparent and non-discriminatory. The requirements shall be published as part of the allocation principles in the network statement, and the Commission shall be informed.

3. The requirements in paragraph 2 may only include the provision of a financial guarantee that must not exceed an appropriate level which shall be proportional to the contemplated level of activity of the applicant, and assurance of the capability to prepare compliant bids for infrastructure capacity.

Article 17
Framework agreements

1. Without prejudice to Articles 81, 82 and 86 of the Treaty, a framework agreement may be concluded with an applicant. Such a framework agreement specifies the characteristics of the infrastructure capacity required by and offered to the applicant over a period of time exceeding one working timetable period. The framework agreement shall not specify a train path in detail, but should be such as to seek to meet the legitimate commercial needs of the applicant. A Member State may require prior approval of such a framework agreement by the regulatory body referred to in Article 30 of this Directive.

2. Framework agreements shall not be such as to preclude the use of the relevant infrastructure by other applicants or services.

3. A framework agreement shall allow for the amendment or limitation of its terms to enable better use to be made of the railway infrastructure.

4. The framework agreement may contain penalties should it be necessary to modify or terminate the agreement.

5. Framework agreements shall in principle be for a period of five years. The infrastructure manager may agree to a shorter or longer period in specific cases. Any period longer than five years shall be justified by the existence of commercial contracts, specialised investments or risks.

Any period longer than 10 years shall be possible only in exceptional cases, in particular, where there is large-scale, long-term investment, and particularly where such investment is covered by contractual commitments.

6. While respecting commercial confidentiality, the general nature of each framework agreement shall be made available to any interested party.

Article 18
Schedule for the allocation process

1. The infrastructure manager shall adhere to the schedule for capacity allocation set out in Annex III.

2. Infrastructure managers shall agree with the other relevant infrastructure managers concerned which international train paths are to be included in the working timetable, before commencing consultation on the draft working timetable. Adjustments shall only be made if absolutely necessary.

Article 19
Application

1. Applicants may apply on the basis of public or private law to the infrastructure manager to request an agreement granting rights to use railway infrastructure against a charge as provided for in chapter II.

2. Requests relating to the regular working timetable must adhere to the deadlines set out in Annex III.

3. An applicant who is a party to a framework agreement shall apply in accordance with that agreement.

4. Applicants may request infrastructure capacity crossing more than one network by applying to one infrastructure manager. That infrastructure manager shall then be permitted to act on behalf of the applicant to seek capacity with the other relevant infrastructure managers.

5. Infrastructure managers shall ensure that, for infrastructure capacity crossing more than one network, applicants may apply direct to any joint body which the infrastructure managers may establish.

Article 20
Scheduling

1. The infrastructure manager shall as far as is possible meet all requests for infrastructure capacity including requests for train paths crossing more than one network, and shall as far as possible take account of all constraints on applicants, including the economic effect on their business.

2. The infrastructure manager may give priority to specific services within the scheduling and coordination process but only as set out in Articles 22 and 24.

3. The infrastructure manager shall consult interested parties about the draft working timetable and allow them at least one month to present their views. Interested parties shall include all those who have requested infrastructure capacity as well as other parties who wish to have the opportunity to comment on how the working timetable may affect their ability to procure rail services during the working timetable period.

4. The infrastructure manager shall take appropriate measures to deal with any concerns that are expressed.

Article 21
Coordination process

1. During the scheduling process referred to in Article 20, when the infrastructure manager encounters conflicts between different requests he shall attempt, through coordination of the requests, to ensure the best possible matching of all requirements.

2. When a situation requiring coordination arises, the infrastructure manager shall have the right, within reasonable limits, to propose infrastructure capacity that differs from that which was requested.

3. The infrastructure manager shall attempt, through consultation with the appropriate applicants, to achieve a resolution of any conflicts.

4. The principles governing the coordination process shall be defined in the network statement. These shall in particular reflect the difficulty of arranging international train paths and the effect that modification may have on other infrastructure managers.

5. When requests for infrastructure capacity cannot be satisfied without coordination, the infrastructure manager shall attempt to accommodate all requests through coordination.

6. Without prejudice to the existing appeal procedures and to the provisions of Article 30, in case of disputes relating to the allocation of infrastructure capacity, a dispute resolution system shall be made available in order to resolve such disputes promptly. If this system is applied, a decision shall be reached within a time limit of 10 working days.

Article 22
Congested infrastructure

1. Where after coordination of the requested paths and consultation with applicants it is not possible to satisfy requests for infrastructure capacity adequately then the infrastructure manager must immediately declare that element of infrastructure on which this has occurred to be congested.

This shall also be done for infrastructure which it can be foreseen will suffer from insufficient capacity in the near future.

2. When infrastructure has been declared to be congested, the infrastructure manager shall carry out a capacity analysis as described in Article 25, unless a capacity enhancement plan as described in Article 26 is already being implemented.

3. When charges in accordance with Article 7(4) have not been levied or have not achieved a satisfactory result and the infrastructure has been declared to be congested, the infrastructure manager may in addition employ priority criteria to allocate infrastructure capacity.

4. The priority criteria shall take account of the importance of a service to society, relative to any other service which will consequently be excluded.

In order to guarantee within this framework the development of adequate transport services, in particular to comply with public-service requirements or promote the development of rail freight, Member States may take any measures necessary, under non-discriminatory conditions, to ensure that such services are given priority when infrastructure capacity is allocated.

Member States may, where appropriate, grant the infrastructure manager compensation corresponding to any loss of revenue related to the need to allocate a given capacity to certain services pursuant to the previous subparagraph.

This shall include taking account of the effect of this exclusion in other Member States.

5. The importance of freight services and in particular international freight services shall be given adequate consideration in determining priority criteria.

6. The procedures which shall be followed and criteria used where infrastructure is congested shall be set out in the network statement.

Article 23
Ad hoc requests

1. The infrastructure manager shall respond to ad hoc requests for individual train paths as quickly as possible, and in any event, within five working days. Information supplied on available spare capacity shall be made available to all applicants who may wish to use this capacity.

2. Infrastructure managers shall where necessary undertake an evaluation of the need for reserve capacity to be kept available within the final scheduled working timetable to enable them to respond rapidly to foreseeable ad hoc requests for capacity. This shall also apply in cases of congested infrastructure.

Article 24
Specialised infrastructure

1. Without prejudice to paragraph 2, infrastructure capacity shall be considered to be available for the use of all types of service which conform to the characteristics necessary for operation on the train path.

2. Where there are suitable alternative routes, the infrastructure manager may, after consultation with interested parties, designate particular infrastructure for use by specified types of traffic. Without prejudice to Articles 81, 82 and 86 of the Treaty, when such designation has occurred, the infrastructure manager may give priority to this type of traffic when allocating infrastructure capacity.

Such designation shall not prevent the use of such infrastructure by other types of traffic when capacity is available and when the rolling stock conforms to the technical characteristics necessary for operation on the line.

3. When infrastructure has been designated pursuant to paragraph 2, this shall be described in the network statement.

Article 25
Capacity analysis

1. The objective of capacity analysis is to determine the restrictions on infrastructure capacity which prevent requests for capacity from being adequately met, and to propose methods of enabling

additional requests to be satisfied. This analysis shall identify the reasons for the congestion and what measures might be taken in the short and medium term to ease the congestion.

2. The analysis shall consider the infrastructure, the operating procedures, the nature of the different services operating and the effect of all these factors on infrastructure capacity. Measures to be considered shall include in particular re-routing of services, re-timing services, speed alterations and infrastructure improvements.

3. A capacity analysis shall be completed within six months of the identification of infrastructure as congested.

Article 26
Capacity enhancement plan

1. Within six months of the completion of a capacity analysis, the infrastructure manager shall produce a capacity enhancement plan.

2. A capacity enhancement plan shall be developed after consultation with users of the relevant congested infrastructure.

It shall identify:

a) the reasons for the congestion;
b) the likely future development of traffic;
c) the constraints on infrastructure development;
d) the options and costs for capacity enhancement, including likely changes to access charges.

It shall also, on the basis of a cost benefit analysis of the possible measures identified, determine what action shall be taken to enhance infrastructure capacity, including a calendar for implementation of the measures.

The plan may be subject to prior approval by the Member State.

3. The infrastructure manager shall cease to levy any fees which are levied for the relevant infrastructure under Article 7(4) in cases where:

a) he does not produce a capacity enhancement plan; or
b) he does not make progress with the action plan identified in the capacity enhancement plan.

However, the infrastructure manager may, subject to the approval of the regulatory body referred to in Article 30 continue to levy those fees if:

a) the capacity enhancement plan cannot be realised for reasons beyond his control; or
b) the options available are not economically or financially viable.

Article 27
Use of train paths

1. In particular for congested infrastructure the infrastructure manager shall require the surrender of a train path which, over a period of at least one month, has been used less than a threshold quota to be laid down in the network statement, unless this was due to non-economic reasons beyond the operator's control.

2. An infrastructure manager may specify in the network statement conditions whereby it will take account of previous levels of utilisation of train paths in determining priorities for the allocation process.

Article 28
Infrastructure capacity for scheduled maintenance

1. Requests for infrastructure capacity to enable maintenance to be performed shall be submitted during the scheduling process.

2. Adequate account shall be taken by the infrastructure manager of the effect of infrastructure capacity reserved for scheduled track maintenance on applicants.

Article 29
Special measures to be taken in the event of disturbance

1. In the event of disturbance to train movements caused by technical failure or accident the infrastructure manager must take all necessary steps to restore the normal situation. To that end he shall draw up a contingency plan listing the various public bodies to be informed in the event of serious incidents or serious disturbance to train movements.

2. In an emergency and where absolutely necessary on account of a breakdown making the infrastructure temporarily unusable, the paths allocated may be withdrawn without warning for as long as is necessary to repair the system.

The infrastructure manager may, if he deems it necessary, require railway undertakings to make available to him the resources which he feels are the most appropriate to restore the normal situation as soon as possible.

3. Member States may require railway undertakings to be involved in assuring the enforcement and monitoring of their own compliance of the safety standards and rules.

CHAPTER IV
GENERAL MEASURES

Article 30
Regulatory body

1. Without prejudice to Article 21(6), Member States shall establish a regulatory body. This body, which can be the Ministry responsible for transport matters or any other body, shall be independent in its organisation, funding decisions, legal structure and decision-making from any infrastructure manager, charging body, allocation body or applicant. The body shall function according to the principles outlined in this Article whereby appeal and regulatory functions may be attributed to separate bodies.

2. An applicant shall have a right to appeal to the regulatory body if it believes that it has been unfairly treated, discriminated against or is in any other way aggrieved, and in particular against decisions adopted by the infrastructure manager or where appropriate the railway undertaking concerning:

a) the network statement;
b) criteria contained within it;
c) the allocation process and its result;
d) the charging scheme;
e) level or structure of infrastructure fees which it is, or may be, required to pay;
[f) arrangements for access in accordance with Article 10 of Council Directive 91/440/EEC of 29 July 1991 on the development of the Community's railways[1] as amended by Directive 2004/51/EC of the European Parliament and of the Council of 30 April 2004 amending Council Directive 91/440/EEC on the development of the Community's railways.[2]]

Notes
[[1] OJ L 237, 24.8.1991, p. 25.]
[[2] OJ L 164, 30.4.2004, p. 164.]
The amendments shown in square brackets were made by Directive 2004/49/EC (OJ L 164, 30.4.2004, as corrected at OJ L 220, 21.6.2004, p. 16), Article 30, with effect from 30 April 2004.

---

3. The regulatory body shall ensure that charges set by the infrastructure manager comply with chapter II and are non-discriminatory. Negotiation between applicants and an infrastructure manager concerning the level of infrastructure charges shall only be permitted if these are carried out under the supervision of the regulatory body. The regulatory body shall intervene if negotiations are likely to contravene the requirements of this Directive.

4. The regulatory body shall have the power to request relevant information from the infrastructure manager, applicants and any third party involved within the Member State concerned, which must be supplied without undue delay.

5. The regulatory body shall be required to decide on any complaints and take action to remedy the situation within a maximum period of two months from receipt of all information.

Notwithstanding paragraph 6, a decision of the regulatory body shall be binding on all parties covered by that decision.

In the event of an appeal against a refusal to grant infrastructure capacity, or against the terms of an offer of capacity, the regulatory body shall either confirm that no modification of the infrastructure manager's decision is required, or it shall require modification of that decision in accordance with directions specified by the regulatory body.

6. Member States shall take the measures necessary to ensure that decisions taken by the regulatory body are subject to judicial review.

Commentary
Art 30: F&N: 14.227

Article 31
Cooperation of regulatory bodies

The national regulatory bodies shall exchange information about their work and decision-making principles and practice for the purpose of coordinating their decision-making principles across the Community. The Commission shall support them in this task.

[*Article 32*]

Notes
Article 32 was deleted by Directive 2004/49/EC (OJ L 164, 30.4.2004, as corrected at OJ L 220, 21.6.2004, p. 16), Article 30, with effect from 30 April 2004.

Article 33
Derogations

1. For a period of five years from 15 March 2003, the following Member States:
— Ireland, as a Member State located on an island, with a rail link to only one other Member State,
— the United Kingdom, in respect of Northern Ireland, on the same basis, and
— Greece, as a Member State that does not have any direct rail link to any other Member State,
do not need to apply the requirements set out in:

a) Articles 3, 4(2), 13, 14, 17, 21(4), 21(6), 22, 24(3), 25 to 28 and 30 on the condition that decisions on the allocation of infrastructure capacity or the charging of fees are open to appeal, when so requested in writing by a railway undertaking, before an independent body which shall take its decision within two months of the submission of all relevant information and whose decision shall be subject to judicial review, and

b) Article 32 in so far as rail transport services falling outside the scope of Article 10 of Directive 91/440/EEC are concerned.

2. However, where:

a) more than one railway undertaking licensed in accordance with Article 4 of Directive 95/18/EC, or, in the case of Ireland and Northern Ireland, a railway company so licensed elsewhere submits an official application to operate competing railway services in, to or from Ireland, Northern Ireland or Greece, the continued applicability of this derogation will be decided upon in accordance with the advisory procedure referred to in Article 35(2); or

b) a railway undertaking operating railway services in Ireland, Northern Ireland or Greece submits an official application to operate railway services on, to or from the territory of another Member State (in the case of Ireland, or the United Kingdom, in respect of Northern Ireland, or both, another Member State outside their territories), the derogations referred to in paragraph 1 shall not apply.

Within one year from the receipt of either the decision referred to in point (a) adopted in accordance with the advisory procedure referred to in Article 35(2), or notification of the official application referred to in point (b), the Member State or States concerned (Ireland, the United Kingdom with respect to Northern Ireland, or Greece) shall put in place legislation to implement the Articles referred to in paragraph 1.

3. A derogation referred to in paragraph 1 may be renewed for periods not longer than five years. Not later than 12 months before the expiry date of the derogation a Member State availing itself of such derogation may address a request to the Commission for a renewed derogation. Any such request must be substantiated. The Commission shall examine such a request and adopt a decision in accordance with the advisory procedure referred to in Article 35(2). The said advisory procedure shall apply to any decision related to the request.

When adopting its decision the Commission shall take into account any development in the geo-political situation and the development of the rail market in, from and to the Member State having requested the renewed derogation.

4. Luxembourg as a Member State with a relatively small rail network does not need to apply until 31 August 2004 the requirement to award to an independent body the functions determining equitable and non-discriminatory access to infrastructure, as provided for in Articles 4 and 14 in so far as they oblige Member States to establish independent bodies performing the tasks referred to in those Articles.

CHAPTER V
FINAL PROVISIONS

Article 34
Implementing measures

1. Member States may bring any question concerning the implementation of this Directive to the attention of the Commission. Appropriate decisions shall be adopted in accordance with the advisory procedure referred to in Article 35(2).

[2. At the request of a Member State or on its own initiative the Commission shall, in a specific case, examine the application and enforcement of provisions concerning charging, capacity allocation, and within two months of receipt of such a request decide in accordance with the procedure referred to in Article 35(2) whether the related measure may continue to be applied. The Commission shall communicate its decision to the European Parliament, the Council and to the Member States.]

3. The amendments necessary to adapt the Annexes shall be adopted in accordance with the regulatory procedure referred to in Article 35(3).

Notes
The amendments shown in square brackets was made by Directive 2004/49/EC (OJ L 164, 30.4.2004, as corrected at OJ L 220, 21.6.2004, p. 16), Article 30, with effect from 30 April 2004.

Article 35
Committee procedures

1. The Commission shall be assisted by a Committee.

2. Where reference is made to this paragraph, Articles 3 and 7 of Decision 1999/468/EC shall apply, having regard to the provisions of Article 8 thereof.

3. Where reference is made to this paragraph, Articles 5 and 7 of Decision 1999/468/EC shall apply, having regard to the provisions of Article 8 thereof.

The period laid down in Article 5(6) of Decision 1999/468/EC shall be set at three months.

4. The Committee shall adopt its rules of procedure.

Article 36
Report

The Commission shall by 15 March 2005 submit to the European Parliament and to the Council a report on the implementation of this Directive, accompanied if necessary by proposals for further Community action.

Article 37
Repeals

Regulation (EEC) No 2830/77, Regulation (EEC) No 2183/78, Decision 82/529/EEC, Decision 83/418/EEC and Directive 95/19/EC are hereby repealed.

Article 38
Implementation

The Member States shall bring into force the laws, regulations and administrative provisions necessary to comply with this Directive by 15 March 2003. They shall forthwith inform the Commission thereof.

When Member States adopt those provisions, they shall contain a reference to this Directive or be accompanied by such reference on the occasion of their official publication. Member States shall determine how such reference is to be made.

Article 39
Entry into force

This Directive shall enter into force on the date of its publication in the Official Journal of the European Communities.

Notes
Date of entry into force: 15 March 2001.

Article 40
Addressees

This Directive is addressed to the Member States.

Done at Brussels, 26 February 2001.

ANNEX I
CONTENTS OF THE NETWORK STATEMENT

The network statement referred to in Article 3 shall contain the following information:

1. A section setting out the nature of the infrastructure which is available to railway undertakings and the conditions of access to it.
2. A section on charging principles and tariffs. This shall contain appropriate details of the charging scheme as well as sufficient information on charges that apply to the services listed in Annex II which are provided by only one supplier. It shall detail the methodology, rules and, where applicable, scales used for the application of Article 7(4) and (5) and Articles 8 and 9. It shall contain information on changes in charges already decided upon or foreseen.
3. A section on the principles and criteria for capacity allocation. This shall set out the general capacity characteristics of the infrastructure which is available to railway undertakings and any restrictions relating to its use, including likely capacity requirements for maintenance. It shall also specify the procedures and deadlines which relate to the capacity allocation process. It shall contain specific criteria which are employed during that process, in particular:
   a) the procedures according to which applicants may request capacity from the infrastructure manager;
   b) the requirements governing applicants;
   c) the schedule for the application and allocation processes;
   d) the principles governing the coordination process;

e) the procedures which shall be followed and criteria used where infrastructure is congested;

f) details of restrictions on the use of infrastructure;

g) any conditions by which account is taken of previous levels of utilisation of capacity in determining priorities for the allocation process.

It shall detail the measures taken to ensure the adequate treatment of freight services, international services and requests subject to the ad hoc procedure.

Annex II
Services to be Supplied to the Railway Undertakings

1. The minimum access package shall comprise:
   a) handling of requests for infrastructure capacity;
   b) the right to utilise capacity which is granted;
   c) use of running track points and junctions;
   d) train control including signalling, regulation, dispatching and the communication and provision of information on train movement;
   e) all other information required to implement or operate the service for which capacity has been granted.
2. Track access to services facilities and supply of services shall comprise:
   a) use of electrical supply equipment for traction current, where available;
   b) refuelling facilities;
   c) passenger stations, their buildings and other facilities;
   d) freight terminals;
   e) marshalling yards;
   f) train formation facilities;
   g) storage sidings;
   h) maintenance and other technical facilities.
3. Additional services may comprise:
   a) traction current;
   b) pre-heating of passenger trains;
   c) supply of fuel, shunting, and all other services provided at the access services facilities mentioned above;
   d) tailor-made contracts for:
      — control of transport of dangerous goods,
      — assistance in running abnormal trains.
4. Ancillary services may comprise:
   a) access to telecommunication network;
   b) provision of supplementary information;
   c) technical inspection of rolling stock.

Annex III
Schedule for the Allocation Process

1. The working timetable shall be established once per calendar year.
[2. The change of working timetable shall take place at midnight on the second Saturday in December. Where a change or adjustment is carried out after the winter, in particular to take account, where appropriate, of changes in regional passenger traffic timetables, it shall take place at midnight on the second Saturday in June and at such other intervals between these dates as are required. Infrastructure managers may agree on different dates and in this case they shall inform the Commission if international traffic may be affected.]
3. The final date for receipt of requests for capacity to be incorporated into the working timetable shall be no more than 12 months in advance of the entry into force of the working timetable.
4. No later than 11 months before the working timetable comes into force, the infrastructure managers shall ensure that provisional international train paths have been established in cooperation

with other relevant allocation bodies as set out in Article 15. Infrastructure managers shall ensure that as far as possible these are adhered to during the subsequent processes.

5.   No later than four months after the deadline for submission of bids by applicants, the infrastructure manager shall prepare a draft timetable.

Notes

The amendment shown in square brackets was made by Commission Decision 202/844/EC of 23 October 2002 (OJ L 289, 26.10.2002, p. 30) with effect from 14 December 2002. Because of the specific regulatory system in Great Britain, the United Kingdom was entitled to apply paragraph 2 from the 2004 timetable, starting in December 2003, provided that the other provisions of the Directive, and in particular those relating to international cooperation, were not affected.

E4

PROPOSAL FOR A REGULATION OF THE EUROPEAN PARLIAMENT AND OF THE COUNCIL

applying rules of competition to transport by rail, road and inland waterway (Codified version)

Notes

This proposal was presented by the Commission on 27 November 2006. The text is available on the Europa website at the following address:
http://eur-lex.europa.eu/LexUriServ/site/en/com/2006/com2006_0722en01.pdf

THE EUROPEAN PARLIAMENT AND THE COUNCIL OF THE EUROPEAN UNION,

Having regard to the Treaty establishing the European Community, and in particular

Articles 71 and 83 thereof,

Having regard to the proposal from the Commission,

Having regard to the opinion of the European Economic and Social Committee,[1]

Having regard to the opinion of the Committee of the Regions,[2]

Acting in accordance with the procedure laid down in Article 251 of the Treaty,[3]

Notes
[1] OJ C [...], [...], p. [...].
[2] OJ C [...], [...], p. [...].
[3] OJ C [...], [...], p. [...].

Whereas:

(1)   Regulation (EEC) No 1017/68 of the Council of 19 July 1968 applying rules of competition to transport by rail, road and inland waterway[4] has been substantially amended several times.[5] In the interests of clarity and rationality the said Regulation should be codified.

Notes
[4]   OJ L 175, 23.7.1968, p. 1. Regulation as last amended by the 2003 Act of Accession.
[5]   See Annex I.

(2) Rules of competition for transport by rail, road and inland waterway are part of the common transport policy and of general economic policy.

(3) Rules of competition for those sectors should take account of the distinctive features of transport.

(4) Since the rules of competition for transport derogate from the general rules of competition, it must be made possible for undertakings to ascertain what rules apply in any particular case.

(5) The system of rules on competition for transport should apply equally to the joint financing or acquisition of transport equipment for the joint operation of services by certain groupings of undertakings, and also to certain operations in connection with transport by rail, road or inland waterway of providers of services ancillary to transport.

(6) In order to ensure that trade between Member States is not affected or competition within the internal market distorted, it is necessary to prohibit in principle for the three modes of transport specified above all agreements between undertakings, decisions of associations of undertakings and concerted practices between undertakings and all instances of abuse of a dominant position within the internal market which could have such effects.

(7) Certain types of agreement, decision and concerted practice in the transport sector the object and effect of which is merely to apply technical improvements or to achieve technical co-operation may be exempted from the prohibition on restrictive agreements since they contribute to improving productivity. In the light of experience following application of this Regulation, the Council may, on a proposal from the Commission, amend the list of such types of agreement.

(8) In order that an improvement may be fostered in the sometimes too dispersed structure of the industry in the road and inland waterway sectors, exemption from the prohibition on restrictive agreements should also be granted in the case of those agreements, decisions and concerted practices providing for the creation and operation of groupings of undertakings in these two transport sectors whose object is the carrying on of transport operations, including the joint financing or acquisition of transport equipment for the joint operation of services. Such overall exemption can be granted only on condition that the total carrying capacity of a grouping does not exceed a fixed maximum, and that the individual capacity of undertakings belonging to the grouping does not exceed certain limits so fixed as to ensure that no one undertaking can hold a dominant position within the grouping. The Commission must, however, have power to intervene if, in specific cases, such agreements should have effects incompatible with the conditions under which a restrictive agreement may be recognised as lawful, and should constitute an abuse of the exemption. Nevertheless, the fact that a grouping has a total carrying capacity greater than the fixed maximum, or cannot claim the overall exemption because of the individual capacity of the undertakings belonging to the grouping, does not in itself prevent such a grouping from constituting a lawful agreement, decision or concerted practice if it satisfies the relevant conditions laid down in this Regulation.

(9) It is for the undertakings themselves, in the first instance, to judge whether the predominant effects of their agreements, decisions or concerted practices are the restriction of competition or the economic benefits acceptable as justification for such restriction and to decide accordingly, on their own responsibility, as to the illegality or legality of such agreements, decisions or concerted practices.

(10) Therefore, undertakings should be allowed to conclude or operate agreements without declaring them. This exposes such agreements to the risk of being declared void with retroactive effect should they be examined following a complaint or on the Commission's own initiative, but does not prevent their being retroactively declared lawful in the event of such subsequent examination,

HAVE ADOPTED THIS REGULATION:

Article 1
Scope

The provisions of this Regulation shall, in the field of transport by rail, road and inland waterway, apply both to all agreements, decisions and concerted practices which have as their object or effect the fixing of transport rates and conditions, the limitation or control of the supply of transport, the sharing of transport markets, the application of technical improvements or technical co-opera-tion, or the joint financing or acquisition of transport equipment or supplies where such operations are directly related to the provision of transport services and are necessary for the joint operation of services by a grouping within the meaning of Article 3 of road or inland waterway transport under-takings, and to the abuse of a dominant position on the transport market. These provisions shall apply also to operations of providers of services ancillary to transport which have any of those objects or effects.

Article 2
Exception for technical agreements

1. The prohibition in Article 81(1) of the Treaty shall not apply to agreements, decisions or concerted practices the object and effect of which is to apply technical improvements or to achieve technical co-operation by means of:

(a) the standardisation of equipment, transport supplies, vehicles or fixed installations;
(b) the exchange or pooling, for the purpose of operating transport services, of staff, equipment, vehi-cles or fixed installations;
(c) the organisation and execution of successive, complementary, substitute or combined transport operations, and the fixing and application of inclusive rates and conditions for such operations, including special competitive rates;
(d) the use, for journeys by a single mode of transport, of the routes which are most rational from the operational point of view;
(e) the co-ordination of transport timetables for connecting routes;
(f) the grouping of single consignments;
(g) the establishment of uniform rules as to the structure of tariffs and their conditions of application, provided such rules do not lay down transport rates and conditions.

2. The Commission shall, where appropriate, submit proposals to the Council with a view to extend-ing or reducing the list in paragraph 1.

Article 3
Exemption for groups of small and medium-sized undertakings

1. Agreements, decisions and concerted practices as referred to in Article 81(1) of the Treaty shall be exempt from the prohibition in that Article where their purpose is:

(a) the constitution and operation of groupings of road or inland waterway transport undertakings with a view to carrying on transport activities;
(b) the joint financing or acquisition of transport equipment or supplies, where these operations are directly related to the provision of transport services and are necessary for the joint operations of the aforesaid groupings;

always provided that the total carrying capacity of any grouping does not exceed:

(i) 10,000 metric tons in the case of road transport;
(ii) 500,000 metric tons in the case of transport by inland waterway.

The individual capacity of each undertaking belonging to a grouping shall not exceed 1,000 metric tons in the case of road transport or 50,000 metric tons in the case of transport by inland waterway.

2. If the implementation of any agreement, decision or concerted practice covered by paragraph 1 has, in a given case, effects which are incompatible with the requirements of Article 81(3) of the Treaty, undertakings or associations of undertakings may be required to make such effects cease.

Article 4
Repeal

Regulation (EEC) No 1017/68 is repealed, with the exception of Article 13(3), which continues to apply to decisions adopted pursuant to Article 5 of Regulation (EEC) No 1017/68 prior to 1 May 2004 until the date of expiration of those decisions. References to the repealed Regulation shall be construed as references to this Regulation and shall be read in accordance with the correlation table in Annex II.

Article 5
Entry into force, existing agreements

1. This Regulation shall enter into force on the twentieth day following that of its publication in the *Official Journal of the European Union*.

2. The prohibition in Article 81(1) of the Treaty shall not apply to agreements, decisions and concerted practices which were in existence at the date of accession of Austria, Finland and Sweden or at the date of accession of the Czech Republic, Estonia, Cyprus, Latvia, Lithuania, Hungary, Malta, Poland, Slovenia and Slovakia and which, by reason of accession, fall within the scope of Article 81(1) if, within six months from the date of accession, they are so amended that they comply with the conditions laid down in Article 3 of this Regulation. This paragraph does not apply to agreements, decisions and concerted practices which at the date of accession already fall under Article 53(1) of the EEA Agreement.

This Regulation shall be binding in its entirety and directly applicable in all Member States.

Done at Brussels,

ANNEX I

PART A
REPEALED REGULATION WITH ITS SUCCESSIVE AMENDMENT

Regulation (EEC) No 1017/68 of the Council
(OJ L 175, 23.7.1968, p. 1)

Council Regulation (EC) No 1/2003   Article 36 only
(OJ L 1, 4.1.2003, p. 1)

PART B
NON-REPEALED SUCCESSIVE AMENDMENTS

1972 Act of Accession
1979 Act of Accession
1994 Act of Accession
2003 Act of Accession

ANNEX II
CORRELATION TABLE

Regulation (EEC) No 1017/68	This Regulation
Article 1	Article 1
Article 3	Article 2
Article 4(1), first subparagraph, first introductory phrase, first indent	Article 3(1), first subparagraph, first introductory phrase, (a)
Article 4(1), first subparagraph, first introductory phrase, second indent	Article 3(1), first subparagraph, first introductory phrase, (b)
Article 4(1), first subparagraph, second introductory phrase, first indent	Article 3(1), first subparagraph, second introductory phrase, (i)
Article 4(1), first subparagraph, second introductory phrase, second indent	Article 3(1), first subparagraph, second introductory phrase, (ii)
Article 4(1), second subparagraph	Article 3(1), second subparagraph

Article 4(2)	Article 3(2)
—	Article 4
Article 30(1)	Article 5(1)
Article 30(3), second subparagraph	Article 5(2)
Article 31	—
—	Annex I
—	Annex II

E5

COUNCIL REGULATION (EEC) NO 4056/86

of 22 December 1986
laying down detailed rules for the application of Articles [81] and [82] of the
Treaty to maritime transport

Official Journal L 378, 31.12.1986, p. 4

Celex No: 31986R4056

Notes

Council Regulation (EEC) No 4056/86 was repealed with effect from 18 October 2006 by Council Regulation (EC) No 1419/2006 (OJ L 269, 28.9.2006, p. 1), Article 1. However, Article 1(3)(b) and (c), Articles 3 to 7, Article 8(2) and Article 26 continue to apply in respect of liner shipping conferences satisfying the requirements of Regulation 4056/86/EEC on 18 October 2006, for a transitional period of two years from that date (Council Regulation (EC) No 1419/2006, Article 1).

EEA application: see EEA Agreement Annex XIV, Chapter G, Point 11 (as amended by the EEA Enlargement Agreement (OJ L 130, 29.4.2004, p. 3 and EEA Supplement No 23, 29.4.2004, p. 1), EEA Joint Committee Decision No 130/2004 of 24 September 2004 (OJ L 64, 10.3.2005, p. 57 and EEA Supplement No 12, 10.3.2005, p. 42) and Decision No 43/2005 (OJ No L 198, 28.7.2005, p. 45 and EEA Supplement No 38, 28.7.2005, p. 26)).

Commentary

Regulation 4056/86/EEC: B&C: 3.008, 3.083, 3.086–3.087, 3.093, 5.033, 5.050, 5.096, 7.015, 10.008, 10.048, 10.082, 10.149, 12.006–12.007, 12.011, 12.019, 12.028–12.029, 13.015, 13.169, 14.085 **F&N:** 8.594, 8.777, 14.08, 14.10, 14.77, 14.93, 14.100, 14.104, 14.119, 14.123–14.125, 14.127–14.128, 14.134, 14.139, 14.147
Arts 3–6: B&C: 3.074
Arts 3–7: B&C: 12.022

THE COUNCIL OF THE EUROPEAN COMMUNITIES,

Having regard to the Treaty establishing the European Economic Community, and in particular Articles [80](2) and [83] thereof,

Having regard to the proposal from the Commission,

Having regard to the opinion of the European Parliament,[1]

Having regard to the opinion of the Economic and Social Committee,[2]

Notes
[1] OJ No C 172, 2.7.1984, p. 178; OJ No C 255, 13.10.1986, p. 169.
[2] OJ No C 77, 21.3.1983, p. 13; OJ No C 344, 31.12.1985, p. 31.

Commentary
Preamble: **B&C:** 3.041

[1] Whereas the rules on competition form part of the Treaty's general provisions which also apply to maritime transport; whereas detailed rules for applying those provisions are set out in the Chapter of the Treaty dealing with the rules on competition or are to be determined by the procedures laid down therein;

[2] Whereas according to Council Regulation No 141,[1] Council Regulation No 17[2] does not apply to transport; whereas Council Regulation (EEC) No 1017/68[3] applies to inland transport only; whereas, consequently, the Commission has no means at present of investigating directly cases of suspected infringement of Articles [81] and [82] in maritime transport; whereas, moreover, the Commission lacks such powers of its own to take decisions or impose penalties as are necessary for it to bring to an end infringements established by it;

Notes
[1] OJ No 124, 28.11.1962, p. 2751/62.
[2] OJ No 13, 21.2.1962, p. 204/62.
[3] OJ No L 175, 23.7.1968, p. 1.

[3] Whereas this situation necessitates the adoption of a Regulation applying the rules of competition to maritime transport; whereas Council Regulation (EEC) No 954/79 of 15 May 1979 concerning the ratification by Member States of, or their accession to, the United Nations Convention on a Code of Conduct for Liner Conference[1] will result in the application of the Code of Conduct to a considerable number of conferences serving the Community; whereas the Regulation applying the rules of competition to maritime transport foreseen in the last recital of Regulation (EEC) No 954/79 should take account of the adoption of the Code;

Notes
[1] OJ No L 121, 17.5.1979, p. 1.

Commentary
Recital 3: **B&C:** 12.021

[4] Whereas, as far as conferences subject to the Code of Conduct are concerned, the Regulation should supplement the Code or make it more precise;

[5] Whereas it appears preferable to exclude tramp vessel services from the scope of this Regulation, rates for these services being freely negotiated on a case-by-case basis in accordance with supply and demand conditions;

[6] Whereas this Regulation should take account of the necessity, on the one hand to provide for implementing rules that enable the Commission to ensure that competition is not unduly distorted within the common market, and on the other hand to avoid excessive regulation of the sector;

[7] Whereas this Regulation should define the scope of the provisions of Articles [81] and [82] of the Treaty, taking into account the distinctive characteristics of maritime transport; whereas trade between Member States may be affected where restrictive practices or abuses concern international maritime transport, including intra-Community transport, from or to Community ports; whereas such restrictive practices or abuses may influence competition, firstly, between ports in different Member States by altering their respective catchment areas, and secondly, between activities in those catchment areas, and disturb trade patterns within the common market;

Commentary
Recital 7: **B&C:** 12.020

[8] Whereas certain types of technical agreement, decisions and concerted practices may be excluded from the prohibition on restrictive practices on the ground that they do not, as a general rule, restrict competition;

Commentary
Recital 8: B&C: 12.021 **F&N:** 14.102, 14.106

---

[9] Whereas provision should be made for block exemption of liner conferences; whereas liner conferences have a stabilizing effect, assuring shippers of reliable services; whereas they contribute generally to providing adequate efficient scheduled maritime transport services and give fair consideration to the interests of users; whereas such results cannot be obtained without the cooperation that shipping companies promote within conferences in relation to rates and, where appropriate, availability of capacity or allocation of cargo for shipment, and income; whereas in most cases conferences continue to be subject to effective competition from both non-conference scheduled services and, in certain circumstances, from tramp services and from other modes of transport; whereas the mobility of fleets, which is a characteristic feature of the structure of availability in the shipping field, subjects conferences to constant competition which they are unable as a rule to eliminate as far as a substantial proportion of the shipping services in question is concerned;

[10] Whereas, however, in order to prevent conferences from engaging in practices which are incompatible with Article [81](3) of the Treaty, certain conditions and obligations should be attached to the exemption;

Commentary
Recital 10: B&C: 12.025

---

[11] Whereas the aim of the conditions should be to prevent conferences from imposing restrictions on competition which are not indispensable to the attainment of the objectives on the basis of which exemption is granted; whereas, to this end, conferences should not, in respect of a given route, apply rates and conditions of carriage which are differentiated solely by reference to the country of origin or destination of the goods carried and thus cause within the Community deflections of trade that are harmful to certain ports, shippers, carriers or providers of services ancillary to transport; whereas, furthermore, loyalty arrangements should be permitted only in accordance with rules which do not restrict unilaterally the freedom of users and consequently competition in the shipping industry, without prejudice, however, to the right of a conference to impose penalties on users who seek by improper means to evade the obligation of loyalty required in exchange for the rebates, reduced freight rates or commission granted to them by the conference; whereas users must be free to determine the undertakings to which they have recourse in respect of inland transport or quayside services not covered by the freight charge or by other charges agreed with the shipping line;

[12] Whereas certain obligations should also attached to the exemption; whereas in this respect users must at all times be in a position to acquaint themselves with the rates and conditions of carriage applied by members of the conference, since in the case of inland transports organized by shippers, the latter continue to be subject to Regulation (EEC) No 1017/68; whereas provision should be made that awards given at arbitration and recommendations made by conciliators and accepted by the parties be notified forthwith to the Commission in order to enable it to verify that conferences are not thereby exempted from the conditions provided for in the Regulation and thus do not infringe the provisions of Articles [81] and [82];

[13] Whereas consultations between users or associations of users and conferences are liable to secure a more efficient operation of maritime transport services which takes better account of users" requirements; whereas, consequently, certain restrictive practices which could ensue from such consultations should be exempted;

[14] Whereas there can be no exemption if the conditions set out in Article [81](3) are not satisfied; whereas the Commission must therefore have power to take the appropriate measures where an

agreement or concerted practice owing to special circumstances proves to have certain effects incompatible with Article [81](3); whereas, in view of the specific role fulfilled by the conferences in the sector of the liner services, the reaction of the Commission should be progressive and proportionate; whereas the Commission should consequently have the power first to address recommendations, then to take decisions;

[15] Whereas the automatic nullity provided for in Article [81](3) in respect of agreements or decisions which have not been granted exemption pursuant to Article [81](3) owing to their discriminatory or other features applies only to the elements of the agreement covered by the prohibition of Article [81](1) and applies to the agreement in its entirety only if those elements do not appear to be severable from the whole of the agreement whereas the Commission should therefore, if it finds an infringement of the block exemption, either specify what elements of the agreement are by the prohibition and consequently automatically void, or indicate the reasons why those elements are not severable from the rest of the agreement and why the agreement is therefore void in its entirety;

[16] Whereas, in view of the characteristics of international maritime transport, account should be taken of the fact that the application of this Regulation to certain restrictive practices or abuses may result in conflicts with the laws and rules of certain third countries and prove harmful to important Community trading and shipping interests; whereas consultations and, where appropriate, negotiations authorized by the Council should be undertaken by the Commission with those countries in pursuance of the maritime transport policy of the Community;

[17] Whereas this Regulation should make provision for the procedures, decision-making powers and penalties that are necessary to ensure compliance with the prohibitions laid down in Article [81](1) and Article [82], as well as the conditions governing the application of Article [81](3);

[18] Whereas account should be taken in this respect of the procedural provisions of Regulation (EEC) No 1017/68 applicable to inland transport operations which takes account of certain distinctive features of transport operations viewed as a whole;

[19] Whereas, in particular, in view of the special characteristics of maritime transport, it is primarily the responsibility of undertakings to see to it that their agreements, decisions and concerted practices conform to the rules on competition, and consequently their notification to the Commission need not be made compulsory;

[20] Whereas in certain circumstances undertakings may, however, wish to apply to the Commission for confirmation that their agreements, decisions and concerted practices are in conformity with the provisions in force; whereas a simplified procedure should be laid down for such cases,

HAS ADOPTED THIS REGULATION:

SECTION I

Article 1
Subject-matter and scope of the Regulation

[. . .]

3. For the purposes of this Regulation:

[. . .]

(b) "liner conference" means a group of two or more vessel-operating carriers which provides international liner services for the carriage of cargo on a particular route or routes within specified geographical limits and which has an agreement or arrangement, whatever its nature, within the framework of which they operate under uniform or common freight rates and any other agreed conditions with respect to the provision of liner services;

(c) "transport user" means an undertaking (e.g. shippers, consignees, forwarders, etc.) provided it has entered into, or demonstrates an intention to enter into, a contractual or other arrangement with a conference or shipping line for the shipment of goods, or any association of shippers.

911

Notes

Article 1 was repealed with effect from 18 October 2006 by Council Regulation (EC) No 1419/2006 (OJ L 269, 28.9.2006, p. 1). However, Article 1(3)(b) and (c), Articles 3 to 7, Article 8(2) and Article 26 continue to apply in respect of liner shipping conferences satisfying the requirements of Regulation 4056/86/EEC on 18 October 2006, for a transitional period of two years from that date.

Commentary

Art 1: B&C: 12.022
Art 1(2): B&C: 12.007, 12.023 F&N: 14.105
Art 1(3): F&N: 14.128
Art 1(3)(a): B&C: 12.007 F&N: 14.128
Art 1(3)(b): B&C: 12.022–12.023 F&N: 14.101, 14.128
Art 1(3)(c): B&C: 12.022, 12.025

[*Article 2*]

Notes

Article 2 was repealed with effect from 18 October 2006 by Council Regulation (EC) No 1419/2006 (OJ L 269, 28.9.2006, p. 1).

Commentary

Art 2: B&C: 3.074, 12.020 F&N: 14.125, 14.213

Article 3
Exemption for agreements between carriers concerning the operation of scheduled maritime transport services

Agreements, decisions and concerted practices of all or part of the members of one or more liner conferences are hereby exempted from the prohibition in Article [81](1) of the Treaty, subject to the condition imposed by Article 4 of this Regulation, when they have as their objective the fixing of rates and conditions of carriage, and, as the case may be, one or more of the following objectives:

(a) *the coordination of shipping timetables, sailing dates or dates of calls;*
(b) *the determination of the frequency of sailings or calls;*
(c) *the coordination or allocation of sailings or calls among members of the conference;*
(d) *the regulation of the carrying capacity offered by each member;*
(e) *the allocation of cargo or revenue among members.*

Notes

Article 3 was repealed with effect from 18 October 2006 by Council Regulation (EC) No 1419/2006 (OJ L 269, 28.9.2006, p. 1). However, Article 1(3)(b) and (c), Articles 3 to 7, Article 8(2) and Article 26 continue to apply in respect of liner shipping conferences satisfying the requirements of Regulation 4056/86/EEC on 18 October 2006, for a transitional period of two years from that date.

Commentary

Art 3: B&C: 12.023–12.024 F&N: 3.156, 8.04, 14.101, 14.128
Art 3(d): F&N: 14.109

Article 4
Condition attaching to exemption

The exemption provided for in Articles 3 and 6 shall be granted subject to the condition that the agreement, decision or concerted practice shall not, within the common market, cause detriment to certain ports, transport users or carriers by applying for the carriage of the same goods and in the area covered by the agreement, decision or concerted practice, rates and conditions of carriage which differ according to the country of origin or destination or port of loading or discharge, unless such rates or conditions can be economically justified.

Any agreement or decision or, if it is severable, any part of such an agreement or decision not complying with the preceding paragraph shall automatically be void pursuant to Article [81](2) of the Treaty.

Notes
Article 4 was repealed with effect from 18 October 2006 by Council Regulation (EC) No 1419/2006 (OJ L 269, 28.9.2006, p. 1). However, Article 1(3)(b) and (c), Articles 3 to 7, Article 8(2) and Article 26 continue to apply in respect of liner shipping conferences satisfying the requirements of Regulation 4056/86/EEC on 18 October 2006, for a transitional period of two years from that date.

Commentary
Art 4: B&C: 12.026–12.027

Article 5
Obligations attaching to exemption

The following obligations shall be attached to the exemption provided for in Article 3:

1. Consultations

There shall be consultations for the purpose of seeking solutions on general issues of principle between transport users on the one hand and conferences on the other concerning the rates, conditions and quality of scheduled maritime transport services.

These consultations shall take place whenever requested by any of the abovementioned parties.

2. Loyalty arrangements

The shipping lines' members of a conference shall be entitled to institute and maintain loyalty arrangements with transport users, the form and terms of which shall be matters for consultation between the conference and transport users' organizations. These loyalty arrangements shall provide safeguards making explicit the rights of transport users and conference members. These arrangements shall be based on the contract system or any other system which is also lawful.

Loyalty arrangements must comply with the following conditions:

(a) Each conference shall offer transport users a system of immediate rebates or the choice between such a system and a system of deferred rebates:

— under the system of immediate rebates each of the parties shall be entitled to terminate the loyalty arrangement at any time without penalty and subject to a period of notice of not more than six months; this period shall be reduced to three months when the conference rate is the subject of a dispute;

— under the system of deferred rebates neither the loyalty period on the basis of which the rebate is calculated nor the subsequent loyalty period required before payment of the rebate may exceed six months; this period shall be reduced to three months where the conference rate is the subject of a dispute.

(b) The conference shall, after consulting the transport users concerned, set out:

(i) a list of cargo and any portion of cargo agreed with transport users which is specifically excluded from the scope of the loyalty arrangement; 100% loyalty arrangements may be offered but may not be unilaterally imposed;

(ii) a list of circumstances in which transport users are released from their obligation of loyalty; these shall include:

— circumstances in which consignments are dispatched from or to a port in the area covered by the conference but not advertised and where the request for a waiver can be justified, and

— those in which waiting time at a port exceeds a period to be determined for each port and for each commodity or class of commodities following consultation of the transport users directly concerned with the proper servicing of the port.

The conference must, however, be informed in advance by the transport user, within a specified period, of his intention to dispatch the consignment from a port not advertised by the conference or to make use of a non-conference vessel at a port served by the conference as soon as he has been able to establish from the published schedule of sailings that the maximum waiting period will be exceeded.

3. Services not covered by the freight charges

Transport users shall be entitled to approach the undertakings of their choice in respect of inland transport operations and quayside services not covered by the freight charge or charges on which the shipping line and the transport user have agreed.

4. Availability of tariffs

Tariffs, related conditions, regulations and any amendments thereto shall be made available on request to transport users at reasonable cost, or they shall be available for examination at offices of shipping lines and their agents. They shall set out all the conditions concerning loading and discharge, the exact extent of the services covered by the freight charge in proportion to the sea transport and the land transport or by any other charge levied by the shipping line and customary practice in such matters.

5. Notification to the Commission of awards at arbitration and recommendations

Awards given at arbitration and recommendations made by conciliators that are accepted by the parties shall be notified forthwith to the Commission when they resolve disputes relating to the practices of conferences referred to in Article 4 and in points 2 and 3 above.

Notes

Article 5 was repealed with effect from 18 October 2006 by Council Regulation (EC) No 1419/2006 (OJ L 269, 28.9.2006, p. 1). However, Article 1(3)(b) and (c), Articles 3 to 7, Article 8(2) and Article 26 continue to apply in respect of liner shipping conferences satisfying the requirements of Regulation 4056/86/EEC on 18 October 2006, for a transitional period of two years from that date.

Commentary
Art 5: **B&C:** 12.026 **F&N:** 14.120
Art 5(1): **B&C:** 12.027
Art 5(2): **B&C:** 12.027

Article 6
Exemption for agreements between transport users and conferences concerning the use of scheduled maritime transport services

Agreements, decisions and concerned practices between transport users, on the one hand, and conferences, on the other hand, and agreements between transport users which may be necessary to that end, concerning the rates, conditions and quality of liner services, as long as they are provided for in Article 5(1) and (2) are hereby exempted from the prohibition laid down in Article [81](1) of the Treaty.

Notes

Article 6 was repealed with effect from 18 October 2006 by Council Regulation (EC) No 1419/2006 (OJ L 269, 28.9.2006, p. 1). However, Article 1(3)(b) and (c), Articles 3 to 7, Article 8(2) and Article 26 continue to apply in respect of liner shipping conferences satisfying the requirements of Regulation 4056/86/EEC on 18 October 2006, for a transitional period of two years from that date.

Commentary
Art 6: **B&C:** 3.083, 12.023, 12.027 **F&N:** 14.120

Article 7
Monitoring of exempted agreements

[1. Breach of an obligation

Where the persons concerned are in breach of an obligation which, pursuant to Article 5, attaches to the exemption provided for in Article 3, the Commission may, in order to put an end to such breach and under the conditions laid down in Council Regulation (EC) No 1/2003 of 16 December 2002 on the implementation of the rules on competition laid down in Articles [81] and [82] of the Treaty[1] adopt a decision that either prohibits them from carrying out or requires them to perform certain specific acts, or withdraws the benefit of the block exemption which they enjoyed.]

2. Effects incompatible with Article [81](3)

(a) Where, owing to special circumstances as described below, agreements, decisions and concerted practices which qualify for the exemption provided for in Articles 3 and 6 have nevertheless effects which are incompatible with the conditions laid down in Article [81](3) of the Treaty, the Commission, on receipt of a complaint or on its own initiative, [under the conditions laid down in Regulation (EC) No 1/2003], shall take the measures described in (c) below. The severity of these measures must be in proportion to the gravity of the situation.

(b) Special circumstances are, inter alia, *created by:*

(i) *acts of conferences or a change of market conditions in a given trade resulting in the absence or elimination of actual or potential competition such as restrictive practices whereby the trade is not available to competition; or*

(ii) *acts of conference which may prevent technical or economic progress or user participation in the benefits;*

(iii) *acts of third countries which:*

— *prevent the operation of outsiders in a trade,*

— *impose unfair tariffs on conference members,*

— *impose arrangements which otherwise impede technical or economic progress (cargo-sharing, limitations on types of vessels).*

(c) (i) *If actual or potential competition is absent or may be eliminated as a result of action by a third country, the Commission shall enter into consultations with the competent authorities of the third country concerned, followed if necessary by negotiations under directives to be given by the Council, in order to remedy the situation.*

If the special circumstances result in the absence or elimination of actual or potential competition contrary to Article [81](3)(b) of the Treaty the Commission shall withdraw the benefit of the block exemption. [At the same time it shall decide, in accordance with Article 9 of Regulation (EC) No 1/2003, whether to accept commitments offered by the undertakings concerned with a view, inter alia, *to obtaining access to the market for non-conference lines.];*

(ii) *If, as a result of special circumstances as set out in (b), there are effects other than those referred to in (i) hereof, the Commission shall take one or more of the measures described in paragraph 1.*

Notes

[1] OJ L 1, 4.1.2003, p. 1.

The amendments shown in square brackets were made with effect from 1 May 2004 by Council Regulation (EC) No 1/2003 (OJ L 1, 4.1.2003, p. 1).

Article 7 was repealed with effect from 18 October 2006 by Council Regulation (EC) No 1419/2006 (OJ L 269, 28.9.2006, p. 1). However, Article 1(3)(b) and (c), Articles 3 to 7, Article 8(2) and Article 26 continue to apply in respect of liner shipping conferences satisfying the requirements of Regulation 4056/86/EEC on 18 October 2006, for a transitional period of two years from that date.

Commentary

Art 7: F&N: 14.121

Art 7(1): B&C: 3.086

Art 7(2): B&C: 3.086

Article 8
Effects incompatible with Article [82] of the Treaty

2. Where the Commission, either on its own initiative or at the request of a Member State or of natural or legal persons claiming a legitimate interest, finds that in any particular case the conduct of conferences benefiting from the exemption laid down in Article 3 nevertheless has effects which are incompatible with Article [82] of the Treaty, it may withdraw the benefit of the block exemption and take, [pursuant to Regulation (EC) No 1/2003], all appropriate measures for the purpose of bringing to an end infringements of Article [82] of the Treaty.

Notes

Paragraphs 1 and 3 were deleted and paragraph 2 was amended with effect from 1 May 2004 by Council Regulation (EC) No 1/2003 (OJ L 1, 4.1.2003, p.1). Article 8 was repealed with effect from 18 October 2006 by Council Regulation (EC) No 1419/2006 (OJ L 269, 28.9.2006, p. 1). However, Article 1(3)(b) and (c), Articles 3 to 7, Article 8(2) and Article 26 continue to apply in respect of liner shipping conferences satisfying the requirements of Regulation 4056/86/EEC on 18 October 2006, for a transitional period of two years from that date.

Commentary

Art 8: B&C: 3.086 **F&N:** 4.420, 14.121

Art 8(2): F&N: 14.121

[Article 9]

Notes

Article 9 was repealed with effect from 18 October 2006 by Council Regulation (EC) No 1419/2006 (OJ L 269, 28.9.2006, p. 1).

Commentary

Art 9: **B&C:** 12.020 **F&N:** 14.99, 14.125

SECTION II
RULES OF PROCEDURE

[Articles 10 to 12]

Notes

Articles 10 to 12 were repealed with effect from 1 May 2004 by Council Regulation (EC) No 1/2003 (OJ L1, 4.1.2003, p. 1).

[Article 13]

Notes

Article 13(1) and (2) were repealed with effect from 1 May 2004 by Council Regulation (EC) No 1/2003 (OJ L 1, 4.1.2003, p. 1).

The remainder of Article 13 was repealed with effect from 18 October 2006 by Council Regulation (EC) No 1419/2006 (OJ L 269, 28.9.2006, p. 1).

Commentary

Art 13(3): **B&C:** 3.008

[Article 14 to Article 25]

Notes

Articles 14 to 25 were repealed with effect from 1 May 2004 by Regulation (EC) No 1/2003 (OJ L 1, 4.1.2003, p. 1).

Commentary

Art 18: **B&C:** 13.033 **F&N:** 8.263
Art 19(2): **F&N:** 8.594, 8.777, 8.780

Article 26
Implementing provisions

The Commission shall have power to adopt implementing provisions concerning the scope of the obligation of communication pursuant to Article 5 (5) [. . .].

Notes

The words indicated in square brackets were deleted with effect from 1 May 2004 by Council Regulation (EC) No 1/2003 (OJ L1, 4.1.2003, p. 1).

Article 26 was repealed with effect from 18 October 2006 by Council Regulation 1419/2006/EC (OJ L 269, 28.9.2006, p. 1). However, Article 1(3)(b) and (c), Articles 3 to 7, Article 8(2) and Article 26 continue to apply in respect of liner shipping conferences satisfying the requirements of Regulation 4056/86/EEC on 18 October 2006, for a transitional period of two years from that date.

[Article 26a, Article 27]

Notes

Articles 26a and 27 were repealed with effect from 18 October 2006 by Council Regulation (EC) No 1419/2006 (OJ L 269, 28.9.2006, p. 1).

E6

COUNCIL REGULATION (EEC) NO 479/92

of 25 February 1992
on the application of Article [81](3) of the Treaty to certain categories of agreements, decisions and concerted practices between liner shipping companies (consortia)

Official Journal L 55, 29.2.1992, p. 3

Celex No: 31992R0479

THE COUNCIL OF THE EUROPEAN COMMUNITIES,

Having regard to the Treaty establishing the European Economic Community, and in particular Article [83] thereof,

Having regard to the proposal from the Commission,[1]

Having regard to the opinion of the European Parliament,[2]

Having regard to the opinion of the Economic and Social Committee,[3]

Notes
[1] OJ No C 167, 10.7.1990, p. 9.
[2] OJ No C 305, 25.11.1991, p. 39.
[3] OJ No C 69, 18.3.1991, p. 16.

Commentary
Regulation 479/92: B&C: 3.075, 12.029 **F&N:** 3.416, 14.134

---

[1]   Whereas Article [81](1) of the Treaty may in accordance with Article [81](3) thereof be declared inapplicable to categories of agreements, decisions and concerted practices which fulfil the conditions contained in Article [81](3);

[2]   Whereas, pursuant to Article [83] of the Treaty, the provisions for the application of Article [81](3) of the Treaty should be adopted by way of Regulation; whereas, according to Article [83](2)(b), such a Regulation must lay down detailed rules for the application of Article [81](3), taking into account the need to ensure effective supervision, on the one hand, and to simplify administration to the greatest possible extent on the other; whereas, according to Article [83](2)(d), such a Regulation is required to define the respective functions of the Commission and of the Court of Justice;

[3]   Whereas liner shipping is a capital intensive industry; whereas containerization has increased pressures for cooperation and rationalization; whereas the Community shipping industry needs to attain the necessary economies of scale in order to compete successfully on the world liner shipping market;

[4]   Whereas joint-service agreements between liner shipping companies with the aim of rationalizing their operations by means of technical, operational and/or commercial arrangements (described in shipping circles as consortia) can help to provide the necessary means for improving the productivity of liner shipping services and promoting technical and economic progress;

[5]   Having regard to the importance of maritime transport for the development of the Community's trade and the role which consortia agreements can fulfil in this respect, taking account of the special features of international liner shipping;

[6]   Whereas the legalization of these agreements is a measure which can make a positive contribution to improving the competitiveness of shipping in the Community;

[7]   Whereas users of the shipping services offered by consortia can obtain a share of the benefits resulting from the improvements in productivity and service, by means of, *inter alia*, regularity, cost reductions derived from higher levels of capacity utilization, and better service quality stemming from improved vessels and equipment;

[8] Whereas the Commission should be enabled to declare by way of Regulation that the provisions of Article [81](1) of the Treaty do not apply to certain categories of consortia agreements, decisions and concerted practices, in order to make it easier for undertakings to cooperate in ways which are economically desirable and without adverse effect from the point of view of competition policy;

[9] Whereas the Commission, in close and constant liaison with the competent authorities of the Member States, should be able to define precisely the scope of these exemptions and the conditions attached to them;

[10] Whereas consortia in liner shipping are a specialized and complex type of joint venture; whereas there is a great variety of different consortia agreements operating in different circumstances; whereas the scope, parties, activities or terms of consortia are frequently altered; whereas the Commission should therefore be given the responsibility of defining from time to time the consortia to which a group exemption should apply;

[11] Whereas, in order to ensure that all the conditions of Article [81](3) of the Treaty are met, conditions should be attached to group exemptions to ensure in particular that a fair share of the benefits will be passed on to shippers and that competition is not eliminated;

[12] Whereas pursuant to Article 11(4) of Council Regulation (EEC) No 4056/86 of 22 December 1986 laying down detailed rules for the application of Articles [81] and [82] of the Treaty to maritime transport[1] the Commission may provide that a decision taken in accordance with Article [81](3) of the Treaty shall apply with retroactive effect; whereas it is desirable that the Commission be empowered to adopt, by Regulation, provisions to that effect;

Notes
[1] OJ No L 378, 31.12.1986, p. 4.

---

[13] Whereas notification of agreements, decisions and concerted practices falling within the scope of this Regulation must not be made compulsory, it being primarily the responsibility of undertakings to see to it that they conform to the rules on competition, and in particular to the conditions laid down by the subsequent Commission Regulation implementing this Regulation;

[14] Whereas there can be no exemption if the conditions set out in Article [81](3) of the Treaty are not satisfied; whereas the Commission should therefore have power to take the appropriate measures where an agreement proves to have effects incompatible with Article [81](3) of the Treaty; whereas the Commission should be able first to address recommendations to the parties and then to take decisions,

HAS ADOPTED THIS REGULATION:

Article 1

1. Without prejudice to the application of Regulation (EEC) No 4056/86, the Commission may by regulation and in accordance with Article [81](3) of the Treaty, declare that Article [81](1) of the Treaty shall not apply to certain categories of agreements between undertakings, decisions of associations of undertakings and concerted practices that have as an object to promote or establish cooperation in the joint operation of maritime transport services between liner shipping companies, for the purpose of rationalizing their operations by means of technical, operational and/or commercial arrangements — with the exception of price fixing (consortia).

2. Such regulation adopted pursuant to paragraph 1 shall define the categories of agreements, decisions and concerted practices to which it applies and shall specify the conditions and obligations under which, pursuant to Article [81](3) of the Treaty, they shall be considered exempted from the application of Article [81](1) of the Treaty.

Article 2

1. The regulation adopted pursuant to Article 1 shall apply for a period of five years, calculated as from the date of its entry into force.

2. It may be repealed or amended where circumstances have changed with respect to any of the facts which were basic to its adoption.

Article 3

The regulation adopted pursuant to Article 1 may include a provision stating that it applies with retroactive effect to agreements, decisions and concerted practices which were in existence at the date of entry into force of such regulation, provided they comply with the conditions established in that regulation.

[Article 3a

A Regulation pursuant to Article 1 may stipulate that the prohibition contained in Article [81](1) of the Treaty shall not apply, for such period as fixed by that Regulation, to agreements, decisions and concerted practices already in existence at the date of accession to which Article [81](1) applies by virtue of the accession of Austria, Finland, Norway and Sweden and which do not satisfy the conditions of Article [81](3). However, this Article shall not apply to agreements, decisions and concerted practices which at the date of accession already fall under Article 53(1) of the EEA Agreement.]

Notes

Article 3a was inserted by the Act concerning the conditions of accession of the Kingdom of Norway, the Republic of Austria, the Republic of Finland and the Kingdom of Sweden and the adjustments to the Treaties on which the European Union is founded, ANNEX I — List referred to in Article 29 of the Act of Accession — III. COMPETITION — A. ENABLING REGULATIONS (OJ C 241, 29.8.1994, p. 56) with effect from 1 October 1995.

Article 4

Before adopting its regulation, the Commission shall publish a draft thereof to enable all the persons and organizations concerned to submit their comments within such reasonable time limit as the Commission shall fix, but in no case less than one month.

[Article 5

Before publishing the draft Regulation and before adopting the Regulation, the Commission shall consult the Advisory Committee referred to in Article 14 of Council Regulation (EC) No 1/2003 of 16 December 2002 on the implementation of the rules on competition laid down in Articles 81 and 82 of the Treaty.[1]]

Notes

[[1] OJ L 1, 4.1.2003, p. 1.]
The amendments shown in square brackets were made by Council Regulation (EC) No 1/2003 (OJ L 1, 4.1.2003, p. 1) Article 36, with effect from 1 May 2004.

[Article 6]

Notes

Article 6 was repealed by Council Regulation (EC) No 1/2003 (OJ L1, 4.1.2003, p. 1) Article 36, with effect from 1 May 2004.

Article 7

This Regulation shall enter into force on the day following its publication in the Official Journal of the European Communities. This Regulation shall be binding in its entirety and directly applicable in all Member States.

Notes

Date of entry into force: 1 March 1992.

Done at Brussels, 25 February 1992.

E7

COMMISSION REGULATION
(EC) No 823/2000

of 19 April 2000
on the application of Article 81(3) of the Treaty to certain
categories of agreements, decisions and concerted practices between
liner shipping companies (consortia)

(Text with EEA relevance)

Official Journal L 100, 20.4.2000, p. 24

Celex No: 32000R0823

Notes

EEA application: this Regulation was adopted with appropriate adaptations by EEA Joint Committee Decision No 49/2000 (OJ L 237, 21.9.2000, p. 60 and EEA Supplement No 42, 21.9.2000, p. 3): see the EEA Agreement, Annex XIV, Chapter G, Point 11c (as subsequently amended by the EEA Enlargement Agreement (OJ L 130, 29.4.2004, p. 3 and EEA Supplement No 23, 29.4.2004, p. 1), EEA Joint Committee Decision No 17/2005 (OJ No L 161, 23.6.2005, p. 39 and EEA Supplement No 32, 23.6.2005, p. 23) and Decision No 106/2005 (OJ No L 306, 24.11.2005, p. 43 and EEA Supplement No 60, 24.11.2005, p. 27).

Commentary

Regulation 823/2000/EC: B&C: 3.084, 3.093, 12.030, 12.032–12.033 **F&N:** 14.94, 14.133, 14.134, 14.137, 14.139, 14.148

THE COMMISSION OF THE EUROPEAN COMMUNITIES,

Having regard to the Treaty establishing the European Community,

Having regard to Council Regulation (EEC) No 479/92 of 25 February 1992 on the application of Article [81](3) of the Treaty to certain categories of agreements, decisions and concerted practices between liner shipping companies (consortia),[1] as amended by the Act of Accession of Austria, Finland and Sweden, and in particular Article 1 thereof,

Having published a draft of this Regulation,[2]

Having consulted the Advisory Committee on Restrictive Practices and Dominant Positions in Maritime Transport,

---

Notes
[1] OJ L 55, 29.2.1992, p. 3.
[2] OJ C 379, 31.12.1999, p. 13.

Whereas:

(1) Regulation (EEC) No 479/92 empowers the Commission to apply Article 81(3) of the Treaty to certain categories of agreements, decisions and concerted practices between shipping companies (consortia) relating to the joint operation of liner transport services, which, through the cooperation they bring about between the shipping companies that are parties thereto, are liable to restrict competition within the common market and to affect trade between Member States and may therefore be caught by the prohibition contained in Article 81(1) of the Treaty.

(2) The Commission has made use of this power by adopting Commission Regulation (EC) No 870/95.[1] In the light of experience thus acquired so far, it is possible to define a category of consortia which are capable of falling within the scope Article 81(1) but which can normally be regarded as satisfying the conditions laid down in Article 81(3).

Part E Sectoral Regimes

(3) The Commission has taken due account of the special features of maritime transport. Those features will also constitute a material factor in any Commission assessment of consortia not covered by this block exemption.

(4) Consortia, as defined in this Regulation, generally help to improve the productivity and quality of available liner shipping services by reason of the rationalisation they bring to the activities of member companies and through the economies of scale they allow in the operation of vessels and utilisation of port facilities. They also help to promote technical and economic progress by facilitating and encouraging greater utilisation of containers and more efficient use of vessel capacity.

(5) Users of the shipping services provided by consortia generally obtain a fair share of the benefits resulting from the improvements in productivity and service quality which they bring about. Those benefits may also take the form of an improvement in the frequency of railings and port calls, or an improvement in scheduling as well as better quality and personalised services through the use of more modern vessels and other equipment, including port facilities. Users can benefit effectively from consortia only if there is sufficient competition in the trades in which the consortia operate.

(6) Those agreements should therefore enjoy a block exemption, provided that they do not give the companies concerned the possibility of eliminating competition in a substantial part of the trades in question. In order to take account of the constant fluctuations in the maritime transport market and the frequent changes made by the parties to the terms of consortium agreements or to the activities covered by the agreements, one of the objects of this Regulation is to clarify the conditions to be met by consortia in order to benefit from the block exemption it grants.

(7) For the purpose of establishing and running a joint service, an essential feature inherent in consortia is the ability to make capacity adjustments. The non-utilisation of a certain percentage of vessel capacity within a consortium is not an essential feature of consortia.

(8) The block exemption granted by this Regulation should cover both consortia operating within a liner conference and consortia operating outside such conferences, except that it does not cover the joint fixing of freight rates.

Commentary
Recital 8: F&N: 14.139

(9) Rate-fixing activities come under Council Regulation (EEC) No 4056/86 of 22 December 1986 laying down detailed rules for the application of Articles [81] and [82] of the Treaty to maritime transport,[1] as amended by the Act of Accession of Austria, Finland and Sweden. Consortium members that wish to fix rates jointly and do not satisfy the criteria of Regulation (EEC) No 4056/86 must apply for individual exemption.

(10) The first of the conditions attaching to the block exemption should be that a fair share of the benefits resulting from the improved efficiency, as well as the other benefits offered by consortia, are passed on to transport users.

(11) This requirement of Article 81(3) should be regarded as being met when a consortium is in one or more of the three situations described below:

— there is effective price competition between the members of the conference within which the consortium operates as a result of independent rate action,

— there exists within the conference within which the consortium operates a sufficient degree of effective competition in terms of services provided between consortium members and other conference members that are not members of the consortium, as a result of the fact that the conference agreement expressly allows consortia to offer their own service arrangements, e.g. the provision by the consortium. alone of a "just-in-time delivery" service or an advanced "electronic data interchange" (EDI) service allowing users to be kept informed at all times of

the whereabouts of their goods, or a significant increase in the frequency of sailings and calls in the service offered by a consortium compared with that offered by the conference,
— consortium members are subject to effective, actual or potential competition from non-consortium lines, whether or not a conference operates in the trade or trades in question.

(12) In order to satisfy this same requirement of Article 81(3), provision should be made for a further condition aimed at promoting individual competition as to quality of service between consortium members as well as between consortium members and other shipping companies operating in the trade or trades.

(13) It should be a condition that consortia and their members do not, in respect of a given route, apply rates and conditions of carriage which are differentiated solely by reference to the country of origin or destination of the goods carried and thus cause within the Community deflections of trade that are harmful to certain ports, shippers, carriers or providers of services ancillary to transport, unless such rates or conditions can be economically justified.

(14) The aim of the conditions should also be to prevent consortia from imposing restrictions on competition which are not indispensable to the attainment of the objectives justifying the grant of the exemption. To this end, consortium agreements should contain a provision enabling each shipping line party to the agreement to withdraw from the consortium provided that it gives reasonable notice. However, provision should be made for a longer notice period in the case of highly integrated and/or high-investment consortia in order to take account of the higher investments undertaken to set them up and the more extensive reorganisation entailed in the event of a member's leaving. It should also be stipulated that, where a consortium operates with a joint marketing structure, each member should have the right to engage in independent marketing activities provided that it gives reasonable notice.

(15) Exemption must be limited to consortia which do not have the possibility of eliminating competition in a substantial part of the services in question.

(16) In order to determine for the purposes of exemption whether exemption competition exists on each market upon which the consortium operates, account should be taken not only of direct trade between the ports served by a consortium but also of any competition from other liner services sailing from ports which may be substituted for those served by the consortium and, where appropriate, of other modes of transport.

(17) The block exemption granted by this Regulation is therefore applicable only on condition that on each market upon which the consortium operates the market share held by a consortium does not exceed a given size.

(18) The market share held by a consortium within a conference should be smaller in view of the fact that the agreements is question are superimposed on an existing restrictive agreement.

(19) However, it is appropriate to offer consortia which exceed the limits laid down in this Regulation by a given percentage but which continue to be subject to effective competition in the trades in which they operate a simplified procedure so that they may benefit from the legal certainty afforded by block exemptions. Such a procedure should also enable the Commission to carry out effective monitoring and simplify the administrative control of agreements.

(20) However, consortia which exceed the limit should be able to obtain exemption by individual decision, provided that they satisfy the tests of Article 81(3), regard being had to the special features of maritime transport.

(21) This Regulation should apply only to agreements concluded between the members of a consortium. Therefore, the block exemption should not cover restrictive agreements concluded between, on the one hand, consortia or one or more of their members, and, on the other hand, other shipping companies. Nor should it apply to restrictive agreements between different consortia operating in the same trade or between the members of such consortia.

Commentary
Recital 21: F&N: 14.137

---

(22) Certain obligations should also be attached to the exemption. In this respect, transport users should at all times be in a position to acquaint themselves with the conditions for the provision of the maritime transport services jointly operated by the members of the consortium.

Provision should be made for real and effective consultations between the consortia and transport users on the activities covered by the agreements. This Regulation also specifies what is meant by "real and effective consultations" and what main procedural stages are to be followed for such consultations. Provision should be made for such mandatory consultation, limited to the activities of consortia as such.

Commentary
Recital 22: **B&C:** 12.031

(23) Such consultations are likely to secure a more efficient operation of maritime transport services which takes account of users" requirements. Consequently, certain restrictive practices which could ensue from such consultations should be exempted.

(24) For the purposes of this Regulation, the concept of *force majeure* is that laid down by the Court of Justice of the European Communities in its established case-law.

(25) Provision should be made whereby awards given at arbitration and recommendations made by conciliators and accepted by the parties are to he notified to the Commission forthwith, in order to enable it to verify that consortia are not thereby exempted from the conditions and obligations provided for in the Regulation and thus do not infringe the provisions of Articles 81 and 82.

(26) It is necessary to specify, in accordance with Article 6 of Regulation (EEC) No 479/92, the cases in which the Commission may withdraw from companies the benefit of the block exemption.

(27) 11 consortia benefited from the block exemption contained in Regulation (EC) No 870/95 by application of the opposition procedure in that Regulation which enabled the Commission in particular to check that they were subject to effective competition. There is no indication that circumstances have since become such that those consortia are no longer subject to effective competition. Those consortia should therefore continue to be exempted on the terms laid down in this Regulation.

(28) No applications under Article 12 of Regulation (EEC) No 4056/86 should need to be made in respect of agreements automatically exempted by this Regulation. However, when real doubts exist, companies should be permitted to request the Commission to declare whether their agreements comply with this Regulation.

(29) This Regulation is without prejudice to the application of Article 82 of the Treaty.

(30) In view of the expiry of Regulation (EC) No 870/95, it is appropriate to adopt a new Regulation renewing the block exemption,

HAS ADOPTED THIS REGULATION:

CHAPTER I
SCOPE AND DEFINITIONS

Article 1
Scope

This Regulation shall apply to consortia only in so far as they provide international liner transport services from or to one or more Community ports.

Commentary
Art 1: **F&N:** 14.181

Article 2
Definitions

For the purposes of this Regulation:

1. "consortium" means an agreement between two or more vessel-operating carriers which provide international liner shipping services exclusively for the carriage of cargo, chiefly by container, relating to one or more trades, and the object of which is to bring about cooperation in the joint operation of a maritime transport service, and which improves the service that would be offered individually by each of its members in the absence of the consortium, in order to rationalise their

923

operations by means of technical, operational and/or commercial arrangements, with the exception of price fixing;

2. "liner shipping" means the transport of goods on a regular basis on a particular route or routes between ports and in accordance with timetables and sailing dates advertised in advance and available, even on an occasional basis, to any transport user against payment;

3. "service arrangement" means a contractual arrangement concluded between one or more transport users and an individual member of a consortium or a consortium itself under which, in return for an undertaking to commission the transportation of a certain quantity of goods over a given period of time, a user receives an individual undertaking from the consortium member or the consortium to provide an individualised service which is of a given quality and specially tailored to its needs;

4. "transport user" means any undertaking (such as shipper, consignee, forwarder) which has entered into, or demonstrated an intention to enter into, a contractual agreement with a consortium (or one of its members) for the shipment of goods, or any association of shippers;

5. "independent rate action" means the right of a maritime conference member to offer, on a case-by-case basis and in respect of goods, freight rates which differ from those laid down in the conference tariff, provided that notice is given to the other conference members.

[6. "commencement of the service" means the date on which the first vessel sails on the service or, when there has been substantial new investment, the date on which the first vessel sails under the conditions directly arising from that substantial new investment;]

[7. "substantial new investment" means investment which results in the building, purchase or long-term charter of vessels, which are specifically designed, required and substantial for the operation of the service and which constitutes at least half of the total investment made by the consortium members in relation to the maritime transport service offered by the consortium.]

Notes

Points 6 and 7 shown in square brackets were added by Commission Regulation (EC) No 611/2005 (OJ L 101, 21.4.2005, p. 10) with effect from 26 April 2005.

Commentary

Art 2: F&N: 14.177–14.178, 14.180
Art 2(1): B&C: 12.031

CHAPTER II
EXEMPTIONS

Article 3
Exempted agreements

1. Pursuant to Article 81(3) of the Treaty and subject to the conditions and obligations laid down in this Regulation, it is hereby declared that Article 81(1) of the Treaty shall not apply to the activities listed in paragraph 2 of this Article when contained in consortium agreements as defined in Articles 1 and 2 of this Regulation.

2. The declaration of non-applicability shall apply only to the following activities:

(a) the joint operation of liner shipping transport services which comprise solely the following activities:

    (i) the coordination and/or joint fixing of sailing timetables and the determination of ports of call;

    (ii) the exchange, sale or cross-chartering of space or slots on vessels;

    (iii) the pooling of vessels and/or port installations;

    (iv) the use of one or more joint operations offices;

    (v) the provision of containers, chassis and other equipment and/or the rental, leasing or purchase contracts for such equipment;

    (vi) the use of a computerised data exchange system and/or joint documentation system;

(b) temporary capacity adjustments;

(c) the joint operation or use of port terminals and related services (such as lighterage or stevedoring services);

(d) the participation in one or more of the following pools: cargo, revenue or net revenue;

(e) the joint exercise of voting rights held by the consortium in the conference within which its members operate, in so far as the vote being jointly exercised concerns the consortium"s activities as such;

(f) a joint marketing structure and/or the issue of a joint bill of lading;

(g) any other activity ancillary to those referred to above in points (a) to (f) which is necessary for their implementation.

3. The following clauses shall in particular be considered ancillary activities within the meaning of paragraph 2(g):

(a) an obligation on members of the consortium to use on the trade or trades in question vessels allocated to the consortium and to refrain from chartering space on vessels belonging to third parties;

(b) an obligation on members of the consortium not to assign or charter space to other vessel-operating carriers on the trade or trades in question except with the prior consent of the other members of the consortium.

Commentary
Art 3: B&C: 3.084, 12.030–12.031 F&N: 14.138, 14.181
Art 3(2): F&N: 14.138
Art 3(2)(c): F&N: 14.140
Art 3(2)(g): F&N: 14.140
Art 3(3): F&N: 14.140

Article 4
Non-utilisation of capacity

The exemption provided for in Article 3 shall not apply to a consortium when the consortium includes arrangements concerning the non-utilisation of existing capacity whereby shipping line members of the consortium refrain from using a certain percentage of the capacity of vessels operated within the framework of the consortium.

Commentary
Art 4: B&C: 12.031 F&N: 14.138, 14.181

CHAPTER III
CONDITIONS FOR EXEMPTION

Article 5
Basic condition for the grant of exemption

The exemption provided for in Article 3 shall apply only if one or more of the conditions set out below are met:

[(a) there is effective price competition between the members of the conference within which the consortium operates, due to the fact that the members are expressly authorised by the conference agreement, whether by virtue of a statutory obligation or otherwise, to apply independent rate action to any freight rate provided for in the conference tariff and/or to enter into individual confidential contracts; or]

(b) there exists within the conference within which the consortium operates a sufficient degree of effective competition between the conference members in terms of the services provided, due to the fact that the conference agreement expressly allows the consortium to offer its own service arrangements, irrespective of form, concerning the frequency and quality of transport services provided as well as freedom at all times to adapt the services it offers in response to [specific] requests from transport users; or

(c) whether or not a conference operates in the trade or trades in question, the consortium members are subject to effective competition, actual or potential, from shipping lines which are not members of that consortium.

Notes

Point (a) was replaced as shown in square brackets by Commission Regulation (EC) No 611/2005 (OJ L 101, 21.4.2005, p.10) with effect from 26 April 2005.

Commentary
Art 5: B&C: 12.031 F&N: 14.139, 14.142

Article 6
Conditions relating to market share

1. In order to qualify for the exemption provided for in Article 3, a consortium must possess on each market upon which it operates a market share of under 30% calculated by reference to the volume of goods carried (freight tonnes or 20-foot equivalent units) when it operates within a conference, and under 35% when it operates outside a conference.

2. The exemption provided for in Article 3 shall continue to apply if the market share referred to in paragraph 1 of this Article is exceeded during any period of two consecutive calendar years by not more than one tenth.

3. Where one of the limits specified in paragraphs 1 and 2 is exceeded, the exemption provided for in Article 3 shall continue to apply for a period of six months following the end of the calendar year during which it was exceeded. This period shall be extended to 12 months if the excess is due to the withdrawal from the market of a carrier which is not a member of the consortium.

Commentary
Art 6: B&C: 12.031

[Article 7]

Notes

Article 7 was deleted by Commission Regulation (EC) No 463/2004 of 12 March 2004 (OJ L77, 13.3.2004, p. 23) with effect from 1 May 2004.

Commentary
Art 7: B&C: 12.031, 13.014 F&N: 14.145

Article 8
Other conditions

Eligibility for the exemptions provided for in Articles 3 and 10 shall be subject to the following conditions:

(a) the consortium must allow each of its members to offer, on the basis of an individual contract, its own service arrangements;

[(b) the consortium agreement must give member companies the right to withdraw from the consortium without financial or other penalty such as, in particular, an obligation to cease all transport activity in the trade or trades in question, whether or not coupled with the condition that such activity may be resumed only after a certain period has elapsed. This right shall be subject to a maximum notice period of six months which may be given after an initial period of 18 months starting from the date of entry into force of the consortium agreement or the agreement to make a substantial new investment in the joint maritime service. If the date of entry into force of the agreement is earlier than the date of commencement of the service, the initial period shall not be more than 24 months starting from the date of entry into force of the consortium agreement or the date of entry into force of the agreement to make a substantial new investment in the joint maritime service.

However, in the case of a highly integrated consortium which has a net revenue pool and/or high level of investment due to the purchase or charter by its members of vessels specifically for the purpose of setting up the consortium, the maximum notice period shall be six months, which may be given after an initial period of 30 months starting from the date of entry into force of the consortium agreement or the agreement to make a substantial new investment in the joint maritime service. If the date of entry into force of the agreement is earlier than the date of commencement of the service, the initial period shall not be more than 36 months starting from the date of entry into force of the consortium agreement or the date of entry into force of the agreement to make a substantial new investment in the joint maritime service.]

(c) where a consortium operates with a joint marketing structure, each member of the consortium must be free to engage in independent marketing without penalty subject to a maximum period of notice of six months;

(d) neither the consortium nor consortia members shall, within the common market, cause detriment to certain ports, users or carriers by applying to the carnage of the same goods and in the area covered by the agreement, rates and conditions of carriage which differ according to the country of origin or destination or port of loading or discharge, unless such rates or conditions can be economically justified.

Notes

Point (b) was replaced as shown in square brackets by Commission Regulation (EC) No 611/2005 (OJ L 101, 21.4.2005, p. 10) with effect from 26 April 2005.

Commentary

Art 8: B&C: 12.031 F&N: 14.146

Art 8(b): F&N: 14.146

CHAPTER IV

OBLIGATIONS

Article 9

Obligations attaching to exemption

1. The obligations provided for in paragraphs 2 to of this Article shall be attached to the exemptions provided for in Article 3 and Article 13(1).

2. There shall be real and effective consultations between users or their representative organisations, on the one hand, and the consortium, on the other hand, for the purpose of seeking solutions on all important matters, other than purely operational matters of minor importance, concerning the conditions and quality of scheduled maritime transport services offered by the consortium or its members.

These consultations shall take place whenever requested by any of the abovementioned parties.

The consultations must take place, except in cases of force majeure, prior to the implementation of the measure forming the subject of the consultation. if, for reasons of force majeure, the members of the consortium are obliged to put a decision into effect before consultations have taken place, any consultations requested shall take place within 10 working days of the date of the request. Save in the case of such force majeure, to which reference shall be made in the notice announcing the measure, no public announcement of the measure shall be made before the consultations.

The consultations shall take place in accordance with the following procedural stages:

(a) prior to the consultation, details of the subject matter of the consultation shall be notified in writing by the consortium to the other party;

(b) an exchange of views shall take place between the parties either in writing or at meetings or both in the course of which the representatives of the consortium members and of the shippers taking part shall have authority to reach a common point of view and the parties shall use their best efforts to achieve that end;

(c) where no common point of view can be reached despite the efforts of both parties, the disagreement shall be acknowledged and publicly announced. It may be brought to the Commission's attention by either party;

(d) a reasonable period for the completion of consultations may be fixed, if possible, by common agreement between the two parties. That period shall be not less than one month, save in exceptional cases or by agreement between the parties.

3. The conditions concerning the maritime transport services provided by the consortium and its members, including those relating to the quality of such services and all relevant modifications, shall be made available on request to transport users at reasonable cost and shall be available for examination without cost at the offices of the consortium members, or the consortium itself, and their agents.

[4. ...]

[5. Any consortium claiming the benefit of this Regulation must be able, on being given a period of notice which the Commission or the Member States' competition authorities shall determine on a case-by-case basis and which shall be not less than one month, to demonstrate at the request of the Commission or the Member States' competition authorities that the conditions and obligations imposed by Articles 5 to 8 and paragraphs 2 and 3 of this Article are met. It must submit the consortium agreement in question to the Commission or the Member States' competition authorities as appropriate within that period.]

Notes

Paragraph 4 was deleted as indicated in square brackets and paragraph 5 was replaced as shown in square brackets by Commission Regulation (EC) No 463/2004 (OJ L77, 13.3.2004, p. 23) with effect from 1 May 2004.

Commentary

Art 9: B&C: 12.031 F&N: 14.147, 14.179
Art 9(5): B&C: 12.031

Article 10

Exemption for agreements between transport users and consortia on the use of scheduled maritime transport services

Agreements, decisions and concerted practices between transport users or their representative organisations, on the one hand, and a consortium exempted under Article 3, on the other hand, concerning the conditions and quality of liner shipping services provided by the consortium and all general questions connected with such services in so far as they arise out of the consultations provided for in paragraph 2 of Article 9, are hereby exempted from the prohibition laid down in Article 81(1) of the Treaty.

Commentary

Art 10: B&C: 12.031 F&N: 14.147

CHAPTER V
MISCELLANEOUS PROVISIONS

Article 11

Professional secrecy

[1. Information acquired as a result of the application of Article 9(5) shall be used only for the purposes of this Regulation.]

2. The Commission and the authorities of the Member States, their officials and other servants shall not disclose information acquired by them as a result of the application of this Regulation which is of the kind covered by the obligation of professional secrecy.

3. The provisions of paragraphs 1 and 2 shall not prevent publication of general information or studios which do not contain information relating to particular undertakings or associations of undertakings.

Notes

Paragraph 1 was replaced as shown in square brackets by Commission Regulation (EC) No 463/2004 (OJ L77, 13.3.2004, p. 23) with effect from 1 May 2004.

[*Article 12*
Withdrawal in individual cases

1. The Commission may withdraw the benefit of this Regulation, in accordance with Article 29 of Council Regulation (EC) No 1/2003,[1] where it finds in a particular case that an agreement, decision by an association of undertakings or concerted practice to which Article 3 or Article 13(1) of this Regulation apply nevertheless has certain effects which are incompatible with Article 81(3) in particular where:

(a) in a given trade, competition from outside the conference within which the consortium operates or from outside a particular consortium is not effective;

(b) a consortium fails repeatedly to comply with the obligations provided for in Article 9 of this Regulation;

(c) such effects result from an arbitration award.

2. Where, in any particular case, an agreement, decision by an association of undertakings or concerted practice referred to in paragraph 1 has effects which are incompatible with Article 81(3) of the Treaty in the territory of a Member State, or in a part thereof, which has all the characteristics of a distinct geographic market, the competition authority of that Member State may withdraw the benefit of this Regulation in respect of that territory.]

Notes
[[1] OJ L 1, 4.1.2003, p. 1.]

Article 12 was replaced as shown in square brackets by Commission Regulation (EC) No 463/2004 (OJ L77, 13.3.2004, p. 23) with effect from 1 May 2004.

Commentary
Art 12: **B&C:** 3.086
Art 12(1): **B&C:** 3.086
Art 12(2): **B&C:** 3.087

Article 13
Transitional provisions

1. Article 81(1) of the Treaty shall not apply to agreements in force on 25 April 2000 which fulfil, on that date, the exemption requirements laid down by Regulation (EC) No 870/95 and to which the opposition procedure provided for by Article 7 of that Regulation was applied.

[2. A notification made pursuant to Article 7 in respect of which the period of six months referred to in the second subparagraph of paragraph 1 of that Article has not expired shall lapse as from 1 May 2004.]

Notes
Paragraph 2 was replaced as shown in square brackets by Commission Regulation (EC) No 463/2004 (OJ L 77, 13.3.2004, p. 23) with effect from 1 May 2004.

Article 14
Entry into force

This Regulation shall enter into force on 26 April 2000.

It shall apply until [25 April 2010].

This Regulation shall be binding in its entirety and directly applicable in all Member States.

Notes
The amendment shown in square brackets was made by Commission Regulation (EC) No 611/2005 (OJ L 101, 21.4.2005, p. 10).

Commentary
Art 14: **B&C:** 3.084

Done at Brussels, 19 April 2000.

E8

COUNCIL REGULATION (EEC) No 3975/87

of 14 December 1987
laying down the procedure for the application of the rules on
competition to undertakings in the air transport sector

Official Journal L 374, 31.12.1987, p. 1

Celex No: 31987R3975

Notes

Regulation 3975/87/EEC was repealed with effect from 1 May 2004, with the exception of Article 6(3), which shall continue to apply to decisions adopted pursuant to Article 81(3) prior to 1 May 2004 until the date of expiry of those decisions: Council Regulation (EC) No 411/2004 of 26 February 2004 (OJ L 68, 6.3.2004, p. 1), Article 1.
EEA application: for residual application, see the Surveillance and Court Agreement, Protocol 4, Part I, Chapter II, Section XI, Article 38.

Commentary

Regulation 3975/87/EEC: B&C: 1.023, 3.002, 7.133, 12.007, 12.047, 14.010 **F&N:** 8.263, 14.08, 14.10, 14.13–14.14, 14.187–14.188

Article 6
Duration and revocation of decisions applying Article [81](3)

3. The Commission may revoke or amend its decision or prohibit specific acts by the parties:

(a) where there has been a change in any of the facts which were basic to the making of the decision; or

(b) where the parties commit a breach of any obligation attached to the decision; or

(c) where the decision is based on incorrect information or was induced by deceit; or

(d) where the parties abuse the exemption from the provisions of Article 85(1) of the Treaty granted to them by the decision.

In cases falling under subparagraphs (b), (c) or (d), the decision may be revoked with retroactive effect.

E9

COUNCIL REGULATION (EEC) No 3976/87

of 14 December 1987
on the application of Article [81](3) of the Treaty to certain categories of
agreements and concerted practices in the air transport sector

Official Journal L 374, 31.12.1987, p. 9

Celex No: 31987R3976

THE COUNCIL OF THE EUROPEAN COMMUNITIES,

Having regard to the Treaty establishing the European Economic Community and in particular Article [83] thereof,

Having regard to the proposal from the Commission,[1]

Having regard to the opinions of the European Parliament,[2]

Having regard to the opinions of the Economic and Social Committee,[3]

Notes
[1] OJ C 182, 9.7.1984, p. 3.
[2] OJ C 262, 14.10.1985, p. 44; OJ C 190, 20.7.1987, p. 182 and OJ C 345, 21.12.1987.
[3] OJ C 303, 25.11.1985, p. 31 and OJ C 333, 29.12.1986, p. 27.

Commentary
Regulation 3976/87/EEC: B&C: 3.075, 12.040–12.041 **F&N:** 3.416, 14.13, 14.15, 14.72–14.73

[1] Whereas Council Regulation (EEC) No. 3975/87[1] lays down the procedure for the application of the rules on competition to undertakings in the air transport sector; whereas Regulation No. 17 of the Council[2] lays down the procedure for the application of these rules to agreements, decisions and concerted practices other than those directly relating to the provision of air transport services;

Notes
[1] [OJ L 374, 31.12.1987, p. 1.]
[2] OJ No 13, 21.2.1962, p. 204/62.

[2] Whereas Article [81](1) of the Treaty may be declared inapplicable to certain categories of agreements, decisions and concerted practices which fulfil the conditions contained in Article [81](3);

[3] Whereas common provisions for the application of Article [81](3) should be adopted by way of Regulation pursuant to Article [83]; whereas, according to Article [83](2)(b), such a Regulation must lay down detailed rules for the application of Article [81](3), taking into account the need to ensure effective supervision, on the one hand, and to simplify administration to the greatest possible extent, on the other; whereas, according to Article [83](2)(d), such a Regulation is required to define the respective functions of the [Commission] and of the Court of Justice;

[4] Whereas the air transport sector has to date been governed by a network of international agreements, bilateral agreement between States and bilateral and multilateral agreements between air carriers; whereas the changes required to this international regulatory system to ensure increased competition should be effected gradually so as to provide time for the air-transport sector to adapt;

[5] Whereas the Commission should be enabled for this reason to declare by way of Regulation that the provisions of Article [81](1) do not apply to certain categories of agreements between undertakings, decisions by associations of undertakings and concerted practices;

931

[6] Whereas it should be laid down under what specific conditions and in what circumstances the Commission may exercise such powers in close and constant liaison with the competent authorities of the Member States;

[7] Whereas it is desirable, in particular, that block exemptions be granted for certain categories of agreements, decisions and concerted practices; whereas these exemptions should be granted for a limited period during which air carriers can adapt to a more competitive environment; whereas the Commission, in close liaison with the Member States, should be able to define precisely the scope of these exemptions and the conditions attached to them;

[8] Whereas there can be no exemption if the conditions set out in Article [81](3) are not satisfied; whereas the Commission should therefore have power to take the appropriate measures where an agreement proves to have effects incompatible with Article [81](3); whereas the Commission should consequently be able first to address recommendations to the parties and then to take decisions;

[9] Whereas this Regulation does not prejudge the application of Article [86] of the Treaty;

[10] Whereas the Heads of State and Government, at their meeting in June 1986, agreed that the internal market in air transport should be completed by 1992 in pursuance of Community actions leading to the strengthening of its economic and social cohesion; whereas the provisions of this Regulation, together with those of Council Directive 87/601/EEC of 14 December 1987 on fares for scheduled air services between Member States[1] and those of Council Decision 87/602/EEC of 14 December 1987 on the sharing of passenger capacity between air carriers on scheduled air services between Member States and on access for air carriers to scheduled air service routes between Member States,[2] are a first step in this direction and the Council will therefore, in order to meet the objective set by the Heads of State and Government, adopt further measures of liberalization at the end of a three year initial period,

Notes
[1] [OJ L 374, 31.12.1987, p. 12.]
[2] [OJ L 374, 31.12.1987, p. 19.]

HAS ADOPTED THIS REGULATION:

Article 1

This Regulation shall apply to [...]¹ [air transport] [...]².

Notes
[1] The words indicated by square brackets were deleted by Council Regulation (EEC) No 2411/92 (OJ L 240, 24.8.1992, p. 19) with effect from 27 July 1992.
[2] The words indicated by square brackets were deleted by Council Regulation (EC) No 411/2004 (OJ L 68, 6.3.2004, p. 1) with effect from 1 May 2004.

Article 2

1. Without prejudice to the application of Regulation (EEC) No 3975/87 and in accordance with Article [81](3) of the Treaty, the Commission may by regulation declare that Article [81](1) shall not apply to certain categories of agreements between undertakings, decisions of associations of undertakings and concerted practices.

[2. The Commission may, in particular, adopt such Regulations in respect of agreements, decisions or concerted practices which have as their object any of the following:

— joint planning and coordination of airline schedules,
— consultations on tariffs for the carriage of passengers and baggage and of freight on scheduled air services,
— joint operations on new less busy scheduled air services,
— slot allocation at airports and airport scheduling; the [Commision] shall take care to ensure consistency with the Code of Conduct adopted by the Council,

— common purchase, development and operation of computer reservation systems relating to timetabling, reservations and ticketing by air transport undertakings; the Commission shall take care to ensure consistency with the Code of Conduct adopted by the Council.]

3. Without prejudice to paragraph 2, such Commission regulations shall define the categories of agreements, decisions or concerted practices to which they apply and shall specify in particular:

(a) the restrictions or clauses which may, or may not, appear in the agreements, decisions and concerted practices;

(b) the clauses which must be contained in the agreements, decisions and concerted practices, or any other conditions which must be satisfied.

Notes

Article 2(2) was replaced as shown in square brackets by Council Regulation (EEC) No 2411/92 (OJ L 240, 24.8.1992, p. 19) with effect from 27 July 1992.

Commentary

Art 2(2): **B&C:** 12.041

[Article 3

Any Regulation adopted pursuant to Article 2 shall be for a specified period.

It may be repealed or amended where circumstances have changed with respect to any of the factors which prompted its adoption; in such case, a period shall be fixed for amendment of the agreements and concerted practices to which the earlier Regulation applied before repeal or amendment.]

Notes

Article 3 was replaced as shown in square brackets by Council Regulation (EEC) No 2411/92 (OJ L 240, 24.8.1992, p. 19) with effect from 27 July 1992.

Commentary

Art 3: **B&C:** 12.041

Article 4

Regulations adopted pursuant to Article 2 shall include a provision that they apply with retroactive effect to agreements, decisions and concerted practices which were in existence at the date of the entry into force of such Regulations.

[Article 4a

[A Regulation pursuant to Article 2 may stipulate that the prohibition contained in Article [81](1) of the Treaty shall not apply, for such period as fixed by that Regulation, to agreements, decisions and concerted practices already in existence at the date of accession to which Article [81](1) applies by virtue of the accession of Austria, Finland, Norway and Sweden and which do not satisfy the conditions of Article [81](3). However, this Article shall not apply to agreements, decisions and concerted practices which at the date of accession already fall under Article 53(1) of the EEA Agreement.]

Notes

Article 4a was inserted as shown in square brackets by the Act of Accession of Norway, Austria, Finland and Sweden, Annex I(III)(A) (OJ C 241, 29.8.1994, p. 56), with effect from 1 January 1995.

Article 5

Before adopting a regulation, the Commission shall publish a draft thereof and invite all persons and organizations concerned to submit their comments within such reasonable time limit, being not less than one month, as the Commission shall fix.

[Article 6

The Commission shall consult the Advisory Committee referred to in Article 14 of Council Regulation (EC) No 1/2003 of 16 December 2002 on the implementation of the rules on competition laid down in Articles 81 and 82 of the Treaty[1] before publishing a draft Regulation and before adopting a Regulation.]

Notes

[[1] OJ L 1, 4.1.2003, p. 1.]
Article 6 was replaced as shown in square brackets by Council Regulation (EC) No 1/2003 (OJ L 1, 4.1.2003, p. 1), Article 41, with effect from 1 May 2004.

[*Article 7*]

Notes

Article 7 was repealed by Council Regulation (EC) No 1/2003 (OJ L 1, 4.1.2003, p. 1), Article 41, with effect from 1 May 2004.

[*Article 8*]

Notes

Article 8 was deleted by Council Regulation (EEC) No 2411/92 (OJ L 240, 24.8.1992, p. 19) with effect from 27 July 1992.

Article 9

This Regulation shall enter into force on 1 January 1988.

This Regulation shall be binding in its entirety and directly applicable in all Member States.

Done at Brussels, 14 December 1987

E10

COUNCIL REGULATION (EEC) No 2299/89

of 24 July 1989
on a code of conduct for computerized reservation systems

Official Journal L 220, 29.7.1989, p. 1

Celex No: 31989R2299

Notes

EEA application: see the EEA Agreement, Annex XIII, Chapter VI, Point 63 (as amended by EEA Joint Committee Decision No 7/94 and Decision No 148/1999 (OJ No L 15, 18.1.2001, p. 45)).

THE COUNCIL OF THE EUROPEAN COMMUNITIES,

Having regard to the Treaty establishing the European Economic Community, and in particular Article [80](2) thereof,

Having regard to the proposal from the Commission,[1]

Having regard to the opinion of the European Parliament,[2]

Having regard to the opinion of the Economic and Social Committee,[3]

Notes

[1] OJ No C 294, 18.11.1988, p. 12.

[2] OJ No C 158, 26.6.1989.
[3] OJ No C 56, 6.3.1989, p. 32.

Commentary
Regulation 2299/89: B&C: 12.049

[1] Whereas the bulk of airline reservations are made through computerized reservation systems;

[2] Whereas such systems can, if properly used, provide an important and useful service to air carriers, travel agents and the travelling public by affording easy access to up-to-date and accurate information on flights, fares and seat availability, making reservations and, in some cases, issuing tickets and boarding passes;

[3] Whereas abuses in the form of denial of access to the systems or discrimination in the provision, loading or display of data or unreasonable conditions imposed on participants or subscribers can seriously disadvantage air carriers, travel agents and ultimately consumers;

[4] Whereas this Regulation is without prejudice to the application of Articles [81] and [82] of the Treaty;

[5] Whereas Commission Regulation (EEC) No 2672/88[1] exempts for the provisions of Article [81](1) of the Treaty agreements for the common purchase, development and operation of computerized reservation systems;

Notes
[1] OJ No L 239, 30.8.1988, p. 13. [Regulation 2672/88/EEC expired on 31 October 1991.]

[6] Whereas a mandatory code of conduct applicable to all computerized reservation systems and/or distribution facilities offered for use and/or used in the Community could ensure that such systems are used in a non-discriminatory and transparent way, subject to certain safeguards, so avoiding their misuse while reinforcing undistorted competition between air carriers and between computerized reservation systems and thereby protecting the interests of consumers;

[7] Whereas it would not be appropriate to impose obligations on a computerized reservation system vendor or on a parent or participating carrier in respect of an air carrier of a third country which, alone or jointly with others, owns and/or controls another such system which does not conform with this code or offer equivalent treatment;

[8] Whereas a complaints investigation and enforcement procedure for non-compliance with such a code is desirable,

Commentary
Recital 8: B&C: 12.049

HAS ADOPTED THIS REGULATION:

[Article 1

This Regulation shall apply to any computerised reservation system, insofar as it contains air-transport products and insofar as rail-transport products are incorporated in its principal display, when offered for use or used in the territory of the Community, irrespective of:

— the status or nationality of the system vendor,
— the source of the information used or the location of the relevant central data processing unit,
— the geographical location of the airports between which air carriage takes place.]

Notes
Article 1 was replaced as shown in square brackets by Council Regulation (EC) No 323/1999 (OJ L 40, 13.2.1999, p. 1) with effect from 15 March 1999.

[Article 2

For the purposes of this Regulation:

(a) "unbundled air transport product" means the carriage by air of a passenger between two airports, including any related ancillary services and additional benefits offered for sale and/or sold as an integral part of that product;

(b) "bundled air transport product" means a prearranged combination of an unbundled air transport product with other services not ancillary to air transport, offered for sale and/or sold at an inclusive price;

(c) "air transport product" means both unbundled and bundled air transport products;

(d) "scheduled air service" means a series of flights all possessing the following characteristics:
— performed by aircraft for the transport of passengers or passengers and cargo and/or mail for remuneration, in such a manner that seats are available on each flight for individual purchase by consumers either directly from the air carrier or from its authorized agents),
— operated so as to serve traffic between the same two or more points, either:

1. according to a published timetable; or

2. with flights so regular or frequent that they constitute a recognizably systematic series;

(e) "fare" means the price to be paid for unbundled air transport products and the conditions under which this price applies;

(f) "computerized reservation system" (CRS) means a computerized system containing information about, *inter alia*, air carriers"
— schedules,
— availability,
— fares, and
— related services,

with or without facilities through which:

— reservations may be made, or
— tickets may be issued,

to the extent that some or all of these services are made available to subscribers;

(g) "distribution facilities" means facilities provided by a system vendor for the provision of information about air carriers" schedules, availability, fares and related services and for making reservations and/or issuing tickets, and for any other related services;

(h) "system vendor" means any entity and its affiliates which is or are responsible for the operation or marketing of a CRS;

(i) "parent carrier" means any air carrier which directly or indirectly, alone or jointly with others, owns or effectively controls a system vendor, as well as any air carrier which it owns or effectively controls;

(j) "effective control" means a relationship constituted by rights, contracts or any other means which, either separately or jointly and having regard to the considerations of fact or law involved, confer the possibility of directly or indirectly exercising a decisive influence on an undertaking, in particular by:
— the right to use all or part of the assets of an undertaking,
— rights or contracts which confer a decisive influence on the composition, voting or decisions of the bodies of an undertaking or otherwise confer a decisive influence on the running of the business of the undertaking;

(k) "participating carrier" means an air carrier which has an agreement with a system vendor for the distribution of air transport products through a CRS. To the extent that a parent carrier uses the facilities of its own CRS which are covered by this Regulation, it shall be considered a participating carrier;]¹

[(l) "subscriber" shall mean a person, other than a consumer, or an undertaking, other than a participating carrier, using a CRS under contract or other financial arrangement with a system vendor. A financial arrangement shall be deemed to exist where a specific payment is made for the services of the system vendor or where an air-transport product is purchased;

(m) "consumer" shall mean any person seeking information about or intending to purchase an air-transport product for private use;]²

[(n) "principal display" means a comprehensive neutral display of data concerning air services between city-pairs, within a specified time period;

(o) "elapsed journey time" means the time difference between scheduled departure and arrival time;

(p) "service enhancement" means any product or service offered by a system vendor on its own behalf to subscribers in conjunction with a CRS, other than distribution facilities;]¹

[(q) "unbundled rail-transport product" shall mean the carriage of a passenger between two stations by rail, including any related ancillary services and additional benefits offered for sale or sold as an integral part of that product;

(r) "bundled rail-transport product" shall mean a pre-arranged combination of an unbundled rail-transport product with other services not ancillary to rail transport, offered for sale or sold at an inclusive price;

(s) "rail-transport product" shall mean both unbundled and bundled rail transport products;

(t) "ticket" shall mean a valid document giving entitlement to transport or an equivalent in paperless, including electronic, form issued or authorised by the carrier or its authorised agent;

(u) "duplicate reservation" shall mean a situation which arises when two or more reservations are made for the same passenger when it is evident that the passenger will not be able to use more than one.]²

Notes

¹ Article 2 was replaced as shown in square brackets by Council Regulation (EEC) No 3089/93 (OJ L 278, 11.11.1993, p. 1) with effect from 11 December 1993.

² Paragraphs (l) and (m) were replaced and paragraphs (q) to (u) were added as shown in square brackets by Council Regulation (EC) No 323/1999 (OJ L 40, 13.2.1999, p. 1) with effect from 15 March 1999.

[Article 3

1. A system vendor shall have the capacity, in its own name as a separate entity from the parent carrier, to have rights and obligations of all kinds, to make contracts, *inter alia* with parent carriers, participating carriers and subscribers, or to accomplish other legal acts and to sue and be sued.

2. A system vendor shall allow any air carrier the opportunity to participate, on an equal and non-discriminatory basis, in its distribution facilities within the available capacity of the system concerned and subject to any technical constraints outside the control of the system vendor.

3. (a) A system vendor shall not:
   — attach unreasonable conditions to any contract with a participating carrier,
   — require the acceptance of supplementary conditions which, by their nature or according to commercial usage, have no connection with participation in its CRS and shall apply the same conditions for the same level of service.
   (b) A system vendor shall not make it a condition of participation in its CRS that a participating carrier may not at the same time be a participant in another system.
   (c) A participating carrier may terminate its contract with a system vendor on giving notice which need not exceed six months, to expire not before the end of the first year. In such a case a system the vendor shall not be entitled to recover more than the costs directly related to the termination of the contract.

4. If a system vendor has decided to add any improvement to the distribution facilities provided or the equipment used in the provision of the facilities, it shall provide information on and offer these improvements to all participating carriers, including parent carriers, with equal time lines and on the same terms and conditions, subject to any technical constraints outside the control of the system vendor, and in such a way that there will be no difference in lead-time for the implementation of the new improvements between parent and participating carriers.]

Notes

Article 3 was replaced as shown in square brackets by Council Regulation (EEC) No 3089/93 (OJ L 278, 11.11.1993, p. 1) with effect from 11 June 1994 (Article 3(1)) and 11 December 1993 (remainder).

[Article 3a

1. (a) A parent carrier may not discriminate against a competing CRS by refusing to provide the latter, on request and with equal timeliness, with the same information on schedules, fares and availability relating to its own air services as that which it provides to its own CRS or to distribute its air transport products through another CRS, or by refusing to accept or to confirm with equal timeliness a reservation made through a competing CRS for any of its air transport products which are distributed through its own CRS. The parent carrier shall be obliged to accept and to confirm only those bookings which are in conformity with its fares and conditions.][1]

[(b) The parent carrier shall not be obliged to accept any costs in this connection except for reproduction of the information to be provided and for accepted bookings. The booking fee payable to a CRS for an accepted booking made in accordance with this Article shall not exceed the fee charged by the same CRS to participating carriers for an equivalent transaction.][2]

[(c) The parent carrier shall be entitled to carry out controls to ensure that Article 5 (1) is respected by the competing CRS.][1]

[2. The obligation imposed by this Article shall not apply in favour of a competing CRS when, in accordance with the procedures of Article 11, it has been decided that that CRS is in breach of Article 4a or of Article 6 concerning parent carriers" unauthorised access to information.][2]

Notes

[1] Article 3a was added as shown in square brackets by Council Regulation (EEC) No 3089/93 (OJ L 278, 11.11.1993, p. 1) with effect from 11 December 1993.

[2] Paragraph 1(b) and paragraph 2 were replaced as shown in square brackets by Council Regulation (EC) No 323/1999 (OJ L 40, 13.2.1999, p. 1) with effect from 15 March 1999.

[Article 4

1. Participating carriers and other providers of air transport products shall ensure that the data which they decide to submit to a CRS are accurate, non-misleading, transparent and no less comprehensive than for any other CRS. The data shall, *inter alia*, enable a system vendor to meet the requirements of the ranking criteria as set out in the Annex.

Data submitted via intermediaries shall not be manipulated by them in a manner which would lead to inaccurate, misleading or discriminatory information.][1]

[The principles stated in the first and second subparagraphs shall apply to rail services in respect of data provided for inclusion in the principal display.][2]

[2. A system vendor shall not manipulate the material referred to in paragraph 1 in a manner which would lead to the provision of inaccurate, misleading or discriminatory information.

3. A system vendor shall load and process data provided by participating carriers with equal care and timeliness, subject only to the constraints of the loading method selected by individual participating carriers and to the standard formats used by the said vendor.][1]

Notes

[1] Article 4 was replaced as shown in square brackets by Council Regulation (EEC) No 3089/93 (OJ L 278, 11.11.1993, p. 1) with effect from 11 December 1993.

[2] Article 4(1) was subsequently amended as shown in square brackets by Council Regulation (EC) No 323/1999 (OJ L 40, 13.2.1999, p. 1) with effect from 15 March 1999.

[Article 4a

1. Loading and/or processing facilities provided by a system vendor shall be offered to all parent and participating carriers without discrimination. Where relevant and generally accepted air transport industry standards are available, system vendors shall offer facilities compatible with them.

2. A system vendor shall not reserve any specific loading and/or processing procedure or any other distribution facility for one or more of its parent carrier(s).

3. A system vendor shall ensure that its distribution facilities are separated, in a clear and verifiable manner, from any carrier's private inventory and management and marketing facilities. Separation may be established either logically by means of software or physically in such a way that any connection between the distribution facilities and the private facilities may be achieved by means of an application-to application interface only. Irrespective of the method of separation adopted, any such interface shall be made available to all parent and participating carriers on a non-discriminatory basis and shall provide equality of treatment in respect of procedures, protocols, inputs and outputs. Where relevant and generally accepted air transport industry standards are available, system vendors shall offer interfaces compatible with them.][1]

[4. The system vendor shall ensure that any third parties providing CRS services in whole or in part on its behalf comply with the relevant provisions of this Regulation.][2]

Notes

[1] Article 4a as shown in square brackets was added by Council Regulation (EEC) No 3089/93 (OJ L 278, 11.11.1993, p. 1) with effect from 11 December 1993.

[2] Paragraph 4 as shown in square brackets was added by Council Regulation (EC) No 323/1999 (OJ L 40, 13.2.1999, p. 1) with effect from 15 March 1999.

[*Article 5*

1. (a) Displays generated by a CRS shall be clear and non-discriminatory.
   (b) A system vendor shall not intentionally or negligently display inaccurate or misleading information in its CRS.

2. (a) A system vendor shall provide a principal display or displays for each individual transaction through its CRS and shall include therein the data provided by participating carriers on flight schedules, fare types and seat availability in a clear and comprehensive manner and without discrimination or bias, in particular as regards the order in which information is presented.
   (b) A consumer shall be entitled to have, on request, a principal display limited to scheduled or non-scheduled services only.
   (c) No discrimination on the basis of airports serving the same city shall be exercised in constructing and selecting flights for a given city-pair for inclusion in a principal display.
   (d) Ranking of flight options in a principal display shall be as set out in the Annex.
   (e) Criteria to be used for ranking shall not be based on any factor directly or indirectly relating to carrier identity and shall be applied on a non-discriminatory basis to all participating carriers.

3. Where a system vendor provides information on fares, the display shall be neutral and non-discriminatory and shall contain at least the fares provided for all flights of participating carriers shown in the principal display. The source of such information shall be acceptable to the participating carrier(s) and system vendor concerned.

4. Information on bundled products regarding, *inter alia*, who is organizing the tour, availability and prices, shall not be featured in the principal display.

5. A CRS shall not be considered in breach of this Regulation to the extent that it changes a display in order to meet the specific request(s) of a consumer.]

Notes

Article 5 as shown in square brackets was added by Council Regulation (EEC) No 3089/93 (OJ L 278, 11.11.1993, p. 1) with effect from 11 June 1994 (Article 5(2)(b)) and 11 December 1993 (remainder).

[*Article 6*

1. The following provisions shall govern the availability of information, statistical or otherwise, by a system vendor from its CRS:][1]

[(a) information concerning identifiable individual bookings shall be provided on an equal basis and only to the air carrier or carriers participating in the service covered by and to the subscribers involved in the booking.

Information under the control of the system vendor concerning identifiable individual bookings shall be archived off-line within seventy-two hours of the completion of the last element in the individual booking and destroyed within three years. Access to such data shall be allowed only for billing-dispute reasons.]²

[(b) any marketing, booking and sales data made available shall be on the basis that:

    (i) such data are offered with equal timeliness and on a non-discriminatory basis to all participating carriers, including parent carriers;]¹

    [(ii) such data may and, on request, shall cover all participating carriers and/or subscribers, but shall include no identification, either directly or indirectly, of, or personal information on a passenger or a corporate user;]²

    [(iii) all requests for such data are treated with equal care and timeless, subject to the transmission method selected by the individual carrier;]¹

    [(iv) information is made available on request to participating carriers and subscribers both globally and selectively with regard to the market in which they operate;

    (v) a group of airlines and/or subscribers is entitled to purchase data for common processing.]²

[2. A system vendor shall not make personal information concerning a passenger available to others not involved in the transaction without the consent of the passenger.

3. A system vendor shall ensure that the provisions in paragraphs 1 and 2 above are complied with, by technical means and/or appropriate safeguards regarding at least software, in such a way that information provided by or created for air carriers can in no way be accessed by one or more of the parent carriers except as permitted by this Article.]¹

[…]²

Notes

¹ Article 6 was replaced as shown in square brackets by Council Regulation (EEC) No 3089/93 (OJ L 278, 11.11.1993, p. 1) with effect from 11 December 1993.

² Article 6(1)(a) was replaced and Article 6(1)(b) was amended as shown in square brackets and paragraphs 4 and 5 were deleted as indicated by square brackets by Council Regulation (EC) No 323/1999 (OJ L 40, 13.2.1999, p. 1) with effect from 15 March 1999.

Article 7

[1. The obligations of a system vendor under Articles 3 and 4 to 6 shall not apply in respect of a parent carrier of a third country to the extent that its CRS outside the territory of the Community does not offer Community air carriers equivalent treatment to that provided under this Regulation and under Commission Regulation (EEC) No 83/91.¹

2. The obligations of parent or participating carriers under Articles 3a, 4 and 8 shall not apply in respect of a CRS controlled by (an) air carrier(s) of one or more third country (countries) to the extent that outside the territory of the Community the parent or participating carrier(s) is (are) not accorded equivalent treatment to that provided under this Regulation and under Commission Regulation (EEC) No 83/ 91.]

3. A system vendor or an air carrier proposing to avail itself of the provisions of paragraphs 1 or 2 must notify the Commission of its intentions and the reasons therefor at least 14 days in advance of such action. In exceptional circumstances, the Commission may, at the request of the vendor or the air carrier concerned, grant a waiver from the 14-day rule.

4. Upon receipt of a notification, the Commission shall without delay determine whether discrimination within the meaning of paragraphs 1 and 2 exists. If this is found to be the case, the Commission shall so inform all system vendors or the air carriers concerned in the Community as well as Member States. If discrimination within the meaning of paragraph 1 or 2 does not exist, the Commission shall so inform the system vendor or air carriers concerned.

[5. (a) In cases where serious discrimination within the meaning of paragraph 1 or 2 is found to exist, the Commission may by decision instruct CRSs to modify their operations appropriately in order to terminate such discrimination. The Commission shall immediately inform Member States of such a decision.

(b) Unless the Council, at the request of a Member State, takes another decision within two months of the date of the Commission's decision, the latter shall enter into force.]

Notes

[¹ OJ No L 10, 15.1.1991, p. 9.]

Paragraphs 1 and 2 were replaced and paragraph 5 was added as shown in square brackets by Council Regulation (EEC) No 3089/93 (OJ L 278, 11.11.1993, p. 1) with effect from 11 December 1993.

[*Article 8*

1. A parent carrier shall neither directly nor indirectly link the use of any specific CRS by a subscriber with the receipt of any commission or other incentive or disincentive for the sale of air transport products available on its flights.

2. A parent carrier shall neither directly nor indirectly require use of any specific CRS by a subscriber for sale or issue of tickets for any air transport products provided either directly or indirectly by itself.

3. Any condition which an air carrier may require of a travel agent when authorizing it to sell and issue tickets for its air transport products shall be without prejudice to paragraphs 1 and 2.]

Notes

Article 8 was replaced as shown in square brackets by Council Regulation (EEC) No 3089/93 (OJ L 278, 11.11.1993, p. 1) with effect from 11 December 1993.

Article 9

1. A system vendor shall make any of the distribution facilities of a CRS available to any subscriber on a non-discriminatory basis.

2. A system vendor shall not require a subscriber to sign an exclusive contract, nor directly or indirectly prevent a subscriber from subscribing to, or using, any other system or systems.

3. A service enhancement offered to any other subscriber shall be offered by the system vendor to all subscribers on a non-discriminatory basis.

[4. (a) A system vendor shall not attach unreasonable conditions to any subscriber contract allowing for the use of its CRS and, in particular, a subscriber may terminate its contract with a system vendor by giving notice which need not exceed three months, to expire not before the end of the first year. In such a case, a system vendor shall not be entitled to recover more than the costs directly related to the termination of the contract.

(b) Subject to paragraph 2, the supply of technical equipment is not subject to the conditions set out in (a).

5. A system vendor shall provide in each subscriber contract for:

(a) the principal display, conforming to Article 5, to be accessed for each individual transaction, except where a consumer requests information for only one air carrier or where the consumer requests information for bundled air transport products alone;

(b) the subscriber not to manipulate material supplied by CRSs in a manner which would lead to inaccurate, misleading or discriminatory presentation of information to consumers.

6. A system vendor shall not impose an obligation on a subscriber to accept an offer of technical equipment or software, but may require that equipment and software used be compatible with its own system.]

Notes

Articles 9(4), 9(5) and 9(6) were replaced as shown in square brackets by Council Regulation (EEC) No 3089/93 (OJ L 278, 11.11.1993, p. 1) with effect from 11 December 1993.

[*Article 9a*

1. (a) In the case of information provided by a CRS, a subscriber shall use a neutral display in accordance with Article 5(2)(a) and (b) unless another display is required to meet a preference indicated by a consumer.

941

(b) No subscriber shall manipulate information provided by a CRS in a manner that leads to inaccurate, misleading or discriminatory presentation of that information to any consumer.

(c) A subscriber shall make reservations and issue tickets in accordance with the information contained in the CRS used, or as authorised by the carrier concerned.

(d) A subscriber shall inform each consumer of any en route changes of equipment, the number of scheduled en route stops, the identity of the air carrier actually operating the flight, and of any changes of airport required in any itinerary provided, to the extent that that information is present in the CRS. The subscriber shall inform the consumer of the name and address of the system vendor, the purposes of the processing, the duration of the retention of individual data and the means available to the data subject of exercising his access rights.

(e) A consumer shall be entitled at any time to have a print-out of the CRS display or to be given access to a parallel CRS display reflecting the image that is being displayed to the subscriber.

(f) A person shall be entitled to have effective access free of charge to his own data regardless of whether the data is stored by the CRS or by the subscriber.

2. A subscriber shall use the distribution facilities of a CRS in accordance with Annex II.]

Notes

Article 9a as shown in square brackets was inserted by Council Regulation (EC) No 323/1999 (OJ L 40, 13.2.1999, p. 1) with effect from 15 March 1999.

Article 10

[1. (a) Any fee charged to a participating carrier by a system vendor shall be non-discriminatory, reasonably structured and reasonably related to the cost of the service provided and used and shall, in particular, be the same for the same level of service. The billing for the services of a CRS shall be sufficiently detailed to allow the participating carriers to see exactly which services have been used and the fees therefor; as a minimum, booking fee bills shall include the following information for each segment:
— type of CRS booking,
— passenger name,
— country,
— IATA/ARC agency identification code,
— city-code,
— city pair of segment,
— booking date (transaction date),
— flight date,
— flight number,
— status code (booking status),
— service type (class of service),
— passenger name record (PNR) locator, and
— booking/cancellation indicator.

The billing information shall be offered on magnetic media. The fee to be charged for the billing information provided in the form chosen by the carrier shall not exceed the cost of the medium itself together with its transportation costs.

A participating air carrier shall be offered the facility of being informed when any booking or transaction is made for which a booking fee will be charged. Where a carrier elects to be so informed, it shall be offered the option of disallowing any such booking or transaction, unless the latter has already been accepted. In the event of such a disallowance, the air carrier shall not be charged for that booking or transaction.

(b) Any fee for equipment rental or other service charged to a subscriber by a system vendor shall be non-discriminatory, reasonably structured and reasonably related to the cost of the service provided and used and shall, in particular, be the same for the same level of service. Productivity benefits awarded to subscribers by system vendors in the form of discount on rental charges or commission payments shall be deemed to be distribution costs of the system vendors and shall be based on ticketed segments. When, subject to paragraph 5 of Annex II the system vendor does not know whether a ticket has been issued or not, then that system vendor shall be entitled to rely upon notification of the ticket number from the subscriber.

The billing for the services of a CRS shall be sufficiently detailed to allow subscribers to see exactly which services have been used and what fees have been charged therefor.

2. A system vendor shall, on request, provide interested parties, including consumers, with details of current procedures, fees and system facilities, including interfaces, editing and display criteria used. For consumers that information shall be free of charge and cover the processing of individual data. This provision shall not, however, require a system vendor to disclose proprietary information such as software.]

3. Any changes to fee levels, conditions or facilities offered and the basis therefor shall be communicated to all participating carriers and subscribers on a non-discriminatory basis.

Notes

Paragraphs 1 and 2 were replaced as shown in square brackets by Council Regulation (EC) No 323/1999 (OJ L 40, 13.2.1999, p. 1) with effect from 13 August 1999 (Article 10(1)(b)) and 15 March 1999 (remainder).

Article 11

1. Acting on receipt of a complaint or on its own initiative, the Commission shall initiate procedures to terminate infringement of the provisions of this Regulation.

2. Complaints may be submitted by:

(a) Member States;

(b) natural or legal persons who claim a legitimate interest.

3. The Commission shall immediately forward to the Member States copies of the complaints and applications and of all relevant documents sent to it or which it sends out in the course of such procedures.

Article 12

1. In carrying out the duties assigned to it by this Regulation, the Commission may obtain all necessary information from the Member States and from undertakings and associations of undertakings.

2. The Commission may fix a time limit of not less than one month for the communication of the information requested.

3. When sending a request for information to an undertaking or association of undertakings, the Commission shall forward a copy of the request at the same time to the Member State in whose territory the head office of the undertaking or association of undertakings is situated.

4. In its request, the Commission shall state the legal basis and purpose of the request and also the penalties for supplying incorrect information provided for in Article 16(1).

5. The owners of the undertakings or their representatives and, in the case of legal persons or of companies, firms or associations not having legal personality, the person authorized to represent them by law or by their rules shall be bound to supply the information requested.

Article 13

1. In carrying out the duties assigned to it by this Regulation, the Commission may undertake all necessary investigations into undertakings and associations of undertakings. To this end, officials authorized by the Commission shall be empowered:

(a) to examine the books and other business records;

(b) to take copies of, or extracts from, the books and business records;

(c) to ask for oral explanations on the spot;

(d) to enter any premises, land and vehicles used by undertakings or associations of undertakings.

2. The authorized officials of the Commission shall exercise their powers upon production of an authorization in writing specifying the subject matter and purpose of the investigation and the penalties provided for in Article 16(1) in cases where production of the required books or other business records is incomplete. In good time before the investigation, the Commission shall inform the Member State, in whose territory the same is to be made, of the investigation and the identity of the authorized officials.

3. Undertakings and associations of undertakings shall submit to investigations ordered by decision of the Commission. The decision shall specify the subject matter and purpose of the investigation, appoint the date on which it is to begin and indicate the penalties provided for in Article 16(1) and the right to have the decision reviewed in the Court of Justice.

4. The Commission shall take the decisions mentioned in paragraph 3 after consultation with the Member State in the territory of which the investigation is to be made.

5. Officials of the Member State in the territory of which investigation is to be made may assist the Commission officials in carrying out their duties, at the request of the Member State or of the Commission.

6. Where an undertaking opposes an investigation ordered pursuant to this Article, the Member State concerned shall afford the necessary assistance to the officials authorized by the Commission to enable them to make their investigation.

Article 14

1. Information acquired as a result of the application of Articles 12 and 13 shall be used only for the purposes of the relevant request or investigation.

2. Without prejudice to Articles 11 and 20, the Commission and the competent authorities of the Member States, their officials and other servants shall not disclose information of a kind covered by the obligation of professional secrecy which has been acquired by them as a result of the application of this Regulation.

3. Paragraphs 1 and 2 shall not prevent publication of general information or of surveys which do not contain information relating to particular undertakings or associations of undertakings.

Article 15

1. When an undertaking or association of undertakings does not supply the information requested within the time limit fixed by the Commission or supplies incomplete information, the Commission shall by decision require the information to be supplied. The decision shall specify what information is required, fix an appropriate time limit within which it is to be supplied and indicate the penalties provided for in Article 16(1) as well as the right to have the decision reviewed by the Court of Justice.

2. At the same time the Commission shall send a copy of its decision to the competent authority of the Member State in the territory of which the head office of the undertaking or association of undertakings is situated.

Article 16

1. The Commission may, by decision, impose fines on undertakings or associations of undertakings from €1 000 to 50 000 where, intentionally or negligently:

(a) they supply incorrect information in response to a request made pursuant to Article 12 or do not supply information within the time limit fixed;

(b) they produce the required books or other business records in incomplete form during investigations or refuse to submit to an investigation pursuant to Article 13(1).

2. The Commission may, by decision, impose fines on system vendors, parent carriers, participating carriers and/or subscribers for infringements of this Regulation up to a maximum of 10% of the annual turnover for the relevant activity of the undertaking concerned. In fixing the amount of the fine, regard shall be had both to the seriousness and to the duration of the infringement.

3. Decisions taken pursuant to paragraphs 1 and 2 shall not be of a penal nature.

Commentary
Art 16(2): B&C: 12.049

Article 17

The Court of Justice shall have unlimited jurisdiction within the meaning of Article [229] of the Treaty to review decisions whereby the Commission has imposed a fine; it may cancel, reduce or increase the fine.

Article 18

For the purposes of applying Article 16, the euro shall be that adopted in drawing up the general budget of the European Communities in accordance with Articles [277] and [279] of the Treaty.

Article 19

[1. Before taking decisions pursuant to Article 11 or 16, the Commission shall give the undertakings or associations of undertakings concerned the opportunity of being heard on the matters to which the Commission takes or has taken objection.]

2. Should the Commission or the competent authorities of the Member States consider it necessary, they may also hear other natural or legal persons. Applications by such persons to be heard shall be granted when they show a sufficient interest.

Notes

Article 19(1) was replaced as shown in square brackets by Council Regulation (EC) No 323/1999 (OJ L 40, 13.2.1999, p. 1) with effect from 15 March 1999.

Article 20

1. The Commission shall publish the decisions which it adopts pursuant to Article 16.

2. Such publication shall state the names of the parties and the main content of the decision; it shall have regard to the legitimate interest of undertakings in the protection of their business secrets.

[Article 21

1. Neither Article 5, Article 9(5) nor the Annexes shall apply to a CRS used by an air carrier or a group of air carriers:

(a) in its or their own office or offices and sales counters clearly identified as such; or

(b) to provide information and/or distribution facilities accessible through a public telecommunications network, clearly and continuously identifying the information provider or providers as such.

2. Where booking is performed directly by an air carrier, that air carrier shall be subject to Article 9a(d) and (f).]

Notes

Article 21 was replaced as shown in square brackets by Council Regulation (EC) No 323/1999 (OJ L 40, 13.2.1999, p. 1) with effect from 15 March 1999.

[Article 21a][1]

[1. The system vendor shall ensure that the technical compliance of its CRS with Articles 4a and 6 is monitored by an independent auditor on a calendar year basis. For that purpose, the auditor shall be granted access at all times to any programmes, procedures, operations and safeguards used on the computers or computer systems through which the system vendor provides its distribution facilities. Each system vendor shall submit its auditor's report on his inspection and findings to the Commission within four months of the end of the calendar year under review. The Commission shall examine those reports with a view to taking any action necessary in accordance with Article 11(1).][2]

[2. The system vendor shall inform participating carriers and the Commission of the identity of the auditor at least three months before confirmation of an appointment and at least three months before each annual reappointment. If, within one month of notification, any of the participating carriers objects to the capability of the auditor to carry out the tasks as required under this Article, the Commission shall, within a further two months and after consultation with the auditor, the system vendor and any other party claiming a legitimate interest, decide whether or not the auditor is to be replaced.]

Notes

[1] Article 21a was added as shown in square brackets by Council Regulation (EEC) No 3089/93 (OJ L 278, 11.11.1993, p. 1) with effect from 11 December 1993.

[2] Article 21a(1) was replaced as shown in square brackets by Council Regulation (EC) No 323/1999 (OJ L 40, 13.2.1999, p. 1) with effect from 15 March 1999.

[Article 21b

1. Subject to this Article, this Regulation shall apply to the inclusion of rail-transport products.

2. A system vendor may decide to include rail services in the principal display of its CRS.

3. Where a system vendor decides to include rail products in the principal display of its CRS, it shall choose to include certain well defined categories of rail services, while respecting the principles stated in Article 3(2).

4. A rail-transport operator shall be deemed to be a participating or parent carrier, as appropriate, for the purposes of the code, insofar as it has an agreement with a system vendor for the distribution of its products through the principal display of a CRS or its own reservation system is a CRS as defined in Article 2(f). Subject to paragraph 5, those products shall be treated as air-transport products and shall be incorporated in the principal display in accordance with the criteria set out in Annex I.

5. (a) When applying the rules laid down in paragraphs 1 and 2 of Annex I to rail services the system vendor shall adjust the ranking principles for the principal display in order to take due account of the needs of consumers to be adequately informed of rail services that represent a competitive alternative to the air services. In particular, system vendors may rank rail services with a limited number of short stops with non-stop direct air services.

   (b) System vendors shall define clear criteria for the application of this Article to rail services. Such criteria shall cover elapsed journey time and reflect the need to avoid excessive screen padding. At least two months before their application those criteria shall be submitted to the Commission for information.

6. For the purposes of this Article, all references to "flights" in this Regulation shall be deemed to include references to "rail services" and references to "air-transport products" shall be deemed to include references to "rail products".

7. Particular attention shall be given to an assessment of the application of this Article in the Commission's report under Article 23(1).]

Notes

Article 21b as shown in square brackets was added by Council Regulation (EC) No 323/1999 (OJ L 40, 13.2.1999, p. 1) with effect from 15 March 1999.

[Article 22]¹

[1. This Regulation shall be without prejudice to national legislation on security, public-order and data-protection measures taken in implementation of Directive 95/46/EC.¹]²

[2. The beneficiaries of rights arising under Article 3(4), Articles 4a, 6 and 21a cannot renounce these rights by contractual or any other means.]¹

Notes

[¹ OJ L 281, 23.11.1995, p. 31.]

¹ Article 22 was replaced as shown in square brackets by Council Regulation (EEC) No 3089/93 (OJ L 278, 11.11.1993, p. 1) with effect from 11 December 1993.

² Article 22(1) was subsequently replaced as shown in square brackets by Council Regulation (EC) No 323/1999 (OJ L 40, 13.2.1999, p. 1) with effect from 15 March 1999.

[Article 23

Within two years of the entry into force of this Regulation, the Commission shall draw up a report on the application of this Regulation which shall, *inter alia*, take account of economic developments in the relevant market. That report may be accompanied by proposals for the revision of this Regulation.]

Notes

Article 23 was replaced as shown in square brackets by Council Regulation (EC) No 323/1999 (OJ L 40, 13.2.1999, p. 1) with effect from 15 March 1999.

This Regulation shall be binding in its entirety and directly applicable in all Member States.

Done at Brussels, 24 July 1989

[ANNEX I

PRINCIPAL DISPLAY RANKING CRITERIA FOR FLIGHTS[1] OFFERING
UNBUNDLED AIR TRANSPORT PRODUCTS

1. Ranking of flight options in a principal display, for the day or days requested, must be in the following order unless requested in a different way by a consumer for an individual transaction:

(i)   all non-stop direct flights between the city-pairs concerned;
(ii) all other direct flights, not involving a change of aircraft or train, between the city pairs concerned;
(iii) connecting flights.

2. A consumer must at least be afforded the possibility of having, on request, a principal display ranked by departure or arrival time and/or elapsed journey time. Unless otherwise requested by a consumer, a principal display must be ranked by departure time for group (i) and elapsed journey time for groups (ii) and (iii).

3. Where a system vendor chooses to display information for any city-pair in relation to the schedules or fares of non-participating carriers, but not necessarily all such carriers, such information must be displayed in an accurate, non-misleading and non-discriminatory manner between carriers displayed.

4. If, to the system vendor's knowledge, information on the number of direct scheduled air services and the identity of the air carriers concerned is not comprehensive, that must be clearly stated on the relevant display.

5. Flights other than scheduled air services must be clearly identified.

6. Flights involving stops en route must be clearly identified.

7. Where flights are operated by an air carrier which is not the air carrier identified by the carrier designator code, the actual operator of the flight must be clearly identified. That requirement will apply in all cases, except for short-term *ad hoc* arrangements.

8. A system vendor must not use the screen space in a principal display in a manner which gives excessive exposure to one particular travel option or which displays unrealistic travel options.

9. Except as provided in paragraph 10, the following will apply:

(a) for direct services, no flight may be featured more than once in any principal display;
(b) for multi-sector services involving a change of aircraft, no combination of flights may be featured more than once in any principal display;
(c) flights involving a change of aircraft must be treated and displayed as connecting flights, with one line per aircraft segment. Nevertheless, where the flights are operated by the same carrier with the same flight number and where a carrier requires only one flight coupon and one reservation, a CRS should issue only one coupon and should charge for only one reservation.

10. 1. Where participating carriers have joint-venture or other contractual arrangements requiring two or more of them to assume separate responsibility for the offer and sale of air-transport products on a flight or combination of flights, the terms "flight" (for direct services) and "combination of flights" (for multi-sector services) used in paragraph 9 must be interpreted as allowing each of the carriersconcerned — not more than two — to have a separate display using its individual carrier designator code.

    2. Where more than two carriers are involved, designation of the two carriers entitled to avail themselves of the exception provided for in subparagraph 1 must be a matter for the carrier actually operating the flight. In the absence of information from the operating carrier sufficient to identify the two carriers to be designated, a system vendor must designate the carriers on a non-discriminatory basis.

11. A principal display must, wherever practicable, include connecting flights on scheduled services which are operated by participating carriers and are constructed by using a minimum number of nine connecting points. A system vendor must accept a request by a participating carrier to include an indirect service, unless the routing is in excess of 130% of the great circle distance between the two airports or unless that would lead to the exclusion of services with a shorter elapsed journey time. Connecting points with routings in excess of 130% of that great circle distance need not be used.]

Notes

[¹ All references to flights in this Annex are in accordance with Article 21b(6).]

Annex I as shown in square brackets was inserted by Council Regulation (EC) No 323/1999 (OJ L 40, 13.2.1999, p. 1) with effect from 15 March 1999.

[ANNEX II

USE OF DISTRIBUTION FACILITIES BY SUBSCRIBERS

1. A subscriber must keep accurate records covering all CRS reservation transactions. Those records must include flight numbers, reservations booking designators, date of travel, departure and arrival times, status of segments, names and initials of passengers with their contact addresses and/or telephone numbers and ticketing status. When booking or cancelling space, the subscriber must ensure that the reservation designator being used corresponds to the fare paid by the passenger.

2. A subscriber should not deliberately make duplicate reservations for the same passenger. Where confirmed space is not available on the customer's choice, the passenger may be wait-listed on that flight (if wait-list is available) and confirmed on an alternative flight.

3. When a passenger cancels a reservation, the subscriber must immediately release that space.

4. When a passenger changes an itinerary, the subscriber must ensure that all space and supplementary services are cancelled when the new reservations are made.

5. A subscriber must, where practicable, request or process all reservations for a specific itinerary and all subsequent changes through the same CRS.

6. No subscriber may request or sell airline space unless requested to do so by a consumer.

7. A subscriber must ensure that a ticket is issued in accordance with the reservation status of each segment and in accordance with the applicable time limit. A subscriber must not issue a ticket indicating a definite reservation and a particular flight unless confirmation of that reservation has been received.]

Notes

Annex II as shown in square brackets was inserted by Council Regulation (EC) No 323/1999 (OJ L 40, 13.2.1999, p. 1) with effect from 15 March 1999.

E11

EXPLANATORY NOTE ON THE EEC CODE OF CONDUCT FOR COMPUTER RESERVATION SYSTEMS

(90/C 184/02)

Official Journal C184, 25.7.1990, p. 2.

1. Introduction

During the first few months of the implementation phase of Regulation (EEC) No 2299/89 on a code of conduct for computerized reservation systems¹ a number of questions have been raised on the way in which the provisions of the code have to be applied in practical terms with respect to the programming and operation of systems. The resulting clarification would seem to be of interest to system vendors in general since it would give some guidelines in particular to the programming by the system vendors. However, the solutions outlined may not be exhaustive and other approaches may in some instances comply with the provisions of the Annex. Furthermore, other elements in a total system may well influence unfavourably solutions which otherwise would be acceptable. The Commission, therefore, must reserve to itself the possibility of examining any system in its totality with a view to assessing its total compatibility with the code of conduct. It is important, therefore, that the Commission is kept up to date with the problems and the solutions found to them in the application of the code of conduct.

Reference is made to the block exemption Regulation[2] on the application of Article [81](3) of the [EC] Treaty to certain categories of agreements between undertakings relating to computer reservation systems for air transport services.

Notes
[1] OJ No L 220, 29.7.89
[2] OJ No L 239, 30.8.89

2. Existing contracts

Existing contracts with air carriers, travel agents and subscribers may not be fully in compliance with the code. How should they be treated?

Since the code of conduct is a Regulation and directly legally binding in the Community, all relevant contracts will have to be brought in line with the provisions of the code. This does not essentially mean a renegotiation of these contracts. An additional clause to the contract sent by the system vendors to the other contracting parties, referring to the direct applicability of the code of conduct and indicating the way in which certain clauses of the contracts would consequently have to be understood, is sufficient to bring all contracting parties up to date with the effects of the code on their contractual situation.

It goes without saying that the abovementioned procedure can only be followed for amendments to those provisions in the contracts which are in contravention of the code of conduct.

3. Responsibility for information

According to Article 4(1), participating carriers and other providers of information (eg OAG or ABC) are responsible for the quality of the information. The system vendors might, in their contracts with information suppliers, adopt a clause in this respect.

It is, for example, the responsibility of participating carriers and others to ensure that system vendors can recognize and consequently indicate that there is a change of aircraft and not just a stop en route (otherwise a connecting flight might be displayed as an indirect flight).

This would mean that participating carriers and others are responsible for the submission of data in such a way that the system vendors are given sufficient information to enable them to rank the services in accordance with the requirements of the code.

If a system vendor is aware or should be aware of inaccurate or misleading information, Article 5(2) of the code of conduct comes into play.

The system vendor should ensure that the information concerning direct flights of participating carriers is comprehensive. If schedules of non-participating carriers are not displayed and it can be reasonably expected that the system vendor is aware that services of non-participating carriers on the requested route exist (that is the case when these flights are mentioned in ABC/OAG guides), then this must be clearly indicated. A general statement is not sufficient; specific messages should be displayed wherever this is the case.

4. Secondary displays

The code applies primarily to principal displays. However, the responsibility of system vendors, in respect of displays, is not limited to principal displays. In particular Article 4(2) applies to secondary displays.

5. Use of principal displays

The system vendor shall ensure that the principal display is accessed first by the subscribers, either by technical means or through the contract. Unless a consumer, that is, any person seeking information about and/or intending to purchase an air transport product, expressly requests another display, the principal displays shall be used for the provision of information and consequent transactions.

When preference has been expressed for a specific flight, then a direct access display may be used to indicate a certain seat availability even when this display does not respect the display principles. A consumer can express a preference for a specific secondary display for more than one transaction, eg a company can request a travel agent to book its employees only on a specific airline for their business travel. This can be considered as an express request for each individual booking. In such cases secondary displays can be used for information and booking purposes.

6. Information on fares

Information on fares in relation to the principal display must be complete and not misleading. This means that all publicly available air fares for the air services displayed must be included in the database (see paragraph 3) and must be displayed on a non-discriminatory basis.

7. Exclusive use of computerized reservation systems

The code of conduct does not create ticketing authorization for system vendors. A system vendor may get that authorization through the agreement with the participating air carrier. Article 8 stipulates that the basic ticketing authorization is a matter for agreement between the airline in question and the travel agent. When an agent has been given authorization to issue printed tickets by an air carrier he can then use stock for that purpose which the air carrier either has given to him or which the authorization indicates he can use (eg bank settlement plan tickets). For the purpose of printing the tickets the agent can use any printer which can do the job, and the air carrier cannot specify only the use of its own printer. However, no printing fee to the system vendor can be incurred for the air carrier which is not participating. In other words, the ticket is issued by the travel agent and not by the system vendor.

If an air carrier does participate fully in a computerized reservation system, then an authorized travel agent is free to use that computerized reservation system for ticketing on that airline. However, if an air carrier does not participate in or accept reservations or tickets from a computerized reservation system, then Article 8 does not create a right for the travel agent to use that computerized reservation system for those purposes anyway. Neither does Article 8 in any way create a right for a travel agent to make reservations or issue tickets for an air carrier.

8. Exclusivity clauses

A system vendor can link in its contracts with subscribers the fee levels with the number of bookings processed through its computerized reservation system, as long as the fee levels are cost-related.

The linkage of fee levels with a certain percentage of bookings made by the subscriber is not permitted, since the difference in fee level could not be justified by differences in costs.

9. Termination of contracts

Article 9(4) gives subscribers the right to terminate contracts with system vendors without any penalty on three months' notice irrespective of the agreed termination date. Contracts may be concluded for a period exceeding one year. If a contract is terminated before the first year has expired, real damages may be claimed. In other cases system vendors can only charge the costs directly related to the termination of the contract.

10. Relationship of fees to costs

It should be acknowledged that some costs may differ in different countries. Therefore, in order to comply with the provision of Article 10(1), it is possible, for example, to make a distinction between costs for the service and costs for communication. The fee level should be the same for the same level of service, but communication and other costs can differ from one country to another. Fee levels may reflect the differences in such costs only if these differences can be adequately demonstrated.

11. Sample for display

The system vendor should always bear in mind that the purpose is to provide the consumer with accurate and non-misleading information. It is this basic criterion which prohibits the subscribers and/or the system vendors from constructing or displaying flight options with the purpose of discriminating against and/or of giving advantage to one or more carriers or airports.

The selection of the sample of flights of participating carriers which is to be displayed on one or more pages in response to a consumer request must respect at least the following principles:

— all direct services within the time limits between the two airports or cities in question must be included, ie both nonstop services and services with intermediate stops;
— the time limits within which the sample of connecting flights is to be selected may be a specific departure time around which a bracket is then constructed or the same principle applied to arrival time. It is also possible for a system to sample according to elapsed journey time on the day in question.

A minimum number of nine connecting points shall, if possible, be used for the construction of connecting flights for inclusion in the sample for the principal display. This does not mean, however, that unrealistic travel options are included.

A routing with an elapsed journey time which is considerably longer than alternative connections and which does not offer specific advantages may be considered as unrealistic, for example.

A system vendor is obliged to include in a sample for a principal display indirect services requested by participating carriers and falling within the time limits of the consumer request, unless the routing is in excess of 130% of the great circle distance between the two airports.

Routing in excess of 130% may, at the option of the system vendor, be included. However, this must be done in a non-discriminatory way. This means in fact that objective parameters should be set to determine which of these routes are to be included. The system vendor must take all practical measures to ensure that no unrealistic travel options are included.

Paragraph 2 of the general part of the Annex is aimed to prohibit the so-called "screen padding" practice. A system vendor is not allowed to give excessive exposure to one particular travel option or to display unrealistic travel options. This means in practice that similar flights should be displayed in a comparable format; that flight options should be displayed without discrimination and without giving advantage to particular carriers or airports and that unnecessary information should be avoided, for example, when a code-shared flight is displayed then the basic individual flights of the two carriers should not be sampled and shown as well as a connection; likewise when a through flight is displayed with one flight number.

A system vendor has the option to sample and display information of any non-participating carrier in any or all of the three categories of flights set out in the Annex to the code. This information has to be displayed in an accurate, non-misleading and non-discriminatory manner as between the non-participating carriers. Within the three different categories of flights, participating carriers may be treated more favourably then non-participating carriers. Since the non-participating carrier is not providing information directly to the system vendor, it cannot be held directly responsible for the quality of the data. However, Article 4(1) of the code also refers to other information providers such as OAG or ABC. These information providers should ensure the quality of the information of non-participating airlines if they are providing the information under contract to the system vendor (see paragraph 3).

12. Ranking and quality of information in display

The ranking of the sample shall, unless the consumer requests otherwise, be in the following order:

first group: all direct non-stop flights in order of departure time;

second group: all direct flights with intermediate stop(s) in order of elapsed journey time:

— no change of aircraft may take place,
— only one flight number must be used,
— the fact that there are intermediate stops must be clearly indicated;

third group: all connecting flights in order of elapsed journey time:

— all on-line flights including a change of aircraft or a change of flight number, all interline and all code-shared flights fall within this category,

— change of aircraft and/or intermediate stops and/or change of airport must be clearly indicated. Special attention should be given to flights involving a change of aircraft where the same type of equipment is used for the different segments,

— code sharing is possible, but should be clearly indicated,

— code-shared flights may be displayed on one line or two lines but a system must be consistent in its practice. It must be quite clear that more than one airline is involved. The clearest way of doing this would be by displaying the flights on two or more lines,

— one flight number may be used for connecting flights, unless the different segments are displayed separately on a connection,

— one flight number may be used if there is a change of aircraft and/or change of terminal building involved,

— the use of one flight number when there is a change of airport included is not acceptable.

It should be noted that elapsed journey time should be realistic. The participating carriers are primarily responsible for the accurate and non-misleading scheduling of departure and arrival time. The use of penalty points by the system vendor is not in conformity with the provisions of the code, for instance for a change of terminal. However, it is the responsibility of the airline or the vendor to consider a realistic connecting time when providing or constructing a connection.

In addition to the abovementioned default display there shall be a possibility for the consumer to request displays:

1. ranked by departure time,
2. ranked by arrival time, and
3. ranked by elapsed journey time;

or any combination of:

1. departure time and elapsed journey time, and
2. arrival time and elapsed journey time is also possible.

E12

COMMISSION REGULATION (EC) No 1459/2006

of 28 September 2006
on the application of Article 81(3) of the Treaty to certain categories of agreements
and concerted practices concerning consultations on passenger tariffs on scheduled
air services and slot allocation at airports

Official Journal L 272, 3.10.2006, p. 3

Celex No: 32006R1459

THE COMMISSION OF THE EUROPEAN COMMUNITIES,

Having regard to the Treaty establishing the European Community,

Having regard to Council Regulation (EEC) No 3976/87 of 14 December 1987 on the application of Article [81](3) of the Treaty to certain categories of agreements and concerted practices in the air transport sector,[1] and in particular Article 2 thereof,

Having published a draft of this Regulation,[2]

After consulting the Advisory Committee on Restrictive Practices and Dominant Positions,

Notes
[1] OJ L 374, 31.12.1987, p. 9. Regulation as last amended by Regulation (EC) No 411/2004 (OJ L 68, 6.3.2004, p. 1).
[2] OJ C 42, 18.2.2006, p. 15.

Commentary
Regulation 1459/2006/EC: B&C: 3.085, 3.093, 12.043–12.044 **F&N:** 14.83

Whereas:

(1) Since 1 May 2004, the air transport sector has been subject to the generally applicable provisions of Council Regulation (EC) No 1/2003 of 16 December 2002 on the implementation of the rules on competition laid down in Articles 81 and 82 of the Treaty.[1]

Notes
[1] OJ L 1, 4.1.2003, p. 1. Regulation as amended by Regulation (EC) No 411/2004 (OJ L 68, 6.3.2004, p. 1).

(2) Regulation (EC) No 1/2003 provides that agreements which fall under Article 81(1) of the Treaty which satisfy the conditions of Article 81(3) are not prohibited, no prior decision to that effect being required. In principle, undertakings and associations must now assess for themselves whether their agreements, concerted practices and decisions are compatible with Article 81 of the Treaty.

(3) Regulation (EEC) No 3976/87 empowers the Commission to apply Article 81(3) of the Treaty by Regulation to certain categories of agreements, decisions or concerted practices relating directly or indirectly to the provision of air transport services on routes between Community airports and on routes between the Community and third countries.

(4) Agreements, decisions or concerted practices concerning consultations on passenger tariffs on scheduled air services and slot allocation and airport scheduling are liable to restrict competition and affect trade between Member States.

(5) However, since such agreements, decisions or concerted practices may benefit air transport users and/or air carriers, Commission Regulation (EEC) No 1617/93 of 25 June 1993 on the application of Article [81](3) of the Treaty to certain categories of agreements and concerted practices concerning joint planning and coordination of schedules, joint operations, consultations on passenger and cargo tariffs on scheduled air services and slot allocation at airports[1] declared that Article 81(1) of the Treaty did not apply, *inter alia*, to certain agreements, decisions or concerted practices concerning consultations on tariffs and slot allocation at airports for air services between Community airports. Regulation (EEC) No 1617/93 expired on 30 June 2005.

Notes
[1] OJ L 155, 26.6.1993, p. 18. Regulation as last amended by the 2003 Act of Accession.

(6) In June 2004 the Commission initiated a consultation on the revision of Regulation (EEC) No 1617/93 to determine whether the block exemption should be discontinued, maintained in its original form or extended in scope. The Commission received responses from Member States, airlines, travel agents and consumer groups.

(7) In view of the results of the consultation and the directly applicable exception system introduced by Regulation (EC) No 1/2003, there are not sufficient grounds to continue to declare by Regulation Article 81(1) inapplicable to consultations on slot allocation and airport scheduling agreements or to consultations on tariffs for the carriage of passengers, with their baggage, on scheduled air services between Community airports. However, the airline industry should be allowed sufficient time to adapt to the new situation and to assess for themselves whether their agreements and practices are compatible with Article 81 of the Treaty and, if necessary, to amend them. Since Regulation (EEC) No 1617/93 has already expired, it is necessary to adopt a new block exemption regulation for a transitional period.

(8) Arrangements on slot allocation at airports and airport scheduling can improve the efficient utilization of airport capacity and airspace, facilitate air-traffic control and help to spread the supply of air transport services from the airport. Entry to congested airports must remain possible if competition is not to be eliminated. In order to provide a satisfactory degree of security and transparency, arrangements in this respect can only be accepted if all air carriers concerned can

participate in the negotiations, and if the allocation is made on a non-discriminatory and transparent basis.

(9) A block exemption should be granted until 31 December 2006 in respect of consultations on slot allocation and airport scheduling in so far as they concern air services the point of origin and/or point of destination of which is located in the Community. After 31 December 2006, the airline industry should assess for itself whether agreements and concerted practices between undertakings and decisions of associations of undertakings caught by Article 81(1) of the Treaty satisfy the conditions of Article 81(3). The assessment should, *inter alia*, consider whether all carriers concerned can participate in the consultations on slot allocation and airport scheduling, and whether these consultations are conducted in a non-discriminatory and transparent manner. This Regulation is without prejudice to Council Regulation (EEC) No 95/93 of 18 January 1993 on common rules for the allocation of slots at Community airports.[1]

Notes

[1] OJ L 14, 22.1.1993, p. 1. Regulation as last amended by Regulation (EC) No 793/2004 of the European Parliament and of the Council (OJ L 138, 30.4.2004, p. 50).

(10) Consultations on passenger tariffs may contribute to the generalised acceptance of interlinable passenger tariffs to the benefit of air carriers as well as air transport users. However, consultations must not exceed the aim of facilitating interlining.

(11) The results of the consultation initiated by the Commission in June 2004 for the review of Regulation (EEC) No 1617/93 indicate that the intra-Community air transport market has evolved in such a way that the degree of assurance that consultations on tariffs will continue to meet all the criteria of Article 81(3) of the Treaty is declining.

(12) A block exemption should therefore be granted until 31 December 2006 in respect of consultations on tariffs for the carriage of passengers, with their baggage, on scheduled air services between Community airports. After that date, the airline industry should assess for itself whether agreements and concerted practices between undertakings and decisions of associations of undertakings caught by Article 81(1) of the Treaty satisfy the conditions of Article 81(3) of the Treaty.

(13) Since 1 May 2004, the Commission has been empowered to apply Article 81(3) of the Treaty by Regulation in respect of air services on routes between the Community and third countries, as well as on routes between Community airports.

(14) In contrast to intra-Community air-traffic, air services between Member States and third countries are, in general, governed by bilateral air services agreements. The nature and level of detail of regulatory requirements set out in these agreements vary widely. Without prejudice to Community law, including Regulation (EC) No 847/2004 of the European Parliament and of the Council of 29 April 2004 on the negotiation and implementation of air service agreements between Member States and third countries,[1] it is common for air services agreements to restrict and/or regulate market access and/or pricing, which may impede competition between air carriers on routes between the Community and third countries. Moreover, it is common for air services agreements to restrict the ability of carriers to enter into the kind of bilateral cooperation agreements which provide consumers with alternatives to the International Air Transport Association (IATA) interlining system.

Notes

[1] OJ L 157, 30.4.2004, p. 7, as corrected by OJ L 195, 2.6.2004, p. 3.

(15) On routes between the Community and third countries, the proportion of passenger journeys involving a connection is appreciably higher than on intra-Community international flights. Therefore, the benefits of interlining for consumers obtained through tariff consultations should be greater on routes between the Community and third countries.

(16) It can be assumed with sufficient certainty that consultations on tariffs for the carriage of passengers, with their baggage, on scheduled air services between points in the Community and points in third countries currently satisfy the conditions of Article 81(3) of the Treaty.

However, markets for air transport are undergoing rapid developments. A short block exemption should therefore be granted in respect of such consultations until 31 October 2007.

(17) The competent authorities in the United States of America and Australia are reviewing their respective antitrust policies in respect of IATA tariff conferences. These reviews are likely to be completed by June 2007. It is, therefore, appropriate that the Commission should review the block exemption for passenger tariff conferences with respect to routes between the Community and these countries by that time.

Commentary
Recital 17: **B&C:** 12.045

(18) Data should be collected to enhance the Commission's knowledge on the relative use of the passenger tariffs set in the consultations and their relative importance for actual interlining on scheduled services between the Community and third countries. The data should also enable the Commission to better assess the effects of regulatory restrictions flowing from bilateral air services agreements. Air carriers participating in consultations should therefore be required to collect data for all fare classes in which interlinable fares are agreed, for each IATA season starting from 1 May 2004.

(19) In accordance with Article 4 of Regulation (EEC) No 3976/87, this Regulation should apply with retroactive effect to agreements, decisions and concerted practices in existence on the date of entry into force of this Regulation, provided that they meet the conditions for exemption set out in this Regulation.

(20) Community law in the field of civil aviation that is relevant for the internal market was extended to the area comprising the Community and Norway, Iceland and Liechtenstein through the Agreement on the European Economic Area. Therefore, flights between the Community and Norway, Iceland and Liechtenstein should be treated in the same manner as intra-Community flights. Community legislation is extended to the territory covered by the EEA Agreement through decisions by the EEA Joint Committee. For the purposes of this Regulation, however, it is necessary to stipulate that the block exemption provided for in respect of extra-Community flights does not apply to flights between points in the Community and points in Norway, Iceland and Liechtenstein.

Commentary
Recital 20: **B&C:** 12.045

(21) Community law in the field of civil aviation that is relevant for the internal market was extended to the area comprising the Community and Switzerland through the Agreement between the European Community and the Swiss Confederation on Air Transport.[1] As long as that agreement remains in force, therefore, flights between the Community and Switzerland should be treated in the same manner as intra-Community flights. Community legislation is extended to the territory covered by the Agreement through decisions by the Joint Committee set up under the Agreement. For the purposes of this Regulation, however, it is necessary to stipulate that the block exemption provided for in respect of routes between the Community and third countries does not apply to flights between points in the Community and points in Switzerland.

Notes
[1] Agreement between the European Community and the Swiss Confederation on Air Transport (OJ L 114, 30.4.2002, p. 73).

(22) This Regulation is without prejudice to the application of Article 82 of the Treaty,

Commentary
Recital 22: **B&C:** 12.045

HAS ADOPTED THIS REGULATION:

Article 1
Exemptions

Pursuant to Article 81(3) of the Treaty and subject to the provisions of this Regulation, it is hereby declared that Article 81(1) of the Treaty shall not apply to agreements between undertakings in the air transport sector, decisions by associations of such undertakings and concerted practices between such undertakings which have as their purpose one or more of the following:

(a) the holding of consultations on slot allocation and airport scheduling in so far as they concern air services the point of origin and/or point of destination of which is located in the Community;

(b) the holding of consultations on tariffs for the carriage of passengers, with their baggage, on scheduled air services between points in the Community or between points in the Community, on the one hand, and points in Switzerland, Norway, Iceland or Liechtenstein, on the other;

(c) the holding of consultations on tariffs for the carriage of passengers, with their baggage, on scheduled air services between points in the Community, on the one hand, and points in Australia or the United States of America, on the other;

(d) the holding of consultations on tariffs for the carriage of passengers, with their baggage, on scheduled air services between points in the Community, on the one hand, and points in third countries other than those referred to in points (b) and (c), on the other.

Article 2
Slot allocation and airport scheduling

1. Article 1(a) shall apply only if the following conditions are fulfilled:

(a) the consultations are open to all air carriers having expressed an interest in the slots which are the subject of the consultations;

(b) rules of priority are established and applied without discrimination, whether direct or indirect, on the grounds of carrier identity, nationality or category of service, which take into account constraints or air traffic distribution rules laid down by competent national or international authorities and give due consideration to the needs of the travelling publics and of the airport concerned; subject to point (c), such rules of priority may take account of rights acquired by air carriers through the use of particular slots in the previous corresponding season;

(c) slots are allocated to new entrants, as defined in Article 2(b) of Regulation (EEC) No 95/93 as follows:

   (i) at Community airports, a 50% share of newly created or unused slots and slots which have been given up by a carrier during or by the end of the season or which otherwise become available to enable new entrants to be able to compete effectively with established carriers on routes to/from the airport in question; the share allocated to new entrants may be less than 50% if requests by new entrants represent less than 50% of all applications for such new slots;

   (ii) at third country airports, a sufficient share of such available slots for entry at congested airports to remain possible on routes between such airports and points located in the Community;

(d) the rules of priority, once established, are made available on request to any interested party;

(e) air carriers participating in the consultations have access, at the time of the consultations at the latest, to information relating to:

   (i) historical slots by air carrier, in chronological order, for all air carriers at the airport;

   (ii) requested slots (initial submissions) by air carrier, in chronological order, for all air carriers;

   (iii) allocated slots, and outstanding slot requests listed individually in chronological order, by air carrier, for all air carriers;

   (iv) remaining slots available;

   (v) full details of the criteria used in the allocation;

(f) if a request for slots is not accepted, the air carrier concerned is entitled to a statement of the reasons therefor.

2. The Commission and the Member States concerned shall be entitled to send observers to consultations on slot allocation and airport scheduling held in the context of a multilateral meeting in advance of each season. For this purpose, air carriers shall give the Member States concerned and the Commission the same notice as is given to participants of the date, venue and subject matter of the consultations. The notice given to the Member States concerned and to the Commission shall not be less than 10 days. Such notice shall be given:

(a) to the Member States concerned according to procedures to be established by the competent authorities of those Member States;

(b) to the Commission according to procedures to be published in the *Official Journal of the European Union*.

Commentary
Art 2: **B&C:** 12.044
Art 2(2): **B&C:** 3.085, 12.043

Article 3
Consultations on passenger tariffs

1. Article 1(b), (c) and (d) shall apply only if the following conditions are fulfilled:

(a) the participants in the consultations only discuss air fares to be paid by air transport users directly to a participating air carrier or to its authorised agents, for carriage as passengers on a scheduled service, and the conditions relating to those passenger tariffs; the consultations do not extend to the capacity for which such tariffs are to be available;

(b) the consultations give rise to interlining, that is to say, air transport users are able, in respect of the types of passenger tariffs and of the seasons which were the subject of the consultations:

(i) to combine on a single ticket the service which was the subject of the consultations, with services on the same or on connecting routes operated by other air carriers, whereby the applicable passenger tariffs and conditions are set by the airline or airlines effecting carriage; and

(ii) in so far as is permitted by the conditions governing the initial reservation, to change a reservation on a service which was the subject of the consultations onto a service on the same route operated by another air carrier at the passenger tariffs and conditions applied by that other carrier;

(c) an air carrier is entitled to refuse to allow combinations and changes of reservation for objective and non-discriminatory reasons of a technical or commercial nature, in particular where the air carrier effecting carriage is concerned about the credit worthiness of the air carrier who would be collecting payment for this carriage, in which case the latter air carrier must be notified thereof in writing;

(d) the passenger tariffs which are the subject of the consultations are applied by participating air carriers without discrimination on grounds of passenger nationality or place of residence;

(e) participation in the consultations is voluntary and open to any air carrier who operates or intends to operate direct or indirect services on the route concerned;

(f) the consultations are not binding on participants, that is to say, following the consultations the participants retain the right to act independently in respect of passenger tariffs;

(g) the consultations do not entail agreement on agents' remuneration or other elements of the tariffs discussed.

2. Air carriers participating in consultations on passenger tariffs for scheduled air services between points in the Community and points in third countries other than those referred to in Article 1(b) shall collect data with regard to:

(a) the number of tickets issued at tariffs set in the consultations in the total number of tickets issued for travel between the Community and third countries other than those referred to in Article 1(b);

(b) the extent to which tickets at tariffs set in the consultations are issued for travel on a journey where the passenger interlines;

(c) the extent to which tickets which are not at tariffs set in the consultations are issued for travel on a journey where the passenger interlines.

That data shall be collected for all types of ticket and fare which are the subject of the consultations. The data shall make it possible to distinguish between the various forms of cooperation between air carriers that enable passengers to combine services operated by more than one carrier onto a single ticket. The data collected shall be provided to the Commission by or on behalf of the air carriers involved for each IATA season, starting from 1 May 2004. The data may be made available to the competent authorities of the Member States.

3. The Commission and the Member States concerned shall be entitled to send observers to consultations on passenger tariffs. For this purpose, air carriers shall give the Member States concerned and the Commission the same notice as is given to participants of the date, venue and subject matter of the consultations. The notice given to the Member States concerned and to the Commission shall not be less than 10 days.

Such notice shall be given:

(a) to the Member States concerned according to procedures to be established by the competent authorities of those Member States;

(b) to the Commission according to procedures to be published in the *Official Journal of the European Union*. A full report on the consultations shall be submitted to the Commission by or on behalf of the air carriers involved at the same time as it is submitted to participants, but not later than six weeks after the consultations were held.

Commentary
Art 3: **B&C:** 12.045
Art 3(3): **B&C:** 3.085, 12.043

Article 4
Entry into force

This Regulation shall enter into force on the 20th day following its publication in the *Official Journal of the European Union*.

Exemptions granted pursuant to Article 1(a) and (b) shall apply until 31 December 2006.

Exemptions granted pursuant to Article 1(c) shall apply until 30 June 2007.

Exemptions granted pursuant to Article 1(d) shall apply until 31 October 2007.

This Regulation shall apply with retroactive effect to agreements, decisions and concerted practices in existence on the day on which it enters into force, with effect from the time when the conditions set out in this Regulation were fulfilled.

Notes
Date of entry into force: 23 October 2006.

Commentary
Art 4: **B&C:** 3.085, 12.044

This Regulation shall be binding in its entirety and directly applicable in all Member States.

Done at Brussels, 28 September 2006.

E13

CLARIFICATION OF THE COMMISSION RECOMMENDATIONS ON THE APPLICATION OF THE COMPETITION RULES TO NEW TRANSPORT INFRASTRUCTURE PROJECTS

(97/C 298/05)

(Text with EEA relevance)

Official Journal C 298, 30.9.1997, p. 5

Celex No: 31997Y0930(01)

INTRODUCTION

1. Accelerating the implementation of the trans-European transport network is one of the Community's objectives for developing competitiveness and growth in Europe. The high-level group on public-private partnership financing of trans-European network transport projects has stressed the need to create a legal environment that facilitates public–private partnerships.

2. Application of the competition rules is often seen as a factor of uncertainty that impedes the investment of private capital into trans-European network transport projects at an early stage. This is because, in applying the competition rules, the specific features of each project have to be taken into consideration and a case-by-case analysis carried out, in particular where individual exemptions are to be granted within the meaning of Article [81](3).

3. So as to ensure that all the parties involved in creating such infrastructures are better informed, the Commission has already presented to the Council and the European Parliament recommendations on the application of the competition rules to transport infrastructure projects (see the annual report drawn up in December 1995, COM(95) 571, published on 30 May 1996, and in particular Annex II to the chapter on the trans-European transport network).

4. As a follow-up to the conclusions of the high-level group, which underlined the usefulness of clarifying those recommendations, the Commission in this communication further explains the application of the competition rules, in particular as regards:

— the general objectives that are being pursued in this field,
— the procedure for examining trans-European network transport projects,
— the conditions for exemption of capacity reservation agreements,

and attempts to reconcile the need to maximize the financial viability of rail projects with the provision of free and non-discriminatory access to infrastructure.

The objectives that are being pursued

5. In order to promote competitiveness and job-creation, the Commission's policy is to ensure effective competition and the development of intra-Community trade, while at the same time ensuring that the measures proposed or adopted are compatible with the tasks in the general economic interest performed by public services.

6. The various Community policies relating to the development of competition in the transport sector are interrelated, in particular through implementation of the principle of freedom to provide services, application of the competition rules laid down in the Treaty and the rules governing the award of contracts.

7. Public-private partnership projects must in all cases take account of the general framework provided by the common transport policy and, as regards rail projects in particular, the Commission's White Paper published in December 1992 (COM(92) 494).

8. The integration process involved in the establishment of the single market shapes the economic context in which competition policy is applied. The principle of freedom to provide transport services, laid down in the Treaty, is implemented through the establishment of the common transport policy.

9. For example, with regard to railways, Directive 91/440/EEC gives railway undertakings and international groupings of railway undertakings, subject to certain conditions, right of access to Member States' railway networks in providing international rail transport services. Directive 91/440/EEC establishes a legal framework within which the rules on competition between undertakings can operate. Within this legal framework, undertakings can conclude agreements, whose lawfulness has to be assessed in the light of the competition rules.

10. A distinction should be made here between the competition rules and the rules governing public procurement, which are often confused: the Community's competition rules as laid down in the Treaty, particularly Articles [81] and [82], do not contain any specific provisions on procedures for calls for tenders in public procurement.

11. As pointed out in the Commission's December 1995 annual report and the final report of the high-level group on public-private partnership financing of trans-European network transport projects, two distinct sets of rules governing public procurement apply at Community level to transport infrastructure work, namely Directive 93/37/EEC, which concerns the award of public works contracts, and Directive 93/38/EEC, which concerns entities operating in the water, electricity, transport and telecommunications sectors.

12. This Communication does not set out to deal with the application of the rules governing the award of public works contracts to trans-European network transport projects. It sets out only to clarify the Commission's recommendations regarding the application of the competition rules laid down in Articles [81] and [82] of the Treaty to trans-European network transport projects.

13. Competition policy comprises three main areas, namely restrictive agreements and practices (anti-trust), the regulated or monopoly sectors and State aid. The Commission has a whole range of interdependent instruments at its disposal in implementing competition policy. The rules governing restrictive agreements and abuses of dominant positions, the provisions on merger control and State aid and the rules on market liberalization all have the same objective: preventing distortions of competition within the single market.

14. In implementing the Community competition rules, the Commission is particularly vigilant to ensure that firms do not try to neutralize the pro-competitive effects of the single market through agreements that introduce or maintain market partitioning. Such practices include certain types of vertical agreements and/or distribution systems and unjustified refusals to allow third parties non-discriminatory access to essential infrastructure.

15. The Commission pursues its policy here through application of the rules governing restrictive agreements and abuses of dominant positions, i.e. Articles [81] and [82] of the Treaty.

16. Article [81] of the Treaty prohibits anti-competitive agreements between firms which may affect trade between Member States and which have as their object or effect the prevention, restriction or distortion of competition within the common market.

17. However, this prohibition may be declared inapplicable to agreements which fulfil each of the following four conditions:

— they contribute to improving the production or distribution of goods or to promoting technical or economic progress;
— they allow consumers a fair share of the resulting benefit,
— they do not impose on the undertakings concerned restrictions which are not indispensable to the attainment of these objectives;
— they do not afford the undertakings the possibility of eliminating competition in respect of a substantial part of the products in question.

18. Article [82] of the Treaty prohibits any abuse by one or more undertakings of a dominant position within the common market or in a substantial part of it in so far as it may affect trade between Member States. In contrast to Article [81] of the Treaty, Article [82] does not provide for any exemption from this prohibition.

19. The Commission is prepared to help make more information available to all parties involved in infrastructure projects (the public authorities, transport companies, banks and private investors). Project promoters are therefore invited to contact the Commission if they require any information and advice. The Commission will examine the projects in full confidentiality. If they wish to obtain any information on the competition rules, projects leaders may contract Directorate-General IV in the Commission or the Commission's "One-stop help desk" (fax: 32-2 295 65 04).

20. Project promoters should also contact their national competition authorities who will be able to provide them with all necessary information on the competition rules.

The Procedure for Examining Projects

21. In the conclusions to its report, the high-level group on public-private partnership financing of trans-European network transport projects stressed the importance of a legal environment that encourages the development of public–private partnerships.

22. In this perspective and in respecting the application of the competition rules, the Commission takes account of the specific features of each project on the basis of a case-by-case assessment.

23. A large number of trans-European network transport projects require participation agreements from the outset that bring together a large number of operators. Projects involving new railway infrastructure call for particular attention because of developments in the railways sector and the financing difficulties associated with projects having a low level of profitability.

24. Participants in any project requiring large amounts of investment require particular legal certainty regarding their commitments as from the very outset of the project. This is why project promoters would like to have the Commission's formal position on the eligibility of their project within a reasonable period of time.

25. The Commission departments, and in particular Directorate-General IV, which is responsible for competition policy, encourage parties to contact them early on, when the project is at the discussion and planning stage and before any agreements are signed. This should prevent difficulties arising after the notification of the agreements and thereby slowing down the processing of applications. It will also ensure that the Commission departments are fully informed about projects from the very start and are therefore able to process the applications more rapidly, in particular with a view to an exemption pursuant to Article [81](3) of the Treaty.

26. So that parties are able to predict when they can expect to receive a reply from the Commission, the latter in its December 1995 recommendations stated that it would do its utmost to take a final decision within a maximum period of six months of the notification of agreements, provided the parties had contacted it before finalizing the agreements and provided that it had all the necessary information for assessing the project.

Reconciling Financial Profitability and Freedom of Access to Infrastructure

27. The information obtained by the Commission from railway infrastructure project promoters indicates a number of issues regarding the application of the competition rules and the financial profitability of projects. The main issues are taking account of the different competing modes of transport, the question of infrastructure access, and the prices charged for such access.

(a) Taking account of the different competing modes of transport

28. The in-depth analysis of a project requires a definition of the relevant market. Such a definition naturally means that the different modes of transport are taken into account to establish their substitutability or their complementarity (see in particular the night services Decision of 21 September 1994 OJ L 259, 7.10.1994, p. 20, points 19, et seq.).

(b) Access to infrastructure

29. Application of the competition rules, taking due account of the specific rules applicable to the rail transport sector, is intended to prevent market partitioning through anti-competitive practices such

as unjustified refusals to allow third parties non-discriminatory access to facilities which they need in order to carry on their activity.

30. A clear distinction should be drawn between two concepts: firstly, the concept of freedom of access deriving from the principle of freedom to provide services and, secondly, the concept of capacity reservation agreement for operational requirements planned over a reasonable period.

31. The issuing of access rights to railway companies is the responsibility of the public authorities, which act in accordance with the Community and national rules in force (in particular, as regards railways, Article 10 of Directive 91/440/EEC and Directive 95/19/EC). One of the objectives of these provisions is to ensure competition and the development of intra-Community trade without jeopardizing the public services' performance of their tasks in the general economic interest.

32. The reservation of infrastructure capacity for an operator providing transport services planned in advance represents an agreement concluded between the infrastructure manager or the entity responsible for capacity allocation and the transport undertaking. Any such agreement differs from the issuing of a right of access by the competent public authority. Moreover, it may be caught by Article [81] or Article [82] of the Treaty.

33. In the consultations carried out in drawing up the Commission's December 1995 recommendations and the report of the high-level group on public–private partnership financing of trans-European network transport projects, the participants stressed that the infrastructure manager must be able, if he so wishes, to reserve at least part of the capacity for transport companies, which contribute to the financial equilibrium of the project. There is also the question of the use of the transport equipment purchased by companies which are also project promoters.

34. The infrastructure in question requires a high level of investment, repayable over very long periods, and with a generally low level of profitability. Project promoters should therefore be able to obtain certain guarantees as regards the utilization of the new infrastructure and the payment of user charges.

35. Project promoters nevertheless recognize that the reservation of capacity over a long period is contrary to the principles of freedom of access to infrastructure and of competition.

36. Where there is congestion on the infrastructure, capacity reservation agreements that are not essential to the operation of transport services may become a means of prohibiting access to other transport companies that have the necessary rights of access. The competition rules do not allow such practices. It must be ensured that specific agreements concluded by participants in an infrastructure project do not prevent infrastructure access for transport services authorized to have such access within the meaning of the provisions of Directive 91/440/EEC and Directive 95/19/EC.

37. In addition, allowing infrastructure access to various users providing competing transport services or services on separate markets can facilitate the financing of the infrastructure by ensuring greater revenue from its use. For example, if several transport companies providing freight transport services on one and the same line or different transport services such as freight and passenger services are allowed access to one and the same rail infrastructure, this will mean that a larger number of user charges will be paid.

38. For these reasons, the recommendations put forward by the Commission in December 1995 are based on the following general criteria:

  (i) if infrastructure operator wishes to give transport companies the opportunity of reserving capacity from the very start of the project, this opportunity should be offered to all Community undertakings that may be interested;

  (ii) the capacity reserved for a company should be proportional to the direct or indirect financial commitments entered into by that company and should correspond to the operational requirements planned over a reasonable period;

  (iii) a new infrastructure is generally not congested as soon as it is put into service. A company, or a group of companies within the meaning of Article 3 of Directive 91/440/EEC, should therefore not have all the capacity available reserved for it. Some of the capacity should remain available so as to allow competing services to be operated by other companies;

  (iv) the companies awarded user rights may not object to these rights being withdrawn if they are not used;

(v) the duration of capacity reservation agreements must not exceed a reasonable period of time, to be agreed in each particular instance.

39. These recommendations do not take the place of case-by-case assessment of projects, in accordance with the procedural rules laid down for this purpose.

40. So as to clarify the scope of the December 1995 recommendations, it is none the less useful to make the following specific points:

— the recommendations are without prejudice to the rules applicable to the award of contracts, and in particular the provisions of Directives 93/37/EEC and 93/38/EEC. Consequently, they do not create any new obligation as regards tendering, but are simply intended to make project promoters aware of the advantages of providing prior information to potential users. Such an approach makes it possible to attract the largest number of infrastructure users and to decrease the risk of complaints on the part of transport operators, who might feel discriminated against if sufficient information were not provided,

— in principle, capacity reservation agreements that are justified by operational requirements do not pose any difficulty under the competition rules as long as the infrastructure is not congested, since no entry barrier is created,

— if there is congestion, an agreement reserving capacity that is essential for the effective operation of transport services planned over a reasonable period may justify the granting of an exemption pursuant to Article [81](3), where all the conditions laid down therein are fulfilled.

41. The purpose of the recommendations is to inform infrastructure project promoters of the need to provide for capacity systems that are sufficiently flexible over time and do not create distortions of competition between users, while at the same time safeguarding over a reasonable period the legitimate interests of each of the users, and in particular those who have supported the project from the outset.

42. A clear separation of responsibilities for the allocation of capacity may facilitate examination of notified projects. For example, the following separations may prevent conflicts of interest as regards capacity allocation:

— the infrastructure manager is responsible for allocating capacity on a non-discriminatory basis and does not himself operate transport services on the infrastructure

— the manager operates transport services on the infrastructure (or controls users), but an independent body is responsible for allocating capacity on a non-discriminatory basis.

(c) The prices charged for access to infrastructure

43. As regards the prices charged for access to infrastructure, the infrastructure manager may pursue the aim of attracting the largest possible number of users from the outset by charging low prices during an initial period. In principle, the competition rules do not oppose any such commercial policy on the part of the infrastructure manager provided that the prices charged apply, over one and the same period, in a non-discriminatory manner to all competing users. The competition rules laid down in the Treaty do not allow the application of dissimilar conditions to equivalent transactions, since this creates distortions of competition that may affect trade between Member States.

44. If project promoters require any further information on these questions, they should contact the Commission and, in particular, Directorate-General IV, which is responsible for competition policy (see point 19).

E14

DIRECTIVE 2003/54/EC OF THE EUROPEAN PARLIAMENT AND OF THE COUNCIL

of 26 June 2003
concerning common rules for the internal market in electricity
and repealing Directive 96/92/EC

Official Journal L 176, 15.7.2003, p. 37

Celex No: 32003L0054

Notes

EEA application: this Directive was adopted with appropriate adaptations by EEA Joint Committee Decision No 146/2005 (OJ No L 53, 23.2.2006, p. 43 and EEA Supplement No 10, 23.2.2005, p. 17), entry into force pending: see the EEA Agreement, Annex IV, Point 22.

Commentary

Directive 2003/54/EC: B&C: 12.060, 12.075 F&N: 12.49, 12.55, 12.108, 12.348, 12.362, 12.393, 12.426
Recitals 24–26: F&N: 12.109

THE EUROPEAN PARLIAMENT AND THE COUNCIL OF THE EUROPEAN UNION,

Having regard to the Treaty establishing the European Community, and in particular Article 47(2), Article 55 and Article 95 thereof,

Having regard to the proposals from the Commission,[1]

Having regard to the Opinion of the European Economic and Social Committee,[2]

Having consulted the Committee of the Regions,

Acting in accordance with the procedure laid down in Article 251 of the Treaty,[3]

Notes

[1] OJ C 240 E, 28.8.2001, p. 60, and OJ C 227 E, 24.9.2002, p. 393.

[2] OJ C 36, 8.2.2002, p. 10.

[3] Opinion of the European Parliament of 13 March 2002 (OJ C 47 E, 27.2.2003, p. 350), Council Common Position of 3 February 2003 (OJ C 50 E, 4.3.2003, p. 15) and Decision of the European Parliament of 4 June 2003 [OJ C 68 E, 18.3.2004, p. 148–211E].

Whereas:

(1) Directive 96/92/EC of the European Parliament and of the Council of 19 December 1996 concerning common rules for the internal market in electricity[1] has made significant contributions towards the creation of an internal market for electricity.

Notes

[1] OJ L 27, 30.1.1997, p. 20.

---

(2) Experience in implementing this Directive shows the benefits that may result from the internal market in electricity, in terms of efficiency gains, price reductions, higher standards of service and increased competitiveness. However, important shortcomings and possibilities for improving the functioning of the market remain, notably concrete provisions are needed to ensure a level playing field in generation and to reduce the risks of market dominance and predatory behaviour, ensuring non-discriminatory transmission and distribution tariffs, through access to the network on the basis of tariffs published prior to their entry into force, and ensuring that the rights of small

and vulnerable customers are protected and that information on energy sources for electricity generation is disclosed, as well as reference to sources, where available, giving information on their environmental impact.

(3) At its meeting in Lisbon on 23 and 24 March 2000, the European Council called for rapid work to be undertaken to complete the internal market in both electricity and gas sectors and to speed up liberalisation in these sectors with a view to achieving a fully operational internal market. The European Parliament, in its Resolution of 6 July 2000 on the Commission's second report on the state of liberalisation of energy markets, requested the Commission to adopt a detailed timetable for the achievement of accurately defined objectives with a view to gradually but completely liberalising the energy market.

(4) The freedoms which the Treaty guarantees European citizens — free movement of goods, freedom to provide services and freedom of establishment — are only possible in a fully open market, which enables all consumers freely to choose their suppliers and all suppliers freely to deliver to their customers.

(5) The main obstacles in arriving at a fully operational and competitive internal market relate amongst other things to issues of access to the network, tarification issues and different degrees of market opening between Member States.

(6) For competition to function, network access must be non-discriminatory, transparent and fairly priced.

Commentary
Recital 6: F&N: 12.389

---

(7) In order to complete the internal electricity market, non-discriminatory access to the network of the transmission or the distribution system operator is of paramount importance. A transmission or distribution system operator may comprise one or more undertakings.

(8) In order to ensure efficient and non-discriminatory network access it is appropriate that the distribution and transmission systems are operated through legally separate entities where vertically integrated undertakings exist. The Commission should assess measures of equivalent effect, developed by Member States to achieve the aim of this requirement, and, where appropriate, submit proposals to amend this Directive. It is also appropriate that the transmission and distribution system operators have effective decision-making rights with respect to assets necessary to maintain, operate and develop networks when the assets in question are owned and operated by vertically integrated undertakings. It is necessary that the independence of the distribution system operators and the transmission system operators be guaranteed especially with regard to generation and supply interests. Independent management structures must therefore be put in place between the distribution system operators and the transmission system operators and any generation/supply companies.

It is important however to distinguish between such legal separation and ownership unbundling. Legal separation does not imply a change of ownership of assets and nothing prevents similar or identical employment conditions applying throughout the whole of the vertically integrated undertakings. However, a non-discriminatory decision-making process should be ensured through organisational measures regarding the independence of the decision-makers responsible.

(9) In the case of small systems the provision of ancillary services may have to be ensured by transmission system operators (TSOs) interconnected with small systems.

(10) While this Directive is not addressing ownership issues it is recalled that in case of an undertaking performing transmission or distribution and which is separated in its legal form from those undertakings performing generation and/or supply activities, the designated system operators may be the same undertaking owning the infrastructure.

(11) To avoid imposing a disproportionate financial and administrative burden on small distribution companies, Member States should be able, where necessary, to exempt such companies from the legal distribution unbundling requirements.

(12) Authorisation procedures should not lead to an administrative burden disproportionate to the size and potential impact of electricity producers.

(13) Further measures should be taken in order to ensure transparent and non discriminatory tariffs for access to networks. Those tariffs should be applicable to all system users on a non discriminatory basis.

(14) In order to facilitate the conclusion of contracts by an electricity undertaking established in a Member State for the supply of electricity to eligible customers in another Member State, Member States and, where appropriate, national regulatory authorities should work towards more homogenous conditions and the same degree of eligibility for the whole of the internal market.

(15) The existence of effective regulation, carried out by one or more national regulatory authorities, is an important factor in guaranteeing non-discriminatory access to the network. Member States specify the functions, competences and administrative powers of the regulatory authorities. It is important that the regulatory authorities in all Member States share the same minimum set of competences. Those authorities should have the competence to fix or approve the tariffs, or at least, the methodologies underlying the calculation of transmission and distribution tariffs. In order to avoid uncertainty and costly and time consuming disputes, these tariffs should be published prior to their entry into force.

(16) The Commission has indicated its intention to set up a European Regulators Group for Electricity and Gas which would constitute a suitable advisory mechanism for encouraging cooperation and coordination of national regulatory authorities, in order to promote the development of the internal market for electricity and gas, and to contribute to the consistent application, in all Member States, of the provisions set out in this Directive and Directive 2003/55/EC of the European Parliament and of the Council of 26 June 2003 concerning common rules for the internal market in natural gas[1] and in Regulation (EC) No 1228/2003 of the European Parliament and of the Council of 26 June 2003 on conditions for access to the network for cross-border exchanges in electricity.[2]

Notes
[1] See [OJ L 176, 15.7.2003, p. 57].
[2] See [OJ L 176, 15.7.2003, p. 1].

Commentary
Recital 16: B&C: 12.062

(17) In order to ensure effective market access for all market players, including new entrants, non discriminatory and cost-reflective balancing mechanisms are necessary. As soon as the electricity market is sufficiently liquid, this should be achieved through the setting up of transparent market-based mechanisms for the supply and purchase of electricity needed in the framework of balancing requirements. In the absence of such a liquid market, national regulatory authorities should play an active role to ensure that balancing tariffs are non discriminatory and cost-reflective. At the same time, appropriate incentives should be provided to balance in-put and off-take of electricity and not to endanger the system.

(18) National regulatory authorities should be able to fix or approve tariffs, or the methodologies underlying the calculation of the tariffs, on the basis of a proposal by the transmission system operator or distribution system operator(s), or on the basis of a proposal agreed between these operator(s) and the users of the network. In carrying out these tasks, national regulatory authorities should ensure that transmission and distribution tariffs are non-discriminatory and cost-reflective, and should take account of the long-term, marginal, avoided network costs from distributed generation and demand-side management measures.

(19) All Community industry and commerce, including small and medium-sized enterprises, and all Community citizens that enjoy the economic benefits of the internal market should also be able to enjoy high levels of consumer protection, and in particular households and, where Member States deem it appropriate, small enterprises should also be able to enjoy public service guarantees, in particular with regard to security of supply and reasonable tariffs, for reasons of fairness, competitiveness and indirectly to create employment.

(20) Electricity customers should be able to choose their supplier freely. Nonetheless a phased approach should be taken to completing the internal market for electricity to enable industry to

adjust and ensure that adequate measures and systems are in place to protect the interests of customers and ensure they have a real and effective right to choose their supplier.

Commentary
Recital 20: F&N: 12.63

(21) Progressive market opening towards full competition should as soon as possible remove differences between Member States. Transparency and certainty in the implementation of this Directive should be ensured.

(22) Nearly all Member States have chosen to ensure competition in the electricity generation market through a transparent authorisation procedure. However, Member States should ensure the possibility to contribute to security of supply through the launching of a tendering procedure or an equivalent procedure in the event that sufficient electricity generation capacity is not built on the basis of the authorisation procedure. Member States should have the possibility, in the interests of environmental protection and the promotion of infant new technologies, of tendering for new capacity on the basis of published criteria. New capacity includes *inter alia* renewables and combined heat and power (CHP).

(23) In the interest of security of supply, the supply/demand balance in individual Member States should be monitored, and monitoring should be followed by a report on the situation at Community level, taking account of interconnection capacity between areas. Such monitoring should be carried out sufficiently early to enable appropriate measures to be taken if security of supply is compromised. The construction and maintenance of the necessary network infrastructure, including interconnection capacity, should contribute to ensuring a stable electricity supply. The maintenance and construction of the necessary network infrastructure, including interconnection capacity and decentralised electricity generation, are important elements in ensuring a stable electricity supply.

(24) Member States should ensure that household customers and, where Member States deem it appropriate, small enterprises, enjoy the right to be supplied with electricity of a specified quality at clearly comparable, transparent and reasonable prices. In order to ensure the maintenance of the high standards of public service in the Community, all measures taken by Member States to achieve the objectives of this Directive should be regularly notified to the Commission. The Commission should regularly publish a report analysing measures taken at national level to achieve public service objectives and comparing their effectiveness, with a view to making recommendations as regards measures to be taken at national level to achieve high public service standards. Member States should take the necessary measures to protect vulnerable customers in the context of the internal electricity market. Such measures can differ according to the particular circumstances in the Member States in question and may include specific measures relating to the payment of electricity bills, or more general measures taken in the social security system. When universal service is also provided to small enterprises, measures to ensure that this universal service is provided may differ according to households and small enterprises.

(25) The Commission has indicated its intention to take initiatives especially as regards the scope of the labelling provision and notably on the manner in which the information on the environmental impact in terms of at least emissions of CO_2 and the radioactive waste resulting from electricity production from different energy sources, could be made available in a transparent, easily accessible and comparable manner throughout the European Union and on the manner in which the measures taken in the Member States to control the accuracy of the information provided by suppliers could be streamlined.

(26) The respect of the public service requirements is a fundamental requirement of this Directive, and it is important that common minimum standards, respected by all Member States, are specified in this Directive, which take into account the objectives of common protection, security of supply, environmental protection and equivalent levels of competition in all Member States. It is important that the public service requirements can be interpreted on a national basis, taking into account national circumstances and subject to the respect of Community law.

(27) Member States may appoint a supplier of last resort. This supplier may be the sales division of a vertically integrated undertaking, that also performs the functions of distribution, provided that it meets the unbundling requirements of this Directive.

(28) Measures implemented by Member States to achieve the objectives of social and economic cohesion may include, in particular, the provision of adequate economic incentives, using, where appropriate, all existing national and Community tools. These tools may include liability mechanisms to guarantee the necessary investment.

(29) To the extent to which measures taken by Member States to fulfil public service obligations constitute State aid under Article 87(1) of the Treaty, there is an obligation according to Article 88(3) of the Treaty to notify them to the Commission.

(30) The requirement to notify the Commission of any refusal to grant authorisation to construct new generation capacity has proven to be an unnecessary administrative burden and should therefore be dispensed with.

(31) Since the objective of the proposed action, namely the creation of a fully operational internal electricity market, in which fair competition prevails, cannot be sufficiently achieved by the Member States and can therefore, by reason of the scale and effects of the action, be better achieved at Community level, the Community may adopt measures in accordance with the principle of subsidiarity as set out in Article 5 of the Treaty. In accordance with the principle of proportionality, as set out in that Article, this Directive does not go beyond what is necessary in order to achieve that objective.

(32) In the light of the experience gained with the operation of Council Directive 90/547/EEC of 29 October 1990 on the transit of electricity through transmission grids,[1] measures should be taken to ensure homogeneous and non-discriminatory access regimes for transmission, including cross-border flows of electricity between Member States. To ensure homogeneity in the treatment of access to the electricity networks, also in the case of transit, that Directive should be repealed.

Notes

[1] OJ L 313, 13.11.1990, p. 30. Directive as last amended by Commission Directive 98/75/EC (OJ L 276, 13.10.1998, p. 9).

---

(33) Given the scope of the amendments that are being made to Directive 96/92/EC, it is desirable, for reasons of clarity and rationalisation, that the provisions in question should be recast.

(34) This Directive respects the fundamental rights, and observes the principles, recognised in particular by the Charter of Fundamental Rights of the European Union,

HAVE ADOPTED THIS DIRECTIVE:

CHAPTER I
SCOPE AND DEFINITIONS

Article 1
Scope

This Directive establishes common rules for the generation, transmission, distribution and supply of electricity. It lays down the rules relating to the organisation and functioning of the electricity sector, access to the market, the criteria and procedures applicable to calls for tenders and the granting of authorisations and the operation of systems.

Article 2
Definitions

For the purposes of this Directive:

1. "generation" means the production of electricity;
2. "producer" means a natural or legal person generating electricity;
3. "transmission" means the transport of electricity on the extra high-voltage and high-voltage interconnected system with a view to its delivery to final customers or to distributors, but not including supply;

4. "transmission system operator" means a natural or legal person responsible for operating, ensuring the maintenance of and, if necessary, developing the transmission system in a given area and, where applicable, its interconnections with other systems, and for ensuring the long term ability of the system to meet reasonable demands for the transmission of electricity;

5. "distribution" means the transport of electricity on high-voltage, medium voltage and low voltage distribution systems with a view to its delivery to customers, but not including supply;

6. "distribution system operator" means a natural or legal person responsible for operating, ensuring the maintenance of and, if necessary, developing the distribution system in a given area and, where applicable, its interconnections with other systems and for ensuring the long term ability of the system to meet reasonable demands for the distribution of electricity;

7. "customers" means wholesale and final customers of electricity;

8. "wholesale customers" means any natural or legal persons who purchase electricity for the purpose of resale inside or outside the system where they are established;

9. "final customers" means customers purchasing electricity for their own use;

10. "household customers" means customers purchasing electricity for their own household consumption, excluding commercial or professional activities;

11. "non-household customers" means any natural or legal persons purchasing electricity which is not for their own household use and shall include producers and wholesale customers;

12. "eligible customers" means customers who are free to purchase electricity from the supplier of their choice within the meaning of Article 21 of this Directive;

13. "interconnectors" means equipment used to link electricity systems;

14. "interconnected system" means a number of transmission and distribution systems linked together by means of one or more interconnectors;

15. "direct line" means either an electricity line linking an isolated production site with an isolated customer or an electricity line linking an electricity producer and an electricity supply undertaking to supply directly their own premises, subsidiaries and eligible customers;

16. "economic precedence" means the ranking of sources of electricity supply in accordance with economic criteria;

17. "ancillary services" means all services necessary for the operation of a transmission or distribution system;

18. "system users" means any natural or legal persons supplying to, or being supplied by, a transmission or distribution system;

19. "supply" means the sale, including resale, of electricity to customers;

20. "integrated electricity undertaking" means a vertically or horizontally integrated undertaking;

21. "vertically integrated undertaking" means an undertaking or a group of undertakings whose mutual relationships are defined in Article 3(3) of Council Regulation (EEC) No 4064/89 of 21 December 1989 on the control of concentrations between undertakings[1] and where the undertaking/group concerned is performing at least one of the functions of transmission or distribution and at least one of the functions of generation or supply of electricity;

22. "related undertaking" means affiliated undertakings, within the meaning of Article 41 of the Seventh Council Directive 83/349/EEC of 13 June 1983 based on Article 44(2)(g)[2] of the Treaty on consolidated accounts,[3] and/or associated undertakings, within the meaning of Article 33(1) thereof, and/or undertakings which belong to the same shareholders;

23. "horizontally integrated undertaking" means an undertaking performing at least one of the functions of generation for sale, or transmission, or distribution, or supply of electricity, and another non electricity activity;

24. "tendering procedure" means the procedure through which planned additional requirements and replacement capacity are covered by supplies from new or existing generating capacity;

25. "long-term planning" means the planning of the need for investment in generation and transmission and distribution capacity on a long term basis, with a view to meeting the demand of the system for electricity and securing supplies to customers;

26. "small isolated system" means any system with consumption of less than 3000 GWh in the year 1996, where less than 5% of annual consumption is obtained through interconnection with other systems;

27. "micro isolated system" means any system with consumption less than 500 GWh in the year 1996, where there is no connection with other systems;

28. "security" means both security of supply and provision of electricity, and technical safety;

29. "energy efficiency/demand-side management" means a global or integrated approach aimed at influencing the amount and timing of electricity consumption in order to reduce primary energy consumption and peak loads by giving precedence to investments in energy efficiency measures, or other measures, such as interruptible supply contracts, over investments to increase generation capacity, if the former are the most effective and economical option, taking into account the positive environmental impact of reduced energy consumption and the security of supply and distribution cost aspects related to it;

30. "renewable energy sources" means renewable non-fossil energy sources (wind, solar, geothermal, wave, tidal, hydropower, biomass, landfill gas, sewage treatment plant gas and biogases);

31. "distributed generation" means generation plants connected to the distribution system.

Notes

[1] OJ L 395, 30.12.1989, p. 1. Regulation as last amended by Regulation (EC) No 1310/97 (OJ L 180, 9.7.1997, p. 1).

[2] The title of Directive 83/349/EEC has been adjusted to take account of the renumbering of the Articles of the Treaty establishing the European Community in accordance with Article 12 of the Treaty of Amsterdam; the original reference was to Article 54(3)(g).

[3] OJ L 193, 18.7.1983, p. 1. Directive as last amended by Directive 2001/65/EC of the European Parliament and of the Council (OJ L 283, 27.10.2001, p. 28).

Commentary

Art 2(9): B&C: 12.061
Art 2(10): B&C: 12.061
Art 2(12): B&C: 12.061

CHAPTER II
GENERAL RULES FOR THE ORGANISATION OF THE SECTOR

Article 3
Public service obligations and customer protection

1. Member States shall ensure, on the basis of their institutional organisation and with due regard to the principle of subsidiarity, that, without prejudice to paragraph 2, electricity undertakings are operated in accordance with the principles of this Directive with a view to achieving a competitive, secure and environmentally sustainable market in electricity, and shall not discriminate between these undertakings as regards either rights or obligations.

2. Having full regard to the relevant provisions of the Treaty, in particular Article 86 thereof, Member States may impose on undertakings operating in the electricity sector, in the general economic interest, public service obligations which may relate to security, including security of supply, regularity, quality and price of supplies and environmental protection, including energy efficiency and climate protection. Such obligations shall be clearly defined, transparent, non discriminatory, verifiable and shall guarantee equality of access for EU electricity companies to national consumers. In relation to security of supply, energy efficiency/demand-side management and for the fulfilment of environmental goals, as referred to in this paragraph, Member States may introduce the implementation of long term planning, taking into account the possibility of third parties seeking access to the system.

3. Member States shall ensure that all household customers, and, where Member States deem it appropriate, small enterprises, (namely enterprises with fewer than 50 occupied persons and an annual turnover or balance sheet not exceeding EUR 10 million), enjoy universal service, that is the right to be supplied with electricity of a specified quality within their territory at reasonable, easily and clearly comparable and transparent prices. To ensure the provision of universal service, Member States may appoint a supplier of last resort. Member States shall impose on distribution companies an obligation to connect customers to their grid under terms, conditions and tariffs set in accordance with the procedure laid down in Article 23(2). Nothing in this Directive shall

prevent Member States from strengthening the market position of the domestic, small and medium-sized consumers by promoting the possibilities of voluntary aggregation of representation for this class of consumers.

The first subparagraph shall be implemented in a transparent and non-discriminatory way and shall not impede the opening of the market provided for in Article 21.

4. When financial compensation, other forms of compensation and exclusive rights which a Member State grants for the fulfilment of the obligations set out in paragraphs 2 and 3 are provided, this shall be done in a non-discriminatory and transparent way.

5. Member States shall take appropriate measures to protect final customers, and shall in particular ensure that there are adequate safeguards to protect vulnerable customers, including measures to help them avoid disconnection. In this context, Member States may take measures to protect final customers in remote areas. They shall ensure high levels of consumer protection, particularly with respect to transparency regarding contractual terms and conditions, general information and dispute settlement mechanisms. Member States shall ensure that the eligible customer is in fact able to switch to a new supplier. As regards at least household customers, these measures shall include those set out in Annex A.

6. Member States shall ensure that electricity suppliers specify in or with the bills and in promotional materials made available to final customers:

(a) the contribution of each energy source to the overall fuel mix of the supplier over the preceding year;
(b) at least the reference to existing reference sources, such as web-pages, where information on the environmental impact, in terms of at least emissions of CO_2 and the radioactive waste resulting from the electricity produced by the overall fuel mix of the supplier over the preceding year is publicly available.

With respect to electricity obtained via an electricity exchange or imported from an undertaking situated outside the Community, aggregate figures provided by the exchange or the undertaking in question over the preceding year may be used.

Member States shall take the necessary steps to ensure that the information provided by suppliers to their customers pursuant to this Article is reliable.

7. Member States shall implement appropriate measures to achieve the objectives of social and economic cohesion, environmental protection, which may include energy efficiency/demand-side management measures and means to combat climate change, and security of supply. Such measures may include, in particular, the provision of adequate economic incentives, using, where appropriate, all existing national and Community tools, for the maintenance and construction of the necessary network infrastructure, including interconnection capacity.

8. Member States may decide not to apply the provisions of Articles 6, 7, 20 and 22 insofar as their application would obstruct the performance, in law or in fact, of the obligations imposed on electricity undertakings in the general economic interest and insofar as the development of trade would not be affected to such an extent as would be contrary to the interests of the Community. The interests of the Community include, amongst others, competition with regard to eligible customers in accordance with this Directive and Article 86 of the Treaty.

9. Member States shall, upon implementation of this Directive, inform the Commission of all measures adopted to fulfil universal service and public service obligations, including consumer protection and environmental protection, and their possible effect on national and international competition, whether or not such measures require a derogation from this Directive. They shall inform the Commission subsequently every two years of any changes to such measures, whether or not they require a derogation from this Directive.

Commentary
Art 3: F&N: 12.110
Art 3(2): B&C: 12.065
Art 3(3): B&C: 12.061
Art 3(5): B&C: 12.061

Article 4
Monitoring of security of supply

Member States shall ensure the monitoring of security of supply issues. Where Member States consider it appropriate they may delegate this task to the regulatory authorities referred to in Article 23(1). This monitoring shall, in particular, cover the supply/demand balance on the national market, the level of expected future demand and envisaged additional capacity being planned or under construction, and the quality and level of maintenance of the networks, as well as measures to cover peak demand and to deal with shortfalls of one or more suppliers. The competent authorities shall publish every two years, by 31 July at the latest, a report outlining the findings resulting from the monitoring of these issues, as well as any measures taken or envisaged to address them and shall forward this report to the Commission forthwith.

Article 5
Technical rules

Member States shall ensure that technical safety criteria are defined and that technical rules establishing the minimum technical design and operational requirements for the connection to the system of generating installations, distribution systems, directly connected consumers' equipment, interconnector circuits and direct lines are developed and made public. These technical rules shall ensure the interoperability of systems and shall be objective and non discriminatory. They shall be notified to the Commission in accordance with Article 8 of Directive 98/34/EC of the European Parliament and of the Council of 22 June 1998 laying down a procedure for the provision of information in the field of technical standards and regulations and of rules on Information Society Services.[1]

Notes

[1] OJ L 204, 21.7.1998, p. 37. Directive as amended by Directive 98/48/EC (OJ L 217, 5.8.1998, p. 18).

CHAPTER III
GENERATION

Article 6
Authorisation procedure for new capacity

1. For the construction of new generating capacity, Member States shall adopt an authorisation procedure, which shall be conducted in accordance with objective, transparent and non discriminatory criteria.

2. Member States shall lay down the criteria for the grant of authorisations for the construction of generating capacity in their territory. These criteria may relate to:

(a) the safety and security of the electricity system, installations and associated equipment;
(b) protection of public health and safety;
(c) protection of the environment;
(d) land use and siting;
(e) use of public ground;
(f) energy efficiency;
(g) the nature of the primary sources;
(h) characteristics particular to the applicant, such as technical, economic and financial capabilities;
(i) compliance with measures adopted pursuant to Article 3.

3. Member States shall ensure that authorisation procedures for small and/or distributed generation take into account their limited size and potential impact.

4. The authorisation procedures and criteria shall be made public. Applicants shall be informed of the reasons for any refusal to grant an authorisation. The reasons must be objective, non-discriminatory, well founded and duly substantiated. Appeal procedures shall be made available to the applicant.

Article 7
Tendering for new capacity

1. Member States shall ensure the possibility, in the interests of security of supply, of providing for new capacity or energy efficiency/demand-side management measures through a tendering procedure or any procedure equivalent in terms of transparency and non-discrimination, on the basis of published criteria. These procedures can, however, only be launched if on the basis of the authorisation procedure the generating capacity being built or the energy efficiency/demand-side management measures being taken are not sufficient to ensure security of supply.

2. Member States may ensure the possibility, in the interests of environmental protection and the promotion of infant new technologies, of tendering for new capacity on the basis of published criteria. This tender may relate to new capacity or energy efficiency/demand-side management measures. A tendering procedure can, however, only be launched if on the basis of the authorisation procedure the generating capacity being built or the measures being taken are not sufficient to achieve these objectives.

3. Details of the tendering procedure for means of generating capacity and energy efficiency/demand-side management measures shall be published in the *Official Journal of the European Union* at least six months prior to the closing date for tenders.

The tender specifications shall be made available to any interested undertaking established in the territory of a Member State so that it has sufficient time in which to submit a tender.

With a view to ensuring transparency and non-discrimination the tender specifications shall contain a detailed description of the contract specifications and of the procedure to be followed by all tenderers and an exhaustive list of criteria governing the selection of tenderers and the award of the contract, including incentives, such as subsidies, which are covered by the tender. These specifications may also relate to the fields referred to in Article 6(2).

4. In invitations to tender for the requisite generating capacity, consideration must also be given to electricity supply offers with long term guarantees from existing generating units, provided that additional requirements can be met in this way.

5. Member States shall designate an authority or a public body or a private body independent from electricity generation, transmission, distribution and supply activities, which may be a regulatory authority referred to in Article 23(1), to be responsible for the organisation, monitoring and control of the tendering procedure referred to in paragraphs 1 to 4. Where a transmission system operator is fully independent from other activities not relating to the transmission system in ownership terms, the transmission system operator may be designated as the body responsible for organising, monitoring and controlling the tendering procedure. This authority or body shall take all necessary steps to ensure confidentiality of the information contained in the tenders.

CHAPTER IV
TRANSMISSION SYSTEM OPERATION

Article 8
Designation of Transmission System Operators

Member States shall designate, or shall require undertakings which own transmission systems to designate, for a period of time to be determined by Member States having regard to considerations of efficiency and economic balance, one or more transmission system operators. Member States shall ensure that transmission system operators act in accordance with Articles 9 to 12.

Article 9
Tasks of Transmission System Operators

Each transmission system operator shall be responsible for:

(a) ensuring the long-term ability of the system to meet reasonable demands for the transmission of electricity;
(b) contributing to security of supply through adequate transmission capacity and system reliability;
(c) managing energy flows on the system, taking into account exchanges with other interconnected systems. To that end, the transmission system operator shall be responsible for ensuring a secure,

reliable and efficient electricity system and, in that context, for ensuring the availability of all necessary ancillary services insofar as this availability is independent from any other transmission system with which its system is interconnected;

(d) providing to the operator of any other system with which its system is interconnected sufficient information to ensure the secure and efficient operation, coordinated development and interoperability of the interconnected system;

(e) ensuring non-discrimination as between system users or classes of system users, particularly in favour of its related undertakings;

(f) providing system users with the information they need for efficient access to the system.

Commentary
Art 9: B&C: 12.061

Article 10
Unbundling of Transmission System Operators

1. Where the transmission system operator is part of a vertically integrated undertaking, it shall be independent at least in terms of its legal form, organisation and decision making from other activities not relating to transmission. These rules shall not create an obligation to separate the ownership of assets of the transmission system from the vertically integrated undertaking.

2. In order to ensure the independence of the transmission system operator referred to in paragraph 1, the following minimum criteria shall apply:

(a) those persons responsible for the management of the transmission system operator may not participate in company structures of the integrated electricity undertaking responsible, directly or indirectly, for the day-to-day operation of the generation, distribution and supply of electricity;

(b) appropriate measures must be taken to ensure that the professional interests of the persons responsible for the management of the transmission system operator are taken into account in a manner that ensures that they are capable of acting independently;

(c) the transmission system operator shall have effective decision-making rights, independent from the integrated electricity undertaking, with respect to assets necessary to operate, maintain or develop the network. This should not prevent the existence of appropriate coordination mechanisms to ensure that the economic and management supervision rights of the parent company in respect of return on assets, regulated indirectly in accordance with Article 23(2), in a subsidiary are protected. In particular, this shall enable the parent company to approve the annual financial plan, or any equivalent instrument, of the transmission system operator and to set global limits on the levels of indebtedness of its subsidiary. It shall not permit the parent company to give instructions regarding day-to-day operations, nor with respect to individual decisions concerning the construction or upgrading of transmission lines, that do not exceed the terms of the approved financial plan, or any equivalent instrument;

(d) the transmission system operator shall establish a compliance programme, which sets out measures taken to ensure that discriminatory conduct is excluded, and ensure that observance of it is adequately monitored. The programme shall set out the specific obligations of employees to meet this objective. An annual report, setting out the measures taken, shall be submitted by the person or body responsible for monitoring the compliance programme to the regulatory authority referred to in Article 23(1) and shall be published.

Commentary
Art 10: F&N: 12.234

Article 11
Dispatching and balancing

1. Without prejudice to the supply of electricity on the basis of contractual obligations, including those which derive from the tendering specifications, the transmission system operator shall, where it has this function, be responsible for dispatching the generating installations in its area and for determining the use of interconnectors with other systems.

2. The dispatching of generating installations and the use of interconnectors shall be determined on the basis of criteria which may be approved by the Member State and which must be objective, published and applied in a non discriminatory manner which ensures the proper functioning of the internal market in electricity. They shall take into account the economic precedence of electricity from available generating installations or interconnector transfers and the technical constraints on the system.

3. A Member State may require the system operator, when dispatching generating installations, to give priority to generating installations using renewable energy sources or waste or producing combined heat and power.

4. A Member State may, for reasons of security of supply, direct that priority be given to the dispatch of generating installations using indigenous primary energy fuel sources, to an extent not exceeding in any calendar year 15% of the overall primary energy necessary to produce the electricity consumed in the Member State concerned.

5. Member States may require transmission system operators to comply with minimum standards for the maintenance and development of the transmission system, including interconnection capacity.

6. Transmission system operators shall procure the energy they use to cover energy losses and reserve capacity in their system according to transparent, non-discriminatory and market-based procedures, whenever they have this function.

7. Rules adopted by transmission system operators for balancing the electricity system shall be objective, transparent and non-discriminatory, including rules for the charging of system users of their networks for energy imbalance. Terms and conditions, including rules and tariffs, for the provision of such services by transmission system operators shall be established pursuant to a methodology compatible with Article 23(2) in a non-discriminatory and cost-reflective way and shall be published.

Commentary
Art 11: F&N: 12.78

Article 12
Confidentiality for Transmission System Operators

Without prejudice to Article 18 or any other legal duty to disclose information, the transmission system operator shall preserve the confidentiality of commercially sensitive information obtained in the course of carrying out its business. Information disclosed regarding its own activities, which may be commercially advantageous, shall be made available in a non-discriminatory manner.

CHAPTER V
DISTRIBUTION SYSTEM OPERATION

Article 13
Designation of Distribution System Operators

Member States shall designate or shall require undertakings that own or are responsible for distribution systems to designate, for a period of time to be determined by Member States having regard to considerations of efficiency and economic balance, one or more distribution system operators. Member States shall ensure that distribution system operators act in accordance with Articles 14 to 16.

Article 14
Tasks of Distribution System Operators

1. The distribution system operator shall maintain a secure, reliable and efficient electricity distribution system in its area with due regard for the environment.

2. In any event, it must not discriminate between system users or classes of system users, particularly in favour of its related undertakings.

3. The distribution system operator shall provide system users with the information they need for efficient access to the system.

4. A Member State may require the distribution system operator, when dispatching generating instal-lations, to give priority to generating installations using renewable energy sources or waste or produc-ing combined heat and power.

5. Distribution system operators shall procure the energy they use to cover energy losses and reserve capacity in their system according to transparent, non-discriminatory and market based procedures, whenever they have this function. This requirement shall be without prejudice to using electricity acquired under contracts concluded before 1 January 2002.

6. Where distribution system operators are responsible for balancing the electricity distribution sys-tem, rules adopted by them for that purpose shall be objective, transparent and non discriminatory, including rules for the charging of system users of their networks for energy imbalance. Terms and conditions, including rules and tariffs, for the provision of such services by distribution system opera-tors shall be established in accordance with Article 23(2) in a non-discriminatory and cost-reflective way and shall be published.

7. When planning the development of the distribution network, energy efficiency/demand-side management measures and/or distributed generation that might supplant the need to upgrade or replace electricity capacity shall be considered by the distribution system operator.

Commentary
Art 14(2): B&C: 12.061 F&N: 12.389

Article 15
Unbundling of Distribution System Operators

1. Where the distribution system operator is part of a vertically integrated undertaking, it shall be independent at least in terms of its legal form, organisation and decision making from other activities not relating to distribution. These rules shall not create an obligation to separate the ownership of assets of the distribution system operator from the vertically integrated undertaking.

2. In addition to the requirements of paragraph 1, where the distribution system operator is part of a vertically integrated undertaking, it shall be independent in terms of its organisation and decision making from the other activities not related to distribution. In order to achieve this, the following minimum criteria shall apply:

(a) those persons responsible for the management of the distribution system operator may not partic-ipate in company structures of the integrated electricity undertaking responsible, directly or indi-rectly, for the day-to-day operation of the generation, transmission or supply of electricity;

(b) appropriate measures must be taken to ensure that the professional interests of the persons respon-sible for the management of the distribution system operator are taken into account in a manner that ensures that they are capable of acting independently;

(c) the distribution system operator shall have effective decision-making rights, independent from the integrated electricity undertaking, with respect to assets necessary to operate, maintain or develop the network. This should not prevent the existence of appropriate coordination mecha-nisms to ensure that the economic and management supervision rights of the parent company in respect of return on assets, regulated indirectly in accordance with Article 23(2), in a subsidiary are protected. In particular, this shall enable the parent company to approve the annual financial plan, or any equivalent instrument, of the distribution system operator and to set global limits on the levels of indebtedness of its subsidiary. It shall not permit the parent company to give instruc-tions regarding day-to-day operations, nor with respect to individual decisions concerning the construction or upgrading of distribution lines, that do not exceed the terms of the approved financial plan, or any equivalent instrument;

(d) the distribution system operator shall establish a compliance programme, which sets out mea-sures taken to ensure that discriminatory conduct is excluded, and ensure that observance of it is adequately monitored. The programme shall set out the specific obligations of employees to meet this objective. An annual report, setting out the measures taken, shall be submitted by the person or body responsible for monitoring the compliance programme to the regulatory authority referred to in Article 23(1) and published.

Member States may decide not to apply paragraphs 1 and 2 to integrated electricity undertakings serving less than 100000 connected customers, or serving small isolated systems.

Commentary
Art 15: F&N: 12.234

Article 16
Confidentiality for Distribution System Operators

Without prejudice to Article 18 or any other legal duty to disclose information, the distribution system operator must preserve the confidentiality of commercially sensitive information obtained in the course of carrying out its business, and shall prevent information about its own activities which may be commercially advantageous being disclosed in a discriminatory manner.

Commentary
Art 16: F&N: 12.78

Article 17
Combined operator

The rules in Articles 10(1) and 15(1) do not prevent the operation of a combined transmission and distribution system operator, which is independent in terms of its legal form, organisation and decision making from other activities not relating to transmission or distribution system operation and which meets the requirements set out in points (a) to (d). These rules shall not create an obligation to separate the ownership of assets of the combined system from the vertically integrated undertaking:

(a) those persons responsible for the management of the combined system operator may not participate in company structures of the integrated electricity undertaking responsible, directly or indirectly, for the day-to-day operation of the generation, or supply of electricity;

(b) appropriate measures must be taken to ensure that the professional interests of the persons responsible for the management of the combined system operator are taken into account in a manner that ensures that they are capable of acting independently;

(c) the combined system operator shall have effective decision-making rights, independent from the integrated electricity undertaking, with respect to assets necessary to operate, maintain and develop the network. This should not prevent the existence of appropriate coordination mechanisms to ensure that the economic and management supervision rights of the parent company in respect of return on assets, regulated indirectly in accordance with Article 23(2), in a subsidiary are protected. In particular, this shall enable the parent company to approve the annual financial plan, or any equivalent instrument, of the combined system operator and to set global limits on the levels of indebtedness of its subsidiary. It shall not permit the parent company to give instructions regarding day-to-day operations, nor with respect to individual decisions concerning the construction or upgrading of transmission and distribution lines, that do not exceed the terms of the approved financial plan, or any equivalent instrument;

(d) the combined system operator shall establish a compliance programme which sets out measures taken to ensure that discriminatory conduct is excluded, and ensure that observance of it is adequately monitored. The programme shall set out the specific obligations of employees to meet this objective. An annual report, setting out the measures taken, shall be submitted by the person or body responsible for monitoring the compliance programme to the regulatory authority referred to in Article 23(1) and published.

CHAPTER VI
UNBUNDLING AND TRANSPARENCY OF ACCOUNTS

Article 18
Right of access to accounts

1. Member States or any competent authority they designate, including the regulatory authorities referred to in Article 23, shall, insofar as necessary to carry out their functions, have right of access to the accounts of electricity undertakings as set out in Article 19.

2. Member States and any designated competent authority, including the regulatory authorities referred to in Article 23, shall preserve the confidentiality of commercially sensitive information. Member States may provide for the disclosure of such information where this is necessary in order for the competent authorities to carry out their functions.

Article 19
Unbundling of accounts

1. Member States shall take the necessary steps to ensure that the accounts of electricity undertakings are kept in accordance with paragraphs 2 to 3.

2. Electricity undertakings, whatever their system of ownership or legal form, shall draw up, submit to audit and publish their annual accounts in accordance with the rules of national law concerning the annual accounts of limited liability companies adopted pursuant to the Fourth Council Directive 78/660/EC of 25 July 1978 based on Article 44(2)(g)[1] of the Treaty on the annual accounts of certain types of companies.[2]

Undertakings which are not legally obliged to publish their annual accounts shall keep a copy of these at the disposal of the public in their head office.

3. Electricity undertakings shall, in their internal accounting, keep separate accounts for each of their transmission and distribution activities as they would be required to do if the activities in question were carried out by separate undertakings, with a view to avoiding discrimination, cross subsidisation and distortion of competition. They shall also keep accounts, which may be consolidated, for other electricity activities not relating to transmission or distribution. Until 1 July 2007, they shall keep separate accounts for supply activities for eligible customers and supply activities for non-eligible customers. Revenue from ownership of the transmission/distribution system shall be specified in the accounts. Where appropriate, they shall keep consolidated accounts for other, non-electricity activities. The internal accounts shall include a balance sheet and a profit and loss account for each activity.

4. The audit referred to in paragraph 2 shall, in particular, verify that the obligation to avoid discrimination and cross-subsidies referred to in paragraph 3, is respected.

Notes

[1] The title of Directive 78/660/EEC has been adjusted to take account of the renumbering of the Articles of the Treaty establishing the European Community in accordance with Article 12 of the Treaty of Amsterdam; the original reference was to Article 54(3)(g).

[2] OJ L 222, 14.8.1978, p. 11. Directive as last amended by Directive 2001/65/EC of the European Parliament and of the Council (OJ L 283, 27.10.2001, p. 28).

Commentary
Art 19(3): F&N: 12.391

CHAPTER VII
ORGANISATION OF ACCESS TO THE SYSTEM

Article 20
Third party access

1. Member States shall ensure the implementation of a system of third party access to the transmission and distribution systems based on published tariffs, applicable to all eligible customers and applied objectively and without discrimination between system users. Member States shall ensure that these tariffs, or the methodologies underlying their calculation, are approved prior to their entry

into force in accordance with Article 23 and that these tariffs, and the methodologies — where only methodologies are approved — are published prior to their entry into force.

2. The operator of a transmission or distribution system may refuse access where it lacks the necessary capacity. Duly substantiated reasons must be given for such refusal, in particular having regard to Article 3. Member States shall ensure, where appropriate and when refusal of access takes place, that the transmission or distribution system operator provides relevant information on measures that would be necessary to reinforce the network. The party requesting such information may be charged a reasonable fee reflecting the cost of providing such information.

Commentary
Art 20: F&N: 12.389
Art 20(2): F&N: 12.404

Article 21
Market opening and reciprocity

1. Member States shall ensure that the eligible customers are:

(a) until 1 July 2004, the eligible customers as specified in Article 19(1) to (3) of Directive 96/92/EC. Member States shall publish by 31 January each year the criteria for the definition of these eligible customers;
(b) from 1 July 2004, at the latest, all non-household customers;
(c) from 1 July 2007, all customers.

2. To avoid imbalance in the opening of electricity markets:

(a) contracts for the supply of electricity with an eligible customer in the system of another Member State shall not be prohibited if the customer is considered as eligible in both systems involved;
(b) in cases where transactions as described in point (a) are refused because of the customer being eligible only in one of the two systems, the Commission may oblige, taking into account the situation in the market and the common interest, the refusing party to execute the requested supply at the request of the Member State where the eligible customer is located.

Article 22
Direct lines

1. Member States shall take the measures necessary to enable:

(a) all electricity producers and electricity supply undertakings established within their territory to supply their own premises, subsidiaries and eligible customers through a direct line;
(b) any eligible customer within their territory to be supplied through a direct line by a producer and supply undertakings.

2. Member States shall lay down the criteria for the grant of authorisations for the construction of direct lines in their territory. These criteria must be objective and non discriminatory.

3. The possibility of supplying electricity through a direct line as referred to in paragraph 1 shall not affect the possibility of contracting electricity in accordance with Article 20.

4. Member States may make authorisation to construct a direct line subject either to the refusal of system access on the basis, as appropriate, of Article 20 or to the opening of a dispute settlement procedure under Article 23.

5. Member States may refuse to authorise a direct line if the granting of such an authorisation would obstruct the provisions of Article 3. Duly substantiated reasons must be given for such refusal.

Article 23
Regulatory authorities

1. Member States shall designate one or more competent bodies with the function of regulatory authorities. These authorities shall be wholly independent from the interests of the electricity industry.

They shall, through the application of this Article, at least be responsible for ensuring non-discrimination, effective competition and the efficient functioning of the market, monitoring in particular:

(a) the rules on the management and allocation of interconnection capacity, in conjunction with the regulatory authority or authorities of those Member States with which interconnection exists;

(b) any mechanisms to deal with congested capacity within the national electricity system;

(c) the time taken by transmission and distribution undertakings to make connections and repairs;

(d) the publication of appropriate information by transmission and distribution system operators concerning interconnectors, grid usage and capacity allocation to interested parties, taking into account the need to treat non-aggregated information as commercially confidential;

(e) the effective unbundling of accounts, as referred to in Article 19, to ensure that there are no cross subsidies between generation, transmission, distribution and supply activities;

(f) the terms, conditions and tariffs for connecting new producers of electricity to guarantee that these are objective, transparent and non-discriminatory, in particular taking full account of the costs and benefits of the various renewable energy sources technologies, distributed generation and combined heat and power;

(g) the extent to which transmission and distribution system operators fulfil their tasks in accordance with Articles 9 and 14;

(h) the level of transparency and competition.

The authorities established pursuant to this Article shall publish an annual report on the outcome of their monitoring activities referred to in points (a) to (h).

2. The regulatory authorities shall be responsible for fixing or approving, prior to their entry into force, at least the methodologies used to calculate or establish the terms and conditions for:

(a) connection and access to national networks, including transmission and distribution tariffs. These tariffs, or methodologies, shall allow the necessary investments in the networks to be carried out in a manner allowing these investments to ensure the viability of the networks;

(b) the provision of balancing services.

3. Notwithstanding paragraph 2, Member States may provide that the regulatory authorities shall submit, for formal decision, to the relevant body in the Member State the tariffs or at least the methodologies referred to in that paragraph as well as the modifications in paragraph 4. The relevant body shall, in such a case, have the power to either approve or reject a draft decision submitted by the regulatory authority. These tariffs or the methodologies or modifications thereto shall be published together with the decision on formal adoption. Any formal rejection of a draft decision shall also be published, including its justification.

4. Regulatory authorities shall have the authority to require transmission and distribution system operators, if necessary, to modify the terms and conditions, tariffs, rules, mechanisms and methodologies referred to in paragraphs 1, 2 and 3, to ensure that they are proportionate and applied in a non-discriminatory manner.

5. Any party having a complaint against a transmission or distribution system operator with respect to the issues mentioned in paragraphs 1, 2 and 4 may refer the complaint to the regulatory authority which, acting as dispute settlement authority, shall issue a decision within two months after receipt of the complaint. This period may be extended by two months where additional information is sought by the regulatory authority. This period may be further extended with the agreement of the complainant. Such a decision shall have binding effect unless and until overruled on appeal.

Where a complaint concerns connection tariffs for major new generation facilities, the two-month period may be extended by the regulatory authority.

6. Any party who is affected and has a right to complain concerning a decision on methodologies taken pursuant to paragraphs 2, 3 or 4 or, where the regulatory authority has a duty to consult, concerning the proposed methodologies, may, at the latest within two months, or a shorter time period as provided by Member States, following publication of the decision or proposal for a decision, submit a complaint for review. Such a complaint shall not have suspensive effect.

7. Member States shall take measures to ensure that regulatory authorities are able to carry out their duties referred to in paragraphs 1 to 5 in an efficient and expeditious manner.

8. Member States shall create appropriate and efficient mechanisms for regulation, control and transparency so as to avoid any abuse of a dominant position, in particular to the detriment of consumers, and any predatory behaviour. These mechanisms shall take account of the provisions of the Treaty, and in particular Article 82 thereof.

Until 2010, the relevant authorities of the Member States shall provide, by 31 July of each year, in conformity with competition law, the Commission with a report on market dominance, predatory and anti competitive behaviour. This report shall, in addition, review the changing ownership patterns and any practical measures taken at national level to ensure a sufficient variety of market actors or practical measures taken to enhance interconnection and competition. From 2010 onwards, the relevant authorities shall provide such a report every two years.

9. Member States shall ensure that the appropriate measures are taken, including administrative action or criminal proceedings in conformity with their national law, against the natural or legal persons responsible where confidentiality rules imposed by this Directive have not been respected.

10. In the event of cross border disputes, the deciding regulatory authority shall be the regulatory authority which has jurisdiction in respect of the system operator which refuses use of, or access to, the system.

11. Complaints referred to in paragraphs 5 and 6 shall be without prejudice to the exercise of rights of appeal under Community and national law.

12. National regulatory authorities shall contribute to the development of the internal market and of a level playing field by cooperating with each other and with the Commission in a transparent manner.

Commentary

Art 23: F&N: 12.68
Art 23(1): B&C: 12.062
Art 23(2): B&C: 12.062

Chapter VIII
Final Provisions

Article 24
Safeguard measures

In the event of a sudden crisis in the energy market and where the physical safety or security of persons, apparatus or installations or system integrity is threatened, a Member State may temporarily take the necessary safeguard measures.

Such measures must cause the least possible disturbance in the functioning of the internal market and must not be wider in scope than is strictly necessary to remedy the sudden difficulties which have arisen.

The Member State concerned shall without delay notify these measures to the other Member States, and to the Commission, which may decide that the Member State concerned must amend or abolish such measures, insofar as they distort competition and adversely affect trade in a manner which is at variance with the common interest.

Article 25
Monitoring of imports of electricity

Member States shall inform the Commission every three months of imports of electricity, in terms of physical flows, that have taken place during the previous three months from third countries.

Article 26
Derogations

1. Member States which can demonstrate, after the Directive has been brought into force, that there are substantial problems for the operation of their small isolated systems, may apply for derogations from the relevant provisions of Chapters IV, V, VI, VII, as well as Chapter III, in the case of micro isolated systems, as far as refurbishing, upgrading and expansion of existing capacity are concerned, which may be granted to them by the Commission. The latter shall inform the Member States of those applications prior to taking a decision, taking into account respect for confidentiality. This decision

shall be published in the *Official Journal of the European Union*. This Article shall also be applicable to Luxembourg.

2. A Member State which, after the Directive has been brought into force, for reasons of a technical nature has substantial problems in opening its market for certain limited groups of the non-household customers referred to in Article 21(1)(b) may apply for derogation from this provision, which may be granted to it by the Commission for a period not exceeding 18 months after the date referred to in Article 30(1). In any case, such derogation shall end on the date referred to in Article 21(1)(c).

[3. Estonia shall be granted a temporary derogation from the application of Article 21(1)(b) and (c) until 31 December 2012. Estonia shall take the measures necessary to ensure the opening of its electricity market. This shall be carried out gradually over the reference period with the aim of complete opening of the market by 1 January 2013. On 1 January 2009, the opening of the market must represent at least 35% of consumption. Estonia shall communicate annually to the Commission the consumption thresholds extending eligibility to final customers.]

Notes

Article 26(3) as shown in square brackets inserted by Council Directive 2004/85/EC (OJ L 236, 7.7.2004, p. 1), with effect from 8 July 2004.
Derogations:
2004/920/EC: Commission Decision of 20 December 2004 on a derogation from certain provisions of Directive 2003/54/EC of the European Parliament and of the Council concerning the archipelago of the Azores (notified under document number C(2004) 4880) (OJ L 389, 30.12.2004, p. 31).
2006/375/EC: Commission Decision of 23 May 2006 — Derogation from certain provisions of Directive 2003/54/EC concerning the archipelago of Madeira (notified under document number C(2006) 2008) (OJ L 142, 30.5.2006, p. 35).
2006/653/EC: Commission Decision of 25 September 2006 granting the Republic of Cyprus a derogation from certain provisions of Directive 2003/54/EC (notified under document number C(2006) 4177) (OJ L 270, 29.9.2006, p. 7).

Article 27
Review procedure

In the event that the report referred to in Article 28(3) reaches the conclusion whereby, given the effective manner in which network access has been carried out in a Member State — which gives rise to fully effective, non-discriminatory and unhindered network access — the Commission concludes that certain obligations imposed by this Directive on undertakings (including those with respect to legal unbundling for distribution system operators) are not proportionate to the objective pursued, the Member State in question may submit a request to the Commission for exemption from the requirement in question.

The request shall be notified, without delay, by the Member State to the Commission, together with all the relevant information necessary to demonstrate that the conclusion reached in the report on effective network access being ensured will be maintained.

Within three months of its receipt of a notification, the Commission shall adopt an opinion with respect to the request by the Member State concerned, and where appropriate, submit proposals to the European Parliament and to the Council to amend the relevant provisions of the Directive. The Commission may propose, in the proposals to amend the Directive, to exempt the Member State concerned from specific requirements, subject to that Member State implementing equally effective measures as appropriate.

Article 28
Reporting

1. The Commission shall monitor and review the application of this Directive and submit an overall progress report to the European Parliament and the Council before the end of the first year following the entry into force of this Directive, and thereafter on an annual basis. The report shall cover at least:

(a) the experience gained and progress made in creating a complete and fully operational internal market in electricity and the obstacles that remain in this respect, including aspects of market dominance, concentration in the market, predatory or anti-competitive behaviour and the effect of this in terms of market distortion;

(b) the extent to which the unbundling and tarification requirements contained in this Directive have been successful in ensuring fair and non-discriminatory access to the Community's electricity system and equivalent levels of competition, as well as the economic, environmental and social consequences of the opening of the electricity market for customers;

(c) an examination of issues relating to system capacity levels and security of supply of electricity in the Community, and in particular the existing and projected balance between demand and supply, taking into account the physical capacity for exchanges between areas;

(d) special attention will be given to measures taken in Member States to cover peak demand and to deal with shortfalls of one or more suppliers;

(e) the implementation of the derogation provided under Article 15(2) with a view to a possible revision of the threshold;

(f) a general assessment of the progress achieved with regard to bilateral relations with third countries which produce and export or transport electricity, including progress in market integration, the social and environmental consequences of the trade in electricity and access to the networks of such third countries;

(g) the need for possible harmonisation requirements that are not linked to the provisions of this Directive;

(h) the manner in which Member States have implemented in practice the requirements regarding energy labelling contained in Article 3(6), and the manner in which any Commission Recommendations on this issue have been taken into account.

Where appropriate, this report may include recommendations especially as regards the scope and modalities of labelling provisions including e.g. the way in which reference is made to existing reference sources and the content of these sources, and notably on the manner in which the information on the environmental impact in terms of at least emissions of CO_2 and the radioactive waste resulting from the electricity production from different energy sources could be made available in a transparent, easily accessible and comparable manner throughout the European Union and on the manner in which the measures taken by the Member States to control the accuracy of the information provided by suppliers could be streamlined, and measures to counteract negative effects of market dominance and market concentration.

2. Every two years, the report referred to in paragraph 1 shall also cover an analysis of the different measures taken in the Member States to meet public service obligations, together with an examination of the effectiveness of those measures and, in particular, their effects on competition in the electricity market. Where appropriate, this report may include recommendations as to the measures to be taken at national level to achieve high public service standards, or measures intended to prevent market foreclosure.

3. The Commission shall, no later than 1 January 2006, forward to the European Parliament and Council, a detailed report outlining progress in creating the internal electricity market. The report shall, in particular, consider:

— the existence of non-discriminatory network access;
— effective regulation;
— the development of interconnection infrastructure and the security of supply situation in the Community;
— the extent to which the full benefits of the opening of markets are accruing to small enterprises and households, notably with respect to public service and universal service standards;
— the extent to which markets are in practice open to effective competition, including aspects of market dominance, market concentration and predatory or anti-competitive behaviour;
— the extent to which customers are actually switching suppliers and renegotiating tariffs;
— price developments, including supply prices, in relation to the degree of the opening of markets;
— the experience gained in the application of the Directive as far as the effective independence of system operators in vertically integrated undertakings is concerned and whether other measures in addition to functional independence and separation of accounts have been developed which have effects equivalent to legal unbundling.

Where appropriate, the Commission shall submit proposals to the European Parliament and the Council, in particular to guarantee high public service standards.

Where appropriate, the Commission shall submit proposals to the European Parliament and the Council, in particular to ensure full and effective independence of distribution system operators before 1 July 2007. When necessary, these proposals shall, in conformity with competition law, also concern measures to address issues of market dominance, market concentration and predatory or anti-competitive behaviour.

Commentary
Art 28: B&C: 12.063

Article 29
Repeals

Directive 90/547/EEC shall be repealed with effect from 1 July 2004.

Directive 96/92/EC shall be repealed from 1 July 2004 without prejudice to the obligations of Member States concerning the deadlines for transposition and application of the said Directive. References made to the repealed Directive shall be construed as being made to this Directive and should be read in accordance with the correlation table in Annex B.

Article 30
Implementation

1. Member States shall bring into force the laws, regulations and administrative provisions necessary to comply with this Directive not later than 1 July 2004. They shall forthwith inform the Commission thereof.

2. Member States may postpone the implementation of Article 15(1) until 1 July 2007. This shall be without prejudice to the requirements contained in Article 15(2).

3. When Member States adopt these measures, they shall contain a reference to this Directive or shall be accompanied by such reference on the occasion of their official publication. The methods of making such reference shall be laid down by Member States.

Article 31
Entry into force

This Directive shall enter into force on the twentieth day following that of its publication in the *Official Journal of the European Union.*

Notes
Date of entry into force: 4 August 2003.

Article 32
Addressees

This Directive is addressed to the Member States.

Done at Brussels, 26 June 2003.

ANNEX A
MEASURES ON CONSUMER PROTECTION

Without prejudice to Community rules on consumer protection, in particular Directives 97/7/EC of the European Parliament and of the Council[1] and Council Directive 93/13/EC,[2] the measures referred to in Article 3 are to ensure that customers:

(a) have a right to a contract with their electricity service provider that specifies:
   — the identity and address of the supplier;
   — the services provided, the service quality levels offered, as well as the time for the initial connection;
   — if offered, the types of maintenance service offered;
   — the means by which up-to-date information on all applicable tariffs and maintenance charges may be obtained;

— the duration of the contract, the conditions for renewal and termination of services and of the contract, the existence of any right of withdrawal;

— any compensation and the refund arrangements which apply if contracted service quality levels are not met; and

— the method of initiating procedures for settlement of disputes in accordance with point (f).

Conditions shall be fair and well known in advance. In any case, this information should be provided prior to the conclusion or confirmation of the contract. Where contracts are concluded through intermediaries, the above information shall also be provided prior to the conclusion of the contract;

(b) are given adequate notice of any intention to modify contractual conditions and are informed about their right of withdrawal when the notice is given. Service providers shall notify their subscribers directly of any increase in charges, at an appropriate time no later than one normal billing period after the increase comes into effect. Member States shall ensure that customers are free to withdraw from contracts if they do not accept the new conditions notified to them by their electricity service provider;

(c) receive transparent information on applicable prices and tariffs and on standard terms and conditions, in respect of access to and use of electricity services;

(d) are offered a wide choice of payment methods. Any difference in terms and conditions shall reflect the costs to the supplier of the different payment systems. General terms and conditions shall be fair and transparent. They shall be given in clear and comprehensible language. Customers shall be protected against unfair or misleading selling methods;

(e) shall not be charged for changing supplier;

(f) benefit from transparent, simple and inexpensive procedures for dealing with their complaints. Such procedures shall enable disputes to be settled fairly and promptly with provision, where warranted, for a system of reimbursement and/or compensation. They should follow, wherever possible, the principles set out in Commission Recommendation 98/257/EC;[3]

(g) when having access to universal service under the provisions adopted by Member States pursuant to Article 3(3), are informed about their rights regarding universal service.

Notes
[1] OJ L 144, 4.6.1997, p. 19.
[2] OJ L 95, 21.4.1993, p. 29.
[3] OJ L 115, 17.4.1998, p. 31.

ANNEX B
CORRELATION TABLE

Directive 96/92/EC	*This Directive*
Article 1	Article 1 Scope
Article 2	Article 2 Definitions
Article 3 and 10(1)	Article 3 PSOs and Customer protection
—	Article 4 Monitoring of security of supply
Article 7(2)	Article 5 Technical rules
Article 4 and 5	Article 6 Authorisation procedure for new capacity
Article 4 and 6	Article 7 Tendering for new capacity
Article 7(1)	Article 8 Designation of TSOs
Article 7(3)–(5)	Article 9 Tasks of TSOs
Article 7(6)	Article 10 Unbundling of TSOs
Article 8	Article 11 Dispatching and balancing
Article 9	Article 12 Confidentiality for TSOs
Article 10(2) and (3)	Article 13 Designation of DSOs

Directive 96/92/EC	This Directive
Article 11	Article 14 Tasks of DSOs
—	Article 15 Unbundling of DSOs
Article 12	Article 16 Confidentiality for DSOs
—	Article 17 Combined operator
Article 13	Article 18 Right of access to accounts
Article 14	Article 19 Unbundling of accounts
Article 15–18	Article 20 Third Party Access
Article 19	Article 21 Market opening and reciprocity
Article 21	Article 22 Direct lines
Article 20(3)–(4) and 22	Article 23 Regulatory authorities
Article 23	Article 24 Safeguard measures
—	Article 25 Monitoring of imports of electricity
Article 24	Article 26 Derogations
—	Article 27 Review procedure
Article 25 and 26	Article 28 Reporting
—	Article 29 Repeals
Article 27	Article 30 Implementation
Article 28	Article 31 Entry into force
Article 29	Article 32 Addressees
	Annex A Measures on consumer protection

STATEMENTS MADE WITH REGARD TO DECOMMISSIONING AND WASTE MANAGEMENT ACTIVITIES

Interinstitutional statement

"The European Parliament, the Council and the Commission underline the need for Member States to ensure that adequate financial resources for decommissioning and waste management activities, which are audited in Member States, are actually available for the purpose for which they have been established and are managed in a transparent way, thus avoiding obstacles to fair competition in the energy market".

Commission statement

"The Commission notes the importance of ensuring that funds established for the purpose of decommissioning and waste management activities, which relate to the objectives of the Euratom Treaty, are managed in a transparent way, and used only for the said purpose. In this context, it intends, within the scope of its responsibilities of the Euratom Treaty to publish an annual report on the use of decommissioning and waste management funds. It shall pay particular attention to ensuring the full application of the relevant provisions of Community law".

E15

DIRECTIVE 2003/55/EC OF THE EUROPEAN PARLIAMENT AND OF THE COUNCIL

of 26 June 2003

concerning common rules for the internal market in natural gas and repealing Directive 98/30/EC

Official Journal L 176, 15.7.2003, p. 57

Celex No: 32003L0055

Notes

This document is reproduced as corrected by the corrigendum published at OJ L 16, 23.1.2004, p. 74.

EEA application: this Directive was adopted with appropriate adaptations by EEA Joint Committee Decision No 146/2005 (OJ No L 53, 23.2.2006, p. 43 and EEA Supplement No 10, 23.2.2005, p. 17), entry into force pending: see the EEA Agreement, Annex IV, Point 23.

Commentary

Directive 2003/55 EC: **B&C:** 10.143, 12.056, 12.075 **F&N:** 5.270, 12.19, 12.34, 12.49, 12.55, 12.108, 12.143, 12.278, 12.362, 12.394

THE EUROPEAN PARLIAMENT AND THE COUNCIL OF THE EUROPEAN UNION,

Having regard to the Treaty establishing the European Community, and in particular Article 47(2), Article 55 and Article 95 thereof,

Having regard to the proposals from the Commission,[1]

Having regard to the Opinion of the European Economic and Social Committee,[2]

Having consulted the Committee of the Regions,

Acting in accordance with the procedure laid down in Article 251 of the Treaty,[3]

Notes

[1] OJ C 240 E, 28.8.2001, p. 60 and OJ C 227 E, 24.9.2002, p. 393.

[2] OJ C 36, 8.2.2002, p. 10.

[3] Opinion of the European Parliament of 13 March 2002 (OJ C 47 E, 27.2.2003, p. 367), Council Common Position of 3 February 2003 (OJ C 50 E, 4.3.2003, p. 36) and Decision of the European Parliament of 4 June 2003 [OJ C 68 E, 18.3.2004, p. 148–211].

Whereas:

(1) Directive 98/30/EC of the European Parliament and of the Council of 22 June 1998 concerning common rules for the internal market in natural gas[1] has made significant contributions towards the creation of an internal market for gas.

Notes

[1] OJ L 204, 21.7.1998, p. 1.

---

(2) Experience in implementing this Directive shows the benefits that may result from the internal market in gas, in terms of efficiency gains, price reductions, higher standards of service and increased competitiveness. However, significant shortcomings and possibilities for improving the functioning of the market remain, notably concrete provisions are needed to ensure a level playing field and to reduce the risks of market dominance and predatory behaviour, ensuring non-discriminatory transmission and distribution tariffs, through access to the network on the basis of

tariffs published prior to their entry into force, and ensuring that the rights of small and vulnerable customers are protected.

(3) At its meeting in Lisbon on 23 and 24 March 2000, the European Council called for rapid work to be undertaken to complete the internal market in both electricity and gas sectors and to speed up liberalisation in these sectors with a view to achieving a fully operational internal market. The European Parliament, in its Resolution of 6 July 2000 on the Commission's second report on the state of liberalisation of energy markets, requested the Commission to adopt a detailed timetable for the achievement of accurately defined objectives with a view to gradually but completely liberalising the energy market.

(4) The freedoms which the Treaty guarantees European citizens — free movement of goods, freedom to provide services and freedom of establishment — are only possible in a fully open market, which enables all consumers freely to choose their suppliers and all suppliers freely to deliver to their customers.

(5) In view of the anticipated increase in dependency as regards natural gas consumption, consideration should be given to initiatives and measures to encourage reciprocal arrangements for access to third-country networks and market integration.

(6) The main obstacles in arriving at a fully operational and competitive internal market relate to, amongst other things, issues of access to the network, access to storage, tarification issues, interoperability between systems and different degrees of market opening between Member States.

(7) For competition to function, network access must be non-discriminatory, transparent and fairly priced.

(8) In order to complete the internal gas market, non-discriminatory access to the network of the transmission and distribution system operators is of paramount importance. A transmission or distribution system operator may consist of one or more undertakings.

Commentary
Recital 8: F&N: 12.389

---

(9) In case of a gas undertaking performing transmission, distribution, storage or liquefied natural gas (LNG) activities and which is separate in its legal form from those undertakings performing production and/or supply activities, the designated system operators may be the same undertaking owning the infrastructure.

(10) In order to ensure efficient and non-discriminatory network access it is appropriate that the transmission and distribution systems are operated through legally separate entities where vertically integrated undertakings exist. The Commission should assess measures of equivalent effect, developed by Member States to achieve the aim of this requirement, and, where appropriate, submit proposals to amend this Directive.
It is also appropriate that the transmission and distribution system operators have effective decision making rights with respect to assets necessary to maintain and operate and develop networks when the assets in question are owned and operated by vertically integrated undertakings.
It is important however to distinguish between such legal separation and ownership unbundling. Legal separation implies neither a change of ownership of assets and nothing prevents similar or identical employment conditions applying throughout the whole of the vertically integrated undertakings. However, a non-discriminatory decision-making process should be ensured through organisational measures regarding the independence of the decision-makers responsible.

(11) To avoid imposing a disproportionate financial and administrative burden on small distribution companies, Member States should be able, where necessary, to exempt such companies from the legal distribution unbundling requirements.

(12) In order to facilitate the conclusion of contracts by a gas undertaking established in a Member State for the supply of gas to eligible customers in another Member State, Member States and, where appropriate, national regulatory authorities should work towards more homogenous conditions and the same degree of eligibility for the whole of the internal market.

(13) The existence of effective regulation, carried out by one or more national regulatory authorities, is an important factor in guaranteeing non-discriminatory access to the network. Member States specify the functions, competences and administrative powers of the regulatory authorities. It is

important that the regulatory authorities in all Member States share the same minimum set of competences. Those authorities should have the competence to fix or approve the tariffs, or at least, the methodologies underlying the calculation of transmission and distribution tariffs and tariffs for access to liquefied natural gas (LNG) facilities. In order to avoid uncertainty and costly and time consuming disputes, these tariffs should be published prior to their entry into force.

(14) The Commission has indicated its intention to set up a European Regulators Group for Electricity and Gas which would constitute a suitable advisory mechanism for encouraging cooperation and coordination of national regulatory authorities, in order to promote the development of the internal market for electricity and gas, and to contribute to the consistent application, in all Member States, of the provisions set out in this Directive and Directive 2003/54/EC of the European Parliament and of the Council of 26 June 2003 concerning common rules for the internal market in electricity[1] and in Regulation (EC) No 1228/2003 of the European Parliament and of the Council of 26 June 2003 on conditions for access to the network for cross-border exchanges in electricity.[2]

Notes
1 See [OJ L 176, 15.7.2003, p. 37].
2 See [OJ L 176, 15.7.2003, p. 1].

(15) In order to ensure effective market access for all market players including new entrants, non discriminatory and cost-reflective balancing mechanisms are necessary. As soon as the gas market is sufficiently liquid, this should be achieved through the setting up of transparent market-based mechanisms for the supply and purchase of gas needed in the framework of balancing requirements. In the absence of such a liquid market, national regulatory authorities should play an active role to ensure that balancing tariffs are non-discriminatory and cost-reflective. At the same time, appropriate incentives should be provided to balance in-put and off-take of gas and not to endanger the system.

(16) National regulatory authorities should be able to fix or approve tariffs, or the methodologies underlying the calculation of the tariffs, on the basis of a proposal by the transmission system operator or distribution system operator(s) or LNG system operator, or on the basis of a proposal agreed between these operator(s) and the users of the network. In carrying out these tasks, national regulatory authorities should ensure that transmission and distribution tariffs are non-discriminatory and cost-reflective, and should take account of the long-term, marginal, avoided network costs from demand-side management measures.

(17) The benefits resulting from the internal market should be available to all Community industry and commerce, including small and medium-sized enterprises, and to all Community citizens as quickly as possible, for reasons of fairness, competitiveness, and indirectly, to create employment as a result of the efficiency gains that will be enjoyed by enterprises.

(18) Gas customers should be able to choose their supplier freely. Nonetheless a phased approach should be taken to completing the internal market for gas, coupled with a specific deadline, to enable industry to adjust and ensure that adequate measures and systems are in place to protect the interests of customers and ensure they have a real and effective right to choose their supplier.

(19) Progressive opening of markets towards full competition should as soon as possible remove differences between Member States. Transparency and certainty in the implementation of this Directive should be ensured.

(20) Directive 98/30/EC contributes to access to storage as part of the gas system. In the light of the experience gained in implementing the internal market, additional measures should be taken to clarify the provisions for access to storage and ancillary services.

(21) Storage facilities are essential means, amongst other things of implementing public service obligations such as security of supply. This should not lead to distortion of competition or discrimination in the access to storage.

(22) Further measures should be taken in order to ensure transparent and non discriminatory tariffs for access to transportation. Those tariffs should be applicable to all users on a non discriminatory basis. Where a storage facility, linepack or ancillary service operates in a sufficiently

competitive market, access could be allowed on the basis of transparent and non-discriminatory market-based mechanisms.

(23) In the interest of security of supply, the supply/demand balance in individual Member States should be monitored, and monitoring should be followed by a report on the situation at Community level, taking account of interconnection capacity between areas. Such monitoring should be carried out sufficiently early to enable appropriate measures to be taken if security of supply is compromised. The construction and maintenance of the necessary network infrastructure, including interconnection capacity, should contribute to ensuring a stable gas supply.

(24) Member States should ensure that, taking into account the necessary quality requirements, biogas and gas from biomass or other types of gas are granted non-discriminatory access to the gas system, provided such access is permanently compatible with the relevant technical rules and safety standards. These rules and standards should ensure, that these gases can technically and safely be injected into, and transported through the natural gas system and should also address the chemical characteristics of these gases.

(25) Long-term contracts will continue to be an important part of the gas supply of Member States and should be maintained as an option for gas supply undertakings in so far as they do not undermine the objectives of this Directive and are compatible with the Treaty, including competition rules. It is therefore necessary to take them into account in the planning of supply and transportation capacity of gas undertakings.

(26) In order to ensure the maintenance of high standards of public service in the Community, all measures taken by Member States to achieve the objectives of this Directive should be regularly notified to the Commission. The Commission should regularly publish a report analysing measures taken at national level to achieve public service objectives and comparing their effectiveness, with a view to making recommendations as regards measures to be taken at national level to achieve high public service standards.

Member States should ensure that when they are connected to the gas system customers are informed about their rights to be supplied with natural gas of a specified quality at reasonable prices. Measures taken by Member States to protect final customers may differ according to households and small and medium sized enterprises.

(27) The respect of the public service requirements is a fundamental requirement of this Directive, and it is important that common minimum standards, respected by all Member States, are specified in this Directive, which take into account the objectives of consumer protection, security of supply, environmental protection and equivalent levels of competition in all Member States. It is important that the public service requirements can be interpreted on a national basis, taking into account national circumstances and subject to the observance of Community law.

Commentary
Recital 27: F&N: 12.109

---

(28) Measures implemented by Member States to achieve the objectives of social and economic cohesion may include, in particular, the provision of adequate economic incentives, using, where appropriate, all existing national and Community tools. These tools may include liability mechanisms to guarantee the necessary investment.

(29) To the extent to which measures taken by Member States to fulfil public service obligations constitute State aid under Article 87(1) of the Treaty, there is an obligation according to Article 88(3) of the Treaty to notify them to the Commission

(30) Since the objective of the proposed action, namely the creation of a fully operational internal gas market, in which fair competition prevails, cannot be sufficiently achieved by the Member States and can therefore, by reason of the scale and effects of the action, be better achieved at Community level, the Community may adopt measures in accordance with the principle of subsidiarity and proportionality as set out in Article 5 of the Treaty. In accordance with the principle of proportionality, as set out in that Article, this Directive does not go beyond what is necessary in order to achieve that objective.

(31) In the light of the experience gained with the operation of Council Directive 91/296/EEC of 31 May 1991 on the transit of natural gas through grids,[1] measures should be taken to ensure homogeneous and non-discriminatory access regimes for transmission, including cross-border

flows of gas between Member States. To ensure homogeneity in the treatment of access to the gas networks, also in the case of transit, that Directive should be repealed, without prejudice to the continuity of contracts concluded under the said Directive. The repeal of Directive 91/296/EEC should not prevent long-term contracts being concluded in the future.

Notes
[1] OJ L 147, 12.6.1991, p. 37. Directive as last amended by Commission Directive 95/49/EC (OJ L 233, 30.9.1995, p. 86).

(32) Given the scope of the amendments that are being made to Directive 98/30/EC, it is desirable, for reasons of clarity and rationalisation, that the provisions in question should be recast.
(33) This Directive respects the fundamental rights, and observes the principles, recognised in particular by the Charter of Fundamental Rights of the European Union.
(34) The measures necessary for the implementation of this Directive should be adopted in accordance with Council Decision 1999/468/EC of 28 June 1999 laying down the procedures for the exercise of implementing powers conferred on the Commission,[1]

Notes
[1] OJ L 184, 17.7.1999, p. 23.

HAVE ADOPTED THIS DIRECTIVE:

CHAPTER I
SCOPE AND DEFINITIONS

Article 1
Scope

1. This Directive establishes common rules for the transmission, distribution, supply and storage of natural gas. It lays down the rules relating to the organisation and functioning of the natural gas sector, access to the market, the criteria and procedures applicable to the granting of authorisations for transmission, distribution, supply and storage of natural gas and the operation of systems.

2. The rules established by this Directive for natural gas, including liquefied natural gas (LNG), shall also apply to biogas and gas from biomass or other types of gas in so far as such gases can technically and safely be injected into, and transported through, the natural gas system.

Commentary
Art 1: F&N: 12.29

Article 2
Definitions

For the purposes of this Directive:

1. "natural gas undertaking" means any natural or legal person carrying out at least one of the following functions: production, transmission, distribution, supply, purchase or storage of natural gas, including LNG, which is responsible for the commercial, technical and/or maintenance tasks related to those functions, but shall not include final customers;
2. "upstream pipeline network" means any pipeline or network of pipelines operated and/or constructed as part of an oil or gas production project, or used to convey natural gas from one or more such projects to a processing plant or terminal or final coastal landing terminal;
3. "transmission" means the transport of natural gas through a high pressure pipeline network other than an upstream pipeline network with a view to its delivery to customers, but not including supply;
4. "transmission system operator" means a natural or legal person who carries out the function of transmission and is responsible for operating, ensuring the maintenance of, and, if necessary, developing the transmission system in a given area and, where applicable, its interconnections with other systems, and for ensuring the long-term ability of the system to meet reasonable demands for the transportation of gas;

5. "distribution" means the transport of natural gas through local or regional pipeline networks with a view to its delivery to customers, but not including supply;

6. "distribution system operator" means a natural or legal person who carries out the function of distribution and is responsible for operating, ensuring the maintenance of, and, if necessary, developing the distribution system in a given area and, where applicable, its interconnections with other systems, and for ensuring the long-term ability of the system to meet reasonable demands for the distribution of gas;

7. "supply" means the sale, including resale, of natural gas, including LNG, to customers;

8. "supply undertaking" means any natural or legal person who carries out the function of supply;

9. "storage facility" means a facility used for the stocking of natural gas and owned and/or operated by a natural gas undertaking, including the part of LNG facilities used for storage but excluding the portion used for production operations, and excluding facilities reserved exclusively for transmission system operators in carrying out their functions;

10. "storage system operator" means a natural or legal person who carries out the function of storage and is responsible for operating a storage facility;

11. "LNG facility" means a terminal which is used for the liquefaction of natural gas or the importation, offloading, and re-gaseification of LNG, and shall include ancillary services and temporary storage necessary for the re-gaseification process and subsequent delivery to the transmission system, but shall not include any part of LNG terminals used for storage;

12. "LNG system operator" means a natural or legal person who carries out the function of liquefaction of natural gas, or the importation, offloading, and re-gaseification of LNG and is responsible for operating a LNG facility;

13. "system" means any transmission networks, distribution networks, LNG facilities and/or storage facilities owned and/or operated by a natural gas undertaking, including linepack and its facilities supplying ancillary services and those of related undertakings necessary for providing access to transmission, distribution and LNG;

14. "ancillary services" means all services necessary for access to and the operation of transmission and/or distribution networks and/or LNG facilities and/or storage facilities including load balancing and blending, but excluding facilities reserved exclusively for transmission system operators carrying out their functions;

15. "linepack" means the storage of gas by compression in gas transmission and distribution systems, but excluding facilities reserved for transmission system operators carrying out their functions;

16. "interconnected system" means a number of systems which are linked with each other;

17. "interconnector" means a transmission line which crosses or spans a border between Member States for the sole purpose of connecting the national transmission systems of these Member States;

18. "direct line" means a natural gas pipeline complementary to the interconnected system;

19. "integrated natural gas undertaking" means a vertically or horizontally integrated undertaking;

20. "vertically integrated undertaking" means a natural gas undertaking or a group of undertakings whose mutual relationships are defined in Article 3(3) of Council Regulation (EEC) No 4064/89 of 21 December 1989 on the control of concentrations between undertakings[1] and where the undertaking/group concerned is performing at least one of the functions of transmission, distribution, LNG or storage, and at least one of the functions of production or supply of natural gas;

21. "horizontally integrated undertaking" means an undertaking performing at least one of the functions of production, transmission, distribution, supply or storage of natural gas, and a non-gas activity;

22. "related undertakings" means affiliated undertakings, within the meaning of Article 41 of the Seventh Council Directive 83/349/EEC of 13 June 1983 based on the Article 44(2)(g)[2] of the Treaty on consolidated accounts,[3] and/or associated undertakings, within the meaning of Article 33(1) thereof, and/or undertakings which belong to the same shareholders;

23. "system users" means any natural or legal persons supplying to, or being supplied by, the system;

24. "customers" means wholesale and final customers of natural gas and natural gas undertakings which purchase natural gas;

25. "household customers" means customers purchasing natural gas for their own household consumption;

26. "non-household customers" means customers purchasing natural gas which is not for their own household use;

27. "final customers" means customers purchasing natural gas for their own use;

28. "eligible customers" means customers who are free to purchase gas from the supplier of their choice, within the meaning of Article 23 of this Directive;

29. "wholesale customers" means any natural or legal persons other than transmission system operators and distribution system operators who purchase natural gas for the purpose of resale inside or outside the system where they are established;

30. "long-term planning" means the planning of supply and transportation capacity of natural gas undertakings on a long-term basis with a view to meeting the demand for natural gas of the system, diversification of sources and securing supplies to customers;

31. "emergent market" means a Member State in which the first commercial supply of its first long-term natural gas supply contract was made not more than 10 years earlier;

32. "security" means both security of supply of natural gas and technical safety;

33. "new infrastructure" means an infrastructure not completed by the entry into force of this Directive.

Notes

[1] OJ L 395, 30.12.1989, p. 1. Regulation as last amended by Regulation (EC) No 1310/97 (OJ L 180, 9.7.1997, p. 1).

[2] The title of Directive 83/349/EEC has been adjusted to take account of the renumbering of the Articles of the Treaty establishing the European Community in accordance with Article 12 of the Treaty of Amsterdam; the original reference was to Article 54(3)(g).

[3] OJ L 193, 18.7.1983, p. 1. Directive as last amended by Directive 2001/65/EC of the European Parliament and of the Council (OJ L 283, 27.10.2001, p. 28).

Chapter II
General Rules for the Organisation of the Sector

Article 3
Public service obligations and customer protection

1. Member States shall ensure, on the basis of their institutional organisation and with due regard to the principle of subsidiarity, that, without prejudice to paragraph 2, natural gas undertakings are operated in accordance with the principles of this Directive with a view to achieving a competitive, secure and environmentally sustainable market in natural gas, and shall not discriminate between these undertakings as regards either rights or obligations.

2. Having full regard to the relevant provisions of the Treaty, in particular Article 86 thereof, Member States may impose on undertakings operating in the gas sector, in the general economic interest, public service obligations which may relate to security, including security of supply, regularity, quality and price of supplies, and environmental protection, including energy efficiency and climate protection. Such obligations shall be clearly defined, transparent, non discriminatory, verifiable and shall guarantee equality of access for EU gas companies to national consumers. In relation to security of supply, energy efficiency/demand-side management and for the fulfilment of environmental goals, as referred to in this paragraph, Member States may introduce the implementation of long term planning, taking into account the possibility of third parties seeking access to the system.

3. Member States shall take appropriate measures to protect final customers and to ensure high levels of consumer protection, and shall, in particular, ensure that there are adequate safeguards to protect vulnerable customers, including appropriate measures to help them avoid disconnection. In this context, they may take appropriate measures to protect customers in remote areas who are connected to the gas system. Member States may appoint a supplier of last resort for customers connected to the gas network. They shall ensure high levels of consumer protection, particularly with respect to transparency regarding general contractual terms and conditions, general information and dispute settlement mechanisms. Member States shall ensure that the eligible customer is effectively able to switch to a new supplier. As regards at least household customers these measures shall include those set out in Annex A.

4. Member States shall implement appropriate measures to achieve the objectives of social and economic cohesion, environmental protection, which may include means to combat climate change, and security of supply. Such measures may include, in particular, the provision of adequate economic incentives, using, where appropriate, all existing national and Community tools, for the maintenance and construction of necessary network infrastructure, including interconnection capacity.

5. Member States may decide not to apply the provisions of Article 4 with respect to distribution insofar as their application would obstruct, in law or in fact, the performance of the obligations imposed on natural gas undertakings in the general economic interest and insofar as the development of trade would not be affected to such an extent as would be contrary to the interests of the Community. The interests of the Community include, *inter alia*, competition with regard to eligible customers in accordance with this Directive and Article 86 of the Treaty.

6. Member States shall, upon implementation of this Directive, inform the Commission of all measures adopted to fulfil public service obligations, including consumer and environmental protection, and their possible effect on national and international competition, whether or not such measures require a derogation from the provisions of this Directive. They shall notify the Commission subsequently every two years of any changes to such measures, whether or not they require a derogation from this Directive.

Article 4
Authorisation procedure

1. In circumstances where an authorisation (e.g. licence, permission, concession, consent or approval) is required for the construction or operation of natural gas facilities, the Member States or any competent authority they designate shall grant authorisations to build and/or operate such facilities, pipelines and associated equipment on their territory, in accordance with paragraphs 2 to 4. Member States or any competent authority they designate may also grant authorisations on the same basis for the supply of natural gas and for wholesale customers.

2. Where Member States have a system of authorisation, they shall lay down objective and non discriminatory criteria which shall be met by an undertaking applying for an authorisation to build and/or operate natural gas facilities or applying for an authorisation to supply natural gas. The non discriminatory criteria and procedures for the granting of authorisations shall be made public.

3. Member States shall ensure that the reasons for any refusal to grant an authorisation are objective and non discriminatory and are given to the applicant. Reasons for such refusals shall be forwarded to the Commission for information. Member States shall establish a procedure enabling the applicant to appeal against such refusals.

4. For the development of newly supplied areas and efficient operation generally, and without prejudice to Article 24, Member States may decline to grant a further authorisation to build and operate distribution pipeline systems in any particular area once such pipeline systems have been or are proposed to be built in that area and if existing or proposed capacity is not saturated.

Commentary
Art 4(4): **B&C:** 12.075 **F&N:** 12.20

Article 5
Monitoring of security of supply

Member States shall ensure the monitoring of security of supply issues. Where Member States consider it appropriate, they may delegate this task to the regulatory authorities referred to in Article 25(1). This monitoring shall, in particular, cover the supply/demand balance on the national market, the level of expected future demand and available supplies, envisaged additional capacity being planned or under construction, and the quality and level of maintenance of the networks, as well as measures to cover peak demand and to deal with shortfalls of one or more suppliers. The competent authorities shall publish, by 31 July each year at the latest a report outlining the findings resulting from the monitoring of these issues, as well as any measures taken or envisaged to address them and shall forward this report to the Commission forthwith.

Commentary
Art 5: F&N: 12.415

Article 6
Technical rules

Member States shall ensure that technical safety criteria are defined and that technical rules establishing the minimum technical design and operational requirements for the connection to the system of LNG facilities, storage facilities, other transmission or distribution systems, and direct lines, are developed and made public. These technical rules shall ensure the interoperability of systems and shall be objective and non-discriminatory. They shall be notified to the Commission in accordance with Article 8 of Directive 98/34/EC of the European Parliament and of the Council of 22 June 1998 laying down a procedure for the provision of information in the field of technical standards and regulations and of rules on Information Society Services.[1]

Notes
[1] OJ L 204, 21.7.1998, p. 37. Directive as amended by Directive 98/48/EC (OJ L 217, 5.8.1998, p. 18).

CHAPTER III
TRANSMISSION, STORAGE AND LNG

Article 7
Designation of system operators

Member States shall designate or shall require natural gas undertakings which own transmission, storage or LNG facilities to designate, for a period of time to be determined by Member States having regard to considerations of efficiency and economic balance, one or more system operators. Member States shall take the measures necessary to ensure that transmission, storage and LNG system operators act in accordance with Articles 8 to 10.

Commentary
Art 7: B&C: 12.075

Article 8
Tasks of system operators

1. Each transmission, storage and/or LNG system operator shall:

(a) operate, maintain and develop under economic conditions secure, reliable and efficient transmission, storage and/or LNG facilities, with due regard to the environment;

(b) refrain from discriminating between system users or classes of system users, particularly in favour of its related undertakings;

(c) provide any other transmission system operator, any other storage system operator, any other LNG system operator and/or any distribution system operator, sufficient information to ensure that the transport and storage of natural gas may take place in a manner compatible with the secure and efficient operation of the interconnected system;

(d) provide system users with the information they need for efficient access to the system.

2. Rules adopted by transmission system operators for balancing the gas transmission system shall be objective, transparent and non-discriminatory, including rules for the charging of system users of their networks for energy imbalance. Terms and conditions, including rules and tariffs, for the provision of such services by transmission system operators shall be established pursuant to a methodology compatible with Article 25(2) in a non-discriminatory and cost-reflective way and shall be published.

3. Member States may require transmission system operators to comply with minimum requirements for the maintenance and development of the transmission system, including interconnection capacity.

4. Transmission system operators shall procure the energy they use for the carrying out of their functions according to transparent, non-discriminatory and market based procedures.

Article 9
Unbundling of transmission system operators

1. Where the transmission system operator is part of a vertically integrated undertaking, it shall be independent at least in terms of its legal form, organisation and decision making from other activities not relating to transmission. These rules shall not create an obligation to separate the ownership of assets of the transmission system from the vertically integrated undertaking.

2. In order to ensure the independence of the transmission system operator referred to in paragraph 1, the following minimum criteria shall apply:

(a) those persons responsible for the management of the transmission system operator may not participate in company structures of the integrated natural gas undertaking responsible, directly or indirectly, for the day-to-day operation of the production, distribution and supply of natural gas;

(b) appropriate measures must be taken to ensure that the professional interests of persons responsible for the management of the transmission system operator are taken into account in a manner that ensures that they are capable of acting independently;

(c) the transmission system operator shall have effective decision-making rights, independent from the integrated gas undertaking, with respect to assets necessary to operate, maintain or develop the network. This should not prevent the existence of appropriate coordination mechanisms to ensure that the economic and management supervision rights of the parent company in respect of return on assets regulated indirectly in accordance with Article 25(2) in a subsidiary are protected. In particular, this shall enable the parent company to approve the annual financial plan, or any equivalent instrument, of the transmission system operator and to set global limits on the levels of indebtedness of its subsidiary. It shall not permit the parent company to give instructions regarding day-to-day operations, nor with respect to individual decisions concerning the construction or upgrading of transmission lines, that do not exceed the terms of the approved financial plan, or any equivalent instrument;

(d) the transmission system operator shall establish a compliance programme, which sets out measures taken to ensure that discriminatory conduct is excluded, and ensure that observance of it is adequately monitored. The programme shall set out the specific obligations of employees to meet this objective. An annual report, setting out the measures taken, shall be submitted by the person or body responsible for monitoring the compliance programme to the regulatory authority referred to in Article 25(1) and shall be published.

Commentary
Art 9: B&C: 12.075 F&N: 12.234

Article 10
Confidentiality for transmission system operators

1. Without prejudice to Article 16 or any other legal duty to disclose information, each transmission, storage and/or LNG system operator shall preserve the confidentiality of commercially sensitive information obtained in the course of carrying out its business, and shall prevent information about its own activities which may be commercially advantageous from being disclosed in a discriminatory manner.

2. Transmission system operators shall not, in the context of sales or purchases of natural gas by related undertakings, abuse commercially sensitive information obtained from third parties in the context of providing or negotiating access to the system.

Commentary
Art 10: B&C: 12.075

Chapter IV
Distribution and Supply

Article 11
Designation of distribution system operators

Member States shall designate, or shall require undertakings which own or are responsible for distribution systems to designate, for a period of time to be determined by Member States, having regard to considerations of efficiency and economic balance, one or more distribution system operators and shall ensure that those operators act in accordance with Articles 12 to 14.

Article 12
Tasks of distribution system operators

1. Each distribution system operator shall operate, maintain and develop under economic conditions a secure, reliable and efficient system, with due regard for the environment.

2. In any event, the distribution system operator shall not discriminate between system users or classes of system users, particularly in favour of its related undertakings.

3. Each distribution system operator shall provide any other distribution system operator, and/or any transmission, and/or LNG system operator, and/or storage system operator with sufficient information to ensure that the transport and storage of natural gas takes place in a manner compatible with the secure and efficient operation of the interconnected system.

4. Each distribution system operator shall provide system users with the information they need for efficient access to the system.

5. Where distribution system operators are responsible for balancing the gas distribution system, rules adopted by them for that purpose shall be objective, transparent and non-discriminatory, including rules for the charging of system users for energy imbalance. Terms and conditions, including rules and tariffs, for the provision of such services by system operators shall be established pursuant to a methodology compatible with Article 25(2) in a non-discriminatory and cost-reflective way and shall be published.

Commentary
Art 12(2): F&N: 12.389

Article 13
Unbundling of distribution system operators

1. Where the distribution system operator is part of a vertically integrated undertaking, it shall be independent at least in terms of its legal form, organisation and decision making from other activities not relating to distribution. These rules shall not create an obligation to separate the ownership of assets of the distribution system from the vertically integrated undertaking.

2. In addition to the requirements of paragraph 1, where the distribution system operator is part of a vertically integrated undertaking, it shall be independent in terms of its organisation and decision making from the other activities not related to distribution. In order to achieve this, the following minimum criteria shall apply:

(a) those persons responsible for the management of the distribution system operator may not participate in company structures of the integrated natural gas undertaking responsible, directly or indirectly, for the day-to-day operation of the production, transmission and supply of natural gas;

(b) appropriate measures must be taken to ensure that the professional interests of persons responsible for the management of the distribution system operator are taken into account in a manner that ensures that they are capable of acting independently;

(c) the distribution system operator shall have effective decision-making rights, independent from the integrated gas undertaking, with respect to assets necessary to operate, maintain or develop the network. This should not prevent the existence of appropriate coordination mechanisms to ensure that the economic and management supervision rights of the parent company in respect of return on assets, regulated indirectly in accordance with Article 25(2), in a subsidiary are protected. In particular, this shall enable the parent company to approve the annual financial plan, or any equivalent instrument, of the distribution system operator and to set global limits on the levels of indebtedness of its subsidiary. It shall not permit the parent company to give instructions regarding day-to-day operations, nor with respect to individual decisions concerning the construction or upgrading of distribution lines, that do not exceed the terms of the approved financial plan, or any equivalent instrument;

(d) the distribution system operator shall establish a compliance programme, which sets out measures taken to ensure that discriminatory conduct is excluded, and ensure that observance of it is adequately monitored. The programme shall set out the specific obligations of employees to meet this objective. An annual report, setting out the measures taken, shall be submitted by the person or body responsible for monitoring the compliance programme to the regulatory authority referred to in Article 25(1) and shall be published.

Member States may decide not to apply paragraphs 1 and 2 to integrated natural gas undertakings serving less than 100000 connected customers.

Commentary
Art 13: B&C: 12.075 F&N: 12.234

Article 14
Confidentiality for distribution system operators

1. Without prejudice to Article 16 or any other legal duty to disclose information, each distribution system operator shall preserve the confidentiality of commercially sensitive information obtained in the course of carrying out its business, and shall prevent information about its own activities which may be commercially advantageous from being disclosed in a discriminatory manner.

2. Distribution system operators shall not, in the context of sales or purchases of natural gas by related undertakings, abuse commercially sensitive information obtained from third parties in the context of providing or negotiating access to the system.

Article 15
Combined operator

The rules in Articles 9(1) and Article 13(1) shall not prevent the operation of a combined transmission, LNG, storage and distribution system operator, which is independent in terms of its legal form, organisation and decision making from other activities not relating to transmission LNG, storage and distribution system operations and which meets the requirements set out in points (a) to (d). These rules shall not create an obligation to separate the ownership of assets of the combined system from the vertically integrated undertaking:

(a) those persons responsible for the management of the combined system operator may not participate in company structures of the integrated natural gas undertaking responsible, directly or indirectly, for the day-to-day operation of the production and supply of natural gas;

(b) appropriate measures must be taken to ensure that the professional interests of persons responsible for the management of the combined system operator are taken into account in a manner that ensures that they are capable of acting independently;

(c) the combined system operator shall have effective decision-making rights, independent from the integrated gas undertaking, with respect to assets necessary to operate, maintain or develop the network. This should not prevent the existence of appropriate coordination mechanisms to ensure that the economic and management supervision rights of the parent company in respect of return on assets, regulated indirectly in accordance with Article 25(2) in a subsidiary are protected. In particular, this shall enable the parent company to approve the annual financial plan, or any equivalent instrument, of the combined system operator and to set global limits on the levels of indebtedness of its subsidiary. It shall not permit the parent company to give instructions regarding day-to-day operations, nor with respect to individual decisions concerning the construction or upgrading of transmission and distribution lines, that do not exceed the terms of the approved financial plan, or any equivalent instrument;

(d) the combined system operator shall establish a compliance programme, which sets out measures taken to ensure that discriminatory conduct is excluded, and ensure that observance of it is adequately monitored. The programme shall set out the specific obligations of employees to meet this objective. An annual report, setting out the measures taken, shall be submitted by the person or body responsible for monitoring the compliance programme to the regulatory authority referred to in Article 25(1) and shall be published.

CHAPTER V

UNBUNDLING AND TRANSPARENCY OF ACCOUNTS

Article 16
Right of access to accounts

1. Member States or any competent authority they designate, including the regulatory authorities referred to in Article 25(1) and the dispute settlement authorities referred to in Article 20(3), shall, insofar as necessary to carry out their functions, have right of access to the accounts of natural gas undertakings as set out in Article 17.

2. Member States and any designated competent authority, including the regulatory authorities referred to in Article 25(1) and the dispute settlement authorities, shall preserve the confidentiality of commercially sensitive information. Member States may provide for the disclosure of such information where this is necessary in order for the competent authorities to carry out their functions.

Commentary
Art 16: **B&C:** 12.075

Article 17
Unbundling of accounts

1. Member States shall take the necessary steps to ensure that the accounts of natural gas undertakings are kept in accordance with paragraphs 2 to 5. Where undertakings benefit from a derogation from this provision on the basis of Article 28(2) and (4), they shall at least keep their internal accounts in accordance with this Article.

2. Natural gas undertakings, whatever their system of ownership or legal form, shall draw up, submit to audit and publish their annual accounts in accordance with the rules of national law concerning the annual accounts of limited liability companies adopted pursuant to the Fourth Council Directive 78/660/EEC of 25 July 1978 based on Article 44(2)(g)[1] of the Treaty on the annual accounts of certain types of companies.[2] Undertakings which are not legally obliged to publish their annual accounts shall keep a copy of these at the disposal of the public at their head office.

3. Natural gas undertakings shall, in their internal accounting, keep separate accounts for each of their transmission, distribution, LNG and storage activities as they would be required to do if the activities in question were carried out by separate undertakings, with a view to avoiding discrimination, cross-subsidisation and distortion of competition. They shall also keep accounts, which may be consolidated, for other gas activities not relating to transmission, distribution, LNG and storage. Until 1 July 2007, they shall keep separate accounts for supply activities for eligible customers and supply activities for non-eligible customers. Revenue from ownership of the transmission/distribution network shall be specified in the accounts. Where appropriate, they shall keep consolidated accounts for other, non-gas activities. The internal accounts shall include a balance sheet and a profit and loss account for each activity.

4. The audit, referred to in paragraph 2, shall, in particular, verify that the obligation to avoid discrimination and cross-subsidies referred to in paragraph 3, is respected.

5. Undertakings shall specify in their internal accounting the rules for the allocation of assets and liabilities, expenditure and income as well as for depreciation, without prejudice to nationally applicable accounting rules, which they follow in drawing up the separate accounts referred to in paragraph 3. These internal rules may be amended only in exceptional cases. Such amendments shall be mentioned and duly substantiated.

999

6. The annual accounts shall indicate in notes any transaction of a certain size conducted with related undertakings.

Notes

[1] The title of Directive 78/660/EEC has been adjusted to take account of the renumbering of the Articles of the Treaty establishing the European Community in accordance with Article 12 of the Treaty of Amsterdam; the original reference was to Article 54(3)(g).

[2] OJ L 222, 14.8.1978, p. 11. Directive as last amended by Directive 2001/65/EC of the European Parliament and of the Council (OJ L 283, 27.10.2001, p. 28).

Commentary
Art 17: B&C: 12.075

CHAPTER VI
ORGANISATION OF ACCESS TO THE SYSTEM

Article 18
Third party access

1. Member States shall ensure the implementation of a system of third party access to the transmission and distribution system, and LNG facilities based on published tariffs, applicable to all eligible customers, including supply undertakings, and applied objectively and without discrimination between system users. Member States shall ensure that these tariffs, or the methodologies underlying their calculation shall be approved prior to their entry into force by a regulatory authority referred to in Article 25(1) and that these tariffs — and the methodologies, where only methodologies are approved — are published prior to their entry into force.

2. Transmission system operators shall, if necessary for the purpose of carrying out their functions including in relation to cross-border transmission, have access to the network of other transmission system operators.

3. The provisions of this Directive shall not prevent the conclusion of long-term contracts in so far as they comply with Community competition rules

Commentary
Art 18: F&N: 12.389

Article 19
Access to storage

1. For the organisation of access to storage facilities and linepack when technically and/or economically necessary for providing efficient access to the system for the supply of customers, as well as for the organisation of access to ancillary services, Member States may choose either or both of the procedures referred to in paragraphs 3 and 4. These procedures shall operate in accordance with objective, transparent and non-discriminatory criteria.

2. The provisions of paragraph 1 shall not apply to ancillary services and temporary storage that are related to LNG facilities and are necessary for the re-gaseification process and subsequent delivery to the transmission system.

3. In the case of negotiated access, Member States shall take the necessary measures for natural gas undertakings and eligible customers either inside or outside the territory covered by the interconnected system to be able to negotiate access to storage and linepack, when technically and/or economically necessary for providing efficient access to the system, as well as for the organisation of access to other ancillary services. The parties shall be obliged to negotiate access to storage, linepack and other ancillary services in good faith.

Contracts for access to storage, linepack and other ancillary services shall be negotiated with the relevant storage system operator or natural gas undertakings. Member States shall require storage system operators and natural gas undertakings to publish their main commercial conditions for the use of storage, linepack and other ancillary services within the first six months following implementation of this Directive and on an annual basis every year thereafter.

4. In the case of regulated access Member States shall take the necessary measures to give natural gas undertakings and eligible customers either inside or outside the territory covered by the interconnected system a right to access to storage, linepack and other ancillary services, on the basis of published tariffs and/or other terms and obligations for use of that storage and linepack, when technically and/or economically necessary for providing efficient access to the system, as well as for the organisation of access to other ancillary services. This right of access for eligible customers may be given by enabling them to enter into supply contracts with competing natural gas undertakings other than the owner and/or operator of the system or a related undertaking.

Commentary
Art 19: B&C: 12.076

Article 20
Access to upstream pipeline networks

1. Member States shall take the necessary measures to ensure that natural gas undertakings and eligible customers, wherever they are located, are able to obtain access to upstream pipeline networks, including facilities supplying technical services incidental to such access, in accordance with this Article, except for the parts of such networks and facilities which are used for local production operations at the site of a field where the gas is produced. The measures shall be notified to the Commission in accordance with the provisions of Article 33.

2. The access referred to in paragraph 1 shall be provided in a manner determined by the Member State in accordance with the relevant legal instruments. Member States shall apply the objectives of fair and open access, achieving a competitive market in natural gas and avoiding any abuse of a dominant position, taking into account security and regularity of supplies, capacity which is or can reasonably be made available, and environmental protection. The following may be taken into account:

(a) the need to refuse access where there is an incompatibility of technical specifications which cannot be reasonably overcome;

(b) the need to avoid difficulties which cannot be reasonably overcome and could prejudice the efficient, current and planned future production of hydrocarbons, including that from fields of marginal economic viability;

(c) the need to respect the duly substantiated reasonable needs of the owner or operator of the upstream pipeline network for the transport and processing of gas and the interests of all other users of the upstream pipeline network or relevant processing or handling facilities who may be affected; and

(d) the need to apply their laws and administrative procedures, in conformity with Community law, for the grant of authorisation for production or upstream development.

3. Member States shall ensure that they have in place dispute settlement arrangements, including an authority independent of the parties with access to all relevant information, to enable disputes relating to access to upstream pipeline networks to be settled expeditiously, taking into account the criteria in paragraph 2 and the number of parties which may be involved in negotiating access to such networks.

4. In the event of cross border disputes, the dispute settlement arrangements for the Member State having jurisdiction over the upstream pipeline network which refuses access shall be applied. Where, in cross border disputes, more than one Member State covers the network concerned, the Member States concerned shall consult with a view to ensuring that the provisions of this Directive are applied consistently.

Commentary
Art 20: F&N: 12.38

Article 21
Refusal of access

1. Natural gas undertakings may refuse access to the system on the basis of lack of capacity or where the access to the system would prevent them from carrying out the public service obligations

referred to in Article 3(2) which are assigned to them or on the basis of serious economic and financial difficulties with take-or-pay contracts having regard to the criteria and procedures set out in Article 27 and the alternative chosen by the Member State in accordance with paragraph 1 of that Article. Duly substantiated reasons shall be given for such a refusal.

2. Member States may take the measures necessary to ensure that the natural gas undertaking refusing access to the system on the basis of lack of capacity or a lack of connection makes the necessary enhancements as far as it is economic to do so or when a potential customer is willing to pay for them. In circumstances where Member States apply Article 4(4), Member States shall take such measures.

Commentary
Art 21: F&N: 12.404
Art 21(2): F&N: 12.410

Article 22
New infrastructure

1. Major new gas infrastructures, i.e. interconnectors between Member States, LNG and storage facilities, may, upon request, be exempted from the provisions of Articles 18, 19, 20, and 25(2), (3) and (4) under the following conditions:

(a) the investment must enhance competition in gas supply and enhance security of supply;
(b) the level of risk attached to the investment is such that the investment would not take place unless an exemption was granted;
(c) the infrastructure must be owned by a natural or legal person which is separate at least in terms of its legal form from the system operators in whose systems that infrastructure will be built;
(d) charges are levied on users of that infrastructure;
(e) the exemption is not detrimental to competition or the effective functioning of the internal gas market, or the efficient functioning of the regulated system to which the infrastructure is connected.

2. Paragraph 1 shall apply also to significant increases of capacity in existing infrastructures and to modifications of such infrastructures which enable the development of new sources of gas supply.

3. (a) The regulatory authority referred to in Article 25 may, on a case by case basis, decide on the exemption referred to in paragraphs 1 and 2. However, Member States may provide that the regulatory authorities shall submit, for formal decision, to the relevant body in the Member State its opinion on the request for an exemption. This opinion shall be published together with the decision.

    (b)   (i) The exemption may cover all or parts of, respectively, the new infrastructure, the existing infrastructure with significantly increased capacity or the modification of the existing infrastructure.

        (ii) In deciding to grant an exemption consideration shall be given, on a case by case basis, to the need to impose conditions regarding the duration of the exemption and non-discriminatory access to the interconnector.

        (iii) When deciding on the conditions in this subparagraph account shall, in particular, be taken of the duration of contracts, additional capacity to be built or the modification of existing capacity, the time horizon of the project and national circumstances.

(c) When granting an exemption the relevant authority may decide upon the rules and mechanisms for management and allocation of capacity insofar as this does not prevent the implementation of long term contracts.

(d) The exemption decision, including any conditions referred to in (b), shall be duly reasoned and published.

(e) In the case of an interconnector any exemption decision shall be taken after consultation with the other Member States or regulatory authorities concerned.

4. The exemption decision shall be notified, without delay, by the competent authority to the Commission, together with all the relevant information with respect to the decision. This information may be submitted to the Commission in aggregate form, enabling the Commission to reach a well-founded decision.

In particular, the information shall contain:

(a) the detailed reasons on the basis of which the regulatory authority, or Member State, granted the exemption, including the financial information justifying the need for the exemption;

(b) the analysis undertaken of the effect on competition and the effective functioning of the internal gas market resulting from the grant of the exemption;

(c) the reasons for the time period and the share of the total capacity of the gas infrastructure in question for which the exemption is granted;

(d) in case the exemption relates to an interconnector, the result of the consultation with the Member States concerned or regulatory authorities;

(e) the contribution of the infrastructure to the diversification of gas supply.

Within two months after receiving a notification, the Commission may request that the regulatory authority or the Member State concerned amend or withdraw the decision to grant an exemption. The two month period may be extended by one additional month where additional information is sought by the Commission.

If the regulatory authority or Member State concerned does not comply with the request within a period of four weeks, a final decision shall be taken in accordance with the procedure referred to in Article 30(2).

The Commission shall preserve the confidentiality of commercially sensitive information.

Commentary
Art 22: B&C: 12.061 F&N: 12.71, 12.273, 12.276, 12.281, 12.358

Article 23
Market opening and reciprocity

1. Member States shall ensure that the eligible customers are:

(a) until 1 July 2004, the eligible customers as specified in Article 18 of Directive 98/30/EC. Member States shall publish by 31 January each year the criteria for the definition of these eligible customers;

(b) from 1 July 2004, at the latest, all non-household customers;

(c) from 1 July 2007, all customers.

2. To avoid imbalance in the opening of gas markets:

(a) contracts for the supply with an eligible customer in the system of another Member State shall not be prohibited if the customer is eligible in both systems involved;

(b) in cases where transactions as described in point (a) are refused because the customer is eligible in only one of the two systems, the Commission may, taking into account the situation in the market and the common interest, oblige the refusing party to execute the requested supply, at the request of one of the Member States of the two systems.

Commentary
Art 23: B&C: 12.076

Article 24
Direct lines

1. Member States shall take the necessary measures to enable:

(a) natural gas undertakings established within their territory to supply the eligible customers through a direct line;

(b) any such eligible customer within their territory to be supplied through a direct line by natural gas undertakings.

2. In circumstances where an authorisation (e.g. licence, permission, concession, consent or approval) is required for the construction or operation of direct lines, the Member States or any competent authority they designate shall lay down the criteria for the grant of authorisations for the construction or operation of such lines in their territory. These criteria shall be objective, transparent and non-discriminatory.

3. Member States may make authorisations to construct a direct line subject either to the refusal of system access on the basis of Article 21 or to the opening of a dispute settlement procedure under Article 25.

Commentary
Art 24: F&N: 12.273

Article 25
Regulatory authorities

1. Member States shall designate one or more competent bodies with the function of regulatory authorities. These authorities shall be wholly independent of the interests of the gas industry. They shall, through the application of this Article, at least be responsible for ensuring non-discrimination, effective competition and the efficient functioning of the market, monitoring in particular:

(a) the rules on the management and allocation of interconnection capacity, in conjunction with the regulatory authority or authorities of those Member States with which interconnection exists;

(b) any mechanisms to deal with congested capacity within the national gas system;

(c) the time taken by transmission and distribution system operators to make connections and repairs;

(d) the publication of appropriate information by transmission and distribution system operators concerning interconnectors, grid usage and capacity allocation to interested parties, taking into account the need to treat non-aggregated information as commercially confidential;

(e) the effective unbundling of accounts as referred to in Article 17, to ensure there are no cross subsidies between transmission, distribution, storage, LNG and supply activities;

(f) the access conditions to storage, linepack and to other ancillary services as provided for in Article 19;

(g) the extent to which transmission and distribution system operators fulfil their tasks in accordance with Articles 8 and 12;

(h) the level of transparency and competition.

The authorities established pursuant to this Article shall publish an annual report on the outcome of their monitoring activities referred to in points (a) to (h).

2. The regulatory authorities shall be responsible for fixing or approving prior to their entry into force, at least the methodologies used to calculate or establish the terms and conditions for:

(a) connection and access to national networks, including transmission and distribution tariffs, and terms, conditions and tariffs for access to LNG facilities. These tariffs, or methodologies, shall allow the necessary investments in the networks and LNG facilities to be carried out in a manner allowing these investments to ensure the viability of the networks and LNG facilities;.

(b) the provision of balancing services.

3. Notwithstanding paragraph 2, Member States may provide that the regulatory authorities shall submit, for formal decision, to the relevant body in the Member State the tariffs or at least the methodologies referred to in that paragraph as well as the modifications in paragraph 4. The relevant body shall, in such a case, have the power to either approve or reject a draft decision submitted by the regulatory authority.

These tariffs or the methodologies or modifications thereto shall be published together with the decision on formal adoption. Any formal rejection of a draft decision shall also be published, including its justification.

4. Regulatory authorities shall have the authority to require transmission, LNG and distribution system operators, if necessary, to modify the terms and conditions, including tariffs and methodologies referred to in paragraphs 1, 2 and 3, to ensure that they are proportionate and applied in a non-discriminatory manner.

5. Any party having a complaint against a transmission, LNG or distribution system operator with respect to the issues mentioned in paragraphs 1, 2 and 4 and in Article 19 may refer the complaint to the regulatory authority which, acting as dispute settlement authority, shall issue a decision within two months after receipt of the complaint. This period may be extended by two months where additional

information is sought by the regulatory authorities. This period may be extended with the agreement of the complainant. Such a decision shall have binding effect unless and until overruled on appeal.

6. Any party who is affected and who has a right to complain concerning a decision on methodologies taken pursuant to paragraphs 2, 3 or 4 or, where the regulatory authority has a duty to consult, concerning the proposed methodologies, may, at the latest within two months, or a shorter time period as provided by Member States, following publication of the decision or proposal for a decision, submit a complaint for review. Such a complaint shall not have suspensive effect.

7. Member States shall take measures to ensure that regulatory authorities are able to carry out their duties referred to in paragraphs 1 to 5 in an efficient and expeditious manner.

8. Member States shall create appropriate and efficient mechanisms for regulation, control and transparency so as to avoid any abuse of a dominant position, in particular to the detriment of consumers, and any predatory behaviour. These mechanisms shall take account of the provisions of the Treaty, and in particular Article 82 thereof.

9. Member States shall ensure that the appropriate measures are taken, including administrative action or criminal proceedings in conformity with their national law, against the natural or legal persons responsible where confidentiality rules imposed by this Directive have not been respected.

10. In the event of cross border disputes, the deciding regulatory authority shall be the regulatory authority which has jurisdiction in respect of the system operator, which refuses use of, or access to, the system.

11. Complaints referred to in paragraphs 5 and 6 shall be without prejudice to the exercise of rights of appeal under Community and national law.

12. National regulatory authorities shall contribute to the development of the internal market and of a level playing field by cooperating with each other and with the Commission in a transparent manner.

Commentary
Art 25: F&N: 12.68

CHAPTER VII
FINAL PROVISIONS

Article 26
Safeguard measures

1. In the event of a sudden crisis in the energy market or where the physical safety or security of persons, apparatus or installations or system integrity is threatened, a Member State may temporarily take the necessary safeguard measures.

2. Such measures shall cause the least possible disturbance to the functioning of the internal market and shall not be wider in scope than is strictly necessary to remedy the sudden difficulties which have arisen.

3. The Member State concerned shall without delay notify these measures to the other Member States, and to the Commission, which may decide that the Member State concerned must amend or abolish such measures, insofar as they distort competition and adversely affect trade in a manner which is at variance with the common interest.

Article 27
Derogations in relation to take-or-pay commitments

1. If a natural gas undertaking encounters, or considers it would encounter, serious economic and financial difficulties because of its take-or-pay commitments accepted in one or more gas-purchase contracts, an application for a temporary derogation from Article 18 may be sent to the Member State concerned or the designated competent authority. Applications shall, according to the choice of Member States, be presented on a case-by-case basis either before or after refusal of access to the system. Member States may also give the natural gas undertaking the choice of presenting an application either before or after refusal of access to the system. Where a natural gas undertaking has refused access, the application shall be presented without delay. The applications shall be accompanied by all relevant

information on the nature and extent of the problem and on the efforts undertaken by the natural gas undertaking to solve the problem.

If alternative solutions are not reasonably available, and taking into account the provisions of paragraph 3, the Member State or the designated competent authority may decide to grant a derogation.

2. The Member State, or the designated competent authority, shall notify the Commission without delay of its decision to grant a derogation, together with all the relevant information with respect to the derogation. This information may be submitted to the Commission in an aggregated form, enabling the Commission to reach a well-founded decision. Within eight weeks of its receipt of this notification, the Commission may request that the Member State or the designated competent authority concerned amend or withdraw the decision to grant a derogation.

If the Member State or the designated competent authority concerned does not comply with this request within a period of four weeks, a final decision shall be taken expeditiously in accordance with the procedure referred to in Article 30(2).

The Commission shall preserve the confidentiality of commercially sensitive information.

3. When deciding on the derogations referred to in paragraph 1, the Member State, or the designated competent authority, and the Commission shall take into account, in particular, the following criteria:

(a) the objective of achieving a competitive gas market;
(b) the need to fulfil public service obligations and to ensure security of supply;
(c) the position of the natural gas undertaking in the gas market and the actual state of competition in this market;
(d) the seriousness of the economic and financial difficulties encountered by natural gas undertakings and transmission undertakings or eligible customers;
(e) the dates of signature and terms of the contract or contracts in question, including the extent to which they allow for market changes;
(f) the efforts made to find a solution to the problem;
(g) the extent to which, when accepting the take-or-pay commitments in question, the undertaking could reasonably have foreseen, having regard to the provisions of this Directive, that serious difficulties were likely to arise;
(h) the level of connection of the system with other systems and the degree of interoperability of these systems; and
(i) the effects the granting of a derogation would have on the correct application of this Directive as regards the smooth functioning of the internal natural gas market.

A decision on a request for a derogation concerning take or pay contracts concluded before the entry into force of this Directive should not lead to a situation in which it is impossible to find economically viable alternative outlets. Serious difficulties shall in any case be deemed not to exist when the sales of natural gas do not fall below the level of minimum offtake guarantees contained in gas purchase take or pay contracts or in so far as the relevant gas purchase take-or-pay contract can be adapted or the natural gas undertaking is able to find alternative outlets.

4. Natural gas undertakings which have not been granted a derogation as referred to in paragraph 1 shall not refuse, or shall no longer refuse, access to the system because of take-or-pay commitments accepted in a gas purchase contract. Member States shall ensure that the relevant provisions of Chapter VI namely Articles 18 to 25 are complied with.

5. Any derogation granted under the above provisions shall be duly substantiated. The Commission shall publish the decision in the *Official Journal of the European Union*.

6. The Commission shall, within five years of the entry into force of this Directive, submit a review report on the experience gained from the application of this Article, so as to allow the European Parliament and the Council to consider, in due course, the need to adjust it.

Commentary
Art 27: F&N: 12.93, 12.232, 12.404

Article 28
Emergent and isolated markets

1. Member States not directly connected to the interconnected system of any other Member State and having only one main external supplier may derogate from Articles 4, 9, 23 and/or 24 of this Directive. A supply undertaking having a market share of more than 75% shall be considered to be a main supplier. This derogation shall automatically expire from the moment when at least one of these conditions no longer applies. Any such derogation shall be notified to the Commission.

2. A Member State, qualifying as an emergent market, which because of the implementation of this Directive would experience substantial problems may derogate from Articles 4, 7, 8(1) and (2), 9, 11, 12(5), 13, 17, 18, 23(1) and/or 24 of this Directive. This derogation shall automatically expire from the moment when the Member State no longer qualifies as an emergent market. Any such derogation shall be notified to the Commission.

3. On the date at which the derogation referred to in paragraph 2 expires, the definition of eligible customers shall result in an opening of the market equal to at least 33% of the total annual gas consumption of the national gas market. Two years thereafter, Article 23(1)(b) shall apply, and three years thereafter, Article 23(1)(c). Until Article 23(1)(b) applies the Member State referred to in paragraph 2 may decide not to apply Article 18 as far as ancillary services and temporary storage for the re-gaseification process and its subsequent delivery to the transmission system are concerned.

4. Where implementation of this Directive would cause substantial problems in a geographically limited area of a Member State, in particular concerning the development of the transmission and major distribution infrastructure, and with a view to encouraging investments, the Member State may apply to the Commission for a temporary derogation from Article 4, Article 7, Article 8(1) and (2), Article 9, Article 11, Article 12(5), Article 13, Article 17, Article 18, Article 23(1) and/or Article 24 for developments within this area.

5. The Commission may grant the derogation referred to in paragraph 4, taking into account, in particular, the following criteria:

— the need for infrastructure investments, which would not be economic to operate in a competitive market environment,
— the level and pay-back prospects of investments required,
— the size and maturity of the gas system in the area concerned,
— the prospects for the gas market concerned,
— the geographical size and characteristics of the area or region concerned, and socioeconomic and demographic factors.

(a) For gas infrastructure other than distribution infrastructure a derogation may be granted only if no gas infrastructure has been established in this area, or has been so established for less than 10 years. The temporary derogation may not exceed 10 years from the time gas is first supplied in the area.

(b) For distribution infrastructure a derogation may be granted for a time period which may not exceed 20 years for the distribution infrastructure from the time gas is first supplied through the said system in the area.

6. Luxembourg may benefit from a derogation from Articles 8(3) and 9 for a period of five years from 1 July 2004. Such a derogation shall be reviewed before the end of the five year period and any decision to renew the derogation for another five years shall be taken in accordance with the procedure referred to in Article 30(2). Any such derogation shall be notified to the Commission.

7. The Commission shall inform the Member States of applications made under paragraph 4 prior to taking a decision pursuant to paragraph 5, taking into account respect for confidentiality. This decision, as well as the derogations referred to in paragraphs 1 and 2, shall be published in the *Official Journal of the European Union*.

8. Greece may derogate from Articles 4, 11, 12, 13, 18, 23 and/or 24 of this Directive for the geographical areas and time periods specified in the licences issued by it, prior to 15 March 2002 and in accordance with Directive 98/30/EC, for the development and exclusive exploitation of distribution networks in certain geographical areas.

Commentary
Art 28: F&N: 12.19, 12.327

Article 29
Review procedure

In the event that the report referred to in Article 31(3) reaches the conclusion whereby, given the effective manner in which network access has been carried out in a Member State — which gives rise to fully effective, non-discriminatory and unhindered network access — the Commission concludes that certain obligations imposed by this Directive on undertakings (including those with respect to legal unbundling for distribution system operators) are not proportionate to the objective pursued, the Member State in question may submit a request to the Commission for exemption from the requirement in question.

The request shall be notified, without delay, by the Member State to the Commission, together with all the relevant information necessary to demonstrate that the conclusion reached in the report on effective network access being ensured will be maintained.

Within three months of its receipt of a notification, the Commission shall adopt an opinion with respect to the request by the Member State concerned, and where appropriate, submit proposals to the European Parliament and to the Council to amend the relevant provisions of the Directive. The Commission may propose, in the proposals to amend the Directive, to exempt the Member State concerned from specific requirements subject to that Member State implementing equally effective measures as appropriate.

Article 30
Committee

1. The Commission shall be assisted by a Committee.

2. Where reference is made to this paragraph, Articles 3 and 7 of Decision 1999/468/EC shall apply, having regard to the provisions of Article 8 thereof.

3. The Committee shall adopt its rules of procedure.

Article 31
Reporting

1. The Commission shall monitor and review the application of this Directive and submit an overall progress report to the European Parliament and the Council before the end of the first year following the entry into force of this Directive, and thereafter on an annual basis. The report shall cover at least:

(a) the experience gained and progress made in creating a complete and fully operational internal market in natural gas and the obstacles that remain in this respect including aspects of market dominance, concentration in the market, predatory or anti-competitive behaviour;

(b) the derogations granted under this Directive, including implementation of the derogation provided for in Article 13(2) with a view to a possible revision of the threshold;

(c) the extent to which the unbundling and tarification requirements contained in this Directive have been successful in ensuring fair and non-discriminatory access to the Community's gas system and equivalent levels of competition, as well as the economic, environmental and social consequences of the opening of the gas market for customers;

(d) an examination of issues relating to system capacity levels and security of supply of natural gas in the Community, and in particular the existing and projected balance between demand and supply, taking into account the physical capacity for exchanges between areas and the development of storage (including the question of the proportionality of market regulation in this field);

(e) special attention will be given to the measures taken in Member States to cover peak demand and to deal with shortfalls of one or more suppliers;

(f) a general assessment of the progress achieved with regard to bilateral relations with third countries which produce and export or transport natural gas, including progress in market integration, trade and access to the networks of such third countries;

(g) the need for possible harmonisation requirements which are not linked to the provisions of this Directive.

Where appropriate, this report may include recommendations and measures to counteract negative effects of market dominance and market concentration.

2. Every two years, the report referred to in paragraph 1 shall also cover an analysis of the different measures taken in Member States to meet public service obligations, together with an examination of the effectiveness of those measures, and in particular their effects on competition in the gas market. Where appropriate, the report may include recommendations as to the measures to be taken at national level to achieve high public service standards or measures intended to prevent market foreclosure.

3. The Commission shall, no later than 1 January 2006, forward to the European Parliament and Council, a detailed report outlining progress in creating the internal gas market. The report shall, in particular, consider:

— the existence of non-discriminatory network access;
— effective regulation;
— the development of interconnection infrastructure, the conditions of transit, and the security of supply situation in the Community;
— the extent to which the full benefits of the opening of the market are accruing to small enterprises and households, notably with respect to public service standards;
— the extent to which markets are in practice open to effective competition, including aspects of market dominance, market concentration and predatory or anti-competitive behaviour;
— the extent to which customers are actually switching suppliers and renegotiating tariffs;
— price developments, including supply prices, in relation to the degree of the opening of markets;
— whether effective and non-discriminatory third party access to gas storage exists when technically and/or economically necessary for providing efficient access to the system;
— the experience gained in the application of the Directive as far as the effective independence of system operators in vertically integrated undertakings is concerned and whether other measures in addition to functional independence and separation of accounts have been developed which have effects equivalent to legal unbundling.

Where appropriate, the Commission shall submit proposals to the European Parliament and the Council, in particular to guarantee high public service standards.

Where appropriate, the Commission shall submit proposals to the European Parliament and the Council, in particular to ensure full and effective independence of distribution system operators before 1 July 2007. When necessary, these proposals shall, in conformity with competition law, also concern measures to address issues of market dominance, market concentration and predatory or anti-competitive behaviour.

Article 32
Repeals

1. Directive 91/296/EEC shall be repealed with effect from 1 July 2004, without prejudice to contracts concluded pursuant to Article 3(1) of Directive 91/296/EEC, which shall continue to be valid and to be implemented under the terms of the said Directive.

2. Directive 98/30/EC shall be repealed from 1 July 2004, without prejudice to the obligations of Member States concerning the deadlines for transposition and application of the said Directive. References made to the repealed Directive shall be construed as being made to this Directive and should be read in accordance with the correlation table in Annex B.

Article 33
Implementation

1. Member States shall bring into force the laws, regulations and administrative provisions necessary to comply with this Directive not later than 1 July 2004. They shall forthwith inform the Commission thereof.

2. Member States may postpone the implementation of Article 13(1) until 1 July 2007. This shall be without prejudice to the requirements contained in Article 13(2).

3. When Member States adopt these measures, they shall contain a reference to this Directive or shall be accompanied by such reference on the occasion of their official publication. The methods of making such reference shall be laid down by Member States.

Commentary
Art 33: B&C: 12.074

Article 34
Entry into force

This Directive shall enter into force on the twentieth day following that of its publication in the *Official Journal of the European Union*.

Notes
Date of entry into force: 4 August 2003.

Article 35
Addressees

This Directive is addressed to the Member States.

Done at Brussels, 26 June 2003.

ANNEX A
MEASURES ON CONSUMER PROTECTION

Without prejudice to Community rules on consumer protection, in particular Directives 97/7/EC of the European Parliament and of the Council[1] and Council Directive 93/13/EC,[2] the measures referred to in Article 3 are to ensure that customers:

(a) have a right to a contract with their gas service provider that specifies:
— the identity and address of the supplier;
— the services provided, the service quality levels offered, as well as the time for the initial connection;
— if offered, the types of maintenance service offered;
— the means by which up to date information on all applicable tariffs and maintenance charges may be obtained;
— the duration of the contract, the conditions for renewal and termination of services and of the contract, the existence of any right of withdrawal;
— any compensation and the refund arrangements which apply if contracted service quality levels are not met; and
— the method of initiating procedures for settlement of disputes in accordance with point (f).
Conditions shall be fair and well known in advance. In any case, this information should be provided prior to the conclusion or confirmation of the contract. Where contracts are concluded through intermediaries, the above information shall also be provided prior to the conclusion of the contract;

(b) are given adequate notice of any intention to modify contractual conditions and are informed about their right of withdrawal when the notice is given. Service providers shall notify their subscribers directly of any increase in charges, at an appropriate time no later than one normal billing period after the increase comes into effect. Member States shall ensure that customers are free to withdraw from contracts if they do not accept the new conditions, notified to them by their gas service provider;

(c) receive transparent information on applicable prices and tariffs and on standard terms and conditions, in respect of access to and use of gas services;

(d) are offered a wide choice of payment methods. Any difference in terms and conditions shall reflect the costs to the supplier of the different payment systems. General terms and conditions shall be fair and transparent. They shall be given in clear and comprehensible language. Customers shall be protected against unfair or misleading selling methods;

(e) shall not be charged for changing supplier;

(f) benefit from transparent, simple and inexpensive procedures for dealing with their complaints. Such procedures shall enable disputes to be settled fairly and promptly with provision, where warranted, for a system of reimbursement and/or compensation. They should follow, wherever possible, the principles set out in Commission Recommendation 98/257/EC;[3]

(g) connected to the gas system are informed about their rights to be supplied, under the national legislation applicable, with natural gas of a specified quality at reasonable prices.

Notes
[1] OJ L 144, 4.6.1997, p. 19.
[2] OJ L 95, 21.4.1993, p. 29.
[3] OJ L 115, 17.4.1998, p. 31.

ANNEX B
CORRELATION TABLE

Directive 98/30/EC	*This Directive*
Article 1	Article 1 Scope
Article 2	Article 2 Definitions
Article 3	Article 3 PSOs and Customer protection
Article 4	Article 4 Authorisation procedure
—	Article 5 Monitoring of security of supply
Article 5	Article 6 Technical rules
Article 6	Article 7 Designation of TSOs
Article 7	Article 8 Tasks of TSOs
—	Article 9 Unbundling of TSOs
Article 8	Article 10 Confidentiality for TSOs
Article 9(1)	Article 11 Designation of DSOs
Article 10	Article 12 Tasks of DSOs
—	Article 13 Unbundling of DSOs
Article 11	Article 14 Confidentiality for DSOs
—	Article 15 Combined operator
Article 12	Article 16 Right of access to accounts
Article 13	Article 17 Unbundling of accounts
Article 14–16	Article 18 Third Party Access
—	Article 19 Access to storage
Article 23	Article 20 Access to upstream pipeline networks
Article 17	Article 21 Refusal of access
—	Article 22 New infrastructure
Article 18 and 19	Article 23 Market opening and reciprocity
Article 20	Article 24 Direct lines
Article 21(2)–(3) and 22	Article 25 Regulatory authorities
Article 24	Article 26 Safeguard measures
Article 25	Article 27 Derogations in relation to take-or-pay commitments
Article 26	Article 28 Emergent and Isolated Markets
—	Article 29 Review procedure
—	Article 30 Committee

Directive 98/30/EC	*This Directive*
Article 27 and 28	Article 31 Reporting
—	Article 32 Repeals
Article 29	Article 33 Implementation
Article 30	Article 34 Entry into force
Article 31	Article 35 Addressees
	Annex A Measures on consumer protection

E16

COMMISSION DIRECTIVE

of 16 May 1988

on competition in the markets in telecommunications terminal equipment

(88/301/EEC)

Official Journal L 131, 27.5.1988, p. 73

Celex No: 31988L0301

Notes

EEA application: see the EEA Agreement, Annex XIV, Chapter H, Point 12 (as amended by EEA Joint Committee Decision No 25/95 (OJ No L 251, 19.10.1995, p. 31 and EEA Supplement No 39, 19.10.1995, p. 1).

Commentary
Directive 88/301/EEC: B&C: 12.089 **F&N:** 6.105, 6.245

THE COMMISSION OF THE EUROPEAN COMMUNITIES,

Having regard to the Treaty establishing the European Economic Community, and in particular Article [86](3) thereof,

Whereas:

1. In all the Member States, telecommunications are, either wholly or partly, a State monopoly generally granted in the form of special or exclusive rights to one or more bodies responsible for providing and operating the network infrastructure and related services. Those rights, however, often go beyond the provision of network utilization services and extend to the supply of user terminal equipment for connection to the network. The last decades have seen considerable technical developments in networks, and the pace of development has been especially striking in the area of terminal equipment.

2. Several Member States have, in response to technical and economic developments, reviewed their grant of special or exclusive rights in the telecommunications sector. The proliferation of types of terminal equipment and the possibility of the multiple use of terminals means that users must be allowed a free choice between the various types of equipment available if they are to benefit fully from the technological advances made in the sector.

3. Article [28] of the Treaty prohibits quantitative restrictions on imports from other Member States and all measures having equivalent effect. The grant of special or exclusive rights to import and market goods to one organization can, and often does, lead to restrictions on imports from other Member States.

4. Article [31] of the Treaty states that "Member States shall progressively adjust any State monopolies of a commercial character so as to ensure that when the transitional period has ended no discrimination regarding the conditions under which goods are procured and marketed exists between nationals of Member States.

The provisions of this Article shall apply to any body through which a Member State, in law or in fact, either directly or indirectly supervises, determines or appreciably influences imports or exports between Member States. These provisions shall likewise apply to monopolies delegated by the State to others." Paragraph 2 of Article [31] prohibits Member States from introducing any new measure contrary to the principles laid down in Article [31](1).

Notes

Following amendment and renumbering of the Treaty by the Treaty of Amsterdam, Article 31 of the Treaty states that "Member States shall adjust any State monopolies of a commercial character so as to ensure that no discrimination regarding the conditions under which goods are procured and marketed exists between nationals of Member States. The provisions of this Article shall apply to any body through which a Member State, in law or in fact, either directly or indirectly supervises, determines or appreciably influences imports or exports between Member States. These provisions shall likewise apply to monopolies delegated by the State to others.".

5. The special or exclusive rights relating to terminal equipment enjoyed by national telecommunications monopolies are exercised in such a way as, in practice, to disadvantage equipment from other Member States, notably by preventing users from freely choosing the equipment that best suits their needs in terms of price and quality, regardless of its origin. The exercise of these rights is therefore not compatible with Article [31] in all the Member States except Spain and Portugal, where the national monopolies are to be adjusted progressively before the end of the transitional period provided for by the Act of Accession.

6. The provision of installation and maintenance services is a key factor in the purchasing or rental of terminal equipment. The retention of exclusive rights in this field would be tantamount to retention of exclusive marketing rights. Such rights must therefore also be abolished if the abolition of exclusive importing and marketing rights is to have any practical effect.

7. Article [49] of the Treaty provides that "restrictions on freedom to provide services within the Community shall be progressively abolished during the transitional period in respect of nationals of Member States who are established in a State of the Community other than that of the person for whom the services are intended." Maintenance of terminals is a service within the meaning of Article [50] of the Treaty. As the transitional period has ended, the service in question, which cannot from a commercial point of view be dissociated from the marketing of the terminals, must be provided freely and in particular when provided by qualified operators.

Notes

Following amendment and renumbering of the Treaty by the Treaty of Amsterdam, Article 49 of the Treaty states that "restrictions on freedom to provide services within the Community shall be prohibited in respect of nationals of Member States who are established in a State of the Community other than that of the person for whom the services are intended."

8. Article [86](1) of the Treaty provides that "in the case of public undertakings and undertakings to which Member States grant special or exclusive rights, Member States shall neither enact nor maintain in force any measure contrary to the rules contained in this Treaty, in particular to those rules provided for in Article 7 and Articles [81] to [89]."

Notes

Article 7 of the Treaty was repealed by the Treaty of Amsterdam.

9. The market in terminal equipment is still as a rule governed by a system which allows competition in the common market to be distorted; this situation continues to produce infringements of the competition rules laid down by the Treaty and to affect adversely the development of trade to such an extent as would be contrary to the interests of the Community. Stronger competition in the terminal equipment market requires the introduction of transparent technical specifications and type-approval procedures which meet the essential requirements mentioned in Council Directive 86/361/EEC[1]

and allow the free movement of terminal equipment. In turn, such transparency necessarily entails the publication of technical specifications and typeapproval procedures. To ensure that the latter are applied transparently, objectively and without discrimination, the drawing-up and application of such rules should be entrusted to bodies independent of competitors in the market in question. It is essential that the specifications and type-approval procedures are published simultaneously and in an orderly fashion. Simultaneous publication will also ensure that behaviour contrary to the Treaty is avoided. Such simultaneous, orderly publication can be achieved only by means of a legal instrument that is binding on all the Member States. The most appropriate instrument to this end is a directive.

Notes
[1] OJ L 217, 5.8.1986, p. 21.

10. The Treaty entrusts the Commission with very clear tasks and gives it specific powers with regard to the monitoring of relations between the Member States and their public undertakings and enterprises to which they have delegated special or exclusive rights, in particular as regards the elimination of quantitative restrictions and measures having equivalent effect, discrimination between nationals of Member States, and competition. The only instrument, therefore, by which the Commission can efficiently carry out the tasks and powers assigned to it, is a Directive based on Article [86](3).

11. Telecommunications bodies or enterprises are undertakings within the meaning of Article [86](1) because they carry on an organized business activity involving the production of goods or services. They are either public undertakings or private enterprises to which the Member States have granted special or exclusive rights for the importation, marketing, connection, bringing into service of telecommunications terminal equipment and/or maintenance of such equipment. The grant and maintenance of special and exclusive rights for terminal equipment constitute measures within the meaning of that Article. The conditions for applying the exception of Article [86](2) are not fulfilled. Even if the provision of a telecommunications network for the use of the general public is a service of general economic interest entrusted by the State to the telecommunications bodies, the abolition of their special or exclusive rights to import and market terminal equipment would not obstruct, in law or in fact, the performance of that service. This is all the more true given that Member States are entitled to subject terminal equipment to type-approval procedures to ensure that they conform to the essential requirements.

12. Article [82] of the Treaty prohibits as incompatible with the common market any conduct by one or more undertakings that involves an abuse of a dominant position within the common market or a substantial part of it.

13. The telecommunications bodies hold individually or jointly a monopoly on their national telecommunications network. The national networks are markets. Therefore, the bodies each individually or jointly hold a dominant position in a substantial part of the market in question within the meaning of Article [82].

The effect of the special or exclusive rights granted to such bodies by the State to import and market terminal equipment is to:

— restrict users to renting such equipment, when it would often be cheaper for them, at least in the long term, to purchase this equipment. This effectively makes contracts for the use of networks subject to acceptance by the user of additional services which have no connection with the subject of the contracts,

— limit outlets and impede technical progress since the range of equipment offered by the telecommunications bodies is necessarily limited and will not be the best available to meet the requirements of a significant proportion of users.

Such conduct is expressly prohibited by Article [82](d) and (b), and is likely significantly to affect trade between Member States.

At all events, such special or exclusive rights in regard to the terminal equipment market give rise to a situation which is contrary to the objective of Article 3(f) of the Treaty, which provides for the institution of a system ensuring that competition in the common market is not distorted, and requires a fortiori that competition must not be eliminated. Member States have an obligation under

Article [10] of the Treaty to abstain from any measure which could jeopardize the attainment of the objectives of the Treaty, including Article 3 (f).

The exclusive rights to import and market terminal equipment must therefore be regarded as incompatible with Article [82] in conjunction with Article 3, and the grant or maintenance of such rights by a Member State is prohibited under Article [86](1).

14. To enable users to have access to the terminal equipment of their choice, it is necessary to know and make transparent the characteristics of the termination points of the network to which the terminal equipment is to be connected. Member States must therefore ensure that the characteristics are published and that users have access to termination points.

15. To be able to market their products, manufacturers of terminal equipment must know what technical specifications they must satisfy. Member States should therefore formalize and publish the specifications and type-approval rules, which they must notify to the Commission in draft form, in accordance with Council Directive 83/189/EEC.[1] The specifications may be extended to products imported from other Member States only insofar as they are necessary to ensure conformity with the essential requirements specified in Article 2(17) of Directive 86/361/EEC that can legitimately be required under Community law. Member States must, in any event, comply with Articles [28] and [30] of the Treaty, under which an importing Member State must allow terminal equipment legally manufactured and marketed in another Member State to be imported on to its territory, and may only subject it to such type-approval and possibly refuse approval for reasons concerning conformity with the abovementioned essential requirements.

Notes
[1] OJ L 109, 28.3.1983, p. 8.

---

16. The immediate publication of these specifications and procedures cannot be considered in view of their complexity. On the other hand, effective competition is not possible without such publication, since potential competitors of the bodies or enterprises with special or exclusive rights are unaware of the precise specifications with which their terminal equipment must comply and of the terms of the type-approval procedures and hence their cost and duration. A deadline should therefore be set for the publication of specifications and the type-approval procedures. A period of two-and-a-half years will also enable the telecommunications bodies with special or exclusive rights to adjust to the new market conditions and will enable economic operators, especially small and medium-sized enterprises, to adapt to the new competitive environment.

17. Monitoring of type-approval specifications and rules cannot be entrusted to a competitor in the terminal equipment market in view of the obvious conflict of interest. Member States should therefore ensure that the responsibility for drawing up type-approval specifications and rules is assigned to a body independent of the operator of the network and of any other competitor in the market for terminals.

18. The holders of special or exclusive rights in the terminal equipment in question have been able to impose on their customers long-term contracts preventing the introduction of free competition from having a practical effect within a reasonable period. Users must therefore be given the right to obtain a revision of the duration of their contracts,

HAS ADOPTED THIS DIRECTIVE:

Article 1

For the purposes of this Directive:

— "terminal equipment" means equipment directly or indirectly connected to the termination of a public telecommunications network to send, process or receive information. A connection is indirect if equipment is placed between the terminal and the termination of the network. In either case (direct or indirect), the connection may be made by wire, optical fibre or electromagnetically.

[Terminal equipment also means satellite earth station equipment],

— "undertaking" means a public or private body, to which a Member State grants special or exclusive rights for the importation, marketing, connection, bringing into service of telecommunications terminal equipment and/or maintenance of such equipment,

[— "special rights" means rights that are granted by a Member State to a limited number of undertakings, through any legislative, regulatory or administrative instrument, which, within a given geographical area,
— limits to two or more the number of such undertakings, otherwise than according t objective, proportional and non-discriminatory criteria, or
— designates, otherwise than according to such criteria, several competing undertakings, or
— confers on any undertaking or undertakings, otherwise than according to such criteria, any legal or regulatory advantages which substantially affect the ability of any other undertaking to import, market, connect, bring into service and/or maintain telecommunication terminal equipment in the same geographical area under substantially equivalent conditions,
— "satellite earth station equipment" means equipment which is capable of being used for the transmission only, or for the transmission and reception ("transmit/receive"), or for the reception only ("receive-only") of radiocommunication signals by means of satellites or other space-based systems.]

Notes

Article 1 was amended as shown in square brackets by Commission Directive 94/46/EC (OJ L 268, 19.10.1994, p. 15).

Article 2

[Member States which have granted special or exclusive rights to undertakings shall ensure that all exclusive rights are withdrawn, as well as those special rights which

(a) limit two or more the number of undertakings within the meaning of Article 1, otherwise than according to objective, proportional and non-discriminatory criteria, or
(b) designate, otherwise than according to such criteria, several competing undertakings within the meaning of Article 1.]

They shall, not later than three months following the notification of this Directive, inform the Commission of the measures taken or draft legislation introduced to that end.

Notes

Article 2 was amended as shown in square brackets by Commission Directive 94/46/EC (OJ L 268, 19.10.1994, p. 15).

Commentary

Art 2: **B&C:** 12.089

Article 3

Member States shall ensure that economic operators have the right to import, market, connect, bring into service and maintain terminal equipment. However, Member States may:

[— in the case of satellite earth station equipment, refuse to allow such equipment to be connected to the public telecommunications network and/or to be brought into service where it does not satisfy the relevant common technical regulations adopted in pursuance of Council Directive 93/97/EEC (8)[1] or, in the absence thereof, the essential requirements laid down in Article 4 of that Directive. In the absence of common technical rules of harmonized regulatory conditions, national rules shall be proportionate to those essential requirements and shall be notified to the Commission in pursuance of Directive 83/189/EEC where that Directive so requires.
— in the case of other terminal equipment, refuse to allow such equipment to be connected to the public telecommunications network where it does not satisfy the relevant common technical regulations adopted in pursuance of Council Directive 91/263/EEC (9)[2] or, in the absence thereof, the essential requirements laid down in Article 4 of that Directive.]
— require economic operators to possess the technical qualifications needed to connect, bring into service and maintain terminal equipment on the basis of objective, non-discriminatory and publicly available criteria.

Notes

[1] OJ No L 290, 24.11.1993, p. 1.
[2] OJ No L 128, 23.5.1991, p. 1.]

Article 3 was amended as shown in square brackets by Commission Directive 94/46/EC (OJ L 268, 19.10.1994, p. 15).

Commentary
Art 3: **B&C:** 12.089

Article 4

Member States shall ensure that users have access to new public network termination points and that the physical characteristics of these points are published not later than 31 December 1988.

Access to public network termination points existing at 31 December 1988 shall be given within a reasonable period to any user who so requests.

Article 5

1. Member States shall, not later than the date mentioned in Article 2, communicate to the Commission a list of all technical specifications and type-approval procedures which are used for terminal equipment, and shall provide the publication references.

Where they have not as yet been published in a Member State, the latter shall ensure that they are published not later than the dates referred to in Article 8.

2. Member States shall ensure that all other specifications and type-approval procedures for terminal equipment are formalized and published. Member States shall communicate the technical specifications and type-approval procedures in draft form to the Commission in accordance with Directive 83/189/EEC and according to the timetable set out in Article 8.

Article 6

Member States shall ensure that, from 1 July 1989, responsibility for drawing up the specifications referred to in Article 5, monitoring their application and granting type-approval is entrusted to a body independent of public or private undertakings offering goods and/or services in the telecommunications sector.

Article 7

Member States shall take the necessary steps to ensure that undertakings within the meaning of Article 1 make it possible for their customers to terminate, with maximum notice of one year, leasing or maintenance contracts which concern terminal equipment subject to exclusive or special rights at the time of the conclusion of the contracts.

For terminal equipment requiring type-approval, Member States shall ensure that this possibility of termination is afforded by the undertakings in question no later than the dates provided for in Article 8. For terminal equipment not requiring type-approval, Member States shall introduce this possibility no later than the date provided for in Article 2.

Article 8

Member States shall inform the Commission of the draft technical specifications and type-approval procedures referred to in Article 5(2):

— not later than 31 December 1988 in respect of equipment in category A of the list in Annex I,
— not later than 30 September 1989 in respect of equipment in category B of the list in Annex I,
— not later than 30 June 1990 in respect of other terminal equipment in category C of the list in Annex I.

Member States shall bring these specifications and type-approval procedures into force after expiry of the procedure provided for by Directive 83/189/EEC.

Article 9

Member States shall provide the Commission at the end of each year with a report allowing it to monitor compliance with the provisions of Articles 2, 3, 4, 6 and 7.

An outline of the report is attached as Annex II.

Article 10

The provisions of this Directive shall be without prejudice to the provisions of the instruments of accession of Spain and Portugal, and in particular Articles 48 and 208 of the Act of Accession.

Article 11

This Directive is addressed to the Member States.

Done at Brussels, 16 May 1988.

ANNEX I
LIST OF TERMINAL EQUIPMENT REFERRED TO IN ARTICLE 8

	Category
Additional telephone set; private automatic branch exchanges (PABXs):	A
Modems:	A
Telex terminals:	B
Data-transmission terminals:	B
Mobile telephones:	B
Receive-only satellite stations not reconnected to the public network of a Member State:	B
First telephone set:	C
Other terminal equipment:	C

ANNEX II
OUTLINE OF THE REPORT PROVIDED FOR IN ARTICLE 9

Implementation of Article 2

1. Terminal equipment for which legislation is being or has been modified.

By category of terminal equipment:

— date of adoption of the measure or,
— date of introduction of the bill or,
— date of entry into force of the measure.

2. Terminal equipment still subject to special or exclusive rights:

— type of terminal equipment and rights concerned.

Implementation of Article 3

— terminal equipment, the connection and/or commissioning of which has been restricted,
— technical qualifications required, giving reference of their publication.

Implementation of Article 4

— references of publications in which the physical characteristics are specified,
— number of existing network termination points,
— number of network termination points now accessible.

Implementation of Article 6

— independent body or bodies appointed.

Implementation of Article 7

— measures put into force, and
— number of terminated contracts.

E17

DIRECTIVE 2002/21/EC OF THE EUROPEAN PARLIAMENT AND OF THE COUNCIL

of 7 March 2002

on a common regulatory framework for electronic communications networks and services
(Framework Directive)

Official Journal L 108, 24.4.2002, p. 33

Celex No: 32002L0021

Notes

EEA application: this Directive was adopted with appropriate adaptations by EEA Joint Committee Decision No 11/2004 (OJ No L 116, 22.4.2004, p. 60 and EEA Supplement No 20, 22.4.2004, p. 14): see EEA Agreement, Annex XI, Point 5cl.

Commentary

Directive 2002/21/EC: B&C: 4.013, 4.094, 10.053, 12.089, 12.092, 12.110 **F&N:** 13.14, 13.173, 13.315
Arts 14–16: B&C: 4.013, 12.125

THE EUROPEAN PARLIAMENT AND THE COUNCIL OF THE EUROPEAN UNION,

Having regard to the Treaty establishing the European Community, and in particular Article 95 thereof,

Having regard to the proposal from the Commission,[1]

Having regard to the opinion of the Economic and Social Committee,[2]

Acting in accordance with the procedure laid down in Article 251 of the Treaty,[3]

Notes

[1] OJ C 365 E, 19.12.2000, p. 198 and OJ C 270 E, 25.9.2001, p. 199.

[2] OJ C 123, 25.4.2001, p. 56.

[3] Opinion of the European Parliament of 1 March 2001 (OJ C 277, 1.10.2001, p. 91), Council Common Position of 17 September 2001 (OJ C 337, 30.11.2001, p. 34) and Decision of the European Parliament of 12 December 2001 [OJ C 177 E, 25.7.2002, p. 81]. Council Decision of 14 February 2002.

Whereas:

(1) The current regulatory framework for telecommunications has been successful in creating the conditions for effective competition in the telecommunications sector during the transition from monopoly to full competition.

(2) On 10 November 1999, the Commission presented a communication to the European Parliament, the Council, the Economic and Social Committee and the Committee of the Regions entitled "Towards a new framework for electronic communications infrastructure and associated services — the 1999 communications review". In that communication, the Commission reviewed the existing regulatory framework for telecommunications, in accordance with its obligation under Article 8 of Council Directive 90/387/EEC of 28 June 1990 on the establishment of the internal market for telecommunications services through the implementation of open network provision.[1] It also presented a series of policy proposals for a new regulatory framework for electronic communications infrastructure and associated services for public consultation.

Notes

[1] OJ L 192, 24.7.1990, p. 1. Directive as amended by Directive 97/51/EC of the European Parliament and of the Council (OJ L 295, 29.10.1997, p. 23).

---

(3) On 26 April 2000 the Commission presented a communication to the European Parliament, the Council, the Economic and Social Committee and the Committee of the Regions on the results of the public consultation on the 1999 communications review and orientations for the new regulatory framework. The communication summarised the public consultation and set out certain key orientations for the preparation of a new framework for electronic communications infrastructure and associated services.

(4) The Lisbon European Council of 23 and 24 March 2000 highlighted the potential for growth, competitiveness and job creation of the shift to a digital, knowledge-based economy. In particular, it emphasised the importance for Europe's businesses and citizens of access to an inexpensive, world-class communications infrastructure and a wide range of services.

(5) The convergence of the telecommunications, media and information technology sectors means all transmission networks and services should be covered by a single regulatory framework. That regulatory framework consists of this Directive and four specific Directives: Directive 2002/20/EC of the European Parliament and of the Council of 7 March 2002 on the authorisation of electronic communications networks and services (Authorisation Directive),[1] Directive 2002/19/EC of the European Parliament and of the Council of 7 March 2002 on access to, and interconnection of, electronic communications networks and associated facilities (Access Directive),[2] Directive 2002/22/EC of the European Parliament and of the Council of 7 March 2002 on universal service and users' rights relating to electronic communications networks and services (Universal Service Directive),[3] Directive 97/66/EC of the European Parliament and of the Council of 15 December 1997 concerning the processing of personal data and the protection of privacy in the telecommunications sector,[4] (hereinafter referred to as "the Specific Directives"). It is necessary to separate the regulation of transmission from the regulation of content. This framework does not therefore cover the content of services delivered over electronic communications networks using electronic communications services, such as broadcasting content, financial services and certain information society services, and is therefore without prejudice to measures taken at Community or national level in respect of such services, in compliance with Community law, in order to promote cultural and linguistic diversity and to ensure the defence of media pluralism. The content of television programmes is covered by Council Directive 89/552/EEC of 3 October 1989 on the coordination of certain provisions laid down by law, regulation or administrative action in Member States concerning the pursuit of television broadcasting activities.[5] The separation between the regulation of transmission and the regulation of content does not prejudice the taking into account of the links existing between them, in particular in order to guarantee media pluralism, cultural diversity and consumer protection.

Notes

[1] See [OJ L 108, 24.4.2002, p. 21].
[2] See [OJ L 108, 24.4.2002, p. 7].
[3] See [OJ L 108, 24.4.2002, p. 51].
[4] OJ L 24, 30.1.1998, p. 1.
[5] OJ L 298, 17.10.1989, p. 23. Directive as amended by Directive 97/36/EC of the European Parliament and of the Council (OJ L 202, 30.7.1997, p. 60).

Commentary
Recital 5: B&C: 12.089, 12.094, 12.095

(6) Audiovisual policy and content regulation are undertaken in pursuit of general interest objectives, such as freedom of expression, media pluralism, impartiality, cultural and linguistic diversity, social inclusion, consumer protection and the protection of minors. The Commission communication "Principles and guidelines for the Community's audio-visual policy in the digital age", and the Council conclusions of 6 June 2000 welcoming this communication, set out the key actions to be taken by the Community to implement its audio-visual policy.

(7) The provisions of this Directive and the Specific Directives are without prejudice to the possibility for each Member State to take the necessary measures to ensure the protection of its essential security interests, to safeguard public policy and public security, and to permit the investigation, detection and prosecution of criminal offences, including the establishment by national

regulatory authorities of specific and proportional obligations applicable to providers of electronic communications services.

Commentary
Recital 7: B&C: 12.096

(8) This Directive does not cover equipment within the scope of Directive 1999/5/EC of the European Parliament and of the Council of 9 March 1999 on radio equipment and telecommunications terminal equipment and the mutual recognition of their conformity,[1] but does cover consumer equipment used for digital television. It is important for regulators to encourage network operators and terminal equipment manufacturers to cooperate in order to facilitate access by disabled users to electronic communications services.

Notes
[1] OJ L 91, 7.4.1999, p. 10.

(9) Information society services are covered by Directive 2000/31/EC of the European Parliament and of the Council of 8 June 2000 on certain legal aspects of information society services, in particular electronic commerce, in the internal market (Directive on electronic commerce).[1]

Notes
[1] OJ L 178, 17.7.2000, p. 1.

(10) The definition of "information society service" in Article 1 of Directive 98/34/EC of the European Parliament and of the Council of 22 June 1998 laying down a procedure for the provision of information in the field of technical standards and regulations and of rules of information society services[1] spans a wide range of economic activities which take place on-line. Most of these activities are not covered by the scope of this Directive because they do not consist wholly or mainly in the conveyance of signals on electronic communications networks. Voice telephony and electronic mail conveyance services are covered by this Directive. The same undertaking, for example an Internet service provider, can offer both an electronic communications service, such as access to the Internet, and services not covered under this Directive, such as the provision of web-based content.

Notes
[1] OJ L 204, 21.7.1998, p. 37. Directive as amended by Directive 98/48/EC (OJ L 217, 5.8.1998, p. 18).

Commentary
Recital 10: B&C: 12.095

(11) In accordance with the principle of the separation of regulatory and operational functions, Member States should guarantee the independence of the national regulatory authority or authorities with a view to ensuring the impartiality of their decisions. This requirement of independence is without prejudice to the institutional autonomy and constitutional obligations of the Member States or to the principle of neutrality with regard to the rules in Member States governing the system of property ownership laid down in Article 295 of the Treaty. National regulatory authorities should be in possession of all the necessary resources, in terms of staffing, expertise, and financial means, for the performance of their tasks.

Commentary
Recital 11: B&C: 12.092

(12) Any party who is the subject of a decision by a national regulatory authority should have the right to appeal to a body that is independent of the parties involved. This body may be a court. Furthermore, any undertaking which considers that its applications for the granting of rights to install facilities have not been dealt with in accordance with the principles set out in this Directive should be entitled to appeal against such decisions. This appeal procedure is without prejudice to the division of competences within national judicial systems and to the rights of legal entities or natural persons under national law.

(13) National regulatory authorities need to gather information from market players in order to carry out their tasks effectively. Such information may also need to be gathered on behalf of the Commission, to allow it to fulfil its obligations under Community law. Requests for information should be proportionate and not impose an undue burden on undertakings. Information gathered by national regulatory authorities should be publicly available, except in so far as it is confidential in accordance with national rules on public access to information and subject to Community and national law on business confidentiality.

(14) Information that is considered confidential by a national regulatory authority, in accordance with Community and national rules on business confidentiality, may only be exchanged with the Commission and other national regulatory authorities where such exchange is strictly necessary for the application of the provisions of this Directive or the Specific Directives. The information exchanged should be limited to that which is relevant and proportionate to the purpose of such an exchange.

(15) It is important that national regulatory authorities consult all interested parties on proposed decisions and take account of their comments before adopting a final decision. In order to ensure that decisions at national level do not have an adverse effect on the single market or other Treaty objectives, national regulatory authorities should also notify certain draft decisions to the Commission and other national regulatory authorities to give them the opportunity to comment. It is appropriate for national regulatory authorities to consult interested parties on all draft measures which have an effect on trade between Member States. The cases where the procedures referred to in Articles 6 and 7 apply are defined in this Directive and in the Specific Directives. The Commission should be able, after consulting the Communications Committee, to require a national regulatory authority to withdraw a draft measure where it concerns definition of relevant markets or the designation or not of undertakings with significant market power, and where such decisions would create a barrier to the single market or would be incompatible with Community law and in particular the policy objectives that national regulatory authorities should follow. This procedure is without prejudice to the notification procedure provided for in Directive 98/34/EC and the Commission's prerogatives under the Treaty in respect of infringements of Community law.

(16) National regulatory authorities should have a harmonised set of objectives and principles to underpin, and should, where necessary, coordinate their actions with the regulatory authorities of other Member States in carrying out their tasks under this regulatory framework.

Commentary
Recital 16: B&C: 12.092

(17) The activities of national regulatory authorities established under this Directive and the Specific Directives contribute to the fulfilment of broader policies in the areas of culture, employment, the environment, social cohesion and town and country planning.

(18) The requirement for Member States to ensure that national regulatory authorities take the utmost account of the desirability of making regulation technologically neutral, that is to say that it neither imposes nor discriminates in favour of the use of a particular type of technology, does not preclude the taking of proportionate steps to promote certain specific services where this is justified, for example digital television as a means for increasing spectrum efficiency.

Commentary
Recital 18: B&C: 12.094

(19) Radio frequencies are an essential input for radio-based electronic communications services and, in so far as they relate to such services, should therefore be allocated and assigned by national regulatory authorities according to a set of harmonised objectives and principles governing their action as well as to objective, transparent and non-discriminatory criteria, taking into account the democratic, social, linguistic and cultural interests related to the use of frequency. It is important that the allocation and assignment of radio frequencies is managed as efficiently as possible. Transfer of radio frequencies can be an effective means of increasing efficient use of spectrum, as long as there are sufficient safeguards in place to protect the public

interest, in particular the need to ensure transparency and regulatory supervision of such transfers. Decision No 676/2002/EC of the European Parliament and of the Council of 7 March 2002 on a regulatory framework for radio spectrum policy in the European Community (Radio Spectrum Decision)[1] establishes a framework for harmonisation of radio frequencies, and action taken under this Directive should seek to facilitate the work under that Decision.

Notes
[1] See [OJ L 108, 24.4.2002, p. 1].

(20) Access to numbering resources on the basis of transparent, objective and non-discriminatory criteria is essential for undertakings to compete in the electronic communications sector. All elements of national numbering plans should be managed by national regulatory authorities, including point codes used in network addressing. Where there is a need for harmonisation of numbering resources in the Community to support the development of pan-European services, the Commission may take technical implementing measures using its executive powers. Where this is appropriate to ensure full global interoperability of services, Member States should coordinate their national positions in accordance with the Treaty in international organisations and fora where numbering decisions are taken. The provisions of this Directive do not establish any new areas of responsibility for the national regulatory authorities in the field of Internet naming and addressing.

(21) Member States may use, *inter alia*, competitive or comparative selection procedures for the assignment of radio frequencies as well as numbers with exceptional economic value. In administering such schemes, national regulatory authorities should take into account the provisions of Article 8.

(22) It should be ensured that procedures exist for the granting of rights to install facilities that are timely, non-discriminatory and transparent, in order to guarantee the conditions for fair and effective competition. This Directive is without prejudice to national provisions governing the expropriation or use of property, the normal exercise of property rights, the normal use of the public domain, or to the principle of neutrality with regard to the rules in Member States governing the system of property ownership.

(23) Facility sharing can be of benefit for town planning, public health or environmental reasons, and should be encouraged by national regulatory authorities on the basis of voluntary agreements. In cases where undertakings are deprived of access to viable alternatives, compulsory facility or property sharing may be appropriate. It covers *inter alia*: physical co-location and duct, building, mast, antenna or antenna system sharing. Compulsory facility or property sharing should be imposed on undertakings only after full public consultation.

(24) Where mobile operators are required to share towers or masts for environmental reasons, such mandated sharing may lead to a reduction in the maximum transmitted power levels allowed for each operator for reasons of public health, and this in turn may require operators to install more transmission sites to ensure national coverage.

(25) There is a need for *ex ante* obligations in certain circumstances in order to ensure the development of a competitive market. The definition of significant market power in the Directive 97/33/EC of the European Parliament and of the Council of 30 June 1997 on interconnection in telecommunications with regard to ensuring universal service and interoperability through application of the principles of open network provision (ONP)[1] has proved effective in the initial stages of market opening as the threshold for *ex ante* obligations, but now needs to be adapted to suit more complex and dynamic markets. For this reason, the definition used in this Directive is equivalent to the concept of dominance as defined in the case law of the Court of Justice and the Court of First Instance of the European Communities.

Notes
[1] OJ L 199, 26.7.1997, p. 32. Directive as amended by Directive 98/61/EC (OJ L 268, 3.10.1998, p. 37).

Commentary
Recital 25: B&C: 12.099

(26) Two or more undertakings can be found to enjoy a joint dominant position not only where there exist structural or other links between them but also where the structure of the relevant market is conducive to coordinated effects, that is, it encourages parallel or aligned anti-competitive behaviour on the market.

(27) It is essential that *ex ante* regulatory obligations should only be imposed where there is not effective competition, i.e. in markets where there are one or more undertakings with significant market power, and where national and Community competition law remedies are not sufficient to address the problem. It is necessary therefore for the Commission to draw up guidelines at Community level in accordance with the principles of competition law for national regulatory authorities to follow in assessing whether competition is effective in a given market and in assessing significant market power. National regulatory authorities should analyse whether a given product or service market is effectively competitive in a given geographical area, which could be the whole or a part of the territory of the Member State concerned or neighbouring parts of territories of Member States considered together. An analysis of effective competition should include an analysis as to whether the market is prospectively competitive, and thus whether any lack of effective competition is durable. Those guidelines will also address the issue of newly emerging markets, where *de facto* the market leader is likely to have a substantial market share but should not be subjected to inappropriate obligations. The Commission should review the guidelines regularly to ensure that they remain appropriate in a rapidly developing market. National regulatory authorities will need to cooperate with each other where the relevant market is found to be transnational.

Commentary
Recital 27: **B&C:** 12.099–12.100 **F&N:** 13.57

(28) In determining whether an undertaking has significant market power in a specific market, national regulatory authorities should act in accordance with Community law and take into the utmost account the Commission guidelines.

(29) The Community and the Member States have entered into commitments in relation to standards and the regulatory framework of telecommunications networks and services in the World Trade Organisation.

(30) Standardisation should remain primarily a market-driven process. However there may still be situations where it is appropriate to require compliance with specified standards at Community level to ensure interoperability in the single market. At national level, Member States are subject to the provisions of Directive 98/34/EC. Directive 95/47/EC of the European Parliament and of the Council of 24 October 1995 on the use of standards for the transmission of television signals[1] did not mandate any specific digital television transmission system or service requirement. Through the Digital Video Broadcasting Group, European market players have developed a family of television transmission systems that have been standardised by the European Telecommunications Standards Institute (ETSI) and have become International Telecommunication Union recommendations. Any decision to make the implementation of such standards mandatory should follow a full public consultation. Standardisation procedures under this Directive are without prejudice to the provisions of Directive 1999/5/EC, Council Directive 73/23/EEC of 19 February 1973 on the harmonisation of the laws of Member States relating to electrical equipment designed for use within certain voltage limits[2] and Council Directive 89/336/EEC of 3 May 1989 on the approximation of the laws of the Member States relating to electromagnetic compatibility.[3]

Notes
[1] OJ L 281, 23.11.1995, p. 51.
[2] OJ L 77, 26.3.1973, p. 29.
[3] OJ L 139, 23.5.1989, p. 19.

(31) Interoperability of digital interactive television services and enhanced digital television equipment, at the level of the consumer, should be encouraged in order to ensure the free flow of information, media pluralism and cultural diversity. It is desirable for consumers to have the

capability of receiving, regardless of the transmission mode, all digital interactive television services, having regard to technological neutrality, future technological progress, the need to promote the take-up of digital television, and the state of competition in the markets for digital television services. Digital interactive television platform operators should strive to implement an open application program interface (API) which conforms to standards or specifications adopted by a European standards organisation. Migration from existing APIs to new open APIs should be encouraged and organised, for example by Memoranda of Understanding between all relevant market players. Open APIs facilitate interoperability, i.e. the portability of interactive content between delivery mechanisms, and full functionality of this content on enhanced digital television equipment. However, the need not to hinder the functioning of the receiving equipment and to protect it from malicious attacks, for example from viruses, should be taken into account.

(32) In the event of a dispute between undertakings in the same Member State in an area covered by this Directive or the Specific Directives, for example relating to obligations for access and interconnection or to the means of transferring subscriber lists, an aggrieved party that has negotiated in good faith but failed to reach agreement should be able to call on the national regulatory authority to resolve the dispute. National regulatory authorities should be able to impose a solution on the parties. The intervention of a national regulatory authority in the resolution of a dispute between undertakings providing electronic communications networks or services in a Member State should seek to ensure compliance with the obligations arising under this Directive or the Specific Directives.

(33) In addition to the rights of recourse granted under national or Community law, there is a need for a simple procedure to be initiated at the request of either party in a dispute, to resolve cross-border disputes which lie outside the competence of a single national regulatory authority.

(34) A single Committee should replace the "ONP Committee" instituted by Article 9 of Directive 90/387/EEC and the Licensing Committee instituted by Article 14 of Directive 97/13/EC of the European Parliament and of the Council of 10 April 1997 on a common framework for general authorisations and individual licences in the field of telecommunications services.[1]

Notes
[1] OJ L 117, 7.5.1997, p. 15.

(35) National regulatory authorities and national competition authorities should provide each other with the information necessary to apply the provisions of this Directive and the Specific Directives, in order to allow them to cooperate fully together. In respect of the information exchanged, the receiving authority should ensure the same level of confidentiality as the originating authority.

(36) The Commission has indicated its intention to set up a European regulators group for electronic communications networks and services which would constitute a suitable mechanism for encouraging cooperation and coordination of national regulatory authorities, in order to promote the development of the internal market for electronic communications networks and services, and to seek to achieve consistent application, in all Member States, of the provisions set out in this Directive and the Specific Directives, in particular in areas where national law implementing Community law gives national regulatory authorities considerable discretionary powers in application of the relevant rules.

(37) National regulatory authorities should be required to cooperate with each other and with the Commission in a transparent manner to ensure consistent application, in all Member States, of the provisions of this Directive and the Specific Directives. This cooperation could take place, *inter alia*, in the Communications Committee or in a group comprising European regulators. Member States should decide which bodies are national regulatory authorities for the purposes of this Directive and the Specific Directives.

(38) Measures that could affect trade between Member States are measures that may have an influence, direct or indirect, actual or potential, on the pattern of trade between Member States in a manner which might create a barrier to the single market. They comprise measures that have a significant impact on operators or users in other Member States, which include, *inter alia*: measures which affect prices for users in other Member States; measures which affect the ability

of an undertaking established in another Member State to provide an electronic communications service, and in particular measures which affect the ability to offer services on a transnational basis; and measures which affect market structure or access, leading to repercussions for undertakings in other Member States.

(39) The provisions of this Directive should be reviewed periodically, in particular with a view to determining the need for modification in the light of changing technological or market conditions.

(40) The measures necessary for the implementation of this Directive should be adopted in accordance with Council Decision 1999/468/EC of 28 June 1999 laying down the procedures for the exercise of implementing powers conferred on the Commission.[1]

Notes
[1] OJ L 184, 17.7.1999, p. 23.

(41) Since the objectives of the proposed action, namely achieving a harmonised framework for the regulation of electronic communications services, electronic communications networks, associated facilities and associated services cannot be sufficiently achieved by the Member States and can therefore, by reason of the scale and effects of the action, be better achieved at Community level, the Community may adopt measures in accordance with the principle of subsidiarity as set out in Article 5 of the Treaty. In accordance with the principle of proportionality, as set out in that Article, this Directive does not go beyond what is necessary for those objectives.

(42) Certain directives and decisions in this field should be repealed.

(43) The Commission should monitor the transition from the existing framework to the new framework, and may in particular, at an appropriate time, bring forward a proposal to repeal Regulation (EC) No 2887/2000 of the European Parliament and of the Council of 18 December 2000 on unbundled access to the local loop,[1]

Notes
[1] OJ L 336, 30.12.2000, p. 4.

HAVE ADOPTED THIS DIRECTIVE:

CHAPTER I
SCOPE, AIM AND DEFINITIONS

Article 1
Scope and aim

1. This Directive establishes a harmonised framework for the regulation of electronic communications services, electronic communications networks, associated facilities and associated services. It lays down tasks of national regulatory authorities and establishes a set of procedures to ensure the harmonised application of the regulatory framework throughout the Community.

2. This Directive as well as the Specific Directives are without prejudice to obligations imposed by national law in accordance with Community law or by Community law in respect of services provided using electronic communications networks and services.

3. This Directive as well as the Specific Directives are without prejudice to measures taken at Community or national level, in compliance with Community law, to pursue general interest objectives, in particular relating to content regulation and audio-visual policy.

4. This Directive and the Specific Directives are without prejudice to the provisions of Directive 1999/5/EC.

[5. This Directive and the Specific Directive shall be without prejudice to any specific measure adapted for the regulation of international roaming on public mobile telephone networks within the Community.]

Notes
Article 1(5) shown in square brackets was inserted by Regulation (EC) 717/2007 (OJ L 171 29.6.2007) with effect from 30 June 2007.

Commentary
Art 1: **B&C:** 12.096
Art 1(2): **B&C:** 12.090
Art 1(3): **B&C:** 12.090
Art 1(4): **B&C:** 12.090

Article 2
Definitions

For the purposes of this Directive:

(a) "electronic communications network" means transmission systems and, where applicable, switching or routing equipment and other resources which permit the conveyance of signals by wire, by radio, by optical or by other electromagnetic means, including satellite networks, fixed (circuit- and packet-switched, including Internet) and mobile terrestrial networks, electricity cable systems, to the extent that they are used for the purpose of transmitting signals, networks used for radio and television broadcasting, and cable television networks, irrespective of the type of information conveyed;

(b) "transnational markets" means markets identified in accordance with Article 15(4) covering the Community or a substantial part thereof;

(c) "electronic communications service" means a service normally provided for remuneration which consists wholly or mainly in the conveyance of signals on electronic communications networks, including telecommunications services and transmission services in networks used for broadcasting, but exclude services providing, or exercising editorial control over, content transmitted using electronic communications networks and services; it does not include information society services, as defined in Article 1 of Directive 98/34/EC, which do not consist wholly or mainly in the conveyance of signals on electronic communications networks;

(d) "public communications network" means an electronic communications network used wholly or mainly for the provision of publicly available electronic communications services;

(e) "associated facilities" means those facilities associated with an electronic communications network and/or an electronic communications service which enable and/or support the provision of services via that network and/or service. It includes conditional access systems and electronic programme guides;

(f) "conditional access system" means any technical measure and/or arrangement whereby access to a protected radio or television broadcasting service in intelligible form is made conditional upon subscription or other form of prior individual authorisation;

(g) "national regulatory authority" means the body or bodies charged by a Member State with any of the regulatory tasks assigned in this Directive and the Specific Directives;

(h) "user" means a legal entity or natural person using or requesting a publicly available electronic communications service;

(i) "consumer" means any natural person who uses or requests a publicly available electronic communications service for purposes which are outside his or her trade, business or profession;

(j) "universal service" means the minimum set of services, defined in Directive 2002/22/EC (Universal Service Directive), of specified quality which is available to all users regardless of their geographical location and, in the light of specific national conditions, at an affordable price;

(k) "subscriber" means any natural person or legal entity who or which is party to a contract with the provider of publicly available electronic communications services for the supply of such services;

(l) "Specific Directives" means Directive 2002/20/EC (Authorisation Directive), Directive 2002/19/EC (Access Directive), Directive 2002/22/EC (Universal Service Directive) and Directive 97/66/EC;

(m) "provision of an electronic communications network" means the establishment, operation, control or making available of such a network;

(n) "end-user" means a user not providing public communications networks or publicly available electronic communications services.

(o) "enhanced digital television equipment" means set-top boxes intended for connection to television sets or integrated digital television sets, able to receive digital interactive television services;

(p) "application program interface (API)" means the software interfaces between applications, made available by broadcasters or service providers, and the resources in the enhanced digital television equipment for digital television and radio services.

Commentary
Art 2: B&C: 12.094 F&N: 13.150

CHAPTER II
NATIONAL REGULATORY AUTHORITIES

Article 3
National regulatory authorities

1. Member States shall ensure that each of the tasks assigned to national regulatory authorities in this Directive and the Specific Directives is undertaken by a competent body.

2. Member States shall guarantee the independence of national regulatory authorities by ensuring that they are legally distinct from and functionally independent of all organisations providing electronic communications networks, equipment or services. Member States that retain ownership or control of undertakings providing electronic communications networks and/or services shall ensure effective structural separation of the regulatory function from activities associated with ownership or control.

3. Member States shall ensure that national regulatory authorities exercise their powers impartially and transparently.

4. Member States shall publish the tasks to be undertaken by national regulatory authorities in an easily accessible form, in particular where those tasks are assigned to more than one body. Member States shall ensure, where appropriate, consultation and cooperation between those authorities, and between those authorities and national authorities entrusted with the implementation of competition law and national authorities entrusted with the implementation of consumer law, on matters of common interest. Where more than one authority has competence to address such matters, Member States shall ensure that the respective tasks of each authority are published in an easily accessible form.

5. National regulatory authorities and national competition authorities shall provide each other with the information necessary for the application of the provisions of this Directive and the Specific Directives. In respect of the information exchanged, the receiving authority shall ensure the same level of confidentiality as the originating authority.

6. Member States shall notify to the Commission all national regulatory authorities assigned tasks under this Directive and the Specific Directives, and their respective responsibilities.

Commentary
Art 3: B&C: 12.092
Art 3(3): B&C: 12.093

Article 4
Right of appeal

1. Member States shall ensure that effective mechanisms exist at national level under which any user or undertaking providing electronic communications networks and/or services who is affected by a decision of a national regulatory authority has the right of appeal against the decision to an appeal body that is independent of the parties involved. This body, which may be a court, shall have the appropriate expertise available to it to enable it to carry out its functions. Member States shall ensure that the merits of the case are duly taken into account and that there is an effective appeal mechanism. Pending the outcome of any such appeal, the decision of the national regulatory authority shall stand, unless the appeal body decides otherwise.

2. Where the appeal body referred to in paragraph 1 is not judicial in character, written reasons for its decision shall always be given. Furthermore, in such a case, its decision shall be subject to review by a court or tribunal within the meaning of Article 234 of the Treaty.

Commentary
Art 4: B&C: 12.092–12.093 F&N: 13.58

Article 5
Provision of information

1. Member States shall ensure that undertakings providing electronic communications networks and services provide all the information, including financial information, necessary for national regulatory authorities to ensure conformity with the provisions of, or decisions made in accordance with, this Directive and the Specific Directives. These undertakings shall provide such information promptly on request and to the timescales and level of detail required by the national regulatory authority. The information requested by the national regulatory authority shall be proportionate to the performance of that task. The national regulatory authority shall give the reasons justifying its request for information.

2. Member States shall ensure that national regulatory authorities provide the Commission, after a reasoned request, with the information necessary for it to carry out its tasks under the Treaty. The information requested by the Commission shall be proportionate to the performance of those tasks. Where the information provided refers to information previously provided by undertakings at the request of the national regulatory authority, such undertakings shall be informed thereof. To the extent necessary, and unless the authority that provides the information has made an explicit and reasoned request to the contrary, the Commission shall make the information provided available to another such authority in another Member State.

Subject to the requirements of paragraph 3, Member States shall ensure that the information submitted to one national regulatory authority can be made available to another such authority in the same or different Member State, after a substantiated request, where necessary to allow either authority to fulfil its responsibilities under Community law.

3. Where information is considered confidential by a national regulatory authority in accordance with Community and national rules on business confidentiality, the Commission and the national regulatory authorities concerned shall ensure such confidentiality.

4. Member States shall ensure that, acting in accordance with national rules on public access to information and subject to Community and national rules on business confidentiality, national regulatory authorities publish such information as would contribute to an open and competitive market.

5. National regulatory authorities shall publish the terms of public access to information as referred to in paragraph 4, including procedures for obtaining such access.

Commentary
Art 5: B&C: 12.092
Art 5(3): B&C: 12.093

Article 6
Consultation and transparency mechanism

Except in cases falling within Articles 7(6), 20 or 21 Member States shall ensure that where national regulatory authorities intend to take measures in accordance with this Directive or the Specific Directives which have a significant impact on the relevant market, they give interested parties the opportunity to comment on the draft measure within a reasonable period. National regulatory authorities shall publish their national consultation procedures. Member States shall ensure the establishment of a single information point through which all current consultations can be accessed. The results of the consultation procedure shall be made publicly available by the national regulatory authority, except in the case of confidential information in accordance with Community and national law on business confidentiality.

Commentary
Art 6: B&C: 12.093, 12.104

Article 7
Consolidating the internal market for electronic communications

1. In carrying out their tasks under this Directive and the Specific Directives, national regulatory authorities shall take the utmost account of the objectives set out in Article 8, including in so far as they relate to the functioning of the internal market.

2. National regulatory authorities shall contribute to the development of the internal market by cooperating with each other and with the Commission in a transparent manner to ensure the consistent application, in all Member States, of the provisions of this Directive and the Specific Directives. To this end, they shall, in particular, seek to agree on the types of instruments and remedies best suited to address particular types of situations in the market place.

3. In addition to the consultation referred to in Article 6, where a national regulatory authority intends to take a measure which:

(a) falls within the scope of Articles 15 or 16 of this Directive, Articles 5 or 8 of Directive 2002/19/EC (Access Directive) or Article 16 of Directive 2002/22/EC (Universal Service Directive), and
(b) would affect trade between Member States,

it shall at the same time make the draft measure accessible to the Commission and the national regulatory authorities in other Member States, together with the reasoning on which the measure is based, in accordance with Article 5(3), and inform the Commission and other national regulatory authorities thereof. National regulatory authorities and the Commission may make comments to the national regulatory authority concerned only within one month or within the period referred to in Article 6 if that period is longer. The one-month period may not be extended.

4. Where an intended measure covered by paragraph 3 aims at:

(a) defining a relevant market which differs from those defined in the recommendation in accordance with Article 15(1), or
(b) deciding whether or not to designate an undertaking as having, either individually or jointly with others, significant market power, under Article 16(3), (4) or (5),

and would affect trade between Member States and the Commission has indicated to the national regulatory authority that it considers that the draft measure would create a barrier to the single market or if it has serious doubts as to its compatibility with Community law and in particular the objectives referred to in Article 8, then the draft measure shall not be adopted for a further two months. This period may not be extended. Within this period the Commission may, in accordance with the procedure referred to in Article 22(2), take a decision requiring the national regulatory authority concerned to withdraw the draft measure. This decision shall be accompanied by a detailed and objective analysis of why the Commission considers that the draft measure should not be adopted together with specific proposals for amending the draft measure.

5. The national regulatory authority concerned shall take the utmost account of comments of other national regulatory authorities and the Commission and may, except in cases covered by paragraph 4, adopt the resulting draft measure and, where it does so, shall communicate it to the Commission.

6. In exceptional circumstances, where a national regulatory authority considers that there is an urgent need to act, by way of derogation from the procedure set out in paragraphs 3 and 4, in order to safeguard competition and protect the interests of users, it may immediately adopt proportionate and provisional measures. It shall, without delay, communicate those measures, with full reasons, to the Commission and the other national regulatory authorities. A decision by the national regulatory authority to render such measures permanent or extend the time for which they are applicable shall be subject to the provisions of paragraphs 3 and 4.

Commentary
Art 7: **B&C:** 4.095, 12.092, 12.104, 12.126 **F&N:** 2.64, 13.35, 13.40, 13.184, 13.198, 13.236
Art 7(3): **B&C:** 12.104
Art 7(4): **B&C:** 12.101, 12.104

Part E Sectoral Regimes

CHAPTER III
TASKS OF NATIONAL REGULATORY AUTHORITIES

Article 8
Policy objectives and regulatory principles

1. Member States shall ensure that in carrying out the regulatory tasks specified in this Directive and the Specific Directives, the national regulatory authorities take all reasonable measures which are aimed at achieving the objectives set out in paragraphs 2, 3 and 4. Such measures shall be proportionate to those objectives.

Member States shall ensure that in carrying out the regulatory tasks specified in this Directive and the Specific Directives, in particular those designed to ensure effective competition, national regulatory authorities take the utmost account of the desirability of making regulations technologically neutral.

National regulatory authorities may contribute within their competencies to ensuring the implementation of policies aimed at the promotion of cultural and linguistic diversity, as well as media pluralism.

2. The national regulatory authorities shall promote competition in the provision of electronic communications networks, electronic communications services and associated facilities and services by *inter alia*:

(a) ensuring that users, including disabled users, derive maximum benefit in terms of choice, price, and quality;

(b) ensuring that there is no distortion or restriction of competition in the electronic communications sector;

(c) encouraging efficient investment in infrastructure, and promoting innovation; and

(d) encouraging efficient use and ensuring the effective management of radio frequencies and numbering resources.

3. The national regulatory authorities shall contribute to the development of the internal market by *inter alia*:

(a) removing remaining obstacles to the provision of electronic communications networks, associated facilities and services and electronic communications services at European level;

(b) encouraging the establishment and development of trans-European networks and the interoperability of pan-European services, and end-to-end connectivity;

(c) ensuring that, in similar circumstances, there is no discrimination in the treatment of undertakings providing electronic communications networks and services;

(d) cooperating with each other and with the Commission in a transparent manner to ensure the development of consistent regulatory practice and the consistent application of this Directive and the Specific Directives.

4. The national regulatory authorities shall promote the interests of the citizens of the European Union by *inter alia*:

(a) ensuring all citizens have access to a universal service specified in Directive 2002/22/EC (Universal Service Directive);

(b) ensuring a high level of protection for consumers in their dealings with suppliers, in particular by ensuring the availability of simple and inexpensive dispute resolution procedures carried out by a body that is independent of the parties involved;

(c) contributing to ensuring a high level of protection of personal data and privacy;

(d) promoting the provision of clear information, in particular requiring transparency of tariffs and conditions for using publicly available electronic communications services;

(e) addressing the needs of specific social groups, in particular disabled users; and

(f) ensuring that the integrity and security of public communications networks are maintained.

Commentary

Art 8: B&C: 12.092–12.094, 12.125 F&N: 13.35, 13.40, 13.47
Art 8(2): B&C: 12.093
Art 8(2)(d): B&C: 12.117
Art 8(3)(c): B&C: 12.093
Art 8(4)(e): B&C: 12.125

Management of radio frequencies for electronic communications services

1. Member States shall ensure the effective management of radio frequencies for electronic communication services in their territory in accordance with Article 8. They shall ensure that the allocation and assignment of such radio frequencies by national regulatory authorities are based on objective, transparent, non-discriminatory and proportionate criteria.

2. Member States shall promote the harmonisation of use of radio frequencies across the Community, consistent with the need to ensure effective and efficient use thereof and in accordance with the Decision No 676/2002/EC (Radio Spectrum Decision).

3. Member States may make provision for undertakings to transfer rights to use radio frequencies with other undertakings.

4. Member States shall ensure that an undertaking's intention to transfer rights to use radio frequencies is notified to the national regulatory authority responsible for spectrum assignment and that any transfer takes place in accordance with procedures laid down by the national regulatory authority and is made public. National regulatory authorities shall ensure that competition is not distorted as a result of any such transaction. Where radio frequency use has been harmonised through the application of Decision No 676/2002/EC (Radio Spectrum Decision) or other Community measures, any such transfer shall not result in change of use of that radio frequency.

Commentary
Art 9: **B&C:** 12.092, 12.117
Art 9(1): **B&C:** 12.093
Art 9(2): **B&C:** 12.117
Art 9(3): **B&C:** 12.117

Article 10
Numbering, naming and addressing

1. Member States shall ensure that national regulatory authorities control the assignment of all national numbering resources and the management of the national numbering plans. Member States shall ensure that adequate numbers and numbering ranges are provided for all publicly available electronic communications services. National regulatory authorities shall establish objective, transparent and non-discriminatory assigning procedures for national numbering resources.

2. National regulatory authorities shall ensure that numbering plans and procedures are applied in a manner that gives equal treatment to all providers of publicly available electronic communications services. In particular, Member States shall ensure that an undertaking allocated a range of numbers does not discriminate against other providers of electronic communications services as regards the number sequences used to give access to their services.

3. Member States shall ensure that the national numbering plans, and all subsequent additions or amendments thereto, are published, subject only to limitations imposed on the grounds of national security.

4. Member States shall support the harmonisation of numbering resources within the Community where that is necessary to support the development of pan European services. The Commission may, in accordance with the procedure referred to in Article 22(3), take the appropriate technical implementing measures on this matter.

5. Where this is appropriate in order to ensure full global interoperability of services, Member States shall coordinate their positions in international organisations and forums in which decisions are taken on issues relating to the numbering, naming and addressing of electronic communications networks and services.

Commentary
Art 10: **B&C:** 12.092
Art 10(1): **B&C:** 12.093

Article 11
Rights of way

1. Member States shall ensure that when a competent authority considers:

— an application for the granting of rights to install facilities on, over or under public or private property to an undertaking authorised to provide public communications networks, or

— an application for the granting of rights to install facilities on, over or under public property to an undertaking authorised to provide electronic communications networks other than to the public,

the competent authority:

— acts on the basis of transparent and publicly available procedures, applied without discrimination and without delay, and

— follows the principles of transparency and non-discrimination in attaching conditions to any such rights.

The abovementioned procedures can differ depending on whether the applicant is providing public communications networks or not.

2. Member States shall ensure that where public or local authorities retain ownership or control of undertakings operating electronic communications networks and/or services, there is effective structural separation of the function responsible for granting the rights referred to in paragraph 1 from activities associated with ownership or control.

3. Member States shall ensure that effective mechanisms exist to allow undertakings to appeal against decisions on the granting of rights to install facilities to a body that is independent of the parties involved.

Commentary
Art 11: **B&C:** 12.092

Article 12
Co-location and facility sharing

1. Where an undertaking providing electronic communications networks has the right under national legislation to install facilities on, over or under public or private property, or may take advantage of a procedure for the expropriation or use of property, national regulatory authorities shall encourage the sharing of such facilities or property.

2. In particular where undertakings are deprived of access to viable alternatives because of the need to protect the environment, public health, public security or to meet town and country planning objectives, Member States may impose the sharing of facilities or property (including physical co-location) on an undertaking operating an electronic communications network or take measures to facilitate the coordination of public works only after an appropriate period of public consultation during which all interested parties must be given an opportunity to express their views. Such sharing or coordination arrangements may include rules for apportioning the costs of facility or property sharing.

Commentary
Art 12: **B&C:** 12.097 **F&N:** 13.159

Article 13
Accounting separation and financial reports

1. Member States shall require undertakings providing public communications networks or publicly available electronic communications services which have special or exclusive rights for the provision of services in other sectors in the same or another Member State to:

(a) keep separate accounts for the activities associated with the provision of electronic communications networks or services, to the extent that would be required if these activities were carried out by legally independent companies, so as to identify all elements of cost and revenue, with the basis of their calculation and the detailed attribution methods used, related to their activities associated with the provision of electronic communications networks or services including an itemised breakdown of fixed asset and structural costs, or

(b) have structural separation for the activities associated with the provision of electronic communications networks or services.

Member States may choose not to apply the requirements referred to in the first subparagraph to undertakings the annual turnover of which in activities associated with electronic communications networks or services in the Member States is less than EUR 50 million.

2. Where undertakings providing public communications networks or publicly available electronic communications services are not subject to the requirements of company law and do not satisfy the small and medium-sized enterprise criteria of Community law accounting rules, their financial reports shall be drawn up and submitted to independent audit and published. The audit shall be carried out in accordance with the relevant Community and national rules.

This requirement shall also apply to the separate accounts required under paragraph 1(a).

Commentary
Art 13: B&C: 12.097

CHAPTER IV
GENERAL PROVISIONS

Article 14
Undertakings with significant market power

1. Where the Specific Directives require national regulatory authorities to determine whether operators have significant market power in accordance with the procedure referred to in Article 16, paragraphs 2 and 3 of this Article shall apply.

2. An undertaking shall be deemed to have significant market power if, either individually or jointly with others, it enjoys a position equivalent to dominance, that is to say a position of economic strength affording it the power to behave to an appreciable extent independently of competitors, customers and ultimately consumers.

In particular, national regulatory authorities shall, when assessing whether two or more undertakings are in a joint dominant position in a market, act in accordance with Community law and take into the utmost account the guidelines on market analysis and the assessment of significant market power published by the Commission pursuant to Article 15. Criteria to be used in making such an assessment are set out in Annex II.

3. Where an undertaking has significant market power on a specific market, it may also be deemed to have significant market power on a closely related market, where the links between the two markets are such as to allow the market power held in one market to be leveraged into the other market, thereby strengthening the market power of the undertaking.

Commentary
Art 14(2): B&C: 12.099

Article 15
Market definition procedure

1. After public consultation and consultation with national regulatory authorities the Commission shall adopt a recommendation on relevant product and service markets (hereinafter "the recommendation"). The recommendation shall identify in accordance with Annex I hereto those product and service markets within the electronic communications sector, the characteristics of which may be such as to justify the imposition of regulatory obligations set out in the Specific Directives, without prejudice to markets that may be defined in specific cases under competition law. The Commission shall define markets in accordance with the principles of competition law.

The Commission shall regularly review the recommendation.

2. The Commission shall publish, at the latest on the date of entry into force of this Directive, guidelines for market analysis and the assessment of significant market power (hereinafter "the guidelines") which shall be in accordance with the principles of competition law.

3. National regulatory authorities shall, taking the utmost account of the recommendation and the guidelines, define relevant markets appropriate to national circumstances, in particular relevant geographic markets within their territory, in accordance with the principles of competition law. National regulatory authorities shall follow the procedures referred to in Articles 6 and 7 before defining the markets that differ from those defined in the recommendation.

4. After consultation with national regulatory authorities the Commission may, acting in accordance with the procedure referred to in Article 22(3), adopt a Decision identifying transnational markets.

Commentary
Art 15: **B&C:** 12.126 **F&N:** 13.53
Art 15(1): **B&C:** 4.013, 4.023, 12.126
Art 15(3): **B&C:** 12.101–12.102

Article 16
Market analysis procedure

1. As soon as possible after the adoption of the recommendation or any updating thereof, national regulatory authorities shall carry out an analysis of the relevant markets, taking the utmost account of the guidelines. Member States shall ensure that this analysis is carried out, where appropriate, in collaboration with the national competition authorities.

2. Where a national regulatory authority is required under Articles 16, 17, 18 or 19 of Directive 2002/22/EC (Universal Service Directive), or Articles 7 or 8 of Directive 2002/19/EC (Access Directive) to determine whether to impose, maintain, amend or withdraw obligations on undertakings, it shall determine on the basis of its market analysis referred to in paragraph 1 of this Article whether a relevant market is effectively competitive.

3. Where a national regulatory authority concludes that the market is effectively competitive, it shall not impose or maintain any of the specific regulatory obligations referred to in paragraph 2 of this Article. In cases where sector specific regulatory obligations already exist, it shall withdraw such obligations placed on undertakings in that relevant market. An appropriate period of notice shall be given to parties affected by such a withdrawal of obligations.

4. Where a national regulatory authority determines that a relevant market is not effectively competitive, it shall identify undertakings with significant market power on that market in accordance with Article 14 and the national regulatory authority shall on such undertakings impose appropriate specific regulatory obligations referred to in paragraph 2 of this Article or maintain or amend such obligations where they already exist.

5. In the case of transnational markets identified in the Decision referred to in Article 15(4), the national regulatory authorities concerned shall jointly conduct the market analysis taking the utmost account of the guidelines and decide on any imposition, maintenance, amendment or withdrawal of regulatory obligations referred to in paragraph 2 of this Article in a concerted fashion.

6. Measures taken according to the provisions of paragraphs 3, 4 and 5 of this Article shall be subject to the procedures referred to in Articles 6 and 7.

Commentary
Art 16: **B&C:** 12.098, 12.101 **F&N:** 13.53
Art 16(1): **B&C:** 4.023
Art 16(3): **B&C:** 12.098

Article 17
Standardisation

1. The Commission, acting in accordance with the procedure referred to in Article 22(2), shall draw up and publish in the *Official Journal of the European Communities* a list of standards and/or specifications to serve as a basis for encouraging the harmonised provision of electronic communications networks, electronic communications services and associated facilities and services. Where necessary, the Commission may, acting in accordance with the procedure referred to in Article 22(2) and following consultation of the Committee established by Directive 98/34/EC, request that standards

be drawn up by the European standards organisations (European Committee for Standardisation (CEN), European Committee for Electrotechnical Standardisation (CENELEC), and European Telecommunications Standards Institute (ETSI)).

2. Member States shall encourage the use of the standards and/or specifications referred to in paragraph 1, for the provision of services, technical interfaces and/or network functions, to the extent strictly necessary to ensure interoperability of services and to improve freedom of choice for users.

As long as standards and/or specifications have not been published in accordance with paragraph 1, Member States shall encourage the implementation of standards and/or specifications adopted by the European standards organisations.

In the absence of such standards and/or specifications, Member States shall encourage the implementation of international standards or recommendations adopted by the International Telecommunication Union (ITU), the International Organisation for Standardisation (ISO) or the International Electrotechnical Commission (IEC).

Where international standards exist, Member States shall encourage the European standards organisations to use them, or the relevant parts of them, as a basis for the standards they develop, except where such international standards or relevant parts would be ineffective.

3. If the standards and/or specifications referred to in paragraph 1 have not been adequately implemented so that interoperability of services in one or more Member States cannot be ensured, the implementation of such standards and/or specifications may be made compulsory under the procedure laid down in paragraph 4, to the extent strictly necessary to ensure such interoperability and to improve freedom of choice for users.

4. Where the Commission intends to make the implementation of certain standards and/or specifications compulsory, it shall publish a notice in the *Official Journal of the European Communities* and invite public comment by all parties concerned. The Commission, acting in accordance with the procedure referred to in Article 22(3), shall make implementation of the relevant standards compulsory by making reference to them as compulsory standards in the list of standards and/or specifications published in the *Official Journal of the European Communities*.

5. Where the Commission considers that standards and/or specifications referred to in paragraph 1 no longer contribute to the provision of harmonised electronic communications services, or that they no longer meet consumers' needs or are hampering technological development, it shall, acting in accordance with the procedure referred to in Article 22(2), remove them from the list of standards and/or specifications referred to in paragraph 1.

6. Where the Commission considers that standards and/or specifications referred to in paragraph 4 no longer contribute to the provision of harmonised electronic communications services, or that they no longer meet consumers' needs or are hampering technological development, it shall, acting in accordance with the procedure referred to in Article 22(3), remove them from this list of standards and/or specifications referred to in paragraph 1.

7. This Article does not apply in respect of any of the essential requirements, interface specifications or harmonised standards to which the provisions of Directive 1999/5/EC apply.

Commentary
Art 17: B&C: 12.092

Article 18
Interoperability of digital interactive television services

1. In order to promote the free flow of information, media pluralism and cultural diversity, Member States shall encourage, in accordance with the provisions of Article 17(2):

(a) providers of digital interactive television services for distribution to the public in the Community on digital interactive television platforms, regardless of the transmission mode, to use an open API;

(b) providers of all enhanced digital television equipment deployed for the reception of digital interactive television services on interactive digital television platforms to comply with an open API in accordance with the minimum requirements of the relevant standards or specifications.

2. Without prejudice to Article 5(1)(b) of Directive 2002/19/ EC (Access Directive), Member States shall encourage proprietors of APIs to make available on fair, reasonable and non-discriminatory terms, and against appropriate remuneration, all such information as is necessary to enable providers of digital interactive television services to provide all services supported by the API in a fully functional form.

3. Within one year after the date of application referred to in Article 28(1), second subparagraph, the Commission shall examine the effects of this Article. If interoperability and freedom of choice for users have not been adequately achieved in one or more Member States, the Commission may take action in accordance with the procedure laid down in Article 17(3) and (4).

Commentary
Art 18: **B&C:** 12.092

Article 19
Harmonisation procedures

1. Where the Commission, acting in accordance with the procedure referred to in Article 22(2), issues recommendations to Member States on the harmonised application of the provisions in this Directive and the Specific Directives in order to further the achievement of the objectives set out in Article 8, Member States shall ensure that national regulatory authorities take the utmost account of those recommendations in carrying out their tasks. Where a national regulatory authority chooses not to follow a recommendation, it shall inform the Commission giving the reasoning for its position.

2. Where the Commission finds that divergence at national level in regulations aimed at implementing Article 10(4) creates a barrier to the single market, the Commission may, acting in accordance with the procedure referred to in Article 22(3), take the appropriate technical implementing measures.

Commentary
Art 19: **B&C:** 12.092

Article 20
Dispute resolution between undertakings

1. In the event of a dispute arising in connection with obligations arising under this Directive or the Specific Directives between undertakings providing electronic communications networks or services in a Member State, the national regulatory authority concerned shall, at the request of either party, and without prejudice to the provisions of paragraph 2, issue a binding decision to resolve the dispute in the shortest possible time frame and in any case within four months except in exceptional circumstances. The Member State concerned shall require that all parties cooperate fully with the national regulatory authority.

2. Member States may make provision for national regulatory authorities to decline to resolve a dispute through a binding decision where other mechanisms, including mediation, exist and would better contribute to resolution of the dispute in a timely manner in accordance with the provisions of Article 8. The national regulatory authority shall inform the parties without delay. If after four months the dispute is not resolved, and if the dispute has not been brought before the courts by the party seeking redress, the national regulatory authority shall issue, at the request of either party, a binding decision to resolve the dispute in the shortest possible time frame and in any case within four months.

3. In resolving a dispute, the national regulatory authority shall take decisions aimed at achieving the objectives set out in Article 8. Any obligations imposed on an undertaking by the national regulatory authority in resolving a dispute shall respect the provisions of this Directive or the Specific Directives.

4. The decision of the national regulatory authority shall be made available to the public, having regard to the requirements of business confidentiality. The parties concerned shall be given a full statement of the reasons on which it is based.

5. The procedure referred to in paragraphs 1, 3 and 4 shall not preclude either party from bringing an action before the courts.

Commentary
Art 20: B&C: 12.093 F&N: 13.47, 13.50
Art 20(4): B&C: 12.093

Article 21
Resolution of cross-border disputes

1. In the event of a cross-border dispute arising under this Directive or the Specific Directives between parties in different Member States, where the dispute lies within the competence of national regulatory authorities from more than one Member State, the procedure set out in paragraphs 2, 3 and 4 shall be applicable.

2. Any party may refer the dispute to the national regulatory authorities concerned. The national regulatory authorities shall coordinate their efforts in order to bring about a resolution of the dispute, in accordance with the objectives set out in Article 8. Any obligations imposed on an undertaking by the national regulatory authority in resolving a dispute shall respect the provisions of this Directive or the Specific Directives.

3. Member States may make provision for national regulatory authorities jointly to decline to resolve a dispute where other mechanisms, including mediation, exist and would better contribute to resolution of the dispute in a timely manner in accordance with the provisions of Article 8. They shall inform the parties without delay. If after four months the dispute is not resolved, if the dispute has not been brought before the courts by the party seeking redress, and if either party requests it, the national regulatory authorities shall coordinate their efforts in order to bring about a resolution of the dispute, in accordance with the provisions set out in Article 8.

4. The procedure referred to in paragraph 2 shall not preclude either party from bringing an action before the courts.

Article 22
Committee

1. The Commission shall be assisted by a Committee ("the Communications Committee").

2. Where reference is made to this paragraph, Articles 3 and 7 of Decision 1999/468/EC shall apply, having regard to the provisions of Article 8 thereof.

3. Where reference is made to this paragraph, Articles 5 and 7 of Decision 1999/468/EC shall apply, having regard to the provisions of Article 8 thereof.

The period laid down in Article 5(6) of Decision 1999/468/EC shall be three months.

4. The Committee shall adopt its rules of procedure.

Article 23
Exchange of information

1. The Commission shall provide all relevant information to the Communications Committee on the outcome of regular consultations with the representatives of network operators, service providers, users, consumers, manufacturers and trade unions, as well as third countries and international organisations.

2. The Communications Committee shall, taking account of the Community's electronic communications policy, foster the exchange of information between the Member States and between the Member States and the Commission on the situation and the development of regulatory activities regarding electronic communications networks and services.

Article 24
Publication of information

1. Member States shall ensure that up-to-date information pertaining to the application of this Directive and the Specific Directives is made publicly available in a manner that guarantees all interested parties easy access to that information. They shall publish a notice in their national official gazette describing how and where the information is published. The first such notice shall be

published before the date of application referred to in Article 28(1), second subparagraph, and thereafter a notice shall be published whenever there is any change in the information contained therein.

2.   Member States shall send to the Commission a copy of all such notices at the time of publication. The Commission shall distribute the information to the Communications Committee as appropriate.

Article 25
Review procedures

1. The Commission shall periodically review the functioning of this Directive and report to the European Parliament and to the Council, on the first occasion not later than three years after the date of application referred to in Article 28(1), second subparagraph. For this purpose, the Commission may request information from the Member States, which shall be supplied without undue delay.

CHAPTER V
FINAL PROVISIONS

Article 26
Repeal

The following Directives and Decisions are hereby repealed with effect from the date of application referred to in Article 28(1), second subparagraph:

— Directive 90/387/EEC,
— Council Decision 91/396/EEC of 29 July 1991 on the introduction of a single European emergency call number,[1]
— Council Directive 92/44/EEC of 5 June 1992 on the application of open network provision to leased lines,[2]
— Council Decision 92/264/EEC of 11 May 1992 on the introduction of a standard international telephone access code in the Community,[3]
— Directive 95/47/EC,
— Directive 97/13/EC,
— Directive 97/33/EC,
— Directive 98/10/EC of the European Parliament and of the Council of 26 February 1998 on the application of open network provision (ONP) to voice telephony and on universal service for telecommunications in a competitive environment.[4]

Notes
[1] OJ L 217, 6.8.1991, p. 31.
[2] OJ L 165, 19.6.1992, p. 27. Directive as last amended by Commission Decision 98/80/EC (OJ L 14, 20.1.1998, p. 27).
[3] OJ L 137, 20.5.1992, p. 21.
[4] OJ L 101, 1.4.1998, p. 24.

Article 27
Transitional measures

Member States shall maintain all obligations under national law referred to in Article 7 of Directive 2002/19/EC (Access Directive) and Article 16 of Directive 2002/22/EC (Universal Service Directive) until such time as a determination is made in respect of those obligations by a national regulatory authority in accordance with Article 16 of this Directive.

Operators of fixed public telephone networks that were designated by their national regulatory authority as having significant market power in the provision of fixed public telephone networks and services under Annex I, Part 1 of Directive 97/33/EC or Directive 98/10/EC shall continue to be considered "notified operators" for the purposes of Regulation (EC) No 2887/2000 until such a time as the market analysis procedure referred to in Article 16 has been completed. Thereafter they shall cease to be considered "notified operators" for the purposes of the Regulation.

Article 28
Transposition

1. Member States shall adopt and publish the laws, regulations and administrative provisions necessary to comply with this Directive not later than 24 July 2003. They shall forthwith inform the Commission thereof.

They shall apply those measures from 25 July 2003.

2. When Member States adopt these measures, they shall contain a reference to this Directive or be accompanied by such a reference on the occasion of their official publication. The methods of making such a reference shall be laid down by the Member States.

3. Member States shall communicate to the Commission the text of the provisions of national law which they adopt in the field governed by this Directive and of any subsequent amendments to those provisions.

Article 29
Entry into force

This Directive shall enter into force on the day of its publication in the *Official Journal of the European Communities*.

Notes
Date of entry into force: 24 April 2002.

Article 30
Addressees

This Directive is addressed to the Member States.

Done at Brussels, 7 March 2002.

ANNEX I
LIST OF MARKETS TO BE INCLUDED IN THE INITIAL COMMISSION
RECOMMENDATION ON RELEVANT PRODUCT AND SERVICE MARKETS
REFERRED TO IN ARTICLE 15

1. *Markets referred to in Directive 2002/22/EC (Universal Service Directive)*
   Article 16 — Markets defined under the former regulatory framework, where obligations should be reviewed.
   The provision of connection to and use of the public telephone network at fixed locations.
   The provision of leased lines to end users.

2. *Markets referred to in Directive 2002/19/EC (Access Directive)*
   Article 7 — Markets defined under the former regulatory framework, where obligations should be reviewed.

   Interconnection (Directive 97/33/EC)
      call origination in the fixed public telephone network
      call termination in the fixed public telephone network
      transit services in the fixed public telephone network
      call origination on public mobile telephone networks
      call termination on public mobile telephone networks
      leased line interconnection (interconnection of part circuits)

   Network access and special network access (Directive 97/33/EC, Directive 98/10/EC)
      access to the fixed public telephone network, including unbundled access to the local loop
      access to public mobile telephone networks, including carrier selection

   Wholesale leased line capacity (Directive 92/44/EEC)
      wholesale provision of leased line capacity to other suppliers of electronic communications networks or services

3. Markets referred to in Regulation (EC) No 2887/2000
Services provided over unbundled (twisted metallic pair) loops.

4. Additional markets
The national market for international roaming services on public mobile telephone networks.

ANNEX II
CRITERIA TO BE USED BY NATIONAL REGULATORY AUTHORITIES IN MAKING AN ASSESSMENT OF JOINT DOMINANCE IN ACCORDANCE WITH ARTICLE 14(2), SECOND SUBPARAGRAPH

Two or more undertakings can be found to be in a joint dominant position within the meaning of Article 14 if, even in the absence of structural or other links between them, they operate in a market the structure of which is considered to be conducive to coordinated effects. Without prejudice to the case law of the Court of Justice on joint dominance, this is likely to be the case where the market satisfies a number of appropriate characteristics, in particular in terms of market concentration, transparency and other characteristics mentioned below:

— mature market,
— stagnant or moderate growth on the demand side,
— low elasticity of demand,
— homogeneous product,
— similar cost structures,
— similar market shares,
— lack of technical innovation, mature technology,
— absence of excess capacity,
— high barriers to entry,
— lack of countervailing buying power,
— lack of potential competition,
— various kinds of informal or other links between the undertakings concerned,
— retaliatory mechanisms,
— lack or reduced scope for price competition.

The above is not an exhaustive list, nor are the criteria cumulative. Rather, the list is intended to illustrate only the sorts of evidence that could be used to support assertions concerning the existence of joint dominance.

Commentary
Annex II: F&N: 13.194, 13.195

E18

DIRECTIVE 2002/19/EC OF THE EUROPEAN PARLIAMENT AND OF THE COUNCIL

of 7 March 2002

on access to, and interconnection of, electronic communications
networks and associated facilities

(Access Directive)

Official Journal L 108, 24.4.2002, p. 7

Celex No: 32002L0019

Notes

EEA application: this Directive was adopted with appropriate adaptations by EEA Joint Committee Decision No 11/2004 (OJ No L 116, 22.4.2004, p. 60 and EEA Supplement No 20, 22.4.2004, p. 14): see EEA Agreement, Annex XI, Point 5cj.

Commentary

Directive 2002/19/EC: B&C: 12.089, 12.106, 12.125 F&N: 13.14, 13.19, 13.23, 13.248
Arts 8–13: B&C: 12.109
Arts 9–13: B&C: 12.098
Chap III: B&C: 12.109
Chap IV: B&C: 12.109

THE EUROPEAN PARLIAMENT AND THE COUNCIL OF THE EUROPEAN UNION,

Having regard to the Treaty establishing the European Community, and in particular Article 95 thereof,

Having regard to the proposal from the Commission,[1]

Having regard to the opinion of the Economic and Social Committee,[2]

Acting in accordance with the procedure laid down in Article 251 of the Treaty,[3]

Notes

[1] OJ C 365 E, 19.12.2000, p. 215 and OJ C 270 E, 25.9.2001, p. 161.
[2] OJ C 123, 25.4.2001, p. 50.
[3] Opinion of the European Parliament of 1 March 2001 (OJ C 277, 1.10.2001, p. 72), Council Common Position of 17 September 2001 (OJ C 337, 30.11.2001, p. 1) and Decision of the European Parliament of 12 December 2001 [OJ C 177 E, 25.7.2002, p.82]. Council Decision of 14 February 2002.

Whereas:

(1) Directive 2002/21/EC of the European Parliament and of the Council of 7 March 2002 on a common regulatory framework for electronic communications networks and services (Framework Directive)[1] lays down the objectives of a regulatory framework to cover electronic communications networks and services in the Community, including fixed and mobile telecommunications networks, cable television networks, networks used for terrestrial broadcasting, satellite networks and Internet networks, whether used for voice, fax, data or images. Such networks may have been authorised by Member States under Directive 2002/20/EC of the European Parliament and of the Council of 7 March 2002 on the authorisation of electronic communications networks and services (Authorisation Directive)[2] or have been authorised under previous regulatory measures. The provisions of this Directive apply to those networks that are used for the provision of publicly available electronic communications services. This Directive covers access and interconnection arrangements between service suppliers. Non-public networks do not have obligations under this

Directive except where, in benefiting from access to public networks, they may be subject to conditions laid down by Member States.

Notes
[1] See [OJ L 108, 24.4.2002, p. 33].
[2] See [OJ L 108, 24.4.2002, p. 21].

(2) Services providing content such as the offer for sale of a package of sound or television broadcasting content are not covered by the common regulatory framework for electronic communications networks and services.

(3) The term "access" has a wide range of meanings, and it is therefore necessary to define precisely how that term is used in this Directive, without prejudice to how it may be used in other Community measures. An operator may own the underlying network or facilities or may rent some or all of them.

(4) Directive 95/47/EC of the European Parliament and of the Council of 24 October 1995 on the use of standards for the transmission of television signals[1] did not mandate any specific digital television transmission system or service requirement, and this opened up an opportunity for the market actors to take the initiative and develop suitable systems. Through the Digital Video Broadcasting Group, European market actors have developed a family of television transmission systems that have been adopted by broadcasters throughout the world. These transmissions systems have been standardised by the European Telecommunications Standards Institute (ETSI) and have become International Telecommunication Union recommendations. In relation to wide-screen digital television, the 16:9 aspect ratio is the reference format for wide-format television services and programmes, and is now established in Member States' markets as a result of Council Decision 93/424/EEC of 22 July 1993 on an action plan for the introduction of advanced television services in Europe.[2]

Notes
[1] OJ L 281, 23.11.1995, p. 51.
[2] OJ L 196, 5.8.1993, p. 48.

(5) In an open and competitive market, there should be no restrictions that prevent undertakings from negotiating access and interconnection arrangements between themselves, in particular on cross-border agreements, subject to the competition rules of the Treaty. In the context of achieving a more efficient, truly pan-European market, with effective competition, more choice and competitive services to consumers, undertakings which receive requests for access or interconnection should in principle conclude such agreements on a commercial basis, and negotiate in good faith.

(6) In markets where there continue to be large differences in negotiating power between undertakings, and where some undertakings rely on infrastructure provided by others for delivery of their services, it is appropriate to establish a framework to ensure that the market functions effectively. National regulatory authorities should have the power to secure, where commercial negotiation fails, adequate access and interconnection and interoperability of services in the interest of end-users. In particular, they may ensure end-to-end connectivity by imposing proportionate obligations on undertakings that control access to end-users. Control of means of access may entail ownership or control of the physical link to the end-user (either fixed or mobile), and/or the ability to change or withdraw the national number or numbers needed to access an end-user's network termination point. This would be the case for example if network operators were to restrict unreasonably end-user choice for access to Internet portals and services.

Commentary
Recital 6: **B&C:** 12.103, 12.107

(7) National legal or administrative measures that link the terms and conditions for access or interconnection to the activities of the party seeking interconnection, and specifically to the degree of its investment in network infrastructure, and not to the interconnection or access services

provided, may cause market distortion and may therefore not be compatible with competition rules.

Commentary
Recital 7: B&C: 12.107

(8) Network operators who control access to their own customers do so on the basis of unique numbers or addresses from a published numbering or addressing range. Other network operators need to be able to deliver traffic to those customers, and so need to be able to interconnect directly or indirectly to each other. The existing rights and obligations to negotiate interconnection should therefore be maintained. It is also appropriate to maintain the obligations formerly laid down in Directive 95/47/EC requiring fully digital electronic communications networks used for the distribution of television services and open to the public to be capable of distributing wide-screen television services and programmes, so that users are able to receive such programmes in the format in which they were transmitted.

Commentary
Recital 8: B&C: 12.105

(9) Interoperability is of benefit to end-users and is an important aim of this regulatory framework. Encouraging interoperability is one of the objectives for national regulatory authorities as set out in this framework, which also provides for the Commission to publish a list of standards and/or specifications covering the provision of services, technical interfaces and/or network functions, as the basis for encouraging harmonisation in electronic communications. Member States should encourage the use of published standards and/or specifications to the extent strictly necessary to ensure interoperability of services and to improve freedom of choice for users.

(10) Competition rules alone may not be sufficient to ensure cultural diversity and media pluralism in the area of digital television. Directive 95/47/EC provided an initial regulatory framework for the nascent digital television industry which should be maintained, including in particular the obligation to provide conditional access on fair, reasonable and non-discriminatory terms, in order to make sure that a wide variety of programming and services is available. Technological and market developments make it necessary to review these obligations on a regular basis, either by a Member State for its national market or the Commission for the Community, in particular to determine whether there is justification for extending obligations to new gateways, such as electronic programme guides (EPGs) and application program interfaces (APIs), to the extent that is necessary to ensure accessibility for end-users to specified digital broadcasting services. Member States may specify the digital broadcasting services to which access by end-users must be ensured by any legislative, regulatory or administrative means that they deem necessary.

Commentary
Recital 10: B&C: 12.125

(11) Member States may also permit their national regulatory authority to review obligations in relation to conditional access to digital broadcasting services in order to assess through a market analysis whether to withdraw or amend conditions for operators that do not have significant market power on the relevant market. Such withdrawal or amendment should not adversely affect access for end-users to such services or the prospects for effective competition.

(12) In order to ensure continuity of existing agreements and to avoid a legal vacuum, it is necessary to ensure that obligations for access and interconnection imposed under Articles 4, 6, 7, 8, 11, 12, and 14 of Directive 97/33/EC of the European Parliament and of the Council of 30 June 1997 on interconnection in telecommunications with regard to ensuring universal service and interoperability through application of the principles of open network provision (ONP),[1] obligations on special access imposed under Article 16 of Directive 98/10/EC of the European Parliament and of the Council of 26 February 1998 on the application of open network provision (ONP) to voice telephony and on universal service for telecommunications in a competitive environment,[2] and obligations concerning the provision of leased line transmission capacity under Council Directive 92/44/EEC of 5 June 1992 on the application of open

network provision to leased lines,[3] are initially carried over into the new regulatory framework, but are subject to immediate review in the light of prevailing market conditions. Such a review should also extend to those organisations covered by Regulation (EC) No 2887/2000 of the European Parliament and of the Council of 18 December 2000 on unbundled access to the local loop.[4]

Notes

[1] OJ L 199, 26.7.1997, p. 32. Directive as last amended by Directive 98/61/EC (OJ L 268, 3.10.1998, p. 37).

[2] OJ L 101, 1.4.1998, p. 24.

[3] OJ L 165, 19.6.1992, p. 27. Directive as last amended by Commission Decision No 98/80/EC (OJ L 14, 20.1.1998, p. 27).

[4] OJ L 366, 30.12.2000, p. 4.

(13)   The review should be carried out using an economic market analysis based on competition law methodology. The aim is to reduce *ex ante* sector specific rules progressively as competition in the market develops. However the procedure also takes account of transitional problems in the market such as those related to international roaming and of the possibility of new bottlenecks arising as a result of technological development, which may require *ex ante* regulation, for example in the area of broadband access networks. It may well be the case that competition develops at different speeds in different market segments and in different Member States, and national regulatory authorities should be able to relax regulatory obligations in those markets where competition is delivering the desired results. In order to ensure that market players in similar circumstances are treated in similar ways in different Member States, the Commission should be able to ensure harmonised application of the provisions of this Directive. National regulatory authorities and national authorities entrusted with the implementation of competition law should, where appropriate, coordinate their actions to ensure that the most appropriate remedy is applied. The Community and its Member States have entered into commitments on interconnection of telecommunications networks in the context of the World Trade Organisation agreement on basic telecommunications and these commitments need to be respected.

Commentary
Recital 13: B&C: 12.100

(14)   Directive 97/33/EC laid down a range of obligations to be imposed on undertakings with significant market power, namely transparency, non-discrimination, accounting separation, access, and price control including cost orientation. This range of possible obligations should be maintained but, in addition, they should be established as a set of maximum obligations that can be applied to undertakings, in order to avoid over-regulation. Exceptionally, in order to comply with international commitments or Community law, it may be appropriate to impose obligations for access or interconnection on all market players, as is currently the case for conditional access systems for digital television services.

(15)   The imposition of a specific obligation on an undertaking with significant market power does not require an additional market analysis but a justification that the obligation in question is appropriate and proportionate in relation to the nature of the problem identified.

(16)   Transparency of terms and conditions for access and interconnection, including prices, serve to speed-up negotiation, avoid disputes and give confidence to market players that a service is not being provided on discriminatory terms. Openness and transparency of technical interfaces can be particularly important in ensuring interoperability. Where a national regulatory authority imposes obligations to make information public, it may also specify the manner in which the information is to be made available, covering for example the type of publication (paper and/or electronic) and whether or not it is free of charge, taking into account the nature and purpose of the information concerned.

(17)   The principle of non-discrimination ensures that undertakings with market power do not distort competition, in particular where they are vertically integrated undertakings that supply services to undertakings with whom they compete on downstream markets.

(18)   Accounting separation allows internal price transfers to be rendered visible, and allows national regulatory authorities to check compliance with obligations for non-discrimination where

applicable. In this regard the Commission published Recommendation 98/322/EC of 8 April 1998 on interconnection in a liberalised telecommunications market (Part 2 — accounting separation and cost accounting).[1]

Notes
[1] OJ L 141, 13.5.1998, p. 6.

(19) Mandating access to network infrastructure can be justified as a means of increasing competition, but national regulatory authorities need to balance the rights of an infrastructure owner to exploit its infrastructure for its own benefit, and the rights of other service providers to access facilities that are essential for the provision of competing services. Where obligations are imposed on operators that require them to meet reasonable requests for access to and use of networks elements and associated facilities, such requests should only be refused on the basis of objective criteria such as technical feasibility or the need to maintain network integrity. Where access is refused, the aggrieved party may submit the case to the dispute resolutions procedure referred to in Articles 20 and 21 of Directive 2002/21/EC (Framework Directive). An operator with mandated access obligations cannot be required to provide types of access which are not within its powers to provide. The imposition by national regulatory authorities of mandated access that increases competition in the short-term should not reduce incentives for competitors to invest in alternative facilities that will secure more competition in the long-term. The Commission has published a Notice on the application of the competition rules to access agreements in the telecommunications sector[1] which addresses these issues. National regulatory authorities may impose technical and operational conditions on the provider and/or beneficiaries of mandated access in accordance with Community law. In particular the imposition of technical standards should comply with Directive 98/34/EC of the European Parliament and of the Council of 22 June 1998 laying down a procedure for the provision of information in the field of technical standards and regulations and of rules of Information Society Services.[2]

Notes
[1] OJ C 265, 22.8.1998, p. 2.
[2] OJ L 204, 21.7.1998, p. 37. Directive as amended by Directive 98/48/EC (OJ L 217, 5.8.1998, p. 18).

(20) Price control may be necessary when market analysis in a particular market reveals inefficient competition. The regulatory intervention may be relatively light, such as an obligation that prices for carrier selection are reasonable as laid down in Directive 97/33/EC, or much heavier such as an obligation that prices are cost oriented to provide full justification for those prices where competition is not sufficiently strong to prevent excessive pricing. In particular, operators with significant market power should avoid a price squeeze whereby the difference between their retail prices and the interconnection prices charged to competitors who provide similar retail services is not adequate to ensure sustainable competition. When a national regulatory authority calculates costs incurred in establishing a service mandated under this Directive, it is appropriate to allow a reasonable return on the capital employed including appropriate labour and building costs, with the value of capital adjusted where necessary to reflect the current valuation of assets and efficiency of operations. The method of cost recovery should be appropriate to the circumstances taking account of the need to promote efficiency and sustainable competition and maximise consumer benefits.

(21) Where a national regulatory authority imposes obligations to implement a cost accounting system in order to support price controls, it may itself undertake an annual audit to ensure compliance with that cost accounting system, provided that it has the necessary qualified staff, or it may require the audit to be carried out by another qualified body, independent of the operator concerned.

(22) Publication of information by Member States will ensure that market players and potential market entrants understand their rights and obligations, and know where to find the relevant detailed information. Publication in the national gazette helps interested parties in other Member States to find the relevant information.

(23) In order to ensure that the pan-European electronic communications market is effective and efficient, the Commission should monitor and publish information on charges which contribute to determining prices to end-users.

(24) The development of the electronic communications market, with its associated infrastructure, could have adverse effects on the environment and the landscape. Member States should therefore monitor this process and, if necessary, take action to minimise any such effects by means of appropriate agreements and other arrangements with the relevant authorities.

(25) In order to determine the correct application of Community law, the Commission needs to know which undertakings have been designated as having significant market power and what obligations have been placed upon market players by national regulatory authorities. In addition to national publication of this information, it is therefore necessary for Member States to send this information to the Commission. Where Member States are required to send information to the Commission, this may be in electronic form, subject to appropriate authentication procedures being agreed.

(26) Given the pace of technological and market developments, the implementation of this Directive should be reviewed within three years of its date of application to determine if it is meeting its objectives.

(27) The measures necessary for the implementation of this Directive should be adopted in accordance with Council Decision 1999/468/EC of 28 June 1999 laying down the procedures for the exercise of implementing powers conferred on the Commission.[1]

Notes
[1] OJ L 184, 17.7.1999, p. 23.

(28) Since the objectives of the proposed action, namely establishing a harmonised framework for the regulation of access to and interconnection of electronic communications networks and associated facilities, cannot be sufficiently achieved by the Member States and can therefore, by reason of the scale and effects of the action, be better achieved at Community level, the Community may adopt measures, in accordance with the principle of subsidiarity as set out in Article 5 of the Treaty. In accordance with the principle of proportionality, as set out in that Article, this Directive does not go beyond what is necessary in order to achieve those objectives,

HAVE ADOPTED THIS DIRECTIVE:

CHAPTER I
SCOPE, AIM AND DEFINITIONS

Article 1
Scope and aim

1. Within the framework set out in Directive 2002/21/EC(Framework Directive), this Directive harmonises the way in which Member States regulate access to, and interconnection of, electronic communications networks and associated facilities. The aim is to establish a regulatory framework, in accordance with internal market principles, for the relationships between suppliers of networks and services that will result in sustainable competition, interoperability of electronic communications services and consumer benefits.

2. This Directive establishes rights and obligations for operators and for undertakings seeking interconnection and/or access to their networks or associated facilities. It sets out objectives for national regulatory authorities with regard to access and interconnection, and lays down procedures to ensure that obligations imposed by national regulatory authorities are reviewed and, where appropriate, withdrawn once the desired objectives have been achieved. Access in this Directive does not refer to access by end-users.

Commentary
Art 1: B&C: 12.106

Article 2
Definitions

For the purposes of this Directive the definitions set out in Article 2 of Directive 2002/21/EC (Framework Directive) shall apply.

The following definitions shall also apply:

(a) "access" means the making available of facilities and/or services, to another undertaking, under defined conditions, on either an exclusive or non-exclusive basis, for the purpose of providing electronic communications services. It covers *inter alia*: access to network elements and associated facilities, which may involve the connection of equipment, by fixed or non-fixed means (in particular this includes access to the local loop and to facilities and services necessary to provide services over the local loop), access to physical infrastructure including buildings, ducts and masts; access to relevant software systems including operational support systems, access to number translation or systems offering equivalent functionality, access to fixed and mobile networks, in particular for roaming, access to conditional access systems for digital television services; access to virtual network services;

(b) "interconnection" means the physical and logical linking of public communications networks used by the same or a different undertaking in order to allow the users of one undertaking to communicate with users of the same or another undertaking, or to access services provided by another undertaking. Services may be provided by the parties involved or other parties who have access to the network. Interconnection is a specific type of access implemented between public network operators;

(c) "operator" means an undertaking providing or authorised to provide a public communications network or an associated facility;

(d) "wide-screen television service" means a television service that consists wholly or partially of programmes produced and edited to be displayed in a full height wide-screen format. The 16:9 format is the reference format for wide-screen television services;

(e) "local loop" means the physical circuit connecting the network termination point at the subscriber's premises to the main distribution frame or equivalent facility in the fixed public telephone network.

Commentary
Art 2(a): **B&C:** 12.105
Art 2(b): **B&C:** 12.105
Art 2(c): **B&C:** 12.107
Art 2(d): **B&C:** 12.106
Art 2(e): **F&N:** 13.156

CHAPTER II
GENERAL PROVISIONS

Article 3
General framework for access and interconnection

1. Member States shall ensure that there are no restrictions which prevent undertakings in the same Member State or in different Member States from negotiating between themselves agreements on technical and commercial arrangements for access and/or interconnection, in accordance with Community law. The undertaking requesting access or interconnection does not need to be authorised to operate in the Member State where access or interconnection is requested, if it is not providing services and does not operate a network in that Member State.

2. Without prejudice to Article 31 of Directive 2002/22/EC of the European Parliament and of the Council of 7 March 2002 on universal service and users' rights relating to electronic communications networks and services (Universal Service Directive),[1] Member States shall not maintain legal or administrative measures which oblige operators, when granting access or interconnection, to offer different terms and conditions to different undertakings for equivalent services and/or imposing

obligations that are not related to the actual access and interconnection services provided without prejudice to the conditions fixed in the Annex of Directive 2002/20/EC (Authorisation Directive).

Notes
[1] See [OJ L 108, 24.4.2002, p. 51].

Commentary
Art 3: **B&C:** 12.107

Article 4
Rights and obligations for undertakings

1. Operators of public communications networks shall have a right and, when requested by other undertakings so authorised, an obligation to negotiate interconnection with each other for the purpose of providing publicly available electronic communications services, in order to ensure provision and interoperability of services throughout the Community. Operators shall offer access and interconnection to other undertakings on terms and conditions consistent with obligations imposed by the national regulatory authority pursuant to Articles 5, 6, 7 and 8.

2. Public electronic communications networks established for the distribution of digital television services shall be capable of distributing wide-screen television services and programmes. Network operators that receive and redistribute wide-screen television services or programmes shall maintain that wide-screen format.

3. Without prejudice to Article 11 of Directive 2002/20/EC (Authorisation Directive), Member States shall require that undertakings which acquire information from another undertaking before, during or after the process of negotiating access or interconnection arrangements use that information solely for the purpose for which it was supplied and respect at all times the confidentiality of information transmitted or stored. The received information shall not be passed on to any other party, in particular other departments, subsidiaries or partners, for whom such information could provide a competitive advantage.

Commentary
Art 4(1): **B&C:** 12.108
Art 4(2): **B&C:** 12.106
Art 4(3): **B&C:** 12.108

Article 5
Powers and responsibilities of the national regulatory authorities with regard to access and interconnection

1. National regulatory authorities shall, acting in pursuit of the objectives set out in Article 8 of Directive 2002/21/EC (Framework Directive), encourage and where appropriate ensure, in accordance with the provisions of this Directive, adequate access and interconnection, and interoperability of services, exercising their responsibility in a way that promotes efficiency, sustainable competition, and gives the maximum benefit to end-users.

In particular, without prejudice to measures that may be taken regarding undertakings with significant market power in accordance with Article 8, national regulatory authorities shall be able to impose:

(a) to the extent that is necessary to ensure end-to-end connectivity, obligations on undertakings that control access to end-users, including in justified cases the obligation to interconnect their networks where this is not already the case;

(b) to the extent that is necessary to ensure accessibility for end-users to digital radio and television broadcasting services specified by the Member State, obligations on operators to provide access to the other facilities referred to in Annex I, Part II on fair, reasonable and non-discriminatory terms.

2. When imposing obligations on an operator to provide access in accordance with Article 12, national regulatory authorities may lay down technical or operational conditions to be met by the provider and/or beneficiaries of such access, in accordance with Community law, where necessary to

ensure normal operation of the network. Conditions that refer to implementation of specific technical standards or specifications shall respect Article 17 of Directive 2002/21/EC (Framework Directive).

3. Obligations and conditions imposed in accordance with paragraphs 1 and 2 shall be objective, transparent, proportionate and non-discriminatory, and shall be implemented in accordance with the procedures referred to in Articles 6 and 7 of Directive 2002/21/EC (Framework Directive).

4. With regard to access and interconnection, Member States shall ensure that the national regulatory authority is empowered to intervene at its own initiative where justified or, in the absence of agreement between undertakings, at the request of either of the parties involved, in order to secure the policy objectives of Article 8 of Directive 2002/21/EC (Framework Directive), in accordance with the provisions of this Directive and the procedures referred to in Articles 6 and 7, 20 and 21 of Directive 2002/21/EC (Framework Directive).

Commentary
Art 5: B&C: 12.109 F&N: 13.26
Art 5(1): B&C: 12.109
Art 5(2): B&C: 12.109
Art 5(3): B&C: 12.103
Art 5(4): B&C: 12.109
Art 5(4)(a): B&C: 12.125

CHAPTER III
OBLIGATIONS ON OPERATORS AND MARKET REVIEW PROCEDURES

Article 6
Conditional access systems and other facilities

1. Member States shall ensure that, in relation to conditional access to digital television and radio services broadcast to viewers and listeners in the Community, irrespective of the means of transmission, the conditions laid down in Annex I, Part I apply.

2. In the light of market and technological developments, Annex I may be amended in accordance with the procedure referred to in Article 14(3).

3. Notwithstanding the provisions of paragraph 1, Member States may permit their national regulatory authority, as soon as possible after the entry into force of this Directive and periodically thereafter, to review the conditions applied in accordance with this Article, by undertaking a market analysis in accordance with the first paragraph of Article 16 of Directive 2002/21/EC (Framework Directive) to determine whether to maintain, amend or withdraw the conditions applied.

Where, as a result of this market analysis, a national regulatory authority finds that one or more operators do not have significant market power on the relevant market, it may amend or withdraw the conditions with respect to those operators, in accordance with the procedures referred to in Articles 6 and 7 of Directive 2002/21/EC (Framework Directive), only to the extent that:

(a) accessibility for end-users to radio and television broadcasts and broadcasting channels and services specified in accordance with Article 31 of Directive 2002/22/EC (Universal Service Directive) would not be adversely affected by such amendment or withdrawal, and

(b) the prospects for effective competition in the markets for:
   (i) retail digital television and radio broadcasting services, and
   (ii) conditional access systems and other associated facilities,
   would not be adversely affected by such amendment or withdrawal.

An appropriate period of notice shall be given to parties affected by such amendment or withdrawal of conditions.

4. Conditions applied in accordance with this Article are without prejudice to the ability of Member States to impose obligations in relation to the presentational aspect of electronic programme guides and similar listing and navigation facilities.

Commentary
Art 6: B&C: 12.109

Article 7
Review of former obligations for access and interconnection

1. Member States shall maintain all obligations on undertakings providing public communications networks and/or services concerning access and interconnection that were in force prior to the date of entry into force of this Directive under Articles 4, 6, 7, 8, 11, 12, and 14 of Directive 97/33/EC, Article 16 of Directive 98/10/EC, and Articles 7 and 8 of Directive 92/44/EC, until such time as these obligations have been reviewed and a determination made in accordance with paragraph 3.

2. The Commission will indicate relevant markets for the obligations referred to in paragraph 1 in the initial recommendation on relevant product and service markets and the Decision identifying trans-national markets to be adopted in accordance with Article 15 of Directive 2002/21/EC (Framework Directive).

3. Member States shall ensure that, as soon as possible after the entry into force of this Directive, and periodically thereafter, national regulatory authorities undertake a market analysis, in accordance with Article 16 of Directive 2002/21/EC (Framework Directive) to determine whether to maintain, amend or withdraw these obligations. An appropriate period of notice shall be given to parties affected by such amendment or withdrawal of obligations.

Commentary
Art 7: B&C: 12.109

Article 8
Imposition, amendment or withdrawal of obligations

1. Member States shall ensure that national regulatory authorities are empowered to impose the obligations identified in Articles 9 to 13.

2. Where an operator is designated as having significant market power on a specific market as a result of a market analysis carried out in accordance with Article 16 of Directive 2002/21/EC (Framework Directive), national regulatory authorities shall impose the obligations set out in Articles 9 to 13 of this Directive as appropriate.

3. Without prejudice to:

— the provisions of Articles 5(1), 5(2) and 6,
— the provisions of Articles 12 and 13 of Directive 2002/21/EC (Framework Directive), Condition 7 in Part B of the Annex to Directive 2002/20/EC (Authorisation Directive) as applied by virtue of Article 6(1) of that Directive, Articles 27, 28 and 30 of Directive 2002/22/EC (Universal Service Directive) and the relevant provisions of Directive 97/66/EC of the European Parliament and of the Council of 15 December 1997 concerning the processing of personal data and the protection of privacy in the telecommunications sector[1] containing obligations on undertakings other than those designated as having significant market power, or
— the need to comply with international commitments,

national regulatory authorities shall not impose the obligations set out in Articles 9 to 13 on operators that have not been designated in accordance with paragraph 2.

In exceptional circumstances, when a national regulatory authority intends to impose on operators with significant market power other obligations for access or interconnection than those set out in Articles 9 to 13 in this Directive it shall submit this request to the Commission. The Commission, acting in accordance with Article 14(2), shall take a decision authorising or preventing the national regulatory authority from taking such measures.

4. Obligations imposed in accordance with this Article shall be based on the nature of the problem identified, proportionate and justified in the light of the objectives laid down in Article 8 of Directive 2002/21/EC (Framework Directive). Such obligations shall only be imposed following consultation in accordance with Articles 6 and 7 of that Directive.

5. In relation to the third indent of the first subparagraph of paragraph 3, national regulatory authorities shall notify decisions to impose, amend or withdraw obligations on market players to

the Commission, in accordance with the procedure referred to in Article 7 of Directive 2002/21/EC (Framework Directive).

Notes
[1] OJ L 24, 30.1.1998, p. 1.

Commentary
Art 8: **B&C:** 12.109
Art 8(2): **B&C:** 12.103
Art 8(4): **B&C:** 12.103

Article 9
Obligation of transparency

1. National regulatory authorities may, in accordance with the provisions of Article 8, impose obligations for transparency in relation to interconnection and/or access, requiring operators to make public specified information, such as accounting information, technical specifications, network characteristics, terms and conditions for supply and use, and prices.

2. In particular where an operator has obligations of non-discrimination, national regulatory authorities may require that operator to publish a reference offer, which shall be sufficiently unbundled to ensure that undertakings are not required to pay for facilities which are not necessary for the service requested, giving a description of the relevant offerings broken down into components according to market needs, and the associated terms and conditions including prices. The national regulatory authority shall, *inter alia*, be able to impose changes to reference offers to give effect to obligations imposed under this Directive.

3. National regulatory authorities may specify the precise information to be made available, the level of detail required and the manner of publication.

4. Notwithstanding paragraph 3, where an operator has obligations under Article 12 concerning unbundled access to the twisted metallic pair local loop, national regulatory authorities shall ensure the publication of a reference offer containing at least the elements set out in Annex II.

5. In the light of market and technological developments, Annex II may be amended in accordance with the procedure referred to in Article 14(3).

Commentary
Art 9: **B&C:** 12.098, 12.103

Article 10
Obligation of non-discrimination

1. A national regulatory authority may, in accordance with the provisions of Article 8, impose obligations of non-discrimination, in relation to interconnection and/or access.

2. Obligations of non-discrimination shall ensure, in particular, that the operator applies equivalent conditions in equivalent circumstances to other undertakings providing equivalent services, and provides services and information to others under the same conditions and of the same quality as it provides for its own services, or those of it subsidiaries or partners.

Commentary
Art 10: **B&C:** 12.098, 12.103 **F&N:** 13.32, 13.236, 13.252

Article 11
Obligation of accounting separation

1. A national regulatory authority may, in accordance with the provisions of Article 8, impose obligations for accounting separation in relation to specified activities related to interconnection and/or access.

In particular, a national regulatory authority may require a vertically integrated company to make transparent its wholesale prices and its internal transfer prices *inter alia* to ensure compliance where there is a requirement for non-discrimination under Article 10 or, where necessary, to prevent unfair cross-subsidy. National regulatory authorities may specify the format and accounting methodology to be used.

2. Without prejudice to Article 5 of Directive 2002/21/EC (Framework Directive), to facilitate the verification of compliance with obligations of transparency and non-discrimination, national regulatory authorities shall have the power to require that accounting records, including data on revenues received from third parties, are provided on request. National regulatory authorities may publish such information as would contribute to an open and competitive market, while respecting national and Community rules on commercial confidentiality.

Commentary
Art 11: **B&C:** 12.098, 12.103

Article 12
Obligations of access to, and use of, specific network facilities

1. A national regulatory authority may, in accordance with the provisions of Article 8, impose obligations on operators to meet reasonable requests for access to, and use of, specific network elements and associated facilities, *inter alia* in situations where the national regulatory authority considers that denial of access or unreasonable terms and conditions having a similar effect would hinder the emergence of a sustainable competitive market at the retail level, or would not be in the end-user's interest.

Operators may be required *inter alia*:

(a) to give third parties access to specified network elements and/or facilities, including unbundled access to the local loop;
(b) to negotiate in good faith with undertakings requesting access;
(c) not to withdraw access to facilities already granted;
(d) to provide specified services on a wholesale basis for resale by third parties;
(e) to grant open access to technical interfaces, protocols or other key technologies that are indispensable for the interoperability of services or virtual network services;
(f) to provide co-location or other forms of facility sharing, including duct, building or mast sharing;
(g) to provide specified services needed to ensure interoperability of end-to-end services to users, including facilities for intelligent network services or roaming on mobile networks;
(h) to provide access to operational support systems or similar software systems necessary to ensure fair competition in the provision of services;
(i) to interconnect networks or network facilities.

National regulatory authorities may attach to those obligations conditions covering fairness, reasonableness and timeliness.

2. When national regulatory authorities are considering whether to impose the obligations referred in paragraph 1, and in particular when assessing whether such obligations would be proportionate to the objectives set out in Article 8 of Directive 2002/21/EC (Framework Directive), they shall take account in particular of the following factors:

(a) the technical and economic viability of using or installing competing facilities, in the light of the rate of market development, taking into account the nature and type of interconnection and access involved;
(b) the feasibility of providing the access proposed, in relation to the capacity available;
(c) the initial investment by the facility owner, bearing in mind the risks involved in making the investment;
(d) the need to safeguard competition in the long term;
(e) where appropriate, any relevant intellectual property rights;
(f) the provision of pan-European services.

Commentary
Art 12: **B&C:** 12.098, 12.103

Article 13
Price control and cost accounting obligations

1. A national regulatory authority may, in accordance with the provisions of Article 8, impose obligations relating to cost recovery and price controls, including obligations for cost orientation of prices and obligations concerning cost accounting systems, for the provision of specific types of interconnection and/or access, in situations where a market analysis indicates that a lack of effective competition means that the operator concerned might sustain prices at an excessively high level, or apply a price squeeze, to the detriment of end-users. National regulatory authorities shall take into account the investment made by the operator and allow him a reasonable rate of return on adequate capital employed, taking into account the risks involved.

2. National regulatory authorities shall ensure that any cost recovery mechanism or pricing methodology that is mandated serves to promote efficiency and sustainable competition and maximise consumer benefits. In this regard national regulatory authorities may also take account of prices available in comparable competitive markets.

3. Where an operator has an obligation regarding the cost orientation of its prices, the burden of proof that charges are derived from costs including a reasonable rate of return on investment shall lie with the operator concerned. For the purpose of calculating the cost of efficient provision of services, national regulatory authorities may use cost accounting methods independent of those used by the undertaking. National regulatory authorities may require an operator to provide full justification for its prices, and may, where appropriate, require prices to be adjusted.

4. National regulatory authorities shall ensure that, where implementation of a cost accounting system is mandated in order to support price controls, a description of the cost accounting system is made publicly available, showing at least the main categories under which costs are grouped and the rules used for the allocation of costs. Compliance with the cost accounting system shall be verified by a qualified independent body. A statement concerning compliance shall be published annually.

Commentary
Art 13: B&C: 12.098, 12.103

CHAPTER IV
PROCEDURAL PROVISIONS

Article 14
Committee

1. The Commission shall be assisted by the Communications Committee set up by Article 22 of Directive 2002/21/EC (Framework Directive).

2. Where reference is made to this paragraph, Articles 3 and 7 of Decision 1999/468/EC shall apply, having regard to the provisions of Article 8 thereof.

3. Where reference is made to this paragraph, Articles 5 and 7 of Decision 1999/468/EC shall apply, having regard to the provisions of Article 8 thereof.

The period laid down in Article 5(6) of Decision 1999/468/EC shall be set at three months.

4. The Committee shall adopt its rules of procedure.

Article 15
Publication of, and access to, information

1. Member States shall ensure that the specific obligations imposed on undertakings under this Directive are published and that the specific product/service and geographical markets are identified. They shall ensure that up-to-date information, provided that the information is not confidential and, in particular, does not comprise business secrets, is made publicly available in a manner that guarantees all interested parties easy access to that information.

2. Member States shall send to the Commission a copy of all such information published. The Commission shall make this information available in a readily accessible form, and shall distribute the information to the Communications Committee as appropriate.

Article 16
Notification

1. Member States shall notify to the Commission by at the latest the date of application referred to in Article 18(1) second subparagraph the national regulatory authorities responsible for the tasks set out in this Directive.

2. National regulatory authorities shall notify to the Commission the names of operators deemed to have significant market power for the purposes of this Directive, and the obligations imposed upon them under this Directive. Any changes affecting the obligations imposed upon undertakings or of the undertakings affected under the provisions of this Directive shall be notified to the Commission without delay.

Article 17
Review procedures

The Commission shall periodically review the functioning of this Directive and report to the European Parliament and to the Council, on the first occasion not later than three years after the date of application referred to in Article 18(1), second subparagraph. For this purpose, the Commission may request from the Member States information, which shall be supplied without undue delay.

Article 18
Transposition

1. Member States shall adopt and publish the laws, regulations and administrative provisions necessary to comply with this Directive by not later than 24 July 2003. They shall forthwith inform the Commission thereof.

They shall apply those measures from 25 July 2003.

When Member States adopt these measures, they shall contain a reference to this Directive or be accompanied by such a reference on the occasion of their official publication. The methods of making such reference shall be laid down by Member States.

2. Member States shall communicate to the Commission the text of the provisions of national law which they adopt in the field governed by this Directive and of any subsequent amendments to those provisions.

Article 19
Entry into force

This Directive shall enter into force on the day of its publication in the *Official Journal of the European Communities*.

Notes

Date of entry into force: 24 April 2002.

Article 20
Addressees

This Directive is addressed to the Member States.

Done at Brussels, 7 March 2002.

ANNEX I
CONDITIONS FOR ACCESS TO DIGITAL TELEVISION AND RADIO SERVICES BROADCAST TO VIEWERS AND LISTENERS IN THE COMMUNITY

Part I: Conditions for Conditional Access Systems to be Applied in Accordance with Article 6(1)

In relation to conditional access to digital television and radio services broadcast to viewers and listeners in the Community, irrespective of the means of transmission, Member States must ensure in accordance with Article 6 that the following conditions apply:

(a) conditional access systems operated on the market in the Community are to have the necessary technical capability for cost-effective transcontrol allowing the possibility for full control by network operators at local or regional level of the services using such conditional access systems;

(b) all operators of conditional access services, irrespective of the means of transmission, who provide access services to digital television and radio services and whose access services broadcasters depend on to reach any group of potential viewers or listeners are to:
— offer to all broadcasters, on a fair, reasonable and non-discriminatory basis compatible with Community competition law, technical services enabling the broadcasters" digitally-transmitted services to be received by viewers or listeners authorised by means of decoders administered by the service operators, and comply with Community competition law,
— keep separate financial accounts regarding their activity as conditional access providers.
(c) when granting licences to manufacturers of consumer equipment, holders of industrial property rights to conditional access products and systems are to ensure that this is done on fair, reasonable and non-discriminatory terms. Taking into account technical and commercial factors, holders of rights are not to subject the granting of licences to conditions prohibiting, deterring or discouraging the inclusion in the same product of:
— a common interface allowing connection with several other access systems, or
— means specific to another access system, provided that the licensee complies with the relevant and reasonable conditions ensuring, as far as he is concerned, the security of transactions of conditional access system operators.

Part II: Other Facilities to which Conditions may be Applied under Article 5(1)(b)

(a) Access to application program interfaces (APIs);
(b) Access to electronic programme guides (EPGs).

Commentary
Annex I, Part 2: B&C: 12.109

Annex II

Minimum List of Items to be Included in a Reference Offer for Unbundled Access to the Twisted Metallic Pair Local Loop to be Published by Notified Operators

For the purposes of this Annex the following definitions apply:

(a) "local sub-loop" means a partial local loop connecting the network termination point at the subscriber's premises to a concentration point or a specified intermediate access point in the fixed public telephone network;
(b) "unbundled access to the local loop" means full unbundled access to the local loop and shared access to the local loop; it does not entail a change in ownership of the local loop;
(c) "full unbundled access to the local loop" means the provision to a beneficiary of access to the local loop or local sub-loop of the notified operator authorising the use of the full frequency spectrum of the twisted metallic pair;
(d) "shared access to the local loop" means the provision to a beneficiary of access to the local loop or local sub-loop of the notified operator, authorising the use of the non-voice band frequency spectrum of the twisted metallic pair; the local loop continues to be used by the notified operator to provide the telephone service to the public;

A. Conditions for unbundled access to the local loop

1. Network elements to which access is offered covering in particular the following elements:
   (a) access to local loops;
   (b) access to non-voice band frequency spectrum of a local loop, in the case of shared access to the local loop;
2. Information concerning the locations of physical access sites,[1] availability of local loops in specific parts of the access network;
3. Technical conditions related to access and use of local loops, including the technical characteristics of the twisted metallic pair in the local loop;
4. Ordering and provisioning procedures, usage restrictions.

Notes

[1] Availability of this information may be restricted to interested parties only, in order to avoid public security concerns.

B. Co-location services

1. Information on the notified operator's relevant sites.[1]
2. Co-location options at the sites indicated under point 1 (including physical co-location and, as appropriate, distant co-location and virtual co-location).
3. Equipment characteristics: restrictions, if any, on equipment that can be co-located.
4. Security issues: measures put in place by notified operators to ensure the security of their locations.
5. Access conditions for staff of competitive operators.
6. Safety standards.
7. Rules for the allocation of space where co-location space is limited.
8. Conditions for beneficiaries to inspect the locations at which physical co-location is available, or sites where co-location has been refused on grounds of lack of capacity.

Notes

[1] Availability of this information may be restricted to interested parties only, in order to avoid public security concerns.

C. Information systems

Conditions for access to notified operator's operational support systems, information systems or databases for pre-ordering, provisioning, ordering, maintenance and repair requests and billing.

D. Supply conditions

1. Lead time for responding to requests for supply of services and facilities; service level agreements, fault resolution, procedures to return to a normal level of service and quality of service parameters.
2. Standard contract terms, including, where appropriate, compensation provided for failure to meet lead times.
3. Prices or pricing formulae for each feature, function and facility listed above.

E19

DIRECTIVE 2002/20/EC OF THE EUROPEAN PARLIAMENT AND OF THE COUNCIL

of 7 March 2002

on the authorisation of electronic communications networks and services

(Authorisation Directive)

Official Journal L 108, 24.4.2002, p. 21

Celex No: 32002L0020

Notes

EEA application: this Directive was adopted with appropriate adaptations by EEA Joint Committee Decision No 11/2004 (OJ No L 116, 22.4.2004, p. 60 and EEA Supplement No 20, 22.4.2004, p. 14): see EEA Agreement, Annex XI, Point 5ck.

Commentary

Directive 2002/20/EC: **B&C:** 12.089, 12.110 **F&N:** 13.14
Recitals 11–14: **B&C:** 12.112

THE EUROPEAN PARLIAMENT AND THE COUNCIL OF THE EUROPEAN UNION,

Having regard to the Treaty establishing the European Community, and in particular Article 95 thereof,

Having regard to the proposal from the Commission,[1]

Having regard to the opinion of the Economic and Social Committee,[2]

Acting in accordance with the procedure laid down in Article 251 of the Treaty,[3]

Notes

[1] OJ C 365 E, 19.12.2000, p. 230 and OJ C 270 E, 25.9.2001, p. 182.

[2] OJ C 123, 25.4.2001, p. 55.

[3] Opinion of the European Parliament of 1 March 2001 (OJ C 277, 1.10.2001, p. 116), Council Common Position of 17 September 2001 (OJ C 337, 30.11.2001, p. 18) and Decision of the European Parliament of 12 December 2001 [OJ C 177 E, 25.7.2002, p. 82]. Council Decision of 14 February 2002.

Whereas:

(1) The outcome of the public consultation on the 1999 review of the regulatory framework for electronic communications, as reflected in the Commission communication of 26 April 2000, and the findings reported by the Commission in its communications on the fifth and sixth reports on the implementation of the telecommunications regulatory package, has confirmed the need for a more harmonised and less onerous market access regulation for electronic communications networks and services throughout the Community.

(2) Convergence between different electronic communications networks and services and their technologies requires the establishment of an authorisation system covering all comparable services in a similar way regardless of the technologies used.

(3) The objective of this Directive is to create a legal framework to ensure the freedom to provide electronic communications networks and services, subject only to the conditions laid down in this Directive and to any restrictions in conformity with Article 46(1) of the Treaty, in particular measures regarding public policy, public security and public health.

(4) This Directive covers authorisation of all electronic communications networks and services whether they are provided to the public or not. This is important to ensure that both categories of

providers may benefit from objective, transparent, non-discriminatory and proportionate rights, conditions and procedures.

(5) This Directive only applies to the granting of rights to use radio frequencies where such use involves the provision of an electronic communications network or service, normally for remuneration. The self-use of radio terminal equipment, based on the non-exclusive use of specific radio frequencies by a user and not related to an economic activity, such as use of a citizen's band by radio amateurs, does not consist of the provision of an electronic communications network or service and is therefore not covered by this Directive. Such use is covered by the Directive 1999/5/EC of the European Parliament and of the Council of 9 March 1999 on radio equipment and telecommunications terminal equipment and the mutual recognition of their conformity.[1]

Notes
[1] OJ L 91, 7.4.1999, p. 10.

Commentary
Recital 5: B&C: 12.110, 12.112

(6) Provisions regarding the free movement of conditional access systems and the free provision of protected services based on such systems are laid down in Directive 98/84/EC of the European Parliament and of the Council of 20 November 1998 on the legal protection of services based on, or consisting of, conditional access.[1] The authorisation of such systems and services therefore does not need to be covered by this Directive.

Notes
[1] OJ L 320, 28.11.1998, p. 54.

Commentary
Recital 6: B&C: 12.110

(7) The least onerous authorisation system possible should be used to allow the provision of electronic communications networks and services in order to stimulate the development of new electronic communications services and pan-European communications networks and services and to allow service providers and consumers to benefit from the economies of scale of the single market.

Commentary
Recital 7: B&C: 12.111

(8) Those aims can be best achieved by general authorisation of all electronic communications networks and services without requiring any explicit decision or administrative act by the national regulatory authority and by limiting any procedural requirements to notification only. Where Member States require notification by providers of electronic communication networks or services when they start their activities, they may also require proof of such notification having been made by means of any legally recognised postal or electronic acknowledgement of receipt of the notification. Such acknowledgement should in any case not consist of or require an administrative act by the national regulatory authority to which the notification must be made.

Commentary
Recital 8: B&C: 12.097

(9) It is necessary to include the rights and obligations of undertakings under general authorisations explicitly in such authorisations in order to ensure a level playing field throughout the Community and to facilitate cross-border negotiation of interconnection between public communications networks.

Commentary
Recital 9: B&C: 12.110

(10) The general authorisation entitles undertakings providing electronic communications networks and services to the public to negotiate interconnection under the conditions of Directive 2002/19/EC

of the European Parliament and of the Council of 7 March 2002 on access to, and interconnection of, electronic communication networks and associated facilities (Access Directive).[1] Undertakings providing electronic communications networks and services other than to the public can negotiate interconnection on commercial terms.

Notes

[1] See [OJ L 108, 24.4.2002, p. 7].

(11) The granting of specific rights may continue to be necessary for the use of radio frequencies and numbers, including short codes, from the national numbering plan. Rights to numbers may also be allocated from a European numbering plan, including for example the virtual country code "3883" which has been attributed to member countries of the European Conference of Post and Telecommunications (CEPT). Those rights of use should not be restricted except where this is unavoidable in view of the scarcity of radio frequencies and the need to ensure the efficient use thereof.

Commentary
Recital 11: B&C: 12.112

(12) This Directive does not prejudice whether radio frequencies are assigned directly to providers of electronic communication networks or services or to entities that use these networks or services. Such entities may be radio or television broadcast content providers. Without prejudice to specific criteria and procedures adopted by Member States to grant rights of use for radio frequencies to providers of radio or television broadcast content services, to pursue general interest objectives in conformity with Community law, the procedure for assignment of radio frequencies should in any event be objective, transparent, non-discriminatory and proportionate. In accordance with case law of the Court of Justice, any national restrictions on the rights guaranteed by Article 49 of the Treaty should be objectively justified, proportionate and not exceed what is necessary to achieve general interest objectives as defined by Member States in conformity with Community law. The responsibility for compliance with the conditions attached to the right to use a radio frequency and the relevant conditions attached to the general authorisation should in any case lie with the undertaking to whom the right of use for the radio frequency has been granted.

(13) As part of the application procedure for granting rights to use a radio frequency, Member States may verify whether the applicant will be able to comply with the conditions attached to such rights. For this purpose the applicant may be requested to submit the necessary information to prove his ability to comply with these conditions. Where such information is not provided, the application for the right to use a radio frequency may be rejected.

(14) Member States are neither obliged to grant nor prevented from granting rights to use numbers from the national numbering plan or rights to install facilities to undertakings other than providers of electronic communications networks or services.

(15) The conditions, which may be attached to the general authorisation and to the specific rights of use, should be limited to what is strictly necessary to ensure compliance with requirements and obligations under Community law and national law in accordance with Community law.

(16) In the case of electronic communications networks and services not provided to the public it is appropriate to impose fewer and lighter conditions than are justified for electronic communications networks and services provided to the public.

Commentary
Recital 16: B&C: 12.111

(17) Specific obligations which may be imposed on providers of electronic communications networks and services in accordance with Community law by virtue of their significant market power as defined in Directive 2002/21/EC of the European Parliament and of the Council of 7 March 2002 on a common regulatory framework for electronic communications networks and services (Framework Directive)[1] should be imposed separately from the general rights and obligations under the general authorisation.

Notes
[1] See [OJ L 108, 24.4.2002, p. 33].

(18) The general authorisation should only contain conditions which are specific to the electronic communications sector. It should not be made subject to conditions which are already applicable by virtue of other existing national law which is not specific to the electronic communications sector. Nevertheless, the national regulatory authorities may inform network operators and service providers about other legislation concerning their business, for instance through references on their websites.

(19) The requirement to publish decisions on the granting of rights to use frequencies or numbers may be fulfilled by making these decisions publicly accessible via a website.

(20) The same undertaking, for example a cable operator, can offer both an electronic communications service, such as the conveyance of television signals, and services not covered under this Directive, such as the commercialisation of an offer of sound or television broadcasting content services, and therefore additional obligations can be imposed on this undertaking in relation to its activity as a content provider or distributor, according to provisions other than those of this Directive, without prejudice to the list of conditions laid in the Annex to this Directive.

Commentary
Recital 20: B&C: 12.110

(21) When granting rights of use for radio frequencies, numbers or rights to install facilities, the relevant authorities may inform the undertakings to whom they grant such rights of the relevant conditions in the general authorisation.

(22) Where the demand for radio frequencies in a specific range exceeds their availability, appropriate and transparent procedures should be followed for the assignment of such frequencies in order to avoid any discrimination and optimise use of those scarce resources.

(23) National regulatory authorities should ensure, in establishing criteria for competitive or comparative selection procedures, that the objectives in Article 8 of Directive 2002/21/EC (Framework Directive) are met. It would therefore not be contrary to this Directive if the application of objective, non-discriminatory and proportionate selection criteria to promote the development of competition would have the effect of excluding certain undertakings from a competitive or comparative selection procedure for a particular radio frequency.

(24) Where the harmonised assignment of radio frequencies to particular undertakings has been agreed at European level, Member States should strictly implement such agreements in the granting of rights of use of radio frequencies from the national frequency usage plan.

(25) Providers of electronic communications networks and services may need a confirmation of their rights under the general authorisation with respect to interconnection and rights of way, in particular to facilitate negotiations with other, regional or local, levels of government or with service providers in other Member States. For this purpose the national regulatory authorities should provide declarations to undertakings either upon request or alternatively as an automatic response to a notification under the general authorisation. Such declarations should not by themselves constitute entitlements to rights nor should any rights under the general authorisation or rights of use or the exercise of such rights depend upon a declaration.

(26) Where undertakings find that their applications for rights to install facilities have not been dealt with in accordance with the principles set out in Directive 2002/21/EC (Framework Directive) or where such decisions are unduly delayed, they should have the right to appeal against decisions or delays in such decisions in accordance with that Directive.

(27) The penalties for non-compliance with conditions under the general authorisation should be commensurate with the infringement. Save in exceptional circumstances, it would not be proportionate to suspend or withdraw the right to provide electronic communications services or the right to use radio frequencies or numbers where an undertaking did not comply with one or more of the conditions under the general authorisation. This is without prejudice to urgent measures which the relevant authorities of the Member States may need to take in case of serious threats to public safety, security or health or to economic and operational interests of

other undertakings. This Directive should also be without prejudice to any claims between undertakings for compensation for damages under national law.

(28) Subjecting service providers to reporting and information obligations can be cumbersome, both for the undertaking and for the national regulatory authority concerned. Such obligations should therefore be proportionate, objectively justified and limited to what is strictly necessary. It is not necessary to require systematic and regular proof of compliance with all conditions under the general authorisation or attached to rights of use. Undertakings have a right to know the purposes for which the information they should provide will be used. The provision of information should not be a condition for market access. For statistical purposes a notification may be required from providers of electronic communication networks or services when they cease activities.

(29) This Directive should be without prejudice to Member States' obligations to provide any information necessary for the defence of Community interests within the context of international agreements. This Directive should also be without prejudice to any reporting obligations under legislation which is not specific to the electronic communications sector such as competition law.

(30) Administrative charges may be imposed on providers of electronic communications services in order to finance the activities of the national regulatory authority in managing the authorisation system and for the granting of rights of use. Such charges should be limited to cover the actual administrative costs for those activities. For this purpose transparency should be created in the income and expenditure of national regulatory authorities by means of annual reporting about the total sum of charges collected and the administrative costs incurred. This will allow undertakings to verify that administrative costs and charges are in balance.

(31) Systems for administrative charges should not distort competition or create barriers for entry into the market. With a general authorisation system it will no longer be possible to attribute administrative costs and hence charges to individual undertakings except for the granting of rights to use numbers, radio frequencies and for rights to install facilities. Any applicable administrative charges should be in line with the principles of a general authorisation system. An example of a fair, simple and transparent alternative for these charge attribution criteria could be a turnover related distribution key. Where administrative charges are very low, flat rate charges, or charges combining a flat rate basis with a turnover related element could also be appropriate.

(32) In addition to administrative charges, usage fees may be levied for the use of radio frequencies and numbers as an instrument to ensure the optimal use of such resources. Such fees should not hinder the development of innovative services and competition in the market. This Directive is without prejudice to the purpose for which fees for rights of use are employed. Such fees may for instance be used to finance activities of national regulatory authorities that cannot be covered by administrative charges. Where, in the case of competitive or comparative selection procedures, fees for rights of use for radio frequencies consist entirely or partly of a one-off amount, payment arrangements should ensure that such fees do not in practice lead to selection on the basis of criteria unrelated to the objective of ensuring optimal use of radio frequencies. The Commission may publish on a regular basis benchmark studies with regard to best practices for the assignment of radio frequencies, the assignment of numbers or the granting of rights of way.

(33) Member States may need to amend rights, conditions, procedures, charges and fees relating to general authorisations and rights of use where this is objectively justified. Such changes should be duly notified to all interested parties in good time, giving them adequate opportunity to express their views on any such amendments.

(34) The objective of transparency requires that service providers, consumers and other interested parties have easy access to any information regarding rights, conditions, procedures, charges, fees and decisions concerning the provision of electronic communications services, rights of use of radio frequencies and numbers, rights to install facilities, national frequency usage plans and national numbering plans. The national regulatory authorities have an important task in providing such information and keeping it up to date. Where such rights are administered by other levels of government the national regulatory authorities should endeavour to create a user-friendly instrument for access to information regarding such rights.

(35) The proper functioning of the single market on the basis of the national authorisation regimes under this Directive should be monitored by the Commission.

(36) In order to arrive at a single date of application of all elements of the new regulatory framework for the electronic communications sector, it is important that the process of national transposition of this Directive and of alignment of the existing licences with the new rules take place in parallel. However, in specific cases where the replacement of authorisations existing on the date of entry into force of this Directive by the general authorisation and the individual rights of use in accordance with this Directive would lead to an increase in the obligations for service providers operating under an existing authorisation or to a reduction of their rights, Member States may avail themselves of an additional nine months after the date of application of this Directive for alignment of such licences, unless this would have a negative effect on the rights and obligations of other undertakings.

(37) There may be circumstances under which the abolition of an authorisation condition regarding access to electronic communications networks would create serious hardship for one or more undertakings that have benefited from the condition. In such cases further transitional arrangements may be granted by the Commission, upon request by a Member State.

(38) Since the objectives of the proposed action, namely the harmonisation and simplification of electronic communications rules and conditions for the authorisation of networks and services cannot be sufficiently achieved by the Member States and can therefore, by reason of the scale and effects of the action, be better achieved at Community level, the Community may adopt measures in accordance with the principle of subsidiarity as set out in Article 5 of the Treaty. In accordance with the principle of proportionality, as set out in that Article, this Directive does not go beyond what is necessary for those objectives,

HAVE ADOPTED THIS DIRECTIVE:

Article 1
Objective and scope

1. The aim of this Directive is to implement an internal market in electronic communications networks and services through the harmonisation and simplification of authorisation rules and conditions in order to facilitate their provision throughout the Community.

2. This Directive shall apply to authorisations for the provision of electronic communications networks and services.

Commentary
Art 1: **B&C:** 12.110

Article 2
Definitions

1. For the purposes of this Directive, the definitions set out in Article 2 of Directive 2002/21/EC (Framework Directive) shall apply.

2. The following definitions shall also apply:

(a) "general authorisation" means a legal framework established by the Member State ensuring rights for the provision of electronic communications networks or services and laying down sector specific obligations that may apply to all or to specific types of electronic communications networks and services, in accordance with this Directive;

(b) "harmful interference" means interference which endangers the functioning of a radionavigation service or of other safety services or which otherwise seriously degrades, obstructs or repeatedly interrupts a radiocommunications service operating in accordance with the applicable Community or national regulations.

Commentary
Art 2: **B&C:** 12.110

Article 3
General authorisation of electronic communications networks and services

1. Member States shall ensure the freedom to provide electronic communications networks and services, subject to the conditions set out in this Directive. To this end, Member States shall not prevent an undertaking from providing electronic communications networks or services, except where this is necessary for the reasons set out in Article 46(1) of the Treaty.

2. The provision of electronic communications networks or the provision of electronic communications services may, without prejudice to the specific obligations referred to in Article 6(2) or rights of use referred to in Article 5, only be subject to a general authorisation. The undertaking concerned may be required to submit a notification but may not be required to obtain an explicit decision or any other administrative act by the national regulatory authority before exercising the rights stemming from the authorisation. Upon notification, when required, an undertaking may begin activity, where necessary subject to the provisions on rights of use in Articles 5, 6 and 7.

3. The notification referred to in paragraph 2 shall not entail more than a declaration by a legal or natural person to the national regulatory authority of the intention to commence the provision of electronic communication networks or services and the submission of the minimal information which is required to allow the national regulatory authority to keep a register or list of providers of electronic communications networks and services. This information must be limited to what is necessary for the identification of the provider, such as company registration numbers, and the provider's contact persons, the provider's address, a short description of the network or service, and an estimated date for starting the activity.

Article 4
Minimum list of rights derived from the general authorisation

1. Undertakings authorised pursuant to Article 3, shall have the right to:

(a) provide electronic communications networks and services;
(b) have their application for the necessary rights to install facilities considered in accordance with Article 11 of Directive 2002/21/EC (Framework Directive).

2. When such undertakings provide electronic communications networks or services to the public the general authorisation shall also give them the right to:

(a) negotiate interconnection with and where applicable obtain access to or interconnection from other providers of publicly available communications networks and services covered by a general authorisation anywhere in the Community under the conditions of and in accordance with Directive 2002/19/EC (Access Directive);
(b) be given an opportunity to be designated to provide different elements of a universal service and/ or to cover different parts of the national territory in accordance with Directive 2002/22/EC of the European Parliament and of the Council of 7 March 2002 on universal service and users' rights relating to electronic communications networks and services (Universal Service Directive).[1]

Notes
[1] See [OJ L 108, 24.4.2002, p. 51].

Commentary
Art 4: B&C: 12.110

Article 5
Rights of use for radio frequencies and numbers

1. Member States shall, where possible, in particular where the risk of harmful interference is negligible, not make the use of radio frequencies subject to the grant of individual rights of use but shall include the conditions for usage of such radio frequencies in the general authorisation.

2. Where it is necessary to grant individual rights of use for radio frequencies and numbers, Member States shall grant such rights, upon request, to any undertaking providing or using networks or services under the general authorisation, subject to the provisions of Articles 6, 7 and 11(1)(c) of this

Directive and any other rules ensuring the efficient use of those resources in accordance with Directive 2002/21/EC (Framework Directive).

Without prejudice to specific criteria and procedures adopted by Member States to grant rights of use of radio frequencies to providers of radio or television broadcast content services with a view to pursuing general interest objectives in conformity with Community law, such rights of use shall be granted through open, transparent and non-discriminatory procedures. When granting rights of use, Member States shall specify whether those rights can be transferred at the initiative of the right holder, and under which conditions, in the case of radio frequencies, in accordance with Article 9 of Directive 2002/21/EC (Framework Directive). Where Member States grant rights of use for a limited period of time, the duration shall be appropriate for the service concerned.

3. Decisions on rights of use shall be taken, communicated and made public as soon as possible after receipt of the complete application by the national regulatory authority, within three weeks in the case of numbers that have been allocated for specific purposes within the national numbering plan and within six weeks in the case of radio frequencies that have been allocated for specific purposes within the national frequency plan. The latter time limit shall be without prejudice to any applicable international agreements relating to the use of radio frequencies or of orbital positions.

4. Where it has been decided, after consultation with interested parties in accordance with Article 6 of Directive 2002/21/EC (Framework Directive), that rights for use of numbers of exceptional economic value are to be granted through competitive or comparative selection procedures, Member States may extend the maximum period of three weeks by up to three weeks.

With regard to competitive or comparative selection procedures for radio frequencies Article 7 shall apply.

5. Member States shall not limit the number of rights of use to be granted except where this is necessary to ensure the efficient use of radio frequencies in accordance with Article 7.

Commentary
Art 5: B&C: 12.112 F&N: 13.34

Article 6
**Conditions attached to the general authorisation and to the rights of use for
radio frequencies and for numbers, and specific obligations**

1. The general authorisation for the provision of electronic communications networks or services and the rights of use for radio frequencies and rights of use for numbers may be subject only to the conditions listed respectively in parts A, B and C of the Annex. Such conditions shall be objectively justified in relation to the network or service concerned, non-discriminatory, proportionate and transparent.

2. Specific obligations which may be imposed on providers of electronic communications networks and services under Articles 5(1), 5(2), 6 and 8 of Directive 2002/19/EC (Access Directive) and Articles 16, 17, 18 and 19 of Directive 2002/22/EC (Universal Service Directive) or on those designated to provide universal service under the said Directive shall be legally separate from the rights and obligations under the general authorisation. In order to achieve transparency for undertakings, the criteria and procedures for imposing such specific obligations on individual undertakings shall be referred to in the general authorisation.

3. The general authorisation shall only contain conditions which are specific for that sector and are set out in Part A of the Annex and shall not duplicate conditions which are applicable to undertakings by virtue of other national legislation.

4. Member States shall not duplicate the conditions of the general authorisation where they grant the right of use for radio frequencies or numbers.

Commentary
Art 6: F&N: 13.34, 13.159
Art 6(1): B&C: 12.112
Art 6(2): B&C: 12.110

Article 7
Procedure for limiting the number of rights of use to be granted for radio frequencies

1. Where a Member State is considering whether to limit the number of rights of use to be granted for radio frequencies, it shall *inter alia*:

(a) give due weight to the need to maximise benefits for users and to facilitate the development of competition;

(b) give all interested parties, including users and consumers, the opportunity to express their views on any limitation in accordance with Article 6 of Directive 2002/21/EC (Framework Directive);

(c) publish any decision to limit the granting of rights of use, stating the reasons therefor;

(d) after having determined the procedure, invite applications for rights of use; and

(e) review the limitation at reasonable intervals or at the reasonable request of affected undertakings.

2. Where a Member State concludes that further rights of use for radio frequencies can be granted, it shall publish that conclusion and invite applications for such rights.

3. Where the granting of rights of use for radio frequencies needs to be limited, Member States shall grant such rights on the basis of selection criteria which must be objective, transparent, non-discriminatory and proportionate. Any such selection criteria must give due weight to the achievement of the objectives of Article 8 of Directive 2002/21/EC (Framework Directive).

4. Where competitive or comparative selection procedures are to be used, Member States may extend the maximum period of six weeks referred to in Article 5(3) for as long as necessary to ensure that such procedures are fair, reasonable, open and transparent to all interested parties, but by no longer than eight months.

These time limits shall be without prejudice to any applicable international agreements relating to the use of radio frequencies and satellite coordination.

5. This Article is without prejudice to the transfer of rights of use for radio frequencies in accordance with Article 9 of Directive 2002/21/EC (Framework Directive).

Commentary
Art 7: B&C: 12.112

Article 8
Harmonised assignment of radio frequencies

Where the usage of radio frequencies has been harmonised, access conditions and procedures have been agreed, and undertakings to which the radio frequencies shall be assigned have been selected in accordance with international agreements and Community rules, Member States shall grant the right of use for such radio frequencies in accordance therewith. Provided that all national conditions attached to the right to use the radio frequencies concerned have been satisfied in the case of a common selection procedure, Member States shall not impose any further conditions, additional criteria or procedures which would restrict, alter or delay the correct implementation of the common assignment of such radio frequencies.

Commentary
Art 8: B&C: 12.112

Article 9
Declarations to facilitate the exercise of rights to install facilities and rights of interconnection

At the request of an undertaking, national regulatory authorities shall, within one week, issue standardised declarations, confirming, where applicable, that the undertaking has submitted a notification under Article 3(2) and detailing under what circumstances any undertaking providing electronic communications networks or services under the general authorisation has the right to apply for rights to install facilities, negotiate interconnection, and/or obtain access or interconnection in order to facilitate the exercise of those rights for instance at other levels of government or in relation to other undertakings. Where appropriate such declarations may also be issued as an automatic reply following the notification referred to in Article 3(2).

Commentary
Art 9: B&C: 12.110

Article 10
Compliance with the conditions of the general authorisation or of rights of use and with specific obligations

1. National regulatory authorities may require undertakings providing electronic communications networks or services covered by the general authorisation or enjoying rights of use for radio frequencies or numbers to provide information necessary to verify compliance with the conditions of the general authorisation or of rights of use or with the specific obligations referred to in Article 6(2), in accordance with Article 11.

2. Where a national regulatory authority finds that an undertaking does not comply with one or more of the conditions of the general authorisation, or of rights of use or with the specific obligations referred to in Article 6(2), it shall notify the undertaking of those findings and give the undertaking a reasonable opportunity to state its views or remedy any breaches within:

— one month after notification, or
— a shorter period agreed by the undertaking or stipulated by the national regulatory authority in case of repeated breaches, or
— a longer period decided by the national regulatory authority.

3. If the undertaking concerned does not remedy the breaches within the period as referred to in paragraph 2, the relevant authority shall take appropriate and proportionate measures aimed at ensuring compliance. In this regard, Member States may empower the relevant authorities to impose financial penalties where appropriate. The measures and the reasons on which they are based shall be communicated to the undertaking concerned within one week of their adoption and shall stipulate a reasonable period for the undertaking to comply with the measure.

4. Notwithstanding the provisions of paragraphs 2 and 3, Member States may empower the relevant authority to impose financial penalties where appropriate on undertakings for failure to provide information in accordance with obligations imposed under Article 11(1)(a) or (b) of this Directive or Article 9 of Directive 2002/19/EC (Access Directive) within a reasonable period stipulated by the national regulatory authority.

5. In cases of serious and repeated breaches of the conditions of the general authorisation, the rights of use or specific obligations referred to in Article 6(2), where measures aimed at ensuring compliance as referred to in paragraph 3 of this Article have failed, national regulatory authorities may prevent an undertaking from continuing to provide electronic communications networks or services or suspend or withdraw rights of use.

6. Irrespective of the provisions of paragraphs 2, 3 and 5, where the relevant authority has evidence of a breach of the conditions of the general authorisation, rights of use or specific obligations referred to in Article 6(2) that represents an immediate and serious threat to public safety, public security or public health or will create serious economic or operational problems for other providers or users of electronic communications networks or services, it may take urgent interim measures to remedy the situation in advance of reaching a final decision. The undertaking concerned shall thereafter be given a reasonable opportunity to state its view and propose any remedies. Where appropriate, the relevant authority may confirm the interim measures.

7. Undertakings shall have the right to appeal against measures taken under this Article in accordance with the procedure referred to in Article 4 of Directive 2002/21/EC (Framework Directive).

Commentary
Art 10: B&C: 12.110

Article 11
Information required under the general authorisation, for rights of use and for the specific obligations

1. Without prejudice to information and reporting obligations under national legislation other than the general authorisation, national regulatory authorities may only require undertakings to provide information under the general authorisation, for rights of use or the specific obligations referred to in Article 6(2) that is proportionate and objectively justified for:

(a) systematic or case-by-case verification of compliance with conditions 1 and 2 of Part A, condition 6 of Part B and condition 7 of Part C of the Annex and of compliance with obligations as referred to in Article 6(2);

(b) case-by-case verification of compliance with conditions as set out in the Annex where a complaint has been received or where the national regulatory authority has other reasons to believe that a condition is not complied with or in case of an investigation by the national regulatory authority on its own initiative;

(c) procedures for and assessment of requests for granting rights of use;

(d) publication of comparative overviews of quality and price of services for the benefit of consumers;

(e) clearly defined statistical purposes;

(f) market analysis for the purposes of Directive 2002/19/EC (Access Directive) or Directive 2002/22/EC (Universal Service Directive).

The information referred to in points (a), (b), (d), (e) and (f) of the first subparagraph may not be required prior to or as a condition for market access.

2. Where national regulatory authorities require undertakings to provide information as referred to in paragraph 1, they shall inform them of the specific purpose for which this information is to be used.

Commentary
Art 11: B&C: 12.110

Article 12
Administrative charges

1. Any administrative charges imposed on undertakings providing a service or a network under the general authorisation or to whom a right of use has been granted shall:

(a) in total, cover only the administrative costs which will be incurred in the management, control and enforcement of the general authorisation scheme and of rights of use and of specific obligations as referred to in Article 6(2), which may include costs for international cooperation, harmonisation and standardisation, market analysis, monitoring compliance and other market control, as well as regulatory work involving preparation and enforcement of secondary legislation and administrative decisions, such as decisions on access and interconnection; and

(b) be imposed upon the individual undertakings in an objective, transparent and proportionate manner which minimises additional administrative costs and attendant charges.

2. Where national regulatory authorities impose administrative charges, they shall publish a yearly overview of their administrative costs and of the total sum of the charges collected. In the light of the difference between the total sum of the charges and the administrative costs, appropriate adjustments shall be made.

Commentary
Art 12: B&C: 12.110

Article 13
Fees for rights of use and rights to install facilities

Member States may allow the relevant authority to impose fees for the rights of use for radio frequencies or numbers or rights to install facilities on, over or under public or private property which reflect the need to ensure the optimal use of these resources. Member States shall ensure that such fees shall be objectively justified, transparent, non-discriminatory and proportionate in relation to their intended purpose and shall take into account the objectives in Article 8 of Directive 2002/21/EC (Framework Directive).

Commentary
Art 13: **B&C**: 12.110

Article 14
Amendment of rights and obligations

1. Member States shall ensure that the rights, conditions and procedures concerning general authorisations and rights of use or rights to install facilities may only be amended in objectively justified cases and in a proportionate manner. Notice shall be given in an appropriate manner of the intention to make such amendments and interested parties, including users and consumers, shall be allowed a sufficient period of time to express their views on the proposed amendments, which shall be no less than four weeks except in exceptional circumstances.

2. Member States shall not restrict or withdraw rights to install facilities before expiry of the period for which they were granted except where justified and where applicable in conformity with relevant national provisions regarding compensation for withdrawal of rights.

Article 15
Publication of information

1. Member States shall ensure that all relevant information on rights, conditions, procedures, charges, fees and decisions concerning general authorisations and rights of use is published and kept up to date in an appropriate manner so as to provide easy access to that information for all interested parties.

2. Where information as referred to in paragraph 1 is held at different levels of government, in particular information regarding procedures and conditions on rights to install facilities, the national regulatory authority shall make all reasonable efforts, bearing in mind the costs involved, to create a user-friendly overview of all such information, including information on the relevant levels of government and the responsible authorities, in order to facilitate applications for rights to install facilities.

Article 16
Review procedures

The Commission shall periodically review the functioning of the national authorisation systems and the development of cross-border service provision within the Community and report to the European Parliament and to the Council on the first occasion not later than three years after the date of application of this Directive referred to in Article 18(1), second subparagraph. For this purpose, the Commission may request from the Member States information, which shall be supplied without undue delay.

Article 17
Existing authorisations

1. Member States shall bring authorisations already in existence on the date of entry into force of this Directive into line with the provisions of this Directive by at the latest the date of application referred to in Article 18(1), second subparagraph.

2. Where application of paragraph 1 results in a reduction of the rights or an extension of the obligations under authorisations already in existence, Member States may extend the validity of those rights and obligations until at the latest nine months after the date of application referred to in Article 18(1), second subparagraph, provided that the rights of other undertakings under Community law are not affected thereby. Member States shall notify such extensions to the Commission and state the reasons therefor.

3. Where the Member State concerned can prove that the abolition of an authorisation condition regarding access to electronic communications networks, which was in force before the date of entry into force of this Directive, creates excessive difficulties for undertakings that have benefited from mandated access to another network, and where it is not possible for these undertakings to negotiate new agreements on reasonable commercial terms before the date of application referred to in

Article 18(1), second subparagraph, Member States may request a temporary prolongation of the relevant condition(s). Such requests shall be submitted by the date of application referred to in Article 18(1), second subparagraph, at the latest, and shall specify the condition(s) and period for which the temporary prolongation is requested.

The Member State shall inform the Commission of the reasons for requesting a prolongation. The Commission shall consider such a request, taking into account the particular situation in that Member State and of the undertaking(s) concerned, and the need to ensure a coherent regulatory environment at a Community level. It shall take a decision on whether to grant or reject the request, and where it decides to grant the request, on the scope and duration of the prolongation to be granted. The Commission shall communicate its decision to the Member State concerned within six months after receipt of the application for a prolongation. Such decisions shall be published in the *Official Journal of the European Communities*.

Article 18
Transposition

1. Member States shall adopt and publish the laws, regulations and administrative provisions necessary to comply with this Directive by 24 July 2003 at the latest. They shall forthwith inform the Commission thereof.

They shall apply those measures from 25 July 2003.

When Member States adopt these measures, they shall contain a reference to this Directive or be accompanied by such reference on the occasion of their official publication. The methods of making such reference shall be laid down by Member States.

2. Member States shall communicate to the Commission the text of the provisions of national law which they adopt in the field governed by this Directive and of any subsequent amendments to those provisions.

Article 19
Entry into force

This Directive shall enter into force on the day of its publication in the *Official Journal of the European Communities*.

Notes
Date of entry into force: 24 April 2002.

Article 20
Addressees

This Directive is addressed to the Member States.

Done at Brussels, 7 March 2002.

ANNEX

Commentary
Annex: F&N: 3.34, 13.159

The conditions listed in this Annex provide the maximum list of conditions which may be attached to general authorisations (Part A), rights to use radio frequencies (Part B) and rights to use numbers (Part C) as referred to in Article 6(1) and Article 11(1)(a).

A. Conditions which may be attached to a general authorisation

1. Financial contributions to the funding of universal service in conformity with Directive 2002/22/EC (Universal Service Directive).
2. Administrative charges in accordance with Article 12 of this Directive.
3. Interoperability of services and interconnection of networks in conformity with Directive 2002/19/EC (Access Directive).

4. Accessibility of numbers from the national numbering plan to end-users including conditions in conformity with Directive 2002/22/EC (Universal Service Directive).
5. Environmental and town and country planning requirements, as well as requirements and conditions linked to the granting of access to or use of public or private land and conditions linked to co-location and facility sharing in conformity with Directive 2002/22/EC (Framework Directive) and including, where applicable, any financial or technical guarantees necessary to ensure the proper execution of infrastructure works.
6. "Must carry" obligations in conformity with Directive 2002/22/EC (Universal Service Directive).
7. Personal data and privacy protection specific to the electronic communications sector in conformity with Directive 97/66/EC of the European Parliament and of the Council of 15 December 1997 concerning the processing of personal data and the protection of privacy in the telecommunications sector.[1]

Notes
[1] OJ L 24, 30.1.1998, p. 1.

8. Consumer protection rules specific to the electronic communications sector including conditions in conformity with Directive 2002/22/EC (Universal Service Directive).
9. Restrictions in relation to the transmission of illegal content, in accordance with Directive 2000/31/EC of the European Parliament and of the Council of 8 June 2000 on certain legal aspects of information society services, in particular electronic commerce, in the internal market[1] and restrictions in relation to the transmission of harmful content in accordance with Article 2a(2) of Council Directive 89/552/EEC of 3 October 1989 on the coordination of certain provisions laid down by law, regulation or administrative action in Member States concerning the pursuit of television broadcasting activities.[2]

Notes
[1] OJ L 178, 17.7.2000, p. 1.
[2] OJ L 298, 17.10.1989, p. 23. Directive as amended by Directive 97/36/EC of the European Parliament and of the Council (OJ L 202, 30.7.1997, p. 60).

10. Information to be provided under a notification procedure in accordance with Article 3(3) of this Directive and for other purposes as included in Article 11 of this Directive.
11. Enabling of legal interception by competent national authorities in conformity with Directive 97/66/EC and Directive 95/46/EC of the European Parliament and of the Council of 24 October 1995 on the protection of individuals with regard to the processing of personal data and on the free movement of such data.[1]

Notes
[1] OJ L 281, 23.11.1995, p. 31.

12. Terms of use during major disasters to ensure communications between emergency services and authorities and broadcasts to the general public.
13. Measures regarding the limitation of exposure of the general public to electromagnetic fields caused by electronic communications networks in accordance with Community law.
14. Access obligations other than those provided for in Article 6(2) of this Directive applying to undertakings providing electronic communications networks or services, in conformity with Directive 2002/19/EC (Access Directive).
15. Maintenance of the integrity of public communications networks in accordance with Directive 2002/19/EC (Access Directive) and Directive 2002/22/EC (Universal Service Directive) including by conditions to prevent electromagnetic interference between electronic communications networks and/or services in accordance with Council Directive 89/336/EEC of 3 May 1989 on the approximation of the laws of the Member States relating to electromagnetic compatibility.[1]

Notes
[1] OJ L 139, 23.5.1989, p. 19. Directive as last amended by Directive 93/68/EEC (OJ L 220, 30.8.1993, p. 1).

16. Security of public networks against unauthorised access according to Directive 97/66/EC.
17. Conditions for the use of radio frequencies, in conformity with Article 7(2) of Directive 1999/5/EC, where such use is not made subject to the granting of individual rights of use in accordance with Article 5(1) of this Directive.
18. Measures designed to ensure compliance with the standards and/or specifications referred to in Article 17 of Directive 2002/21/EC (Framework Directive).

Commentary
Part A: B&C: 12.111

B. Conditions which may be attached to rights of use for radio frequencies

1. Designation of service or type of network or technology for which the rights of use for the frequency has been granted, including, where applicable, the exclusive use of a frequency for the transmission of specific content or specific audiovisual services.
2. Effective and efficient use of frequencies in conformity with Directive 2002/21/EC (Framework Directive), including, where appropriate, coverage requirements.
3. Technical and operational conditions necessary for the avoidance of harmful interference and for the limitation of exposure of the general public to electromagnetic fields, where such conditions are different from those included in the general authorisation.
4. Maximum duration in conformity with Article 5 of this Directive, subject to any changes in the national frequency plan.
5. Transfer of rights at the initiative of the right holder and conditions for such transfer in conformity with Directive 2002/21/EC (Framework Directive).
6. Usage fees in accordance with Article 13 of this Directive.
7. Any commitments which the undertaking obtaining the usage right has made in the course of a competitive or comparative selection procedure.
8. Obligations under relevant international agreements relating to the use of frequencies.

Commentary
Part B: B&C: 12.112

C. Conditions which may be attached to rights of use for numbers

1. Designation of service for which the number shall be used, including any requirements linked to the provision of that service.
2. Effective and efficient use of numbers in conformity with Directive 2002/21/EC (Framework Directive).
3. Number portability requirements in conformity with Directive 2002/22/EC (Universal Service Directive).
4. Obligation to provide public directory subscriber information for the purposes of Articles 5 and 25 of Directive 2002/22/EC (Universal Service Directive).
5. Maximum duration in conformity with Article 5 of this Directive, subject to any changes in the national numbering plan.
6. Transfer of rights at the initiative of the right holder and conditions for such transfer in conformity with Directive 2002/21/EC (Framework Directive).
7. Usage fees in accordance with Article 13 of this Directive.
8. Any commitments which the undertaking obtaining the usage right has made in the course of a competitive or comparative selection procedure.
9. Obligations under relevant international agreements relating to the use of numbers.

Commentary
Part C: B&C: 12.112

E20

DIRECTIVE 2002/22/EC OF THE EUROPEAN PARLIAMENT AND OF THE COUNCIL

of 7 March 2002
on universal service and users' rights relating to electronic communications networks and services
(Universal Service Directive)

Official Journal L 108, 24.4.2002, p. 51

Celex No: 32002L0022

Notes

EEA application: this Directive was adopted with appropriate adaptations by EEA Joint Committee Decision No 11/2004 (OJ No L 116, 22.4.2004, p. 60 and EEA Supplement No 20, 22.4.2004, p. 14): see EEA Agreement, Annex XI, Point 5cm.

Commentary

Directive 2002/22/EC: **B&C:** 12.089, 12.113 **F&N:** 13.14, 13.16, 13.222, 13.318
Chap II: **B&C:** 12.114
Chap III: **B&C:** 12.114
Chap IV: **B&C:** 12.114
Chap V: **B&C:** 12.114
Arts 3–15: **B&C:** 12.114
Arts 16–19: **B&C:** 12.098, 12.114
Arts 17–19: **B&C:** 12.103
Arts 20–31: **B&C:** 12.114
Arts 32–40: **B&C:** 12.114

THE EUROPEAN PARLIAMENT AND THE COUNCIL OF THE EUROPEAN UNION,

Having regard to the Treaty establishing the European Community, and in particular Article 95 thereof,

Having regard to the proposal from the Commission,[1]

Having regard to the opinion of the Economic and Social Committee,[2]

Having regard to the opinion of the Committee of the Regions,[3]

Acting in accordance with the procedure laid down in Article 251 of the Treaty,[4]

Notes

[1] OJ C 365 E, 19.12.2000, p. 238 and OJ C 332 E, 27.11.2001, p. 292.
[2] OJ C 139, 11.5.2001, p. 15.
[3] OJ C 144, 16.5.2001, p. 60.
[4] Opinion of the European Parliament of 13 June 2001 [OJ C 53 E, 28.2.2002, p. 133], Council Common Position of 17 September 2001 (OJ C 337, 30.11.2001, p. 55) and Decision of the European Parliament of 12 December 2001 [OJ C 177 E, 25.7.2002, p. 83].

Whereas:

(1) The liberalisation of the telecommunications sector and increasing competition and choice for communications services go hand in hand with parallel action to create a harmonised regulatory framework which secures the delivery of universal service. The concept of universal service should evolve to reflect advances in technology, market developments and changes in user demand. The regulatory framework established for the full liberalisation of the telecommunications market in 1998 in the Community defined the minimum scope of universal service obligations and established rules for its costing and financing.

(2) Under Article 153 of the Treaty, the Community is to contribute to the protection of consumers.

(3) The Community and its Member States have undertaken commitments on the regulatory framework of telecommunications networks and services in the context of the World Trade Organisation (WTO) agreement on basic telecommunications. Any member of the WTO has the right to define the kind of universal service obligation it wishes to maintain. Such obligations will not be regarded as anti-competitive per se, provided they are administered in a transparent, non-discriminatory and competitively neutral manner and are not more burdensome than necessary for the kind of universal service defined by the member.

(4) Ensuring universal service (that is to say, the provision of a defined minimum set of services to all end-users at an affordable price) may involve the provision of some services to some end-users at prices that depart from those resulting from normal market conditions. However, compensating undertakings designated to provide such services in such circumstances need not result in any distortion of competition, provided that designated undertakings are compensated for the specific net cost involved and provided that the net cost burden is recovered in a competitively neutral way.

Commentary
Recital 4: B&C: 12.113, 12.125

---

(5) In a competitive market, certain obligations should apply to all undertakings providing publicly available telephone services at fixed locations and others should apply only to undertakings enjoying significant market power or which have been designated as a universal service operator.

(6) The network termination point represents a boundary for regulatory purposes between the regulatory framework for electronic communication networks and services and the regulation of telecommunication terminal equipment. Defining the location of the network termination point is the responsibility of the national regulatory authority, where necessary on the basis of a proposal by the relevant undertakings.

Commentary
Recital 6: B&C: 12.089

---

(7) Member States should continue to ensure that the services set out in Chapter II are made available with the quality specified to all end-users in their territory, irrespective of their geographical location, and, in the light of specific national conditions, at an affordable price. Member States may, in the context of universal service obligations and in the light of national conditions, take specific measures for consumers in rural or geographically isolated areas to ensure their access to the services set out in the Chapter II and the affordability of those services, as well as ensure under the same conditions this access, in particular for the elderly, the disabled and for people with special social needs. Such measures may also include measures directly targeted at consumers with special social needs providing support to identified consumers, for example by means of specific measures, taken after the examination of individual requests, such as the paying off of debts.

(8) A fundamental requirement of universal service is to provide users on request with a connection to the public telephone network at a fixed location, at an affordable price. The requirement is limited to a single narrowband network connection, the provision of which may be restricted by Member States to the end-user's primary location/residence, and does not extend to the Integrated Services Digital Network (ISDN) which provides two or more connections capable of being used simultaneously. There should be no constraints on the technical means by which the connection is provided, allowing for wired or wireless technologies, nor any constraints on which operators provide part or all of universal service obligations. Connections to the public telephone network at a fixed location should be capable of supporting speech and data communications at rates sufficient for access to online services such as those provided via the public Internet. The speed of Internet access experienced by a given user may depend on a number of factors including the provider(s) of Internet connectivity as well as the given application for which a connection is being used. The data rate that can be supported by a single narrowband connection to the public telephone network depends on the capabilities of the subscriber's terminal equipment as well as the connection. For this reason it is not appropriate to mandate a

specific data or bit rate at Community level. Currently available voice band modems typically offer a data rate of 56 kbit/s and employ automatic data rate adaptation to cater for variable line quality, with the result that the achieved data rate may be lower than 56 kbit/s. Flexibility is required on the one hand to allow Member States to take measures where necessary to ensure that connections are capable of supporting such a data rate, and on the other hand to allow Member States where relevant to permit data rates below this upper limit of 56 kbits/s in order, for example, to exploit the capabilities of wireless technologies (including cellular wireless networks) to deliver universal service to a higher proportion of the population. This may be of particular importance in some accession countries where household penetration of traditional telephone connections remains relatively low. In specific cases where the connection to the public telephony network at a fixed location is clearly insufficient to support satisfactory Internet access, Member States should be able to require the connection to be brought up to the level enjoyed by the majority of subscribers so that it supports data rates sufficient for access to the Internet. Where such specific measures produce a net cost burden for those consumers concerned, the net effect may be included in any net cost calculation of universal service obligations.

(9) The provisions of this Directive do not preclude Member States from designating different undertakings to provide the network and service elements of universal service. Designated undertakings providing network elements may be required to ensure such construction and maintenance as are necessary and proportionate to meet all reasonable requests for connection at a fixed location to the public telephone network and for access to publicly available telephone services at a fixed location.

(10) Affordable price means a price defined by Member States at national level in the light of specific national conditions, and may involve setting common tariffs irrespective of location or special tariff options to deal with the needs of low-income users. Affordability for individual consumers is related to their ability to monitor and control their expenditure.

(11) Directory information and a directory enquiry service constitute an essential access tool for publicly available telephone services and form part of the universal service obligation. Users and consumers desire comprehensive directories and a directory enquiry service covering all listed telephone subscribers and their numbers (including fixed and mobile numbers) and want this information to be presented in a non-preferential fashion. Directive 97/66/EC of the European Parliament and of the Council of 15 December 1997 concerning the processing of personal data and the protection of privacy in the telecommunications sector[1] ensures the subscribers' right to privacy with regard to the inclusion of their personal information in a public directory.

Notes
[1] OJ L 24, 30.1.1998, p. 1.

(12) For the citizen, it is important for there to be adequate provision of public pay telephones, and for users to be able to call emergency telephone numbers and, in particular, the single European emergency call number ("112") free of charge from any telephone, including public pay telephones, without the use of any means of payment. Insufficient information about the existence of "112" deprives citizens of the additional safety ensured by the existence of this number at European level especially during their travel in other Member States.

(13) Member States should take suitable measures in order to guarantee access to and affordability of all publicly available telephone services at a fixed location for disabled users and users with special social needs. Specific measures for disabled users could include, as appropriate, making available accessible public telephones, public text telephones or equivalent measures for deaf or speech-impaired people, providing services such as directory enquiry services or equivalent measures free of charge for blind or partially sighted people, and providing itemised bills in alternative format on request for blind or partially sighted people. Specific measures may also need to be taken to enable disabled users and users with special social needs to access emergency services "112" and to give them a similar possibility to choose between different operators or service providers as other consumers. Quality of service standards have been developed for a range of parameters to assess the quality of services received by subscribers and how well undertakings designated with universal service obligations perform in achieving these standards. Quality of

service standards do not yet exist in respect of disabled users. Performance standards and relevant parameters should be developed for disabled users and are provided for in Article 11 of this Directive. Moreover, national regulatory authorities should be enabled to require publication of quality of service performance data if and when such standards and parameters are developed. The provider of universal service should not take measures to prevent users from benefiting fully from services offered by different operators or service providers, in combination with its own services offered as part of universal service.

(14) The importance of access to and use of the public telephone network at a fixed location is such that it should be available to anyone reasonably requesting it. In accordance with the principle of subsidiarity, it is for Member States to decide on the basis of objective criteria which undertakings have universal service obligations for the purposes of this Directive, where appropriate taking into account the ability and the willingness of undertakings to accept all or part of the universal service obligations. It is important that universal service obligations are fulfilled in the most efficient fashion so that users generally pay prices that correspond to efficient cost provision. It is likewise important that universal service operators maintain the integrity of the network as well as service continuity and quality. The development of greater competition and choice provide more possibilities for all or part of the universal service obligations to be provided by undertakings other than those with significant market power. Therefore, universal service obligations could in some cases be allocated to operators demonstrating the most cost-effective means of delivering access and services, including by competitive or comparative selection procedures. Corresponding obligations could be included as conditions in authorisations to provide publicly available services.

(15) Member States should monitor the situation of consumers with respect to their use of publicly available telephone services and in particular with respect to affordability. The affordability of telephone service is related to the information which users receive regarding telephone usage expenses as well as the relative cost of telephone usage compared to other services, and is also related to their ability to control expenditure. Affordability therefore means giving power to consumers through obligations imposed on undertakings designated as having universal service obligations. These obligations include a specified level of itemised billing, the possibility for consumers selectively to block certain calls (such as high-priced calls to premium services), the possibility for consumers to control expenditure via pre-payment means and the possibility for consumers to offset up-front connection fees. Such measures may need to be reviewed and changed in the light of market developments. Current conditions do not warrant a requirement for operators with universal service obligations to alert subscribers where a predetermined limit of expenditure is exceeded or an abnormal calling pattern occurs. Review of the relevant legislative provisions in future should consider whether there is a possible need to alert subscribers for these reasons.

(16) Except in cases of persistent late payment or non-payment of bills, consumers should be protected from immediate disconnection from the network on the grounds of an unpaid bill and, particularly in the case of disputes over high bills for premium rate services, should continue to have access to essential telephone services pending resolution of the dispute. Member States may decide that such access may continue to be provided only if the subscriber continues to pay line rental charges.

(17) Quality and price are key factors in a competitive market and national regulatory authorities should be able to monitor achieved quality of service for undertakings which have been designated as having universal service obligations. In relation to the quality of service attained by such undertakings, national regulatory authorities should be able to take appropriate measures where they deem it necessary. National regulatory authorities should also be able to monitor the achieved quality of services of other undertakings providing public telephone networks and/or publicly available telephone services to users at fixed locations.

(18) Member States should, where necessary, establish mechanisms for financing the net cost of universal service obligations in cases where it is demonstrated that the obligations can only be provided at a loss or at a net cost which falls outside normal commercial standards. It is important to ensure that the net cost of universal service obligations is properly calculated and that any

financing is undertaken with minimum distortion to the market and to undertakings, and is compatible with the provisions of Articles 87 and 88 of the Treaty.

(19) Any calculation of the net cost of universal service should take due account of costs and revenues, as well as the intangible benefits resulting from providing universal service, but should not hinder the general aim of ensuring that pricing structures reflect costs. Any net costs of universal service obligations should be calculated on the basis of transparent procedures.

(20) Taking into account intangible benefits means that an estimate in monetary terms, of the indirect benefits that an undertaking derives by virtue of its position as provider of universal service, should be deducted from the direct net cost of universal service obligations in order to determine the overall cost burden.

(21) When a universal service obligation represents an unfair burden on an undertaking, it is appropriate to allow Member States to establish mechanisms for efficiently recovering net costs. Recovery via public funds constitutes one method of recovering the net costs of universal service obligations. It is also reasonable for established net costs to be recovered from all users in a transparent fashion by means of levies on undertakings. Member States should be able to finance the net costs of different elements of universal service through different mechanisms, and/or to finance the net costs of some or all elements from either of the mechanisms or a combination of both. In the case of cost recovery by means of levies on undertakings, Member States should ensure that that the method of allocation amongst them is based on objective and non-discriminatory criteria and is in accordance with the principle of proportionality. This principle does not prevent Member States from exempting new entrants which have not yet achieved any significant market presence. Any funding mechanism should ensure that market participants only contribute to the financing of universal service obligations and not to other activities which are not directly linked to the provision of the universal service obligations. Recovery mechanisms should in all cases respect the principles of Community law, and in particular in the case of sharing mechanisms those of non-discrimination and proportionality. Any funding mechanism should ensure that users in one Member State do not contribute to universal service costs in another Member State, for example when making calls from one Member State to another.

(22) Where Member States decide to finance the net cost of universal service obligations from public funds, this should be understood to comprise funding from general government budgets including other public financing sources such as state lotteries.

(23) The net cost of universal service obligations may be shared between all or certain specified classes of undertaking. Member States should ensure that the sharing mechanism respects the principles of transparency, least market distortion, non-discrimination and proportionality. Least market distortion means that contributions should be recovered in a way that as far as possible minimises the impact of the financial burden falling on end-users, for example by spreading contributions as widely as possible.

(24) National regulatory authorities should satisfy themselves that those undertakings benefiting from universal service funding provide a sufficient level of detail of the specific elements requiring such funding in order to justify their request. Member States' schemes for the costing and financing of universal service obligations should be communicated to the Commission for verification of compatibility with the Treaty. There are incentives for designated operators to raise the assessed net cost of universal service obligations. Therefore Member States should ensure effective transparency and control of amounts charged to finance universal service obligations.

(25) Communications markets continue to evolve in terms of the services used and the technical means used to deliver them to users. The universal service obligations, which are defined at a Community level, should be periodically reviewed with a view to proposing that the scope be changed or redefined. Such a review should take account of evolving social, commercial and technological conditions and the fact that any change of scope should be subject to the twin test of services that become available to a substantial majority of the population, with a consequent risk of social exclusion for those who can not afford them. Care should be taken in any change of the scope of universal service obligations to ensure that certain technological choices are not artificially promoted above others, that a disproportionate financial burden is not imposed on sector undertakings (thereby endangering market developments and innovation) and that any financing burden does not fall unfairly on consumers with lower incomes. Any change of scope

automatically means that any net cost can be financed via the methods permitted in this Directive. Member States are not permitted to impose on market players financial contributions which relate to measures which are not part of universal service obligations. Individual Member States remain free to impose special measures (outside the scope of universal service obligations) and finance them in conformity with Community law but not by means of contributions from market players.

(26) More effective competition across all access and service markets will give greater choice for users. The extent of effective competition and choice varies across the Community and varies within Member States between geographical areas and between access and service markets. Some users may be entirely dependent on the provision of access and services by an undertaking with significant market power. In general, for reasons of efficiency and to encourage effective competition, it is important that the services provided by an undertaking with significant market power reflect costs. For reasons of efficiency and social reasons, end-user tariffs should reflect demand conditions as well as cost conditions, provided that this does not result in distortions of competition. There is a risk that an undertaking with significant market power may act in various ways to inhibit entry or distort competition, for example by charging excessive prices, setting predatory prices, compulsory bundling of retail services or showing undue preference to certain customers. Therefore, national regulatory authorities should have powers to impose, as a last resort and after due consideration, retail regulation on an undertaking with significant market power. Price cap regulation, geographical averaging or similar instruments, as well as non-regulatory measures such as publicly available comparisons of retail tariffs, may be used to achieve the twin objectives of promoting effective competition whilst pursuing public interest needs, such as maintaining the affordability of publicly available telephone services for some consumers. Access to appropriate cost accounting information is necessary, in order for national regulatory authorities to fulfil their regulatory duties in this area, including the imposition of any tariff controls. However, regulatory controls on retail services should only be imposed where national regulatory authorities consider that relevant wholesale measures or measures regarding carrier selection or pre-selection would fail to achieve the objective of ensuring effective competition and public interest.

Commentary
Recital 26: **B&C:** 12.103, 12.125

---

(27) Where a national regulatory authority imposes obligations to implement a cost accounting system in order to support price controls, it may itself undertake an annual audit to ensure compliance with that cost accounting system, provided that it has the necessary qualified staff, or it may require the audit to be carried out by another qualified body, independent of the operator concerned.

(28) It is considered necessary to ensure the continued application of the existing provisions relating to the minimum set of leased line services in Community telecommunications legislation, in particular in Council Directive 92/44/EEC of 5 June 1992 on the application of open network provision to leased lines,[1] until such time as national regulatory authorities determine, in accordance with the market analysis procedures laid down in Directive 2002/21/EC of the European Parliament and of the Council of 7 March 2002 on a common regulatory framework for electronic communications networks and services (Framework Directive),[2] that such provisions are no longer needed because a sufficiently competitive market has developed in their territory. The degree of competition is likely to vary between different markets of leased lines in the minimum set, and in different parts of the territory. In undertaking the market analysis, national regulatory authorities should make separate assessments for each market of leased lines in the minimum set, taking into account their geographic dimension. Leased lines services constitute mandatory services to be provided without recourse to any compensation mechanisms. The provision of leased lines outside of the minimum set of leased lines should be covered by general retail regulatory provisions rather than specific requirements covering the supply of the minimum set.

(29) National regulatory authorities may also, in the light of an analysis of the relevant market, require mobile operators with significant market power to enable their subscribers to access the services of any interconnected provider of publicly available telephone services on a call-by-call basis or by means of pre-selection.

(30) Contracts are an important tool for users and consumers to ensure a minimum level of transparency of information and legal security. Most service providers in a competitive environment will conclude contracts with their customers for reasons of commercial desirability. In addition to the provisions of this Directive, the requirements of existing Community consumer protection legislation relating to contracts, in particular Council Directive 93/13/EEC of 5 April 1993 on unfair terms in consumer contracts[1] and Directive 97/7/EC of the European Parliament and of the Council of 20 May 1997 on the protection of consumers in respect of distance contracts,[2] apply to consumer transactions relating to electronic networks and services. Specifically, consumers should enjoy a minimum level of legal certainty in respect of their contractual relations with their direct telephone service provider, such that the contractual terms, conditions, quality of service, condition for termination of the contract and the service, compensation measures and dispute resolution are specified in their contracts. Where service providers other than direct telephone service providers conclude contracts with consumers, the same information should be included in those contracts as well. The measures to ensure transparency on prices, tariffs, terms and conditions will increase the ability of consumers to optimise their choices and thus to benefit fully from competition.

(31) End-users should have access to publicly available information on communications services. Member States should be able to monitor the quality of services which are offered in their territories. National regulatory authorities should be able systematically to collect information on the quality of services offered in their territories on the basis of criteria which allow comparability between service providers and between Member States. Undertakings providing communications services, operating in a competitive environment, are likely to make adequate and up-to-date information on their services publicly available for reasons of commercial advantage. National regulatory authorities should nonetheless be able to require publication of such information where it is demonstrated that such information is not effectively available to the public.

(32) End-users should be able to enjoy a guarantee of interoperability in respect of all equipment sold in the Community for the reception of digital television. Member States should be able to require minimum harmonised standards in respect of such equipment. Such standards could be adapted from time to time in the light of technological and market developments.

(33) It is desirable to enable consumers to achieve the fullest connectivity possible to digital television sets. Interoperability is an evolving concept in dynamic markets. Standards bodies should do their utmost to ensure that appropriate standards evolve along with the technologies concerned. It is likewise important to ensure that connectors are available on television sets that are capable of passing all the necessary elements of a digital signal, including the audio and video streams, conditional access information, service information, application program interface (API) information and copy protection information. This Directive therefore ensures that the functionality of the open interface for digital television sets is not limited by network operators, service providers or equipment manufacturers and continues to evolve in line with technological developments. For display and presentation of digital interactive television services, the realisation of a common standard through a market-driven mechanism is recognised as a consumer benefit.

Member States and the Commission may take policy initiatives, consistent with the Treaty, to encourage this development.

(34) All end-users should continue to enjoy access to operator assistance services whatever organisation provides access to the public telephone network.

(35) The provision of directory enquiry services and directories is already open to competition. The provisions of this Directive complement the provisions of Directive 97/66/EC by giving subscribers a right to have their personal data included in a printed or electronic directory. All service providers which assign telephone numbers to their subscribers are obliged to make relevant information available in a fair, cost-oriented and non-discriminatory manner.

(36) It is important that users should be able to call the single European emergency number "112", and any other national emergency telephone numbers, free of charge, from any telephone, including public pay telephones, without the use of any means of payment. Member States should have already made the necessary organisational arrangements best suited to the national organisation of the emergency systems, in order to ensure that calls to this number are adequately answered and handled. Caller location information, to be made available to the emergency services, will improve the level of protection and the security of users of "112" services and assist the emergency services, to the extent technically feasible, in the discharge of their duties, provided that the transfer of calls and associated data to the emergency services concerned is guaranteed. The reception and use of such information should comply with relevant Community law on the processing of personal data. Steady information technology improvements will progressively support the simultaneous handling of several languages over the networks at a reasonable cost. This in turn will ensure additional safety for European citizens using the "112" emergency call number.

(37) Easy access to international telephone services is vital for European citizens and European businesses. "00" has already been established as the standard international telephone access code for the Community. Special arrangements for making calls between adjacent locations across borders between Member States may be established or continued. The ITU has assigned, in accordance with ITU Recommendation E.164, code "3883" to the European Telephony Numbering Space (ETNS). In order to ensure connection of calls to the ETNS, undertakings operating public telephone networks should ensure that calls using "3883" are directly or indirectly interconnected to ETNS serving networks specified in the relevant European Telecommunications Standards Institute (ETSI) standards. Such interconnection arrangements should be governed by the provisions of Directive 2002/19/EC of the European Parliament and of the Council of 7 March 2002 on access to, and interconnection of, electronic communications networks and associated facilities (Access Directive).[1]

Notes
[1] See [OJ L 108, 24.4.2002, p. 7].

(38) Access by end-users to all numbering resources in the Community is a vital pre-condition for a single market. It should include freephone, premium rate, and other non-geographic numbers, except where the called subscriber has chosen, for commercial reasons, to limit access from certain geographical areas. Tariffs charged to parties calling from outside the Member State concerned need not be the same as for those parties calling from inside that Member State.

(39) Tone dialling and calling line identification facilities are normally available on modern telephone exchanges and can therefore increasingly be provided at little or no expense. Tone dialling is increasingly being used for user interaction with special services and facilities, including value added services, and the absence of this facility can prevent the user from making use of these services. Member States are not required to impose obligations to provide these facilities when they are already available. Directive 97/66/EC safeguards the privacy of users with regard to itemised billing, by giving them the means to protect their right to privacy when calling line identification is implemented. The development of these services on a pan-European basis would benefit consumers and is encouraged by this Directive.

(40) Number portability is a key facilitator of consumer choice and effective competition in a competitive telecommunications environment such that end-users who so request should be able to

retain their number(s) on the public telephone network independently of the organisation providing service. The provision of this facility between connections to the public telephone network at fixed and non-fixed locations is not covered by this Directive. However, Member States may apply provisions for porting numbers between networks providing services at a fixed location and mobile networks.

(41) The impact of number portability is considerably strengthened when there is transparent tariff information, both for end-users who port their numbers and also for end-users who call those who have ported their numbers. National regulatory authorities should, where feasible, facilitate appropriate tariff transparency as part of the implementation of number portability.

(42) When ensuring that pricing for interconnection related to the provision of number portability is cost-oriented, national regulatory authorities may also take account of prices available in comparable markets.

(43) Currently, Member States impose certain "must carry" obligations on networks for the distribution of radio or television broadcasts to the public. Member States should be able to lay down proportionate obligations on undertakings under their jurisdiction, in the interest of legitimate public policy considerations, but such obligations should only be imposed where they are necessary to meet general interest objectives clearly defined by Member States in conformity with Community law and should be proportionate, transparent and subject to periodical review. "Must carry" obligations imposed by Member States should be reasonable, that is they should be proportionate and transparent in the light of clearly defined general interest objectives, and could, where appropriate, entail a provision for proportionate remuneration. Such "must carry" obligations may include the transmission of services specifically designed to enable appropriate access by disabled users.

(44) Networks used for the distribution of radio or television broadcasts to the public include cable, satellite and terrestrial broadcasting networks. They might also include other networks to the extent that a significant number of end-users use such networks as their principal means to receive radio and television broadcasts.

(45) Services providing content such as the offer for sale of a package of sound or television broadcasting content are not covered by the common regulatory framework for electronic communications networks and services. Providers of such services should not be subject to universal service obligations in respect of these activities. This Directive is without prejudice to measures taken at national level, in compliance with Community law, in respect of such services.

(46) Where a Member State seeks to ensure the provision of other specific services throughout its national territory, such obligations should be implemented on a cost efficient basis and outside the scope of universal service obligations. Accordingly, Member States may undertake additional measures (such as facilitating the development of infrastructure or services in circumstances where the market does not satisfactorily address the requirements of end-users or consumers), in conformity with Community law. As a reaction to the Commission's e-Europe initiative, the Lisbon European Council of 23 and 24 March 2000 called on Member States to ensure that all schools have access to the Internet and to multimedia resources.

(47) In the context of a competitive environment, the views of interested parties, including users and consumers, should be taken into account by national regulatory authorities when dealing with issues related to end-users' rights. Effective procedures should be available to deal with disputes between consumers, on the one hand, and undertakings providing publicly available communications services, on the other. Member States should take full account of Commission Recommendation 98/257/EC of 30 March 1998 on the principles applicable to the bodies responsible for out-of-court settlement of consumer disputes.[1]

Notes
[1] OJ L 115, 17.4.1998, p. 31.

(48) Co-regulation could be an appropriate way of stimulating enhanced quality standards and improved service performance. Co-regulation should be guided by the same principles as formal regulation, i.e. it should be objective, justified, proportional, non-discriminatory and transparent.

(49) This Directive should provide for elements of consumer protection, including clear contract terms and dispute resolution, and tariff transparency for consumers. It should also encourage the extension of such benefits to other categories of end-users, in particular small and medium-sized enterprises.

(50) The provisions of this Directive do not prevent a Member State from taking measures justified on grounds set out in Articles 30 and 46 of the Treaty, and in particular on grounds of public security, public policy and public morality.

(51) Since the objectives of the proposed action, namely setting a common level of universal service for telecommunications for all European users and of harmonising conditions for access to and use of public telephone networks at a fixed location and related publicly available telephone services and also achieving a harmonised framework for the regulation of electronic communications services, electronic communications networks and associated facilities, cannot be sufficiently achieved by the Member States and can therefore by reason of the scale or effects of the action be better achieved at Community level, the Community may adopt measures in accordance with the principles of subsidiarity as set out in Article 5 of the Treaty. In accordance with the principle of proportionality, as set out in that Article, this Directive does not go beyond what is necessary in order to achieve those objectives.

(52) The measures necessary for the implementation of this Directive should be adopted in accordance with Council Decision 1999/468/EC of 28 June 1999 laying down the procedures for the exercise of implementing powers conferred on the Commission,[1]

Notes
[1] OJ L 184, 17.7.1999, p. 23.

HAVE ADOPTED THIS DIRECTIVE:

Chapter I
Scope, Aims and Definitions

Article 1
Scope and aims

1. Within the framework of Directive 2002/21/EC (Framework Directive), this Directive concerns the provision of electronic communications networks and services to end-users. The aim is to ensure the availability throughout the Community of good quality publicly available services through effective competition and choice and to deal with circumstances in which the needs of end-users are not satisfactorily met by the market.

2. This Directive establishes the rights of end-users and the corresponding obligations on undertakings providing publicly available electronic communications networks and services. With regard to ensuring provision of universal service within an environment of open and competitive markets, this Directive defines the minimum set of services of specified quality to which all end-users have access, at an affordable price in the light of specific national conditions, without distorting competition. This Directive also sets out obligations with regard to the provision of certain mandatory services such as the retail provision of leased lines.

Commentary
Art 1(1): **B&C:** 12.113
Art 1(2): **B&C:** 12.113

Article 2
Definitions

For the purposes of this Directive, the definitions set out in Article 2 of Directive 2002/21/EC (Framework Directive) shall apply.

The following definitions shall also apply:

(a) "public pay telephone" means a telephone available to the general public, for the use of which the means of payment may include coins and/or credit/debit cards and/or pre-payment cards, including cards for use with dialling codes;

(b) "public telephone network" means an electronic communications network which is used to provide publicly available telephone services; it supports the transfer between network termination points of speech communications, and also other forms of communication, such as facsimile and data;

(c) "publicly available telephone service" means a service available to the public for originating and receiving national and international calls and access to emergency services through a number or numbers in a national or international telephone numbering plan, and in addition may, where relevant, include one or more of the following services: the provision of operator assistance, directory enquiry services, directories, provision of public pay phones, provision of service under special terms, provision of special facilities for customers with disabilities or with special social needs and/or the provision of non-geographic services;

(d) "geographic number" means a number from the national numbering plan where part of its digit structure contains geographic significance used for routing calls to the physical location of the network termination point (NTP);

(e) "network termination point" (NTP) means the physical point at which a subscriber is provided with access to a public communications network; in the case of networks involving switching or routing, the NTP is identified by means of a specific network address, which may be linked to a subscriber number or name;

(f) "non-geographic numbers" means a number from the national numbering plan that is not a geographic number. It includes inter alia mobile, freephone and premium rate numbers.

Commentary
Art 2: B&C: 12.113 F&N: 13.150

CHAPTER II
UNIVERSAL SERVICE OBLIGATIONS INCLUDING SOCIAL OBLIGATIONS

Article 3
Availability of universal service

1. Member States shall ensure that the services set out in this Chapter are made available at the quality specified to all end-users in their territory, independently of geographical location, and, in the light of specific national conditions, at an affordable price.

2. Member States shall determine the most efficient and appropriate approach for ensuring the implementation of universal service, whilst respecting the principles of objectivity, transparency, non-discrimination and proportionality. They shall seek to minimise market distortions, in particular the provision of services at prices or subject to other terms and conditions which depart from normal commercial conditions, whilst safeguarding the public interest.

Commentary
Art 3: B&C: 12.114

Article 4
Provision of access at a fixed location

1. Member States shall ensure that all reasonable requests for connection at a fixed location to the public telephone network and for access to publicly available telephone services at a fixed location are met by at least one undertaking.

2. The connection provided shall be capable of allowing end-users to make and receive local, national and international telephone calls, facsimile communications and data communications, at data rates that are sufficient to permit functional Internet access, taking into account prevailing technologies used by the majority of subscribers and technological feasibility.

Commentary
Art 4: B&C: 12.114

Article 5
Directory enquiry services and directories

1. Member States shall ensure that:

(a) at least one comprehensive directory is available to end-users in a form approved by the relevant authority, whether printed or electronic, or both, and is updated on a regular basis, and at least once a year;

(b) at least one comprehensive telephone directory enquiry service is available to all end-users, including users of public pay telephones.

2. The directories in paragraph 1 shall comprise, subject to the provisions of Article 11 of Directive 97/66/EC, all subscribers of publicly available telephone services.

3. Member States shall ensure that the undertaking(s) providing the services referred to in paragraph 1 apply the principle of non-discrimination to the treatment of information that has been provided to them by other undertakings.

Article 6
Public pay telephones

1. Member States shall ensure that national regulatory authorities can impose obligations on undertakings in order to ensure that public pay telephones are provided to meet the reasonable needs of end-users in terms of the geographical coverage, the number of telephones, the accessibility of such telephones to disabled users and the quality of services.

2. A Member State shall ensure that its national regulatory authority can decide not to impose obligations under paragraph 1 in all or part of its territory, if it is satisfied that these facilities or comparable services are widely available, on the basis of a consultation of interested parties as referred to in Article 33.

3. Member States shall ensure that it is possible to make emergency calls from public pay telephones using the single European emergency call number "112" and other national emergency numbers, all free of charge and without having to use any means of payment.

Commentary
Art 6: B&C: 12.114

Article 7
Special measures for disabled users

1. Member States shall, where appropriate, take specific measures for disabled end-users in order to ensure access to and affordability of publicly available telephone services, including access to emergency services, directory enquiry services and directories, equivalent to that enjoyed by other end-users.

2. Member States may take specific measures, in the light of national conditions, to ensure that disabled end-users can also take advantage of the choice of undertakings and service providers available to the majority of end-users.

Commentary
Art 7: B&C: 12.114

Article 8
Designation of undertakings

1. Member States may designate one or more undertakings to guarantee the provision of universal service as identified in Articles 4, 5, 6 and 7 and, where applicable, Article 9(2) so that the whole of the national territory can be covered. Member States may designate different undertakings or sets of

undertakings to provide different elements of universal service and/or to cover different parts of the national territory.

2. When Member States designate undertakings in part or all of the national territory as having universal service obligations, they shall do so using an efficient, objective, transparent and non-discriminatory designation mechanism, whereby no undertaking is a priori excluded from being designated. Such designation methods shall ensure that universal service is provided in a cost-effective manner and may be used as a means of determining the net cost of the universal service obligation in accordance with Article 12.

Commentary
Art 8(1): B&C: 12.115

Article 9
Affordability of tariffs

1. National regulatory authorities shall monitor the evolution and level of retail tariffs of the services identified in Articles 4, 5, 6 and 7 as falling under the universal service obligations and provided by designated undertakings, in particular in relation to national consumer prices and income.

2. Member States may, in the light of national conditions, require that designated undertakings provide tariff options or packages to consumers which depart from those provided under normal commercial conditions, in particular to ensure that those on low incomes or with special social needs are not prevented from accessing or using the publicly available telephone service.

3. Member States may, besides any provision for designated undertakings to provide special tariff options or to comply with price caps or geographical averaging or other similar schemes, ensure that support is provided to consumers identified as having low incomes or special social needs.

4. Member States may require undertakings with obligations under Articles 4, 5, 6 and 7 to apply common tariffs, including geographical averaging, throughout the territory, in the light of national conditions or to comply with price caps.

5. National regulatory authorities shall ensure that, where a designated undertaking has an obligation to provide special tariff options, common tariffs, including geographical averaging, or to comply with price caps, the conditions are fully transparent and are published and applied in accordance with the principle of non-discrimination. National regulatory authorities may require that specific schemes be modified or withdrawn.

Commentary
Art 9: B&C: 12.114
Art 9(5): B&C: 12.103

Article 10
Control of expenditure

1. Member States shall ensure that designated undertakings, in providing facilities and services additional to those referred to in Articles 4, 5, 6, 7 and 9(2), establish terms and conditions in such a way that the subscriber is not obliged to pay for facilities or services which are not necessary or not required for the service requested.

2. Member States shall ensure that designated undertakings with obligations under Articles 4, 5, 6, 7 and 9(2) provide the specific facilities and services set out in Annex I, Part A, in order that subscribers can monitor and control expenditure and avoid unwarranted disconnection of service.

3. Member States shall ensure that the relevant authority is able to waive the requirements of paragraph 2 in all or part of its national territory if it is satisfied that the facility is widely available.

Commentary
Art 10: B&C: 12.114

Article 11
Quality of service of designated undertakings

1. National regulatory authorities shall ensure that all designated undertakings with obligations under Articles 4, 5, 6, 7 and 9(2) publish adequate and up-to-date information concerning their performance in the provision of universal service, based on the quality of service parameters, definitions and measurement methods set out in Annex III. The published information shall also be supplied to the national regulatory authority.

2. National regulatory authorities may specify, inter alia, additional quality of service standards, where relevant parameters have been developed, to assess the performance of undertakings in the provision of services to disabled end-users and disabled consumers. National regulatory authorities shall ensure that information concerning the performance of undertakings in relation to these parameters is also published and made available to the national regulatory authority.

3. National regulatory authorities may, in addition, specify the content, form and manner of information to be published, in order to ensure that end-users and consumers have access to comprehensive, comparable and user-friendly information.

4. National regulatory authorities shall be able to set performance targets for those undertakings with universal service obligations at least under Article 4. In so doing, national regulatory authorities shall take account of views of interested parties, in particular as referred to in Article 33.

5. Member States shall ensure that national regulatory authorities are able to monitor compliance with these performance targets by designated undertakings.

6. Persistent failure by an undertaking to meet performance targets may result in specific measures being taken in accordance with Directive 2002/20/EC of the European Parliament and of the Council of 7 March 2002 on the authorisation of electronic communications networks and services (Authorisation Directive).[1] National regulatory authorities shall be able to order independent audits or similar reviews of the performance data, paid for by the undertaking concerned, in order to ensure the accuracy and comparability of the data made available by undertakings with universal service obligations.

Notes
[1] See [OJ L 108, 24.4.2002, p. 21].

Commentary
Art 11: B&C: 12.114

Article 12
Costing of universal service obligations

1. Where national regulatory authorities consider that the provision of universal service as set out in Articles 3 to 10 may represent an unfair burden on undertakings designated to provide universal service, they shall calculate the net costs of its provision.

For that purpose, national regulatory authorities shall:

(a) calculate the net cost of the universal service obligation, taking into account any market benefit which accrues to an undertaking designated to provide universal service, in accordance with Annex IV, Part A; or

(b) make use of the net costs of providing universal service identified by a designation mechanism in accordance with Article 8(2).

2. The accounts and/or other information serving as the basis for the calculation of the net cost of universal service obligations under paragraph 1(a) shall be audited or verified by the national regulatory authority or a body independent of the relevant parties and approved by the national regulatory authority. The results of the cost calculation and the conclusions of the audit shall be publicly available.

Article 13
Financing of universal service obligations

1. Where, on the basis of the net cost calculation referred to in Article 12, national regulatory authorities find that an undertaking is subject to an unfair burden, Member States shall, upon request from a designated undertaking, decide:

(a) to introduce a mechanism to compensate that undertaking for the determined net costs under transparent conditions from public funds; and/or

(b) to share the net cost of universal service obligations between providers of electronic communications networks and services.

2. Where the net cost is shared under paragraph 1(b), Member States shall establish a sharing mechanism administered by the national regulatory authority or a body independent from the beneficiaries under the supervision of the national regulatory authority. Only the net cost, as determined in accordance with Article 12, of the obligations laid down in Articles 3 to 10 may be financed.

3. A sharing mechanism shall respect the principles of transparency, least market distortion, non-discrimination and proportionality, in accordance with the principles of Annex IV, Part B. Member States may choose not to require contributions from undertakings whose national turnover is less than a set limit.

4. Any charges related to the sharing of the cost of universal service obligations shall be unbundled and identified separately for each undertaking. Such charges shall not be imposed or collected from undertakings that are not providing services in the territory of the Member State that has established the sharing mechanism.

Commentary
Art 13: **B&C:** 12.115

Article 14
Transparency

1. Where a mechanism for sharing the net cost of universal service obligations as referred to in Article 13 is established, national regulatory authorities shall ensure that the principles for cost sharing, and details of the mechanism used, are publicly available.

2. Subject to Community and national rules on business confidentiality, national regulatory authorities shall ensure that an annual report is published giving the calculated cost of universal service obligations, identifying the contributions made by all the undertakings involved, and identifying any market benefits, that may have accrued to the undertaking(s) designated to provide universal service, where a fund is actually in place and working.

Article 15
Review of the scope of universal service

1. The Commission shall periodically review the scope of universal service, in particular with a view to proposing to the European Parliament and the Council that the scope be changed or redefined. A review shall be carried out, on the first occasion within two years after the date of application referred to in Article 38(1), second subparagraph, and subsequently every three years.

2. This review shall be undertaken in the light of social, economic and technological developments, taking into account, inter alia, mobility and data rates in the light of the prevailing technologies used by the majority of subscribers. The review process shall be undertaken in accordance with Annex V. The Commission shall submit a report to the European Parliament and the Council regarding the outcome of the review.

CHAPTER III

REGULATORY CONTROLS ON UNDERTAKINGS WITH SIGNIFICANT
MARKET POWER IN SPECIFIC MARKETS

Article 16
Review of obligations

1. Member States shall maintain all obligations relating to:

(a) retail tariffs for the provision of access to and use of the public telephone network, imposed under Article 17 of Directive 98/10/EC of the European Parliament and of the Council of 26 February 1998 on the application of open network provision (ONP) to voice telephony and on universal service for telecommunications in a competitive environment;[1]

(b) carrier selection or pre-selection, imposed under Directive 97/33/EC of the European Parliament and of the Council of 30 June 1997 on interconnection in telecommunications with regard to ensuring universal service and interoperability through application of the principles of open network provision (ONP);[2]

(c) leased lines, imposed under Articles 3, 4, 6, 7, 8 and 10 of Directive 92/44/EEC,

until a review has been carried out and a determination made in accordance with the procedure in paragraph 3 of this Article.

2. The Commission shall indicate relevant markets for the obligations relating to retail markets in the initial recommendation on relevant product and service markets and the Decision identifying transnational markets to be adopted in accordance with Article 15 of Directive 2002/21/EC (Framework Directive).

3. Member States shall ensure that, as soon as possible after the entry into force of this Directive, and periodically thereafter, national regulatory authorities undertake a market analysis, in accordance with the procedure set out in Article 16 of Directive 2002/21/EC (Framework Directive) to determine whether to maintain, amend or withdraw the obligations relating to retail markets. Measures taken shall be subject to the procedure referred to in Article 7 of Directive 2002/21/EC (Framework Directive).

Notes
[1] OJ L 101, 1.4.1998, p. 24.
[2] OJ L 199, 26.7.1997, p. 32. Directive as amended by Directive 98/61/EC (OJ L 268, 3.10.1998, p. 37).

Commentary
Art 16: B&C: 12.098

Article 17
Regulatory controls on retail services

1. Member States shall ensure that, where:

(a) as a result of a market analysis carried out in accordance with Article 16(3) a national regulatory authority determines that a given retail market identified in accordance with Article 15 of Directive 2002/21/EC (Framework Directive) is not effectively competitive, and

(b) the national regulatory authority concludes that obligations imposed under Directive 2002/19/EC (Access Directive), or Article 19 of this Directive would not result in the achievement of the objectives set out in Article 8 of Directive 2002/21/EC (Framework Directive),

national regulatory authorities shall impose appropriate regulatory obligations on undertakings identified as having significant market power on a given retail market in accordance with Article 14 of Directive 2002/21/EC (Framework Directive).

2. Obligations imposed under paragraph 1 shall be based on the nature of the problem identified and be proportionate and justified in the light of the objectives laid down in Article 8 of Directive 2002/21/EC (Framework Directive). The obligations imposed may include requirements that the identified undertakings do not charge excessive prices, inhibit market entry or restrict competition by setting predatory prices, show undue preference to specific end-users or unreasonably bundle services. National regulatory authorities may apply to such undertakings appropriate retail price cap measures,

measures to control individual tariffs, or measures to orient tariffs towards costs or prices on comparable markets, in order to protect end-user interests whilst promoting effective competition.

3. National regulatory authorities shall, on request, submit information to the Commission concerning the retail controls applied and, where appropriate, the cost accounting systems used by the undertakings concerned.

4. National regulatory authorities shall ensure that, where an undertaking is subject to retail tariff regulation or other relevant retail controls, the necessary and appropriate cost accounting systems are implemented. National regulatory authorities may specify the format and accounting methodology to be used. Compliance with the cost accounting system shall be verified by a qualified independent body. National regulatory authorities shall ensure that a statement concerning compliance is published annually.

5. Without prejudice to Article 9(2) and Article 10, national regulatory authorities shall not apply retail control mechanisms under paragraph 1 of this Article to geographical or user markets where they are satisfied that there is effective competition.

Commentary
Art 17: **B&C:** 12.098, 12.103
Art 17(2): **B&C:** 12.103

Article 18
Regulatory controls on the minimum set of leased lines

1. Where, as a result of the market analysis carried out in accordance with Article 16(3), a national regulatory authority determines that the market for the provision of part or all of the minimum set of leased lines is not effectively competitive, it shall identify undertakings with significant market power in the provision of those specific elements of the minimum set of leased lines services in all or part of its territory in accordance with Article 14 of Directive 2002/21/EC (Framework Directive). The national regulatory authority shall impose obligations regarding the provision of the minimum set of leased lines, as identified in the list of standards published in the *Official Journal of the European Communities* in accordance with Article 17 of Directive 2002/21/EC (Framework Directive), and the conditions for such provision set out in Annex VII to this Directive, on such undertakings in relation to those specific leased line markets.

2. Where as a result of the market analysis carried out in accordance with Article 16(3), a national regulatory authority determines that a relevant market for the provision of leased lines in the minimum set is effectively competitive, it shall withdraw the obligations referred to in paragraph 1 in relation to this specific leased line market.

3. The minimum set of leased lines with harmonised characteristics, and associated standards, shall be published in the *Official Journal of the European Communities* as part of the list of standards referred to in Article 17 of Directive 2002/21/EC (Framework Directive). The Commission may adopt amendments necessary to adapt the minimum set of leased lines to new technical developments and to changes in market demand, including the possible deletion of certain types of leased line from the minimum set, acting in accordance with the procedure referred to in Article 37(2) of this Directive.

Commentary
Art 18: **B&C:** 12.098, 12.103

Article 19
Carrier selection and carrier pre-selection

1. National regulatory authorities shall require undertakings notified as having significant market power for the provision of connection to and use of the public telephone network at a fixed location in accordance with Article 16(3) to enable their subscribers to access the services of any interconnected provider of publicly available telephone services:

(a) on a call-by-call basis by dialling a carrier selection code; and
(b) by means of pre-selection, with a facility to override any pre-selected choice on a call-by-call basis by dialling a carrier selection code.

2. User requirements for these facilities to be implemented on other networks or in other ways shall be assessed in accordance with the market analysis procedure laid down in Article 16 of Directive 2002/21/EC (Framework Directive) and implemented in accordance with Article 12 of Directive 2002/19/EC (Access Directive).

3. National regulatory authorities shall ensure that pricing for access and interconnection related to the provision of the facilities in paragraph 1 is cost oriented and that direct charges to subscribers, if any, do not act as a disincentive for the use of these facilities.

Commentary
Art 19: B&C: 12.098, 12.103

CHAPTER IV
END-USER INTERESTS AND RIGHTS

Article 20
Contracts

1. Paragraphs 2, 3 and 4 apply without prejudice to Community rules on consumer protection, in particular Directives 97/7/EC and 93/13/EC, and national rules in conformity with Community law.

2. Member States shall ensure that, where subscribing to services providing connection and/or access to the public telephone network, consumers have a right to a contract with an undertaking or undertakings providing such services. The contract shall specify at least:

(a) the identity and address of the supplier;
(b) services provided, the service quality levels offered, as well as the time for the initial connection;
(c) the types of maintenance service offered;
(d) particulars of prices and tariffs and the means by which up-to-date information on all applicable tariffs and maintenance charges may be obtained;
(e) the duration of the contract, the conditions for renewal and termination of services and of the contract;
(f) any compensation and the refund arrangements which apply if contracted service quality levels are not met; and
(g) the method of initiating procedures for settlement of disputes in accordance with Article 34.
   Member States may extend these obligations to cover other end-users.

3. Where contracts are concluded between consumers and electronic communications services providers other than those providing connection and/or access to the public telephone network, the information in paragraph 2 shall also be included in such contracts. Member States may extend this obligation to cover other end-users.

4. Subscribers shall have a right to withdraw from their contracts without penalty upon notice of proposed modifications in the contractual conditions. Subscribers shall be given adequate notice, not shorter than one month, ahead of any such modifications and shall be informed at the same time of their right to withdraw, without penalty, from such contracts, if they do not accept the new conditions.

Article 21
Transparency and publication of information

1. Member States shall ensure that transparent and up-to-date information on applicable prices and tariffs, and on standard terms and conditions, in respect of access to and use of publicly available telephone services is available to end-users and consumers, in accordance with the provisions of Annex II.

2. National regulatory authorities shall encourage the provision of information to enable end-users, as far as appropriate, and consumers to make an independent evaluation of the cost of alternative usage patterns, by means of, for instance, interactive guides.

Article 22
Quality of service

1. Member States shall ensure that national regulatory authorities are, after taking account of the views of interested parties, able to require undertakings that provide publicly available electronic communications services to publish comparable, adequate and up-to-date information for end-users

1090

on the quality of their services. The information shall, on request, also be supplied to the national regulatory authority in advance of its publication.

2. National regulatory authorities may specify, inter alia, the quality of service parameters to be measured, and the content, form and manner of information to be published, in order to ensure that end-users have access to comprehensive, comparable and user-friendly information. Where appropriate, the parameters, definitions and measurement methods given in Annex III could be used.

Article 23

Integrity of the network

Member States shall take all necessary steps to ensure the integrity of the public telephone network at fixed locations and, in the event of catastrophic network breakdown or in cases of force majeure, the availability of the public telephone network and publicly available telephone services at fixed locations. Member States shall ensure that undertakings providing publicly available telephone services at fixed locations take all reasonable steps to ensure uninterrupted access to emergency services.

Article 24

Interoperability of consumer digital television equipment

In accordance with the provisions of Annex VI, Member States shall ensure the interoperability of the consumer digital television equipment referred to therein.

Article 25

Operator assistance and directory enquiry services

1. Member States shall ensure that subscribers to publicly available telephone services have the right to have an entry in the publicly available directory referred to in Article 5(1)(a).

2. Member States shall ensure that all undertakings which assign telephone numbers to subscribers meet all reasonable requests to make available, for the purposes of the provision of publicly available directory enquiry services and directories, the relevant information in an agreed format on terms which are fair, objective, cost oriented and non-discriminatory.

3. Member States shall ensure that all end-users provided with a connection to the public telephone network can access operator assistance services and directory enquiry services in accordance with Article 5(1)(b).

4. Member States shall not maintain any regulatory restrictions which prevent end-users in one Member State from accessing directly the directory enquiry service in another Member State.

5. Paragraphs 1, 2, 3 and 4 apply subject to the requirements of Community legislation on the protection of personal data and privacy and, in particular, Article 11 of Directive 97/66/EC.

Article 26

Single European emergency call number

1. Member States shall ensure that, in addition to any other national emergency call numbers specified by the national regulatory authorities, all end-users of publicly available telephone services, including users of public pay telephones, are able to call the emergency services free of charge, by using the single European emergency call number "112".

2. Member States shall ensure that calls to the single European emergency call number "112" are appropriately answered and handled in a manner best suited to the national organisation of emergency systems and within the technological possibilities of the networks.

3. Member States shall ensure that undertakings which operate public telephone networks make caller location information available to authorities handling emergencies, to the extent technically feasible, for all calls to the single European emergency call number "112".

4. Member States shall ensure that citizens are adequately informed about the existence and use of the single European emergency call number "112".

Article 27
European telephone access codes

1. Member States shall ensure that the "00" code is the standard international access code. Special arrangements for making calls between adjacent locations across borders between Member States may be established or continued. The end-users of publicly available telephone services in the locations concerned shall be fully informed of such arrangements.

2. Member States shall ensure that all undertakings that operate public telephone networks handle all calls to the European telephony numbering space, without prejudice to the need for an undertaking that operates a public telephone network to recover the cost of the conveyance of calls on its network.

Article 28
Non-geographic numbers

Member States shall ensure that end-users from other Member States are able to access non-geographic numbers within their territory where technically and economically feasible, except where a called subscriber has chosen for commercial reasons to limit access by calling parties located in specific geographical areas.

Article 29
Provision of additional facilities

1. Member States shall ensure that national regulatory authorities are able to require all undertakings that operate public telephone networks to make available to end-users the facilities listed in Annex I, Part B, subject to technical feasibility and economic viability.

2. A Member State may decide to waive paragraph 1 in all or part of its territory if it considers, after taking into account the views of interested parties, that there is sufficient access to these facilities.

3. Without prejudice to Article 10(2), Member States may impose the obligations in Annex I, Part A, point (e), concerning disconnection as a general requirement on all undertakings.

Article 30
Number portability

1. Member States shall ensure that all subscribers of publicly available telephone services, including mobile services, who so request can retain their number(s) independently of the undertaking providing the service:

(a) in the case of geographic numbers, at a specific location; and
(b) in the case of non-geographic numbers, at any location.

This paragraph does not apply to the porting of numbers between networks providing services at a fixed location and mobile networks.

2. National regulatory authorities shall ensure that pricing for interconnection related to the provision of number portability is cost oriented and that direct charges to subscribers, if any, do not act as a disincentive for the use of these facilities.

3. National regulatory authorities shall not impose retail tariffs for the porting of numbers in a manner that would distort competition, such as by setting specific or common retail tariffs.

Notes
By way of derogation from Article 30(1), Bulgaria may postpone the introduction of number portability to no later than 1 January 2009: Protocol concerning the conditions and arrangements for admission of the Republic of Bulgaria and Romania to the European Union —Annex VI: List referred to in Article 20 of the Protocol: transitional measures, Bulgaria — 9.Telecommunications and information technologies (OJ L 157, 21.6.2005, p. 118) and Act concerning the conditions of accession of the Republic of Bulgaria and Romania and the adjustments to the Treaties on which the European Union is founded — Annex VI: List referred to in Article 23 of the Act of Accession: transitional measures, Bulgaria — 9.Telecommunications and information technologies (OJ L 157, 21.6.2005, p. 292).

Article 31
"Must carry" obligations

1. Member States may impose reasonable "must carry" obligations, for the transmission of specified radio and television broadcast channels and services, on undertakings under their jurisdiction providing electronic communications networks used for the distribution of radio or television broadcasts to the public where a significant number of end-users of such networks use them as their principal means to receive radio and television broadcasts. Such obligations shall only be imposed where they are necessary to meet clearly defined general interest objectives and shall be proportionate and transparent. The obligations shall be subject to periodical review.

2. Neither paragraph 1 of this Article nor Article 3(2) of Directive 2002/19/EC (Access Directive) shall prejudice the ability of Member States to determine appropriate remuneration, if any, in respect of measures taken in accordance with this Article while ensuring that, in similar circumstances, there is no discrimination in the treatment of undertakings providing electronic communications networks. Where remuneration is provided for, Member States shall ensure that it is applied in a proportionate and transparent manner.

CHAPTER V
GENERAL AND FINAL PROVISIONS

Article 32
Additional mandatory services

Member States may decide to make additional services, apart from services within the universal service obligations as defined in Chapter II, publicly available in its own territory but, in such circumstances, no compensation mechanism involving specific undertakings may be imposed.

Article 33
Consultation with interested parties

1. Member States shall ensure as far as appropriate that national regulatory authorities take account of the views of end-users, and consumers (including, in particular, disabled users), manufacturers, undertakings that provide electronic communications networks and/or services on issues related to all end-user and consumer rights concerning publicly available electronic communications services, in particular where they have a significant impact on the market.

2. Where appropriate, interested parties may develop, with the guidance of national regulatory authorities, mechanisms, involving consumers, user groups and service providers, to improve the general quality of service provision by, inter alia, developing and monitoring codes of conduct and operating standards.

Article 34
Out-of-court dispute resolution

1. Member States shall ensure that transparent, simple and inexpensive out-of-court procedures are available for dealing with unresolved disputes, involving consumers, relating to issues covered by this Directive. Member States shall adopt measures to ensure that such procedures enable disputes to be settled fairly and promptly and may, where warranted, adopt a system of reimbursement and/or compensation. Member States may extend these obligations to cover disputes involving other end-users.

2. Member States shall ensure that their legislation does not hamper the establishment of complaints offices and the provision of on-line services at the appropriate territorial level to facilitate access to dispute resolution by consumers and end-users.

3. Where such disputes involve parties in different Member States, Member States shall coordinate their efforts with a view to bringing about a resolution of the dispute.

4. This Article is without prejudice to national court procedures.

Article 35
Technical adjustment

Amendments necessary to adapt Annexes I, II, III, VI and VII to technological developments or to changes in market demand shall be adopted by the Commission, acting in accordance with the procedure referred to in Article 37(2).

Article 36
Notification, monitoring and review procedures

1. National regulatory authorities shall notify to the Commission by at the latest the date of application referred to in Article 38(1), second subparagraph, and immediately in the event of any change thereafter in the names of undertakings designated as having universal service obligations under Article 8(1).

The Commission shall make the information available in a readily accessible form, and shall distribute it to the Communications Committee referred to in Article 37.

2. National regulatory authorities shall notify to the Commission the names of operators deemed to have significant market power for the purposes of this Directive, and the obligations imposed upon them under this Directive. Any changes affecting the obligations imposed upon undertakings or of the undertakings affected under the provisions of this Directive shall be notified to the Commission without delay.

3. The Commission shall periodically review the functioning of this Directive and report to the European Parliament and to the Council, on the first occasion not later than three years after the date of application referred to in Article 38(1), second subparagraph. The Member States and national regulatory authorities shall supply the necessary information to the Commission for this purpose.

Article 37
Committee

1. The Commission shall be assisted by the Communications Committee, set up by Article 22 of Directive 2002/21/EC (Framework Directive).

2. Where reference is made to this paragraph, Articles 5 and 7 of Decision 1999/468/EC shall apply, having regard to the provisions of Article 8 thereof.

The period laid down in Article 5(6) of Decision 1999/468/EC shall be three months.

3. The Committee shall adopt its rules of procedure.

Article 38
Transposition

1. Member States shall adopt and publish the laws, regulations and administrative provisions necessary to comply with this Directive by 24 July 2003 at the latest. They shall forthwith inform the Commission thereof.

They shall apply those measures from 25 July 2003.

2. When Member States adopt these measures, they shall contain a reference to this Directive or be accompanied by such a reference on the occasion of their official publication. The methods of making such a reference shall be laid down by the Member States.

3. Member States shall communicate to the Commission the text of the provisions of national law which they adopt in the field governed by this Directive and of any subsequent modifications to those provisions.

Article 39
Entry into force

This Directive shall enter into force on the day of its publication in the *Official Journal of the European Communities.*

Notes
Date of entry into force: 24 April 2002.

Part E Sectoral Regimes

Article 40

Addressees

This Directive is addressed to the Member States.

Done at Brussels, 7 March 2002.

ANNEX I

DESCRIPTION OF FACILITIES AND SERVICES REFERRED TO IN ARTICLE 10 (CONTROL OF EXPENDITURE) AND ARTICLE 29 (ADDITIONAL FACILITIES)

Part A: Facilities and services referred to in Article 10

(a) Itemised billing

Member States are to ensure that national regulatory authorities, subject to the requirements of relevant legislation on the protection of personal data and privacy, may lay down the basic level of itemised bills which are to be provided by designated undertakings (as established in Article 8) to consumers free of charge in order that they can:

(i) allow verification and control of the charges incurred in using the public telephone network at a fixed location and/or related publicly available telephone services, and

(ii) adequately monitor their usage and expenditure and thereby exercise a reasonable degree of control over their bills.

Where appropriate, additional levels of detail may be offered to subscribers at reasonable tariffs or at no charge.

Calls which are free of charge to the calling subscriber, including calls to helplines, are not to be identified in the calling subscriber's itemised bill.

(b) Selective call barring for outgoing calls, free of charge

I.e. the facility whereby the subscriber can, on request to the telephone service provider, bar outgoing calls of defined types or to defined types of numbers free of charge.

(c) Pre-payment systems

Member States are to ensure that national regulatory authorities may require designated undertakings to provide means for consumers to pay for access to the public telephone network and use of publicly available telephone services on pre-paid terms.

(d) Phased payment of connection fees

Member States are to ensure that national regulatory authorities may require designated undertakings to allow consumers to pay for connection to the public telephone network on the basis of payments phased over time.

(e) Non-payment of bills

Member States are to authorise specified measures, which are to be proportionate, non-discriminatory and published, to cover non-payment of telephone bills for use of the public telephone network at fixed locations. These measures are to ensure that due warning of any consequent service interruption or disconnection is given to the subscriber beforehand. Except in cases of fraud, persistent late payment or non-payment, these measures are to ensure, as far as is technically feasible, that any service interruption is confined to the service concerned. Disconnection for non-payment of bills should take place only after due warning is given to the subscriber. Member States may allow a period of limited service prior to complete disconnection, during which only calls that do not incur a charge to the subscriber (e.g. "112" calls) are permitted.

Part B: List of facilities referred to in Article 29

(a) Tone dialling or DTMF (dual-tone multi-frequency operation)

I.e. the public telephone network supports the use of DTMF tones as defined in ETSI ETR 207 for end-to-end signalling throughout the network both within a Member State and between Member States.

1095

(b) Calling-line identification

I.e. the calling party's number is presented to the called party prior to the call being established.

This facility should be provided in accordance with relevant legislation on protection of personal data and privacy, in particular Directive 97/66/EC.

To the extent technically feasible, operators should provide data and signals to facilitate the offering of calling-line identity and tone dialling across Member State boundaries.

ANNEX II

INFORMATION TO BE PUBLISHED IN ACCORDANCE WITH ARTICLE 21
(TRANSPARENCY AND PUBLICATION OF INFORMATION)

The national regulatory authority has a responsibility to ensure that the information in this Annex is published, in accordance with Article 21. It is for the national regulatory authority to decide which information is to be published by the undertakings providing public telephone networks and/or publicly available telephone services and which information is to be published by the national regulatory authority itself, so as to ensure that consumers are able to make informed choices.

1. Name(s) and address(es) of undertaking(s)
I.e. names and head office addresses of undertakings providing public telephone networks and/or publicly available telephone services.

2. Publicly available telephone services offered

2.1. Scope of the publicly available telephone service
Description of the publicly available telephone services offered, indicating what is included in the subscription charge and the periodic rental charge (e.g. operator services, directories, directory enquiry services, selective call barring, itemised billing, maintenance, etc.).

2.2. Standard tariffs covering access, all types of usage charges, maintenance, and including details of standard discounts applied and special and targeted tariff schemes.

2.3. Compensation/refund policy, including specific details of any compensation/refund schemes offered.

2.4. Types of maintenance service offered.

2.5. Standard contract conditions, including any minimum contractual period, if relevant.

3. Dispute settlement mechanisms including those developed by the undertaking.

4. Information about rights as regards universal service, including the facilities and services mentioned in Annex I.

ANNEX III
QUALITY OF SERVICE PARAMETERS

Supply-time and Quality-of-service Parameters, Definitions and Measurement Methods Referred to in Articles 11 and 22

Parameter[1]	*Definition*	*Measurement method*
Supply time for initial connection	ETSI EG 201 769-1	ETSI EG 201 769-1
Fault rate per access line	ETSI EG 201 769-1	ETSI EG 201 769-1
Fault repair time	ETSI EG 201 769-1	ETSI EG 201 769-1
Unsuccessful call ratio[2]	ETSI EG 201 769-1	ETSI EG 201 769-1
Call set up time[2]	ETSI EG 201 769-1	ETSI EG 201 769-1
Response times for operator services	ETSI EG 201 769-1	ETSI EG 201 769-1
Response times for directory enquiry services	ETSI EG 201 769-1	ETSI EG 201 769-1
Proportion of coin and card operated public pay telephones in working order	ETSI EG 201 769-1	ETSI EG 201 769-1
Bill correctness complaints	ETSI EG 201 769-1	ETSI EG 201 769-1

Notes

[1] Parameters should allow for performance to be analysed at a regional level (i.e. no less than Level 2 in the Nomenclature of Territorial Units for Statistics (NUTS) established by Eurostat).

[2] Member States may decide not to require that up-to-date information concerning the performance for these two parameters be kept, if evidence is available to show that performance in these two areas is satisfactory.

Note: Version number of ETSI EG 201 769-1 is 1.1.1 (April 2000).

Annex IV

Calculating the Net Cost, if any, of Universal Service Obligations and Establishing any Recovery or Sharing Mechanism in Accordance with Articles 12 and 13

Part A: Calculation of net cost

Universal service obligations refer to those obligations placed upon an undertaking by a Member State which concern the provision of a network and service throughout a specified geographical area, including, where required, averaged prices in that geographical area for the provision of that service or provision of specific tariff options for consumers with low incomes or with special social needs.

National regulatory authorities are to consider all means to ensure appropriate incentives for undertakings (designated or not) to provide universal service obligations cost efficiently. In undertaking a calculation exercise, the net cost of universal service obligations is to be calculated as the difference between the net cost for a designated undertaking of operating with the universal service obligations and operating without the universal service obligations. This applies whether the network in a particular Member State is fully developed or is still undergoing development and expansion. Due attention is to be given to correctly assessing the costs that any designated undertaking would have chosen to avoid had there been no universal service obligation. The net cost calculation should assess the benefits, including intangible benefits, to the universal service operator.

The calculation is to be based upon the costs attributable to:

(i) elements of the identified services which can only be provided at a loss or provided under cost conditions falling outside normal commercial standards.

This category may include service elements such as access to emergency telephone services, provision of certain public pay telephones, provision of certain services or equipment for disabled people, etc;

(ii) specific end-users or groups of end-users who, taking into account the cost of providing the specified network and service, the revenue generated and any geographical averaging of prices imposed by the Member State, can only be served at a loss or under cost conditions falling outside normal commercial standards.

This category includes those end-users or groups of end-users which would not be served by a commercial operator which did not have an obligation to provide universal service.

The calculation of the net cost of specific aspects of universal service obligations is to be made separately and so as to avoid the double counting of any direct or indirect benefits and costs. The overall net cost of universal service obligations to any undertaking is to be calculated as the sum of the net costs arising from the specific components of universal service obligations, taking account of any intangible benefits. The responsibility for verifying the net cost lies with the national regulatory authority.

Part B: Recovery of any net costs of universal service obligations

The recovery or financing of any net costs of universal service obligations requires designated undertakings with universal service obligations to be compensated for the services they provide under non-commercial conditions. Because such a compensation involves financial transfers, Member States are to ensure that these are undertaken in an objective, transparent, non-discriminatory and proportionate manner. This means that the transfers result in the least distortion to competition and to user demand.

In accordance with Article 13(3), a sharing mechanism based on a fund should use a transparent and neutral means for collecting contributions that avoids the danger of a double imposition of contributions falling on both outputs and inputs of undertakings.

The independent body administering the fund is to be responsible for collecting contributions from undertakings which are assessed as liable to contribute to the net cost of universal service obligations in the Member State and is to oversee the transfer of sums due and/or administrative payments to the undertakings entitled to receive payments from the fund.

ANNEX V
PROCESS FOR REVIEWING THE SCOPE OF UNIVERSAL SERVICE IN ACCORDANCE WITH ARTICLE 15

In considering whether a review of the scope of universal service obligations should be undertaken, the Commission is to take into consideration the following elements:
— social and market developments in terms of the services used by consumers,
— social and market developments in terms of the availability and choice of services to consumers,
— technological developments in terms of the way services are provided to consumers.
In considering whether the scope of universal service obligations be changed or redefined, the Commission is to take into consideration the following elements:
— are specific services available to and used by a majority of consumers and does the lack of availability or non-use by a minority of consumers result in social exclusion, and
— does the availability and use of specific services convey a general net benefit to all consumers such that public intervention is warranted in circumstances where the specific services are not provided to the public under normal commercial circumstances?

ANNEX VI
INTEROPERABILITY OF DIGITAL CONSUMER EQUIPMENT REFERRED TO IN ARTICLE 24

1. *The common scrambling algorithm and free-to-air reception*
   All consumer equipment intended for the reception of digital television signals, for sale or rent or otherwise made available in the Community, capable of descrambling digital television signals, is to possess the capability to:
   — allow the descrambling of such signals according to the common European scrambling algorithm as administered by a recognised European standards organisation, currently ETSI;
   — display signals that have been transmitted in clear provided that, in the event that such equipment is rented, the rentee is in compliance with the relevant rental agreement.
2. *Interoperability for analogue and digital television sets*
   Any analogue television set with an integral screen of visible diagonal greater than 42 cm which is put on the market for sale or rent in the Community is to be fitted with at least one open interface socket, as standardised by a recognised European standards organisation, e.g. as given in the CENELEC EN 50 049-1:1997 standard, permitting simple connection of peripherals, especially additional decoders and digital receivers.
   Any digital television set with an integral screen of visible diagonal greater than 30 cm which is put on the market for sale or rent in the Community is to be fitted with at least one open interface socket (either standardised by, or conforming to a standard adopted by, a recognised European standards organisation, or conforming to an industry-wide specification) e.g. the DVB common interface connector, permitting simple connection of peripherals, and able to pass all the elements of a digital television signal, including information relating to interactive and conditionally accessed services.

Annex VII
Conditions for the Minimum Set of Leased Lines Referred to in Article 18

Note: In accordance with the procedure in Article 18, provision of the minimum set of leased lines under the conditions established by Directive 92/44/EC should continue until such time as the national regulatory authority determines that there is effective competition in the relevant leased lines market.

National regulatory authorities are to ensure that provision of the minimum set of leased lines referred to in Article 18 follows the basic principles of non-discrimination, cost orientation and transparency.

1. Non discrimination

National regulatory authorities are to ensure that the organisations identified as having significant market power pursuant to Article 18(1) adhere to the principle of non-discrimination when providing leased lines referred to in Article 18. Those organisations are to apply similar conditions in similar circumstances to organisations providing similar services, and are to provide leased lines to others under the same conditions and of the same quality as they provide for their own services, or those of their subsidiaries or partners, where applicable.

2. Cost orientation

National regulatory authorities are, where appropriate, to ensure that tariffs for leased lines referred to in Article 18 follow the basic principles of cost orientation.

To this end, national regulatory authorities are to ensure that undertakings identified as having significant market power pursuant to Article 18(1) formulate and put in practice a suitable cost accounting system.

National regulatory authorities are to keep available, with an adequate level of detail, information on the cost accounting systems applied by such undertakings. They are to submit this information to the Commission on request.

3. Transparency

National regulatory authorities are to ensure that the following information in respect of the minimum set of leased lines referred to in Article 18 is published in an easily accessible form.

3.1. Technical characteristics, including the physical and electrical characteristics as well as the detailed technical and performance specifications which apply at the network termination point.

3.2. Tariffs, including the initial connection charges, the periodic rental charges and other charges. Where tariffs are differentiated, this must be indicated.
Where, in response to a particular request, an organisation identified as having significant market power pursuant to Article 18(1) considers it unreasonable to provide a leased line in the minimum set under its published tariffs and supply conditions, it must seek the agreement of the national regulatory authority to vary those conditions in that case.

3.3. Supply conditions, including at least the following elements:
— information concerning the ordering procedure,
— the typical delivery period, which is the period, counted from the date when the user has made a firm request for a leased line, in which 95% of all leased lines of the same type have been put through to the customers.
This period will be established on the basis of the actual delivery periods of leased lines during a recent time interval of reasonable duration. The calculation must not include cases where late delivery periods were requested by users,
— the contractual period, which includes the period which is in general laid down in the contract and the minimum contractual period which the user is obliged to accept,
— the typical repair time, which is the period, counted from the time when a failure message has been given to the responsible unit within the undertaking identified as having significant market power pursuant to Article 18(1) up to the moment in which 80% of all leased lines of the same type have been re-established and in appropriate cases notified back in operation

to the users. Where different classes of quality of repair are offered for the same type of leased lines, the different typical repair times shall be published,
— any refund procedure.

In addition where a Member State considers that the achieved performance for the provision of the minimum set of leased lines does not meet users' needs, it may define appropriate targets for the supply conditions listed above.

E21

COMMISSION DIRECTIVE 2002/77/EC

of 16 September 2002
on competition in the markets for electronic communications networks and services
(Text with EEA relevance)

Official Journal L 249, 17.9.2002, p. 21

Celex No: 32002L0077

Notes

EEA application: this Directive was adopted with appropriate adaptations by EEA Joint Committee Decision No 153/2003 (OJ No L 41, 12.02.2004, p. 45 and EEA Supplement No 7, 12.02.2004, p. 32): see EEA Agreement, Annex XIV, Chapter H, Point 13a.

Commentary
Directive 2002/77/EC: **B&C:** 12.089, 12.116 **F&N:** 6.38, 6.245, 13.19, 13.21, 13.23
Recitals 1–6: **B&C:** 12.116
Arts 3–8: **B&C:** 12.116

THE COMMISSION OF THE EUROPEAN COMMUNITIES,

Having regard to the Treaty establishing the European Community, and in particular Article 86(3) thereof,

Whereas:

(1) Commission Directive 90/388/EEC of 28 June 1990 on competition in the markets for telecommunications services,[1] as last amended by Directive 1999/64/EC,[2] has been substantially amended several times. Since further amendments are to be made, it should be recast in the interest of clarity.

Notes
[1] OJ L 192, 24.7.1990, p. 10.
[2] OJ L 175, 10.7.1999, p. 39.

---

(2) Article 86 of the Treaty entrusts the Commission with the task of ensuring that, in the case of public undertakings and undertakings enjoying special or exclusive rights, Member States comply with their obligations under Community law. Pursuant to Article 86(3), the Commission can specify and clarify the obligations arising from that Article and, in that framework, set out the conditions which are necessary to allow the Commission to perform effectively the duty of surveillance imposed upon it by that paragraph.

(3) Directive 90/388/EEC required Member States to abolish special and exclusive rights for the provision of telecommunications services, initially for other services than voice telephony, satellite

services and mobile radio communications, and then it gradually established full competition in the telecommunications market.

(4) A number of other Directives in this field have also been adopted under Article 95 of the Treaty by the European Parliament and the Council aiming, principally, at the establishment of an internal market for telecommunications services through the implementation of open network provision and the provision of a universal service in an environment of open and competitive markets. Those Directives should be repealed with effect from 25 July 2003 when the new regulatory framework for electronic communications networks and services is applied.

(5) The new electronic communications regulatory framework consists of one general Directive, Directive 2002/21/EC of the European Parliament and of the Council of 7 March 2002 on a common regulatory framework for electronic communications networks and services (Framework Directive)[1] and four specific Directives: Directive 2002/20/EC of the European Parliament and of the Council of 7 March 2002 on the authorisation of electronic communications networks and services (Authorisation Directive),[2] Directive 2002/19/EC of the European Parliament and of the Council of 7 March 2002 on access to, and interconnection of, electronic communications networks and associated facilities (Access Directive),[3] Directive 2002/22/EC of the European Parliament and of the Council of 7 March 2002 on universal service and users' rights relating to electronic communications networks and services (Universal Service Directive),[4] and Directive 2002/58/EC of the European Parliament and of the Council of 12 July 2002 concerning the processing of personal data and the protection of privacy in the electronic communications (Directive on privacy and electronic communications) sector.[5]

Notes
[1] OJ L 108, 24.4.2002, p. 33.
[2] OJ L 108, 24.4.2002, p. 21.
[3] OJ L 108, 24.4.2002, p. 7.
[4] OJ L 108, 24.4.2002, p. 51.
[5] OJ L 201, 31.7.2002, p. 37.

(6) In the light of the developments which have marked the liberalisation process and the gradual opening of the telecommunications markets in Europe since 1990, certain definitions used in Directive 90/388/EEC and its amending acts should be adjusted in order to reflect the latest technological developments in the telecommunications field, or replaced in order to take account of the convergence phenomenon which has shaped the information technology, media and telecommunications industries over recent years. The wording of certain provisions should, where possible, be clarified in order to facilitate their application, taking into account, where appropriate, the relevant Directives adopted under Article 95 of the Treaty, and the experience acquired through the implementation of Directive 90/388/EEC as amended.

(7) This Directive makes reference to "electronic communications services" and "electronic communications networks" rather than the previously used terms "telecommunications services" and "telecommunications networks". These new definitions are indispensable in order to take account of the convergence phenomenon by bringing together under one single definition all electronic communications services and/or networks which are concerned with the conveyance of signals by wire, radio, optical or other electromagnetic means (i.e. fixed, wireless, cable television, satellite networks). Thus, the transmission and broadcasting of radio and television programmes should be recognised as an electronic communication service and networks used for such transmission and broadcasting should likewise be recognised as electronic communications networks. Furthermore, it should be made clear that the new definition of electronic communications networks also covers fibre networks which enable third parties, using their own switching or routing equipment, to convey signals.

(8) In this context, it should be made clear that Member States must remove (if they have not already done so) exclusive and special rights for the provision of all electronic communications networks, not just those for the provision of electronic communications services and should ensure that undertakings are entitled to provide such services without prejudice to the provisions of Directives 2002/19/EC, 2002/20/EC, 2002/21/EC and 2002/22/EC. The definition of electronic communications networks should also mean that Member States are not permitted to restrict the right

of an operator to establish, extend and/or provide a cable network on the ground that such network could also be used for the transmission of radio and television programming. In particular, special or exclusive rights which amount to restricting the use of electronic communications networks for the transmission and distribution of television signals are contrary to Article 86(1), read in conjunction with Article 43 (right of establishment) and/or Article 82(b) of the EC Treaty insofar as they have the effect of permitting a dominant undertaking to limit "production, markets or technical development to the prejudice of consumers". This is, however, without prejudice to the specific rules adopted by the Member States in accordance with Community law, and, in particular, in accordance with Council Directive 89/552/EEC of 3 October 1989,[1] on the coordination of certain provisions laid down by law, regulation or administrative action in Member States concerning the pursuit of television broadcasting activities, as amended by Directive 97/36/EC of the European Parliament and of the Council,[2] governing the distribution of audiovisual programmes intended for the general public.

Notes
[1] OJ L 298, 17.10.1989, p. 23.
[2] OJ L 202, 30.7.1997, p. 60.

(9) Pursuant to the principle of proportionality, Member States should no longer make the provision of electronic communications services and the establishment and provision of electronic communications networks subject to a licensing regime but to a general authorisation regime. This is also required by Directive 2002/20/EC, according to which electronic communications services or networks should be provided on the basis of a general authorisation and not on the basis of a license. An aggrieved party should have the right to challenge a decision preventing him from providing electronic communications services or networks before an independent body and, ultimately, before a court or a tribunal. It is a fundamental principle of Community law that an individual is entitled to effective judicial protection whenever a State measure violates rights conferred upon him by the provisions of a Directive.

(10) Public authorities may exercise a dominant influence on the behaviour of public undertakings, as a result either of the rules governing the undertaking or of the manner in which the shareholdings are distributed. Therefore, where Member States control vertically integrated network operators which operate networks which have been established under special or exclusive rights, those Member States should ensure that, in order to avoid potential breaches of the Treaty competition rules, such operators, when they enjoy a dominant position in the relevant market, do not discriminate in favour of their own activities. It follows that Member States should take all measures necessary to prevent any discrimination between such vertically integrated operators and their competitors.

(11) This Directive should also clarify the principle derived from Commission Directive 96/2/EC of 16 January 1996 amending Directive 90/388/EC with regard to mobile and personal communications,[1] by providing that Member States should not grant exclusive or special rights of use of radio frequencies and that the rights of use of those frequencies should be assigned according to objective, non-discriminatory and transparent procedures. This should be without prejudice to specific criteria and procedures adopted by Member States to grant such rights to providers of radio or television broadcast content services with a view to pursuing general interest objectives in conformity with Community law.

Notes
[1] OJ L 20, 26.1.1996, p. 59.

(12) Any national scheme pursuant to Directive 2002/22/EC, serving to share the net cost of the provision of universal service obligations shall be based on objective, transparent and non-discriminatory criteria and shall be consistent with the principles of proportionality and of least market distortion. Least market distortion means that contributions should be recovered in a way that as far as possible minimises the impact of the financial burden falling on end-users, for example by spreading contributions as widely as possible.

(13) Where rights and obligations arising from international conventions setting up international satellite organisations are not compatible with the competition rules of the Treaty, Member States should take, in accordance with Article 307 of the EC Treaty, all appropriate steps to eliminate such incompatibilities. This Directive should clarify this obligation because Article 3 of Directive 94/46/EC,[1] merely required Member States to "communicate to the Commission" the information they possessed on such incompatibilities. Article 11 of this Directive should clarify the obligation on Member States to remove any restrictions which could still be in force because of those international conventions.

Notes
[1] OJ L 268, 19.10.1994, p. 15.

(14) This Directive should maintain the obligation imposed on Member States by Directive 1999/64/EC, so as to ensure that dominant providers of electronic communications networks and publicly available telephone services operate their public electronic communication network and cable television network as separate legal entities.

(15) This Directive should be without prejudice to obligations of the Member States concerning the time limits set out in Annex I, Part B, within which the Member States are to comply with the preceding Directives.

(16) Member States should supply to the Commission any information which is necessary to demonstrate that existing national implementing legislation reflects the clarifications provided for in this Directive as compared with Directives 90/388/EC, 94/46/EC, 95/51/EC,[1] 96/2/EC, 96/19/EC[2] and 1999/64/EC.

Notes
[1] OJ L 256, 26.10.1995, p. 49.
[2] OJ L 74, 22.3.1996, p. 13.

(17) In the light of the above, Directive 90/388/EC should be repealed,

HAS ADOPTED THIS DIRECTIVE:

Article 1
Definitions

For the purposes of this Directive the following definitions shall apply:

1. "electronic communications network" shall mean transmission systems and, where applicable, switching or routing equipment and other resources which permit the conveyance of signals by wire, by radio, by optical or by other electromagnetic means, including satellite networks, fixed (circuit - and packet - switched, including Internet) and mobile terrestrial networks, and electricity cable systems, to the extent that they are used for the purpose of transmitting signals, networks used for radio and television broadcasting, and cable television networks, irrespective of the type of information conveyed;

2. "public communications network" shall mean an electronic communications network used wholly or mainly for the provision of public electronic communications services;

3. "electronic communications services" shall mean a service normally provided for remuneration which consists wholly or mainly in the conveyance of signals on electronic communications networks, including telecommunications services and transmission services in networks used for broadcasting but exclude services providing or exercising editorial control over, content transmitted using electronic communications networks and services; it does not include information society services as defined in Article 1 of Directive 98/34/EC which do not consist wholly or mainly in the conveyance of signals on electronic communications networks;

4. "publicly available electronic communications services" shall mean electronic communications services available to the public;

5. "exclusive rights" shall mean the rights that are granted by a Member State to one undertaking through any legislative, regulatory or administrative instrument, reserving it the right to provide an electronic communications service or to undertake an electronic communications activity within a given geographical area;

6. "special rights" shall mean the rights that are granted by a Member State to a limited number of undertakings through any legislative, regulatory or administrative instrument which, within a given geographical area:

    (a) designates or limits to two or more the number of such undertakings authorised to provide an electronic communications service or undertake an electronic communications activity, otherwise than according to objective, proportional and non-discriminatory criteria, or

    (b) confers on undertakings, otherwise than according to such criteria, legal or regulatory advantages which substantially affect the ability of any other undertaking to provide the same electronic communications service or to undertake the same electronic communications activity in the same geographical area under substantially equivalent conditions;

7. "satellite earth station network" shall mean a configuration of two or more earth stations which interwork by means of a satellite;

8. "cable television networks" shall mean any mainly wire-based infrastructure established primarily for the delivery or distribution of radio or television broadcast to the public.

Commentary
Art 1(6): F&N: 6.38

Article 2
Exclusive and special rights for electronic communications networks and electronic communications services

1. Member States shall not grant or maintain in force exclusive or special rights for the establishment and/or the provision of electronic communications networks, or for the provision of publicly available electronic communications services.

2. Member States shall take all measures necessary to ensure that any undertaking is entitled to provide electronic communications services or to establish, extend or provide electronic communications networks.

3. Member States shall ensure that no restrictions are imposed or maintained on the provision of electronic communications services over electronic communications networks established by the providers of electronic communications services, over infrastructures provided by third parties, or by means of sharing networks, other facilities or sites without prejudice to the provisions of Directives 2002/19/EC, 2002/20/EC, 2002/21/EC and 2002/22/EC.

4. Member States shall ensure that a general authorisation granted to an undertaking to provide electronic communications services or to establish and/or provide electronic communications networks, as well as the conditions attached thereto, shall be based on objective, non-discriminatory, proportionate and transparent criteria.

5. Reasons shall be given for any decision taken on the grounds set out in Article 3(1) of Directive 2002/20/EC preventing an undertaking from providing electronic communications services or networks.

Any aggrieved party should have the possibility to challenge such a decision before a body that is independent of the parties involved and ultimately before a court or a tribunal.

Commentary
Art 2: F&N: 13.34

Article 3
Vertically integrated public undertakings

In addition to the requirements set out in Article 2(2), and without prejudice to Article 14 of Directive 2002/21/EC, Member States, shall ensure that vertically integrated public undertakings which provide electronic communications networks and which are in a dominant position do not discriminate in favour of their own activities.

Commentary
Art 3: F&N: 13.32, 13.236

Article 4
Rights of use of frequencies

Without prejudice to specific criteria and procedures adopted by Member States to grant rights of use of radio frequencies to providers of radio or television broadcast content services with a view to pursuing general interest objectives in conformity with Community law:

1. Member States shall not grant exclusive or special rights of use of radio frequencies for the provision of electronic communications services.
2. The assignment of radio frequencies for electronic communication services shall be based on objective, transparent, non-discriminatory and proportionate criteria.

Article 5
Directory services

Member States shall ensure that all exclusive and/or special rights with regard to the establishment and provision of directory services on their territory, including both the publication of directories and directory enquiry services, are abolished.

Article 6
Universal service obligations

1. Any national scheme pursuant to Directive 2002/22/EC, serving to share the net cost of the provision of universal service obligations shall be based on objective, transparent and non-discriminatory criteria and shall be consistent with the principle of proportionality and of least market distortion. In particular, where universal service obligations are imposed in whole or in part on public undertakings providing electronic communications services, this shall be taken into consideration in calculating any contribution to the net cost of universal service obligations.

2. Member States shall communicate any scheme of the kind referred to in paragraph 1 to the Commission.

Article 7
Satellites

1. Member States shall ensure that any regulatory prohibition or restriction on the offer of space segment capacity to any authorised satellite earth station network operator are abolished, and shall authorise within their territory any space-segment supplier to verify that the satellite earth station network for use in connection with the space segment of the supplier in question is in conformity with the published conditions for access to such person's space segment capacity.

2. Member States which are party to international conventions setting up international satellite organisations shall, where such conventions are not compatible with the competition rules of the EC Treaty, take all appropriate steps to eliminate such incompatibilities.

Article 8
Cable television networks

1. Each Member State shall ensure that no undertaking providing public electronic communications networks operates its cable television network using the same legal entity as it uses for its other public electronic communications network, when such undertaking:

(a) is controlled by that Member State or benefits from special rights; and
(b) is dominant in a substantial part of the common market in the provision of public electronic communications networks and publicly available telephone services; and
(c) operates a cable television network which has been established under special or exclusive right in the same geographic area.

2. The term "publicly available telephone services" shall be considered synonymous with the term "public voice telephony services" referred to in Article 1 of Directive 1999/64/EC.

3. Member States which consider that there is sufficient competition in the provision of local loop infrastructure and services in their territory shall inform the Commission accordingly.

Such information shall include a detailed description of the market structure. The information provided shall be made available to any interested party on demand, regard being had to the legitimate interest of undertakings in the protection of their business secrets.

4. The Commission shall decide within a reasonable period, after having heard the comments of these parties, whether the obligation of legal separation may be ended in the Member State concerned.

5. The Commission shall review the application of this Article not later than 31 December 2004.

Article 9

Member States shall supply to the Commission not later than 24 July 2003 such information as will allow the Commission to confirm that the provisions of this Directive have been complied with.

Article 10
Repeal

Directive 90/388/EC, as amended by the Directives listed in Annex I, Part A, is repealed with effect from 25 July 2003, without prejudice to the obligations of the Member States in respect of the time limits for transposition laid down in Annex I, Part B.

References to the repealed Directives shall be construed as references to this Directive and shall be read in accordance with the correlation table in Annex II.

Article 11

This Directive shall enter into force on the 20th day following that of its publication in the *Official Journal of the European Communities*.

Article 12

This Directive is addressed to the Member States.

Done at Brussels, 16 September 2002.

ANNEX I

PART A
LIST OF DIRECTIVES TO BE REPEALED

Directive 90/388/EEC (OJ L 192, 24.7.1990, p. 10)

Articles 2 and 3 of Directive 94/46/EC (OJ L 268, 19.1.1994, p. 15)

Directive 95/51/EC (OJ L 256, 26.10.1995, p. 49)

Directive 96/2/EC (OJ L 20, 26.1.1996, p. 59)

Directive 96/19/EC (OJ L 74, 22.3.1996, p. 13)

Directive 1999/64/EC (OJ L 175, 10.7.1999, p. 39)

PART B
TRANSPOSITION DATES FOR THE ABOVE DIRECTIVES

Directive 90/388/EEC: transposition date:	31 December 1990
Directive 94/46/EC: transposition date:	8 August 1995
Directive 95/51/EC: transposition date:	1 October 1996
Directive 96/2/EC: transposition date:	15 November 1996
Directive 96/19/EC: transposition date:	11 January 1997
Directive 1999/64/EC: transposition date:	30 April 2000

ANNEX II
CORRELATION TABLE

This Directive	Directive 90/388/EEC
Article 1 (Definitions)	Article 1
Article 2 (withdrawal of exclusive/special rights)	Article 2
Article 3 (vertically integrated public undertakings)	Article 3(a)(ii)
Article 4 (rights of use of radio frequencies)	Article 3(b)
Article 5 (directory services)	Article 4(b)
Article 6 (universal service obligations)	Article 4(c)
Article 7 (satellites)	Article 3 of Directive 94/46/EC
Article 8 (cable networks)	Article 9

E22

COMMISSION RECOMMENDATION

of 11 February 2003

on relevant product and service markets within the electronic communications sector susceptible to *ex ante* regulation in accordance with Directive 2002/21/EC of the European Parliament and of the Council on a common regulatory framework for electronic communication networks and services

(notified under document number C(2003) 497)

(Text with EEA relevance)

(2003/311/EC)

Official Journal L 114, 8.5.2003, p. 45

Celex No: 32003H0311

THE COMMISSION OF THE EUROPEAN COMMUNITIES,

Having regard to the Treaty establishing the European Community,

Having regard to Directive 2002/21/EC of the European Parliament and of the Council on a common regulatory framework for electronic communication networks and services,[1] and in particular Article 15 thereof,

---

Notes
[1] OJ L 108, 24.4.2002, p. 33.

Commentary
Recommendation: F&N: 13.24, 13.198

Whereas:

(1) Directive 2002/21/EC (hereinafter the Framework Directive), establishes a new legislative framework for the electronic communications sector that seeks to respond to convergence trends by covering all electronic communications networks and services within its scope The aim is to reduce *ex ante* sector-specific rules progressively as competition in the market develops.

(2) The purpose of this Recommendation is to identify those product and service markets in which *ex ante* regulation may be warranted. However, this first Recommendation has to be consistent with the transition from the 1998 regulatory framework to the new regulatory framework. Directive 2002/19/EC of the European Parliament and of the Council on access to, and interconnection of, electronic communications networks and associated facilities,[1] hereinafter the Access Directive, and Directive 2002/22/EC of the European Parliament and of the Council on universal service and users' rights relating to electronic communications networks and services[2] hereinafter the Universal service Directive already identify specific market areas which need to be analysed by national regulatory authorities in addition to the markets listed in this Recommendation. In accordance with the Framework Directive, it is for national regulatory authorities to define relevant geographic markets within their territory.

Notes
[1] OJ L 108, 24.4.2002, p. 7.
[2] OJ L 108, 24.4.2002, p. 51.

(3) Under the 1998 regulatory framework, several areas in the telecommunications sector are subject to *ex ante* regulation. These areas have been delineated in the applicable directives, but are not always "markets" within the meaning of competition law and practice. Annex I of the Framework Directive provides a list of such market areas to be included in the initial version of the Recommendation.

(4) As the title of Annex I of the Framework Directive makes clear, all the market areas listed therein need to be included in the initial version of the Recommendation in order that NRAs can carry out a review of existing obligations imposed under the 1998 regulatory framework.

(5) Article 15(1) of the Framework Directive requires the Commission to define markets in accordance with the principles of competition law. The Commission has therefore defined markets (corresponding to the market areas listed in Annex I of the Framework Directive) in accordance with competition law principles.

(6) There are in the electronic communications sector at least two main types of relevant markets to consider: markets for services or products provided to end users (retail markets), and markets for the inputs which are necessary for operators to provide services and products to end users (wholesale markets). Within these two types of markets, further market distinctions may be made depending on demand and supply side characteristics.

(7) The starting point for the definition and identification of markets is a characterisation of retail markets over a given time horizon, taking into account demand-side and supply-side substitutability. Having characterised and defined retail markets which are markets involving the supply and demand of end users, it is then appropriate to identify relevant wholesale markets which are markets involving the demand of products of, and supply of products to, a third party wishing to supply end users.

(8) Defining markets in accordance with the principles of competition law means that some of the market areas in Annex I of the Framework Directive comprise a number of separate individual markets on the basis of demand side characteristics. This is the case of products for retail access to the public telephone network at a fixed location and for telephone services provided at a fixed location. The market area in Annex I referring to wholesale leased lines is defined as separate markets for wholesale terminating segments and wholesale trunk segments on the basis of both demand side and supply side characteristics.

(9) In identifying markets in accordance with competition law principles, recourse should be had to the following three criteria. The first criterion is the presence of high and non-transitory entry barriers whether of structural, legal or regulatory nature. However, given the dynamic character and functioning of electronic communications markets, possibilities to overcome barriers within a relevant time horizon have also to be taken into consideration when carrying out a prospective analysis to identify the relevant markets for possible *ex ante* regulation. Therefore the second criterion admits only those markets the structure of which does not tend towards effective competition within the relevant time horizon. The application of this criterion involves examining the state of competition behind the barriers of entry. The third criterion is that application of competition law alone would not adequately address the market failure(s) concerned.

(10) In particular, as far as entry barriers are concerned, two types of entry barriers are relevant for the purpose of this Recommendation: structural barriers and legal or regulatory barriers.

(11) Structural barriers to entry result from original cost or demand conditions that create asymmetric conditions between incumbents and new entrants impeding or preventing market entry of the latter. For instance, high structural barriers may be found to exist when the market is characterised by substantial economies of scale and/or economies of scope and high sunk cost. To date, such barriers can still be identified with respect to the widespread deployment and/or provision of local access networks to fixed locations. A related structural barrier can also exist where the provision of service requires a network component that cannot be technically duplicated or only duplicated at a cost that makes it uneconomic for competitors.

(12) Legal or regulatory barriers are not based on economic conditions, but result from legislative, administrative or other state measures that have a direct effect on the conditions of entry and/or the positioning of operators on the relevant market. Examples are legal or regulatory barriers preventing entry into a market where there is a limit on the number of undertakings that have access to spectrum for the provision of underlying services. Other examples of legal or regulatory barriers are price controls or other price related measures imposed on undertakings, which affect not only entry but also the positioning of undertakings on the market.

(13) Entry barriers may also become less relevant with regard to innovation-driven markets characterised by ongoing technological progress. In such markets, competitive constraints often come from innovative threats from potential competitors that are not currently in the market. In such innovation-driven markets, dynamic or longer term competition can take place among firms that are not necessarily competitors in an existing "static" market. This Recommendation does not identify markets where entry barriers are not expected to persist over a foreseeable period.

(14) Even when a market is characterised by high barriers to entry, other structural factors in that market may mean that the market tends towards an effectively competitive outcome within the relevant time horizon. This may for instance be the case in markets with a limited, but sufficient, number of undertakings having diverging cost structures and facing price-elastic market demand. There may also be excess capacity in a market that would allow rival firms to expand output very rapidly in response to any price increase. In such markets, market shares may change over time and/or falling prices may be observed.

(15) The decision to identify a market as justifying possible *ex ante* regulation should also depend on an assessment of the sufficiency of competition law in reducing or removing such barriers or in restoring effective competition. Furthermore, new and emerging markets, in which market power may be found to exist because of "first-mover" advantages, should not in principle be subject to *ex ante* regulation.

(16) In undertaking periodic reviews of the markets identified in this Recommendation, the three criteria should be used. These criteria should be applied cumulatively, so that failing any one of them means that the market should not be identified in subsequent recommendations. Thus, whether an electronic communications market continues to be identified by subsequent versions of the Recommendation as justifying possible *ex ante* regulation would depend on the persistence of high entry barriers, on the second criterion measuring the dynamic state of competitiveness and thirdly on the sufficiency of competition law (absent *ex ante* regulation) to address persistent market failures. A market could also be removed from a recommendation once there is evidence of sustainable and effective competition on that market within the Community, provided that the removal of existing regulation obligations would not reduce competition on that market.

(17) The Annex to this Recommendation indicates how each market in the Recommendation is linked to the market areas in Annex I to the Framework Directive. When reviewing existing obligations imposed under the previous regulatory framework, in order to determine whether to maintain, amend or withdraw them, NRAs should undertake the analysis on the basis of the markets identified in this Recommendation, in order to give effect to the requirement that market definition for the purposes of *ex ante* regulation should be based on competition law principles. Pending the first market analysis by NRAs under the new regulatory framework, existing obligations remain in force.

(18) The identification of markets in this Recommendation is without prejudice to markets that may be defined in specific cases under competition law.

(19) The range of different network topologies and technologies deployed across the Community means that in some cases national regulatory authorities must decide the precise boundaries between, or elements within, particular markets identified in the Recommendation, while adhering to competition law principles. National regulatory authorities may identify markets that differ from those of the Recommendation, provided they act in accordance with Article 7 of the Framework Directive. Since the imposition of *ex ante* regulation on a market could affect trade between Member States as described in recital 38 of the Framework Directive, the Commission considers that the identification of any market that differs from those of the Recommendation are likely to be subject to the appropriate procedure in Article 7 of the Framework Directive. Failure to notify a market which affects trade between Member States may result in infringement proceedings being taken. Any market identified by national regulatory authorities should be based on the competition principles developed in the Commission Notice on the definition of relevant market for the purposes of Community competition law,[1] and be consistent with the Commission Guidelines on market analysis and the assessment of significant market power and satisfy the three criteria set out above. Should an NRA consider that demand and supply patterns may justify an alternative market definition of a market listed in this Recommendation, it should then follow the appropriate procedures set out in Article 6 and 7 of the Framework Directive.

Notes
[1] OJ C 372, 9.12.1997, p. 5.

---

(20) The fact that this Recommendation identifies those product and service markets in which *ex ante* regulation may be warranted does not mean that regulation is always warranted or that these markets will be subject to the imposition of regulatory obligations set out in the specific Directives. Regulation will not be warranted if there is effective competition on these markets. In particular, regulatory obligations must be appropriate and be based on the nature of the problem identified, proportionate and justified in the light of the objectives laid down in the Framework Directive, in particular maximising benefits for users, ensuring no distortion or restriction of competition, encouraging efficient investment in infrastructure and promoting innovation, and encouraging efficient use and management of radio frequencies and numbering resources.

(21) The Commission will review the need for any update of this Recommendation no later than 30 June 2004 on the basis of market developments.

(22) This Recommendation has been subject to a public consultation and to consultation with national regulatory authorities and national competition authorities.

HAS ADOPTED THIS RECOMMENDATION:

1. In defining relevant markets in accordance with Article 15(3) of Directive 2002/21/EC, national regulatory authorities are recommended to analyse the product and service markets identified in the Annex.

2. This Recommendation is addressed to the Member States.

Done at Brussels, 11 February 2003.

ANNEX

Retail level

1. Access to the public telephone network at a fixed location for residential customers.
2. Access to the public telephone network at a fixed location for non-residential customers.
3. Publicly available local and/or national telephone services provided at a fixed location for residential customers.
4. Publicly available international telephone services provided at a fixed location for residential customers.
5. Publicly available local and/or national telephone services provided at a fixed location for non-residential customers.
6. Publicly available international telephone services provided at a fixed location for non-residential customers.

These six markets are identified for the purpose of analysis in respect of Article 17 of the Universal Service Directive.

Together, markets 1 through 6 correspond to "the provision of connection to and use of the public telephone network at fixed locations", referred to in Annex I(1) of the Framework Directive. This combined market is also referred to in Article 19 of the Universal Service Directive (for possible imposition of carrier call-by-call selection or carrier selection).

7. The minimum set of leased lines (which comprises the specified types of leased lines up to and including 2Mb/sec as referenced in Article 18 and Annex VII of the Universal Service Directive).

   This market is referred to in Annex I(1) of the Framework Directive in respect of Article 16 of the Universal Service Directive (the provision of leased lines to end users).

   A market analysis must be undertaken for the purposes of Article 18 of the Universal Service Directive which covers regulatory controls on the provision of the minimum set of leased lines.

Wholesale level

8. Call origination on the public telephone network provided at a fixed location. For the purposes of this Recommendation, call origination is taken to include local call conveyance and delineated in such a way as to be consistent with the delineated boundaries for the markets for call transit and for call termination on the public telephone network provided at a fixed location.

   This market corresponds to that referred to in Annex I(2) of the Framework Directive in respect of Directive 97/33/EC (call origination in the fixed public telephone network).

9. Call termination on individual public telephone networks provided at a fixed location.

   For the purposes of this Recommendation, call termination is taken to include local call conveyance and delineated in such a way as to be consistent with the delineated boundaries for the markets for call origination and for call transit on the public telephone network provided at a fixed location.

   This market corresponds to the one referred to in Annex I(2) of the Framework Directive in respect of Directive 97/33/EC (call termination in the fixed public telephone network).

10. Transit services in the fixed public telephone network.

    For the purposes of this Recommendation, transit services are taken as being delineated in such a way as to be consistent with the delineated boundaries for the markets for call origination and for call termination on the public telephone network provided at a fixed location.

    This market corresponds to the one referred to in Annex I(2) of the Framework Directive in respect of Directive 97/33/EC (transit services in the fixed public telephone network).

11. Wholesale unbundled access (including shared access) to metallic loops and sub-loops for the purpose of providing broadband and voice services.

    This market corresponds to that referred to in Annex I(2) of the Framework Directive in respect of Directive 97/33/EC and Directive 98/10/EC (access to the fixed public telephone network, including unbundled access to the local loop) and to that referred to in Annex I (3) of the Framework Directive in respect of Regulation No 2887/2000.

12. Wholesale broadband access.

    This market covers "bit-stream" access that permit the transmission of broadband data in both directions and other wholesale access provided over other infrastructures, if and when they offer facilities equivalent to bit-stream access. It includes "Network access and special network access" referred to in Annex I(2) of the Framework Directive, but does not cover the market in point 11 above, nor the market in point 18.

13. Wholesale terminating segments of leased lines.

14. Wholesale trunk segments of leased lines.

    Together, the wholesale markets 13 and 14 correspond to those referred to in Annex I(2) of the Framework Directive in respect of Directive 97/33/EC and Directive 98/10/EC (leased line interconnection) and to those referred to in Annex I(2) of the Framework Directive in respect of Directive 92/44/EEC (wholesale provision of leased line capacity to other suppliers of electronic communications networks or services).

15. Access and call origination on public mobile telephone networks, referred to (separately) in Annex I(2) of the Framework Directive in respect of Directives 97/33/EC and 98/10/EC.

16. Voice call termination on individual mobile networks.
    This market corresponds to the one referred to in Annex I(2) of the Framework Directive in respect of Directive 97/33/EC (call termination on public mobile telephone networks).
17. The wholesale national market for international roaming on public mobile networks.
    This market corresponds to the one referred to in Annex I(4) of the Framework Directive.
18. Broadcasting transmission services, to deliver broadcast content to end users.

Note

National regulatory authorities have discretion with respect to the analysis of the market for "Conditional access systems to digital television and radio services broadcast" in accordance with Article 6(3) of the Access Directive. Article 6(3) of the Access Directive provides that Member States may permit their NRAs to review the market for conditional access system to digital television and radio services broadcast, irrespective of the means of transmission.

E23

GUIDELINES ON THE APPLICATION OF EEC COMPETITION RULES IN THE TELECOMMUNICATIONS SECTOR

(91/C 233/02)

Official Journal C 233, 6.9.1991, p. 2

Celex No: 51991XC0906(02)

Notes

EEA application: the EFTA Surveillance Authority has adopted a parallel notice under Article 5(2)(b) of the Surveillance and Court Agreement: OJ L 153, 18.6.1994, p. 35 and EEA Supplement to the OJ No 15, 18.6.1994, p. 34. Footnote numbering in this document is taken from the offered Journal version not the Eurlex HTML version

Commentary

Guidelines: B&C: 10.087, 12.122, 12.127, 12.148
points 41–42: B&C: 12.131
points 44–46: B&C: 12.132
points 57–58: B&C: 12.131
points 95–98: B&C: 10.087
points 116–120: B&C: 12.167

PREFACE

These guidelines aim at clarifying the application of Community competition rules to the market participants in the telecommunications sector. They must be viewed in the context of the special conditions of the telecommunications sector, and the overall Community telecommunications policy will be taken into account in their application. In particular, account will have to be taken of the actions the Commission will be in a position to propose for the telecommunications industry as a whole, actions deriving from the assessment of the state of play and issues at stake for this industry, as has already been the case for the European electronics and information technology industry in the communication of the Commission of 3 April 1991.[1]

A major political aim, as emphasized by the Commission, the Council, and the European Parliament, must be the development of efficient Europe-wide networks and services, at the lowest cost and of the highest quality, to provide the European user in the single market of 1992 with a basic infrastructure for efficient operation.

The Commission has made it clear in the past that in this context it is considered that liberalization and harmonization in the sector must go hand in hand.

Given the competition context in the telecommunications sector, the telecommunications operators should be allowed, and encouraged, to establish the necessary cooperation mechanisms, in order to create — or ensure — Community-wide full interconnectivity between public networks, and where required between services to enable European users to benefit from a wider range of better and cheaper telecommunications services.

This can and has to be done in compliance with, and respect of, EEC competition rules in order to avoid the diseconomies which otherwise could result. For the same reasons, operators and other firms that may be in a dominant market position should be made aware of the prohibition of abuse of such positions.

The guidelines should be read in the light of this objective. They set out to clarify, *inter alia*, which forms of cooperation amount to undesirable collusion, and in this sense they list what is *not* acceptable. They should therefore be seen as one aspect of an overall Community policy towards telecommunications, and notably of policies and actions to encourage and stimulate those forms of cooperation which promote the development and availability of advanced communications for Europe.

The full application of competition rules forms a major part of the Community's overall approach to telecommunications. These guidelines should help market participants to shape their strategies and arrangements for Europe-wide networks and services from the outset in a manner which allows them to be fully in line with these rules. In the event of significant changes in the conditions which prevailed when the guidelines were drawn up, the Commission may find it appropriate to adapt the guidelines to the evolution of the situation in the telecommunications sector.

Notes

1 The European electronics and information technology industry: state of play, issues at stake and proposals for action, SEC(91) 565, 3 April 1991.

I. Summary

1. The Commission of the European Communities in its Green Paper on the development of the common market for telecommunications services and equipment (COM(87)290) dated 30 June 1987 proposed a number of Community positions. Amongst these, positions (H) and (I) are as follows:

    "(H) strict continuous review of operational (commercial) activities of telecommunications administrations according to Articles [81], [82] and [86] of the [EC] Treaty. This applies in particular to practices of cross-subsidization of activities in the competitive services sector and of activities in manufacturing;

    (I) strict continuous review of all private providers in the newly opened sectors according to Articles [81] and [82], in order to avoid the abuse of dominant positions;".

2. These positions were restated in the Commission's document of 9 February 1988 "Implementing the Green Paper on the development of the common market for telecommunications services and equipment/state of discussions and proposals by the Commission" (COM(88)48). Among the areas where the development of concrete policy actions is now possible, the Commission indicated the following:

    "Ensuring fair conditions of competition:

    Ensuring an open competitive market makes continuous review of the telecommunications sector necessary.

    The Commission intends to issue guidelines regarding the application of competition rules to the telecommunications sector and on the way that the review should be carried out."

This is the objective of this communication.

The telecommunications sector in many cases requires cooperation agreements, *inter alia*, between telecommunications organizations (TOs) in order to ensure network and services interconnectivity, one-stop shopping and one-stop billing which are necessary to provide for Europe-wide services and to offer optimum service to users. These objectives can be achieved, *inter alia*, by TOs cooperating — for example, in those areas where exclusive or special rights for provision may continue in accordance with Community law, including competition law, as well as in areas where optimum service will require certain features of cooperation. On the other hand the overriding objective to develop the conditions for the market to provide European users with a greater variety of telecommunications services, of better quality and at lower cost requires the introduction and safeguarding of a strong competitive structure. Competition plays a central role for the Community, especially in view of the completion of the single market for 1992. This role has already been emphasized in the Green Paper.

The single market will represent a new dimension for telecoms operators and users. Competition will give them the opportunity to make full use of technological development and to accelerate it, and encouraging them to restructure and reach the necessary economies of scale to become competitive not only on the Community market, but worldwide.

With this in mind, these guidelines recall the main principles which the Commission, according to its mandate under the Treaty's competition rules, has applied and will apply in the sector without prejudging the outcome of any specific case which will have to be considered on the facts.

The objective is, *inter alia*, to contribute to more certainty of [conditions] for investment in the sector and the development of Europe-wide services.

The mechanisms for creating certainty for individual cases (apart from complaints and ex-officio investigations) are provided for by the notification and negative clearance procedures provided under Regulation No 17, which give a formal procedure for clearing cooperation agreements in this area whenever a formal clearance is requested. This is set out in further detail in this communication.

II. Introduction

3. The fundamental technological development worldwide in the telecommunications sector[1] has caused considerable changes in the competition conditions. The traditional monopolistic administrations cannot alone take up the challenge of the technological revolution. New economic forces have appeared on the telecoms scene which are capable of offering users the numerous enhanced services generated by the new technologies. This has given rise to and stimulated a wide deregulation process propagated in the Community with various degrees of intensity.

   This move is progressively changing the face of the European market structure. New private suppliers have penetrated the market with more and more transnational value-added services and equipment. The telecommunications administrations, although keeping a central role as public services providers, have acquired a business-like way of thinking. They have started competing dynamically with private operators in services and equipment. Wide restructuring, through mergers and joint ventures, is taking place in order to compete more effectively on the deregulated market through economies of scale and rationalization. All these events have a multiplier effect on technological progress.

Notes

[1] Telecommunications embraces any transmission, emission or reception of signs, signals, writing, images and sounds or intelligence of any nature by wire, radio, optical and other electromagnetic systems (Article 2 of WATTC Regulation of 9 December 1988).

---

4. In the light of this, the central role of competition for the Community appears clear, especially in view of the completion of the single market for 1992. This role has already been emphasized in the Green Paper.

5. In the application of competition rules the Commission endeavours to avoid the adopting of State measures or undertakings erecting or maintaining artificial barriers incompatible with the single market. But it also favours all forms of cooperation which foster innovation and economic progress, as contemplated by competition law. Pursuing effective competition in telecoms is not a matter of political choice. The choice of a free market and a competition-oriented economy was already envisaged in the EEC Treaty, and the competition rules of the Treaty are directly applicable within the Community. The abovementioned fundamental changes make necessary the full application of competition law.

6. There is a need for more certainty as to the application of competition rules. The telecommunication administrations together with keeping their duties of public interest, are now confronted with the application of these rules practically without transition from a long tradition of legal protection.

Their scope and actual implications are often not easily perceivable. As the technology is fast-moving and huge investments are necessary, in order to benefit from the new possibilities on the market-place, all the operators, public or private, have to take quick decisions, taking into account the competition regulatory framework.

7. This need for more certainty regarding the application of competition rules is already met by assessments made in several individual cases. However, assessments of individual cases so far have enabled a response to only some of the numerous competition questions which arise in telecommunications. Future cases will further develop the Commission's practice in this sector.

Purpose of these guidelines

8. These guidelines are intended to advise public telecommunications operators, other telecommunications service and equipment suppliers and users, the legal profession and the interested members of the public about the general legal and economic principles which have been and are being followed by the Commission in the application of competition rules to undertakings in the telecommunications sector, based on experience gained in individual cases in compliance with the rulings of the Court of Justice of the European Communities.

9. The Commission will apply these principles also to future individual cases in a flexible way, and taking the particular context of each case into account. These guidelines do not cover all the general principles governing the application of competition rules, but only those which are of specific relevance to telecommunication issues. The general principles of competition rules not specifically connected with telecommunications but entirely applicable to these can be found, *inter alia*, in the regulatory acts, the Court judgments and the Commission decisions dealing with the individual cases, the Commission's yearly reports on competition policy, press releases and other public information originating from the Commission.

10. These guidelines do not create enforceable rights. Moreover, they do not prejudice the application of EEC competition rules by the Court of Justice of the European Communities and by national authorities (as these rules may be directly applied in each Member State, by the national authorities, administrative or judicial).

11. A change in the economic and legal situation will not automatically bring about a simultaneous amendment to the guidelines. The Commission, however, reserves the possibility to make such an amendment when it considers that these guidelines no longer satisfy their purpose, because of fundamental and/or repeated changes in legal precedents, methods of applying competition rules, and the regulatory, economic and technical context.

12. These guidelines essentially concern the direct application of competition rules to undertakings, i.e. Articles [81] and [82] of the [EC] Treaty. They do not concern those applicable to the Member States, in particular Articles [10] and [86](1) and (3). Principles ruling the application of Article [86] in telecommunications are expressed in Commission Directives adopted under Article [86](3) for the implementation of the Green Paper.[2]

Notes

[2] Commission Directive 88/301/EEC of 16 May 1988 on competition in the markets in telecommunications terminal equipment (OJ No L 131, 27.5.1988, p. 73).
Commission Directive 90/388/EEC of 28 June 1990 on competition in the markets for telecommunications services (OJ No L 192, 24.7.1990, p. 10). [Directive 90/388/EEC was repealed by Commission Directive 2002/77/EC of 16 September 2002 (OJ L 249, 17.9.2002, p. 21).]

Relationship between competition rules applicable to undertakings and those applicable to Member States

13. The Court of Justice of the European Communities[3] has ruled that while it is true that Articles [81] and [82] of the Treaty concern the conduct of undertakings and not the laws or regulations of the Member States, by virtue of Article [10](2) of the [EC] Treaty, Member States must not adopt or maintain in force any measure which could deprive those provisions of their effectiveness. The Court has stated that such would be the case, in particular, if a Member State were to require or favour prohibited cartels or reinforce the effects thereof or to encourage abuses by dominant undertakings.
If those measures are adopted or maintained in force *vis-à-vis* public undertakings or undertakings to which a Member State grants special or exclusive rights, Article [86] might also apply.

Notes

³ Judgment of 10.1.1985 in Case 229/83, *Leclerc/gasoline* [1985] ECR 17; Judgment of 11.7.1985 in Case 299/83, *Leclerc/books* [1985] ECR 2517; Judgment of 30.4.1986 in Cases from 209 to 213/84, *Ministère public v Asjes* [1986] ECR 1425; Judgment of 1.10.1987 in Case 311/85, *Vereniging van Vlaamse Reisbureaus v Sociale Dienst van de Plaatselijke en Gewestelijke Overheidsdiensten* [1987] ECR 3801.

14. When the conduct of a public undertaking or an undertaking to which a Member State grants special or exclusive rights arises entirely as a result of the exercise of the undertaking's autonomous behaviour, it can only be caught by Articles [81] and [82].

    When this behaviour is imposed by a mandatory State measure (regulative or administrative), leaving no discretionary choice to the undertakings concerned, Article [86] may apply to the State involved in association with Articles [81] and [82]. In this case Articles [81] and [82] apply to the undertakings' behaviour taking into account the constraints to which the undertakings are submitted by the mandatory State measure.

    Ultimately, when the behaviour arises from the free choice of the undertakings involved, but the State has taken a measure which encourages the behaviour or strengthens its effects, Articles [81] and/or [82] apply to the undertakings' behaviour and Article [86] may apply to the State measure. This could be the case, *inter alia*, when the State has approved and/or legally endorsed the result of the undertakings' behaviour (for instance tariffs).

    These guidelines and the Article [86] Directives complement each other to a certain extent in that they cover the principles governing the application of the competition rules: Articles [81] and [82] on the one hand, Article [86] on the other.

    Application of competition rules and other Community law, including open network provision (ONP) rules

15. Articles [81] and [82] and Regulations implementing those Articles in application of Article [83] of the [EC] Treaty constitute law in force and enforceable throughout the Community. Conflicts should not arise with other Community rules because Community law forms a coherent regulatory framework. Other Community rules, and in particular those specifically governing the telecommunications sector, cannot be considered as provisions implementing Articles [81] and [82] in this sector. However it is obvious that Community acts adopted in the telecommunications sector are to be interpreted in a way consistent with competition rules, so to ensure the best possible implementation of all aspects of the Community telecommunications policy.

16. This applies, *inter alia*, to the relationship between competition rules applicable to undertakings and the ONP rules. According to the Council Resolution of 30 June 1988 on the development of the common market for telecommunications services and equipment up to 1992,⁴ ONP comprises the "rapid definition, by Council Directives, of technical conditions, usage conditions, and tariff principles for open network provision, starting with harmonized conditions for the use of leased lines". The details of the ONP procedures have been fixed by Directive 90/387/EEC⁵ on the establishment of the internal market for telecommunications services through the implementation of open network provision, adopted by Council on 28 June 1990 under Article [95] of the [EC] Treaty.

Notes

⁴ OJ No C 257, 4.10.1988, p. 1.
⁵ OJ No L 192, 24.7.1990, p. 1.

17. ONP has a fundamental role in providing European-wide access to Community-wide interconnected public networks. When ONP harmonization is implemented, a network user will be offered harmonized access conditions throughout the EEC, whichever country they address. Harmonized access will be ensured in compliance with the competition rules as mentioned above, as the ONP rules specifically provide.

    ONP rules cannot be considered as competition rules which apply to States and/or to undertakings" behaviour. ONP and competition rules therefore constitute two different but coherent sets of rules. Hence, the competition rules have full application, even when all ONP rules have been adopted.

18. Competition rules are and will be applied in a coherent manner with Community trade rules in force. However, competition rules apply in a non-discriminatory manner to EEC undertakings and to non-EEC ones which have access to the EEC market.

III. COMMON PRINCIPLES OF APPLICATION OF ARTICLES [81] AND [82]

Equal application of Articles [81] and [82]

19. Articles [81] and [82] apply directly and throughout the Community to all undertakings, whether public or private, on equal terms and to the same extent, apart from the exception provided in Article [86](2).[6]

    The Commission and national administrative and judicial authorities are competent to apply these rules under the conditions set out in Council Regulation No 17.[7]

Notes

[6] Article 86(2) states: "Undertakings entrusted with the operation of services of general economic interest or having the character of a revenue-producing monopoly shall be subject to the rules contained in this Treaty, in particular to the rules on competition, in so far as the application of such rules does not obstruct the performance, in law or in fact, of the particular tasks assigned to them. The development of trade must not be affected to such an extent as would be contrary to the interests of the Community".

[7] OJ No 13, 21.2.1962, p. 204/62 (Special Edition 1959–62, p. 87).

20. Therefore, Articles [81] and [82] apply both to private enterprises and public telecommunications operators embracing telecommunications administrations and recognized private operating agencies, hereinafter called "telecommunications organizations" (TOs).

    TOs are undertakings within the meaning of Articles [81] and [82] to the extent that they exert an economic activity, for the manufacturing and/or sale of telecommunications equipment and/or for the provision of telecommunications services, regardless of other facts such as, for example, whether their nature is economic or not and whether they are legally distinct entities or form part of the State organization.[8] Associations of TOs are associations of undertakings within the meaning of Article [81], even though TOs participate as undertakings in organizations in which governmental authorities are also represented.

    Articles [81] and [82] apply also to undertakings located outside the EEC when restrictive agreements are implemented or intended to be implemented or abuses are committed by those undertakings within the common market to the extent that trade between Member States is affected.[9]

Notes

[8] See Judgment of the Court of 16.6.1987 in Case 118/85, *Commission v Italy — Transparency of Financial Relations between Member States and Public Undertakings* [1987] ECR 2599.

[9] See Judgment of the Court of 27.9.1988 in Joined Cases 89, 104, 114, 116, 117, 125, 126, 127, 129/85, *Ålström & others v Commission ("Woodpulp")* [1988] ECR 5193.

Competition restrictions justified under Article [86](2) or by essential requirements

21. The exception provided in Article [86](2) may apply both to State measures and to practices by undertakings. The Services Directive 90/388/EEC, in particular in Article 3, makes provision for a Member State to impose specified restrictions in the licences which it can grant for the provision of certain telecommunications services. These restrictions may be imposed under Article [86](2) or in order to ensure the compliance with State essential requirements specified in the Directive.

22. As far as Article [86](2) is concerned, the benefit of the exception provided by this provision may still be invoked for a TO's behaviour when it brings about competition restrictions which its Member State did not impose in application of the Services Directive. However, the fact should be taken into account that in this case the State whose function is to protect the public and the general economic interest, did not deem it necessary to impose the said restrictions. This makes particularly hard the burden of proving that the Article [86](2) exception still applies to an [undertaking's] behaviour involving these restrictions.

23. The Commission infers from the case law of the Court of Justice[10] that it has exclusive competence, under the control of the Court, to decide that the exception of Article [86](2) applies. The national authorities including judicial authorities can assess that this exception does not apply, when they find that the competition rules clearly do not obstruct the performance of the task of general economic interest assigned to undertakings. When those authorities cannot make a clear assessment in this sense they should suspend their decision in order to enable the Commission to find that the conditions for the application of that provision are fulfilled.

Notes
[10] Case 10/71, *Mueller-Hein* [1971] ECR 723; Judgment of 11.4.1989 in Case 66/86, *Ahmed Saeed* [1989] ECR 803.

24. As to measures aiming at the compliance with "essential requirements" within the meaning of the Services Directive, under Article 1 of the latter,[11] they can only be taken by Member States and not by undertakings.

Notes
[11] "… the non-economic reasons in the general interest which may cause a Member State to restrict access to the public telecommunications network or public telecommunications services."

The relevant market

25. In order to assess the effects of an agreement on competition for the purposes of Article [81] and whether there is a dominant position on the market for the purposes of Article [82], it is necessary to define the relevant market(s), product or service market(s) and geographic market(s), within the domain of telecommunications. In a context of fast-moving technology the relevant market definition is dynamic and variable.

(a) The product market

26. A product market comprises the totality of the products which, with respect to their characteristics, are particularly suitable for satisfying constant needs and are only to a limited extent interchangeable with other products in terms of price, usage and consumer preference. An examination limited to the objective characteristics only of the relevant products cannot be sufficient: the competitive conditions and the structure of supply and demand on the market must also be taken into consideration.[12]

   The Commission can precisely define these markets only within the framework of individual cases.

Notes
[12] Case 322/81, *Michelin v Commission*, 9 November 1983 [1983] ECR 3529, Ground 37.

27. For the guidelines' purpose it can only be indicated that distinct service markets could exist at least for terrestrial network provision, voice communication, data communication and satellites. With regard to the equipment market, the following areas could all be taken into account for the purposes of market definition: public switches, private switches, transmission systems and more particularly, in the field of terminals, telephone sets, modems, telex terminals, data transmission terminals and mobile telephones. The above indications are without prejudice to the definition of further narrower distinct markets. As to other services — such as value-added ones — as well as terminal and network equipment, it cannot be specified here whether there is a market for each of them or for an aggregate of them, or for both, depending upon the interchangeability existing in different geographic markets. This is mainly determined by the supply and the requirements in those markets.

28. Since the various national public networks compete for the installation of the telecommunication hubs of large users, market definition may accordingly vary. Indeed, large telecommunications users, whether or not they are service providers, locate their premises depending, *inter alia*, upon the features of the telecommunications services supplied by each TO. Therefore, they compare national public networks and other services provided by the TOs in terms of characteristics and prices.

29. As to satellite provision, the question is whether or not it is substantially interchangeable with terrestrial network provision:

   (a) communication by satellite can be of various kinds: fixed service (point to point communication), multipoint (point to multipoint and multipoint to multipoint), one-way or two-way;

   (b) satellites' main characteristics are: coverage of a wide geographic area not limited by national borders, insensitivity of costs to distance, flexibility and ease of networks deployment, in particular in the very small aperture terminals (VSAT) systems;

   (c) satellites' uses can be broken down into the following categories: public switched voice and data transmission, business value-added services and broadcasting;

   (d) a satellite provision presents a broad interchangeability with the terrestrial transmission link for the basic voice and data transmission on long distance. Conversely, because of its characteristics it is not substantially interchangeable but rather complementary to terrestrial transmission links for several specific voice and data transmission uses. These uses are: services to peripheral or lessdeveloped regions, links between non-contiguous countries, reconfiguration of capacity and provision of routing for traffic restoration. Moreover, satellites are not currently substantially interchangeable for direct broadcasting and multipoint private networks for value-added business services. Therefore, for all those uses satellites should constitute distinct product markets. Within satellites, there may be distinct markets.

30. In mobile communications distinct services seem to exist such as cellular telephone, paging, telepoint, cordless voice and cordless data communication. Technical development permits providing each of these systems with more and more enhanced features. A consequence of this is that the differences between all these systems are progressively blurring and their interchangeability increasing. Therefore, it cannot be excluded that in future for certain uses several of those systems be embraced by a single product market. By the same token, it is likely that, for certain uses, mobile systems will be comprised in a single market with certain services offered on the public switched network.

(b) The geographic market

31. A geographic market is an area:
   — where undertakings enter into competition with each other, and
   — where the objective conditions of competition applying to the product or service in question are similar for all traders.[13]

Notes

[13] Judgment of 14.2.1978 in Case 27/76, United Brands v Commission [1978] ECR 207, Ground 44. In the telecommunications sector: Judgment of 5.10.1988 in Case 247/86, Alsatel-Novasam [1988] ECR 5987.

---

32. Without prejudice to the definition of the geographic market in individual cases, each national territory within the EEC seems still to be a distinct geographic market as regards those relevant services or products, where:
   — the customer's needs cannot be satisfied by using a non-domestic service,
   — there are different regulatory conditions of access to services, in particular special or exclusive rights which are apt to isolate national territories,
   — as to equipment and network, there are no Community-common standards, whether mandatory or voluntary, whose absence could also isolate the national markets. The absence of voluntary Community-wide standards shows different national customers' requirements.
   However, it is expected that the geographic market will progressively extend to the EEC territory at the pace of the progressive realization of a single EEC market.

33. It has also to be ascertained whether each national market or a part thereof is a substantial part of the common market. This is the case where the services of the product involved represent a substantial percentage of volume within the EEC. This applies to all services and products involved.

34. As to satellite uplinks, for cross-border communication by satellite the uplink could be provided from any of several countries. In this case, the geographic market is wider than the national territory and may cover the whole EEC.
   As to space segment capacity, the extension of the geographic market will depend on the power of the satellite and its ability to compete with other satellites for transmission to a given area, in other words on its range. This can be assessed only case by case.

35. As to services in general as well as terminal and network equipment, the Commission assesses the market power of the undertakings concerned and the result for EEC competition of the undertakings' conduct, taking into account their interrelated activities and interaction between the EEC and world markets. This is even more necessary to the extent that the EEC market is progressively being opened. This could have a considerable effect on the structure of the markets in the EEC, on the overall competitivity of the undertakings operating in those markets, and in the long run, on their capacity to remain independent operators.

IV. Application of Article [81]

36. The Commission recalls that a major policy target of the Council Resolution of 30 June 1988 on the development of the common market for telecommunications services and equipment up to 1992 was that of:

> "... stimulating European cooperation at all levels, as far as compatible with Community competition rules, and particularly in the field of research and development, in order to secure a strong European presence on the telecommunications markets and to ensure the full participation of all Member States".

In many cases Europe-wide services can be achieved by TOs' cooperation — for example, by ensuring interconnectivity and interoperability

   (i) in those areas where exclusive or special rights for provision may continue in accordance with Community law and in particular with the Services Directive 90/388/EEC; and

   (ii) in areas where optimum service will require certain features of cooperation, such as so-called "one-stop shopping" arrangements, i.e. the possibility of acquiring Europe-wide services at a single sales point.

The Council is giving guidance, by Directives, Decisions, recommendations and resolutions on those areas where Europe-wide services are most urgently needed: such as by recommendation [90]/659/EEC on the coordinated introduction of the integrated services digital network (ISDN) in the European Community[14] and by recommendation 87/371/EEC on the coordinated introduction of public pan-European cellular digital land-based mobile communications in the Community.[15]

The Commission welcomes and fully supports the necessity of cooperation particularly in order to promote the development of trans-European services and strengthen the competitivity of the EEC industry throughout the Community and in the world markets. However, this cooperation can only attain that objective if it complies with Community competition rules. Regulation No 17 provides well-defined clearing procedures for such cooperation agreements. The procedures foreseen by Regulation No 17 are:

   (i) the application for negative clearance, by which the Commission certifies that the agreements are not caught by Article [81], because they do not restrict competition and/or do not affect trade between Member States; and

   (ii) the notification of agreements caught by Article [81] in order to obtain an exemption under Article [81](3). Although if a particular agreement is caught by Article [81], an exemption can be granted by the Commission under Article [81](3), this is only so when the agreement brings about economic benefits — assessed on the basis of the criteria in the said paragraph 3 — which outweigh its restrictions on competition. In any event competition may not be eliminated for a substantial part of the products in question. Notification is not an obligation; but if, for reasons of legal certainty, the parties decide to request an exemption pursuant to Article 4 of Regulation No 17 the agreements may not be exempted until they have been notified to the Commission.

Notes
[14] OJ No L 382, 31.12.1986, p. 36.
[15] OJ No L 196, 17.7.1987, p. 81.

Commentary
para 36: B&C: 12.144

---

37. Cooperation agreements may be covered by one of the Commission block exemption Regulations or Notices.[16] In the first case the agreement is automatically exempted under Article [81](3). In the latter case, in the Commission's view, the agreement does not appreciably restrict competition and trade between Member States and therefore does not justify a Commission action. In either case, the agreement does not need to be notified; but it may be notified in case of doubt. If the Commission receives a multitude of notifications of similar cooperation agreements in the telecommunications sector, it may consider whether a specific block exemption regulation for such agreements would be appropriate.

38. The categories of agreements[17] which seem to be typical in telecommunications and may be caught by Article [81] are listed below. This list provides examples only and is, therefore, not exhaustive. The Commission is thereby indicating possible competition restrictions which could be caught by Article [81] and cases where there may be the possibility of an exemption.

39. These agreements may affect trade between Member States for the following reasons:
    (i)   services other than services reserved to TOs, equipment and spatial segment facilities are traded throughout the EEC; agreements on these services and equipment are therefore likely to affect trade. Although at present cross-frontier trade is limited, there is potentially no reason to suppose that suppliers of such facilities will in future confine themselves to their national market;
    (ii) as to reserved network services, one can consider that they also are traded throughout the Community. These services could be provided by an operator located in one Member State to customers located in other Member States, which decide to move their telecommunications hub into the first one because it is economically or qualitatively advantageous. Moreover, agreements on these matters are likely to affect EEC trade at least to the extent they influence the conditions under which the other services and equipment are supplied throughout the EEC.

40. Finally, to the extent that the TOs hold dominant positions in facilities, services and equipment markets, their behaviour leading to - and including the conclusion of - the agreements in question could also give rise to a violation of Article [82], if agreements have or are likely to have as their effect hindering the maintenance of the degree of competition still existing in the market or the growth of that competition, or causing the TOs to reap trading benefits which they would not have reaped if there had been normal and sufficiently effective competition.

A. Horizontal agreements concerning the provision of terrestrial facilities and reserved services

41. Agreements concerning terrestrial facilities (public switched network or leased circuits) or services (e.g. voice telephony for the general public) can currently only be concluded between TOs because of this legal regime providing for exclusive or special rights. The fact that the Services Directive recognizes the possibility for a Member State to reserve this provision to certain operators does not exempt those operators from complying with the competition rules in providing these facilities or services. These agreements may restrict competition within a Member State only where such exclusive rights are granted to more than one provider.

42. These agreements may restrict the competition between TOs for retaining or attracting large telecommunications users for their telecommunications centres. Such "hub competition` is substantially based upon favourable rates and other conditions, as well as the quality of the services. Member States are not allowed to prevent such competition since the Directive allows only the granting of exclusive and special rights by each Member State in its own territory.

Commentary
para 42: B&C: 12.131

43. Finally, these agreements may restrict competition in non-reserved services from third party undertakings, which are supported by the facilities in question, for example if they impose discriminatory or inequitable trading conditions on certain users.

44. (aa) *Price agreements*: all TOs' agreements on prices, discounting or collection charges for international services, are apt to restrict the hub competition to an appreciable extent. Coordination on or prohibition of discounting could cause particularly serious restrictions. In situations of public

knowledge such as exists in respect of the tariff level, discounting could remain the only possibility of effective price competition.

45. In several cases the Court of Justice and the Commission have considered price agreements among the most serious infringements of Article [81].[18]

    While harmonization of tariff structures may be a major element for the provision of Community-wide services, this goal should be pursued as far as compatible with Community competition rules and should include definition of efficient pricing principles throughout the Community. Price competition is a crucial, if not the principal, element of customer choice and is apt to stimulate technical progress. Without prejudice to any application for individual exemption that may be made, the justification of any price agreement in terms of Article [81](3) would be the subject of very rigorous examination by the Commission.

Notes

[18] *PVC*, Commission Decision 89/190/EEC, OJ No L 74, 17.3.1989, p. 1; Case 123/85, *BNIC v Clair* [1985] ECR 391; Case 8/72, *Cementhandelaren v Commission* [1972] ECR 977; *Polypropylene*, Commission Decision 86/398/EEC (OJ No L 230/1, 18.8.1986, p. 1) on appeal Case179/86.

Commentary
para 45: B&C: 12.132

46. Conversely, where the agreements concern only the setting up of common tariff structures or principles, the Commission may consider whether this would not constitute one of the economic benefits under Article [81](3) which outweigh the competition restriction. Indeed, this could provide the necessary transparency on tariff calculations and facilitate users' decisions about traffic flow or the location of headquarters or premises. Such agreements could also contribute to achieving one of the Green Paper's economic objectives — more cost-orientated tariffs.

    In this connection, following the intervention of the Commission, the CEPT has decided to abolish recommendation PGT/10 on the general principles for the lease of international telecommunications circuits and the establishment of private international networks. This recommendation recommended, *inter alia*, the imposition of a 30% surcharge or an access charge where third-party traffic was carried on an international telecommunications leased circuit, or if such a circuit was interconnected to the public telecommunications network. It also recommended the application of uniform tariff coefficients in order to determine the relative price level of international telecommunications leased circuits. Thanks to the CEPT's cooperation with the Commission leading to the abolition of the recommendation, competition between telecoms operators for the supply of international leased circuits is re-established, to the benefit of users, especially suppliers of non-reserved services. The Commission had found that the recommendation amounted to a price agreement between undertakings under Article [81] of the Treaty which substantially restricted competition within the European Community.[19]

Notes

[19] See Commission press release IP(90) 188 of 6 March 1990.

Commentary
para 46: B&C: 12.132

47. (ab) *Agreements on other conditions for the provision of facilities*

    These agreements may limit hub competition between the partners. Moreover, they may limit the access of users to the network, and thus restrict third undertakings' competition as to non-reserved services. This applies especially to the use of leased circuits. The abolished CEPT recommendation PGT/10 on tariffs had also recommended restrictions on conditions of sale which the Commission objected to. These restrictions were mainly:

    — making the use of leased circuits between the customer and third parties subject to the condition that the communication concern exclusively the activity for which the circuit has been granted,
    — a ban on subleasing,

— authorization of private networks only for customers tied to each other by economic links and which carry out the same activity,

— prior consultation between the TOs for any approval of a private network and of any modification of the use of the network, and for any interconnection of private networks.

For the purpose of an exemption under Article [81](3), the granting of special conditions for a particular facility in order to promote its development could be taken into account among other elements. This could foster technologies which reduce the costs of services and contribute to increasing competitiveness of European industry structures. Naturally, the other Article [81](3) requirements should also be met.

48. (ac) *Agreements on the choice of telecommunication routes.*

These may have the following restrictive effects:

(i)   to the extent that they coordinate the TOs' choice of the routes to be set up in international services, they may limit competition between TOs as suppliers to users' communications hubs, in terms of investments and production, with a possible effect on tariffs. It should be determined whether this restriction of their business autonomy is sufficiently appreciable to be caught by Article [81]. In any event, an argument for an exemption under Article [81](3) could be more easily sustained if common routes designation were necessary to enable interconnections and, therefore, the use of a Europe-wide network;

(ii) to the extent that they reserve the choice of routes already set up to the TOs, and this choice concerns one determined facility, they could limit the use of other facilities and thus services provision possibly to the detriment of technological progress. By contrast, the choice of routes does not seem restrictive in principle to the extent that it constitutes a technical requirement.

49. (ad) *Agreements on the imposition of technical and quality standards on the services provided on the public network*

Standardization brings substantial economic benefits which can be relevant under Article [81](3). It facilitates *inter alia* the provision of pan-European telecommunications services. As set out in the framework of the Community's approach to standardization, products and services complying with standards may be used Community-wide. In the context of this approach, European standards institutions have developed in this field (ETSI and CEN-Cenelec). National markets in the EC would be opened up and form a Community market. Service and equipment markets would be enlarged, hence favouring economies of scale. Cheaper products and services are thus available to users. Standardization may also offer an alternative to specifications controlled by undertakings dominant in the network architecture and in non-reserved services. Standardization agreements may, therefore, lessen the risk of abuses by these undertakings which could block the access to the markets for non-reserved services and for equipment. However, certain standardization agreements can have restrictive effects on competition: hindering innovation, freezing a particular stage of technical development, blocking the network access of some users/service providers. This restriction could be appreciable, for example when deciding to what extent intelligence will in future be located in the network or continue to be permitted in customers" equipment. The imposition of specifications other than those provided for by Community law could have restrictive effects on competition. Agreements having these effects are, therefore, caught by Article [81].

The balance between economic benefits and competition restrictions is complex. In principle, an exemption could be granted if an agreement brings more openness and facilitates access to the market, and these benefits outweigh the restrictions caused by it.

Commentary
para 49: B&C: 12.135

50. Standards jointly developed and/or published in accordance with the ONP procedures carry with them the presumption that the cooperating TOs which comply with those standards fulfil the requirement of open and efficient access (see the ONP Directive mentioned in paragraph 16). This presumption can be rebutted, *inter alia*, if the agreement contains restrictions which are not foreseen by Community law and are not indispensable for the standardization sought.

51. One important Article [81](3) requirement is that users must also be allowed a fair share of the resulting benefit. This is more likely to happen when users are directly involved in the standardization process in order to contribute to deciding what products or services will meet their needs. Also, the involvement of manufacturers or service providers other than TOs seems a positive element for Article [81](3) purposes. However, this involvement must be open and widely representative in order to avoid competition restrictions to the detriment of excluded manufacturers or service providers. Licensing other manufacturers may be deemed necessary, for the purpose of granting an exemption to these agreements under Article [81](3).

52. (ae) *Agreements foreseeing special treatment for TOs' terminal equipment or other companies' equipment for the interconnection or interoperation of terminal equipment with reserved services and facilities*

53. (af) *Agreements on the exchange of information*
A general exchange of information could indeed be necessary for the good functioning of international telecommunications services, and for cooperation aimed at ensuring interconnectivity or one-stop shopping and billing. It should not be extended to competition-sensitive information, such as certain tariff information which constitutes business secrets, discounting, customers and commercial strategy, including that concerning new products. The exchange of this information would affect the autonomy of each TO's commercial policy and it is not necessary to attain the said objectives.

Commentary
para 53: B&C: 12.138

B. Agreements concerning the provision of non-reserved services and terminal equipment

54. Unlike facilities markets, where only the TOs are the providers, in the services markets the actual or potential competitors are numerous and include, besides the TOs, international private companies, computer companies, publishers and others. Agreements on services and terminal equipment could therefore be concluded between TOs, between TOs and private companies, and between private companies.

55. The liberalizing process has led mostly to strategic agreements between (i) TOs, and (ii) TOs and other companies. These agreements usually take the form of joint ventures.

56. (ba) *Agreements between TOs*
The scope of these agreements, in general, is the provision by each partner of a value-added service including the management of the service. Those agreements are mostly based on the "one-stop shopping" principle, i.e. each partner offers to the customer the entire package of services which he needs. These managed services are called managed data network services (MDNS). An MDNS essentially consists of a broad package of services including facilities, value-added services and management. The agreements may also concern such basic services as satellite uplink.

57. *These agreements could restrict competition in the MDNS market and also in the markets for a service or a group of services included in the MDNS:*
   (i)   between the participating TOs themselves; and
   (ii) vis-à-vis other actual or potential third-party providers.

58. (i) *Restrictions of competition between TOs*
Cooperation between TOs could limit the number of potential individual MDNS offered by each participating TO.
The agreements may affect competition at least in certain aspects which are contemplated as specific examples of prohibited practices under Article [81](1)(a) to (c), in the event that:
   — they fix or recommend, or at least lead (through the exchange of price information) to coordination of prices charged by each participant to customers,
   — they provide for joint specification of MDNS products, quotas, joint delivery, specification of customers' systems; all this would amount to controlling production, markets, technical development and investments,
   — they contemplate joint purchase of MDNS hardware and/or software, which would amount to sharing markets or sources of supply.

59. (ii) *Restrictive effects on third party undertakings*

Third parties' market entry could be precluded or hampered if the participating TOs:
— refuse to provide facilities to third party suppliers of services,
— apply usage restrictions only to third parties and not to themselves (e.g. a private provider is precluded from placing multiple customers on a leased line facility to obtain lower unit costs),
— favour their MDNS offerings over those of private suppliers with respect to access, availability, quality and price of leased circuits, maintenance and other services,
— apply especially low rates to their MDNS offerings, cross-subsidizing them with higher rates for monopoly services.

Examples of this could be the restrictions imposed by the TOs on private network operators as to the qualifications of the users, the nature of the messages to be exchanged over the network or the use of international private leased circuits.

Commentary
para 59: B&C: 12.131

60. Finally, as the participating TOs hold, individually or collectively, a dominant position for the creation and the exploitation of the network in each national market, any restrictive behaviour described in paragraph 59 could amount to an abuse of a dominant position under Article [82] (see V below).

61. On the other hand, agreements between TOs may bring economic benefits which could be taken into account for the possible granting of an exemption under Article [81](3). *Inter alia*, the possible benefits could be as follows:
— a European-wide service and "one-stop shopping" could favour business in Europe. Large multinational undertakings are provided with a European communication service using only a single point of contact,
— the cooperation could lead to a certain amount of European-wide standardization even before further EEC legislation on this matter is adopted,
— the cooperation could bring a cost reduction and consequently cheaper offerings to the advantage of consumers,
— a general improvement of public infrastructure could arise from a joint service provision.

62. Only by notification of the cases in question, in accordance with the appropriate procedures under Regulation No 17, will the Commission be able, where requested, to ascertain, on the merits, whether these benefits outweigh the competition restrictions. But in any event, restrictions on access for third parties seem likely to be considered as not indispensable and to lead to the elimination of competition for a substantial part of the products and services concerned within the meaning of Article [81](3), thus excluding the possibility of an exemption. Moreover, if an MDNS agreement strengthens appreciably a dominant position which a participating TO holds in the market for a service included in the MDNS, this is also likely to lead to a rejection of the exemption.

Commentary
para 62: B&C: 12.131

63. The Commission has outlined the conditions for exempting such forms of cooperation in a case concerning a proposed joint venture between 22 TOs for the provision of a Europe-wide MDNS, later abandoned for commercial reasons,[20] The Commission considered that the MDNS project presented the risks of restriction of competition between the operators themselves and private service suppliers but it accepted that the project also offered economic benefits to telecommunications users such as access to Europe-wide services through a single operator. Such cooperation could also have accelerated European standardization, reduced costs and increased the quality of the services. The Commission had informed the participants that approval of the project would have to be subject to guarantees designed to prevent undue restriction of competition in the telecommunications services markets, such as discrimination against private services suppliers and cross-subsidization. Such guarantees would be essential conditions for the granting

of an exemption under the competition rules to cooperation agreements involving TOs. The requirement for an appropriate guarantee of non-discrimination and non-cross-subsidization will be specified in individual cases according to the examples of discrimination indicated in Section V below concerning the application of Article [82].

Notes

[20] Commission press release IP(89) 948 of 14.12.1989.

Commentary
para 63: B&C: 12.147

64. (bb) *Agreements between TOs and other service providers*
    Cooperation between TOs and other operators is increasing in telecommunications services. It frequently takes the form of a joint venture. The Commission recognizes that it may have beneficial effects. However, this cooperation may also adversely affect competition and the opening up of services markets. Beneficial and harmful effects must therefore be carefully weighed.

65. Such agreements may restrict competition for the provision of telecommunications services:
    (i) between the partners; and
    (ii) from third parties.

66. (i) Competition between the partners may be restricted when these are actual or potential competitors for the relevant telecommunications service. This is generally the case, even when only the other partners and not the TOs are already providing the service. Indeed, TOs may have the required financial capacity, technical and commercial skills to enter the market for non-reserved services and could reasonably bear the technical and financial risk of doing it. This is also generally the case as far as private operators are concerned, when they do not yet provide the service in the geographical market covered by the cooperation, but do provide this service elsewhere. They may therefore be potential competitors in this geographic market.

67. (ii) The cooperation may restrict competition from third parties because:
    — there is an appreciable risk that the participant TO, i.e. the dominant network provider, will give more favourable network access to its cooperation partners than to other service providers in competition with the partners,
    — potential competitors may refrain from entering the market because of this objective risk or, in any event, because of the presence on the market-place of a cooperation involving the monopolist for the network provision. This is especially the case when market entry barriers are high: the market structure allows only few suppliers and the size and the market power of the partners are considerable.

68. On the other hand, the cooperation may bring economic benefits which outweigh its harmful effect and therefore justify the granting of an exemption under Article [81](3). The economic benefits can consist, *inter alia*, of the rationalization of the production and distribution of telecommunication services, in improvements in existing services or development of new services, or transfer of technology which improves the efficiency and the competitiveness of the European industrial structures.

69. In the absence of such economic benefits a complementarity between partners, i.e. between the provision of a reserved activity and that of a service under competition, is not a benefit as such. Considering it as a benefit would be equal to justifying an involvement through restrictive agreements of TOs in any non-reserved service provision. This would be to hinder a competitive structure in this market.
    In certain cases, the cooperation could consolidate or extend the dominant position of the TOs concerned to a non-reserved services market, in violation of Article [82].

70. The imposition or the proposal of cooperation with the service provider as a condition for the provision of the network may be deemed abusive (see paragraph 98(vi)).

71. (bc) *Agreements between service providers other than TOs*
    The Commission will apply the same principles indicated in (ba) and (bb) above also to agreements between private service providers, *inter alia*, agreements providing quotas, price fixing, market and/or customer allocation. In principle, they are unlikely to qualify for an exemption. The Commission will be particularly vigilant in order to avoid cooperation on services leading

to a strengthening of dominant positions of the partners or restricting competition from third parties. There is a danger of this occurring for example when an undertaking is dominant with regard to the network architecture and its proprietary standard is adopted to support the service contemplated by the cooperation. This architecture enabling interconnection between computer systems of the partners could attract some partners to the dominant partner. The dominant position for the network architecture will be strengthened and Article [82] may apply.

72. In any exemption of agreements between TOs and other services and/or equipment providers, or between these providers, the Commission will require from the partners appropriate guarantees of non-cross-subsidization and non-discrimination. The risk of cross-subsidization and discrimination is higher when the TOs or the other partners provide both services and equipment, whether within or outside the Community.

C. Agreements on research and development (R&D)

73. As in other high technology based sectors, R&D in telecommunications is essential for keeping pace with technological progress and being competitive on the market-place to the benefit of users. R&D requires more and more important financial, technical and human resources which only few undertakings can generate individually. Cooperation is therefore crucial for attaining the above objectives.

Commentary
para 73: B&C: 12.142

74. The Commission has adopted a Regulation for the block exemption under Article [81](3) of R&D agreements in all sectors, including telecommunications.[21]

Notes
[21] Regulation (EEC) No 418/85, OJ No L 53, 22.2.1985, p. 5. [See now Commission Regulation (EC) No 2659/2000 (OJ L 304, 5.12.2001, p.7.]

75. Agreements which are not covered by this Regulation (or the other Commission block exemption Regulations) could still obtain an individual exemption from the Commission if Article [81](3) requirements are met individually. However, not in all cases do the economic benefits of an R&D agreement outweigh its competition restrictions. In telecommunications, one major asset, enabling access to new markets, is the launch of new products or services. Competition is based not only on price, but also on technology. R&D agreements could constitute the means for powerful undertakings with high market shares to avoid or limit competition from more innovative rivals. The risk of excessive restrictions of competition increases when the cooperation is extended from R&D to manufacturing and even more to distribution.

76. The importance which the Commission attaches to R&D and innovation is demonstrated by the fact that it has launched several programmes for this purpose. The joint companies' activities which may result from these programmes are not automatically cleared or exempted as such in all aspects from the application of the competition rules. However, most of those joint activities may be covered by the Commission's block exemption Regulations. If not, the joint activities in question may be exempted, where required, in accordance with the appropriate criteria and procedures.

77. In the Commission's experience joint distribution linked to joint R&D which is not covered by the Regulation on R&D does not play the crucial role in the exploitation of the results of R&D. Nevertheless, in individual cases, provided that a competitive environment is maintained, the Commission is prepared to consider full-range cooperation even between large firms. This should lead to improving the structure of European industry and thus enable it to meet strong competition in the world market place.

Commentary
para 77: B&C: 12.143

V. Application of Article [82]

78. Article [82] applies when:
    (i) the undertaking concerned holds an individual or a joint dominant position;
    (ii) it commits an abuse of that dominant position; and
    (iii) the abuse may affect trade between Member States.

Dominant position

79. In each national market the TOs hold individually orcollectively a dominant position for the creation and the exploitation of the network, since they are protected by exclusive or special rights granted by the State. Moreover, the TOs hold a dominant position for some telecommunications services, in so far as they hold exclusive or special rights with respect to those services.[22]

Notes

[22] Commission Decision 82/861/EEC in the "*British Telecommunications*" case, point 26, OJ No L 360, 21.12.1982, p. 36, confirmed in the Judgment of 20.3.1985 in Case 41/83, *Italian Republic v Commission* [1985] ECR 873, generally known as "*British Telecom*".

Commentary
para 79: **B&C:** 12.147

80. The TOs may also hold dominant positions on the markets for certain equipment or services, even though they no longer hold any exclusive rights on those markets. After the elimination of these rights, they may have kept very important market shares in this sector. When the market share in itself does not suffice to give the TOs a dominant position, it could do it in combination with the other factors such as the monopoly for the network or other related services and a powerful and wide distribution network. As to the equipment, for example terminal equipment, even if the TOs are not involved in the equipment manufacturing or in the services provision, they may hold a dominant position in the market as distributors.

81. Also, firms other than TOs may hold individual or collective dominant positions in markets where there are no exclusive rights. This may be the case especially for certain non-reserved services because of either the market shares alone of those undertakings, or because of a combination of several factors. Among these factors, in addition to the market shares, two of particular importance are the technological advance and the holding of the information concerning access protocols or interfaces necessary to ensure interoperability of software and hardware. When this information is covered by intellectual property rights this is a further factor of dominance.

82. Finally, the TOs hold, individually or collectively, dominant positions in the demand for some telecommunication equipment, works or software services. Being dominant for the network and other services provisions they may account for a purchaser's share high enough to give them dominance as to the demand, i.e. making suppliers dependent on them. Dependence could exist when the supplier cannot sell to other customers a substantial part of its production or change a production. In certain national markets, for example in large switching equipment, big purchasers such as the TOs face big suppliers. In this situation, it should be weighed up case by case whether the supplier or the customer position will prevail on the other to such an extent as to be considered dominant under Article [82].
    With the liberalization of services and the expansion of new forces on the services markets, dominant positions of undertakings other than the TOs may arise for the purchasing of equipment.

Abuse

83. Commission's activity may concern mainly the following broad areas of abuses:
    A. *TOs' abuses*: in particular, they may take advantage of their monopoly or at least dominant position to acquire a foothold or to extend their power in non-reserved neighbouring markets, to the detriment of competitors and customers.

B. *Abuses by undertaking other than TOs*: these may take advantage of the fundamental information they hold, whether or not covered by intellectual property rights, with the object and/or effect of restricting competition.

C. *Abuses of a dominant purchasing position*: for the time being this concerns mainly the TOs, especially to the extent that they hold a dominant position for reserved activities in the national market. However, it may also increasingly concern other undertakings which have entered the market.

A. TOs' Abuses

84. The Commission has recognized in the Green Paper the central role of the TOs, which justifies the maintenance of certain monopolies to enable them to perform their public task. This public task consists in the provision and exploitation of a universal network or, where appropriate, universal service, i.e. one having general coverage and available to all users (including service providers and the TOs themselves) upon request on reasonable and non-discriminatory conditions.
This fundamental obligation could justify the benefit of the exception provided in Article [86](2) under certain circumstances, as laid down in the Services Directive.

85. In most cases, however, the competition rules, far from obstructing the fulfilment of this obligation, contribute to ensuring it. In particular, Article [82] can apply to behaviour of dominant undertakings resulting in a refusal to supply, discrimination, restrictive tying clauses, unfair prices or other inequitable conditions.
If one of these types of behaviour occurs in the provision of one of the monopoly services, the fundamental obligation indicated above is not performed. This could be the case when a TO tries to take advantage of its monopoly for certain services (for instance: network provision) in order to limit the competition they have to face in respect of non-reserved services, which in turn are supported by those monopoly services.
It is not necessary for the purpose of the application of Article [82] that competition be restricted as to a service which is supported by the monopoly provision in question. It would suffice that the behaviour results in an appreciable restriction of competition in whatever way. This means that an abuse may occur when the company affected by the behaviour is not a service provider but an end user who could himself be disadvantaged in competition in the course of his own business.

86. The Court of Justice has set out this fundamental principle of competition in telecommunications in one of its judgments.[23] An abuse within the meaning of Article [82] is committed where, without any objective necessity, an undertaking holding a dominant position on a particular market reserves to itself or to an undertaking belonging to the same group an ancillary activity which might be carried out by another undertaking as part of its activities on a neighbouring but separate market, with the possibility of eliminating all competition from such undertaking.
The Commission believes that this principle applies, not only when a dominant undertaking monopolizes other markets, but also when by anti-competitive means it extends its activity to other markets.
Hampering the provision of non-reserved services could limit production, markets and above all the technical progress which is a key factor of telecommunications. The Commission has already shown these adverse effects of usage restrictions on monopoly provision in its decision in the "*British Telecom*" case.[24] In this Decision it was found that the restrictions imposed by British Telecom on telex and telephone networks usage, namely on the transmission of international messages on behalf of third parties:
(i) limited the activity of economic operators to the detriment of technological progress;
(ii) discriminated against these operators, thereby placing them at a competitive disadvantage *vis-à-vis* TOs not bound by these restrictions; and
(iii) made the conclusion of the contracts for the supply of telex circuits subject to acceptance by the other parties of supplementary obligations which had no connection with such contracts. These were considered abuses of a dominant position identified respectively in Article [82](b), (c) and (d).
This could be done:
(a) as above, by refusing or restricting the usage of the service provided under monopoly so as to limit the provision of non-reserved services by third parties; or

(b) by predatory behaviour, as a result of cross-subsidization.

Notes

[23] Case 311/84, *Centre belge d'études de marché Télémarketing (CBEM) SA v Compagnie luxembourgeoise de télédiffusion SA and Information Publicité Benelux SA*, 3 October 1985 [1985] ECR 3261, Grounds 26 and 27.

[24] See Note 22.

---

87. The separation of the TOs' regulatory power from their business activity is a crucial matter in the context of the application of Article [82]. This separation is provided in the Article [86] Directives on terminals and on services mentioned in Note 2 above.

(a) Usage restrictions

88. Usage restrictions on provisions of reserved services are likely to correspond to the specific examples of abuses indicated in Article [82]. In particular:

   — they may limit the provision of telecommunications services in free competition, the investments and the technical progress, to the prejudice of telecommunications consumers (Article [82](b)),

   — to the extent that these usage restrictions are not applied to all users, including the TOs themselves as users, they may result in discrimination against certain users, placing them at a competitive disadvantage (Article [82](c)),

   — they may make the usage of the reserved services subject to the acceptance of obligations which have no connection with this usage (Article [82](d)).

89. The usage restrictions in question mainly concern public networks (public switched telephone network (PSTN) or public switched data networks (PSDN)) and especially leased circuits. They may also concern other provisions such as satellite uplink, and mobile communication networks. The most frequent types of behaviour are as follows:

   (i) Prohibition imposed by TOs on third parties:

   (a) to connect private leased circuits by means of concentrator, multiplexer or other equipment to the public switched network; and/or

   (b) to use private leased circuits for providing services, to the extent that these services are not reserved, but under competition.

90. To the extent that the user is granted a licence by State regulatory authorities under national law in compliance with EEC law, these prohibitions limit the user's freedom of access to the leased circuits, the provision of which is a public service. Moreover, it discriminates between users, depending upon the usage (Article [82](c)). This is one of the most serious restrictions and could substantially hinder the development of international telecommunications services (Article [82](b)).

91. When the usage restriction limits the provision of non-reserved service in competition with that provided by the TO itself the abuse is even more serious and the principles of the abovementioned "*Télémarketing*" judgment (Note 23 *supra*) apply.

92. In individual cases, the Commission will assess whether the service provided on the leased circuit is reserved or not, on the basis of the Community regulatory acts interpreted in the technical and economic context of each case. Even though a service could be considered reserved according to the law, the fact that a TO actually prohibits the usage of the leased circuit only to some users and not to others could constitute a discrimination under Article [82](c).

93. The Commission has taken action in respect of the Belgian Régie des télégraphes et téléphones after receiving a complaint concerning an alleged abuse of dominant position from a private supplier of value-added telecommunications services relating to the conditions under which telecommunications circuits were being leased. Following discussions with the Commission, the RTT authorized the private supplier concerned to use the leased telecommunications circuits subject to no restrictions other than that they should not be used for the simple transport of data.

Moreover, pending the possible adoption of new rules in Belgium, and without prejudice to any such rules, the RTT undertook that all its existing and potential clients for leased telecommunications circuits to which third parties may have access shall be governed by the same conditions as those which were agreed with the private sector supplier mentioned above.[25]

Notes

[25] Commission Press release IP(90) 67 of 29.1.1990.

(ii) Refusal by TOs to provide reserved services (in particular the network and leased circuits) to third parties

94. Refusal to supply has been considered an abuse by the Commission and the Court of Justice.[26] This behaviour would make it impossible or at least appreciably difficult for third parties to provide non-reserved services. This, in turn, would lead to a limitation of services and of technical development (Article [82](b)) and, if applied only to some users, result in discrimination (Article [82](c)).

Notes

[26] Cases 6 and 7/73 *Commercial Solvents v Commission* [1974] ECR 223; *United Brands v Commission* (Note 13, above).

(iii) Imposition of extra charges or other special conditions for certain usages of reserved services

95. An example would be the imposition of access charges to leased circuits when they are connected to the public switched network or other special prices and charges for service provision to third parties. Such access charges may discriminate between users of the same service (leased circuits provision) depending upon the usage and result in imposing unfair trading conditions. This will limit the usage of leased circuits and finally non-reserved service provision. Conversely, it does not constitute an abuse provided that it is shown, in each specific case, that the access charges correspond to costs which are entailed directly for the TOs for the access in question. In this case, access charges can be imposed only on an equal basis to all users, including TOs themselves.

96. Apart from these possible additional costs which should be covered by an extra charge, the interconnection of a leased circuit to the public switched network is already remunerated by the price related to the use of this network. Certainly, a leased circuit can represent a subjective value for a user depending on the profitability of the enhanced service to be provided on that leased circuit. However, this cannot be a criterion on which a dominant undertaking, and above all a public service provider, can base the price of this public service.

97. The Commission appreciates that the substantial difference between leased circuits and the public switched network causes a problem of obtaining the necessary revenues to cover the costs of the switched network. However, the remedy chosen must not be contrary to law, i.e. the EEC Treaty, as discriminatory pricing between customers would be.

(iv) Discriminatory price or quality of the service provided

98. This behaviour may relate, *inter alia*, to tariffs or to restrictions or delays in connection to the public switched network or leased circuits provision, in installation, maintenance and repair, in effecting interconnection of systems or in providing information concerning network planning, signalling protocols, technical standards and all other information necessary for an appropriate interconnection and interoperation with the reserved service and which may affect the interworking of competitive services or terminal equipment offerings.

(v) Tying the provision of the reserved service to the supply by the TOs or others of terminal equipment to be interconnected or interoperated, in particular through imposition, pressure, offer of special prices or other trading conditions for the reserved service linked to the equipment.

(vi) Tying the provision of the reserved service to the agreement of the user to enter into cooperation with the reserved service provider himself as to the non-reserved service to be carried on the network

(vii) Reserving to itself for the purpose of non-reserved service provision or to other service providers information obtained in the exercise of a reserved service in particular information concerning users of a reserved services providers more favourable conditions for the supply of this information

This latter information could be important for the provision of services under competition to the extent that it permits the targeting of customers of those services and the definition of business strategy. The behaviour indicated above could result in a discrimination against undertakings to which the use of this information is denied in violation of Article [82](c). The information in question can only be disclosed with the agreement of the users concerned and in accordance with relevant data protection legislation (see the proposal for a Council Directive concerning the protection of personal data and privacy in the context of public digital telecommunications networks, in particular the integrated services digital network (ISDN) and public digital mobile networks).[27]

Notes
[27] Commission document COM(90) 314 of 13.9.1990.

(viii) Imposition of unneeded reserved services by supplying reserved and/or non-reserved services when the former reserved services are reasonably separable from the others

Commentary
para 98: B&C: 12.160–12.161

99. The practices under (v) (vi) (vii) and (viii) result in applying conditions which have no connection with the reserved service, contravening Article [82](d).

100. Most of these practices were in fact identified in the Services Directive as restrictions on the provision of services within the meaning of Article [49] and Article [82] of the Treaty brought about by State measures. They are therefore covered by the broader concept of "restrictions" which under Article 6 of the Directive have to be removed by Member States.

101. The Commission believes that the Directives on terminals and on services also clarify some principles of application of Articles [81] and [82] in the sector.
The Services Directive does not apply to important sectors such as mobile communications and satellites; however, competition rules apply fully to these sectors. Moreover, as to the services covered by the Directive it will depend very much on the degree of precision of the licences given by the regulatory body whether the TOs still have a discretionary margin for imposing conditions which should be scrutinized under competition rules. Not all the conditions can be regulated in licences: consequently, there could be room for discretionary action. The application of competition rules to companies will therefore depend very much on a case-by-case examination of the licences. Nothing more than a class licence can be required for terminals.

(b) Cross-subsidization

102. Cross-subsidization means that an undertaking allocates all or part of the costs of its activity in one product or geographic market to its activity in another product or geographic market. Under certain circumstances, cross-subsidization in telecommunications could distort competition, i.e. lead to beating other competitors with offers which are made possible not by efficiency and performance but by artificial means such as subsidies. Avoiding cross-subsidization leading to unfair competition is crucial for the development of service provision and equipment supply.

103. Cross-subsidization does not lead to predatory pricing and does not restrict competition when it is the costs of reserved activities which are subsidized by the revenue generated by other reserved activities since there is no competition possible as to these activities. This form of subsidization is even necessary, as it enables the TOs holders of exclusive rights to perform their obligation to provide a public service universally and on the same conditions to everybody. For instance, telephone provision in unprofitable rural areas is subsidized through revenues from telephone provision in profitable urban areas or long-distance calls. The same could be said of subsidizing the provision of reserved services through revenues generated by activities under competition. The application of the general principle of cost-orientation should be the ultimate goal, in order, *inter alia*, to ensure that prices are not inequitable as between users.

104. Subsidizing activities under competition, whether concerning services or equipment, by allocating their costs to monopoly activities, however, is likely to distort competition in violation of Article [82]. It could amount to an abuse by an undertaking holding a dominant position within the Community. Moreover, users of activities under monopoly have to bear unrelated costs for the provision of these activities. Cross-subsidization can also exist between monopoly provision and equipment manufacturing and sale. Cross-subsidization can be carried out through:
    — funding the operation of the activities in question with capital remunerated substantially below the market rate;
    — providing for those activities premises, equipment, experts and/or services with a remuneration substantially lower than the market price.

105. As to funding through monopoly revenues or making available monopoly material and intellectual means for the starting up of new activities under competition, this constitutes an investment whose costs should be allocated to the new activity. Offering the new product or service should normally include a reasonable remuneration of such investment in the long run. If it does not, the Commission will assess the case on the basis of the remuneration plans of the undertaking concerned and of the economic context.

106. Transparency in the TOs' accounting should enable the Commission to ascertain whether there is cross-subsidization in the cases in which this question arises. The ONP Directive provides in this respect for the definition of harmonized tariff principles which should lessen the number of these cases.

     This transparency can be provided by an accounting system which ensures the fully proportionate distribution of all costs between reserved and non-reserved activities. Proper allocation of costs is more easily ensured in cases of structural separation, i.e. creating distinct entities for running each of these two categories of activities.

     An appropriate accounting system approach should permit the identification and allocation of all costs between the activities which they support. In this system all products and services should bear proportionally all the relevant costs, including costs of research and development, facilities and overheads. It should enable the production of recorded figures which can be verified by accountants.

107. As indicated above (paragraph 59), in cases of cooperation agreements involving TOs a guarantee of no cross-subsidization is one of the conditions required by the Commission for exemption under Article [81](3). In order to monitor properly compliance with that guarantee, the Commission now envisages requesting the parties to ensure an appropriate accounting system as described above, the accounts being regularly submitted to the Commission. Where the accounting method is chosen, the Commission will reserve the possibility of submitting the accounts to independent audit, especially if any doubt arises as to the capability of the system to ensure the necessary transparency or to detect any cross-subsidization. If the guarantee cannot be properly monitored, the Commission may withdraw the exemption.

108. In all other cases, the Commission does not envisage requiring such transparency of the TOs. However, if in a specific case there are substantial elements converging in indicating the existence of an abusive cross-subsidization and/or predatory pricing, the Commission could establish a presumption of such cross-subsidization and predatory pricing. An appropriate separate accounting system could be important in order to counter this presumption.

109. Cross-subsidization of a reserved activity by a non-reserved one does not in principle restrict competition. However, the application of the exception provided in Article [86](2) to this non-reserved activity could not as a rule be justified by the fact that the financial viability of the TO in question rests on the non-reserved activity. Its financial viability and the performance of its task of general economic interest can only be ensured by the State where appropriate by the granting of an exclusive or special right and by imposing restrictions on activities competing with the reserved ones.

110. Also cross-subsidization by a public or private operator outside the EEC may be deemed abusive in terms of Article [82] if that operator holds a dominant position for equipment or non-reserved services within the EEC. The existence of this dominant position, which allows the holder to behave to an appreciable extent independently of its competitors and custom-

ers and ultimately of consumers, will be assessed in the light of all elements in the EEC and outside.

B. Abuses by undertakings other than the TOs

111. Further to the liberalization of services, undertakings other than the TOs may increasingly extend their power to acquire dominant positions in non-reserved markets. They may already hold such a position in some services markets which had not been reserved. When they take advantage of their dominant position to restrict competition and to extend their power, Article [82] may also apply to them. The abuses in which they might indulge are broadly similar to most of those previously described in relation to the TOs.

112. Infringements of Article [82] may be committed by the abusive exercise of industrial property rights in relation with standards, which are of crucial importance for telecommunications. Standards may be either the results of international standardization, or *de facto* standards and the property of undertakings.

113. Producers of equipment or suppliers of services are dependent on proprietary standards to ensure the interconnectivity of their computer resources. An undertaking which owns a dominant network architecture may abuse its dominant position by refusing to provide the necessary information for the interconnection of other architecture resources to its architecture products. Other possible abuses — similar to those indicated as to the TOs — are, *inter alia*, delays in providing the information, discrimination in the quality of the information, discriminatory pricing or other trading conditions, and making the information provision subject to the acceptance by the producer, supplier or user of unfair trading conditions.

114. On 1 August 1984, the Commission accepted a unilateral undertaking from IBM to provide other manufacturers with the technical interface information needed to permit competitive products to be used with IBM's then most powerful range of computers, the System/370. The Commission thereupon suspended the proceedings under Article [82] which it had initiated against IBM in December 1980. The IBM Undertaking[28] also contains a commitment relating to SNA formats and protocols.

Notes

[28] Reproduced in full in EC Bulletin 10-1984 (point 3.4.1). As to its continued application, see Commission press release No IP(88) 814 of 15 December 1988.

115. The question how to reconcile copyrights on standards with the competition requirements is particularly difficult. In any event, copyright cannot be used unduly to restrict competition.

C. Abuses of dominant purchasing position

116. Article [82] also applies to behaviour of undertakings holding a dominant purchasing position. The examples of abuses indicated in that Article may therefore also concern that behaviour.

117. The Council Directive 90/531/EEC[29] based on Articles [54](2), [55], [95] and [133] of the [EC] Treaty on the procurement procedures of entities operating in *inter alia* the telecommunications sector regulates essentially:

  (i) procurement procedures in order to ensure on a reciprocal basis non-discrimination on the basis of nationality; and

  (ii) for products or services for use in reserved markets, not in competitive markets. That Directive, which is addressed to States, does not exclude the application of Article [82] to the purchasing of products within the scope of the Directive. The Commission will decide case by case how to ensure that these different sets of rules are applied in a coherent manner.

Notes

[29] OJ No L 297, 29.10.1990, p. 1.

118. Furthermore, both in reserved and competitive markets, practices other than those covered by the Directive may be established in violation of Article [82]. One example is taking advantage of a dominant purchasing position for imposing excessively favourable prices or other trading conditions, in comparison with other purchasers and suppliers (Article [82](a)). This could result in discrimination under Article [82](c). Also obtaining, whether or not through imposition, an

exclusive distributorship for the purchased product by the dominant purchaser may constitute an abusive extension of its economic power to other markets (see "*Télémarketing*' Court judgment (Note 23 *supra*)).

119. Another abusive practice could be that of making the purchase subject to licensing by the supplier of standards for the product to be purchased or for other products, to the purchaser itself, or to other suppliers (Article [82](d)).

120. Moreover, even in competitive markets, discriminatory procedures on the basis of nationality may exist, because national pressures and traditional links of a non-economic nature do not always disappear quickly after the liberalization of the markets. In this case, a systematic exclusion or considerably unfavourable treatment of a supplier, without economic necessity, could be examined under Article [82], especially (b) (limitation of outlets) and (c) (discrimination). In assessing the case, the Commission will substantially examine whether the same criteria for awarding the contract have been followed by the dominant undertaking for all suppliers. The Commission will normally take into account criteria similar to those indicated in Article 27 (1) of the Directive.[31] The purchases in question being outside the scope of the Directive, the Commission will not require that transparent purchasing procedures be pursued.

Notes

[30] (See Note 26) Article 27(1)(a) and (b). The criteria on which the contracting entities shall base the award of the contracts shall be: (a) the most economically advantageous tender involving various criteria such as delivery date, period for completion, running costs, cost-effectiveness, quality, aesthetic and functional characteristics, technical merit, after-sales services and technical assistance, commitments with regard to spare parts, security of supplies and price; or (b) the lowest price only.

D. Effect on trade between Member States

121. The same principle outlined regarding Article [81] applies here. Moreover, in certain circumstances, such as the case of the elimination of a competitor by an undertaking holding a dominant position, although trade between Member States is not directly affected, for the purposes of Article [82] it is sufficient to show that there will be repercussions on the competitive structure of the common market.

VI. APPLICATION OF ARTICLES [81] AND [82] IN THE FIELD OF SATELLITES

122. The development of this sector is addressed globally by the Commission in the "Green Paper on a common approach in the field of satellite communications in the European Community" of 20 November 1990 (Doc. COM(90) 490 final). Due to the increasing importance of satellites and the particular uncertainty among undertakings as to the application of competition rules to individual cases in this sector, it is appropriate to address the sector in a distinct section in these guidelines.

123. State regulations on satellites are not covered by the Commission Directives under Article [86] of the [EC] Treaty respectively on terminals and services mentioned above except in the Directive on terminals which contemplates receive-only satellite stations not connected to a public network. The Commission's position on the regulatory framework compatible with the Treaty competition rules is stated in the Commission Green Paper on satellites mentioned above.

124. In any event the Treaty competition rules fully apply to the satellites domain, *inter alia*, Articles [81] and [82] to undertakings. Below is indicated how the principles set out above, in particular in Sections IV and V, apply to satellites.

125. Agreements between European TOs in particular within international conventions may play an important role in providing European satellites systems and a harmonious development of satellite services throughout the Community. These benefits are taken into consideration under competition rules, provided that the agreements do not contain restrictions which are not indispensable for the attainment of these objectives.

126. Agreements between TOs concerning the operation of satellite systems in the broadest sense may be caught by Article [81]. As to space segment capacity, the TOs are each other's competitors, whether actual or potential. In pooling together totally or partially their supplies of space segment capacity they may restrict competition between themselves. Moreover, they are likely to

restrict competition vis-à-vis third parties to the extent that their agreements contain provisions with this object or effect: for instance provisions limiting their supplies in quality and/or quantity, or restricting their business autonomy by imposing directly or indirectly a coordination between these third parties and the parties to the agreements. It should be examined whether such agreements could qualify for an exemption under Article [81](3) provided that they are notified. However, restrictions on third parties' ability to compete are likely to preclude such an exemption. It should also be examined whether such agreements strengthen any individual or collective dominant position of the parties, which also would exclude the granting of an exemption. This could be the case in particular if the agreement provides that the parties are exclusive distributors of the space segment capacity provided by the agreement.

127. Such agreements between TOs could also restrict competition as to the uplink with respect to which TOs are competitors. In certain cases the customer for satellite communication has the choice between providers in several countries, and his choice will be substantially determined by the quality, price and other sales conditions of each provider. This choice will be even ampler since uplink is being progressively liberalized and to the extent that the application of EEC rules to State legislations will open up the uplink markets. Community-wide agreements providing directly or indirectly for coordination as to the parties' uplink provision are therefore caught by Article [81].

128. Agreements between TOs and private operators on space segment capacity may be also caught by Article [81], as that provision applies, *inter alia*, to cooperation, and in particular joint venture agreements. These agreements could be exempted if they bring specific benefits such as technology transfer, improvement of the quality of the service or enabling better marketing, especially for a new capacity, outweighing the restrictions. In any event, imposing on customers the bundled uplink and space segment capacity provision is likely to exclude an exemption since it limits competition in uplink provision to the detriment of the customer's choice, and in the current market situation will almost certainly strengthen the TOs' dominant position in violation of Article [82]. An exemption is unlikely to be granted also when the agreement has the effect of reducing substantially the supply in an oligopolistic market, and even more clearly when an effect of the agreement is to prevent the only potential competitor of a dominant provider in a given market from offering its services independently. This could amount to a violation of Article [82]. Direct or indirect imposition of any kind of agreement by a TO, for instance by making the uplink subject to the conclusion of an agreement with a third party, would constitute an infringement of Article [82].

VII. Restructuring in Telecommunications

129. Deregulation, the objective of a single market for 1992 and the fundamental changes in the telecommunications technology have caused wide strategic restructuring in Europe and throughout the world as well. They have mostly taken the form of mergers and joint ventures.

(a) Mergers

130. In assessing telecom mergers in the framework of Council Regulation (EEC) No 4064/89 on the control of concentrations between undertakings[31] the Commission will take into account, *inter alia*, the following elements.

Notes

[31] OJ No L 395, 30.12.1989, p. 1; Corrigendum OJ No L 257, 21.9.1990, p. 13.

---

131. Restructuring moves are in general beneficial to the European telecommunications industry. They may enable the companies to rationalize and to reach the critical mass necessary to obtain the economies of scale needed to make the important investments in research and development. These are necessary to develop new technologies and to remain competitive in the world market.

However, in certain cases they may also lead to the anti-competitive creation or strengthening of dominant positions.

132. The economic benefits resulting from critical mass must be demonstrated. The concentration operation could result in a mere aggregation of market shares, unaccompanied by restructuring

measures or plans. This operation may create or strengthen Community or national dominant positions in a way which impedes competition.

133. When concentration operations have this sole effect, they can hardly be justified by the objective of increasing the competitivity of Community industry in the world market. This objective, strongly pursued by the Commission, rather requires competition in EEC domestic markets in order that the EEC undertakings acquire the competitive structure and attitude needed to operate in the world market.

134. In assessing concentration cases in telecommunications, the Commission will be particularly vigilant to avoid the strengthening of dominant positions through integration. If dominant service providers are allowed to integrate into the equipment market by way of mergers, access to this market by other equipment suppliers may be seriously hindered. A dominant service provider is likely to give preferential treatment to its own equipment subsidiary.

Moreover, the possibility of disclosure by the service provider to its subsidiary of sensitive information obtained from competing equipment manufacturers can put the latter at a competitive disadvantage.

The Commission will examine case by case whether vertical integration has such effects or rather is likely to reinforce the competitive structure in the Community.

135. The Commission has enforced principles on restructuring in a case concerning the GEC and Siemens joint bid for Plessey.[32]

Notes

[32] Commission Decision rejecting Plessey's complaint against the GEC-Siemens bid (Case IV/33.018 *GEC-Siemens/Plessey*), OJ No C 239, 25.9.1990, p. 2.

136. Article [81](1) applies to the acquisition by an undertaking of a minority shareholding in a competitor where, *inter alia*, the arrangements involve the creation of a structure of cooperation between the investor and the other undertakings, which will influence these undertakings' competitive conduct.[33]

Notes

[33] *British American Tobacco Company Ltd and RJ Reynolds Industries Inc. v Commission* (Joined Cases 142 and 156/84) of 17.11.1987, [1987] ECR 4487.

(b) Joint ventures

137. A joint venture can be of a cooperative or a concentrative nature. It is of a cooperative nature when it has as its object or effect the coordination of the competitive behaviour of undertakings which remain independent. The principles governing cooperative joint ventures are to be set out in Commission guidelines to that effect. Concentrative joint ventures fall under Regulation (EEC) No 4064/89.[34]

Notes

[34] OJ No C 203, 14.8.1990, p. 10.

138. In some of the latest joint venture cases the Commission granted an exemption under Article [81](3) on grounds which are particularly relevant to telecommunications. Precisely in a decision concerning telecommunications, the "*Optical Fibres*" case,[35] the Commission considered that the joint venture enabled European companies to produce a high technology product, promoted technical progress, and facilitated technology transfer. Therefore, the joint venture permits European companies to withstand competition from non-Community producers, especially in the USA and Japan, in an area of fast-moving technology characterized by international markets. The Commission confirmed this approach in the "*Canon-Olivetti*" case.[36]

Notes

[35] Decision 86/405/EEC, OJ No L 236, 22.8.86, p. 30.
[36] Decision 88/88/EEC, OJ No L 52, 26.2.1988, p. 51.

VIII. Impact of the International Conventions on the Application of EEC Competition Rules to Telecommunications

139. International conventions (such as the Convention of International Telecommunication Union (ITU) or Conventions on Satellites) play a fundamental role in ensuring worldwide cooperation for the provision of international services. However, application of such international conventions on telecommunications by EEC Member States must not affect compliance with the EEC law, in particular with competition rules.

140. Article [307] of the [EC] Treaty regulates this matter.[37] The relevant obligations provided in the various conventions or related Acts do not pre-date the entry into force of the Treaty. As to the ITU and World Administrative Telegraph and Telephone Conference (WATTC), whenever a revision or a new adoption of the ITU Convention or of the WATTC Regulations occurs, the ITU or WATTC members recover their freedom of action. The Satellites Conventions were adopted much later.

    Moreover, as to all conventions, the application of EEC rules does not seem to affect the fulfilment of obligations of Member States vis-à-vis third countries. Article [307] does not protect obligations between EEC Member States entered into in international treaties. The purpose of Article [307] is to protect the right of third countries only and it is not intended to crystallize the acquired international treaty rights of Member States to the detriment of the EEC Treaty's objectives or of the Community interest. Finally, even if Article [307](1) did apply, the Member States concerned would nevertheless be obliged to take all appropriate steps to eliminate incompatibility between their obligations vis-à-vis third countries and the EEC rules. This applies in particular where Member States acting collectively have the statutory possibility to modify the international convention in question as required, e.g. in the case of the Eutelsat Convention.

Notes

[37] "The rights and obligations arising from agreements concluded before the entry into force of this Treaty between one or more Member States on the one hand and one or more third countries on the other, shall not be affected by the provisions of this Treaty. To the extent that such agreements are not compatible with this Treaty, the Member State or States concerned shall take all appropriate steps to eliminate the incompatibilities established. Member States shall, where necessary, assist each other to this end and shall, where appropriate, adopt a common attitude ..."

---

141. As to the WATTC Regulations, the relevant provisions of the Regulations in force from 9 December 1988 are flexible enough to give the parties the choice whether or not to implement them or how to implement them.

    In any event, EEC Member States, by signing the Regulations, have made a joint declaration that they will apply them in accordance with their obligations under the EEC Treaty.

142. As to the International Telegraph and Telephone Consultative Committee (CCITT) recommendations, competition rules apply to them.

143. Members of the CCITT are, pursuant to Article 11(2) of the International Telecommunications Convention, "administrations" of the Members of the ITU and recognized private operating agencies ("RPOAs`) which so request with the approval of the ITU members which have recognized them. Unlike the members of the ITU or the Administrative Conferences which are States, the members of the CCITT are telecommunications administrations and RPOAs. Telecommunications administrations are defined in Annex 2 to the International Telecommunications Conventions as "tout service ou département gouvernemental responsable des mesures à prendre pour exécuter les obligations de la Convention Internationale des télécommunications et des règlements" [any government service or department responsible for the measures to be taken to fulfil the obligations laid down in the International Convention on Telecommunications and Regulations]. The CCITT meetings are in fact attended by TOs. Article 11(2) of the International Telecommunications Convention clearly provides that telecommunications administrations and RPOAs are members of the CCITT by themselves. The fact that, because of the ongoing process of separation of the regulatory functions from the business activity, some national authorities participate in the CCITT is not in contradiction with the nature of undertakings of other members. Moreover, even if the CCITT membership became governmental as a result of the separation of regulatory and operational activities of

the telecommunications administrations, Article [86] in association with Article [81] could still apply either against the State measures implementing the CCITT recommendations and the recommendations themselves on the basis of Article [86](1), or if there is no such national implementing measure, directly against the telecommunications organizations which followed the recommendation.[38]

Notes

[38] See Commission Decision 87/3/EEC *ENI/Montedison*, OJ No L 5, 7.1.1987, p. 13.

144. In the Commission's view, the CCITT recommendations are adopted, *inter alia*, by undertakings. Such CCITT recommendations, although they are not legally binding, are agreements between undertakings or decisions by an association of undertakings. In any event, according to the case law of the Commission and the European Court of Justice[39] a statutory body entrusted with certain public functions and including some members appointed by the government of a Member State may be an "association of undertakings' if it represents the trading interests of other members and takes decisions or makes agreements in pursuance of those interests.

The Commission draws attention to the fact that the application of certain provisions in the context of international conventions could result in infringements of the EEC competition rules:

— As to the WATTC Regulations, this is the case for the respective provisions for mutual agreement between TOs on the supply of international telecommunications services (Article 1(5)), reserving the choice of telecommunications routes to the TOs (Article 3(3)), recommending practices equivalent to price agreements (Articles [6(1)(1), 6(1)(2)]), and limiting the possibility of special arrangements to activities meeting needs within and/or between the territories of the Members concerned (Article 9) and only where existing arrangements cannot satisfactorily meet the relevant telecommunications needs (Opinion PL A).

— CCITT recommendations D1 and D2 as they stand at the date of the adoption of these guidelines could amount to a collective horizontal agreement on prices and other supply conditions of international leased lines to the extent that they lead to a coordination of sales policies between TOs and therefore limit competition between them. This was indicated by the Commission in a CCITT meeting on 23 May 1990. The Commission reserves the right to examine the compatibility of other recommendations with Article [81].

— The agreements between TOs concluded in the context of the Conventions on Satellites are likely to limit competition contrary to Article [81] and/or [82] on the grounds set out in paragraphs 126 to 128 above.

Notes

[39] See *Pabst & Richarz/BNIA*, OJ No L 231, 21.8.1976, p. 24, *AROW/BNIC*, OJ No L 379, 31.12.1982, p. 1, and Case 123/83 *BNIC v Clair* [1985] ECR 391.

E24

NOTICE ON THE APPLICATION OF THE COMPETITION RULES TO ACCESS AGREEMENTS IN THE TELECOMMUNICATIONS SECTOR

Framework, Relevant Markets and Principles
(98/C 265/02)
(Text with EEA relevance)

Official Journal C 265, 22.8.1998, p. 2

Celex No 31998Y0[82]2(01)

PREFACE

In the telecommunications industry, access agreements are central in allowing market participants the benefits of liberalisation.

The purpose of this notice is threefold:

— to set out access principles stemming from Community competition law as shown in a large number of Commission decisions in order to create greater market certainty and more stable conditions for investment and commercial initiative in the telecoms and multimedia sectors;

— to define and clarify the relationship between competition law and sector specific legislation under the Article [95] framework (in particular this relates to the relationship between competition rules and open network provision legislation);

— to explain how competition rules will be applied in a consistent way across the sectors involved in the provision of new services, and in particular to access issues and gateways in this context.

INTRODUCTION

1. The timetable for full liberalisation in the telecommunications sector has now been established, and most Member States had to remove the last barriers to the provision of telecommunications networks and services in a competitive environment to consumers by 1 January 1998.[1] As a result of this liberalisation a second set of related products or services will emerge as well as the need for access to facilities necessary to provide these services. In this sector, interconnection to the public switched telecommunications network is a typical, but not the only, example of such access.

The Commission has stated that it will define the treatment of access agreements in the telecommunications sector under the competition rules.[2] This notice, therefore, addresses the issue of how competition rules and procedures apply to access agreements in the context of harmonised EC and national regulation in the telecommunications sector.

Notes

[1] According to Commission Directives 96/19/EC and 96/2/EC (cited in footnote 3), certain Member States may request a derogation from full liberalisation for certain limited periods. This notice is without prejudice to such derogations, and the Commission will take account of the existence of any such derogation when applying the competition rules to access agreements, as described in this notice.

See: Commission Decision 97/114/EC of 27 November 1996 concerning the additional implementation periods requested by Ireland for the implementation of Commission Directives 90/388/EEC and 96/2/EC as regards full competition in the telecommunications markets (OJ L 41, 12.2.1997, p. 8); Commission Decision 97/310/EC of 12 February 1997 concerning the granting of additional implementation periods to the Portuguese Republic for the implementation of Commission Directives 90/388/EEC and 96/2/EC as regards full competition in the telecommunications markets (OJ L 133, 24.5.1997, p. 19); Commission Decision 97/568/EC of 14 May 1997 on the granting of additional implementation periods to Luxembourg for the implementation of Directive 90/388/EEC as regards full competition in the telecommunications markets (OJ L 234, 26.8.1997, p. 7); Commission Decision 97/603/EC of 10 June 1997 concerning the granting of additional implementation periods to Spain for the implementation of Commission Directive 90/388/EEC as regards full competition in the telecommunications markets (OJ L 243, 5.9.1997, p. 48); Commission Decision 97/607/EC of 18 June 1997 concerning the granting of additional implementation periods to Greece for the implementation of Directive 90/388/EEC as regards full competition in the telecommunications markets (OJ L 245, 9.9.1997, p. 6).

[2] Communication by the Commission of 3 May 1995 to the European Parliament and the Council, Consultation on the Green Paper on the liberalisation of telecommunications infrastructure and cable television networks, COM(95) 158 final.

2. The regulatory framework for the liberalisation of telecommunications consists of the liberalisation directives issued under Article [86] of the Treaty and the harmonisation Directives under Article [95], including in particular the open network provision (ONP) framework. The ONP framework provides harmonised rules for access and interconnection to the telecommunications networks and the voice telephony services. The legal framework provided by the liberalisation and harmonisation legislation is the background to any action taken by the Commission in its application of the competition rules. Both the liberalisation legislation (the Article [86] Directives)[3] and the harmonisation legislation (the ONP Directives)[4] are aimed at ensuring the attainment of the objectives of the Community as laid out in Article 3 of the Treaty, and specifically, the establishment of "a system ensuring that competition in the internal market is not distorted" and "an internal market characterised by the abolition, as between Member States, of obstacles to the free movement of goods, persons, services and capital".

Notes

[3] Commission Directive 88/301/EEC of 16 May 1988, on competition in the markets in telecommunications terminal equipment (OJ L 131, 27.5.1988, p. 73); Commission Directive 90/388/EEC of 28 June 1990 on competition in the markets for telecommunications services (OJ L 192, 24.7.1990, p. 10) (the "Services Directive")[*]; Commission Directive 94/46/EC of 13 October 1994, amending Directive 88/301/EEC and Directive 90/388/EEC in particular with regard to satellite communications (OJ L 268, 19.10.1994, p. 15); Commission Directive 95/51/EC of 18 October 1995 amending Directive 90/388/EEC with regard to the abolition of the restrictions on the use of cable television networks for the provision of already liberalised telecommunications services (OJ L 256, 26.10.1995, p. 49) [*]; Commission Directive 96/2/EC of 16 January 1996 amending Directive 90/388/EEC with regard to mobile and personal communications (OJ L 20, 26.1.1996, p. 59) [*]; Commission Directive 96/19/EC of 13 March 1996 amending Directive 90/388/EEC with regard to the implementation of full competition in the telecommunications markets (OJ L 74, 22.3.1996, p. 13) (the "Full Competition Directive")[*].

[* Directive 90/388/EEC was repealed by Commission Directive 2002/77/EC of 16 September 2002 (OJ L 249, 17.9.2002).]

4 Interconnection agreements are the most significant form of access agreement in the telecommunications sector. A basic framework for interconnection agreements is set up by the rules on open network provision (ONP), and the application of competition rules must be seen against this background: Directive 97/13/EC of the European Parliament and of the Council of 10 April 1997 on a common framework for authorisations and individual licences in the field of telecommunications services (OJ L 117, 7.5.1997, p. 15) (the "Licensing Directive")[*]; Directive 97/33/EC of the European Parliament and of the Council of 30 June 1997 on interconnection in Telecommunications with regard to ensuring universal service and interoperability through application of the principles of open network

1141

Part E   Sectoral Regimes

provision (ONP) (OJ L 199, 26.7.1997, p. 32) (the "Interconnection Directive")[*]; Council Directive 90/387/EEC of 28 June 1990 on the establishment of the internal market for telecommunications services through the implementation of open network provision (OJ L 192, 24.7.1990, p. 1) (the "Framework Directive")[*]; Council Directive 92/44/EEC of 5 June 1992 on the application of open network provision to leased lines (OJ L 165, 19.6.1992, p. 27) (the "Leased Lines Directive")[*]; Directive 95/62/EEC of the European Parliament and of the Council of 13 December 1995 on the application of open network provision to voice telephony (OJ L 321, 30.12.1995, p. 6) replaced by Directive 98/10/EC of the European Parliament and of the Council of 26 February 1998 on the application of open network provision (ONP) to voice telephony and on universal service for telecommunications in a competitive environment (OJ L 101, 1.4.1998, p. 24) (the "Voice Telephony Directive")[*]; Directive 97/66/EC of the European Parliament and of the Council of 15 December 1997 concerning the processing of personal data and the protection of privacy in the telecommunications sector (OJ L 24, 30.1.1998, p. 1) (the "Data Protection Directive").[**]

[*These Directives were repealed by Directive 2002/21/EC of 7 March 2002 on a common regulatory framework for electronic communications networks and services (Framework Directive) (OJ L 108, 24.4.2002).]

[** Directive 97/66/EC was repealed by Directive 2002/58/EC of 12 July 2002 concerning the processing of personal data and the protection of privacy in the electronic communications sector (Directive on privacy and electronic communications) (OJ L 201, 31.7.2002).]

3. The Commission has published Guidelines on the application of EEC competition rules in the telecommunications sector.[5] The present notice is intended to build on those Guidelines, which do not deal explicitly with access issues.

Notes
[5] OJ C 233, 6.9.1991, p. 2.

4. In the telecommunications sector, liberalisation and harmonisation legislation permit and simplify the task of Community firms in embarking on new activities in new markets and consequently allow users to benefit from increased competition. These advantages must not be jeopardised by restrictive or abusive practices of undertakings: the Community's competition rules are therefore essential to ensure the completion of this development. New entrants must in the initial stages be guaranteed the right to have access to the networks of incumbent telecommunications operators (TOs). Several authorities, at the regional, national and Community levels, have a role in regulating this sector. If the competition process is to work well in the internal market, effective coordination between these institutions must be ensured.

5. Part I of the notice sets out the legal framework and details how the Commission intends to avoid unnecessary duplication of procedures while safeguarding the rights of undertakings and users under the competition rules. In this context, the Commission's efforts to encourage decentralised application of the competition rules by national courts and national authorities aim at achieving remedies at a national level, unless a significant Community interest is involved in a particular case. In the telecommunications sector, specific procedures in the ONP framework likewise aim at resolving access problems in the first place at a decentralised, national level, with a further possibility for conciliation at Community level in certain circumstances. Part II defines the Commission's approach to market definition in this sector. Part III details the principles that the Commission will follow in the application of the competition rules: it aims to help telecommunications market participants shape their access agreements by explaining the competition law requirements. The principles set out in this Notice apply not only to traditional fixed line telecommunications, but also to all telecommunications, including areas such as satellite communications and mobile communications.

6. The notice is based on the Commission's experience in several cases,[6] and certain studies into this area carried out on behalf of the Commission.[7] As this notice is based on the generally applicable competition rules, the principles set out in this Notice will, to extent that comparable problems arise, be equally applicable in other areas, such as access issues in digital communications sectors generally. Similarly, several of the principles contained in the Treaty will be of relevance to any company occupying a dominant position including those in fields other than telecommunications.

Notes

[6] In the telecommunications area, notably: Commission Decision 91/562/EEC of 18 October 1991, *Eirpage* (OJ L 306, 7.11.1991, p. 22); Commission Decisions 96/546/EC and 96/547/EC of 17 July 1996, *Atlas and Phoenix* (OJ L 239, 19.9.1996, p. 23 and p. 57); and Commission Decision 97/780/EC of 29 October 1997, *Unisource* (OJ L 318, 20.11.1997, p. 1). There are also a number of pending cases involving access issues.

[7] Competition aspects of interconnection agreements in the telecommunications sector, June 1995; Competition aspects of access by service providers to the resources of telecommunications operators, December 1995. See also Competition Aspects of Access Pricing, December 1995.

Commentary

point 6: F&N: 12.400

7. The present notice is based on issues which have arisen during the initial stages of transition from monopolies to competitive markets. Given the convergence of the telecommunications, broadcasting and information technology sectors,[8] and the increased competition on these markets, other issues will emerge. This may make it necessary to adapt the scope and principles set out in this notice to these new sectors.

Notes

[8] See the Commission's Green Paper of 3 December 1997 on the Convergence of the Telecommunications, Media and Information Technology sectors and the implications for Regulation — Towards an information society approach (COM(97) 623).

8. The principles set out in this document will apply to practices outside the Community to the extent that such practices have an effect on competition within the Community and affect trade between Member States. In applying the competition rules, the Commission is obliged to comply with the Community's obligations under the WTO telecommunications agreement.[9] The Commission also notes that there are continuing discussions with regard to the international accounting rates system in the context of the ITU. The present notice is without prejudice to the Commission's position in these discussions.

Notes

[9] See Council Decision 97/838/EC of 28 November 1997 concerning the conclusion on behalf of the European Community, as regards matters within its competence, of the results of the WTO negotiations on basic telecommunications services (OJ L 347, 18.12.1997, p. 45).

9. This notice does not in any way restrict the rights conferred on individuals or undertakings by Community law, and is without prejudice to any interpretation of the Community competition rules that may be given by the Court of Justice or the Court of First Instance of the European Communities. This notice does not purport to be a comprehensive analysis of all possible competition problems in this sector: other problems already exist and more are likely to arise in the future.

10. The Commission will consider whether the present notice should be amended or added to in the light of experience gained during the first period of a liberalised telecommunications environment.

Part i — Framework

1. Competition rules and sector specific regulation

11. Access problems in the broadest sense of the word can be dealt with at different levels and on the basis of a range of legislative provisions, of both national and Community origin. A service provider faced with an access problem such as a TO's unjustified refusal to supply (or on reasonable terms) a leased line needed by the applicant to provide services to its customers could therefore contemplate a number of routes to seek a remedy. Generally speaking, aggrieved parties will experience a number of benefits, at least in an initial stage, in seeking redress at a national level. At a national level, the applicant has two main choices, namely (1) specific national regulatory procedures now established in accordance with Community law and harmonised under Open Network Provision (see footnote 4), and (2) an action under national and/or Community law before a national court or national competition authority.[10]

12. Complaints made to the Commission under the competition rules in the place of or in addition to national courts, national competition authorities and/or to national regulatory authorities under ONP procedures will be dealt with according to the priority which they deserve in view of the urgency, novelty and transnational nature of the problem involved and taking into account the need to avoid duplicate proceedings (see points 23 *et seq.*).

13. The Commission recognises that national regulatory authorities (NRAs)[11] have different tasks, and operate in a different legal framework from the Commission when the latter is applying the competition rules. First, the NRAs operate under national law, albeit often implementing European law. Secondly, that law, based as it is on considerations of telecommunications policy, may have objectives different to, but consistent with, the objectives of Community competition policy. The Commission cooperates as far as possible with the NRAs, and NRAs also have to cooperate between themselves in particular when dealing with cross-border issues.[12] Under Community law, national authorities, including regulatory authorities and competition authorities, have a duty not to approve any practice or agreement contrary to Community competition law.

14. Community competition rules are not sufficient to remedy all of the various problems in the telecommunications sector. NRAs therefore have a significantly wider ambit and a significant and far-reaching role in the regulation of the sector. It should also be noted that as a matter of Community law, the NRAs must be independent.[13]

15. It is also important to note that the ONP Directives impose on TOs having significant market power certain obligations of transparency and non-discrimination that go beyond those that would normally be imposed under Article [82] of the Treaty. ONP Directives lay down obligations relating to transparency, obligations to supply and pricing practices. These obligations are enforced by the NRAs, which also have jurisdiction to take steps to ensure effective competition.[14]

16. In relation to Article [82], this notice is written, for convenience, in most respects as if there was one telecommunications operator occupying a dominant position. This will not necessarily be the case in all Member States: for example new telecommunications networks offering increasingly wide coverage will develop progressively. These alternative telecommunications networks may, or may ultimately, be large and extensive enough to be partly or even wholly substitutable for the existing national networks, and this should be kept in mind. The existence and the position on the market of competing operators will be relevant in determining whether sole or joint dominant positions exist: references to the existence of a dominant position in this notice should be read with this in mind.

17. Given the Commission's responsibility for the Community's competition policy, the Commission must serve the Community's general interest. The administrative resources at the Commission's disposal to perform its task are necessarily limited and cannot be used to deal with all the cases brought to its attention. The Commission is therefore obliged, in general, to take all organisational measures necessary for the performance of its task and, in particular, to establish priorities.[15]

Notes

15 Judgments of the Court of First Instance of the European Communities: Case T-24/90, Automec v Commission [1992] ECR II-2223, at paragraph 77 and Case T-114/92 BEMIM [1995] ECR II-147.

18. The Commission has therefore indicated that it intends, in using its decision-making powers, to concentrate on notifications, complaints and own-initiative proceedings having particular political, economic or legal significance for the Community.[16] Where these features are absent in a particular case, notifications will not normally be dealt with by means of a formal decision, but rather a comfort letter (subject to the consent of the parties), and complaints should, as a rule, be handled by national courts or other relevant authorities. In this context, it should be noted that the competition rules are directly effective[17] so that Community competition law is enforceable in the national courts. Even where other Community legislation has been respected, this does not remove the need to comply with the Community competition rules.[18]

Notes

[16] Notice on cooperation between national courts and the Commission in applying Articles [81] and [82] of the EC Treaty (OJ C 39, 13.2.1993, p. 6, at paragraph 14). [See now Commission Notice on the co-operation between the Commission and the courts of the EU Member States in the application of Articles 81 and 82 EC (OJ C 101, 27.4.2004, p. 54.]
Notice on cooperation between national competition authorities and the Commission (OJ C 313, 15.10.1997, p. 3). [See now Commission Notice on cooperation within the Network of Competition Authorities (OJ C 101, 27.4.2004, p. 43.]
[17] Case 127/73, *BRT v SABAM* [1974] ECR 51.
[18] Case 66/86, *Ahmed Saeed* [1989] ECR 838.

19. Other national authorities, in particular NRAs acting within the ONP framework, have jurisdiction over certain access agreements (which must be notified to them). However, notification of an agreement to an NRA does not make notification of an agreement to the Commission unnecessary. The NRAs must ensure that actions taken by them are consistent with Community competition law.[19] This duty requires them to refrain from action that would undermine the effective protection of Community law rights under the competition rules.[20] Therefore, they may not approve arrangements which are contrary to the competition rules.[21] If the national authorities act so as to undermine those rights, the Member State may itself be liable for damages to those harmed by this action.[22] In addition, NRAs have jurisdiction under the ONP directives to take steps to ensure effective competition.[23]

Notes

[19] They must not, for example, encourage or reinforce or approve the results of anti-competitive behaviour:
— *Ahmed Saeed*, see footnote 18;
— Case 153/93, *Federal Republic of Germany v Delta Schiffahrtsges* [1994] ECR I-2517,
— Case 267/86, *Van Eycke* [1988] ECR 4769.

[20] Case 13/77, GB-Inno-BM/ATAB [1977] ECR 2115, at paragraph 33:
"while it is true that Article [82] is directed at undertakings, nonetheless it is also true that the Treaty imposes a duty on Member States not to adopt or maintain in force any measure which could deprive the provision of its effectiveness."

[21] For further duties of national authorities see: Case 103/88, Fratelli Costanzo [1989] ECR 1839. See Ahmed Saeed, cited in footnote 18:
"Articles [10] and [86] of the [EC] Treaty must be interpreted as (i) prohibiting the national authorities from encouraging the conclusion of agreements on tariffs contrary to Article [81](1) or Article [82] of the Treaty, as the case may be; (ii) precluding the approval by those authorities of tariffs resulting from such agreements".

[22] Joined Cases C-6/90, and C-9/90 *Francovich* [1991] ECR I-5357; Joined Cases C-46/93, *Brasserie de Pêcheur v Germany* and Case C-48/93, *R v Secretary of State for Transport ex parte Factortame and others* [1996] ECR I-1029.

[23] For example, recital 18 of the Leased Lines Directive and Article 9(3) of the ONP Interconnection Directive, see footnote 4.

Commentary
point 19: F&N: 13.35

20. Access agreements in principle regulate the provision of certain services between independent undertakings and do not result in the creation of an autonomous entity which would be distinct from the parties to the agreements. Access agreements are thus generally outside the scope of the Merger Regulation.[24]

Notes

[24] Council Regulation (EEC) No 4064/89 of 21 December 1989 on the control of concentrations between undertakings (OJ L 395, 30.12.1989, p. 1); corrected version (OJ L 257, 21.9.1990, p. 13). (See now Council Regulation (EC) No 139/2004 (OJ L 24, 29.1.2004, p.1).]

21. Under Regulation No 17,[25] the Commission could be seised of an issue relating to access agreements by way of a notification of an access agreement by one or more of the parties involved,[26] by way of a complaint against a restrictive access agreement or against the behaviour of a dominant company in granting or refusing access,[27] by way of a Commission own-initiative procedure into such a grant or refusal, or by way of a sector inquiry.[28] In addition, a complainant may request that the Commission take interim measures in circumstances where there is an urgent risk of serious and irreparable harm to the complainant or to the public interest.[29] It should however, be noted in cases of great urgency that procedures before national courts can usually result more quickly in an order to end the infringements than procedures before the Commission.[30]

Notes

[25] Council Regulation No 17 of 6 February 1962, First Regulation implementing Articles [81] and [82] of the Treaty (OJ 13, 21.2.1962, p. 204). [See now Council Regulation (EC) No 1/2003 (OJ L 1, 4.1.2003, p.1).]

[26] Articles 2 and 4(1) of Regulation No 17.

[27] Article 3 of Regulation No 17.

[28] Articles 3 and 12 of Regulation No 17.

[29] Case 792/79R, *Camera Care v Commission* [1980] ECR 119. See also Case T-44/90, *La Cinq v Commission* [1992] ECR II-1.

[30] See point 16 of the Notice cited in footnote 16.

22. There are a number of areas where agreements will be subject to both the competition rules and national or European sector specific measures, most notably Internal Market measures. In the telecommunications sector, the ONP Directives aim at establishing a regulatory regime for access agreements. Given the detailed nature of ONP rules and the fact that they may go beyond the requirements of Article [82], undertakings operating in the telecommunications sector should be aware that compliance with the Community competition rules does not absolve them of their duty to abide by obligations imposed in the ONP context, and vice versa.

2. Commission action in relation to access agreements[31]

Notes
[31] Article 2 or Article 4(1) of Regulation No 17.

23. Access agreements taken as a whole are of great significance, and it is therefore appropriate for the Commission to spell out as clearly as possible the Community legal framework within which these agreements should be concluded. Access agreements having restrictive clauses will involve issues under Article [81]. Agreements which involve dominant, or monopolist, undertakings involve Article [82] issues: concerns arising from the dominance of one or more of the parties will generally be of greater significance in the context of a particular agreement than those under Article [81].
Notifications

24. In applying the competition rules, the Commission will build on the ONP Directives which set a framework for action at the national level by the NRAs. Where agreements fall within Article [81](1), they must be notified to the Commission if they are to benefit from an exemption under Article [81](3). Where agreements are notified, the Commission intends to deal with some notifications by way of formal decisions, following appropriate publicity in the Official Journal of the European Communities, and in accordance with the principles set out below. Once the legal principles have been clearly established, the Commission then proposes to deal by way of comfort letter with other notifications raising the same issues.

3. Complaints

25. Natural or legal persons with a legitimate interest may, under certain circumstances, submit a complaint to the Commission, requesting that the Commission by decision require that an infringement of Article [81] or Article [82] of the Treaty be brought to an end. A complainant may additionally request that the Commission take interim measures where there is an urgent risk of serious and irreparable harm.[32] A prospective complainant has other equally or even more effective options, such as an action before a national court. In this context, it should be noted that procedures before the national courts can offer considerable advantages for individuals and companies, such as in particular:[33]
    — national courts can deal with and award a claim for damages resulting from an infringement of the competition rules,
    — national courts can usually adopt interim measures and order the termination of an infringement more quickly than the Commission is able to do,
    — before national courts, it is possible to combine a claim under Community law with a claim under national law,
    — legal costs can be awarded to the successful applicant before a national court.
    Furthermore, the specific national regulatory principles as harmonised under ONP Directives can offer recourse both at the national level and, if necessary, at the Community level.

Notes
[32] *Camera Care* and *La Cinq*, referred to at footnote 29.
[33] See point 16 of the Notice cited in footnote 16.

Commentary
point 25: F&N: 13.44

3.1. Use of national and ONP procedures

26. As referred to above[34] the Commission will take into account the Community interest of each case brought to its attention. In evaluating the Community interest, the Commission examines ". . . the significance of the alleged infringement as regards the functioning of the common market, the probability of establishing the existence of the infringement and the scope of the investigation required in order to fulfil, under the best possible conditions, its task of ensuring that Articles [81] and [82] are complied with . . .".[35]

Another essential element in this evaluation is the extent to which a national judge is in a position to provide an effective remedy for an infringement of Article [81] or [82]. This may prove difficult, for example, in cases involving extra-territorial elements.

Notes
[34] See point 18.
[35] See *Automec*, cited in footnote 15, at paragraph 86.

27. Article [81](1) and Article [82] of the Treaty produce direct effects in relations between individuals which must be safeguarded by national courts.[36] As regards actions before the NRA, the ONP Interconnection Directive provides that such an authority has power to intervene and order changes in relation to both the existence and content of access agreements. NRAs must take into account "the need to stimulate a competitive market" and may impose conditions on one or more parties, inter alia, "to ensure effective competition".[37]

Notes
[36] *BRT v SABAM*, cited in footnote 17.
[37] Article 9(1) and (3) of the ONP Interconnection Directive[*]. [* See note 4 above.]

Commentary
point 27: F&N: 13.44

28. The Commission may itself be seised of a dispute either pursuant to the competition rules, or pursuant to an ONP conciliation procedure. Multiple proceedings might lead to unnecessary duplication of investigative efforts by the Commission and the national authorities. Where complaints are lodged with the Commission under Article 3 of Regulation No 17 while there are related actions before a relevant national or European authority or court, the Directorate-General for Competition will generally not initially pursue any investigation as to the existence of an infringement under Article [81] or [82] of the Treaty. This is subject, however, to the following points.

Commentary
point 28: F&N: 13.46

3.2. Safeguarding complainant's rights

29. Undertakings are entitled to effective protection of their Community law rights.[38] Those rights would be undermined if national proceedings were allowed to lead to an excessive delay of the Commission's action, without a satisfactory resolution of the matter at a national level. In the telecommunications sector, innovation cycles are relatively short, and any substantial delay in resolving an access dispute might in practice be equivalent to a refusal of access, thus prejudging the proper determination of the case.

Notes
[38] Case 14/83, *Von Colson* [1984] ECR 1891.

30. The Commission therefore takes the view that an access dispute before an NRA should be resolved within a reasonable period of time, normally speaking not extending beyond six months of the matter first being drawn to the attention of that authority. This resolution could take the form of either a final determination of the action or another form of relief which would safeguard the rights of the complainant. If the matter has not reached such a resolution then, *prima facie*, the rights of the parties are not being effectively protected, and the Commission would in principle, upon request by the complainant, begin its investigations into the case in accordance with its normal procedures, after consultation and in cooperation with the national authority in question. In general, the Commission will not begin such investigations where there is already an ongoing action under ONP conciliation procedures.

Commentary
point 30: F&N: 13.50

31. In addition, the Commission must always look at each case on its merits: it will take action if it feels that in a particular case, there is a substantial Community interest affecting, or likely to affect, competition in a number of Member States.

Commentary
point 31: F&N: 13.52

3.3. Interim measures

32. As regards any request for interim measures, the existence or possibility of national proceedings is relevant to the question of whether there is a risk of serious and irreparable harm. Such proceedings should, *prima facie*, remove the risk of such harm and it would therefore not be appropriate for the Commission to grant interim measures in the absence of evidence that the risk would nevertheless remain.

33. The availability of and criteria for interim injunctive relief is an important factor which the Commission must take into account in reaching this *prima facie* conclusion. If interim injunctive relief were not available, or if such relief was not likely adequately to protect the complainant's rights under Community law, the Commission would consider that the national proceedings did not remove the risk of harm, and could therefore commence its examination of the case.

4. *Own-initiative investigation and sector inquiries*

34. If it appears necessary, the Commission will open an own-initiative investigation. It can also launch a sector inquiry, subject to consultation of the Advisory Committee of Member State competition authorities.

5. *Fines[*]*

35. The Commission may impose fines of up to 10% of the annual worldwide turnover of undertakings which intentionally or negligently breach Article [81](1) or Article [82].[39] Where agreements have been notified pursuant to Regulation No 17 for an exemption under Article [81](3), no fine may be levied by the Commission in respect of activities described in the notification[40] for the period following notification. However, the Commission may withdraw the immunity from fines by informing the undertakings concerned that, after preliminary examination, it is of the opinion that Article [81](1) of the Treaty applies and that application of Article [81](3) is not justified.[41]

Notes
[39] Article 15(2) of Regulation No 17.
[40] Article 15(5) of Regulation No 17.
[41] Article 15(6) of Regulation No 17.
[* See now Council Regulation (EC) No 1/2003 (OJ L 1, 4.1.2003, p. 1), Article 23.]

36. The ONP Interconnection Directive has two particular provisions which are relevant to fines under the competition rules. First, it provides that interconnection agreements must be communicated to the relevant NRAs and made available to interested third parties, with the exception of those parts which deal with the commercial strategy of the parties.[42] Secondly, it provides that the NRA must have a number of powers which it can use to influence or amend the interconnection agreements.[43] These provisions ensure that appropriate publicity is given to the agreements, and provide the NRA with the opportunity to take steps, where appropriate, to ensure effective competition on the market.

Notes
[42] Article 6(c) of the ONP Interconnection Directive[*].
[43] Inter alia, at Article 9 of the ONP Interconnection Directive[*].
   [* See note 4 above.]

37. Where an agreement has been notified to an NRA, but has not been notified to the Commission, the Commission does not consider it would be generally appropriate as a matter of policy to impose a fine in respect of the agreement, even if the agreement ultimately proves to contain

conditions in breach of Article [81]. A fine would, however, be appropriate in some cases, for example where:

(a) the agreement proves to contain provisions in breach of Article [82]; and/or

(b) the breach of Article [81] is particularly serious.

The Commission has recently published Guidelines on how fines will be calculated.[44]

Notes

[44] Guidelines on the method of setting fines imposed pursuant to Article 15(2) of Regulation No 17 and Article 65(5) of the ECSC Treaty (OJ C 9, 14.1.1998, p. 3). [See now Guidelines on the method of setting fines imposed pursuant to Article 23(2)(a) of Regulation No 1/2003 (OJ C 210, 1.9.2006, p. 2).]

38. Notification to the NRA is not a substitute for a notification to the Commission and does not limit the possibility for interested parties to submit a complaint to the Commission, or for the Commission to begin an own-initiative investigation into access agreements. Nor does such notification limit the rights of a party to seek damages before a national court for harm caused by anti-competitive agreements.[45]

Notes

[45] See footnote 22.

PART II — RELEVANT MARKETS

39. In the course of investigating cases within the framework set out in Part I above, the Commission will base itself on the approach to the definition of relevant markets set out in the Commission's Notice on the definition of the relevant market for the purposes of Community competition law.[46]

Notes

[46] OJ C 372, 9.12.1997, p. 5.

40. Firms are subject to three main sources of competitive constraints; demand substitutability, supply substitutability and potential competition, with the first constituting the most immediate and effective disciplinary force on the suppliers of a given product or service. Demand substitutability is therefore the main tool used to define the relevant product market on which restrictions of competition for the purposes of Article [81](1) and Article [82] can be identified.

41. Supply substitutability may in appropriate circumstances be used as a complementary element to define relevant markets. In practice it cannot be clearly distinguished from potential competition. Supply side substitutability and potential competition are used for the purpose of determining whether the undertaking has a dominant position or whether the restriction of competition is significant within the meaning of Article [81], or whether there is elimination of competition.

42. In assessing relevant markets it is necessary to look at developments in the market in the short term.

The following sections set out some basic principles of particular relevance to the telecommunications sector.

1. Relevant product market

43. Section 6 of Form A/B defines the relevant product market as follows:

"A relevant product market comprises all those products and/or services which are regarded as interchangeable or substitutable by the consumer, by reason of the products" characteristics, their prices and their intended use".

44. Liberalisation of the telecommunications sector will lead to the emergence of a second type of market, that of access to facilities which are currently necessary to provide these liberalised services. Interconnection to the public switched telecommunications network would be a typical example of such access. Without interconnection, it will not be commercially possible for third parties to provide, for example, comprehensive voice telephony services.

45. It is clear, therefore, that in the telecommunications sector there are at least two types of relevant markets to consider — that of a service to be provided to end users and that of access to those

facilities necessary to provide that service to end users (information, physical network, etc.). In the context of any particular case, it will be necessary to define the relevant access and services markets, such as interconnection to the public telecommunications network, and provision of public voice telephony services, respectively.

46. When appropriate, the Commission will use the test of a relevant market which is made by asking whether, if all the suppliers of the services in question raised their prices by 5 to 10%, their collective profits would rise. According to this test, if their profits would rise, the market considered is a separate relevant market.

47. The Commission considers that the principles under competition law governing these markets remain the same regardless of the particular market in question. Given the pace of technological change in this sector, any attempt to define particular product markets in this notice would run the risk of rapidly becoming inaccurate or irrelevant. The definition of particular product markets — for example, the determination of whether call origination and call termination facilities are part of the same facilities market — is best done in the light of a detailed examination of an individual case.

1.1. Services market

48. This can be broadly defined as the provision of any telecommunications service to users. Different telecommunications services will be considered substitutable if they show a sufficient degree of interchangeability for the end-user, which would mean that effective competition can take place between the different providers of these services.

1.2. Access to facilities

49. For a service provider to provide services to end-users it will often require access to one or more (upstream or downstream) facilities. For example, to deliver physically the service to end-users, it needs access to the termination points of the telecommunications network to which these end-users are connected. This access can be achieved at the physical level through dedicated or shared local infrastructure, either self provided or leased from a local infrastructure provider. It can also be achieved either through a service provider who already has these end-users as subscribers, or through an interconnection provider who has access directly or indirectly to the relevant termination points.

Commentary
point 49: F&N: 13.215

---

50. In addition to physical access, a service provider may need access to other facilities to enable it to market its service to end users: for example, a service provider must be able to make end-users aware of its services. Where one organisation has a dominant position in the supply of services such as directory information, similar concerns arise as with physical access issues.

51. In many cases, the Commission will be concerned with physical access issues, where what is necessary is access to the network facilities of the dominant TO.[47]

Notes

[47] Interconnection is defined in the Full Competition Directive as ". . . the physical and logical linking of the telecommunications facilities of organisations providing telecommunications networks and/or telecommunications services, in order to allow the users of one organisation to communicate with the users of the same or another organisation or to access services provided by third organisations."

In the Full Competition Directive and ONP Directives, telecommunications services are defined as "services, whose provision consists wholly or partly in the transmission and/or routing of signals on a telecommunications network." It therefore includes the transmission of broadcasting signals and CATV networks."

A telecommunications network is itself defined as ". . . the transmission equipment and, where applicable, switching equipment and other resources which permit the conveyance of signals between defined termination points by wire, by radio, by optical or by other electromagnetic means".

52. Some incumbent TOs may be tempted to resist providing access to third party service providers or other network operators, particularly in areas where the proposed service will be in competition with a service provided by the TO itself. This resistance will often manifest itself as unjustified delay in giving access, a reluctance to allow access or a willingness to allow it only under disadvantageous conditions. It is the role of the competition rules to ensure that these prospective access markets are allowed to develop, and that incumbent TOs are not permitted to use their control over access to stifle developments on the services markets.

53. It should be stressed that in the telecommunications sector, liberalisation can be expected to lead to the development of new, alternative networks which will ultimately have an impact on access market definition involving the incumbent telecommunications operator.

2. *Relevant geographic market*

54. Relevant geographic markets are defined in Form A/B as follows:

"The relevant geographic market comprises the area in which the undertakings concerned are involved in the supply and demand of products or services, in which the conditions of competition are sufficiently homogeneous and which can be distinguished from neighbouring areas because the conditions of competition are appreciably different in those areas."

55. As regards the provision of telecommunication services and access markets, the relevant geographic market will be the area in which the objective conditions of competition applying to service providers are similar, and competitors are able to offer their services. It will therefore be necessary to examine the possibility for these service providers to access an end-user in any part of this area, under similar and economically viable conditions. Regulatory conditions such as the terms of licences, and any exclusive or special rights owned by competing local access providers are particularly relevant.[48]

Notes
[48] Commission Decision 94/894/EC of 13 December 1994, *Eurotunnel* (OJ L 354, 21.12.1994, p. 66).

PART III — PRINCIPLES

56. The Commission will apply the following principles in cases before it.

57. The Commission has recognised that "Articles [81] and [82] . . . constitute law in force and enforceable throughout the Community. Conflicts should not arise with other Community rules because Community law forms a coherent regulatory framework . . . it is obvious that Community acts adopted in the telecommunications sector are to be interpreted in a way consistent with competition rules, so as to ensure the best possible implementation of all aspects of the Community telecommunications policy . . . This applies, inter alia, to the relationship between competition rules applicable to undertakings and the ONP rules".[49]

Notes
[49] See Guidelines cited in footnote 5, at paragraphs 15 and 16.

58. Thus, competition rules continue to apply in circumstances where other Treaty provisions or secondary legislation are applicable. In the context of access agreements, the internal market and competition provisions of Community law are both important and mutually reinforcing for the proper functioning of the sector. Therefore in making an assessment under the competition rules, the Commission will seek to build as far as possible on the principles established in the harmonisation legislation. It should also be borne in mind that a number of the competition law principles set out below are also covered by specific rules in the context of the ONP framework. Proper application of these rules should often avoid the need for the application of the competition rules.

Commentary
point 58: F&N: 13.28

59. As regards the telecommunications sector, attention should be paid to the cost of universal service obligations. Article [86](2) of the Treaty may justify exceptions to the principles of Articles [81] and [82]. The details of universal service obligations are a regulatory matter. The field of application of Article [86](2) has been specified in the Article [86] Directives in the telecommunications sector, and the Commission will apply the competition rules in this context.

60. Articles [81] and [82] of the Treaty apply in the normal manner to agreements or practices which have been approved or authorised by a national authority,[50] or where the national authority has required the inclusion of terms in an agreement at the request of one or more of the parties involved.

Notes

[50] Commission Decision 82/896/EEC of 15 December 1982, *AROW/BNIC* (OJ L 379, 31.12.1982, p. 19).

61. However, if a NRA were to require terms which were contrary to the competition rules, the undertakings involved would in practice not be fined, although the Member State itself would be in breach of Article 3(g) and Article [10] of the Treaty[51] and therefore subject to challenge by the Commission under Article [226]. Additionally, if an undertaking having special or exclusive rights within the meaning of Article [86], or a State-owned undertaking, were required or authorised by a national regulator to engage in behaviour constituting an abuse of its dominant position, the Member State would also be in breach of Article [86](1) and the Commission could adopt a decision requiring termination of the infringement.[52]

Notes

[51] See footnote 18.

[52] Joined Cases C-48 and 66/90 *Netherlands and others v Commission* [1992] ECR I-565.

62. NRAs may require strict standards of transparency, obligations to supply and pricing practices on the market, particularly where this is necessary in the early stages of liberalisation. When appropriate, legislation such as the ONP framework will be used as an aid in the interpretation of the competition rules.[53] Given the duty resting on NRAs to ensure that effective competition is possible, application of the competition rules is likewise required for an appropriate interpretation of the ONP principles. It should also be noted that many of the issues set out below are also covered by rules under the Full Competition Directive and the ONP Licensing and Data protection Directives: effective enforcement of this regulatory framework should prevent many of the competition issues set out below from arising.

Notes

[53] See *Ahmed Saeed*, cited in footnote 18, where internal market legislation relating to pricing was used as an aid in determining what level of prices should be regarded as unfair for the purposes of Article [82].

1. Dominance (Article [82])

63. In order for an undertaking to provide services in the telecommunications services market, it may need to obtain access to various facilities. For the provision of telecommunications services, for example, interconnection to the public switched telecommunications network will usually be necessary. Access to this network will almost always be in the hands of a dominant TO. As regards access agreements, dominance stemming from control of facilities will be the most relevant to the Commission's appraisal.

64. Whether or not a company is dominant does not depend only on the legal rights granted to that company. The mere ending of legal monopolies does not put an end to dominance. Indeed, notwithstanding the liberalisation Directives, the development of effective competition from alternative network providers with adequate capacity and geographic reach will take time.

65. The judgment of the Court of Justice in *Tetra Pak*[54] is also likely to prove important in the telecommunications sector. The Court held that given the extremely close links between the dominated and non-dominated market, and given the extremely high market share on the dominated market, Tetra Pak was "in a situation comparable to that of holding a dominant position on the markets in question as a whole."

The *Tetra Pak* case concerned closely related horizontal markets: the analysis is equally applicable, however, to closely related vertical markets which will be common in the telecommunications sector. In the telecommunications sector, it is often the case that a particular operator has an extremely strong position on infrastructure markets, and on markets downstream of that infrastructure. Infrastructure costs also typically constitute the single largest cost of the downstream operations. Further, operators will often face the same competitors on both the infrastructure and downstream markets.

Notes

[54] On each market, Tetra Pak was faced with the same potential customers and actual competitors. Case C-333/94 P, *Tetra Pak International SA v Commission* [1996] ECR I-5951.

66. It is therefore possible to envisage a number of situations where there will be closely related markets, together with an operator having a very high degree of market power on at least one of those markets.
67. It these circumstances are present, it may be appropriate for the Commission to find that the particular operator was in a situation comparable to that of holding a dominant position on the markets in question as a whole.
68. In the telecommunications sector, the concept of "essential facilities" will in many cases be of relevance in determining the duties of dominant TOs. The expression essential facility is used to describe a facility or infrastructure which is essential for reaching customers and/or enabling competitors to carry on their business, and which cannot be replicated by any reasonable means.[55]

Notes

55 See also the definition included in the "Additional commitment on regulatory principles by the European Communities and their Member States" used by the Group on basic telecommunications in the context of the World Trade Organisation (WTO) negotiations:
  "Essential facilities mean facilities of a public telecommunications transport network and service that:
  (a) are exclusively or predominantly provided by a single or limited number of suppliers; and
  (b) cannot feasibly be economically or technically substituted in order to provide a service."

Commentary
point 68: F&N: 4.193

69. A company controlling the access to an essential facility enjoys a dominant position within the meaning of Article [82]. Conversely, a company may enjoy a dominant position pursuant to Article [82] without controlling an essential facility.

1.1. Services market

70. One of the factors used to measure the market power of an undertaking is the sales attributable to that undertaking, expressed as a percentage of total sales in the market for substitutable services in the relevant geographic area. As regards the services market, the Commission will assess, inter alia, the turnover generated by the sale of substitutable services, excluding the sale or internal usage of interconnection services and the sale or internal usage of local infrastructure,[56] taking into consideration the competitive conditions and the structure of supply and demand on the market.

Notes
56 Case 6/72 *Continental Can* [1973] ECR 215.

1.2. Access to facilities

71. The concept of "access" as referred to in point 45 can relate to a range of situations, including the availability of leased lines enabling a service provider to build up its own network, and interconnection in the strict sense, that is interconnecting two telecommunication networks, for example mobile and fixed. In relation to access it is probable that the incumbent operator will remain dominant for some time after the legal liberalisation has taken place. The incumbent operator, which controls the facilities, is often also the largest service provider, and it has in the past not needed to distinguish between the conveyance of telecommunications services and the provision of these services to end-users. Traditionally, an operator who is also a service provider

has not required its downstream operating arm to pay for access, and therefore it has not been easy to calculate the revenue to be allocated to the facility. In a case where an operator is providing both access and services it is necessary to separate so far as possible the revenues as the basis for the calculation of the company's share of whichever market is involved. Article 8(2) of the Interconnection Directive addresses this issue by introducing a requirement for separate accounting for "activities related to interconnection — covering both interconnection services provided internally and interconnection services provided to others — and other activities". The proposed Commission Recommendation on Accounting Separation in the context of Interconnection will also be helpful in this regard.

72. The economic significance of obtaining access also depends on the coverage of the network with which interconnection is sought. Therefore, in addition to using turnover figures, the Commission will, where possible, also take into account the number of customers who have subscribed to services offered by the dominant company comparable with those which the service provider requesting access intends to provide. Accordingly, market power for a given undertaking will be measured partly by the number of subscribers who are connected to termination points of the telecommunications network of that undertaking expressed as a percentage of the total number of subscribers connected to termination points in the relevant geographic area.

Supply-side substitutability

73. As stated in point 41, supply-side substitutability is also relevant to the question of dominance. A market share of over 50%[57] is usually sufficient to demonstrate dominance although other factors will be examined. For example, the Commission will examine the existence of other network providers, if any, in the relevant geographic area to determine whether such alternative infrastructures are sufficiently dense to provide competition to the incumbent's network and the extent to which it would be possible for new access providers to enter the market.

Notes

57 It should be noted in this context that under the ONP framework an organisation may be notified as having significant market power. The determination of whether an organisation does or does not have significant market power depends on a number of factors, but the starting presumption is that an organisation with a market share of more than 25% will normally be considered to have significant market power. The Commission will take account of whether an undertaking has been notified as having significant market power under the ONP rules in its appraisal under the competition rules. It is clear, however, that the notion of significant market power generally describes a position of economic power on a market less than that of dominance: the fact that an undertaking has significant market power under the ONP rules will generally therefore not lead to a presumption of dominance, although in a particular situation, this may prove to be the case. One important factor to be taken into consideration, however, will be whether the market definition used in the ONP procedures is appropriate for use in applying the competition rules.

Other relevant factors

74. In addition to market share data, and supply-side substitutability, in determining whether an operator is dominant the Commission will also examine whether the operator has privileged access to facilities which cannot reasonably be duplicated within an appropriate time frame, either for legal reasons or because it would cost too much.

75. As competing access providers appear and challenge the dominance of the incumbent, the scope of the rights they receive from Member States' authorities, and notably their territorial reach, will play an important part in the determination of market power. The Commission will closely follow market evolution in relation to these issues and will take account of any altered market conditions in its assessment of access issues under the competition rules.

1.3. Joint dominance

76. The wording of Article [82] makes it clear that the Article also applies when more than one company shares a dominant position. The circumstances in which a joint dominant position exists, and in which it is abused, have not yet been fully clarified by the case law of the Community judicature or the practice of the Commission, and the law is still developing.

77. The words of Article [82] ("abuse by one or more undertakings") describe something different from the prohibition of anti-competitive agreements or concerted practices in Article [81].

To hold otherwise would be contrary to the usual principles of interpretation of the Treaty, and would render the words pointless and without practical effect. This does not, however, exclude the parallel application of Articles [81] and [82] to the same agreement or practice, which has been upheld by the Commission and the Court in a number of cases,[58] nor is there anything to prevent the Commission from taking action only under one of the provisions, when both apply.

Notes
[58] Case 85/76 *Hoffmann-La Roche* [1979] ECR 461. Commission Decision 89/113/EEC of 21 December 1988, Decca Navigator System (OJ L 43, 15.2.1989, p. 27).

78. Two companies, each dominant in a separate national market, are not the same as two jointly dominant companies. For two or more companies to be in a joint dominant position, they must together have substantially the same position vis-à-vis their customers and competitors as a single company has if it is in a dominant position. With specific reference to the telecommunications sector, joint dominance could be attained by two telecommunications infrastructure operators covering the same geographic market.

Commentary
point 78: F&N: 4.112

79. In addition, for two or more companies to be jointly dominant it is necessary, though not sufficient, for there to be no effective competition between the companies on the relevant market. This lack of competition may in practice be due to the fact that the companies have links such as agreements for cooperation, or interconnection agreements. The Commission does not, however, consider that either economic theory or Community law implies that such links are legally necessary for a joint dominant position to exist.[59] It is a sufficient economic link if there is the kind of interdependence which often comes about in oligopolistic situations. There does not seem to be any reason in law or in economic theory to require any other economic link between jointly dominant companies. This having been said, in practice such links will often exist in the telecommunications sector where national TOs nearly inevitably have links of various kinds with one another.

Notes
[59] Commission Decision 92/553/EEC of 22 July 1992, Nestlé/Perrier (OJ L 356, 5.12.1992, p. 1).

Commentary
point 79: B&C: 10.053   F&N: 4.110, 4.112, 13.190

80. To take as an example access to the local loop, in some Member States this could well be controlled in the near future by two operators — the incumbent TO and a cable operator. In order to provide particular services to consumers, access to the local loop of either the TO or the cable television operator is necessary. Depending on the circumstances of the case and in particular on the relationship between them, it is possible that neither operator holds a dominant position: together, however, they may hold a joint monopoly of access to these facilities. In the longer term, technological developments may lead to other local loop access mechanisms being viable, such as energy networks: the existence of such mechanisms will be taken into account in determining whether dominant positions or joint dominant positions exist.

2. Abuse of dominance

81. Application of Article [82] presupposes the existence of a dominant position and some link between the dominant position and the alleged abusive conduct. It will often be necessary in the telecommunications sector to examine a number of associated markets, one or more of which may be dominated by a particular operator. In these circumstances, there are a number of possible situations where abuses could arise:
   — conduct on the dominated market having effects on the dominated market,[60]
   — conduct on the dominated market having effects on markets other than the dominated market,[61]
   — conduct on a market other than the dominated market and having effects on the dominated market,[62]

— conduct on a market other than the dominated market and having effects on a market other than the dominated market.[63]

Notes

[60] The most common situation.

[61] Joined Cases 6/73 and 7/73 *Commercial Solvents v Commission* [1974] ECR 223 and Case 311/84 *CBEM v CLT and IPB* [1985] ECR 3261.

[62] Case C-62/86, *AKZO v Commission* [1991] ECR I-3359 and Case T-65/89 *BPB Industries and British Gypsum v Commission* [1993] ECR II-389.

[63] Case C-333/94 P, *Tetra Pak International v Commission* [1996] ECR I-5951. In this fourth case, application of Article [82] can only be justified by special circumstances (*Tetra Pak*, at paragraphs 29 and 30).

82. Although the factual and economic circumstances of the telecommunications sector are often novel, in many cases it is possible to apply established competition law principles. When looking at competition problems in this sector, it is important to bear in mind existing case law and Commission decisional practice on, for example, leveraging market power, discrimination and bundling.

2.1. Refusal to grant access to facilities and application of unfavourable terms

83. A refusal to give access may be prohibited under Article [82] if the refusal is made by a company which is dominant because of its control of facilities, as incumbent TOs will usually be for the foreseeable future. A refusal may have "the effect of hindering the maintenance of the degree of competition still existing in the market or the growth of that competition".[64]

A refusal will only be abusive if it has exploitative or anti-competitive effects. Service markets in the telecommunications sector will initially have few competitive players and refusals will therefore generally affect competition on those markets. In all cases of refusal, any justification will be closely examined to determine whether it is objective.

Notes

[64] Case 85/76, *Hoffmann-La Roche* [1979] ECR 461.

Commentary
point 83: B&C: 12.153

84. Broadly there are three relevant scenarios:
   (a) a refusal to grant access for the purposes of a service where another operator has been given access by the access provider to operate on that services market;
   (b) a refusal to grant access for the purposes of a service where no other operator has been given access by the access provider to operate on that services market;
   (c) a withdrawal of access from an existing customer.

Commentary
point 84: F&N: 13.249

Discrimination

85. As to the first of the above scenarios, it is clear that a refusal to supply a new customer in circumstances where a dominant facilities owner is already supplying one or more customers operating in the same downstream market would constitute discriminatory treatment which, if it would restrict competition on that downstream market, would be an abuse. Where network operators offer the same, or similar, retail services as the party requesting access, they may have both the incentive and the opportunity to restrict competition and abuse their dominant position in this way. There may, of course, be justifications for such refusal — for example, vis-à-vis applicants which represent a potential credit risk. In the absence of any objective justifications, a refusal would usually be an abuse of the dominant position on the access market.

86. In general terms, the dominant company's duty is to provide access in such a way that the goods and services offered to downstream companies are available on terms no less favourable than those given to other parties, including its own corresponding downstream operations.

Commentary
point 86: F&N: 13.262

Essential facilities

87. As to the second of the above situations, the question arises as to whether the access provider should be obliged to contract with the service provider in order to allow the service provider to operate on a new service market. Where capacity constraints are not an issue and where the company refusing to provide access to its facility has not provided access to that facility, either to its downstream arm or to any other company operating on that services market, then it is not clear what other objective justification there could be.

88. In the transport field,[65] the Commission has ruled that a firm controlling an essential facility must give access in certain circumstances.[66] The same principles apply to the telecommunications sector. If there were no commercially feasible alternatives to the access being requested, then unless access is granted, the party requesting access would not be able to operate on the service market. Refusal in this case would therefore limit the development of new markets, or new products on those markets, contrary to Article [82](b), or impede the development of competition on existing markets. A refusal having these effects is likely to have abusive effects.

Notes

[65] Commission Decision 94/19/EC of 21 December 1993, *Sea Containers v. Stena Sealink* — Interim measure (OJ L 15, 18.1.1994, p. 8). Commission Decision 94/119/EEC of 21 December 1993, *Port of Rødby (Denmark)* (OJ L 55, 26.2.1994, p. 52).

[66] See also (among others):
Judgments of the Court of Justice and the Court of First Instance: Cases 6 and 7/73 Commercial Solvents v Commission [1974] ECR 223; Case 311/84, Télémarketing [1985] ECR 3261; Case C-18/88 RTT v GB-Inno [1991] ECR I-5941; Case C-260/89, Elliniki Radiophonia Teleorassi [1991] ECR I-2925; Cases T-69, T-70 and T-76/89, RTE, BBC and ITP v Commission [1991] ECR II-485, 535, 575; Case C-271/90, Spain v Commission [1992] ECR I-5833; Cases C-241 and 242/91 P, RTE and ITP Ltd v Commission (Magill), [1995] ECR I-743.
Commission Decisions: Commission Decision 76/185/ECSC of 29 October 1975, *National Carbonising Company* (OJ L 35, 10.2.1976, p. 6). Commission Decision 88/589/EEC of 4 November 1988, *London European/Sabena* (OJ L 317, 24.11.1988, p. 47). Commission Decision 92/213/EEC of 26 February 1992, *British Midland v. Aer Lingus* (OJ L 96, 10.4.1992, p. 34); B&I v Sealink [1992] 5 CMLR 255; EC Bulletin, No 6-1992, point 1.3.30.

89. The principle obliging dominant companies to contract in certain circumstances will often be relevant in the telecommunications sector. Currently, there are monopolies or virtual monopolies in the provision of network infrastructure for most telecom services in the Community. Even where restrictions have already been, or will soon be, lifted, competition in downstream markets will continue to depend upon the pricing and conditions of access to upstream network services that will only gradually reflect competitive market forces. Given the pace of technological change in the telecommunications sector, it is possible to envisage situations where companies would seek to offer new products or services which are not in competition with products or services already offered by the dominant access operator, but for which this operator is reluctant to provide access.

90. The Commission must ensure that the control over facilities enjoyed by incumbent operators is not used to hamper the development of a competitive telecommunications environment. A company which is dominant on a market for services and which commits an abuse contrary to Article [82] on that market may be required, in order to put an end to the abuse, to supply access to its facility to one or more competitors on that market. In particular, a company may abuse its dominant position if by its actions it prevents the emergence of a new product or service.

91. The starting point for the Commission's analysis will be the identification of an existing or potential market for which access is being requested. In order to determine whether access should be ordered under the competition rules, account will be taken of a breach by the dominant company of its duty not to discriminate (see below) or of the following elements, taken cumulatively:

(a) access to the facility in question is generally essential in order for companies to compete on that related market.[67]
    The key issue here is therefore what is essential. It will not be sufficient that the position of the company requesting access would be more advantageous if access were granted — but refusal

of access must lead to the proposed activities being made either impossible or seriously and unavoidably uneconomic.

Although, for example, alternative infrastructure may as from 1 July 1996 be used for liberalised services, it will be some time before this is in many cases a satisfactory alternative to the facilities of the incumbent operator. Such alternative infrastructure does not at present offer the same dense geographic coverage as that of the incumbent TO's network;

(b) there is sufficient capacity available to provide access;

(c) the facility owner fails to satisfy demand on an existing service or product market, blocks the emergence of a potential new service or product, or impedes competition on an existing or potential service or product market;

(d) the company seeking access is prepared to pay the reasonable and non-discriminatory price and will otherwise in all respects accept non-discriminatory access terms and conditions;

(e) there is no objective justification for refusing to provide access.

Relevant justifications in this context could include an overriding difficulty of providing access to the requesting company, or the need for a facility owner which has undertaken investment aimed at the introduction of a new product or service to have sufficient time and opportunity to use the facility in order to place that new product or service on the market. However, although any justification will have to be examined carefully on a case-by-case basis, it is particularly important in the telecommunications sector that the benefits to end-users which will arise from a competitive environment are not undermined by the actions of the former State monopolists in preventing competition from emerging and developing.

Notes

[67] It would be insufficient to demonstrate that one competitor needed access to a facility in order to compete in the downstream market. It would be necessary to demonstrate that access is necessary for all except exceptional competitors in order for access to be made compulsory.

Commentary
point 91: F&N: 4.202, 13.218

92. In determining whether an infringement of Article [82] has been committed, account will be taken both of the factual situation in that and other geographic areas, and, where relevant, the relationship between the access requested and the technical configuration of the facility.

Commentary
point 92: F&N: 13.138, 13.141

93. The question of objective justification will require particularly close analysis in this area. In addition to determining whether difficulties cited in any particular case are serious enough to justify the refusal to grant access, the relevant authorities must also decide whether these difficulties are sufficient to outweigh the damage done to competition if access is refused or made more difficult and the downstream service markets are thus limited.

94. Three important elements relating to access which could be manipulated by the access provider in order, in effect, to refuse to provide access are timing, technical configuration and price.

95. Dominant TOs have a duty to deal with requests for access efficiently: undue and inexplicable or unjustified delays in responding to a request for access may constitute an abuse. In particular, however, the Commission will seek to compare the response to a request for access with:

(a) the usual time frame and conditions applicable when the responding party grants access to its facilities to its own subsidiary or operating branch;

(b) responses to requests for access to similar facilities in other Member States;

(c) the explanations given for any delay in dealing with requests for access.

Commentary
point 95: F&N: 4.176, 13.51

96. Issues of technical configuration will similarly be closely examined in order to determine whether they are genuine. In principle, competition rules require that the party requesting access must be granted access at the most suitable point for the requesting party, provided that this point is

technically feasible for the access provider. Questions of technical feasibility may be objective justifications for refusing to supply — for example, the traffic for which access is sought must satisfy
the relevant technical standards for the infrastructure — or there may be questions of capacity
restraints, where questions of rationing may arise.[68]

Notes
[68] As noted in point 91.

97. Excessive pricing for access, as well as being abusive in itself,[69] may also amount to an effective
refusal to grant access.

Notes
[69] See point 105.

Commentary
point 97: F&N: 4.176

98. There are a number of elements of these tests which require careful assessment. Pricing questions
in the telecommunications sector will be facilitated by the obligations under ONP Directives to
have transparent cost-accounting systems.

Commentary
point 98: B&C: 12.155

Withdrawal of supply

99. As to the third of the situations referred to in point 84, some previous Commission decisions and
the case law of the Court have been concerned with the withdrawal of supply from downstream
competitors. In Commercial Solvents, the Court held that "an undertaking which has a dominant
position on the market in raw materials and which, with the object of reserving such raw material
for manufacturing its own derivatives, refuses to supply a customer, which is itself a manufacturer
of these derivatives, and therefore risks eliminating all competition on the part of this customer,
is abusing its dominant position within the meaning of Article [82]".[70]

Notes
[70] Cases 6 and 7/73, *Commercial Solvents* [1974] ECR 223.

100. Although this case dealt with the withdrawal of a product, there is no difference in principle
between this case and the withdrawal of access. The unilateral termination of access agreements
raises substantially similar issues to those examined in relation to refusals. Withdrawal of access
from an existing customer will usually be abusive. Again, objective reasons may be provided to
justify the termination. Any such reasons must be proportionate to the effects on competition
of the withdrawal.

2.2. Other forms of abuse

101. Refusals to provide access are only one form of possible abuse in this area. Abuses may also arise
in the context of access having been granted. An abuse may occur inter alia where the operator is
behaving in a discriminatory manner or the operator's actions otherwise limit markets or technical development. The following are non-exhaustive examples of abuse which can take place.

Network configuration

102. Network configuration by a dominant network operator which makes access objectively more
difficult for service providers[71] could constitute an abuse unless it were objectively justifiable.
One objective justification would be where the network configuration improves the efficiency
of the network generally.

Notes
[71] That is to say, to use the network to reach their own customers.

Tying

103. This is of particular concern where it involves the tying of services for which the TO is dominant with those for which it is not.[72] Where the vertically integrated dominant network operator obliges the party requesting access to purchase one or more services[73] without adequate
justification, this may exclude rivals of the dominant access provider from offering those elements of the package independently. This requirement could thus constitute an abuse under
Article [82].

The Court has further held that "... even where tied sales of two products are in accordance
with commercial usage or there is a natural link between the two products in question, such
sales may still constitute abuse within the meaning of Article [82] unless they are objectively
justified...".[74]

Notes

72 This is also dealt with under the ONP framework: see Article 7(4) of the Interconnection Directive, Article 12(4) of
the Voice telephony Directive and Annex II to the ONP Framework Directive.
[73] Including those which are superfluous to the party requesting access, or indeed those which may constitute services
which that party itself would like to provide for its customers.
[74] *Tetra Pak International*, cited in footnote 63.

Commentary
point 103: F&N: 13.239

Pricing

104. In determining whether there is a pricing problem under the competition rules, it will be necessary to demonstrate that costs and revenues are allocated in an appropriate way. Improper allocation of costs and interference with transfer pricing could be used as mechanisms for disguising
excessive pricing, predatory pricing or a price squeeze.

Excessive pricing

105. Pricing problems in connection with access for service providers to a dominant operator's facilities will often revolve around excessively high prices:[75] In the absence of another viable alternative to the facility to which access is being sought by service providers, the dominant or
monopolistic operator may be inclined to charge excessive prices.

Notes

75 The Commission Communication of 27 November 1996 on Assessment Criteria for National Schemes for the
Costing and Financing of Universal Service and Guidelines for the Operation of such Schemes will be relevant for the
determination of the extent to which the universal service obligation can be used to justify additional charges related
to the sharing of the net cost in the provision of universal service (COM(96) 608). See also the reference to the universal service obligation in point 59.

106. An excessive price has been defined by the Court of Justice as being "excessive in relation to the
economic value of the service provided".[76] In addition the Court has made it clear that one of
the ways this could be calculated is as follows:

"This excess could, inter alia, be determined objectively if it were possible for it to be calculated
by making a comparison between the selling price of the product in question and its cost of
production".[77]

Notes

76 Case 26/75, *General Motors Continental v Commission* [1975] ECR 1367, at paragraph 12.
[77] Case 27/76, *United Brands Company and United Brands Continental BV v Commission* [1978] ECR 207.

107. It is necessary for the Commission to determine what the actual costs for the relevant product
are. Appropriate cost allocation is therefore fundamental to determining whether a price is
excessive. For example, where a company is engaged in a number of activities, it will be necessary to allocate relevant costs to the various activities, together with an appropriate contribution
towards common costs. It may also be appropriate for the Commission to determine the proper
cost allocation methodology where this is a subject of dispute.

108. The Court has also indicated that in determining what constitutes an excessive price, account may be taken of Community legislation setting out pricing principles for the particular sector.[78]

Notes

[78] *Ahmed Saeed*, cited in footnote 18, at paragraph 43.

109. Further, comparison with other geographic areas can also be used as an indicator of an excessive price: the Court has held that if possible a comparison could be made between the prices charged by a dominant company, and those charged on markets which are open to competition.[79] Such a comparison could provide a basis for assessing whether or not the prices charged by the dominant company were fair.[80] In certain circumstances, where comparative data are not available, regulatory authorities have sought to determine what would have been the competitive price were a competitive market to exist.[81] In an appropriate case, such an analysis may be taken into account by the Commission in its determination of an excessive price.

Notes

79 Case 30-87, Corinne Bodson v Pompes funèbres des régions libérées [1988] ECR 2479. See also: Joined Cases 110/88, 241/88 and 242/88 François Lucazeau and others v Société des Auteurs, Compositeurs et Editeurs de Musique (SACEM) and others [1989] ECR 2881, at paragraph 25: "When an undertaking holding a dominant position imposes scales of fees for its services which are appreciably higher than those charged in other Member States and where a comparison of the fee levels has been made on a consistent basis, that difference must be regarded as indicative of an abuse of a dominant position. In such a case it is for the undertaking in question to justify the difference by reference to objective dissimilarities between the situation in the Member State concerned and the situation prevailing in all the other Member States."

80 See ONP rules and Commission Recommendation on Interconnection in a liberalised telecommunications market (OJ L 73, 12.3.1998, p. 42 (Text of Recommendation) and OJ C 84, 19.3.1998, p. 3 (Communication on Recommendation)).

81 For example, in their calculation of interconnection tariffs.

Predatory pricing

110. Predatory pricing occurs, inter alia, where a dominant firm sells a good or service below cost for a sustained period of time, with the intention of deterring entry, or putting a rival out of business, enabling the dominant firm to further increase its market power and later its accumulated profits. Such unfairly low prices are in breach of Article [82](a). Such a problem could, for example, arise in the context of competition between different telecommunications infrastructure networks, where a dominant operator may tend to charge unfairly low prices for access in order to eliminate competition from other (emerging) infrastructure providers. In general a price is abusive if it is below the dominant company's average variable costs or if it is below average total costs and part of an anti-competitive plan.[82] In network industries a simple application of the above rule would not reflect the economic reality of network industries.

Notes

[82] *AKZO*, cited in footnote 62.

111. This rule was established in the AKZO case where the Court of Justice defined average variable costs as "those which vary depending on the quantities produced"[83] and explained the reasoning behind the rule as follows:

"A dominant undertaking has no interest in applying such prices except that of eliminating competitors so as to enable it subsequently to raise its prices by taking advantage of its monopolistic position, since each sale generates a loss, namely the total amount of the fixed costs (that is to say, those which remain constant regardless of the quantities produced) and, at least, part of the variable costs relating to the unit produced."

Notes

[83] *AKZO*, paragraph 71.

112. In order to trade a service or group of services profitably, an operator must adopt a pricing strategy whereby its total additional costs in providing that service or group of services are covered by the additional revenues earned as a result of the provision of that service or group of services. Where a dominant operator sets a price for a particular product or service which is below its average total costs of providing that service, the operator should justify this price in commercial terms: a dominant operator which would benefit from such a pricing policy only if one or more of its competitors was weakened would be committing an abuse.

113. As indicated by the Court of Justice in AKZO, the Commission must determine the price below which a company could only make a profit by weakening or eliminating one or more competitors. Cost structures in network industries tend to be quite different to most other industries since the former have much larger common and joint costs.

114. For example, in the case of the provision of telecommunications services, a price which equates to the variable cost of a service may be substantially lower than the price the operator needs in order to cover the cost of providing the service. To apply the AKZO test to prices which are to be applied over time by an operator, and which will form the basis of that operator's decisions to invest, the costs considered should include the total costs which are incremental to the provision of the service. In analysing the situation, consideration will have to be given to the appropriate time frame over which costs should be analysed. In most cases, there is reason to believe that neither the very short nor very long run are appropriate.

115. In these circumstances, the Commission will often need to examine the average incremental costs of providing a service, and may need to examine average incremental costs over a longer period than one year.

116. If a case arises, the ONP rules and Commission recommendations concerning accounting requirements and transparency will help to ensure the effective application of Article [82] in this context.

Price squeeze

117. Where the operator is dominant in the product or services market, a price squeeze could constitute an abuse. A price squeeze could be demonstrated by showing that the dominant company's own downstream operations could not trade profitably on the basis of the upstream price charged to its competitors by the upstream operating arm of the dominant company. A loss-making downstream arm could be hidden if the dominant operator has allocated costs to its access operations which should properly be allocated to the downstream operations, or has otherwise improperly determined the transfer prices within the organisation. The Commission Recommendation on Accounting Separation in the context of Interconnection addresses this issue by recommending separate accounting for different business areas within a vertically integrated dominant operator. The Commission may, in an appropriate case, require the dominant company to produce audited separated accounts dealing with all necessary aspects of the dominant company's business. However, the existence of separated accounts does not guarantee that no abuse exists: the Commission will, where appropriate, examine the facts on a case-by-case basis.

118. In appropriate circumstances, a price squeeze could also be demonstrated by showing that the margin between the price charged to competitors on the downstream market (including the dominant company's own downstream operations, if any) for access and the price which the network operator charges in the downstream market is insufficient to allow a reasonably efficient service provider in the downstream market to obtain a normal profit (unless the dominant company can show that its downstream operation is exceptionally efficient).[84]

Notes

84 Commission Decision 88/518/EEC of 18 July 1988, *Napier Brown/British Sugar* (OJ L 284, 19.10.1988, p. 41): the margin between industrial and retail prices was reduced to the point where the wholesale purchaser with packaging operations as efficient as those of the wholesale supplier could not profitably serve the retail market. See also *National Carbonising Company*, cited in footnote 66.

119. If either of these scenarios were to arise, competitors on the downstream market would be faced with a price squeeze which could force them out of the market.

Discrimination

120. A dominant access provider may not discriminate between the parties to different access agreements where such discrimination would restrict competition. Any differentiation based on the use which is to be made of the access rather than differences between the transactions for the access provider itself, if the discrimination is sufficiently likely to restrict or distort actual or potential competition, would be contrary to Article [82]. This discrimination could take the form of imposing different conditions, including the charging of different prices, or otherwise differentiating between access agreements, except where such discrimination would be objectively justified, for example on the basis of cost or technical considerations or the fact that the users are operating at different levels. Such discrimination could be likely to restrict competition in the downstream market on which the company requesting access was seeking to operate, in that it might limit the possibility for that operator to enter the market or expand its operations on that market.[85]

Notes

[85] However, when infrastructure capacity is under-utilised, charging a different price for access depending on the demand in the different downstream markets may be justified to the extent that such differentiation permits a better development of certain markets, and where such differentiation does not restrict or distort competition. In such a case, the Commission will analyse the global effects of such price differentiation on all of the downstream markets.

121. Such discrimination could similarly have an effect an competition where the discrimination was between operators on closely related downstream markets. Where two distinct downstream product markets exist, but one product would be regarded as substitutable for another save for the fact that there was a price difference between the two products, discriminating in the price charged to the providers of these two products could decrease existing or potential competition. For example, although fixed and mobile voice telephony services at present probably constitute separate product markets, the markets are likely to converge. Charging higher interconnection prices to mobile operators as compared to fixed operators would tend to hamper this convergence, and would therefore have an effect on competition. Similar effects on competition are likely in other telecommunications markets.

Such discrimination would in any event be difficult to justify given the obligation to set cost-related prices.

Commentary
point 121: F&N: 13.237

122. With regard to price discrimination, Article [82](c) prohibits unfair discrimination by a dominant firm between customers of that firm[86] including discriminating between customers on the basis of whether or not they agree to deal exclusively with that dominant firm.

Notes

[86] Case C-310/93 P, *BPB Industries und British Gypsum v Commission* [1995] ECR I-865, at p. 904, applying to discrimination by BPB among customers in the related market for dry plaster.

123. Article 7 of the Interconnection Directive provides that "different tariffs, terms and conditions for interconnection may be set for different categories of organisations which are authorised to provide networks and services, where such differences can be objectively justified on the basis of the type of interconnection provided and/or the relevant national licensing conditions . . ." (provided that such differences do not result in distortions of competition).

124. A determination of whether such differences result in distortions of competition must be made in the particular case. It is important to remember that Articles [81] and [82] deal with competition and not regulatory matters. Article [82] cannot require a dominant company to treat different categories of customers differently, except where this is the result of market conditions and the principles of Article [82]. On the contrary, Article [82] prohibits dominant companies from discriminating between similar transactions where such a discrimination would have an effect on competition.

125. Discrimination without objective justification as regards any aspects or conditions of an access agreement may constitute an abuse. Discrimination may relate to elements such as pricing, delays, technical access, routing,[87] numbering, restrictions on network use exceeding essential requirements and use of customer network data. However, the existence of discrimination can only be determined on a case-by-case basis. Discrimination is contrary to Article [82] whether or not it results from or is apparent from the terms of a particular access agreement.

Notes
[87] That is to say, to a preferred list of correspondent network operators.

Commentary
point 125: F&N: 13.51

126. There is, in this context, a general duty on the network operator to treat independent customers in the same way as its own subsidiary or downstream service arm. The nature of the customer and its demands may play a significant role in determining whether transactions are comparable. Different prices for customers at different levels (for example, wholesale and retail) do not necessarily constitute discrimination.

127. Discrimination issues may arise in respect of the technical configuration of the access, given its importance in the context of access.

The degree of technical sophistication of the access: restrictions on the type or "level" in the network hierarchy of exchange involved in the access or the technical capabilities of this exchange are of direct competitive significance. These could be the facilities available to support a connection or the type of interface and signalling system used to determine the type of service available to the party requesting access (for example, intelligent network facilities).

The number and/or location of connection points: the requirement to collect and distribute traffic for particular areas at the switch which directly serves that area rather than at a higher level of the network hierarchy may be important. The party requesting access incurs additional expense by either providing links at a greater distance from its own switching centre or being liable to pay higher conveyance charges.

Equal access: the possibility for customers of the party requesting access to obtain the services provided by the access provider using the same number of dialled digits as are used by the customers of the latter is a crucial feature of competitive telecommunications.

Objective justification

128. Justifications could include factors relating to the actual operation of the network owned by the access provider, or licensing restrictions consistent with, for example, the subject matter of intellectual property rights.

2.3. Abuses of joint dominant positions

129. In the case of joint dominance (see points 76 *et seq.*) behaviour by one of several jointly dominant companies may be abusive even if others are not behaving in the same way.

130. In addition to remedies under the competition rules, if no operator was willing to grant access, and if there was no technical or commercial justification for the refusal, one would expect that the NRA would resolve the problem by ordering one or more of the companies to offer access, under the terms of the relevant ONP Directive or under national law.

3. Access agreements (Article [81])

131. Restrictions of competition included in or resulting from access agreements may have two distinct effects: restriction of competition between the two parties to the access agreement, or restriction of competition from third parties, for example through exclusivity for one or both of the parties to the agreement. In addition, where one party is dominant, conditions of the access agreement may lead to a strengthening of that dominant position, or to an extension of that dominant position to a related market, or may constitute an unlawful exploitation of the dominant position through the imposition of unfair terms.

132. Access agreements where access is in principle unlimited are not likely to be restrictive of competition within the meaning of Article [81](1). Exclusivity obligations in contracts

providing access to one company are likely to restrict competition because they limit access to infrastructure for other companies. Since most networks have more capacity than any single user is likely to need, this will normally be the case in the telecommunications sector.

133. Access agreements can have significant pro-competitive effects as they can improve access to the downstream market. Access agreements in the context of interconnection are essential to interoperability of services and infrastructure, thus increasing competition in the downstream market for services, which is likely to involve higher added value than local infrastructure.

134. There is, however, obvious potential for anti-competitive effects of certain access agreements or clauses therein. Access agreements may, for example:

   (a) serve as a means of coordinating prices;

   (b) serve as a means of market sharing;

   (c) have exclusionary effects on third parties;[88]

   (d) lead to an exchange of commercially sensitive information between the parties.

Notes

[88] Commission Decision 94/663/EC of 21 September 1994, *Night Services* (OJ L 259, 7.10.1994, p. 20); Commission Decision 94/894/EC, see footnote 48.

---

135. The risk of price coordination is particularly acute in the telecommunications sector since interconnection charges often amount to 50% or more of the total cost of the services provided, and where interconnection with a dominant operator will usually be necessary. In these circumstances, the scope for price competition is limited and the risk (and the seriousness) of price coordination correspondingly greater.

136. Furthermore, interconnection agreements between network operators may under certain circumstances be an instrument of market sharing between the network operator providing access and the network operator seeking access, instead of the emergence of network competition between them.

137. In a liberalised telecommunications environment, the above types of restrictions of competition will be monitored by the national authorities and the Commission under the competition rules. The right of parties who suffer from any type of anti-competitive behaviour to complain to the Commission is unaffected by national regulation.

Clauses falling within Article [81](1)

138. The Commission has identified certain types of restriction which would potentially infringe Article [81](1) of the Treaty and therefore require individual exemption. These clauses will most commonly relate to the commercial framework of the access.

139. In the telecommunications sector, it is inherent in interconnection that parties will obtain certain customer and traffic information about their competitors. This information exchange could in certain cases influence the competitive behaviour of the undertakings concerned, and could easily be used by the parties for collusive practices, such as market sharing.[89] The Interconnection Directive requires that information received from an organisation seeking interconnection be used only for the purposes for which it was supplied. In order to comply with the competition rules and the Interconnection Directives, operators will have to introduce safeguards to ensure that confidential information is only disclosed to those parts of the companies involved in making the interconnection agreements, and to ensure that the information is not used for anti-competitive purposes. Provided that these safeguards are complete and function correctly, there should be no reason in principle why simple interconnection agreements should be caught by Article [81](1).

Notes

[89] Case T-34/92, *Fiatagri UK and New Holland Ford v Commission* [1994] ECR II-905; Case C-8/95 P, *New Holland Ford v Commission*, judgment of 28 May 1988, [[1998] ECR I-3175]; Case T-35/92, *John Deere v Commission* [1994] ECR II-957; Case C-7/95 P, *John Deere v Commission*, judgment of 28 May 1988, [[1998] ECR I-3111] (Cases involving applications brought against Commission Decision 92/157/EEC of 17 February 1992, *UK Agricultural Tractor Registration Exchange*) (OJ L 68, 13.3.1992, p. 19).

---

140. Exclusivity arrangements, for example where traffic would be conveyed exclusively through the telecommunications network of one or both parties rather than to the network of other parties

with whom access agreements have been concluded will similarly require analysis under Article [81](3). If no justification is provided for such routing, such clauses will be prohibited. Such exclusivity clauses are not, however, an inherent part of interconnection agreements.

141. Access agreements that have been concluded with an anti-competitive object are extremely unlikely to fulfil the criteria for an individual exemption under Article [81](3).

142. Furthermore, access agreements may have an impact on the competitive structure of the market. Local access charges will often account for a considerable portion of the total cost of the services provided to end-users by the party requesting access, thus leaving limited scope for price competition. Because of the need to safeguard this limited degree of competition, the Commission will therefore pay particular attention to scrutinising access agreements in the context of their likely effects on the relevant markets in order to ensure that such agreements do not serve as a hidden and indirect means for fixing or coordinating end-prices for end-users, which constitutes one of the most serious infringements of Article [81] of the Treaty.[90] This would be of particular concern in oligopolistic markets.

Notes

[90] Case 8/72, *Vereniging van Cementhandelaaren v Commission* [1972] ECR 977; Case 123/85, *Bureau National Interprofessionnel du Cognac v Clair* [1985] ECR 391.

143. In addition, clauses involving discrimination leading to the exclusion of third parties are similarly restrictive of competition. The most important is discrimination with regard to price, quality or other commercially significant aspects of the access to the detriment of the party requesting access, which will generally aim at unfairly favouring the operations of the access provider.

4. Effect on trade between Member States

144. The application of both Article [81] and Article [82] presupposes an effect on trade between Member States.

145. In order for an agreement to have an effect on trade between Member States, it must be possible for the Commission to "foresee with a sufficient degree of probability on the basis of a set of objective factors of law or of fact that the agreement in question may have an influence, direct or indirect, actual or potential, on the pattern of trade between Member States".[91]

It is not necessary for each of the restrictions of competition within the agreement to be capable of affecting trade,[92] provided the agreement as a whole does so.

Notes

[91] Case 56/65, *STM* [1966] ECR 235, p. 249.
[92] Case 193/83, *Windsurfing International v Commission* [1986] ECR 611.

146. As regards access agreements in the telecommunications sector, the Commission will consider not only the direct effect of restrictions of competition on inter-state trade in access markets, but also the effects on inter-State trade in downstream telecommunications services. The Commission will also consider the potential of these agreements to foreclose a given geographic market which could prevent undertakings already established in other Member States from competing in this geographic market.

147. Telecommunications access agreements will normally affect trade between Member States as services provided over a network are traded throughout the Community and access agreements may govern the ability of a service provider or an operator to provide any given service. Even where markets are mainly national, as is generally the case at present given the stage of development of liberalisation, abuses of dominance will normally speaking affect market structure, leading to repercussions on trade between Member States.

148. Cases in this area involving issues under Article [82] are likely to relate either to abusive clauses in access agreements, or a refusal to conclude an access agreement on appropriate terms or at all. As such, the criteria listed above for determining whether an access agreement is capable of affecting trade between Member States would be equally relevant here.

CONCLUSIONS

149. The Commission considers that competition rules and sector specific regulation form a coherent set of measures to ensure a liberalised and competitive market environment for telecommunications markets in the Community.

150. In taking action in this sector, the Commission will aim to avoid unnecessary duplication of procedures, in particular competition procedures and national/Community regulatory procedures as set out under the ONP framework.

151. Where competition rules are invoked, the Commission will consider which markets are relevant and will apply Articles [81] and [82] in accordance with the principles set out above.

E25

COMMISSION GUIDELINES

on market analysis and the assessment of significant market power under the community
regulatory framework for electronic communications networks and services

(2002/C 165/03)

(Text with EEA relevance)

Official Journal C 165, 11.7.2002, p. 6

Celex No: 52002XC0711(02)

Commentary
Guidelines: **B&C:** 4.013, 4.016, 4.025, 4.054, 4.093, 10.026, 12.100, 12.101, 12.148, 12.149 **F&N:** 13.177, 13.195
paras 24–28: **B&C:** 12.126
paras 24–31: **F&N:** 13.28
paras 24–32: **F&N:** 13.56
paras 25–27: **B&C:** 4.013
paras 55–60: **F&N:** 13.339
para 72–106: **B&C:** 12.102
paras 81–82: **F&N:** 13.30
paras 83–85: **B&C:** 12.149
paras 83–100: **B&C:** 12.153
paras 86–101: **B&C:** 12.150
paras 86–106: **F&N:** 13.194
paras 102–106: **B&C:** 12.150
paras 135–143: **F&N:** 13.39

I. INTRODUCTION

1.1. Scope and purpose of the guidelines

1. These guidelines set out the principles for use by national regulatory authorities (NRAs) in the analysis of markets and effective competition under the new regulatory framework for electronic communications networks and services.

2. This new regulatory framework comprises five Directives: Directive 2002/21/EC of the European Parliament and of the Council of 7 March 2002 on a common regulatory framework for electronic communications networks and services,[1] hereinafter the framework Directive; Directive 2002/20/EC of the European Parliament and of the Council of 7 March 2002 on the authorisation of electronic communications networks and services,[2] hereinafter the authorisation Directive;

Directive 2002/19/EC of the European Parliament and of the Council of 7 March 2002 on access to, and interconnection of, electronic communications networks and associated facilities,[3] hereinafter the access Directive; Directive 2002/22/EC of the European Parliament and of the Council of 7 March 2002 on universal service and users' rights relating to electronic communications networks and services,[4] hereinafter the universal service Directive; a Directive of the European Parliament and of the Council concerning the processing of personal data and the protection of privacy in the electronic communications sector.[5] However, until this last Directive is formally adopted, Directive 97/66/EC of the European Parliament and the Council concerning the processing of personal data and protection of privacy in the telecommunications sector,[6] hereinafter the data protection Directive, remains the relevant Directive.

Notes
[1] OJ L 108, 24.4.2002, p. 33.
[2] OJ L 108, 24.4.2002, p. 21.
[3] OJ L 108, 24.4.2002, p. 7.
[4] OJ L 108, 24.4.2002, p. 51.
[5] [Directive 2002/58/EC of the European Parliament and of the Council of 12 July 2002 concerning the processing of personal data and the protection of privacy in the electronic communications sector (Directive on privacy and electronic communications), OJ L 201, 31.7.2002, p. 37.]
[6] OJ L 24, 30.1.1998, p. 1.

3. Under the 1998 regulatory framework, the market areas of the telecommunications sector that were subject to *ex-ante* regulation were laid down in the relevant directives, but were not markets defined in accordance with the principles of competition law. In these areas defined under the 1998 regulatory framework, NRAs had the power to designate undertakings as having significant market power when they possessed 25% market share, with the possibility to deviate from this threshold taking into account the undertaking's ability to influence the market, its turnover relative to the size of the market, its control of the means of access to end-users, its access to financial resources and its experience in providing products and services in the market.

4. Under the new regulatory framework, the markets to be regulated are defined in accordance with the principles of European competition law. They are identified by the Commission in its recommendation on relevant product and service markets pursuant to Article 15(1) of the framework Directive (hereinafter "the Recommendation"). When justified by national circumstances, other markets can also be identified by the NRAs, in accordance with the procedures set out in Articles 6 and 7 of the framework Directive. In case of transnational markets which are susceptible to *ex-ante* regulation, they will where appropriate be identified by the Commission in a decision on relevant transnational markets pursuant to Article 15(4) of the framework Directive (hereinafter "the Decision on transnational markets").

5. On all of these markets, NRAs will intervene to impose obligations on undertakings only where the markets are considered not to be effectively competitive[7] as a result of such undertakings being in a position equivalent to dominance within the meaning of Article 82 of the EC Treaty.[8] The notion of dominance has been defined in the case-law of the Court of Justice as a position of economic strength affording an undertaking the power to behave to an appreciable extent independently of competitors, customers and ultimately consumers. Therefore, under the new regulatory framework, in contrast with the 1998 framework, the Commission and the NRAs will rely on competition law principles and methodologies to define the markets to be regulated *ex-ante* and to assess whether undertakings have significant market power ("SMP") on those markets.

Notes
[7] Except where the new regulatory framework expressly permits obligations to be imposed independently of the competitive state of the market.
[8] Article 14 of the framework Directive.

6. These guidelines are intended to guide NRAs in the exercise of their new responsibilities for defining markets and assessing SMP. They have been adopted by the Commission in accordance with Article 15(2) of the framework Directive, after consultation of the relevant national authorities and following a public consultation, the results of which have been duly taken into account.

7. Under Article 15(3) of the framework Directive, NRAs should take the utmost account of these guidelines. This will be an important factor in any assessment by the Commission of the proportionality and legality of proposed decisions by NRAs, taking into account the policy objectives laid down in Article 8 of the framework Directive.

8. These guidelines specifically address the following subjects: (a) market definition; (b) assessment of SMP; (c) SMP designation; and (d) procedural issues related to all of these subjects.

9. The guidelines have been designed for NRAs to use as follows:
   — to define the geographical dimension of those product and service markets identified in the Recommendation. NRAs will not define the geographic scope of any transnational markets, as any Decision on transnational markets will define their geographic dimension,
   — to carry out, using the methodology set out in Section 3 of the guidelines, a market analysis of the conditions of competition prevailing in the markets identified in the Recommendation and Decision and by NRAs,
   — to identify relevant national or sub-national product and service markets which are not listed in the Recommendation when this is justified by national circumstances and following the procedures set out in Articles 6 and 7 of the framework Directive,
   — to designate, following the market analysis, undertakings with SMP in the relevant market and to impose proportionate *ex-ante* measures consistent with the terms of the regulatory framework as described in Sections 3 and 4 of the guidelines,
   — to assist Member States and NRAs in applying Article 11(1f) of the authorisation Directive, and Article 5(1) of the framework Directive, and thus ensure that undertakings comply with the obligation to provide information necessary for NRAs to determine relevant markets and assess significant market power thereon,
   — to guide NRAs when dealing with confidential information, which is likely to be provided by:
      — undertakings under Article 11(1f) of the authorisation Directive and Article 5(1) of the framework Directive,
      — national competition authorities (NCAs) as part of the cooperation foreseen in Article 3(5) of the framework Directive, and
      — the Commission and a NRA in another Member State as part of the cooperation foreseen in Article 5(2) of the framework Directive.

10. The guidelines are structured in the following way:
    Section 1 provides an introduction and overview of the background, purpose, scope and content of the guidelines. **Section 2** describes the methodology to be used by NRAs to define the geographic scope of the markets identified in the market Recommendation as well as to define relevant markets outside this Recommendation. **Section 3** describes the criteria for assessing SMP in a relevant market. **Section 4** outlines the possible conclusions that NRAs may reach in their market analyses and describes the possible actions that may result. **Section 5** describes the powers of investigation of NRAs, suggests procedures for coordination between NRAs and between NRAs and NCAs, and describes coordination and cooperation procedures between NRAs and the Commission. Finally, **Section 6** describes procedures for public consultation and publication of NRAs' proposed decisions.

11. The major objective of these guidelines is to ensure that NRAs use a consistent approach in applying the new regulatory framework, and especially when designating undertakings with SMP in application of the provisions of the regulatory framework.

12. By issuing these guidelines, the Commission also intends to explain to interested parties and undertakings operating in the electronic communications sector how NRAs should undertake their assessments of SMP under the framework Directive, thereby maximising the transparency and legal certainty of the application of the sector specific legislation.

13. The Commission will amend these guidelines, whenever appropriate, taking into account experience with the application of the regulatory framework and future developments in the jurisprudence of the Court of First Instance and the European Court of Justice.

14. These guidelines do not in any way restrict the rights conferred by Community law on individuals or undertakings. They are entirely without prejudice to the application of Community law, and in particular of the competition rules, by the Commission and the relevant national authorities, and to its interpretation by the European Court of Justice and the Court of First Instance.

These guidelines do not prejudice any action the Commission may take or any guidelines the Commission may issue in the future with regard to the application of European competition law.

1.2. Principles and policy objectives behind sector specific measures

15. NRAs must seek to achieve the policy objectives identified in Article 8(2), (3) and (4) of the framework Directive. These fall into three categories:
    — promotion of an open and competitive market for electronic communications networks, services and associated facilities,
    — development of the internal market, and
    — promotion of the interests of European citizens.

16. The purpose of imposing *ex-ante* obligations on undertakings designated as having SMP is to ensure that undertakings cannot use their market power either to restrict or distort competition on the relevant market, or to leverage such market power onto adjacent markets.

17. These regulatory obligations should only be imposed on those electronic communications markets whose characteristics may be such as to justify sector-specific regulation and in which the relevant NRA has determined that one or more operators have SMP.

18. The product and service markets whose characteristics may be such as to justify sector-specific regulation are identified by the Commission in its Recommendation and, when the definition of different relevant markets is justified by national circumstances, by the NRAs following the procedures set out in Articles 6 and 7 of the framework Directive.[9] In addition, certain other markets are specifically identified in Article 6 of the access Directive and Articles 18 and 19 of the universal service Directive.

Notes

[9] In addition, transnational markets whose characteristics may be such as to justify sector-specific regulation may be identified by the Commission in a Decision on transnational markets.

---

19. In respect of each of these relevant markets, NRAs will assess whether the competition is effective. A finding that effective competition exists on a relevant market is equivalent to a finding that no operator enjoys a single or joint dominant position on that market. Therefore, for the purposes of applying the new regulatory framework, effective competition means that there is no undertaking in the relevant market which holds alone or together with other undertakings a single or collective dominant position. When NRAs conclude that a relevant market is not effectively competitive, they will designate undertakings with SMP on that market, and will either impose appropriate specific obligations, or maintain or amend such obligations where they already exist, in accordance with Article 16(4) of the framework Directive.

20. In carrying out the market analysis under the terms of Article 16 of the framework Directive, NRAs will conduct a forward looking, structural evaluation of the relevant market, based on existing market conditions. NRAs should determine whether the market is prospectively competitive, and thus whether any lack of effective competition is durable,[10] by taking into account expected or foreseeable market developments over the course of a reasonable period. The actual period used should reflect the specific characteristics of the market and the expected timing for the next review of the relevant market by the NRA. NRAs should take past data into account in their analysis when such data are relevant to the developments in that market in the foreseeable future.

Notes

[10] Recital 27 of the framework Directive.

Commentary
para 20: B&C: 12.102

---

21. If NRAs designate undertakings as having SMP, they must impose on them one or more regulatory obligations, in accordance with the relevant Directives and taking into account the principle of proportionality. Exceptionally, NRAs may impose obligations for access and interconnection that go beyond those specified in the access Directive, provided this is done with the prior agreement of the Commission, as provided by Article 8(3) of that Directive.

22. In the exercise of their regulatory tasks under Article 15 and 16 of the framework Directive, NRAs enjoy discretionary powers which reflect the complexity of all the relevant factors that must be assessed (economic, factual and legal) when identifying the relevant market and determining the existence of undertakings with SMP. These discretionary powers remain subject, however, to the procedures provided for in Article 6 and 7 of the framework Directive.

Commentary
para 22: **B&C:** 12.102

23. Regulatory decisions adopted by NRAs pursuant to the Directives will have an impact on the development of the internal market. In order to prevent any adverse effects on the functioning of the internal market, NRAs must ensure that they implement the provisions to which these guidelines apply in a consistent manner. Such consistency can only be achieved by close coordination and cooperation with other NRAs, with NCAs and with the Commission, as provided in the framework Directive and as recommended in Section 5.3 of these guidelines.

1.3. Relationship with competition law

24. Under the regulatory framework, markets will be defined and SMP will be assessed using the same methodologies as under competition law. Therefore the definition of the geographic scope of markets identified in the Recommendation, the definition where necessary of relevant product/services markets outside the Recommendation, and the assessment of effective competition by NRAs should be consistent with competition case-law and practice. To ensure such consistency, these guidelines are based on (1) existing case-law of the Court of First Instance and the European Court of Justice concerning market definition and the notion of dominant position within the meaning of Article 82 of the EC Treaty and Article 2 of the merger control Regulation;[11] (2) the "Guidelines on the application of EEC competition rules in the telecommunications sector';[12] (3) the "Commission notice on the definition of relevant markets for the purposes of Community competition law",[13] hereinafter the "Notice on market definition"; and (4) the "Notice on the application of competition rules to access agreements in the telecommunications sector",[14] hereinafter the "Access notice".

Notes

[11] Regulation (EEC) No 4064/89 on the control of concentrations between undertakings (OJ L 395, 30.12.1989, p. 1), as last amended by Regulation (EC) No 1310/97 of 30 June 1997 (OJ L 180, 9.7.1997, p. 1) (hereafter the merger control Regulation). [See now Council Regulation (EC) No 139/2004 (OJ L 24, 29.1.2004, p.1).]

[12] Guidelines on the application of EEC competition rules in the telecommunications sector (OJ C 233, 6.9.1991, p. 2).

[13] Commission notice on the definition of relevant market for the purposes of Community competition law (OJ C 372, 9.12.1997, p. 5).

[14] Notice on the application of the competition rules to access agreements in the telecommunications sector (OJ C 265, 22.8.1998, p. 2).

Commentary
para 24: **B&C:** 12.127

25. The use of the same methodologies ensures that the relevant market defined for the purpose of sector-specific regulation will in most cases correspond to the market definitions that would apply under competition law. In some cases, and for the reasons set out in Section 2 of these guidelines, markets defined by the Commission and competition authorities in competition cases may differ from those identified in the Recommendation and Decision, and/or from markets defined by NRAs under Article 15(3) of the framework Directive. Article 15(1) of the framework Directive makes clear that the markets to be defined by NRAs for the purpose of *ex-ante* regulation are without prejudice to those defined by NCAs and by the Commission in the exercise of their respective powers under competition law in specific cases.

26. For the purposes of the application of Community competition law, the Commission's Notice on market definition explains that the concept of the relevant market is closely linked to the objectives pursued under Community policies. Markets defined under Articles 81 and 82 EC Treaty are generally defined on an ex-post basis. In these cases, the analysis will consider events that have

already taken place in the market and will not be influenced by possible future developments. Conversely, under the merger control provisions of EC competition law, markets are generally defined on a forward-looking basis.

Commentary
para 26: B&C: 12.126

27. On the other hand, relevant markets defined for the purposes of sector-specific regulation will always be assessed on a forward looking basis, as the NRA will include in its assessment an appreciation of the future development of the market. However, NRAs' market analyses should not ignore, where relevant, past evidence when assessing the future prospects of the relevant market (see also Section 2, below). The starting point for carrying out a market analysis for the purpose of Article 15 of the framework Directive is not the existence of an agreement or concerted practice within the scope of Article 81 EC Treaty, nor a concentration within the scope of the Merger Regulation, nor an alleged abuse of dominance within the scope of Article 82 EC Treaty, but is based on an overall forward-looking assessment of the structure and the functioning of the market under examination. Although NRAs and competition authorities, when examining the same issues in the same circumstances and with the same objectives, should in principle reach the same conclusions, it cannot be excluded that, given the differences outlined above, and in particular the broader focus of the NRAs' assessment, markets defined for the purposes of competition law and markets defined for the purpose of sector-specific regulation may not always be identical.

Commentary
para 27: B&C: 12.102

28. Although merger analysis is also applied *ex ante*, it is not carried out periodically as is the case with the analysis of the NRAs under the new regulatory framework. A competition authority does not, in principle, have the opportunity to conduct a periodic review of its decision in the light of market developments, whereas NRAs are bound to review their decisions periodically under Article 16(1) of the framework Directive. This factor can influence the scope and breadth of the market analysis and the competitive assessment carried out by NRAs, and for this reason, market definitions under the new regulatory framework, even in similar areas, may in some cases, be different from those markets defined by competition authorities.

Commentary
para 28: B&C: 4.023

29. It is considered that markets which are not identified in the Recommendation will not warrant *ex-ante* sector specific regulation, except where the NRA is able to justify such regulation of an additional or different relevant market in accordance with the procedure in Article 7 of the framework Directive.

30. The designation of an undertaking as having SMP in a market identified for the purpose of *ex-ante* regulation does not automatically imply that this undertaking is also dominant for the purpose of Article 82 EC Treaty or similar national provisions. Moreover, the SMP designation has no bearing on whether that undertaking has committed an abuse of a dominant position within the meaning of Article 82 of the EC Treaty or national competition laws. It merely implies that, from a structural perspective, and in the short to medium term, the operator has and will have, on the relevant market identified, sufficient market power to behave to an appreciable extent independently of competitors, customers, and ultimately consumers, and this, solely for purposes of Article 14 of the framework Directive.

Commentary
para 30: B&C: 12.126

31. In practice, it cannot be excluded that parallel procedures under *ex-ante* regulation and competition law may arise with respect to different kinds of problems in relevant markets.[15] Competition authorities may therefore carry out their own market analysis and impose appropriate

competition law remedies alongside any sector specific measures applied by NRAs. However, it must be noted that such simultaneous application of remedies by different regulators would address different problems in such markets. *Ex-ante* obligations imposed by NRAs on undertakings with SMP aim to fulfil the specific objectives set out in the relevant directives, whereas competition law remedies aim to sanction agreements or abusive behaviour which restrict or distort competition in the relevant market.

Notes

[15] It is expected that effective cooperation between NRAs and NCAs would prevent the duplication of procedures concerning identical market issues.

32. As far as emerging markets are concerned, recital 27 of the framework Directive notes that emerging markets, where *de facto* the market leader is likely to have a substantial market share, should not be subject to inappropriate *ex-ante* regulation. This is because premature imposition of *ex-ante* regulation may unduly influence the competitive conditions taking shape within a new and emerging market. At the same time, foreclosure of such emerging markets by the leading undertaking should be prevented. Without prejudice to the appropriateness of intervention by the competition authorities in individual cases, NRAs should ensure that they can fully justify any form of early, *ex-ante* intervention in an emerging market, in particular since they retain the ability to intervene at a later stage, in the context of the periodic re-assessment of the relevant markets.

2. MARKET DEFINITION

2.1. Introduction

33. In the Competition guidelines issued in 1991,[16] the Commission recognised the difficulties inherent in defining the relevant market in an area of rapid technological change, such as the telecommunications sector. Whilst this statement still holds true today as far as the electronic communications sector is concerned, the Commission since the publication of those guidelines has gained considerable experience in applying the competition rules in a dynamic sector shaped by constant technological changes and innovation, as a result of its role in managing the transition from monopoly to competition in this sector. It should however be recalled that the present guidelines do not purport to explain how the competition rules apply, generally, in the electronic communications sector, but focus only on issues related to (i) market definition; and (ii) the assessment of significant market power within the meaning of Article 14 of the framework Directive (hereafter SMP).

Notes

[16] Guidelines on the application of EEC competition rules in the telecommunications sector (OJ C 233, 6.9.1991, p. 2).

34. In assessing whether an undertaking has SMP, that is whether it "enjoys a position of economic strength affording it the power to behave to an appreciable extent independently of its competitors, customers and ultimately consumers",[17] the definition of the relevant market is of fundamental importance since effective competition can only be assessed by reference to the market thus defined.[18] The use of the term "relevant market" implies the description of the products or services that make up the market and the assessment of the geographical scope of that market (the terms "products" and "services" are used interchangeably throughout this text). In that regard, it should be recalled that relevant markets defined under the 1998 regulatory framework were distinct from those identified for competition-law purposes, since they were based on certain specific aspects of end-to-end communications rather than on the demand and supply criteria used in a competition law analysis.[19]

Notes

[17] Article 14(2) of the framework Directive.

[18] Case C-209/98, *Entreprenørforeningens Affalds* [2000] ECR I-3743, paragraph 57, and Case C-242/95 *GT-Link* [1997] ECR I-4449, paragraph 36. It should be recognised that the objective of market definition is not an end in itself, but part of a process, namely assessing the degree of a firm's market power.

[19] See Directive 97/33/EC of the European Parliament and of the Council of 30 June 1997 on interconnection in telecommunications with regard to ensuring universal service and interoperability through application of the principles of open network provision (ONP) (OJ L 199, 26.7.1997, p. 32) (the interconnection Directive); Council Directive 90/387/EEC of 28 June 1990 on the establishment of the internal market for telecommunications services through the implementation of open network provision (OJ L 192, 24.7.1990, p. 1) (the ONP framework Directive); Council Directive 92/44/EEC of 5 June 1992 on the application of open network provision to leased lines (OJ L 165, 19.6.1992, p. 27) (the leased lines Directive); Directive 95/62/EC of the European Parliament and of the Council of 13 December 1995 on the application of open network provision (ONP) to voice telephony (OJ L 321, 30.12.1995, p. 6), replaced by Directive 98/10/EC of the European Parliament and of the Council of 26 February 1998 on the application of open network provision (ONP) to voice telephony and on universal service for telecommunications in a competitive environment (OJ L 101, 1.4.1998, p. 24) (the ONP voice telephony Directive).

35. Market definition is not a mechanical or abstract process but requires an analysis of any available evidence of past market behaviour and an overall understanding of the mechanics of a given sector. In particular, a dynamic rather than a static approach is required when carrying out a prospective, or forward-looking, market analysis.[20] In this respect, any experience gained by NRAs, NCAs and the Commission through the application of competition rules to the telecommunication sector clearly will be of particular relevance in applying Article 15 of the framework Directive. Thus, any information gathered, any findings made and any studies or reports commissioned or relied upon by NRAs (or NCAs) in the exercise of their tasks, in relation to the conditions of competition in the telecommunications markets (provided of course that market conditions have since remained unchanged), should serve as a starting point for the purposes of applying Article 15 of the framework Directive and carrying out a prospective market analysis.[21]

Notes

[20] Joined Cases C-68/94 and C-30/95, *France and Others v Commission* [1998] ECR I-1375. See, also, Notice on market definition, at paragraph 12.

[21] To the extent that the electronic communications sector is technology and innovation-driven, any previous market definition may not necessarily be relevant at a later point in time.

36. The main product and service markets whose characteristics may be such as to justify the imposition of *ex-ante* regulatory obligations are identified in the Recommendation which the Commission is required to adopt pursuant to Article 15(1) of the framework Directive, as well as any Decision on transnational markets which the Commission decides to adopt pursuant to Article 15(4) of the framework Directive. Therefore, in practice the task of NRAs will normally be to define the geographical scope of the relevant market, although NRAs have the possibility under Article 15(3) of the framework Directive to define markets other than those listed in the Recommendation in accordance with Article 7 of the framework Directive (see below, Section 6).

Commentary
para 36: B&C: 13.170

37. Whilst a prospective analysis of market conditions may in some cases lead to a market definition different from that resulting from a market analysis based on past behaviour,[22] NRAs should nonetheless seek to preserve, where possible, consistency in the methodology adopted between, on the one hand, market definitions developed for the purposes of *ex-ante* regulation, and on the other hand, market definitions developed for the purposes of the application of the competition rules. Nevertheless, as stated in Article 15(1) of the framework Directive and Section 1 of the guidelines, markets defined under sector-specific regulation are defined without prejudice to markets that may be defined in specific cases under competition law.

Notes
[22] Notice on market definition, paragraph 12.

Commentary
para 37: B&C: 12.102

2.2. Main criteria for defining the relevant market

38. The extent to which the supply of a product or the provision of a service in a given geographical area constitutes the relevant market depends on the existence of competitive constraints on the price-setting behaviour of the producer(s) or service provider(s) concerned. There are two main competitive constraints to consider in assessing the behaviour of undertakings on the market, (i) demand-side; and (ii) supply-side substitution. A third source of competitive constraint on an operator's behaviour exists, namely potential competition. The difference between potential competition and supply-substitution lies in the fact that supply-side substitution responds promptly to a price increase whereas potential entrants may need more time before starting to supply the market. Supply substitution involves no additional significant costs whereas potential entry occurs at significant sunk costs.[23] The existence of potential competition should thus be examined for the purpose of assessing whether a market is effectively competitive within the meaning of the framework Directive, that is whether there exist undertakings with SMP.[24]

Notes
[23] See, also, Notice on market definition, paragraphs 20–23, Case IV/M.1225 — *Enso/Stora*, (OJ L 254, 29.9.1999), paragraph 40.
[24] See Notice on market definition, paragraph 24. Distinguishing between supply-side substitution and potential competition in electronic communications markets may be more complicated than in other markets given the dynamic character of the former. What matters, however, is that potential entry from other suppliers is taken into consideration at some stage of the relevant market analysis, that is, either at the initial market definition stage or at the subsequent stage of the assessment of market power (SMP).

39. Demand-side substitutability is used to measure the extent to which consumers are prepared to substitute other services or products for the service or product in question,[25] whereas supply-side substitutability indicates whether suppliers other than those offering the product or services in question would switch in the immediate to short term their line of production or offer the relevant products or services without incurring significant additional costs.

Notes
[25] It is not necessary that all consumers switch to a competing product; it suffices that enough or sufficient switching takes place so that a relative price increase is not profitable. This requirement corresponds to the principle of "sufficient interchangeability" laid down in the case-law of the Court of Justice; see below, footnote 32.

40. One possible way of assessing the existence of any demand and supply-side substitution is to apply the so-called "hypothetical monopolist test".[26] Under this test, an NRA should ask what would happen if there were a small but significant, lasting increase in the price of a given product or service, assuming that the prices of all other products or services remain constant (hereafter, "relative price increase"). While the significance of a price increase will depend on each individual case, in practice, NRAs should normally consider customers' (consumers or undertakings) reactions to a permanent price increase of between 5 to 10%.[27] The responses by consumers or undertakings concerned will aid in determining whether substitutable products do exist and, if so, where the boundaries of the relevant product market should be delineated.[28]

Notes
[26] See, also, Access notice, paragraph 46, and Case T-83/91, *Tetra Pak v Commission*, [1994] ECR II-755, paragraph 68. This test is also known as "SSNIP" (small but significant non transitory increase in price). Although the SSNIP test is but one example of methods used for defining the relevant market and notwithstanding its formal econometric nature, or its margins for errors (the so-called "cellophane fallacy", see below), its importance lies primarily in its use as a conceptual tool for assessing evidence of competition between different products or services.
[27] See Notice on market definition, paragraphs 17–18.

[28] In other words, where the cross-price elasticity of demand between two products is high, one may conclude that consumers view these products as close substitutes. Where consumer choice is influenced by considerations other than price increases, the SSNIP test may not be an adequate measurement of product substitutability; see Case T-25/99, *Colin Arthur Roberts and Valerie Ann Roberts v Commission*, [2001] ECR II-1881.

41. As a starting point, an NRA should apply this test firstly to an electronic communications service or product offered in a given geographical area, the characteristics of which may be such as to justify the imposition of regulatory obligations, and having done so, add additional products or areas depending on whether competition from those products or areas constrains the price of the main product or service in question. Since a relative price increase of a set of products[29] is likely to lead to some sales being lost, the key issue is to determine whether the loss of sales would be sufficient to offset the increased profits which would otherwise be made from sales made following the price increase. Assessing the demand-side and supply-side substitution provides a way of measuring the quantity of the sales likely to be lost and consequently of determining the scope of the relevant market.

Notes

[29] Within the context of market definition under Article 82 of the EC Treaty, a competition authority or a court would estimate the "starting price" for applying the SSNIP on the basis of the price charged by the alleged monopolist. Likewise, under the prospective assessment of the effects which a merger may have on competition, the starting price would be based on the prevailing prices of the merging parties. However, where an NRA carries out a market analysis for the purposes of applying Article 14 of the framework Directive the service or product in question may be offered by several firms. In such a case, the starting price should be the industry "average price".

42. In principle, the "hypothetical monopolist test" is relevant only with regard to products or services, the price of which is freely determined and not subject to regulation. Thus, the working assumption will be that current prevailing prices are set at competitive levels. If, however, a service or product is offered at a regulated, cost-based price, then such price is presumed, in the absence of indications to the contrary, to be set at what would otherwise be a competitive level and should therefore be taken as the starting point for applying the "hypothetical monopolist test".[30] In theory, if the demand elasticity of a given product or service is significant, even at relative competitive prices, the firm in question lacks market power. If, however, elasticity is high even at current prices, that may mean only that the firm in question has already exercised market power to the point that further price increases will not increase its profits. In this case, the application of the hypothetical monopoly test may lead to a different market definition from that which would be produced if the prices were set at a competitive level.[31] Any assessment of market definition must therefore take into account this potential difficulty. However, NRAs should proceed on the basis that the prevailing price levels provide a reasonable basis from which to start the relevant analysis unless there is evidence that this is not in fact the case.

Notes

[30] It is worth noting that prices which result from price regulation which does not aim at ensuring that prices are cost-based, but rather at ensuring an affordable offer within the context of the provision of universal services, may not be presumed to be set at a competitive level, nor should they serve as a starting point for applying the SSNIP test.

[31] Indeed, one of the drawbacks of the application of the SSNIP test is that in some cases, a high-demand cross-price elasticity may mean that a firm has already exercised market power, a situation known in competition law and practice as the "cellophane fallacy". In such cases, the prevailing price does not correspond to a competitive price. Determining whether the prevailing price is set above the competitive level is admittedly one of the most difficult aspects of the SSNIP test. NRAs faced with such difficulties could rely on other criteria for assessing demand and supply substitution such as functionality of services, technical characteristics, etc. Clearly, if evidence exist to show that in the past a firm has engaged in anti-competitive behaviour (price-fixing) or has enjoyed market power, then this may serve as an indication that its prices are not under competitive constraint and accordingly are set above the competitive level.

Commentary
para 42: **B&C:** 4.029

43. If an NRA chooses to have recourse to the hypothetical monopolist test, it should then apply this test up to the point where it can be established that a relative price increase within the geographic and product markets defined will not lead consumers to switch to readily available substitutes or to suppliers located in other areas.

2.2.1. The relevant product/service market

44. According to settled case-law, the relevant product/ service market comprises all those products or services that are sufficiently interchangeable or substitutable, not only in terms of their objective characteristics, by virtue of which they are particularly suitable for satisfying the constant needs of consumers, their prices or their intended use, but also in terms of the conditions of competition and/or the structure of supply and demand on the market in question.[32] Products or services which are only to a small, or relative degree interchangeable with each other do not form part of the same market.[33] NRAs should thus commence the exercise of defining the relevant product or service market by grouping together products or services that are used by consumers for the same purposes (end use).

Notes

[32] Case C-333/94 P, *Tetra Pak v Commission* [1996] ECR I-5951, paragraph 13, Case 31/80 *L'Oréal* [1980] ECR3775, paragraph 25, Case 322/81, *Michelin v Commission* [1983] ECR 3461, paragraph 37, Case C-62/86, *AkzoChemie v Commission* [1991] ECR I-3359, Case T-504/93, *Tiercé Ladbroke v Commission* [1997] ECR II-923, paragraph 81, T-65/96, *Kish Glass v Commission* [2000] ECR II-1885, paragraph 62, Case C-475/99, *Ambulanz Glöckner and Landkreis Südwestpfalz*, [2001] ECR I-[8089], paragraph 33. The test of sufficient substitutability or interchangeability was first laid down by the Court of Justice in Case 6/72, *Europemballage and Continental Can v Commission*, [1973] ECR 215, paragraph 32 and Case 85/76, *Hoffmann La-Roche v Commission* [1979] ECR 461, paragraph 23.

[33] Case C-333/94 P, *Tetra Pak v Commission* [1996] ECR I-5951, paragraph 13, Case 66/86, *Ahmed Saeed* [1989] ECR 803, paragraphs 39 and 40, Case *United Brands v Commission* [1978] ECR207, paragraphs 22 and 29, and 12; Case T-229/94, *Deutsche Bahn v Commission* [1997] ECR II-1689, paragraph 54. In *Tetra Pak*, the Court confirmed that the fact that demand for aseptic and non-aseptic cartons used for packaging fruit juice was marginal and stable over time relative to the demand for cartons used for packaging milk was evidence of a very little interchangeability between the milk and the non-milk packaging sector, idem, paragraphs 13 and 15.

45. Although the aspect of the end use of a product or service is closely related to its physical characteristics, different kind of products or services may be used for the same end. For instance, consumers may use dissimilar services such as cable and satellite connections for the same purpose, namely to access the Internet. In such a case, both services (cable and satellite access services) may be included in the same product market. Conversely, paging services and mobile telephony services, which may appear to be capable of offering the same service, that is, dispatching of two-way short messages, may be found to belong to distinct product markets in view of their different perceptions by consumers as regards their functionality and end use.

Commentary
para 45: B&C: 4.034

46. Differences in pricing models and offerings for a given product or service may also imply different groups of consumers. Thus, by looking into prices, NRAs may define separate markets for business and residential customers for essentially the same service. For instance, the ability of operators engaged in providing international retail electronic communications services to discriminate between residential and business customers, by applying different sets of prices and discounts, has led the Commission to decide that these two groups form separate markets as far as such services are concerned (see below). However, in order for products to be viewed as demand-side substitutes it is not necessary that they are offered at the same price. A low quality product or service sold at a low price could well be an effective substitute to a higher quality product sold at higher prices. What matters in this case is the likely responses of consumers following a relative price increase.[34]

Notes

[34] For example, in the case of a relative price increase, consumers of a lower quality/price service may switch to a higher quality/price service if the cost of doing so (the premium paid) is offset by the price increase. Conversely, consumers

of a higher quality product may no longer accept a higher premium and switch to a lower quality service. In such cases, low and high quality products would appear to be effective substitutes.

Commentary
para 46: B&C: 4.042

47. Furthermore, product substitutability between different electronic communications services will arise increasingly through the convergence of various technologies. Use of digital systems leads to an increasing similarity in the performance and characteristics of network services using distinct technologies. A packet-switched network, for instance, such as Internet, may be used to transmit digitised voice signals in competition with traditional voice telephony services.[35]

Notes
[35] Communication from the Commission — Status of voice on the Internet under Community law, and in particular, under Directive 90/388/EEC — Supplement to the Communication by the Commission to the European Parliament and the Council on the status and implementation of Directive 90/388/EEC on competition in the markets for telecommunications services (OJ C 369, 22.12.2000, p. 3). Likewise, it cannot be excluded that in the future xDSL technology and multipoint video distribution services based on wireless local loops may be used for the transmission of TV materials in direct competition with other existing TV delivery systems based on cable systems, direct-to-home satellite transmission and terrestrial analogue or digital transmission platforms.

48. In order, therefore, to complete the market-definition analysis, an NRA, in addition to considering products or services whose objective characteristics, prices and intended use make them sufficiently interchangeable, should also examine, where necessary, the prevailing conditions of demand and supply substitution by applying the hypothetical monopolist test.

Commentary
para 48: B&C: 4.018

2.2.1.1. Demand-side substitution

49. Demand-side substitution enables NRAs to determine the substitutable products or range of products to which consumers could easily switch in case of a relative price increase. In determining the existence of demand substitutability, NRAs should make use of any previous evidence of consumers' behaviour. Where available, an NRA should examine historical price fluctuations in potentially competing products, any records of price movements, and relevant tariff information. In such circumstances evidence showing that consumers have in the past promptly shifted to other products or services, in response to past price changes, should be given appropriate consideration. In the absence of such records, and where necessary, NRAs will have to seek and assess the likely response of consumers and suppliers to a relative price increase of the service in question.

50. The possibility for consumers to substitute a product or a service for another because of a small, but significant lasting price increase may, however, be hindered by considerable switching costs. Consumers who have invested in technology or made any other necessary investments in order to receive a service or use a product may be unwilling to incur any additional costs involved in switching to an otherwise substitutable service or product. In the same vein, customers of existing providers may also be "locked in" by long-term contracts or by the prohibitively high cost of switching terminals. Accordingly, in a situation where end users face significant switching costs in order to substitute product A for product B, these two products should not be included in the same relevant market.[36]

Notes
[36] Switching costs which stem from strategic choices by undertakings rather than from exogenous factors should be considered, together with some other form of entry barriers, at the subsequent stage of SMP assessment. Where a market is still growing, total switching costs for already "captured" consumers may not be significant and may not thus deter demand or supply-side substitution.

51. Demand substitutability focuses on the interchangeable character of products or services from the buyer's point of view. Proper delineation of the product market may, however, require further consideration of potential substitutability from the supply side.

2.2.1.2. Supply-side substitution

52. In assessing the scope for supply substitution, NRAs may also take into account the likelihood that undertakings not currently active on the relevant product market may decide to enter the market, within a reasonable time frame,[37] following a relative price increase, that is, a small but significant, lasting price increase. In circumstances where the overall costs of switching production to the product in question are relatively negligible, then that product may be incorporated into the product market definition. The fact that a rival firm possesses some of the assets required to provide a given service is immaterial if significant additional investment is needed to market and offer profitably the services in question.[38] Furthermore, NRAs will need to ascertain whether a given supplier would actually use or switch its productive assets to produce the relevant product or offer the relevant service (for instance, whether their capacity is committed under long-term supply agreements, etc.). Mere hypothetical supply-side substitution is not sufficient for the purposes of market definition.

Notes

[37] The time frame to be used to assess the likely responses of other suppliers in case of a relative price increase will inevitably depend on the characteristics of each market and should be decided on a case-by-case basis.

[38] See, also, Case C-333/94, *Tetra Pak v Commission*, op. cit., paragraph 19. As mentioned above, the required investments should also be undertaken within a reasonable time frame.

53. Account should also be taken of any existing legal, statutory or other regulatory requirements which could defeat a time-efficient entry into the relevant market and as a result discourage supply-side substitution. For instance, delays and obstacles in concluding interconnection or co-location agreements, negotiating any other form of network access, or obtaining rights of ways for network expansion,[39] may render unlikely in the short term the provision of new services and the deployment of new networks by potential competitors.

Notes

[39] See, also, Case COMP/M.2574 — *Pirelli/Edizione/Olivetti/Telecom Italia*, paragraph 58.

54. As can been seen from the above considerations, supply substitution may serve not only for defining the relevant market but also for identifying the number of market participants.

2.2.2. Geographic market

55. Once the relevant product market is identified, the next step to be undertaken is the definition of the geographical dimension of the market. It is only when the geographical dimension of the product or service market has been defined that a NRA may properly assess the conditions of effective competition therein.

56. According to established case-law, the relevant geographic market comprises an area in which the undertakings concerned are involved in the supply and demand of the relevant products or services, in which area the conditions of competition are similar or sufficiently homogeneous and which can be distinguished from neighbouring areas in which the prevailing conditions of competition are appreciably different.[40] The definition of the geographic market does not require the conditions of competition between traders or providers of services to be perfectly homogeneous. It is sufficient that they are similar or sufficiently homogeneous, and accordingly, only those areas in which the conditions of competition are "heterogeneous" may not be considered to constitute a uniform market.[41]

Notes

[40] *United Brands*, op. cit., paragraph 44, *Michelin*, op. cit., paragraph 26, Case 247/86 *Alsatel v Novasam* [1988] ECR 5987, paragraph 15; *Tiercé Ladbroke v Commission*, op. cit., paragraph 102.

[41] *Deutsche Bahn v Commission*, op. cit., paragraph 92. Case T-139/98 *AAMS v Commission*, [2001] ECR [II-3413], paragraph 39.

57. The process of defining the limits of the geographic market proceeds along the same lines as those discussed above in relation to the assessment of the demand and supply-side substitution in response to a relative price increase.

58. Accordingly, with regard to demand-side substitution, NRAs should assess mainly consumers' preferences as well as their current geographic patterns of purchase. In particular, linguistic reasons may explain why certain services are not available or marketed in different language areas. As far as supply-side substitution is concerned, where it can be established that operators which are not currently engaged or present on the relevant market, will, however, decide to enter that market in the short term in the event of a relative price increase, then the market definition should be expanded to incorporate those "outside" operators.

59. In the electronic communications sector, the geographical scope of the relevant market has traditionally been determined by reference to two main criteria:[42]

    (a) the area covered by a network;[43] and

    (b) the existence of legal and other regulatory instruments.[44]

Notes

[42] See, for instance, Case IV/M.1025 — *Mannesmann/Olivetti/Infostrada*, paragraph 17, and Case COMP/JV.23 — *Telefónica Portugal Telecom/Médi Telecom*.

[43] In practice, this area will correspond to the limits of the area in which an operator is authorised to operate. In Case COMP/M.1650 — *ACEA/Telefónica*, the Commission pointed out that since the notified joint venture would have a licence limited to the area of Rome, the geographical market could be defined as local; at paragraph 16.

[44] The fact that mobile operators can provide services only in the areas where they have been authorised to and the fact that a network architecture reflects the geographical dimension of the mobile licences explains why mobile markets are considered to be national in scope. The extra connection and communications costs that consumers face when roaming abroad, coupled with the loss of certain additional service functionalities (i.e. lack of voice mail abroad) further supports this definition; see Case IV/M.1439 — *Telia/Telenor*, paragraph 124, Case IV/M.1430 — *Vodafone/Airtouch*, paragraphs 13-17, Case COMP/JV.17 — *Mannesmann/Bell Atlantic/Omnitel*, paragraph 15.

60. On the basis of these two main criteria,[45] geographic markets can be considered to be local, regional, national or covering territories of two or more countries (for instance, pan-European, EEA-wide or global markets).

Notes

[45] Physical interconnection agreements may also be taken into consideration for defining the geographical scope of the market, Case IV/M.570 — *TBT/BT/TeleDanmark/Telenor*, paragraph 35.

2.2.3. Other issues of market definition

61. For the purposes of *ex-ante* regulation, in certain exceptional cases, the relevant market may be defined on a route-by-route basis. In particular, when considering the dimension of markets for international retail or wholesale electronic communications services, it may be appropriate to treat paired countries or paired cities as separate markets.[46] Clearly, from the demand side, the delivery of a call to one country is not a substitute for the delivery of the same to another country. On the other hand, the question of whether indirect transmission services, that is, re-routing or transit of the same call via a third country, represent effective supply-side substitutes depends on the specificities of the market and should be decided on a case-by-case basis.[47] However, a market for the provision of services on a bilateral route would be national in scope since supply and demand patterns in both ends of the route would most likely correspond to different market structures.[48]

Notes

[46] Case IV/M.856 — *British Telecom/MCI (II)*, paragraph 19s., Case IV/JV.15 — *BT/AT & T*, paragraph 84 and 92, Case COMP/M.2257 — *France Telecom/Equant*, paragraph 32, It is highly unlikely that the provision of electronic communications services could be segmented on the basis of national (or local) bilateral routes.

[47] Reference may be made, for instance, to the market for backhaul capacity in international routes (i.e. cable station serving country A to country E) where a potential for substitution between cable stations serving different countries (i.e., cable stations connecting Country A to B, A to C and A to D) may exist where a supplier of backhaul capacity in relation to the route A to E is or would be constrained by the ability of consumers to switch to any of the other "routes", also able to deal with traffic from or to country E.

[48] Where a market is defined on the basis of a bilateral route, its geographical scope could be wider than national if suppliers are present in both ends of the market and can satisfy demand coming from both ends of the relevant route.

62. In its Notice on market definition, the Commission drew attention to certain cases where the boundaries of the relevant market may be expanded to take into consideration products or geographical areas which, although not directly substitutable, should be included in the market definition because of so-called "chain substitutability".[49] In essence, chain substitutability occurs where it can be demonstrated that although products A and C are not directly substitutable, product B is a substitute for both product A and product C and therefore products A and C may be in the same product market since their pricing might be constrained by the substitutability of product B. The same reasoning also applies for defining the geographic market. Given the inherent risk of unduly widening the scope of the relevant market, findings of chain substitutability should be adequately substantiated.[50]

Notes

[49] See Notice on market definition, paragraphs 57 and 58. For instance, chain substitutability could occur where an undertaking providing services at national level constraints the prices charged by undertakings providing services in separate geographical markets. This may be the case where the prices charged by undertakings providing cable networks in particular areas are constrained by a dominant undertaking operating nationally; see also, Case COMP/M.1628 — *TotalFina/Elf* (OJ L 143, 29.5.2001, p. 1), paragraph 188.

[50] Evidence should show clear price interdependence at the extremes of the chain and the degree of substitutability between the relevant products or geographical areas should be sufficiently strong.

2.3. The Commission's own practice

63. The Commission has adopted a number of decisions under Regulation No 17 and the merger control Regulation relating to the electronic communications sector. These decisions may be of particular relevance for NRAs with regard to the methodology applied by the Commission in defining the relevant market.[51] As stated above, however, in a sector characterised by constant innovation and rapid technological convergence, it is clear that any current market definition runs the risk of becoming inaccurate or irrelevant in the near future.[52] Furthermore, markets defined under competition law are without prejudice to markets defined under the new regulatory framework as the context and the timeframe within which a market analysis is conducted may be different.[53]

Notes

51 The Commission has, inter alia, made references in its decisions to the existence of the following markets: international voice-telephony services (Case IV/M.856 — *British Telecommunications/MCI* (II), OJ L 336, 8.12.1997), advanced telecommunications services to corporate users (Case IV/35.337, *Atlas*, OJ L 239, 19.9.1996, paragraphs 5-7, Case IV/35617, *Phoenix/Global/One*, OJ L 239, 19.9.1996, paragraph 6, Case IV/34.857, *BT-MCI (I)*, OJ L 223, 27.8.1994), standardised low-level packet-switched data-communications services, resale of international transmission capacity (Case IV/M.975 — *Albacom/BT/ENI*, paragraph 24) audioconferencing (*Albacom/BT/ENI*, paragraph 17), satellite services (Case IV/350518 — *Iridium*, OJ L 16, 18.1.1997), (enhanced) global telecommunications services (Case IV/JV.15 — *BT/AT & T*, Case COMP/M.1741 — *MCI WorldCom/Sprint*, paragraph 84, Case COMP/M.2257 — *France Telecom/Equant*, paragraph 18), directory-assistance services (Case IV/M.2468 — *SEAT Pagine Gialle/ENIRO*, paragraph 19, Case COMP/M.1957 — *VIAG Interkom/Telenor Media*, paragraph 8), Internet-access services to end users (Case IV/M.1439 — *Telia/Telenor*, Case COMP/JV.46 — *Blackstone/CDPQ/ Kabel Nordrhein/Westfalen*, paragraph 26, Case COMP/M.1838 — *BT/Esat*, paragraph 7), top-level or universal Internet connectivity (Case COMP/M.1741 — *MCI WorldCom/Sprint*, paragraph 52), seamless pan-European mobile telecommunications services to internationally mobile customers (Case COMP/M.1975 — *Vodafone Airtouch/Mannesmann*, Case COMP/M.2016 — *France Telecom/Orange*, paragraph 15), wholesale roaming services (Case COMP/M.1863 — *Vodafone/Airtel*, paragraph 17), and market for connectivity to the international signalling network (Case COMP/2598 — *TDC/CMG/Migway JV*, paragraphs 17–18).

52 See, also, Joined Cases T-125/97 and T-127/97, *The Coca-Cola Company and Others v Commission* [2000] ECR II-1733, at paragraphs 81 and 82.

53 See, also, Article 15 of the framework Directive.

64. As stated in the Access notice, there are in the electronic communications sector at least two main types of relevant markets to consider, that of services provided to end users (services market) and that of access to facilities necessary to provide such services (access market).[54] Within these two broad market definitions further market distinctions may be made depending on demand and supply side patterns.

Part E Sectoral Regimes

Notes
[54] Access notice, paragraph 45.

65. In particular, in its decision-making practice, the Commission will normally make a distinction between the provision of services and the provision of underlying network infrastructure. For instance, as regards the provision of infrastructure, the Commission has identified separate markets for the provision of local loop, long distance and international infrastructure.[55] As regards fixed services, the Commission has distinguished between subscriber (retail) access to switched voice telephony services (local, long distance and international), operator (wholesale) access to networks (local, long distance and international) and business data communications services.[56] In the market for fixed telephony retail services, the Commission has also distinguished between the initial connection and the monthly rental.[57] Retail services are offered to two distinct classes of consumers, namely, residential and business users, the latter possibly being broken down further into a market for professional, small and medium sized business customers and another for large businesses.[58] With regard to fixed telephony retail services offered to residential users, demand and supply patterns seem to indicate that two main types of services are currently being offered, traditional fixed telephony services (voice and narrowband data transmissions) on the one hand, and high speed communications services (currently in the form of xDSL services) on the other hand.[59]

Notes
[55] See Case COMP/M.1439 — *Telia/Telenor*.
[56] See *Telia/Telenor, BT/AT & T, France Télécom/Equant*, op. cit. See also Commission Decision of 20 May 1999, *Cégétel + 4* (OJ L 218, 18.8.1999), paragraph 22. With regard to the emerging market for "Global broadband data communications services — GBDS", the Commission has found that such services can be supported by three main network architectures: (i) terrestrial wireline systems; (ii) terrestrial wireless systems; and (iii) satellite-based systems, and that from a demand side, satellite-based GBDS can be considered as a separate market, Case COMP/M.1564 — *Astrolink*, paragraphs 20–23.
[57] Directive 96/19/EC, recital 20 (OJ L 74, 22.3.1996, p. 13). See, also, communication from the Commission, "Unbundled access to the local loop: enabling the competitive provision of a full range of electronic communication services, including broadband multimedia and high speed Internet" (OJ C 272, 23.9.2000, p. 55). Pursuant to point 3.2, "While categories of services have to be monitored closely, particularly given the speed of technological change, and regularly reassessed on a case-by-case basis, these services are presently normally not substitutable for one another, and would therefore be considered as forming different relevant markets".
[58] The Commission has identified separate markets for services to large multinational corporations (MNCs) given the significant differences in the demand (and supply) of services to this group of customers compared to other retail (business) customers, see Case IV/JV.15 — *BT/AT & T*, Case COMP/M.1741 — *MCI WorldCom/Sprint*, Case COMP/M.2257 — *France Télécom/Equant*.
[59] See communication on "Unbundled access to the local loop", op.cit, point 3.2. The market for "high-speed" communications services could possibly be further divided into distinct segments depending on the nature of the services offered (i.e. Internet services, video-on-demand, etc.).

66. As regards the provision of mobile communications services, the Commission has found that, from a demand-side point of view, mobile telephony services and fixed telephony services constitute separate markets.[60] Within the mobile market, evidence gathered from the Commission has indicated that the market for mobile communications services encompasses both GSM 900 and GSM 1800 and possibly analogue platforms.[61]

Notes
[60] Case COMP/M.2574 — *Pirelli/Edizione/Olivetti/Telecom Italia*, paragraph 33. It could also be argued that dial-up access to the Internet via existing 2G mobile telephones is a separate market from dial-up access via the public switched telecommunications network. According to the Commission, accessing the Internet via a mobile phone is unlikely to be a substitute for existing methods of accessing the Internet via a PC due to difference in sizes of the screen and the format of the material that can be obtained through the different platforms; see Case COMP/M.1982 — *Telia/Oracle/Drutt*, paragraph 15, and Case COMP/JV.48 *Vodafone/Vivendi/Canal+*.
[61] Case COMP/M.2469 — *Vodafone/Airtel*, paragraph 7, Case IV/M.1430 — *Vodafone/Airtouch*, Case IV/M.1669, *Deutsche Telecom/One2One*, paragraph 7. Whether this market can be further segmented into a carrier (network operator) market and a downstream service market should be decided on a case-by-case basis; see Case IV/M.1760 — *Mannesmann/Orange*, paragraphs 8-10, and Case COMP/M.2053 — *Telenor/BellSouth/Sonofon*, paragraphs 9–10.

Commentary
para 66: F&N: 13.178

67. The Commission has found that with regard to the "access" market, the latter comprises all types of infrastructure that can be used for the provision of a given service.[62] Whether the market for network infrastructures should be divided into as many separate submarkets as there are existing categories of network infrastructure, depends clearly on the degree of substitutability among such (alternative) networks.[63] This exercise should be carried out in relation to the class of users to which access to the network is provided. A distinction should, therefore, be made between provision of infrastructure to other operators (wholesale level) and provision to end users (retail level).[64] At the retail level, a further segmentation may take place between business and residential customers.[65]

Notes

[62] For instance, in *British Interactive Broadcasting/Open*, the Commission noted that for the provision of basic voice services to consumers, the relevant infrastructure market included not only the traditional copper network of BT but also the cable networks of the cable operators, which were capable of providing basic telephony services, and possibly wireless fixed networks, Case IV/36.359, (OJ L 312, 6.12.1999, paragraphs 33–38). In Case IV/M.1113 — *Nortel/ Norweb*, the Commission recognised that electricity networks using "digital power line" technology could provide an alternative to existing traditional local telecommunications access loop, paragraphs 28–29.

[63] In assessing the conditions of network competition in the Irish market that would ensue following full liberalisation, the Commission also relied on the existence of what, at that period of time, were perceived as potential alternative infrastructure providers, namely, cable TV and electricity networks, *Telecom Eireann*, cit., paragraph 30. The Commission left open the question whether the provision of transmission capacity by an undersea network infrastructure constitutes a distinct market from terrestrial or satellite transmissions networks, Case COMP/M.1926 — *Telefonica/Tyco/JV*, at paragraph 8.

[64] Case COMP/M.1439, *Telia/Telenor*, paragraph 79. For instance, an emerging pan-European market for wholesale access (SMS) to mobile infrastructure has been identified by the Commission in Case COMP/2598 — *TDC/CMG/ Migway* JV, at paragraphs 28–29.

[65] In applying these criteria, the Commission has found that, as far as the fixed infrastructure is concerned, demand for the lease of transmission capacity and the provision of related services to other operators occurs at wholesale level (the market for carrier's carrier services; see Case IV/M.683 — *GTS-Hermes Inc./HIT Rail BV*, paragraph 14, Case IV/ M.1069 — *WorldCom/MCI* (OJ L 116, 4.5.1999, p. 1), *Unisource* (OJ L 318, 20.11.1997, p. 1), *Phoenix/Global One* (OJ L 239, 19.9.1996, p. 57), Case IV/JV.2 — *Enel/FT/DT*. In Case COMP/M.1439 — *Telia/Telenor*, the Commission identified distinct patterns of demand for wholesale and retail (subscriber) access to network infrastructure (provision or access to the local loop, and provision or access to long distance and international network infrastructure), paragraphs 75–83.

68. When the service to be provided concerns only end users subscribed to a particular network, access to the termination points of that network may well constitute the relevant product market. This will not be the case if it can be established that the same services may be offered to the same class of consumers by means of alternative, easily accessible competing networks. For example, in its Communication on unbundling the local loop,[66] the Commission stated that although alternatives to the PSTN for providing high speed communications services to residential consumers exist (fibre optic networks, wireless local loops or upgradable TV networks), none of these alternatives may be considered as a substitute to the fixed local loop infrastructure.[67] Future innovative and technological changes may, however, justify different conclusions.[68]

Notes

[66] See footnote 58.

[67] Fibre optics are currently competitive only on upstream transmission markets whereas wireless local loops which are still to be deployed will target mainly professionals and individuals with particular communications needs. With the exception of certain national markets, existing cable TV networks need costly upgrades to support two ways broadband communications, and, compared with xDLS technologies, they do not offer a guaranteed bandwidth since customers share the same cable channel.

[68] See also Case IV/JV.11 — *@Home Benelux BV*.

69. Access to mobile networks may also be defined by reference to two potentially separate markets, one for call origination and another for call termination. In this respect, the question whether the access market to mobile infrastructure relates to access to an individual mobile network or to

all mobile networks, in general, should be decided on the basis of an analysis of the structure and functioning of the market.[69]

Notes

[69] For example, if a fixed operator wants to terminate calls to the subscribers of a particular network, in principle, it will have no other choice but to call or interconnect with the network to which the called party has subscribed. For instance, in light of the "calling party pays" principle, mobile operators have no incentives to compete on prices for terminating traffic to their own network. See also, OECD, "Competition issues in telecommunications-background note for the secretariat", DAFFE/CLP/WP2(2001)3, and Commission's press release IP/02/483.

3. Assessing Significant Market Power (Dominance)

70. According to Article 14 of the framework Directive "an undertaking shall be deemed to have significant market power if, either individually or jointly with others, it enjoys a position equivalent to dominance, that is to say a position of economic strength affording it the power to behave to an appreciable extent independently of competitors customers and ultimately consumers". This is the definition that the Court of Justice case-law ascribes to the concept of dominant position in Article 82 of the Treaty.[70] The new framework has aligned the definition of SMP with the Court's definition of dominance within the meaning of Article 82 of the Treaty.[71] Consequently, in applying the new definition of SMP, NRAs will have to ensure that their decisions are in accordance with the Commission's practice and the relevant jurisprudence of the Court of Justice and the Court of First Instance on dominance.[72] However, the application of the new definition of SMP, *ex-ante*, calls for certain methodological adjustments to be made regarding the way market power is assessed. In particular, when assessing *ex-ante* whether one or more undertakings are in a dominant position in the relevant market, NRAs are, in principle, relying on different sets of assumptions and expectations than those relied upon by a competition authority applying Article 82, *ex post*, within a context of an alleged committed abuse.[73] Often, the lack of evidence or of records of past behaviour or conduct will mean that the market analysis will have to be based mainly on a prospective assessment. The accuracy of the market analysis carried out by NRAs will thus be conditioned by information and data existing at the time of the adoption of the relevant decision.

Notes

[70] Case 27/76 *United Brands v Commission* [1978] ECR 207.
[71] See, also, recital 25 of the framework Directive.
[72] See Article 14, paragraph 2, and recital 28 of the framework Directive.
[73] It should be noted that NRAs do not have to find an abuse of a dominant position in order to designate an undertaking as having SMP.

71. The fact that an NRA's initial market predictions do not finally materialise in a given case does not necessarily mean that its decision at the time of its adoption was inconsistent with the Directive. In applying *ex ante* the concept of dominance, NRAs must be accorded discretionary powers correlative to the complex character of the economic, factual and legal situations that will need to be assessed. In accordance with the framework Directive, market assessments by NRAs will have to be undertaken on a regular basis. In this context, therefore, NRAs will have the possibility to react at regular intervals to any market developments and to take any measure deemed necessary.

3.1. Criteria for assessing SMP

72. As the Court has stressed, a finding of a dominant position does not preclude some competition in the market. It only enables the undertaking that enjoys such a position, if not to determine, at least to have an appreciable effect on the conditions under which that competition will develop, and in any case to act in disregard of any such competitive constraint so long as such conduct does not operate to its detriment.[74]

Notes

[74] Case 85/76, *Hoffmann-La Roche v Commission* [1979] ECR 461, paragraph 39. It should be stressed here that for the purposes of *ex-ante* regulation, if an undertaking has already been imposed regulatory obligations, the fact that competition may have been restored in the relevant market as a result precisely of the obligations thus imposed, this does

not mean that that undertaking is no longer in a dominant position and that it should no longer continue being designated as having SMP.

73. In an *ex-post* analysis, a competition authority may be faced with a number of different examples of market behaviour each indicative of market power within the meaning of Article 82. However, in an *ex-ante* environment, market power is essentially measured by reference of the power of the undertaking concerned to raise prices by restricting output without incurring a significant loss of sales or revenues.

74. The market power of an undertaking can be constrained by the existence of potential competitors.[75] An NRA should thus take into account the likelihood that undertakings not currently active on the relevant product market may in the medium term decide to enter the market following a small but significant non-transitory price increase. Undertakings which, in case of such a price increase, are in a position to switch or extend their line of production/services and enter the market should be treated by NRAs as potential market participants even if they do not currently produce the relevant product or offer the relevant service.

Notes

[75] The absence of any substitutable service or product may justify a finding of a situation of economic dependence which is characteristic of the existence of a dominant position. See Commission decisions, *Decca Navigator System* (OJ L 43, 15.2.1987, p. 27) and *Magill TV Guide: ITP, BBC, RTE* (OJ L 78, 21.3.1989, p. 43). See also, Case 22/78 *Hugin v Commission* 1979 [ECR] 1869, Case 226/84, British Leyland v Commission 1986 [ECR] 3263.

75. As explained in the paragraphs below, a dominant position is found by reference to a number of criteria and its assessment is based, as stated above, on a forward-looking market analysis based on existing market conditions. Market shares are often used as a proxy for market power. Although a high market share alone is not sufficient to establish the possession of significant market power (dominance), it is unlikely that a firm without a significant share of the relevant market would be in a dominant position. Thus, undertakings with market shares of no more than 25% are not likely to enjoy a (single) dominant position on the market concerned.[76] In the Commission's decision-making practice, single dominance concerns normally arise in the case of undertakings with market shares of over 40%, although the Commission may in some cases have concerns about dominance even with lower market shares,[77] as dominance may occur without the existence of a large market share. According to established case-law, very large market shares — in excess of 50% — are in themselves, save in exceptional circumstances, evidence of the existence of a dominant position.[78] An undertaking with a large market share may be presumed to have SMP, that is, to be in a dominant position, if its market share has remained stable over time.[79] The fact that an undertaking with a significant position on the market is gradually losing market share may well indicate that the market is becoming more competitive, but it does not preclude a finding of significant market power. On the other hand, fluctuating market shares over time may be indicative of a lack of market power in the relevant market.

Notes

[76] See, also, recital 15 of Council Regulation (EEC) No 4064/89.

[77] *United Brands v Commission*, op. cit. The greater the difference between the market share of the undertaking in question and that of its competitors, the more likely will it be that the said undertaking is in a dominant position. For instance, in Case COMP/M.1741 — *MCI WorldCom/Sprint* it was found that the merged entity would have in the market for the provision of top-level Internet connectivity an absolute combined market share of more than [35–45]%, several times larger than its closest competitor, enabling it to behave independently of its competitors and customers (see paragraphs 114, 123, 126, 146, 155 and 196).

[78] Case C-62/86, *AKZO v Commission*, [1991] ECR I-3359, paragraph 60; Case T-228/97, *Irish Sugar v Commission*, [1999] ECR II-2969, paragraph 70, Case *Hoffmann-La Roche v Commission*, op. cit, paragraph 41, Case T-139/98, *AAMS and Others v Commission* [2001 ECR II-[3413], paragraph 51. However, large market shares can become accurate measurements only on the assumption that competitors are unable to expand their output by sufficient volume to meet the shifting demand resulting from a rival's price increase.

[79] Case *Hoffmann-La Roche v Commission*, op. cit., paragraph 41, Case C-62/86, *Akzo v Commission* [1991] ECR I-3359, paragraphs 56, 59. "An undertaking which has a very large market share and holds it for some time, by means of the volume of production and the sale of the supply which it stands for — without holders of much smaller market shares being able to meet rapidly the demand from those who would like to break away from the undertaking which has largest market share — is by virtue of that share in a position of strength which makes it an unavoidable trading partner and

which, because of this alone, secures for it, at the very least during relatively long periods, that freedom of action which is the special feature of a dominant position", Case *AAMS and Others v Commission*, op. cit., paragraph 51.

76. As regards the methods used for measuring market size and market shares, both volume sales and value sales provide useful information for market measurement.[80] In the case of bulk products preference is given to volume whereas in the case of differentiated products (i.e. branded products) sales in value and their associated market share will often be considered to reflect better the relative position and strength of each provider. In bidding markets the number of bids won and lost may also be used as approximation of market shares.[81]

Notes

[80] Notice on market definition, op. cit., at p. 5.

[81] See Case COMP/M.1741 — *MCI WorldCom/Sprint*, paragraph 239–240. In bidding markets, however, it is important not to rely only on market shares as they in themselves may not be representative of the undertakings actual position, for further discussion, see, also, Case COMP/M.2201 — *MAN/Aüwarter*.

77. The criteria to be used to measure the market share of the undertaking(s) concerned will depend on the characteristics of the relevant market. It is for NRAs to decide which are the criteria most appropriate for measuring market presence. For instance, leased lines revenues, leased capacity or numbers of leased line termination points are possible criteria for measuring an undertaking's relative strength on leased lines markets. As the Commission has indicated, the mere number of leased line termination points does not take into account the different types of leased lines that are available on the market — ranging from analogue voice quality to high-speed digital leased lines, short distance to long distance international leased lines. Of the two criteria, leased lines revenues may be more transparent and less complicated to measure. Likewise, retail revenues, call minutes or numbers of fixed telephone lines or subscribers of public telephone network operators are possible criteria for measuring the market shares of undertakings operating in these markets.[82] Where the market defined is that of interconnection, a more realistic measurement parameter would be the revenues accrued for terminating calls to customers on fixed or mobile networks. This is so because the use of revenues, rather than for example call minutes, takes account of the fact that call minutes can have different values (i.e. local, long distance and international) and provides a measure of market presence that reflects both the number of customers and network coverage.[83] For the same reasons, the use of revenues for terminating calls to customers of mobile networks may be the most appropriate means to measure the market presence of mobile network operators.[84]

Notes

[82] See, Determination of organisations with significant power (SMP) for the implementation of the ONP Directive, DG XIII, 1 March 1999, at http://europa.eu.int/ISPO/infosoc/telecompolicy/en/SMPdeter.pdf, at paragraph 3.2.

[83] Idem, at paragraph 5.2.

[84] With regard to the interconnection market of fixed and mobile networks, the termination traffic to be measured should include own network traffic and interconnection traffic received from all other fixed and mobile networks, national or international.

78. It is important to stress that the existence of a dominant position cannot be established on the sole basis of large market shares. As mentioned above, the existence of high market shares simply means that the operator concerned might be in a dominant position. Therefore, NRAs should undertake a thorough and overall analysis of the economic characteristics of the relevant market before coming to a conclusion as to the existence of significant market power. In that regard, the following criteria can also be used to measure the power of an undertaking to behave to an appreciable extent independently of its competitors, customers and consumers. These criteria include amongst others:
— overall size of the undertaking,
— control of infrastructure not easily duplicated,
— technological advantages or superiority,
— absence of or low countervailing buying power,
— easy or privileged access to capital markets/financial resources,

— product/services diversification (e.g. bundled products or services),
— economies of scale,
— economies of scope,
— vertical integration,
— a highly developed distribution and sales network,
— absence of potential competition,
— barriers to expansion.

Commentary
para 78: B&C: 12.149

79. A dominant position can derive from a combination of the above criteria, which taken separately may not necessarily be determinative.

80. A finding of dominance depends on an assessment of ease of market entry. In fact, the absence of barriers to entry deters, in principle, independent anti-competitive behaviour by an undertaking with a significant market share. In the electronic communications sector, barriers to entry are often high because of existing legislative and other regulatory requirements which may limit the number of available licences or the provision of certain services (i.e. GSM/DCS or 3G mobile services). Furthermore, barriers to entry exist where entry into the relevant market requires large investments and the programming of capacities over a long time in order to be profitable.[85] However, high barriers to entry may become less relevant with regard to markets characterised by on-going technological progress. In electronic communications markets, competitive constraints may come from innovative threats from potential competitors that are not currently in the market. In such markets, the competitive assessment should be based on a prospective, forward-looking approach.

Notes

[85] *Hoffmann-La Roche v Commission*, op. cit., at paragraph 48. One of the most important types of entry barriers is sunk costs. Sunk costs are particularly relevant to the electronic communications sector in view of the fact that large investments are necessary to create, for instance, an efficient electronic communications network for the provision of access services and it is likely that little could be recovered if a new entrant decides to exit the market. Entry barriers are exacerbated by further economies of scope and density which generally characterise such networks. Thus, a large network is always likely to have lower costs than a smaller one, with the result that an entrant in order to take a large share of the market and be able to compete would have to price below the incumbent, making it thus difficult to recover sunk costs.

81. As regards the relevance of the notion of "essential facilities" for the purposes of applying the new definition of SMP, there is for the moment no jurisprudence in relation to the electronic communications sector. However, this notion, which is mainly relevant with regard to the existence of an abuse of a dominant position under Article 82 of the EC Treaty, is less relevant with regard to the *ex-ante* assessment of SMP within the meaning of Article 14 of the framework Directive. In particular, the doctrine of "essential facilities" is complementary to existing general obligations imposed on dominant undertaking, such as the obligation not to discriminate among customers and has been applied in cases under Article 82 in exceptional circumstances, such as where the refusal to supply or to grant access to third parties would limit or prevent the emergence of new markets, or new products, contrary to Article 82(b) of the Treaty. It has thus primarily been associated with access issues or cases involving a refusal to supply or to deal under Article 82 of the Treaty, without the presence of any discriminatory treatment. Under existing case-law, a product or service cannot be considered "necessary" or "essential" unless there is no real or potential substitute. Whilst it is true that an undertaking which is in possession of an "essential facility" is by definition in a dominant position on any market for that facility, the contrary is not always true. The fact that a given facility is not "essential" or "indispensable" for an economic activity on some distinct market, within the meaning of the existing case-law[86] does not mean that the owner of this facility might not be in a dominant position. For instance, a network operator can be in a dominant position despite the existence of alternative competing networks if the size or importance of its network affords him the possibility to behave independently from other network operators.[87] In other words, what matters is to establish whether a given facility affords its owner significant

market power in the market without thus being necessary to further establish that the said facility can also be considered "essential" or "indispensable" within the meaning of existing case-law.

Notes

[86] Joined Cases C-241/91 P and C-242/91 P, *RTE and ITP v Commission*, [1995] ECR I-743, Case C-7/97, *Oscar Bronner* [1998] ECR I-7791, and Joined Cases T-374/94, T-375/94, T-384/94 and T-388/94, *European Night Services and others v Commission* [1998] ECR II-3141.

[87] Case COMP/M.1741 — *MCI WorldCom/Sprint*, paragraph 196.

82. It follows from the foregoing that the doctrine of the "essential facilities" is less relevant for the purposes of applying *ex ante* Article 14 of the framework Directive than applying ex-post Article 82 of the EC Treaty.

3.1.1. *Leverage of market power*

83. According to Article 14(3) of the framework Directive, "where an undertaking has significant market power on a specific market, it may also be deemed to have significant market power on a closely related market, where the links between the two markets are such as to allow the market power held in one market to be leveraged into the other market, thereby strengthening the market power of the undertaking".

84. This provision is intended to address a market situation comparable to the one that gave rise to the Court's judgment in *Tetra Pak II*.[88] In that case, the Court decided that an undertaking that had a dominant position in one market, and enjoyed a leading position on a distinct but closely associated market, was placed as a result in a situation comparable to that of holding a dominant position on the markets in question taken as a whole. Thanks to its dominant position on the first market, and its market presence on the associated, secondary market, an undertaking may thus leverage the market power which it enjoys in the first market and behave independently of its customers on the latter market.[89] Although in *Tetra Pak* the markets taken as a whole in which Tetra Pak was found to be dominant were horizontal, close associative links, within the meaning of the Court's case-law, will most often be found in vertically integrated markets. This is often the case in the telecommunications sector, where an operator often has a dominant position on the infrastructure market and a significant presence on the downstream, services market.[90] Under such circumstances, an NRA may consider it appropriate to find that such operator has SMP on both markets taken together. However, in practice, if an undertaking has been designated as having SMP on an upstream wholesale or access market, NRAs will normally be in a position to prevent any likely spill-over or leverage effects downstream into the retail or services markets by imposing on that undertaking any of the obligations provided for in the access Directive which may be appropriate to avoid such effects. Therefore, it is only where the imposition of *ex-ante* obligations on an undertaking which is dominant in the (access) upstream market would not result in effective competition on the (retail) downstream market that NRAs should examine whether Article 14(3) may apply.

Notes

[88] Case C-333/94 P, *Tetra Pak v Commission* [1996] ECR I-5951.

[89] See, also, Case COMP/M.2146 — *Tetra Laval/Sidel*, paragraphs 325–389, *subjudice*, T-5/02. [See now Case T-5/02 *Tetra Laval BV v Commission* [2002] ECR II-4381; case C-12/03 P *Commission v Tetra Laval BV* [2005] ECR I-987.]

[90] See Access notice, paragraph 65.

85. The foregoing considerations are also relevant in relation to horizontal markets.[91] Moreover, irrespective of whether the markets under consideration are vertical or horizontal, both markets should be electronic communications markets within the meaning of Article 2 of the framework Directive and both should display such characteristics as to justify the imposition of *ex-ante* regulatory obligations.[92]

Notes

[91] In the case of horizontal markets, the market analysis should focus on establishing the existence of close associative links which will enable an undertaking dominant in one market to behave independently of its competitors in a

neighbouring market. Such links may be found to exist by reference to the type of conduct of suppliers and users in the markets under consideration (same customers and/or suppliers in both markets, i.e. customers buying both retail voice calls and retail Internet access) or the fact that the input product or service is essentially the same (i.e. provision by a fixed operator of network infrastructure to ISPs for wholesale call origination and wholesale call termination); see, also, Case T-83/91, *Tetra Pak v Commission*, op. cit., paragraph 120 and Case COMP/M.2416 — *Tetra Laval/Sidel*.

92 Article 14(3) of the framework Directive is not intended to apply in relation to market power leveraged from a "regulated" market into an emerging, "non-regulated" market. In such cases, any abusive conduct in the "emerging" market would normally be dealt with under Article 82 of the EC Treaty.

3.1.2. Collective dominance

86. Under Article 82 of the EC Treaty, a dominant position can be held by one or more undertakings ("collective dominance"). Article 14(2) of the framework Directive also provides that an undertaking may enjoy significant market power, that is, it may be in a dominant position, either individually or jointly with others.

87. In the Access notice, the Commission had stated that, although at the time both its own practice and the case-law of the Court were still developing, it would consider two or more undertakings to be in a collective dominant position when they had substantially the same position vis-à-vis their customers and competitors as a single company has if it is in a dominant position, provided that no effective competition existed between them. The lack of competition could be due, in practice, to the existence of certain links between those companies. The Commission had also stated, however, that the existence of such links was not a prerequisite for a finding of joint dominance.[93]

Notes
93 See Access notice, paragraph 79.

88. Since the publication of the Access notice, the concept of collective dominance has been tested in a number of decisions taken by the Commission under Regulation No 17 and under the merger control Regulation. In addition, both the Court of First Instance (CFI) and the Court of Justice of the European Communities (ECJ) have given judgments which have contributed to further clarifying the exact scope of this concept.

3.1.2.1. The jurisprudence of the CFI/ECJ

89. The expression "one or more undertakings" in Article 82 of the EC Treaty implies that a dominant position may be held by two or more economic entities which are legally and economically independent of each other.[94]

Notes
94 Joined Cases C-395/96 P and C-396/96 P, *Compagnie maritime belge and others v Commission* [2000] ECR I-1365.

90. Until the ruling of the ECJ in *Compagnie maritime belge*[95] and the ruling of the CFI in *Gencor*[96] (see below), it might have been argued that a finding of collective dominance was based on the existence of economic links, in the sense of structural links, or other factors which could give rise to a connection between the undertakings concerned.[97] The question of whether collective dominance could also apply to an oligopolistic market, that is a market comprised of few sellers, in the absence of any kind of links among the undertakings present in such a market, was first raised in *Gencor*. The case concerned the legality of a decision adopted by the Commission under the merger control Regulation prohibiting the notified transaction on the grounds that it would lead to the creation of a duopoly market conducive to a situation of oligopolistic dominance.[98] Before the CFI, the parties argued that the Commission had failed to prove the existence of "links" between the members of the duopoly within the meaning of the existing case-law.

Notes
95 Idem, at paragraph 39.
96 Case T102/96, *Gencor v Commission* [1999] ECR II-753.

[97] See Joined Cases T-68/89, T-77/89 and T-78/89, *SIV and Others v Commission* [1992] ECR II-1403, paragraph 358, Case C-393/92 *Almelo* [1994] ECR I-1477, paragraph 43, Case C-96/94, *Centro Servizi Spediporto* [1995] ECR I-2883, paragraph 33, Joined Cases C-140/94, 141/94, and C-142/94, *DIP*, [1995] ECR I-3257, paragraph 62, Case C-70/95, *Sodemare* [1997] ECR I-3395, paragraph 46, and Joined Cases C-68/94 and C-30/95 *France and Others v Commission* [1998] ECR I-1375, paragraph 221.

[98] Case IV/M.619 — *Gencor Lonhro* (OJ L 11, 14.1.1997, p. 30).

91. The CFI dismissed the application by stating, *inter alia*, that there was no legal precedent suggesting that the notion of "economic links" was restricted to the notion of structural links between the undertakings concerned: According to the CFI, "there is no reason whatsoever in legal or economic terms to exclude from the notion of economic links the relationship of interdependence existing between the parties to a tight oligopoly within which, in a market with the appropriate characteristics, in particular in terms of market concentration, transparency and product homogeneity, those parties are in a position to anticipate one another's behaviour and are therefore strongly encouraged to align their conduct in the market, in particular in such a way as to maximise their joint profits by restricting production with a view to increasing prices. In such a context, each trader is aware that highly competitive action on its part designed to increase its market share (for example a price cut) would provoke identical action by the others, so that it would derive no benefit from its initiative. All the traders would thus be affected by the reduction in price *levels*".[99] As the Court pointed out, market conditions may be such that "each undertaking may become aware of common interests and, in particular, cause prices to increase without having to enter into an agreement or resort to concerted practice".[100]

Notes

[99] *Gencor v Commission*, op. cit., at paragraph 276.
[100] Idem, at paragraph 277.

92. The CFI's ruling in *Gencor* was later endorsed by the ECJ in *Compagnie maritime belge*, where the Court gave further guidance as to how the term of collective dominance should be understood and as to which conditions must be fulfilled before such finding can be made. According to the Court, in order to show that two or more undertakings hold a joint dominant position, it is necessary to consider whether the undertakings concerned together constitute a collective entity vis-à-vis their competitors, their trading partners and their consumers on a particular market.[101] This will be the case when (i) there is no effective competition among the undertakings in question; and (ii) the said undertakings adopt a uniform conduct or common policy in the relevant market.[102] Only when that question is answered in the affirmative, is it appropriate to consider whether the collective entity actually holds a dominant position.[103] In particular, it is necessary to ascertain whether economic links exist between the undertakings concerned which enable them to act independently of their competitors, customers and consumers. The Court recognised that an implemented agreement, decision or concerted practice (whether or not covered by an exemption under Article 81(3) of the Treaty) may undoubtedly result in the undertakings concerned being linked in a such way that their conduct on a particular market on which they are active results in them being perceived as a collective entity vis-à-vis their competitors, their trading partners and consumers.[104]

Notes

[101] *Compagnie maritime belge transports and Others*, op. cit., at paragraph 39, see, also, Case T-342/99 *Airtours/Commission* [2002] ECR II-[2585], paragraph 76.
[102] See, in particular, *France and Others v Commission*, op. cit., paragraph 221.
[103] *Compagnie maritime belge*, at paragraph 39.
[104] Idem at paragraph 44.

93. The mere fact, however, that two or more undertakings are linked by an agreement, a decision of associations of undertakings or a concerted practice within the meaning of Article 81(1) of the Treaty does not, of itself, constitute a necessary basis for such a finding. As the Court stated, "a finding of a collective dominant position may also be based on other connecting factors and

would depend on an economic assessment and, in particular, on an assessment of the structure of the market in question".[105]

Notes
[105] Idem at paragraph 45.

94. It follows from the *Gencor* and *Compagnie maritime belge* judgments that, although the existence of structural links can be relied upon to support a finding of a collective dominant position, such a finding can also be made in relation to an oligopolistic or highly concentrated market whose structure alone in particular, is conducive to coordinated effects on the relevant market.[106]

Notes
[106] The use here of the term "coordinated effects" is no different from the term "parallel anticompetitive behaviour" also used in Commission's decisions applying the concept of collective (oligopolistic) dominance.

3.1.2.2.   The Commission's decision-making practice and Annex II of the framework Directive

95. In a number of decisions adopted under the merger control Regulation, the Commission considered the concept of collective dominance. It sought in those cases to ascertain whether the structure of the oligopolistic markets in question was conducive to coordinated effects on those markets.[107]

Notes
[107] See in particular, Cases COMP/M.2498 — *UPM-Kymmene/Haindl*, and COMP/M.2499 — *Norske Skog/Parenco/Walsum*, Case COMP/M.2201 — *MAN/Auwärter*, Case COMP/M.2097 — *SCA/Matsä Tissue*, Case COMP/M.1882 — *Pirelli/BICC*, Case COMP/M.1741 — *MCI WorldCom/Sprint*, *subjudice*, T-310/00 [see now [2004] ECR II-3253] Case IV/M.1524 — *Airtours/First Choice* (OJ L 93, 13.4.2000, p. 1), *subjudice* T-342/99 [see now [2002] ECR II-2585], Case IV/M.1383 — *Exxon/Mobil*, Case IV/M.1313 — *Danish Crown/Vestjyske Slagterier* (OJ L 20, 25.1.2000, p. 1), Case IV/M.1225 — *Enso/Stora* (OJ L 254, 29.9.1999, p. 9), Case IV/M.1016 — *Price Waterhouse/Coopers & Lybrand* (OJ L 50, 26.2.1999, p. 27), Case IV/M.619 — *Gencor/Lonrho*, cit., Case IV/M.308, *Kali + Salz/MdK/Treuhand* (OJ L 186, 21.7.1994, p. 38) and Case IV/M.190 — *Nestlé/Perrier* (OJ L 356, 5.12.1992, p. 1).

96. When assessing *ex-ante* the likely existence or emergence of a market which is or could become conducive to collective dominance in the form of tacit coordination, NRAs, should analyse:
    (a) whether the characteristics of the market makes it conducive to tacit coordination; and
    (b) whether such form of coordination is sustainable that is, (i) whether any of the oligopolists have the ability and incentive to deviate from the coordinated outcome, considering the ability and incentives of the non-deviators to retaliate; and (ii) whether buyers/ fringe competitors/potential entrants have the ability and incentive to challenge any anti-competitive coordinated outcome.[108]

Notes
[108] This is in essence the type of analysis carried out by the Commission in past decisions related to collective dominance, see, for instance, Case IV/M.190 — *Nestlé/Perrier*, (OJ L 356, 5.12.1992, p. 1), *Gencor/Lonrho*, cit., Case IV/M.1383 — *Exxon/Mobil*, paragraph 259, Case IV/M.1524 — *Airtours/First Choice* (OJ L 93, 13.4.2000, p. 1), and Case COMP/M.2499 — *Norske Skog/Parenco/Walsum*, paragraph 76; see, also, *Airtours v Commission*, op. cit., paragraph 62.

97. This analysis is facilitated by looking at a certain number of criteria which are summarised in Annex II of the framework Directive, which have also been used by the Commission in applying the notion of collective dominance under the merger control Regulation. According to this Annex, "two or more undertakings can be found to be in a joint dominant position within the meaning of Article 14 if, even in the absence of structural or other links between them, they operate in a market, the structure of which is considered to be conducive to coordinated effects.[109] Without prejudice to the case-law of the Court of Justice on joint dominance, this is likely to be the case where the market satisfies a number of appropriate characteristics, in particular in terms of market concentration, transparency and other characteristics mentioned below:
— mature market,

— stagnant or moderate growth on the demand side,

— low elasticity of demand,

— homogeneous product,

— similar cost structures,

— similar market shares,

— lack of technical innovation, mature technology,

— absence of excess capacity,

— high barriers to entry,

— lack of countervailing buying power,

— lack of potential competition,

— various kind of informal or other links between the undertakings concerned,

— retaliatory mechanisms,

— lack or reduced scope for price competition".

Notes

109 See, also, recital 26 of the framework Directive: "two or more undertakings can be found to enjoy a joint dominant position not only where there exist structural or other links between them but also where the structure of the relevant market is conducive to coordinated effects, that is, it encourages parallel or aligned anticompetitive behaviour on the market".

98. Annex II of the framework Directive expressly states that the above is not an exhaustive list, nor are the criteria cumulative. Rather, the list is intended to illustrate the sorts of evidence that could be used to support assertions concerning the existence of a collective (oligopolistic) dominance in the form of tacit coordination.[110] As stated above, the list also shows that the existence of structural links among the undertakings concerned is not a prerequisite for finding a collective dominant position. It is however clear that where such links exist, they can be relied upon to explain, together with any of the other abovementioned criteria, why in a given oligopolistic market coordinated effects are likely to arise. In the absence of such links, in order to establish whether a market is conducive to collective dominance in the form of tacit coordination, it is necessary to consider a number of characteristics of the market. While these characteristics are often presented in the form of the abovementioned list, it is necessary to examine all of them and to make an overall assessment rather than mechanistically applying a "check list". Depending on the circumstances of the case, the fact that one or another of the structural elements usually associated with collective dominance may not be clearly established is not in itself decisive to exclude the likelihood of a coordinated outcome.[111]

Notes

110 See Case COMP/M.2498 — *UPM-Kymmene/Haindl*, and Case COMP/M.2499 — *Norske Skog/Parenco/Walsum*, at paragraph 77.

111 See, for instance, Case COMP/M.2097 — *SCA/Metsä Tissue*.

99. In an oligopolistic market where most, if not all, of the abovementioned criteria are met, it should be examined whether, in particular, the market operators have a strong incentive to converge to a coordinated market outcome and refrain from reliance on competitive conduct. This will be the case where the long-term benefits of an anti-competitive conduct outweigh any short-term gains resulting from a resort to a competitive behaviour.

100. It must be stressed that a mere finding that a market is concentrated does not necessarily warrant a finding that its structure is conducive to collective dominance in the form of tacit coordination.[112]

Notes

112 For instance, in Case COMP/M.2201 — *MAN/Auwärter*, despite the fact that two of the parties present in the German city-bus market in Germany, MAN/Auwärter and EvoBus, would each supply just under half of that market, the Commission concluded that there was no risk of joint dominance. In particular, the Commission found that any tacit division of the market between EvoBus and MAN/Auwärter was not likely as there would be no viable coordination mechanism. Secondly, significant disparities between EvoBus and MAN/Auwärter, such as different cost structures, would make it likely that the companies would compete rather than collude. Likewise, in the Alcoa/ British Aluminium case, the Commission found that despite the fact that two of the parties present in the relevant

market accounted for almost 80% of the sales, the market could not be said to be conducive to oligopolistic dominance since (i) market shares were volatile and unstable; and (ii) demand was quite irregular making it difficult for the parties to be able to respond to each other's action in order to tacitly coordinate their behaviour. Furthermore, the market was not transparent in relation to prices and purchasers had significant countervailing power. The Commission's conclusions were further reinforced by the absence of any credible retaliation mechanism likely to sustain any tacit coordination and the fact that competition in the market was not only based on prices but depended to a large extent on technological innovation and after-sales follow-up, Case COMP/M.2111 — *Alcoa/British Aluminium*.

101. Ultimately, in applying the notion of collective dominance in the form of tacit coordination, the criteria which will carry the most sway will be those which are critical to a coordinated outcome in the specific market under consideration. For instance, in Case COMP/M.2499 — *Norske Skog/Parenco/Walsum*, the Commission came to the conclusion that even if the markets for newsprint and wood-containing magazine paper were concentrated, the products were homogeneous, demand was highly inelastic, buyer power was limited and barriers to entry were high, nonetheless the limited stability of market shares, the lack of symmetry in costs structures and namely, the lack of transparency of investments decisions and the absence of a credible retaliation mechanism rendered unlikely and unsustainable any possibility of tacit coordination among the oligopolists.[113]

Notes

[113] Likewise, in Case COMP/M.2348 — *Outokumpu/Norzink*, the Commission found that even if the zinc market was composed of few players, entry barriers were high and demand growth perspectives low, the likelihood of the emergence of a market structure conducive to coordinated outcome was unlikely if it could be shown that (i) parties could not manipulate the formation of prices; (ii) producers had asymmetric cost structures and there was no credible retaliation mechanism in place.

3.1.2.3. Collective dominance and the telecommunications sector

102. In applying the notion of collective dominance, NRAs may also take into consideration decisions adopted under the merger control Regulation in the electronic communications sector, in which the Commission has examined whether any of the notified transactions could give rise to a finding of collective dominance.

103. In *MCI WorldCom/Sprint*, the Commission examined whether the merged entity together with Concert Alliance could be found to enjoy a collective dominant position on the market for global telecommunications services (GTS). Given that operators on that market competed on a bid basis where providers were selected essentially in the first instances of the bidding process on the basis of their ability to offer high quality, tailor-made sophisticated services, and not on the basis of prices, the Commission's investigation was focused on the incentives for market participants to engage in parallel behaviour as to who wins what bid (and who had won what bids).[114] After having examined in depth the structure of the market (homogenous product, high barriers of entry, customers countervailing power, etc.) the Commission concluded that it was not able to show absence of competitive constraints from actual competitors, a key factor in examining whether parallel behaviour can be sustained, and thus decided not to pursue further its objections in relation to that market.[115]

Notes

[114] See Case COMP/M.1741 — *MCI WorldCom/Sprint*, paragraph 263.
[115] Idem, paragraphs 257–302.

104. In *BT/Esat*,[116] one of the issues examined by the Commission was whether market conditions in the Irish market for dial-up Internet access lent themselves to the emergence of a duopoly consisting of the incumbent operator, Eircom, and the merged entity. The Commission concluded that this was not the case for the following reasons. First, market shares were not stable; second, demand was doubling every six months; third, internet access products were not considered homogeneous; and finally, technological developments were one of the main characteristics of the market.[117]

Notes
[116] Case COMP/M.1838 — *BT/Esat*.
[117] Idem, paragraphs 10 to 14.

105. In *Vodafone/Airtouch*,[118] the Commission found that the merged entity would have joint control of two of the four mobile operators present on the German mobile market (namely D2 and E-Plus, the other two being T-Mobil and VIAG Interkom). Given that entry into the market was highly regulated, in the sense that licences were limited by reference to the amount of available radio frequencies, and that market conditions were transparent, it could not be ruled out that such factors could lead to the emergence of a duopoly conducive to coordinated effects.[119]

Notes
[118] Case IV/M.1430 — *Vodafone/Airtouch*.
[119] Idem, at paragraph 28. The likely emergence of a duopolistic market concerned only the three largest mobile operators, that is D2 and E-Plus, on the one hand, and T-Mobil on the other hand, given that VIAG Interkom's market share was below 5%. The Commission's concerns were finally removed after the parties proposed to divest Vodafone's entire stake in E-Plus.

106. In *France Telecom/Orange* the Commission found that, prior to the entry of Orange into the Belgian mobile market, the two existing players, Proximus and Mobistar, were in a position to exercise joint dominance. As the Commission noted, for the four years preceding Orange's entry, both operators had almost similar and transparent pricing, their prices following exactly the same trends.[120] In the same decision the Commission further dismissed claims by third parties as to the risk of a collective dominant position of Vodafone and France Telecom in the market for the provision of pan-European mobile services to internationally mobile customers. Other than significant asymmetries between the market shares of the two operators, the market was considered to be emerging, characterised by an increasing demand and many types of different services on offer and on price.[121]

Notes
[120] Case COMP/M.2016 — *France Telecom/Orange*, at paragraph 26.
[121] Idem, at paragraphs 39–40. In its working document "On the initial findings of the sector inquiry into mobile roaming charges", the Commission made reference to (i) the likely existence of a number of economic links between mobile operators, namely through their interconnection agreements, their membership of the GSM Association, the WAP and the UMTS forum, the fact that terms and conditions of roaming agreements were almost standardised; and (ii) the likely existence of high barriers to entry. In its preliminary assessment the Commission also stressed that the fact that the mobile market is, in general, technology driven, did not seem to have affected the conditions of competition prevailing on the wholesale international roaming market, see: http://europa.eu.int/comm/competition/antitrust/others/sector_inquiries/roaming/, at pages 24 and 25.

4. Imposition, Maintenance, Amendment or Withdrawal of Obligations under the Regulatory Framework

107. Section 3 of these guidelines dealt with the analysis of relevant markets that NRAs must carry out under Article 16 of the framework Directive to determine whether a market is effectively competitive, i.e. whether there are undertakings in that market who are in a dominant position. This section aims to provide guidance for NRAs on the action they should take following that analysis, i.e. the imposition, maintenance, amendment or withdrawal, as appropriate, of specific regulatory obligations on undertakings designated as having SMP. This section also describes the circumstances in which similar obligations than those that can be imposed on SMP operators may, exceptionally, be imposed on undertakings who have not been designated as having SMP.

108. The specific regulatory obligations which may be imposed on SMP undertakings can apply both to wholesale and retail markets. In principle, the obligations related to wholesale markets are set out in Articles 9 to 13 of the access Directive. The obligations related to retail markets are set out in Articles 17 to 19 of the universal service Directive.

109. The obligations set out in the access Directive are: transparency (Article 9); non-discrimination (Article 10); accounting separation (Article 11), obligations for access to and use of specific network facilities (Article 12), and price control and cost accounting obligations (Article 13). In addition, Article 8 of the access Directive provides that NRAs may impose obligations outside this list. In order to do so, they must submit a request to the Commission, which will take a decision, after seeking the advice of the Communications Committee, as to whether the NRA concerned is permitted to impose such obligations.

110. The obligations set out in the universal service Directive are: regulatory controls on retail services (Article 17), availability of the minimum set of leased lines (Article 18 and Annex VII) and carrier selection and preselection (Article 19).

111. Under the regulatory framework, these obligations should only be imposed on undertakings which have been designated as having SMP in a relevant market, except in certain defined cases, listed in Section 4.3.

4.1. Imposition, maintenance, amendment or withdrawal of obligations on SMP operators

112. As explained in Section 1, the notion of effective competition means that there is no undertaking with dominance on the relevant market. In other words, a finding that a relevant market is effectively competitive is, in effect, a determination that there is neither single nor joint dominance on that market. Conversely, a finding that a relevant market is not effectively competitive is a determination that there is single or joint dominance on that market.

113. If an NRA finds that a relevant market is subject to effective competition, it is not allowed to impose obligations on any operator on that relevant market under Article 16. If the NRA has previously imposed regulatory obligations on undertaking(s) in that market, the NRA must withdraw such obligations and may not impose any new obligation on that undertaking(s). As stipulated in Article 16(3) of the framework Directive, where the NRA proposes to remove existing regulatory obligations, it must give parties affected a reasonable period of notice.

114. If an NRA finds that competition in the relevant market is not effective because of the existence of an undertaking or undertakings in a dominant position, it must designate in accordance with Article 16(4) of the framework Directive the undertaking or undertakings concerned as having SMP and impose appropriate regulatory obligations on the undertaking(s) concerned. However, merely designating an undertaking as having SMP on a given market, without imposing any appropriate regulatory obligations, is inconsistent with the provisions of the new regulatory framework, notably Article 16(4) of the framework Directive. In other words, NRAs must impose at least one regulatory obligation on an undertaking that has been designated as having SMP. Where an NRA determines the existence of more than one undertaking with dominance, i.e. that a joint dominant position exists, it should also determine the most appropriate regulatory obligations to be imposed, based on the principle of proportionality.

115. If an undertaking was previously subject to obligations under the 1998 regulatory framework, the NRA must consider whether similar obligations continue to be appropriate under the new regulatory framework, based on a new market analysis carried out in accordance with these guidelines. If the undertaking is found to have SMP in a relevant market under the new framework, regulatory obligations similar to those imposed under the 1998 regulatory framework may therefore be maintained. Alternatively, such obligations could be amended, or new obligations provided in the new framework might also be imposed, as the NRA considers appropriate.

116. Except where the Community's international commitments under international treaties prescribe the choice of regulatory obligation (see Section 4.4) or when the Directives prescribe particular remedies as under Article 18 and 19 of the universal service Directive, NRAs will have to choose between the range of regulatory obligations set out in the Directives in order to remedy a particular problem in a market found not to be effectively competitive. Where NRAs intend to impose other obligations for access and interconnection than those listed in the access Directive, they must submit a request for Commission approval of their proposed course of action. The Commission must seek the advice of the Communications Committee before taking its decision.

117. Community law, and in particular Article 8 of the framework Directive, requires NRAs to ensure that the measures they impose on SMP operators under Article 16 of the framework

Directive are justified in relation to the objectives set out in Article 8 and are proportionate to the achievement of those objectives. Thus any obligation imposed by NRAs must be proportionate to the problem to be remedied. Article 7 of the framework Directive requires NRAs to set out the reasoning on which any proposed measure is based when they communicate that measure to other NRAs and to the Commission. Thus, in addition to the market analysis supporting the finding of SMP, NRAs need to include in their decisions a justification of the proposed measure in relation to the objectives of Article 8, as well as an explanation of why their decision should be considered proportionate.

118. Respect for the principle of proportionality will be a key criterion used by the Commission to assess measures proposed by NRAs under the procedure of Article 7 of framework Directive. The principle of proportionality is well-established in Community law. In essence, the principle of proportionality requires that the means used to attain a given end should be no more than what is appropriate and necessary to attain that end. In order to establish that a proposed measure is compatible with the principle of proportionality, the action to be taken must pursue a legitimate aim, and the means employed to achieve the aim must be both necessary and the least burdensome, i.e. it must be the minimum necessary to achieve the aim.

119. However, particularly in the early stages of implementation of the new framework, the Commission would not expect NRAs to withdraw existing regulatory obligations on SMP operators which have been designed to address legitimate regulatory needs which remain relevant, without presenting clear evidence that those obligations have achieved their purpose and are therefore no longer required since competition is deemed to be effective on the relevant market. Different remedies are available in the new regulatory framework to address different identified problems and remedies should be tailored to these specified problems.

120. The Commission, when consulted as provided for in Article 7(3) of the framework Directive, will also check that any proposed measure taken by the NRAs is in conformity with the regulatory framework as a whole, and will assess the impact of the proposed measure on the single market.

121. The Commission will assist NRAs to ensure that as far as possible they adopt consistent approaches in their choice of remedies where similar situations exist in different Member States. Moreover, as noted in Article 7(2) of the framework Directive, NRAs shall seek to agree on the types of remedies best suited to address particular situations in the marketplace.

4.2. Transnational markets: joint analysis by NRAs

122. Article 15(4) of the framework Directive gives the Commission the power to issue a Decision identifying product and service markets that are transnational, covering the whole of the Community or a substantial part thereof. Under the terms of Article 16(5) of the framework Directive, the NRAs concerned must jointly conduct the market analysis and decide whether obligations need to be imposed. In practice, the European Regulators Group is expected to provide a suitable forum for such a joint analysis.

123. In general, joint analysis by NRAs would follow similar procedures (e.g. for public consultation) to those required when a single national regulatory authority is conducting a market analysis. Precise arrangements for collective analysis and decision-making will need to be drawn up.

4.3. Imposition of certain specific regulatory obligations on non-SMP operators

124. The preceding parts of this section set out the procedures whereby certain specific obligations may be imposed on SMP undertakings, under Articles 7 and 8 of the access Directive and Article 16–19 of the universal service Directive. Exceptionally, similar obligations may be imposed on operators other than those that have been designated as having SMP, in the following cases, listed in Article 8(3) of the access Directive:
   — obligations covering *inter alia* access to conditional access systems, obligations to interconnect to ensure end-to-end interoperability, and access to application program interfaces and electronic programme guides to ensure accessibility to specified digital TV and radio broadcasting services (Article 5(1), 5(2) and 6 of the access Directive),

1197

— obligations that NRAs may impose for co-location where rules relating to environmental protection, health, security or town and country planning deprive other undertakings of viable alternatives to co-location (Article 12 of the framework Directive),

— obligations for accounting separation on undertakings providing electronic communications services who enjoy special or exclusive rights in other sectors (Article 13 of the framework Directive),

— obligations relating to commitments made by an undertaking in the course of a competitive or comparative selection procedure for a right of use of radio frequency (Condition B7 of the Annex to the authorisation Directive, applied via Article 6(1) of that Directive),

— obligations to handle calls to subscribers using specific numbering resources and obligations necessary for the implementation of number portability (Articles 27, 28 and 30 of the universal service Directive),

— obligations based on the relevant provisions of the data protection Directive, and

— obligations to be imposed on non-SMP operators in order to comply with the Community's international commitments.

4.4. Relationship to WTO commitments

125. The EC and its Member States have given commitments in the WTO in relation to undertakings that are "major suppliers" of basic telecommunications services.[122] Such undertakings are subject to all of the obligations set out in the EC's and its Member States' commitments in the WTO for basic telecommunications services. The provisions of the new regulatory framework, in particular relating to access and interconnection, ensure that NRAs continue to apply the relevant obligations to undertakings that are major suppliers in accordance with the WTO commitments of the EC and its Member States.

Notes

122 GATS commitments taken by EC on telecommunications: http://gats-info.eu.int/gats-info/swtosvc.pl?&SECCODE=02.C.

5. POWERS OF INVESTIGATION AND COOPERATION PROCEDURES FOR THE PURPOSE OF MARKET ANALYSIS

5.1. Overview

126. This section of the guidelines covers procedures in respect of an NRA's powers to obtain the information necessary to conduct a market analysis.

127. The regulatory framework contains provisions to enable NRAs to require undertakings that provide electronic communications networks and services to supply all the information, including confidential information, necessary for NRAs to assess the state of competition in the relevant markets and impose appropriate *ex-ante* obligations and thus to ensure compliance with the regulatory framework.

128. This section of the guidelines also includes guidance as to measures to ensure effective cooperation between NRAs and NCAs at national level, and among NRAs and between NRAs and the Commission at Community level. In particular this section deals with the exchange of information between those authorities.

129. Many electronic communication markets are fast-moving and their structures are changing rapidly. NRAs should ensure that the assessment of effective competition, the public consultation, and the designation of operators having SMP are all carried out within a reasonable period. Any unnecessary delay in the decision could have harmful effects on incentives for investment by undertakings in the relevant market and therefore on the interests of consumers.

5.2. Market analysis and powers of investigation

130. Under Article 16(1) of the framework Directive, NRAs must carry out an analysis of the relevant markets identified in the Recommendation and any Decision as soon as possible after their adoption or subsequent revision. The conclusions of the analysis of each of the relevant markets, together with the proposed regulatory action, must be published and a public consultation must be conducted, as described in Section 6.

131. In order to carry out their market analysis, NRAs will first need to collect all the information they consider necessary to assess market power in a given market. To the extent that such information needs to be obtained directly from undertakings, Article 11 of the authorisation Directive provides that undertakings are required by the terms of their general authorisation to supply the information necessary for NRAs to conduct a market analysis within the meaning of Article 16(2) of the framework Directive. This is reinforced by the more general obligation in Article 5(1) of the framework Directive which provides that Member States shall ensure that undertakings providing electronic communications networks and services provide all the information necessary for NRAs to ensure conformity with Community law.

132. When NRAs request information from an undertaking, they should state the reasons justifying the request and the time limit within which the information is to be provided. As provided for in Article 10(4) of the authorisation Directive, NRAs may be empowered to impose financial penalties on undertakings for failure to provide information.

133. In accordance with Article 5(4) of the framework Directive, NRAs must publish all information that would contribute to an open and competitive market, acting in accordance with national rules on public access to information and subject to Community and national rules on commercial confidentiality.

134. However, as regards information that is confidential in nature, the provisions of Article 5(3) of the framework Directive, require NRAs to ensure the confidentiality of such information in accordance with Community and national rules on business confidentiality. This confidentiality obligation applies equally to information that has been received in confidence from another public authority.

5.3. Cooperation procedures

Between NRAs and NCAs

135. Article 16(1) of the framework Directive requires NRAs to associate NCAs with the market analyses as appropriate. Member States should put in place the necessary procedures to guarantee that the analysis under Article 16 of the framework Directive is carried out effectively. As the NRAs conduct their market analyses in accordance with the methodologies of competition law, the views of NCAs in respect of the assessment of competition are highly relevant. Cooperation between NRAs and NCAs will be essential, but NRAs remain legally responsible for conducting the relevant analysis. Where under national law the tasks assigned under Article 16 of the framework Directive are carried out by two or more separate regulatory bodies, Member States should ensure clear division of tasks and set up procedures for consultation and cooperation between regulators in order to assure coherent analysis of the relevant markets.

136. Article 3(5) of the framework Directive requires NRAs and NCAs to provide each other with the information necessary for the application of the regulatory framework, and the receiving authority must ensure the same level of confidentiality as the originating authority. NCAs should therefore provide NRAs with all relevant information obtained using the former's investigatory and enforcement powers, including confidential information.

137. Information that is considered confidential by an NCA, in accordance with Community and national rules on business confidentiality, should only be exchanged with NRAs where such exchange is necessary for the application of the provisions of the regulatory framework. The information exchanged should be limited to that which is relevant and proportionate to the purpose of such exchange.

Between the Commission and NRAs

138. For the regulatory framework to operate efficiently and effectively, it is vital that there is a high level of cooperation between the Commission and the NRAs. It is particularly important that effective informal cooperation takes place. The European Regulators Group will be of great importance in providing a framework for such cooperation, as part of its task of assisting and advising the Commission. Cooperation is likely to be of mutual benefit, by minimising the

likelihood of divergences in approach between different NRAs, in particular divergent remedies to deal with the same problem.[123]

Notes

[123] The Communications Committee in Article 22 of the framework Directive also aims at ensuring effective cooperation between the Commission and the Member States.

---

139. In accordance with Article 5(2) of the framework Directive, NRAs must supply the Commission with information necessary for it to carry out its tasks under the Treaty. This covers information relating to the regulatory framework (to be used in verifying compatibility of NRA action with the legislation), but also information that the Commission might require, for example, in considering compliance with WTO commitments.

140. NRAs must ensure that, where they submit information to the Commission which they have requested undertakings to provide, they inform those undertakings that they have submitted it to the Commission.

141. The Commission can also make such information available to another NRA, unless the original NRA has made an explicit and reasoned request to the contrary. Although there is no legal requirement to do so, the Commission will normally inform the undertaking which originally provided the information that it has been passed on to another NRA.

Between NRAs

142. It is of the utmost importance that NRAs develop a common regulatory approach across Member States that will contribute to the development of a true single market for electronic communications. To this end, NRAs are required under Article 7(2) of the framework Directive to cooperate with each other and with the Commission in a transparent manner to ensure the consistent application, in all Member States, of the new regulatory framework. The European Regulators" Group is expected to serve as an important forum for cooperation.

143. Article 5(2) of the framework Directive also foresees that NRAs will exchange information directly between each other, as long as there is a substantiated request. This will be particularly necessary where a transnational market needs to be analysed, but it will also be required within the framework of cooperation in the European Regulators' Group. In all exchanges of information, the NRAs are required to maintain the confidentiality of information received.

6. PROCEDURES FOR CONSULTATION AND PUBLICATION OF PROPOSED NRA DECISIONS

6.1. Public consultation mechanism

144. Except in the urgent cases as explained below, an NRA that intends to take a measure which would have a significant impact on the relevant market should give the interested parties the opportunity to comment on the draft measure. To this effect, the NRA must hold a public consultation on its proposed measure. Where the draft measure concerns a decision relating to an SMP designation or non-designation it should include the following:
   — the market definition used and reasons therefor, with the exception of information that is confidential in accordance with European and national law on business confidentiality,
   — evidence relating to the finding of dominance, with the exception of information that is confidential in accordance with European and national law on business confidentiality together with the identification of any undertakings proposed to be designated as having SMP,
   — full details of the sector-specific obligations that the NRA proposes to impose, maintain, modify or withdraw on the abovementioned undertakings together with an assessment of the proportionality of that proposed measure.

145. The period of the consultation should be reasonable. However, NRAs' decisions should not be delayed excessively as this can impede the development of the market. For decisions related to the existence and designation of undertakings with SMP, the Commission considers that a period of two months would be reasonable for the public consultation. Different periods could be used in some cases if justified. Conversely, where a draft SMP decision is proposed on the

basis of the results of an earlier consultation, the length of consultation period for these decisions may well be shorter than two months.

6.2. Mechanisms to consolidate the internal market for electronic communications

146. Where an NRA intends to take a measure which falls within the scope of the market definition or market analysis procedures of Articles 15 and 16 of the framework Directive, as well as when NRAs apply certain other specific Articles in the regulatory framework[124] and where the measures have an effect on trade between Member States, the NRAs must communicate the measures, together with their reasoning, to NRAs in other Member States and to the Commission in accordance with Article 7(3) of the framework Directive. It should do this at the same time as it begins its public consultation. The NRA must then give other NRAs and the Commission the chance to comment on the NRA's proposed measures, before adopting any final decision. The time available for other NRAs and the Commission to comment should be the same time period as that set by the NRA for its national public consultation, unless the latter is shorter than the minimum period of one month provided for in Article 7(3). The Commission may decide in justified circumstances to publish its comments.

Notes

124 The specific Articles covered are as follows: Articles 15 and 16 of the framework Directive (the latter of which refers to Articles 16–19 of the universal service Directive and Articles 7 and 8 of the access Directive), Articles 5 and 8 of the access Directive (the latter of which refers to the obligations provided for in Articles 9–13 of the access Directive) and Article 16 of the universal service Directive (which refers to Articles 17–19 of universal service Directive). In addition, Article 6 of the access Directive, although not explicitly referenced in Article 7 of the framework Directive, itself contains cross-reference to Article 7 of the framework Directive and is therefore covered by the procedures therein.

147. With regard to measures that could affect trade between Member States, this should be understood as meaning measures that may have an influence, direct or indirect, actual or potential, on the pattern of trade between Member States in a manner which might create a barrier to the single European market.[125] Therefore, the notion of an effect on trade between Member States is likely to cover a broad range of measures.

Notes

125 Recital 38 of the framework Directive.

148. NRAs must make public the results of the public consultation, except in the case of information that is confidential in accordance with Community and national law on business confidentiality.

149. With the exception of two specific cases, explained in the following paragraph, the NRA concerned may adopt the final measure after having taken account of views expressed during its mandatory consultation. The final measure must then be communicated to the Commission without delay.

6.3. Commission power to require the withdrawal of NRAs' draft measures

150. Under the terms of Article 7(4) of the framework Directive, there are two specific situations where the Commission has the possibility to require an NRA to withdraw a draft measure which falls within the scope of Article 7(3):
    — the draft measure concerns the definition of a relevant market which differs from that identified in the Recommendation, or
    — the draft measure concerns a decision as to whether to designate, or not to designate, an undertaking as having SMP, either individually or jointly with others.

151. In respect of the above two situations, where the Commission has indicated to the NRA in the course of the consultation process that it considers that the draft measure would create a barrier to the single European market or where the Commission has serious doubts as to the compatibility of the draft measure with Community law, the adoption of the measure must be delayed by a maximum of an additional two months.

152. During this two-month period, the Commission may, after consulting the Communications Committee following the advisory procedure,[126] take a decision requiring the NRA to withdraw

the draft measure. The Commission's decision will be accompanied by a detailed and objective analysis of why it considers that the draft measure should not be adopted together with specific proposals for amending the draft measure. If the Commission does not take a decision within that period, the draft measure may be adopted by the NRA.

Notes

[126] As provided for in Article 3 of Council Decision 1999/468/EC laying the procedure for the exercising of implementing powers conferred on the Commission, the Commission shall take the utmost account of the opinion delivered by the Committee, but shall not be bound by the opinion.

6.4. Urgent cases

153. In exceptional circumstances, NRAs may act urgently in order to safeguard competition and protect the interest of users. An NRA may therefore, exceptionally, adopt proportionate and provisional measures without consulting either interested parties, the NRAs in other Member States, or the Commission. Where an NRA has taken such urgent action, it must, without delay, communicate these measures, with full reasons, to the Commission, and to the other NRAs. The Commission will verify the compatibility of those measures with Community law and in particular will assess their proportionality in relation to the policy objectives of Article 8 of the framework Directive.

154. If the NRA wishes to make the provisional measures permanent, or extends the time for which it is applicable, the NRA must go through the normal consultation procedure set out above. It is difficult to foresee any circumstances that would justify urgent action to define a market or designate an SMP operator, as such measure are not those that can be carried out immediately. The Commission therefore does not expect NRAs to use the exceptional procedures in such cases.

6.5. Adoption of the final decision

155. Once an NRA's decision has become final, NRAs should notify the Commission of the names of the undertakings that have been designated as having SMP and the obligations imposed on them, in accordance with the requirements of Article 36(2) of the universal service Directive and Articles 15(2) and 16(2) of the access Directive. The Commission will thereafter make this information available in a readily accessible form, and will transmit the information to the Communications Committee as appropriate.

156. Likewise, NRAs should publish the names of undertakings that they have designated as having SMP and the obligations imposed on them. They should ensure that up-to-date information is made publicly available in a manner that guarantees all interested parties easy access to that information.

E26

COUNCIL REGULATION (EEC) No 1534/91

of 31 May 1991
on the application of Article [81](3) of the Treaty to certain categories of agreements, decisions and concerted practices in the insurance sector

Official Journal L 143, 7.6.1991, p. 1

Celex No: 31991R1534

Commentary
Regulation 1534/91/EEC: B&C: 1.022, 3.075, 12.170 F&N: 3.416, 11.98, 11.105, 11.128

THE COUNCIL OF THE EUROPEAN COMMUNITIES,

Having regard to the Treaty establishing the European Economic Community, and in particular Article [83] thereof,

Having regard to the proposal from the Commission,[1]

Having regard to the opinion of the European Parliament,[2]

Having regard to the opinion of the Economic and Social Committee,[3]

Notes

[1] OJ C 16, 23.1.1990, p. 13

[2] OJ C 260, 15.10.1990, p. 57

[3] OJ C 182, 23.7.1990, p. 27

---

[1] Whereas Article [81](1) of the Treaty may, in accordance with Article [81](3), be declared inapplicable to categories of agreements, decisions and concerted practices when satisfy the requirements of Article [81](3);

[2] Whereas the detailed rules for the application of Article [81](3) of the Treaty must be adopted by way of a Regulation based on Article [83] of the Treaty;

[3] Whereas cooperation between undertakings in the insurance sector is, to a certain extent, desirable to ensure the proper functioning of this sector and may at the same time promote consumers' interests;

[4] Whereas the application of Council Regulation (EEC) No 4064/89 of 21 December 1989 on the control of concentrations between undertakings[1] enables the Commission to exercise close supervision on issues arising from concentrations in all sectors, including the insurance sector;

Notes

[1] OJ L 395, 30.12.1989, p. 1. [See now Council Regulation (EC) No 139/2004 (OJ L 24, 29.1.2004, p.1).]

---

[5] Whereas exemptions granted under Article [81](3) of the Treaty cannot themselves affect Community and national provisions safeguarding consumers' interests in this sector;

[6] Whereas agreements, decisions and concerted practices serving such aims may, in so far as they fall within the prohibition contained in Article [81](1) of the Treaty, be exempted therefrom under certain conditions; whereas this applies in particular to agreements, decisions and concerted practices relating to the establishment of common risk premium tariffs based on collectively ascertained statistics or the number of claims, the establishment of standard policy conditions, common coverage of certain types of risks, the settlement of claims, the testing and acceptance of security devices, and registers of, and information on, aggravated risks;

[7] Whereas in view of the large number of notifications submitted pursuant to Council Regulation No 17 of 6 February 1962: First Regulation implementing Articles [81] and [82] of the Treaty,[1] as last amended by the Act of Accession of Spain and Portugal, it is desirable that in order to facilitate the Commission's task, it should be enabled to declare, by way of Regulation, that the provisions of Article [81](1) of the Treaty are inapplicable to certain categories of agreements, decisions and concerted practices;

Notes

[1] OJ 13, 21.2.1962, p. 204/62. [See now Council Regulation (EC) No 1/2003 (OJ L 1, 4.1.2003, p.1).]

---

[8] Whereas it should be laid down under which conditions the Commission, in close and constant liaison with the competent authorities of the Member States, may exercise such powers;

[9] Whereas, in the exercise of such powers, the Commission will take account not only of the risk of competition being eliminated in a substantial part of the relevant market and of any benefit that might be conferred on policyholders resulting from the agreements, but also of the risk which the proliferation of restrictive clauses and the operation of accommodation companies would entail for policyholders;

[10] Whereas the keeping of registers and the handling of information on aggravated risks should be carried out subject to the proper protection of confidentiality;

[11] Whereas, under Article 6 of Regulation No 17, the Commission may provide that a decision taken in accordance with Article [81](3) of the Treaty shall apply with retroactive effect; whereas the Commission should also be able to adopt provisions to such effect in a Regulation;

[12] Whereas, under Article 7 of Regulation No 17, agreements, decisions and concerted practices may, by decision of the Commission, be exempted from prohibition, in particular if they are modified in such manner that they satisfy the requirements of Article [81](3) of the Treaty; whereas it is desirable that the Commission be enabled to grant by Regulation like exemption to such agreements, decisions and concerted practices if they are modified in such manner as to fall within a category defined in an exempting Regulation;

[13] Whereas it cannot be ruled out that, in specific cases, the conditions set out in Article [81](3) of the Treaty may not be fulfilled; whereas the Commission must have the power to regulate such cases pursuant to Regulation No 17 by way of a Decision having effect for the future,

HAS ADOPTED THIS REGULATION:

Article 1

1. Without prejudice to the application of Regulation No 17, the Commission may, by means of a Regulation and in accordance with Article [81](3) of the Treaty, declare that Article [81](1) shall not apply to categories of agreements between undertakings, decisions of associations of undertakings and concerted practices in the insurance sector which have as their object cooperation with respect to:

(a) the establishment of common risk premium tariffs based on collectively ascertained statistics or the number of claims;
(b) the establishment of common standard policy conditions;
(c) the common coverage of certain types of risks;
(d) the settlement of claims;
(e) the testing and acceptance of security devices;
(f) registers of, and information on, aggravated risks, provided that the keeping of these registers and the handling of this information is carried out subject to the proper protection of confidentiality.

2. The Commission Regulation referred to in paragraph 1, shall define the categories of agreements, decisions and concerted practices to which it applies and shall specify in particular:

(a) the restrictions or clauses which may, or may not, appear in the agreements, decisions and concerted practices;
(b) the clauses which must be contained in the agreements, decisions and concerted practices or the other conditions which must be satisfied.

Article 2

Any Regulation adopted pursuant to Article 1 shall be of limited duration.

It may be repealed or amended where circumstances have changed with respect to any of the facts which were essential to its being adopted; in such case, a period shall be fixed for modification of the agreements, decisions and concerted practices to which the earlier Regulation applies.

Article 3

A Regulation adopted pursuant to Article 1 may provide that it shall apply with retroactive effect to agreements, decisions and concerted practices to which, at the date of entry into force of the said Regulation, a Decision taken with retroactive effect pursuant to Article 6 of Regulation No 17 would have applied.

Article 4

1. A Regulation adopted pursuant to Article 1 may provide that the prohibition contained in Article [81](1) of the Treaty shall not apply, for such period as shall be fixed in that Regulation, to agreements, decisions and concerted practices already in existence on 13 March 1962 which do not satisfy the conditions of Article [81](3) where:

— within six months from the entry into force of the said Regulation, they are so modified as to satisfy the said conditions in accordance with the provisions of the said Regulation and

— the modifications are brought to the notice of the Commission within the time limit fixed by the said Regulation.

The provisions of the first subparagraph shall apply in the same way to those agreements, decisions and concerted practices existing at the date of accession of new Member States to which Article [81](1) of the Treaty applies by virtue of accession and which do not satisfy the conditions of Article [81](3).

2. Paragraph 1 shall apply to agreements, decisions and concerted practices which had to be notified before 1 February 1963, in accordance with Article 5 of Regulation No 17, only where they have been so notified before that date.

Paragraph 1 shall not apply to agreements, decisions and concerted practices existing at the date of accession of new Member States to which Article [81](1) of the Treaty applies by virtue of accession and which had to be notified within six months from the date of accession in accordance with Articles 5 and 25 of Regulation No 17, unless they have been so notified within the said period.

3. The benefit of provisions adopted pursuant to paragraph 1 may not be invoked in actions pending at the date of entry into force of a Regulation adopted pursuant to Article 1; neither may it be invoked as grounds for claims for damages against third parties.

Article 5

Where the Commission proposes to adopt a Regulation, it shall publish a draft thereof to enable all persons and organizations concerned to submit to it their comments within such time limit, being not less than one month, as it shall fix.

Article 6

1. The Commission shall consult the Advisory Committee on Restrictive Practices and Monopolies:

(a) before publishing a draft Regulation;

(b) before adopting a Regulation.

2. Article 10(5) and (6) of Regulation No 17, relating to consultation of the Advisory Committee, shall apply. However, joint meetings with the Commission shall take place not earlier than one month after dispatch of the notice convening them.

Article 7

[...]

Notes

Article 7 was repealed by Council Regulation (EC) No 1/2003 (OJ L 1, 4.1.2003, p. 1), Article 40, with effect from 1 May 2004

Article 8

Not later than six years after the entry into force of the Commission Regulation provided for in Article 1, the Commission shall submit to the European Parliament and the Council a report on the functioning of this Regulation, accompanied by such proposals for amendments to this Regulation as may appear necessary in the light of experience. This Regulation shall be binding in its entirety and directly applicable in all Member States.

Done at Brussels, 31 May 1991.

E27

COMMISSION REGULATION (EC) No 358/2003

of 27 February 2003

on the application of Article 81(3) of the Treaty to certain categories of agreements,
decisions and concerted practices in the insurance sector

(Text with EEA relevance)

Official Journal L 53, 28.2.2003, p. 8

Celex No: 32003R0358

Notes

EEA application: this Instrument was adopted with appropriate adaptations by EEA Joint Committee Decision
No 82/2003, OJ L 257, 9.10.2003, p. 37 and EEA Supplement No 51/24: see EEA Agreement, Annex XIV, Chapter J,
Point 15b (as subsequently amended by Decision No 107/2005, OJ L 306, 24.11.2005, p. 45 and EEA Supplement
No 60, 24.11.2005, p. 28, and Decision 130/2004, OJ L 64, 10.3.2005, p. 57 and EEA Supplement No 12, 10.3.2005,
p. 42).

Commentary

Regulation 358/2003: B&C: 3.081, 3.093, 5.017, 5.096, 5.144, 12.170–12.171, 12.174, 12.176 F&N: 11.98,
11.109, 11.126
Chapter II: F&N: 11.109
Recitals 10–13: B&C: 12.172

THE COMMISSION OF THE EUROPEAN COMMUNITIES,

Having regard to the Treaty establishing the European Community,

Having regard to Council Regulation (EEC) No 1534/91 of 31 May 1991 on the application of
Article 81(3) of the Treaty to certain categories of agreements, decisions and concerted practices in the
insurance sector,[1] and in particular Article 1(1)(a), (b), (c) and (e) thereof,

Having published a draft of this Regulation,[2]

Having consulted the Advisory Committee on Restrictive Practices and Dominant Positions,

---

Notes
[1] OJ L 143, 7.6.1991, p. 1.
[2] OJ C 163, 9.7.2002, p. 7.

Whereas:

(1) Regulation (EEC) No 1534/91 empowers the Commission to apply Article 81(3) of the Treaty by
regulation to certain categories of agreements, decisions and concerted practices in the insurance
sector which have as their object cooperation with respect to:

— the establishment of common risk premium tariffs based on collectively ascertained statistics
or the number of claims,

— the establishment of common standard policy conditions,

— the common coverage of certain types of risks,

— the settlement of claims,

— the testing and acceptance of security devices,

— registers of, and information on, aggravated risks.

(2) Pursuant to Council Regulation (EEC) No 1534/91, the Commission adopted Regulation (EEC)
No 3932/92 of 21 December 1992 on the application of Article 81(3) of the Treaty to certain categories of agreements, decisions and concerted practices in the insurance sector.[1] Regulation

(EEC) No 3932/92, as amended by the Act of Accession of Austria, Finland and Sweden, expires on 31 March 2003.

Notes
[1] OJ L 398, 31.12.1992, p. 7.

(3) Regulation (EEC) No 3932/92 does not grant an exemption to agreements concerning the settlement of claims and registers of, and information on, aggravated risks. The Commission considered that it lacked sufficient experience in handling individual cases to make use of the power conferred by Council Regulation (EEC) No 1534/91 in those fields. This situation has not changed.

Commentary
Recital 3: B&C: 12.170 F&N: 11.128

(4) On 12 May 1999, the Commission adopted a Report[1] to the Council and the European Parliament on the operation of Regulation (EEC) No 3932/92. On 15 December 1999, the Economic and Social Committee adopted an opinion on the Commission's report.[2] On 19 May 2000, the Parliament adopted a Resolution on the Commission's report.[3] On 28 June 2000, the Commission held a consultation meeting with interested parties, including representatives of the insurance sector and national competition authorities, on the Regulation. On 9 July 2002, the Commission published in the *Official Journal* a draft of the present Regulation, with an invitation to interested parties to submit comments not later than 30 September 2002.

Notes
[1] COM(1999) 192 final.
[2] CES 1139/99.
[3] PE A5-0104/00.

(5) A new Regulation should meet the two requirements of ensuring effective protection of competition and providing adequate legal security for undertakings. The pursuit of these objectives should take account of the need to simplify administrative supervision to as great an extent as possible. Account must also be taken of the Commission's experience in this field since 1992, and the results of the consultations on the 1999 Report and consultations leading up to the adoption of this Regulation.

(6) Regulation (EEC) No 1534/91 requires the exempting regulation of the Commission to define the categories of agreements, decisions and concerted practices to which it applies, to specify the restrictions or clauses which may, or may not, appear in the agreements, decisions and concerted practices, and to specify the clauses which must be contained in the agreements, decisions and concerted practices or the other conditions which must be satisfied.

(7) Nevertheless, it is appropriate to move away from the approach of listing exempted clauses and to place greater emphasis on defining categories of agreements which are exempted up to a certain level of market power and on specifying the restrictions or clauses which are not to be contained in such agreements. This is consistent with an economics based approach which assesses the impact of agreements on the relevant market. However, it should be recognised that in the insurance sector there are certain types of collaboration involving all the undertakings on a relevant insurance market which can be regarded as normally satisfying the conditions laid down in Article 81(3) of the Treaty.

(8) For the application of Article 81(3) of the Treaty by regulation, it is not necessary to define those agreements which are capable of falling within Article 81(1). In the individual assessment of agreements under Article 81(1), account has to be taken of several factors, and in particular the market structure on the relevant market.

(9) The benefit of the block exemption should be limited to those agreements for which it can be assumed with sufficient certainty that they satisfy the conditions of Article 81(3) of the Treaty.

(10) Collaboration between insurance undertakings or within associations of undertakings in the calculation of the average cost of covering a specified risk in the past or, for life insurance, tables

of mortality rates or of the frequency of illness, accident and invalidity, makes it possible to improve the knowledge of risks and facilitates the rating of risks for individual companies. This can in turn facilitate market entry and thus benefit consumers. The same applies to joint studies on the probable impact of extraneous circumstances that may influence the frequency or scale of claims, or the yield of different types of investments. It is, however, necessary to ensure that such collaboration is only exempted to the extent to which it is necessary to attain these objectives. It is therefore appropriate to stipulate that agreements on commercial premiums are not exempted; indeed, commercial premiums may be lower than the amounts indicated by the results of the calculations tables or studies in question, since insurers can use the revenues from their investments in order to reduce their premiums. Moreover, the calculations, tables or studies in question should be non-binding and serve only for reference purposes.

(11) Moreover, the broader the categories into which statistics on the cost of covering a specified risk in the past are grouped, the less leeway insurance undertakings have to calculate premiums on a narrower basis. It is therefore appropriate to exempt joint calculations of the past cost of risks on condition that the available statistics are provided with as much detail and differentiation as is actuarially adequate.

(12) Furthermore, since access to such calculations, tables and studies is necessary both for insurance undertakings active on the geographic or product market in question and also for those considering entering that market, such insurance undertakings must be granted access to such calculations tables and studies on reasonable and non-discriminatory terms, as compared with insurance undertakings already present on that market. Such terms might for example include a commitment from an insurance undertaking not yet present on the market to provide statistical information on claims, should it ever enter the market. They might also include membership of the association of insurers responsible for producing the calculations, as long as access to such membership is itself available on reasonable and non-discriminatory terms to insurance undertakings not yet active on the market in question. However, any fee charged for access to such calculations or related studies to insurance undertakings which have not contributed to them, would not be considered reasonable for this purpose if it were so high as to constitute a barrier to entry on the market.

(13) The reliability of joint calculations, tables and studies becomes greater as the amount of statistics on which they are based is increased. Insurers with high market shares may generate sufficient statistics internally to be able to make reliable calculations, but those with small market shares will not be able to do so, much less new entrants. The inclusion in such joint calculations, tables and studies of information from all insurers on a market, including large ones, promotes competition by helping smaller insurers, and facilitates market entry. Given this specificity of the insurance sector, it is not appropriate to subject any exemption for such joint calculations and joint studies to market share thresholds.

(14) Standard policy conditions or standard individual clauses and standard models illustrating the profits of a life assurance policy can produce benefits. For example, they can bring efficiency gains for insurers; they can facilitate market entry by small or inexperienced insurers; they can help insurers to meet legal obligations; and they can be used by consumer organisations as a benchmark to compare insurance policies offered by different insurers.

Commentary
Recital 14: B&C: 12.173

---

(15) However, standard policy conditions must not lead either to the standardisation of products or to the creation of a significant imbalance between the rights and obligations arising from the contract. Accordingly, the exemption should only apply to standard policy conditions on condition that they are not binding, and expressly mention that participating undertakings are free to offer different policy conditions to their customers. Moreover, standard policy conditions may not contain any systematic exclusion of specific types of risk without providing for the express possibility of including that cover by agreement and may not provide for the contractual relationship with the policyholder to be maintained for an excessive period or go beyond the initial

object of the policy. This is without prejudice to obligations arising from Community or national law to include certain risks in certain policies.

(16) In addition, it is necessary to stipulate that the common standard policy conditions must be generally available to any interested person, and in particular to the policyholder, so as to ensure that there is real transparency and therefore benefit for consumers.

(17) The inclusion in an insurance policy of risks to which a significant number of policyholders is not simultaneously exposed may hinder innovation, given that the bundling of unrelated risks can be a disincentive for insurers to offer separate and specific insurance cover for them. A clause which imposes such comprehensive cover should therefore not be covered by the block exemption. Where there is a legal requirement on insurers to include in policies cover for risks to which a significant number of policyholders are not simultaneously exposed, then the inclusion in an non-binding model contract of a standard clause reflecting such a legal requirement does not constitute a restriction of competition and falls outside the scope of Article 81(1) of the Treaty.

(18) Co-insurance or co-reinsurance groups (often called "pools"), can allow insurers and reinsurers to provide insurance or reinsurance for risks for which they might only offer insufficient cover in the absence of the pool. They can also help insurance and reinsurance undertakings to acquire experience of risks with which they are unfamiliar. However, such groups can involve restrictions of competition, such as the standardisation of policy conditions and even of amounts of cover and premiums. It is therefore appropriate to lay down the circumstances in which such groups can benefit from exemption.

(19) For genuinely new risks it is not possible to know in advance what subscription capacity is necessary to cover the risk, nor whether two or more such groups could co-exist for the purposes of providing this type of insurance. A pooling arrangement which is for the co-insurance or co-reinsurance exclusively of such new risks (not of a mixture of new risks and existing risks) can therefore be exempted for a limited period of time. Three years should constitute an adequate period for the constitution of sufficient historical information on claims to assess the necessity or otherwise of one single pool. This Regulation therefore grants an exemption to any such group which is newly-created in order to cover a new risk, for the first three years of its existence.

Commentary
Recital 19: F&N: 11.117

---

(20) The definition of "new risks" clarifies that only risks which did not exist before are [included] in the definition, thus excluding for example risks which hitherto existed but were not insured. Moreover, a risk whose nature changes significantly (for example a considerable increase in terrorist activity) falls outside the definition, as the risk itself is not new in that case. A new risk, by its nature, requires an entirely new insurance product, and cannot be covered by additions or modifications to an existing insurance product.

(21) For risks which are not new, it is recognised that such co-insurance and co-reinsurance groups which involve a restriction of competition can also, in certain limited circumstances, involve benefits such as to justify an exemption under Article 81(3) of the Treaty, even if they could be replaced by two or more competing insurance entities. They may for example, allow their members to gain the necessary experience of the sector of insurance involved, they may allow cost savings, or reduction of premiums through joint reinsurance on advantageous terms. However, any exemption for such groups is not justified if the group in question benefits from a significant level of market power, since in those circumstances the restriction of competition deriving from the existence of the pool would normally outweigh any possible advantages.

(22) This Regulation therefore grants an exemption to any such co-insurance or co-reinsurance group which has existed for more than three years, or which is not created in order to cover a new risk, on condition that the insurance products underwritten within the group by its members do not exceed the following thresholds: 25% of the relevant market in the case of co-reinsurance groups, and 20% in the case of co-insurance groups. The threshold for co-insurance groups is lower because the co-insurance pools may involve uniform policy conditions and commercial premiums. These exemptions however only apply if the group in question meets the further

conditions laid out in this Regulation, which are intended to keep to a minimum the restrictions of competition between the members of the group.

(23) Pools falling outside the scope of this Regulation may be eligible for an individual exemption, depending on the details of the pool itself and the specific conditions of the market in question. Considering that many insurance markets are constantly evolving, an individual analysis would be necessary in such cases in order to determine whether or not the conditions of Article 81(3) of the Treaty are met.

(24) The adoption by an association or associations of insurance or reinsurance undertakings of technical specifications, rules or codes of practice concerning safety devices, and of procedures for evaluating the compliance of safety devices with those technical specifications, rules or codes of practice, can be beneficial in providing a benchmark to insurers and reinsurers when assessing the extent of the risk they are asked to cover in a specific case, which depends on the quality of security equipment and of its installation and maintenance. However, where there exist Community-level technical specifications, classification systems, rules, procedures or codes of practice harmonised in line with Community legislation covering the free movement of goods, it is not appropriate to exempt by regulation any agreements among insurers on the same subject, since the objective of such harmonisation at European level is to lay down exhaustive and adequate levels of security for security devices which apply uniformly across the Community. Any agreement among insurers on different requirements for safety devices could undermine the achievement of that objective.

(25) As concerns the installation and maintenance of security devices, in so far as no such Community-level harmonisation exists, agreements between insurers laying down technical specifications or approval procedures that are used in one or several Member States can be exempted by regulation; however, the exemption should be subjected to certain conditions, in particular that each insurance undertaking must remain free to accept for insurance, on whatever terms and conditions it wishes, devices and installation and maintenance undertakings not approved jointly.

(26) If individual agreements exempted by this Regulation nevertheless have effects which are incompatible with Article 81(3) of the Treaty, as interpreted by the administrative practice of the Commission and the case-law of the Court of Justice, the Commission may withdraw the benefit of the block exemption. This may occur in particular where studies on the impact of future developments are based on unjustifiable hypotheses; or where recommended standard policy conditions contain clauses which create, to the detriment of the policyholder, a significant imbalance between the rights and obligations arising from the contract; or where groups are used or managed in such a way as to give one or more participating undertakings the means of acquiring or reinforcing a position of significant market power on the relevant market, or if these groups result in market sharing.

(27) In order to facilitate the conclusion of agreements, some of which can involve significant investment decisions, the period of validity of this Regulation should be fixed at seven years.

(28) This Regulation is without prejudice to the application of Article 82 of the Treaty.

(29) In accordance with the principle of the primacy of Community law, no measure taken pursuant to national laws on competition should prejudice the uniform application throughout the common market of the Community competition rules or the full effect of any measures adopted in implementation of those rules, including this Regulation,

HAS ADOPTED THIS REGULATION:

CHAPTER I
EXEMPTION AND DEFINITIONS

Article 1
Exemption

Pursuant to Article 81(3) of the Treaty and subject to the provisions of this Regulation, it is hereby declared that Article 81(1) of the Treaty shall not apply to agreements entered into between two or more undertakings in the insurance sector (hereinafter referred to as "the parties") with respect to:

(a) the joint establishment and distribution of:

— calculations of the average cost of covering a specified risk in the past (hereinafter "calculations");

— in connection with insurance involving an element of capitalisation, mortality tables, and tables showing the frequency of illness, accident and invalidity (hereinafter "tables");

(b) the joint carrying-out of studies on the probable impact of general circumstances external to the interested undertakings, either on the frequency or scale of future claims for a given risk or risk category or on the profitability of different types of investment (hereinafter "studies"), and the distribution of the results of such studies;

(c) the joint establishment and distribution of non-binding standard policy conditions for direct insurance (hereinafter "standard policy conditions");

(d) the joint establishment and distribution of non-binding models illustrating the profits to be realised from an insurance policy involving an element of capitalisation (hereinafter "models");

(e) the setting-up and operation of groups of insurance undertakings or of insurance undertakings and reinsurance undertakings for the common coverage of a specific category of risks in the form of co-insurance or co-reinsurance; and

(f) the establishment, recognition and distribution of:

— technical specifications, rules or codes of practice concerning those types of security devices for which there do not exist at Community level technical specifications, classification systems, rules, procedures or codes of practice harmonised in line with Community legislation covering the free movement of goods, and procedures for assessing and approving the compliance of security devices with such specifications, rules or codes of practice,

— technical specifications, rules or codes of practice for the installation and maintenance of security devices, and procedures for assessing and approving the compliance of undertakings which install or maintain security devices with such specifications, rules or codes of practice.

Commentary
Art 1: B&C: 3.081, 12.171–12.172
Art 1(a): B&C: 12.172
Art 1(b): B&C: 12.172
Art 1(c): B&C: 12.173
Art 1(d): B&C: 12.173
Art 1(e): B&C: 12.174
Art 1(f): B&C: 12.178

Article 2
Definitions

For the purposes of the present Regulation, the following definitions shall apply:

1. "Agreement" means an agreement, a decision of an association of undertakings or a concerted practice;

2. "Participating undertakings" means undertakings party to the agreement and their respective connected undertakings;

3. "Connected undertakings" means:

(a) undertakings in which a party to the agreement, directly or indirectly:
   (i) has the power to exercise more than half the voting rights, or
   (ii) has the power to appoint more than half the members of the supervisory board, board of management or bodies legally representing the undertaking, or
   (iii) has the right to manage the undertaking's affairs;

(b) undertakings which directly or indirectly have, over a party to the agreement, the rights or powers listed in (a);

(c) undertakings in which an undertaking referred to in (b) has, directly or indirectly, the rights or powers listed in (a);

(d) undertakings in which a party to the agreement together with one or more of the undertakings referred to in (a), (b) or (c), or in which two or more of the latter undertakings, jointly have the rights or powers listed in (a);

(e) undertakings in which the rights or the powers listed in (a) are jointly held by:
  (i) parties to the agreement or their respective connected undertakings referred to in (a) to (d), or
  (ii) one or more of the parties to the agreement or one or more of their connected undertakings referred to in (a) to (d) and one or more third parties.

4. "Standard policy conditions" refers to any clauses contained in model or reference insurance policies prepared jointly by insurers or by bodies or associations of insurers;

5. "Co-insurance groups" means groups set up by insurance undertakings which:
  (i) agree to underwrite in the name and for the account of all the participants the insurance of a specified risk category; or
  (ii) entrust the underwriting and management of the insurance of a specified risk category in their name and on their behalf to one of the insurance undertakings, to a common broker or to a common body set up for this purpose;

6. "Co-reinsurance groups" means groups set up by insurance undertakings, possibly with the assistance of one or more re-insurance undertakings:
  (i) in order to reinsure mutually all or part of their liabilities in respect of a specified risk category;
  (ii) incidentally, to accept in the name and on behalf of all the participants the re-insurance of the same category of risks;

7. "New risks" means risks which did not exist before, and for which insurance cover requires the development of an entirely new insurance product, not involving an extension, improvement or replacement of an existing insurance product.

8. "Security devices" means components and equipment designed for loss prevention and reduction, and systems formed from such elements.

9. "Commercial premium" means the price which is charged to the purchaser of an insurance policy.

Commentary
Art 2(5): **B&C:** 12.171
Art 2(6): **B&C:** 12.171
Art 2(7): **B&C:** 12.175 **F&N:** 11.117

CHAPTER II
JOINT CALCULATIONS, TABLES, AND STUDIES

Article 3
Conditions for exemption

1. The exemption provided for in Article 1(a) shall apply on condition that the calculations or tables:

(a) are based on the assembly of data, spread over a number of risk-years chosen as an observation period, which relate to identical or comparable risks in sufficient number to constitute a base which can be handled statistically and which will yield figures on (inter alia):
  — the number of claims during the said period,
  — the number of individual risks insured in each risk-year of the chosen observation period,
  — the total amounts paid or payable in respect of claims arisen during the said period,
  — the total amount of capital insured for each risk-year during the chosen observation period;

(b) include as detailed a breakdown of the available statistics as is actuarially adequate;

(c) do not include in any way elements for contingencies, income deriving from reserves, administrative or commercial costs or fiscal or para-fiscal contributions, and take into account neither revenues from investments nor anticipated profits.

2. The exemptions provided for in both Article 1(a) and Article 1(b) shall apply on condition that the calculations, tables or study results:

(a) do not identify the insurance undertakings concerned or any insured party;

(b) when compiled and distributed, include a statement that they are non-binding;

(c) are made available on reasonable and non-discriminatory terms, to any insurance undertaking which requests a copy of them, including insurance undertakings which are not active on the geographical or product market to which those calculations, tables or study results refer.

Commentary
Art 3: B&C: 12.172
Art 3(1)(b): F&N: 11.109
Art 3(1)(c): F&N: 11.109
Art 3(2)(a): F&N: 11.109
Art 3(2)(b): F&N: 11.109
Art 3(2)(c): F&N: 11.109

Article 4
Agreements not covered by the exemption

The exemption provided for in Article 1 shall not apply where participating undertakings enter into an undertaking or commitment among themselves, or oblige other undertakings, not to use calculations or tables that differ from those established pursuant to Article 1(a), or not to depart from the results of the studies referred to in Article 1(b).

Commentary
Art 4: B&C: 12.172 F&N: 11.109

CHAPTER III
STANDARD POLICY CONDITIONS AND MODELS

Article 5
Conditions for exemption

1. The exemption provided for in Article 1(c) shall apply on condition that the standard policy conditions:

(a) are established and distributed with an explicit statement that they are non-binding and that their use is not in any way recommended;

(b) expressly mention that participating undertakings are free to offer different policy conditions to their customers; and

(c) are accessible to any interested person and provided simply upon request.

2. The exemption provided for in Article 1(d) shall apply on condition that the non-binding models are established and distributed only by way of guidance.

Commentary
Art 5: B&C: 12.173 F&N: 11.132
Art 5(1): F&N: 11.112

Article 6
Agreements not covered by the exemption

1. The exemption provided for in Article 1(c) shall not apply where the standard policy conditions contain clauses which:

(a) contain any indication of the level of commercial premiums;

(b) indicate the amount of the cover or the part which the policyholder must pay himself (the "excess");

(c) impose comprehensive cover including risks to which a significant number of policyholders are not simultaneously exposed;

(d) allow the insurer to maintain the policy in the event that he cancels part of the cover, increases the premium without the risk or the scope of the cover being changed (without prejudice to indexation clauses), or otherwise alters the policy conditions without the express consent of the policyholder;

(e) allow the insurer to modify the term of the policy without the express consent of the policyholder;

(f) impose on the policyholder in the non-life assurance sector a contract period of more than three years;

(g) impose a renewal period of more than one year where the policy is automatically renewed unless notice is given upon the expiry of a given period;

(h) require the policyholder to agree to the reinstatement of a policy which has been suspended on account of the disappearance of the insured risk, if he is once again exposed to a risk of the same nature;

(i) require the policyholder to obtain cover from the same insurer for different risks;

(j) require the policyholder, in the event of disposal of the object of insurance, to make the acquirer take over the insurance policy;

(k) exclude or limit the cover of a risk if the policyholder uses security devices, or installing or maintenance undertakings, which are not approved in accordance with the relevant specifications agreed by an association or associations of insurers in one or several other Member States or at the European level.

2. The exemption provided for in Article 1(c) shall not benefit undertakings or associations of undertakings which agree, or agree to oblige other undertakings, not to apply conditions other than standard policy conditions established pursuant to an agreement between the participating undertakings.

3. Without prejudice to the establishment of specific insurance conditions for particular social or occupational categories of the population, the exemption provided for in Article 1(c) shall not apply to agreements decisions and concerted practices which exclude the coverage of certain risk categories because of the characteristics associated with the policyholder.

4. The exemption provided for in Article 1(d) shall not apply where, without prejudice to legally imposed obligations, the non-binding models include only specified interest rates or contain figures indicating administrative costs;

5. The exemption provided for in Article 1(d) shall not benefit undertakings or associations of undertakings which concert or undertake among themselves, or oblige other undertakings, not to apply models illustrating the benefits of an insurance policy other than those established pursuant to an agreement between the participating undertakings.

Commentary
Art 6: B&C: 12.173 F&N: 11.112, 11.114, 11.132
Art 6(2): F&N: 11.113
Art 6(3): F&N: 11.113

CHAPTER IV
COMMON COVERAGE OF CERTAIN TYPES OF RISKS

Article 7
Application of exemption and market share thresholds

1. As concerns co-insurance or co-reinsurance groups which are created after the date of entry into force of the present Regulation in order exclusively to cover new risks, the exemption provided for in Article 1(e) shall apply for a period of three years from the date of the first establishment of the group, regardless of the market share of the group.

2. As concerns co-insurance or co-reinsurance groups which do not fall within the scope of the first paragraph (for the reason that they have been in existence for over three years or have not been created in order to cover a new risk), the exemption provided for in Article 1(e) shall apply as long as the present Regulation remains in force, on condition that the insurance products underwritten within the grouping arrangement by the participating undertakings or on their behalf do not, in any of the markets concerned, represent:

1214

(a) in the case of co-insurance groups, more than 20% of the relevant market;

(b) in the case of co-reinsurance groups, more than 25% of the relevant market.

3. For the purposes of applying the market share threshold provided for in the second paragraph the following rules shall apply:

(a) the market share shall be calculated on the basis of the gross premium income; if gross premium income data are not available, estimates based on other reliable market information, including insurance cover provided or insured risk value, may be used to establish the market share of the undertaking concerned;

(b) the market share shall be calculated on the basis of data relating to the preceding calendar year;

(c) the market share held by the undertakings referred to in Article 2(3)(e) shall be apportioned equally to each undertaking having the rights or the powers listed in Article 2(3)(a).

4. If the market share referred to in point (a) of the second paragraph is initially not more than 20% but subsequently rises above this level without exceeding 22%, the exemption provided for in Article 1(e) shall continue to apply for a period of two consecutive calendar years following the year in which the 20% threshold was first exceeded.

5. If the market share referred to in point (a) of the second paragraph is initially not more than 20% but subsequently rises above 22%, the exemption provided for in Article 1(e) shall continue to apply for one calendar year following the year in which the level of 22% was first exceeded.

6. The benefit of paragraphs 4 and 5 may not be combined so as to exceed a period of two calendar years.

7. If the market share referred to in point (b) of the second paragraph is initially not more than 25% but subsequently rises above this level without exceeding 27%, the exemption provided for in Article 1(e) shall continue to apply for a period of two consecutive calendar years following the year in which the 25% threshold was first exceeded.

8. If the market share referred to in point (b) of the second paragraph is initially not more than 25% but subsequently rises above 27%, the exemption provided for in Article 1(e) shall continue to apply for one calendar year following the year in which the level of 27% was first exceeded.

9. The benefit of paragraphs 7 and 8 may not be combined so as to exceed a period of two calendar years.

Commentary
Art 7(1): **B&C:** 12.175 **F&N:** 11.117
Art 7(2): **B&C:** 12.176 **F&N:** 11.118

Article 8
Conditions for exemption

The exemption provided for in Article 1(e) shall apply on condition that:

(a) each participating undertaking has the right to withdraw from the group, subject to a period of notice of not more than one year, without incurring any sanctions;

(b) the rules of the group do not oblige any member of the group to insure or re-insure through the group, in whole or in part, any risk of the type covered by the group;

(c) the rules of the group do not restrict the activity of the group or its members to the insurance or reinsurance of risks located in any particular geographical part of the European Union;

(d) the agreement does not limit output or sales;

(e) the agreement does not allocate markets or customers;

(f) the members of a co-reinsurance group do not agree on the commercial premiums which they charge in direct insurance; and

(g) no member of the group, or undertaking which exercises a determining influence on the commercial policy of the group, is also a member of, or exercises a determining influence on the commercial policy of, a different group active on the same relevant market.

Commentary
Art 8: **B&C:** 12.176 **F&N:** 11.119

CHAPTER V
SECURITY DEVICES

Article 9
Conditions for exemption

The exemption provided for in Article 1(f) shall apply on condition that:

(a) the technical specifications and compliance assessment procedures are precise, technically justified and in proportion to the performance to be attained by the security device concerned;

(b) the rules for the evaluation of installation undertakings and maintenance undertakings are objective, relate to their technical competence and are applied in a non-discriminatory manner;

(c) such specifications and rules are established and distributed with an accompanying statement that insurance undertakings are free to accept for insurance, on whatever terms and conditions they wish, other security devices or installation and maintenance undertakings which do not comply with these technical specifications or rules;

(d) such specifications and rules are provided simply upon request to any interested person;

(e) any lists of security devices and installation and maintenance undertakings compliant with specifications include a classification based on the level of performance obtained;

(f) a request for an assessment may be submitted at any time by any applicant;

(g) the evaluation of conformity does not impose on the applicant any expenses that are disproportionate to the costs of the approval procedure;

(h) the devices and installation undertakings and maintenance undertakings that meet the assessment criteria are certified to this effect in a non-discriminatory manner within a period of six months of the date of application, except where technical considerations justify a reasonable additional period;

(i) the fact of compliance or approval is certified in writing;

(j) the grounds for a refusal to issue the certificate of compliance are given in writing by attaching a duplicate copy of the records of the tests and controls that have been carried out;

(k) the grounds for a refusal to take into account a request for assessment are provided in writing; and

(l) the specifications and rules are applied by bodies accredited to norms in the series EN 45 000 and EN ISO/IEC 17025.

CHAPTER VI
MISCELLANEOUS PROVISIONS

Article 10
Withdrawal

The Commission may withdraw the benefit of this Regulation, pursuant to Article 7 of Council Regulation (EEC) No 1534/91, where either on its own initiative or at the request of a Member State or of a natural or legal person claiming a legitimate interest, it finds in a particular case that an agreement to which the exemption provided for in Article 1 applies nevertheless has effects which are incompatible with the conditions laid down in Article 81(3) of the Treaty, and in particular where,

(a) studies to which the exemption in Article 1(b) applies are based on unjustifiable hypotheses;

(b) standard policy conditions to which the exemption in Article 1(c) applies contain clauses which create, to the detriment of the policyholder, a significant imbalance between the rights and obligations arising from the contract;

(c) in relation to the common coverage of certain types of risks to which the exemption in Article 1(e) applies, the setting-up or operation of a group results, through the conditions governing admission, the definition of the risks to be covered, the agreements on retrocession or by any other means, in the sharing of the markets for the insurance products concerned or for neighbouring products.

Commentary
Art 10: B&C: 3.086

Article 11
Transitional period

The prohibition laid down in Article 81(1) of the Treaty shall not apply during the period from 1 April 2003 to 31 March 2004 in respect of agreements already in force on 31 March 2003 which do not satisfy the conditions for exemption provided for in this Regulation but which satisfy the conditions for exemption provided for in Regulation (EEC) No 3932/92.

[*Article 11a*

The prohibition in Article 81(1) of the Treaty shall not apply to agreements which were in existence at the date of accession of the Czech Republic, Estonia, Cyprus, Latvia, Lithuania, Hungary, Malta, Poland, Slovenia and Slovakia and which, by reason of accession, fall within the scope of Article 81(1) if, within six months from the date of accession, they are so amended that they comply with the conditions laid down in this Regulation.]

Notes

Article 11a, shown in square brackets, was added by Commission Regulation (EC) No 886/2004 of 4 March 2004 adapting certain regulations and decisions in the field of free movement of goods, competition policy, agriculture, environment and external relations by reason of the accession of the Czech Republic, Estonia, Cyprus, Latvia, Lithuania, Hungary, Malta, Poland, Slovenia and Slovakia (OJ L 168, 1.5.2004, p. 14).

Article 12
Period of validity

This Regulation shall enter into force on 1 April 2003. It shall expire on 31 March 2010.

This Regulation shall be binding in its entirety and directly applicable in all Member States.

Done at Brussels, 27 February 2003.

E28

DIRECTIVE 97/67/EC
OF THE EUROPEAN PARLIAMENT AND OF
THE COUNCIL

of 15 December 1997
on common rules for the development of the internal market of Community
postal services and the improvement of quality of service

Official Journal L15, 21.1.1998, p.14

Celex No: 31997L0067

Commentary
Directive 97/67: B&C: 12.183
Arts 12–14: B&C: 12.185
Arts 16–19: B&C: 12.185

THE EUROPEAN PARLIAMENT AND THE COUNCIL OF THE EUROPEAN UNION,

Having regard to the Treaty establishing the European Community, and in particular Articles [47](2), [55] and [95] thereof,

Having regard to the proposal from the Commission,[1]

Having regard to the opinion of the Economic and Social Committee,[2]

Having regard to the opinion of the Committee of the Regions,[3]

Having regard to the resolution of the European Parliament of 22 January 1993 concerning the green paper on the development of the single market for postal services,[4]

Having regard to the Council resolution of 7 February 1994 on the development of Community postal services,[5]

Acting in accordance with the procedure laid down in Article [251] of the Treaty, in the light of the joint text approved by the Conciliation Committee on 7 November 1997,[6]

Notes
[1] OJ C 322, 2.12.1995, p. 22, and OJ C 300, 10.10.1996, p. 22.
[2] OJ C 174, 17.6.1996, p. 41.
[3] OJ C 337, 11.11.1996, p. 28.
[4] OJ C 42, 15.2.1993, p. 240.
[5] OJ C 48, 16.2.1994, p. 3.
[6] Opinion of the European Parliament of 9 May 1996 (OJ C 152, 27.5.1996, p. 20), Council Common Position of 29 April 1997 (OJ C 188, 19.6.1997, p. 9) and Decision of the European Parliament of 16 September 1997 (OJ C 304, 6.10.1997, p. 34); Decision of the European Parliament of 19 November 1997 and Decision of the Council of 1 December 1997.

(1) Whereas measures should be adopted with the aim of establishing the internal market in accordance with Article [14] of the Treaty; whereas this market comprises an area without internal frontiers in which the free movement of goods, persons, services and capital is ensured;

(2) Whereas the establishment of the internal market in the postal sector is of proven importance for the economic and social cohesion of the Community, in that postal services are an essential instrument of communication and trade;

(3) Whereas on 11 June 1992 the Commission presented a Green Paper on the development of the single market for postal services and, on 2 June 1993, a Communication on the guidelines for the development of Community postal services;

(4) Whereas the Commission has conducted wide-ranging public consultation on those aspects of postal services that are of interest to the Community and the interested parties in the postal sector have communicated their observations to the Commission;

(5) Whereas the current extent of the universal postal service and the conditions governing its provision vary significantly from one Member State to another; whereas, in particular, performance in terms of quality of services is very unequal amongst Member States;

(6) Whereas cross-border postal links do not always meet the expectations of users and European citizens, and performance, in terms of quality of service with regard to Community cross-border postal services, is at the moment unsatisfactory;

(7) Whereas the disparities observed in the postal sector have considerable implications for those sectors of activity which rely especially on postal services and effectively impede the progress towards internal Community cohesion, in that the regions deprived of postal services of sufficiently high quality find themselves at a disadvantage as regards both their letter service and the distribution of goods;

(8) Whereas measures seeking to ensure the gradual and controlled liberalisation of the market and to secure a proper balance in the application thereof are necessary in order to guarantee, throughout the Community, and subject to the obligations and rights of the universal service providers, the free provision of services in the postal sector itself;

(9) Whereas action at Community level to ensure greater harmonisation of the conditions governing the postal sector is therefore necessary and steps must consequently be taken to establish common rules;

(10) Whereas, in accordance with the principle of subsidiarity, a set of general principles should be adopted at Community level, whilst the choice of the exact procedures should be a matter for the Member States, which should be free to choose the system best adapted to their own circumstances;

(11) Whereas it is essential to guarantee at Community level a universal postal service encompassing a minimum range of services of specified quality to be provided in all Member States at an affordable price for the benefit of all users, irrespective of their geographical location in the Community;

(12) Whereas the aim of the universal services is to offer all users easy access to the postal network through the provision, in particular, of a sufficient number of access points and by ensuring satisfactory conditions with regard to the frequency of collections and deliveries; whereas the provision of the universal service must meet the fundamental need to ensure continuity of operation, whilst at the same time remaining adaptable to the needs of users as well as guaranteeing them fair and non-discriminatory treatment;

(13) Whereas universal service must cover national services as well as cross-border services;

(14) Whereas users of the universal service must be given adequate information on the range of services offered, the conditions governing their supply and use, the quality of the services provided, and the tariffs;

(15) Whereas the provisions of this Directive relating to universal service provision are without prejudice to the right of universal service operators to negotiate contracts with customers individually;

(16) Whereas the maintenance of a range of those services that may be reserved, in compliance with the rules of the Treaty and without prejudice to the application of the rules on competition, appears justified on the grounds of ensuring the operation of the universal service under financially balanced conditions; whereas the process of liberalisation should not curtail the continuing supply of certain free services for blind and partially sighted persons introduced by the Member States;

(17) Whereas items of correspondence weighing 350 grammes and over represent less than 2% of letter volume and less than 3% of the receipts of the public operators; whereas the criteria of price (five times the basic tariff) will better permit the distinction between the reserved service and the express service, which is liberalised;

(18) Whereas, in view of the fact that the essential difference between express mail and universal postal services lies in the value added (whatever form it takes) provided by express services and perceived by customers, the most effective way of determining the extra value perceived is to

consider the extra price that customers are prepared to pay, without prejudice, however, to the price limit of the reserved area which must be respected;

(19) Whereas it is reasonable to allow, on an interim basis, for direct mail and cross-border mail to continue to be capable of reservation within the price and weight limits provided; whereas, as a further step towards the completion of the internal market of postal services, a decision on the further gradual controlled liberalisation of the postal market, in particular with a view to the liberalisation of cross-border and direct mail as well as on a further review of the price and weight limits, should be taken by the European Parliament and the Council not later than 1 January 2000, on a proposal from the Commission following a review of the sector;

(20) Whereas, for reasons of public order and public security, Member States may have a legitimate interest in conferring on one or more entities designated by them the right to site on the public highway letter-boxes intended for the reception of postal items; whereas, for the same reasons, they are entitled to appoint the entity or entities responsible for issuing postage stamps identifying the country of origin and those responsible for providing the registered mail service used in the course of judicial or administrative procedures in accordance with their national legislation; whereas they may also indicate membership of the European Union by integrating the 12-star symbol;

(21) Whereas new services (services quite distinct from conventional services) and document exchange do not form part of the universal service and consequently there is no justification for their being reserved to the universal service providers; whereas this applies equally to self-provision (provision of postal services by the natural or legal person who is the originator of the mail, or collection and routing of these items by a third party acting solely on behalf of that person), which does not fall within the category of services;

(22) Whereas Member States should be able to regulate, by appropriate authorization procedures, on their territory, the provision of postal services which are not reserved to the universal service providers; whereas those procedures must be transparent, non-discriminatory, proportionate and based on objective criteria;

(23) Whereas the Member States should have the option of making the grant of licences subject to universal service obligations or contributions to a compensation fund intended to compensate the universal service provider for the provision of services representing an unfair financial burden; whereas Member States should be able to include in the authorisations an obligation that the authorised activities must not infringe the exclusive or special rights granted to the universal service providers for the reserved services; whereas an identification system for direct mail may be introduced for the purposes of supervision where direct mail is liberalised;

(24) Whereas measures necessary for the harmonisation of authorisation procedures laid down by the Member States governing the commercial provision to the public of non-reserved services will have to be adopted;

(25) Whereas, should this prove necessary, measures shall be adopted to ensure the transparency and non-discriminatory nature of conditions governing access to the public postal network in Member States;

(26) Whereas, in order to ensure sound management of the universal service and to avoid distortions of competition, the tariffs applied to the universal service should be objective, transparent, non-discriminatory and geared to costs;

(27) Whereas the remuneration for the provision of the intra-Community cross-border mail service, without prejudice to the minimum set of obligations derived from Universal Postal Union acts, should be geared to cover the costs of delivery incurred by the universal service provider in the country of destination; whereas this remuneration should also provide an incentive to improve or maintain the quality of the cross-border service through the use of quality-of-service targets; whereas this would justify suitable systems providing for an appropriate coverage of costs and related specifically to the quality of service achieved;

(28) Whereas separate accounts for the different reserved services and non-reserved services are necessary in order to introduce transparency into the actual costs of the various services and in order to ensure that cross-subsidies from the reserved sector to the non-reserved sector do not adversely affect the competitive conditions in the latter;

(29) Whereas, in order to ensure the application of the principles set out in the previous three recitals, universal service providers should implement, within a reasonable time limit, cost accounting systems, which can be independently verified, by which costs can be allocated to services as accurately as possible on the basis of transparent procedures; whereas such requirements can be fulfilled, for example, by implementation of the principle of fully distributed costing; whereas such cost accounting systems may not be required in circumstances where genuine conditions of open competition exist;

(30) Whereas consideration should be given to the interests of users, who are entitled to services of a high quality; whereas, therefore, every effort must be made to improve and enhance the quality of services provided at Community level; whereas such improvements in quality require Member States to lay down standards, to be attained or surpassed by the universal service providers, in respect of the services forming part of the universal service;

(31) Whereas the quality of service expected by users constitutes an essential aspect of the services provided; whereas the evaluation standards for this quality of service and the levels of quality achieved must be published in the interests of users; whereas it is necessary to have available harmonised quality-of-service standards and a common methodology for measurement in order to be able to evaluate the convergence of the quality of service throughout the Community;

(32) Whereas national quality standards consistent with Community standards must be determined by Member States; whereas, in the case of intra-Community cross-border services requiring the combined efforts of at least two universal service providers from two different Member States, quality standards must be defined at Community level;

(33) Whereas compliance with these standards must be independently verified at regular intervals and on a harmonised basis; whereas users must have the right to be informed of the results of this verification and Member States should ensure that corrective action is taken where those results demonstrate that the standards are not being met;

(34) Whereas Council Directive 93/13/EEC of 5 April 1993 on unfair terms in consumer contracts [1] applies to postal operators;

Notes
[1] OJ L 95, 21.4.1993, p. 29.

(35) Whereas the need for improvement of quality of service means that disputes have to be settled quickly and efficiently; whereas, in addition to the forms of legal redress available under national and Community law, a procedure dealing with complaints should be provided, which should be transparent, simple and inexpensive and should enable all relevant parties to participate;

(36) Whereas progress in the interconnection of postal networks and the interests of users require that technical standardisation be encouraged; whereas technical standardisation is indispensable for the promotion of interoperability between national networks and for an efficient Community universal service;

(37) Whereas guidelines on European harmonisation provide for specialised technical standardisation activities to be entrusted to the European Committee for Standardisation;

(38) Whereas a committee should be established to assist the Commission with the implementation of this Directive, particularly in relation to the future work on the development of measures relating to the quality of Community cross-border service and technical standardisation;

(39) Whereas, in order to ensure the proper functioning of the universal service and to ensure undistorted competition in the non-reserved sector, it is important to separate the functions of the regulator, on the one hand, and the operator, on the other; whereas no postal operator may be both judge and interested party; whereas it is for the Member State to define the statute of one or more national regulatory authorities, which may be chosen from public authorities or independent entities appointed for that purpose;

(40) Whereas the effects of the harmonised conditions on the functioning of the internal market in postal services will need to be the subject of an assessment; whereas, therefore, the Commission will present a report to the European Parliament and the Council on the application of this Directive, including the appropriate information on developments in the sector, particularly concerning economic, social, employment and technological aspects, as well as on quality of

service, three years following the date of its entry into force, and in any event no later than 31 December 2000;

(41) Whereas this Directive does not affect the application of the rules of the Treaty, and in particular its rules on competition and the freedom to provide services;

(42) Whereas nothing shall prevent Member States from maintaining in force or introducing measures for the postal sector which are more liberal than those provided for by this Directive, nor, should this Directive lapse, from maintaining in force measures which they have introduced in order to implement it, provided in each case that such measures are compatible with the Treaty;

(43) Whereas it is appropriate that this Directive should apply until 31 December 2004 unless otherwise decided by the European Parliament and the Council on the basis of a proposal from the Commission;

(44) Whereas this Directive does not apply to any activity which falls outside the scope of Community law, such as those provided for by Titles V and VI of the Treaty on European Union, and in any case to activities concerning public security, defence, State security (including the economic well-being of the State when the activities relate to State security matters) and the activities of the State in areas of criminal law;

(45) Whereas this Directive does not, in the case of undertakings which are not established in the Community, prevent the adoption of measures in accordance with both Community law and existing international obligations designed to ensure that nationals of the Member States enjoy similar treatment in third countries; whereas Community undertakings should benefit in third countries from treatment and effective access that is comparable to the treatment and access to the market which is conferred on nationals of the countries concerned within the Community context,

HAVE ADOPTED THIS DIRECTIVE:

CHAPTER I
Objective and scope

Article 1

This Directive establishes common rules concerning:
— the provision of a universal postal service within the Community,
— the criteria defining the services which may be reserved for universal service providers and the conditions governing the provision of non-reserved services,
— tariff principles and transparency of accounts for universal service provision,
— the setting of quality standards for universal service provision and the setting-up of a system to ensure compliance with those standards,
— the harmonisation of technical standards,
— the creation of independent national regulatory authorities.

Commentary
Art 1: **B&C:** 12.183

Article 2

For the purposes of this Directive, the following definitions shall apply:

1. *postal services*: services involving the clearance, sorting, transport and delivery of postal items;

2. *public postal network*: the system of organisation and resources of all kinds used by the universal service provider(s) for the purposes in particular of:
— the clearance of postal items covered by a universal service obligation from access points throughout the territory,
— the routing and handling of those items from the postal network access point to the distribution centre,
— distribution to the addresses shown on items;

3. *access points*: physical facilities, including letter boxes provided for the public either on the public highway or at the premises of the universal service provider, where postal items may be deposited with the public postal network by customers;

4. *clearance*: the operation of collecting postal items deposited at access points;

5. *distribution*: the process from sorting at the distribution centre to delivery of postal items to their addressees;

6. *postal item*: an item addressed in the final form in which it is to be carried by the universal service provider. In addition to items of correspondence, such items also include for instance books, catalogues, newspapers, periodicals and postal packages containing merchandise with or without commercial value;

7. *item of correspondence*: a communication in written form on any kind of physical medium to be conveyed and delivered at the address indicated by the sender on the item itself or on its wrapping. Books, catalogues, newspapers and periodicals shall not be regarded as items of correspondence;

8. *direct mail*: a communication consisting solely of advertising, marketing or publicity material and comprising an identical message, except for the addressee's name, address and identifying number as well as other modifications which do not alter the nature of the message, which is sent to a significant number of addressees, to be conveyed and delivered at the address indicated by the sender on the item itself or on its wrapping. The national regulatory authority shall interpret the term "significant number of addressees` within each Member State and shall publish an appropriate definition. Bills, invoices, financial statements and other non-identical messages shall not be regarded as direct mail. A communication combining direct mail with other items within the same wrapping shall not be regarded as direct mail. Direct mail shall include cross-border as well as domestic direct mail;

9. *registered item*: a service providing a flat-rate guarantee against risks of loss, theft or damage and supplying the sender, where appropriate upon request, with proof of the handing in of the postal item and/or of its delivery to the addressee;

10. *insured item*: a service insuring the postal item up to the value declared by the sender in the event of loss, theft or damage;

11. *cross-border mail*: mail from or to another Member State or from or to a third country;

12. *document exchange*: provision of means, including the supply of ad hoc premises as well as transportation by a third party, allowing self-delivery by mutual exchange of postal items between users subscribing to this service;

13. *universal service provider*: the public or private entity providing a universal postal service or parts thereof within a Member State, the identity of which has been notified to the Commission in accordance with Article 4;

14. *authorisations*: means any permission setting out rights and obligations specific to the postal sector and allowing undertakings to provide postal services and, where applicable, to establish and/or operate postal networks for the provision of such services, in the form of a "general authorisation` or "individual licence" as defined below:

— "general authorisation" means an authorisation, regardless of whether it is regulated by a "class licence" or under general law and regardless of whether such regulation requires registration or declaration procedures, which does not require the undertaking concerned to obtain an explicit decision by the national regulatory authority before exercising the rights stemming from the authorisation,

— "individual licence" means an authorisation which is granted by a national regulatory authority and which gives an undertaking specific rights, or which subjects that undertaking's operations to specific obligations supplementing the general authorisation where applicable, where the undertaking is not entitled to exercise the rights concerned until it has received the decision by the national regulatory authority;

15. *terminal dues*: the remuneration of universal service providers for the distribution of incoming cross-border mail comprising postal items from another Member State or from a third country;

16. *sender*: a natural or legal person responsible for originating postal items;

17. *users*: any natural or legal person benefiting from universal service provision as a sender or an addressee;

18. *national regulatory authority*: the body or bodies, in each Member State, to which the Member State entrusts, inter alia, the regulatory functions falling within the scope of this Directive;

19. *essential requirements*: general non-economic reasons which can induce a Member State to impose conditions on the supply of postal services. These reasons are the confidentiality of correspondence, security of the network as regards the transport of dangerous goods and, where justified, data protection, environmental protection and regional planning.

Data protection may include personal data protection, the confidentiality of information transmitted or stored and protection of privacy.

Commentary
Art 2(13): B&C: 12.183

CHAPTER 2
Universal service

Article 3

1. Member States shall ensure that users enjoy the right to a universal service involving the permanent provision of a postal service of specified quality at all points in their territory at affordable prices for all users.

2. To this end, Member States shall take steps to ensure that the density of the points of contact and of the access points takes account of the needs of users.

3. They shall take steps to ensure that the universal service provider(s) guarantee(s) every working day and not less than five days a week, save in circumstances or geographical conditions deemed exceptional by the national regulatory authorities, as a minimum:

— one clearance,
— one delivery to the home or premises of every natural or legal person or, by way of derogation, under conditions at the discretion of the national regulatory authority, one delivery to appropriate installations.

Any exception or derogation granted by a national regulatory authority in accordance with this paragraph must be communicated to the Commission and to all national regulatory authorities.

4. Each Member State shall adopt the measures necessary to ensure that the universal service includes the following minimum facilities:

— the clearance, sorting, transport and distribution of postal items up to two kilograms,
— the clearance, sorting, transport and distribution of postal packages up to 10 kilograms,
— services for registered items and insured items.

5. The national regulatory authorities may increase the weight limit of universal service coverage for postal packages to any weight not exceeding 20 kilograms and may lay down special arrangements for the door-to-door delivery of such packages.

Notwithstanding the weight limit of universal service coverage for postal packages established by a given Member State, Member States shall ensure that postal packages received from other Member States and weighing up to 20 kilograms are delivered within their territories.

6. The minimum and maximum dimensions for the postal items in question shall be those laid down in the Convention and the Agreement concerning Postal Parcels adopted by the Universal Postal Union.

7. The universal service as defined in this Article shall cover both national and cross-border services.

Commentary
Art 3: B&C: 12.185
Art 3(3): B&C: 12.185
Art 3(4): B&C: 12.185
Art 3(5): B&C: 12.185

Article 4

Each Member State shall ensure that the provision of the universal service is guaranteed and shall notify the Commission of the steps it has taken to fulfil this obligation and, in particular, the identity of its universal service provider(s). Each Member State shall determine in accordance with Community law the obligations and rights assigned to the universal service provider(s) and shall publish them.

Article 5

1. Each Member State shall take steps to ensure that universal service provision meets the following requirements:

— it shall offer a service guaranteeing compliance with the essential requirements,
— it shall offer an identical service to users under comparable conditions,
— it shall be made available without any form of discrimination whatsoever, especially without discrimination arising from political, religious or ideological considerations,
— it shall not be interrupted or stopped except in cases of force majeure,
— it shall evolve in response to the technical, economic and social environment and to the needs of users.

2. The provisions of paragraph 1 shall not preclude measures which the Member States take in accordance with requirements relating to public interest recognized by the Treaty, in particular Articles [30] and [46] thereof, concerning, inter alia, public morality, public security, including criminal investigations, and public policy.

Commentary
Art 5: **B&C:** 12.185

Article 6

Member States shall take steps to ensure that users are regularly given sufficiently detailed and up-to-date information by the universal service provider(s) regarding the particular features of the universal services offered, with special reference to the general conditions of access to these services as well as to prices and quality standard levels. This information shall be published in an appropriate manner.

Member States shall notify the Commission, within 12 months of the date of entry into force of this Directive, how the information to be published in accordance with the first subparagraph is being made available. Any subsequent modifications shall be notified to the Commission at the earliest opportunity.

Commentary
Art 6: **B&C:** 12.185

CHAPTER 3
Harmonization of the services which may be reserved

[Article 7

1. To the extent necessary to ensure the maintenance of universal service, Member States may continue to reserve services to universal service provider(s). Those services shall be limited to the clearance, sorting, transport and delivery of items of domestic correspondence and incoming cross-border correspondence, whether by accelerated delivery or not, within both of the following weight and price limits. The weight limit shall be 100 grams from 1 January 2003 and 50 grams from 1 January 2006. These weight limits shall not apply as from 1 January 2003 if the price is equal to, or more than, three times the public tariff for an item of correspondence in the first weight step of the fastest category, and, as from 1 January 2006, if the price is equal to, or more than, two and a half times this tariff.

In the case of the free postal service for blind and partially sighted persons, exceptions to the weight and price restrictions may be permitted.

To the extent necessary to ensure the provision of universal service, direct mail may continue to be reserved within the same weight and price limits.

To the extent necessary to ensure the provision of universal service, for example when certain sectors of postal activity have already been liberalised or because of the specific characteristics particular to the postal services in a Member State, outgoing cross-border mail may continue to be reserved within the same weight and price limits.

2. Document exchange may not be reserved.

3. The Commission shall finalise a prospective study which will assess, for each Member State, the impact on universal service of the full accomplishment of the postal internal market in 2009. Based on the study's conclusions, the Commission shall submit by 31 December 2006 a report to the European Parliament and the Council accompanied by a proposal confirming, if appropriate, the date of 2009 for the full accomplishment of the postal internal market or determining any other step in the light of the study's conclusions.]

Notes

Article 7 was replaced as shown in square brackets by Directive 2002/39/EC (OJ L 176, 5.7.2002, p.21) with effect from 5 July 2002.

Article 8

The provisions of Article 7 shall be without prejudice to Member States' right to organise the siting of letter boxes on the public highway, the issue of postage stamps and the registered mail service used in the course of judicial or administrative procedures in accordance with their national legislation.

CHAPTER 4
Conditions governing the provision of non-reserved services and access to the network

Article 9

1. For non-reserved services which are outside the scope of the universal service as defined in Article 3, Member States may introduce general authorisations to the extent necessary in order to guarantee compliance with the essential requirements.

2. For non-reserved services which are within the scope of the universal service as defined in Article 3, Member States may introduce authorisation procedures, including individual licences, to the extent necessary in order to guarantee compliance with the essential requirements and to safeguard the universal service.

The granting of authorisations may:

— where appropriate, be made subject to universal service obligations,
— if necessary, impose requirements concerning the quality, availability and performance of the relevant services,
— be made subject to the obligation not to infringe the exclusive or special rights granted to the universal service provider(s) for the reserved postal services under Article 7(1) and (2).

3. The procedures described in paragraphs 1 and 2 shall be transparent, non-discriminatory, proportionate and based on objective criteria. Member States must ensure that the reasons for refusing an authorisation in whole or in part are communicated to the applicant and must establish an appeal procedure.

4. In order to ensure that the universal service is safeguarded, where a Member State determines that the universal service obligations, as provided for by this Directive, represent an unfair financial burden for the universal service provider, it may establish a compensation fund administered for this purpose by a body independent of the beneficiary or beneficiaries. In this case, it may make the granting of authorisation subject to an obligation to make a financial contribution to that fund. The Member State must ensure that the principles of transparency, non-discrimination and proportionality are respected in establishing the compensation fund and when fixing the level of the financial contributions. Only those services set out in Article 3 may be financed in this way.

5. Member States may provide for an identification system for direct mail, allowing the supervision of such services where they are liberalised.

Article 10

1. The European Parliament and the Council, acting on a proposal from the Commission and on the basis of Articles [47](2), [55] and [95] of the Treaty, shall adopt the measures necessary for the harmonisation of the procedures referred to in Article 9 governing the commercial provision to the public of non-reserved postal services.

2. The harmonisation measures referred to in paragraph 1 shall concern, in particular, the criteria to be observed and the procedures to be followed by the postal operator, the manner of publication of those criteria and procedures, as well as the appeal procedures to be followed.

Article 11

The European Parliament and the Council, acting on a proposal from the Commission and on the basis of Articles [47](2), [55] and [95] of the Treaty, shall adopt such harmonisation measures as are necessary to ensure that users and the universal service provider(s) have access to the public postal network under conditions which are transparent and non-discriminatory.

CHAPTER 5
Tariff principles and transparency of accounts

Article 12

Member States shall take steps to ensure that the tariffs for each of the services forming part of the provision of the universal service comply with the following principles:

— prices must be affordable and must be such that all users have access to the services provided,
— prices must be geared to costs; Member States may decide that a uniform tariff should be applied throughout their national territory,
— the application of a uniform tariff does not exclude the right of the universal service provider(s) to conclude individual agreements on prices with customers,
— tariffs must be transparent and non-discriminatory.
[— whenever universal service providers apply special tariffs, for example for services for businesses, bulk mailers or consolidators of mail from different customers, they shall apply the principles of transparency and non-discrimination with regard both to the tariffs and to the associated conditions. The tariffs shall take account of the avoided costs, as compared to the standard service covering the complete range of features offered for the clearance, transport, sorting and delivery of individual postal items and, together with the associated conditions, shall apply equally both as between different third parties and as between third parties and universal service providers supplying equivalent services. Any such tariffs shall also be available to private customers who post under similar conditions,
— cross-subsidisation of universal services outside the reserved sector out of revenues from services in the reserved sector shall be prohibited except to the extent to which it is shown to be strictly necessary to fulfil specific universal service obligations imposed in the competitive area; except in Member States where there are no reserved services, rules shall be adopted to this effect by the national regulatory authorities who shall inform the Commission of such measures.]

Notes

The indents shown in square brackets were inserted by Directive 2002/39/EC (OJ L 176, 5.7.2002, p.21) with effect from 5 July 2002.

Article 13

1. In order to ensure the cross-border provision of the universal service, Member States shall encourage their universal service providers to arrange that in their agreements on terminal dues for intra-Community cross-border mail, the following principles are respected:

— terminal dues shall be fixed in relation to the costs of processing and delivering incoming cross-border mail,
— levels of remuneration shall be related to the quality of service achieved,
— terminal dues shall be transparent and non-discriminatory.

2. The implementation of these principles may include transitional arrangements designed to avoid undue disruption on postal markets or unfavourable implications for economic operators provided there is agreement between the operators of origin and receipt; such arrangements shall, however, be restricted to the minimum required to achieve these objectives.

Article 14

1. Member States shall take the measures necessary to ensure, within two years of the date of entry into force of this Directive, that the accounting of the universal service providers is conducted in accordance with the provisions of this Article.

2. The universal service providers shall keep separate accounts within their internal accounting systems at least for each of the services within the reserved sector on the one hand and for the non-reserved services on the other. The accounts for the non-reserved services should clearly distinguish between services which are part of the universal service and services which are not. Such internal accounting systems shall operate on the basis of consistently applied and objectively justifiable cost accounting principles.

3. The accounting systems referred to in paragraph 2 shall, without prejudice to paragraph 4, allocate costs to each of the reserved and to the non-reserved services respectively in the following manner:

(a) costs which can be directly assigned to a particular service shall be so assigned;
(b) common costs, that is costs which cannot be directly assigned to a particular service, shall be allocated as follows:
    (i) whenever possible, common costs shall be allocated on the basis of direct analysis of the origin of the costs themselves;
    (ii) when direct analysis is not possible, common cost categories shall be allocated on the basis of an indirect linkage to another cost category or group of cost categories for which a direct assignment or allocation is possible; the indirect linkage shall be based on comparable cost structures;
    (iii) when neither direct nor indirect measures of cost allocation can be found, the cost category shall be allocated on the basis of a general allocator computed by using the ratio of all expenses directly or indirectly assigned or allocated, on the one hand, to each of the reserved services and, on the other hand, to the other services.

4. Other cost accounting systems may be applied only if they are compatible with paragraph 2 and have been approved by the national regulatory authority. The Commission shall be informed prior to their application.

5. National regulatory authorities shall ensure that compliance with one of the cost accounting systems described in paragraphs 3 or 4 is verified by a competent body which is independent of the universal service provider. Member States shall ensure that a statement concerning compliance is published periodically.

6. The national regulatory authority shall keep available, to an adequate level of detail, information on the cost accounting systems applied by a universal service provider, and shall submit such information to the Commission on request.

7. On request, detailed accounting information arising from these systems shall be made available in confidence to the national regulatory authority and to the Commission.

8. Where a given Member State has not reserved any of the services reservable under Article 7 and as not established a compensation fund for universal service provision, as permitted under Article 9(4), and where the national regulatory authority is satisfied that none of the designated universal service providers in that Member State is in receipt of State subvention, hidden or otherwise, the national regulatory authority may decide not to apply the requirements of paragraphs 2, 3, 4, 5, 6 and 7 of this Article. The national regulatory authority shall inform the Commission of all such decisions.

Article 15

The financial accounts of all universal service providers shall be drawn up, submitted to audit by an independent auditor and published in accordance with the relevant Community and national legislation to commercial undertakings.

CHAPTER 6
Quality of services

Article 16

Member States shall ensure that quality-of-service standards are set and published in relation to universal service in order to guarantee a postal service of good quality.

Quality standards shall focus, in particular, on routing times and on the regularity and reliability of services.

These standards shall be set by:

— the Member States in the case of national services,
— the European Parliament and the Council in the case of intra-Community cross-border services (see Annex). Future adjustment of these standards to technical progress or market developments shall be made in accordance with the procedure laid down in Article 21.

Independent performance monitoring shall be carried out at least once a year by external bodies having no links with the universal service providers under standardised conditions to be specified in accordance with the procedure laid down in Article 21 and shall be the subject of reports published at least once a year.

Article 17

Member States shall day down quality standards for national mail and shall ensure that they are compatible with those laid down for intra-Community cross-border services.

Member States shall notify their quality standards for national services to the Commission, who will publish them in the same manner as the standards for intra-Community cross-border services referred to in Article 18.

National regulatory authorities shall ensure that independent performance monitoring is carried out in accordance with the fourth subparagraph of Article 16, that the results are justified, and that corrective action is taken where necessary.

Article 18

1. In accordance with Article 16, quality standards for intra-Community cross-border services are laid down in the Annex.

2. Where exceptional situations relating to infrastructure or geography so require, the national regulatory authorities may determine exemptions from the quality standards provided for in the Annex. Where national regulatory authorities determine exemptions in this manner, they shall notify the Commission forthwith. The Commission shall submit an annual report of the notifications received during the previous 12 months to the Committee established under Article 21 for its information.

3. The Commission shall publish in the *Official Journal of the European Communities* any adjustments made to the quality standards for intra-Community cross-border services and shall take steps to ensure the regular independent monitoring and the publication of performance levels certifying compliance with these standards and the progress accomplished. National regulatory authorities shall ensure that corrective action is taken where necessary.

Article 19

[Member States shall ensure that transparent, simple and inexpensive procedures are drawn up for dealing with users" complaints, particularly in cases involving loss, theft, damage or non-compliance with service quality standards (including procedures for determining where responsibility lies in cases where more than one operator is involved).

Member States may provide that this principle is also applied to beneficiaries of services which are:

— outside the scope of the universal service as defined in Article 3, and
— within the scope of the universal service as defined in Article 3, but which are not provided by the universal service provider.

Member States shall adopt measures to ensure that the procedures referred to in the first subparagraph enable disputes to be settled fairly and promptly with provision, where warranted, for a system of reimbursement and/or compensation.]

Without prejudice to other possibilities of appeal under national and Community legislation, Member States shall ensure that users, acting individually or, where permitted by national law, jointly with organisations representing the interests of users and/or consumers, may bring before the competent national authority cases where users" complaints to the universal service provider have not been satisfactory resolved.

In accordance with Article 16, Member States shall ensure that the universal service providers publish, together with the annual report on the monitoring of their performance, information on the number of complaints and the manner in which they have been dealt with.

Notes

The amendments shown in square brackets were made by Directive 2002/39/EC (OJ L 176, 5.7.2002, p.21) with effect from 5 July 2002.

CHAPTER 7

Harmonisation of technical standards

Article 20

The harmonisation of technical standards shall be continued, taking into account in particular the interests of users.

The European Committee for Standardisation shall be entrusted with drawing up technical standards applicable in the postal sector on the basis of remits to it pursuant to the principles set out in Council Directive 83/189/EEC of 28 March 1983 laying down a procedure for the provision of information in the field of technical standards and regulations.[1]

This work shall take account of the harmonisation measures adopted at international level and in particular those decided upon within the Universal Postal Union.

The standards applicable shall be published in the Official Journal of the European Communities once a year.

Member States shall ensure that universal service providers refer to the standards published in the Official Journal where necessary in the interests of users and in particular when they supply the information referred to in Article 6.

The Committee provided for in Article 21 shall be kept informed of the discussions within the European Committee for Standardisation and the progress achieved in this area by that body.

Notes

[1] OJ L 109, 26.4.1983, p. 8. Directive as last amended by Commission Decision 96/139/EC (OJ L 32, 10.2.1996, p. 31).

CHAPTER 8

[The committee

[Article 21

1. The Commission shall be assisted by a committee.

2. Where reference is made to this Article, Articles 5 and 7 of Decision 1999/468/EC[1] shall apply, having regard to the provisions of Article 8 thereof.

The period laid down in Article 5(6) of Decision 1999/468/EC shall be set at three months.

3. The Committee shall adopt its rules of procedure.]

Notes

[¹ Council Decision 1999/468/EC of 28 June 1999 laying down the procedures for the exercise of implementing powers conferred on the Commission (OJ L 184, 17.7.1999, p. 23).]

Article 21 was replaced as shown in square brackets by Regulation (EC) No 1882/2003 of 29 September 2003 (OJ L 284, 31.10.2003, p.1) with effect from 20 November 2003.

CHAPTER 9
The national regulatory authority

Article 22

Each Member State shall designate one or more national regulatory authorities for the postal sector that are legally separate from and operationally independent of the postal operators.

Member States shall inform the Commission which national regulatory authorities they have designated to carry out the tasks arising from this Directive.

[The national regulatory authorities shall have as a particular task ensuring compliance with the obligations arising from this Directive and shall, where appropriate, establish controls and specific procedures to ensure that the reserved services are respected. They may also be charged with ensuring compliance with competition rules in the postal sector.]

Notes

The amendments shown in square brackets were made by Directive 2002/39/EC (OJ L 176, 5.7.2002, p.21) with effect from 5 July 2002.

Commentary
Art 22: **B&C:** 12.185

CHAPTER 10
Final provisions

[Article 23

Without prejudice to Article 7, every two years, on the first occasion no later than 31 December 2004, the Commission shall submit a report to the European Parliament and the Council on the application of this Directive, including the appropriate information about developments in the sector, particularly concerning economic, social, employment and technological aspects, as well as about quality of service. The report shall be accompanied where appropriate by proposals to the European Parliament and the Council.]

Notes

Article 23 was replaced as shown in square brackets by Directive 2002/39/EC (OJ L 176, 5.7.2002, p.21) with effect from 5 July 2002.

Commentary
Art 23: **B&C:** 12.186

Article 24

Member States shall bring into force the laws, regulations and administrative provisions necessary to comply with this Directive not later than 12 months after the date of its entry into force. They shall forthwith inform the Commission thereof.

When Member States adopt these measures, they shall contain a reference to this Directive or be accompanied by such reference on the occasion of their official publication.

Article 25

This Directive shall enter into force on the 20th day following that of its publication in the Official Journal of the European Communities.

Notes
Date of entry into force: 10 February 1998

Article 26

1. This Directive shall not prevent any Member State from maintaining or introducing measures which are more liberal than those provided for by this Directive. Such measures must be compatible with the Treaty.

2. Should this Directive lapse, the measures taken by the Member States to implement it may be maintained, to the extent that they are compatible with the Treaty.

[*Article 27*

The provisions of this Directive, with the exception of Article 26, shall expire on 31 December 2008 unless otherwise decided in accordance with Article 7(3). The authorisation procedures described in Article 9 shall not be affected by this date.]

Notes
Article 27 was replaced as shown in square brackets by Directive 2002/39/EC (OJ L 176, 5.7.2002, p.21) with effect from 5 July 2002.

Commentary
Art 23: B&C: 12.186

Article 28

This Directive is addressed to the Member States.

Done at Brussels, 15 December 1997.

ANNEX
Quality standards for intra-Community cross-border mail

The quality standards for intra-Community cross-border mail in each country are to be established in relation to the time limit for routing measured from end to end* for postal items of the fastest standard category according to the formula D + n, where D represents the date of deposit** and n the number of working days which elapse between that date and that delivery to the addressee.

Quality standards for intra-Community cross-border mail	
Time limit	Objective
D + 3	85 % of items
D + 5	97 % of items

The standards must be achieved not only for the entirety of intra-Community traffic but also for each of the bilateral flows between two Member States.

Notes
* End-to-end routing is measured from the access point to the network to the point of delivery to the addressee.
** The date of deposit to be taken into account shall be the same day as that on which the item is deposited, provided that deposit occurs before the last collection time notified from the access point to the network in question. When deposit takes place after this time limit, the date of deposit to be taken into consideration will be that of the following day of collection.

E29

NOTICE FROM THE COMMISSION

on the application of the competition rules to the postal sector and on the assessment of certain
State measures relating to postal services

(98/C 39/02)

(Text with EEA relevance)

Official Journal C 39, 6.2.1998, p. 2

Celex No: 31998Y0206(01)

Commentary
Notice: B&C: 11.110, 15.059 F&N: 4.344, 4.346

PREFACE

Subsequent to the submission by the Commission of a Green Paper on the development of the single
market for postal services[1] and of a communication to the European Parliament and the Council,
setting out the results of the consultations on the Green Paper and the measures advocated by
the Commission,[2] a substantial discussion has taken place on the future regulatory environment
for the postal sector in the Community. By Resolution of 7 February 1994 on the development of
Community postal services,[3] the Council invited the Commission to propose measures defining
a harmonised universal service and the postal services which could be reserved. In July 1995, the
Commission proposed a package of measures concerning postal services which consisted of a proposal
for a Directive of the European Parliament and the Council on common rules for the development
of Community postal services and the improvement of quality of service[4] and a draft of the present
Notice on the application of the competition rules.[5]

Notes
[1] COM(91) 476 final.
[2] "Guidelines for the development of Community postal services" (COM(93) 247 of 2 June 1993).
[3] OJ C 48, 16.2.1994, p. 3.
[4] OJ C 322, 2.12.1995, p. 22.
[5] OJ C 322, 2.12.1995, p. 3.

This notice, which complements the harmonisation measures proposed by the Commission, builds
on the results of those discussions in accordance with the principles established in the Resolution of
7 February 1994. It takes account of the comments received during the public consultation on the
draft of this notice published in December 1995, of the European Parliament's resolution[6] on this
draft adopted on 12 December 1996, as well as of the discussions on the proposed Directive in the
European Parliament and in Council.

Notes
[6] OJ C 20, 20.1.1997, p. 159.

The Commission considers that because they are an essential vehicle of communication and trade,
postal services are vital for all economic and social activities. New postal services are emerging and
market certainty is needed to favour investment and the creation of new employment in the sector. As
recognized by the Court of Justice of the European Communities, Community law, and in particular
the competition rules of the EC Treaty, apply to the post sector.[7] The Court stated that "in the case
of public undertakings to which Member States grant special or exclusive rights, they are neither to
enact nor to maintain in force any measure contrary to the rules contained in the Treaty with regard

to competition' and that those rules "must be read in conjunction with Article [86](2) which provides that undertakings entrusted with the operation of services of general economic interest are to be subject to the rules on competition in so far as the application of such rules does not obstruct the performance, in law or in fact, of the particular tasks assigned to them." Questions are therefore frequently put to the Commission on the attitude it intends to take, for purposes of the implementation of the competition rules contained in the Treaty, with regard to the behaviour of postal operators and with regard to State measures relating to public undertakings and undertakings to which the Member States grant special or exclusive rights in the postal sector.

Notes
[7] In particular in Joined Cases C-48/90 and C-66/90, *Netherlands and Koninklijke PTT Nederland and PTT Post BV v Commission* [1992] ECR I-565 and Case C-320/91 *Procureur du Roi v Paul Corbeau* [1993] ECR I-2533.

This notice sets out the Commission's interpretation of the relevant Treaty provisions and the guiding principles according to which the Commission intends to apply the competition rules of the Treaty to the postal sector in individual cases, while maintaining the necessary safeguards for the provision of a universal service, and gives to enterprises and Member States clear guidelines so as to avoid infringements of the Treaty. This Notice is without prejudice to any interpretation to be given by the Court of Justice of the European Communities.

Furthermore, this Notice sets out the approach the Commission intends to take when applying the competition rules to the behaviour of postal operators and when assessing the compatibility of State measures restricting the freedom to provide service and/or to compete in the postal markets with the competition rules and other rules of the Treaty. In addition, it addresses the issue of non-discriminatory access to the postal network and the safeguards required to ensure fair competition in the sector.

Especially on account of the development of new postal services by private and public operators, certain Member States have revised, or are revising, their postal legislation in order to restrict the monopoly of their postal organisations to what is considered necessary for the realisation of the public-interest objective. At the same time, the Commission is faced with a growing number of complaints and cases under competition law on which it must take position. At this stage, a notice is therefore the appropriate instrument to provide guidance to Member States and postal operators, including those enjoying special or exclusive rights, to ensure correct implementation of the competition rules. This Notice, although it cannot be exhaustive, aims to provide the necessary guidance for the correct interpretation, in particular, of Articles [49], [81], [82], [86], and [87] of the Treaty in individual cases. By issuing the present notice, the Commission is taking steps to bring transparency and to facilitate investment decisions of all postal operators, in the interest of the users of postal services in the European Union.

As the Commission explained in its communication of 11 September 1996 on "Services of general interest in Europe",[8] solidarity and equal treatment within a market economy are fundamental Community objectives. Those objectives are furthered by services of general interest. Europeans have come to expect high-quality services at affordable prices, and many of them even view services of general interest as social rights.

Notes
[8] COM(96) 443 final. [See now Communication from the commission "Services of general interest in Europe" (2001/C17/04), OJ C 17, 19.1.2001, p.4.]

As regards, in particular, the postal sector, consumers are becoming increasingly assertive in exercising their rights and wishes. Worldwide competition is forcing companies using such services to seek out better price deals comparable to those enjoyed by their competitors. New technologies, such as fax or electronic mail, are putting enormous pressures on the traditional postal services. Those developments have given rise to worries about the future of those services accompanied by concerns over employment and economic and social cohesion. The economic importance of those services is considerable. Hence the importance of modernising and developing services of general interest, since they contribute so much to European competitiveness, social solidarity and quality of life.

The Community's aim is to support the competitiveness of the European economy in an increasingly competitive world and to give consumers more choice, better quality and lower prices, while at the same time helping, through its policies, to strengthen economic and social cohesion between the Member States and to reduce certain inequalities. Postal services have a key role to play here. The Community is committed to promoting their functions of general economic interest, as solemnly confirmed in the new Article [16], introduced by the Amsterdam Treaty, while improving their efficiency. Market forces produce a better allocation of resources and greater effectiveness in the supply of services, the principal beneficiary being the consumer, who gets better quality at a lower price. However, those mechanisms sometimes have their limits; as a result the potential benefits might not extend to the entire population and the objective of promoting social and territorial cohesion in the Union may not be attained. The public authority must then ensure that the general interest is taken into account.

The traditional structures of some services of general economic interest, which are organised on the basis of national monopolies, constitute a challenge for European economic integration. This includes postal monopolies, even where they are justified, which may obstruct the smooth functioning of the market, in particular by sealing off a particular market sector.

The real challenge is to ensure smooth interplay between the requirements of the single market in terms of free movement, economic performance and dynamism, free competition, and the general interest objectives. This interplay must benefit individual citizens and society as a whole. This is a difficult balancing act, since the goalposts are constantly moving: the single market is continuing to expand and public services, far from being fixed, are having to adapt to new requirements.

The basic concept of universal service, which was originated by the Commission,[9] is to ensure the provision of high-quality service to all prices everyone can afford. Universal service is defined in terms of principles: equality, universality, continuity and adaptability; and in terms of sound practices: openness in management, price-setting and funding and scrutiny by bodies independent of those operating the services. Those criteria are not always all met at national level, but where they have been introduced using the concept of European universal service, there have been positive effects for the development of general interest services. Universal service is the expression in Europe of the requirements and special features of the European model of society in a policy which combines a dynamic market, cohesion and solidarity.

Notes
[9] See footnote 8.

High-quality universal postal services are of great importance for private and business customers alike. In view of the development of electronic commerce their importance will even increase in the very near future. Postal services have a valuable role to play here.

As regards the postal sector, Directive 97/67/EC has been adopted by the European Parliament and the Council (hereinafter referred to as "the Postal Directive"). It aims to introduce common rules for developing the postal sector and improving the quality of service, as well as gradually opening up the markets in a controlled way.

The aim of the Postal Directive is to safeguard the postal service as a universal service in the long term. It imposes on Member States a minimum harmonised standard of universal services including a high-quality service countrywide with regular guaranteed deliveries at prices everyone can afford. This involves the collection, transport, sorting and delivery of letters as well as catalogues and parcels within certain price and weight limits. It also covers registered and insured (valeur déclarée) items and applies to both domestic and cross-border deliveries. Due regard is given to considerations of continuity, confidentiality, impartiality and equal treatment as well as adaptability.

To guarantee the funding of the universal service, a sector may be reserved for the operators of this universal service. The scope of the reserved sector has been harmonised in the Postal Directive According to the Postal Directive, Member States can only grant exclusive rights for the provision of postal services to the extent that this is necessary to guarantee the maintenance of the universal service. Moreover, the Postal Directive establishes the maximum scope that Member States may reserve in order to achieve this objective. Any additional funding which may be required for the universal service may be found by writing certain obligations into commercial operator's franchises; for example, they may be required to make financial contributions to a compensation fund administered for this purpose by a body independent of the beneficiary or beneficiaries, as foreseen in Article 9 of the Postal Directive.

The Postal Directive lays down a minimum common standard of universal services and establishes common rules concerning the reserved area. It therefore increases legal certainty as regards the legality of some exclusive and special rights in the postal sector. There are, however State measures that are not dealt with in it and that can be in conflict with the Treaty rules addressed to Member States. The autonomous behaviour of the postal operators also remains subject to the competition rules in the Treaty.

Article [86](2) of the Treaty provides that suppliers of services of general interest may be exempted from the rules in the Treaty, to the extent that the application of those rules would obstruct the performance of the general interest tasks for which they are responsible. That exemption from the Treaty rules is however subject to the principle of proportionality. That principle is designed to ensure the best match between the duty to provide general interest services and the way in which the services are actually provided, so that the means used are in proportion to the ends pursued. The principle is formulated to allow for a flexible and context-sensitive balance that takes account of the technical and budgetary constraints that may vary from one sector to another. It also makes for the best possible interaction between market efficiency and general interest requirements, by ensuring that the means used to satisfy the requirements do not unduly interfere with the smooth running of the single European market and do not affect trade to an extent that would be contrary to the Community interest.[10]

Notes

[10] See judgment of 23 October 1997 in Cases C-157/94 to C-160/94 *"Member State Obligations — Electricity"* *Commission v Netherlands* (157/94), *Italy* (158/94), *France* (154/94), *Spain* (160/94).

The application of the Treaty rules, including the possible application of the Article [86](2) exemption, as regards both behaviour of undertakings and State measures can only be done on a case-by-case basis. It seems, however, highly desirable, in order to increase legal certainty as regards measures not covered by the Postal Directive, to explain the Commission's interpretation of the Treaty and the approach that it aims to follow in its future application of those rules. In particular, the Commission considers that, subject to the provisions of Article [86](2) in relation to the provision of the universal service, the application of the Treaty rules would promote the competitiveness of the undertakings active in the postal sector, benefit consumers and contribute in a positive way to the objectives of general interest.

The postal sector in the European Union is characterised by areas which Member States have reserved in order to guarantee universal service and which are now being harmonised by the Postal Directive in order to limit distortive effects between Member States. The Commission must, according to the Treaty, ensure that postal monopolies comply with the rules of the Treaty, and in particular the competition rules, in order to ensure maximum benefit and limit any distortive effects for the consumers. In pursuing this objective by applying the competition rules to the sector on a case-by-case-basis, the Commission will ensure that monopoly power is not used for extending a protected dominant position into liberalised activities or for unjustified discrimination in favour of big accounts at the expense of small users. The Commission will also ensure that postal monopolies granted in the area of cross-border services are not used for creating or maintaining illicit price cartels harming the interest of companies and consumers in the European Union.

This notice explains to the players on the market the practical consequences of the applicability of the competition rules to the postal sector, and the possible derogations from the principles. It sets out the position the Commission would adopt, in the context set by the continuing existence of special and exclusive rights as harmonised by the Postal Directive, in assessing individual cases or before the Court of Justice in cases referred to the Court by national courts under Article [234] of the Treaty.

1. DEFINITIONS

In the context of this notice, the following definitions shall apply:[11]

"*postal services*": services involving the clearance, sorting, transport and delivery of postal items;

"*public postal network*": the system of organisation and resources of all kinds used by the universal service provider(s) for the purposes in particular of:

— the clearance of postal items covered by a universal service obligation from access points throughout the territory,

— the routing and handling of those items from the postal network access point to the distribution centre,

— distribution to the addresses shown on items;

"*access points*": physical facilities, including letter boxes provided for the public either on the public highway or at the premises of the universal service provider, where postal items may be deposited with the public postal network by customers;

"*clearance*": the operation of collecting postal items deposited at access points;

"*distribution*": the process from sorting at the distribution centre to delivery of postal items to their addresses;

"*postal item*": an item addressed in the final form in which it is to be carried by the universal service provider. In addition to items of correspondence, such items also include for instance books, catalogues, newspapers, periodicals and postal packages containing merchandise with or without commercial value;

"*item of [correspondence]*": a communication in written form on any kind of physical medium to be conveyed and delivered at the address indicated by the sender on the item itself or on its wrapping. Books, catalogues, newspapers and periodicals shall not be regarded as items of correspondence;

"*direct mail*": a communication consisting solely of advertising, marketing or publicity material and comprising an identical message, except for the addressee's name, address and identifying number as well as other modifications which do not alter the nature of the message, which is sent to a significant number of addresses, to be conveyed and delivered at the address indicated by the sender on the item itself or on its wrapping. The National Regulatory Authority should interpret the term "significant number of addressees" within each Member State and publish an appropriate definition. Bills, invoices, financial statements and other non-identical messages should not be regarded as direct mail. A communication combining direct mail with other items within the same wrapping should not be regarded as direct mail. Direct mail includes cross-border as well as domestic direct mail;

"*document exchange*": provision of means, including the supply of *ad hoc* premises as well as transportation by a third party, allowing self-delivery by mutual exchange of postal items between users subscribing to this service;

"*express mail service*": a service featuring, in addition to greater speed and reliability in the collection, distribution, and delivery of items, all or some of the following supplementary facilities: guarantee of delivery by a fixed date; collection from point of origin; personal delivery to addressee; possibility of changing the destination and address in transit; confirmation to sender of receipt of the item dispatched; monitoring and tracking of items dispatched; personalised service for customers and provision of an *à la carte service*, as and when required. Customers are in principle prepared to pay a higher price for this service;

"*universal service provider*": the public or private entity providing a universal postal service or parts thereof within a Member State, the identity of which has been notified to the Commission;

"*exclusive rights*": rights granted by a Member State which reserve the provision of postal services to one undertaking through any legislative, regulatory or administrative instrument and reserve to it the right to provide a postal service, or to undertake an activity, within a given geographical area;

"special rights": rights granted by a Member State to a limited number of undertakings through any legislative, regulatory or administrative instrument which, within a given geographical area:

— limits, on a discretionary basis, to two or more the number of such undertakings authorised to provide a service or undertake an activity, otherwise than according to objective, proportional and non-discriminatory criteria, or

— designates, otherwise than according to such criteria, several competing undertakings as undertakings authorised to provide a service or undertake an activity, or

— confers on any undertaking or undertakings, otherwise than according to such criteria, legal or regulatory advantages which substantially affect the ability of any other undertaking to provide the same service or undertake the same activity in the same geographical area under substantially comparable conditions;

"terminal dues": the remuneration of universal service providers for the distribution of incoming cross-border mail comprising postal items from another Member State or from a third country;

"intermediary": any economical operator who acts between the sender and the universal service provider, by clearing, routing and/or pre-sorting postal items, before channelling them into the public postal network of the same or of another country;

"national regulatory authority": the body or bodies, in each Member State, to which the Member State entrusts, inter alia, the regulatory functions falling within the scope of the Postal Directive;

"essential requirements": general non-economic reasons which can induce a Member State to impose conditions on the supply of postal services.[12] These reasons are: the confidentiality of correspondence, security of the network as regards the transport of dangerous goods and, where justified, data protection, environmental protection and regional planning.

Data protection may include personal data protection, the confidentiality of information transmitted or stored and protection of privacy.

Notes

[11] The definitions will be interpreted in the light of the Postal Directive and any changes resulting from review of that Directive.

[12] The meaning of this important phrase in the context of Community competition law is explained in paragraph 5.3.

---

2. MARKET DEFINITION AND POSITION ON THE POSTAL MARKET

(a) Geographical and product market definition

2.1. Articles [81] and [82] of the Treaty prohibit as incompatible with the common market any conduct by one or more undertakings that may negatively affect trade between Member States which involves the prevention, restriction, or distortion of competition and/or an abuse of a dominant position within the common market or a substantial part of it. The territories of the Member States constitute separate geographical markets with regard to the delivery of domestic mail and also with regard to the domestic delivery of inward cross-border mail, owing primarily to the exclusive rights of the operators referred to in point 4.2 and to the restrictions imposed on the provision of postal services. Each of the geographical markets constitutes a substantial part of the common market. For the determination of "relevant market`, the country of origin of inward cross-border mail is immaterial.

2.2. As regards the product markets, the differences in practice between Member States demonstrate that recognition of several distinct markets is necessary in some cases. Separation of different product-markets is relevant, among, other things, to special or exclusive rights granted. In its assessment of individual cases on the basis of the different market and regulatory situations in the Member States and on the basis of a harmonised framework provided by the Postal Directive, the Commission will in principle consider that a number of distinct product markets exist, like the clearance, sorting, transport and delivery of mail, and for example direct mail, and cross-border mail. The Commission will take into account the fact that these markets are wholly or partly liberalised in a number of Member States. The Commission will consider the following markets when assessing individual cases.

2.3. The general letter service concerns the delivery of items of correspondence to the addresses shown on the items.

It does not include self-provision, that is the provision of postal services by the natural or legal person (including a sister or subsidiary organisation) who is the originator of the mail.

Also excluded, in accordance with practice in many Member States, are such postal items as are not considered items of correspondence, since they consist of identical copies of the same written communication and have not been altered by additions, deletions or indications other than the name of the addressee and his address. Such items are magazines, newspapers, printed periodicals catalogues, as well as goods or documents accompanying and relating to such items.

Direct mail is covered by the definition of items of correspondence. However, direct mail items do not contain personalised messages. Direct mail addresses the needs of specific operators for commercial communications services, as a complement to advertising in the media. Moreover, the senders of direct mail do not necessarily require the same short delivery times, priced at first-class letter tariffs, asked for by customers requesting services on the market as referred to above. The fact that both services are not always directly interchangeable indicates the possibility of distinct markets.

2.4. Other distinct markets include, for example, the express mail market, the document exchange market, as well as the market for new services (services quite distinct from conventional services). Activities combining the new telecommunications technologies and some elements of the postal services may be, but are not necessarily, new services within the meaning of the Postal Directive. Indeed, they may reflect the adaptability of traditional services.

A document exchange differs from the market referred to in point 2.3 since it does not include the collection and the delivery to the addressee of the postal items transported. It involves only means, including the supply of ad hoc premises as well as transportation by a third party, allowing self-delivery by mutual exchange of postal items between users subscribing to this service. The users of a document exchange are members of a closed user group.

The express mail service also differs from the market referred to in point 2.3 owing to the value added by comparison with the basic postal service.[13] In addition to faster and more reliable collection, transportation and delivery of the postal items, an express mail service is characterised by the provision of some or all of the following supplementary services: guarantee of delivery by a given date; collection from the sender's address; delivery to the addressee in person; possibility of a change of destination and addressee in transit; conformation to the sender of delivery; tracking and tracing; personalised treatment for customers and the offer of a range of services according to requirements. Customers are in principle prepared to pay a higher price for this service. The reservable services as defined in the Postal Directive may include accelerated delivery of items of domestic correspondence falling within the prescribed price and weight limits.

Notes
[13] Commission Decisions 90/16/EEC (OJ L 10, 12.1.1990, p. 47) and 90/456/EEC (OJ L 233, 28.8.1990, p. 19).

2.5. Without prejudice to the definition of reservable services given in the Postal Directive, different activities can be recognised, within the general letter service, which meet distinct needs and should in principle be considered as different markets; the markets for the clearance and for the sorting of mail, the market for the transport of mail and, finally, the delivery of mail (domestic or inward cross-border). Different categories of customers must be distinguished in this respect. Private customers demand the distinct products or services as one integrated service. However, business customers, which represent most of the revenues of the operators referred to in point 4.2, actively pursue the possibilities of substituting for distinct components of the final service alternative solutions (with regard to quality of service levels and/or costs incurred) which are in some cases provided by, or sub-contracted to, different operators. Business customers want to balance the advantages and disadvantages of self-provision versus provision by the postal operator. The existing monopolies limit the external supply of those individual services, but they would otherwise limit the external supply of those individual according to market conditions. That market reality supports the opinion that clearance, sorting, transport and delivery of postal items constitute different markets.[14] From a competition-law point of view, the distinction between the four markets may be relevant.

That is the case for cross-border mail where the clearance and transport will be done by a postal operator other than the one providing the distribution. This is also the case as regards domestic mail, since most postal operators permit major customers to undertake sorting of bulk traffic in return for discounts, based on their public tariffs. The deposit and collection of mail and method of payment also vary in these circumstances. Mail rooms of larger companies are now often operated by intermediaries, which prepare and pre-sort mail before handing it over to the postal operator for final distribution. Moreover, all postal operators allow some kind of downstream access to distribution. Moreover, all postal operators allow some kind of downstream access to their postal network, for instance by allowing or even demanding (sorted) mail to be deposited at an expediting or sorting centre. This permits in many cases a higher reliability (quality of service) by bypassing any sources of failure in the postal network upstream.

Notes

[14] See Commission Notice on the definition of the relevant market for the purpose of the application of Community competition law (OJ C 372, 9.12.1997, p. 5).

(b) Dominant position

2.6. Since in most Member States the operator referred to in point 4.2 is, by virtue of the exclusive rights granted to him, the only operator controlling a public postal network covering the whole territory of the Member State, such an operator has a dominant position within the meaning of Article [82] of the Treaty on the national market for the distribution of items of correspondence. Distribution is the service to the user which allows for important economies of scale, and the operator providing this service is in most cases also dominant on the markets for the clearance, sorting and transport of mail. In addition, the enterprise which provides distribution, particularly if it also operates post office premises, has the important advantage of being regarded by the users as the principal postal enterprise, because it is the most conspicuous one, and is therefore the natural first choice. Moreover, this dominant position also includes, in most Member States, services such as registered mail or special delivery services, and/or some sectors of the parcels market.

(c) Duties of dominant postal operators

2.7. According to point (b) of the second paragraph of Article [82] of the Treaty, an abuse may consist in limiting the performance of the relevant service to the prejudice of its consumers. Where a Member State grants exclusive rights to an operator referred to in point 4.2 for services which it does not offer, or offers in conditions not satisfying the needs of customers in the same way as the services which competitive economic operators would have offered, the Member State induces those operators, by the simple exercise of the exclusive right which has been conferred on them, to limit the supply of the relevant service, as the effective exercise of those activities by private companies is, in this case, impossible. This is particularly the case where measures adopted to protect the postal service restrict the provision of other distinct services on distinct or neighbouring markets such as the express mail market. The Commission has requested several Member States to abolish restrictions resulting from exclusive rights regarding the provision of express mail services by international couriers.[15]

Another type of possible abuse involves providing a seriously inefficient service and failing to take advantage of technical developments. This harms customers who are prevented from choosing between alternative suppliers. For instance, a report prepared for the Commission[16] in 1994 showed that, where they have not been subject to competition, the public postal operators in the Member States have not made any significant progress since 1990 in the standardisation of dimensions and weights. The report also showed that some postal operators practised hidden cross-subsidies between reserved and non-reserved services (see points 3.1 and 3.4), which explained, according to that study, most of the price disparities between Member States in 1994, especially penalising residential users who do not qualify for any discounts schemes, since they make use of reserved services that are priced at a higher level than necessary.

The examples given illustrate the possibility that, where they are granted special or exclusive rights, postal operators may let the quality of the service decline[17] and omit to take necessary steps to improve service quality. In such cases, the Commission may be induced to act taking account of the conditions explained in point 8.3.

As regards cross-border postal services, the study referred to above showed that the quality of those services needed to be improved significantly in order to meet the needs of customers, and in particular of residential customers who cannot afford to use the services of courier companies or facsimile transmission instead. Independent measurements carried out in 1995 and 1996 show an improvement of quality of service since 1994. However, those measurements only concern first class mail, and the most recent measurements show that the quality has gone down slightly again.

The majority of Community public postal operators have notified an agreement on terminal dues to the Commission for assessment under the competition rules of the Treaty. The parties to the agreement have explained that their aim is to establish fair compensation for the delivery of cross-border mail reflecting more closely the real costs incurred and to improve the quality of cross-border mail services.

Notes

[15] See footnote 13.

[16] UFC — Que Choisir, Postal services in the European Union, April 1994.

[17] In many Member States users could, some decades ago, still rely on this service to receive in the afternoon, standard letters posted in the morning. Since then, a continuous decline in the quality of the service has been observed, and in particular of the number of daily rounds of the postmen, which were reduced from five to one (or two in some cities of the European Union). The exclusive rights of the postal organisations favoured a fall in quality, since they prevented other companies from entering the market. As a consequence the postal organisations failed to compensate for wage increases and reduction of the working hours by introducing modern technology, as was done by enterprises in industries open to competition.

2.8. Unjustified refusal to supply is also an abuse prohibited by Article [82] of the Treaty. Such behaviour would lead to a limitation of services within the meaning of Article [82], second paragraph, (b) and, if applied only to some users, result in discrimination contrary to Article [82], second paragraph, (c), which requires that no dissimilar conditions be applied to equivalent transactions. In most of the Member States, the operators referred to in point 4.2 provide access at various access points of their postal networks to intermediaries. Conditions of access, and in particular the tariffs applied, are however, often confidential and may facilitate the application of discriminatory conditions, Member States should ensure that their postal legislation does not encourage postal operators to differentiate unjustifiably as regards the conditions applied or to exclude certain companies.

2.9. While a dominant firm is entitled to defend its position by competing with rivals, it has a special responsibility not to further diminish the degree of competition remaining on the market. Exclusionary practices may be directed against existing competitors on the market or intended to impede market access by new entrants. Examples of such illegal behaviour include: refusal to deal as a means of eliminating a competitor by a firm which is the sole or dominant source of supply of a product or controls access to an essential technology or infrastructure; predatory pricing and selective price cutting (see section 3); exclusionary dealing agreements; discrimination as part of a wider pattern of monopolizing conduct designed to exclude competitors; and exclusionary rebate schemes.

3. Cross-subsidisation

(a) Basic principles

3.1. Cross-subsidisation means that an undertaking bears or allocates all or part of the costs of its activity in one geographical or product market to its activity in another geographical or product market. Under certain circumstances, cross-subsidisation in the postal sector, where nearly all operators provide reserved and non-reserved services, can distort competition and lead to competitors being beaten by offers which are made possible not by efficiency (including economies of scope) and performance but by cross-subsidies. Avoiding cross-subsidisation leading to unfair competition is crucial for the development of the postal sector.

3.2. Cross-subsidisation does not distort competition when the costs of reserved activities are subsidised by the revenue generated by other reserved services since there is no competition possible as to these services. This form of subsidisation may sometimes be necessary, to enable the operators referred to in point 4.2 to perform their obligation to provide a service universally, and on the same conditions to everybody.[18] For instance, unprofitable mail delivery in rural areas is subsidised through revenues from profitable mail delivery in urban areas. The same could be said of subsidising the provision of reserved services through revenues generated by activities open to competition. Moreover, cross-subsidisation between non-reserved activities is not in itself abusive.

Notes

[18] See [the] Postal Directive, recitals 16 and 28, and Chapter 5.

3.3. By contrast, subsidising activities open to competition by allocating their costs to reserved services is likely to distort competition in breach of Article [82]. It could amount to an abuse by an undertaking holding a dominant position within the Community. Moreover, users of activities covered by a monopoly would have to bear costs which are unrelated to the provision of those activities. Nonetheless, dominant companies too many compete on price, or improve their cash flow and obtain only partial contribution to their fixed (overhead) costs, unless the prices are predatory or go against relevant national or Community regulations.

(b) Consequences

3.4. A reference to cross-subsidisation was made in point 2.7; duties of dominant postal operators. The operators referred to in point 4.2 should not use the income from the reserved area to cross-subsidise activities in areas open to competition. Such a practice could prevent, restrict or distort competition in the non-reserved area. However, in some justified cases, subject to the provisions of Article [86](2), cross-subsidisation can be regarded as lawful, for example for cultural mail,[19] as long as it is applied in a non discriminatory manner, or for particular services to the socially, medically and economically disadvantaged. When necessary, the Commission will indicate what other exemptions the Treaty would allow to be made. In all other cases, taking into account the indications given in point 3.3, the price of competitive services offered by the operator referred to in point 4.2 should, because of the difficulty of allocating common costs, in principle be at least equal to the average total costs of provision. This means covering the direct costs plus an appropriate proportion of the common and overhead costs of the operator. Objective criteria, such as volumes, time (labour) usage, or intensity of usage, should be used to determine the appropriate proportion. When using the turnover generated by the services involved as a criterion in a case of cross-subsidisation, allowance should be made for the fact that in such a scenario the turnover of the relevant activity is being kept artificially low. Demand-influenced factors, such as revenues or profits, are themselves influenced by predation. If services were offered systematically and selectively at a price below average total cost, the Commission would, on a case-by-case basis, investigate the matter under Article [82], or under Article [82] and Article [86](1) or under Article [87].

Notes

[19] Referred to by UPU as "work of the mind", comprising books, newspapers, periodicals and journals.

---

4. PUBLIC UNDERTAKINGS AND SPECIAL OR EXCLUSIVE RIGHTS

4.1. The treaty obliges the Member States, in respect of public undertakings and undertakings to which they grant special or exclusive rights, neither to enact nor maintain in force any measures contrary to the Treaty rules (Article [86](1)). The expression "undertaking" includes every person or legal entity exercising an economic activity, irrespective of the legal status of the entity and the way in which it is financed. The clearance, sorting, transportation and distribution of postal items constitute economic activities, and these services are normally supplied for reward.

The term "public undertaking" includes every undertaking over which the public authorities may exercise directly or indirectly a dominant influence by virtue of ownership of it, their financial participation in it or the rules which govern it.[20] A dominant influence on the part of the public authorities may in particular be presumed when the public authorities hold, directly or indirectly, the majority of the subscribed capital of the undertaking, control the majority of the voting rights attached to shares issued by the undertaking or can appoint more than half of the members of the administrative, managerial or supervisory body. Bodies which are part of the Member State's administration and which provide in an organised manner postal services for third parties against remuneration are to be regarded as such undertakings. Undertakings to which special or exclusive rights are granted can, according to Article [86](1), be public as well as private.

Notes
[20] Commission Directive 80/723/EEC on the transparency of financial relations between Member States and public undertakings, OJ L 195, 29.7.1980, p. 35.

4.2. National regulations concerning postal operators to which the Member States have granted special or exclusive rights to provide certain postal services are "measures" within the meaning of Article [86](1) of the Treaty and must be assessed under the Treaty provisions to which that Article refers.

In addition to Member States' obligations under Article [86](1), public undertakings and undertakings that have been granted special or exclusive rights are subject to Articles [81] and [82].

4.3. In most Member States, special and exclusive rights apply to services such as the clearance, transportation and distribution of certain postal items, as well as the way in which those services are provided, such as the exclusive right to place letter boxes along the public highway or to issue stamps bearing the name of the country in question.

Commentary
point 4: B&C: 11.110

5. FREEDOM TO PROVIDE SERVICES

(a) Basic principles

5.1. The granting of special or exclusive rights to one or more operators referred to in point 4.2 to carry out the clearance, including public collection, transport and distribution of certain categories of postal items inevitably restricts the provision of such services, both by companies established in other Member States and by undertakings established in the Member State concerned. This restriction has a trans-border character when the addresses or the senders of the postal items handled by those undertakings are established in other Member States. In practice, restrictions on the provision of postal services, within the meaning of Article [49] of the Treaty,[21] comprise prohibiting the conveyance of certain categories of postal items to other Member States including by intermediaries, as well as the prohibition on distributing gross-border mail. The Postal Directive lays down the justified restrictions on the provision of postal services.

Notes
[21] For a general explanation of the principles deriving from Article [49], see Commission interpretative communication concerning the free movement of services across frontiers (OJ C 334, 9.12.1993, p. 3).

5.2. Article [55], read in conjunction with Article [45] and [46] of the Treaty, sets out exceptions from Article [49]. Since they are exceptions to a fundamental principle, they must be interpreted restrictively. As regards postal services, the exception under Article [45] only applies to the conveyance and distribution of a special kind of mail, that is mail generated in the curse of judicial or administrative procedures, connected, even occasionally, with the exercise of official authority, in particular notifications in pursuance of any judicial or administrative procedures. The conveyance and distribution of such items on a Member State's territory may therefore be subjected at a licensing requirement (see point 5.5) in order to protect the public interest. The conditions of the other derogations from the Treaty listed in those provisions will not normally be fulfilled in relation to postal services. Such services cannot, in themselves, threaten public policy and cannot affect public health.

5.3. The case-law of the Court of Justice allows, in principle, further derogations on the basis of mandatory requirements, provided that they fulfil non-economic essential requirements in the general interest, are applied without discrimination, and are appropriate and proportionate to the objective to be achieved. As regards postal services, the essential requirements which the Commission would consider as justifying restrictions on the freedom to provide postal services are data protection subject to approximation measures taken in this field, the confidentiality of correspondence, security of the network as regards the transport of dangerous goods, as well as, where justified under the provisions of the Treaty, environmental protection and regional planning. Conversely, the Commission would not consider it justified to impose restrictions on the freedom to provide postal services for reasons of consumer protection since this general interest requirement can be met by the general legislation on fair trade practices and consumer protection. Benefits to consumers are enhanced by the freedom to provide postal services, provided that universal service obligations are well defined on the basis of the Postal Directive and can be fulfilled.

5.4. The Commission therefore considers that the maintenance of any special or exclusive right which limits cross-border provision of postal services needs to be justified in the light of Articles [86] and [49] of the Treaty. At present, the special or exclusive rights whose scope does not go beyond the reserved services as defined in the Postal Directive are prima facie justified under Article [86](2). Outward cross-border mail is de jure or de facto liberalised in some Member States, such as Denmark, the Netherlands, Finland, Sweden, and the United Kingdom.

(b) Consequences

5.5. The adoption of the measures contained in the Postal Directive requires Member States to regulate postal services. Where Member States restrict postal services to ensure the achievement of universal service and essential requirements, the content of such regulation must correspond to the objective pursued. Obligations should, as a general rule, be enforced within the framework of class licences and declaration procedures by which operators of postal services supply their name, legal form, title and address as well as a short description of the services they offer to the public. Individual licensing should only be applied for specific postal services, where it is demonstrated that less restrictive procedures cannot ensure those objectives. Member States may be invited, on a case-by-case basis, to notify the measures they adopt to the Commission to enable it to assess their proportionality.

6. Measures Adopted by Member States

(a) Basic principles

6.1. Member States have the freedom to define what are general interest services, to grant the special or exclusive rights that are necessary for providing them, to regulate their management and, where appropriate, to fund them. However, under Article [86](1) of the Treaty, Member States must, in the case of public undertakings and undertakings to which they have granted special or exclusive rights, neither enact nor maintain in force any measure contrary to the Treaty rules, and in particular its competition rules.

(b) Consequences

6.2. The operation of a universal clearance and distribution network confers significant advantages on the operator referred to in point 4.2 in offering not only reserved or liberalised services falling within the definition of universal service, but also other (non-universal postal) services. The prohibition under Article [86](1), read in conjunction with Article [82](b), applies to the use, without objective justification, of a dominant position on one market to obtain market power on related or neighbouring markets which are distinct from the former, at the risk of eliminating competition on those markets. In countries where local delivery of items of correspondence is liberalised, such as Spain, and the monopoly is limited to inter-city transport and delivery, the use of a dominant position to extend the monopoly from the latter market to the former would therefore be incompatible with the Treaty provisions, in the absence of specific justification, if the functioning of services in the general economic interest was not previously endangered. The Commission considers that it would be appropriate for Member States to inform the Commission of any extension of special or exclusive rights and of the justification therefor.

6.3. There is a potential effect on the trade between Member States from restrictions on the provision of postal services, since the postal services offered by operators other than the operators referred to in point 4.2 can cover mailings to or from other Member States, and restrictions may impede cross-border activities of operators in other Member States.

6.4. As explained in point 8(b)(vii), Member States must monitor access conditions and the exercise of special and exclusive rights. They need not necessarily set up new bodies to do this but they should not give to their operator[22] as referred to in point 4.2, or to a body which is related (legally, administratively and structurally) to that operator, the power of supervision of the exclusive rights granted and of the activities of postal operators generally. An enterprise in a dominant position must not be allowed to have such a power over its competitors. The independence, both in theory and in practice, of the supervisory authority from all the enterprise supervised is essential. The system of undistorted competition required by the Treaty can only be ensured if equal opportunities for the different economic operators, including confidentiality of sensitive business information, are guaranteed. To allow an operator to check the declarations of its competitors or to assign to an undertaking the power to supervise the activities of its competitors or to be associated in the granting of licences means that such undertaking is given commercial information about its competitors and thus has the opportunity to influence the activity of those competitors.

Notes

[22] See in particular, Case C-18/88 *RTT v GB-Inno-BM* [1991] ECR I-5981, paragraphs 25 to 28.

7. POSTAL OPERATORS AND STATE AID

(a) Principles

While a few operators referred to in point 4.2 are highly profitable, the majority appear to be operating either in financial deficit or at close to break-even in postal operations, although information on underlying financial performance is limited, as relatively few operators publish relevant information of an auditable standard on a regular basis. However, direct financial support in the form of subsidies or indirect support such as tax exemptions is being given to fund some postal services, even if the actual amounts are often not transparent.

The Treaty makes the Commission responsible for enforcing Article [87], which declares State aid that affects trade between Member States of the Community to be incompatible with the common market except in certain circumstances where an exemption is, or may be, granted. Without prejudice to Article [86](2), Articles [87] and [88] are applicable to postal services.[23]

Pursuant to Article [88](3), Member States are required to notify to the Commission for approval all plans to grant aid or to alter existing aid arrangements. Moreover, the Commission is required to monitor aid which it has previously authorised or which dates from before the entry into force of the Treaty or before the accession of the Member State concerned.

All universal service providers currently fall within the scope of Commission Directive 80/723/EEC of 25 June 1980 on the transparency of financial relations between Member States and public undertakings,[24] as last amended by Directive 93/84/EEC.[25] In addition to the general transparency requirement for the accounts of operators referred to in point 4.2 as discussed in point 8(b)(vi), Member States must therefore ensure that financial relations between them and those operators are transparent as required by the Directive, so that the following are clearly shown:

(a) public funds made available directly, including tax exemptions or reductions;
(b) public funds made available through other public undertakings or financial institutions;
(c) the use to which those public funds are actually put.

The Commission regards, in particular, the following as making available public funds:

(a) the setting-off of operating losses;
(b) the provision of capital;
(c) non-refundable grants or loans on privileged terms;
(d) the granting of financial advantages by forgoing profits or the recovery of sums due;
(e) the forgoing of a normal return on public funds used;
(f) compensation for financial burdens imposed by the public authorities.

Notes

[23] Case C-387/92 *Banco de Credito Industrial v. Ayuntamiento Valencia* [1994] ECR I-877.
[24] OJ L 195, 29.7.1980, p. 35.
[25] OJ L 254, 12.10.1993, p. 16. [See now Commission Directive 2005/81/EC of 28 November 2005 amending Directive 80/723/EEC (OJ L 312, 29.11.2005).]

(b) Application of Articles [86] and [87]

The Commission has been called upon to examine a number of tax advantages granted to a postal operator on the basis of Article [87] in connection with Article [86] of the Treaty. The Commission sought to check whether that privileged tax treatment could be used to cross-subsidize that operator's operations in sectors open to competition. At that time, the postal operator did not have an analytical cost-accounting system serving to enable the Commission to distinguish between the reserved activities and the competitive ones. Accordingly, the Commission, on the basis of the findings of studies carried out in that area, assessed the additional costs due to universal-service obligations borne by that postal operator and compared those costs with the tax advantages. The Commission concluded that the costs exceeded those advantages and therefore decided that the tax system under examination could not lead to cross-subsidization of that operator's operations in the competitive areas.[26]

It is worth noting that in its decision the Commission invited the Member State concerned to make sure that the postal operator adopted an analytical cost-accounting system and requested an annual report which would allow the monitoring of compliance with Community law.

The Court of First Instance ha endorsed the Commission's decision and has stated that the tax advantages to that postal operator are State aid which benefit from an exemption from the prohibition set out in Article [87](1) on the basis of Article [86](2).[27]

Notes

[26] Case NN 135/92, OJ C 262, 7.10.1995, p. 11.
[27] Case T-106/95 *FFSA v Commission* [1997] ECR II-229.

---

8. Service of General Economic Interest

(a) Basic principles

8.1. Article [86](2) of the Treaty allows an exception from the application of the Treaty rules where the application of those rules obstructs, in law or in fact, the performance of the particular task assigned to the operators referred to in point 4.2 for the provision of a service of general economic interest. Without prejudice to the rights of the Member States to define particular requirements of services of general interest, that task consists primarily in the provision and the maintenance of a universal public postal service, guaranteeing at affordable, cost-effective and transparent tariffs nationwide access to the public postal network within a reasonable distance and during adequate opening hours, including the clearance of postal items from accessible postal boxes or collection points throughout the territory and the timely delivery of such items to the address indicated, as well as associated services entrusted by measures of a regulatory nature to those operators for universal delivery at a specified quality. The universal service is to evolve in response to the social, economical and technical environment and to the demands of users.

The general interest involved requires the availability in the Community of a genuinely integrated public postal network, allowing efficient circulation of information and thereby fostering, on the one hand, the competitiveness of European industry and the development of trade and greater cohesion between the regions and Member States, and on the other, the improvement of social contacts between the citizens of the Union. The definition of the reserved area has to take into account the financial resources necessary for the provision of the service of general economic interest.

8.2. The financial resources for the maintenance and improvement of that public network still derive mainly from the activities referred to in point 2.3. Currently, and in the absence of harmonisation at Community level, most Member States have fixed the limits of the monopoly by reference to the weight of the item. Some Member States apply a combined weight and price limit whereas one Member State applies a price limit only. Information collected by the Commission on the revenues obtained from mail flows in the Member States seems to indicate that the maintenance of special or exclusive rights with regard to this market could, in the absence of exceptional circumstances, be sufficient to guarantee the improvement an maintenance of the public postal network.

The service for which Member States can reserve exclusive or special rights, to the extent necessary to ensure the maintenance of the universal service, is harmonised in the Postal Directive. To the extent to which Member States grant special or exclusive rights for this service, the service is to be considered a separate product-market in the assessment of individual cases in particular with regard to direct mail, the distribution of inward cross-border mail, outward cross-border mail, as well as with regard to the collection, sorting and transport of mail. The Commission will take account of the fact that those markets are wholly or partly liberalised in a number of Member States.

8.3. When applying the competition rules and other relevant Treaty rules to the postal sector, the Commission, acting upon a complaint or upon its own initiative, will take account of the harmonized definition set out in the Postal Directive in assessing whether the scope of the reserved area can be justified under Article [86](2). The point of departure will be a presumption that, to the extent that they fall within the limits of the reserved area as defined in the Postal Directive, the special or exclusive rights will be prima facie justified under Article [86](2). That presumption can, however, be rebutted if the facts in a case show that a restriction does not fulfil the conditions of Article [86](2).[28]

Notes

28 In relation to the limits on the application of the exception set out in Article [86](2), see the position taken by the Court of Justice in the following cases: Case C-179/90 Merci convenzionali porto di Genova v Siderurgica Gabrielli [1991] ECR I-1979; Case C-41/90 Klaus Höfner and Fritz Elser v Macroton [1991] ECR I-5889.

8.4. The direct mail market is still developing at a different pace from one Member State to the other, which makes it difficult for the Commission, at this stage, to specify in a general way the obligations of the Member States regarding that service. The two principal issues in relation to direct mail are potential abuse by customers of its tariffication and of its liberalisation (reserved items being delivered by an alternative operators as if they were non-reserved direct mail items) so as to circumvent the reserved services referred to in point 8.2. Evidence from the Member States which do not restrict direct mail services, such as Spain, Italy, the Netherlands, Austria, Sweden and Finland, is still inconclusive and does not yet allow a definitive general assessment. In view of that uncertainty, it is considered appropriate to proceed temporarily on a case-by-case basis. If particular circumstances make it necessary, and without prejudice to point 8.3, Member States may maintain certain existing restrictions on direct mail services or introduce licensing in order to avoid artificial traffic distortions and substantial destabilization of revenues.

8.5. As regards the distribution of inward cross-border mail, the system of terminal dues received by the postal operator of the Member State of delivery of cross-border mail from the operator of the Member State of origin is currently under revision to adapt terminal dues, which are in many cases too low, to actual costs of delivery.
Without prejudice to point 8.3, Member States may maintain certain existing restrictions on the distribution of inward cross-border mail,[29] so as to avoid artificial diversion of traffic, which would inflate the share of cross-border mail in Community traffic. Such restrictions may only concern items falling under the reservable area of services. In assessing the situation in the framework of individual cases, the Commission will take into account the relevant, specific circumstances in the Member States.

Notes

29 This may in particular concern mail from one State which has been conveyed by commercial companies to another State to be introduced in the public postal network via a postal operator of that other State.

8.6. The clearance, sorting and transport of postal items has been or is currently increasingly being opened up to third parties by postal operators in a number of Member States. Given that the revenue effects of such opening up may vary according to the situation in the different Member States, certain Member States may, if particular circumstances make it necessary, and without prejudice to point 8.3, maintain certain existing restrictions on the clearance, sorting and transport of postal items by intermediaries,[30] so as to allow for the necessary restructuring of the operator referred to in point 4.2. However, such restrictions should in principle be applied only to postal items covered by the existing monopolies, should not limit what is already accepted in the Member State concerned, and should be compatible with the principle of non-discriminatory access to the postal network as set out in point 8(b)(vii).

Notes

[30] Even in a monopoly situation, senders will have the freedom to make use of particular services provided by an inter-mediary, such as (pre-)sorting before deposit with the postal operator.

(b) Conditions for the application of Article [86](2) to the postal sector

Commentary
point 8(b): F&N: 4.346

The following conditions should apply with regard to the exception under Article [86](2):

(i) Liberalisation of other postal services

Except for those services for which reservation is necessary, and which the Postal Directive allows to be reserved, Member States should withdraw all special or exclusive rights for the supply of postal services to the extent that the performance of the particular task assigned to the operators referred to in point 4.2 for the provision of a service of a general economic interest is not obstructed in law or in fact, with the exception of mail connected to the exercise of official authority, and they should take all necessary measures to guarantee the right of all economic operators to supply postal services.

This does not prevent Member States from making, where necessary, the supply of such services subject to declaration procedures or class licences and, when necessary, to individual licensing procedures aimed at the enforcement of essential requirements and at safeguarding the universal service. Member States should, in that event, ensure that the conditions set out in those procedures are transparent, objective, and without discriminatory effect, and that there is an efficient procedure of appealing to the courts against any refusal.

(ii) Absence of less restrictive means to ensure the services in the general economic interest

Exclusive rights may be granted or maintained only where they are indispensable for ensuring the functioning of the tasks of general economic interest. In many areas the entry of new companies into the market could, on the basis of their specific skills and expertise, contribute to the realisation of the services of general economic interest.

If the operator referred to in point 4.2 fails to provide satisfactorily all of the elements of the universal service required by the Postal Directive (such as the possibility of every citizen in the Member State concerned, and in particular those living in remote areas, to have access to newspapers, magazines and books), even with the benefit of a universal postal network and of special or exclusive rights, the Member State concerned must take action.[31] Instead of extending the rights already granted, Member States should create the possibility that services are provided by competitors and for this purpose may impose obligations on those competitors in addition to essential requirements. All of those obligations should be objective, non-discriminatory and transparent.

Notes

[31] According to Article 3 of the Postal Directive, Member States are to ensure that users enjoy the right to a universal service.

(iii) Proportionality

Member States should moreover ensure that the scope of any special and exclusive rights granted is in proportion to the general economic interest which is pursued through those rights. Prohibiting self-delivery, that is the provision of postal services by the natural or legal person (including a sister or subsidiary organisation) who is the originator of the mail, or collection and transport of such items by a third party acting solely on its behalf, would for example not be proportionate to the objective of guaranteeing adequate resources for the public postal network. Member States must also adjust the scope of those special or exclusive rights, according to changes in the needs and the conditions under which postal services are provided and taking account of any State aid granted to the operator referred to in point 4.2.

(iv) Monitoring by an independent regulatory body

The monitoring of the performance of the public-service tasks of the operators referred to in point 4.2 and of open access to the public postal network and, where applicable, the grant of licences or the control of declarations as well as the observance by economic operators of the special or exclusive rights of operators referred to in point 4.2 should be ensured by a body or bodies independent of the latter.[32]

That body should in particular ensure: that contracts for the provision of reserved services are made fully transparent, are separately invoiced and distinguished from non-reserved services, such as printing, labelling and enveloping; that terms and conditions for services which are in part reserved and in part liberalised are separate; and that the reserved element is open to all postal users, irrespective of whether or not the non-reserved component is purchased.

Notes

[32] See in particular Articles 9 and 22 of the Postal Directive.

(v) Effective monitoring of reserved services

The tasks excluded from the scope of competition should be effectively monitored by the Member State according to published service targets and performance levels and there should be regular and public reporting on their fulfilment.

(vi) Transparency of accounting

Each operator referred to in point 4.2 uses a single postal network to compete in a variety of markets. Price and service discrimination between or within classes of customers can easily be practised by operators running a universal postal network, given the significant overheads which cannot be fully and precisely assigned to any one service in particular. It is therefore extremely difficult to determine cross-subsidies within them, both between the different stages of the handling of postal items in the public postal network and between the reserved services and the services provided under conditions of competition. Moreover, a number of operators offer preferential tariffs for cultural items which clearly do not cover the average total costs. Member States are obliged by Article [10] and [86] to ensure that Community law is fully complied with. The Commission considers that the most appropriate way of fulfilling that obligation would be for Member States to require operators referred to in point 4.2 to keep separate financial records, identifying separately, inter alia, costs and revenues associated with the provision of the services supplied under their exclusive rights and those provided under competitive conditions, and making it possible to assess fully the conditions applied at the various access points of the public postal network. Services made up of elements falling within the reserved and competitive services should also distinguish between the costs of each element. Internal accounting systems should operate on the basis of consistently applied and objectively justified cost-accounting principles. The financial accounts should be drawn up, audited by an independent auditor, which may be appointed by the National Regulatory Authority, and be published in accordance with the relevant Community and national legislation applying to commercial organisations.

(vii) Non-discriminatory access to the postal network

Operators should provide the universal postal service by affording non-discriminatory access to customers or intermediaries at appropriate public points of access, in accordance with the needs of those users. Access conditions including contracts (when offered) should be transparent, published in an appropriate manner and offered on a non-discriminatory basis.

Preferential tariffs appear to be offered by some operators to particular groups of customers in a non-transparent fashion. Member States should monitor the access conditions to the network with a view to ensuring that there is no discrimination either in the conditions of use or in the charges payable. It should in particular be ensured that intermediaries, including operators from other Member States, can choose from amongst available access points to the public postal network and obtain access within a reasonable period at price conditions based on costs, that take into account the actual services required.

The obligation to provide non-discriminatory access to the public postal network does not mean that Member States are required to ensure access for items of correspondence from its territory, which were conveyed by commercial companies to another State, in breach of a postal monopoly, to be introduced in the public postal network via a postal operator of that other State, for the sole purpose of taking advantage of lower postal tariffs. Other economic reasons, such as production costs and facilities, added values or the level of service offered in other Member States are not regarded as improper. Fraud can be made subject to penalties by the independent regulatory body.

At present cross-border access to postal networks is occasionally rejected, or only allowed subject to conditions, for postal items whose production process includes cross-border data transmission before those postal items were given physical form. Those cases are usually called non-physical remail. In the present circumstances there may indeed be an economic problem for the postal operator that delivers the mail, due to the level of terminal dues applied between postal operators. The operators seek to resolve this problem by the introduction of an appropriate terminal dues system.

The Commission may request Member States, in accordance with the first paragraph of Article [10] of the Treaty, to inform the Commission of the conditions of access applied and of the reasons for them. The Commission is not to disclose information acquired as a result of such requests to the extent that it is covered by the obligation of professional secrecy.

9. REVIEW

This notice is adopted at Community level to facilitate the assessment of certain behaviour of undertakings and certain State measures relating to postal services. It is appropriate that after a certain period of development, possibly by the year 2000, the Commission should carry out an evaluation of the postal sector with regard to the Treaty rules, to establish whether modifications of the views set out in this notice are required on the basis of social, economic or technological considerations and on the basis of experience with cases in the postal sector. In due time the Commission will carry out a global evaluation of the situation in the postal sector in the light of the aims of this notice.

E30

COUNCIL REGULATION (EC) No 1184/2006

of 24 July 2006

applying certain rules of competition to the production of, and trade in, agricultural products

(Codified version)

Official Journal L 214, 4.8.2006, p. 7

Celex No: 32006R1184

Commentary
Regulation 1184/2006: **B&C:** 12.197–12.198, 14.044

THE COUNCIL OF THE EUROPEAN UNION,

Having regard to the Treaty establishing the European Community, and in particular Articles 36 and 37 thereof,

Having regard to the proposal from the Commission,

Having regard to the opinion of the European Parliament.[1]

Notes
[1] Opinion of the European Parliament of 27 April 2006 (not yet published in the Official Journal).

Whereas:

(1) The content of Council Regulation No 26 of 4 April 1962 applying certain rules of competition to production of and trade in agricultural products[1] has been amended.[2] In the interests of clarity and rationality the said Regulation should be codified.

Notes
[1] OJ 30, 20.4.1962, p. 993/62. Regulation as amended by Regulation No 49 (OJ 53, 1.7.1962, p. 1571/62).
[2] See Annex I.

Commentary
Recital 1: B&C: 12.198

(2) By virtue of Article 36 of the Treaty one of the matters to be decided under the common agricultural policy is whether the rules on competition laid down in the Treaty are to apply to the production of, and trade in, agricultural products. Accordingly, the provisions of this Regulation should be supplemented in the light of developments in that policy.

(3) The rules on competition relating to the agreements, decisions and practices referred to in Article 81 of the Treaty and to the abuse of dominant positions are to be applied to the production of, and trade in, agricultural products, in so far as their application does not impede the functioning of national organisations of agricultural markets or jeopardise attainment of the objectives of the common agricultural policy.

(4) Special attention is warranted in the case of farmers' organisations the particular objective of which is the joint production or marketing of agricultural products or the use of joint facilities, unless such joint action excludes competition or jeopardises attainment of the objectives of Article 33 of the Treaty.

(5) In order both to avoid compromising the development of a common agricultural policy and to ensure certainty in the law and non-discriminatory treatment of the undertakings concerned, the Commission should have sole power, subject to review by the Court of Justice, to determine whether the conditions provided for in the two preceding recitals are fulfilled as regards the agreements, decisions and practices referred to in Article 81 of the Treaty.

(6) In order to implement, as part of the development of the common agricultural policy, the rules on aid for production of, or trade in, agricultural products, the Commission should be in a position to draw up a list of existing, new or proposed types of aid, to make appropriate observations to the Member States and to propose suitable measures to them,

HAS ADOPTED THIS REGULATION:

Article 1

Articles 81 to 86 of the Treaty and provisions made for their implementation shall, subject to Article 2 of this Regulation, apply to all agreements, decisions and practices referred to in Articles 81(1) and 82 of the Treaty which relate to production of, or trade in, the products listed in Annex I to the Treaty.

Commentary
Art 1: B&C: 12.200

Article 2

1. Article 81(1) of the Treaty shall not apply to such of the agreements, decisions and practices referred to in Article 1 of this Regulation as form an integral part of a national market organisation or are necessary for attainment of the objectives set out in Article 33 of the Treaty.

In particular, it shall not apply to agreements, decisions and practices of farmers, farmers' associations, or associations of such associations belonging to a single Member State which concern the production or sale of agricultural products or the use of joint facilities for the storage, treatment or processing of agricultural products, and under which there is no obligation to charge identical prices, unless the

Commission finds that competition is thereby excluded or that the objectives of Article 33 of the Treaty are jeopardised.

2. After consulting the Member States and hearing the undertakings or associations of undertakings concerned and any other natural or legal person that it considers should be heard, the Commission shall have sole power, subject to review by the Court of Justice, to determine, by decision which shall be published, which agreements, decisions and practices fulfil the conditions specified in paragraph 1.

The Commission shall so determine either on its own initiative or at the request of a competent authority of a Member State or of an interested undertaking or association of undertakings.

3. The publication shall state the names of the parties and the main content of the decision. It shall have regard to the legitimate interest of undertakings in the protection of their business secrets.

Commentary

Art 2: **B&C:** 12.200, 12.204
Art 2(1): **B&C:** 12.200–12.204, 12.207, 12.209, 14.044
Art 2(2): **B&C:** 12.207–12.208
Art 2(3): **B&C:** 12.207

Article 3

The provisions of Article 88(1) and of the first sentence of Article 88(3) of the Treaty shall apply to aid granted for production of, or trade in, the products listed in Annex I to the Treaty.

Article 4

Regulation No 26 shall be repealed.

References to the repealed Regulation shall be construed as references to this Regulation and shall be read in accordance with the correlation table in Annex II.

Article 5

This Regulation shall enter into force on the 20th day following its publication in the Official Journal of the European Union.

Notes

Date of entry into force: 24 August 2006.

This Regulation shall be binding in its entirety and directly applicable in all Member States.

Done at Brussels, 24 July 2006.

ANNEX I
Repealed Regulation with its Amendment

Council Regulation No 26	(OJ 30, 20.4.1962, p. 993/62)
Council Regulation No 49	(OJ 53, 1.7.1962, p. 1571/62)
	Only Article 1(1)(g)

ANNEX II
Correlation Table

Regulation No 26	*This Regulation*
Article 1	Article 1
Article 2(1)	Article 2(1)
Article 2(2)	Article 2(2), first subparagraph
Article 2(3)	Article 2(2), second subparagraph
Article 2(4)	Article 2(3)

Regulation No 26	*This Regulation*
Article 3	—
Article 4	Article 3
—	Article 4
Article 5	Article 5
—	Annex I
—	Annex II

PUBLIC UNDERTAKINGS

F1

COMMISSION DECISION 2005/842/EC

of 28 November 2005

on the application of Article 86(2) of the EC Treaty to State aid in the form of public service compensation granted to certain undertakings entrusted with the operation of services of general economic interest

(notified under document number C(2005) 2673)

Official Journal L 312, 29.11.2005, p. 67

Celex No: 32005D0842

Notes

EEA application: this Instrument was adopted with appropriate adaptations by EEA Joint Committee Decision No 91/2006 (OJ No L 289, 19.10.2006, p. 31 and EEA Supplement No 52, 19.10.2006, p. 24) with effect from 8 July 2006: see EEA Agreement, Annex XV, Point 1h.

Commentary

Decision 2005/842/EC: B&C: 11.056, 15.068 F&N: 6.159, 6.215, 6.246

THE COMMISSION OF THE EUROPEAN COMMUNITIES,

Having regard to the Treaty establishing the European Community, and in particular Article 86(3) thereof,

Whereas:

(1) Article 16 of the Treaty requires the Community, without prejudice to Articles 73, 86 and 87, to use its powers in such a way as to make sure that services of general economic interest operate on the basis of principles and conditions which enable them to fulfil their missions.

(2) For certain services of general economic interest to operate on the basis of principles and under conditions that enable them to fulfil their missions, financial support from the State intended to cover some or all of the specific costs resulting from the public service obligations may prove necessary. In accordance with Article 295 of the Treaty, as interpreted by the case-law of the Court of Justice and Court of First Instance of the European Communities, it is irrelevant from the viewpoint of Community law whether such services of general economic interest are operated by public or private undertakings.

(3) Article 86(2) of the Treaty states in this respect that undertakings entrusted with the operation of services of general economic interest or having the character of a revenue-producing monopoly are subject to the rules contained in the Treaty, in particular to the rules on competition. However, Article 86(2) allows an exception from the rules contained in the Treaty, provided that a number of criteria are met. Firstly, there must be an act of entrustment, whereby the State confers responsibility for the execution of a certain task to an undertaking. Secondly, the entrustment must relate to a service of general economic interest. Thirdly, the exception has to be necessary for the performance of the tasks assigned and proportional to that end (hereinafter the necessity requirement). Finally, the development of trade must not be affected to such an extent as would be contrary to the interests of the Community.

(4) In its judgment in the case of *Altmark Trans GmbH and Regierungspräsidium Magdeburg v Nahverkehrsgesellschaft Altmark GmbH*[1] (*Altmark*), the Court of Justice held that public service compensation does not constitute State aid within the meaning of Article 87 of the Treaty provided that four cumulative criteria are met. First, the recipient undertaking must actually have public service obligations to discharge, and the obligations must be clearly defined. Second, the parameters on the basis of which the compensation is calculated must be established in advance in an objective and transparent manner. Third, the compensation cannot exceed what is necessary to

cover all or part of the costs incurred in the discharge of the public service obligations, taking into account the relevant receipts and a reasonable profit. Finally, where the undertaking which is to discharge public service obligations, in a specific case, is not chosen pursuant to a public procurement procedure which would allow for the selection of the tenderer capable of providing those services at the least cost to the community, the level of compensation needed must be determined on the basis of an analysis of the costs which a typical undertaking, well run and adequately provided with means of transport, would have incurred.

Notes
[1] [2003] ECR I-7747.

(5) Where those four criteria are met, public service compensation does not constitute State aid, and Articles 87 and 88 of the Treaty do not apply. If the Member States do not respect those criteria and if the general criteria for the applicability of Article 87(1) of the Treaty are met, public service compensation constitutes State aid that is subject to Articles 73, 86, 87 and 88 of the Treaty. This Decision should therefore only apply to public service compensation in so far as it constitutes State aid.

(6) Article 86(3) of the Treaty allows the Commission to specify the meaning and extent of the exception under Article 86(2) of the Treaty, and to set out rules intended to enable effective monitoring of the fulfilment of the criteria set out in Article 86(2), where necessary. The conditions under which certain systems of compensation are compatible with Article 86(2) and are not subject to the prior notification requirement of Article 88(3) of the Treaty should therefore be specified.

(7) Such aid may be declared compatible only if it is granted in order to ensure the provision of services that are services of general economic interest as referred to in Article 86(2) of the Treaty. It is clear from the case-law that, with the exception of the sectors in which there are Community rules governing the matter, Member States have a wide margin of discretion in the definition of services that could be classified as being services of general economic interest. Thus, with the exception of the sectors in which there are Community rules governing the matter, the Commission's task is to ensure that there is no manifest error as regards the definition of services of general economic interest.

(8) In order for Article 86(2) of the Treaty to apply, the undertaking beneficiary of the aid must have been specifically entrusted by the Member State with the operation of a particular service of general economic interest. According to the case-law on the interpretation of Article 86(2) of the Treaty, such act or acts of entrustment must specify, at least, the precise nature, scope and duration of the public service obligations imposed and the identity of the undertakings concerned.

(9) In order to ensure that the criteria set out in Article 86(2) of the Treaty are met, it is necessary to lay down more precise conditions which must be fulfilled in respect of the entrustment of the operation of services of general economic interest. Indeed the amount of compensation can be properly calculated and checked only if the public service obligations incumbent on the undertakings and any obligations incumbent on the State are clearly set out in a formal act of the competent public authorities within the Member State concerned. The form of the instrument may vary from one Member State to another but it should specify, at least, the precise nature, scope and duration of the public service obligations imposed and the identity of undertakings concerned, and the costs to be borne by the undertaking concerned.

(10) When defining public service obligations and in assessing whether those obligations are met by the undertakings concerned, the Member States are invited to consult widely, with particular emphasis on users.

(11) Moreover, in order to avoid unjustified distortions of competition, Article 86(2) of the Treaty requires that compensation does not exceed what is necessary to cover the costs incurred by the undertaking in discharging the public service obligations, account being taken of the relevant receipts and a reasonable profit. This should be understood as referring to the actual costs incurred by the undertaking concerned.

(12) Compensation in excess of what is necessary to cover the costs incurred by the undertaking concerned is not necessary for the operation of the service of general economic interest, and consequently constitutes incompatible State aid that should be repaid to the State. Compensation granted for the operation of a service of general economic interest but actually used by the undertaking concerned to operate on another market is also not necessary for the operation of the service of general economic interest, and consequently also constitutes incompatible State aid that should be repaid.

(13) In order to ensure compliance with the necessity requirement set out in Article 86(2) of the Treaty it is necessary to lay down provisions relating to the calculation and monitoring of the amount of compensation granted. Member States should check regularly that the compensation granted does not lead to overcompensation. Nevertheless, in order to allow a minimum of flexibility for undertakings and Member States, where the amount of overcompensation does not exceed 10% of the amount of annual compensation, it should be possible for such overcompensation to be carried forward to the next period and be deducted from the amount of compensation which would otherwise have been payable. The revenue of undertakings entrusted with the operation of services of general economic interest in the field of social housing may vary dramatically, in particular due to the risk of insolvency of leaseholders. Consequently, where such undertakings only operate services of general economic interest, it should be possible for any overcompensation during one period to be carried forward to the next period, up to 20% of the annual compensation.

(14) To the extent that compensation is granted to undertakings entrusted with the operation of services of general economic interest, the amount of the compensation does not go beyond the costs of the services, and the thresholds laid down in this Decision are respected, the Commission considers that the development of trade is not affected to such an extent as would be contrary to the interests of the Community. In such circumstances, the Commission considers that the compensation should be deemed to constitute State aid compatible with Article 86(2) of the Treaty.

(15) Small amounts of compensation granted to undertakings providing services of general economic interest whose turnover is limited do not affect the development of trade and competition to such an extent as would be contrary to the interests of the Community. When the conditions set out in this Decision are fulfilled, prior notification should therefore not be required. For the purpose of defining the scope of the exemption from notification, the turnover of undertakings receiving public service compensation and the level of such compensation should be taken into consideration.

(16) Hospitals and undertakings in charge of social housing which are entrusted with tasks involving services of general economic interest have specific characteristics that need to be taken into consideration. In particular, account should be taken of the fact that at the current stage of development of the internal market, the intensity of distortion of competition in those sectors is not necessarily proportionate to the level of turnover and compensation. Accordingly, hospitals providing medical care, including, where applicable, emergency services and ancillary services directly related to the main activities, notably in the field of research, and undertakings in charge of social housing providing housing for disadvantaged citizens or socially less advantaged groups, which due to solvability constraints are unable to obtain housing at market conditions, should benefit from the exemption from notification provided for in this Decision, even if the amount of compensation they receive exceeds the thresholds laid down in this Decision, if the services performed are qualified as services of general economic interest by the Member States.

(17) Article 73 of the Treaty constitutes a *lex specialis* with regard to Article 86(2). It lays down the rules applicable to public service compensation in the land transport sector. That Article has been developed by Council Regulation (EEC) No 1191/69 of 26 June 1969 on action by Member States concerning the obligations inherent in the concept of a public service in transport by rail, road and inland waterway,[1] which lays down general conditions for public service obligations in the land transport sector and imposes methods for calculating compensation. Regulation (EEC) No 1191/69 exempts all compensation in the land transport sector that fulfils the conditions of notification under Article 88(3) of the Treaty. It also allows Member States to derogate

from its provisions in the case of undertakings providing exclusively urban, suburban or regional transport. Where that derogation is applied, any compensation for public service obligations is, in so far as it constitutes State aid, governed by Council Regulation (EEC) No 1107/70 of 4 June 1970 on the granting of aids for transport by rail, road and inland waterway.[2] According to the judgment in *Altmark*, compensation which does not respect the provisions of Article 73 cannot be declared compatible with the Treaty on the basis of Article 86(2), or on the basis of any other Treaty provision. Consequently, such compensation should not be covered by this Decision.

Notes

[1] OJ L 156, 28.6.1969, p. 1. Regulation as last amended by Regulation (EEC) No 1893/91 (OJ L 169, 29.6.1991, p. 1).
[2] OJ L 130, 15.6.1970, p. 1. Regulation as last amended by Regulation (EC) No 543/97 (OJ L 84, 26.3.1997, p. 6).

(18) Unlike land transport, the maritime and air transport sectors are subject to Article 86(2) of the Treaty. Certain rules applicable to public service compensation in the air and maritime transport sectors are to be found in Council Regulation (EEC) No 2408/92 of 23 July 1992 on access for Community air carriers to intra-Community air routes[1] and Council Regulation (EEC) No 3577/92 of 7 December 1992 applying the principle of freedom to provide services to maritime transport within Member States (maritime cabotage).[2] However, contrary to Regulation (EEC) No 1191/69, these Regulations do not refer to the compatibility of the possible State aid elements nor contain an exemption from the obligation to notify under Article 88(2) of the Treaty. It is therefore appropriate to apply this Decision to public service compensation in the air and maritime transport sectors provided that, in addition to fulfilling the conditions set out in this Decision, such compensation also respects the sectoral rules contained in Regulation (EEC) No 2408/92 and Regulation (EEC) No 3577/92 when applicable.

Notes

[1] OJ L 240, 24.8.1992, p. 8. Regulation as last amended by 2003 Act of Accession.
[2] OJ L 364, 12.12.1992, p. 7.

(19) The thresholds applicable to public service compensation in the air and maritime transport sectors should normally be the same as those applicable in general. However, in the specific cases of public service compensation for air or maritime links to islands and for airports and ports which constitute services of general economic interest as referred to in Article 86(2) of the Treaty it is more appropriate to also provide alternative thresholds based on average annual number of passengers as this more accurately reflects the economic reality of these activities.

(20) This Decision is to a large extent a specification of the meaning and extent of the exception under Article 86(2) of the Treaty as it has been consistently applied in the past by the Court of Justice and the Court of First Instance and by the Commission. To the extent that it does not modify the material law applicable in this area it should apply immediately. However, certain provisions of this Decision go beyond the status quo by setting out additional requirements aimed at enabling effective monitoring of the criteria set out in Article 86(2). In order to allow Member States to take the necessary measures in this respect, it is appropriate to foresee a period of one year prior to the application of those specific provisions.

(21) Exemption from the requirement of prior notification for certain services of general economic interest does not rule out the possibility for Member States to notify a specific aid project. Such notification will be assessed in accordance with the principles of the Community framework for State aid in the form of public service compensation.[1]

Notes

[1] OJ C 297, 29.11.2005.

(22) This Decision applies without prejudice to the provisions of Commission Directive 80/723/EEC of 25 June 1980 on the transparency of financial relations between Member States and public undertakings as well as on financial transparency within certain undertakings.[1]

Notes
[1] OJ L 195, 29.7.1980, p. 35. Directive as last amended by Directive 2000/52/EC (OJ L 193, 29.7.2000, p. 75). [See now Commission Directive 2006/111/EC of 16 November 2006 on the transparency of financial relations between Member States and public undertakings as well as on financial transparency within certain undertakings (Codified version), OJ L 318, 17.11.2006, p. 17.]

(23) This Decision applies without prejudice to the Community provisions in force in the fields of public procurement and of competition, in particular Articles 81 and 82 of the Treaty.

(24) This Decision applies without prejudice to stricter specific provisions relating to public service obligations that are contained in sectoral Community legislation,

HAS ADOPTED THIS DECISION:

Article 1
Subject matter

This Decision sets out the conditions under which State aid in the form of public service compensation granted to certain undertakings entrusted with the operation of services of general economic interest is to be regarded as compatible with the common market and exempt from the requirement of notification laid down in Article 88(3) of the Treaty.

Article 2
Scope

1. This Decision applies to State aid in the form of public service compensation granted to undertakings in connection with services of general economic interest as referred to in Article 86(2) of the Treaty which falls within one of the following categories:

(a) public service compensation granted to undertakings with an average annual turnover before tax, all activities included, of less than EUR 100 million during the two financial years preceding that in which the service of general economic interest was assigned, which receive annual compensation for the service in question of less than EUR 30 million;

(b) public service compensation granted to hospitals and social housing undertakings carrying out activities qualified as services of general economic interest by the Member State concerned;

(c) public service compensation for air or maritime links to islands on which average annual traffic during the two financial years preceding that in which the service of general economic interest was assigned does not exceed 300,000 passengers;

(d) public service compensation for airports and ports for which average annual traffic during the two financial years preceding that in which the service of general economic interest was assigned does not exceed 1,000,000 passengers, in the case of airports, and 300,000 passengers, in the case of ports.

The threshold of EUR 30 million in point (a) of the first subparagraph may be determined by taking an annual average representing the value of compensation granted during the contract period or over a period of five years. For credit institutions, the threshold of EUR 100 million of turnover shall be replaced by a threshold of EUR 800 million in terms of balance sheet total.

2. In the field of air and maritime transport, this Decision shall only apply to State aid in the form of public service compensation granted to undertakings in connection with services of general economic interest as referred to in Article 86(2) of the Treaty which complies with Regulation (EEC) No 2408/92 and Regulation (EEC) No 3577/92, when applicable.

This Decision shall not apply to State aid in the form of public service compensation granted to undertakings in the field of land transport.

Article 3
Compatibility and exemption from notification

State aid in the form of public service compensation that meets the conditions laid down in this Decision shall be compatible with the common market and shall be exempt from the obligation of prior notification provided for in Article 88(3) of the Treaty, without prejudice to the application of stricter provisions relating to public service obligations contained in sectoral Community legislation.

Article 4
Entrustment

In order for this Decision to apply, responsibility for operation of the service of general economic interest shall be entrusted to the undertaking concerned by way of one or more official acts, the form of which may be determined by each Member State. The act or acts shall specify, in particular:

(a) the nature and the duration of the public service obligations;
(b) the undertaking and territory concerned;
(c) the nature of any exclusive or special rights assigned to the undertaking;
(d) the parameters for calculating, controlling and reviewing the compensation;
(e) the arrangements for avoiding and repaying any overcompensation.

Article 5
Compensation

1. The amount of compensation shall not exceed what is necessary to cover the costs incurred in discharging the public service obligations, taking into account the relevant receipts and a reasonable profit on any own capital necessary for discharging those obligations. The compensation must be actually used for the operation of the service of general economic interest concerned, without prejudice to the undertaking's ability to enjoy a reasonable profit.

The amount of compensation shall include all the advantages granted by the State or through State resources in any form whatsoever. The reasonable profit shall take account of all or some of the productivity gains achieved by the undertakings concerned during an agreed limited period without reducing the level of quality of the services entrusted to the undertaking by the State.

2. The costs to be taken into consideration shall comprise all the costs incurred in the operation of the service of general economic interest. They shall be calculated, on the basis of generally accepted cost accounting principles, as follows:

(a) where the activities of the undertaking in question are confined to the service of general economic interest, all its costs may be taken into consideration;
(b) where the undertaking also carries out activities falling outside the scope of the service of general economic interest, only the costs associated with the service of general economic interest shall be taken into consideration;
(c) the costs allocated to the service of general economic interest may cover all the variable costs incurred in providing the service of general economic interest, a proportionate contribution to fixed costs common to both service of general economic interest and other activities and a reasonable profit;
(d) the costs linked with investments, notably concerning infrastructure, may be taken into account when necessary for the operation of the service of general economic interest.

3. The revenue to be taken into account shall include at least the entire revenue earned from the service of general economic interest. If the undertaking in question holds special or exclusive rights linked to another service of general economic interest that generates profit in excess of the reasonable profit, or benefits from other advantages granted by the State, these shall be included in its revenue, irrespective of their classification for the purposes of Article 87. The Member State concerned may decide that the profits accruing from other activities outside the scope of the service of general economic interest are to be assigned in whole or in part to the financing of the service of general economic interest.

4. For the purposes of this Decision "reasonable profit" means a rate of return on own capital that takes account of the risk, or absence of risk, incurred by the undertaking by virtue of the intervention by the Member State, particularly if the latter grants exclusive or special rights. This rate shall not normally exceed the average rate for the sector concerned in recent years. In sectors where there is no undertaking comparable to the undertaking entrusted with the operation of the service of general economic interest, a comparison may be made with undertakings situated in other Member States, or if necessary, in other sectors, provided that the particular characteristics of each sector are taken

into account. In determining what constitutes a reasonable profit, the Member States may introduce incentive criteria relating, in particular, to the quality of service provided and gains in productive efficiency.

5. When a company carries out activities falling both inside and outside the scope of services of general economic interest, the internal accounts shall show separately the costs and receipts associated with the service of general economic interest and those of other services, as well as the parameters for allocating costs and revenues.

The costs linked to any activities outside the scope of the service of general economic interest shall cover all the variable costs, an appropriate contribution to common fixed costs and an adequate return on capital. No compensation shall be granted in respect of those costs.

Article 6
Control of overcompensation

Member States shall carry out regular checks, or ensure that such checks are carried out, to ensure that undertakings are not receiving compensation in excess of the amount determined in accordance with Article 5.

Member States shall require the undertaking concerned to repay any overcompensation paid, and the parameters for the calculation of the compensation shall be updated for the future. Where the amount of overcompensation does not exceed 10 % of the amount of the annual compensation, such overcompensation may be carried forward to the next annual period and deducted from the amount of compensation payable in respect of that period.

In the sector of social housing, Member States shall carry out regular checks, or ensure that such checks are carried out, at the level of each undertaking, to ensure that the undertaking concerned is not receiving compensation in excess of the amount determined in accordance with Article 5. Any overcompensation may be carried forward to the next period up to 20% of the annual compensation, provided that the undertaking concerned only operates services of general economic interest.

Article 7
Availability of information

The Member States shall keep available for a period of at least 10 years, all the elements necessary to determine whether the compensation granted is compatible with this Decision.

Upon a written request from the Commission, Member States shall provide the Commission with all the information that the latter considers necessary to determine whether the systems of compensation in force are compatible with this Decision.

Article 8
Reports

Periodic reports on the implementation of this Decision, comprising a detailed description of the conditions of application in all sectors, including the social housing and the hospital sectors, shall be submitted to the Commission by each Member State every three years.

The first report shall be submitted by 19 December 2008.

Article 9
Evaluation

By 19 December 2009 at the latest, the Commission will undertake an impact assessment based on factual information and the results of wide consultations conducted by the Commission on the basis, notably, of data provided by the Member States in accordance with Article 8.

The results of the impact assessment will be made available to the European Parliament, the Committee of Regions, the European Economic and Social Committee and the Member States.

Part F Public Undertakings

Article 10
Entry into force

This Decision shall enter into force on 19 December 2005.

Points (c), (d) and (e) of Article 4, and Article 6 shall apply from 29 November 2006.

Article 11
Addressees

This Decision is addressed to the Member States.

Done at Brussels, 28 November 2005.

F2

COMMISSION DIRECTIVE 2006/111/EC

of 16 November 2006

on the transparency of financial relations between Member States and public undertakings as well
as on financial transparency within certain undertakings

(Text with EEA relevance)

(Codified version)

Official Journal L318, 17.11.2006, p. 17

Celex No: 32006L0111

Commentary
Directive 2006/111: B&C: 11.026, 11.110, 15.016

THE COMMISSION OF THE EUROPEAN COMMUNITIES,

Having regard to the Treaty establishing the European Community, and in particular Article 86(3)
thereof,

Whereas:

(1) Commission Directive 80/723/EEC of 25 June 1980 on the transparency of financial relations
between Member States and public undertakings as well as on financial transparency within certain undertakings[1] has been substantially amended several times.[2] In the interests of clarity and
rationality the said Directive should be codified.

Notes
[1] OJ L 195, 29.7.1980, p. 35. Directive as last amended by Directive 2005/81/EC (OJ L 312, 29.11.2005, p. 47).
[2] See Annex I, Part A.

---

(2) Public undertakings play a substantial role in the national economy of the Member States.

(3) Member States sometimes grant special or exclusive rights to particular undertakings, or make
payments or give some other kind of compensation to particular undertakings entrusted with the
operation of services of general economic interest. These undertakings are often also in competition with other undertakings.

(4) Article 295 of the Treaty provides that the Treaty is in no way to prejudice the rules in Member
States governing the system of property ownership. There should be no unjustified discrimination

between public and private undertakings in the application of the rules on competition. This Directive should apply to both public and private undertakings.

(5) The Treaty requires the Commission to ensure that Member States do not grant undertakings, public or private, aids incompatible with the common market.

(6) However, the complexity of the financial relations between national public authorities and public undertakings tends to hinder the performance of this duty.

(7) A fair and effective application of the aid rules in the Treaty to both public and private undertakings will be possible only if these financial relations are made transparent.

(8) Such transparency applied to public undertakings should enable a clear distinction to be made between the role of the State as public authority and its role as proprietor.

(9) Article 86(1) of the Treaty imposes obligations on Member States in the case of public undertakings and undertakings to which Member States grant special or exclusive rights. Article 86(2) of the Treaty applies to undertakings entrusted with the operation of services of general economic interest. Article 86(3) of the Treaty requires the Commission to ensure the application of the provisions of that Article and provides it with the requisite means to this end. In order to ensure the application of the provisions of Article 86 of the Treaty the Commission must have the necessary information. This entails defining the conditions for ensuring such transparency.

(10) It should be made clear what is to be understood by the terms "public authorities" and "public undertakings".

(11) The Member States have differing administrative territorial structures. This Directive should cover public authorities at all levels in each Member State.

(12) Public authorities may exercise a dominant influence on the behaviour of public undertakings not only where they are the proprietor or have a majority participation but also by virtue of powers they hold in management or supervisory bodies as a result either of the rules governing the undertaking or of the manner in which the shareholdings are distributed.

(13) The provision of public funds to public undertakings may take place either directly or indirectly. Transparency must be achieved irrespective of the manner in which such provision of public funds is made. It may also be necessary to ensure that adequate information is made available as regards the reasons for such provision of public funds and their actual use.

(14) Complex situations linked to the diverse forms of public and private undertakings granted special or exclusive rights or entrusted with the operation of services of general economic interest as well as the range of activities that might be carried on by a single undertaking and the different degrees of market liberalisation in the various Member States could complicate application of the competition rules, and particularly Article 86 of the Treaty. It is therefore necessary for Member States and the Commission to have detailed data about the internal and financial and organisational structure of such undertakings, in particular separate and reliable accounts relating to different activities carried on by the same undertaking.

(15) The accounts should show the distinction between different activities, the costs and revenues associated with each activity and the methods of cost and revenue assignment and allocation. Such separate accounts should be available in relation to, on the one hand, products and services in respect of which the Member State has granted a special or exclusive right or entrusted the undertaking with the operation of a service of general economic interest, as well as, on the other hand, for each other product or service in respect of which the undertaking is active. The obligation of separation of accounts should not apply to undertakings whose activities are limited to the provision of services of general economic interest and which do not operate activities outside the scope of these services of general economic interest. It does not seem necessary to require separation of accounts within the area of services of general economic interest or within the area of the special or exclusive rights, as far as this is not necessary for the cost and revenue allocation between these services and products and those outside the services of general economic interest or the special or exclusive rights.

(16) Requiring Member States to ensure that the relevant undertakings maintain such separate accounts is the most efficient means by which fair and effective application of the rules of competition to such undertakings can be assured. In 1996 the Commission adopted a Communication on services of general interest in Europe,[1] which was supplemented by another Communication in 2001,[2] in which it emphasised the importance of such services. It is necessary

to take account of the importance of the sectors concerned, which may involve services of general interest, the strong market position that the relevant undertakings may have and the vulnerability of emerging competition in the sectors being liberalised. In accordance with the principle of proportionality it is necessary and appropriate for the achievement of the basic objective of transparency to lay down rules on such separate accounts. This Directive does not go beyond what is necessary in order to achieve the objectives pursued, in accordance with the provisions of the third paragraph of Article 5 of the Treaty.

Notes
[1] OJ C 281, 26.9.1996, p. 3.
[2] OJ C 17, 19.1.2001, p. 4.

(17) In certain sectors provisions adopted by the Community require Member States and certain undertakings to maintain separate accounts. It is necessary to ensure an equal treatment for all economic activities throughout the Community and to extend the requirement to maintain separate accounts to all comparable situations. This Directive should not amend specific rules established for the same purpose in other Community provisions and should not apply to activities of undertakings covered by those provisions.

(18) Certain undertakings should be excluded from the application of this Directive by virtue of the size of their turnover. This applies to those public undertakings whose business is not conducted on such a scale as to justify the administrative burden of ensuring transparency. In view of the limited potential for an effect on trade between Member States, it is not necessary, at this time, to require separate accounts in relation to the supply of certain categories of services.

(19) This Directive is without prejudice to other provisions of the Treaty, notably Articles 86(2), 88 and 296, and to any other rules concerning the provision of information by Member States to the Commission.

(20) In cases where the compensation for the fulfilment of services of general economic interest has been fixed for an appropriate period following an open, transparent and non-discriminatory procedure it does not seem necessary to require such undertakings to maintain separate accounts.

(21) The undertakings in question being in competition with other undertakings, information acquired should be covered by the obligation of professional secrecy.

(22) A reporting system based on *ex post facto* checks of the financial flows between public authorities and public undertakings operating in the manufacturing sector will enable the Commission to fulfil its obligations. That system of control must cover specific financial information.

(23) In order to limit the administrative burden on Member States, the reporting system should make use of both publicly available data and information available to majority shareholders. The presentation of consolidated reports is to be permitted. Incompatible aid to major undertakings operating in the manufacturing sector will have the greatest distortive effect on competition in the common market. Therefore, such a reporting system may at present be limited to undertakings with a yearly turnover of more than EUR 250 million.

(24) This Directive should be without prejudice to the obligations of the Member States relating to the time-limits for transposition into national law of the Directives set out in Annex I, Part B,

HAS ADOPTED THIS DIRECTIVE:

Article 1

1. The Member States shall ensure that financial relations between public authorities and public undertakings are transparent as provided in this Directive, so that the following emerge clearly:

(a) public funds made available directly by public authorities to the public undertakings concerned;
(b) public funds made available by public authorities through the intermediary of public undertakings or financial institutions;
(c) the use to which these public funds are actually put.

2. Without prejudice to specific provisions laid down by the Community the Member States shall ensure that the financial and organisational structure of any undertaking required to maintain separate accounts is correctly reflected in the separate accounts, so that the following emerge clearly:

(a) the costs and revenues associated with different activities;

(b) full details of the methods by which costs and revenues are assigned or allocated to different activities.

Article 2

For the purpose of this Directive:

(a) "public authorities" means all public authorities, including the State and regional, local and all other territorial authorities;

(b) "public undertakings" means any undertaking over which the public authorities may exercise directly or indirectly a dominant influence by virtue of their ownership of it, their financial participation therein, or the rules which govern it.

 A dominant influence on the part of the public authorities shall be presumed when these authorities, directly or indirectly in relation to an undertaking:

 (i) hold the major part of the undertaking's subscribed capital; or
 (ii) control the majority of the votes attaching to shares issued by the undertakings; or
 (iii) can appoint more than half of the members of the undertaking's administrative, managerial or supervisory body;

(c) "public undertakings operating in the manufacturing sector" means all undertakings whose principal area of activity, defined as being at least 50% of total annual turnover, is in manufacturing. These undertakings are those whose operations fall under Section D — Manufacturing being subsection DA up to and including subsection DN of the NACE (Rev. 1) classification;[1]

(d) "undertaking required to maintain separate accounts" means any undertaking that enjoys a special or exclusive right granted by a Member State pursuant to Article 86(1) of the Treaty or is entrusted with the operation of a service of general economic interest pursuant to Article 86(2) of the Treaty, that receives public service compensation in any form whatsoever in relation to such service and that carries on other activities;

(e) "different activities" means, on the one hand, all products or services in respect of which a special or exclusive right is granted to an undertaking or all services of general economic interest with which an undertaking is entrusted and, on the other hand, each other separate product or service in respect of which the undertaking is active;

(f) "exclusive rights" means rights that are granted by a Member State to one undertaking through any legislative, regulatory or administrative instrument, reserving it the right to provide a service or undertake an activity within a given geographical area;

(g) "special rights" means rights that are granted by a Member State to a limited number of undertakings, through any legislative, regulatory or administrative instrument, which, within a given geographical area:

 (i) limits to two or more the number of such undertakings, authorised to provide a service or undertake an activity, otherwise than according to objective, proportional and non-discriminatory criteria; or
 (ii) designates, otherwise than according to such criteria, several competing undertakings, as being authorised to provide a service or undertake an activity; or
 (iii) confers on any undertaking or undertakings, otherwise than according to such criteria, any legal or regulatory advantages which substantially affect the ability of any other undertaking to provide the same service or to operate the same activity in the same geographical area under substantially equivalent conditions.

Notes
[1] OJ L 83, 3.4.1993, p. 1.

Part F Public Undertakings

Article 3

The transparency referred to in Article 1(1) shall apply in particular to the following aspects of financial relations between public authorities and public undertakings:

(a) the setting-off of operating losses;
(b) the provision of capital;
(c) non-refundable grants, or loans on privileged terms;
(d) the granting of financial advantages by forgoing profits or the recovery of sums due;
(e) the forgoing of a normal return on public funds used;
(f) compensation for financial burdens imposed by the public authorities.

Commentary
Art 3: **B&C:** 15.016

Article 4

1. To ensure the transparency referred to in Article 1(2), the Member States shall take the measures necessary to ensure that for any undertaking required to maintain separate accounts:

(a) the internal accounts corresponding to different activities are separate;
(b) all costs and revenues are correctly assigned or allocated on the basis of consistently applied and objectively justifiable cost accounting principles;
(c) the cost accounting principles according to which separate accounts are maintained are clearly established. 2. Paragraph 1 shall only apply to activities which are not covered by specific provisions laid down by the Community and shall not affect any obligations of Member States or undertakings arising from the Treaty or from such specific provisions.

Article 5

1. As far as the transparency referred to in Article 1(1) is concerned, this Directive shall not apply to financial relations between the public authorities and:

(a) public undertakings, as regards services the supply of which is not liable to affect trade between Member States to an appreciable extent;
(b) central banks;
(c) public credit institutions, as regards deposits of public funds placed with them by public authorities on normal commercial terms;
(d) public undertakings whose total annual net turnover over the period of the two financial years preceding that in which the funds referred to in Article 1(1) are made available or used has been less than EUR 40 million. However, for public credit institutions the corresponding threshold shall be a balance sheet total of EUR 800 million.

2. As far as the transparency referred to in Article 1(2) is concerned, this Directive shall not apply:

(a) to undertakings, as regards services the supply of which is not liable to affect trade between Member States to an appreciable extent;
(b) to undertakings whose total annual net turnover over the period of the two financial years preceding any given year in which it enjoys a special or exclusive right granted by a Member State pursuant to Article 86(1) of the Treaty, or in which it is entrusted with the operation of a service of general economic interest pursuant to Article 86(2) of the Treaty is less than EUR 40 million; however, for public credit institutions the corresponding threshold shall be a balance sheet total of EUR 800 million;
(c) to undertakings which have been entrusted with the operation of services of general economic interest pursuant to Article 86(2) of the Treaty if the compensation they receive, in any form whatsoever, was fixed for an appropriate period following an open, transparent and non-discriminating procedure.

Commentary
Art 5: **B&C:** 11.026, 15.016
Art 5(2)(b): **B&C:** 11.026
Art 5(2)(c): **B&C:** 11.026

Article 6

1. Member States shall ensure that information concerning the financial relations referred to in Article 1(1) be kept at the disposal of the Commission for five years from the end of the financial year in which the public funds were made available to the public undertakings concerned. However, where the same funds are used during a later financial year, the five-year time limit shall run from the end of that financial year.

2. Member States shall ensure that information concerning the financial and organisational structure of undertakings referred to in Article 1(2) be kept at the disposal of the Commission for five years from the end of the financial year to which the information refers.

3. Member States shall, where the Commission considers it necessary so to request, supply to it the information referred to in paragraphs 1 and 2, together with any necessary background information, notably the objectives pursued.

Commentary
Art 6: **B&C:** 11.026

Article 7

The Commission shall not disclose such information supplied to it pursuant to Article 6(3) as is of a kind covered by the obligation of professional secrecy. The first paragraph shall not prevent publication of general information or surveys which do not contain information relating to particular public undertakings to which this Directive applies.

Article 8

1. Member States whose public undertakings operate in the manufacturing sector shall supply the financial information as set out in paragraphs 2 and 3 to the Commission on an annual basis within the timetable contained in paragraph 5.

2. The financial information required for each public undertaking operating in the manufacturing sector and in accordance with paragraph 4 shall be the annual report and annual accounts, in accordance with the definition of Council Directive 78/660/EEC.[1] The annual accounts and annual report include the balance sheet and profit/loss account, explanatory notes, together with accounting policies, statements by directors, segmental and activity reports. Moreover, notices of shareholders' meetings and any other pertinent information shall be provided.

The reports required shall be provided for each individual public undertaking separately, as well as for the holding or subholding company which consolidates several public undertakings in so far as the consolidated sales of the holding or subholding company lead to its being classified as "manufacturing".

3. The following details, in so far as not disclosed in the annual report and annual accounts of each public undertaking, shall be provided in addition to the information referred to in paragraph 2:

(a) the provision of any share capital or quasi-capital funds similar in nature to equity, specifying the terms of its or their provision (whether ordinary, preference, deferred or convertible shares and interest rates; the dividend or conversion rights attaching thereto);

(b) non-refundable grants, or grants which are only refundable in certain circumstances;

(c) the award to the enterprise of any loans, including overdrafts and advances on capital injections, with a specification of interest rates and the terms of the loan and its security, if any, given to the lender by the enterprise receiving the loan;

(d) guarantees given to the enterprise by public authorities in respect of loan finance (specifying terms and any charges paid by enterprises for these guarantees);

(e) dividends paid out and profits retained;

(f) any other forms of State intervention, in particular, the forgoing of sums due to the State by a public undertaking, including *inter alia* the repayment of loans, grants, payment of corporate or social taxes or any similar charges.

The share capital referred to in (a) shall include share capital contributed by the State directly and any share capital received contributed by a public holding company or other public undertaking, including financial institutions, whether inside or outside the same group, to a given public undertaking. The relationship between the provider of the finance and the recipient shall always be specified.

4. The information required by paragraphs 2 and 3 shall be provided for all public undertakings whose turnover for the most recent financial year was more than EUR 250 million. The information required above shall be supplied separately for each public undertaking including those located in other Member States, and shall include, where appropriate, details of all intra- and inter-group transactions between different public undertakings, as well as transactions conducted directly between public undertakings and the State.

Certain public enterprises split their activities into several legally distinct undertakings. For such enterprises the Commission is willing to accept one consolidated report. The consolidation should reflect the economic reality of a group of enterprises operating in the same or closely related sectors. Consolidated reports from diverse, and purely financial, holdings shall not be sufficient.

5. The information required under paragraphs 2 and 3 shall be supplied to the Commission on an annual basis.

The information shall be provided within 15 working days of the date of publication of the annual report of the public undertaking concerned. In any case, and specifically for undertakings which do not publish an annual report, the required information shall be submitted not later than nine months following the end of the undertaking's financial year.

6. In order to assess the number of companies covered by this reporting system, Member States shall supply to the Commission a list of the companies covered by this Article and their turnover. The list is to be updated by 31 March of each year.

7. Member States will furnish the Commission with any additional information that it deems necessary in order to complete a thorough appraisal of the data submitted.

Notes
[1] OJ L 222, 14.8.1978, p. 11.

Commentary
Art 8: B&C: 11.026, 15.016

Article 9

The Commission shall regularly inform the Member States of the results of the operation of this Directive.

Article 10

Directive 80/723/EEC, as amended by the Directives listed in Annex I, Part A, is repealed, without prejudice to the obligations of the Member States relating to the time-limits for transposition into national law of the Directives set out in Annex I, Part B.

References to the repealed Directive shall be construed as references to this Directive and shall be read in accordance with the correlation table in Annex II.

Commentary
Art 10: B&C: 11.026

Article 11

This Directive shall enter into force on 20 December 2006.

Article 12

This Directive is addressed to the Member States.

Done at Brussels, 16 November 2006.

ANNEX I

PART A

REPEALED DIRECTIVE WITH ITS SUCCESSIVE AMENDMENTS

(referred to in Article 10)

Commission Directive 80/723/EEC	(OJ L 195, 29.7.1980, p. 35)
Commission Directive 85/413/EEC	(OJ L 229, 28.8.1985, p. 20)
Commission Directive 93/84/EEC	(OJ L 254, 12.10.1993, p. 16)
Commission Directive 2000/52/EC	(OJ L 193, 29.7.2000, p. 75)
Commission Directive 2005/81/EC	(OJ L 312, 29.11.2005, p. 47)

PART B

LIST OF TIME LIMITS FOR TRANSPOSITION INTO NATIONAL LAW

(referred to in Article 10)

Directive	Time limit for transposition
80/723/EEC	31 December 1981
85/413/EEC	1 January 1986
93/84/EEC	1 November 1993
2000/52/EC	31 July 2001
2005/81/EC	19 December 2006

ANNEX II

CORRELATION TABLE

Directive 80/723/EEC	*This Directive*
Article 1	Article 1
Article 2(1), introductory sentence	Article 2, introductory sentence
Article 2(1), point (a)	Article 2, point (a)
Article 2(1), point (b)	Article 2, point (b), first subparagraph
Article 2(1), points (c) to (f)	Article 2, points (c) to (f)
Article 2(1), point (g), introductory words	Article 2, point (g), introductory words
Article 2(1), point (g), first indent	Article 2, point (g)(i)
Article 2(1), point (g), second indent	Article 2, point (g)(ii)
Article 2(1), point (g), third indent	Article 2, point (g)(iii)
Article 2(2), introductory sentence	Article 2, point (b), second subparagraph, introductory sentence
Article 2(2), point (a)	Article 2, point (b), second subparagraph, point (i)
Article 2(2), point (b)	Article 2, point (b), second subparagraph, point (ii)
Article 2(2), point (c)	Article 2, point (b), second subparagraph, point (iii)
Article 3	Article 3
Article 3a	Article 4
Article 4	Article 5
Article 5	Article 6

Directive 80/723/EEC	This Directive
Article 5a(1)	Article 8(1)
Article 5a(2), first subparagraph, introductory sentence	Article 8(2), first subparagraph
Article 5a(2), first subparagraph, point (i)	Article 8(2), first subparagraph
Article 5a(2), second subparagraph, introductory sentence	Article 8(3), first subparagraph, introductory sentence
Article 5a(2), second subparagraph, point (ii)	Article 8(3), first subparagraph, point (a)
Article 5a(2), second subparagraph, point (iii)	Article 8(3), first subparagraph, point(b)
Article 5a(2), second subparagraph, point (iv)	Article 8(3), first subparagraph, point (c)
Article 5a(2), second subparagraph, point (v)	Article 8(3), first subparagraph, point(d)
Article 5a(2), second subparagraph, point (vi)	Article 8(3), first subparagraph, point (e)
Article 5a(2), second subparagraph, point (vii)	Article 8(3), first subparagraph, point (f)
Article 5a(3), first subparagraph	Article 8(4), first subparagraph
Article 5a(3), second subparagraph, first sentence	Article 8(4), second subparagraph
Article 5a(3), second subparagraph, second sentence	Article 8(3), second subparagraph, first sentence
Article 5a(3), second subparagraph, third sentence	Article 8(3), second subparagraph, second sentence
Article 5a(3), second subparagraph, last sentence	Article 8(2), second subparagraph
Article 5a(3), third subparagraph	Article 8(4), third subparagraph
Article 5a(4), first subparagraph	Article 8(5), first subparagraph
Article 5a(4), second subparagraph	Article 8(5), second subparagraph
Article 5a(4), third subparagraph	Article 8(6)
Article 5a(5)	—
Article 5a(6)	Article 8(7)
Article 6(1)	Article 7, first paragraph
Article 6(2)	Article 7, second paragraph
Article 7	Article 9
Article 8	—
—	Article 10
—	Article 11
Article 9	Article 12
—	Annex I
—	Annex II

Commentary
Annex II: B&C: 11.026

F3

APPLICATION OF ARTICLES [87] AND [88] OF THE [EC] TREATY TO PUBLIC AUTHORITIES' HOLDINGS

(Bulletin EC 9-1984)

Notes

EEA application: for the corresponding EEA provision, see the EEA Agreement, Annex XV, Point 9 and the EFTA Surveillance Authority's Procedural and Substantive Rules in the Field of State Aid (Guidelines on the application and interpretation of Articles 61 and 62 of the EEA Agreement and Article 1 of Protocol 3 to the Surveillance and Court Agreement), Part IV, Chapter 19 (OJ L 231, 03.09.1994, and EEA Supplement No 32).

THE COMMISSION'S POSITION

The Commission has sent Member States a paper explaining its general approach to the acquisition of shareholdings by the public authorities and setting out Member States' obligations in the field.

"Public holding" means a direct holding of central, regional or local government, or a direct holding of financial institutions or other national, regional or industrial agencies[1] which are funded from State resources within the meaning of Article [87](1) of the EC Treaty, or over which central, regional or local government exercises a dominant influence.

The Commission has already had occasion in the past to consider the question of public holdings in company capital from the angle of policy on State aid; in most cases, in view of the particular circumstances, it has regarded them as constituting State aid. This position is spelt out clearly in the steel and shipbuilding codes.

The steel code states that "the concept of aid includes . . . any aid elements contained in the financing measures taken by Member States in respect of the steel undertakings which they directly or indirectly control and which do not count as the provision of equity capital according to standard company practice in a market economy" (Commission Decision No 2320/81/ECSC of 7 April 1981 establishing Community rules for aid to the steel industry:[2] recital II, last paragraph, and Article 1). Pursuant to that Decision the Commission has usually regarded any contribution of capital to companies as State aid.

The shipbuilding code contains a formula identical to the one in the steel code (Council Directive No 81/363/EEC of 28 April 1981 on aid to shipbuilding:[3] last recital and Article 1(e)).

Notes

[1] This includes public undertakings as defined in Article 2 of Commission Directive 80/723/EEC of 25 June 1980 on the transparency of financial relations between Member States and public undertakings (OJ L 195, 29.7.1980). [Directive 80/723/EEC was repealed with effect from 20 December 2006 by Commission Directive 2006/111/EC of 16 November 2006 on the transparency of financial relations between Member States and public undertakings as well as on financial transparency within certain undertakings (Codified version), OJ L318, 17.11.2006, p. 17. Article 10 of Directive 2006/111/EC provides that references to the repealed Directive shall be construed as references to Directive 2006/111/EC and shall be read in accordance with the correlation table in Annex II to Directive 2006/111/EC.]

[2] OJ L 228, 13.8.1981.

[3] OJ L 137, 23.5.1981.

---

1. The Treaty establishes both the principle of impartiality with regard to the system of property ownership (Article [295] and the principle of equality between public and private undertakings. This means that Commission action may neither penalize nor favour public authorities which provide companies with equity capital. Nor is it for the Commission to express any opinion as to the choice companies make between methods of financing — loan or equity — whether the funds are of private or public origin.

Where, applying the guidelines laid down in this paper, it is apparent that a public authority which injects capital by acquiring a holding in a company is not merely providing equity capital under normal market economy conditions, the case has to be assessed in the light of Article [87] of the EC Treaty.

2. Four types of situation can be distinguished in which public authorities may have occasion to acquire a holding in the capital of companies:

   (a) the setting up of a company,

   (b) partial or total transfer of ownership from the private to the public sector,

   (c) in an existing public enterprise, injection of fresh capital or conversion of endowment funds into capital,

   (d) in an existing private sector company, participation in an increase in share capital.

3. On this basis four cases can be distinguished.

3.1. Straightforward partial or total acquisition of a holding in the capital of an existing company, without any injection of fresh capital, does not constitute aid to the company.

3.2. Nor is State aid involved where fresh capital is contributed in circumstances that would be acceptable to a private investor operating under normal market economy conditions. This can be taken to apply:

   (i) where a new company is set up with the public authorities holding the entire capital or a majority or minority interest, provided the authorities apply the same criteria as provider of capital under normal market economy conditions;

   (ii) where fresh capital is injected into a public enterprise, provided this fresh capital corresponds to new investment needs and to costs directly linked to them, that the industry in which the enterprise operates does not suffer from structural overcapacity in the common market, and that the enterprise's financial position is sound;

   (iii) where the public holding in a company is to be increased, provided the capital injected is proportionate to the number of shares held by the authorities and goes together with the injection of capital by a private shareholder; the private investor's holding must have real economic significance;

   (iv) where, even though the holding is acquired in the manner referred to in either of the last two indents of Section 3.3 below, it is in a small or medium-sized enterprise which because of its size is unable to provide adequate security on the private financial market, but whose prospects are such as to warrant a public holding exceeding its net assets or private investment;

   (v) where the strategic nature of the investment in terms of markets or supplies is such that acquisition of a shareholding could be regarded as the normal behaviour of a provider of capital, although profitability is delayed;

   (vi) where the recipient company's development potential, reflected in innovative capacity from investment of all kinds, is such that the operation may be regarded as an investment involving a special risk but likely to pay off ultimately.

3.3. On the other hand, there is State aid where fresh capital is contributed in circumstances that would not be acceptable to a private investor operating under normal market economy conditions. This is the case:

   (i) where the financial position of the company, and particularly the structure and volume of its debt, is such that a normal return (in dividends or capital gains) cannot be expected within a reasonable time from the capital invested;

   (ii) where, because of its inadequate cash flow if for no other reason, the company would be unable to raise the funds needed for an investment programme on the capital market;

   (iii) where the holding is a short-term one, with duration and selling price fixed in advance, so that the return to the provider of capital is considerably less than he could have expected from a capital market investment for a similar period;

   (iv) where the public authorities' holding involves the taking over or the continuation of all or part of the nonviable operations[4] of an ailing company through the formation of a new legal entity;

   (v) where the injection of capital into companies whose capital is divided between private and public shareholders makes the public holding reach a significantly higher level than originally and the relative disengagement of private shareholders is largely due to the companies' poor profit outlook;

(vi) where the amount of the holding exceeds the real value (net assets plus value of any goodwill or know-how) of the company, except in the case of companies of the kind referred to in the fourth indent of Section 3.2. above.

Notes

[4] Excluding the straightforward takeover of the assets of a company which has become insolvent or gone into liquidation.

3.4. Some acquisitions may not fall within the categories indicated in Sections 3.2 and 3.3 so that it cannot be decided from the outset whether they do, or do not constitute State aid.

In certain circumstances, however, there is a presumption that there is indeed State aid.

This is the case where:

(i) the authorities' intervention takes the form of acquisition of a holding combined with other types of intervention which need to be notified pursuant to Article [88](3);

(ii) the holding is taken in an industry experiencing particular difficulties, without the circumstances being covered by Section 3.3; accordingly, where the Commission finds that an industry is suffering from structural overcapacity and even though most such cases will be within the scope of Section 3.3, it may consider it necessary to monitor all holdings in that industry, including those coming under Section 3.2.

4. Leaving aside the fact that the Commission has at all times the right to request information from the Member States case-by-case, the obligations devolving on Member States in the light of the Commission's practice to date and the approach outlined here should be set out anew and specified in detail.

4.1. In the case referred to at 3.1, there is no need to place any particular obligations on Member States.

4.2. In the cases referred to at 3.2, the Commission would ask Member States to inform it retrospectively by means of regular, and normally annual, reports on holdings acquired by financial institutions and directly by public authorities. The information given should include the following at least, possibly as part of the financial institutions' reports:

(i) name of the institution or authority which acquired the holding,

(ii) name of the company involved,

(iii) amount of the holding,

(iv) capital of the company before the holding was acquired,

(v) industry in which the company operates,

(vi) number of employees.

4.3. As regards the cases referred to in Section 3.3, since these do constitute State aid, Member States are required to notify the Commission pursuant to Article [88](3) of the EC Treaty before they are put into effect.

4.4. With regard to the cases referred to in Section 3.4 in which it is not clear from the outset whether or not they involve State aid, Member States should inform the Commission retrospectively by means of regular and normally annual reports in the manner described in Section 4.2.

In cases of the kind described in Section 3.4 where there is a presumption of State aid, the Commission should be informed in advance. On the basis of an examination of the information received, it will decide within 15 working days whether the information should be regarded as notification for the purposes of Article [88](3) of the EC Treaty.

4.5. Without prejudice to the Commission's right to ask for information on specific cases, the obligation to supply regular retrospective information only applies to shareholdings in companies where one of the following thresholds is exceeded:

(i) balance-sheet total: ECU 4 million,

(ii) net turnover: ECU 8 million,

(iii) number of employees: 250.

The Commission may review these thresholds in the light of future experience.

5. Member States also use certain forms of intervention which, while not having all the features of a capital contribution in the form of acquisition of a public holding, resemble this sufficiently to be treated in the same way. This is the case notably with capital contributions taking the form of convertible debenture loans or of loans where the financial yield is, at least in part, dependent on the company's financial performance.

   The criteria in Section 3 also apply in respect of these forms of intervention, and Member States are under the obligations set out in Section 4.

6. In certain cases the Commission has authorized aid measures which also include the acquisition of holdings in certain circumstances. The various procedural clauses in the authorization decisions are not affected by the provisions in this paper.

7. This paper also applies to holdings in agricultural undertakings. It may be adapted to take account of any new circumstances arising from the accession of new Member States.

F4

COMMISSION COMMUNICATION TO THE MEMBER STATES

Application of Articles [87] and [88] of the [EC] Treaty and of Article 5 of Commission Directive 80/723/EEC to public undertakings in the manufacturing sector

Official Journal C 307, 13.11.1993, p. 3

Celex No: 31993Y1113(01)

Notes

Directive 80/723/EEC was repealed with effect from 20 December 2006 by Commission Directive 2006/111/EC of 16 November 2006 on the transparency of financial relations between Member States and public undertakings as well as on financial transparency within certain undertakings (Codified version), OJ L318, 17.11.2006, p. 17. Article 10 of Directive 2006/111/EC provides that references to the repealed Directive shall be construed as references to Directive 2006/111/EC and shall be read in accordance with the correlation table in Annex II to Directive 2006/111/EC. Unless otherwise indicated, Article numbers in the new Directive are the same as in the old Directive.

EEA application: for the corresponding EEA provision, see the EFTA Surveillance Authority's Procedural and Substantive Rules in the Field of State Aid (Guidelines on the application and interpretation of Articles 61 and 62 of the EEA Agreement and Article 1 of Protocol 3 to the Surveillance and Court Agreement), Part IV, Chapter 20 (OJ L 231, 03.09.1994, and EEA Supplement No 32).

I. INTRODUCTION

1. A reinforced application of policy towards State aid is necessary for the successful completion of the internal market. One of the areas identified as worthy of attention in this respect is public undertakings. There is need for both increased transparency and development of policy for public undertakings because they have not been sufficiently covered by State aid disciplines:

   — in many cases only capital injections and not other forms of public funds have been fully included in aid disciplines for public undertakings;

   — in addition, these disciplines in general only cover loss-making public undertakings;

   — finally it also appears that there is a considerable volume of aid to public undertakings given other than through approved aid schemes (which are also available to private undertakings) which have not been notified under Article [88](3).

2. This communication is designed to remedy this situation. In the first place it explains the legal background of the Treaty and outlines the aid policy and case-law of the Council, Parliament, Commission and Court of Justice for public enterprises. This will, in particular, focus, on the one hand, on Directive 80/723/EC[*] on the transparency of the financial relationship between public undertakings and the State, and, on the other hand, it will develop the well established principle that where the State provides finances to a company in circumstances that would not be acceptable to an investor operating under normal market economy conditions, State aid is involved. The communication then explains how the Commission intends to increase transparency by applying this principle to all forms of public funds and to companies in all situations.

Notes
[* See now Directive 2006/111/EC, OJ L 318, 17.11.2006, p. 17.]

3. This communication does not deal with the question of the compatibility under one of the derogations provided for in the EEC Treaty because no change is envisaged in this policy. Finally, this communication is limited to the manufacturing sector. This will not, however, preclude the Commission from using the approach described by this communication in individual cases or sectors outside manufacturing to the extent that the principles in this communication apply in these excluded sectors and where it feels that it is essential to determine if State aid is involved.

II. PUBLIC UNDERTAKINGS AND THE RULES OF COMPETITION

4. Article [295] states: "This Treaty shall in no way prejudice the rules in Member States governing the system of property ownership". In other words the Treaty is neutral in the choice a Member State may make between public and private ownership and does not prejudice a Member State's right to run a mixed economy. However, these rights do not absolve public undertakings from the rules of competition because the institution of a system ensuring that competition in the common market is not distorted is one of the bases on which the Treaty is built (Article [3(1)(g)]). The Treaty also provides the general rules for ensuring such a system (Articles [81] to [89]). In addition the Treaty lays down that these general rules of competition shall apply to public undertakings (Article [86](1)). There is a specific derogation in Article [86](2) from the general rule of Article [86](1) in that the rules of competition apply to all public undertakings including those entrusted with the operation of services of general economic interest or having the character of a revenue-producing monopoly in so far as the application of such rules does not obstruct the performance in law or in fact of the particular tasks assigned to them. The development of trade must not be affected to such an extent as would be contrary to the interests of the Community. In the context of the State aid rules (Articles [87] to [89]), this means that aid granted to public undertakings must, like any other State aid to private undertakings, be notified in advance to the Commission (Article [88](3)) to ascertain whether or not it falls within the scope of Article [87](1), i.e. aid that affects trade and competition between Member States. If it falls within Article [87](1), it is for the Commission to determine whether one of the general derogations provided for in the Treaty is applicable such that the aid becomes compatible with the common market. It is the Commission's role to ensure that there is no discrimination against either public or private undertakings when it applies the rules of competition.

5. It was to ensure this principle of non-discrimination, or neutrality of treatment that, in 1980, the Commission adopted a Directive on the transparency of financial relations between Member States and public undertakings.[1] The Commission was motivated by the fact that the complexity of the financial relations between national public authorities and public undertakings tended to hinder its duty of ensuring that aid incompatible with the common market was not granted. It further considered that the State aid rules could only be applied fairly to both public and private undertakings when the financial relations between public authorities and public undertakings were made transparent.

Notes
[1] Directive 80/723/EEC (OJ L 195, 29.7.1980, p. 35) as amended by Directive 85/413/EEC (OJ L 229, 28.8.1985, p. 20) which included previously excluded sectors. [See now Commission Directive 2006/111/EC of 16 November 2006 on the transparency of financial relations between Member States and public undertakings as well as on financial transparency within certain undertakings (Codified version), OJ L318, 17.11.2006, p. 17.]

6. The Directive obliged Member States to ensure that the flow of all public funds to public undertakings and the uses to which these funds are put are made transparent (Article 1). Member States shall, when the Commission considers it necessary so to request, supply to it the information referred to in Article 1, together with any necessary background information, notably the objectives pursued (Article 5[*]). Although the transparency in question applied to all public funds, the following were particularly mentioned as falling within its scope:
   — the setting-off of operating losses,
   — the provision of capital,
   — non-refundable grants or loans on privileged terms,
   — the granting of financial advantages by forgoing profits or the recovery of sums due,
   — the forgoing of a normal return on public funds used,
   — compensation for financial burdens imposed by the public authorities.

Notes

[* See now Directive 2006/111/EC (OJ L 318, 17.11.2006, p. 17), Article 6.]

7. The Commission further considered that transparency of public funds must be achieved irrespective of the manner in which such provision of public funds is made. Thus, not only were the flows of funds directly from public authorities to public enterprises deemed to fall within the scope of the transparency Directive but also the flows of funds indirectly from other public undertakings over which the public authority holds a dominant influence (Article 2).
8. The legality of the transparency Directive was upheld by the Court of Justice in its judgment of 6 July 1982.[2]

Notes

[2] Joined Cases 188 to 190/80 *France, Italy and the United Kingdom v Commission* [1982] ECR 2545.

8.1. On the argument that there was no necessity for the Directive and that it infringed the rule of proportionality, the Court held as follows (paragraph 18): "In view of the diverse forms of public undertakings in the various Member States and the ramifications of their activities, it is inevitable that their financial relations with public authorities should themselves be very diverse, often complex and therefore difficult to supervise, even with the assistance of the sources of published information to which the applicant governments have referred. In those circumstances there is an undeniable need for the Commission to seek additional information on those relations by establishing common criteria for all the Member States and for all the undertakings in question".
8.2. On the argument that the Directive in question infringed the principle of neutrality of Article [295] of the Treaty, the Court held that (paragraph 21), "it should be borne in mind that the principle of equality, to which the governments refer in connection with the relationship between public and private undertakings in general, presupposes that the two are in comparable situations. . . . private undertakings determine their industrial and commercial strategy by taking into account, in particular, requirements of profitability. Decisions of public undertakings, on the other hand, may be affected by factors of a different kind within the framework of the pursuit of objectives of public interest by public authorities which may exercise an influence over those decisions. The economic and financial consequences of the impact of such factors lead to the establishment between those undertakings and public authorities of financial relations of a special kind which differ from those existing between public authorities and private undertakings. As the Directive concerns precisely those special financial relations, the submission relating to discrimination cannot be accepted."
8.3. On the argument that the Directive's list of public funds to be made transparent (Article 3) was an attempt to define the notion of aid within the meaning of Articles [87] and [88], the Court stated as follows (paragraph 23): "In relation to the definition contained in Article 3 of the financial relations which are subject to the rules contained in the Directive, it is sufficient to state that it is not an attempt by the Commission to define the concept of aid which appears in Articles [87] and [88] of the Treaty, but only a statement of the financial transactions of which the Commission considers that it must be informed in order to check whether a Member State

has granted aids to the undertakings in question, without complying with its obligation to notify the Commission under Article [88](3)".

8.4. On the argument that the public enterprises on which information was to be provided (Article 2) was an attempt to define the notion of public undertakings within the meaning of Article [86] of the Treaty, the Court stated that (paragraph 24), "it should be emphasized that the object of those provisions is not to define the concept as it appears in Article [86] of the Treaty, but to establish the necessary criteria to delimit the group of undertakings whose financial relations with the public authorities are to be subject to the duty laid down by the Directive to supply information". It continued in paragraph 25 as follows: "According to Article 2 of the Directive, the expression "public undertakings" means any undertaking over which the public authorities may exercise directly or indirectly a dominant influence. According to the second paragraph, such influence is not to be presumed when the public authorities directly or indirectly hold the major part of the undertaking"s subscribed capital, control the majority of the votes, or can appoint more than half of the members of its administrative, managerial of supervisory body". It continued in paragraph 26 as follows: "As the Court has already stated, the reason for the inclusion in the Treaty of the provisions of Article [86] is precisely the influence which the public authorities are able to exert over the commercial decisions of public undertakings. That influence may be exerted on the basis of financial participation or of rules governing the management of the undertaking. By choosing the same criteria to determine the financial relations on which it must be able to obtain information in order to perform its duty of surveillance under Article [86](3), the Commission has remained within the limits of the discretion conferred upon it by that provision".

9. The principles developed by the Court of Justice with respect to the transparency Directive are now part of the established jurisprudence and of particular importance is the fact that the Court has confirmed that:
— making financial relations transparent and the provision, on request, of information under the Directive is necessary and respects the principle of proportionality;
— the Directive respects the principle of neutrality of treatment of public and private undertakings;
— for the purposes of monitoring compliance with Articles [87] and [88] the Commission has a legitimate interest to be informed of all the types of flows of public funds to public enterprises;
— for the purposes of monitoring compliance with Articles [87] and [88] the Commission has a legitimate interest in the flows of public funds to public undertakings that come either directly from the public authorities or indirectly from other public undertakings.

III. PRINCIPLES TO BE USED IN DETERMINING WHETHER AID IS INVOLVED

10. Having established over which enterprises and over which funds the Commission has a legitimate interest for the purposes of Articles [86] and [87], it is necessary to examine the principles to be used in determining whether any aid is involved. Only if aid is involved is there any question of any prior notification. Where aid is involved it is necessary to then examine whether any of the derogations provided for in the Treaty are applicable.[3] This analysis of determining on the one hand whether aid is involved and on the other whether the aid is compatible under one of the derogations of the Treaty, must be kept as a two stage process if full transparency is to be assured.

Notes
[3] See also points 32 and 33 below.

11. When public undertakings, just like private ones, benefit from monies granted under transparent aid schemes approved by the Commission, then it is clear that aid is involved and under what conditions the Commission has authorized its approval. However, the situation with respect to the other forms of public funds listed in the transparency Directive is not always so clear. In certain circumstances public enterprises can derive an advantage from the nature of their relationship with public authorities through the provision of public funds when this latter provides funds in circumstances that go beyond its simple role as proprietor. To ensure respect for the principle of neutrality the aid must be assessed as the difference between the terms on which the funds

were made available by the State to the public enterprise, and the terms which a private investor would find acceptable in providing funds to a comparable private undertaking when the private investor is operating under normal market economy conditions (hereinafter "market economy investor principle"). As the Commission points out in its communication on Industrial policy in an open and competitive environment (COM (90) 556) "competition is becoming ever more global and more intense both on the world and on Community markets". This trend has many implications for European companies, for example with regards to R&D, investment strategies and their financing. Both public and private enterprises in similar sectors and in comparable economic and financial situations must be treated equally with respect to this financing. However, if any public funds are provided on terms more favourable (i.e. in economic terms more cheaply) than a private owner would provide them to a private undertaking in a comparable financial and competitive position, then the public undertaking is receiving an advantage not available to private undertakings from their proprietors. Unless the more favourable provision of public funds is treated as aid, and evaluated with respect to one of the derogations of the Treaty, then the principle of neutrality of treatment between public and private undertakings is infringed.

12. This principle of using an investor operating under normal market conditions as a benchmark to determine both whether aid is involved and if so to quantify it, has been adopted by the *Council* and the *Commission* in the steel and shipbuilding sectors, and has been endorsed by the *Parliament* in this context. In addition the Commission has adopted and applied this principle in numerous individual cases. The principle has also been accepted by the *Court* in every case submitted to it as a yardstick for the determination of whether aid was involved.

13. In 1981 the Council adopted the principle of the market economy investor principle on two occasions. Firstly it approved unanimously the Commission decision establishing Community rules for aid to the steel industry,[4] and secondly it approved, by a qualified majority, the shipbuilding code.[5] In both cases the Council stated that the concept of aid includes any aid elements contained in the financing measures taken by Member States in respect of the steel/shipbuilding undertakings which they *directly or indirectly control* and which do not count as the provision of equity capital *according to standard company practice in a market economy*. Thus not only did the Council approve or adopt the market economy principle, it went along the same lines as the Commission in the abovementioned transparency Directive, which brought within its scope not only the direct provision of funds but also their indirect provision.

Notes

[4] Decision 81/2320/ECSC of 7 August 1981 (OJ L 228, 13.8.1981, p. 14.). See, in particular, the second recital and Article 1.

[5] Council Directive 81/363/EEC of 28 April 1981 (OJ L 137, 23.5.1981, p. 39). See, in particular, the last recital and Article 1(e).

---

14. The Council has maintained this general principle, most recently in 1989 in the case of steel,[6] and in 1990 in the case of shipbuilding.[7] In fact in the 1989 steel aid code the Council agreed to prior notification of all provisions of capital or similar financing in order to allow the Commission to decide whether they constituted aid, i.e. could "be regarded as a genuine provision of risk capital *according to usual investment practice in a market economy*" (Article 1(2)). The Council also reaffirmed and approved unanimously this principle in Commission Decision 89/218/ECSC concerning new aid to Finsider/ILVA.[8]

Notes

[6] Commission Decision 322/89/ECSC of 1 February 1989 (OJ L 38, 10.2.1989, p. 8).

[7] Council Directive 90/684/EEC of 21 December 1990, (OJ L 380, 31.12.1990, p. 27).

[8] OJ L 86, 31.3.1989, p. 76.

---

15. The Parliament has been called upon to give its opinion on the market economy investor principle contained in the shipbuilding Directives. For these Directives the Parliament agreed to the Commission drafts which included this principle.[9]

Notes

[9] See, for example, OJ C 28, 9.2.1981, p. 23, and OJ C 7, 12.1.1987, p. 320.

---

16. The Commission adopted the same market economy investor principle when it laid down its position in general on public holdings in company capital which still remains valid.[10] It stated "where it is apparent that a public authority which injects capital . . . in a company is not merely providing equity capital under normal market economy conditions, the case has to be assessed in the light of Article [87] of the [EC] Treaty" (paragraph 1). It considered in particular that State aid was involved "where the financial position of the company and particularly the structure and volume of its debts, is such that a normal return (in dividends or capital gains) cannot be expected within a reasonable time from the capital invested".

Notes
[10] Communication to the Member States concerning public authorities holdings in company capital. (Bul. EC 91984).

17. The Commission has moreover applied this market economy investor principle in many individual cases to determine whether any aid was involved. The Commission examined in each case the financial circumstances of the company which received the public funds to see if a market economy investor would have made the monies available on similar terms. In the Leeuwarden Decision the Commission established that the capital injections constituted aid because "the overcapacity in the . . . industry constituted handicaps indicating that the firm would *probably* have been unable to raise on the private capital market the funds essential to its survival. The situation on the market provides *no reasonable grounds* for hope that a firm urgently needing large-scale restructuring could generate sufficient cash flow to finance the replacement investment necessary . . . ".[11] This policy has been applied consistently over a number of years. More recently in the CDF v Orkem decision,[12] the Commission established that the public authority "injected capital into an undertaking in conditions that are not those of a market economy". In fact, the company in question "had very little chance of obtaining sufficient capital from the private market to ensure its survival and long-term stability". In the ENI/Lanerossi Decision,[13] the Commission stated that "finance was granted in circumstances that would not be acceptable to a private investor operating under normal market economy conditions, as in the present case the financial and economic position of these factories, particularly in view of the duration and volumes of their losses, was such that a normal return in dividends or capital gains could not be expected for the capital invested".[14] There have also been a number of cases where the Commission has clearly stated that capital injections by the State have not constituted aid because a reasonable return by way of dividends or capital growth could normally be expected.[15]

Notes
[11] OJ L 277, 29.9.1982, p. 15.
[12] OJ C 198, 7.8.1990, p. 2.
[13] OJ L 16, 20.1.1989, p. 52.
[14] Decisions *Meura* (OJ L 276, 19.10.1984, p. 34), *Leeuwarden* (OJ L 277, 29.9.1982, p. 15), *Intermills I* (OJ L 280, 2.10.1982, p. 30), *Boch/Noviboch* (OJ L 59, 27.2.1985, p. 21), *Boussac* (OJ L 352, 15.12.1987, p. 42), *Alfa-Fiat* (OJ L 394, 31.5.1989, p. 9), *Pinault-Isoroy* (OJ L 119, 7.5.1988, p. 38), *Fabelta* (OJ L 62, 3.3.1984, p. 18) *Ideal Spun* (OJ L 283, 27.10.1984, p. 42), *Renault* (OJ L 220, 11.8.1988, p. 30), *Veneziana Vetro* (OJ L 166, 16.6.1989, p. 60), *Quimigal* (OJ C 188, 28.7.1990, p. 3) and *IOR/Finalp* [OJ L 183, 3.7.1992, p. 30] where the same reasoning can be found.
[15] Decisions *CDF/Orkem*, in parts, (op. cit.), *Quimigal*, in parts, (op. cit.), *Intermills II* (Bulletin EC 4-1990, point 1.1.34) and *Ernaelsteen* (Eighteenth Competition Report, points 212 and 213).

18. The Commission has also applied the market economy investor principle to many individual cases under the shipbuilding Directives and steel aid codes. In shipbuilding, for example in Bremer Vulkan,[16] the Commission considered that a bridging loan and the purchase of new shares constituted State aid because it did "not accept the argument put forward by the German Government that [it] . . . only acted like a private investor who happened to be better at foreseeing future market developments than anyone else." In steel, for example, it took decisions in several individual cases where capital injections were considered as aid.[17]

Part F Public Undertakings

1281

Notes

[16] [OJ L 185, 28.7.1993, p. 43.]

[17] OJ L 227, 19.8.1983, p. 1. See also, in particular, cases relating to Arbed, Sidmar, ALZ, Hoogovens, Irish Steel, Sacilor v Usinor and British Steel where the same reasoning can be found. In all these steel cases the aid was held to be compatible. More recently, the Council unanimously approved this principle in the Finsider/ILVA case — see point 26 below.

19. It is noteworthy that in many of the above described cases the capital injected into the public undertakings came not directly from the State but indirectly from State holding companies or other public undertakings.

20. The Court has been called upon to examine a number of cases decided by the Commission in its application of the market economy investor principle set out in the 1984 guidelines. In each case submitted to it, the Court accepted the principle as an appropriate one to be used to determine whether or not aid was involved. It then examined whether the Commission decision sufficiently proved its application in the specific circumstances of the case in question. For example, in its judgment in Case 40/85[18] (*Boch*), the Court stated (paragraph 13):

"An appropriate way of establishing whether [the] measure is a State aid is to apply the criterion, which was mentioned in the Commission's decision and, moreover, was not contested by the Belgian Government, of determining to what extent the undertaking would be able to obtain the sums in question on the private capital markets. In the case of an undertaking whose capital is almost entirely held by the public authorities, the test is, in particular, whether in similar circumstances a private shareholder, having regard to the foreseeability of obtaining a return and leaving aside all social, regional policy and sectoral considerations, would have subscribed the capital in question".

The Court has recently reaffirmed this principle in the *Boussac* judgment,[19] where it stated (paragraphs 39 and 40): "In order to determine if the measures constitute State aid, it is necessary to apply the criterion in the Commission's decision, which was not contested by the French Government, whether it would have been possible for the undertaking to obtain the funds on the private capital market", and "the financial situation of the company was such that it would not expect an acceptable return on the investment within a reasonable time period and that Boussac would not have been able to find the necessary funds on the market" (unofficial translation).[20] The Court has recently further refined the market economy investor principle by making a distinction between a private investor whose time horizon is a short-term even speculative one, and that of a private holding group with a longer-term perspective (*Alfa/Fiat and Lanerossi*).[21] "It is necessary to make clear that the behaviour of a private investor with which the intervention of the public investor . . . must be compared, while not necessarily that of an ordinary investor placing his capital with a more or less short-term view of its profitability, must at least be that of a private holding or group of enterprises which pursue a structural, global or sectoral policy and which are guided by a longer-term view of profitability". On the basis of the facts of the case "the Commission was able to correctly conclude that a private investor, even if taking decisions at the level of the whole group in a wider economic context, would not, under normal market economy conditions, have been able to expect an acceptable rate of profitability (even in the long term) on the capital invested . . . " (unofficial translation). "A private investor may well inject new capital to ensure the survival of a company experiencing temporary difficulties, but which after, if necessary, a restructuring will become profitable again. A parent company may also, during a limited time, carry the losses of a subsidiary in order to allow this latter to withdraw from the sector under the most favourable conditions. Such decisions can be motivated not only by the possibility to get a direct profit, but also by other concerns such as maintaining the image of the whole group or to redirect its activities. However, when the new injections of capital are divorced from all possibility of profitability, even in the long term, these injections must be considered as aid . . . " (unofficial translation).

Notes

[18] *Belgium v Commission* [1986] ECR 2321.

[19] Case C-301/87 [[1990] ECR I-307].

[20] See also *Intermills* Case 323/82, *Leeuwarden* Joined Cases 296/318/82, *Meura* Case 234/84 where the same reasoning can be found.
[21] Cases C-305/89 [[1991] ECR I-1603] and C-303/88 [[1991] ECR I-1433] respectively [. . .].

21. The fact that in many of the cases decided by the Court the injections came indirectly from State holding companies or from other public undertakings and not directly from the State, did not alter the aid character of the monies in question. The Court has always examined the economic reality of the situation to determine whether State resources were involved. In the *Steinicke* and *Weinlig* judgment,[22] the Court stated that " . . . save for the reservation in Article [86](2) of the Treaty, Article [87] covers all private and public undertakings and all their production" and that "in applying Article [87] regard must primarily be had to the effects of aid on the undertakings or producers favoured and not the status of the institutions entrusted with the distribution and administration of the aid". More recently in the *Crédit Agricole* judgment,[23] the Court confirmed this and added that " . . . aid need not necessarily be financed from State resources to be classified as State aid . . . there is no necessity to draw any distinction according to whether the aid is granted directly by the State or by public or private bodies established or appointed by it to administer aid."

Notes

[22] Case 78/76.
[23] Case 290/83.

IV. Increased Transparency of Policy

22. To date most but by no means all of the cases which have come before the Council, the Commission and the Court where the market economy investor principle has been applied have concerned capital injections in loss-making or even near-bankrupt companies. One of the aims of this communication is to increase transparency by more systematically applying aid disciplines:
    — to public undertakings in all situations, not just those making losses as is the case at present,
    — to all the forms of public funds mentioned in the transparency Directive (Article 3 — see points 6 and 8.3 above), in particular, for loans, guarantees and the rate of return, not just for capital injections as is the case at present.
23. This increased transparency of policy is to be brought about by clearly applying the market economy investor principle to public undertakings in all situations and all public funds covered by the transparency Directive. The market economy investor principle is used because:
    — it is an appropriate yardstick both for measuring any financial advantage a public undertaking may enjoy over an equivalent private one and for ensuring neutrality of treatment between public and private undertakings;
    — it has proved itself practical to the Commission in numerous cases;
    — it has been confirmed by the Court (see particularly points 20 and 21 above), and
    — t has been approved by the Council in the steel and shipbuilding sector.

    Unless this clarification is implemented there is a danger not only of lack of transparency, but also of discrimination against private undertakings which do not have the same links with the public authorities nor the same access to public funds. The current communication is a logical development of existing policy rather than any radical new departure and is necessary to explain the application of the principle to a wider number of situations and a wider range of funds. In fact the Court, the Commission and the Council have already applied the principle of the market economy investor in a limited number of cases to the forms of public funds other than equity which are also the object of this communication — i.e. guarantees, loans, return on capital.[24]

Notes

[24] It should be noted that this is not an exhaustive list of the different forms of financing which may entail aid. The Commission will act against the provision of any other advantages to public undertakings in a tangible or intangible form that may constitute aid.

24. *Guarantee.* In IOR/Finalp (op. cit.) the Commission considered that when a State holding company became the one and only owner of an ailing company (thereby exposing it to unlimited liability under Italian commercial law) this was equivalent to taking extra risk by giving, in effect, an open-ended guarantee. The Commission using its well established principle stated that a market economy investor would normally be reluctant to become the one and only shareholder of a company if as a consequence he must assume unlimited liability for it; he will make sure that this additional risk is outweighed by additional gains.

25. *Loan.* In *Boch* (op. cit.) the Court stated (paragraphs 12 and 13): "By virtue of Article [87](1) ... the provisions of the Treaty concerning State aid apply to aid granted by a Member State or through State resources in any form whatsoever. It follows ... that no distinction can be drawn between aid granted in the form of *loans* and aid granted in the form of a subscription of capital of an undertaking. An appropriate way of establishing whether such a measure is a State aid is to apply the criterion ... of determining to what extent the undertaking would be able to obtain the sums in question on the private capital markets."

26. *Return on capital.* When it opened the Article 88 procedure of the ECSC Treaty (letter to the Italian Government of 6 May 1988) in the Finsider/ILVA case, the Commission considered that the loans granted by State credit institutions were not granted to the undertaking in question under conditions acceptable to a private investor operating under normal market conditions, but were dependent on an (*implicit*) *guarantee* of the State and as such constituted State aid. In fact at a later date this implicit guarantee was made explicit when the debts were honoured. The opening of the procedure led to a decision with the unanimous approval of the Council[25] which imposed conditions on the enterprise in question to ensure that its *viability* would be re-established, and a *minimum return on capital* should be earned.

Notes

[25] OJ L 86, 31.3.1989, p. 76. See also the Commission communication to the Council of 25 October 1988 — SEC(88) 1485 final, and point 207 of the Fourteenth Competition Report. In fact, the whole aim of the steel code for all Member States was to restore viability through a minimum return and self-financing according to market principles.

V. Practicality of the Market Economy Investor Principle

27. The practical experience gained by the Commission from the application of State aid rules to public enterprises and the general support among the Community institutions for the basic themes of the market economy investor principle confirm the Commission's view that it is, as such, an appropriate yardstick to determine whether, or not aid exists. However, it is noted that the majority of cases to which the mechanism has been applied have been of a particular nature and the wider application of the mechanism may appear to cause certain difficulties. Some further explanations are therefore warranted. In addition, the fear has been expressed that the application of the market economy investor principle could lead to the Commission's judgment replacing the investor and his appreciation of investment projects. In the first place this criticism can be refuted by the fact that this principle has already shown itself to be both an appropriate and practical yardstick for determining which public funds constitute aid in numerous individual cases. Secondly it is not the aim of the Commission in the future, just as it has not been in the past, to replace the investor's judgment. Any requests for extra finance naturally call for public undertakings and public authorities, just as they do for private undertakings and the private providers of finance, to analyse the risk and the likely outcome of the project.

In turn, the Commission realizes that this analysis of risk requires public undertakings, like private undertakings, to exercise entrepreneurial skills, which by the very nature of the problem implies a wide margin of judgment on the part of the investor. Within that wide margin the exercise of judgment by the investor cannot be regarded as involving State aid. It is in evaluation of the justification for the provision of funds that the Member State has to decide if a notification is necessary in conformity with its obligation under Article [88](3). In this context, it is useful to recall the arrangements of the 1984 communication on public authorities" holdings which stated that where there is a presumption that a financial flow from the State to a public holding constitutes aid, the Commission shall be informed in advance. On the basis of an examination of the information received it will decide within 15 working days whether the information should be regarded as notification for the purposes of Article [88](3) (point 4.4.2). Only where there are no objective grounds to reasonably expect that an investment will give an adequate rate of return that would be acceptable to a private investor in a comparable private undertaking operating under normal market conditions, is State aid involved even when this is financed wholly or partially by public funds. It is not the Commission's intention to analyse investment projects on an *ex-ante* basis (unless notification is received in advance in conformity with Article [88](3)).

28. There is no question of the Commission using the benefit of hindsight to state that the provision of public funds constituted State aid on the sole basis that the outturn rate of return was not adequate. Only projects where the Commission considers that there were no objective or bona fide grounds to reasonably expect an adequate rate of return in a comparable private undertaking *at the moment the investment/financing* decision is made can be treated as State aid. It is only in such cases that funds are being provided more cheaply than would be available to a private undertaking, i.e. a subsidy is involved. It is obvious that, because of the inherent risks involved in any investment, not all projects will be successful and certain investments may produce a subnormal rate of return or even be a complete failure. This is also the case for private investors whose investment can result in subnormal rates of return or failures. Moreover such an approach makes no discrimination between projects which have short or long-term payback periods, as long as the risk are adequately and objectively assessed and discounted at the time the decision to invest is made, in the way that a private investor would.

29. This communication, by making clearer how the Commission applies the market economy investor principle and the criteria used to determine when aid is involved, will reduce uncertainty in this field. It is not the Commission's intention to apply the principles in this communication (in what is necessarily a complex field) in a dogmatic or doctrinaire fashion. It understands that a wide margin of judgment must come into entrepreneurial investment decisions. The principles have however to be applied when it is beyond reasonable doubt that there is no other plausible explanation for the provision of public funds other than considering them as State aid. This approach will also have to be applied to any cross-subsidization by a profitable part of a public group of undertakings of an unprofitable part. This happens in private undertakings when either the undertaking in question has a strategic plan with good hopes of long-term gain, or that the cross-subsidy has a net benefit to the group as a whole. In cases where there is cross-subsidization in public holding companies the Commission will take account of similar strategic goals. Such cross-subsidization will be considered as aid only where the Commission considers that there is no other reasonable explanation to explain the flow of funds other than that they constituted aid. For fiscal or other reasons certain enterprises, be they public or private, are often split into several legally distinct subsidiaries. However, the Commission will not normally ask for information of the flow of funds between such legally distinct subsidiaries of companies for which one consolidated report is required.

30. The Commission is also aware of the differences in approach a market economy investor may have between his minority holding in a company on the one hand and full control of a large group on the other hand. The former relationship may often be characterized as more of a speculative or even short-term interest, whereas the latter usually implies a longer-term interest. Therefore, where the public authority controls an individual public undertaking or group of undertakings it will normally be less motivated by purely short-term profit considerations than if it had merely a minority/non-controlling holding and its time horizon will accordingly be longer. The Commission will take account of the nature of the public authorities" holding in comparing their behaviour with the benchmark of the equivalent market economy investor. This remark is also valid for the evaluation of calls for extra funds to financially restructure a company as opposed to calls for funds required to finance specific projects.[26] In addition the Commission is also aware that a market economy investor's attitude is generally more favourably disposed towards calls for extra finance when the undertaking or group requiring the extra finance has a good record of providing adequate returns by way of dividends or capital accumulation on past investments. Where a company has underperformed in this respect in comparison with equivalent companies, this request for finance will normally be examined more sceptically by the private investor/owner called upon to provide the extra finance. Where this call for finance is necessary to protect the

value of the whole investment the public authority like a private investor can be expected to take account of this wider context when examining whether the commitment of new funds is commercially justified. Finally where a decision is made to abandon a line of activity because of its lack of medium/long-term commercial viability, a public group, like a private group, can be expected to decide the timing and scale of its run down in the light of the impact on the overall credibility and structure of the group.

Notes

[26] This may be particularly important for public undertakings that have been deliberately undercapitalized by the public authority owner for reasons extraneous to commercial justifications (e.g. public expenditure restrictions).

31. In evaluating any calls for extra finance a shareholder would typically have at his disposal the information necessary to judge whether he is justified in responding to these calls for additional finance. The extent and detail of the information provided by the undertaking requiring finance may vary according to the nature and volume of the funding required, to the relationship between the undertaking and the shareholder and even to the past performance of the undertaking in providing an adequate return.[27] A market economy investor would not usually provide any additional finance without the appropriate level of information. Similar considerations would normally apply to public undertakings seeking finance. This financial information in the form of the relevant documentation should be made available at the specific request of the Commission if it is considered that it would help in evaluating the investment proposals from the point of view of deciding whether or not their financing constitutes aid.[28] The Commission will not disclose, information supplied to it as it is covered by the obligation of professional secrecy. Therefore, investment projects will not be scrutinized by the Commission in advance except where aid is involved and prior notification in conformity with Article [88](3) is required. However, where it has reasonable grounds to consider that aid may be granted in the provision of finance to public undertakings, the Commission, pursuant to its responsibilities under Articles [87] and [88], may ask for the information from Member States necessary to determine whether aid is involved in the specific case in question.

Notes

[27] Minority shareholders who have no "inside" information on the running of the company may require a more formal justification for providing funds than a controlling owner who may in fact be involved at board level in formulating strategies and is already party to detailed information on the undertaking's financial situation.

[28] The provision of this information on request falls within scope of the Commission's powers of investigation of aid under Articles [87] and [88] in combination with Article [10] of the [EC] Treaty and under Article 1(c) of the Transparency Directive which states that the use to which public funds are put should be made transparent.

VI. Compatibility of Aid

32. Each Member State is free to choose the size and nature of its public sector and to vary it over time. The Commission recognizes that when the State decides to exercise its right to public ownership, commercial objectives are not always the essential motivation. Public enterprises are sometimes expected to fulfil non-commercial functions alongside, or in addition to, their basic commercial activities. For example, in some Member States public companies may be used as a locomotive for the economy, as part of efforts to counter recession, to restructure troubled industries or to act as catalysts for regional development. Public companies may be expected to locate in less developed regions where costs are higher or to maintain employment at levels beyond purely commercial levels. The Treaty enables the Commission to take account of such considerations where they are justified in the Community interest. In addition the provision of some services may entail a public service element, which may even be enforced by political or legal constraints. These non-commercial objectives/functions (i.e. social goods) have a cost which ultimately has to be financed by the State (i.e. taxpayers) either in the form of new finance (e.g. capital injections) or a reduced rate of return on capital invested. This aiding of the provision of public services can, in certain circumstances, distort competition. Unless one of the derogations of the Treaty is

applicable, public undertakings are not exempted from the rules of competition by the imposition of these non-commercial objectives.

33. If the Commission is to carry out its duties under the Treaty, it must have the information available to determine whether the financial flows to public undertakings constitute aid, to quantify such aid and then to determine if one of the derogations provided for in the Treaty is applicable. This communication limits itself to the objective of increasing transparency for the financial flows in question which is an essential first step. To decide, as a second step, whether any aid that is identified is compatible, is a question which is not dealt with because such a decision will be in accordance with the well known principles used by the Commission in the area to which no change is envisaged. (It should be stressed that the Commission is concerned with aid only when it has an impact on intra-Community trade and competition. Thus, if aid is granted for a non-commercial purpose to a public undertaking which has no impact on intra-Community trade and competition, Article [87](1) is not applicable.) This obligation of submitting to Community control all aid having a Community dimension is the necessary counterpart to the right of Member States being able to export freely to other Member States and is the basis of a common market.

VII. Different Forms of State Intervention

34. In deciding whether any public funds to public undertakings constitute aid, the Commission must take into account the factors discussed below for each type of intervention covered by this communication — capital injections, guarantees, loans, return on investment.[29] These factors are given as a guide to Member States of the likely Commission attitude in individual cases. In applying this policy the Commission will bear in mind the practicability of the market economy investor principle described above. This communication takes over the definition of public funds and public undertakings used in the transparency Directive. This is given as guidance for Member States as to the general attitude of the Commission. However, the Commission will obviously have to prove in individual cases of application of this policy that public undertakings within the meaning of Article [86] and State resources within the meaning of Article [87](1) are involved, just as it has in individual cases in the past. As far as any provision of information under the transparency Directive is concerned, these definitions have been upheld by the Court for the purposes of the Directive and there is no further obligation on the Commission to justify them.

Notes

[29] This list is not exhaustive.

Capital injections

35. A capital injection is considered to be an aid when it is made in circumstances which would not be acceptable to an investor operating under normal market conditions. This is normally taken to mean a situation where the structure and future prospects for the company are such that a normal return (by way of dividend payments or capital appreciation) by reference to a comparable private enterprise cannot be expected within a reasonable time. Thus, the 1984 communication on capital injections remains valid.

A market economy investor would normally provide equity finance if the present value[30] of expected future cash flows from the intended project (accruing to the investor by way of dividend payments and/or capital gains and adjusted for risk) exceed the new outlay. The context within which this will have to be interpreted was explained above in paragraphs 27 to 31.

Notes

[30] Future cash flows discounted at the company's cost of capital (in-house discount rate).

---

36. In certain Member States investors are obliged by law to contribute additional equity to firms whose capital base has been eroded by continuous losses to below a predetermined level. Member States have claimed that these capital injections cannot be considered as aid as they are merely fulfilling a legal obligation. However, this "obligation" is more apparent than real. Commercial investors faced with such a situation must also consider all other options including the possibility of liquidating or otherwise running down their investment. If this liquidation or running down

proves to be the more financially sound option taking into account the impact on the group and is not followed, then any subsequent capital injection or any other State intervention has to be considered as constituting aid.

37. When comparing the actions of the State and those of a market economy investor in particular when a company is not making a loss, the Commission will evaluate the financial position of the company at the time it is/was proposed to inject additional capital. On the basis of an evaluation of the following items the Commission will examine whether there is an element of aid contained in the amount of capital invested. This aid element consists in the cost of the investment less the value of the investment, appropriately discounted. It is stressed that the items listed below are indispensable to any analysis but not necessarily sufficient since account must also be taken of the principles set out in paragraphs 27 to 31 above and of the question whether the funds required are for investment projects or a financial restructuring.

37.1. *Profit and loss situation.* An analysis of the results of the company spread over several years. Relevant profitability ratios would be extracted and the underlying trends subject to evaluation.

37.2. *Financial indicators.* The debt/equity ratio (gearing of the company) would be compared with generally accepted norms, industry-sector averages and those of close competitors, etc. The calculation of various liquidity and solvency ratios would be undertaken to ascertain the financial standing of the company (this is particularly relevant in relation to the assessment of the loan finance potential of a company operating under normal market conditions). The Commission is aware of the difficulties involved in making such comparisons between Member States due in particular to different accounting practices or standards. It will bear this in mind when choosing the appropriate reference points to be used as a comparison with the public undertakings receiving funds.

37.3. *Financial projections.* In cases where funding is sought to finance an investment programme then obviously this programme and the assumptions upon which it is based have to be studied in detail to see if the investment is justified.

37.4. *Market situation.* Market trends (past performance and most importantly future prospects) and the company's market share over a reasonable time period should be examined and future projections subjected to scrutiny.

Guarantees

38. The position currently adopted by the Commission in relation to loan guarantees has recently been communicated to Member States.[31] It regards all guarantees given by the State directly or by way of delegation through financial institutions as falling within the scope of Article [87](1) of the [EC] Treaty. It is only if guarantees are assessed at the granting stage that all the distortions or potential distortions of competition can be detected. The fact that a firm receives a guarantee even if it is never called in may enable it to continue trading, perhaps forcing competitors who do not enjoy such facilities to go out of business. The firm in question has therefore received support which has disadvantaged its competitors i.e. it has been aided and this has had an effect on competition. An assessment of the aid element of guarantees will involve an analysis of the borrower's financial situation (see point 37 above). The aid element of these guarantees would be the difference between the rate which the borrower would pay in a free market and that actually obtained with the benefit of the guarantee, net of any premium paid for the guarantee. Creditors can only safely claim against a government guarantee where this is made and given explicitly to either a public or a private undertaking. If this guarantee is deemed incompatible with the common market following evaluation with respect to the derogations under the Treaty, reimbursement of the value of any aid will be made by the undertaking to the government even if this means a declaration of bankruptcy but creditors" claims will be honoured. These provisions apply equally to public and private undertakings and no additional special arrangements are necessary for public enterprises other than the remarks made below.

Notes
[31] Communication to all Member States dated 5 April 1989, as amended by letter of 12 October 1989.

38.1. Public enterprises whose legal status does not allow bankruptcy are in effect in receipt of permanent aid on all borrowings equivalent to a guarantee when such status allows the enterprises in question to obtain credit on terms more favourable than would otherwise be available.

38.2. Where a public authority takes a hold in a public undertaking of a nature such that it is exposed to unlimited liability instead of the normal limited liability, the Commission will treat this as a guarantee on all the funds which are subject to unlimited liability.[32] It will then apply the above described principles to this guarantee.

Notes
[32] See point 24 above.

Loans

39. When a lender operating under normal market economy conditions provides loan facilities for a client, he is aware of the inherent risk involved in any such venture. The risk is of course that the client will be unable to repay the loan. The potential loss extends to the full amount advanced (the capital) and any interest due but unpaid at the time of default. The risk attached to any loan arrangement is usually reflected in two distinct parameters:

(a) the interest rate charged;
(b) the security sought to cover the loan.

40. Where the perceived risk attached to the loan is high then *ceteris paribus* both (a) and (b) above can be expected to reflect this fact. It is when this does not take place in practice that the Commission will consider that the firm in question has had an advantage conferred on it, i.e. has been aided. Similar considerations apply where the assets pledged by a fixed or floating charge on the company would be insufficient to repay the loan in full. The Commission will in future examine carefully the security used to cover loan finance. This evaluation process would be similar to that proposed for capital injections (see point 37 above).

41. The aid element amounts to the difference between the rate which the firm should pay (which itself is dependent on its financial position and the security which it can offer on foot of the loan) and that actually paid. (This one-stage analysis of the loan is based on the presumption that in the event of default the lender will exercise his legal right to recover any monies due to him). In the extreme case, i.e. where an unsecured loan is given to a company which under normal circumstances would be unable to obtain finance (for example because its prospects of repaying the loan are poor) then the loan effectively equates a grant payment and the Commission would evaluate it as such.

42. The situation would be viewed from the point of view of the lender at the moment the loan is approved. If he chooses to lend (or is directly or indirectly forced to do so as may be the case with State-controlled banks) on conditions which could not be considered as normal in banking terms, then there is an element of aid involved which has to be quantified. These provisions would of course also apply to private undertakings obtaining loans from public financial institutions.

Return on investments

43. The State, in common with any other market economy investor, should expect a normal return obtained by comparable private undertakings on its capital investments by way of dividends or capital appreciation.[33] The rate of return will be measured by the profit (after depreciation but before taxation and disposals) expressed as a percentage of assets employed. It is therefore a measure that is neutral with respect to the form of finance used in each undertaking (i.e. debt or equity) which for public undertakings may be decided for reasons extraneous to purely commercial considerations. If this normal return is neither forthcoming beyond the short term nor is likely to be forthcoming in the long term (with the uncertainty of this longer-term future gain not appropriately accounted for) and no remedial action has been taken by the public undertaking to rectify the situation, then it can be assumed that the entity is being indirectly aided as the State is foregoing the benefit which a market economy investor would expect from a similar investment. A normal rate of return will be defined with reference where possible being made to comparable private companies. The Commission is aware of the difficulties involved in making such comparisons between Member States — see particularly point 37. In addition the

difference in capital markets, currency fluctuations and interest rates between Member States further complicate international comparisons of such ratios. Where accounting practices even within a single Member State make accurate asset valuation hazardous, thereby undermining rate of return calculations, the Commission will examine the possibility of using either adjusted valuations or other simpler criteria such as operating cash flow (after depreciation but before disposals) as a proxy of economic performance.

When faced with an inadequate rate of return a private undertaking would either take action to remedy the situation or be obliged to do so by its shareholders. This would normally involve the preparation of a detailed plan to increase overall profitability. If a public undertaking has an inadequate rate of return, the Commission could consider that this situation contains elements of aid, which should be analysed with respect to Article [87]. In these circumstances, the public undertaking is effectively getting its capital cheaper than the market rate, i.e. equivalent to a subsidy.

Notes

[33] The foregoing of a normal return on public funds falls within the scope of the Transparency Directive.

44. Similarly, if the State forgoes dividend income from a public undertaking and the resultant retained profits do not earn a normal rate of return as defined above then the company in question is effectively being subsidized by the State. It may well be that the State sees it as preferable for reasons not connected with commercial considerations to forgo dividends (or accept reduced dividend payments) rather than make regular capital injections into the company. The end result is the same and this regular "funding" has to be treated in the same way as new capital injections and evaluated in accordance with the principles set out above.

45. **Duration**

After an initial period of five years, the Commission will review the application of the policy described in this communication. On the basis of this review, and after consulting Member States, the Commission may propose any modifications which it considers appropriate.

F5

COMMUNICATION FROM THE COMMISSION

Services of general interest in Europe

(2001/C 17/04)

Official Journal C 17, 19.1.2001, p. 4

Celex No: 52001XC0119(02)

Commentary
Communication: B&C: 11.002 F&N: 6.171

EXECUTIVE SUMMARY

Services of general interest are a key element in the European model of society. The new Article 16 in the EC Treaty now confirms their place among the shared values of the Union and their role in promoting social and territorial cohesion. These services also contribute to the overall competitiveness of the European economy and are provided in the context of continuously evolving markets and technologies. The globalisation of trade, the completion of the internal market and rapid technological change bring about increasing pressure to open new sectors to competition. It is against this background that the European Council of Lisbon requested the Commission to update its Communication of 1996 on services of general interest in Europe.

It is above all the responsibility of public authorities at the appropriate local, regional or national level and in full transparency to define the missions of services of general interest and the way they will be fulfilled. The Community will ensure in the application of the Treaty rules and with the instruments at its disposal that the performance of such services, in terms of quality and prices, responds best to the needs of their users and of citizens at large.

In some sectors, whose dimension and network structure give them a natural European dimension, Community action has already been taken. The Communication provides currently available information on the positive impact of this action on the availability, quality and affordability of services of general interest in the sectors concerned.

The experience gained so far also confirms the full compatibility of the Treaty rules on competition and the internal market with high standards in the provision of services of general interest. In certain circumstances, in particular where market forces alone do not result in a satisfactory provision of services, public authorities may entrust certain operators of services with obligations of general interest and where necessary grant them special or exclusive rights and/or devise a funding mechanism for their provision.

Member States and the operators concerned need legal certainty. The Communication clarifies both the scope and criteria of application of internal market and competition rules. First of all, such rules apply only inasmuch as activities concerned are economic activities that affect trade between Member States. Where the rules apply, compatibility with those rules is based on three principles:
— neutrality with regard to the public or private ownership of companies,
— Member States' freedom to define services of general interest, subject to control for manifest error,
— proportionality requiring that restrictions of competition and limitations of the freedoms of the single market do not exceed what is necessary to guarantee effective fulfilment of the mission.

As the context continues to evolve and the Commission gains further experience in the application of internal market and competition rules, it will provide further clarification.

The communication also gives perspectives on how, building upon Article 16, the Community in partnership with local, regional and national authorities can develop a proactive policy at European level to ensure that all the citizens of Europe have access to the best services.

1. INTRODUCTION

1. In 1996 the Commission presented a Communication on services of general interest in Europe.[1] In that communication, the Commission stressed the importance of missions of general interest in order to attain the fundamental objectives of the European Union. It advocated that a reference be inserted in this sense in the EC Treaty. The definitions of terms,[2] the views and the objectives laid down in the 1996 communication on the future role of these services in the context of the single market remain valid today. This communication updates that of 1996.

Notes
[1] OJ C 281, 26.9.1996, p. 3.
[2] See Annex II.

---

2. Since the adoption of the first communication, a number of developments have occurred. As suggested by the Commission, the Amsterdam Treaty introduced a reference to the role of services of general interest. The new Article 16 of the EC Treaty recognises the fundamental character of the values underpinning such services and the need for the Community to take into account their function in devising and implementing all its policies, placing it among the principles of the Treaty: "Without prejudice to Articles 73, 86 and 87, and given the place occupied by services of general economic interest in the shared values of the Union as well as their role in promoting social and territorial cohesion, the Community and the Member States, each within their respective

powers and within the scope of application of this Treaty, shall take care that such services operate on the basis of principles and conditions, which enable them to fulfil their missions."

3. The 1996 communication stated that, from the point of view of the Commission, far from being incompatible, services of general economic interest, internal market and Community competition policy were complementary in the pursuit of the fundamental objectives of the Treaty. Their interplay must benefit individual citizens and society as a whole.

4. Since 1996, markets, technology and user needs have continued to develop apace. Experience has been gained with those sectors that were then in the process of liberalisation under the single market programme. Further liberalisation occurred at Community level, while securing and in some cases improving the level of quality and protection for users. As the internal market deepened, new issues have arisen relating to the delimitation of certain services that were previously supplied primarily on a non-competitive basis, but which now elicit, or may elicit, competitors. Moreover, technological developments and in particular the advent of the Information Society lead to the conclusion that the territorial approach to some of these services is outdated and that they should be considered from a cross-border perspective.

5. In spite of the positive effects of liberalisation, concerns have continued to be expressed concerning services of general interest and the Community action. Linked to changes in technology and the overall regulatory environment as well as evolving consumer demand, a concern exists on the part of citizens that the quality of services of general interest might suffer. Building on this concern, traditional providers and the public authorities that support them claim that the application of Community law could jeopardise the structures for the provision of such services, which have proved their worth over a long period, and with them the quality of services to the public. Competing providers in the private sector on the contrary claim that existing arrangements give an unfair advantage to the organisation entrusted by the public authorities with the provision of such services and infringe Community law.

6. Against that background and at the request of the European Council of Lisbon, reiterated by that of Feira, the Commission has undertaken to update its communication of 1996. The objective is twofold:
   — to provide further clarification on the respective roles of different levels of public authorities and of the competition and internal market provisions applied to services of general interest in order to respond to the request for greater legal certainty on the part of operators. Of special concern is the field of application of the rules on State aid,
   — to further develop the European framework relating to the good functioning of services of general interest, in which local, regional and national authorities as well as the Community have their role to play, in line with Article 16 of the EC Treaty.

7. The communication is organised in several sections. In Section 2 the Commission sets out its views on the mission fulfilled by services of general interest. Section 3 provides clarification on the application of competition and single market rules to services of general interest. Section 4 presents some preliminary results from experience with the application of the universal service principle in sectors liberalised under the single market programme. Further information on the situation of individual sectors is provided in Annex I. Section 5 provides orientation for further action to enhance the quality and efficient provision of services of general interest as a key element in the European model of society.

2. The Mission of Services of General Interest

8. At the heart of Community policy on services of general interest lies the interest of citizens. Services of general interest make an important contribution to the overall competitiveness of European industry and to economic, social and territorial cohesion. As users of these services, European citizens have come to expect high quality services at affordable prices. It is thus users and their requirements that are the main focus of public action in this domain. The Community protects the objectives of general interest and the mission of serving the public.

9. In order to fulfil their mission, it is necessary for the relevant public authorities to act in full transparency, by stipulating with some precision the needs of users for which services of general interest are being established, who is in charge of setting up and enforcing the relevant obligations and how these obligations are going to be fulfilled. Action at the appropriate level, Community, national,

regional or local level, needs to be taken to establish criteria for services of general interest. Such action must be mutually supportive and coherent.

10. The needs of users should be defined widely. Those of consumers clearly play an important role. For consumers, a guarantee of universal access, high quality and affordability constitutes the basis of their needs. Enterprises, and in particular, small and medium-sized enterprises, are also major users of services of general interest, whose needs must be met. Citizens" concerns are also of a wider nature, such as:
    — that for a high level of environment protection,
    — specific needs of certain categories of the population, such as the handicapped and those on low incomes,
    — complete territorial coverage of essential services in remote or inaccessible areas.

Commentary
para 10: F&N: 6.141

---

11. A number of principles can help define users" requirements for services of general interest. These principles include:
    — clear definition of basic obligations to ensure good quality service provision, high levels of public health and physical safety of services,
    — full transparency, e.g. on tariffs, terms and conditions of contracts, choice and financing of providers,
    — choice of service and where appropriate, choice of supplier and effective competition between suppliers,
    — existence, where justified, of regulatory bodies independent of operators and redress in the form of complaint handling and dispute settlement mechanisms.
    They may also include representation and active participation of users in the definition of services and choice of forms of payment.

12. Suppliers of services of general interest also play an important role and through their long experience in meeting the needs of users have much to contribute to the further development of such services. They therefore require adequate consultation alongside that of users.[3] However, when organising consultation, public authorities need to clearly separate the needs of users from those of suppliers.

Notes
[3] The ETUC and the CEEP have proposed a "Charter of services of general interest", which represents an important contribution to the current debate on the future of services of general interest.

---

13. Public authorities are faced with the question of how to ensure that the missions they assign to services of general interest are executed according to a high standard of quality and in the most efficient manner. There are several ways in which such missions can be fulfilled. The choice will be made taking into account in particular:
    — technical and economic characteristics of the service in question,
    — the specific requirements of users,
    — cultural and historical specificity in the Member State concerned.
    The choice of different means for different services — or even for the same service where circumstances vary from one Member State to another or within a Member State — should therefore not be seen as contradictory, but on the contrary as an essential feature of effectiveness.

3. Services of General Interest and the Single Market

14. Services of general economic interest are different from ordinary services in that public authorities consider that they need to be provided even where the market may not have sufficient incentives to do so. This is not to deny that in many cases the market will be the best mechanism for providing such services. Many basic requirements, such as food, clothing, shelter, are provided exclusively or overwhelmingly by the market. However, if the public authorities consider that certain services are in the general interest and market forces may not result in a satisfactory provision, they can lay down a number of specific service provisions to meet these needs in the form

of service of general interest obligations. The fulfilment of these obligations may trigger, albeit not necessarily, the granting of special or exclusive rights, or the provision of specific funding mechanisms. The definition of a specific mission of general interest and the attendant service required to fulfil that mission need not imply any specific method of service provision. The classical case is the universal service obligation,[4] i.e. the obligation to provide a certain service throughout the territory at affordable tariffs and on similar quality conditions, irrespective of the profitability of individual operations.

Notes

[4] The notion of universal service and that of public service obligation have been acknowledged by the case-law of the Court (Case C-320/91 *Corbeau* [1993]; Case C-393/92 *Almelo* [1994]) and developed in Community legislation for those services, for which a common regulatory framework has been put in place to achieve a single European market (see below, Section 4).

15. Public authorities may decide to apply general interest obligations on all operators in a market or, in some cases, to designate one or a limited number of operators with specific obligations, without granting special or exclusive rights. In this way, the greatest competition is allowed and users retain maximum freedom with regard to choice of service provider. Where only one or a limited number of all operators competing in a certain market are charged with public service obligations while the others are not, it may be appropriate to involve all operators active in that market in the financing of the net extra costs of the service of general interest by a system of additional charges or a public service fund. In this case, it is important that the share borne by any undertaking should be proportionate to its activity in the market and be clearly separated from other charges that it may bear in the normal exercise of its activities.

16. Today, public voice telephony, for example, is provided throughout the Community under universal service obligations defined in Community legislation, notwithstanding the complete liberalisation of the telecom sector in 1998. Indeed, the decisions taken in the early 1990s in favour of gradual liberalisation were themselves a reflection of market and technological developments, which meant that retaining special and exclusive rights in the sector was no longer an effective and proportionate means of securing the revenue needed by operators to provide universal service. Within a competitive market, the Community framework allowed Member States to put in place mechanisms to share the costs of providing universal service as defined at Community level. However, most Member States have in fact not found it necessary to activate such schemes, given the relatively low costs involved.

17. However, certain services of general interest do not lend themselves to a plurality of providers, for instance where only one single provider can be economically viable. In these circumstances, public authorities will usually grant exclusive and special rights for providing the service of general interest by awarding concessions for limited periods through tendering procedures. Competition at the moment of the award of the tender is meant to ensure that the missions assigned to a service of general interest are met at low cost to the public.

Commentary
para 17: B&C: 11.002

18. Where neither of the first two options allows for satisfactory fulfilment of the mission of general interest, it may be necessary to combine entrustment of one single operator or a limited number of operators with the particular public service task, with the granting or maintaining of special or exclusive rights in favour of that single operator or group of operators. In this situation, as well as in the above-described situation where exclusive rights have been granted subject to a tendering procedure, public authorities may ensure appropriate funding enabling the entrusted operators to perform the particular public service task assigned to them.

Commentary
para 18: B&C: 11.050 F&N: 6.135

19. Observing the EC Treaty provisions and in particular those on competition and the internal market is fully compatible with ensuring the provision of services of general interest. Article 86 of

the Treaty, and in particular Article 86(2), is the central provision for reconciling the Community objectives, including those of competition and internal market freedoms on the one hand, with the effective fulfilment of the mission of general economic interest entrusted by public authorities on the other hand. This Article reads:

"1. In the case of public undertakings or undertakings to which Member States grant special or exclusive rights, Member States shall neither enact or maintain in force any measure contrary to the rules contained in this Treaty, in particular to those rules provided in Article 12 and Articles 81 to 89.

2. Undertakings entrusted with the operation of services of general economic interest or having the character of a revenue-producing monopoly shall be subject to the rules contained in this Treaty, in particular to the rules on competition, in so far as the application of such rules does not obstruct the performance, in law or in fact, of the particular tasks assigned to them. The development of trade must not be affected to such an extent as would be contrary to the interest of the Community.

3. The Commission shall ensure the application of the provisions of this Article, and shall, where necessary, address appropriate directives or decisions to Member States."

20. To understand how these provisions affect the arrangements made by the public authorities to ensure that certain services are provided to the public, it is useful to articulate three principles that underlie the application of Article 86. They are: neutrality, freedom to define, and proportionality.

21. Neutrality as regards the public or private ownership of companies is guaranteed by Article 295 of the EC Treaty. On the one hand, the Commission does not question whether undertakings responsible for providing general interest services should be public or private. Therefore, it does not require privatisation of public undertakings. On the other hand, the rules of the Treaty and in particular competition and internal market rules apply regardless of the ownership of an undertaking (public or private).

22. Member States' freedom to define means that Member States are primarily responsible for defining what they regard as services of general economic interest on the basis of the specific features of the activities. This definition can only be subject to control for manifest error. They may grant special or exclusive rights that are necessary to the undertakings entrusted with their operation, regulate their activities and, where appropriate, fund them. In areas that are not specifically covered by Community regulation Member States enjoy a wide margin for shaping their policies, which can only be subject to control for manifest error. Whether a service is to be regarded as a service of general interest and how it should be operated are issues that are first and foremost decided locally. The role of the Commission is to ensure that the means employed are compatible with Community law. However, in every case, for the exception provided for by Article 86(2) to apply, the public service mission needs to be clearly defined and must be explicitly entrusted through an act of public authority (including contracts).[5] This obligation is necessary to ensure legal certainty as well as transparency vis-à-vis the citizens and is indispensable for the Commission to carry out its proportionality assessment.

Notes

[5] Case C-159/94 *EDF* [1997].

23. Proportionality under Article 86(2) implies that the means used to fulfil the general interest mission shall not create unnecessary distortions of trade. Specifically, it has to be ensured that any restrictions to the rules of the EC Treaty, and in particular, restrictions of competition and limitations of the freedoms of the internal market do not exceed what is necessary to guarantee effective fulfilment of the mission. The performance of the service of general economic interest must be ensured and the entrusted undertakings must be able to carry the specific burden and the net extra costs of the particular task assigned to them. The Commission exercises this control of proportionality, subject to the judicial review of the Court of Justice, in a way that is reasonable and realistic, as illustrated by the use it actually makes of the decision-making powers conferred to it by Article 86(3).[6]

Notes
[6] See the Commission's annual reports on competition policy.

24. The principles formulated in Article 86 allow for a flexible and context-sensitive balance that takes account of the Member States' different circumstances and objectives as well as the technical constraints that may vary from one sector to another.

25. Experience provides a sufficiently large typology, concerning the specific ways of reconciling the requirements of general interest and those of competition and internal market.[7] As described above, Member States have several options for ensuring the provision of services of general interest, ranging from opening up the market to competition over imposing public service obligations up to conferring exclusive or special rights to a single operator or a limited number of operators, with or without provision of funding.

Notes
[7] As an example for the compatibility of funding public service broadcasting with competition law on the basis of Article 86(2) see Commission Decision of 24.2.1999 in case NN 70/98 *Kinderkanal and Phoenix* OJ 1999 C 238/3, and Commission Decision of 29.9.1999 in case NN 88/98 *BBC News* 24 OJ 2000 C 78/6.

26. Concerning the particular issue of funding, the European Court of First Instance recently decided that compensation granted by the State to an undertaking for the performance of general interest duties constitutes State aid within the meaning of Article 87(1) of the EC Treaty.[8] In so far as it does not benefit from the exemptions foreseen in Article 73 or 87, it may, however, be compatible with the EC Treaty on the basis of Article 86(2). This is the case where all conditions of this provision are fulfilled and, in particular, the compensation does not exceed the net extra costs of the particular task entrusted to the undertaking. The Commission considers that whenever the compensation is fixed for an appropriate period following an open, transparent and non-discriminating procedure, there is the presumption that such aid is compatible with the State aid rules of the Treaty.[9]

Notes
[8] Case T-106/95 *FFSA* [1997]; case T-46/97 *SIC* [2000]; case C-174/97P *FFSA* [1998].
[9] For an application of the same principle, see the draft Regulation on land transport COM(7) 2000/9 of 26 July 2000 and the directive on transparency Commission Directive 2000/52/EC of 26.7.2000 amending Directive 80/723/EEC (OJ L193 of 29.7.2000).

27. Even before delimiting the extent of the derogation from competition and internal market rules afforded by Article 86, it is worth assessing whether such Community rules apply at all. In making this assessment, one should bear in mind three considerations: the distinction between economic and non-economic activities, the effect on trade between Member States and the Community policy towards cases of minor importance.

28. The conditions of Article 86 refer to services of general <u>economic</u> interest. In general, internal market and competition rules do not apply to non-economic activities and therefore have no impact on services of general interest to the extent to which these services constitute non-economic activities. This means in the first place that matters which are intrinsically prerogatives of the State (such as ensuring internal and external security, the administration of justice, the conduct of foreign relations and other exercises of official authority) are excluded from the application of competition and internal market rules. Therefore, Article 86 and its conditions do not come into play. The European Court of Justice has held, for example, that an organism controlling and supervising the air space and collecting charges for the use of its air navigation system,[10] or a private law body carrying out anti-pollution surveillance in a sea port,[11] exercise powers which are typically those of a public authority and which are not of an economic nature.

Notes
[10] Case C-364/92 *SAT/Eurocontrol* [1994].
[11] Case C-343/95 *Diego Calí* [1997].

29. In the second place, services such as national education and compulsory basic social security schemes are also excluded from the application of competition and internal market rules. With regard to the

former, the European Court of Justice ruled that the State, in establishing and maintaining such a system, is not seeking to engage in gainful activity but is fulfilling its duty towards its own population in the social, cultural and educational fields.[12] With regard to the latter, the European Court of Justice held that organisations charged with the management of State-imposed social security schemes, such as compulsory sickness insurance, which are based on the principle of solidarity, non-profit making and where the benefits paid are not proportional to the amount of the compulsory contributions, fulfil an exclusively social function and do not exercise an economic activity.[13]

Notes

[12] Case 263/86 *Humbel* [1988].
[13] Cases C-159/91 and C-160/91 *Poucet* [1993].

30. More generally, according to the case law of the Court of Justice,[14] many activities conducted by organisations performing largely social functions, which are not profit oriented and which are not meant to engage in industrial or commercial activity, will normally be excluded from the Community competition and internal market rules. This takes into account several non-economic activities of organisations such as trade unions, political parties, churches and religious societies, consumer associations, learned societies, charities as well as relief and aid organisations. However, whenever such an organisation, in performing a general interest task, engages in economic activities, application of Community rules to these economic activities will be guided by the principles in this Communication respecting in particular the social and cultural environment in which the relevant activities take place. Moreover, where Community law would apply to these activities, the Commission will also examine, in the light of a more general reflection on the use of its discretionary powers, whether the interests of the Community require to proceed with regard to these cases, subject to its legal obligations established in the EC Treaty.

Notes

[14] Case C-109/92 *Wirth* [1993].

31. It should also be pointed out that Community competition law only applies where the conduct in question is liable to affect trade between Member States. Likewise, the rules in the Treaty establishing the freedom to provide services do not apply when all the aspects of such activities are confined within a single Member State.

32. Concerning antitrust rules (Articles 81 and 82 of the EC Treaty), an activity which affects the market only insignificantly — and this may be the case of a number of services of general interest of local character — will normally not affect trade between Member States and therefore will not be subject to the Community rules.[15] Reference should also be made to the policy of not pursuing under the Community competition rules, cases of minor importance, which the Commission has explained in detail.[16] Again, many local services are likely to be considered cases of minor importance and therefore the Commission will not have to pursue alleged violations of antitrust rules in this context.

Notes

[15] According to the European Court of Justice (Cases C-215/96 and C-216/96 *Bagnasco* [1999]), there is effect on trade between Member States where it is possible to foresee with a sufficient degree of probability on the basis of a set of objective factors of law or fact that the conduct in question may have an influence on the pattern of trade between Member States, such as might prejudice the realisation of the aim of a single market in all the Member States. In establishing these criteria, reference must be made to the position and the importance of the parties on the relevant market.
[16] Notice concerning agreements of minor importance falling outside Article 81(1) (OJ C 372, 9.12.1997, p. 13). [See now Commission Notice on agreements of minor importance which do not appreciably restrict competition under Article 81(1) of the Treaty establishing the European Community (*de minimis*), 2001/C 368/07 (OJ C 368, 22.12.01, p.13).]

33. As for the assessment under the State aid rules of the EC Treaty, it is true that the relatively small amount of aid or the relatively small size of the undertaking which receives it does not as such exclude the possibility that intra-Community trade might be affected. However, under settled case-law, the criterion of trade being affected is only met if the recipient undertaking carries on

an economic activity involving trade between Member States. The Commission also sets ceilings, under which it considers that State aid rules do not apply.[17] As a result, many local services are likely to be excluded from the scope of State aid rules.

Notes

[17] Notice on the *de minimis* rule for State aid (OJ C 68, 6.3.1996, p. 9), to be succeeded by a *de minimis* Regulation on State aid, draft published in OJ C 89, 28.3.2000, p. 6. [See now Commission Regulation (EC) No 1998/2006 of 15 December 2006 on the application of Articles 87 and 88 of the EC Treaty to *de minimis* aid (OJ L379, 12.12.2006, p. 5).]

34. Moreover, public funding for services of general economic interest that may be liable to affect trade must be examined in the light of the specific provisions on State aid in the Treaty to see whether it is nevertheless permissible. Besides the exception provided for by Article 86(2) explained above, a number of specific exemptions from the ban on State aid are available. Of particular interest are, for instance, the derogations provided under Article 73 for aid to transport and under Article 87(3)(d) for aid to promote culture and heritage conservation.[18] Conditions for compatibility under Article 87(3) have been laid down in frameworks or guidelines such as those for State aids for small and medium-sized enterprises [19] (SMEs), undertakings in deprived urban areas,[20] employment[21] and training,[22] national regional aid,[23] environmental protection[24] and research and development.[25]

Notes

[18] In order to be able to benefit from the derogation to the general prohibition of State aid laid down in Art. 87(3)(d), the aid must be used for cultural purposes, e.g. film production. See for instance the Commission Decision of 29 July 1998 not to raise objections to the French support scheme for the production of films (N 3/98, OJ 1998 C 279) and the subsequent decisions not to raise objections to the support schemes for the production of films in Germany (Bund) (N 4/1998, Decision of 21.4.1999, OJ 1999 C 272/4), Ireland (N 237/2000, Decision of 28.6.2000, not yet published in the OJ), The Netherlands (N 486/1997, Decision of 25.11.1998, OJ 1999 C 120/2) and Sweden (N 748/1999, Decision of 2.2.2000, OJ 2000 C 134/3). As can be seen from these decisions, Art. 87(3)(d) allows aid to be granted to film production according to the specific circumstances in each Member State, and notably for the flexibility in the assessment of aid to difficult and low budget films. Pending the outcome of the review of the support schemes in other Member States, the Commission will assess the need for a more precise framework. This will be done in close consultation with the Member States (see the Commission Communication of 14 December 1999 on "The principles and guidelines for the Community's audiovisual policy in the digital age", COM(1999) 657 final).

[19] Guidelines on State aid for SMEs (OJ C 213, 23.7.1996, p. 4); to be succeeded by a block exemption. Regulation for State aid to SMEs, draft published in OJ C 89, 28.3.2000, p. 15. [See now Commission Regulation (EC) No 70/2001 of 12 January 2001 on the application of Articles 87 and 88 of the EC Treaty to State aid to small and medium-sized enterprises (OJ L 10, 13.1.2001, p.33).]

[20] Guidelines on State aid for undertakings in deprived urban areas (OJ C 146, 14.5.1997, p. 6).

[21] Guidelines on aid to employment (OJ C 334, 12.12.1995, p. 4). [See now Commission Regulation (EC) No 2204/2002 of 12 December 2002 on the application of Articles 87 and 88 of the EC Treaty to State aid for employment (OJ L 337, 13.12.2002, p. 3).]

[22] Framework on training aid (OJ C 343, 11.11.98, p. 10); to be succeeded by a block exemption Regulation for State aid for training, draft published in OJ C 89, 28.3.2000. [See now Commission Regulation (EC) No 68/2001 of 12 January 2001 on the application of Articles 87 and 88 of the EC Treaty to training aid (OJ L 10, 13.1.2001, p. 20).]

[23] Guidelines on national regional aid (OJ C 74, 10.3.1998, p. 9). [See now Guidelines on national regional aid for 2007–2013 (OJ C 54, 4.3.2006, p 13).]

[24] Community guidelines on State aid for environmental protection (OJ C 72, 10.3.1994, p. 3). [See now Community guidelines on State aid for environmental protection, 2001/C 37/03 (OJ C 37, 3.2.2001, p. 3).]

[25] Community framework for State aid for research and development, (OJ C 45, 17.2.1996, p. 5). [See now Community framework for State aid for research and development and innovation (OJ C 323, 30.12.2006, p 1).]

35. The principles laid down in this communication apply to any economic sector. For example, following a request of the European Council, the Commission adopted in 1998 a Report to the Council of Ministers on services of general economic interest in the banking sector,[26] based on a questionnaire addressed to all Member States. The result of the Commission's investigation was that a number of Member States consider that certain credit institutions fulfil specific tasks that constitute services of general economic interest. These tasks comprise mainly the promotion of small and medium-sized enterprises, the granting or guaranteeing of export credits, social housing loans, municipal financing, financing of infrastructure projects and regional development.

Two Member States consider the supplying by a certain group of credit institutions of a comprehensive financial infrastructure providing territorial coverage as indicated in paragraph 10 as being a service of general economic interest. The Report concludes that the compatibility of each of these systems and tasks with Article 86(2) of the EC Treaty has to be examined on a case-to-case basis.

Notes

[26] Report of the European Commission to the Council of Ministers, "Services of general economic interest in the banking sector", adopted by the Commission on 17 June 1998 and presented to the ECOFIN Council on 23 November 1998.

36. Finally, as technologies and markets evolve, public authorities and operators are progressively faced with new uncertainties regarding the application of EC law to their activities. The Commission will therefore continue to reflect on the best use it can make of the instruments at its disposal to increase legal certainty. Once it will have gained experience in dealing with new situations arising in the field of services of general interest, the Commission will endeavour to further clarify the scope of the application and the criteria for compatibility with EC rules. This will be done, in conformity with established practice, in close consultation with Member States. Instruments for doing so include communications, guidelines and block exemption regulations.

4. Experience with the Liberalisation of Certain Services of General Interest

37. At the time of the 1996 Communication, liberalisation of the markets for several major services of general interest had been decided under the single market programme, but it was too early to judge what the effects in terms of quality, price and availability of services might be. In certain sectors, particularly telecommunications, this is no longer the case. Generally, however, availability of good quality, timely data on key dimensions with which to evaluate experience in these services is still lacking. The most comprehensive information relates to telecommunications followed by air transport. With respect to energy, considerable data exist regarding price levels, and the Commission has now launched a study, building on the work already undertaken by Eurostat to constantly monitor "competition indicators", a number of factors indicating the real level of competition on the market. Furthermore, the Commission has now received replies by Member States regarding public service levels and objectives in the gas and electricity sectors, and on this basis is preparing a Communication that will serve as a benchmarking tool to maintain and increase public service standards to the higher level.

38. On the basis of currently available information, liberalisation of services under the single market programme appears to have had a positive impact on the availability, quality and affordability of services of general interest. However, this does not mean that such services are necessarily functioning satisfactorily. Other factors come in to play, such as the price of equipment required for connection, congestion or various anti-competitive practices which have not yet been adequately addressed or the lack of effective redress mechanisms for users when services do not function properly. As a result, the full benefits of liberalisation have yet to be reaped for all sections of society and all parts of the Community.

39. Universal service, in particular the definition of specific universal service obligations is a key accompaniment to market liberalisation of service sectors such as telecommunications in the European Union. The definition and guarantee of universal service ensures that the continuous accessibility and quality of established services is maintained for all users and consumers during the process of passing from monopoly provision to openly competitive markets. Universal service, within an environment of open and competitive telecommunications markets, is defined as the minimum set of services of specified quality to which all users and consumers have access in the light of specific national conditions, at an affordable price. These provisions set the starting point for competition-driven improvements in service quality and price.

4.1. Telecommunications

40. Universal service as currently defined in Community telecommunication legislation includes the provision of voice telephony, fax and voice band data transmission via modems (i.e. access

to the Internet). Users must have access at a fixed location to international and national calls, as well as emergency services. The definition also covers the provision of operator assistance, directory services, public pay phones and special facilities for customers with disabilities or with special social needs. It does not cover mobile telephony or broadband access to the Internet.

41. Concerning voice telephony, according to a recent study[27] 96% of European households have voice telephony access at home. Just over half of the remaining households either are not interested or have alternative means of access. Less than 2% do not have access to voice telephony for financial reasons. Since the beginning of 1998, all consumers have profited from significant price reductions: in the first year alone, prices went down by 40% for international, 30% for long-distance and 30% for regional calls; however, local calls have seen no major price decreases. On average, over the period 1997–1999, prices have decreased by more than 40% for residential consumers.

Notes

[27] Gallup Europe, Report: "The situation of telecommunications services in the regions of the European Union', April 2000.

42. Competition has boosted the development of mobile telephony. Penetration rates have gone up since liberalisation from 11% to 48% of the population. Low income households are more likely to rely exclusively on mobile telephony than high income ones (6% of households compared to 2%) even though the overall rate of usage rises with income. This shows that, for substantial numbers of low income households, mobile telephones constitute an acceptable alternative to fixed telephony, even in the absence of universal service obligations.

43. As Internet access via third generation mobile telephony and Internet over TV will break the dependency on computers (33% of EU households) to obtain Internet access, penetration rates are expected to grow extremely rapidly over the next five years.

44. Rural subscribers do not appear to be disadvantaged in terms of the spatial distribution of essential services. Overall, rural households have in fact more telephone equipment than households in metropolitan areas. It appears that income has much more influence on services than does rural/urban distinctions.

4.2. Transport

45. The process of gradual market opening for air transport was completed by 1 July 1998. In its Communication adopted last year, the Commission assessed the consequences of 10 years of liberalisation.[28] Liberalisation of air transport has led to an increase in the number of carriers from 132 in 1993 to 164 in 1998. The market share of incumbent national carriers has been declining steadily and the number of routes with more than two operators has trebled since 1992. An increasingly large number of promotional fares have increased the range of attractive fares for users. Flexible fares in contrast have kept on increasing. They are twice the level of promotional ones.

Notes

[28] COM(1999) 182 final of 20 July 1999.

46. The degree of competition on a route has a substantial impact on the price of air transport. The level of fares decreases when a market passes from monopoly to duopoly or towards more than two carriers. The price reduction for business fares from monopoly towards three or more carrier routes is 10%, that for full economy fares 17% and for promotional fares 24%.

47. A number of factors retard or diminish the impact of liberalisation. Access to slots and limitations on airport capacity represent a real problem for new entrants. Loyalty schemes such as frequent flier programmes favour airlines with large networks, which offer passengers greater chances to accumulate and use FFP points. This discriminates particularly against cost-effective, small-scale airlines. The high cost and low quality of ground handling services adds a fixed cost element which diminishes the ability of new entrants to compete on price. Finally, congestion and poor use of available air space means that the quality of service suffers and delays become more frequent.

48. Through the imposition of public service obligations, some of these difficulties may be overcome. Choice of the route and standards imposed are subject to control of the Commission. Since 1993, public service obligations have been imposed on more than one hundred routes within the Community, mainly in France, Ireland and Portugal but also in Sweden, Germany, Italy and the United Kingdom. But this represents only a very low percentage of the total air traffic of the Community.

49. Driven by market developments, the provision of passenger services in the rail and road sectors are undergoing important changes at present. Several operators have started to play an active role in other Member States. In parallel, Member States have started to open home markets to competition. Harmonisation of a basic level of competition and minimum requirements for transparency when awarding service contracts were considered necessary to guarantee high levels of quality. The Commission has proposed a new framework,[29] which will ensure that public transport operators are under competitive pressure to offer passengers better services, keep costs under control and ensure the highest safety level.

Notes
[29] COM(2000) 9 of 26 July 2000.

4.3. Energy

50. Compared with telecommunications or air transport, much less information is available on the impact of energy liberalisation on services of general interest. The opening to competition of the electricity and gas sectors is indeed too recent to draw operational conclusions. In most countries with the exception of Belgium, Denmark and Ireland households have benefited from a reduction in price between July 1996 and January 2000 averaging 5,2% in the EU. Small enterprises have benefited from larger reductions averaging 7,9%, albeit with substantial increases in Denmark and Greece.

4.4. The appreciation of services of general interest by consumers

51. As part of the Eurobarometer series of polls of public opinion,[30] a number of questions were asked to the households surveyed concerning their opinion about a number of services of general interest. The survey complements the more detailed data available for telecommunications from the residential report presented above. The results are of interest because they enable a comparison to be made across different types of service. However, no indication of how services have developed over time is possible. Substantial differences in the nature of responses between Member States would seem to indicate that expectations concerning services constitute an important determinant of the perceived level of satisfaction. For this reason comparisons between the different types of services are probably more illuminating than the absolute values of responses.

Notes
[30] Eurobarometer No 53 of July 2000, "The Europeans and services of general interest".

52. Consumer satisfaction on a number of dimensions (access, price, quality, information available, terms and conditions, complaints) was measured individually for a fixed basket of services, composed of telephony, electricity, gas and water supply, postal services, urban transport and intercity rail services. Both access and take up of the different services varied considerably. For instance nearly 13% do not have access to gas. Even nearly 7% claimed to have no access to intercity rail services and nearly 5% to local transport services. Electricity, the post and water supply were the services most nearly of truly universal availability. Based on the reply "not applicable" to subsequent questions, it would appear that the actual take up of services follows quite closely physical availability.

53. In terms of price, postal services received the most positive rating, followed by public utilities. Even so, substantial dissatisfaction with the current level of prices can be deduced from the fact that over 30% of respondents considered them to be unfair or excessive in every case. Telephony and long-distance rail services elicited the most unfavourable response. Quality ratings for services are generally good with the exception of transport and to a lesser extent postal services.

Combining the appreciation of price with quality, long-distance rail services clearly do not appear to be performing well. Consumers consider public utilities (electricity, gas and water) to best meet their expectations, with communications and local transport more mixed. Treatment of complaints receive also a very low level of satisfaction, deduced from the fact that for every service measured, over 45% of respondents considered the treatment to have been either bad or very bad.

5. A EUROPEAN PERSPECTIVE

54. The Community's aims remain: supporting the competitiveness of the European economy in increasingly open world markets; contributing to a high level of consumer protection and confidence by among others giving consumers more choice, better quality and lower prices, strengthening economic, social and territorial cohesion. General interest services have a key role to play in achieving these aims. Efficient services are a major determinant in the location of production activities, on account of the benefits both for the firms using them and the workers living in the area. The existence of a network of services of general interest is an essential element of social cohesion; conversely, the disappearance of such services is a telling sign of the desertification of a rural area or the degradation of a town. The Community is committed to maintaining the function of these services intact, while improving their efficiency.

55. In pursuing these aims, the Community takes due account of the principle of subsidiarity. Respect of this principle, in particular Member States' freedom to define what constitutes a service of general interest, requires a careful examination of the appropriate roles of the different levels of government in the regulation of such services. The Commission will further elaborate its position on the subject in the context of the forthcoming White Paper on Governance.

56. The new Article 16 of the Treaty explicitly recognises the economic, social and territorial cohesion role of services of general economic interest and envisages a Community duty to facilitate the achievement of their mission. The importance of these provisions was brought out by the Heads of State or Government at their summit in Lisbon in March 2000:[31]

> "The European Council considers it essential that, in the framework of the internal market and of a knowledge-based economy, full account is taken of the Treaty provisions relating to services of general economic interest, and to the undertakings entrusted with operating such services."

Notes
[31] Lisbon European Council, 23–24 March 2000, Conclusions of the Presidency, SN 100/00, point 19.

57. Both this political statement and the changes currently under way point to the need for a proactive stance on general interest services, which incorporates and goes beyond the approach based on the single market. In this vein, the Commission, in partnership with the national, regional and local levels, will continue to promote a European perspective on general interest services for the benefit of citizens on three fronts: by making the most of market opening; by strengthening European coordination and solidarity; and by developing other Community contributions in support of services of general interest.

5.1. Making the most of market opening

58. The opening up of markets for economic services, notably networked services, and the corresponding introduction of universal or public service obligations, need to be pursued in accordance with the characteristics of each sector, including the degree of market integration already achieved. The common objective is to benefit Europe's citizens through the development of a competitive single market. This objective was strongly reaffirmed by the European Council of Lisbon, which called for an acceleration of liberalisation in the areas of gas, electricity, transport and postal services and asked the Commission to prepare a progress report and appropriate proposals for its meeting in the spring of 2001.

59. The Commission will continue to pursue the following principles in its policy of opening up markets:

    — using evaluation tools to assess the operation, performance and competitiveness of general interest services, so that the regulation can be adapted in line with technological changes (which increase the cross-border possibilities of providing services within the internal market), new consumer needs and new public interest demands. The broad economic policy guidelines together with the report on their implementation and the annual Commission Communication on "Economic reform — report on the functioning of product and capital markets" (Cardiff Report)[32] provide the framework for, among other things, assessing on a regular basis the functioning of services of general economic interest in the single market. For specific sectors, notably telecommunications, reviews of regulatory reform and its effects are made available on a regular basis;[33] the practice of periodic reviews could be usefully generalised to all sectors for which a common framework exists at Community level;[34]

— maintaining a step-by-step approach based on evaluation of reform and consultation with the various parties concerned, including consumers. The Commission will continue to follow the practice of preparing for changes in the regulatory framework through the issue of Green Papers[35] accompanied or complemented by further stages of public consultation;[36]

— enforcing transparency in the operation of the suppliers of services of general economic interest, be they public or private, notably as regards possible distortions of competition. The Commission Directive amending the so-called Transparency Directive[37] aims at enforcing such transparency by extending the rules on separation of accounts, currently applicable to specific sectors, to any undertaking that enjoys a special or exclusive right granted by a Member State pursuant to Article 86(1) of the Treaty, or that is entrusted with the operation of a service of general economic interest pursuant to Article 86(2) of the Treaty and receives State aid in any form whatsoever, including any grant, support or compensation, in relation to such service and which carries on other activities.

Notes

[32] COM(1999) 10 of 20 January 1999, COM(2000) 26 of 26 January 2000.

[33] "Fifth Report on the implementation of the telecommunications regulatory package, COM(1999) 537 of 11 November 1999."

[34] The Commission is currently preparing a review of regulatory reform and service standards in the gas and electricity industries.

[35] Examples of Green Papers include: "The citizen's network: Fulfilling the potential of public passenger transport in Europe", COM(95) 601; "Towards fair and efficient pricing in transport — Policy options for internalising the external cost of transport in the European Union", COM(95) 691; "Green Paper on a numbering policy for telecommunications services in Europe" COM(96) 590; "Green Paper on the convergence of the telecommunications, media and information-technology sectors, and the implications for regulation — Towards an information-society approach", COM(97) 623.

[36] See, for example, the communication on "The public consultation on the draft notice on the application of the competition rules to the postal sector and in particular on the assessment of certain State measures relating to postal services", COM(1996) 480 following the Commission Green Paper on "The development of the single market for postal services", COM(1991) 476; the communication on "The results of the public consultation on the 1999 communications review and orientations for the new regulatory framework", COM(2000) 239.

[37] Commission Directive 2000/52/EC of 26 July 2000 amending Directive 80/723/EEC (OJ L 193, 29.7.2000, p. 75).

60. If the European economy is to make the most of the opportunities afforded by the opening of the markets, it is important that the decisions on the Commission's pending proposals should be taken as soon as possible. The Commission expects the new regulatory framework for telecommunications, based on its proposals for a framework Directive and four specific Directives,[38] to be adopted in the course of 2001, in accordance with the timetable set by the European Council in Lisbon[39] for the completion of the internal market. The Commission is also counting on the Council and the European Parliament to adopt as soon as possible its proposals on postal services and transport.[40]

Notes

[38] See Annex I.

[39] Lisbon European Council, 23–24 March 2000, Conclusions of the Presidency, SN 100/00, point 17.

[40] COM(2000) 319 of 30 May 2000 and Annex I on transport.

61. Following the same reasoning, and in particular to ensure that public and private operators are put on an equal footing, the Commission has submitted a proposal[41] allowing, *inter alia*, to

exempt from the scope of Directive 93/38/EEC those sectors or services to which it applies (water, energy, transport and telecommunications) which, in a given Member State, operate in conditions of effective competition, after the relevant activity has been effectively liberalised according to relevant EC legislation. The telecommunications liberalisation has already had an impact on the application of procurement rules. By virtue of specific provisions in Directive 93/38/EEC, the Commission stated in a Communication[42] that it regards most of the services in this field within the EU to be exempted (with some exceptions) from the scope of Directive 93/38/EEC.

Notes

[41] Proposal for a Directive of the European Parliament and of the Council coordinating the procedure of entities operating in the water, energy and transport sectors, COM(2000) 276, 10 May 2000.

[42] OJ C 156, 3.6.1999, p. 3.

5.2. *Strengthening European coordination and solidarity*

62. Increasing European integration in certain sectors suggests a parallel increase in European coordination for monitoring the activities of regulators and operators. The appropriate institutional arrangements will vary depending on the degree of market integration achieved and the potential failures to be addressed, including in the performance of existing national regulators.

63. In order to facilitate the evaluation of services of general economic interest the Commission could envisage an examination of the results achieved overall in the Member States in the operation of these services and the effectiveness of the regulatory frameworks. Such an examination should take into particular account the interactions between different infrastructure networks, and the objectives of both economic efficiency, consumer protection and economic, social and territorial cohesion.

64. The special place of services of general economic interest in the shared values of the Union, recognised by Article 16 of the Treaty, calls for a parallel recognition of the link between access to services of general interest and European citizenship. While Member States retain ample freedom as to means by which the objectives of solidarity served by services of general interest are to be accomplished, a core common concept of such general interest may be necessary to sustain allegiance to the Union. The Commission considers the provisions on access to services of general economic interest in the draft Charter of Fundamental Rights as an important step in this direction.

5.3. *Other Community contributions in support of services of general interest*

65. The Community involvement with services of general interest goes beyond developing the single market, including providing for instruments to ensure standards of quality, the coordination of regulators and the evaluation of operations. Other Community policy instruments and actions share the same objectives of consumer protection, economic, social and territorial cohesion and help services of general economic interest in fulfilling their mission. Such contributions are meant to enhance, and by no means replace, the national, regional and local roles in their respective fields. Specific developments since the 1996 Communication on services of general interest include:

    — the adoption, by the Commission and the Member States, of a European spatial development perspective setting out the framework and the key policy options for the development of the European territory,

    — the implementation of the trans-European networks programme, in line with the commitments made by the Heads of States or Government and the sectoral guidelines adopted by the Council and the European Parliament. A revision of the guidelines for the transport networks is expected to further advance the achievement of the objectives in that area,

    — the initiative for the creation of a European research area to improve the coordination between national and Community policies,[43] including aspects on the "territorialisation" of research and electronic networks,

    — the adoption by the Commission of the 1999–2001 action plan on consumer policy, establishing as a priority the area of services of general interest,

— the e-Europe action plan for an information society for all aimed at accelerating the uptake of digital technologies across Europe. To this purpose, the action plan focuses on affordable access, the development of the necessary skills and on measures to stimulate Internet use (such as eLearning, eHealth, eGovernment).

Notes
[43] "Towards a European research area", COM(2000) 6 of 18 January 2000.

66. Horizontal consumer protection legislation also applies to all services of general interest. This horizontal legislation deals with issues of basic consumer protection such as unfair contract terms, distance selling, etc. However, there is a need to develop effective and non-discriminatory enforcement of horizontal and sectoral consumer legislation across the EU. This will require a systematic effort by all concerned, including closer administrative cooperation between Member States, national regulatory authorities, service providers and consumer representatives.

67. In the context of the World Trade Organisation, and more particularly the General Agreement on Trade in Services, the Community is also committed to maintain its services of general economic interest. It should be noted that the GATS Agreement preserves WTO Members' sovereign right to regulate economic and non-economic activities within their territory and to guarantee the achievement of legitimate public objectives. Thus, even in areas where commitments have been entered into, countries have the possibility to maintain the quality standards and the social objectives which are at the basis of their system. This being said, the legitimate right for Members to establish an adequate regulatory framework to ensure an effective functioning of the services sector must not be used as an inappropriate barrier to trade.

68. General interest services linked to the function of welfare and social protection are a matter of national or regional responsibility. Nevertheless, there is a recognised role for the Community in promoting cooperation and coordination in these areas. A particular concern of the Commission is promoting the cooperation by Member States in matters related to the reform of social protection. Following the endorsement by the Council of the Communication on the modernisation of social protection[44] and the mandate from the European Council of Lisbon to the high-level group on social protection, the Commission will develop its activities in monitoring reform and animating the debate on policies as a means toward establishing a European consensus in this area.

Notes
[44] "A concerted strategy for modernising social protection", COM(1999) 347 of 14 July 1999.

ANNEX I
STATE OF PLAY FOR INDIVIDUAL SECTORS

Certain services of general interest have been subject to market opening through the application of single market legislation and EU competition policy. This section reviews developments in sectors subject to Community rules. It does not cover the entire range of services of general interest. In particular non-economic services are excluded.[45]

Notes
[45] See paragraphs 28 to 30.

Electronic Communications

Since 1990, the European Commission has progressively put in place a comprehensive regulatory framework for the liberalisation of the telecommunications market. By allowing competition to thrive, this policy has had a major impact on the development of the market, contributing to the emergence of a strong communication sector in Europe, and allowing consumers and business users to take advantage of greater choice, lower prices and innovative services and applications.

The provisions of the existing framework liberalised all telecommunications services and networks from January 1998. This has transformed a sector traditionally characterised by State monopolies into a dynamic industry ready to take full advantage of the global market.

Underpinning the resulting regulatory framework has been the political objective of promoting growth, employment creation and competitiveness, protecting the interests of consumers, ensuring a wide choice of providers and services for all users and fostering innovation, competitive prices and quality of service.

The regulatory framework put in place for the 1998 liberalisation has been reviewed in the light of market and technological developments and the experience of the implementation process. Many areas of the EU telecommunications market remain dominated by incumbent operators in Member States, notwithstanding a growing number of operators and service providers. The Review provides an opportunity to re-assess existing regulation, to ensure that it reinforces the development of competition and consumer choice, and to continue to safeguard objectives of general interest. To this end the new framework, which would be effective from 1st January 2002, proposes five new directives[46] including one which specially addresses services of general public interest, namely "universal service and users" rights relating to electronic communications networks and services".

Universal service obligations, which the Community has asked Member States to impose on operators, ensure the provision of a wide range of basic services. The current regulatory framework on universal service requires that a defined minimum set of services of specified quality are available to all users, independent of their geographical location, at an affordable price. The legislation goes into detail on the services covered, the process for designating operators with specific obligations where this is necessary and the framework for the financing of any net costs relating to these service obligations by market actors. This approach to universal service is maintained in the proposed new directive.

The evidence from Member States is that this balancing of universal service obligations alongside the continuing opening up of the market has encouraged operators to take a dynamic view of the notion of universal service. Whilst the formal legislative framework effectively provides minimum guaranteed provision, the competitive process has encouraged undertakings to offer new tariff packages and contract terms which further enhance the services which consumers can expect as standard throughout the Community. This is already evident in the provision of mobile communications services which are not subject to specific universal service obligations but where extensive competition has produced rapid service innovation including the widespread provision of pre-paid service options to users. The latest survey evidence[47] in the Community shows that significant proportions of residential users are now opting for mobile telephone service only (in place of fixed line service) and that, if anything, lower income households are as likely or more likely to have mobile only subscriptions as are higher income households.

Notes

[46] See http://www.ispo.cec.be/infosoc/telecompolicy/review99/Welcome.html [Address no longer valid.]
[47] Commission studies, "The situation of telecommunications services in the regions of the EU", April 2000, undertaken by EOS Gallup.

Postal Services

The existing regulatory framework[48] has opened approximately 3% of the European market for postal services (i.e. items of correspondence weighing more than 350 gr or priced more than five times the basic tariff). Seven Member States (Denmark, Germany, Finland, Italy, Netherlands, Sweden, Spain) have gone further in some respects in the market opening than required by the postal Directive.

On 30 May 2000, the European Commission adopted a new proposal for a Directive proposing to further open on average 20% of the market for postal services in 2003 (i.e. full market opening of the express mail and outgoing cross-border mail, weight/price limits decreased to 50 gr and 2,5 times the basic tariff for all other items of correspondence). It also expands existing consumer protection rights with regards to redress and complaint handling mechanisms to include all postal service providers and not only public service ones.

The existing Directive defines a "universal service" as one accessible to all users "involving the permanent provision of a postal service of a specified quality at all points of the Member States territory at affordable prices for users". Moreover, the postal Directive defines more specifically a minimum universal service involving daily clearance and delivery (at least five days a week) of postal items up to

2 kg and packages up to 10 kg as well as registered and insured items. The Member States have to ensure that cross-border packages up to 20 kg are delivered and are free to expand the minimum domestic universal service in order to include packages weighing up to 20 kg. Finally, the postal Directive also defined European standards for quality of service for the cross-border mail of the "fastest delivery category" available. A national regulatory authority, independent of the postal operators, is in charge of ensuring compliance with the obligations of the Directive.

For non-reserved services which are outside the scope of the universal service, Member States can introduce general authorisation procedures to the extent necessary to guarantee compliance with essential requirements. For non-reserved services which are within the scope of the universal service, Member States may introduce individual licences, to the extent necessary to guarantee compliance with essential requirements and to safeguard the universal service. Member States can also award licenses to alternative operators to provide the universal service in particular geographic areas. Finally, a compensation fund can be established in order to ensure that the universal service is safeguarded in case the universal service obligations create an unfair financial burden for the universal service providers.

Experience so far has shown that the universal service is maintained throughout the Union, including in the seven Member States that have gone further in some respects in the market opening than required by the postal Directive. Overall, postal operators including universal service providers are more efficient and the services have improved compared with several years ago (e.g. range of services, quality of service for both domestic and cross-border mail). A good example of such an improvement is the quality of service for cross-border priority mail that have improved from 84% delivery in D+3 to 91% delivery in D+3 over the period 1997 to 1999.

The postal sector is likely to evolve quite rapidly over the coming years because the development of electronic mail can replace traditional mail to a certain extent, automation of mail processing allows productivity to increase and the need to develop new or improved services (e-commerce will require efficient logistics networks to deliver goods and services throughout the Union). The evolutive character of universal service will allow access to all users of those services.

Notes
[48] EC Directive 97/67 (OJ L 15, 21.1.1998, p. 14).

Transport

1. Liberalisation

The Treaty reflects the specific challenges faced in opening transport markets to Community-wide competition, by creating, in Article 70, the Common Transport Policy. In so doing, the Member States recognised the fact that the creation of Internal transport markets, liberalisation, and the attainment of public service objectives are all central parts of what is, in fact, an integrated policy approach. Thus, the Community has taken a gradual approach to liberalising transport markets, in order to ensure that security standards are met, and to guarantee essential public service objectives. Considerable progress has been made in opening markets to EU-wide competition:

Air transport:

The process of gradual opening up of the markets started in 1987 and was finalised by the "Third aviation package"[49] entering into force in 1993. The package fully liberalised intra-Community traffic by 1 April 1997 when air carriers were permitted cabotage rights in a Member State in which the company was not established.

Ground handling of airport services has been liberalised for airline self-handling by Community legislation from 1996[50] for airports with more than 1 million passengers a year as of 1 January 1998. Third-party handling is liberalised since 1 January 1999 (3 million passengers, further step 2 million passengers as of 1 January 2001).

Notes
[49] Council Regulation (EEC) No 2407/92 of 23 July 1992 on licensing of air carriers, Regulation (EEC) No 2409/92 of 23 July 1992 on access for Community carriers to intra-Community air routes, Regulation (EEC) No 2409/92 of 23 July 1992 on fares and rates for air services.

[50] Council Directive 96/67/EC of 15 October 1996 on access to the groundhandling at Community airports (OJ L 272, 25.10.1996, p. 36).

Maritime transport:

Liberalisation is complete in international transport as between Member States. Community legislation[51] liberalised maritime cabotage services as of 1 January 1993. Temporary exemptions were granted to France, Italy, Spain, Portugal and Greece. The last sector to have been liberalised in these Member States has been that of island cabotage services, which became open on 1 January 1999 with the exception of two sectors in Greece which enjoy an additional temporary exemption until 1 January 2004. In the port sector future Community legislation will undertake to tackle the problem of market access and financing.

Notes

[51] Council Regulation (EEC) No 3577/92 of 7 December 1992 applying the principle of freedom to provide services to maritime transport within a Member State (maritime cabotage).

Road transport:

Community competition was first introduced in 1969 through a system of Community quotas for international journeys. In 1992 this system was replaced by Community authorisation[52] allowing access to the EU markets under objective quality criteria. Community legislation lead to a complete abolition of any quantitative restrictions on the provision of cabotage services by 1 July 1998.[53]

Access to the international market for the carriage of persons has been liberalised since 1 June 1992.[54] The respective regulation lays down market access conditions for each type of road passenger transport service (occasional, regular, shuttle and special regular services). Cabotage rights, except for national regular services, were introduced by two regulations[55] and grant free access under an authorisation system since 1 January 1996.

The market for providing combined transport services (rigid definition, intending to avoid that transport by road becomes the major leg of a combined transport journey) has now been fully liberalised since 1 July 1993.[56]

Notes

[52] Council Regulation abolishing quantitative restrictions on access to the market in the international carriage of goods by road (OJ L 95/1, 9.4.1992, p. 1).
[53] Council Regulation (EEC) No 4059/89 (OJ L 390, 30.12.1989, p. 3), Regulation (EEC) No 3118/93 (OJ L 279, 12.11.1993, p. 1.).
[54] Council Regulation (EEC) 684/92 of 16 March 1992 on common rules for the international carriage of passengers by coach and bus (OJ L 74, 20.3.1992, p. 1).
[55] Council Regulation (EEC) No 2454/92 of 23 July 1992 laying down the conditions under which non-resident carriers may operate national road passenger transport services within a Member State (OJ L 251, 29.8.1992) replaced by Regulation (EEC) No 12/98 of 11 December 1997 laying down the conditions under which non-resident carriers may operate national road passenger transport services within a Member State (OJ L 4, 8.1.1998, p. 10).
[56] Council Directive 92/106/EEC on the establishment of common rules for certain types of combined transport of goods between Member States (OJ L 368, 17.12.1992, p. 38).

Inland waterways:

Historically, national systems of "chartering by rotation" have existed. Community legislation[57] required Member States to abolish such systems from 1 January 2000 from which time contracts in the field of national and international inland waterway transport in the Community are to be freely concluded and prices freely negotiated.

Notes

[57] Council Directive 96/75/EEC of 19 November 1996 (OJ L 304, 27.11.1996, p. 12).

Rail transport:

It became clear that existing Community legislation on market access and the organisational and financial structure of railway companies as well as on licensing and allocation of tracks were too vague to be effective. The Commission has responded with a package of proposals[58] to strengthen these elements. It extends the licensing rules to all railway undertakings in the Community and establishes clear and extensive rules and processes for setting charges and allocation of capacity. And most importantly, it opens access for goods transport to the core Community railway net. The package was adopted by the Commission in July 1998 and is forwarded to the Council for adoption in early 2001.

Notes

[58] COM(1998) 480 final, adopted by the Commission on 22 July 1998 (OJ C 321, 20.10.98, p. 6), and amended proposal COM(1999) 616 final, adopted by the Commission on 25 November 1999; Proposal for a Council Directive amending Directive 91/440/EEC on the development of the Community's railways; Proposal for a Council Directive amending Directive 95/18/EC on the licensing of railway undertakings; Proposal for a Council Directive relating to the allocation of railway infrastructure capacity and the levying of charges for the use of railway infrastructure and safety certification.

2. General principles for public service instruments

In all cases of liberalisation introduced by Community legislation, a high level of transport services in the general interest was safeguarded in practice. The legislation provided for instruments to be applied when minimum standards of quality have to be ensured. Intense competition in the air and maritime industries has not endangered the provision of services meeting public needs as Member States have adopted appropriate safeguard measures.

It is clear that a key element in this process has been the adoption of a series of measures and policies that ensure that essential public service standards are maintained and improved within the context of this gradual market opening, notably with respect to the following:

— Guaranteeing service on non-profitable routes. When liberalisation takes place, it is often necessary to take measures to ensure the continued service of routes that are not profitable. This can be done in two ways. First, through direct subsidy, available to all carriers operating the route on a non-discriminatory basis. Second, through the award of exclusive rights to operate a service, with or without compensation.

Examples of such awards concern services feeding airports or ports of islands or remote regions. These arrangements ensure the essential mobility for residents as well as businesses situated in such areas and allow the supply of necessary goods.

In many circumstances, such arrangements require approval under the State aid rules. The Commission has, in such cases, consistently accepted such schemes, providing that they are designed in a manner least likely to distort trade and competition and are reasonably necessary in the case in question. For example, if exclusive rights are put out to open non-discriminatory tender, they are viewed as, in principle, compatible with the Treaty;

— Guaranteeing continued minimum service standards on any given route. When opening markets to competition it is often necessary in the transport sector to ensure that service standards do not fall, as companies may sacrifice quality and regularity for cost reduction. This can be contrary to public service objectives. To cover this, Member States typically have recourse to minimum access conditions for the grant of an operating license, applied in a non-discriminatory manner to all potential entrants. Access by sea, between islands and the EU mainland is often ensured through certain minimum requirements on regularity, capacity and pricing for services for passengers and for goods. Direct subsidies may have to be made available to balance incremental costs caused by such conditions. Those subsidies would for example reduce the ticket price per passenger or per goods carried. They are supposed to be granted to all operators of the same route on a non-discriminatory basis.

The application of these principles in practice can, for example, be seen in the air and inland transport sectors.

3. Examples from transport sectors

Air transport:

The aviation sector is an excellent example of how a full liberalisation process can be compatible with the maintenance of public service obligations. This liberalisation was accompanied by the right for Member States to impose a public service obligation when it considers that this route is vital for the economic development of the region in which the airport is located. This may concern routes serving an airport in a peripheral or development region in its territory or on a thin route to any regional airport in its territory. The standards imposed under the public service obligation may concern prices, the number of seats offered, frequencies etc., where a similar level of service would not be provided if air carriers were solely considering their commercial interest. Choice of the route and standards imposed are subject to the control of the Commission.

Once a public service obligation is imposed on a route, the access to this route remains opened to any air carrier under the constraint of respecting the public service obligation. However, if nobody is willing to operate on the route because it is not commercially interesting, Member States may limit access to the route to only one air carrier for a period of maximum three years. In this case the right to operate such services is offered by public tender at Community level.

Apart from the possibility of imposing public service obligations, Member States may also give aid of a social character. Spain, Portugal and France have used this way of subsidising non viable routes. This approach may be combined with the imposition of a public service obligation guaranteeing a level of service on the route concerned. The aid has a social character if it covers only specific categories of passengers travelling on the route, like children or handicapped people. In the case of underprivileged regions like islands, the aid may cover the entire population of the region in question.

These two types of system for maintaining minimum service standards on non commercial routes have so far proved to be quite satisfactory in air transport.

Inland transport:

Harmonisation of a basic level of competition and minimum requirements for transparency when awarding service contracts are considered necessary to guaranty high levels of quality. The Commission has adopted a draft Regulation on public services in passenger transport,[59] which will ensure that public transport operators are under competitive pressure to offer passengers better services, keep costs under control and ensure the highest safety level. It also establishes an explicit obligation for transport authorities to pursue adequate services in order to protect quality, integration of services and interests of the employees. Efficient public transport is considered as playing an essential role in beating congestion and cleaning up the environment.

Notes
[59] COM(7) 2000 of 26 July 2000.

Energy

The electricity Directive[60] requires Member States to open up a minimum of 30% of domestic demand to EU-wide competition in 2000, the gas Directive[61] requires a 20% minimum market opening. In creating an open and competitive internal gas and electricity market, the Community has taken a gradual approach. The first liberalisation Directives in these sectors had to be implemented by Member States by February 1999[62,63] and August 2000[64] respectively. This approach was taken to enable industry to adapt to the change, and to ensure that necessary measures can be taken to ensure the maintenance and increase of services of general interest in these areas.

Although the two Directives reflect the particular differences of the sectors concerned, they both follow similar approaches; introducing phased minimum opening levels of liberalisation of demand,[65] requiring non-discriminatory third-party access to networks and essential facilities such as gas storage, requiring unbundling measures for transmission and distribution facilities, and requiring effective regulation to prevent discrimination.

In fact, however, liberalisation has progressed much more quickly across the Community than either required by the Directives, or expected. Around 65% of electricity demand and 80% of total

European gas demand is already fully open to EU-wide competition, and, in most Member States, it has been decided to move to complete liberalisation within the next few years.[66] Furthermore, whilst the Directives provided choices for Member States in their implementation, for example with respect to types of third-party access and unbundling methods, almost all Member States, both with respect to gas and electricity, have chosen approaches widely accepted as being most likely to develop effective competition.

Evidently, public service issues are central to the liberalisation of these markets. Indeed, in many respects the guaranteed supply of electricity at reasonable prices to all EU customers, and where connected gas, is one of the most essential public services. Both Directives, therefore, provide a number of provisions and safeguards to ensure that essential public service objectives, such as guaranteeing security of supply, universal connection to the electricity grid at reasonable prices, and protection of vulnerable citizens from disconnection, are safeguarded. In a liberalised market, these objectives are met through the setting of strict licence conditions on market operators.

The maintenance of the highest possible standards throughout the Community in these areas has therefore been, and will remain, an essential precondition for liberalisation. For this reason, both the gas and electricity Directives provide the possibility for Member States to take the necessary measures to ensure that services of general interest are maintained, and that service standards are maintained and improved.

Notes

[60] Directive 96/92/EC concerning common rules for the internal market in electricity. [See now Directive 2003/54/EC of 26 June 2003 concerning common rules for the internal market in electricity and repealing Directive 96/92/EC (OJ L 176, 15.7.2003, p.37)]

[61] Directive 98/30/EC concerning common rules for the internal market for natural gas. [See now Directive 2003/55/EC of 26 June 2003 concerning common rules for the internal market in natural gas and repealing Directive 98/30/EC (OJ L 176, 15.7.2003, p. 57)]

[62] Belgium and Ireland had one additional year, Greece two.

[63] Directive 96/92/EC concerning common rules for the internal market in electricity. [See now Directive 2003/54/EC of 26 June 2003 concerning common rules for the internal market in electricity and repealing Directive 96/92/EC (OJ L 176, 15.7.2003, p.37)]

[64] Directive 98/30/EC concerning common rules for the internal market for natural gas. [See now Directive 2003/55/EC of 26 June 2003 concerning common rules for the internal market in natural gas and repealing Directive 98/30/EC (OJ L 176, 15.7.2003, p. 57)]

[65] Regarding electricity, Member States had to open 28% of demand in 1999, and 35% by 2003. Regarding gas, Member States had to open a minimum of 20% of demand in 2000, and 28% by 2003.

[66] With respect to electricity, for example, UK, FIN, SV, D have already opened 100% of demand. B, NL, DK, ES will completely open up their demand in the medium term.

The following mechanisms to ensure the proper provision of services of general interest are becoming the norm throughout Europe:

— *Network security and reliability*

   The transmission and distribution grids remain[67] monopoly operators. As such the situation is substantially unchanged pre- and post-liberalisation. Member States remain free to entrust the management and operation of this task to a public company,[68] or to a private company. In both cases, Member States commonly provide for independent review and control of standards either by an independent regulator, or by Government. Network security and reliability has been and continues to be high in Europe, and is unaffected by liberalisation.

— *Security of supply*

   Under the Directives, Member States remain free to take the measures necessary, as they always have been, to ensure the security of supply of electricity and gas. Any measures taken must, however, be necessary to meet the objectives in question, and may not be discriminatory in nature. Member States may, for example, specify the fuel for new electricity generation in the event that reliance on one source becomes excessive, or may take measures to ensure an adequate variety in the source of gas supplies.

— *Right to be connected to the grid*

   Only with respect to electricity is the right to be connected commonly viewed as necessary by Member States. In this case the Directive specifically provides that "Member States may impose on distribution companies an obligation to supply customers located in a given area. The tariff for such supplies may be regulated, for instance to ensure equal treatment to customers concerned". Where final consumers are liberalised, owners of the distribution grid can remain obliged to provide universal connection. It is then for each Member State to decide whether they wish to make it a licence condition for companies selling electricity to final clients that they be obliged to supply all similar customers within a given area at identical prices.

— *Special consumer protection*

As electricity and gas are essential services, special provisions are necessary to ensure that vulnerable members of society are not disconnected from supply. Where markets are fully liberalised, public service standards are maintained through minimum licence conditions. If these conditions are not met, the license to supply electricity or gas would be withdrawn.

— *Service standards*

It is clearly in the public interest to ensure that service <u>standards</u> related to the supply of electricity and gas, such as the speed with which requests for connection are met and repairs are effected, the accuracy of billing and the quality of other customer services, are the highest possible, and continually improving. It is vital that these standards are maintained and increased in a liberalised market. Where liberalisation — particularly at the domestic level — has taken place, experience indicates that such standards increase, for two reasons. First, the grant of a license to sell electricity is always made subject to conditions. Some of the conditions provide minimum service standards. National regulators, year-by-year, increase and expand these standards. Second, as service standards represent one important area upon which companies compete, competition leads to their improvements. This results in standards increasing above those minimum levels set by regulators or governments.

Thus, the legislative framework within which the progressive liberalisation of the electricity and gas industry is taking place in Europe has the dual objective of lowering prices and maintaining and even increasing services of public interest. Experience clearly demonstrates that with, where necessary, appropriate regulatory measures in place, such services of public interest can not only be maintained, but increased in a competitive market place. Indeed, whilst the Directives provide[69] for the possibility to derogate from their requirements if no other less restrictive way can be found to achieve legitimate public service objectives, no Member State has in fact found it necessary to do so.

Of course, in order to achieve the objectives mentioned above, active monitoring and, where necessary, regulation is necessary. Whilst many of these issues are left to subsidiarity — it is for example for each Member State to determine the level of protection given from disconnection — the Commission's objective is to ensure the highest levels of all forms of services of general public interest throughout the Community.

Notes

[67] With the exception of certain overlaps of the gas networks, notably in Germany.

[68] Some countries, such as Spain, are in the process of bringing into public ownership the transmission network.

[69] Article 3(2) of both Directives.

Radio and Television

Private television services have developed mainly since the 1980s, establishing the current public/private dual system of broadcasting. The need for a coexistence of public service and private commercial broadcasting is recognised and supported by both the Member States and the Community. At present, the television and radio sector is liberalised at Community level.

The broadcast media play a central role in the functioning of modern democratic societies, in particular in the development and transmission of social values. Therefore, the broadcasting sector has, since its inception, been subject to specific regulation in the general interest. This regulation has been based on common values, such as freedom of expression and the right of reply, pluralism, protection of copyright, promotion of cultural and linguistic diversity, protection of minors and of human dignity, consumer protection.

Regulation to ensure that these values are respected is enacted first and foremost by the Member States in conformity with EC law. The Protocol on the system of public broadcasting in the Member States, which was annexed to the Treaty establishing the European Community by the Treaty of Amsterdam, recognises the role and the importance of public service broadcasting and confirms that the Member States are competent to define and organise the public service remit and its financing, provided that this does not affect the trading conditions and competition in the Community to an extent which would be contrary to the common interest, while the realisation of the public service remit shall be taken into account.

At Community level, the "Television without frontiers" Directive establishes a legal framework ensuring the freedom to provide television broadcasting services in the internal market, taking due account of the relevant general interest. However, the transposition of the amended "Television without frontiers" Directive has yet to be completed by all Member States. In addition, the competition rules of the Treaty establishing the European Community entrust the Commission with the task of preventing anti-competitive behaviour to the detriment of the consumers, notably the abuse of dominant positions and, on the basis of merger control, the creation of oligopolistic or monopolistic market structures.

It is for the Member States, in conformity with EC law, to decide whether they want to establish a system of public service broadcasting, to define its exact remit and to decide on the modalities of its financing. Due to the nature of their funding, public service broadcasters may become subject to the State aid rules of the EC Treaty. The Commission must notably ensure that public funding of public service broadcasters is proportional to the public service remit as defined by the Member State concerned, i.e. in particular that any State-granted compensation does not exceed the net extra costs of the particular task assigned to the public service broadcaster in question.

The funding by Member States of public service broadcasters has been the subject of a number of complaints to the Commission by private commercial broadcasters, notably about the presence of public service broadcasters on the advertising market.[70] It is worth noting that the problems raised by these complaints relate in general to the implementation of financing schemes that include advertising revenues and public funding. The choice of the financing scheme falls within the competence of the Member State, and there can be no objection in principle to the choice of a dual financing scheme (combining public funds and advertising revenue) rather than a single funding scheme (solely public funds) as long as competition in the relevant markets (e.g. advertising, acquisition and/or sale of programmes) is not affected to an extent which is contrary to the Community interest. The Commission intends to conclude its analysis of the pending complaints in the coming months. In doing so, it will closely consult with the Member States.

The Commission considers that the digital revolution does not call into question the need for audiovisual policy to identify relevant general interests and, where necessary, to protect them through the regulatory process. Technological developments, however, call for ongoing evaluation of the means and methods used, in order to ensure that they continue to be proportionate to the objectives to be achieved.

Whilst the means of distribution (and notably whether point to multipoint or point to point) clearly remains crucial, some new types of service may also require other factors to be taken into consideration when assessing the necessity and proportionality of any regulatory approach (e.g. "encryption or in the clear").

Notes

[70] See the Commission's "XXIXth Report on Competition Policy (1999)", p. 89.

ANNEX II
DEFINITION OF TERMS

Services of general interest

This term covers market and non-market services which the public authorities class as being of general interest and subject to specific public service obligations.

Services of general economic interest

This is the term used in Article 86 of the Treaty and refers to market services which the Member States subject to specific public service obligations by virtue of a general interest criterion. This would tend to cover such things as transport networks, energy and communications.

Public service

This is an ambiguous term since it may refer either to the actual body providing the service or to the general interest role assigned to the body concerned. It is with a view to promoting or facilitating the performance of the general interest role that specific public service obligations may be imposed by the public authorities on the body rendering the service, for instance in the matter of inland, air or rail transport and energy. These obligations can be applied at national or regional level. There is often confusion between the term public service, which relates to the vocation to render a service to the public in terms of what service is to be provided, and the term public sector (including the civil service), which relates to the legal status of those providing the service in terms of who owns the services.

Universal service

Universal service, in particular the definition of specific universal service obligations is a key accompaniment to market liberalisation of service sectors such as telecommunications in the European Union. The definition and guarantee of universal service ensures that the continuous accessibility and quality of established services is maintained for all users and consumers during the process of passing from monopoly provision to openly competitive markets. Universal service, within an environment of open and competitive telecommunications markets, is defined as the minimum set of services of specified quality to which all users and consumers have access in the light of specific national conditions, at an affordable price.

F6

COMMUNITY FRAMEWORK FOR STATE AID IN THE FORM OF PUBLIC SERVICE COMPENSATION

(2005/C 297/04)

Official Journal C 297, 29.11.2005, p. 4

Celex No: 52005XC1129(01)

Notes

EEA application: for the corresponding EEA provision, see the EFTA Surveillance Authority's Procedural and Substantive Rules in the Field of State Aid (Guidelines on the application and interpretation of Articles 61 and 62 of the EEA Agreement and Article 1 of Protocol 3 to the Surveillance and Court Agreement), Part III, Chapter 18C (as introduced by EFTA Surveillance Authority Decision No 328/05/COL of 20 December 2005 (OJ L 109, 26.4.2007, p. 44).

Commentary
Framework: B&C: 15.136

1. Purpose and Scope

1. It is apparent from the case-law of the Court of Justice of the European Communities,[1] that public service compensation does not constitute State aid within the meaning of Article 87(1) of the EC Treaty if it fulfils certain conditions. However, if public service compensation does not meet these conditions and if the general criteria for the applicability of Article 87(1) are satisfied, such compensation constitutes State aid.

Notes

[1] Judgments in Case C-280/00 *Altmark Trans GmbH and Regierungspräsidium Magdeburg v Nahverkehrsgesellschaft Altmark GmbH ("Altmark")* [2003] ECR I-7747 and Joined Cases C-34/01 to C-38/01 *Enirisorse SpA v Ministero delle Finanze* [2003] ECR I-14243.

2. Commission Decision 2005/842/EC of 28 November 2005 on the application of Article 86(2) of the EC Treaty to State aid in the form of public service compensation granted to certain undertakings entrusted with the operation of services of general economic interest[1] lays down the conditions under which certain types of public service compensation constitute State aid compatible with Article 86(2) of the EC Treaty and exempts compensation satisfying those conditions from the prior notification requirement. Public service compensation which constitutes State aid and does not fall within the scope of Decision 2005/842/EC *on the application of Article 86(2) of the EC Treaty to State aid in the form of public service compensation granted to certain undertakings entrusted with the operation of services of general economic interest* will still be subject to the prior notification requirement. The purpose of this framework is to spell out the conditions under which such State aid can be found compatible with the common market pursuant to Article 86(2).

Notes

[1] OJ L 312, 29.11.2005, p. 67.

3. This framework is applicable to public service compensation granted to undertakings in connexion with activities subject to the rules of the EC Treaty, with the exception of the transport sector, and the public service broadcasting sector covered by the Communication from the Commission on the application of State aid rules to public service broadcasting.[1]

Notes

[1] OJ C 320, 15.11.2001, p. 5.

4. The provisions of this framework apply without prejudice to the stricter specific provisions relating to public service obligations contained in sectoral Community legislation and measures.
5. This framework applies without prejudice to the Community provisions in force in the field of public procurement and competition (in particular Articles 81 and 82 of the EC Treaty).

2. Conditions Governing the Compatibility of Public Service Compensation that Constitutes State Aid

2.1. General provisions

6. In its judgment in *Altmark*, the Court laid down the conditions under which public service compensation does not constitute State aid as follows:
"[. . .] First, the recipient undertaking must actually have public service obligations to discharge, and the obligations must be clearly defined. [. . .].
[. . .] Second, the parameters on the basis of which the compensation is calculated must be established in advance in an objective and transparent manner, to avoid it conferring an economic advantage which may favour the recipient undertaking over competing undertakings. [. . .] Payment by a Member State of compensation for the loss incurred by an

1315

undertaking without the parameters of such compensation having been established before-hand, where it turns out after the event that the operation of certain services in connection with the discharge of public service obligations was not economically viable, therefore constitutes a financial measure which falls within the concept of State aid within the meaning of Article 87(1) of the Treaty.

[. . .] Third, the compensation cannot exceed what is necessary to cover all or part of the costs incurred in the discharge of public service obligations, taking into account the relevant receipts and a reasonable profit [. . .].

[. . .] Fourth, where the undertaking which is to discharge public service obligations, in a specific case, is not chosen pursuant to a public procurement procedure which would allow for the selection of the tenderer capable of providing those services at the least cost to the community, the level of compensation needed must be determined on the basis of an analysis of the costs which a typical undertaking, well run and adequately provided with means of transport so as to be able to meet the necessary public service requirements, would have incurred in discharging those obligations, taking into account the relevant receipts and a reasonable profit for discharging the obligations."

7. Where these four criteria are met, public service compensation does not constitute State aid, and Articles 87 and 88 of the EC Treaty do not apply. If the Member States do not respect these criteria and if the general criteria for the applicability of Article 87(1) of the EC Treaty are met, public service compensation constitutes State aid.

8. The Commission considers that at the current stage of development of the common market, such State aid may be declared compatible with the Treaty under Article 86(2) of the EC Treaty if it is necessary to the operation of the services of general economic interest and does not affect the development of trade to such an extent as would be contrary to the interests of the Community. The following conditions should be met in order to achieve such balance.

2.2. Genuine service of general economic interest within the meaning of Article 86 of the EC Treaty

9. It is apparent from the case-law of the Court of Justice that with the exception of the sectors in which there are Community rules governing the matter, Member States have a wide margin of discretion regarding the nature of services that could be classified as being services of general economic interest. Thus, the Commission's task is to ensure that this margin of discretion is applied without manifest error as regards the definition of services of general economic interest.

10. It transpires from Article 86(2) that undertakings[1] entrusted with the operation of services of general economic interest are undertakings entrusted with "a particular task". When defining public service obligations and in assessing whether those obligations are met by the undertakings concerned, the Member States are encouraged to consult widely, with a particular emphasis on users.

Notes

[1] "Undertaking" is to be understood as any entity engaged in an economic activity, regardless of the legal status of the entity and the way in which it is financed. "Public undertaking" is to be understood as any undertaking over which the public authorities may exercise directly or indirectly a dominant influence by virtue of their ownership of it, their financial participation therein, or the rules which govern it, as defined in Article 2(1)(b) of Commission Directive 80/723/EEC of 25 June 1980 on the transparency of financial relations between Member States and public undertakings as well as on financial transparency within certain undertakings (OJ L 195, 29.7.1980, p. 35. Directive as last amended by Directive 2000/52/EC, OJ L 193, 29.7.2000, p. 75). [See now Commission Directive 2006/111/EC of 16 November 2006 (OJ L 318, 17.11.2006, p. 17).]

2.3. Need for an instrument specifying the public service obligations and the methods of calculating compensation

11. The concept of service of general economic interest within the meaning of Article 86 of the EC Treaty means that the undertakings in question have been entrusted with a special task by the State.[1] Public authorities remain responsible — with the exception of the sectors in which there are Community rules governing the matter — for setting the framework of criteria and conditions for the provision of services, regardless of the legal status of the provider and of whether the

service is provided on the basis of free competition. Accordingly, a public service assignment is necessary in order to define the obligations of the undertakings in question and of the State. The term "State" covers the central, regional and local authorities.

Notes
[1] See, in particular, the judgment in Case C-127/73 *BRT v SABAM* [1974] ECR-313.

12. Responsibility for operation of the service of general economic interest must be entrusted to the undertaking concerned by way of one or more official acts, the form of which may be determined by each Member State. The act or acts must specify, in particular:
    (a) the precise nature and the duration of the public service obligations;
    (b) the undertakings and territory concerned;
    (c) the nature of any exclusive or special rights assigned to the undertaking;
    (d) the parameters for calculating, controlling and reviewing the compensation;
    (e) the arrangements for avoiding and repaying any over-compensation.
13. When defining public service obligations and in assessing whether those obligations are met by the undertakings concerned, Member States are invited to consult widely, with particular emphasis on users.

2.4. *Amount of compensation*

14. The **amount of compensation** may not exceed what is necessary to cover the costs incurred in discharging the public service obligations, taking into account the relevant receipts and reasonable profit for discharging those obligations. The amount of compensation includes all the advantages granted by the State or through State resources in any form whatsoever. The reasonable profit may include all or some of the productivity gains achieved by the undertakings concerned during an agreed limited period without reducing the level of quality of the services entrusted to the undertaking by the State.
15. In any event, compensation must be actually used for the operation of the service of general economic interest concerned. Public service compensation granted for the operation of a service of general economic interest, but actually used to operate on other markets is not justified, and consequently constitutes incompatible State aid. The undertaking receiving public service compensation may, however, enjoy a reasonable profit.
16. The **costs to be taken into consideration** include all the costs incurred in the operation of the service of general economic interest. Where the activities of the undertaking in question are confined to the service of general economic interest, all its costs may be taken into consideration. Where the undertaking also carries out activities falling outside the scope of the service of general economic interest, only the costs associated with the service of general economic interest may be taken into consideration. The costs allocated to the service of general economic interest may cover all the variable costs incurred in providing the service of general economic interest, an appropriate contribution to fixed costs common to both the service of general economic interest and other activities and an adequate return on the own capital assigned to the service of general economic interest.[1] The costs linked with investments, notably concerning infrastructure, may be taken into account when necessary for the functioning of the service of general economic interest. The costs linked to any activities outside the scope of the service of general economic interest must cover all the variable costs, an appropriate contribution to fixed common costs and an adequate return on capital. These costs may, under no circumstances, be imputed to the service of general economic interest. The calculation of costs must follow criteria which have previously been defined and be based on generally accepted cost accounting principles which must be brought to the knowledge of the Commission in the context of the notification pursuant to Article 88(3) of the EC Treaty.

Notes
[1] See Joined Cases C-83/01P, C-93/01P and C-94/01P *Chronopost SA* [2003] ECR I-6993.

17. The **revenue to be taken into account** must include at least the entire revenue earned from the service of general economic interest. If the undertaking in question holds special or exclusive

rights linked to a service of general economic interest that generates profit in excess of the reasonable profit, or benefits from other advantages granted by the State, these must be taken into consideration, irrespective of their classification for the purposes of Article 87 of the EC Treaty, and are added to its revenue. The Member State may also decide that the profits accruing from other activities outside the scope of the service of general economic interest must be allocated in whole or in part to the financing of the service of general economic interest.

18. "**Reasonable profit**" should be taken to mean a rate of return on own capital that takes account of the risk, or absence of risk, incurred by the undertaking by virtue of the intervention by the Member State, particularly if the latter grants exclusive or special rights. This rate must normally not exceed the average rate for the sector concerned in recent years. In sectors where there is no undertaking comparable to the undertaking entrusted with the operation of the service of general economic interest, a comparison may be made with undertakings situated in other Member States, or if necessary, in other sectors, provided that the particular characteristics of each sector are taken into account. In determining what amounts to a reasonable profit, the Member State may introduce incentive criteria relating, among other things, to the quality of service provided and gains in productive efficiency.

19. When a company carries out activities falling both inside and outside the scope of the service of general economic interest, the internal accounts must show separately the costs and receipts associated with the service of general economic interest and those associated with other services, as well as the parameters for allocating costs and revenues. Where an undertaking is entrusted with the operation of several services of general economic interest either because the authority assigning the service of general economic interest is different or because the nature of the service of general economic interest is different, the undertaking's internal accounts must make it possible to ensure that there is no over-compensation at the level of each service of general economic interest. These principles are without prejudice to the provisions of Directive 80/723/EEC in cases where that Directive applies.

3. Over-compensation

20. Member States must check regularly, or arrange for checks to be made, to ensure that there has been no over-compensation. Since over-compensation is not necessary for the operation of the service of general economic interest, it constitutes incompatible State aid that must be repaid to the State, and for the future, the parameters for the calculation of the compensation must be updated.

21. Where the amount of over-compensation does not exceed 10% of the amount of annual compensation, such over-compensation may be carried forward to the next year. Some services of general economic interest may have costs that vary significantly each year, notably as regards specific investments. In such cases, exceptionally, over-compensation in excess of 10% in certain years may prove necessary for the operation of the service of general economic interest. The specific situation which may justify over-compensation in excess of 10% should be explained in the notification to the Commission. However, the situation should be reviewed at intervals determined on the basis of the situation in each sector which, in any event, should not exceed four years. All over-compensation discovered at the end of that period should be repaid.

22. Any over-compensation may be used to finance another service of general economic interest operated by the same undertaking, but such a transfer must be shown in the undertaking's accounts and be carried out in accordance with the rules and principles set out in this framework, notably as regards prior notification The Member States must ensure that such transfers are subjected to proper control. The transparency rules laid down in Directive 80/723/EEC apply.

23. The amount of over-compensation cannot remain available to an undertaking on the ground that it would rank as aid compatible with the Treaty (for example, environmental aid, employment aid and aid for small and medium-sized enterprises). If a Member State wishes to grant such aid, the prior notification procedure laid down in Article 88(3) of the EC Treaty should be complied with. Aid may be disbursed only if it has been authorised by the Commission. If such aid is compatible with a block exemption Regulation, the conditions of the relevant block exemption Regulation must be fulfilled.

4. CONDITIONS AND OBLIGATIONS ATTACHED TO COMMISSION DECISIONS

24. According to Article 7(4) of Council Regulation (EC) No 659/1999 of 22 March 1999 laying down detailed rules for the application of Article [88] of the EC Treaty,[1] the Commission may attach to a positive decision conditions subject to which an aid may be considered compatible with the common market, and lay down obligations to enable compliance with the decision to be monitored. In the field of services of general economic interest, conditions and obligations may be necessary notably to ensure that aid granted to the undertakings concerned does not actually lead to over-compensations. In this context, periodical reports or other obligations may be necessary, in the light of the specific situation of each service of general economic interest.

Notes
[1] OJ L 83, 27.3.1999, p. 1. Regulation as amended by the 2003 Act of Accession.

5. APPLICATION OF THE FRAMEWORK

25. This framework will apply for a period of six years from the date of its publication in the Official Journal of the European Union. The Commission may, after consulting the Member States, amend the framework before it expires, for important reasons linked to the development of the common market. Four years after the date of publication of this framework, the Commission will undertake an impact assessment based on factual information and the results of wide consultations conducted by the Commission on the basis, notably, of data provided by the Member States. The results of the impact assessment will be made available to the European Parliament, the Committee of Regions and the Economic and Social Committee and to the Member States.

26. The Commission will apply the provisions of this framework to all aid projects notified to it and will take a decision on those projects after the framework is published in the Official Journal, even if the projects were notified prior to such publication. In the case of non-notified aid, the Commission will apply:

    (a) the provisions of this framework, if the aid was granted after publication of the framework in the Official Journal;
    (b) the provisions in force at the time the aid was granted, in all other cases.

6. APPROPRIATE MEASURES

27. The Commission proposes as appropriate measures for the purposes of Article 88(1) of the EC Treaty that Member States bring their existing schemes regarding public service compensation into line with this framework, within 18 months following its publication in the Official Journal. Member States should confirm to the Commission within one month of publication of the framework in the Official Journal that they agree to the appropriate measures proposed. In the absence of any reply, the Commission will take it that the Member State concerned does not agree.

PART G

STATE AIDS

G1

COUNCIL REGULATION (EC) No 659/1999

of 22 March 1999
laying down detailed rules for the application of Article [88] of the EC Treaty

Official Journal L 83, 27.3.1999, p. 1

Celex No: 31999R0659

Notes

EEA application: this Regulation was adopted with appropriate adaptations by an agreement between EFTA States of 10 December 2001 amending Protocol 3 to the Surveillance and Court Agreement, with effect from 28 August 2003. See also EEA Agreement, Protocol 26, Article 2, Point 1 (as amended by EEA Joint Committee Decision No 164/2001 (OJ L 65, 7.3.2002, p. 46 and EEA Supplement No 13, 7.3.2002, p. 26) and Decision No 123/2005 (OJ L 339, 22.12.2005, p. 32, and EEA Supplement No 66, 22.12.2005, p. 18)).

Commentary

Regulation 659/99/EC: B&C: 1.022, 15.069–15.070 F&N: 8.262, 16.210, 16.274, 16.386

THE COUNCIL OF THE EUROPEAN UNION,

Having regard to the Treaty establishing the European Community, and in particular Article [89] thereof,

Having regard to the proposal from the Commission,[1]

Having regard to the opinion of the European Parliament,[2]

Having regard to the opinion of the Economic and Social Committee,[3]

Notes

[1] OJ C 116, 16.4.1998, p. 13.
[2] Opinion delivered on 14 January 1999 (not yet published in the Official Journal).
[3] OJ C 284, 14.9.1998, p. 10.

---

(1) Whereas, without prejudice to special procedural rules laid down in regulations for certain sectors, this Regulation should apply to aid in all sectors; whereas, for the purpose of applying Articles [73] and [87] of the Treaty, the Commission has specific competence under Article [88] thereof to decide on the compatibility of State aid with the common market when reviewing existing aid, when taking decisions on new or altered aid and when taking action regarding non-compliance with its decisions or with the requirement as to notification;

(2) Whereas the Commission, in accordance with the case-law of the Court of Justice of the European Communities, has developed and established a consistent practice for the application of Article [88] of the Treaty and has laid down certain procedural rules and principles in a number of communications; whereas it is appropriate, with a view to ensuring effective and efficient procedures pursuant to Article [88] of the Treaty, to codify and reinforce this practice by means of a regulation;

(3) Whereas a procedural regulation on the application of Article [88] of the Treaty will increase transparency and legal certainty;

(4) Whereas, in order to ensure legal certainty, it is appropriate to define the circumstances under which aid is to be considered as existing aid; whereas the completion and enhancement of the internal market is a gradual process, reflected in the permanent development of State aid policy; whereas, following these developments, certain measures, which at the moment they were put into effect did not constitute State aid, may since have become aid;

(5) Whereas, in accordance with Article [88](3) of the Treaty, any plans to grant new aid are to be notified to the Commission and should not be put into effect before the Commission has authorised it;

(6) Whereas, in accordance with Article [10] of the Treaty, Member States are under an obligation to cooperate with the Commission and to provide it with all information required to allow the Commission to carry out its duties under this Regulation;

(7) Whereas the period within which the Commission is to conclude the preliminary examination of notified aid should be set at two months from the receipt of a complete notification or from the receipt of a duly reasoned statement of the Member State concerned that it considers the notification to be complete because the additional information requested by the Commission is not available or has already been provided; whereas, for reasons of legal certainty, that examination should be brought to an end by a decision;

(8) Whereas in all cases where, as a result of the preliminary examination, the Commission cannot find that the aid is compatible with the common market, the formal investigation procedure should be opened in order to enable the Commission to gather all the information it needs to assess the compatibility of the aid and to allow the interested parties to submit their comments; whereas the rights of the interested parties can best be safeguarded within the framework of the formal investigation procedure provided for under Article [88](2) of the Treaty;

(9) Whereas, after having considered the comments submitted by the interested parties, the Commission should conclude its examination by means of a final decision as soon as the doubts have been removed; whereas it is appropriate, should this examination not be concluded after a period of 18 months from the opening of the procedure, that the Member State concerned has the opportunity to request a decision, which the Commission should take within two months;

(10) Whereas, in order to ensure that the State aid rules are applied correctly and effectively, the Commission should have the opportunity of revoking a decision which was based on incorrect information;

(11) Whereas, in order to ensure compliance with Article [88] of the Treaty, and in particular with the notification obligation and the standstill clause in Article [88](3), the Commission should examine all cases of unlawful aid; whereas, in the interests of transparency and legal certainty, the procedures to be followed in such cases should be laid down; whereas when a Member State has not respected the notification obligation or the standstill clause, the Commission should not be bound by time limits;

(12) Whereas in cases of unlawful aid, the Commission should have the right to obtain all necessary information enabling it to take a decision and to restore immediately, where appropriate, undistorted competition; whereas it is therefore appropriate to enable the Commission to adopt interim measures addressed to the Member State concerned; whereas the interim measures may take the form of information injunctions, suspension injunctions and recovery injunctions; whereas the Commission should be enabled in the event of non-compliance with an information injunction, to decide on the basis of the information available and, in the event of non-compliance with suspension and recovery injunctions, to refer the matter to the Court of Justice direct, in accordance with the second subparagraph of Article [88](2) of the Treaty;

(13) Whereas in cases of unlawful aid which is not compatible with the common market, effective competition should be restored; whereas for this purpose it is necessary that the aid, including interest, be recovered without delay; whereas it is appropriate that recovery be effected in accordance with the procedures of national law; whereas the application of those procedures should not, by preventing the immediate and effective execution of the Commission decision, impede the restoration of effective competition; whereas to achieve this result, Member States should take all necessary measures ensuring the effectiveness of the Commission decision;

(14) Whereas for reasons of legal certainty it is appropriate to establish a period of limitation of 10 years with regard to unlawful aid, after the expiry of which no recovery can be ordered;

(15) Whereas misuse of aid may have effects on the functioning of the internal market which are similar to those of unlawful aid and should thus be treated according to similar procedures; whereas unlike unlawful aid, aid which has possibly been misused is aid which has been previously approved by the Commission; whereas therefore the Commission should not be allowed to use a recovery injunction with regard to misuse of aid;

(16) Whereas it is appropriate to define all the possibilities in which third parties have to defend their interests in State aid procedures;

(17) Whereas in accordance with Article [88](1) of the Treaty, the Commission is under an obligation, in cooperation with Member States, to keep under constant review all systems of existing aid; whereas in the interests of transparency and legal certainty, it is appropriate to specify the scope of cooperation under that Article;

(18) Whereas, in order to ensure compatibility of existing aid schemes with the common market and in accordance with Article [88](1) of the Treaty, the Commission should propose appropriate measures where an existing aid scheme is not, or is no longer, compatible with the common market and should initiate the procedure provided for in Article [88](2) of the Treaty if the Member State concerned declines to implement the proposed measures;

(19) Whereas, in order to allow the Commission to monitor effectively compliance with Commission decisions and to facilitate cooperation between the Commission and Member States for the purpose of the constant review of all existing aid schemes in the Member States in accordance with Article [88](1) of the Treaty, it is necessary to introduce a general reporting obligation with regard to all existing aid schemes;

(20) Whereas, where the Commission has serious doubts as to whether its decisions are being complied with, it should have at its disposal additional instruments allowing it to obtain the information necessary to verify that its decisions are being effectively complied with; whereas for this purpose on-site monitoring visits are an appropriate and useful instrument, in particular for cases where aid might have been misused; whereas therefore the Commission must be empowered to undertake on-site monitoring visits and must obtain the cooperation of the competent authorities of the Member States where an undertaking opposes such a visit;

(21) Whereas, in the interests of transparency and legal certainty, it is appropriate to give public information on Commission decisions while, at the same time, maintaining the principle that decisions in State aid cases are addressed to the Member State concerned; whereas it is therefore appropriate to publish all decisions which might affect the interests of interested parties either in full or in a summary form or to make copies of such decisions available to interested parties, where they have not been published or where they have not been published in full; whereas the Commission, when giving public information on its decisions, should respect the rules on professional secrecy, in accordance with Article [214] of the Treaty;

(22) Whereas the Commission, in close liaison with the Member States, should be able to adopt implementing provisions laying down detailed rules concerning the procedures under this Regulation; whereas, in order to provide for cooperation between the Commission and the competent authorities of the Member States, it is appropriate to create an Advisory Committee on State aid to be consulted before the Commission adopts provisions pursuant to this Regulation,

HAS ADOPTED THIS REGULATION:

CHAPTER I
GENERAL

Article 1
Definitions

For the purpose of this Regulation:

(a) "aid" shall mean any measure fulfilling all the criteria laid down in Article [87](1) of the Treaty;

(b) "existing aid" shall mean:

[(i) without prejudice to Articles 144 and 172 of the Act of Accession of Austria, Finland and Sweden, to Annex IV, point 3 and the Appendix to said Annex of the Act of Accession of the Czech Republic, Estonia, Cyprus, Latvia, Lithuania, Hungary, Malta, Poland, Slovenia and Slovakia, and to Annex V, point 2 and 3(b) and the Appendix to said Annex of the Act of Accession of Bulgaria and Romania, all aid which existed prior to the entry into force of the Treaty in the respective Member States, that is to say, aid schemes and individual aid which were put into effect before, and are still applicable after, the entry into force of the Treaty;]

(ii) authorised aid, that is to say, aid schemes and individual aid which have been authorised by the Commission or by the Council;

(iii) aid which is deemed to have been authorised pursuant to Article 4(6) of this Regulation or prior to this Regulation but in accordance with this procedure;

(iv) aid which is deemed to be existing aid pursuant to Article 15;

(v) aid which is deemed to be an existing aid because it can be established that at the time it was put into effect it did not constitute an aid, and subsequently became an aid due to the evolution of the common market and without having been altered by the Member State. Where certain measures become aid following the liberalisation of an activity by Community law, such measures shall not be considered as existing aid after the date fixed for liberalisation;

(c) "new aid" shall mean all aid, that is to say, aid schemes and individual aid, which is not existing aid, including alterations to existing aid;

(d) "aid scheme" shall mean any act on the basis of which, without further implementing measures being required, individual aid awards may be made to undertakings defined within the act in a general and abstract manner and any act on the basis of which aid which is not linked to a specific project may be awarded to one or several undertakings for an indefinite period of time and/or for an indefinite amount;

(e) "individual aid" shall mean aid that is not awarded on the basis of an aid scheme and notifiable awards of aid on the basis of an aid scheme;

(f) "unlawful aid" shall mean new aid put into effect in contravention of Article [88](3) of the Treaty;

(g) "misuse of aid" shall mean aid used by the beneficiary in contravention of a decision taken pursuant to Article 4(3) or Article 7(3) or (4) of this Regulation;

(h) "interested party" shall mean any Member State and any person, undertaking or association of undertakings whose interests might be affected by the granting of aid, in particular the beneficiary of the aid, competing undertakings and trade associations.

Notes

Article 1(b)(i) as shown in square brackets was inserted by Council Regulation (EC) No 1791/2006 of 20 November 2006 (OJ L 363, 20.12.2006, p. 1), Article 1 and Annex, part 4, with effect from 1 January 2007.

Commentary

Art 1(a): **B&C:** 15.074
Art 1(b)(i)–(v): **B&C:** 15.070
Art 1(c): **B&C:** 15.074
Art 1(d): **B&C:** 15.070
Art 1(e): **B&C:** 15.070
Art 1(f): **B&C:** 15.091, 15.098 **F&N:** 16.278
Art 1(g): **B&C:** 15.086, 15.091
Art 1(h): **B&C:** 15.081 **F&N:** 16.295, 16.379

CHAPTER II
PROCEDURE REGARDING NOTIFIED AID

Article 2
Notification of new aid

1. Save as otherwise provided in regulations made pursuant to Article [89] of the Treaty or to other relevant provisions thereof, any plans to grant new aid shall be notified to the Commission in sufficient time by the Member State concerned. The Commission shall inform the Member State concerned without delay of the receipt of a notification.

2. In a notification, the Member State concerned shall provide all necessary information in order to enable the Commission to take a decision pursuant to Articles 4 and 7 (hereinafter referred to as "complete notification").

Commentary
Art 2: **B&C:** 15.074

Art 2(1): B&C: 15.077
Art 2(2): B&C: 15.075, 15.094

Article 3
Standstill clause

Aid notifiable pursuant to Article 2(1) shall not be put into effect before the Commission has taken, or is deemed to have taken, a decision authorising such aid.

Commentary
Art 3: B&C: 15.077 F&N: 16.276

Article 4
Preliminary examination of the notification and decisions of the Commission

1. The Commission shall examine the notification as soon as it is received. Without prejudice to Article 8, the Commission shall take a decision pursuant to paragraphs 2, 3 or 4.

2. Where the Commission, after a preliminary examination, finds that the notified measure does not constitute aid, it shall record that finding by way of a decision.

3. Where the Commission, after a preliminary examination, finds that no doubts are raised as to the compatibility with the common market of a notified measure, in so far as it falls within the scope of Article [87](1) of the Treaty, it shall decide that the measure is compatible with the common market (hereinafter referred to as a "decision not to raise objections"). The decision shall specify which exception under the Treaty has been applied.

4. Where the Commission, after a preliminary examination, finds that doubts are raised as to the compatibility with the common market of a notified measure, it shall decide to initiate proceedings pursuant to Article [88](2) of the Treaty (hereinafter referred to as a "decision to initiate the formal investigation procedure").

5. The decisions referred to in paragraphs 2, 3 and 4 shall be taken within two months. That period shall begin on the day following the receipt of a complete notification. The notification will be considered as complete if, within two months from its receipt, or from the receipt of any additional information requested, the Commission does not request any further information. The period can be extended with the consent of both the Commission and the Member State concerned. Where appropriate, the Commission may fix shorter time limits.

6. Where the Commission has not taken a decision in accordance with paragraphs 2, 3 or 4 within the period laid down in paragraph 5, the aid shall be deemed to have been authorised by the Commission. The Member State concerned may thereupon implement the measures in question after giving the Commission prior notice thereof, unless the Commission takes a decision pursuant to this Article within a period of 15 working days following receipt of the notice.

Commentary
Art 4(1): B&C: 15.078
Art 4(2): B&C: 15.080
Art 4(2)–(4): B&C: 15.078
Art 4(3): B&C: 15.080, 15.091
Art 4(4): B&C: 15.080, 15.119
Art 4(5): B&C: 15.078, 15.119 F&N: 16.291
Art 4(6): B&C: 15.080

Article 5
Request for information

1. Where the Commission considers that information provided by the Member State concerned with regard to a measure notified pursuant to Article 2 is incomplete, it shall request all necessary additional information. Where a Member State responds to such a request, the Commission shall inform the Member State of the receipt of the response.

2. Where the Member State concerned does not provide the information requested within the period prescribed by the Commission or provides incomplete information, the Commission shall send a reminder, allowing an appropriate additional period within which the information shall be provided.

3. The notification shall be deemed to be withdrawn if the requested information is not provided within the prescribed period, unless before the expiry of that period, either the period has been extended with the consent of both the Commission and the Member State concerned, or the Member State concerned, in a duly reasoned statement, informs the Commission that it considers the notification to be complete because the additional information requested is not available or has already been provided. In that case, the period referred to in Article 4(5) shall begin on the day following receipt of the statement. If the notification is deemed to be withdrawn, the Commission shall inform the Member State thereof.

Commentary
Art 5: B&C: 15.075 **F&N:** 16.293
Art 5(1): B&C: 15.094
Art 5(2): B&C: 15.094

Article 6
Formal investigation procedure

1. The decision to initiate the formal investigation procedure shall summarise the relevant issues of fact and law, shall include a preliminary assessment of the Commission as to the aid character of the proposed measure and shall set out the doubts as to its compatibility with the common market. The decision shall call upon the Member State concerned and upon other interested parties to submit comments within a prescribed period which shall normally not exceed one month. In duly justified cases, the Commission may extend the prescribed period.

2. The comments received shall be submitted to the Member State concerned. If an interested party so requests, on grounds of potential damage, its identity shall be withheld from the Member State concerned. The Member State concerned may reply to the comments submitted within a prescribed period which shall normally not exceed one month. In duly justified cases, the Commission may extend the prescribed period.

Commentary
Art 6: F&N: 16.295, 16.387, 16.388, 16.410
Art 6(1): B&C: 15.081, 15.119
Art 6(2): B&C: 15.083

Article 7
Decisions of the Commission to close the formal investigation procedure

1. Without prejudice to Article 8, the formal investigation procedure shall be closed by means of a decision as provided for in paragraphs 2 to 5 of this Article.

2. Where the Commission finds that, where appropriate following modification by the Member State concerned, the notified measure does not constitute aid, it shall record that finding by way of a decision.

3. Where the Commission finds that, where appropriate following modification by the Member State concerned, the doubts as to the compatibility of the notified measure with the common market have been removed, it shall decide that the aid is compatible with the common market (hereinafter referred to as a "positive decision"). That decision shall specify which exception under the Treaty has been applied.

4. The Commission may attach to a positive decision conditions subject to which an aid may be considered compatible with the common market and may lay down obligations to enable compliance with the decision to be monitored (hereinafter referred to as a "conditional decision").

5. Where the Commission finds that the notified aid is not compatible with the common market, it shall decide that the aid shall not be put into effect (hereinafter referred to as a "negative decision").

6. Decisions taken pursuant to paragraphs 2, 3, 4 and 5 shall be taken as soon as the doubts referred to in Article 4(4) have been removed. The Commission shall as far as possible endeavour to adopt a decision within a period of 18 months from the opening of the procedure. This time limit may be extended by common agreement between the Commission and the Member State concerned.

7. Once the time limit referred to in paragraph 6 has expired, and should the Member State concerned so request, the Commission shall, within two months, take a decision on the basis of the information available to it. If appropriate, where the information provided is not sufficient to establish compatibility, the Commission shall take a negative decision.

Commentary
Art 7: B&C: 15.091
Art 7(1): B&C: 15.083
Art 7(2): B&C: 15.085
Art 7(3): B&C: 15.085
Art 7(4): B&C: 15.085–15.086
Art 7(5): B&C: 15.085 F&N: 16.344
Art 7(6): B&C: 15.083, 15.119 F&N: 16.297
Art 7(7): B&C: 15.083

Article 8
Withdrawal of notification

1. The Member State concerned may withdraw the notification within the meaning of Article 2 in due time before the Commission has taken a decision pursuant to Article 4 or 7.

2. In cases where the Commission initiated the formal investigation procedure, the Commission shall close that procedure.

Article 9
Revocation of a decision

The Commission may revoke a decision taken pursuant to Article 4(2) or (3), or Article 7(2), (3), (4), after having given the Member State concerned the opportunity to submit its comments, where the decision was based on incorrect information provided during the procedure which was a determining factor for the decision. Before revoking a decision and taking a new decision, the Commission shall open the formal investigation procedure pursuant to Article 4(4). Articles 6, 7 and 10, Article 11(1), Articles 13, 14 and 15 shall apply *mutatis mutandis.*

CHAPTER III
PROCEDURE REGARDING UNLAWFUL AID

Article 10
Examination, request for information and information injunction

1. Where the Commission has in its possession information from whatever source regarding alleged unlawful aid, it shall examine that information without delay.

2. If necessary, it shall request information from the Member State concerned. Article 2(2) and Article 5(1) and (2) shall apply *mutatis mutandis.*

3. Where, despite a reminder pursuant to Article 5(2), the Member State concerned does not provide the information requested within the period prescribed by the Commission, or where it provides incomplete information, the Commission shall by decision require the information to be provided (hereinafter referred to as an "information injunction"). The decision shall specify what information is required and prescribe an appropriate period within which it is to be supplied.

Commentary
Art 10: B&C: 15.072
Art 10(1): F&N: 16.402

Article 11
Injunction to suspend or provisionally recover aid

1. The Commission may, after giving the Member State concerned the opportunity to submit its comments, adopt a decision requiring the Member State to suspend any unlawful aid until the Commission has taken a decision on the compatibility of the aid with the common market (hereinafter referred to as a "suspension injunction").

2. The Commission may, after giving the Member State concerned the opportunity to submit its comments, adopt a decision requiring the Member State provisionally to recover any unlawful aid until the Commission has taken a decision on the compatibility of the aid with the common market (hereinafter referred to as a "recovery injunction"), if the following criteria are fulfilled:

— according to an established practice there are no doubts about the aid character of the measure concerned

and

— there is an urgency to act

and

— there is a serious risk of substantial and irreparable damage to a competitor.

Recovery shall be effected in accordance with the procedure set out in Article 14(2) and (3). After the aid has been effectively recovered, the Commission shall take a decision within the time limits applicable to notified aid.

The Commission may authorise the Member State to couple the refunding of the aid with the payment of rescue aid to the firm concerned.

The provisions of this paragraph shall be applicable only to unlawful aid implemented after the entry into force of this Regulation.

Commentary

Article 12
Non-compliance with an injunction decision

If the Member State fails to comply with a suspension injunction or a recovery injunction, the Commission shall be entitled, while carrying out the examination on the substance of the matter on the basis of the information available, to refer the matter to the Court of Justice of the European Communities direct and apply for a declaration that the failure to comply constitutes an infringement of the Treaty.

Commentary

Article 13
Decisions of the Commission

1. The examination of possible unlawful aid shall result in a decision pursuant to Article 4(2), (3) or (4). In the case of decisions to initiate the formal investigation procedure, proceedings shall be closed by means of a decision pursuant to Article 7. If a Member State fails to comply with an information injunction, that decision shall be taken on the basis of the information available.

2. In cases of possible unlawful aid and without prejudice to Article 11(2), the Commission shall not be bound by the time-limit set out in Articles 4(5), 7(6) and 7(7).

3. Article 9 shall apply *mutatis mutandis*.

Commentary
Art 13: **B&C:** 15.094
Art 13(1): **F&N:** 16.402
Art 13(2): **B&C:** 15.078

Article 14
Recovery of aid

1. Where negative decisions are taken in cases of unlawful aid, the Commission shall decide that the Member State concerned shall take all necessary measures to recover the aid from the beneficiary (hereinafter referred to as a "recovery decision"). The Commission shall not require recovery of the aid if this would be contrary to a general principle of Community law.

2. The aid to be recovered pursuant to a recovery decision shall include interest at an appropriate rate fixed by the Commission. Interest shall be payable from the date on which the unlawful aid was at the disposal of the beneficiary until the date of its recovery.

3. Without prejudice to any order of the Court of Justice of the European Communities pursuant to Article [242] of the Treaty, recovery shall be effected without delay and in accordance with the procedures under the national law of the Member State concerned, provided that they allow the immediate and effective execution of the Commission's decision. To this effect and in the event of a procedure before national courts, the Member States concerned shall take all necessary steps which are available in their respective legal systems, including provisional measures, without prejudice to Community law.

Commentary
Art 14: **B&C:** 15.098
Art 14(1): **B&C:** 15.098
Art 14(2): **B&C:** 15.100 **F&N:** 16.339
Art 14(3): **B&C:** 15.102, 15.127

Article 15
Limitation period

1. The powers of the Commission to recover aid shall be subject to a limitation period of ten years.

2. The limitation period shall begin on the day on which the unlawful aid is awarded to the beneficiary either as individual aid or as aid under an aid scheme. Any action taken by the Commission or by a Member State, acting at the request of the Commission, with regard to the unlawful aid shall interrupt the limitation period. Each interruption shall start time running afresh. The limitation period shall be suspended for as long as the decision of the Commission is the subject of proceedings pending before the Court of Justice of the European Communities.

3. Any aid with regard to which the limitation period has expired, shall be deemed to be existing aid.

Commentary
Art 15: **B&C:** 15.101 **F&N:** 16.280

CHAPTER IV
PROCEDURE REGARDING MISUSE OF AID

Article 16
Misuse of aid

Without prejudice to Article 23, the Commission may in cases of misuse of aid open the formal investigation procedure pursuant to Article 4(4). Articles 6, 7, 9 and 10, Article 11(1), Articles 12, 13, 14 and 15 shall apply *mutatis mutandis*.

Commentary
Art 16: **B&C:** 15.086, 15.093–15.095

CHAPTER V
PROCEDURE REGARDING EXISTING AID SCHEMES

Article 17
Cooperation pursuant to Article [88](1) of the Treaty

1. The Commission shall obtain from the Member State concerned all necessary information for the review, in cooperation with the Member State, of existing aid schemes pursuant to Article [88](1) of the Treaty.

2. Where the Commission considers that an existing aid scheme is not, or is no longer, compatible with the common market, it shall inform the Member State concerned of its preliminary view and give the Member State concerned the opportunity to submit its comments within a period of one month. In duly justified cases, the Commission may extend this period.

Commentary
Art 17(1): **B&C:** 15.071
Art 17(2): **B&C:** 15.073

Article 18
Proposal for appropriate measures

Where the Commission, in the light of the information submitted by the Member State pursuant to Article 17, concludes that the existing aid scheme is not, or is no longer, compatible with the common market, it shall issue a recommendation proposing appropriate measures to the Member State concerned. The recommendation may propose, in particular:

(a) substantive amendment of the aid scheme,
   or

(b) introduction of procedural requirements,
   or

(c) abolition of the aid scheme.

Commentary
Art 18: **B&C:** 15.073

Article 19
Legal consequences of a proposal for appropriate measures

1. Where the Member State concerned accepts the proposed measures and informs the Commission thereof, the Commission shall record that finding and inform the Member State thereof. The Member State shall be bound by its acceptance to implement the appropriate measures.

2. Where the Member State concerned does not accept the proposed measures and the Commission, having taken into account the arguments of the Member State concerned, still considers that those measures are necessary, it shall initiate proceedings pursuant to Article 4(4). Articles 6, 7 and 9 shall apply *mutatis mutandis*.

Commentary
Art 19(1): **B&C:** 15.073
Art 19(2): **B&C:** 15.073

CHAPTER VI
INTERESTED PARTIES

Article 20
Rights of interested parties

1. Any interested party may submit comments pursuant to Article 6 following a Commission decision to initiate the formal investigation procedure. Any interested party which has submitted

such comments and any beneficiary of individual aid shall be sent a copy of the decision taken by the Commission pursuant to Article 7.

2. Any interested party may inform the Commission of any alleged unlawful aid and any alleged misuse of aid. Where the Commission considers that on the basis of the information in its possession there are insufficient grounds for taking a view on the case, it shall inform the interested party thereof. Where the Commission takes a decision on a case concerning the subject matter of the information supplied, it shall send a copy of that decision to the interested party.

3. At its request, any interested party shall obtain a copy of any decision pursuant to Articles 4 and 7, Article 10(3) and Article 11.

Commentary
Art 20(1): F&N: 16.297, 16.387, 16.388
Art 20(2): B&C: 15.112 **F&N:** 16.390

Chapter VII
Monitoring

Article 21
Annual reports

1. Member States shall submit to the Commission annual reports on all existing aid schemes with regard to which no specific reporting obligations have been imposed in a conditional decision pursuant to Article 7(4).

2. Where, despite a reminder, the Member State concerned fails to submit an annual report, the Commission may proceed in accordance with Article 18 with regard to the aid scheme concerned.

Commentary
Art 21: B&C: 15.089

Article 22
On-site monitoring

1. Where the Commission has serious doubts as to whether decisions not to raise objections, positive decisions or conditional decisions with regard to individual aid are being complied with, the Member State concerned, after having been given the opportunity to submit its comments, shall allow the Commission to undertake on-site monitoring visits.

2. The officials authorised by the Commission shall be empowered, in order to verify compliance with the decision concerned:

(a) to enter any premises and land of the undertaking concerned;
(b) to ask for oral explanations on the spot;
(c) to examine books and other business records and take, or demand, copies.

The Commission may be assisted if necessary by independent experts.

3. The Commission shall inform the Member State concerned, in good time and in writing, of the on-site monitoring visit and of the identities of the authorised officials and experts. If the Member State has duly justified objections to the Commission's choice of experts, the experts shall be appointed in common agreement with the Member State. The officials of the Commission and the experts authorised to carry out the on-site monitoring shall produce an authorisation in writing specifying the subject-matter and purpose of the visit.

4. Officials authorised by the Member State in whose territory the monitoring visit is to be made may be present at the monitoring visit.

5. The Commission shall provide the Member State with a copy of any report produced as a result of the monitoring visit.

6. Where an undertaking opposes a monitoring visit ordered by a Commission decision pursuant to this Article, the Member State concerned shall afford the necessary assistance to the officials and experts authorised by the Commission to enable them to carry out the monitoring visit. To this end the Member States shall, after consulting the Commission, take the necessary measures within eighteen months after the entry into force of this Regulation.

Commentary
Art 22: F&N: 8.262
Art 22(1): B&C: 15.089
Art 22(3): B&C: 15.089
Art 22(6): B&C: 15.089

Article 23
Non-compliance with decisions and judgments

1. Where the Member State concerned does not comply with conditional or negative decisions, in particular in cases referred to in Article 14, the Commission may refer the matter to the Court of Justice of the European Communities direct in accordance with Article [88](2) of the Treaty.

2. If the Commission considers that the Member State concerned has not complied with a judgment of the Court of Justice of the European Communities, the Commission may pursue the matter in accordance with Article [228] of the Treaty.

Commentary
Art 23: B&C: 15.113

CHAPTER VIII
COMMON PROVISIONS

Article 24
Professional secrecy

The Commission and the Member States, their officials and other servants, including independent experts appointed by the Commission, shall not disclose information which they have acquired through the application of this Regulation and which is covered by the obligation of professional secrecy.

Commentary
Art 24: F&N: 16.391

Article 25
Addressee of decisions

Decisions taken pursuant to Chapters II, III, IV, V and VII shall be addressed to the Member State concerned. The Commission shall notify them to the Member State concerned without delay and give the latter the opportunity to indicate the Commission which information it considers to be covered by the obligation of professional secrecy.

Article 26
Publication of decisions

1. The Commission shall publish in the *Official Journal of the European Communities* a summary notice of the decisions which it takes pursuant to Article 4(2) and (3) and Article 18 in conjunction with Article 19(1). The summary notice shall state that a copy of the decision may be obtained in the authentic language version or versions.

2. The Commission shall publish in the *Official Journal of the European Communities* the decisions which it takes pursuant to Article 4(4) in their authentic language version. In the Official Journal published in languages other than the authentic language version, the authentic language version will be accompanied by a meaningful summary in the language of that Official Journal.

3. The Commission shall publish in the *Official Journal of the European Communities* the decisions which it takes pursuant to Article 7.

4. In cases where Article 4(6) or Article 8(2) applies, a short notice shall be published in the *Official Journal of the European Communities*.

5. The Council, acting unanimously, may decide to publish decisions pursuant to the third subparagraph of Article [88](2) of the Treaty in the *Official Journal of the European Communities*.

Commentary
Art 26: **B&C:** 15.089

Article 27
Implementing provisions

The Commission, acting in accordance with the procedure laid down in Article 29, shall have the power to adopt implementing provisions concerning the form, content and other details of notifications, the form, content and other details of annual reports, details of time-limits and the calculation of time-limits, and the interest rate referred to in Article 14(2).

Commentary
Art 27: **F&N:** 16.275

Article 28
Advisory Committee on State aid

An Advisory Committee on State aid (hereinafter referred to as the "Committee`) shall be set up. It shall be composed of representatives of the Member States and chaired by the representative of the Commission.

Article 29
Consultation of the Committee

1. The Commission shall consult the Committee before adopting any implementing provision pursuant to Article 27.

2. Consultation of the Committee shall take place at a meeting called by the Commission. The drafts and documents to be examined shall be annexed to the notification. The meeting shall take place no earlier than two months after notification has been sent. This period may be reduced in the case of urgency.

3. The Commission representative shall submit to the Committee a draft of the measures to be taken. The Committee shall deliver an opinion on the draft, within a time-limit which the chairman may lay down according to the urgency of the matter, if necessary by taking a vote.

4. The opinion shall be recorded in the minutes; in addition, each Member State shall have the right to ask to have its position recorded in the minutes. The Committee may recommend the publication of this opinion in the *Official Journal of the European Communities*.

5. The Commission shall take the utmost account of the opinion delivered by the Committee. It shall inform the Committee on the manner in which its opinion has been taken into account.

Article 30
Entry into force

This Regulation shall enter into force on the twentieth day following that of its publication in the *Official Journal of the European Communities*.

Notes
Date of entry in force: 16 April 1999.

This Regulation shall be binding in its entirety and directly applicable in all Member States.

Done at Brussels, 22 March 1999.

G2

COMMISSION REGULATION (EC)
No 794/2004

of 21 April 2004

implementing Council Regulation (EC) No 659/1999 laying down detailed rules for the application of Article [88] of the EC Treaty

Official Journal L 140, 30.4.2004, p. 1

Celex No: 32004R0794

Notes

This regulation is reproduced as corrected by the corrigenda published at OJ L 25, 28.1.2005, p. 75 and OJ L 131, 25.5.2005, p. 45.

On 13 July 2007 the Commission published proposed amendments to Regulation 794/2004/EC. The proposed amendments are published on the Europa website at the following address:

http://ec.europa.eu/comm/competition/state_aid/reform/procrules_notif_en.doc

EEA application: the EFTA Surveillance Authority has adopted a corresponding instrument under Article 5(2)(b) of the Surveillance and Court Agreement: see EFTA Surveillance Authority Decision No 195/04/COL (OJ L 139, 25.5.2006, p. 37) as subsequently amended by Decision No 319/05/COL of 14 December 2005 (OJ L 113, 27.4.2006, p. 24). See also EEA Agreement, Protocol 26, Article 2, Point 2 (as amended by EEA Joint Committee Decision No 164/2001 (OJ L 65, 7.3.2002, p. 46 and EEA Supplement No 13, 7.3.2002, p. 26) and Decision No 123/2005 (OJ L 339, 22.12.2005, p. 32, and EEA Supplement No 66, 22.12.2005, p. 18)).

Commentary

Regulation 794/2004/EC: B&C: 15.074 F&N: 16.274
Chap V: B&C: 15.100
Arts 9–11: F&N: 16.331, 16.339, 16.342

THE COMMISSION OF THE EUROPEAN COMMUNITIES,

Having regard to the Treaty establishing the European Community,

Having regard to Council Regulation (EC) No 659/1999 of 22 March 1999 laying down detailed rules for the application of Article [88] of the EC Treaty,[1] and in particular Article 27 thereof,

After consulting the Advisory Committee on State Aid,

Notes

[1] OJ L 83, 27.3.1999, p. 1. Regulation as amended by the 2003 Act of Accession.

Whereas:

(1) In order to facilitate the preparation of State aid notifications by Member States, and their assessment by the Commission, it is desirable to establish a compulsory notification form. That form should be as comprehensive as possible.

(2) The standard notification form as well as the summary information sheet and the supplementary information sheets should cover all existing guidelines and frameworks in the state aid field. They should be subject to modification or replacement in accordance with the further development of those texts.

(3) Provision should be made for a simplified system of notification for certain alterations to existing aid. Such simplified arrangements should only be accepted if the Commission has been regularly informed on the implementation of the existing aid concerned.

(4) In the interests of legal certainty it is appropriate to make it clear that small increases of up to 20% of the original budget of an aid scheme, in particular to take account of the effects of inflation, should not need to be notified to the Commission as they are unlikely to affect the Commission's

original assessment of the compatibility of the scheme, provided that the other conditions of the aid scheme remain unchanged.

(5) Article 21 of Regulation (EC) No 659/1999 requires Member States to submit annual reports to the Commission on all existing aid schemes or individual aid granted outside an approved aid scheme in respect of which no specific reporting obligations have been imposed in a conditional decision.

(6) For the Commission to be able to discharge its responsibilities for the monitoring of aid, it needs to receive accurate information from Member States about the types and amounts of aid being granted by them under existing aid schemes. It is possible to simplify and improve the arrangements for the reporting of State aid to the Commission which are currently described in the joint procedure for reporting and notification under the EC Treaty and under the World Trade Organisation (WTO) Agreement set out in the Commission's letter to Member States of 2 August 1995. The part of that joint procedure relating to Member States reporting obligations for subsidy notifications under Article 25 of the WTO Agreement on Subsidies and Countervailing measures and under Article XVI of GATT 1994, adopted on 21 July 1995 is not covered by this Regulation.

(7) The information required in the annual reports is intended to enable the Commission to monitor overall aid levels and to form a general view of the effects of different types of aid on competition. To this end, the Commission may also request Member States to provide, on an ad hoc basis, additional data for selected topics. The choice of subject matter should be discussed in advance with Member States.

(8) The annual reporting exercise does not cover the information, which may be necessary in order to verify that particular aid measures respect Community law. The Commission should therefore retain the right to seek undertakings from Member States, or to attach to decisions conditions requiring the provision of additional information.

(9) It should be specified that time-limits for the purposes of Regulation (EC) No 659/1999 should be calculated in accordance with Regulation (EEC, Euratom) No 1182/71 of the Council of 3 June 1971 determining the rules applicable to periods, dates and time limits,[1] as supplemented by the specific rules set out in this Regulation. In particular, it is necessary to identify the events, which determine the starting point for time-limits applicable in State aid procedures. The rules set out in this Regulation should apply to pre-existing time-limits which will continue to run after the entry into force of this Regulation.

Notes
[1] OJ L 124, 8.6.1971, p. 1.

(10) The purpose of recovery is to re-establish the situation existing before aid was unlawfully granted. To ensure equal treatment, the advantage should be measured objectively from the moment when the aid is available to the beneficiary undertaking, independently of the outcome of any commercial decisions subsequently made by that undertaking.

(11) In accordance with general financial practice it is appropriate to fix the recovery interest rate as an annual percentage rate.

(12) The volume and frequency of transactions between banks results in an interest rate that is consistently measurable and statistically significant, and should therefore form the basis of the recovery interest rate. The inter-bank swap rate should, however, be adjusted in order to reflect general levels of increased commercial risk outside the banking sector. On the basis of the information on inter-bank swap rates the Commission should establish a single recovery interest rate for each Member State. In the interest of legal certainty and equal treatment, it is appropriate to fix the precise method by which the interest rate should be calculated, and to provide for the publication of the recovery interest rate applicable at any given moment, as well as relevant previously applicable rates.

(13) A State aid grant may be deemed to reduce a beneficiary undertaking's medium-term financing requirements. For these purposes, and in line with general financial practice, the medium-term may be defined as five years. The recovery interest rate should therefore correspond to an annual percentage rate fixed for five years.

(14) Given the objective of restoring the situation existing before the aid was unlawfully granted, and in accordance with general financial practice, the recovery interest rate to be fixed by the Commission should be annually compounded. For the same reasons, the recovery interest rate applicable in the first year of the recovery period should be applied for the first five years of the recovery period, and the recovery interest rate applicable in the sixth year of the recovery period for the following five years.

(15) This Regulation should apply to recovery decisions notified after the date of entry into force of this Regulation,

HAS ADOPTED THIS REGULATION:

CHAPTER I
SUBJECT MATTER AND SCOPE

Article 1
Subject matter and scope

1. This Regulation sets out detailed provisions concerning the form, content and other details of notifications and annual reports referred to in Regulation (EC) No 659/1999. It also sets out provisions for the calculation of time limits in all procedures concerning State aid and of the interest rate for the recovery of unlawful aid.

2. This Regulation shall apply to aid in all sectors.

CHAPTER II
NOTIFICATIONS

Article 2
Notification forms

Without prejudice to Member States' obligations to notify state aids in the coal sector under Commission Decision 2002/871/CE,[1] notifications of new aid pursuant to Article 2(1) of Regulation (EC) No 659/1999, other than those referred to in Article 4(2), shall be made on the notification form set out in Part I of Annex I to this Regulation.

Supplementary information needed for the assessment of the measure in accordance with regulations, guidelines, frameworks and other texts applicable to State aid shall be provided on the supplementary information sheets set out in Part III of Annex I.

Whenever the relevant guidelines or frameworks are modified or replaced, the Commission shall adapt the corresponding forms and information sheets.

Notes
[1] OJ L 300, 5.11.2002, p. 42.

Article 3
Transmission of notifications

1. The notification shall be transmitted to the Commission by the Permanent Representative of the Member State concerned. It shall be addressed to the Secretary-General of the Commission.

If the Member State intends to avail itself of a specific procedure laid down in any regulations, guidelines, frameworks and other texts applicable to State aid, a copy of the notification shall be addressed to the Director-General responsible. The Secretary-General and the Directors-General may designate contact points for the receipt of notifications.

2. All subsequent correspondence shall be addressed to the Director-General responsible or to the contact point designated by the Director-General.

3. The Commission shall address its correspondence to the Permanent Representative of the Member State concerned, or to any other address designated by that Member State.

4. Until 31 December 2005 notifications shall be transmitted by the Member State on paper. Whenever possible an electronic copy of the notification shall also be transmitted.

With effect from 1 January 2006 notifications shall be transmitted electronically, unless otherwise agreed by the Commission and the notifying Member State.

All correspondence in connection with a notification which has been submitted after 1 January 2006 shall be transmitted electronically.

5. The date of transmission by fax to the number designated by the receiving party shall be considered to be the date of transmission on paper, if the signed original is received no later than ten days thereafter.

6. By 30 September 2005 at the latest, after consulting Member States, the Commission shall publish in the *Official Journal of the European Union* details of the arrangements for the electronic transmission of notifications, including addresses together with any necessary arrangements for the protection of confidential information.

Commentary
Art 3(1): F&N: 16.288

Article 4
Simplified notification procedure for certain alterations to existing aid

1. For the purposes of Article 1(c) of Regulation (EC) No 659/1999, an alteration to existing aid shall mean any change, other than modifications of a purely formal or administrative nature which cannot affect the evaluation of the compatibility of the aid measure with the common market. However an increase in the original budget of an existing aid scheme by up to 20% shall not be considered an alteration to existing aid.

2. The following alterations to existing aid shall be notified on the simplified notification form set out in Annex II:

    (a) increases in the budget of an authorised aid scheme exceeding 20%;
    (b) prolongation of an existing authorised aid scheme by up to six years, with or without an increase in the budget;
    (c) tightening of the criteria for the application of an authorised aid scheme, a reduction of aid intensity or a reduction of eligible expenses.

The Commission shall use its best endeavours to take a decision on any aid notified on the simplified notification form within a period of one month.

3. The simplified notification procedure shall not be used to notify alterations to aid schemes in respect of which Member States have not submitted annual reports in accordance with Article 5, 6, and 7, unless the annual reports for the years in which the aid has been granted are submitted at the same time as the notification.

Commentary
Art 4: F&N: 16.313

Chapter III
Annual reports

Article 5
Form and content of annual reports

1. Without prejudice to the second and third subparagraphs of this Article and to any additional specific reporting requirements laid down in a conditional decision adopted pursuant to Article 7(4) of Regulation (EC) No 659/1999, or to the observance of any undertakings provided by the Member State concerned in connection with a decision to approve aid, Member States shall compile the annual reports on existing aid schemes referred to in Article 21(1) of Regulation (EC) No 659/1999 in respect

of each whole or part calendar year during which the scheme applies in accordance with the standardised reporting format set out in Annex IIIA.

Annex IIIB sets out the format for annual reports on existing aid schemes relating to the production, processing and marketing of agricultural products listed in Annex I of the Treaty.

Annex IIIC sets out the format for annual reports on existing aid schemes for state aid relating to the production, processing or marketing of fisheries products listed in Annex I of the Treaty.

2. The Commission may ask Member States to provide additional data for selected topics, to be discussed in advance with Member States.

Article 6
Transmission and publication of annual reports

1. Each Member State shall transmit its annual reports to the Commission in electronic form no later than 30 June of the year following the year to which the report relates.

In justified cases Member States may submit estimates, provided that the actual figures are transmitted at the very latest with the following year's data.

2. Each year the Commission shall publish a State aid synopsis containing a synthesis of the information contained in the annual reports submitted during the previous year.

Article 7
Status of annual reports

The transmission of annual reports shall not be considered to constitute compliance with the obligation to notify aid measures before they are put into effect pursuant to Article 88(3) of the Treaty, nor shall such transmission in any way prejudice the outcome of an investigation into allegedly unlawful aid in accordance with the procedure laid down in Chapter III of Regulation (EC) No 659/1999.

CHAPTER IV
TIME-LIMITS

Article 8
Calculation of time-limits

1. Time-limits provided for in Regulation (EC) No 659/1999 and in this Regulation or fixed by the Commission pursuant to Article 88 of the Treaty shall be calculated in accordance with Regulation (EEC, Euratom) No 1182/71, and the specific rules set out in paragraphs 2 to 5 of this Article. In case of conflict, the provisions of this regulation shall prevail.

2. Time limits shall be specified in months or in working days.

3. With regard to time-limits for action by the Commission, the receipt of the notification or subsequent correspondence in accordance with Article 3(1) and Article 3(2) of this Regulation shall be the relevant event for the purpose of Article 3(1) of Regulation (EEC, Euratom) No 1182/71.

As far as notifications transmitted after 31 December 2005, and correspondence relating to them are concerned, the receipt of the electronic notification or communication at the relevant address published in the *Official Journal of the European Union* shall be the relevant event.

4. With regard to time-limits for action by Member States, the receipt of the relevant notification or correspondence from the Commission in accordance with [Article] 3(3) of this Regulation shall be the relevant event for the purposes of Article 3(1) of Regulation (EEC, Euratom) No 1182/71.

5. With regard to the time-limit for the submission of comments following initiation of the formal investigation procedure referred to in [Article] 6(1) of Regulation (EC) No 659/1999 by third parties and those Member States which are not directly concerned by the procedure, the publication of the notice of initiation in the *Official Journal of the European Union* shall be the relevant event for the purposes of Article 3(1) of Regulation (EEC, Euratom) No 1182/71.

6. Any request for the extension of a time-limit shall be duly substantiated, and shall be submitted in writing to the address designated by the party fixing the time-limit at least two working days before expiry.

CHAPTER V
INTEREST RATE FOR THE RECOVERY OF UNLAWFUL AID

Article 9
Method for fixing the interest rate

1. Unless otherwise provided for in a specific decision the interest rate to be used for recovering State aid granted in breach of Article 88(3) of the Treaty shall be an annual percentage rate fixed for each calendar year.

It shall be calculated on the basis of the average of the five-year inter-bank swap rates for September, October and November of the previous year, plus 75 basis points. In duly justified cases, the Commission may increase the rate by more than 75 basis points in respect of one or more Member States.

2. If the latest three-month average of the five-year inter-bank swap rates available, plus 75 basis points, differs by more than 15% from the State aid recovery interest rate in force, the Commission shall recalculate the latter.

The new rate shall apply from the first day of the month following the recalculation by the Commission. The Commission shall inform Member States by letter of the recalculation and the date from which it applies.

3. The interest rate shall be fixed for each Member State individually, or for two or more Member States together.

4. In the absence of reliable or equivalent data or in exceptional circumstances the Commission may, in close co-operation with the Member State(s) concerned, fix a State aid recovery interest rate, for one or more Member States, on the basis of a different method and on the basis of the information available to it.

Article 10
Publication

The Commission shall publish current and relevant historical State aid recovery interest rates in the *Official Journal of the European Union* and for information on the Internet.

Article 11
Method for applying interest

1. The interest rate to be applied shall be the rate applicable on the date on which unlawful aid was first put at the disposal of the beneficiary.

2. The interest rate shall be applied on a compound basis until the date of the recovery of the aid. The interest accruing in the previous year shall be subject to interest in each subsequent year.

3. The interest rate referred to in paragraph 1 shall be applied throughout the whole period until the date of recovery. However, if more than five years have elapsed between the date on which the unlawful aid was first put at the disposal of the beneficiary and the date of the recovery of the aid, the interest rate shall be recalculated at five yearly intervals, taking as a basis the rate in force at the time of recalculation.

CHAPTER VI
FINAL PROVISIONS

Article 12
Review

The Commission shall in consultation with the Member States, review the application of this Regulation within four years after its entry into force.

Article 13
Entry into force

This Regulation shall enter into force on the twentieth day following that of its publication in the *Official Journal of the European Union.*

Chapter II shall apply only to those notifications transmitted to the Commission more than five months after the entry into force of this Regulation.

Chapter III shall apply to annual reports covering aid granted from 1 January 2003 onwards.

Chapter IV shall apply to any time limit, which has been fixed but which has not yet expired on the date of entry into force of this Regulation.

Articles 9 and 11 shall apply in relation to any recovery decision notified after the date of entry into force of this Regulation.

This Regulation shall be binding in its entirety and be directly applicable in all Member States.

Done at Brussels, 21 April 2004.

Notes
Date of entry into force: 20 May 2004.

Commentary
Art 13: F&N: 16.342

ANNEX I
Standard Form for Notification of State Aids Pursuant to Article 88(3) EC Treaty and for the Provision of Information on Unlawful Aid

---

Notes
Owing to the length of the Standard Form, Annex I is not reproduced in this volume. Annex I was amended by Commission Regulation (EC) No 1627/2006 of 24 October 2006, OJ L 302, 1.11.2006, p. 10, which replaced Supplementary Information sheets 4 and 5 in Part III of Annex I. An electronic version of Annex I (in its unamended form) is published on the Europa website at the following address: <http://ec.europa.eu/comm/competition/state_aid/legislation/forms.html>
On 13 July 2007 the Commission published proposed amendments to Regulation 794/2004/EC, including an amended version of Annex I. The proposed amendment is published on the Europa website at the following address: http://ec.europa.eu/comm/competition/state_aid/reform/procrules_notif_en.doc

Commentary
Annex I: F&N: 16.307

ANNEX II
SIMPLIFIED NOTIFICATION FORM

Notes
An electronic version of Annex II is published on the Europa website at the following address:
<http://ec.europa.eu/comm/competition/state_aid/legislation/forms.html>
On 13 July 2007 the Commission published proposed amendments to Regulation 794/2004/EC, including a new Annex II. The proposed amendment is published on the Europa website at the following address:
http://ec.europa.eu/comm/competition/state_aid/reform/procrules_notif_en.doc

Commentary
Annex II: F&N: 16.313

This form may be used for the simplified notification pursuant to Article 4(2) of the Commission Implementation Regulation [Commission Regulation (EC) No 794/2004 (OJ L 140, 30.4.2004, p. 1] implementing Council Regulation (EC) No 659/1999.[1]

1. *Prior approved aid scheme²*
   1.1. Aid number allocated by the Commission:
   1.2. Title:
   1.3. Date of approval [by reference to the letter of the Commission SG(. .)D/…]:
   1.4. Publication in the *Official Journal of the European Union*:
   1.5. Primary objective (please specify one):
   1.6. Legal basis:
   1.7. Overall budget:
   1.8. Duration:
2. *Instrument subject to notification*
   • new budget (please specify the overall as well as the annual budget in the respective national currency):
   • new duration (please specify the starting date from which the aid may be granted and the last date until which the aid may be granted):
   • tightening of criteria (please indicate if the amendment concerns a reduction of aid intensity or eligible expenses and specify details):
   Please attach a copy (or a web link) of the relevant extracts of the final text(s) of the legal basis.

Notes

[1] Council Regulation (EC) No 659/1999 laying down detailed rules for the application of Article [88] of the EC Treaty, OJ L 83, 27.3.1999, p. 1.

[2] If the aid scheme has been notified to the Commission on more than one occasion, please provide details for the latest complete notification that has been approved by the Commission

---

Annex IIIA
Standardised Reporting Format for Existing State Aid

(This format covers all sectors except agriculture)

Notes

An electronic version of Annex III is published on the Europa website at the following address:
<http://ec.europa.eu/comm/competition/state_aid/legislation/forms.html>

With a view to simplifying, streamlining and improving the overall reporting system for State aid, the existing Standardised Reporting Procedure shall be replaced by an annual updating exercise. The Commission shall send a pre-formatted spreadsheet, containing detailed information on all existing aid schemes and individual aid, to the Member States by 1 March each year. Member States shall return the spreadsheet in an electronic format to the Commission by 30 June of the year in question. This will enable the Commission to publish State aid data in year t for the reporting period t-1.[1]

The bulk of the information in the pre-formatted spreadsheet shall be pre-completed by the Commission on the basis of data provided at the time of approval of the aid. Member States shall be required to check and, where necessary, modify the details for each scheme or individual aid, and to add the annual expenditure for the latest year (t-1). In addition, Member States shall indicate which schemes have expired or for which all payments have stopped and whether or not a scheme is co-financed by Community Funds.

Information such as the objective of the aid, the sector to which the aid is directed, etc shall refer to the time at which the aid is approved and not to the final beneficiaries of the aid. For example, the primary objective of a scheme which, at the time the aid is approved, is exclusively earmarked for small and medium-sized enterprises shall be aid for small and medium-sized enterprises. However, another scheme for which all aid is ultimately awarded to small and medium-sized enterprises shall not be regarded as such if, at the time the aid is approved, the scheme is open to all enterprises.

Part G State Aids

The following parameters shall be included in the spreadsheet. Parameters 1–3 and 6–12 shall be pre-completed by the Commission and checked by the Member States. Parameters 4, 5 and 13 shall be completed by the Member States.

(1) Title
(2) Aid number
(3) All previous aid numbers (e.g., following the renewal of a scheme)
(4) Expiry
      Member States should indicate those schemes which have expired or for which all payments have stopped
(5) Co-financing
      Although Community funding itself is excluded, total State aid for each Member State shall include aid measures that are co-financed by Community funding. In order to identify which schemes are co-financed and estimate how much such aid represents in relation to overall State aid, Member States are required to indicate whether or not the scheme is co-financed and if so the percentage of aid that is co-financed. If this is not possible, an estimate of the total amount of aid that is co-financed shall be provided.
(6) Sector
      The sectoral classification shall be based largely on NACE[2] at the [three-digit level.]
(7) Primary objective
(8) Secondary objective
      A secondary objective is one for which, in addition to the primary objective, the aid (or a distinct part of it) was exclusively earmarked at the time the aid was approved. For example, a scheme for which the primary objective is research and development may have as a secondary objective small and medium-sized enterprises (SMEs) if the aid is earmarked exclusively for SMEs. Another scheme for which the primary objective is SMEs may have as secondary objectives training and employment if, at the time the aid was approved, the aid is earmarked for x% training and y% employment.
(9) Region(s)
      Aid may, at the time of approval, be exclusively earmarked for a specific region or group of regions. Where appropriate, a distinction should be made between the Article 87(3)a regions and the Article 87(3)c regions. If the aid is earmarked for one particular region, this should be specified at NUTS[3] level II.
(10) Category of aid instrument(s)
      A distinction shall be made between six categories (Grant, Tax reduction/exemption, Equity participation, Soft loan, Tax deferral, Guarantee)
(11) Description of aid instrument in national language
(12) Type of aid
      A distinction shall be made between three categories: Scheme, Individual application of a scheme, Individual aid awarded outside of a scheme (ad hoc aid)
(13) Expenditure
      As a general rule, figures should be expressed in terms of actual expenditure (or actual revenue foregone in the case of tax expenditure). Where payments are not available, commitments or budget appropriations shall be provided and flagged accordingly. Separate figures shall be provided for each aid instrument within a scheme or individual aid (e.g. grant, soft loans, etc.) Figures shall be expressed in the national currency in application at the time of the reporting period. Expenditure shall be provided for t-1, t-2, t-3, t-4, t-5.

Notes
[1] t is the year in which the data are requested.
[2] NACE Rev.1.1 is the Statistical classification of economic activities in the European Community.
[3] NUTS is the nomenclature of territorial units for statistical purposes in the Community.

ANNEX IIIB

STANDARDISED REPORTING FORMAT FOR EXISTING STATE AID

(This format covers the agricultural sector)

Notes

An electronic version of Annex III is published on the Europa website at the following address:
<http://ec.europa.eu/comm/competition/state_aid/legislation/forms.html>

With a view to simplifying, streamlining and improving the overall reporting system for State aid, the existing Standardised Reporting Procedure shall be replaced by an annual updating exercise. The Commission shall send a pre-formatted spreadsheet, containing detailed information on all existing aid schemes and individual aid, to the Member States by 1 March each year. Member States shall return the spreadsheet in an electronic format to the Commission by 30 June of the year in question. This will enable the Commission to publish State aid data in year t for the reporting period t-1.[1]

The bulk of the information in the pre-formatted spreadsheet shall be pre-completed by the Commission on the basis of data provided at the time of approval of the aid. Member States shall be required to check and, where necessary, modify the details for each scheme or individual aid, and to add the annual expenditure for the latest year (t-1). In addition, Member States shall indicate which schemes have expired or for which all payments have stopped and whether or not a scheme is co-financed by Community Funds.

Information such as the objective of the aid, the sector to which the aid is directed, etc shall refer to the time at which the aid is approved and not to the final beneficiaries of the aid. For example, the primary objective of a scheme which, at the time the aid is approved, is exclusively earmarked for small and medium-sized enterprises shall be aid for small and medium-sized enterprises. However, another scheme for which all aid is ultimately awarded to small and medium-sized enterprises shall not be regarded as such if, at the time the aid is approved, the scheme is open to all enterprises.

The following parameters shall be included in the spreadsheet. Parameters 1–3 and 6–12 shall be pre-completed by the Commission and checked by the Member States. Parameters 4, 5, 13 and 14 shall be completed by the Member States.

1. Title
2. Aid number
3. All previous aid numbers (e.g., following the renewal of a scheme)
4. Expiry
   Member States should indicate those schemes which have expired or for which all payments have stopped
5. Co-financing
   Although Community funding itself is excluded, total State aid for each Member State shall include aid measures that are co-financed by Community funding. In order to identify which schemes are co-financed and estimate how much such aid represents in relation to overall State aid, Member States are required to indicate whether or not the scheme is co-financed and if so the percentage of aid that is co-financed. If this is not possible, an estimate of the total amount of aid that is co-financed shall be provided.
6. Sector
   The sectoral classification shall be based largely on NACE[2] at the [three-digit level.]
7. Primary objective
8. Secondary objective
   A secondary objective is one for which, in addition to the primary objective, the aid (or a distinct part of it) was exclusively earmarked at the time the aid was approved. For example, a scheme for which the primary objective is research and development may have as a secondary objective small and medium-sized enterprises (SMEs) if the aid is earmarked exclusively for SMEs. Another scheme for which the primary objective is SMEs may have as secondary objectives training and employment aid if, at the time the aid was approved the aid is earmarked for x% training and y% employment.

1345

9. Region(s)

Aid may, at the time of approval, be exclusively earmarked for a specific region or group of regions. Where appropriate, a distinction should be made between Objective 1 regions and less-favoured areas.

10. Category of aid instrument(s)

A distinction shall be made between six categories (Grant, Tax reduction/exemption, Equity participation, Soft loan, Tax deferral, Guarantee)

11. Description of aid instrument in national language

12. Type of aid

A distinction shall be made between three categories: Scheme, Individual application of a scheme, Individual aid awarded outside of a scheme (ad hoc aid)

13. Expenditure

As a general rule, figures should be expressed in terms of actual expenditure (or actual revenue foregone in the case of tax expenditure). Where payments are not available, commitments or budget appropriations shall be provided and flagged accordingly. Separate figures shall be provided for each aid instrument within a scheme or individual aid (e.g. grant, soft loans, etc.) Figures shall be expressed in the national currency in application at the time of the reporting period. Expenditure shall be provided for t-1, t-2, t-3, t-4, t-5.

14. Aid intensity and beneficiaries

Member States should indicate:

— the effective aid intensity of the support actually granted per type of aid and of region
— the number of beneficiaries
— the average amount of aid per beneficiary.

Notes

[1] t is the year in which the data are requested.
[2] NACE Rev.1.1 is the Statistical classification of economic activities in the European Community.

Annex IIIC
Information to be Contained in the Annual Report to be Provided to the Commission

---

Notes

An electronic version of Annex III is published on the Europa website at the following address:
<http://ec.europa.eu/comm/competition/state_aid/legislation/forms.html>

The reports shall be provided in computerised form. They shall contain the following information:

1. Title of aid scheme, Commission aid number and reference of the Commission decision
2. Expenditure. The figures have to be expressed in euros or, if applicable, national currency. In the case of tax expenditure, annual tax losses have to be reported. If precise figures are not available, such losses may be estimated. For the year under review indicate separately for each aid instrument within the scheme (e.g. grant, soft loan, guarantee, etc.):
   2.1. amounts committed, (estimated) tax losses or other revenue forgone, data on guarantees, etc. for new assisted projects. In the case of guarantee schemes, the total amount of new guarantees handed out should be provided;
   2.2. actual payments, (estimated) tax losses or other revenue forgone, data on guarantees, etc. for new and current projects. In the case of guarantee schemes, the following should be provided: total amount of outstanding guarantees, premium income, recoveries, indemnities paid out, operating result of the scheme under the year under review;
   2.3. number of assisted projects and/or enterprises;
   2.4. estimated overall amount of:
       — aid granted for the permanent withdrawal of fishing vessels through their transfer to third countries;
       — aid granted for the temporary cessation of fishing activities;
       — aid granted for the renewal of fishing vessels;

— aid granted for modernisation of fishing vessels;

— aid granted for the purchase of used vessels;

— aid granted for socio-economic measures;

— aid granted to make good damage caused by natural disasters or exceptional occurrences;

— aid granted to outermost regions;

— aid granted through parafiscal charges;

2.5. regional breakdown of amounts under point 2.1. by regions defined as Objective 1 regions and other areas;

3. Other information and remarks.

G3

COMMISSION NOTICE

on cooperation between national courts and the Commission in the State aid field

Official Journal C 312, 23.11.1995, p. 8

Celex No: 51995XC1123(01)

Notes

EEA application: for the corresponding EEA provision, see the EFTA Surveillance Authority's Procedural and Substantive Rules in the Field of State Aid (Guidelines on the application and interpretation of Articles 61 and 62 of the EEA Agreement and Article 1 of Protocol 3 to the Surveillance and Court Agreement), Part II, Chapter 9A (as introduced by EFTA Surveillance Authority Decision No 32/00/COL of 16 February 2000 (OJ L 274, 26.10.2000, p. 19 and EEA Supplement No 48)).

See also now Notice from the Commission: Towards an effective implementation of Commission decisions ordering Member States to recover unlawful and incompatible State aid (adopted by the Commission on 27 October 2007, net yet published in the Official Journal).

Commentary

Notice: **B&C:** 15.111 **F&N:** 16.429

The purpose of this notice is to offer guidance on cooperation between national courts and the Commission in the State aid field. The notice does not in any way limit the rights conferred on Member States, individuals or undertakings by Community law. It is without prejudice to any interpretation of Community law which may be given by the Court of Justice and the Court of First Instance of the European Communities. Finally, it does not seek to interfere in any way with the fulfilment by national courts of their duties.

I. Introduction

1. The elimination of internal frontiers between Member States enables undertakings in the Community to expand their activities throughout the internal market and consumers to benefit from increased competition. These advantages must not be jeopardized by distortions of competition caused by aid granted unjustifiably to undertakings. The completion of the internal market thus reaffirms the importance of enforcement of the Community's competition policy.

2. The Court of Justice has delivered a number of important judgments on the interpretation and application of Articles [87] and [88] of the EC Treaty. The Court of First Instance now has jurisdiction over actions by private parties against the Commission's State aid decisions and will thus also

contribute to the development of case-law in this field. The Commission is responsible for the day-to-day application of the competition rules under the supervision of the Court of First Instance and the Court of Justice. Public authorities and courts in the Member States, together with the Community's courts and the Commission each assume their own tasks and responsibilities for the enforcement of the EC Treaty's State aid rules, in accordance with the principles laid down by the case-law of the Court of Justice.

3. The proper application of competition policy in the internal market may require effective cooperation between the Commission and national courts. This notice explains how the Commission intends to assist national courts by instituting closer cooperation in the application of Articles [87] and [88] in individual cases. Concern is frequently expressed that the Commission's final decisions in State aid cases are reached some time after the distortions of competition have damaged the interests of third parties. While the Commission is not always in a position to act promptly to safeguard the interests of third parties in State aid matters, national courts may be better placed to ensure that breaches of the last sentence of Article [88](3) are dealt with and remedied.

II. Powers[1]

Notes

[1] The Court of Justice has described the roles of the Commission and the national courts in the following way:

"9. As far as the role of the Commission is concerned, the Court pointed out in its judgment in Case 78/96, *Steinlike and Weinlig v Germany* [1977] ECR 595, at paragraph 9, that the intention of the Treaty, in providing through Article [88] for aid to be kept under constant review and supervised by the Commission, is that the finding that aid may be incompatible with the common market is to be arrived at, subject to review by the Court, by means of an appropriate procedure which it is the Commission's responsibility to set in motion.

10. As far as the role of national courts is concerned, the Court held in the same judgment that proceedings may be commenced before national courts requiring those courts to interpret and apply the concept of aid contained in Article [87] in order to determine whether State aid introduced without observance of the preliminary examination procedure provided for in Article [88](3) ought to have been subject to this procedure.

11. The involvement of national courts is the result of the direct effect which the last sentence of Article [88] (3) of the Treaty has been held to have. In this respect, the Court stated in its judgment of 11 December 1973 in Case 120/73, *Lorenz v Germany*, [1973] ECR p. 1471 that the immediate enforceability of the prohibition on implementation referred to in that Article extends to all aid which has been implemented without being notified and, in the event of notification, operates during the preliminary period, and if the Commission sets in motion the contentious procedure, until the final decision.

14. ... The principal and exclusive role conferred on the Commission by Articles [87] and [88] of the Treaty, which is to hold aid to be incompatible with the common market where this is appropriate, is fundamentally different from the role of national courts in safeguarding rights which individuals enjoy as a result of the direct effect of the prohibition laid down in the last sentence of Article [88](3) of the Treaty. Whilst the Commission must examine the compatibility of the proposed aid with the common market, even where the Member State has acted in breach of the prohibition on giving effect to aid, national courts do no more than preserve, until the final decision of the Commission, the rights of individuals faced with a possible breach by State authorities of the prohibition laid down by the last sentence of Article [88](3)."

Case C-354/90 *Fédération nationale du commerce extérieur des produits alimentaires and Syndicat national des négociants et transformateurs de saumon v France* [1991] ECR I-5505, paragraphs 9, 10, 11 and 14, at pp. 5527 and 5528.

4. The Commission is the administrative authority responsible for the implementation and development of competition policy in the Community's public interest. National courts are responsible for the protection of rights and the enforcement of duties, usually at the behest of private parties. The Commission must examine all aid measures which fall under Article [87](1) in order to assess their compatibility with the common market. National courts must make sure that Member States comply with their procedural obligations.

5. The last sentence of Article [88](3) (in bold below) has direct effect in the legal order of the Member States:

"The Commission shall be informed, in sufficient time to enable it to submit its comments, of any plans to grant or alter aid. If it considers that any such plan is not compatible with the common market having regard to Article [87], it shall without delay initiate the procedure provided for in paragraph 2. **The Member State concerned shall not put its proposed measures into effect until this procedure has resulted in a final decision.**"

6. The prohibition on implementation referred to in the last sentence of Article [88](3) extends to all aid which has been implemented without being notified[2] and, in the event of notification, operates during the preliminary period and, if the Commission sets in motion the contentious procedure, until the final decision.[3]

Notes

[2] With the exception of "existing" aid. Such aid may be implemented until the Commission has decided that is it incompatible with the common market: see Case C-387/92, *Banco de Crédito Industrial*, now *Banco Exterior de Espana v Ayuntamiento de Valencia* [1994] ECR I-877 and Case C-44/93, *Namur-Les Assurances du Crédit v Office National du Ducroire and Belgium* [1994] ECR I-3829.

[3] Case C-354/90, cited at footnote 1, paragraph 11 at p. 5527.

7. Of course a court will have to consider whether the "proposed measures" constitute State aid within the meaning of Article [87](1)[4] before reaching a decision under the last sentence of Article [88](3). The Commission's Decisions and the Court's case-law devote considerable attention to this important question. Accordingly, the notion of State aid must be interpreted widely to encompass not only subsidies, but also tax concessions and investments from public funds made in circumstances in which a private investor would have withheld support.[5] The aid must come from the "State", which includes all levels, manifestations and emanations of public authority.[6] The aid must favour certain undertakings or the production of certain goods: this serves to distinguish State aid to which Article [87](1) applies from general measures to which it does not.[7] For example, measures which have neither as their object nor as their effect the favouring of certain undertakings or the production of certain goods, or which apply to persons in accordance with objective criteria without regard to the location, sector or undertaking in which the beneficiary may be employed, are not considered to be State aid.

Notes

[4] See the Court of Justice's judgment in Case 78/76, *Steinlike and Weinlig v Germany* [1977] ECR 595, paragraph 14: ". . . a national court may have cause to interpret and apply the concept of aid contained in Article [87] in order to determine whether State aid introduced without observance of the preliminary examination procedure provided for in Article [88](3) ought to have been subject to this procedure".

[5] For a recent formulation, see Advocate-General Jacob's opinion in Joined Cases C-278/92, C-279/92 and C-280/92, *Spain v Commission*, paragraph 28: ". . . State aid is granted whenever a Member State makes available to an undertaking funds which in the normal course of events would not be provided by a private investor applying normal commercial criteria and disregarding other considerations of a social, political or philanthropic nature".

[6] The Court of Justice held in Case 290/83, *Commission v France* [1985] ECR p. 439, that ". . . The prohibition contained in Article [87] covers all aid granted by a Member State or through State resources and there is no necessity to draw any distinction according to whether the aid is granted directly by the State or by public or private bodies established or appointed by it to administer the aid" (paragraph 14 at p. 449).

[7] A clear statement of this distinction is to be found in Advocate-General Darmon's opinion in Joined Cases C-72 and C-73/91, *Sloman Neptun*, [1993] ECR I-887.

8. Only the Commission can decide that State aid is "compatible with the common market", i.e. authorized.

9. In applying Article [87](1), national courts may of course refer preliminary questions to the Court of Justice pursuant to Article [234] of the EC Treaty and indeed must do so in certain circumstances. They must also request assistance from the Commission by asking it for "legal or economic information" by analogy with the Court's *Delimitis*[8] judgment in respect of Article [81] of the EC Treaty.

Notes

[8] Case C-234/89, *Delimitis v Henninger Bräu* [1991] ECR I-935; Commission notice on cooperation between national courts and the Commission in applying Articles [81] and [82] of the EC Treaty (OJ No C 39, 13. 12. 1993, p. 6) [see now Commission Notice on the co-operation between the Commission and the courts of the EU Member States in the application of Articles 81 and 82 EC (OJ C 101, 27.4.2004, p. 54). See Advocate-General Lenz's opinion in Case C-44/93, cited at footnote 2 (paragraph 106). See also Case C-2/88, *Imm, Zwartveld* [1990] ECR I-3365 and

I-4405: "the Community institutions are under a duty of sincere cooperation with the judicial authorities of the Member States, which are responsible for ensuring that Community law is applied and respected in the national legal system" (paragraph 1 at p. I-3366 and paragraph 10 at pp. 4410 and 4411, respectively).

10. The national court's role is to safeguard rights which individuals enjoy as a result of the direct effect of the prohibition laid down in the last sentence of Article [88](3). The court should use all appropriate devices and remedies and apply all relevant provisions of national law to implement the direct effect of this obligation placed by the Treaty on Member States.[9] A national court must, in a case within its jurisdiction, apply Community law in its entirety and protect rights which that law confers on individuals; it must therefore set aside any provision of national law which may conflict with it, whether prior or subsequent to the Community rule.[10] The judge may, as appropriate and in accordance with applicable rules of national law and the developing case-law of the Court of Justice,[11] grant interim relief, for example by ordering the freezing or return of monies illegally paid, and award damages to parties whose interests are harmed.

Notes

[9] As the Court of Justice held in Case C-354/90, cited at footnote 1, paragraph 12 at p. 5528: "... the validity of measures giving effect to aid is affected if national authorities act in breach of the last sentence of Article [88](3) of the Treaty. National courts must offer to individuals in a position to rely on such breach the certain prospect that all the necessary inferences will be drawn, in accordance with their national law, as regards the validity of measures giving effect to the aid, the recovery of financial support granted in disregard of that provision and possible interim measures."

[10] Case 106/77, *Amministrazione delle Finanze dello Stato v Simmenthal*, [1978] ECR 629 (paragraph 21 at p. 644). See also Case C-213/89, *The Queen v Secretary of State for Transport, ex parte: Factortame Ltd et al.*, [1990] ECR I-2433, at p. 2475.

[11] Joined Cases C-6/90 and C-9/90, *Andrea Francovich et al. v Italy*, [1991] ECR I-5357. Other important cases are pending before the Court concerning the responsibilities of national courts in the application of Community law: Case C-48/93, *The Queen v Secretary of State for Transport, ex parte: Factortame Ltd. and others* (OJ No C 94, 3.4.1993, p. 13) [see now [1996] ECR I-1029]; Case C-46/93, *Brasserie du Pêcheur SA v Germany* (OJ No C 92, 2.4.1993, p. 4) [see now [1996] ECR I-1029]; Case C-312/93, *SCS Peterbroeck, Van Campenhout & Cie v Belgian State* (OJ No C 189, 13.7.1993, p. 9) [see now [1995] ECR I-4599]; Cases C-430 and C-431/93, *J. Van Schindel and J. N. C. Van Veen v Stichting Pensioenfonds voor Fysiotherapeuten* (OJ No C 338, 15.12.1993, p. 10) [see now [1995] ECR I-4705].

11. The Court of Justice has held that the full effectiveness of Community rules would be impaired and the protection of the rights which they grant would be weakened if individuals were unable to obtain redress when their rights are infringed by a breach of Community law for which a Member State can be held responsible;[12] the principle whereby a State must be liable for loss and damage caused to individuals as a result of breaches of Community law for which the State can be held responsible is inherent in the system of the Treaty;[13] a national court which considers, in a case concerning Community law, that the sole obstacle precluding it from granting interim relief is a rule of national law, must set aside that rule.[14]

Notes

[12] *Francovich*, cited at footnote 11, paragraph 33 at p. 5414.

[13] *Francovich*, cited at footnote 11, paragraph 35 at p. 5414.

[14] *The Queen v Secretary of State for Transport, ex parte: Factortame Ltd. et al.*, cited at footnote 10.

12. These principles apply in the event of a breach of the Community's competition rules. Individuals and undertakings must have access to all procedural rules and remedies provided for by national law on the same conditions as would apply if a comparable breach of national law were involved. This equality of treatment concerns not only the definitive finding of a breach of directly effective Community law, but extends also to all legal means capable of contributing to effective legal protection.

III. THE COMMISSION'S LIMITED POWERS

13. The application of Community competition law by the national courts has considerable advantages for individuals and undertakings. The Commission cannot award damages for loss suffered as a result of an infringement of Article [88](3). Such claims may be brought only before the national courts. National courts can usually adopt interim measures and order the termination of infringements quickly. Before national courts, it is possible to combine a claim under Community law with

a claim under national law. This is not possible in a procedure before the Commission. In addition, courts may award costs to the successful applicant. This is never possible in the administrative procedure before the Commission.

IV. Application of Article [88](3)

14. Member States are required to notify to the Commission all plans to grant aid or to alter aid plans already approved. This also applies to aid that may qualify for automatic approval under Article [87](2), because the Commission has to check that the requisite conditions are met. The only exception to the notification obligation is for aid classed as *de minimis* because it does not affect trade between Member States significantly and thus does not fall within Article [87](1).[15]

Notes

[15] See point 3.2 of the Community guidelines on State aid for SMEs (OJ No C 213, 19.8.1992, p. 2) and the letter to the Member States ref. IV/D/06878 of 23 March 1993, Competition Law in the European Communities, Volume II.

15. The Commission receives notification of general schemes or programmes of aid, as well as of plans to grant aid to individual firms. Once a scheme has been authorized by the Commission, individual awards of aid under the scheme do not normally have to be notified. However, under some of the aid codes or frameworks for particular industries or particular types of aid, individual notification is required of all awards of aid or of awards exceeding a certain amount. Individual notification may also be required in some cases by the terms of the Commission's authorization of a given scheme. Member States must notify aid which they wish to grant outside the framework of an authorized scheme. Notification is required in respect of planned measures, including plans to make financial transfers from public funds to public or private sector enterprises, which may involve aid within the meaning of Article [87](1).

16. The first question which national courts have to consider in an action under the last sentence of Article [88](3) is whether the measure constitutes new or existing State aid within the meaning aid of Article [87](1). The second question to be answered is whether the measure has been notified either individually or under a scheme and if so, whether the Commission has had sufficient time to come to a decision.[16]

Notes

[16] Case 120/73, *Lorenz v Germany*, [1973] ECR 1471.

17. With respect to aid schemes, a period of two months is considered by the Court of Justice to be "sufficient time", after which the Member State concerned may, after giving the Commission prior notice, implement the notified measure.[17] This period is reduced by the Commission voluntarily to 30 working days for individual cases and 20 working days under the "accelerated" procedure. The periods run from the time the Commission is satisfied that the information provided by the Member State is sufficient to enable it to reach a decision.[18]

Notes

[17] Case 120/73, *Lorenz v Germany*, cited at footnote 16, paragraph 4 at p. 1481; see also Case 84/42, *Germany v Commission*, [1984] ECR 1451, paragraph 11 at p. 1488.

[18] The Commission has issued a guide to its procedures in State aid cases: see Competition Law in the European Communities, Volume II.

18. If the Commission has decided to initiate the procedure provided for in Article [88](2), the period during which the implementation of an aid measure is prohibited runs until the Commission has reached a positive decision. For non-notified aid measures, no deadline exists for the Commission's decision-making process, although the Commission will act as speedily as possible. Aid may not be awarded before the Commission's final decision.

19. If the Commission has not ruled on an aid measure, national courts can always be guided, in interpreting Community law, by the case-law of the Court of First Instance and the Court of Justice,

as well as by decisions issued by the Commission. The Commission has published a number of general notices which may be of assistance in this regard.[19]

Notes

[19] The Commission publishes and updates from time to time a compendium of State aid rules (Competition Law in the European Communities, Volume II).

20. National courts should thus be able to decide whether or not the measure at issue is illegal under Article [88](3). Where national courts have doubts, they may and in some cases must request a preliminary ruling from the Court of Justice in accordance with Article [234].

21. Where national courts give judgment finding that Article [88](3) has not been complied with, they must rule that the measure at issue infringes Community law and take the appropriate measures to safeguard the rights enjoyed by individuals and undertakings.

V. Effects of Commission Decisions

22. The Court of Justice has held[20] that a national court is bound by a Commission Decision addressed to a Member State under Article [88](2) where the beneficiary of the aid in question seeks to question the validity of the decision of which it had been informed in writing by the Member State concerned and where it had failed to bring an action for annulment of the decision within the time limits prescribed by Article [230] of the EC Treaty.

Notes

[20] Case C-188/92, *TWD Textilwerke Deggendorf GmbH v Germany*, [1994] ECR I-833; see also Case 77/72, *Capolongo v Maya*, [1973] ECR 611.

VI. Cooperation between National Courts and the Commission

23. The Commission realizes that the principles set out above for the application of Articles [87] and [88] by national courts are complex and may sometimes be insufficiently developed to enable them to carry out their judicial duties properly. National courts may therefore ask the Commission for assistance.

24. Article [10] of the EC Treaty establishes the principle of loyal and constant cooperation between the Community institutions and the Member States with a view to attaining the objectives of the Treaty, including implementation of Article 3(g), which provides for the establishment of a system ensuring that competition in the internal market is not distorted. This principle involves obligations and duties of mutual assistance, both for the Member States and for the Community institutions. Under Article [10], the Commission has a duty of cooperation with the judicial authorities of the Member States which are responsible for ensuring that Community law is applied and respected in the national legal order.

25. The Commission considers that such cooperation is essential in order to guarantee the strict, effective and consistent application of Community competition law. In addition, participation by the national courts in the application of competition law in the field of State aid is necessary to give effect to Article [88](3). The Treaty obliges the Commission to follow the procedure laid down in Article [88](2) before it can order reimbursement of aid which is incompatible with the common market.[21] The Court has ruled that Article [88](3) has direct effect and that the illegality of an aid measure, and the consequences that flow therefrom, can never be validated retroactively by a positive decision of the Commission on an aid measure. Application of the rules on notification in the field of State aid therefore constitutes an essential link in the chain of possible legal action by individuals and undertakings.

Notes

[21] The Commission has informed the Member States that " . . . in appropriate cases it may—after giving the Member State concerned the opportunity to comment and to consider alternatively the granting of rescue aid, as defined by the Community guidelines—adopt a provisional decision ordering the Member State to recover any monies which have been disbursed in infringement of the procedural requirements. The aid would have to be recovered in accordance

with the requirements of domestic law; the sum repayable would carry interest running from the time the aid was paid out." (Commission communication to the Member States supplementing the Commission's letter No SG(91) D/4577 of 4 March 1991 concerning the procedures for the notification of aid plans and procedures applicable when aid is provided in breach of the rules of Article [88](3) of the EC Treaty), not yet published. [See now Council Regulation (EC) No 659/1999 (OJ L 83, 27.3.1999, p. 1) and Commission Regulation (EC) No 794/2004 (OJ L 140, 30.4.2004, p. 1).]

26. In the light of these considerations, the Commission intends to work towards closer cooperation with national courts in the following manner.

27. The Commission is committed to a policy of openness and transparency. The Commission conducts its policy so as to give the parties concerned useful information on the application of competition rules. To this end, it will continue to publish as much information as possible about State aid cases and policy. The case-law of the Court of Justice and Court of First Instance, general texts on State aid published by the Commission, decisions taken by the Commission, the Commission's annual reports on competition policy and the monthly Bulletin of the European Union may assist national courts in examining individual cases.

28. If these general pointers are insufficient, national courts may, within the limits of their national procedural law, ask the Commission for information of a procedural nature to enable them to discover whether a certain case is pending before the Commission, whether a case has been the subject of a notification or whether the Commission has officially initiated a procedure or taken any other decision.

29. National courts may also consult the Commission where the application of Article [87](1) or Article [88](3) causes particular difficulties. As far as Article [87](1) is concerned, these difficulties may relate in particular to the characterization of the measure as State aid, the possible distortion of competition to which it may give rise and the effect on trade between Member States. Courts may therefore consult the Commission on its customary practice in relation to these issues.

They may obtain information from the Commission regarding factual data, statistics, market studies and economic analyses. Where possible, the Commission will communicate these data or will indicate the source from which they can be obtained.

30. In its answer, the Commission will not go into the substance of the individual case or the compatibility of the measure with the common market. The answer given by the Commission will not be binding on the requesting court. The Commission will make it clear that its view is not definitive and that the court's right to request a preliminary ruling from the Court of Justice pursuant to Article [234] is unaffected.

31. It is in the interests of the proper administration of justice that the Commission should answer requests for legal and factual information in the shortest possible time. Nevertheless, the Commission cannot accede to such requests unless several conditions are met. The requisite data must actually be at its disposal and the Commission may communicate only non-confidential information.

32. Article [287] of the EC Treaty requires the Commission not to disclose information of a confidential nature. In addition, the duty of loyal cooperation under Article [10] applies to the relationship between courts and the Commission, and does not concern the parties to the dispute pending before those courts. The Commission is obliged to respect legal neutrality and objectivity. Consequently, it will not accede to requests for information unless they come from a national court, either directly, or indirectly through parties which have been ordered by the court concerned to request certain information.

VII. Final Remarks

33. This notice applies *mutatis mutandis* to relevant State aid rules, in so far as they have direct effect in the legal order of Member States, of:

— the Treaty establishing the European Coal and Steel Community and provisions adopted thereunder, and
— the Agreement on the European Economic Area.

34. This notice is issued for guidance and does not in any way limit the rights conferred on Member States, individuals or undertakings by Community law.

Part G State Aids

35. This notice is without prejudice to any interpretation of Community law which may be given by the Court of Justice and Court of First Instance of the European Communities.

36. A summary of the answers given by the Commission pursuant to this notice will be published annually in the Report on Competition Policy.

G4

COMMISSION NOTICE

on the determination of the applicable rules for the assessment of unlawful State aid
(notified under document number C(2002) 458)

(2002/C 119/12)

Text with EEA relevance

Official Journal C 119, 22.5.2002, p. 22

Celex No: 52002XC0522(04)

Notes

EEA application: for the corresponding EEA provision, see the EFTA Surveillance Authority's Procedural and Substantive Rules in the Field of State Aid (Guidelines on the application and interpretation of Articles 61 and 62 of the EEA Agreement and Article 1 of Protocol 3 to the Surveillance and Court Agreement), as amended by EFTA Surveillance Authority Decision of 25 April 2007 (not yet published)).

A number of instruments approved by the Commission over the years contain a provision to the effect that unlawful State aid, i.e. aid put into effect in contravention of Article 88(3) of the EC Treaty, shall be assessed in accordance with the texts in force at the time when the aid was granted. This is for example the case for the Community guidelines on State aid for environmental protection[1] and the multisectoral framework on regional aid for large investment projects.[2]

For the purpose of transparency and legal certainty, the Commission informs Member States and third parties that it has decided to apply the same rule in respect of all instruments indicating how the Commission will exercise its discretion in order to assess the compatibility of State aid with the common market (frameworks, guidelines, communications, notices). Therefore, the Commission shall always assess the compatibility of unlawful State aid with the common market in accordance with the substantive criteria set out in any instrument in force at the time when the aid was granted.

The present notice is without prejudice to the more specific rules contained in the Community guidelines on State aid for rescuing and restructuring firms in difficulty.[3]

The present notice is without prejudice to the interpretation of Council and Commission regulations in the field of State aid.

Notes
[1] OJ C 37, 3.2.2001, p. 3.
[2] OJ C 70, 19.3.2002, p. 8.
[3] OJ C 288, 9.10.1999, p. 2.

G5

FORM FOR THE SUBMISSION OF COMPLAINTS CONCERNING ALLEGED UNLAWFUL STATE AID

(2003/C 116/03)

Official Journal C 116, 16.5.2003, p. 3

Celex No: 52003XC0516(02)

Notes

An electronic version of this form is published on the Europa website at the following address:
<http://ec.europa.eu/comm/competition/state_aid/legislation/rules.html#complaints>

EEA application: for the corresponding EEA provision, see the EFTA Surveillance Authority's Procedural and Substantive Rules in the Field of State Aid (Guidelines on the application and interpretation of Articles 61 and 62 of the EEA Agreement and Article 1 of Protocol 3 to the Surveillance and Court Agreement), Part II, Chapter 9B and Annex I, section 3 (as added by EFTA Surveillance Authority Decision No 196/03/COL of 5 November 2003 (OJ L 139, 25.5.2006, p. 28 and EEA Supplement No 25)).

Article 88(3) of the EC Treaty provides that the Commission shall be informed, in sufficient time to enable it to submit its comments, of any plans to grant or alter aid. Member States shall not put its proposed measures into effect until this procedure has resulted in a final decision.

Aid that has been put into effect in contravention of Article 88(3) of the Treaty constitutes "unlawful aid".

In accordance with Article 10(1) of Council Regulation (EC) No 659/1999,[1] where the Commission has in its possession information from whatever source regarding alleged unlawful aid, it shall examine that information without delay.

Notes

[1] OJ L 83, 27.3.1999, p. 1.

Furthermore, according to Article 20(2) of the abovementioned Regulation, any interested party may inform the Commission of any alleged unlawful aid and any alleged misuse of aid (hereinafter referred to as a complaint).

Any person or company may submit a complaint to the Commission. The procedure is free. However, when investigating complaints the Commission is obliged to respect the procedural rules set out in Regulation (EC) No 659/1999, and in particular the rights of defence of the Member State.

Moreover, as an alternative, or as well as submitting a complaint to the Commission, it is usually possible for third parties whose interests have been adversely affected by the grant of an unlawful aid to pursue the matter before the national courts. A report on the application of State aid rules by the national courts is available on

http://europa.eu.int/comm/competition/state_aid/legislation/app_by_member_states/

However, the Commission cannot offer advice about the national procedures available in individual cases.

The annexed form sets out the information the Commission needs in order to be able to follow-up a complaint about alleged unlawful aid. If you are not able to complete all the sections of the form, please give the reasons.

The form is accessible in all Community languages on the Internet server of the European Commission at the following addresses:
[http://ec.europa.eu/comm/competition/state_aid/legislation/rules.html#complaint]. The Europa website also contains much useful information about the Community's State aid rules which may help you or your adviser to complete the form.

You can send this form to the following addresses:

For complaints relating to possible unlawful State aid in the sector of the production, processing and marketing of Annex I agricultural products:

European Commission
Directorate-General for Agriculture
Directorate H
Office: Loi 130 5–128
B-1049 Brussels
Fax (32–2) 296 76 72
e-mail: Agri-State-Aids@cec.eu.int

For complaints relating to possible unlawful State aid in the sector of the production, processing and marketing of fisheries and aquaculture products:

European Commission
Directorate-General for Fisheries
Directorate D
Rue Joseph II 99 B-1049
Brussels Fax (32–2) 295 19 42
e-mail: fish-aidesdetat@cec.eu.int

For complaints relating to possible unlawful State aid in the transport sector or the coal sector:

European Commission
Directorate-General for Energy and Transport
Directorate A
Unit 4 — Internal Market, Public Service, Competition and Users' Rights
B-1049 Brussels
Fax (32–2) 296 41 04
e-mail: stateaid.transport@cec.eu.int

For complaints relating to possible unlawful State aid in other sectors:

European Commission
Directorate General for Competition
State aid Greffe
J-70, (4/136)
B-1049 Brussels
Fax (32–2) 295 36 10
e-mail: Stateaidgreffe@cec.eu.int

If you are not sure which department is responsible, you may address your complaint to the

Secretary General
European Commission
B-1049
Brussels
e-mail: Aidesdetat@cec.eu.int

I.A. Information Regarding the Complainant

I.1. Surname and forename of complainant, or corporate name:
I.2. Address or Registered Office:
I.3. Telephone, fax, e-mail address:

I.4. Name, address, telephone, fax, e-mail address of a contact person:

I.5. If the complainant is an enterprise, a brief description of the complainant and its field(s) and place(s) of activity:

I.6. Please summarise briefly how the award of the alleged aid affects the complainant's interests.

I.B. Information Regarding the Representative of the Complainant

I.7. If the complaint is submitted on behalf of someone else (a person or a firm), please also provide the name, address, fax, e-mail address of the representative and attach written proof that the representative is authorized to act.

II. Information Regarding the Member State

II.1. Member State:

II.2. Level at which the alleged unlawful State aid has been granted:
— central government
— region (please specify)
— other (please specify)

III. Information Regarding the Alleged Aid Measures Complained of

III.1. Are you complaining about an alleged aid scheme, or an alleged individual aid?

III.2. When was the alleged aid given or the alleged aid scheme implemented? What is the duration of the alleged aid scheme (if known)?

III.3. In which economic sector(s) does this alleged aid apply?

III.4. What is the amount of the alleged aid? In what form is it given (loans, grants, guarantees, tax incentives or exemptions etc)?

III.5. Who is the beneficiary? In the case of a scheme, who is eligible for the alleged aid?
Please give as much information as possible, including a description of the main activities of the firm(s) concerned.

III.6. For what purpose was the alleged aid given (if known)?

IV. Grounds of Complaint

Please explain in detail the grounds for your complaint, including the reasons why you have complained, what rules of community law you think have been infringed by the granting of the alleged aid in question and how this has affected conditions of competition in the common market and trade between Member States.

If the alleged aid has damaged your own commercial interests, please explain how.

V. Information on Other Procedures

V.1. Details of any approaches already made to the Commission's services (if possible, attach copies of correspondence):

V.2. Approaches already made to national authorities (e.g. central, regional or local government bodies, ombudsman, etc.; if possible, attach copies of correspondence):

V.3. Recourse to national courts or other procedures (e.g. arbitration or conciliation). (Indicate whether there has already been a decision or award and attach a copy if appropriate):

VI. Supporting Documents

List any documents or evidence which is submitted in support of the complaint, and attach copies.

Whenever possible, a copy of the national law or other measure which provides the legal basis for the payment of the alleged aid should be provided.

VII. Confidentiality

You should be aware that in order to protect the rights of defence of the Member State concerned, the Commission may have to disclose your identity and any supporting documents, or their contents, to the Member State. If you do not wish your identity or certain documents or information to be disclosed, please indicate this clearly, clearly identify the confidential parts of any documents and give your reasons.

Place, date and signature of complainant.

Part G   State Aids

G6

COMMISSION COMMUNICATION
C(2003) 4582

of 1 December 2003
on professional secrecy in State aid decisions
(2003/C 297/03)

Official Journal C 297, 9.12.2003, p. 6

Celex No: 52003XC1209(02)

Notes

EEA application: for the corresponding EEA provision, see the EFTA Surveillance Authority's Procedural and Substantive Rules in the Field of State Aid (Guidelines on the application and interpretation of Articles 61 and 62 of the EEA Agreement and Article 1 of Protocol 3 to the Surveillance and Court Agreement), Part II, Chapter 9C (as added by EFTA Surveillance Authority Decision No 15/04/COL of 18 February 2004 (OJ L 154, 8.6.2006, p. 27)).

---

1. INTRODUCTION

(1) This Communication sets out how the Commission intends to deal with requests by Member States, as addressees of State aid decisions, to consider parts of such decisions as covered by the obligation of professional secrecy and thus not to be disclosed when the decision is published.

(2) This involves two aspects, namely:
   (a) the identification of the information which might be covered by the obligation of professional secrecy; and
   (b) the procedure to be followed for dealing with such requests.

2. LEGAL FRAMEWORK

(3) Article 287 of the Treaty states that: "The members of the institutions of the Community, the members of committees, and the officials and other servants of the Community shall be required, even after their duties have ceased, not to disclose information of the kind covered by the obligation of professional secrecy, in particular information about undertakings, their business relations or their cost components".

(4) This is also reflected in Articles 24 and 25 of Council Regulation (EC) No 659/1999 of 22 March 1999 laying down detailed rules for the application of Article [88] of the EC Treaty.[1]

Notes
[1] OJ L 83, 27.3.1999, p. 1.

---

(5) Article 253 of the Treaty states: "Regulations, directives and decisions adopted jointly by the European Parliament and the Council, and such acts adopted by the Council or the Commission, shall state the reasons on which they are based and shall refer to any proposals or opinions which were required to be obtained pursuant to this Treaty".

(6) Article 6(1), first sentence of Regulation (EC) No 659/1999 further stipulates with regard to decisions to initiate the formal investigation procedures: "The decision to initiate the formal investigation procedure shall summarise the relevant issues of fact and law, shall include a preliminary assessment of the Commission as to the aid character of the proposed measure and shall set out the doubts as to its compatibility with the common market [. . .]".

3. Identification of Information which can be Covered by Professional Secrecy

(7) The Court of Justice has established that although Article 287 of the Treaty primarily refers to information gathered from undertakings, the expression "in particular" shows that the principle in question is a general one which applies also to other confidential information.[1]

Notes

[1] Case 145/83 *Adams v Commission* [1985] ECR 3539, paragraph 34, and Case T-353/94 *Postbank v Commission* [1996] ECR II-921, paragraph 86.

---

(8) It follows that professional secrecy covers both business secrets and other confidential information.

(9) There is no reason why the notions of business secret and other confidential information should be interpreted differently from the meaning given to these terms in the context of antitrust and merger procedures. The fact that in antitrust and merger procedures the addressees of the Commission decision are undertakings, while in State aid procedures the addressees are Member States, does not constitute an obstacle to a uniform approach as to the identification of what can constitute business secrets or other confidential information.

3.1. Business secrets

(10) Business secrets can only concern information relating to a business which has actual or potential economic value, the disclosure or use of which could result in economic benefits for other companies. Typical examples are methods of assessing manufacturing and distribution costs, production secrets (that is to say, a secret, commercially valuable plan, formula, process or device that is used for the making, preparing, compounding, or processing of trade commodities and that can be said to be the end product of either innovation or substantial effort) and processes, supply sources, quantities produced and sold, market shares, customer and distributor lists, marketing plans, cost price structure, sales policy, and information on the internal organisation of the undertaking.

(11) It would appear that in principle business secrets can only relate to the beneficiary of the aid (or other third party) and can only concern information submitted by the Member State (or third party). Hence, statements from the Commission itself (for example, expressing doubts about feasibility of a restructuring plan) cannot be covered by the obligation of professional secrecy.

(12) The simple fact that disclosure of information might cause harm to the company is not of itself sufficient grounds to consider that such information should be considered as business secret. For example, a Commission decision to initiate the formal investigation procedure in the case of a restructuring aid may cast doubt on certain aspects of the restructuring plan in the light of information the Commission has received. Such a decision could (further) affect the credit-position of that company. However, that would not necessarily lead to the conclusion that the information on which that decision was based must be considered as business secrets.

(13) In general, the Commission will apply the following non-exhaustive list of criteria to determine whether information can be deemed to constitute business secrets:

(a) the extent to which the information is known outside the company;

(b) the extent to which measures have been taken to protect the information within the company, for example, through non compete clauses or non-disclosure agreements imposed on employees or agents, etc;

(c) the value of the information for the company and its competitors;

(d) the effort or investment which the undertaking had to undertake to acquire the information;

(e) the effort which others would need to undertake to acquire or copy the information;

(f) the degree of protection offered to such information under the legislation of the Member State concerned.

(14) In principle, the Commission considers that the following information would not normally be covered by the obligation of professional secrecy:
   (a) information which is publicly available, including information available only upon payment through specialised information services or information which is common knowledge among specialists in the field (for example common knowledge among engineers or medical doctors). Likewise, turnover is not normally considered as a business secret, as it is a figure published in the annual accounts or otherwise known to the market. Reasons must be given for requests for confidentiality concerning turnover figures which are not in the public domain and the requests must be evaluated on a case-by-case basis. The fact that information is not publicly available does not necessarily mean that the information can be regarded as a business secret;
   (b) historical information, in particular information at least five years old;
   (c) statistical or aggregate information;
   (d) names of aid recipients, sector of activity, purpose and amount of the aid, etc.
(15) Detailed reasons must be given for any request to derogate from these principles in exceptional cases.

3.2. Other confidential information

(16) In antitrust and merger cases, confidential information includes certain types of information communicated to the Commission on condition that confidentiality is observed (for example a market study commissioned by an undertaking which is party to the procedure and forming part of its property). It seems that a similar approach could be retained for State aid decisions.
(17) In the field of State aid, there may, however, be some forms of confidential information, which would not necessarily be present in antitrust and merger procedures, referring specifically to secrets of the State or other confidential information relating to its organisational activity. Generally, in view of the Commission's obligation to state the reasons for its decisions and the transparency requirement, such information can only in very exceptional circumstances be covered by the obligation of professional secrecy. For example, information regarding the organisation and costs of public services will not normally be considered "other confidential information" (although it may constitute a business secret, if the criteria laid down in section 3.1 are met).

4. APPLICABLE PROCEDURE

4.1. General principles

(18) The Commission's main task is to reconcile two opposing obligations, namely the requirement to state the reasons for its decisions under Article 253 of the Treaty and therefore ensure that its decisions contain all the essential elements on which they are based, and that of safeguarding the obligation of professional secrecy.
(19) Besides the basic obligation to state the reasons for its decisions, the Commission has to take into account the need for effective application of the State aid rules (inter alia, by giving Member States, beneficiaries and interested parties the possibility to comment on or challenge its decisions) and for transparency of its policy. There is therefore an overriding interest in making public the full substance of its decisions. As a general principle, requests for confidential treatment can only be granted where strictly necessary to protect business secrets or other confidential information meriting similar protection.
(20) Business secrets and other confidential information do not enjoy an absolute protection: this means for example that they could be divulged when they are essential for the Commission's statement of the reasons for its decisions. This means that information necessary for the identification of an aid measure and its beneficiary cannot normally be covered by the obligation of professional secrecy. Similarly, information necessary to demonstrate that the conditions of Article 87(1) of the Treaty are met, cannot normally be covered by the obligation of professional secrecy. However, the Commission will have to consider carefully whether the need for publication is more important, given the specific circumstances of a case, than the prejudice that might be generated for that Member State or undertaking involved.

(21) The public version of a Commission decision can only feature deletions from the adopted version for reasons of professional secrecy. Paragraphs cannot be moved, and no sentence can be added or altered. Where the Commission considers that certain information cannot be disclosed, a footnote may be added, paraphrasing the non-disclosed information or indicating a range of magnitude or size, if useful to assure the comprehensibility and coherence of the decision.

(22) Requests not to disclose the full text of a decision or substantial parts of it which would undermine the understanding of the Commission's statement of reasons cannot be accepted.

(23) If there is a complainant involved, the Commission will take into account the complainant's interest in ascertaining the reasons why the Commission adopted a certain decision, without the need to have recourse to Court proceedings.[1] Hence, requests by Member States for parts of the decision which address concerns of complainants to be covered by the obligation of professional secrecy will need to be particularly well reasoned and persuasive. On the other hand, the Commission will not normally be inclined to disclose information alleged to be of the kind covered by the obligation of professional secrecy where there is a suspicion that the complaint has been lodged primarily to obtain access to the information.

Notes
[1] Case C-367/95 P *Commission v Sytraval* [ECR] 1998 I-1719, paragraph 64.

(24) Member States cannot invoke professional secrecy to refuse to provide information to the Commission which the Commission considers necessary for the examination of aid measures. In this respect, reference is made to the procedure set out in Regulation (EC) No 659/1999 (in particular Articles 2(2), 5, 10 and 16).

4.2. Procedure

(25) The Commission currently notifies its decisions to the Member State concerned without delay and gives the latter the opportunity to indicate, normally within a time period of 15 working days, which information it considers to be covered by the obligation of professional secrecy. This time period may be extended by agreement between the Commission and the Member State concerned.

(26) Where the Member State concerned does not indicate which information it considers to be covered by the obligation of professional secrecy within the period prescribed by the Commission, the decision will normally be disclosed in full.

(27) Where the Member State concerned wishes certain information to be covered by the obligation of professional secrecy, it must indicate the parts it considers to be covered and provide a justification in respect of each part for which non-disclosure is requested.

(28) The Commission will then examine the request from the Member State without delay. If the Commission does not accept that certain parts of the decision are covered by the obligation of professional secrecy, it will state the reasons why in its view those parts cannot be left out of the public version of the decision. In the absence of an acceptable justification by the Member State for its request (i.e. reasoning which is not manifestly irrelevant or manifestly wrong), the Commission need not further specify the reasons why those parts cannot be left out of the public version of the decision other than by referring to the absence of justification.

(29) If the Commission decides to accept that certain parts are covered by the obligation of professional secrecy without agreeing in full with the Member State's request, it will notify its decision with a new draft to the Member State indicating the parts which have been omitted. If the Commission accepts that the parts indicated by the Member State are covered by the obligation of professional secrecy, the text of the decision will be published pursuant to Article 26 of Regulation (EC) No 659/1999, with the omission of the parts covered by the obligation of professional secrecy. Such omissions will be indicated in the text.[1]

Notes
[1] Using square brackets [. . .] and indicating in a footnote "covered by the obligation of professional secrecy".

(30) The Member State will have 15 working days following receipt of the Commission's decision stating the reasons for its refusal to accept the non-disclosure of certain parts, to react and provide additional elements to justify its request.

Part G State Aids

(31) If the Member State concerned does not react further within the period prescribed by the Commission, the Commission will normally publish the decision as indicated in its reply to the original request made by the Member State.

(32) If the Member State concerned does submit any additional elements within the prescribed period, those elements will be examined by the Commission without delay. If the Commission accepts that the parts indicated by the Member State are covered by the obligation of professional secrecy, the text of the decision will be published as set out in paragraph (29).

(33) In the event that it is not possible to reach agreement, the Commission will proceed with the publication of its decision to initiate the formal investigation procedure forthwith. Such decisions must summarise the relevant issues of fact and law, include a preliminary assessment of the aid character of the proposed measure and set out the doubts as to its compatibility with the common market. Clearly certain essential information must be included in order to enable third parties and the other Member States to comment usefully. The duty of the Commission to provide such essential information will normally prevail over any claim to the protection of business secrets or other confidential information. Furthermore, it is in the interest of the beneficiary as well as interested parties to have access to such a decision as quickly as possible. Permitting any delay in this respect would jeopardise the process of State aid control.

(34) In the event that it is not possible to reach agreement on requests for certain information in decisions not to raise objections and decisions to close the formal investigation procedure to be covered by the obligation of professional secrecy, the Commission will notify its final decision to the Member State together with the text it intends to publish, giving the Member State another 15 working days to react. In the absence of an answer which the Commission considers pertinent, the Commission will normally proceed with the publication of the text.

(35) The Commission is currently reviewing its State aid notification forms. In order to avoid unnecessary correspondence with Member States and delay in the publication of decisions, it intends, in the future, to include in the form a question asking whether the notification contains information which should not be published, and the reasons for non-publication. Only if that question is answered in the affirmative will the Commission enter into correspondence with the Member State in respect of specific cases. Similarly, if additional information is required by the Commission, the Member State will have to indicate at the moment it provides the information requested whether such information should not be published, and the reasons for non-publication. If the Commission uses the information thus identified by the Member State in its decision, it will communicate the adopted decision to the Member State, stating the reasons why in its view these parts cannot be left out from the public version of the decision as laid down in paragraph (28).

(36) Once the Commission has decided what text it will publish and notified the Member State of its final decision, it is for the Member State to decide whether or not to make use of any judicial procedures available to it, including any interim measures, within the time limits provided for in Article 230 of the EC Treaty.

4.3. Third parties

(37) Where third parties other than the Member State concerned (for example, complainants, other Member States or the beneficiary) submit information in the context of State aid procedures, these guidelines will be applied mutatis mutandis.

4.4. Application in time

(38) These guidelines cannot establish binding legal rules and do not purport to do so. They merely set out in advance, in the interests of sound administration, the manner in which the Commission intends to address the issue of confidentiality in State aid procedures. As a rule, if agreement cannot be reached, the Commission's decision to publish may be the subject of specific judicial review proceedings. As these guidelines merely pertain to procedural matters (and to a large extent set out existing practice), they will be applied with immediate effect, including for decisions not to raise objections[1] adopted before the entry into force of Regulation (EC) No 659/1999 to which third parties seek access.

Notes

[1] Decisions to initiate the formal investigation procedure and final decisions adopted before that date were already published in full in the *Official Journal of the European Communities*. Prior to publication, Member States could indicate whether any information was covered by the obligation of professional secrecy.

G7

COMMISSION COMMUNICATION CONCERNING THE OBSOLESCENCE OF CERTAIN STATE AID POLICY DOCUMENTS

(2004/C 115/01)
(Text with EEA relevance)

Official Journal C 115, 30.4.2004, p. 1

Celex No: 52004XC0430(04)

Over the years, the Commission has adopted a number of texts concerning procedural issues in the field of State aid. Some of these texts have taken the form of Commission Communications to the Member States and have been published in the *Official Journal of the European Union*. Other texts have been published in volume IIA of the Competition Law in the European Communities series, Rules applicable to State aid, situation at 30 June 1998 (ISBN 92–828–4008–5).

Following the adoption by the Commission of Commission Regulation (EC) No 794/2004[1] implementing Council Regulation (EC) No 659/1999 of 22 March 1999 laying down detailed rules for the application of Article [88] of the EC Treaty,[2] a number of these texts have become obsolete. These texts concern the notification obligation, notification procedures, including accelerated notifications, annual reporting, timelimits and recovery of unlawful aid.

Notes

[1] OJ L 140, 30.4.2004, p. 1.
[2] OJ L 83, 27.3.1999, p. 1.

Accordingly the Commission wishes to inform Member States and interested parties that from the date of publication of this communication in the *Official Journal of the European Union*, the Commission no longer intends to apply, in relation to any matter, the following documents, irrespective of their legal status:

1. Commission communication on the notification of State aid to the Commission pursuant to Article [88](3) of the EEC Treaty: the failure of Member States to respect their obligations;[1]
2. Commission communication (on the notification obligation);[2]
3. Commission communication on the cumulation of aids for different purposes;[3]
4. Commission letter to Member States SG(89) D/5521 of 27 April 1989 (on the definition of putting an aid into effect);[4]
5. Commission letter to Member States SG(91) D/4577 of 4 March 1991 (Communication to Member States concerning the procedures for the notification of aid plans and procedures applicable when aid is provided in breach of the rules of Article [88](3) of the EEC Treaty);[5]
6. Guidance note on use of the de minimis facility provided for in the SME guidelines (letter of 23 March 1993, IV/D/6878 from DG IV to the Member States);[6]

7. Commission letter to Member States of 22 February 1995 (interest rates to be applied when aid granted unlawfully is being recovered);[7]
8. Commission communication to the Member States (on the recovery of aid granted unlawfully);[8]
9. Commission letter to Member States of 22 February 1994 (concerning notifications);[9]
10. Section A of the joint procedure for reporting and notification under the EC Treaty and under the WTO Agreement as identified in Commission letter to Member States of 2 August 1995;[10]
11. Commission letter to Member States SG(81) 12740 of 2 October 1981 (time limits for decisions);[11]
12. Commission letter to Member States of 30 April 1987 (Procedure pursuant to Article [88](2) of the EEC Treaty — time-limits);[12]
13. Commission communication to the Member States on the accelerated clearance of aid schemes for SMEs and of amendments of existing schemes;[13]
14. Accelerated procedure for processing notifications of employment aid Standard notification form;[14]
15. Commission letter to Member States of 27 June 1989 (Procedure pursuant to Article [88](2) of the EEC Treaty — Notice to Member States and other parties concerned to submit their comments);[15]
16. Commission Letter to Member States of 11 October 1990 (Notice to Member States and other parties about aid cases not objected to by the Commission);[16]
17. "Guide to procedures in State aid cases".[17]

Notes

[1] OJ C 252, 30.9.1980, p. 2.
[2] OJ C 318, 24.11.1983, p. 3.
[3] OJ C 3, 05.01.1985, p. 2.
[4] Competition Law in the European Communities, Volume IIA, Rules applicable to State aid, Brussels–Luxembourg 1999, ISBN 92–828–4008–5, English Version p. 58.
[5] Competition Law in the European Communities, Volume IIA, Rules applicable to State aid, Brussels–Luxembourg 1999, ISBN 92–828–4008–5, English Version p. 59.
[6] Competition Law in the European Communities, Volume IIA, Rules applicable to State aid, Brussels–Luxembourg 1999, ISBN 92–828–4008–5, English Version p. 64.
[7] Competition Law in the European Communities, Volume IIA, Rules applicable to State aid, Brussels–Luxembourg 1999, ISBN 92–828–4008–5, English Version p. 68.
[8] OJ C 156, 22.6.1995, p. 5.
[9] Competition Law in the European Communities, Volume IIA, Rules applicable to State aid, Brussels–Luxembourg 1999, ISBN 92–828–4008–5, English Version p. 70.
[10] Competition Law in the European Communities, Volume IIA, Rules applicable to State aid, Brussels–Luxembourg 1999, ISBN 92–828–4008–5, English Version p. 72. Section B of this letter, which covers reporting to the WTO under Article 25 of the Agreement on Subsidies and Countervailing Measures, remains applicable.
[11] Competition Law in the European Communities, Volume IIA, Rules applicable to State aid, Brussels–Luxembourg 1999, ISBN 92–828–4008–5, English Version p. 89.
[12] Competition Law in the European Communities, Volume IIA, Rules applicable to State aid, Brussels–Luxembourg 1999, ISBN 92–828–4008–5, English Version p. 90.
[13] OJ C 213, 19.08.1992, p. 10.
[14] OJ C 218, 27.07.1996, p. 4.
[15] Competition Law in the European Communities, Volume IIA, Rules applicable to State aid, Brussels–Luxembourg 1999, ISBN 92–828–4008–5, English Version p. 99.
[16] Competition Law in the European Communities, Volume IIA, Rules applicable to State aid, Brussels–Luxembourg 1999, ISBN 92–828–4008–5, English Version p. 100.
[17] Competition Law in the European Communities, Volume IIA, Rules applicable to State aid, Brussels–Luxembourg 1999, ISBN 92–828–4008–5, English Version p. 23.

However, the Commission also wishes to inform Member States and interested parties that in so far as the provisions of Chapter V of Regulation (EC) 794/2004 only apply to decisions ordering the recovery of unlawful aid notified to Member States after the date of entry into force of the Regulation, the Commission communication of 8 May 2003 on the interest rates to be applied when aid granted unlawfully is being recovered[1] remains in effect as regards the execution by Member States of recovery orders notified before that date.

Notes
[1] OJ C 110, 8.5.2003, p. 21.

G8

DETAILS OF ARRANGEMENT FOR THE ELECTRONIC TRANSMISSION OF STATE AID NOTIFICATIONS INCLUDING ADDRESSES TOGETHER WITH THE ARRANGEMENTS FOR THE PROTECTION OF CONFIDENTIAL INFORMATION

Article 3(6) of Commission Regulation (EC) No 794/2004 of 21 April 2004 implementing Council Regulation (EC) No 659/1999 laying down detailed rules for the application of Article [88] of the EC Treaty

(2005/C 237/03)

Text with EEA relevance

Official Journal C 237, 27.9.2005, p. 3

Celex No: 52005XC0927(01)

Notes
EEA application: the EFTA Surveillance Authority has adopted a corresponding instrument: see OJ C 286, 23.11.2006, p.8 and EEA Supplement No 57, 23.11.2006, p. 31.

1. The present notice sets out the detailed arrangements for the transmission of the electronic notification forms, which will be compulsory as of 1 January 2006. It is based on Article 3(6) of Commission Regulation (EC) No 794/2004 of 21 April 2004 implementing Council Regulation (EC) No 659/1999 laying down detailed rules for the application of Article [88] of the Treaty. Article 3(6) requests the Commission to publish these arrangements before 30 September 2005. The advisory Committee for State aids has been consulted.

2. The notifications forms of Annexe I Part 1 and 2 of Regulation (EC) No 794/2004 will be made available in a Web-application, the different supplementary information sheets (part III of Annexe I) will be annexed as a word document. The address of the web application will be the following:

https://webgate.cec.eu.int/competition/sani

3. Member States are requested to nominate a Local Administrator as well as the person authorized to validate notifications as well as a replacement. The Commission will grant them a login and password for the web-application which will make sure that the incoming notifications are authorized.

Member States will have the possibility to sub-delegate certain access rights to other persons depending on the internal organisation of the Member States administration for the State aid notifications. The sub-delegation shall not modify the authorization to validate the notification.

4. Subsequent correspondence between the Member States and the Commission relating o the same notification will be sent electronically via a PKI (Public Key Infrastructure) encrypted e-mail system.

The address for this e-mail system will be a functional mailbox established within each DG responsible for the treatment of State aid notifications. Each DG will introduce a certification system which will make the e-mail correspondence secure and confidential.

5. Upon validation of the notification form and the corresponding Supplementary Information Sheet (SIS), the system will dispatch the notification to the Sec. Gen. and transfer the core data into the ISIS (Integrated State Aid Information System) database. Following that a notification of receipt will automatically be send to the notifying Member State indicating the delay within which the Commission intends to assess the case preliminary as well as the DG which the case has been attributed to by the system.

The delay will depend upon whether the Member State avails himself of the simplified procedure of Article 4 of Regulation (EC) No 794/2004.

6. In the case of the simplified procedures, the Commission will use its best endeavours to preliminarily assess the case within a month's period.

In all other cases, the delay will be fixed at two months.

Subsequent correspondence relating to the particular notification will be exchanged between the Member State and the DG responsible via a PKI (Public Key Infrastructure) secured system. Member States will inform the Commission of their representative authorized to receive the key and to manage the security system. Two keys will be available per Member State. Member States are responsible for the security guarantee of their own e-mailing system between the sending point and the Authorized Disclosure Officer (ADO).

7. Withdrawal of notifications should be done via the same secured e-mail system. Decisions that a notification is deemed to be withdrawn are decisions of the Commission; they will be communicated to the Member State through the secured e-mail system.

8. Pre-notifications shall not be submitted via the web-based system, but shall be sent by e-mail. Upon finalisation of the informal contacts Member States will be requested to fill in the formal notification through the web-application.

9. The Commission will establish a functional mailbox where all suggestions for improvements of the functioning of the system and the Web based application shall/could be sent to by Member States.

G9

COUNCIL REGULATION (EC) No 994/98

of 7 May 1998

on the application of Articles [87] and [88] of the Treaty establishing the European Community
to certain categories of horizontal State aid

Official Journal L 142, 14.5.1998, p. 1

Celex No: 31998R0994

Notes

On 5 October 2006 the Commission presented a proposal to amend this Regulation. That proposal is published on the Europa website at:
<http://ec.europa.eu/comm/competition/state_aid/reform/reform.cfm>

Commentary

Regulation 994/98/EC: B&C: 1.022, 1.065, 15.028, 15.067, 15.076 F&N: 16.58, 16.283

THE COUNCIL OF THE EUROPEAN UNION,

Having regard to the Treaty establishing the European Community, and in particular Article [89] thereof,

Having regard to the proposal from the Commission,[1]

After consulting the European Parliament,[2]

Having regard to the opinion of the Economic and Social Committee,[3]

Notes

[1] OJ C 262, 28.8.1997, p. 6.
[2] OJ C 138, 4.5.1998.
[3] OJ C 129, 27.4.1998, p. 70.

---

(1) Whereas, pursuant to Article [89] of the Treaty, the Council may make any appropriate regulations for the application of Articles [87] and [88] and may, in particular, determine the conditions in which Article [88](3) shall apply and the categories of aid exempted from this procedure;

(2) Whereas, under the Treaty, the assessment of compatibility of aid with the common market essentially rests with the Commission;

(3) Whereas the proper functioning of the internal market requires strict and efficient application of the rules of competition with regard to State aids;

(4) Whereas the Commission has applied Articles [87] and [88] of the Treaty in numerous decisions and has also stated its policy in a number of communications; whereas, in the light of the Commission's considerable experience in applying Articles [87] and [88] of the Treaty and the general texts issued by the Commission on the basis of those provisions, it is appropriate, with a view to ensuring efficient supervision and simplifying administration, without weakening Commission monitoring, that the Commission should be enabled to declare by means of regulations, in areas where the Commission has sufficient experience to define general compatibility criteria, that certain categories of aid are compatible with the common market pursuant to one or more of the provisions of Article [87](2) and (3) of the Treaty and are exempted from the procedure provided for in Article [88](3) thereof;

(5) Whereas group exemption regulations will increase transparency and legal certainty; whereas they can be directly applied by national courts, without prejudice to Articles [10] and [234] of the Treaty;

(6) Whereas it is appropriate that the Commission, when it adopts regulations exempting categories of aid from the obligation to notify provided for in Article [88](3) of the Treaty, specifies the purpose of the aid, the categories of beneficiaries and thresholds limiting the exempted aid, the conditions governing the cumulation of aid and the conditions of monitoring, in order to ensure the compatibility with the common market of aid covered by this Regulation;

(7) Whereas it is appropriate to enable the Commission, when it adopts regulations exempting certain categories of aid from the obligation to notify in Article [88](3) of the Treaty, to attach further detailed conditions in order to ensure the compatibility with the common market of aid covered by this Regulation;

(8) Whereas it may be useful to set thresholds of other appropriate conditions requiring the notification of awards of aid in order to allow the Commission to examine individually the effect of certain aid on competition and trade between Member States and its compatibility with the common market;

(9) Whereas the Commission, having regard to the development and the functioning of the common market, should be enabled to establish by means of a regulation that certain aid does not fulfil all the criteria of Article [87](1) of the Treaty and is therefore exempted from the notification procedure laid down in Article [88](3), provided that aid granted to the same undertaking over a given period of time does not exceed a certain fixed amount;

(10) Whereas in accordance with Article [88](1) of the Treaty the Commission is under an obligation, in cooperation with Member States, to keep under constant review all systems of existing aid; whereas for this purpose and in order to ensure the largest possible degree of transparency and adequate control it is desirable that the Commission ensures the establishment of a reliable system of recording and storing information about the application of the regulations it adopts, to which all Member States have access, and that it receives all necessary information from the Member States on the implementation of aid exempted from notification to fulfil this obligation, which may be examined and evaluated with the Member States within the Advisory Committee; whereas for this purpose it is also desirable that the Commission may require such information to be supplied as is necessary to ensure the efficiency of such review;

(11) Whereas the control of the granting of aid involves factual, legal and economic issues of a very complex nature and great variety in a constantly evolving environment; whereas the Commission should therefore regularly review the categories of aid which should be exempted from notification; whereas the Commission should be able to repeal or amend regulations it has adopted pursuant to this Regulation where circumstances have changed with respect to any important element which constituted grounds for their adoption or where the progressive development or the functioning of the common market so requires;

(12) Whereas the Commission, in close and constant liaison with the Member States, should be able to define precisely the scope of these regulations and the conditions attached to them; whereas, in order to provide for cooperation between the Commission and the competent authorities of the Member States, it is appropriate to set up an advisory committee on State aid to be consulted before the Commission adopts regulations pursuant to this Regulation,

HAS ADOPTED THIS REGULATION:

Article 1
Group exemptions

1. The Commission may, by means of regulations adopted in accordance with the procedures laid down in Article 8 of this Regulation and in accordance with Article [87] of the Treaty, declare that the following categories of aid should be compatible with the common market and shall not be subject to the notification requirements of Article [88](3) of the Treaty:

(a) aid in favour of:

   (i) small and medium-sized enterprises;
   (ii) research and development;
   (iii) environmental protection;
   (iv) employment and training;

(b) aid that complies with the map approved by the Commission for each Member State for the grant of regional aid.

2. The Regulations referred to in paragraph 1 shall specify for each category of aid:

(a) the purpose of the aid;
(b) the categories of beneficiaries;
(c) thresholds expressed either in terms of aid intensities in relation to a set of eligible costs or in terms of maximum aid amounts;
(d) the conditions governing the cumulation of aid;
(e) the conditions of monitoring as specified in Article 3.

3. In addition, the regulations referred to in paragraph 1 may, in particular:

(a) set thresholds or other conditions for the notification of awards of individual aid;
(b) exclude certain sectors from their scope;
(c) attach further conditions for the compatibility of aid exempted under such regulations.

Commentary
Art 1(1): **B&C:** 15.076
Art 1(2): **B&C:** 15.076
Art 1(3): **B&C:** 15.076

Article 2
De minimis

1. The Commission may, by means of a Regulation adopted in accordance with the procedure laid down in Article 8 of this Regulation, decide that, having regard to the development and functioning of the common market, certain aids do not meet all the criteria of Article [88](1) and that they are therefore exempted from the notification procedure provided for in Article [88](3), provided that aid granted to the same undertaking over a given period of time does not exceed a certain fixed amount.

2. At the Commission's request, Member States shall, at any time, communicate to it any additional information relating to aid exempted under paragraph 1.

Commentary
Art 2: **B&C:** 15.028

Article 3
Transparency and monitoring

1. When adopting regulations pursuant to Article 1, the Commission shall impose detailed rules upon Member States to ensure transparency and monitoring of the aid exempted from notification in accordance with those regulations. Such rules shall consist, in particular, of the requirements laid down in paragraphs 2, 3 and 4.

2. On implementation of aid systems or individual aids granted outside any system, which have been exempted pursuant to such regulations, Member States shall forward to the Commission, with a view to publication in the *Official Journal of the European Communities*, summaries of the information regarding such systems of aid or such individual aids as are not covered by exempted aid systems.

3. Member States shall record and compile all the information regarding the application of the group exemptions. If the Commission has information which leads it to doubt that an exemption regulation is being applied properly, the Member States shall forward to it any information it considers necessary to assess whether an aid complies with that regulation.

4. At least once a year, Member States shall supply the Commission with a report on the application of group exemptions, in accordance with the Commission's specific requirements, preferably in computerised form. The Commission shall make access to those reports available to all the Member States. The Advisory Committee referred to in Article 7 shall examine and evaluate those reports once a year.

Part G **State Aids**

Article 4
Period of validity and amendment of regulations

1. Regulations adopted pursuant to Articles 1 and 2 shall apply for a specific period. Aid exempted by a regulation adopted pursuant to Articles 1 and 2 shall be exempted for the period of validity of that regulation and for the adjustment period provided for in paragraphs 2 and 3.

2. Regulations adopted pursuant to Articles 1 and 2 may be repeated or amended where circumstances have changed with respect to any important element that constituted grounds for their adoption or where the progressive development or the functioning of the common market so requires. In that case the new regulation shall set a period of adjustment of six months for the adjustment of aid covered by the previous regulation.

3. Regulations adopted pursuant to Articles 1 and 2 shall provide for a period as referred to in paragraph 2, should their application not be extended when they expire.

Article 5
Evaluation report

Every five years the Commission shall submit a report to the European Parliament and to the Council on the application of this Regulation. It shall submit a draft report for consideration by the Advisory Committee referred to in Article 7.

Article 6
Hearing of interested parties

Where the Commission intends to adopt a regulation, it shall publish a draft thereof to enable all interested persons and organisations to submit their comments to it within a reasonable time limit to be fixed by the Commission and which may not under any circumstances be less than one month.

Article 7
Advisory committee

An advisory committee, hereinafter referred to as the Advisory Committee on State Aid, shall be set up. It shall be composed of representatives of the Member States and chaired by the representative of the Commission.

Article 8
Consultation of the Advisory Committee

1. The Commission shall consult the Advisory Committee on State Aid:

(a) before publishing any draft regulation;
(b) before adopting any regulation.

2. Consultation of the Committee shall take place at a meeting called by the Commission. The drafts and documents to be examined shall be annexed to the notification. The meeting shall take place no earlier than two months after notification has been sent.

This period may be reduced in the case of the consultations referred to in paragraph 1(b), when urgent or for simple extension of a regulation.

3. The representative of the Commission shall submit to the Committee a draft of the measures to be taken. The Committee shall deliver its opinion on the draft, within a time limit which the Chairman may lay down according to the urgency of the matter, if necessary by taking a vote.

4. The opinion shall be recorded in the minutes; in addition, each Member State shall have the right to ask to have its position recorded in the minutes. The Advisory Committee may recommend publication of the opinion in the *Official Journal of the European Communities*.

5. The Commission shall take the utmost account of the opinion delivered by the Committee. It shall inform the Committee of the manner in which its opinion has been taken into account.

Article 9
Final provisions

This Regulation shall enter into force on the day following its publication in the *Official Journal of the European Communities*.

This Regulation shall be binding in its entirety and directly applicable in all Member States.

Done at Brussels, 7 May 1998.

Notes

Date of entry into force: 15 May 1998.

G10

COMMISSION REGULATION (EC) No 68/2001

of 12 January 2001
on the application of Articles 87 and 88 of the EC Treaty to training aid

Official Journal L 10, 13.1.2001, p. 20

Celex No: 32001R0068

Notes

EEA application: this Regulation was incorporated with appropriate adaptations by EEA Joint Committee Decision No 88/2002 (OJ L 266, 3.10.2002, p. 37 and EEA Supplement No 49, 3.10.2002, p. 13): see EEA Agreement Annex XV, Point 1d (as subsequently amended by Decision No 131/2004 (OJ No L 64, 10.3.2005, p. 67 and EEA Supplement No 12, 10.3.2005, p. 49)).

Commentary

Regulation 68/2001/EC: B&C: 15.067 F&N: 16.74–16.78, 16.284

THE COMMISSION OF THE EUROPEAN COMMUNITIES,

Having regard to the Treaty establishing the European Community,

Having regard to Council Regulation (EC) No 994/98 of 7 May 1998 on the application of Articles [87] and [88] of the Treaty establishing the European Community to certain categories of horizontal State aid,[1] and in particular point (a)(iv) of Article 1(1) thereof,

Having published a draft of this Regulation,[2]

Having consulted the Advisory Committee on State Aid,

Notes

[1] OJ L 142, 14.5.1998, p. 1.
[2] OJ C 89, 28.3.2000, p. 8.

Whereas:

(1) Regulation (EC) No 994/98 empowers the Commission to declare, in accordance with Article 87 of the Treaty, that under certain conditions training aid is compatible with the common market and not subject to the notification requirement of Article 88(3) of the Treaty.

(2) The Commission has applied Articles 87 and 88 of the Treaty to training aid in numerous decisions and has also stated its policy, most recently in the Community framework on training aid.[1] In the light of the Commission's considerable experience in applying those Articles to training aid, it is appropriate, with a view to ensuring efficient supervision and simplifying administration without weakening Commission monitoring, that the Commission should make use of the powers conferred by Regulation (EC) No 994/98.

Notes
[1] OJ C 343, 11.11.1998, p. 10.

(3) In order to establish a transparent and coherent policy for all sectors, it is appropriate that the scope of this Regulation be as broad as possible and include the agricultural sector, fisheries and aquaculture.

(4) This Regulation is without prejudice to the possibility for Member States to notify training aid. Such notifications will be assessed by the Commission in particular in the light of the criteria set out in this Regulation, or in accordance with the applicable Community guidelines and frameworks, if such guidelines and frameworks exist. This is currently the case for activities relating to the production, processing and marketing of products listed in Annex I to the Treaty and for the sector of maritime transport. The framework on training aid should be abolished from the date of entry into force of this Regulation, since its contents are replaced by this Regulation.

(5) For reasons of transparency, it should be recalled that in accordance with the second subparagraph of Article 51(1), of Council Regulation (EC) No 1257/1999 of 17 May 1999 on support for rural development from the European Agricultural Guidance and Guarantee Fund (EAGGF) and amending and repealing certain Regulations,[1] Articles 87 to 89 of the Treaty do not apply to financial contributions provided by the Member States for measures subject to Community support for training according to Article 9 of the said Regulation.

Notes
[1] OJ L 160, 26.6.1999, p. 80.

(6) For reasons of transparency it should be underlined that this Regulation should only apply to training measures which constitute State aid within the meaning of Article 87(1) of the Treaty. Many training measures are not caught by that Article, but constitute general measures because they are open to all enterprises in all sectors without discrimination and without discretionary power for the authorities applying the measure, e.g. general tax incentive schemes, such as automatic tax credits, open to all firms investing in employee training. Other training measures do not fall within the scope of Article 87(1) of the Treaty because they directly benefit people everywhere and do not grant an advantage to certain enterprises or sectors. Examples are: schooling and initial training (such as apprenticeships and day-release schemes); the training or re-training of unemployed people, including traineeships in enterprises; measures directly targeted at workers or even at certain categories of workers, affording them the opportunity of receiving training unconnected with the firm or industry in which they work (for example the "learning account"). On the other hand, it should be recalled that contributions from sectoral funds, if they are made compulsory by the State, are not considered as private resources, but constitute State resources within the meaning of Article 87(1) of the Treaty.

(7) This Regulation should exempt any aid that meets all the relevant requirements of this Regulation, and any aid scheme, provided that any aid that could be granted under such scheme meets all the relevant requirements of this Regulation. With a view to ensuring efficient supervision and simplifying administration without weakening Commission monitoring, aid schemes and individual grants, outside any aid scheme, should contain an express reference to this Regulation.

(8) In order to eliminate differences that might give rise to distortions of competition, in order to facilitate coordination between different Community and national initiatives concerning small and medium-sized enterprises, and for reasons of administrative clarity and legal certainty, the definition of "small and medium-sized enterprises" used in this Regulation should be that laid down in Commission Recommendation 96/280/EC of 3 April 1996 concerning the definition of small and medium-sized enterprises.[1]

Notes
[1] OJ L 107, 30.4.1996, p. 4.

(9) In order to determine whether or not aid is compatible with the common market pursuant to this Regulation, it is necessary to take into consideration the aid intensity and thus the aid amount expressed as a grant equivalent. Calculation of the grant equivalent of aid payable in

several instalments, and calculation of aid in the form of a soft loan, require the use of market interest rates prevailing at the time of grant. With a view to a uniform, transparent and simple application of the State aid rules, the market rates for the purposes of this Regulation should be deemed to be the reference rates, provided that, in the case of a soft loan, the loan is backed by normal security and does not involve abnormal risk. The reference rates should be those which are periodically fixed by the Commission on the basis of objective criteria and published in the *Official Journal of the European Communities* and on the Internet.

(10) Training usually has positive external effects for society as a whole since it increases the pool of skilled workers from which other firms may draw, improves the competitiveness of Community industry and plays an important role in employment strategy. In view of the fact that enterprises in the Community generally underinvest in the training of their workers, State aid might help to correct this market imperfection and therefore can be considered under certain conditions to be compatible with the common market and therefore exempted from prior notification.

(11) In order to ensure that State aid is limited to the minimum necessary to obtain the Community objective which market forces alone would not make possible, the permissible intensities of exempted aid should be modulated according to the type of training provided, the size of the enterprise and its geographical location.

(12) General training provides transferable qualifications and substantially improves the employability of the trained worker. Aid for this purpose has less distortive effects on competition, so that higher intensities of aid can be considered compatible with the common market and exempted from prior notification. Specific training, on the other hand, which mainly benefits the enterprise, involves a greater risk of distortion of competition so that the intensity of aid which can be considered compatible and exempted from prior notification should be much lower.

(13) In view of the handicaps with which SMEs are confronted and the higher relative costs that they have to bear when they invest in the training of their workers, the intensities of aid exempted by this Regulation should be increased for SMEs.

(14) In assisted areas under Article 87(3)(a) and (c) of the Treaty, training has a relatively greater external impact, since there is a substantial underinvestment in training in those regions and a higher unemployment rate. Consequently, the intensities of aid exempted by this Regulation should be increased for those areas.

(15) The characteristics of training in the maritime transport sector justify a specific approach for that sector.

(16) It is appropriate that large amounts of aid remain subject to an individual assessment by the Commission before they are put into effect. Accordingly, aid amounts exceeding a fixed amount, which should be set at EUR 1,000,000, are excluded from the exemption provided for in this Regulation and remain subject to the requirements of Article 88(3) of the Treaty.

(17) This Regulation should not exempt aid cumulated with other State aid, including aid granted by national, regional and local authorities, or with Community assistance, in relation to the same eligible costs when such cumulation exceeds the thresholds fixed in this Regulation.

(18) In order to ensure transparency and effective monitoring in accordance with Article 3 of Regulation (EC) No 994/98, it is appropriate to establish a standard format in which Member States should provide the Commission with summary information whenever, in pursuance of this Regulation, an aid scheme is implemented or an individual aid outside such schemes is granted, with a view to publication in the *Official Journal of the European Communities*. For the same reasons, it is appropriate to establish rules concerning the records that Member States should keep regarding the aid exempted by this Regulation. For the purposes of the annual reports to be submitted to the Commission by Member States, it is appropriate for the Commission to establish its specific requirements, including, in view of the wide availability of the necessary technology, information in computerised form.

(19) Having regard to the Commission's experience and in particular the frequency with which it is generally necessary to revise State aid policy, it is appropriate to limit the period of application of this Regulation. Should this Regulation expire without being extended, aid schemes already exempted by this Regulation should continue to be exempted for six months,

HAS ADOPTED THIS REGULATION:

[*Article 1*
Scope

This Regulation applies to training aid in all sectors, including the activities relating to the production, processing and marketing of products listed in Annex I of the Treaty, with the exception of aid falling within the scope of Council Regulation (EC) No 1407/2002.[1]]

Notes

[[1] OJ L 205, 2.8.2002, p. 1.]

Article 1 was amended as shown in square brackets by Commission Regulation (EC) No 363/2004 of 25 February 2004 (OJ L 63, 28.2.2004, p. 63), Article 1(1), with effect from 19 March 2004.

Article 2
Definitions

For the purpose of this Regulation:

(a) "aid" shall mean any measure fulfilling all the criteria laid down in Article 87(1) of the Treaty;

[(b) "small and medium-sized enterprises" shall mean enterprises as defined in Annex I to Commission Regulation (EC) No 70/2001;[1]

(c) "large enterprises" shall mean enterprises not coming under the definition of small and medium-sized enterprises;]

(d) "specific training" shall mean training involving tuition directly and principally applicable to the employee's present or future position in the assisted firm and providing qualifications which are not or only to a limited extent transferable to other firms or fields of work;

(e) "general training" shall mean training involving tuition which is not applicable only or principally to the employee's present or future position in the assisted firm, but which provides qualifications that are largely transferable to other firms or fields of work and thereby substantially improve the employability of the employee. Training shall be considered "general" if, for example,

— it is jointly organised by different independent enterprises, or if employees of different enterprises may avail themselves of the training,

— it is recognised, certified or validated by public authorities or bodies or by other bodies or institutions on which a Member State or the Community has conferred the necessary powers;

(f) "aid intensity" shall mean the gross aid amount expressed as a percentage of the project's eligible costs. All figures used shall be taken before any deduction for direct taxation. Where aid is awarded in a form other than a grant, the aid amount shall be the grant equivalent of the aid. Aid payable in several instalments shall be discounted to its value at the time of granting. The interest rate to be used for discounting purposes and for calculating the aid amount in a soft loan shall be the reference rate applicable at the time of grant;

(g) "disadvantaged worker" shall mean:

— any young person under 25 who has not previously obtained his first regular paid employment,

— any person with serious disabilities which result from physical, mental or psychological impairments and yet capable of entering the labour market,

— any migrant worker who moves or has moved within the Community or becomes resident in the Community to take up work and who needs professional and/or language training,

— any person wishing to re-enter working life after a break of at least three years, and particularly any person who gave up work on account of the difficulty of reconciling his working life and family life, for the first six months after recruitment,

— any person older than 45 who has not attained an upper secondary educational qualification or its equivalent,

— any long-term unemployed person, i.e. any person who was without work for 12 consecutive months, for the first six months after recruitment.

Notes

[[1] OJ L 10, 13.1.2002, p. 33.]

Article 2 was amended as shown in square brackets by Commission Regulation (EC) No 363/2004 of 25 February 2004 (OJ L 63, 28.2.2004, p. 63), Article 1(2), with effect from 19 March 2004.

Article 3
Conditions for exemption

1. Individual aid outside any scheme, fulfilling all the conditions of this Regulation, shall be compatible with the common market within the meaning of Article 87(3) of the Treaty and shall be exempt from the notification requirement of Article 88(3) of the Treaty provided that it contains an express reference to this Regulation, by citing its title and publication reference in the *Official Journal of the European Communities*.

2. Aid schemes fulfilling all the conditions of this Regulation shall be compatible with the common market within the meaning of Article 87(3) of the Treaty and shall be exempt from the notification requirement of Article 88(3) of the Treaty provided that:

(a) any aid that could be awarded under such scheme fulfils all the conditions of this Regulation;
(b) the scheme contains an express reference to this Regulation, by citing its title and publication reference in the *Official Journal of the European Communities*.

3. Aid granted under the schemes referred to in paragraph 2 shall be compatible with the common market within the meaning of Article 87(3) of the Treaty and shall be exempt from the notification requirement of Article 88(3) of the Treaty provided that the aid granted directly fulfils all the conditions of this Regulation.

Article 4
Exempted training aid

1. Aid schemes and individual aid for training must fulfil the conditions laid down in paragraphs 2 to 7.

2. Where the aid is granted for specific training, its intensity shall not exceed 25% for large enterprises and 35% for small and medium-sized enterprises.

These intensities shall be increased by five percentage points for enterprises in areas which qualify for regional aid pursuant to Article 87(3)(c) of the Treaty and by 10 percentage points for enterprises in areas which qualify for regional aid pursuant to Article 87(3)(a) of the Treaty.

3. Where the aid is granted for general training, its intensity shall not exceed 50% for large enterprises and 70% for small and medium-sized enterprises.

These intensities shall be increased by five percentage points for enterprises in areas which qualify for regional aid pursuant to Article 87(3)(c) of the Treaty and by 10 percentage points for enterprises in areas which qualify for regional aid pursuant to Article 87(3)(a) of the Treaty.

4. The maximum intensities referred to in paragraphs 2 and 3 shall be increased by 10 percentage points if the training is given to disadvantaged workers.

5. In cases where the aid project involves both specific and general training components which cannot be separated for the calculation of the aid intensity, and in cases where the specific or general character of the training aid project cannot be established, the intensities applicable to specific training pursuant to paragraph 2 shall apply.

6. Where the aid is granted in the maritime transport sector, it may reach an intensity of 100%, whether the training project concerns specific or general training, provided that the following conditions are met:

(a) the trainee shall not be an active member of the crew but shall be supernumerary on board, and
(b) the training shall be carried out on board ships entered on Community registers.

7. The eligible costs of a training aid project shall be:

(a) trainers' personnel costs,
(b) trainers' and trainees' travel expenses,
(c) other current expenses such as materials and supplies,
(d) depreciation of tools and equipment, to the extent that they are used exclusively for the training project,

(e) cost of guidance and counselling services with regard to the training project,

(f) trainees' personnel costs up to the amount of the total of the other eligible costs referred to in (a) to (e). Only the hours during which the trainees actually participate in the training, after deduction of any productive hours or of their equivalent, may be taken into account.

The eligible costs shall be supported by documentary evidence, which shall be transparent and itemised.

Article 5
Large individual aid grants

The exemption shall not apply if the amount of aid granted to one enterprise for a single training project exceeds EUR 1,000,000.

Article 6
Cumulation

1. The aid ceilings fixed in Articles 4 and 5 shall apply regardless of whether the support for the project is financed entirely from State resources or is partly financed by the Community.

2. Aid exempted by this Regulation shall not be cumulated with any other State aid within the meaning of Article 87(1) of the Treaty, or with other Community funding, in relation to the same eligible costs, if such cumulation would result in an aid intensity exceeding that fixed by this Regulation.

Article 7
Transparency and monitoring

1. On implementation of an aid scheme, or grant of individual aid outside any scheme, exempted by this Regulation, Member States shall, within 20 working days, forward to the Commission, with a view to its publication in the *Official Journal of the European Communities*, a summary of the information regarding such aid scheme or individual aid according to the model laid down in Annex II.

2. Member States shall maintain detailed records regarding the aid schemes exempted by this Regulation, the individual aid granted under those schemes, and the individual aid exempted by this Regulation that is granted outside any existing aid scheme. Such records shall contain all information necessary to establish that the conditions for exemption, as laid down in this Regulation, are fulfilled. Member States shall keep a record regarding an individual aid for 10 years from the date on which it was granted, and regarding an aid scheme, for 10 years from the date on which the last individual aid was granted under such scheme. On written request, the Member State concerned shall provide the Commission, within a period of 20 working days or such longer period as may be fixed in the request, with all the information which the Commission considers necessary to assess whether the conditions of this Regulation have been complied with.

[3. Member States shall compile an annual report on the application of this Regulation in accordance with the implementing provisions concerning the form and content of annual reports which are laid down pursuant to Article 27 of Council Regulation (EC) No 659/1999.[1]

Until such provisions enter into force, Member States shall compile an annual report on the application of this Regulation in respect of the whole or part of each calendar year during which this Regulation applies, in the form laid down in Annex III, also in computerised form. Member States shall provide the Commission with such report no later than three months after the expiry of the period to which the report relates.]

Notes

[[1] OJ L 83, 27.3.1999, p. 1.]

Article 7 was amended as shown in square brackets by Commission Regulation (EC) No 363/2004 of 25 February 2004 (OJ L 63, 28.2.2004, p. 63), Article 1(3), with effect from 19 March 2004.

Commentary
Art 7(1): **F&N:** 16.286

[*Article 7a*
Transitional provisions

Aid schemes implemented before the date of entry into force of this Regulation, and aid granted under such schemes, in the absence of a Commission authorisation and in breach of the notification requirement of Article 88(3) of the Treaty, shall be compatible with the common market within the meaning of Article 87(3) of the Treaty and shall be exempt if they fulfil the conditions laid down in Article 3(2)(a) and Article 3(3) of this Regulation.

Individual aid outside any scheme granted before the date of entry into force of this Regulation, in the absence of a Commission authorisation and in breach of the notification requirement of Article 88(3) of the Treaty, shall be compatible with the common market within the meaning of Article 87(3) of the Treaty and shall be exempt if it fulfils all the conditions of this Regulation, except the requirement in Article 3(1) that express reference be made to this Regulation.

Any aid which does not fulfil these conditions shall be assessed by the Commission in accordance with the relevant frameworks, guidelines, communications and notices.]

Notes

Article 7a as shown in square brackets was inserted by Commission Regulation (EC) No 363/2004 of 25 February 2004 (OJ L 63, 28.2.2004, p. 63), Article 1(4), with effect from 19 March 2004.

Article 8
Entry into force and period of validity

1. This Regulation shall enter into force on the 20th day following its publication in the *Official Journal of the European Communities.*

[It shall apply until 30 June 2008]

2. At the end of the period of validity of this Regulation, aid schemes exempted under this Regulation shall remain exempted during an adjustment period of six months.

Notes

Date of entry into force: 2 February 2001.
Article 8 was amended as shown in square brackets by Commission Regulation (EC) No 1976/2006 of 20 December 2006 (OJ L 368, 23.12.2006, p. 85), Article 3.

This Regulation shall be binding in its entirety and directly applicable in all Member States.

Done at Brussels, 12 January 2001.

[ANNEX I]

Notes

Annex I was deleted by Commission Regulation (EC) No 363/2004 of 25 February 2004 (OJ L 63, 28.2.2004, p. 63), Article 1(5), with effect from 19 March 2004.

ANNEX II

FORM OF SUMMARY INFORMATION TO BE PROVIDED WHENEVER AN AID SCHEME EXEMPTED BY THIS REGULATION IS IMPLEMENTED AND WHENEVER AN INDIVIDUAL AID EXEMPTED BY THIS REGULATION IS GRANTED OUTSIDE ANY AID SCHEME

Notes

Annex II is available in electronic form from the Europa website at the following address:
http://ec.europa.eu/comm/competition/state_aid/legislation/forms.html

Summary Information on State Aid Granted in Conformity with Commission Regulation (EC) No 68/2001

Summary information to be filled in	Explanatory remarks
Member State	
Region	Indicate the name of the region if the aid is granted by a subcentral authority
Title of aid scheme or name of company receiving an individual aid	Indicate the name of the aid scheme or in the case of individual aid, the name of the beneficiary. In the latter case, no subsequent annual report is necessary!
Legal basis	Indicate the precise national legal reference for the aid scheme or for the individual aid
Annual expenditure planned under the scheme or overall amount of individual aid granted to the company	Amounts are to be given in euro or, if applicable, national currency. In the case of an aid scheme: indicate the annual overall amount of the budget appropriation(s) or the estimated tax loss per year for all aid instruments contained in the scheme. In the case of an individual aid award: indicate the overall aid amount/tax loss. If appropriate, indicate also for how many years the aid will be paid in instalments or over how many years tax losses will be incurred. For guarantees in both cases, indicate the (maximum) amount of loans guaranteed
Maximum aid intensity	Indicate the maximum aid intensity or the maximum aid amount per eligible item
Date of implementation	Indicate the date from which aid may be granted under the scheme or when the individual aid is granted
Duration of scheme or individual aid award	Indicate the date (year and month) until which aid may be granted under the scheme or in the case of an individual aid and if appropriate the expected date (year and month) of the last instalment to be paid
Objective of aid	In the case of training aid, indicate whether the training is specific or general. In the case of general training, documentary evidence (e.g. description of the contents of the training) must be attached regarding the qualification of the training as general

Summary information to be filled in	Explanatory remarks
Economic sector(s) concerned	Choose from the list, where relevant
☐ All sectors	
or	
☐ Agriculture	
☐ Fisheries and Aquaculture	
☐ Coalmining	
☐ All manufacturing	
or	
☐ Steel	
☐ Shipbuilding	
☐ Synthetic fibres	
☐ Motor vehicles	
☐ Other manufacturing	
☐ All services	
or	
☐ Maritime transport services	
☐ Other transport services	
☐ Financial services	
☐ Other services	
Remarks:	
Name and address of the granting authority	
Other information	

ANNEX III
FORM OF THE PERIODIC REPORT TO BE PROVIDED TO THE COMMISSION

ANNUAL REPORTING FORMAT ON AID SCHEMES EXEMPTED UNDER A GROUP
EXEMPTION REGULATION ADOPTED PURSUANT TO ARTICLE I OF COUNCIL
REGULATION (EC) No 994/98

Member States are required to use the format below for their reporting obligations to the Commission under group exemption regulations adopted on the basis of Council Regulation (EC) No 994/98.

The reports should also be provided in computerised form.

Information required for all aid schemes exempted under group exemption regulations adopted pursuant to Article 1 of Council Regulation (EC) No 994/98

1. Title of aid scheme
2. Commission exemption regulation applicable
3. Expenditure

Separate figures have to be provided for each aid instrument within a scheme or individual aid (e.g. grant, soft loans, etc). The figures have to be expressed in euro or, if applicable, national currency. In the case of tax expenditure, annual tax losses have to be reported. If precise figures are not available, such losses may be estimated.

These expenditure figures should be provided on the following basis:

for the year under review indicate separately for each aid instrument within the scheme (e.g. grant, soft loan, guarantee, etc.):

3.1. amounts committed, (estimated) tax losses or other revenue forgone, data on guarantees, etc. for new assisted projects. In the case of guarantee schemes, the total amount of new guarantees handed out should be provided;

3.2. actual payments, (estimated) tax losses or other revenue forgone, data on guarantees, etc. for new and current projects. In the case of guarantee schemes, the following should be provided: total amount of outstanding guarantees, premium income, recoveries, indemnities paid out, operating result of the scheme under the year under review;

3.3. number of new assisted projects;

3.4. estimated overall number of jobs created or maintained by new projects (if appropriate);

3.5. estimated overall amount of investment aided by new projects;

3.6. regional breakdown of amounts under point 3.1 either by regions defined at NUTS[1] level 2 or below or by Article 87(3)(a) regions, Article 87(3)(c) regions and non-assisted regions;

3.7. sectorial breakdown of amounts under point 3.1. by beneficiaries' sectors of activity (if more than one sector is covered, indicate the share of each):

— agriculture
— fisheries and/or aquaculture
— coalmining
— manufacturing
of which:
steel
shipbuilding
synthetic fibres
motor vehicles
other manufacturing (please specify)
— services
of which:
maritime transport services
other transport services
financial services
other services (please specify)
— other sectors (please specify)

4. Other information and remarks

Notes
[1] NUTS is the nomenclature of territorial units for statistical purposes in the EC.

G11

COMMISSION REGULATION (EC) No 70/2001

of 12 January 2001

on the application of Articles 87 and 88 of the EC Treaty to State aid to small and medium-sized enterprises

Official Journal L 10, 13.1.2001, p. 33

Celex No: 32001R0070

Notes

EEA application: this Regulation was incorporated with appropriate adaptations by EEA Joint Committee Decision No 88/2002 (OJ L 266, 3.10.2002, p. 56 and EEA Supplement No 49, 3.10.2002, p. 42): see EEA Agreement, Annex XV, Point 1f (as subsequently amended by Decision No 131/2004 (OJ No L 64, 10.3.2005, p. 67 and EEA Supplement No 12, 10.3.2005, p. 49)).

Commentary

Regulation 70/2001/EC: B&C: 15.067 **F&N:** 16.60, 16.62–16.65, 16.284

THE COMMISSION OF THE EUROPEAN COMMUNITIES,

Having regard to the Treaty establishing the European Community,

Having regard to Council Regulation (EC) No 994/98 of 7 May 1998 on the application of Articles [87] and [88] of the Treaty establishing the European Community to certain categories of horizontal State aid,[1] and in particular points (a)(i) and (b) of Article 1(1) thereof,

Having published a draft of this Regulation,[2]

Having consulted the Advisory Committee on State Aid,

Notes
[1] OJ L 142, 14.5.1998, p. 1.
[2] OJ C 89, 28.3.2000, p. 15.

Whereas:

(1) Regulation (EC) No 994/98 empowers the Commission to declare, in accordance with Article 87 of the Treaty, that under certain conditions aid to small and medium-sized enterprises is compatible with the common market and not subject to the notification requirement of Article 88(3) of the Treaty.

(2) Regulation (EC) No 994/98 also empowers the Commission to declare, in accordance with Article 87 of the Treaty, that aid that complies with the map approved by the Commission for each Member State for the grant of regional aid is compatible with the common market and is not subject to the notification requirement of Article 88(3) of the Treaty.

(3) The Commission has applied Articles 87 and 88 of the Treaty to small and medium-sized enterprises in and outside assisted areas in numerous decisions and has also stated its policy, most recently in the Community guidelines on State aid for small and medium-sized enterprises[1] and in the guidelines on national regional aid.[2] In the light of the Commission's considerable experience in applying those Articles to small and medium-sized enterprises and in the light of the general texts relating to small and medium-sized enterprises and to regional aid issued by the Commission on the basis of those provisions, it is appropriate, with a view to ensuring efficient supervision and simplifying administration without weakening Commission monitoring, that the Commission should make use of the powers conferred by Regulation (EC) No 994/98.

Notes
¹ OJ C 213, 23.7.1996, p. 4.
² OJ C 74, 10.3.1998, p. 9.

(4) This Regulation is without prejudice to the possibility for Member States of notifying aid to small and medium-sized enterprises. Such notifications will be assessed by the Commission in particular in the light of the criteria set out in this Regulation. The guidelines on State aid for small and medium-sized enterprises should be abolished from the date of entry into force of this Regulation, since their contents are replaced by this Regulation.

(5) Small and medium-sized enterprises play a decisive role in job creation and, more generally, act as a factor of social stability and economic drive. However, their development may be limited by market imperfections. They often have difficulties in obtaining capital or credit, given the risk-shy nature of certain financial markets and the limited guarantees that they may be able to offer. Their limited resources may also restrict their access to information, notably regarding new technology and potential markets. Having regard to those considerations, the purpose of the aid exempted by this Regulation should be to facilitate the development of the economic activities of small and medium-sized enterprises, provided that such aid does not adversely affect trading conditions to an extent contrary to the common interest.

(6) This Regulation should exempt any aid that meets all the relevant requirements of this Regulation, and any aid scheme, provided that any aid that could be granted under such scheme meets all the relevant requirements of this Regulation. With a view to ensuring efficient supervision and simplifying administration without weakening Commission monitoring, aid schemes and individual grants outside any aid scheme should contain an express reference to this Regulation.

(7) This Regulation should apply without prejudice to special rules in regulations and directives concerning State aid in certain sectors, such as currently exist for shipbuilding, and should not apply to agriculture and fisheries and aquaculture.

(8) In order to eliminate differences that might give rise to distortions of competition, in order to facilitate coordination between different Community and national initiatives concerning small and medium-sized enterprises, and for reasons of administrative clarity and legal certainty, the definition of "small and medium-sized enterprises" used in this Regulation should be that laid down in Commission Recommendation 96/280/EC of 3 April 1996 concerning the definition of small and medium-sized enterprises.[1] That definition was also used in the Community guidelines on State aid for small and medium-sized enterprises.[2]

Notes
¹ OJ L 107, 30.4.1996, p. 4.
² [OJ C 213, 23.7.1996, p. 4.]

(9) In accordance with the established practice of the Commission, and with a view to better ensuring that aid is proportionate and limited to the amount necessary, thresholds should be expressed in terms of aid intensities in relation to a set of eligible costs, rather than in terms of maximum aid amounts.

(10) In order to determine whether or not aid is compatible with the common market pursuant to this Regulation, it is necessary to take into consideration the aid intensity and thus the aid amount expressed as a grant equivalent. The calculation of the grant equivalent of aid payable in several instalments and aid in the form of a soft loan requires the use of market interest rates prevailing at the time of grant. With a view to a uniform, transparent, and simple application of the State aid rules, the market rates for the purposes of this Regulation should be deemed to be the reference rates, provided that, in the case of a soft loan, the loan is backed by normal security and does not involve abnormal risk. The reference rates should be those which are periodically fixed by the Commission on the basis of objective criteria and published in the *Official Journal of the European Communities* and on the Internet.

(11) Having regard to the differences between small enterprises and medium-sized enterprises, different ceilings of aid intensity should be set for small enterprises and for medium-sized enterprises.

(12) The ceilings of aid intensity should be fixed, in the light of the Commission's experience, at a level that strikes the appropriate balance between minimising distortions of competition in the aided sector and the objective of facilitating the development of the economic activities of small and medium-sized enterprises.

(13) It is appropriate to establish further conditions that should be fulfilled by any aid scheme or individual aid exempted by this Regulation. Having regard to Article 87(3)(c) of the Treaty, such aid should not normally have the sole effect of continuously or periodically reducing the operating costs which the beneficiary would normally have to bear, and should be proportionate to the handicaps that have to be overcome in order to secure the socioeconomic benefits deemed to be in the Community interest. It is therefore appropriate to limit the scope of this Regulation to aid granted in relation to certain tangible and intangible investments, certain services supplied to beneficiaries and certain other activities. In the light of Community overcapacity in the transport sector, with the exception of railway rolling stock, eligible investment costs for enterprises having their main economic activity in the transport sector should not include transport means and equipment.

(14) This Regulation should exempt aid to small and medium-sized enterprises regardless of location. Investment and job creation can contribute to the economic development of less favoured regions in the Community. Small and medium-sized enterprises in those regions suffer from both the structural disadvantage of the location and the difficulties deriving from their size. It is therefore appropriate that small and medium-sized enterprises in assisted regions should benefit from higher ceilings.

(15) In order not to favour the capital factor of an investment over the labour factor, provision should be made for the possibility of measuring aid to investment on the basis of either the costs of the investment or the costs of new employment linked to the carrying-out of the investment project.

(16) In the light of the World Trade Organisation (WTO) Agreement on Subsidies and Countervailing Measures,[1] this Regulation should not exempt export aid or aid favouring domestic over imported products. Aid towards the costs of participation in trade fairs or of studies or consultancy services needed for the launch of a new or existing product on a new market does not normally constitute export aid.

Notes
[1] OJ L 336, 23.12.1994, p. 156.

---

(17) Having regard to the need to strike the appropriate balance between minimising distortions of competition in the aided sector and the objectives of this Regulation, it should not exempt individual aid grants which exceed a fixed maximum amount, whether or not made under an aid scheme exempted by this Regulation.

(18) In order to ensure that the aid is necessary and acts as an incentive to develop certain activities, this Regulation should not exempt aid for activities in which the beneficiary would already engage under market conditions alone.

(19) This Regulation should not exempt aid cumulated with other State aid, including aid granted by national, regional or local authorities, or with Community assistance, in relation to the same eligible costs, when such cumulation exceeds the thresholds fixed in this Regulation.

(20) In order to ensure transparency and effective monitoring, in accordance with Article 3 of Regulation (EC) No 994/98, it is appropriate to establish a standard format in which Member States should provide the Commission with summary information whenever, in pursuance of this Regulation, an aid scheme is implemented or an individual aid outside such schemes is granted, with a view to publication in the *Official Journal of the European Communities*. For the same reasons, it is appropriate to establish rules concerning the records that Member States should keep regarding the aid exempted by this Regulation. For the purposes of the annual report to be submitted to the Commission by Member States, it is appropriate for the Commission to establish its specific requirements, including, in view of the wide availability of the necessary technology, information in computerised form.

(21) Having regard to the Commission's experience in this area, and in particular the frequency with which it is generally necessary to revise State aid policy, it is appropriate to limit the period of application of this Regulation. Should this Regulation expire without being extended, aid schemes already exempted by this Regulation should continue to be exempted for six months,

HAS ADOPTED THIS REGULATION:

Article 1
Scope

1. Without prejudice to special Community Regulations or Directives under the EC Treaty govern-ing the granting of State aid in specific sectors, whether more or less restrictive than this Regulation, this Regulation applies to aid granted to small and medium-sized enterprises in all sectors.

2. This Regulation shall not apply:

[(a) to fishery and acquaculture products covered by Council Regulation (EC) No 104/2000[1] and to activities linked to the primary production (farming) of agricultural products; to the manufacture and marketing of products intended to imitate or substitute for milk and milk products;][1]
(b) to aid to export-related activities, namely aid directly linked to the quantities exported, to the establishment and operation of a distribution network or to other current expenditure linked to the export activity;
(c) to aid contingent upon the use of domestic over imported goods.
[(d) to aid falling within the scope of Council Regulation (EC) No 1407/2002.[2]][2]

Notes
[[1] OJ L 17, 21.1.2000, p. 22.]
[[2] OJ L 205, 2.8.2002, p. 1.]
[1] Article 1(2), point (a) was amended as shown in square brackets by Commission Regulation (EC) No 1857/2006 of 15 December 2006 (OJ L 358, 16.12.2006, p. 3), Article 21, with effect from 1 January 2007.
[2] Article 1(2), point (d) was added by Commission Regulation (EC) No 364/2004 of 25 February 2004 (OJ L 63, 28.2.2004, p. 2), Article 1(1), with effect from 19 March 2004.

Article 2
Definitions

For the purpose of this Regulation:

(a) "aid" shall mean any measure fulfilling all the criteria laid down in Article 87(1) of the Treaty;
(b) "small and medium-sized enterprises" shall mean enterprises as defined in Annex I;
(c) "investment in tangible assets" shall mean an investment in fixed physical assets relating to the creation of a new establishment, the extension of an existing establishment, or the engagement in an activity involving a fundamental change in the product or production process of an existing establishment (in particular through rationalisation, diversification or modernisation). An investment in fixed assets undertaken in the form of the takeover of an establishment which has closed or which would have closed had it not been purchased shall also be regarded as tangible investment;
(d) "investment in intangible assets" shall mean investment in transfer of technology by the acquisi-tion of patent rights, licences, know-how or unpatented technical knowledge;
(e) "gross aid intensity" shall mean the aid amount expressed as a percentage of the project's eligible costs. All figures used shall be taken before any deduction for direct taxation. Where aid is awarded in a form other than a grant, the aid amount shall be the grant equivalent of the aid. Aid payable in several instalments shall be discounted to its value at the moment of granting. The interest rate to be used for discounting purposes and for calculating the aid amount in a soft loan shall be the reference rate applicable at the time of grant;

[For aid for research and development (R&D), the gross aid intensity for an R&D project being carried out in collaboration between public research establishments and enterprises shall be cal-culated on the basis of the combined aid deriving from direct government support for a specific research project and, where they constitute aid, contributions from public non-profit-making higher education or research establishments to the project.][1]

1384

(f) "net aid intensity" shall mean the aid amount net of tax expressed as a percentage of the project's eligible costs;

(g) "number of employees" shall mean the number of annual labour units (ALU), namely the number of persons employed full time in one year, part-time and seasonal work being ALU fractions.

[(h) "fundamental research" shall mean an activity designed to broaden scientific and technical knowledge not linked to industrial or commercial objectives;

(i) "industrial research" shall mean planned research or critical investigation aimed at the acquisition of new knowledge, the objective being that such knowledge may be useful in developing new products, processes or services or in bringing about a significant improvement in existing products, processes or services;

(j) "pre-competitive development" shall mean the shaping of the results of industrial research into a plan, arrangement or design for new, altered or improved products, processes or services, whether they are intended to be sold or used, including the creation of an initial prototype which could not be used commercially. This may also include the conceptual formulation and design of other products, processes or services and initial demonstration projects or pilot projects, provided that such projects cannot be converted or used for industrial applications or commercial exploitation. It does not include the routine or periodic changes made to products, production lines, manufacturing processes, existing services and other operations in progress, even if such changes may represent improvements.][1]

[(k) "agricultural product" means:

  (i) the products listed in Annex I of the Treaty, except fishery and acquaculture products covered by Regulation (EC) No 104/2000;

  (ii) products falling under CN codes 4502, 4503 and 4505 (cork products);

  (iii) products intended to imitate or substitute milk and milk products, as referred to in Article 3(2) of Council Regulation (EEC) No 1898/87[1];

(l) "products intended to imitate or substitute milk and milk products" means products which could be confused with milk and/or milk products but whose composition differs from such products in that they contain fat and/or protein of non-milk origin with or without protein derived from milk ("products other than milk products" as referred to in Article 3(2) of Regulation (EEC) No 1898/87);

(m) "processing of agricultural products" means any operation on an agricultural product resulting in a product which is also an agricultural product, except on farm activities necessary for preparing an animal or plant product for the first sale;

(n) "marketing of agricultural products" means holding or display with a view to sale, offering for sale, delivery or any other manner of placing on the market, except the first sale by a primary producer to resellers or processors and any activity preparing a product for such first sale; a sale by a primary producer to final consumers shall be considered as marketing if it takes place in separate premises reserved for that purpose.][2]

Notes

[[1] OJ L 182, 3.7.1987, p. 36.][2]

[1] Point (e) was amended and points (h), (i) and (j) were added by Commission Regulation (EC) No 364/2004 of 25 February 2004 (OJ L 63, 28.2.2004, p. 2), Article 1(2), with effect from 19 March 2004.

[2] Points (k) to (n) and footnote, shown in square brackets, were added by Commission Regulation (EC) No 1857/2006 of 15 December 2006 (OJ L 358, 16.12.2006, p. 3), Article 21, with effect from 1 January 2007.

Article 3
Conditions for exemption

1. Individual aid outside any scheme, fulfilling all the conditions of this Regulation, shall be compatible with the common market within the meaning of Article 87(3) of the Treaty and shall be exempt from the notification requirement of Article 88(3) of the Treaty provided that it contains an express reference to this Regulation, by citing its title and publication reference in the *Official Journal of the European Communities.*

Part G State Aids

2. Aid schemes fulfilling all the conditions of this Regulation shall be compatible with the common market within the meaning of Article 87(3) of the Treaty and shall be exempt from the notification requirement of Article 88(3) of the Treaty provided that:

(a) any aid that could be awarded under such scheme fulfils all the conditions of this Regulation;
(b) the scheme contains an express reference to this Regulation, by citing its title and publication reference in the *Official Journal of the European Communities.*

3. Aid granted under the schemes referred to in paragraph 2 shall be compatible with the common market within the meaning of Article 87(3) of the Treaty and shall be exempt from the notification requirement of Article 88(3) of the Treaty provided that the aid granted directly fulfils all the conditions of this Regulation.

Article 4
Investment

1. Aid for investment in tangible and intangible assets inside or outside the Community shall be compatible with the common market within the meaning of Article 87(3) of the Treaty and shall be exempt from the notification requirement of Article 88(3) of the Treaty if it fulfils the conditions of paragraphs 2 to 6.

[2. Where the investment takes place in areas or in sectors which do not qualify for regional aid pursuant to Article 87(3)(a) and (c) of the Treaty at the moment the aid is granted, the gross aid intensity shall not exceed:

(a) 15% in the case of small enterprises;
(b) 7,5% in the case of medium-sized enterprises.

3. Where the investment takes place in areas and in sectors which qualify for regional aid at the moment the aid is granted, the aid intensity shall not exceed the ceiling of regional investment aid determined in the map approved by the Commission for each Member State by more than:

(a) 10 percentage points gross in areas covered by Article 87(3)(c), provided that the total net aid intensity does not exceed 30%; or
(b) 15 percentage points gross in areas covered by Article 87(3)(a), provided that the total net aid intensity does not exceed 75%.

The higher regional aid ceilings shall only apply if the aid is granted under the condition that the investment is maintained in the recipient region for at least five years and the beneficiary's contribution to its financing is at least 25%.]¹

4. The ceilings fixed in paragraphs 2 and 3 shall apply to intensity of the aid calculated either as a percentage of the investment's eligible costs or as a percentage of the wage costs of employment created by the carrying-out of an investment (aid to job creation) or a combination thereof, provided the aid does not exceed the most favourable amount resulting from the application of either calculation.

5. In cases where the aid is calculated on the basis of the investment's costs, the eligible costs of tangible investment shall be the costs relating to investment in land, buildings, machinery and equipment. In the transport sector, except for railway rolling stock, transport means and transport equipment shall not be included in the eligible costs. The eligible costs of intangible investment shall be the costs of acquisition of the technology.

6. In cases where the aid is calculated on the basis of jobs created, the amount of the aid shall be expressed as a percentage of the wage costs over a period of two years relating to the employment created under the following conditions:

(a) job creation shall be linked to the carrying-out of a project of investment in tangible or intangible assets. Jobs shall be created within three years of the investment's completion;
(b) the investment project shall lead to a net increase in the number of employees in the establishment concerned, compared with the average over the previous twelve months; and
(c) the employment created shall be maintained during a minimum period of five years.

[7. Where the investment concerns the processing and marketing of agricultural products listed in Annex I to the Treaty, the gross aid intensity may not exceed:

(a) 75 % of eligible investments in the outermost regions;

(b) 65 % of eligible investments in the smaller Aegean Islands within the meaning of Council Regulation (EEC) No 2019/93 ([1]);
(c) 50 % of eligible investments in regions eligible under Article 87(3)(a) EC;
(d) 40 % of eligible investments in all other regions.

Notes

[1] OJ L 184, 27.7.1993, p. 1.][2]

[1] Paragraphs 2 and 3 were replaced as shown in square brackets by Commission Regulation (EC) No 364/2004 of 25 February 2004 (OJ L 63, 28.2.2004, p. 2), Article 1(3), with effect from 19 March 2004.

[2] Paragraph 7 and footnote, shown in square brackets, were added by Commission Regulation (EC) No 1857/2006 of 15 December 2006 (OJ L 358, 16.12.2006, p. 3), Article 21, with effect from 1 January 2007.

Commentary
Art 4: B&C: 15.067
Art 4(3): B&C: 15.067

Article 5
Consultancy and other services and activities

Aid to small and medium-sized enterprises that fulfil the following conditions shall be compatible with the common market within the meaning of Article 87(3) of the Treaty and shall be exempt from the notification requirement of Article 88(3) of the Treaty:

(a) for services provided by outside consultants, the gross aid shall not exceed 50% of the costs of such services. The services concerned shall not be a continuous or periodic activity nor relate to the enterprise's usual operating expenditure, such as routine tax consultancy services, regular legal services, or advertising;
(b) for participation in fairs and exhibitions, the gross aid shall not exceed 50% of the additional costs incurred for renting, setting up and running the stand. This exemption shall only apply to the first participation of an enterprise in a particular fair or exhibition.

[Article 5a
Aid for research and development

1. Aid for research and development shall be compatible with the common market within the meaning of Article 87(3)(c) of the Treaty and shall be exempt from the notification requirement of Article 88(3) of the Treaty if it fulfils the conditions set out in paragraphs 2 to 5.

2. The aided project must completely fall within the stages of research and development defined in Article 2(h), (i) and (j).

3. The gross aid intensity, as calculated on the basis of the eligible costs of the project, shall not exceed:

(a) 100% for fundamental research;
(b) 60% for industrial research;
(c) 35% for pre-competitive development.

If a project includes different stages of research and development, the permissible aid intensity shall be established on the basis of the weighted average of the respective permissible aid intensities, calculated on the basis of the eligible costs involved.

In the case of collaborative projects, the maximum amount of aid for each beneficiary shall not exceed the permitted aid intensity calculated by reference to the eligible costs incurred by the beneficiary concerned.

4. The ceilings in paragraph 3 may be increased as follows up to a maximum gross aid intensity of 75% for industrial research and 50% for pre-competitive development:

(a) where the project takes place in an area which, at the time when the aid is granted, qualifies for regional aid, the maximum aid intensity may be increased by 10 percentage points gross in areas covered by Article 87(3)(a) of the Treaty and by five percentage points gross in areas covered by Article 87(3)(c) of the Treaty;
(b) where the project aims at carrying out research with potential multi-sectoral application and focuses on a multidisciplinary approach in accordance with the objective, tasks and technical

targets of a specific project or programme undertaken under the Sixth Framework Programme for research and development, established by Decision No 1513/2002/EC of the European Parliament and of the Council[1] or any subsequent Framework Programme for research and development or Eureka, the maximum aid intensity may be increased by 15 percentage points gross;

(c) the maximum aid intensity may be increased by 10 percentage points if one of the following conditions is satisfied:

    (i) the project involves effective cross-border cooperation between at least two independent partners in two Member States, particularly in the context of coordinating national R&D policies; no single company in the Member State granting the aid may bear more than 70% of the eligible costs; or

    (ii) the project involves effective cooperation between a company and a public research body, particularly in the context of coordination of national R&D policies, where the public research body bears at least 10% of the eligible project costs and has the right to publish the results insofar as they stem from research implemented by that body; or

    (iii) the results of the project are widely disseminated through technical and scientific conferences or published in peer-reviewed scientific and technical journals.

For the purposes of points (i) and (ii) subcontracting is not considered to be effective cooperation.

5. Eligible costs for the purposes of this Article shall be the following:

(a) personnel costs (researchers, technicians and other supporting staff to the extent employed on the research project);

(b) costs of instruments and equipment to the extent and for the duration used for the research project. If such instruments and equipment are not used for their full life for the research project, only the depreciation costs corresponding to the life of the research project, as calculated on the basis of good accounting practice, are considered as eligible;

(c) costs for buildings and land, to the extent and for the duration used for the research project. With regard to buildings, only the depreciation costs corresponding to the life of the research project, as calculated on the basis of good accounting practice, are considered as eligible. For land, costs of commercial transfer or actually incurred capital costs are eligible;

(d) cost of consultancy and equivalent services used exclusively for the research activity, including research, technical knowledge and patents bought or licensed from outside sources at market prices, where the transaction has been carried out at arm's length and there is no element of collusion involved. These costs are only considered eligible up to 70% of total eligible project costs;

(e) additional overheads incurred directly as a result of the research project;

(f) other operating expenses, including costs of materials, supplies and similar products incurred directly as a result of the research activity.]

Notes

[1 OJ L 232, 29.8.2002, p. 1.]

Article 5a as shown in square brackets was inserted by Commission Regulation (EC) No 364/2004 of 25 February 2004 (OJ L 63, 28.2.2004, p. 2), Article 1(4), with effect from 19 March 2004.

[*Article 5b*
Aid for technical feasibility studies

Aid for technical feasibility studies preparatory to industrial research activities or pre-competitive development activities shall be compatible with the common market within the meaning of Article 87(3)(c) of the Treaty and shall be exempt from the notification requirement of Article 88(3) of the Treaty provided that the gross aid intensity, as calculated on the basis of study costs, does not exceed 75%.]

Notes

Article 5b as shown in square brackets was inserted by Commission Regulation (EC) No 364/2004 of 25 February 2004 (OJ L 63, 28.2.2004, p. 2), Article 1(4), with effect from 19 March 2004.

Part G State Aids

[*Article 5c*
Aid for patenting costs

1. Aid for the costs associated with obtaining and validating patents and other industrial property rights shall be compatible with the common market within the meaning of Article 87(3)(c) of the Treaty and shall be exempt from the notification requirement of Article 88(3) of the Treaty up to the same level of aid as would have qualified as R&D aid in respect of the research activities which first led to the industrial property rights concerned.

2. Eligible costs for the purposes of paragraph 1 shall be the following:

(a) all costs preceding the grant of the right in the first legal jurisdiction, including costs relating to the preparation, filing and prosecution of the application as well as costs incurred in renewing the application before the right has been granted;

(b) translation and other costs incurred in order to obtain the granting or validation of the right in other legal jurisdictions;

(c) costs incurred in defending the validity of the right during the official prosecution of the application and possible opposition proceedings, even if such costs occur after the right is granted.]

Notes

Article 5c as shown in square brackets was inserted by Commission Regulation (EC) No 364/2004 of 25 February 2004 (OJ L 63, 28.2.2004, p. 2), Article 1(4), with effect from 19 March 2004.

[*Article 6*
Large individual aid grants

1. In the case of aid covered by Articles 4 and 5, this Regulation shall not exempt an individual aid grant where one of the following thresholds is met:

(a) the total eligible costs of the whole project are at least EUR 25,000,000; and
  (i) in areas or in sectors which do not qualify for regional aid, the gross aid intensity is at least 50% of the ceilings laid down in Article 4(2);
  (ii) in areas and in sectors which qualify for regional aid, the net aid intensity is at least 50% of the net aid ceiling as determined in the regional aid map for the area concerned; or

(b) the total gross aid amount is at least EUR 15,000,000.

2. In the case of aid covered by Articles 5a, 5b and 5c, this Regulation shall not exempt an individual aid grant where the following thresholds are met:

(a) the total eligible costs of the whole project incurred by all companies participating in the project are at least EUR 25,000,000; and

(b) it is proposed to provide aid with a gross grant equivalent of at least EUR 5,000,000 to one or more of the individual companies.

In the case of aid granted to a Eureka project, the thresholds in the first subparagraph shall be replaced by the following:

(a) the total eligible costs of the Eureka project incurred by all companies participating in the project are at least EUR 40,000,000; and

(b) it is proposed to provide aid with a gross grant equivalent of at least EUR 10,000,000 to one or more of the individual companies.]

Notes

Article 6 was replaced as shown in square brackets by Commission Regulation (EC) No 364/2004 of 25 February 2004 (OJ L 63, 28.2.2004, p. 2), Article 1(5), with effect from 19 March 2004.

[*Article 6a*
Aid remaining subject to prior notification to the Commission

1. This Regulation shall not exempt any aid, whether individual aid or aid granted under an aid scheme, in the form of one or more advances that are repayable only in the event of a successful outcome

of research activities, where the total amount of the advances expressed as a percentage of the eligible costs exceeds the intensities provided for in Articles 5a, 5b or 5c or the limit fixed in Article 6(2).

2. This Regulation is without prejudice to any obligation on a Member State to notify individual grants of aid under other State aid instruments, and in particular the obligation to notify, or to inform the Commission of, aid to an enterprise receiving restructuring aid within the meaning of the Community guidelines on State aid for rescuing and restructuring firms in difficulty[1] and the obligation to notify regional aid for large investment projects under the applicable multisectoral Framework.]

Notes
[[1] OJ C 288, 9.10.1999, p. 2.]

Article 6a was inserted by Commission Regulation (EC) No 364/2004 of 25 February 2004 (OJ L 63, 28.2.2004, p. 2), Article 1(6), with effect from 19 March 2004.

Article 7
Necessity for the aid

This Regulation shall only exempt aid if, before work on the aided project is started:

— either an application for aid has been submitted to the Member State by the beneficiary, or
— the Member State has adopted legal provisions establishing a legal right to aid according to objective criteria and without further exercise of discretion by the Member State.

Article 8
Cumulation

[1. The aid ceilings fixed in Articles 4 to 6 shall apply regardless of whether the support for the aided project is financed entirely from State resources or is partly financed by the Community.]

2. Aid exempted by this Regulation shall not be cumulated with any other State aid within the meaning of Article 87(1) of the Treaty, or with other Community funding, in relation to the same eligible costs, if such cumulation would result in an aid intensity exceeding that fixed by this Regulation.

Notes
Paragraph 1 of Article 8 was replaced as shown in square brackets by Commission Regulation (EC) No 364/2004 of 25 February 2004 (OJ L 63, 28.2.2004, p. 2), Article 1(7), with effect from 19 March 2004.

Article 9
Transparency and monitoring

1. On implementation of an aid scheme, or grant of individual aid outside any scheme, exempted by this Regulation, Member States shall, within 20 working days, forward to the Commission, with a view to its publication in the *Official Journal of the European Communities*, a summary of the information regarding such aid scheme or individual aid in the form laid down in Annex II.

2. Member States shall maintain detailed records regarding the aid schemes exempted by this Regulation, the individual aid granted under those schemes, and the individual aid exempted by this Regulation that is granted outside any existing aid scheme. Such records shall contain all information necessary to establish that the conditions for exemption, as laid down in this Regulation, are fulfilled, including information on the status of the company as an SME. Member States shall keep a record regarding an individual aid for 10 years from the date on which it was granted, and regarding an aid scheme, for 10 years from the date on which the last individual aid was granted under such scheme. On written request, the Member State concerned shall provide the Commission, within a period of 20 working days or such longer period as may be fixed in the request, with all the information which the Commission considers necessary to assess whether the conditions of this Regulation have been complied with.

[3. Member States shall compile an annual report on the application of this Regulation in accordance with the implementing provisions concerning the form and content of annual reports provisions which are laid down pursuant to Article 27 of Council Regulation (EC) No 659/1999.[1]

Until such provisions enter into force, Member States shall compile an annual report on the application of this Regulation in respect of the whole or part of each calendar year during which this

Regulation applies, in the form laid down in Annex III, also in computerised form. Member States shall provide the Commission with such report no later than three months after the expiry of the period to which the report relates.]

Notes
[¹ OJ L 83, 27.3.1999, p. 1.]
Paragraph 3 of Article 9 was replaced as shown in square brackets by Commission Regulation (EC) No 364/2004 of 25 February 2004 (OJ L 63, 28.2.2004, p. 2), Article 1(8), with effect from 19 March 2004.

Commentary
Art 9(1): **F&N**: 16.286

[*Article 9a*
Transitional provisions

1. Notifications concerning aid for Research and Development pending on 19 March 2004 shall continue to be assessed under the Framework for State aid for Research and Development, while all other pending notifications shall be assessed in accordance with the provisions of this regulation.

2. Aid schemes implemented before the date of entry into force of this Regulation, and aid granted under such schemes in the absence of a Commission authorisation and in breach of the notification requirement of Article 88(3) of the Treaty, shall be compatible with the common market within the meaning of Article 87(3) of the Treaty and shall be exempt if they fulfil the conditions laid down in Article 3(2)(a) and Article 3(3) of this Regulation.

Individual aid outside any scheme granted before the date of entry into force of this Regulation in the absence of a Commission authorisation and in breach of the notification requirement of Article 88(3) of the Treaty, shall be compatible with the common market within the meaning of Article 87(3) of the Treaty and shall be exempt if it fulfils all the conditions of this Regulation, except the requirement in Article 3(1) that express reference be made to this Regulation.

Any aid which does not fulfil these conditions shall be assessed by the Commission in accordance with the relevant frameworks, guidelines, communications and notices.]

Notes
Article 9(a) as shown in square brackets was inserted by Commission Regulation (EC) No 364/2004 of 25 February 2004 (OJ L 63, 28.2.2004, p. 2), Article 1(9), with effect from 19 March 2004.

Article 10
Entry into force and period of validity

1. This Regulation shall enter into force on the 20th day following that of its publication in the *Official Journal of the European Communities*.

[It shall apply until 30 June 2008].

2. At the end of the period of validity of this Regulation, aid schemes exempted under this Regulation shall remain exempted during an adjustment period of six months.

Notes
Article 10 was amended as shown in square brackets by Commission Regulation (EC) No 1976/2006 of 20 December 2006 (OJ L 368, 23.12.06, p. 86), Article 2.

This Regulation shall be binding in its entirety and directly applicable in all Member States.

Done at Brussels, 12 January 2001.

Notes
Date of entry into force: 2 February 2001.

Part G State Aids

1391

ANNEX I

DEFINITION OF SMALL AND MEDIUM-SIZED ENTERPRISES

(Extract from Commission Recommendation 2003/361/EC of 6 May 2003 concerning the definition of small and medium sized enterprises, OJ L 124, 20.5.2003, p. 36)

DEFINITION OF MICRO, SMALL AND MEDIUM-SIZED ENTERPRISES ADOPTED BY THE COMMISSION

Notes

Annex I was replaced by Commission Regulation (EC) No 364/2004 of 25 February 2004 (OJ L 63, 28.2.2004, p. 2), Article 1(10), with effect from 1 January 2005. Annex I, as amended, incorporates the definition of micro, small and medium-sized enterprises annexed to Commission Recommendation 2003/361/EC of 6 May 2003 (reproduced at C15, page 455 above).

ANNEX II

FORM OF SUMMARY INFORMATION TO BE PROVIDED WHENEVER AN AID SCHEME EXEMPTED BY THIS REGULATION IS IMPLEMENTED AND WHENEVER AN INDIVIDUAL AID EXEMPTED BY THIS REGULATION IS GRANTED OUTSIDE ANY AID SCHEME

Notes

Annex II is available in electronic form from the Europa website at the following address: http://ec.europa.eu/comm/competition/state_aid/legislation/forms.html

---

Summary Information on State Aid Granted in conformity with Commission Regulation (EC) No 70/2001

Summary information to be filled in	Explanatory remarks
Member State	
Region	Indicate the name of the region if the aid is granted by a subcentral authority
Title of aid scheme or name of company receiving an individual aid	Indicate the name of the aid scheme or in the case of individual aid, the name of the beneficiary.
	In the latter case, no subsequent annual report is necessary!
Legal basis	Indicate the precise national legal reference for the aid scheme or for the individual aid
Annual expenditure planned under the scheme or overall amount of individual aid granted to the company	Amounts are to be given in euro or, if applicable, national currency.
	In the case of an aid scheme:
	indicate the annual overall amount of the budget appropriation(s) or the estimated tax loss per year for all aid instruments contained in the scheme.
	In the case of an individual aid award:
	indicate the overall aid amount/tax loss. If appropriate, indicate also for how many years the aid will be paid in instalments or over how many years tax losses will be incurred.
	For guarantees in both cases, indicate the (maximum) amount of loans guaranteed

Summary information to be filled in	Explanatory remarks
Maximum aid intensity	Indicate the maximum aid intensity or the maximum aid amount per eligible item
Date of implementation	Indicate the date from which aid may be granted under the scheme or when the individual aid is granted
Duration of scheme or individual aid award	Indicate the date (year and month) until which aid may be granted under the scheme or in case of an individual aid and if appropriate the expected date (year and month) of the last instalment to be paid
Objective of aid	It is understood that the primary objective is aid to SME. This field gives the opportunity to indicate further (secondary) objectives pursued (e.g. small enterprises only or SME: investment aid/consultancy)
Economic sector(s) concerned	Choose from the list, where relevant

□ All sectors
 or
  □ Coalmining
  □ All manufacturing
   or
    □ Steel
    □ Shipbuilding
    □ Synthetic fibres
    □ Motor vehicles
    □ Other manufacturing
  [□ Processing and marketing of
    agricultural products]¹
  □ All services
   or
    □ Transport services
    □ Financial services
    □ Other services

Remarks:

Name and address of the granting
authority

Other information

Notes

[¹ As defined in Article 2(k) of this Regulation.]

The amendments shown in square brackets were made by Commission Regulation (EC) No 1857/2006 of 15 December 2006 (OJ L 358, 16.12.2006, p. 3), Article 21, with effect from 1 January 2007.

ANNEX III

FORM OF THE PERIODIC REPORT TO BE PROVIDED TO THE COMMISSION

Annual Reporting Format on Aid Schemes Exempted under a Group Exemption Regulation Adopted pursuant to Article 1 of Council Regulation (EC) No 994/98

Member States are required to use the format below for their reporting obligations to the Commission under group exemption regulations adopted on the basis of Council Regulation (EC) No 994/98.

The reports should also be provided in computerised form.

Information required for all aid schemes exempted under group exemption regulations adopted pursuant to Article 1 of Council Regulation (EC) No 994/98

1. Title of aid scheme

2. Commission exemption regulation applicable

3. Expenditure

Separate figures have to be provided for each aid instrument within a scheme or individual aid (e.g. grant, soft loans, etc.) The figures have to be expressed in euro or, if applicable, national currency. In the case of tax expenditure, annual tax losses have to be reported. If precise figures are not available, such losses may be estimated.

These expenditure figures should be provided on the following basis.

For the year under review indicate separately for each aid instrument within the scheme (e.g. grant, soft loan, guarantee, etc.):

3.1. amounts committed, (estimated) tax losses or other revenue forgone, data on guarantees, etc. for new assisted projects. In the case of guarantee schemes, the total amount of new guarantees handed out should be provided;

3.2. actual payments, (estimated) tax losses or other revenue forgone, data on guarantees, etc. for new and current projects. In the case of guarantee schemes, the following should be provided: total amount of outstanding guarantees, premium income, recoveries, indemnities paid out, operating result of the scheme under the year under review;

3.3. number of new assisted projects;

3.4. estimated overall number of jobs created or maintained by new projects (if appropriate);

3.5. estimated overall amount of investment aided by new projects;

3.6. Regional breakdown of amounts under point 3.1 either by regions defined at NUTS[1] level 2 or below or by Article 87(3)(a) regions, Article 87(3)(c) regions and non-assisted regions;

3.7. Sectorial breakdown of amounts under point 3.1. by beneficiaries' sectors of activity (if more than one sector is covered, indicate the share of each):

    coalmining

    manufacturing

    of which:

        steel

        shipbuilding

        synthetic fibres

        motor vehicles

        other manufacturing (please specify)

    services

    of which:

        transport services

        financial services

        other services (please specify)

    other sectors (please specify)

4. Other information and remarks.

Notes

[1] NUTS is the nomenclature of territorial units for statistical purposes in the Community.

G12

COMMISSION REGULATION (EC) No 2204/2002

of 5 December 2002
on the application of Articles 87 and 88 of the EC Treaty to State aid for employment

Official Journal L 337, 13.12.2002, p. 3

Celex No: 32002R2204

Notes

The text of this Regulation is reproduced as corrected by the Corrigendum at OJ L 349, 24.12.2002, p. 126.

EEA application: this Regulation was incorporated with appropriate adaptations by EEA Joint Committee Decision No 83/2003 (OJ No L 257, 9.10.2003 and EEA Supplement No 51, p. 25): see EEA Agreement, Annex XV, Point 1g.

Commentary

Regulation 2201/2002/EC: B&C: 15.067, 15.076 F&N: 16.66, 16.67–16.73, 16.284

THE COMMISSION OF THE EUROPEAN COMMUNITIES,

Having regard to the Treaty establishing the European Community,

Having regard to Council Regulation (EC) No 994/98 of 7 May 1998 on the application of Articles [87] and [88] of the Treaty establishing the European Community to certain categories of horizontal State aid,[1] and in particular point (a)(iv) and point (b) of Article 1(1) thereof,

Having published a draft of this Regulation,[2]

Having consulted the Advisory Committee on State Aid,

Notes
[1] OJ L 142, 14.5.1998, p. 1.
[2] OJ C 88, 12.4.2002, p. 2.

Whereas:

(1) Regulation (EC) No 994/98 empowers the Commission to declare, in accordance with Article 87 of the Treaty, that under certain conditions aid for employment is compatible with the common market and not subject to the notification requirement of Article 88(3) of the Treaty.

(2) Regulation (EC) No 994/98 also empowers the Commission to declare, in accordance with Article 87 of the Treaty, that aid that complies with the map approved by the Commission for each Member State for the grant of regional aid is compatible with the common market and is not subject to the notification requirement of Article 88(3) of the Treaty.

(3) The Commission has applied Articles 87 and 88 of the Treaty to employment aid in and outside assisted areas in numerous decisions and has also stated its policy, in the guidelines on aid to employment,[1] in the notice on monitoring of State aid and reduction of labour costs,[2] in the guidelines on national regional aid[3] and in Commission Regulation (EC) No 70/2001 of 12 January 2001 on the application of Articles 87 and 88 of the EC Treaty to State aid to small and medium-sized enterprises.[4] In the light of the Commissions experience in applying those provisions, it is appropriate, with a view to ensuring efficient supervision and simplifying administration without weakening Commission monitoring, that the Commission should make use of the powers conferred by Regulation (EC) No 994/98.

Notes
[1] OJ C 334, 12.12.1995, p. 4.
[2] OJ C 1, 3.1.1997, p. 10.
[3] OJ C 74, 10.3.1998, p. 9.
[4] OJ L 10, 13.1.2001, p. 33.

(4) This Regulation is without prejudice to the possibility for Member States to notify aid for employment. Such notifications will be assessed by the Commission in particular in the light of the criteria set out in this Regulation, in Regulation (EC) No 70/2001 or in accordance with any relevant Community guidelines or frameworks. This is currently the case for the sector of maritime transport. The guidelines on State aid for employment[1] cease to apply from the date of entry into force of this Regulation, as do the notice on monitoring of State aid and reduction of labour costs and the notice on an accelerated procedure for processing notifications of employment aid.[2] Notifications pending at the entry into force of this Regulation will be assessed in accordance with its provisions. It is appropriate to lay down transitional provisions concerning the application of this Regulation to employment aid granted before its entry into force and in breach of the obligation in Article 88(3) of the Treaty.

Notes
[1] OJ C 371, 23.12.2000, p. 12.
[2] OJ C 218, 27.7.1996, p. 4.

(5) The promotion of employment is a central aim for the economic and social policies of the Community and of its Member States. The Community has developed a European employment strategy in order to promote this objective. Unemployment remains a significant problem in some parts of the Community, and certain categories of worker still find particular difficulty in entering the labour market. For this reason there is a justification for public authorities to apply measures providing incentives to enterprises to increase their levels of employment, in particular of workers from these disadvantaged categories.

(6) This Regulation applies only to employment measures which fulfil all the conditions of Article 87(1) of the Treaty and thus constitute State aid. A number of employment policy measures do not constitute State aid within the meaning of Article 87(1) because they constitute aid to individuals that does not favour certain undertakings or the production of certain goods, or because they do not affect trade between Member States or because they are general measures to promote employment which do not distort or threaten to distort competition by favouring certain undertakings or the production of certain goods. Such general measures, which may include general reduction of the taxation of labour and social costs, boosting investment in general education and training, measures to provide guidance and counselling, general assistance and training for the unemployed and improvements in labour law are therefore unaffected by this Regulation. This is also the case of measures which are deemed not to meet all the criteria of Article 87(1) of the Treaty and therefore do not fall under the notification requirement of Article 88(3) of the Treaty by virtue of Commission Regulation (EC) No 69/2001 of 12 January 2001 on the application of Articles 87 and 88 of the EC Treaty to *de minimis* aid.[1]

Notes
[1] OJ L 10, 13.1.2001, p. 30. [See now Commission Regulation (EC) No 1998/2006 of 15 December 2006 (OJ L 379, 28.12.2006, p. 5).

(7) Having regard to those considerations, the purpose and effect of the aid exempted by this Regulation should be to promote employment in accordance with the European employment strategy, in particular of workers from disadvantaged categories, without adversely affect trading conditions to an extent contrary to the common interest. Employment aid granted to a firm on an individual basis may have a major impact on competition in the relevant market because it favours that firm over others which have not received such aid. By being granted only to a single firm, such aid is likely to have only a limited effect on employment. For this reason individual awards of employment aid should continue to be notified to the Commission, and this Regulation should exempt aid only if given in the form of schemes.

(8) This Regulation should exempt any aid granted under a scheme that meets all the relevant requirements of this Regulation. With a view to ensuring efficient supervision and simplifying administration without weakening Commission monitoring, aid schemes should contain an express reference to this Regulation.

(9) This Regulation should not exempt from notification State aid in the shipbuilding and coalmining sectors, for which special rules are laid down in, respectively, Council Regulation (EC) No 1540/98[1] and Council Regulation (EC) No 1407/2002.[2]

Notes
[1] OJ L 202, 18.7.1998, p. 1.
[2] OJ L 205, 2.8.2002, p. 1.

(10) This Regulation should apply in the transport sector. However, having regard to the particular characteristics of competition in that sector, it is not appropriate to exempt aid for the creation of employment.

(11) The Commission has a consistently less favourable view of aid targeted at particular sectors, including, but not limited to, sensitive sectors experiencing overcapacity or crisis. Aid schemes which are targeted at specific sectors should not therefore be covered by the exemption from notification provided by this Regulation.

(12) In accordance with the established practice of the Commission, and with a view to better ensuring that aid is proportionate and limited to the amount necessary, thresholds should be expressed in terms of aid intensities in relation to a set of eligible costs, rather than in terms of maximum aid amounts.

(13) In order to determine whether or not aid is compatible with the common market pursuant to this Regulation, it is necessary to take into consideration the aid intensity and thus the aid amount expressed as a grant equivalent. The calculation of the grant equivalent of aid payable in several instalments and aid in the form of a soft loan requires the use of market interest rates prevailing at the time of grant. With a view to a uniform, transparent, and simple application of the State aid rules, the market rates for the purposes of this Regulation should be deemed to be the reference rates, provided that, in the case of a soft loan, the loan is backed by normal security and does not involve abnormal risk. The reference rates should be those which are periodically fixed by the Commission on the basis of objective criteria and published in the *Official Journal of the European Communities* and on the Internet.

(14) Having regard to the differences between enterprises of different sizes, different ceilings of aid intensity for the creation of employment should be set for small and medium sized enterprises and large enterprises. In order to eliminate differences that might give rise to distortions of competition, in order to facilitate coordination between different Community and national initiatives, and for reasons of administrative clarity and legal certainty, the definition of "small and medium-sized enterprises" (SMEs) used in this Regulation should be that laid down in Commission Recommendation 96/280/EC of 3 April 1996 concerning the definition of small and medium-sized enterprises.[1] That definition was also used in Regulation (EC) No 70/2001.

Notes
[1] OJ L 107, 30.4.1996, p. 4.

(15) The ceilings of aid intensity should be fixed, in the light of the Commissions experience, at a level that strikes the appropriate balance between minimising distortions of competition and the objective of promoting employment. In the interests of coherence, the ceilings should be harmonised with those fixed in the guidelines on national regional aid and in Regulation (EC) No 70/2001, which allowed aid to be calculated by reference to the creation of employment linked to investment projects.

(16) Employment costs form part of the normal operating costs of any enterprise. It is therefore particularly important that aid should have a positive effect on employment and should not merely enable enterprises to reduce costs which they would otherwise bear.

(17) Without rigorous controls and strict limits, employment aid can have harmful effects which cancel out its immediate effects on job creation. If the aid is used to protect firms exposed to

intra-Community competition, it could have the effect of delaying adjustments needed to ensure the competitiveness of Community industry. In the absence of rigorous controls, such aid may be concentrated in the most prosperous regions, contrary to the objective of economic and social cohesion. Within the single market, aid granted to reduce costs of employment can lead to distortions of intra-Community competition and deflections in the allocation of resources and mobile investment, to the shifting of unemployment from one country to another, and to relocation.

(18) Aid to create jobs should be subject to the condition that the created job should be maintained for a certain minimum period. The period set in this regulation should override the five-year rule set out in point 4.14 of the guidelines on national regional aid.

(19) Aid to maintain jobs, meaning financial support given to a firm to persuade it not to lay off its workers, is similar to operating aid. Subject to any sectoral rules, therefore, such as those which exist in the sector of maritime transport, it should be authorised only in specific circumstances and for a limited period. It should continue to be notified to the Commission and should not be covered by the exemption from such notification provided by this Regulation. The limited circumstances in which it can be authorised include those where, in accordance with Article 87(2)(b) of the Treaty, it is intended to make good the damage caused by natural disasters or exceptional occurrences; another instance is under the conditions applying to operating aid in the guidelines on national regional aid, in regions eligible for the derogation under Article 87(3)(a) of the Treaty concerning the economic development of areas where the standard of living is abnormally low or where there is serious underemployment, including ultra-peripheral regions; a third instance is where such aid is granted in the context of the rescue and restructuring of a company in difficulty, in accordance with the provisions of the relevant Community guidelines.[1]

Notes

[1] OJ C 288, 9.10.1999, p. 2. [See now OJ C 244, 1.10.2004, p.2.]

---

(20) A particular type of aid is aid granted to employers for the conversion of temporary or fixed-term employment contracts into contracts of indeterminate duration. Such measures should not be covered by the exemption from such notification provided by this Regulation and should be notified so that the Commission can determine whether they have positive employment effects. It should in particular be ensured that such measures do not allow the employment to be aided both at the creation of the post and at the conversion of the contract, in such a way that the ceiling for aid for initial investment or for creation of employment is exceeded.

(21) Small and medium-sized enterprises play a decisive role in job creation. At the same time, their size may present a handicap to the creation of new employment because of the risks and administrative burden involved in the recruitment of new personnel. Similarly, job creation can contribute to the economic development of less favoured regions in the Community and thus improve economic and social cohesion. Enterprises in those regions suffer from the structural disadvantage of the location. It is therefore appropriate that small and medium-sized enterprises, and enterprises in assisted regions, should be able to benefit from aid to create employment.

(22) Large firms in non-assisted areas do not suffer from particular difficulties and employment costs are part of their normal operating expenses. For this reason, and in order to maximise the incentive effect of aid to create jobs in SMEs and in regions eligible for the derogations under Article 87(3)(a) and (c) of the Treaty, large firms in regions not eligible for these derogations should not be eligible for aid to create employment.

(23) Certain categories of worker experience particular difficulty in finding work, because employers consider them to be less productive. This perceived lower productivity may be due either to lack of recent experience of employment (for example, young workers, long-term unemployed) or to permanent handicap. Employment aid intended to encourage firms to recruit such individuals is justified by the fact that the lower productivity of these workers reduces the financial advantage accruing to the firm and by the fact that the workers also benefit from the measure and are likely to be excluded from the labour market unless employers are offered such incentives. It is

therefore appropriate to allow schemes providing such aid, whatever the size or location of the beneficiary.

(24) The categories of worker considered to be disadvantaged should be defined, but it should be possible for Member States to notify aid to promote the recruitment of other categories they consider to be disadvantaged, with supporting arguments.

(25) Workers with a disability may need permanent help to enable them to remain in the labour market, going beyond aid for initial recruitment and possibly including participation in sheltered employment. Schemes providing aid for such purposes should be exempted from notification provided that the aid can be shown to be no more than necessary to compensate for the lower productivity of the workers concerned, the ancillary costs of employing them or the costs of establishing or maintaining sheltered employment. This condition is designed to prevent enterprises benefiting from such aid from selling below competitive prices in markets also served by other enterprises.

(26) This Regulation should not prevent the cumulation of aid for the recruitment of disadvantaged workers or for the recruitment or employment of disabled workers with other aid granted in respect of employment costs, since in such cases it is legitimate to provide an incentive for workers from these categories to be employed in preference to others.

(27) In order to ensure that the aid is necessary and acts as an incentive to employment, this Regulation should not exempt aid for the creation of employment or for recruitment which the beneficiary would already undertake under market conditions alone.

(28) This Regulation should not exempt aid for the creation of employment where this is cumulated with other State aid, including aid granted by national, regional or local authorities, or with Community assistance, in relation to the same eligible costs or to the costs of investments to which the employment concerned is linked, when such cumulation exceeds the thresholds fixed in this Regulation or in the Community rules on State aid for investment, in particular the Guidelines on national regional aid and Regulation (EC) No 70/2001. The only exceptions to this principle should be for aid for the recruitment of disadvantaged workers or for the recruitment or employment of disabled workers.

(29) It is appropriate that large amounts of aid should remain subject to an individual assessment by the Commission before they are put into effect. Accordingly, aid amounts exceeding a fixed amount over a certain period to a single enterprise or establishment are excluded from the exemption provided for in this Regulation and remain subject to the requirements of Article 88(3) of the Treaty.

(30) Aid measures to promote employment or other aid with objectives connected with employment and labour markets may be of a different nature from measures exempted by this Regulation. Such measures should be notified under Article 88(3).

(31) In the light of the World Trade Organisation (WTO) Agreement on Subsidies and Countervailing Measures, this Regulation should not exempt export aid or aid favouring domestic over imported products. Such aid would be incompatible with the Community's international obligations under that Agreement and should not therefore be exempted from notification, nor authorised if so notified.

(32) In order to ensure transparency and effective monitoring, in accordance with Article 3 of Regulation (EC) No 994/98, it is appropriate to establish a standard format in which Member States should provide the Commission with summary information whenever, in pursuance of this Regulation, an aid scheme is implemented, with a view to publication in the *Official Journal of the European Communities*. For the same reasons, it is appropriate to establish rules concerning the records that Member States should keep regarding the aid scheme exempted by this Regulation. For the purposes of the annual report to be submitted to the Commission by Member States, it is appropriate for the Commission to establish its specific requirements. In order to facilitate administrative treatment and in view of the wide availability of the necessary technology, the summary information and the annual report should be provided in computerised form.

(33) Having regard to the Commissions experience in this area, and in particular the frequency with which it is generally necessary to revise State aid policy, it is appropriate to limit the period of application of this Regulation. Pursuant to Article 4(2) of Regulation (EC) No 994/98, it is

Part G State Aids

1399

necessary to include transitional arrangements whereby aid schemes already exempted by this Regulation will, on its expiry, continue to be exempted for another six months,

HAS ADOPTED THIS REGULATION

Article 1
Scope

1. This Regulation shall apply to schemes which constitute State aid within the meaning of Article 87(1) of the Treaty and which provide aid for the creation of employment, provide aid for the recruitment of disadvantaged and disabled workers or provide aid to cover the additional costs of employing disabled workers.

2. This Regulation shall apply to aid in all sectors, including the activities relating to the production, processing and marketing of products listed in Annex I to the Treaty.

It shall not apply to any aid granted in the coal or shipbuilding sectors, nor to any aid for the creation of employment, within the meaning of Article 4, granted in the transport sector. Such aid shall remain subject to prior notification to the Commission in accordance with Article 88(3) of the Treaty.

3. This Regulation shall not apply:

(a) to aid to export-related activities, namely aid directly linked to the quantities exported, to the establishment and operation of a distribution network or to other current expenditure linked to the export activity;

(b) to aid contingent upon the use of domestic in preference to imported goods.

Commentary
Art 1(2): **B&C:** 15.067

Article 2
Definitions

For the purpose of this Regulation:

(a) "aid" means any measure fulfilling all the criteria laid down in Article 87(1) of the Treaty;

(b) "small and medium-sized enterprises" means enterprises as defined in Annex I to Regulation (EC) No 70/2001;

(c) "gross aid intensity" means the aid amount expressed as a percentage of the relevant costs. All figures used shall be taken before any deduction for direct taxation. Where aid is awarded in a form other than a grant, the aid amount shall be the grant equivalent of the aid. Aid payable in several instalments shall be discounted to its value at the moment of granting. The interest rate to be used for discounting purposes and for calculating the aid amount in a soft loan shall be the reference rate applicable at the time of grant;

(d) "net aid intensity" means the discounted aid amount net of tax expressed as a percentage of the relevant costs;

(e) "number of employees" means the number of annual working units (AWU), namely the number of persons employed full time in one year, part-time and seasonal work being AWU fractions;

(f) "disadvantaged worker" means any person who belongs to a category which has difficulty entering the labour market without assistance, namely a person meeting at least one of the following criteria:

    (i) any person who is under 25 or is within two years after completing full-time education and who has not previously obtained his or her first regular paid employment;

    (ii) any migrant worker who moves or has moved within the Community or becomes resident in the Community to take up work;

    (iii) any person who is a member of an ethnic minority within a Member State and who requires development of his or her linguistic, vocational training or work experience profile to enhance prospects of gaining access to stable employment;

    (iv) any person who wishes to enter or to re-enter working life and who has been absent both from work and from education for at least two years, and particularly any person who gave up work on account of the difficulty of reconciling his or her working life and family life;

(v) any person living as a single adult looking after a child or children;
(vi) any person who has not attained an upper secondary educational qualification or its equivalent, who does not have a job or who is losing his or her job;
(vii) any person older than 50, who does not have a job or who is losing his or her job;
(viii) any long-term unemployed person, i.e. any person who has been unemployed for 12 of the previous 16 months, or six of the previous eight months in the case of persons under 25;
(ix) any person recognised to be or to have been an addict in accordance with national law;
(x) any person who has not obtained his or her first regular paid employment since beginning a period of imprisonment or other penal measure;
(xi) any woman in a NUTS II geographical area where average unemployment has exceeded 100% of the Community average for at least two calendar years and where female unemployment has exceeded 150% of the male unemployment rate in the area concerned for at least two of the past three calendar years;
(g) "disabled worker" means any person either:
(i) recognised as disabled under national law; or
(ii) having a recognised, serious, physical, mental or psychological impairment;
(h) "sheltered employment" means employment in an establishment where at least 50% of the employees are disabled workers who are unable to take up work in the open labour market;
(i) "wage cost" comprises the following components actually payable by the beneficiary of the State aid in respect of the employment concerned:
(i) the gross wage, i.e. before tax; and
(ii) the compulsory social security contributions.
(j) a job is "linked to the carrying-out of a project of investment" if it concerns the activity to which the investment relates and if it is created within three years of the investment's completion. During this period, the jobs created following an increase in the utilisation rate of the capacity created by the investment are also linked to the investment;
(k) "investment in tangible assets" means an investment in fixed physical assets relating to the creation of a new establishment, the extension of an existing establishment, or the engagement in an activity involving a fundamental change in the product or production process of an existing establishment (in particular through rationalisation, diversification or modernisation). An investment in fixed assets undertaken in the form of the takeover of an establishment which has closed or which would have closed had it not been purchased shall also be regarded as tangible investment;
(l) "investment in intangible assets" means investment in transfer of technology by the acquisition of patent rights, licences, know-how or unpatented technical knowledge.

Article 3
Conditions for exemption

1. Subject to Article 9, aid schemes fulfilling all the conditions of this Regulation shall be compatible with the common market within the meaning of Article 87(3) of the Treaty and shall be exempt from the notification requirement of Article 88(3) of the Treaty provided that:

(a) any aid that could be awarded under such scheme fulfils all the conditions of this Regulation;
(b) the scheme contains an express reference to this Regulation, by citing its title and publication reference in the *Official Journal of the European Communities*.

2. Aid granted under the schemes referred to in paragraph 1 shall be compatible with the common market within the meaning of Article 87(3) of the Treaty and shall be exempt from the notification requirement of Article 88(3) provided that the aid granted fulfils all the conditions of this Regulation.

Article 4
Creation of employment

1. Aid schemes for the creation of employment and any aid that could be awarded under such scheme shall fulfil the conditions of paragraphs 2, 3 and 4.

Part G State Aids

2. Where the employment is created in areas or in sectors which do not qualify for regional aid pursuant to Article 87(3)(a) and (c) at the moment the aid is granted, the gross aid intensity shall not exceed:

(a) 15% in the case of small enterprises;

(b) 7,5% in the case of medium-sized enterprises.

3. Where the employment is created in areas and in sectors which qualify for regional aid pursuant to Article 87(3)(a) and (c) at the moment at which the aid is awarded, the net aid intensity shall not exceed the corresponding ceiling of regional investment aid determined in the map applying at the time the aid is granted, as approved by the Commission for each Member State: for this purpose, regard shall be had, inter alia, to the multisectoral framework for regional aid for large investment projects.[1]

In the case of small and medium-sized enterprises, and unless the map provides otherwise for such enterprises, this ceiling shall be increased by:

(a) 10 percentage points gross in areas covered by Article 87(3)(c), provided that the total net aid intensity does not exceed 30%; or

(b) 15 percentage points gross in areas covered by Article 87(3)(a), provided that the total net aid intensity does not exceed 75%.

The higher regional aid ceilings shall only apply if the beneficiary's contribution to financing is at least 25% and if the employment is maintained within the qualifying region.

When employment is created in the production, processing and marketing of products listed in Annex I to the Treaty, in areas which qualify as less favoured areas under Council Regulation (EC) No 1257/1999,[2] these higher aid ceilings or, if applicable, the higher aid ceilings of that Regulation, shall apply.

4. The ceilings fixed in paragraphs 2 and 3 shall apply to the intensity of the aid calculated as a percentage of the wage costs over a period of two years relating to the employment created under the following conditions:

(a) the employment created must represent a net increase in the number of employees, both in the establishment and in the enterprise concerned, compared with the average over the past 12 months;

(b) the employment created shall be maintained for a minimum period of three years, or two years in the case of SMEs; and

(c) the new workers employed as a result of the creation of employment must have never had a job or have lost or be losing their previous job.

5. Where aid is granted for the creation of employment under a scheme exempted under this Article, additional aid may be granted in case of recruitment of a disadvantaged or disabled worker in accordance with the terms of Articles 5 or 6.

Notes
[1] OJ C 70, 19.3.2002, p. 8.
[2] OJ L 160, 26.6.1999, p. 80.

Article 5
Recruitment of disadvantaged and disabled workers

1. Aid schemes for the recruitment by any enterprise of disadvantaged and disabled workers and any aid that could be awarded under such scheme shall fulfil the conditions of paragraphs 2 and 3.

2. The gross intensity of all aid relating to the employment of the disadvantaged or disabled worker or workers concerned, calculated as a percentage of the wage costs over a period of one year following recruitment, shall not exceed 50% for disadvantaged workers or 60% for disabled workers.

3. The following conditions shall apply:

(a) where the recruitment does not represent a net increase in the number of employees in the establishment concerned, the post or posts must have fallen vacant following voluntary departure,

retirement on grounds of age, voluntary reduction of working time or lawful dismissal for misconduct and not as a result of redundancy, and

(b) except in the case of lawful dismissal for misconduct the worker or workers must be entitled to
continuous employment for a minimum of 12 months.

Article 6
Additional costs of employment of disabled workers

1. Aid schemes for the employment of disabled workers and any aid that could be awarded under
such a scheme shall fulfil the conditions of paragraphs 2 and 3.

2. The aid, together with any aid provided under Article 5, shall not exceed the level needed to compensate for any reduced productivity resulting from the disabilities of the worker or workers, and for
any of the following costs:

(a) costs of adapting premises;
(b) costs of employing staff for time spent solely on the assistance of the disabled worker or workers;
(c) costs of adapting or acquiring equipment for their use,

which are additional to those which the beneficiary would have incurred if employing workers who are
not disabled, over any period for which the disabled worker or workers are actually employed.

Where the beneficiary provides sheltered employment, aid may in addition cover, but shall not
exceed, the costs of constructing, installing or expanding the establishment concerned, and any costs
of administration and transport which result from the employment of disabled workers.

3. Schemes exempted by this Article shall provide that aid be subject to the condition that the beneficiary maintain records allowing verification that the aid granted to it meets the provisions of this
Article and Article 8(4).

Article 7
Necessity for the aid

1. This Regulation shall only exempt aid under Article 4 if before the employment concerned is
created:

(a) either an application for aid has been submitted to the Member State by the beneficiary; or
(b) the Member State has adopted legal provisions establishing a legal right to aid according to objective criteria and without further exercise of discretion by the Member State.

2. Aid shall enjoy exemption under Article 4 in cases where:

(a) the employment created is linked to the carrying-out of a project of investment in tangible or
intangible assets; and
(b) the employment is created within three years of the investment's completion,

only if the application referred in paragraph 1(a), or the adoption referred to in paragraph 1(b), takes
place before work on the project is started.

Article 8
Cumulation

1. The aid ceilings fixed in Articles 4, 5 and 6 shall apply regardless of whether the support for the
aided employment or recruitment is financed entirely from State resources or is partly financed by
the Community.

2. Aid under schemes exempted by Article 4 of this Regulation shall not be cumulated with any other
State aid within the meaning of Article 87(1) of the Treaty, or with other Community funding, in
relation to the same wage costs, if such cumulation would result in an aid intensity exceeding that
fixed by this Regulation.

3. Aid under schemes exempted by Article 4 of this Regulation shall not be cumulated:

(a) with any other State aid within the meaning of Article 87(1) of the Treaty, or with other Community
funding, in relation to costs of any investment to which the created employment is linked and
which has not yet been completed at the time the employment is created, or which was completed
in the three years before the employment is created; or

Part G State Aids

(b) with any such aid or funding in relation to the same wage costs or to other employment linked to the same investment,

if such cumulation would result in an aid intensity exceeding the relevant ceiling of regional invest-ment aid determined in the guidelines on national regional aid and in the map approved by the Commission for each Member State or the ceiling in Regulation (EC) No 70/2001. Where the rel-evant ceiling has been adapted in a particular case, in particular by the application of State aid rules applying in a particular sector, or by an instrument applying to large investment projects, such as the applicable multisectoral framework for regional aid for large investment projects, the adapted ceiling shall apply for the purposes of this paragraph.

4. By way of derogation from paragraphs 2 and 3, aid under schemes exempted by Articles 5 and 6 of this Regulation may be cumulated with other State aid within the meaning of Article 87(1) of the Treaty, or with other Community funding, in relation to the same costs, including with aid under schemes exempted by Article 4 of this Regulation which complies with paragraphs 2 and 3, provided that such cumulation does not result in a gross aid intensity exceeding 100% of the wage costs over any period for which the worker or workers are employed.

The first subparagraph shall be without prejudice to any lower limits on aid intensity that may have been set pursuant to the Community framework for State aid for research and development.[1]

Notes
[1] OJ C 45, 17.2.1996, p. 5.

Article 9
Aid subject to prior notification to the Commission

1. Aid schemes which are targeted at particular sectors shall not be exempted from notification under this Regulation and shall remain subject to the notification requirement of Article 88(3) of the Treaty.

2. This Regulation shall not exempt from notification the grant of aid to a single enterprise or estab-lishment exceeding a gross aid amount of EUR 15 million over any three-year period. The Commission shall assess such aid, if granted under a scheme which is otherwise exempted by this Regulation, by reference solely to the criteria of this Regulation.

3. This Regulation is without prejudice to any obligation on a Member State to notify individual grants of aid under obligations entered into in the context of other State aid Instruments, and in particular the obligation to notify, or to inform the Commission of, aid to an enterprise receiving restructuring aid within the meaning of the Community guidelines on State aid for rescuing and restructuring firms in difficulty and the obligation to notify regional aid for large investment projects under the applicable multisectoral Framework.

4. Aid schemes to promote the recruitment of categories of worker who are not disadvantaged within the meaning of Article 2(f) shall remain subject to the notification requirement of Article 88(3) of the Treaty unless exempted under Article 4. On notification, Member States shall submit, for appraisal by the Commission, arguments showing that the workers concerned are disadvantaged. In this respect, Article 5 shall apply.

5. Aid to maintain jobs, namely financial support given to an undertaking to retain workers who would otherwise be laid off, shall remain subject to the notification requirement of Article 88(3) of the Treaty. Subject to any sectoral rules, such aid may be authorised by the Commission only where, in accordance with Article 87(2)(b) of the Treaty, it is intended to make good the damage caused by natural disasters or exceptional occurrences or, under the conditions applying to operating aid in the guidelines on national regional aid, in regions eligible for the derogation under Article 87(3)(a) con-cerning the economic development of areas where the standard of living is abnormally low or where there is serious underemployment.

6. Aid for the conversion of temporary or fixed-term employment contracts into contracts of indeter-minate duration shall remain subject to the notification requirement of Article 88(3) of the Treaty.

7. Aid schemes for job-sharing, for provision of support for working parents and similar employment measures which promote employment but which do not result in a net increase in employment, in the recruitment of disadvantaged workers, or in the recruitment or employment of disabled workers shall remain subject to the notification requirement of Article 88(3) of the Treaty and shall be assessed by the Commission in accordance with Article 87.

8. Other aid measures with objectives connected with employment and labour markets, such as measures to encourage early retirement, shall also remain subject to the notification requirement of Article 88(3) of the Treaty and shall be assessed by the Commission in accordance with Article 87.

9. Individual cases of employment aid granted independently of any scheme shall remain subject to the notification requirement of Article 88(3) of the Treaty. Such aid will be assessed in the light of this Regulation and may be authorised by the Commission only if it is compatible with any specific applicable rules which may have been laid down in respect of the sector in which the beneficiary operates and only if it can be shown that the effects of the aid on employment outweigh the impact on competition in the relevant market.

Article 10
Transparency and monitoring

1. On implementation of an aid scheme exempted by this Regulation, Member States shall, within 20 working days, forward to the Commission, with a view to its publication in the *Official Journal of the European Communities*, a summary of the information regarding such aid scheme in the form laid down in Annex I. This shall be provided in computerised form.

2. Member States shall maintain detailed records regarding the aid schemes exempted by this Regulation and the individual aid granted under those schemes. Such records shall contain all information necessary to establish that the conditions for exemption, as laid down in this Regulation, are fulfilled, including information on the status of any company whose entitlement to aid depends on its status as an SME. Member States shall keep a record regarding an aid scheme for 10 years from the date on which the last individual aid was granted under such scheme. On written request, the Member State concerned shall provide the Commission, within a period of 20 working days or such longer period as may be fixed in the request, with all the information which the Commission considers necessary to assess whether the conditions of this Regulation have been complied with.

3. Member States shall compile a report on the application of this Regulation in respect of each whole or part calendar year during which this Regulation applies, in the form laid down in Annex II, in computerised form. Member States shall provide the Commission with such report no later than three months after the expiry of the period to which the report relates.

Commentary
Art 10(1): F&N: 16.286

Article 11
Entry into force, period of validity, and transitional arrangements

1. This Regulation shall enter into force on the 20th day following its publication in the *Official Journal of the European Communities*.

[It shall apply until 30 June 2008.]

2. Notifications pending at the time of entry into force of this Regulation shall be assessed in accordance with its provisions.

Aid schemes implemented before the date of entry into force of this Regulation, and aid granted under these schemes, in the absence of a Commission authorisation and in breach of the obligation in Article 88(3) of the Treaty, shall be compatible with the common market within the meaning of Article 87(3) of the Treaty and shall be exempted under this Regulation if they fulfil the conditions laid down in Article 3(1)(a) and Article 3(2). Any aid which does not fulfil these conditions shall be assessed by the Commission in accordance with the relevant frameworks, guidelines, communications and notices.

3. At the end of the period of validity of this Regulation, aid schemes exempted under this Regulation shall remain exempted during an adjustment period of six months.

Notes

Date of entry into force: 2 January 2003.

Article 11 was amended as shown in square brackets by Commission Regulation (EC) No 1976/2006 of 20 December 2006 (OJ L 368, 23.12.2006, p. 85), Article 1.

This Regulation shall be binding in its entirety and directly applicable in all Member States.

Done at Brussels, 5 December 2002.

ANNEX I

INFORMATION COMMUNICATED BY MEMBER STATES REGARDING STATE AID GRANTED UNDER REGULATION (EC) NO 2204/2002 OF 12 DECEMBER 2002 ON THE APPLICATION OF ARTICLES 87 AND 88 OF THE EC TREATY TO STATE AID FOR EMPLOYMENT

(to be provided in computerised form, by electronic mail, to stateaidgreffe@cec.eu.int)

Notes

Annex I is available in electronic form at the following address:
http://ec.europa.eu/comm/competition/state_aid/legislation/forms.html

Aid No:

Explanatory remark: This number will be filled in by DG COMP.

Member State:

Region:

Explanatory remark: Indicate the name of the region if the aid is granted by a sub-central authority.

Title of aid scheme:

Explanatory remark: Indicate the name of the aid scheme.

Legal basis:

Explanatory remark: Indicate the precise national legal reference for the aid and a publication reference.

Annual expenditure planned under the scheme:

Explanatory remarks: Amounts are to be given in euro or, if applicable, national currency. Indicate the annual overall amount of the budget appropriation(s) or the estimated tax loss per year for all aid instruments contained in the scheme. For guarantees, indicate the (maximum) amount of loans guaranteed.

Maximum aid intensity under:

— Article 4: creation of employment:
— Article 5: recruitment of disadvantaged and disabled workers:
— Article 6: additional costs of employment of disabled workers:

Explanatory remark: Indicate the maximum aid intensity distinguishing between aid under Articles 4, 5 and 6 of the Regulation.

Date of implementation:

Explanatory remark: Indicate the date from which aid may be granted under the scheme.

Duration of scheme:

Explanatory remark: Indicate the date (year and month) until which aid may be granted under the scheme.

Objective of aid:

— Article 4: creation of employment:
— Article 5: recruitment of disadvantaged and disabled workers:
— Article 6: employment of disabled workers:

Explanatory remark: The primary objective(s) of the measure should be identified from among the three options. This field also gives the opportunity to indicate further (secondary) objectives pursued.

Economic sector(s) concerned:

— all Community sectors[1]
— all manufacturing[1]
— all services[1]
— other (please specify)

Explanatory remarks: Choose from the list, where relevant. Aid schemes which are targeted at specific sectors are not covered by the exemption from notification provided by this Regulation.

Name and address of the granting authority:

Explanatory remark: Please include the telephone No and where possible the address for electronic mail.

Other information:

Explanatory remarks: If the scheme is co-financed by Community funds, please add the following sentence:

"The aid scheme is co-financed under [reference]."

If the scheme's duration extends beyond the date of validity of this Regulation, please add the following sentence:

"The exemption regulation expires on 31 December 2006 followed by a transitional period of six months."

Notes

[1] With the exception of the shipbuilding sector, and other sectors which are the subjects of special rules in regulations and directives governing all State aid within the sector.

ANNEX II
FORM OF THE PERIODIC REPORT TO BE PROVIDED TO THE COMMISSION

Annual Reporting Format on Aid Schemes Exempted under a Group Exemption Regulation Adopted pursuant to Article 1 of Regulation (EC) No 994/98

Member States are required to use the format below for their reporting obligations to the Commission under group exemption regulations adopted on the basis of Regulation (EC) No 994/98.

The reports should be provided in computerised form to:

stateaidgreffe@cec.eu.int

Information required for all aid schemes exempted under group exemption regulations adopted pursuant to Article 1 of Regulation (EC) No 994/98

1. Title and No of aid scheme
2. Commission exemption regulation applicable
3. Expenditure
   Separate figures have to be provided for each aid instrument within a scheme (e.g. grant, soft loans, etc.). The figures have to be expressed in euro or, if applicable, national currency. In the case of tax expenditure, annual tax losses have to be reported. If precise figures are not available, such losses may be estimated.

These expenditure figures should be provided on the following basis:

For the year under review indicate separately for each aid instrument within the scheme (e.g. grant, soft loan, guarantee, etc.):

3.1. Amounts committed, (estimated) tax losses or other revenue forgone, data on guarantees, etc. for new decisions to grant aid. In the case of guarantee schemes, the total amount of new guarantees handed out should be provided.

3.2. Actual payments, (estimated) tax losses or other revenue forgone, data on guarantees, etc. for new and current grants of aid. In the case of guarantee schemes, the following should be provided: total amount of outstanding guarantees, premium income, recoveries, indemnities paid out, operating result of the scheme under the year under review.

3.3. Number of new decisions to grant aid.

3.4. Estimated overall number of jobs created or disadvantaged or disabled workers recruited or employed under new decisions to grant aid (as appropriate). Aid for the recruitment of disadvantaged workers should be broken down by the categories in Article 2(f).

3.5. [Blank]

3.6. Regional breakdown of amounts under point 3.1 either by regions defined at NUTS[1] level II or below or by Article 87(3)(a) regions, Article 87(3)(c) regions and non-assisted regions.

Notes

[1] NUTS is the nomenclature of territorial units for statistical purposes in the European Community.

3.7. Sectoral breakdown of amounts under point 3.1 by beneficiaries' sectors of activity (If more than one sector is covered, indicate the amount for each):

— coalmining
— manufacturing of which:
  — steel
  — shipbuilding
  — synthetic fibres
  — motor vehicles
  — other manufacturing
— services of which:
  — transport services
  — financial services
  — other services
— other sectors (please specify)

4. Other information and remarks.

G13

COMMISSION REGULATION (EC)
No 1857/2006

of 15 December 2006

on the application of Articles 87 and 88 of the Treaty to State aid to small and medium-sized enterprises active in the production of agricultural products and amending Regulation (EC) No 70/2001

Official Journal L 358, 16.12.2006, p. 3

Celex No: 32001R0070

Commentary

Regulation 1857/2006: **B&C:** 15.059, 15.067

THE COMMISSION OF THE EUROPEAN COMMUNITIES,

Having regard to the Treaty establishing the European Community,

Having regard to Council Regulation (EC) No 994/98 of 7 May 1998 on the application of Articles [87] and [88] of the Treaty establishing the European Community to certain categories of horizontal State aid,[1] and in particular Article 1(1)(a)(i) thereof,

Having published a draft of this Regulation,

Having consulted the Advisory Committee on State Aid,

Notes

[1] OJ L 142, 14.5.1998, p. 1.

Whereas:

(1) Regulation (EC) No 994/98 empowers the Commission to declare, in accordance with Article 87 of the Treaty, that, under certain conditions, aid to small and medium-sized enterprises is compatible with the common market and not subject to the notification requirement of Article 88(3) of the Treaty.

(2) Commission Regulation (EC) No 70/2001 of 12 January 2001 on the application of Articles 87 and 88 of the EC Treaty to State aid to small and medium-sized enterprises[2] does not apply to activities linked to the production, processing or marketing of products listed in Annex I to the Treaty.

Notes

[2] OJ L 10, 13.1.2001, p. 33. Regulation as last amended by Regulation (EC) No 1040/2006 (OJ L 187, 8.7.2006, p. 8).

---

(3) The Commission has applied Articles 87 and 88 of the Treaty to small and medium-sized enterprises active in the production, processing and marketing of agricultural products in numerous decisions and has also stated its policy, most recently in the Community guidelines for State aid in the agriculture sector.[3] In the light of the Commission's considerable experience in applying those Articles to small and medium-sized enterprises active in the production of agricultural products, it is appropriate, with a view to ensuring efficient supervision and simplifying administration without weakening Commission monitoring, that the Commission should also make use of the powers conferred by Regulation (EC) No 994/98 for small and medium-sized enterprises active in the production of agricultural products, insofar as Article 89 of the Treaty has been declared applicable to such products.

Notes
3 OJ C 28, 1.2.2000, p. 2. Corrected version (OJ C 232, 12.8.2000, p. 17).

(4) Over the coming years, agriculture will have to adapt to new realities and further changes in terms of market evolution, market policy and trade rules, consumer demand and preferences and the enlargement of the Community. These changes will affect not only agricultural markets but also local economies in rural areas in general. Rural development policy should aim at restoring and enhancing the competitiveness of rural areas and, therefore, contribute to the maintenance and creation of employment in those areas.

(5) Small and medium-sized enterprises play a decisive role in job creation and, more generally, act as a factor of social stability and economic drive. However, their development may be limited by market imperfections. They often have difficulties in obtaining capital or credit, given the risk-shy nature of certain financial markets and the limited guarantees that they may be able to offer. Their limited resources may also restrict their access to information, notably regarding new technology and potential markets. Having regard to those considerations, the purpose of the aid exempted by this Regulation should be to facilitate the development of the economic activities of small and medium-sized enterprises, provided that such aid does not adversely affect trading conditions to an extent contrary to the common interest. These developments should be encouraged and supported by simplification of the existing rules, as far as they apply to small and medium-sized enterprises.

(6) The production, processing and marketing of agricultural products in the Community is largely dominated by small and medium-sized enterprises. However, there are considerable differences between the structure of primary production, on the one hand, and processing and marketing of agricultural products, on the other hand. The processing and marketing of agricultural products would often appear similar to that of industrial products. Therefore, it would appear more appropriate to have a different approach for processing and marketing of agricultural products and include those activities in the rules for industrial products. Consequently, and contrary to the approach taken in Commission Regulation (EC) No 1/2004 of 23 December 2003 on the application of Articles 87 and 88 of the EC Treaty to State aid to small and medium-sized enterprises active in the production, processing and marketing of agricultural products,[4] it appears useful to set up an exemption regulation targeted at the specific needs of primary agricultural production.

Notes
4 OJ L 1, 3.1.2004, p. 1.

(7) Council Regulation (EC) No 1257/1999 of 17 May 1999 on support for rural development from the European Agricultural Guidance and Guarantee Fund (EAGGF) and amending and repealing certain Regulations[5] and Council Regulation (EC) No 1698/2005 of 20 September 2005 on support for rural development by the European Agricultural Fund for Rural Development (EAFRD)[6] have introduced specific State aid rules for certain rural development measures receiving Member State support without any Community financing.

Notes
5 OJ L 160, 26.6.1999, p. 80.
6 OJ L 277, 21.10.2005, p. 1. Regulation as last amended by Regulation (EC) No 1698/2005 (OJ L 277, 21.10.2005, p. 1).

(8) This Regulation should exempt any aid that meets all the requirements it lays down, and any aid scheme, provided that any aid that could be granted under such scheme meets all the requirements of this Regulation. With a view to ensuring efficient supervision and simplifying administration without weakening Commission monitoring, aid schemes and individual grants outside any aid scheme should contain an express reference to this Regulation.

(9) In view of the need to strike the appropriate balance between minimising distortions of competition in the aided sector and the objectives of this Regulation, it should not exempt individual grants which exceed a fixed maximum amount, whether or not made under an aid scheme exempted by this Regulation.

(10) This Regulation should not exempt export aid or aid contingent upon the use of domestic over imported products. Such aid may be incompatible with the Community's international obligations. Aid towards the costs of participation in trade fairs or of studies or consultancy services needed for the launch of a new or existing product on a new market should not normally constitute export aid.

(11) In order to eliminate differences that might give rise to distortions of competition, to facilitate coordination between different Community and national initiatives concerning small and medium-sized enterprises and for reasons of administrative clarity and legal certainty, the definition of "small and medium-sized enterprises" used in this Regulation should be that set out in Annex I to Regulation (EC) No 70/2001.

(12) In accordance with established practice of the Commission, and with a view to ensuring that aid is proportionate and limited to the amount necessary, thresholds should normally be expressed in terms of aid intensities in relation to a set of eligible costs, rather than in terms of maximum aid amounts.

(13) In order to determine whether or not aid is compatible with the common market pursuant to this Regulation, it is necessary to take into consideration the aid intensity and thus the aid amount expressed as a grant equivalent. The calculation of the grant equivalent of aid payable in several instalments requires the use of market interest rates prevailing at the time of grant. With a view to a uniform, transparent, and simple application of the State aid rules, the market rates for the purposes of this Regulation should be deemed to be the reference rates periodically fixed by the Commission on the basis of objective criteria and published in the *Official Journal of the European Union* and on the Internet.

(14) In order to ensure transparency and effective monitoring, this Regulation should apply only to aid measures which are transparent. These are aid measures in which it is possible to calculate precisely the gross grant equivalent as a percentage of eligible expenditure *ex ante* without a need to undertake a risk assessment (for example, grants, interest rate subsidies and capped fiscal measures). Public loans should be considered to be transparent provided that they are backed by normal security and do not involve abnormal risk and are therefore not considered to contain a State guarantee element. In principle, aid measures involving State guarantees or public loans with a State guarantee element should not be considered as transparent. However, such aid measures should be considered as transparent if, before the implementation of the measure, the methodology used to calculate the aid intensity of the State guarantee has been accepted by the Commission following notification to the Commission after adoption of this Regulation. The methodology will be assessed by the Commission in line with the Notice on the application of Article 87 and 88 of the EC Treaty to State aid in the Forms of Guarantees.[7] Public participation and aid comprised in risk capital measures should not be considered as transparent aid. Aid measures which are not transparent should always be notified to the Commission. Notifications of non-transparent aid measures will be assessed by the Commission in particular in the light of the criteria set out in the Community guidelines for State aid in the agriculture and forestry sector 2007–2013.

Notes
[7] OJ C 71, 11.3.2000, p. 14.

(15) In accordance with established practice of the Commission for the evaluation of State aid in the agricultural sector, no differentiation between small enterprises and medium-sized enterprises is necessary. For certain types of aid, the establishment of maximum amounts of aid which a beneficiary may receive is appropriate.

(16) Aid ceilings should be fixed, in the light of the Commission's experience, at a level that strikes the appropriate balance between minimising distortions of competition in the aided sector and the objective of facilitating the development of the economic activities of small and medium-sized enterprises in the agriculture sector. In the interests of coherence with Community-financed support measures, the ceilings should be harmonised with those fixed in Regulation (EC) No 1257/1999 and in Regulation (EC) No 1698/2005.

(17) It is appropriate to establish further conditions that should be fulfilled by any aid scheme or individual aid exempted by this Regulation. Any restrictions on production or limitations of Community support under the common market organisations should be taken into account. Having regard to Article 87(3)(c) of the Treaty, aid should not have the sole effect of continuously or periodically reducing the operating costs which the beneficiary would normally have to bear, and should be proportionate to the handicaps that have to be overcome in order to secure the socio-economic benefits deemed to be in the Community interest. Unilateral State aid measures which simply seek to improve the financial situation of producers but which in no way contribute to the development of the sector, and in particular aids which are granted solely on the basis of price, quantity, unit of production or unit of the means of production are considered to constitute operating aids which are incompatible with the common market. Furthermore, such aids are also likely to interfere with the mechanisms of the common organisations of the markets. It is therefore appropriate to limit the scope of this Regulation to certain types of aid.

(18) This Regulation should exempt aid to small and medium-sized agricultural holdings (farms) regardless of location. Investment and job creation can contribute to the economic development of less favoured regions and areas as referred to in Article 36(a)(i), (ii) and (iii) of Regulation (EC) No 1698/2005. Small and medium-sized agricultural holdings (farms) in those areas suffer from both the structural disadvantage of the location and the difficulties deriving from their size. It is therefore appropriate that small and medium-sized enterprises in such areas should benefit from higher ceilings.

(19) Because of the risk of distortions resulting from targeted investment aid and in order to offer farmers freedom to decide about products invested in, investment aid exempted under this Regulation should not be limited to specific agricultural products. This condition should not prevent a Member State from excluding certain agricultural products from such aid or aid schemes, notably where no normal market outlets can be found. Also, certain types of investment should per se be excluded from this Regulation.

(20) Where aid is granted to adapt to newly introduced standards at Community level, Member States should not be able to lengthen the adaptation period for farmers by delaying implementation of such rules. Therefore, the date from which new legislation can no longer be considered new should be clearly set out.

(21) Certain Council Regulations in the field of agriculture provide for specific authorisations for the payment of aid by Member States, often in combination with or in addition to Community financing. However, those provisions usually do not provide for an exemption from the duty to notify under Article 88 of the Treaty, insofar as such aid fulfils the conditions of Article 87(1) of the Treaty. Since the conditions for such aids are clearly specified in those Regulations, and/or there is a duty to communicate such measures to the Commission under the special provisions of those Regulations, no further and separate notification under Article 88(3) of the Treaty is necessary in order to allow for an assessment of these measures by the Commission. For reasons of legal certainty, a reference to those provisions should be included in this Regulation, and therefore notification of those measures under Article 88 of the Treaty should not be necessary, insofar as it can be ascertained in advance that such aid is exclusively granted to small and medium-sized enterprises.

(22) In order to ensure that the aid is necessary and acts as an incentive to develop certain activities, this Regulation should not exempt aid for activities in which the beneficiary would already engage under market conditions alone. No aid should be granted retroactively in respect of activities which have already been undertaken by the beneficiary.

(23) This Regulation should not exempt aid cumulated with other State aid, including aid granted by national, regional or local authorities, with public support granted within the framework of Regulation (EC) No 1698/2005 or with Community assistance, in relation to the same eligible costs, when such cumulation exceeds the thresholds fixed in this Regulation. Aid exempted under this Regulation should not be cumulated with *de minimis* support within the meaning of Commission Regulation (EC) No 1860/2004 of 6 October 2004 on the application of Articles 87 and 88 of the EC Treaty to *de minimis* aid in the agriculture and fisheries sectors[8] in respect of the same eligible expenditure or investment project, if such cumulation would result in an aid intensity exceeding that fixed by this Regulation.

Notes
8 OJ L 325, 28.10.2004, p. 4.

(24) In order to ensure transparency and effective monitoring, in accordance with Article 3 of Regulation (EC) No 994/98, it is appropriate to establish a standard format in which Member States should provide the Commission with summary information whenever, in accordance with this Regulation, an aid scheme is implemented or individual aid is granted outside such a scheme, with a view to publication in the *Official Journal of the European Union*. For the same reasons, it is appropriate to establish rules concerning the records that Member States should keep regarding the aid exempted by this Regulation. For the purposes of the annual report to be submitted to the Commission by Member States, it is appropriate for the Commission to establish its specific requirements. In view of the wide availability of the necessary technology, the summary information and the annual report should be in computerised form.

(25) Failure by a Member State to comply with the reporting obligations established in this Regulation may make it impossible for the Commission to perform its monitoring task under Article 88(1) of the Treaty and, in particular, to assess whether the cumulative economic effect of the aids exempted under this Regulation is such as to adversely affect trading conditions to an extent contrary to the common interest. The need to evaluate the cumulative effect of State aid is particularly high where the same beneficiary may receive aid granted by several sources, as is increasingly the case in the field of agriculture. It is therefore of primary importance that the Member State rapidly submits appropriate information before implementing aid under this Regulation.

(26) Aid to companies active in the processing and marketing of agricultural products should be covered by the rules governing aid to small and medium-sized enterprises in other sectors laid down in Regulation (EC) No 70/2001. Regulation (EC) No 70/2001 should therefore be amended accordingly.

(27) State aid exempted under Regulation (EC) No 1/2004 should continue to be exempted if it fulfils all the conditions of this Regulation.

(28) It is appropriate to lay down transitional provisions for aid which was granted before the entry into force of this Regulation and was not notified in breach of the obligation in Article 88(3) of the Treaty.

(29) This Regulation is without prejudice to the possibility for Member States to notify aid to small and medium-sized enterprises active in the production of agricultural products. Such notifications will be assessed by the Commission in the light of this Regulation and on the basis of the Community guidelines for State aid in the agriculture and forestry sector 2007–2013. Notifications pending on the date of entry into force of this Regulation should be assessed first in the light of this Regulation and, if the conditions it lays down are not fulfilled, then on the basis of the Community guidelines for State aid in the agriculture and forestry sector 2007–2013.

(30) In the light of the Commission's experience in this area, and in particular the frequency with which it is generally necessary to revise State aid policy, it is appropriate to limit the period of application of this Regulation. Should this Regulation expire without being extended, aid schemes already exempted by this Regulation should continue to be exempt for a further period of six months, in order to give Member States time to adapt,

HAS ADOPTED THIS REGULATION:

CHAPTER 1

SCOPE, DEFINITIONS AND CONDITIONS

Article 1

Scope

1. This Regulation shall apply to transparent aid granted to small and medium-sized agricultural holdings (farms) active in the primary production of agricultural products. Without prejudice to Article 9, it shall not apply to aid granted for expenditure linked to the processing or marketing of agricultural products.

2. Without prejudice to Article 16(1)(a), this Regulation shall not apply to:

(a) aid to export-related activities, namely aid directly linked to the quantities exported, to the establishment and operation of a distribution network or to other current expenditure linked to the export activity;

(b) aid contingent upon the use of domestic over imported goods.

Article 2

Definitions

For the purpose of this Regulation:

1. "aid" means any measure fulfilling all the criteria laid down in Article 87(1) of the Treaty;
2. "agricultural product" means:

(a) the products listed in Annex I of the Treaty, except fishery and acquaculture products covered by Council Regulation (EC) No 104/2000;[9]

(b) products falling under CN codes 4502, 4503 and 4504 (cork products);

(c) products intended to imitate or substitute milk and milk products, as referred to in Article 3(2) of Council Regulation (EEC) No 1898/87;[10]

3. "processing of agricultural products" means any operation on an agricultural product resulting in a product which is also an agricultural product, except on farm activities necessary for preparing an animal or plant product for the first sale;
4. "marketing of agricultural products" means holding or display with a view to sale, offering for sale, delivery or any other manner of placing on the market, except the first sale by a primary producer to resellers or processors and any activity preparing a product for such first sale; a sale by a primary producer to final consumers shall be considered as marketing if it takes place in separate premises reserved for that purpose;
5. "small and medium-sized enterprises" (SME) means small and medium-sized enterprises as defined in Annex I to Regulation (EC) No 70/2001;
6. "gross aid intensity" means the aid amount expressed as a percentage of the project's eligible costs. All figures used shall be taken before any deduction for direct taxation. Where aid is awarded in a form other than a grant, the aid amount shall be the grant equivalent of the aid. Aid payable in several instalments shall be discounted to its value at the moment of granting. The interest rate to be used for discounting purposes and for calculating the aid amount in a soft loan shall be the reference rate applicable at the time of grant;
7. "quality product" is a product fulfilling the criteria to be defined pursuant to Article 32 of Regulation (EC) No 1698/2005;
8. "adverse climatic event which can be assimilated to a natural disaster" means weather conditions such as frost, hail, ice, rain or drought which destroy more than 30% of the average of annual production of a given farmer in the preceding three-year period or a three-year average based on the preceding five-year period, excluding the highest and lowest entry;
9. "less favoured areas" means areas as defined by Member States on the basis of Article 17 of Regulation (EC) No 1257/1999;
10. "investment made to comply with newly introduced minimum standards" means:

(a) in the case of standards which do not provide for any transitional period, investments actually started not more than two years after the date on which the standards are to be made compulsory vis-à-vis operators; or

(b) in the case of standards which provides for a transitional period, investments actually started before the date on which the standards are to be made compulsory vis-à-vis operators;

11. "young farmers" means producers of agricultural products fulfilling the criteria laid down in Article 22 of Regulation (EC) No 1698/2005;
12. "producer group" means a group which is set up for the purpose of jointly adapting, within the objectives of the common market organisations, the production and output of its members to market requirements, in particular by concentrating supply;
13. "producer association" means an association which consists of recognised producer groups and pursues the same objectives on a larger scale;

14. "fallen stock" means animals which have been killed by euthanasia with or without definite diagnosis or have died (including stillborn and unborn animals) on a farm or any premise or during transport, but have not been slaughtered for human consumption;

15. "TSE and BSE test costs" means all costs, including those for test kits, taking, transporting, testing, storing and destruction of samples necessary for tests undertaken in accordance with Annex X, Chapter C to Regulation (EC) No 999/2001 of the European Parliament and of the Council;[11]

16. "enterprises in difficulty" means enterprises considered in difficulty within the meaning of the Community guidelines on State aid for rescuing and restructuring firms in difficulty;[12]

17. "replacement investment" means an investment that simply replaces an existing building or machine, or parts of it, by a new up-to date building or machine, without expanding the production capacity by at least 25% or without fundamentally changing the nature of production or the technology involved. Neither the complete demolition of a farm building at least 30 years old and replacement by an up-to date building, nor the fundamental renovation of a farm building, are considered as replacement investments. Renovation is considered as fundamental when its cost amounts to at least 50% of the value of the new building.

18. "transparent aid" means aid measures in which it is possible to calculate precisely the gross grant equivalent as a percentage of eligible expenditure ex ante without need to undertake a risk assessment (for example measures which use grants, interest rate subsidies, capped fiscal measures).

Notes
[9] OJ L 17, 21.1.2000, p. 22.
[10] OJ L 182, 3.7.1987, p. 36.
[11] OJ L 147, 31.5.2001, p. 1.
[12] OJ C 244, 1.10.2004, p. 2.

Article 3
Conditions for exemption

1. Transparent individual aid outside any scheme, fulfilling all the conditions of this Regulation, shall be compatible with the common market within the meaning of Article 87(3)(c) of the Treaty and shall be exempt from the notification requirement of Article 88(3) of the Treaty provided that the summary information provided for in Article 20(1) has been submitted and that the aid contains an express reference to this Regulation, by citing its title and publication reference in the *Official Journal of the European Union*.

2. Transparent aid schemes fulfilling all the conditions set out in this Regulation shall be compatible with the common market within the meaning of Article 87(3)(c) of the Treaty and shall be exempt from the notification requirement of Article 88(3) of the Treaty provided that:

(a) any aid that could be awarded under such scheme fulfils all the conditions set out in this Regulation;

(b) the scheme contains an express reference to this Regulation, citing its title and publication reference in the *Official Journal of the European Union*;

(c) the summary information provided for in Article 20(1) has been submitted.

3. Aid granted under the schemes referred to in paragraph 2 shall be compatible with the common market within the meaning of Article 87(3)(c) of the Treaty and shall be exempt from the notification requirement of Article 88(3) of the Treaty provided that the aid granted directly fulfils all the conditions of this Regulation.

4. Aid which does not fall within the scope of this Regulation, or of other Regulations adopted pursuant to Article 1 of Regulation (EC) No 994/98 or Regulations listed in Article 17 of this Regulation, shall be notified to the Commission in accordance with Article 88(3) of the Treaty. Such aid shall be assessed in accordance with the criteria laid down in the Community guidelines for State aid in the agriculture and forestry sector 2007–2013.

Chapter 2
Categories of aid

Article 4
Investment in agricultural holdings

1. Aid for investments in agricultural holdings within the Community for primary production of agricultural products, shall be compatible with the common market within the meaning of Article 87(3)(c) of the Treaty and shall be exempt from the notification requirement of Article 88(3) of the Treaty if it fulfils the conditions set out in paragraphs 2 to 10 of this Article.

2. The gross aid intensity must not exceed:

(a) 50% of eligible investments in less favoured areas or in areas referred to in Article 36(a)(i), (ii) and (iii) of Regulation (EC) No 1698/2005, as designated by Member States in accordance with Articles 50 and 94 of that Regulation;

(b) 40% of eligible investments in other regions;

(c) 60% of eligible investments in less-favoured areas or in areas referred to in Article 36(a)(i), (ii) and (iii) of Regulation (EC) No 1698/2005, as designated by Member States in accordance with Articles 50 and 94 of that Regulation, and 50% in other regions, in the case of investments made by young farmers within five years of setting up;

(d) 75% of eligible investments in the outermost regions and the small Aegean Islands within the meaning of Council Regulation (EEC) No 2019/93;[13]

(e) 75% of eligible investments in regions referred to in point (a) and 60% in other regions where investments result in extra costs relating to the protection and improvement of the environment, the improvement of hygiene conditions of livestock enterprises or the welfare of farm animals. This increase may only be granted for investments which go beyond the minimum Community requirements in force, or for investments made to comply with newly introduced minimum standards. The increase must be limited to the extra eligible costs necessary and must not apply in the case of investments which result in an increase in production capacity.

3. The investment must pursue notably the following objectives:

(a) reduction of production costs;

(b) improvement and re-deployment of production;

(c) improvement in quality;

(d) preservation and improvement of the natural environment, or the improvement of hygiene conditions or animal welfare standards.

4. The eligible expenses may include:

(a) the construction, acquisition or improvement of immovable property;

(b) the purchase or lease-purchase of machinery and equipment, including computer software up to the market value of the asset;

(c) general costs linked to expenditure under points (a) and (b), such as architects, engineers and consultation fees, feasibility studies, the acquisition of patents and licences. Costs connected with a leasing contract other than those listed in point (b) of the first subparagraph, such as tax, lessor's margin, interest refinancing costs, overheads insurance, charges, etc. are not eligible expenditure.

5. Aid may only be granted to agricultural holdings which are not enterprises in difficulty.

Aid may be granted in order to enable the beneficiary to reach newly introduced minimum standards regarding the environment, hygiene and animal welfare.

6. The aid must not be granted in contravention of any prohibitions or restrictions laid down in Council Regulations establishing common organisations of the market, even where such prohibitions and restrictions only refer to Community support.

7. The aid must not be limited to specific agricultural products and must therefore be open to all sectors of agriculture, unless a Member State excludes certain products because of overcapacity or a lack of market outlets. Aid must not be granted in respect of the following:

(a) the purchase of production rights, animals and annual plants;

(b) the planting of annual plants;

1416

(c) drainage works or irrigation equipment and irrigation works, unless such investment leads to a reduction of previous water use of at least 25%;

(d) simple replacement investments.

8. Aid may be granted for a purchase of land other than land for construction purposes costing up to 10% of the eligible expenses of the investment.

9. The maximum amount of aid granted to an individual enterprise must not exceed EUR 400,000 over any period of three fiscal years, or EUR 500,000 if the enterprise is situated in a less favoured area or in an area referred to in Article 36(a)(i), (ii) or (iii) of Regulation (EC) No 1698/2005, as designated by Member States in accordance with Articles 50 and 94 of that Regulation.

10. The aid must not be granted in respect of the manufacture of products which imitate or substitute for milk and milk products.

Notes

[13] OJ L 184, 27.7.1993, p. 1.

Article 5

Conservation of traditional landscapes and buildings

1. Aid for conservation of traditional landscapes and buildings shall be compatible with the common market within the meaning of Article 87(3)(c) of the Treaty and shall be exempt from the notification requirement of Article 88(3) of the Treaty if it complies with the provisions of paragraphs 2 and 3 of this Article.

2. Aid may be granted up to 100% of the real costs incurred as regards investments or capital works intended for the conservation of non-productive heritage features located on agricultural holdings, such as archaeological or historical features. These costs may include reasonable compensation for the work undertaken by the farmer himself, or his workers, up to a limit of EUR 10,000 a year.

3. Aid may be granted up to 60%, or 75% in less favoured areas or in areas referred to in Article 36(a)(i), (ii) or (iii) of Regulation (EC) No 1698/2005, as designated by Member States in accordance with Articles 50 and 94 of that Regulation, of the real costs incurred as regards investments or capital works intended for the conservation of heritage features of productive assets on farms, such as farm buildings, provided that the investment does not entail any increase in the production capacity of the farm.

Where there is an increase in production capacity, the aid rates for investment established in Article 4(2) shall apply as regards eligible expenses resulting from undertaking the relevant work using normal contemporary materials. Additional aid may be granted at a rate of up to 100% to cover the extra costs incurred by using traditional materials necessary to maintain the heritage features of the building.

Article 6

Relocation of farm buildings in the public interest

1. Aid for the relocation of farm buildings shall be compatible with the common market within the meaning of Article 87(3)(c) of the Treaty and shall be exempt from the notification requirement of Article 88(3) of the Treaty if it is in the public interest and fulfils the conditions set out in paragraphs 2, 3 and 4 of this Article.

The public interest invoked to justify the granting of aid under this Article shall be specified in the relevant provisions of the Member State.

2. Aid may be granted up to 100% of the actual costs incurred where a relocation in the public interest simply consists of the dismantling, removal and re-erection of existing facilities.

3. Where the relocation in the public interest results in the farmer benefiting from more modern facilities, the farmer must contribute at least 60%, or 50% in less favoured areas or in areas referred to in Article 36(a)(i), (ii) or (iii) of Regulation (EC) No 1698/2005, as designated by Member States in accordance with Articles 50 and 94 of that Regulation, of the increase in the value of the facilities concerned after relocation. If the beneficiary is a young farmer, this contribution shall be at least 55% or 45% respectively.

Part G State Aids

4. Where the relocation in the public interest results in an increase in production capacity, the contribution from the beneficiary must be at least equal to 60%, or 50% in less favoured areas or in areas referred to in Article 36(a)(i), (ii) or (iii) of Regulation (EC) No 1698/2005, as designated by Member States in accordance with Articles 50 and 94 of that Regulation, of the expenses relating to this increase. If the beneficiary is a young farmer, this contribution shall be at least 55% or 45%.

Article 7
Aid for setting up of young farmers

Aid for the setting up of young farmers shall be compatible with the common market within the meaning of Article 87(3)(c) of the Treaty and shall be exempt from the notification requirement of Article 88(3) of the Treaty if the criteria set out in Article 22 of Regulation (EC) No 1698/2005 are fulfilled.

Article 8
Aid for early retirement

Aid for early retirement of farmers shall be compatible with the common market within the meaning of Article 87(3)(c) of the Treaty and shall be exempt from the notification requirement of Article 88(3) of the Treaty under the following conditions:

(a) the criteria set out in Article 23 of Regulation (EC) No 1698/2005 and any rules adopted by the Commission to implement that Article must be fulfilled;
(b) the cessation of commercial farming activities must be permanent and definitive.

Article 9
Aid for producer groups

1. Start-up aid for the constitution of producer groups or producer associations shall be compatible with the common market within the meaning of Article 87(3)(c) of the Treaty and shall be exempt from the notification requirement of Article 88(3) of the Treaty if it complies with the provisions of paragraphs 2 to 8 of this Article.

2. The following shall be eligible for the aid referred to in paragraph 1, provided that they are entitled to financial assistance under the legislation of the Member State concerned:

(a) producer groups or producer associations involved in the production of agricultural products; and/or
(b) associations of producers responsible for the supervision of the use of geographical indications and designations of origin or quality marks in conformity with Community law.

The internal rules of the producer group or association must provide an obligation on members to market production in accordance with the rules on supply and placing on the market drawn up by the group or association. Those rules may permit a proportion of the production to be marketed directly by the producer. They must require producers joining the group or association to remain members for at least three years and to give at least 12 months notice of withdrawal. In addition they must provide common rules on production, in particular relating to product quality, or use of organic practices or other practices designed to protect the environment, common rules for placing goods on the market and rules on product information, with particular regard to harvesting and availability. However, producers must remain responsible for managing their holdings. The agreements concluded in the framework of the producer group or association must comply fully with all relevant provisions of competition law, in particular Articles 81 and 82 of the Treaty.

3. The eligible expenses may include the rental of suitable premises, the acquisition of office equipment, including computer hardware and software, administrative staff costs, overheads and legal and administrative fees. If premises are purchased, the eligible expenses for premises must be limited to rental costs at market rates.

4. The aid must not be paid in respect of costs incurred after the fifth year, or paid following the seventh year after recognition of the producer organisation. This is without prejudice to grant aid towards eligible expenses limited to and resulting from a year-on-year increase in turnover of a beneficiary of at least 30% where this is due to the accession of new members and/or the coverage of new products.

5. The aid must not be granted to production organisations such as companies or co-operatives, the objective of which is the management of one or more agricultural holdings and which are therefore in effect single producers.

6. The aid must not be granted to other agricultural associations, which undertake tasks at the level of agricultural production, such as mutual support and farm relief and farm management services, in the members' holdings without being involved in the joint adaptation of supply to the market.

7. The total amount of aid granted to a producer group or association under this Article must not exceed EUR 400 000.

8. The aid must not be granted to producer groups or associations the objectives of which are incompatible with a Council Regulation setting up a common market organisation.

Article 10
Aid in respect of animal and plant diseases and pest infestations

1. Aid to compensate farmers for the costs of prevention and eradication of animal or plant diseases or pest infestations incurred for the costs of health checks, tests and other screening measures, purchase and administration of vaccines, medicines and plant protection products, slaughter and destruction costs of animals and costs of destruction of crops shall be compatible with the common market within the meaning of Article 87(3)(c) of the Treaty and shall be exempt from the notification requirement of Article 88(3) of the Treaty if it fulfils the following conditions and the conditions set out in paragraphs 4 to 8 of this Article:

(a) the gross aid intensity must not exceed 100%;
(b) the aid shall be granted in kind by means of subsidised services and must not involve direct payments of money to producers.

2. Aid to compensate farmers for losses caused by animal or plant diseases or pest infestations shall be compatible with the common market within the meaning of Article 87(3)(c) of the Treaty and shall be exempt from the notification requirement of Article 88(3) of the Treaty if it fulfils the following conditions and the conditions set out in paragraphs 4 to 8 of this Article:

(a) compensation must be calculated only in relation to:
    (i) the market value of animals killed or plants destroyed by the disease or pest infestation or of animals killed or plants destroyed by public order as part of a compulsory public prevention or eradication programme;
    (ii) income losses due to quarantine obligations and difficulties in restocking or replanting;
(b) the gross aid intensity must not exceed 100%;
(c) the aid must be limited to losses caused by diseases for which an outbreak has been formally recognised by public authorities.

3. The maximum amount of costs or loss eligible for aid pursuant to paragraphs 1 and 2 must be reduced by:

(a) any amount received under insurance schemes; and
(b) costs not incurred because of the disease, which would otherwise have been incurred.

4. Payments must be made in relation to diseases or pests for which Community or national provisions exist, whether laid down by law, regulation or administrative action. Payments must thus be made as part of a public programme at Community, national or regional level for the prevention, control or eradication of the disease or pest concerned. The diseases or pest infestation must be clearly identified in the programme, which must also contain a description of the measures concerned.

5. The aid must not relate to a disease in respect of which Community legislation provides for specific charges for control measures.

6. The aid must not relate to measures in respect of which Community legislation provides that the cost of such measures is to be borne by the agricultural holding, unless the cost of such aid measures is entirely offset by compulsory charges on producers.

7. As regards animal diseases, the aid must be granted in respect of diseases mentioned in the list of animal diseases established by the World Organisation for Animal Health and/or in the Annex to Council Decision 90/424/EEC.[14]

Part G   State Aids

1419

8. Aid schemes must be introduced within three years following the occurrence of the expense or loss. Aid must be paid out within four years following the occurrence.

Notes
[14] OJ L 224, 18.8.1990, p. 19.

Article 11
Aid for losses due to adverse climatic events

1. Aid to compensate farmers for losses of plants or animals or farm buildings caused by adverse climatic events which can be assimilated to natural disasters shall be compatible with the common market within the meaning of Article 87(3)(c) of the Treaty and shall be exempt from the notification requirement of Article 88(3) of the Treaty if it fulfils the conditions set out in paragraphs 2 to 6, 9 and 10 of this Article as far as plants or animals are concerned, and paragraphs 3 to 8 and 10 of this Article as far as farm buildings are concerned.

2. Gross aid intensity must not exceed 80%, and 90% in less favoured areas or in areas referred to in Article 36(a)(i), (ii) or (iii) of Regulation (EC) No 1698/2005, as designated by Member States in accordance with Articles 50 and 94 of that Regulation, of the reduction in income from the sale of the product resulting from the adverse climatic event. That reduction in income shall be calculated by subtracting:

(a) the result of multiplying the quantity of product produced in the year of the adverse climatic event by the average selling price obtained during that year;
(b) the result of multiplying the average annual quantity produced in the preceding three-year period (or a three-year average based on the preceding five-year period, excluding the highest and lowest entry) by the average selling price obtained.

The amount thus eligible for aid may be increased by other costs specifically incurred by the farmer because of non-harvesting due to the adverse event.

3. The maximum amount of loss eligible for aid pursuant to paragraph 1 must be reduced by:

(a) any amount received under insurance schemes; and
(b) costs not incurred because of the adverse climatic event.

4. The calculation of loss must be made at the level of the individual holding.

5. Aid must be paid directly to the farmer concerned or to a producer organisation of which the farmer is a member. If the aid is paid to a producer organisation, the amount of aid must not exceed the amount of aid that could be granted to the farmer.

6. Compensation for damages to farm buildings and farm equipment caused by adverse climatic events which can be assimilated to natural disasters must not exceed gross aid intensity of 80%, and 90% in less favoured areas or in areas referred to in Article 36(a)(i), (ii) or (iii) of Regulation (EC) No 1698/2005, as designated by Member States in accordance with Articles 50 and 94 of that Regulation.

7. The adverse climatic event which can be assimilated to a natural disaster must be formally recognised as such by public authorities.

8. From 1 January 2010, compensation offered must be reduced by 50% unless it is given to farmers who have taken out insurance covering at least 50% of their average annual production or production-related income and the statistically most frequent climatic risks in the Member State or region concerned.

9. From 1 January 2011, aid for losses caused by drought may be paid only by a Member State which has fully implemented Article 9 of Directive 2000/60/EC of the European Parliament and of the Council[15] in respect of agriculture, and ensures that the costs of water services provided to agriculture are recovered through an adequate contribution from that sector.

10. Aid schemes must be introduced within three years following the occurrence of the expense or loss. Aid must be paid out within four years following the occurrence.

Notes
[15] OJ L 327, 22.12.2000, p. 1.

Article 12
Aid towards the payment of insurance premiums

1. Aid for insurance premiums shall be compatible with the common market within the meaning of Article 87(3)(c) of the Treaty and shall be exempt from the notification requirement of Article 88(3) of the Treaty if it fulfils the conditions set out in paragraphs 2 and 3 of this Article.

2. The gross aid intensity must not exceed:

(a) 80% of the cost of insurance premiums, where the policy specifies that it provides cover only against losses caused by adverse climatic events which can be assimilated to natural disasters;

(b) 50% of the cost of insurance premiums, where the policy specifies that it provides cover against:

  (i) losses referred to in point (a) and against other losses caused by climatic events; and/or
  (ii) losses caused by animal or plant diseases or pest infestations.

3. The aid must not constitute a barrier to the operation of the internal market for insurance services. The aid must not be limited to insurance provided by a single insurance company or group of companies, or be made subject to the condition that the insurance contract be taken out with a company established in the Member State concerned.

Article 13
Aid for land reparcelling

Aid for land reparcelling shall be compatible with the common market within the meaning of Article 87(3)(c) of the Treaty and shall be exempt from the notification requirement of Article 88(3) of the Treaty if it is granted towards and limited to the legal and administrative costs, including survey costs, up to 100% of actual costs incurred.

Article 14
Aid to encourage the production of quality agricultural products

1. Aid to encourage the production of quality agricultural products shall be compatible with the common market within the meaning of Article 87(3)(c) of the Treaty and shall be exempt from the notification requirement of Article 88(3) of the Treaty if it is granted towards the eligible costs listed in paragraph 2 and fulfils the conditions set out in paragraphs 3 to 6 of this Article.

2. Aid may be granted to cover the costs of the following service activities, insofar as they are related to the development of quality agricultural products:

(a) up to 100% of the costs of market research activities, product conception and design, including aid granted for the preparation of applications for recognition of geographical indications and designations of origin or certificates of specific character in accordance with the relevant Community regulations;

(b) up to 100% of the costs of the introduction of quality assurance schemes such as ISO 9000 or 14000 series, systems based on hazard analysis and critical control points (HACCP), traceability systems, systems to assure respect of authenticity and marketing norms or environmental audit systems;

(c) up to 100% of the costs of training personnel to apply schemes and systems as referred to in point (b);

(d) up to 100% of the costs of the charges levied by recognised certifying bodies for the initial certification of quality assurance and similar systems;

(e) up to 100% of the costs of compulsory control measures undertaken pursuant to Community or national legislation by or on behalf of the competent authorities, unless Community legislation requires enterprises to bear such costs;

(f) up to the amounts laid down in the Annex to Regulation (EC) No 1698/2005 for support concerning measures referred to in Article 32 of that Regulation.

3. The aid may be granted only in respect of costs of services provided by third parties and/or controls undertaken by or on behalf of third parties, such as the competent regulatory authorities, or bodies

acting on their behalf, or independent organisms responsible for the control and supervision of the use of geographical indications and designations of origin, organic labels, or quality labels, provided these denominations and labels are in conformity with Community legislation. The aid must not be granted towards expenditure for investment.

4. The aid must not be granted towards the cost of controls undertaken by the farmer or manufacturer himself, or where Community legislation provides that the cost of control is to be met by producers, without specifying the actual level of charges.

5. With the exception of the aid referred to in paragraph 2(f), the aid shall be granted in kind by means of subsidised services and must not involve direct payments of money to producers.

6. The aid must be accessible to all those eligible in the area concerned, based on objectively defined conditions. Where the provision of services listed in paragraph 2 is undertaken by producer groups or other agricultural mutual support organisations, membership of such groups or organisations must not be a condition for access to the service. Any contribution of non-members towards the administrative costs of the group or organisation concerned must be limited to the proportional costs of providing the service.

Article 15
Provision of technical support in the agricultural sector

1. Aid shall be compatible with the common market within the meaning of Article 87(3)(c) of the Treaty and shall be exempt from the notification requirement of Article 88(3) of the Treaty if it is granted towards the eligible costs of the technical support activities listed in paragraph 2 and fulfils the conditions set out in paragraphs 3 and 4 of this Article.

2. Aid may be granted to cover the following eligible costs:

(a) concerning education and training of farmers and farm workers:

    (i) costs of organising the training programme;
    (ii) travel and subsistence expenses of participants;
    (iii) cost of the provision of replacement services during the absence of the farmer or the farm worker;

(b) concerning farm replacement services, the actual costs of the replacement of a farmer, the farmer's partner, or a farm worker, during illness and holidays;

(c) concerning consultancy services provided by third parties, the fees for services which do not constitute a continuous or periodic activity nor relate to the enterprise's usual operating expenditure, such as routine tax consultancy services, regular legal services, or advertising;

(d) concerning the organisation of and participation in forums to share knowledge between businesses, competitions, exhibitions and fairs:

    (i) participation fees;
    (ii) travel costs;
    (iii) costs of publications;
    (iv) the rent of exhibition premises;
    (v) symbolic prizes awarded in the framework of competitions, up to a value of EUR 250 per prize and winner;

(e) provided that individual companies, brands or origin are not named:

    (i) the vulgarisation of scientific knowledge;
    (ii) factual information on quality systems open to products from other countries, on generic products and on the nutritional benefits of generic products and suggested uses for them.

    Aid may also be granted to cover the costs referred to in point (e) if the origin of products covered by Council Regulation (EC) No 510/2006[16] and by Articles 54 to 58 of Council Regulation (EC) No 1493/1999[17] is indicated, provided that the references to the origin correspond exactly to those references which have been registered by the Community.

(f) publications such as catalogues or websites presenting factual information about producers from a given region or producers of a given product, provided the information and presentation is neutral and that all producers concerned have equal opportunities to be represented in the publication.

3. The aid may cover 100% of the costs listed in paragraph 2. The aid must be granted in kind by means of subsidised services and must not involve direct payments of money to producers.

4. The aid must be accessible to all those eligible in the area concerned, based on objectively defined conditions. Where the provision of technical support is undertaken by producer groups or other organisations, membership of such groups or organisations must not be a condition for access to the service. Any contribution of non-members towards the administrative costs of the group or organisation concerned must be limited to the costs of providing the service.

Notes
[16] OJ L 93, 31.3.2006, p. 12.
[17] OJ L 179, 14.7.1999, p. 1.

Article 16
Support for the livestock sector

1. The following aid to enterprises active in the livestock sector shall be compatible with the common market within the meaning of Article 87(3)(c) of the Treaty and shall be exempt from the notification requirement of Article 88(3) of the Treaty:

(a) aid at a rate of up to 100% to cover the administrative costs of the establishment and maintenance of herd books;

(b) aid at a rate of up to 70% of the costs of tests performed by or on behalf of third parties, to determine the genetic quality or yield of livestock, with the exception of controls undertaken by the owner of the livestock and routine controls of milk quality;

(c) until 31 December 2011, aid at a rate of up to 40% for the introduction at farm level of innovative animal breeding techniques or practices, with the exception of costs relating to the introduction or performance of artificial insemination;

(d) aid at a rate of up to 100% of costs of removal of fallen stock, and 75% of the costs of destruction of such carcasses; alternatively, aid up to an equivalent amount towards the costs of premiums paid by farmers for insurance covering the costs of removal and destruction of fallen stock;

(e) aid at a rate of up to 100% for costs of removal and destruction of carcasses where the aid is financed through fees or through compulsory contributions destined for the financing of the destruction of such carcasses, provided that such fees or contributions are limited to and directly imposed on the meat sector;

(f) aid of 100% for the costs of removal and destruction of fallen stock where there is an obligation to perform TSE tests on the fallen stock concerned;

(g) aid at a rate of up to 100% towards the costs of TSE tests.

As far as compulsory BSE testing of bovine animals slaughtered for human consumption is concerned, total direct and indirect support, including Community payments, must not be more than EUR 40 per test. This amount refers to the total costs of testing, comprising test-kit, taking, transporting, testing, storing and destruction of the sample. The obligation to test may be based on Community or national legislation.

2. The exemption provided for in paragraph 1(d), (e), (f) and (g) shall be conditional upon the existence of a consistent programme monitoring and ensuring safe disposal of all fallen stock in the Member State. In order to facilitate administration of such State aid, payment may be made to economic operators active downstream from the farmer, providing services linked to the removal and/or destruction of fallen stock, if it can be properly demonstrated that the full amount of State aid paid is passed on to the farmer.

3. The aid shall not involve direct payments of money to producers.

Article 17
Aid provided for in certain Council Regulations

The following aid to small and medium-sized enterprises shall be compatible with the common market within the meaning of Article 87(3)(c) of the Treaty and shall be exempt from the notification requirement of Article 88(3) of the Treaty:

(a) aid granted by Member States fulfilling all the conditions laid down in Council Regulation (EC) No 1255/1999,[18] in particular Article 14(2) thereof;

(b) aid granted by Member States fulfilling all the conditions laid down in Council Regulation (EC) No 1782/2003,[19] in particular Article 87, Article 107(3) and the first subparagraph of Article 125(5) thereof;

(c) aid granted by Member States in accordance with Article 15(6) of Council Regulation (EC) No 2200/96.[20]

Notes

[18] OJ L 160, 26.6.1999, p. 48.

[19] OJ L 270, 21.10.2003, p. 1.

[20] OJ L 297, 21.11.1996, p. 1.

CHAPTER 3

COMMON AND FINAL PROVISIONS

Article 18

Steps preceding grant of aid

1. In order to qualify for exemption under this Regulation, aid shall only be granted under an aid scheme in respect of activities undertaken or services received after the aid scheme has been set up and published in accordance with this Regulation.

If the aid scheme creates an automatic right to receive the aid, requiring no further action at administrative level, the aid itself shall only be granted in respect of activities undertaken or services received after the aid scheme has been set up and published in accordance with this Regulation.

If the aid scheme requires an application to be submitted to the competent authority concerned, the aid itself shall only be granted in respect of activities undertaken or services received after the following conditions have been fulfilled:

(a) the aid scheme must have been set up and published in accordance with this Regulation;

(b) an application for the aid must have been properly submitted to the competent authority concerned;

(c) the application must have been accepted by the competent authority concerned in a manner which obliges that authority to grant the aid, clearly indicating the amount of aid to be granted or how this amount will be calculated; such acceptance by the competent authority may only be made if the budget available for the aid or aid scheme not exhausted.

2. In order to qualify for exemption under this Regulation, individual aid outside any aid scheme shall only be granted in respect of activities undertaken or services received after the criteria in points (b) and (c) of the third subparagraph of paragraph 1 have been satisfied.

3. This Article shall not apply to aid covered by Article 17.

Article 19

Cumulation

1. The aid ceilings fixed in Articles 4 to 16 shall apply regardless of whether the support for the aided project or activity is financed entirely from State resources or is partly financed by the Community.

2. Aid exempted by this Regulation shall not be cumulated with any other State aid within the meaning of Article 87(1) of the Treaty, or financial contributions provided by Member States, including those covered by the second subparagraph of Article 88(1) of Regulation (EC) No 1698/2005, or financial contributions by the Community in relation to the same eligible costs, if such cumulation would result in an aid intensity exceeding the maximum laid down in this Regulation.

3. Aid exempted by this Regulation shall not be cumulated with *de minimis* support within the meaning of Regulation (EC) No 1860/2004 in respect of the same eligible expenditure or investment project, if such cumulation would result in an aid intensity exceeding that fixed by this Regulation.

Article 20

Transparency and monitoring

1. At the latest 10 working days before the entry into force of an aid scheme exempted by this Regulation, or the granting of individual aid exempted by this Regulation outside any scheme,

Member States shall forward to the Commission, with a view to its publication in the *Official Journal of the European Union*, a summary of the information regarding such aid scheme or individual aid in the form laid down in Annex I. This shall be provided in computerised form. Within 10 working days of receipt of that summary, the Commission will send a notice of receipt with an identification number and publish the summary on the internet.

2. Member States shall maintain detailed records regarding the aid schemes exempted by this Regulation, the individual aid granted under those schemes, and the individual aid exempted by this Regulation that is granted outside any existing aid scheme. Such records shall contain all information necessary to establish that the conditions for exemption, as laid down in this Regulation, are fulfilled, including information on the status of the company as an SME. Member States shall keep a record regarding each individual aid for 10 years from the date on which it was granted and, regarding an aid scheme, for 10 years from the date on which the last individual aid was granted under such scheme. On written request, the Member State concerned shall provide the Commission, within a period of 20 working days or such longer period as may be fixed in the request, with all the information which the Commission considers necessary to assess whether the conditions of this Regulation have been complied with.

3. Member States shall compile a report on the application of this Regulation in respect of each whole or part calendar year during which this Regulation applies, in the form laid down in Annex II. This report may be integrated into the annual report to be submitted by Member States pursuant to Article 21(1) of Council Regulation (EC) No 659/1999,[21] and shall be submitted by 30 June of the year following the calendar year covered by the report. By the same date, the Member State shall submit a separate report relating to payments made under Articles 10 and 11 of this Regulation, describing the amounts paid in that calendar year, the conditions for payment, the diseases concerned under Article 10 and, in relation to Article 11, the appropriate meteorological information proofing type, timing, relative magnitude and location of the climatic events and on its consequences on the production for which compensation has been granted.

4. As soon as an aid scheme exempted by this Regulation enters into force, or an individual aid exempted by this Regulation is granted outside an aid scheme, Member States shall publish on the internet the full text of such aid scheme, or the criteria and conditions under which such individual aid is granted.

The address of the web-sites including a direct link to the text of the scheme shall be communicated to the Commission together with the summary of the information regarding the aid required pursuant to paragraph 1. It shall also be contained in the annual report submitted pursuant to paragraph 3.

5. Paragraph 1 shall not apply to aid covered by Article 17.

Notes
[21] OJ L 83, 27.3.1999, p. 1.

Article 21
Amendment of Regulation (EC) No 70/2001

. . .

Notes
The amendments made by Article 21 to Regulation (EC) No 70/2001 are incorporated in the text of that Regulation, reproduced elsewhere in this volume (G11, p. 1381 above).

Article 22
Transitional measures

Aid schemes exempted under Regulation (EC) No 1/2004 which fulfil all the conditions of this Regulation shall continue to be exempted until the date mentioned in Article 23(1) of this Regulation.

Article 23
Entry into force and applicability

1. This Regulation shall enter into force on the 20th day following its publication in the *Official Journal of the European Union*.

It shall apply from 1 January 2007 until 31 December 2013.

2. Notifications pending at the time of entry into force of this Regulation shall be assessed in accordance with its provisions. Where the conditions of this Regulation are not fulfilled, the Commission will examine such pending notifications under the Community guidelines for State aid in the agriculture sector.

Individual aid and aid schemes implemented before the date of entry into force of this Regulation and aid granted under those schemes in the absence of a Commission authorisation and in breach of the notification requirement of Article 88(3) of the Treaty shall be compatible with the common market within the meaning of Article 87(3)(c) of the Treaty and shall be exempt if they fulfil the conditions laid down in Article 3 of this Regulation, except the requirements in paragraph 1 and paragraph 2 (b) and (c) of that Article that express reference be made to this Regulation, and that the summary provided for in Article 20(1) has been submitted before granting aid. Any aid which does not fulfil those conditions will be assessed by the Commission in accordance with the relevant frameworks, guidelines, communications and notices.

3. Aid schemes exempted under this Regulation shall remain exempt for a period of six months following the date of expiry of this Regulation.

Notes
Date of entry into force: 5 January 2007.

This Regulation shall be binding in its entirety and directly applicable in all Member States.

Done at Brussels, 15 December 2006.

ANNEX I
FORM OF SUMMARY INFORMATION TO BE PROVIDED WHENEVER AN AID SCHEME EXEMPTED BY THIS REGULATION IS IMPLEMENTED AND WHENEVER AN INDIVIDUAL AID EXEMPTED BY THIS REGULATION IS GRANTED OUTSIDE ANY AID SCHEME

Summary Information On State Aid Granted In Conformity With Commission Regulation (EC) No 1857/2006

Member State

Region (Indicate the name of the region if the aid is granted by a subcentral authority).

Title of aid scheme or name of company receiving an individual aid (Indicate the name of the aid scheme or in case of individual aid, the name of the beneficiary).

Legal basis (Indicate the precise national legal reference for the aid scheme or for the individual aid).

Annual expenditure planned under the scheme or overall amount of individual aid granted to the company (Amounts are to be given in euros or, if applicable, national currency. In case of an aid scheme, indicate the annual overall amount of the budget appropriation(s) or the estimated tax loss per year for all aid instruments contained in the scheme. In case of an individual aid award: indicate the overall aid amount/tax loss. If appropriate, indicate also for how many years the aid will be paid in instalments or over how many years tax losses will be incurred. For guarantees in both cases, indicate the (maximum) amount of loans guaranteed).

Maximum aid intensity (Indicate the maximum aid intensity or the maximum aid amount per eligible item).

Date of implementation (Indicate the date from which aid may be granted under the scheme or when the individual aid is granted).

Duration of scheme or individual aid award (Indicate the date (year and month) until which aid may be granted under the scheme or in case of an individual aid and if appropriate the expected date (year and month) of the last instalment to be paid).

Objective of aid (It is understood that the primary objective is aid to SME. Indicate the further (secondary) objectives pursued. Indicate which one of (Articles(s) 4 to 17) is used and the eligible costs covered by the scheme or individual aid).

Sector(s) concerned (Indicate the sub sectors by mentioning the type of animal production (e.g. pig/poultry) or type of plant production (e.g. apple/tomato) concerned).

Name and address of the granting authority

Web-address (Indicate the internet address where the full text of the scheme or the criteria and conditions under which individual aid is granted outside of an aid scheme can be found).

Other information.

ANNEX II

FORM OF THE PERIODIC REPORT TO BE PROVIDED TO THE COMMISSION

Annual reporting format on aid schemes exempted under a group exemption regulation adopted pursuant to Article 1 of Council Regulation (EC) No 994/98

Member States are required to use the format below for their reporting obligations to the Commission under group exemption regulations adopted on the basis of Regulation (EC) No 994/98.

The reports shall be provided in computerised form.

Information required for all aid schemes exempted under group exemption regulations adopted pursuant to Article 1 of Regulation (EC) No 994/98.

1. *Title of aid scheme*
2. *Commission exemption regulation applicable*
3. *Expenditure*

    (Separate figures have to be provided for each aid instrument within a scheme or individual aid (e.g. grant, soft loans, etc.)). The figures have to be expressed in euros or, if applicable, national currency. In the case of tax expenditure, annual tax losses have to be reported. If precise figures are not available, such losses may be estimated.

    These expenditure figures should be provided on the following basis.

    For the year under review indicate separately for each aid instrument within the scheme (e.g. grant, soft loan, guarantee, etc.):

3.1. amounts committed, (estimated) tax losses or other revenue forgone, data on guarantees, etc. for new assisted projects. In the case of guarantee schemes, the total amount of new guarantees handed out should be provided;

3.2. actual payments, (estimated) tax losses or other revenue forgone, data on guarantees, etc. for new and current projects. In the case of guarantee schemes, the following should be provided: total amount of outstanding guarantees, premium income, recoveries, and indemnities paid out, operating result of the scheme under the year under review;

3.3. number of assisted projects and/or enterprises;

3.4. [Leave blank]

3.5. estimated overall amount of:

    — investment aided,
    — expenditure for conservation of traditional landscapes and buildings aided,
    — expenditure for relocation of farm buildings in the public interest aided,
    — aid granted for setting up of young farmers,
    — aid granted for early retirement,
    — expenditure of producer groups aided,
    — expenditure for diseases,
    — expenditure for bad weather compensation,
    — expenditure for insurance premiums aided,

— aid granted for land reparcelling,
— aid granted to encourage the production of quality agricultural products,
— expenditure for technical support aided,
— expenditure for support for the animal sector;

3.6. regional breakdown of amounts under points 3.1. by less favoured areas or by areas referred to in Article 36(a)(i), (ii) and (iii) of Council Regulation (EC) No 1698/2005 and other areas;

3.7. sectoral breakdown of amounts under 3.1. by beneficiaries' sectors of activity (if more than one sector is covered, indicate the share of each):
— type of animal product,
— type of plant product.

4. *Other information and remarks.*

G14

COMMISSION REGULATION (EC) No 1998/2006

of 15 December 2006
on the application of Articles 87 and 88 of the Treaty to *de minimis* aid

Official Journal L 379, 28.12.2006, p. 5

Celex No: 32006R1998

THE COMMISSION OF THE EUROPEAN COMMUNITIES,

Having regard to the Treaty establishing the European Community,

Having regard to Council Regulation (EC) No 994/98 of 7 May 1998 on the application of Articles [87] and [88] of the Treaty establishing the European Community to certain categories of horizontal State aid,[1] and in particular Article 2 thereof,

Having published a draft of this Regulation,[2]

Having consulted the Advisory Committee on State aid,

Notes
[1] OJ L 142, 14.5.1998, p. 1.
[2] OJ C 137, 10.6.2006, p. 4.

Commentary
Regulation 1998/2006/EC: B&C: 1.115, 15.028, 15.076

Whereas:

(1) Regulation (EC) No 994/98 empowers the Commission to set out in a Regulation a threshold under which aid measures are deemed not to meet all the criteria of Article 87(1) of the Treaty and therefore do not fall under the notification procedure provided for in Article 88(3) of the Treaty.

(2) The Commission has applied Articles 87 and 88 of the Treaty and has, in particular, clarified in numerous decisions the notion of aid within the meaning of Article 87(1) of the Treaty. The Commission has also stated its policy with regard to a *de minimis* ceiling, below which Article 87(1) can be considered not to apply, initially in its notice on the *de minimis* rule for State aid[1] and subsequently in Commission Regulation (EC) No 69/2001 of 12 January 2001 on the application of Articles 87 and 88 of the EC Treaty to *de minimis* aid.[2] In the light of the experience gained in applying that Regulation and in order to take account of the evolution of inflation and gross domestic product in the Community up to and including 2006 and of the likely developments

through the period of validity of this Regulation, it appears appropriate to revise some of the conditions laid down in Regulation (EC) No 69/2001 and to replace that Regulation.

Notes
[1] OJ C 68, 6.3.1996, p. 9.
[2] OJ L 10, 13.1.2001, p. 30.

(3) In view of the special rules which apply in the sectors of primary production of agricultural products, fisheries and aquaculture and of the risk that smaller amounts of aid than those set out in this Regulation could fulfil the criteria of Article 87(1) of the Treaty in those sectors, this Regulation should not apply to those sectors. Given the evolution of the transport sector, in particular the restructuring of many transport activities following their liberalisation, it is no longer appropriate to exclude the transport sector from the scope of the *de minimis* Regulation. The scope of this Regulation should therefore be extended to the whole of the transport sector. The general *de minimis* ceiling should however be adapted in order to take account of the average small size of undertakings active in the road freight and passengers transport sector. For the same reasons, and also in view of the overcapacity of the sector and of the objectives of transport policy as regards road congestion and freight transports, aid for the acquisition of road freight transport vehicles by undertakings performing road freight transport for hire and reward should be excluded. This does not call into question the Commission's favourable approach with regard to State aid for cleaner and more environmentally friendly vehicles in Community instruments other than this Regulation. In view of Council Regulation (EC) No 1407/2002 of 23 July 2002 on State aid to the coal industry,[1] this Regulation should not apply to the coal sector.

Notes
[1] OJ L 205, 02.08.2002, p. 1.

(4) Considering the similarities between the processing and marketing of agricultural products, on the one hand, and of non-agricultural products, on the other hand, this Regulation should apply to the processing and marketing of agricultural products, provided that certain conditions are met. Neither on-farm activities necessary for preparing a product for the first sale, such as harvesting, cutting and threshing of cereals, packing of eggs etc., nor the first sale to resellers or processors should be considered as processing or marketing in this respect. As from the entry into force of this Regulation, aid granted in favour of undertakings active in the processing or marketing of agricultural products should no longer be subject to Commission Regulation (EC) No 1860/2004 of 6 October 2004 on the application of Articles 87 and 88 of the EC Treaty to *de minimis* aid in the agriculture and fisheries sector.[1] Regulation (EC) No 1860/2004 should therefore be amended accordingly.

Notes
[1] OJ L 325, 28.10.2004, p. 4.

(5) The Court of Justice of the European Communities has established that, once the Community has legislated for the establishment of a common organisation of the market in a given sector of agriculture, Member States are under an obligation to refrain from taking any measure which might undermine or create exceptions to it. For this reason, this Regulation should not apply to aid, the amount of which is fixed on the basis of price or quantity of products purchased or put on the market. Nor should it apply to *de minimis* support which is linked to an obligation to share the aid with primary producers.

(6) This Regulation should not apply to *de minimis* export aid or *de minimis* aid favouring domestic over imported products. In particular, it should not apply to aid financing the establishment and operation of a distribution network in other countries. Aid towards the cost of participating in trade fairs, or of studies or consultancy services needed for the launch of a new or existing product on a new market does not normally constitute export aid.

(7) This Regulation should not apply to undertakings in difficulty within the meaning of the Community guidelines on State aid for rescuing and restructuring firms in difficulty[1] in view of the

difficulties linked to determining the gross grant equivalent of aid granted to this type of undertaking.

Notes
[1] OJ C 244, 1.10.2004, p. 2.

(8) In the light of the Commission's experience, it can be established that aid not exceeding a ceiling of EUR 200,000 over any period of three years does not affect trade between Member States and/or does not distort or threaten to distort competition and therefore does not fall under Article 87(1) of the Treaty. As regards undertakings active in the road transport sector, this ceiling should be set at EUR 100 000.

(9) The years to take into account for this purpose are the fiscal years as used for fiscal purposes by the undertaking in the Member State concerned. The relevant period of three years should be assessed on a rolling basis so that, for each new grant of *de minimis* aid, the total amount of *de minimis* aid granted in the fiscal year concerned, as well as during the previous two fiscal years, needs to be determined. Aid granted by a Member State should be taken into account for this purpose even when financed entirely or partly by resources of Community origin. It should not be possible for aid measures exceeding the *de minimis* ceiling to be broken down into a number of smaller parts in order to bring such parts within the scope of this Regulation.

(10) In accordance with the principles governing aid falling within Article 87(1) of the Treaty, *de minimis* aid should be considered to be granted at the moment the legal right to receive the aid is conferred on the undertaking under the applicable national legal regime.

(11) In order to avoid circumvention of maximum aid intensities provided in different Community instruments, *de minimis* aid should not be cumulated with State aid in respect of the same eligible costs if such cumulation would result in an aid intensity exceeding that fixed in the specific circumstances of each case by a block exemption Regulation or Decision adopted by the Commission.

(12) For the purposes of transparency, equal treatment and the correct application of the *de minimis* ceiling, all Member States should apply the same method of calculation. In order to facilitate this calculation and in accordance with the present practice of application of the *de minimis* rule, aid amounts not taking the form of a cash grant should be converted into their gross grant equivalent. Calculation of the grant equivalent of transparent types of aid other than grants or of aid payable in several instalments requires the use of market interest rates prevailing at the time of granting such aid. With a view to a uniform, transparent and simple application of the State aid rules, the market rates for the purposes of this Regulation should be deemed to be the reference rates periodically fixed by the Commission on the basis of objective criteria and published in the *Official Journal of the European Union* or on the Internet. It may, however, be necessary to add additional basis points on top of the floor rate in view of the securities provided or the risk associated with the beneficiary.

(13) For the purposes of transparency, equal treatment and effective monitoring, this Regulation should apply only to *de minimis* aid which is transparent. Transparent aid is aid for which it is possible to calculate precisely the gross grant equivalent *ex ante* without a need to undertake a risk assessment. Such precise calculation can, for instance, be realised as regards grants, interest rate subsidies and capped tax exemptions. Aid comprised in capital injections should not be considered as transparent *de minimis* aid, unless the total amount of the public injection is lower than the *de minimis* ceiling. Aid comprised in risk capital measures as referred to in the Community guidelines on State aid to promote risk capital investments in small and medium-sized enterprises[1] should not be considered as transparent *de minimis* aid, unless the risk capital scheme concerned provides capital only up to the *de minimis* ceiling to each target undertaking. Aid comprised in loans should be treated as transparent *de minimis* aid when the gross grant equivalent has been calculated on the basis of market interest rates prevailing at the time of grant.

Notes
[1] OJ C 194, 18.8.2006, p. 2.

(14) This Regulation does not exclude the possibility that a measure, adopted by a Member State, might not be considered as State aid within the meaning of Article 87(1) of the Treaty on the

basis of other grounds than those set out in this Regulation, for instance, in the case of capital injections, because such measure has been decided in conformity with the market investor principle.

(15) It is necessary to provide legal certainty for guarantee schemes which do not have the potential to affect trade and distort competition and in respect of which sufficient data is available to assess any potential effects reliably. This Regulation should therefore transpose the general *de minimis* ceiling of EUR 200,000 into a guarantee-specific ceiling based on the guaranteed amount of the individual loan underlying such guarantee. It is appropriate to calculate this specific ceiling using a methodology assessing the State aid amount included in guarantee schemes covering loans in favour of viable undertakings. The methodology and the data used to calculate the guarantee-specific ceiling should exclude undertakings in difficulty as referred to in the Community guidelines on State aid for rescuing and restructuring firms in difficulty. This specific ceiling should therefore not apply to ad hoc individual aid granted outside the scope of a guarantee scheme, to aid granted to undertakings in difficulty, or to guarantees on underlying transactions not constituting a loan, such as guarantees on equity transactions. The specific ceiling should be determined on the basis of the fact that taking account of a cap rate (net default rate) of 13%, representing a worst case scenario for guarantee schemes in the Community, a guarantee amounting to EUR 1,500,000 can be considered as having a gross grant equivalent identical to the general *de minimis* ceiling. This amount should be reduced to EUR 750,000 as regards undertakings active in the road transport sector. Only guarantees covering up to 80% of the underlying loan should be covered by these specific ceilings. A methodology accepted by the Commission following notification of such methodology on the basis of a Commission Regulation in the State aid area, like Commission Regulation (EC) No 1628/2006 of 24 October 2006 on the application of Articles 87 and 88 of the Treaty to national regional investment aid,[1] may also be used by Member States for the purpose of assessing the gross grant equivalent contained in a guarantee, if the approved methodology explicitly addresses the type of guarantees and the type of underlying transactions at stake in the context of the application of the present Regulation.

Notes

[1] OJ L 302, 1.11.2006, p. 29.

(16) Upon notification by a Member State, the Commission may examine whether an aid measure which does not consist in a grant, loan, guarantee, capital injection or risk capital measure leads to a gross grant equivalent that does not exceed the *de minimis* ceiling and could therefore be covered by the provisions of this Regulation.

(17) The Commission has a duty to ensure that State aid rules are respected and in particular that aid granted under the *de minimis* rules adheres to the conditions thereof. In accordance with the cooperation principle laid down in Article 10 of the Treaty, Member States should facilitate the achievement of this task by establishing the necessary machinery in order to ensure that the total amount of *de minimis* aid, granted to the same undertaking under the *de minimis* rule, does not exceed the ceiling of EUR 200,000 over a period of three fiscal years. To that end, when granting a *de minimis* aid, Member States should inform the undertaking concerned of the amount of the aid and of its *de minimis* character, by referring to this Regulation. Moreover, prior to granting such aid the Member State concerned should obtain from the undertaking a declaration about other *de minimis* aid received during the fiscal year concerned and the two previous fiscal years and carefully check that the *de minimis* ceiling will not be exceeded by the new *de minimis* aid. Alternatively it should be possible to ensure that the ceiling is respected by means of a central register, or, in the case of guarantee schemes set up by the European Investment Fund, the latter may establish itself a list of beneficiaries and require Member States to inform the beneficiaries of the *de minimis* aid received.

(18) Regulation (EC) No 69/2001 expires on 31 December 2006. This Regulation should therefore apply from 1 January 2007. In view of the fact that Regulation (EC) No 69/2001 did not apply to the transport sector, which was not subject to *de minimis* so far; given also the very limited *de minimis* amount applicable in the sector of processing and marketing of agricultural products, and provided that certain conditions are met, this Regulation should apply to aid granted before

its entry into force to undertakings active in the transport sector, and in the sector of processing and marketing of agricultural products. Moreover, any individual aid granted in accordance with Regulation (EC) No 69/2001 during the period of application of that Regulation should remain unaffected by this Regulation.

(19) Having regard to the Commission's experience and in particular the frequency with which it is generally necessary to revise State aid policy, it is appropriate to limit the period of application of this Regulation. Should this Regulation expire without being extended, Member States should have an adjustment period of six months with regard to *de minimis* aid covered by this Regulation,

HAS ADOPTED THIS REGULATION:

Article 1
Scope

1. This Regulation applies to aid granted to undertakings in all sectors, with the exception of:

(a) aid granted to undertakings active in the fishery and aquaculture sectors, as covered by Council Regulation (EC) No 104/2000;[1]

(b) aid granted to undertakings active in the primary production of agricultural products as listed in Annex I to the Treaty;

(c) aid granted to undertakings active in the processing and marketing of agricultural products as listed in Annex I to the Treaty, in the following cases:
  (i) when the amount of the aid is fixed on the basis of the price or quantity of such products purchased from primary producers or put on the market by the undertakings concerned,
  (ii) when the aid is conditional on being partly or entirely passed on to primary producers;

(d) aid to export-related activities towards third countries or Member States, namely aid directly linked to the quantities exported, to the establishment and operation of a distribution network or to other current expenditure linked to the export activity;

(e) aid contingent upon the use of domestic over imported goods;

(f) aid granted to undertakings active in the coal sector, as defined in Regulation (EC) No 1407/2002;

(g) aid for the acquisition of road freight transport vehicles granted to undertakings performing road freight transport for hire or reward;

(h) aid granted to undertakings in difficulty.

2. For the purposes of this Regulation:

(a) "agricultural products" means products listed in Annex I to the EC Treaty, with the exception of fishery products;

(b) "processing of agricultural products" means any operation on an agricultural product resulting in a product which is also an agricultural product, except on farm activities necessary for preparing an animal or plant product for the first sale;

(c) "marketing of agricultural products" means holding or display with a view to sale, offering for sale, delivery or any other manner of placing on the market, except the first sale by a primary producer to resellers or processors and any activity preparing a product for such first sale; a sale by a primary producer to final consumers shall be considered as marketing if it takes place in separate premises reserved for that purpose.

Notes
[1] OJ L 17, 21.1.2000, p. 22.

Article 2
De minimis aid

1. Aid measures shall be deemed not to meet all the criteria of Article 87(1) of the Treaty and shall therefore be exempt from the notification requirement of Article 88(3) of the Treaty, if they fulfil the conditions laid down in paragraphs 2 to 5 of this Article.

2. The total *de minimis* aid granted to any one undertaking shall not exceed EUR 200 000 over any period of three fiscal years. The total *de minimis* aid granted to any one undertaking active in the road transport sector shall not exceed EUR 100,000 over any period of three fiscal years. These ceilings

shall apply irrespective of the form of the *de minimis* aid or the objective pursued and regardless of whether the aid granted by the Member State is financed entirely or partly by resources of Community origin. The period shall be determined by reference to the fiscal years used by the undertaking in the Member State concerned.

When an overall aid amount provided under an aid measure exceeds this ceiling, that aid amount cannot benefit from this Regulation, even for a fraction not exceeding that ceiling. In such a case, the benefit of this Regulation cannot be claimed for this aid measure either at the time the aid is granted or at any subsequent time.

3. The ceiling laid down in paragraph 2 shall be expressed as a cash grant. All figures used shall be gross, that is, before any deduction of tax or other charge. Where aid is awarded in a form other than a grant, the aid amount shall be the gross grant equivalent of the aid.

Aid payable in several instalments shall be discounted to its value at the moment of its being granted. The interest rate to be used for discounting purposes and to calculate the gross grant equivalent shall be the reference rate applicable at the time of grant.

4. This Regulation shall apply only to aid in respect of which it is possible to calculate precisely the gross grant equivalent of the aid *ex ante* without need to undertake a risk assessment ("transparent aid"). In particular:

(a) Aid comprised in loans shall be treated as transparent *de minimis* aid when the gross grant equivalent has been calculated on the basis of market interest rates prevailing at the time of the grant.

(b) Aid comprised in capital injections shall not be considered as transparent *de minimis* aid, unless the total amount of the public injection does not exceed the *de minimis* ceiling.

(c) Aid comprised in risk capital measures shall not be considered as transparent *de minimis* aid, unless the risk capital scheme concerned provides capital only up to the *de minimis* ceiling to each target undertaking.

(d) Individual aid provided under a guarantee scheme to undertakings which are not undertakings in difficulty shall be treated as transparent *de minimis* aid when the guaranteed part of the underlying loan provided under such scheme does not exceed EUR 1 500 000 per undertaking. Individual aid provided under a guarantee scheme in favour of undertakings active in the road transport sector which are not undertakings in difficulty shall be treated as transparent *de minimis* aid when the guaranteed part of the underlying loan provided under such scheme does not exceed EUR 750 000 per undertaking. If the guaranteed part of the underlying loan only accounts for a given proportion of this ceiling, the gross grant equivalent of that guarantee shall be deemed to correspond to the same proportion of the applicable ceiling laid down in Article 2(2). The guarantee shall not exceed 80% of the underlying loan. Guarantee schemes shall also be considered as transparent if (i) before the implementation of the scheme, the methodology to calculate the gross grant equivalent of the guarantees has been accepted following notification of this methodology to the Commission under another Regulation adopted by the Commission in the State aid area and (ii) the approved methodology explicitly addresses the type of guarantees and the type of underlying transactions at stake in the context of the application of this Regulation.

5. *De minimis* aid shall not be cumulated with State aid in respect of the same eligible costs if such cumulation would result in an aid intensity exceeding that fixed in the specific circumstances of each case by a block exemption Regulation or Decision adopted by the Commission.

Article 3
Monitoring

1. Where a Member State intends to grant *de minimis* aid to an undertaking, it shall inform that undertaking in writing of the prospective amount of the aid (expressed as gross grant equivalent) and of its *de minimis* character, making express reference to this Regulation, and citing its title and publication reference in the *Official Journal of the European Union*. Where the *de minimis* aid is granted to different undertakings on the basis of a scheme and different amounts of individual aid are granted to those undertakings under the scheme, the Member State concerned may choose to fulfil this obligation by informing the undertakings of a fixed sum corresponding to the maximum aid amount to be granted under the scheme. In such case, the fixed sum shall be used for determining whether the

ceiling laid down in Article 2(2) is met. Prior to granting the aid, the Member State shall also obtain a declaration from the undertaking concerned, in written or electronic form, about any other *de minimis* aid received during the previous two fiscal years and the current fiscal year.

The Member State shall only grant the new *de minimis* aid after having checked that this will not raise the total amount of *de minimis* aid received by the undertaking during the period covering the fiscal year concerned, as well as the previous two fiscal years in that Member State, to a level above the ceiling laid down in Article 2(2).

2. Where a Member State has set up a central register of *de minimis* aid containing complete information on all *de minimis* aid granted by any authority within that Member State, the first subparagraph of paragraph 1 shall cease to apply from the moment the register covers a period of three years.

Where an aid is provided by a Member State on the basis of a guarantee scheme providing a guarantee which is financed from the EU budget under mandate through the European Investment Fund, the first subparagraph of paragraph 1 of this Article may cease to apply.

In such cases, the following monitoring system shall apply:

(a) the European Investment Fund shall establish, on a yearly basis, on the basis of information that financial intermediaries must provide to the EIF, a list of beneficiaries of aid and of the gross grant equivalent received by each of them. The European Investment Fund shall send this information to the Member State concerned and to the Commission; and

(b) the Member State concerned shall disseminate that information to the final beneficiaries within three months of receipt of such information from the European Investment Fund; and

(c) the Member State concerned shall obtain a declaration from each beneficiary that the overall *de minimis* aid it has received does not exceed the ceiling laid down in Article 2(2). In case the ceiling is exceeded with respect to one or more beneficiaries, the Member State concerned shall ensure that the aid measure leading to the ceiling being exceeded is either notified to the Commission or recovered from the beneficiary.

3. Member States shall record and compile all the information regarding the application of this Regulation. Such records shall contain all information necessary to demonstrate that the conditions of this Regulation have been complied with. Records regarding individual *de minimis* aid shall be maintained for 10 years from the date on which it was granted. Records regarding a *de minimis* aid scheme shall be maintained for 10 years from the date on which the last individual aid was granted under such scheme. On written request the Member State concerned shall provide the Commission, within a period of 20 working days, or such longer period as may be fixed in the request, with all the information that the Commission considers necessary for assessing whether the conditions of this Regulation have been complied with, in particular the total amount of *de minimis* aid received by any undertaking.

Article 4
Amendment

Article 2 of Regulation (EC) No 1860/2004 is amended as follows:

(a) in point 1, the words "processing and marketing" are deleted;
(b) point 3 is deleted.

Article 5
Transitional measures

1. This Regulation shall apply to aid granted before its entry into force to undertakings active in the transport sector and undertakings active in the processing and marketing of agricultural products if the aid fulfils all the conditions laid down in Articles 1 and 2. Any aid which does not fulfil those conditions will be assessed by the Commission in accordance with the relevant frameworks, guidelines, communications and notices.

2. Any individual *de minimis* aid granted between 2 February 2001 and 30 June 2007, which fulfils the conditions of Regulation (EC) No 69/2001, shall be deemed not to meet all the criteria of Article 87(1) of the Treaty and shall therefore be exempt from the notification requirement of Article 88(3) of the Treaty.

3. At the end of the period of validity of this Regulation, any *de minimis* aid which fulfils the conditions of this Regulation may be validly implemented for a further period of six months.

Article 6
Entry into force and period of validity

1. This Regulation shall enter into force on the 20th day following that of its publication in the *Official Journal of the European Union*.

It shall apply from 1 January 2007 until 31 December 2013.

2. This Regulation shall be binding in its entirety and directly applicable in all Member States.

Done at Brussels, 15 December 2006.

Notes

Date of entry into force: 29 December 2006.

G15

COMMISSION REGULATION (EC) No 1628/2006

of 24 October 2006
on the application of Articles 87 and 88 of the Treaty to national regional investment aid
(Text with EEA relevance)

Official Journal L 302, 1.11.2006, p. 29

Celex No: 32006R1628

THE COMMISSION OF THE EUROPEAN COMMUNITIES,

Having regard to the Treaty establishing the European Community,

Having regard to Council Regulation (EC) No 994/98 of 7 May 1998 on the application of Articles [87] and [88] of the Treaty establishing the European Community to certain categories of horizontal State aid,[1] and in particular points (a)(i) and (b) of Article 1(1) thereof,

Having published a draft of this Regulation,[2]

After consulting the Advisory Committee on State Aid,

Notes

[1] OJ L 142, 14.5.1998, p. 1.
[2] OJ C 120, 20.5.2006, p. 2.

Commentary
Regulation 1628/2006: B&C: 15.052

Whereas:

(1) Regulation (EC) No 994/98 empowers the Commission to declare, in accordance with Article 87 of the Treaty, that under certain conditions aid that complies with the map approved by the Commission for each Member State for the grant of regional aid is compatible with the common market and is not subject to the notification requirement of Article 88(3) of the Treaty.

(2) The Commission has applied Articles 87 and 88 of the Treaty to regional investment aid schemes in assisted areas in numerous decisions and has also stated its policy, in particular in the guidelines on national regional aid for 2007–2013[3] as well as in Commission Regulation (EC) No 70/2001

Part G State Aids

of 12 January 2001 on the application of Articles 87 and 88 of the EC Treaty to State aid to small and medium-sized enterprises.[4] In the light of the Commission's considerable experience in applying Articles 87 and 88 of the Treaty to regional investment aid and in the light of the guidelines on national regional aid issued by the Commission on the basis of those provisions, it is appropriate, with a view to ensuring efficient supervision and simplifying administration without weakening Commission monitoring, that the Commission should make use of the powers conferred by Regulation (EC) No 994/98.

Notes
[3] OJ C 54, 4.3.2006, p. 13.
[4] OJ L 10, 13.1.2001, p. 33. Regulation as amended by Regulation (EC) No 364/2004 (OJ L 63, 28.2.2004, p. 22).

(3) By addressing the handicaps of the disadvantaged regions, national regional aid promotes the economic, social and territorial cohesion of Member States and the Community as a whole. National regional investment aid is designed to assist the development of the most disadvantaged regions by supporting investment and job creation in a sustainable context. It promotes the expansion, rationalisation, modernisation and diversification of the economic activities of undertakings located in the less-favoured regions, in particular by encouraging firms to set up new establishments there.

(4) In order to determine whether or not aid is compatible with the common market pursuant to this Regulation, it is necessary to take into consideration the aid intensity and thus the aid amount expressed as a grant equivalent. The calculation of the grant equivalent of aid payable in several instalments requires the use of market interest rates prevailing at the time of grant. With a view to a uniform, transparent, and simple application of the State aid rules, the market rates for the purposes of this Regulation should be deemed to be the reference rates which are periodically fixed by the Commission on the basis of objective criteria and published in the *Official Journal of the European Union* and on the Internet.

(5) In order to ensure transparency and effective monitoring, this Regulation should apply only to regional investment aid schemes which are transparent. These are aid schemes in which it is possible to calculate precisely the gross grant equivalent as a percentage of eligible expenditure *ex ante* without a need to undertake a risk assessment (for example grants, interest rate subsidies and capped fiscal measures). Public loans should be considered to be transparent provided that they are backed by normal security and do not involve abnormal risk and are therefore not considered to contain a state guarantee element. In principle, aid schemes involving state guarantees or public loans with a state guarantee element should not be considered as transparent. However, such aid schemes should be considered as transparent if, before the implementation of the scheme, the methodology used to calculate the aid intensity of the state guarantee has been accepted by the Commission following notification to the Commission after adoption of this Regulation. The methodology will be assessed by the Commission in accordance with the Notice on the application of Article 87 and 88 of the EC treaty to State aid in the Forms of Guarantees.[5] Public participation and aid comprised in risk capital measures should not be considered as transparent aid. Regional aid schemes which are not transparent should always be notified to the Commission. Notifications of non transparent regional aid schemes will be assessed by the Commission in particular in the light of the criteria set out in the Guidelines on national regional aid for 2007–2013.

Notes
[5] OJ C 71, 11.3.2000, p. 14.

(6) This Regulation should also apply to ad hoc aid, that is to say, individual aid that is not awarded on the basis of an aid scheme, if the ad hoc aid is used to supplement aid granted on the basis of a transparent regional investment aid scheme and the ad hoc component does not exceed 50% of the total aid to be granted for the investment. It should be recalled that individual aid to small and medium-sized enterprises granted outside of any aid scheme in accordance with Article 3(1) of Regulation (EC) No 70/2001 is compatible with the common market within the meaning of Article 87(3) of the Treaty and is exempted from the notification requirement of Article 88(3) of the Treaty.

(7) Any aid that meets all the requirements of this Regulation should be exempted from the notification requirement. Regional aid schemes exempted under this Regulation should contain an express reference to this Regulation.

(8) This Regulation should not apply to certain sectors in which special rules apply. Aid awarded in these sectors remains subject to prior notification to the Commission in accordance with Article 88(3) of the Treaty. This is the case for the coal and steel industry, the synthetic fibres and shipbuilding sectors, fisheries and aquaculture. In the agricultural sector, this Regulation should not apply to activities linked to the primary production of agricultural products listed in Annex I to the Treaty. It should apply to the processing and marketing of agricultural products with the exception of the manufacture and marketing of products which imitate or substitute for milk and milk products, as referred to in Article 3(2) of Council Regulation (EEC) No 1898/87 of 2 July 1987 on the protection of designations used in marketing of milk and milk products.[6] On-farm activities necessary for preparing a product for the first sale, as well as the first sale to resellers and processors should not be regarded as processing or marketing in this respect. This Regulation should ensure that the aid intensities in favour of undertakings processing and marketing agricultural products set out in Article 28(3) of Council Regulation (EC) No 1698/2005 of 20 September 2005 on support for rural development by the European Agricultural Fund for Rural Development (EAFRD)[7] can always be attained.

Notes

[6] OJ L 182, 3.7.1987, p. 36. Regulation as last amended by 1994 Act of Accession.

[7] OJ L 277, 21.10.2005, p. 1.

(9) The Commission has a consistently less favourable view of aid targeted at particular sectors. Investment aid schemes which are targeted at specific sectors of economic activity within manufacturing or services should not therefore be covered by the exemption from notification provided by this Regulation. However, regional investment aid schemes aimed at tourism activities should not be considered as targeted at specific sectors and should be exempt from the notification requirement of Article 88(3) of the Treaty, provided that the aid awarded fulfils all the conditions of this Regulation.

(10) Aid to small and medium-sized enterprises for consultancy and other services awarded in accordance with Article 5(a) of Regulation (EC) No 70/2001 is compatible with the common market within the meaning of Article 87(3) of the Treaty and is exempted from the notification requirement of Article 88(3) of the Treaty. Such aid should therefore not fall within the scope of this Regulation.

(11) In accordance with the established practice of the Commission, and with a view to better ensuring that aid is proportionate and limited to the amount necessary, thresholds should be expressed in terms of aid intensities in relation to a set of eligible costs, rather than in terms of maximum aid amounts.

(12) It is appropriate to establish further conditions that should be fulfilled by any aid scheme or individual aid exempted by this Regulation. Having regard to Article 87(3)(c) of the Treaty, such aid should not normally have the sole effect of continuously or periodically reducing the operating costs which the beneficiary would normally have to bear, and should be proportionate to the handicaps that have to be overcome in order to secure the socioeconomic benefits deemed to be in the Community interest. It is therefore appropriate to limit the scope of this Regulation to regional aid granted in relation to initial investments within the meaning of this Regulation. Regional aid schemes which provide for operating aid remain subject to the notification requirements of Article 88(3) of the Treaty. Aid to newly created small undertakings, other than investment or consultancy aid, also remains subject to the notification requirements of Article 88(3) of the Treaty.

(13) Since the Commission has to ensure that authorised aid does not alter trading conditions in a way contrary to the general interest, investment aid awarded in favour of a beneficiary which is subject to an outstanding recovery order following a previous Commission decision declaring the aid illegal and incompatible with the common market, should be excluded from the scope of this Regulation. Such aid therefore remains subject to the notification requirements of Article 88(3) of the Treaty.

(14) In order not to favour the capital factor of an investment over the labour factor, provision should be made for the possibility of measuring aid to investment on the basis of either the investment costs or the costs of new employment directly linked to the carrying-out of the investment project.

(15) Large amounts of aid should remain subject to an individual assessment by the Commission before they are put into effect. Accordingly, aid amounts exceeding a certain threshold granted to a single undertaking or establishment on the basis of an existing aid scheme should be excluded from the exemption provided for in this Regulation and remain subject to the notification requirements of Article 88(3) of the Treaty. In order to prevent large investment projects being artificially divided into sub-projects, a large investment project should be considered to be a single investment project if the initial investment is undertaken within a period of three years by the same undertaking or undertakings and consists of fixed assets combined in an economically indivisible way. To assess whether an initial investment is economically indivisible, the Commission will take into account the technical, functional and strategic links and the immediate geographical proximity. The economic indivisibility will be assessed independently from ownership. This implies that to establish whether a large investment project constitutes a single investment project, the assessment should be the same irrespective of whether the project is carried out by one undertaking, by more than one undertaking sharing the investment costs or by more undertakings bearing the costs of separate investments within the same investment project (for example in the case of a joint venture).

(16) It is important to ensure that regional aid produces a real incentive effect and encourages investments which would not otherwise be made in the assisted areas and acts as an incentive to develop new activities. Before the start of work on the aided project, the responsible authorities should therefore confirm in writing that the project prima facie meets the conditions of eligibility. Confirmation in writing should be taken to include communication by fax or e-mail.

(17) In view of the specificities of regional aid, this Regulation should not exempt aid cumulated with other State aid, including aid granted by national, regional or local authorities or with Community assistance, in relation to the same eligible costs, when such cumulation exceeds the thresholds fixed in this Regulation. Regional investment aid exempted under this Regulation should not be cumulated with *de minimis* support within the meaning of Commission Regulation (EC) No 69/2001 of 12 January 2001 on the application of Articles 87 and 88 of the EC Treaty to *de minimis* aid[8] in respect of the same eligible expenditure, if such cumulation would result in an aid intensity exceeding that fixed by this Regulation.

Notes

[8] OJ L 10, 13.1.2001, p. 30. [See now Commission Regulation (EC) No 1998/2006 (OJ L 379, 28.12.2006, p. 5).]

---

(18) This Regulation should not apply to aid to export-related activities towards third countries or Member States, namely aid directly linked to the quantities exported, to the establishment and operation of a distribution network or to other current expenditure linked to export activities and aid contingent upon the use of domestic over imported goods.

(19) In order to ensure transparency and effective monitoring in accordance with Article 3 of Regulation (EC) No 994/98, it is appropriate to establish a standard format to be used by Member States to provide the Commission with summary information whenever, in accordance with this Regulation, an aid scheme is implemented, or an ad hoc aid is granted, with a view to publication in the *Official Journal of the European Union*. For the same reasons, it is appropriate to establish rules concerning the records that Member States should keep regarding the aid schemes exempted by this Regulation. In order to facilitate administrative treatment and in view of the wide availability of the necessary technology, the summary information should be provided in computerised form. In order to improve the transparency of regional aid in an enlarged Community, Member States should publish the full text of the aid scheme and communicate to the Commission the internet address of the publication.

(20) In the light of the Commission's experience in this area, and in particular the frequency with which it is generally necessary to revise State aid policy, it is appropriate to limit the period of application of this Regulation.

(21) This Regulation is without prejudice to any obligation on a Member State to notify individual grants of aid under obligations entered into in the context of other State aid instruments, and in particular the obligation to notify, or to inform the Commission of, aid to an undertaking receiving rescue and restructuring aid within the meaning of the Community guidelines on State aid for rescuing and restructuring firms in difficulty,[9]

Notes

[9] OJ C 244, 1.10.2004, p. 2.

HAS ADOPTED THIS REGULATION:

Article 1

Scope

1. This Regulation shall apply to transparent regional investment aid schemes which constitute State aid within the meaning of Article 87(1) of the Treaty. It shall also apply to ad hoc aid which constitutes State aid within the meaning of Article 87(1) of the Treaty if the ad hoc aid is used to supplement aid granted on the basis of a transparent regional investment aid scheme, and the ad hoc component does not exceed 50% of the total aid to be granted for the investment.

2. This Regulation shall not apply to aid in the following sectors:

(a) the fisheries and aquaculture sector;
(b) the shipbuilding sector;
(c) the coal industry;
(d) the steel industry;
(e) the synthetic fibres sector.

It shall not apply to activities linked to the primary production of agricultural products listed in Annex I to the Treaty. It shall apply to the processing and marketing of agricultural products to the exclusion of the manufacture and marketing of products which imitate or substitute for milk and milk products, as referred to in Article 3(2) of Regulation (EEC) No 1898/87.

3. This Regulation shall not apply to the following types of aid:

(a) aid to export related activities towards third countries or Member States, namely aid directly linked to the quantities exported, to the establishment and operation of a distribution network or to the other current expenditure linked to export activity;
(b) aid contingent upon the use of domestic in preference to imported goods.

Article 2

Definitions

1. For the purpose of this Regulation the following definitions shall apply:

(a) "aid" means any measure fulfilling all the criteria laid down in Article 87(1) of the Treaty;
(b) "small and medium-sized enterprises (SMEs)" means small and medium-sized enterprises as defined in Annex I to Regulation (EC) No 70/2001;
(c) "initial investment" means:

    (i) an investment in material and immaterial assets relating to the setting-up of a new establishment, the extension of an existing establishment, diversification of the output of an establishment into new additional products or a fundamental change in the overall production process of an existing establishment; or

    (ii) the acquisition of the capital assets directly linked to an establishment, where the establishment has closed or would have closed had it not been purchased, and the assets are bought by an independent investor. The sole acquisition of the shares of an undertaking does not constitute initial investment;

(d) "ad hoc aid" means individual aid that is not awarded on the basis of an aid scheme;

(e) "material assets" means assets relating to land, buildings and plant/machinery;

(f) "immaterial assets" means assets entailed by the transfer of technology through the acquisition of patent rights, licences, know-how or unpatented technical knowledge;

(g) "large investment project" means an initial investment in capital assets with an eligible expenditure above EUR 50 million, calculated at prices and exchange rates on the date when the aid is granted; a large investment project will be considered to be a single investment project when the initial investment is undertaken within a period of three years by the same undertaking or undertakings and consists of fixed assets combined in an economically indivisible way;

(h) "aid intensity in present gross grant equivalent (GGE)" means the discounted value of the aid expressed as a percentage of the discounted value of the eligible costs;

(i) "transparent regional investment aid schemes" means regional investment aid schemes in which it is possible to calculate precisely the Gross grant equivalent as a percentage of eligible expenditure ex ante without need to undertake a risk assessment (for example schemes which use grants, interest rate subsidies, capped fiscal measures);

(j) "start of work" means either the start of construction work or the first legally binding commitment to order equipment, excluding preliminary feasibility studies, whichever is the earlier;

(k) "job creation" means a net increase in the number of annual labour units (ALU) directly employed in a particular establishment compared with the average over the previous 12 months; ALU are the number of persons employed full time in one year, part-time and seasonal work being ALU fractions;

(l) "wage cost" means the total amount actually payable by the beneficiary of the aid in respect of the employment concerned, comprising the gross wage, before tax, and the compulsory contributions such as social security charges;

(m) "jobs directly created by an investment project" means jobs concerning the activity to which the investment relates and created within three years of completion of the investment, including jobs created following an increase in the utilisation rate of the capacity created by the investment;

(n) "agricultural product" means

(i) the products listed in Annex I of the Treaty, except fishery and acquaculture products covered by Council Regulation (EC) No 104/2000;[10]

(ii) products falling under CN codes 4502, 4503 and 4504 (cork products);

(iii) products intended to imitate or substitute milk and milk products, as referred to in Article 3(2) of Regulation (EEC) No 1898/87;

(o) "products intended to imitate or substitute milk and milk products" mean products which could be confused with milk and/or milk products but whose composition differs from such products in that they contain fat and/or protein of non-milk origin with or without protein derived from milk ("products other than milk products" as referred to in Article 3(2) of Regulation (EEC) No 1898/87);

(p) "processing of agricultural products" means any operation on an agricultural product resulting in a product which is also an agricultural product, except on-farm activities necessary for preparing an animal or plant product for the first sale;

(q) "marketing of an agricultural product" means holding or displaying with a view to sale, offering for sale, delivery or any other manner of placing on the market, except the first sale by a primary producer to resellers and processors and any activity preparing a product for such first sale; a sale by a farmer to final consumers shall only be considered as marketing if it takes places in separate premises reserved for that purpose;

(r) "tourism activities" means the following business activities in terms of NACE Rev. 1.1:[11]

(i) NACE 55: Hotels and restaurants,

(ii) NACE 63.3: Activities of travel agencies & tour operators, tourist assistance activities,

(iii) NACE 92: Recreational, cultural and sporting activities.

2. Schemes which use public loans are considered as transparent regional investment aid schemes within the meaning of paragraph 1(i) if they are backed by normal security and do not involve abnormal risk, and are therefore not considered to contain a state guarantee element; schemes which use state guarantees or public loans with a state guarantee element, are considered as transparent if, before the

implementation of the scheme, the methodology to calculate the aid intensity of the state guarantee has been accepted following notification to the Commission after adoption of this Regulation. Public participations and aid comprised in risk capital measures shall not be considered as transparent.

Notes
[10] OJ L 17, 21.1.2000, p. 22.
[11] Classification of Economic Activities in the European Community.

Article 3
Conditions for exemption

1. Transparent regional investment aid schemes fulfilling all the conditions of this Regulation shall be compatible with the common market within the meaning of Article 87(3) of the Treaty and shall be exempt from the notification requirement of Article 88(3) of the Treaty provided that:

(a) any aid awarded under such a scheme fulfils all the conditions of this Regulation;
(b) the scheme contains an express reference to this Regulation, citing its title and publication reference in the *Official Journal of the European Union.*

2. Aid up to the amount determined in accordance with Article 7(e) awarded on the basis of schemes referred to in paragraph 1 of this Article shall be compatible with the common market within the meaning of Article 87(3) of the Treaty and shall be exempt from the notification requirement of Article 88(3) of the Treaty provided that the aid awarded directly fulfils all the conditions of this Regulation.

3. Ad hoc aid which is only used to supplement aid granted on the basis of transparent regional investment aid schemes and which does not exceed 50% of the total aid to be granted for the investment, shall be compatible with the common market within the meaning of Article 87(3) of the Treaty and shall be exempt from the notification requirement of Article 88(3) of the Treaty provided that the ad hoc aid awarded directly fulfils all the conditions of this Regulation.

Article 4
Aid for initial investment

1. Aid for initial investment shall be compatible with the common market within the meaning of Article 87(3) of the Treaty and shall be exempt from the notification requirement of Article 88(3) of the Treaty provided that:

(a) the aid is granted in regions eligible for regional aid, as determined in the approved regional aid map for the Member State concerned for the period 2007–2013; and
(b) the aid intensity in present gross grant equivalent does not exceed the regional aid ceiling which is in force at the time the aid is granted for the region in which the investment takes place, as determined in the approved regional aid map for the Member State concerned for the period 2007–2013. With the exception of aid granted in favour of large investment projects and aid for the transport sector, the ceilings in point (b) may be increased by 20 percentage points for aid for initial investment awarded to small enterprises and by 10 percentage points for aid awarded to medium-sized enterprises.

2. In addition to the general conditions for exemption laid down in this Regulation, aid for initial investment shall satisfy the following specific conditions:

(a) the investment must be maintained in the recipient region for at least five years, or three years in the case of SMEs, after the whole investment has been completed;
(b) to be eligible, immaterial assets must:

   (i) be used exclusively in the establishment receiving the regional aid;
   (ii) be regarded as amortizable assets;
   (iii) be purchased from third parties under market conditions;
   (iv) be included in the assets of the firm and remain in the establishment receiving the regional aid for at least five years or three years in the case of SMEs;

(c) where the aid is calculated on the basis of material or immaterial investment costs, or of acquisition costs in case of takeovers, the beneficiary must provide a financial contribution of at least 25%

of the eligible costs, either through its own resources or by external financing, in a form which is free of any public support. However, where the maximum aid intensity approved under the national regional aid map for the Member State concerned, increased in accordance with the second subparagraph of paragraph 1, if appropriate, exceeds 75%, the financial contribution of the beneficiary is reduced accordingly. The condition in point (a) of the first subparagraph shall not prevent the replacement of plant or equipment which has become out-dated within the period referred to in that point due to rapid technological change, provided the economic activity is retained in the region concerned for the minimum period.

3. The ceilings fixed in paragraph 1 shall apply to the intensity of the aid calculated either as a percentage of the investment's eligible material and immaterial costs or as a percentage of the estimated wage costs of the person hired, calculated over a period of two years, for jobs directly created by the investment project, or a combination thereof, provided the aid does not exceed the most favourable amount resulting from the application of either calculation.

4. The eligible investment costs shall be discounted to their value at the moment of granting of the aid. Aid payable in several instalments shall be discounted to its value at the moment of granting of the aid. The interest rate to be used for discounting purposes shall be the reference rate applicable at the time of grant. In cases where aid is awarded by means of tax exemptions or reductions on future taxes due, subject to the respect of a certain aid intensity defined in GGE, discounting of aid tranches takes place on the basis of the reference rates applicable at the various times the tax advantages become effective.

5. In case of acquisition of an establishment, only the costs of buying assets from third parties shall be taken into consideration, provided the transaction has taken place under market conditions. Where the acquisition is accompanied by other initial investment, the expenditure relating to the latter shall be added to the cost of the purchase.

6. Costs related to the acquisition of assets under lease, other than land and buildings, shall only be taken into consideration if the lease takes the form of financial leasing and contains an obligation to purchase the asset at the expiry of the term of the lease. For the lease of land and buildings, the lease must continue for at least five years after the anticipated date of the completion of the investment project or three years in the case of SMEs.

7. In the transport sector, expenditure on the purchase of transport equipment (movable assets) shall not be eligible for aid for initial investment.

8. Except in the case of SMEs and takeovers, the assets acquired shall be new. In the case of takeovers, assets for the acquisition of which aid has already been granted prior to the purchase shall be deducted. For SMEs, the full costs of investments in immaterial assets may also be taken into consideration. For large undertakings, such costs are eligible only up to a limit of 50% of the total eligible investment expenditure for the project.

9. Where the aid is calculated on the basis of wage costs, the following conditions shall be satisfied:

(a) jobs must be directly created by an investment project;
(b) the job creation must occur within three years of the completion of the investment and each job shall be maintained for a minimum period of five years, or three years in the case of SMEs.

10. By way of derogation from paragraph 1, the maximum aid intensities for investments in the processing and marketing of agricultural products may be increased to:

(a) 50% of eligible investments in regions eligible under 87(3)(a) of the Treaty and 40% of eligible investments in other regions eligible for regional aid, as determined in the regional aid map approved for the Member States concerned for the period 2007–2013, if the beneficiary is a small or medium-sized enterprise;
(b) 25% of eligible investments in regions eligible under 87(3)(a) of the Treaty and 20% of eligible investments in other regions eligible for regional aid, as determined in the regional aid map approved for the Member States concerned for the period 2007–2013, if the beneficiary has less than 750 employees and/or less than EUR 200 million turnover, calculated in line with Commission Recommendation 2003/361/EC,[12] and if such beneficiary fulfils all other conditions of that Recommendation.

Notes
[12] OJ L 124, 20.5.2003, p. 36.

Article 5
Necessity for the aid

1. This Regulation shall only exempt aid awarded under regional investment aid schemes if, before the start of work on the project, the beneficiary has submitted an application to the national or regional authorities for aid and, in respect of applications submitted from 1 January 2007, the authority responsible for administering the scheme has confirmed in writing that, subject to the final outcome of a detailed verification, the project meets the conditions of eligibility laid down by the scheme. An express reference to both conditions must also be included in the aid scheme. If work begins before the conditions laid down in this Article are fulfilled, the whole project shall not be eligible for regional aid.

2. Paragraph 1 shall not apply to aid schemes where a tax exemption or reduction is granted automatically to eligible expenditure without any discretion on the part of the authorities.

Article 6
Cumulation

1. The aid ceilings fixed in Article 4 shall apply to the total amount of public support for the aided project regardless of whether that support is financed from local, regional, national or Community sources.

2. Aid exempted by this Regulation shall not be cumulated with any other State aid within the meaning of Article 87(1) of the Treaty or with other Community or national funding, in relation to the same eligible costs, if such cumulation would result in an aid intensity exceeding that fixed by this Regulation.

3. Regional investment aid exempted by this Regulation shall not be cumulated with *de minimis* support within the meaning of Regulation (EC) No 69/2001 in respect of the same eligible expenditure, if such cumulation would result in an aid intensity exceeding that fixed by this Regulation.

Article 7
Aid subject to prior notification to the Commission

The following aid shall not be exempted from notification under this Regulation and shall remain subject to the notification requirement of Article 88(3) of the Treaty:

(a) non transparent regional investment aid schemes;

(b) regional aid schemes targeted at specific sectors of economic activity within manufacturing or services. Regional investment aid schemes aimed at tourism activities are not considered as targeted at specific sectors;

(c) regional aid schemes which provide for operating aid;

(d) regional aid schemes which provide for aid other than investment or consultancy aid to newly created small undertakings;

(e) regional aid awarded in favour of large investment projects on the basis of existing aid schemes if the total amount of aid from all sources exceeds 75% of the maximum amount of aid an investment with eligible expenditure of EUR 100 million could receive, applying the standard aid ceiling in force for large undertakings in the approved regional aid map on the date the aid is to be granted;

(f) ad hoc regional aid, other than that exempted pursuant to Article 3(1) of Regulation (EC) No 70/2001 and Article 3(3) of this Regulation;

(g) investment aid in favour of a beneficiary which is subject to an outstanding recovery order following a previous Commission decision declaring the aid illegal and incompatible with the common market.

Article 8
Transparency and monitoring

1. On implementation of an aid scheme or grant of ad hoc aid exempted by this Regulation, Member States shall, within 20 working days, forward to the Commission, with a view to its publication in the

Official Journal of the European Union, a summary of the information regarding such aid in the form laid down in Annex I. This shall be provided electronically in computerised form.

2. Whenever regional aid is granted on the basis of an existing aid scheme for large investment projects which fall below the threshold for individual notification laid down by Article 7(e), the Member States shall, within 20 working days starting from the day on which the aid is granted by the competent authority, provide the Commission with the information requested in the standard form laid down in Annex II, electronically in computerised form. The Commission will make the summary information available to the public through its website (http://ec.europa.eu./comm/competition/).

3. Member States shall maintain detailed records regarding the aid schemes exempted by this Regulation and the individual aid awarded under those schemes. Such records shall contain all information necessary to establish that the conditions for exemption, as laid down in this Regulation, are fulfilled, including information on the status of any undertaking whose entitlement to aid depends on its status as an SME. Member States shall keep a record regarding an aid scheme, for 10 years from the date on which the last individual aid was awarded under such scheme. On written request, the Member State concerned shall provide the Commission, within a period of 20 working days or such longer period as may be fixed in the request, with all the information which the Commission considers necessary to assess whether the conditions of this Regulation have been complied with.

4. Member States shall submit a report to the Commission on the application of this Regulation in respect of each whole or part calendar year during which this Regulation applies, in the form laid down in Chapter III of Commission Regulation (EC) No 794/2004.[13]

5. Member State shall publish the full text of the aid schemes which fall within the scope of this Regulation and shall communicate to the Commission the internet address of the publication. That information shall also be contained in the annual report submitted pursuant to paragraph 4. Projects for which expenses were incurred before the date of publication of the aid scheme shall not be eligible for regional aid.

Notes
[13] OJ L 140, 30.4.2004, p. 1.

Article 9
Entry into force and period of validity

1. This Regulation shall enter into force on the twentieth day following that of its publication in the *Official Journal of the European Union*. It shall apply to aid schemes which enter into force, or are put into effect, after 31 December 2006.

It shall remain in force until 31 December 2013.

2. Notifications pending at the time of entry into force of this Regulation shall be assessed in accordance with its provisions. Aid schemes put into effect before the date of entry into force of this Regulation and aid granted under those schemes, in the absence of a Commission authorisation and in breach of the obligation to notify laid down in Article 88(3) of the Treaty, shall be compatible with the common market within the meaning of Article 87(3) of the Treaty and shall be exempted under this Regulation if they fulfil all the conditions of this Regulation.

At the end of the period of validity of this Regulation, the exemption for aid schemes exempted under this Regulation shall expire at the date of expiry of the approved regional aid maps.

This Regulation shall be binding in its entirety and directly applicable in all Member States.

Done at Brussels, 24 October 2006

Notes
Date of entry into force: 21 November 2006.

Annex I

Annex I

INFORMATION COMMUNICATED BY MEMBER STATES REGARDING STATE AID GRANTED UNDER COMMISSION REGULATION (EC) NO 1628/2006 ON THE APPLICATION OF ARTICLES 87 AND 88 OF THE TREATY TO NATIONAL REGIONAL INVESTMENT AID

(to be provided in computerised form, by electronic mail, to stateaidgreffe@ec.europa.eu)

Aid No	XR *(to be completed by DG COMP)/year*
Member state	
Region in which the scheme applies (NUTS II)	
Title of aid scheme or the name of the undertaking receiving ad hoc aid supplement	
Legal basis	
(for the scheme or for the ad hoc aid)	
Annual expenditure planned under the <u>scheme</u> Amounts are to be given in € or, if applicable, in national currency. Indicate the annual overall amount of the budget appropriation(s) or the estimated tax loss per year for all aid instruments contained in the scheme.	<u>Annual</u> overall amount under the scheme EUR...million
In case of <u>ad hoc aid,</u> indicate the overall aid amount. If appropriate, indicate also for how many years the ad hoc aid will be paid in instalments or how many years tax losses will be incurred.	Overall amount of ad hoc aid EUR...million Paid over...years
Maximum aid intensity Please specify the %	In conformity with Article 4 of the Regulation Yes No
Date of implementation (indicate the date from which aid may be granted under the scheme or when the ad hoc aid is granted)	../../20..
Duration (indicate the date until which aid may be granted under the scheme or in case of an ad hoc aid the expected date of the last instalment to be paid)	Until ../../20..
Economic sectors concerned	All sectors eligible for regional investment aid Yes
	Limited to specify sectors Yes/No Please specify which according to NACE Rev.1.1 classification[:1]
Name and address of the granting authority (Include the telephone No and the address for electronic mail) Indicate the internet address of the publication of the aid scheme.	Name Address

ANNEX II
FORM FOR THE PROVISION OF SUMMARY INFORMATION FOR AID FOR LARGE INVESTMENTS PROJECTS WHERE THE AID DOES NOT EXCEED THE THRESHOLDS REFERRED TO IN ARTICLE 7(E)

1. Aid in favour of (name of the undertaking(s) receiving the aid):
2. Aid scheme reference (Commission reference of the existing scheme or schemes under which the aid is awarded):
3. Public entity/entities providing the assistance (name and co-ordinates of the granting authority or authorities):
4. Member State where the investment takes place:
5. Region (NUTS 3 level) where the investment takes place:
6. Municipality (previously NUTS 5 level, now LAU 2) where the investment takes place:
7. Type of project (setting-up of a new establishment, extension of existing establishment, diversification of the output of an establishment into new additional products or a fundamental change in the overall production process of an existing establishment):
8. Products manufactured or services provided on the basis of the investment project (with PRODCOM/NACE nomenclature or CPA nomenclature for projects in the service sectors):
9. Short description of investment project:
10. Discounted eligible cost of investment project (in EUR).
11. Discounted aid amount (gross) in EUR:
12. Aid intensity (% in GGE):
13. Conditions attached to the payment of the proposed assistance (if any):
14. Planned start and end date of the project:
15. Date of award of the aid:

G16

REVISED DRAFT COMMISSION REGULATION (EC) NO . . ./ . . .

of . . . 2007
on the application of Articles 87 and 88 of the EC Treaty declaring certain categories of aid compatible with the common market

Notes
This document was originally published by the Commission for consultation on 24 April 2007. On 8 September 2007, the Commission published a revised draft in the Official Journal, with an invitation to submit comments on the revised draft (OJ C 210, 8.9.2007, p.14). The revised draft is reproduced here. The revised draft should be read in conjuction with the Commission's "Second Memorandum on the revised draft general block exemption Regulation", September 2007, published on the Europa website at http://ec.europa.eu/comm/competition/state_aid/reform/revised_final_memorandum_gber.pdf, which was published too late to be included in this volume.

THE COMMISSION OF THE EUROPEAN COMMUNITIES

Having regard to the Treaty establishing the European Community,

Having regard to Council Regulation (EC) 994/98 of 7 May 1998 on the application of Articles [87] and [88] of the Treaty establishing the European Community to certain categories of horizontal State aid,[1] and in particular Article 1 points (a) and (b) thereof,

Having published a draft of this Regulation,[2]

After consulting the Advisory Committee on State Aid,

Notes

[1] OJ L 142, 14.5.1998, p. 1.
[2] OJ C 210, 8.9.2007, p.14

Whereas:

(1) Regulation (EC) No 994/98 empowers the Commission to declare, in accordance with Article 87 of the Treaty that under certain conditions aid to small and medium-sized enterprises ("SMEs"), aid in favour of research and development, aid in favour of environmental protection, employment and training aid, and aid that complies with the map approved by the Commission for each Member State for the grant of regional aid is compatible with the common market and not subject to the notification requirement of Article 88 (3) of the Treaty.

(2) The Commission has applied Articles 87 and 88 of the Treaty in numerous decisions and gained sufficient experience to define general compatibility criteria as regards aid in favour of SMEs, in the form of investment aid in and outside assisted areas, in the form of risk capital schemes and in the area of research and development, in particular in the context of the implementation of Commission Regulation (EC) No 70/2001 of 12 January 2001 on the application of Articles 87 and 88 of the EC Treaty to State aid to small and medium-sized enterprises,[3] the implementation of Commission Regulation (EC) No 364/2004 of 25 February 2004 amending Regulation (EC) No 70/2001 as regards the extension of its scope to include aid for research and development[4] and the implementation of the Commission communication on State aid and risk capital[5] and Community guidelines on State aid to promote risk capital investments in small and medium-sized enterprises.[6]

Notes

[3] OJ L 10, 13.1.2001, p. 33.
[4] OJ L 63, 28.2.2004, p. 22.
[5] OJ C 235, 21.8.2001, p. 3.
[6] OJ C 194, 18.8.2006, p. 2.

---

(3) The Commission has also gained sufficient experience in the application of Articles 87 and 88 of the Treaty in the fields of training aid, employment aid, environmental aid, research and development aid and regional aid with respect to both SMEs and large enterprises, in particular in the context of the implementation of Commission Regulation (EC) No 68/2001 of 12 January 2001 on the application of Articles 87 and 88 of the EC Treaty to training aid,[7] Commission Regulation (EC) No 2204/2002 of 12 December 2002 on the application of Articles 87 and 88 of the EC Treaty to State aid for employment,[8] the Community framework for State aid for research and development,[9] the Community Framework for State aid for research and development and innovation,[10] the Community guidelines on State aid for environmental protection[11] and the Guidelines on national regional aid.[12]

Notes

[7] OJ L 10, 13.1.2001, p. 20
[8] OJ L 337, 13.12.2002, p. 3
[9] OJ C 45, 17.2.1996, p. 5.
[10] OJ C 323, 30.12.2006, p. 1.
[11] OJ C 37, 3.2.2001, p. 3.
[12] OJ C 54, 4.3.2006, p. 13.

---

(4) In the light of this experience, it is necessary to adapt some of the conditions laid down in the regulations mentioned above. For reasons of simplification and to ensure more efficient monitoring of aid by the Commission, they should be replaced by a single Regulation.

(5) This Regulation should exempt any aid that fulfils all the relevant conditions of this Regulation, and any aid scheme, provided that any aid that could be granted under such scheme fulfils all the relevant conditions of this Regulation. In order to ensure more efficient monitoring of the aid individual aid granted under an aid scheme and *ad hoc* individual aid granted outside any aid scheme, but to the exclusion of aid schemes, should contain an express reference to this Regulation and to the identification number attributed to any such measure by the Commission. In order to monitor the implementation of this Regulation, the Commission should also be in a position to obtain all necessary information from Member States concerning the measures implemented under the benefit of this Regulation. A failure of the Member State to provide information within a reasonable deadline on these aid measures may therefore be considered as an indication that the conditions of this Regulation are not being respected. A failure by a Member State to provide information allowing for monitoring of an aid measure may therefore lead the Commission to decide that the Regulation, or the relevant part of the Regulation, should be withdrawn as regards the Member State concerned. As soon as the Member State has provided correct and complete information, the Commission should allow the Regulation to be fully applicable again.

(6) State aid within the meaning of Article 87(1) of the Treaty not covered by this Regulation should remain subject to the notification requirement of Article 88(3) of the Treaty. This Regulation is without prejudice to the possibility for Member States to notify aid the objectives of which correspond to objectives covered by this Regulation. Such aid will be assessed by the Commission in particular on the basis of the conditions set out in this Regulation and in accordance with the criteria laid down in specific guidelines or frameworks adopted by the Commission wherever the aid measure at stake falls within the scope of application of such specific instrument.

(7) This Regulation should not apply to export aid or aid favouring domestic over imported products. In particular, it should not apply to aid financing the establishment and operation of a distribution network in other countries. Aid towards the cost of participating in trade fairs, or of studies or consultancy services needed for the launch of a new or existing product on a new market does not normally constitute export aid.

(8) This Regulation should apply across virtually all sectors. In the sector of fisheries and aquaculture, this Regulation should only exempt aid in the fields of research and development, aid in the form of risk capital, training aid and aid for disadvantaged and disabled workers.

(9) In the agricultural sector, in view of the special rules which apply in the primary production of agricultural products, this Regulation should only exempt aid in the fields of research and development, aid in the form of risk capital, training aid, environmental aid and aid for disadvantaged and disabled workers.

(10) In view of the similarities between the processing and marketing of agricultural products and of non-agricultural products this Regulation should apply to the processing and marketing of agricultural products, provided that certain conditions are met.

(11) Neither on-farm activities necessary for preparing a product for the first sale, nor the first sale to resellers or processors should be considered as processing or marketing for the purposes of this Regulation. The Court of Justice of the European Communities has established that, once the Community has legislated for the establishment of a common organisation of the market in a given sector of agriculture, Member States are under an obligation to refrain from taking any measure which might undermine or create exceptions to it. This Regulation should therefore not apply to aid, the amount of which is fixed on the basis of price or quantity of products purchased or put on the market, nor should it apply to aid which is linked to an obligation to share it with primary producers.

(12) In view of Council Regulation (EC) No 1407/2002 of 23 July 2002 on State aid to the coal industry,[13] this Regulation should not apply to aid granted to undertakings active in the coal sector with the exception of training aid, research and development aid and environmental aid.

Notes

[13] OJ L 205, 2.8.2002, p. 1.

(13) Where a regional aid scheme purports to realise regional objectives, but is targeted at particular sectors of the economy, the objective and likely effects of the scheme may be sectoral rather than

horizontal. Therefore, regional aid schemes targeted at specific sectors of economic activity should not be covered by the exemption from notification. However, the tourism sector plays an important role in national economies and in general has a particularly positive effect on regional development. Regional aid schemes aimed at tourism activities should therefore be exempt from the notification requirement.

(14) Aid granted to undertakings in difficulty within the meaning of the Community guidelines on State aid for rescuing and restructuring firms in difficulty[14] should be assessed under those Guidelines in order to avoid their circumvention. SMEs which are incorporated since less than three years and whose business plan foresees losses in those first three years shall not be considered as being in difficulty for this period for the purposes of this Regulation.

Notes
[14] OJ C 244, 1.10.2004, p. 2.

---

(15) The Commission has to ensure that authorised aid does not alter trading conditions in a way contrary to the general interest. Therefore, aid in favour of a beneficiary which is subject to an outstanding recovery order following a previous Commission decision declaring an aid illegal and incompatible with the common market, should be excluded from the scope of this Regulation. As a consequence, any individual *ad hoc* aid granted to such a beneficiary and any aid scheme not containing a provision explicitly excluding such beneficiaries remains subject to the notification requirements of Article 88(3) of the Treaty. This provision shall not affect the legitimate expectations of beneficiaries of aid schemes which are not subject to outstanding recovery orders.

(16) In order to ensure the consistent application of Community State aid rules, as well as for reasons of administrative simplification, the definitions of terms which are relevant in context of different categories of aid covered by this Regulation should be harmonised.

(17) For the purposes of transparency, equal treatment and effective monitoring, this Regulation should apply only to aid which is transparent. Transparent aid is aid for which it is possible to calculate precisely the gross grant equivalent *ex ante* without a need to undertake a risk assessment. Such precise calculation can, for instance, be realised as regards grants, interest rate subsidies and capped tax exemptions.

(18) Aid comprised in guarantee schemes should be considered as transparent when the methodology to calculate the gross grant equivalent has been approved following notification of this methodology to the Commission, and, in the case of regional aid, also when the Commission has approved such methodology after adoption of Commission Regulation (EC) No 1628/2006 on the application of Articles 87 and 88 of the Treaty to national regional aid.[15] The Commission will examine such notifications on the basis of the Commission Notice on the application of Articles 87 and 88 of the EC Treaty to State aid in the form of guarantees.[16] In view of the difficulty in calculating the grant equivalent of aid in the form of repayable advances such aid should be covered by this Regulation only if the total amount of the repayable advance is inferior to the applicable individual notification threshold under this Regulation.

Notes
[15] OJ L 302, 1.11.2006, p. 29.
[16] OJ C 71, 11.3.2000, p. 14.

---

(19) Due to the higher risk of distortion of competition, large amounts of aid should continue to be assessed by the Commission on an individual basis. Thresholds should therefore be set for each type of aid within the scope of this Regulation, at a level which takes into account the type of aid concerned and its likely effects on competition. Any aid granted above those thresholds remains subject to the notification requirement of Article 88(3) of the Treaty.

(20) With a view to ensuring that aid is proportionate and limited to the amount necessary, thresholds should, whenever possible, be expressed in terms of aid intensities in relation to a set of eligible costs. For the purpose of calculating aid intensities, aid payable in several instalments should be discounted to its value at the moment of granting. The interest rate to be used for discounting purposes and for calculating the aid amount in aid not taking the form of a grant, should be the reference rate applicable at the time of grant. Because it is based on a form of aid

for which eligible costs are difficult to identify, the threshold with regard to aid in the form of risk capital should be formulated in terms of maximum aid amounts.

(21) The thresholds in terms of aid intensity or aid amount should be fixed, in the light of the Commission's experience, at a level that strikes the appropriate balance between minimising distortions of competition in the aided sector and tackling the market failure or cohesion issue concerned. With respect to regional aid, this threshold should be set at a level taking into account the allowable aid intensities under the regional aid maps.

(22) In order to determine whether the individual notification thresholds and the maximal aid intensities laid down in this Regulation are respected, the total amount of public support for the aided activity or project should be taken into account, regardless of whether that support is financed from local, regional, national or Community sources.

(23) Moreover, this Regulation should specify the circumstances under which different categories of aid covered by this Regulation may be cumulated. As regards cumulation of aid covered by this Regulation with State aid not covered by this Regulation, regard should be had to the decision of the Commission approving the aid not covered by this Regulation, as well as the State aid rules on which this decision is based. Special provisions should apply in respect to cumulation of aid for disadvantaged and disabled workers with other types of aid. This Regulation should also make provision for cumulation of aid measures with identifiable eligible costs and aid measures without identifiable eligible costs.

(24) In order to ensure that the aid is necessary and acts as an incentive to develop further activities or projects, this Regulation should not apply to aid for activities in which the beneficiary would already engage under market conditions alone. As regards any aid covered by this Regulation granted to SMEs, such incentive should be considered present when, before the activities relating to the implementation of the aided project or activities are initiated, the SME has submitted an application to the Member State. [As regards any aid covered by this regulation granted to beneficiaries which are large enterprises, the Member State should, in addition to the conditions applying to SMEs, also verify that that the beneficiary has analysed, in an internal document, the feasibility of the aided project or activity with aid and without aid. This analysis should be realised by the beneficiary *ex ante* on the basis of quantitative and qualitative indicators. The Member State should verify that analysis and keep such documents in its records. Moreover, as the incentive effect of *ad hoc* aid granted to large enterprises is considered to be difficult to establish, this form of aid should be excluded from the scope of application of this Regulation. The Commission will examine the existence of such incentive effect in the context of the notification of the aid concerned on the basis of the criteria established in the applicable guidelines, frameworks or other Community instruments.]

(25) In order to ensure transparency and effective monitoring in accordance with Article 3 of Regulation (EC) No 994/98, it is appropriate to establish a standard form to be used by Member States to provide the Commission with summary information whenever, in pursuance of this Regulation, an aid scheme or *ad hoc* individual aid are implemented. The summary information form shall be used for the publication of the measure in the *Official Journal of the European Union* and on the internet. The summary information should be sent to the Commission in electronic format making use of the established IT application before the measure is implemented. The Commission will attribute an identification number to each aid measure which is communicated to it. The fact that such number is attributed to an aid measure does not imply that the Commission has examined whether the aid fulfils the conditions of this Regulation. It creates therefore no legitimate expectations for the Member State or beneficiary as regards the compatibility of the aid measure with this Regulation.

(26) For the same reasons, the Commission should establish specific requirements as regards the form and the content of the annual reports to be submitted to the Commission by Member States. Moreover, it is appropriate to establish rules concerning the records that Member States should keep regarding the aid schemes and individual aid exempted by this Regulation.

(27) It is necessary to establish further conditions that should be fulfilled by any aid scheme or individual aid exempted by this Regulation. Indeed, having regard to Articles 87(3)(a) and 87(3)(c) of the Treaty, such aid should be proportionate to the market failures or handicaps that have to be overcome in order to be in the Community interest. It is therefore appropriate to limit the

scope of this Regulation, as far as it concerns investment aid to SMEs, environmental investment aid and regional aid, to aid granted in relation to certain tangible and intangible investments. In the light of Community overcapacity and the specific problems of distortion of
competition in the road freight and air transport sectors eligible investment costs for undertakings having their main economic activity in these transport sectors should not include transport
means and equipment. Special provisions apply as regards the definition of tangible assets for the
purpose of environmental aid.

(28) Consistent with the principles governing the aid falling within Article 87(1) of the Treaty, aid
should be considered to be granted at the moment the legal right to receive the aid is conferred
on the beneficiary under the applicable national legal regime.

(29) In order not to favour the capital factor of an investment over the labour factor, provision should
be made for the possibility of measuring aid to investment in favour of SMEs and regional aid
on the basis of either the costs of the investment or the costs of employment directly created by
an investment project.

(30) Environmental aid in the form of tax reductions, aid for disadvantaged or disabled workers,
regional aid or aid in the form of risk capital granted to a beneficiary on an *ad hoc* basis may have
a major impact on competition in the relevant market because it favours the beneficiary over
other undertakings which have not received such aid. Because it is granted only to a single
undertaking, *ad hoc* aid is likely to have only a limited positive structural effect on the environment, the employment of disabled and disadvantaged workers regional cohesion or the risk capital market failure. For this reason, aid schemes providing environmental aid in the form of tax
reductions regional aid or aid in the form of risk capital should be exempted under this Regulation, whilst individual *ad hoc* awards should be notified to the Commission. This Regulation
should however exempt *ad hoc* regional aid when this *ad hoc* aid is used to supplement aid
granted on the basis of a regional aid scheme, with a maximum limit for the *ad hoc* component
of 50 % of the total aid to be granted for the investment.

(31) The provisions relating to SME investment aid do not provide, as was the case in Regulation
(EC) No 70/2001, any possibility for increasing the maximum aid intensities by means of a
regional bonus. However, the maximum aid intensities provided in the section concerning
regional aid can be granted also to SMEs as long as the conditions for granting regional aid are
fulfilled. Similarly, the provisions relating to environmental investment aid do not provide any
possibility for increasing the maximum aid intensities by means of a regional bonus. The maximum aid intensities provided for under the section concerning regional aid can however also be
applied to projects which have a positive impact on the environment, as long as the conditions
for granting regional aid are fulfilled.

(32) By addressing the handicaps of the disadvantaged regions, national regional aid promotes the
economic, social and territorial cohesion of Member States and the Community as a whole.
National regional aid is designed to assist the development of the most disadvantaged regions by
supporting investment and job creation in a sustainable context. It promotes the expansion,
rationalization, modernization and diversification of the economic activities of undertakings
located in the less favoured regions, in particular by encouraging firms to set up new establishments there.

(33) In order to prevent large regional investment projects from being artificially divided into sub-
projects, thereby escaping the notification thresholds provided under this Regulation, a large
investment project should be considered to be a single investment project if the investment is
undertaken within a period of three years by the same undertaking or undertakings and consists
of fixed assets combined in an economically indivisible way. To assess whether an investment is
economically indivisible, Member States should take into account the technical, functional and
strategic links and the immediate geographical proximity. The economic indivisibility should be
assessed independently from ownership. This means that to establish whether a large investment
project constitutes a single investment project, the assessment should be the same irrespective of
whether the project is carried out by one undertaking, by more than one undertaking sharing
the investment costs or by more undertakings bearing the costs of separate investments within
the same investment project (for example in the case of a joint venture).

(34) In contrast to regional aid, which may be granted in assisted areas only, SME investment aid may be granted both in assisted and in non-assisted areas. The Member States may thus provide, in assisted areas, investment aid as long as they respect either all conditions applying to the section concerning regional aid or all conditions applying to the section concerning SME investment aid.

(35) Sustainable development is one of the main pillars in the Lisbon Strategy for Growth and Jobs, together with competitiveness and security of energy supplies. Sustainable development is based, amongst others, on a high level of protection and improvement of the quality of the environment. Promoting environmental sustainability and combating climate change leads as well to increasing security of supply and ensuring the competitiveness of European economies and the availability of affordable energy. The area of environmental protection is often confronted with market failures in the form of negative externalities. Under normal market conditions, undertakings may not necessarily have an incentive to reduce their pollution since such reduction may increase their costs. When undertakings are not obliged to internalise the costs of pollution, society as a whole bears these costs. This internalisation of environmental costs can be ensured by imposing environmental regulation or taxes. The lack of full harmonization of environmental standards at Community level creates an uneven playing field. Furthermore, an even higher level of environmental protection can be achieved by the initiatives to go beyond the mandatory Community standards, which may harm the competitive position of the undertakings concerned.

(36) In view of the sufficient experience gathered in the application of the Community guidelines on State aid for environmental protection, investment aid for environmental protection improving on Community standards or in the absence of Community standards (for example in the case of retrofitting existing vehicles), aid for early adaptation to future Community standards by SMEs, environmental aid for investment in energy saving, environmental aid for investment in high efficiency cogeneration, environmental aid for investments to promote renewable energy sources and environmental aid in the form of tax reductions should be exempt from the notification requirement. In particular, aid for the acquisition of new transport vehicles complying with adopted Community standards is permissible before their entry into force when the new standards, once mandatory, do not apply retroactively to already purchased vehicles.

(37) A correct calculation of the extra investment or production costs to achieve environmental protection is essential to determine whether or not aid is compatible with Article 87(3) of the Treaty. Such calculation should take place on the basis of a comparable reference investment not providing the environmental benefits concerned, with the same capacity in terms of effective production. In view of the difficulties which may arise, in particular, with respect to the deduction of benefits deriving from extra investment, provision should be made for a simplified method of calculation of the extra investment costs. Therefore, and with the exception of environmental aid for investment in energy saving measures, these costs should, for the purpose of applying this Regulation, be calculated without taking into account operating benefits, cost savings or additional ancillary production and without taking into account operating costs engendered during the life of the investment. The maximum aid intensities provided for the different types of environmental investment aid concerned have been determined accordingly.

(38) As regards environmental aid for investment in cogeneration and environmental aid for investments to promote renewable energy sources, the extra costs should, for the purpose of the application of this Regulation, be calculated without taking into account other support measures granted for the same eligible costs, with the exception of other environmental investment aid.

(39) In order to eliminate differences that might give rise to distortions of competition and to facilitate coordination between different Community and national initiatives concerning SMEs, as well as for reasons of administrative clarity and legal certainty, the definition of SME used for the purpose of this Regulation should be based on the definition in Commission Recommendation 2003/361/EC of 6 May 2003 concerning the definition of small and medium sized enterprises.[17]

Notes

[17] OJ L 124, 20.5.2003, p. 36.

---

(40) SMEs play a decisive role in job creation and, more generally, act as a factor of social stability and economic drive. However, their development may be limited by market failures, leading to these SMEs suffering from typical handicaps. SMEs often have difficulties in obtaining capital, risk capital or loans, given the risk-averse nature of certain financial markets and the limited collateral that they may be able to offer. Their limited resources may also restrict their access to information, notably regarding new technology and potential markets. In order to facilitate the development of the economic activities of SMEs, this Regulation should therefore exempt certain categories of aid when they are granted in favour of SMEs. Consequently, it is justified to exempt such aid from prior notification and to consider that, for the purposes of application of this Regulation, when a beneficiary fulfils the conditions of the SME definition provided in annex to this Regulation, that SME can be presumed, when the aid amount does not exceed the applicable notification threshold, to be limited in its development by the typical SME handicaps prompted by market failures.

(41) Having regard to the differences between small enterprises and medium-sized enterprises, different basic aid intensities and different bonuses should be set for small enterprises and for medium-sized enterprises. Market failures affecting SMEs in general, amongst others as regards access to finance, result in even greater obstacles to the development of small enterprises as compared to medium-sized enterprises.

(42) On the basis of the experience gained in applying the Communication on State aid and risk capital,[18] there appear to be a number of specific risk capital market failures in the Community in respect of certain types of investments at certain stages of undertakings' development. These market failures result from an imperfect matching of supply and demand of risk capital. As a result, the level of risk capital provided in the market may be too restricted, and undertakings do not obtain funding despite having a valuable business model and growth prospects. The main source of market failure relevant to risk capital markets, which particularly affects access to capital by SMEs and which may justify public intervention, relates to imperfect or asymmetric information. Consequently, risk capital schemes taking the form of investment funds in which a sufficient proportion of the funds are considered as private equity should be exempt from the notification requirement under certain conditions. This regulation will not affect the EIF and EIB status as defined in the Community guidelines on risk capital.

Notes
[18] OJ C 194, 18.8.2006, p. 2.

(43) Aid for research and development can contribute to economic growth, strengthening competitiveness and boosting employment. On the basis of its experience with the application of Regulation (EC) No 364/2004, the Community framework for State aid for research and development,[19] the Community Framework for State aid for research and development and innovation,[20] it appears that given the available research and development capabilities of both SMEs and large enterprises, market failures may prevent the market from reaching the optimal output and lead to an inefficient outcome. Such inefficient outcomes generally relate to positive externalities/knowledge spill-overs, public goods/knowledge spill-overs, imperfect and asymmetric information and coordination and network failures.

Notes
[19] OJ C 45, 17.2.1996, p. 5.
[20] OJ C 323, 30.12.2006, p. 1.

(44) Aid for research and development for SMEs is of particular importance, because one of the structural disadvantages of SMEs lies in the difficulty they may experience in gaining access to new technological developments, technology transfers or highly qualified personnel. Therefore, aid for research and development projects, aid for technical feasibility studies and aid to cover industrial property rights costs for SMEs should be exempt from the requirement of prior notification, under certain conditions.

(45) As regards project aid for research and development, the aided part of the research project must completely fall within the categories of fundamental research, industrial research or

experimental development. When a project encompasses different tasks, each task must be qualified as falling under the categories of fundamental research, industrial research or experimental development or as not falling under any of those categories at all. This qualification need not necessarily follow a chronological approach, moving sequentially over time from fundamental research to activities closer to the market. Accordingly, a task which is carried out at a late stage of a project may be qualified as industrial research. Similarly, it is not excluded that an activity carried out at an earlier stage of the project may constitute experimental development.

(46)   In the agricultural sector, on the basis of the experience gained in particular when applying the Commission communication amending the Community framework for State aid for research and development,[21] certain aid for research and development should be exempted if conditions similar to those provided in the specific provisions laid down for the agricultural sector in the Community framework for State aid for research and development and innovation are fulfilled. If those specific conditions are not fulfilled, aid may be exempted if it fulfils the conditions set out in the general provisions related to research and development in this regulation.

Notes
[21] OJ C 48, 13.2.1998, p. 2.

(47)   The promotion of training and the recruitment of disadvantaged and disabled workers and compensation of additional costs for the employment of disabled workers constitute a central objective of the economic and social policies of the Community and of its Member States.

(48)   Training usually has positive externalities for society as a whole since it increases the pool of skilled workers from which other firms may draw, improves the competitiveness of Community industry and plays an important role in the Community employment strategy. Training, including e-learning, is also essential for the constitution, the acquisition and the diffusion of knowledge, a public good of primary importance. In view of the fact that undertakings in the Community generally under-invest in the training of their workers, especially when this training is general in nature and does not lead to an immediate and concrete advantage for the undertaking concerned, State aid can help to correct this market failure. Therefore such aid should be exempt, under certain conditions, from prior notification. In view of the particular handicaps with which SMEs are confronted and the higher relative costs that they have to bear when they invest in training, the intensities of aid exempted by this Regulation should be increased for SMEs.

(49)   A distinction can be drawn between general and specific training. The permissible aid intensities should differ according to the type of training provided and the size of the undertaking. General training provides transferable qualifications and substantially improves the employability of the trained worker. Aid for this purpose has less distortive effects on competition, meaning that higher intensities of aid can be exempted from prior notification. Specific training, which mainly benefits the undertaking, involves a greater risk of distortion of competition and the intensity of aid which can be exempted from prior notification should therefore be much lower. Training shall be considered to be general in nature also when it relates to environmental management, eco-innovation or corporate social responsibility and thereby increases the capacity of the beneficiary to contribute to general objectives in the environment field.

(50)   Certain categories of disabled or disadvantaged workers still experience particular difficulty in entering the labour market. For this reason there is a justification for public authorities to apply measures providing incentives to undertakings to increase their levels of employment, in particular of workers from these disadvantaged categories. Employment costs form part of the normal operating costs of any undertaking. It is therefore particularly important that aid for the employment of disabled and disadvantaged workers should have a positive effect on employment levels of these categories of workers and should not merely enable undertakings to reduce costs which they would otherwise have to bear. Consequently, such aid should be exempt from prior notification when it is likely to assist these categories of workers in re-entering the job market or, as regards disabled workers, re-entering and staying in the job market.

(51) It is appropriate to lay down transitional provisions for aid which was granted before the entry into force of this Regulation and was not notified in breach of the obligation in Article 88(3) of the Treaty. With the repeal of Commission Regulation (EC) No o1628/2006 on the application of Articles 87 and 88 of the EC Treaty to national regional aid, the existing regional investment schemes as approved will be allowed to continue being implemented under the conditions foreseen by that Regulation, in line with article 9, paragraph 2, last indent, of that Regulation.

(52) In the light of the Commission's experience in this area, and in particular the frequency with which it is generally necessary to revise State aid policy, it is appropriate to limit the period of application of this Regulation. Should this Regulation expire without being extended, aid schemes already exempted by this Regulation should continue to be exempted for a further period of six months, in order to give Member States time to adapt.

(53) The following regulations should be repealed: Regulation (EC) No 70/2001, Regulation (EC) No 68/2001, Regulation (EC) No 2204/2002 and Regulation (EC) No 1628/2006.

HAS ADOPTED THIS REGULATION:

CHAPTER I
COMMON PROVISIONS

Article 1
Scope

1. This Regulation shall apply to the following types of aid:

(a) regional investment and employment aid;
(b) SME investment and employment aid
(c) aid for environmental protection;
(d) aid for consultancy and SME participation in fairs
(e) aid in the form of risk capital;
(f) aid for research and development;
(g) training aid;
(h) aid for disadvantaged or disabled workers.

2. It shall not apply to:

(a) aid to export-related activities, namely aid directly linked to the quantities exported, to the establishment and operation of a distribution network or to other current costs linked to the export activity;
(b) aid contingent upon the use of domestic over imported goods.

3. This Regulation shall apply to aid in all sectors of the economy with the exception of the following:

(a) aid granted to undertakings active in the fishery and aquaculture sectors, as covered by Council Regulation (EC) No 104/2000,[22] except for training aid, aid in the form of risk capital, aid for research and development and aid for disadvantaged and disabled workers;
(b) aid granted to undertakings active in the primary production of agricultural products as listed in Annex I to the Treaty, except for training aid, aid in the form of risk capital, aid for research and development, environmental aid, and aid for disadvantaged and disabled workers;
(c) aid granted to undertakings active in the processing and marketing of agricultural products as listed in Annex I to the Treaty, in the following cases:
  (i) when the amount of the aid is fixed on the basis of the price or quantity of such products purchased from primary producers or put on the market by the undertakings concerned, or
  (ii) when the aid is conditional on being partly or entirely passed on to primary producers;
(d) aid granted to undertakings active in the coal sector with the exception of training aid, research and development aid and environmental aid;
(e) aid granted to undertakings active in the steel sector, with the exception of environmental aid, training aid and aid for disadvantaged and disabled workers;

(f) regional aid granted to undertakings active in the shipbuilding sector;

(g) regional aid granted to undertakings active in the synthetic fibres[23] sector.

4. This Regulation shall not apply to regional aid schemes which are targeted at specific sectors of economic activity within manufacturing or services. Schemes aimed at tourism activities are not considered as targeted at specific sectors.

5. This Regulation shall not apply to *ad hoc* individual aid granted to large enterprises, except as provided for in Article 11(1).

6. This Regulation shall not apply to the following aid:

(a) aid schemes which do not explicitly exclude the payment of individual aid in favour of an undertaking which is subject to an outstanding recovery order following a previous Commission decision declaring an aid illegal and incompatible with the common market;

(b) *ad hoc* individual aid in favour of an undertaking which is subject to an outstanding recovery order following a previous Commission decision declaring an aid illegal and incompatible with the common market;

(c) aid to undertakings in difficulty.

Notes

[22] OJ L 17, 21.1.2000, p. 22.

[23] NACE code XXX.

Article 2
Definitions

For the purposes of this Regulation the following definitions shall apply:

1. "aid" means any measure fulfilling all the criteria laid down in Article 87(1) of the Treaty;

2. "aid scheme" means any act on the basis of which, without further implementing measures being required, individual aid awards may be made to undertakings defined within the act in a general and abstract manner and any act on the basis of which aid which is not linked to a specific project may be awarded to one or several undertakings for an indefinite period of time and/or for an indefinite amount;

3. "*ad hoc* individual aid" means individual aid not awarded on the basis of an aid scheme;

4. "aid intensity" means the aid amount expressed as a percentage of the eligible costs;

5. "transparent aid" means aid in respect of which it is possible to calculate precisely the gross grant equivalent *ex ante* without need to undertake a risk assessment;

6. "small and medium-sized enterprises" or "SME" shall mean undertakings fulfilling the criteria laid down in Annex I;

7. "large enterprises" shall mean undertakings not fulfilling the criteria laid down in Annex I;

8. "assisted areas" means regions eligible for regional aid, as determined in the approved regional aid map for the Member State concerned for the period 2007–2013;

9. "tangible assets" means assets relating to land, buildings and plant, machinery and equipment. In the transport sector, except for the road freight and air transport, transport means and transport equipment shall be considered as eligible assets except as regards regional aid;

10. "intangible assets" means assets entailed in by transfer of technology by the acquisition of patent rights, licences, know-how or unpatented technical knowledge;

11. "large investment project" means an investment in capital assets with eligible costs above EUR 50 million, calculated at prices and exchange rates on the date when the aid is granted;

12. "number of employees" means the number of annual labour units (ALU), namely the number of persons employed full time in one year, part-time and seasonal work being ALU fractions;

13. "employment directly created by an investment project" means employment concerning the activity to which the investment relates, including employment created following an increase in the utilisation rate of the capacity created by the investment;

14. "wage cost" means the total amount actually payable by the beneficiary of the aid in respect of the employment concerned, comprising:

(a) the gross wage, before tax; and
(b) the compulsory contributions, such as social security charges;

15. "SME investment and employment aid" means aid fulfilling the conditions provided in Article 12;

16. "investment aid" includes the types of aid foreseen in the following articles: Article 11 concerning regional investment and employment aid; Article 12 concerning SME investment and employment aid and Articles 14 to 18 concerning investment aid for environmental protection;

17. "disadvantaged worker" means any person who belongs to any of the following categories:

(a) any person who has not been in regular paid employment for the previous 6 months;
(b) any person who has not attained an upper secondary educational or vocational qualification (ISCED 3);
(c) any person over the age of 50 years;
(d) any person living as a single adult with one or more dependents;
(e) any woman working in a sector or profession characterised by a gender imbalance which is 25 % more significant than the average national gender imbalance;
(f) any person who is a member of an ethnic minority within a Member State and who requires development of his or her linguistic, vocational training or work experience profile to enhance prospects of gaining access to stable employment;

18. "disabled worker" means any person:

(a) recognised as disabled under national law; or
(b) having a recognised limitation which results from physical, mental or psychological impairment;

19. "sheltered employment" means employment in an establishment where at least 50 % of workers are disabled;

20. "supported employment" means employment of disabled workers in an establishment which offers personal assistance or support, but is not a "sheltered employment" environment;

21. "agricultural product" means:

(a) the products listed in Annex I of the Treaty, except fishery and aquaculture products covered by Regulation (EC) No 104/2000;
(b) products falling under CN codes 4502, 4503 and 4504 (cork products);
(c) products intended to imitate or substitute milk and milk products, as referred to in Article 3(2) of Council Regulation (EEC) No 1898/87;[24]

22. "processing of agricultural products" means any operation on an agricultural product resulting in a product which is also an agricultural product, except on farm activities necessary for preparing an animal or plant product for the first sale;

23. "marketing of agricultural products" means holding or display with a view to sale, offering for sale, delivery or any other manner of placing on the market, except the first sale by a primary producer to resellers or processors and any activity preparing a product for such first sale; a sale by a primary producer to final consumers shall be considered as marketing if it takes place in separate premises reserved for that purpose;

24. "tourism activities" means the following business activities in terms of NACE Rev. 1.1:

(a) NACE 55: Hotels and restaurants;
(b) NACE 63.3: Activities of travel agencies & tour operators, tourist assistance activities;
(c) NACE 92: Recreational, cultural and sporting activities;

25. "repayable advance" means a loan for a project which is paid in one or more instalments and the conditions for the reimbursement of which depend on the outcome of the research and development project;

26. "risk capital" means finance provided through equity and quasi-equity financing to undertakings during their early-growth stages (seed, start-up and expansion phases);

27. "steel sector" means the sectors covered by Annex I of the guidelines on national regional aid for 2007–2013;[25]

Notes
[24] OJ L 182, 3.7.1987, p. 36.
[25] OJ C 54, 4.3.2006, p. 13.

Article 3
Conditions for exemption

1. Aid schemes fulfilling all the conditions of chapter I of this Regulation, as well as the relevant provisions of chapter II of this Regulation shall be compatible with the common market within the meaning of Article 87(3) of the Treaty and shall be exempt from the notification requirement of Article 88(3) of the Treaty provided that any individual aid awarded under such scheme fulfils all the conditions of this Regulation, and the scheme contains an express reference to this Regulation by citing its title and publication reference in the *Official Journal of the European Union*.

2. Individual aid granted under a scheme referred to in paragraph 1 shall be compatible with the common market within the meaning of Article 87(3) of the Treaty and shall be exempt from the notification requirement of Article 88(3) of the Treaty provided that the aid fulfils all the conditions of chapter I of this Regulation, as well as the relevant provisions of chapter II of this Regulation, and that the individual aid measure contains an express reference to this Regulation, by citing its title and publication reference in the *Official Journal of the European Union* and an express reference to the Commission identification number provided for in Article 9(1).

3. *Ad hoc* individual aid fulfilling all the conditions of chapter I of this Regulation, as well as the relevant provisions of chapter II of this Regulation shall be compatible with the common market within the meaning of Article 87(3) of the Treaty and shall be exempt from the notification requirement of Article 88(3) of the Treaty provided that the aid contains an express reference to this Regulation, by citing its title and publication reference in the *Official Journal of the European Union* and an express reference to the Commission identification number provided for in Article 9(1).

Article 4
Aid intensity and eligible costs

1. For the purposes of calculating aid intensity, all figures used shall be taken before any deduction of tax or other charge. Where aid is awarded in a form other than a grant, the aid amount shall be the grant equivalent of the aid. Aid payable in several instalments shall be discounted to its value at the moment of granting. The interest rate to be used for discounting purposes shall be the reference rate applicable at the time of grant. In cases where aid is awarded by means of tax exemptions or reductions on future taxes due, subject to the respect of a certain aid intensity defined in gross grant equivalent, discounting of aid tranches takes place on the basis of the reference rates applicable at the various times the tax advantages become effective.

2. The eligible costs shall be supported by documentary evidence which shall be clear and itemised.

Article 5
Transparency of aid

1. This Regulation shall apply only to transparent aid.

In particular, the following types of aid shall be considered to be transparent:

(a) aid comprised in loans, where the gross grant equivalent has been calculated on the basis of the reference rate prevailing at the time of the grant and taking into account the existence of normal security and/or abnormal risk associated with the loan;

(b) aid comprised in guarantee schemes, where the methodology to calculate the gross grant equivalent has been accepted following notification of this methodology to the Commission in the context of the application of this Regulation or Regulation (EC) No 1628/2006 and the approved methodology explicitly addresses the type of guarantees and the type of underlying transactions at stake;

(c) aid comprised in fiscal measures, where the measure provides for a cap ensuring that the applicable threshold is not exceeded.

2. The following types of aid shall not be considered to be transparent:

(a) aid comprised in capital injections;

(b) aid comprised in risk capital measures, with the exception of aid fulfilling the conditions of Article 23.

3. Aid in the form of repayable advances shall only be considered to be transparent aid if the total amount of the repayable advance does not exceed the applicable thresholds under this Regulation. If the threshold is expressed in terms of aid intensity, the total amount of the repayable advance, expressed as a percentage of the eligible costs, shall not exceed the applicable aid intensity.

Article 6
Individual notification thresholds

1. This Regulation shall not apply to any individual aid, whether granted *ad hoc* or on the basis of a scheme, the grant equivalent of which exceeds the following thresholds:

(a) SME investment aid: EUR 7,5 million per undertaking per investment project;
(b) investment aid for environmental protection: EUR 5 million per undertaking per investment project;
(c) aid for consultancy in favour of SMEs and aid for SME participation in fairs: EUR 2 million per undertaking per project;
(d) research and development project aid and feasibility studies:
    (i)   if the project is predominantly fundamental research, EUR 20 million per undertaking, per project/feasibility study;
    (ii) if the project is predominantly industrial research, EUR 10 million per undertaking, per project/feasibility study;
    (iii) for all other projects, EUR 7,5 million per undertaking, per project/feasibility study;
    (iv) if the project is a EUREKA project, twice the amounts laid down in points (i), (ii) and (iii) respectively.
    A project shall be considered to consist "predominantly" of fundamental research or "predominantly" of industrial research, if more than 50% of the eligible project costs are incurred through activities which fall within the category of fundamental research, respectively industrial research. In cases where the predominant character of the project cannot be established, the lower threshold shall apply.
(e) aid for industrial property rights costs for SMEs: EUR 5 million per undertaking per project;
(f) training aid: EUR 2 million per training project;
(g) aid for the recruitment of disadvantaged workers: EUR 5 million per undertaking per year;
(h) aid for the employment of disabled workers in the form of wage costs: EUR 10 million per undertaking per year.
(i) aid for the employment of disabled workers compensating for additional expenses: EUR 10 million per undertaking per year.

2. Regional aid awarded in favour of large investment projects shall be notified to the Commission if the total amount of aid from all sources exceeds 75% of the maximum amount of aid an investment with eligible costs of EUR 100 million could receive, applying the standard aid threshold in force for large enterprises in the approved regional aid map on the date the aid is to be granted.

Article 7
Cumulation

1. In determining whether the individual notification thresholds laid down in Article 6 and the maximum aid intensities laid down in Chapter II are respected, the total amount of public support measures for the aided activity or project shall be taken into account, regardless of whether that support is financed from local, regional, national or Community sources.

2. Aid exempted by this Regulation may be cumulated with any other aid exempted under this Regulation as long as those aid measures concern different identifiable eligible costs.

3. Aid exempted by this Regulation shall not be cumulated with any other aid exempted under this Regulation or de minimis aid fulfilling the conditions laid down in Commission Regulation (EC) No 1998/2006 [26] or with other Community funding in relation to the same – partly or fully overlapping – eligible costs if such cumulation would result in exceeding the highest aid intensity or aid amount applicable to this aid under this Regulation.

4. By way of derogation from paragraph 3, aid in favour of disabled workers, as foreseen in Articles 32 and 33, may be cumulated with aid exempted under this Regulation in relation to the same eligible costs above the highest applicable threshold under this Regulation, provided that such cumulation does not result in an aid intensity exceeding 100 % of the wage costs over any period for which the workers concerned are employed.

5. As regards the cumulation of aid measures exempted under this Regulation with identifiable eligible costs and aid measures exempted under this Regulation without identifiable eligible costs, the conditions laid down in the second subparagraph shall apply.

Where a target undertaking has received capital under a risk capital measure within the scope of Article 23 and subsequently applies, during the first three years after the first risk capital investment, for aid within the scope of this Regulation, the relevant aid thresholds or maximum eligible amounts under this Regulation will be reduced by 50% in general and by 20% for target undertakings located in assisted areas. The reduction shall not exceed the total amount of risk capital received. This reduction does not apply to aid for research and development exempted under Articles 25 to 27.

Notes
[26] OJ L 379, 28.12.2006, p. 5.

Article 8
Incentive effect

1. This Regulation shall only exempt aid which has an incentive effect.

Aid shall be considered to have an incentive effect if it enables the beneficiary to carry out activities or projects which it would not have carried out as such in the absence of the aid.

Regional aid shall be considered to have an incentive effect also if, in the absence of the aid, the investment project would not have been carried out in the assisted area concerned.

2. As regards aid to SMEs, covered by this Regulation, the condition laid down in paragraph 1 shall be considered to be fulfilled if, before work on the project or activity has started, the beneficiary has submitted an application for the aid to the Member State concerned.

[3. As regards aid to large enterprises, covered by this Regulation, the condition laid down in paragraph 1 shall be considered to be fulfilled if, in addition to fulfilling the condition laid down in paragraph 2, the Member State has verified, before granting the individual aid concerned, that documentation prepared by the beneficiary establishes the incentive effect of the aid on the basis of one or more of the following criteria:

(a) the increased size of the project/activity due to the aid;
(b) the increased scope of the project/activity due to the aid;
(c) the increased total amount spent by the beneficiary on the project/activity due to the aid.]

4. The conditions laid down in paragraphs 2 [and 3] shall not apply as regards fiscal measures establishing a legal right to aid in accordance with objective criteria and without further exercise of discretion by the Member State if these fiscal measures have been adopted before work on the aided project or activity has started.

5. If the conditions of paragraphs 1 to 4 are not fulfilled, the entire aid measure will not be exempted under this Regulation.

Article 9
Transparency and monitoring

1. At the latest 10 working days before granting individual aid Member States shall forward to the Commission a summary of the information regarding such aid in electronic form, via the established Commission IT application and in the form laid down in [Annex III], with a view to its publication in the *Official Journal of the European Union* and on the Commission's website. Within five working days of receipt of that summary, the Commission shall send an acknowledgment of receipt to the Member State with the identification number of the aid measure concerned.

2. As soon as an aid scheme enters into force, or an *ad hoc* individual aid is granted on the basis of this Regulation, Member States shall publish on the internet the full text of such aid measure, indicating the criteria and conditions under which such aid is granted and the identity of the granting authority. The address of the website shall be communicated to the Commission together with the summary of the information regarding the aid required pursuant to paragraph 1. It shall also be contained in the annual report submitted pursuant to paragraph 5.

3. Member States shall refer to the identification number provided by the Commission pursuant to paragraph 1 in each aid granting measure addressed to a final beneficiary, with the exception of aid taking the form of fiscal measures.

4. Whenever individual aid is granted under an existing aid scheme for research and development projects covered by Article 25 and the individual aid exceeds EUR 3 million or whenever individual regional aid is granted, on the basis of an existing aid scheme for large investment projects, which is not individually notifiable pursuant to Article 6, the Member States shall, within 20 working days from the day on which the aid is granted by the competent authority, provide the Commission with the information requested in the standard form laid down in Annex II, via the established IT application.

5. In accordance with Chapter III of Council Regulation (EC) No 794/2004,[27] Member States shall compile a report in electronic form on the application of this Regulation in respect of each whole year or each part of the year during which this Regulation applies.

6. Member States shall maintain detailed records regarding any individual aid or aid scheme exempted under this Regulation. Such records shall contain all information necessary to establish that the conditions laid down in this Regulation, are fulfilled, including information on the status of any undertaking whose entitlement to aid or a bonus depends on its status as an SME, information on the incentive effect of the aid and information making it possible to establish the precise amount of eligible costs for the purpose of applying this Regulation.

Records regarding individual aid shall be maintained for 10 years from the date on which the aid was granted. Records regarding an aid scheme shall be maintained for 10 years from the date on which the last aid was granted under such scheme.

7. The Commission shall regularly monitor aid measures of which it has been informed pursuant to paragraph 1.

8. On written request, the Member State concerned shall provide the Commission within the period fixed in the request, with all the information which the Commission considers necessary to monitor the application of this Regulation.

If such information is not provided within that period or a commonly agreed period, the Commission shall send a reminder setting a new deadline for the submission of the information. If, despite such reminder, the Member State concerned does not provide the information requested, the Commission may, after having provided the Member State concerned with the possibility to make its views known, adopt a decision stating that all future aid measures to which this Regulation applies are to be notified to the Commission.

Notes
[27] OJ L 140, 30.4.2004, p. 1.

Article 10
Specific conditions applicable to investment aid

1. In order to be considered an eligible cost for the purposes of this Regulation, investments shall consist of the following:

(a) an investment in tangible and/or intangible assets relating to the setting-up of a new establishment, the extension of an existing establishment, diversification of the output of an establishment into new additional products or a fundamental change in the overall production process of an existing establishment, or

(b) the acquisition of the capital assets directly linked to an establishment, where the establishment has closed or would have closed had it not been purchased, and the assets are bought by an independent investor.

The sole acquisition of the shares of an undertaking shall not constitute investment.

2. In order to be considered eligible costs for the purposes of this Regulation, intangible assets shall fulfil the following conditions:

(a) they must be used exclusively in the establishment receiving the aid;

(b) they must be regarded as amortizable assets;

(c) they must be purchased from third parties under market conditions, without the acquirer being in a position to exercise control, within the meaning of Article 3 of Council Regulation (EC) No 139/2004,[28] on the seller, or vice versa;

(d) they must be included in the assets of the undertaking and remain in the establishment receiving the aid for at least five years or three years in the case of SMEs.

3. In order to be considered an eligible cost for the purposes of this Regulation, employment directly created by an investment project shall fulfil the following conditions:

(a) employment shall be created within three years of completion of the investment; and

(b) the investment project shall lead to a net increase in the number of employees in the establishment concerned, compared with the average over the previous twelve months; and

(c) the employment created shall be maintained during a minimum period of five years in case of large enterprise and a minimum period of three years in case of SMEs.

Notes

[28] OJ L 24, 29.01.2004, p. 1.

CHAPTER II
SPECIFIC PROVISIONS FOR THE DIFFERENT CATEGORIES OF AID

SECTION 1
Regional Aid

Article 11
Regional investment and employment aid

1. Regional investment and employment aid schemes shall be compatible with the common market within the meaning of Article 87(3) of the EC Treaty and shall be exempt from the notification requirement of Article 88(3) of the Treaty, provided that the conditions laid down in this Article are fulfilled.

Ad hoc aid which is only used to supplement aid granted on the basis of regional investment and employment aid schemes and which does not exceed 50 % of the total aid to be granted for the investment, shall be compatible with the common market within the meaning of Article 87(3) of the Treaty and shall be exempt from the notification requirement of Article 88(3) of the Treaty provided that the *ad hoc* aid awarded directly fulfils all the conditions of this Regulation.

2. The aid shall be granted in regions eligible for regional aid, as determined in the approved regional aid map for the Member State concerned for the period 2007–2013. The investment must be maintained in the recipient region for at least five years, or three years in the case of SMEs, after the whole investment has been completed. This shall not prevent the replacement of plant or equipment which has become out-dated due to rapid technological change, provided the economic activity is retained in the region concerned for the minimum period.

3. The aid intensity in present gross grant equivalent shall not exceed the regional aid threshold which is in force at the time the aid is granted for the region in which the investment takes place, as determined in the approved regional aid map for the Member State concerned for the period 2007–2013.

4. With the exception of aid granted in favour of large investment projects and regional aid for the transport sector, the thresholds fixed in paragraph 3 may be increased by 20 percentage points

for aid awarded to small enterprises and by 10 percentage points for aid awarded to medium-sized enterprises.

5. The thresholds fixed in paragraph 3 shall apply to the intensity of the aid calculated either as a percentage of the investment's eligible tangible and intangible costs or as a percentage of the estimated wage costs of the person hired, calculated over a period of two years, for employment directly created by the investment project or a combination thereof, provided that the aid does not exceed the most favourable amount resulting from the application of either calculation.

6. Where the aid is calculated on the basis of tangible or intangible investment costs, or of acquisition costs in case of takeovers, the beneficiary must provide a financial contribution of at least 25% of the eligible costs, either through its own resources or by external financing, in a form which is free of any public support. However, where the maximum aid intensity approved under the national regional aid map for the Member State concerned, increased in accordance with paragraph 4, exceeds 75%, the financial contribution of the beneficiary is reduced accordingly. If the aid is calculated on the basis of tangible or intangible investment costs, the conditions set out in paragraph 7 shall also apply.

7. In the case of acquisition of an establishment, only the costs of buying assets from third parties shall be taken into consideration, provided that the transaction has taken place under market conditions. Where the acquisition is accompanied by other investment, the costs relating to the latter shall be added to the cost of the purchase;

Costs related to the acquisition of assets under lease, other than land and buildings, shall only be taken into consideration if the lease takes the form of financial leasing and contains an obligation to purchase the asset at the expiry of the term of the lease; for the lease of land and buildings, the lease must continue for at least five years after the anticipated date of the completion of the investment project or three years in the case of SMEs.

Except in the case of SMEs and takeovers, the assets acquired shall be new. In the case of takeovers, assets for the acquisition of which aid has already been granted prior to the purchase shall be deducted. For SMEs, the full costs of investments in intangible assets may also be taken into consideration. For large enterprises, such costs are eligible only up to a limit of 50% of the total eligible investment costs for the project.

8. Where the aid is calculated on the basis of wage costs, the employment shall be directly created by the investment project.

9. By way of derogation from paragraphs 3 and 4, the maximum aid intensities for investments in the processing and marketing of agricultural products may be set at:

(a) 50% of eligible investments in regions eligible under Article 87(3)(a) of the Treaty and 40% of eligible investments in other regions eligible for regional aid, as determined in the regional aid map approved for the Member States concerned for the period 2007–2013, if the beneficiary is a small or medium-sized enterprise;

(b) 25% of eligible investments in regions eligible under Article 87(3)(a) of the Treaty and 20% of eligible investments in other regions eligible for regional aid, as determined in the regional aid map approved for the Member States concerned for the period 2007–2013, if the beneficiary has less than 750 employees and less than EUR 200 million turnover, calculated in accordance with Annex I.

10. In order to prevent a large investment being artificially divided into sub-projects, a large investment project will be considered to be a single investment project when investments are undertaken during a period of three years by the same undertaking or undertakings and consists of fixed assets combined in an economically indivisible way.

Part G State Aids

SECTION 2
SME Investment and Employment Aid

Article 12
SME Investment and employment Aid

1. Investment aid in favour of small and medium-sized enterprises shall be compatible with the common market within the meaning of Article 87(3) of the Treaty and shall be exempt from the notification requirement of Article 88(3) of the Treaty, provided that the conditions laid down in paragraphs 2, 3 and 4 are fulfilled.

2. The aid intensity shall not exceed:

(a) 20% in the case of small enterprises;
(b) 10% in the case of medium-sized enterprises.

3. The eligible costs shall be the following:

(a) the investment's eligible tangible and intangible costs, or
(b) the estimated wage costs of employment directly created by the investment project, calculated over a period of two years.

4. Where the investment concerns the processing and marketing of agricultural products listed in Annex I to the Treaty, the aid intensity shall not exceed:

(a) 75% of eligible investments in the outermost regions;
(b) 65% of eligible investments in the smaller Aegean Islands within the meaning of Council Regulation (EEC) No 2019/93;[29]
(c) 50% of eligible investments in regions eligible under Article 87(3)(a) of the Treaty;
(d) 40% of eligible investments in all other regions.

Notes
[29] OJ L, 27.7.1993, p. 1.

SECTION 3
Aid for Environmental Protection

Article 13
Definitions

For the purposes of this section, the following definitions shall apply:

(a) "environmental protection" means any action designed to remedy or prevent damage to physical surroundings or natural resources by the beneficiary's own activities, to reduce risk of such damage or to lead to a more efficient use of natural resources, including energy-saving measures and the use of renewable sources of energy;
(b) "energy-saving measures" means action which enables undertakings to reduce the amount of energy used in their production cycle, to the exclusion of the design and manufacture of machines or means of transport which can be operated with fewer natural resources and to the exclusion of action taken with a view to improving safety or hygiene;
(c) "Community standard" means a mandatory Community standard setting the level to be attained in environmental terms. Obligations provided under Council Directive No 96/61/EC [30] shall not be regarded as a Community standard for the purpose of this regulation;
(d) "renewable energy sources" means renewable, non-fossil energy sources (wind, solar, geothermal, wave, tidal, hydropower installations with a capacity below 10MW, direct biomass burning, landfill gas, sewage treatment plant gas and biogases);
(e) "energy generation from renewable energy sources" means energy generated by processes using only renewable energy sources, as well as the proportion in terms of calorific value of energy produced from renewable energy sources in hybrid installations – like co-firing - also using conventional energy sources, including renewable electricity used for filling storage systems and excluding electricity produced as a result of storage systems;

1464

(f) "cogeneration" means the simultaneous generation in one process of thermal energy and electrical and/or mechanical energy;

(g) "high efficiency cogeneration" means cogeneration meeting the criteria of Annex II and Annex III to Directive 2004/8/EC of the European Parliament and of the Council[31] and satisfying the harmonised efficiency reference values as defined in the Article 4 of that Directive;

(h) "environmental tax" means a tax whose specific taxable base has a clear negative effect on the environment and which seeks to tax certain goods or services so that the environmental costs may be included in their price and/or so that producers and consumers are oriented towards activities which better respect the environment;

(i) "tangible assets": for the purpose of section 3 of this regulation and by derogation to article 2.9, road freight transport means and equipment shall be considered as eligible tangible assets.

Notes
[30] OJ L 257, 10.10.1996, p. 26.
[31] OJ L 52, 21.2.2004, p.50.

Article 14
Investment aid for environmental protection improving on Community standards

1. Investment aid for environmental protection shall be compatible with the common market within the meaning of Article 87(3)(c) of the Treaty and shall be exempt from the notification requirement of Article 88 (3) of the Treaty, provided that the conditions laid down in paragraphs 2 to 5 are fulfilled.

2. The aided investment shall fulfil one of the following conditions:

(a) the investment enables the beneficiary to reduce the pollution resulting from its activities by means of improving on the Community standards applicable, irrespective of the presence of mandatory national standards that are more stringent than the Community standard;

(b) the investment enables the beneficiary to reduce the pollution resulting from its existing activities in the absence of Community standards.

3. The aid intensity shall not exceed 25%.[32]

However, the aid intensity may be increased by 20 percentage points for aid awarded to small enterprises and by 10 percentage points for aid awarded to medium-sized enterprises.

4. The eligible costs shall be the extra investment costs necessary to achieve a level of environmental protection higher than the level required by the Community standards.

5. Aid for investments relating to waste management shall not be exempted under this Article.

Notes
[32] This proposal does not prejudge the Commission positions in the context of the ongoing revision of the environmental guidelines, in particular with regard to intensities. In any event, given the simplified calculation methods retained for the purposes of this Regulation, the maximum aid intensities provided under this Regulation will necessarily have to stay below the maximum aid intensities provided under the guidelines which are based on more detailed calculation methods.

Article 15
Aid for early adaptation to future Community standards for SMEs

1. Aid allowing SMEs to comply with new Community standards improving on environmental protection shall be compatible with the common market within the meaning of Article 87(3)(c) of the Treaty and shall be exempt from the notification requirement of Article 88(3) of the Treaty, provided that the conditions laid down in paragraphs 2, 3 and 4 are fulfilled:

2. The Community standards shall have been adopted, but the date of mandatory transposition must not have expired.

The investment shall be implemented and finalised at least one year before the mandatory date of transposition.

3. The aid intensity shall not exceed 15 percentage points[33] for small enterprises and 10 percentage points[34] for medium-sized enterprises.

4. The eligible costs shall be the extra investment costs necessary to achieve the level of environmental protection required by the Community standard.

Notes
[33] See footnote 32.
[34] See footnote 32.

Article 16
Environmental aid for investment in energy saving measures

1. Environmental investment aid enabling undertakings to realise energy savings shall be compatible with the common market within the meaning of Article 87(3)(c) of the Treaty and shall be exempt from the notification requirement of Article 88(3) of the Treaty, provided that the conditions laid down in the paragraphs 2 and 3 are fulfilled.

2. The aid intensity shall not exceed 35 %.[35]

However, the aid intensity may be increased by 20 percentage points for aid awarded to small enterprises and by 10 percentage points for aid awarded to medium-sized enterprises.

3. The eligible costs shall be the extra investment costs necessary to achieve a level of energy savings higher than the level required by the Community standards. The eligible costs shall be calculated on the basis of the extra investment costs minus the operating benefits accruing from the reduced energy consumption during the first five years of the life of the investment.

Notes
[35] See footnote 32.

Article 17
Environmental aid for investment in high efficiency cogeneration

1. Environmental aid enabling undertakings to invest in high efficiency cogeneration shall be compatible with the common market within the meaning of Article 87(3)(c) of the Treaty and shall be exempt from the notification requirement of Article 88(3) of the Treaty, provided that the conditions laid down in paragraphs 2 and 3 are fulfilled.

2. The aid intensity shall not exceed 35%.[36]

However, the aid intensity may be increased by 20 percentage points for aid awarded to small enterprises and by 10 percentage points for aid awarded to medium-sized enterprises.

3. The eligible costs shall be the extra investment costs necessary to realise a high efficiency cogeneration plant.

Notes
[36] See footnote 32.

Article 18
Environmental aid for investments to exploit renewable energy sources

1. Environmental aid enabling undertakings to realise investments for the production of energy from renewable energy sources shall be compatible with the common market within the meaning of Article 87(3)(c) of the Treaty and shall be exempt from the notification requirement of Article 88(3) of the Treaty, provided that the conditions laid down in paragraphs 2 and 3 are fulfilled.

2. The aid intensity shall not exceed 35%.[37]

However, the aid intensity may be increased by 20 percentage points for aid awarded to small enterprises and by 10 percentage points for aid awarded to medium-sized enterprises.

3. The eligible costs shall be the extra costs borne by the beneficiary compared with a conventional power plant or with a conventional heating system with the same capacity in terms of the effective production of energy.

Article 19
Environmental aid in the form of tax reductions

1. Environmental aid in the form of tax reduction on environmental tax schemes fulfilling the conditions of Council Directive 2003/96/EC[38] shall be compatible with the common market within the meaning of Article 87(3)(c) of the Treaty and shall be exempt from the notification requirement of Article 88(3) of the Treaty, provided the conditions laid down in paragraphs 2 and 3 are fulfilled.

2. The aid shall not exceed the difference between the Community minimum tax level and the national tax without reduction.

The Community minimum tax level shall be considered to be the minimum level of taxation foreseen in Directive 2003/96/EC.

3. Tax reductions shall be granted for periods no longer than ten years.

Notes
[38] OJ L 283, 31.10.2003, p. 51.

SECTION 4

Aid for Consultancy in Favour of SMEs and SME Participation in Fairs

Article 20
Aid for consultancy in favour of SMEs

1. Aid to small and medium-sized enterprises for consultancy shall be compatible with the common market within the meaning of Article 87(3) of the Treaty and shall be exempt from the notification requirement of Article 88(3) of the Treaty, provided that the conditions laid down in paragraphs 2 and 3 are fulfilled.

2. The aid intensity shall not exceed 50%.

3. The eligible costs shall be the consultancy costs of services provided by outside consultants.

The services concerned shall not be a continuous or periodic activity nor relate to the undertaking's usual operating costs, such as routine tax consultancy services, regular legal services, or advertising.

Article 21
Aid for SME participation in fairs

1. Aid to small and medium-sized enterprises for participation in fairs shall be compatible with the common market within the meaning of Article 87(3) of the Treaty and shall be exempt from the notification requirement of Article 88(3) of the Treaty provided the conditions laid down in paragraphs 2 and 3 are fulfilled.

2. The aid intensity shall not exceed 50%.

3. The eligible costs shall be the costs incurred for renting, setting up and running the stand for the first participation of an undertaking in a particular fair or exhibition.

SECTION 5

Aid in the Form of Risk Capital

Article 22
Definitions

For the purposes of this section, the following definitions shall apply:

(a) "equity" means ownership interest in an undertaking, represented by the shares issued to investors;

(b) "quasi-equity" means financial instruments whose return for the holder is predominantly based on the profits or losses of the underlying target undertaking and are unsecured in the event of default;

(c) "private equity" means private – as opposed to public – equity or quasi-equity investment in undertakings not listed on a stock-market, including venture capital;

(d) "seed capital" means financing provided to study, assess and develop an initial concept, preceding the start-up phase;

(e) "start-up capital" means financing provided to undertakings, which have not sold their product or service commercially and are not yet generating a profit for product development and initial marketing;

(f) "expansion capital" means financing provided for the growth and expansion of an undertaking, which may or may not break even or trade profitably, for the purposes of increasing production capacity, market or product development or the provision of additional working capital;

(g) "exit strategy" means a strategy for the liquidation of holdings by a venture capital or private equity fund in accordance with a plan to achieve maximum return, including trade sale, write-offs, repayment of preference shares/loans, sale to another venture capitalist, sale to a financial institution and sale by public offering, including Initial Public Offerings;

(h) "target undertaking" means an undertaking in which an investor or investment fund is considering investing.

Article 23
Aid in the form of risk capital

1. Risk capital aid schemes in favour of SMEs shall be compatible with the common market within the meaning of Article 87(3) of the Treaty and shall be exempt from the notification requirement of Article 88 (3) of the Treaty, provided the conditions laid down in paragraphs 2 to 8 are fulfilled:

2. The aid shall takes the form of participation into a profit driven investment fund, managed on a commercial basis.

3. The tranches of finance realised by the investment fund shall not exceed EUR 1,000,000 per target undertaking over any period of twelve months.

4. For SMEs located in assisted areas, as well as for small undertakings located in non-assisted areas, the risk capital measure shall be restricted to providing financing for seed capital, start-up capital and/or expansion capital. For medium-sized undertakings located in non-assisted areas, the risk capital measure shall be restricted to providing financing for seed capital and/or start-up capital, to the exclusion of expansion capital.

5. The risk capital measure shall provide at least 70% of its total budget in the form of equity or quasi-equity into the target undertakings. The maximum duration of the period during which aid may be granted on the basis of the risk capital aid scheme to target undertakings shall be limited to six years.

6. At least 50% of the funding of the investment funds shall be provided through funding by private equity, or at least 30% in the case of investment funds targeting exclusively SMEs located in assisted areas. The providers of private equity shall be selected by the Member State either on the basis of a public tender or on the basis of on open invitation to participate in investment funds if the Member State has no discretionary powers of limiting the number of private equity investors participating.

7. To ensure that the risk capital measure is profit-driven, the following conditions shall be fulfilled:

(a) a business plan shall exist for each investment, containing details of product, sales and profitability development and establishing the *ex ante* viability of the project; and

(b) a clear and realistic exit strategy shall exist for each investment.

8. To ensure that the management of the investment fund is effected on a commercial basis, the following conditions shall be fulfilled:

(a) there shall be an agreement between a professional fund manager or a management company and participants in the fund, providing that the manager's remuneration is linked to performance and setting out the objectives of the fund and proposed timing of investments; and

(b) private equity investors shall be represented in the fund investment structure, such as through an investors' or advisory committee; and

(c) best practices and regulatory supervision shall apply to the management of funds.

SECTION 6
Aid for Research and Development

Article 24
Definitions

For the purposes of this section, the following definitions shall apply:

(a) "research organisation" means an entity, such as a university or research institute, irrespective of its legal status (organised under public or private law) or way of financing whose primary goal is to conduct fundamental research, industrial research or experimental development and to disseminate their results by way of teaching, publication or technology transfer. All profits must be reinvested in these activities, the dissemination of their results or teaching. Undertakings that can exert influence upon such an organisation, for instance in their capacity of shareholders or members of the organisation, shall enjoy no preferential access to the research capacities of such an organisation or to the research results generated by it;

(b) "fundamental research" means experimental or theoretical work undertaken primarily to acquire new knowledge of the underlying foundations of phenomena and observable facts, without any direct practical application or use in view;

(c) "industrial research" means the planned research or critical investigation aimed at the acquisition of new knowledge and skills for developing new products, processes or services or for bringing about a significant improvement in existing products, processes or services. It comprises the creation of components parts to complex systems, which is necessary for the industrial research, notably for generic technology validation, to the exclusion of prototypes;

(d) "experimental development" means the acquiring, combining, shaping and using existing scientific, technological, business and other relevant knowledge and skills for the purpose of producing plans and arrangements or designs for new, altered or improved products, processes or services. These may also include, for instance, other activities aiming at the conceptual definition, planning and documentation of new products, processes or services. The activities may comprise producing drafts, drawings, plans and other documentation, provided that they are not intended for commercial use.

The development of commercially usable prototypes and pilot projects is also included where the prototype is necessarily the final commercial product and where it is too expensive to produce for it to be used only for demonstration and validation purposes. In case of a subsequent commercial use of demonstration or pilot projects, any revenue generated from such use must be deducted from the eligible costs.

The experimental production and testing of products, processes and services are also eligible, provided that these cannot be used or transformed to be used in industrial applications or commercially.

Experimental development does not include routine or periodic changes made to products, production lines, manufacturing processes, existing services and other operations in progress, even if such changes may represent improvements.

Article 25
Aid for research and development projects

1. Aid for research and development projects shall be compatible with the common market within the meaning of Article 87(3) of the Treaty and shall be exempt from the notification requirement of Article 88 (3) of the Treaty provided that the conditions laid down in paragraphs 2 to 5 are fulfilled:

2. The aided part of the research project shall completely fall within one or more of the following research categories:

(a) fundamental research;
(b) industrial research;
(c) experimental development.

When a project encompasses different tasks, each task shall be qualified as falling under one of the categories listed in the first subparagraph, or as not falling under any of those categories.

Part G State Aids

3. The basic aid intensity shall not exceed:

(a) 100% for fundamental research;
(b) 50% for industrial research;
(c) 25% for experimental development.

The aid intensity shall be established for each beneficiary of aid, including in a collaboration project, as provided in paragraph 4(b)(i).

In the case of State aid for a research and development project being carried out in collaboration between research organisations and undertakings, the combined aid deriving from direct government support for a specific research project and, where they constitute aid, contributions from research organisations to that project may not exceed the applicable aid intensities for each benefiting undertaking.

4. The basic aid intensities set for industrial research and experimental development in paragraph 3 may be increased as follows:

(a) where the aid is given to SMEs, the aid intensity may be increased by 10 percentage points for medium-sized enterprises and by 20 percentage points for small enterprises; and
(b) a bonus of 15 percentage points may be added, up to a maximum aid intensity of 80%, if:

    (i) the project involves effective collaboration between at least two undertakings which are independent of each other and the following conditions are fulfilled:
        — no single undertaking bears more than 70% of the eligible costs of the collaboration project,
        — the project involves collaboration with at least one SME or is carried out in at least two different Member States; or
    (ii) the project involves effective collaboration between an undertaking and a research organisation and the following conditions are fulfilled:
        — the research organisation bears at least 10% of the eligible project costs; and
        — the research organisation has the right to publish the results of the research projects insofar as they stem from research implemented by that organisation; or
    (iii) in the case of industrial research, the results of the project are widely disseminated through technical and scientific conferences or through publication in scientific or technical journals or in open access repositories (databases where raw research data can be accessed by anyone, or through free or open source software.

For the purposes of points (b)(i) and (ii) of the first subparagraph subcontracting shall not be considered to be effective collaboration.

5. The eligible costs shall be the following:

(a) personnel costs (researchers, technicians and other supporting staff to the extent employed on the research project);
(b) costs of instruments and equipment to the extent and for the period used for the research project. If such instruments and equipment are not used for their full life for the research project, only the depreciation costs corresponding to the life of the research project, as calculated on the basis of good accounting practice, are considered as eligible;
(c) costs for building and land, to the extent and for the duration used for the research project. With regard to buildings, only the depreciation costs corresponding to the life of the research project, as calculated on the basis of good accounting practice are considered as eligible. For land, costs of commercial transfer or actually incurred capital costs are eligible;
(d) cost of contractual research, technical knowledge and patents bought or licensed from outside sources at market prices, where the transaction has been carried out at arm's length and there is no element of collusion involved, as well as costs of consultancy and equivalent services used exclusively for the research activity;
(e) additional overheads incurred directly as a result of the research project;
(f) other operating expenses, including costs of materials, supplies and similar products incurred directly as a result of the research activity.

6. All eligible costs shall be allocated to a specific category of research and development.

Article 26
Aid for technical feasibility studies

1. Aid for technical feasibility studies preparatory to industrial research or experimental development activities shall be compatible with the common market within the meaning of Article 87(3)(c) of the Treaty and shall be exempt from the notification requirement of Article 88(3) of the Treaty, provided that the conditions laid down in paragraphs 2 and 3 are fulfilled.

2. The aid intensity shall not exceed:

(a) for SMEs, 75% for studies preparatory to industrial research activities and 50 % for studies preparatory to experimental development activities;
(b) for large enterprises, 65% for studies preparatory to industrial research activities and 40 % for studies preparatory to experimental development activities.

3. The eligible costs shall be the costs of the study.

Article 27
Aid for industrial property rights costs for SMEs

1. Aid to SMEs for the costs associated with obtaining and validating patents and other industrial property rights shall be compatible with the common market within the meaning of Article 87(3)(c) of the Treaty and shall be exempt from the notification requirement of Article 88(3) of the Treaty, provided the conditions laid down in paragraphs 2 and 3 are fulfilled.

2. The aid intensity shall not exceed the intensity which would have qualified as project aid covered by Article 25(3) and (4), in respect of the research activities which first led to the industrial property rights concerned.

3. The eligible costs shall be the following:

(a) all costs preceding the grant of the right in the first jurisdiction, including costs relating to the preparation, filing and prosecution of the application as well as costs incurred in renewing the application before the right has been granted;
(b) translation and other costs incurred in order to obtain the granting or validation of the right in other legal jurisdictions;
(c) costs incurred in defending the validity of the right during the official prosecution of the application and possible opposition proceedings, even if such costs occur after the right is granted.

Article 28
Aid for research and development in the agricultural sector

1. Aid for research and development concerning products listed in Annex I to the EC Treaty shall be compatible with the common market within the meaning of Article 87(3)(c) of the EC Treaty and shall be exempt from the notification requirement of Article 88(3) of the EC Treaty, provided all the following conditions are fulfilled:

(a) it is of general interest to the particular sector or sub-sector concerned;
(b) information that research will be carried out, and with which goal, is published on the internet, prior to the commencement of the research. An approximate date of expected results and their place of publication on the internet, as well as a mention that the result will be available at no cost, must be included;
(c) the results of the research are made available on internet, for a period of at least 5 years. This information on the internet shall be published no later than any information which may be given to members of any particular organisation;
(d) aid shall be granted directly to the researching institution or body and must not involve the direct granting of non-research related aid to a company producing, processing or marketing agricultural products, nor provide price support to producers of such products.

2. The aid intensity shall not exceed 100 %.

3. Aid for research and development concerning products listed in Annex I to the EC and not fulfilling the conditions laid down in paragraph 1 shall be compatible with the common market within the

meaning of Article 87(3)(c) of the EC Treaty and shall be exempt from the notification requirement of Article 88(3) of the Treaty, provided the conditions laid down in Articles 24 to 27 are fulfilled.

SECTION 7
Training Aid

Article 29
Definitions

For the purposes of this section, the following definitions shall apply:

1. "specific training" means training involving tuition directly and principally applicable to the employee's present or future position in the undertaking and providing qualifications which are not or only to a limited extent transferable to other undertakings or fields of work;

2. "general training" means training involving tuition which is not applicable directly and principally to the employee's present or future position in the undertaking, but which provides qualifications that are largely transferable to other undertakings or fields of work.

   Training shall be considered "general" if, for example:

   (a) it is jointly organised by different independent undertakings, or if employees of different undertakings may avail themselves of the training; or
   (b) it is recognised, certified or validated by public authorities or bodies or by other bodies or institutions on which a Member State or the Community has conferred the necessary powers.

Article 30
Training aid

1. Training aid shall be compatible with the common market within the meaning of Article 87(3) of the Treaty and shall be exempt from the notification requirement of Article 88(3) of the Treaty, provided that the conditions laid down in paragraphs 2, 3 and 4 are fulfilled.

2. The aid intensity shall not exceed:

(a) 25% for specific training, and
(b) 60% for general training.

However, the aid intensity may be increased, up to a maximum aid intensity of 80 %, as follows:

(a) by 10 percentage points if the training is given to disabled or disadvantaged workers;
(b) by 10 percentage points if the aid is awarded to medium-sized enterprises and by 20 percentage points if the aid is awarded to small enterprises.

3. In cases where the aid project involves both specific and general training components which cannot be separated for the calculation of the aid intensity, and in cases where the specific or general character of the training aid project cannot be established, the intensities applicable to specific training shall apply.

4. The eligible costs of a training aid project shall be:

(a) trainers' personnel costs;
(b) trainers' and trainees' travel expenses, including accommodation;
(c) other current expenses such as materials and supplies directly related to the project;
(d) depreciation of tools and equipment, to the extent that they are used exclusively for the training project;
(e) cost of guidance and counselling services with regard to the training project;
(f) trainees' personnel costs and general indirect costs (administrative costs, rent, overheads) up to the amount of the total of the other eligible costs referred to in (a) to (e). As regards the former type of costs, only the hours during which the trainees actually participate in the training, after deduction of any productive hours, may be taken into account.

SECTION 8
Aid for Disadvantaged and Disabled Workers

Article 31
Aid for the recruitment of disadvantaged workers in the form of wage subsidies

1. Aid schemes for the recruitment of disadvantaged workers shall be compatible with the common market within the meaning of Article 87(3) of the Treaty and shall be exempt from the notification requirement of Article 88 (3) of the Treaty, provided the conditions laid down in paragraphs 2 to 5 are fulfilled.

2. The aid intensity shall not exceed 50 % of the eligible costs.

3. Eligible costs shall the wage costs over a maximum period of 12 months following recruitment.

4. Where the recruitment does not represent a net increase in the number of employees in the undertaking concerned, the post or posts shall have fallen vacant following voluntary departure, disability, retirement on grounds of age, voluntary reduction of working time or lawful dismissal for misconduct and not as a result of redundancy.

5. Except in the case of lawful dismissal for misconduct, the disadvantaged worker shall be entitled to continuous employment for a minimum period of 12 months. By way of derogation, Member States may limit the minimum period of employment consistent with their national legislation governing employment contracts, in which case the aid shall be reduced *pro rata* accordingly.

Article 32
Aid for the employment of disabled workers in the form of wage subsidies

1. Aid schemes for the employment of disabled workers in the form of wage subsidies shall be compatible with the common market within the meaning of Article 87(3) of the Treaty and shall be exempt from the notification requirement of Article 88 (3) of the Treaty, provided the conditions laid down in paragraphs 2 to 5 are fulfilled:

2. The aid intensity shall not exceed 60 % of the eligible costs.

3. Eligible costs shall be the wage costs over any given duration during which the disabled worker is being employed.

4. Where the recruitment does not represent a net increase in the number of employees in the undertaking concerned, the post or posts shall have fallen vacant following voluntary departure, disability, retirement on grounds of age, voluntary reduction of working time or lawful dismissal for misconduct and not as a result of redundancy.

5. Except in the case of lawful dismissal for misconduct the disabled workers shall be entitled to continuous employment for a minimum period of 12 months. By way of derogation, Member States may limit the minimum period of employment consistent with their national legislation governing employment contracts, in which case the aid shall be reduced pro rata accordingly.

Article 33
Aid for the employment of disabled workers compensating for additional expenses

1. Aid schemes for compensating the additional costs of employing disabled workers shall be compatible with the common market within the meaning of Article 87(3) of the Treaty and shall be exempt from the notification requirement of Article 88(3) of the Treaty, provided the conditions laid down in paragraphs 2 and 3 are fulfilled:

2. The aid intensity shall not exceed 100 % of the eligible costs.

3. Eligible costs shall be costs other than wage costs, which the employer has to bear and which are additional to those which the undertaking would have incurred if employing workers who are not disabled, over any given duration during which the disabled worker is being employed.

The following costs shall be eligible:

(a) costs of adapting premises;
(b) costs of employing staff for time spent solely on the assistance of the disabled workers;

Part G State Aids

(c) costs of adapting or acquiring equipment, or acquiring and validating software for their use by disabled workers, including adapted or assistive technology facilities, which are additional to those which the beneficiary would have incurred if employing workers who are not disabled;

(d) where the beneficiary undertaking provides sheltered employment, the costs of constructing, installing or expanding the establishment concerned, and any costs of administration and transport which result directly from the employment of disabled workers;

(e) where the beneficiary provides supported employment, any costs of administration and transport which result directly from the employment of disabled workers.

CHAPTER III
FINAL PROVISIONS

Article 34
Repeal

Regulation (EC) No 70/2001, Regulation (EC) No 68/2001, Regulation (EC) No 2204/2002 and Regulation (EC) No 1628/2006 are repealed.

Any references to the repealed Regulations shall be construed as references to this Regulation.

Article 35
Transitional provisions

1. This Regulation shall apply to aid granted before its entry into force, if the aid fulfils all the conditions laid down in this Regulation, with the exception of Article 9, paragraphs 1 to 3.

2. Any aid granted before [31 December 2008], which does not fulfil the conditions laid down in this Regulation but fulfils the conditions laid down in Regulation (EC) No 70/2001, Regulation (EC) No 68/2001, Regulation (EC) No 2204/2002 or Regulation (EC) No 1628/2006 shall be exempt from the notification requirement of Article 88(3) of the Treaty.

Any other aid granted before the entry into force of this Regulation aid which fulfils neither the conditions laid down in this Regulation nor the conditions laid down in one of the Regulations mentioned in the previous paragraph, will be assessed by the Commission in accordance with the relevant frameworks, guidelines, communications and notices.

3. At the end of the period of validity of this Regulation, any aid schemes exempted under this Regulation shall remain exempted during an adjustment period of six month, with the exception of regional aid schemes. The exemption of regional aid schemes under Regulation (EC) No 1628/2006 shall expire at the date of expiry of the approved regional aid maps.

Article 36
Entry into force and applicability

1. This Regulation shall enter into force on the twentieth day following that of its publication in the *Official Journal of the European Union.*

It shall apply until 31 December 2013.

This Regulation shall be binding in its entirety and directly applicable in all Member States.

Done at Brussels, . . .

ANNEX I
Definition of SME

Article 1
Enterprise

An enterprise is considered to be any entity engaged in an economic activity, irrespective of its legal form. This includes, in particular, self-employed persons and family businesses engaged in craft or other activities, and partnerships or associations regularly engaged in an economic activity.

1474

Article 2
Staff headcount and financial thresholds determining enterprise categories

1. The category of micro, small and medium-sized enterprises (SMEs) is made up of enterprises which employ fewer than 250 persons and which have an annual turnover not exceeding 50 million euro, and/or an annual balance sheet total not exceeding EUR 43 million.

2. Within the SME category, a small enterprise is defined as an enterprise which employ fewer than 50 persons and whose annual turnover and/or annual balance sheet total does not exceed EUR 10 million.

3. Within the SME category, a micro-enterprise is defined as an enterprise which employs fewer than 10 persons and whose annual turnover and/or annual balance sheet total does not exceed EUR 2 million.

Article 3
Types of enterprise taken into consideration in calculating staff numbers and financial amounts

1. An "autonomous enterprise" is any enterprise which is not classified as a partner enterprise within the meaning of paragraph 2 or as a linked enterprise within the meaning of paragraph 3.

2. "Partner enterprises" are all enterprises which are not classified as linked enterprises within the meaning of paragraph 3 and between which there is the following relationship: an enterprise (upstream enterprise) holds, either solely or jointly with one or more linked enterprises within the meaning of paragraph 3, 25 % or more of the capital or voting rights of another enterprise (downstream enterprise).

However, an enterprise may be ranked as autonomous, and thus as not having any partner enterprises, even if this 25 % threshold is reached or exceeded by the following investors, provided that those investors are not linked, within the meaning of paragraph 3, either individually or jointly to the enterprise in question:

(a) public investment corporations, venture capital companies, individuals or groups of individuals with a regular venture capital investment activity who invest equity capital in unquoted businesses (business angels), provided the total investment of those business angels in the same enterprise is less than EUR 1,250,000;
(b) universities or non-profit research centres;
(c) institutional investors, including regional development funds;
(d) autonomous local authorities with an annual budget of less than EUR 10 million and less than 5000 inhabitants.

3. "Linked enterprises" are enterprises which have any of the following relationships with each other:

(a) an enterprise has a majority of the shareholders' or members' voting rights in another enterprise;
(b) an enterprise has the right to appoint or remove a majority of the members of the administrative, management or supervisory body of another enterprise;
(c) an enterprise has the right to exercise a dominant influence over another enterprise pursuant to a contract entered into with that enterprise or to a provision in its memorandum or articles of association;
(d) an enterprise, which is a shareholder in or member of another enterprise, controls alone, pursuant to an agreement with other shareholders in or members of that enterprise, a majority of shareholders' or members' voting rights in that enterprise.

There is a presumption that no dominant influence exists if the investors listed in the second subparagraph of paragraph 2 are not involving themselves directly or indirectly in the management of the enterprise in question, without prejudice to their rights as stakeholders.

Enterprises having any of the relationships described in the first subparagraph through one or more other enterprises, or any one of the investors mentioned in paragraph 2, are also considered to be linked.

Enterprises which have one or other of such relationships through a natural person or group of natural persons acting jointly are also considered linked enterprises if they engage in their activity or in part of their activity in the same relevant market or in adjacent markets.

An "adjacent market" is considered to be the market for a product or service situated directly upstream or downstream of the relevant market.

4. Except in the cases set out in paragraph 2, second subparagraph an enterprise cannot be considered an SME if 25% or more of the capital or voting rights are directly or indirectly controlled, jointly or individually, by one or more public bodies.

5. Enterprises may make a declaration of status as an autonomous enterprise, partner enterprise or linked enterprise, including the data regarding the thresholds set out in Article 2. The declaration may be made even if the capital is spread in such a way that it is not possible to determine exactly by whom it is held, in which case the enterprise may declare in good faith that it can legitimately presume that it is not owned as to 25% or more by one enterprise or jointly by enterprises linked to one another. Such declarations are made without prejudice to the checks and investigations provided for by national or Community rules.

Article 4

Data used for the staff headcount and the financial amounts and reference period

1. The data to apply to the headcount of staff and the financial amounts are those relating to the latest approved accounting period and calculated on an annual basis. They are taken into account from the date of closure of the accounts. The amount selected for the turnover is calculated excluding value added tax (VAT) and other indirect taxes.

2. Where, at the date of closure of the accounts, an enterprise finds that, on an annual basis, it has exceeded or fallen below the headcount or financial thresholds stated in Article 2, this will not result in the loss or acquisition of the status of medium-sized, small or micro-enterprise unless those thresholds are exceeded over two consecutive accounting periods.

3. In the case of newly-established enterprises whose accounts have not yet been approved, the data to apply is to be derived from a bona fide estimate made in the course of the financial year.

Article 5

Staff headcount

The headcount corresponds to the number of annual work units (AWU), i.e. the number of persons who worked full-time within the enterprise in question or on its behalf during the entire reference year under consideration. The work of persons who have not worked the full year, the work of those who have worked part-time, regardless of duration, and the work of seasonal workers are counted as fractions of AWU. The staff consists of:

(a) employees;
(b) persons working for the enterprise being subordinated to it and deemed to be employees under national law;
(c) owner-managers;
(d) partners engaging in a regular activity in the enterprise and benefiting from financial advantages from the enterprise.

Apprentices or students engaged in vocational training with an apprenticeship or vocational training contract are not included as staff. The duration of maternity or parental leaves is not counted.

Article 6

Establishing the data of an enterprise

1. In the case of an autonomous enterprise, the data, including the number of staff, are determined exclusively on the basis of the accounts of that enterprise.

2. The data, including the headcount, of an enterprise having partner enterprises or linked enterprises are determined on the basis of the accounts and other data of the enterprise or, where they exist, the consolidated accounts of the enterprise, or the consolidated accounts in which the enterprise is included through consolidation.

To the data referred to in the first subparagraph are added the data of any partner enterprise of the enterprise in question situated immediately upstream or downstream from it. Aggregation is proportional to the percentage interest in the capital or voting rights (whichever is greater). In the case of cross-holdings, the greater percentage applies.

1476

To the data referred to in the first and second subparagraph are added 100 % of the data of any enterprise, which is linked directly or indirectly to the enterprise in question, where the data were not already included through consolidation in the accounts.

3. For the application of paragraph 2, the data of the partner enterprises of the enterprise in question are derived from their accounts and their other data, consolidated if they exist. To these are added 100% of the data of enterprises which are linked to these partner enterprises, unless their accounts data are already included through consolidation.

For the application of the same paragraph 2, the data of the enterprises which are linked to the enterprise in question are to be derived from their accounts and their other data, consolidated if they exist. To these are added, pro rata, the data of any possible partner enterprise of that linked enterprise, situated immediately upstream or downstream from it, unless it has already been included in the consolidated accounts with a percentage at least proportional to the percentage identified under the second subparagraph of paragraph 2.

4. Where in the consolidated accounts no staff data appear for a given enterprise, staff figures are calculated by aggregating proportionally the data from its partner enterprises and by adding the data from the enterprises to which the enterprise in question is linked.

Annex II
Form For The Provision Of Summary Information For Research And Development Under The Extended Reporting Obligation Laid Down In Article 9(4)

1. Aid in favour of (name of the undertaking(s) receiving the aid, SME or not):

2. Aid scheme reference (Commission reference of the existing scheme or schemes under which the aid is awarded):

3. Public entity/entities providing the assistance (name and co-ordinates of the granting authority or authorities):

4. Member State where the aided project or measure is carried out:

5. Type of project or measure:

6. Short description of project or measure:

7. Where applicable, eligible costs (in EUR):

8. Discounted aid amount (gross) in EUR:

9. Aid intensity (% in gross grant equivalent):

10. Conditions attached to the payment of the proposed aid (if any):

11. Planned start and end date of the project or measure:

12. Date of award of the aid:

Form For The Provision of Summary Information For Aid For Large Investment Projects Where The Aid Does Not Exceed The Thresholds Referred To In Article 9(4)

1. Aid in favour of (name of the undertaking(s) receiving the aid):

2. Aid scheme reference (Commission reference of the existing scheme or schemes under which the aid is awarded):

3. Public entity/entities providing the assistance (name and co-ordinates of the granting authority or authorities):

4. Member State where the investment takes place:

5. Region (NUTS 3 level) where the investment takes place:

6. Municipality (previously NUTS 5 level, now LAU 2) where the investment takes place:

7. Type of project (setting-up of a new establishment, extension of existing establishment, diversification of the output of an establishment into new additional products or a fundamental change in the overall production process of an existing establishment):

8. Products manufactured or services provided on the basis of the investment project (with PRODCOM/NACE nomenclature or CPA nomenclature for projects in the service sectors):

9. Short description of investment project:

10. Discounted eligible cost of investment project (in EUR):

11. Discounted aid amount (gross) in EUR:

12. Aid intensity (% in GGE):

13. Conditions attached to the payment of the proposed assistance (if any):

14. Planned start and end date of the project:

15. Date of award of the aid:

G17

SECOND MEMORANDUM ON THE REVISED DRAFT GENERAL BLOCK EXEMPTION REGULATION[1] SEPTEMBER 2007

Notes

[1] A first version of this memorandum was published by the Commission's Competition Services in June 2007, explaining the policy choices made in the draft GBER published on 24/4/2007. The present memorandum explains the policy choices presented in a second version of the draft GBER published in OJ C 210 of 8/9/2007, p. 14. Annex I contains a list of the recitals and provisions which have been amended as compared to the first draft published by the Commission in April 2007.

This document, which was published on 28 September 2007, is available on the Europa website at the following address: http://ec.europa.eu/comm/competition/state_aid/reform/revised_final_memorandum_gber.pdf

LEGAL NOTICE

Table of contents

1. **Introduction and framework**

1.1 The GBER in the context of the SAAP

1. One of the main objectives of the reform of state aid policy, as set out in the *"State Aid Action Plan"* (SAAP) adopted by the Commission in 2005,[2] is to create a simple, user-friendly and coherent set of legislative rules applying to those types of aid which can be considered to fulfil the conditions of compatibility outlined in Article 87(3) of the EC Treaty. As a consequence, the Commission announced that in order to enhance readability and allow for better prioritization of cases within the Commission, it would simplify the existing Block exemption regulations (BERs) and consolidate them into one single instrument: the general block exemption (GBER).[3] Block exemptions have the particularity that all state aid measures fulfilling the substantive and procedural conditions provided under said regulation are *exempted from the prior notification obligation* laid down in Article 88 of the Treaty. This seriously reduces the administrative cost of handling the aid measures concerned for the beneficiary, the Member State concerned and the Commission.

Notes

[2] See http://ec.europa.eu/comm/competition/state_aid/reform/reform.html.

[3] See point 35 of SAAP.

---

2. As the GBER will constitute one of the cornerstones of the future state aid architecture, it is essential to get the balance right between, on the one hand, the *simplification objective*, and, on the other hand, the need to ensure respect of the State aid rules, while at the same time taking into account the need for a refined economic analysis in the State aid area. By so doing, the GBER should contribute to achieving that *"less and better targeted aid"* would be granted.

3. The draft GBER is based on *Enabling Regulation No 994/98*[4] and can only cover aid measures for which the Council has explicitly provided legislative powers to the Commission. When adopting the different drafts of the GBER, the Commission took into account the experience gained from the application of the existing BERs. This experience has been set out, amongst others, in a report from the Commission to the Council and the European Parliament entitled "Evaluation report on the application of the Council Regulation (EC) No 994/98 of 7 May 1998 regarding the application of Articles 87 (ex-Article 92) and 88 (ex-Article 93) of the EC Treaty to certain categories of horizontal State aid, pursuant to Article 5 of this Regulation".[5]

Notes

[4] Council Regulation (EC) No 994/98 of 7 May 1998 on the application of Articles [87] and [88] of the Treaty establishing the European Community to certain categories of horizontal State aid, OJ L 142, 14.5.1998, p.1.

[5] Document COM/2006/0831 final, available at: http://eurlex. europa.eu/LexUriServ/LexUriServ.do?uri=CELEX: 52006DC0831:EN:NOT.

Part G State Aids

4. Aid measures will be exempted under the GBER only if the Commission has sufficient experience with respect to the type of aid concerned and is confident that the outcome of the "balancing test" is clearly positive.[6] Indeed, the Commission should retain the competence of deciding, upon notification, all those cases where the outcome of the balancing test is unsure. The text of the GBER is available at the following website: http://ec.europa.eu/comm/competition/state_aid/reform/reform.html.

Notes

[6] The balancing test measures the economic risks and benefits of the aid measures and weighs the positive against the negative effects of the aid. The Commission normally carries out this test on a case by case basis. Its application is illustrated, amongst others, in the recently adopted Community Framework for State aid for Research and Development and Innovation, OJ C 323 of 30.12.2006, p. 1.

1.2 Structure and overview of the content of the GBER

5. The GBER is essentially *subdivided into two main parts*: a first horizontal part largely of a procedural nature (chapter I) which applies to all types of aid covered by the GBER. A second, more substantive part (chapter II) contains the detailed substantive conditions applying to each of the types of aids contained in the GBER (e.g. training aid, environmental aid, . . .).

6. In the *first chapter*, the draft essentially intends, in line with the agenda on "Better Regulation",[7] to harmonise, as far as possible, all horizontal and procedural aspects applying to the different aid areas concerned. This chapter proposes, amongst others, common definitions of standard concepts, common requirements as regards the transparency of the aid, shared provisions on incentive effect, a comprehensive overview of the sectorial exclusions applying to the different types of aid and uniform requirements as regards transparency & monitoring.

Notes

[7] http://ec.europa.eu/governance/better_regulation/br_what_en.htm.

7. The *second chapter* contains the material conditions applying to different types of aid which – when fulfilling a certain number of conditions – the Commission considers as compatible with Article 87(3) EC Treaty and can therefore be exempted from the notification obligation. This second chapter covers, firstly, certain horizontal types of aid already contained in *existing block exemption regulations*: aid to SMEs, research and development aid for SMEs, aid for disadvantaged and disabled workers, training aid and regional aid.[8] The content of the sector-specific BER regulations in the transport, agriculture and fisheries area have not been included into the scope of the GBER.[9]

Notes

[8] For a complete list of the existing block exemptions, see http://ec.europa.eu/comm/competition/state_aid/legislation/block.html.
[9] This is without prejudice to the fact that certain sectorial limitations may apply to the GBER.

8. In the second chapter, the Commission also proposes to integrate into the GBER *two types of aid, not previously included in any existing block exemption*: environmental aid and aid in the form of risk capital. A third important extension of the material scope of BERs stems from the fact that the *R&D section will also apply to large enterprises*. The conditions imposed on these new categories of aid are largely inspired by the requirements of the existing R&D&I framework, risk capital guidelines[10] and the future environmental guidelines.[11] More details will be provided in this respect in the following chapters.

Notes

[10] See section 4 of the guidelines on risk capital, available at http://ec.europa.eu/comm/competition/state_aid/legislation/horizontal.html
[11] Member States will be consulted separately on these draft environmental guidelines.

9. Chapter 2 of the GBER is organised by objectives of aid, since Member States seem generally to design aid measures on the basis of objectives pursued – for instance, to increase employment or

to promote regional development – rather than in terms of investment aid versus operating aid. The types of aid which can be considered as "investment aid" have however been grouped in the beginning of the chapter in order to underline their proximity and their common features,[12] just after article 10, which contains common provisions applying to investment aid.

Notes

[12] Articles 11 to 19 of the GBER.

10. It must be highlighted that the GBER applies only to measures which are to be considered as State aid in the meaning of Article 87(1) of the EC Treaty. Some stakeholders have underlined, in their comments on the GBER, that some of the measures covered by the GBER,[13] under a given number of conditions, may not constitute State aid at all. This might be the case occasionally. The GBER can however, as clearly results from article 1.1 of Enabling Regulation no 994/1998, not be understood as providing a legislative interpretation of 87(1) of the Treaty. It limits itself to indicating under which conditions a given measure can be considered compatible in the meaning of Article 87(3) of the EC Treaty.[14] In cases where the state aid nature of a given measure may be in doubt it may be in the interest of a Member State to have that aid measure comply with the conditions of the GBER so as to ensure legal certainty for itself and the interested stakeholders.

Notes

[13] For instance, measures concerning disabled workers or measures which could also be covered by Commission Decision of 28 November 2005 on the application of Article 86(2) of the EC Treaty to State aid in the form of public service compensation granted to certain undertakings entrusted with the operation of services of general economic interest (OJ L 312, 29.11.2005, p. 67).

[14] See, in this sense, the wording of article 3 GBER.

11. The *third chapter* of the draft GBER contains the final provisions relating, amongst others, to transitional measures and entry into force. Annex I integrates the Community's SME-definition[15] unchanged into State aid rules. It replaces the identical annex I of BER 364/2004.[16]

Notes

[15] Commission Recommendation of 6 May 2003 concerning the definition of micro, small and medium-sized enterprises, OJ L 124, 20.05.2003, p. 36.

[16] Commission Regulation (EC) No 364/2004 of 25 February 2004 amending Regulation (EC) No 70/2001 as regards the extension of its scope to include aid for research and development, OJ L 63, 28.2.2004, p. 22.

12. *Annex II* contains the forms for providing information to the Commission on large projects under regional aid[17] and R&D&I provisions.

Notes

[17] Annex identical to annex II of Regulation 1628/2006.

2 Content of the horizontal part (Chapter I)

13. Chapter I (articles 1 to 10 of the GBER) contains the common provisions generally applying to all types of aid contained in the GBER. It includes common definitions, common provisions on excluded sectors, excluded beneficiaries and excluded types of aid, harmonised rules on transparency, a list of individual notification ceilings applying to large cases in each of the areas covered by the GBER, common provisions on "incentive effect", an exhaustive provision concerning the possibilities to cumulate different types of aid covered by the GBER and common provisions on transparency and monitoring.

14. In line with the Commission's most recent policy[18] and for reasons of simplification, the SME bonuses have been harmonised throughout the text: the bonus for small enterprises is set at 20 percentage points and for medium enterprises at 10 percentage points. No economic evidence has been provided either that would indicate the necessity of maintaining different SME bonuses for the different types of aid included in the GBER.

Notes
[18] See amongst others regional BER 1628/2006.

2.1 Sectorial scope

15. Each of the existing BERs and of the existing guidelines contains specific provisions on its sectorial scope and excludes some industrial sectors from its scope of application[19] either because more specific provisions are included in sectorial regulations[20] or because the economic features of the sector – for instance the declining nature of the industry concerned – leads to aid measures having different effects as compared to other sectors of industry. The draft GBER contains a consolidation and simplification of all of these sectorial exceptions (article 1.3).
    Under this provision, the following types of aid are excluded from the GBER:
    — Aid granted to undertakings active in the fishery and aquaculture sectors and aid granted to undertakings active in the primary production of agricultural products. Training aid, aid in the form of risk capital, aid for research and development and aid for disadvantaged and disabled workers can however be granted in those sectors.
    — Aid granted to undertakings active in the processing and marketing of agricultural products are excluded in a limited number of scenarios.
    — Aid granted to undertakings active in the coal sector are excluded from the GBER with the sole exception of training aid, research and development aid and environmental aid. Aid granted to undertakings active in the steel sector are excluded from the GBER with the sole exception of training aid and aid for disadvantaged and disabled workers.
    — Regional aid may not be granted under the GBER to undertakings active in the shipbuilding sector or active in the synthetic fibres sector.

Notes
[19] For instance, article 1 of SME BER 70/2001, as amended by BER 364/2004 excludes a number of sectors (agricultural production, agricultural processing, coal, . . .) from its scope of application.
[20] See amongst others specific rules applying to the agricultural and fisheries sector.

16. Moreover, a number of existing BERs also include certain sectoral reservations, indicating that their material scope of application is without prejudice to other sectorial instruments[21]. For reasons of simplicity and readability, the draft GBER does not any longer contain any such general and unspecific reservations: the exclusions are those explicitly mentioned in the GBER itself without need for the reader to consult any other Community instrument.

Notes
[21] See e.g. article 1.1 of SME BER 70/2001.

2.2 Other exclusions

17. In order to avoid state aid measures unravelling the internal market and more specifically the free movement of goods, as well as in order to ensure the Community's respect of its international WTO obligations, the proposal excludes export aid from its scope of application (article 1.2), in line with earlier BERs, including the recently adopted regional BER and de minimis regulation.[22]

Notes
[22] See article 1.1 of *de minimis* Regulation no 1998/2006.

18. The proposal excludes from the scope of the GBER aid to undertakings which are subject to an outstanding "*Deggendorf*"[23] recovery order (article 1.6). This proposal builds further on a similar line taken in the regional BER.[24] It intends to exclude both a) individual ad hoc aid to such beneficiaries and b) *the full scheme* which would not explicitly and formally exclude such beneficiaries from its national scope of application. The latter part of the prohibition merely implies that if the text of the scheme adopted at Member States level does not explicitly exclude such beneficiaries, the entire scheme is considered as not being block exempted, without prejudice to the existing rights of companies which are not subject to recovery orders.[25] This proposal intends,

in line with the State Aid Action Plan (SAAP), to ensure a proper enforcement of state aid rules by reinforcing the effectiveness of recovery orders.[26]

Notes

[23] Judgment of the ECJ of 15 May 1997, *Deggendorf/Commission*, C-355/95 P, ECR, p. I-2549.
[24] Article 7 (g) of Regulation 1628/2006.
[25] See in this sense, recital 15.
[26] See SAAP, points 53 and following.

19. The text also completely *excludes enterprises in difficulty* from its scope of application (article 1.6.c). This is in line with our constant policy, since any aid going to an enterprise in difficulty – as defined in the rescue and restructuring guidelines[27] – will necessarily adopt the character of rescue and restructuring aid. The new provision makes this clear for all types of aid covered by the GBER. However, in order to avoid the risk that young start-up companies, which may be loss-making in their first years of existence, would be ineligible for aid under the GBER, recital 14 of the revised draft GBER clarifies that SMEs which have been incorporated for less than three years and whose business plan foresees losses in those first three years shall not be considered as an undertaking in difficulty. This statement is made purely for the purposes of the GBER and does not affect the interpretation to be given to the definition of "enterprises in difficulty," when applying the rescue and restructuring guidelines.

Notes

[27] Communication from the Commission — Community guidelines on State aid for rescuing and restructuring firms in difficulty, OJ C 244, 1.10.2004, p. 2.

20. Finally, article 1.5 excludes all *ad hoc individual aid*[28] *to large enterprises* from its scope of application. As explained in recital 24, this exclusion is due to the fact that the incentive effect of these types of measures is often difficult to identify. The Commission thus considers that it should be in a position to examine the presence of such incentive effect upon notification. Recital 30 of the revised GBER also contains an exhaustive list of the aid measures covered by the GBER which can only be granted in the form of schemes, irrespective of the type of beneficiaries: such limitations exist as regards regional aid (article 12), aid in the form of risk capital (article 23), aid in the form of environmental tax reductions (article 19) and aid for employing disadvantaged and disabled workers (articles 31 to 33).

Notes

[28] "Ad hoc individual aid", as defined in article 2.3.

2.3 Definitions

21. Definitions of concepts contained in the GBER are included in article 2 when the concept concerned is used in different sections of chapter II. A typical example would be the concept of "intangible assets", which is used in the context of regional aid, SME aid and environmental aid. By so doing, a harmonisation and simplification of the concepts is achieved, whereas, in the past, the same term was sometimes defined differently in different BERs.[29] It should be noted that a certain number of specific provisions apply as regards what is to be considered as "tangible assets" for the purpose of aid granted to beneficiaries which are active in the transport sector.[30]

Notes

[29] See, for instance, the definition of "disadvantaged worker" in the BER on training aid (Regulation 68/2001) and in the BER on employment aid (Regulation 2204/2002).
[30] See more particularly articles 2.9 and 13 (i), as well as recital 27 of the revised GBER.

22. Where they are only relevant for one single type of aid, definitions are provided in specific provisions of *chapter II*. This is the case, for specific definitions concerning environmental aid (article 13), risk capital (article 22),[31] R&D (article 24)[32] and training aid (article 28).[33] An example of concepts used only in one provision would be the definitions of general training and specific training, both concepts which are not used outside the context of the specific training aid provisions.

Notes
[31] Definitions inspired by the Risk capital guidelines of 2006.
[32] Definitions inspired by the R&D&I Framework of 2006.
[33] Definitions inspired by existing BER 68/2001.

2.4 Aid intensity and eligible costs

23. Article 4 contains a harmonised provision on aid intensity and eligible costs, indicating amongst others the principles to apply for the purpose of calculating the so-called gross grant equivalent. The second paragraph, inspired by the existing training BER,[34] recalls the general obligation for Member States and beneficiaries to keep evidence of the eligible cost on the basis of which the allowable aid intensities are calculated.

Notes
[34] See article 4.7 of BER 68/2001.

24. The principles outlined in article 4 are to be used in order to ensure that the maximal allowable aid intensities provided in the provisions of chapter II of the GBER are respected.

2.5 Requirement of "Transparent" aid

25. The attached draft expands the line on transparency, already adopted in both the regional BER and de minimis regulation, into the GBER (article 5). It is considered that it is possible to calculate a gross grant equivalent, along the principles defined in article 4, only with respect to transparent aid.

26. This implies:
    — *Loans* are transparent if the grant equivalent has been calculated in line with the reference rate methodology. It is indicated however that this implies that the basic reference rate applies only in the absence of abnormal risk (i.e. with normal security). In other words, loans which imply an abnormal risk or loans not covered by normal security may indeed still be considered as "transparent" for the purpose of the GBER on the condition that the gross grant equivalent is determined, on the basis of the basic reference rate (floor rate), increased with the appropriate number of additional basis points.[35]
    — *Capital injections and risk capital measures* are not considered as transparent. This is without prejudice to the provision explicitly devoted to risk capital (article 23).
    — *Guarantees* are transparent only if the methodology has been approved by the Commission upon notification. This approach is in line with the approach already decided in the context of the regional BER and the de minimis regulation.
    — The fact that the list of forms of aid to be regarded as un-transparent also explicitly includes *repayable advances and fiscal measures* is new. The approach regarding repayable advances is however inspired by the line already taken with respect to this form of aid in R&D BER 364/2004.[36] Similarly, the approach on fiscal measures is in line with what has already been decided by the Commission in the de minimis regulation.[37] This approach is also consistent with the recent case law of the Court of Justice:[38] as a consequence, only capped fiscal measures qualify for being block exempted.
    — The revised draft also clarifies that a certain number of measures are "transparent" per se. Recital 17 – inspired by recital 13 of the de minimis regulation – provides that: "Transparent aid is aid for which it is possible to calculate precisely the gross grant equivalent ex ante without a need to undertake a risk assessment. Such precise calculation can, for instance, be realised as regards grants, interest rate subsidies and capped tax exemptions."

Notes
[35] See in this respect, the Commission notice on the method for setting the reference and discount rates available at http://ec.europa.eu/comm/competition/state_aid/legislation/reference.html.
[36] See article 6a of SME R&D BER 364/2004.
[37] See recital 13 of Regulation 1998/2006.
[38] Judgment of the ECJ of 3 March 2005, *Heiser*, C-172/03, ECR, p.I-1627.

2.6 Individual notification ceilings

27. As announced in the SAAP, the Commission should concentrate its resources on the most distortive cases and simplify the administrative treatment of aid which is clearly compatible with Article 87(3) of the EC Treaty. In this context, individual aid covered by the GBER should be subject to an *individual notification obligation* only if, in light of the large amount of aid, it is considered that a notification remains necessary to check whether the positive effects of the aid exceed the negative impacts on competition (so-called "balancing test" mentioned above).

28. In order to simplify the rules, *only one notification threshold* will apply for each category of aid (article 6). Each of them will be purely based on a single aid amount.

29. The proposal regarding notification ceilings is the following:

	Threshold GBER/per year	Threshold existing BER/guidelines
Training	2M €	1M €
Disadvantaged workers	5M €	15M €/3 years
Disabled workers	10M €	
Environment	5M €	25M€ eligible costs and 5 M€ aid[39]
SME investment aid	7.5 M €	Variable ceiling:+/– 2M €[40]
RAG	75% of maximum aid amount for an investment of 100 M €[41]	75% of maximum aid amount for an investment of 100 M €
R&D	20M € fundamental research 10M € industrial research 7.5 M € other research[42]	20 M € fundamental research 10 M € industrial research 7.5 M € other research

Notes

[39] See point 76 of the environmental guidelines 2001.

[40] Article 6.2 of Regulation 364/2004.

[41] The notification ceiling is the same as the one provided in article 7 (e) of regulation 1628/2006. This also implies that aid granted under article 11 is to be individually notified only if it exceeds the ceiling as provided in article 6.2 GBER. In other words, individual notifications of regional aid measures, as foreseen in article 11, provided to an SME shall not be affected by the notification ceiling provided in article 6.1.(a), which applies only to aid measures covered by article 12 GBER.

[42] The notification ceiling is the same as the one provided in section 7.1 of the R&D&I framework.

30. It is should be noted that sub-paragraph 6.1. (h) of the first draft GBER, has been subdivided into two separate sub-paragraphs 6.1. (h) and 6.1.(i) in the revised draft. This modification intends to clarify that the ceiling of 10 Million € applies separately to each of articles 31 and 32 GBER. In other words, up to 10 Million € can be provided under the GBER under each of those provisions.

31. Each notification will lead to a detailed economic analysis[43] of the positive and negative effects of the aid measure in question. Such detailed economic analysis will however be undertaken by the Commission under a "rule of reason": if a first assessment of the measure does not result in the finding of serious problems by the Commission, the measure should be rapidly approved. It is however not for the GBER itself to provide guidance on the precise treatment to be given by the Commission to cases notified to it. Such guidance will be laid down either in the specific guidelines where they exist (environment, R&D&I) or in a future general economic methodology to be issued by the Commission at a later stage.

Notes

[43] See, as regards the distinction between, standard economic assessment and detailed economic assessment the risk capital guidelines and the R&D&I framework: the ceilings provided in section 7.1 of the R&D&I framework correspond to the ceilings provided in article 6.1(d) of the GBER.

32. The Commission proposes to undertake a review of the practical impact of these simplified thresholds on the number of notifications received by the Commission 3 years after their entry into force, i.e. in the course of 2010. If necessary, amendments of the thresholds will be proposed.

Part G State Aids

2.7 Cumulation provisions

33. The GBER contains a comprehensive set of cumulation rules which apply with respect to measures which are *all* covered by the GBER itself, to the exclusion of those measures covered by guidelines but not exempted by the GBER.[44] Whereas the text of the first draft was not completely straightforward in this respect, the revised text of article 7.3 and recital 23 GBER leaves no doubt as regards the fact that the GBER itself does not intend to provide mandatory rules with respect to the cumulation of aid under the GBER, on the one hand, with aid not covered by the GBER, on the other hand.

Notes

[44] See, for instance, regional aid for newly created small enterprises, points 84 and following of the 2006 regional aid guidelines.

34. The draft regulation thus contains cumulation provisions for two broad hypotheses: on the one hand, cumulation of two types of aid both of which have clearly identifiable costs and, on the other hand, cumulation of aid with identifiable costs with another aid measure without clearly identifiable costs.

35. All existing BERs contain provisions regarding the cumulation of State aid with other State aid with respect to *the same eligible costs*.[45] Such cumulation is prohibited if it leads to aid intensities exceeding the highest applicable aid intensity beyond the maximum aid intensity under that BER. This approach is generally maintained in the GBER (article 7.3). Article 7.5 contains specific rules with regard to the cumulation between the types of aid covered by the GBER which have clearly identifiable eligible costs,[46] on the one hand, and aid in the form of *risk capital* – currently the only type of aid contained in the GBER without clearly identifiable eligible costs – on the other hand. The cumulation provisions applying to risk capital are inspired by section 6 of the Risk capital guidelines

Notes

[45] See, for instance, article 8.2 of SME BER 70/2001.

[46] This category includes all types of investment aid as defined [in] article 2.16, as well as all other types of aid covered by the GBER, with the sole exception of aid in the form of risk capital, as foreseen in article 23 GBER.

36. In line with the regional BER and the *de minimis* regulation,[47] cumulation of *de minimis* aid and state aid with respect to the same eligible costs is prohibited if this leads to the highest applicable aid intensity under the GBER being exceeded.

Notes

[47] Article 2.5 of regulation 1998/2006.

2.8 Incentive effect

37. The majority of the *existing BERs*[48] foresee as a minimum requirement that the beneficiary should apply to the authority for the aid before that beneficiary has initiated the subsidised project/activity, unless the aid scheme concerned provides a legal right to obtain the aid concerned without Member State's discretion (e.g. tax exemption).[49]

Notes

[48] The exception is training BER 68/2001 which does not foresee anything explicitly with respect to incentive effect/ necessity of aid. The recently adopted regional BER 1628/2006 goes beyond the traditional necessity criterion by requiring (Article 5§1 of regional BER) that a letter from the Member States indicating that prima facie the project is eligible be received by the beneficiary before work on the project is initiated.

[49] See e.g. article 7 of SME BER 70/2001.

38. The draft GBER proposes to impose a new *"positive" requirement of demonstration of the incentive effect of the aid for large enterprises*. Demonstration of an "incentive effect" is indeed considered, under the SAAP,[50] to be one of the cornerstones of the refined economic analysis to be implemented in the state aid area. Large enterprises would have to produce a document – typically a business plan – established before obtaining the aid, indicating why the aid should be considered

to have an incentive effect. This analysis should be realised on the basis of a number of qualitative criteria identified in the text and inspired largely from the criteria established in the R&D&I framework.[51] This type of document should, in practice, not imply any substantial increase in workload for the large undertakings concerned, as they can be presumed to realise this type of analysis anyhow for their own financial purposes. These new conditions do not apply to SMEs: the traditional criteria – already contained in the existing BERs – will continue to apply as regards SMEs. The positive, but rebuttable, presumption of an incentive effect in favour of SMEs applies not only to the provisions of the GBER which are expressly addressed to SMEs - like articles 12 or 20 for instance - but also to all other provisions of the GBER which apply to all types of undertakings, such as articles 11 or 30, - as long as the beneficiary of the aid provided under that provision is an SME under the definition provided in Annex I of the GBER.

Notes
[50] See, amongst others, points 20 to 25 of the State Aid Action Plan.
[51] See section 6 of the R&D&I framework 2006.

39. A number of Member States have, in the course of the Advisory Committee of 3 and 4 July 2007, expressed concerns as regards the fact that the criteria proposed by the Commission would create legal uncertainty and would not be operational. In the light of these comments, the Commission's Competition services intend to re-assess this provision. As such re-assessment could however not be realised in time to be reflected in the revised draft to be published in the Official Journal, the relevant provisions concerning incentive effect – recital 24 and article 8.3 GBER – have been put between square brackets.

2.9 Transparency and monitoring

40. Article 9 consolidates and updates the transparency and monitoring provisions contained in the existing BERs.[52]

Notes
[52] See, for instance, article 9 of SME BER 70/2001.

41. A first important change is the proposal to introduce a unique *identification number* which any aid measure claiming the benefit of the GBER must have obtained. Such system of ID numbers will clearly improve transparency: all interested stakeholders will be in a position to check whether or not the Commission has been informed about the implementation of an aid measure on the basis of the presence of an ID number in the national legislation and subsequent implementing measures. Transparency will also be increased by means of publication of the measures on the internet. The importance of this ID number is underlined by the fact that it is explicitly mentioned as a condition for exemption in article 3 of the GBER.

42. Under the revised draft GBER,[53] Member States will be required to submit a summary information sheet at the latest 10 days before the measure concerned is implemented. This implies, as regards aid schemes, which are often adopted by legislative bodies within the Member States internal legal order, that the ID number does not need to be mentioned in the legislative act itself. However, the aid scheme cannot be implemented before an ID number has been obtained for the scheme. This ID number will subsequently have to be mentioned in all individual aid measures implementing the scheme. As regards ad hoc individual aid, the draft remains unchanged: the act through which the ad hoc aid is granted should mention the ID number. As regards fiscal measures, there is no individual granting act of an authority to an identified beneficiary. Therefore the ID cannot be included in any such act. For this reason the revised draft GBER exempts fiscal measures from the obligation to include an ID number.[54] In this respect, the GBER builds further on practice already established in BERs for agricultural products.[55] This change does not imply that aid falling under the GBER would have to be "notified" to the Commission in advance. Nor does it imply some kind of compatibility check to be realised by the Commission.[56]

Notes
[53] See, in this sense, especially the revised articles 3.1 and 9.1 GBER.
[54] See in this sense the revised article 9.3 GBER.

43. A second important change, contained in article 9.8, concerns the procedural consequences of a refusal by the Member State concerned to provide information on an aid measure implemented under the GBER. In such case, it is now foreseen that the Commission may *withdraw the benefit of the GBER* for the Member State concerned for the future. The revised draft GBER includes a number of clarifications with respect to the spirit in which the Commission intends to apply this provision. The revised draft firstly no longer provides for a minimum deadline of 20 days within which the Member States is to reply to request for information of the Commission. Secondly, recital 5 clarifies that the Commission need not necessarily withdraw the benefit of the entire GBER in case of a failure to provide information. This implies, in practice, that if a Member State is not able to provide information with respect to training aid schemes, the Commission may limit itself to withdrawing the benefit of article 30 GBER for that Member State. Recital 5 of the revised draft also clearly spells out that as soon as the Member States has provided correct and complete information and the Commission has ensured that the measures at stake are compatible with the common market, the Commission shall allow the Regulation to be fully applicable again. Article 9.8 GBER is also without prejudice to the possibility for the Commission to open the procedure foreseen in Article 88 EC Treaty in respect of the past implementation of the aid scheme or of past ad hoc individual measures and without prejudice to the possibility for the Commission to initiate the procedure of Article 226 EC Treaty for lack of cooperation.

44. It is noteworthy that Article 9.4 contains specific information obligations for large projects which are identical to those contained in the existing regional BER and in the recent R&D&I framework.

2.10 SME bonus

45. The existing BERs contain different SME-bonuses.⁵⁷ The GBER provides for a harmonised bonus of 20 percentage points for small undertakings (in the past often 15 %) and 10 percentage points for medium enterprises (in the past often 7.5 %). The basic aid intensity of SME investment aid has also been aligned to this. This approach is in line with the recent regional BER and the R&D&I framework.⁵⁸

46. Both as regards R&D aid and as regards training aid, a maximum cap of 80 % aid intensity has been introduced so as to make sure – in the light of the necessity to keep an incentive effect – that at least 20 % of the project/activities concerned would be financed by the beneficiary himself without any public support, which corresponds to general Commission policy.⁵⁹

2.11 Regional bonus

47. The attached draft excludes regional bonuses from all areas covered by the GBER. In this respect, the draft follows the line already adopted by the Commission in the guidelines on risk capital and in the R&D&I Framework. The main reason for this approach is that regional policies should be circumscribed to the instrument explicitly devoted to this policy. Instruments devoted to other horizontal objectives (SME policy, environment, . . .) should be kept to develop those objectives. This much clearer distinction should make the rules easier to understand and apply.

This simplification does obviously not prohibit the cumulation of different types of aid – for instance training aid and regional investment aid – as long as the cumulation rules (article 7 GBER) are respected.

48. This approach should also be seen in the light of the fact that since 2006 regional investment aid measures may be implemented without notification to the Commission under regulation 1628/2006. These measures will be incorporated in the GBER. Member States which want to promote regional objectives may therefore grant such regional aid, possibly in combination with types of aid which do not have the same eligible costs like training aid or R&D project aid, and thereby realise their regional development objectives within a simplified regulatory framework.[60]

Notes
[60] See, in this sense, recital 31 of the GBER.

49. It should finally be reminded that the R&D&I framework and risk capital guidelines indicate that, when assessing the market failure and the incentive effect in the context of the detailed assessment of notified aid measures, the regional aspects will be taken into account.[61]

Notes
[61] See points 7.3.1 and 7.3.3 of R&D&I guidelines.

2.12 *Common provisions relating to so-called "investment aid"*

50. Article 10 contains a certain number of provisions which are included in chapter I not because they apply systematically to all types of aid contained in chapter II, but because they contain common rules applying to all types of "investment aid". In the revised draft GBER an additional definition of "investment aid" has been included in article 2.16 in order to clarify the scope of application of article 10: it applies to regional investment and employment aid, as set out in article 11, to SME investment and employment aid, as set out in article 12 and to aid for environmental protection as set out in articles 14 to 18.

51. Moreover, as compared to the earlier draft, the provision relating to replacement of "tangible" assets has been moved from article 10 – where it was erroneously included in a provision concerning "intangible" assets – to article 11.2, in line with what is currently provided in article 4.2 of Regional block exemption Regulation no 1628/2006.

3 Content of the substantive part (Chapter II)

3.1 *Regional aid*

52. Article 11 of the GBER contains the particular rules applying to what has been traditionally called "regional investment aid" and which has been renamed in the GBER regional investment and employment aid, in view of the fact that the investment costs can be calculated also on the basis of the number of jobs created.[62] This provision will replace regional BER 1628/2006. The repeal of this regulation by the GBER will not lead to Member States needing to adapt their schemes implemented under the regional BER.[63] These schemes may continue to be implemented unaffected. New schemes – adopted after the entry into force of the GBER – will however have to be in line with the GBER.

Notes
[62] See articles 10.3 and 11.8 of the GBER.
[63] See, in this sense, recital 51 of the GBER.

53. The differences between the GBER and regulation 1628/2006 are reduced in scope and relate to the definition of tangible and intangible assets, the monitoring requirements, the precise content of the requirement of "transparent aid" and the provision on incentive effect.[64] In all of these respects, the proposed changes relate to provisions which have been harmonised throughout the different areas of aid concerned.

Notes

[64] This implies that the conditions contained in article 8 GBER apply in full to regional aid provided under article 12 GBER. As a consequence, article 5.1 of RAG BER no 1628/2006 concerning the condition of "necessity of aid" will be replaced by the uniform conditions foreseen article 8.3 GBER concerning "incentive effect".

3.2 SME investment and employment aid

54. Article 12 of the GBER intends to update the existing provision of the SME BER.[65] The *five main differences* between the substantive conditions of the GBER and the existing BER 70/2001 are the following:

    a) Increase of the maximal aid intensity, in line with the modification of the SME bonus: 20 % for small enterprises and 10 % for medium-sized enterprises.

    b) Abolition of the regional bonus.
    The possibility of granting investment aid to an SME with an aid intensity higher than 10/20 % is still possible under the regional aid provisions of the GBER. For doing so the envisaged measure should fulfil all conditions of article 11. Article 12 however preserves the Member States' possibility of operating uniform SME investment aid programs throughout their entire territory, containing both assisted and non-assisted regions[66]

    c) Definition of tangible and intangible assets has been harmonised throughout aid areas (article 10).

    d) The duration of the obligation to maintain employment with the beneficiary has been reduced to 3 years, in line with the recent regional BER (article 10.3).

    e) The notification ceiling has been simplified and set at 7.5 million € (article 6.1.a). This ceiling corresponds to the lowest possible notification ceiling under the regional BER and the RAG Guidelines[67] and intends to ensure consistency between the notification ceilings of SME aid and regional aid.

Notes

[65] Article 4 of SME BER 70/2001.
[66] See in this respect recital 34.
[67] See point 64 of RAG Guidelines.

55. This type of aid has traditionally been called "SME investment aid". In the GBER, it has been systematically renamed "SME investment and employment aid", in view of the fact that the investment costs can be calculated also on the basis of the number of jobs created.[68]

Notes

[68] See articles 10.3 and 11.8 of the GBER.

3.3 Environmental aid

56. The inclusion of environmental aid into the scope of the GBER constitutes the *main enlargement of the scope of this regulation*, as compared to existing BERs. The types of environmental aid which have been included are, firstly, different types of environmental investment aid[69] and, secondly, environmental aid in the form of tax reductions. The proposals made in this context have to be seen also in the light of the ongoing revision of the existing environmental guidelines, which has been announced in the State aid action plan.[70] A separate consultation is organised with respect to these revised environmental guidelines.[71] The Commission will ensure that a consistent approach is taken in the GBER and the guidelines, once the final version of the environmental guidelines has been adopted and before the final adoption of the GBER.

Notes

[69] See paragraphs 28 to 37 of the Community guidelines on State aid for environmental protection, OJ C 37, 3.2.2001, p. 3.
[70] See State aid action plan, points 37 and 45–47.
[71] See the first draft published on 10/5/2007 on the Commission website: http//ec.europa.eu/comm/competition/state_aid/reform/reform.cfm [Note: the second draft was published on 5.10.2007 and is available at: http://ec.europa.eu/comm/competition/state_aid/reform/guidelines_environment_en_2.pdf]

57. The provisions on *environmental investment aid* (articles 14 to 18) are largely inspired by the environmental guidelines from 2001 and based on the experience gained by the Commission in the application of these guidelines. Although the different forms of investment aid are inspired by said guidelines, the calculation method for the eligible costs has been substantially simplified for the purpose of the GBER. This also the reason why the aid intensities provided in the GBER are lower than those found in the current environmental guidelines. The proposal of aid intensities in the GBER does not prejudge the Commission positions in the context of the ongoing revision of the environmental guidelines, in particular with regard to intensities.

58. Whereas the basic principle has been maintained that only extra investment costs necessary to meet the environmental objective concerned are to be included in the eligible costs, for most categories of investment aid, the *GBER allows disregarding the benefits engendered by the investment.*[72] This simplification can however be applied only partly as regards investment in energy saving measures (article 16) in view of the importance of the cost savings concerned. With respect to this type of aid the simplification would involve too high a risk of overcompensation, thereby unravelling the accuracy of the balancing test.[73] This would also go against the need for companies to realise a full internalisation of the environmental costs of their economic activities.

Notes

[72] See point 37 of the environmental guidelines 2001 and recital 37 of the GBER.
[73] See for a description of this balancing test, the R&D&I framework, section 1.3.1.

59. Moreover, it is to be noted that the *SME aid for early adaptation to future standards* (article 15) differs from what is provided in the environmental guidelines 2001[74] to the extent it introduces a period of one year before the mandatory date of transposition during which no such aid can be granted any more.[75] This is justified by the fact that during this last year the companies concerned have no other choice than to realise the necessary investments to comply with mandatory legislation. In the absence of such condition, the aid concerned could not systematically be considered to have the incentive effect which is required to include it in a BER.

Notes

[74] See, more particularly, point 28 of the environmental guidelines 2001.
[75] See article 15.2 second indent of the GBER.

60. The provisions on *environmental aid in form of tax reductions* include only a part of the provisions contained in the 2001 guidelines. Indeed, only the tax reductions on environmental taxes harmonized by the Energy Tax Directive[76] and exceeding the Community minimum tax level prescribed by this Directive are included in the GBER. Tax schemes concerning non-harmonised taxes, taxes harmonised under other Directives than the Energy Tax Directive, reductions or exemptions on existing taxes, as well as taxes harmonised under the Energy Tax Directive, but allowing tax levels for some categories below the Community minimum tax level are not included in the GBER. Such measures will continue to be notified to the Commission and be examined in the light of the environmental guidelines. These exclusions are justified by the fact that, in all these cases, the risks of distortion of competition are higher and the environmental benefits unclear.

Notes

[76] Council Directive 2003/96/EC of 27 October 2003 restructuring the Community framework for the taxation of energy products and electricity, OJ L 283, 31.10.2003, p. 51.

3.4 Aid for consultancy and SME participation in fairs

61. Articles 20 and 21 of the GBER intend to update the existing provision of the SME BER. The only difference is that for reasons of clarity, the old article 5 of SME BER 70/2001 has been subdivided into two separate provisions. Moreover, in line with the general simplification of notification thresholds, this particular notification ceiling has also been simplified to a single figure of 2 Million €,[77] which corresponds, in practice, to the standard scenario under the existing SME BER.[78]

Part G State Aids

Notes
[77] See article 6.1.(c) of the GBER.
[78] 25 M€ x 50% x 15% (basic aid intensity for small enterprises) = 1.8 M € (article 6 (a) of Regulation no 70/2001).

3.5 *Aid in the form of risk capital*

62. The inclusion of risk capital into the GBER constitutes, after the inclusion of environmental aid, the *second main enlargement of the scope of this regulation*.

63. The content of article 23 of the GBER corresponds largely to the safe harbour of the risk capital guidelines.[79] Indeed, this category of risk capital measures is the one which comprises the least risks of distortions of competition and for which the result of the balancing test is most straight-forward. However, in view of the fact that only categories of aid which are clearly compatible with Article 87 (3) EC Treaty and relating to which the Commission has sufficient experience can be included in the GBER, this regulation contains safeguards which are not present in section 4 of the guidelines. These safeguards are essentially the following:

    a) only participations in *investment funds* are covered, as compared to all other forms mentioned in point 4.2 of the guidelines. This excludes, amongst others, risk capital measures in the form of fiscal incentives from the scope of article 23 GBER.

    b) *equity and quasi-equity* measures should constitute the cornerstone of exempted risk capital measures, as opposed to other measures envisaged in point 4.3.3 of the guidelines.

    c) a limitation as to the duration of the period during which the fund may decide to start invest-ing into target companies has been introduced. This is without prejudice to the possibility that investment periods into specific target companies may be longer than 6 years.

    d) Additional safeguards as regards the fact that "private investors" are indeed stemming from the private sector. For this reason, the concept of "private investor"[80] has been replaced by the concept of "*private equity*", as defined in article 22 of the GBER.[81] The GBER does not affect however the way in which the European Investment Bank and the European Investment Fund are to be treated under the risk capital guidelines.[82]

    e) the maximal aid that can be provided on a yearly basis has been set at *1 million €*.

    f) The GBER contains, in article 23.6, a specific requirement concerning the applicable selection procedure for choosing private equity partners participating in the risk capital investment fund. Two options are envisaged under this requirement: either a full fledged public tender, or a more flexible open invitation. Only in the latter case of an open invitation procedure does the condition of absence of discretionary powers – as provided in article 23.6, last sentence of the GBER – apply, as these types of concerns are generally catered for in formal tender procedures.

Notes
[79] Section 4 of the Community guidelines on state aid to promote risk capital investments in small and medium-sized enterprises, OJ C 194, 18.8.2006, p. 2.
[80] See in this respect point 3.2 of the risk capital guidelines.
[81] This definition is inspired by the definition provided in 2.2 of the guidelines.
[82] See in this sense, the last sentence of recital 42 of the GBER.

---

64. It should be noted that article 23.4 has been re-worded in the revised draft GBER. The new provision intends to clarify the precise content of point 4.3.2 of the Risk capital guidelines as regards the precise stages in the evolution of risk capital measures which may be subsidised under the GBER, the types of beneficiaries and the regions of the Community concerned. This clarifi-cation does not intend to change the substance of the rules concerned. The amended provision now provides that 1) for SMEs located in assisted areas, as well as for small undertakings located in non-assisted areas, the risk capital measure shall be restricted to providing financing for seed capital, start-up capital and/or expansion capital. 2) For medium-sized undertakings located in non-assisted areas, the risk capital measure shall be restricted to providing financing for seed capital and/or start-up capital, to the exclusion of expansion capital.

65. The Commission's Competition services have received a number of questions relating to the issue whether articles 7.5 and 23.4 GBER allow the same beneficiary to receive several grants of

risk capital aid under the GBER. In the light of the provisions of the Risk capital guidelines, and more particularly section 5.1.(c) of these guidelines concerning so-called "follow-on investments," the same beneficiary may indeed receive several times risk capital under article 23 GBER, as long as all conditions of the GBER are fulfilled for each separate grant of aid. This would imply for instance, that a beneficiary located in an assisted region could receive under the GBER in a first period of 12 months "seed capital" up to an amount of 1 Million € from an investment fund, and in a subsequent period of 12 months, also receive "start-up capital" up to an amount of 1 Million €. This scenario would lead to a total amount of 2 Million € risk capital being granted under the benefit of the GBER. This approach is also in line with the cumulation provision contained in the Risk Capital guidelines.[83]

Notes
[83] See section 6 of Risk capital guidelines, cited above.

66. The risk capital-related definitions contained in article 22 of the GBER largely correspond to the definitions contained in point 20 of the risk capital guidelines. They have merely been clarified, shortened or simplified occasionally to the extent necessary for an inclusion into an act of binding legal nature.

3.6 R&D aid

67. The current SME BER, as amended by Commission Regulation 364/2004, covers R&D *project aid* (fundamental/industrial and pre-competitive research), as well as *aid for technical feasibility studies*, and aid for covering IPR costs. The provisions of this BER however do only apply to SMEs. The GBER proposes to extend the scope of both R&D project aid (article 25) and aid for technical feasibility studies (article 26) to *large enterprises*, under conditions identical to those provided in section 5 of the R&D&I framework 2006. This constitutes the third main extension of the scope of the GBER. This extension should allow for well targeted R&D aid to be granted more easily, in line with Lisbon objectives and the principle of "better targeted aid".

68. The provision with respect to aid for industrial property rights costs for SMEs (article 27) is identical with the provisions in R&D BER 364/2004 and the R&D&I framework.

69. A *simplified notification ceiling* has been introduced with respect to aid for industrial property rights costs for SMEs.[84] With respect to the two other types of R&D aid contained in the GBER, the notification ceilings already decided in the context of the R&D&I framework have been used for reasons of consistency.[85]

Notes
[84] Article 6.1. (e) of the GBER.
[85] See point 7.1 of the R&D&I framework.

70. Moreover, in line with the provisions of the R&D&I Framework,[86] a specific provision has been included allowing for R&D aid in the agricultural sector. As explained in recital 46 of the GBER, if the specific conditions of article 28 of the GBER are not fulfilled, the aid measure concerned may still be exempted if it fulfils the conditions set out in the general provisions (articles 25 and 26).

Notes
[86] See section 9 of the R&D&I Framework.

71. It should be noted that the revised draft GBER has been aligned, more clearly than its predecessor, to the R&D&I Framework, in that the definition of "experimental development" has been harmonised with the one set out in point 2.2.(g) of the R&D&I Framework.

72. Finally, it should be highlighted that, in a similar fashion to the Community framework for State aid for research and development and innovation,[87] the GBER should be applied in accordance with provisions of the EC Treaty other than Articles 87 and 88 of that Treaty. Indeed, according to the case-law of the ECJ, it results from the general scheme of the Treaty that a state aid procedure must never produce a result which is contrary to the specific provisions of the Treaty.[88] More particularly, according to general Treaty principles, State aid cannot be considered compatible

in the meaning of [Article 87(3)] of the Treaty if the aid measure at stake is discriminatory to an extent not justified by its State aid character. With regard to R&D&I, the Commission has announced in the R&D&I Framework[89] that it will not approve an aid measure which excludes the possibility of exploitation of R&D&I results in other Member States. Similarly, the draft GBER should be interpreted as not covering aid measures containing such limitations. In particular, requirements that all aspects of a subsidised R&D project would have to be realised within the geographical territory of the granting authority are incompatible with internal market rules.[90] However, some requirements as regards the domiciliation of beneficiaries may be compatible with internal market rules in the context of the assessment of a state aid case: the Member State concerned may indeed require that the beneficiary would have, at the moment of granting the aid, economic activity realised in the territory of the granting authority. Such economic activity may be evidenced by the presence of a branch, site or agency of the beneficiary, without going as far as requiring a registered office in the territory concerned.[91]

Notes

[87] See more particularly point 2.1 of this Framework, available at http://eurlex.europa.eu/LexUriServ/site/en/oj/2006/c_323/c_32320061230en00010026.pdf.
[88] See, amongst others, Judgment of the ECJ of 15 June 1993, *Matra/Commission*, C-225/91, ECR, p. I-3203, point 41.
[89] See section 2.1 of the R&D&I Framework.
[90] See, in this sense, judgment of the ECJ of 10 March 2005, C-39/04, not yet reported.
[91] See, for instance, decision of the Commission of 26/10/2006, N625/06 Italia (*Piemonte*), available at http://ec.europa.eu/community_law/state_aids/comp-2006/n625-06.pdf

3.7 Training aid

73. The Report from the Commission on the application of the Council Regulation (EC) No 994/98[92] pointed to a number of concerns relating to the implementation of training BER 68/2001. As a consequence and in order to clarify and facilitate the calculation of the eligible costs, article 29.4 (f) of the GBER now includes a *new category of "general indirect costs". It should be noted that this additional category does not imply abolishing the pre-existing category of current expenses directly linked to the training project, which is maintained in article 30.4.c).* It rather creates additional flexibility for Member States, whilst ensuring that no abuse is made of the new category of indirect costs by capping the amount of costs that can be included under this point.

Notes

[92] Report from the Commission to the Council and the European Parliament - Evaluation report on the application of the Council Regulation (EC) No 994/98 of 7 May 1998 regarding the application of Articles 87 (ex-Article 92) and 88 (ex-Article 93) of the EC Treaty to certain categories of horizontal State aid, pursuant to Article 5 of this Regulation, COM/2006/0831 final, points 3.2, available at http://eurlex. europa.eu/LexUriServ/LexUriServ.do?uri=CELEX:52006DC0831:EN:NOT.

74. Furthermore, the definitions of *general and specific training* (article 29) have been amended in order to ensure that the two categories would fully complement each other: the same criteria are now used – in the negative and positive respectively – for the two categories so as to ensure that any training activity can be considered either as general or as specific in nature.
75. Moreover, the maximal *aid intensity for general training aid* has, in view of the extent of the market failure affecting this type of projects, been increased to 60 %. In view of the different bonuses which may be added up to this basic aid intensity, a cap has been introduced at 80%, to ensure a minimal participation of the beneficiary in the project costs. Finally, the Commission proposes to increase the *notification ceiling of individual aid measures to 2 million €* (article 6.1.f).
76. Finally, some stakeholders have suggested inserting some specific provisions regarding the training of disabled workers in article 30 GBER. In this respect it has to be highlighted that a training aid measure covering some specific costs related to disabled workers may include those costs within the category of current expenses directly related to the training project mentioned in article 23.4.(c). Alternatively, the aid measure could be exempted from notification because it is

based on the double basis of articles 30 and 33 of the GBER, which can be cumulated within the conditions outlined in article 7 GBER.

3.8 Aid to disadvantaged and disabled persons

77. The main change between the section on aid to disadvantaged and disabled persons (articles 31 to 33 of the GBER) and employment BER 2204/2002 relates to the fact that the aid measures contained in article 4 of that BER are not included in the GBER: in practice, the provision relating to *job creation aid* was largely overlapping with the possibilities provided under SME investment & employment aid and regional investment & employment aid.[93] Indeed, both of these provisions allow calculating the eligible costs on the basis of the wage costs of the employment created by the investment. By merging the categories of investment and employment aid, the legibility of the GBER is seriously improved.

Notes
[93] Articles 11 and 12 of the GBER.

78. The existing employment BER provides for aid for the recruitment of disabled and disadvantaged persons (article 5). The precise *duration of the period during which the wage costs of the workers concerned could be subsidised* under the BER was not always considered very clear. Therefore this provision has been clarified and subdivided into two separate parts: one part concerns aid for the recruitment of disadvantaged workers and allows for aid only for one year period (article 31), whereas the other part allows for aid for the employment of disabled persons for an unlimited period (article 32). Thereby clarity is created as regards the precise scope of both new provisions. The latter provision should also allow Member States to incentivise companies to hire disabled persons.

79. Moreover, the *definition of "disadvantaged" worker* has been largely simplified in article 2 (16) of the GBER, as compared to the lists of disadvantaged workers currently included in article 2 (g) of BER 68/2001 and article 2 (f) of BER 2204/2002. It is should be noted in this respect that although no longer explicitly mentioned in the GBER, several categories of "disadvantaged" workers - like unemployed persons younger than 25 years or addicts – which were mentioned explicitly in Regulation 2204/2002 are likely to be included in the larger categories created under the GBER. More particularly, the new category of "persons who have not been in regular paid employment for the previous six months" (article 2.16(a) GBER) is likely to encompass all previous detailed categories, including, amongst others: young people who have not obtained a first employment (article 2.f.i of Regulation 2204/2002); migrant workers and members of an ethnic minority without a job (article 2(.f)(ii) and 2(f)(.iii) of Regulation 2204/2002); . . . .

80. As regards the *definition of "disabled" worker*, the revised draft GBER comes back to the traditional definition currently found in the existing BERs. The condition contained in the first draft GBER that a competent authority of a Member State should determine the precise level of disability as compared with the particular job position at stake, has been abandoned. Similarly, the definition of "sheltered employment" in article 2. 19 of the revised GBER is now in line with the definition of this concept in article 2.(h) of Regulation 2204/2002.

81. Finally, with respect to aid for the recruitment of disadvantaged workers and the employment of disabled workers, a number of stakeholders have argued that the requirement of a minimal recruitment period of 12 months was counter-productive and occasionally blocked access to the labour market for the workers concerned. Therefore, this condition has been made more flexible, allowing Member States to reduce it to the minimum employment period at national level (articles 31.5 and 32.5).

4 Transitional provisions

82. Article 35 GBER contains a number of transitional provisions which are largely inspired by the transitional provisions of de minimis Regulation 1998/2006.

83. The first paragraph (35.1) provides the possibility of invoking the benefit of the GBER as regards (illegal) individual aid granted – on the basis of an aid scheme or on an ad hoc basis[94] – before its entry into force. As it was not possible, before the entry into force of the GBER, to obtain an

ID number as provided in article 9 of the GBER, that condition is waived for aid granted before the entry into force of the Regulation.

Notes

[94] The restrictions applying in the context of the GBER to aid granted on an ad hoc basis, as foreseen amongst others in article 1.5 GBER, will have to be taken into account in this respect.

---

84. The second paragraph (35.2), as amended in the revised GBER, provides that there will be an overlapping period between that date of entry into force of the Regulation (presumed to be 1/7/2008) and 31/12/2008, during which Member States will have the choice of applying to a given aid measure either the provisions of one of the existing BERs (e.g. SME BER 70/2001) or the provisions of the GBER. The choice implies however that either *all* conditions of the existing BERs are respected (including the lower notification ceilings and aid intensities) or *all* conditions of the GBER. This overlapping period is a consequence of the fact that article 4.2 of the Enabling Regulation includes an obligation for a so-called "adjustment period" in order to allow Member States to adapt their administrative practices to the new requirements.

5 Appropriate measures to accompany the GBER

85. A BER defines the conditions under which aid measures may be put into effect without the need for prior notification to the Commission. The adoption of the GBER, coinciding with the repeal of the existing BERs (see article 34 GBER) implies that the *schemes covered by the existing BERs* can no longer be validly implemented under those instruments as from the end of the transition period.[95] The adoption of the GBER does not however create ipso facto any obligation for Member States to amend *existing aid schemes not covered by existing BERs*, even if these schemes fulfil objectives identical or similar to those pursued by the BER.[96] More particularly, aid schemes which have been individually approved in a Commission decision, following notification by the Member State concerned, remain unaffected by the adoption of the GBER. If the Commission considered it necessary that Member States should amend these existing aid schemes to bring them in line with the new GBER, it must bring forward a separate proposal for appropriate measures in accordance with Article 88(1) of the Treaty.

Notes

[95] See section 4 above.
[96] See Judgement of the Court of Justice of 14.4.2005, *Belgium v Commission*, C-110/03, especially at § 73.

---

86. Since Training BER no 68/2001, SME BER no 70/2001 and employment BER no 2204/2002 contained largely similar rules to those laid down in the pre-existing frameworks, the Commission did not consider it necessary, at the moment of adopting these BERs, to propose appropriate measures accompanying the adoption of these BERs. In contrast, the GBER will lead to a series of substantial changes, both regarding the general conditions imposed in chapter I (conditions on transparency contained in article 5 GBER, conditions on incentive effect contained in article 8 GBER, harmonised conditions applying to investment aid, contained in article 10 GBER. . .), as well as regarding specific substantive conditions imposed in chapter II to specific categories of aid (see, for instance, new rules for calculating the extra investment costs for environmental aid contained in articles 14 to 18 GBER).

87. For these reasons, the services of the Commission consider that the GBER may have to be accompanied by a separate Commission proposal for appropriate measures to require existing aid schemes – not covered by an existing BER - to be brought into line with the principles and conditions outlined in the GBER and amended accordingly where necessary, at a date to be fixed. The precise terms and scope of this proposal for appropriate measures will be presented to Member States and discussed at a later stage.

88. These appropriate measures are likely to address essentially existing aid schemes in support of training, employment and SMEs, to the exclusion of regional aid schemes and R&D aid schemes. Indeed, as regards regional aid, the conditions of the GBER are largely inspired by those of regional BER no 1628/2006, which is itself based on Commission's guidelines for regional

aid 2007–2013.[97] In this respect, the Commission proposed appropriate measures, in 2005, asking Member States to end all their existing regional aid schemes by the end of 2006 and to replace them with aid schemes which comply with the Commission's guidelines for regional aid 2007–2013.[98] The R&D measures covered by the GBER closely follow the provisions of the 2006 R&D&I framework. Since point 10.2 of this framework already contains proposals for appropriate measures to bring existing R&D aid schemes in line with the new rules, a further proposal for appropriate measures does not appear necessary in the context of the adoption of the GBER.

Notes

[97] OJ C 54, 04.03.2006, p. 13–45.

[98] This is in line with the fact that recital 51 GBER foresees that Member States will not, upon adoption of the GBER, need to review regional aid schemes which are exempted under the recently adopted BER no 1628/2006.

89. Finally, regarding environmental aid, it has already been pointed out above in section 3.3 of this memorandum, that the environmental provisions of the GBER will be carefully coordinated with the ongoing review of the environmental aid guidelines. The need for proposals for appropriate measures will be considered in the context of the guidelines.[99] The need for additional proposals of appropriate measures in the context of the adoption of the GBER will be examined in the light of the final version of the environmental guidelines.

Notes

[99] See currently point 6.2 of the draft Community guidelines for State aid for environmental protection dated 10.05.2007, that can be found at: http://ec.europa.eu/comm/competition/state_aid/reform/. [Note: the second draft of the Community guidelines for State aid for environmental protection was published on 5.10.2007 and is available at: http://ec.europa.eu/comm/competition/state_aid/reform/guidelines_environment_en_2.pdf]

6 Applicable legislative procedure and timeframe

90. The legislative procedure that the Commission needs to follow is outlined in article 8 of Enabling Regulation no 994/1998.

91. After its adoption by the College on 24/4/2007, the draft GBER has been sent to Member States in order to be discussed in a first Advisory Committee with Member States on 3& 4 July 2007.

92. The draft has subsequently been published in the Official Journal for the mandatory consultation of interested third parties provided for in the Enabling Regulation no 994/98. (OJ C 210 of 8/9/2007, p. 14[100]).

Notes

[100] lex.europa.eu/LexUriServ/site/en/oj/2007/c_210/c_21020070908en00140040.pdf

93. After having taken into account comments of interested stakeholders, the draft will be re-assessed within the Commission, before being re-discussed with Member States in a second Advisory Committee.

94. The adoption and publication of the final version of the regulation is scheduled for spring 2008, as the existing block exemptions expire on 30/6/2008.[101]

Notes

[101] See Commission Regulation (EC) No 1976/2006 of 20 December 2006 amending Regulations (EC) No 2204/2002, (EC) No 70/2001 and (EC) No 68/2001 as regards the extension of the periods of application.

Contact person:

Harold Nyssens
DG COMP A-3
Tel: 00 32 2 296 87 02
Harold.Nyssens@ec.europa.eu

Part G State Aids

ANNEX I

List of the recitals and provisions of the revised draft GBER as published in the Official Journal which have been amended since the first draft GBER published on the Commission website on 24/4/2007:

— Recitals: 4, 5, 8, 14, 17, 18 23, 24, 27, 30, 31, 37, 49, 50, 51
— Provisions: 1.1, 1.3(e), 2.9, 2.15, 2.16, 2.18, 2.19, 2.20, 2.26, 2.27, 3, 4.2, 5.1.(a), 5.3, 6.1.(a), 6.1.(e), 6.1.(h), 6.1.(i), 7.3, 7.5, 8.3, 9, 10.1, 10.2.(d), 10.4, 13.(i), 19.1, 22.(d), 22.(f), 23.4, 23.5, 24.(d), 31, 32.5, 35.1, 35.2.

G18

COMMUNITY GUIDELINES ON STATE AID FOR ENVIRONMENTAL PROTECTION

(2001/C 37/03)

Official Journal C 37, 3.2.2001, p. 3

Celex No: 32001Y0203(02)

Notes

On 5 October 2007 OG Competition published for consultation a secondary preliminary draft of new community guidelines for State aid for environmental protection. That draft is not reproduced in this volume. It is published on the Europa website at the following address: http://ec.europa.eu/comm/competition/state_aid/reform/guidelines_environment_en_2.pdf.

EEA application: for the corresponding EEA provision, see the EFTA Surveillance Authority's Procedural and Substantive Rules in the Field of State Aid (Guidelines on the application and interpretation of Articles 61 and 62 of the EEA Agreement and Article 1 of Protocol 3 to the Surveillance and Court Agreement), Part III, Chapter 15 (as amended by EFTA Surveillance Authority Decision No 152/01/COL of 23 May 2001 (OJ L 21, 24.1.2002, p. 32 and EEA Supplement No 6)).

Commentary
Guidelines: B&C: 15.003, 15.060 F&N: 16.114

A. INTRODUCTION

1. In 1994 the Commission adopted the Community guidelines on State aid for environmental protection,[1] which expired on 31 December 1999. In accordance with point 4.3 of the guidelines, it conducted a review in 1996 and concluded that there was no need to make any amendments in the meantime. On 22 December 1999 it decided to extend the validity of the guidelines until 30 June 2000.[2] On 28 June 2000 the Commission decided to extend the validity of the guidelines to 31 December 2000.[3]

Notes
[1] OJ C 72, 10.3.1994, p. 3.
[2] OJ C 14, 19.1.2000, p. 8.
[3] OJ C 184, 1.7.2000, p. 25.

---

2. Since the guidelines were adopted in 1994, action in the field of the environment has evolved at the initiative of the Member States and the Community and at world level, in particular following

the adoption of the Kyoto Protocol. Member States are granting State aid more frequently in the energy sector, for example, and the aid they provide is frequently in forms which have been rather uncommon until recently, such as tax reductions and exemptions. New forms of operating aid are also on the increase. The Commission ought therefore to adopt new guidelines, which will be needed in order to familiarise Member States and firms with the criteria that it will apply in deciding whether or not aid measures planned by the Member States are compatible with the common market.

3. Under Article 6 of the EC Treaty, environmental policy objectives must be integrated into the Commission's policy on aid controls in the environmental sector, in particular with a view to promoting sustainable development. Accordingly, competition policy and environmental policy are not mutually antagonistic, but the requirements of environmental protection need to be integrated into the definition and implementation of competition policy, in particular so as to promote sustainable development.[4]

Notes

[4] The Commission also set out its commitment to integrating environmental policy into other policy areas in its working paper of 26 May 1999 entitled "Integrating environmental aspects into all relevant policy areas" and in its report to the Helsinki European Council on integrating environmental concerns and sustainable development into Community policies (SEC(1999) 1941 final).

---

4. However, taking long-term environmental requirements into account does not mean that all aid must be authorised. Consideration has to be given to the effects the aid may have in terms of sustainable development and full application of the "polluter pays" principle. Some forms of aid certainly do satisfy these tests, particularly where they make it possible to achieve a high level of environmental protection while avoiding any conflict with the principle of the internalisation of costs. But other forms of aid, as well as having adverse effects on trade between Member States and on competition, may run counter to the "polluter pays" principle and may hinder the establishment of a process of sustainable development. This might be the case, for example, where aid is designed merely to facilitate compliance with new mandatory Community standards.

5. The Commission's approach in these guidelines therefore consists in determining whether, and under what conditions, State aid may be regarded as necessary to ensure environmental protection and sustainable development without having disproportionate effects on competition and economic growth. This analysis must be carried out in the light of the lessons that can be drawn from the functioning of the 1994 guidelines and in the light of the changes in environmental policy that have occurred since then.

B. Definitions and Scope

6. The concept of environmental protection: for the purposes of these guidelines, the Commission takes "environmental protection" to mean any action designed to remedy or prevent damage to our physical surroundings or natural resources, or to encourage the efficient use of these resources.

The Commission regards energy-saving measures and the use of renewable sources of energy as action to protect the environment. Energy-saving measures should be understood as meaning among other things action which enables companies to reduce the amount of energy used in their production cycle. The design and manufacture of machines or means of transport which can be operated with fewer natural resources are not covered by these guidelines. Action taken within plants or other production units with a view to improving safety or hygiene is important and may be eligible for certain types of aid, but it is not covered by these guidelines.

The concept of the internalisation of costs: in these guidelines the "internalisation of costs" means the principle that all costs associated with the protection of the environment should be included in firms' production costs.

The "polluter pays" principle: this is the principle that the costs of measures to deal with pollution should be borne by the polluter who causes the pollution.

Polluter: a polluter is someone who directly or indirectly damages the environment or who creates conditions leading to such damage.[5]

<u>Prices to reflect costs</u>: this principle states that the prices of goods or services should incorporate the external costs associated with the negative impact on the environment of their production and marketing.

<u>Community standard</u>: mandatory Community standard setting the levels to be attained in environmental terms and the obligation under Community law to use the best available techniques (BAT)[6] which do not entail excessive costs.

<u>Renewable energy sources</u>: renewable non-fossil energy sources, viz. wind energy, solar energy, geothermal energy, wave energy, tidal energy, hydroelectric installations with a capacity below 10 MW and biomass, where biomass is defined as products from agriculture and forestry, vegetable waste from agriculture, forestry and the food production industry, and untreated wood waste and cork waste.[7]

<u>Electric power generated from renewable energy sources</u>: electric power generated by plant using only renewable energy sources, and that share of electric power generated from renewable energy sources in hybrid plant using traditional energy sources, in particular for contingency purposes.[8]

<u>Environmental tax</u>: "One likely feature for a levy to be considered as environmental would be that the taxable base of the levy has a clear negative effect on the environment. However, a levy could also be regarded as environmental if it has a less clear, but nevertheless discernible positive environmental effect. [. . .] In general, it is up to the Member State to show the estimated environmental effect of the levy [. . .].".[9]

Notes

[5] Council Recommendation of 3 March 1975 regarding cost allocation and action by public authorities on environmental matters (OJ L 194, 25.7.1975, p. 1).

[6] The concept of best available techniques was introduced into Community legislation by Council Directive 76/464/EEC of 4 May 1976 on pollution caused by certain dangerous substances discharged into the aquatic environment of the Community (OJ L 129, 18.5.1976, p. 23) and appeared again, in slightly amended form, in Council Directive 84/360/EEC of 28 June 1984 on the combating of air pollution from industrial plants (OJ L 188, 16.7.1984, p. 20). Council Directive 96/61/EEC of 24 September 1996 concerning integrated pollution prevention and control (OJ L 257, 10.10.1996, p. 26; "the IPPC Directive") developed and confirmed this concept. The scope of the IPPC Directive covers industrial installations with a high pollution potential. The Directive has applied since November 1999 to new installations or existing installations which have undergone substantial changes. Existing installations must comply with the rules of the IPPC Directive by October 2007. Until that date the provisions of the two above-mentioned directives relating to the concept of BAT continue to apply. As a rule, the concrete standards — i.e. the emission or consumption limit values based on the use of the best available techniques — are not set by the Community but by the national authorities.

[7] This definition is contained in the Commission proposal for a Parliament and Council Directive on the promotion of electricity from renewable sources in the internal electricity market (OJ C 311 E, 31.10.2000, p. 320). Once the Directive has been adopted by Parliament and the Council, the Commission will apply the definition given in the final text.

[8] Same observation as for footnote 7.

[9] Environmental taxes and charges in the single market (COM(97) 9 final, 26.3.1997).

---

7. <u>Scope</u>: These guidelines apply to aid[10] to protect the environment in all sectors governed by the EC Treaty, including those subject to specific Community rules on State aid (steel processing,[11] shipbuilding, motor vehicles, synthetic fibres, transport, and fisheries), but excluding the field covered by the Community guidelines for State aid in the agriculture sector.[12] These guidelines apply to fisheries and aquaculture, without prejudice to the application of the provisions set out in Council Regulation (EC) No 2792/99 of 17 December 1999 laying down the detailed rules and arrangements regarding Community structural assistance in the fisheries sector[13] and in the guidelines for examining State aid in the fisheries and aquaculture sector.[14] State aid for R&D in the environmental field is subject to the rules set out in the Community framework for State aid for research and development.[15] Similarly, the Commission considers that the characteristics of aid for environmental training activities do not justify such aid being treated separately, and it will therefore examine it in accordance with the provisions of Commission Regulation (EC) No 68/2001 of 12 January 2001 on the application of Articles 87 and 88 of the EC Treaty to training aid.[16]

By virtue of Article 3 of Commission Decision No 2496/96/ECSC of 18 December 1996 establishing Community rules for State aid to the steel industry,[17] aid for environmental protection in the steel industry will continue to be analysed in accordance with the Community guidelines on

State aid for environmental protection published in Official Journal C 72 of 10 March 1994 until the expiry of the ECSC Treaty.

These guidelines do not apply to stranded costs, which will be dealt with separately.[18] The Commission would point out that, by virtue of Commission Regulation (EC) No 69/2001 of 12 January 2001 on the application of Articles 87 and 88 of the EC Treaty to *de minimis*[19] aid, aid of not more than EUR 100,000 granted to a firm for a period of three years is not caught by Article 87. That Regulation does not, however, apply to agriculture, fisheries, and transport, nor to the sectors covered by the ECSC Treaty.

Notes

[10] The purpose of these guidelines is not to discuss the concept of State aid, which derives from Article 87(1) of the EC Treaty and from the case law of the Court of Justice and the Court of First Instance.

[11] Within the limits laid down in the second paragraph of point 7.

[12] OJ C 28, 1.2.2000, p. 2.

[13] OJ L 337, 30.12.1999, p. 10.

[14] The Commission would point out that these guidelines concern only environmental aid, without prejudice to the applicability of other provisions governing State aid, subject to the limitations of the rules on combinations of aid in point 74 below.

[15] OJ C 45, 17.2.1996, p. 5.

[16] OJ L 10, 13.1.2001, p. 20.

[17] OJ L 338, 28.12.1996, p. 42.

[18] Stranded costs are costs which firms must bear because of commitments they made and are no longer able to honour as a result of the liberalisation of the sector in question.

[19] OJ L 10, 13.1.2001, p. 30.

C. Policy for Controlling State Aid and Environmental Policy

8. During the 1970s and 1980s Community policy on the environment took an essentially corrective approach. The emphasis was on standards intended to reflect the main concerns of environmental policy.

9. The fifth action programme on the environment, entitled "Towards sustainability" and adopted in 1993,[20] represents something of a break with that approach. It emphasises the need to conduct a long-term policy with the aim of promoting sustainable development. The objective is to reconcile on a lasting basis the development of the European economy with the need to protect the environment. Community action must no longer be limited to reacting to environmental problems but, as explicitly provided for in Article 6 of the EC Treaty as amended by the Treaty of Amsterdam, environmental protection requirements must be integrated into the definition and implementation of all Community policies and activities, and must foster the active involvement of socioeconomic operators.

Notes

[20] OJ C 138, 17.5.1993, p. 1.

10. Article 174 of the Treaty also provides for Community policy to be based on the "polluter pays" principle. The costs associated with protecting the environment should be internalised by firms just like other production costs. In order to implement this policy, the Community will have to use a series of instruments: regulation, and in particular the adoption of standards, but also voluntary agreements or economic instruments.

11. In 1996 the Commission drew up a progress report on the fifth action programme on the environment. The report states that the programme's overall strategy and objectives are still valid. There can be no doubt that progress has been made in integrating environmental and sustainability aspects into the other Community policies. However, what has still not occurred is a genuine change in attitude on the part of all the interested parties: policymakers, firms and the general public. It is important to develop the concept of shared responsibility for the environment and to make the general public aware of the issues at stake.

12. In 1999 the Commission adopted a global assessment of the fifth action programme. The assessment noted that, although the programme raised awareness of the need for stakeholders, citizens

and decision-makers in other sectors to pursue environmental objectives actively, less progress had been made overall in changing economic trends and modes of conduct which were harmful to the environment.

13. The assessment also noted that "it is increasingly clear that damages to the environment have costs to society as a whole and, conversely, that environmental action can generate benefits in the form of economic growth, employment and competitiveness" and that "the effective application of the "polluter pays" principle and the full internalisation of environmental costs onto polluters remains a critical process".[21]

Notes

[21] Europe's environment: what directions for the future? The global assessment of the European Community programme of policy and action in relation to the environment and sustainable development, "Towards sustainability" (COM(1999) 543 final of 24.11.1999).

14. The Commission's policy on the control of State aid for environmental purposes therefore needs to satisfy a double imperative:
    (a) to ensure the competitive functioning of markets, while promoting the completion of the single market and increased competitiveness in firms;
    (b) to ensure that the requirements of environmental protection are integrated into the definition and implementation of competition policy, in particular in order to promote sustainable development. The Commission here believes that internalisation of costs is a priority objective that can be achieved in various ways, including by way of instruments based on market laws or those based on a regulatory approach, these being the most effective tools for achieving the objectives described above.

15. Cost internalisation helps to ensure that prices accurately reflect costs in so far as economic operators allocate their financial resources on the basis of the prices of the goods and services they wish to buy. The progress report on the fifth programme emphasises that this aim has not been realised because prices do not reflect ecological costs. This in turn makes it more difficult to raise public awareness and promotes overexploitation of natural resources.

16. Ensuring that prices reflect costs at all stages of the economic process is the best way of making all parties aware of the cost of protecting the environment. Apart from its potentially adverse effects on trade and competition, State aid generally undermines that aim because it enables certain firms to reduce costs artificially and not to reveal the costs of environmental protection to consumers. In the long term, therefore, some forms of State aid run counter to the objectives of sustainable development.

17. The Community guidelines on State aid adopted by the Commission in 1994 form an integral part of this Community policy. In general, the "polluter pays" principle and the need for firms to internalise the costs associated with protecting the environment would appear to militate against the granting of State aid.

18. Nevertheless, the guidelines state that aid can be justified in two instances:
    (a) in certain specific circumstances in which it is not yet possible for all costs to be internalised by firms and the aid can therefore represent a **temporary second-best solution** by encouraging firms to adapt to standards;
    (b) the aid may also act as an **incentive** to firms to improve on standards or to undertake further investment designed to reduce pollution from their plants.

19. In the Community guidelines adopted in 1994, the Commission took the view that, in certain cases, total cost internalisation was not yet possible and that aid might be necessary on a temporary basis. The following changes have nevertheless taken place since 1994:
    (a) since the adoption of the fifth action programme on the environment, which was already based on the "polluter pays" principle and cost internalisation, firms have had seven years in which to adapt to the gradual application of the principle;
    (b) the Commission's 1996 progress report on the fifth action programme and the 1999 evaluation report restate the need to provide for cost internalisation and to use market instruments in order to make significant progress in improving the environment;
    (c) the use of market instruments and proper pricing is also advocated by the Kyoto Protocol on climate change.

20. The Commission's position is therefore that aid should no longer be used to make up for the absence of cost internalisation. If environmental requirements are to be taken into account in the long term, prices must accurately reflect costs and environmental protection costs must be fully internalised. Consequently, the Commission takes the view that aid is not justified in the case of investments designed merely to bring companies into line with new or existing Community technical standards. In its view, however, in order to address the special difficulties encountered by SMEs, it should be possible to grant them aid for adapting to new Community standards for a period of three years from the adoption of such standards. Aid may though be useful where it serves as an incentive to achieve levels of protection which are higher than those required by Community standards. This is the case when a Member State decides to adopt standards which are more stringent than the Community standards so as to achieve a higher level of environmental protection. It will also apply when a firm invests in environmental protection over and above the strictest existing Community standards or where no Community standards exist.

21. However, it has not been shown that aid has an incentive effect of this kind where it is designed merely to help firms to comply with existing or new Community technical standards. Such standards constitute the ordinary law with which firms must comply, and it is not necessary to provide them with aid in order to encourage them to obey the law.[22]

Notes
[22] With the exception of SMEs, as provided for in point 20.

Specific case of the energy sector and tax reductions

22. Since the guidelines were adopted in 1994, the energy sector has undergone major changes which need to be taken into consideration.

23. Certain Member States have adopted, are in the process of adopting or might consider adopting taxes the effects of which are conducive to environmental protection. In some cases, exemptions from or reductions in taxes are granted to firms in particular categories in order to avoid placing them in a difficult competitive situation. The Commission takes the view that such measures may constitute State aid within the meaning of Article 87 of the Treaty. However, the adverse effects of such aid can be offset by the positive effects of adopting taxes. Accordingly, if such exemptions are necessary to ensure the adoption or continued application of taxes applicable to all products, the Commission takes the view that they are acceptable, subject to certain conditions and for a limited period of time. This period may last for 10 years if the conditions are met. Thereafter, Member States will remain free to renotify the measures in question to the Commission, which could adopt the same approach in its analysis while taking into consideration the positive results obtained in environmental terms.

24. Member States have also taken action in recent years to promote the use of renewable sources of energy and combined heat and energy production, which has the encouragement of the Commission given the major advantages for the environment. The Commission therefore takes the view that, where measures to promote renewable sources of energy and the combined production of electric power and heat constitute State aid, they are acceptable subject to certain conditions. It must be certain, however, that such aid is not in breach of other provisions of the Treaty or secondary legislation.

D. Relative Importance of Environmental Aid

25. The data in the eighth survey on State aid in the European Union in the manufacturing and certain other sectors[23] show that between 1996 and 1998 environmental aid accounted on average for only 1,85% of total aid granted to the manufacturing and service sectors.

Notes
[23] COM(2000) 205 final, 11.4.2000.

26. In the period 1994–1999 environmental aid was provided predominantly in the form of grants. Proportionally speaking, little use was made of the other forms of aid: low-interest loans, State guarantees, etc.

27. As to the sectors receiving aid, the period 1998–1999 saw an increase in aid for measures in the energy sector, whether in support of energy saving or to promote the use of new or renewable sources of energy, especially in the form of ecotaxes.

E. General Conditions for Authorising Environmental Aid

E.1. Investment aid

E.1.1. *Transitional investment aid to help SMEs adapt to new Community standards*

28. For a period of three years from the adoption of new compulsory Community standards, investment aid to help SMEs meet new standards may be authorised up to a maximum of 15% gross of eligible costs.

E.1.2. *General conditions for authorising investment aid to firms improving on Community standards*

29. Investment aid enabling firms to improve on the Community standards applicable may be authorised up to not more than 30% gross of the eligible investment costs as defined in point 37. These conditions also apply to aid where firms undertake investment in the absence of mandatory Community standards or where they have to undertake investment in order to comply with national standards that are more stringent than the applicable Community standards.

E.1.3. *Investment in energy*

30. Investments in energy saving as defined in point 6 are deemed equivalent to investments to promote environmental protection. Such investments play a major role in achieving economically the Community objectives for the environment.[24] They are, therefore, eligible for investment aid at the basic rate of 40% of eligible costs.

Notes

[24] Action plan to improve energy efficiency in the European Community (COM(2000) 247 final, 26.4.2000).

---

31. Investments in the combined production of electric power and heat may also qualify under these guidelines if it can be shown that the measures beneficial in terms of the protection of the environment because the conversion efficiency[25] is particularly high, because the measures will allow energy consumption to be reduced or because the production process will be less damaging to the environment. In this connection, the Commission will take into particular consideration the type of primary energy used in the production process. It should also be borne in mind that increased energy use from combined production of heat and power is a Community priority for the environment.[26] Such investment may, therefore, be given aid at the basic rate of 40% of eligible cost.

Notes

[25] By "conversion efficiency" is meant the ratio between the quantity of primary energy used to produce a secondary form of energy and the quantity of secondary energy actually produced. It is calculated as follows: electric energy produced + thermal energy produced/energy used.

[26] Council Resolution of 18 December 1997 on a Community strategy to promote combined heat and power (OJ C 4, 8.1.1998, p. 1).

---

32. Investments to promote renewable sources of energy are deemed equivalent to environmental investments undertaken in the absence of mandatory Community standards. It should also be borne in mind that measures in support of renewable sources of energy are one of the Community's environmental priorities[27] and one of the long-term objectives that should be encouraged most. The rate of aid for investment in support of these forms of energy is therefore 40% of eligible costs.

The Commission takes the view that renewable energy installations serving all the needs of an entire community such as an island or residential area should also benefit. Investments made in this connection may qualify for a bonus of 10 percentage points on top of the basic rate of 40% of eligible costs.

The Commission considers that, where it can be shown to be necessary, Member States will be able to grant investment aid to support renewable energy, up to 100% of eligible costs. The installations concerned will not be entitled to receive any further support.

Notes

[27] Council Resolution of 8 June 1998 on renewable sources of energy (OJ C 198, 24.6.1998, p. 1).

E.1.4. *Bonus for firms located in assisted regions*

33. In regions which are eligible for national regional aid, firms may receive aid to promote regional development. To encourage them to invest further in the environment, it should be possible, where appropriate, to provide additional aid towards any environmental investment carried out in accordance with point 29.[28]

Notes

[28] These bonuses are not available where the Member State grants investment aid in accordance with the third paragraph of point 32 (aid of up to 100% of eligible costs).

34. Consequently, in regions eligible for regional aid, the maximum rate of environmental aid applicable to eligible costs as defined in point 37 below is determined as follows.

In assisted regions the maximum rate of aid applicable is the higher of the following two options:

(a) either the basic rate for environmental investment aid, i.e. 30 % gross (standard system), 40% gross (investments in energy saving, in renewable sources of energy or to promote the combined production of electric power and heat) or 50% gross (investments in renewable sources of energy that supply an entire community), plus 5 percentage points gross in the regions covered by Article 87(3)(c) and 10 percentage points in the regions covered by Article 87(3)(a);[29]

(b) or the regional aid rate plus 10 percentage points gross.

Notes

[29] Investments in assisted regions are eligible for investment aid if the conditions of the guidelines on regional State aid (OJ C 74, 10.3.1998, p. 9) are met.

E.1.5. *Bonus for SMEs*

35. Where investments of the kind referred to in points 29 to 32 are carried out by small or medium-sized enterprises, an increase of 10 percentage points gross may be authorised.[30] For the purposes of these guidelines, the definition of SMEs is that given by the relevant Community texts.[31]

The above bonuses for assisted regions and SMEs may be combined, but the maximum rate of environmental aid may never exceed 100% gross of the eligible costs. SMEs do not qualify for a double bonus either under the provisions applicable to regional aid or under those applicable in the environmental field.[32]

Notes

[30] This bonus is not available where the Member State grants investment aid in accordance with the third paragraph of point 32 (aid of up to 100% of eligible costs).

[31] Commission Recommendation 96/280/EC of 3 April 1996 concerning the definition of small and medium-sized enterprises (OJ L 107, 30.4.1996, p. 4).

[32] Investments by SMEs are eligible for investment aid under the provisions of Commission Regulation (EC) No 70/2001 of 12 January 2001 on the application of Articles 87 and 88 of the EC Treaty to State aid for small and medium-sized enterprises (OJ L 10, 13.1.2001, p. 33).

E.1.6. *The investments concerned*

36. The investments concerned are investments in land which are strictly necessary in order to meet environmental objectives, investments in buildings, plant and equipment intended to reduce or eliminate pollution and nuisances, and investments to adapt production methods with a view to protecting the environment.

Spending on technology transfer through the acquisition of operating licences or of patented and non-patented know-how may also qualify. But any such intangible asset must satisfy the following tests:

(a) it must be regarded as a depreciable asset;

(b) it must be purchased on market terms, from a firm in which the acquirer has no power of direct or indirect control;

(c) it must be included in the assets of the firm, and remain in the establishment of the recipient of the aid and be used there for at least five years. This condition does not apply if these intangible assets are technically out of date. If it is sold during those five years, the yield from the sale must be deducted from the eligible costs and all or part of the amount of aid must, where appropriate, be reimbursed.

E.1.7. Eligible costs

37. Eligible costs must be confined strictly to the extra investment costs necessary to meet the environmental objectives.

This has the following consequences: where the cost of investment in environmental protection cannot be easily identified in the total cost, the Commission will take account of objective and transparent methods of calculation, e.g. the cost of a technically comparable investment that does not though provide the same degree of environmental protection.

In all cases, eligible costs must be calculated net of the benefits accruing from any increase in capacity, cost savings engendered during the first five years of the life of the investment and additional ancillary production during that five-year period.[33]

For renewable energy, eligible investment costs are normally the extra costs borne by the firm compared with a conventional power plant with the same capacity in terms of the effective production of energy.

Where SMEs adapt to new Community standards, eligible costs include additional investments needed to attain the level of environmental protection required by those standards.

Where the firm is adapting to national standards adopted in the absence of Community standards, the eligible costs consist of the additional investment costs necessary to achieve the level of environmental protection required by the national standards.

Where the firm is adapting to national standards which are more stringent than the Community standards or undertakes a voluntary improvement on Community standards, the eligible costs consist of the additional investment costs necessary to achieve a level of environmental protection higher than the level required by the Community standards. The cost of investments needed to reach the level of protection required by the Community standards is not eligible.

Where no standards exist, eligible costs consist of the investment costs necessary to achieve a higher level of environmental protection than that which the firm or firms in question would achieve in the absence of any environmental aid.

Notes

[33] If the investments are concerned solely with environmental protection without any other economic benefits, no additional reduction will be applied in determining the eligible costs.

E.1.8. Rehabilitation of polluted industrial sites

38. Interventions made by firms repairing environmental damage by rehabilitating polluted industrial sites may come within the scope of these guidelines.[34] The environmental damage concerned may be damage to the quality of the soil or of surface water or groundwater.[35]

Where the person responsible for the pollution is clearly identified, that person must finance the rehabilitation in accordance with the "polluter pays" principle, and no State aid may be given. By "person responsible for the pollution" is meant the person liable under the law applicable in each Member State, without prejudice to the adoption of Community rules in the matter.

Where the person responsible for the pollution is not identified or cannot be made to bear the cost, the person responsible for the work may receive aid.[36]

Aid for the rehabilitation of polluted industrial sites may amount to up to 100% of the eligible costs, plus 15% of the cost of the work. The eligible costs are equal to the cost of the work less the increase in the value of the land.

The total amount of aid may under no circumstances exceed the actual expenditure incurred by the firm.

Notes

[34] The Commission would point out that rehabilitation work carried out by public authorities is not as such caught by Article 87 of the Treaty. Problems of State aid may, however, arise if the land is sold after rehabilitation at a price below its market value.

[35] All expenditure incurred by a firm in rehabilitating its site, whether or not such expenditure can be shown as a fixed asset on its balance sheet, ranks as eligible investment in the case of the rehabilitation of polluted sites.

[36] The person responsible for performing the work need not necessarily be the person responsible for the pollution in the meaning in which that expression is used here.

E.1.9. Relocation of firms

39. The Commission takes the view that as a rule the relocation of firms to new sites does not constitute environmental protection and does not therefore give entitlement to aid under these guidelines.

The granting of aid may, however, be justified when a firm established in an urban area or in a Natura 2000 designated area lawfully carries on an activity that creates major pollution and must, on account of this location, move from its place of establishment to a more suitable area.

All the following criteria must be satisfied at the same time:

(a) The change of location must be dictated on environmental protection grounds and must have been ordered by administrative or judicial decision.

(b) The firm must comply with the strictest environmental standards applicable in the new region where it is located.

A firm satisfying the above conditions may receive investment aid in accordance with point 29. The provisions of point 35 concerning the granting of a bonus for SMEs will apply.

In order to determine the amount of eligible costs in the case of relocation aid, the Commission will take into account the yield from the sale or renting of the plant or land abandoned, the compensation paid in the event of expropriation and the costs connected with the purchase of land or the construction or purchase of new plant of the same capacity as the plant abandoned. Account may also be taken of any other gains connected with the transfer of the plant, notably gains resulting from an improvement, on the occasion of the transfer, in the technology used and accounting gains associated with better use of the plant. Investments relating to any capacity increase may not be taken into consideration in calculating the eligible costs conferring entitlement to the granting of environmental aid.

If the administrative or judicial decision ordering the change of location results in the early termination of a contract for the renting of land or buildings, any penalties imposed on the firm for having terminated the contract may be taken into consideration in calculating the eligible costs.

E.1.10. Common rules

40. Aid for investment to improve on Community standards or undertaken where no Community standards exist may not be granted where such improvements merely bring companies into line with Community standards already adopted but not yet in force. A firm may be given aid to enable it to comply with national standards which are more stringent than Community standards or where no Community standards exist only if it complies with the national standards by the final date laid down in the relevant national measures. Investments carried out after that date do not qualify.[37]

Notes

[37] The rules set out in this point are without prejudice to point 28 concerning aid for SMEs.

Part G State Aids

E.2. Aid to SMEs for advisory/consultancy services in the environmental field

41. Advisory/consultancy services play an important part in helping SMEs to make progress in environmental protection. The Commission therefore takes the view that aid may be granted under the provisions of Regulation (EC) No 70/200138.[38]

Notes
[38] Reference given in footnote 32.

E.3. Operating aid
E.3.1. *Rules applicable to all operating aid to promote waste management and energy saving*

42. The following rules apply to two types of operating aid, namely:
    (a) aid for the management of waste where such management is in line with the hierarchical classification of the principles of waste management;[39]
    (b) aid in the energy-saving field.

Notes
[39] Classification given in the Community strategy for waste management (COM(96) 399 final of 30.7.1996). In this communication, the Commission recalls that waste management is a priority objective for the Community in order to reduce the risks to the environment. The concept of waste treatment must be looked at from three angles: re-utilisation, recycling and recovery. Waste whose production is unavoidable must be treated and eliminated without danger.

43. Where such aid is shown to be absolutely necessary, it should be strictly limited to compensating for extra production costs by comparison with the market prices of the relevant products or services.[40] Such aid must also be temporary and, as a general rule, must be wound down over time, so as to provide an incentive for prices to reflect costs reasonably rapidly.

Notes
[40] The concept of production costs must be understood as being net of any aid but inclusive of a normal level of profit.

44. The Commission takes the view that firms should normally bear the costs of treating industrial waste in accordance with the "polluter pays" principle. However, operating aid may be necessary where national standards are introduced which are more stringent than the applicable Community rules, or where national standards are introduced in the absence of Community rules, so that firms temporarily lose competitiveness at international level.
    Firms receiving operating aid towards the treatment of industrial or non-industrial waste must finance the service provided in proportion to the amount of waste they produce and/or the cost of treatment.
45. All such operating aid is subject to a limited duration of five years where the aid is "degressive". Its intensity may amount to 100% of the extra costs in the first year but must have fallen in a linear fashion to zero by the end of the fifth year.
46. In the case of "non-degressive" aid, its duration is limited to five years and its intensity must not exceed 50% of the extra costs.

E.3.2. *Rules applicable to all operating aid in the form of tax reductions or exemptions*

47. When adopting taxes that are to be levied on certain activities for reasons of environmental protection, Member States may deem it necessary to make provision for temporary exemptions for certain firms notably because of the absence of harmonisation at European level or because of the temporary risks of a loss of international competitiveness. In general, such exemptions constitute operating aid caught by Article 87 of the EC Treaty. In analysing these measures, it has to be ascertained among other things whether the tax is to be levied as the result of a Community decision or an autonomous decision on the part of a Member State.
48. If the tax is to be levied as the result of an autonomous decision on the part of a Member State, the firms affected may have some difficulty in adapting rapidly to the new tax burden. In such circumstances there may be justification for a temporary exemption enabling certain firms to adapt to the new situation.

49. If the tax is to be levied as the result of a Community directive, there are two possible scenarios:
    (a) a Member State applies tax to certain products at a rate higher than the minimum rate laid down in the Community directive and grants an exemption to certain firms, which, as a result, pay tax at a rate which is lower but nevertheless at least equal to the minimum rate set by the directive. The Commission takes the view that, in those circumstances, a temporary exemption may be justified to enable firms to adapt to higher taxation and to provide them with an incentive to act in a more environmentally friendly manner;
    (b) a Member State applies tax to certain products at the minimum rate laid down in the Community directive and grants an exemption to certain firms, which are thus subject to taxation at a rate below the minimum rate. If such an exemption is not authorised by the directive in question, it will constitute aid which is incompatible with Article 87 of the Treaty. If it is authorised by the directive, the Commission may take the view that it is compatible with Article 87 in so far as it is necessary and is not disproportionate in the light of the Community objectives pursued. The Commission will be specially concerned to ensure that any such exemption is strictly limited in time.

50. In general, the tax measures in question should make a significant contribution to protecting the environment. Care should be taken to ensure that the exemptions do not, by their very nature, undermine the general objectives pursued.

51. These exemptions can constitute operating aid which may be authorised on the following conditions:
    1. When, for environmental reasons, a Member State introduces **a new tax** in a sector of activity or on products in respect of which no Community tax harmonisation has been carried out or when the tax envisaged by the Member State exceeds that laid down by Community legislation, the Commission takes the view that exemption decisions covering a 10-year period with no degressivity may be justified in two cases:
        (a) these exemptions are conditional on the conclusion of agreements between the Member State concerned and the recipient firms whereby the firms or associations of firms undertake to achieve environmental protection objectives during the period for which the exemptions apply or when firms conclude voluntary agreements which have the same effect. Such agreements or undertakings may relate, among other things, to a reduction in energy consumption, a reduction in emissions or any other environmental measure. The substance of the agreements must be negotiated by each Member State and will be assessed by the Commission when the aid projects are notified to it. Member States must ensure strict monitoring of the commitments entered into by the firms or associations of firms. The agreements concluded between a Member State and the firms concerned must stipulate the penalty arrangements applicable if the commitments are not met.

        These provisions also apply where a Member State makes a tax reduction subject to conditions that have the same effect as the agreements or commitments referred to above;
        (b) these exemptions need not be conditional on the conclusion of agreements between the Member State concerned and the recipient firms if the following alternative conditions are satisfied:
            — where the reduction concerns a Community tax, the amount effectively paid by the firms after the reduction must remain higher than the Community minimum in order to provide the firms with an incentive to improve environmental protection,
            — where the reduction concerns a domestic tax imposed in the absence of a Community tax, the firms eligible for the reduction must nevertheless pay a significant proportion of the national tax.
    2. The provisions in point 51.1 may be applied to existing taxes if the following two conditions are satisfied at the same time:
        (a) the tax in question must have an appreciable positive impact in terms of environmental protection;
        (b) the derogations for the firms concerned must have been decided on when the tax was adopted or must have become necessary as a result of a significant change in economic conditions that placed the firms in a particularly difficult competitive situation. In the

latter instance, the amount of the reduction may not exceed the increase in costs resulting from the change in economic conditions. Once there is no longer any increase in costs, the reduction must no longer apply.

3. Member States may also encourage the development of processes for producing electric power from conventional energy sources such as gas that have an energy efficiency very much higher than the energy efficiency obtained with conventional production processes. In such cases, given the importance of such techniques for environmental protection and provided that the primary energy used reduces significantly the negative effects in terms of environmental protection, the Commission takes the view that total exemptions from taxes may be justified for a period of five years where aid is non-degressive. Derogations for 10 years may also be granted in accordance with the conditions set out in points 51.1 and 51.2.

52. Where an existing tax is increased significantly and where the Member State concerned takes the view that derogations are needed for certain firms, the conditions set out in point 51.1 as regards new taxes are applicable by analogy.

53. When the reductions concern a tax that has not been harmonised at Community level and when the domestic tax is lower than or equal to the Community minimum, the Commission takes the view that long-term exemptions are not justified. In this case, any exemptions granted must satisfy the conditions laid down in points 45 and 46 and must, in any event, be covered by an express authorisation to derogate from the Community minimum.

In all cases of reduction of tax, the Member State may grant operating aid in accordance with points 45 and 46.

E.3.3. *Rules applicable to operating aid for renewable energy sources*

54. As regards the production of renewable energy, operating aid will usually be allowable under these guidelines.

55. The Commission takes the view that such aid qualifies for special treatment because of the difficulties these sources of energy have sometimes encountered in competing effectively with conventional sources. It must also be borne in mind that it is Community policy to encourage the development of these sources of energy, notably on environmental grounds. Aid may be necessary in particular where the technical processes available do not allow energy to be produced at unit costs comparable to those of conventional sources.

56. Operating aid may be justified here in order to cover the difference between the cost of producing energy from renewable energy sources and the market price of that energy. The form of such aid may vary depending on the kind of energy involved and the support mechanism worked out by the Member State. Moreover, when studying cases, the Commission will take account of the competitive position of each form of energy involved.

57. Member States may grant aid for renewable energy sources as follows:

E.3.3.1. *Option 1*

58. In the renewable energy field, unit investment costs are particularly high and generally account for a significant proportion of firms' costs and do not allow firms to charge competitive prices on the markets where they sell energy.

59. In order to take better account of this market-access barrier for renewable energies, Member States may grant aid to compensate for the difference between the production cost of renewable energy and the market price of the form of power concerned. Any operating aid may then be granted only for plant depreciation. Any further energy produced by the plant will not qualify for any assistance. However, the aid may also cover a fair return on capital if Member States can show that this is indispensable given the poor competitiveness of certain renewable energy sources.

In determining the amount of operating aid, account should also be taken of any investment aid granted to the firm in question in respect of the new plant.

When notifying aid schemes to the Commission, Member States must state the precise support mechanisms and in particular the methods of calculating the amount of aid. If the Commission authorises the scheme, the Member State must then apply those mechanisms and methods of calculation when it comes to granting aid to firms.

60. Unlike most other renewable sources of energy, biomass requires relatively less investment but brings higher operating costs. The Commission will, therefore, be amenable to operating aid exceeding the amount of investment where Member States can show that the aggregate costs borne by the firms after plant depreciation are still higher than the market prices of the energy.

E.3.3.2. *Option 2*

61. Member States may grant support for renewable energy sources by using market mechanisms such as green certificates or tenders. These systems allow all renewable energy producers to benefit indirectly from guaranteed demand for their energy, at a price above the market price for conventional power. The price of these green certificates is not fixed in advance but depends on supply and demand.

62. Where they constitute State aid, these systems may be authorised by the Commission if Member States can show that support is essential to ensure the viability of the renewable energy sources concerned, does not in the aggregate result in overcompensation for renewable energy and does not dissuade renewable energy producers from becoming more competitive. With a view to verifying that these criteria are met, the Commission intends to authorise these aid systems for a period of ten years, after which it will have to be assessed whether the support measure needs to be continued.

E.3.3.3. *Option 3*

63. Member States may grant operating aid to new plants producing renewable energy that will be calculated on the basis of the external costs avoided. These are the environmental costs that society would have to bear if the same quantity of energy were produced by a production plant operating with conventional forms of energy. They will be calculated on the basis of the difference between, on the one hand, the external costs produced and not paid by renewable energy producers and, on the other hand, the external costs produced and not paid by non-renewable energy producers. To carry out these calculations, the Member State will have to use a method of calculation that is internationally recognised and has been communicated to the Commission. It will have to provide among other things a reasoned and quantified comparative cost analysis, together with an assessment of competing energy producers' external costs, so as to demonstrate that the aid does genuinely compensate for external costs not covered.

At any event, the amount of the aid thus granted to the renewable energy producer must not exceed EUR 0,05 per kWh.

Furthermore, the amount of aid granted to producers that exceeds the amount of aid resulting from option 1 must be reinvested by the firms in renewable sources of energy. It will be taken into account by the Commission if this activity also qualifies for State aid.

64. If Option 3 is to remain consistent with the general rules on competition, the Commission must be certain that the aid does not give rise to any distortion of competition contrary to the common interest. In other words, it must be certain that the aid will result in an actual overall increase in the use of renewable energy sources at the expense of conventional energy sources, and not in a simple transfer of market shares between renewable energy sources. The following conditions will therefore have to be met:
    — aid granted under this option must form part of a scheme which treats firms in the renewable energy sector on an equal footing;
    — the scheme must provide for aid to be granted without discrimination as between firms producing the same renewable energy;
    — the scheme must be re-examined by the Commission every five years.

E.3.3.4. *Option 4*

65. Member States may still grant operating aid in accordance with the general rules governing such aid in points 45 and 46.

E.3.4. *Rules applicable to operating aid for the combined production of electric power and heat*

66. The Commission takes the view that operating aid for the combined production of electric power and heat may be justified provided that the conditions set out in point 31 are met. Such aid may be granted to firms distributing electric power and heat to the public where the costs of producing

such electric power or heat exceed its market price. In similar circumstances, operating aid may be granted in accordance with the rules in points 58 to 65. The decision as to whether the aid is essential will take account of the costs and revenue resulting from the production and sale of the electric power or heat.

67. Operating aid may be granted on the same conditions as for the industrial use of the combined production of electric power and heat where it can be shown that the production cost of one unit of energy using that technique exceeds the market price of one unit of conventional energy. The production cost may include the plant's normal return on capital, but any gains by the firm in terms of heat production must be deducted from production costs.

F. Policies, Measures and Instruments for Reducing Greenhouse Gases

68. The Kyoto Protocol, signed by the Member States and by the Community, provides that the parties undertake to limit or reduce greenhouse gas emissions during the period 2008–2012. For the Community as a whole, the target is to reduce greenhouse gas emissions by 8% of their 1990 level.

69. Member States and the Community, as parties to the Protocol, will have to achieve the greenhouse gas reductions by means of common and coordinated policies and measures,[41] including economic instruments, and also by means of the instruments established by the Kyoto Protocol itself, namely international emissions trading, joint implementation, and the clean development mechanism.

Notes

[41] For details of common and coordinated policies and measures see in particular "Preparing for Implementation of the Kyoto Protocol" (COM(1999) 230 of 19.5.1999).

---

70. In the absence of any Community provisions in this area and without prejudice to the Commission's right of initiative in proposing such provisions, it is for each Member State to formulate the policies, measures and instruments it wishes to adopt in order to comply with the targets set under the Kyoto Protocol.

71. The Commission takes the view that some of the means adopted by Member States to comply with the objectives of the Protocol could constitute State aid but it is still too early to lay down the conditions for authorising any such aid.

G. Basis of Exemption for all Projects Examined by the Commission

72. Subject to the limits and conditions set out in these guidelines, environmental aid will be authorised by the Commission pursuant to Article 87(3)(c) of the EC Treaty for "aid to facilitate the development of certain economic activities or of certain economic areas, where such aid does not adversely affect trading conditions to an extent contrary to the common interest".

73. Aid to promote the execution of important projects of common European interest which are an environmental priority and will often have beneficial effects beyond the frontiers of the Member State(s) concerned can be authorised under the exemption provided for in Article 87(3)(b) of the EC Treaty. However, the aid must be necessary for the project to proceed, and the project must be specific, well defined and qualitatively important and must make an exemplary and clearly identifiable contribution to the common European interest. When this exemption is applied, the Commission may authorise aid at higher rates than the limits laid down for aid authorised pursuant to Article 87(3)(c).

H. Overlapping Aid from Different Sources

74. The aid ceilings stipulated in these guidelines are applicable irrespective of whether the aid in question is financed wholly or in part from State resources or from Community resources. Aid authorised under these guidelines may not be combined with other forms of State aid within the meaning of Article 87(1) of the Treaty or with other forms of Community financing if such overlapping produces an aid intensity higher than that laid down in these guidelines.

In the case of aid serving different purposes and involving the same eligible costs, the most favourable aid ceiling will apply.

I. "Appropriate Measures" within the Meaning of Article 88(1) of the EC Treaty

75. Acting under Article 88(1) of the Treaty, the Commission will propose the following appropriate measures to the Member States in respect of their existing systems of aid.

76. In order to enable it to assess any substantial amounts of aid granted under authorised schemes and to decide whether such aid is compatible with the common market, the Commission will propose, as an appropriate measure under Article 88(1) of the Treaty, that Member States should notify it in advance of any individual case of investment aid granted under an authorised scheme where the eligible costs exceed EUR 25 million and where the aid exceeds the gross grant equivalent of EUR 5 million. Notification will be given by means of the form of which a model is shown in the Annex.

77. The Commission will also propose, as an appropriate measure under Article 88(1), that Member States should bring their existing environmental aid schemes into line with these guidelines before 1 January 2002.

78. The Commission will ask the Member States to confirm within one month of receipt of the proposed measures referred to in points 75 to 77 that they agree to the proposals. In the absence of any reply, the Commission will take it that the relevant Member State does not agree.

79. The Commission would point out that, with the exception of aid classed as *de minimis* aid under Regulation (EC) No 69/2001,[42] these guidelines do not affect the obligation incumbent on Member States under Article 88(3) of the Treaty to notify any aid schemes, any changes to those schemes and any individual aid granted to firms outside the framework of authorised schemes.

Notes
[42] OJ L 10, 13.1.2001, p. 30.

80. The Commission intends to ensure that any authorisation for a future scheme complies with these guidelines.

J. Application of the Guidelines

81. These guidelines will become applicable when they are published in the Official Journal of the European Communities. They will cease to be applicable on 31 December 2007. After consulting the Member States, the Commission may amend them before that date on the basis of important competition policy or environmental policy considerations or in order to take account of other Community policies or international commitments.

82. The Commission will apply these guidelines to all aid projects notified in respect of which it is called upon to take a decision after the guidelines are published in the Official Journal, even where the projects were notified prior to their publication.
    In the case of non-notified aid, the Commission will apply:
    (a) these guidelines if the aid was granted after their publication in the Official Journal of the European Communities;
    (b) the guidelines in force when aid is granted in all other cases.

K. Integration of Environmental Policy into Other State Aid Guidelines

83. Article 6 of the Treaty states that: "Environmental protection requirements must be integrated into the definition and implementation of the Community policies and activities referred to in Article 3, in particular with a view to promoting sustainable development."
    When the Commission adopts or revises other Community guidelines or frameworks on State aid, it will consider how those requirements can best be taken into account. It will also examine whether it would not be expedient to ask the Member States to provide an environmental impact study whenever they notify it of an important aid project, irrespective of the sector involved.

ANNEX

ADDITIONAL INFORMATION ORDINARILY TO BE SUPPLIED WHEN NOTIFYING STATE AID FOR ENVIRONMENTAL PURPOSES UNDER ARTICLE 88(3) OF THE TREATY

(Schemes, Cases of Aid Granted under an Approved Scheme, and One-off Aid Measures)

To be attached to the general questionnaire in Section A of Annex II to the Commission letter to Member States of 2 August 1995 on notifications and standardised annual reports:

1. Objectives.
   Detailed description of the objectives of the measure, and of the type of environmental protection it is intended to promote.
2. Description of the measure.
   Detailed description of the measure and of the recipients.
   Description of the total costs of the investments involved and of the eligible costs.
   If the measure in question has already been applied in the past, what environmental results have been obtained?
   If the measure is a new one, what environmental results are anticipated, and over what period?
   If the aid is to be granted towards an improvement on standards, what are the standards applicable, and in what way does the measure allow an appreciably higher level of environmental protection to be achieved?
   If the aid is to be granted in the absence of mandatory standards, please give a detailed description of the way.

G19

COMMUNICATION FROM THE COMMISSION

Community guidelines on State aid for rescuing and restructuring firms in difficulty

(2004/C 244/02)

Text with EEA relevance

Official Journal C 244, 1.10.2004, p. 2

Celex No: 52004XC1001(01)

EEA application: for the corresponding EEA provision, see the EFTA Surveillance Authority's Procedural and Substantive Rules in the Field of State Aid (Guidelines on the application and interpretation of Articles 61 and 62 of the EEA Agreement and Article 1 of Protocol 3 to the Surveillance and Court Agreement), Part III, Chapter 16 (as amended by EFTA Surveillance Authority Decision No 305/04/COL of 1 December 2004 (OJ L 97, 15.4.2005, p. 41))

Commentary
Guidelines: **B&C:** 15.061, 15.077 **F&N:** 16.157, 16.158, 16.172, 16.182, 16.190
points 9–141: **F&N:** 16.159
points 31–71: **F&N:** 16.174
points 32–54: **F&N:** 16.195
points 38–39: **B&C:** 15.063
points 43–44: **B&C:** 15.063
points 49–51: **F&N:** 16.194
points 52–54: **F&N:** 16.195
points 55–56: **B&C:** 15.063 **F&N:** 16.195
points 57–59: **F&N:** 16.196
points 60–67: **F&N:** 16.197
points 68–71: **F&N:** 16.198
points 72–73: **B&C:** 15.063
points 78–86: **F&N:** 16.199
points 87–98: **F&N:** 16.200
points 99–101: **F&N:** 16.201

---

1. INTRODUCTION

1. The Commission adopted its original Community Guidelines on State aid for rescuing and restructuring firms in difficulty[1] in 1994. In 1997, the Commission added specific rules for agriculture.[2] A new version of the guidelines was adopted in 1999[3] and will expire on 9 October 2004.

Notes
[1] OJ C 368, 23.12.1994, p. 12.
[2] OJ C 283, 19.9.1997, p. 2. See also the footnote relating to the heading of Chapter 5.
[3] OJ C 288, 9.10.1999, p. 2.

---

2. The Commission wishes through this version of the Guidelines, the text of which builds on previous versions, to make certain changes and clarifications prompted by a number of factors.

3. First, in the light of conclusions of the meetings of the European Councils of Stockholm on 23 and 24 March 2001 and of Barcelona on 15 and 16 March 2002, which called on Member States to continue to reduce State aid as a percentage of gross domestic product while redirecting it towards more horizontal objectives of common interest including cohesion objectives, closer scrutiny of the distortion created by allowing aid for rescue and restructuring operations seems warranted. This is also consistent with the conclusions of the European Council held in Lisbon on 23 and 24 March 2000 aimed at increasing the competitiveness of the European economy.

4. The exit of inefficient firms is a normal part of the operation of the market. It cannot be the norm that a company which gets into difficulties is rescued by the State. Aid for rescue and restructuring operations has given rise to some of the most controversial State aid cases in the past and is among the most distortive types of State aid. Hence, the general principle of the prohibition of State aid as laid down in the Treaty should remain the rule and derogation from that rule should be limited.

Commentary
point 4: B&C: 15.061

5. The "one time, last time" principle is further reinforced, to avoid the use of repeated rescue or restructuring aids to keep firms artificially alive.
6. The 1999 guidelines made a distinction between rescue aid and restructuring aid, whereby rescue aid was defined as temporary assistance to keep an ailing firm afloat for the time needed to work out a restructuring and/or a liquidation plan. In principle, restructuring measures financed through State aid could not be undertaken during this phase. However, such strict distinction between rescue and restructuring has given rise to difficulties. Firms in difficulty may already need to take certain urgent structural measures to halt or reduce a worsening of the financial situation in the rescue phase. These guidelines therefore widen the concept of "rescue aid" in order to allow the beneficiary to undertake urgent measures, even of a structural nature, such as an immediate closure of a branch or other form of abandonment of loss-making activities. Given the urgent character of such aids, the Member States should be given the opportunity to opt for a simplified procedure to obtain their approval.
7. As regards restructuring aids, building on the 1994 guidelines, the 1999 guidelines continued to require a substantial contribution from the beneficiary to the restructuring. Within this revision, it is appropriate to reaffirm with greater clarity the principle that this contribution must be real and free of aid. The beneficiary's contribution has a twofold purpose: on the one hand, it will demonstrate that the markets (owners, creditors) believe in the feasibility of the return to viability within a reasonable time period. On the other hand, it will ensure that restructuring aid is limited to the minimum required to restore viability while limiting distortion of competition. In this respect the Commission will also request compensatory measures to minimise the effect on competitors.
8. The provision of rescue or restructuring aid to firms in difficulty may only be regarded as legitimate subject to certain conditions. It may be justified, for instance, by social or regional policy considerations, by the need to take into account the beneficial role played by small and medium-sized enterprises (SMEs) in the economy or, exceptionally, by the desirability of maintaining a competitive market structure when the demise of firms could lead to a monopoly or to a tight oligopolistic situation. On the other hand, it would not be justified to keep a firm artificially alive in a sector with long-term structural overcapacity or when it can only survive as a result of repeated State interventions.

2. Definitions and Scope of the Guidelines and Links with Other Texts on State Aid

2.1. Meaning of "a firm in difficulty"

9. There is no Community definition of what constitutes "a firm in difficulty". However, for the purposes of these Guidelines, the Commission regards a firm as being in difficulty where it is unable, whether through its own resources or with the funds it is able to obtain from its owner/shareholders or creditors, to stem losses which, without outside intervention by the public authorities, will almost certainly condemn it to going out of business in the short or medium term.

Commentary
point 9: B&C: 15.061

10. In particular, a firm is, in principle and irrespective of its size, regarded as being in difficulty for the purposes of these Guidelines in the following circumstances:
    (a) in the case of a limited liability company,[1] where more than half of its registered capital has disappeared[2] and more than one quarter of that capital has been lost over the preceding 12 months;
    (b) in the case of a company where at least some members have unlimited liability for the debt of the company,[3] where more than half of its capital as shown in the company accounts has disappeared and more than one quarter of that capital has been lost over the preceding 12 months;
    (c) whatever the type of company concerned, where it fulfils the criteria under its domestic law for being the subject of collective insolvency proceedings.

Notes
[1] This refers in particular to the types of company mentioned in the first subparagraph of Article 1(1) of Council Directive 78/660/EEC (OJ L 222, 14.8.1978, p. 11) as last amended by Directive 2003/51/EC of the European Parliament and of the Council (OJ L 178, 17.7.2003, p. 16).
[2] By analogy with the provisions of Article 17 of Council Directive 77/91/EEC (OJ L 26, 30.1.1977, p. 1) as last amended by the 2003 Act of Accession.
[3] This refers in particular to the types of company mentioned in the second subparagraph of Article 1(1) of Council Directive 78/660/EEC.

Commentary
point 10: F&N: 16.172
point 10(a): F&N: 16.160
point 10(b): F&N: 16.160
point 10(c): F&N: 16.160

11. Even when none of the circumstances set out in point 10 are present, a firm may still be considered to be in difficulties, in particular where the usual signs of a firm being in difficulty are present, such as increasing losses, diminishing turnover, growing stock inventories, excess capacity, declining cash flow, mounting debt, rising interest charges and falling or nil net asset value. In acute cases the firm may already have become insolvent or may be the subject of collective insolvency proceedings brought under domestic law. In the latter case, these Guidelines apply to any aid granted in the context of such proceedings which leads to the firm's continuing in business. In any event, a firm in difficulty is eligible only where, demonstrably, it cannot recover through its own resources or with the funds it obtains from its owners/shareholders or from market sources.

Commentary
point 11: F&N: 16.161

12. For the purposes of these Guidelines, a newly created firm is not eligible for rescue or restructuring aid even if its initial financial position is insecure. This is the case, for instance, where a new firm emerges from the liquidation of a previous firm or merely takes over such firm's assets. A firm will in principle be considered as newly created for the first three years following the start of operations in the relevant field of activity. Only after that period will it become eligible for rescue or restructuring aid, provided that:
    (a) it qualifies as a firm in difficulty within the meaning of these Guidelines, and
    (b) it does not form part of a larger business group[1] except under the conditions laid down in point 13.

Notes
[1] To determine whether a company is independent or forms part of a group, the criteria laid down in Annex I to Commission Regulation (EC) No 68/2001 (OJ L 10, 13.1.2001, p. 20), as amended by Regulation (EC) No 363/2004 (OJ L 63, 28.2.2004, p. 20) will be taken into account.

Commentary
point 12: B&C: 15.063 F&N: 16.162

13. A firm belonging to or being taken over by a larger business group is not normally eligible for rescue or restructuring aid, except where it can be demonstrated that the firm's difficulties are

intrinsic and are not the result of an arbitrary allocation of costs within the group, and that the difficulties are too serious to be dealt with by the group itself. Where a firm in difficulty creates a subsidiary, the subsidiary, together with the firm in difficulty controlling it, will be regarded as a group and may receive aid under the conditions laid down in this point.

Commentary
point 13: F&N: 16.163

2.2. Definition of "rescue and restructuring aid"

14. Rescue aid and restructuring aid are covered by the same set of guidelines, because in both cases the public authorities are faced with a firm in difficulty and the rescue and restructuring are often two parts of a single operation, even if they involve different processes.
15. Rescue aid is by nature temporary and reversible assistance. Its primary objective is to make it possible to keep an ailing firm afloat for the time needed to work out a restructuring or liquidation plan. The general principle is that rescue aid makes it possible temporarily to support a company confronted with an important deterioration of its financial situation reflected by an acute liquidity crisis or technical insolvency. Such temporary support should allow time to analyse the circumstances which gave rise to the difficulties and to develop an appropriate plan to remedy those difficulties. Moreover, the rescue aid must be limited to the minimum necessary. In other words, rescue aid offers a short respite, not exceeding six months, to a firm in difficulty. The aid must consist of reversible liquidity support in the form of loan guarantees or loans, with an interest rate at least comparable to those observed for loans to healthy firms and in particular the reference rates adopted by the Commission. Structural measures which do not require immediate action, such as, the irremediable and automatic participation of the State in the own funds of the firm, cannot be financed through rescue aid.

Commentary
point 15: B&C: 15.062 F&N: 16.167, 16.169

16. Once a restructuring or liquidation plan for which aid has been requested has been established and is being implemented, all further aid will be considered as restructuring aid. Measures which need to be implemented immediately to stem losses, including structural measures (for example, immediate withdrawal from a loss-making field of activity), can be undertaken with the rescue aid, subject to the conditions mentioned in Section 3.1 for individual aids and section 4.3 for aid schemes. Except where use is made of the simplified procedure set out in section 3.1.2, a Member State will need to demonstrate that such structural measures must be undertaken immediately. Rescue aid cannot normally be granted for financial restructuring.

Commentary
point 16: B&C: 15.062 F&N: 16.176

17. Restructuring, on the other hand, will be based on a feasible, coherent and far-reaching plan to restore a firm's long-term viability. Restructuring usually involves one or more of the following elements: the reorganisation and rationalisation of the firm's activities on to a more efficient basis, typically involving the withdrawal from loss-making activities, the restructuring of those existing activities that can be made competitive again and, possibly, diversification in the direction of new and viable activities. Financial restructuring (capital injections, debt reduction) usually has to accompany the physical restructuring. Restructuring operations within the scope of these Guidelines cannot, however, be limited to financial aid designed to make good past losses without tackling the reasons for those losses.

Commentary
point 17: F&N: 16.175, 16.178

2.3. Scope

18. These Guidelines apply to firms in all sectors, except to those operating in the coal[1] or steel sector,[2] without prejudice to any specific rules relating to firms in difficulty in the sector concerned.[3] With the exception of point 79,[4] they apply to the fisheries and aquaculture sector, subject to compliance with the specific rules laid down in the Guidelines for the examination of State aid to fisheries and aquaculture.[5] Chapter 5 contains some additional rules for agriculture.

Notes

[1] Article 3 of Council Regulation (EC) No 1407/2002 (OJ L 205, 2.8.2002, p. 1), as amended by the 2003 Act of Accession.

[2] Point 19 of the Communication from the Commission concerning certain aspects of the treatment of competition cases resulting from the expiry of the ECSC Treaty (OJ C 152, 26.6.2002, p. 5). Point 1 of the communication from the Commission on rescue and restructuring aid and closure aid for the steel sector (OJ C 70, 19.3.2002, p. 21). Appropriate measures adopted in the context of the Multisectoral Framework on regional aid for large investment projects (OJ C 70, 19.3.2002, p. 8).

[3] Specific rules of this nature exist for the aviation sector (OJ C 350, 10.12.1994, p. 5).

[4] In other words, awards of aid to SMEs that do not fulfil the conditions set out in this point 0 may nevertheless be exempted from individual notification.

[5] OJ C 19, 20.1.2001, p. 7.

Commentary
point 18: F&N: 16.164

2.4. Compatibility with the common market

19. Article 87(2) and (3) of the Treaty provide for the possibility that aid falling within the scope of Article 87(1) will be regarded as compatible with the common market. Apart from cases of aid envisaged by Article 87(2), in particular aid to make good the damage caused by natural disasters or exceptional occurrences, which are not covered here, the only basis on which aid for firms in difficulty can be deemed compatible is Article 87(3)(c). Under that provision the Commission has the power to authorise "aid to facilitate the development of certain economic activities (. . .) where such aid does not adversely affect trading conditions to an extent contrary to the common interest." In particular, this could be the case where the aid is necessary to correct disparities caused by market failures or to ensure economic and social cohesion.

20. Given that its very existence is in danger, a firm in difficulty cannot be considered an appropriate vehicle for promoting other public policy objectives until such time as its viability is assured. Consequently, the Commission considers that aid to firms in difficulty may contribute to the development of economic activities without adversely affecting trade to an extent contrary to the Community interest only if the conditions set out in these Guidelines are met. Where the firms which are to receive rescue or restructuring aid are located in assisted areas, the Commission will take the regional considerations referred to in Article 87(3)(a) and (c) of the Treaty into account as described in points 55 and 56.

21. The Commission will pay particular attention to the need to prevent the use of these Guidelines to circumvent the principles laid down in existing frameworks and Guidelines.

22. The assessment of rescue or restructuring aid should not be affected by changes in the ownership of the business aided.

2.5. Recipients of previous unlawful aid

23. Where unlawful aid has previously been granted to the firm in difficulty, in respect of which the Commission has adopted a negative decision with a recovery order, and where no such recovery has taken place in compliance with Article 14 of Council Regulation (EC) No 659/1999 of 22 March 1999 laying down detailed rules for the application of Article [88] of the EC Treaty,[1] the assessment of any rescue and restructuring aid to be granted to the same undertaking shall take into account, first, the cumulative effect of the old aid and of the new aid and, secondly, the fact that the old aid has not been repaid.[2]

Notes
¹ OJ L 83, 27.3.1999, p. 1. Regulation as amended by the 2003 Act of Accession.
² Case C-355/95 P, *Textilwerke Deggendorf v Commission and others* [1997] ECR I-2549.

Commentary
point 23: F&N: 16.166

3. General Conditions for the Authorisation of Rescue and/or Restructuring Aid Notified Individually to the Commission

24. This Chapter deals exclusively with aid measures that are notified individually to the Commission. Under certain conditions, the Commission may authorise rescue or restructuring aid schemes: those conditions are set out in Chapter 4.

3.1. Rescue aid

3.1.1. Conditions

25. In order to be approved by the Commission, rescue aid as defined in point 15 must:
    (a) consist of liquidity support in the form of loan guarantees or loans;¹ in both cases, the loan must be granted at an interest rate at least comparable to those observed for loans to healthy firms, and in particular the reference rates adopted by the Commission; any loan must be reimbursed and any guarantee must come to an end within a period of not more than six months after the disbursement of the first instalment to the firm;
    (b) be warranted on the grounds of serious social difficulties and have no unduly adverse spillover effects on other Member States;
    (c) be accompanied, on notification, by an undertaking given by the Member State concerned to communicate to the Commission, not later than six months after the rescue aid measure has been authorised, a restructuring plan or a liquidation plan or proof that the loan has been reimbursed in full and/or that the guarantee has been terminated; in the case of non-notified aid the Member State must communicate, no later than six months after the first implementation of a rescue aid measure, a restructuring plan or a liquidation plan or proof that the loan has been reimbursed in full and /or that the guarantee has been terminated;
    (d) be restricted to the amount needed to keep the firm in business for the period during which the aid is authorised; such an amount may include aid for urgent structural measures in accordance with point 16; the amount necessary should be based on the liquidity needs of the company stemming from losses; in determining that amount regard will be had to the outcome of the application of the formula set out in the Annex; any rescue aid exceeding the result of that calculation will need to be duly explained;
    (e) respect the condition set out in section 3.3 (one time, last time).

Notes
¹ An exception may be made in the case of rescue aid in the banking sector, in order to enable the credit institution in question to continue temporarily carrying on its banking business in accordance with the prudential legislation in force (Directive 2000/12/EC of the European Parliament and of the Council, OJ L 126, 26.5.2000, p. 1). At any rate, aid granted in a form other than loan guarantees or loans fulfilling the conditions set out in point (a), should fulfil the general principles of rescue aid and cannot consist in structural financial measures related to the bank's own funds. Any aid granted in a form other than loan guarantees or loans fulfilling the conditions set out in point (a), will be taken into account when any compensatory measures under a restructuring plan are examined in accordance with points 38 to 42.

Commentary
point 25(a): F&N: 16.169
point 25(b): B&C: 15.062 F&N: 16.167
point 25(c): F&N: 16.170
point 25(d): F&N: 16.171

26. Where the Member State has submitted a restructuring plan within six months of the date of authorisation or, in the case of non-notified aid, of implementation of the measure, the deadline for reimbursing the loan or for putting an end to the guarantee is extended until the Commission reaches its decision on the plan, unless the Commission decides that such an extension is not justified.

Commentary
point 26: **F&N:** 16.170

27. Without prejudice to Article 23 of Regulation (EC) No 659/1999 and to the possibility of an action before the Court of Justice, in accordance with the second subparagraph of Article 88(2) of the Treaty, the Commission will initiate proceedings under Article 88(2) of the Treaty if the Member State fails to communicate:
    (a) a credible and substantiated restructuring plan or a liquidation plan, or
    (b) proof that the loan has been reimbursed in full and/or that the guarantee has been terminated before the six-month deadline has expired.
28. In any event, the Commission may decide to initiate such proceedings, without prejudice to Article 23 of Regulation (EC) No 659/1999 and to the possibility of an action before the Court of Justice in accordance with the second subparagraph of Article 88(2) of the Treaty, if it considers that the loan or the guarantee has been misused, or that, after the six-month deadline has expired, the failure to reimburse the aid is no longer justified.
29. The approval of rescue aid does not necessarily mean that aid under a restructuring plan will subsequently be approved; such aid will have to be assessed on its own merits.

3.1.2. Simplified procedure

30. The Commission will as far as possible endeavour to take a decision within a period of one month in respect of rescue aids fulfilling all conditions set out in section 3.1.1 and the following cumulative requirements:
    (a) the firm concerned satisfies at least one of the three criteria set out in point 10;
    (b) the rescue aid is limited to the amount resulting from the application of the formula set out in the Annex and does not exceed EUR 10 million.

Commentary
point 30: **B&C:** 15.062 **F&N:** 16.172

3.2. Restructuring aid

3.2.1. Basic principle

31. Aid for restructuring raises particular competition concerns as it can shift an unfair share of the burden of structural adjustment and the attendant social and economic problems onto other producers who are managing without aid, and to other Member States. The general principle should therefore be to allow the grant of restructuring aid only in circumstances in which it can be demonstrated that it does not run counter to the Community interest. This will only be possible if strict criteria are met, and if it is certain that any distortions of competition will be offset by the benefits flowing from the firm's survival (for instance, where it is clear that the net effect of redundancies resulting from the firm's going out of business, combined with the effects on its suppliers, would exacerbate employment problems or, exceptionally, where the firm's disappearance would result in a monopoly or tight oligopolistic situation) and that, in principle, there are adequate compensatory measures in favour of competitors.

Commentary
point 31: **B&C:** 15.062 **F&N:** 16.181

3.2.2. Conditions for the authorisation of aid

32. Subject to the special provisions for assisted areas, SMEs and the agricultural sector (see points 55, 56, 57, 59 and Chapter 5), the Commission will approve aid only under the following conditions:

Eligibility of the firm

33. The firm must qualify as a firm in difficulty within the meaning of these Guidelines (see points 9 to 13).

Restoration of long-term viability

34. The grant of the aid must be conditional on implementation of the restructuring plan which must be endorsed by the Commission in all cases of individual aid, except in the case of SMEs, as laid down in section 3.2.5.

35. The restructuring plan, the duration of which must be as short as possible, must restore the long-term viability of the firm within a reasonable timescale and on the basis of realistic assumptions as to future operating conditions. Restructuring aid must therefore be linked to a viable restructuring plan to which the Member State concerned commits itself. The plan must be submitted in all relevant detail to the Commission and include, in particular, a market survey. The improvement in viability must derive mainly from internal measures contained in the restructuring plan; it may be based on external factors such as variations in prices and demand over which the company has no great influence, but only if the market assumptions made are generally acknowledged. Restructuring must involve the abandonment of activities which would remain structurally loss-making even after restructuring.

Commentary
point 35: F&N: 16.179

36. The restructuring plan must describe the circumstances that led to the company's difficulties, thereby providing a basis for assessing whether the proposed measures are appropriate. It must take account, inter alia, of the present state of and future prospects for supply and demand on the relevant product market, with scenarios reflecting best-case, worst-case and intermediate assumptions and the firm's specific strengths and weaknesses. It must enable the firm to progress towards a new structure that offers it prospects for long-term viability and enables it to stand on its own feet.

37. The plan must provide for a turnaround that will enable the company, after completing its restructuring, to cover all its costs including depreciation and financial charges. The expected return on capital must be enough to enable the restructured firm to compete in the marketplace on its own merits. Where the firm's difficulties stem from flaws in its corporate governance system, appropriate adaptations will have to be introduced.

Commentary
point 37: F&N: 16.179

Avoidance of undue distortions of competition

38. In order to ensure that the adverse effects on trading conditions are minimized as much as possible, so that the positive effects pursued outweigh the adverse ones, compensatory measures must be taken. Otherwise, the aid will be regarded as "contrary to the common interest" and therefore incompatible with the common market. The Commission will have regard to the objective of restoring the long-term viability in determining the adequacy of the compensatory measures.

Commentary
point 38: F&N: 16.183

39. These measures may comprise divestment of assets, reductions in capacity or market presence and reduction of entry barriers on the markets concerned. When assessing whether the compensatory measures are appropriate the Commission will take account of the market structure and the conditions of competition to ensure that any such measure does not lead to a deterioration in the structure of the market, for example by having the indirect effect of creating a monopoly or a tight oligopolistic situation. If a Member State is able to prove that such a situation would arise, the compensatory measures should be construed in such a way to avoid this situation.

Commentary
point 39: F&N: 16.184, 16.185

40. The measures must be in proportion to the distortive effects of the aid and, in particular, to the size[1] and the relative importance of the firm on its market or markets. They should take place in particular in the market(s) where the firm will have a significant market position after restructuring. The degree of reduction must be established on a case-by-case basis. The Commission will determine the extent of the measures necessary on the basis of the market survey attached to the restructuring plan and, where appropriate on the basis of any other information at the disposal of the Commission including that supplied by interested parties. The reduction must be an integral part of the restructuring as laid down in the restructuring plan. This principle applies irrespective of whether the divestitures take place before or after the granting of the State aid, as long as they are part of the same restructuring. Write-offs and closure of loss-making activities which would at any rate be necessary to restore viability will not be considered reduction of capacity or market presence for the purpose of the assessment of the compensatory measures. Such an assessment will take account of any rescue aid granted beforehand.

Notes

[1] In this respect the Commission may also take into account whether the company in question is a medium-sized enterprise or a large one.

Commentary
point 40: F&N: 16.186

41. However, this condition will not normally apply to small enterprises, since it can be assumed that ad hoc aid to small enterprises does not normally distort competition to an extent contrary to the common interest, except where otherwise provided by rules on State aid in a particular sector or when the beneficiary is active in a market suffering from long-term overcapacity.
42. When the beneficiary is active in a market suffering from long-term structural overcapacity, as defined in the context of the Multisectoral framework on regional aid for large investments,[1] the reduction in the company's capacity or market presence may have to be as high as 100%.[2]

Notes

[1] OJ C 70, 19.3.2002, p. 8.
[2] In such cases, the Commission will only allow aid to alleviate the social costs of the restructuring, in line with section 3.2.6 and environmental aid to clean up polluted sites which might otherwise be abandoned.

Commentary
point 42: F&N: 16.184

Aid limited to the minimum: real contribution, free of aid

43. The amount and intensity of the aid must be limited to the strict minimum of the restructuring costs necessary to enable restructuring to be undertaken in the light of the existing financial resources of the company, its shareholders or the business group to which it belongs. Such assessment will take account of any rescue aid granted beforehand. Aid beneficiaries will be expected to make a significant contribution to the restructuring plan from their own resources, including the sale of assets that are not essential to the firm's survival, or from external financing at market conditions. Such contribution is a sign that the markets believe in the feasibility of the return to viability. Such contribution must be real, i.e., actual, excluding all future expected profits such as cash flow, and must be as high as possible.

Commentary
point 43: F&N: 16.188

44. The Commission will normally consider the following contributions[1] to the restructuring to be appropriate: at least 25% in the case of small enterprises, at least 40%, for medium-sized enterprises and at least 50% for large firms. In exceptional circumstances and in cases of particular hardship, which must be demonstrated by the Member State, the Commission may accept a lower contribution.

Commentary
point 44: F&N: 16.190

45. To limit the distortive effect, the amount of the aid or the form in which it is granted must be such as to avoid providing the company with surplus cash which could be used for aggressive, market-distorting activities not linked to the restructuring process. The Commission will accordingly examine the level of the firm's liabilities after restructuring, including the situation after any postponement or reduction of its debts, particularly in the context of its continuation in business following collective insolvency proceedings brought against it under national law.[1] None of the aid should go to finance new investment that is not essential for restoring the firm's viability.

Notes
[1] See point 10(c).

Specific conditions attached to the authorisation of aid

46. In addition to the compensatory measures described in points 38 to 42, the Commission may impose any conditions and obligations it considers necessary in order to ensure that the aid does not distort competition to an extent contrary to the common interest, in the event that the Member State concerned has not given a commitment that it will adopt such provisions. For example, it may require the Member State:
    (a) to take certain measures itself (for example, to open up certain markets directly or indirectly linked to the company's activities to other Community operators with due respect to Community law);
    (b) to impose certain obligations on the recipient firm;
    (c) to refrain from granting other types of aid to the recipient firm during the restructuring period.

Commentary
point 46: F&N: 16.192

Full implementation of restructuring plan and observance of conditions

47. The company must fully implement the restructuring plan and must discharge any other obligations laid down in the Commission decision authorising the aid. The Commission will regard any failure to implement the plan or to fulfil the other obligations as misuse of the aid, without prejudice to Article 23 of Regulation (EC) No 659/1999 and to the possibility of an action before the Court of Justice in accordance with the second subparagraph of Article 88(2) of the Treaty.

Commentary
point 47: F&N: 16.193

48. Where restructuring operations cover several years and involve substantial amounts of aid, the Commission may require payment of the restructuring aid to be split into instalments and may make payment of each instalment subject to:
    (i) confirmation, prior to each payment, of the satisfactory implementation of each stage in the restructuring plan, in accordance with the planned timetable; or
    (ii) its approval, prior to each payment, after verification that the plan is being satisfactorily implemented.

Commentary
point 48: F&N: 16.192

Monitoring and annual report

49. The Commission must be put in a position to make certain that the restructuring plan is being implemented properly, through regular detailed reports communicated by the Member State concerned.

50. In the case of aid to large firms, the first of these reports will normally have to be submitted to the Commission not later than six months after approval of the aid. Reports will subsequently have to be sent to the Commission at least once a year, at a fixed date, until the objectives of the restructuring plan can be deemed to have been achieved. They must contain all the information the Commission needs in order to be able to monitor the implementation of the restructuring programme, the timetable for payments to the company and its financial position and the observance of any conditions or obligations laid down in the decision approving the aid. They must in particular include all relevant information on any aid for any purpose which the company has received, either on an individual basis or under a general scheme, during the restructuring period (see points 68 to 71). Where the Commission needs prompt confirmation of certain key items of information, for example, on closures or capacity reductions, it may require more frequent reports.

51. In the case of aid to SMEs, transmission each year of a copy of the recipient firm's balance sheet and profit-and-loss account will normally be sufficient, except where stricter conditions have been laid down in the decision approving the aid.

3.2.3. Amendment of the restructuring plan

52. Where restructuring aid has been approved, the Member State concerned may, during the restructuring period, ask the Commission to agree to changes to the restructuring plan and the amount of the aid. The Commission may allow such changes where they meet the following conditions:
    (a) the revised plan must still show a return to viability within a reasonable time scale;
    (b) if the amount of the aid is increased, any requisite compensatory measures must be more extensive than those initially imposed;
    (c) if the proposed compensatory measures are smaller than those initially planned, the amount of the aid must be correspondingly reduced;
    (d) the new timetable for implementation of the compensatory measures may be delayed with respect to the timetable initially adopted only for reasons outside the company's or the Member State's control: if that is not the case, the amount of the aid must be correspondingly reduced.

53. If the conditions imposed by the Commission or the commitments given by the Member State are relaxed, the amount of aid must be correspondingly reduced or other conditions may be imposed.

54. Should the Member State introduce changes to an approved restructuring plan without duly informing the Commission, the Commission will initiate proceedings under Article 88(2) of the Treaty, as provided for by Article 16 of Regulation (EC) No 659/1999 (misuse of aid), without prejudice to Article 23 of Regulation (EC) No 659/1999 and to the possibility of an action before the Court of Justice in accordance with the second subparagraph of Article 88(2) of the Treaty.

3.2.4. Restructuring aid in assisted areas

55. Economic and social cohesion being a priority objective of the Community under Article 158 of the Treaty and other policies being required to contribute to this objective under Article 159,[1] the Commission must take the needs of regional development into account when assessing restructuring aid in assisted areas. The fact that an ailing firm is located in an assisted area does not, however, justify a permissive approach to aid for restructuring: in the medium to long term it does not help a region to prop up companies artificially. Furthermore, in order to promote regional development it is in the regions own best interest to apply its resources to develop as soon as possible activities that are viable and sustainable. Finally, distortions of competition must be minimised even in the case of aid to firms in assisted areas. In this context, regard must also be had to possible harmful spill-over effects which could take place in the area concerned and other assisted areas.

Notes
[1] Article 159 of the EC Treaty provides, inter alia, that "the formulation and implementation of the Community's policies and actions and the implementation of the internal market shall take into account the objectives set out in Article
158 and shall contribute to their achievement".

56. Thus, the criteria listed in points 32 to 54 are equally applicable to assisted areas, even when the
needs of regional development are considered. In assisted areas, however, and unless otherwise
stipulated in rules on State aid in a particular sector, the conditions for authorising aid may be
less stringent as regards the implementation of compensatory measures and the size of the beneficiary's contribution. If needs of regional development justify it, in cases in which a reduction of
capacity or market presence appear to be the most appropriate measure to avoid undue distortions
of competition, the required reduction will be smaller in assisted areas than in non-assisted areas.
In those cases, which need to be demonstrated by the Member State concerned, a distinction will
be drawn between areas eligible for regional aid under Article 87(3)(a) of the Treaty and those
eligible under Article 87(3)(c) so as to take account of the greater severity of the regional problems
in the former areas.

3.2.5. Aid for restructuring SMEs

57. Aid to small enterprises[1] tends to affect trading conditions less than that granted to medium-sized
and large firms. This also applies to aid to help restructuring, so that the conditions laid down in
points 32 to 54 are applied less strictly in the following respects:
    (a) the grant of restructuring aid to small enterprises will not usually be linked to compensatory
    measures (see point 41), unless this is otherwise stipulated in rules on State aid in a particular
    sector.
    (b) the requirements regarding the content of reports will be less stringent for SMEs (see
    points 49, 50 and 51).

Notes
[1] As defined in the Commission Recommendation 2003/361/EC (OJ L 124, 20.5.2003, p. 36). Until 31 December
2004, the relevant definition is to be found in the Commission Recommendation 96/280/EC (OJ L 107, 30.4.1996,
p. 4).

58. However, the "one time, last time" principle (section 3.3) applies in full to SMEs.
59. For SMEs the restructuring plan does not need to be endorsed by the Commission. However,
the plan must meet the requirements laid down in points 35, 36 and 37 and be approved by
the Member State concerned and communicated to the Commission. The grant of aid must be
conditional on full implementation of the restructuring plan. The obligation to verify that these
conditions are fulfilled lies with the Member State.

3.2.6. Aid to cover the social costs of restructuring

60. Restructuring plans normally entail reductions in or abandonment of the affected activities. Such
retrenchments are often necessary in the interests of rationalisation and efficiency, quite apart
from any capacity reductions that may be required as a condition for granting aid. Whatever the
reason for them, such measures will generally lead to reductions in the company's workforce.
61. Member States' labour legislation may comprise general social security schemes under which
redundancy benefits and early retirement pensions are paid direct to redundant employees. Such
schemes are not to be regarded as State aid falling within the scope of Article 87(1) of the Treaty.
62. Besides direct redundancy benefit and early retirement provision for employees, general social
support schemes frequently provide for the government to cover the cost of benefits which the
company grants to redundant workers and which go beyond its statutory or contractual obligations. Where such schemes are available generally without sectoral limitations to any worker
meeting predefined and automatic eligibility conditions, they are not deemed to involve aid
under Article 87(1) for firms undertaking restructuring. On the other hand, if the schemes are
used to support restructuring in particular industries, they may well involve aid because of the
selective way in which they are used.[1]

Notes

[1] In its judgment in Case C-241/94 *France v Commission* [1996] ECR I-4551 (Kimberly Clark Sopalin), the Court of Justice confirmed that the system of financing on a discretionary basis by the French authorities, through the National Employment Fund, was liable to place certain firms in a more favourable situation than others and thus to qualify as aid within the meaning of Article 87(1) of the Treaty. (The Court's judgment did not call into question the Commission's conclusion that the aid was compatible with the common market.)

63. The obligations a company itself bears under employment legislation or collective agreements with trade unions, to provide redundancy benefits and/or early retirement pensions are part of the normal costs of a business which a firm has to meet from its own resources. That being so, any contribution by the State to these costs must be counted as aid. This is true regardless of whether the payments are made direct to the firm or are administered through a government agency to the employees.

64. The Commission has no a priori objection to such aid when it is granted to firms in difficulty, for it brings economic benefits above and beyond the interests of the firm concerned, facilitating structural change and reducing hardship.

65. Besides meeting the cost of redundancy payments and early retirement, aid is commonly provided in connection with a particular restructuring scheme for training, counselling and practical help with finding alternative employment, assistance with relocation, and professional training and assistance for employees wishing to start new businesses. The Commission consistently takes a favourable view of such aid when it is granted to firms in difficulty.

66. The type of aid described in points 62 to 65 must be clearly identified in the restructuring plan, since aid for social measures exclusively for the benefit of redundant employees is disregarded for the purposes of determining the extent of the compensatory measures referred to in points 38 to 42.

67. In the common interest, the Commission will ensure in the context of the restructuring plan that social effects of the restructuring in Member States other than the one granting aid are kept to the minimum.

3.2.7. Need to inform the Commission of any aid granted to the recipient firm during the restructuring period

68. Where restructuring aid received by a large or medium-sized enterprise is examined under these Guidelines, the grant of any other aid during the restructuring period, even in accordance with a scheme that has already been authorised, is liable to influence the Commission's assessment of the extent of the compensatory measures required.

69. Notifications of aid for restructuring a large or medium-sized enterprise must indicate all other aid of any kind which is planned to be granted to the recipient firm during the restructuring period, unless it is covered by the de minimis rule or by exemption regulations. The Commission shall take such aid into account when assessing the restructuring aid.

70. Any aid actually granted to a large or medium-sized enterprise during the restructuring period, including aid granted in accordance with an approved scheme, must be notified individually to the Commission to the extent that the latter was not informed thereof at the time of its decision on the restructuring aid.

71. The Commission shall ensure that the grant of aid under approved schemes is not liable to circumvent the requirements of these Guidelines.

3.3. "One time, last time"

72. Rescue aid is a one-off operation primarily designed to keep a company in business for a limited period, during which its future can be assessed. It should not be possible to allow repeated granting of rescue aids that would merely maintain the status quo, postpone the inevitable and in the meantime shift economic and social problems on to other, more efficient producers or other Member States. Hence, rescue aid should be granted only once (one time, last time condition). In accordance with the same principle, in order to prevent firms from being unfairly assisted when they can only survive thanks to repeated State support, restructuring aid should be granted once only. Finally, if rescue aid is granted to a firm that has already received restructuring aid, it can be considered that the beneficiary's difficulties are of a recurrent nature and that repeated State

interventions give rise to distortions of competition that are contrary to the common interest. Such repeated State interventions should not be permitted.

73. When planned rescue or restructuring aid is notified to the Commission, the Member State must specify whether the firm concerned has already received rescue or restructuring aid in the past, including any such aid granted before the date of application of these Guidelines and any unnotified aid.[1] If so, and where less than 10 years have elapsed since the rescue aid was granted or the restructuring period came to an end or implementation of the restructuring plan has been halted (whichever is the latest), the Commission will not allow further rescue or restructuring aid. Exceptions to that rule are permitted in the following cases:

    (a) where restructuring aid follows the granting of rescue aid as part of a single restructuring operation;

    (b) where rescue aid has been granted in accordance with the conditions in section [3.1], and this aid was not followed by a State supported restructuring, if:

        (i) the firm could reasonably be believed to be viable in the long-term following the granting of rescue aid, and

        (ii) new rescue or restructuring aid becomes necessary after at least five years due to unforeseeable circumstances[2] for which the company is not responsible;

    (c) in exceptional and unforeseeable circumstances for which the company is not responsible.

    In the cases set out in points (b) and (c), the simplified procedure mentioned in section 3.1.2 cannot be used.

Notes

[1] With regard to unnotified aid, the Commission will take account in its appraisal of the possibility that the aid could have been declared compatible with the common market other than as rescue or restructuring aid.

[2] An unforeseeable circumstance is one which could in no way be anticipated by the company's management when the restructuring plan was drawn up and which is not due to negligence or errors of the company's management or decisions of the group to which it belongs.

Commentary
point 73: F&N: 16.165

74. The application of this rule will in no way be affected by any changes in ownership of the recipient firm following the grant of aid or by any judicial or administrative procedure which has the effect of putting its balance sheet on a sounder footing, reducing its liabilities or wiping out its previous debts where it is the same firm that is continuing in business.

75. Where a business group has received rescue or restructuring aid, the Commission will normally not allow further rescue or restructuring aid to the group itself or any of the entities belonging to the group unless 10 years have elapsed since the rescue aid was granted or the restructuring period came to an end or implementation of the restructuring plan has been halted, whichever is the latest. Where an entity belonging to a business group has received rescue or restructuring aid, the group as a whole as well as the other entities of the group remain eligible for rescue or restructuring aid (subject to compliance with the other provisions of these Guidelines), with the exception of the earlier beneficiary of the aid. Member States must ensure that no aid will be passed on from the group or other group entities to the earlier beneficiary of the aid.

76. Where a firm takes over assets of another firm, and in particular one that has been the subject of one of the procedures referred to in point 74 or of collective insolvency proceedings brought under national law and has already received rescue or restructuring aid, the purchaser is not subject to the "one time, last time" requirement, provided that the following cumulative conditions are met:

    (a) the purchaser is clearly separate from the old firm;

    (b) the purchaser has acquired the old firm's assets at market prices;

    (c) the winding-up or court-supervised administration and purchase of the old company are not merely devices aimed at evading application of the "one time, last time" principle: the Commission may determine that this was the case if, for example, the difficulties encountered by the purchaser were clearly foreseeable when it took over the assets of the old company.

77. It should, however, be stressed here that, since it constitutes aid for initial investment, aid for the purchase of the assets cannot be authorised under these Guidelines.

4. AID SCHEMES FOR SMEs

4.1. General principles

78. The Commission will authorise schemes for providing rescue and/or restructuring aid to small or medium-sized enterprises in difficulty only where the firms concerned correspond to the Community definition of SMEs. Subject to the following specific provisions, the compatibility of such schemes will be assessed in the light of the conditions set out in Chapters 2 and 3, with the exception of Section 3.1.2 which does not apply to aid schemes. Any aid which is granted under a scheme but does not meet any of those conditions must be notified individually and approved in advance by the Commission.

4.2. Eligibility

79. Unless otherwise stipulated in rules on State aid in a particular sector, awards of aid under schemes authorised from the date of application of these Guidelines, to small or medium-sized enterprises will be exempted from individual notification only where the enterprise concerned meets at least one of the three criteria set out in point 10. Aid to enterprises that do not meet any of those three criteria must be notified individually to the Commission so that it can assess whether they qualify as firms in difficulty. Aid to enterprises active in a market suffering from long-term structural overcapacity, irrespective of the size of the beneficiary, must also be notified individually to the Commission so that it can assess the application of point 42.

Commentary
point 79: B&C: 15.061

4.3. Conditions for the authorisation of rescue aid schemes

80. In order to be approved by the Commission, rescue aid schemes must satisfy the conditions set out in points (a), (b), (d) and (e) of point 25. Furthermore, rescue aid may not be granted for more than six months, during which time an analysis must be made of the firm's position. Before the end of that period the Member State must either approve a restructuring plan or a liquidation plan, or demand reimbursement of the loan and the aid corresponding to the risk premium from the beneficiary.

81. Any rescue aid granted for longer than six months or not reimbursed after six months must be individually notified to the Commission.

4.4. Conditions for the authorisation of restructuring aid schemes

82. The Commission will authorise restructuring aid schemes only if the grant of aid is conditional on full implementation by the recipient of a restructuring plan that has been approved by the Member State concerned and meets the following conditions:
   (a) restoration of viability: the criteria set out in points 34 to 37 apply;
   (b) avoidance of undue distortions of competition: since aid to small enterprises tends to distort competition less, the principle set out in points 38 to 42 does not apply unless it is otherwise stipulated in rules on State aid in a particular sector; schemes should nevertheless provide that recipient firms must not increase their capacity during the restructuring; for medium-sized enterprises points 38 to 42 apply;
   (c) aid limited to the minimum necessary: the principles set out in points 43, 44 and 45 apply;
   (d) amendment of the restructuring plan: any changes to the plan must comply with the rules set out in points 52, 53 and 54.

4.5. Common conditions for the authorisation of rescue and/or restructuring aid schemes

83. Schemes must specify the maximum amount of aid that can be awarded to any one firm as part of an operation to provide rescue and/or restructuring aid, including where the plan is modified. Any aid exceeding that amount must be notified individually to the Commission. The maximum amount of aid granted for the combined rescue and restructuring aid of any one firm may not be more than EUR 10 million, including any aid obtained from other sources or under other schemes.

84. In addition, the "one time, last time" principle must be respected. The rule laid down in section 3.3 applies.

85. Member States must also notify measures individually to the Commission where one firm takes over assets of another firm which has itself already received rescue or restructuring aid.

4.6. Monitoring and annual reports

86. Points 49, 50 and 51 do not apply to aid schemes. However, it will be a condition of approval that reports are presented on the scheme's operation, normally on an annual basis, containing the information specified in the Commission's instructions on standardised reports.[1] The reports must also include a list of all beneficiary companies, indicating for each of them:
   (a) company name;
   (b) the company's sectoral code, using the NACE[2] three-digit sectoral classification codes;
   (c) number of employees;
   (d) annual turnover and balance sheet value;
   (e) amount of aid granted;
   (f) amount and form of the beneficiary's contribution;
   (g) where appropriate, the form and the degree of the compensatory measures;
   (h) where appropriate, any restructuring aid, or other support treated as such, which it has received in the past;
   (i) whether or not the beneficiary company has been wound up or subject to collective insolvency proceedings before the end of the restructuring period.

Notes

1 See Annex III. A and B (standardised reporting format for existing State aid) to Commission Regulation (EC) No 794/2004 of 21 April 2004 adopting provisions for the implementation of Council Regulation (EC) No 659/1999 laying down detailed rules for the application of Article [88] of the EC Treaty (OJ L 140, 30.4.2004, p. 1).
2 Statistical classification of economic activities in the European Community, published by the Statistical Office of the European Communities.

5. PROVISIONS APPLICABLE TO AID FOR RESTRUCTURING IN THE AGRICULTURAL SECTOR[1]

Notes

1 This covers, for the purpose of these Guidelines, all operators involved in the primary production of agricultural products of Annex I to the Treaty (farming). Aid measures in favour of enterprises processing and marketing agricultural products are not covered by this Chapter. Aid to processing and marketing companies is to be assessed in line with the general rules of these Guidelines. Fisheries and aquaculture are not covered by this chapter.

5.1. Compensatory measures

87. Points 38 to 42, and 57 and 82(b) provide that the requirement for compensatory measures is not normally applied in the case of small enterprises, unless otherwise stipulated in sector-specific State aid rules. In the agricultural sector, the Commission will normally require compensatory measures, in accordance with the principles set out in points 38 to 42, to be carried out by all recipients of restructuring aid, whatever their size.

5.2. Definition of excess capacity

88. For the purposes of these Guidelines, structural excess capacity in the agricultural sector will be defined by the Commission on a case-by-case basis taking account in particular of the extent and trend for the relevant product category over the past three years, of market stabilisation measures, especially export refunds and withdrawals from the market, of development of world market prices, and of the presence of sectoral limits in Community legislation.

Commentary
point 88: F&N: 16.200

5.3. Eligibility for rescue and restructuring aid schemes

89. By way of derogation from point 79, the Commission may also exempt aid to SMEs from individual notification if the SME concerned does not meet at least one of the three criteria set out in point 10.

5.4. Capacity reductions

90. Where there is a structural excess of production capacity, the requirement of irreversibly reducing or closing capacity set out in points 38 to 42 applies. Open farmland may be re-used after 15 years following effective capacity closure. Until then, it has to be maintained in good agricultural and environmental condition for land no longer used for production purposes, in accordance with Article 5 of Council Regulation (EC) No 1782/2003 of 29 September 2003 establishing common rules for direct support schemes under the common agricultural policy and establishing certain support schemes for farmers,[1] and with the relevant implementation rules.

Notes

[1] OJ L 270, 21.10. 2003, p. 1. Regulation as last amended by Regulation (EC) No 864/2004 (OJ L 161, 30.4.2004, p. 48).

91. Where the aid measure is targeted on particular products or operators, the production capacity reduction must attain at least 10% of that for which the restructuring aid is effectively granted. For measures not so targeted, the production capacity reduction must attain at least 5%. For restructuring aid granted in less favoured areas,[1] the capacity reduction requirement will be reduced by two percentage points. The Commission will waive these capacity reduction requirements where the decisions to grant restructuring aid taken in favour of beneficiaries in a given sector over any consecutive 12-month period do not together involve more than 1% of the production capacity of that sector in the Member State concerned. This rule may be applied at regional level in the case of an aid regime limited to a given region.

Notes

[1] As defined in Articles 13 and following of Council Regulation (EC) No 1257/1999 (OJ L 160, 26.6.1999, p. 80), as last amended by Regulation (EC) No 583/2004 (OJ L 91, 30.3.2004, p. 1).

Commentary
point 91: F&N: 16.200

92. The requirement of irreversibly reducing capacity may be achieved at the relevant market level (not necessarily involving reductions by the beneficiaries of the restructuring aid). Subject to compliance with common agricultural policy provisions, Member States may choose whatever capacity reduction system they wish.
93. The Member State must demonstrate that the capacity reduction would be supplementary to any reduction which would be applied in the absence of the restructuring aid.
94. Where the capacity reduction is not sought at the level of the beneficiary of the aid, measures to achieve the reduction must be implemented no later than one year after the aid has been granted.
95. In order to ensure the effectiveness of the closure of capacity undertaken at the relevant market level, the Member State must give a commitment not to grant State aid for capacity increases in the sector concerned. This commitment shall remain in force for a period of five years from the date where the required capacity reduction actually has been achieved.
96. In determining eligibility for and amounts of restructuring aid, no account shall be taken of the burdens of compliance with Community quota and related provisions at the level of individual operators.

5.5. "One time, last time" condition

97. The principle that rescue or restructuring aid should be granted once only also applies to the agricultural sector. However, instead of the period of 10 years set out in section 3.3 a five-year period will apply.

5.6. Monitoring and annual report

98. The rules set out in Chapters 3 and 4 apply to monitoring and annual reports in the agricultural sector, except for the obligation to supply a list of all aid beneficiaries and certain items of information on each of them (see point 86). Where recourse has been had to the provisions of points 90 to 96, the report must also include data showing the production capacity which has effectively benefited from restructuring aid and the capacity reduction achieved.

6. Appropriate Measures as Referred to in Article 88(1)

99. The Commission will propose, by separate letter, pursuant to Article 88(1) of the Treaty, that the Member States adopt appropriate measures as set out in points 100 and 101, with regard to their existing aid schemes. The Commission will make authorisation of any future scheme conditional on compliance with those provisions.
100. Member States which have accepted the Commission's proposal must adapt their existing aid schemes which are to remain in operation after 9 October 2004 within six months in order to bring them into line with these Guidelines.
101. Member States must indicate their acceptance of these appropriate measures within one month following receipt of said letter proposing appropriate measures.

7. Date of Application and Duration

102. The Commission will apply these Guidelines with effect from 10 October 2004 until 9 October 2009.
103. Notifications registered by the Commission prior to 10 October 2004 will be examined in the light of the criteria in force at the time of notification.
104. The Commission will examine the compatibility with the common market of any rescue or restructuring aid granted without its authorisation and therefore in breach of Article 88(3) of the Treaty on the basis of these Guidelines if some or all of the aid is granted after their publication in the Official Journal of the European Union.
   In all other cases it will conduct the examination on the basis of the Guidelines which apply at the time the aid is granted.

Annex

Formula[1] to calculate maximum amount of rescue aid to qualify for the simplified procedure:

$$\frac{EBIT_t + depreciation_t + (working\ capital_t - working\ capital_{t-1})}{2}$$

The formula is based on the operating results of the company (EBIT, earnings before interest and taxes) recorded in the year before granting/notifying the aid (indicated as t). To this amount depreciation has been added. Then changes in working capital must be added to the total. The change in working capital is calculated as the difference between the current assets and current liabilities[2] for the latest closed accounting periods. Similarly, if there would be provisions at the level of the operating result, this will need to be clearly indicated and the result should not include such provisions.

The formula aims at estimating the negative operating cash flow of the company in the year preceding the application for the aid (or before the award of the aid in case of non-notified aids). Half of this amount should keep the company in business for a six-month period. Thus the result of the formula has to be divided by 2.

This formula can only be applied where the result is a negative amount.

In case the formula leads to a positive result, a detailed explanation will need to be submitted demonstrating that the firm is in difficulty as defined in points 10 and 11.

Example:

Earnings before interest and taxes (EUR million)	(12)	
Depreciation (EUR million)	(2)	
Balance sheet (EUR million)	December 31, X	December 31, XO
Current assets		
Cash or equivalents	10	5
Accounts receivable	30	20
Inventories	50	45
Prepaid expenses	20	10
Other current assets	20	20
Total current assets	130	100
Current liabilities		
Accounts payable	20	25
Accrued expenses	15	10
Deferred income	5	5
Total current liabilities	40	40
Working capital	90	60
Change in working capital	(30)	

Maximum amount of rescue aid = [−12 + 2 + (−30)] / 2 = −EUR 20 million.

As the outcome of the formula is higher than EUR 10 million, the simplified procedure described in point 30 cannot be used. If this limit is exceeded, the Member State should provide an explanation of how the future cash-flow needs of the company and the amount of rescue aid have been determined.

Notes

[1] EBIT (earnings before interest and taxes as set out in the annual accounts of the year before the application, indicated as t) must be increased with depreciation in the same period plus the changes in working capital over a two-year period (year before the application and preceding year), divided by two to determine an amount over six months, i.e. normal period for permitting rescue aid.

[2] Current assets: liquid funds, receivables (client and debtor accounts), other current assets and prepaid expenses, inventories. Current liabilities: financial debt, trade accounts payable (supplier and creditor accounts) and other current liabilities, deferred income, other accrued liabilities, tax liabilities.

Commentary
Annex: F&N: 16.172, 16.200

G20

GUIDELINES ON NATIONAL REGIONAL AID FOR 2007–2013

(2006/C 54/08)

(Text with EEA relevance)

Official Journal C 54, 4.3.2006, p. 13

Celex No: 52006XC0304(02)

Notes

EEA application: for the corresponding EEA provision, see the EFTA Surveillance Authority's Procedural and Substantive Rules in the Field of State Aid (Guidelines on the application and interpretation of Articles 61 and 62 of the EEA Agreement and Article 1 of Protocol 3 to the Surveillance and Court Agreement), Part VI, Chapter 25B (as introduced by EFTA Surveillance Authority Decision No. 85/06/COL of 6 April 2006, not yet published).

Commentary
Guidelines: **B&C:** 15.046, 15.048
paras 1–3: **B&C:** 15.047
paras 18–20: **B&C:** 15.049
paras 21–32: **B&C:** 15.050, 15.055
paras 60–70: **B&C:** 15.051
paras 80–83: **B&C:** 15.051
paras 84–91: **B&C:** 15.051

---

1. Introduction

1. On the basis of Article 87(3)(a) and (c) of the Treaty, State aid granted to promote the economic development of certain disadvantaged areas within the European Union may be considered to be compatible with the common market by the Commission. This kind of State aid is known as national regional aid. National regional aid consists of aid for investment granted to large companies, or in certain limited circumstances, operating aid, which in both cases are targeted on specific regions in order to redress regional disparities. Increased levels of investment aid granted to small and medium-sized enterprises located within the disadvantaged regions over and above what is allowed in other areas are also considered as regional aid.

2. By addressing the handicaps of the disadvantaged regions, national regional aid promotes the economic, social and territorial cohesion of Member States and the European Union as a whole. This geographical specificity distinguishes regional aid from other forms of horizontal aid, such as aid for research, development and innovation, employment, training or the environment, which pursue other objectives of common interest in accordance with Article 87(3) of the Treaty, albeit sometimes with higher rates of aid in the disadvantaged areas in recognition of the specific difficulties which they face.[1]

Notes
[1] Regional top-ups for aid granted for such purposes are therefore not considered as regional aid.

---

3. National regional investment aid is designed to assist the development of the most disadvantaged regions by supporting investment and job creation. It promotes the expansion and diversification of the economic activities of enterprises located in the less-favoured regions, in particular by encouraging firms to set up new establishments there.

4. The criteria applied by the Commission when examining the compatibility of national regional aid with the common market under Articles 87(3)(a) and 87(3)(c) of the EC Treaty have been codified

in the 1998 guidelines on national regional aid[2] which cover the period 2000–2006.[3] The specific rules governing aid for large investment projects have been codified in the 2002 Multisectoral Framework.[4] However, important political and economic developments since 1998, including the enlargement of the European Union on 1 May 2004, the anticipated accession of Bulgaria and Romania and the accelerated process of integration following the introduction of the single currency, have created the need for a comprehensive review in order to prepare new guidelines which will apply from 2007 to 2013.

Notes

[2] OJ C 74 10.3.1998, p. 9, modified in OJ C 288 9.10.1999, p. 2, and OJ C 285 9.9.2000, p. 5.

[3] Point 4.4 of the regional aid guidelines was amended by the Community Guidelines on State aid for rescuing and restructuring firms in difficulty, OJ C 288, 9.10.1999, p. 2.

[4] OJ C 70, 19.3.2002, p. 8, as amended in OJ C 263, 1.11.2003, p. 3.

Commentary

para 4: **B&C:** 15.046

5. Regional aid can only play an effective role if it is used sparingly and proportionately and is concentrated on the most disadvantaged regions of the European Union. In particular the permissible aid ceilings should reflect the relative seriousness of the problems affecting the development of the regions concerned. Furthermore, the advantages of the aid in terms of the development of a less-favoured region must outweigh the resulting distortions of competition.[5] The weight given to the advantages of the aid is likely to vary according to the derogation applied, so that a greater distortion of competition can be accepted in the case of the most disadvantaged regions covered by Article 87(3)(a) than in those covered by Article 87(3)(c).[6]

Notes

[5] See in this respect the judgment of the Court of Justice in Case 730/79, *Philip Morris* [1980] ECR 2671, paragraph 17 and in Case C-169/95, *Spain v Commission* [1997] ECR I-135, paragraph 20.

[6] See in this respect the judgment of the Court of First Instance in T-380/94, *AIUFFASS and AKT* [1996] ECR II- 2169, paragraph 54.

Commentary

para 5: **B&C:** 15.046, 15.055

6. In certain very limited, well-defined cases, the structural handicaps of a region may be so severe that regional investment aid, together with a comprehensive horizontal aid regime may not be sufficient to trigger a process of regional development. Only in such cases may regional investment aid be supplemented by regional operating aid.

7. An increasing body of evidence suggests that there are significant barriers to the formation of new enterprises in the Community which are more acute inside the disadvantaged regions. The Commission has therefore decided to introduce a new aid instrument in these guidelines to encourage small business start-ups in disadvantaged regions with differentiated aid ceilings according to the regions concerned.

2. Scope

8. The Commission will apply these Guidelines to regional aid granted in every sector of the economy apart from the fisheries sector and the coal industry[7] which are subject to special rules laid down by specific legal instruments. In the agricultural sector, these guidelines do not apply to the production of agricultural products listed in Annex I of the Treaty. They do apply to the processing and marketing of such products, but only to the extent laid down in the Community guidelines for State aid in the agriculture sector,[8] or any replacement Guidelines. In addition, some other sectors are also subject to specific rules which take account of the particular situation of the sectors concerned and which may totally or partially derogate from these guidelines.[9] As regards the steel industry, in accordance with its long-established practice, the Commission considers that regional aid to the steel industry as defined in Annex I is not compatible with the common market. This incompatibility also applies to large individual aid grants made in this sector to small and medium-sized enterprises within the meaning of Article 6 of Regulation (EC) No 70/2001,[10] or

any successor regulation, which are not exempted by the same Regulation. In addition, due to its specific characteristics, no regional investment aid may be granted in the synthetic fibres sector as defined in Annex II.

Notes
7 For the purposes of these guidelines "coal" means high-grade, medium-grade and low-grade category A and B coal within the meaning of the international codification system for coal laid down by the United Nations Economic Commission for Europe.
8 OJ C 28 of 1.2.2000, p.2. Corrigendum OJ C 232 12.8.2000, p. 17.
9 The sectors covered by special rules over and above those set out here are currently: transport and shipbuilding.
10 OJ L 10, 13.1.2001, p. 33. Regulation as amended by Regulation (EC) No 364/2004 (OJ L 63, 28.2.2004, p. 22).

9. Aid may only be granted to firms in difficulties within the meaning of the Community guide-lines on State aid for rescuing and restructuring firms in difficulty[11] in accordance with the latter guidelines.[12]

Notes
11 OJ C 244, 1.10.2004, p. 2.
12 In particular, aid granted to large or medium-sized enterprises during the restructuring period must always be noti-fied individually to the Commission, even if it is granted as part of an approved scheme.

10. As a general rule, regional aid should be granted under a multi-sectoral aid scheme which forms an integral part of a regional development strategy with clearly defined objectives. Such a scheme may also enable the competent authorities to prioritise investment projects according to their interest for the region concerned. Where, exceptionally, it is envisaged to grant individual ad hoc aid to a single firm, or aid confined to one area of activity, it is the responsibility of the Member State to demonstrate that the project contributes towards a coherent regional development strat-egy and that, having regard to the nature and size of the project, it will not result in unacceptable distortions of competition. If aid granted under a scheme appears to be unduly concentrated on a particular sector of activity, the Commission may review the scheme pursuant to Article 17 of Regulation (EC) No 659/1999 of 22 March 1999 on modalities for the application of Article [88] of the EC Treaty[13] and may propose, in line with Article 18 (c) of this Regulation, to abolish the scheme.

Notes
13 OJ L 83, 27.3.1999, p. 1.

Commentary
para 10: B&C: 15.046

11. Member States do not have to notify national regional aid schemes which fulfil all the conditions laid down in the group exemption Regulations adopted by the Commission pursuant to Article 1 of Council Regulation (EC) No 994/98 of 7 May 1998 on the application of Articles [87] and [88] of the EC Treaty establishing the European Community to certain categories of horizontal State aid.[14]

Notes
14 OJ L 142, 14.5.1998, p. 1.

3. Demarcation of regions

3.1. Population coverage eligible for regional aid, 2007–2013

12. In the light of the principle of the exceptional nature of regional aid, the Commission considers that the total population coverage of assisted regions in the Community must be substantially less than that of unassisted regions.
13. Having regard to the conclusions of different European Councils calling for a reduction in overall levels of State aid, and in view of the widely shared concerns about the distortive effects of invest-ment aid for large companies, the Commission considers that the overall population coverage of

the regional aid guidelines for 2007–2013 should be limited to that which is necessary to allow coverage of the most disadvantaged regions, as well as a limited number of regions which are disadvantaged in relation to the national average in the Member State concerned. Accordingly, it has decided to fix the limit for the overall population coverage to 42% of the population of the current Community of 25 Member States, which is similar to the limit fixed on the basis of a Community of 15 members in 1998. This limit will provide for an appropriate level of concentration of regional aid in EU-25, while allowing a sufficient degree of flexibility for the accession of Bulgaria and Romania, the entire territory of which will normally be eligible for regional aid.[15]

Notes

[15] This 42% limit is estimated to rise to 45.5% on an EU-27 basis following the Accession of Bulgaria and Romania.

14. This notwithstanding, in order to ensure a sufficient degree of continuity for the existing Member States, the Commission has also decided to apply an additional safety net to ensure that no Member State loses more than 50% of the coverage of its population covered during the period 2000–2006.[16]

Notes

[16] Application of the safety net will lead to a total population coverage of about 43.1% on an EU-25 basis, or 46.6% on an EU-27 basis.

3.2. The derogation in Article 87(3)(a)

15. Article 87(3)(a) provides that aid to promote the economic development of areas where the standard of living is abnormally low or where there is serious underemployment may be considered compatible with the common market. As the Court of Justice of the European Communities has held, "the use of the words "abnormally" and "serious" in the exemption contained in [Article 87(3)(a)] shows that it concerns only areas where the economic situation is extremely unfavourable in relation to the Community as a whole".[17]

Notes

[17] Case 248/84, *Germany v Commission* [1987] ECR 4013, paragraph 19.

16. The Commission accordingly considers that the conditions laid down are fulfilled if the region, being a NUTS[18] level II geographical unit, has a per capita gross domestic product (GDP), measured in purchasing power standards (PPS), of less than 75% of the Community average.[19] The GDP per capita[20] of each region and the Community average to be used in the analysis are determined by the Statistical Office of the European Communities. In the interest of ensuring the maximum possible coherence between the designation of regions eligible for the derogation under Article 87(3)(a) under the regional aid guidelines, and the regions eligible for the convergence objective under the structural fund regulations, the Commission has used the same GDP per capita data to designate the Article 87(3)(a) regions as that used to designate the convergence regions under the structural fund regulations.[21]

Notes

[18] Regulation (EC) No 1059/2003 of the European Parliament and of the Council of 26 May 2003 on the establishment of a common classification of territorial units for statistics (NUTS) OJ L 154, 21.6.2003, p. 1. The NUTS nomenclature is used by EUROSTAT as a reference for the collection, development and harmonisation of EU regional statistics and for socio-economic analyses of the regions.

[19] The underlying assumption being that the GDP indicator is capable of reflecting synthetically both the phenomena mentioned.

[20] In this, and all subsequent references to GDP per capita in these guidelines, GDP is measured in terms of purchasing power standards.

[21] The data cover the period 2000–2002.

Commentary
para 16: **B&C:** 15.046

17. In recognition of the special handicaps which they face by reason of their remoteness and specific constraints in integrating into the internal market, the Commission considers that regional aid for the outermost regions covered by Article 299(2) of the Treaty[22] also falls within the scope of the derogation in Article 87(3)(a), whether or not the regions concerned have a GDP per capita of less than 75% of the Community average.

Notes

[22] Azores, Madeira, Canary Islands, Guadeloupe, Martinique, Réunion and French Guyana.

3.3. *Phasing out arrangements for the "statistical effect" regions*

18. For certain regions, the GDP per capita exceeds 75% of the Community average solely because of the statistical effect of enlargement. These are regions at NUTS II level which have a GDP per capita of more than 75% of the EU-25 average, but less than 75% of the EU-15 average.[23][24]

Notes

[23] In practice, 75% of the average EU-15 GDP per capita corresponds to 82.2% of the average EU-25 GDP per capita.
[24] These regions are subsequently referred to as the "statistical effect" regions.

19. In order to ensure that the past progress of these regions is not undermined by too rapid change, in terms of aid intensities and the availability of operating aid, the Commission considers that they should continue to remain eligible for the derogation in Article 87(3)(a) on a transitional basis until 31 December 2010.

20. In 2010 the Commission will review the position of these regions on the basis of the three-year average of the most recent GDP data available from Eurostat. If the relative GDP per capita of any of the regions has declined below 75% of the EU-25 average, the regions concerned will continue to be eligible for the derogation under Article 87(3)(a). Otherwise the statistical effect regions will become eligible for aid under the derogation of Article 87(3)(c) from 1 January 2011.

3.4. *The derogation in Article 87(3)(c)*

21. The Court of Justice, in Case 248/84,[25] has expressed its views on the range of problems covered by this derogation and the reference framework for the analysis as follows: "The exemption in [Article 87(3)(c)], on the other hand, is wider in scope inasmuch as it permits the development of certain areas without being restricted by the economic conditions laid down in [Article 87(3)(a)], provided such aid "does not adversely affect trading conditions to an extent contrary to the common interest". That provision gives the Commission power to authorize aid intended to further the economic development of areas of a Member State which are disadvantaged in relation to the national average".

Notes

[25] Footnote 17, supra.

22. The regional aid covered by the derogation in Article 87(3)(c) must, however, form part of a well-defined regional policy of the Member State and adhere to the principle of geographical concentration. Inasmuch as it is intended for regions which are less disadvantaged than those to which Article 87(3)(a) relates, both the geographic scope of the exception and the aid intensity allowed must be strictly limited. This being so, only a small part of the national territory of a Member State may normally qualify for the aid in question.

23. So as to afford national authorities sufficient latitude when it comes to choosing eligible regions without jeopardizing the effectiveness of the system of checks and balances operated by the Commission in respect of this type of aid and the equal treatment of all Member States, the selection of the regions eligible under the derogation in question should be undertaken by a two-step process which consists, first, of the determination by the Commission of the maximum population coverage for each Member State[26] for such aid, and, secondly, of the selection of eligible regions.

3.4.1. Determination of eligible national population coverage

24. As a first step, the determination of the national population coverage eligible for aid under the derogation in Article 87(3)(c) must be made by a method which is objective, fair and transparent. Furthermore, the final outcome must remain within the overall limit for coverage of regional aid determined by the Commission under section 3.1, taking account also of the safety net. In order to achieve this, the Commission determines the population ceiling for each Member State on the basis of the following method.

25. First, Member States automatically receive an allocation equivalent to the population of any regions which were eligible for aid under the derogation in Article 87(3)(a) of the Treaty but which no longer meet the conditions for eligibility under that Article and which are not covered by the arrangements for the statistical effect regions described in section 3.3. These are the regions which had a GDP per capita of less than 75% on an EU-15 basis when the 1998 regional aid guidelines were adopted, but which as a result of their economic development no longer meet that condition on an EU-15 basis. Since these regions[27] have previously benefited from a relatively high level of aid, the Commission considers it necessary to allow Member States the flexibility, if they so wish, to continue to support these regions for the duration of these guidelines, under the derogation in Article 87(3)(c).[28]

26. Second, in order to allow for the continued support of low population density regions, the Member States concerned also receive an allocation based on the population of low population density regions.[29]

27. After deducting the population coverage resulting from the application of the objective criteria set out in sections 3.2 and 3.3, as well as the allocations referred to in the two preceding paragraphs from the upper limit of 42% of EU-25 population determined in section 3.1, the balance is available for distribution between the Member States using a distribution key that takes account of variations in GDP per capita and unemployment between the regions, both in a national and a Community context. The detailed formula is set out in Annex IV.[30]

28. Finally, as indicated in section 3.1, a safety net is applied to ensure that no Member State loses more than 50% of the coverage of its population under the 1998 guidelines.

29. The resulting allocations are set out in Annex V, together with the lists of regions eligible for support under Article 87(3)(a), the statistical effect regions and the economic development regions.

3.4.2. Selection of eligible regions[31]

30. The eligibility criteria for the selection of regions by the Member States must be sufficiently flexible to allow for the wide diversity of situations in which the granting of national regional aid may potentially be justified but at the same time they must be transparent and provide sufficient safeguards that the award of regional aid will not distort trade and competition to an extent contrary to the common interest. Accordingly, the Commission considers that the following regions may

be eligible for selection by the Member States concerned for the award of regional investment aid pursuant to the derogation under Article 87(3)(c) :[32]

(a) the "economic development" regions;

(b) the low population density regions: such areas are made up essentially of NUTS-II geographic regions with a population density of less than 8 inhabitants per km², or NUTS-III geographic regions with a population density of less than 12.5 inhabitants per km².[33] However, a certain flexibility is allowed in the selection of these areas, subject to the following limitations:

— flexibility in the selection of areas must not mean an increase in the population covered;

— the NUTS III parts qualifying for flexibility must have a population density of less than 12.5 inhabitants per square kilometre;

— they must be contiguous with NUTS III regions which satisfy the low population density test;

(c) regions which form contiguous zones with a minimum population of at least 100,000 and which are located within either NUTS-II or NUTS-III regions which have either a GDP per capita of less than the EU-25 average, **or** which have an unemployment rate which is higher than 115% of the national average, (both calculated on the average of the most recent 3 years of Eurostat data);

(d) NUTS-III regions with less than 100,000 population which have either a GDP per capita of less than the EU-25 average **or** which have an unemployment rate which is higher than 115% of the national average, (both calculated on the average of the most recent three years of Eurostat data);

(e) islands and other regions categorised by similar geographical isolation[34] which have either a GDP per capita of less than the EU-25 average, **or** which have an unemployment rate which is higher than 115% of the national average, (both calculated on the average of the most recent three years of Eurostat data);

(f) islands with fewer than 5,000 inhabitants and other communities with fewer than 5,000 inhabitants categorised by similar geographical isolation;

(g) NUTS-III regions or parts thereof adjacent to a region which is eligible for support under Article 87(3)(a) as well as NUTS-III regions or parts thereof which share a land border, or a sea border of less than 30 kilometres with a country which is not a Member State of the European Economic Area or EFTA.

(h) In duly justified cases, Member States may also designate other regions which form contiguous zones with a minimum population of at least 50,000 which are undergoing major structural change, or are in serious relative decline, when compared with other comparable regions. It will be the task of Member States which wish to use this possibility to demonstrate that the award of regional investment aid in the region concerned is justified, using recognised economic indicators and comparisons with the situation at Community level.

Notes

[31] Those statistical effect regions which from 1 January 2011 are not eligible for the derogation under Article 87(3)(a) are automatically eligible under Article 87(3)(c).

[32] Taking account of their small size, for Cyprus and Luxembourg it is sufficient that the regions designated have either a GDP per capita which is less than the EU average, or an unemployment rate which is higher than 115% of the national average, and have a minimum population of 10,000 inhabitants.

[33] In order to prevent double counting, this criterion should be applied on a residual basis, after taking account of the relative wealth of the regions concerned.

[34] For example peninsulas and mountainous regions.

---

31. In addition, in order to allow Member States greater flexibility to target very localised regional disparities, below the NUTS-III level, Member States may also designate other smaller areas which do not meet the conditions described above provided they have a minimum population of 20,000.[35] It will be the task of Member States which wish to use this possibility to demonstrate that the areas proposed are relatively more in need of economic development than other areas in that region, using recognised economic indicators such as GDP per capita, employment or unemployment levels, local productivity or skills indicators. Regional aid will be approved

by the Commission in these areas for SMEs, and the relevant SME bonus will also apply. However, because of the potential distortion of competition resulting from the spill-over effect into the more prosperous surrounding regions, the Commission will not approve aid for investments by large companies in these areas, or aids for investments with eligible expenses exceeding EUR 25 million.

Notes

[35] This minimum limit may be reduced in the case of islands and other areas categorised by similar geographical isolation.

32. Compliance with the total coverage allowed for each Member State will be determined by the actual population of the regions concerned, on the basis of the most recent recognised statistical information available.

4. Regional investment aid

4.1. Form of aid and aid ceilings

4.1.1. Form of aid

33. Regional investment aid is aid awarded for an initial investment project.

34. *Initial investment* means an investment in material and immaterial assets relating to:
    — the setting-up of a new establishment;
    — the extension of an existing establishment;
    — diversification of the output of an establishment into new, additional products;
    — a fundamental change in the overall production process of an existing establishment.
    "Material assets" means assets relating to land, buildings and plant/machinery. In case of acquisition of an establishment, only the costs of buying assets from third parties should be taken into consideration, provided the transaction has taken place under market conditions.
    "Immaterial assets" means assets entailed by the transfer of technology through the acquisition of patent rights, licences, know-how or unpatented technical knowledge.
    Replacement investment which does not meet any of these conditions is thus excluded from the concept.[36]

Notes

[36] Replacement investment may however qualify as operating aid under certain conditions as set out in section 5.

35. The acquisition of the assets directly linked to an establishment may also be regarded as initial investment provided the establishment has closed or would have closed had it not been purchased, and is bought by an independent investor.[37]

Notes

[37] Consequently, the sole acquisition of the shares of the legal entity of an enterprise does not qualify as initial investment.

36. Regional investment aid is calculated either in reference to material and immaterial investment costs resulting from the initial investment project or to (estimated) wage costs for jobs directly created by the investment project.[38]

Notes

[38] A job is deemed to be directly created by an investment project if it concerns the activity to which the investment relates and is created within three years of completion of the investment, including jobs created following an increase in the utilisation rate of the capacity created by the investment.

37. The form of the aid is variable. It may, for example, take the form of grants, low-interest loans or interest rebates, state guarantees, the purchase of a share-holding or an alternative provision of capital on favourable terms, exemptions or reductions in taxes, social security or other compulsory charges, or the supply of land, goods or services at favourable prices.

38. It is important to ensure that regional aid produces a real incentive effect to undertake investments which would not otherwise be made in the assisted areas. Therefore aid may only be granted under aid schemes if the beneficiary has submitted an application for aid and the authority responsible for administering the scheme has subsequently confirmed in writing[39] that, subject to detailed verification, the project in principle meets the conditions of eligibility laid down by the scheme before the start of work on the project.[40] An express reference to both conditions must also be included in all aid schemes.[41] In the case of ad hoc aid, the competent authority must have issued a letter of intent, conditional on Commission approval of the measure, to award aid before work starts on the project. If work begins before the conditions laid down in this paragraph are fulfilled, the whole project will not be eligible for aid.

Notes

[39] In the case of aid which is subject to individual notification to and approval by the Commission, confirmation of eligibility must be made conditional on the Commission decision approving the aid.

[40] "Start of work" means either the start of construction work or the first firm commitment to order equipment, excluding preliminary feasibility studies.

[41] The only exception to these rules is in the case of approved tax aid schemes where a tax exemption or reduction is granted automatically to qualifying expenditure without any discretion on the part of the authorities.

39. Where the aid is calculated on the basis of material or immaterial investment costs, or of acquisition costs in the case referred to in paragraph 35, to ensure that the investment is viable and sound and respecting the applicable aid ceilings, the beneficiary must provide a financial contribution of at least 25% of the eligible costs, either through its own resources or by external financing, in a form which is free of any public support.[42]

Notes

[42] This is for example not the case for a subsidised loan, public equity-capital loans or public participations which do not meet the market economy investor principle, state guarantees containing elements of aid, as well as public support granted within the scope of the *de minimis* rule.

40. Furthermore, in order to ensure that the investment makes a real and sustained contribution to regional development, aid must be made conditional, through the conditions attached to the aid, or its method of payment, on the maintenance of the investment in question in the region concerned for a minimum period of at least five years after its completion.[43] In addition, where the aid is calculated on the basis of wage costs, the posts must be filled within three years of the completion of the works. Each of the jobs created through the investment must be maintained within the region concerned for a period of five years from the date the post was first filled. In the case of SMEs, Member States may reduce these five-year periods for the maintenance of an investment or jobs created to a minimum of three years.

Notes

[43] This rule shall not prevent the replacement of plant or equipment which has become out-dated within this five year period due to rapid technological change, provided the economic activity is retained in the region concerned for the minimum period.

41. The level of the aid is defined in terms of intensity compared with reference costs. All aid intensities must be calculated in terms of gross grant equivalents (GGE).[44] The aid intensity in gross grant equivalent is the discounted value of the aid expressed as a percentage of the discounted value of the eligible costs. For aid which is individually notified to the Commission, the gross grant equivalent is calculated at the moment of notification. In other cases, the eligible investment costs are discounted to their value at the moment of the granting of the aid. Aid payable in several instalments shall be discounted to its value at the moment of its being notified or granted, as appropriate. The interest rate to be used for discounting purposes and to calculate the aid amount in a soft loan is the reference rate applicable at the time of grant. In cases where aid is awarded by means of tax exemptions or reductions on future taxes due, discounting of aid tranches takes place on the basis of the reference rates applicable at the various times the tax advantages become effective.

[44] The Commission is discontinuing its former practice of converting regional aid notified by Member States into net grant equivalents in order to take account of the judgment of the Court of First Instance of 15 June 2000 in Case T- 298/97, *Alzetta*. In that case the Court of First Instance ruled: "The Commission is not empowered, under the State aid monitoring system established by the Treaty, to take into consideration the incidence of tax on the amount of financial aid allocated when it assesses whether it is compatible with the Treaty. Such charges are not levied specifically on the aid itself but are levied downstream, and apply to the aid in question in the same way as to any income received. They cannot therefore be relevant when assessing the specific effect of the aid on trade and competition and, in particular, when estimating the benefit obtained by the recipients of such aid by comparison with competing undertakings which have not received such aid and whose income is also liable to tax." Furthermore, the Commission considers that the use of GGEs, which are also used to calculate the intensities of other types of State aid, will contribute to increasing the simplicity and transparency of the State aid control system, and also takes account of the increased proportion of State aid which is awarded in the form of tax exemptions.

4.1.2. Aid ceilings (maximum aid intensities) for aid to large companies

42. The intensity of the aid must be adapted to take account of the nature and intensity of the regional problems that are being addressed. This means that the admissible aid intensities are from the outset less high in regions qualifying for exemption under Article 87(3)(c) than in those qualifying under Article 87(3)(a).
43. The Commission must also take account of the fact that following recent enlargements the disparities in the relative wealth of the regions qualifying under Article 87(3)(a) have increased substantially. In fact, a significant number of regions and indeed entire Member States now have a per capita GDP of below 45% of the EU-25 average, which was not the case in 1998. The existence of these greater disparities of wealth within the Community requires the Commission to introduce a greater categorisation of the regions concerned.
44. In the case of regions falling under Article 87(3)(a), the Commission thus considers that the intensity of regional aid must not exceed:
    — 30% GGE for regions with less than 75% of average EU-25 GDP per capita, for outermost regions with higher GDP per capita and until 1 January 2011 statistical effect regions;
    — 40% GGE for regions with less than 60% of average EU-25 GDP per capita;
    — 50% GGE for regions with less than 45% of average EU-25 GDP per capita.

Commentary
para 44: **B&C:** 15.049

45. In recognition of their specific handicaps, the outermost regions will be eligible for a further bonus of 20% GGE if their GDP per capita falls below 75% of the EU-25 average and 10% GGE in other cases.
46. The statistical effect regions which fall under the derogation under Article 87(3)(c) from 1 January 2011 will be eligible for an aid intensity of 20%.
47. In the other Article 87(3)(c) regions, the ceiling on regional aid must not exceed 15% GGE. This is reduced to 10% GGE in the case of regions with both more than 100% of average EU-25 GDP per capita and a lower unemployment rate than the EU-25 average, measured at NUTS-III level (based on averages for the last three years, using Eurostat data).[45]

[45] By way of exception, a higher aid intensity may be permitted in the case of a NUTS-III region, or smaller, adjacent to an Article 87(3)(a) region if this is necessary to ensure that the differential between the two regions does not exceed 20 percentage points.

Commentary
para 47: **B&C:** 15.050, 15.055

48. However, the low population density regions and regions (corresponding to NUTS-III level or smaller) adjoining a region with Article 87(3)(a) status selected by Member States for coverage under Article 87(3)(c), as well as NUTS-III regions or parts thereof which share a land border with a country which is not a Member State of the European Economic Area or EFTA, are always eligible for an aid intensity of 15% GGE.

Commentary
para 48: B&C: 15.055

4.1.3. Bonuses for small and medium-sized enterprises

49. In the case of aid awarded to small and medium-sized enterprises,[46] the ceilings in section 4.1.2 may be increased by 20% GGE for aid granted to small enterprises and by 10% GGE for aid granted to medium-sized enterprises.[47]

Notes

[46] Annex I of Commission Regulation (EC) No 364/2004 of 25 February 2004 amending Regulation (EC) No 70/2001, OJ L 63, 28.2.2004, p. 22, or any successor regulation.

[47] These bonuses do not apply to aid awarded in the transport sector.

Commentary
para 49: B&C: 15.051

4.2. Eligible expenses

4.2.1. Aid calculated on the basis of investment costs

50. Expenditures on land, buildings and plant/machinery[48] are eligible for aid for initial investment.

Notes

[48] In the transport sector, expenditure on the purchase of transport equipment (movable assets) is not eligible for aid for initial investment.

51. For SMEs, the costs of preparatory studies and consultancy costs linked to the investment may also be taken into account up to an aid intensity of 50% of the actual costs incurred.

52. In the event of an acquisition of the type referred to in paragraph 35, only the costs of buying assets[49] from third parties should be taken into consideration.[50] The transaction must take place under market conditions.

Notes

[49] Where the acquisition is accompanied by other initial investment, the expenditure relating to the latter should be added to the cost of the purchase.

[50] In exceptional cases, the aid may alternatively be calculated by reference to the (estimated) wage costs for the jobs safeguarded or newly created by the acquisition. These cases have to be individually notified to the Commission.

53. Costs related to the acquisition of assets other than land and buildings under lease can only be taken into consideration if the lease takes the form of financial leasing and contains an obligation to purchase the asset at the expiry of the term of the lease. For the lease of land and buildings, the lease must continue for at least five years after the anticipated date of the completion of the investment project for large companies, and three years for SMEs.

54. Except in the case of SMEs and takeovers, the assets acquired should be new. In the case of takeovers, assets for whose acquisition aid has already been granted prior to the purchase should be deducted.

55. For SMEs, the full costs of investments in intangible assets by the transfer of technology through the acquisition of patent rights, licences, know-how or unpatented technical knowledge may always be taken into consideration. For large companies, such costs are eligible only up to a limit of 50% of the total eligible investment expenditure for the project.

56. In all cases, eligible intangible assets will be subject to the necessary conditions for ensuring that they remain associated with the recipient region eligible for the regional aid and, consequently, that they are not the subject of a transfer benefiting other regions, especially other regions not eligible for regional aid. To this end, eligible intangible assets will have to satisfy the following conditions in particular:

— they must be used exclusively in the establishment receiving the regional aid;

— they must be regarded as amortizable assets;

— they must be purchased from third parties under market conditions;

— they must be included in the assets of the firm and remain in the establishment receiving the regional aid for at least five years (three years for SMEs).

4.2.2. Aid calculated on the basis of wage costs

57. As was indicated in section 4.1.1, regional aid may also be calculated by reference to the expected wage costs[51] arising from job creation as a result of an initial investment project.

Notes
[51] The wage cost means the total amount actually payable by the beneficiary of the aid in respect of the employment concerned, comprising the gross wage, before tax, and the compulsory social security contributions.

58. *Job creation* means a *net* increase in the number of employees[52] directly employed in a particular establishment compared with the average over the previous 12 months. Any jobs lost during that 12 month period must therefore be deducted from the apparent number of jobs created during the same period.[53]

Notes
[52] The number of employees means the number of annual labour units, namely the number of persons employed full time in one year, part-time and seasonal work being ALU fractions.
[53] Such a definition holds true as much for an existing establishment as for a new establishment.

59. The amount of aid must not exceed a certain percentage of the wage cost of the person hired, calculated over a period of two years. The percentage is equal to the intensity allowed for investment aid in the area in question.

4.3. Aid for large investment projects

60. For the purpose of these guidelines, a "*large investment project*" is an "initial investment" as defined by these guidelines with an eligible expenditure above EUR 50 million.[54] In order to prevent that a large investment project being artificially divided into sub-projects in order to escape the provisions of these guidelines, a large investment project will be considered to be a single investment project when the initial investment is undertaken in a period of three years by one or more companies and consists of fixed assets combined in an economically indivisible way.[55]

Notes
[54] The EUR 50 million must be calculated at prices and exchange rates on the date when the aid is granted, or in the case of large investment projects where individual notification is required, at prices and exchange rates at the date of the notification.
[55] To assess whether an initial investment is economically indivisible, the Commission will take into account the technical, functional and strategic links and the immediate geographical proximity. The economic indivisibility will be assessed independently from ownership. This implies that to establish whether a large investment project constitutes a single investment project, the assessment should be the same irrespective of whether the project is carried out by one undertaking, by more than one undertakings sharing the investment costs or by more undertakings bearing the costs of separate investments within the same investment project (for example in the case of a joint venture).

61. To calculate whether the eligible expenditure for large investment projects reaches the various thresholds in these guidelines, the eligible expenditure to be taken into account is either the traditional investment costs or the wage cost, whichever is the higher.

62. In two successive Multisectoral frameworks on regional aid for large investment projects in 1998[56] and 2002,[57] the Commission reduced the maximum aid intensities for large investment projects to limit distortions of competition. In the interests of simplification and transparency, the Commission has decided to integrate the provisions of the 2002 Multisectoral framework (MSF-2002) into the Regional aid guidelines for the period 2007–13.

Notes
[56] OJ C 107, 7.4.1998, p. 7.
[57] OJ C 70, 19.3.2002, p. 8 as amended by OJ C 263, 1.11.2003, p. 1.

63. MSF-2002 will therefore cease to apply to aid awarded or notified[58] after 31 December 2006 and will be replaced by these guidelines.[59]

Notes
58 Individually notifiable investment projects will be assessed in accordance with the rules in force at the time of notification.
59 Given the wide general scope of these guidelines, the Commission decided that it is not technically feasible to proceed with the establishment of a list of sectors where serious structural difficulties prevail.

4.3.1. Increased transparency and monitoring of large investment projects

64. Member States are required to notify individually to the Commission any aid to be awarded to investment projects under an existing aid scheme if the aid proposed from all sources is more than the maximum allowable amount of aid that an investment with eligible expenditure EUR 100 million can receive under the scale and the rules laid down in paragraph 67.[60] The notification thresholds for different regions with the most commonly encountered aid intensities under these guidelines are summarised in the table below.

Aid intensity	10%	15%	20%	30%	40%	50%
Notification threshold	EUR 7.5 million	EUR 11.25 million	EUR 15.0 million	EUR 22.5 million	EUR 30.0 million	EUR 37.5 million

Notes
60 Ad hoc individual aid must always be notified to the Commission. Because of its clear effect on the conditions of trade and competition, the need for a specific justification for the link with regional development applies with greater force to ad hoc individual aid for large individual investment projects.

65. Whenever regional aid is granted on the basis of existing aid schemes for non-notifiable large investments projects, Member States must, within 20 working days starting from the granting of the aid by the competent authority, provide the Commission with the information requested in the standard form laid down in Annex III. The Commission will make summary information available to the public through its website (http://europa.eu.int/comm/competition/).

66. Member States must maintain detailed records regarding the granting of aid for all large investment projects. Such records, which must contain all information necessary to establish that the maximum allowable aid intensity has been observed, must be maintained for 10 years from the date on which the aid was granted.

4.3.2. Rules for the assessment of large investment projects

67. Regional investment aid for large investment projects is subject to an adjusted regional aid ceiling,[61] on the basis of the following scale:

Eligible expenditure	*Adjusted aid ceiling*
Up to EUR 50 million	100% of regional ceiling
For the part between EUR 50 million and EUR 100 million	50% of regional ceiling
For the part exceeding EUR 100 million	34% of regional ceiling

Thus, the allowable aid amount for a large investment project will be calculated according to the following formula: maximum aid amount = R × (50 + 0.50 × B + 0.34 × C), where R is the unadjusted regional aid ceiling, B is the eligible expenditure between EUR 50 million and EUR 100 million, and C is the eligible expenditure above EUR 100 million. This is calculated on the basis of the official exchange rates prevailing on the date of the grant of aid, or in the case of aid subject to individual notification, on the date of notification.

Notes
61 The starting point for the calculation of the adjusted aid ceiling is always the maximum aid intensity allowed for aid for large enterprises in accordance with section 4.1.2 above. No SME bonuses may be granted to large investment projects.

68. Where the total amount of aid from all sources exceeds 75% of the maximum amount of aid an investment with eligible expenditure of EUR 100 million could receive, applying the standard aid ceiling in force for large enterprises in the approved regional aid map on the date the aid is to be granted, and where

    (a) the aid beneficiary accounts for more than 25% of the sales of the product(s) concerned on the market(s) concerned before the investment or will account for more than 25% after the investment, or

    (b) the production capacity created by the project is more than 5% of the market measured using apparent consumption data[62] for the product concerned, unless the average annual growth rate of its apparent consumption over the last five years is above the average annual growth rate of the European Economic Area's GDP, the Commission will approve regional investment aid only after a detailed verification, following the opening of the procedure provided for in Article 88(2) of the Treaty, that the aid is necessary to provide an incentive effect for the investment and that the benefits of the aid measure outweigh the resulting distortion of competition and effect on trade between Member States.[63]

Notes

[62] Apparent consumption of the product concerned is production plus imports minus exports.

[63] Before the entry into force of these guidelines the Commission will draw up further guidance on the criteria it will take into account during this assessment.

69. The product concerned is normally the product covered by the investment project.[64] When the project concerns an intermediate product and a significant part of the output is not sold on the market, the product concerned may be the downstream product. The relevant product market includes the product concerned and its substitutes considered to be such either by the consumer (by reason of the product's characteristics, prices and intended use) or by the producer (through flexibility of the production installations).

Notes

[64] Where an investment project involves the production of several different products, each of the products needs to be considered.

70. The burden of proof that the situations to which paragraphs 68(a) and (b) refer do not apply, lies with the Member State.[65] For the purpose of applying points (a) and (b), sales and apparent consumption will be defined at the appropriate level of the Prodcom classification,[66] normally in the EEA, or, if such information is not available or relevant, on the basis of any other generally accepted market segmentation for which statistical data are readily available.

Notes

[65] If the Member State demonstrates that the aid beneficiary creates a new product market, the tests laid down in paragraph 68(a) and (b) do not need to be carried out, and the aid will be authorised under the scale in paragraph 67.

[66] Council Regulation (EEC) No 3924/91 of 19 December 1991 on the establishment of a Community survey of industrial production (OJ L 374, 31.12.1991, p. 1).

4.4. Rules on the cumulation of aid

71. The aid intensity ceilings laid down in sections 4.1 and 4.3 above apply to the total aid:
    — where assistance is granted concurrently under several regional schemes or in combination with ad hoc aid;
    — whether the aid comes from local, regional, national or Community sources.

72. Where aid calculated on the basis of material or immaterial investment costs is combined with aid calculated on the basis of wage costs, the intensity ceiling laid down for the region concerned must be respected.[67]

Notes

[67] This condition is deemed to be met if the sum of the aid for the initial investment, expressed as a percentage of the investment, and of the job creation aid, expressed as a percentage of wage costs, does not exceed the most favourable amount resulting from application of either the ceiling set for the region in accordance with the criteria indicated at section 4.1 or the ceiling set for the region in accordance with the criteria indicated at section 4.3.

73. Where the expenditure eligible for regional aid is eligible in whole or in part for aid for other purposes, the common portion will be subject to the most favourable ceiling under the applicable rules.

74. Where the Member State lays down that State aid under one scheme may be combined with aid under other schemes, it must specify, in each scheme, the method by which it will ensure compliance with the conditions listed above.

75. Regional investment aid shall not be cumulated with *de minimis* support in respect of the same eligible expenses in order to circumvent the maximum aid intensities laid down in these guidelines.

5. Operating aid[68]

76. Regional aid aimed at reducing a firm's current expenses (operating aid) is normally prohibited. Exceptionally, however, such aid may be granted in regions eligible under the derogation in Article 87(3)(a) provided that (i) it is justified in terms of its contribution to regional development and its nature and (ii) its level is proportional to the handicaps it seeks to alleviate.[69] It is for the Member State to demonstrate the existence and importance of any handicaps.[70] In addition, certain specific forms of operating aid can be accepted in the low population density regions and the least populated areas.

Notes

[68] Like other forms of regional aid, the granting of operating aid is always subject to the specific rules which may apply in particular sectors.

[69] Operating aid takes the form in particular of tax exemptions or reductions in social security contributions which are not linked to eligible investment costs.

[70] The Commission is currently studying the feasibility of establishing a methodology for evaluating the additional costs in the outermost regions.

Commentary
para 76: B&C: 15.051

77. Operating aid should in principle only be granted in respect of a predefined set of eligible expenditures or costs [71] and limited to a certain proportion of those costs.

Notes

[71] For example, replacement investments, transport costs or labour costs.

78. Because of the specific nature of financial and intra-group activities, as defined in Section J (codes 65, 66 and 67) and intra-group activities falling within the scope of Section K (code 74) of the NACE code, operating aid granted for these activities has only a very limited likelihood of promoting regional development but a very high risk of distorting competition, as stated in the Commission notice on the application of the State aid rules to measures relating to direct business taxation.[72] The Commission will therefore not approve any operating aid to the financial services sector, or for intra-group activities under these guidelines unless such aid is granted under general schemes which are open to all sectors and which are designed to offset additional transport or employment costs. Operating aid intended to promote exports is likewise excluded.

Notes

[72] OJ C 384, 10.12.1998, p. 3.

79. Because it is intended to overcome delays and bottlenecks in regional development, except as provided for in paragraphs 80 and 81, operating aid should always be temporary and reduced over time, and should be phased out when the regions concerned achieve real convergence with the wealthier areas of the EU.[73]

Notes

[73] This principle of degressivity must also be respected when new operating aid schemes are notified to replace existing ones. However, flexibility as regards the application of this principle may be permitted in the case of operating aid schemes designed to address the geographical handicaps of particular areas located within Article 87(3)(a) regions.

80. In derogation from the previous paragraph, operating aid which is not both progressively reduced and limited in time may only be authorised:
    — in the outermost regions, in so far as it is intended to offset the additional costs arising in the pursuit of economic activity from the factors identified in Article 299(2) of the Treaty, the permanence and combination of which severely restrain the development of such regions (remoteness, insularity, small size, difficult topography and climate, and economic dependence on a few products);[74]
    — in the least populated regions, in so far as it is intended to prevent or reduce the continuing depopulation of these regions.[75] The least populated regions represent or belong to regions at NUTS-II level with a population density of 8 inhabitants per km2 or less and extend to adjacent and contiguous smaller areas meeting the same population density criterion.

Notes

[74] In view of the constraints faced by the outermost regions, except in the cases referred to in paragraph 78, the Commission considers that operating aid of up to 10% of the turnover of the beneficiary may be awarded without the need for specific justification. It is the task of the Member State to demonstrate that any proposed aid above this amount is justified in terms of its contribution to regional development, and that its level is proportional to the additional costs linked to the factors identified in Article 299(2) which it is intended to offset.

[75] It is the task of the Member State to demonstrate that the aid proposed is necessary and appropriate to prevent or reduce continuing depopulation.

Commentary
para 80: B&C: 15.051

81. In addition, in the outermost regions and low population density regions, aid which is not both progressively reduced and limited in time and which is intended partly to offset additional transport costs may be authorized under the following conditions:
    — aid may serve only to compensate for the additional cost of transport, taking into account other schemes of assistance to transport. While the amount of aid may be calculated on a representative basis, systematic overcompensation must be avoided;
    — aid may be given only in respect of the extra cost of transport of goods produced in the outermost regions and low population density regions inside the national borders of the country concerned. It must not be allowed to become export aid. No aid may be given towards the transport or transmission of the products of businesses without an alternative location (products of the extractive industries, hydroelectric power stations, etc.);
    — for the outermost regions only, aid may also cover the cost of transporting primary commodities, raw materials or intermediate products from the place of their production to the place of final processing in the region concerned;
    — the aid must be objectively quantifiable in advance, on the basis of an aid-per-passenger or aid per-ton/kilometre ratio, and there must be an annual report drawn up which, among other things, shows the operation of the ratio or ratios;
    — the estimate of additional cost must be based on the most economical form of transport and the shortest route between the place of production or processing and commercial outlets using that form of transport; external costs to the environment should also be taken into account.

Commentary
para 81: B&C: 15.051

82. In all cases, the need for and level of operating aid should be regularly re-examined to ensure its long-term relevance to the region concerned. The Commission will therefore only approve operating aid schemes for the duration of these guidelines.

83. In order to verify the effects on trade and competition of operating aid schemes, Member States will be required to provide each year a single report in respect of each NUTS-II region in which operating aid is granted which provides a breakdown of total expenditure, or estimated income forgone, for each operating aid scheme approved in the region concerned and identifies the ten largest beneficiaries of operating aid in the region concerned,[76] specifying the sector(s) of activity of the beneficiaries and the amount of aid received by each.

Part G State Aids

6. Aid for newly created small enterprises

84. While newly created small enterprises encounter difficulties throughout the EU, it appears that the economic development of the assisted regions is hindered by relatively low levels of entrepreneurial activity and in particular by even lower than average rates of business start-ups. It therefore appears necessary to introduce a new form of aid, which can be granted in addition to regional investment aid, in order to provide incentives to support business start-ups and the early stage development of small enterprises in the assisted areas.

85. In order to ensure that it is effectively targeted, it appears that this type of aid should be graduated according to the difficulties faced by each category of region. Furthermore, in order to avoid an unacceptable risk of distortions of competition, including the risk of crowding-out existing enterprises, the aid should, for an initial period at least, be strictly limited to small enterprises, limited in amount and degressive.

86. The Commission will accordingly approve aid schemes which provide aid of up to a total of EUR 2 million per enterprise[77] for small enterprises with their economic activity in regions eligible for the derogation in Article 87(3)(a), and up to EUR 1 million per enterprise for small enterprises with their economic activity in regions eligible for the derogation in Article 87(3)(c). Annual amounts of aid awarded for newly created small enterprises must not exceed 33% of the above-mentioned total amounts of aid per enterprise.

87. The eligible expenses are legal, advisory, consultancy and administrative costs directly related to the creation of the enterprise, as well as the following costs, insofar as they are actually incurred within the first five years of the creation of the enterprise thereafter:[78]
    — interests on external finance and a dividend on own capital employed not exceeding the reference rate;
    — fees for renting production facilities/equipment;
    — energy, water, heating, taxes (other than VAT and corporate taxes on business income) and administrative charges;
    — depreciation, fees for leasing production facilities/equipment as well as wage costs including compulsory social charges may also be included provided that the underlying investments or job creation and recruitment measures have not benefited from other forms of aid.

88. The aid intensity may not exceed
    — in Article 87(3)(a) regions, 35% of eligible expenses incurred in the first three years after the creation of the enterprise, and 25% in the two years thereafter;
    — in Article 87(3)(c) regions, 25% of eligible expenses incurred in the first three years after the creation of the enterprise, and 15% in the two years thereafter.

89. These intensities are increased by 5% in Article 87(3)(a) regions with a GDP per capita of less than 60% of the EU-25 average, in regions with a population density of less than 12.5 inhabitants/km² and in small islands with a population of less than 5,000, and other communities of the same size suffering from similar isolation.

90. The Member State shall put in place the necessary system to ensure that the upper limits for the amount of aid and the relevant aid intensity in relation to the eligible costs concerned are not exceeded. In particular, the aid provided for in this chapter shall not be cumulated with other public support (including *de minimis* support) in order to circumvent the maximum aid intensities or amounts laid down.

91. Granting aid designed exclusively for newly created small enterprises may produce perverse incentives for existing small enterprises to close down and re-open in order to receive this type of aid. Member States should be aware of this risk and should design aid schemes in such a way as to avoid this problem, for example by placing limits on applications from owners of recently closed firms.

7. Transitional arrangements

7.1. Reductions of aid intensities for regions remaining within Article 87(3)(a) on 1 January 2007

92. Where the implementation of these guidelines will result in a reduction in maximum aid intensities of more than 15 percentage points, net to gross,[79] the reduction may be implemented in two stages with the initial reduction of a minimum of 10 percentage points being applied on 1 January 2007, and the balance on 1 January 2011.

Notes

[79] I.e. from 50% net grant equivalent to 30% gross grant equivalent.

7.2. Reductions of aid intensities in the economic development regions

93. Provided the areas concerned are proposed by the Member State as eligible for regional aid under Article 87(3)(c) for the whole period 2007–2013, the reduction of aid intensities for the economic development regions may take place in two stages. A reduction of at least 10 percentage points net to gross shall be applied on 1 January 2007. As necessary to meet the new aid intensities allowed under these guidelines, a final reduction shall be applied at the latest on 1 January 2011.[80]

Notes

[80] Since Northern Ireland benefited from a specific provision in the regional aid guidelines for the period 2000–2006, the application of the same transitional arrangement is also justified.

7.3. Phasing-out of operating aid

94. For regions which lose their capacity to grant operating aid as a result of the loss of eligibility under Article 87(3)(a), the Commission can accept a linear phasing out of operating aid schemes over a two-year period from the date of the loss of eligibility to grant such aid.

7.4. Phasing out of Article 87(3)(c) regions

95. Following the entry into force of these guidelines, a number of regions will lose their eligibility for regional investment aid. In order to facilitate the smooth transition of these regions to the reformed horizontal State aid regime which is progressively being put in place through the implementation of the State aid action plan, Member States may exceptionally designate additional regions to be eligible for regional aid under Article 87(3)(c) until 1 January 2009, provided that the following conditions are met:
— the regions concerned were eligible for regional aid under Article 87(3)(c) on 31 December 2006;
— the combined total population of the regions eligible for regional investment aid under Article 87(3)(c) pursuant to the allocation of population coverages referred to in paragraphs 27 and 28 and those designated in accordance with this provision shall not exceed 66% of the national population eligible for regional aid under Article 87(3)(c) on 31 December 2006;[81]
— the maximum aid intensity permitted in the additional regions designated in accordance with this provision shall not exceed 10%.

Notes

[81] After exclusion of those regions which were eligible for regional aid under Article 87(3)(c) on 31 December 2006 and which qualify for aid under the present guidelines by virtue of other provisions (statistical effect regions, economic development regions, low population density regions). The resulting allocations are set out in Annex V.

Part G State Aids

8. Regional aid maps and declaration of compatibility

96. The regions of a Member State eligible for regional investment aid under the derogations and the ceilings on the intensity of aid for initial investment[82] approved for each region together form a Member State's regional aid map. The regional aid map also defines the regions eligible to grant enterprise aid. Operating aid schemes are not covered by the regional aid maps, and are assessed on a case by case basis on the basis of a notification by the Member State concerned pursuant to Article 88(3) of the Treaty.

Notes

[82] As adjusted in accordance with paragraph 67 in the case of individually notifiable aid for large investment projects.

97. The Court of Justice has ruled that the "decisions" by which the Commission adopts the regional aid maps for each Member State should be construed as forming an integral part of the guidelines on regional aid and as having binding force only on condition that they have been accepted by Member States.[83]

Notes

[83] Judgment of 18 June 2002 in Case C-242/00 *Germany v Commission*.

98. Furthermore, it should be recalled that the regional aid maps also define the scope of any group exemption exempting regional aid from the notification obligation under Article 88(3) of the Treaty, whether such aid is granted on the basis of Regulation (EC) No 70/2001,[84] or on the basis of a possible future exemption regulation for other forms of regional aid. Article 1(1)(b) of Regulation (EC) No 994/98[85] provides only for the exemption of "aid that complies with the map approved by the Commission for each Member State for the grant of regional aid".

Notes

[84] Commission Regulation (EC) No 70/2001 of 12 January 2001 on the application of Articles 87 and 88 of the EC Treaty to State aid to small and medium-sized enterprises (OJ L 10, 13.1.2001, p. 33), as amended by Commission Regulation (EC) No 364/2004 of 25 February 2004 amending Regulation (EC) No 70/2001 as regards the extension of its scope to include aid for research and development (OJ L 63, 28.2.2004, p. 22).
[85] Council Regulation (EC) No 994/98 of 7 May 1998 on the application of Articles [87] and [88] of the Treaty establishing the European Community to certain categories of horizontal State aid OJ L 142, 14.5.1998, p. 1.

99. Under these guidelines, depending on the socio-economic situation of the Member States, the regional aid map will include:
    (1) regions which can be identified on the basis of the criteria set out in these guidelines and in respect of which maximum aid intensities are defined by these guidelines. These are the regions eligible for the derogation under Article 87(3)(a) and the statistical effect regions.
    (2) regions which are to be designated by Member States for eligibility for regional aid in accordance with Article 87(3)(c) up to the limit for population coverage determined in accordance with section 3.4.1.

100. Of course, provided they respect the conditions set out in these guidelines, it is the responsibility of the Member States themselves to decide whether they wish to grant regional investment aid and up to what level. As soon as possible after the publication of these guidelines, each Member State should accordingly notify to the Commission, in accordance with Article 88(3) of the Treaty, a single regional aid map covering its entire national territory.

101. The Commission will examine the notifications in accordance with the procedure set out in Article 88(3) of the Treaty. At the conclusion of its examination, it will publish the approved regional aid maps in the *Official Journal of the European Union*. These maps will take effect on 1 January 2007, or their date of publication if later, and will be considered an integral part of the present guidelines.

102. The notification should clearly identify the regions proposed for eligibility under Article 87(3)(a) or (c), and the aid intensities envisaged for large companies, taking account of adjustments in the regional aid ceiling for large investment projects. Where for certain regions, transitional rules will apply, or where a change of aid intensity is anticipated, the relevant periods and aid intensities should be detailed.

103. Given that the regions eligible for support under Article 87(3)(a) and the statistical effect regions are determined exogenously at the NUTS-II level, it will not normally be necessary to provide detailed supporting socio-economic data. On the other hand detailed supporting information should be given to explain the designation of the Article 87(3)(c) regions, other than the economic development, the low population density and the border regions, including the detailed identification of the regions concerned, population data, information on GDP and unemployment levels in the regions concerned, and any other relevant information.

104. In order to ensure continuity, which is essential for long-term regional development, the list of regions notified by Member States should in principle apply throughout the period 2007-2013. It may, however, be subject to a mid-term review in 2010. Any Member State wishing to amend the list of regions eligible for aid under Article 87(3)(c) or the applicable aid intensities must submit a notification to the Commission before 1 April 2010 at the latest. Any changes of region in this context may not exceed 50% of the total coverage allowed for the Member State under Article 87(3)(c). With the exception of the statistical effect regions, regions which loose their eligibility for regional aid coverage as a result of this mid-term review will not be eligible for any transitional support. Moreover, Member States may at any time notify to the Commission a request to add further regions to the list until such time as the relevant population coverage is reached.

9. Entry into force, implementation, transparency and review

105. The Commission intends to apply these guidelines to all regional aid to be granted after 31 December 2006. Regional aid awarded or to be granted before 2007 will be assessed in accordance with the 1998 guidelines on national regional aid.

Commentary
para 105: B&C: 15.046

106. Since they must be coherent with the regional aid map, notifications of regional aid schemes, or ad hoc aid to be granted after 31 December 2006, cannot normally be considered complete until the regional aid map has been adopted for the Member State concerned in accordance with the arrangements described in section 8. Accordingly, the Commission will not normally examine notifications of regional aid schemes which are to apply after 31 December 2006, or ad hoc aid to be granted after that date, until the adoption of the regional aid map for the Member State concerned.[86] The same applies to aid schemes for newly created small enterprises covered by section 6 of these guidelines.

Notes

[86] The Commission informs the Member States that in order to reduce that burden of the obligation of notification to the maximum extent possible, it intends to make use of the powers conferred on it by Regulation (EC) No 994/98 to exempt from notification under Article 88(3) of the Treaty all transparent regional investment aid schemes which comply with the national regional aid map approved for the Member State concerned. Ad hoc individual aid and operating aid schemes will not be exempt from notification. Moreover, the information and individual notification requirements for large individual aid projects set out in section 4.3 of these guidelines will continue to apply, including in the case of aid which is granted under exempted schemes.

107. The Commission considers that the implementation of these guidelines will lead to substantial changes in the rules applicable to regional aid throughout the Community. Furthermore, in the light of the changed economic and social conditions prevailing in the EU, it appears necessary to review the continuing justification for and effectiveness of all regional aid schemes, including both investment aid and operating aid schemes. For these reasons, the Commission will propose the following appropriate measures to Member States pursuant to Article 88(1) of the Treaty:

— without prejudice to Article 10(2) of Regulation (EC) No 70/2001[87] on the application of Articles 87 and 88 of the Treaty to State aid for small and medium-sized enterprises, as amended by Regulation (EC) No 364/2004[88] and to Article 11(2) of Regulation (EC) No 2204/2002 on the application of Articles 87 and 88 of the EC Treaty to State aid for employment,[89] Member States shall limit the application in time of all existing regional aid schemes to aid to be granted on or before 31 December 2006;

— where environment aid schemes allow regional investment aid to be granted for environmental investments pursuant to footnote 29 of the Community guidelines on State aid for environmental protection,[90] Member States shall amend the relevant schemes in order to ensure that aid may only be granted after 31 December 2006 if it complies with the regional aid map in force on the date the aid is granted;

— Member States shall as necessary amend other existing aid schemes in order to ensure that any regional bonuses such as those allowed for training aid, aid for research and development or environment aid may only be granted after 31 December 2006 in areas which are eligible for support under Article 87(3)(a) or (c) in accordance with the regional aid map adopted by the Commission in force on the date the aid is granted.

The Commission will invite Member States to confirm their acceptance of these proposals within one month.

Notes
[87] OJ L 10, 13.1.2001, p. 33.
[88] OJ L 63, 28.2.2004, p. 22.
[89] OJ L 337, 13.12.2002, p. 3.
[90] OJ C 37, 3.2.2001, p. 3.

108. In addition, the Commission considers that further measures are necessary to improve the transparency of regional aid in an enlarged union. In particular, it appears necessary to ensure that the Member States, economic operators, interested parties and indeed the Commission itself should have easy access to the full text of all applicable regional aid schemes in the EU. The Commission considers that this can easily be achieved through the establishment of linked internet sites. For this reason, when examining regional aid schemes, the Commission will systematically seek an undertaking from the Member State that the full text of the final aid scheme will be published on the internet and that the internet address of the publication will be communicated to the Commission. Projects for which expenses were incurred before the date of publication of the scheme will not be eligible for regional aid.

109. The Commission may decide to review or amend these guidelines at any time if this should be necessary for reasons associated with competition policy or in order to take account of other Community policies and international commitments.

Annex I

Definition of the Steel Industry

The steel industry, for the purposes of these guidelines consists of the undertakings engaged in the production of the steel products listed below:

Product Combined	Nomenclature Code[1]
Pig iron	7201
Ferro-alloys	7202 11 20, 7202 11 80, 7202 99 11
Ferrous products obtained by direct reduction of iron ore and other spongy ferrous products	7203
Iron and non-alloy steel	7206
Semi-finished products of iron or non-alloy steel	7207 11 11, 7207 11 14, 7207 11 16, 7207 12 10, 7207 19 11, 7207 19 14, 7207 19 16, 7207 19 31, 7207 20 11, 7207 20 15, 7207 20 17, 7207 20 32, 7207 20 51, 7207 20 55, 7207 20 57, 7207 20 71

Product Combined	Nomenclature Code[1]
Flat rolled products of iron and non-alloy steel	7208 10 00, 7208 25 00, 7208 26 00, 7208 27 00, 7208 36 00, 7208 37, 7208 38, 7208 39, 7208 40, 7208 51, 7208 52, 7208 53, 7208 54, 7208 90 10, 7209 15 00, 7209 16, 7209 17, 7209 18, 7209 25 00, 7209 26, 7209 27, 7209 28, 7209 90 10, 7210 11 10, 7210 12 11, 7210 12 19, 7210 20 10, 7210 30 10, 7210 41 10, 7210 49 10, 7210 50 10, 7210 61 10, 7210 69 10, 7210 70 31, 7210 70 39, 7210 90 31, 7210 90 33, 7210 90 38, 7211 13 00, 7211 14, 7211 19, 7211 23 10, 7211 23 51, 7211 29 20, 7211 90 11, 7212 10 10, 7212 10 91, 7212 20 11, 7212 30 11, 7212 40 10, 7212 40 91, 7212 50 31, 7212 50 51, 7212 60 11, 7212 60 91
Bars and rods, hot rolled, in irregularly wound coils, of iron or non alloy steel	7213 10 00, 7213 20 00, 7213 91, 7213 99
Other bars and rods or iron and non-alloy steel	7214 20 00, 7214 30 00, 7214 91, 7214 99, 7215 90 10
Angles, shapes and sections of iron or non-alloy steel	7216 10 00, 7216 21 00, 7216 22 00, 7216 31, 7216 32, 7216 33, 7216 40, 7216 50, 7216 99 10
Stainless steel	7218 10 00, 7218 91 11, 7218 91 19, 7218 99 11, 7218 99 20
Flat-rolled products of stainless steel	7219 11 00, 7219 12, 7219 13, 7219 14, 7219 21, 7219 22, 7219 23 00, 7219 24 00, 7219 31 00, 7219 32, 7219 33, 7219 34, 7219 35, 7219 90 10, 7220 11 00, 7220 12 00, 7220 20 10, 7220 90 11, 7220 90 31
Bars and rods of stainless steel	7221 00, 7222 11, 7222 19, 7222 30 10, 7222 40 10, 7222 40 30
Flat rolled products of other alloy steel	7225 11 00, 7225 19, 7225 20 20, 7225 30 00, 7225 40, 7225 50 00, 7225 91 10, 7225 92 10, 7225 99 10, 7226 11 10, 7226 19 10, 7226 19 30, 7226 20 20, 7226 91, 7226 92 10, 7226 93 20, 7226 94 20, 7226 99 20
Bars and rods of other alloys steels	7224 10 00, 7224 90 01, 7224 90 05, 7224 90 08, 7224 90 15, 7224 90 31, 7224 90 39, 7227 10 00, 7227 20 00, 7227 90, 7228 10 10, 7228 10 30, 7228 20 11, 7228 20 19, 7228 20 30, 7228 30 20, 7228 30 41, 7228 30 49, 7228 30 61, 7228 30 69, 7228 30 70, 7228 30 89, 7228 60 10, 7228 70 10, 7228 70 31, 7228 80
Sheet piling	7301 10 00
Rails and cross ties	7302 10 31, 7302 10 39, 7302 10 90, 7302 20 00, 7302 40 10, 7302 10 20
Seamless tubes, pipes and hollow profiles	7303, 7304
Welded iron or steel tubes and pipes, the external diameter of which exceeds 406.4 mm	7305

Notes
[1] OJ L 279, 23.10.2001, p. 1.

ANNEX II
DEFINITION OF THE SYNTHETIC FIBRES INDUSTRY

The synthetic fibres industry is defined, for the purposes of these guidelines, as:

— extrusion/texturisation of all generic types of fibre and yarn based on polyester, polyamide, acrylic or polypropylene, irrespective of their end-uses, or

— polymerisation (including polycondensation) where it is integrated with extrusion in terms of the machinery used, or

— any ancillary process linked to the contemporaneous installation of extrusion/texturisation capacity by the prospective beneficiary or by another company in the group to which it belongs and which, in the specific business activity concerned, is normally integrated with such capacity in terms of the machinery used.

ANNEX III
FORM FOR THE PROVISION OF SUMMARY INFORMATION FOR AID FOR LARGE INVESTMENT PROJECTS REQUESTED IN PARAGRAPH 65

(1) Aid in favour of (name of the company/companies receiving the aid):

(2) Aid scheme reference (Commission reference of the existing scheme or schemes under which the aid is awarded):

(3) Public entity/entities providing the assistance (name and co-ordinates of the granting authority or authorities):

(4) Member State where the investment takes place:

(5) Region (NUTS-III level) where the investment takes place:

(6) Municipality (previously NUTS-V level, now LAU 2) where the investment takes place:

(7) Type of project (setting-up of a new establishment, extension of existing establishment, diversification of output of existing establishment into new, additional products, fundamental change in the overall production process of an existing establishment):

(8) Products manufactured or services provided on the basis of the investment project (with PRODCOM/NACE nomenclature or CPA nomenclature for projects in the service sectors):

(9) Short description of investment project:

(10) Discounted eligible cost of investment project (in EUR):

(11) Discounted aid amount (gross) in EUR:

(12) Aid intensity (% in GGE):

(13) Conditions attached to the payment of the proposed assistance (if any):

(14) Planned start and end date of the project:

(15) Date of award of the aid:

ANNEX IV
METHOD FOR ALLOCATION OF POPULATION SHARES IN ASSISTED ARTICLE 87(3)(C) AREAS ACROSS MEMBER STATES

The guiding principle behind the allocation of eligible population figures is to attribute them according to the observed **degree of regional disparities** within and between different Member States.

These disparities are captured through two indicators the Gross Domestic Product per capita in Purchasing Power Standard (**GDP per capita in PPS**) and the **unemployment** level. The method calculates the disparities leaving aside all assisted Article 87(3)(a) regions and the "statistical effect" as well as the economic development regions and the low population density regions. The data employed in the calculation is the average for the last three years for which data is available, 2000–2002 for GDP per capita and 2001–2003 for unemployment at national and EU-25 level.

The methodology is applied in three sequential steps:

Step I

In order to verify the referred disparity two **thresholds are used**. Regions at the NUTS-III level definition must have a GDP per capita below 85% or an unemployment level of more than 115% of the national average (MS = 100). As far as the unemployment level is concerned, it is considered that sufficient disparity is attained if the region in question has an unemployment figure that is 50% higher than the national average.

Step II

To take into account the relative position of the Member State with respect to the EU-25 average the thresholds of 85 for GDP per capita and 115 for unemployment are modified according to the following formulas:

$$\text{Adjusted GDP threshold } GDP = 85 \times \left(\frac{1 + \dfrac{100}{RMS}}{2} \right)$$

$$\text{Adjust unemployment threshold } Unemployment = MIN \left[150; 115 \times \left(\frac{1 + \dfrac{100}{RMS}}{2} \right) \right]$$

where *RMS* is the relative position of the MS to the EU 25 average in %.

The introduction of these corrections implies that regions in richer Member States should show a lower GDP per capita in comparison with the national average in order to qualify for the criteria of sufficient disparity. Regions in Member States with a low unemployment should have to show a higher level of unemployment although capped at the 150% unemployment level. On the contrary, regions in poorer Member States can have a higher GDP per capita than 85 and regions in Member States with a high unemployment can prove sufficient disparity with an unemployment level below 115.

Examples of application of correction formulas

Relative position of the Netherlands (EU-25 =100): GDP per capita 122.5, Unemployment 32.9.

After application of the mentioned correction formulas the thresholds for the Netherlands shift from 85 to 77.2 for GDP per capita and from 115 to 150 for unemployment.

Relative position of Greece (EU-25 =100): GDP per capita 74.5, Unemployment 111.7

After application of the mentioned correction formulas the thresholds employed for Greece shift from 85 to 99.5 for GDP per capita and from 115 to 109.0 for unemployment.

Step III

The next step is to verify which areas not eligible for regional aid pursuant to Article 87(3)(a) or not specifically allocated as areas eligible for Article 87(3)(c) qualify for the sufficient disparity criteria. The population for all the NUTS-III areas that verify these criteria are added together for each

Member State. Then the total population figure of all areas fulfilling these criteria for the EU-25 is calculated as well as the percentage that each Member State represents in this total. These respective percentages are then considered to be the **Repartition Key** for shares of population coverage allowed.

If the decision of the Commission is to allow coverage of 42% of the EU-25 population to live in assisted areas, the population of all assisted Article 87(3)(a) and earmarked Article 87(3)(c) areas are deducted from this figure. The remaining quantity is distributed among the Member States according to the **Repartition Key**.

In addition and also since it is not feasible to prove any internal disparity for Member States with no NUTS-III regional breakdown (Luxemburg and Cyprus) a safety net is applied to guarantees that no Member State can have its assisted areas coverage reduced by more than 50% [(]Article 87(3)(a) and (c) areas taken together) than that under the 1998 Regional Aid Guidelines. The aim is to ensure that all Member States are allocated a margin providing sufficient flexibility for an effective regional development policy.

ANNEX V
REGIONAL AID COVERAGE, 2007–2013

Belgium	Regions	GDP/CAP[1]	Population covered
Article 87(3)(a)	. . .		
Statistical effect	Hainaut	75.45	
			12.4%
Article 87(3)(c)			13.5%
Total population coverage 2007–2013			25.9%

Notes
[1] GDP per capita 2000–2002, PPS, EU-25 = 100 (Eurostat news release 47/2005 of 7.4.2005).

Czech Republic	Regions	GDP/CAP	Population covered
Article 87(3)(a)	Strední Morava	52.03	
	Severozápad	53.29	
	Strední Cechy	54.35	
	Moravskoslezsko	55.29	
	Severovýchod	55.59	
	Jihovýchod	58.17	
	Jihozápad	60.41	
			88.6%
Statistical effect . . .			
Article 87(3)(c)			
Total population coverage 2007–2013			88.6%
Transitional additional coverage 2007–2008 under Article 87(3)(c)			7.7 %

Denmark	Population covered
Article 87(3)(a) . . .	
Statistical effect . . .	
Article 87(3)(c)	8.6%
Total population coverage 2007–2013	8.6%
Transitional additional coverage 2007–2008 under Article 87(3)(c)	2.7%

Germany	Regions	GDP/CAP	Population covered
Article 87(3)(a)	Dessau	65.99	
	Chemnitz	69.63	
	Brandenburg-Nordost	70.64	
	Magdeburg	72.27	
	Mecklenburg-Vorpommern	72.56	
	Thüringen	73.10	
	Dresden	74.95	12.5%
Statistical effect	Halle	75.07	
	Leipzig	77.12	
	Brandenburg-Südwest	77.45	
	Lüneburg	81.80	
			6.1%
Article 87(3)(c)			11.0%
Total population coverage 2007–2013			29.6%

Estonia	Regions	GDP/CAP	Population covered
Article 87(3)(a)	Estonia	44.94	100%

Greece	Regions	GDP/CAP	Population covered
Article 87(3)(a)	Dytiki Ellada	56.30	
	Anatoliki Makedonia, Thraki	57.40	
	Ipeiros	59.30	
	Thessalia	62.90	
	Ionia Nisia	65.53	
	Kriti	72.27	
	Peloponnisos	73.71	
	Voreio Aigaio	74.29	
			36.6%

Greece	Regions	GDP/CAP	Population covered
Statistical effect	Kentriki Makedonia	75.89	
	Dytiki Makedonia	76.77	
	Attiki	78.98	
			55.5%
Article 87(3)(c)			7.9%
Total population coverage 2007–2013			100.0%

Spain	Regions	GDP/CAP	Population covered
Article 87(3)(a)	Extremadura	59.89	
	Andalucia	69.29	
	Galicia	73.36	
	Castilla-La Mancha	74.75	
	Canarias	87.79	
			36.2%
Statistical effect	Asturias	79.33	
	Murcia	79.37	
	Ceuta	79.64	
	Melilla	79.72	
			5.8%
Article 87(3)(c)			17.7%
Total population coverage 2007–2013			59.6%
Transitional additional coverage 2007–2008 under Article 87(3)(c)			12.4%

France	Regions	GDP/CAP	Population covered
Article 87(3)(a)	Guyane	56.76	
	Réunion	60.63	
	Guadeloupe	67.32	
	Martinique	74.88	
			2.9%
Statistical effect . . .			
Article 87(3)(c)			15.5%
Total population coverage 2007–2013			18.4%
Transitional additional coverage 2007–2008 under Article 87(3)(c)			6.9%

Ireland	Population covered
Article 87(3)(a) . . .	
Statistical effect . . .	
Article 87(3)(c)	50.0%
Total population coverage 2007–2013	50.0%
Transitional additional coverage 2007–2008 under Article 87(3)(c)	25.0%

Italy	Regions	GDP/CAP	Population covered
Article 87(3)(a)	Calabria	67.93	
	Campania	71.78	
	Sicilia	71.98	
	Puglia	72.49	
			29.2%
Statistical effect	Basilicata	77.54	
			1.0%
Article 87(3)(c)			3.9%
Total population coverage 2007–2013			34.1%
Transitional additional coverage 2007–2008 under Article 87(3)(c)			5.6%

Cyprus	Population covered
Article 87(3)(a) . . .	
Statistical effect . . .	
Article 87(3)(c)	50.0%
Total population coverage 2007–2013	50.0%
Transitional additional coverage 2007–2008 under Article 87(3)(c)	16.0%

Latvia	Regions	GDP/CAP	Population covered
Article 87(3)(a)	Latvia	37.28	100%

Lithuania	Regions	GDP/CAP	Population covered
Article 87(3)(a)	Lithuania	40.57	100%

Luxembourg	Population covered
Article 87(3)(a) . . .	
Statistical effect . . .	
Article 87(3)(c)	16.0%
Total population coverage 2007–2013	16.0%
Transitional additional coverage 2007–2008 under Article 87(3)(c)	5.1%

Hungary	Regions	GDP/CAP	Population covered
Article 87(3)(a)	Észak Magyaroszág	36.10	
	Észak Alföld	36.31	
	Dél Alföld	39.44	
	Dél Dunántúl	41.36	

Part G State Aids

1561

Hungary	Regions	GDP/CAP	Population covered
	Közép Dunántúl	52.28	
	Nyugat Dunántúl	60.37	
			72.2%
Statistical effect . . .			
Article 87(3)(c) . . .			27.8%
Total population coverage 2007–2013			100.0%

Malta	Regions	GDP/CAP	Population covered
Article 87(3)(a)	Malta	74.75	100%

Netherlands	Population covered
Article 87(3)(a) . . .	
Statistical effect . . .	
Article 87(3)(c)	7.5%
Total population coverage 2007–2013	7.5%
Transitional additional coverage 2007–2008 under Article 87(3)(c)	2.4%

Austria	Regions	GDP/CAP	Population covered
Article 87(3)(a) . . .			
Statistical effect	Burgenland	81.50	3.4%
Article 87(3)(c)			19.1%
Total population coverage 2007–2013			22.5%

Poland	Regions	GDP/CAP	Population covered
Article 87(3)(a)	Lubelskie	32.23	
	Podkarpackie	32.80	
	Warminsko-Mazurskie	34.70	
	Podlaskie	35.05	
	Swietokrzyskie	35.82	
	Opolskie	38.28	
	Malopolskie	39.81	
	Lubuskie	41.09	
	Lódzkie	41.45	
	Kujawsko-Pomorskie	41.80	
	Pomorskie	45.75	
	Zachodniopomorskie	46.29	
	Dolnoslaskie	47.52	
	Wielkopolskie	48.18	

Poland	Regions	GDP/CAP	Population covered
	Slaskie	50.62	
	Mazowieckie	68.77	
			100%

Portugal	Regions	GDP/CAP	Population covered
Article 87(3)(a)	Norte	61.94	
	Centro (PT)	63.08	
	Alentejo	65.72	
	Açores	61.61	
	Madeira	87.84	
			70.1
Statistical effect	Algarve	80.05	3.8%
Article 87(3)(c) . . .			2.8%
Total population coverage 2007–2013			76.7%
Transitional additional coverage 2007–2008 under Article 87(3)(c)			19.2%

Slovenia	Regions	GDP/CAP	Population covered
Article 87(3)(a)	Slovenia	74.40	100%

Slovakia	Regions	GDP/CAP	Population covered
Article 87(3)(a)	Východné Slovensko	37.21	
	Stredné Slovensko	40.72	
	Západné Slovensko	45.42	
			88.9%
Statistical effect . . .			
Article 87(3)(c) . . .			
Total population coverage 2007–2013			88.9%
Transitional additional coverage 2007–2008 under Article 87(3)(c)			7.5%

Finland		Population covered
Article 87(3)(a) . . .		
Statistical effect . . .		
Article 87(3)(c)		33.0%
Total population coverage 2007–2013		33.0%

Part G State Aids

1563

Sweden			Population covered
Article 87(3)(a) . . .			
Article 87(3)(c)			15.3%
Total population coverage 2007–2013			15.3%

United Kingdom	Regions	GDP/CAP	Population covered
Article 87(3)(a)	Cornwall & Isles of Scilly	70.16	
	West Wales and the Valleys	73.98	
			4.0%
Statistical effect	Highlands and Islands	77.71	0.6%
Article 87(3)(c)			19.3%
Total population coverage 2007–2013			23.9%

G21

COMMUNITY GUIDELINES ON STATE AID TO PROMOTE RISK CAPITAL INVESTMENTS IN SMALL AND MEDIUM-SIZED ENTERPRISES

(2006/C 194/02)

(Text with EEA relevance)

Official Journal C 194, 18.8.2006, p. 2

Celex No: 52006XC0818(01)

Notes

EEA application: for the corresponding EEA provision, see the EFTA Surveillance Authority's Procedural and Substantive Rules in the Field of State Aid (Guidelines on the application and interpretation of Articles 61 and 62 of the EEA Agreement and Article 1 of Protocol 3 to the Surveillance and Court Agreement), Part III, Chapter 10A (as substituted by EFTA Surveillance Authority Decision of 25 October 2006 (not yet published)).

Commentary
Guidelines: **B&C:** 15.003, 15.060

1 Introduction
    1.1 Risk capital as a Community objective
    1.2 Experience in the field of State aid to risk capital
    1.3 The balancing test for State aid supporting risk capital investments
        1.3.1 The State Aid Action Plan and the balancing test
        1.3.2 Market failures
        1.3.3 Appropriateness of the instrument

1 Introduction

1.1 Risk capital as a Community objective

Risk capital relates to the equity financing of companies with perceived high-growth potential during their early growth stages. The demand for risk capital typically comes from companies with growth potential that do not have sufficient access to capital markets, while the offer of risk capital comes from investors ready to take high risk in exchange of potentially above average returns from the equity invested. In its Communication to the Spring European Council, Working together for growth and jobs — A new start for the Lisbon strategy,[1] the Commission has recognised the insufficient level of risk capital available for start-up, innovative young businesses. The Commission has taken initiatives, like the Joint European Resources for Micro- to Medium Enterprises (JEREMIE) which

Part G State Aids

is a joint initiative of the Commission and the European Investment Fund to tackle the lack of risk capital for small and medium-sized enterprises in some regions. Building on the experience gained with the financial instruments under the multiannual programme for enterprise and entrepreneurship, and in particular for small and medium-sized enterprises (MAP) adopted by Council Decision 2000/819/EC[2] the Commission has proposed a High Growth and Innovative SME Facility (GIF) under the Competitiveness and Innovation Programme (CIP), which is currently being adopted and will cover the period 2007–2013.[3] The Facility will increase the supply of equity to innovative SMEs by investing on market terms into venture capital funds focused on SMEs in their early stages and in the expansion phase.

The Commission addressed the issue of risk capital financing in its Communication on "Financing SME Growth — Adding European Value" adopted on 29 June 2006.[4] The Commission has also stressed the importance of reducing and redirecting State aids to address market failures in order to increase economic efficiency and to stimulate research, development and innovation. In this context, the Commission has undertaken to reform the State aid rules, inter alia, with the aim of facilitating access to finance and risk capital.

In fulfilment of its commitment, the Commission published the "State Aid Action Plan — Less and better targeted State aid: A roadmap for State aid reform 2005-2009 ("the State Aid Action Plan")"[5] in June 2005. The State Aid Action Plan has highlighted the importance of improving the business climate and facilitating the rapid start-up of new enterprises. In this context, the State Aid Action Plan announced the review of the Communication on State aid and risk capital[6] to tackle the market failures affecting the provision of risk capital to start-ups and young, innovative small and medium-sized enterprises ("SMEs"), in particular by increasing the flexibility of the rules contained in the Communication on State aid and risk capital.

While it is the primary role of the market to provide sufficient risk capital in the Community, there is an "equity gap" in the risk capital market, a persistent capital market imperfection preventing supply from meeting demand at a price acceptable to both sides, which negatively affects European SMEs. The gap concerns mainly high-tech innovative and mostly young firms with high growth potential. However, a wider range of firms of different ages and in different sectors with smaller growth potential that cannot find financing for their expansion projects without external risk capital may also be affected. The existence of the equity gap may justify the granting of State aid in certain limited circumstances. If properly targeted, State aid in support of risk capital provision can be an effective means to alleviate the identified market failures in this field and to leverage private capital.

These guidelines replace the Communication on State aid and risk capital by setting out the conditions under which State aid supporting risk capital investments may be considered compatible with the common market. The guidelines explain the conditions under which State aid is present in accordance with Article 87(1) of the EC Treaty and the criteria that the Commission will apply in the compatibility assessment of the risk capital measures in accordance with Article 87(3) of the EC Treaty.

Notes

[1] COM(2005) 24.

[2] OJ L 333, 29.12.2000, p. 84. Decision as last amended by Decision No 1776/2005/EC of the European Parliament and of the Council (OJ L 289, 3.11.2005, p. 14).

[3] COM(2005) 121 final.

[4] COM(2006) 349.

[5] COM(2005) 107 final – SEC(2005) 795.

[6] OJ C 235, 21.8.2001, p. 3.

1.2 Experience in the field of State aid to risk capital

These guidelines have been prepared in the light of the experience gained in the application of the Communication on State aid and risk capital. Comments from public consultations of Member States and stakeholders on the revision of the Communication on State aid and risk capital, on the State aid Action Plan and on the Communication on State aid to innovation[1] have also been taken into account.

The experience of the Commission and the comments received in the consultations have shown that the Communication on State aid and risk capital has generally worked well in practice, but also revealed a need to increase the flexibility in the application of the rules and to adjust the rules to reflect the changed situation of the risk capital market. In addition, experience has shown that for some types of risk capital investments in some areas it was not always possible to fulfil the conditions set out in the Communication on State aid and risk capital, and, as a result, risk capital could not be adequately supported with State aid in these cases. Furthermore, experience has also shown a low overall profitability of the aided risk capital funds.

To remedy these problems, these guidelines adopt a more flexible approach in certain circumstances so as to allow Member States to better target their risk capital measures to the relevant market failure. These guidelines also set out a refined economic approach for the assessment of the compatibility of risk capital measures with the EC Treaty. Under the Communication on State aid and risk capital the assessment of the compatibility of schemes was already based on a relatively sophisticated economic analysis focussing on the size of the market failure and the targeting of the measure. Hence, the Communication on State aid and risk capital already reflected the key focus of a refined economic approach. However, some fine-tuning was still needed in respect of some of the criteria to ensure that the measure better target the relevant market failure. In particular, the guidelines contain elements to ensure that profit-driven and professional investment decisions are strengthened in order to further encourage private investors to co-invest with the State. Finally, an effort has been made to provide clarity where the experience with the Communication on State aid and risk capital has shown that this was needed.

Notes
[1] COM(2005) 436 final.

1.3 The balancing test for State aid supporting risk capital investments

1.3.1 The State Aid Action Plan and the balancing test

In the State Aid Action Plan the Commission underlined the importance of strengthening the economic approach to State aid analysis. This translates into a balancing the potential positive effects of the measure in reaching an objective of common interest against its potential negative effects in terms of distortion of competition and trade. The balancing test, as outlined in the State Aid Action Plan, is composed of three steps, the first two relating to the positive effects and the last one to the negative effects and the resulting balance:

(1) Is the aid measure aimed at a well-defined objective of common interest, such as growth, employment, cohesion and environment?
(2) Is the aid well designed to deliver the objective of common interest, that is does the proposed aid address the market failure or other objective?
  (i) Is State aid an appropriate policy instrument?
  (ii) Is there an incentive effect, i.e. does the aid change the behaviour of firms and/or investors?
  (iii) Is the aid measure proportional, i.e. could the same change in behaviour be obtained with less aid?
(3) Are the distortions of competition and effect on trade limited, so that the overall balance is positive?

The balancing test is equally relevant for the design of State aid rules and for the assessment of cases falling within their scope.

1.3.2 Market failures

On the basis of the experience gained in applying the Communication on State aid and risk capital, the Commission considers that there is no general risk capital market failure in the Community. It does, however, accept that there are market gaps for some types of investments at certain stages of enterprises" development. These gaps result from an imperfect matching of supply and demand of risk capital and can generally be described as an equity gap.

The provision of equity finance, in particular to smaller businesses, presents numerous challenges both to the investor and to the enterprise invested in. On the supply side, the investor needs to make a careful analysis not merely of any collateral being offered (as is the case of a lender) but of the entire business strategy in order to estimate the possibilities of making a profit on the investment and the risks associated with it. The investor also needs to be able to monitor that the business strategy is well implemented by the enterprise's managers. The investor finally needs to plan and execute an exit strategy, in order to generate a risk-adjusted return on investment from selling its equity stake in the company in which the investment is made.

On the demand side, the enterprise must understand the benefits and risks associated with external equity investment to pursue the venture and to prepare sound business plans to secure the necessary resources and mentoring. Owing to a lack of internal capital or the collateral needed to obtain debt funding and/or a solid credit history, the enterprise may face very tight funding constraints. In addition, the enterprise must share control with an outside investor, who usually has an influence over company decisions in addition to a portion of the equity.

As a result, the matching of supply and demand of risk capital may be inefficient so that the level of risk capital provided in the market is too restricted, and enterprises do not obtain funding despite having a valuable business model and growth prospects. The Commission considers that the main source of market failure relevant to risk capital markets, which particularly affects access to capital by SMEs and companies at the early stages of their development and which may justify public intervention, relates to imperfect or asymmetric information. Imperfect or asymmetric information may result notably in:

(a) Transaction and agency costs: potential investors face more difficulties in gathering reliable information on the business prospects of an SME or a new company and subsequently in monitoring and supporting the enterprise's development. This is in particular the case for highly innovative projects or risky projects. Furthermore, small deals are less attractive to investment funds due to relatively high costs for investment appraisal and other transaction costs.

(b) Risk aversion: investors may become more reluctant to provide risk capital to SMEs, the more the provision of risk capital is subject to imperfect of asymmetric information. In other words, imperfect or asymmetric information tends to exacerbate risk aversion.

1.3.3 Appropriateness of the instrument

The Commission considers that State aid to risk capital measures may constitute an appropriate instrument within the limits and conditions set out in these guidelines. However, it must be borne in mind that risk capital provision is essentially a commercial activity involving commercial decisions. In this context, more general structural measures not constituting State aid may also contribute to an increase in the provision of risk capital, such as promoting a culture of entrepreneurship, introducing a more neutral taxation of the different forms of SME financing (for example new equity, retained earnings and debt), fostering market integration, and easing regulatory constraints, including limitations on investments by certain types of financial institutions (for example, pension funds) and administrative procedures for setting up companies.

1.3.4 Incentive effect and necessity

State aid for risk capital must result in a net increase in the availability of risk capital to SMEs, in particular by leveraging investments by private investors. The risk of "dead weight", or lack of incentive effect, means that some enterprises funded through publicly supported measures would have obtained finance on the same terms even in the absence of State aid (crowding out). There is evidence of this happening, although such evidence is inevitably anecdotal. In those circumstances public resources are ineffective.

The Commission considers that aid in the form of risk capital satisfying the conditions laid down in these guidelines ensures the presence of an incentive effect. The need to provide incentives depends on the size of the market failure related to the different types of measures and beneficiaries. Therefore different criteria are expressed in terms of size of investment tranches per target enterprise, degree of involvement of private investors, and consideration of notably the size of the company and the business stage financed.

1.3.5 Proportionality of aid

The need to provide incentives depends on the size of the market failure related to the different types of measures, beneficiaries and development stage of the SMEs. A risk capital measure is well designed if the aid is necessary in all its elements to create the incentives to provide equity to SMEs in their seed, start-up and early stages. State aid will be inefficient if it goes beyond what is needed to induce more risk capital provision. In particular, to ensure that aid is limited to the minimum, it is crucial that there is significant private participation and that the investments are profit-driven and are managed on a commercial basis.

1.3.6 Negative effects and overall balance

The EC Treaty requires the Commission to control State aid within the Community. This is why the Commission has to be vigilant in order to ensure that measures are well targeted and to avoid severe distortions of competition. When deciding whether the grant of public funds for measures designed to promote risk capital is compatible with the common market, the Commission will seek to limit as far as possible the following categories of risk:

(a) the risk of "crowding out". The presence of publicly supported measures may discourage other potential investors from providing capital. This could, over the longer term, further discourage private investment in young SMEs and thus end up widening the equity gap, while at the same time creating the need for additional public funding;

(b) the risk that advantages to the investors and/or investment funds create an undue distortion of competition in the venture capital market relative to their competitors that do not receive the same advantages;

(c) the risk that an oversupply of public risk capital for target enterprises not invested according to a commercial logic could help inefficient firms stay afloat and could cause an artificial inflation of their valuations, making it all the less attractive for private investors to supply risk capital to these firms.

1.4 Approach for State aid control in the area of risk capital

Provision of risk capital funding to enterprises cannot be linked to the traditional concept of "eligible costs" used for State aid control, which relies on certain specified costs for which aid is allowed and the setting of maximum aid intensities. The diversity of possible models for risk capital measures devised by Member States also means that the Commission is not in a position to define rigid criteria by which to determine whether such measures are compatible with the common market. The assessment of risk capital therefore implies a departure from the traditional way in which State aid control is carried out.

However, since the Communication on State aid and risk capital has proved to work well in practice in the area of risk capital, the Commission has decided to continue and thereby ensure continuity with the approach of the Communication.

2 SCOPE AND DEFINITIONS

2.1 Scope

These guidelines only apply to risk capital schemes targeting SMEs. They are not intended to constitute the legal basis for declaring an ad hoc measure providing capital to an individual enterprise compatible with the common market.

Nothing in these guidelines should be taken to call into question the compatibility of State aid measures which meet the criteria laid down in any other guidelines, frameworks or regulations adopted by the Commission. The Commission will pay particular attention to the need to prevent the use of these guidelines to circumvent the principles laid down in existing frameworks, guidelines and Regulations. Risk capital measures must specifically exclude the provision of aid to enterprises:

(a) in difficulty, within the meaning of the Community guidelines on State aid for rescuing and restructuring firms in difficulty;[1]

(b) in the shipbuilding,[2] coal[3] and steel industry.[4]

These Guidelines do not apply to aid to export-related activities, namely aid directly linked to the quantities exported, to the establishment and operation of a distribution network or to other current expenditure linked to the export activity, as well as aid contingent upon the use of domestic in preference to imported goods.

Notes

[1] OJ C 244, 1.10.2004, p. 2.

[2] For the purpose of these Guidelines, the definitions laid down in the Framework on State aid to shipbuilding OJ C317, 30.12.2003, p. 11, apply.

[3] For the purpose of these Guidelines, "coal" means high-grade, medium-grade and low–grade category A and B coal within the meaning of the international codification system for coal laid down by the United Nations Economic Commission for Europe.

[4] For the purpose of these Guidelines, the definition laid down in Annex I in the Guidelines on national regional aid for 2007–2013 (OJ C 54, 4.3.2006, p. 13) applies.

2.2 Definitions

For the purposes of these guidelines, the following definitions shall apply:

(a) "**equity**" means ownership interest in a company, represented by the shares issued to investors;

(b) "**private equity**" means private (as opposed to public) equity investment in companies not listed on a stock-market, including venture capital, replacement capital and buy-outs;

(c) "**quasi-equity investment instruments**" means instruments whose return for the holder (investor/ lender) is predominantly based on the profits or losses of the underlying target company, are unsecured in the event of default. This definition is based on a substance over form approach;

(d) "**debt investment instruments**" means loans and other funding instruments which provide the lender/investor with a predominant component of fixed minimum remuneration and are at least partly secured. This definition is based on a substance over form approach;

(e) "**seed capital**" means financing provided to study, assess and develop an initial concept, preceding the start-up phase;

(f) "**start-up capital**" means financing provided to companies, which have not sold their product or service commercially and are not yet generating a profit, for product development and initial marketing;

(g) "**early-stage capital**" means seed and start-up capital;

(h) "**expansion capital**" means financing provided for the growth and expansion of a company, which may or may not break even or trade profitably, for the purposes of increasing production capacity, market or product development or the provision of additional working capital;

(i) "**venture capital**" means investment in unquoted companies by investment funds (venture capital funds) that, acting as principals, manage individual, institutional or in-house money and includes early-stage and expansion financing, but not replacement finance and buy-outs;

(j) "**replacement capital**" means the purchase of existing shares in a company from another private equity investment organisation or from another shareholder or shareholders. Replacement capital is also called secondary purchase;

(k) "**risk capital**" means equity and quasi-equity financing to companies during their early-growth stages (seed, start-up and expansion phases), including informal investment by business angels, venture capital and alternative stock markets specialised in SMEs including high-growth companies (hereafter referred to as investment vehicles);

(l) "**risk capital measures**" means schemes to provide or promote aid in the form of risk capital;

(m) "**Initial Public Offering**" ("**IPO**") means the process of launching the sale or distribution of a company"s shares to the public for the first time;

(n) "**follow-on investment**" means an additional investment in a company subsequent to an initial investment;

(o) "**buyout**" means the purchase of at least a controlling percentage of a company's equity from the current shareholders to take over its assets and operations through negotiation or a tender offer;

(p) "**exit strategy**" means a strategy for the liquidation of holdings by a venture capital or private equity fund according to a plan to achieve maximum return, including trade sale, write-offs, repayment of preference shares/loans, sale to another venture capitalist, sale to a financial institution and sale by public offering (including Initial Public Offerings);

(q) **"small and medium-sized enterprises"** ("SMEs") means small enterprises and medium-sized enterprises within the meaning of Commission Regulation (EC) No 70/2001 of 12 January 2001 on the application of Articles 87 and 88 of the EC Treaty to State aid to small and medium-sized enterprises[1] or any Regulation replacing that Regulation;

(r) **"target enterprise or company"** means an enterprise or company in which an investor or investment fund is considering investing;

(s) **"business angels"** means wealthy private individuals who invest directly in young new and growing unquoted business (seed finance) and provide them with advice, usually in return for an equity stake in the business, but may also provide other long-term finance;

(t) **"assisted areas"** means regions falling within the scope of the derogations contained in Article 87(3)(a) or (c) of the EC Treaty;

Notes

[1] OJ L 10, 13.1.2001, p. 33: Regulation as last amended by Regulation (EC) No 1040/2006 (OJ L 187, 8.7.2006, p. 8).

3 Applicability of Article 87(1) in the Field of Risk Capital

3.1 General applicable texts

There are already a number of published Commission texts which provide interpretation on whether individual measures fall within the definition of State aid and which may be relevant to risk capital measures. These include the 1984 communication on government capital injections,[1] the 1998 notice on the application of the State aid rules to measures relating to direct business taxation[2] and the notice on the application of Articles 87 and 88 of the EC Treaty to State aid in the form of guarantees.[3] The Commission will continue to apply these texts, when assessing whether risk capital measures constitute State aid.

Notes

[1] Bulletin EC 9-1984, reproduced in "Competition law in the European Communities", Volume IIA, p. 133.

[2] OJ C 384, 10.12.1998, p. 3.

[3] OJ C 71, 11.3.2000, p. 14.

3.2 Presence of aid at three levels

Risk capital measures often involve complex constructions devised to promote risk capital because the public authorities create incentives for one set of economic operators (investors) in order to provide finance to another set (target SMEs). Depending on the design of the measure, and even if the intention of the public authorities may be only to provide benefits to the latter group, enterprises at either or both levels may benefit from State aid. Moreover, in most cases the measure provides for the creation of a fund or other investment vehicle which has an existence separate from that of the investors and the enterprises in which the investment is made. In such cases it is also necessary to consider whether the fund or vehicle can be considered to be an enterprise benefiting from State aid.

In this context, funding with resources, which are not State resources within the meaning of Article 87(1) of the EC Treaty, is considered to be provided by private investors. This is, in particular, the case for funding by the European Investment Bank and the European Investment fund.

The Commission will take into account the following specific factors in determining whether State aid is present at each of the different levels.[1]

Aid to investors. Where a measure allows private investors to effect equity or quasi-equity investments into a company or set of companies on terms more favourable than public investors, or than if they had undertaken such investments in the absence of the measure, then those private investors will be considered to receive an advantage. Such advantage may take different forms, as specified in section 4.2 of these guidelines. This remains the case even if the private investor is persuaded by the measure to confer an advantage on the company or companies concerned. In contrast, the Commission will consider the investment to be effected *pari passu* between public and private investors, and thus not to constitute State aid, where its terms would be acceptable to a normal economic operator in a market economy in the absence of any State intervention. This is assumed to be the case only if public and private investors share exactly the same upside and downside risks and rewards and hold the same level of subordination, and normally where at least 50 percent of the funding of the measure is provided by private investors, which are independent from the companies in which they invest.

Aid to an investment fund, investment vehicle and/or its manager. In general, the Commission considers that an investment fund or an investment vehicle is an intermediary vehicle for the transfer of aid to investors and/or enterprises in which investment is made, rather than being a beneficiary of aid itself. However, measures such as fiscal measures or other measures involving direct transfers in favour of an investment vehicle or an existing fund with numerous and diverse investors with the character of an independent enterprise may constitute aid unless the investment is made on terms which would be acceptable to a normal economic operator in a market economy and therefore provide no advantage to the beneficiary. Likewise, aid to the fund"s managers or the management company will be considered to be present if their remuneration does not fully reflect the current market remuneration in comparable situations.

On the other hand, there is a presumption of no aid if the managers or management company are chosen through an open and transparent public tender procedure or if they do not receive any other advantages granted by the State.

Aid to the enterprises in which investment is made. In particular, where aid is present at the level of the investors, the investment vehicle or the investment fund, the Commission will normally consider that it is at least partly passed on to the target enterprises and thus that it is also present at their level. This is the case even where investment decisions are being taken by the managers of the fund with a purely commercial logic.

In cases where the investment is made on terms which would be acceptable to a private investor in a market economy in the absence of any State intervention the enterprises in which the investment is made will not be considered as aid recipients. For this purpose, the Commission will consider whether such investment decisions are exclusively profit-driven and are linked to a reasonable business plan and projections, as well as to a clear and realistic exit strategy. Also important will be the choice and investment mandate of the fund's managers or the management company as well as the percentage and degree of involvement of private investors.

Notes

[1] It should, however, be noted that guarantees granted by the State in favour of investments in risk capital are more likely to include an element of aid to the investor than is the case with traditional loan guarantees, which are normally considered to constitute aid to the borrower rather than to the lender.

3.3 *De minimis* amounts

Where all financing in the form of risk capital provided to beneficiaries is *de minimis* within the meaning of Commission Regulation (EC) No 69/2001 of 12 January 2001 on the application of Articles 87 and 88 of the EC Treaty to de minimis aid[1] and Commission Regulation (EC) No 1860/2004 on the application of Articles 87 and 88 of the EC Treaty to de minimis aid in the agriculture and fisheries sectors,[2] then it is deemed not to fall under Article 87(1) of the EC Treaty. In risk capital measures the application of the *de minimis* rule is made more complicated by difficulties in the calculation of the aid and also by the fact that measures may provide aid not only to the target enterprises but also to other investors. Where these difficulties can be overcome, however, the *de minimis* rule remains applicable. Therefore, if a scheme provides public capital only up to the relevant *de minimis* threshold to each enterprise over a three-year period, then it is certain that any aid to these enterprises and/or the investors is within the prescribed limits.

Notes

[1] OJ L 10, 13.1.2001, p. 30.
[2] OJ L 325, 28.10.2004, p. 4.

4 ASSESSMENT OF THE COMPATIBILITY OF RISK CAPITAL AID UNDER ARTICLE 87(3)(C) OF THE EC TREATY

4.1 General principles

Article 87(3)(c) of the EC Treaty provides that aid to facilitate the development of certain economic activities may be considered to be compatible with the common market where such aid does not adversely affect trading conditions to an extent contrary to the common interest. On the basis of the balancing test set out in section 1.3, the Commission will declare a risk capital measure compatible only if it concludes that the aid measure leads to an increased provision of risk capital without adversely affecting trading conditions to an extent contrary to the common interest. This section sets out a set of conditions under which the Commission will consider that aid in the form of risk capital is compatible with Article 87(3)(c).

Where the Commission is in possession of a complete notification which shows that all the conditions laid down in this section are met, it will try to make a rapid assessment of the aid within the time limits laid down in Council Regulation (EC) No 659/1999 of 22 March 1999 laying down detailed rules for the application of Article [88] of the EC Treaty.[1] For certain types of measures which do not fulfil all the conditions set out in this section, the Commission will undertake a more detailed assessment of the risk capital measure as set out in detail in section 5.

Where there is also aid at the level of target enterprises and the provision of risk capital is linked to costs which are eligible for aid under another regulation or framework or other guidelines, that text may be applied to consider whether the aid is compatible with the common market.

Notes
[1] OJ L 83, 27.3.1999, p. 1.

4.2 Form of aid

The choice of form of an aid measure lies in general with the Member State and this applies equally to risk capital measures. However, the Commission's assessment of such measures will include whether they encourage market investors to provide risk capital to the target enterprises and are likely to result in investment decisions being taken on a commercial (that is, a profit-driven) basis, as further explained in section 4.3.

The Commission believes that the types of measure capable of producing this result include the following:

(a) constitution of investment funds ("venture capital funds") in which the State is a partner, investor or participant, even if on less advantageous terms than other investors;

(b) guarantees to risk capital investors or to venture capital funds against a proportion of investment losses, or guarantees given in respect of loans to investors/funds for investment in risk capital, provided the public cover for the potential underlying losses does not exceed 50% of the nominal amount of the investment guaranteed;

(c) other financial instruments in favour of risk capital investors or venture capital funds to provide extra capital for investment;

(d) fiscal incentives to investment funds and/or their managers, or to investors to undertake risk capital investment.

4.3 Conditions for compatibility

To ensure that the incentive effect and the necessity of aid as set out in section 1.3.4 are present in a risk capital measure a number of indicators are relevant. The rationale is that State aid must target a specific market failure for the existence of which there is sufficient evidence. For this purpose, these guidelines lay down specific safe-harbour thresholds relating to tranches of investment in target SMEs in their early stages of business activity. Furthermore, so that aid is limited to the minimum necessary, it is crucial that aided investments into target SMEs are profit-driven and are managed on a commercial basis. The Commission will consider that the incentive effect, the necessity and proportionality of

Part G State Aids

aid are present in a risk capital measure and that the overall balance is positive where all the following conditions are met. Measures specifically involving investment vehicles will be assessed under section 5 of these guidelines and not under the conditions in this section.

4.3.1 *Maximum level of investment tranches*

The risk capital measure must provide for tranches of finance, whether wholly or partly financed through State aid, not exceeding EUR 1.5 million per target SME over each period of twelve months.

4.3.2 *Restriction to seed, start-up and expansion financing*

The risk capital measure must be restricted to provide financing up to the expansion stage for small enterprises, or for medium-sized enterprises located in assisted areas. It must be restricted to provide financing up to the start-up stage for medium-sized enterprises located in non-assisted areas.

4.3.3 *Prevalence of equity and quasi-equity investment instruments*

The risk capital measure must provide at least 70% of its total budget in the form of equity and quasi-equity investment instruments into target SMEs. In assessing the nature of such instruments, the Commission will have regard to the economic substance of the instrument rather than to its name and the qualification attributed to it by the investors. In particular, the Commission will take into account the degree of risk in the target company's venture borne by the investor, the potential losses borne by the investor, the predominance of profit-dependent remuneration versus fixed remuneration, and the level of subordination of the investor in the event of the company's bankruptcy. The Commission may also take into account the treatment applicable to the investment instrument under the prevalent domestic legal, regulatory, financial, and accounting rules, if these are consistent and relevant for the qualification.

4.3.4 *Participation by private investors*

At least 50% of the funding of the investments made under the risk capital measure must be provided by private investors, or for at least 30% in the case of measures targeting SMEs located in assisted areas.

4.3.5 *Profit-driven character of investment decisions*

The risk capital measure must ensure that decisions to invest into target companies are profit-driven. This is the case where the motivation to effect the investment is based on the prospects of a significant profit potential and constant assistance to target companies for this purpose. This criterion is considered to be met if all the following conditions are fulfilled:

(a) the measures have significant involvement of private investors as described in section 4.3.4, providing investments on a commercial basis (that is, only for profit) directly or indirectly in the equity of the target enterprises; and

(b) a business plan exists for each investment containing details of product, sales and profitability development and establishing the *ex ante* viability of the project; and

(c) a clear and realistic exit strategy exists for each investment.

4.3.6 *Commercial management*

The management of a risk capital measure or fund must be effected on a commercial basis. The management team must behave as managers in the private sector, seeking to optimise the return for their investors. This criterion is considered to be present where all the following conditions are fulfilled:

(a) there is an agreement between a professional fund manager or a management company and participants in the fund, providing that the manager's remuneration is linked to performance and setting out the objectives of the fund and proposed timing of investments; and

(b) private market investors are represented in decision-making, such as through an investors" or advisory committee; and

(c) best practices and regulatory supervision apply to the management of funds.

4.3.7 Sectoral focus

To the extent that many private sector funds focus on specific innovative technologies or even sectors (such as health, information technology, biotechnology) the Commission may accept a sectoral focus for risk capital measures, provided the measure falls within the scope of these guidelines as set out in section 2.1.

5 COMPATIBILITY OF RISK CAPITAL AID MEASURES SUBJECT TO A DETAILED ASSESSMENT

This section applies to risk capital measures which do not satisfy all the conditions laid down in section 4. A more detailed compatibility assessment based on the balancing test outlined in section 1.3 is necessary for these measures due to the need to ensure the targeting of the relevant market failure and due to the higher risks of potential crowding-out of private investors and of distortion of competition.

The analysis of compatibility of the measures with the EC Treaty will be based on a number of positive and negative elements. No single element is determinant, nor can any set of elements be regarded as sufficient on its own to ensure compatibility. In some cases their applicability, and the weight attached to them, may depend on the form of the measure. Member States will have to provide all the elements and the evidence they consider useful for the assessment of a measure. The level of evidence required and the Commission assessment will depend on the features of each case and will be proportionate to the level of market failure tackled and to the risk of crowding out private investment.

5.1 Aid measures subject to a detailed assessment

The following types of risk capital measures not complying with one or more of the conditions set out in section 4 will be subject to a more detailed assessment given the less obvious evidence of a market failure and the higher potential for crowding out of private investment and/or distortion of competition.

(a) Measures providing for investment tranches beyond the safe-harbour threshold of EUR 1.5 million per target SME over each period of twelve months

The Commission is aware of the constant fluctuation of the risk capital market and of the equity gap over time, as well as of the different degree by which enterprises are affected by the market failure depending on their size, on their stage of business development, and on their economic sector. Therefore, the Commission is prepared to consider declaring risk capital measures providing for investment tranches exceeding the threshold of EUR 1.5 million per enterprise per year compatible with the common market, provided the necessary evidence of the market failure is submitted.

(b) Measures providing finance for the expansion stage for medium-sized enterprises in non-assisted areas

The Commission recognises that certain medium-sized enterprises in non-assisted areas may have insufficient access to risk capital even in their expansion stage despite the availability of finance to enterprises having a significant turnover and/or total balance. Therefore, the Commission is prepared to consider declaring measures partly covering the expansion stage of medium-sized enterprises compatible with the common market in certain cases, provided the necessary evidence is submitted.

(c) Measures providing for follow-on investments into target companies that already received aided capital injections to fund subsequent financing rounds even beyond the general safe-harbour thresholds and the companies' early-growth financing

The Commission recognises the importance of follow-on investments into target companies that already received aided capital injections in their early stages to finance financing rounds even beyond the maximum safe-harbour investment tranches and the companies" early-growth financing up to the exit of the initial investment. This may be necessary to avoid dilution of the public participation in these financing rounds while ensuring continuity of financing for the target enterprises so that both public and private investors can fully benefit from the risky investments. In these circumstances and taking into account the specificities of the targeted sector and enterprises, the Commission is prepared to consider declaring follow-on investment compatible with the common market provided the amount of this investment is consistent with the initial investment and with the size of the fund.

(d) Measures providing for a participation by private investors below 50% in non-assisted areas or below 30% in assisted areas

In the Community the level of development of the private risk capital market varies to a significant extent in the various Member States. In some cases, it might be difficult to find private investors, and therefore the Commission is prepared to consider declaring measures with a private participation below the thresholds set out in section 4.3.4 compatible with the common market, if Member States submit the necessary evidence.

This problem may be even greater for risk capital measures targeting SMEs in assisted areas. In these cases there may be an additional shortage of capital available for them given their remote location from venture capital centres, the lower population density, and the increased risk-aversion of private investors. These SMEs may also be affected by demand-side issues such as the difficulty in drawing up a viable, investment-ready business proposition, a more limited equity culture, and particular reluctance to lose management control as a result of venture capital intervention.

(e) Measures providing seed capital to small enterprises which may foresee (i) less or no private participation by private investors, and/or (ii) predominance of debt investment instruments as opposed to equity and quasi-equity

The market failures affecting enterprises in their seed stage are more pronounced due to the high degree of risk involved by the potential investment and the need to closely mentor the entrepreneur in this crucial phase. This is also reflected by the reluctance and near absence of private investors to provide seed capital, which implies no or very limited risk of crowding-out. Furthermore, there is reduced potential for distortion of competition due to the significant distance from the market of these small-size enterprises. These reasons may justify a more favourable stance of the Commission towards measures targeting the seed stage, also in light of their potentially crucial importance to generate growth and jobs in the Community.

(f) Measures specifically involving an investment vehicle

An investment vehicle may facilitate the matching between investors and target SMEs for which it may therefore improve the access to risk capital. In case of market failures related to the enterprises targeted by the vehicle, the vehicle may not function efficiently without financial incentives. For instance, investors may not find the type of investments targeted by the vehicle attractive compared to investments of higher tranches of investments or investments in more established enterprises or more established market places, despite a clear potential for profitability of the target enterprises. Therefore, the Commission is prepared to consider declaring measures specifically involving an investment vehicle compatible with the common market, provided the necessary evidence for a clearly defined market failure is submitted.

(g) Costs linked to the first screening of companies in view of the conclusion of the investments, up to the due diligence phase ("scouting costs")

Risk capital funds or their managers may incur "scouting costs" in identifying SMEs, prior to the due diligence phase. Grants covering part of these scouting costs must encourage the funds or their managers to carry out more "scouting" activities than would otherwise be the case. This may also be beneficial for the SMEs concerned, even if the search does not lead to an investment, since it enables those SMEs to acquire more experience with risk capital financing. These reasons may justify a more favourable stance of the Commission towards grants covering part of the scouting costs of risk capital funds or their managers, subject to the following conditions: The eligible costs must be limited to the scouting costs related to SMEs mainly in their seed or start-up stage, where such costs do not lead to investment, and the costs must exclude legal and administrative costs of the funds. In addition, the grant must not exceed 50% of the eligible costs.

5.2 Positive effects of the aid

5.2.1 Existence and evidence of market failure

For risk capital measures envisaging investment tranches into target enterprises beyond the conditions laid down in section 4, in particular those providing for tranches above EUR 1.5 million per target SME over each period of twelve months, follow-on investments or financing of the expansion stage for medium-sized enterprises in non-assisted areas as well as for measures specifically involving an investment vehicle, the Commission will require additional evidence of the market failure being tackled at each level where aid may be present before declaring the proposed risk capital measure compatible with the common market. Such evidence must be based on a study showing the level of the "equity gap" with regard to the enterprises and sectors targeted by the risk capital measure. The relevant information concerns the supply of risk capital and the fundraising capital, as well as the significance of the venture capital industry in the local economy. It should ideally be provided for periods of three to five years preceding the implementation of the measure and also for the future, on the basis of reasonable projections, if available. The evidence submitted could also include the following elements:

(a) development of the fundraising over the past five years, also in comparison with the correspondent national and/or European averages;
(b) the current overhang of money;
(c) the share of government aided investment programs in the total venture capital investment over the preceding three to five years;
(d) the percentage of new start-ups receiving venture capital;
(e) the distribution of investments by categories of amount of investment;
(f) a comparison of the number of business plans presented with the number of investments made by segment (amount of investment, sector, round of financing, etc.).

For measures targeting SMEs located in assisted areas, the relevant information must be supplemented by any other relevant evidence proving the regional specificities which justify the features of the measure envisaged.

The following elements may be relevant:

(a) estimation of the additional size of the equity gap caused by the peripherality and other regional specificities, in particular in terms of total amount of risk capital invested, number of funds or investment vehicles present in the territory or at a short distance, availability of skilled managers, number of deals and average and minimum size of deals if available;
(b) specific local economic data, social and/or historic reasons for an underprovision of risk capital, in comparison with the relevant average data and/or situation at national and/or Community level as appropriate;
(c) any other relevant indicator showing an increased degree of market failure. Member States may resubmit the same evidence several times provided that the underlying market conditions have not changed. The Commission reserves the right to question the validity of the submitted evidence.

5.2.2 Appropriateness of the instrument

An important element in the balancing test is whether and to what extent State aid in the field of risk capital can be considered as an appropriate instrument to encourage private risk capital investment. This assessment is closely related to the assessment of the incentive effect and the necessity of aid, as set out in section 5.2.3.

In its detailed assessment, the Commission will take particular account of any impact assessment of the proposed measure which the Member State has made. Where the Member State has considered other policy options and the advantages of using a selective instrument such as State aid have been established and submitted to the Commission, the measures concerned are considered to constitute an appropriate instrument. The Commission will also assess evidence of other measures taken or to be taken to address the "equity gap" notably *ex post* evaluations and both supply and demand side issues affecting the targeted SMEs, to see how they would interact with the proposed risk capital measure.

5.2.3 Incentive effect and necessity of aid

The incentive effect of the risk capital aid measures plays a crucial role in the compatibility assessment. The Commission believes that the incentive effect is present for measures meeting all the conditions in section 4. However, as for the measures covered in this section the presence of the incentive effect becomes less obvious. Therefore, the Commission will also take into account the following additional criteria showing the profit-driven character of investment decisions and the commercial management of the measure, where relevant.

5.2.3.1 Commercial management

In addition to the conditions laid down in section 4.3.6 the Commission will consider it positively that the risk capital measure or fund is managed by professionals from the private sector or by independent professionals chosen according to a transparent, non-discriminatory procedure, preferably an open tender, with proven experience and a track record in capital market investments ideally in the same sector(s) targeted by the fund, as well as an understanding of the relevant legal and accounting background for the investment.

5.2.3.2 Presence of an investment committee

A further positive element would be the existence of an investment committee, independent of the fund management company and composed of independent experts coming from the private sector with significant experience in the targeted sector, and preferably also of representatives of investors, or independent experts chosen according to a transparent, non-discriminatory procedure, preferably an open tender. These experts would provide the managers or management company with analyses of the existing and the expected future market situation and would scrutinise and propose to them potential target enterprises with good investment prospects.

5.2.3.3 Size of the measure/fund

The Commission will consider it positively where a risk capital measure has a budget for investments into target SMEs of a sufficient size to take advantage of economies of scale in administering a fund and the possibility of diversifying risk via a pool of a sufficient number of investments. The size of the fund should be such as to ensure the possibility of absorbing the transaction costs and/or financing the later more profitable financing stages of target companies. Larger funds will be considered positively also taking into account the sector targeted, and provided the risks of crowding-out private investment and distorting competition are minimised.

5.2.3.4 Presence of business angels

For measures targeting seed capital, in view of the more pronounced level of market failure that can be perceived in this phase, the Commission will consider positively the direct or indirect involvement of business angels in investments in the seed stage. In such circumstances, it is therefore prepared to consider declaring measures compatible with the common market even if they foresee a predominance of debt instruments, including a higher degree of subordination of the State funds and a right of first profit for business angels or higher remuneration for their provision of capital and active involvement in the management of the measure/fund and/or of the target enterprises.

5.2.4 Proportionality

Compatibility requires that the aid amount is limited to the minimum necessary. The way to achieve this aspect of proportionality will necessarily depend on the form of the measure in question. However in the absence of any mechanism to check that investors are not overcompensated, or a measure where the risk of losses is borne entirely by the public sector and/or where the benefits flow entirely to the other investors, the measure will not be considered proportionate.

The Commission will consider that the following elements positively influence the assessment of proportionality as they represent a best-practice approach:

(a) **Open tender for managers.** A transparent, non-discriminatory open tender for the choice of the managers or management company ensuring the best combination of quality and value for money will be considered positively, as it will limit the cost (and possibly aid) level at the minimum necessary and will also minimise distortion of competition.

(b) **Call for tender or public invitation to investors.** A call for tender for the establishment of any "preferential terms" given to investors, or the availability of any such terms to other investors. This availability might take the form of a public invitation to investors at the launch of an investment fund or investment vehicle, or might take the form of a scheme (such as a guarantee scheme) which remained open to new entrants over an extended period.

5.3 Negative effects of the aid

The Commission will balance the potential negative effects in terms of distortion of competition and risk of crowding-out private investment against the positive effects when assessing the compatibility of risk capital measures. These potentially negative effects will have to be analysed at each of the three levels where aid may be present. Aid to investors, to investment vehicles and to investment funds may negatively affect competition in the market for the provision of risk capital. Aid to target enterprises may negatively affect the product markets on which these enterprises compete.

5.3.1 Crowding-out

At the level of the market for the provision of risk capital, State aid may result in crowding out private investment. This might reduce the incentives of private investors to provide funding for target SMEs and encourage them to wait until the State provides aid for such investments. This risk becomes more relevant, the higher the amount of an investment tranche invested into an enterprise, the larger the size of an enterprise, and the later the business stage, as private risk capital becomes progressively available in these circumstances. Therefore, the Commission will require specific evidence regarding the risk of crowding-out for measures providing for larger investment tranches in target SMEs, for follow-on investments or for financing of the expansion stage in medium-sized enterprises in non-assisted areas or for measures with low participation by private investors or measures involving specifically an invest-ment vehicle. In addition, Member States will have to provide evidence to show that there is no risk of crowding-out, specifically concerning the targeted segment, sector and/or industry structure. The following elements may be relevant:

(a) the number of venture capital firms/funds/investment vehicles present at national level or in the area in case of a regional fund and the segments in which they are active;
(b) the targeted enterprises in terms of size of companies, growth stage, and business sector;
(c) the average deal size and possibly the minimum deal size the funds or investors would scrutinise;
(d) the total amount of venture capital available for the target enterprises, sector and stage targeted by the relevant measure.

5.3.2 Other distortions of competition

As most target SMEs are recently established, at the level of the market where they are present, it is unlikely that these SMEs will have significant market power and thus that there will be a significant distortion of competition in this respect. However, it can not be excluded that risk capital measures might have the effect of keeping inefficient firms or sectors afloat, which would otherwise disappear. Furthermore, an over-supply of risk capital funding to inefficient enterprises may artificially increase their valuation and thus distort the risk capital market at the level of fund providers, which would have to pay higher prices to buy these enterprises. Sector specific aid may also maintain production in non-competitive sectors, whereas region-specific aid may build up an inefficient allocation of produc-tion factors between regions.

In its analysis of these risks, the Commission will examine, in particular, the following factors:

(a) overall profitability of the firms invested in over time and prospects of future profitability;
(b) rate of enterprise failure targeted by the measure;
(c) maximum size of investment tranche envisaged by the measure as compared to the turnover and costs of the target SMEs;
(d) over-capacity of the sector benefiting from the aid.

5.4 Balancing and decision

In the light of the above positive and negative elements, the Commission will balance the effects of the risk capital measure and determine whether the resulting distortions adversely affect trading conditions to an extent contrary to the common interest. The analysis in each particular case will be based on an overall assessment of the foreseeable positive and negative impact of the State aid. For that purpose the Commission will not use the criteria set out in these guidelines mechanically but will make an overall assessment of their relative importance.

The Commission may raise no objections to the notified aid measure without entering into the formal investigation procedure or, following the formal investigation procedure laid down in Article 6 of Regulation (EC) No 659/1999, it may close the procedure with a decision pursuant to Article 7 of that Regulation. If it adopts a conditional decision pursuant to Article 7(4) of Regulation (EC) No 659/1999 closing a formal investigation procedure, it may in particular attach the following conditions to limit the potential distortion of competition and ensure proportionality:

(a) if higher thresholds of investment tranches per target enterprise are foreseen, it may lower the maximum amount proposed per investment tranche or set an overall maximum amount of finance per target enterprise;

(b) if investments in the expansion stage in medium-sized enterprises in non-assisted areas are foreseen, it may limit investments predominantly to the seed and start-up stage and/or limit the investments to one or two rounds and/or limit the tranches to a maximum threshold per target enterprise;

(c) if follow-on investment is foreseen, it may set specific limits to the maximum amount to be invested into each target enterprise, to the investment stage eligible for intervention, and/or to the period during which aid may be granted, having also regard to the sector concerned and to the size of the fund;

(d) if a lower participation of private investors is foreseen, it may require a progressive increase of the participation of private investors over the life of the fund, having particular regard to the business stage, the sector, the respective levels of profit-sharing and subordination, and possibly the localisation in assisted areas of the target enterprises;

(e) for measures providing seed capital only, it may require Member States to ensure that the State receives an adequate return on its investment commensurate with the risks incurred for these investments, in particular where the State finances the investment in the form of quasi-equity or debt instruments, the return on which should, for instance, be linked to potential rights of exploitation (for example, royalties) generated by intellectual property rights created as a result of the investment;

(f) require a different balancing between respective profit- and loss-sharing arrangements and level of subordination between the State and private investors;

(g) require more stringent commitments as regards cumulation of risk capital aid with aid granted under other State aid regulations or frameworks, by way of derogation from section 6.

6 CUMULATION

Where capital provided to a target enterprise under a risk capital measure covered by these guidelines is used to finance initial investment or other costs eligible for aid under other block exemption regulations, guidelines, frameworks, or other State aid documents, the relevant aid ceilings or maximum eligible amounts will be reduced by 50% in general and by 20% for target enterprises located in assisted areas during the first three years of the first risk capital investment and up to the total amount received. This reduction does not apply to aid intensities provided for in the Community Framework for State aid for Research and Development[1] or any successor framework or block exemption regulation in this field.

Notes
[1] OJ C 45, 17.2.1996, p. 5.

---

7 FINAL PROVISIONS

7.1 Monitoring and reporting

Regulation (EC) No 659/1999 and Commission Regulation (EC) No 794/2004 of 21 April 2004 implementing Council Regulation (EC) No 659/1999 laying down detailed rules for the application of Article [88] of the EC Treaty[1] require Member States to submit annual reports to the Commission.

In respect of risk capital measures the reports must contain a summary table with a breakdown of the investments effected by the fund or under the risk capital measure including a list of all the enterprise beneficiaries of risk capital measures. The report must also give a brief description of the activity of investments funds with details of potential deals scrutinised and of the transactions actually undertaken as well as the performance of investment vehicles with aggregate information about the amount of capital raised through the vehicle. The Commission may request additional information regarding the aid granted, to check whether the conditions of the Commission's decision approving the aid measure have been respected.

The annual reports will be published on the internet site of the Commission.

In addition, the Commission considers that further measures are necessary to improve the transparency of State aid in the Community. In particular, it appears necessary to ensure that the Member States, economic operators, interested parties and the Commission itself have easy access to the full text of all applicable risk capital aid schemes. This can easily be achieved through the establishment of linked internet sites. For this reason, when examining risk capital aid schemes, the Commission will systematically require the Member State concerned to publish the full text of all final aid schemes on the internet and to communicate the internet address of the publication to the Commission. The scheme must not be applied before the information is published on the internet. Member States must maintain detailed records regarding the granting of aid for all risk capital measures. Such records must contain all information necessary to establish that the conditions laid down in the guidelines have been observed, notably as regards the size of the tranche, the size of the company (small or medium-sized), the development stage of the company (seed, start-up or expansion), its sector of activity (preferably at 4 digit level of the NACE classification) as well as information on the management of the funds and on the other criteria mentioned in these guidelines. This information must be maintained for 10 years from the date on which the aid is granted.

The Commission will ask Member States to provide this information in order to carry out an impact assessment of these guidelines three years after their entry into force.

Notes
[1] OJ L 140, 30.4.2004, p. 1.

7.2 Entry into force and validity

The Commission will apply these guidelines from the date of their publication in the *Official Journal of the European Union*. These guidelines will replace the 2001 Communication on State aid and risk capital These guidelines will cease to be valid on 31 December 2013. After consulting Member States, the Commission may amend it before that date on the basis of important competition policy or risk capital policy considerations or in order to take account of other Community policies or international commitments.

Where this would be helpful the Commission may also provide further clarifications of its approach to particular issues. The Commission intends to carry out a review of these guidelines three years after their entry into force.

The Commission will apply these guidelines to all notified risk capital measures in respect of which it must take a decision after the guidelines are published in the *Official Journal of the* European *Union*, even where the measures were notified prior to the publication of the guidelines. In accordance with the Commission notice on the determination of the applicable rules for the assessment of unlawful State aid ("*consecutio legis*"),[1] the Commission will apply the following in respect of non-notified aid:

(a) these guidelines, if the aid was granted after their publication in the *Official Journal of the European Union*;

(b) the Communication on State aid and risk capital in all other cases.

Notes
[1] OJ C 119, 22.5.2002, p. 22.

7.3 Appropriate Measures

The Commission hereby proposes to Member States, on the basis of Article 88(1) of the EC Treaty, the following appropriate measures concerning their respective existing risk capital measures. Member States should amend, where necessary, their existing risk capital measures in order to bring them into line with these guidelines within twelve months after the publication of the guidelines. The Member States are invited to give their explicit unconditional agreement to these proposed appropriate measures within two months from the date of publication of these guidelines. In the absence of any reply, the Commission will assume that the Member State in question does not agree with the proposed measures.

G22

COMMUNITY FRAMEWORK FOR STATE AID FOR RESEARCH AND DEVELOPMENT AND INNOVATION

(2006/C 323/01)

Official Journal C323, 30.12.2006, p. 1

Celex No: 52006XC1230(01)

Notes

EEA application: for the corresponding EEA provision, see the EFTA Surveillance Authority"s Procedural and Substantive Rules in the Field of State Aid (Guidelines on the application and interpretation of Articles 61 and 62 of the EEA Agreement and Article 1 of Protocol 3 to the Surveillance and Court Agreement), Part III, Chapter 14 (as substituted by EFTA Surveillance Authority Decision of 7 February 2007 (not yet published)).

Commentary
Communication: B&C: 15.003

---

1. Introduction
    1.1. Objectives of State aid for Research and Development and Innovation
    1.2. State aid policy and R&D&I
    1.3. The balancing test and its application to aid to Research and Development and Innovation
        1.3.1. The State Aid Action Plan: less and better targeted aid, balancing test for the assessment of aid
        1.3.2. The objective of common interest addressed by the framework
        1.3.3. Appropriate instrument
        1.3.4. Incentive effect and necessity of aid
        1.3.5. Proportionality of the aid
        1.3.6. Negative effects of the aid to R&D&I must be limited so that the overall balance is positive
    1.4. Implementing the balancing test: legal presumptions and need for more specific assessment
    1.5. Motivation for specific measures covered by this framework

Part G **State Aids**

1. Introduction

1.1. Objectives of State aid for Research and Development and Innovation

Promoting Research and Development and Innovation (hereinafter: R&D&I) is an important objective of common interest. Article 163 of the EC Treaty stipulates that "The Community shall have the objective of strengthening the scientific and technological bases of Community industry and encouraging it to become more competitive at international level, while promoting all the research activities deemed necessary . . .". Articles 164 to 173 of the EC Treaty determine the activities to be carried out in this respect and the scope and implementation of the multi-annual framework programme.

When meeting in Barcelona in March 2002, the European Council adopted a clear goal for the future development of research spending. It agreed that overall spending on Research and Development (hereinafter: R&D) and innovation in the Community should be increased with the aim of approaching 3% of gross domestic product by 2010. It further clarified that two-thirds of this new investment should come from the private sector. To reach this objective, research investment should grow at an average rate of 8% every year, shared between a 6% growth rate for public expenditure[1] and a 9% yearly growth rate for private investment.[2]

The objective is through State aid to enhance economic efficiency[3] and thereby, contribute to sustainable growth and jobs. Therefore, State aid for R&D&I shall be compatible if the aid can be expected to lead to additional R&D&I and if the distortion of competition is not considered to be contrary to the common interest, which the Commission equates for the purposes of this framework with economic efficiency. The aim of this framework is to ensure this objective and in particular, to make it easier for Member States to better target the aid to the relevant market failures.[4]

Article 87(1) of the EC Treaty lays down the principle that State aid is prohibited. In certain cases, however, such aid may be compatible with the common market on the basis of Article 87 (2) and (3). Aid for R&D&I will primarily be justified on the basis of Article 87(3)(b) and 87(3)(c). In this framework the Commission lays down rules which it will apply in the assessment of aid notified to it, thereby exercising its discretion and increasing legal certainty and transparency of its decision-making.

Notes

[1] It must be kept in mind that only a part of the public expenditure on R&D will qualify as State aid.

[2] Cf. "Investing in research: an action plan for Europe": Communication from the Commission to the Council, the European Parliament, the European Economic and Social Committee and the Committee of the Regions, COM(2003)226 final, p. 7.

[3] In economics, the term "efficiency" (or "economic efficiency") refers to the extent to which total welfare is optimised in a particular market or in the economy at large. Additional R&D&I increases economic efficiency by shifting market demand towards new or improved products, processes or services, which is equivalent to a decrease in the quality adjusted price of these goods.

[4] A "market failure" is said to exist when the market, if left to its own devices, does not lead to an economically efficient outcome. It is in those circumstances that state intervention, including state aid, has the potential to improve the market outcome in terms of prices, output and use of resources.

1.2. State aid policy and R&D&I

In the context of the Lisbon strategy the level of R&D&I is considered not to be optimal for the economy in the Community, implying that an increase in the level of R&D&I would lead to higher growth in the Community. The Commission considers that the existing rules for State aid to R&D have to be modernised and enhanced to meet this challenge.

First, the Commission, in this framework, expands the existing possibilities of aid to R&D to new activities supporting innovation. Innovation is related to a process connecting knowledge and technology with the exploitation of market opportunities for new or improved products, services and business processes compared to those already available on the common market, and encompassing a certain degree of risk. For the purpose of State aid rules, the Commission considers however that State aid for innovation should be authorised not on the basis of an abstract definition of innovation but only to the extent that it relates to precise activities, which clearly address the market failures that are hampering innovation and for which the benefits of State aid are likely to outweigh any possible harm to competition and trade

Second, the Commission aims at supporting a better administration of State aid to R&D&I. It intends to extend the scope of the block-exemption for R&D, which is currently limited to aid to small and medium-sized enterprises (hereafter: SMEs).[5] A future general block exemption regulation (hereafter: BER) will cover the less problematic aid measures in the area of R&D&I. This framework will continue to apply for all measures notified to the Commission whether because the measure is not covered by the BER, because of an obligation in the BER to notify aid individually, or because the Member State decides to notify a measure which could in principle have been exempted under the BER, as well as for the assessment of all non-notified aid.

Third, in order to better focus the Commission's scrutiny, this framework provides, for the assessment of measures falling within its scope, not only rules on the compatibility of certain aid measure (Chapter 5 below) but also, due to the increased risk of certain aid measures distorting competition and trade, additional elements concerning the analysis of the incentive effect and necessity of aid (Chapter 6 below) and an additional methodology to be applied in case of detailed assessment (Chapter 7 below).

In this context the Commission underlines that competitive markets should in principle, on their own, lead to the most efficient outcome in terms of R&D&I. However, this may not always be the case in the field of R&D&I and government intervention might then improve the outcome. Undertakings will invest more in research only to the extent that they can draw concrete commercial benefits from the results and are aware of the possibilities to do so. There are many reasons for low levels of R&D&I, which are partly due to structural barriers, and partly to the presence of market failures. Structural barriers should preferably be handled by structural measures,[6] whereas State aid may play a role in counter-weighing inefficiencies due to market failures. Furthermore, empirical evidence indicates that for State aid to be efficient it must be accompanied by favourable framework conditions, such as adequate intellectual property right systems, a competitive environment with research and innovation-friendly regulations and supportive financial markets.

However, State aid also distorts competition, and strong competition is at the same time a crucial factor for the market-driven stimulation of investment in R&D&I. Therefore, State aid measures must be carefully designed in order to limit the distortions. Otherwise, State aid can become counterproductive and reduce the overall level of R&D&I and economic growth.

The main concern related to R&D&I aid to undertakings is that rival undertakings' dynamic incentives to invest are distorted and possibly reduced. When an undertaking receives aid, this generally strengthens its position on the market and reduces the return on investment for other undertakings. When the reduction is significant enough, it is possible that rivals will cut back on their R&D&I activity. In addition, when the aid results in a soft budget constraint for the beneficiary, it may also reduce the incentive to innovate at the level of the beneficiary. Furthermore, the aid can support inefficient undertakings or enable the beneficiary to enhance exclusionary practices or market power.

Notes

[5] State Aid Action Plan. Less and better targeted State aid: a roadmap for State aid reform 2005–2009. COM(2005) 107 final — SEC (2005) 795: adopted on 7 June 2005.

[6] Including: university education, research programmes and public research facilities, IPR rules favouring innovation, attractive framework conditions for undertakings to do R&D&I.

1.3. The balancing test and its application to aid to Research and Development and Innovation

1.3.1. *The State Aid Action Plan: less and better targeted aid, balancing test for the assessment of aid*

In the State Aid Action Plan,[7] the Commission announced that "to best contribute to the re-launched Lisbon Strategy for growth and jobs, the Commission will, when relevant, strengthen its economic approach to State aid analysis. An economic approach is an instrument to better focus and target certain State aid towards the objectives of the re-launched Lisbon Strategy". In assessing whether an aid measure can be deemed compatible with the common market, the Commission balances the positive impact of the aid measure in reaching an objective of common interest against its potentially negative side effects by distortion of trade and competition. The State Aid Action Plan, building on existing practice, has formalised this balancing exercise in what has been termed a "balancing test".[8] It operates in three steps to decide upon the approval of a State aid measure; the first two steps are addressing the positive effects of State aid and the third is addressing the negative effects and resulting balancing of the positive and negative effects:

(1) Is the aid measure aimed at a well-defined objective of common interest (eg growth, employment, cohesion, environment)?

(2) Is the aid well designed to deliver the objective of common interest i.e. does the proposed aid address the market failure or other objective?

    (i) Is State aid an appropriate policy instrument?

    (ii) Is there an incentive effect, i.e. does the aid change the behaviour of firms?

    (iii) Is the aid measure proportional, i.e. could the same change in behaviour be obtained with less aid?

(3) Are the distortions of competition and effect on trade limited, so that the overall balance is positive?

This balancing test is applicable to the design of State aid rules as well as for the assessment of cases.

For a block exemption regulation, the State aid is compatible if the conditions laid down are fulfilled. The same applies in general to most cases addressed in this framework. However, for the individual aid measures which may have a high distortive potential due to high aid amounts, the Commission will make an overall assessment of the positive and negative effects of the aid based on the proportionality principle.

Notes

[7] State aid Action Plan (footnote), paragraph 21.

[8] Cf. State Aid Action Plan (footnote 5), paragraph 11 and 20, as elaborated in more detail already in the Communication on Innovation, COM(2005) 436 final of 21 September 2005.

1.3.2. The objective of common interest addressed by the framework

This framework addresses the objective of common interest of promoting Research and Development and Innovation. It aims at enhancing economic efficiency by tackling well defined market failures, which prevent the economy in the Community from reaching the optimal level of R&D&I.

To establish rules ensuring that aid measures achieve this objective, it is, first of all, necessary to identify the market failures hampering R&D&I. R&D&I takes place through a series of activities, which are upstream to a number of product markets, and which exploit available R&D&I capabilities to develop new or improved products[9] and processes in these product markets, thus fostering growth in the economy. However, given the available R&D&I capabilities, market failures may prevent the market from reaching the optimal output and lead to an inefficient outcome for the following reasons:

— **Positive externalities/knowledge spill-overs:** R&D&I often generate benefits for society in the form of knowledge spill-overs. However, left to the market, a number of projects may have an unattractive rate of return from a private perspective, even though the projects would be beneficial for society because profit seeking undertakings neglect the external effects of their actions when deciding how much R&D&I they should undertake. Consequently, projects in the common interest may not be pursued unless the government intervenes.

— **Public good/knowledge spill-overs:** For the creation of general knowledge, like fundamental research, it is impossible to prevent others from using the knowledge (public good), whereas more specific knowledge related to production can be protected, for example through patents allowing the inventor a higher return on their invention. To find the appropriate policy to support R&D&I, it is important to distinguish between creation of general knowledge and knowledge that can be protected. Undertakings tend to free ride on the general knowledge created by others, which makes undertakings unwilling to create the knowledge themselves. In fact, the market may not only be inefficient but completely absent. If more general knowledge was produced, the whole society could benefit from the knowledge spill-overs throughout the economy. For this purpose, governments may have to support the creation of knowledge by undertakings. In the case of fundamental research, they may have to pay fully for companies" efforts to conduct fundamental research.

— **Imperfect and asymmetric information**: R&D&I are characterised by a high degree of risk and uncertainty. Due to imperfect and/or asymmetric information, private investors may be reluctant to finance valuable projects; highly-qualified personnel may be unaware of recruitment possibilities in innovative undertakings. As a result, the allocation of human resources and financial resources may not be adequate in these markets and valuable projects for the economy may not be carried out.

— **Coordination and network failures**. The ability of undertakings to coordinate with each other or at least interact, and thus deliver R&D&I may be impaired. Problems may arise for various reasons, including difficulties in coordinating R&D and finding adequate partners.

Notes
[9] This includes services.

1.3.3. *Appropriate instrument*

It is important to keep in mind that there may be other, better placed instruments to increase the level of R&D&I in the economy, for example regulation, increase in funding of universities, general tax measures in favour of R&D&I.[10] The appropriateness of a policy instrument in a given situation is normally linked to the main reasons behind the problem. Reducing market barriers may be more appropriate than State aid to deal with the difficulty of a new entrant to appropriate R&D&I results. Increased investment in universities may be more appropriate to deal with a lack of qualified R&D&I personnel than granting State aid to R&D&I projects. Member States should therefore choose State aid when it is an appropriate instrument on the basis of the problem they are trying to address. This means it is necessary to clearly identify the market failure they intend to target with the aid measure.

Notes
[10] See the Notice on the application of the State aid rules to measures relating to direct business taxation: OJ C 384, 10.12.1998, p. 3.

1.3.4. *Incentive effect and necessity of aid*

State aid for R&D&I must lead to the recipient of aid changing its behaviour so that it increases its level of R&D&I activity and R&D&I projects or activities take place which would not otherwise be carried out, or which would be carried out in a more restricted manner. The Commission considers that as a result of aid, R&D&I activity should be increased in size, scope, amount spent or speed. Incentive effect is identified by counterfactual analysis, comparing the levels of intended activity with aid and without aid. Member States must clearly demonstrate how they intend to ensure that the incentive effect is present.

1.3.5. *Proportionality of the aid*

Aid is considered to be proportional only if the same result could not be reached with a less distortive aid measure. In particular, the amount and intensity of the aid must be limited to the minimum needed for the aided R&D&I activity to take place.

1.3.6. *Negative effects of the aid to R&D&I must be limited so that the overall balance is positive*

The possible distortions of competition resulting from State aid for R&D&I can be categorised as:

— disrupting the dynamic incentives of undertakings and crowding out;
— supporting inefficient production;
— exclusionary practices and enhancing market power;
— effects on the localisation of economic activities across Member States;
— effects on trade flows within the internal market.

The negative effects are normally higher for higher aid amounts and for aid granted to activities which are close to commercialisation of the product or the service. Therefore aid intensities should generally be lower for activities linked to development and innovation than for research related activities. Furthermore, in the definition of eligible costs it is important to ensure that costs that can be considered to cover routine company activities are not eligible for aid. Also, characteristics of the beneficiary and the relevant markets have an influence on the level of distortion. Such aspects will be taken into account in more detail for the cases which will undergo a detailed assessment.

1.4. Implementing the balancing test: legal presumptions and need for more specific assessment

This framework will be used for the assessment of aid for research and development and innovation which is notified to the Commission. The Commission's compatibility assessment will be conducted on the basis of the balancing test presented in Chapter 1. Accordingly, a measure will only be approved if, considering each of the elements in the balancing test, this leads to an overall positive evaluation. However, the Commission's assessment may differ in the way this evaluation is conducted, as in each case the risks for competition and trade associated with certain types of measures may differ. Without prejudice to Articles 4 to 7 of Council Regulation (EC) No 659/1999 of 22 March 1999 laying down detailed rules for the application of Article [88] of the EC Treaty,[11] the Commission applies different legal presumptions according to the type of State aid measure notified.

All notified aid will be assessed first under the provisions in Chapter 5. In that chapter, the Commission has identified a series of measures for which it considers *a priori* that State aid targeting these measures will address a specific market failure hampering R&D&I. The Commission has furthermore elaborated a series of conditions and parameters, which aim at ensuring that State aid targeting these measures actually presents an incentive effect, is proportionate and has a limited negative impact on competition and trade. Chapter 5 thus contains parameters in respect of the aided activity, aid intensities and conditions attached to compatibility. In principle, only measures which fulfil the criteria specified in Chapter 5 are eligible for compatibility under Article 87(3)(c) of the EC Treaty on the basis of this framework.

In Chapter 6, the Commission presents more specifically how it will assess the necessity and incentive effect of the aid.

In Chapter 7, the Commission presents more specifically in which cases and how it will conduct a detailed assessment. This translates into different levels of assessment described in more detail below. For the first level, the Commission considers that it is in principle sufficient that the measures concerned are in line with the conditions described in Chapter 5, provided that the conditions in Chapter 6 to presume the incentive effect are fulfilled. For all other measures, the Commission considers that additional scrutiny is necessary, because of higher risks for competition and trade, due to the activity, aid amount, or type of beneficiary. The additional scrutiny will generally consist in further and more detailed factual analysis of the case in line with the provisions set out in Chapter 6 in respect of necessity and incentive effect or in Chapter 7, in respect of the assessment for aid exceeding the threshold set in section 7.1. of this framework. As a result of this additional scrutiny, the Commission may approve the aid, declare it incompatible with the common market or declare that it is compatible with the common market subject to conditions.

Firstly, the Commission considers that for certain aid measures, fulfilling the provisions set out in Chapters 5 and 6 will generally be sufficient for securing compatibility, as it is presumed that for such a measure the result of the application of the balancing test would be positive. Whether a measure falls into this category depends upon the type of beneficiary, the activity aided and the amount of aid granted. The Commission considers that the following measures will be declared compatible on the basis of Chapters 5 and 6 if (i) they fulfil all the conditions and parameters mentioned in Chapter 5 and (ii) the aid is only granted after the aid application has been made to the national authorities:

— project aid and feasibility studies where the aid beneficiary is an SME and where the aid amount is below EUR 7.5 million per SME for a project (project aid plus aid for feasibility study);
— aid for industrial property rights costs for SMEs;
— aid for young innovative enterprises;

— aid for innovation advisory services; aid for innovation support services;
— aid for the loan of highly qualified personnel.

For the measures listed above, Chapter 6 clarifies that the incentive effect is presumed to be present if the condition mentioned above in (ii) is fulfilled.

Second, for notified aid **below** the thresholds set in section 7.1. of this framework, the additional scrutiny consists in a demonstration of the incentive effect and necessity as set out in Chapter 6. Such measures will therefore be declared compatible on the basis of Chapter 5 and Chapter 6 only if (i) they fulfil all the conditions and parameters mentioned in Chapter 5 and (ii) the incentive effect and necessity have been demonstrated in accordance with Chapter 6. Third, for notified aid **above** the thresholds set in section 7.1. of this framework, the additional scrutiny consists in a detailed assessment according to Chapter 7. These measures will therefore be declared compatible on the basis of Chapters 5, 6 and 7 only if (i) they fulfil all the conditions and parameters mentioned in Chapter 5 and (ii) the balancing test pursuant to Chapter 7 results in an overall positive evaluation.

Notes
[11] OJ L 83, 27.3.1999, p. 1.

1.5. Motivation for specific measures covered by this framework

Applying these criteria to R&D&I, the Commission has identified a series of measures for which State aid may, under specific conditions, be compatible with Article 87(3) (c) of the EC Treaty.

Aid for projects covering fundamental and industrial research and experimental development is mainly targeted at the market failure related to positive externalities (knowledge spillovers), including public goods. The Commission considers it useful to maintain different categories of R&D&I activities regardless of the fact that the activities may follow an interactive model of innovation rather than a linear model. Different aid intensities reflect different sizes of market failures and how close the activity is to commercialisation. Furthermore, compared to the previous State aid rules in this field, certain innovation activities have been included in experimental development. In addition, the bonus system has been simplified. Due to expected larger implications of market failures and expected higher positive externalities, bonuses appear justified for SMEs, collaboration by and collaboration with SMEs, cross-border collaboration as well as public-private partnerships (collaborations of undertakings with public research organisations).

Aid for technical feasibility studies related to R&D&I projects aims at overcoming the market failure related to imperfect and asymmetric information. These studies are considered to be further away from the market than the project itself, and therefore relatively high aid intensities can be accepted.

Aid for industrial property rights costs for SMEs is targeted at the market failure related to positive externalities (knowledge spillovers). The aim is to increase the possibilities for SMEs to sufficiently appropriate returns, thereby giving them greater incentive to undertake R&D&I.

Aid for young innovative enterprises has been introduced to deal with the market failures linked with imperfect and asymmetric information, which harm these undertakings in a particularly acute way, damaging their ability to receive appropriate funding for innovative ventures.

Aid for process and organisational innovation in services targets the market failures linked to imperfect information and positive externalities. It is meant to tackle the problem that innovation in services activities may not fit in the R&D categories. Innovation in service activities often results from interactions with customers and confrontation with the market, rather than from the exploitation and use of existing scientific, technological or business knowledge. Furthermore, innovation in service activities tends to be based on new processes and organisation rather than technological development. To that extent, process and organisational innovation in services is not properly covered by R&D project aid and requires an additional and specific aid measure to address the market failures that hamper it.

Aid for advisory services and innovation support services, provided by innovation intermediaries, targets market failures linked with insufficient information dissemination, externalities and lack of coordination. State aid is an appropriate solution to change the incentives for SMEs to buy such services and to increase the supply and demand of the services provided by innovation intermediaries.

Aid for the loan of highly qualified personnel addresses the market failure linked with imperfect information in the labour market in the Community. Highly qualified personnel in the Community are more likely to be hired by large undertakings, because they tend to perceive large undertakings as offering better working conditions, and more secure and more attractive careers. By contrast, SMEs could benefit from important knowledge transfer and from increased innovation capabilities, if they were able to recruit highly qualified personnel to conduct R&D&I activities. Creating bridges between large undertakings or universities and SMEs may also contribute to addressing coordination market failures, and supporting clustering.

Aid for innovation clusters aims at tackling market failures linked with coordination problems hampering the development of clusters, or limiting the interaction and knowledge flows within clusters. State aid could contribute in two ways to this problem: first by supporting the investment in open and shared infrastructures for innovation clusters, and secondly by supporting cluster animation, so that collaboration, networking and learning is enhanced.

2. Scope of Application and Definitions

2.1 Scope of application of the framework

This framework applies to State aid for research and development and innovation. It will be applied in accordance with other Community policies on State aid, other provisions of the Treaties founding the European Communities and legislation adopted pursuant to those Treaties.

According to general Treaty principles, State aid cannot be approved if the aid measure is discriminatory to an extent not justified by its State aid character. With regard to R&D&I, it should in particular be underlined that the Commission will not approve an aid measure which excludes the possibility of exploitation of R&D&I results in other Member States.

Public authorities may commission R&D from companies or buy the results of R&D from them. If such R&D is not procured at market price, this will normally involve State aid within the meaning of Article 87(1) of the EC Treaty. If, on the other hand, these contracts are awarded according to market conditions, an indication for which may be that a tender procedure in accordance with the applicable directives on public procurement, in particular Directive 2004/17/EC of the European Parliament and of the Council of 31 March 2004 coordinating the procurement procedures of entities operating in the water, energy, transport and postal services sectors[12] and Directive 2004/18/EC of the European Parliament and of the Council of 31 March 2004 on the coordination of procedures for the award of public works contracts, public supply contracts and public service contracts[13] has been carried out, the Commission will normally consider that no State aid within the meaning of Article 87(1) of the EC Treaty is involved.

This framework applies to aid to support research and development and innovation in all sectors governed by the EC Treaty. It also applies to those sectors which are subject to specific Community rules on State aid, unless such rules provide otherwise.[14]

This framework applies to State aid for R&D&I in the environmental field,[15] as there are many synergies to exploit between innovation for quality and performance and innovation to optimise energy use, waste and safety.

Following the entry into force of Commission Regulation (EC) No 364/2004 of 25 February 2004 amending Regulation (EC) No 70/2001 as regards the extension of its scope to include aid for research and development,[16] aid for research and development to SMEs is exempt from the notification requirement under the conditions stipulated in Commission Regulation (EC) No 70/2001 of 12 January 2001 on the application of Articles 87 and 88 of the EC Treaty to State aid to small and medium-sized enterprises.[17] Member States, however, remain free to notify such aid. If they decide to do so, this framework will continue to be used for the assessment of such notified aid.

While personnel costs are eligible in several of the measures covered by this framework and a measure on aid for the loan of highly qualified personnel has been introduced, general employment and training aid for researchers continue to fall under the specific State aid instruments for employment and training aid, currently Commission Regulation (EC) No 68/2001 of 12 January 2001 on the application of Articles 87 and 88 of the EC Treaty to training aid[18] and Commission Regulation (EC)

No 2204/ 2002 of 12 December 2002 on the application of Articles 87 and 88 of the EC Treaty to State aid for employment.[19] Aid for research and development and innovation for undertakings in difficulty within the meaning of the Community Guidelines on State aid for rescue and restructuring undertakings in difficulty[20] is excluded from the scope of this framework.

Notes

[12] OJ L 134, 30.4.2004, p. 1.

[13] OJ L 134, 30.4.2004, p. 114.

[14] For example, Article 3 of Regulation (EEC) No 1107/70 of the Council of 4 June 1970 on the granting of aids for transport by rail, road and inland waterway provides special rules for the compatibility of State aid to R&D in the sector of transport by rail, road and inland waterway.

[15] See current Community guidelines on State aid for environmental protection, OJ C 37, 3.2.2001, p. 3, point 7. In addition, in the context of the revision of the environmental guidelines, the Commission will consider the opportunity to integrate new measures that can also cover eco-innovation.

[16] OJ L 63, 28.2.2004, p. 22.

[17] OJ L 10, 13.1.2001, p. 33. Regulation as amended by Regulation (EC) No 364/2004.

[18] OJ L 10, 13.1.2001, p. 20. Regulation as amended by Regulation (EC) No 363/2004 (OJ L 63, 28.2.2004, p. 20).

[19] OJ L 337, 13.12.2002, p. 3.

[20] Currently OJ C 244, 1.10.2004, p. 2.

2.2. Definitions

For the purpose of this framework the following definitions apply:

(a) **"small and medium-sized enterprises"**, or **"SMEs"**, **"small enterprises"** and **"medium-sized enterprises"** means such undertakings within the meaning of Regulation (EC) No 70/2001, or any regulation replacing that regulation;

(b) **"large enterprises"** means undertakings not coming under the definition of small and medium-sized enterprises;

(c) **"aid intensity"** means the gross aid amount expressed as a percentage of the project's eligible costs. All figures used shall be taken before any deduction of tax or other charge. Where aid is awarded in a form other than a grant, the aid amount shall be the grant equivalent of the aid. Aid payable in several instalments shall be discounted to its value at the moment of granting. The interest rate to be used for discounting purposes and for calculating the aid amount in a soft loan shall be the reference rate applicable at the time of grant. The aid intensity is calculated per beneficiary;

(d) **"research organisation"** means an entity, such as university or research institute, irrespective of its legal status (organised under public or private law) or way of financing, whose primary goal is to conduct fundamental research, industrial research or experimental development and to disseminate their results by way of teaching, publication or technology transfer; all profits are reinvested in these activities, the dissemination of their results or teaching; undertakings that can exert influence upon such an entity, in the quality of, for example, shareholders or members, shall enjoy no preferential access to the research capacities of such an entity or to the research results generated by it;

(e) **"fundamental research"** means experimental or theoretical work undertaken primarily to acquire new knowledge of the underlying foundations of phenomena and observable facts, without any direct practical application or use in view;

(f) **"industrial research"** means the planned research or critical investigation aimed at the acquisition of new knowledge and skills for developing new products, processes or services or for bringing about a significant improvement in existing products, processes or services. It comprises the creation of components of complex systems, which is necessary for the industrial research, notably for generic technology validation, to the exclusion of prototypes as covered by point (g);

(g) **"experimental development"** means the acquiring, combining, shaping and using of existing scientific, technological, business and other relevant knowledge and skills for the purpose of producing plans and arrangements or designs for new, altered or improved products, processes or services. These may also include, for example, other activities aiming at the conceptual definition, planning and documentation of new products, processes and services. The activities may comprise producing drafts, drawings, plans and other documentation, provided that they are not intended for commercial use.

The development of commercially usable prototypes and pilot projects is also included where the prototype is necessarily the final commercial product and where it is too expensive to produce for it to be used only for demonstration and validation purposes. In case of a subsequent commercial use of demonstration or pilot projects, any revenue generated from such use must be deducted from the eligible costs.

The experimental production and testing of products, processes and services are also eligible, provided that these cannot be used or transformed to be used in industrial applications or commercially.

Experimental development does not include the routine or periodic changes made to products, production lines, manufacturing processes, existing services and other operations in progress, even if such changes may represent improvements;

(h) **"repayable advance"** means a loan for a project which is paid in one or more instalments and the conditions for the reimbursement of which depend on the outcome of the R&D&I project,

(i) **"process innovation"**[21] means the implementation of a new or significantly improved production or delivery method (including significant changes in techniques, equipment and/or software). Minor changes or improvements, an increase in production or service capabilities through the addition of manufacturing or logistical systems which are very similar to those already in use, ceasing to use a process, simple capital replacement or extension, changes resulting purely from changes in factor prices, customisation, regular seasonal and other cyclical changes, trading of new or significantly improved products are not considered innovations;

(j) **"organisational innovation"**[22] means the implementation of a new organisational method in the undertaking's business practices, workplace organisation or external relations. Changes in business practices, workplace organisation or external relations that are based on organisational methods already in use in the undertaking, changes in management strategy, mergers and acquisitions, ceasing to use a process, simple capital replacement or extension, changes resulting purely from changes in factor prices, customisation, regular seasonal and other cyclical changes, trading of new or significantly improved products are not considered innovations;

(k) **"highly qualified personnel"** means researchers, engineers, designers and marketing managers with tertiary education degree and at least 5 years of relevant professional experience. Doctoral training may count as relevant professional experience;

(l) **"secondment"** means temporary employment of personnel by a beneficiary during a period of time, after which the personnel has the right to return to its previous employer;

(m) **"innovation clusters"** means groupings of independent undertakings — innovative start-ups, small, medium and large undertakings as well as research organisations — operating in a particular sector and region and designed to stimulate innovative activity by promoting intensive interactions, sharing of facilities and exchange of knowledge and expertise and by contributing effectively to technology transfer, networking and information dissemination among the undertakings in the cluster. Preferably, the Member State should intend to create a proper balance of SMEs and large undertakings in the cluster, to achieve a certain critical mass, notably through specialisation in a certain area of R&D&I and taking into account existing clusters in the Member State and at Community-level.

Notes

[21] Cf. definition in the OSLO manual, Guidelines for Collecting and Interpreting Innovation Data, 3rd Edition, Organisation for Economic Co-operation and Development, 2005, page 49.

[22] Cf. definition in the OSLO manual, page 51.

3. State Aid within the Meaning of Article 87(1) of the EC Treaty

Generally, any funding meeting the criteria of 87(1) of the EC Treaty will be considered to be State aid. For the sake of providing further guidance, situations typically arising in the field of Research, Development and Innovation activities are considered below.

3.1. Research organisations and innovation intermediaries as recipients of State aid within the meaning of Article 87(1) of the EC Treaty

The question whether research organisations are recipients of State aid must be answered in accordance with general State aid principles.

In line with Article 87(1) of the EC Treaty and the case-law of the Court, public financing of R&D&I activities by research organisations will qualify as State aid, if all conditions of Article 87(1) of the EC Treaty are fulfilled. In accordance with the case-law, this requires inter alia that the research organisation qualifies as an undertaking within the meaning of Article 87(1) of the EC Treaty. This does not depend upon its legal status (organized under public or private law) or economic nature (i.e. profit making or not). What is decisive for its qualification as an undertaking is whether the research organisation carries out an economic activity, which is an activity consisting of offering goods and/or services on a given market.[23] Accordingly, any public funding of economic activities falls under Article 87(1) of the EC Treaty, should all other conditions be fulfilled.

Notes

[23] Case 118/85 *Commission v Italy* [1987] ECR 2599, paragraph 7, Case C-35/96 *Commission v Italy* [1998] ECR I-3851, CNSD, paragraph 36: Case C-309/99 *Wouters* [2002] ECR I-1577 paragraph 46.

3.1.1. *Public funding of non-economic activities*

If the same entity carries out activities of both economic and non-economic nature, in order to avoid cross-subsidisation of the economic activity, the public funding of the non-economic activities will not fall under Article 87(1) of the EC Treaty, if the two kinds of activities and their costs and funding can be clearly separated.[24] Evidence that the costs have been allocated correctly can consist of annual financial statements of the universities and research organisations.

The Commission nevertheless considers that the primary activities of research organisations are normally of a non-economic character, notably:

— education for more and better skilled human resources;
— the conduct of independent R&D for more knowledge and better understanding, including collaborative R&D;
— the dissemination of research results.

The Commission furthermore considers that technology transfer activities (licensing, spin-off creation or other forms of management of knowledge created by the research organisation) are of non-economic character if these activities are of an internal nature[25] and all income from these activities is reinvested in the primary activities of the research organisations.[26]

Notes

[24] Economic activities comprise in particular research carried out under contract with industry, the renting out of research infrastructure and consultancy work.

[25] By internal nature, the Commission means a situation where the management of the knowledge of the research organisation(s) is conducted either by a department or a subsidiary of the research organisation or jointly with other research organisations. Contracting the provision of specific services to third parties by way of open tenders does not jeopardise the internal nature of such activities.

[26] For all remaining kinds of technology transfer receiving State funding, the Commission does not consider itself in a position, on the basis of its current knowledge, to decide in a general manner upon the State aid character of the funding of such activities. It underlines the obligation of the Member States under Article 88(3) of the EC Treaty to assess the character of such measures in each case and to notify them to the Commission, in case they consider them to represent State aid.

3.1.2. *Public funding of economic activities*

If research organisations or other not-for-profit innovation intermediaries (for example, technology centres, incubators, chambers of commerce) perform economic activities, such as renting out infra-structures, supplying services to business undertakings or performing contract research, this should be done on normal market conditions, and public funding of these economic activities will generally entail State aid.

However, if the research organisation or not-for-profit innovation intermediary can prove that the totality of the State funding that it received to provide certain services has been passed on to the final recipient, and that there is no advantage granted to the intermediary, the intermediary organisation may not be recipient of State aid.

For aid to the final recipients, normal State aid rules apply.

3.2. Indirect State aid within the meaning of Article 87(1) of the EC Treaty to undertakings through publicly funded research organisations

This section is intended to clarify under which conditions undertakings obtain an advantage within the meaning of Article 87(1) of the EC Treaty in cases of contract research by a research organisation or collaboration with a research organisation. As far as the other elements of Article 87(1) of the EC Treaty are concerned, the normal rules apply. In particular, it will have to be assessed in accordance with the relevant case-law whether the behaviour of the research organisation can be attributed to the State.[27]

Notes

[27] Cf. Case C-482/99 *France v Commission* [2002] ECR I-4397, on the issue of imputability to the State.

3.2.1. *Research on behalf of undertakings (Contract research or research services)*

This point concerns the situation in which a project is carried out by a research organisation on behalf of an undertaking. The research organisation, acting as an agent, renders a service to the undertaking acting as principal in situations where (i) the agent receives payment of an adequate remuneration for its service and (ii) the principal specifies the terms and conditions of this service. Typically, the principal will own the results of the project and carry the risk of failure. When a research organisation carries out such a contract, there will normally be no State aid passed to the undertaking through the research organisation, if one of the following conditions is fulfilled:

(1) the research organisation provides its service at market price; or

(2) if there is no market price, the research organisation provides its service at a price which reflects its full costs plus a reasonable margin.

3.2.2. *Collaboration of undertakings and research organisations*

In a collaboration project, at least two partners participate in the design of the project, contribute to its implementation and share the risk and the output of the project.

In the case of collaboration projects carried out jointly by undertakings and research organisations, the Commission considers that no indirect State aid is granted to the industrial partner through the research organisation due to the favourable conditions of the collaboration if one of the following conditions is fulfilled:

(1) the participating undertakings bear the full cost of the project.

(2) the results which do not give rise to intellectual property rights may be widely disseminated and any intellectual property rights to the R&D&I results which result from the activity of the research organisation are fully allocated[28] to the research organisation.

(3) the research organisation receives from the participating undertakings compensation equivalent to the market price for the intellectual property rights[29] which result from the activity of the research organisation carried out in the project and which are transferred to the participating undertakings. Any contribution of the participating undertakings to the costs of the research organisation shall be deducted from such compensation.

If none of the previous conditions are fulfilled, the Member State may rely on an individual assessment of the collaboration project.[30] There may also be no State aid where the assessment of the contractual agreement between the partners leads to the conclusion that any intellectual property rights to the R&D&I results as well as access rights to the results are allocated to the different partners of the collaboration and adequately reflect their respective interests, work packages, and financial and other contributions to the project. If conditions (1), (2) and (3) are not fulfilled and the individual assessment of the collaboration project does not lead to the conclusion that there is no State aid, the Commission will consider the full value of the contribution of the research organisation to the project as aid to undertakings.

Notes

[28] "Full allocation" means that the research organisation enjoys the full economic benefit of those rights by retaining full disposal of them, notably the right of ownership and the right to license. These conditions may also be fulfilled if the organisation decides to conclude further contracts concerning these rights including licensing them to the collaboration partner.

[29] "Compensation equivalent to the market price for the intellectual property rights" refers to compensation for the full economic benefit of those rights. In line with general State aid principles and given the inherent difficulty to establish objectively the market price for intellectual property rights, the Commission will consider this condition fulfilled if the research organisation as seller negotiates in order to obtain the maximum benefit at the moment when the contract is concluded.

[30] This provision does not intend to modify the obligation of the Member States to notify certain measures on the basis of Article 88(3) of the EC Treaty.

---

4. Compatibility of Aid under Article 87(3)(b) of the EC Treaty

Aid for R&D&I to promote the execution of an important project of common European interest may be considered to be compatible with the common market pursuant to Article 87(3)(b) of the EC Treaty.

The Commission will conclude that Article 87(3)(b) of the EC Treaty applies if the following cumulative conditions are fulfilled:

(1) the aid proposal concerns a project which is clearly defined in respect of the terms of its implementation including its participants as well as its objectives. The Commission may also consider a group of projects as together constituting a project.

(2) the project must be in the common European interest: the project must contribute in a concrete, clear and identifiable manner to the Community interest. The advantage achieved by the objective of the project must not be limited to one Member State or the Member States implementing it, but must extend to the Community as a whole. The project must present a substantive leap forward for the Community objectives, for instance by being of great importance for the European Research Area or being a lead project for European industry. The fact that the project is carried out by undertakings in different countries is not sufficient. The positive effects of the aid could be shown for example by important spill-overs for society, through the contribution of the measure to the improvement of the Community situation regarding R&D&I in the international context, through creation of new markets or the development of new technologies. The benefits of the project should not be confined to the industry directly concerned but its results should be of wider relevance and application to the economy within the Community (up- or downstream markets, alternative uses in other sectors, etc.).

(3) the aid is necessary to achieve the defined objective of common interest and presents an incentive for the execution of the project, which must also involve a high level of risk. This could be shown by looking at the level of profitability of the project, at the amount of investment and time path of cash flows and at feasibility studies, risk assessments and expert opinions.

(4) the project is of great importance with respect to its character and its volume: it must be a meaningful project with regard to its objective and a project of substantial size.

The Commission will consider notified projects more favourably if they include a significant own contribution of the beneficiary to the project. It will equally consider more favourably notified projects involving undertakings or research entities from a significant number of Member States.

In order to allow for the Commission to properly assess the case, the common European interest must be demonstrated in practical terms: for example, it must be demonstrated that the project enables significant progress to be made towards achieving specific Community objectives.

5. Compatibility of Aid under Article 87(3)(c) of the EC Treaty

State aid for research and development and innovation shall be compatible with the common market within the meaning of Article 87(3)(c) of the EC Treaty, if, on the basis of the balancing test, it leads to increased R&D&I-activities without adversely affecting trading conditions to an extent contrary to the common interest. The Commission will view favourably notifications of aid measures which are supported by rigorous evaluations of similar past aid measures demonstrating the incentive effect of the aid. The following measures are eligible for compatibility under Article 87(3)(c) of the EC Treaty.

5.1. Aid for R&D projects

Aid for R&D projects will be considered compatible with the common market within the meaning of Article 87(3)(c) of the EC Treaty provided that the conditions set out in this section are fulfilled.

5.1.1. Research categories

The aided part of the research project must completely fall within one or more of the following research categories: fundamental research, industrial research, experimental development.

When classifying different activities, the Commission will refer to its own practice as well as the specific examples and explanations provided in the Frascati Manual on the Measurement of Scientific and technological Activities, Proposed Standard Practice for Surveys on Research and Experimental Development.[31]

When a project encompasses different tasks, each task must be qualified as falling under the categories of fundamental research, industrial research or experimental development or as not falling under any of those categories at all.

This qualification need not necessarily follow a chronological approach, moving sequentially over time from fundamental research to activities closer to the market. Accordingly, nothing will prevent the Commission from qualifying a task which is carried out at a late stage of a project as industrial research, while finding that an activity carried out at an earlier stage of the project constitutes experimental development or is not research at all.

Notes
[31] Organisation for Economic Co-operation and Development, 2002.

5.1.2. Basic aid intensities

The aid intensity, as calculated on the basis of the eligible costs of the project, shall not exceed:

(a) 100% for fundamental research;
(b) 50% for industrial research;
(c) 25% for experimental development.

The aid intensity must be established for each beneficiary of aid, including in a collaboration project.

In the case of State aid for an R&D project being carried out in collaboration between research organisations and undertakings, the combined aid deriving from direct government support for a specific research project and, where they constitute aid (see section), contributions from research organisations to that project may not exceed the applicable aid intensities for each benefiting undertaking.

5.1.3. Bonuses

The ceilings fixed for industrial research and experimental development may be increased as follows:

(a) where the aid is to be given to SMEs, the aid intensity may be increased by 10 percentage points for medium-sized enterprises and by 20 percentage points for small enterprises;

(b) up to a maximum aid intensity of 80%, a bonus of 15 percentage points may be added if:[32]

   (i) the project involves effective collaboration between at least two undertakings which are independent of each other and the following conditions are fulfilled:

      — no single undertaking must bear more than 70% of the eligible costs of the collaboration project;

      — the project must involve collaboration with at least one SME or be cross-border, that is to say, the research and development activities are carried out in at least two different Member States.

  (ii) the project involves effective collaboration between an undertaking and a research organisation, particularly in the context of co-ordination of national R&D policies, and the following conditions are fulfilled:

      — the research organisation bears at least 10% of the eligible project costs;

      — the research organisation has the right to publish the results of the research projects insofar as they stem from research implemented by that organisation.

 (iii) only in case of industrial research, if the results of the project are widely disseminated through technical and scientific conferences or published in scientific or technical journals or in open access repositories (databases where raw research data can be accessed by anyone), or through free or open source software.

For the purposes of points (i) and (ii) subcontracting is not considered to be effective collaboration. In case of collaboration between an undertaking and a research organisation, the maximum aid intensities and bonuses specified in this Framework do not apply to the research organisation.

Table illustrating the aid intensities:

	Small enterprise	Medium sized enterprise	Large Enterprise
Fundamental research	100%	100%	100%
Industrial research	70%	60%	50%
Industrial research	80%	75%	65%
Subject to:			
— collaboration between undertakings;			
for large undertakings: cross-border or with at least one SME			
or			
— collaboration of an undertaking with a research organisation			
or			
— dissemination of results			
Experimental development	45%	35%	25%
Experimental development	60%	50%	40%
subject to			
— collaboration between undertakings;			
for large undertakings: cross-border or at least one SME			
or			
— collaboration of an undertaking with a research organisation			

5.1.4. Eligible costs

The aid intensity will be calculated on the basis of the costs of the research project to the extent that they can be considered as eligible. All eligible costs must be allocated to a specific category of R&D.

The following costs shall be eligible:

(a) personnel costs (researchers, technicians and other supporting staff to the extent employed on the research project);

(b) costs of instruments and equipment to the extent and for the period used for the research project. If such instruments and equipment are not used for their full life for the research project, only the depreciation costs corresponding to the life of the research project, as calculated on the basis of good accounting practice, are considered as eligible;

(c) costs for building and land, to the extent and for the duration used for the research project. With regard to buildings, only the depreciation costs corresponding to the life of the research project, as calculated on the basis of good accounting practice are considered as eligible. For land, costs of commercial transfer or actually incurred capital costs are eligible;

(d) cost of contractual research, technical knowledge and patents bought or licensed from outside sources at market prices, where the transaction has been carried out at arm's length and there is no element of collusion involved, as well as costs of consultancy and equivalent services used exclusively for the research activity;

(e) additional overheads incurred directly as a result of the research project;

(f) other operating expenses, including costs of materials, supplies and similar products incurred directly as a result of the research activity.

5.1.5. Repayable advance

If a Member State grants a repayable advance which qualifies as State aid within the meaning of Article 87(1) of the EC Treaty, the following rules shall apply.

Where a Member State can demonstrate, on the basis of a valid methodology based on sufficient verifiable data, that it is possible to calculate the gross grant equivalent of such aid granted in the form of a repayable advance and to accordingly design a scheme where this gross grant equivalent fulfils the conditions on maximum intensities in this section, it may notify this scheme and the associated methodology to the Commission. If the Commission accepts the methodology and deems the scheme compatible, the aid may be granted on the basis of the gross grant equivalent of the repayable advance, up to the aid intensities permissible under this section.

In all other cases, the repayable advance is expressed as a percentage of the eligible costs; it may then exceed the rates indicated in this section. provided that the following rules are fulfilled.

In order to allow the Commission to assess the measure, it must provide for detailed provisions on the repayment in case of success and clearly define what will be considered as a successful outcome of the research activities. All these elements must be notified to the Commission. The Commission will examine that the definition of a successful outcome has been established on the basis of a reasonable and prudent hypothesis. In case of a successful outcome, the measure must provide that the advance is repaid with an interest rate at least equal to the applicable rate resulting from the application of the Commission notice on the method for setting the reference and discount rates.[33]

In case of a success exceeding the outcome defined as successful, the Member State concerned should be entitled to request payments beyond repayment of the advance amount including interest according to the reference rate foreseen by the Commission.

In case the project fails, the advance does not have to be fully repaid. In case of partial success, the Commission will normally require that the repayment secured is in proportion to the degree of success achieved.

The advance may cover up to a maximum of 40% of the eligible costs for the experimental development phase of the project and up to 60% for the industrial research phase, to which bonuses can be added.

Notes
[33] OJ C 273, 9.9.1997, p. 3. Also published under:
http://ec.europa.eu/comm/competition/state_aid/legislation/reference.html.

5.1.6. Fiscal measures

On the basis of evaluation studies[34] provided by Member States in the notification, the Commission will consider that R&D&I fiscal aid schemes have an incentive effect by stimulating higher R&D&I-spending by undertakings.

The aid intensity of an R&D&I fiscal State aid measure can be calculated either on the basis of individual R&D&I projects or, at the level of an undertaking, as the ratio between the overall tax relief and the sum of all eligible R&D&I costs incurred in a period not exceeding three consecutive fiscal years. In the latter case, the R&D&I fiscal State aid measure may apply without distinction to all eligible R&D&I activities; the applicable aid intensity for experimental development must then not be exceeded.[35]

At the time of notification, the Member State must provide an estimate of the number of beneficiaries.

Notes
[34] Even though this may not be possible *ex ante* for a newly introduced fiscal State aid measure, Member States will be expected to provide evaluation studies on the incentive effects of their own fiscal measures.
[35] Conversely, where an R&D&I fiscal State aid measure distinguishes between different R&D&I categories, the relevant aid intensities must not be exceeded.

5.1.7. Matching clause

In order to address actual or potential direct or indirect distortions of international trade, higher intensities than generally permissible under this section may be authorized if — directly or indirectly — competitors located outside the Community have received (in the last three years) or are going to receive, aid of an equivalent intensity for similar projects, programmes, research, development or technology. However, where distortions of international trade are likely to occur after more than three years, given the particular nature of the sector in question, the reference period may be extended accordingly.

If at all possible, the Member State concerned will provide the Commission with sufficient information to enable it to assess the situation, in particular regarding the need to take account of the competitive advantage enjoyed by a third-country competitor. If the Commission does not have evidence concerning the granted or proposed aid, it may also base its decision on circumstantial evidence.

5.2. Aid for technical feasibility studies

Aid for technical feasibility studies preparatory to industrial research or experimental development activities shall be compatible with the common market within the meaning of Article 87(3)(c) of the EC Treaty provided that the aid intensity, as calculated on the basis of the study costs, does not exceed the following aid intensities:

(a) for SMEs, 75% for studies preparatory to industrial research activities and 50% for studies preparatory to experimental development activities,
(b) for large undertakings, 65% for studies preparatory to industrial research activities and 40% for studies preparatory to experimental development activities.

5.3. Aid for industrial property rights costs for SMEs

Aid to SMEs for the costs associated with obtaining and validating patents and other industrial property rights shall be compatible with the common market within the meaning of Article 87(3)(c) of the

EC Treaty up to the same level of aid as would have qualified as R&D aid in respect of the research activities which first led to the industrial property rights concerned.

Eligible costs are:

(a) all costs preceding the grant of the right in the first legal jurisdiction, including costs relating to the preparation, filing and prosecution of the application as well as costs incurred in renewing the application before the right has been granted;

(b) translation and other costs incurred in order to obtain the granting or validation of the right in other legal jurisdictions;

(c) costs incurred in defending the validity of the right during the official prosecution of the application and possible opposition proceedings, even if such costs occur after the right is granted.

5.4. Aid for young innovative enterprises

Aid to young innovative enterprises shall be compatible with the common market within the meaning of Article 87(3)(c) of the EC Treaty if the following conditions are fulfilled:[36]

(a) the beneficiary is a small enterprise that has been of existence for less than 6 years at the time when the aid is granted and

(b) the beneficiary is an innovative enterprise, on the basis that:
  (i) the Member State can demonstrate, by means of an evaluation carried out by an external expert, notably on the basis of a business plan, that the beneficiary will in the foreseeable future develop products, services or processes which are technologically new or substantially improved compared to the state of the art in its industry in the Community, and which carry a risk of technological or industrial failure, or
  (ii) the R&D expenses of the beneficiary represent at least 15% of its total operating expenses in at least one of the three years preceding the granting of the aid or in the case of a start-up enterprise without any financial history, in the audit of its current fiscal period, as certified by an external auditor.

(c) the aid is not higher than EUR 1 million. This aid may not exceed EUR 1.5 million in regions eligible for the derogation in Article 87(3)(a) of the EC Treaty, and EUR 1.25 million in regions eligible for the derogation in Article 87(3)(c) of the EC Treaty.

The beneficiary may receive the aid only once during the period in which it qualifies as a young innovative enterprise This aid may be cumulated with other aid under this framework, with aid for research and development and innovation exempted by Regulation (EC) No 364/2004 or any successor regulation and with aid approved by the Commission under the risk capital guidelines.

The beneficiary may receive State aid other than R&D&I aid and risk capital aid only 3 years after the granting of the young innovative enterprise aid.

Notes

[36] This is without prejudice to the application of the Guidelines on national regional aid for 2007–2013, OJ C 54, 4.3.2006, p. 13, and notably the granting of aid for newly created small enterprises up to a total of EUR 2 million per small enterprise located in regions eligible for the derogation in Article 87(3)(a) of the Treaty.

5.5. Aid for process and organisational innovation in services

Innovation in services may not always fall within the research categories defined in section 5.1 but is typically less systematic and stems frequently from customer interaction, market demand, adoption of business and organisational models and practices from more innovative sectors or from other similar sources.

Aid for process and organisational innovation in services shall be compatible with the common market within the meaning of Article 87(3)(c) of the EC Treaty with a maximum aid intensity of 15% for large enterprises, 25% for medium enterprises and 35% for small enterprises. Large enterprises are only eligible for such aid if they collaborate with SMEs in the aided activity, whereby the collaborating SMEs must incur at least 30% of the total eligible costs.

Routine or periodic changes made to products, production lines, manufacturing processes, existing services and other operations in progress, even if such changes may represent improvements, do not qualify for State aid.

The following conditions must be fulfilled:

(a) organisational innovation must always be related to the use and exploitation of Information and Communication Technologies (ICT) to change the organisation;

(b) the innovation must be formulated as a project with an identified and qualified project manager, as well as identified project costs;

(c) the result of the aided project must be the development of a standard, of a business model, methodology or concept, which can be systematically reproduced, possibly certified, and possibly patented;

(d) the process or organisational innovation must be new or substantially improved compared to the state of the art in its industry in the Community. The novelty could be demonstrated by the Member States for instance on the basis of a precise description of the innovation, comparing it with state of the art process or organisational techniques used by other undertakings in the same industry;

(e) the process or organisational innovation project must entail a clear degree of risk. This risk could be demonstrated by the Member State for instance in terms of: project costs in relation to company turnover, time required to develop the new process, expected gains from the process innovation by comparison with the project costs, probability of failure. Eligible costs are the same as for aid to R&D projects (cf. section). In case of organisational innovation, however, costs of instruments and equipment cover costs of ICT instruments and equipment only.

5.6. Aid for innovation advisory services and for innovation support services

Aid for innovation advisory services and for innovation support services shall be compatible with the common market within the meaning of Article 87(3)(c) of the EC Treaty if each of the following conditions are fulfilled:

(1) the beneficiary is an SME;

(2) the aid does not exceed a maximum of EUR 200 000 per beneficiary within any three year period;[37]

(3) the service provider benefits from a national or European certification. If the service provider does not benefit from a national or European certification, the aid may not cover more than 75% of the eligible costs;

(4) the beneficiary must use the State aid to buy the services at market price (or if the service provider is a non-for-profit entity, at a price which reflects its full costs plus a reasonable margin).

The following costs shall be eligible:

— as regards innovation advisory services the following costs: management consulting; technological assistance; technology transfer services; training; consultancy for acquisition, protection and trade in Intellectual Property Rights and for licensing agreements; consultancy on the use of standards[;]

— as regards innovation support services the following costs: office space; data banks; technical libraries; market research; use of laboratory; quality labelling, testing and certification.

If the service provider is a not-for-profit entity, the aid may be given in the form of a reduced price, as the difference between the price paid and the market price (or a price which reflects full costs plus a reasonable margin). In such a case, the Member States shall set up a system ensuring transparency about the full costs of the innovation advisory and innovation support services provided, as well as about the price paid by the beneficiary, so that the aid received can be measured and monitored.

Notes

[37] Without prejudice to the possibility of also receiving *de minimis* aid in respect of other eligible expenses.

5.7. Aid for the loan of highly qualified personnel

Aid for the loan of highly qualified personnel seconded from a research organisation or a large enterprise to an SME shall be compatible with the common market within the meaning of Article 87(3)(c) of the EC Treaty, provided the following conditions are fulfilled:

The seconded personnel must not be replacing other personnel, but must be employed in a newly created function within the beneficiary undertaking and must have been employed for at least two years in the research organisation or the large enterprise, which is sending the personnel on secondment. The seconded personnel must work on R&D&I activities within the SME receiving the aid.

Eligible costs are all personnel costs for borrowing and employing highly qualified personnel, including the costs of using a recruitment agency, as well as a mobility allowance for the seconded personnel. The maximum aid intensity shall be 50% of the eligible costs, for a maximum of 3 years per undertaking and per person borrowed.

This provision does not allow covering consultancy costs (payment of the service rendered by the expert, without employing the expert in the undertaking) as such, which are covered under the rules for SME-aid.[38]

Notes
[38] Currently Regulation (EC) No 70/2001.

5.8. Aid for innovation clusters

Investment aid may be granted for the setting up, expansion and animation of innovation clusters exclusively to the legal entity operating the innovation cluster. This entity shall be in charge of managing the participation and access to the cluster's premises, facilities and activities. Access to the cluster's premises, facilities and activities must not be restricted and the fees charged for using the cluster's facilities and for participating in the cluster's activities should reflect their costs. Such aid may be granted for the following facilities:

— facilities for training and research centre;
— open-access research infrastructures: laboratory, testing facility;
— broadband network infrastructures.

The maximum aid intensity is 15%. In the case of regions falling under Article 87(3)(a) of the EC Treaty, the Commission considers that the intensity must not exceed:

— 30% for regions with less than 75% of average EU-25 GDP per capita, for outermost regions with higher GDP per capita and until 1 January 2011 statistical effect regions,[39]
— 40% for regions with less than 60% of average EU-25 GDP per capita,
— 50% for regions with less than 45% of average EU-25 GDP per capita.

In recognition of their specific handicaps, the outermost regions will be eligible for a further bonus of 20% if their GDP per capita falls below 75% of the EU-25 average and 10 % in other cases.

The statistical effect regions which fall under the derogation under Article 87(3)(c) of the EC Treaty from 1 January 2011 will be eligible for an aid intensity of 20%.

In the case of aid being granted to an SME, the maximum intensities shall be increased by 20 percentage points for aid granted to a small enterprise and by 10 percentage points for aid granted to a medium-sized enterprise.

The eligible costs shall be the costs relating to investment in land, buildings, machinery and equipment.

Operating aid for cluster animation may be granted to the legal entity operating the innovation cluster. Such aid must be temporary and, as a general rule, must be abolished over time, so as to provide an incentive for prices to reflect costs reasonably rapidly.

Such aid may be granted for a limited duration of five years where the aid is degressive. Its intensity may amount to 100% the first year but must have fallen in a linear fashion to zero by the end of the fifth year. In the case of non-degressive aid, its duration is limited to five years and its intensity must not exceed 50% of the eligible costs. In duly justified cases, and on the basis of convincing evidence provided by the notifying Member State, aid for cluster animation may be granted for a longer period of time, not exceeding 10 years.

The eligible costs shall be the personnel and administrative costs relating to the following activities:

— marketing of the cluster to recruit new companies to take part in the cluster,
— management of the cluster's open-access facilities,
— organisation of training programmes, workshops and conferences to support knowledge sharing and networking between the members of the cluster.

When notifying investment aid or aid for cluster animation, the Member State must provide an analysis of the technological specialisation of the innovation cluster, existing regional potential, existing research capacity, presence of clusters in the Community with similar purposes and potential market volumes of the activities in the cluster.

Cases where Member States fund innovation infrastructure to be operated on an open access basis within not for profit research organisations should be assessed using the provisions set out in section 3.1.

Notes
[39] Cf. Guidelines on national regional aid for 2007–2013, para. 18–20.

---

6. INCENTIVE EFFECT AND NECESSITY OF AID

State aid must have an incentive effect, i.e. result in the recipient changing its behaviour so that it increases its level of R&D&I activity. As a result of the aid, the R&D&I activity should be increased in size, scope, amount spent or speed. The Commission considers that the aid does not present an incentive for the beneficiary in all cases in which the R&D&I activity[40] has already commenced prior to the aid application by the beneficiary to the national authorities. If the aided R&D&I-project has not started before the application, the Commission considers that the incentive effect is **automatically met** for the following aid measures:

— project aid and feasibility studies where the aid beneficiary is an SME and where the aid amount is below EUR 7.5 million for a project per SME,
— aid for industrial property rights costs for SMEs,
— aid for young innovative enterprises,
— aid for innovation advisory services and innovation support services,
— aid for the loan of highly qualified personnel.

For all other measures,[41] the Commission will require that an incentive effect is demonstrated by the notifying Member States.

In order to verify that the planned aid will induce the aid recipient to change its behaviour so that it increases its level of R&D&I activity, the Member States shall provide an *ex-ante* evaluation of the increased R&D&I activity **for all individual measures assessed by the Commission**, on the basis of an analysis comparing a situation without aid and a situation with aid being granted. The following criteria may be used, together with other relevant quantitative and/or qualitative factors submitted by the Member State that made the notification:

increase in project size: increase in the total project costs (without decreased spending by the aid beneficiary by comparison with a situation without aid); increase in the number of people assigned to R&D&I activities;

increase in scope: increase in the number of the expected deliverables from the project; more ambitious project illustrated by a higher probability of a scientific or technological breakthrough or a higher risk of failure (notably linked to the higher risk involved in the research project, to the long-term nature of the project and uncertainty about its results);

increase in speed: shorter time before completion of the project as compared to the same project being carried out without aid;

increase in total amount spent on R&D&I: increase in total R&D&I spending by the aid beneficiary; changes in the committed budget for the project (without corresponding decrease in the budget of other projects); increase in R&D&I spending by the aid beneficiary as a proportion of total turnover.

If a significant effect on *at least one* of these elements can be demonstrated, taking account of the normal behaviour of an undertaking in the respective sector, the Commission will normally conclude that the aid proposal has an incentive effect.

If the Commission undertakes a **detailed assessment** of an individual measure, these indicators may not be considered sufficient demonstration of an incentive effect, and the Commission may need to be provided with complementary evidence.

When **assessing an aid scheme,** the conditions relating to the incentive effect shall be deemed to be satisfied if the Member State has committed itself to grant individual aid under the approved aid scheme only after it has verified that an incentive effect is present and to submit annual reports on the implementation of the approved aid scheme. In the annual reports, the Member State must demonstrate how it has assessed the incentive effect of the aid before granting the aid through the use of the quantitative and qualitative indicators given above.

Notes

[40] If the aid proposal is to grant aid for an R&D&I-project, this does not exclude that the potential beneficiary has already carried out feasibility studies which are not covered by the request for State aid.

[41] I.e. project aid for large undertakings and for SMEs for aid exceeding EUR 7.5 million: aid for process and organisational innovation in services and aid for innovation clusters.

---

7. COMPATIBILITY OF AID SUBJECT TO A DETAILED ASSESSMENT

The Commission considers that an increase in the level of R&D&I activity in the Community is in the common interest of the Community as it can be expected to significantly contribute to growth, prosperity and sustainable development. In this context, the Commission recognises that State aid has a positive role to play when it is well targeted and creates the right incentive for undertakings to increase R&D&I. Nevertheless, State aid may also lead to significant distortions of competition which must be taken into consideration.

7.1. Measures subject to a detailed assessment

For the following measures, due to the higher risk of distortion of competition, the Commission will carry out a more detailed assessment.

For measures covered by a BER

— for all cases notified to the Commission following **a duty to notify aid individually** as prescribed in the BER.

For measures covered by this framework

Where the aid amount exceeds:

— for **project aid**[42] and **feasibility studies**:
  — if the project is predominantly fundamental research,[43] EUR 20 million per undertaking, per project/feasibility study;
  — if the project is predominantly industrial research,[44] EUR 10 million per undertaking, per project/feasibility study;
  — for all other projects, EUR 7.5 million per undertaking, per project/feasibility study.
— for **process or organisational innovation** in services activities, EUR 5 million per project per undertaking;
— for innovation clusters (per cluster), EUR 5 million.

The purpose of this detailed assessment is to ensure that high amounts of aid for R&D&I do not distort competition to an extent contrary to the common interest, but actually contribute to the common interest. This happens when the benefits of State aid in terms of additional R&D&I outweigh the harm for competition and trade.

The detailed assessment is a proportionate assessment, depending on the distortion potential of the case. Accordingly, the fact that a detailed assessment will be carried out does not necessarily imply the need to open a formal investigation procedure, although this may be the case for certain measures.

Provided Member States ensure full co-operation and provide adequate information in a timely manner, the Commission will use its best endeavours to conduct the investigation in a timely manner.

Notes

42 For EUREKA projects, this ceiling is set at twice the amount.

43 A project is considered to consist "predominantly" of fundamental research, if more than half of the eligible project costs is incurred through activities which fall within the category of fundamental research.

44 A project is considered to consist "predominantly" of industrial research, if more than half of the eligible project costs is incurred through activities which fall within the categories of industrial research or fundamental research.

7.2. Methodology of the detailed assessment: R&D&I criteria for economic assessment of certain individual cases

Below, the Commission presents guidance as to the kind of information it may require and the methodology it would follow for measures subject to a detailed assessment. This guidance is intended to make the Commission's decisions and their reasoning transparent and foreseeable in order to create predictability and legal certainty.

Detailed assessment will be conducted on the basis of the following positive and negative elements which will apply in addition to the criteria set out in Chapter 5. In some cases, the applicability and the weight attached to these elements may depend on the form or objective of the aid. The level of the Commission's assessment will be proportional to the risk of distortion of competition. This means that the scope of the analysis will depend on the nature of the case. State aid for activities that are far away from the market is therefore less likely to give rise to very extensive scrutiny.

Member States are invited to provide all the elements that they consider useful for the assessment of the case. The Member States are, in particular, invited to rely on evaluations of past State aid schemes or measures, impact assessments made by the granting authority, risk assessments, financial reports, internal business plans that any company should realise for important projects, expert opinions and other studies related to R&D&I.

7.3. Positive effects of the aid

The fact that the aid induces undertakings to pursue R&D&I in the Community which they would not otherwise have pursued constitutes the main positive element to take into consideration when assessing the compatibility of the aid.

In this context, the Commission will notably pay attention to the following elements:

— the net increase of R&D&I conducted by the undertaking,
— the contribution of the measure to the global improvement of the sector concerned as regards the level of R&D&I,
— the contribution of the measure to the improvement of the Community situation regarding R&D&I in the international context.

7.3.1. Existence of a market failure

As indicated in Chapter 1, State aid may be necessary to increase R&D&I in the economy only to the extent that the market, on its own, fails to deliver an optimal outcome. It is established that certain market failures hamper the overall level of R&D&I in the Community. However, not all undertakings and sectors in the economy are confronted to these market failures to the same extent. Consequently, as regards measures subject to a detailed assessment, the Member State should provide adequate information whether the aid refers to a general market failure regarding R&D&I in the Community, or to a specific market failure. Depending on the specific market failure addressed, the Commission will take into consideration the following elements:

— **Knowledge spillovers:** the level of information dissemination foreseen; the specificity of the knowledge created; the availability of IPR protection.

— **Imperfect and asymmetric information:** level of risk and complexity of research; need for external finance; characteristics of the aid beneficiary to receive external finance.

— **Coordination failures:** number of collaborating undertakings; intensity of collaboration; diverging interest between collaborating partners; problems in designing contracts; problems of third parties to coordinate collaboration.

For State aid targeting R&D&I projects or activities located in assisted areas, the Commission will take into account: (i) disadvantages caused by the peripherality and other regional specificities, (ii) specific local economic data, social and/or historic reasons for a low level of R&D&I activity in comparison with the relevant average data and/or situation at national and/or Community level as appropriate; and (iii) any other relevant indicator showing an increased degree of market failure.

7.3.2. *Appropriate Instrument*

State aid for R&D&I can be authorised under Article 87(3)(c) of the EC Treaty when it is necessary to achieve an objective of common interest, as an exception to the general prohibition of State aid. An important element in the balancing test is whether and to what extent State aid for R&D&I can be considered an appropriate instrument to increase R&D&I activities, given that other less distortive instruments may achieve the same results.

In its compatibility analysis, the Commission will take particular account of any impact assessment of the proposed measure which the Member State has made. Measures for which the Member State has considered other policy options and for which the advantages of using a selective instrument such as State aid are established and submitted to the Commission, are considered to constitute an appropriate instrument.

7.3.3. *Incentive effect and necessity of aid*

Analysing the incentive effect of the aid measure is the most important condition in analysing State aid for R&D&I. Identifying the incentive effect **translates** into assessing whether the planned aid will induce undertakings to pursue R&D&I which they would not otherwise have pursued.

Chapter 6 provides a series of indicators that can be used by Member States to demonstrate an incentive effect. However, when a measure undergoes a detailed assessment, the Commission will require that the incentive effect of the aid is substantiated more precisely, to avoid undue distortions of competition.

In its analysis, the Commission will, in addition to the indicators mentioned in Chapter 6, take into consideration the following elements:

— **Specification of intended change:** the intended change in behaviour State aid aims at in the notified case has to be well specified (new project triggered, size, scope or speed of a project enhanced).

— **Counterfactual analysis:** the change of behaviour has to be identified by counterfactual analysis: what would be the level of intended activity with and without aid? The difference of the two scenarios is considered to be the impact of the aid measure and describes the incentive effect.

— **Level of profitability:** if a project would not, in itself, be profitable to undertake for a private undertaking, but would generate important benefits for society, it is more likely that the aid has an incentive effect. To evaluate the overall profitability (or lack thereof) of the project, evaluation methodologies can be used which are standard practice in the particular industry concerned.[45]

— **Amount of investment and time path of cash flows:** High start-up investment, low level of appropriable cash flows and a significant fraction of cash flows arising in the very far future will be considered positive elements in assessing the incentive effect.

— **Level of risk involved in the research project:** On the basis of e.g. feasibility studies, risk assessments and expert opinions, the assessment of risk will in particular take into account the irreversibility of the investment, the probability of commercial failure, the risk that the project will be less productive than expected, the risk that conducting the project would undermine other activities and the risk that the project costs undermine the undertaking's financial viability. For State aid targeting R&D&I projects or activities located in assisted areas, the Commission will take into account disadvantages caused by the peripherality and other regional specificities, which negatively impact on the level of risk in the research project.

— **Continuous evaluation:** measures for which (low scale) pilot projects are foreseen, or which define well specified milestones resulting in termination of the project in case of failure and where a publicly available *ex post* monitoring is foreseen will be considered more positively as regards the assessment of the incentive effect.

Notes

[45] These may include methods to evaluate the Net Present Value of the project (that is to say, the sum of the discounted expected cash flow resulting from the investment minus the investment cost), the internal rate of return (IRR) or the return of capital employed (ROCE). Financial reports and internal business plans containing information on demand forecasts: cost forecasts: financial forecasts (for example, NPV, IRR, ROCE), documents that are submitted to an investment committee and that elaborate on various investment scenarios or documents provided to the financial markets could serve as evidence.

7.3.4. *Proportionality of the aid*

Independently of the criteria mentioned in Chapter 5, the Member State concerned should provide the additional following information:

— **Open selection process:** Where there are multiple (potential) candidates for undertaking the R&D&I project in a Member State, the proportionality requirement is more likely to be met if the project has been allocated on the basis of transparent, objective and non-discriminatory criteria.

— **Aid to the minimum:** Member States have to explain how the amount given has been calculated to ensure that it is limited to the minimum necessary.

7.4. Analysis of the distortion of competition and trade

State aid for R&D&I may impact on competition at two levels: (i) competition in the innovation process, i.e. competition in terms of R&D&I which takes place upstream of product markets and (ii) competition in the product markets where the results of the R&D&I activities are exploited.

In assessing the negative effects of the aid measure, the Commission will focus its analysis of the distortions of competition on the foreseeable impact the R&D&I aid has on competition between undertakings in the product markets concerned. The Commission will give more weight to risks for competition and trade that arise in a predictable future and with particular likelihood.

The impact on competition in the innovation process will be relevant insofar as it has a foreseeable impact on the outcome of future product market competition. In certain cases the results of R&D&I, for example, in the form of intellectual property rights, are themselves traded in so-called technology markets, for instance through patent licensing. In these cases, the Commission may also consider the effect of the aid on competition in the technology markets.

The impact of R&D&I on product markets is largely dynamic and the analysis will therefore be of a forward-looking nature. Frequently, the same innovative activity will be associated with multiple future product markets. If so, the impact of State aid will be looked upon on the set of markets concerned.

There are three distinct ways in which R&D&I aid can distort competition in product markets:

(1) R&D&I aid can distort the dynamic incentives of market players to invest (crowding out effect);

(2) R&D&I aid can create or maintain positions of market power;

(3) R&D&I aid can maintain an inefficient market structure.

State aid may also have a negative effect on trade in the common market. In particular where R&D&I aid leads to the crowding out of competitors, the aid measures may essentially result in a shift of trade flows and location of economic activity.

7.4.1. *Distorting dynamic incentives*

The main concern related to R&D&I aid to undertakings is that competitors' dynamic incentives to invest are distorted. When an undertaking receives aid, this generally increases the likelihood of successful R&D&I on the part of this undertaking leading to an increased presence on the product market(s) in the future. This increased presence may lead competitors to reduce the scope of their original investment plans (crowding out effect).

In its analysis, the Commission will consider the following elements:

— **Aid amount.** Aid measures which involve significant amounts of aid are more likely to lead to significant crowding out effects. The significance of the aid amount will be measured with reference to total private R&D expenditure in the sector, and the amount spent by the main players.
— **Closeness to the market/category of the aid.** The more the aid measure is aimed at R&D&I activity close to the market, the more it is liable to develop significant crowding out effects.
— **Open selection process:** Where the grant is given on the basis of objective and non-discriminatory criteria, the Commission will take a more positive stance.
— **Exit barriers:** Competitors are more likely to maintain (or even to increase) their investment plans when exit barriers to the innovation process are high. This may be the case when many of the competitors' past investments are locked in to a particular R&D&I trajectory.
— **Incentives to compete for a future market:** R&D&I aid may lead to a situation where competitors to the aid beneficiary renounce competing for a future market, because the advantage provided by the aid (in terms of the degree of technological advance or in terms of timing) reduces the possibility for them to profitably enter this future market.
— **Product differentiation and intensity of competition:** Where product innovation is rather about developing differentiated products (related, for example, to distinct brands, standards, technologies, consumer groups) competitors are less likely to be affected. The same is true if there are many effective competitors in the market.

7.4.2. *Creating market power*

Aid in support of R&D&I may have distortive effects in terms of increasing or maintaining the degree of market power in product markets. Market power is the power to influence market prices, output, the variety or quality of goods and services, or other parameters of competition on the market for a significant period of time, to the detriment of consumers. The Commission will assess the market power before the aid is granted, and the change in market power, which can be expected as a result of the aid.

The Commission is concerned mainly about those R&D&I measures allowing the aid beneficiary to transfer or strengthen market power held on existing product markets to future product markets. The Commission is therefore unlikely to identify competition concerns related to market power in markets where each aid beneficiary has a market share below 25% and in markets having a market concentration with Herfindahl-Hirschman Index (HHI) below 2 000. In its analysis, the Commission will consider the following elements:

— **Market power of aid beneficiary and market structure:** Where the recipient is already dominant on a product market, the aid measure may reinforce this dominance by further weakening the competitive constraint that competitors can exert on the recipient undertaking. Similarly, State aid measures may have significant impact in oligopolistic markets where only a few players are active.
— **Level of entry barriers:** In the field of R&D&I, significant entry barriers may exist for new entrants. These barriers include legal entry barriers (in particular intellectual property rights), economies of scale and scope, access barriers to networks and infrastructure, and other strategic barriers to entry or expansion.
— **Buyer power:** The market power of an undertaking may also be limited by the market position of the buyers. The presence of strong buyers can serve to counter a finding of a strong market position if it is likely that the buyers will seek to preserve sufficient competition in the market.
— **Selection process:** Aid measures which allow undertakings with a strong market position to influence the selection process, for example, by having the right to recommend undertakings in the selection process or influencing the research path in a way which disfavours alternatives path on unjustified grounds, is liable to raise concern by the Commission.

7.4.3. *Maintaining inefficient market structures*

R&D&I aid may, if not correctly targeted, support inefficient undertakings and hence lead to market structures where many market players operate significantly below efficient scale. In its analysis, the Commission will consider whether the aid is granted in markets featuring overcapacity, in declining industries or in sensitive sectors. Concerns are less likely in situations where State aid for R&D&I aims at changing the growth dynamics of the sector, notably by introducing new technologies.

7.5. Balancing and decision

In the light of these positive and negative elements, the Commission balances the effects of the measure and determines whether the resulting distortions adversely affect trading conditions to an extent contrary to the common interest. The analysis in each particular case will be based on an overall assessment of the foreseeable positive and negative impacts of the State aid. For that purpose the Commission will not use the criteria set out in sections 7.3 and 7.4 mechanically but will make an overall assessment based on the proportionality principle.

The Commission may raise no objections to the notified aid measure without entering into the formal investigation procedure or, following the formal investigation procedure laid down in Article 6 of Regulation (EC) No 659/1999, decide to close the procedure with a decision pursuant to Article 7 of that Regulation. If it takes a conditional decision within the meaning of Article 7(4) of Regulation (EC) No 659/1999, it may in particular consider attaching the following conditions, which must reduce the resulting distortions or effect on trade and be proportionate:

— lower aid intensities than the maximum intensities allowed in Chapter 5, including claw-back mechanisms and different conditions for repaying reimbursable advances,
— diffusion of results, collaboration and other behavioural commitments,
— separation of accounts in order to avoid cross-subsidization from one market to another market, when the beneficiary is active in multiple markets,
— no discrimination against other potential beneficiaries (reduce selectivity).

8. Cumulation

As regards cumulation, the aid ceilings fixed under this framework shall apply regardless of whether the support for the aided project is financed entirely from State resources or is partly financed by the Community, except in the specific and limited context of the conditions established for Community funding under the RTD Framework Programmes, adopted respectively in accordance with Title XVIII of the EC Treaty or Title II of the Euratom Treaty.

Where the expenditure eligible for aid for R&D&I is eligible in whole or in part for aid for other purposes, the common portion will be subject to the most favourable ceiling under the applicable rules. This limitation does not apply to aid granted in accordance with the Community guidelines on State aid to promote risk capital investments in SME.[46]

Aid for R&D&I shall not be cumulated with *de minimis* support in respect of the same eligible expenses in order to circumvent the maximum aid intensities laid down in this framework.

Notes
[46] OJ C 194, 18.8.2006, p. 2.

---

9. Special Rules for Agriculture and Fisheries

As regards R&D aid concerning products listed in Annex I to the EC Treaty, and by way of derogation from aid intensity limitations or supplements specified elsewhere in this framework, the Commission will continue to allow an aid intensity of up to 100%, subject to fulfilment in each case of the four following conditions:

— it is of general interest to the particular sector or sub-sector concerned;
— information that research will be carried out, and with which goal, is published on the internet, prior to the commencement of the research. An approximate date of expected results and their

place of publication on the internet, as well as a mention that the result will be available at no cost, must be included;

— the results of the research are made available on internet, for a period of at least 5 years. This information on the internet shall be published no later than any which may be given to members of any particular organisation;

— aid shall be granted directly to the researching institution or body and must not involve the direct granting of non-research related aid to a company producing, processing or marketing agricultural products, nor provide price support to producers of such products.

The Commission will allow State aid for cooperation pursuant to Article 29 of Council Regulation (EC) No 1698/2005 of 20 September 2005 on support for rural development by the European Agricultural Fund for Rural Development (EAFRD)[47] if such cooperation has been approved for Community co-financing under that Article and/or the State aid is granted as additional financing pursuant to Article 89 of Regulation (EC) No 1698/2005 under the same conditions and at the same intensity as the co-financing.

Cases of R&D aid for products listed in Annex I to the EC Treaty not fulfilling the conditions in this chapter are to be examined under the normal rules of this framework.

Notes

[47] OJ L 277, 21.10.2005, p. 1. Regulation as amended by Regulation (EC) No 1463/2006 (OJ L 277, 9.10.2006, p. 1).

---

10. FINAL PROVISIONS

10.1. Reporting and monitoring

10.1.1. Annual reports

In line with the requirements of Regulation (EC) No 659/1999 and Commission Regulation (EC) No 794/2004 of 21 April 2004 implementing Council Regulation (EC) No 659/1999 laying down detailed rules for the application of Article [88] of the EC Treaty,[48] Member States must submit annual reports to the Commission.

Beyond the requirements stipulated in those provisions, annual reports for R&D&I-aid measures shall contain for each measure, including the granting of aid under an approved scheme, the following information:

— the name of the beneficiary,
— the aid amount per beneficiary,
— the aid intensity,
— the sectors of activity where the aided projects are undertaken.

In case of fiscal aid, the Member State must only provide a list of those beneficiaries who have received an annual tax relief in excess of 200 000 EUR.

In case of clusters, the report must also give a brief description of the activity of the cluster and its effectiveness in attracting R&D&I activity. The Commission may request additional information regarding the aid granted, to check whether the conditions of the Commission's decision approving the aid measure have been respected.

The annual reports will be published on the internet site of the Commission.

For all aid granted under an approved scheme to large undertakings, Member States must also explain in the annual report how the incentive effect has been respected for aid given to such undertakings, notably using the indicators and criteria mentioned in Chapter 6 above.

Notes

[48] OJ L 140, 30.4.2004, p. 1. Regulation as amended by Regulation (EC) No 1627/2006 (OJ L 302, 1.11.2006, p. 10).

10.1.2. *Access to full text of schemes*

The Commission considers that further measures are necessary to improve the transparency of State aid in the Community. In particular, it appears necessary to ensure that the Member States, economic operators, interested parties and the Commission itself have easy access to the full text of all applicable R&D&I aid schemes.

This can easily be achieved through the establishment of linked internet sites. For this reason, when examining R&D&I aid schemes, the Commission will systematically require the Member State concerned to publish the full text of all final aid schemes on the internet and to communicate the internet address of the publication to the Commission. The scheme must not be applied before the information is published on the internet.

10.1.3. *Information sheets*

Besides, whenever aid for R&D&I is granted on the basis of aid schemes without falling under the duty for individual notification, and exceeds EUR 3 million, Member States must, within 20 working days starting from the granting of the aid by the competent authority, provide the Commission with the information requested in the standard form laid down in the Annex to this framework. The Commission will make summary information available to the public through its website (http://ec.europa. eu/comm/competition/index_en.html).

Member States must ensure that detailed records regarding the granting of aid for all R&D&I measures are maintained. Such records, which must contain all information necessary to establish that the eligible costs and maximum allowable aid intensity have been observed, must be maintained for 10 years from the date on which the aid was granted.

The Commission will ask Member States to provide this information in order to carry out an impact assessment of this framework three years after its entry into force.[49]

Notes

[49] In that process, Member States may want to support the Commission by providing their own *ex post* assessment of schemes and individual measures.

10.2. Appropriate Measures

The Commission herewith proposes to Member States, on the basis of Article 88(1) of the EC Treaty, the following appropriate measures concerning their respective existing research and development aid schemes:

In order to comply with the provisions of this framework, Member States should amend, where necessary, such schemes in order to bring them into line with this framework within twelve months after its entry into force, with the following exceptions:

— Member States have twenty four months to introduce amendments regarding the provisions covered in point 3.1.1 of this framework;
— the new threshold for large individual projects will apply as from the entry into force of this framework;
— the duty to provide more detailed annual reports pursuant to point 10.1.1. and the duty to submit information sheets pursuant to point 10.1.3. will apply to existing aid schemes six months after the entry into force of this framework.

The Member States are invited to give their explicit unconditional agreement to these proposed appropriate measures within two months from the date of publication of this framework. In the absence of any reply, the Commission will assume that the Member State in question does not agree with the proposed measures.

10.3. Entry into force, validity and revision

This framework will enter into force on 1 January 2007 or, if it has not been published in the *Official Journal of the European Union* before that date, on the first day following its publication therein and will replace the Community Framework for State aid for Research and Development.

This framework will be applicable until 31 December 2013. After consulting the Member States, the Commission may amend it before that date on the basis of important competition policy or research policy considerations or in order to take account of other Community policies or international commitments. The Commission intends to carry out a review of the framework 3 years after its entry into force.

The Commission will apply this framework to all aid projects notified in respect of which it is called upon to take a decision after the framework is published in the *Official Journal*, even where the projects were notified prior to its publication. This includes individual aid granted under approved aid schemes and notified to the Commission following an obligation to notify such aid individually.

In line with the Commission notice on the determination of the applicable rules for the assessment of unlawful State aid,[50] the Commission will apply in the case of non-notified aid,

— this framework if the aid was granted after its entry into force,

— the framework in force when the aid was granted in all other cases.

Notes
[50]   OJ C 119 of 22.5.2002, p. 22.

ANNEX
Form for the Provision of Summary Information for Aid under the Extended Reporting Obligation (Section 10.1)

(1) Aid in favour of (name of the undertaking/undertakings receiving the aid, SME or not): ....
....

(2) Aid scheme reference (Commission reference of the existing scheme or schemes under which the aid is awarded):...

(3) Public entity/entities providing the assistance (name and co-ordinates of the granting authority or authorities): ....

(4) Member State where the aided project or measure is carried out: ....

(5) Type of project or measure: ....

(6) Short description of project or measure: ....
....
....
....

(7) Where applicable, eligible costs (in EUR): ....

(8) Discounted aid amount (gross) in EUR:..

(9) Aid intensity (% in gross grant equivalent):..

(10) Conditions attached to the payment of the proposed aid (if any):...
....

(11) Planned start and end date of the project or measure:...

(12) Date of award of the aid: ....

G23

COMMISSION COMMUNICATION

on State aid elements in sales of land and buildings by public authorities

(97/C 209/03)

(Text with EEA relevance)

Official Journal C 209, 10.7.1997, p. 3

Celex No: 31997Y0710(01)

Notes

EEA application: for the corresponding EEA provision, see the EFTA Surveillance Authority's Procedural and Substantive Rules in the Field of State Aid (Guidelines on the application and interpretation of Articles 61 and 62 of the EEA Agreement and Article 1 of Protocol 3 to the Surveillance and Court Agreement), Part III, Chapter 18B (as introduced by EFTA Surveillance Authority Decision No 275/99/COL of 17 November 1999 (OJ L 137, 8.6.2000, p. 28 and EEA Supplement No 26, 8.6.2000)).

Commentary

Communication: B&C: 15.036, 15.060

---

1. INTRODUCTION

On a number of occasions in recent years the Commission has investigated sales of publicly owned land and buildings in order to establish whether there was an element of State aid in favour of the buyers. The Commission has drawn up general guidance to Member States in order to make its general approach with regard to the problem of State aid through sales of land and buildings by public authorities transparent and to reduce the number of cases it has to examine.

The following guidance to Member States:

— describes a simple procedure that allows Member States to handle sales of land and buildings in a way that automatically precludes the existence of State aid,

— specifies clearly cases of sales of land and buildings that should be notified to the Commission to allow for assessment of whether or not a certain transaction contains aid and, if so, whether or not the aid is compatible with the common market,

— enables the Commission to deal expeditiously with any complaints or submissions from third parties drawing its attention to cases of alleged aid connected to sales of land and buildings.

This guidance takes account of the fact that in most Member States budgetary provisions exist to ensure that public property is in principle not sold below its value. Therefore, the procedural precautions recommended to avoid State aid rules coming into play are formulated in a way that should normally allow Member States to comply with the guidance without changing their domestic procedures.

The guidance concerns only sales of publicly owned land and buildings. It does not concern the public acquisition of land and buildings or the letting or leasing of land and buildings by public authorities. Such transactions may also include State aid elements.

The guidance does not affect specific provisions or practices of Member States intended to promote the quality of and access to private housing.

2. PRINCIPLES

1. Sale through an unconditional bidding procedure

A sale of land and buildings following a sufficiently well-publicized, open and unconditional bidding procedure, comparable to an auction, accepting the best or only bid is by definition at market

value and consequently does not contain State aid. The fact that a different valuation of the land and buildings existed prior to the bidding procedure, e.g. for accounting purposes or to provide a proposed initial minimum bid, is irrelevant.

(a) An offer is "sufficiently well-publicized" when it is repeatedly advertised over a reasonably long period (two months or more) in the national press, estate gazettes or other appropriate publications and through real-estate agents addressing a broad range of potential buyers, so that it can come to the notice of all potential buyers.

The intended sale of land and buildings, which in view of their high value or other features may attract investors operating on a Europe-wide or international scale, should be announced in publications which have a regular international circulation. Such offers should also be made known through agents addressing clients on a Europe-wide or international scale.

(b) An offer is "unconditional" when any buyer, irrespective of whether or not he runs a business or of the nature of his business, is generally free to acquire the land and buildings and to use it for his own purposes, Restrictions may be imposed for the prevention of public nuisance, for reasons of environmental protection or to avoid purely speculative bids. Urban and regional planning restrictions imposed on the owner pursuant to domestic law on the use of the land and buildings do not affect the unconditional nature of an offer.

(c) If it is a condition of the sale that the future owner is to assume special obligations —other than those arising from general domestic law or decision of the planning authorities or those relating to the general protection and conservation of the environment and to public health — for the benefit of the public authorities or in the general public interest, the offer is to be regarded as "unconditional" within the meaning of the above definition only if all potential buyers would have to, and be able to, meet that obligation, irrespective of whether or not they run a business or of the nature of their business.

2. Sale without an unconditional bidding procedure

(a) Independent expert evaluation

If public authorities intend not to use the procedure described under 1, an independent evaluation should be carried out by one or more independent asset valuers prior to the sale negotiations in order to establish the market value on the basis of generally accepted market indicators and valuation standards. The market price thus established is the minimum purchase price that can be agreed without granting State aid.

An "asset valuer" is a person of good repute who:

— has obtained an appropriate degree at a recognized centre of learning or an equivalent academic qualification,
— has suitable experience and is competent in valuing land and buildings in the location and of the category of the asset.

If in any Member State there are not appropriate established academic qualifications, the asset valuer should be a member of a recognized professional body concerned with the valuation of land and buildings and either:

— be appointed by the courts or an authority of equivalent status,
— have as a minimum a recognized certificate of secondary education and sufficient level of training with at least three years post-qualification practical experience in, and with knowledge of, valuing land and buildings in that particular locality.

The valuer should be independent in the carrying out of his tasks, i.e. public authorities should not be entitled to issue orders as regards the result of the valuation. State valuation offices and public officers or employees are to be regarded as independent provided that undue influence on their findings is effectively excluded.

"Market value" means the price at which land and buildings could be sold under private contract between a willing seller and an arm's length buyer on the date of valuation, it being assumed that the property is publicly exposed to the market, that market conditions permit orderly disposal and that a normal period, having regard to the nature of the property, is available for the negotiation of the sale.[1]

Notes
[1] Article 49(2) of Council Directive 91/674/EEC (OJ No L 374, 31.12.1991, p. 7).

(b) Margin

If, after a reasonable effort to sell the land and buildings at the market value, it is clear that the value set by the valuer cannot be obtained, a divergence of up to 5% from that value can be deemed to be in line with market conditions. If, after a further reasonable time, it is clear that the land and buildings cannot be sold at the value set by the valuer less this 5% margin, a new valuation may be carried out which is to take account of the experience gained and of the offers received.

(c) Special obligations

Special obligations that relate to the land and buildings and not to the purchaser or his economic activities may be attached to the sale in the public interest provided that every potential buyer is required, and in principle is able, to fulfil them, irrespective of whether or not he runs a business or of the nature of his business. The economic disadvantage of such obligations should be evaluated separately by independent valuers and may be set off against the purchase price. Obligations whose fulfilment would at least partly be in the buyer's own interest should be evaluated with that fact in mind: there may, for example, be an advantage in terms of advertising, sport or arts sponsorship, image, improvement of the buyer's own environment, or recreational facilities for the buyer's own staff.

The economic burden related to obligations incumbent on all landowners under the ordinary law are not to be discounted from the purchase price (these would include, for example, care and maintenance of the land and buildings as part of the ordinary social obligations of property ownership or the payment of taxes and similar charges).

(d) Cost to the authorities

The primary cost to the public authorities of acquiring land and buildings is an indicator for the market value unless a significant period of time elapsed between the purchase and the sale of the land and buildings. In principle, therefore, the market value should not be set below primary costs during a period of at least three years after acquisition unless the independent valuer specifically identified a general decline in market prices for land and buildings in the relevant market.

3. Notification

Member States should consequently notify to the Commission, without prejudice to the *de minimis* rule,[2] the following transactions to allow it to establish whether State aid exists and, if so, to assess its compatibility with the common market.

(a) any sale that was not concluded on the basis of an open and unconditional bidding procedure, accepting the best or only bid; and

(b) any sale that was, in the absence of such procedure, conducted at less than market value as established by independent valuers.

Notes
[2] OJ No C 68, 6.3.1996, p. 9.

4. Complaints

When the Commission receives a complaint or other submission from third parties alleging that there was a State aid element in an agreement for the sale of land and buildings by public authorities, it will assume that no State aid is involved if the information supplied by the Member State concerned shows that the above principles were observed.

Commentary
Section II: **B&C:** 15.036
Section II(2): **B&C:** 15.036

G24

COMMUNICATION OF THE COMMISSION TO THE MEMBER STATES

pursuant to Article [88](1) of the EC Treaty applying Articles [87] and [88] of the
Treaty to short-term export-credit insurance

(97/C 281/03)

(Text with EEA relevance)

Official Journal C 281, 17.9.1997, p. 4

Celex No: 31997Y0917(01)

Notes

EEA application: for the corresponding EEA provision, see the EFTA Surveillance Authority's Procedural and Substantive Rules in the Field of State Aid (Guidelines on the application and interpretation of Articles 61 and 62 of the EEA Agreement and Article 1 of Protocol 3 to the Surveillance and Court Agreement), Part III, Chapter 17A and Annex XI (as introduced by EFTA Surveillance Authority Decision No 45/98/COL of 4 March 1998 (OJ L 120, 23.4.1998, p. 27 and EEA Supplement No 16), as subsequently re-enacted and amended).

Commentary
Communication: **B&C**: 15.060

---

1. INTRODUCTION

1.1. Member States maintain an active policy of supporting their export industry. Of the total aid given by Member States to their manufacturing industry over the period 1992 to 1994, 7% went on supporting exports, largely in the form of favourable terms for export credits and export-credit insurance.[1]

Notes

[1] Source: Fifth survey on State aids in the European Community, EC Commission, 1997, p. 20. From 1992 onwards the cutbacks in subsidized export credits agreed in the Helsinki package are likely to reduce this figure.

1.2. Export subsidies directly affect competition in the market place between rival potential suppliers of goods and services. Recognizing their pernicious effects, the Commission, as the guardian of competition under the Treaty, has always strictly condemned export aid in intra-Community trade.[2] However, although Member States' support for their exports outside the Community can also affect competition within the Community,[3] the Commission has not systematically intervened in this field under the State aid rules in Articles [87], [88] and [89] of the Treaty. There have been several reasons for this. First, this area is partly governed by the provisions of the Treaty relating to external trade, Articles 112 and 113, and Article 112 does indeed provide for harmonization of export aid. Secondly, in is not only competition within the Community that is affected by aid for extra-Community exports, but also the competitiveness of Community exporters vis-à-vis those of the Community's trading partners, which give similar aid. Finally, progress in controlling aid has been achieved under the Treaty's trade provisions and in the OECD and WTO.

Notes

[2] In its seventh report on competition policy (1977), point 242, the Commission stated that export aids in intra-Community trade "cannot qualify for derogation whatever their intensity, form, grounds or purpose".

[3] See judgment of the Court of Justice in Case C-142/87 *Belgium v Commission* [1990] ECR I-959. See also Case C-44/93 *Assurances du Crédit v OND and Belgium* [1994] ECR I-3829, paragraph 30.

1.3. While the Commission has so far refrained from exercising its State aid control powers in the areas of export credits and export-credit insurance, work by the Council's Export Credits Group[4] and cases before the Court of Justice of the European Communities[5] have shown that in one area at least, that of short-term export-credit insurance, the actual or potential distortions of competition in the Community may justify action by the Commission under the State aid rules without waiting for progress on other fronts. The distortions of competition can occur not only between exporters in different Member States in their trade within and outside the Community, but also between export-credit insurers offering their services in the Community.

Notes

[4] "L'assurance crédit et le marché unique 1992 (court-terme)", report presented to the coordination group, rapporteur, P. Callut.

[5] See Case C-63/89 *Assurances du Crédit and Cobac v Council and Commission* [1991] ECR I-1799, and Case C-44/93 *Assurances du Crédit v OND and Belgium* [1994] ECR I-3829.

1.4. The purpose of this Communication is to remove such distortions due to State aid in that sector of the export-credit insurance business in which there is competition between public or publicly supported export-credit insurers and private export-credit insurers. This commercial sector of export-credit insurance relates to the insurance of short-term export-credit risks on trade within the Community and with many countries outside it. Such risks are termed "marketable" and will be defined in Section 2 below. The definition currently comprises only so-called "commercial", as opposed to "political", risks in trade within the Community and with the majority of OECD countries, listed in the Annex. While Member States have made considerable efforts to eliminate aid from the commercial sector of export-credit insurance in anticipation of action by the Community, the Single Market requires safeguards to ensure a level playing field in all circumstances.

This Communication will not deal with the insurance of medium and long-term export-credit risks which are largely non-marketable at the present time. In that area the factors which have led the Commission to refrain from extensive use of its State aid control powers still militate against such action. Instead, efforts are being made to harmonize the terms of export-credit insurance, premiums and country-cover policy, taking due account of the programmes in third countries so as not to undermine the competitiveness of Community exporters.

1.5. Section 2 of this communication describes the structure of the export-credit insurance market and distinguishes the commercial or market sector, in which private insurers operate and which is covered by this communication between private and public or publicly supported export-credit insurers and explains why and to what extent the State aid Articles of the Treaty apply. Finally, in Section 4, the Commission states what action it considers necessary to ensure that any remaining State aid of the types listed in Section 3 is removed from the market sector and requests the Member States pursuant to Article [88](1) of the Treaty to take such action, if required.

2. Market and Non-market Sectors of Short-term Export-credit Insurance

2.1. The Report of the Council's Export Credit Group (hereinafter referred to as "the Report"), complaints by private export-credit insurers and cases before the Court of Justice of the European Communities, have shown that in some Member States the same "official" export-credit agencies that insure the medium and long-term risks of exporters for the account or with the guarantee[6] of the State also operate for the account or with the guarantee of the State in parts of the short-term export-credit insurance market where they are in competition with private export-credit insurers that have no such links with the State. The "official" export-credit agencies in question may be government departments, State-owned or State-controlled companies or wholly privately-owned and controlled companies. For the purposes of this communication, such agencies will be termed "public or publicly supported export-credit insurers". As well as the "official" agencies operating in both the medium/long and short-term fields, some privately owned and controlled export-credit insurers that only provide short-term insurance may be supported by their governments through guarantees or equivalent reinsurance arrangements for some segments of their business. These insurers, too, must be categorized as "public or publicly supported". On the other hand, export-credit insurers mainly

1617

or exclusively engaged in the short term that do not operate for the account or with the guarantee[7] of the State for any of their business will be termed "private export-credit insurers".

The Report showed that when public or publicly supported export-credit insurers operated for the account or with the guarantee of the State on parts of the short-term market where they were in competition with private insurers, they enjoyed certain financial advantages which could distort competition against private insurers. In no country did public or publicly supported export-credit insurers have a monopoly for short-term business.

One of the most difficult areas dealt with by the Report was the provision of reinsurance by the State, either directly or indirectly. The Report identified reinsurance arrangements which provide 100% cover and are equivalent to guarantees as a subsidy. It is now recognized that reinsurance facilities whereby the State only participates in or supplements a private-sector reinsurance treaty may also give insurers benefiting from them an advantage over private insurers not receiving such cover, thereby distorting competition.

Notes

[6] In some cases, such as in The Netherlands, medium and long-term business is conducted not under a guarantee, but under a comprehensive reinsurance agreement with the government.

[7] Or with equivalent reinsurance arrangements.

2.2. Despite the recent improvements made—with public or publicly supported export-credit insurers increasingly hiving off their short-term business to separate companies or introducing separate accounting — it has been noted above that action is still needed to create the desired level playing field. The first task is to identify the sector in which a competitive market exists. The Report used as the decisive criterion for distinguishing the market sector, whether or not private reinsurance was available generally, rather than only in individual cases. It was observed that the answer was generally "yes" for commercial risks on non-public buyers, but that for political risks (including risks on public buyers, currency transfer risks and non-commercial, catastrophe risks) the capacity available was so inadequate that cover for such risks was clearly to be regarded as a market activity. On the basis of an analysis of the private reinsurance market by reference to the three criteria of duration, location and nature of risks insured, the Report considered "marketable" risks to involve commercial risks with a risk period of normally a maximum of three years for exports worldwide

2.3. Subsequent comments from Member States, business associations and insurers indicated that generally speaking that definition was too broad. Most of those submissions agreed with the Report that political risks should be excluded because the private reinsurance market was not large enough, and they preferred a maximum risk period of two years for commercial risks. Also, it appeared to be very difficult to reinsure on the private market the commercial risk of protracted default in non-OECD countries.

2.4. In view of the close links between protracted default and insolvency — protracted default risks being liable to turn into insolvency — and the resulting need to classify both risks in the same category (marketable or non-marketable), it is prudent to exclude all commercial risks on non-OECD countries from the definition of marketable risks and from the scope of this communication for the time being. Finally, it appears that at present there are still difficulties in obtaining private reinsurance of commercial risk in some OECD countries.

2.5. [In view of the above, "marketable" risks are defined for the purposes of this communication as commercial and political risks on public and non-public debtors established in the countries listed in the Annex. For such risks the maximum risk period (that is, manufacturing plus credit period with normal Berne Union starting point and usual credit term) is less than two years. All other risks (that is, catastrophe risks[9] and commercial and political risks on countries not listed in the Annex) are considered to be not yet marketable.][1]

[Notwithstanding the definition of "marketable" risks contained in the first sentence of the previous paragraph, if and to the extent that no private insurance market exists in a Member State, commercial and political risks incurred on public and non-public debtors established in the countries listed in the Annex are considered to be temporarily non-marketable if incurred by small and medium-sized enterprises falling within the relevant EU definition[1] and having a total annual export turnover not exceeding EUR 2 million.[2] In such circumstances, a public or publicly supported export-credit insurer shall, as far as possible, align its premium rates for such "non-marketable" risks with the rates charged elsewhere by export-credit insurers for the type of risk in question, namely taking into account the limited spread of foreign buyers, the characteristics of the insured enterprises, and the associated costs. Member States intending to submit a notification to the Commission on the application of this clause shall be subject to the same procedure and the same conditions as set out in point 4.4 below for the application of the escape clause. The Commission reserves the right to discontinue this clause or to revise the conditions of its application in consultation with Member States if it finds that the capacity of the private insurance market in this segment changes during the period of validity of this Communication.]²

"Commercial risks" are defined for the purposes of this communication as:

— arbitrary repudiation of a contract by a debtor, that is, any arbitrary decision by a non-public debtor to interrupt or terminate the contract without legitimate reason,

— arbitrary refusal by a non-public debtor to accept the goods covered by the contract without legitimate reason,

— insolvency of a non-public debtor or his guarantor,

— non-payment by a non-public debtor or by a guarantor of a debt resulting from the contract, that is, protracted default.

Notes

[⁸ ...

⁹ That is, war, revolution, natural disasters, nuclear accidents, and so forth, not so-called "commercial, catastrophe risks" (catastrophic accumulations of loss on individual buyers or countries) which may be covered by excess of loss reinsurance and are commercial risks.]¹

[¹ [*sic*] Commission Recommendation 2003/361/EC of 6 May 2003 concerning the definition of small and medium-sized enterprises, OJ L 124, 20.5.2003, p. 36, as may be amended in the future.

² [*sic*] The calculation of the relevant annual export turnover will be effected according to Article 4 of Annex I of Commission Recommendation 2003/361/EC of 6 May 2003, as may be amended in the future. The provisions laid down in Article 4(2) of Annex I will apply mutatis mutandis with respect to the annual export turnover of the relevant enterprise.]²

¹ The amendments to point 2.5 shown in the first square brackets were made by Communication of the Commission to Member States amending the communication pursuant to Article [88](1) of the EC Treaty applying Articles [87] and [88] of the Treaty to short-term export-credit insurance (OJ C 217, 2.8.2001, p. 2), with effect from 1 January 2002.

² The amendments to point 2.5 shown in the second square brackets were made by Communication of the Commission to Member States amending the communication pursuant to Article [88](1) of the EC Treaty applying Articles [87] and [88] of the Treaty to short-term export-credit insurance (OJ C 325, 22.12.2005, p. 22), with effect from 1 January 2006.

2.6. [The capacity of the private reinsurance market varies. This means that the definition of marketable risks is not immutable and may change over time. The definition may, therefore, be reviewed, notably at the expiry of this communication. The Commission will consult Member States' representatives with relevant experience in this field and other interested parties on such reviews. In so far as necessary, changes to the definition will have to take account of the scope of Community legislation governing export-credit insurance, in order to avoid any conflict or legal uncertainty.]

Notes

[¹⁰ ...]

The amendments to point 2.6 shown in square brackets were made by Communication of the Commission to Member States amending the communication pursuant to Article [88] (1) of the EC Treaty applying Articles [87] and [88] of the Treaty to short-term export-credit insurance (OJ C 325, 22.12.2005, p. 22), with effect from 1 January 2006.

3. FACTORS DISTORTING COMPETITION BETWEEN PRIVATE AND PUBLIC OR PUBLICLY SUPPORTED EXPORT-CREDIT INSURERS

3.1. The factors that may distort competition in favour of public or publicly supported export-credit insurers insuring marketable risks include:[11]

— *de jure* or *de facto* State guarantees of borrowing and losses. Such guarantees enable insures to borrow at rates lower than the normal market rates or make it possible for them to borrow money at all. Furthermore, they obviate the need for insurers to reinsure themselves on the private market,

— any difference in obligations, compared with private insurers, to maintain adequate provisions. It should be noted than when Council Directive 73/239/EEC[12] was amended by Directive 87/343/EC[13] it was understood that the exclusion of export-credit insurance operations for the account of or guaranteed by the State (Article 2(2)(d) of the original Directive) did not include operations in the field of short-term commercial risks which public or publicly supported export-credit insurers effected for their own account and not guaranteed by the State.[14] This means that to insure short-term commercial risks, public or publicly supported insurers must have a certain amount of own funds (solvency margin, including guarantee fund) and technical provisions (notably and equalization reserve) and must have obtained authorization in accordance with Article 6 et seq. of Directive 73/239/EEC,

— relief or exemption from taxes normally payable (such as company taxes and taxes levied on insurance policies),

— awards of aid or provisions of capital by the State. With regard to the latter, the principle should be observed that, unless the State is acting as would a private investor in a market economy, capital injections involve State aid;[15] provision by the State of services in kind, such as access to and use of State infrastructure, facilities or privileged information (for instance, information about debtors gathered by embassies) on terms not reflecting their cost; and reinsurance by the State, either directly, or indirectly via a public or publicly supported export-credit insurer, on terms more favourable than those available from the private reinsurance market, which leads either to under-pricing of the reinsurance or to the artificial creation of capacity that would not be forthcoming from the private market.

Notes

[11] The tying by a public or publicly supported export-credit insurer of insurance of non-marketable risks to the acceptance of cover for marketable risks might infringe Article 86 of the EC Treaty. Such action could both be the subject of proceedings by the Commission and challenged in the courts and before national competition authorities.

[12] First Council Directive 73/239/EEC of 24 July 1973 on the coordination of laws, regulations and administrative provisions relating to the taking-up and pursuit of the business of direct insurance other than life assurance (OJ L 228, 16.8.1973, p. 3).

[13] Council Directive 87/343/EEC of 22 June 1987 amending Council Directive 73/239/EEC on the coordination of laws, regulations and administrative provisions relating to the taking-up and pursuit of the business of direct insurance other than life assurance (OJ L 185, 4.7.1987, p. 72).

[14] See judgment of the Court of Justice in Case C-63/89, *Assurances du Credit and Cobac v Council and Commission*, cited in footnote 5, p. 1848 (paragraph 22).

[15] See communication of the Commission to the Member States concerning public authorities' holdings in company capital (EC Bulletin 9–1984) and communication of the Commission on the application of Articles [87] and [88] of the EC Treaty to public undertakings in the manufacturing sector (OJ C 307, 13.11.1993, p. 3).

3.2. The types of treatment listed in paragraph 3.1 give, or may give, the export-credit insurers that receive them a financial advantage over other export-credit insurers. Such financial advantages granted to certain enterprises distort competition and constitute State aid within the meaning of Article [87](1) of the Treaty.

Article [87](1) is applicable to all measures which grant a financial or economic advantage to certain enterprises or products and involve a charge on or a loss to public funds, whether actual or contingent, and for which nothing or little is required from the beneficiary concerned, in so far as such measures affect trade between Member States and distort or threaten to distort competition by favouring certain undertakings or the production of certain goods.[16]

The financial advantages listed in paragraph 3.1 in respect of marketable risks as defined in paragraph 2.5 affect intra-Community trade in services. Moreover, they lead to variations in the insurance cover available for marketable risks in different Member States, thereby distorting competition between companies in Member States and having secondary effects on intra-Community trade regardless of whether intra-Community exports outside the Community are concerned.[17] The exceptions provided for in Article [87] of the Treaty do not apply to aid for the insurance of marketable risks. The distorting effects of such aid in the Community outweigh any possible national or Community interest in supporting exports. That views has been confirmed by the judgment of the Court of Justice Case C-63/89 which was directly concerned with the issue addressed by this communication. The Court held that although the Directive on partial harmonization of equalization reserves for insurance companies, which exempted export-credit insurance operatings for the account of or guaranteed by the State, was not unlawful, the factors distorting competition between private and public or publicly supported export-credit insurers "might justify recourse to legal action to penalize infringement of the provisions (of Article [87])".[18] In its judgment in Case C-44/93,[19] the Court assumed that the advantages in question constitute State aid and confirmed that the Commission might take action to secure their withdrawal.

Notes

[16] See judgments of the Court of Justice in Case 30/59 *Steenkolenmijnen v High Authority* [1961] ECR p. 1, paragraph 19: Case 173/73 *Italy v Commission* [1974] ECR p. 709, Case 730/79 *Philip Morris v Commission* [1980] ECR p. 2671.

[17] In its judgment in Case C-142/87 *Belgium v Commission*, cited in footnote 3, the Court held that not only aid for intra-Community exports, but also aid for exports outside the Community can influence intra-Community competition and trade. Both types of operation are insured by export-credit insurers and aid with respect to both can therefore have effects on intra-Community competition and trade.

[18] Cited in footnote 5: see paragraph 24. Advocate-General Tesauro, in his opinion in the case, considered that when there is competition between private and public or publicly backed export-credit insurers, "it is highly doubtful whether the Member States can legitimately provide financial backing for public operators. Intervention of that kind could be incompatible with the rules on public aid" ([1991] ECR I-1835, point 15).

[19] Cited in footnote 3: see especially paragraph 34.

4. ACTION REQUIRED TO ELIMINATE DISTORTIONS OF COMPETITION IN SHORT-TERM EXPORT-CREDIT INSURANCE WITH RESPECT TO MARKETABLE RISKS

4.1. State aid of the types listed in paragraph 3.1, which is enjoyed by public supported export-credit insurers for the marketable risks defined in paragraph 2.5, may distort competition and would therefore be ineligible for exemption under the State aid rules of the Treaty.

4.2. Member States are therefore requested under Article [88](1) of the Treaty to amend, where necessary, their export-credit insurance systems for marketable risks in such a way that the granting of State aid of the following types to public or publicly supported export-credit insurers in respect of such risks is ended within one year of the publication of this Communication:

    (a) State guarantees for borrowing or losses;

    (b) exemption from the requirement to constitute adequate reserves and the other requirements listed in the second indent of paragraph 3.1;

    (c) relief or exemption from taxes or other charges normally payable;

    (d) award of aid or provisions of capital or other forms of finance in circumstances in which a private investor acting under normal market conditions would not invest in the company or on terms a private investor would not accept;

    (e) provision by the State of services in kind, such as access to and use of State infrastructure, facilities or privileged information (for instance, information about debtors gathered by embassies), on terms not reflecting their cost; and

    (f) reinsurance by the State, either directly, or indirectly via a public or publicly supported export-credit insurer, on terms more favourable than those available from the private reinsurance market, which leads either to under-pricing of the reinsurance cover or to the artificial creation of capacity that would not be forthcoming from the private market.

However, pending the outcome of the review mentioned in paragraph 4.3, existing complementary State reinsurance arrangements remain permissible for an interim period, provided that:

— the State reinsurance is a minority element in the insurer's overall reinsurance package,

— where the reinsurance treaties of the insurer combine marketable and non-marketable risks, and any State reinsurance thus unavoidably attaches to marketable risk, the level of State reinsurance for marketable risks must not exceed that which would have been available from the private reinsurance market if reinsurance had been sought for those risks in isolation,

— the State reinsurance does not act so as to enable the insurer to insure business on individual buyers beyond the limits set by the participating private-market reinsurers,

— the premium for State reinsurance demonstrably reflects the risk, is calculated using commercial market techniques and, where an equivalent market premium rate is available, is at least equal to that rate,

— the State reinsurance for marketable risks is open to all credit insurers who are able to satisfy the common eligibility criteria.

4.3. For the purposes of complying with paragraph 4.2, public or publicly supported export-credit insurers will, at the very least, have to keep a separate administration and separate accounts for their insurance of marketable risks and non-marketable risks for the account or with the guarantee of the State, demonstrating that they do not enjoy State aid in their insurance of marketable risks. The accounts for business insured on the insurer's own account should comply with Council Directive 91/674/EC.[20]

Furthermore, any Member State providing reinsurance cover to an export-credit insurer by way of participation or involvement in private sector reinsurance treaties covering both marketable and non-marketable risks will have to demonstrate that its arrangements do not involve State aid within the meaning of paragraph 4.2(f).

For this purpose the Commission, in close liaison with the Member States, will continuously, as from the publication of this Communication, monitor such arrangements on the basis of six-monthly reports submitted by Member States concerned and by the end of 1998 will carry out a complete review of such arrangements. The review will take into account all the knowledge and experience acquired in the meantime about the operation of the short-term export-credit insurance market, and Member States' intervention therein, from the reports on implementation supplied under paragraph 4.5 from the first of the annual reviews to be undertaken under paragraph 4.6 and from any notifications of use of the escape clause under paragraph 4.4. Should the review find that the arrangements in a Member State involve State aid, then the Member State will be required to terminate them by the end of 1999 at the latest.

Notes

[20] Council Directive 91/674/EEC of 19 December 1991 on the annual accounts and consolidated accounts of insurance undertakings (OJ L 374, 31. 12. 1991, p. 7).

4.4. The principle that export-credit insurance for marketable risks should be provided by public or publicly supported export-credit insurers only if the financial advantages listed in paragraph 4.2 are withdrawn from them may be departed from in the circumstances set out below.

In certain countries, cover for marketable export-credit risks may be temporarily unavailable from private export-credit insurers or from public or publicly supported export-credit insurers operating for their own account, owing to a lack of insurance or reinsurance capacity. Therefore those risks are temporarily considered to be non-marketable.

In such circumstances, those temporarily non-marketable risks may be taken on to the account of a public or publicly supported export-credit insurer for non-marketable risks insured for the account of or with the guarantee of the State. The insurer should, as far as possible, align its premium rates for such risks with the rates charged elsewhere by private export-credit insurers for the type of risk in question.

Any Member State intending to use that escape clause should immediately notify the Commission of its draft decision. That notification should contain a market report demonstrating the unavailability of cover for the risks in the private insurance market by producing evidence thereof from two large, well-known international private export-credit insurers as well as a national credit insurer, thus justifying the use of the escape clause. It should, moreover, contain a description of the conditions which the public or publicly supported export-credit insurer intends to apply in respect of such risks.

Within two months of the receipt of such notification, the Commission will examine whether the use of the escape clause is in conformity with the above conditions and compatible with the Treaty.

If the Commission finds that the conditions for the use of the escape clause are fulfilled, its decision on compatibility is limited to two years from the date of the decision, provided that the market conditions justifying the use of the escape clause do not change during that period.

Furthermore, the Commission may, in consultation with the other Member States, revise the conditions for the use of the escape clause; it may also decide to discontinue it or replace it with another appropriate system.

4.5. [This Communication will apply until 31 December 2010]. Member States are requested to inform the Commission within two months of notification of this communication, whether they accept its recommendations. By 1 January 1999 at the latest, Member States must inform the Commission of the action they have taken to comply herewith. Should it appear either through those reports or otherwise that the systems in operation in the Member States still involve State aid, the Commission will assess such aid pursuant to Articles [87] and [88] of the Treaty, in accordance with the policy set out above.

Notes
The period of validity of this instrument shown in square brackets, was extended by Communication of the Commission to Member States amending the communication pursuant to Article [88](1) of the EC Treaty applying Articles [87] and [88] of the Treaty to short-term export-credit insurance (OJ C 325, 22.12.2005, p. 22).

4.6. In cooperation with the Member States and interested parties, the Commission will review the definition of marketable risks and the operation of the present communication in the light of market developments and possible Community legislation. All information received by the Commission from Member States and interested parties in connection with such reviews will with the permission of the supplier of the information, be made available to all the other participants in the review.

[ANNEX
LIST OF MARKETABLE RISK COUNTRIES

European Union	*Countries which are members of the OECD*
All the Member States	Australia
	Canada
	Iceland
	Japan
	New Zealand
	Norway
	Switzerland
	United States of America.]

Notes
The annex ws replaced as shown in square brackets by Communication of the Commission to Member States amending the communication pursuant to Article [88](1) of the EC Treaty applying Articles [87] and [88] of the Treaty to short-term export-credit insurance (OJ C 217, 2.8.2001, p. 2), with effect from 1 January 2002.

Part G State Aids

G25

COMMISSION NOTICE

on the application of the State aid rules to measures relating to direct business taxation

(98/C 384/03)

(Text with EEA relevance)

Official Journal C 384, 10.12.1998, p. 3

Celex No: 31998Y1210(01)

Notes

EEA application: for the corresponding EEA provision, see the EFTA Surveillance Authority's Procedural and Substantive Rules in the Field of State Aid (Guidelines on the application and interpretation of Articles 61 and 62 of the EEA Agreement and Article 1 of Protocol 3 to the Surveillance and Court Agreement), Part III, Chapter 17B (as introduced by EFTA Surveillance Authority Decision No 149/99/COL of 30 June 1999 (OJ L 137, 8.6.2000, p. 20 and EEA Supplement No 26, 8.6.2000)).

Commentary

Notice: **B&C:** 15.031–15.060 F&N: 16.34

Introduction

1. On 1 December 1997, following a wide-ranging discussion on the need for coordinated action at Community level to tackle harmful tax competition, the Council (Ecofin) adopted a series of conclusions and agreed a resolution on a code of conduct for business taxation (hereinafter "code of conduct").[1] On that occasion, the Commission undertook to draw up guidelines on the application of Articles [87] and [88] of the Treaty to measures relating to direct business taxation and committed itself "to the strict application of the aid rules concerned". The code of conduct aims to improve transparency in the tax area through a system of information exchanges between Member States and of assessment of any tax measures that may be covered by it. For their part, the State aid provisions of the Treaty will also contribute through their own mechanism to the objective of tackling harmful tax competition.

Notes

[1] OJ C 2, 6.1.1998, p. 1.

---

2. The Commission's undertaking regarding State aid in the form of tax measures forms part of the wider objective of clarifying and reinforcing the application of the State aid rules in order to reduce distortions of competition in the single market. The principle of incompatibility with the common market and the derogations from that principle apply to aid "in any form whatsoever", including certain tax measures. However, the question whether a tax measure can be qualified as aid under Article [87](1) of the Treaty calls for clarification which this notice proposes to provide. Such clarification is particularly important in view of the procedural requirements that stem from designation as aid and of the consequences where Member States fail to comply with such requirements.

Commentary

para 2: **B&C:** 15.031

---

3. Following the completion of the single market and the liberalisation of capital movements, it has also become apparent that there is a need to examine the particular effects of aid granted in the form of tax measures and to spell out the consequences as regards assessment of the aid's compatibility with the common market.[2] The establishment of economic and monetary union and the consolidation of national budgets which it entails will make it even more essential to have strict control

---

of State aid in whatever form it may take. Similarly, account must also be taken, in the common interest, of the major repercussions which some aid granted through tax systems may have on the revenue of other Member States.

Notes
2 See action plan for the single market, CSE(97) 1, 4 June 1997, strategic target 2, action 1.

4. In addition to the objective of ensuring that Commission decisions are transparent and predictable, this notice also aims to ensure consistency and equality of treatment between Member States. The Commission intends, as the code of conduct notes, to examine or re-examine case by case, on the basis of this notice, the tax arrangements in force in the Member States.

A. Community powers of action

5. The Treaty empowers the Community to take measures to eliminate various types of distortion that harm the proper functioning of the common market. It is thus essential to distinguish between the different types of distortion.
6. Some general tax measures may impede the proper functioning of the internal market. In the case of such measures, the Treaty provides, on the one hand, for the possibility of harmonising Member States' tax provisions on the basis of Article [94] (Council directives, adopted unanimously). On the other, some disparities between planned or existing general provisions in Member States may distort competition and create distortions that need to be eliminated on the basis of Articles [96] and [97] (consultation of the relevant Member States by the Commission; if necessary, Council directives adopted by a qualified majority).
7. The distortions of competition deriving from State aid fall under a system of prior Commission authorisation, subject to review by the Community judicature. Pursuant to Article [88](3), State aid measures must be notified to the Commission. Member States may not put their proposed aid measures into effect until the Commission has approved them. The Commission examines the compatibility of aid not in terms of the form which it may take, but in terms of its effect. It may decide that the Member State must amend or abolish aid which the Commission finds to be incompatible with the common market. Where aid has already been implemented in breach of the procedural rules, the Member State must in principle recover it from the recipient(s).

B. Application of Article [87](1) of the EC Treaty to tax measures

8. Article [87](1) states that "any aid granted by a Member State or through State resources in any form whatsoever which distorts or threatens to distort competition by favouring certain undertakings or the production of certain goods shall, in so far as it affects trade between Member States, be incompatible with the common market". In applying the Community rules on State aid, it is irrelevant whether the measure is a tax measure, since Article [87] applies to aid measures "in any form whatsoever". To be termed aid, within the meaning of Article [87], a measure must meet the cumulative criteria described below.
9. Firstly, the measure must confer on recipients an advantage which relieves them of charges that are normally borne from their budgets. The advantage may be provided through a reduction in the firm's tax burden in various ways, including:
— a reduction in the tax base (such as special deductions, special or accelerated depreciation arrangements or the entering of reserves on the balance sheet),
— a total or partial reduction in the amount of tax (such as exemption or a tax credit),
— deferment, cancellation or even special rescheduling of tax debt.
10. Secondly, the advantage must be granted by the State or through State resources. A loss of tax revenue is equivalent to consumption of State resources in the form of fiscal expenditure. This criterion also applies to aid granted by regional or local bodies in the Member States.[3] Furthermore, State support may be provided just as much through tax provisions of a legislative, regulatory or administrative nature as through the practices of the tax authorities.

Notes
3 Judgment of the Court of Justice in Case 248/84 *Germany v Commission* [1987] ECR 4013.

Part G State Aids

11. Thirdly, the measure must affect competition and trade between Member States. This criterion presupposes that the beneficiary of the measure exercises an economic activity, regardless of the beneficiary's legal status or means of financing. Under settled case-law, for the purposes of this provision, the criterion of trade being affected is met if the recipient firm carries on an economic activity involving trade between Member States. The mere fact that the aid strengthens the firm's position compared with that of other firms which are competitors in intra-Community trade is enough to allow the conclusion to be drawn that intra-Community trade is affected. Neither the fact that aid is relatively small in amount,[4] nor the fact that the recipient is moderate in size or its share of the Community market very small,[5] nor indeed the fact that the recipient does not carry out exports[6] or exports virtually all its production outside the Community[7] do anything to alter this conclusion.

Notes

[4] With the exception, however, of aid meeting the tests of the *de minimis* rule. See the Commission notice published in OJ C 68, 6.3.1996, p. 9. [See now Commission Regulation (EC) No 1998/2006 of 15 November 2006 on the application of Articles 87 and 88 of the EC Treaty to *de minimis* aid (OJ L 379 28.12.2006, p. 5)

[5] Joined Cases C-278/92, C-279/92 and C-280/92 *Spain v Commission* [1994] ECR I-4103.

[6] Case 102/87 *France v Commission* [1998] ECR 4067.

[7] Case C-142/87 *Belgium v Commission* [1990] ECR I-959.

12. Lastly, the measure must be specific or selective in that it favours "certain undertakings or the production of certain goods`. The selective advantage involved here may derive from an exception to the tax provisions of a legislative, regulatory or administrative nature or from a discretionary practice on the part of the tax authorities. However, the selective nature of a measure may be justified by "the nature or general scheme of the system".[8] If so, the measure is not considered to be aid within the meaning of Article [87](1) of the Treaty. These various aspects are looked at below.

Notes

[8] Case 173/73 *Italy v Commission* [1974] ECR 709.

Distinction between State aid and general measures

13. Tax measures which are open to all economic agents operating within a Member State are in principle general measures. They must be effectively open to all firms on an equal access basis, and they may not *de facto* be reduced in scope through, for example, the discretionary power of the State to grant them or through other factors that restrict their practical effect. However, this condition does not restrict the power of Member States to decide on the economic policy which they consider most appropriate and, in particular, to spread the tax burden as they see fit across the different factors of production. Provided that they apply without distinction to all firms and to the production of all goods, the following measures do not constitute State aid:

— tax measures of a purely technical nature (for example, setting the rate of taxation, depreciation rules and rules on loss carry-overs; provisions to prevent double taxation or tax avoidance),

— measures pursuing general economic policy objectives through a reduction of the tax burden related to certain production costs (research and development (R&D), the environment, training, employment).

Commentary
para 13: B&C: 15.031

14. The fact that some firms or some sectors benefit more than others from some of these tax measures does not necessarily mean that they are caught by the competition rules governing State aid. Thus, measures designed to reduce the taxation of labour for all firms have a relatively greater effect on labour-intensive industries than on capital-intensive industries, without necessarily constituting State aid. Similarly, tax incentives for environmental, R&D or training investment favour only the firms which undertake such investment, but again do not necessarily constitute State aid.

Commentary
para 14: B&C: 15.031

15. In a judgment delivered in 1974,[9] the Court of Justice held that any measure intended partially or wholly to exempt firms in a particular sector from the charges arising from the normal application of the general system "without there being any justification for this exemption on the basis of the nature or general scheme of this system" constituted State aid. The judgment also states that "Article [87] does not distinguish between the measures of State intervention concerned by reference to their causes or aims but defines them in relation to their effects". The judgment also points out that the fact that the measure brings charges in the relevant sector more into line with those of its competitors in other Member States does not alter the fact that it is aid. Such divergences between tax systems, which, as pointed out above, are covered by Articles [94] to [97], cannot be corrected by unilateral measures that target the firms which are most affected by the disparities between tax systems.

Notes

[9] See footnote 8.

16. The main criterion in applying Article [87](1) to a tax measure is therefore that the measure provides in favour of certain undertakings in the Member State an exception to the application of the tax system. The common system applicable should thus first be determined. It must then be examined whether the exception to the system or differentiations within that system are justified "by the nature or general scheme" of the tax system, that is to say, whether they derive directly from the basic or guiding principles of the tax system in the Member State concerned. If this is not the case, then State aid is involved.

The selectivity or specificity criterion

17. The Commission's decision-making practice so far shows that only measures whose scope extends to the entire territory of the State escape the specificity criterion laid down in Article [87](1). Measures which are regional or local in scope may favour certain undertakings, subject to the principles outlined in paragraph 16. The Treaty itself qualifies as aid measures which are intended to promote the economic development of a region. Article [87](3)(a) and (c) explicitly provides, in the case of this type of aid, for possible derogations from the general principle of incompatibility laid down in Article [87](1).

18. The Treaty clearly provides that a measure which is sectorally specific is caught by Article [87](1). Article [87](1) expressly includes the phrase "the production of certain goods" among the criteria determining whether there is aid that is subject to Commission monitoring. According to well-established practice and case-law, a tax measure whose main effect is to promote one or more sectors of activity constitutes aid. The same applies to a measure that favours only national products which are exported.[10] Furthermore, the Commission has taken the view that a measure which targets all of the sectors that are subject to international competition constitutes aid.[11] A derogation from the base rate of corporation tax for an entire section of the economy therefore constitutes, except for certain cases,[12] State aid, as the Commission decided for a measure concerning the whole of the manufacturing sector.[13]

Notes

[10] Joined Cases 6 and 11/69 *Commission v. France* [1969] ECR 561.

[11] Commission Decision 97/239/EC of 4 December 1996 in the "*Maribel bis/ter*" case (OJ L 95, 10.4.1997, p. 25) (currently *sub judice*, Case C-75/97). [See now Case C-75/97 *Belgium v Commission* [1999] ECR I- 3671.]

[12] In particular, agriculture and fisheries, see paragraph 27.

[13] Commission decision of 22 July 1998 in the "Irish corporation tax" case (SG(98) D/7209) not yet published.

19. In several Member States, different tax rules apply depending on the status of the undertakings. Some public undertakings, for example, are exempt from local taxes or from company taxes. Such rules, which accord preferential treatment to undertakings having the legal status of public undertaking and carrying out an economic activity, may constitute State aid within the meaning of Article [87] of the Treaty.

20. Some tax benefits are on occasion restricted to certain types of undertaking, to some of their functions (intra-group services, intermediation or coordination) or to the production of certain goods. In so far as they favour certain undertakings or the production of certain goods, they may constitute State aid as referred to in Article [87](1).

Discretionary administrative practices

21. The discretionary practices of some tax authorities may also give rise to measures that are caught by Article [87]. The Court of Justice acknowledges that treating economic agents on a discretionary basis may mean that the individual application of a general measure takes on the features of a selective measure, in particular where exercise of the discretionary power goes beyond the simple management of tax revenue by reference to objective criteria.[14]

Notes

[14] Case C-241/94 *France v Commission (Kimberly Clark Sopalin)* [1996] ECR I-4551.

22. If in daily practice tax rules need to be interpreted, they cannot leave room for a discretionary treatment of undertakings. Every decision of the administration that departs from the general tax rules to the benefit of individual undertakings in principle leads to a presumption of State aid and must be analysed in detail. As far as administrative rulings merely contain an interpretation of general rules, they do not give rise to a presumption of aid. However, the opacity of the decisions taken by the authorities and the room for manoeuvre which they sometimes enjoy support the presumption that such is at any rate their effect in some instances. This does not make Member States any less able to provide their taxpayers with legal certainty and predictability on the application of general tax rules.

Justification of a derogation by "the nature or general scheme of the system"

23. The differential nature of some measures does not necessarily mean that they must be considered to be State aid. This is the case with measures whose economic rationale makes them necessary to the functioning and effectiveness of the tax system.[15] However, it is up to the Member State to provide such justification.

Notes

[15] Commission decision 96/369/EC of 13 March 1996 concerning fiscal aid given to German airlines in the form of a depreciation facility (OJ L 146, 20.6.1996, p. 42).

Commentary
para 23: B&C: 15.033

24. The progressive nature of an income tax scale or profit tax scale is justified by the redistributive purpose of the tax. Calculation of asset depreciation and stock valuation methods vary from one Member State to another, but such methods may be inherent in the tax systems to which they belong. In the same way, the arrangements for the collection of fiscal debts can differ from one Member State to the other. Lastly, some conditions may be justified by objective differences between taxpayers. However, if the tax authority has discretionary freedom to set different depreciation periods or different valuation methods, firm by firm, sector by sector, there is a presumption of aid. Such a presumption also exists when the fiscal administration handles fiscal debts on a case by case basis with an objective different from the objective of optimising the recovery of tax debts from the enterprise concerned.

25. Obviously, profit tax cannot be levied if no profit is earned. It may thus be justified by the nature of the tax system that non-profit-making undertakings, such as foundations or associations, are specifically exempt from the taxes on profits if they cannot actually earn any profits. Furthermore, it may also be justified by the nature of the tax system that cooperatives which distribute all their profits to their members are not taxed at the level of the cooperative when tax is levied at the level of their members.

26. A distinction must be made between, on the one hand, the external objectives assigned to a particular tax scheme (in particular, social or regional objectives) and, on the other, the objectives which are inherent in the tax system itself. The whole purpose of the tax system is to collect revenue to finance State expenditure. Each firm is supposed to pay tax once only. It is therefore

inherent in the logic of the tax system that taxes paid in the State in which the firm is resident for tax purposes should be taken into account. Certain exceptions to the tax rules are, however, difficult to justify by the logic of a tax system. This is, for example, the case if non-resident companies are treated more favourably than resident ones or if tax benefits are granted to head offices or to firms providing certain services (for example, financial services) within a group.

27. Specific provisions that do not contain discretionary elements, allowing for example tax to be determined on a fixed basis (for example, in the agriculture or fisheries sectors), may be justified by the nature and general scheme of the system where, for example, they take account of specific accounting requirements or of the importance of land in assets which are specific to certain sectors; such provisions do not therefore constitute State aid. Lastly, the logic underlying certain specific provisions on the taxation of small and medium-sized enterprises (including small agricultural enterprises)[16] is comparable to that underlying the progressiveness of a tax scale.

Notes
[16] Operators in the agricultural sector with no more than 10 annual work units.

C. Compatibility with the Common Market of State Aid in the Form of Tax Measures

28. If a tax measure constitutes aid that is caught by Article [87](1), it can nevertheless, like aid granted in other forms, qualify for one of the derogations from the principle of incompatibility with the common market provided for in Article [87](2) and (3). Furthermore, where the recipient, whether a private or public undertaking, has been entrusted by the State with the operation of services of general economic interest, the aid may also qualify for application of the provisions of Article [86] of the Treaty.[17]

Notes
[17] Judgment of the Court of First Instance in Case T-106/95 *FFSA and others v Commission* [1997] ECR II-229. Order of the Court of Justice in Case C-174/97 P [1998] I-1303.

29. The Commission could not, however, authorise aid which proved to be in breach both of the rules laid down in the Treaty, particularly those relating to the ban on discrimination and to the right of establishment, and of the provisions of secondary law on taxation.[18] Such aspects may, in parallel, be the object of a separate procedure on the basis of Article [226]. As is clear from case-law, those aspects of aid which are indissolubly linked to the object of the aid and which contravene specific provisions of the Treaty other than Articles [87] and [88] must however be examined in the light of the procedure under Article [88] as part of an overall examination of the compatibility or the incompatibility of the aid.

Notes
[18] Case 74/76 *Iannelli v Meroni* [1977] ECR 557. See also Cases 73/79 *"Sovraprezzo"* [1980] ECR 1533, T-49/93 *"SIDE"* [1995] ECR II-2501 and Joined Cases C 142 and 143/80 *"Salengo"* [1981] ECR 1413.

30. The qualification of a tax measure as harmful under the code of conduct does not affect its possible qualification as a State aid. However the assessment of the compatibility of fiscal aid with the common market will have to be made, taking into account, *inter alia*, the effects of aid that are brought to light in the application of the code of conduct.

31. Where a fiscal aid is granted in order to provide an incentive for firms to embark on certain specific projects (investment in particular) and where its intensity is limited with respect to the costs of carrying out the project, it is no different from a subsidy and may be accorded the same treatment. Nevertheless, such arrangements must lay down sufficiently transparent rules to enable the benefit conferred to be quantified.

32. In most cases, however, tax relief provisions are general in nature: they are not linked to the carrying-out of specific projects and reduce a firm's current expenditure without it being possible to assess the precise volume involved when the Commission carries out its ex ante examination. Such measures constitute "operating aid`. Operating aid is in principle prohibited. The Commission authorises it at present only in exceptional cases and subject to certain conditions, for example in shipbuilding, certain types of environmental protection aid[19] and in regions, including

Part G State Aids

ultra-peripheral regions, covered by the Article [87](3)(a) aid derogation provided that they are duly justified and their level is proportional to the handicaps they are intended to offset.[20] It must in principle (with the exception of the two categories of aid mentioned below) be degressive and limited in time. At present, operating aid can also be authorised in the form of transport aid in ultra-peripheral regions and in certain Nordic regions that are sparsely populated and are seriously handicapped in terms of accessibility. Operating aid may not be authorised where it represents aid for exports between Member States. As for State aid in favour of the maritime transport sector the specific rules for that sector apply.[21]

Notes

[19] Community guidelines on State aid for environmental protection (OJ C 72, 10.3.1994, p. 3). [See now Community guidelines on State aid for environmental protection (OJ C 37, 3.2.2001, p. 3).]

[20] Guidelines on national regional aid (OJ C 74, 10.3.1998, p. 9). [See Guidelines on National Regional Aid for 2007–2013 (OJ C 54, 4.3.2006, p. 13).]

[21] Community guidelines on State aid to maritime transport (OJ C 205, 5.7.1997, p. 5). [See now Commission communication C(2004) 43 — Community guidelines on State aid to maritime transport (OJ C 13, 17.1.2004, p. 3).]

---

33. If it is to be considered by the Commission to be compatible with the common market, State aid intended to promote the economic development of particular areas must be "in proportion to, and targeted at, the aims sought'. For the examination of regional aid the criteria allow account to be taken of other possible effects, in particular of certain effects brought to light by the code of conduct. Where a derogation is granted on the basis of regional criteria, the Commission must ensure in particular that the relevant measures:
    — contribute to regional development and relate to activities having a local impact. The establishment of off-shore activities does not, to the extent that their externalities on the local economy are low, normally provide satisfactory support for the local economy,
    — relate to real regional handicaps. It is open to question whether there are any real regional handicaps for activities for which the additional costs have little incidence, such as for example the transport costs for financing activities, which lend themselves to tax avoidance,
    — are examined in a Community context.[22] The Commission must in this respect take account of any negative effects which such measures may have on other Member States.

Notes

[22] Case 730/79 *Philip Morris v Commission* [1980] ECR 2671.

D. Procedures

34. Article [88](3) requires Member States to notify the Commission of all their "plans to grant or alter aid" and provides that any proposed measures may not be put into effect without the Commission's prior approval. This procedure applies to all aid, including tax aid.
35. If the Commission finds that State aid which has been put into effect in breach of this rule does not qualify for any of the exemptions provided for in the Treaty and is therefore incompatible with the common market, it requires the Member State to recover it, except where that would be contrary to a general principle of Community law, in particular legitimate expectations to which the Commission's behaviour can give rise. In the case of State aid in the form of tax measures, the amount to be covered is calculated on the basis of a comparison between the tax actually paid and the amount which should have been paid if the generally applicable rule had been applied. Interest is added to this basic amount. The interest rate to be applied is equivalent to the reference rate used to calculate the grant equivalent of regional aid.
36. Article [88](1) states that the Commission "shall in cooperation with Member States, keep under constant review all systems of aid existing in those States". Such review extends to State aid in the form of tax measures. So as to allow such review to be carried out, the Member States are required to submit to the Commission every year reports on their existing State aid systems. In the case of tax relief or full or partial tax exemption, the reports must provide an estimate of budgetary revenue lost. Following its review, the Commission may, if it considers that the scheme is

not or is no longer compatible with the common market, propose that the Member State amend or abolish it.

E. Implementation

37. The Commission will, on the basis of the guidelines set out in this notice and as from the time of its publication, examine the plans for tax aid notified to it and tax aid illegally implemented in the Member States and will review existing systems. This notice is published for guidance purposes and is not exhaustive. The Commission will take account of all the specific circumstances in each individual case.

38. The Commission will review the application of this notice two years after its publication.

G26

COMMISSION NOTICE

on the application of Articles 87 and 88 of the EC Treaty to State aid in the form of guarantees

(2000/C 71/07)

Official Journal C 71, 11.3.2000, p. 14

Celex No: 32000Y0311(03)

Notes

This document is reproduced with the misspellings in the original corrected.

On 27 June 2007, DG Competition published for consultation a preliminary draft revised Commission Notice on the application of Articles 87 and 88 of the EC Treaty to State aid in the form of guarantees. That draft is not reproduced in this volume. The draft is published on the Europa website at the following address: http://ec.europa.eu/comm/competition/state_aid/reform/draft_guarantee_notice_18072007_en.pdf

EEA application: for the corresponding EEA provision, see the EFTA Surveillance Authority's Procedural and Substantive Rules in the Field of State Aid (Guidelines on the application and interpretation of Articles 61 and 62 of the EEA Agreement and Article 1 of Protocol 3 to the Surveillance and Court Agreement), Part III, Chapter 17 (as introduced by EFTA Surveillance Authority Decision No 78/00/COL of 12 April 2000 (OJ L 274, 26.10.2000, p. 29 and EEA Supplement No 48)).

Commentary

Notice: B&C: 15.030

---

1. INTRODUCTION

1.1. This notice outlines the Commission's approach to State aid granted in the form of guarantees. Guarantees are usually associated with a loan or other financial obligation to be contracted by a borrower with a lender. However, this notice covers all forms of guarantees, irrespective of their legal basis and the transaction covered. Guarantees may be granted as individual guarantees or within guarantee schemes. If aid is involved, this aid in most cases benefits the borrower. However, in certain circumstances, there may also be an aid to the lender.

1.2. This notice applies without prejudice to Article 295 and thus does not prejudice the rules in Member States governing the system of property ownership. The Commission is neutral as regards public or private ownership. This notice does not apply to export credit guarantees.

1.3. In 1989 the Commission addressed two letters on State guarantees to the Member States. In the first letter[1] it pointed out that it regards all guarantees given by a State as falling within the scope of Article 87(1). According to this letter, the Commission must therefore be notified of any plans to give or alter such guarantees in sufficient time to enable it to submit its comments. In the second letter[2] the Commission made it clear that it intended to examine the establishment of State guarantee schemes, and that individual guarantees given under an approved scheme would not need to be notified. In 1993 the Commission adopted a communication[3] which addressed the subject of guarantees as well.

Notes

[1] Commission letter to the Member States, SG(89) D/4328 of 5 April 1989.

[2] Commission letter to the Member States, SG(89) D/12772 of 12 October 1989.

[3] Commission Communication to the Member States on the application of Articles [87] and [88] of the EEC Treaty and of Article 5 of Commission Directive 80/723/EEC to public undertakings in the manufacturing sector (OJ C 307, 13.11.1993, p. 3).

1.4. Experience gained in the meantime suggests that the Commission's policy in this area should be reviewed. This notice replaces the two Commission letters of 1989 and paragraph 38 of the Commission communication of 1993. Its purpose is to give Member States more detailed explanations about the principles on which the Commission intends to base its interpretation of Articles 87 and 88 and their application to State guarantees. The Commission intends in this way to make its policy in this area as transparent as possible, thereby ensuring that its decisions are predictable and that equal treatment is guaranteed.

2. APPLICABILITY OF ARTICLE 87(1)

2.1. Aid to the borrower

2.1.1. Usually, the aid beneficiary is the borrower. The State guarantee enables the borrower to obtain better financial terms for a loan than those normally available on the financial markets. Typically, with the benefit of the State guarantee, the borrower can obtain lower rates and/or offer less security. In some cases, the borrower would not, without a State guarantee, find a financial institution prepared to lend on any terms. State guarantees may thus facilitate the creation of new businesses and enable certain undertakings to raise money in order to pursue new activities or simply remain active instead of being eliminated or restructured, thereby creating distortions of competition. State guarantees thus generally fall within the scope of Article 87(1), if trade between Member States is affected and no market premium is paid.

2.1.2. The benefit of a State guarantee is that the risk associated with the guarantee is carried by the State. This carrying of a risk by the State should normally be remunerated by an appropriate premium. Where the State forgoes such a premium, there is both a benefit for the undertaking and a drain on the resources of the State. Thus, even if no payments are ever made by the State under a guarantee, there may nevertheless be a State aid under Article 87(1). The aid is granted at the moment when the guarantee is given, not the moment at which the guarantee is invoked or the moment at which payments are made under the terms of the guarantee. Whether or not a guarantee constitutes State aid, and, if so, what the amount of that State aid may be, must be assessed at the moment the guarantee is given.

2.1.3. The Commission also regards as aid in the form of a guarantee, the more favourable funding terms obtained by enterprises whose legal form rules out bankruptcy or other insolvency procedures or provides an explicit State guarantee or coverage of losses by the State. The same applies to the acquisition by a State of a holding in an enterprise if unlimited liability is accepted instead of the usual limited liability.[4]

Notes

[4] See footnote 3, paragraph 38.1 and 38.2.

2.1.4. Article 87(1) covers aid granted by a Member State or through State resources. Therefore, in the same way as other forms of potential aid, guarantees given by the State directly, namely by central, regional or local authorities, as well as guarantees given by undertakings under the dominant influence of public authorities, may constitute State aid.

2.2. Aid to the lender

2.2.1. Even if usually the aid beneficiary is the borrower it cannot be ruled out that under certain circumstances the lender, too, will benefit from the aid. In such a case the Commission will certainly pursue the matter accordingly.

2.2.2. In particular, for example, if a State guarantee is given ex post in respect of a loan or other financial obligation already entered into without the terms of this loan or financial obligation being adjusted, or if one guaranteed loan is used to pay back another, non-guaranteed loan to the same credit institution, then there may also be an aid to the lender, in so far as the security of the loans is increased. Such aid is capable of favouring the lender and distorting competition, and generally falls within the scope of Article 87(1), if trade between Member States is affected.

3. Amount of the Aid

3.1. In the case of an individual State guarantee, the aid element must be assessed by reference to the details of the guarantee and loan (or other financial obligation). The relevant factors include in particular the duration and amount of the guarantee and loan, the risk of default by the borrower, the price paid by the borrower for the guarantee, the nature of any security given, how and when the State could be called upon to pay a debt and the means (e.g. declaration of bankruptcy) to be used by the State to recover amounts owed by the borrower once the guarantee has been invoked.

3.2. The cash grant equivalent of a loan guarantee in a given year can be:

— calculated in the same way as the grant equivalent of a soft loan, the interest subsidy representing the difference between the market rate and the rate obtained thanks to the State guarantee after any premiums paid have been deducted, or

— taken to be the difference between (a) the outstanding sum guaranteed, multiplied by the risk factor (the probability of default) and (b) any premium paid, i.e. (guaranteed sum x risk) – premium, or

— calculated by any other objectively justifiable and generally accepted method.

For individual guarantees, the first method should in principle be the standard form of calculation, for guarantee schemes the second one.

The risk factor should be based on the past experience of defaults on loans given in similar circumstances (sector, size of firm, level of general economic activity). The yearly grant equivalents should be discounted to their present value using the reference rate, then added up to obtain the total grant equivalent.

Where, at the time the loan is granted, there is a strong probability that the borrower will default, e.g. because he is in financial difficulty, the value of the guarantee may be as high as the amount effectively covered by that guarantee.

3.3. If a financial obligation is wholly covered by a State guarantee, the lender has less incentive to assess properly, secure and minimise the risk arising from the lending operation, and in particular to assess properly the borrower's creditworthiness. Such risk assessment might also not always be taken over by the guarantor, for lack of means. This lack of incentive to minimise the risk of non-repayment of the loan might encourage lenders to contract loans with a greater than normal commercial risk and could thus increase the amount of higher-risk guarantees in the State's portfolio.

3.4. The Commission suggests that a percentage of at least 20% not covered by a State guarantee will serve as an appropriate limit for inducing the lender to properly assess the creditworthiness of the borrower,[5] to properly secure its loans and to minimise the risk associated with the transaction.[6] The Commission will therefore, in general, examine critically any guarantees covering the entirety (or nearly the entirety) of a financial transaction.

3.5. In the case of State guarantee schemes, the specific features of the individual cases may not be known at the time when the scheme is to be assessed. In these circumstances, the aid element must be assessed by reference to the provisions of the scheme concerning amongst others the maximum amount and duration of loans, the category of enterprise and type of project eligible, the security required from the borrowers, the premium to be paid and the interest rates obtained by them.

4. CONDITIONS EXCLUDING THE EXISTENCE OF AID

4.1. An individual guarantee or a guarantee scheme entered into by the State will be outside the scope of Article 87(1) when there is no aid which favours certain undertakings or the production of certain goods. In such cases, notification by the Member State is not necessary. Also, a guarantee does not constitute State aid under Article 87(1) when the measure does not affect trade between Member States.

4.2. The Commission considers that the fulfilment of all the following conditions ensures that an individual State guarantee does not constitute State aid under Article 87(1):
  (a) the borrower is not in financial difficulty;
  (b) the borrower would in principle be able to obtain a loan on market conditions from the financial markets without any intervention by the State;
  (c) the guarantee is linked to a specific financial transaction, is for a fixed maximum amount, does not cover more than 80 % of the outstanding loan or other financial obligation (except for bonds and similar instruments) and is not open-ended;
  (d) the market price for the guarantee is paid (which reflects, amongst others, the amount and duration of the guarantee, the security given by the borrower, the borrower's financial position, the sector of activity and the prospects, the rates of default, and other economic conditions).

Commentary
point 4.2: F&N: 16.23

4.3. The Commission considers that the fulfilment of all the following conditions ensures that a State guarantee scheme does not constitute State aid under Article 87(1):
  (a) the scheme does not allow guarantees to be granted to borrowers who are in financial difficulty;
  (b) the borrowers would in principle be able to obtain a loan on market conditions from the financial markets without any intervention by the State;
  (c) the guarantees are linked to a specific financial transaction, are for a fixed maximum amount, do not cover more than 80% of each outstanding loan or other financial obligation (except for bonds and similar instruments) and are not open-ended;
  (d) the terms of the scheme are based on a realistic assessment of the risk so that the premiums paid by the beneficiary enterprises make it, in all probability, self-financing;
  (e) the scheme provides for the terms on which future guarantees are granted and the overall financing of the scheme to be reviewed at least once a year;
  (f) the premiums cover both the normal risks associated with granting the guarantee and the administrative costs of the scheme, including, where the State provides the initial capital for the start-up of the scheme, a normal return on that capital.

4.4. Failure to comply with any one of the above conditions set out in points 4.2 and 4.3 does not mean that such guarantee or guarantee scheme is automatically regarded as State aid. If there is any doubt as to whether a planned guarantee or scheme does constitute State aid, it should be notified.

4.5. There may be circumstances in which it is planned to use State guarantees to enable enterprises, and in particular small and medium-sized enterprises, to obtain loans that the market would not supply. The enterprises may be starting up, expanding fast or be small and hence unable to furnish the necessary security to secure a loan or obtain a guarantee. They may fall into the category of high-risk enterprises (expected to move into profitability only in the long term and/or having a particularly high failure rate). This may be the case, for example, with projects concerning new, innovative products or processes. The Commission considers that such circumstances will generally not take State guarantees outside the scope of Article 87(1). State guarantees given in such circumstances should therefore be notified to the Commission in sufficient time, in the same way as State guarantees given in other circumstances.

5. Compatibility of State Aid in the Form of Guarantees with the Common Market

5.1. State guarantees within the scope of Article 87(1) must be examined by the Commission with a view to determining whether or not they are compatible with the common market. Before such assessment of compatibility can be made, the beneficiary of the aid must be identified. As has been explained under point 2, this can be either the borrower, or the lender, or both.

5.2. In most cases the guarantee contains aid to the borrower (point 2.1). Whether or not this aid is compatible with the common market will be examined by the Commission according to the same rules as are applied to aid measures taking other forms. The concrete criteria for the compatibility assessment have been clarified and detailed by the Commission in frameworks and guidelines concerning horizontal, regional and sectoral aid.[7] The examination will take into account, in particular, the aid intensity, the characteristics of the beneficiaries and the objectives pursued.

Notes

[7] See Competition law in the European Community, Volume IIA, Rules applicable to State aid, published by the Office for Official Publications of the European Communities. Certain texts have also been published in the *Official Journal of the European Communities* and are available on the Internet.

5.3. The Commission will accept guarantees only if their mobilisation is contractually linked to specific conditions which may go as far as the compulsory declaration of bankruptcy of the beneficiary undertaking, or any similar procedure. These conditions will have to be agreed at the initial examination by the Commission of the proposed guarantee within the normal procedures of Article 88(3), at the stage when it is granted. In the event that a Member State wants to mobilise the guarantee under conditions other than those initially agreed at the granting stage, then the Commission will regard the mobilisation of the guarantee as creating a new aid which has to be notified under Article 88(3).

5.4. Where the guarantee contains aid to the lender (point 2.2), attention should be drawn to the fact that such aid might, in principle, constitute operating aid.

6. Consequences of the Infringement of Article 88(3)

6.1. Where Member States do not observe the obligations of prior notification and suspension laid down in Article 88(3), the aid element of the guarantee is to be qualified as unlawful in accordance with Article 1(f) of Council Regulation (EC) No 659/1999 of 22 March 1999 laying down detailed rules for the application of Article [88] of the EC Treaty.[8] As to the consequences of infringement of the third sentence of Article 88(3), various distinctions should be drawn. In the following the position of the aid beneficiary and that of lenders not being a beneficiary will be examined in turn.

Notes

[8] OJ L 83, 27.3.1999, p. 1.

6.2. First, where aid has been illegally granted, the beneficiaries of the aid contained in the guarantee will run a risk. The Commission may take interim measures in accordance with Article 11 of Regulation (EC) No 659/1999 pending the outcome of the examination as to the compatibility of the aid. If, after this examination, the Commission finds that the State aid is incompatible with the common market, it shall be recovered from the beneficiary in accordance with Article 14 of Regulation (EC) No 659/1999, even if this means the declaration of bankruptcy of the enterprise.

6.3. Moreover, aid beneficiaries also run a risk at national level, inasmuch as the third sentence of Article 88(3) has direct effect. The Court of Justice of the European Communities has repeatedly confirmed that it is the duty of national courts to safeguard the rights of the individuals concerned, such as competitors of firms receiving illegal aid, against breaches of the third sentence of Article 88(3). National courts have to draw all the appropriate conclusions from the illegality of State aid granted in breach of the procedural rules of the Treaty. If a national court is requested to order recovery of the unlawful aid, it must normally grant that application.[9]

Notes

[9] See Case C-39/94 *Syndicat Français de l'Express International (SFEI) and Others v La Poste and Others* [1996] ECR I-3547.

6.4. Secondly, guarantees differ from other State aid measures, such as grants or tax exemptions, in the sense that in the case of a guarantee the State also enters into a legal relation with the lender. Therefore, consideration has to be given to whether the fact that a State aid has been illegally granted also has consequences for third parties. In the case of State guarantees for loans, this concerns mainly the financial lending institutions. In the case of guarantees for bonds issued to obtain financing for undertakings, this concerns the financial institutions involved in the issuance of the bonds.

6.5. The question whether the illegality of the aid affects the legal relations between the State and third parties is a matter which has to be examined under national law. National courts may have to examine whether national law prevents the guarantee contracts from being honoured, and in that assessment the Commission considers that they should take account of the breach of Community law. Accordingly, lenders may have an interest in verifying, as a standard precaution, that the Community rules on State aid have been observed, whenever guarantees are granted. The Member State should be able to provide a case number issued by the Commission for an individual case or a scheme and eventually a non-confidential copy of the Commission's decision together with the relevant reference to the *Official Journal of the European Communities*. The Commission for its part will do its utmost to make available in a transparent manner information on cases and schemes approved by it.

7. Reports to be Presented to the Commission by the Member States

7.1. As there may be new developments on the financial markets and as the value of State guarantees is difficult to assess, the constant review pursuant to Article 88(1) of State guarantee schemes approved by the Commission is of particular importance. In addition to the usual data on expenditure, the reports to be presented annually to the Commission should give (for schemes and individual guarantees as well) data on the total amount of State guarantees outstanding, the total amount paid in the preceding year by the State to defaulting debtors (net of any funds recovered), and the premiums paid for State guarantees in the same year. This information will help in calculating the rate of default and will be used to reassess the value of future guarantees and, if necessary, the premium to be paid in the future.

7.2. The Commission does not intend to use information supplied in the abovementioned reports and not known or foreseeable when it took an earlier decision, in order to revise its initial conclusions concerning the existence or scale of aid contained in State guarantee schemes. The Commission may, however, use such information to propose appropriate measures to a Member State under Article 88(1) in order to alter an existing State guarantee scheme.

G27

COMMISSION NOTICE

on the method for setting the reference and discount rates

(97/C 273/03)

(Text with EEA relevance)

Official Journal C 273, 9.9.1997, p. 3

Celex No: 51997XC0909(01)

Notes

EEA application: for the corresponding EEA provision, see the EFTA Surveillance Authority's Procedural and Substantive Rules in the Field of State Aid (Guidelines on the application and interpretation of Articles 61 and 62 of the EEA Agreement and Article 1 of Protocol 3 to the Surveillance and Court Agreement), Part VII, Chapter 34 (as added by EFTA Surveillance Authority Decision No 197/03/COL of 5 November 2003 (OJ L 139, 25.5.2006, p. 33 and EEA Supplement No 25) and as subsequently amended by EFTA Surveillance Authority Decision No 69/06/COL of 22 March 2006 (OJ L 324, 23.11.2006, p. 34)).

Commentary

Notice: B&C: 13.182, 13.186, 13.197, 13.200

(This notice replaces the previous notices on the method for setting the reference and discount rates, and in particular the Commission notice[1] of 10 August 1996)

For the purposes of Community monitoring of State aid as required by the EC Treaty, the Commission uses various parameters, including the reference and discount rates.

Those rates are used to measure the grant equivalent of aid that is disbursed in several instalments and to calculate the aid element resulting from interest subsidy schemes for loans. They are also used in implementing the *de minimis* rule[2] and for the repayment of illegal aid.[3]

The reference rates are supposed to reflect the average level of interest rates charged, in the various Member States, on medium and long-term loans (five to ten years) backed by normal security.

The Commission has decided to replace the current system of setting the reference rates, and to use instead one based on the five-year interbank swap rates, plus a premium.

As from 1 August 1997, the reference rates will be set as follows:

— in the case of all Member States except Italy, Portugal and Greece, the indicative rate is defined as the five-year interbank swap rate, in the relevant currency, plus a premium of 0,75 point (75 basis points),
In the case of Italy and Portugal, the indicative rate is defined as the five-year interbank swap rate, in the relevant currency, plus a premium of 200 basis points.
In the case of Greece, the indicative rate is defined as the one-year interbank rate (Athibor), in drachmas, plus a premium of 300 basis points;

— the reference rate is deemed to be equal to the average of the indicative rates recorded in the preceding September, October and November,

— the reference rate is adjusted again in the course of the year if it differs by more than 15% from the average of the indicative rates recorded over the last known three months.

It should also be noted that:

— the reference rate thus determined is a floor rate which may be increased in situations involving a particular risk (for example, an undertaking in difficulty, or where the security normally required by banks is not provided). In such cases, the premium may amount to 400 basis points or more if no private bank would have agreed to grant the relevant loan,

— the Commission reserves the right, if necessary for examining certain cases, to use a shorter base rate (for example, Libor one-year rate) or a longer base rate (for example, the rate on ten-year bonds) than the five-year interbank swap rate,

— in cases where the five-year interbank swap rate is not available, the base rate will be set at the level of the rate of yield on five-year State bonds, plus a premium of 25 basis points.

Reference rates will be made known by the Commission on Internet at the following address:

http://europa.eu.int/en/comm/dg04/aid/tauxref.htm[1]

Notes

[1] OJ C 232, 10.8.1996, p. 10.

[2] OJ C 68, 6.3.1996, p. 9.

[3] OJ C 156, 22.6.1995, p. 5.

[1] Historical and current reference/discount and recovery rates are published on the Europa website at the following address: http://ec.europa.eu/comm/competition/state_aid/legislation/reference.html

G28

COMMISSION COMMUNICATION

on the interest rates to be applied when aid granted unlawfully is being recovered

(2003/C 110/08)

Official Journal C 110, 8.5.2003, p. 21

Celex No: 52003XC0508(07)

Notes

This document is reproduced as corrected by the corrigendum at OJ C 150, 27.6.2003, p. 3.

EEA application: for the corresponding EEA provision, see the EFTA Surveillance Authority's Procedural and Substantive Rules in the Field of State Aid (Guidelines on the application and interpretation of Articles 61 and 62 of the EEA Agreement and Article 1 of Protocol 3 to the Surveillance and Court Agreement), Part VII, Chapter 34 (as added by EFTA Surveillance Authority Decision No 197/03/COL of 5 November 2003 (OJ L 139, 25.5.2006, p. 33 and EEA Supplement No 25) and as subsequently amended by EFTA Surveillance Authority Decision No 69/06/COL of 22 March 2006 (OJ L 324, 23.11.2006, p. 34)).

Article 14 of Council Regulation (EC) No 659/1999 of 22 March 1999 laying down detailed rules for the application of Article [88] of the EC Treaty[1] provides that when negative decisions are taken in cases of unlawful aid, the Commission shall decide that the Member State concerned shall take all necessary measures to recover the aid from the beneficiary. The aid to be recovered shall include interest at an appropriate rate fixed by the Commission. Interest shall be payable from the date the unlawful aid was at the disposal of the beneficiary until the date of its recovery.

In a letter to Member States of 22 February 1995 the Commission took the view that for the purpose of restoring the status quo commercial rates provide a better measure of the advantage improperly conferred on the recipient of unlawful aid. Accordingly, the Commission informed the Member States that in any decisions it might adopt ordering the recovery of aid unlawfully granted, it would apply the reference rate used in the calculation of the net grant equivalent of regional aid measures as the basis for the commercial rate. Thus for several years it has been the standard practice of the Commission to include in its recovery decisions a clause requiring interest to be calculated on the basis of the reference rate used for calculating the net grant equivalent of regional aids.

As part of the process of loyal collaboration between the Commission and Member States during the execution of certain recovery decisions, the question has arisen whether this interest rate should be applied on a simple basis or on a compound basis.[2] The Commission accordingly considers it necessary to clarify urgently its position on the matter, having regard to the objectives of the recovery of unlawful aid and its place in the system of State aid control laid down by the Treaty.

In accordance with a great number of decisions of the Community judiciary,[3] recovery is the logical consequence of the illegality of aid. The objective of recovery is to re-establish the previously existing situation. By repaying the aid, the beneficiary forfeits the unfair advantage which it enjoyed over its competitors on the market and the conditions of competition which existed prior to the payment of the aid are restored.

In market practice, simple interest would normally be calculated where the beneficiary of the funds does not have use of the interest amount before the end of the period, for example where interest is only paid at the end of the period. Compound interest would normally be calculated if each year (or period) the amount of interest can be considered as being paid to the beneficiary and so accruing to the initial capital amount. In this case, the beneficiary would earn interest on the interest paid for each period.

In practice, the type of aid which has been granted and the situation of the individual beneficiary may differ. If the aid consists in overcompensation, the benefit which the company took from it can be assimilated to a deposit which would normally attract compound interest. If the aid was an investment aid for a certain eligible cost, the aid may have replaced an alternative source of financing, which would also normally bear compound interest at commercial rates. If the aid was an operating aid, it would have direct effects on the profit and loss accounts, and hence the balance sheet, leading to the availability of funds for deposit. Thus despite the variety of situations, it appears that the effects of an unlawful aid are to provide funding to the beneficiary on similar conditions to a medium term non-interest bearing loan. Accordingly, the use of compound interest appears necessary to ensure that the financial advantages resulting from this situation are fully neutralised.

Accordingly, the Commission wishes to inform the Member States and interested parties that in any future decisions it may adopt ordering the recovery of aid unlawfully granted, it will apply the reference rate used for calculating the net grant equivalent of regional aids on a compound basis. In accordance with normal market practice, compounding should take place on an annual basis. Likewise, the Commission will expect the Member States to apply compound interest in the execution of pending recovery decisions, unless this would be contrary to a general principle of Community law.

Notes

[1] OJ L 83, 27.3.1999, p. 1.

[2] The calculation of simple interest uses the formula Interest = (Capital x Interest rate x Number of years). The calculation of compound interest, compounding on a yearly basis uses the formula Interest = (Capital $(1 + $ Interest rate$)^{\text{Number of years}}$– Capital.

[3] See in particular Case C-24/95 *Land Rheinland-Pfalz v Alcan* [1997] ECR I-1591 and Case T-459/93 *Siemens v Commission* [1995] ECR II-1675.

Part G State Aids

G29

COMMISSION NOTICE

on current State aid recovery interest rates and reference/discount rates for 15 Member States
applicable as from 1 January 2005 and historic recovery interest rates and reference/discount rates
applicable from 1 August 1997

*Published in accordance with Article 10 of Commission Regulation (EC) No 794/2004
of 21 April 2004 (OJ L 140, 30.4.2004, p. 1) and the Commission notice on the method
for setting the reference and discount rates (OJ C 273, 9.9.1997, p. 3)*

(2005/C 88/04)

Official Journal C 88, 12.4.2005, p. 5

Celex No: 52005XC0412(01)

The current recovery interest rates and reference/discount rates for the other Member States and the
historic interest rates applicable from 1 May 2004 will be published separately.

Notes

Historic and current reference/discount and recovery rates are published on the Europa website at the following address:
http://ec.europa.eu/comm/competition/state_aid/legislation/reference.html

---

From	to	BE	DK	DE	EL	ES	FR	IE	IT	LU	NL	AT	PT	FI	SE	UK
1.1.2005	...		4,23	4,08	4,08	4,08	4,08	4,08	4,08	4,08	4,08	4,08	4,08	4,08	4,69	5,81
1.1.2004	31.12.2004	4,43	4,58	4,43	4,43	4,43	4,43	4,43	4,43	4,43	4,43	4,43	4,43	4,43	5,30	5,68
1.9.2003	31.12.2003	3,95	4,15	3,95	3,95	3,95	3,95	3,95	3,95	3,95	3,95	3,95	3,95	3,95	4,69	5,42
1.8.2003	31.8.2003	3,95	4,15	3,95	3,95	3,95	3,95	3,95	3,95	3,95	3,95	3,95	3,95	3,95	5,68	5,42
1.1.2003	31.7.2003	4,80	5,03	4,80	4,80	4,80	4,80	4,80	4,80	4,80	4,80	4,80	4,80	4,80	5,68	5,42
1.1.2002	31.12.2002	5,06	5,54	5,06	5,06	5,06	5,06	5,06	5,06	5,06	5,06	5,06	5,06	5,06	5,85	6,01
1.12.2001	31.12.2001	5,23	6,70	5,23	5,23	5,23	5,23	5,23	5,23	5,23	5,23	5,23	5,23	5,23	6,40	7,06
1.1.2001	30.11.2001	6,33	6,70	6,33	6,33	6,33	6,33	6,33	6,33	6,33	6,33	6,33	6,33	6,33	6,40	7,06
1.4.2000	31.12.2000	5,70	6,21	5,70	10,40	5,70	5,70	5,70	5,70	5,70	5,70	5,70	5,70	5,70	6,85	7,64
1.1.2000	31.3.2000	5,70	6,21	5,70	12,24	5,70	5,70	5,70	5,70	5,70	5,70	5,70	5,70	5,70	6,85	7,64
1.11.1999	31.12.1999	5,61	5,44	5,61	12,71	5,61	5,61	5,61	5,61	5,61	5,61	5,61	5,61	5,61	6,71	6,86
1.10.1999	31.10.1999	4,76	5,44	4,76	12,71	4,76	4,76	4,76	4,76	4,76	4,76	4,76	4,76	4,76	6,71	6,86
1.8.1999	30.9.1999	4,76	5,44	4,76	12,71	4,76	4,76	4,76	4,76	4,76	4,76	4,76	4,76	4,76	5,76	6,86
1.5.1999	31.7.1999	4,71	5,44	4,73	12,71	4,72	4,77	4,69	6,18	4,71	4,76	4,77	6,02	4,75	4,96	6,86
1.3.1999	30.4.1999	4,71	5,44	4,73	15,24	4,72	4,77	4,69	6,18	4,71	4,76	4,77	6,02	4,75	4,96	6,86
1.1.1999	28.2.1999	4,71	5,44	4,73	15,24	4,72	4,77	4,69	6,18	4,71	4,76	4,77	6,02	4,75	5,90	6,86
1.12.1998	31.12.1998	4,87	5,44	4,87	15,91	5,13	4,94	4,97	6,95	4,87	4,93	5,05	7,56	5,13	5,79	7,77
1.11.1998	30.11.1998	4,87	6,46	4,87	15,91	5,13	4,94	4,97	6,95	4,87	4,93	5,05	7,56	5,13	5,79	7,77
1.10.1998	31.10.1998	5,97	6,46	5,94	15,91	5,13	5,83	6,14	6,95	5,97	5,95	5,05	7,56	5,13	5,79	7,77
1.9.1998	30.9.1998	5,97	6,46	5,94	15,91	6,20	5,83	6,14	6,95	5,97	5,95	5,96	7,56	6,21	5,79	7,77
1.6.1998	31.8.1998	5,97	6,46	5,94	15,91	6,20	5,83	6,14	6,95	5,97	5,95	5,96	7,56	6,21	7,03	7,77
1.2.1998	31.5.1998	5,97	6,46	5,94	19,95	6,20	5,83	6,14	8,20	5,97	5,95	5,96	7,56	6,21	7,03	7,77
1.1.1998	31.1.1998	5,97	6,46	5,94	16,54	6,20	5,83	6,14	8,20	5,97	5,95	5,96	7,56	6,21	7,03	7,77
1.8.1997	31.12.1997	5,55	6,04	5,54	14,22	6,22	5,53	6,72	8,21	5,55	5,56	5,57	7,37	5,96	6,86	8,15

Part G State Aids

G30

REFERENCE AND RECOVERY RATES IN THE FIELD OF STATE AID

(2005/C 136/18)

Text with EEA relevance

Official Journal C 136, 3.6.2005, p. 40

Celex No: 52005XC0603(04)

Notes

Historic and current reference/discount and recovery rates are published on the Europa website at the following address: http://ec.europa.eu/comm/competition/state_aid/legislation/reference.html

---

1. Reference Rate

The Commission adopts the following reference rates for the new Member States:

In force from:	CY	CZ	EE	HU	LV	LT	MT	PL	SK	SI
1.6.2005	6,33	4,05	5,50	8,59	6,64	6,49	7,00	6,24	7,55	5,10
1.4.2005	6,33	4,05	5,50	8,59	6,64	6,49	7,00	7,62	7,55	5,10
1.1.2005	6,33	4,86	5,50	8,59	6,64	6,49	7,00	7,62	7,55	5,10
1.5.2004	6,33	5,00	5,50	8,59	6,64	6,49	7,00	9,56	7,55	5,10

These rates are fixed on the basis of the method for setting and updating the reference/discount rates published in the Official Journal C 273, 9.9.1997, p. 3. Technical adaptations to this method were made by Commission notice published in Official Journal C 241, 26.8.1999, p. 9. This is the first time this method is applied for Poland and the Czech Republic.

For Estonia, Cyprus, Latvia, Lithuania, Hungary, Malta, Slovakia and Slovenia, the method is not applicable due to the unavailability of inter-banking swap rates for their currencies. For these Member states the reference/discount rate is still this which was communicated by these Member States for use at the moment of accession.

2. Recovery Rate

The Commission adopts the following recovery rates pursuant to Article 9 of Regulation (EC) No 794/2004 for the following new Member States:

In force from:	CZ	PL
1.6.2005	4,05	6,24
1.4.2005	4,05	7,62
1.5.2004	4,86	7,62

3. Publication

These figures will be published in the Official Journal of the European Union and on the internet site of DG COMP.

G31

COMMISSION NOTICE

on current State aid recovery interest rates and reference/discount rates for 25 Member States
applicable as from 1 October 2007

*(Published in accordance with Article 10 of Commission Regulation (EC) 794/2004 of 21 April 2004
(OJ L 140, 30.4.2004, p 1) and the Commission notice on the method for setting the reference and
discount rates (OJ C 273, 9.9.1997, p.3))*

(2007/C 205/02)

Official Journal C 205, 4.9.2007, p. 2

Celex No: 52007XC0904(01)

Notes

Historic and current reference/discount and recovery rates are published on the Europa website at the following address:
http://ec.europa.eu/comm/competition/state_aid/legislation/reference.html.

From	To	AT	BE	CY	CZ	DE	DK	EE	EL	ES	FI	FR	HU	IE	IT	LT	LU	LV	MT	NL	PL	PT	SE	SI	SK	UK
1.1.2007	...		4,62	6,34	4,24	4,62	4,76	5,50	4,62	4,62	4,62	4,62	8,54	4,62	4,62	6,49	4,62	6,64	7,00	4,62	5,94	4,62	4,68	4,62	5,20	5,90
1.9.2006	31.12.2006	4,36	4,36	6,34	4,34	4,36	4,49	5,50	4,36	4,36	4,36	4,36	8,12	4,36	4,36	6,49	4,36	6,64	7,00	4,36	5,56	4,36	4,31	4,43	5,62	5,33
1.6.2006	31.8.2006	4,36	4,36	6,34	3,72	4,36	4,49	5,50	4,36	4,36	4,36	4,36	7,04	4,36	4,36	6,49	4,36	6,64	7,00	4,36	5,56	4,36	4,31	4,43	4,77	5,33
1.3.2006	31.5.2006	3,70	3,70	6,34	3,72	3,70	3,74	5,50	3,70	3,70	3,70	3,70	7,04	3,70	3,70	6,49	3,70	6,64	7,00	3,70	5,56	3,70	3,74	4,43	3,98	5,33
1.1.2006	28.2.2006	3,70	3,70	7,53	3,72	3,70	3,74	5,50	3,70	3,70	3,70	3,70	8,59	3,70	3,70	6,49	3,70	6,64	7,00	3,70	5,56	3,70	3,74	5,10	7,55	5,33
1.9.2005	31.12.2005	4,08	4,08	7,53	3,40	4,08	3,54	5,50	4,08	4,08	4,08	4,08	8,59	4,08	4,08	6,49	4,08	6,64	7,00	4,08	6,24	4,08	3,96	5,10	7,55	5,81
1.7.2005	31.8.2005	4,08	4,08	7,53	4,05	4,08	4,23	5,50	4,08	4,08	4,08	4,08	8,59	4,08	4,08	6,49	4,08	6,64	7,00	4,08	6,24	4,08	3,96	5,10	7,55	5,81
1.6.2005	30.6.2005	4,08	4,08	7,53	4,05	4,08	4,23	5,50	4,08	4,08	4,08	4,08	8,59	4,08	4,08	6,49	4,08	6,64	7,00	4,08	6,24	4,08	4,69	5,10	7,55	5,81
1.4.2005	31.5.2005	4,08	4,08	6,33	4,05	4,08	4,23	5,50	4,08	4,08	4,08	4,08	8,59	4,08	4,08	6,49	4,08	6,64	7,00	4,08	7,62	4,08	4,69	5,10	7,55	5,81
1.1.2005	31.3.2005	4,08	4,08	6,33	4,86	4,08	4,23	5,50	4,08	4,08	4,08	4,08	8,59	4,08	4,08	6,49	4,08	6,64	7,00	4,08	7,62	4,08	4,69	5,10	7,55	5,81
01.09.2007	.....	5,42	5,42	5,49	4,24	5,42	5,58	5,50	5,42	5,42	5,42	5,42	8,54	5,42	5,42	6,49	5,42	6,64	7,00	5,42	5,94	5,42	5,49	5,42	5,20	5,90
01.01.2007	31.08.2007	4,62	4,62	5,49	4,24	4,62	4,76	5,50	4,62	4,62	4,62	4,62	8,54	4,62	4,62	6,49	4,62	6,64	7,00	4,62	5,94	4,62	4,68	4,62	5,20	5,90
01.12.2006	31.12.2006	4,36	4,36	6,34	4,34	4,36	4,49	5,50	4,36	4,36	4,36	4,36	8,12	4,36	4,36	6,49	4,36	6,64	7,00	4,36	5,56	4,36	4,31	4,43	5,62	5,33
01.09.2006	30.11.2006	4,36	4,36	6,34	4,34	4,36	4,49	5,50	4,36	4,36	4,36	4,36	8,12	4,36	4,36	6,49	4,36	6,64	7,00	4,36	5,56	4,36	4,31	4,43	5,62	5,33
01.06.2006	31.08.2006	4,36	4,36	6,34	3,72	4,36	4,49	5,50	4,36	4,36	4,36	4,36	7,04	4,36	4,36	6,49	4,36	6,64	7,00	4,36	5,56	4,36	4,31	4,43	3,98	5,33
01.03.2006	31.05.2006	3,70	3,70	6,34	3,72	3,70	3,74	5,50	3,70	3,70	3,70	3,70	7,04	3,70	3,70	6,49	3,70	6,64	7,00	3,70	5,56	3,70	3,74	4,43	3,98	5,33
01.01.2006	28.02.2006	3,70	3,70	6,34	3,72	3,70	3,74	5,50	3,70	3,70	3,70	3,70	7,04	3,70	3,70	6,49	3,70	6,64	7,00	3,70	5,56	3,70	3,74	4,43	3,98	5,33
01.12.2005	31.12.2005	4,08	4,08	6,34	3,40	4,08	3,54	5,50	4,08	4,08	4,08	4,08	8,59	4,08	4,08	6,49	4,08	6,64	7,00	4,08	6,24	4,08	3,96	5,10	7,55	5,81
01.09.2005	30.11.2005	4,08	4,08	7,53	3,40	4,08	3,54	5,50	4,08	4,08	4,08	4,08	8,59	4,08	4,08	6,49	4,08	6,64	7,00	4,08	6,24	4,08	3,96	5,10	7,55	5,81
01.07.2005	31.08.2005	4,08	4,08	7,53	4,05	4,08	4,23	5,50	4,08	4,08	4,08	4,08	8,59	4,08	4,08	6,49	4,08	6,64	7,00	4,08	6,24	4,08	3,96	5,10	7,55	5,81
01.06.2005	30.06.2005	4,08	4,08	7,53	4,05	4,08	4,23	5,50	4,08	4,08	4,08	4,08	8,59	4,08	4,08	6,49	4,08	6,64	7,00	4,08	6,24	4,08	4,69	5,10	7,55	5,81
01.04.2005	31.05.2005	4,08	4,08	7,88	4,05	4,08	4,23	5,50	4,08	4,08	4,08	4,08	8,59	4,08	4,08	6,49	4,08	6,64	7,00	4,08	6,24	4,08	4,69	5,10	7,55	5,81
01.01.2005	31.03.2005	4,08	4,08	7,88	4,86	4,08	4,23	5,50	4,08	4,08	4,08	4,08	8,59	4,08	4,08	6,49	4,08	6,64	7,00	4,08	7,62	4,08	4,69	5,10	7,55	5,81
01.05.2004	31.12.2004	4,43	4,43	6,33	(a)	4,43	4,58	5,50	4,43	4,43	4,43	4,43	8,59	4,43	4,43	6,49	4,43	6,64	7,00	4,43	(b)	4,43	5,30	5,10	7,55	5,68

(a) For the Czech Republic the reference/discount rate for this period was 5,00%, the recovery rate was 4,86%

(b) For Poland the reference/discount rate for this period was 9,56%, the recovery rate was 7,62%